FAR AMT

Federal Aviation Regulations for Aviation Maintenance Technicians

2006

U.S. Department of Transportation: From Title 14 of the Code of Federal Regulations (14 CFR)

Federal Aviation Regulations for Aviation Maintenance Technicians Includes Parts 1, 13, 21, 23, 27, 33, 34, 35, 39, 43, 45, 47, 65, 91, 119, 121 J&L, 125, 135, 145, 147, and 183, Advisory Circulars 20-62D, 20-109A, 21-12B, 39-7C, 43-9C, 43.9-1E, 65-30A, and FAA-G-8082-11A

Updated and Published by

Aviation Supplies & Academics, Inc.
7005 132nd Place SE
Newcastle, WA 98059-3153

ASA-06-FAR-AMT

FAR-AMT
(Federal Aviation Regulations for Aviation Maintenance Technicians)
2006 Edition

Aviation Supplies & Academics, Inc.
7005 132nd Place SE
Newcastle, WA 98059-3153

This publication contains current regulations as of August 11, 2005.
None of the material in this publication supersedes any documents, procedures, or regulations issued by the Federal Aviation Administration.

Visit the FAA's website to review changes to the regulations:
http://www.faa.gov/regulations_policies/faa_regulations/

ASA-06-FAR-AMT
ISBN 1-56027-563-4

Printed in the United States of America

06 05 9 8 7 6 5 4 3 2 1

ASA's 2006 FAR and AIM Series

FAR/AIM *FAR Flight Crew* *FAR AMT*

ASA has been supplying the standard reference of the industry, the FAR/AIM series, for more than two decades. The 2006 series continues to provide information directly from the Federal Aviation Regulations and the *Aeronautical Information Manual*, along with these important features:

- Regulation and AIM changes are posted on the ASA website as a free download; sign up to have Update notices automatically emailed to you as a free service from ASA
- All changes since last printing are clearly identified
- Includes suggested study list of AIM paragraphs and regulations pertinent to specific pilot certificates and ratings
- Index includes both FAR and AIM terms to provide an alphabetized listing of subject matter for quick look-up
- AIM produced with full-color graphics

Each regulation Part is preceded by a table of contents. Changes since last year's printing are identified on Page v and in the table of contents for each regulation Part (in bold and marked with an asterisk), as well as within the text for quick reference (changed text is indicated with a bold line in the margin). In the AIM, changes are explained in lists at the beginning, and with bold lines in the margins. It is recommended you familiarize yourself with all the changes to identify those that affect your aviation activities.

Changes affecting the regulations take place daily; the AIM changes every 6 months. ASA tracks all changes and offers you **two options for *FREE* Updates**:

- Updates are posted on the ASA website that you can download for free
- You may sign up on our website for ASA's free service to have Update notices automatically emailed to you

You may also visit the FAA website at http://www.faa.gov/certification/aircraft/av-info/dst/default.htm to review advisory circulars, Notice of Proposed Regulations (NPRMs), current regulations, and FAA Orders and publications.

You'll find a Reader Response page in the back of this book which you can fill out and mail or fax to us. We welcome your suggestions and comments, as they help generate further improvements to future editions.

Although ASA is not a government agency, and we do not write the regulations or the AIM, we do work closely with the FAA. Questions or concerns can be forwarded to our attention, and we will in turn pass the comments on to the FAA. They are interested in user-feedback and your comments could foster improvements in the regulations which affect the whole industry.

FAR/AIM Comments
ASA, Inc.
7005 132nd Place SE
Newcastle, WA 98059-3153

Internet: www.asa2fly.com
Fax: 425.235.0128
E-mail: asa@asa2fly.com

What's Changed Since Last Year?

Changes since last year's printing of the book are noted in the table of contents of each Part with an asterisk and bold title:

Example:

***61.5 Certificates and rating issued under this part.**

The updated text within the context of the regulation is indicated by a bold line in the margin:

(a) The following certificates are issued under this part to an applicant who satisfactorily accomplishes the training and certification requirements for the certificate sought:
(1) Pilot certificates—
(i) Student pilot.
(ii) Recreational pilot.
(iii) Private pilot.
(iv) Commercial pilot.
(v) Airline transport pilot.
(2) Flight instructor certificates.
(3) Ground instructor certificates.

How to Identify the Currency of the Regulations

In each Part following the Table of Contents is a Source, with the date of origin for that regulation.

Example:

Docket number within the Federal Registers, where original text can be found

Federal Register volume 38, page 3161

SOURCE: Docket No. 11802, 38 FR 3161, Feb. 1, 1973, unless otherwise noted.

Date regulation was written

If a change has taken place since the original Regulation was written, it is noted at the end of the regulation.

Example:

Docket number within the Federal Registers

Federal Register volume 38, page 3161, where the original text of regulation is

Date original regulation was written

[Doc. No. 11802, 38, FR 3161, Feb. 1, 1973, as amended by Amdt. 61-77, 51 FR 40703, Nov. 7, 1986]

Amendment number, the change to regulation; in the Federal Register

Federal Register Volume 51, page number 40703, where Amendment can be found

Date change took place

Summary of Changes Since September 2004

Parts 119, 121, 135 and 183

- Adopts the rule published December 6, 2002 which imposed statutory requirements from the Aging Aircraft Safety Act of 1991 for certain airplanes to undergo inspections and records reviews after their 14th year in service and at specified intervals after that, as well as imposes supplemental inspections by specified deadlines in the maintenance programs for these airplanes.

Part 13

- The FAA is adopting procedures for administratively assessing civil penalties for violations of the FARs.
- Editorial and technical corrections to a recent amendment which changed procedures concerning initiating and adjudicating a civil penalty against an individual acting as a pilot, flight engineer, mechanic, or repairman.
- Investigative and enforcement procedures are updated to account for technical changes such as employee functions, addresses, office organization, filing instructions, and internet accessibility of documents and FAA decisions.

Part 21

- An error relating to type certification of large reciprocating-engine powered airplanes is corrected.

Part 43

- This change is the result of the Bilateral Aviation Safety Agreement (BASA) between the United States and Canada; it amends the regulations governing maintenance, preventive maintenance, and alterations performed on U.S. aeronautical products by certain Canadian persons and removes specific regulatory references and other requirements unique to that work when performed in Canada.

Part 47

- Revisions to the regulations concerning registering aircraft and recording security documents to comply with a new International Registry.

Part 65

- SFAR No. 103. In response to the increased hiring needs, the FAA has established a new rule by which air traffic controllers may request a waiver of the mandatory separation age.
- Part 65, SFAR No. 100: Allows Flight Standards District Offices (FSDO) to accept expired flight instructor certificates, expired inspection authorizations for renewals, and expired airman written test reports for certain practical tests from U.S. military and civilian personnel (U.S. personnel) who are assigned outside the United States in support of U.S. Armed Forces operations.

Part 91

- SFAR No. 65–1 is removed from Part 91.
- Editorial changes were made (which do not change the intent of the rule) regarding Temporary Flight Restrictions (TFRs).
- This change removes the requirement for a pyrotechnic signaling device for aircraft operated for hire over water and beyond power-off gliding distance from shore for air carriers operating under part 121 unless it is part of a required life raft.
- This final rule allows an aircraft operator to transport State and local candidates for compensation, without having to comply with FAA safety rules applicable to air carriers and other commercial operators.
- Correction was made to the Subpart K (Fractional Ownership Operations) compliance date.
- Establishes a new noise standard for subsonic jet airplanes and subsonic transport category large airplanes.

Part 121

- Revisions to allow certain alternative procedures in conducting full-scale emergency evacuation demonstrations for transport category airplanes.

Part 145

- The FAA is delaying the effective date of the final rule requiring each repair station to have an approved training program until April 6, 2006 because applicable guidance material is not yet available to assist repair stations in developing their programs.

Inspection Authorization Knowledge Test Guide (FAA-G-8082-11) was revised effective 2004.

To view the rules currently in effect, visit ASA's online Update:

www.asa2fly.com / farupdate.html

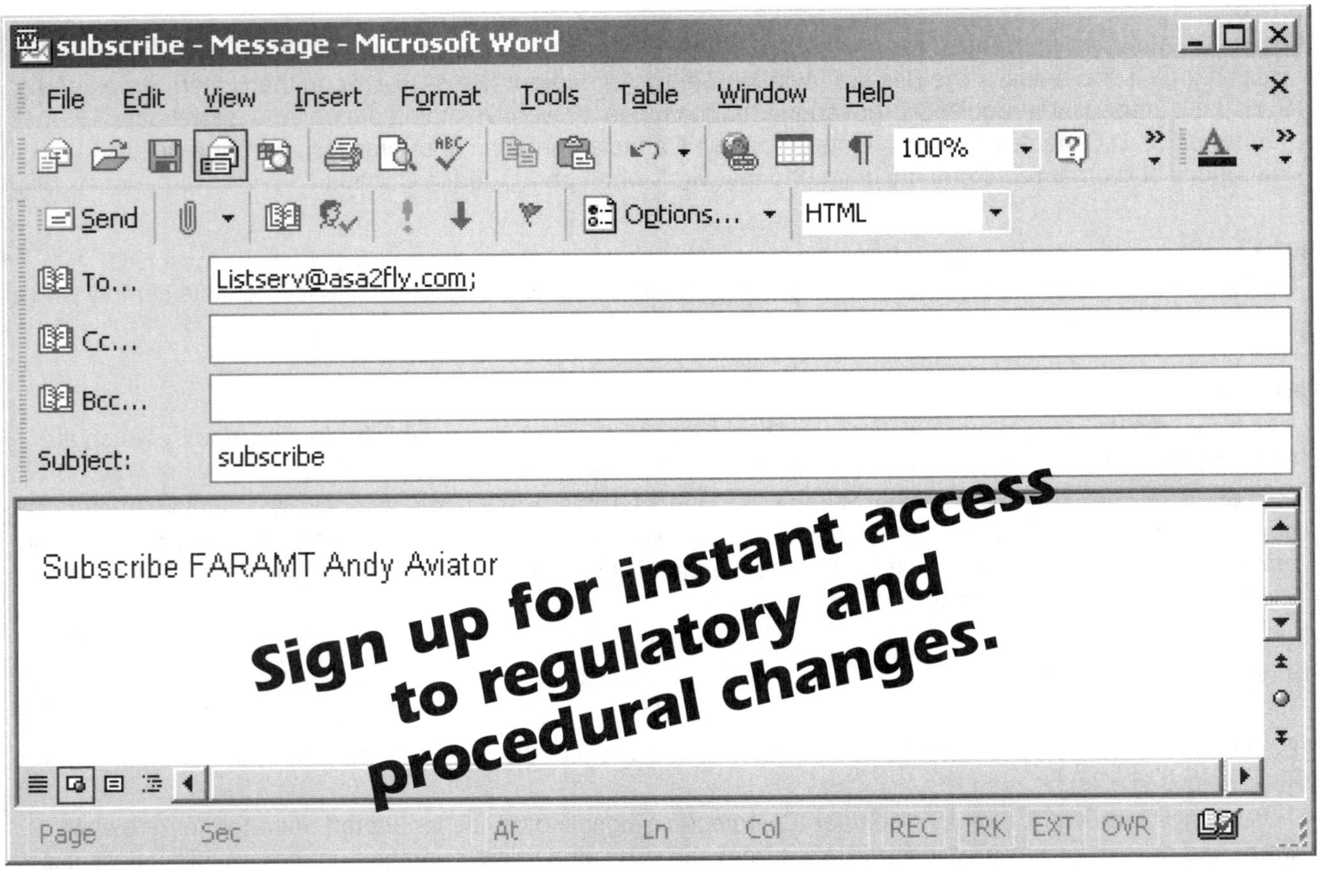

Note: Changes affecting the regulations take place daily, and the AIM changes twice a year. ASA tracks all changes and posts them on the ASA website so you always have the most current information. Follow these steps to have Update notices automatically emailed to you—

Send a plain text e-mail to:	**Listserv@asa2fly.com**
Subject line:	**subscribe**
Body of message:	**Subscribe FARAMT Your Name**

FAR Parts Listed in Titles 14 and 49 of the Code of Federal Regulations

Location Key

ALL................. Published in ASA's *FAR/AIM*, *FAR-FC*, and *FAR-AMT* books
FAR/AIM.......... *FAR/AIM* combination book
FAR-FC .... *FAR for Flight Crew* book
FAR-AMT .... *FAR for Aviation Maintenance Technicians* book
FAA .... Available from the Government Printing Office or at www.faa.gov
CD-FL-PRO .... Available in electronic form on ASA's Pro-Flight Library CD

Part	Title	Location
	Subchapter A—Definitions	
1	Definitions and abbreviations	ALL, CD-FL-PRO
	Subchapter B—Procedural Rules	
11	General rulemaking procedures	FAA, CD-FL-PRO
13	Investigative and enforcement procedures	FAR-AMT, CD-FL-PRO
14	Rules implementing the Equal Access to Justice Act of 1980	FAA, CD-FL-PRO
15	Administrative claims under Federal Tort Claims Act	FAA, CD-FL-PRO
16	Rules of practice for Federally-assisted airport enforcement proceedings	FAA, CD-FL-PRO
	Subchapter C—Aircraft	
21	Certification procedures for products and parts	FAR-AMT, CD-FL-PRO
23	Airworthiness standards: normal, utility, acrobatic, and commuter category airplanes	FAR-AMT, CD-FL-PRO
25	Airworthiness standards: transport category airplanes	FAR-FC, CD-FL-PRO
27	Airworthiness standards: normal category rotorcraft	FAR-AMT, CD-FL-PRO
29	Airworthiness standards: transport category rotorcraft	FAA, CD-FL-PRO
31	Airworthiness standards: manned free balloons	FAA, CD-FL-PRO
33	Airworthiness standards: aircraft engines	FAR-AMT, CD-FL-PRO
34	Fuel venting and exhaust emission requirements for turbine engine powered airplanes	FAR-AMT, CD-FL-PRO
35	Airworthiness standards: propellers	FAR-AMT, CD-FL-PRO
36	Noise standards: aircraft type and airworthiness certification	FAA, CD-FL-PRO
39	Airworthiness directives	FAR-AMT, CD-FL-PRO
43	Maintenance, preventive maintenance, rebuilding, and alteration	FAR/AIM, FAR-AMT, CD-FL-PRO
45	Identification and registration marking	FAR-AMT, CD-FL-PRO
47	Aircraft registration	FAR-AMT, CD-FL-PRO
49	Recording of aircraft titles and security documents	FAA, CD-FL-PRO
50-59	*[Reserved]*	

Subchapter D — Airmen

60 *[Reserved]*

61 Certification: Pilots, flight instructors, and ground instructors .... FAR/AIM, CD-FL-PRO

63 Certification: Flight crewmembers other than pilots .... FAR-FC, CD-FL-PRO

65 Certification: Airmen other than flight crewmembers .... FAR-AMT, FAR-FC, CD-FL-PRO

67 Medical standards and certification .... FAR/AIM, CD-FL-PRO

Subchapter E — Airspace

71 Designation of class A, B, C, D, and E airspace areas; air traffic service routes; and reporting points .... FAR/AIM, CD-FL-PRO

73 Special use airspace .... FAR/AIM, CD-FL-PRO

75 *[Reserved]*

77 Objects affecting navigable airspace .... FAA, CD-FL-PRO

Subchapter F — Air Traffic and General Operating Rules

91 General operating and flight rules .... ALL (FAR-FC Subpart K only), CD-FL-PRO

93 Special air traffic rules and airport traffic patterns .... FAA, CD-FL-PRO

95 IFR altitudes .... FAA, CD-FL-PRO

97 Standard instrument approach procedures .... FAR/AIM, CD-FL-PRO

99 Security control of air traffic .... FAA, CD-FL-PRO

101 Moored balloons, kites, unmanned rockets and unmanned free balloons .... FAA, CD-FL-PRO

103 Ultralight vehicles .... FAR/AIM, CD-FL-PRO

105 Parachute operations .... FAR/AIM, CD-FL-PRO

107 Airport security .... FAA, CD-FL-PRO

108 Airplane operator security .... FAA, CD-FL-PRO

109 Indirect air carrier security .... FAA, CD-FL-PRO

Subchapter G — Air Carriers and Operators for Compensation or Hire: Certification and Operations

119 Certification: Air carriers and commercial operators .... FAR/AIM, FAR-AMT, CD-FL-PRO

121 Operating requirements: Domestic, flag, and supplemental operations .... FAR-FC, FAR-AMT (Subparts J & L only), CD-FL-PRO

125 Certification and operations: Airplanes having a seating capacity of 20 or more passengers or a maximum payload capacity of 6,000 pounds or more; and rules governing persons on board such aircraft .... FAR-AMT, CD-FL-PRO

129 Operations: Foreign air carriers and foreign operators of U.S.-registered aircraft engaged in common carriage .... FAA, CD-FL-PRO

133 Rotorcraft external-load operations .... FAA, CD-FL-PRO

135 Operating requirements: Commuter and on-demand operations and rules governing persons on board such aircraft .... FAR/AIM, FAR-AMT, CD-FL-PRO

136 National Parks Air Tour Management .... FAR/AIM, CD-FL-PRO
137 Agricultural aircraft operations .... FAR/AIM, CD-FL-PRO
139 Certification and operations:
Land airports serving certain air carriers .... FAA, CD-FL-PRO

Subchapter H — Schools and Other Certificated Agencies

140 *[Reserved]*
141 Pilot schools .... FAR/AIM, CD-FL-PRO
142 Training centers .... FAR/AIM, CD-FL-PRO
143 *[Reserved]*
145 Repair stations .... FAR-AMT, CD-FL-PRO
147 Aviation maintenance technician schools .... FAR-AMT, CD-FL-PRO

Subchapter I — Airports

150 Airport noise compatibility planning .... FAA, CD-FL-PRO
151 Federal aid to airports .... FAA, CD-FL-PRO
152 Airport aid program .... FAA, CD-FL-PRO
155 Release of airport property from surplus property disposal restrictions .... FAA, CD-FL-PRO
156 State block grant pilot program .... FAA, CD-FL-PRO
157 Notice of construction, alteration, activation, and deactivation of airports .... FAA, CD-FL-PRO
158 Passenger facility charges (PFCs) .... FAA, CD-FL-PRO
161 Notice and approval of airport noise and access restrictions .... FAA, CD-FL-PRO
169 Expenditure of Federal funds for nonmilitary airports or air navigation facilities thereon .... FAA, CD-FL-PRO

Subchapter J — Navigational Facilities

170 Establishment and discontinuance criteria for air traffic control services and navigational facilities .... FAA, CD-FL-PRO
171 Non-Federal navigation facilities .... FAA, CD-FL-PRO

Subchapter K—Administrative Regulations

183 Representatives of the Administrator .... FAR-AMT, CD-FL-PRO
185 Testimony by employees and production of records in legal proceedings, and service of legal process and pleadings .... FAA, CD-FL-PRO
187 Fees .... FAA, CD-FL-PRO
189 Use of Federal Aviation Administration communications system .... FAA, CD-FL-PRO
191 Protection of sensitive security information .... FAA, CD-FL-PRO
193 Protection of voluntarily submitted information .... FAA, CD-FL-PRO

Subchapters L through M *[Reserved]*

Subchapter N — War Risk Insurance

198 Aviation insurance .... FAA, CD-FL-PRO

49 CFR Subtitle B — Other Regulations Pertaining to Transportation

830 Notification and Reporting of Aircraft Accidents or Incidents and Overdue Aircraft, and Preservation of Aircraft Wreckage, Mail, Cargo, and Records .... FAR/AIM, FAA, CD-FL-PRO

1552 Flight Schools .... FAR/AIM, FAA, CD-FL-PRO

FAR-AMT Contents

		Page
Part 1	Definitions and Abbreviations	1
Part 13	Investigative and Enforcement Procedures	11
Part 21	Certification Procedures for Products and Parts	43
Part 23	Airworthiness Standards: Normal, Utility, Acrobatic, and Commuter Category Airplanes	79
Part 27	Airworthiness Standards: Normal Category Rotorcraft	203
Part 33	Airworthiness Standards: Aircraft Engines	261
Part 34	Fuel Venting and Exhaust Emission Requirements for Turbine Engine Powered Airplanes	285
Part 35	Airworthiness Standards: Propellers	293
Part 39	Airworthiness Directives	297
Part 43	Maintenance, Preventive Maintenance, Rebuilding, and Alteration	299
Part 45	Identification and Registration Marking	313
Part 47	Aircraft Registration	317
Part 65	Certification: Airmen Other Than Flight Crewmembers	327
Part 91	General Operating and Flight Rules	349
Part 119	Certification: Air Carriers and Commercial Operators	447
Part 121	Certification and Operations: Subparts J & L	463
Part 125	Certification and Operations: Airplanes Having a Seating Capacity of 20 or More Passengers or a Maximum Payload Capacity of 6,000 Pounds or More	475
Part 135	Operating Requirements: Commuter and On-Demand Operations	523
Part 145	Repair Stations	617
Part 147	Aviation Maintenance Technician Schools	627
Part 183	Representatives of the Administrator	635
Advisory Circulars		639
FAR Index		795

SUBCHAPTER A DEFINITIONS

PART 1 DEFINITIONS AND ABBREVIATIONS

Sec.
1.1 General definitions.
1.2 Abbreviations and symbols.
1.3 Rules of construction.

Authority: 49 U.S.C. 106(g), 40113, 44701.

§1.1 General definitions.

As used in Subchapters A through K of this chapter, unless the context requires otherwise:

Administrator means the Federal Aviation Administrator or any person to whom he has delegated his authority in the matter concerned.

Aerodynamic coefficients means nondimensional coefficients for aerodynamic forces and moments.

Air carrier means a person who undertakes directly by lease, or other arrangement, to engage in air transportation.

Air commerce means interstate, overseas, or foreign air commerce or the transportation of mail by aircraft or any operation or navigation of aircraft within the limits of any Federal airway or any operation or navigation of aircraft which directly affects, or which may endanger safety in, interstate, overseas, or foreign air commerce.

Aircraft means a device that is used or intended to be used for flight in the air.

Aircraft engine means an engine that is used or intended to be used for propelling aircraft. It includes turbosuperchargers, appurtenances, and accessories necessary for its functioning, but does not include propellers.

Airframe means the fuselage, booms, nacelles, cowlings, fairings, airfoil surfaces (including rotors but excluding propellers and rotating airfoils of engines), and landing gear of an aircraft and their accessories and controls.

Airplane means an engine-driven fixed-wing aircraft heavier than air, that is supported in flight by the dynamic reaction of the air against its wings.

Airport means an area of land or water that is used or intended to be used for the landing and takeoff of aircraft, and includes its buildings and facilities, if any.

Airship means an engine-driven lighter-than-air aircraft that can be steered.

Air traffic means aircraft operating in the air or on an airport surface, exclusive of loading ramps and parking areas.

Air traffic clearance means an authorization by air traffic control, for the purpose of preventing collision between known aircraft, for an aircraft to proceed under specified traffic conditions within controlled airspace.

Air traffic control means a service operated by appropriate authority to promote the safe, orderly, and expeditious flow of air traffic.

Air Traffic Service (ATS) route is a specified route designated for channeling the flow of traffic as necessary for the provision of air traffic services. The term "ATS route" refers to a variety of airways, including jet routes, area navigation (RNAV) routes, and arrival and departure routes. An ATS route is defined by route specifications, which may include:

(1) An ATS route designator;

(2) The path to or from significant points;

(3) Distance between significant points;

(4) Reporting requirements; and

(5) The lowest safe altitude determined by the appropriate authority.

Air transportation means interstate, overseas, or foreign air transportation or the transportation of mail by aircraft.

Alert Area. An alert area is established to inform pilots of a specific area wherein a high volume of pilot training or an unusual type of aeronautical activity is conducted.

Alternate airport means an airport at which an aircraft may land if a landing at the intended airport becomes inadvisable.

Altitude engine means a reciprocating aircraft engine having a rated takeoff power that is producible from sea level to an established higher altitude.

Appliance means any instrument, mechanism, equipment, part, apparatus, appurtenance, or accessory, including communications equipment, that is used or intended to be used in operating or controlling an aircraft in flight, is installed in or attached to the aircraft, and is not part of an airframe, engine, or propeller.

Approved, unless used with reference to another person, means approved by the Administrator.

Area navigation (RNAV) is a method of navigation that permits aircraft operations on any desired flight path.

Area navigation (RNAV) route is an ATS route based on RNAV that can be used by suitably equipped aircraft.

Armed Forces means the Army, Navy, Air Force, Marine Corps, and Coast Guard, including their regular and reserve components and members serving without component status.

Autorotation means a rotorcraft flight condition in which the lifting rotor is driven entirely by action of the air when the rotorcraft is in motion.

Auxiliary rotor means a rotor that serves either to counteract the effect of the main rotor torque on a rotorcraft or to maneuver the rotorcraft about one or more of its three principal axes.

Balloon means a lighter-than-air aircraft that is not engine driven, and that sustains flight through the use of either gas buoyancy or an airborne heater.

Brake horsepower means the power delivered at the propeller shaft (main drive or main output) of an aircraft engine.

Calibrated airspeed means the indicated airspeed of an aircraft, corrected for position and instrument error. Calibrated airspeed is equal to true airspeed in standard atmosphere at sea level.

Canard means the forward wing of a canard configuration and may be a fixed, movable, or variable geometry surface, with or without control surfaces.

Canard configuration means a configuration in which the span of the forward wing is substantially less than that of the main wing.

Category:

(1) As used with respect to the certification, ratings, privileges, and limitations of airmen, means a broad classifica-

tion of aircraft. Examples include: airplane; rotorcraft; glider; and lighter-than-air; and

(2) As used with respect to the certification of aircraft, means a grouping of aircraft based upon intended use or operating limitations. Examples include: transport, normal, utility, acrobatic, limited, restricted, and provisional.

Category A, with respect to transport category rotorcraft, means multiengine rotorcraft designed with engine and system isolation features specified in Part 29 and utilizing scheduled takeoff and landing operations under a critical engine failure concept which assures adequate designated surface area and adequate performance capability for continued safe flight in the event of engine failure.

Category B, with respect to transport category rotorcraft, means single-engine or multiengine rotorcraft which do not fully meet all Category A standards. Category B rotorcraft have no guaranteed stay-up ability in the event of engine failure and unscheduled landing is assumed.

Category II operations, with respect to the operation of aircraft, means a straight-in ILS approach to the runway of an airport under a Category II ILS instrument approach procedure issued by the Administrator or other appropriate authority.

Category III operations, with respect to the operation of aircraft, means an ILS approach to, and landing on, the runway of an airport using a Category III ILS instrument approach procedure issued by the Administrator or other appropriate authority.

Category IIIa operations, an ILS approach and landing with no decision height (DH), or a DH below 100 feet (30 meters), and controlling runway visual range not less than 700 feet (200 meters).

Category IIIb operations, an ILS approach and landing with no DH, or with a DH below 50 feet (15 meters), and controlling runway visual range less than 700 feet (200 meters), but not less than 150 feet (50 meters).

Category IIIc operations, an ILS approach and landing with no DH and no runway visual range limitation.

Ceiling means the height above the earth's surface of the lowest layer of clouds or obscuring phenomena that is reported as "broken", "overcast", or "obscuration", and not classified as "thin" or "partial".

Civil aircraft means aircraft other than public aircraft.

Class:

(1) As used with respect to the certification, ratings, privileges, and limitations of airmen, means a classification of aircraft within a category having similar operating characteristics. Examples include: single engine; multiengine; land; water; gyroplane; helicopter; airship; and free balloon; and

(2) As used with respect to the certification of aircraft, means a broad grouping of aircraft having similar characteristics of propulsion, flight, or landing. Examples include: airplane; rotorcraft; glider; balloon; landplane; and seaplane.

Clearway means:

(1) For turbine engine powered airplanes certificated after August 29, 1959, an area beyond the runway, not less than 500 feet wide, centrally located about the extended centerline of the runway, and under the control of the airport authorities. The clearway is expressed in terms of a clearway plane, extending from the end of the runway with an upward slope not exceeding 1.25 percent, above which no object nor any terrain protrudes. However, threshold lights may protrude above the plane if their height above the end of the runway is 26 inches or less and if they are located to each side of the runway.

(2) For turbine engine powered airplanes certificated after September 30, 1958, but before August 30, 1959, an area beyond the takeoff runway extending no less than 300 feet on either side of the extended centerline of the runway, at an elevation no higher than the elevation of the end of the runway, clear of all fixed obstacles, and under the control of the airport authorities.

Climbout speed, with respect to rotorcraft, means a referenced airspeed which results in a flight path clear of the height-velocity envelope during initial climbout.

Commercial operator means a person who, for compensation or hire, engages in the carriage by aircraft in air commerce of persons or property, other than as an air carrier or foreign air carrier or under the authority of Part 375 of this title. Where it is doubtful that an operation is for "compensation or hire", the test applied is whether the carriage by air is merely incidental to the person's other business or is, in itself, a major enterprise for profit.

Consensus standard means, for the purpose of certificating light-sport aircraft, an industry-developed consensus standard that applies to aircraft design, production, and airworthiness. It includes, but is not limited to, standards for aircraft design and performance, required equipment, manufacturer quality assurance systems, production acceptance test procedures, operating instructions, maintenance and inspection procedures, identification and recording of major repairs and major alterations, and continued airworthiness.

Controlled airspace means an airspace of defined dimensions within which air traffic control service is provided to IFR flights and to VFR flights in accordance with the airspace classification.

NOTE—Controlled airspace is a generic term that covers Class A, Class B, Class C, Class D, and Class E airspace.

Controlled Firing Area. A controlled firing area is established to contain activities, which if not conducted in a controlled environment, would be hazardous to nonparticipating aircraft.

Crewmember means a person assigned to perform duty in an aircraft during flight time.

Critical altitude means the maximum altitude at which, in standard atmosphere, it is possible to maintain, at a specified rotational speed, a specified power or a specified manifold pressure. Unless otherwise stated, the critical altitude is the maximum altitude at which it is possible to maintain, at the maximum continuous rotational speed, one of the following:

(1) The maximum continuous power, in the case of engines for which this power rating is the same at sea level and at the rated altitude.

(2) The maximum continuous rated manifold pressure, in the case of engines, the maximum continuous power of which is governed by a constant manifold pressure.

Critical engine means the engine whose failure would most adversely affect the performance or handling qualities of an aircraft.

Decision height, with respect to the operation of aircraft, means the height at which a decision must be made, during an ILS or PAR instrument approach, to either continue the approach or to execute a missed approach.

Enhanced flight visibility (EFV) means the average forward horizontal distance, from the cockpit of an aircraft in flight, at which prominent topographical objects may be clearly distinguished and identified by day or night by a pilot using an enhanced flight vision system.

Enhanced flight vision system (EFVS) means an electronic means to provide a display of the forward external scene topography (the natural or manmade features of a place or region especially in a way to show their relative positions and elevation) through the use of imaging sensors, such as a forward looking infrared, millimeter wave radiometry, millimeter wave radar, low light level image intensifying.

Equivalent airspeed means the calibrated airspeed of an aircraft corrected for adiabatic compressible flow for the particular altitude. Equivalent airspeed is equal to calibrated airspeed in standard atmosphere at sea level.

Extended over-water operation means—

(1) With respect to aircraft other than helicopters, an operation over water at a horizontal distance of more than 50 nautical miles from the nearest shoreline; and

(2) With respect to helicopters, an operation over water at a horizontal distance of more than 50 nautical miles from the nearest shoreline and more than 50 nautical miles from an off-shore heliport structure.

External load means a load that is carried, or extends, outside of the aircraft fuselage.

External-load attaching means the structural components used to attach an external load to an aircraft, including external-load containers, the backup structure at the attachment points, and any quick-release device used to jettison the external load.

Final takeoff speed means the speed of the airplane that exists at the end of the takeoff path in the en route configuration with one engine inoperative.

Fireproof—

(1) With respect to materials and parts used to confine fire in a designated fire zone, means the capacity to withstand at least as well as steel in dimensions appropriate for the purpose for which they are used, the heat produced when there is a severe fire of extended duration in that zone; and

(2) With respect to other materials and parts, means the capacity to withstand the heat associated with fire at least as well as steel in dimensions appropriate for the purpose for which they are used.

Fire resistant—

(1) With respect to sheet or structural members means the capacity to withstand the heat associated with fire at least as well as aluminum alloy in dimensions appropriate for the purpose for which they are used; and

(2) With respect to fluid-carrying lines, fluid system parts, wiring, air ducts, fittings, and powerplant controls, means the capacity to perform the intended functions under the heat and other conditions likely to occur when there is a fire at the place concerned.

Flame resistant means not susceptible to combustion to the point of propagating a flame, beyond safe limits, after the ignition source is removed.

Flammable, with respect to a fluid or gas, means susceptible to igniting readily or to exploding.

Flap extended speed means the highest speed permissible with wing flaps in a prescribed extended position.

Flash resistant means not susceptible to burning violently when ignited.

Flight crewmember means a pilot, flight engineer, or flight navigator assigned to duty in an aircraft during flight time.

Flight level means a level of constant atmospheric pressure related to a reference datum of 29.92 inches of mercury. Each is stated in three digits that represent hundreds of feet. For example, flight level 250 represents a barometric altimeter indication of 25,000 feet; flight level 255, an indication of 25,500 feet.

Flight plan means specified information, relating to the intended flight of an aircraft, that is filed orally or in writing with air traffic control.

Flight time means:

(1) Pilot time that commences when an aircraft moves under its own power for the purpose of flight and ends when the aircraft comes to rest after landing; or

(2) For a glider without self-launch capability, pilot times that commences when the glider is towed for the purpose of flight and ends when the glider comes to rest after landing.

Flight visibility means the average forward horizontal distance, from the cockpit of an aircraft in flight, at which prominent unlighted objects may be seen and identified by day and prominent lighted objects may be seen and identified by night.

Foreign air carrier means any person other than a citizen of the United States, who undertakes directly, by lease or other arrangement, to engage in air transportation.

Foreign air commerce means the carriage by aircraft of persons or property for compensation or hire, or the carriage of mail by aircraft, or the operation or navigation of aircraft in the conduct or furtherance of a business or vocation, in commerce between a place in the United States and any place outside thereof; whether such commerce moves wholly by aircraft or partly by aircraft and partly by other forms of transportation.

Foreign air transportation means the carriage by aircraft of persons or property as a common carrier for compensation or hire, or the carriage of mail by aircraft, in commerce between a place in the United States and any place outside of the United States, whether that commerce moves wholly by aircraft or partly by aircraft and partly by other forms of transportation.

Forward wing means a forward lifting surface of a canard configuration or tandem-wing configuration airplane. The surface may be a fixed, movable, or variable geometry surface, with or without control surfaces.

Glider means a heavier-than-air aircraft, that is supported in flight by the dynamic reaction of the air against its lifting surfaces and whose free flight does not depend principally on an engine.

Go-around power or thrust setting means the maximum allowable in-flight power or thrust setting identified in the performance data.

Ground visibility means prevailing horizontal visibility near the earth's surface as reported by the United States National Weather Service or an accredited observer.

Gyrodyne means a rotorcraft whose rotors are normally engine-driven for takeoff, hovering, and landing, and for forward flight through part of its speed range, and whose means of propulsion, consisting usually of conventional propellers, is independent of the rotor system.

Gyroplane means a rotorcraft whose rotors are not engine-driven, except for initial starting, but are made to rotate by action of the air when the rotorcraft is moving; and whose means of propulsion, consisting usually of conventional propellers, is independent of the rotor system.

Helicopter means a rotorcraft that, for its horizontal motion, depends principally on its engine-driven rotors.

Heliport means an area of land, water, or structure used or intended to be used for the landing and takeoff of helicopters.

Idle thrust means the jet thrust obtained with the engine power control level set at the stop for the least thrust position at which it can be placed.

IFR conditions means weather conditions below the minimum for flight under visual flight rules.

IFR over-the-top, with respect to the operation of aircraft, means the operation of an aircraft over-the-top on an IFR flight plan when cleared by air traffic control to maintain "VFR conditions" or "VFR conditions on top".

Indicated airspeed means the speed of an aircraft as shown on its pitot static airspeed indicator calibrated to reflect standard atmosphere adiabatic compressible flow at sea level uncorrected for airspeed system errors.

Instrument means a device using an internal mechanism to show visually or aurally the attitude, altitude, or operation of an aircraft or aircraft part. It includes electronic devices for automatically controlling an aircraft in flight.

Interstate air commerce means the carriage by aircraft of persons or property for compensation or hire, or the carriage of mail by aircraft, or the operation or navigation of aircraft in the conduct or furtherance of a business or vocation, in commerce between a place in any State of the United States, or the District of Columbia, and a place in any other State of the United States, or the District of Columbia; or between places in the same State of the United States through the airspace over any place outside thereof; or between places in the same territory or possession of the United States, or the District of Columbia.

Interstate air transportation means the carriage by aircraft of persons or property as a common carrier for compensation or hire, or the carriage of mail by aircraft in commerce:

(1) Between a place in a State or the District of Columbia and another place in another State or the District of Columbia;

(2) Between places in the same State through the airspace over any place outside that State; or

(3) Between places in the same possession of the United States;

Whether that commerce moves wholly by aircraft of partly by aircraft and partly by other forms of transportation.

Intrastate air transportation means the carriage of persons or property as a common carrier for compensation or hire, by turbojet-powered aircraft capable of carrying thirty or more persons, wholly within the same State of the United States.

Kite means a framework, covered with paper, cloth, metal, or other material, intended to be flown at the end of a rope or cable, and having as its only support the force of the wind moving past its surfaces.

Landing gear extended speed means the maximum speed at which an aircraft can be safely flown with the landing gear extended.

Landing gear operating speed means the maximum speed at which the landing gear can be safely extended or retracted.

Large aircraft means aircraft of more than 12,500 pounds, maximum certificated takeoff weight.

Lighter-than-air aircraft means aircraft that can rise and remain suspended by using contained gas weighing less than the air that is displaced by the gas.

Light-sport aircraft means an aircraft, other than a helicopter or powered-lift that, since its original certification, has continued to meet the following:

(1) A maximum takeoff weight of not more than—

(i) 660 pounds (300 kilograms) for lighter-than-air aircraft;

(ii) 1,320 pounds (600 kilograms) for aircraft not intended for operation on water; or

(iii) 1,430 pounds (650 kilograms) for an aircraft intended for operation on water.

(2) A maximum airspeed in level flight with maximum continuous power (V_H) of not more than 120 knots CAS under standard atmospheric conditions at sea level.

(3) A maximum never-exceed speed (V_{NE}) of not more than 120 knots CAS for a glider.

(4) A maximum stalling speed or minimum steady flight speed without the use of lift-enhancing devices (V_{S1}) of not more than 45 knots CAS at the aircraft's maximum certificated takeoff weight and most critical center of gravity.

(5) A maximum seating capacity of no more than two persons, including the pilot.

(6) A single, reciprocating engine, if powered.

(7) A fixed or ground-adjustable propeller if a powered aircraft other than a powered glider.

(8) A fixed or autofeathering propeller system if a powered glider.

(9) A fixed-pitch, semi-rigid, teetering, two-blade rotor system, if a gyroplane.

(10) A nonpressurized cabin, if equipped with a cabin.

(11) Fixed landing gear, except for an aircraft intended for operation on water or a glider.

(12) Fixed or repositionable landing gear, or a hull, for an aircraft intended for operation on water.

(13) Fixed or retractable landing gear for a glider.

Load factor means the ratio of a specified load to the total weight of the aircraft. The specified load is expressed in terms of any of the following: aerodynamic forces, inertia forces, or ground or water reactions.

Long-range communication system (LRCS). A system that uses satellite relay, data link, high frequency, or another approved communication system which extends beyond line of sight.

Long-range navigation system (LRNS). An electronic navigation unit that is approved for use under instrument flight rules as a primary means of navigation, and has at least one source of navigational input, such as inertial navigation system, global positioning system, Omega/very low frequency, or Loran C.

Mach number means the ratio of true airspeed to the speed of sound.

Main rotor means the rotor that supplies the principal lift to a rotorcraft.

Maintenance means inspection, overhaul, repair, preservation, and the replacement of parts, but excludes preventive maintenance.

Major alteration means an alteration not listed in the aircraft, aircraft engine, or propeller specifications—

(1) That might appreciably affect weight, balance, structural strength, performance, powerplant operation, flight characteristics, or other qualities affecting airworthiness; or

(2) That is not done according to accepted practices or cannot be done by elementary operations.

Major repair means a repair:

(1) That, if improperly done, might appreciably affect weight, balance, structural strength, performance, powerplant operation, flight characteristics, or other qualities affecting airworthiness; or

(2) That is not done according to accepted practices or cannot be done by elementary operations.

Manifold pressure means absolute pressure as measured at the appropriate point in the induction system and usually expressed in inches of mercury.

Maximum speed for stability characteristics, V_{FC}/M_{FC} means a speed that may not be less than a speed midway between maximum operating limit speed (V_{MO}/M_{MO}) and demonstrated flight diving speed (V_{DF}/M_{DF}), except that, for altitudes where the Mach number is the limiting factor, M_{FC} need not exceed the Mach number at which effective speed warning occurs.

Medical certificate means acceptable evidence of physical fitness on a form prescribed by the Administrator.

Military operations area. A military operations area (MOA) is airspace established outside Class A airspace to separate or segregate certain nonhazardous military activities from IFR Traffic and to identify for VFR traffic where theses activities are conducted.

Minimum descent altitude means the lowest altitude, expressed in feet above mean sea level, to which descent is authorized on final approach or during circle-to-land maneuvering in execution of a standard instrument approach procedure, where no electronic glide slope is provided.

Minor alteration means an alteration other than a major alteration.

Minor repair means a repair other than a major repair.

Navigable airspace means airspace at and above the minimum flight altitudes prescribed by or under this chapter, including airspace needed for safe takeoff and landing.

Night means the time between the end of evening civil twilight and the beginning of morning civil twilight, as published in the American Air Almanac, converted to local time.

Nonprecision approach procedure means a standard instrument approach procedure in which no electronic glide slope is provided.

Operate, with respect to aircraft, means use, cause to use or authorize to use aircraft, for the purpose (except as provided in § 91.13 of this chapter) of air navigation including the piloting of aircraft, with or without the right of legal control (as owner, lessee, or otherwise).

Operational control, with respect to a flight, means the exercise of authority over initiating, conducting or terminating a flight.

Overseas air commerce means the carriage by aircraft of persons or property for compensation or hire, or the carriage of mail by aircraft, or the operation or navigation of aircraft in the conduct or furtherance of a business or vocation, in commerce between a place in any State of the United States, or the District of Columbia, and any place in a territory or possession of the United States; or between a place in a territory or possession of the United States, and a place in any other territory or possession of the United States.

Overseas air transportation means the carriage by aircraft of persons or property as a common carrier for compensation or hire, or the carriage of mail by aircraft, in commerce:

(1) Between a place in a State or the District of Columbia and a place in a possession of the United States; or

(2) Between a place in a possession of the United States and a place in another possession of the United States; whether that commerce moves wholly by aircraft or partly by aircraft and partly by other forms of transportation.

Over-the-top means above the layer of clouds or other obscuring phenomena forming the ceiling.

Parachute means a device used or intended to be used to retard the fall of a body or object through the air.

Person means an individual, firm, partnership, corporation, company, association, joint-stock association, or governmental entity. It includes a trustee, receiver, assignee, or similar representative of any of them.

Pilotage means navigation by visual reference to landmarks.

Pilot in command means the person who:

(1) Has final authority and responsibility for the operation and safety of the flight;

(2) Has been designated as pilot in command before or during the flight; and

(3) Holds the appropriate category, class, and type rating, if appropriate, for the conduct of the flight.

Pitch setting means the propeller blade setting as determined by the blade angle measured in a manner, and at a radius, specified by the instruction manual for the propeller.

Positive control means control of all air traffic, within designated airspace, by air traffic control.

Powered-lift means a heavier-than-air aircraft capable of vertical takeoff, vertical landing, and low speed flight that depends principally on engine-driven lift devices or engine thrust for lift during these flight regimes and on nonrotating airfoil(s) for lift during horizontal flight.

Powered parachute means a powered aircraft comprised of a flexible or semi-rigid wing connected to a fuselage so that the wing is not in position for flight until the aircraft is in motion. The fuselage of a powered parachute contains the aircraft engine, a seat for each occupant and is attached to the aircraft's landing gear.

Precision approach procedure means a standard instrument approach procedure in which an electronic glide slope is provided, such as ILS and PAR.

Preventive maintenance means simple or minor preservation operations and the replacement of small standard parts not involving complex assembly operations.

Prohibited area. A prohibited area is airspace designated under part 73 within which no person may operate an aircraft without the permission of the using agency.

Propeller means a device for propelling an aircraft that has blades on an engine-driven shaft and that, when rotated, produces by its action on the air, a thrust approximately perpendicular to its plane of rotation. It includes control components normally supplied by its manufacturer, but does not include main and auxiliary rotors or rotating airfoils of engines.

Public aircraft means any of the following aircraft when not being used for a commercial purpose or to carry an individual other than a crewmember or qualified non-crewmember:

(1) An aircraft used only for the United States Government; an aircraft owned by the Government and operated by any person for purposes related to crew training, equipment development, or demonstration; an aircraft owned and operated by the government of a State, the District of Columbia, or a territory or possession of the United States or a political subdivision of one of these governments; or an aircraft exclusively leased for at least 90 continuous days by the government of a State, the District of Columbia, or a territory or possession of the United States or a political subdivision of one of these governments.

(i) For the sole purpose of determining public aircraft status, commercial purposes means the transportation of persons or property for compensation or hire, but does not include the operation of an aircraft by the armed forces for reimbursement when that reimbursement is required by any Federal statute, regulation, or directive, in effect on November 1, 1999, or by one government on behalf of another government under a cost reimbursement agreement if the government on whose behalf the operation is conducted certifies to the Administrator of the Federal Aviation Administration that the operation is necessary to respond to a significant and imminent threat to life or property (including natural resources) and that no service by a private operator is reasonably available to meet the threat.

(ii) For the sole purpose of determining public aircraft status, governmental function means an activity undertaken by a government, such as national defense, intelligence missions, firefighting, search and rescue, law enforcement (including transport of prisoners, detainees, and illegal aliens), aeronautical research, or biological or geological resource management.

(iii) For the sole purpose of determining public aircraft status, qualified non-crewmember means an individual, other than a member of the crew, aboard an aircraft operated by the armed forces or an intelligence agency of the United States Government, or whose presence is required to perform, or is associated with the performance of, a governmental function.

(2) An aircraft owned or operated by the armed forces or chartered to provide transportation to the armed forces if—

(i) The aircraft is operated in accordance with title 10 of the United States Code;

(ii) The aircraft is operated in the performance of a governmental function under title 14, 31, 32, or 50 of the United States Code and the aircraft is not used for commercial purposes; or

(iii) The aircraft is chartered to provide transportation to the armed forces and the Secretary of Defense (or the Secretary of the department in which the Coast Guard is operating) designates the operation of the aircraft as being required in the national interest.

(3) An aircraft owned or operated by the National Guard of a State, the District of Columbia, or any territory or possession of the United States, and that meets the criteria of paragraph (2) of this definition, qualifies as a public aircraft only to the extent that it is operated under the direct control of the Department of Defense.

Rated continuous OEI power, with respect to rotorcraft turbine engines, means the approved brake horsepower developed under static conditions at specified altitudes and temperatures within the operating limitations established for the engine under Part 33 of this chapter, and limited in use to the time required to complete the flight after the failure of one engine of a multiengine rotorcraft.

Rated maximum continuous augmented thrust, with respect to turbojet engine type certification, means the approved jet thrust that is developed statically or in flight, in standard atmosphere at a specified altitude, with fluid injection or with the burning of fuel in a separate combustion chamber, within the engine operating limitations established under Part 33 of this chapter, and approved for unrestricted periods of use.

Rated maximum continuous power, with respect to reciprocating, turbopropeller, and turbo-shaft engines, means the approved brake horsepower that is developed statically or in flight, in standard atmosphere at a specified altitude, within the engine operating limitations established under Part 33, and approved for unrestricted periods of use.

Rated maximum continuous thrust, with respect to turbojet engine type certification, means the approved jet thrust that is developed statically or in flight, in standard atmosphere at a specified altitude, without fluid injection and without the burning of fuel in a separate combustion chamber, within the engine operating limitations established under Part 33 of this chapter, and approved for unrestricted periods of use.

Rated takeoff augmented thrust, with respect to turbojet engine type certification, means the approved jet thrust that is developed statically under standard sea level conditions, with fluid injection or with the burning of fuel in a separate combustion chamber, within the engine operating limitations established under Part 33 of this chapter, and limited in use to periods of not over 5 minutes for takeoff operation.

Rated takeoff power, with respect to reciprocating, turbopropeller, and turboshaft engine type certification, means the approved brake horsepower that is developed statically under standard sea level conditions, within the engine operating limitations established under Part 33, and limited in use to periods of not over 5 minutes for takeoff operation.

Rated takeoff thrust, with respect to turbojet engine type certification, means the approved jet thrust that is developed statically under standard sea level conditions, without fluid injection and without the burning of fuel in a separate combustion chamber, within the engine operating limitations established under Part 33 of this chapter, and limited in use to periods of not over 5 minutes for takeoff operation.

Rated 30-minute OEI power, with respect to rotorcraft turbine engines, means the approved brake horsepower developed under static conditions at specified altitudes and temperatures within the operating limitations established for the engine under Part 33 of this chapter, and limited in use to a period of not more than 30 minutes after the failure of one engine of a multiengine rotorcraft.

Rated 30-second OEI power, with respect to rotorcraft turbine engines, means the approved brake horsepower developed under static conditions at specified altitudes and temperatures within the operating limitations established for the engine under Part 33 of this chapter, for continued one-flight operation after the failure of one engine in multiengine rotorcraft, limited to three periods of use no longer than 30 seconds each in any one flight, and followed by mandatory inspection and prescribed maintenance action.

Rated 2-minute OEI power, with respect to rotorcraft turbine engines, means the approved brake horsepower developed under static conditions at specified altitudes and temperatures within the operating limitations established for the engine under Part 33 of this chapter, for continued one-flight operation after the failure of one engine in multiengine rotorcraft, limited to three periods of use no longer than 2 minutes each in any one flight, and followed by mandatory inspection and prescribed maintenance action.

Rated 2½-minute OEI power, with respect to rotorcraft turbine engines, means the approved brake horsepower developed under static conditions at specified altitudes and temperatures within the operating limitations established for the engine under Part 33 of this chapter, and limited in use to a period of not more than 2½ minutes after the failure of one engine of a multiengine rotorcraft.

Rating means a statement that, as a part of a certificate, sets forth special conditions, privileges, or limitations.

Reference landing speed means the speed of the airplane, in a specified landing configuration, at the point where it descends through the 50 foot height in the determination of the landing distance.

Reporting point means a geographical location in relation to which the position of an aircraft is reported.

Restricted area. A restricted area is airspace designated under Part 73 within which the flight of aircraft, while not wholly prohibited, is subject to restriction.

Rocket means an aircraft propelled by ejected expanding gases generated in the engine from self-contained propellants and not dependent on the intake of outside substances. It includes any part which becomes separated during the operation.

Rotorcraft means a heavier-than-air aircraft that depends principally for its support in flight on the lift generated by one or more rotors.

Rotorcraft-load combination means the combination of a rotorcraft and an external-load, including the external-load attaching means. Rotorcraft-load combinations are designated as Class A, Class B, Class C, and Class D, as follows:

(1) Class A rotorcraft-load combination means one in which the external load cannot move freely, cannot be jettisoned, and does not extend below the landing gear.

(2) Class B rotorcraft-load combination means one in which the external load is jettisonable and is lifted free of land or water during the rotorcraft operation.

(3) Class C rotorcraft-load combination means one in which the external load is jettisonable and remains in contact with land or water during the rotorcraft operation.

(4) Class D rotorcraft-load combination means one in which the external-load is other than a Class A, B, or C and has been specifically approved by the Administrator for that operation.

Route segment is a portion of a route bounded on each end by a fix or navigation aid (NAVAID).

Sea level engine means a reciprocating aircraft engine having a rated takeoff power that is producible only at sea level.

Second in command means a pilot who is designated to be second in command of an aircraft during flight time.

Show, unless the context otherwise requires, means to show to the satisfaction of the Administrator.

Small aircraft means aircraft of 12,500 pounds or less, maximum certificated takeoff weight.

Special VFR conditions mean meteorological conditions that are less than those required for basic VFR flight in controlled airspace and in which some aircraft are permitted flight under visual flight rules.

Special VFR operations means aircraft operating in accordance with clearances within controlled airspace in meteorological conditions less than the basic VFR weather minima. Such operations must be requested by the pilot and approved by ATC.

Standard atmosphere means the atmosphere defined in U.S. Standard Atmosphere, 1962 (Geopotential altitude tables).

Stopway means an area beyond the takeoff runway, no less wide than the runway and centered upon the extended centerline of the runway, able to support the airplane during an aborted takeoff, without causing structural damage to the airplane, and designated by the airport authorities for use in decelerating the airplane during an aborted takeoff.

Synthetic vision means a computer-generated image of the external scene topography from the perspective of the flight deck that is derived from aircraft attitude, high-precision navigation solution, and database of terrain, obstacles and relevant cultural features.

Synthetic vision system means an electronic means to display a synthetic vision image of the external scene topography to the flight crew.

Takeoff power:

(1) With respect to reciprocating engines, means the brake horsepower that is developed under standard sea level conditions, and under the maximum conditions of crankshaft rotational speed and engine manifold pressure approved for the normal takeoff, and limited in continuous use to the period of time shown in the approved engine specification; and

(2) With respect to turbine engines, means the brake horsepower that is developed under static conditions at a specified altitude and atmospheric temperature, and under the maximum conditions of rotor shaft rotational speed and gas temperature approved for the normal takeoff, and limited

in continuous use to the period of time shown in the approved engine specification.

Takeoff safety speed means a referenced airspeed obtained after lift-off at which the required one-engine-inoperative climb performance can be achieved.

Takeoff thrust, with respect to turbine engines, means the jet thrust that is developed under static conditions at a specific altitude and atmospheric temperature under the maximum conditions of rotorshaft rotational speed and gas temperature approved for the normal takeoff, and limited in continuous use to the period of time shown in the approved engine specification.

Tandem wing configuration means a configuration having two wings of similar span, mounted in tandem.

TCAS I means a TCAS that utilizes interrogations of, and replies from, airborne radar beacon transponders and provides traffic advisories to the pilot.

TCAS II means a TCAS that utilizes interrogations of, and replies from airborne radar beacon transponders and provides traffic advisories and resolution advisories in the vertical plane.

TCAS III means a TCAS that utilizes interrogation of, and replies from, airborne radar beacon transponders and provides traffic advisories and resolution advisories in the vertical and horizontal planes to the pilot.

Time in service, with respect to maintenance time records, means the time from the moment an aircraft leaves the surface of the earth until it touches it at the next point of landing.

True airspeed means the airspeed of an aircraft relative to undisturbed air. True airspeed is equal to equivalent airspeed multiplied by $(\rho 0/\rho)^{1/2}$.

Traffic pattern means the traffic flow that is prescribed for aircraft landing at, taxiing on, or taking off from, an airport.

Type:

(1) As used with respect to the certification, ratings, privileges, and limitations of airmen, means a specific make and basic model of aircraft, including modifications thereto that do not change its handling or flight characteristics. Examples include: DC-7, 1049, and F-27; and

(2) As used with respect to the certification of aircraft, means those aircraft which are similar in design. Examples include: DC-7 and DC-7C; 1049G and 1049H; and F-27 and F-27F.

(3) As used with respect to the certification of aircraft engines means those engines which are similar in design. For example, JT8D and JT8D-7 are engines of the same type, and JT9D-3A and JT9D-7 are engines of the same type.

United States, in a geographical sense, means (1) the States, the District of Columbia, Puerto Rico, and the possessions, including the territorial waters, and (2) the airspace of those areas.

United States air carrier means a citizen of the United States who undertakes directly by lease, or other arrangement, to engage in air transportation.

VFR over-the-top, with respect to the operation of aircraft, means the operation of an aircraft over-the-top under VFR when it is not being operated on an IFR flight plan.

Warning area. A warning area is airspace of defined dimensions, extending from 3 nautical miles outward from the coast of the United States, that contains activity that may be hazardous to nonparticipating aircraft. The purpose of such warning areas is to warn nonparticipating pilots of the potential danger. A warning area may be located over domestic or international waters or both.

Weight-shift-control aircraft means a powered aircraft with a framed pivoting wing and a fuselage controllable only in pitch and roll by the pilot's ability to change the aircraft's center of gravity with respect to the wing. Flight control of the aircraft depends on the wing's ability to flexibly deform rather than the use of control surfaces.

Winglet or tip fin means an out-of-plane surface extending from a lifting surface. The surface may or may not have control surfaces.

[Docket No. 1150, 27 FR 4588, May 15, 1962; as amended by Amdt. 1–39, 60 FR 5075, Jan. 25, 1995; Amdt. No. 1–40, 60 FR 30749, June 9, 1995; Amdt. No. 1–42, 61 FR 2081, Jan. 24, 1996; Amdt. No. 1–43, 61 FR 5183, Feb. 9, 1996; Amdt. No. 1–44, 61 FR 7190, Feb. 26, 1996; Amdt. 1–46, 61 FR 31328, June 19, 1996; Amdt. 1–45, 61 FR 34547, July 2, 1996; Amdt. 1–47, 62 FR 16298, April 4, 1997; Amdt. 1–49, 67 FR 70825, Nov. 26, 2002; Amdt. 1–50, 68 FR 16947, April 8, 2003; Amdt. 1–51, 68 FR 25487, May 13, 2003; Amdt. 1–52, 69 FR 1639, Jan. 9, 2004; Amdt. 1–53, 69 FR 44861, July 27, 2004]

§1.2 Abbreviations and symbols.

In Subchapters A through K of this chapter:

"AGL" means above ground level.
"ALS" means approach light system.
"ASR" means airport surveillance radar.
"ATC" means air traffic control.
"CAS" means calibrated airspeed.
"CAT II" means Category II.
"CONSOL or CONSOLAN" means a kind of low or medium frequency long range navigational aid.
"DH" means decision height.
"DME" means distance measuring equipment compatible with TACAN.
"EAS" means equivalent airspeed.
"EFVS" means enhanced flight vision system.
"FAA" means Federal Aviation Administration.
"FM" means fan marker.
"GS" means glide slope.
"HIRL" means high-intensity runway light system.
"IAS" means indicated airspeed.
"ICAO" means International Civil Aviation Organization.
"IFR" means instrument flight rules.
"ILS" means instrument landing system.
"IM" means ILS inner marker.
"INT" means intersection.
"LDA" means localizer-type directional aid.
"LFR" means low-frequency radio range.
"LMM" means compass locator at middle marker.
"LOC" means ILS localizer.
"LOM" means compass locator at outer marker.
"M" means mach number.
"MAA" means maximum authorized IFR altitude.
"MALS" means medium intensity approach light system.
"MALSR" means medium intensity approach light system with runway alignment indicator lights.
"MCA" means minimum crossing altitude.
"MDA" means minimum descent altitude.
"MEA" means minimum en route IFR altitude.
"MM" means ILS middle marker.

"MOCA" means minimum obstruction clearance altitude.
"MRA" means minimum reception altitude.
"MSL" means mean sea level.
"NDB (ADF)" means nondirectional beacon (automatic direction finder).
"NOPT" means no procedure turn required.
"OEI" means one engine inoperative.
"OM" means ILS outer marker.
"PAR" means precision approach radar.
"RAIL" means runway alignment indicator light system.
"RBN" means radio beacon.
"RCLM" means runway centerline marking.
"RCLS" means runway centerline light system.
"REIL" means runway end identification lights.
"RR" means low or medium frequency radio range station.
"RVR" means runway visual range as measured in the touchdown zone area.
"SALS" means short approach light system.
"SSALS" means simplified short approach light system.
"SSALSR" means simplified short approach light system with runway alignment indicator lights.
"TACAN" means ultra-high frequency tactical air navigational aid.
"TAS" means true airspeed.
"TCAS" means a traffic alert and collision avoidance system.
"TDZL" means touchdown zone lights.
"TVOR" means very high frequency terminal omnirange station.
V_A means design maneuvering speed.
V_B means design speed for maximum gust intensity.
V_C means design cruising speed.
V_D means design diving speed.
V_{DF}/M_{DF} means demonstrated flight diving speed.
V_{EF} means the speed at which the critical engine is assumed to fail during takeoff.
V_F means design flap speed.
V_{FC}/M_{FC} means maximum speed for stability characteristics.
V_{FE} means maximum flap extended speed.
V_{FTO} means final takeoff speed.
V_H means maximum speed in level flight with maximum continuous power.
V_{LE} means maximum landing gear extended speed.
V_{LO} means maximum landing gear operating speed.
V_{LOF} means lift-off speed.
V_{MC} means minimum control speed with the critical engine inoperative.
V_{MO}/M_{MO} means maximum operating limit speed.
V_{MU} means minimum unstick speed.
V_{NE} means never-exceed speed.
V_{NO} means maximum structural cruising speed.
V_R means rotation speed.
V_{REF} means reference landing speed.
V_S means the stalling speed or the minimum steady flight speed at which the airplane is controllable.
V_{S0} means the stalling speed or the minimum steady flight speed in the landing configuration.
V_{S1} means the stalling speed or the minimum steady flight speed obtained in a specific configuration.
V_{SR} means reference stall speed.
V_{SR0} means reference stall speed in the landing configuration.
V_{SR1} means reference stall speed in a specific configuration.
V_{SW} means speed at which onset of natural or artificial stall warning occurs.
V_{TOSS} means takeoff safety speed for Category A rotorcraft.
V_X means speed for best angle of climb.
V_Y means speed for best rate of climb.
V_1 means the maximum speed in the takeoff at which the pilot must take the first action (e.g., apply brakes, reduce thrust, deploy speed brakes) to stop the airplane within the accelerate-stop distance. V_1 also means the minimum speed in the takeoff, following a failure of the critical engine at V_{EF}, at which the pilot can continue the takeoff and achieve the required height above the takeoff surface within the takeoff distance.
V_2 means takeoff safety speed.
V_{2min} means minimum takeoff safety speed.
"VFR" means visual flight rules.
"VHF" means very high frequency.
"VOR" means very high frequency omnirange station.
"VORTAC" means collocated VOR and TACAN.

[Docket No. 1150, 27 FR 4590, May 15, 1962; as amended by Amdt. 1–48, 63 FR 8318, Feb. 18, 1998; Amdt. 1–49, 67 FR 70825, Nov. 26, 2002; Amdt. 1–52, 69 FR 1639, Jan. 9, 2004]

§1.3 Rules of construction.

(a) In Subchapters A through K of this chapter, unless the context requires otherwise:

(1) Words importing the singular include the plural;

(2) Words importing the plural include the singular; and

(3) Words importing the masculine gender include the feminine.

(b) In Subchapters A through K of this chapter, the word:

(1) "Shall" is used in an imperative sense;

(2) "May" is used in a permissive sense to state authority or permission to do the act prescribed, and the words "no person may * * *" or "a person may not * * *" mean that no person is required, authorized, or permitted to do the act prescribed; and

(3) "Includes" means "includes but is not limited to."

[Docket No. 1150, 27 FR 4590, May 15, 1962, as amended by Amdt. 1–10, 31 FR 5055, March 29, 1966]

PART 13
INVESTIGATIVE AND ENFORCEMENT PROCEDURES

SPECIAL FEDERAL AVIATION REGULATION

SFAR No. 72

Subpart A — Investigative Procedures

Sec.
13.1 Reports of violations.
13.3 Investigations (general).
13.5 Formal complaints.
13.7 Records, documents and reports.

Subpart B — Administrative Actions

13.11 Administrative disposition of certain violations.

Subpart C — Legal Enforcement Actions

13.13 Consent orders.
***13.14 Civil penalties: General.**
***13.15 Civil penalties: Other than by administrative assessment.**
***13.16 Civil penalties: Administrative assessment against a person other than an individual acting as a pilot, flight engineer, mechanic, or repairman. Administrative assessment against all persons for hazardous materials violations.**
13.17 Seizure of aircraft.
***13.18 Civil penalties: Administrative assessment against an individual acting as a pilot, flight engineer, mechanic, or repairman.**
13.19 Certificate action.
13.20 Orders of compliance, cease and desist orders, orders of denial, and other orders.
13.21 Military personnel.
13.23 Criminal penalties.
13.25 Injunctions.
13.27 Final order of Hearing Officer in certificate of aircraft registration proceedings.
13.29 Civil penalties: Streamlined enforcement procedures for certain security violations.

Subpart D — Rules of Practice for FAA Hearings

13.31 Applicability.
13.33 Appearances.
13.35 Request for hearing.
13.37 Hearing Officer's powers.
13.39 Disqualification of Hearing Officer.
13.41 [Reserved]
13.43 Service and filing of pleadings, motions, and documents.
13.44 Computation of time and extension of time.
13.45 Amendment of notice and answer.
13.47 Withdrawal of notice or request for hearing.
13.49 Motions.
13.51 Intervention.
13.53 Depositions.
13.55 Notice of hearing.
13.57 Subpoenas and witness fees.
13.59 Evidence.
13.61 Argument and submittals.
13.63 Record.

Subpart E — Orders of Compliance Under the Hazardous Materials Transportation Act

13.71 Applicability.
13.73 Notice of proposed order of compliance.
13.75 Reply or request for hearing.
13.77 Consent order of compliance.
13.79 Hearing.
13.81 Order of immediate compliance.
13.83 Appeal.
13.85 Filing, service, and computation of time.
13.87 Extension of time.

Subpart F — Formal Fact-Finding Investigation Under an Order of Investigation

13.101 Applicability.
13.103 Order of investigation.
13.105 Notification.
13.107 Designation of additional parties.
13.109 Convening the investigation.
13.111 Subpoenas.
13.113 Noncompliance with the investigative process.
13.115 Public proceedings.
13.117 Conduct of investigative proceeding or deposition.
13.119 Rights of persons against self-incrimination.
13.121 Witness fees.
13.123 Submission by party to the investigation.
13.125 Depositions.
13.127 Reports, decisions and orders.
13.129 Post-investigation action.
13.131 Other procedures.

Subpart G — Rules of Practice in FAA Civil Penalty Actions

***13.201 Applicability.**
***13.202 Definitions.**
***13.203 Separation of functions.**
13.204 Appearances and rights of parties.
13.205 Administrative law judges.
13.206 Intervention.
13.207 Certification of documents.
13.208 Complaint.
***13.209 Answer.**
***13.210 Filing of documents.**
13.211 Service of documents.
13.212 Computation of time.
13.213 Extension of time.
13.214 Amendment of pleadings.
13.215 Withdrawal of complaint or request for a hearing.
13.216 Waivers.
13.217 Joint procedural or discovery schedule.
13.218 Motions.
13.219 Interlocutory appeals.
13.220 Discovery.
13.221 Notice of hearing.
13.222 Evidence.
13.223 Standard of proof.
13.224 Burden of proof.

13.225 Offer of proof.
13.226 Public disclosure of evidence.
13.227 Expert or opinion witnesses.
13.228 Subpoenas.
13.229 Witness fees.
***13.230 Record.**
13.231 Argument before the administrative law judge.
13.232 Initial decision.
***13.233 Appeal from initial decision.**
13.234 Petition to reconsider or modify a final decision and order of the FAA decisionmaker on appeal.
13.235 Judicial review of final decision and order.

Subpart H— Civil Monetary Penalty Inflation Adjustment

13.301 Scope and purpose.
13.303 Definitions.
13.305 Cost of Living Adjustments of Civil Monetary Penalties.

Subpart I— Flight Operational Quality Assurance Programs

13.401 Flight operational quality assurance program: prohibition against use of data for enforcement purposes.

Authority: 18 U.S.C. 6002; 28 U.S.C. 2461 (note); 49 U.S.C. 106(g), 5121–5124, 40113–40114, 44103–44106, 44702–44703, 44709–44710, 44713, 46101–46110, 46301–46316, 46318, 46501–46502, 46504–46507, 47106, 47111, 47122, 47306, 47531–47532; 49 CFR 1.47.

Source: Docket No. 18884, 44 FR 63723, Nov. 5, 1979, unless otherwise noted.

SFAR No. 72 to Part 13

Civil Penalties: Streamlined Enforcement Test and Evaluation Program

This FAR may be used, at the agency's discretion, in enforcement actions involving individuals presenting dangerous or deadly weapons for screening at airports or in checked baggage where the amount of the proposed civil penalty is less than $5,000. In these cases, §§13.16(a), 13.16(c), and 13.16(f) through (l) of this chapter are used, as well as sections (A) through (D) below:

(A) *Delegation of authority.* The authority of the Administrator, under section 901 of the Federal Aviation Act of 1958, as amended, to initiate the assessment of civil penalties for a violation of the Act, or a rule, regulation, or order issued thereunder, is delegated to the regional Office of Civil Aviation Security Division Manager and the regional Office of Civil Aviation Security Deputy Division Manager for the purpose of issuing notices of violation in cases involving violations of the Federal Aviation Act and the FAA's regulations by individuals presenting dangerous or deadly weapons for screening at airport checkpoints or in checked baggage. This authority may not be delegated below the level of the Office of Civil Aviation Security Deputy Division Manager.

(B) *Notice of violation.* A civil penalty action is initiated by sending a notice of violation to the person charged with the violation. The notice of violation contains a statement of the charges and the amount of the proposed civil penalty. Not later than 30 days after receipt of the notice of violation, the person charged with a violation shall:

(1) Submit the amount of the proposed civil penalty or an agreed-upon amount, in which case either an order assessing a civil penalty or a compromise order shall be issued in that amount;

(2) Submit to the regional Office of the Assistant Chief Counsel any of the following:

(i) Written information, including documents and witness statements, demonstrating that a violation of the regulations did not occur or that a penalty or the penalty amount is not warranted by the circumstances;

(ii) A written request to reduce the proposed civil penalty, the amount of reduction, and the reasons and any documents supporting a reduction of the proposed civil penalty, including records indicating a financial inability to pay or records showing that payment of the proposed civil penalty would prevent the person from continuing in business; or

(iii) A written request for an informal conference to discuss the matter with an agency attorney and submit relevant information or documents; or

(3) Request a hearing in which case a complaint shall be filed with the hearing docket clerk.

(C) *Final notice of violation and civil penalty assessment order.* A final notice of violation and civil penalty assessment order ("final notice and order") may be issued after participation in any informal proceedings as provided in paragraph (B)(2) of this section, or after failure of the respondent to respond in a timely manner to a notice of violation. A final notice and order will be sent to the individual charged with a violation. The final notice and order will contain a statement of the charges and the amount of the proposed civil penalty and, as a result of information submitted to the agency attorney during any informal procedures, may modify an allegation or a proposed civil penalty contained in the notice of violation.

A final notice and order may be issued—

(1) If the person charged with a violation fails to respond to the notice of violation within 30 days after receipt of that notice; or

(2) If the parties participated in any informal procedures under paragraph (B)(2) of this section and the parties have not agreed to compromise the action or the agency attorney has not agreed to withdraw the notice of violation.

(D) *Order assessing civil penalty.* An order assessing civil penalty may be issued after notice and opportunity for a hearing. A person charged with a violation may be subject to an order assessing civil penalty in the following circumstances:

(1) An order assessing civil penalty may be issued if a person charged with a violation submits, or agrees to submit, the amount of civil penalty proposed in the notice of violation.

(2) An order assessing civil penalty may be issued if a person charged with a violation submits, or agrees to submit, an agreed-upon amount of civil penalty that is not reflected in either the notice of violation or the final notice and order.

(3) The final notice and order becomes (and contains a statement so indicating) an order assessing a civil penalty when the person charged with a violation submits the

amount of the proposed civil penalty that is reflected in the final notice and order.

(4) The final notice and order becomes (and contains a statement so indicating) an order assessing a civil penalty 16 days after receipt of the final notice and order, unless not later than 15 days after receipt of the final notice and order, the person charged with a violation does one of the following—

(i) Submits an agreed-upon amount of civil penalty that is not reflected in the final notice and order, in which case an order assessing civil penalty or a compromise order shall be issued in that amount; or

(ii) Requests a hearing in which case a complaint shall be filed with the hearing docket clerk.

(5) Unless an appeal is filed with the FAA decisionmaker in a timely manner, an initial decision or order of an administrative law judge shall be considered an order assessing civil penalty if an administrative law judge finds that an alleged violation occurred and determines that a civil penalty, in an amount found to be appropriate by the administrative law judge, is warranted.

(6) Unless a petition for review is filed with a U.S. Court of Appeals in a timely manner, a final decision and order of the Administrator shall be considered an order assessing civil penalty if the FAA decisionmaker finds that an alleged violation occurred and a civil penalty is warranted.

[Docket No. 27873, 59 FR 44269, Aug. 26, 1994]

Subpart A — Investigative Procedures

§13.1 Reports of violations.

(a) Any person who knows of a violation of the Federal Aviation Act of 1958, as amended, the Hazardous Materials Transportation Act relating to the transportation or shipment by air of hazardous materials, the Airport and Airway Development Act of 1970, the Airport and Airway Improvement Act of 1982, the Airport and Airway Improvement Act of 1982 as amended by the Airport and Airway Safety and Capacity Expansion Act of 1987, or any rule, regulation, or order issued thereunder, should report it to appropriate personnel of any FAA regional or district office.

(b) Each report made under this section, together with any other information the FAA may have that is relevant to the matter reported, will be reviewed by FAA personnel to determine the nature and type of any additional investigation or enforcement action the FAA will take.

[Docket No. 18884, 44 FR 63723, Nov. 5, 1979; as amended by Amdt. 13–17, 53 FR 33783, Aug. 31, 1988]

§13.3 Investigations (general).

(a) Under the Federal Aviation Act of 1958, as amended, (49 U.S.C. 1301 *et seq.*), the Hazardous Materials Transportation Act (49 U.S.C. 1801 *et seq.*), the Airport and Airway Development Act of 1970 (49 U.S.C. 1701 *et seq.*), the Airport and Airway Improvement Act of 1982 (49 U.S.C. 2201 *et seq.*), the Airport and Airway Improvement Act of 1982 (as amended, 49 U.S.C. App. 2201 *et seq.*, Airport and Airway Safety and Capacity Expansion Act of 1987), and the Regulations of the Office of the Secretary of Transportation (49 CFR 1 *et seq.*), the Administrator may conduct investigations, hold hearings, issue subpoenas, require the production of relevant documents, records, and property, and take evidence and depositions.

(b) For the purpose of investigating alleged violations of the Federal Aviation Act of 1958, as amended the Hazardous Materials Transportation Act, the Airport and Airway Development Act of 1970, the Airport and Airway Improvement Act of 1982, the Airport and Airway Improvement Act of 1982 as amended by the Airport and Airway Safety and Capacity Expansion Act of 1987, or any rule, regulation, or order issued thereunder, the Administrator's authority has been delegated to the various services and or offices for matters within their respective areas for all routine investigations. When the compulsory processes of sections 313 and 1004 (49 U.S.C. 1354 and 1484) of the Federal Aviation Act, or section 109 of the Hazardous Materials Transportation Act (49 U.S.C. 1808) are invoked, the Administrator's authority has been delegated to the Chief Counsel, the Deputy Chief Counsel, each Assistant Chief Counsel, each Regional Counsel, the Aeronautical Center Counsel, and the Technical Center Counsel.

(c) In conducting formal investigations, the Chief Counsel, the Deputy Chief Counsel, each Assistant Chief Counsel, each Regional Counsel, the Aeronautical Center Counsel, and the Technical Center Counsel may issue an order of investigation in accordance with Subpart F of this part.

(d) A complaint against the sponsor, proprietor, or operator of a Federally-assisted airport involving violations of the legal authorities listed in §16.1 of this chapter shall be filed in accordance with the provisions of part 16 of this chapter, except in the case of complaints, investigations, and proceedings initiated before December 16, 1996, the effective date of part 16 of this chapter.

[Docket No. 18884, 44 FR 63723, Nov. 5, 1979; as amended by Amdt. 13–17, 53 FR 33783, Aug. 31, 1988; 53 FR 35255, Sept. 12, 1988; Amdt. 13–19, 54 FR 39290, Sept. 25, 1989; Amdt. 13–27, 61 FR 54004, Oct. 16, 1996; Amdt. 13–29, 62 FR 46865, Sept. 4, 1997]

§13.5 Formal complaints.

(a) Any person may file a complaint with the Administrator with respect to anything done or omitted to be done by any person in contravention of any provision of any Act or of any regulation or order issued under it, as to matters within the jurisdiction of the Administrator. This section does not apply to complaints against the Administrator or employees of the FAA acting within the scope of their employment.

(b) Complaints filed under this section must—

(1) Be submitted in writing and identified as a complaint filed for the purpose of seeking an appropriate order or other enforcement action;

(2) Be submitted to the Federal Aviation Administration, Office of the Chief Counsel, Attention: Enforcement Docket (AGC-10), 800 Independence Avenue S.W., Washington, D.C. 20591;

(3) Set forth the name and address, if known, of each person who is the subject of the complaint and, with respect to each person, the specific provisions of the Act or regulation or order that the complainant believes were violated;

(4) Contain a concise but complete statement of the facts relied upon to substantiate each allegation;

(5) State the name, address and telephone number of the person filing the complaint; and

(6) Be signed by the person filing the complaint or a duly authorized representative.

(c) Complaints which do not meet the requirements of paragraph (b) of this section will be considered reports under §13.1.

(d) Complaints which meet the requirements of paragraph (b) of this section will be docketed and a copy mailed to each person named in the complaint.

(e) Any complaint filed against a member of the Armed Forces of the United States acting in the performance of official duties shall be referred to the Secretary of the Department concerned for action in accordance with the procedures set forth in §13.21 of this part.

(f) The person named in the complaint shall file an answer within 20 days after service of a copy of the complaint.

(g) After the complaint has been answered or after the allotted time in which to file an answer has expired, the Administrator shall determine if there are reasonable grounds for investigating the complaint.

(h) If the Administrator determines that a complaint does not state facts which warrant an investigation or action, the complaint may be dismissed without a hearing and the reason for the dismissal shall be given, in writing, to the person who filed the complaint and the person named in the complaint.

(i) If the Administrator determines that reasonable grounds exist, an informal investigation may be initiated or an order of investigation may be issued in accordance with Subpart F of this part, or both. Each person named in the complaint shall be advised which official has been delegated the responsibility under §13.3(b) or (c) for conducting the investigation.

(j) If the investigation substantiates the allegations set forth in the complaint, a notice of proposed order may be issued or other enforcement action taken in accordance with this part.

(k) The complaint and other pleadings and official FAA records relating to the disposition of the complaint are maintained in current docket form in the Enforcement Docket (AGC-10), Office of the Chief Counsel, Federal Aviation Administration, 800 Independence Avenue SW, Washington, DC 20591. Any interested person may examine any docketed material at that office, at any time after the docket is established, except material that is ordered withheld from the public under applicable law or regulations, and may obtain a photostatic or duplicate copy upon paying the cost of the copy.

(Secs. 313(a), 314(a), 601 through 610, and 1102 of the Federal Aviation Act of 1958 (49 U.S.C. 1354(a), 1421 through 1430, 1502); sec. 6(c), Dept. of Transportation Act (49 U.S.C. 1655(c)))

[Docket No 13–14, 44 FR 63723, Nov. 5, 1979; as amended by Amdt. 13–16, 45 FR 35307, May 27, 1980; Amdt. 13–19, 54 FR 39290, Sept. 25, 1989]

§13.7 Records, documents and reports.

Each record, document and report that the Federal Aviation Regulations require to be maintained, exhibited or submitted to the Administrator may be used in any investigation conducted by the Administrator; and, except to the extent the use may be specifically limited or prohibited by the section which imposes the requirement, the records, documents and reports may be used in any civil penalty action, certificate action, or other legal proceeding.

Subpart B— Administrative Actions

§13.11 Administrative disposition of certain violations.

(a) If it is determined that a violation or an alleged violation of the Federal Aviation Act of 1958, or an order or regulation issued under it, or of the Hazardous Materials Transportation Act, or an order or regulation issued under it, does not require legal enforcement action, an appropriate official of the FAA field office responsible for processing the enforcement case or other appropriate FAA official may take administrative action in disposition of the case.

(b) An administrative action under this section does not constitute a formal adjudication of the matter, and may be taken by issuing the alleged violator—

(1) A "Warning Notice" which recites available facts and information about the incident or condition and indicates that it may have been a violation; or

(2) A "Letter of Correction" which confirms the FAA decision in the matter and states the necessary corrective action the alleged violator has taken or agrees to take. If the agreed corrective action is not fully completed, legal enforcement action may be taken.

Subpart C— Legal Enforcement Actions

§13.13 Consent orders.

(a) At any time before the issuance of an order under this subpart, the official who issued the notice and the person subject to the notice may agree to dispose of the case by the issuance of a consent order by the official.

(b) A proposal for a consent order, submitted to the official who issued the notice, under this section must include—

(1) A proposed order;

(2) An admission of all jurisdictional facts;

(3) An express waiver of the right to further procedural steps and of all rights to judicial review; and

(4) An incorporation by reference of the notice and an acknowledgment that the notice may be used to construe the terms of the order.

(c) If the issuance of a consent order has been agreed upon after the filing of a request for hearing in accordance with Subpart D of this part, the proposal for a consent order shall include a request to be filed with the Hearing Officer withdrawing the request for a hearing and requesting that the case be dismissed.

§13.14 Civil penalties: General.

(a) Any person who violates any of the following statutory provisions, or any rule, regulation, or order issued thereunder, is subject to a civil penalty of not more than the amount specified in 49 U.S.C. chapter 463 for each violation:

(1) Chapter 401 (except sections 40103(a) and (d), 40105, 40116, and 40117);

(2) Chapter 441 (except section 44109);

(3) Section 44502(b) or (c);

(4) Chapter 447 (except sections 44717 and 44719–44723);

(5) Chapter 451;

(6) Sections 46301(b), 46302, 46303, 46318, or 46319; or

(7) Sections 47528 through 47530.

(b) Any person who knowingly commits an act in violation of 49 U.S.C. chapter 51 or a regulation prescribed or order issued under that chapter, is subject to a civil penalty under 49 U.S.C. 5123.

(c) The minimum and maximum amounts of civil penalties for violations of the statutory provisions specified in paragraphs (a) and (b) of this section, or rules, regulations, or orders issued thereunder, are periodically adjusted for inflation in accordance with the formula established in 28 U.S.C. 2461 note and implemented in 14 CFR part 13, subpart H.

[Docket No. 27854, 69 FR 59495, Oct. 4, 2004; as amended by Amdt. 13–32, 70 FR 1813, Jan. 11, 2005]

§13.15 Civil penalties: Other than by administrative assessment.

(a) The FAA uses the procedures in this section when it seeks a civil penalty other than by the administrative assessment procedures in §§13.16 or 13.18.

(b) The authority of the Administrator, under 49 U.S.C. chapter 463, to seek a civil penalty for a violation cited in §§13.14(a), and the ability to refer cases to the United States Attorney General, or the delegate of the Attorney General, for prosecution of civil penalty actions sought by the Administrator is delegated to the Chief Counsel; the Deputy Chief Counsel for Operations; the Assistant Chief Counsel for Enforcement; the Assistant Chief Counsel, Europe, Africa, and Middle East Area Office; the Regional Counsel; the Aeronautical Center Counsel; and the Technical Center Counsel. This delegation applies to cases involving:

(1) An amount in controversy in excess of:

(i) $50,000, if the violation was committed by any person before December 12, 2003;

(ii) $400,000, if the violation was committed by a person other than an individual or small business concern on or after December 12, 2003;

(iii) $50,000, if the violation was committed by an individual or small business concern on or after December 12, 2003; or

(2) An in rem action, seizure of aircraft subject to lien, suit for injunctive relief, or for collection of an assessed civil penalty.

(c) The Administrator may compromise any civil penalty proposed under this section, before referral to the United States Attorney General, or the delegate of the Attorney General, for prosecution.

(1) The Administrator, through the Chief Counsel; the Deputy Chief Counsel for Operations; the Assistant Chief Counsel for Enforcement; the Assistant Chief Counsel, Europe, Africa, and Middle East Area Office; the Regional Counsel; the Aeronautical Center Counsel; or the Technical Center Counsel sends a civil penalty letter to the person charged with a violation cited in §§13.14(a). The civil penalty letter contains a statement of the charges, the applicable law, rule, regulation, or order, the amount of civil penalty that the Administrator will accept in full settlement of the action or an offer to compromise the civil penalty.

(2) Not later than 30 days after receipt of the civil penalty letter, the person charged with a violation may present any material or information in answer to the charges to the agency attorney, either orally or in writing, that may explain, mitigate, or deny the violation or that may show extenuating circumstances. The Administrator will consider any material or information submitted in accordance with this paragraph to determine whether the person is subject to a civil penalty or to determine the amount for which the Administrator will compromise the action.

(3) If the person charged with the violation offers to compromise for a specific amount, that person must send to the agency attorney a certified check or money order for that amount, payable to the Federal Aviation Administration. The Chief Counsel; the Deputy Chief Counsel for Operations; the Assistant Chief Counsel for Enforcement; the Assistant Chief Counsel, Europe, Africa, and Middle East Area Office; the Regional Counsel; Aeronautical Center Counsel; or the Technical Center Counsel may accept the certified check or money order or may refuse and return the certified check or money order.

(4) If the offer to compromise is accepted by the Administrator, the agency attorney will send a letter to the person charged with the violation stating that the certified check or money order is accepted in full settlement of the civil penalty action.

(5) If the parties cannot agree to compromise the civil penalty action or the offer to compromise is rejected and the certified check or money order submitted in compromise is returned, the Administrator may refer the civil penalty action to the United States Attorney General, or the delegate of the Attorney General, to begin proceedings in a United States district court, pursuant to the authority in 49 U.S.C. 46305, to prosecute and collect the civil penalty.

[Docket No. 18884, 44 FR 63723, Nov. 5, 1979; as amended by Amdt. 13–18, 53 FR 34653, Sept. 7, 1988; Amdt. 13–20, 55 FR 15128, April 20, 1990; Amdt. 13–29, 62 FR 46865, Sept. 4, 1997; Amdt. 13–32, 69 FR 59495, Oct. 4, 2004]

§13.16 Civil Penalties: Administrative assessment against a person other than an individual acting as a pilot, flight engineer, mechanic, or repairman. Administrative assessment against all persons for hazardous materials violations.

(a) The FAA uses these procedures when it assesses a civil penalty against a person other than an individual acting as a pilot, flight engineer, mechanic, or repairman for a violation cited in 49 U.S.C. 46301(d)(2) or 47531.

(b) ***District court jurisdiction.*** Notwithstanding the provisions of paragraph (a) of this section, the United States district courts have exclusive jurisdiction of any civil penalty action initiated by the FAA for violations described in those paragraphs, under 49 U.S.C. 46301(d)(4), if—

(1) The amount in controversy is more than $50,000 for a violation committed by any person before December 12, 2003;

(2) The amount in controversy is more than $400,000 for a violation committed by a person other than an individual or small business concern on or after December 12, 2003;

(3) The amount in controversy is more than $50,000 for a violation committed by an individual or a small business concern on or after December 12, 2003;

(4) The action is in rem or another action in rem based on the same violation has been brought;

(5) The action involves an aircraft subject to a lien that has been seized by the Government; or

(6) Another action has been brought for an injunction based on the same violation.

(c) *Hazardous materials violations.* The FAA may assess a civil penalty against any person who knowingly commits an act in violation of 49 U.S.C. chapter 51 or a regulation prescribed or order issued under that chapter, under 49 U.S.C. 5123 and 49 CFR 1.47(k). An order assessing a civil penalty for a violation under 49 U.S.C. chapter 51, or a rule, regulation, or order issued thereunder, is issued only after the following factors have been considered:

(1) The nature, circumstances, extent, and gravity of the violation;

(2) With respect to the violator, the degree of culpability, any history of prior violations, the ability to pay, and any effect on the ability to continue to do business; and

(3) Such other matters as justice may require.

(d) *Order assessing civil penalty.* An order assessing civil penalty may be issued for a violation described in paragraphs (a) or (c) of this section, or as otherwise provided by statute, after notice and opportunity for a hearing. A person charged with a violation may be subject to an order assessing civil penalty in the following circumstances:

(1) An order assessing civil penalty may be issued if a person charged with a violation submits or agrees to submit a civil penalty for a violation.

(2) An order assessing civil penalty may be issued if a person charged with a violation does not request a hearing under paragraph (g)(2)(ii) of this section within 15 days after receipt of a final notice of proposed civil penalty.

(3) Unless an appeal is filed with the FAA decisionmaker in a timely manner, an initial decision or order of an administrative law judge shall be considered an order assessing civil penalty if an administrative law judge finds that an alleged violation occurred and determines that a civil penalty, in an amount found appropriate by the administrative law judge, is warranted.

(4) Unless a petition for review is filed with a U.S. Court of Appeals in a timely manner, a final decision and order of the Administrator shall be considered an order assessing civil penalty if the FAA decisionmaker finds that an alleged violation occurred and a civil penalty is warranted.

(e) *Delegation of authority.*

(1) The authority of the Administrator under 49 U.S.C. 46301(d), 47531, and 5123, and 49 CFR 1.47(k) to initiate and assess civil penalties for a violation of those statutes or a rule, regulation, or order issued thereunder, is delegated to the Deputy Chief Counsel for Operations; the Assistant Chief Counsel for Enforcement; the Assistant Chief Counsel, Europe, Africa, and Middle East Area Office; the Regional Counsel; the Aeronautical Center Counsel; and the Technical Center Counsel.

(2) The authority of the Administrator under 49 U.S.C. 5123, 49 CFR 1.47(k), 49 U.S.C. 46301(d), and 49 U.S.C. 46305 to refer cases to the Attorney General of the United States, or the delegate of the Attorney General, for collection of civil penalties is delegated to the Deputy Chief Counsel for Operations; the Assistant Chief Counsel for Enforcement; Assistant Chief Counsel, Europe, Africa, and Middle East Area Office; the Regional Counsel; the Aeronautical Center Counsel; and the Technical Center Counsel.

(3) The authority of the Administrator under 49 U.S.C. 46301(f) to compromise the amount of a civil penalty imposed is delegated to the Deputy Chief Counsel for Operations; the Assistant Chief Counsel for Enforcement; Assistant Chief Counsel, Europe, Africa, and Middle East Area Office; the Regional Counsel; the Aeronautical Center Counsel; and the Technical Center Counsel.

(4) The authority of the Administrator under 49 U.S.C. 5123 (e) and (f) and 49 CFR 1.47(k) to compromise the amount of a civil penalty imposed is delegated to the Deputy Chief Counsel for Operations; the Assistant Chief Counsel for Enforcement; Assistant Chief Counsel, Europe, Africa, and Middle East Area Office; the Regional Counsel; the Aeronautical Center Counsel; and the Technical Center Counsel.

(f) *Notice of proposed civil penalty.* A civil penalty action is initiated by sending a notice of proposed civil penalty to the person charged with a violation or to the agent for services for the person under 49 U.S.C. 46103. A notice of proposed civil penalty will be sent to the individual charged with a violation or to the president of the corporation or company charged with a violation. In response to a notice of proposed civil penalty, a corporation or company may designate in writing another person to receive documents in that civil penalty action. The notice of proposed civil penalty contains a statement of the charges and the amount of the proposed civil penalty. Not later than 30 days after receipt of the notice of proposed civil penalty, the person charged with a violation shall—

(1) Submit the amount of the proposed civil penalty or an agreed-upon amount, in which case either an order assessing civil penalty or compromise order shall be issued in that amount;

(2) Submit to the agency attorney one of the following:

(i) Written information, including documents and witness statements, demonstrating that a violation of the regulations did not occur or that a penalty or the amount of the penalty is not warranted by the circumstances.

(ii) A written request to reduce the proposed civil penalty, the amount of reduction, and the reasons and any documents supporting a reduction of the proposed civil penalty, including records indicating a financial inability to pay or records showing that payment of the proposed civil penalty would prevent the person from continuing in business.

(iii) A written request for an informal conference to discuss the matter with the agency attorney and to submit relevant information or documents; or

(3) Request a hearing, in which case a complaint shall be filed with the hearing docket clerk.

(g) *Final notice of proposed civil penalty.* A final notice of proposed civil penalty may be issued after participation in informal procedures provided in paragraph (f)(2) of this section or failure to respond in a timely manner to a notice of proposed civil penalty. A final notice of proposed civil penalty will be sent to the individual charged with a violation, to the president of the corporation or company charged with a violation, or a person previously designated in writing by the individual, corporation, or company to receive documents in that civil penalty action. If not previously done in response to a notice of proposed civil penalty, a corporation or company may designate in writing another person to receive documents in that civil penalty action. The final notice of proposed civil penalty contains a statement of the charges and the amount of the proposed civil penalty and, as a result of information submitted to the agency attorney during informal procedures, may modify an allegation or a proposed civil penalty contained in a notice of proposed civil penalty.

(1) A final notice of proposed civil penalty may be issued—

(i) If the person charged with a violation fails to respond to the notice of proposed civil penalty within 30 days after receipt of that notice; or

(ii) If the parties participated in any informal procedures under paragraph (f)(2) of this section and the parties have not agreed to compromise the action or the agency attorney has not agreed to withdraw the notice of proposed civil penalty.

(2) Not later than 15 days after receipt of the final notice of proposed civil penalty, the person charged with a violation shall do one of the following—

(i) Submit the amount of the proposed civil penalty or an agreed-upon amount, in which case either an order assessing civil penalty or a compromise order shall be issued in that amount; or

(ii) Request a hearing, in which case a complaint shall be filed with the hearing docket clerk.

(h) *Request for a hearing.* Any person charged with a violation may request a hearing, pursuant to paragraph (f)(3) or paragraph (g)(2)(ii) of this section, to be conducted in accordance with the procedures in subpart G of this part. A person requesting a hearing shall file a written request for a hearing with the hearing docket clerk, using the appropriate address as set forth in §13.210(a) of this part, and shall mail a copy of the request to the agency attorney. The request for a hearing may be in the form of a letter but must be dated and signed by the person requesting a hearing. The request for a hearing may be typewritten or may be legibly handwritten.

(i) *Hearing.* If the person charged with a violation requests a hearing pursuant to paragraph (f)(3) or paragraph (g)(2)(ii) of this section, the original complaint shall be filed with the hearing docket clerk and a copy shall be sent to the person requesting the hearing. The procedural rules in subpart G of this part apply to the hearing and any appeal. At the close of the hearing, the administrative law judge shall issue, either orally on the record or in writing, an initial decision, including the reasons for the decision, that contains findings or conclusions on the allegations contained, and the civil penalty sought, in the complaint.

(j) *Appeal.* Either party may appeal the administrative law judge's initial decision to the FAA decisionmaker pursuant to the procedures in subpart G of this part. If a party files a notice of appeal pursuant to §13.233 of subpart G, the effectiveness of the initial decision is stayed until a final decision and order of the Administrator have been entered on the record. The FAA decisionmaker shall review the record and issue a final decision and order of the Administrator that affirm, modify, or reverse the initial decision. The FAA decisionmaker may assess a civil penalty but shall not assess a civil penalty in an amount greater than that sought in the complaint.

(k) *Payment.* A person shall pay a civil penalty by sending a certified check or money order, payable to the Federal Aviation Administration, to the agency attorney.

(l) *Collection of civil penalties.* If an individual does not pay a civil penalty imposed by an order assessing civil penalty or other final order, the Administrator may take action provided under the law to collect the penalty.

(m) *Exhaustion of administrative remedies and judicial review.*

(1) Cases under the FAA statute. A party may petition for review only of a final decision and order of the FAA decisionmaker to the courts of appeals of the United States for the circuit in which the individual charged resides or has his or her principal place of business or the United States Court of Appeals for the District of Columbia Circuit, under 49 U.S.C. 46110, 46301(d)(6), and 46301(g). Neither an initial decision or order issues by an administrative law judge that has not been appealed to the FAA decisionmaker, nor an order compromising a civil penalty action, may be appealed under those sections.

(2) Cases under the Federal hazardous materials transportation law. A party may seek judicial review only of a final decision and order of the FAA decisionmaker involving a violation of the Federal hazardous materials transportation law or a regulation or order issued thereunder to an appropriate district court of the United States, under 5 U.S.C. 703 and 704 and 28 U.S.C. 1331. Neither an initial decision or order issued by an administrative law judge that has not been appealed to the FAA decisionmaker, nor an order compromising a civil penalty action, may be appealed under these sections.

(n) *Compromise.* The FAA may compromise the amount of any civil penalty imposed under this section, under 49 U.S.C. 5123(e), 46031(f), 46303(b), or 46318 at any time before referring the action to the United States Attorney General, or the delegate of the Attorney General, for collection.

(1) An agency attorney may compromise any civil penalty action where a person charged with a violation agrees to pay a civil penalty and the FAA agrees not to make a finding of violation. Under such agreement, a compromise order is issued following the payment of the agreed-on amount or the signing of a promissory note. The compromise order states the following:

(i) The person has paid a civil penalty or has signed a promissory note providing for installment payments.

(ii) The FAA makes no finding of a violation.

(iii) The compromise order shall not be used as evidence of a prior violation in any subsequent civil penalty proceeding or certificate action proceeding.

(2) An agency attorney may compromise the amount of an civil penalty proposed in a notice, assessed in an order, or imposed in a compromise order.

[Docket No. 27854, 70 FR 1813, Jan. 11, 2005; as amended at 70 FR 8238, Feb. 18, 2005]

§13.17 Seizure of aircraft.

(a) Under section 903 of the Federal Aviation Act of 1958 (49 U.S.C. 1473), a State or Federal law enforcement officer, or a Federal Aviation Administration safety inspector, authorized in an order of seizure issued by the Regional Administrator of the region, or by the Chief Counsel, may summarily seize an aircraft that is involved in a violation for which a civil penalty may be imposed on its owner or operator.

(b) Each person seizing an aircraft under this section shall place it in the nearest available and adequate public storage facility in the judicial district in which it was seized.

(c) The Regional Administrator or Chief Counsel, without delay, sends a written notice and a copy of this section, to the registered owner of the seized aircraft, and to each other persons shown by FAA records to have an interest in it, stating the—

(1) Time, date, and place of seizure;

(2) Name and address of the custodian of the aircraft;

(3) Reasons for the seizure, including the violations believed, or judicially determined, to have been committed; and

(4) Amount that may be tendered as—

(i) A compromise of a civil penalty for the alleged violation; or

(ii) Payment for a civil penalty imposed by a Federal court for a proven violation.

(d) The Chief Counsel, or the Regional Counsel or Assistant Chief Counsel for the region or area in which an aircraft is seized under this section, immediately sends a report to the United States District Attorney for the judicial district in which it was seized, requesting the District Attorney to institute proceedings to enforce a lien against the aircraft.

(e) The Regional Administrator or Chief Counsel directs the release of a seized aircraft whenever—

(1) The alleged violator pays a civil penalty or an amount agreed upon in compromise, and the costs of seizing, storing, and maintaining the aircraft;

(2) The aircraft is seized under an order of a Federal Court in proceedings in rem to enforce a lien against the aircraft, or the United States District Attorney for the judicial district concerned notifies the FAA that the District Attorney refuses to institute those proceedings; or

(3) A bond in the amount and with the sureties prescribed by the Chief Counsel, the Regional Counsel, or the Assistant Chief Counsel is deposited, conditioned on payment of the penalty, or the compromise amount, and the costs of seizing, storing, and maintaining the aircraft.

[Docket No. 18884, 44 FR 63723, Nov. 5, 1979; as amended by Amdt. 13–19, 54 FR 39290, Sept. 25, 1989; Amdt. 13–29, 62 FR 46865, Sept. 4, 1997]

§13.18 Civil penalties: Administrative assessment against an individual acting as a pilot, flight engineer, mechanic, or repairman.

(a) ***General.***

(1) This section applies to each action in which the FAA seeks to assess a civil penalty by administrative procedures against an individual acting as a pilot, flight engineer, mechanic, or repairman, under 49 U.S.C. 46301(d)(5), for a violation listed in 49 U.S.C. 46301(d)(2). This section does not apply to a civil penalty assessed for violation of 49 U.S.C. chapter 51, or a rule, regulation, or order issued thereunder.

(2) *District court jurisdiction.* Notwithstanding the provisions of paragraph (a)(1) of this section, the United States district courts have exclusive jurisdiction of any civil penalty action involving an individual acting as a pilot, flight engineer, mechanic, or repairman for violations described in that paragraph, under 49 U.S.C. 46301(d)(4), if:

(i) The amount in controversy is more than $50,000.

(ii) The action involves an aircraft subject to a lien that has been seized by the Government; or

(iii) Another action has been brought for an injunction based on the same violation.

(b) ***Definitions.*** As used in this part, the following definitions apply:

(1) Flight engineer means an individual who holds a flight engineer certificate issued under part 63 of this chapter.

(2) Individual acting as a pilot, flight engineer, mechanic, or repairman means an individual acting in such capacity, whether or not that individual holds the respective airman certificate issued by the FAA.

(3) Mechanic means an individual who holds a mechanic certificate issued under part 65 of this chapter.

(4) Pilot means an individual who holds a pilot certificate issued under part 61 of this chapter.

(5) Repairman means an individual who holds a repairman certificate issued under part 65 of this chapter.

(c) ***Delegation of authority.***

(1) The authority of the Administrator under 49 U.S.C. 46301(d)(5), to initiate and assess civil penalties is delegated to the Chief Counsel; the Deputy Chief Counsel for Operations; the Assistant Chief Counsel for Enforcement; Assistant Chief Counsel, Europe, Africa, and Middle East Area Office; the Regional Counsel; the Aeronautical Center Counsel; and the Technical Center Counsel.

(2) The authority of the Administrator to refer cases to the Attorney General of the United States, or the delegate of the Attorney General, for collection of civil penalties is delegated to the Chief Counsel; the Deputy Chief Counsel for Operations; the Assistant Chief Counsel for Enforcement; Assistant Chief Counsel, Europe, Africa, and Middle East Area Office; the Regional Counsel; the Aeronautical Center Counsel; and the Technical Center Counsel.

(3) The authority of the Administrator to compromise the amount of a civil penalty under 49 U.S.C. 46301(f) is delegated to the Chief Counsel; the Deputy Chief Counsel for Operations; the Assistant Chief Counsel for Enforcement; Assistant Chief Counsel, Europe, Africa, and Middle East Area Office; the Regional Counsel; the Aeronautical Center Counsel; and the Technical Center Counsel.

(d) ***Notice of proposed assessment.*** A civil penalty action is initiated by sending a notice of proposed assessment to the individual charged with a violation specified in paragraph (a) of this section. The notice of proposed assessment contains a statement of the charges and the amount of the proposed civil penalty. The individual charged with a violation may do the following:

(1) Submit the amount of the proposed civil penalty or an agreed-on amount, in which case either an order of assessment or a compromise order will be issued in that amount.

(2) Answer the charges in writing.

(3) Submit a written request for an informal conference to discuss the matter with an agency attorney and submit relevant information or documents.

(4) Request that an order be issued in accordance with the notice of proposed assessment so that the individual charged may appeal to the National Transportation Safety Board.

(e) ***Failure to respond to notice of proposed assessment.*** An order of assessment may be issued if the individual charged with a violation fails to respond to the notice of proposed assessment within 15 days after receipt of that notice.

(f) ***Order of assessment.*** An order of assessment, which assesses a civil penalty, may be issued for a violation described in paragraph (a) of this section after notice and an opportunity to answer any charges and be heard as to why such order should not be issued.

(g) ***Appeal.*** Any individual who receives an order of assessment issued under this section may appeal the order to the National Transportation Safety Board. The appeal stays the effectiveness of the Administrator's order.

(h) ***Exhaustion of administrative remedies.*** An individual substantially affected by an order of the NTSB or the Administrator may petition for review only of a final decision and order of the National Transportation Safety Board to a court of appeals of the United States for the circuit in which the individual charged resides or has his or her principal place of business or the United States Court of Appeals for the District of Columbia Circuit, under 49 U.S.C. 46110 and 46301(d)(6). Neither an order of assessment that has not been appealed to the National Transportation Board, nor an order compromising a civil penalty action, may be appealed under those sections.

(i) ***Compromise.*** The FAA may compromise any civil penalty action initiated under this section, in accordance with 49 U.S.C. 46301(f).

(1) An agency attorney may compromise any civil penalty action where an individual charged with a violation agrees to pay a civil penalty and the FAA agrees to make no finding of violation. Under such agreement, a compromise order is issued following the payment of the agreed-on amount or the signing of a promissory note. The compromise order states the following:

(i) The individual has paid a civil penalty or has signed a promissory note providing for installment payments;

(ii) The FAA makes no finding of violation; and

(iii) The compromise order will not be used as evidence of a prior violation in any subsequent civil penalty proceeding or certificate action proceeding.

(2) An agency attorney may compromise the amount of any civil penalty proposed or assessed in an order.

(j) ***Payment.***

(1) An individual must pay a civil penalty by:

(i) Sending a certified check or money order, payable to the Federal Aviation Administration, to the FAA office identified in the order of assessment, or

(ii) Making an electronic funds transfer according to the directions specified in the order of assessment.

(2) The civil penalty must be paid within 30 days after service of the order of assessment, unless an appeal is filed with the National Transportation Safety Board. The civil penalty must be paid within 30 days after a final order of the Board or the Court of Appeals affirms the order of assessment in whole or in part.

(k) ***Collection of civil penalties.*** If an individual does not pay a civil penalty imposed by an order of assessment or other final order, the Administrator may take action provided under the law to collect the penalty.

[Docket No. 27854, 69 FR 59497, Oct. 4, 2004]

§13.19 Certificate action.

(a) Under section 609 of the Federal Aviation Act of 1958 (49 U.S.C. 1429), the Administrator may reinspect any civil aircraft, aircraft engine, propeller, appliance, air navigation facility, or air agency, and may re-examine any civil airman. Under section 501(e) of the FAA Act, any Certificate of Aircraft Registration may be suspended or revoked by the Administrator for any cause that renders the aircraft ineligible for registration.

(b) If, as a result of such a reinspection re-examination, or other investigation made by the Administrator under section 609 of the FAA Act, the Administrator determines that the public interest and safety in air commerce requires it, the Administrator may issue an order amending, suspending, or revoking, all or part of any type certificate, production certificate, airworthiness certificate, airman certificate, air carrier operating certificate, air navigation facility certificate, or air agency certificate. This authority may be exercised for remedial purposes in cases involving the Hazardous Materials Transportation Act (49 U.S.C. 1801 et seq.) or regulations issued under that Act. This authority is also exercised by the Chief Counsel, the Assistant Chief Counsel, Enforcement, the Assistant Chief Counsel, Regulations, the Assistant Chief Counsel, Europe, Africa, and Middle East Area Office, each Regional Counsel, and the Aeronautical Center Counsel. If the Administrator finds that any aircraft registered under Part 47 of this chapter is ineligible for registration or if the holder of a Certificate of Aircraft Registration has refused or failed to submit AC Form 8050-73, as required by §47.51 of this chapter, the Administrator issues an order suspending or revoking that certificate. This authority as to aircraft found ineligible for registration is also exercised by each Regional Counsel, the Aeronautical Center Counsel, and the Assistant Chief Counsel, Europe, Africa, and Middle East Area Office.

(c) Before issuing an order under paragraph (b) of this section, the Chief Counsel, the Assistant Chief Counsel, Enforcement, the Assistant Chief Counsel, Regulations, the Assistant Chief Counsel, Europe, Africa, and Middle East Area Office, each Regional Counsel, or the Aeronautical Center Counsel advises the certificate holder of the charges or other reasons upon which the Administrator bases the proposed action and, except in an emergency, allows the holder to answer any charges and to be heard as to why the certificate should not be amended, suspended, or revoked. The holder may, by checking the appropriate box on the form that is sent to the holder with the notice of proposed certificate action, elect to—

(1) Admit the charges and surrender his or her certificate;

(2) Answer the charges in writing;

(3) Request that an order be issued in accordance with the notice of proposed certificate action so that the certificate holder may appeal to the National Transportation Safety Board, if the charges concerning a matter under Title VI of the FA Act;

(4) Request an opportunity to be heard in an informal conference with the FAA counsel; or

(5) Request a hearing in accordance with Subpart D of this part if the charges concern a matter under Title V of the FA Act.

Except as provided in §13.35(b), unless the certificate holder returns the form and, where required, an answer or motion, with a postmark of not later than 15 days after the date of receipt of the notice, the order of the Administrator is issued as proposed. If the certificate holder has requested an informal conference with the FAA counsel and the charges concern a matter under Title V of the FA Act, the holder may after that conference also request a formal hearing in writing with a postmark of not later than 10 days after the close of the conference. After considering any information submitted by the certificate holder, the Chief Counsel, the Assistant Chief Counsel for Regulations and Enforcement, the Regional Counsel concerned, or the Aeronautical Center Counsel (as to matters under Title V of the FA Act) issues the order of the Administrator, except that if the holder has made a valid request for a formal hearing on a matter under Title V of the FA Act initially or after an informal conference, Subpart D of this part governs further proceedings.

(d) Any person whose certificate is affected by an order issued under this section may appeal to the National Transportation Safety Board. If the certificate holder files an appeal with the Board, the Administrator's order is stayed unless the Administrator advises the Board that an emergency exists and safety in air commerce requires that the order become effective immediately. If the Board is so advised, the order remains effective and the Board shall finally dispose of the appeal within 60 days after the date of the advice. This paragraph does not apply to any person whose Certificate of Aircraft Registration is affected by an order issued under this section.

[Docket No. 13–14, 44 FR 63723, Nov. 5, 1979; as amended by Amdt. 13–15, 45 FR 20773, March 31, 1980; Amdt. 13–19, 54 FR 39290, Sept. 25, 1989; Amdt. 13–29, 62 FR 46865, Sept. 4, 1997]

§13.20 Orders of compliance, cease and desist orders, orders of denial, and other orders.

(a) This section applies to orders of compliance, cease and desist orders, orders of denial, and other orders issued by the Administrator to carry out the provisions of the Federal Aviation Act of 1958, as amended, the Hazardous Materials Transportation Act, the Airport and Airway Development Act of 1970, and the Airport and Airway Improvement Act of 1982, or the Airport and Airway Improvement Act of 1982 as amended by the Airport and Airway Safety and Capacity Expansion Act of 1987. This section does not apply to orders issued pursuant to section 602 or section 609 of the Federal Aviation Act of 1958, as amended.

(b) Unless the Administrator determines that an emergency exists and safety in air commerce requires the immediate issuance of an order under this section, the person subject to the order shall be provided with notice prior to issuance.

(c) Within 30 days after service of the notice, the person subject to the order may reply in writing or request a hearing in accordance with Subpart D of this part.

(d) If a reply is filed, as to any charges not dismissed or not subject to a consent order, the person subject to the order may, within 10 days after receipt of notice that the remaining charges are not dismissed, request a hearing in accordance with Subpart D of this part.

(e) Failure to request a hearing within the period provided in paragraphs (c) or (d) of this section—

(1) Constitutes a waiver of the right to appeal and the right to a hearing, and

(2) Authorizes the official who issued the notice to find the facts to be as alleged in the notice, or as modified as the official may determine necessary based on any written response, and to issue an appropriate order, without further notice or proceedings.

(f) If a hearing is requested in accordance with paragraph (c) or (d) of this section, the procedure of Subpart D of this part applies. At the close of the hearing, the Hearing Officer, on the record or subsequently in writing, shall set forth findings and conclusions and the reasons therefor, and either—

(1) Dismiss the notice; or

(2) Issue an order.

(g) Any party to the hearing may appeal from the order of the Hearing Officer by filing a notice of appeal with the Administrator within 20 days after the date of issuance of the order.

(h) If a notice of appeal is not filed from the order issued by a Hearing Officer, such order is the final agency order.

(i) Any person filing an appeal authorized by paragraph (g) of this section shall file an appeal brief with the Administrator within 40 days after the date of issuance of the order, and serve a copy on the other party. A reply brief must be filed within 20 days after service of the appeal brief and a copy served on the appellant.

(j) On appeal the Administrator reviews the available record of the proceeding, and issues an order dismissing, reversing, modifying or affirming the order. The Administrator's order includes the reasons for the Administrator's action.

(k) For good cause shown, requests for extensions of time to file any document under this section may be granted by—

(1) The official who issued the order, if the request is filed prior to the designation of a Hearing Officer; or

(2) The Hearing Officer, if the request is filed prior to the filing of a notice of appeal; or

(3) The Administrator, if the request is filed after the filing of a notice of appeal.

(l) Except in the case of an appeal from the decision of a Hearing Officer, the authority of the Administrator under this section is also exercised by the Chief Counsel, Deputy Chief Counsel, each Assistant Chief Counsel, each Regional

Counsel, and the Aeronautical Center Counsel (as to matters under Title V of the Federal Aviation Act of 1958).

(m) Filing and service of documents under this section shall be accomplished in accordance with §13.43; and the periods of time specified in this section shall be computed in accordance with §13.44.

[Docket No. 18884, 44 FR 63723, Nov. 5, 1979; as amended by Amdt. 13–17, 53 FR 33783, Aug. 31, 1988; Amdt. 13–19, 54 FR 39290, Sept. 25, 1989; Amdt. 13–29, 62 FR 46865, Sept. 4, 1997]

§13.21 Military personnel.

If a report made under this part indicates that, while performing official duties, a member of the Armed Forces, or a civilian employee of the Department of Defense who is subject to the Uniform Code of Military Justice (10 U.S.C. Ch. 47), has violated the Federal Aviation Act of 1958, or a regulation or order issued under it, the Chief Counsel, the Assistant Chief Counsel, Enforcement, the Assistant Chief Counsel, Regulations, the Assistant Chief Counsel, Europe, Africa, and Middle East Area Office, each Regional Counsel, and the Aeronautical Center Counsel sends a copy of the report to the appropriate military authority for such disciplinary action as that authority considers appropriate and a report to the Administrator thereon.

[Docket No. 18884, 44 FR 63723, Nov. 5, 1979; as amended by Amdt. 13–19, 54 FR 39290, Sept. 25, 1989; Amdt. 13–29, 62 FR 46866, Sept. 4, 1997]

§13.23 Criminal penalties.

(a) Sections 902 and 1203 of the Federal Aviation Act of 1958 (49 U.S.C. 1472 and 1523), provide criminal penalties for any person who knowingly and willfully violates specified provisions of that Act, or any regulation or order issued under those provisions. Section 110(b) of the Hazardous Materials Transportation Act (49 U.S.C. 1809(b)) provides for a criminal penalty of a fine of not more than $25,000, imprisonment for not more than five years, or both, for any person who willfully violates a provision of that Act or a regulation or order issued under it.

(b) If an inspector or other employee of the FAA becomes aware of a possible violation of any criminal provision of the Federal Aviation Act of 1958 (except a violation of section 902 (i) through (m) which is reported directly to the Federal Bureau of Investigation), or of the Hazardous Materials Transportation Act, relating to the transportation or shipment by air of hazardous materials, he or she shall report it to the Office of the Chief Counsel or the Regional Counsel or Assistant Chief Counsel for the region or area concerned. If appropriate, that office refers the report to the Department of Justice for criminal prosecution of the offender. If such an inspector or other employee becomes aware of a possible violation of a Federal statute that is within the investigatory jurisdiction of another Federal agency, he or she shall immediately report it to that agency according to standard FAA practices.

[Docket No. 18884, 44 FR 63723, Nov. 5, 1979; as amended by Amdt. 13–19, 54 FR 39290, Sept. 25, 1989; Amdt. 13–29, 62 FR 46866, Sept. 4, 1997]

§13.25 Injunctions.

(a) Whenever it is determined that a person has engaged, or is about to engage, in any act or practice constituting a violation of the Federal Aviation Act of 1958, or any regulation or order issued under it for which the FAA exercises enforcement responsibility, or, with respect to the transportation or shipment by air of any hazardous materials, in any act or practice constituting a violation of the Hazardous Materials Transportation Act, or any regulation or order issued under it for which the FAA exercises enforcement responsibility, the Chief Counsel, the Assistant Chief Counsel, Enforcement, the Assistant Chief Counsel, Regulations, the Assistant Chief Counsel, Europe, Africa, and Middle East Area Office, each Regional Counsel, and the Aeronautical Center Counsel may request the United States Attorney General, or the delegate of the Attorney General, to bring an action in the appropriate United States District Court for such relief as is necessary or appropriate, including mandatory or prohibitive injunctive relief, interim equitable relief, and punitive damages, as provided by section 1007 of the Federal Aviation Act of 1958 (49 U.S.C. 1487) and section 111(a) of the Hazardous Materials Transportation Act (49 U.S.C. 1810).

(b) Whenever it is determined that there is substantial likelihood that death, serious illness, or severe personal injury, will result from the transportation by air of a particular hazardous material before an order of compliance proceeding, or other administrative hearing or formal proceeding to abate the risk of the harm can be completed, the Chief Counsel, the Assistant Chief Counsel, Enforcement, the Assistant Chief Counsel, Regulations, the Assistant Chief Counsel, Europe, Africa, and Middle East Area Office, each Regional Counsel, and the Aeronautical Center Counsel may bring, or request the United States Attorney General to bring, an action in the appropriate United States District Court for an order suspending or restricting the transportation by air of the hazardous material or for such other order as is necessary to eliminate or ameliorate the imminent hazard, as provided by section 111(b) of the Hazardous Materials Transportation Act (49 U.S.C. 1810).

[Docket No. 18884, 44 FR 63723, Nov. 5, 1979; as amended by Amdt. 13–19, 54 FR 39290, Sept. 25, 1989; Amdt. 13–29, 62 FR 46866, Sept. 4, 1997]

§13.27 Final order of Hearing Officer in certificate of aircraft registration proceedings.

(a) If, in proceedings under section 501(b) of the Federal Aviation Act of 1958 (49 USC 1401), the Hearing Officer determines that the holder of the Certificate of Aircraft Registration has refused or failed to submit AC Form 8050-73, as required by §47.51 of this chapter, or that the aircraft is ineligible for a Certificate of Aircraft Registration, the Hearing Officer shall suspend or revoke the respondent's certificate, as proposed in the notice of proposed certificate action.

(b) If the final order of the Hearing Officer makes a decision on the merits, it shall contain a statement of the findings and conclusions of law on all material issues of fact and law. If the Hearing Officer finds that the allegations of the notice have been proven, but that no sanction is required, the Hearing Officer shall make appropriate findings and issue an order terminating the notice. If the Hearing Officer finds that the allegations of the notice have not been proven, the Hearing Officer shall issue an order dismissing the notice. If the Hearing Officer finds it to be equitable and in the public interest, the Hearing Officer shall issue an order terminating the proceeding upon payment by the respondent of a civil penalty in an amount agreed upon by the parties.

(c) If the order is issued in writing, it shall be served upon the parties.

[Docket No. 13–14, 44 FR 63723, Nov. 5, 1979; as amended by Amdt. 13–15, 45 FR 20773, March 31, 1980]

§13.29 Civil penalties: Streamlined enforcement procedures for certain security violations.

This section may be used, at the agency's discretion, in enforcement actions involving individuals presenting dangerous or deadly weapons for screening at airports or in checked baggage where the amount of the proposed civil penalty is less than $5,000. In these cases, sections 13.16(a), 13.16(c), and 13.16 (f) through (l) of this chapter are used, as well as paragraphs (a) through (d) of this section:

(a) *Delegation of authority.* The authority of the Administrator, under 49 U.S.C. 46301, to initiate the assessment of civil penalties for a violation of 49 U.S.C. Subtitle VII, or a rule, regulation, or order issued thereunder, is delegated to the regional Civil Aviation Security Division Manager and the regional Civil Aviation Security Deputy Division Manager for the purpose of issuing notices of violation in cases involving violations of 49 U.S.C. Subtitle VII and the FAA's regulations by individuals presenting dangerous or deadly weapons for screening at airport checkpoints or in checked baggage. This authority may not be delegated below the level of the regional Civil Aviation Security Deputy Division Manager.

(b) *Notice of violation.* A civil penalty action is initiated by sending a notice of violation to the person charged with the violation. The notice of violation contains a statement of the charges and the amount of the proposed civil penalty. Not later than 30 days after receipt of the notice of violation, the person charged with a violation shall:

(1) Submit the amount of the proposed civil penalty or an agreed-upon amount, in which case either an order assessing a civil penalty or a compromise order shall be issued in that amount; or

(2) Submit to the agency attorney identified in the material accompanying the notice of any of the following:

(i) Written information, including documents and witness statements, demonstrating that a violation of the regulations did not occur or that a penalty or the penalty amount is not warranted by the circumstances; or

(ii) A written request to reduce the proposed civil penalty, the amount of reduction, and the reasons and any documents supporting a reduction of the proposed civil penalty, including records indicating a financial inability to pay or records showing that payment of the proposed civil penalty would prevent the person from continuing in business; or

(iii) A written request for an informal conference to discuss the matter with an agency attorney and submit relevant information or documents; or

(3) Request a hearing in which case a complaint shall be filed with the hearing docket clerk.

(c) *Final notice of violation and civil penalty assessment order.* A final notice of violation and civil penalty assessment order ("final notice and order") may be issued after participation in any informal proceedings as provided in paragraph (b)(2) of this section, or after failure of the respondent to respond in a timely manner to a notice of violation. A final notice and order will be sent to the individual charged with a violation. The final notice and order will contain a statement of the charges and the amount of the proposed civil penalty and, as a result of information submitted to the agency attorney during any informal procedures, may reflect a modified allegation or proposed civil penalty.

A final notice and order may be issued—

(1) If the person charged with a violation fails to respond to the notice of violation within 30 days after receipt of that notice; or

(2) If the parties participated in any informal procedures under paragraph (b)(2) of this section and the parties have not agreed to compromise the action or the agency attorney has not agreed to withdraw the notice of violation.

(d) *Order assessing civil penalty.* An order assessing civil penalty may be issued after notice and opportunity for a hearing. A person charged with a violation may be subject to an order assessing civil penalty in the following circumstances:

(1) An order assessing civil penalty may be issued if a person charged with a violation submits, or agrees to submit, the amount of civil penalty proposed in the notice of violation.

(2) An order assessing civil penalty may be issued if a person charged with a violation submits, or agrees to submit, an agreed-upon amount of civil penalty that is not reflected in either the notice of violation or the final notice and order.

(3) The final notice and order becomes (and contains a statement so indicating) an order assessing a civil penalty when the person charged with a violation submits the amount of the proposed civil penalty that is reflected in the final notice and order.

(4) The final notice and order becomes (and contains a statement so indicating) an order assessing a civil penalty 16 days after receipt of the final notice and order, *unless* not later than 15 days after receipt of the final notice and order, the person charged with a violation does one of the following—

(i) Submits an agreed-upon amount of civil penalty that is not reflected in the final notice and order, in which case an order assessing civil penalty or a compromise order shall be issued in that amount; or

(ii) Requests a hearing in which case a complaint shall be filed with the hearing docket clerk.

(5) Unless an appeal is filed with the FAA decisionmaker in a timely manner, an initial decision or order of an administrative law judge shall be considered an order assessing civil penalty if an administrative law judge finds that an alleged violation occurred and determines that a civil penalty in an amount found to be appropriate by the administrative law judge, is warranted.

(6) Unless a petition for review is filed with a U.S. Court of Appeals in a timely manner, a final decision and order of the Administrator shall be considered an order assessing civil penalty if the FAA decisionmaker finds that an alleged violation occurred and a civil penalty is warranted.

[Docket No. 27873, FR 61 44155, Aug. 28, 1996]

Subpart D—Rules of Practice for FAA Hearings

§13.31 Applicability.

This subpart applies to proceedings in which a hearing has been requested in accordance with §§13.19(c)(5), 13.20(c), 13.20(d), 13.75(a)(2), 13.75(b), or 13.81(e).

[Docket No. 18884, 44 FR 63723, Nov. 5, 1979; as amended by Amdt. 13–18, 53 FR 34655, Sept. 7, 1988]

§13.33 Appearances.

Any party to a proceeding under this subpart may appear and be heard in person or by attorney.

§13.35 Request for hearing.

(a) A request for hearing must be made in writing to the Hearing Docket, Room 924A, Federal Aviation Administration, 800 Independence Avenue SW, Washington, D.C. 20591. It must describe briefly the action proposed by the FAA, and must contain a statement that a hearing is requested. A copy of the request for hearing and a copy of the answer required by paragraph (b) of this section must be served on the official who issued the notice of proposed action.

(b) An answer to the notice of proposed action must be filed with the request for hearing. All allegations in the notice not specifically denied in the answer are deemed admitted.

(c) Within 15 days after service of the copy of the request for hearing, the official who issued the notice of proposed action forwards a copy of that notice, which serves as the complaint, to the Hearing Docket.

[Docket No. 18884, 44 FR 63723, Nov. 5, 1979; as amended by Amdt. 13–19, 54 FR 39290, Sept. 25, 1989]

§13.37 Hearing Officer's powers.

Any Hearing Officer may—

(a) Give notice concerning, and hold, prehearing conferences and hearings;

(b) Administrator oaths and affirmations;

(c) Examine witnesses;

(d) Adopt procedures for the submission of evidence in written form;

(e) Issue subpoenas and take depositions or cause them to be taken;

(f) Rule on offers of proof;

(g) Receive evidence;

(h) Regulate the course of the hearing;

(i) Hold conferences, before and during the hearing, to settle and simplify issues by consent of the parties;

(j) Dispose of procedural requests and similar matters; and

(k) Issue decisions, make findings of fact, make assessments, and issue orders, as appropriate.

§13.39 Disqualification of Hearing Officer.

If disqualified for any reason, the Hearing Officer shall withdraw from the case.

§13.41 [Reserved]

§13.43 Service and filing of pleadings, motions, and documents.

(a) Copies of all pleadings, motions, and documents filed with the Hearing Docket must be served upon all parties to the proceedings by the person filing them.

(b) Service may be made by personal delivery or by mail.

(c) A certificate of service shall accompany all documents when they are tendered for filing and shall consist of a certificate of personal delivery or a certificate of mailing, executed by the person making the personal delivery or mailing the document.

(d) Whenever proof of service by mail is made, the date of mailing or the date as shown on the postmark shall be the date of service, and where personal service is made, the date of personal delivery shall be the date of service.

(e) The date of filing is the date the document is actually received.

§13.44 Computation of time and extension of time.

(a) In computing any period of time prescribed or allowed by this subpart, the date of the act, event, default, notice or order after which the designated period of time begins to run is not to be included in the computation. The last day of the period so computed is to be included unless it is a Saturday, Sunday, or legal holiday for the FAA, in which event the period runs until the end of the next day which is neither a Saturday, Sunday nor a legal holiday.

(b) Upon written request filed with the Hearing Docket and served upon all parties, and for good cause shown, a Hearing Officer may grant an extension of time to file any documents specified in this subpart.

§13.45 Amendment of notice and answer.

At any time more than 10 days before the date of hearing, any party may amend his or her notice, answer, or other pleading, by filing the amendment with the Hearing Officer and serving a copy of it on each other party. After that time, amendments may be allowed only in the discretion of the Hearing Officer. If an amendment to an initial pleading has been allowed, the Hearing Officer shall allow the other parties a reasonable opportunity to answer.

§13.47 Withdrawal of notice or request for hearing.

At any time before the hearing, the FAA counsel may withdraw the notice of proposed action, and the party requesting the hearing may withdraw the request for hearing.

§13.49 Motions.

(a) *Motion to dismiss for insufficiency.* A respondent who requests a formal hearing may, in place of an answer, file a motion to dismiss for failure of the allegations in the notice of proposed action to state a violation of the FA Act or of this chapter or to show lack of qualification of the respondent. If the Hearing Officer denies the motion, the respondent shall file an answer within 10 days.

(b) [Reserved]

(c) *Motion for more definite statement.* The certificate holder may, in place of an answer, file a motion that the allegations in the notice be made more definite and certain. If the Hearing Officer grants the motion, the FAA counsel shall comply within 10 days after the date it is granted. If the Hearing Officer denies the motion the certificate holder shall file an answer within 10 days after the date it is denied.

(d) *Motion for judgment on the pleadings.* After the pleadings are closed, either party may move for a judgment on the pleadings.

(e) *Motion to strike.* Upon motion of either party, the Hearing Officer may order stricken, from any pleadings, any insufficient allegation or defense, or any immaterial, impertinent, or scandalous matter.

(f) *Motion for production of documents.* Upon motion of any party showing good cause, the Hearing Officer may, in the manner provided by Rule 34, Federal Rules of Civil Procedure, order any party to produce any designated document, paper, book, account, letter, photograph, object, or other tangible thing, that is not privileged, that constitutes or contains evidence relevant to the subject matter of the hearings, and that is in the party's possession, custody, or control.

(g) *Consolidation of motions.* A party who makes a motion under this section shall join with it all other motions that are then available to the party. Any objection that is not so raised is considered to be waived.

(h) *Answers to motions.* Any party may file an answer to any motion under this section within 5 days after service of the motion.

§13.51 Intervention.

Any person may move for leave to intervene in a proceeding and may become a party thereto, if the Hearing Officer, after the case is sent to the Hearing Officer for hearing, finds that the person may be bound by the order to be issued in the proceedings or has a property or financial interest that may not be adequately represented by existing parties, and that the intervention will not unduly broaden the issues or delay the proceedings. Except for good cause shown, a motion for leave to intervene may not be considered if it is filed less than 10 days before the hearing.

§13.53 Depositions.

After the respondent has filed a request for hearing and an answer, either party may take testimony by deposition in accordance with section 1004 of the Federal Aviation Act of 1958.

(49 U.S.C. 1484) or Rule 26, Federal Rules of Civil Procedure.

§13.55 Notice of hearing.

The Hearing Officer shall set a reasonable date, time, and place for the hearing, and shall give the parties adequate notice thereof and of the nature of the hearing. Due regard shall be given to the convenience of the parties with respect to the place of the hearing.

§13.57 Subpoenas and witness fees.

(a) The Hearing Officer to whom a case is assigned may, upon application by any party to the proceeding, issue subpoenas requiring the attendance of witnesses or the production of documentary or tangible evidence at a hearing or for the purpose of taking depositions. However, the application for producing evidence must show its general relevance and reasonable scope. This paragraph does not apply to the attendance of FAA employees or to the production of documentary evidence in the custody of such an employee at a hearing.

(b) A person who applies for the production of a document in the custody of an FAA employee must follow the procedure in §13.49(f). A person who applies for the attendance of an FAA employee must send the application, in writing, to the Hearing Officer setting forth the need for that employee's attendance.

(c) A witness in a proceeding under this subpart is entitled to the same fees and mileage as is paid to a witness in a court of the United States under comparable circumstances. The party at whose instance the witness is subpoenaed or appears shall pay the witness fees.

(d) Notwithstanding the provisions of paragraph (c) of this section, the FAA pays the witness fees and mileage if the Hearing Officer who issued the subpoena determines, on the basis of a written request and good cause shown, that—

(1) The presence of the witness will materially advance the proceeding; and

(2) The party at whose instance the witness is subpoenaed would suffer a serious hardship if required to pay the witness fees and mileage.

§13.59 Evidence.

(a) Each party to a hearing may present the party's case or defense by oral or documentary evidence, submit evidence in rebuttal, and conduct such cross-examination as may be needed for a full disclosure of the facts.

(b) Except with respect to affirmative defenses and orders of denial, the burden of proof is upon the FAA counsel.

(c) The Hearing Officer may order information contained in any report or document filed or in any testimony given pursuant to this subpart withheld from public disclosure when, in the judgment of the Hearing Officer, disclosure would adversely affect the interests of any person and is not required in the public interest or is not otherwise required by statute to be made available to the public. Any person may make written objection to the public disclosure of such information, stating the ground for such objection.

§13.61 Argument and submittals.

The Hearing Officer shall give the parties adequate opportunity to present arguments in support of motions, objections, and the final order. The Hearing Officer may determine whether arguments are to be oral or written. At the end of the hearing the Hearing Officer may, in the discretion of the Hearing Officer, allow each party to submit written proposed findings and conclusions and supporting reasons for them.

§13.63 Record.

The testimony and exhibits presented at a hearing, together with all papers, requests, and rulings filed in the proceedings are the exclusive basis for the issuance of an order. Either party may obtain a transcript from the official reporter upon payment of the fees fixed therefor.

Subpart E— Orders of Compliance Under the Hazardous Materials Transportation Act

§13.71 Applicability.

Whenever the Chief Counsel, the Assistant Chief Counsel, Enforcement, the Assistant Chief Counsel, Europe, Africa, and Middle East Area Office, or a Regional Counsel has reason to believe that a person is engaging in the transportation or shipment by air of hazardous materials in violation of the Hazardous Materials Transportation Act, or any regulation or order issued under it for which the FAA exercises enforcement responsibility, and the circumstances do not require the issuance of an order of immediate compliance, he may conduct proceedings pursuant to section 109 of that Act (49 U.S.C. 1808) to determine the nature and extent of the violation, and may thereafter issue an order directing compliance.

[Docket No. 18884, 44 FR 63723, Nov. 5, 1979; as amended by Amdt. 13–19, 54 FR 39290, Sept. 25, 1989; Amdt. 13–29, 62 FR 46866, Sept. 4, 1997]

§13.73 Notice of proposed order of compliance.

A compliance order proceeding commences when the Chief Counsel, the Assistant Chief Counsel, Enforcement, the Assistant Chief Counsel, Europe, Africa, and Middle East Area Office, or a Regional Counsel sends the alleged violator a notice of proposed order of compliance advising the alleged violator of the charges and setting forth the remedial action sought in the form of a proposed order of compliance.

[Docket No. 18884, 44 FR 63723, Nov. 5, 1979; as amended by Amdt. 13–19, 54 FR 39290, Sept. 25, 1989; Amdt. 13–29, 62 FR 46866, Sept. 4, 1997]

§13.75 Reply or request for hearing.

(a) Within 30 days after service upon the alleged violator of a notice of proposed order of compliance, the alleged violator may—

(1) File a reply in writing with the official who issued the notice; or

(2) Request a hearing in accordance with Subpart D of this part.

(b) If a reply is filed, as to any charges not dismissed or not subject to a consent order of compliance, the alleged violator may, within 10 days after receipt of notice that the remaining charges are not dismissed, request a hearing in accordance with Subpart D of this part.

(c) Failure of the alleged violator to file a reply or request a hearing within the period provided in paragraph (a) or (b) of this section—

(1) Constitutes a waiver of the right to a hearing and the right to an appeal, and

(2) Authorizes the official who issued the notice to find the facts to be as alleged in the notice and to issue an appropriate order directing compliance, without further notice or proceedings.

§13.77 Consent order of compliance.

(a) At any time before the issuance of an order of compliance, the official who issued the notice and the alleged violator may agree to dispose of the case by the issuance of a consent order of compliance by the official.

(b) A proposal for a consent order submitted to the official who issued the notice under this section must include—

(1) A proposed order of compliance;

(2) An admission of all jurisdictional facts;

(3) An express waiver of right to further procedural steps and of all rights to judicial review;

(4) An incorporation by reference of the notice and an acknowledgment that the notice may be used to construe the terms of the order of compliance; and

(5) If the issuance of a consent order has been agreed upon after the filing of a request for hearing in accordance with Subpart D of this part, the proposal for a consent order shall include a request to be filed with the Hearing Officer withdrawing the request for a hearing and requesting that the case be dismissed.

§13.79 Hearing.

If an alleged violator requests a hearing in accordance with §13.75, the procedure of Subpart D of this part applies. At the close of the hearing, the Hearing Officer, on the record or subsequently in writing, sets forth the Hearing Officer's findings and conclusion and the reasons therefor, and either—

(a) Dismisses the notice of proposed order of compliance; or

(b) Issues an order of compliance.

§13.81 Order of immediate compliance.

(a) Notwithstanding §§13.73 through 13.79, the Chief Counsel, the Assistant Chief Counsel, Enforcement, the Assistant Chief Counsel, Europe, Africa, and Middle East Area Office, or a Regional Counsel may issue an order of immediate compliance, which is effective upon issuance, if the person who issues the order finds that—

(1) There is strong probability that a violation is occurring or is about to occur;

(2) The violation poses a substantial risk to health or to safety of life or property; and

(3) The public interest requires the avoidance or amelioration of that risk through immediate compliance and waiver of the procedures afforded under §§13.73 through 13.79.

(b) An order of immediate compliance is served promptly upon the person against whom the order is issued by telephone or telegram, and a written statement of the relevant facts and the legal basis for the order, including the findings required by paragraph (a) of this section, is served promptly by personal service or by mail.

(c) The official who issued the order of immediate compliance may rescind or suspend the order if it appears that the criteria set forth in paragraph (a) of this section are no longer satisfied, and, when appropriate, may issue a notice of proposed order of compliance under §13.73 in lieu thereof.

(d) If at any time in the course of a proceeding commenced in accordance with §13.73 the criteria set forth in paragraph (a) of this section are satisfied, the official who issued the notice may issue an order of immediate compliance, even if the period for filing a reply or requesting a hearing specified in §13.75 has not expired.

(e) Within three days after receipt of service of an order of immediate compliance, the alleged violator may request a hearing in accordance with Subpart D of this part and the procedure in that subpart will apply except that—

(1) The case will be heard within fifteen days after the date of the order of immediate compliance unless the alleged violator requests a later date;

(2) The order will serve as the complaint; and

(3) The Hearing Officer shall issue his decision and order dismissing, reversing, modifying, or affirming the order of immediate compliance on the record at the close of the hearing.

(f) The filing of a request for hearing in accordance with paragraph (e) of this section does not stay the effectiveness of an order of immediate compliance.

(g) At any time after an order of immediate compliance has become effective, the official who issued the order may request the United States Attorney General, or the delegate of the Attorney General, to bring an action for appropriate relief in accordance with §13.25.

[Docket No. 18884, 44 FR 63723, Nov. 5, 1979; as amended by Amdt. 13–19, 54 FR 39290, Sept. 25, 1989; Amdt. 13–29, 62 FR 46866, Sept. 4, 1997]

§13.83 Appeal.

(a) Any party to the hearing may appeal from the order of the Hearing Officer by filing a notice of appeal with the Administrator within 20 days after the date of issuance of the order.

(b) Any person against whom an order of immediate compliance has been issued in accordance with §13.81 or the official who issued the order of immediate compliance may appeal from the order of the Hearing Officer by filing a notice of appeal with the Administrator within three days after the date of issuance of the order by the Hearing Officer.

(c) Unless the Administrator expressly so provides, the filing of a notice of appeal does not stay the effectiveness of an order of immediate compliance.

(d) If a notice of appeal is not filed from the order of compliance issued by a Hearing Officer, such order is the final agency order of compliance.

(e) Any person filing an appeal authorized by paragraph (a) of this section shall file an appeal brief with the Administrator within 40 days after the date of the issuance of the order, and serve a copy on the other party. Any reply brief must be filed within 20 days after service of the appeal brief. A copy of the reply brief must be served on the appellant.

(f) Any person filing an appeal authorized by paragraph (b) of this section shall file an appeal brief with the Administrator with the notice of appeal and serve a copy on the other party. Any reply brief must be filed within 3 days after receipt of the appeal brief. A copy of the reply brief must be served on the appellant.

(g) On appeal the Administrator reviews the available record of the proceeding, and issues an order dismissing, reversing, modifying or affirming the order of compliance or the order of immediate compliance. The Administrator's order includes the reasons for the action.

(h) In cases involving an order of immediate compliance, the Administrator's order on appeal is issued within ten days after the filing of the notice of appeal.

§13.85 Filing, service, and computation of time.

Filing and service of documents under this subpart shall be accomplished in accordance with §13.43 except service of orders of immediate compliance under §13.81(b); and the periods of time specified in this subpart shall be computed in accordance with §13.44.

§13.87 Extension of time.

(a) The official who issued the notice of proposed order of compliance, for good cause shown, may grant an extension of time to file any document specified in this subpart, except documents to be filed with the Administrator.

(b) Extensions of time to file documents with the Administrator may be granted by the Administrator upon written request, served upon all parties, and for good cause shown.

Subpart F— Formal Fact-Finding Investigation Under an Order of Investigation

§13.101 Applicability.

(a) This subpart applies to fact-finding investigations in which an order of investigation has been issued under §13.3(c) or §13.5(i) of this part.

(b) This subpart does not limit the authority of duly designated persons to issue subpoenas, administer oaths, examine witnesses and receive evidence in any informal investigation as provided for in sections 313 and 1004(a) of the Federal Aviation Act (49 U.S.C. 1354 and 1484(a)) and section 109(a) of the Hazardous Materials Transportation Act (49 U.S.C. 1808(a)).

§13.103 Order of investigation.

The order of investigation—

(a) Defines the scope of the investigation by describing the information sought in terms of its subject matter or its relevancy to specified FAA functions;

(b) Sets forth the form of the investigation which may be either by individual deposition or investigative proceeding or both; and

(c) Names the official who is authorized to conduct the investigation and serve as the Presiding Officer.

§13.105 Notification.

Any person under investigation and any person required to testify and produce documentary or physical evidence during the investigation will be advised of the purpose of the investigation, and of the place where the investigative proceeding or deposition will be convened. This may be accomplished by a notice of investigation or by a subpoena. A copy of the order of investigation may be sent to such persons, when appropriate.

§13.107 Designation of additional parties.

(a) The Presiding Officer may designate additional persons as parties to the investigation, if in the discretion of the Presiding Officer, it will aid in the conduct of the investigation.

(b) The Presiding Officer may designate any person as a party to the investigation if that person—

(1) Petitions the Presiding Officer to participate as a party; and

(2) Is so situated that the disposition of the investigation may as a practical matter impair the ability to protect that person's interest unless allowed to participate as a party, and

(3) Is not adequately represented by existing parties.

§13.109 Convening the investigation.

The investigation shall be conducted at such place or places designated by the Presiding Officer, and as convenient to the parties involved as expeditious and efficient handling of the investigation permits.

§13.111 Subpoenas.

(a) Upon motion of the Presiding Officer, or upon the request of a party to the investigation, the Presiding Officer may issue a subpoena directing any person to appear at a designated time and place to testify or to produce documentary or physical evidence relating to any matter under investigation.

(b) Subpoenas shall be served by personal service, or upon an agent designated in writing for the purpose, or by registered or certified mail addressed to such person or agent. Whenever service is made by registered or certified mail, the date of mailing shall be considered as the time when service is made.

(c) Subpoenas shall extend in jurisdiction throughout the United States or any territory or possession thereof.

§13.113 Noncompliance with the investigative process.

If any person fails to comply with the provisions of this subpart or with any subpoena or order issued by the Presiding Officer or the designee of the Presiding Officer, judicial enforcement may be initiated against that person under applicable statutes.

§13.115 Public proceedings.

(a) All investigative proceedings and depositions shall be public unless the Presiding Officer determines that the public interest requires otherwise.

(b) The Presiding Officer may order information contained in any report or document filed or in any testimony given pursuant to this subpart withheld from public disclosure when, in the judgment of the Presiding Officer, disclosure would adversely affect the interests of any person and is not required in the public interest or is not otherwise required by statute to be made available to the public. Any person may make written objection to the public disclosure of such information, stating the grounds for such objection.

§13.117 Conduct of investigative proceeding or deposition.

(a) The Presiding Officer or the designee of the Presiding Officer may question witnesses.

(b) Any witness may be accompanied by counsel.

(c) Any party may be accompanied by counsel and either the party or counsel may—

(1) Question witnesses, provided the questions are relevant and material to the matters under investigation and would not unduly impede the progress of the investigation; and

(2) Make objections on the record and argue the basis for such objections.

(d) Copies of all notices or written communications sent to a party or witness shall upon request be sent to that person's attorney of record.

§13.119 Rights of persons against self-incrimination.

(a) Whenever a person refuses, on the basis of a privilege against self-incrimination, to testify or provide other information during the course of any investigation conducted under this subpart, the Presiding Officer may, with the approval of the Attorney General of the United States, issue an order requiring the person to give testimony or provide other information. However, no testimony or other information so compelled (or any information directly or indirectly derived from such testimony or other information) may be used against the person in any criminal case, except in a prosecution for perjury, giving a false statement, or otherwise failing to comply with the order.

(b) The Presiding Officer may issue an order under this section if—

(1) The testimony or other information from the witness may be necessary to the public interest; and

(2) The witness has refused or is likely to refuse to testify or provide other information on the basis of a privilege against self-incrimination.

(c) Immunity provided by this section will not become effective until the person has refused to testify or provide other information on the basis of a privilege against self-incrimination, and an order under this section has been issued. An order, however, may be issued prospectively to become effective in the event of a claim of the privilege.

§13.121 Witness fees.

All witnesses appearing shall be compensated at the same rate as a witness appearing before a United States District Court.

§13.123 Submission by party to the investigation.

(a) During an investigation conducted under this subpart, a party may submit to the Presiding Officer—

(1) A list of witnesses to be called, specifying the subject matter of the expected testimony of each witness, and

(2) A list of exhibits to be considered for inclusion in the record.

(b) If the Presiding Officer determines that the testimony of a witness or the receipt of an exhibit in accordance with paragraph (a) of this section will be relevant, competent and material to the investigation, the Presiding Officer may subpoena the witness or use the exhibit during the investigation.

§13.125 Depositions.

Depositions for investigative purposes may be taken at the discretion of the Presiding Officer with reasonable notice to the party under investigation. Such depositions shall be taken before the Presiding Officer or other person authorized to administer oaths and designated by the Presiding Officer. The testimony shall be reduced to writing by the person taking the deposition, or under the direction of that person, and where possible shall then be subscribed by the deponent. Any person may be compelled to appear and testify and to produce physical and documentary evidence.

§13.127 Reports, decisions and orders.

The Presiding Officer shall issue a written report based on the record developed during the formal investigation, including a summary of principal conclusions. A summary of principal conclusions shall be prepared by the official who issued the order of investigation in every case which results in no action, or no action as to a particular party to the investigation. All such reports shall be furnished to the parties to the investigation and filed in the public docket. Insertion of the report in the Public Docket shall constitute "entering of record" and publication as prescribed by section 313(b) of the Federal Aviation Act.

§13.129 Post-investigation action.

A decision on whether to initiate subsequent action shall be made on the basis of the record developed during the formal investigation and any other information in the possession of the Administrator.

§13.131 Other procedures.

Any question concerning the scope or conduct of a formal investigation not covered in this subpart may be ruled on by the Presiding Officer on motion of the Presiding Officer, or on the motion of a party or a person testifying or producing evidence.

Subpart G—Rules of Practice in FAA Civil Penalty Actions

Source: Amdt. 13–21, 55 FR 27575, July 3, 1990, unless otherwise noted.

§13.201 Applicability.

(a) This subpart applies to all civil penalty actions initiated under §§13.16 of this part in which a hearing has been requested.

(b) This subpart applies only to proceedings initiated after September 7, 1988. All other cases, hearings, or other proceedings pending or in progress before September 7, 1988, are not affected by the rules in this subpart.

[Amdt. 13–21, 55 FR 27575, July 3, 1990, as amended by Amdt. 13–32, 69 FR 59498, Oct. 4, 2004]

§13.202 Definitions.

Administrative law judge means an administrative law judge appointed pursuant to the provisions of 5 U.S.C. 3105.

Agency attorney means the Deputy Chief Counsel for Operations, the Assistant Chief Counsel, Enforcement, the Assistant Chief Counsel, Europe, Africa, and Middle East Area Office, each Regional Counsel, the Aeronautical Center Counsel, or the Technical Center Counsel, or an attorney on the staff of the Assistant Chief Counsel, Enforcement, the Assistant Chief Counsel, Europe, Africa, and Middle East Area Office, each Regional Counsel, the Aeronautical Center Counsel, or the Technical Center Counsel who prosecutes a civil penalty action. An agency attorney shall not include:

(1) The Chief Counsel, the Deputy Chief Counsel for Policy and Adjudication, or the Assistant Chief Counsel for Litigation;

(2) Any attorney on the staff of the Assistant Chief Counsel for Litigation;

(3) Any attorney who is supervised in a civil penalty action by a person who provides such advice to the FAA decisionmaker in that action or a factually-related action.

Attorney means a person licensed by a state, the District of Columbia, or a territory of the United States to practice law or appear before the courts of that state or territory.

Complaint means a document issued by an agency attorney alleging a violation of the Federal Aviation Act of 1958, as amended, or a rule, regulation, or order issued thereunder, or the Hazardous Materials Transportation Act, or a rule, regulation, or order issued thereunder that has been filed with the hearing docket after a hearing has been requested pursuant to §13.16(d)(3) or §13.16(e)(2)(ii) of this part.

FAA decisionmaker means the Administrator of the Federal Aviation Administration, acting in the capacity of the decisionmaker on appeal, or any person to whom the Administrator has delegated the Administrator's decisionmaking authority in a civil penalty action. As used in this subpart, the FAA decisionmaker is the official authorized to issue a final decision and order of the Administrator in a civil penalty action.

Mail includes U.S. certified mail, U.S. registered mail, or use of an overnight express courier service.

Order assessing civil penalty means a document that contains a finding of violation of the Federal Aviation Act of 1958, as amended, or a rule, regulation, or order issued thereunder, or the Hazardous Materials Transportation Act, or a rule, regulation, or order issued thereunder and may direct payment of a civil penalty. Unless an appeal is filed with the FAA decisionmaker in a timely manner, an initial decision or order of an administrative law judge shall be considered an order assessing civil penalty if an administrative law judge finds that an alleged violation occurred and determines that a civil penalty, in an amount found appropriate by the administrative law judge, is warranted. Unless a petition for review is filed with a U.S. Court of Appeals in a timely manner, a final decision and order of the Administrator shall be considered an order assessing civil penalty if the FAA decisionmaker finds that an alleged violation occurred and a civil penalty is warranted.

Party means the respondent or the Federal Aviation Administration (FAA).

Personal delivery includes hand-delivery or use of a contract or express messenger service. "Personal delivery" does not include the use of Government interoffice mail service.

Pleading means a complaint, an answer, and any amendment of these documents permitted under this subpart.

Properly addressed means a document that shows an address contained in agency records, a residential, business, or other address submitted by a person on any document provided under this subpart, or any other address shown by other reasonable and available means.

Respondent means a person, corporation, or company named in a complaint.

[Docket No. 18884, 44 FR 63723, Nov. 5, 1979; as amended by Amdt. 13–21, 55 FR 27575, July 3, 1990; Amdt. 13–24, 58 FR 50241, Sept. 24, 1993; Amdt. 13–29, 62 FR 46866, Sept. 4, 1997; 70 FR 8238, Feb. 18, 2005]

§13.203 Separation of functions.

(a) Civil penalty proceedings, including hearings, shall be prosecuted by an agency attorney.

(b) An agency employee engaged in the performance of investigative or prosecutorial functions in a civil penalty action shall not, in that case or a factually-related case, participate or give advice in a decision by the administrative law judge or by the FAA decisionmaker on appeal, except as counsel or a witness in the public proceedings.

(c) The Chief Counsel, the Deputy Chief Counsel for Policy and Adjudication, and the Assistant Chief Counsel for Litigation, or an attorney on the staff of the Assistant Chief Counsel for Litigation will advise the FAA decisionmaker regarding an initial decision or any appeal of a civil penalty action to the FAA decisionmaker.

[Amdt. 13–21, 55 FR 27575, July 3, 1990; as amended by Amdt. 13–24, 58 FR 50241, Sept. 24, 1993; 70 FR 8238, Feb. 18, 2005]

§13.204 Appearances and rights of parties.

(a) Any party may appear and be heard in person.

(b) Any party may be accompanied, represented, or advised by an attorney or representative designated by the party and may be examined by that attorney or representative in any proceeding governed by this subpart. An attorney or representative who represents a party may file a notice of appearance in the action, in the manner provided in §13.210 of this subpart, and shall serve a copy of the notice of appearance on each party, in the manner provided in §13.211 of this subpart, before participating in any proceeding governed by this subpart. The attorney or representative shall include the name, address, and telephone number of the attorney or representative in the notice of appearance.

(c) Any person may request a copy of a document upon payment of reasonable costs. A person may keep an original document, data, or evidence, with the consent of the administrative law judge, by substituting a legible copy of the document for the record.

§13.205 Administrative law judges.

(a) *Powers of an administrative law judge.* In accordance with the rules of this subpart, an administrative law judge may:

(1) Give notice of, and hold, prehearing conferences and hearings;

(2) Administer oaths and affirmations;

(3) Issue subpoenas authorized by law and issue notices of deposition requested by the parties;

(4) Rule on offers of proof;

(5) Receive relevant and material evidence;

(6) Regulate the course of the hearing in accordance with the rules of this subpart;

(7) Hold conferences to settle or to simplify the issues by consent of the parties;

(8) Dispose of procedural motions and requests; and

(9) Make findings of fact and conclusions of law, and issue an initial decision.

(b) *Limitations on the power of the administrative law judge.* The administrative law judge shall not issue an order of contempt, award costs to any party, or impose any sanction not specified in this subpart. If the administrative law judge imposes any sanction not specified in this subpart, a party may file an interlocutory appeal of right with the FAA decisionmaker pursuant to §13.219(c)(4) of this subpart. This section does not preclude an administrative law judge from issuing an order that bars a person from a specific proceeding based on a finding of obstreperous or disruptive behavior in that specific proceeding.

(c) *Disqualification.* The administrative law judge may disqualify himself or herself at any time. A party may file a motion, pursuant to §13.218(f)(6), requesting that an administrative law judge be disqualified from the proceedings.

[Amdt. 13–21, 55 FR 27575, July 3, 1990; 55 FR 29293, July 18, 1990]

§13.206 Intervention.

(a) A person may submit a motion for leave to intervene as a party in a civil penalty action. Except for good cause shown, a motion for leave to intervene shall be submitted not later than 10 days before the hearing.

(b) If the administrative law judge finds that intervention will not unduly broaden the issues or delay the proceedings, the administrative law judge may grant a motion for leave to intervene if the person will be bound by any order or decision entered in the action or the person has a property, financial, or other legitimate interest that may not be addressed adequately by the parties. The administrative law judge may determine the extent to which an intervenor may participate in the proceedings.

§13.207 Certification of documents.

(a) *Signature required.* The attorney of record, the party, or the party's representative shall sign each document tendered for filing with the hearing docket clerk, the administrative law judge, the FAA decisionmaker on appeal, or served on each party.

(b) *Effect of signing a document.* By signing a document, the attorney of record, the party, or the party's representative certifies that the attorney, the party, or the party's representative has read the document and, based on reasonable inquiry and to the best of that person's knowledge, information, and belief, the document is—

(1) Consistent with these rules;

(2) Warranted by existing law or that a good faith argument exists for extension, modification, or reversal of existing law; and

(3) Not unreasonable or unduly burdensome or expensive, not made to harass any person, not made to cause unnecessary delay, not made to cause needless increase in the cost of the proceedings, or for any other improper purpose.

(c) *Sanctions.* If the attorney of record, the party, or the party's representative signs a document in violation of this section, the administrative law judge or the FAA decisionmaker shall:

(1) Strike the pleading signed in violation of this section;

(2) Strike the request for discovery or the discovery response signed in violation of this section and preclude further discovery by the party;

(3) Deny the motion or request signed in violation of this section;

(4) Exclude the document signed in violation of this section from the record;

(5) Dismiss the interlocutory appeal and preclude further appeal on that issue by the party who filed the appeal until an initial decision has been entered on the record; or

(6) Dismiss the appeal of the administrative law judge's initial decision to the FAA decisionmaker.

§13.208 Complaint.

(a) *Filing.* The agency attorney shall file the original and one copy of the complaint with the hearing docket clerk, or may file a written motion pursuant to §l3.218(f)(2)(i) of this subpart instead of filing a complaint, not later than 20 days after receipt by the agency attorney of a request for hearing.

The agency attorney should suggest a location for the hearing when filing the complaint.

(b) *Service.* An agency attorney shall personally deliver or mail a copy of the complaint on the respondent, the president of the corporation or company named as a respondent, or a person designated by the respondent to accept service of documents in the civil penalty action.

(c) *Contents.* A complaint shall set forth the facts alleged, any regulation allegedly violated by the respondent, and the proposed civil penalty in sufficient detail to provide notice of any factual or legal allegation and proposed civil penalty.

(d) *Motion to dismiss allegations or complaint.* Instead of filing an answer to the complaint, a respondent may move to dismiss the complaint, or that part of the complaint, alleging a violation that occurred on or after August 2, 1990, and more than 2 years before an agency attorney issued a notice of proposed civil penalty to the respondent.

(1) An administrative law judge may not grant the motion and dismiss the complaint or part of the complaint if the administrative law judge finds that the agency has shown good cause for any delay in issuing the notice of proposed civil penalty.

(2) If the agency fails to show good cause for any delay, an administrative law judge may dismiss the complaint, or that part of the complaint, alleging a violation that occurred more than 2 years before an agency attorney issued the notice of proposed civil penalty to the respondent.

(3) A party may appeal the administrative law judge's ruling on the motion to dismiss the complaint or any part of the complaint in accordance with §13.219(b) of this subpart.

[Amdt. 13–21, 55 FR 27575, July 3, 1990; as amended by Amdt. 13–22, 55 FR 31176, Aug. 1, 1990]

§13.209 Answer.

(a) *Writing required.* A respondent shall file a written answer to the complaint, or may file a written motion pursuant to §13.208(d) or §13.218(f)(1-4) of this subpart instead of filing an answer, not later than 30 days after service of the complaint. The answer may be in the form of a letter but must be dated and signed by the person responding to the complaint. An answer may be typewritten or may be legibly handwritten.

(b) *Filing and address.* A person filing an answer shall personally deliver or mail the original and one copy of the answer for filing with the hearing docket clerk, not later than 30 days after service of the complaint to the Hearing Docket at the appropriate address set forth in §13.210(a) of this subpart. The person filing an answer should suggest a location for the hearing when filing the answer.

(c) *Service.* A person filing an answer shall serve a copy of the answer on the agency attorney who filed the complaint.

(d) *Contents.* An answer shall specifically state any affirmative defense that the respondent intends to assert at the hearing. A person filing an answer may include a brief statement of any relief requested in the answer.

(e) *Specific denial of allegations required.* A person filing an answer shall admit, deny, or state that the person is without sufficient knowledge or information to admit or deny, each numbered paragraph of the complaint. Any statement or allegation contained in the complaint that is not specifically denied in the answer may be deemed an admission of the truth of that allegation. A general denial of the complaint is deemed a failure to file an answer.

(f) *Failure to file answer.* A person's failure to file an answer without good cause shall be deemed an admission of the truth of each allegation contained in the complaint.

[Amdt. 13–21, 55 FR 27575, July 3, 1990; as amended at 70 FR 8238, Feb. 18, 2005]

§13.210 Filing of documents.

(a) *Address and method of filing.* A person tendering a document for filing shall personally deliver or mail the signed original and one copy of each document to the Hearing Docket using the appropriate address:

(1) If delivery is in person, or via expedited courier service: Federal Aviation Administration, 600 Independence Avenue, SW, Wilbur Wright Building—Room 2014, Washington, DC 20591; Att: Hearing Docket Clerk, AGC-430.

(2) If delivery is via U.S. Mail: Federal Aviation Administration, 800 Independence Avenue, SW, Washington, DC 20591; Att: Hearing Docket Clerk, AGC-430, Wilbur Wright Building—Room 2014.

(b) *Date of filing.* A document shall be considered to be filed on the date of personal delivery; or if mailed, the mailing date shown on the certificate of service, the date shown on the postmark if there is no certificate of service, or other mailing date shown by other evidence if there is no certificate of service or postmark.

(c) *Form.* Each document shall be typewritten or legibly handwritten.

(d) *Contents.* Unless otherwise specified in this subpart, each document must contain a short, plain statement of the facts on which the person's case rests and a brief statement of the action requested in the document.

(e) *Internet accessibility of documents filed in the Hearing Docket.*

(1) Unless protected from public disclosure by an order of the ALJ under §13.226, all documents filed in the Hearing Docket are accessible through the DOT's Docket Management System (DMS): http://dms.dot.gov.

To access a particular case file, use the DMS number assigned to the case.

(2) Decisions and orders issued by the Administrator in civil penalty cases, as well as indexes of decisions and other pertinent information are available through the FAA civil penalty adjudication Web site at http://www.faa.gov/agc/website.

[Amdt. 13–21, 55 FR 27575, July 3, 1990; as amended by 55 FR 29293, July 18, 1990; 70 FR 8238, Feb. 18, 2005]

§13.211 Service of documents.

(a) *General.* A person shall serve a copy of any document filed with the Hearing Docket on each party at the time of filing. Service on a party's attorney of record or a party's designated representative may be considered adequate service on the party.

(b) *Type of service.* A person may serve documents by personal delivery or by mail.

(c) *Certificate of service.* A person may attach a certificate of service to a document tendered for filing with the hearing docket clerk. A certificate of service shall consist of a statement, dated and signed by the person filing the document, that the document was personally delivered or mailed to each party on a specific date.

(d) *Date of service.* The date of service shall be the date of personal delivery; or if mailed, the mailing date shown on the certificate of service, the date shown on the postmark if there is no certificate of service, or other mailing date shown by other evidence if there is no certificate of service or postmark.

(e) *Additional time after service by mail.* Whenever a party has a right or a duty to act or to make any response within a prescribed period after service by mail, or on a date certain after service by mail, 5 days shall be added to the prescribed period.

(f) *Service by the administrative law judge.* The administrative law judge shall serve a copy of each document including, but not limited to, notices of prehearing conferences and hearings, rulings on motions, decisions, and orders, upon each party to the proceedings by personal delivery or by mail.

(g) *Valid service.* A document that was properly addressed, was sent in accordance with this subpart, and that was returned, that was not claimed, or that was refused, is deemed to have been served in accordance with this subpart. The service shall be considered valid as of the date and the time that the document was deposited with a contract or express messenger, the document was mailed, or personal delivery of the document was refused.

(h) *Presumption of service.* There shall be a presumption of service where a party or a person, who customarily receives mail, or receives it in the ordinary course of business, at either the person's residence or the person's principal place of business, acknowledges receipt of the document.

§13.212 Computation of time.

(a) This section applies to any period of time prescribed or allowed by this subpart, by notice or order of the administrative law judge, or by any applicable statute.

(b) The date of an act, event, or default, after which a designated time period begins to run, is not included in a computation of time under this subpart.

(c) The last day of a time period is included in a computation of time unless it is a Saturday, Sunday, or a legal holiday. If the last day of the time period is a Saturday, Sunday, or legal holiday, the time period runs until the end of the next day that is not a Saturday, Sunday, or legal holiday.

§13.213 Extension of time.

(a) *Oral requests.* The parties may agree to extend for a reasonable period the time for filing a document under this subpart. If the parties agree, the administrative law judge shall grant one extension of time to each party. The party seeking the extension of time shall submit a draft order to the administrative law judge to be signed by the administrative law judge and filed with the hearing docket clerk. The administrative law judge may grant additional oral requests for an extension of time where the parties agree to the extension.

(b) *Written motion.* A party shall file a written motion for an extension of time with the administrative law judge not later than 7 days before the document is due unless good cause for the late filing is shown. A party filing a written motion for an extension of time shall serve a copy of the motion on each party. The administrative law judge may grant the extension of time if good cause for the extension is shown.

(c) *Failure to rule.* If the administrative law judge fails to rule on a written motion for an extension of time by the date the document was due, the motion for an extension of time is deemed granted for no more than 20 days after the original date the document was to be filed.

§13.214 Amendment of pleadings.

(a) *Filing and service.* A party shall file the amendment with the administrative law judge and shall serve a copy of the amendment on all parties to the proceeding.

(b) *Time.* A party shall file an amendment to a complaint or an answer within the following:

(1) Not later than 15 days before the scheduled date of a hearing, a party may amend a complaint or an answer without the consent of the administrative law judge.

(2) Less than 15 days before the scheduled date of a hearing, the administrative law judge may allow amendment of a complaint or an answer only for good cause shown in a motion to amend.

(c) *Responses.* The administrative law judge shall allow a reasonable time, but not more than 20 days from the date of filing, for other parties to respond if an amendment to a complaint, answer, or other pleading has been filed with the administrative law judge.

§13.215 Withdrawal of complaint or request for hearing.

At any time before or during a hearing, an agency attorney may withdraw a complaint or a party may withdraw a request for a hearing without the consent of the administrative law judge. If an agency attorney withdraws the complaint or a party withdraws the request for a hearing and the answer, the administrative law judge shall dismiss the proceedings under this subpart with prejudice.

§13.216 Waivers.

Waivers of any rights provided by statute or regulation shall be in writing or by stipulation made at a hearing and entered into the record. The parties shall set forth the precise terms of the waiver and any conditions.

§13.217 Joint procedural or discovery schedule.

(a) *General.* The parties may agree to submit a schedule for filing all prehearing motions, a schedule for conducting discovery in the proceedings, or a schedule that will govern all prehearing motions and discovery in the proceedings.

(b) *Form and content of schedule.* If the parties agree to a joint procedural or discovery schedule, one of the parties shall file the joint schedule with the administrative law judge, setting forth the dates to which the parties have agreed, and shall serve a copy of the joint schedule on each party.

(1) The joint schedule may include, but need not be limited to, requests for discovery, any objections to discovery requests, responses to discovery requests to which there are no objections, submission of prehearing motions, responses to prehearing motions, exchange of exhibits to be introduced at the hearing, and a list of witnesses that may be called at the hearing.

(2) Each party shall sign the original joint schedule to be filed with the administrative law judge.

(c) *Time.* The parties may agree to submit all prehearing motions and responses and may agree to close discovery in the proceedings under the joint schedule within a reasonable time before the date of the hearing, but not later than 15 days before the hearing.

(d) *Order establishing joint schedule.* The administrative law judge shall approve the joint schedule filed by the parties. One party shall submit a draft order establishing a joint schedule to the administrative law judge to be signed by the administrative law judge and filed with the hearing docket clerk.

(e) *Disputes.* The administrative law judge shall resolve disputes regarding discovery or disputes regarding compliance with the joint schedule as soon as possible so that the parties may continue to comply with the joint schedule.

(f) *Sanctions for failure to comply with joint schedule.* If a party fails to comply with the administrative law judge's order establishing a joint schedule, the administrative law judge may direct that party to comply with a motion to discovery request or, limited to the extent of the party's failure to comply with a motion or discovery request, the administrative law judge may:

(1) Strike that portion of a party's pleadings;

(2) Preclude prehearing or discovery motions by that party;

(3) Preclude admission of that portion of a party's evidence at the hearing, or

(4) Preclude that portion of the testimony of that party's witnesses at the hearing.

§13.218 Motions.

(a) *General.* A party applying for an order or ruling not specifically provided in this subpart shall do so by motion. A party shall comply with the requirements of this section when filing a motion with the administrative law judge. A party shall serve a copy of each motion on each party.

(b) *Form and contents.* A party shall state the relief sought by the motion and the particular grounds supporting that relief. If a party has evidence in support of a motion, the party shall attach any supporting evidence, including affidavits, to the motion.

(c) *Filing of motions.* A motion made prior to the hearing must be in writing. Unless otherwise agreed by the parties or for good cause shown, a party shall file any prehearing motion, and shall serve a copy on each party, not later than 30 days before the hearing. Motions introduced during a hearing may be made orally on the record unless the administrative law judge directs otherwise.

(d) *Answers to motions.* Any party may file an answer, with affidavits or other evidence in support of the answer, not later than 10 days after service of a written motion on that party. When a motion is made during a hearing, the answer may be made at the hearing on the record, orally or in writing, within a reasonable time determined by the administrative law judge.

(e) *Rulings on motions.* The administrative law judge shall rule on all motions as follows:

(1) *Discovery motions.* The administrative law judge shall resolve all pending discovery motions not later than 10 days before the hearing.

(2) *Prehearing motions.* The administrative law judge shall resolve all pending prehearing motions not later than 7 days before the hearing. If the administrative law judge issues a ruling or order orally, the administrative law judge shall serve a written copy of the ruling or order, within 3 days, on each party. In all other cases, the administrative law judge shall issue rulings and orders in writing and shall serve a copy of the ruling or order on each party.

(3) *Motions made during the hearing.* The administrative law judge may issue rulings and orders on motions made

during the hearing orally. Oral rulings or orders on motions must be made on the record.

(f) *Specific motions.* A party may file the following motions with the administrative law judge:

(1) *Motion to dismiss for insufficiency.* A respondent may file a motion to dismiss the complaint for insufficiency instead of filing an answer. If the administrative law judge denies the motion to dismiss the complaint for insufficiency, the respondent shall file an answer not later than 10 days after service of the administrative law judge's denial of the motion. A motion to dismiss the complaint for insufficiency must show that the complaint fails to state a violation of the Federal Aviation Act of 1958, as amended, or a rule, regulation, or order issued thereunder, or a violation of the Hazardous Materials Transportation Act, or a rule, regulation, or order issued thereunder.

(2) *Motion to dismiss.* A party may file a motion to dismiss, specifying the grounds for dismissal. If an administrative law judge grants a motion to dismiss in part, a party may appeal the administrative law judge's ruling on the motion to dismiss under §13.219(b) of this subpart.

(i) *Motion to dismiss a request for a hearing.* An agency attorney may file a motion to dismiss a request for a hearing instead of filing a complaint. If the motion to dismiss is not granted, the agency attorney shall file the complaint and shall serve a copy of the complaint on each party not later than 10 days after service of the administrative law judge's ruling or order on the motion to dismiss. If the motion to dismiss is granted and the proceedings are terminated without a hearing, the respondent may file an appeal pursuant to §13.233 of this subpart. If required by the decision on appeal, the agency attorney shall file a complaint and shall serve a copy of the complaint on each party not later than 10 days after service of the decision on appeal.

(ii) *Motion to dismiss a complaint.* A respondent may file a motion to dismiss a complaint instead of filing an answer. If the motion to dismiss is not granted, the respondent shall file an answer and shall serve a copy of the answer on each party not later than 10 days after service of the administrative law judge's ruling or order on the motion to dismiss. If the motion to dismiss is granted and the proceedings are terminated without a hearing, the agency attorney may file an appeal pursuant to §13.233 of this subpart. If required by the decision on appeal, the respondent shall file an answer and shall serve a copy of the answer on each party not later than 10 days after service of the decision on appeal.

(3) *Motion for more definite statement.* A party may file a motion for more definite statement of any pleading which requires a response under this subpart. A party shall set forth, in detail, the indefinite or uncertain allegations contained in a complaint or response to any pleading and shall submit the details that the party believes would make the allegation or response definite and certain.

(i) *Complaint.* A respondent may file a motion requesting a more definite statement of the allegations contained in the complaint instead of filing an answer. If the administrative law judge grants the motion, the agency attorney shall supply a more definite statement not later than 15 days after service of the ruling granting the motion. If the agency attorney fails to supply a more definite statement, the administrative law judge shall strike the allegations in the complaint to which the motion is directed. If the administrative law judge denies the motion, the respondent shall file an answer and shall serve a copy of the answer on each party not later than 10 days after service of the order of denial.

(ii) *Answer.* An agency attorney may file a motion requesting a more definite statement if an answer fails to respond clearly to the allegations in the complaint. If the administrative law judge grants the motion, the respondent shall supply a more definite statement not later than 15 days after service of the ruling on the motion. If the respondent fails to supply a more definite statement, the administrative law judge shall strike those statements in the answer to which the motion is directed. The respondent's failure to supply a more definite statement may be deemed an admission of unanswered allegations in the complaint.

(4) *Motion to strike.* Any party may make a motion to strike any insufficient allegation or defense, or any redundant, immaterial, or irrelevant matter in a pleading. A party shall file a motion to strike with the administrative law judge and shall serve a copy on each party before a response is required under this subpart or, if a response is not required, not later than 10 days after service of the pleading.

(5) *Motion for decision.* A party may make a motion for decision, regarding all or any part of the proceedings, at any time before the administrative law judge has issued an initial decision in the proceedings. The administrative law judge shall grant a party's motion for decision if the pleadings, depositions, answers to interrogatories, admissions, matters that the administrative law judge has officially noticed, or evidence introduced during the hearing show that there is no genuine issue of material fact and that the party making the motion is entitled to a decision as a matter of law. The party making the motion for decision has the burden of showing that there is no genuine issue of material fact disputed by the parties.

(6) *Motion for disqualification.* A party may file a motion for disqualification with the administrative law judge and shall serve a copy on each party. A party may file the motion at any time after the administrative law judge has been assigned to the proceedings but shall make the motion before the administrative law judge files an initial decision in the proceedings.

(i) *Motion and supporting affidavit.* A party shall state the grounds for disqualification, including, but not limited to, personal bias, pecuniary interest, or other factors showing disqualification, in the motion for disqualification. A party shall submit an affidavit with the motion for disqualification that sets forth, in detail, the matters alleged to constitute grounds for disqualification.

(ii) *Answer.* A party shall respond to the motion for disqualification not later than 5 days after service of the motion for disqualification.

(iii) *Decision on motion for disqualification.* The administrative law judge shall render a decision on the motion for disqualification not later than 15 days after the motion has been filed. If the administrative law judge finds that the motion for disqualification and supporting affidavit show a basis for disqualification, the administrative law judge shall withdraw from the proceedings immediately. If the administrative law judge finds that disqualification is not warranted, the administrative law judge shall deny the motion and state the grounds for the denial on the record. If the administrative law judge fails to rule on a party's motion for disqualification within 15 days after the motion has been filed, the motion is deemed granted.

(iv) *Appeal.* A party may appeal the administrative law judge's denial of the motion for disqualification in accordance with §13.219(b) of this subpart.

§13.219 Interlocutory appeals.

(a) *General.* Unless otherwise provided in this subpart, a party may not appeal a ruling or decision of the administrative law judge to the FAA decisionmaker until the initial decision has been entered on the record. A decision or order of the FAA decisionmaker on the interlocutory appeal does not constitute a final order of the Administrator for the purposes of judicial appellate review under section 1006 of the Federal Aviation Act of 1958, as amended.

(b) *Interlocutory appeal for cause.* If a party files a written request for an interlocutory appeal for cause with the administrative law judge, or orally requests an interlocutory appeal for cause, the proceedings are stayed until the administrative law judge issues a decision on the request. If the administrative law judge grants the request, the proceedings are stayed until the FAA decisionmaker issues a decision on the interlocutory appeal. The administrative law judge shall grant an interlocutory appeal for cause if a party shows that delay of the appeal would be detrimental to the public interest or would result in undue prejudice to any party.

(c) *Interlocutory appeals of right.* If a party notifies the administrative law judge of an interlocutory appeal of right, the proceedings are stayed until the FAA decisionmaker issues a decision on the interlocutory appeal. A party may file an interlocutory appeal with the FAA decisionmaker, without the consent of the administrative law judge, before an initial decision has been entered in the case of:

(1) A ruling or order by the administrative law judge barring a person from the proceedings.

(2) Failure of the administrative law judge to dismiss the proceedings in accordance with §13.215 of this subpart.

(3) A ruling or order by the administrative law judge in violation of §13.205(b) of this subpart.

(d) *Procedure.* A party shall file a notice of interlocutory appeal, with supporting documents, with the FAA decisionmaker and the hearing docket clerk, and shall serve a copy of the notice and supporting documents on each party and the administrative law judge, not later than 10 days after the administrative law judge's decision forming the basis of an interlocutory appeal of right or not later than 10 days after the administrative law judge's decision granting an interlocutory appeal for cause, whichever is appropriate. A party shall file a reply brief, if any, with the FAA decisionmaker and serve a copy of the reply brief on each party, not later than 10 days after service of the appeal brief. The FAA decisionmaker shall render a decision on the interlocutory appeal, on the record and as a part of the decision in the proceedings, within a reasonable time after receipt of the interlocutory appeal.

(e) The FAA decisionmaker may reject frivolous, repetitive, or dilatory appeals, and may issue an order precluding one or more parties from making further interlocutory appeals in a proceeding in which there have been frivolous, repetitive, or dilatory interlocutory appeals.

[Amdt. 13–21, 55 FR 27575, July 3, 1990; as amended by Amdt. 13–23, 55 FR 45983, Oct. 31, 1990]

§13.220 Discovery.

(a) *Initiation of discovery.* Any party may initiate discovery described in this section, without the consent or approval of the administrative law judge, at any time after a complaint has been filed in the proceedings.

(b) *Methods of discovery.* The following methods of discovery are permitted under this section: depositions on oral examination or written questions of any person; written interrogatories directed to a party; requests for production of documents or tangible items to any person; and requests for admission by a party. A party is not required to file written interrogatories and responses, requests for production of documents or tangible items and responses, and requests for admission and response with the administrative law judge or the hearing docket clerk. In the event of a discovery dispute, a party shall attach a copy of these documents in support of a motion made under this section.

(c) *Service on the agency.* A party shall serve each discovery request directed to the agency or any agency employee on the agency attorney of record.

(d) *Time for response to discovery requests.* Unless otherwise directed by this subpart or agreed by the parties, a party shall respond to a request for discovery, including filing objections to a request for discovery, not later than 30 days of service of the request.

(e) *Scope of discovery.* Subject to the limits on discovery set forth in paragraph (f) of this section, a party may discover any matter that is not privileged and that is relevant to the subject matter of the proceeding. A party may discover information that relates to the claim or defense of any party including the existence, description, nature, custody, condition, and location of any document or other tangible item and the identity and location of any person having knowledge of discoverable matter. A party may discover facts known, or opinions held, by an expert who any other party expects to call to testify at the hearing. A party has no ground to object to a discovery request on the basis that the information sought would not be admissible at the hearing if the information sought during discovery is reasonably calculated to lead to the discovery of admissible evidence.

(f) *Limiting discovery.* The administrative law judge shall limit the frequency and extent of discovery permitted by this section if a party shows that—

(1) The information requested is cumulative or repetitious;

(2) The information requested can be obtained from another less burdensome and more convenient source;

(3) The party requesting the information has had ample opportunity to obtain the information through other discovery methods permitted under this section; or

(4) The method or scope of discovery requested by the party is unduly burdensome or expensive.

(g) *Confidential orders.* A party or person who has received a discovery request for information that is related to a trade secret, confidential or sensitive material, competitive or commercial information, proprietary data, or information on research and development, may file a motion for a confidential order with the administrative law judge and shall serve a copy of the motion for a confidential order on each party.

(1) The party or person making the motion must show that the confidential order is necessary to protect the information from disclosure to the public.

(2) If the administrative law judge determines that the requested material is not necessary to decide the case, the administrative law judge shall preclude any inquiry into the matter by any party.

(3) If the administrative law judge determines that the requested material may be disclosed during discovery, the administrative law judge may order that the material may be discovered and disclosed under limited conditions or may be used only under certain terms and conditions.

(4) If the administrative law judge determines that the requested material is necessary to decide the case and that a confidential order is warranted, the administrative law judge shall provide:

(i) An opportunity for review of the document by the parties off the record;

(ii) Procedures for excluding the information from the record; and

(iii) Order that the parties shall not disclose the information in any manner and the parties shall not use the information in any other proceeding.

(h) *Protective orders.* A party or a person who has received a request for discovery may file a motion for protective order with the administrative law judge and shall serve a copy of the motion for protective order on each party. The party or person making the motion must show that the protective order is necessary to protect the party or the person from annoyance, embarrassment, oppression, or undue burden or expense. As part of the protective order, the administrative law judge may:

(1) Deny the discovery request;

(2) Order that discovery be conducted only on specified terms and conditions, including a designation of the time or place for discovery or a determination of the method of discovery; or

(3) Limit the scope of discovery or preclude any inquiry into certain matters during discovery.

(i) *Duty to supplement or amend responses.* A party who has responded to a discovery request has a duty to supplement or amend the response, as soon as the information is known, as follows:

(1) A party shall supplement or amend any response to a question requesting the identity and location of any person having knowledge of discoverable matters.

(2) A party shall supplement or amend any response to a question requesting the identity of each person who will be called to testify at the hearing as an expert witness and the subject matter and substance of that witness' testimony.

(3) A party shall supplement or amend any response that was incorrect when made or any response that was correct when made but is no longer correct, accurate, or complete.

(j) *Depositions.* The following rules apply to depositions taken pursuant to this section:

(1) *Form.* A deposition shall be taken on the record and reduced to writing. The person being deposed shall sign the deposition unless the parties agree to waive the requirement of a signature.

(2) *Administration of oaths.* Within the United States, or a territory or possession subject to the jurisdiction of the United States, a party shall take a deposition before a person authorized to administer oaths by the laws of the United States or authorized by the law of the place where the examination is held. In foreign countries, a party shall take a deposition in any manner allowed by the Federal Rules of Civil Procedure.

(3) *Notice of deposition.* A party shall serve a notice of deposition, stating the time and place of the deposition and the name and address of each person to be examined, on the person to be deposed, on the administrative law judge, on the hearing docket clerk, and on each party not later than 7 days before the deposition. A party may serve a notice of deposition less than 7 days before the deposition only with consent of the administrative law judge. If a subpoena *duces tecum* is to be served on the person to be examined, the party shall attach a copy of the subpoena *duces tecum* that describes the materials to be produced at the deposition to the notice of deposition.

(4) *Use of depositions.* A party may use any part or all of a deposition at a hearing authorized under this subpart only upon a showing of good cause. The deposition may be used against any party who was present or represented at the deposition or who had reasonable notice of the deposition.

(k) *Interrogatories.* A party, the party's attorney, or the party's representative may sign the party's responses to interrogatories. A party shall answer each interrogatory separately and completely in writing. If a party objects to an interrogatory, the party shall state the objection and the reasons for the objection. An opposing party may use any part or all of a party's responses to interrogatories at a hearing authorized under this subpart to the extent that the response is relevant, material, and not repetitious.

(1) A party shall not serve more than 30 interrogatories to each other party. Each subpart of an interrogatory shall be counted as a separate interrogatory.

(2) A party shall file a motion for leave to serve additional interrogatories on a party with the administrative law judge before serving additional interrogatories on a party. The administrative law judge shall grant the motion only if the party shows good cause for the party's failure to inquire about the information previously and that the information cannot reasonably be obtained using less burdensome discovery methods or be obtained from other sources.

(l) *Requests for admission.* A party may serve a written request for admission of the truth of any matter within the scope of discovery under this section or the authenticity of any document described in the request. A party shall set forth each request for admission separately. A party shall serve copies of documents referenced in the request for admission unless the documents have been provided or are reasonably available for inspection and copying.

(1) *Time.* A party's failure to respond to a request for admission, in writing and signed by the attorney or the party, not later than 30 days after service of the request, is deemed an admission of the truth of the statement or statements contained in the request for admission. The administrative law judge may determine that a failure to respond to a request for admission is not deemed an admission of the truth

if a party shows that the failure was due to circumstances beyond the control of the party or the party's attorney.

(2) *Response.* A party may object to a request for admission and shall state the reasons for objection. A party may specifically deny the truth of the matter or describe the reasons why the party is unable to truthfully deny or admit the matter. If a party is unable to deny or admit the truth of the matter, the party shall show that the party has made reasonable inquiry into the matter or that the information known to, or readily obtainable by, the party is insufficient to enable the party to admit or deny the matter. A party may admit or deny any part of the request for admission. If the administrative law judge determines that a response does not comply with the requirements of this rule or that the response is insufficient, the matter is deemed admitted.

(3) *Effect of admission.* Any matter admitted or deemed admitted under this section is conclusively established for the purpose of the hearing and appeal.

(m) *Motion to compel discovery.* A party may make a motion to compel discovery if a person refuses to answer a question during a deposition, a party fails or refuses to answer an interrogatory, if a person gives an evasive or incomplete answer during a deposition or when responding to an interrogatory, or a party fails or refuses to produce documents or tangible items. During a deposition, the proponent of a question may complete the deposition or may adjourn the examination before making a motion to compel if a person refuses to answer.

(n) *Failure to comply with a discovery order or order to compel.* If a party fails to comply with a discovery order or an order to compel, the administrative law judge, limited to the extent of the party's failure to comply with the discovery order or motion to compel, may:

(1) Strike that portion of a party's pleadings;

(2) Preclude prehearing or discovery motions by that party;

(3) Preclude admission of that portion of a party's evidence at the hearing; or

(4) Preclude that portion of the testimony of that party's witnesses at the hearing.

[Amdt. 13–21, 55 FR 27575, July 3, 1990; as amended by Amdt. 13–23, 55 FR 45983, Oct. 31, 1990]

§13.221 Notice of hearing.

(a) *Notice.* The administrative law judge shall give each party at least 60 days notice of the date, time, and location of the hearing.

(b) *Date, time, and location of the hearing.* The administrative law judge to whom the proceedings have been assigned shall set a reasonable date, time, and location for the hearing. The administrative law judge shall consider the need for discovery and any joint procedural or discovery schedule submitted by the parties when determining the hearing date. The administrative law judge shall give due regard to the convenience of the parties, the location where the majority of the witnesses reside or work, and whether the location is served by a scheduled air carrier.

(c) *Earlier hearing.* With the consent of the administrative law judge, the parties may agree to hold the hearing on an earlier date than the date specified in the notice of hearing.

§13.222 Evidence.

(a) *General.* A party is entitled to present the party's case or defense by oral, documentary, or demonstrative evidence, to submit rebuttal evidence, and to conduct any cross-examination that may be required for a full and true disclosure of the facts.

(b) *Admissibility.* A party may introduce any oral, documentary, or demonstrative evidence in support of the party's case or defense. The administrative law judge shall admit any oral, documentary, or demonstrative evidence introduced by a party but shall exclude irrelevant, immaterial, or unduly repetitious evidence.

(c) *Hearsay evidence.* Hearsay evidence is admissible in proceedings governed by this subpart. The fact that evidence submitted by a party is hearsay goes only to the weight of the evidence and does not affect its admissibility.

§13.223 Standard of proof.

The administrative law judge shall issue an initial decision or shall rule in a party's favor only if the decision or ruling is supported by, and in accordance with, the reliable, probative, and substantial evidence contained in the record. In order to prevail, the party with the burden of proof shall prove the party's case or defense by a preponderance of reliable, probative, and substantial evidence.

§13.224 Burden of proof.

(a) Except in the case of an affirmative defense, the burden of proof is on the agency.

(b) Except as otherwise provided by statute or rule, the proponent of a motion, request, or order has the burden of proof.

(c) A party who has asserted an affirmative defense has the burden of proving the affirmative defense.

§13.225 Offer of proof.

A party whose evidence has been excluded by a ruling of the administrative law judge may offer the evidence for the record on appeal.

§13.226 Public disclosure of evidence.

(a) The administrative law judge may order that any information contained in the record be withheld from public disclosure. Any person may object to disclosure of information in the record by filing a written motion to withhold specific information with the administrative law judge and serving a copy of the motion on each party. The party shall state the specific grounds for nondisclosure in the motion.

(b) The administrative law judge shall grant the motion to withhold information in the record if, based on the motion and any response to the motion, the administrative law judge determines that disclosure would be detrimental to aviation safety, disclosure would not be in the public interest, or that the information is not otherwise required to be made available to the public.

§13.227 Expert or opinion witnesses.

An employee of the agency may not be called as an expert or opinion witness, for any party other than the FAA, in any proceeding governed by this subpart. An employee of a respondent may not be called by an agency attorney as an expert or opinion witness for the FAA in any proceeding governed by this subpart to which the respondent is a party.

§13.228 Subpoenas.

(a) *Request for subpoena.* A party may obtain a subpoena to compel the attendance of a witness at a deposition or hearing or to require the production of documents or tangible items from the hearing docket clerk. The hearing docket clerk shall deliver the subpoena, signed by the hearing docket clerk or an administrative law judge but otherwise in blank, to the party. The party shall complete the subpoena, stating the title of the action and the date and time for the witness' attendance or production of documents or items. The party who obtained the subpoena shall serve the subpoena on the witness.

(b) *Motion to quash or modify the subpoena.* A party, or any person upon whom a subpoena has been served, may file a motion to quash or modify the subpoena with the administrative law judge at or before the time specified in the subpoena for compliance. The applicant shall describe, in detail, the basis for the application to quash or modify the subpoena including, but not limited to, a statement that the testimony, document, or tangible evidence is not relevant to the proceeding, that the subpoena is not reasonably tailored to the scope of the proceeding, or that the subpoena is unreasonable and oppressive. A motion to quash or modify the subpoena will stay the effect of the subpoena pending a decision by the administrative law judge on the motion.

(c) *Enforcement of subpoena.* Upon a showing that a person has failed or refused to comply with a subpoena, a party may apply to the local Federal district court to seek judicial enforcement of the subpoena in accordance with section 1004 of the Federal Aviation Act of 1958, as amended.

§13.229 Witness fees.

(a) *General.* Unless otherwise authorized by the administrative law judge, the party who applies for a subpoena to compel the attendance of a witness at a deposition or hearing, or the party at whose request a witness appears at a deposition or hearing, shall pay the witness fees described in this section.

(b) *Amount.* Except for an employee of the agency who appears at the direction of the agency, a witness who appears at a deposition or hearing is entitled to the same fees and mileage expenses as are paid to a witness in a court of the United States in comparable circumstances.

§13.230 Record.

(a) *Exclusive record.* The transcript of all testimony in the hearing, all exhibits received into evidence, and all motions, applications, requests, and rulings shall constitute the exclusive record for decision of the proceedings and the basis for the issuance of any orders in the proceeding. Any proceedings regarding the disqualification of an administrative law judge shall be included in the record.

(b) *Examination and copying of record.* Any person may examine the record at the Hearing Docket, Federal Aviation Administration, 600 Independence Avenue, SW, Wilbur Wright Building—Room 2014, Washington, DC 20591. Documents may also be examined and copied at the Docket Management Facility, Department of Transportation, 400 Seventh Street SW, Room PL-401, Washington, DC 20590. Any person may have a copy of the record after payment of reasonable costs to copy the record.

[Amdt. 13–21, 55 FR 27575, July 3, 1990; as amended at 70 FR 8238, Feb. 18, 2005]

§13.231 Argument before the administrative law judge.

(a) *Arguments during the hearing.* During the hearing, the administrative law judge shall give the parties a reasonable opportunity to present arguments on the record supporting or opposing motions, objections, and rulings if the parties request an opportunity for argument. The administrative law judge may request written arguments during the hearing if the administrative law judge finds that submission of written arguments would be reasonable.

(b) *Final oral argument.* At the conclusion of the hearing and before the administrative law judge issues an initial decision in the proceedings, the parties are entitled to submit oral proposed findings of fact and conclusions of law, exceptions to rulings of the administrative law judge, and supporting arguments for the findings, conclusions, or exceptions. At the conclusion of the hearing, a party may waive final oral argument.

(c) *Posthearing briefs.* The administrative law judge may request written posthearing briefs before the administrative law judge issues an initial decision in the proceedings if the administrative law judge finds that submission of written arguments would be reasonable. If a party files a written posthearing brief, the party shall include proposed findings of fact and conclusions of law, exceptions to rulings of the administrative law judge, and supporting arguments for the findings, conclusions, or exceptions. The administrative law judge shall give the parties a reasonable opportunity, not more than 30 days after receipt of the transcript, to prepare and submit the briefs.

§13.232 Initial decision.

(a) *Contents.* The administrative law judge shall issue an initial decision at the conclusion of the hearing. In each oral or written decision, the administrative law judge shall include findings of fact and conclusions of law, and the grounds supporting those findings and conclusions, upon all material issues of fact, the credibility of witnesses, the applicable law, any exercise of the administrative law judge's discretion, the amount of any civil penalty found appropriate by the administrative law judge, and a discussion of the basis for any order issued in the proceedings. The administrative law judge is not required to provide a written explanation for rulings on objections, procedural motions, and other matters not directly relevant to the substance of the initial decision. If the administrative law judge refers to any previous unreported or unpublished initial decision, the administrative law judge shall make copies of that initial decision available to all parties and the FAA decisionmaker.

(b) *Oral decision.* Except as provided in paragraph (c) of this section, at the conclusion of the hearing, the administrative law judge shall issue the initial decision and order orally on the record.

(c) *Written decision.* The administrative law judge may issue a written initial decision not later than 30 days after the conclusion of the hearing or submission of the last posthearing brief if the administrative law judge finds that issuing a written initial decision is reasonable. The administrative law judge shall serve a copy of any written initial decision on each party.

(d) *Order assessing civil penalty.* Unless appealed pursuant to §13.233 of this subpart, the initial decision issued by the administrative law judge shall be considered an order assessing civil penalty if the administrative law judge finds that an alleged violation occurred and determines that a civil penalty, in an amount found appropriate by the administrative law judge, is warranted.

§13.233 Appeal from initial decision.

(a) *Notice of appeal.* A party may appeal the initial decision, and any decision not previously appealed pursuant to §13.219, by filing a notice of appeal with the FAA decisionmaker. A party must file the notice of appeal in the FAA Hearing Docket using the appropriate address listed in §13.210(a). A party shall file the notice of appeal not later than 10 days after entry of the oral initial decision on the record or service of the written initial decision on the parties and shall serve a copy of the notice of appeal on each party.

(b) *Issues on appeal.* In any appeal from a decision of an administrative law judge, the FAA decisionmaker considers only the following issues:

(1) Whether each finding of fact is supported by a preponderance of reliable, probative, and substantial evidence;

(2) Whether each conclusion of law is made in accordance with applicable law, precedent, and public policy; and

(3) Whether the administrative law judge committed any prejudicial errors that support the appeal.

(c) *Perfecting an appeal.* Unless otherwise agreed by the parties, a party shall perfect an appeal, not later than 50 days after entry of the oral initial decision on the record or service of the written initial decision on the party, by filing an appeal brief with the FAA decisionmaker.

(1) *Extension of time by agreement of the parties.* The parties may agree to extend the time for perfecting the appeal with the consent of the FAA decisionmaker. If the FAA decisionmaker grants an extension of time to perfect the appeal, the appellate docket clerk shall serve a letter confirming the extension of time on each party.

(2) *Written motion for extension.* If the parties do not agree to an extension of time for perfecting an appeal, a party desiring an extension of time may file a written motion for an extension with the FAA decisionmaker and shall serve a copy of the motion on each party. The FAA decisionmaker may grant an extension if good cause for the extension is shown in the motion.

(d) *Appeal briefs.* A party shall file the appeal brief with the FAA decisionmaker and shall serve a copy of the appeal brief on each party.

(1) A party shall set forth, in detail, the party's specific objections to the initial decision or rulings in the appeal brief. A party also shall set forth, in detail, the basis for the appeal, the reasons supporting the appeal, and the relief requested in the appeal. If the party relies on evidence contained in the record for the appeal, the party shall specifically refer to the pertinent evidence contained in the transcript in the appeal brief.

(2) The FAA decisionmaker may dismiss an appeal, on the FAA decisionmaker's own initiative or upon motion of any other party, where a party has filed a notice of appeal but fails to perfect the appeal by timely filing an appeal brief with the FAA decisionmaker.

(e) *Reply brief.* Unless otherwise agreed by the parties, any party may file a reply brief with the FAA decisionmaker not later than 35 days after the appeal brief has been served on that party. The party filing the reply brief shall serve a copy of the reply brief on each party. If the party relies on evidence contained in the record for the reply, the party shall specifically refer to the pertinent evidence contained in the transcript in the reply brief.

(1) *Extension of time by agreement of the parties.* The parties may agree to extend the time for filing a reply brief with the consent of the FAA decisionmaker. If the FAA decisionmaker grants an extension of time to file the reply brief, the appellate docket clerk shall serve a letter confirming the extension of time on each party.

(2) *Written motion for extension.* If the parties do not agree to an extension of time for filing a reply brief, a party desiring an extension of time may file a written motion for an extension with the FAA decisionmaker and shall serve a copy of the motion on each party. The FAA decisionmaker may grant an extension if good cause for the extension is shown in the motion.

(f) *Other briefs.* The FAA decisionmaker may allow any person to submit an *amicus curiae* brief in an appeal of an initial decision. A party may not file more than one appeal brief or reply brief. A party may petition the FAA decisionmaker, in writing, for leave to file an additional brief and shall serve a copy of the petition on each party. The party may not file the additional brief with the petition. The FAA decisionmaker may grant leave to file an additional brief if the party demonstrates good cause for allowing additional argument on the appeal. The FAA decisionmaker will allow a reasonable time for the party to file the additional brief.

(g) *Number of copies.* A party shall file the original appeal brief or the original reply brief, and two copies of the brief, with the FAA decisionmaker.

(h) *Oral argument.* The FAA decisionmaker has sole discretion to permit oral argument on the appeal. On the FAA decisionmaker's own initiative or upon written motion by any party, the FAA decisionmaker may find that oral argument will contribute substantially to the development of the issues on appeal and may grant the parties an opportunity for oral argument.

(i) *Waiver of objections on appeal.* If a party fails to object to any alleged error regarding the proceedings in an appeal or a reply brief, the party waives any objection to the alleged error. The FAA decisionmaker is not required to consider any objection in an appeal brief or any argument in the reply brief if a party's objection is based on evidence contained on the record and the party does not specifically refer to the pertinent evidence from the record in the brief.

(j) FAA decisionmaker's decision on appeal. The FAA decisionmaker will review the record, the briefs on appeal, and the oral argument, if any, when considering the issues on appeal. The FAA decisionmaker may affirm, modify, or reverse the initial decision, make any necessary findings, or may remand the case for any proceedings that the FAA decisionmaker determines may be necessary.

(1) The FAA decisionmaker may raise any issue, on the FAA decisionmaker's own initiative, that is required for proper disposition of the proceedings. The FAA decisionmaker will give the parties a reasonable opportunity to submit arguments on the new issues before making a decision on appeal. If an issue raised by the FAA decisionmaker requires the consideration of additional testimony or evidence, the FAA decisionmaker will remand the case to the administrative law judge for further proceedings and an initial decision related to that issue. If an issue raised by the FAA decisionmaker is solely an issue of law or the issue was addressed at the hearing but was not raised by a party in the briefs on appeal, a remand of the case to the administrative law judge for further proceedings is not required but may be provided in the discretion of the FAA decisionmaker.

(2) The FAA decisionmaker will issue the final decision and order of the Administrator on appeal in writing and will serve a copy of the decision and order on each party. Unless a petition for review is filed pursuant to §13.235, a final decision and order of the Administrator shall be considered an order assessing civil penalty if the FAA decisionmaker finds that an alleged violation occurred and a civil penalty is warranted.

(3) A final decision and order of the Administrator after appeal is precedent in any other civil penalty action. Any issue, finding or conclusion, order, ruling, or initial decision of an administrative law judge that has not been appealed to the FAA decisionmaker is not precedent in any other civil penalty action.

[Amdt. 13–21, 55 FR 27575, July 3, 1990; as amended by Amdt. 13–32, 69 FR 59498, Oct. 4, 2004; Amdt. 13–32, 70 FR 13345, March 21, 2005]

§13.234 Petition to reconsider or modify a final decision and order of the FAA decisionmaker on appeal.

(a) *General.* Any party may petition the FAA decisionmaker to reconsider or modify a final decision and order issued by the FAA decision-maker on appeal from an initial decision. A party shall file a petition to reconsider or modify with the FAA decisionmaker not later than 30 days after service of the FAA decisionmaker's final decision and order on appeal and shall serve a copy of the petition on each party. The FAA decisionmaker will not reconsider or modify an initial decision and order issued by an administrative law judge that has not been appealed by any party to the FAA decisionmaker.

(b) *Form and number of copies.* A party shall file a petition to reconsider or modify, in writing, with the FAA decisionmaker. The party shall file the original petition with the FAA decisionmaker and shall serve a copy of the petition on each party.

(c) *Contents.* A party shall state briefly and specifically the alleged errors in the final decision and order on appeal, the relief sought by the party, and the grounds that support, the petition to reconsider or modify.

(1) If the petition is based, in whole or in part, on allegations regarding the consequences of the FAA decisionmaker's decision, the party shall describe these allegations and shall describe, and support, the basis for the allegations.

(2) If the petition is based, in whole or in part, on new material not previously raised in the proceedings, the party shall set forth the new material and include affidavits of prospective witnesses and authenticated documents that would be introduced in support of the new material. The party shall explain, in detail, why the new material was not discovered through due diligence prior to the hearing.

(d) *Repetitious and frivolous petitions.* The FAA decisionmaker will not consider repetitious or frivolous petitions. The FAA decisionmaker may summarily dismiss repetitious or frivolous petitions to reconsider or modify.

(e) *Reply petitions.* Any other party may reply to a petition to reconsider or modify, not later than 10 days after service of the petition on that party, by filing a reply with the FAA decisionmaker. A party shall serve a copy of the reply on each party.

(f) *Effect of filing petition.* Unless otherwise ordered by the FAA decisionmaker, filing of a petition pursuant to this section will not stay or delay the effective date of the FAA decisionmaker's final decision and order on appeal and shall not toll the time allowed for judicial review.

(g) *FAA decisionmaker's decision on petition.* The FAA decisionmaker has sole discretion to grant or deny a petition to reconsider or modify. The FAA decisionmaker will grant or deny a petition to reconsider or modify within a reasonable time after receipt of the petition or receipt of the reply petition, if any. The FAA decisionmaker may affirm, modify, or reverse the final decision and order on appeal, or may remand the case for any proceedings that the FAA decisionmaker determines may be necessary.

[Amdt. 13–21, 55 FR 27575, July 3, 1990; 55 FR 29293, July 18, 1990; Amdt. 13–23, 55 FR 45983, Oct. 31, 1990]

§13.235 Judicial review of a final decision and order.

A person may seek judicial review of a final decision and order of the Administrator as provided in section 1006 of the Federal Aviation Act of 1958, as amended. A party seeking judicial review of a final decision and order shall file a petition for review not later than 60 days after the final decision and order has been served on the party.

Subpart H—Civil Monetary Penalty Inflation Adjustment

Source: Docket No. 28762, 61 FR 67445, Dec. 20, 1996 unless otherwise noted.

§13.301 Scope and purpose.

(a) This subpart provides a mechanism for the regular adjustment for inflation of civil monetary penalties in conformity with the Federal Civil Penalties Inflation Adjustment Act of 1990, 28 U.S.C. 2461 (note), as amended by the Debt Collection Improvement Act of 1996, Public Law 104–134, April 26, 1996, in order to maintain the deterrent effect of civil monetary penalties and to promote compliance with the law. This subpart also sets out the current adjusted maximum civil monetary penalties or range of minimum and maximum civil monetary penalties for each statutory civil penalty subject to the FAA's jurisdiction.

(b) Each adjustment to the maximum civil monetary penalty or the range of minimum and maximum civil monetary penalties, as applicable, made in accordance with this subpart applies prospectively from the date it becomes effective to actions initiated under this part, notwithstanding references to a specific maximum civil monetary penalty or range of minimum and maximum civil monetary penalties contained elsewhere in this part.

§13.303 Definitions.

(a) *Civil Monetary Penalty* means any penalty, fine, or other sanction that:

(1) Is for a specific monetary amount as provided by Federal law or has a maximum amount provided by Federal law;

(2) Is assessed or enforced by the FAA pursuant to Federal law; and

(3) Is assessed or enforced pursuant to an administrative proceeding or a civil action in the Federal courts.

(b) *Consumer Price Index* means the Consumer Price Index for all urban consumers published by the Department of Labor.

§13.305 Cost of Living Adjustments of Civil Monetary Penalties.

(a) Except for the limitation to the initial adjustment to statutory maximum civil monetary penalties or range of minimum and maximum civil monetary penalties set forth in paragraph (c) of this section, the inflation adjustment under this subpart is determined by increasing the maximum civil monetary penalty or range of minimum and maximum civil monetary penalty for each civil monetary penalty by the cost-of-living adjustment. Any increase determined under paragraph (a) of this section is rounded to the nearest:

(1) Multiple of $10 in the case of penalties less than or equal to $100;

(2) Multiple of $100 in the case of penalties greater than $100 but less than or equal to $1,000;

(3) Multiple of $1,000 in the case of penalties greater than $1,000 but less than or equal to $10,000;

(4) Multiple of $5,000 in the case of penalties greater than $10,000 but less than or equal to $100,000;

(5) Multiple of $10,000 in the case of penalties greater than $100,000 but less than or equal to $200,000; and

(6) Multiple of $25,000 in the case of penalties greater than $200,000.

(b) For purposes of paragraph (a) of this section, the term "cost-of-living adjustment" means the percentage (if any) for each civil monetary penalty by which the Consumer Price Index for the month of June of the calendar year preceding the adjustment exceeds the Consumer Price Index for the month of June of the calendar year in which the amount of such civil monetary penalty was last set or adjusted pursuant to law.

(c) *Limitation on initial adjustment.* The initial adjustment of maximum civil penalty or range of minimum and maximum civil monetary penalties made pursuant to this subpart does not exceed 10 percent of the statutory maximum civil penalty before an adjustment under this subpart is made. This limitation applies only to the initial adjustment, effective on January 21, 1997.

(d) *Inflation adjustment.* Minimum and maximum civil monetary penalties within the jurisdiction of the FAA are adjusted for inflation as follows:

[See table on the next page]

MINIMUM AND MAXIMUM CIVIL PENALTIES—ADJUSTED FOR INFLATION, EFFECTIVE MARCH 13, 2002

United States Code citation	Civil monetary penalty description	Minimum penalty amount	New adjusted minimum penalty amount	Maximum penalty amount when last set or adjusted pursuant to law	New or Adjusted Maximum penalty amount
49 U.S.C. 5123(a)	Violations of hazardous materials transportation law, regulations, or orders.	$250 per violation adjusted 1/27/1997	$250 per violation.	$27,500 per violation, adjusted 1/21/1997.	$30,000 per violation, adjusted effective 3/30/02.
49 U.S.C. 46301(a)(1)	Violations of statutory provisions listed in 49 U.S.C. 46301(a)(1), regulations prescribed, or orders issued under those provisions.	N/A	N/A	$1,100 per violation, adjusted 1/21/1997.	$1,100 per violation, adjusted 1/21/1997.
49 U.S.C. 46301(a)(2)	Violations of statutory provisions listed in 49 U.S.C. 46301(a)(2), regulations prescribed, or orders issued under those provisions by a person operating an aircraft for the transportation of passengers or property for compensation.	N/A	N/A	$11,000 per violation, adjusted 1/21/1997.	$11,000 per violation, adjusted 1/21/1997.
49 U.S.C. 46301(a)(3)(A)	Violations of statutory provisions listed in 49 U.S.C. 46301(a)(1), regulations prescribed, or orders issued under those provisions relating to the transportation of hazardous materials by air.	N/A	N/A	$11,000 per violation, adjusted 1/21/1997.	$11,000 per violation, adjusted 1/21/1997.
49 U.S.C. 46301(a)(3)(B)	Violations of statutory provisions listed in 49 U.S.C. 46301(a)(1), regulations prescribed, or orders issued under those provisions relating to the registration or recordation under chapter 441 of Title 49, United States Code, or an aircraft not used to provide air transportation.	N/A	N/A	$11,000 per violation, adjusted 1/21/1997.	$11,000 per violation, adjusted 1/21/1997.
49 U.S.C. 46301(a)(3)(C)	Violations of 49 U.S.C. 44718(d), or regulations prescribed or orders issued under it, relating to limiting construction or establishment of landfills.	N/A	N/A	$10,000, set 10/9/1996.	$10,000, set 10/9/1996.
49 U.S.C. 46301(a)(3)(D)	Violations of 49 U.S.C. 44725, or regulations prescribed or orders issued under it, relating to the safe disposal of life-limited aircraft parts.	N/A	N/A	$10,000, adopted 4/5/2000.	$10,000, adopted 4/5/2000.
49 U.S.C. 46301(b)	Tampering with a smoke alarm device.	N/A	N/A	$2,200 per violation, adjusted 1/21/1997.	$2,200 per violation, adjusted 1/21/1997.
49 U.S.C. 46302	Knowingly providing false information about alleged violations involving the special aircraft jurisdiction of the United States.	N/A	N/A	$11,000 per violation, adjusted 1/21/1997.	$11,000 per violation, adjusted 1/21/1997.
49 U.S.C. 46303	Carrying a concealed dangerous weapon.	N/A	N/A	$11,000 per violation, adjusted 1/21/1997.	$11,000 per violation, adjusted 1/21/1997.
49 U.S.C 46318	Interference with cabin or flight crew.	N/A	N/A	$25,000 per violation, adopted 4/5/2000.	$25,000 per violation, adopted 4/5/2000.

[Docket No. 28762, 61 FR 67445, Dec. 20, 1996; as amended by Amdt. 13–28, 62 FR 4134, Jan. 29, 1997; Amdt. 13–31, 67 FR 6366, Feb. 11, 2002]

Subpart I — Flight Operational Quality Assurance Programs

Source: Docket No. FAA–2000–7554, 66 FR 55048, Oct. 31, 2001, unless otherwise noted.

§13.401 Flight Operational Quality Assurance Program: Prohibition Against Use of Data for Enforcement Purposes

(a) *Applicability.* This section applies to any operator of an aircraft who operates such aircraft under an approved Flight Operational Quality Assurance (FOQA) program.

(b) *Definitions.* For the purpose of this section, the terms—

(1) Flight Operational Quality Assurance (FOQA) program means an FAA-approved program for the routine collection and analysis of digital flight data gathered during aircraft operations, including data currently collected pursuant to existing regulatory provisions, when such data is included in an approved FOQA program.

(2) FOQA data means any digital flight data that has been collected from an individual aircraft pursuant to an FAA-approved FOQA program, regardless of the electronic format of that data.

(3) Aggregate FOQA data means the summary statistical indices that are associated with FOQA event categories, based on an analysis of FOQA data from multiple aircraft operations.

(c) *Requirements.* In order for paragraph (e) of this section to apply, the operator must submit, maintain, and adhere to a FOQA Implementation and Operation Plan that is approved by the Administrator and which contains the following elements:

(1) A description of the operator's plan for collecting and analyzing flight recorded data from line operations on a routine basis, including identification of the data to be collected;

(2) Procedures for taking corrective action that analysis of the data indicates is necessary in the interest of safety;

(3) Procedures for providing the FAA with aggregate FOQA data;

(4) Procedures for informing the FAA as to any corrective action being undertaken pursuant to paragraph (c)(2) of this section.

(d) *Submission of aggregate data.* The operator will provide the FAA with aggregate FOQA data in a form and manner acceptable to the Administrator.

(e) *Enforcement.* Except for criminal or deliberate acts, the Administrator will not use an operator's FOQA data or aggregate FOQA data in an enforcement action against that operator or its employees when such FOQA data or aggregate FOQA data is obtained from a FOQA program that is approved by the Administrator.

(f) *Disclosure.* FOQA data and aggregate FOQA data, if submitted in accordance with an order designating the information as protected under part 193 of this chapter, will be afforded the nondisclosure protections of part 193 of this chapter.

(g) *Withdrawal of program approval.* The Administrator may withdraw approval of a previously approved FOQA program for failure to comply with the requirements of this chapter. Grounds for withdrawal of approval may include, but are not limited to—

(1) Failure to implement corrective action that analysis of available FOQA data indicates is necessary in the interest of safety; or

(2) Failure to correct a continuing pattern of violations following notice by the agency; or also

(3) Willful misconduct or willful violation of the FAA regulations in this chapter.

SUBCHAPTER C AIRCRAFT

PART 21
CERTIFICATION PROCEDURES FOR PRODUCTS AND PARTS

SPECIAL FEDERAL AVIATION REGULATION

SFAR No. 88

Subpart A — General

Sec.
21.1 Applicability.
21.2 Falsification of applications, reports or records.
21.3 Reporting of failures, malfunctions, and defects.
21.5 Airplane or Rotorcraft Flight Manual.

Subpart B — Type Certificates

21.11 Applicability.
21.13 Eligibility.
21.15 Application for type certificate.
21.16 Special conditions.
21.17 Designation of applicable regulations.
21.19 Changes requiring a new type certificate.
21.21 Issue of type certificate: normal, utility, acrobatic, commuter, and transport category aircraft; manned free balloons; special classes of aircraft; aircraft engines; propellers.
21.23 [Reserved]
21.24 Issuance of type certificate: primary category aircraft.
21.25 Issue of type certificate: Restricted category aircraft.
***21.27 Issue of type certificate: surplus aircraft of the Armed Forces.**
21.29 Issue of type certificate: import products.
21.31 Type design.
21.33 Inspection and tests.
21.35 Flight tests.
21.37 Flight test pilot.
21.39 Flight test instrument calibration and correction report.
21.41 Type certificate.
21.43 Location of manufacturing facilities.
21.45 Privileges.
21.47 Transferability.
21.49 Availability.
21.50 Instructions for continued airworthiness and manufacturer's maintenance manuals having airworthiness limitations sections.
21.51 Duration.
21.53 Statement of conformity.

Subpart C — Provisional Type Certificates

21.71 Applicability.
21.73 Eligibility.
21.75 Application.
21.77 Duration.
21.79 Transferability.
21.81 Requirements for issue and amendment of Class I provisional type certificates.
21.83 Requirements for issue and amendment of Class II provisional type certificates.
21.85 Provisional amendments to type certificates.

Subpart D — Changes to Type Certificates

21.91 Applicability.
21.93 Classification of changes in type design.
21.95 Approval of minor changes in type design.
21.97 Approval of major changes in type design.
21.99 Required design changes.
21.101 Designation of applicable regulations.

Subpart E — Supplemental Type Certificates

21.111 Applicability.
21.113 Requirement of supplemental type certificate.
21.115 Applicable requirements.
21.117 Issue of supplemental type certificates.
21.119 Privileges.

Subpart F — Production Under Type Certificate Only

21.121 Applicability.
21.123 Production under type certificate.
21.125 Production inspection system: Materials Review Board.
21.127 Tests: aircraft.
21.128 Tests: aircraft engines.
21.129 Tests: propellers.
21.130 Statement of conformity.

Subpart G — Production Certificates

21.131 Applicability.
21.133 Eligibility.
21.135 Requirements for issuance.
21.137 Location of manufacturing facilities.
21.139 Quality control.
21.143 Quality control data requirements; prime manufacturer.
21.147 Changes in quality control system.
21.149 Multiple products.
21.151 Production limitation record.
21.153 Amendment of the production certificates.
21.155 Transferability.
21.157 Inspections and tests.
21.159 Duration.
21.161 Display.
21.163 Privileges.
21.165 Responsibility of holder.

Subpart H — Airworthiness Certificates

21.171 Applicability.
21.173 Eligibility.
21.175 Airworthiness certificates: classification.
21.177 Amendment or modification.
21.179 Transferability.
21.181 Duration.
21.182 Aircraft identification.

21.183 Issue of standard airworthiness certificates for normal, utility, acrobatic, commuter, and transport category aircraft; manned free balloons; and special classes of aircraft.
21.184 Issue of special airworthiness certificates for primary category aircraft.
21.185 Issue of airworthiness certificates for restricted category aircraft.
21.187 Issue of multiple airworthiness certification.
21.189 Issue of airworthiness certificate for limited category aircraft.
21.190 Issue of a special airworthiness certificate for a light-sport category aircraft.
21.191 Experimental certificates.
21.193 Experimental certificates: general.
21.195 Experimental certificates: Aircraft to be used for market surveys, sales demonstrations, and customer crew training.
21.197 Special flight permits.
21.199 Issue of special flight permits.

Subpart I— Provisional Airworthiness Certificates

21.211 Applicability.
21.213 Eligibility.
21.215 Application.
21.217 Duration.
21.219 Transferability.
21.221 Class I provisional airworthiness certificates.
21.223 Class II provisional airworthiness certificates.
21.225 Provisional airworthiness certificates corresponding with provisional amendments to type certificates.

Subpart J— Delegation Option Authorization Procedures

21.231 Applicability.
21.235 Application.
21.239 Eligibility.
21.243 Duration.
21.245 Maintenance of eligibility.
21.247 Transferability.
21.249 Inspections.
21.251 Limits of applicability.
21.253 Type certificates: application.
21.257 Type certificates: issue.
21.261 Equivalent safety provisions.
21.267 Production certificates.
21.269 Export airworthiness approvals.
21.271 Airworthiness approval tags.
21.273 Airworthiness certificates other than experimental.
21.275 Experimental certificates.
21.277 Data review and service experience.
21.289 Major repairs, rebuilding and alteration.
21.293 Current records.

Subpart K— Approval of Materials, Parts, Processes, and Appliances

21.301 Applicability.
21.303 Replacement and modification parts.
21.305 Approval of materials, parts, processes, and appliances.

Subpart L— Export Airworthiness Approvals

21.321 Applicability.
21.323 Eligibility.
21.325 Export airworthiness approvals.
21.327 Application.
21.329 Issue of export certificates of airworthiness for Class I products.
21.331 Issue of airworthiness approval tags for Class II products.
21.333 Issue of export airworthiness approval tags for Class III products.
21.335 Responsibilities of exporters.
21.337 Performance of inspections and overhauls.
21.339 Special export airworthiness approval for aircraft.

Subpart M— Designated Alteration Station Authorization Procedures

21.431 Applicability.
21.435 Application.
21.439 Eligibility.
21.441 Procedure manual.
21.443 Duration.
21.445 Maintenance of eligibility.
21.447 Transferability.
21.449 Inspections.
21.451 Limits of applicability.
21.461 Equivalent safety provisions.
21.463 Supplemental type certificates.
21.473 Airworthiness certificates other than experimental.
21.475 Experimental certificates.
21.477 Data review and service experience.
21.493 Current records.

Subpart N— Approval of Engines, Propellers, Materials, Parts, and Appliances: Import

21.500 Approval of engines and propellers.
21.502 Approval of materials, parts, and appliances.

Subpart O— Technical Standard Order Authorizations

21.601 Applicability.
21.603 TSO marking and privileges.
21.605 Application and issue.
21.607 General rules governing holders of TSO authorizations.
21.609 Approval for deviation.
21.611 Design changes.
21.613 Recordkeeping requirements.
21.615 FAA inspection.
21.617 Issue of letters of TSO design approval: import appliances.
21.619 Noncompliance.
21.621 Transferability and duration.

Authority: 42 U.S.C. 7572; 49 U.S.C. 106(g), 40105, 40113, 44701–44702, 44707, 44709, 44711, 44713, 44715, 45303.

EDITORIAL NOTE: FOR MISCELLANEOUS AMENDMENTS TO CROSS REFERENCES IN THIS PART 21 SEE AMDT. 21–10, 31 FR 9211, JULY 6, 1966.

SPECIAL FEDERAL AVIATION REGULATION

SFAR No. 88 TO PART 21

FUEL TANK SYSTEM FAULT TOLERANCE EVALUATION REQUIREMENTS

1. *Applicability.* This SFAR applies to the holders of type certificates, and supplemental type certificates that may affect the airplane fuel tank system, for turbine-powered transport category airplanes, provided the type certificate was issued after January 1, 1958, and the airplane has either a maximum type certificated passenger capacity of 30 or more, or a maximum type certificated payload capacity of 7,500 pounds or more. This SFAR also applies to applicants for type certificates, amendments to a type certificate, and supplemental type certificates affecting the fuel tank systems for those airplanes identified above, if the application was filed before June 6, 2001, the effective date of this SFAR, and the certificate was not issued before June 6, 2001.

2. *Compliance:* Each type certificate holder, and each supplemental type certificate holder of a modification affecting the airplane fuel tank system, must accomplish the following within the compliance times specified in paragraph (e) of this section:

(a) Conduct a safety review of the airplane fuel tank system to determine that the design meets the requirements of §§25.901 and 25.981(a) and (b) of this chapter. If the current design does not meet these requirements, develop all design changes to the fuel tank system that are necessary to meet these requirements. The FAA (Aircraft Certification Office (ACO), or office of the Transport Airplane Directorate, having cognizance over the type certificate for the affected airplane) may grant an extension of the 18-month compliance time for development of design changes if:

(1) The safety review is completed within the compliance time;

(2) Necessary design changes are identified within the compliance time; and

(3) Additional time can be justified, based on the holder's demonstrated aggressiveness in performing the safety review, the complexity of the necessary design changes, the availability of interim actions to provide an acceptable level of safety, and the resulting level of safety.

(b) Develop all maintenance and inspection instructions necessary to maintain the design features required to preclude the existence or development of an ignition source within the fuel tank system of the airplane.

(c) Submit a report for approval to the FAA Aircraft Certification Office (ACO), or office of the Transport Airplane Directorate, having cognizance over the type certificate for the affected airplane, that:

(1) Provides substantiation that the airplane fuel tank system design, including all necessary design changes, meets the requirements of §§25.901 and 25.981(a) and (b) of this chapter; and

(2) Contains all maintenance and inspection instructions necessary to maintain the design features required to preclude the existence or development of an ignition source within the fuel tank system throughout the operational life of the airplane.

(d) The Aircraft Certification Office (ACO), or office of the Transport Airplane Directorate, having cognizance over the type certificate for the affected airplane, may approve a report submitted in accordance with paragraph 2(c) if it determines that any provisions of this SFAR not compiled with are compensated for by factors that provide an equivalent level of safety.

(e) Each type certificate holder must comply no later than December 6, 2002, or within 18 months after the issuance of a type certificate for which application was filed before June 6, 2001, whichever is later; and each supplemental type certificate holder of a modification affecting the airplane fuel tank system must comply no later than June 6, 2003, or within 18 months after the issuance of a supplemental type certificate for which application was filed before June 6, 2001, whichever is later.

[Docket No. FAA–1999–6411, 66 FR 23129, May 7, 2001; as amended by Amdt. 21–82, 67 FR 57493, Sept. 10, 2002; Amdt. 21–83, 67 FR 72833, Dec. 9, 2002]

Subpart A—General

§21.1 Applicability.

(a) This part prescribes—

(1) Procedural requirements for the issue of type certificates and changes to those certificates; the issue of production certificates; the issue of airworthiness certificates; and the issue of export airworthiness approvals.

(2) Rules governing the holders of any certificate specified in paragraph (a)(1) of this section; and

(3) Procedural requirements for the approval of certain materials, parts, processes, and appliances.

(b) For the purposes of this part, the word "product" means an aircraft, aircraft engine, or propeller. In addition, for the purposes of Subpart L only, it includes components and parts of aircraft, of aircraft engines, and of propellers; also parts, materials, and appliances, approved under the Technical Standard Order system.

[Docket No. 5085, 29 FR 14563, Oct. 24, 1964; as amended by Amdt. 21–2, 30 FR 8465, July 2, 1965; Amdt. 21–6, 30 FR 11379, Sept. 8, 1965]

§21.2 Falsification of applications, reports, or records.

(a) No person shall make or cause to be made–

(1) Any fraudulent of intentionally false statement on any application for a certificate or approval under this part;

(2) Any fraudulent or intentionally false entry in any record or report that is required to be kept, made, or used to show compliance with any requirement for the issuance or the exercise of the privileges of any certificate or approval issued under this part;

(3) Any reproduction for a fraudulent purpose of any certificate or approval issued under this part.

(4) Any alteration of any certificate or approval issued under this part.

(b) The commission by any person of an act prohibited under paragraph (a) of this section is a basis for suspending of revoking any certificate or approval issued under this part and held by that person.

[Docket No. 23345, 57 FR 41367, Sept. 9, 1992]

§21.3 Reporting of failures, malfunctions, and defects.

(a) Except as provided in paragraph (d) of this section, the holder of a Type Certificate (including a Supplemental Type Certificate), a Parts Manufacturer Approval (PMA), or a TSO authorization, or the licensee of a Type Certificate shall report any failure, malfunction, or defect in any product, part, process, or article manufactured by it that it determines has resulted in any of the occurrences listed in paragraph (c) of this section.

(b) The holder of a Type Certificate (including a Supplemental Type Certificate), a Parts Manufacturer Approval (PMA), or a TSO authorization, or the licensee of a Type of Certificate shall report any defect in any product, part, or article manufactured by it that has left its quality control system and that it determines could result in any of the occurrences listed in paragraph (c) of this section.

(c) The following occurrences must be reported as provided in paragraphs (a) and (b) of this section:

(1) Fires caused by a system or equipment failure, malfunction, or defect.

(2) An engine exhaust system failure, malfunction, or defect which causes damage to the engine, adjacent aircraft structure, equipment, or components.

(3) The accumulation or circulation of toxic or noxious gases in the crew compartment or passenger cabin.

(4) A malfunction, failure, or defect of a propeller control system.

(5) A propeller or rotorcraft hub or blade structural failure.

(6) Flammable fluid leakage in areas where an ignition source normally exists.

(7) A brake system failure caused by structural or material failure during operation.

(8) A significant aircraft primary structural defect or failure caused by any autogenous condition (fatigue, understrength, corrosion, etc.).

(9) Any abnormal vibration or buffeting caused by a structural or system malfunction, defect, or failure.

(10) An engine failure.

(11) Any structural or flight control system malfunction, defect, or failure which causes an interference with normal control of the aircraft for which derogates the flying qualities.

(12) A complete loss of more than one electrical power generating system or hydraulic power system during a given operation of the aircraft.

(13) A failure or malfunction of more than one attitude, airspeed, or altitude instrument during a given operation of the aircraft.

(d) The requirements of paragraph (a) of this section do not apply to—

(1) Failures, malfunctions, or defects that the holder of a Type Certificate (including a Supplemental Type Certificate), Parts Manufacturer Approval (PMA), or TSO authorization, or the licensee of a Type Certificate—

(i) Determines were caused by improper maintenance, or improper usage;

(ii) Knows were reported to the FAA by another person under the Federal Aviation Regulations; or

(iii) Has already reported under the accident reporting provisions of Part 430 of the regulations of the National Transportation Safety Board.

(2) Failures, malfunctions, or defects in products, parts, or articles manufactured by a foreign manufacturer under a U.S. Type Certificate issued under §21.29 or §21.617, or exported to the United States under §21.502.

(e) Each report required by this section—

(1) Shall be made to the Aircraft Certification Office in the region in which the person required to make the report is located within 24 hours after it has determined that the failure, malfunction, or defect required to be reported has occurred. However, a report that is due on a Saturday or a Sunday may be delivered on the following Monday and one that is due on a holiday may be delivered on the next workday;

(2) Shall be transmitted in a manner and form acceptable to the Administrator and by the most expeditious method available; and

(3) Shall include as much of the following information as is available and applicable:

(i) Aircraft serial number.

(ii) When the failure, malfunction, or defect is associated with an article approved under a TSO authorization, the article serial number and model designation, as appropriate.

(iii) When the failure, malfunction, or defect is associated with an engine or propeller, the engine or propeller serial number, as appropriate.

(iv) Product model.

(v) Identification of the part, component, or system involved. The identification must include the part number.

(vi) Nature of the failure, malfunction, or defect.

(f) Whenever the investigation of an accident or service difficulty report shows that an article manufactured under a TSO authorization is unsafe because of a manufacturing or design defect, the manufacturer shall, upon request of the Administrator, report to the Administrator the results of its investigation and any action taken or proposed by the manufacturer to correct that defect. If action is required to correct the defect in existing articles, the manufacturer shall submit the data necessary for the issuance of an appropriate airworthiness directive to the Manager of the Aircraft Certification Office for the geographic area of the FAA regional office in the region in which it is located.

[Amdt. 21–36, 35 FR 18187, Nov. 28, 1970; as amended by Amdt. 21–37, 35 FR 18450, Dec. 4, 1970; Amdt. 21–50, 45 FR 38346, June 9, 1980; Amdt. 21–67, 54 FR 39291, Sept. 25, 1989]

§21.5 Airplane or Rotorcraft Flight Manual.

(a) With each airplane or rotorcraft that was not type certificated with an Airplane or Rotorcraft Flight Manual and that has had no flight time prior to March 1, 1979, the holder of a Type Certificate (including a Supplemental Type Certificate) or the licensee of a Type Certificate shall make available to the owner at the time of delivery of the aircraft a current approved Airplane or Rotorcraft Flight Manual.

(b) The Airplane or Rotorcraft Flight Manual required by paragraph (a) of this section must contain the following information:

(1) The operating limitations and information required to be furnished in an Airplane or Rotorcraft Flight Manual or in manual material, markings, and placards, by the applicable regulations under which the airplane or rotorcraft was type certificated.

(2) The maximum ambient atmospheric temperature for which engine cooling was demonstrated must be stated in the performance information section of the Flight Manual, if the applicable regulations under which the aircraft was type certificated do not require ambient temperature on engine cooling operating limitations in the Flight Manual.

[Amdt. 21–46, 43 FR 2316, Jan. 16, 1978]

Subpart B—Type Certificates

Source: Docket No. 5085, 29 FR 14564, Oct. 24, 1964, unless otherwise noted.

§21.11 Applicability.

This subpart prescribes—

(a) Procedural requirements for the issue of type certificates for aircraft, aircraft engines, and propellers; and

(b) Rules governing the holders of those certificates.

§21.13 Eligibility.

Any interested person may apply for a type certificate.

[Amdt. 21–25, 34 FR 14068, Sept. 5, 1969]

§21.15 Application for type certificate.

(a) An application for a type certificate is made on a form and in a manner prescribed by the Administrator and is submitted to the appropriate Aircraft Certification Office.

(b) An application for an aircraft type certificate must be accompanied by a three-view drawing of that aircraft and available preliminary basic data.

(c) An application for an aircraft engine type certificate must be accompanied by a description of the engine design features, the engine operating characteristics, and the proposed engine operating limitations.

[Docket No. 5085, 29 FR 14564, Oct. 24, 1964; as amended by Amdt. 21–40, 39 FR 35459, Oct. 1, 1974; Amdt. 21–67, 54 FR 39291, Sept. 25, 1989]

§21.16 Special conditions.

If the Administrator finds that the airworthiness regulations of this subchapter do not contain adequate or appropriate safety standards for an aircraft, aircraft engine, or propeller because of a novel or unusual design feature of the aircraft, aircraft engine or propeller, he prescribes special conditions and amendments thereto for the product. The special conditions are issued in accordance with Part 11 of this chapter and contain such safety standards for the aircraft, aircraft engine or propeller as the Administrator finds necessary to establish a level of safety equivalent to that established in the regulations.

[Amdt. 21–19, 32 FR 17851, Dec. 13, 1967; as amended by Amdt. 21–51, 45 FR 60170, Sept. 11, 1980]

§21.17 Designation of applicable regulations.

(a) Except as provided in §23.2, §25.2, §27.2, §29.2 and in parts 34 and 36 of this chapter, an applicant for a type certificate must show that the aircraft, aircraft engine, or propeller concerned meets—

(1) The applicable requirements of this subchapter that are effective on the date of application for that certificate unless—

(i) Otherwise specified by the Administrator; or

(ii) Compliance with later effective amendments is elected or required under this section; and

(2) Any special conditions prescribed by the Administrator.

(b) For special classes of aircraft, including the engines and propellers installed thereon (e.g., gliders, airships, and other nonconventional aircraft), for which airworthiness standards have not been issued under this subchapter, the applicable requirements will be the portions of those other airworthiness requirements contained in Parts 23, 25, 27, 29, 31, 33, and 35 found by the Administrator to be appropriate for the aircraft and applicable to a specific type design, or such airworthiness criteria as the Administrator may find provide an equivalent level of safety to those parts.

(c) An application for type certification of a transport category aircraft is effective for 5 years and an application for any other type certificate is effective for 3 years, unless an applicant shows at the time of application that his product requires a longer period of time for design, development, and testing, and the Administrator approves a longer period.

(d) In a case where a type certificate has not been issued, or it is clear that a type certificate will not be issued, within the time limit established under paragraph (c) of this section, the applicant may—

(1) File a new application for a type certificate and comply with all the provisions of paragraph (a) of this section applicable to an original application; or

(2) File for an extension of the original application and comply with the applicable airworthiness requirements of this subchapter that were effective on a date, to be selected by the applicant, not earlier than the date which precedes the date of issue of the type certificate by the time limit established under paragraph (c) of this section for the original application.

(e) If an applicant elects to comply with an amendment to this subchapter that is effective after the filing of the application for a type certificate, he must also comply with any other amendment that the Administrator finds is directly related.

(f) For primary category aircraft, the requirements are:

(1) The applicable airworthiness requirements contained in parts 23, 27, 31, 33, and 35 of this subchapter, or such other airworthiness criteria as the Administrator may find appropriate and applicable to the specific design and intended use and provide a level of safety acceptable the Administrator.

(2) The noise standards of part 36 applicable to primary category aircraft.

[Docket No. 5085, 29 FR 14564, Oct. 24, 1964; as amended by Amdt. 21–19, 32 FR 17851, Dec. 13, 1967; Amdt. 21–24, 34 FR 364, Jan. 10, 1969; Amdt. 21–42, 40 FR 1033, Jan. 6, 1975; Amdt. 21–58, 50 FR 46877, Nov. 13, 1985; Amdt. 21–60, 52 FR 8042, March 13, 1987; Amdt. 21–68, 55 FR 32860, Aug. 10, 1990; Amdt. 21–69, 56 FR 41051, Aug. 16, 1991; Amdt. 21–70, 57 FR 41367, Sept. 9, 1992]

§21.19 Changes requiring a new type certificate.

Each person who proposes to change a product must apply for a new type certificate if the Administrator finds that the proposed change in design, power, thrust, or weight is so extensive that a substantially complete investigation of compliance with the applicable regulations is required.

[Docket No. 28903, 65 FR 36265, June 7, 2000; as amended by Amdt. 21–77, 66 FR 56989, Nov. 14, 2001]

§21.21 Issue of type certificate: normal, utility, acrobatic, commuter, and transport category aircraft; manned free balloons; special classes of aircraft; aircraft engines; propellers.

An applicant is entitled to a type certificate for an aircraft in the normal, utility, acrobatic, commuter, or transport category, or for a manned free balloon, special class of aircraft, or an aircraft engine or propeller, if—

(a) The product qualifies under §21.27; or

(b) The applicant submits the type design, test reports, and computations necessary to show that the product to be certificated meets the applicable airworthiness, aircraft noise, fuel venting, and exhaust emission requirements of the Federal Aviation Regulations and any special conditions prescribed by the Administrator, and the Administrator finds—

(1) Upon examination of the type design, and after completing all tests and inspections, that the type design and the product meet the applicable noise, fuel venting, and emissions requirements of the Federal Aviation Regulations, and further finds that they meet the applicable airworthiness requirements of the Federal Aviation Regulations or that any airworthiness provisions not complied with are compensated for by factors that provide an equivalent level of safety; and

(2) For an aircraft, that no feature or characteristic makes it unsafe for the category in which certification is requested.

[Docket No. 5085, 29 FR 14564, Oct. 24, 1964; as amended by Amdt. 21–15, 32 FR 3735, March 4, 1967; Amdt. 21–27, 34 FR 18368, Nov. 18, 1969; Amdt. 21–60, 52 FR 8042, March 13, 1987; Amdt. 21–68, 55 FR 32860, Aug. 10, 1990]

§21.23 [Reserved]

§21.24 Issuance of type certificate: primary category aircraft.

(a) The applicant is entitled to a type certificate for an aircraft in the primary category if—

(1) The aircraft—

(i) Is unpowered; is an airplane powered by a single, naturally aspirated engine with a 61-knot or less V_{SO} stall speed as defined in §23.49; or is a rotorcraft with a 6-pound per square foot main rotor disc loading limitation, under sea level standard day conditions;

(ii) Weighs not more than 2,700 pounds; or, for seaplanes, not more than 3,375 pounds;

(iii) Has a maximum seating capacity of not more than four persons, including the pilot; and

(iv) Has an unpressurized cabin.

(2) The applicant has submitted—

(i) Except as provided by paragraph (c) of this section, a statement, in a form and manner acceptable to the Administrator, certifying that: the applicant has completed the engineering analysis necessary to demonstrate compliance with the applicable airworthiness requirements; the applicant has conducted appropriate flight, structural, propulsion, and systems tests necessary to show that the aircraft, its components, and its equipment are reliable and function properly; the type design complies with the airworthiness standards and noise requirements established for the aircraft under §21.17(f); and no feature or characteristic makes it unsafe for its intended use;

(ii) The flight manual required by §21.5(b), including any information required to be furnished by the applicable airworthiness standards;

(iii) Instructions for continued airworthiness in accordance with §21.50(b); and

(iv) A report that: summarizes how compliance with each provision of the type certification basis was determined; lists the specific documents in which the type certification data information is provided; lists all necessary drawings and documents used to define the type design; and lists all the engineering reports on tests and computations that the applicant must retain and make available under §21.49 to substantiate compliance with the applicable airworthiness standards.

(3) The Administrator finds that—

(i) The aircraft complies with those applicable airworthiness requirements approved under §21.17(f) of this part; and

(ii) The aircraft has no feature or characteristic that makes it unsafe for its intended use.

(b) An applicant may include a special inspection and preventive maintenance program as part of the aircraft's type design or supplemental type design.

(c) For aircraft manufactured outside of the United States in a country with which the United States has a bilateral airworthiness agreement for the acceptance of these aircraft, and from which the aircraft is to be imported into the United States—

(1) The statement required by paragraph (a)(2)(i) of this section must be made by the civil airworthiness authority of the exporting country; and

(2) The required manuals, placards, listings, instrument markings, and documents required by paragraphs (a) and (b) of this section must be submitted in English.

[Docket No. 23345, 57 FR 41367, Sept. 9, 1992; as amended by Amdt. 21–75, 62 FR 62808, Nov. 25, 1997]

§21.25 Issue of type certificate: Restricted category aircraft.

(a) An applicant is entitled to a type certificate for an aircraft in the restricted category for special purpose operations if he shows compliance with the applicable noise requirements of Part 36 of this chapter, and if he shows that no feature or characteristic of the aircraft makes it unsafe when it is operated under the limitations prescribed for its intended use, and that the aircraft—

(1) Meets the airworthiness requirements of an aircraft category except those requirements that the Administrator finds inappropriate for the special purpose for which the aircraft is to be used; or

(2) Is of a type that has been manufactured in accordance with the requirements of and accepted for use by, an Armed Force of the United States and has been later modified for a special purpose.

(b) For the purposes of this section, "special purpose operations" includes—

(1) Agricultural (spraying, dusting, and seeding, and livestock and predatory animal control);

(2) Forest and wildlife conservation;

(3) Aerial surveying (photography, mapping, and oil and mineral exploration);

(4) Patrolling (pipelines, power lines, and canals);

(5) Weather control (cloud seeding);

(6) Aerial advertising (skywriting, banner towing, airborne signs and public address systems); and

(7) Any other operation specified by the Administrator.

[Docket No. 5085, 29 FR 14564, Oct. 24, 1964; as amended by Amdt. 21–42, 40 FR 1033, Jan. 6, 1975]

§21.27 Issue of type certificate: surplus aircraft of the Armed Forces.

(a) Except as provided in paragraph (b) of this section an applicant is entitled to a type certificate for an aircraft in the normal, utility, acrobatic, commuter, or transport category that was designed and constructed in the United States, accepted for operational use, and declared surplus by, an Armed Force of the United States, and that is shown to comply with the applicable certification requirements in paragraph (f) of this section.

(b) An applicant is entitled to a type certificate for a surplus aircraft of the Armed Forces of the United States that is a counterpart of a previously type certificated civil aircraft, if he shows compliance with the regulations governing the original civil aircraft type certificate.

(c) Aircraft engines, propellers, and their related accessories installed in surplus Armed Forces aircraft, for which a type certificate is sought under this section, will be approved for use on those aircraft if the applicant shows that on the basis of the previous military qualifications, acceptance, and service record, the product provides substantially the same level of airworthiness as would be provided if the engines or propellers were type certificated under Part 33 or 35 of the Federal Aviation Regulations.

(d) The Administrator may relieve an applicant from strict compliance with a specific provision of the applicable requirements in paragraph (f) of this section, if the Administrator finds that the method of compliance proposed by the applicant provides substantially the same level of airworthiness and that strict compliance with those regulations would impose a severe burden on the applicant. The Administrator may use experience that was satisfactory to an Armed Force of the United States in making such a determination.

(e) The Administrator may require an applicant to comply with special conditions and later requirements than those in paragraphs (c) and (f) of this section, if the Administrator finds that compliance with the listed regulations would not ensure an adequate level of airworthiness for the aircraft.

(f) Except as provided in paragraphs (b) through (e) of this section, an applicant for a type certificate under this section must comply with the appropriate regulations listed in the following table:

Type of aircraft	Date accepted for operational use by the Armed Forces of the United States	Regulations that apply[1]
Small reciprocating-engine powered airplanes	Before May 16, 1956 After May 15, 1956	CAR Part 3, as effective May 15, 1956 CAR Part 3, or FAR Part 23
Small turbine engine-powered airplanes	Before Oct. 2, 1959 After Oct. 1, 1959	CAR Part 3 as effective Oct. 1, 1959 CAR Part 3 or FAR Part 23
Commuter category airplanes	After (Feb. 17, 1987) FAR Part 23 as of (Feb. 17, 1987)	
Large reciprocating-engine powered airplanes	Before Aug. 26, 1955 After Aug. 25, 1955	CAR Part 4b, as effective Aug. 25, 1955 CAR Part 4b or FAR Part 25
Large turbine engine-powered airplanes	Before Oct. 2, 1959 After Oct. 1, 1959	CAR Part 4b, as effective Oct. 1, 1959 CAR Part 4b or FAR Part 25
Rotorcraft with maximum certificated takeoff weight of:		
6,000 pounds or less	Before Oct. 2, 1959 After Oct. 1, 1959	CAR Part 6, as effective Oct. 1, 1959 CAR Part 6 or FAR Part 27
Over 6,000 pounds	Before Oct. 2, 1959 After Oct., 1959	CAR Part 7, as effective Oct. 1, 1959 CAR Part 7 or FAR Part 29

[1] Where no specific date is listed, the applicable regulations are those in effect on the date that the first aircraft of the particular model was accepted for operational use by the Armed Forces.

[Docket No. 5085, 29 FR 14564, Oct. 24, 1964; as amended by Amdt. 21–59, 52 FR 1835, Jan. 15, 1987; 52 FR 7262, March 9, 1987]

§21.29 Issue of type certificate: import products.

(a) A type certificate may be issued for a product that is manufactured in a foreign country with which the United States has an agreement for the acceptance of these products for export and import and that is to be imported into the United States if—

(1) The country in which the product was manufactured certifies that the product has been examined, tested, and found to meet—

(i) The applicable aircraft noise, fuel venting and exhaust emissions requirements of this subchapter as designated in §21.17, or the applicable aircraft noise, fuel venting and exhaust emissions requirements of the country in which the product was manufactured, and any other requirements the Administrator may prescribe to provide noise, fuel venting and exhaust emission levels no greater than those provided by the applicable aircraft noise, fuel venting, and exhaust emission requirements of this subchapter as designated in §21.17; and

(ii) The applicable airworthiness requirements of this subchapter as designated in §21.17, or the applicable airworthiness requirements of the country in which the product was manufactured and any other requirements the Administrator may prescribe to provide a level of safety equivalent to that provided by the applicable airworthiness requirements of this subchapter as designated in §21.17;

(2) The applicant has submitted the technical data, concerning aircraft noise and airworthiness, respecting the product required by the Administrator; and

(3) The manuals, placards, listings, and instrument markings required by the applicable airworthiness (and noise, where applicable) requirements are presented in the English language.

(b) A product type certificated under this section is considered to be type certificated under the noise standards of part 36, and the fuel venting and exhaust emission standards of part 34, of the Federal Aviation Regulations where compliance therewith is certified under paragraph (a)(1)(i) of this section, and under the airworthiness standards of that part of the Federal Aviation Regulations with which compliance is certified under paragraph (a)(1)(ii) of this section or to which an equivalent level of safety is certified under paragraph (a)(1)(ii) of this section.

[Amdt. 21–27, 34 FR 18363, Nov. 18, 1969; as amended by Amdt. 21–68, 55 FR 32860, Aug. 10, 1990; 55 FR 37287, Sept. 10, 1990]

§21.31 Type design.

The type design consists of—

(a) The drawings and specifications, and a listing of those drawings and specifications, necessary to define the configuration and the design features of the product shown to comply with the requirements of that part of this subchapter applicable to the product;

(b) Information on dimensions, materials, and processes necessary to define the structural strength of the product;

(c) The Airworthiness Limitations section of the Instructions for Continued Airworthiness as required by Parts 23, 25, 27, 29, 31, 33, and 35 of this chapter; or as otherwise required by the Administrator; and as specified in the applicable airworthiness criteria for special classes of aircraft defined in §21.17(b); and

(d) For primary category aircraft, if desired, a special inspection and preventive maintenance program designed to be accomplished by an appropriately rated and trained pilot-owner.

(e) Any other data necessary to allow, by comparison, the determination of the airworthiness, noise characteristics, fuel venting, and exhaust emissions (where applicable) of later products of the same type.

[Docket No. 5085, 29 FR 14564, Oct. 24, 1964; as amended by Amdt. 21–27, 34 FR 18363, Nov. 18, 1969; Amdt. 21–51, 45 FR 60170, Sept. 11, 1980; Amdt. 21–60, 52 FR 8042, March 13, 1987; Amdt. 21–68, 55 FR 32860, Aug. 10, 1990; Amdt. 21–70, 57 FR 41368, Sept. 9, 1992]

§21.33 Inspection and tests.

(a) Each applicant must allow the Administrator to make any inspection and any flight and ground test necessary to determine compliance with the applicable requirements of the Federal Aviation Regulations. However, unless otherwise authorized by the Administrator—

(1) No aircraft, aircraft engine, propeller, or part thereof may be presented to the Administrator for test unless compliance with paragraphs (b)(2) through (b)(4) of this section has been shown for that aircraft, aircraft engine, propeller, or part thereof; and

(2) No change may be made to an aircraft, aircraft engine, propeller, or part thereof between the time that compliance with paragraphs (b)(2) through (b)(4) of this section is shown for that aircraft, aircraft engine, propeller, or part thereof and the time that it is presented to the Administrator for test.

(b) Each applicant must make all inspections and tests necessary to determine—

(1) Compliance with the applicable airworthiness, aircraft noise, fuel venting, and exhaust emission requirements;

(2) That materials and products conform to the specifications in the type design;

(3) That parts of the products conform to the drawings in the type design; and

(4) That the manufacturing processes, construction and assembly conform to those specified in the type design.

[Docket No. 5085, 29 FR 14564, Oct. 24, 1964; as amended by Amdt. 21–17, 32 FR 14926, Oct. 28, 1967; Amdt. 21–27, 34 FR 18363, Nov. 18, 1969; Amdt. 21–44, 41 FR 55463, Dec. 20, 1976; Amdt. 21–68, 55 FR 32860, Aug. 10, 1990; Amdt. 21–68, 55 FR 32860, Aug. 10, 1990]

§21.35 Flight tests.

(a) Each applicant for an aircraft type certificate (other than under §§21.24 through 21.29) must make the tests listed in paragraph (b) of this section. Before making the tests the applicant must show—

(1) Compliance with the applicable structural requirements of this subchapter;

(2) Completion of necessary ground inspections and tests;

(3) That the aircraft conforms with the type design; and

(4) That the Administrator received a flight test report from the applicant (signed, in the case of aircraft to be certificated under Part 25 [New] of this chapter, by the applicant's test pilot) containing the results of his tests.

(b) Upon showing compliance with paragraph (a) of this section, the applicant must make all flight tests that the Administrator finds necessary—

(1) To determine compliance with the applicable requirements of this subchapter; and

(2) For aircraft to be certificated under this subchapter, except gliders and except airplanes of 6,000 lbs. or less maximum certificated weight that are to be certificated under Part 23 of this chapter, to determine whether there is reasonable assurance that the aircraft, its components, and its equipment are reliable and function properly.

(c) Each applicant must, if practicable, make the tests prescribed in paragraph (b)(2) of this section upon the aircraft that was used to show compliance with—

(1) Paragraph (b)(1) of this section; and

(2) For rotorcraft, the rotor drive endurance tests prescribed in §27.923 or §29.923 of this chapter, as applicable.

(d) Each applicant must show for each flight test (except in a glider or a manned free balloon) that adequate provision is made for the flight test crew for emergency egress and the use of parachutes.

(e) Except in gliders and manned free balloons, an applicant must discontinue flight tests under this section until he shows that corrective action has been taken, whenever—

(1) The applicant's test pilot is unable or unwilling to make any of the required flight tests; or

(2) Items of noncompliance with requirements are found that may make additional test data meaningless or that would make further testing unduly hazardous.

(f) The flight tests prescribed in paragraph (b)(2) of this section must include—

(1) For aircraft incorporating turbine engines of a type not previously used in a type certificated aircraft, at least 300 hours of operation with a full complement of engines that conform to a type certificate; and

(2) For all other aircraft, at least 150 hours of operation.

[Docket No. 5085, 29 FR 14564, Oct. 24, 1964; as amended by Amdt. 21–40, 39 FR 35459, Oct. 1, 1974; Amdt. 21–51, 45 FR 60170, Sept. 11, 1980; Amdt. 21–70, 57 FR 41368, Sept. 9, 1992]

§21.37 Flight test pilot.

Each applicant for a normal, utility, acrobatic, commuter, or transport category aircraft type certificate must provide a person holding an appropriate pilot certificate to make the flight tests required by this part.

[Docket No. 5085, 29 FR 14564, Oct. 24, 1964; as amended by Amdt. 21–59, 52 FR 1835, Jan. 15, 1987]

§21.39 Flight test instrument calibration and correction report.

(a) Each applicant for a normal, utility, acrobatic, commuter, or transport category aircraft type certificate must submit a report to the Administrator showing the computations and tests required in connection with the calibration of instruments used for test purposes and in the correction of test results to standard atmospheric conditions.

(b) Each applicant must allow the Administrator to conduct any flight tests that he finds necessary to check the accuracy of the report submitted under paragraph (a) of this section.

[Docket No. 5085, 29 FR 14564, Oct. 24, 1964; as amended by Amdt. 21–59, 52 FR 1835, Jan. 15, 1987]

§21.41 Type certificate.

Each type certificate is considered to include the type design, the operating limitations, the certificate data sheet, the applicable regulations of this subchapter with which the Administrator records compliance, and any other conditions or limitations prescribed for the product in this subchapter.

§21.43 Location of manufacturing facilities.

Except as provided in §21.29, the Administrator does not issue a type certificate if the manufacturing facilities for the product are located outside of the United States, unless the Administrator finds that the location of the manufacturer's facilities places no undue burden on the FAA in administering applicable airworthiness requirements.

§21.45 Privileges.

The holder or licensee of a type certificate for a product may—

(a) In the case of aircraft, upon compliance with §§21.173 through 21.189, obtain airworthiness certificates;

(b) In the case of aircraft engines or propellers, obtain approval for installation or certified aircraft;

(c) In the case of any product, upon compliance with §§21.133 through 21.163, obtain a production certificate for the type certificated product;

(d) Obtain approval of replacement parts for that product.

§21.47 Transferability.

A type certificate may be transferred to or made available to third persons by licensing agreements. Each grantor shall, within 30 days after the transfer of a certificate or execution or termination of a licensing agreement, notify in writing the appropriate Aircraft Certification Office. The notification must state the name and address of the transferee or licensee, date of the transaction, and in the case of a licensing agreement, the extent of authority granted the licensee.

[Docket No. 5085, 29 FR 14564, Oct. 24, 1964; as amended by Amdt. 21–67, 54 FR 39291, Sept. 25, 1989]

§21.49 Availability.

The holder of a type certificate shall make the certificate available for examination upon the request of the Administrator or the National Transportation Safety Board.

[Docket No. 5085, 29 FR 14564, Oct. 24, 1964; as amended by Docket No. 8084, 32 FR 5769, April 11, 1967]

§21.50 Instructions for continued airworthiness and manufacturer's maintenance manuals having airworthiness limitations sections.

(a) The holder of a type certificate for a rotorcraft for which a Rotorcraft Maintenance Manual containing an "Airworthiness Limitations" section has been issued under §27.1529 (a)(2) or §29.1529 (a)(2) of this chapter, and who obtains approval of changes to any replacement time, inspection interval, or related procedure in that section of the manual, shall make those changes available upon request to any operator of the same type of rotorcraft.

(b) The holder of a design approval, including either the type certificate or supplemental type certificate for an aircraft, aircraft engine, or propeller for which application was made after January 28, 1981, shall furnish at least one set of complete Instructions for Continued Airworthiness, prepared in accordance with §§23.1529, 25.1529, 27.1529, 29.1529, 31.82, 33.4, or 35.4 of this chapter, or as specified in the applicable airworthiness criteria for special classes of aircraft defined in §21.17(b), as applicable, to the owner of each type of aircraft, aircraft engine, or propeller upon its delivery, or upon issuance of the first standard airworthiness certificate for the affected aircraft, whichever occurs later, and thereafter make those instructions available to any other person required by this chapter to comply with any of the terms of these instructions. In addition, changes to the Instructions for Continued Airworthiness shall be made available to any person required by this chapter to comply with any of those instructions.

[Amdt. 21–23, 33 FR 14105, Sept. 18, 1968; as amended by Amdt. 21–51, 45 FR 60170, Sept. 11, 1980; Amdt. 21–60, 52 FR 8042, March 13, 1987]

§21.51 Duration.

A type certificate is effective until surrendered, suspended, revoked, or a termination date is otherwise established by the Administrator.

§21.53 Statement of conformity.

(a) Each applicant must submit a statement of conformity (FAA Form 317) to the Administrator for each aircraft engine and propeller presented to the Administrator for type certification. This statement of conformity must include a statement that the aircraft engine or propeller conforms to the type design therefor.

(b) Each applicant must submit a statement of conformity to the Administrator for each aircraft or part thereof presented to the Administrator for tests. This statement of conformity must include a statement that the applicant has complied with §21.33(a) (unless otherwise authorized under that paragraph).

[Amdt. 21–17, 32 FR 14926, Oct. 28, 1967]

Subpart C— Provisional Type Certificates

Source: Docket No. 5085, 29 FR 14566, Oct. 24, 1964, unless otherwise noted.

§21.71 Applicability.

This subpart prescribes—

(a) Procedural requirements for the issue of provisional type certificates, amendments to provisional type certificates, and provisional amendments to type certificates; and

(b) Rules governing the holders of those certificates.

§21.73 Eligibility.

(a) Any manufacturer of aircraft manufactured within the United States who is a United States citizen may apply for Class I or Class II provisional type certificates, for amendments to provisional type certificates held by him, and for provisional amendments to type certificates held by him.

(b) Any manufacturer of aircraft manufactured in a foreign country with which the United States has an agreement for the acceptance of those aircraft for export and import may apply for a Class II provisional type certificate, for amendments to provisional type certificates held by him, and for provisional amendments to type certificates held by him.

(c) An aircraft engine manufacturer who is a United States citizen and who has altered a type certificated aircraft by installing different type certificated aircraft engines manufactured by him within the United States may apply for a Class I provisional type certificate for the aircraft, and for amendments to Class I provisional type certificates held by him, if the basic aircraft, before alteration, was type certificated in the normal, utility, acrobatic, commuter, or transport category.

[Docket No. 5085, 29 FR 14566, Oct. 24, 1964; as amended by Amdt. 21–12, 31 FR 13380, Oct. 15, 1966; Amdt. 21–59, 52 FR 1836, Jan. 15, 1987]

§21.75 Application.

Applications for provisional type certificates, for amendments thereto, and for provisional amendments to type certificates must be submitted to the Manager of the Aircraft Certification Office for the geographic area in which the applicant is located (or in the case of European, African, Middle East Region, the Manager, Aircraft Engineering Division), and must be accompanied by the pertinent information specified in this subpart.

[Amdt. 21–67, 54 FR 39291, Sept. 25, 1989]

§21.77 Duration.

(a) Unless sooner surrendered, superseded, revoked, or otherwise terminated, provisional type certificates and amendments thereto are effective for the periods specified in this section.

(b) A Class I provisional type certificate is effective for 24 months after the date of issue.

(c) A Class II provisional type certificate is effective for twelve months after the date of issue.

(d) An amendment to a Class I or Class II provisional type certificate is effective for the duration of the amended certificate.

(e) A provisional amendment to a type certificate is effective for six months after its approval or until the amendment of the type certificate is approved, whichever is first.

[Docket No. 5085, 29 FR 14566, Oct. 24, 1964 as amended by Amdt. 21–7, 30 FR 14311, Nov. 16, 1965]

§21.79 Transferability.

Provisional type certificates are not transferable.

§21.81 Requirements for issue and amendment of Class I provisional type certificates.

(a) An applicant is entitled to the issue or amendment of a Class I provisional type certificate if he shows compliance with this section and the Administrator finds that there is no feature, characteristic, or condition that would make the aircraft unsafe when operated in accordance with the limitations established in paragraph (e) of this section and in §91.317 of this chapter.

(b) The applicant must apply for the issue of a type or supplemental type certificate for the aircraft.

(c) The applicant must certify that—

(1) The aircraft has been designed and constructed in accordance with the airworthiness requirements applicable to the issue of the type or supplemental type certificate applied for;

(2) The aircraft substantially meets the applicable flight characteristic requirements for the type or supplemental type certificate applied for; and

(3) The aircraft can be operated safely under the appropriate operating limitations specified in paragraph (a) of this section.

(d) The applicant must submit a report showing that the aircraft had been flown in all maneuvers necessary to show compliance with the flight requirements for the issue of the type or supplemental type certificate applied for, and to establish that the aircraft can be operated safely in accordance with the limitations contained in this subchapter.

(e) The applicant must establish all limitations required for the issue of the type or supplemental type certificate applied for, including limitations on weights, speeds, flight maneuvers, loading, and operation of controls and equipment unless, for each limitation not so established, appropriate operating restrictions are established for the aircraft.

(f) The applicant must establish an inspection and maintenance program for the continued airworthiness of the aircraft.

(g) The applicant must show that a prototype aircraft has been flown for at least 50 hours under an experimental certificate issued under §§21.191 through 21.195, or under the auspices of an Armed Force of the United States. However, in the case of an amendment to a provisional type certificate, the Administrator may reduce the number of required flight hours.

[Docket No. 5085, 29 FR 14566, Oct. 24, 1964; as amended by Amdt. 21–66, 54 FR 34329, Aug. 18, 1989]

§21.83 Requirements for issue and amendment of Class II provisional type certificates.

(a) An applicant who manufactures aircraft within the United States is entitled to the issue or amendment of a Class II provisional type certificate if he shows compliance with this section and the Administrator finds that there is no feature, characteristic, or condition that would make the aircraft unsafe when operated in accordance with the limitations in paragraph (h) of this section, and §§91.317 and 121.207 of this chapter.

(b) An applicant who manufactures aircraft in a country with which the United States has an agreement for the acceptance of those aircraft for export and import is entitled to the issue or amendment of a Class II provisional type certificate if the country in which the aircraft was manufactured certifies that the applicant has shown compliance with this section, that the aircraft meets the requirements of paragraph (f) of this section and that there is no feature, characteristic, or condition that would make the aircraft unsafe when operated in accordance with the limitations in paragraph (h) of this section and §§91.317 and 121.207 of this chapter.

(c) The applicant must apply for a type certificate, in the transport category, for the aircraft.

(d) The applicant must hold a U.S. type certificate for at least one other aircraft in the same transport category as the subject aircraft.

(e) The FAA's official flight test program or the flight test program conducted by the authorities of the country in which the aircraft was manufactured, with respect to the issue of a type certificate for that aircraft, must be in progress.

(f) The applicant or, in the case of a foreign manufactured aircraft, the country in which the aircraft was manufactured, must certify that—

(1) The aircraft has been designed and constructed in accordance with the airworthiness requirements applicable to the issue of the type certificate applied for;

(2) The aircraft substantially complies with the applicable flight characteristic requirements for the type certificate applied for; and

(3) The aircraft can be operated safely under the appropriate operating limitations in this subchapter.

(g) The applicant must submit a report showing that the aircraft has been flown in all maneuvers necessary to show compliance with the flight requirements for the issue of the type certificate and to establish that the aircraft can be operated safely in accordance with the limitations in this subchapter.

(h) The applicant must prepare a provisional aircraft flight manual containing all limitations required for the issue of the type certificate applied for, including limitations on weights, speeds, flight maneuvers, loading, and operation of controls and equipment unless, for each limitation not so established, appropriate operating restrictions are established for the aircraft.

(i) The applicant must establish an inspection and maintenance program for the continued airworthiness of the aircraft.

(j) The applicant must show that a prototype aircraft has been flown for at least 100 hours. In the case of an amendment to a provisional type certificate, the Administrator may reduce the number of required flight hours.

[Amdt. 21–12, 31 FR 13386, Oct. 15, 1966; as amended by Amdt. 21–66, 54 FR 34329, Aug. 18, 1989]

§21.85 Provisional amendments to type certificates.

(a) An applicant who manufactures aircraft within the United States is entitled to a provisional amendment to a type certificate if he shows compliance with this section and the Administrator finds that there is no feature, characteristic, or condition that would make the aircraft unsafe when operated under the appropriate limitations contained in this subchapter.

(b) An applicant who manufactures aircraft in a foreign country with which the United States has an agreement for the acceptance of those aircraft for export and import is entitled to a provisional amendment to a type certificate if the country in which the aircraft was manufactured certifies that the applicant has shown compliance with this section, that the aircraft meets the requirements of paragraph (e) of this section and that there is no feature, characteristic, or condition that would make the aircraft unsafe when operated under the appropriate limitations contained in this subchapter.

(c) The applicant must apply for an amendment to the type certificate.

(d) The FAA's official flight test program or the flight test program conducted by the authorities of the country in which the aircraft was manufactured, with respect to the amendment of the type certificate, must be in progress.

(e) The applicant or, in the case of foreign manufactured aircraft, the country in which the aircraft was manufactured, must certify that—

(1) The modification involved in the amendment to the type certificate has been designed and constructed in accordance with the airworthiness requirements applicable to the issue of the type certificate for the aircraft;

(2) The aircraft substantially complies with the applicable flight characteristic requirements for the type certificate; and

(3) The aircraft can be operated safely under the appropriate operating limitations in this subchapter.

(f) The applicant must submit a report showing that the aircraft incorporating the modifications involved has been flown in all maneuvers necessary to show compliance with the flight requirements applicable to those modifications and to establish that the aircraft can be operated safely in accordance with the limitations specified in §§91.317 and 121.207 of this chapter.

(g) The applicant must establish and publish, in a provisional aircraft flight manual or other document and on appropriate placards, all limitations required for the issue of the type certificate applied for, including weight, speed, flight maneuvers, loading, and operation of controls and equipment, unless, for each limitation not so established, appropriate operating restrictions are established for the aircraft.

(h) The applicant must establish an inspection and maintenance program for the continued airworthiness of the aircraft.

(i) The applicant must operate a prototype aircraft modified in accordance with the corresponding amendment to the type certificate for the number of hours found necessary by the Administrator.

[Amdt. 21–12, 31 FR 13388, Oct. 15, 1966; as amended by Amdt. 21–66, 54 FR 34329, Aug. 18, 1989]

Subpart D— Changes to Type Certificates

Source: Docket No. 5085, 29 FR 14567, Oct. 24, 1964, unless otherwise noted.

§21.91 Applicability.

This subpart prescribes procedural requirements for the approval of changes to type certificates.

§21.93 Classification of changes in type design.

(a) In addition to changes in type design specified in paragraph (b) of this section, changes in type design are classified as minor and major. A "minor change" is one that has no appreciable effect on the weight, balance, structural strength, reliability, operational characteristics, or other characteristics affecting the airworthiness of the product. All other changes are "major changes" (except as provided in paragraph (b) of this section).

(b) For the purpose of complying with Part 36 of this chapter, and except as provided in paragraphs (b)(2), (b)(3), and (b)(4) of this section, any voluntary change in the type design of an aircraft that may increase the noise levels of that aircraft is an "acoustical change" (in addition to being a minor or major change as classified in paragraph (a) of this section) for the following aircraft:

(1) Transport category large airplanes.

(2) Jet (turbojet powered) airplanes (regardless of category). For airplanes to which this paragraph applies, "acoustical changes" do not include changes in type design that are limited to one of the following—

(i) Gear down flight with one or more retractable landing gear down during the entire flight, or

(ii) Spare engine and nacelle carriage external to the skin of the airplane (and return of the pylon or other external mount), or

(iii) Time-limited engine and/or nacelle changes, where the change in type design specifies that the airplane may not be operated for a period of more than 90 days unless compliance with the applicable acoustical change provisions of Part 36 of this chapter is shown for that change in type design.

(3) Propeller driven commuter category and small airplanes in the primary normal, utility, acrobatic, transport, and restricted categories, except for airplanes that are:

(i) Designated for "agricultural aircraft operations" (as defined in §137.3 of this chapter, effective January 1, 1966) to which §36.1583 of this chapter does not apply, or

(ii) Designated for dispensing fire fighting materials to which §36.1583 of this chapter does not apply, or

(iii) U.S. registered, and that had flight time prior to January 1, 1955 or

(iv) Land configured aircraft reconfigured with floats or skis. This reconfiguration does not permit further exception from the requirements of this section upon any acoustical change not enumerated in §21.93(b).

(4) Helicopters except:

(i) Those helicopters that are designated exclusively:

(A) for "agricultural aircraft operations", as defined in §137.3 of this chapter, as effective on January 1, 1996;

(B) for dispensing fire fighting materials; or

(C) for carrying external loads, as defined in §133.1(b) of this chapter, as effective on December 20, 1976.

(ii) Those helicopters modified by installation or removal of external equipment. For purposes of this paragraph, "external equipment" means any instrument, mechanism, part, apparatus, appurtenance, or accessory that is attached to, or extends from, the helicopter exterior but is not used nor is intended to be used in operating or controlling a helicopter in flight and is not part of an airframe or engine. An "acoustical change" does not include:

(A) addition or removal of external equipment;

(B) changes in the airframe made to accommodate the addition or removal of external equipment, to provide for an external load attaching means, to facilitate the use of external equipment or external loads, or to facilitate the safe operation of the helicopter with external equipment mounted to, or external loads carried by, the helicopter;

(C) reconfiguration of the helicopter by the addition or removal of floats and skis;

(D) flight with one or more doors and/or windows removed or in an open position; or

(E) any changes in the operational limitations placed on the helicopter as a consequence of the addition or removal of external equipment, floats, and skis, or flight operations with doors and/or windows removed or in an open position.

(c) For purposes of complying with part 34 of this chapter, any voluntary change in the type design of the airplane or engine which may increase fuel venting or exhaust emissions is an "emissions change."

[Amdt. 21–27, 34 FR 18363, Nov. 18, 1969; as amended by Amdt. 21–42, 40 FR 1033, Jan. 6, 1975; Amdt. 21–47, 43 FR 28419, June 29, 1978; Amdt. 21–56, 47 FR 758, Jan. 7, 1982; Amdt. 21–61, 53 FR 3539, Feb. 5, 1988; Amdt. 21–62, 53 FR 16365, May 6, 1988; Amdt. 21–63, 53 FR 47399, Nov. 22, 1988; Amdt. 21–68, 55 FR 32860, Aug. 10, 1990; Amdt. 21–70, 57 FR 41368, Sept. 9, 1992; Amdt. 21–73, 61 FR 20699, May 7, 1996; Amdt. 21–81, 67 FR 45211, July 8, 2002]

§21.95 Approval of minor changes in type design.

Minor changes in a type design may be approved under a method acceptable to the Administrator before submitting to the Administrator any substantiating or descriptive data.

§21.97 Approval of major changes in type design.

(a) In the case of a major change in type design, the applicant must submit substantiating data and necessary descriptive data for inclusion in the type design.

(b) Approval of a major change in the type design of an aircraft engine is limited to the specific engine configuration upon which the change is made unless the applicant identifies in the necessary descriptive data for inclusion in the type design the other configurations of the same engine type for which approval is requested and shows that the change is compatible with the other configurations.

[Amdt. 21–40, 39 FR 35459, Oct. 1, 1974]

§21.99 Required design changes.

(a) When an Airworthiness Directive is issued under Part 39 the holder of the type certificate for the product concerned must—

(1) If the Administrator finds that design changes are necessary to correct the unsafe condition of the product, and upon his request, submit appropriate design changes for approval; and

(2) Upon approval of the design changes, make available the descriptive data covering the changes to all operators of products previously certificated under the type certificate.

(b) In a case where there are no current unsafe conditions, but the Administrator or the holder of the type certificate finds through service experience that changes in type design will contribute to the safety of the product, the holder of the type certificate may submit appropriate design changes for approval. Upon approval of the changes, the manufacturer shall make information on the design changes available to all operators of the same type of product.

[Docket No. 5085, 29 FR 14567, Oct. 24, 1964; as amended by Amdt. 21–3, 30 FR 8826, July 24, 1965]

§21.101 Designation of applicable regulations.

(a) An applicant for a change to a type certificate must show that the changed product complies with the airworthiness requirements applicable to the category of the product in effect on the date of the application for the change and with parts 34 and 36 of this chapter. Exceptions are detailed in paragraphs (b) and (c) of this section.

(b) If paragraphs (b)(1), (2), or (3) of this section apply, an applicant may show that the changed product complies with an earlier amendment of a regulation required by paragraph (a) of this section, and of any other regulation the Administrator finds is directly related. However, the earlier amended regulation may not precede either the corresponding regulation incorporated by reference in the type certificate, or any regulation in §§23.2, 25.2, 27.2, or 29.2 of this chapter that is related to the change. The applicant may show compliance with an earlier amendment of a regulation for any of the following:

(1) A change that the Administrator finds not to be significant. In determining whether a specific change is significant, the Administrator considers the change in context with all previous relevant design changes and all related revisions to the applicable regulations incorporated in the type certificate for the product. Changes that meet one of the following criteria are automatically considered significant:

(i) The general configuration or the principles of construction are not retained.

(ii) The assumptions used for certification of the product to be changed do not remain valid.

(2) Each area, system, component, equipment, or appliance that the Administrator finds is not affected by the change.

(3) Each area, system, component, equipment, or appliance that is affected by the change, for which the Administrator finds that compliance with a regulation described in paragraph (a) of this section would not contribute materially to the level of safety of the changed product or would be impractical.

(c) An applicant for a change to an aircraft (other than a rotorcraft) of 6,000 pounds or less maximum weight, or to a non-turbine rotorcraft of 3,000 pounds or less maximum weight may show that the changed product complies with the regulations incorporated by reference in the type certificate. However, if the Administrator finds that the change is significant in an area, the Administrator may designate compliance with an amendment to the regulation incorporated by reference in the type certificate that applies to the change and any regulation that the Administrator finds is directly related, unless the Administrator also finds that compliance with that amendment or regulation would not contribute materially to the level of safety of the changed product or would be impractical.

(d) If the Administrator finds that the regulations in effect on the date of the application for the change do not provide adequate standards with respect to the proposed change because of a novel or unusual design feature, the applicant must also comply with special conditions, and amendments to those special conditions, prescribed under the provisions of §21.16, to provide a level of safety equal to that established by the regulations in effect on the date of the application for the change.

(e) An application for a change to a type certificate for a transport category aircraft is effective for 5 years, and an application for a change to any other type certificate is effective for 3 years. If the change has not been approved, or if it is clear that it will not be approved under the time limit established under this paragraph, the applicant may do either of the following:

(1) File a new application for a change to the type certificate and comply with all the provisions of paragraph (a) of this section applicable to an original application for a change.

(2) File for an extension of the original application and comply with the provisions of paragraph (a) of this section. The applicant must then select a new application date. The new application date may not precede the date the change is approved by more than the time period established under this paragraph (e).

(f) For aircraft certificated under §§21.17(b), 21.24, 21.25, and 21.27 the airworthiness requirements applicable to the category of the product in effect on the date of the application for the change include each airworthiness requirement that the Administrator finds to be appropriate for the type certification of the aircraft in accordance with those sections.

[Docket No. 28903, 65 FR 36266, June 7, 2000; as amended by Amdt. 21–77, 66 FR 56989, Nov. 14, 2001]

Subpart E — Supplemental Type Certificates

Source: Docket No. 5085, 29 FR 14568, Oct. 24, 1964, unless otherwise noted.

§21.111 Applicability.

This subpart prescribes procedural requirements for the issue of supplemental type certificates.

§21.113 Requirement of supplemental type certificate.

Any person who alters a product by introducing a major change in type design, not great enough to require a new application for a type certificate under §21.19, shall apply to the Administrator for a supplemental type certificate, except that the holder of a type certificate for the product may apply for amendment of the original type certificate. The application must be made in a form and manner prescribed by the Administrator.

§21.115 Applicable requirements.

(a) Each applicant for a supplemental type certificate must show that the altered product meets applicable requirements specified in §21.101 and, in the case of an acoustical change described in §21.93(b), show compliance with the applicable noise requirements of part 36 of this chapter and, in the case of an emissions change described in §21.93(c), show compliance with the applicable fuel venting and exhaust emissions requirements of part 34 of this chapter.

(b) Each applicant for a supplemental type certificate must meet §§21.33 and 21.53 with respect to each change in the type design.

[Amdt. 21–17, 32 FR 14927, Oct. 28, 1967; as amended by Amdt. 21–42, 40 FR 1033, Jan. 6, 1975; Amdt. 21–52A, 45 FR 79009, Nov. 28, 1980; Amdt. 21–61, 53 FR 3540, Feb. 5, 1988; Amdt. 21–68, 55 FR 32860, Aug. 10, 1990; Amdt. 21–71, 57 FR 42854, Sept. 16, 1992; Amdt. 21–77, 65 FR 36266, June 7, 2000; Amdt. 21–77, 66 FR 56989, Nov. 14, 2001]

§21.117 Issue of supplemental type certificates.

(a) An applicant is entitled to a supplemental type certificate if he meets the requirements of §§21.113 and 21.115.

(b) A supplemental type certificate consists of—

(1) The approval by the Administrator of a change in the type design of the product; and

(2) The type certificate previously issued for the product.

§21.119 Privileges.

The holder of a supplemental type certificate may—

(a) In the case of aircraft, obtain airworthiness certificates;

(b) In the case of other products, obtain approval for installation on certificated aircraft; and

(c) Obtain a production certificate for the change in the type design that was approved by that supplemental type certificate.

Subpart F — Production Under Type Certificate Only

Source: Docket No. 5085, 29 FR 14568, Oct. 24, 1964, unless otherwise noted.

§21.121 Applicability.

This subpart prescribes rules for production under a type certificate only.

§21.123 Production under type certificate.

Each manufacturer of a product being manufactured under a type certificate only shall—

(a) Make each product available for inspection by the Administrator;

(b) Maintain at the place of manufacture the technical data and drawings necessary for the Administrator to determine whether the product and its parts conform to the type design;

(c) Except as otherwise authorized by the Aircraft Certification Directorate Manager for the geographic area which the manufacturer is located, for products manufactured more than 6 months after the date of issue of the type certificate, establish and maintain an approved production inspection system that insures that each product conforms to the type design and is in condition for safe operation; and

(d) Upon the establishment of the approved production inspection system (as required by paragraph (c) of this section) submit to the Administrator a manual that describes that system and the means for making the determinations required by §21.125(b).

[Docket No. 5085, 29 FR 14568, Oct. 24, 1964; as amended by Amdt. 21–34, 35 FR 13008, Aug. 15, 1970; Amdt. 21–51, 45 FR 60170, Sept. 11, 1980; Amdt. 21–67, 54 FR 39291, Sept. 25, 1989]

§21.125 Production inspection system: Materials Review Board.

(a) Each manufacturer required to establish a production inspection system by §21.123(c) shall—

(1) Establish a Materials Review Board (to include representatives from the inspection and engineering departments) and materials review procedures; and

(2) Maintain complete records of Materials Review Board action for at least two years.

(b) The production inspection system required in §21.123(c) must provide a means for determining at least the following:

(1) Incoming materials, and bought or subcontracted parts, used in the finished product must be as specified in the type design data, or must be suitable equivalents.

(2) Incoming materials, and bought or subcontracted parts, must be properly identified if their physical or chemical properties cannot be readily and accurately determined.

(3) Materials subject to damage and deterioration must be suitably stored and adequately protected.

(4) Processes affecting the quality and safety of the finished product must be accomplished in accordance with acceptable industry or United States specifications.

(5) Parts and components in process must be inspected for conformity with the type design data at points in production where accurate determinations can be made.

(6) Current design drawings must be readily available to manufacturing and inspection personnel, and used when necessary.

(7) Design changes, including material substitutions, must be controlled and approved before being incorporated in the finished product.

(8) Rejected materials and parts must be segregated and identified in a manner that precludes installation in the finished product.

(9) Materials and parts that are withheld because of departures from design data or specifications, and that are to be considered for installation in the finished product, must be processed through the Materials Review Board. Those materials and parts determined by the Board to be serviceable must be properly identified and reinspected if rework or repair is necessary. Materials and parts rejected by the Board must be marked and disposed of to ensure that they are not incorporated in the final product.

(10) Inspection records must be maintained, identified with the completed product where practicable, and retained by the manufacturer for at least two years.

§21.127 Tests: aircraft.

(a) Each person manufacturing aircraft under a type certificate only shall establish an approved production flight test procedure and flight check-off form, and in accordance with that form, flight test each aircraft produced.

(b) Each production flight test procedure must include the following:

(1) An operational check of the trim, controllability, or other flight characteristics to establish that the production aircraft has the same range and degree of control as the prototype aircraft.

(2) An operational check of each part or system operated by the crew while in flight to establish that, during flight, instrument readings are within normal range.

(3) A determination that all instruments are properly marked, and that all placards and required flight manuals are installed after flight test.

(4) A check of the operational characteristics of the aircraft on the ground.

(5) A check on any other items peculiar to the aircraft being tested that can best be done during the ground or flight operation of the aircraft.

§21.128 Tests: aircraft engines.

(a) Each person manufacturing aircraft engines under a type certificate only shall subject each engine (except rocket engines for which the manufacturer must establish a sampling technique) to an acceptable test run that includes the following:

(1) Break-in runs that include a determination of fuel and oil consumption and a determination of power characteristics at rated maximum continuous power or thrust and, if applicable, at rated takeoff power or thrust.

(2) At least five hours of operation at rated maximum continuous power or thrust. For engines having a rated takeoff power or thrust higher than rated maximum continuous power or thrust, the five-hour run must include 30 minutes at rated takeoff power or thrust.

(b) The test runs required by paragraph (a) of this section may be made with the engine appropriately mounted and using current types of power and thrust measuring equipment.

[Docket No. 5085, 29 FR 14568, Oct. 24, 1964; as amended by Amdt. 21–5, 32 FR 3735, March 4, 1967]

§21.129 Tests: propellers.

Each person manufacturing propellers under a type certificate only shall give each variable pitch propeller an acceptable functional test to determine if it operates properly throughout the normal range of operation.

§21.130 Statement of conformity.

Each holder or licensee of a type certificate only, for a product manufactured in the United States, shall, upon the initial transfer by him of the ownership of such product manufactured under that type certificate, or upon application for the original issue of an aircraft airworthiness certificate or an aircraft engine or propeller airworthiness approval tag (FAA Form 8130-3), give the Administrator a statement of conformity (FAA Form 317). This statement must be signed by an authorized person who holds a responsible position in the manufacturing organization, and must include—

(a) For each product, a statement that the product conforms to its type certificate and is in condition for safe operation;

(b) For each aircraft, a statement that the aircraft has been flight checked; and

(c) For each aircraft engine or variable pitch propeller, a statement that the engine or propeller has been subjected by the manufacturer to a final operational check.

However, in the case of a product manufactured for an Armed Force of the United States, a statement of conformity is not required if the product has been accepted by that Armed Force.

[Amdt. 21–25, 34 FR 14068, Sept. 5, 1969]

Subpart G— Production Certificates

Source: Docket No. 5085, 29 FR 14569, Oct. 24, 1964, unless otherwise noted.

§21.131 Applicability.

This subpart prescribes procedural requirements for the issue of production certificates and rules governing the holders of those certificates.

§21.133 Eligibility.

(a) Any person may apply for a production certificate if he holds, for the product concerned, a—

(1) Current type certificate;

(2) Right to the benefits of that type certificate under a licensing agreement; or

(3) Supplemental type certificate.

(b) Each application for a production certificate must be made in a form and manner prescribed by the Administrator.

§21.135 Requirements for issuance.

An applicant is entitled to a production certificate if the Administrator finds, after examination of the supporting data and after inspection of the organization and production facilities, that the applicant has complied with §§21.139 and 21.143.

§21.137 Location of manufacturing facilities.

The Administrator does not issue a production certificate if the manufacturing facilities concerned are located outside the United States, unless the Administrator finds no undue burden on the United States in administering the applicable requirements of the Federal Aviation Act of 1958 or of the Federal Aviation Regulations.

§21.139 Quality control.

The applicant must show that he has established and can maintain a quality control system for any product, for which he requests a production certificate, so that each article will meet the design provisions of the pertinent type certificate.

§21.143 Quality control data requirements; prime manufacturer.

(a) Each applicant must submit, for approval, data describing the inspection and test procedures necessary to ensure that each article produced conforms to the type design and is in a condition for safe operation, including as applicable—

(1) A statement describing assigned responsibilities and delegated authority of the quality control organization, together with a chart indicating the functional relationship of the quality control organization to management and to other organizational components, and indicating the chain of authority and responsibility within the quality control organization;

(2) A description of inspection procedures for raw materials, purchased items, and parts and assemblies produced by manufacturers' suppliers including methods used to ensure acceptable quality of parts and assemblies that cannot be completely inspected for conformity and quality when delivered to the prime manufacturer's plant;

(3) A description of the methods used for production inspection of individual parts and complete assemblies, including the identification of any special manufacturing processes involved, the means used to control the processes, the final test procedure for the complete product, and, in the case of aircraft, a copy of the manufacturer's production flight test procedures and checkoff list;

(4) An outline of the materials review system, including the procedure for recording review board decisions and disposing of rejected parts;

(5) An outline of a system for informing company inspectors of current changes in engineering drawings, specifications, and quality control procedures; and

(6) A list or chart showing the location and type of inspection stations.

(b) Each prime manufacturer shall make available to the Administrator information regarding all delegation of authority to suppliers to make major inspections of parts or assemblies for which the prime manufacturer is responsible.

[Docket No. 5085, 29 FR 14569, Oct. 24, 1964; as amended by Amdt. 21–51, 45 FR 60170, Sept. 11, 1980]

§21.147 Changes in quality control system.

After the issue of a production certificate, each change to the quality control system is subject to review by the Administrator. The holder of a production certificate shall immediately notify the Administrator, in writing of any change that may affect the inspection, conformity, or airworthiness of the product.

§21.149 Multiple products.

The Administrator may authorize more than one type certificated product to be manufactured under the terms of one production certificate, if the products have similar production characteristics.

§21.151 Production limitation record.

A production limitation record is issued as part of a production certificate. The record lists the type certificate of every product that the applicant is authorized to manufacture under the terms of the production certificate.

§21.153 Amendment of the production certificates.

The holder of a production certificate desiring to amend it to add a type certificate or model, or both, must apply therefor in a form and manner prescribed by the Administrator. The applicant must comply with the applicable requirements of §§21.139, 21.143, and 21.147.

§21.155 Transferability.

A production certificate is not transferable.

§21.157 Inspections and tests.

Each holder of a production certificate shall allow the Administrator to make any inspections and tests necessary to determine compliance with the applicable regulations in this subchapter.

§21.159 Duration.

A production certificate is effective until surrendered, suspended, revoked, or a termination date is otherwise established by the Administrator, or the location of the manufacturing facility is changed.

§21.161 Display.

The holder of a production certificate shall display it prominently in the main office of the factory in which the product concerned is manufactured.

§21.163 Privileges.

(a) The holder of a production certificate may—

(1) Obtain an aircraft airworthiness certificate without further showing, except that the Administrator may inspect the aircraft for conformity with the type design; or

(2) In the case of other products, obtain approval for installation on type certificated aircraft.

(b) Notwithstanding the provisions of §147.3 of this chapter, the holder of a production certificate for a primary category aircraft, or for a normal, utility, or acrobatic category aircraft of a type design that is eligible for a special airworthiness certificate in the primary category under §21.184(c), may—

(1) Conduct training for persons in the performance of a special inspection and preventive maintenance program approved as a part of the aircraft's type design under §21.24(b), provided the training is given by a person holding a mechanic certificate with appropriate airframe and powerplant ratings issued under part 65 of this chapter; and

(2) Issue a certificate of competency to persons successfully completing the approved training program, provided the certificate specifies the aircraft make and model to which the certificate applies.

[Docket No. 23345, 57 FR 41368, Sept. 9, 1992]

§21.165 Responsibility of holder.

The holder of a production certificate shall—

(a) Maintain the quality control system in conformity with the data and procedures approved for the production certificate; and

(b) Determine that each part and each completed product, including primary category aircraft assembled under a production certificate by another person from a kit provided by the holder of the production certificate, submitted for airworthiness certification or approval conforms to the approved design and is in a condition for safe operation.

[Docket No. 5085, 29 FR 14569, Oct. 24, 1964; as amended by Amdt. 21–64, 53 FR 48521, Dec. 1, 1988 Amdt. 21–70, 57 FR 41368, Sept. 9, 1992]

Subpart H— Airworthiness Certificates

Source: Docket No. 5085, 29 FR 14569, Oct. 24, 1964, unless otherwise noted.

§21.171 Applicability.

This subpart prescribes procedural requirements for the issue of airworthiness certificates.

§21.173 Eligibility.

Any registered owner of a U.S.-registered aircraft (or the agent of the owner) may apply for an airworthiness certificate for that aircraft. An application for an airworthiness certificate must be made in a form and manner acceptable to the Administrator, and may be submitted to any FAA office.

[Amdt. 21–26, 34 FR 15244, Sept. 30, 1969]

§21.175 Airworthiness certificates: classification.

(a) Standard airworthiness certificates are airworthiness certificates issued for aircraft type certificated in the normal, utility, acrobatic, commuter, or transport category, and for manned free balloons, and for aircraft designated by the Administrator as special classes of aircraft.

(b) Special airworthiness certificates are primary, restricted, limited, light-sport, and provisional airworthiness certificates, special flight permits, and experimental certificates.

[Amdt. 21–21, 33 FR 6858, May 7, 1968; as amended by Amdt. 21–60, 52 FR 8043, March 13, 1987 Amdt. 21–70, 57 FR 41368, Sept. 9, 1992; Amdt. 21–85, 69 FR 44861, July 27, 2004]

§21.177 Amendment or modification.

An airworthiness certificate may be amended or modified only upon application to the Administrator.

§21.179 Transferability.

An airworthiness certificate is transferred with the aircraft.

§21.181 Duration.

(a) Unless sooner surrendered, suspended, revoked, or a termination date is otherwise established by the Administrator, airworthiness certificates are effective as follows:

(1) Standard airworthiness certificates, special airworthiness certificates–primary category, and airworthiness certificates issued for restricted or limited category aircraft are effective as long as the maintenance, preventive maintenance, and alterations are performed in accordance with Parts 43 and 91 of this chapter and the aircraft are registered in the United States.

(2) A special flight permit is effective for the period of time specified in the permit.

(3) A special airworthiness certificate in the light-sport category is effective as long as—

(i) The aircraft meets the definition of a light-sport aircraft;

(ii) The aircraft conforms to its original configuration, except for those alterations performed in accordance with an applicable consensus standard and authorized by the aircraft's manufacturer or a person acceptable to the FAA;

(iii) The aircraft has no unsafe condition and is not likely to develop an unsafe condition; and

(iv) The aircraft is registered in the United States.

(4) An experimental certificate for research and development, showing compliance with regulations, crew training, or market surveys is effective for 1 year after the date of issue or renewal unless the FAA prescribes a shorter period. The duration of an experimental certificate issued for operating amateur-built aircraft, exhibition, air-racing, operating primary kit-built aircraft, or operating light-sport aircraft is unlimited, unless the FAA establishes a specific period for good cause.

(b) The owner, operator, or bailee of the aircraft shall, upon request, make it available for inspection by the Administrator.

(c) Upon suspension, revocation, or termination by order of the Administrator of an airworthiness certificate, the owner, operator, or bailee of an aircraft shall, upon request, surrender the certificate to the Administrator.

[Amdt. 21–21, 33 FR 6858, May 7, 1968; as amended by Amdt. 21–49, 44 FR 46781, Aug. 9, 1979 Amdt. 21–70, 57 FR 41368, Sept. 9, 1992; Amdt. 21–85, 69 FR 44861, July 27, 2004]

§21.182 Aircraft identification.

(a) Except as provided in paragraph (b) of this section, each applicant for an airworthiness certificate under this subpart must show that his aircraft is identified as prescribed in §45.11.

(b) Paragraph (a) of this section does not apply to applicants for the following:

(1) A special flight permit.

(2) An experimental certificate for an aircraft not issued for the purpose of operating amateur-built aircraft, operating primary kit-built aircraft, or operating light-sport aircraft.

(3) A change from one airworthiness classification to another, for an aircraft already identified as prescribed in §45.11.

[Amdt. 21–13, 32 FR 188, Jan. 10, 1967; as amended by Amdt. 21–51, 45 FR 60170, Sept. 11, 1980; Amdt. 21–70, 57 FR 41368, Sept. 9, 1992; Amdt. 21–85, 69 FR 44862, July 27, 2004]

§21.183 Issue of standard airworthiness certificates for normal, utility, acrobatic, commuter, and transport category aircraft; manned free balloons; and special classes of aircraft.

(a) *New aircraft manufactured under a production certificate.* An applicant for a standard airworthiness certificate for a new aircraft manufactured under a production certificate is entitled to a standard airworthiness certificate without further showing, except that the Administrator may inspect the aircraft to determine conformity to the type design and condition for safe operation.

(b) *New aircraft manufactured under type certificate only.* An applicant for a standard airworthiness certificate for a new aircraft manufactured under a type certificate only is entitled to a standard airworthiness certificate upon presentation, by the holder or licensee of the type certificate, of the statement of conformity prescribed in §21.130 if the Administrator finds after inspection that the aircraft conforms to the type design and is in condition for safe operation.

(c) *Import aircraft.* An applicant for a standard airworthiness certificate for an import aircraft type certificated in accordance with §21.29 is entitled to an airworthiness certificate if the country in which the aircraft was manufactured certifies, and the Administrator finds, that the aircraft conforms to the type design and is in condition for safe operation.

(d) *Other aircraft.* An applicant for a standard airworthiness certificate for aircraft not covered by paragraphs (a) through (c) of this section is entitled to a standard airworthiness certificate if—

(1) He presents evidence to the Administrator that the aircraft conforms to a type design approved under a type certificate or a supplemental type certificate and to applicable Airworthiness Directives;

(2) The aircraft (except an experimentally certificated aircraft that previously had been issued a different airworthiness certificate under this section) has been inspected in accordance with the performance rules for 100-hour inspections set forth in §43.15 of this chapter and found airworthy by—

(i) The manufacturer;

(ii) The holder of a repair station certificate as provided in Part 145 of this chapter;

(iii) The holder of a mechanic certificate as authorized in Part 65 of this chapter; or

(iv) The holder of a certificate issued under Part 121 of this chapter, and having a maintenance and inspection organization appropriate to the aircraft type; and

(3) The Administrator finds after inspection, that the aircraft conforms to the type design, and is in condition for safe operation.

(e) *Noise requirements.* Notwithstanding all other provisions of this section, the following must be complied with for the original issuance of a standard airworthiness certificate:

(1) For transport category large airplanes and jet (turbojet powered) airplanes that have not had any flight time before the dates specified in §36.1(d), no standard airworthiness certificate is originally issued under this section unless the Administrator finds that the type design complies with the noise requirements in §36.1(d) in addition to the applicable airworthiness requirements in this section. For import airplanes, compliance with this paragraph is shown if the country in which the airplane was manufactured certifies, and the Administrator finds, that §36.1(d) (or the applicable airplane noise requirements of the country in which the airplane was manufactured and any other requirements the Administrator may prescribe to provide noise levels no greater than those provided by compliance with §36.1(d)) and paragraph (c) of this section are complied with.

(2) For normal, utility, acrobatic, commuter, or transport category propeller driven small airplanes (except for those

airplanes that are designed for "agricultural aircraft operations" (as defined in §137.3 of this chapter, as effective on January 1, 1966) or for dispensing fire fighting materials to which §36.1583 of this chapter does not apply) that have not had any flight time before the applicable date specified in Part 36 of this chapter, no standard airworthiness certificate is originally issued under this section unless the applicant shows that the type design complies with the applicable noise requirements of Part 36 of this chapter in addition to the applicable airworthiness requirements in this section. For import airplanes, compliance with this paragraph is shown if the country in which the airplane was manufactured certifies, and the Administrator finds, that the applicable requirements of Part 36 of this chapter (or the applicable airplane noise requirements of the country in which the airplane was manufactured and any other requirements the Administrator may prescribe to provide noise levels no greater than those provided by compliance with the applicable requirements of Part 36 of this chapter) and paragraph (c) of this section are complied with.

(f) *Passenger emergency exit requirements.* Notwithstanding all other provisions of this section, each applicant for issuance of a standard airworthiness certificate for a transport category airplane manufactured after October 16, 1987, must show that the airplane meets the requirements of §25.807(c)(7) in effect on July 24, 1989. For the purposes of this paragraph, the date of manufacture of an airplane is the date the inspection acceptance records reflect that the airplane is complete and meets the FAA-approved type design data.

(g) *Fuel venting and exhaust emission requirements.* Notwithstanding all other provisions of this section, and irrespective of the date of application, no airworthiness certificate is issued, on and after the dates specified in part 34 for the airplanes specified therein, unless the airplane complies with the applicable requirements of that part.

[Amdt. 21–17, 32 FR 14927, Oct. 28, 1967; as amended by Amdt. 21–20, 33 FR 3055, Feb. 16, 1968; Amdt. 21–25, 34 FR 14068, Sept. 5, 1969; Amdt. 21–42, 40 FR 1033, Jan. 6, 1975; Amdt. 21–47, 43 FR 28419, June 29, 1978; Amdt. 21–52, 45 FR 67066, Oct. 9, 1980; Amdt. 21–59, 52 FR 1836, Jan. 15, 1987; Amdt. 21–60, 52 FR 8043, March 13, 1987; Amdt. 21–65, 54 FR 26695, June 23, 1989; Amdt. 21–68, 55 FR 32860, Aug. 10, 1990; Amdt. 21–79, 66 FR 21065, April 27, 2001; Amdt. 21–81, 67 FR 45211, July 8, 2002]

§21.184 Issue of special airworthiness certificates for primary category aircraft.

(a) *New primary category aircraft manufactured under a production certificate.* An applicant for an original, special airworthiness certificate-primary category for a new aircraft that meets the criteria of §21.24(a)(1), manufactured under a production certificate, including aircraft assembled by another person from a kit provided by the holder of the production certificate and under the supervision and quality control of that holder, is entitled to a special airworthiness certificate without further showing, except that the Administrator may inspect the aircraft to determine conformity to the type design and condition for safe operation.

(b) *Imported aircraft.* An applicant for a special airworthiness certificate-primary category for an imported aircraft type certificated under §21.29 is entitled to a special airworthiness certificate if the civil airworthiness authority of the country in which the aircraft was manufactured certifies, and the Administrator finds after inspection, that the aircraft conforms to an approved type design that meets the criteria of §21.24(a)(1) and is in a condition for safe operation.

(c) *Aircraft having a current standard airworthiness certificate.* An applicant for a special airworthiness certificate-primary category, for an aircraft having a current standard airworthiness certificate that meets the criteria of §21.24(a)(1), may obtain the primary category certificate in exchange for its standard airworthiness certificate through the supplemental type certification process. For the purposes of this paragraph, a current standard airworthiness certificate means that the aircraft conforms to its approved normal, utility, or acrobatic type design, complies with all applicable airworthiness directives, has been inspected and found airworthy within the last 12 calendar months in accordance with §91.409(a)(1) of this chapter, and is found to be in a condition for safe operation by the Administrator.

(d) *Other aircraft.* An applicant for a special airworthiness certificate-primary category for an aircraft that meets the criteria of §21.24(a)(1), and is not covered by paragraph (a), (b), or (c) of this section, is entitled to a special airworthiness certificate if—

(1) The applicant presents evidence to the Administrator that the aircraft conforms to an approved primary, normal, utility, or acrobatic type design, including compliance with all applicable airworthiness directives;

(2) The aircraft has been inspected and found airworthy within the past 12 calendar months in accordance with §91.409(a)(1) of this chapter and;

(3) The aircraft is found by the Administrator to conform to an approved type design and to be in a condition for safe operation.

(e) *Multiple-category airworthiness certificates* in the primary category and any other category will not be issued; a primary category aircraft may hold only one airworthiness certificate.

[Docket No. 23345, 57 FR 41368, Sept. 9, 1992; as amended by Amdt. 21–70, 57 FR 43776, Sept. 22, 1992]

§21.185 Issue of airworthiness certificates for restricted category aircraft.

(a) *Aircraft manufactured under a production certificate or type certificate only.* An applicant for the original issue of a restricted category airworthiness certificate for an aircraft type certificated in the restricted category, that was not previously type certificated in any other category, must comply with the appropriate provisions of §21.183.

(b) *Other aircraft.* An applicant for a restricted category airworthiness certificate for an aircraft type certificated in the restricted category, that was either a surplus aircraft of the Armed Forces or previously type certificated in another category, is entitled to an airworthiness certificate if the aircraft has been inspected by the Administrator and found by him to be in a good state of preservation and repair and in a condition for safe operation.

(c) *Import aircraft.* An applicant for the original issue of a restricted category airworthiness certificate for an import aircraft type certificated in the restricted category only in accordance with §21.29 is entitled to an airworthiness certificate if the country in which the aircraft was manufactured certifies, and the Administrator finds, that the aircraft conforms to the type design and is in a condition for safe operation.

(d) *Noise requirements.* For propeller-driven small airplanes (except airplanes designed for "agricultural aircraft operations," as defined in §137.3 of this chapter, as effective on January 1, 1966, or for dispensing fire fighting materials) that have not had any flight time before the applicable date specified in Part 36 of this chapter, and notwithstanding the other provisions of this section, no original restricted category airworthiness certificate is issued under this section unless the Administrator finds that the type design complies with the applicable noise requirements of Part 36 of this chapter in addition to the applicable airworthiness requirements of this section. For import airplanes, compliance with this paragraph is shown if the country in which the airplane was manufactured certifies, and the Administrator finds, that the applicable requirements of Part 36 of this chapter (or the applicable airplane noise requirements of the country in which the airplane was manufactured and any other requirements the Administrator may prescribe to provide noise levels no greater than those provided by compliance with the applicable requirements of Part 36 of this chapter) and paragraph (c) of this section are complied with.

[Amdt. 21–10, 31 FR 9211, July 6, 1966; as amended by Amdt. 21–32, 35 FR 10202, June 23, 1970; Amdt. 21–42, 40 FR 1034, Jan. 6, 1975]

§21.187 Issue of multiple airworthiness certification.

(a) An applicant for an airworthiness certificate in the restricted category, and in one or more other categories except primary category, is entitled to the certificate, if—

(1) He shows compliance with the requirements for each category, when the aircraft is in the configuration for that category; and

(2) He shows that the aircraft can be converted from one category to another by removing or adding equipment by simple mechanical means.

(b) The operator of an aircraft certificated under this section shall have the aircraft inspected by the Administrator, or by a certificated mechanic with an appropriate airframe rating, to determine airworthiness each time the aircraft is converted from the restricted category to another category for the carriage of passengers for compensation or hire, unless the Administrator finds this unnecessary for safety in a particular case.

(c) The aircraft complies with the applicable requirements of part 34.

[Docket No. 5085, 29 FR 14569, Oct. 24, 1964; as amended by Amdt. 21–68, 55 FR 32860, Aug. 10, 1990; Amdt. 21–70, 57 FR 41369, Sept. 9, 1992]

§21.189 Issue of airworthiness certificate for limited category aircraft.

(a) An applicant for an airworthiness certificate for an aircraft in the limited category is entitled to the certificate when—

(1) He shows that the aircraft has been previously issued a limited category type certificate and that the aircraft conforms to that type certificate; and

(2) The Administrator finds, after inspection (including a flight check by the applicant), that the aircraft is in a good state of preservation and repair and is in a condition for safe operation.

(b) The Administrator prescribes limitations and conditions necessary for safe operation.

[Docket No. 5085, 29 FR 14570, Oct. 24, 1964; as amended by Amdt. 21–4, 30 FR 9437, July 29, 1965]

§21.190 Issue of a special airworthiness certificate for a light-sport category aircraft.

(a) ***Purpose.*** The FAA issues a special airworthiness certificate in the light-sport category to operate a light-sport aircraft, other than a gyroplane.

(b) ***Eligibility.*** To be eligible for a special airworthiness certificate in the light-sport category:

(1) An applicant must provide the FAA with—

(i) The aircraft's operating instructions;

(ii) The aircraft's maintenance and inspection procedures;

(iii) The manufacturer's statement of compliance as described in paragraph (c) of this section; and

(iv) The aircraft's flight training supplement.

(2) The aircraft must not have been previously issued a standard, primary, restricted, limited, or provisional airworthiness certificate, or an equivalent airworthiness certificate issued by a foreign civil aviation authority.

(3) The aircraft must be inspected by the FAA and found to be in a condition for safe operation.

(c) ***Manufacturer's statement of compliance for light-sport category aircraft.*** The manufacturer's statement of compliance required in paragraph (b)(1)(iii) of this section must—

(1) Identify the aircraft by make and model, serial number, class,
date of manufacture, and consensus standard used;

(2) State that the aircraft meets the provisions of the identified consensus standard;

(3) State that the aircraft conforms to the manufacturer's design data, using the manufacturer's quality assurance system that meets the identified consensus standard;

(4) State that the manufacturer will make available to any interested person the following documents that meet the identified consensus standard:

(i) The aircraft's operating instructions.

(ii) The aircraft's maintenance and inspection procedures.

(iii) The aircraft's flight training supplement.

(5) State that the manufacturer will monitor and correct safety-of-flight issues through the issuance of safety directives and a continued airworthiness system that meets the identified consensus standard;

(6) State that at the request of the FAA, the manufacturer will provide unrestricted access to its facilities; and

(7) State that the manufacturer, in accordance with a production acceptance test procedure that meets an applicable consensus standard has—

(i) Ground and flight tested the aircraft;

(ii) Found the aircraft performance acceptable; and

(iii) Determined that the aircraft is in a condition for safe operation.

(d) ***Light-sport aircraft manufactured outside the United States.*** For aircraft manufactured outside of the United States to be eligible for a special airworthiness certificate in the light-sport category, an applicant must meet the

21

requirements of paragraph (b) of this section and provide to the FAA evidence that—

(1) The aircraft was manufactured in a country with which the United States has a Bilateral Airworthiness Agreement concerning airplanes or Bilateral Aviation Safety Agreement with associated Implementation Procedures for Airworthiness concerning airplanes, or an equivalent airworthiness agreement; and

(2) The aircraft is eligible for an airworthiness certificate, flight authorization, or other similar certification in its country of manufacture.

[Docket No. FAA–2001–11133, 69 FR 44862, July 27, 2004]

§21.191 Experimental certificates.

Experimental certificates are issued for the following purposes:

(a) *Research and development.* Testing new aircraft design concepts, new aircraft equipment, new aircraft installations, new aircraft operating techniques, or new uses for aircraft.

(b) *Showing compliance with regulations.* Conducting flight tests and other operations to show compliance with the airworthiness regulations including flights to show compliance for issuance of type and supplemental type certificates, flights to substantiate major design changes, and flights to show compliance with the function and reliability requirements of the regulations.

(c) *Crew training.* Training of the applicant's flight crews.

(d) *Exhibition.* Exhibiting the aircraft's flight capabilities, performance, or unusual characteristics at air shows, motion picture, television, and similar productions, and the maintenance of exhibition flight proficiency, including (for persons exhibiting aircraft) flying to and from such air shows and productions.

(e) *Air racing.* Participating in air races, including (for such participants) practicing for such air races and flying to and from racing events.

(f) *Market surveys.* Use of aircraft for purposes of conducting market surveys, sales demonstrations, and customer crew training only as provided in §21.195.

(g) *Operating amateur-built aircraft.* Operating an aircraft the major portion of which has been fabricated and assembled by persons who undertook the construction project solely for their own education or recreation.

(h) *Operating primary kit-built aircraft.* Operating a primary category aircraft that meets the criteria of §21.24(a)(1) that was assembled by a person from a kit manufactured by the holder of a production certificate for that kit, without the supervision and quality control of the production certificate holder under §21.184(a).

(i) *Operating light-sport aircraft.* Operating a light-sport aircraft that—

(1) Has not been issued a U.S. or foreign airworthiness certificate and does not meet the provisions of §103.1 of this chapter. An experimental certificate will not be issued under this paragraph for these aircraft after August 31, 2008;

(2) Has been assembled—

(i) From an aircraft kit for which the applicant can provide the information required by §21.193(e); and

(ii) In accordance with manufacturer's assembly instructions that meet an applicable consensus standard; or

(3) Has been previously issued a special airworthiness certificate in the light-sport category under §21.190.

[Amdt. 21–21, 38 FR 6858, May 7, 1968; as amended by Amdt. 21–57, 49 FR 39651, Oct. 9, 1984; Amdt. 21–70, 57 FR 41369, Sept. 9, 1992; Amdt. 21–85, 69 FR 44862, July 27, 2004; Amdt. 21–85, 69 FR 53336, Sept. 1, 2004]

§21.193 Experimental certificates: general.

An applicant for an experimental certificate must submit the following information:

(a) A statement, in a form and manner prescribed by the Administrator setting forth the purpose for which the aircraft is to be used.

(b) Enough data (such as photographs) to identify the aircraft.

(c) Upon inspection of the aircraft, any pertinent information found necessary by the Administrator to safeguard the general public.

(d) In the case of an aircraft to be used for experimental purposes—

(1) The purpose of the experiment;

(2) The estimated time or number of flights required for the experiment;

(3) The areas over which the experiment will be conducted; and

(4) Except for aircraft converted from a previously certificated type without appreciable change in the external configuration, three-view drawings or three-view dimensioned photographs of the aircraft.

(e) In the case of a light-sport aircraft assembled from a kit to be certificated in accordance with §21.191(i)(2), an applicant must provide the following:

(1) Evidence that an aircraft of the same make and model was manufactured and assembled by the aircraft kit manufacturer and issued a special airworthiness certificate in the light-sport category.

(2) The aircraft's operating instructions.

(3) The aircraft's maintenance and inspection procedures.

(4) The manufacturer's statement of compliance for the aircraft kit used in the aircraft assembly that meets §21.190(c), except that instead of meeting §21.190(c)(7), the statement must identify assembly instructions for the aircraft that meet an applicable consensus standard.

(5) The aircraft's flight training supplement.

(6) In addition to paragraphs (e)(1) through (e)(5) of this section, for an aircraft kit manufactured outside of the United States, evidence that the aircraft kit was manufactured in a country with which the United States has a Bilateral Airworthiness Agreement concerning airplanes or a Bilateral Aviation Safety Agreement with associated Implementation Procedures for Airworthiness concerning airplanes, or an equivalent airworthiness agreement.

[Docket No. 5085, 29 FR 14569, Oct. 24, 1964; as amended by Amdt. 21–85, 69 FR 44862, July 27, 2004]

§21.195 Experimental certificates: Aircraft to be used for market surveys, sales demonstrations, and customer crew training.

(a) A manufacturer of aircraft manufactured within the United States may apply for an experimental certificate for an aircraft that is to be used for market surveys, sales demonstrations, or customer crew training.

(b) A manufacturer of aircraft engines who has altered a type certificated aircraft by installing different engines, manufactured by him within the United States, may apply for an experimental certificate for that aircraft to be used for market surveys, sales demonstrations, or customer crew training, if the basic aircraft, before alteration, was type certificated in the normal, acrobatic, commuter, or transport category.

(c) A person who has altered the design of a type certificated aircraft may apply for an experimental certificate for the altered aircraft to be used for market surveys, sales demonstrations, or customer crew training if the basic aircraft, before alteration, was type certificated in the normal, utility, acrobatic, or transport category.

(d) An applicant for an experimental certificate under this section is entitled to that certificate if, in addition to meeting the requirements of §21.193—

(1) He has established an inspection and maintenance program for the continued airworthiness of the aircraft; and

(2) He shows that the aircraft has been flown for at least 50 hours, or for at least 5 hours if it is a type certificated aircraft which has been modified.

[Amdt. 21–21, 33 FR 6858, May 7, 1968; as amended by Amdt. 21–28, 35 FR 2818, Feb. 11, 1970; Amdt. 21–57, 49 FR 39651, Oct. 9, 1984; Amdt. 21–59, 52 FR 1836, Jan. 15, 1987]

§21.197 Special flight permits.

(a) A special flight permit may be issued for an aircraft that may not currently meet applicable airworthiness requirements but is capable of safe flight, for the following purposes:

(1) Flying the aircraft to a base where repairs, alterations, or maintenance are to be performed, or to a point of storage.

(2) Delivering or exporting the aircraft.

(3) Production flight testing new production aircraft.

(4) Evacuating aircraft from areas of impending danger.

(5) Conducting customer demonstration flights in new production aircraft that have satisfactorily completed production flight tests.

(b) A special flight permit may also be issued to authorize the operation of an aircraft at a weight in excess of its maximum certificated takeoff weight for flight beyond the normal range over water, or over land areas where adequate landing facilities or appropriate fuel is not available. The excess weight that may be authorized under this paragraph is limited to the additional fuel, fuel-carrying facilities, and navigation equipment necessary for the flight.

(c) Upon application, as prescribed in §§121.79 and 135.17 of this chapter, a special flight permit with a continuing authorization may be issued for aircraft that may not meet applicable airworthiness requirements but are capable of safe flight for the purpose of flying aircraft to a base where maintenance or alterations are to be performed. The permit issued under this paragraph is an authorization, including conditions and limitations for flight, which is set forth in the certificate holder's operations specifications. The permit issued under this paragraph may be issued to—

(1) Certificate holders authorized to conduct operations under Part 121 of this chapter; or

(2) Certificate holders authorized to conduct operations under Part 135 for those aircraft they operate and maintain under a continuous airworthiness maintenance program prescribed by §135.411 (a)(2) or (b) of that part.

The permit issued under this paragraph is an authorization, including any conditions and limitations for flight, which is set forth in the certificate holder's operations specifications.

(3) Management specification holders authorized to conduct operations under part 91, subpart K, for those aircraft they operate and maintain under a continuous airworthiness maintenance program prescribed by §91.1411 of this part.

[Docket No. 5085, 29 FR 14570, Oct. 24, 1964; as amended by Amdt. 21–21, 33 FR 6859, May 7, 1968; Amdt. 21–51, 45 FR 60170, Sept. 11, 1980; Amdt. 21–54, 46 FR 37878, July 23, 1981; Amdt. 21–79, 66 FR 21066, April 27, 2001; Amdt. 21–84, 68 FR 54559, Sept. 17, 2003]

§21.199 Issue of special flight permits.

(a) Except as provided in §21.197(c), an applicant for a special flight permit must submit a statement in a form and manner prescribed by the Administrator, indicating—

(1) The purpose of the flight.

(2) The proposed itinerary.

(3) The crew required to operate the aircraft and its equipment, e.g., pilot, co-pilot, navigator, etc.

(4) The ways, if any, in which the aircraft does not comply with the applicable airworthiness requirements.

(5) Any restriction the applicant considers necessary for safe operation of the aircraft.

(6) Any other information considered necessary by the Administrator for the purpose of prescribing operating limitations.

(b) The Administrator may make, or require the applicant to make appropriate inspections or tests necessary for safety.

[Docket No. 5085, 29 FR 14570, Oct. 24, 1964; as amended by Amdt. 21–21, 33 FR 6859, May 7, 1968; Amdt. 21–22, 33 FR 11901, Aug. 22, 1968]

Subpart I—Provisional Airworthiness Certificates

Source: Docket No. 5085, 29 FR 14571, Oct. 24, 1964, unless otherwise noted.

§21.211 Applicability.

This subpart prescribes procedural requirements for the issue of provisional airworthiness certificates.

§21.213 Eligibility.

(a) A manufacturer who is a United States citizen may apply for a Class I or Class II provisional airworthiness certificate for aircraft manufactured by him within the U.S.

(b) Any holder of an air carrier operating certificate under Part 121 of this chapter who is a United States citizen may apply for a Class II provisional airworthiness certificate for transport category aircraft that meet either of the following:

(1) The aircraft has a current Class II provisional type certificate or an amendment thereto.

(2) The aircraft has a current provisional amendment to a type certificate that was preceded by a corresponding Class II provisional type certificate.

(c) An aircraft engine manufacturer who is a United States citizen and who has altered a type certificated aircraft by installing different type certificated engines, manufactured by him within the United States, may apply for a Class I provisional airworthiness certificate for that aircraft, if the basic aircraft, before alteration, was type certificated in the normal, utility, acrobatic, commuter, or transport category.

[Docket No. 5085, 29 FR 14571, Oct. 24, 1964; as amended by Amdt. 21–59, 52 FR 1836, Jan. 15, 1987; Amdt. 21–79, 66 FR 21066, April 27, 2001]

§21.215 Application.

Applications for provisional airworthiness certificates must be submitted to the Manufacturing Inspection District Office in the geographic area in which the manufacturer or air carrier is located. The application must be accompanied by the pertinent information specified in this subpart.

[Amdt. 21–67, 54 FR 39291, Sept. 25, 1989; 54 FR 52872, Dec. 22, 1989]

§21.217 Duration.

Unless sooner surrendered, superseded, revoked, or otherwise terminated, provisional airworthiness certificates are effective for the duration of the corresponding provisional type certificate, amendment to a provisional type certificate, or provisional amendment to the type certificate.

§21.219 Transferability.

Class I provisional airworthiness certificates are not transferable. Class II provisional airworthiness certificates may be transferred to an air carrier eligible to apply for a certificate under §21.213(b).

§21.221 Class I provisional airworthiness certificates.

(a) Except as provided in §21.225, an applicant is entitled to a Class I provisional airworthiness certificate for an aircraft for which a Class I provisional type certificate has been issued if—

(1) He meets the eligibility requirements of §21.213 and he complies with this section; and

(2) The Administrator finds that there is no feature, characteristic or condition of the aircraft that would make the aircraft unsafe when operated in accordance with the limitations established in §§21.81(e) and 91.317 of this subchapter.

(b) The manufacturer must hold a provisional type certificate for the aircraft.

(c) The manufacturer must submit a statement that the aircraft conforms to the type design corresponding to the provisional type certificate and has been found by him to be in safe operating condition under all applicable limitations.

(d) The aircraft must be flown at least five hours by the manufacturer.

(e) The aircraft must be supplied with a provisional aircraft flight manual or other document and appropriate placards containing the limitations established by §§21.81(e) and 91.317.

[Docket No. 5085, 29 FR 14571, Oct. 24, 1964; as amended by Amdt. 21–66, 54 FR 34329, Aug. 18, 1989]

§21.223 Class II provisional airworthiness certificates.

(a) Except as provided in §21.225, an applicant is entitled to a Class II provisional airworthiness certificate for an aircraft for which a Class II provisional type certificate has been issued if—

(1) He meets the eligibility requirements of §21.213 and he complies with this section; and

(2) The Administrator finds that there is no feature, characteristic, or condition of the aircraft that would make the aircraft unsafe when operated in accordance with the limitations established in §§21.83(h), 91.317, and 121.207 of this chapter.

(b) The applicant must show that a Class II provisional type certificate for the aircraft has been issued to the manufacturer.

(c) The applicant must submit a statement by the manufacturer that the aircraft has been manufactured under a quality control system adequate to ensure that the aircraft conforms to the type design corresponding with the provisional type certificate.

(d) The applicant must submit a statement that the aircraft has been found by him to be in a safe operating condition under the applicable limitations.

(e) The aircraft must be flown at least five hours by the manufacturer.

(f) The aircraft must be supplied with a provisional aircraft flight manual containing the limitations established by §§21.83(h), 91.317, and 121.207 of this chapter.

[Docket No. 5085, 29 FR 14571, Oct. 24, 1964; as amended by Amdt. 21–12, 31 FR 13389, Oct. 15, 1966; Amdt. 21–66, 54 FR 34329, Aug. 18, 1989]

§21.225 Provisional airworthiness certificates corresponding with provisional amendments to type certificates.

(a) An applicant is entitled to a Class I or a Class II provisional airworthiness certificate, for an aircraft, for which a provisional amendment to the type certificate has been issued, if—

(1) He meets the eligibility requirements of §21.213 and he complies with this section; and

(2) The Administrator finds that there is no feature, characteristic, or condition of the aircraft, as modified in accordance with the provisionally amended type certificate, that would make the aircraft unsafe when operated in accordance with the applicable limitations established in §§21.85(g), 91.317, and 121.207 of this chapter.

(b) The applicant must show that the modification was made under a quality control system adequate to ensure that the modification conforms to the provisionally amended type certificate.

(c) The applicant must submit a statement that the aircraft has been found by him to be in a safe operating condition under the applicable limitations.

(d) The aircraft must be flown at least five hours by the manufacturer.

(e) The aircraft must be supplied with a provisional aircraft flight manual or other document and appropriate placards containing the limitations required by §§21.85(g), 91.317, and 121.207 of this chapter.

[Docket No. 5085, 29 FR 14571, Oct. 24, 1964; as amended by Amdt. 21–12, 31 FR 13389, Oct. 15, 1966; Amdt. 21–66, 54 FR 34329, Aug. 18, 1989]

Subpart J—Delegation Option Authorization Procedures

Source: Amdt. 21–5, 30 FR 11375, Sept. 8, 1965, unless otherwise noted.

§21.231 Applicability.

This subpart prescribes procedures for—

(a) Obtaining and using a delegation option authorization for type, production, and airworthiness certification (as applicable) of—

(1) Small airplanes and small gliders;

(2) Commuter category airplanes;

(3) Normal category rotorcraft;

(4) Turbojet engines of not more than 1,000 pounds thrust;

(5) Turbopropeller and reciprocating engines of not more than 500 brake horsepower; and

(6) Propellers manufactured for use on engines covered by paragraph (a)(4) of this section; and

(b) Issuing airworthiness approval tags for engines, propellers, and parts of products covered by paragraph (a) of this section.

[Amdt. 21–5, 30 FR 11375, Sept. 8, 1965; as amended by Amdt. 21–59, 52 FR 1836, Jan. 15, 1987]

§21.235 Application.

(a) An application for a delegation option authorization must be submitted, in a form and manner prescribed by the Administrator, to the Aircraft Certification Office for the area in which the manufacturer is located.

(b) The application must include the names, signatures, and titles of the persons for whom authorization to sign airworthiness certificates, repair and alteration forms, and inspection forms is requested.

[Docket No. 5085, 29 FR 14574, Oct. 24, 1964; as amended by Amdt. 21–67, 54 FR 39291, Sept. 25, 1989]

§21.239 Eligibility.

To be eligible for a delegation option authorization, the applicant must—

(a) Hold a current type certificate, issued to him under the standard procedures, for a product type certificated under the same part as the products for which the delegation option authorization is sought;

(b) Hold a current production certificate issued under the standard procedures;

(c) Employ a staff of engineering, flight test, production and inspection personnel who can determine compliance with the applicable airworthiness requirements of this chapter; and

(d) Meet the requirements of this subpart.

§21.243 Duration.

A delegation option authorization is effective until it is surrendered or the Administrator suspends, revokes, or otherwise terminates it.

§21.245 Maintenance of eligibility.

The holder of a delegation option authorization shall continue to meet the requirements for issue of the authorization or shall notify the Administrator within 48 hours of any change (including a change of personnel) that could affect the ability of the holder to meet those requirements.

§21.247 Transferability.

A delegation option authorization is not transferable.

§21.249 Inspections.

Upon request, each holder of a delegation option authorization and each applicant shall let the Administrator inspect his organization, facilities, product, and records.

§21.251 Limits of applicability.

(a) Delegation option authorizations apply only to products that are manufactured by the holder of the authorization.

(b) Delegation option authorizations may be used for—

(1) Type certification;

(2) Changes in the type design of products for which the manufacturer holds, or obtains, a type certificate;

(3) The amendment of a production certificate held by the manufacturer to include additional models or additional types for which he holds or obtains a type certificate; and

(4) The issue of—

(i) Experimental certificates for aircraft for which the manufacturer has applied for a type certificate or amended type certificate under §21.253, to permit the operation of those aircraft for the purpose of research and development, crew training, market surveys, or the showing of compliance with the applicable airworthiness requirements;

(ii) Airworthiness certificates (other than experimental certificates) for aircraft for which the manufacturer holds a type certificate and holds or is in the process of obtaining a production certificate;

(iii) Airworthiness approval tags (FAA Form 8130-3) for engines and propellers for which the manufacturer holds a type certificate and holds or is in the process of obtaining a production certificate; and

(iv) Airworthiness approval tags (FAA Form 8130-3) for parts of products covered by this section.

(c) Delegation option procedures may be applied to one or more types selected by the manufacturer, who must notify the FAA of each model, and of the first serial number of each model manufactured by him under the delegation option procedures. Other types or models may remain under the standard procedures.

(d) Delegation option authorizations are subject to any additional limitations prescribed by the Administrator after inspection of the applicant's facilities or review of the staff qualifications.

[Amdt. 21–5, 30 FR 11375, Sept. 8, 1965; as amended by Amdt. 21–31, 35 FR 7292, May 9, 1970; Amdt. 21–43, 40 FR 2576, Jan. 14, 1975]

§21.253 Type certificates: application.

(a) To obtain, under the delegation option authorization, a type certificate for a new product or an amended type certificate, the manufacturer must submit to the Administrator—

(1) An application for a type certificate (FAA Form 312);

(2) A statement listing the airworthiness requirements of this chapter (by part number and effective date) that the manufacturer considers applicable;

(3) After determining that the type design meets the applicable requirements, a statement certifying that this determination has been made;

(4) After placing the required technical data and type inspection report in the technical data file required by §21.293(a)(1)(i), a statement certifying that this has been done;

(5) A proposed type certificate data sheet; and

(6) An Aircraft Flight Manual (if required) or a summary of required operating limitations and other information necessary for safe operation of the product.

§21.257 Type certificates: issue.

An applicant is entitled to a type certificate for a product manufactured under a delegation option authorization if the Administrator finds that the product meets the applicable airworthiness, noise, fuel venting, and exhaust emission requirements (including applicable acoustical change or emissions change requirements in the case of changes in type design).

[Amdt. 21–68, 55 FR 32860, Aug. 10, 1990]

§21.261 Equivalent safety provisions.

The manufacturer shall obtain the Administrator's concurrence on the application of all equivalent safety provisions applied under §21.21.

§21.267 Production certificates.

To have a new model or new type certificate listed on his production certificate (issued under Subpart G of this part), the manufacturer must submit to the Administrator—

(a) An application for an amendment to the production certificate;

(b) After determining that the production certification requirements of Subpart G, with respect to the new model or type, are met, a statement certifying that this determination has been made;

(c) A statement identifying the type certificate number under which the product is being manufactured; and

(d) After placing the manufacturing and quality control data required by §21.143 with the data required by §21.293(a)(1)(ii), a statement certifying that this has been done.

§21.269 Export airworthiness approvals.

The manufacturer may issue export airworthiness approvals.

§21.271 Airworthiness approval tags.

(a) A manufacturer may issue an airworthiness approval tag (FAA Form 8130-3) for each engine and propeller covered by §21.251(b)(4), and may issue an airworthiness approval tag for parts of each product covered by that section, if he finds, on the basis of inspection and operation tests, that those products conform to a type design for which he holds a type certificate and are in condition for safe operation.

(b) When a new model has been included on the Production Limitation Record, the production certification number shall be stamped on the engine or propeller identification data place instead of issuing an airworthiness approval tag.

[Amdt. 21–5, 30 FR 11375, Sept. 8, 1965; as amended by Amdt. 21–43, 40 FR 2577, Jan. 14, 1975]

§21.273 Airworthiness certificates other than experimental.

(a) The manufacturer may issue an airworthiness certificate for aircraft manufactured under a delegation option authorization if he finds, on the basis of the inspection and production flight check, that each aircraft conforms to a type design for which he holds a type certificate and is in a condition for safe operation.

(b) The manufacturer may authorize any employee to sign airworthiness certificates if that employee—

(1) Performs, or is in direct charge of, the inspection specified in paragraph (a) of this section; and

(2) Is listed on the manufacturer's application for the delegation option authorization, or on amendments thereof.

[Amdt. 21–5, 30 FR 11375, Sept. 8, 1965; as amended by Amdt. 21–18, 32 FR 15472, Nov. 7, 1967]

§21.275 Experimental certificates.

(a) The manufacturer shall, before issuing an experimental certificate, obtain from the Administration any limitations and conditions that the Administrator considers necessary for safety.

(b) For experimental certificates issued by the manufacturer, under this subpart, for aircraft for which the manufacturer holds the type certificate and which have undergone changes to the type design requiring flight test, the manufacturer may prescribe any operating limitations that he considers necessary.

§21.277 Data review and service experience.

(a) If the Administrator finds that a product for which a type certificate was issued under this subpart does not meet the applicable airworthiness requirements, or that an unsafe feature or characteristic caused by a defect in design or manufacture exists, the manufacturer, upon notification by the Administrator, shall investigate the matter and report to the Administrator the results of the investigation and the action, if any, taken or proposed.

(b) If corrective action by the user of the product is necessary for safety because of any noncompliance or defect specified in paragraph (a) of this section, the manufacturer shall submit the information necessary for the issue of an Airworthiness Directive under Part 39.

§21.289 Major repairs, rebuilding and alteration.

For types covered by a delegation option authorization, a manufacturer may—

(a) After finding that a major repair or major alteration meets the applicable airworthiness requirements of this chapter, approve that repair or alteration; and

(b) Authorize any employee to execute and sign FAA Form 337 and make required log book entries if that employee—

(1) Inspects, or is in direct charge of inspecting, the repair, rebuilding, or alteration; and

(2) Is listed on the application for the delegation option authorization, or on amendments thereof.

§21.293 Current records.

(a) The manufacturer shall maintain at his factory, for each product type certificated under a delegation option authorization, current records containing the following:

(1) For the duration of the manufacturing operating under the delegation option authorization—

(i) A technical data file that includes the type design drawings, specifications, reports on tests prescribed by this part, and the original type inspection report and amendments to that report;

(ii) The data (including amendments) required to be submitted with the original application for each production certificate; and

(iii) A record of any rebuilding and alteration performed by the manufacturer on products manufactured under the delegation option authorization.

(2) For 2 years—

(i) A complete inspection record for each product manufactured, by serial number, and data covering the processes and tests to which materials and parts are subjected; and

(ii) A record of reported service difficulties.

(b) The records and data specified in paragraph (a) of this section shall be—

(1) Made available, upon the Administrator's request, for examination by the Administrator at any time; and

(2) Identified and sent to the Administrator as soon as the manufacturer no longer operates under the delegation option procedures.

Subpart K— Approval of Materials, Parts, Processes, and Appliances

Source: Docket No. 5085, 29 FR 14574, Oct. 24, 1964, unless otherwise noted.

§21.301 Applicability.

This subpart prescribes procedural requirements for the approval of certain materials, parts, processes, and appliances.

§21.303 Replacement and modification parts.

(a) Except as provided in paragraph (b) of this section, no person may produce a modification or replacement part for sale for installation on a type certificated product unless it is produced pursuant to a Parts Manufacturer Approval issued under this subpart.

(b) This section does not apply to the following:

(1) Parts produced under a type or production certificate.

(2) Parts produced by an owner or operator for maintaining or altering his own product.

(3) Parts produced under an FAA Technical Standard Order.

(4) Standard parts (such as bolts and nuts) conforming to established industry or U.S. specifications.

(c) An application for a Parts Manufacturer Approval is made to the Manager of the Aircraft Certification Office for the geographic area in which the manufacturing facility is located and must include the following:

(1) The identity of the product on which the part is to be installed.

(2) The name and address of the manufacturing facilities at which these parts are to be manufactured.

(3) The design of the part, which consists of—

(i) Drawings and specifications necessary to show the configuration of the part; and

(ii) Information on dimensions, materials, and processes necessary to define the structural strength of the part.

(4) Test reports and computations necessary to show that the design of the part meets the airworthiness requirements of the Federal Aviation Regulations applicable to the product on which the part is to be installed, unless the applicant shows that the design of the part is identical to the design of a part that is covered under a type certificate. If the design of the part was obtained by a licensing agreement, evidence of that agreement must be furnished.

(d) An applicant is entitled to a Parts Manufacturer Approval for a replacement or modification part if—

(1) The Administrator finds, upon examination of the design and after completing all tests and inspections, that the design meets the airworthiness requirements of the Federal Aviation Regulations applicable to the product on which the part is to be installed; and

(2) He submits a statement certifying that he has established the fabrication inspection system required by paragraph (h) of this section.

(e) Each applicant for a Parts Manufacturer Approval must allow the Administrator to make any inspection or test necessary to determine compliance with the applicable Federal Aviation Regulations. However, unless otherwise authorized by the Administrator—

(1) No part may be presented to the Administrator for an inspection or test unless compliance with paragraphs (f) (2) through (4) of this section has been shown for that part; and

(2) No change may be made to a part between the time that compliance with paragraphs (f)(2) through (4) of this section is shown for that part and the time that the part is presented to the Administrator for the inspection or test.

(f) Each applicant for a Parts Manufacturer Approval must make all inspections and tests necessary to determine—

(1) Compliance with the applicable airworthiness requirements;

(2) That materials conform to the specifications in the design;

(3) That the part conforms to the drawings in the design; and

(4) That the fabrication processes, construction, and assembly conform to those specified in the design.

(g) The Administrator does not issue a Parts Manufacturer Approval if the manufacturing facilities for the part are located outside of the United States, unless the Administrator finds that the location of the manufacturing facilities places no burden on the FAA in administering applicable airworthiness requirements.

(h) Each holder of a Parts Manufacturer Approval shall establish and maintain a fabrication inspection system that ensures that each completed part conforms to its design data and is safe for installation on applicable type certificated products. The system shall include the following:

(1) Incoming materials used in the finished part must be as specified in the design data.

(2) Incoming materials must be properly identified if their physical and chemical properties cannot otherwise be readily and accurately determined.

(3) Materials subject to damage and deterioration must be suitably stored and adequately protected.

(4) Processes affecting the quality and safety of the finished product must be accomplished in accordance with acceptable specifications.

(5) Parts in process must be inspected for conformity with the design data at points in production where accurate determination can be made. Statistical quality control procedures may be employed where it is shown that a satisfactory level of quality will be maintained for the particular part involved.

(6) Current design drawings must be readily available to manufacturing and inspection personnel, and used when necessary.

(7) Major changes to the basic design must be adequately controlled and approved before being incorporated in the finished part.

(8) Rejected materials and components must be segregated and identified in such a manner as to preclude their use in the finished part.

(9) Inspection records must be maintained, identified with the completed part, where practicable, and retained in the manufacturer's file for a period of at least 2 years after the part has been completed.

(i) A Parts Manufacturer Approval issued under this section is not transferable and is effective until surrendered or withdrawn or otherwise terminated by the Administrator.

(j) The holder of a Parts Manufacturer Approval shall notify the FAA in writing within 10 days from the date the manufacturing facility at which the parts are manufactured is relocated or expanded to include additional facilities at other locations.

(k) Each holder of a Parts Manufacturer Approval shall determine that each completed part conforms to the design data and is safe for installation on type certificated products.

[Amdt. 21–38, 37 FR 10659, May 26, 1972; as amended by Amdt. 21–41, 39 FR 41965, Dec. 4, 1974; Amdt. 21–67, 54 FR 39291, Sept. 25, 1989]

§21.305 Approval of materials, parts, processes, and appliances.

Whenever a material, part, process, or appliance is required to be approved under this chapter, it may be approved—

(a) Under a Parts Manufacturer Approval issued under §21.303;

(b) Under a Technical Standard Order issued by the Administrator. Advisory Circular 20–110 contains a list of Technical Standard Orders that may be used to obtain approval. Copies of the Advisory Circular may be obtained from the U.S. Department of Transportation, Publication Section (M-443.1), Washington, D.C. 20590;

(c) In conjunction with type certification procedures for a product; or

(d) In any other manner approved by the Administrator.

[Amdt. 21–38, 37 FR 10659, May 26, 1972; as amended by Amdt. 21–50, 45 FR 38346, June 9, 1980]

Subpart L—Export Airworthiness Approvals

Source: Amdt. 21–2, 30 FR 8465, July 2, 1965, unless otherwise noted.

§21.321 Applicability.

(a) This subpart prescribes—

(1) Procedural requirements for the issue of export airworthiness approvals; and

(2) Rules governing the holders of those approvals.

(b) For the purposes of this subpart—

(1) A Class I product is a complete aircraft, aircraft engine, or propeller, which—

(i) Has been type certificated in accordance with the applicable Federal Aviation Regulations and for which Federal Aviation Specifications or type certificate data sheets have been issued; or

(ii) Is identical to a type certificated product specified in paragraph (b)(1)(i) of this section in all respects except as is otherwise acceptable to the civil aviation authority of the importing state.

(2) A Class II product is a major component of a Class I product (e.g., wings, fuselages, empennage assemblies, landing gears, power transmissions, control surfaces, etc.), the failure of which would jeopardize the safety of a Class I

product; or any part, material, or appliance, approved and manufactured under the Technical Standard Order (TSO) system in the "C" series.

(3) A Class III product is any part or component which is not a Class I or Class II product and includes standard parts, i.e., those designated as AN, NAS, SAE, etc.

(4) The words "newly overhauled" when used to describe a product means that the product has not been operated or placed in service, except for functional testing, since having been overhauled, inspected and approved for return to service in accordance with the applicable Federal Aviation Regulations.

[Amdt. 21–2, 30 FR 11375, July 2, 1965; as amended by Amdt. 21–48, 44 FR 15649, March 15, 1979]

§21.323 Eligibility.

(a) Any exporter or his authorized representative may obtain an export airworthiness approval for a Class I or Class II product.

(b) Any manufacturer may obtain an export airworthiness approval for a Class III product if the manufacturer—

(1) Has in his employ a designated representative of the Administrator who has been authorized to issue that approval; and

(2) Holds for that product—

(i) A production certificate;

(ii) An approved production inspection system;

(iii) An FAA Parts Manufacturer Approval (PMA); or

(iv) A Technical Standard Order authorization.

§21.325 Export airworthiness approvals.

(a) *Kinds of approvals.*

(1) Export airworthiness approval of Class I products is issued in the form of Export Certificates of Airworthiness, FAA Form 8130-4. Such a certificate does not authorize the operation of aircraft.

(2) Export airworthiness approval of Class II and III products is issued in the form of Airworthiness Approval Tags, FAA Form 8130-3.

(b) *Products which may be approved.* Export airworthiness approvals are issued for—

(1) New aircraft that are assembled and that have been flight-tested, and other Class I products located in the United States, except that export airworthiness approval may be issued for any of the following without assembly or flight-test:

(i) A small airplane type certificated under Part 3 or 4a of the Civil Air Regulations, or Part 23 of the Federal Aviation Regulations, and manufactured under a production certificate;

(ii) A glider type certificated under §21.23 of this part and manufactured under a production certificate; or

(iii) A normal category rotorcraft type certificated under Part 6 of the Civil Air Regulations or Part 27 of the Federal Aviation Regulations and manufactured under a production certificate.

(2) Used aircraft possessing a valid U.S. airworthiness certificate, or other used Class I products that have been maintained in accordance with the applicable CAR's or FAR's and are located in a foreign country, if the Administrator finds that the location places no undue burden upon the FAA in administering the provisions of this regulation.

(3) Class II and III products that are manufactured and located in the United States.

(c) *Export airworthiness approval exceptions.* If the export airworthiness approval is issued on the basis of a written statement by the importing state as provided for in §21.327(e)(4), the requirements that are not met and the differences in configuration, if any, between the product to be exported and the related type certificated product, are listed on the export airworthiness approval as exceptions.

[Amdt. 21–2, 30 FR 8465, July 2, 1965; as amended by Amdt. 21–14, 32 FR 2999, Feb. 17, 1967; Amdt. 21–43, 40 FR 2577, Jan. 14, 1975; Amdt. 21–48, 44 FR 15649, March 15, 1979]

§21.327 Application.

(a) Except as provided in paragraph (b) of this section, an application for export airworthiness approval for a Class I or Class II product is made on a form and in a manner prescribed by the Administrator and is submitted to the appropriate Flight Standards District Office or to the nearest international field office.

(b) A manufacturer holding a production certificate may apply orally to the appropriate Flight Standards District Office or the nearest international field office for export airworthiness approval of a Class II product approved under his production certificate.

(c) Application for export airworthiness approval of Class III products is made to the designated representative of the Administrator authorized to issue those approvals.

(d) A separate application must be made for—

(1) Each aircraft;

(2) Each engine and propeller, except that one application may be made for more than one engine or propeller, if all are of the same type and model and are exported to the same purchaser and country; and

(3) Each type of Class II product, except that one application may be used for more than one type of Class II product when—

(i) They are separated and identified in the application as to the type and model of the related Class I product; and

(ii) They are to be exported to the same purchaser and country.

(e) Each application must be accompanied by a written statement from the importing country that will validate the export airworthiness approval if the product being exported is—

(1) An aircraft manufactured outside the United States and being exported to a country with which the United States has a reciprocal agreement concerning the validation of export certificates;

(2) An unassembled aircraft which has not been flight-tested;

(3) A product that does not meet the special requirement of the importing country; or

(4) A product that does not meet a requirement specified in §§21.329, 21.331, or 21.333, as applicable, for the issuance of an export airworthiness approval. The written statement must list the requirements not met.

(f) Each application for export airworthiness approval of a Class I product must include, as applicable:

(1) A Statement of Conformity, FAA Form 8130-9, for each new product that has not been manufactured under a production certificate.

(2) A weight and balance report, with a loading schedule when applicable, for each aircraft in accordance with Part 43 of this chapter. For transport aircraft and commuter category airplanes this report must be based on an actual weighing of the aircraft within the preceding twelve months, but after any major repairs or alterations to the aircraft. Changes in equipment not classed as major changes that are made after the actual weighing may be accounted for on a "computed" basis and the report revised accordingly. Manufacturers of new nontransport category airplanes, normal category rotorcraft, and gliders may submit reports having computed weight and balance data, in place of an actual weighing of the aircraft, if fleet weight control procedures approved by the FAA have been established for such aircraft. In such a case, the following statement must be entered in each report: "The weight and balance data shown in this report are computed on the basis of Federal Aviation Administration approved procedures for establishing fleet weight averages." The weight and balance report must include an equipment list showing weights and moment arms of all required and optional items of equipment that are included in the certificated empty weight.

(3) A maintenance manual for each new product when such a manual is required by the applicable airworthiness rules.

(4) Evidence of compliance with the applicable airworthiness directives. A suitable notation must be made when such directives are not complied with.

(5) When temporary installations are incorporated in an aircraft for the purpose of export delivery, the application form must include a general description of the installations together with a statement that the installation will be removed and the aircraft restored to the approved configuration upon completion of the delivery flight.

(6) Historical records such as aircraft and engine log books, repair and alteration forms, etc., for used aircraft and newly overhauled products.

(7) For products intended for overseas shipment, the application form must describe the methods used, if any, for the preservation and packaging of such products to protect them against corrosion and damage while in transit or storage. The description must also indicate the duration of the effectiveness of such methods.

(8) The Airplane or Rotorcraft Flight Manual when such material is required by the applicable airworthiness regulations for the particular aircraft.

(9) A statement as to the date when title passed or is expected to pass to a foreign purchaser.

(10) The data required by the special requirements of the importing country.

[Amdt. 21–2, 30 FR 8465, July 2, 1965; as amended by Docket No. 8084, 32 FR 5769, April 11, 1967; Amdt. 21–48, 44 FR 15650, March 15, 1979; Amdt. 21–59, 52 FR 1836, Jan. 15, 1987]

§21.329 Issue of export certificates of airworthiness for Class I products.

An applicant is entitled to an export certificate of airworthiness for a Class I product if that applicant shows at the time the product is submitted to the Administrator for export airworthiness approval that it meets the requirements of paragraphs (a) through (f) of this section, as applicable, except as provided in paragraph (g) of this section:

(a) New or used aircraft manufactured in the United States must meet the airworthiness requirement for a standard U.S. airworthiness certificate under §21.183, or meet the airworthiness certification requirements for a "restricted" airworthiness certificate under §21.185.

(b) New or used aircraft manufactured outside the United States must have a valid U.S. standard airworthiness certificate.

(c) Used aircraft must have undergone an annual type inspection and be approved for return to service in accordance with Part 43 of this chapter. The inspection must have been performed and properly documented within 30 days before the date the application is made for an export certificate of airworthiness. In complying with this paragraph, consideration may be given to the inspections performed on an aircraft maintained in accordance with a continuous airworthiness maintenance program under Part 121 of this chapter or a progressive inspection program under Part 91 of this chapter, within the 30 days prior to the date the application is made for an export certificate of airworthiness.

(d) New engines and propellers must conform to the type design and must be in a condition for safe operation.

(e) Used engines and propellers which are not being exported as part of a certificated aircraft must have been newly overhauled.

(f) The special requirements of the importing country must have been met.

(g) A product need not meet a requirement specified in paragraphs (a) through (f) of this section, as applicable, if acceptable to the importing country and the importing country indicates that acceptability in accordance with §21.327(e)(4) of this part.

[Amdt. 21–2, 30 FR 8465, July 2, 1965; as amended by Amdt. 21–8, 31 FR 2421, Feb. 5, 1966; Amdt. 21–9, 31 FR 3336, March 3, 1966; Amdt. 21–48, 44 FR 15650, March 15, 1979; Amdt. 21–79, 66 FR 21066, April 27, 2001]

§21.331 Issue of airworthiness approval tags for Class II products.

(a) An applicant is entitled to an export airworthiness approval tag for Class II products if that applicant shows, except as provided in paragraph (b) of this section, that—

(1) The products are new or have been newly overhauled and conform to the approved design data;

(2) The products are in a condition for safe operation;

(3) The products are identified with at least the manufacturer's name, part number, model designation (when applicable), and serial number or equivalent; and

(4) The products meet the special requirements of the importing country.

(b) A product need not meet a requirement specified in paragraph (a) of this section if acceptable to the importing country and the importing country indicates that acceptability in accordance with §21.327(e)(4) of this part.

[Amdt. 21–2, 30 FR 8465, July 2, 1965; as amended by Amdt. 21–48, 44 FR 15650, March 15, 1979]

§21.333 Issue of export airworthiness approval tags for Class III products.

(a) An applicant is entitled to an export airworthiness approval tag for Class III products if that applicant shows, except as provided in paragraph (b) of this section, that—

(1) The products conform to the approved design data applicable to the Class I or Class II product of which they are a part;

(2) The products are in a condition for safe operation; and

(3) The products comply with the special requirements of the importing country.

(b) A product need not meet a requirement specified in paragraph (a) of this section if acceptable to the importing country and the importing country indicates that acceptability in accordance with §21.327(e)(4) of this part.

[Amdt. 21–2, 30 FR 8465, July 2, l965; as amended by Amdt. 21–48, 44 FR 15650, March 15, 1979]

§21.335 Responsibilities of exporters.

Each exporter receiving an export airworthiness approval for a product shall—

(a) Forward to the air authority of the importing country all documents and information necessary for the proper operation of the products being exported, e.g., Flight Manuals, Maintenance Manuals, Service Bulletins, and assembly instructions, and such other material as is stipulated in the special requirements of the importing country. The documents, information, and material may be forwarded by any means consistent with the special requirements of the importing country;

(b) Forward the manufacturer's assembly instructions and an FAA-approved flight test checkoff form to the air authority of the importing country when unassembled aircraft are being exported. These instructions must be in sufficient detail to permit whatever rigging, alignment, and ground testing is necessary to ensure that the aircraft will conform to the approved configuration when assembled;

(c) Remove or cause to be removed any temporary installation incorporated on an aircraft for the purpose of export delivery and restore the aircraft to the approved configuration upon completion of the delivery flight;

(d) Secure all proper foreign entry clearances from all the countries involved when conducting sales demonstrations or delivery flights; and

(e) When title to an aircraft passes or has passed to a foreign purchaser—

(1) Request cancellation of the U.S. registration and airworthiness certificates, giving the date of transfer of title, and the name and address of the foreign owner;

(2) Return the Registration and Airworthiness Certificates, AC Form 8050.3 and FAA Form 8100-2, to the FAA; and

(3) Submit a statement certifying that the United States' identification and registration numbers have been removed from the aircraft in compliance with §45.33.

[Amdt. 21–2, 30 FR 8465, July 2, 1965; as amended by Amdt. 21–48, 44 FR 15650, March 15, 1979]

§21.337 Performance of inspections and overhauls.

Unless otherwise provided for in this subpart, each inspection and overhaul required for export airworthiness approval of Class I and Class II products must be performed and approved by one of the following:

(a) The manufacturer of the product.

(b) An appropriately certificated domestic repair station.

(c) An appropriately certificated foreign repair station having adequate overhaul facilities, and maintenance organization appropriate to the product involved, when the product is a Class I product located in a foreign country and an international office of Flight Standards Service has approved the use of such foreign repair station.

(d) The holder of an inspection authorization as provided in Part 65 of this chapter.

(e) An air carrier, when the product is one that the carrier has maintained under its own or another air carrier's continuous airworthiness maintenance program and maintenance manuals as provided in Part 121 of this chapter.

(f) A commercial operator, when the product is one that the operator has maintained under its continuous airworthiness maintenance program and maintenance manual as provided in Part 121 of this chapter.

[Amdt. 21–2, 30 FR 8465, July 2, 1965; as amended by Amdt. 21–8, 31 FR 2421, Feb. 5, 1966; Amdt. 21–79, 66 FR 21066, April 27, 2001]

§21.339 Special export airworthiness approval for aircraft.

A special export certificate of airworthiness may be issued for an aircraft located in the United States that is to be flown to several foreign countries for the purpose of sale, without returning the aircraft to the United States for the certificate if—

(a) The aircraft possesses either—

(1) A standard U.S. certificate of airworthiness; or

(2) A special U.S. certificate of airworthiness in the restricted category issued under §21.185;

(b) The owner files an application as required by §21.327 except that items 3 and 4 of the application (FAA Form 8130-1) need not be completed;

(c) The aircraft is inspected by the Administrator before leaving the United States and is found to comply with all the applicable requirements;

(d) A list of foreign countries in which it is intended to conduct sales demonstrations, together with the expected dates and duration of such demonstration, is included in the application;

(e) For each prospective importing country, the applicant shows that—

(1) He has met that country's special requirements, other than those requiring that documents, information, and materials be furnished; and

(2) He has the documents, information, and materials necessary to meet the special requirements of that country; and

(f) All other requirements for the issuance of a Class I export certificate of airworthiness are met.

[Amdt. 21–12, 31 FR 12565, Sept. 23, 1966; as amended by Amdt. 21–43, 40 FR 2577, Jan. 14, 1975; Amdt. 21–55, 46 FR 44737, Sept. 8, 1981]

Subpart M— Designated Alteration Station Authorization Procedures

Source: Amdt. 21–6, 30 FR 11379, Sept. 8, 1965; 30 FR 11849, Sept. 16, 1965, unless otherwise noted.

§21.431 Applicability.

(a) This subpart prescribes Designated Alteration Station (DAS) authorization procedures for—

(1) Issuing supplemental type certificates;

(2) Issuing experimental certificates; and

(3) Amending standard airworthiness certificates.

(b) This subpart applies to domestic repair stations, air carriers, commercial operators of large aircraft, and manufacturers of products.

[Amdt. 21–6, 30 FR 11379, Sept. 8, 1965; 30 FR 11849, Sept. 16, 1965; Amdt. 21–74, 62 FR 13253, March 19, 1997]

§21.435 Application.

The applicant for a DAS authorization must submit an application, in writing and signed by an official of the applicant, to the Aircraft Certification Office responsible for the geographic area in which the applicant is located. The application must contain—

(a) The repair station certificate number held by the repair station applicant, and the current ratings covered by the certificate;

(b) The air carrier or commercial operator operating certificate number held by the air carrier or commercial operator applicant, and the products that it may operate and maintain under the certificate;

(c) A statement by the manufacturer applicant of the products for which he holds the type certificate;

(d) The names, signatures, and titles of the persons for whom authorization to issue supplemental type certificates or experimental certificates, or amend airworthiness certificates, is requested; and

(e) A description of the applicant's facilities, and of the staff with which compliance with §21.439(a)(4) is to be shown.

[Amdt. 21–6, 30 FR 11379, Sept. 8, 1965; 30 FR 11849, Sept. 16, 1965; as amended by Amdt. 21–67, 54 FR 39291, Sept. 25, 1989]

§21.439 Eligibility.

(a) To be eligible for a DAS authorization, the applicant must—

(1) Hold a current domestic repair station certificate under Part 145, or air carrier or commercial operator operating certificate under Part 121;

(2) Be a manufacturer of a product for which it has alteration authority under §43.3(i) of this subchapter;

(3) Have adequate maintenance facilities and personnel, in the United States, appropriate to the products that it may operate and maintain under its certificate; and

(4) Employ, or have available, a staff of engineering, flight test, and inspection personnel who can determine compliance with the applicable airworthiness requirements of this chapter.

(b) At least one member of the staff required by paragraph (a)(4) of this section must have all of the following qualifications:

(1) A thorough working knowledge of the applicable requirements of this chapter.

(2) A position, on the applicant's staff, with authority to establish alteration programs that ensure that altered products meet the applicable requirements of this chapter.

(3) At least one year of satisfactory experience in direct contact with the FAA (or its predecessor agency (CAA)) while processing engineering work for type certification or alteration projects.

(4) At least eight years of aeronautical engineering experience (which may include the one year required by paragraph (b)(3) of this section).

(5) The general technical knowledge and experience necessary to determine that altered products, of the types for which a DAS authorization is requested, are in condition for safe operation.

§21.441 Procedure manual.

(a) No DAS may exercise any authority under this subpart unless it submits, and obtains approval of, a procedure manual containing—

(1) The procedures for issuing STCs; and

(2) The names, signatures, and responsibilities of officials and of each staff member required by §21.439(a)(4), identifying those persons who—

(i) Have authority to make changes in procedures that require a revision to the procedure manual; and

(ii) Are to conduct inspections (including conformity and compliance inspections) or approve inspection reports, prepare or approve data, plan or conduct tests, approve the results of tests, amend airworthiness certificates, issue experimental certificates, approve changes to operating limitations or Aircraft Flight Manuals, and sign supplemental type certificates.

(b) No DAS may continue to perform any DAS function affected by any change in facilities or staff necessary to continue to meet the requirements of §21.439, or affected by any change in procedures from those approved under paragraph (a) of this section, unless that change is approved and entered in the manual. For this purpose, the manual shall contain a log-of-revisions page with space for the identification of each revised item, page, or date, and the signature of the person approving the change for the Administrator.

§21.443 Duration.

(a) A DAS authorization is effective until it is surrendered or the Administrator suspends, revokes, or otherwise terminates it.

(b) The DAS shall return the authorization certificate to the Administrator when it is no longer effective.

§21.445 Maintenance of eligibility.

The DAS shall continue to meet the requirements for issue of the authorization or shall notify the Administrator within 48 hours of any change (including a change of personnel) that could affect the ability of the DAS to meet those requirements.

§21.447 Transferability.

A DAS authorization is not transferable.

§21.449 Inspections.

Upon request, each DAS and each applicant shall let the Administrator inspect his facilities, products, and records.

§21.451 Limits of applicability.

(a) DAS authorizations apply only to products—

(1) Covered by the ratings of the repair station applicant;

(2) Covered by the operating certificate and maintenance manual of the air carrier or commercial operator applicant; and

(3) For which the manufacturer applicant has alteration authority under §43.3(i) of this subchapter.

(b) DAS authorizations may be used for—

(1) The issue of supplemental type certificates;

(2) The issue of experimental certificates for aircraft that—

(i) Are altered by the DAS under a supplemental type certificate issued by the DAS; and

(ii) Require flight tests in order to show compliance with the applicable airworthiness requirements of this chapter; and

(3) The amendment of standard airworthiness certificates for aircraft altered under this subpart.

(c) DAS authorizations are subject to any additional limitations prescribed by the Administrator after inspection of the applicant's facilities or review of the staff qualifications.

(d) Notwithstanding any other provision of this subpart, a DAS may not issue a supplemental type certificate involving the exhaust emissions change requirements of part 34 or the acoustical change requirements of part 36 of this chapter until the Administrator finds that those requirements are met.

[Amdt. 21–6, 30 FR 11379, Sept. 8, 1965; 30 FR 11849, Sept. 16, 1965; as amended by Amdt. 21–42, 40 FR 1034, Jan. 6, 1975; Amdt. 21–68, 55 FR 32860, Aug. 10, 1990]

§21.461 Equivalent safety provisions.

The DAS shall obtain the Administrator's concurrence on the application of all equivalent safety provisions applied under §21.21.

§21.463 Supplemental type certificates.

(a) For each supplemental type certificate issued under this subpart, the DAS shall follow the procedure manual prescribed in §21.441 and shall, before issuing the certificate—

(1) Submit to the Administrator a statement describing—

(i) The type design change;

(ii) The airworthiness requirements of this chapter (by part and effective date) that the DAS considers applicable; and

(iii) The proposed program for meeting the applicable airworthiness requirements;

(2) Find that each applicable airworthiness requirement is met; and

(3) Find that the type of product for which the STC is to be issued, as modified by the supplemental type design data upon which the STC is based, is of proper design for safe operation.

(b) Within 30 days after the date of issue of the STC, the DAS shall submit to the Administrator—

(1) Two copies of the STC;

(2) One copy of the design data approved by the DAS and referred to in the STC;

(3) One copy of each inspection and test report; and

(4) Two copies of each revision to the Aircraft Flight Manual or to the operating limitations, and any other information necessary for safe operation of the product.

§21.473 Airworthiness certificates other than experimental.

For each amendment made to a standard airworthiness certificate under this subpart, the DAS shall follow the procedure manual prescribed in §21.441 and shall, before making that amendment—

(a) Complete each flight test necessary to meet the applicable airworthiness requirements of this chapter;

(b) Find that each applicable airworthiness requirement of this chapter is met; and

(c) Find that the aircraft is in condition for safe operation.

§21.475 Experimental certificates.

The DAS shall, before issuing an experimental certificate, obtain from the Administrator any limitations and conditions that the Administrator considers necessary for safety.

§21.477 Data review and service experience.

(a) If the Administrator finds that a product for which an STC was issued under this subpart does not meet the applicable airworthiness requirements, or that an unsafe feature or characteristic caused by a defect in design or manufacture exists, the DAS, upon notification by the Administrator, shall investigate the matter and report to the Administrator the results of the investigation and the action, if any, taken or proposed.

(b) If corrective action by the user of the product is necessary for safety because of any noncompliance or defect specified in paragraph (a) of this section, the DAS shall submit the information necessary for the issue of an Airworthiness Directive under Part 39.

§21.493 Current records.

(a) The DAS shall maintain, at its facility, current records containing—

(1) For each product for which it has issued an STC under this subpart, a technical data file that includes any data and amendments thereto (including drawings, photographs, specifications, instructions, and reports) necessary for the STC;

(2) A list of products by make, model, manufacturer's serial number and, if applicable, any FAA identification, that have been altered under the DAS authorization; and

(3) A file of information from all available sources on alteration difficulties of products altered under the DAS authorization.

(b) The records prescribed in paragraph (a) of this section shall be—

(1) Made available by the DAS, upon the Administrator's request, for examination by the Administrator at any time; and

(2) In the case of the data file prescribed in paragraph (a)(1) of this section, identified by the DAS and sent to the Administrator as soon as the DAS no longer operates under this subpart.

Subpart N—Approval of Engines, Propellers, Materials, Parts, and Appliances: Import

§21.500 Approval of engines and propellers.

Each holder or licensee of a U.S. type certificate for an aircraft engine or propeller manufactured in a foreign country with which the United States has an agreement for the acceptance of those products for export and import, shall furnish with each such aircraft engine or propeller imported into this country, a certificate of airworthiness for export issued by the country of manufacture certifying that the individual aircraft engine or propeller—

(a) Conforms to its U.S. type certificate and is in condition for safe operation; and

(b) Has been subjected by the manufacturer to a final operational check.

[Amdt. 21–25, 34 FR 14068, Sept. 5, 1969]

§21.502 Approval of materials, parts, and appliances.

(a) A material, part, or appliance, manufactured in a foreign country with which the United States has an agreement for the acceptance of those materials, parts, or appliances for export and import, is considered to meet the requirements for approval in the Federal Aviation Regulations when the country of manufacture issues a certificate of airworthiness for export certifying that the individual material, part, or appliance meets those requirements, unless the Administrator finds, based on the technical data submitted under paragraph (b) of this section, that the material, part, or appliance is otherwise not consistent with the intent of the Federal Aviation Regulations.

(b) An applicant for approval of a material, part, or appliance must, upon request, submit to the Administrator any technical data respecting that material, part, or appliance.

[Amdt. 21–25, 34 FR 14068, Sept. 5, 1969]

Subpart O—Technical Standard Order Authorizations

Source: Docket No. 19589, 45 FR 38346, June 9, 1980, unless otherwise noted.

§21.601 Applicability.

(a) This subpart prescribes—

(1) Procedural requirements for the issue of Technical Standard Order authorizations;

(2) Rules governing the holders of Technical Standard Order authorizations; and

(3) Procedural requirements for the issuance of a letter of Technical Standard Order design approval.

(b) For the purpose of this subpart—

(1) A Technical Standard Order (referred to in this subpart as "TSO") is issued by the Administrator and is a minimum performance standard for specified articles (for the purpose of this subpart, articles means materials, parts, processes, or appliances) used on civil aircraft.

(2) A TSO authorization is an FAA design and production approval issued to the manufacturer of an article which has been found to meet a specific TSO.

(3) A letter of TSO design approval is an FAA design approval for a foreign-manufactured article which has been found to meet a specific TSO in accordance with the procedures of §21.617.

(4) An article manufactured under a TSO authorization, an FAA letter of acceptance as described in §21.603(b), or an appliance manufactured under a letter of TSO design approval described in §21.617 is an approved article or appliance for the purpose of meeting the regulations of this chapter that require the article to be approved.

(5) An article manufacturer is the person who controls the design and quality of the article produced (or to be produced, in the case of an application), including the parts of them and any processes or services related to them that are procured from an outside source.

(c) The Administrator does not issue a TSO authorization if the manufacturing facilities for the product are located outside of the United States, unless the Administrator finds that the location of the manufacturer's facilities places no undue burden on the FAA in administering applicable airworthiness requirements.

§21.603 TSO marking and privileges.

(a) Except as provided in paragraph (b) of this section and §21.617(c), no person may identify an article with a TSO marking unless that person holds a TSO authorization and the article meets applicable TSO performance standards.

(b) The holder of an FAA letter of acceptance of a statement of conformance issued for an article before July 1, 1962, or any TSO authorization issued after July 1, 1962, may continue to manufacture that article without obtaining a new TSO authorization but shall comply with the requirements of §§21.3, 21.607 through 21.615, 21.619, and 21.621.

(c) Notwithstanding paragraphs (a) and (b) of this section, after August 6, 1976, no person may identify or mark an article with any of the following TSO numbers:

(1) TSO-C18, -C18a, -C18b, -C18c.
(2) TSO-C24.
(3) TSO-C33.
(4) TSO-C61 or C61a.

§21.605 Application and issue.

(a) The manufacturer (or an authorized agent) shall submit an application for a TSO authorization, together with the following documents, to the Manager of the Aircraft Certification Office for the geographic area in which the applicant is located:

(1) A statement of conformance certifying that the applicant has met the requirements of this subpart and that the article concerned meets the applicable TSO that is effective on the date of application for that article.

(2) One copy of the technical data required in the applicable TSO.

(3) A description of its quality control system in the detail specified in §21.143. In complying with this section, the applicant may refer to current quality control data filed with the FAA as part of a previous TSO authorization application.

(b) When a series of minor changes in accordance with §21.611 is anticipated, the applicant may set forth in its application the basic model number of the article and the part number of the components with open brackets after it to denote that suffix change letters or numbers (or combinations of them) will be added from time to time.

(c) After receiving the application and other documents required by paragraph (a) of this section to substantiate compliance with this part, and after a determination has been made of its ability to produce duplicate articles under this part, the Administrator issues a TSO authorization (including all TSO deviations granted to the applicant) to the applicant to identify the article with the applicable TSO marking.

(d) If the application is deficient, the applicant must, when requested by the Administrator, submit any additional information necessary to show compliance with this part. If the applicant fails to submit the additional information within 30 days after the Administrator's request, the application is denied and the applicant is so notified.

(e) The Administrator issues or denies the application within 30 days after its receipt or, if additional information has been requested, within 30 days after receiving that information.

[Docket No. 19589, 45 FR 38346, June 9, 1980; as amended by Amdt. 21–67, 54 FR 39291, Sept. 25, 1989]

§21.607 General rules governing holders of TSO authorizations.

Each manufacturer of an article for which a TSO authorization has been issued under this part shall—

(a) Manufacture the article in accordance with this part and the applicable TSO;

(b) Conduct all required tests and inspections and establish and maintain a quality control system adequate to ensure that the article meets the requirements of paragraph (a) of this section and is in condition for safe operation;

(c) Prepare and maintain, for each model of each article for which a TSO authorization has been issued, a current file of complete technical data and records in accordance with §21.613; and

(d) Permanently and legibly mark each article to which this section applies with the following information:

(1) The name and address of the manufacturer.

(2) The name, type, part number, or model designation of the article.

(3) The serial number or the date of manufacture of the article or both.

(4) The applicable TSO number.

§21.609 Approval for deviation.

(a) Each manufacturer who requests approval to deviate from any performance standard of a TSO shall show that the standards from which a deviation is requested are compensated for by factors or design features providing an equivalent level of safety.

(b) The request for approval to deviate, together with all pertinent data, must be submitted to the Manager of the Aircraft Certification Office for the geographic area in which the manufacturer is located. If the article is manufactured in another country, the request for approval to deviate, together with all pertinent data, must be submitted through the civil aviation authority in that country to the FAA.

[Docket No. 19589, 45 FR 38346, June 9, 1980; as amended by Amdt. 21–67, 54 FR 39291, Sept. 25, 1989]

§21.611 Design changes.

(a) *Minor changes by the manufacturer holding a TSO authorization.* The manufacturer of an article under an authorization issued under this part may make minor design changes (any change other than a major change) without further approval by the Administrator. In this case, the changed article keeps the original model number (part numbers may be used to identify minor changes) and the manufacturer shall forward to the appropriate Aircraft Certification Office for the geographic area, any revised data that are necessary for compliance with §21.605(b).

(b) *Major changes by manufacturer holding a TSO authorization.* Any design change by the manufacturer that is extensive enough to require a substantially complete investigation to determine compliance with a TSO is a major change. Before making such a change, the manufacturer shall assign a new type or model designation to the article and apply for an authorization under §21.605.

(c) *Changes by person other than manufacturer.* No design change by any person (other than the manufacturer who submitted the statement of conformance for the article) is eligible for approval under this part unless the person seeking the approval is a manufacturer and applies under §21.605(a) for a separate TSO authorization. Persons other than a manufacturer may obtain approval for design changes under Part 43 or under the applicable airworthiness regulations.

[Docket No. 19589, 45 FR 38346, June 9, 1980; as amended by Amdt. 21–67, 54 FR 39291, Sept. 25, 1989]

§21.613 Recordkeeping requirements.

(a) *Keeping the records.* Each manufacturer holding a TSO authorization under this part shall, for each article manufactured under that authorization, keep the following records at its factory:

(1) A complete and current technical data file for each type or model article, including design drawings and specifications.

(2) Complete and current inspection records showing that all inspections and tests required to ensure compliance with this part have been properly completed and documented.

(b) *Retention of records.* The manufacturer shall retain the records described in paragraph (a)(1) of this section until it no longer manufactures the article. At that time, copies of these records shall be sent to the Administrator. The manufacturer shall retain the records described in paragraph (a)(2) of this section for a period of at least 2 years.

§21.615 FAA inspection.

Upon the request of the Administrator, each manufacturer of an article under a TSO authorization shall allow the Administrator to—

(a) Inspect any article manufactured under that authorization;

(b) Inspect the manufacturer's quality control system;

(c) Witness any tests;

(d) Inspect the manufacturing facilities; and

(e) Inspect the technical data files on that article.

§21.617 Issue of letters of TSO design approval: import appliances.

(a) A letter of TSO design approval may be issued for an appliance that is manufactured in a foreign country with which the United States has an agreement for the acceptance of these appliances for export and import and that is to be imported into the United States if—

(1) The country in which the appliance was manufactured certifies that the appliance has been examined, tested, and found to meet the applicable TSO designated in §21.305(b) or the applicable performance standards of the country in which the appliance was manufactured and any other performance standards the Administrator may prescribe to provide a level of safety equivalent to that provided by the TSO designated in §21.305(b); and

(2) The manufacturer has submitted one copy of the technical data required in the applicable performance standard through its civil aviation authority.

(b) The letter of TSO design approval will be issued by the Administrator and must list any deviation granted to the manufacturer under §21.609.

(c) After the Administrator has issued a letter of TSO design approval and the country of manufacture issues a Certificate of Airworthiness for Export as specified in §21.502(a), the manufacturer shall be authorized to identify the appliance with the TSO marking requirements described in §21.607(d) and in the applicable TSO. Each appliance must be accompanied by a Certificate of Airworthiness for Export as specified in §21.502(a) issued by the country of manufacture.

§21.619 Noncompliance.

The Administrator may, upon notice, withdraw the TSO authorization or letter of TSO design approval of any manufacturer who identifies with a TSO marking an article not meeting the performance standards of the applicable TSO.

§21.621 Transferability and duration.

A TSO authorization or letter of TSO design approval issued under this part is not transferable and is effective until surrendered, withdrawn, or otherwise terminated by the Administrator.

PART 23

AIRWORTHINESS STANDARDS: NORMAL, UTILITY, ACROBATIC, AND COMMUTER CATEGORY AIRPLANES

SPECIAL FEDERAL AVIATION REGULATION

SFAR No. 23

Subpart A — General

Sec.
23.1 Applicability.
23.2 Special retroactive requirements.
23.3 Airplane categories.

Subpart B — Flight

GENERAL

23.21 Proof of compliance.
23.23 Load distribution limits.
23.25 Weight limits.
23.29 Empty weight and corresponding center of gravity.
23.31 Removable ballast.
23.33 Propeller speed and pitch limits.

PERFORMANCE

23.45 General.
23.49 Stalling period.
23.51 Takeoff speeds.
23.53 Takeoff performance.
23.55 Accelerate-stop distance.
23.57 Takeoff path.
23.59 Takeoff distance and takeoff run.
23.61 Takeoff flight path.
23.63 Climb: General.
23.65 Climb: All engines operating.
23.66 Takeoff climb: One-engine inoperative.
23.67 Climb: One engine inoperative.
23.69 Enroute climb/descent.
23.71 Glide: Single-engine airplanes.
23.73 Reference landing approach speed.
23.75 Landing distance.
23.77 Balked landing.

FLIGHT CHARACTERISTICS

23.141 General.

CONTROLLABILITY AND MANEUVERABILITY

23.143 General.
23.145 Longitudinal control.
23.147 Directional and lateral control.
23.149 Minimum control speed.
23.151 Acrobatic maneuvers.
23.153 Control during landings.
23.155 Elevator control force in maneuvers.
23.157 Rate of roll.

TRIM

23.161 Trim.

STABILITY

23.171 General.
23.173 Static longitudinal stability.
23.175 Demonstration of static longitudinal stability.
23.177 Static directional and lateral stability.
23.181 Dynamic stability.

STALLS

23.201 Wings level stall.
23.203 Turning flight and accelerated turning stalls.
23.207 Stall warning.

SPINNING

23.221 Spinning.

GROUND AND WATER HANDLING CHARACTERISTICS

23.231 Longitudinal stability and control.
23.233 Directional stability and control.
23.235 Operation on unpaved surfaces.
23.237 Operation on water.
23.239 Spray characteristics.

MISCELLANEOUS FLIGHT REQUIREMENTS

23.251 Vibration and buffeting.
23.253 High speed characteristics.

Subpart C — Structure

GENERAL

23.301 Loads.
23.302 Canard or tandem wing configurations.
23.303 Factor of safety.
23.305 Strength and deformation.
23.307 Proof of structure.

FLIGHT LOADS

23.321 General.
23.331 Symmetrical flight conditions.
23.333 Flight envelope.
23.335 Design airspeeds.
23.337 Limit maneuvering load factors.
23.341 Gust loads factors.
23.343 Design fuel loads.
23.345 High lift devices.
23.347 Unsymmetrical flight conditions.
23.349 Rolling conditions.
23.351 Yawing conditions.
23.361 Engine torque.
23.363 Side load on engine mount.
23.365 Pressurized cabin loads.
23.367 Unsymmetrical loads due to engine failure.
23.369 Rear lift truss.
23.371 Gyroscopic and aerodynamic loads.
23.373 Speed control devices.

Control Surface and System Loads

23.391 Control surface loads.
23.393 Loads parallel to hinge line.
23.395 Control system loads.
23.397 Limit control forces and torques.
23.399 Dual control system.
23.405 Secondary control system.
23.407 Trim tab effects.
23.409 Tabs.
23.415 Ground gust conditions.

Horizontal Stabilizing and Balancing Surfaces

23.421 Balancing loads.
23.423 Maneuvering loads.
23.425 Gust loads.
23.427 Unsymmetrical loads.

Vertical Surfaces

23.441 Maneuvering loads.
23.443 Gust loads.
23.445 Outboard fins or winglets.

Ailerons and Special Devices

23.455 Ailerons.
23.459 Special devices.

Ground Loads

23.471 General.
23.473 Ground load conditions and assumptions.
23.477 Landing gear arrangement.
23.479 Level landing conditions.
23.481 Tail down landing conditions.
23.483 One-wheel landing conditions.
23.485 Side load conditions.
23.493 Braked roll conditions.
23.497 Supplementary conditions for tail wheels.
23.499 Supplementary conditions for nose wheels.
23.505 Supplementary conditions for ski planes.
23.507 Jacking loads.
23.509 Towing loads.
23.511 Ground load; unsymmetrical loads on multiple-wheel units.

Water Loads

23.521 Water load conditions.
23.523 Design weights and center of gravity positions.
23.525 Application of loads.
23.527 Hull and main float load factors.
23.529 Hull and main float landing conditions.
23.531 Hull and main float takeoff condition.
23.533 Hull and main float bottom pressures.
23.535 Auxiliary float loads.
23.537 Seawing loads.

Emergency Landing Conditions

23.561 General.
23.562 Emergency landing dynamic conditions.

Fatigue Evaluation

23.571 Metallic pressurized cabin structures.
23.572 Metallic wing, empennage, and associated structures.
23.573 Damage tolerance and fatigue evaluation of structure.
23.574 Metallic damage tolerance and fatigue evaluation of commuter category airplanes.
23.575 Inspections and other procedures.

Subpart D — Design and Construction

23.601 General.
23.603 Materials and workmanship.
23.605 Fabrication methods.
23.607 Fasteners.
23.609 Protection of structure.
23.611 Accessibility provisions.
23.613 Material strength properties and design values.
23.619 Special factors.
23.621 Casting factors.
23.623 Bearing factors.
23.625 Fitting factors.
23.627 Fatigue strength.
23.629 Flutter.

Wings

23.641 Proof of strength.

Control Surfaces

23.651 Proof of strength.
23.655 Installation.
23.657 Hinges.
23.659 Mass balance.

Control Systems

23.671 General.
23.672 Stability augmentation and automatic and power-operated systems.
23.673 Primary flight controls.
23.675 Stops.
23.677 Trim systems.
23.679 Control system locks.
23.681 Limit load static tests.
23.683 Operation tests.
23.685 Control system details.
23.687 Spring devices.
23.689 Cable systems.
23.691 Artificial stall barrier system.
23.693 Joints.
23.697 Wing flap controls.
23.699 Wing flap position indicator.
23.701 Flap interconnection.
23.703 Takeoff warning system.

Landing Gear

23.721 General.
23.723 Shock absorption tests.
23.725 Limit drop tests.
23.726 Ground load dynamic tests.
23.727 Reserve energy absorption drop test.
23.729 Landing gear extension and retraction system.
23.731 Wheels.
23.733 Tires.
23.735 Brakes.
23.737 Skis.
23.745 Nose/tail wheel steering.

Floats and Hulls

23.751 Main float buoyancy.
23.753 Main float design.
23.755 Hulls.
23.757 Auxiliary floats.

Personnel and Cargo Accommodations

23.771 Pilot compartment.
23.773 Pilot compartment view.
23.775 Windshields and windows.
23.777 Cockpit controls.
23.779 Motion and effect of cockpit controls.
23.781 Cockpit control knob shape.
23.783 Doors.
23.785 Seats, berths, litters, safety belts, and shoulder harnesses.
23.787 Baggage and cargo compartments.
23.791 Passenger information signs.
23.803 Emergency evacuation.
23.805 Flightcrew emergency exits.
23.807 Emergency exits.
23.811 Emergency exit marking.
23.812 Emergency lighting.
23.813 Emergency exit access.
23.815 Width of aisle.
23.831 Ventilation.

Pressurization

23.841 Pressurized cabins.
23.843 Pressurization tests.

Fire Protection

23.851 Fire extinguishers.
23.853 Passenger and crew compartment interiors.
23.855 Cargo and baggage compartment fire protection.
23.859 Combustion heater fire protection.
23.863 Flammable fluid fire protection.
23.865 Fire protection of flight controls, engine mounts, and other flight structure.

Electrical Bonding and Lightning Protection

23.867 Electrical bonding and protection against lightning and static electricity.

Miscellaneous

23.871 Leveling means.

Subpart E — Powerplant

General

23.901 Installation.
23.903 Engines.
23.904 Automatic power reserve system.
23.905 Propellers.
23.907 Propeller vibration.
23.909 Turbocharger systems.
23.925 Propeller clearance.
23.929 Engine installation ice protection.
23.933 Reversing systems.
23.934 Turbojet and turbofan engine thrust reverser systems tests.
23.937 Turbopropeller-drag limiting systems.
23.939 Powerplant operating characteristics.
23.943 Negative acceleration.

Fuel System

23.951 General.
23.953 Fuel system independence.
23.954 Fuel system lightning protection.
23.955 Fuel flow.
23.957 Flow between interconnected tanks.
23.959 Unusable fuel supply.
23.961 Fuel system hot weather operation.
23.963 Fuel tanks: general.
23.965 Fuel tank tests.
23.967 Fuel tank installation.
23.969 Fuel tank expansion space.
23.971 Fuel tank sump.
23.973 Fuel tank filler connection.
23.975 Fuel tank vents and carburetor vapor vents.
23.977 Fuel tank outlet.
23.979 Pressure fueling systems.

Fuel System Components

23.991 Fuel pumps.
23.993 Fuel system lines and fittings.
23.994 Fuel system components.
23.995 Fuel valves and controls.
23.997 Fuel strainer or filter.
23.999 Fuel system drains.
23.1001 Fuel jettisoning system.

Oil System

23.1011 General.
23.1013 Oil tanks.
23.1015 Oil tank tests.
23.1017 Oil lines and fittings.
23.1019 Oil strainer or filter.
23.1021 Oil system drains.
23.1023 Oil radiators.
23.1027 Propeller feathering system.

COOLING

23.1041 General.
23.1043 Cooling tests.
23.1045 Cooling test procedures for turbine engine powered airplanes.
23.1047 Cooling test procedures for reciprocating engine powered airplanes.

LIQUID COOLING

23.1061 Installation.
23.1063 Coolant tank tests.

INDUCTION SYSTEM

23.1091 Air induction system.
23.1093 Induction system icing protection.
23.1095 Carburetor deicing fluid flow rate.
23.1097 Carburetor deicing fluid system capacity.
23.1099 Carburetor deicing fluid system detail design.
23.1101 Carburetor air preheater design.
23.1103 Induction system ducts.
23.1105 Induction system screens.
23.1107 Induction system filters.
23.1109 Turbocharger bleed air system.
23.1111 Turbine engine bleed air system.

EXHAUST SYSTEM

23.1121 General.
23.1123 Exhaust system.
23.1125 Exhaust heat exchangers.

POWERPLANT CONTROLS AND ACCESSORIES

23.1141 Powerplant controls: General.
23.1142 Auxiliary power unit controls.
23.1143 Engine controls.
23.1145 Ignition switches.
23.1147 Mixture controls.
23.1149 Propeller speed and pitch controls.
23.1153 Propeller feathering controls.
23.1155 Turbine engine reverse thrust and propeller pitch settings below the flight regime.
23.1157 Carburetor air temperature controls.
23.1163 Powerplant accessories.
23.1165 Engine ignition systems.

POWERPLANT FIRE PROTECTION

23.1181 Designated fire zones; regions included.
23.1182 Nacelle areas behind firewalls.
23.1183 Lines, fittings, and components.
23.1189 Shutoff means.
23.1191 Firewalls.
23.1192 Engine accessory compartment diaphragm.
23.1193 Cowling and nacelle.
23.1195 Fire extinguishing systems.
23.1197 Fire extinguishing agents.
23.1199 Extinguishing agent containers.
23.1201 Fire extinguishing systems materials.
23.1203 Fire detector system.

Subpart F — Equipment

GENERAL

23.1301 Function and installation.
23.1303 Flight and navigation instruments.
23.1305 Powerplant instruments.
23.1307 Miscellaneous equipment.
23.1309 Equipment, systems, and installations.

INSTRUMENTS: INSTALLATION

23.1311 Electronic display instrument systems.
23.1321 Arrangement and visibility.
23.1322 Warning, caution, and advisory lights.
23.1323 Airspeed indicating system.
23.1325 Static pressure system.
23.1326 Pitot heat indication systems.
23.1327 Magnetic direction indicator.
23.1329 Automatic pilot system.
23.1331 Instruments using a power source.
23.1335 Flight director systems.
23.1337 Powerplant instruments installation.

ELECTRICAL SYSTEMS AND EQUIPMENT

23.1351 General.
23.1353 Storage battery design and installation.
23.1357 Circuit protective devices.
23.1359 Electrical system fire protection.
23.1361 Master switch arrangement.
23.1365 Electrical cables and equipment.
23.1367 Switches.

LIGHTS

23.1381 Instrument lights.
23.1383 Taxi and landing lights.
23.1385 Position light system installation.
23.1387 Position light system dihedral angles.
23.1389 Position light distribution and intensities.
23.1391 Minimum intensities in the horizontal plane of position lights.
23.1393 Minimum intensities in any vertical plane of position lights.
23.1395 Maximum intensities in overlapping beams of position lights.
23.1397 Color specifications.
23.1399 Riding light.
23.1401 Anticollision light system.

SAFETY EQUIPMENT

23.1411 General.
23.1415 Ditching equipment.
23.1416 Pneumatic de-icer boot system.
23.1419 Ice protection.

MISCELLANEOUS EQUIPMENT

23.1431 Electronic equipment.
23.1435 Hydraulic systems.
23.1437 Accessories for multiengine airplanes.
23.1438 Pressurization and pneumatic systems.
23.1441 Oxygen equipment and supply.
23.1443 Minimum mass flow of supplemental oxygen.
23.1445 Oxygen distribution system.

23.1447 Equipment standards for oxygen dispensing units.
23.1449 Means for determining use of oxygen.
23.1450 Chemical oxygen generators.
23.1451 Fire protection for oxygen equipment.
23.1453 Protection of oxygen equipment from rupture.
23.1457 Cockpit voice recorders.
23.1459 Flight recorders.
23.1461 Equipment containing high energy rotors.

Subpart G — Operating Limitations and Information

23.1501 General.
23.1505 Airspeed limitations.
23.1507 Operating maneuvering speed.
23.1511 Flap extended speed.
23.1513 Minimum control speed.
23.1519 Weight and center of gravity.
23.1521 Powerplant limitations.
23.1522 Auxiliary power unit limitations
23.1523 Minimum flight crew.
23.1524 Maximum passenger seating configuration.
23.1525 Kinds of operation.
23.1527 Maximum operating altitude.
23.1529 Instructions for Continued Airworthiness.

Markings and Placards

23.1541 General.
23.1543 Instrument markings: General.
23.1545 Airspeed indicator.
23.1547 Magnetic direction indicator.
23.1549 Powerplant and auxiliary power unit instruments.
23.1551 Oil quantity indicator.
23.1553 Fuel quantity indicator.
23.1555 Control markings.
23.1557 Miscellaneous markings and placards.
23.1559 Operating limitations placard.
23.1561 Safety equipment.
23.1563 Airspeed placards.
23.1567 Flight maneuver placard.

Airplane Flight Manual and Approved Manual Material

23.1581 General.
23.1583 Operating limitations.
23.1585 Operating procedures.
23.1587 Performance information.
23.1589 Loading information.

Appendix A to Part 23 — Simplified Design Load Criteria
Appendix B to Part 23 — [Reserved]
Appendix C to Part 23 — Basic Landing Conditions
Appendix D to Part 23 — Wheel Spin-Up and Spring-Back Loads
Appendix E to Part 23 — [Reserved]
Appendix F to Part 23 — Test Procedure
Appendix G to Part 23 — Instructions for Continued Airworthiness
Appendix H to Part 23 — Installation of an Automatic Power Reserve (APR) System
Appendix I to Part 23 — Seaplane Loads

Authority: 49 U.S.C. 106(g), 40113, 44701–44702, 44704.

Source: Docket No. 4080, 29 FR 17955, Dec. 18. 1964; 30 FR 258, Jan. 9, 1965, unless otherwise noted.

SFAR No. 23 to Part 23

1. *Applicability.* An applicant is entitled to a type certificate in the normal category for a reciprocating or turbopropeller multiengine powered small airplane that is to be certificated to carry more than 10 occupants and that is intended for use in operations under Part 135 of the Federal Aviation Regulations if he shows compliance with the applicable requirements of Part 23 of the Federal Aviation Regulations, as supplemented or modified by the additional airworthiness requirements of this regulation.

2. *References.* Unless otherwise provided, all references in this regulation to specific sections of Part 23 of the Federal Aviation Regulations are those sections of Part 23 in effect on March 30, 1967.

Flight Requirements

3. *General.* Compliance must be shown with the applicable requirements of Subpart B of Part 23 of the Federal Aviation Regulations in effect on March 30, 1967, as supplemented or modified in sections 4 through 10 of this regulation.

Performance

4. *General.*

(a) Unless otherwise prescribed in this regulation, compliance with each applicable performance requirement in sections 4 through 7 of this regulation must be shown for ambient atmospheric conditions and still air.

(b) The performance must correspond to the propulsive thrust available under the particular ambient atmospheric conditions and the particular flight condition. The available propulsive thrust must correspond to engine power or thrust, not exceeding the approved power or thrust less—

(1) Installation losses; and

(2) The power or equivalent thrust absorbed by the accessories and services appropriate to the particular ambient atmospheric conditions and the particular flight condition.

(c) Unless otherwise prescribed in this regulation, the applicant must select the take-off, en route, and landing configurations for the airplane.

(d) The airplane configuration may vary with weight, altitude, and temperature, to the extent they are compatible with the operating procedures required by paragraph (e) of this section.

(e) Unless otherwise prescribed in this regulation, in determining the critical engine inoperative takeoff performance, the accelerate-stop distance, takeoff distance, changes in the airplane's configuration, speed, power, and thrust, must be made in accordance with procedures established by the applicant for operation in service.

(f) Procedures for the execution of balked landings must be established by the applicant and included in the Airplane Flight Manual.

(g) The procedures established under paragraphs (e) and (f) of this section must—

(1) Be able to be consistently executed in service by a crew of average skill;

(2) Use methods or devices that are safe and reliable; and

(3) Include allowance for any time delays, in the execution of the procedures, that may reasonably be expected in service.

5. *Takeoff*—

(a) *General.* The takeoff speeds described in paragraph (b), the accelerate-stop distance described in paragraph (c), and the takeoff distance described in paragraph (d), must be determined for—

(1) Each weight, altitude, and ambient temperature within the operational limits selected by the applicant;

(2) The selected configuration for takeoff;

(3) The center of gravity in the most unfavorable position;

(4) The operating engine within approved operating limitation; and

(5) Takeoff data based on smooth, dry, hard-surface runway.

(b) *Takeoff speeds.*

(1) The decision speed V_1 is the calibrated airspeed on the ground at which, as a result of engine failure or other reasons, the pilot is assumed to have made a decision to continue or discontinue the takeoff. The speed V_1 must be selected by the applicant but may not be less than;—

(i) 1.10 V_{S1};

(ii) 1.10 V_{MC};

(iii) A speed that permits acceleration to V_1 and stop in accordance with paragraph (c) allowing credit for an overrun distance equal to that required to stop the airplane from a ground speed of 35 knots utilizing maximum braking; or

(iv) A speed at which the airplane can be rotated for takeoff and shown to be adequate to safely continue the takeoff, using normal piloting skill, when the critical engine is suddenly made inoperative.

(2) Other essential takeoff speeds necessary for safe operation of the airplane must be determined and shown in the Airplane Flight Manual.

(c) *Accelerate-stop distance.*

(1) The accelerate-stop distance is the sum of the distances necessary to—

(i) Accelerate the airplane from a standing start to V_1; and

(ii) Decelerate the airplane from V_1 to a speed not greater than 35 knots, assuming that in the case of engine failure, failure of the critical engine is recognized by the pilot at the speed V_1. The landing gear must remain in the extended position and maximum braking may be utilized during deceleration.

(2) Means other than wheel brakes may be used to determine the accelerate-stop distance if that means is available with the critical engine inoperative and—

(i) Is safe and reliable;

(ii) Is used so that consistent results can be expected under normal operating conditions; and

(iii) Is such that exceptional skill is not required to control the airplane.

(d) *All engines operating takeoff distance.* The all engine operating takeoff distance is the horizontal distance required to takeoff and climb to a height of 50 feet above the takeoff surface according to procedures in FAR 23.51(a).

(e) *One-engine-inoperative takeoff.* The maximum weight must be determined for each altitude and temperature within the operational limits established for the airplane, at which the airplane has takeoff capability after failure of the critical engine at or above V_1 determined in accordance with paragraph (b) of this section. This capability may be established—

(1) By demonstrating a measurably positive rate of climb with the airplane in the takeoff configuration, landing gear extended; or

(2) By demonstrating the capability of maintaining flight after engine failure utilizing procedures prescribed by the applicant.

6. *Climb*—

(a) *Landing climb: All-engines-operating.* The maximum weight must be determined with the airplane in the landing configuration, for each altitude, and ambient temperature within the operational limits established for the airplane and with the most unfavorable center of gravity and out-of-ground effect in free air, at which the steady gradient of climb will not be less than 3.3 percent, with:

(1) The engines at the power that is available 8 seconds after initiation of movement of the power or thrust controls from the minimum flight idle to the takeoff position.

(2) A climb speed not greater than the approach speed established under section 7 of this regulation and not less than the greater of 1.05 V_{MC} or 1.10 V_{S1}.

(b) *En route climb, one-engine-inoperative.*

(1) the maximum weight must be determined with the airplane in the en route configuration, the critical engine inoperative, the remaining engine at not more than maximum continuous power or thrust, and the most unfavorable center of gravity, at which the gradient at climb will be not less than—

(i) 1.2 percent (or a gradient equivalent to 0.20 V_{S02}, if greater) at 5,000 feet and an ambient temperature of 41°F. or

(ii) 0.6 percent (or a gradient equivalent to 0.01 V_{S02}, if greater) at 5,000 feet and ambient temperature of 81°F.

(2) The minimum climb gradient specified in subdivisions (i) and (ii) of subparagraph (1) of this paragraph must vary linearly between 41°F. and 81°F. and must change at the same rate up to the maximum operational temperature approved for the airplane.

7. *Landing.* The landing distance must be determined for standard atmosphere at each weight and altitude in accordance with FAR 23.75(a), except that instead of the gliding approach specified in FAR 23.75(a)(1), the landing may be preceded by a steady approach down to the 50-foot height at a gradient of descent not greater than 5.2 percent (3) at a calibrated airspeed not less than 1.3 V_{S1}.

Trim

8. *Trim*—

(a) *Lateral and directional trim.* The airplane must maintain lateral and directional trim in level flight at a speed of V_H or V_{MO}/M_{MO}, whichever is lower, with landing gear and wing flaps retracted.

(b) *Longitudinal trim.* The airplane must maintain longitudinal trim during the following conditions, except that it need not maintain trim at a speed greater than V_{MO}/M_{MO}:

(1) In the approach conditions specified in FAR 23.161(c) (3) through (5), except that instead of the speeds specified

therein, trim must be maintained with a stick force of not more than 10 pounds down to a speed used in showing compliance with section 7 of this regulation or 1.4 V_{S1} whichever is lower.

(2) In level flight at any speed from V_H or V_{MO}/M_{MO}, whichever is lower, to either V_X or 1.4 V_{S1}, with the landing gear and wing flaps retracted.

Stability

9. *Static longitudinal stability.*

(a) In showing compliance with the provisions of FAR 23.175(b) and with paragraph (b) of this section, the airspeed must return to within $\pm 7\frac{1}{2}$ percent of the trim speed.

(b) *Cruise stability.* The stick force curve must have a stable slope for a speed range of ± 50 knots from the trim speed except that the speeds need not exceed V_{FC}/M_{FC} or be less than 1.4 V_{S1}. This speed range will be considered to begin at the outer extremes of the friction band and the stick force may not exceed 50 pounds with—

(i) Landing gear retracted;

(ii) Wing flaps retracted;

(iii) The maximum cruising power as selected by the applicant as an operating limitation for turbine engines or 75 percent of maximum continuous power for reciprocating engines except that the power need not exceed that required at V_{MO}/M_{MO};

(iv) Maximum takeoff weight; and

(v) The airplane trimmed for level flight with the power specified in subparagraph (iii) of this paragraph.

V_{FC}/M_{FC} may not be less than a speed midway between V_{MO}/M_{MO} and V_{DF}/M_{DF}, except that, for altitudes where Mach number is the limiting factor, M_{FC} need not exceed the Mach number at which effective speed warning occurs.

(c) *Climb stability. For turbopropeller powered airplanes only.* In showing compliance with FAR 23.175(a), an applicant must in lieu of the power specified in FAR 23.175(a)(4), use the maximum power or thrust selected by the applicant as an operating limitation for use during climb at the best rate of climb speed except that the speed need not be less than 1.4 V_{S1}.

Stalls

10. *Stall warning.* If artificial stall warning is required to comply with the requirements of FAR 23.207, the warning device must give clearly distinguishable indications under expected conditions of flight. The use of a visual warning device that requires the attention of the crew within the cockpit is not acceptable by itself.

Control Systems

11. *Electric trim tabs.* The airplane must meet the requirements of FAR 23.677 and in addition it must be shown that the airplane is safely controllable and that a pilot can perform all the maneuvers and operations necessary to effect a safe landing following any probable electric trim tab runaway which might be reasonably expected in service allowing for appropriate time delay after pilot recognition of the runaway. This demonstration must be conducted at the critical airplane weights and center of gravity positions.

Instruments: Installation

12. *Arrangement and visibility.* Each instrument must meet the requirements of FAR 23.1321 and in addition—

(a) Each flight, navigation, and powerplant instrument for use by any pilot must be plainly visible to him from his station with the minimum practicable deviation from his normal position and line of vision when he is looking forward along the flight path.

(b) The flight instruments required by FAR 23.1303 and by the applicable operating rules must be grouped on the instrument panel and centered as nearly as practicable about the vertical plane of each pilot's forward vision. In addition—

(1) The instrument that most effectively indicates the attitude must be on the panel in the top center position;

(2) The instrument that most effectively indicates airspeed must be adjacent to and directly to the left of the instrument in the top center position;

(3) The instrument that most effectively indicates altitude must be adjacent to and directly to the right of the instrument in the top center position; and

(4) The instrument that most effectively indicates direction of flight must be adjacent to and directly below the instrument in the top center position.

13. *Airspeed indicating system.* Each airspeed indicating system must meet the requirements of FAR 23.1323 and in addition—

(a) Airspeed indicating instruments must be of an approved type and must be calibrated to indicate true airspeed at sea level in the standard atmosphere with a minimum practicable instrument calibration error when the corresponding pilot and static pressures are supplied to the instruments.

(b) The airspeed indicating system must be calibrated to determine the system error, i.e., the relation between IAS and CAS, in flight and during the accelerate takeoff ground run. The ground run calibration must be obtained between 0.8 of the minimum value of V_1 and 1.2 times the maximum value of V_1, considering the approved ranges of altitude and weight. The ground run calibration will be determined assuming an engine failure at the minimum value of V_1.

(c) The airspeed error of the installation excluding the instrument calibration error, must not exceed 3 percent or 5 knots whichever is greater, throughout the speed range from V_{MO} to 1.3 S_1 with flaps retracted and from 1.3 V_{S0} to V_{FE} with flaps in the landing position.

(d) Information showing the relationship between IAS and CAS must be shown in the Airplane Flight Manual.

14. *Static air vent system.* The static air vent system must meet the requirements of FAR 23.1325. The altimeter system calibration must be determined and shown in the Airplane Flight Manual.

Operating Limitations and Information

15. *Maximum operating limit speed V_{MO}/M_{MO}.* Instead of establishing operating limitations based on V_{ME} and V_{NO}, the applicant must establish a maximum operating limit speed V_{MO}/M_{MO} in accordance with the following:

(a) The maximum operating limit speed must not exceed the design cruising speed Vc and must be sufficiently below V_D/M_D or V_{DF}/M_{DF} to make it highly improbable that the latter speeds will be inadvertently exceeded in flight.

(b) The speed V_{MO} must not exceed 0.8 V_D/M_D or 0.8 V_{DF}/M_{DF} unless flight demonstrations involving upsets as specified by the Administrator indicates a lower speed margin will not result in speeds exceeding V_D/M_D or V_{DF}. Atmospheric variations, horizontal gusts, and equipment errors, and airframe production variations will be taken into account.

16. *Minimum flight crew.* In addition to meeting the requirements of FAR 23.1523, the applicant must establish the minimum number and type of qualified flight crew personnel sufficient for safe operation of the airplane considering—

(a) Each kind of operation for which the applicant desires approval;

(b) The workload on each crewmember considering the following:

(1) Flight path control.

(2) Collision avoidance.

(3) Navigation.

(4) Communications.

(5) Operation and monitoring of all essential aircraft systems.

(6) Command decisions; and

(c) The accessibility and ease of operation of necessary controls by the appropriate crewmember during all normal and emergency operations when at his flight station.

17. *Airspeed indicator.* The airspeed indicator must meet the requirements of FAR 23.1545 except that, the airspeed notations and markings in terms of V_{NO} and V_{NE} must be replaced by the V_{MO}/M_{MO} notations. The airspeed indicator markings must be easily read and understood by the pilot. A placard adjacent to the airspeed indicator is an acceptable means of showing compliance with the requirements of FAR 23.1545(c).

Airplane Flight Manual

18. *General.* The Airplane Flight Manual must be prepared in accordance with the requirements of FARs 23.1583 and 23.1587, and in addition the operating limitations and performance information set forth in sections 19 and 20 must be included.

19. *Operating limitations.* The Airplane Flight Manual must include the following limitations—

(a) *Airspeed limitations.*

(1) The maximum operating limit speed V_{MO}/M_{MO} and a statement that this speed limit may not be deliberately exceeded in any regime of flight (climb, cruise, or descent) unless a higher speed is authorized for flight test or pilot training;

(2) If an airspeed limitation is based upon compressibility effects, a statement to this effect and information as to any symptoms, the probable behavior of the airplane, and the recommended recovery procedures; and

(3) The airspeed limits, shown in terms of V_{MO}/M_{MO} instead of V_{NO} and V_{NE}.

(b) *Takeoff weight limitations.* The maximum takeoff weight for each airport elevation, ambient temperature, and available takeoff runway length within the range selected by the applicant. This weight may not exceed the weight at which:

(1) The all-engine operating takeoff distance determined in accordance with section 5(d) or the accelerate-stop distance determined in accordance with section 5(c), which ever is greater, is equal to the available runway length;

(2) The airplane complies with the one-engine-inoperative takeoff requirements specified in section 5(e); and

(3) The airplane complies with the one-engine-inoperative en route climb requirements specified in section 6(b), assuming that a standard temperature lapse rate exists from the airport elevation to the altitude of 5,000 feet, except that the weight may not exceed that corresponding to a temperature of 41°F at 5,000 feet.

20. *Performance information.* The Airplane Flight Manual must contain the performance information determined in accordance with the provisions of the performance requirements of this regulation. The information must include the following:

(a) Sufficient information so that the take-off weight limits specified in section 19(b) can be determined for all temperatures and altitudes within the operation limitations selected by the applicant.

(b) The conditions under which the performance information was obtained, including the airspeed at the 50-foot height used to determine landing distances.

(c) The performance information (determined by extrapolation and computed for the range of weights between the maximum landing and takeoff weights) for—

(1) Climb in the landing configuration; and

(2) Landing distance.

(d) Procedure established under section 4 of this regulation related to the limitations and information required by this section in the form of guidance material including any relevant limitations or information.

(e) An explanation of significant or unusual flight or ground handling characteristics of the airplane.

(f) Airspeeds, as indicated airspeeds, corresponding to those determined for takeoff in accordance with section 5(b).

21. *Maximum operating altitudes.* The maximum operating altitude to which operation is permitted, as limited by flight, structural, powerplant, functional, or equipment characteristics, must be specified in the Airplane Flight Manual.

22. *Stowage provision for Airplane Flight Manual.* Provision must be made for stowing the Airplane Flight Manual in a suitable fixed container which is readily accessible to the pilot.

23. *Operating procedures.* Procedures for restarting turbine engines in flight (including the effects of altitude) must be set forth in the Airplane Flight Manual.

Airframe Requirements

Flight loads

24. *Engine torque.*

(a) Each turbopropeller engine mount and its supporting structure must be designed for the torque effects of—

(1) The conditions set forth in FAR 23.361(a).

(2) The limit engine torque corresponding to takeoff power and propeller speed, multiplied by a factor accounting for propeller control system malfunction, including quick feathering action, simultaneously with 1 g level flight loads. In the absence of a rational analysis, a factor of 1.6 must be used.

(b) The limit torque is obtained by multiplying the mean torque by a factor of 1.25.

25. *Turbine engine gyroscopic loads.* Each turbopropeller engine mount and its supporting structure must be designed for the gyroscopic loads that result, with the engines at maximum continuous r.p.m., under either—

(a) The conditions prescribed in FARs 23.351 and 23.423; or

(b) All possible combinations of the following:

(1) A yaw velocity of 2.5 radius per second.

(2) A pitch velocity of 1.0 radians per second.

(3) A normal load factor of 2.5.

(4) Maximum continuous thrust.

26. *Unsymmetrical loads due to engine failure.*

(a) Turbopropeller powered airplanes must be designed for the unsymmetrical loads resulting from the failure of the critical engine including the following conditions in combination with a single malfunction of the propeller drag limiting system, considering the probable pilot corrective action on the flight controls.

(1) At speeds between V_{MC} and V_D, the loads resulting from power failure because of fuel flow interruption are considered to be limit loads.

(2) At speeds between V_{MC} and V_C, the loads resulting from the disconnection of the engine compressor from the turbine or from loss of the turbine blades are considered to be ultimate loads.

(3) The time history of the thrust decay and drag buildup occurring as a result of the prescribed engine failures must be substantiated by test or other data applicable to the particular engine-propeller combination.

(4) The timing and magnitude of the probable pilot corrective action must be conservatively estimated, considering the characteristics of the particular engine-propeller-airplane combination.

(b) Pilot corrective action may be assumed to be initiated at the time maximum yawing velocity is reached, but not earlier than two seconds after the engine failure. The magnitude of the corrective action may be based on the control forces specified in FAR 23.397 except that lower forces may be assumed where it is shown by analysis or test that these forces can control the yaw and roll resulting from the prescribed engine failure conditions.

Ground Loads

27. *Dual wheel landing gear units.* Each dual wheel landing gear unit and its supporting structure must be shown to comply with the following:

(a) *Pivoting.* The airplane must be assumed to pivot about one side of the main gear with the brakes on that side locked. The limit vertical load factor must be 1.0 and the coefficient of friction 0.8. This condition need apply only to the main gear and its supporting structure.

(b) *Unequal tire inflation.* A 60–40 percent distribution of the loads established in accordance with FAR 23.471 through FAR 23.483 must be applied to the dual wheels.

(c) *Flat tire.*

(1) Sixty percent of the loads specified in FAR 23.471 through FAR 23.483 must be applied to either wheel in a unit.

(2) Sixty percent of the limit drag and side loads and 100 percent of the limit vertical load established in accordance with FARs 23.493 and 23.485 must be applied to either wheel in a unit except that the vertical load need not exceed the maximum vertical load in paragraph (c)(1) of this section.

Fatigue Evaluation

28. *Fatigue evaluation of wing and associated structure.* Unless it is shown that the structure, operating stress levels, materials, and expected use are comparable from a fatigue standpoint to a similar design which has had substantial satisfactory service experience, the strength, detail design, and the fabrication of those parts of the wing, wing carrythrough, and attaching structure whose failure would be catastrophic must be evaluated under either—

(a) A fatigue strength investigation in which the structure is shown by analysis, tests, or both to be able to withstand the repeated loads of variable magnitude expected in service; or

(b) A fail-safe strength investigation in which it is shown by analysis, tests, or both that catastrophic failure of the structure is not probable after fatigue, or obvious partial failure, of a principal structural element, and that the remaining structure is able to withstand a static ultimate load factor of 75 percent of the critical limit load factor at V_C. These loads must be multiplied by a factor of 1.15 unless the dynamic effects of failure under static load are otherwise considered.

Design and Construction

29. *Flutter.* For Multiengine turbopropeller powered airplanes, a dynamic evaluation must be made and must include—

(a) The significant elastic, inertia, and aerodynamic forces associated with the rotations and displacements of the plane of the propeller; and

(b) Engine-propeller-nacelle stiffness and damping variations appropriate to the particular configuration.

Landing Gear

30. *Flap operated landing gear warning device.* Airplanes having retractable landing gear and wing flaps must be equipped with a warning device that functions continuously when the wing flaps are extended to a flap position that activates the warning device to give adequate warning before landing, using normal landing procedures, if the landing gear is not fully extended and locked. There may not be a manual shut off for this warning device. The flap position sensing unit may be installed at any suitable location. The system for this device may use any part of the system (including the aural warning device) provided for other landing gear warning devices.

Personnel and Cargo Accommodations

31. *Cargo and baggage compartments.* Cargo and baggage compartments must be designed to meet the requirements of FAR 23.787 (a) and (b), and in addition means must be provided to protect passengers from injury by the contents of any cargo or baggage compartment when the ultimate forward inertia force is 9g.

32. *Doors and exits.* The airplane must meet the requirements of FAR 23.783 and FAR 23.807 (a)(3), (b), and (c), and in addition:

(a) There must be a means to lock and safeguard each external door and exit against opening in flight either inadvertently by persons, or as a result of mechanical failure. Each external door must be operable from both the inside and the outside.

(b) There must be means for direct visual inspection of the locking mechanism by crewmembers to determine whether external doors and exits, for which the initial opening movement is outward, are fully locked. In addition, there must be a visual means to signal to crewmembers when normally used external doors are closed and fully locked.

(c) The passenger entrance door must qualify as a floor level emergency exit. Each additional required emergency exit except floor level exits must be located over the wing or must be provided with acceptable means to assist the occupants in descending to the ground. In addition to the passenger entrance door:

(1) For a total seating capacity of 15 or less, an emergency exit as defined in FAR 23.807(b) is required on each side of the cabin.

(2) For a total seating capacity of 16 through 23, three emergency exits as defined in 23.807(b) are required with one on the same side as the door and two on the side opposite the door.

(d) An evacuation demonstration must be conducted utilizing the maximum number of occupants for which certification is desired. It must be conducted under simulated night conditions utilizing only the emergency exits on the most critical side of the aircraft. The participants must be representative of average airline passengers with no prior practice or rehearsal for the demonstration. Evacuation must be completed within 90 seconds.

(e) Each emergency exit must be marked with the word “Exit” by a sign which has white letters 1 inch high on a red background 2 inches high, be self-illuminated or independently internally electrically illuminated, and have a minimum luminescence (brightness) of at least 160 microlamberts. The colors may be reversed if the passenger compartment illumination is essentially the same.

(f) Access to window type emergency exits must not be obstructed by seats or seat backs.

(g) The width of the main passenger aisle at any point between seats must equal or exceed the values in the following table.

Total seating capacity	Minimum main passenger aisle width	
	Less than 25 inches from floor	25 inches and more from floor
10 through 23	9 inches	15 inches

Miscellaneous

33. *Lightning strike protection.* Parts that are electrically insulated from the basic airframe must be connected to it through lightning arrestors unless a lightning strike on the insulated part—

(a) Is improbable because of shielding by other parts; or

(b) Is not hazardous.

34. *Ice protection.* If certification with ice protection provisions is desired, compliance with the following requirements must be shown:

(a) The recommended procedures for the use of the ice protection equipment must be set forth in the Airplane Flight Manual.

(b) An analysis must be performed to establish, on the basis of the airplane's operational needs, the adequacy of the ice protection system for the various components of the airplane. In addition, tests of the ice protection system must be conducted to demonstrate that the airplane is capable of operating safely in continuous maximum and intermittent maximum icing conditions as described in FAR 25, Appendix C.

(c) Compliance with all or portions of this section may be accomplished by reference, where applicable because of similarity of the designs, to analysis and tests performed by the applicant for a type certificated model.

35. *Maintenance information.* The applicant must make available to the owner at the time of delivery of the airplane the information he considers essential for the proper maintenance of the airplane. That information must include the following:

(a) Description of systems, including electrical, hydraulic, and fuel controls.

(b) Lubrication instructions setting forth the frequency and the lubricants and fluids which are to be used in the various systems.

(c) Pressures and electrical loads applicable to the various systems.

(d) Tolerances and adjustments necessary for proper functioning.

(e) Methods of leveling, raising, and towing.

(f) Methods of balancing control surfaces.

(g) Identification of primary and secondary structures.

(h) Frequency and extent of inspections necessary to the proper operation of the airplane.

(i) Special repair methods applicable to the airplane.

(j) Special inspection techniques, including those that require X-ray, ultrasonic, and magnetic particle inspection.

(k) List of special tools.

Propulsion

General

36. *Vibration characteristics.* For turbopropeller powered airplanes, the engine installation must not result in vibration characteristics of the engine exceeding those established during the type certification of the engine.

37. *In-flight restarting of engine.* If the engine on turbopropeller powered airplanes cannot be restarted at the maximum cruise altitude, a determination must be made of the altitude below which restarts can be consistently accomplished. Restart information must be provided in the Airplane Flight Manual.

38. *Engines*—

(a) *For turbopropeller powered airplanes.* The engine installation must comply with the following requirements:

(1) *Engine isolation.* The powerplants must be arranged and isolated from each other to allow operation, in at least one configuration, so that the failure or malfunction of any engine, or of any system that can affect the engine, will not—

(i) Prevent the continued safe operation of the remaining engines; or

(ii) Require immediate action by any crewmember for continued safe operation.

(2) *Control of engine rotation.* There must be a means to individually stop and restart the rotation of any engine in flight except that engine rotation need not be stopped if continued rotation could not jeopardize the safety of the airplane. Each component of the stopping and restarting system on the engine side of the firewall, and that might be exposed to fire, must be at least fire resistant. If hydraulic propeller feathering systems are used for this purpose, the feathering lines must be at least fire resistant under the operating conditions that may be expected to exist during feathering.

(3) *Engine speed and gas temperature control devices.* The powerplant systems associated with engine control devices, systems, and instrumentation must provide reasonable assurance that those engine operating limitations that adversely affect turbine rotor structural integrity will not be exceeded in service.

(b) *For reciprocating-engine powered airplanes.* To provide engine isolation, the powerplants must be arranged and isolated from each other to allow operation, in at least one configuration, so that the failure or malfunction of any engine, or of any system that can affect that engine, will not—

(1) Prevent the continued safe operation of the remaining engines; or

(2) Require immediate action by any crewmember for continued safe operation.

39. *Turbopropeller reversing systems.*

(a) Turbopropeller reversing systems intended for ground operation must be designed so that no single failure or malfunction of the system will result in unwanted reverse thrust under any expected operating condition. Failure of structural elements need not be considered if the probability of this kind of failure is extremely remote.

(b) Turbopropeller reversing systems intended for in-flight use must be designed so that no unsafe condition will result during normal operation of the system, or from any failure (or reasonably likely combination of failures) of the reversing system, under any anticipated condition of operation of the airplane. Failure of structural elements need not be considered if the probability of this kind of failure is extremely remote.

(c) Compliance with this section may be shown by failure analysis, testing, or both for propeller systems that allow propeller blades to move from the flight low-pitch position to a position that is substantially less than that at the normal flight low-pitch stop position. The analysis may include or be supported by the analysis made to show compliance with the type certification of the propeller and associated installation components. Credit will be given for pertinent analysis and testing completed by the engine and propeller manufacturers.

40. *Turbopropeller drag-limiting systems.* Turbopropeller drag-limiting systems must be designed so that no single failure or malfunction of any of the systems during normal or emergency operation results in propeller drag in excess of that for which the airplane was designed. Failure of structural elements of the drag-limiting systems need not be considered if the probability of this kind of failure is extremely remote.

41. *Turbine engine powerplant operating characteristics.* For turbopropeller powered airplanes, the turbine engine powerplant operating characteristics must be investigated in flight to determine that no adverse characteristics (such as stall, surge, or flameout) are present to a hazardous degree, during normal and emergency operation within the range of operating limitations of the airplane and of the engine.

42. *Fuel flow.*

(a) For turbopropeller powered airplanes—

(1) The fuel system must provide for continuous supply of fuel to the engines for normal operation without interruption due to depletion of fuel in any tank other than the main tank; and

(2) The fuel flow rate for turbopropeller engine fuel pump systems must not be less than 125 percent of the fuel flow required to develop the standard sea level atmospheric conditions takeoff power selected and included as an operating limitation in the Airplane Flight Manual.

(b) For reciprocating engine powered airplanes, it is acceptable for the fuel flow rate for each pump system (main and reserve supply) to be 125 percent of the takeoff fuel consumption of the engine.

Fuel System Components

43. *Fuel pumps.* For turbopropeller powered airplanes, a reliable and independent power source must be provided for each pump used with turbine engines which do not have provisions for mechanically driving the main pumps. It must be demonstrated that the pump installations provide a reliability and durability equivalent to that provided by FAR 23.991(a).

44. *Fuel strainer or filter.* For turbopropeller powered airplanes, the following apply:

(a) There must be a fuel strainer or filter between the tank outlet and the fuel metering device of the engine. In addition, the fuel strainer or filter must be—

(1) Between the tank outlet and the engine-driven positive displacement pump inlet, if there is an engine-driven positive displacement pump;

(2) Accessible for drainage and cleaning and, for the strainer screen, easily removable; and

(3) Mounted so that its weight is not supported by the connecting lines or by the inlet or outlet connections of the strainer or filter itself.

(b) Unless there are means in the fuel system to prevent the accumulation of ice on the filter, there must be means to automatically maintain the fuel flow if ice-clogging of the filter occurs; and

(c) The fuel strainer or filter must be of adequate capacity (with respect to operating limitations established to insure proper service) and of appropriate mesh to insure proper engine operation, with the fuel contaminated to a degree (with respect to particle size and density) that can be reasonably expected in service. The degree of fuel filtering may not be less than that established for the engine type certification.

45. *Lightning strike protection.* Protection must be provided against the ignition of flammable vapors in the fuel vent system due to lightning strikes.

Cooling

46. *Cooling test procedures for turbopropeller powered airplanes.*

(a) Turbopropeller powered airplanes must be shown to comply with the requirements of FAR 23.1041 during takeoff, climb en route, and landing stages of flight that correspond to the applicable performance requirements. The cooling test must be conducted with the airplane in the configuration and operating under the conditions that are critical relative to cooling during each stage of flight. For the cooling tests a temperature is "stabilized" when its rate of change is less than 2°F. per minute.

(b) Temperatures must be stabilized under the conditions from which entry is made into each stage of flight being investigated unless the entry condition is not one during which component and engine fluid temperatures would stabilize, in which case, operation through the full entry condition must be conducted before entry into the stage of flight being investigated in order to allow temperatures to reach their natural levels at the time of entry. The takeoff cooling test must be preceded by a period during which the powerplant component and engine fluid temperatures are stabilized with the engines at ground idle.

(c) Cooling tests for each stage of flight must be continued until—

(1) The component and engine fluid temperatures stabilize;

(2) The stage of flight is completed; or

(3) An operating limitation is reached.

Induction System

47. *Air induction.* For turbopropeller powered airplanes—

(a) There must be means to prevent hazardous quantities of fuel leakage or overflow from drains, vents, or other components of flammable fluid systems from entering the engine intake system; and

(b) The air inlet ducts must be located or protected so as to minimize the ingestion of foreign matter during takeoff, landing, and taxiing.

48. *Induction system icing protection.* For turbopropeller powered airplanes, each turbine engine must be able to operate throughout its flight power range without adverse effect on engine operation or serious loss of power or thrust, under the icing conditions specified in Appendix C of FAR 25. In addition, there must be means to indicate to appropriate flight crewmembers the functioning of the powerplant ice protection system.

49. *Turbine engine bleed air systems.* Turbine engine bleed air systems of turbopropeller powered airplanes must be investigated to determine—

(a) That no hazard to the airplane will result if a duct rupture occurs. This condition must consider that a failure of the duct can occur anywhere between the engine port and the airplane bleed service; and

(b) That if the bleed air system is used for direct cabin pressurization, it is not possible for hazardous contamination of the cabin air system to occur in event of lubrication system failure.

Exhaust System

50. *Exhaust system drains.* Turbopropeller engine exhaust systems having low spots or pockets must incorporate drains at such locations. These drains must discharge clear of the airplane in normal and ground attitudes to prevent the accumulation of fuel after the failure of an attempted engine start.

Powerplant Controls and Accessories

51. *Engine controls.* If throttles or power levers for turbopropeller powered airplanes are such that any position of these controls will reduce the fuel flow to the engine(s) below that necessary for satisfactory and safe idle operation of the engine while the airplane is in flight, a means must be provided to prevent inadvertent movement of the control into this position. The means provided must incorporate a positive lock or stop at this idle position and must require a separate and distinct operation by the crew to displace the control from the normal engine operating range.

52. *Reverse thrust controls.* For turbopropeller powered airplanes, the propeller reverse thrust controls must have a means to prevent their inadvertent operation. The means must have a positive lock or stop at the idle position and must require a separate and distinct operation by the crew to displace the control from the flight regime.

53. *Engine ignition systems.* Each turbopropeller airplane ignition system must be considered an essential electrical load.

54. *Powerplant accessories.* The powerplant accessories must meet the requirements of FAR 23.1163, and if the continued rotation of any accessory remotely driven by the engine is hazardous when malfunctioning occurs, there must be means to prevent rotation without interfering with the continued operation of the engine.

Powerplant Fire Protection

55. *Fire detector system.* For turbopropeller powered airplanes, the following apply:

(a) There must be a means that ensures prompt detection of fire in the engine compartment. An overtemperature switch in each engine cooling air exit is an acceptable method of meeting this requirement.

(b) Each fire detector must be constructed and installed to withstand the vibration, inertia, and other loads to which it may be subjected in operation.

(c) No fire detector may be affected by any oil, water, other fluids, or fumes that might be present.

(d) There must be means to allow the flight crew to check, in flight, the functioning of each fire detector electric circuit.

(e) Wiring and other components of each fire detector system in a fire zone must be at least fire resistant.

56. *Fire protection, cowling and nacelle skin.* For reciprocating engine powered airplanes, the engine cowling must be designed and constructed so that no fire originating in the engine compartment can enter, either through openings or by burn through, any other region where it would create additional hazards.

57. *Flammable fluid fire protection.* If flammable fluids or vapors might be liberated by the leakage of fluid systems in areas other than engine compartments, there must be means to—

(a) Prevent the ignition of those fluids or vapors by any other equipment; or

(b) Control any fire resulting from that ignition.

Equipment

58. *Powerplant instruments.*

(a) The following are required for turbopropeller airplanes:

(1) The instruments required by FAR 23.1305 (a)(1) through (4), (b)(2) and (4).

(2) A gas temperature indicator for each engine.

(3) Free air temperature indicator.

(4) A fuel flowmeter indicator for each engine.

(5) Oil pressure warning means for each engine.

(6) A torque indicator or adequate means for indicating power output for each engine.

(7) Fire warning indicator for each engine.

(8) A means to indicate when the propeller blade angle is below the low-pitch position corresponding to idle operation in flight.

(9) A means to indicate the functioning of the ice protection system for each engine.

(b) For turbopropeller powered airplanes, the turbopropeller blade position indicator must begin indicating when the blade has moved below the flight low-pitch position.

(c) The following instruments are required for reciprocating-engine powered airplanes:

(1) The instruments required by FAR 23.1305.

(2) A cylinder head temperature indicator for each engine.

(3) A manifold pressure indicator for each engine.

Systems and Equipment

General

59. *Function and installation.* The systems and equipment of the airplane must meet the requirements of FAR 23.1301, and the following:

(a) Each item of additional installed equipment must—

(1) Be of a kind and design appropriate to its intended function;

(2) Be labeled as to its identification, function, or operating limitations, or any applicable combination of these factors, unless misuse or inadvertent actuation cannot create a hazard;

(3) Be installed according to limitations specified for that equipment; and

(4) Function properly when installed.

(b) Systems and installations must be designed to safeguard against hazards to the aircraft in the event of their malfunction or failure.

(c) Where an installation, the functioning of which is necessary in showing compliance with the applicable requirements, requires a power supply, such installation must be considered an essential load on the power supply, and the power sources and the distribution system must be capable of supplying the following power loads in probable operation combinations and for probable durations:

(1) All essential loads after failure of any prime mover, power converter, or energy storage device.

(2) All essential loads after failure of any one engine on two-engine airplanes.

(3) In determining the probable operating combinations and durations of essential loads for the power failure conditions described in subparagraphs (1) and (2) of this paragraph, it is permissible to assume that the power loads are reduced in accordance with a monitoring procedure which is consistent with safety in the types of operations authorized.

60. *Ventilation.* The ventilation system of the airplane must meet the requirements of FAR 23.831, and in addition, for pressurized aircraft the ventilating air in flight crew and passenger compartments must be free of harmful or hazardous concentrations of gases and vapors in normal operation and in the event of reasonably probable failures or malfunctioning of the ventilating, heating, pressurization, or other systems, and equipment. If accumulation of hazardous quantities of smoke in the cockpit area is reasonably probable, smoke evacuation must be readily accomplished.

Electrical Systems and Equipment

61. *General.* The electrical systems and equipment of the airplane must meet the requirements of FAR 23.1351, and the following:

(a) *Electrical system capacity.* The required generating capacity, and number and kinds of power sources must—

(1) Be determined by an electrical load analysis, and

(2) Meet the requirements of FAR 23.1301.

(b) *Generating system.* The generating system includes electrical power sources, main power busses, transmission cables, and associated control, regulation, and protective devices. It must be designed so that—

(1) The system voltage and frequency (as applicable) at the terminals of all essential load equipment can be maintained within the limits for which the equipment is designed, during any probable operating conditions;

(2) System transients due to switching, fault clearing, or other causes do not make essential loads inoperative, and do not cause a smoke or fire hazard;

(3) There are means, accessible in flight to appropriate crewmembers, for the individual and collective disconnection of the electrical power sources from the system; and

(4) There are means to indicate to appropriate crewmembers the generating system quantities essential for the safe operation of the system, including the voltage and current supplied by each generator.

62. *Electrical equipment and installation.* Electrical equipment controls, and wiring must be installed so that operation of any one unit or system of units will not adversely affect the simultaneous operation of to the safe operation.

63. *Distribution system.*

(a) For the purpose of complying with this section, the distribution system includes the distribution busses, their associated feeders and each control and protective device.

(b) Each system must be designed so that essential load circuits can be supplied in the event of reasonably probable faults or open circuits, including faults in heavy current carrying cables.

(c) If two independent sources of electrical power for particular equipment or systems are required by this regulation, their electrical energy supply must be insured by means such as duplicate electrical equipment, throwover switching, or multichannel or loop circuits separately routed.

64. *Circuit protective devices.* The circuit protective devices for the electrical circuits of the airplane must meet the requirements of FAR 23.1357, and in addition circuits for loads which are essential to safe operation must have individual and exclusive circuit protection.

[Docket No. 8070, 34 FR 189, Jan. 7, 1969; as amended by SFAR 23–1, 34 FR 20176, Dec. 24, 1969; 35 FR 1102, Jan. 28, 1970]

Subpart A—General

§23.1 Applicability.

(a) This part prescribes airworthiness standards for the issue of type certificates, and changes to those certificates, for airplanes in the normal, utility, acrobatic, and commuter categories.

(b) Each person who applies under Part 21 for such a certificate or change must show compliance with the applicable requirements of this part.

[Docket No. 4080, 29 FR 17955, Dec. 18, 1964; as amended by Amdt. 23–34, 52 FR 1825, Jan. 15, 1987]

§23.2 Special retroactive requirements.

(a) Notwithstanding §§21.17 and 21.101 of this chapter and irrespective of the type certification basis, each normal, utility, and acrobatic category airplane having a passenger seating configuration, excluding pilot seats, of nine or less, manufactured after December 12, 1986, or any such foreign airplane for entry into the United States must provide a safety belt and shoulder harness for each forward- or aft-facing seat which will protect the occupant from serious head injury when subjected to the inertia loads resulting from the ultimate static load factors prescribed in §23.561(b)(2) of this part, or which will provide the occupant protection specified in §23.562 of this part when that section is applicable to the airplane. For other seat orientations, the seat/restraint system must be designed to provide a level of occupant protection equivalent to that provided for forward- or aft-facing seats with a safety belt and shoulder harness installed.

(b) Each shoulder harness installed at a flight crewmember station, as required by this section, must allow the crewmember, when seated with the safety belt and shoulder harness fastened, to perform all functions necessary for flight operations.

(c) For the purpose of this section, the date of manufacture is:

(1) The date the inspection acceptance records, or equivalent, reflect that the airplane is complete and meets the FAA approved type design data; or

(2) In the case of a foreign manufactured airplane, the date the foreign civil airworthiness authority certifies the airplane is complete and issues an original standard airworthiness certificate, or the equivalent in that country.

[Docket No. 4080, 29 FR 17955, Dec. 18. 1964; 30 FR 258, Jan. 9, 1965; as amended by Amdt. 23–36, 53 FR 30812, Aug. 15, 1988]

§23.3 Airplane categories.

(a) The normal category is limited to airplanes that have a seating configuration, excluding pilot seats, of nine or less, a maximum certificated takeoff weight of 12,500 pounds or less, and intended for nonacrobatic operation. Nonacrobatic operation includes:

(1) Any maneuver incident to normal flying;

(2) Stalls (except whip stalls); and

(3) Lazy eights, chandelles, and steep turns, in which the angle of bank is not more than 60 degrees.

(b) The utility category is limited to airplanes that have a seating configuration, excluding pilot seats, of nine or less, a maximum certificated takeoff weight of 12,500 pounds or less, and intended for limited acrobatic operation. Airplanes certificated in the utility category may be used in any of the operations covered under paragraph (a) of this section and in limited acrobatic operations. Limited acrobatic operation includes:

(1) Spins (if approved for the particular type of airplane); and

(2) Lazy eights, chandelles, and steep turns, or similar maneuvers, in which the angle of bank is more than 60 degrees but not more than 90 degrees.

(c) The acrobatic category is limited to airplanes that have a seating configuration, excluding pilot seats, of nine or less, a maximum certificated takeoff weight of 12,500 pounds or less, and intended for use without restrictions, other than those shown to be necessary as a result of required flight tests.

(d) The commuter category is limited to propeller-driven, multiengine airplanes that have a seating configuration, excluding pilot seats, of 19 or less, and a maximum certificated takeoff weight of 19,000 pounds or less. The commuter category operation is limited to any maneuver incident to normal flying, stalls (except whip stalls), and steep turns, in which the angle of bank is not more than 60 degrees.

(e) Except for commuter category, airplanes may be type certificated in more than one category if the requirements of each requested category are met.

[Docket No. 4080, 29 FR 17955, Dec. 18, 1964; as amended by Amdt. 23–4, 32 FR 5934, April 14, 1967; Amdt. 23–34, 52 FR 1825, Jan. 15, 1987; 52 FR 34745, Sept. 14, 1987; Amdt. 23–50, 61 FR 5183, Feb. 9, 1996]

Subpart B—Flight

General

§23.21 Proof of compliance.

(a) Each requirement of this subpart must be met at each appropriate combination of weight and center of gravity within the range of loading conditions for which certification is requested. This must be shown—

(1) By tests upon an airplane of the type for which certification is requested, or by calculations based on, and equal in accuracy to, the results of testing; and

(2) By systematic investigation of each probable combination of weight and center of gravity, if compliance cannot be reasonably inferred from combinations investigated.

(b) The following general tolerances are allowed during flight testing. However, greater tolerances may be allowed in particular tests:

Item	Tolerance
Weight	+5%, -10%
Critical items affected by weight	+5%, -1%
C.G.	±7% total travel

§23.23 Load distribution limits.

(a) Ranges of weights and centers of gravity within which the airplane may be safely operated must be established. If a weight and center of gravity combination is allowable only within certain lateral load distribution limits that could be inadvertently exceeded, these limits must be established for the corresponding weight and center of gravity combinations.

(b) The load distribution limits may not exceed any of the following:

(1) The selected limits;

(2) The limits at which the structure is proven; or

(3) The limits at which compliance with each applicable flight requirement of this subpart is shown.

[Docket No. 26269, 58 FR 42156, Aug. 6, 1993]

§23.25 Weight limits.

(a) *Maximum weight.* The maximum weight is the highest weight at which compliance with each applicable requirement of this part (other than those complied with at the design landing weight) is shown. The maximum weight must be established so that it is—

(1) Not more than the least of—

(i) The highest weight selected by the applicant; or

(ii) The design maximum weight, which is the highest weight at which compliance with each applicable structural loading condition of this part (other than those complied with at the design landing weight) is shown; or

(iii) The highest weight at which compliance with each applicable flight requirement is shown, and

(2) Not less than the weight with—

(i) Each seat occupied, assuming a weight of 170 pounds for each occupant for normal and commuter category airplanes, and 190 pounds for utility and acrobatic category airplanes, except that seats other than pilot seats may be placarded for a lesser weight; and

(A) Oil at full capacity, and

(B) At least enough fuel for maximum continuous power operation of at least 30 minutes for day-VFR approved airplanes and at least 45 minutes for night-VFR and IFR approved airplanes; or

(ii) The required minimum crew, and fuel and oil to full tank capacity.

(b) *Minimum weight.* The minimum weight (the lowest weight at which compliance with each applicable requirement of this part is shown) must be established so that it is not more than the sum of—

(1) The empty weight determined under §23.29;

(2) The weight of the required minimum crew (assuming a weight of 170 pounds for each crewmember); and

(3) The weight of—

(i) For turbojet powered airplanes, 5 percent of the total fuel capacity of that particular fuel tank arrangement under investigation, and

(ii) For other airplanes, the fuel necessary for one-half hour of operation at maximum continuous power.

[Docket No. 4080, 29 FR 17955, Dec. 18, 1964; as amended by Amdt. 23–7, 34 FR 13086, Aug. 13, 1969; Amdt. 23–21, 43 FR 2317, Jan. 16, 1978; Amdt. 23–34, 52 FR 1825, Jan. 15, 1987; Amdt. 23–45, 58 FR 42156, Aug. 6, 1993; Amdt. 23–50, 61 FR 5183, Feb. 9, 1996]

§23.29 Empty weight and corresponding center of gravity.

(a) The empty weight and corresponding center of gravity must be determined by weighing the airplane with—

(1) Fixed ballast;

(2) Unusable fuel determined under 23.959; and

(3) Full operating fluids, including—

(i) Oil;

(ii) Hydraulic fluid; and

(iii) Other fluids required for normal operation of airplane systems, except potable water, lavatory precharge water, and water intended for injection in the engines.

(b) The condition of the airplane at the time of determining empty weight must be one that is well defined and can be easily repeated.

[Docket No. 4080, 29 FR 17955, Dec. 18, 1964; 30 FR 258, Jan. 9, 1965; as amended by Amdt. 23–21, 43 FR 2317, Jan. 16, 1978]

§23.31 Removable ballast.

Removable ballast may be used in showing compliance with the flight requirements of this subpart, if—

(a) The place for carrying ballast is properly designed and installed, and is marked under 23.1557; and

(b) Instructions are included in the airplane flight manual, approved manual material, or markings and placards, for the proper placement of the removable ballast under each loading condition for which removable ballast is necessary.

[Docket No. 4080, 29 FR 17955, Dec. 18, 1964; 30 FR 258, Jan. 9, 1965; as amended by Amdt. 23–13, 37 FR 20023, Sept. 23, 1972]

§23.33 Propeller speed and pitch limits.

(a) *General.* The propeller speed and pitch must be limited to values that will assure safe operation under normal operating conditions.

(b) *Propellers not controllable in flight.* For each propeller whose pitch cannot be controlled in flight—

(1) During takeoff and initial climb at the all engine(s) operating climb speed specified in §23.65, the propeller must limit the engine r.p.m., at full throttle or at maximum allowable takeoff manifold pressure, to a speed not greater than the maximum allowable takeoff r.p.m.; and

(2) During a closed throttle glide, at V_{NE}, the propeller may not cause an engine speed above 110 percent of maximum continuous speed.

(c) *Controllable pitch propellers without constant speed controls.* Each propeller that can be controlled in flight, but that does not have constant speed controls, must have a means to limit the pitch range so that—

(1) The lowest possible pitch allows compliance with paragraph (b)(1) of this section; and

(2) The highest possible pitch allows compliance with paragraph (b)(2) of this section.

(d) *Controllable pitch propellers with constant speed controls.* Each controllable pitch propeller with constant speed controls must have—

(1) With the governor in operation, a means at the governor to limit the maximum engine speed to the maximum allowable takeoff r.p.m.; and

(2) With the governor inoperative, the propeller blades at the lowest possible pitch, with takeoff power, the airplane stationary, and no wind, either—

(i) A means to limit the maximum engine speed to 103 percent of the maximum allowable takeoff r.p.m., or

(ii) For an engine with an approved overspeed, a means to limit the maximum engine and propeller speed to not more than the maximum approved overspeed.

[Docket No. 4080, 29 FR 17955, Dec. 18, 1964; as amended by Amdt. 23–45, 58 FR 42156, Aug. 6, 1993; Amdt. 23–50, 61 FR 5183, Feb. 9, 1996]

PERFORMANCE

§23.45 General.

(a) Unless otherwise prescribed, the performance requirements of this part must be met for—

(1) Still air and standard atmosphere; and

(2) Ambient atmospheric conditions, for commuter category airplanes, for reciprocating engine-powered airplanes of more than 6,000 pounds maximum weight, and for turbine engine-powered airplanes.

(b) Performance data must be determined over not less than the following ranges of conditions—

(1) Airport altitudes from sea level to 10,000 feet; and

(2) For reciprocating engine-powered airplanes of 6,000 pounds, or less, maximum weight, temperature from standard to 30°C above standard; or

(3) For reciprocating engine-powered airplanes of more than 6,000 pounds maximum weight and turbine engine-powered airplanes, temperature from standard to 30°C above standard, or the maximum ambient atmospheric temperature at which compliance with the cooling provisions of §23.1041 to §23.1047 is shown, if lower.

(c) Performance data must be determined with the cowl flaps or other means for controlling the engine cooling air supply in the position used in the cooling tests required by §23.1041 to §23.1047.

(d) The available propulsive thrust must correspond to engine power, not exceeding the approved power, less—

(1) Installation losses; and

(2) The power absorbed by the accessories and services appropriate to the particular ambient atmospheric conditions and the particular flight condition.

(e) The performance, as affected by engine power or thrust, must be based on a relative humidity:

(1) Of 80 percent at and below standard temperature; and

(2) From 80 percent, at the standard temperature, varying linearly down to 34 percent at the standard temperature plus 50°F.

(f) Unless otherwise prescribed, in determining the takeoff and landing distances, changes in the airplane's configuration, speed, and power must be made in accordance with procedures established by the applicant for operation in service. These procedures must be able to be executed consistently by pilots of average skill in atmospheric conditions reasonably expected to be encountered in service.

(g) The following, as applicable, must be determined on a smooth, dry, hard-surfaced runway—

(1) Takeoff distance of §23.53(b);

(2) Accelerate-stop distance of §23.55;

(3) Takeoff distance and takeoff run of §23.59; and

(4) Landing distance of §23.75.

Note: The effect on these distances of operation on other types of surfaces (for example, grass, gravel) when dry, may be determined or derived and these surfaces listed in the Airplane Flight Manual in accordance with §23.1583(p).

(h) For commuter category airplanes, the following also apply:

(1) Unless otherwise prescribed, the applicant must select the takeoff, enroute, approach, and landing configurations for the airplane.

(2) The airplane configuration may vary with weight, altitude, and temperature, to the extent that they are compatible with the operating procedures required by paragraph (h)(3) of this section.

(3) Unless otherwise prescribed, in determining the critical-engine-inoperative takeoff performance, takeoff flight path, and accelerate-stop distance, changes in the airplane's configuration, speed, and power must be made in accordance with procedures established by the applicant for operation in service.

(4) Procedures for the execution of discontinued approaches and balked landings associated with the conditions prescribed in §23.67(c)(4) and §23.77(c) must be established.

(5) The procedures established under paragraphs (h)(3) and (h)(4) of this section must—

(i) Be able to be consistently executed by a crew of average skill in atmospheric conditions reasonably expected to be encountered in service;

(ii) Use methods or devices that are safe and reliable; and

(iii) Include allowance for any reasonably expected time delays in the execution of the procedures.

[Docket No. 4080, 29 FR 17955, Dec. 18. 1964; 30 FR 258, Jan. 9, 1965; as amended by Amdt. 23–21, 43 FR 2317, Jan. 16, 1978; Amdt. 23–34, 52 FR 1826, Jan. 15, 1987; Amdt. 23–45, 58 FR 42156, Aug. 6, 1993; Amdt. 23–50, 61 FR 5184, Feb. 9, 1996]

§23.49 Stalling period.

(a) V_{SO} and V_{S1} are the stalling speeds or the minimum steady flight speeds, in knots (CAS), at which the airplane is controllable with—

(1) For reciprocating engine-powered airplanes, the engine(s) idling, the throttle(s) closed or at not more than the power necessary for zero thrust at a speed not more than 110 percent of the stalling speed;

(2) For turbine engine-powered airplanes, the propulsive thrust not greater than zero at the stalling speed, or, if the resultant thrust has no appreciable effect on the stalling speed, with engine(s) idling and throttle(s) closed;

(3) The propeller(s) in the takeoff position;

(4) The airplane in the condition existing in the test, in which V_{SO} and V_{S1} are being used;

(5) The center of gravity in the position that results in the highest value of V_{SO} and V_{S1}; and

(6) The weight used when V_{SO} and V_{S1} are being used as a factor to determine compliance with a required performance standard.

(b) V_{SO} and V_{S1} must be determined by flight tests, using the procedure and meeting the flight characteristics specified in §23.201.

(c) Except as provided in paragraph (d) of this section, V_{SO} and V_{S1} at maximum weight must not exceed 61 knots for—

(1) Single-engine airplanes; and

(2) Multiengine airplanes of 6,000 pounds or less maximum weight that cannot meet the minimum rate of climb specified in §23.67(a)(1) with the critical engine inoperative.

(d) All single-engine airplanes, and those multiengine airplanes of 6,000 pounds or less maximum weight with a V_{SO}

23

of more than 61 knots that do not meet the requirements of §23.67(a)(1), must comply with §23.562(d).

[Docket No. 27807, 61 FR 5184, Feb. 9, 1996]

§23.51 Takeoff speeds.

(a) For normal, utility, and acrobatic category airplanes, rotation speed, V_R, is the speed at which the pilot makes a control input, with the intention of lifting the airplane out of contact with the runway or water surface.

(1) For multiengine landplanes, V_R, must not be less than the greater of 1.05 V_{MC}; or 1.10 V_{S1};

(2) For single-engine landplanes, V_R, must not be less than V_{S1}; and

(3) For seaplanes and amphibians taking off from water, V_R, may be any speed that is shown to be safe under all reasonably expected conditions, including turbulence and complete failure of the critical engine.

(b) For normal, utility, and acrobatic category airplanes, the speed at 50 feet above the takeoff surface level must not be less than:

(1) or multiengine airplanes, the highest of—

(i) A speed that is shown to be safe for continued flight (or emergency landing, if applicable) under all reasonably expected conditions, including turbulence and complete failure of the critical engine;

(ii) 1.10 V_{MC}; or

(iii) 1.20 V_{S1}.

(2) For single-engine airplanes, the higher of—

(i) A speed that is shown to be safe under all reasonably expected conditions, including turbulence and complete engine failure; or

(ii) 1.20 V_{S1}.

(c) For commuter category airplanes, the following apply:

(l) V_1 must be established in relation to V_{EF} as follows:

(i) V_{EF} is the calibrated airspeed at which the critical engine is assumed to fail. V_{EF} must be selected by the applicant but must not be less than 1.05 V_{MC} determined under §23.149(b) or, at the option of the applicant, not less than V_{MCG} determined under §23.149(f).

(ii) The takeoff decision speed, V_1, is the calibrated airspeed on the ground at which, as a result of engine failure or other reasons, the pilot is assumed to have made a decision to continue or discontinue the takeoff. The takeoff decision speed, V_1, must be selected by the applicant but must not be less than V_{EF} plus the speed gained with the critical engine inoperative during the time interval between the instant at which the critical engine is failed and the instant at which the pilot recognizes and reacts to the engine failure, as indicated by the pilot's application of the first retarding means during the accelerate-stop determination of §23.55.

(2) The rotation speed, V_R, in terms of calibrated airspeed, must be selected by the applicant and must not be less than the greatest of the following:

(i) V_1;

(ii) 1.05 V_{MC} determined under §23.149(b);

(iii) 1.10 V_{S1}; or

(iv) The speed that allows attaining the initial climb-out speed, V_2, before reaching a height of 35 feet above the takeoff surface in accordance with §23.57(c)(2).

(3) For any given set of conditions, such as weight, altitude, temperature, and configuration, a single value of V_R must be used to show compliance with both the one-engine-inoperative takeoff and all-engines-operating takeoff requirements.

(4) The takeoff safety speed, V_2, in terms of calibrated airspeed, must be selected by the applicant so as to allow the gradient of climb required in §23.67 (c)(1) and (c)(2) but must not be less than 1.10 V_{MC} or less than 1.20 V_{S1}.

(5) The one-engine-inoperative takeoff distance, using a normal rotation rate at a speed 5 knots less than V_R, established in accordance with paragraph (c)(2) of this section, must be shown not to exceed the corresponding one-engine-inoperative takeoff distance, determined in accordance with §23.57 and §23.59(a)(1), using the established V_R. The takeoff, otherwise performed in accordance with §23.57, must be continued safely from the point at which the airplane is 35 feet above the takeoff surface and at a speed not less than the established V_2 minus 5 knots.

(6) The applicant must show, with all engines operating, that marked increases in the scheduled takeoff distances, determined in accordance with §23.59(a)(2), do not result from over-rotation of the airplane or out-of-trim conditions.

[Docket No. 27807, 61 FR 5184, Feb. 9, 1996]

§23.53 Takeoff performance.

(a) For normal, utility, and acrobatic category airplanes, the takeoff distance must be determined in accordance with paragraph (b) of this section, using speeds determined in accordance with §23.51 (a) and (b).

(b) For normal, utility, and acrobatic category airplanes, the distance required to takeoff and climb to a height of 50 feet above the takeoff surface must be determined for each weight, altitude, and temperature within the operational limits established for takeoff with—

(1) Takeoff power on each engine;

(2) Wing flaps in the takeoff position(s); and

(3) Landing gear extended.

(c) For commuter category airplanes, takeoff performance, as required by §§23.55 through 23.59, must be determined with the operating engine(s) within approved operating limitations.

[Docket No. 27807, 61 FR 5185, Feb. 9, 1996]

§23.55 Accelerate-stop distance.

For each commuter category airplane, the accelerate-stop distance must be determined as follows:

(a) The accelerate-stop distance is the sum of the distances necessary to—

(1) Accelerate the airplane from a standing start to V_{EF} with all engines operating;

(2) Accelerate the airplane from V_{EF} to V_1, assuming the critical engine fails at V_{EF}; and

(3) Come to a full stop from the point at which V_1 is reached.

(b) Means other than wheel brakes may be used to determine the accelerate-stop distances if that means—

(1) Is safe and reliable;

(2) Is used so that consistent results can be expected under normal operating conditions; and

(3) Is such that exceptional skill is not required to control the airplane.

[Amdt. 23–34, 52 FR 1826, Jan. 15, 1987; as amended by Amdt. 23–50, 61 FR 5185, Feb. 9, 1996]

§23.57 Takeoff path.

For each commuter category airplane, the take-off path is as follows:

(a) The takeoff path extends from a standing start to a point in the takeoff at which the airplane is 1500 feet above the takeoff surface at or below which height the transition from the takeoff to the enroute configuration must be completed; and

(1) The takeoff path must be based on the procedures prescribed in §23.45;

(2) The airplane must be accelerated on the ground to V_{EF} at which point the critical engine must be made inoperative and remain inoperative for the rest of the takeoff; and

(3) After reaching V_{EF}, the airplane must be accelerated to V_2.

(b) During the acceleration to speed V_2, the nose gear may be raised off the ground at a speed not less than V_R. However, landing gear retraction must not be initiated until the airplane is airborne.

(c) During the takeoff path determination, in accordance with paragraphs (a) and (b) of this section—

(1) The slope of the airborne part of the takeoff path must not be negative at any point;

(2) The airplane must reach V_2 before it is 35 feet above the takeoff surface, and must continue at a speed as close as practical to, but not less than V_2, until it is 400 feet above the takeoff surface;

(3) At each point along the takeoff path, starting at the point at which the airplane reaches 400 feet above the takeoff surface, the available gradient of climb must not be less than—

(i) 1.2 percent for two-engine airplanes;

(ii) 1.5 percent for three-engine airplanes;

(iii) 1.7 percent for four-engine airplanes; and

(4) Except for gear retraction and automatic propeller feathering, the airplane configuration must not be changed, and no change in power that requires action by the pilot may be made, until the airplane is 400 feet above the takeoff surface.

(d) The takeoff path to 35 feet above the takeoff surface must be determined by a continuous demonstrated takeoff.

(e) The takeoff path to 35 feet above the takeoff surface must be determined by synthesis from segments; and

(1) The segments must be clearly defined and must be related to distinct changes in configuration, power, and speed;

(2) The weight of the airplane, the configuration, and the power must be assumed constant throughout each segment and must correspond to the most critical condition prevailing in the segment; and

(3) The takeoff flight path must be based on the airplane's performance without utilizing ground effect.

[Amdt. 23–34, 52 FR 1827, Jan. 15, 1987; as amended by Amdt. 23–50, 61 FR 5185, Feb. 9, 1996]

§23.59 Takeoff distance and takeoff run.

For each commuter category airplane—

(a) Takeoff distance is the greater of—

(1) The horizontal distance along the takeoff path from the start of the takeoff to the point at which the airplane is 35 feet above the takeoff surface as determined under §23.57; or

(2) With all engines operating, 115 percent of the horizontal distance from the start of the takeoff to the point at which the airplane is 35 feet above the takeoff surface, determined by a procedure consistent with §23.57.

(b) If the takeoff distance includes a clearway, the takeoff run is the greater of—

(1) The horizontal distance along the takeoff path from the start of the takeoff to a point equidistant between the liftoff point and the point at which the airplane is 35 feet above the takeoff surface as determined under §23.57; or

(2) With all engines operating, 115 percent of the horizontal distance from the start of the takeoff to a point equidistant between the liftoff point and the point at which the airplane is 35 feet above the takeoff surface, determined by a procedure consistent with §23.57.

[Amdt. 23–34, 52 FR 1827, Jan. 15, 1987; as amended by Amdt. 23–50, 61 FR 5185, Feb. 9, 1996]

§23.61 Takeoff flight path.

For each commuter category airplane, the takeoff flight path must be determined as follows:

(a) The takeoff flight path begins 35 feet above the takeoff surface at the end of the takeoff distance determined in accordance with §23.59.

(b) The net takeoff flight path data must be determined so that they represent the actual takeoff flight paths, as determined in accordance with §23.57 and with paragraph (a) of this section, reduced at each point by a gradient of climb equal to—

(1) 0.8 percent for two-engine airplanes;

(2) 0.9 percent for three-engine airplanes; and

(3) 1.0 percent for four-engine airplanes.

(c) The prescribed reduction in climb gradient may be applied as an equivalent reduction in acceleration along that part of the takeoff flight path at which the airplane is accelerated in level flight.

[Amdt. 23–34, 52 FR 1827, Jan. 15, 1987]

§23.63 Climb: General.

(a) Compliance with the requirements of §§23.65, 23.66, 23.67, 23.69, and 23.77 must be shown—

(1) Out of ground effect; and

(2) At speeds that are not less than those at which compliance with the powerplant cooling requirements of §§23.1041 to 23.1047 has been demonstrated; and

(3) Unless otherwise specified, with one engine inoperative, at a bank angle not exceeding 5 degrees.

(b) For normal, utility, and acrobatic category reciprocating engine-powered airplanes of 6,000 pounds or less maximum weight, compliance must be shown with §23.65(a), §23.67(a), where appropriate, and §23.77(a) at maximum takeoff or landing weight, as appropriate, in a standard atmosphere.

(c) For normal, utility, and acrobatic category reciprocating engine-powered airplanes of more than 6,000 pounds maximum weight, and turbine engine-powered airplanes in the normal, utility, and acrobatic category, compliance must be shown at weights as a function of airport altitude and ambient temperature, within the operational limits established for takeoff and landing, respectively, with—

(1) Sections 23.65(b) and 23.67(b) (1) and (2), where appropriate, for takeoff, and

(2) Section 23.67(b)(2), where appropriate, and §23.77(b), for landing.

(d) For commuter category airplanes, compliance must be shown at weights as a function of airport altitude and ambient temperature within the operational limits established for takeoff and landing, respectively, with—

(1) Sections 23.67(c)(1), 23.67(c)(2), and 23.67(c)(3) for takeoff; and

(2) Sections 23.67(c)(3), 23.67(c)(4), and 23.77(c) for landing.

[Docket No. 27807, 61 FR 5186, Feb. 9, 1996]

§23.65 Climb: All engines operating.

(a) Each normal, utility, and acrobatic category reciprocating engine-powered airplane of 6,000 pounds or less maximum weight must have a steady climb gradient at sea level of at least 8.3 percent for landplanes or 6.7 percent for seaplanes and amphibians with—

(1) Not more than maximum continuous power on each engine;

(2) The landing gear retracted;

(3) The wing flaps in the takeoff position(s); and

(4) A climb speed not less than the greater of 1.1 V_{MC} and 1.2 V_{S1} for multiengine airplanes and not less than 1.2 V_{S1} for single-engine airplanes.

(b) Each normal, utility, and acrobatic category reciprocating engine-powered airplane of more than 6,000 pounds maximum weight and turbine engine-powered airplanes in the normal, utility, and acrobatic category must have a steady gradient of climb after takeoff of at least 4 percent with

(1) Take off power on each engine;

(2) The landing gear extended, except that if the landing gear can be retracted in not more than seven seconds, the test may be conducted with the gear retracted;

(3) The wing flaps in the takeoff position(s); and

(4) A climb speed as specified in §23.65(a)(4).

[Docket No. 27807, 61 FR 5186, Feb. 9, 1996]

§23.66 Takeoff climb: One-engine inoperative.

For normal, utility, and acrobatic category reciprocating engine-powered airplanes of more than 6,000 pounds maximum weight, and turbine engine-powered airplanes in the normal, utility, and acrobatic category, the steady gradient of climb or descent must be determined at each weight, altitude, and ambient temperature within the operational limits established by the applicant with—

(a) The critical engine inoperative and its propeller in the position it rapidly and automatically assumes;

(b) The remaining engine(s) at takeoff power;

(c) The landing gear extended, except that if the landing gear can be retracted in not more than seven seconds, the test may be conducted with the gear retracted;

(d) The wing flaps in the takeoff position(s):

(e) The wings level; and

(f) A climb speed equal to that achieved at 50 feet in the demonstration of §23.53.

[Docket No. 27807, 61 FR 5186, Feb. 9, 1996]

§23.67 Climb: One engine inoperative.

(a) For normal, utility, and acrobatic category reciprocating engine-powered airplanes of 6,000 pounds or less maximum weight, the following apply:

(1) Except for those airplanes that meet the requirements prescribed in §23.562(d), each airplane with a V_{SO} of more than 61 knots must be able to maintain a steady climb gradient of at least 1.5 percent at a pressure altitude of 5,000 feet with the—

(i) Critical engine inoperative and its propeller in the minimum drag position;

(ii) Remaining engine(s) at not more than maximum continuous power;

(iii) Landing gear retracted;

(iv) Wing flaps retracted; and

(v) Climb speed not less than 1.2 V_{S1}.

(2) For each airplane that meets the requirements prescribed in §23.562(d), or that has a V_{SO} of 61 knots or less, the steady gradient of climb or descent at a pressure altitude of 5,000 feet must be determined with the—

(i) Critical engine inoperative and its propeller in the minimum drag position;

(ii) Remaining engine(s) at not more than maximum continuous power;

(iii) Landing gear retracted;

(iv) Wing flaps retracted; and

(v) Climb speed not less than 1.2 V_{S1}.

(b) For normal, utility, and acrobatic category reciprocating engine-powered airplanes of more than 6,000 pounds maximum weight, and turbine engine-powered airplanes in the normal, utility, and acrobatic category—

(1) The steady gradient of climb at an altitude of 400 feet above the takeoff must be measurably positive with the—

(i) Critical engine inoperative and its propeller in the minimum drag position;

(ii) Remaining engine(s) at takeoff power;

(iii) Landing gear retracted;

(iv) Wing flaps in the takeoff position(s); and

(v) Climb speed equal to that achieved at 50 feet in the demonstration of §23.53.

(2) The steady gradient of climb must not be less than 0.75 percent at an altitude of 1,500 feet above the takeoff surface, or landing surface, as appropriate, with the—

(i) Critical engine inoperative and its propeller in the minimum drag position;

(ii) Remaining engine(s) at not more than maximum continuous power;

(iii) Landing gear retracted;

(iv) Wing flaps retracted; and

(v) Climb speed not less than 1.2 V_{S1}.

(c) For commuter category airplanes, the following apply:

(1) *Takeoff; landing gear extended.* The steady gradient of climb at the altitude of the takeoff surface must be measurably positive for two-engine airplanes, not less than 0.3 percent for three-engine airplanes, or 0.5 percent for four-engine airplanes with—

23

(i) The critical engine inoperative and its propeller in the position it rapidly and automatically assumes;

(ii) The remaining engine(s) at takeoff power;

(iii) The landing gear extended, and all landing gear doors open;

(iv) The wing flaps in the takeoff position(s);

(v) The wings level; and

(vi) A climb speed equal to V_2.

(2) *Takeoff; landing gear retracted.* The steady gradient of climb at an altitude of 400 feet above the takeoff surface must be not less than 2.0 percent of two-engine airplanes, 2.3 percent for three-engine airplanes, and 2.6 percent for four-engine airplanes with—

(i) The critical engine inoperative and its propeller in the position it rapidly and automatically assumes;

(ii) The remaining engine(s) at takeoff power;

(iii) The landing gear retracted;

(iv) The wing flaps in the takeoff position(s);

(v) A climb speed equal to V_2.

(3) *Enroute.* The steady gradient of climb at an altitude of 1,500 feet above the takeoff or landing surface, as appropriate, must be not less than 1.2 percent for two-engine airplanes, 1.5 percent for three-engine airplanes, and 1.7 percent for four-engine airplanes with—

(i) The critical engine inoperative and its propeller in the minimum drag position;

(ii) The remaining engine(s) at not more than maximum continuous power;

(iii) The landing gear retracted;

(iv) The wing flaps retracted; and

(v) A climb speed not less than 1.2 V_{S1}.

(4) *Discontinued approach.* The steady gradient of climb at an altitude of 400 feet above the landing surface must be not less than 2.1 percent for two-engine airplanes, 2.4 percent for three-engine airplanes, and 2.7 percent for four-engine airplanes, with—

(i) The critical engine inoperative and its propeller in the minimum drag position;

(ii) The remaining engine(s) at takeoff power;

(iii) Landing gear retracted;

(iv) Wing flaps in the approach position(s) in which V_{S1} for these position(s) does not exceed 110 percent of the V_{S1} for the related all-engines-operated landing position(s); and

(v) A climb speed established in connection with normal landing procedures but not exceeding 1.5 V_{S1}.

[Docket No. 27807, 61 FR 5186, Feb. 9, 1996]

§23.69 Enroute climb/descent.

(a) *All engines operating.* The steady gradient and rate of climb must be determined at each weight, altitude, and ambient temperature within the operational limits established by the applicant with—

(1) Not more than maximum continuous power on each engine;

(2) The landing gear retracted;

(3) The wing flaps retracted; and

(4) A climb speed not less than 1.3 V_{S1}.

(b) *One engine inoperative.* The steady gradient and rate of climb/descent must be determined at each weight, altitude, and ambient temperature within the operational limits established by the applicant with—

(1) The critical engine inoperative and its propeller in the minimum drag position;

(2) The remaining engine(s) at not more than maximum continuous power;

(3) The landing gear retracted;

(4) The wing flaps retracted; and

(5) A climb speed not less than 1.2 V_{S1}.

[Docket No. 27807, 61 FR 5187, Feb. 9, 1996]

§23.71 Glide: Single-engine airplanes.

The maximum horizontal distance traveled in still air, in nautical miles, per 1,000 feet of altitude lost in a glide, and the speed necessary to achieve this must be determined with the engine inoperative, its propeller in the minimum drag position, and landing gear and wing flaps in the most favorable available position.

[Docket No. 27807, 61 FR 5187, Feb. 9, 1996]

§23.73 Reference landing approach speed.

(a) For normal, utility, and acrobatic category reciprocating engine-powered airplanes of 6,000 pounds or less maximum weight, the reference landing approach speed, V_{REF}, must not be less than the greater of V_{MC}, determined in §23.149(b) with the wing flaps in the most extended takeoff position, and 1.3 V_{S0}.

(b) For normal, utility, and acrobatic category reciprocating engine-powered airplanes of more than 6,000 pounds maximum weight, and turbine engine-powered airplanes in the normal, utility, and acrobatic category, the reference landing approach speed, V_{REF}, must not be less than the greater of V_{MC}, determined in §23.149(c), and 1.3 V_{S0}.

(c) For commuter category airplanes, the reference landing approach speed, V_{REF} must not be less than the greater of 1.05 V_{MC}, determined in §23.149(c), and 1.3 V_{S0}.

[Docket No. 27807, 61 FR 5187, Feb. 9, 1996]

§23.75 Landing distance.

The horizontal distance necessary to land and come to a complete stop from a point 50 feet above the landing surface must be determined, for standard temperatures at each weight and altitude within the operational limits established for landing, as follows:

(a) A steady approach at not less than V_{REF}, determined in accordance with §23.73 (a), (b), or (c), as appropriate, must be maintained down to the 50 foot height and—

(1) The steady approach must be at a gradient of descent not greater than 5.2 percent (3 degrees) down to the 50-foot height.

(2) In addition, an applicant may demonstrate by tests that a maximum steady approach gradient steeper than 5.2 percent, down to the 50-foot height, is safe. The gradient must be established as an operating limitation and the information necessary to display the gradient must be available to the pilot by an appropriate instrument.

(b) A constant configuration must be maintained throughout the maneuver.

(c) The landing must be made without excessive vertical acceleration or tendency to bounce, nose over, ground loop, porpoise, or water loop.

(d) It must be shown that a safe transition to the balked landing conditions of §23.77 can be made from the conditions that exist at the 50 foot height, at maximum landing weight, or at the maximum landing weight for altitude and temperature of §23.63 (c)(2) or (d)(2), as appropriate.

(e) The brakes must be used so as to not cause excessive wear of brakes or tires.

(f) Retardation means other than wheel brakes may be used if that means—

(1) Is safe and reliable; and

(2) Is used so that consistent results can be expected in service.

(3) Is such that no more than average skill is required to control the airplane.

(g) If any device is used that depends on the operation of any engine, and the landing distance would be increased when a landing is made with that engine inoperative, the landing distance must be determined with that engine inoperative unless the use of other compensating means will result in a landing distance not more than that with each engine operating.

[Amdt. 23–21, 43 FR 2318, Jan. 16, 1978; as amended by Amdt. 23–34, 52 FR 1828, Jan. 15, 1987; Amdt. 23–42, 56 FR 351, Jan. 3, 1991; Amdt. 23–50, 61 FR 5187, Feb. 9, 1996]

§23.77 Balked landing.

(a) Each normal, utility, and acrobatic category reciprocating engine-powered airplane at 6,000 pounds or less maximum weight must be able to maintain a steady gradient of climb at sea level of at least 3.3 percent with—

(1) Takeoff power on each engine;

(2) The landing gear extended;

(3) The wing flaps in the landing position, except that if the flaps may safely be retracted in two seconds or less without loss of altitude and without sudden changes of angle of attack, they may be retracted; and

(4) A climb speed equal to V_{REF}, as defined in §23.73(a).

(b) Each normal, utility, and acrobatic category reciprocating engine-powered airplane of more than 6,000 pounds maximum weight and each normal, utility, and acrobatic category turbine engine-powered airplane must be able to maintain a steady gradient of climb of at least 2.5 percent with—

(1) Not more than the power that is available on each engine eight seconds after initiation of movement of the power controls from minimum flight-idle position;

(2) The landing gear extended;

(3) The wing flaps in the landing position; and

(4) A climb speed equal to V_{REF}, as defined in §23.73(b).

(c) Each commuter category airplane must be able to maintain a steady gradient of climb of at least 3.2 percent with—

(1) Not more than the power that is available on each engine eight seconds after initiation of movement of the power controls from the minimum flight idle position;

(2) Landing gear extended;

(3) Wing flaps in the landing position; and

(4) A climb speed equal to V_{REF}, as defined in §23.73(c).

[Amdt. 23–21, 43 FR 2318, Jan. 16, 1978; as amended by Amdt. 23–34, 52 FR 1828, Jan. 15, 1987; Amdt. 23–24, 52 FR 34745, Sept. 14, 1987; Amdt. 23–50, 61 FR 5187, Feb. 9, 1996]

Flight Characteristics

§23.141 General.

The airplane must meet the requirements of §§23.143 through 23.253 at all practical loading conditions and operating altitudes for which certification has been requested, not exceeding the maximum operating altitude established under §23.1527, and without requiring exceptional piloting skill, alertness, or strength.

[Docket No. 26269, 58 FR 42156, Aug. 6, 1993]

Controllability and Maneuverability

§23.143 General.

(a) The airplane must be safely controllable and maneuverable during all flight phases including—

(1) Takeoff;

(2) Climb;

(3) Level flight;

(4) Descent;

(5) Go-around; and

(6) Landing (power on and power off) with the wing flaps extended and retracted.

(b) It must be possible to make a smooth transition from one flight condition to another (including turns and slips) without danger of exceeding the limit load factor, under any probable operating condition (including, for multiengine airplanes, those conditions normally encountered in the sudden failure of any engine).

(c) If marginal conditions exist with regard to required pilot strength, the control forces necessary must be determined by quantitative tests. In no case may the control forces under the conditions specified in paragraphs (a) and (b) of this section exceed those prescribed in the following table:

Values in pounds force applied to the relevant control	Pitch	Roll	Yaw
(a) For temporary application:			
Stick	60	30	—
Wheel (Two hands on rim)	75	50	—
Wheel (One hand on rim)	50	25	—
Rudder Pedal	—	—	150
(b) For prolonged application	10	5	20

[Docket No, 4080, 29 FR 17955, Dec. 18, 1964; as amended by Amdt. 23–14, 38 FR 31819, Nov. 19, 1973; Amdt. 23–17, 41 FR 55464, Dec. 20, 1976; Amdt. 23–45, 58 FR 42156, Aug. 6, 1993; Amdt. 23–50, 61 FR 5188, Feb. 9, 1996]

§23.145 Longitudinal control.

(a) With the airplane as nearly as possible in trim at 1.3 V_{S1}, it must be possible, at speeds below the trim speed, to pitch the nose downward so that the rate of increase in airspeed allows prompt acceleration to the trim speed with—

(1) Maximum continuous power on each engine

(2) Power off; and

(3) Wing flap and landing gear—

(i) retracted, and

(ii) extended.

(b) Unless otherwise required, it must be possible to carry out the following maneuvers without requiring the application of single-handed control forces exceeding those specified in §23.143(c). The trimming controls must not be adjusted during the maneuvers:

(1) With the landing gear extended, the flaps retracted, and the airplanes as nearly as possible in trim at 1.4 V_{S1}, extend the flaps as rapidly as possible and allow the airspeed to transition from 1.4 V_{S1} to 1.4 V_{SO}:

(i) With power off; and

(ii) With the power necessary to maintain level flight in the initial condition.

(2) With landing gear and flaps extended, power off, and the airplane as nearly as possible in trim at 1.3 V_{SO}, quickly apply takeoff power and retract the flaps as rapidly as possible to the recommended go around setting and allow the airspeed to transition from 1.3 V_{SO} to 1.3 V_{S1}. Retract the gear when a positive rate of climb is established.

(3) With landing gear and flaps extended, in level flight, power necessary to attain level flight at 1.1 V_{SO}, and the airplane as nearly as possible in trim, it must be possible to maintain approximately level flight while retracting the flaps as rapidly as possible with simultaneous application of not more than maximum continuous power. If gated flat positions are provided, the flap retraction may be demonstrated in stages with power and trim reset for level flight at 1.1 V_{S1}, in the initial configuration for each stage—

(i) From the fully extended position to the most extended gated position;

(ii) Between intermediate gated positions, if applicable; and

(iii) From the least extended gated position to the fully retracted position.

(4) With power off, flaps and landing gear retracted and the airplane as nearly as possible in trim at 1.4 V_{S1}, apply takeoff power rapidly while maintaining the same airspeed.

(5) With power off, landing gear and flaps extended, and the airplane as nearly as possible in trim at V_{REF}, obtain and maintain airspeeds between 1.1 V_{SO}, and either 1.7 V_{SO} or V_{FE}, whichever is lower without requiring the application of two-handed control forces exceeding those specified in §23.143(c).

(6) With maximum takeoff power, landing gear retracted, flaps in the takeoff position, and the airplane as nearly as possible in trim at V_{FE} appropriate to the takeoff flap position, retract the flaps as rapidly as possible while maintaining constant speed.

(c) At speeds above V_{MO}/M_{MO}, and up to the maximum speed shown under §23.251, a maneuvering capability of 1.5 g must be demonstrated to provide a margin to recover from upset or inadvertent speed increase.

(d) It must be possible, with a pilot control force of not more than 10 pounds, to maintain a speed of not more than V_{REF} during a power-off glide with landing gear and wing flaps extended, for any weight of the airplane, up to and including the maximum weight.

(e) By using normal flight and power controls, except as otherwise noted in paragraphs (e)(1) and (e)(2) of this section, it must be possible to establish a zero rate of descent at an attitude suitable for a controlled landing without exceeding the operational and structural limitations of the airplane, as follows:

(1) For single-engine and multiengine airplanes, without the use of the primary longitudinal control system.

(2) For multiengine airplanes—

(i) Without the use of the primary directional control; and

(ii) If a single failure of any one connecting or transmitting link would affect both the longitudinal and directional primary control system, without the primary longitudinal and directional control system.

[Docket No. 26269, 58 FR 42157, Aug. 6, 1993; as amended by Amdt. 23–45, 58 FR 51970, Oct. 5, 1993; Amdt. 23–50, 61 FR 5188, Feb. 9, 1996]

§23.147 Directional and lateral control.

(a) For each multiengine airplane, it must be possible, while holding the wings level within five degrees, to make sudden changes in heading safely in both directions. This ability must be shown at 1.4 V_{S1} with heading changes up to 15 degrees, except that the heading change at which the rudder force corresponds to the limits specified in §23.143 need not be exceeded, with the—

(1) Critical engine inoperative and its propeller in the minimum drag position;

(2) Remaining engines at maximum continuous power;

(3) Landing gear—

(i) Retracted; and

(ii) Extended; and

(4) Flaps retracted.

(b) For each multiengine airplane, it must be possible to regain full control of the airplane without exceeding a bank angle of 45 degrees, reaching a dangerous attitude or encountering dangerous characteristics, in the event of a sudden and complete failure of the critical engine, making allowance for a delay of two seconds in the initiation of recovery action appropriate to the situation, with the airplane initially in trim, in the following condition:

(1) Maximum continuous power on each engine;

(2) The wing flaps retracted;

(3) The landing gear retracted;

(4) A speed equal to that at which compliance with §23.69(a) has been shown; and

(5) All propeller controls in the position at which compliance with §23.69(a) has been shown.

(c) For all airplanes, it must be shown that the airplane is safely controllable without the use of the primary lateral control system in any all-engine configuration(s) and at any speed or altitude within the approved operating envelope. It must also be shown that the airplane's flight characteristics are not impaired below a level needed to permit continued safe flight and the ability to maintain attitudes suitable for a controlled landing without exceeding the operational and structural limitations of the airplane. If a single failure of any one connecting or transmitting link in the lateral control system would also cause the loss of additional control system(s), compliance with the above requirement must be shown with those additional systems also assumed to be inoperative.

[Docket No. 27807, 61 FR 5188, Feb. 9, 1996]

§23.149 Minimum control speed.

(a) V_{MC} is the calibrated airspeed at which, when the critical engine is suddenly made inoperative, it is possible to maintain control of the airplane with that engine still inoperative, and thereafter maintain straight flight at the same speed with an angle of bank of not more than 5 degrees. The method used to simulate critical engine failure must represent the most critical mode of powerplant failure expected in service with respect to controllability.

(b) V_{MC} for takeoff must not exceed 1.2 V_{S1}, where V_{S1} is determined at the maximum takeoff weight. V_{MC} must be determined with the most unfavorable weight and center of gravity position and with the airplane airborne and the ground effect negligible, for the takeoff configuration(s) with—

(1) Maximum available takeoff power initially on each engine;

(2) The airplane trimmed for takeoff;

(3) Flaps in the takeoff position(s);

(4) Landing gear retracted; and

(5) All propeller controls in the recommended takeoff position throughout.

(c) For all airplanes except reciprocating engine-powered airplanes of 6,000 pounds or less maximum weight, the conditions of paragraph (a) of this section must also be met for the landing configuration with—

(1) Maximum available takeoff power initially on each engine;

(2) The airplane trimmed for an approach, with all engines operating, at V_{REF} at an approach gradient equal to the steepest used in the landing distance demonstration of §23.75;

(3) Flaps in the landing position;

(4) Landing gear extended; and

(5) All propeller controls in the position recommended for approach with all engines operating.

(d) A minimum speed to intentionally render the critical engine inoperative must be established and designated as the safe, intentional, one-engine-inoperative speed, V_{SSE}.

(e) At V_{MC}, the rudder pedal force required to maintain control must not exceed 150 pounds and it must not be necessary to reduce power of the operative engine(s). During the maneuver, the airplane must not assume any dangerous attitude and it must be possible to prevent a heading change of more than 20 degrees.

(f) At the option of the applicant, to comply with the requirements of §23.51(c)(1), V_{MCG} may be determined. V_{MCG} is the minimum control speed on the ground, and is the calibrated airspeed during the takeoff run at which, when the critical engine is suddenly made inoperative, it is possible to maintain control of the airplane using the rudder control alone (without the use of nosewheel steering), as limited by 150 pounds of force, and using the lateral control to the extent of keeping the wings level to enable the takeoff to be safely continued. In the determination of V_{MCG}, assuming that the path of the airplane accelerating with all engines operating is along the centerline of the runway, its path from the point at which the critical engine is made inoperative to the point at which recovery to a direction parallel to the centerline is completed may not deviate more than 30 feet laterally from the centerline at any point. V_{MCG} must be established with—

(1) The airplane in each takeoff configuration or, at the option of the applicant, in the most critical takeoff configuration;

(2) Maximum available takeoff power on the operating engines;

(3) The most unfavorable center of gravity;

(4) The airplane trimmed for takeoff; and

(5) The most unfavorable weight in the range of takeoff weights.

[Docket No. 27807, 61 FR 5189, Feb. 9, 1996]

§23.151 Acrobatic maneuvers.

Each acrobatic and utility category airplane must be able to perform safely the acrobatic maneuvers for which certification is requested. Safe entry speeds for these maneuvers must be determined.

§23.153 Control during landings.

It must be possible, while in the landing configuration, to safely complete a landing without exceeding the one-hand control force limits specified in §23.143(c) following an approach to land—

(a) At a speed of V_{REF} minus 5 knots;

(b) With the airplane in trim, or as nearly as possible in trim and without the trimming control being moved throughout the maneuver;

(c) At an approach gradient equal to the steepest used in the landing distance demonstration of §23.75; and

(d) With only those power changes, if any, that would be made when landing normally from an approach at V_{REF}.

[Docket No. 27807, 61 FR 5189, Feb. 9, 1996]

§23.155 Elevator control force in maneuvers.

(a) The elevator control force needed to achieve the positive limit maneuvering load factor may not be less than:

(1) For wheel controls, W/100 (where W is the maximum weight) or 20 pounds, whichever is greater, except that it need not be greater than 50 pounds; or

(2) For stick controls, W/140 (where W is the maximum weight) or 15 pounds, whichever is greater, except that it need not be greater than 35 pounds.

(b) The requirement of paragraph (a) of this section must be met at 75 percent of maximum continuous power for reciprocating engines, or the maximum continuous power for turbine engines, and with the wing flaps and landing gear retracted—

(1) In a turn, with the trim setting used for wings level flight at V_O; and

(2) In a turn with the trim setting used for the maximum wings level flight speed, except that the speed may not exceed V_{NE} or V_{MO}/M_{MO}, whichever is appropriate.

(c) There must be no excessive decrease in the gradient of the curve of stick force versus maneuvering load factor with increasing load factor.

[Amdt. 23–14, 38 FR 31819, Nov. 19, 1973; 38 FR 32784, Nov. 28, 1973; as amended by Amdt. 23–45, 58 FR 42158, Aug. 6, 1993; Amdt. 23–50, 61 FR 5189, Feb. 9, 1996]

§23.157 Rate of roll.

(a) *Takeoff.* It must be possible, using a favorable combination of controls, to roll the airplane from a steady 30-degree banked turn through an angle of 60 degrees, so as to reverse the direction of the turn within:

(1) For an airplane of 6,000 pounds or less maximum weight, 5 seconds from initiation of roll; and

(2) For an airplane of over 6,000 pounds maximum weight,

$$(W + 500)/1{,}300$$

seconds, but not more than 10 seconds, where W is the weight in pounds.

(b) The requirement of paragraph (a) of this section must be met when rolling the airplane in each direction with—

(1) Flaps in the takeoff position;

(2) Landing gear retracted;

(3) For a single-engine airplane, at maximum takeoff power; and for a multiengine airplane with the critical engine inoperative and the propeller in the minimum drag position, and the other engines at maximum takeoff power; and

(4) The airplane trimmed at a speed equal to the greater of 1.2 V_{S1} or 1.1 V_{MC}, or as nearly as possible in trim for straight flight.

(c) *Approach.* It must be possible, using a favorable combination of controls, to roll the airplane from a steady 30-degree banked turn through an angle of 60 degrees, so as to reverse the direction of the turn within:

(1) For an airplane of 6,000 pounds or less maximum weight, 4 seconds from initiation of roll; and

(2) For an airplane of over 6,000 pounds maximum weight,

$$(W + 2{,}800)/2{,}200$$

seconds, but not more than 7 seconds, where W is the weight in pounds.

(d) The requirement of paragraph (c) of this section must be met when rolling the airplane in each direction in the following conditions—

(1) Flaps in the landing position(s);

(2) Landing gear extended;

(3) All engines operating at the power for a 3 degree approach; and

(4) The airplane trimmed at V_{REF}.

[Amdt. 23–14, 38 FR 31819, Nov. 19, 1973; as amended by Amdt. 23–45, 58 FR 42158, Aug. 6, 1993; Amdt. 23–50, 61 FR 5189, Feb. 9, 1996]

TRIM

§23.161 Trim.

(a) *General.* Each airplane must meet the trim requirements of this section after being trimmed and without further pressure upon, or movement of, the primary controls or their corresponding trim controls by the pilot or the automatic pilot. In addition, it must be possible, in other conditions of loading, configuration, speed and power to ensure that the pilot will not be unduly fatigued or distracted by the need to apply residual control forces exceeding those for prolonged application of §23.143(c). This applies in normal operation of the airplane and, if applicable, to those conditions associated with the failure of one engine for which performance characteristics are established.

(b) *Lateral and directional trim.* The airplane must maintain lateral and directional trim in level flight with the landing gear and wing flaps retracted as follows:

(1) For normal, utility, and acrobatic category airplanes, at a speed of 0.9 V_H, V_C, or V_{MO}/M_{MO}, whichever is lowest; and

(2) For commuter category airplanes, at all speeds from 1.4 V_{S1} to the lesser of V_H or V_{MO}/M_{MO}.

(c) *Longitudinal trim.* The airplane must maintain longitudinal trim under each of the following conditions:

(1) A climb with—

(i) Takeoff power, landing gear retracted, wing flaps in the takeoff position(s), at the speeds used in determining the climb performance required by §23.65; and

(ii) Maximum continuous power at the speeds and in the configuration used in determining the climb performance required by §23.69(a).

(2) Level flight at all speeds from the lesser of V_H and either V_{NO} or V_{MO}/M_{MO} (as appropriate), to 1.4 V_{S1}, with the landing gear and flaps retracted.

(3) A descent at V_{NO} or V_{MO}/M_{MO}, whichever is applicable, with power off and with the landing gear and flaps retracted.

(4) Approach with landing gear extended and with—

(i) A 3 degree angle of descent, with flaps retracted and at a speed of 1.4 V_{S1};

(ii) A 3 degree angle of descent, flaps in the landing position(s) at V_{REF}; and

(iii) An approach gradient equal to the steepest used in the landing distance demonstrations of §23.75, flaps in the landing position(s) at V_{REF}.

(d) In addition, each multiple airplane must maintain longitudinal and directional trim, and the lateral control force must not exceed 5 pounds at the speed used in complying with §23.67(a), (b)(2), or (c)(3), as appropriate, with—

(1) The critical engine inoperative, and if applicable, its propeller in the minimum drag position;

(2) The remaining engines at maximum continuous power;

(3) The landing gear retracted;

(4) Wing flaps retracted; and

(5) An angle of bank of not more than five degrees.

(e) In addition, each commuter category airplane for which, in the determination of the takeoff path in accordance with §23.57, the climb in the takeoff configuration at V_2 extends beyond 400 feet above the takeoff surface, it must be possible to reduce the longitudinal and lateral control forces to 10 pounds and 5 pounds, respectively, and the directional control force must not exceed 50 pounds at V_2 with—

(1) The critical engine inoperative and its propeller in the minimum drag position;

(2) The remaining engine(s) at takeoff power;

(3) Landing gear retracted;

(4) Wing flaps in the takeoff position(s); and

(5) An angle of bank not exceeding 5 degrees.

[Docket No. 4080, 29 FR 17955, Dec. 18, 1964; as amended by Amdt. 23–21, 43 FR 2318, Jan. 16, 1978; Amdt. 23–34, 52 FR 1828, Jan. 15, 1987; Amdt. 23–42, 56 FR 351, Jan. 3, 1991; 56 FR 5455, Feb. 11, 1991; Amdt. 23–50, 61 FR 5190, Feb. 9, 1996]

STABILITY

§23.171 General.

The airplane must be longitudinally, directionally, and laterally stable under §§23.173 through 23.181. In addition, the airplane must show suitable stability and control "feel" (static stability) in any condition normally encountered in service, if flight tests show it is necessary for safe operation.

§23.173 Static longitudinal stability.

Under the conditions specified in §23.175 and with the airplane trimmed as indicated, the characteristics of the elevator control forces and the friction within the control system must be as follows:

(a) A pull must be required to obtain and maintain speeds below the specified trim speed and a push required to obtain and maintain speeds above the specified trim speed. This must be shown at any speed that can be obtained, except that speeds requiring a control force in excess of 40 pounds or speeds above the maximum allowable speed or below the minimum speed for steady unstalled flight, need not be considered.

(b) The airspeed must return to within the tolerances specified for applicable categories of airplanes when the control force is slowly released at any speed within the speed range specified in paragraph (a) of this section. The applicable tolerances are—

(1) The airspeed must return to within plus or minus 10 percent of the original trim airspeed; and

(2) For commuter category airplanes, the airspeed must return to within plus or minus 7.5 percent of the original trim airspeed for the cruising condition specified in §23.175(b).

(c) The stick force must vary with speed so that any substantial speed change results in a stick force clearly perceptible to the pilot.

[Docket No. 4080, 29 FR 17955, Dec. 18, 1964; as amended by Amdt. 23–14, 38 FR 31820 Nov. 19, 1973; Amdt. 23–34, 52 FR 1828, Jan. 15, 1987]

§23.175 Demonstration of static longitudinal stability.

Static longitudinal stability must be shown as follows:

(a) *Climb.* The stick force curve must have a stable slope at speeds between 85 and 115 percent of the trim speed, with—

(1) Flaps retracted;

(2) Landing gear retracted;

(3) Maximum continuous power; and

(4) The airplane trimmed at the speed used in determining the climb performance required by §23.69(a).

(b) *Cruise.* With flaps and landing gear retracted and the airplane in trim with power for level flight at representative cruising speeds at high and low altitudes, including speeds up to V_{NO} or V_{MO}/M_{MO}, as appropriate, except that the speed need not exceed V_H—

(1) For normal, utility, and acrobatic category airplanes, the stick force curve must have a stable slope at all speeds within a range that is the greater of 15 percent of the trim speed plus the resulting free return speed range, or 40 knots plus the resulting free return speed range, above and below the trim speed, except that the slope need not be stable—

(i) At speeds less than 1.3 V_{S1}; or

(ii) For airplanes with V_{NE} established under §23.1505(a), at speeds greater than V_{NE}; or

(iii) For airplanes with V_{MO}/M_{MO} established under §23.1505(c), at speeds greater than V_{FC}/M_{FC}.

(2) For commuter category airplanes, the stick force curve must have a stable slope at all speeds within a range of 50 knots plus the resulting free return speed range, above and below the trim speed, except that the slope need not be stable—

(i) At speeds less than 1.4 V_{S1}; or

(ii) At speeds greater than V_{FC}/M_{FC}; or

(iii) At speeds that require a stick force greater than 50 pounds.

(c) *Landing.* The stick force curve must have a stable slope at speeds between 1.1 V_{S1} and 1.8 V_{S1} with—

(1) Flaps in the landing position;

(2) Landing gear extended; and

(3) The airplane trimmed at—

(i) V_{REF}, or the minimum trim speed if higher, with power off; and

(ii) V_{REF} with enough power to maintain a 3 degree angle of descent.

[Docket No. 27807, 61 FR 5190, Feb. 9, 1996]

§23.177 Static directional and lateral stability.

(a) The static directional stability, as shown by the tendency to recover from a wings level sideslip with the rudder free, must be positive for any landing gear and flap position appropriate to the takeoff, climb, cruise, approach, and landing configurations. This must be shown with symmetrical power up to maximum continuous power, and at speeds from 1.2 V_{S1} up to the maximum allowable speed for the condition being investigated. The angle of sideslip for these tests must be appropriate to the type of airplane. At larger angles of sideslip, up to that at which full rudder is used or a control force limit in §23.143 is reached, whichever occurs first, and at speeds from 1.2 V_{S1} to V_O, the rudder pedal force must not reverse.

(b) The static lateral stability, as shown by the tendency to raise the low wing in a sideslip, must be positive for all landing gear and flap positions. This must be shown with symmetrical power up to 75 percent of maximum continuous power at speeds above 1.2 V_{S1} in the take off configuration(s) and at speeds above 1.3 V_{S1} in other configurations, up to the maximum allowable speed for the configuration being investigated, in the takeoff, climb, cruise, and approach configurations. For the landing configuration, the power must be that necessary to maintain a 3 degree angle of descent in coordinated flight. The static lateral stability must not be negative at 1.2 V_{S1} in the takeoff configuration, or at 1.3 V_{S1} in other configurations. The angle of sideslip for these tests must be appropriate to the type of airplane, but in no case may the constant heading sideslip angle be less than that obtainable with a 10 degree bank, or if less, the maximum bank angle obtainable with full rudder deflection or 150 pound rudder force.

(c) Paragraph (b) of this section does not apply to acrobatic category airplanes certificated for inverted flight.

(d) In straight, steady slips at 1.2 V_{S1} for any landing gear and flap positions, and for any symmetrical power conditions up to 50 percent of maximum continuous power, the aileron and rudder control movements and forces must increase steadily, but not necessarily in constant proportion, as the angle of sideslip is increased up to the maximum appropriate to the type of airplane. At larger slip angles, up to the angle at which full rudder or aileron control is used or a control force limit contained in §23.143 is reached, the aileron and rudder control movements and forces must not reverse as the angle of sideslip is increased. Rapid entry into, and recovery from, a maximum sideslip considered appropriate for the airplane must not result in uncontrollable flight characteristics.

[Docket No. 27807, 61 FR 5190, Feb. 9, 1996]

§23.181 Dynamic stability.

(a) Any short period oscillation not including combined lateral-directional oscillations occurring between the stalling speed and the maximum allowable speed appropriate to the configuration of the airplane must be heavily damped with the primary controls—

(1) Free; and

(2) In a fixed position.

(b) Any combined lateral-directional oscillations ("Dutch roll") occurring between the stalling speed and the maximum allowable speed appropriate to the configuration of the airplane must be damped to $1/10$ amplitude in 7 cycles with the primary controls—

(1) Free; and

(2) In a fixed position.

(c) If it is determined that the function of a stability augmentation system. reference §23.672, is needed to meet the flight characteristic requirements of this part, the primary control requirements of paragraphs (a)(2) and (b)(2) of this section are not applicable to the tests needed to verify the acceptability of that system.

(d) During the conditions as specified in §23.175, when the longitudinal control force required to maintain speeds differing from the trim speed by at least plus and minus 15 percent is suddenly released, the response of the airplane must not exhibit any dangerous characteristics nor be excessive in relation to the magnitude of the control force released. Any long-period oscillation of flight path, phugoid oscillation, that results must not be so unstable as to increase the pilot's workload or otherwise endanger the airplane.

[Amdt. 23–21, 43 FR 2318, Jan. 16, 1978; as amended by Amdt. 23–45, 58 FR 42158, Aug. 6, 1993]

STALLS

§23.201 Wings level stall.

(a) It must be possible to produce and to correct roll by unreversed use of the rolling control and to produce and to correct yaw by unreversed use of the directional control, up to the time the airplane stalls.

(b) The wings level stall characteristics must be demonstrated in flight as follows. Starting from a speed at least 10 knots above the stall speed, the elevator control must be pulled back so that the rate of speed reduction will not exceed one knot per second until a stall is produced, as shown by either:

(1) An uncontrollable downward pitching motion of the airplane;

(2) A downward pitching motion of the airplane that results from the activation of a stall avoidance device (for example, stick pusher); or

(3) The control reaching the stop.

(c) Normal use of elevator control for recovery is allowed after the downward pitching motion of paragraphs (b)(1) or (b)(2) of this section has unmistakably been produced, or after the control has been held against the stop for not less than the longer of two seconds or the time employed in the minimum steady slight speed determination of §23.49.

(d) During the entry into and the recovery from the maneuver, it must be possible to prevent more than 15 degrees of roll or yaw by the normal use of controls.

(e) Compliance with the requirements of this section must be shown under the following conditions:

(1) *Wing flaps.* Retracted, fully extended, and each intermediate normal operating position.

(2) *Landing gear.* Retracted and extended.

(3) *Cowl flaps.* Appropriate to configuration.

(4) *Power:*

(i) Power off; and

(ii) 75 percent of maximum continuous power. However, if the power-to-weight ratio at 75 percent of maximum continuous power result in extreme nose-up attitudes, the test may be carried out with the power required for level flight in the landing configuration at maximum landing weight and a speed of 1.4 V_{S0}, except that the power may not be less than 50 percent of maximum continuous power.

(5) *Trim.* The airplane trimmed at a speed as near 1.5 V_{S1} as practicable.

(6) *Propeller.* Full increase r.p.m. position for the power off condition.

[Docket No. 27807, 61 FR 5191, Feb. 9, 1996]

§23.203 Turning flight and accelerated turning stalls.

Turning flight and accelerated turning stalls must be demonstrated in tests as follows:

(a) Establish and maintain a coordinated turn in a 30 degree bank. Reduce speed by steadily and progressively tightening the turn with the elevator until the airplane is stalled, as defined in §23.201(b). The rate of speed reduction must be constant, and—

(1) For a turning flight stall, may not exceed one knot per second; and

(2) For an accelerated turning stall, be 3 to 5 knots per second with steadily increasing normal acceleration.

(b) After the airplane has stalled, as defined in §23.201(b), it must be possible to regain wings level flight by normal use of the flight controls, but without increasing power and without—

(1) Excessive loss of altitude;

(2) Undue pitchup;

(3) Uncontrollable tendency to spin;

(4) Exceeding a bank angle of 60 degrees in the original direction of the turn or 30 degrees in the opposite direction in the case of turning flight stalls;

(5) Exceeding a bank angle of 90 degrees in the original direction of the turn or 60 degrees in the opposite direction in the case of accelerated turning stalls; and

(6) Exceeding the maximum permissible speed or allowable limit load factor.

(c) Compliance with the requirements of this section must be shown under the following conditions:

(1) *Wing flaps:* Retracted, fully extended, and each intermediate normal operating position;

(2) *Landing gear:* Retracted and extended;

(3) *Cowl flaps:* Appropriate to configuration;

(4) *Power:*

(i) Power off; and

(ii) 75 percent of maximum continuous power. However, if the power-to-weight ratio at 75 percent of maximum continuous power results in extreme nose-up attitudes, the test may be carried out with the power required for level flight in the landing configuration at maximum landing weight and a speed of 1.4 V_{S0}, except that the power may not be less than 50 percent of maximum continuous power.

(5) *Trim:* The airplane trimmed at a speed as near 1.5 V_{S1} as practicable.

(6) *Propeller.* Full increase rpm position for the power off condition.

[Amdt. 23–14, 38 FR 31820, Nov. 19, 1973; as amended by Amdt. 23–45, 58 FR 42159, Aug. 6, 1993; Amdt. 23–50, 61 FR 5191, Feb. 9, 1996]

§23.207 Stall warning.

(a) There must be a clear and distinctive stall warning, with the flaps and landing gear in any normal position, in straight and turning flight.

(b) The stall warning may be furnished either through the inherent aerodynamic qualities of the airplane or by a device that will give clearly distinguishable indications under expected conditions of flight. However, a visual stall warning device that requires the attention of the crew within the cockpit is not acceptable by itself.

(c) During the stall tests required by §23.201(b) and §23.203(a)(1), the stall warning must begin at a speed exceeding the stalling speed by a margin of not less than 5 knots and must continue until the stall occurs.

(d) When following procedures furnished in accordance with §23.1585, the stall warning must not occur during a takeoff with all engines operating, a takeoff continued with one engine inoperative, or during an approach to landing.

(e) During the stall tests required by §23.203(a)(2), the stall warning must begin sufficiently in advance of the stall for the stall to be averted by pilot action taken after the stall warning first occurs.

(f) For acrobatic category airplanes, an artificial stall warning may be mutable, provided that it is armed automatically during takeoff and rearmed automatically in the approach configuration.

[Amdt. 23–14, 38 FR 31820, Nov. 19, 1973; as amended by Amdt. 23–45, 58 FR 42159, Aug. 6, 1993; Amdt. 23–50, 61 FR 5191, Feb. 9, 1996]

SPINNING

§23.221 Spinning.

(a) *Normal category airplanes.* A single-engine, normal category airplane must be able to recover from a one-turn spin or a three-second spin, whichever takes longer, in not more than one additional turn after initiation of the first control action for recovery, or demonstrate compliance with the optional spin resistant requirements of this section.

(1) The following apply to one turn or three second spins:

(i) For both the flaps-retracted and flaps-extended conditions, the applicable airspeed limit and positive limit maneuvering load factor must not be exceeded;

(ii) No control forces or characteristic encountered during the spin or recovery may adversely affect prompt recovery;

(iii) It must be impossible to obtain unrecoverable spins with any use of the flight or engine power controls either at the entry into or during the spin; and

(iv) For the flaps-extended condition, the flaps may be retracted during the recovery but not before rotation has ceased.

(2) At the applicant's option, the airplane may be demonstrated to be spin resistant by the following:

(i) During the stall maneuver contained in §23.201, the pitch control must be pulled back and held against the stop. Then, using ailerons and rudders in the proper direction, it must be possible to maintain wings-level flight within 15 degrees of bank and to roll the airplane from a 30 degree bank in one direction to a 30 degree bank in the other direction;

(ii) Reduce the airplane speed using pitch control at a rate of approximately one knot per second until the pitch control reaches the stop; then, with the pitch control pulled back and held against the stop, apply full rudder control in a manner to promote spin entry for a period of seven seconds or through a 360 degree heading change, whichever occurs first. If the 360 degree heading change is reached first, it must have taken no fewer than four seconds. This maneuver must be performed first with the ailerons in the neutral position, and then with the ailerons deflected opposite the direction of turn in the most adverse manner. Power and airplane configuration must be set in accordance with §23.201(e) without change during the maneuver. At the end of seven seconds or a 360 degree heading change, the airplane must respond immediately and normally to primary flight controls applied to regain coordinated, unstalled flight without reversal of control effect and without exceeding the temporary control forces specified by §23.143(c); and

(iii) Compliance with §§23.201 and 23.203 must be demonstrated with the airplane in uncoordinated flight, corresponding to one ball width displacement on a slip-skid indicator, unless one ball width displacement cannot be obtained with full rudder, in which case the demonstration must be with full rudder applied.

(b) *Utility category airplanes.* A utility category airplane must meet the requirements of paragraph (a) of this section. In addition, the requirements of paragraph (c) of this section and §23.807(b)(7) must be met if approval for spinning is requested.

(c) *Acrobatic category airplanes.* An acrobatic category airplane must meet the spin requirements of paragraph (a) of this section and §23.807(b)(6). In addition, the following requirements must be met in each configuration for which approval for spinning is requested:

(1) The airplane must recover from any point in a spin up to and including six turns, or any greater number of turns for which certification is requested, in not more than one and one-half additional turns after initiation of the first control action for recovery. However, beyond three turns, the spin may be discontinued if spiral characteristics appear.

(2) The applicable airspeed limits and limit maneuvering load factors must not be exceeded. For flaps-extended con-

figurations for which approval is requested, the flaps must not be retracted during the recovery.

(3) It must be impossible to obtain unrecoverable spins with any use of the flight or engine power controls either at the entry into or during the spin.

(4) There must be no characteristics during the spin (such as excessive rates of rotation or extreme oscillatory motion) that might prevent a successful recovery due to disorientation or incapacitation of the pilot.

[Docket No. 27807, 61 FR 5191, Feb. 9, 1996]

GROUND AND WATER HANDLING CHARACTERISTICS

§23.231 Longitudinal stability and control.

(a) A landplane may have no uncontrollable tendency to nose over in any reasonably expected operating condition, including rebound during landing or takeoff. Wheel brakes must operate smoothly and may not induce any undue tendency to nose over.

(b) A seaplane or amphibian may not have dangerous or uncontrollable porpoising characteristics at any normal operating speed on the water.

§23.233 Directional stability and control.

(a) A 90 degree cross-component of wind velocity, demonstrated to be safe for taxiing, takeoff, and landing must be established and must be not less than 0.2 V_{SO}.

(b) The airplane must be satisfactorily controllable in power-off landings at normal landing speed, without using brakes or engine power to maintain a straight path until the speed has decreased to at least 50 percent of the speed at touchdown.

(c) The airplane must have adequate directional control during taxiing.

(d) Seaplanes must demonstrate satisfactory directional stability and control for water operations up to the maximum wind velocity specified in paragraph (a) of this section.

[Docket No. 4080, 29 FR 17955, Dec. 18, 1964; as amended by Amdt. 23–45, 58 FR 42159, Aug. 6, 1993; Amdt. 23–50, 61 FR 5192, Feb. 9, 1996]

§23.235 Operation on unpaved surfaces.

The airplane must be demonstrated to have satisfactory characteristics and the shock-absorbing mechanism must not damage the structure of the airplane when the airplane is taxied on the roughest ground that may reasonably be expected in normal operation and when takeoffs and landings are performed on unpaved runways having the roughest surface that may reasonably be expected in normal operation.

[Docket No. 27807, 61 FR 5192, Feb. 9, 1996]

§23.237 Operation on water.

A wave height, demonstrated to be safe for operation, and any necessary water handling procedures for seaplanes and amphibians must be established.

[Docket No. 27807, 61 FR 5192, Feb. 9, 1996]

§23.239 Spray characteristics.

Spray may not dangerously obscure the vision of the pilots or damage the propellers or other parts of a seaplane or amphibian at any time during taxiing, takeoff, and landing.

MISCELLANEOUS FLIGHT REQUIREMENTS

§23.251 Vibration and buffeting.

There must be no vibration or buffeting severe enough to result in structural damage, and each part of the airplane must be free from excessive vibration, under any appropriate speed and power conditions up to V_D/M_D. In addition, there must be no buffeting in any normal flight condition severe enough to interfere with the satisfactory control of the airplane or cause excessive fatigue to the flight crew. Stall warning buffeting within these limits is allowable.

[Docket No. 26269, 58 FR 42159, Aug. 6, 1993]

§23.253 High speed characteristics.

If a maximum operating speed V_{MO}/M_{MO} is established under §23.1505(c), the following speed increase and recovery characteristics must be met:

(a) Operating conditions and characteristics likely to cause inadvertent speed increases (including upsets in pitch and roll) must be simulated with the airplane trimmed at any likely speed up to V_{MO}/M_{MO}. These conditions and characteristics include gust upsets, inadvertent control movements, low stick force gradients in relation to control friction, passenger movement, leveling off from climb and descent from Mach to airspeed limit altitude.

(b) Allowing for pilot reaction time after occurrence of the effective inherent or artificial speed warning specified in §23.1303, it must be shown that the airplane can be recovered to a normal attitude and its speed reduced to V_{MO}/M_{MO} without—

(1) Exceeding V_D/M_D, the maximum speed shown under §23.251, or the structural limitations; or

(2) Buffeting that would impair the pilot's ability to read the instruments or to control the airplane for recovery.

(c) There may be no control reversal about any axis at any speed up to the maximum speed shown under §23.251. Any reversal of elevator control force or tendency of the airplane to pitch, roll, or yaw must be mild and readily controllable, using normal piloting techniques.

[Amdt. 23–7, 34 FR 13087, Aug. 13, 1969; as amended by Amdt. 23–26, 45 FR 60170, Sept. 11, 1980; Amdt. 23–45, 58 FR 42160, Aug. 6, 1993; Amdt. 23–50, 61 FR 5192, Feb. 9, 1996]

Subpart C—Structure

GENERAL

§23.301 Loads.

(a) Strength requirements are specified in terms of limit loads (the maximum loads to be expected in service) and ultimate loads (limit loads multiplied by prescribed factors of safety). Unless otherwise provided, prescribed loads are limit loads.

(b) Unless otherwise provided, the air, ground, and water loads must be placed in equilibrium with inertia forces, considering each item of mass in the airplane. These loads must be distributed to conservatively approximate or closely represent actual conditions. Methods used to determine load intensities and distribution on canard and tandem wing configurations must be validated by flight test measurement unless the methods used for determining those loading conditions are shown to be reliable or conservative on the configuration under consideration.

(c) If deflections under load would significantly change the distribution of external or internal loads, this redistribution must be taken into account.

(d) Simplified structural design criteria may be used if they result in design loads not less than those prescribed in §§23.331 through 23.521. For airplane configurations described in appendix A, §23.1, the design criteria of appendix A of this part are an approved equivalent of §§23.321 through 23.459. If appendix A of this part is used, the entire appendix must be substituted for the corresponding sections of this part.

[Docket No. 4080, 29 FR 17955, Dec. 18, 1964; 30 FR 258, Jan. 9, 1965; as amended by Amdt. 23–28, 47 FR 13315, Mar. 29, 1982; Amdt. 23–42, 56 FR 352, Jan. 3, 1991; Amdt. 23–48, 61 FR 5143, Feb. 9, 1996]

§23.302 Canard or tandem wing configurations.

The forward structure of a canard or tandem wing configuration must:

(a) Meet all requirements of subpart C and subpart D of this part applicable to a wing; and

(b) Meet all requirements applicable to the function performed by these surfaces.

[Amdt. 23–42, 56 FR 352, Jan. 3, 1991]

§23.303 Factor of safety.

Unless otherwise provided, a factor of safety of 1.5 must be used.

§23.305 Strength and deformation.

(a) The structure must be able to support limit loads without detrimental, permanent deformation. At any load up to limit loads, the deformation may not interfere with safe operation.

(b) The structure must be able to support ultimate loads without failure for at least three seconds, except local failures or structural instabilities between limit and ultimate load are acceptable only if the structure can sustain the required ultimate load for at least three seconds. However when proof of strength is shown by dynamic tests simulating actual load conditions, the three second limit does not apply.

[Docket No. 4080, 29 FR 17955, Dec. 18, 1964; as amended by Amdt. 23–45, 58 FR 42160, Aug. 6, 1993]

§23.307 Proof of structure.

(a) Compliance with the strength and deformation requirements of §23.305 must be shown for each critical load condition. Structural analysis may be used only if the structure conforms to those for which experience has shown this method to be reliable. In other cases, substantiating load tests must be made. Dynamic tests, including structural flight tests, are acceptable if the design load conditions have been simulated.

(b) Certain parts of the structure must be tested as specified in Subpart D of this part.

Flight Loads

§23.321 General.

(a) Flight load factors represent the ratio of the aerodynamic force component (acting normal to the assumed longitudinal axis of the airplane) to the weight of the airplane. A positive flight load factor is one in which the aerodynamic force acts upward, with respect to the airplane.

(b) Compliance with the flight load requirements of this subpart must be shown—

(1) At each critical altitude within the range in which the airplane may be expected to operate;

(2) At each weight from the design minimum weight to the design maximum weight; and

(3) For each required altitude and weight, for any practicable distribution of disposable load within the operating limitations specified in §§23.1583 through 23.1589.

(c) When significant, the effects of compressibility must be taken into account.

[Docket No. 4080, 29 FR 17955, Dec. 18, 1964; as amended by Amdt. 23–45, 58 FR 42160, Aug. 6, 1993]

§23.331 Symmetrical flight conditions.

(a) The appropriate balancing horizontal tail load must be accounted for in a rational or conservative manner when determining the wing loads and linear inertia loads corresponding to any of the symmetrical flight conditions specified in §§23.333 through 23.341.

(b) The incremental horizontal tail loads due to maneuvering and gusts must be reacted by the angular inertia of the airplane in a rational or conservative manner.

(c) Mutual influence of the aerodynamic surfaces must be taken into account when determining flight loads.

[Docket No. 4080, 29 FR 17955, Dec. 18, 1964; 30 FR 258, Jan. 9, 1965; as amended by Amdt. 23–42, 56 FR 352, Jan. 3, 1991]

§23.333 Flight envelope.

(a) *General.* Compliance with the strength requirements of this subpart must be shown at any combination of airspeed and load factor on and within the boundaries of a flight envelope (similar to the one in paragraph (d) of this section) that represents the envelope of the flight loading conditions specified by the maneuvering and gust criteria of paragraphs (b) and (c) of this section respectively.

(b) *Maneuvering envelope.* Except where limited by maximum (static) lift coefficients, the airplane is assumed to be subjected to symmetrical maneuvers resulting in the following limit load factors:

(1) The positive maneuvering load factor specified in §23.337 at speeds up to V_D;

(2) The negative maneuvering load factor specified in §23.337 at V_C; and

(3) Factors varying linearly with speed from the specified value at V_C to 0.0 at V_D for the normal and commuter category, and -1.0 at V_D for the acrobatic and utility categories.

(c) *Gust envelope.*

23

(1) The airplane is assumed to be subjected to symmetrical vertical gusts in level flight. The resulting limit load factors must correspond to the conditions determined as follows:

(i) Positive (up) and negative (down) gusts of 50 f.p.s. at V_C must be considered at altitudes between sea level and 20,000 feet. The gust velocity may be reduced linearly from 50 f.p.s. at 20,000 feet to 25 f.p.s. at 50,000 feet.

(ii) Positive and negative gusts of 25 f.p.s. at V_D must be considered at altitudes between sea level and 20,000 feet. The gust velocity may be reduced linearly from 25 f.p.s. at 20,000 feet to 12.5 f.p.s. at 50,000 feet.

(iii) In addition, for commuter category airplanes, positive (up) and negative (down) rough air gusts of 66 f.p.s. at V_B must be considered at altitudes between sea level and 20,000 feet. The gust velocity may be reduced linearly from 66 f.p.s. at 20,000 feet to 38 f.p.s. at 50,000 feet.

(2) The following assumptions must be made:

(i) The shape of the gust is—

$$U = \frac{U_{de}}{2}\left(1 - \cos\frac{2\pi s}{25C}\right)$$

Where—

s = Distance penetrated into gust (ft.);

C = Mean geometric chord of wing (ft.); and

U_{de} = Derived gust velocity referred to in subparagraph (1) of this section.

(ii) Gust load factors vary linearly with speed between V_C and V_D.

(d) *Flight envelope.*

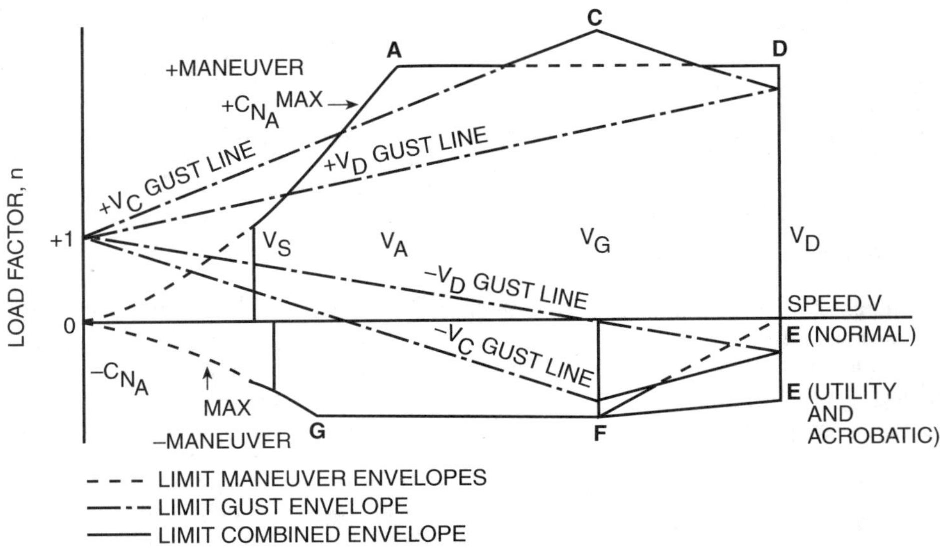

[Docket No. 4080, 29 FR 17955, Dec. 18, 1964; as amended by Amdt. 23–7, 34 FR 13087, Aug. 13, 1969; Amdt. 23–34, 52 FR 1829, Jan. 15, 1987]

§23.335 Design airspeeds.

Except as provided in paragraph (a) (4) of this section, the selected design airspeeds are equivalent airspeeds (EAS).

(a) *Design cruising speed, V_C.* For V_C the following apply:

(1) Where W/S′ = wing loading at the design maximum takeoff weight, V_C (in knots) may not be less than—

(i) 33 √(W/S) (for normal, utility, and commuter category airplanes);

(ii) 36 √(W/S) (for acrobatic category airplanes).

(2) For values of W/S more than 20, the multiplying factors may be decreased linearly with W/S to a value of 28.6 where W/S =100.

(3) V_C need not be more than 0.9 V_H at sea level.

(4) At altitudes where an M_D is established, a cruising speed M_C limited by compressibility may be selected.

(b) *Design dive speed V_D.* For V_D, the following apply:

(1) V_D/M_D may not be less than 1.25 V_C/M_C; and

(2) With $V_{C\,min}$, the required minimum design cruising speed, V_D (in knots) may not be less than—

(i) 1.40 $V_{C\,min}$ (for normal and commuter category airplanes);

(ii) 1.50 $V_{C\,min}$ (for utility category airplanes); and

(iii) 1.55 $V_{C\,min}$ (for acrobatic category airplanes).

(3) For values of W/S more than 20, the multiplying factors in paragraph (b)(2) of this section may be decreased linearly with W/S to a value of 1.35 where W/S = 100.

(4) Compliance with paragraphs (b) (1) and (2) of this section need not be shown if V_D/M_D is selected so that the minimum speed margin between V_C/M_C and V_D/M_D is the greater of the following:

(i) The speed increase resulting when, from the initial condition of stabilized flight at V_C/M_C, the airplane is assumed to be upset, flown for 20 seconds along a flight path 7.5° below the initial path, and then pulled up with a load factor of 1.5 (0.5 g. acceleration increment). At least 75 percent maximum continuous power for reciprocating engines, and maximum cruising power for turbines, or, if less, the power required for V_C/M_C for both kinds of engines, must be assumed until the pullup is initiated, at which point power reduction and pilot-controlled drag devices may be used; and either—

(ii) Mach 0.05 for normal, utility, and acrobatic category airplanes (at altitudes where M_D is established); or

(iii) Mach 0.07 for commuter category airplanes (at altitudes where M_D is established) unless a rational analysis, including the effects of automatic systems, is used to determine a lower margin. If a rational analysis is used, the minimum speed margin must be enough to provide for atmospheric variations (such as horizontal gusts), and the penetration of jet streams or cold fronts), instrument errors, airframe production variations, and must not be less than Mach 0.05.

(c) *Design maneuvering speed V_A.* For V_A, the following applies:

(1) V_A may not be less than $V_S\sqrt{n}$ where—

(i) V_S is a computed stalling speed with flaps retracted at the design weight, normally based on the maximum airplane normal force coefficients, C_{NA}; and

(ii) n is the limit maneuvering load factor used in design

(2) The value of V_A need not exceed the value of V_C used in design.

(d) *Design speed for maximum gust intensity, V_B.* For V_B, the following apply:

(1) V_B may not be less than the speed determined by the intersection of the line representing the maximum positive lift $C_{n\ max}$ and the line representing the rough air gust velocity on the gust V_{-n} diagram, or $V_{S1}\sqrt{n_g}$, whichever is less, where:

(i) n_g the positive airplane gust load factor due to gust, at speed V_C (in accordance with §23.341), and at the particular weight under consideration; and

(ii) V_{S1} is the stalling speed with the flaps retracted at the particular weight under consideration.

(2) V_B need not be greater than V_C.

[Docket No. 4080, 29 FR 17955, Dec. 18, 1964; as amended by Amdt. 23–7, 34 FR 13088, Aug. 13, 1969; Amdt. 23–16, 40 FR 2577, Jan. 14, 1975; Amdt. 23–34, 52 FR 1829, Jan. 15, 1987; Amdt. 23–24, 52 FR 34745, Sept. 14, 1987; Amdt. 23–48, 61 FR 5144, Feb. 9, 1996]

§23.337 Limit maneuvering load factors.

(a) The positive limit maneuvering load factor *n* may not be less than—

(1) 2.1+(24,000 ÷ (W+10,000)) for normal and commuter category airplanes, where W = design maximum takeoff weight, except that n need not be more than 3.8;

(2) 4.4 for utility category airplanes; or

(3) 6.0 for acrobatic category airplanes.

(b) The negative limit maneuvering load factor may not be less than—

(1) 0.4 times the positive load factor for the normal utility and commuter categories; or

(2) 0.5 times the positive load factor for the acrobatic category.

(c) Maneuvering load factors lower than those specified in this section may be used if the airplane has design features that make it impossible to exceed these values in flight.

[Docket No. 4080, 29 FR 17955, Dec. 18, 1964; as amended by Amdt. 23–7, 34 FR 13088, Aug. 13, 1969; Amdt. 23–34, 52 FR 1829, Jan. 15, 1987; Amdt. 23–48, 61 FR 5144, Feb. 9, 1996]

§23.341 Gust loads factors.

(a) Each airplane must be designed to withstand loads on each lifting surface resulting from gusts specified in §23.333(c).

(b) The gust load for a canard or tandem wing configuration must be computed using a rational analysis, or may be computed in accordance with paragraph (c) of this section, provided that the resulting net loads are shown to be conservative with respect to the gust criteria of §23.333(c).

(c) In the absence of a more rational analysis, the gust load factors must be computed as follows—

$$n = 1 + \frac{K_g U_{de} Va}{498(W/S)}$$

Where—

$K_g = 0.88\ \mu g/5.3 + \mu g$ = gust alleviation factor;

$\mu_g = 2(W/S)/\rho\ Cag$ = airplane mass ratio;

U_{de} = Derived gust velocities referred to in §23.333(c) (f.p.s.);

ρ = Density of air (slugs/cu.ft.);

W/S = Wing loading (p.s.f.) due to the applicable weight of the airplane in the particular load case.

C = Mean geometric chord (ft.);

g = Acceleration due to gravity (ft./sec.^{2})

V = Airplane equivalent speed (knots); and

a = Slope of the airplane normal force coefficient curve C_{NA} per radian if the gust loads are applied to the wings and horizontal tail surfaces simultaneously by a rational method. The wing lift curve slope C_L per radian may be used when the gust load is applied to the wings only and the horizontal tail gust loads are treated as a separate condition.

[Amdt. 23–7, 34 FR 13088, Aug. 13, 1969; as amended by Amdt. 23–42, 56 FR 352, Jan. 3, 1991; Amdt. 23–48, 61 FR 5144, Feb. 9, 1996]

§23.343 Design fuel loads.

(a) The disposable load combinations must include each fuel load in the range from zero fuel to the selected maximum fuel load.

(b) If fuel is carried in the wings, the maximum allowable weight of the airplane without any fuel in the wing tank(s) must be established as "maximum zero wing fuel weight," if it is less than the maximum weight.

(c) For commuter category airplanes, a structural reserve fuel condition, not exceeding fuel necessary for 45 minutes of operation at maximum continuous power, may be selected. If a structural reserve fuel condition is selected, it must be used as the minimum fuel weight condition for showing compliance with the flight load requirements prescribed in this part and—

(1) The structure must be designed to withstand a condition of zero fuel in the wing at limit loads corresponding to:

(i) Ninety percent of the maneuvering load factors defined in §23.337, and

(ii) Gust velocities equal to 85 percent of the values prescribed in §23.333(c).

(2) The fatigue evaluation of the structure must account for any increase in operating stresses resulting from the design condition of paragraph (c)(1) of this section.

(3) The flutter, deformation, and vibration requirements must also be met with zero fuel in the wings.

[Docket No. 27805, 61 FR 5144, Feb. 9, 1996]

§23.345 High lift devices.

(a) If flaps or similar high lift devices are to be used for takeoff, approach or landing, the airplane, with the flaps fully extended at V_F, is assumed to be subjected to symmetrical maneuvers and gusts within the range determined by—

(1) Maneuvering, to a positive limit load factor of 2.0; and

(2) Positive and negative gust of 25 feet per second acting normal to the flight path in level flight.

(b) V_F must be assumed to be not less than 1.4 V_S or 1.8 V_{SF}, whichever is greater, where—

(1) V_S is the computed stalling speed with flaps retracted at the design weight; and

(2) V_{SF} is the computed stalling speed with flaps fully extended at the design weight.

(3) If an automatic flap load limiting device is used, the airplane may be designed for the critical combinations of airspeed and flap position allowed by that device.

(c) In determining external loads on the airplane as a whole, thrust, slipstream, and pitching acceleration may be assumed to be zero.

(d) The flaps, their operating mechanism, and their supporting structures, must be designed to withstand the conditions prescribed in paragraph (a) of this section. In addition, with the flaps fully extended at V_F, the following conditions, taken separately, must be accounted for:

(1) A head-on gust having a velocity of 25 feet per second (EAS), combined with propeller slipstream corresponding to 75 percent of maximum continuous power; and

(2) The effects of propeller slipstream corresponding to maximum takeoff power.

[Docket No. 27805, 61 FR 5144, Feb. 9, 1996]

§23.347 Unsymmetrical flight conditions.

(a) The airplane is assumed to be subjected to the unsymmetrical flight conditions of §§23.349 and 23.351. Unbalanced aerodynamic moments about the center of gravity must be reacted in a rational or conservative manner, considering the principal masses furnishing the reacting inertia forces.

(b) Acrobatic category airplanes certified for flick maneuvers (snap roll) must be designed for additional asymmetric loads acting on the wing and the horizontal tail.

[Amended by Amdt. 23–48, 61 FR 5144, Feb. 9, 1996]

§23.349 Rolling conditions.

The wing and wing bracing must be designed for the following loading conditions:

(a) Unsymmetrical wing loads appropriate to the category. Unless the following values result in unrealistic loads, the rolling accelerations may be obtained by modifying the symmetrical flight conditions in §23.333(d) as follows:

(1) For the acrobatic category, in conditions A and F, assume that 100 percent of the semispan wing airload acts on one side of the plane of symmetry and 60 percent of this load acts on the other side.

(2) For normal, utility, and commuter categories, in Condition A, assume that 100 percent of the semispan wing airload acts on one side of the airplane and 75 percent of this load acts on the other side.

(b) The loads resulting from the aileron deflections and speeds specified in §23.455, in combination with an airplane load factor of at least two thirds of the positive maneuvering load factor used for design. Unless the following values result in unrealistic loads, the effect of aileron displacement on wing torsion may be accounted for by adding the following increment to the basic airfoil moment coefficient over the aileron portion of the span in the critical condition determined in §23.333(d):

$$\Delta c_m = -0.01\delta$$

where—

Δc_m is the moment coefficient increment; and

δ is the down aileron deflection in degrees in the critical condition.

[Docket No. 4080, 29 FR 17955, Dec. 18, 1964; as amended by Amdt. 23–7, 34 FR 13088, Aug. 13, 1969; Amdt. 23–34, 52 FR 1829, Jan. 15, 1987; Amdt. 23–48, 61 FR 5144, Feb. 9, 1996]

§23.351 Yawing conditions.

The airplane must be designed for yawing loads on the vertical surfaces resulting from the loads specified in §§23.441 through 23.445.

[Docket No. 4080, 29 FR 17955, Dec. 18, 1964; 30 FR 258, Jan. 9, 1965; as amended by Amdt. 23–42, 56 FR 352, Jan. 3, 1991]

§23.361 Engine torque.

(a) Each engine mount and its supporting structure must be designed for the effects of—

(1) A limit engine torque corresponding to takeoff power and propeller speed acting simultaneously with 75 percent of the limit loads from flight condition A of §23.333(d);

(2) A limit engine torque corresponding to maximum continuous power and propeller speed acting simultaneously with the limit loads from flight condition A of §23.333(d); and

(3) For turbopropeller installations, in addition to the conditions specified in paragraphs (a)(1) and (a)(2) of this section, a limit engine torque corresponding to takeoff power and propeller speed, multiplied by a factor accounting for propeller control system malfunction, including quick feathering, acting simultaneously with 1g level flight loads. In the absence of a rational analysis, a factor of 1.6 must be used.

(b) For turbine engine installations, the engine mounts and supporting structure must be designed to withstand each of the following:

(1) A limit engine torque load imposed by sudden engine stoppage due to malfunction or structural failure (such as compressor jamming).

(2) A limit engine torque load imposed by the maximum acceleration of the engine.

(c) The limit engine torque to be considered under paragraph (a) of this section must be obtained by multiplying the mean torque by a factor of—

(1) 1.25 for turbopropeller installations;

(2) 1.33 for engines with five or more cylinders; and

(3) Two, three, or four, for engines with four, three, or two cylinders, respectively.

[Amdt. 23–26, 45 FR 60171, Sept. 11, 1980; as amended by Amdt. 23–45, 58 FR 42160, Aug. 6, 1993]

§23.363 Side load on engine mount.

(a) Each engine mount and its supporting structure must be designed for a limit load factor in a lateral direction, for the side load on the engine mount, of not less than—

(1) 1.33, or

(2) One-third of the limit load factor for flight condition A.

(b) The side load prescribed in paragraph (a) of this section may be assumed to be independent of other flight conditions.

§23.365 Pressurized cabin loads.

For each pressurized compartment, the following apply:

(a) The airplane structure must be strong enough to withstand the flight loads combined with pressure differential loads from zero up to the maximum relief valve setting.

(b) The external pressure distribution in flight, and any stress concentrations, must be accounted for.

(c) If landings may be made with the cabin pressurized, landing loads must be combined with pressure differential loads from zero up to the maximum allowed during landing.

(d) The airplane structure must be strong enough to withstand the pressure differential loads corresponding to the maximum relief valve setting multiplied by a factor of 1.33, omitting other loads.

(e) If a pressurized cabin has two or more compartments separated by bulkheads or a floor, the primary structure must be designed for the effects of sudden release of pressure in any compartment with external doors or windows. This condition must be investigated for the effects of failure of the largest opening in the compartment. The effects of intercompartmental venting may be considered.

§23.367 Unsymmetrical loads due to engine failure.

(a) Turbopropeller airplanes must be designed for the unsymmetrical loads resulting from the failure of the critical engine including the following conditions in combination with a single malfunction of the propeller drag limiting system, considering the probable pilot corrective action on the flight controls:

(1) At speeds between V_{MC} and V_D, the loads resulting from power failure because of fuel flow interruption are considered to be limit loads.

(2) At speeds between V_{MC} and V_C, the loads resulting from the disconnection of the engine compressor from the turbine or from loss of the turbine blades are considered to be ultimate loads.

(3) The time history of the thrust decay and drag buildup occurring as a result of the prescribed engine failures must be substantiated by test or other data applicable to the particular engine-propeller combination.

(4) The timing and magnitude of the probable pilot corrective action must be conservatively estimated, considering the characteristics of the particular engine-propeller-airplane combination.

(b) Pilot corrective action may be assumed to be initiated at the time maximum yawing velocity is reached, but not earlier than 2 seconds after the engine failure. The magnitude of the corrective action may be based on the limit pilot forces specified in §23.397 except that lower forces may be assumed where it is shown by analysis or test that these forces can control the yaw and roll resulting from the prescribed engine failure conditions.

[Amdt. 23–7, 34 FR 13089, Aug. 13, 1969]

§23.369 Rear lift truss.

(a) If a rear lift truss is used, it must be designed to withstand conditions of reversed airflow at a design speed of—

$V = 8.7 \sqrt{(W/S)} + 8.7$ (knots), where W/S = wing loading at design maximum takeoff weight.

(b) Either aerodynamic data for the particular wing section used, or a value of C_L equaling – 0.8 with a chordwise distribution that is triangular between a peak at the trailing edge and zero at the leading edge, must be used.

[Docket No. 4080, 29 FR 17955, Dec. 18, 1964; as amended by Amdt. 23–7, 34 FR 13089, Aug. 13, 1969; 34 FR 17509, Oct. 30, 1969; Amdt. 23–45, 58 FR 42160, Aug. 6, 1993; Amdt. 23–48, 61 FR 5145, Feb. 9, 1996]

§23.371 Gyroscopic and aerodynamic loads.

(a) Each engine mount and its supporting structure must be designed for the gyroscopic, inertial, and aerodynamic loads that result, with the engine(s) and propeller(s), if applicable, at maximum continuous r.p.m., under either:

(1) The conditions prescribed in §23.351 and §23.423; or

(2) All possible combinations of the following—

(i) A yaw velocity of 2.5 radians per second;

(ii) A pitch velocity of 1.0 radian per second;

(iii) A normal load factor of 2.5; and

(iv) Maximum continuous thrust.

(b) For airplanes approved for aerobatic maneuvers, each engine mount and its supporting structure must meet the requirements of paragraph (a) of this section and be designed to withstand the load factors expected during combined maximum yaw and pitch velocities.

(c) For airplanes certificated in the commuter category, each engine mount and its supporting structure must meet the requirements of paragraph (a) of this section and the gust conditions specified in §23.341 of this part.

[Docket No. 27805, 61 FR 5145, Feb. 9, 1996]

§23.373 Speed control devices.

If speed control devices (such as spoilers and drag flaps) are incorporated for use in enroute conditions—

(a) The airplane must be designed for the symmetrical maneuvers and gusts prescribed in §§23.333, 23.337, and 23.341, and the yawing maneuvers and lateral gusts in §§23.441 and 23.443, with the device extended at speeds up to the placard device extended speed; and

(b) If the device has automatic operating or load limiting features, the airplane must be designed for the maneuver and gust conditions prescribed in paragraph (a) of this section at the speeds and corresponding device positions that the mechanism allows.

[Amdt. 23–7, 34 FR 13089, Aug. 13, 1969]

CONTROL SURFACE AND SYSTEM LOADS

§23.391 Control surface loads.

The control surface loads specified in §§23.397 through 23.459 are assumed to occur in the conditions described in §§23.331 through 23.351.

[Amended by Amdt. 23–48, 61 FR 5145, Feb. 9, 1996]

§23.393 Loads parallel to hinge line.

(a) Control surfaces and supporting hinge brackets must be designed to withstand inertial loads acting parallel to the hinge line.

(b) In the absence of more rational data, the inertial loads may be assumed to be equal to KW, where—

(1) K = 24 for vertical surfaces;

(2) K = 12 for horizontal surfaces; and

(3) W = weight of the movable surfaces.

[Docket No. 27805, 61 FR 5145, Feb. 9, 1996]

§23.395 Control system loads.

(a) Each flight control system and its supporting structure must be designed for loads corresponding to at least 125 percent of the computed hinge moments of the movable control surface in the conditions prescribed in §§23.391 through 23.459. In addition, the following apply:

(1) The system limit loads need not exceed the higher of the loads that can be produced by the pilot and automatic devices operating the controls. However, autopilot forces need not be added to pilot forces. The system must be designed for the maximum effort of the pilot or autopilot, whichever is higher. In addition, if the pilot and the autopilot act in opposition, the part of the system between them may be designed for the maximum effort of the one that imposes the lesser load. Pilot forces used for design need not exceed the maximum forces prescribed in §23.397(b).

(2) The design must, in any case, provide a rugged system for service use, considering jamming, ground gusts, taxiing downwind, control inertia, and friction. Compliance with this subparagraph may be shown by designing for loads resulting from application of the minimum forces prescribed in §23.397(b).

(b) A 125 percent factor on computed hinge moments must be used to design elevator, aileron, and rudder systems. However, a factor as low as 1.0 may be used if hinge moments are based on accurate flight test data, the exact reduction depending upon the accuracy and reliability of the data.

(c) Pilot forces used for design are assumed to act at the appropriate control grips or pads as they would in flight, and to react at the attachments of the control system to the control surface horns.

[Docket No. 4080, 29 FR 17955, Dec. 18, 1964; as amended by Amdt. 23–7, 34 FR 13089, Aug. 13, 1969]

§23.397 Limit control forces and torques.

(a) In the control surface flight loading condition, the airloads on movable surfaces and the corresponding deflections need not exceed those that would result in flight from the application of any pilot force within the ranges specified in paragraph (b) of this section. In applying this criterion, the effects of control system boost and servo-mechanisms, and the effects of tabs must be considered. The automatic pilot effort must be used for design if it alone can produce higher control surface loads than the human pilot.

(b) The limit pilot forces and torques are as follows:

Control	Maximum forces or torques for design weight, weight equal to or less than 5,000 pounds	Minimum forces or torques[2]
Aileron:		
Stick	67 lbs	40 lbs
Wheel[3]	50 D in.-lbs[4]	40 D in.-lbs[4]
Elevator:		
Stick	167 lbs	100 lbs
Wheel (symmetrical)	200 lbs	100 lbs
Wheel (unsymmetrical)[5]		100 lbs
Rudder	200 lbs	150 lbs

[1] For design weight (W) more than 5,000 pounds, the specified maximum values must be increased linearly with weight to 1.18 times the specified values at a design weight of 12,500 pounds and for commuter category airplanes, the specified values must be increased linearly with weight to 1.35 times the specified values at a design weight of 19,000 pounds.

[2] If the design of any individual set of control systems or surfaces makes these specified minimum forces or torques inapplicable, values corresponding to the present hinge moments obtained under §23.415, but not less than 0.6 of the specified minimum forces or torques, may be used.

[3] The critical parts of the aileron control system must also be designed for a single tangential force with a limit value of 1.25 times the couple force determined from the above criteria.

[4] D = wheel diameter (inches).

[5] The unsymmetrical force must be applied at one of the normal handgrip points on the control wheel.

[Docket No. 4080, 29 FR 17955, Dec. 18, 1964; as amended by Amdt. 23–7, 34 FR 13089, Aug. 13, 1969; Amdt. 23–17, 41 FR 55464, Dec. 20, 1976; Amdt. 23–34, 52 FR 1829, Jan. 15, 1987; Amdt. 23–45, 58 FR 42160, Aug. 6, 1993]

§23.399 Dual control system.

(a) Each dual control system must be designed to withstand the force of the pilots operating in opposition, using individual pilot forces not less than the greater of—

(1) 0.75 times those obtained under §23.395; or

(2) The minimum forces specified in §23.397(b).

(b) Each dual control system must be designed to withstand the force of the pilots applied together, in the same direction, using individual pilot forces not less than 0.75 times those obtained under §23.395.

[Docket No. 27805, 61 FR 5145, Feb. 9, 1996]

§23.405 Secondary control system.

Secondary controls, such as wheel brakes, spoilers, and tab controls, must be designed for the maximum forces that a pilot is likely to apply to those controls.

§23.407 Trim tab effects.

The effects of trim tabs on the control surface design conditions must be accounted for only where the surface loads are limited by maximum pilot effort. In these cases, the tabs are considered to be deflected in the direction that would assist the pilot. These deflections must correspond to the maximum degree of "out of trim" expected at the speed for the condition under consideration.

§23.409 Tabs.

Control surface tabs must be designed for the most severe combination of airspeed and tab deflection likely to be obtained within the flight envelope for any usable loading condition.

§23.415 Ground gust conditions.

(a) The control system must be investigated as follows for control surface loads due to ground gusts and taxiing downwind:

(1) If an investigation of the control system for ground gust loads is not required by paragraph (a)(2) of this section, but the applicant elects to design a part of the control system of these loads, these loads need only be carried from control surface horns through the nearest stops or gust locks and their supporting structures.

(2) If pilot forces less than the minimums specified in §23.397(b) are used for design, the effects of surface loads due to ground gusts and taxiing downwind must be investigated for the entire control system according to the formula:

$H = K c S q$

where—

H = limit hinge moment (ft.-lbs.);

c = mean chord of the control surface aft of the hinge line (ft.);

S = area of control surface aft of the hinge line (sq. ft.);

q = dynamic pressure (p.s.f.) based on a design speed not less than $14.6\sqrt{(W/S)} + 14.6$ (f.p.s.) where W/S = wing loading at design maximum weight, except that the design speed need not exceed 88 (f.p.s.);

K = limit hinge moment factor for ground gusts derived in paragraph (b) of this section. (For ailerons and elevators, a positive value of K indicates a moment tending to depress the surface and a negative value of K indicates a moment tending to raise the surface).

(b) The limit hinge moment factor K for ground gusts must be derived as follows:

Surface	*K*	Position of controls
(a) Aileron	0.75	Control column locked lashed in mid-position.
(b) Aileron	±0.50	Ailerons at full throw; + moment on one aileron, – moment on the other.
(c) Elevator	±0.75	(c) Elevator full up (–).
(d) Elevator		(d) Elevator full down (+).
(e) Rudder	±0.75	(e) Rudder in neutral.
(f) Rudder		(f) Rudder at full throw.

(c) At all weights between the empty weight and the maximum weight declared for tie-down stated in the appropriate manual, any declared tie-down points and surrounding structure, control system, surfaces and associated gust locks, must be designed to withstand the limit load conditions that exist when the airplane is tied down and that result from wind speeds of up to 65 knots horizontally from any direction.

[Docket No. 4080, 29 FR 17955, Dec. 18, 1964; as amended by Amdt. 23–7, 34 FR 13089, Aug. 13, 1969; Amdt. 23–45, 58 FR 42160, Aug. 6, 1993; Amdt. 23–48, 61 FR 5145, Feb. 9, 1996]

Horizontal Stabilizing and Balancing Surfaces

§23.421 Balancing loads.

(a) A horizontal surface balancing load is a load necessary to maintain equilibrium in any specified flight condition with no pitching acceleration.

(b) Horizontal balancing surfaces must be designed for the balancing loads occurring at any point on the limit maneuvering envelope and in the flap conditions specified in §23.345.

[Docket No. 4080, 29 FR 17955, Dec. 18, 1964; as amended by Amdt. 23–7, 34 FR 13089, Aug. 13, 1969; Amdt. 23–42, 56 FR 352, Jan. 3, 1991]

§23.423 Maneuvering loads.

Each horizontal surface and its supporting structure, and the main wing of a canard or tandem wing configuration, if that surface has pitch control, must be designed for the maneuvering loads imposed by the following conditions:

(a) A sudden movement of the pitching control, at the speed V_A, to the maximum aft movement, and the maximum forward movement, as limited by the control stops, or pilot effort, whichever is critical.

(b) A sudden aft movement of the pitching control at speeds above V_A, followed by a forward movement of the pitching control resulting in the following combinations of normal and angular acceleration:

Condition	Normal Acceleration (n)	Angular acceleration (radian/sec^2)
Nose-up pitching	1.0	$+39 n_m \times V \times (n_m - 1.5)$
Nose-down pitching	n_m	$-39 n_m \times V \times (n_m - 1.5)$

where—

(1) n_m = positive limit maneuvering load factor used in the design of the airplane; and

(2) V = initial speed in knots.

The conditions in this paragraph involve loads corresponding to the loads that may occur in a "checked maneuver" (a maneuver in which the pitching control is suddenly displaced in one direction and then suddenly moved in the opposite direction). The deflections and timing of the "checked maneuver" must avoid exceeding the limit maneuvering load factor. The total horizontal surface load for both nose-up and nose-down pitching conditions is the sum of the balancing loads at V and the specified value of the normal load factor n, plus the maneuvering load increment due to the specified value of the angular acceleration.

[Amdt. 23–42, 56 FR 353, Jan. 3, 1991; 56 FR 5455, Feb. 11, 1991]

§23.425 Gust loads.

(a) Each horizontal surface, other than a main wing, must be designed for loads resulting from—

(1) Gust velocities specified in §23.333(c) with flaps retracted; and

(2) Positive and negative gusts of 25 f.p.s. nominal intensity at V_F corresponding to the flight conditions specified in §23.345(a)(2).

(b) [Reserved]

(c) When determining the total load on the horizontal surfaces for the conditions specified in paragraph (a) of this section, the initial balancing loads for steady unaccelerated flight at the pertinent design speeds V_F, V_C, and V_D must first be determined. The incremental load resulting from the gusts must be added to the initial balancing load to obtain the total load.

(d) In the absence of a more rational analysis, the incremental load due to the gust must be computed as follows only on airplane configurations with aft-mounted, horizontal surfaces, unless its use elsewhere is shown to be conservative:

$$\Delta L_{ht} = \frac{K_g U_{de} V a_{ht} S_{ht}}{498}\left(1 - \frac{d\varepsilon}{d\alpha}\right)$$

where—

ΔL_{ht} = Incremental horizontal tailload (lbs.);
K_g = Gust alleviation factor defined in §23.341;
U_{de} = Derived gust velocity (f.p.s.);
V = Airplane equivalent speed (knots);
a_{ht} = Slope of aft horizontal lift curve (per radian)
S_{ht} = Area of aft horizontal lift surface (ft^2); and

$$\left(1 - \frac{d\varepsilon}{d\alpha}\right) = \text{Downwash factor}$$

[Docket No. 4080, 20 FR 17955, Dec. 18, 1964; as amended by Amdt. 23–7, 34 FR 13089 Aug. 13, 1969; Amdt. 23–42, 56 FR 353, Jan. 3, 1991]

§23.427 Unsymmetrical loads.

(a) Horizontal surfaces other than main wing and their supporting structure must be designed for unsymmetrical loads arising from yawing and slipstream effects, in combination with the loads prescribed for the flight conditions set forth in §§23.421 through 23.425.

(b) In the absence of more rational data for airplanes that are conventional in regard to location of engines, wings, horizontal surfaces other than main wing, and fuselage shape:

(1) 100 percent of the maximum loading from the symmetrical flight conditions may be assumed on the surface on one side of the plane of symmetry; and

(2) The following percentage of that loading must be applied to the opposite side:

Percent = 100−10(n−1), where n is the specified positive maneuvering load factor, but this value may not be more than 80 percent.

(c) For airplanes that are not conventional (such as airplanes with horizontal surfaces other than main wing having appreciable dihedral or supported by the vertical tail surfaces) the surfaces and supporting structures must be designed for combined vertical and horizontal surface loads resulting from each prescribed flight condition taken separately.

[Amdt. 23–14, 38 FR 31820, Nov. 19, 1973; as amended by Amdt. 23–42, 56 FR 353, Jan. 3, 1991]

Vertical Surfaces

§23.441 Maneuvering loads.

(a) At speeds up to V_A, the vertical surfaces must be designed to withstand the following conditions. In computing the loads, the yawing velocity may be assumed to be zero:

(1) With the airplane in unaccelerated flight at zero yaw, it is assumed that the rudder control is suddenly displaced to the maximum deflection, as limited by the control stops or by limit pilot forces.

(2) With the rudder deflected as specified in paragraph (a)(1) of this section, it is assumed that the airplane yaws to the overswing sideslip angle. In lieu of a rational analysis, an overswing angle equal to 1.5 times the static sideslip angle of paragraph (a)(3) of this section may be assumed.

(3) A yaw angle of 15 degrees with the rudder control maintained in the neutral position (except as limited by pilot strength).

(b) For commuter category airplanes, the loads imposed by the following additional maneuver must be substantiated at speeds from V_A to V_D/M_D. When computing the tail loads—

(1) The airplane must be yawed to the largest attainable steady state sideslip angle, with the rudder at maximum deflection caused by any one of the following:

(i) Control surface stops;

(ii) Maximum available booster effort;

(iii) Maximum pilot rudder force as shown below:

See following figure.

~ME134E.DOC

Maximum Pilot Rudder Force

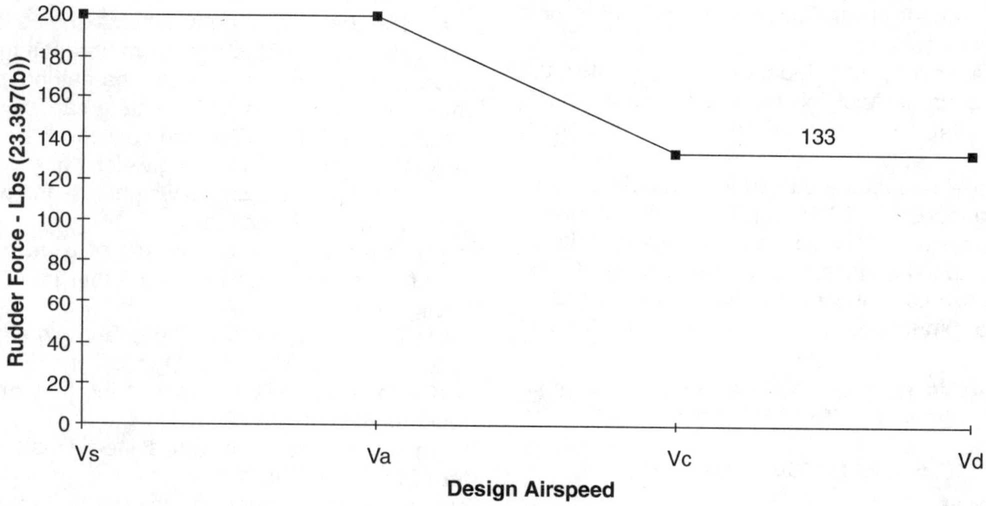

(2) The rudder must be suddenly displaced from the maximum deflection to the neutral position.

(c) The yaw angles specified in paragraph (a)(3) of this section may be reduced if the yaw angle chosen for a particular speed cannot be exceeded in—

(1) Steady slip conditions;

(2) Uncoordinated rolls from steep banks; or

(3) Sudden failure of the critical engine with delayed corrective action.

[Docket No. 4080, 29 FR 17955, Dec. 18, 1964; as amended by Amdt. 23–7, 34 FR 13090, Aug. 13, 1969; Amdt. 23–14, 38 FR 31821, Nov. 19, 1973; Amdt. 23–28, 47 FR 13315, Mar. 29, 1982; Amdt. 23–42, 56 FR 353, Jan. 3, 1991; Amdt. 23–48, 61 FR 5145, Feb. 9, 1996]

§23.443 Gust loads.

(a) Vertical surfaces must be designed to withstand, in unaccelerated flight at speed V_C, lateral gusts of the values prescribed for V_C in §23.333(c).

(b) In addition, for commuter category airplanes, the airplane is assumed to encounter derived gusts normal to the plane of symmetry while in unaccelerated flight at V_B, V_C, V_D, and V_F. The derived gusts and airplane speeds corresponding to these conditions, as determined by §§23.341 and 23.345, must be investigated. The shape of the gust must be as specified in §23.333(c)(2)(i).

(c) In the absence of a more rational analysis, the gust load must be computed as follows:

$$L_{vt} = \frac{K_{gt} U_{de} V a_{vt} S_{vt}}{498}$$

Where—

L_{vt} = Vertical surface loads (lbs.);

$$K_{gt} = \frac{0.88\mu_{gt}}{5.3 + \mu_{gt}} = \text{gust alleviation factor;}$$

$$\mu_{gt} = \frac{2W}{\rho c_t g a_{vt} S_{vt}} \frac{K^2}{l_{vt}} = \text{lateral mass ratio;}$$

U_{de} = Derived gust velocity (f.p.s.);

ρ = Air density (slugs/cu.ft.);

W = the applicable weight of the airplane in the particular load case (lbs.);

S_{vt} = Area of vertical surface (ft.^{2});

c_t = Mean geometric chord of vertical surface (ft.);

a_{vt} = Lift curve slope of vertical surface (per radian);

K = Radius of gyration in yaw (ft.);

l_{vt} = Distance from airplane c.g. to lift center of vertical surface (ft.);

g = Acceleration due to gravity (ft./sec.^{2}); and

V = Equivalent airspeed (knots).

[Amdt. 23–7, 34 FR 13090, Aug. 13, 1969; as amended by Amdt. 23–34, 52 FR 1830, Jan. 15, 1987; 52 FR 7262, Mar. 9, 1987; Amdt. 23–24, 52 FR 34745, Sept. 14, 1987; Amdt. 23–42, 56 FR 353, Jan. 3, 1991; Amdt. 23–48, 61 FR 5147, Feb. 9, 1996]

§23.445 Outboard fins or winglets.

(a) If outboard fins or winglets are included on the horizontal surfaces or wings, the horizontal surfaces or wings must be designed for their maximum load in combination with loads induced by the fins or winglets and moments or forces exerted on the horizontal surfaces or wings by the fins or winglets.

(b) If outboard fins or winglets extend above and below the horizontal surface, the critical vertical surface loading (the load per unit area as determined under §§23.441 and 23.443) must be applied to—

(1) The part of the vertical surfaces above the horizontal surface with 80 percent of that loading applied to the part below the horizontal surface; and

(2) The part of the vertical surfaces below the horizontal surface with 80 percent of that loading applied to the part above the horizontal surface.

(c) The end plate effects of outboard fins or winglets must be taken into account in applying the yawing conditions of §§23.441 and 23.443 to the vertical surfaces in paragraph (b) of this section.

(d) When rational methods are used for computing loads, the maneuvering loads of §23.441 on the vertical surfaces and the one-g horizontal surface load, including induced loads on the horizontal surface and moments or forces exerted on the horizontal surfaces by the vertical surfaces, must be applied simultaneously for the structural loading condition.

[Docket No. 4080, 29 FR 17955, Dec. 18, 1964; Amdt. 23–14, 38 FR 31821, Nov. 19, 1973; Amdt. 23–42, 56 FR 353, Jan. 3, 1991]

AILERONS AND SPECIAL DEVICES

§23.455 Ailerons.

(a) The ailerons must be designed for the loads to which they are subjected—

(1) In the neutral position during symmetrical flight conditions; and

(2) By the following deflections (except as limited by pilot effort), during unsymmetrical flight conditions:

(i) Sudden maximum displacement of the aileron control at V_A. Suitable allowance may be made for control system deflections.

(ii) Sufficient deflection at V_C, where V_C is more than V_A, to produce a rate of roll not less than obtained in paragraph (a)(2)(i) of this section.

(iii)Sufficient deflection at V_D to produce a rate of roll not less than one-third of that obtained in paragraph (a)(2)(i) of this section.

(b) [Reserved]

[Docket No. 4080, 29 FR 17955, Dec. 18, 1964; as amended by Amdt. 23–7, 34 FR 13090, Aug. 13, 1969; Amdt. 23–42, 56 FR 353, Jan. 3, 1991]

§23.459 Special devices.

The loading for special devices using aerodynamic surfaces (such as slots and spoilers) must be determined from test data.

GROUND LOADS

§23.471 General.

The limit ground loads specified in this subpart are considered to be external loads and inertia forces that act upon an airplane structure. In each specified ground load condition, the external reactions must be placed in equilibrium with the linear and angular inertia forces in a rational or conservative manner.

§23.473 Ground load conditions and assumptions.

(a) The ground load requirements of this subpart must be complied with at the design maximum weight except that §§23.479, 23.481, and 23.483 may be complied with at a design landing weight (the highest weight for landing conditions at the maximum descent velocity) allowed under paragraphs (b) and (c) of this section.

(b) The design landing weight may be as low as—

(1) 95 percent of the maximum weight if the minimum fuel capacity is enough for at least one-half hour of operation at maximum continuous power plus a capacity equal to a fuel weight which is the difference between the design maximum weight and the des ˇn landing weight; or

(2) The design maximum weight less the weight of 25 percent of the total fuel capacity.

(c) The design landing weight of a multiengine airplane may be less than that allowed under paragraph (b) of this section if—

(1) The airplane meets the one-engine-inoperative climb requirements of §23.67(b)(1) or (c); and

(2) Compliance is shown with the fuel jettisoning system requirements of §23.1001.

(d) The selected limit vertical inertia load factor at the center of gravity of the airplane for the ground load conditions prescribed in this subpart may not be less than that which would be obtained when landing with a descent velocity (V), in feet per second, equal to $4.4(W/S)^{1/4}$, except that this velocity need not be more than 10 feet per second and may not be less than seven feet per second.

(e) Wing lift not exceeding two-thirds of the weight of the airplane may be assumed to exist throughout the landing impact and to act through the center of gravity. The ground reaction load factor may be equal to the inertia load factor minus the ratio of the above assumed wing lift to the airplane weight.

(f) If energy absorption tests are made to determine the limit load factor corresponding to the required limit descent velocities, these tests must be made under §23.723(a).

(g) No inertia load factor used for design purposes may be less than 2.67, nor may the limit ground reaction load factor be less than 2.0 at design maximum weight, unless these lower values will not be exceeded in taxiing at speeds up to takeoff speed over terrain as rough as that expected in service.

[Docket No. 4080, 29 FR 17955, Dec. 18, 1964; as amended by Amdt. 23–7, 34 FR 13090, Aug. 13, 1969; Amdt. 23–28, 47 FR 13315, Mar. 29, 1982; Amdt. 23–45, 58 FR 42160, Aug. 6, 1993; Amdt. 23–48, 61 FR 5147, Feb. 9, 1996]

§23.477 Landing gear arrangement.

Sections 23.479 through 23.483, or the conditions in Appendix C, apply to airplanes with conventional arrangements of main and nose gear, or main and tail gear.

§23.479 Level landing conditions.

(a) For a level landing, the airplane is assumed to be in the following attitudes:

(1) For airplanes with tail wheels, a normal level flight attitude.

(2) For airplanes with nose wheels, attitudes in which—

(i) The nose and main wheels contact the ground simultaneously; and

(ii) The main wheels contact the ground and the nose wheel is just clear of the ground.

The attitude used in paragraph (a)(2)(i) of this section may be used in the analysis required under paragraph (a)(2)(ii) of this section.

(b) When investigating landing conditions, the drag components simulating the forces required to accelerate the tires and wheels up to the landing speed (spin-up) must be properly combined with the corresponding instantaneous vertical ground reactions, and the forward-acting horizontal loads resulting from rapid reduction of the spin-up drag loads (spring-back) must be combined with vertical ground reactions at the instant of the peak forward load, assuming wing lift and a tire-sliding coefficient of friction of 0.8. However, the drag loads may not be less than 25 percent of the maximum vertical ground reactions (neglecting wing lift).

(c) In the absence of specific tests or a more rational analysis for determining the wheel spin-up and spring-back loads for landing conditions, the method set forth in appendix D of this part must be used. If appendix D of this part is used, the drag components used for design must not be less than those given by appendix C of this part.

(d) For airplanes with tip tanks or large overhung masses (such as turbo-propeller or jet engines) supported by the wing, the tip tanks and the structure supporting the tanks or overhung masses must be designed for the effects of dynamic responses under the level landing conditions of either paragraph (a)(1) or (a)(2)(ii) of this section. In evaluating the effects of dynamic response, an airplane lift equal to the weight of the airplane may be assumed.

[Docket No. 4080, 29 FR 17955, Dec. 18, 1964; as amended by Amdt. 23–17, 41 FR 55464, Dec. 20, 1976; Amdt. 23–45, 58 FR 42160, Aug. 6, 1993]

§23.481 Tail down landing conditions.

(a) For a tail down landing, the airplane is assumed to be in the following attitudes:

(1) For airplanes with tail wheels, an attitude in which the main and tail wheels contact the ground simultaneously.

(2) For airplanes with nose wheels, a stalling attitude, or the maximum angle allowing ground clearance by each part of the airplane, whichever is less.

(b) For airplanes with either tail or nose wheels, ground reactions are assumed to be vertical, with the wheels up to speed before the maximum vertical load is attained.

§23.483 One-wheel landing conditions.

For the one-wheel landing condition, the airplane is assumed to be in the level attitude and to contact the ground on one side of the main landing gear. In this attitude, the ground reactions must be the same as those obtained on that side under §23.479.

§23.485 Side load conditions.

(a) For the side load condition, the airplane is assumed to be in a level attitude with only the main wheels contacting the ground and with the shock absorbers and tires in their static positions.

(b) The limit vertical load factor must be 1.33, with the vertical ground reaction divided equally between the main wheels.

(c) The limit side inertia factor must be 0.83, with the side ground reaction divided between the main wheels so that—

(1) 0.5 (W) is acting inboard on one side; and

(2) 0.33 (W) is acting outboard on the other side.

(d) The side loads prescribed in paragraph (c) of this section are assumed to be applied at the ground contact point and the drag loads may be assumed to be zero.

[Docket No. 4080, 29 FR 17955, Dec. 18, 1964; as amended by Amdt. 23–45, 58 FR 42160, Aug. 6, 1993]

§23.493 Braked roll conditions.

Under braked roll conditions, with the shock absorbers and tires in their static positions, the following apply:

(a) The limit vertical load factor must be 1.33.

(b) The attitudes and ground contacts must be those described in §23.479 for level landings.

(c) A drag reaction equal to the vertical reaction at the wheel multiplied by a coefficient of friction of 0.8 must be applied at the ground contact point of each wheel with brakes, except that the drag reaction need not exceed the maximum value based on limiting brake torque.

§23.497 Supplementary conditions for tail wheels.

In determining the ground loads on the tail wheel and affected supporting structures, the following apply:

(a) For the obstruction load, the limit ground reaction obtained in the tail down landing condition is assumed to act up and aft through the axle at 45 degrees. The shock absorber and tire may be assumed to be in their static positions.

(b) For the side load, a limit vertical ground reaction equal to the static load on the tail wheel, in combination with a side component of equal magnitude, is assumed. In addition—

(1) If a swivel is used, the tail wheel is assumed to be swiveled 90 degrees to the airplane longitudinal axis with the resultant ground load passing through the axle;

(2) If a lock, steering device, or shimmy damper is used, the tail wheel is also assumed to be in the trailing position with the side load acting at the ground contact point; and

(3) The shock absorber and tire are assumed to be in their static positions.

(c) If a tail wheel, bumper, or an energy absorption device is provided to show compliance with §23.925(b), the following apply:

(1) Suitable design loads must be established for the tail wheel, bumper, or energy absorption device; and

(2) The supporting structure of the tail wheel, bumper, or energy absorption device must be designed to withstand the loads established in paragraph (c)(1) of this section.

[Docket No. 4080, 29 FR 17955, Dec. 18, 1964; as amended by Amdt. 23–48, 61 FR 5147, Feb. 9, 1996]

§23.499 Supplementary conditions for nose wheels.

In determining the ground loads on nose wheels and affected supporting structures, and assuming that the shock absorbers and tires are in their static positions, the following conditions must be met:

(a) For aft loads, the limit force components at the axle must be—

(1) A vertical component of 2.25 times the static load on the wheel; and

(2) A drag component of 0.8 times the vertical load.

(b) For forward loads, the limit force components at the axle must be—

(1) A vertical component of 2.25 times the static load on the wheel; and

(2) A forward component of 0.4 times the vertical load.

(c) For side loads, the limit force components at ground contact must be—

(1) A vertical component of 2.25 times the static load on the wheel; and

(2) A side component of 0.7 times the vertical load.

(d) For airplanes with a steerable nose wheel that is controlled by hydraulic or other power, at design takeoff weight with the nose wheel in any steerable position, the application of 1.33 times the full steering torque combined with a vertical reaction equal to 1.33 times the maximum static reaction on the nose gear must be assumed. However, if a torque limiting device is installed, the steering torque can be reduced to the maximum value allowed by that device.

(e) For airplanes with a steerable nose wheel that has a direct mechanical connection to the rudder pedals, the mechanism must be designed to withstand the steering torque for the maximum pilot forces specified in §23.397(b).

[Docket No. 4080, 29 FR 17955, Dec. 18, 1964; as amended by Amdt. 23–48, 61 FR 5147, Feb. 9, 1996]

§23.505 Supplementary conditions for skiplanes.

In determining ground loads for skiplanes, and assuming that the airplane is resting on the ground with one main ski frozen at rest and the other skis free to slide, a limit side force equal to 0.036 times the design maximum weight must be applied near the tail assembly, with a factor of safety of 1.

[Amdt. 23–7, 34 FR 13090, Aug. 13, 1969]

§23.507 Jacking loads.

(a) The airplane must be designed for the loads developed when the aircraft is supported on jacks at the design maximum weight assuming the following load factors for landing gear jacking points at a three-point attitude and for primary flight structure jacking points in the level attitude:

(1) Vertical-load factor of 1.35 times the static reactions.

(2) Fore, aft, and lateral load factors of 0.4 times the vertical static reactions.

(b) The horizontal loads at the jack points must be reacted by inertia forces so as to result in no change in the direction of the resultant loads at the jack points.

(c) The horizontal loads must be considered in all combinations with the vertical load.

[Amdt. 23–14, 38 FR 31821, Nov. 19, 1973]

§23.509 Towing loads.

The towing loads of this section must be applied to the design of tow fittings and their immediate attaching structure.

(a) The towing loads specified in paragraph (d) of this section must be considered separately. These loads must be applied at the towing fittings and must act parallel to the ground. In addition:

(1) A vertical load factor equal to 1.0 must be considered acting at the center of gravity; and

(2) The shock struts and tires must be in there static positions.

(b) For towing points not on the landing gear but near the plane of symmetry of the airplane, the drag and side tow load components specified for the auxiliary gear apply. For towing points located outboard of the main gear, the drag and side tow load components specified for the main gear apply. Where the specified angle of swivel cannot be reached, the maximum obtainable angle must be used.

(c) The towing loads specified in paragraph (d) of this section must be reacted as follows:

(1) The side component of the towing load at the main gear must be reacted by a side force at the static ground line of the wheel to which the load is applied.

(2) The towing loads at the auxiliary gear and the drag components of the towing loads at the main gear must be reacted as follows:

(i) A reaction with a maximum value equal to the vertical reaction must be applied at the axle of the wheel to which the load is applied. Enough airplane inertia to achieve equilibrium must be applied.

(ii) The loads must be reacted by airplane inertia.

(d) The prescribed towing loads are as follows, where W is the design maximum weight:

See following table.

Tow point	Position	Load		
		Magnitude	No.	Direction
Main gear		0.225W	1 2 3 4	Forward, parallel to drag axis Forward, at 30° to drag axis Aft, parallel to drag axis Aft, at 30° to drag axis
Auxiliary gear	Swiveled forward	0.3W	5 6	Forward Aft
	Swiveled aft	0.3W	7 8	Forward Aft
	Swiveled 45° from forward	0.15W	9 10	Forward, in plane of wheel Aft, in plane of wheel
	Swiveled 45° from aft	0.15W	11 12	Forward, in plane of wheel Aft, in plane of wheel

[Amdt. 23–14, 38 FR 31821, November 19, 1973]

§23.511 Ground load; unsymmetrical loads on multiple-wheel units.

(a) *Pivoting loads.* The airplane is assumed to pivot about on side of the main gear with—

(1) The brakes on the pivoting unit locked; and

(2) Loads corresponding to a limit vertical load factor of 1, and coefficient of friction of 0.8 applied to the main gear and its supporting structure.

(b) *Unequal tire loads.* The loads established under §§23.471 through 23.483 must be applied in turn, in a 60/40 percent distribution, to the dual wheels and tires in each dual wheel landing gear unit.

(c) *Deflated tire loads.* For the deflated tire condition—

(1) 60 percent of the loads established under §§23.471 through 23.483 must be applied in turn to each wheel in a landing gear unit; and

(2) 60 percent of the limit drag and side loads, and 100 percent of the limit vertical load established under §§23.485 and 23.493 or lesser vertical load obtained under paragraph (c)(1) of this section, must be applied in turn to each wheel in the dual wheel landing gear unit.

[Amdt. 23–7, 34 FR 13090, Aug. 13, 1969]

WATER LOADS

§23.521 Water load conditions.

(a) The structure of seaplanes and amphibians must be designed for water loads developed during takeoff and landing with the seaplane in any attitude likely to occur in normal operation at appropriate forward and sinking velocities under the most severe sea conditions likely to be encountered.

(b) Unless the applicant makes a rational analysis of the water loads, §§23.523 through 23.537 apply.

[Docket No. 4080, 29 FR 17955, Dec. 18, 1964; as amended by Amdt. 23–45, 58 FR 42160, Aug. 6, 1993; Amdt. 23–48, 61 FR 5147, Feb. 9, 1996]

§23.523 Design weights and center of gravity positions.

(a) *Design weights.* The water load requirements must be met at each operating weight up to the design landing weight except that, for the takeoff condition prescribed in §23.531, the design water takeoff weight (the maximum weight for water taxi and takeoff run) must be used.

(b) *Center of gravity positions.* The critical centers of gravity within the limits for which certification is requested must be considered to reach maximum design loads for each part of the seaplane structure.

[Docket No. 26269, 58 FR 42160, Aug. 6, 1993]

§23.525 Application of loads.

(a) Unless otherwise prescribed, the seaplane as a whole is assumed to be subjected to the loads corresponding to the load factors specified in §23.527.

(b) In applying the loads resulting from the load factors prescribed in §23.527, the loads may be distributed over the hull or main float bottom (in order to avoid excessive local shear loads and bending moments at the location of water load application) using pressures not less than those prescribed in §23.533(c).

(c) For twin float seaplanes, each float must be treated as an equivalent hull on a fictitious seaplane with a weight equal to one-half the weight of the twin float seaplane.

(d) Except in the takeoff condition of §23.531, the aerodynamic lift on the seaplane during the impact is assumed to be ⅔ of the weight of the seaplane.

[Docket No. 26269, 58 FR 42161, Aug. 6, 1993; 58 FR 51970, Oct. 5, 1993]

§23.527 Hull and main float load factors.

(a) Water reaction load factors n_W must be computed in the following manner:

(1) For the step landing case

$$n_w = \frac{C_1 V_{S0}^2}{(Tan^{2/3}\beta)W^{1/3}}$$

(2) For the bow and stern landing cases

$$n_w = \frac{C_1 V_{S0}^2}{(Tan^{2/3}\beta)W^{1/3}} \times \frac{K_1}{(1+r_x^2)^{2/3}}$$

(b) The following values are used:

(1) n_W = water reaction load factor (that is, the water reaction divided by seaplane weight).

(2) C_1 = empirical seaplane operations factor equal to 0.012 (except that this factor may not be less than that necessary to obtain the minimum value of step load factor of 2.33).

(3) V_{SO} = seaplane stalling speed in knots with flaps extended in the appropriate landing position and with no slipstream effect.

(4) β = Angle of dead rise at the longitudinal station at which the load factor is being determined in accordance with figure 1 of appendix I of this part.

(5) W = seaplane landing weight in pounds.

(6) K_1 = empirical hull station weighing factor, in accordance with figure 2 of appendix I of this part.

(7) r_x = ratio of distance, measured parallel to hull reference axis, from the center of gravity of the seaplane to the hull longitudinal station at which the load factor is being computed to the radius of gyration in pitch of the seaplane, the hull reference axis being a straight line, in the plane of symmetry, tangential to the keel at the main step.

(c) For a twin float seaplane, because of the effect of flexibility of the attachment of the floats to the seaplane, the factor K_1 may be reduced at the bow and stern to 0.8 of the value shown in figure 2 of appendix I of this part. This reduction applies only to the design of the carry through and seaplane structure.

[Docket No. 26269, 58 FR 42161, Aug. 6, 1993; 58 FR 51970, Oct. 5, 1993]

§23.529 Hull and main float landing conditions.

(a) *Symmetrical step, bow, and stern landing.* For symmetrical step, bow, and stern landings, the limit water reaction load factors are those computed under §23.527. In addition—

(1) For symmetrical step landings, the resultant water load must be applied at the keel, through the center of gravity, and must be directed perpendicularly to the keel line;

(2) For symmetrical bow landings, the resultant water load must be applied at the keel, one-fifth of the longitudinal distance from the bow to the step, and must be directed perpendicularly to the keel line; and

(3) For symmetrical stern landings, the resultant water load must be applied at the keel, at a point 85 percent of the longitudinal distance from the step to the stern post, and must be directed perpendicularly to the keel line.

(b) *Unsymmetrical landing for hull and single float seaplanes.* Unsymmetrical step, bow, and stern landing conditions must be investigated. In addition—

(1) The loading for each condition consists of an upward component and a side component equal, respectively, to 0.75 and 0.25 tan β times the resultant load in the corresponding symmetrical landing condition, and

(2) The point of application and direction of the upward component of the load is the same as that in the symmetrical condition, and the point of application of the side component is at the same longitudinal station as the upward component but is directed inward perpendicularly to the plane of symmetry at a point midway between the keel and chine lines.

(c) *Unsymmetrical landing; twin float seaplanes.* The unsymmetrical loading consists of an upward load at the step of each float of 0.75 and a side load of 0.25 tan β at one float times the step landing load reached under §23.527. The side load is directed inboard, perpendicularly to the plane of symmetry midway between the keel and chine lines of the float, at the same longitudinal station as the upward load.

[Docket No. 26269, 58 FR 42161, Aug. 6, 1993]

§23.531 Hull and main float takeoff condition.

For the wing and its attachment to the hull or main float—

(a) The aerodynamic wing lift is assumed to be zero; and

(b) A downward inertia load, corresponding to a load factor computed from the following formula, must be applied:

$$n = \frac{C_{TO} V_{S1}^{\ 2}}{(Tan^{2/3}\beta) W^{1/3}}$$

Where—

n = inertia load factor;

C_{TO} = empirical seaplane operations factor equal to 0.004;

V_{S1} = seaplane stalling speed (knots) at the design takeoff weight with the flaps extended in the appropriate takeoff position;

β = angle of dead rise at the main step (degrees); and

W = design water takeoff weight in pounds.

[Docket No. 26269, 58 FR 42161, Aug. 6, 1993]

§23.533 Hull and main float bottom pressures.

(a) *General.* The hull and main float structure, including frames and bulkheads, stringers, and bottom plating, must be designed under this section.

(b) *Local pressures.* For the design of the bottom plating and stringers and their attachments to the supporting structure, the following pressure distributions must be applied:

(1) For an unflawed bottom, the pressure at the chine is 0.75 times the pressure at the keel, and the pressures between the keel and chine vary linearly, in accordance with figure 3 of appendix I of this part. The pressure at the keel (p.s.i.) is computed as follows:

$$P_K = \frac{C_2 K_2 V_{S1}^{\ 2}}{Tan\ \beta_k}$$

where—

P_k = pressure (p.s.i.) at the keel;

C_2 = 0.00213;

K_2 = hull station weighing factor, in accordance with figure 2 of appendix I of this part;.

V_{S1} = seaplane stalling speed (knots) at the design water takeoff weight with flaps extended in the appropriate takeoff position; and

β_K = angle of dead rise at keel, in accordance with figure 1 of appendix I of this part.

(2) For a flared bottom, the pressure at the beginning of the flare is the same as that for an unflared bottom, and the pressure between the chine and the beginning of the flare varies linearly, in accordance with figure 3 of appendix I of this part. The pressure distribution is the same as that prescribed in paragraph (b)(1) of this section for an unflared bottom except that the pressure at the chine is computed as follows:

$$P_{ch} = \frac{C_3 K_2 V_{S1}^{\ 2}}{Tan\,\beta}$$

where—
P_{ch} = pressure (p.s.i.) at the chine
C_3 = 0.0016;
K_2 = hull: station weighing factor, in accordance with figure 2 of appendix I of this part;
V_{S1} = seaplane stalling speed (knots) at the design water takeoff weight with flaps extended in the appropriate takeoff position; and
β = angle of dead rise at appropriate station.

The area over which these pressures are applied must simulate pressures occurring during high localized impacts on the hull or float, but need not extend over an area that would induce critical stresses in the frames or in the overall structure.

(c) *Distributed pressures.* For the design of the frames, keel, and chine structure, the following pressure distributions apply:

(1) Symmetrical pressures are commuted as follows:

$$P = \frac{C_4 K_2 V_{SO}^{\ 2}}{Tan\,\beta}$$

where—
P = pressure (p.s.i.);
C_4 = 0.078 C_1 (with C_1 computed under. §23.527);
K_2 = hull station weighing factor determined in accordance with figure 2 of appendix I of this part;
V_{SO} = seaplane stalling speed (knots) with landing flaps extended in the appropriate position and with no slipstream effect; and
β = angle of dead rise at appropriate station

(2) The unsymmetrical pressure distribution consists of the pressures prescribed in paragraph (c)(1) of this section on one side of the hull or main float centerline and one-half of that pressure on the other side of the hull or main float centerline, in accordance with figure 3 of appendix I of this part.

(3) These pressures are uniform and must be applied simultaneously over the entire hull or main float bottom. The loads obtained must be carried into the sidewall structure of the hull proper, but need not be transmitted in a fore and aft direction as shear and bending loads.

[Docket No. 26269, 58 FR 42161, Aug. 6, 1993; 58 FR 51970, Oct. 5, 1993]

§23.535 Auxiliary float loads.

(a) *General.* Auxiliary floats and their attachments and supporting structures must be designed for the conditions prescribed in this section. In the cases specified in paragraphs (b) through (e) of this section, the prescribed water loads may be distributed over the float bottom to avoid excessive local loads, using bottom pressures not less than those prescribed in paragraph (g) of this section.

(b) *Step loading.* The resultant water load must be applied in the plane of symmetry of the float at a point three-fourths of the distance from the bow to the step and must be perpendicular to the keel. The resultant limit load is computed as follows, except that the value of L need not exceed three times the weight of the displaced water when the float is completely submerged:

$$L = \frac{C_5 V_{SO}^{\ 2} W^{2/3}}{Tan^{2/3}\beta_S (1 + r_y^{\ 2})^{2/3}}$$

where—
L = limit load (lbs.);
C_5 = 0.0053
V_{SO} = seaplane stalling speed (knots) with landing flaps extended in the appropriate position and with no slipstream effect;
W= seaplane design landing weight in pounds;
β = angle of dead rise at a station ¾ of the distance from the bow to the step but need not be less than 15 degrees; and
r_y = ratio of the lateral distance between the center of gravity and the plane of symmetry of the float to the radius of gyration in roll.

(c) *Bow loading.* The resultant limit load must be applied in the plane of symmetry of the float at a point one-fourth of the distance from the bow to the step and must be perpendicular to the tangent to the keel line at that point. The magnitude of the resultant load is that specified in paragraph (b) of this section.

(d) *Unsymmetrical step loading.* The resultant water load consists of a component equal to 0.75 times the load specified in paragraph (a) of this section and a side component equal to 0.025 tan β times the load specified in paragraph (b) of this section. The side load must be applied perpendicularly to the plane of symmetry of the float at a point midway between the keel and the chine;

(e) *Unsymmetrical bow loading.* The resultant water load consists of a component equal to 0.75 times the load specified in paragraph (b) of this section and a side component equal to 0.25 tan β times the load specified in paragraph (c) of this section. The side load must be applied perpendicularly to the plane of symmetry at a point midway between the keel and the chine.

(f) *Immersed float condition.* The resultant load must be applied at the centroid of the cross section of the float at a point one-third of the distance from the bow to the step. The limit load components are as follows:

$$\text{vertical} = PgV$$

$$\text{aft} = \frac{C_X P V^{2/3} (K V_{SO})^2}{2}$$

$$\text{side} = \frac{C_Y P V^{2/3} (K V_{SO})^2}{2}$$

where—
ρ = mass density of water (slugs/ft.[3]):
V = volume of float (ft.[3]);
C_X = coefficient of drag force, equal to 0.133;

C_Y = coefficient of side force, equal to 0.106;
K = 0.8, except that lower values may be used if it is shown that the floats are incapable of submerging at a speed of 0.8 V_{S0} in normal operations;
V_{S0} = seaplane stalling speed ((knots) with landing flaps extended in the appropriate position and with no slipstream effect; and
g = acceleration due to gravity (ft/sec^2).

(g) *Float bottom pressures.* The float bottom pressures must be established under §23.533, except that the value of K_2 in the formulae may be taken as 1.0. The angle of dead rise to be used in determining the float bottom pressures is set forth in paragraph (b) of this section.

[Docket No. 26269, 58 FR 42162, Aug. 6, 1993; 58 FR 51970, Oct. 5, 1993]

§23.537 Seawing loads.

Seawing design loads must be based on applicable test data.

[Docket No. 26269, 58 FR 42163, Aug. 6, 1993]

EMERGENCY LANDING CONDITIONS

§23.561 General.

(a) The airplane, although it may be damaged in emergency landing conditions, must be designed as prescribed in this section to protect each occupant under those conditions.

(b) The structure must be designed to give each occupant every reasonable chance of escaping serious injury when—

(1) Proper use is made of the seats, safety belts, and shoulder harnesses provided for in the design;

(2) The occupant experiences the static inertia loads corresponding to the following ultimate load factors—

(i) Upward, 3.0g for normal, utility, and commuter category airplanes, or 4.5g for acrobatic category airplanes;

(ii) Forward, 9.0g;

(iii) Sideward, 1.5g; and

(iv) Downward, 6.0g when certification to the emergency exit provisions of §23.807(d)(4) is requested; and

(3) The items of mass within the cabin, that could injure an occupant, experience the static inertia loads corresponding to the following ultimate load factors—

(i) Upward, 3.0g;

(ii) Forward, 18.0g; and

(iii) Sideward, 4.5g.

(c) Each airplane with retractable landing gear must be designed to protect each occupant in a landing—

(1) With the wheels retracted;

(2) With moderate descent velocity; and

(3) Assuming, in the absence of a more rational analysis—

(i) A downward ultimate inertia force of 3g; and

(ii) A coefficient of friction of 0.5 at the ground.

(d) If it is not established that a turnover is unlikely during an emergency landing, the structure must be designed to protect the occupants in a complete turnover as follows:

(1) The likelihood of a turnover may be shown by an analysis assuming the following conditions—

(i) The most adverse combination of weight and center of gravity position;

(ii) Longitudinal load factor of 9.0g;

(iii) Vertical load factor of 1.0g; and

(iv) For airplanes with tricycle landing gear, the nose wheel strut failed with the nose contacting the ground.

(2) For determining the loads to be applied to the inverted airplane after a turnover, an upward ultimate inertia load factor of 3.0g and a coefficient of friction with the ground of 0.5 must be used.

(e) Except as provided in §23.787(c), the supporting structure must be designed to restrain, under loads up to those specified in paragraph (b)(3) of this section, each item of mass that could injure an occupant if it came loose in a minor crash landing.

[Docket No. 4080, 29 FR 17955, Dec. 18, 1964; as amended by Amdt. 23–7, 34 FR 13090, Aug. 13, 1969; Amdt. 23–24, 52 FR 34745, Sept. 14, 1987; Amdt. 23–36, 53 FR 30812, Aug. 15, 1988; Amdt. 23–46, 59 FR 25772, May 17, 1994; Amdt. 23–48, 61 FR 5147, Feb. 9, 1996]

§23.562 Emergency landing dynamic conditions.

(a) Each seat/restraint system for use in a normal, utility, or acrobatic category airplane must be designed to protect each occupant during an emergency landing when—

(1) Proper use is made of seats, safety belts, and shoulder harnesses provided for in the design; and

(2) The occupant is exposed to the loads resulting from the conditions prescribed in this section.

(b) Except for those seat/restraint systems that are required to meet paragraph (d) of this section, each seat/restraint system for crew or passenger occupancy in a normal, utility, or acrobatic category airplane, must successfully complete dynamic tests or be demonstrated by rational analysis supported by dynamic tests, in accordance with each of the following conditions. These tests must be conducted with an occupant simulated by an anthropomorphic test dummy (ATD) defined by 49 CFR Part 572, Subpart B, or an FAA-approved equivalent, with a nominal weight of 170 pounds and seated in the normal upright position.

(1) For the first test, the change in velocity may not be less than 31 feet per second. The seat/restraint system must be oriented in its nominal position with respect to the airplane and with the horizontal plane of the airplane pitched up 60 degrees, with no yaw, relative to the impact vector. For seat/restraint systems to be installed in the first row of the airplane, peak deceleration must occur in not more than 0.05 seconds after impact and must reach a minimum of 19g. For all other seat/restraint systems, peak deceleration must occur in not more than 0.06 seconds after impact and must reach a minimum of 15g.

(2) For the second test, the change in velocity may not be less than 42 feet per second. The seat/restraint system must be oriented in its nominal position with respect to the airplane and with the vertical plane of the airplane yawed 10 degrees, with no pitch, relative to the impact vector in a direction that results in the greatest load on the shoulder harness. For seat/restraint systems to be installed in the first row of the airplane, peak deceleration must occur in not more than 0.05 seconds after impact and must reach a minimum of 26g. For all other seat/restraint systems, peak deceleration must occur in not more than 0.06 seconds after impact and must reach a minimum of 21g.

(3) To account for floor warpage, the floor rails or attachment devices used to attach the seat/restraint system to the

airframe structure must be preloaded to misalign with respect to each other by at least 10 degrees vertically (i.e., pitch out of parallel) and one of the rails or attachment devices must be preloaded to misalign by 10 degrees in roll prior to conducting the test defined by paragraph (b)(2) of this section.

(c) Compliance with the following requirements must be shown during the dynamic tests conducted in accordance with paragraph (b) of this section:

(1) The seat/restraint system must restrain the ATD although seat/restraint system components may experience deformation, elongation, displacement, or crushing intended as part of the design.

(2) The attachment between the seat/restraint system and the test fixture must remain intact, although the seat structure may have deformed.

(3) Each shoulder harness strap must remain on the ATD's shoulder during the impact.

(4) The safety belt must remain on the ATD's pelvis during the impact.

(5) The results of the dynamic tests must show that the occupant is protected from serious head injury.

(i) When contact with adjacent seats, structure, or other items in the cabin can occur, protection must be provided so that the head impact does not exceed a head injury criteria (HIC) of 1,000.

(ii) The value of HIC is defined as—

$$HIC = \left\{ (t_2 - t_1) \left[\frac{1}{(t_2 - t_1)} \int_{t_1}^{t_2} a(t)dt \right]^{2.5} \right\}_{Max}$$

Where: t_1 is the initial integration time, expressed in seconds, t_2 is the final integration time, expressed in seconds, $(t_2 - t_1)$ is the time duration of the major head impact, expressed in seconds, and a(t) is the resultant deceleration at the center of gravity of the head form expressed as a multiple of g (units of gravity).

(iii) Compliance with the HIC limit must be demonstrated by measuring the head impact during dynamic testing as prescribed in paragraphs (b)(1) and (b)(2) of this section or by a separate showing of compliance with the head injury criteria using test or analysis procedures.

(6) Loads in individual shoulder harness straps may not exceed 1,750 pounds. If dual straps are used for retaining the upper torso, the total strap loads may not exceed 2,000 pounds.

(7) The compression load measured between the pelvis and the lumbar spine of the ATD may not exceed 1,500 pounds.

(d) For all single-engine airplanes with a V_{SO} of more than 61 knots at maximum weight, and those multiengine airplanes of 6,000 pounds or less maximum weight with a V_{SO} of more than 61 knots at maximum weight that do not comply with §23.67(a)(1);

(1) The ultimate load factors of §23.561(b) must be increased by multiplying the load factors by the square of the ratio of the increased stall speed to 61 knots. The increased ultimate load factors need not exceed the values reached at a V_{SO} of 79 knots. The upward ultimate load factor for acrobatic category airplanes need not exceed 5.0g.

(2) The seat/restraint system test required by paragraph (b)(1) of this section must be conducted in accordance with the following criteria:

(i) The change in velocity may not be less than 31 feet per second.

(ii)(A) The peak deceleration (g_p) of 19g and 15g must be increased and multiplied by the square of the ratio of the increased stall speed to 61 knots:

$g_p = 19.0 (V_{SO}/61)^2$ or $g_p = 15.0 (V_{SO}/61)^2$

(B) The peak deceleration need not exceed the value reached at a V_{SO} of 79 knots.

(iii) The peak deceleration must occur in not more than time (t_r), which must be computed as follows:

$$t_r = \frac{31}{32.2(g_p)} = \frac{.96}{g_p}$$

where—

g_p = The peak deceleration calculated in accordance with paragraph (d)(2)(ii) of this section

t_r = The rise time (in seconds) to the peak deceleration.

(e) An alternate approach that achieves an equivalent, or greater, level of occupant protection to that required by this section may be used if substantiated on a rational basis.

[Amdt. 23–36, 53 FR 30812, Aug. 15, 1988; as amended by Amdt. 23–44, 58 FR 38639, July 19, 1993; Amdt. 23–50, 61 FR 5192, Feb. 9, 1996]

Fatigue Evaluation

§23.571 Metallic pressurized cabin structures.

For normal, utility, and acrobatic category airplanes, the strength, detail design, and fabrication of the metallic structure of the pressure cabin must be evaluated under one of the following:

(a) A fatigue strength investigation in which the structure is shown by tests, or by analysis supported by test evidence, to be able to withstand the repeated loads of variable magnitude expected in service; or

(b) A fail safe strength investigation, in which it is shown by analysis, tests, or both that catastrophic failure of the structure is not probable after fatigue failure, or obvious partial failure, of a principal structural element, and that the remaining structures are able to withstand a static ultimate load factor of 75 percent of the limit load factor at V_C, considering the combined effects of normal operating pressures, expected external aerodynamic pressures, and flight loads. These loads must be multiplied by a factor of 1.15 unless the dynamic effects of failure under static load are otherwise considered.

(c) The damage tolerance evaluation of §23.573(b).

[Docket No. 4080, 29 FR 17955, Dec. 18, 1964; as amended by Amdt. 23–14, 38 FR 31821, Nov. 19, 1973; Amdt. 23–45, 58 FR 42163, Aug. 6, 1993; Amdt. 23–48, 61 FR 5147, Feb. 9, 1996]

§23.572 Metallic wing, empennage, and associated structures.

(a) For normal, utility, and acrobatic category airplanes, the strength, detail design, and fabrication of those parts of the airframe structure whose failure would be catastrophic must be evaluated under one of the following unless it is shown that the structure, operating stress level, materials and expected uses are comparable, from a fatigue standpoint, to a similar design that has had extensive satisfactory service experience:

(1) A fatigue strength investigation in which the structure is shown by tests, or by analysis supported by test evidence, to be able to withstand the repeated loads of variable magnitude expected in service; or

(2) A fail-safe strength investigation in which it is shown by analysis, tests, or both, that catastrophic failure of the structure is not probable after fatigue failure, or obvious partial failure, of a principal structural element, and that the remaining structure is able to withstand a static ultimate load factor of 75 percent of the critical limit load factor at V_C. These loads must be multiplied by a factor of 1.15 unless the dynamic effects of failure under static load are otherwise considered.

(3) The damage tolerance evaluation of §23.573(b).

(b) Each evaluation required by this section must—

(1) Include typical loading spectra (e.g. taxi, ground-air-ground cycles, maneuver, gust);

(2) Account for any significant effects due to the mutual influence of aerodynamic surfaces; and

(3) Consider any significant effects from propeller slipstream loading, and buffet from vortex impingements.

[Amdt. 23–7, 34 FR 13090, Aug. 13, 1969; as amended by Amdt. 23–14, 38 FR 31821, Nov. 19, 1973; Amdt. 23–34, 52 FR 1830, Jan. 15, 1987; Amdt. 23–38, 54 FR 39511, Sept. 26, 1989; Amdt. 23–45, 58 FR 42163, Aug. 6, 1993; Amdt. 23–48, 61 FR 5147, Feb. 9, 1996]

§23.573 Damage tolerance and fatigue evaluation of structure.

(a) *Composite airframe structure.* Composite airframe structure must be evaluated under this paragraph instead of §§23.571 and 23.572. The applicant must evaluate the composite airframe structure, the failure of which would result in catastrophic loss of the airplane, in each wing (including canards, tandem wings, and winglets), empennage, their carrythrough and attaching structure, moveable control surfaces and their attaching structure fuselage, and pressure cabin using the damage-tolerance criteria prescribed in paragraphs (a)(1) through (a)(4) of this section unless shown to be impractical. If the applicant establishes that damage tolerance criteria is impractical for a particular structure, the structure must be evaluated in accordance with paragraphs (a)(1) and (a)(6) of this section. Where bonded joints are used the structure must also be evaluated in accordance with paragraph (a)(5) of this section. The effects of material variability and environmental conditions on the strength and durability properties of the composite materials must be accounted for in the evaluations required by this section.

(1) It must be demonstrated by tests, or by analysis supported by tests, that the structure is capable of carrying ultimate load with damage up to the threshold of delectability considering the inspection procedures employed.

(2) The growth rate or no-growth of damage that may occur from fatigue, corrosion, manufacturing flaws or impact damage, under repeated loads expected in service, must be established by tests or analysis supported by tests.

(3) The structure must be shown by residual strength tests, or analyses supported by residual strength tests, to be able to withstand critical limit flight loads, considered as ultimate loads, with the extent of detectable damage consistent with the results of the damage tolerance evaluations. For pressurized cabins, the following loads must be withstood:

(i) Critical limit flight loads with the combined effects of normal operating pressure and expected external aerodynamic pressures.

(ii) The expected external aerodynamic pressures in 1g flight combined with a cabin differential pressure equal to 1.1 times the normal operating differential pressure without any other load.

(4) The damage growth, between initial delectability and the value selected for residual strength demonstrations, factored to obtain inspection intervals, must allow development of an inspection program suitable for application by operation and maintenance personnel.

(5) For any bonded joint, the failure of which would result in catastrophic loss of the airplane, the limit load capacity must be substantiated by one of the following methods—

(i) The maximum disbonds of each bonded joint consistent with the capability to withstand the loads in paragraph (a)(3) of this section must be determined by analysis, tests, or both. Disbonds of each bonded joint greater than this must be prevented by design features; or

(ii) Proof testing must be conducted on each production article that will apply the critical limit design load to each critical bonded joint; or

(iii) Repeatable and reliable non-destructive inspection techniques must be established that ensure the strength of each joint.

(6) Structural components for which the damage tolerance method is shown to be impractical must be shown by component fatigue tests, or analysis supported by tests, to be able to withstand the repeated loads of variable magnitude expected in service. Sufficient component, subcomponent, element, or coupon tests must be done to establish the fatigue scatter factor and the environmental effects. Damage up to the threshold of detectability and ultimate load residual strength capability must be considered in the demonstration.

(b) *Metallic airframe structure.* If the applicant elects to use §23.571(a)(3) or §23.572(a)(3), then the damage tolerance evaluation must include a determination of the probable locations and modes of damage due to fatigue, corrosion, or accidental damage. The determination must be by analysis supported by test evidence and, if available, service experience. Damage at multiple sites due to fatigue must be included where the design is such that this type of damage can be expected to occur. The evaluation must incorporate repeated load and static analyses supported by test evidence. The extent of damage for residual strength evaluation at any time within the operational life of the airplane must be consistent with the initial detectability and subsequent growth under repeated loads. The residual strength evaluation must show that the remaining structure is able to withstand critical limit flight loads, considered as ultimate, with the extent of detectable damage consistent with the results of the damage tolerance evaluations. For pressurized cabins, the following load must be withstood:

(1) The normal operating differential pressure combined with the expected external aerodynamic pressures applied simultaneously with the flight loading conditions specified in this part, and

(2) The expected external aerodynamic pressures in 1g flight combined with a cabin differential pressure equal to 1.1 times the normal operating differential pressure without any other load.

[Docket No. 26269, 58 FR 42163, Aug. 6, 1993; 58 FR 51970, Oct. 5, 1993; Amdt. 23–48, 61 FR 5147, Feb. 9, 1996]

§23.574 Metallic damage tolerance and fatigue evaluation of commuter category airplanes.

For commuter category airplanes—

(a) *Metallic damage tolerance.* An evaluation of the strength, detail design, and fabrication must show that catastrophic failure due to fatigue, corrosion, defects, or damage will be avoided throughout the operational life of the airplane. This evaluation must be conducted in accordance with the provisions of §23.573, except as specified in paragraph (b) of this section, for each part of the structure that could contribute to a catastrophic failure.

(b) *Fatigue (safe-life) evaluation.* Compliance with the damage tolerance requirements of paragraph (a) of this section is not required if the applicant establishes that the application of those requirements is impractical for a particular structure. This structure must be shown, by analysis supported by test evidence, to be able to withstand the repeated loads of variable magnitude expected during its service life without detectable cracks. Appropriate safe-life scatter factors must be applied.

[Docket No. 27805, 61 FR 5148, Feb. 9, 1996]

§23.575 Inspections and other procedures.

Each inspection or other procedure, based on an evaluation required by §§23.571, 23.572, 23.573 or 23.574, must be established to prevent catastrophic failure and must be included in the Limitations Section of the Instructions for Continued Airworthiness required by §23.1529.

[Docket No. 27805, 61 FR 5148, Feb. 9, 1996]

Subpart D—Design and Construction

§23.601 General.

The suitability of each questionable design detail and part having an important bearing on safety in operations, must be established by tests.

§23.603 Materials and workmanship.

(a) The suitability and durability of materials used for parts, the failure of which could adversely affect safety, must—

(1) Be established by experience or tests;

(2) Meet approved specifications that ensure their having the strength and other properties assumed in the design data; and

(3) Take into account the effects of environmental conditions, such as temperature and humidity, expected in service.

(b) Workmanship must be of a high standard.

[Docket No. 4080, 29 FR 17955, Dec. 18, 1964; as amended by Amdt. 23–17, 41 FR 55464, Dec. 20, 1976; Amdt. 23–23, 43 FR 50592, Oct. 10, 1978]

§23.605 Fabrication methods.

(a) The methods of fabrication used must produce consistently sound structures. If a fabrication process (such as gluing, spot welding, or heat-treating) requires close control to reach this objective, the process must be performed under an approved process specification.

(b) Each new aircraft fabrication method must be substantiated by a test program.

[Docket No. 4080, 29 FR 17955, Dec. 18, 1964; 30 FR 258, Jan. 9, 1965; as amended by Amdt. 23–23, 43 FR 50592, Oct. 10, 1978]

§23.607 Fasteners.

(a) Each removable fastener must incorporate two retaining devices if the loss of such fastener would preclude continued safe flight and landing.

(b) Fasteners and their locking devices must not be adversely affected by the environmental conditions associated with the particular installation.

(c) No self-locking nut may be used on any bolt subject to rotation in operation unless a non-friction locking device is used in addition to the self-locking device.

[Docket No. 27805, 61 FR 5148, Feb. 9, 1996]

§23.609 Protection of structure.

Each part of the structure must—

(a) Be suitably protected against deterioration or loss of strength in service due to any cause, including—

(1) Weathering;

(2) Corrosion; and

(3) Abrasion; and

(b) Have adequate provisions for ventilation and drainage.

§23.611 Accessibility provisions.

For each part that requires maintenance, inspection, or other servicing, appropriate means must be incorporated into the aircraft design to allow such servicing to be accomplished.

[Docket No. 27805, 61 FR 5148, Feb. 9, 1996]

§23.613 Material strength properties and design values.

(a) Material strength properties must be based on enough tests of material meeting specifications to establish design values on a statistical basis.

(b) Design values must be chosen to minimize the probability of structural failure due to material variability. Except as provided in paragraph (e) of this section, compliance with this paragraph must be shown by selecting design values that ensure material strength with the following probability

(1) Where applied loads are eventually distributed through a single member within an assembly, the failure of which would result in loss of structural integrity of the component; 99 percent probability with 95 percent confidence.

(2) For redundant structure, in which the failure of individual elements would result in applied loads being safely distributed to other load carrying members; 90 percent probability with 95 percent confidence.

(c) The effects of temperature on allowable stresses used for design in an essential component or structure must be considered where thermal effects are significant under normal operating conditions.

(d) The design of the structure must minimize the probability of catastrophic fatigue failure, particularly at points of stress concentration.

(e) Design values greater than the guaranteed minimums required by this section may be used where only guaranteed minimum values are normally allowed if a "premium selection" of the materials made in which a specimen of each individual item is tested before use to determine that the actual strength properties of that particular item will equal or exceed those used in design.

[Docket No. 4080, 29 FR 17955, Dec. 18, 1964; 30 FR 258, Jan. 9, 1965; as amended by Amdt. 23–23, 43 FR 50592, Oct. 30, 1978; Amdt. 23–45, 58 FR 42163, Aug. 6, 1993]

§23.619 Special factors.

The factor of safety prescribed in §23.303 must be multiplied by the highest pertinent special factors of safety prescribed in §§23.621 through 23.625 for each part of the structure whose strength is—

(a) Uncertain;

(b) Likely to deteriorate in service before normal replacement; or

(c) Subject to appreciable variability because of uncertainties in manufacturing processes or inspection methods.

[Amdt. 23–7, 34 FR 13091, Aug. 13, 1969]

§23.621 Casting factors.

(a) *General.* The factors, tests, and inspections specified in paragraphs (b) through (d) of this section must be applied in addition to those necessary to establish foundry quality control. The inspections must meet approved specifications. Paragraphs (c) and (d) of this section apply to any structural castings except castings that are pressure tested as parts of hydraulic or other fluid systems and do not support structural loads.

(b) *Bearing stresses and surfaces.* The casting factors specified in paragraphs (c) and (d) of this section—

(1) Need not exceed 1.25 with respect to bearing stresses regardless of the method of inspection used; and

(2) Need not be used with respect to the bearing surfaces of a part whose bearing factor is larger than the applicable casting factor.

(c) *Critical castings.* For each casting whose failure would preclude continued safe flight and landing of the airplane or result in serious injury to occupants, the following apply:

(1) Each critical casting must either—

(i) Have a casting factor of not less than 1.25 and receive 100 percent inspection by visual, radiographic, and either magnetic particle, penetrant or other approved equivalent nondestructive inspection method; or

(ii) Have a casting factor of not less than 2.0 and receive 100 percent visual inspection and 100 percent approved nondestructive inspection. When an approved quality control procedure is established and an acceptable statistical analysis supports reduction, nondestructive inspection may be reduced from 100 percent, and applied on a sampling basis.

(2) For each critical casting with a casting factor less than 1.50, three sample castings must be static tested and shown to meet—

(i) The strength requirements of §23.305 at an ultimate load corresponding to a casting factor of 1.25; and

(ii) The deformation requirements of §23.305 at a load of 1.15 times the limit load.

(3) Examples of these castings are structural attachment fittings, parts of flight control systems, control surface hinges and balance weight attachments, seat, berth, safety belt, and fuel and oil tank supports and attachments, and cabin pressure valves.

(d) *Non-critical castings.* For each casting other than those specified in paragraph (c) or (e) of this section, the following apply:

(1) Except as provided in paragraphs (d) (2) and (3) of this section, the casting factors and corresponding inspections must meet the following table:

Casting factor	Inspection
2.0 or more	100 percent visual
Less than 2.0 but more than 1.5	100 percent visual, and magnetic particle or penetrant or equivalent nondestructive inspection methods
1.25 through 1.50	100 percent visual, magnetic particle or penetrant, and radiographic, or approved equivalent nondestructive inspection methods

(2) The percentage of castings inspected by nonvisual methods may be reduced below that specified in subparagraph (d)(1) of this section when an approved quality control procedure is established.

(3) For castings procured to a specification that guarantees the mechanical properties of the material in the casting

and provides for demonstration of these properties by test of coupons cut from the castings on a sampling basis—

(i) A casting factor of 1.0 may be used; and

(ii) The castings must be inspected as provided in paragraph (d)(1) of this section for casting factors of "1.25 through 1.50" and tested under paragraph (c)(2) of this section.

(e) *Non-structural castings.* Castings used for non-structural purposes do not require evaluation, testing or close inspection.

[Docket No. 4080, 29 FR 17955, Dec. 18, 1964; as amended by Amdt. 23–45, 58 FR 42164, Aug. 6, 1993]

§23.623 Bearing factors.

(a) Each part that has clearance (free fit), and that is subject to pounding or vibration, must have a bearing factor large enough to provide for the effects of normal relative motion.

(b) For control surface hinges and control system joints, compliance with the factors prescribed in §§23.657 and 23.693, respectively, meets paragraph (a) of this section.

[Amdt. 23–7, 34 FR 13091, Aug. 13, 1969]

§23.625 Fitting factors.

For each fitting (a part or terminal used to join one structural member to another), the following apply:

(a) For each fitting whose strength is not proven by limit and ultimate load tests in which actual stress conditions are simulated in the fitting and surrounding structures, a fitting factor of at least 1.15 must be applied to each part of—

(1) The fitting;

(2) The means of attachment; and

(3) The bearing on the joined members.

(b) No fitting factor need be used for joint designs based on comprehensive test data (such as continuous joints in metal plating, welded joints, and scarf joints in wood).

(c) For each integral fitting, the part must be treated as a fitting up to the point at which the section properties become typical of the member.

(d) For each seat, berth, safety belt, and harness, its attachment to the structure must be shown, by analysis, tests, or both, to be able to withstand the inertia forces prescribed in §23.561 multiplied by a fitting factor of 1.33.

[Docket No. 4080, 29 FR 17955, Dec. 18, 1964; as amended by Amdt. 23–7, 34 FR 13091, Aug. 13, 1969]

§23.627 Fatigue strength.

The structure must be designed, as far as practicable, to avoid points of stress concentration where variable stresses above the fatigue limit are likely to occur in normal service.

§23.629 Flutter.

(a) It must be shown by the methods of paragraph (b) and either paragraph (c) or (d) of this section, that the airplane is free from flutter, control reversal, and divergence for any condition of operation within the limit V_{-n} envelope and at all speeds up to the speed specified for the selected method. In addition—

(1) Adequate tolerances must be established for quantities which affect flutter, including speed, damping, mass balance, and control system stiffness; and

(2) The natural frequencies of main structural components must be determined by vibration tests or other approved methods.

(b) Flight flutter tests must be made to show that the airplane is free from flutter, control reversal and divergence and to show that—

(1) Proper and adequate attempts to induce flutter have been made within the speed range up to V_D;

(2) The vibratory response of the structure during the test indicates freedom from flutter;

(3) A proper margin of damping exists at V_D; and

(4) There is no large and rapid reduction in damping as V_D is approached.

(c) Any rational analysis used to predict freedom from flutter, control reversal and divergence must cover all speeds up to 1.2 V_D.

(d) Compliance with the rigidity and mass balance criteria (pages 4-12), in Airframe and Equipment Engineering Report No. 45 (as corrected) "Simplified Flutter Prevention Criteria" (published by the Federal Aviation Administration) may be accomplished to show that the airplane is free from flutter, control reversal, or divergence if—

(1) V_D/M_D for the airplane is less than 260 knots (EAS) and less than Mach 0.5,

(2) The wing and aileron flutter prevention criteria, as represented by the wing torsional stiffness and aileron balance criteria, are limited in use to airplanes without large mass concentrations (such as engines, floats, or fuel tanks in outer wing panels) along the wing span, and

(3) The airplane—

(i) Does not have a T-tail or other unconventional tail configurations;

(ii) Does not have unusual mass distributions or other unconventional design features that affect the applicability of the criteria, and

(iii) Has fixed-fin and fixed-stabilizer surfaces.

(e) For turbopropeller-powered airplanes, the dynamic evaluation must include—

(1) Whirl mode degree of freedom which takes into account the stability of the plane of rotation of the propeller and significant elastic, inertial, and aerodynamic forces, and

(2) Propeller, engine, engine mount, and airplane structure stiffness and damping variations appropriate to the particular configuration.

(f) Freedom from flutter, control reversal, and divergence up to V_D/M_D must be shown as follows:

(1) For airplanes that meet the criteria of paragraphs (d)(1) through (d)(3) of this section, after the failure, malfunction, or disconnection of any single element in any tab control system.

(2) For airplanes other than those described in paragraph (f)(1) of this section, after the failure, malfunction, or disconnection of any single element in the primary flight control system, any tab control system, or any flutter damper.

(g) For airplanes showing compliance with the fail-safe criteria of §§23.571 and 23.572, the airplane must be shown by analysis to be free from flutter up to V_D/M_D after fatigue failure, or obvious partial failure, of a principal structural element.

(h) For airplanes showing compliance with the damage tolerance criteria of §23.573, the airplane must be shown by analysis to be free from flutter up to V_D/M_D with the extent of damage for which residual strength is demonstrated.

(i) For modifications to the type design that could affect the flutter characteristics, compliance with paragraph (a) of this section must be shown, except that analysis based on previously approved data may be used alone to show freedom from flutter, control reversal and divergence, for all speeds up to the speed specified for the selected method.

[Amdt. 23–23, 43 FR 50592, Oct. 30, 1978; as amended by Amdt. 23–31, 49 FR 46867, Nov. 28, 1984; Amdt. 23–45, 58 FR 42164, Aug. 6, 1993; 58 FR 51970, Oct. 5, 1993; Amdt. 23–48, 61 FR 5148, Feb. 9, 1996]

WINGS

§23.641 Proof of strength.

The strength of stressed-skin wings must be proven by load tests or by combined structural analysis and load tests.

CONTROL SURFACES

§23.651 Proof of strength.

(a) Limit load tests of control surfaces are required. These tests must include the horn or fitting to which the control system is attached.

(b) In structural analyses, rigging loads due to wire bracing must be accounted for in a rational or conservative manner.

§23.655 Installation.

(a) Movable surfaces must be installed so that there is no interference between any surfaces, their bracing, or adjacent fixed structure, when one surface is held in its most critical clearance positions and the others are operated through their full movement.

(b) If an adjustable stabilizer is used, it must have stops that will limit its range of travel to that allowing safe flight and landing.

[Docket No. 4080, 29 FR 17955, Dec. 18, 1964; as amended by Amdt. 23–45, 58 FR 42164, Aug. 6, 1993]

§23.657 Hinges.

(a) Control surface hinges, except ball and roller bearing hinges, must have a factor of safety of not less than 6.67 with respect to the ultimate bearing strength of the softest material used as a bearing.

(b) For ball or roller bearing hinges, the approved rating of the bearing may not be exceeded.

[Amended by Amdt. 23–48, 61 FR 5148, Feb. 9, 1996]

§23.659 Mass balance.

The supporting structure and the attachment of concentrated mass balance weights used on control surfaces must be designed for—

(a) 24 *g* normal to the plane of the control surface;

(b) 12 *g* fore and aft; and

(c) 12 *g* parallel to the hinge line.

CONTROL SYSTEMS

§23.671 General.

(a) Each control must operate easily, smoothly, and positively enough to allow proper performance of its functions.

(b) Controls must be arranged and identified to provide for convenience in operation and to prevent the possibility of confusion and subsequent inadvertent operation.

§23.672 Stability augmentation and automatic and power-operated systems.

If the functioning of stability augmentation or other automatic or power-operated systems is necessary to show compliance with the flight characteristics requirements of this part, such systems must comply with §23.671 and the following:

(a) A warning, which is clearly distinguishable to the pilot under expected flight conditions without requiring the pilot's attention, must be provided for any failure in the stability augmentation system or in any other automatic or power-operated system that could result in an unsafe condition if the pilot was not aware of the failure. Warning systems must not activate the control system.

(b) The design of the stability augmentation system or of any other automatic or power-operated system must permit initial counteraction of failures without requiring exceptional pilot skill or strength, by either the deactivation of the system or a failed portion thereof, or by overriding the failure by movement of the flight controls in the normal sense.

(c) It must be shown that, after any single failure of the stability augmentation system or any other automatic or power-operated system—

(1) The airplane is safely controllable when the failure or malfunction occurs at any speed or altitude within the approved operating limitations that is critical for the type of failure being considered:

(2) The controllability and maneuverability requirements of this part are met within a practical operational flight envelope (for example, speed, altitude, normal acceleration, and airplane configuration) that is described in the Airplane Flight Manual (AFM): and

(3) The trim, stability, and stall characteristics are not impaired below a level needed to permit continued safe flight and landing.

[Docket No. 26269, 58 FR 42164, Aug. 6, 1993]

§23.673 Primary flight controls.

Primary flight controls are those used by the pilot for the immediate control of pitch, roll, and yaw.

[Docket No. 4080, 29 FR 17955, Dec. 18, 1964; as amended by Amdt. 23–48, 61 FR 5148, Feb. 9, 1996]

§23.675 Stops.

(a) Each control system must have stops that positively limit the range of motion of each movable aerodynamic surface controlled by the system.

(b) Each stop must be located so that wear, slackness, or takeup adjustments will not adversely affect the control characteristics of the airplane because of a change in the range of surface travel.

(c) Each stop must be able to withstand any loads corresponding to the design conditions for the control system.

[Amdt. 23–17, 41 FR 55464, Dec. 20, 1976]

§23.677 Trim systems.

(a) Proper precautions must be taken to prevent inadvertent, improper, or abrupt trim tab operation. There must be means near the trim control to indicate to the pilot the direction of trim control movement relative to airplane motion. In addition, there must be means to indicate to the pilot the position of the trim device with respect to both the range of adjustment and, in the case of lateral and directional trim, the neutral position. This means must be visible to the pilot and must be located and designed to prevent confusion. The pitch trim indicator must be clearly marked with a position or range within which it has been demonstrated that take-off is safe for all center of gravity positions and each flap position approved for takeoff.

(b) Trimming devices must be designed so that, when any one connecting or transmitting element in the primary flight control system fails, adequate control for safe flight and landing is available with—

(1) For single-engine airplanes, the longitudinal trimming devices; or

(2) For multiengine airplanes, the longitudinal and directional trimming devices.

(c) Tab controls must be irreversible unless the tab is properly balanced and has no unsafe flutter characteristics. Irreversible tab systems must have adequate rigidity and reliability in the portion of the system from the tab to the attachment of the irreversible unit to the airplane structure.

(d) It must be demonstrated that the airplane is safely controllable and that the pilot can perform all maneuvers and operations necessary to effect a safe landing following any probable powered trim system runaway that reasonably might be expected in service, allowing for appropriate time delay after pilot recognition of the trim system runaway. The demonstration must be conducted at critical airplane weights and center of gravity positions.

[Docket No. 4080, 29 FR 17955, Dec. 18, 1964; as amended by Amdt. 23–7, 34 FR 13091, Aug. 13, 1969; Amdt. 23–34, 52 FR 1830, Jan. 15, 1987; Amdt. 23–42, 56 FR 353, Jan. 3, 1991; Amdt. 23–49, 61 FR 5165, Feb. 9, 1996]

§23.679 Control system locks.

If there is a device to lock the control system on the ground or water:

(a) There must be a means to—

(1) Give unmistakable warning to the pilot when lock is engaged; or

(2) Automatically disengage the device when the pilot operates the primary flight controls in a normal manner.

(b) The device must be installed to limit the operation of the airplane so that, when the device is engaged, the pilot receives unmistakable warning at the start of the takeoff.

(c) The device must have a means to preclude the possibility of it becoming inadvertently engaged in flight.

[Docket No. 26269, 58 FR 42164, Aug. 6, 1993]

§23.681 Limit load static tests.

(a) Compliance with the limit load requirements of this part must be shown by tests in which—

(1) The direction of the test loads produces the most severe loading in the control system; and

(2) Each fitting, pulley, and bracket used in attaching the system to the main structure is included.

(b) Compliance must be shown (by analyses or individual load tests) with the special factor requirements for control system joints subject to angular motion.

§23.683 Operation tests.

(a) It must be shown by operation tests that, when the controls are operated from the pilot compartment with the system loaded as prescribed in paragraph (b) of this section, the system is free from—

(1) Jamming;

(2) Excessive friction; and

(3) Excessive deflection.

(b) The prescribed test loads are—

(1) For the entire system, loads corresponding to the limit airloads on the appropriate surface, or the limit pilot forces in §23.397(b), whichever are less; and

(2) For secondary controls, loads not less than those corresponding to the maximum pilot effort established under §23.405.

[Docket No. 4080, 29 FR 17955, Dec. 18, 1964; as amended by Amdt. 23–7, 34 FR 13091, Aug. 13, 1969]

§23.685 Control system details.

(a) Each detail of each control system must be designed and installed to prevent jamming, chafing, and interference from cargo, passengers, loose objects, or the freezing of moisture.

(b) There must be means in the cockpit to prevent the entry of foreign objects into places where they would jam the system.

(c) There must be means to prevent the slapping of cables or tubes against other parts.

(d) Each element of the flight control system must have design features, or must be distinctively and permanently marked, to minimize the possibility of incorrect assembly that could result in malfunctioning of the control system.

[Docket No. 4080, 29 FR 17955, Dec. 18, 1964; as amended by Amdt. 23–17, 41 FR 55464, Dec. 20, 1976]

§23.687 Spring devices.

The reliability of any spring device used in the control system must be established by tests simulating service conditions unless failure of the spring will not cause flutter or unsafe flight characteristics.

§23.689 Cable systems.

(a) Each cable, cable fitting, turnbuckle, splice, and pulley used must meet approved specifications. In addition—

(1) No cable smaller than $\frac{1}{8}$ inch diameter may be used in primary control systems;

(2) Each cable system must be designed so that there will be no hazardous change in cable tension throughout the

range of travel under operating conditions and temperature variations; and

(3) There must be means for visual inspection at each fairlead, pulley, terminal, and turnbuckle.

(b) Each kind and size of pulley must correspond to the cable with which it is used. Each pulley must have closely fitted guards to prevent the cables from being misplaced or fouled, even when slack. Each pulley must lie in the plane passing through the cable so that the cable does not rub against the pulley flange.

(c) Fairleads must be installed so that they do not cause a change in cable direction of more than three degrees.

(d) Clevis pins subject to load or motion and retained only by cotter pins may not be used in the control system.

(e) Turnbuckles must be attached to parts having angular motion in a manner that will positively prevent binding throughout the range of travel.

(f) Tab control cables are not part of the primary control system and may be less than $\frac{1}{8}$-inch diameter in airplanes that are safely controllable with the tabs in the most adverse positions.

[Docket No. 4080, 29 FR 17955, Dec. 18, 1964; as amended by Amdt. 23–7, 34 FR 13091, Aug. 13, 1969]

§23.691 Artificial stall barrier system.

If the function of an artificial stall barrier, for example, stick pusher, is used to show compliance with §23.201(c), the system must comply with the following:

(a) With the system adjusted for operation, the plus and minus airspeeds at which downward pitching control will be provided must be established.

(b) Considering the plus and minus airspeed tolerances established by paragraph (a) of this section, an airspeed must be selected for the activation of the downward pitching control that provides a safe margin above any airspeed at which any unsatisfactory stall characteristics occur.

(c) In addition to the stall warning required §23.07, a warning that is clearly distinguishable to the pilot under all expected flight conditions without requiring the pilot's attention, must be provided for faults that would prevent the system from providing the required pitching motion.

(d) Each system must be designed so that the artificial stall barrier can be quickly and positively disengaged by the pilots to prevent unwanted downward pitching of the airplane by a quick release (emergency) control that meets the requirements of §23.1329(b).

(e) A preflight check of the complete system must be established and the procedure for this check made available in the Airplane Flight Manual (AFM). Preflight checks that are critical to the safety of the airplane must be included in the limitations section of the AFM.

(f) For those airplanes whose design includes an autopilot system:

(1) A quick release (emergency) control installed in accordance with §23.1329(b) may be used to meet the requirements of paragraph (d), of this section, and

(2) The pitch servo for that system may be used to provide the stall downward pitching motion.

(g) In showing compliance with §23.1309, the system must be evaluated to determine the effect that any announced or unannounced failure may have on the continued safe flight and landing of the airplane or the ability of the crew to cope with any adverse conditions that may result from such failures. This evaluation must consider the hazards that would result from the airplane's flight characteristics if the system was not provided, and the hazard that may result from unwanted downward pitching motion, which could result from a failure at airspeeds above the selected stall speed.

[Docket No. 27806, 61 FR 5165, Feb. 9, 1996]

§23.693 Joints.

Control system joints (in push-pull systems) that are subject to angular motion, except those in ball and roller bearing systems, must have a special factor of safety of not less than 3.33 with respect to the ultimate bearing strength of the softest material used as a bearing. This factor may be reduced to 2.0 for joints in cable control systems. For ball or roller bearings, the approved ratings may not be exceeded.

§23.697 Wing flap controls.

(a) Each wing flap control must be designed so that, when the flap has been placed in any position upon which compliance with the performance requirements of this part is based, the flap will not move from that position unless the control is adjusted or is moved by the automatic operation of a flap load limiting device.

(b) The rate of movement of the flaps in response to the operation of the pilot's control or automatic device must give satisfactory flight and performance characteristics under steady or changing conditions of airspeed, engine power, and attitude.

(c) If compliance with §23.145(b)(3) necessitates wing flap retraction to positions that are not fully retracted, the wing flap control lever settings corresponding to those positions must be positively located such that a definite change of direction of movement of the lever is necessary to select settings beyond those settings.

[Docket No. 4080, 29 FR 17955, Dec. 18, 1964; as amended by Amdt. 23–49, 61 FR 5165, Feb. 9, 1996]

§23.699 Wing flap position indicator.

There must be a wing flap position indicator for—

(a) Flap installations with only the retracted and fully extended position, unless—

(1) A direct operating mechanism provides a sense of "feel" and position (such as when a mechanical linkage is employed); or

(2) The flap position is readily determined without seriously detracting from other piloting duties under any flight condition, day or night; and

(b) Flap installation with intermediate flap positions if—

(1) Any flap position other than retracted or fully extended is used to show compliance with the performance requirements of this part; and

(2) The flap installation does not meet the requirements of paragraph (a)(1) of this section.

§23.701 Flap interconnection.

(a) The main wing flaps and related movable surfaces as a system must—

(1) Be synchronized by a mechanical interconnection between the movable flap surfaces that is independent of the flap drive system; or by an approved equivalent means; or

(2) Be designed so that the occurrence of any failure of the flap system that would result in an unsafe flight characteristic of the airplane is extremely improbable; or

(b) The airplane must be shown to have safe flight characteristics with any combination of extreme positions of individual movable surfaces (mechanically interconnected surfaces are to be considered as a single surface).

(c) If an interconnection is used in multiengine airplanes, it must be designed to account for the unsymmetrical loads resulting from flight with the engines on one side of the plane of symmetry inoperative and the remaining engines at takeoff power. For single-engine airplanes, and multi-engine airplanes with no slipstream effects on the flaps, it may be assumed that 100 percent of the critical air load acts on one side and 70 percent on the other.

[Docket No. 4080, 29 FR 17955, Dec. 18, 1964; as amended by Amdt. 23–14, 38 FR 31821, Nov. 19, 1973; Amdt. 23–42, 56 FR 353, Jan. 3, 1991; 56 FR 5455, Feb. 11, 1991; Amdt. 23–49, 61 FR 5165, Feb. 9, 1996]

§23.703 Takeoff warning system.

For commuter category airplanes, unless it can be shown that a lift or longitudinal trim device that affects the takeoff performance of the aircraft would not give an unsafe takeoff configuration when selection out of an approved takeoff position, a takeoff warning system must be installed and meet the following requirements:

(a) The system must provide to the pilots an aural warning that is automatically activated during the initial portion of the takeoff role if the airplane is in a configuration that would not allow a safe takeoff. The warning must continue until—

(1) The configuration is changed to allow safe takeoff, or

(2) Action is taken by the pilot to abandon the takeoff roll.

(b) The means used to activate the system must function properly for all authorized takeoff power settings and procedures and throughout the ranges of takeoff weights, altitudes, and temperatures for which certification is requested.

[Docket No. 27806, 61 FR 5166, Feb. 9, 1996]

LANDING GEAR

§23.721 General.

For commuter category airplanes that have a passenger seating configuration, excluding pilot seats, of 10 or more, the following general requirements for the landing gear apply:

(a) The main landing-gear system must be designed so that if it fails due to overloads during takeoff and landing (assuming the overloads to act in the upward and aft directions), the failure mode is not likely to cause the spillage of enough fuel from any part of the fuel system to constitute a fire hazard.

(b) Each airplane must be designed so that, with the airplane under control, it can be landed on a paved runway with any one or more landing-gear legs not extended without sustaining a structural component failure that is likely to cause the spillage of enough fuel to constitute a fire hazard.

(c) Compliance with the provisions of this section may be shown by analysis or tests, or both.

[Amdt. 23–34, 52 FR 1830, Jan. 15, 1987]

§23.723 Shock absorption tests.

(a) It must be shown that the limit load factors selected for design in accordance with §23.473 for takeoff and landing weights, respectively, will not be exceeded. This must be shown by energy absorption tests except that analysis based on tests conducted on a landing gear system with identical energy absorption characteristics may be used for increases in previously approved takeoff and landing weights.

(b) The landing gear may not fail, but may yield, in a test showing its reserve energy absorption capacity, simulating a descent velocity of 1.2 times the limit descent velocity, assuming wing lift equal to the weight of the airplane.

[Docket No. 4080, 29 FR 17955, Dec. 18, 1964; 30 FR 258, Jan. 9, 1965; as amended by Amdt. 23–23, 43 FR 50593, Oct. 30, 1978; Amdt. 23–49, 61 FR 5166, Feb. 9, 1996]

§23.725 Limit drop tests.

(a) If compliance with §23.723(a) is shown by free drop tests, these tests must be made on the complete airplane, or on units consisting of wheel, tire, and shock absorber, in their proper relation, from free drop heights not less than those determined by the following formula:

h (inches) = $3.6\ (W/S)^{1/2}$

However, the free drop height may not be less than 9.2 inches and need not be more than 18.7 inches.

(b) If the effect of wing lift is provided for in free drop tests, the landing gear must be dropped with an effective weight equal to

$$W_e = W\frac{[h+(1-L)d]}{(h+d)}$$

where—

W_e = the effective weight to be used in the drop test (lbs.);

h = specified free drop height (inches);

d = deflection under impact of the tire (at the approved inflation pressure) plus the vertical component of the axle travel relative to the drop mass (inches);

W = W_M for main gear units (lbs), equal to the static weight on that unit with the airplane in the level attitude (with the nose wheel clear in the case of nose wheel type airplanes);

W = W_T for tail gear units (lbs.), equal to the static weight on the tail unit with the airplane in the tail-down attitude;

W = W_N for nose wheel units lbs.), equal to the vertical component of the static reaction that would exist at the nose wheel, assuming that the mass of the airplane acts at the center of gravity and exerts a force of 1.0 g downward and 0.33 g forward; and

L = the ratio of the assumed wing lift to the airplane weight, but not more than 0.667.

(c) The limit inertia load factor must be determined in a rational or conservative manner, during the drop test, using a landing gear unit attitude, and applied drag loads, that represent the landing conditions.

(d) The value of d used in the computation of W_e in paragraph (b) of this section may not exceed the value actually obtained in the drop test.

(e) The limit inertia load factor must be determined from the drop test in paragraph (b) of this section according to the following formula:

$$n = n_j \frac{W_e}{W} + L$$

where—

n_j = the load factor developed in the drop test (that is, the acceleration (dv/dt) in g's recorded in the drop test) plus 1.0; and

W_e, W, and L are the same as in the drop test computation.

(f) The value of n determined in accordance with paragraph (e) may not be more than the limit inertia load factor used in the landing conditions in §23.473.

[Docket No. 4080, 29 FR 17955, Dec. 18, 1964; as amended by Amdt. 23–7, 34 FR 13091, Aug. 13, 1969; Amdt. 23–48, 61 FR 5148, Feb. 9, 1996]

§23.726 Ground load dynamic tests.

(a) If compliance with the ground load requirements of §§23.479 through 23.483 is shown dynamically by drop test, one drop test must be conducted that meets §23.725 except that the drop height must be—

(1) 2.25 times the drop height prescribed in §23.725(a); or

(2) Sufficient to develop 1.5 times the limit load factor.

(b) The critical landing condition for each of the design conditions specified in §§23.479 through 23.483 must be used for proof of strength.

[Amdt. 23–7, 34 FR 13091, Aug. 13, 1969]

§23.727 Reserve energy absorption drop test.

(a) If compliance with the reserve energy absorption requirement in §23.723(b) is shown by free drop tests, the drop height may not be less than 1.44 times that specified in §23.725.

(b) If the effect of wing lift is provided for, the units must be dropped with an effective mass equal to W_e = Wh/(h+d), when the symbols and other details are the same as in §23.725.

[Docket No. 4080, 29 FR 17955, Dec. 18, 1964; as amended by Amdt. 23–7, 34 FR 13091, Aug. 13, 1969]

§23.729 Landing gear extension and retraction system.

(a) *General.* For airplanes with retractable landing gear, the following apply:

(1) Each landing gear retracting mechanism and its supporting structure must be designed for maximum flight load factors with the gear retracted and must be designed for the combination of friction, inertia, brake torque, and air loads, occurring during retraction at any airspeed up to 1.6 V_{S1} with flaps retracted, and for any load factor up to those specified in §23.345 for the flaps-extended condition.

(2) The landing gear and retracting mechanism, including the wheel well doors, must withstand flight loads, including loads resulting from all yawing conditions specified in §23.351, with the landing gear extended at any speed up to at least 1.6 V_{S1} with the flaps retracted.

(b) *Landing gear lock.* There must be positive means (other than the use of hydraulic pressure) to keep the landing gear extended.

(c) *Emergency operation.* For a landplane having retractable landing gear that cannot be extended manually, there must be means to extend the landing gear in the event of either—

(1) Any reasonably probable failure in the normal landing gear operation system; or

(2) Any reasonably probable failure in a power source that would prevent the operation of the normal landing gear operation system.

(d) *Operation test.* The proper functioning of the retracting mechanism must be shown by operation tests.

(e) *Position indicator.* If a retractable landing gear is used, there must be a landing gear position indicator (as well as necessary switches to actuate the indicator) or other means to inform the pilot that each gear is secured in the extended (or retracted) position. If switches are used, they must be located and coupled to the landing gear mechanical system in a manner that prevents an erroneous indication of either "down and locked" if each gear is not in the fully extended position, or "up and locked" if each landing gear is not in the fully retracted position.

(f) *Landing gear warning.* For landplanes, the following aural or equally effective landing gear warning devices must be provided:

(1) A device that functions continuously when one or more throttles are closed beyond the power settings normally used for landing approach if the landing gear is not fully extended and locked. A throttle stop may not be used in place of an aural device. If there is a manual shutoff for the warning device prescribed in this paragraph, the warning system must be designed so that when the warning has been suspended after one or more throttles are closed, subsequent retardation of any throttle to, or beyond, the position for normal landing approach will activate the warning device.

(2) A device that functions continuously when the wing flaps are extended beyond the maximum approach flap position, using a normal landing procedure, if the landing gear is not fully extended and locked. There may not be a manual shutoff for this warning device. The flap position sensing unit may be installed at any suitable location. The system for this device may use any part of the system (including the aural warning device) for the device required in paragraph (f)(1) of this section.

(g) *Equipment located in the landing gear bay.* If the landing gear bay is used as the location for equipment other than the landing gear, that equipment must be designed and installed to minimize damage from items such as a tire burst, or rocks, water, and slush that may enter the landing gear bay.

[Docket No. 4080, 29 FR 17955, Dec. 18, 1964; as amended by Amdt. 23–7, 34 FR 13091, Aug. 13, 1969; Amdt. 23–21, 43 FR 2318, Jan. 1978; Amdt. 23–26, 45 FR 60171, Sept. 11, 1980; Amdt. 23–45, 58 FR 42164, Aug. 6, 1993; Amdt. 23–49, 61 FR 5166, Feb. 9, 1996]

§23.731 Wheels.

(a) The maximum static load rating of each wheel may not be less than the corresponding static ground reaction with—

(1) Design maximum weight; and

(2) Critical center of gravity.

(b) The maximum limit load rating of each wheel must equal or exceed the maximum radial limit load determined under the applicable ground load requirements of this part.

[Docket No. 4080, 29 FR 17955, Dec. 18, 1964; as amended by Amdt. 23–45, 58 FR 42165, Aug. 6, 1993]

§23.733 Tires.

(a) Each landing gear wheel must have a tire whose approved tire ratings static and dynamic) are not exceeded—

(1) By a load on each main wheel tire (to be compared to the static rating approved for such tires) equal to the corresponding static ground reaction under the design maximum weight and critical center of gravity; and

(2) By a load on nose wheel tires (to be compared with the dynamic rating approved for such tires) equal to the reaction obtained at the nose wheel, assuming the mass of the airplane to be concentrated at the most critical center of gravity and exerting a force of 1.0 W downward and 0.31 W forward (where W is the design maximum weight), with the reactions distributed to the nose and main wheels by the principles of statics and with the drag reaction at the ground applied only at wheels with brakes.

(b) If specially constructed tires are used, the wheels must be plainly and conspicuously marked to that effect. The markings must include the make, size, number of plies, and identification marking of the proper tire.

(c) Each tire installed on a retractable landing gear system must, at the maximum size of the tire type expected in service, have a clearance to surrounding structure and systems that is adequate to prevent contact between the tire and any part of the structure of systems.

[Docket No. 4080, 29 FR 17955, Dec. 18, 1964; as amended by Amdt. 23–7, 34 FR 13092, Aug. 13, 1969; Amdt. 23–17, 41 FR 55464, Dec. 20, 1976; Amdt. 23–45, 58 FR 42165, Aug. 6, 1993]

§23.735 Brakes.

(a) Brakes must be provided. The landing brake kinetic energy capacity rating of each main wheel brake assembly must not be less than the kinetic energy absorption requirements determined under either of the following methods:

(1) The brake kinetic energy absorption requirements must be based on a conservative rational analysis of the sequence of events expected during landing at the design landing weight.

(2) Instead of a rational analysis, the kinetic energy absorption requirements for each main wheel brake assembly may be derived from the following formula:

$$KE = 0.0443WV^2/\mathrm{N}$$

where—

KE = Kinetic energy per wheel (ft.-lb.);

W = Design landing weight (lb.);

V = Airplane speed in knots. V must be not less than V_{S0}, the poweroff stalling speed of the airplane at sea level, at the design landing weight, and in the landing configuration; and

N = Number of main wheels with brakes.

(b) Brakes must be able to prevent the wheels from rolling on a paved runway with takeoff power on the critical engine, but need not prevent movement of the airplane with wheels locked.

(c) During the landing distance determination required by §23.75, the pressure on the wheel braking system must not exceed the pressure specified by the brake manufacturer.

(d) If antiskid devices are installed, the devices and associated systems must be designed so that no single probable malfunction or failure will result in a hazardous loss of braking ability or directional control of the airplane.

(e) In addition, for commuter category airplanes, the rejected takeoff brake kinetic energy capacity rating of each main wheel brake assembly must not be less than the kinetic energy absorption requirements determined under either of the following methods—

(1) The brake kinetic energy absorption requirements must be based on a conservative rational analysis of the sequence of events expected during a rejected takeoff at the design takeoff weight.

(2) Instead of a rational analysis, the kinetic energy absorption requirements for each main wheel brake assembly may be derived from the following formula—

$$KE = 0.0443WV^2N$$

where,

KE = Kinetic energy per wheel (ft.-lbs.);

W = Design takeoff weight (lbs.);

V = Ground speed, in knots, associated with the maximum value of V_1 selected in accordance with §23.51(c)(1);

N = Number of main wheels with brakes.

[Amdt. 23–7, 34 FR 13092, Aug. 13, 1969; as amended by Amdt. 23–24, 44 FR 68742, Nov. 29, 1979; Amdt. 23–42, 56 FR 354, Jan. 3, 1991; Amdt. 23–49, 61 FR 5166, Feb. 9, 1996]

§23.737 Skis.

The maximum limit load rating for each ski must equal or exceed the maximum limit load determined under the applicable ground load requirements of this part.

[Docket No. 26269, 58 FR 42165, Aug. 6, 1993]

§23.745 Nose/tail wheel steering.

(a) If nose/tail wheel steering is installed, it must be demonstrated that its use does not require exceptional pilot skill during takeoff and landing, in crosswinds, or in the event of an engine failure; or its use must be limited to low speed maneuvering.

(b) Movement of the pilot's steering control must not interfere with the retraction or extension of the landing gear.

[Docket No. 27806, 61 FR 5166, Feb. 9, 1996]

FLOATS AND HULLS

§23.751 Main float buoyancy.

(a) Each main float must have—

(1) A buoyancy of 80 percent in excess of the buoyancy required by that float to support its portion of the maximum weight of the seaplane or amphibian in fresh water; and

(2) Enough watertight compartments to provide reasonable assurance that the seaplane or amphibian will stay afloat without capsizing if any two compartments of any main float are flooded.

(b) Each main float must contain at least four watertight compartments approximately equal in volume.

[Docket No. 4080, 29 FR 17955, Dec. 18, 1964; as amended by Amdt. 23–45, 58 FR 42165, Aug. 6, 1993]

§23.753 Main float design.

Each seaplane main float must meet the requirements of §23.521.

[Docket No. 26269, 58 FR 42165, Aug. 6, 1993]

§23.755 Hulls.

(a) The hull of a hull seaplane or amphibian of 1,500 pounds or more maximum weight must have watertight compartments designed and arranged so that the hull auxiliary floats, and tires (if used), will keep the airplane afloat without capsizing in fresh water when—

(1) For airplanes of 5,000 pounds or more maximum weight, any two adjacent compartments are flooded; and

(2) For airplanes of 1,500 pounds up to, but not including, 5,000 pounds maximum weight, any single compartment is flooded.

(b) Watertight doors in bulkheads may be used for communication between compartments.

[Docket No. 4080, 29 FR 17955, Dec. 18, 1964; as amended by Amdt. 23–45, 58 FR 42165, Aug. 6, 1993; Amdt. 23–48, 61 FR 5148, Feb. 9, 1996]

§23.757 Auxiliary floats.

Auxiliary floats must be arranged so that, when completely submerged in fresh water, they provide a righting moment of at least 1.5 times the upsetting moment caused by the seaplane or amphibian being tilted.

PERSONNEL AND CARGO ACCOMMODATIONS

§23.771 Pilot compartment.

For each pilot compartment—

(a) The compartment and its equipment must allow each pilot to perform his duties without unreasonable concentration or fatigue;

(b) Where the flight crew are separated from the passengers by a partition, an opening or openable window or door must be provided to facilitate communication between flight crew and the passengers; and

(c) The aerodynamic controls listed in §23.779, excluding cables and control rods, must be located with respect to the propellers so that no part of the pilot or the controls lies in the region between the plane of rotation of any inboard propeller and the surface generated by a line passing through the center of the propeller hub making an angle of 5 degrees forward or aft of the plane of rotation of the propeller.

[Docket No. 4080, 29 FR 17955, Dec. 18, 1964; as amended by Amdt. 23–14, 38 FR 31821, Nov. 19, 1973]

§23.773 Pilot compartment view.

(a) Each pilot compartment must be—

(1) Arranged with sufficiently extensive, clear and undistorted view to enable the pilot to safely taxi, takeoff, approach, land, and perform any maneuvers within the operating limitations of the airplane.

(2) Free from glare and reflections that could interfere with the pilot's vision. Compliance must be shown in all operations for which certification is requested; and

(3) Designed so that each pilot is protected from the elements so that moderate rain conditions do not unduly impair the pilot's view of the flight path in normal flight and while landing.

(b) Each pilot compartment must have a means to either remove or prevent the formation of fog or frost on an area of the internal portion of the windshield and side windows sufficiently large to provide the view specified in paragraph (a)(1) of this section. Compliance must be shown under all expected external and internal ambient operating conditions, unless it can be shown that the windshield and side windows can be easily cleared by the pilot without interruption of moral pilot duties.

[Docket No. 26269, 58 FR 42165, Aug. 6, 1993]

§23.775 Windshields and windows.

(a) The internal panels of windshields and windows must be constructed of a nonsplintering material, such as nonsplintering safety glass.

(b) The design of windshields, windows, and canopies in pressurized airplanes must be based on factors peculiar to high altitude operation, including—

(1) The effects of continuous and cyclic pressurization loadings;

(2) The inherent characteristics of the material used; and

(3) The effects of temperatures and temperature gradients.

(c) On pressurized airplanes, if certification for operation up to and including 25,000 feet is requested, an enclosure canopy including a representative part of the installation must be subjected to special tests to account for the combined effects of continuous and cyclic pressurization loadings and flight loads, or compliance with the fail-safe requirements of paragraph (d) of this section must be shown.

(d) If certification for operation above 25,000 feet is requested the windshields, window panels, and canopies must be strong enough to withstand the maximum cabin pressure differential loads combined with critical aerodynamic pressure and temperature effects, after failure of any load-carrying element of the windshield, window panel, or canopy.

(e) The windshield and side windows forward of the pilot's back when the pilot is seated in the normal flight position must have a luminous transmittance value of not less than 70 percent.

(f) Unless operation in known or forecast icing conditions is prohibited by operating limitations, a means must be provided to prevent or to clear accumulations of ice from the windshield so that the pilot has adequate view for taxi, takeoff, approach, landing, and to perform any maneuvers within the operating limitations of the airplane.

(g) In the event of any probable single failure, a transparency heating system must be incapable of raising the temperature of any windshield or window to a point where there would be—

(1) Structural failure that adversely affects the integrity of the cabin, or

(2) There would be a danger of fire.

(h) In addition, for commuter category airplanes, the following applies:

(1) Windshield panes directly in front of the pilots in the normal conduct of their duties, and the supporting structures for these panes, must withstand, without penetration, the impact of a two-pound bird when the velocity of the airplane (relative to the bird along the airplane's flight path) is equal to the airplane's maximum approach flap speed.

(2) The windshield panels in front of the pilots must be arranged so that, assuming the loss of vision through any one panel, one or more panels remain available for use by a pilot seated at a pilot station to permit continued safe flight and landing.

[Docket No. 4080, 29 FR 17955, Dec. 18, 1964; as amended by Amdt. 23–7, 34 FR 13092, Aug. 13, 1969; Amdt. 23–45, 58 FR 42165, Aug. 6, 1993; 58 FR 51970, Oct. 5, 1993; Amdt. 23–49, 61 FR 5166, Feb. 9, 1996]

§23.777 Cockpit controls.

(a) Each cockpit control must be located and (except where its function is obvious) identified to provide convenient operation and to prevent confusion and inadvertent operation.

(b) The controls must be located and arranged so that the pilot, when seated, has full and unrestricted movement of each control without interference from either his clothing or the cockpit structure.

(c) Powerplant controls must be located—

(1) For multiengine airplanes, on the pedestal or overhead at or near the center of the cockpit;

(2) For single and tandem seated single-engine airplanes, on the left side console or instrument panel;

(3) For other single-engine airplanes at or near the center of the cockpit, on the pedestal, instrument panel, or overhead; and

(4) For airplanes, with side-by-side pilot seats and with two sets of powerplant controls, on left and right consoles.

(d) The control location order from left to right must be power (thrust) lever, propeller (rpm control), and mixture control (condition lever and fuel cutoff for turbine-powered airplanes). Power (thrust) levers must be at least one inch higher or longer to make them more prominent than propeller (rpm control) or mixture controls. Carburetor heat or alternate air control must be to the left of the throttle or at least eight inches from the mixture control when located other than on a pedestal. Carburetor heat or alternate air control, when located on a pedestal must be aft or below the power (thrust) lever. Supercharger controls must be located below or aft of the propeller controls. Airplanes with tandem seating or single-place airplanes may utilize control locations on the left side of the cabin compartment; however, location order from left to right must be power (thrust) lever, propeller (rpm control) and mixture control.

(e) Identical powerplant controls for each engine must be located to prevent confusion as to the engines they control.

(1) Conventional multiengine powerplant controls must be located so that the left control(s) operates the left engines(s) and the right control(s) operates the right engine(s).

(2) On twin-engine airplanes with front and rear engine locations (tandem), the left powerplant controls must operate the front engine and the right powerplant controls must operate the rear engine.

(f) Wing flap and auxiliary lift device controls must be located—

(1) Centrally, or to the right of the pedestal or powerplant throttle control centerline; and

(2) Far enough away from the landing gear control to avoid confusion.

(g) The landing gear control must be located to the left of the throttle centerline or pedestal centerline.

(h) Each fuel feed selector control must comply with §23.995 and be located and arranged so that the pilot can see and reach it without moving any seat or primary flight control when his seat is at any position in which it can be placed.

(1) For a mechanical fuel selector:

(i) The indication of the selected fuel valve position must be by means of a pointer and must provide positive identification and feel (detent, etc.) of the selected position.

(ii) The position indicator pointer must be located at the part of the handle that is the maximum dimension of the handle measured from the center of rotation.

(2) For electrical or electronic fuel selector:

(i) Digital controls or electrical switches must be properly labeled.

(ii) Means must be provided to indicate to the flight crew the tank or function selected. Selector switch position is not acceptable as a means of indication. The "off" or "closed" position must be indicated in red.

(3) If the fuel valve selector handle or electrical or digital selection is also a fuel shut-off selector, the off position marking must be colored red. If a separate emergency shut-off means is provided, it also must be colored red.

[Docket No. 4080, 29 FR 17955, Dec. 18, 1964; as amended by Amdt. 23–7, 34 FR 13092, Aug. 13, 1969; Amdt. 23–33, 51 FR 26656, July 24, 1986; Amdt. 23–51, 61 FR 5136, Feb. 9, 1996]

23

§ 23.779 Motion and effect of cockpit controls.

Cockpit controls must be designed so that they operate in accordance with the following movement and actuation:

(a) Aerodynamic controls:

	Motion and effect
(1) *Primary controls:*	
Aileron	Right (clockwise) for right wing down.
Elevator	Rearward for nose up.
Rudder	Right pedal forward for nose right.
(2) *Secondary controls:*	
Flaps (or auxiliary lift devices)	Forward or up for flaps up or auxiliary device stowed; rearward or down for flaps down or auxiliary device deployed.
Trim tabs (or equivalent)	Switch motion or mechanical rotation of control to produce similar rotation of the airplane about an axis parallel to the axis control. Axis of roll trim control may be displaced to accommodate comfortable actuation by the pilot. For single-engine airplanes, direction of pilot's hand movement must be in the same sense as airplane response for rudder trim if only a portion of a rotational element is accessible.

(b) Powerplant and auxiliary controls:

	Motion and effect
(1) *Powerplant controls:*	
Power (thrust) lever	Forward to increase forward thrust and rearward to increase rearward thrust
Propellers	Forward to increase rpm
Mixture	Forward or upward for rich
Fuel	Forward for open
Carburetor, air heat or alternate air	Forward or upward for cold
Supercharger	Forward or upward for low blower
Turbosuperchargers	Forward, upward, or clockwise to increase pressure
Rotary controls	Clockwise from off to full on
(2) *Auxiliary controls:*	
Fuel tank selector	Right for right tanks, left for left tanks
Landing gear	Down to extend
Speed brakes	Aft to extend

[Amdt. 23–33, 51 FR 26656, July 24, 1986; as amended by Amdt. 23–51, 61 FR 5136, Feb. 9, 1996]

§ 23.781 Cockpit control knob shape.

(a) Flap and landing gear control knobs must conform to the general shapes (but not necessarily the exact sizes or specific proportions) in the following figure:

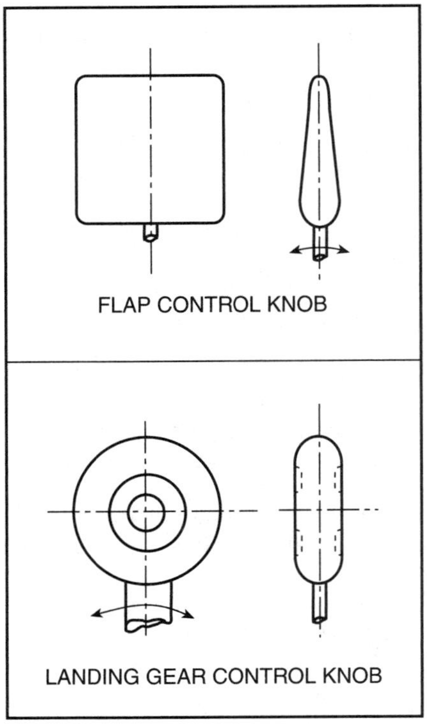

(b) Powerplant control knobs must conform to the general shapes (but not necessarily the exact sizes or specific proportions) in the following figure:

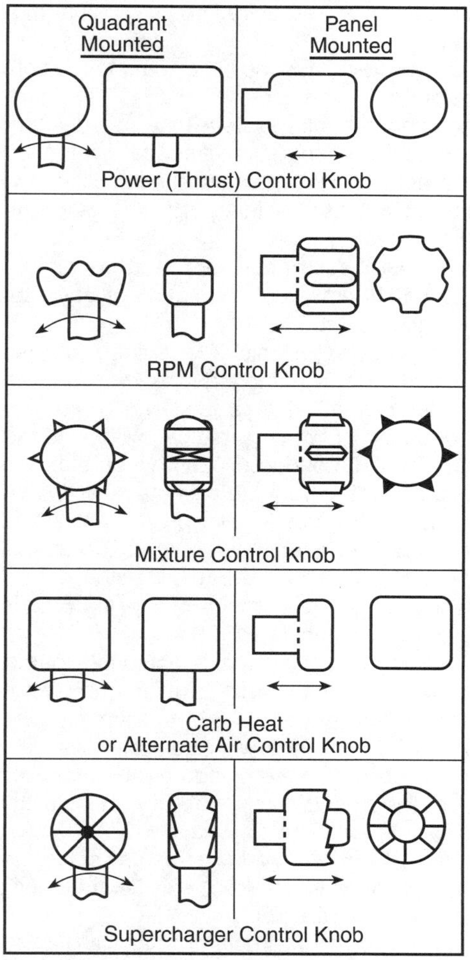

[Docket No. 4080, 29 FR 17955, Dec. 18, 1964; 30 FR 258, Jan. 9, 1965; as amended by Amdt. 23–33, 51 FR 26657, July 24, 1986]

§23.783 Doors.

(a) Each closed cabin with passenger accommodations must have at least one adequate and easily accessible external door.

(b) Passenger doors must not be located with respect to any propeller disk or any other potential hazard so as to endanger persons using the door.

(c) Each external passenger or crew door must comply with the following requirements:

(1) There must be a means to lock and safeguard the door against inadvertent opening during flight by persons, by cargo, or as a result of mechanical failure.

(2) The door must be openable from the inside and the outside when the internal locking mechanism is in the locked position.

(3) There must be a means of opening which is simple and obvious and is arranged and marked inside and outside so that the door can be readily located, unlocked, and opened, even in darkness.

(4) The door must meet the marking requirements of §23.811 of this part.

(5) The door must be reasonably free from jamming as a result of fuselage deformation in an emergency landing.

(6) Auxiliary locking devices that are actuated externally to the airplane may be used but such devices must be overridden by the normal internal opening means.

(d) In addition, each external passenger or crew door, for a commuter category airplane, must comply with the following requirements:

(1) Each door must be openable from both the inside and outside, even though persons may be crowded against the door on the inside of the airplane.

(2) If inward opening doors are used, there must be a means to prevent occupants from crowding against the door to the extent that would interfere with opening the door.

(3) Auxiliary locking devices may be used.

(e) Each external door on a commuter category airplane, each external door forward of any engine or propeller on a normal, utility, or acrobatic category airplane, and each door of the pressure vessel on a pressurized airplane must comply with the following requirements:

(1) There must be a means to lock and safeguard each external door, including cargo and service type doors, against inadvertent opening in flight, by persons, by cargo, or as a result of mechanical failure or failure of a single structural element, either during or after closure.

(2) There must be a provision for direct visual inspection of the locking mechanism to determine if the external door, for which the initial opening movement is not inward, is fully closed and locked. The provisions must be discernible, under operating lighting conditions, by a crewmember using a flashlight or an equivalent lighting source.

(3) There must be a visual warning means to signal a flight crewmember if the external door is not fully closed and locked. The means must be designed so that any failure, or combination of failures, that would result in an erroneous closed and locked indication is improbable for doors for which the initial opening movement is not inward.

(f) In addition, for commuter category airplanes, the following requirements apply:

(1) Each passenger entry door must qualify as a floor level emergency exit. This exit must have a rectangular opening of not less than 24 inches wide by 48 inches high, with corner radii not greater than one-third the width of the exit.

(2) If an integral stair is installed at a passenger entry door, the stair must be designed so that, when subjected to the inertia loads resulting from the ultimate static load factors in §23.561(b)(2) and following the collapse of one or more legs of the landing gear, it will not reduce the effectiveness of emergency egress through the passenger entry door.

(g) If lavatory doors are installed, they must be designed to preclude an occupant from becoming trapped inside the lavatory. If a locking mechanism is installed, it must be capable of being unlocked from outside of the lavatory.

[Docket No. 4080, 29 FR 17955, Dec. 18, 1964; 30 FR 258, Jan. 9, 1965; as amended by Amdt. 23–36, 53 FR 30813, Aug. 15, 1988; Amdt. 23–46, 59 FR 25772, May 17, 1994; Amdt. 23–49, 61 FR 5166, Feb. 9, 1996]

§23.785 Seats, berths, litters, safety belts, and shoulder harnesses.

There must be a seat or berth for each occupant that meets the following:

(a) Each seat/restraint system and the supporting structure must be designed to support occupants weighing at least 215 pounds when subjected to the maximum load factors corresponding to the specified flight and ground load conditions, as defined in the approved operating envelope of the airplane. In addition, these loads must be multiplied by a factor of 1.33 in determining the strength of all fittings and the attachment of—

(1) Each seat to the structure; and

(2) Each safety belt and shoulder harness to the seat or structure.

(b) Each forward-facing or aft-facing seat/restraint system in normal, utility, or acrobatic category airplanes must consist of a seat, a safety belt, and a shoulder harness, with a metal-to-metal latching device, that are designed to provide the occupant protection provisions required in §23.562. Other seat orientations must provide the same level of occupant protection as a forward-facing or aft-facing seat with a safety belt and a shoulder harness, and must provide the protection provisions of §23.562.

(c) For commuter category airplanes, each seat and the supporting structure must be designed for occupants weighing at least 170 pounds when subjected to the inertia loads resulting from the ultimate static load factors prescribed in §23.561(b)(2) of this part. Each occupant must be protected from serious head injury when subjected to the inertia loads resulting from these load factors by a safety belt and shoulder harness, with a metal-to-metal latching device, for the front seats and a safety belt, or a safety belt and shoulder harness, with a metal-to-metal latching device, for each seat other than the front seats.

(d) Each restraint system must have a single-point release for occupant evacuation.

(e) The restraint system for each crewmember must allow the crewmember, when seated with the safety belt and shoulder harness fastened, to perform all functions necessary for flight operations.

(f) Each pilot seat must be designed for the reactions resulting from the application of pilot forces to the primary flight controls as prescribed in §23.395 of this part.

(g) There must be a means to secure each safety belt and shoulder harness, when not in use, to prevent interference with the operation of the airplane and with rapid occupant egress in an emergency.

(h) Unless otherwise placarded, each seat in a utility or acrobatic category airplane must be designed to accommodate an occupant wearing a parachute.

(i) The cabin area surrounding each seat, including the structure, interior walls, instrument panel, control wheel, pedals, and seats within striking distance of the occupant's head or torso (with the restraint system fastened) must be free of potentially injurious objects, sharp edges, protuberances, and hard surfaces. If energy absorbing designs or devices are used to meet this requirement, they must protect the occupant from serious injury when the occupant is subjected to the inertia loads resulting from the ultimate static load factors prescribed in §23.561(b)(2) of this part, or they must comply with the occupant protection provisions of §23.562 of this part, as required in paragraphs (b) and (c) of this section.

(j) Each seat track must be fitted with stops to prevent the seat from sliding off the track.

(k) Each seat/restraint system may use design features, such as crushing or separation of certain components, to reduce occupant loads when showing compliance with the requirements of §23.562 of this part; otherwise, the system must remain intact.

(l) For the purposes of this section, a front seat is a seat located at a flight crewmember station or any seat located alongside such a seat.

(m) Each berth, or provisions for a litter, installed parallel to the longitudinal axis of the airplane, must be designed so that the forward part has a padded end-board, canvas diaphragm, or equivalent means that can withstand the load reactions from a 215-pound occupant when subjected to the inertia loads resulting from the ultimate static load factors of §23.561(b)(2) of this part. In addition—

(1) Each berth or litter must have an occupant restraint system and may not have corners or other parts likely to cause serious injury to a person occupying it during emergency landing conditions; and

(2) Occupant restraint system attachments for the berth or litter must withstand the inertia loads resulting from the ultimate static load factors of §23.561(b)(2) of this part.

(n) Proof of compliance with the static strength requirements of this section for seats and berths approved as part of the type design and for seat and berth installations may be shown by—

(1) Structural analysis, if the structure conforms to conventional airplane types for which existing methods of analysis are known to be reliable;

(2) A combination of structural analysis and static load tests to limit load; or

(3) Static load tests to ultimate loads.

[Amdt. 23–36, 53 FR 30813, Aug. 15, 1988; Amdt. 23–36, 54 FR 50737, Dec. 11, 1989; Amdt. 23–49, 61 FR 5167, Feb. 9, 1996]

§23.787 Baggage and cargo compartments.

(a) Each baggage and cargo compartment must:

(1) Be designed for its placarded maximum weight of contents and for the critical load distributions at the appropriate maximum load factors corresponding to the flight and ground load conditions of this part.

(2) Have means to prevent the contents of any compartment from becoming a hazard by shifting, and to protect any controls, wiring, lines, equipment or accessories whose damage or failure would affect safe operations.

(3) Have a means to protect occupants from injury by the contents of any compartment, located aft of the occupants and separated by structure, when the ultimate forward inertial load factor is 9g and assuming the maximum allowed baggage or cargo weight for the compartment.

(b) Designs that provide for baggage or cargo to be carried in the same compartment as passengers must have a means to protect the occupants from injury when the baggage or cargo is subjected to the inertial loads resulting from the ultimate static load factors of §23.561(b)(3), assuming the maximum allowed baggage or cargo weight for the compartment.

(c) For airplanes that are used only for the carriage of cargo, the flightcrew emergency exits must meet the requirements of §23.807 under any cargo loading conditions.

[Docket No. 27806, 61 FR 5167, Feb. 9, 1996]

§23.791 Passenger information signs.

For those airplanes in which the flightcrew members cannot observe the other occupants' seats or where the flightcrew members' compartment is separated from the passenger compartment, there must be at least one illuminated sign (using either letters or symbols) notifying all passengers when seat belts should be fastened. Signs that notify when seat belts should be fastened must:

(a) When illuminated, be legible to each person seated in the passenger compartment under all probable lighting conditions; and

(b) Be installed so that a flightcrew member can, when seated at the flightcrew member's station, turn the illumination on and off.

[Docket No. 27806, 61 FR 5167, Feb. 9, 1996]

§23.803 Emergency evacuation.

(a) For commuter category airplanes, an evacuation demonstration must be conducted utilizing the maximum number of occupants for which certification is desired. The demonstration must be conducted under simulated night conditions using only the emergency exits on the most critical side of the airplane. The participants must be representative of average airline passengers with no prior practice or rehearsal for the demonstration. Evacuation must be completed within 90 seconds.

(b) In addition, when certification to the emergency exit provisions of §23.807(d)(4) is requested, only the emergency lighting system required by §23.812 may be used to provide cabin interior illumination during the evacuation demonstration required in paragraph (a) of this section.

[Amdt. 23–34, 52 FR 1831, Jan. 15, 1987; as amended by Amdt. 23–46, 59 FR 25773, May 17, 1994]

§23.805 Flightcrew emergency exits.

For airplanes where the proximity of the passenger emergency exits to the flightcrew area does not offer a convenient and readily accessible means of evacuation for the flightcrew, the following apply:

(a) There must be either one emergency exit on each side of the airplane, or a top hatch emergency exit, in the flightcrew area;

(b) Each emergency exit must be located to allow rapid evacuation of the crew and have a size and shape of at least a 19- by 20-inch unobstructed rectangular opening; and

(c) For each emergency exit that is not less than six feet from the ground, an assisting means must be provided. The assisting means may be a rope or any other means demonstrated to be suitable for the purpose. If the assisting means is a rope, or an approved device equivalent to a rope, it must be—

(1) Attached to the fuselage structure at or above the top of the emergency exit opening or, for a device at a pilot's emergency exit window, at another approved location if the stowed device, or its attachment, would reduce the pilot's view; and

(2) Able (with its attachment) to withstand a 400-pound static load.

[Docket No. 26324, 59 FR 25773, May 17, 1994]

§23.807 Emergency exits.

(a) *Number and location.* Emergency exits must be located to allow escape without crowding in any probable crash attitude. The airplane must have at least the following emergency exits:

(1) For all airplanes with a seating capacity of two or more, excluding airplanes with canopies, at least one emergency exit on the opposite side of the cabin from the main door specified in 23.783 of this part.

(2) [Reserved]

(3) If the pilot compartment is separated from the cabin by a door that is likely to block the pilot's escape in a minor crash, there must be an exit in the pilot's compartment. The number of exits required by paragraph (a)(1) of this section must then be separately determined for the passenger compartment, using the seating capacity of that compartment.

(4) Emergency exits must not be located with respect to any propeller disk or any other potential hazard so as to endanger persons using that exit.

(b) *Type and operation.* Emergency exits must be movable windows, panels, canopies, or external doors, openable from both inside and outside the airplane, that provide a clear and unobstructed opening large enough to admit a 19-by-26-inch ellipse. Auxiliary locking devices used to secure the airplane must be designed to be overridden by the normal internal opening means. The inside handles of emergency exits that open outward must be adequately protected against inadvertent operation. In addition, each emergency exit must—

(1) Be readily accessible, requiring no exceptional agility to be used in emergencies;

(2) Have a method of opening that is simple and obvious;

(3) Be arranged and marked for easy location and operation, even in darkness;

(4) Have reasonable provisions against jamming by fuselage deformation; and

(5) In the case of acrobatic category airplanes, allow each occupant to abandon the airplane at any speed between V_{SO} and V_D; and

(6) In the case of utility category airplanes certificated for spinning, allow each occupant to abandon the airplane at the highest speed likely to be achieved in the maneuver for which the airplane is certificated.

(c) *Tests.* The proper functioning of each emergency exit must be shown by tests.

(d) *Doors and exits.* In addition, for commuter category airplanes, the following requirements apply:

(1) In addition to the passenger entry door—

(i) For an airplane with a total passenger seating capacity of 15 or fewer, an emergency exit, as defined in paragraph (b) of this section, is required on each side of the cabin; and

(ii) For an airplane with a total passenger seating capacity of 16 through 19, three emergency exits, as defined in paragraph (b) of this section, are required with one on the same side as the passenger entry door and two on the side opposite the door.

(2) A means must be provided to lock each emergency exit and to safeguard against its opening in flight, either inadvertently by persons or as a result of mechanical failure. In addition, a means for direct visual inspection of the locking mechanism must be provided to determine that each emergency exit for which the initial opening movement is outward is fully locked.

(3) Each required emergency exit, except floor level exits, must be located over the wing or, if not less than six feet from the ground, must be provided with an acceptable means to assist the occupants to descend to the ground. Emergency exits must be distributed as uniformly as practical, taking into account passenger seating configuration.

(4) Unless the applicant has complied with paragraph (d)(1) of this section, there must be an emergency exit on the side of the cabin opposite the passenger entry door, provided that—

(i) For an airplane having a passenger seating configuration of nine or fewer, the emergency exit has a rectangular opening measuring not less than 19 inches by 26 inches high with corner radii not greater than one-third the width of the exit, located over the wing, with a step up inside the airplane of not more than 29 inches and a step down outside the airplane of not more than 36 inches;

(ii) For an airplane having a passenger seating configuration of 10 to 19 passengers, the emergency exit has a rectangular opening measuring not less than 20 inches wide by 36 inches high, with corner radii not greater than one-third the width of the exit, and with a step up inside the airplane of not more than 20 inches. If the exit is located over the wing, the step down outside the airplane may not exceed 27 inches; and

(iii) The airplane complies with the additional requirements of §§23.561(b)(2)(iv), 23.803(b), 23.811(c), 23.812, 23.813(b), and 23.815.

(e) For multiengine airplanes, ditching emergency exits must be provided in accordance with the following requirements, unless the emergency exits required by paragraph (a) or (d) of this section already comply with them:

(1) One exit above the waterline on each side of the airplane having the dimensions specified in paragraph (b) or (d) of this section, as applicable; and

(2) If side exits cannot be above the waterline, there must be a readily accessible overhead hatch emergency exit that has a rectangular opening measuring not less than 20 inches wide by 36 inches long, with corner radii not greater than one-third the width of the exit.

[Docket No. 4080, 29 FR 17955, Dec. 18, 1964; as amended by Amdt. 23–7, 34 FR 13092, Aug. 13, 1969; Amdt. 23–10, 36 FR 2864, Feb. 11, 1971; Amdt. 23–34, 52 FR 1831, Jan. 15, 1987; Amdt. 23–36, 53 FR 30814, Aug. 15, 1988; 53 FR 34194, Sept. 2, 1988; Amdt. 23–46, 59 FR 25773, May 17, 1994; Amdt. 23–49, 61 FR 5167, Feb. 9, 1996]

§23.811 Emergency exit marking.

(a) Each emergency exit and external door in the passenger compartment must be externally marked and readily identifiable from outside the airplane by—

(1) A conspicuous visual identification scheme; and

(2) A permanent decal or placard on or adjacent to the emergency exit which shows the means of opening the emergency exit, including any special instructions, if applicable.

(b) In addition, for commuter category airplanes, these exits and doors must be internally marked with the word "exit" by a sign which has white letters 1 inch high on a red background 2 inches high, be self-illuminated or independently, internally electrically illuminated, and have a minimum brightness of at least 160 microlamberts. The color may be reversed if the passenger compartment illumination is essentially the same.

(c) In addition, when certification to the emergency exit provisions of §23.807(d)(4) is requested, the following apply:

(1) Each emergency exit, its means of access, and its means of opening, must be conspicuously marked;

(2) The identity and location of each emergency exit must be recognizable from a distance equal to the width of the cabin;

(3) Means must be provided to assist occupants in locating the emergency exits in conditions of dense smoke;

(4) The location of the operating handle and instructions for opening each emergency exit from inside the airplane must be shown by marking that is readable from a distance of 30 inches;

(5) Each passenger entry door operating handle must—

(i) Be self-illuminated with an initial brightness of at least 160 microlamberts; or

(ii) Be conspicuously located and well illuminated by the emergency lighting even in conditions of occupant crowding at the door;

(6) Each passenger entry door with a locking mechanism that is released by rotary motion of the handle must be marked—

(i) With a red arrow, with a shaft of at least three-fourths of an inch wide and a head twice the width of the shaft, extending along at least 70 degrees of arc at a radius approximately equal to three-fourths of the handle length;

(ii) So that the center line of the exit handle is with ± one inch of the projected point of the arrow when the handle has reached full travel and has released the locking mechanism;

(iii) With the word "open" in red letters, one inch high, placed horizontally near the head of the arrow; and

(7) In addition to the requirements of paragraph (a) of this section, the external marking of each emergency exit must—

(i) Include a 2-inch colorband outlining the exit; and

(ii) Have a color contrast that is readily distinguishable from the surrounding fuselage surface. The contrast must be such that if the reflection of the darker color is 15 percent or less, the reflectance of the lighter color must be at least 45 percent. "Reflectance" is the ratio of the luminous flux reflected by a body to the luminous flux it receives. When the reflectance of the darker color is greater than 15 percent, at least a 30 percent difference between its reflectance and the reflectance of the lighter color must be provided.

[Amdt. 23–36, 53 FR 30814, Aug. 15, 1988; 53 FR 34194, Sept. 2, 1988; Amdt. 23–46, 59 FR 25773, May 17, 1994]

§23.812 Emergency lighting.

When certification to the emergency exit provisions of §23.807(d)(4) is requested, the following apply:

(a) An emergency lighting system, independent of the main cabin lighting system, must be installed. However, the source of general cabin illumination may be common to both the emergency and main lighting systems if the power supply to the emergency lighting system is independent of the power supply to the main lighting system.

(b) There must be a crew warning light that illuminates in the cockpit when power is on in the airplane and the emergency lighting control device is not armed.

(c) The emergency lights must be operable manually from the flightcrew station and be provided with automatic activation. The cockpit control device must have "on," "off," and "armed" positions so that, when armed in the cockpit, the lights will operate by automatic activation.

(d) There must be a means to safeguard against inadvertent operation of the cockpit control device from the "armed" or "on" positions.

(e) The cockpit control device must have provisions to allow the emergency lighting system to be armed or activated at any time that it may be needed.

(f) When armed, the emergency lighting system must activate and remain lighted when—

(1) The normal electrical power of the airplane is lost; or

(2) The airplane is subjected to an impact that results in a deceleration in excess of 2g and a velocity change in excess of 3.5 feet-per-second, acting along the longitudinal axis of the airplane; or

(3) Any other emergency condition exists where automatic activation of the emergency lighting is necessary to aid with occupant evacuation.

(g) The emergency lighting system must be capable of being turned off and reset by the flightcrew after automatic activation.

(h) The emergency lighting system must provide internal lighting, including—

(1) Illuminated emergency exit marking and locating signs, including those required in §23.811(b);

(2) Sources of general illumination in the cabin that provide an average illumination of not less than 0.05 foot-candle and an illumination at any point of not less than 0.01 foot-candle when measured along the center line of the main passenger aisle(s) and at the seat armrest height; and

(3) Floor proximity emergency escape path marking that provides emergency evacuation guidance for the airplane occupants when all sources of illumination more than 4 feet above the cabin aisle floor are totally obscured.

(i) The energy supply to each emergency lighting unit must provide the required level of illumination for at least 10 minutes at the critical ambient conditions after activation of the emergency lighting system.

(j) If rechargeable batteries are used as the energy supply for the emergency lighting system, they may be recharged from the main electrical power system of the airplane provided the charging circuit is designed to preclude inadvertent battery discharge into the charging circuit faults. If the emergency lighting system does not include a charging circuit, battery condition monitors are required.

(k) Components of the emergency lighting system, including batteries, wiring, relays, lamps, and switches, must be capable of normal operation after being subjected to the inertia forces resulting from the ultimate load factors prescribed in §23.561(b)(2).

(l) The emergency lighting system must be designed so that after any single transverse vertical separation of the fuselage during a crash landing:

(1) At least 75 percent of all electrically illuminated emergency lights required by this section remain operative; and

(2) Each electrically illuminated exit sign required by §23.811(b) and (c) remains operative, except those that are directly damaged by the fuselage separation.

[Docket No. 26324, 59 FR 25774, May 17, 1994]

§23.813 Emergency exit access.

(a) For commuter category airplanes, access to window-type emergency exits may not be obstructed by seats or seat backs.

(b) In addition, when certification to the emergency exit provisions of §23.807(d)(4) is requested, the following emergency exit access must be provided:

(1) The passageway leading from the aisle to the passenger entry door must be unobstructed and at least 20 inches wide.

(2) There must be enough space next to the passenger entry door to allow assistance in evacuation of passengers without reducing the unobstructed width of the passageway below 20 inches.

(3) If it is necessary to pass through a passageway between passenger compartments to reach a required emergency exit from any seat in the passenger cabin, the passageway must be unobstructed; however, curtains may be used if they allow free entry through the passageway.

(4) No door may be installed in any partition between passenger compartments unless that door has a means to latch it in the open position. The latching means must be able to withstand the loads imposed upon it by the door when the door is subjected to the inertia loads resulting from the ultimate static load factors prescribed in §23.561(b)(2).

(5) If it is necessary to pass through a doorway separating the passenger cabin from other areas to reach a required emergency exit from any passenger seat, the door must have a means to latch it in the open position. The latching means must be able to withstand the loads imposed upon it by the door when the door is subjected to the inertia loads resulting from the ultimate static load factors prescribed in §23.561(b)(2).

[Amdt. 23–36, 53 FR 30815, Aug. 15, 1988; Amdt. 23–46, 59 FR 25774, May 17, 1994]

§23.815 Width of aisle.

(a) Except as provided in paragraph (b) of this section, for commuter category airplanes, the width of the main passenger aisle at any point between seats must equal or exceed the values in the following table:

Number of passenger seats	Minimum main passenger aisle width	
	Less than 25 inches from floor	25 inches and more from floor
10 through 19	9 inches	15 inches

(b) When certification to the emergency exit provisions of §23.807(d)(4) is requested, the main passenger aisle width at any point between the seats must equal or exceed the following values:

Number of passenger seats	Minimum main passenger aisle width (inches)	
	Less than 25 inches from floor	25 inches and more from floor
10 or fewer	[1]12	15
11 through 19	12	20

[1]A narrower width not less than 9 inches may be approved when substantiated by tests found necessary by the Administrator.

[Amdt. 23–34, 52 FR 1831, Jan. 15, 1987; Amdt. 23–46, 59 FR 25774, May 17, 1994]

§23.831 Ventilation.

(a) Each passenger and crew compartment must be suitably ventilated. Carbon monoxide concentration may not exceed one part in 20,000 parts of air.

(b) For pressurized airplanes, the ventilating air in the flightcrew and passenger compartments must be free of harmful or hazardous concentrations of gases and vapors in normal operations and in the event of reasonably probable failures or malfunctioning of the ventilating, heating, pressurization, or other systems and equipment. If accumulation of hazardous quantities of smoke in the cockpit area is reasonably probable, smoke evacuation must be readily accomplished starting with full pressurization and without depressurizing beyond safe limits.

[Docket No. 4080, 29 FR 17955, Dec. 18, 1964; 30 FR 258, Jan. 9, 1965; as amended by Amdt. 23–34, 52 FR 1831, Jan. 15, 1987; Amdt. 23–42, 56 FR 354, Jan. 3, 1991]

Pressurization

§23.841 Pressurized cabins.

(a) If certification for operation over 25,000 feet is requested, the airplane must be able to maintain a cabin pressure altitude of not more than 15,000 feet in event of any probable failure or malfunction in the pressurization system.

(b) Pressurized cabins must have at least the following valves, controls, and indicators, for controlling cabin pressure:

(1) Two pressure relief valves to automatically limit the positive pressure differential to a predetermined value at the maximum rate of flow delivered by the pressure source. The combined capacity of the relief valves must be large enough so that the failure of any one valve would not cause an appreciable rise in the pressure differential. The pressure differential is positive when the internal pressure is greater than the external.

(2) Two reverse pressure differential relief valves (or their equivalent) to automatically prevent a negative pressure differential that would damage the structure. However, one valve is enough if it is of a design that reasonably precludes its malfunctioning.

(3) A means by which the pressure differential can be rapidly equalized.

(4) An automatic or manual regulator for controlling the intake or exhaust airflow, or both, for maintaining the required internal pressures and airflow rates.

(5) Instruments to indicate to the pilot the pressure differential, the cabin pressure altitude, and the rate of change of cabin pressure altitude.

(6) Warning indication at the pilot station to indicate when the safe or preset pressure differential is exceeded and when a cabin pressure altitude of 10,000 feet is exceeded.

(7) A warning placard for the pilot if the structure is not designed for pressure differentials up to the maximum relief valve setting in combination with landing loads.

(8) A means to stop rotation of the compressor or to divert airflow from the cabin if continued rotation of an engine-driven cabin compressor or continued flow of any compressor bleed air will create a hazard if a malfunction occurs.

[Amdt. 23–14, 38 FR 31822, Nov. 19, 1973; as amended by Amdt. 23–17, 41 FR 55464, Dec. 20, 1976; Amdt. 23–49, 61 FR 5167, Feb. 9, 1996]

§23.843 Pressurization tests.

(a) *Strength test.* The complete pressurized cabin, including doors, windows, canopy, and valves, must be tested as a pressure vessel for the pressure differential specified in §23.365(d).

(b) *Functional tests.* The following functional tests must be performed:

(1) Tests of the functioning and capacity of the positive and negative pressure differential valves, and of the emergency release valve, to simulate the effects of closed regulator valves.

(2) Tests of the pressurization system to show proper functioning under each possible condition of pressure, temperature, and moisture, up to the maximum altitude for which certification is requested.

(3) Flight tests, to show the performance of the pressure supply, pressure and flow regulators, indicators, and warning signals, in steady and stepped climbs and descents at rates corresponding to the maximum attainable within the operating limitations of the airplane, up to the maximum altitude for which certification is requested.

(4) Tests of each door and emergency exit, to show that they operate properly after being subjected to the flight tests prescribed in paragraph (b)(3) of this section.

Fire Protection

§23.851 Fire extinguishers.

(a) There must be at least one hand fire extinguisher for use in the pilot compartment that is located within easy access of the pilot while seated.

(b) There must be at least one hand fire extinguisher located conveniently in the passenger compartment—

(1) Of each airplane accommodating more than 6 passengers, and

(2) Of each commuter category airplane.

(c) For hand fire extinguishers, the following apply:

(1) The type and quantity of each extinguishing agent used must be appropriate to the kinds of fire likely to occur where that agent is to be used.

(2) Each extinguisher for use in a personnel compartment must be designed to minimize the hazard of toxic gas concentrations.

[Docket No. 26269, 58 FR 42165, Aug. 6, 1993]

§23.853 Passenger and crew compartment interiors.

For each compartment to be used by the crew or passengers:

(a) The materials must be at least flame-resistant;

(b) [Reserved]

(c) If smoking is to be prohibited, there must be a placard so stating, and if smoking is to be allowed—

(1) There must be an adequate number of self-contained, removable ashtrays; and

(2) Where the crew compartment is separated from the passenger compartment, there must be at least one illuminated sign (using either letters or symbols) notifying all passengers when smoking is prohibited. Signs which notify when smoking is prohibited must—

(i) When illuminated, be legible to each passenger seated in the passenger cabin under all probable lighting conditions; and

(ii) Be so constructed that the crew can turn the illumination on and off; and

(d) In addition, for commuter category airplanes the following requirements apply:

(1) Each disposal receptacle for towels, paper, or waste must be fully enclosed and constructed of at least fire resistant materials and must contain fires likely to occur in it under normal use. The ability of the disposal receptacle to contain those fires under all probable conditions of wear, misalignment, and ventilation expected in service must be demonstrated by test. A placard containing the legible words "No Cigarette Disposal" must be located on or near each disposal receptacle door.

(2) Lavatories must have "No Smoking" or "No Smoking in Lavatory" placards located conspicuously on each side of the entry door and self-contained, removable ashtrays located conspicuously on or near the entry side of each lavatory door, except that one ashtray may serve more than one lavatory door if it can be seen from the cabin side of each lavatory door served. The placards must have red letters at least $\frac{1}{2}$ inch high on a white background at least 1 inch high (a "No Smoking" symbol may be included on the placard).

(3) Materials (including finishes or decorative surfaces applied to the materials) used in each compartment occupied by the crew or passengers must meet the following test criteria as applicable:

(i) Interior ceiling panels, interior wall panels, partitions, galley structure, large cabinet walls, structural flooring, and materials used in the construction of stowage compartments (other than underseat stowage compartments and compartments for stowing small items such as magazines and maps) must be self-extinguishing when tested vertically in accordance with the applicable portions of Appendix F of this part or by other equivalent methods. The average burn length may not exceed 6 inches and the average flame time after removal of the flame source may not exceed 15 seconds. Drippings from the test specimen may not continue to flame for more than an average of 3 seconds after falling.

(ii) Floor covering, textiles (including draperies and upholstery), seat cushions, padding, decorative and nondecorative coated fabrics, leather, trays and galley furnishings, electrical conduit, thermal and acoustical insulation and insulation covering, air ducting, joint and edge covering, cargo compartment liners, insulation blankets, cargo covers and transparencies, molded and thermoformed parts, air ducting joints, and trim strips (decorative and chafing), that are constructed of materials not covered in paragraph (d)(3)(iv) of this section must be self extinguishing when tested vertically in accordance with the applicable portions of Appendix F of this part or other approved equivalent methods. The average burn length may not exceed 8 inches and the average flame time after removal of the flame source may not exceed 15 seconds. Drippings from the test specimen may not continue to flame for more than an average of 5 seconds after falling.

(iii) Motion picture film must be safety film meeting the Standard Specifications for Safety Photographic Film PH1.25 (available from the American National Standards Institute, 1430 Broadway, New York, N.Y. 10018) or an FAA approved equivalent. If the film travels through ducts, the ducts must meet the requirements of paragraph (d)(3)(ii) of this section.

(iv) Acrylic windows and signs, parts constructed in whole or in part of elastomeric materials, edge-lighted instrument assemblies consisting of two or more instruments in a common housing, seatbelts, shoulder harnesses, and cargo and baggage tiedown equipment, including containers, bins, pallets, etc., used in passenger or crew compartments, may not have an average burn rate greater than 2.5 inches per minute when tested horizontally in accordance with the applicable portions of Appendix F of this part or by other approved equivalent methods.

(v) Except for electrical wire cable insulation, and for small parts (such as knobs, handles, rollers, fasteners, clips, grommets, rub strips, pulleys, and small electrical parts) that the Administrator finds would not contribute significantly to the propagation of a fire, materials in items not specified in paragraphs (d)(3) (i), (ii), (iii), or (iv) of this section may not have a burn rate greater than 4.0 inches per minute when tested horizontally in accordance with the applicable portions of Appendix F of this part or by other approved equivalent methods.

(e) Lines, tanks, or equipment containing fuel, oil, or other flammable fluids may not be installed in such compartments unless adequately shielded, isolated, or otherwise protected so that any breakage or failure of such an item would not create a hazard.

(f) Airplane materials located on the cabin side of the firewall must be self-extinguishing or be located at such a distance from the firewall, or otherwise protected, so that ignition will not occur if the firewall is subjected to a flame temperature of not less than 2,000 degrees F for 15 minutes. For self-extinguishing materials (except electrical wire and cable insulation and small parts that the Administrator finds would not contribute significantly to the propagation of a fire), a vertical self-extinguishing test must be conducted in accordance with Appendix F of this part or an equivalent method approved by the Administrator. The average burn length of the material may not exceed 6 inches and the average flame time after removal of the flame source may not exceed 15 seconds. Drippings from the material test specimen may not continue to flame for more than an average of 3 seconds after falling.

[Amdt. 23–14, 23 FR 31822, Nov. 19, 1973; as amended by Amdt. 23–23, 43 FR 50593, Oct. 30, 1978; Amdt. 23–25, 45 FR 7755, Feb. 4, 1980; Amdt. 23–34, 52 FR 1831, Jan. 15, 1987; Amdt. 23–49, 61 FR 5167, Feb. 9, 1996]

§23.855 Cargo and baggage compartment fire protection.

(a) Sources of heat within each cargo and baggage compartment that are capable of igniting the compartment contents must be shielded and insulated to prevent such ignition.

(b) Each cargo and baggage compartment must be constructed of materials that meet the appropriate provisions of §23.853(d)(3).

(c) In addition, for commuter category airplanes, each cargo and baggage compartment must:

(1) Be located where the presence of a fire would be easily discovered by the pilots when seated at their duty station, or it must be equipped with a smoke or fire detector system to give a warning at the pilots' station, and provide sufficient access to enable a pilot to effectively reach any part of the compartment with the contents of a hand held fire extinguisher, or

(2) Be equipped with a smoke or fire detector system to give a warning at the pilots' station and have ceiling and sidewall liners and floor panels constructed of materials that have been subjected to and meet the 45 degree angle test of Appendix F of this part. The flame may not penetrate (pass through) the material during application of the flame or subsequent to its removal. The average flame time after removal of the flame source may not exceed 15 seconds, and the average glow time may not exceed 10 seconds. The compartment must be constructed to provide fire protection that is not less than that required of its individual panels; or

(3) Be constructed and sealed to contain any fire within the compartment.

[Docket No. 27806, 61 FR 5167, Feb. 9, 1996]

§23.859 Combustion heater fire protection.

(a) *Combustion heater fire regions.* The following combustion heater fire regions must be protected from fire in accordance with the applicable provisions of §§23.1182 through 23.1191 and 23.1203:

(1) The region surrounding the heater, if this region contains any flammable fluid system components (excluding the heater fuel system) that could—

(i) Be damaged by heater malfunctioning; or

(ii) Allow flammable fluids or vapors to reach the heater in case of leakage.

(2) The region surrounding the heater, if the heater fuel system has fittings that, if they leaked, would allow fuel vapor to enter this region.

(3) The part of the ventilating air passage that surrounds the combustion chamber.

(b) *Ventilating air ducts.* Each ventilating air duct passing through any fire region must be fireproof. In addition—

(1) Unless isolation is provided by fireproof valves or by equally effective means, the ventilating air duct downstream of each heater must be fireproof for a distance great enough to ensure that any fire originating in the heater can be contained in the duct; and

(2) Each part of any ventilating duct passing through any region having a flammable fluid system must be constructed or isolated from that system so that the malfunctioning of any component of that system cannot introduce flammable fluids or vapors into the ventilating airstream.

(c) *Combustion air ducts.* Each combustion air duct must be fireproof for a distance great enough to prevent damage from backfiring or reverse flame propagation. In addition—

(1) No combustion air duct may have a common opening with the ventilating airstream unless flames from backfires or reverse burning cannot enter the ventilating airstream under any operating condition, including reverse flow or malfunctioning of the heater or its associated components; and

(2) No combustion air duct may restrict the prompt relief of any backfire that, if so restricted, could cause heater failure.

(d) *Heater controls: general.* Provision must be made to prevent the hazardous accumulation of water or ice on or in any heater control component, control system tubing, or safety control.

(e) *Heater safety controls.*

(1) Each combustion heater must have the following safety controls:

(i) Means independent of the components for the normal continuous control of air temperature, airflow, and fuel flow must be provided to automatically shut off the ignition and fuel supply to that heater at a point remote from that heater when any of the following occurs:

(A) The heater exchanger temperature exceeds safe limits.

(B) The ventilating air temperature exceeds safe limits.

(C) The combustion airflow becomes inadequate for safe operation.

(D) The ventilating airflow becomes inadequate for safe operation.

(ii) Means to warn the crew when any heater whose heat output is essential for safe operation has been shut off by the automatic means prescribed in paragraph (e)(1)(i) of this section.

(2) The means for complying with paragraph (e)(1)(i) of this section for any individual heater must—

(i) Be independent of components serving any other heater whose heat output is essential for safe operations; and

(ii) Keep the heater off until restarted by the crew.

(f) *Air intakes.* Each combustion and ventilating air intake must be located so that no flammable fluids or vapors can enter the heater system under any operating condition—

(1) During normal operation; or

(2) As a result of the malfunctioning of any other component.

(g) *Heater exhaust.* Heater exhaust systems must meet the provisions of §§23.1121 and 23.1123. In addition, there must be provisions in the design of the heater exhaust system to safely expel the products of combustion to prevent the occurrence of—

(1) Fuel leakage from the exhaust to surrounding compartments;

(2) Exhaust gas impingement on surrounding equipment or structure;

(3) Ignition of flammable fluids by the exhaust, if the exhaust is in a compartment containing flammable fluid lines; and

(4) Restrictions in the exhaust system to relieve backfires that, if so restricted, could cause heater failure.

(h) *Heater fuel systems.* Each heater fuel system must meet each powerplant fuel system requirement affecting safe heater operation. Each heater fuel system component within the ventilating airstream must be protected by shrouds so that no leakage from those components can enter the ventilating airstream.

(i) *Drains.* There must be means to safely drain fuel that might accumulate within the combustion chamber or the heater exchanger. In addition—

(1) Each part of any drain that operates at high temperatures must be protected in the same manner as heater exhausts; and

(2) Each drain must be protected from hazardous ice accumulation under any operating condition.

[Amdt. 23–27, 45 FR 70387, Oct. 23, 1980]

§23.863 Flammable fluid fire protection.

(a) In each area where flammable fluids or vapors might escape by leakage of a fluid system, there must be means to minimize the probability of ignition of the fluids and vapors, and the resultant hazard if ignition does occur.

(b) Compliance with paragraph (a) of this section must be shown by analysis or tests, and the following factors must be considered:

(1) Possible sources and paths of fluid leakage, and means of detecting leakage.

(2) Flammability characteristics of fluids, including effects of any combustible or absorbing materials.

(3) Possible ignition sources, including electrical faults, overheating of equipment, and malfunctioning of protective devices.

(4) Means available for controlling or extinguishing a fire, such as stopping flow of fluids, shutting down equipment, fireproof containment, or use of extinguishing agents.

(5) Ability of airplane components that are critical to safety of flight to withstand fire and heat.

(c) If action by the flight crew is required to prevent or counteract a fluid fire (e.g. equipment shutdown or actuation of a fire extinguisher), quick acting means must be provided to alert the crew.

(d) Each area where flammable fluids or vapors might escape by leakage of a fluid system must be identified and defined.

[Amdt. 23–23, 43 FR 50593, Oct. 30, 1978]

§23.865 Fire protection of flight controls, engine mounts, and other flight structure.

Flight controls, engine mounts, and other flight structure located in designated fire zones, or in adjacent areas that would be subjected to the effects of fire in the designated fire zones, must be constructed of fireproof material or be shielded so that they are capable of withstanding the effects of a fire. Engine vibration isolators must incorporate suitable features to ensure that the engine is retained if the non-fireproof portions of the isolators deteriorate from the effects of a fire.

[Docket No. 27805, 61 FR 5148, Feb. 9, 1996]

ELECTRICAL BONDING AND LIGHTNING PROTECTION

§23.867 Electrical bonding and protection against lightning and static electricity.

(a) The airplane must be protected against catastrophic effects from lightning.

(b) For metallic components, compliance with paragraph (a) of this section may be shown by—

(1) Bonding the components properly to the airframe; or

(2) Designing the components so that a strike will not endanger the airplane.

(c) For nonmetallic components, compliance with paragraph (a) of this section may be shown by—

(1) Designing the components to minimize the effect of a strike; or

(2) Incorporating acceptable means of diverting the resulting electrical current so as not to endanger the airplane.

[Amdt. 23–7, 34 FR 13092, Aug. 13, 1969; as amended by Amdt. 23–49, 61 FR 5168, Feb. 9, 1996]

MISCELLANEOUS

§23.871 Leveling means.

There must be means for determining when the airplane is in a level position on the ground.

[Amdt. 23–7, 34 FR 13092, Aug. 13, 1969]

Subpart E—Powerplant

GENERAL

§23.901 Installation.

(a) For the purpose of this part, the airplane powerplant installation includes each component that—

(1) Is necessary for propulsion; and

(2) Affects the safety of the major propulsive units.

(b) Each powerplant installation must be constructed and arranged to—

(1) Ensure safe operation to the maximum altitude for which approval is requested.

(2) Be accessible for necessary inspections and maintenance.

(c) Engine cowls and nacelles must be easily removable or openable by the pilot to provide adequate access to and exposure of the engine compartment for preflight checks.

(d) Each turbine engine installation must be constructed and arranged to—

(1) Result in carcass vibration characteristics that do not exceed those established during the type certification of the engine.

(2) Ensure that the capability of the installed engine to withstand the ingestion of rain, hail, ice, and birds into the engine inlet is not less than the capability established for the engine itself under §23.903(a)(2).

(e) The installation must comply with—

(1) The instructions provided under the engine type certificate and the propeller type certificate.

(2) The applicable provisions of this subpart.

(f) Each auxiliary power unit installation must meet the applicable portions of this part.

[Docket No. 4080, 29 FR 17955, Dec. 18, 1964; as amended by Amdt. 23–7, 34 FR 13092, Aug. 13, 1969; Amdt. 23–18, 42 FR 15041, Mar. 17, 1977; Amdt. 23–29, 49 FR 6846, Feb. 23, 1984; Amdt. 23–34, 52 FR 1832, Jan. 15, 1987; Amdt. 23–34, 52 FR 34745, Sept. 14, 1987; Amdt. 23–43, 58 FR 18970, April 9, 1993; Amdt. 23–51, 61 FR 5136, Feb. 9, 1996; Amdt. 23– 53, 63 FR 14797, March 26, 1998]

§23.903 Engines.

(a) *Engine type certificate.*

(1) Each engine must have a type certificate and must meet the applicable requirements of part 34 of this chapter.

(2) Each turbine engine and its installation must comply with one of the following:

(i) Sections 33.76, 33.77 and 33.78 of this chapter in effect on December 13, 2000, or as subsequently amended; or.

(ii) Sections 33.77 and 33.78 of this chapter in effect on April 30, 1998, or as subsequently amended before December 13, 2000; or

(iii) Section 33.77 of this chapter in effect on October 31, 1974, or as subsequently amended before April 30, 1998, unless that engine's foreign object ingestion service history has resulted in an unsafe condition; or

(iv) Be shown to have a foreign object ingestion service history in similar installation locations which has not resulted in any unsafe condition.

(b) *Turbine engine installations.* For turbine engine installations—

(1) Design precautions must be taken to minimize the hazards to the airplane in the event of an engine rotor failure or of a fire originating inside the engine which burns through the engine case.

(2) The powerplant systems associated with engine control devices, systems, and instrumentation must be designed to give reasonable assurance that those operating limitations that adversely affect turbine rotor structural integrity will not be exceeded in service.

(c) *Engine isolation.* The powerplants must be arranged and isolated from each other to allow operation, in at least one configuration, so that the failure or malfunction of any engine, or the failure or malfunction (including destruction by fire in the engine compartment) of any system that can affect an engine (other than a fuel tank if only one fuel tank is installed), will not:

(1) Prevent the continued safe operation of the remaining engines; or

(2) Require immediate action by any crewmember for continued safe operation of the remaining engines.

(d) *Starting and stopping (piston engine).*

(1) The design of the installation must be such that risk of fire or mechanical damage to the engine or airplane, as a result of starting the engine in any conditions in which starting is to be permitted, is reduced to a minimum. Any techniques and associated limitations for engine starting must be established and included in the Airplane Flight Manual, approved manual material, or applicable operating placards. Means must be provided for—

(i) Restarting any engine of a multiengine airplane in flight, and

(ii) Stopping any engine in flight, after engine failure, if continued engine rotation would cause a hazard to the airplane.

(2) In addition, for commuter category airplanes, the following apply:

(i) Each component of the stopping system on the engine side of the firewall that might be exposed to fire must be at least fire resistant.

(ii) If hydraulic propeller feathering systems are used for this purpose, the feathering lines must be at least fire resistant under the operating conditions that may be expected to exist during feathering.

(e) *Starting and stopping (turbine engine).* Turbine engine installations must comply with the following:

(1) The design of the installation must be such that risk of fire or mechanical damage to the engine or the airplane, as a result of starting the engine in any conditions in which starting is to be permitted, is reduced to a minimum. Any techniques and associated limitations must be established and included in the Airplane Flight Manual, approved manual material, or applicable operating placards.

(2) There must be means for stopping combustion within any engine and for stopping the rotation of any engine if continued rotation would cause a hazard to the airplane. Each component of the engine stopping system located in any fire zone must be fire resistant. If hydraulic propeller feathering systems are used for stopping the engine, the hydraulic feathering lines or hoses must be fire resistant.

(3) It must be possible to restart an engine in flight. Any techniques and associated limitations must be established and included in the Airplane Flight Manual, approved manual material, or applicable operating placards.

(4) It must be demonstrated in flight that when restarting engines following a false start, all fuel or vapor is discharged in such a way that it does not constitute a fire hazard.

(f) *Restart envelope.* An altitude and airspeed envelope must be established for the airplane for in-flight engine restarting and each installed engine must have a restart capability within that envelope.

(g) *Restart capability.* For turbine engine powered airplanes, if the minimum windmilling speed of the engines, following the in-flight shutdown of all engines, is insufficient to provide the necessary electrical power for engine ignition, a power source independent of the engine-driven electrical power generating system must be provided to permit in-flight engine ignition for restarting.

[Amdt. 23–14, 38 FR 31822, Nov. 19, 1973; as amended by Amdt. 23–17, 41 FR 55464, Dec. 20, 1976; Amdt. 23–26, 45 FR 60171, Sept. 11, 1980; Amdt. 23–29, 49 FR 6847, Feb. 23, 1984; Amdt. 23–34, 52 FR 1832, Jan. 15, 1987; Amdt. 23–40, 55 FR 32861, Aug. 10, 1990; Amdt.

23–43, 58 FR 18970, April 9, 1993; Amdt. 23–51, 61 FR 5136, Feb. 9, 1996; Amdt. 23–53, 63 FR 14798, March 26, 1998; Amdt. 23–54, 65 FR 55854, Sept. 14, 2000; Amdt. 23–54, 68 FR 75391, Dec. 31, 2003]

§23.904 Automatic power reserve system.

If installed, an automatic power reserve (APR) system that automatically advances the power or thrust on the operating engine(s), when any engine fails during takeoff, must comply with appendix H of this part.

[Docket No. 26344, 58 FR 18970, April 9, 1993]

§23.905 Propellers.

(a) Each propeller must have a type certificate.

(b) Engine power and propeller shaft rotational speed may not exceed the limits for which the propeller is certificated.

(c) Each featherable propeller must have a means to unfeather it in flight.

(d) Each component of the propeller blade pitch control system must meet the requirements of §35.42 of this chapter.

(e) All areas of the airplane forward of the pusher propeller that are likely to accumulate and shed ice into the propeller disc during any operating condition must be suitably protected to prevent ice formation, or it must be shown that any ice shed into the propeller disc will not create a hazardous condition.

(f) Each pusher propeller must be marked so that the disc is conspicuous under normal daylight ground conditions.

(g) If the engine exhaust gases are discharged into the pusher propeller disc, it must be shown by tests, or analysis supported by tests, that the propeller is capable of continuous safe operation.

(h) All engine cowling, access doors, and other removable items must be designed to ensure that they will not separate from the airplane and contact the pusher propeller.

[Docket No. 4080, 29 FR 17955, Dec. 18, 1964; as amended by Amdt. 23–26, 45 FR 60171, Sept. 11, 1980; Amdt. 23–29, 49 FR 6847, Feb. 23, 1984; Amdt. 23–43, 58 FR 18970, April 9, 1993]

§23.907 Propeller vibration.

(a) Each propeller other than a conventional fixed-pitch wooden propeller must be shown to have vibration stresses, in normal operating conditions, that do not exceed values that have been shown by the propeller manufacturer to be safe for continuous operation. This must be shown by—

(1) Measurement of stresses through direct testing of the propeller;

(2) Comparison with similar installations for which these measurements have been made; or

(3) Any other acceptable test method or service experience that proves the safety of the installation.

(b) Proof of safe vibration characteristics for any type of propeller, except for conventional, fixed-pitch, wood propellers must be shown where necessary.

[Docket No. 4080, 29 FR 17955, Dec. 18, 1964; 30 FR 258, Jan. 9, 1965; as amended by Amdt. 23–51, 61 FR 5136, Feb. 9, 1996]

§23.909 Turbocharger systems.

(a) Each turbocharger must be approved under the engine type certificate or it must be shown that the turbocharger system, while in its normal engine installation and operating in the engine environment—

(1) Can withstand, without defect, an endurance test of 150 hours that meets the applicable requirements of §33.49 of this subchapter; and

(2) Will have no adverse effect upon the engine.

(b) Control system malfunctions, vibrations, and abnormal speeds and temperatures expected in service may not damage the turbocharger compressor or turbine.

(c) Each turbocharger case must be able to contain fragments of a compressor or turbine that fails at the highest speed that is obtainable with normal speed control devices inoperative.

(d) Each intercooler installation, where provided, must comply with the following—

(1) The mounting provisions of the intercooler must be designed to withstand the loads imposed on the system;

(2) It must be shown that, under the installed vibration environment, the intercooler will not fail in a manner allowing portions of the intercooler to be ingested by the engine; and

(3) Airflow through the intercooler must not discharge directly on any airplane component (e.g., windshield) unless such discharge is shown to cause no hazard to the airplane under all operating conditions.

(e) Engine power, cooling characteristics, operating limits, and procedures affected by the turbocharger system installations must be evaluated. Turbocharger operating procedures and limitations must be included in the Airplane Flight Manual in accordance with §23.1581.

[Amdt. 23–7, 34 FR 13092, Aug. 13, 1969; as amended by Amdt. 23–43, 58 FR 18970, April 9, 1993]

§23.925 Propeller clearance.

Unless smaller clearances are substantiated, propeller clearances, with the airplane at the most adverse combination of weight and center of gravity, and with the propeller in the most adverse pitch position, may not be less than the following:

(a) *Ground clearance.* There must be a clearance of at least seven inches (for each airplane with nose wheel landing gear) or nine inches (for each airplane with tail wheel landing gear) between each propeller and the ground with the landing gear statically deflected and in the level, normal takeoff, or taxing attitude, whichever is most critical. In addition, for each airplane with conventional landing gear struts using fluid or mechanical means for absorbing landing shocks, there must be positive clearance between the propeller and the ground in the level takeoff attitude with the critical tire completely deflated and the corresponding landing gear strut bottomed. Positive clearance for airplanes using leaf spring struts is shown with a deflection corresponding to 1.5g.

(b) *Aft-mounted propellers.* In addition to the clearances specified in paragraph (a) of this section, an airplane with an aft mounted propeller must be designed such that the propeller will not contact the runway surface when the airplane is in the maximum pitch attitude attainable during normal takeoffs and landings.

(1) Suitable design loads must be established for the tail wheel, bumper, or energy absorption device; and

(2) The supporting structure of the tail wheel, bumper, or energy absorption device must be designed to withstand the loads established in paragraph (b)(1) of this section and inspection/replacement criteria must be established for the tail wheel, bumper, or energy absorption device and provided as part of the information required by §23.1529.

(c) *Water clearance.* There must be a clearance of at least 18 inches between each propeller and the water, unless compliance with §23.239 can be shown with a lesser clearance.

(d) *Structural clearance.* There must be—

(1) At least one inch radial clearance between the blade tips and the airplane structure, plus any additional radial clearance necessary to prevent harmful vibration;

(2) At least one-half inch longitudinal clearance between the propeller blades or cuffs and stationary parts of the airplane; and

(3) Positive clearance between other rotating parts of the propeller or spinner and stationary parts of the airplane.

[Docket No. 4080, 29 FR 17955, Dec. 18, 1964; as amended by Amdt. 23–43, 58 FR 18971, April 9, 1993; Amdt. 23–51, 61 FR 5136, Feb. 9, 1996; Amdt. 23–48, 61 FR 5148, Feb. 9, 1996]

§23.929 Engine installation ice protection.

Propellers (except wooden propellers) and other components of complete engine installations must be protected against the accumulation of ice as necessary to enable satisfactory functioning without appreciable loss of thrust when operated in the icing conditions for which certification is requested.

[Amdt. 23–14, 33 FR 31822, Nov. 19, 1973; as amended by Amdt. 23–51, 61 FR 5136, Feb. 9, 1996]

§23.933 Reversing systems.

(a) *For turbojet and turbofan reversing systems.*

(1) Each system intended for ground operation only must be designed so that, during any reversal in flight, the engine will produce no more than flight idle thrust. In addition, it must be shown by analysis or test, or both, that—

(i) Each operable reverser can be restored to the forward thrust position; or

(ii) The airplane is capable of continued safe flight and landing under any possible position of the thrust reverser.

(2) Each system intended for in-flight use must be designed so that no unsafe condition will result during normal operation of the system, or from any failure, or likely combination of failures, of the reversing system under any operating condition including ground operation. Failure of structural elements need not be considered if the probability of this type of failure is extremely remote.

(3) Each system must have a means to prevent the engine from producing more than idle thrust when the reversing system malfunctions; except that it may produce any greater thrust that is shown to allow directional control to be maintained, with aerodynamic means alone, under the most critical reversing condition expected in operation.

(b) *For propeller reversing systems.*

(1) Each system must be designed so that no single failure, likely combination of failures or malfunction of the system will result in unwanted reverse thrust under any operating condition. Failure of structural elements need not be considered if the probability of this type of failure is extremely remote.

(2) Compliance with paragraph (b)(1) of this section must be shown by failure analysis, or testing, or both, for propeller systems that allow the propeller blades to move from the flight low-pitch position to a position that is substantially less than the normal flight, low-pitch position. The analysis may include or be supported by the analysis made to show compliance with §35.21 for the type certification of the propeller and associated installation components. Credit will be given for pertinent analysis and testing completed by the engine and propeller manufacturers.

[Docket No. 26344, 58 FR 18971, April 9, 1993; as amended by Amdt. 23–51, 61 FR 5136, Feb. 9, 1996]

§23.934 Turbojet and turbofan engine thrust reverser systems test.

Thrust reverser systems of turbojet or turbofan engines must meet the requirements of §33.97 of this chapter or it must be demonstrated by tests that engine operation and vibratory levels are not affected.

[Docket No. 26344, 58 FR 18971, April 9, 1993]

§23.937 Turbopropeller-drag limiting systems.

(a) Turbopropeller-powered airplane propeller-drag limiting systems must be designed so that no single failure or malfunction of any of the systems during normal or emergency operation results in propeller drag in excess of that for which the airplane was designed under the structural requirements of this part. Failure of structural elements of the drag limiting systems need not be considered if the probability of this kind of failure is extremely remote.

(b) As used in this section, drag limiting systems include manual or automatic devices that, when actuated after engine power loss, can move the propeller blades toward the feather position to reduce windmilling drag to a safe level.

[Amdt. 23–7, 34 FR 13093, Aug. 13, 1969; as amended by Amdt. 23–43, 58 FR 18971, April 9, 1993]

§23.939 Powerplant operating characteristics.

(a) Turbine engine powerplant operating characteristics must be investigated in flight to determine that no adverse characteristics (such as stall, surge, or flameout) are present, to a hazardous degree, during normal and emergency operation within the range of operating limitations of the airplane and of the engine.

(b) Turbocharged reciprocating engine operating characteristics must be investigated in flight to assure that no adverse characteristics, as a result of an inadvertent overboost, surge, flooding, or vapor lock, are present during normal or emergency operation of the engine(s) throughout the range of operating limitations of both airplane and engine.

(c) For turbine engines, the air inlet system must not, as a result of airflow distortion during normal operation, cause vibration harmful to the engine.

[Amdt. 23–7, 34 FR 13093 Aug. 13, 1969; as amended by Amdt. 23–14, 38 FR 31823, Nov. 19, 1973; Amdt. 23–18, 42 FR 15041, Mar. 17, 1977; Amdt. 23–42, 56 FR 354, Jan. 3, 1991]

§23.943 Negative acceleration.

No hazardous malfunction of an engine, an auxiliary power unit approved for use in flight, or any component or system associated with the powerplant or auxiliary power unit may occur when the airplane is operated at the negative accelerations within the flight envelopes prescribed in §23.333. This must be shown for the greatest value and duration of the acceleration expected in service.

[Amdt. 23–18, 42 FR 15041, Mar. 17, 1977; as amended by Amdt. 23–43, 58 FR 18971, April 9, 1993]

FUEL SYSTEM

§23.951 General.

(a) Each fuel system must be constructed and arranged to ensure fuel flow at a rate and pressure established for proper engine and auxiliary power unit functioning under each likely operating condition, including any maneuver for which certification is requested and during which the engine or auxiliary power unit is permitted to be in operation.

(b) Each fuel system must be arranged so that—

(1) No fuel pump can draw fuel from more than one tank at a time; or

(2) There are means to prevent introducing air into the system.

(c) Each fuel system for a turbine engine must be capable of sustained operation throughout its flow and pressure range with fuel initially saturated with water at 80°F and having 0.75cc of free water per gallon added and cooled to the most critical condition for icing likely to be encountered in operation.

(d) Each fuel system for a turbine engine powered airplane must meet the applicable fuel venting requirements of part 34 of this chapter.

[Amdt. 23–15, 39 FR 35459, Oct. 1, 1974; as amended by Amdt. 23–40, 55 FR 32861, Aug. 10, 1990; Amdt. 23–43, 58 FR 18971, April 9, 1993]

§23.953 Fuel system independence.

(a) Each fuel system for a multiengine airplane must be arranged so that, in at least one system configuration, the failure of any one component (other than a fuel tank) will not result in the loss of power of more than one engine or require immediate action by the pilot to prevent the loss of power of more than one engine.

(b) If a single fuel tank (or series of fuel tanks interconnected to function as a single fuel tank) is used on a multiengine airplane, the following must be provided:

(1) Independent tank outlets for each engine, each incorporating a shut-off valve at the tank. This shutoff valve may also serve as the fire wall shutoff valve required if the line between the valve and the engine compartment does not contain more than one quart of fuel (or any greater amount shown to be safe) that can escape into the engine compartment.

(2) At least two vents arranged to minimize the probability of both vents becoming obstructed simultaneously.

(3) Filler caps designed to minimize the probability of incorrect installation or inflight loss.

(4) A fuel system in which those parts of the system from each tank outlet to any engine are independent of each part of the system supplying fuel to any other engine.

[Docket No. 4080, 29 FR 17955, Dec. 18, 1964; as amended by Amdt. 23–7, 34 FR 13093 Aug. 13, 1969; Amdt. 23–43, 58 FR 18971, April 9, 1993]

§23.954 Fuel system lightning protection.

The fuel system must be designed and arranged to prevent the ignition of fuel vapor within the system by—

(a) Direct lightning strikes to areas having a high probability of stroke attachment;

(b) Swept lightning strokes on areas where swept strokes are highly probable; and

(c) Corona or streamering at fuel vent outlets.

[Amdt. 23–7, 34 FR 13093, Aug. 13, 1969]

§23.955 Fuel flow.

(a) *General.* The ability of the fuel system to provide fuel at the rates specified in this section and at a pressure sufficient for proper engine operation must be shown in the attitude that is most critical with respect to fuel feed and quantity of unusable fuel. These conditions may be simulated in a suitable mockup. In addition—

(1) The quantity of fuel in the tank may not exceed the amount established as the unusable fuel supply for that tank under §23.959(a) plus that quantity necessary to show compliance with this section.

(2) If there is a fuel flowmeter, it must be blocked during the flow test and the fuel must flow through the meter or its bypass.

(3) If there is a flowmeter without a bypass, it must not have any probable failure mode that would restrict fuel flow below the level required for this fuel demonstration.

(4) The fuel flow must include that flow necessary for vapor return flow, jet pump drive flow, and for all other purposes for which fuel is used.

(b) *Gravity systems.* The fuel flow rate for gravity systems (main and reserve supply) must be 150 percent of the takeoff fuel consumption of the engine.

(c) *Pump systems.* The fuel flow rate for each pump system (main and reserve supply) for each reciprocating engine must be 125 percent of the fuel flow required by the engine at the maximum takeoff power approved under this part.

(1) This flow rate is required for each main pump and each emergency pump, and must be available when the pump is operating as it would during takeoff;

(2) For each hand-operated pump, this rate must occur at not more than 60 complete cycles (120 single strokes) per minute.

(3) The fuel pressure, with main and emergency pumps operating simultaneously, must not exceed the fuel inlet pressure limits of the engine unless it can be shown that no adverse effect occurs.

(d) *Auxiliary fuel systems and fuel transfer systems.* Paragraphs (b), (c), and (f) of this section apply to each auxiliary and transfer system, except that—

(1) The required fuel flow rate must be established upon the basis of maximum continuous power and engine rotational speed, instead of takeoff power and fuel consumption; and

(2) If there is a placard providing operating instructions, a lesser flow rate may be used for transferring fuel from any auxiliary tank into a larger main tank. This lesser flow rate must be adequate to maintain engine maximum continuous power but the flow rate must not overfill the main tank at lower engine powers.

(e) *Multiple fuel tanks.* For reciprocating engines that are supplied with fuel from more than one tank, if engine power loss becomes apparent due to fuel depletion from the tank selected, it must be possible after switching to any full tank, in level flight, to obtain 75 percent maximum continuous power on that engine in not more than—

(1) 10 seconds for naturally aspirated single-engine airplanes;

(2) 20 seconds for turbocharged single-engine airplanes, provided that 75 percent maximum continuous naturally aspirated power is regained within 10 seconds; or

(3) 20 seconds for multiengine airplanes.

(f) *Turbine engine fuel systems.* Each turbine engine fuel system must provide at least 100 percent of the fuel flow required by the engine under each intended operation condition and maneuver. The conditions may be simulated in a suitable mockup. This flow must—

(1) Be shown with the airplane in the most adverse fuel feed condition (with respect to altitudes, attitudes, and other conditions) that is expected in operation; and

(2) For multiengine airplanes, notwithstanding the lower flow rate allowed by paragraph (d) of this section, be automatically uninterrupted with respect to any engine until all the fuel scheduled for use by that engine has been consumed. In addition—

(i) For the purposes of this section, "fuel scheduled for use by that engine" means all fuel in any tank intended for use by a specific engine.

(ii) The fuel system design must clearly indicate the engine for which fuel in any tank is scheduled.

(iii) Compliance with this paragraph must require no pilot action after completion of the engine starting phase of operations.

(3) For single-engine airplanes, require no pilot action after completion of the engine starting phase of operations unless means are provided that unmistakenly alert the pilot to take any needed action at least five minutes prior to the needed action; such pilot action must not cause any change in engine operation; and such pilot action must not distract pilot attention from essential flight duties during any phase of operations for which the airplane is approved.

[Docket No. 4080, 29 FR 17955, Dec. 18, 1964; as amended by Amdt. 23–7, 34 FR 13093, Aug. 13, 1969; Amdt. 23–43, 58 FR 18971, April 9, 1993; Amdt. 23–51, 61 FR 5136, Feb. 9, 1996]

§23.957 Flow between interconnected tanks.

(a) It must be impossible, in a gravity feed system with interconnected tank outlets, for enough fuel to flow between the tanks to cause an overflow of fuel from any tank vent under the conditions in §23.959, except that full tanks must be used.

(b) If fuel can be pumped from one tank to another in flight, the fuel tank vents and the fuel transfer system must be designed so that no structural damage to any airplane component can occur because of overfilling of any tank.

[Docket No. 4080, 29 FR 17955, Dec. 18, 1964; as amended by Amdt. 23–43, 58 FR 18972, April 9, 1993]

§23.959 Unusable fuel supply.

(a) The unusable fuel supply for each tank must be established as not less than that quantity at which the first evidence of malfunctioning occurs under the most adverse fuel feed condition occurring under each intended operation and flight maneuver involving that tank. Fuel system component failures need not be considered.

(b) The effect on the usable fuel quantity as a result of a failure of any pump shall be determined.

[Amdt. 23–7, 34 FR 13093, Aug. 13, 1969; as amended by Amdt. 23–18, 42 FR 15041, Mar. 17, 1977; Amdt. 23–51, 61 FR 5136, Feb. 9, 1996]

§23.961 Fuel system hot weather operation.

Each fuel system must be free from vapor lock when using fuel at its critical temperature, with respect to vapor formation, when operating the airplane in all critical operating and environmental conditions for which approval is requested. For turbine fuel, the initial temperature must be 110°F, -0°, +5°F or the maximum outside air temperature for which approval is requested, whichever is more critical.

[Docket No. 26344, 58 FR 18972, April 9, 1993; 58 FR 27060, May 6, 1993]

§23.963 Fuel tanks: General.

(a) Each fuel tank must be able to withstand, without failure, the vibration, inertia, fluid, and structural loads that it may be subjected to in operation.

(b) Each flexible fuel tank liner must be shown to be suitable for the particular application.

(c) Each integral fuel tank must have adequate facilities for interior inspection and repair.

(d) The total usable capacity of the fuel tanks must be enough for at least one-half hour of operation at maximum continuous power.

(e) Each fuel quantity indicator must be adjusted, as specified in §23.1337(b), to account for the unusable fuel supply determined under §23.959(a).

[Docket No. 4080, 29 FR 17955, Dec. 18, 1964; 30 FR 258, Jan. 9, 1965; as amended by Amdt 23–34, 52 FR 1832, Jan. 15, 1987; Amdt. 23–43, 58 FR 18972, April 9, 1993; Amdt. 23–51, 61 FR 5136, Feb. 9, 1996]

§23.965 Fuel tank tests.

(a) Each fuel tank must be able to withstand the following pressures without failure or leakage:

(1) For each conventional metal tank and nonmetallic tank with walls not supported by the airplane structure, a pressure of 3.5 p.s.i., or that pressure developed during maximum ultimate acceleration with a full tank, whichever is greater.

(2) For each integral tank, the pressure developed during the maximum limit acceleration of the airplane with a full tank, with simultaneous application of the critical limit structural loads.

(3) For each nonmetallic tank with walls supported by the airplane structure and constructed in an acceptable manner

using acceptable basic tank material, and with actual or simulated support conditions, a pressure of 2 p.s.i. for the first tank of a specific design. The supporting structure must be designed for the critical loads occurring in the flight or landing strength conditions combined with the fuel pressure loads resulting from the corresponding accelerations.

(b) Each fuel tank with large, unsupported, or unstiffened flat surfaces, whose failure or deformation could cause fuel leakage, must be able to withstand the following test without leakage, failure, or excessive deformation of the tank walls:

(1) Each complete tank assembly and its support must be vibration tested while mounted to simulate the actual installation.

(2) Except as specified in paragraph (b)(4) of this section, the tank assembly must be vibrated for 25 hours at a total displacement of not less than $\frac{1}{32}$ of an inch (unless another displacement is substantiated) while $\frac{2}{3}$ filled with water or other suitable test fluid.

(3) The test frequency of vibration must be as follows:

(i) If no frequency of vibration resulting from any rpm within the normal operating range of engine or propeller speeds is critical, the test frequency of vibration is:

(A) The number of cycles per minute obtained by multiplying the maximum continuous propeller speed in rpm by 0.9 for propeller-driven airplanes, and

(B) For non-propeller driven airplanes the test frequency of vibration is 2,000 cycles per minute.

(ii) If only one frequency of vibration resulting from any rpm within the normal operating range of engine or propeller speeds is critical, that frequency of vibration must be the test frequency.

(iii) If more than one frequency of vibration resulting from any rpm within the normal operating range of engine or propeller speeds is critical, the most critical of these frequencies must be the test frequency.

(4) Under paragraph (b)(3)(ii) and (iii) of this section, the time of test must be adjusted to accomplish the same number of vibration cycles that would be accomplished in 25 hours at the frequency specified in paragraph (b)(3)(i) of this section.

(5) During the test, the tank assembly must be rocked at a rate of 16 to 20 complete cycles per minute, through an angle of 15° on either side of the horizontal (30° total), about an axis parallel to the axis of the fuselage, for 25 hours.

(c) Each integral tank using methods of construction and sealing not previously proven to be adequate by test data or service experience must be able to withstand the vibration test specified in paragraphs (b)(1) through (4) of this section.

(d) Each tank with a nonmetallic liner must be subjected to the sloshing test outlined in paragraph (b)(5) of this section, with the fuel at room temperature. In addition, a specimen liner of the same basic construction as that to be used in the airplane must, when installed in a suitable test tank, withstand the sloshing test with fuel at a temperature of 110°F.

[Docket No. 4080, 29 FR 17955, Dec. 18, 1964; as amended by Amdt. 23–43, 58 FR 18972, April 9, 1993; Amdt. 23–43, 61 FR 253, January 4, 1996; Amdt. 23–51, 61 FR 5136, Feb. 9, 1996]

§23.967 Fuel tank installation.

(a) Each fuel tank must be supported so that tank loads are not concentrated. In addition—

(1) There must be pads, if necessary, to prevent chafing between each tank and its supports;

(2) Padding must be nonabsorbent or treated to prevent the absorption of fuel;

(3) If a flexible tank liner is used, it must be supported so that it is not required to withstand fluid loads;

(4) Interior surfaces adjacent to the liner must be smooth and free from projections that could cause wear, unless—

(i) Provisions are made for protection of the liner at those points; or

(ii) The construction of the liner itself provides such protection; and

(5) A positive pressure must be maintained within the vapor space of each bladder cell under any condition of operation, except for a particular condition for which it is shown that a zero or negative pressure will not cause the bladder cell to collapse; and

(6) Syphoning of fuel (other than minor spillage) or collapse of bladder fuel cells may not result from improper securing or loss of the fuel filler cap.

(b) Each tank compartment must be ventilated and drained to prevent the accumulation of flammable fluids or vapors. Each compartment adjacent to a tank that is an integral part of the airplane structure must also be ventilated and drained.

(c) No fuel tank may be on the engine side of the firewall. There must be at least one-half inch of clearance between the fuel tank and the firewall. No part of the engine nacelle skin that lies immediately behind a major air opening from the engine compartment may act as the wall of an integral tank.

(d) Each fuel tank must be isolated from personnel compartments by a fume-proof and fuel-proof enclosure that is vented and drained to the exterior of the airplane. The required enclosure must sustain any personnel compartment pressurization loads without permanent deformation or failure under the conditions of §§23.365 and 23.843 of this part. A bladder-type fuel cell, if used, must have a retaining shell at least equivalent to a metal fuel tank in structural integrity.

(e) Fuel tanks must be designed, located, and installed so as to retain fuel:

(1) When subjected to the inertia loads resulting from the ultimate static load factors prescribed in §23.561(b)(2) of this part; and

(2) Under conditions likely to occur when the airplane lands on a paved runway at a normal landing speed under each of the following conditions:

(i) The airplane in a normal landing attitude and its landing gear retracted.

(ii) The most critical landing gear leg collapsed and the other landing gear legs extended.

In showing compliance with paragraph (e)(2) of this section, the tearing away of an engine mount must be considered unless all the engines are installed above the wing or on the tail or fuselage of the airplane.

[Docket No. 4080, 29 FR 17955, Dec. 18, 1964; as amended by Amdt. 23–7, 34 FR 13903, Aug. 13, 1969; Amdt. 23–14, 38 FR 31823, Nov. 19, 1973; Amdt. 23–18, 42 FR 15041, Mar. 17, 1977; Amdt. 23–26, 45 FR 60171, Sept. 11, 1980; Amdt. 23–36, 53 FR 30815, Aug. 15, 1988; Amdt. 23–43, 58 FR 18972, April 9, 1993]

§23.969 Fuel tank expansion space.

Each fuel tank must have an expansion space of not less than two percent of the tank capacity, unless the tank vent discharges clear of the airplane (in which case no expansion space is required). It must be impossible to fill the expansion space inadvertently with the airplane in the normal ground attitude.

§23.971 Fuel tank sump.

(a) Each fuel tank must have a drainable sump with an effective capacity, in the normal ground and flight attitudes, of 0.25 percent of the tank capacity, or 1/16 gallon, whichever is greater.

(b) Each fuel tank must allow drainage of any hazardous quantity of water from any part of the tank to its sump with the airplane in the normal ground attitude.

(c) Each reciprocating engine fuel system must have a sediment bowl or chamber that is accessible for drainage; has a capacity of 1 ounce for every 20 gallons of fuel tank capacity; and each fuel tank outlet is located so that, in the normal flight attitude, water will drain from all parts of the tank except the sump to the sediment bowl or chamber.

(d) Each sump, sediment bowl, and sediment chamber drain required by paragraphs (a), (b), and (c) of this section must comply with the drain provisions of §23.999 (b)(1) and (b)(2).

[Docket No. 26344, 58 FR 18972, April 9, 1993; 58 FR 27060, May 6, 1993]

§23.973 Fuel tank filler connection.

(a) Each fuel tank filler connection must be marked as prescribed in §23.1557(c).

(b) Spilled fuel must be prevented from entering the fuel tank compartment or any part of the airplane other than the tank itself.

(c) Each filler cap must provide a fuel-tight seal for the main filler opening. However, there may be small openings in the fuel tank cap for venting purposes or for the purpose of allowing passage of a fuel gauge through the cap provided such openings comply with the requirements of §23.975(a).

(d) Each fuel filling point, except pressure fueling connection points, must have a provision for electrically bonding the airplane to ground fueling equipment.

(e) For airplanes with engines requiring gasoline as the only permissible fuel, the inside diameter of the fuel filler opening must be no larger than 2.36 inches.

(f) For airplanes with turbine engines, the inside diameter of the fuel filler opening must be no smaller than 2.95 inches.

[Docket No. 4080, 29 FR 17955, Dec. 18, 1964; 30 FR 258, Jan. 9, 1965; as amended by Amdt. 23–18, 42 FR 15041, Mar. 17, 1977; Amdt. 23–43, 58 FR 18972, April 9, 1993; Amdt. 23–51, 61 FR 5136, Feb. 9, 1996]

§23.975 Fuel tank vents and carburetor vapor vents.

(a) Each fuel tank must be vented from the top part of the expansion space. In addition—

(1) Each vent outlet must be located and constructed in a manner that minimizes the possibility of its being obstructed by ice or other foreign matter;

(2) Each vent must be constructed to prevent siphoning of fuel during normal operation;

(3) The venting capacity must allow the rapid relief of excessive differences of pressure between the interior and exterior of the tank;

(4) Airspaces of tanks with interconnected outlets must be interconnected;

(5) There may be no point in any vent line where moisture can accumulate with the airplane in either the ground or level flight attitudes, unless drainage is provided. Any drain valve installed must be accessible for drainage;

(6) No vent may terminate at a point where the discharge of fuel from the vent outlet will constitute a fire hazard or from which fumes may enter personnel compartments; and

(7) Vents must be arranged to prevent the loss of fuel, except fuel discharged because of thermal expansion, when the airplane is parked in any direction on a ramp having a one-percent slope.

(b) Each carburetor with vapor elimination connections and each fuel injection engine employing vapor return provisions must have a separate vent line to lead vapors back to the top of one of the fuel tanks. If there is more than one tank and it is necessary to use these tanks in a definite sequence for any reason, the vapor vent line must lead back to the fuel tank to be used first, unless the relative capacities of the tanks are such that return to another tank is preferable.

(c) For acrobatic category airplanes, excessive loss of fuel during acrobatic maneuvers, including short periods of inverted flight, must be prevented. It must be impossible for fuel to siphon from the vent when normal flight has been resumed after any acrobatic maneuver for which certification is requested.

[Docket No. 4080, 29 FR 17955, Dec. 18, 1964; 30 FR 258, Jan. 9, 1965; as amended by Amdt. 23–18, 42 FR 15041, Mar. 17, 1977; Amdt. 23–29, 49 FR 6847, Feb. 23, 1984; Amdt. 23–43, 58 FR 18973, April 9, 1993; Amdt. 23–51, 61 FR 5136, Feb. 9, 1996]

§23.977 Fuel tank outlet.

(a) There must be a fuel strainer for the fuel tank outlet or for the booster pump. This strainer must—

(1) For reciprocating engine powered airplanes, have 8 to 16 meshes per inch; and

(2) For turbine engine powered airplanes, prevent the passage of any object that could restrict fuel flow or damage any fuel system component.

(b) The clear area of each fuel tank outlet strainer must be at least five times the area of the outlet line.

(c) The diameter of each strainer must be at least that of the fuel tank outlet.

(d) Each strainer must be accessible for inspection and cleaning.

[Amdt. 23–17, 41 FR 55465, Dec. 20, 1976; as amended by Amdt. 23–43, 58 FR 18973, April 9, 1993]

§23.979 Pressure fueling systems.

For pressure fueling systems, the following apply:

(a) Each pressure fueling system fuel manifold connection must have means to prevent the escape of hazardous quantities of fuel from the system if the fuel entry valve fails.

(b) An automatic shutoff means must be provided to prevent the quantity of fuel in each tank from exceeding the maximum quantity approved for that tank. This means must—

(1) Allow checking for proper shutoff operation before each fueling of the tank; and

(2) For commuter category airplanes, indicate at each fueling station, a failure of the shutoff means to stop the fuel flow at the maximum quantity approved for that tank.

(c) A means must be provided to prevent damage to the fuel system in the event of failure of the automatic shutoff means prescribed in paragraph (b) of this section.

(d) All parts of the fuel system up to the tank which are subjected to fueling pressures must have a proof pressure of 1.33 times, and an ultimate pressure of at least 2.0 times, the surge pressure likely to occur during fueling.

[Amdt. 23–14, 38 FR 31823, Nov. 19, 1973; as amended by Amdt. 23–51, 61 FR 5137, Feb. 9, 1996]

FUEL SYSTEM COMPONENTS

§23.991 Fuel pumps.

(a) *Main pumps.* For main pumps, the following apply:

(1) For reciprocating engine installations having fuel pumps to supply fuel to the engine, at least one pump for each engine must be directly driven by the engine and must meet 23.955. This pump is a main pump.

(2) For turbine engine installations, each fuel pump required for proper engine operation, or required to meet the fuel system requirements of this subpart (other than those in paragraph (b) of this section), is a main pump. In addition—

(i) There must be at least one main pump for each turbine engine;

(ii) The power supply for the main pump for each engine must be independent of the power supply for each main pump for any other engine; and

(iii) For each main pump, provision must be made to allow the bypass of each positive displacement fuel pump other than a fuel injection pump approved as part of the engine.

(b) *Emergency pumps.* There must be an emergency pump immediately available to supply fuel to the engine if any main pump (other than a fuel injection pump approved as part of an engine) fails. The power supply for each emergency pump must be independent of the power supply for each corresponding main pump.

(c) *Warning means.* If both the main pump and emergency pump operate continuously, there must be a means to indicate to the appropriate flight crewmembers a malfunction of either pump.

(d) Operation of any fuel pump may not affect engine operation so as to create a hazard, regardless of the engine power or thrust setting or the functional status of any other fuel pump.

[Docket No. 4080, 29 FR 17955, Dec. 18, 1964; as amended by Amdt. 23–7, 34 FR 13093, Aug. 13, 1969; Amdt. 23–26, 45 FR 60171, Sept. 11, 1980; Amdt. 23–43, 58 FR 18973, April 9, 1993]

§23.993 Fuel system lines and fittings.

(a) Each fuel line must be installed and supported to prevent excessive vibration and to withstand loads due to fuel pressure and accelerated flight conditions.

(b) Each fuel line connected to components of the airplane between which relative motion could exist must have provisions for flexibility.

(c) Each flexible connection in fuel lines that may be under pressure and subjected to axial loading must use flexible hose assemblies.

(d) Each flexible hose must be shown to be suitable for the particular application.

(e) No flexible hose that might be adversely affected by exposure to high temperatures may be used where excessive temperatures will exist during operation or after engine shutdown.

[Docket No. 4080, 29 FR 17955, Dec. 18, 1964; as amended by Amdt. 23–43, 58 FR 18973, April 9, 1993]

§23.994 Fuel system components.

Fuel system components in an engine nacelle or in the fuselage must be protected from damage which could result in spillage of enough fuel to constitute a fire hazard as a result of a wheels-up landing on a paved runway.

[Amdt. 23–29, 49 FR 6847, Feb. 23, 1984]

§23.995 Fuel valves and controls.

(a) There must be a means to allow appropriate flight crew members to rapidly shut off, in flight, the fuel to each engine individually.

(b) No shutoff valve may be on the engine side of any firewall. In addition, there must be means to—

(1) Guard against inadvertent operation of each shutoff valve; and

(2) Allow appropriate flight crew members to re-open each valve rapidly after it has been closed.

(c) Each valve and fuel system control must be supported so that loads resulting from its operation or from accelerated flight conditions are not transmitted to the lines connected to the valve.

(d) Each valve and fuel system control must be installed so that gravity and vibration will not affect the selected position.

(e) Each fuel valve handle and its connections to the valve mechanism must have design features that minimize the possibility of incorrect installation.

(f) Each check valve must be constructed, or otherwise incorporate provisions, to preclude incorrect assembly or connection of the valve.

(g) Fuel tank selector valves must—

(1) Require a separate and distinct action to place the selector in the "OFF" position; and

(2) Have the tank selector positions located in such a manner that it is impossible for the selector to pass through the "OFF" position when changing from one tank to another.

[Docket No. 4080, 29 FR 17955, Dec. 18, 1964; as amended by Amdt. 23–14, 38 FR 31823, Nov. 19, 1973; Amdt. 23–17, 41 FR 55465, Dec. 20, 1976; Amdt. 23–18, 42 FR 15041, Mar. 17, 1977; Amdt. 23–29, 49 FR 6847, Feb. 23, 1984]

§23.997 Fuel strainer or filter.

There must be a fuel strainer or filter between the fuel tank outlet and the inlet of either the fuel metering device or an engine driven positive displacement pump, whichever is nearer the fuel tank outlet. This fuel strainer or filter must—

(a) Be accessible for draining and cleaning and must incorporate a screen or element which is easily removable;

(b) Have a sediment trap and drain except that it need not have a drain if the strainer or filter is easily removable for drain purposes;

(c) Be mounted so that its weight is not supported by the connecting lines or by the inlet or outlet connections of the strainer or filter itself, unless adequate strength margins under all loading conditions are provided in the lines and connections; and

(d) Have the capacity (with respect to operating limitations established for the engine) to ensure that engine fuel system functioning is not impaired, with the fuel contaminated to a degree (with respect to particle size and density) that is greater than that established for the engine during its type certification.

(e) In addition, for commuter category airplanes, unless means are provided in the fuel system to prevent the accumulation of ice on the filter, a means must be provided to automatically maintain the fuel flow if ice clogging of the filter occurs.

[Amdt. 23–15, 39 FR 35459, Oct. 1, 1974; as amended by Amdt. 23–29, 49 FR 6847, Feb. 23, 1984; Amdt. 23–34, 52 FR 1832, Jan. 15, 1987; Amdt. 23–43, 58 FR 18973, April 9, 1993]

§23.999 Fuel system drains.

(a) There must be at least one drain to allow safe drainage of the entire fuel system with the airplane in its normal ground attitude.

(b) Each drain required by paragraph (a) of this section and §23.971 must—

(1) Discharge clear of all parts of the airplane;

(2) Have a drain valve—

(i) That has manual or automatic means for positive locking in the closed position;

(ii) That is readily accessible;

(iii) That can be easily opened and closed;

(iv) That allows the fuel to be caught for examination;

(v) That can be observed for proper closing; and

(vi) That is either located or protected to prevent fuel spillage in the event of a landing with landing gear retracted.

[Docket No. 4080, 29 FR 17955, Dec. 18, 1964; as amended by Amdt. 23–17, 41 FR 55465, Dec. 20, 1976; Amdt. 23–43, 58 FR 18973, April 9, 1993]

§23.1001 Fuel jettisoning system.

(a) If the design landing weight is less than that permitted under the requirements of §23.473(b), the airplane must have a fuel jettisoning system installed that is able to jettison enough fuel to bring the maximum weight down to the design landing weight. The average rate of fuel jettisoning must be at least 1 percent of the maximum weight per minute, except that the time required to jettison the fuel need not be less than 10 minutes.

(b) Fuel jettisoning must be demonstrated at maximum weight with flaps and landing gear up and in—

(1) A power-off glide at 1.4 V_{S1};

(2) A climb, at the speed at which the one-engine-inoperative enroute climb data have been established in accordance with §23.69(b), with the critical engine inoperative and the remaining engines at maximum continuous power; and

(3) Level flight at 1.4 V_{S1}, if the results of the tests in the conditions specified in paragraphs (b)(1) and (2) of this section show that this condition could be critical.

(c) During the flight tests prescribed in paragraph (b) of this section, it must be shown that—

(1) The fuel jettisoning system and its operation are free from fire hazard;

(2) The fuel discharges clear of any part of the airplane;

(3) Fuel or fumes do not enter any parts of the airplane; and

(4) The jettisoning operation does not adversely affect the controllability of the airplane.

(d) For reciprocating engine powered airplanes, the jettisoning system must be designed so that it is not possible to jettison the fuel in the tanks used for takeoff and landing below the level allowing 45 minutes flight at 75 percent maximum continuous power. However, if there is an auxiliary control independent of the main jettisoning control, the system may be designed to jettison all the fuel.

(e) For turbine engine powered airplanes, the jettisoning system must be designed so that it is not possible to jettison fuel in the tanks used for takeoff and landing below the level allowing climb from sea level to 10,000 feet and thereafter allowing 45 minutes cruise at a speed for maximum range.

(f) The fuel jettisoning valve must be designed to allow flight crewmembers to close the valve during any part of the jettisoning operation.

(g) Unless it is shown that using any means (including flaps, slots, and slats) for changing the airflow across or around the wings does not adversely affect fuel jettisoning, there must be a placard, adjacent to the jettisoning control, to warn flight crewmembers against jettisoning fuel while the means that change the airflow are being used.

(h) The fuel jettisoning system must be designed so that any reasonably probable single malfunction in the system will not result in a hazardous condition due to unsymmetrical jettisoning of, or inability to jettison, fuel.

[Amdt. 23–7, 34 FR 13094, Aug. 13, 1969; as amended by Amdt. 23–43, 58 FR 18973, April 9, 1993; Amdt. 23–51, 61 FR 5137, Feb. 9, 1996]

OIL SYSTEM

§23.1011 General.

(a) For oil systems and components that have been approved under the engine airworthiness requirements and where those requirements are equal to or more severe than the corresponding requirements of subpart E of this part, that approval need not be duplicated. Where the requirements of subpart E of this part are more severe, substantiation must be shown to the requirements of subpart E of this part.

(b) Each engine must have an independent oil system that can supply it with an appropriate quantity of oil at a temperature not above that safe for continuous operation.

(c) The usable oil tank capacity may not be less than the product of the endurance of the airplane under critical operating conditions and the maximum oil consumption of the engine under the same conditions, plus a suitable margin to ensure adequate circulation and cooling.

(d) For an oil system without an oil transfer system, only the usable oil tank capacity may be considered. The amount of oil in the engine oil lines, the oil radiator, and the feathering reserve, may not be considered.

(e) If an oil transfer system is used, and the transfer pump can pump some of the oil in the transfer lines into the main engine oil tanks, the amount of oil in these lines that can be pumped by the transfer pump may be included in the oil capacity.

[Docket No. 4080, 29 FR 17955, Dec. 18, 1964; as amended by Amdt. 23–43, 58 FR 18973, April 9, 1993]

§23.1013 Oil tanks.

(a) *Installation.* Each oil tank must be installed to—

(1) Meet the requirements of §23.967 (a) and (b); and

(2) Withstand any vibration, inertia, and fluid loads expected in operation.

(b) *Expansion space.* Oil tank expansion space must be provided so that—

(1) Each oil tank used with a reciprocating engine has an expansion space of not less than the greater of 10 percent of the tank capacity or 0.5 gallon, and each oil tank used with a turbine engine has an expansion space of not less than 10 percent of the tank capacity; and

(2) It is impossible to fill the expansion space inadvertently with the airplane in the normal ground attitude.

(c) *Filler connection.* Each oil tank filler connection must be marked as specified in §23.1557(c). Each recessed oil tank filler connection of an oil tank used with a turbine engine, that can retain any appreciable quantity of oil, must have provisions for fitting a drain.

(d) *Vent.* Oil tanks must be vented as follows:

(1) Each oil tank must be vented to the engine from the top part of the expansion space so that the vent connection is not covered by oil under any normal flight condition.

(2) Oil tank vents must be arranged so that condensed water vapor that might freeze and obstruct the line cannot accumulate at any point.

(3) For acrobatic category airplanes, there must be means to prevent hazardous loss of oil during acrobatic maneuvers, including short periods of inverted flight.

(e) *Outlet.* No oil tank outlet may be enclosed by any screen or guard that would reduce the flow of oil below a safe value at any operating temperature. No oil tank outlet diameter may be less than the diameter of the engine oil pump inlet. Each oil tank used with a turbine engine must have means to prevent entrance into the tank itself, or into the tank outlet, of any object that might obstruct the flow of oil through the system. There must be a shutoff valve at the outlet of each oil tank used with a turbine engine, unless the external portion of the oil system (including oil tank supports) is fireproof.

(f) *Flexible liners.* Each flexible oil tank liner must be of an acceptable kind.

(g) Each oil tank filler cap of an oil tank that is used with an engine must provide an oiltight seal.

[Docket No. 4080, 29 FR 17955, Dec. 18, 1964; as amended by Amdt. 23–15, 39 FR 35459 Oct. 1, 1974; Amdt. 23–43, 58 FR 18973, April 9, 1993; Amdt. 23–51, 61 FR 5137, Feb. 9, 1996]

§23.1015 Oil tank tests.

Each oil tank must be tested under §23.965, except that—

(a) The applied pressure must be five p.s.i. for the tank construction instead of the pressures specified in §23.965(a);

(b) For a tank with a nonmetallic liner the test fluid must be oil rather than fuel as specified in §23.965(d), and the slosh test on a specimen liner must be conducted with the oil at 250°F.; and

(c) For pressurized tanks used with a turbine engine, the test pressure may not be less than 5 p.s.i. plus the maximum operating pressure of the tank.

[Docket No. 4080, 29 FR 17955, Dec. 18, 1964; as amended by Amdt. 23–15, 39 FR 35460, Oct. 1, 1974]

§23.1017 Oil lines and fittings.

(a) *Oil lines.* Oil lines must meet §23.993 and must accommodate a flow of oil at a rate and pressure adequate for proper engine functioning under any normal operating condition.

(b) *Breather lines.* Breather lines must be arranged so that—

(1) Condensed water vapor or oil that might freeze and obstruct the line cannot accumulate at any point;

(2) The breather discharge will not constitute a fire hazard if foaming occurs, or cause emitted oil to strike the pilot's windshield;

(3) The breather does not discharge into the engine air induction system; and

(4) For acrobatic category airplanes, there is no excessive loss of oil from the breather during acrobatic maneuvers, including short periods of inverted flight.

(5) The breather outlet is protected against blockage by ice or foreign matter.

[Docket No. 4080, 29 FR 17955, Dec. 18, 1964; as amended by Amdt. 23–7, 34 FR 13094, Aug. 13, 1969; Amdt. 23–14, 38 FR 31823, Nov. 19, 1973]

§23.1019 Oil strainer or filter.

(a) Each turbine engine installation must incorporate an oil strainer or filter through which all of the engine oil flows and which meets the following requirements:

(1) Each oil strainer or filter that has a bypass, must be constructed and installed so that oil will flow at the normal rate through the rest of the system with the strainer or filter completely blocked.

(2) The oil strainer or filter must have the capacity (with respect to operating limitations established for the engine) to ensure that engine oil system functioning is not impaired when the oil is contaminated to a degree (with respect to particle size and density) that is greater than that established for the engine for its type certification.

(3) The oil strainer or filter, unless it is installed at an oil tank outlet, must incorporate a means to indicate contamination before it reaches the capacity established in accordance with paragraph (a)(2) of this section.

(4) The bypass of a strainer or filter must be constructed and installed so that the release of collected contaminants is minimized by appropriate location of the bypass to ensure that collected contaminants are not in the bypass flow path.

(5) An oil strainer or filter that has no bypass, except one that is installed at an oil tank outlet, must have a means to connect it to the warning system required in §23.1305(c)(9).

(b) Each oil strainer or filter in a powerplant installation using reciprocating engines must be constructed and installed so that oil will flow at the normal rate through the rest of the system with the strainer or filter element completely blocked.

[Amdt. 23–15, 39 FR 35460, Oct. 1, 1974; as amended by Amdt. 23–29, 49 FR 6847, Feb. 23, 1984; Amdt. 23–43, 58 FR 18973, April 9, 1993]

§23.1021 Oil system drains.

A drain (or drains) must be provided to allow safe drainage of the oil system. Each drain must—

(a) Be accessible;

(b) Have drain valves, or other closures, employing manual or automatic shut-off means for positive locking in the closed position; and

(c) Be located or protected to prevent inadvertent operation.

[Amdt. 23–29, 49 FR 6847, Feb. 23, 1984; as amended by Amdt. 23–43, 58 FR 18973, April 9, 1993]

§23.1023 Oil radiators.

Each oil radiator and its supporting structures must be able to withstand the vibration, inertia, and oil pressure loads to which it would be subjected in operation.

§23.1027 Propeller feathering system.

(a) If the propeller feathering system uses engine oil and that oil supply can become depleted due to failure of any part of the oil system, a means must be incorporated to reserve enough oil to operate the feathering system.

(b) The amount of reserved oil must be enough to accomplish feathering and must be available only to the feathering pump.

(c) The ability of the system to accomplish feathering with the reserved oil must be shown.

(d) Provision must be made to prevent sludge or other foreign matter from affecting the safe operation of the propeller feathering system.

[Docket No. 4080, 29 FR 17955, Dec. 18, 1964; as amended by Amdt. 23–14, 38 FR 31823, Nov. 19, 1973; Amdt. 23–43, 58 FR 18973, April 9, 1993]

Cooling

§23.1041 General.

The powerplant and auxiliary power unit cooling provisions must maintain the temperatures of powerplant components and engine fluids, and auxiliary power unit components and fluids within the limits established for those components and fluids under the most adverse ground, water, and flight operations to the maximum altitude and maximum ambient atmospheric temperature conditions for which approval is requested, and after normal engine and auxiliary power unit shutdown.

[Docket No. 26344, 58 FR 18973, April 9, 1993; as amended by Amdt. 23–51, 61 FR 5137, Feb. 9, 1996]

§23.1043 Cooling tests.

(a) *General.* Compliance with §23.1041 must be shown on the basis of tests, for which the following apply:

(1) If the tests are conducted under ambient atmospheric temperature conditions deviating from the maximum for which approval is requested, the recorded powerplant temperatures must be corrected under paragraphs (c) and (d) of this section, unless a more rational correction method is applicable.

(2) No corrected temperature determined under paragraph (a)(1) of this section may exceed established limits.

(3) The fuel used during the cooling tests must be of the minimum grade approved for the engine.

(4) For turbocharged engines, each turbocharger must be operated through that part of the climb profile for which operation with the turbocharger is requested.

(5) For a reciprocating engine, the mixture settings must be the leanest recommended for climb.

(b) *Maximum ambient atmospheric temperature.* A maximum ambient atmospheric temperature corresponding to sea level conditions of at least 100 degrees F must be established. The assumed temperature lapse rate is 3.6 degrees F per thousand feet of altitude above sea level until a temperature of –69.7 degrees F is reached, above which altitude the temperature is considered constant at –69.7 degrees F. However, for winterization installations, the applicant may select a maximum ambient atmospheric temperature corresponding to sea level conditions of less than 100 degrees F.

(c) Correction factor (except cylinder barrels). Temperatures of engine fluids and powerplant components (except cylinder barrels) for which temperature limits are established, must be corrected by adding to them the difference between the maximum ambient atmospheric temperature for the relevant altitude for which approval has been requested and the temperature of the ambient air at the time of the first occurrence of the maximum fluid or component temperature recorded during the cooling test.

(d) Correction factor for cylinder barrel temperatures. Cylinder barrel temperatures must be corrected by adding to them 0.7 times the difference between the maximum ambient atmospheric temperature for the relevant altitude for which approval has been requested and the temperature of the ambient air at the time of the first occurrence of the maximum cylinder barrel temperature recorded during the cooling test.

[Docket No. 4080, 29 FR 17955, Dec. 18, 1964; as amended by Amdt. 23–7, 34 FR 13094, Aug. 13, 1969; Amdt. 23–21, 43 FR 2319, Jan. 16, 1978; Amdt. 23–51, 61 FR 5137, Feb. 9, 1996]

§23.1045 Cooling test procedures for turbine engine powered airplanes.

(a) Compliance with §23.1041 must be shown for all phases of operation. The airplane must be flown in the configurations, at the speeds, and following the procedures recommended in the Airplane Flight Manual for the relevant stage of flight, that correspond to the applicable performance requirements that are critical to cooling.

(b) Temperatures must be stabilized under the conditions from which entry is made into each stage of flight being investigated, unless the entry condition normally is not one during which component and engine fluid temperatures would stabilize (in which case, operation through the full entry condition must be conducted before entry into the stage of flight being investigated in order to allow temperatures to reach their natural levels at the time of entry). The takeoff cooling test must be preceded by a period during which the powerplant component and engine fluid temperatures are stabilized with the engines at ground idle.

(c) Cooling tests for each stage of flight must be continued until—

(1) The component and engine fluid temperatures stabilize;

(2) The stage of flight is completed; or

(3) An operating limitation is reached.

[Amdt. 23–7, 34 FR 13094, Aug. 13, 1969; as amended by Amdt. 23–51, 61 FR 5137, Feb. 9, 1996]

§23.1047 Cooling test procedures for reciprocating engine powered airplanes.

Compliance with §23.1041 must be shown for the climb (or, for multiengine airplanes with negative one-engine-inoperative rates of climb, the descent) stage of flight. The airplane must be flown in the configurations, at the speeds and following the procedures recommended in the Airplane Flight Manual, that correspond to the applicable performance requirements that are critical to cooling.

[Amdt. 23–7, 34 FR 13094, Aug. 13, 1969; as amended by Amdt. 23–21, 43 FR 2319, Jan. 16, 1978; Amdt. 23–42, 56 FR 354, Jan. 3, 1991; Amdt. 23–43, 58 FR 18973, April 9, 1993; Amdt. 23–51, 61 FR 5137, Feb. 9, 1996]

Liquid Cooling

§23.1061 Installation.

(a) *General.* Each liquid-cooled engine must have an independent cooling system (including coolant tank) installed so that—

(1) Each coolant tank is supported so that tank loads are distributed over a large part of the tank surface;

(2) There are pads or other isolation means between the tank and its supports to prevent chafing.

(3) Pads or any other isolation means that is used must be nonabsorbent or must be treated to prevent absorption of flammable fluids; and

(4) No air or vapor can be trapped in any part of the system, except the coolant tank expansion space, during filling or during operation.

(b) *Coolant tank.* The tank capacity must be at least one gallon, plus 10 percent of the cooling system capacity. In addition—

(1) Each coolant tank must be able to withstand the vibration, inertia, and fluid loads to which it may be subjected in operation;

(2) Each coolant tank must have an expansion space of at least 10 percent of the total cooling system capacity; and

(3) It must be impossible to fill the expansion space inadvertently with the airplane in the normal ground attitude.

(c) *Filler connection.* Each coolant tank filler connection must be marked as specified in §23.1557(c). In addition—

(1) Spilled coolant must be prevented from entering the coolant tank compartment or any part of the airplane other than the tank itself; and

(2) Each recessed coolant filler connection must have a drain that discharges clear of the entire airplane.

(d) *Lines and fittings.* Each coolant system line and fitting must meet the requirements of §23.993, except that the inside diameter of the engine coolant inlet and outlet lines may not be less than the diameter of the corresponding engine inlet and outlet connections.

(e) *Radiators.* Each coolant radiator must be able to withstand any vibration, inertia, and coolant pressure load to which it may normally be subjected. In addition—

(1) Each radiator must be supported to allow expansion due to operating temperatures and prevent the transmittal of harmful vibration to the radiator; and

(2) If flammable coolant is used, the air intake duct to the coolant radiator must be located so that (in case of fire) flames from the nacelle cannot strike the radiator.

(f) *Drains.* There must be an accessible drain that—

(1) Drains the entire cooling system (including the coolant tank, radiator, and the engine) when the airplane is in the normal ground altitude;

(2) Discharges clear of the entire airplane; and

(3) Has means to positively lock it closed.

[Docket No. 4080, 29 FR 17955, Dec. 18, 1964; as amended by Amdt. 23–43, 58 FR 18973, April 9, 1993]

§23.1063 Coolant tank tests.

Each coolant tank must be tested under §23.965, except that—

(a) The test required by §23.965(a) (1) must be replaced with a similar test using the sum of the pressure developed during the maximum ultimate acceleration with a full tank or a pressure of 3.5 pounds per square inch, whichever is greater, plus the maximum working pressure of the system; and

(b) For a tank with a nonmetallic liner the test fluid must be coolant rather than fuel as specified in §23.965(d), and the slosh test on a specimen liner must be conducted with the coolant at operating temperature.

Induction System

§23.1091 Air induction system.

(a) The air induction system for each engine and auxiliary power unit and their accessories must supply the air required by that engine and auxiliary power unit and their accessories under the operating conditions for which certification is requested.

(b) Each reciprocating engine installation must have at least two separate air intake sources and must meet the following:

(1) Primary air intakes may open within the cowling if that part of the cowling is isolated from the engine accessory section by a fire-resistant diaphragm or if there are means to prevent the emergence of backfire flames.

(2) Each alternate air intake must be located in a sheltered position and may not open within the cowling if the emergence of backfire flames will result in a hazard.

(3) The supplying of air to the engine through the alternate air intake system may not result in a loss of excessive power in addition to the power loss due to the rise in air temperature.

(4) Each automatic alternate air door must have an override means accessible to the flight crew.

(5) Each automatic alternate air door must have a means to indicate to the flight crew when it is not closed.

(c) For turbine engine powered airplanes—

(1) There must be means to prevent hazardous quantities of fuel leakage or overflow from drains, vents, or other components of flammable fluid systems from entering the engine intake system; and

(2) The airplane must be designed to prevent water or slush on the runway, taxiway, or other airport operating surfaces from being directed into the engine or auxiliary power unit air intake ducts in hazardous quantities. The air intake ducts must be located or protected so as to minimize the hazard of ingestion of foreign matter during takeoff, landing, and taxiing.

[Docket No. 4080, 29 FR 17955, Dec. 18, 1964; as amended by Amdt. 23–7, 34 FR 13095, Aug. 13, 1969; Amdt. 23–43, 58 FR 18973, April 9, 1993; 58 FR 27060, May 6, 1993; Amdt. 23–51, 61 FR 5137, Feb. 9, 1996]

§23.1093 Induction system icing protection.

(a) *Reciprocating engines.* Each reciprocating engine air induction system must have means to prevent and eliminate icing. Unless this is done by other means, it must be shown that, in air free of visible moisture at a temperature of 30°F.—

(1) Each airplane with sea level engines using conventional venturi carburetors has a preheater that can provide a heat rise of 90°F. with the engines at 75 percent of maximum continuous power;

(2) Each airplane with altitude engines using conventional venturi carburetors has a preheater that can provide a heat rise of 120°F. with the engines at 75 percent of maximum continuous power;

(3) Each airplane with altitude engines using fuel metering device tending to prevent icing has a preheater that, with the engines at 60 percent of maximum continuous power, can provide a heat rise of—

(i) 100°F.; or

(ii) 40°F., if a fluid deicing system meeting the requirements of §§23.1095 through 23.1099 is installed;

(4) Each airplane with sea level engine(s) using fuel metering device tending to prevent icing has a sheltered alternate source of air with a preheat of not less than 60°F with the engines at 75 percent of maximum continuous power;

(5) Each airplane with sea level or altitude engine(s) using fuel injection systems having metering components on which impact ice may accumulate has a preheater capable of providing a heat rise of 75°F when the engine is operating at 75 percent of its maximum continuous power; and

(6) Each airplane with sea level or altitude engine(s) using fuel injection systems not having fuel metering components projecting into the airstream on which ice may form, and introducing fuel into the air induction system downstream of any components or other obstruction on which ice produced by fuel evaporation may form, has a sheltered alternate source of air with a preheat of not less than 60°F with the engines at 75 percent of its maximum continuous power.

(b) *Turbine engines.*

(1) Each turbine engine and its air inlet system must operate throughout the flight power range of the engine (including idling), without the accumulation of ice on engine or inlet system components that would adversely affect engine operation or cause a serious loss of power or thrust—

(i) Under the icing conditions specified in appendix C of part 25 of this chapter, and

(ii) In snow, both falling and blowing, within the limitations established for the airplane for such operation.

(2) Each turbine engine must idle for 30 minutes on the ground, with the air bleed available for engine icing protection at its critical condition, without adverse effect, in an atmosphere that is at a temperature between 15° and 30°F (between -9° and -1°C) and has a liquid water content not less than 0.3 grams per cubic meter in the form of drops having a mean effective diameter not less than 20 microns, followed by momentary operation at takeoff power or thrust. During the 30 minutes of idle operation, the engine may be run up periodically to a moderate power or thrust setting in a manner acceptable to the Administrator.

(c) *Reciprocating engines with Superchargers.* For airplanes with reciprocating engines having superchargers to pressurize the air before it enters the fuel metering device, the heat rise in the air caused by that supercharging at any altitude may be utilized in determining compliance with paragraph (a) of this section if the heat rise utilized is that which will be available, automatically, for the applicable altitudes and operating condition because of supercharging.

[Amdt. 23–7, 34 FR 13095, Aug. 13, 1969; as amended by Amdt. 23–15, 39 FR 35460, Oct. 1, 1974; Amdt. 23–17, 41 FR 55465, Dec. 20, 1976; Amdt. 23–18, 42 FR 15041, Mar. 17, 1977; Amdt. 23–29, 49 FR 6847, Feb. 23, 1984; Amdt. 23–43, 58 FR 18973, April 9, 1993; Amdt. 23–51, 61 FR 5137, Feb. 9, 1996]

§23.1095 Carburetor deicing fluid flow rate.

(a) If a carburetor deicing fluid system is used, it must be able to simultaneously supply each engine with a rate of fluid flow, expressed in pounds per hour, of not less than 2.5 times the square root of the maximum continuous power of the engine.

(b) The fluid must be introduced into the air induction system—

(1) Close to, and upstream of, the carburetor; and

(2) So that it is equally distributed over the entire cross section of the induction system air passages.

§23.1097 Carburetor deicing fluid system capacity.

(a) The capacity of each carburetor deicing fluid system—

(1) May not be less than the greater of—

(i) That required to provide fluid at the rate specified in §23.1095 for a time equal to three percent of the maximum endurance of the airplane; or

(ii) 20 minutes at that flow rate; and

(2) Need not exceed that required for two hours of operation.

(b) If the available preheat exceeds 50°F. but is less than 100°F., the capacity of the system may be decreased in proportion to the heat rise available in excess of 50°F.

§23.1099 Carburetor deicing fluid system detail design.

Each carburetor deicing fluid system must meet the applicable requirements for the design of a fuel system, except as specified in §§23.1095 and 23.1097.

§23.1101 Induction air preheater design.

Each exhaust-heated, induction air preheater must be designed and constructed to—

(a) Ensure ventilation of the preheater when the induction air preheater is not being used during engine operation;

(b) Allow inspection of the exhaust manifold parts that it surrounds; and

(c) Allow inspection of critical parts of the preheater itself.

[Docket No. 4080, 29 FR 17955, Dec. 18, 1964; as amended by Amdt. 23–43, 58 FR 18974, April 9, 1993]

§23.1103 Induction system ducts.

(a) Each induction system duct must have a drain to prevent the accumulation of fuel or moisture in the normal ground and flight attitudes. No drain may discharge where it will cause a fire hazard.

(b) Each duct connected to components between which relative motion could exist must have means for flexibility.

(c) Each flexible induction system duct must be capable of withstanding the effects of temperature extremes, fuel, oil, water, and solvents to which it is expected to be exposed in service and maintenance without hazardous deterioration or delamination.

(d) For reciprocating engine installations, each induction system duct must be—

(1) Strong enough to prevent induction system failures resulting from normal backfire conditions; and

(2) Fire resistant in any compartment for which a fire extinguishing system is required.

(e) Each inlet system duct for an auxiliary power unit must be—

(1) Fireproof within the auxiliary power unit compartment;

(2) Fireproof for a sufficient distance upstream of the auxiliary power unit compartment to prevent hot gas reverse flow from burning through the duct and entering any other compartment of the airplane in which a hazard would be created by the entry of the hot gases;

(3) Constructed of materials suitable to the environmental conditions expected in service, except in those areas requiring fireproof or fire resistant materials; and

(4) Constructed of materials that will not absorb or trap hazardous quantities of flammable fluids that could be ignited by a surge or reverse-flow condition.

(f) Induction system ducts that supply air to a cabin pressurization system must be suitably constructed of material that will not produce hazardous quantities of toxic gases or isolated to prevent hazardous quantities of toxic gases from entering the cabin during a powerplant fire.

[Docket No. 4080, 29 FR 17955, Dec. 18, 1964; as amended by Amdt. 23–7, 34 FR 13095, Aug. 13, 1969; Amdt. 23–43, 58 FR 18974, April 9, 1993]

§23.1105 Induction system screens.

If induction system screens are used—

(a) Each screen must be upstream of the carburetor or fuel injection system.

(b) No screen may be in any part of the induction system that is the only passage through which air can reach the engine, unless—

(1) The available preheat is at least 100°F.; and

(2) The screen can be deiced by heated air;

(c) No screen may be deiced by alcohol alone; and

(d) It must be impossible for fuel to strike any screen.

[Docket No. 4080, 29 FR 17955, Dec. 18, 1964; 30 FR 258, Jan. 9, 1996; as amended by Amdt. 23–51, 61 FR 5137, Feb. 9, 1996]

§23.1107 Induction system filters.

If an air filter is used to protect the engine against foreign material particles in the induction air supply—

(a) Each air filter must be capable of withstanding the effects of temperature extremes, rain, fuel, oil, and solvents to which it is expected to be exposed in service and maintenance; and

(b) Each air filter shall have a design feature to prevent material separated from the filter media from interfering with proper fuel metering operation.

[Docket No. 26344, 58 FR 18974, April 9, 1993; as amended by Amdt. 23–51, 61 FR 5137, Feb. 9, 1996]

§23.1109 Turbocharger bleed air system.

The following applies to turbocharged bleed air systems used for cabin pressurization:

(a) The cabin air system may not be subject to hazardous contamination following any probable failure of the turbocharger or its lubrication system.

(b) The turbocharger supply air must be taken from a source where it cannot be contaminated by harmful or hazardous gases or vapors following any probable failure or malfunction of the engine exhaust, hydraulic, fuel, or oil system.

[Amdt. 23–42, 56 FR 354, Jan. 3, 1991]

§23.1111 Turbine engine bleed air system.

For turbine engine bleed air systems, the following apply:

(a) No hazard may result if duct rupture or failure occurs anywhere between the engine port and the airplane unit served by the bleed air.

(b) The effect on airplane and engine performance of using maximum bleed air must be established.

(c) Hazardous contamination of cabin air systems may not result from failures of the engine lubricating system.

[Amdt. 23–7, 34 FR 13095, Aug. 13, 1969; as amended by Amdt. 23–17, 41 FR 55465, Dec. 20, 1976]

Exhaust System

§23.1121 General.

For powerplant and auxiliary power unit installations, the following apply—

(a) Each exhaust system must ensure safe disposal of exhaust gases without fire hazard or carbon monoxide contamination in any personnel compartment.

(b) Each exhaust system part with a surface hot enough to ignite flammable fluids or vapors must be located or shielded so that leakage from any system carrying flammable fluids or vapors will not result in a fire caused by impingement of the fluids or vapors on any part of the exhaust system including shields for the exhaust system.

(c) Each exhaust system must be separated by fireproof shields from adjacent flammable parts of the airplane that are outside of the engine and auxiliary power unit compartments.

(d) No exhaust gases may discharge dangerously near any fuel or oil system drain.

(e) No exhaust gases may be discharged where they will cause a glare seriously affecting pilot vision at night.

(f) Each exhaust system component must be ventilated to prevent points of excessively high temperature.

(g) If significant traps exist, each turbine engine and auxiliary power unit exhaust system must have drains discharging clear of the airplane, in any normal ground and flight attitude, to prevent fuel accumulation after the failure of an attempted engine or auxiliary power unit start.

(h) Each exhaust heat exchanger must incorporate means to prevent blockage of the exhaust port after any internal heat exchanger failure.

(i) For the purpose of compliance with §23.603, the failure of any part of the exhaust system will be considered to adversely affect safety.

[Docket No. 4080, 29 FR 17955, Dec. 18, 1964; as amended by Amdt. 23–7, 34 FR 13095, Aug. 13, 1969; Amdt. 23–18, 42 FR 15042, Mar. 17, 1977; Amdt. 23–43, 58 FR 18974, April 9, 1993; Amdt. 23–51, 61 FR 5137, Feb. 9, 1996]

§23.1123 Exhaust system.

(a) Each exhaust system must be fireproof and corrosion-resistant, and must have means to prevent failure due to expansion by operating temperatures.

(b) Each exhaust system must be supported to withstand the vibration and inertia loads to which it may be subjected in operation.

(c) Parts of the system connected to components between which relative motion could exist must have means for flexibility.

[Docket No. 4080, 29 FR 17955, Dec. 18, 1964; as amended by Amdt. 23–43, 58 FR 18974, April 9, 1993]

§23.1125 Exhaust heat exchangers.

For reciprocating engine powered airplanes the following apply:

(a) Each exhaust heat exchanger must be constructed and installed to withstand the vibration, inertia, and other loads that it may be subjected to in normal operation. In addition—

(1) Each exchanger must be suitable for continued operation at high temperatures and resistant to corrosion from exhaust gases;

(2) There must be means for inspection of critical parts of each exchanger; and

(3) Each exchanger must have cooling provisions wherever it is subject to contact with exhaust gases.

(b) Each heat exchanger used for heating ventilating air must be constructed so that exhaust gases may not enter the ventilating air.

[Docket No. 4080, 29 FR 17955, Dec. 18, 1964; as amended by Amdt. 23–17, 41 FR 55465, Dec. 20, 1976]

Powerplant Controls and Accessories

§23.1141 Powerplant controls: General.

(a) Powerplant controls must be located and arranged under §23.777 and marked under §23.1555(a).

(b) Each flexible control must be shown to be suitable for the particular application.

(c) Each control must be able to maintain any necessary position without—

(1) Constant attention by flight crew members; or

(2) Tendency to creep due to control loads or vibration.

(d) Each control must be able to withstand operating loads without failure or excessive deflection.

(e) For turbine engine powered airplanes, no single failure or malfunction, or probable combination thereof, in any powerplant control system may cause the failure of any powerplant function necessary for safety.

(f) The portion of each powerplant control located in the engine compartment that is required to be operated in the event of fire must be at least fire resistant.

(g) Powerplant valve controls located in the cockpit must have—

(1) For manual valves, positive stops or in the case of fuel valves suitable index provisions, in the open and closed position; and

(2) For power-assisted valves, a means to indicate to the flight crew when the valve—

(i) Is in the fully open or fully closed position; or

(ii) Is moving between the fully open and fully closed position.

[Docket No. 4080, 29 FR 17955, Dec. 18, 1964; as amended by Amdt. 23–7, 34 FR 13095, Aug. 13, 1969; Amdt. 23–14, 38 FR 31823, Nov. 19, 1973; Amdt. 23–18, 42 FR 15042, Mar. 17, 1977; Amdt. 23–51, 61 FR 5137, Feb. 9, 1996]

§23.1142 Auxiliary power unit controls.

Means must be provided on the flight deck for the starting, stopping, monitoring, and emergency shutdown of each installed auxiliary power unit.

[Docket No. 26344, 58 FR 18974, April 9, 1993]

§23.1143 Engine controls.

(a) There must be a separate power or thrust control for each engine and a separate control for each supercharger that requires a control.

(b) Power, thrust, and supercharger controls must be arranged to allow—

(1) Separate control of each engine and each supercharger; and

(2) Simultaneous control of all engines and all superchargers.

(c) Each power, thrust, or supercharger control must give a positive and immediate responsive means of controlling its engine or supercharger.

(d) The power, thrust, or supercharger controls for each engine or supercharger must be independent of those for every other engine or supercharger.

(e) For each fluid injection (other than fuel) system and its controls not provided and approved as part of the engine, the applicant must show that the flow of the injection fluid is adequately controlled.

(f) If a power, thrust, or a fuel control (other than a mixture control) incorporates a fuel shutoff feature, the control must have a means to prevent the inadvertent movement of the control into the off position. The means must—

(1) Have a positive lock or stop at the idle position; and

(2) Require a separate and distinct operation to place the control in the shutoff position.

(g) For reciprocating single-engine airplanes, each power or thrust control must be designed so that if the control separates at the engine fuel metering device, the airplane is capable of continued safe flight and landing.

[Amdt. 23–7, 34 FR 13095, Aug. 13, 1969; as amended by Amdt. 23–17, 41 FR 55465, Dec. 20, 1976; Amdt. 23–29, 49 FR 6847, Feb. 23, 1984; Amdt. 23–43, 58 FR 18974, April 9, 1993; Amdt. 23–51, 61 FR 5137, Feb. 9, 1996]

§23.1145 Ignition switches.

(a) Ignition switches must control and shut off each ignition circuit on each engine.

(b) There must be means to quickly shut off all ignition on multiengine airplanes by the grouping of switches or by a master ignition control.

(c) Each group of ignition switches, except ignition switches for turbine engines for which continuous ignition is not required, and each master ignition control must have a means to prevent its inadvertent operation.

[Docket No. 4080, 29 FR 17955, Dec. 18, 1964; 30 FR 258, Jan. 9, 1965; as amended by Amdt. 23–18, 42 FR 15042, Mar. 17, 1977; Amdt. 23–43, 58 FR 18974, April 9, 1993]

§23.1147 Mixture controls.

(a) If there are mixture controls, each engine must have a separate control, and each mixture control must have guards or must be shaped or arranged to prevent confusion by feel with other controls.

(1) The controls must be grouped and arranged to allow—

(i) Separate control of each engine; and

(ii) Simultaneous control of all engines.

(2) The controls must require a separate and distinct operation to move the control toward lean or shut-off position.

(b) For reciprocating single-engine airplanes, each manual engine mixture control must be designed so that, if the control separates at the engine fuel metering device, the airplane is capable of continued safe flight and landing.

[Docket No. 4080, 29 FR 17955, Dec. 18, 1964; as amended by Amdt. 23–7, 34 FR 13096, Aug. 13, 1969; Amdt. 23–33, 51 FR 26657, July 24, 1986; Amdt. 23–43, 58 FR 18974, April 9, 1993]

§23.1149 Propeller speed and pitch controls.

(a) If there are propeller speed or pitch controls, they must be grouped and arranged to allow—

(1) Separate control of each propeller; and

(2) Simultaneous control of all propellers.

(b) The controls must allow ready synchronization of all propellers on multiengine airplanes.

§23.1153 Propeller feathering controls.

If there are propeller feathering controls installed, it must be possible to feather each propeller separately. Each control must have a means to prevent inadvertent operation.

[Docket No. 27804, 61 FR 5138, Feb. 9, 1996]

§23.1155 Turbine engine reverse thrust and propeller pitch settings below the flight regime.

For turbine engine installations, each control for reverse thrust and for propeller pitch settings below the flight regime must have means to prevent its inadvertent operation. The means must have a positive lock or stop at the flight idle position and must require a separate and distinct operation by the crew to displace the control from the flight regime (forward thrust regime for turbojet powered airplanes).

[Amdt. 23–7, 34 FR 13096, Aug. 13, 1969]

§23.1157 Carburetor air temperature controls.

There must be a separate carburetor air temperature control for each engine.

§23.1163 Powerplant accessories.

(a) Each engine mounted accessory must—

(1) Be approved for mounting on the engine involved and use the provisions on the engines for mounting; or

(2) Have torque limiting means on all accessory drives in order to prevent the torque limits established for those drives from being exceeded; and

(3) In addition to paragraphs (a)(1) or (a)(2) of this section, be sealed to prevent contamination of the engine oil system and the accessory system.

(b) Electrical equipment subject to arcing or sparking must be installed to minimize the probability of contact with any flammable fluids or vapors that might be present in a free state.

(c) Each generator rated at or more than 6 kilowatts must be designed and installed to minimize the probability of a fire hazard in the event it malfunctions.

(d) If the continued rotation of any accessory remotely driven by the engine is hazardous when malfunctioning occurs, a means to prevent rotation without interfering with the continued operation of the engine must be provided.

(e) Each accessory driven by a gearbox that is not approved as part of the powerplant driving the gearbox must—

(1) Have torque limiting means to prevent the torque limits established for the affected drive from being exceeded;

(2) Use the provisions on the gearbox for mounting; and

(3) Be sealed to prevent contamination of the gearbox oil system and the accessory system.

[Docket No. 4080, 29 FR 17955, Dec. 18, 1964; as amended by Amdt. 23–14, 38 FR 31823, Nov. 19, 1973; Amdt. 23–29, 49 FR 6847, Feb. 23, 1984; Amdt. 23–34, 52 FR 1832, Jan. 15, 1987; Amdt. 23–42, 56 FR 354, Jan. 3, 1991]

§23.1165 Engine ignition systems.

(a) Each battery ignition system must be supplemented by a generator that is automatically available as an alternate source of electrical energy to allow continued engine operation if any battery becomes depleted.

(b) The capacity of batteries and generators must be large enough to meet the simultaneous demands of the engine ignition system and the greatest demands of any electrical system components that draw from the same source.

(c) The design of the engine ignition system must account for—

(1) The condition of an inoperative generator;

(2) The condition of a completely depleted battery with the generator running at its normal operating speed; and

(3) The condition of a completely depleted battery with the generator operating at idling speed, if there is only one battery.

(d) There must be means to warn appropriate crewmembers if malfunctioning of any part of the electrical system is causing the continuous discharge of any battery used for engine ignition.

(e) Each turbine engine ignition system must be independent of any electrical circuit that is not used for assisting, controlling, or analyzing the operation of that system.

(f) In addition, for commuter category airplanes, each turbopropeller ignition system must be an essential electrical load.

[Docket No. 4080, 29 FR 17955, Dec. 18, 1964; as amended by Amdt. 23–17, 41 FR 55465 Dec. 20, 1976; Amdt. 23–34, 52 FR 1833, Jan. 15, 1987]

POWERPLANT FIRE PROTECTION

§23.1181 Designated fire zones; regions included.

Designated fire zones are—

(a) For reciprocating engines—

(1) The power section;

(2) The accessory section;

(3) Any complete powerplant compartment in which there is no isolation between the power section and the accessory section.

(b) For turbine engines—

(1) The compressor and accessory sections;

(2) The combustor, turbine and tailpipe sections that contain lines or components carrying flammable fluids or gases.

(3) Any complete powerplant compartment in which there is no isolation between compressor, accessory, combustor, turbine, and tailpipe sections.

(c) Any auxiliary power unit compartment; and

(d) Any fuel-burning heater, and other combustion equipment installation described in §23.859.

[Docket No. 26344, 58 FR 18975, April 9, 1993; as amended by Amdt. 23–51, 61 FR 5138, Feb. 9, 1996]

§23.1182 Nacelle areas behind firewalls.

Components, lines, and fittings, except those subject to the provisions of §23.1351(e), located behind the engine-compartment firewall must be constructed of such materials and located at such distances from the firewall that they will not suffer damage sufficient to endanger the airplane if a portion of the engine side of the firewall is subjected to a flame temperature of not less than 2,000°F for 15 minutes.

[Amdt. 23–14, 38 FR 31816, Nov. 19, 1973]

§23.1183 Lines, fittings, and components.

(a) Except as provided in paragraph (b) of this section, each component, line, and fitting carrying flammable fluids, gas, or air in any area subject to engine fire conditions must be at least fire resistant, except that flammable fluid tanks and supports which are part of and attached to the engine must be fireproof or be enclosed by a fireproof shield unless damage by fire to any non-fireproof part will not cause leakage or spillage of flammable fluid. Components must be shielded or located so as to safeguard against the ignition of leaking flammable fluid. Flexible hose assemblies (hose and end fittings) must be shown to be suitable for the particular application. An integral oil sump of less than 25-quart capacity on a reciprocating engine need not be fireproof nor be enclosed by a fireproof shield.

(b) Paragraph (a) of this section does not apply to—

(1) Lines, fittings, and components which are already approved as part of a type certificated engine; and

(2) Vent and drain lines, and their fittings, whose failure will not result in, or add to, a fire hazard.

[Docket No. 4080, 29 FR 17955, Dec. 18, 1964; as amended by Amdt. 23–5, 32 FR 6912, May 5, 1967; Amdt. 23–15, 39 FR 35460, Oct. 1, 1974; Amdt. 23–29, 49 FR 6847, Feb. 23, 1984; Amdt. 23–51, 61 FR 5138, Feb. 9, 1996]

§23.1189 Shutoff means.

(a) For each multiengine airplane, the following must apply:

(1) Each engine installation must have means to shut off or otherwise prevent hazardous quantities of fuel, oil, deicing fluid, and other flammable liquids from flowing into, within, or through any engine compartment, except in lines, fittings, and components forming an integral part of an engine.

(2) The closing of the fuel shutoff valve for any engine may not make any fuel unavailable to the remaining engines that would be available to those engines with that valve open.

(3) Operation of any shutoff means may not interfere with the later emergency operation of other equipment such as propeller feathering devices.

(4) Each shutoff must be outside of the engine compartment unless an equal degree of safety is provided with the shutoff inside the compartment.

(5) Not more than one quart of flammable fluid may escape into the engine compartment after engine shutoff. For those installations where the flammable fluid that escapes after shutdown cannot be limited to one quart, it must be demonstrated that this greater amount can be safely contained or drained overboard.

(6) There must be means to guard against inadvertent operation of each shutoff means, and to make it possible for the crew to reopen the shutoff means in flight after it has been closed.

(b) Turbine engine installations need not have an engine oil system shutoff if—

(1) The oil tank is integral with, or mounted on, the engine; and

(2) All oil system components external to the engine are fireproof or located in areas not subject to engine fire conditions.

(c) Power operated valves must have means to indicate to the flight crew when the valve has reached the selected position and must be designed so that the valve will not move from the selected position under vibration conditions likely to exist at the valve location.

[Docket No. 4080, 29 FR 17955, Dec. 18, 1964; as amended by Amdt. 23–7, 34 FR 13096, Aug. 13, 1969; Amdt. 23–14, 38 FR 31823, Nov. 19, 1973; Amdt. 23–29, 49 FR 6847, Feb. 23, 1984; Amdt. 23–43, 58 FR 18975, April 9, 1993]

§23.1191 Firewalls.

(a) Each engine, auxiliary power unit, fuel burning heater, and other combustion equipment, must be isolated from the rest of the airplane by firewalls, shrouds, or equivalent means.

(b) Each firewall or shroud must be constructed so that no hazardous quantity of liquid, gas, or flame can pass from the compartment created by the firewall or shroud to other parts of the airplane.

(c) Each opening in the firewall or shroud must be sealed with close fitting, fireproof grommets, bushings, or firewall fittings.

(d) [Reserved]

(e) Each firewall and shroud must be fireproof and protected against corrosion.

(f) Compliance with the criteria for fireproof materials or components must be shown as follows:

(1) The flame to which the materials or components are subjected must be 2,000 ± 150°F.

(2) Sheet materials approximately 10 inches square must be subjected to the flame from a suitable burner.

(3) The flame must be large enough to maintain the required test temperature over an area approximately five inches square.

(g) Firewall materials and fittings must resist flame penetration for at least 15 minutes.

(h) The following materials may be used in firewalls or shrouds without being tested as required by this section:

(1) Stainless steel sheet, 0.015 inch thick.

(2) Mild steel sheet (coated with aluminum or otherwise protected against corrosion) 0.018 inch thick.

(3) Terne plate, 0.018 inch thick.

(4) Monel metal, 0.018 inch thick.

(5) Steel or copper base alloy firewall fittings.

(6) Titanium sheet, 0.016 inch thick.

[Docket No. 4080, 29 FR 17955, Dec. 18, 1964; as amended by Amdt. 23–43, 58 FR 18975, April 9, 1993; 58 FR 27060, May 6, 1993; Amdt. 23–51, 61 FR 5138, Feb. 9, 1996]

§23.1192 Engine accessory compartment diaphragm.

For aircooled radial engines, the engine power section and all portions of the exhaust system must be isolated from the engine accessory compartment by a diaphragm that meets the firewall requirements of §23.1191.

[Amdt. 23–14, 38 FR 31823, Nov. 19, 1973]

§23.1193 Cowling and nacelle.

(a) Each cowling must be constructed and supported so that it can resist any vibration, inertia, and air loads to which it may be subjected in operation.

(b) There must be means for rapid and complete drainage of each part of the cowling in the normal ground and flight attitudes. Drain operation may be shown by test, analysis, or both, to ensure that under normal aerodynamic pressure distribution expected in service each drain will operate as designed. No drain may discharge where it will cause a fire hazard.

(c) Cowling must be at least fire resistant.

(d) Each part behind an opening in the engine compartment cowling must be at least fire resistant for a distance of at least 24 inches aft of the opening.

(e) Each part of the cowling subjected to high temperatures due to its nearness to exhaust system ports or exhaust gas impingement, must be fire proof.

(f) Each nacelle of a multiengine airplane with supercharged engines must be designed and constructed so that with the landing gear retracted, a fire in the engine compartment will not burn through a cowling or nacelle and enter a nacelle area other than the engine compartment.

(g) In addition, for commuter category airplanes, the airplane must be designed so that no fire originating in any engine compartment can enter, either through openings or by burn-through, any other region where it would create additional hazards.

[Docket No. 4080, 29 FR 17955, Dec. 18, 1964; 30 FR 258, Jan. 9, 1965; as amended by Amdt. 23–18, 42 FR 15042, Mar. 17, 1977; Amdt. 23–34, 52 FR 1833, Jan. 15, 1987; 58 FR 18975, April 9, 1993]

§23.1195 Fire extinguishing systems.

(a) For commuter category airplanes, fire extinguishing systems must be installed and compliance shown with the following:

(1) Except for combustor, turbine, and tailpipe sections of turbine-engine installations that contain lines or components carrying flammable fluids or gases for which a fire originating in these sections is shown to be controllable, a fire extinguisher system must serve each engine compartment;

(2) The fire extinguishing system, the quantity of the extinguishing agent, the rate of discharge, and the discharge distribution must be adequate to extinguish fires. An individual "one shot" system may be used.

(3) The fire extinguishing system for a nacelle must be able to simultaneously protect each compartment of the nacelle for which protection is provided.

(b) If an auxiliary power unit is installed in any airplane certificated to this part, that auxiliary power unit compartment must be served by a fire extinguishing system meeting the requirements of paragraph (a)(2) of this section.

[Amdt. 23–34, 52 FR 1833, Jan. 15, 1987; as amended by Amdt. 23–43, 58 FR 18975, April 9, 1993]

§23.1197 Fire extinguishing agents.

For commuter category airplanes, the following applies:

(a) Fire extinguishing agents must—

(1) Be capable of extinguishing flames emanating from any burning of fluids or other combustible materials in the area protected by the fire extinguishing system; and

(2) Have thermal stability over the temperature range likely to be experienced in the compartment in which they are stored.

(b) If any toxic extinguishing agent is used, provisions must be made to prevent harmful concentrations of fluid or fluid vapors (from leakage during normal operation of the airplane or as a result of discharging the fire extinguisher on the ground or in flight) from entering any personnel compartment, even though a defect may exist in the extinguishing system. This must be shown by test except for built-in carbon dioxide fuselage compartment fire extinguishing systems for which—

(1) Five pounds or less of carbon dioxide will be discharged, under established fire control procedures, into any fuselage compartment; or

(2) Protective breathing equipment is available for each flight crewmember on flight deck duty.

[Amdt. 23–34, 52 FR 1833, Jan. 15, 1987]

§23.1199 Extinguishing agent containers.

For commuter category airplanes, the following applies:

(a) Each extinguishing agent container must have a pressure relief to prevent bursting of the container by excessive internal pressures.

(b) The discharge end of each discharge line from a pressure relief connection must be located so that discharge of the fire extinguishing agent would not damage the airplane. The line must also be located or protected to prevent clogging caused by ice or other foreign matter.

(c) A means must be provided for each fire extinguishing agent container to indicate that the container has discharged or that the charging pressure is below the established minimum necessary for proper functioning.

(d) The temperature of each container must be maintained, under intended operating conditions, to prevent the pressure in the container from—

(1) Falling below that necessary to provide an adequate rate of discharge; or

(2) Rising high enough to cause premature discharge.

(e) If a pyrotechnic capsule is used to discharge the extinguishing agent, each container must be installed so that temperature conditions will not cause hazardous deterioration of the pyrotechnic capsule.

[Amdt. 23–34, 52 FR 1833, Jan. 15, 1987; 52 FR 34745, Sept. 14, 1987]

§23.1201 Fire extinguishing system materials.

For commuter category airplanes, the following apply:

(a) No material in any fire extinguishing system may react chemically with any extinguishing agent so as to create a hazard.

(b) Each system component in an engine compartment must be fireproof.

[Amdt. 23–34, 52 FR 1833, Jan. 15, 1987; 52 FR 7262, Mar. 9, 1987]

§23.1203 Fire detector system.

(a) There must be means that ensure the prompt detection of a fire in—

(1) An engine compartment of—

(i) Multiengine turbine powered airplanes;

(ii) Multiengine reciprocating engine powered airplanes incorporating turbochargers;

(iii) Airplanes with engine(s) located where they are not readily visible from the cockpit; and

(iv) All commuter category airplanes.

(2) The auxiliary power unit compartment of any airplane incorporating an auxiliary power unit.

(b) Each fire detector must be constructed and installed to withstand the vibration, inertia, and other loads to which it may be subjected in operation.

(c) No fire detector may be affected by any oil, water, other fluids, or fumes that might be present.

(d) There must be means to allow the crew to check, in flight, the functioning of each fire detector electric circuit.

(e) Wiring and other components of each fire detector system in a designated fire zone must be at least fire resistant.

[Amdt. 23–18, 42 FR 15042, Mar. 17, 1977; as amended by Amdt. 23–34, 52 FR 1833, Jan. 15, 1987; Amdt. 23–43, 58 FR 18975, April 9, 1993; Amdt. 23–51, 61 FR 5138, Feb. 9, 1996]

Subpart F—Equipment

GENERAL

§23.1301 Function and installation.

Each item of installed equipment must—

(a) Be of a kind and design appropriate to its intended function.

(b) Be labeled as to its identification, function, or operating limitations, or any applicable combination of these factors;

(c) Be installed according to limitations specified for that equipment; and

(d) Function properly when installed.

[Amdt. 23–20, 42 FR 36968, July 18, 1977]

§23.1303 Flight and navigation instruments.

The following are the minimum required flight and navigation instruments:

(a) An airspeed indicator.

(b) An altimeter.

(c) A direction indicator (nonstabilized magnetic compass).

(d) For reciprocating engine-powered airplanes of more than 6,000 pounds maximum weight and turbine engine powered airplanes, a free air temperature indicator or an air-temperature indicator which provides indications that are convertible to free-air.

(e) A speed warning device for—

(1) Turbine engine powered airplanes; and

(2) Other airplanes for which V_{MO}/M_{MO} and V_D/M_D are established under §§23.335(b)(4) and 23.1505(c) if V_{MO}/M_{MO} is greater than 0.8 V_D/M_D.

The speed warning device must give effective aural warning (differing distinctively from aural warnings used for other purposes) to the pilots whenever the speed exceeds V_{MO} plus 6 knots or M_{MO}+0.01. The upper limit of the production tolerance for the warning device may not exceed the prescribed warning speed. The lower limit of the warning device must be set to minimize nuisance warning.

(f) When an attitude display is installed, the instrument design must not provide any means, accessible to the flightcrew, of adjusting the relative positions of the attitude reference symbol and the horizon line beyond that necessary for parallax correction.

(g) In addition, for commuter category airplanes:

(1) If airspeed limitations vary with altitude, the airspeed indicator must have a maximum allowable airspeed indicator showing the variation of V_{MO} with altitude.

(2) The altimeter must be a sensitive type.

(3) Having a passenger seating configuration of 10 or more, excluding the pilot's seats and that are approved for IFR operations, a third attitude instrument must be provided that:

(i) Is powered from a source independent of the electrical generating system;

(ii) Continues reliable operation for a minimum of 30 minutes after total failure of the electrical generating system;

(iii) Operates independently of any other attitude indicating system;

(iv) Is operative without selection after total failure of the electrical generating system;

(v) Is located on the instrument panel in a position acceptable to the Administrator that will make it plainly visible to and usable by any pilot at the pilot's station; and

(vi) Is appropriately lighted during all phases of operation.

[Docket No. 4080, 29 FR 17955, Dec. 18, 1964; as amended by Amdt. 23–17, 41 FR 55465, Dec. 20, 1976; Amdt. 23–43, 58 FR 18975, April 9, 1993; Amdt. 23–49, 61 FR 5168, Feb. 9, 1996]

§23.1305 Powerplant instruments.

The following are required powerplant instruments:

(a) *For all airplanes.*

(1) A fuel quantity indicator for each fuel tank, installed in accordance with §23.1337(b).

(2) An oil pressure indicator for each engine.

(3) An oil temperature indicator for each engine.

(4) An oil quantity measuring device for each oil tank which meets the requirements of §23.1337(d).

(5) A fire warning means for those airplanes required to comply with §23.1203.

(b) *For reciprocating engine-powered airplanes.* In addition to the powerplant instruments required by paragraph (a) of this section, the following powerplant instruments are required:

(1) An induction system air temperature indicator for each engine equipped with a preheater and having induction air temperature limitations that can be exceeded with preheat.

(2) A tachometer indicator for each engine.

(3) A cylinder head temperature indicator for—

(i) Each air-cooled engine with cowl flaps;

(ii) [Reserved]

(iii) Each commuter category airplane

(4) For each pump-fed engine, a means:

(i) That continuously indicates, to the pilot, the fuel pressure or fuel flow; or

(ii) That continuously monitors the fuel system and warns the pilot of any fuel flow trend that could lead to engine failure.

(5) A manifold pressure indicator for each altitude engine and for each engine with a controllable propeller.

(6) For each turbocharger installation:

(i) If limitations are established for either carburetor (or manifold) air inlet temperature or exhaust gas or turbocharger turbine inlet temperature, indicators must be furnished for each temperature for which the limitation is established unless it is shown that the limitation will not be exceeded in all intended operations.

(ii) If its oil system is separate from the engine oil system, oil pressure and oil temperature indicators must be provided.

(7) A coolant temperature indicator for each liquid-cooled engine.

(c) *For turbine engine-powered airplanes.* In addition to the powerplant instruments required by paragraph (a) of this section, the following powerplant instruments are required:

(1) A gas temperature indicator for each engine.

(2) A fuel flowmeter indicator for each engine.

(3) A fuel low pressure warning means for each engine.

(4) A fuel low level warning means for any fuel tank that should not be depleted of fuel in normal operations.

(5) A tachometer indicator (to indicate the speed of the rotors with established limiting speeds) for each engine.

(6) An oil low pressure warning means for each engine.

(7) An indicating means to indicate the functioning of the powerplant ice protection system for each engine.

(8) For each engine, an indicating means for the fuel strainer or filter required by §23.997 to indicate the occurrence of contamination of the strainer or filter before it reaches the capacity established in accordance with §23.997(d).

(9) For each engine, a warning means for the oil strainer or filter required by §23.1019, if it has no bypass, to warn the pilot of the occurrence of contamination of the strainer or filter screen before it reaches the capacity established in accordance with §23.1019(a)(5).

(10) An indicating means to indicate the functioning of any heater used to prevent ice clogging of fuel system components.

(d) *For turbojet/turbofan engine-powered airplanes.* In addition to the powerplant instruments required by paragraphs (a) and (c) of this section, the following powerplant instruments are required:

(1) For each engine, an indicator to indicate thrust or to indicate a parameter that can be related to thrust, including a free air temperature indicator if needed for this purpose.

(2) For each engine, a position indicating means to indicate to the flight crew when the thrust reverser, if installed, is in the reverse thrust position.

(e) *For turbopropeller-powered airplanes.* In addition to the powerplant instruments required by paragraphs (a) and (c) of this section, the following powerplant instruments are required:

(1) A torque indicator for each engine.

(2) A position indicating means to indicate to the flight crew when the propeller blade angle is below the flight low pitch position, for each propeller, unless it can be shown that such occurrence is highly improbable.

[Docket No. 26344, 58 FR 18975, April 9, 1993; 58 FR 27060, May 6, 1993; as amended by Amdt. 23–51, 61 FR, Feb. 9, 1996; Amdt. 23–52, 61 FR 13644, March 27, 1996]

§23.1307 Miscellaneous equipment.

The equipment necessary for an airplane to operate at the maximum operating altitude and in the kinds of operations and meteorological conditions for which certification is requested and is approved in accordance with §23.1559 must be included in the type design.

[Docket No. 4080, 29 FR 17955, Dec. 18, 1964; 30 FR 258, Jan. 9, 1965; as amended by Amdt. 23–23, 43 FR 50593, Oct. 30, 1978; Amdt. 23–43, 58 FR 18976, April 9, 1993; Amdt. 23–49, 61 FR 5168, Feb. 9, 1996]

§23.1309 Equipment, systems, and installations.

(a) Each item of equipment, each system, and each installation:

(1) When performing its intended function, may not adversely affect the response, operation, or accuracy of any—

(i) Equipment essential to safe operation; or

(ii) Other equipment unless there is a means to inform the pilot of the effect.

(2) In a single-engine airplane, must be designed to minimize hazards to the airplane in the event of a probable malfunction or failure.

(3) In a multiengine airplane, must be designed to prevent hazards to the airplane in the event of a probable malfunction or failure.

(4) In a commuter category airplane, must be designed to safeguard against hazards to the airplane in the event of their malfunction or failure.

(b) The design of each item of equipment, each system, and each installation must be examined separately and in relationship to other airplane systems and installations to determine if the airplane is dependent upon its function for continued safe flight and landing and, for airplanes not limited to VFR conditions, if failure of a system would significantly reduce the capability of the airplane or the ability of the crew to cope with adverse operating conditions. Each item of equipment, each system, and each installation identified by this examination as one upon which the airplane is dependent for proper functioning to ensure continued safe flight and landing, or whose failure would significantly reduce the capability of the airplane or the ability of the crew to cope with adverse operating conditions, must be designed to comply with the following additional requirements:

(1) It must perform its intended function under any foreseeable operating condition.

(2) When systems and associated components are considered separately and in relation to other systems—

(i) The occurrence of any failure condition that would prevent the continued safe flight and landing of the airplane must be extremely improbable; and

(ii) The occurrence of any other failure condition that would significantly reduce the capability of the airplane or the ability of the crew to cope with adverse operating conditions must be improbable.

(3) Warning information must be provided to alert the crew to unsafe system operating conditions and to enable them to take appropriate corrective action. Systems, controls, and associated monitoring and warning means must be designed to minimize crew errors that could create additional hazards.

(4) Compliance with the requirements of paragraph (b)(2) of this section may be shown by analysis and, where necessary, by appropriate ground, flight, or simulator tests. The analysis must consider—

(i) Possible modes of failure, including malfunctions and damage from external sources;

(ii) The probability of multiple failures, and the probability of undetected faults;

(iii) The resulting effects on the airplane and occupants, considering the stage of flight and operating conditions; and

(iv) The crew warning cues, corrective action required, and the crew's capability of determining faults.

(c) Each item of equipment, each system, and each installation whose functioning is required by this chapter and that requires a power supply is an "essential load" on the power supply. The power sources and the system must be able to supply the following power loads in probable operating combinations and for probable durations:

(1) Loads connected to the power distribution system with the system functioning normally.

(2) Essential loads after failure of—

(i) Any one engine on two-engine airplanes; or

(ii) Any two engines on an airplane with three or more engines; or

(iii) Any power converter or energy storage device.

(3) Essential loads for which an alternate source of power is required, as applicable, by the operating rules of this chapter, after any failure or malfunction in any one power supply system, distribution system, or other utilization system.

(d) In determining compliance with paragraph (c)(2) of this section, the power loads may be assumed to be reduced under a monitoring procedure consistent with safety in the kinds of operations authorized. Loads not required in controlled flight need not be considered for the two-engine-inoperative condition on airplanes with three or more engines.

(e) In showing compliance with this section with regard to the electrical power system and to equipment design and installation, critical environmental and atmospheric conditions, including radio frequency energy and the effects (both direct and indirect) of lightning strikes, must be considered. For electrical generation, distribution, and utilization equipment required by or used in complying with this chapter, the ability to provide continuous, safe service under foreseeable environmental conditions may be shown by environmental tests, design analysis, or reference to previous comparable service experience on other airplanes.

(f) As used in this section, "system" refers to all pneumatic systems, fluid systems, electrical systems, mechanical systems, and powerplant systems included in the airplane design, except for the following:

(1) Powerplant systems provided as part of the certificated engine.

(2) The flight structure (such a wing, empennage, control surfaces and their systems, the fuselage, engine mounting, and landing gear and their related primary attachments) whose requirements are specific in subparts C and D of this part.

[Amdt. 23–41, 55 FR 43309, Oct. 26, 1990; 55 FR 47028, Nov. 8, 1990; as amended by Amdt. 23–49, 61 FR 5168, Feb. 9, 1996]

INSTRUMENTS: INSTALLATION

§23.1311 Electronic display instrument systems.

(a) Electronic display indicators, including those with features that make isolation and independence between powerplant instrument systems impractical, must:

(1) Meet the arrangement and visibility requirements of §23.1321.

(2) Be easily legible under all lighting conditions encountered in the cockpit, including direct sunlight, considering the expected electronic display brightness level at the end of an electronic display indictor's useful life. Specific limitations on display system useful life must be contained in the Instructions for Continued Airworthiness required by §23.1529.

(3) Not inhibit the primary display of attitude, airspeed, altitude, or powerplant parameters needed by any pilot to set power within established limitations, in any normal mode of operation.

(4) Not inhibit the primary display of engine parameters needed by any pilot to properly set or monitor powerplant limitations during the engine starting mode of operation.

(5) Have an independent magnetic direction indicator and either an independent secondary mechanical altimeter, airspeed indicator, and attitude instrument or individual electronic display indicators for the altitude, airspeed, and attitude that are independent from the airplane's primary electrical power system. These secondary instruments may be installed in panel positions that are displaced from the primary positions specified by §23.1321(d), but must be located where they meet the pilot's visibility requirements of §23.1321(a).

(6) Incorporate sensory cues for the pilot that are equivalent to those in the instrument being replaced by the electronic display indicators.

(7) Incorporate visual displays of instrument markings, required by §§23.1541 through 23.1553, or visual displays that alert the pilot to abnormal operational values or approaches to established limitation values, for each parameter required to be displayed by this part.

(b) The electronic display indicators, including their systems and installations, and considering other airplane systems, must be designed so that one display of information essential for continued safe flight and landing will remain available to the crew, without need for immediate action by any pilot for continued safe operation, after any single failure or probable combination of failures.

(c) As used in this section, "instrument" includes devices that are physically contained in one unit, and devices that are composed of two or more physically separate units or components connected together (such as a remote indicating gyroscopic direction indicator that includes a magnetic sensing element, a gyroscopic unit, an amplifier, and an indicator connected together). As used in this section, "primary" display refers to the display of a parameter that is located in the instrument panel such that the pilot looks at it first when wanting to view that parameter.

[Docket No. 27806, 61 FR 5168, Feb. 9, 1996]

§23.1321 Arrangement and visibility.

(a) Each flight, navigation, and powerplant instrument for use by any required pilot during takeoff, initial climb, final approach, and landing must be located so that any pilot seated at the controls can monitor the airplane's flight path and these instruments with minimum head and eye movement. The powerplant instruments for these flight conditions are those needed to set power within powerplant limitations.

(b) For each multiengine airplane, identical powerplant instruments must be located so as to prevent confusion as to which engine each instrument relates.

(c) Instrument panel vibration may not damage, or impair the accuracy of, any instrument.

(d) For each airplane, the flight instruments required by §23.1303, and, as applicable, by the operating rules of this chapter, must be grouped on the instrument panel and centered as nearly as practicable about the vertical plane of each required pilot's forward vision. In addition:

(1) The instrument that most effectively indicates the attitude must be on the panel in the top center position;

(2) The instrument that most effectively indicates airspeed must be adjacent to and directly to the left of the instrument in the top center position;

(3) The instrument that most effectively indicates altitude must be adjacent to and directly to the right of the instrument in the top center position;

(4) The instrument that most effectively indicates direction of flight, other than the magnetic direction indicator required by §23.1303(c), must be adjacent to and directly below the instrument in the top center position; and

(5) Electronic display indicators may be used for compliance with paragraphs (d)(1) through (d)(4) of this section when such displays comply with requirements in §23.1311.

(e) If a visual indicator is provided to indicate malfunction of an instrument, it must be effective under all probable cockpit lighting conditions.

[Docket No. 4080, 29 FR 17955, Dec. 18, 1964; as amended by Amdt. 23–14, 38 FR 31824, Nov. 19, 1973; Amdt. 23–20, 42 FR 36968, July 18, 1977; Amdt. 23–41, 55 FR 43310, Oct. 26, 1990; 55 FR 46888, Nov. 7, 1990; Amdt. 23–49, 61 FR 5168, Feb. 9, 1996]

§23.1322 Warning, caution, and advisory lights.

If warning, caution, or advisory lights are installed in the cockpit, they must, unless otherwise approved by the Administrator, be—

(a) Red, for warning lights (lights indicating a hazard which may require immediate corrective action);

(b) Amber, for caution lights (lights indicating the possible need for future corrective action);

(c) Green, for safe operation lights; and

(d) Any other color, including white, for lights not described in paragraphs (a) through (c) of this section, provided the color differs sufficiently from the colors prescribed in paragraphs (a) through (c) of this section to avoid possible confusion.

(e) Effective under all probable cockpit lighting conditions.

[Amdt. 23–17, 41 FR 55465, Dec. 20, 1976; as amended by Amdt. 23–43, 58 FR 18976, April 9, 1993]

§23.1323 Airspeed indicating system.

(a) Each airspeed indicating instrument must be calibrated to indicate true airspeed (at sea level with a standard atmosphere) with a minimum practicable instrument calibration error when the corresponding pitot and static pressures are applied.

(b) Each airspeed system must be calibrated in flight to determine the system error. The system error, including position error, but excluding the airspeed indicator instrument calibration error, may not exceed three percent of the calibrated airspeed or five knots, whichever is greater, throughout the following speed ranges:

(1) 1.3 V_{S1} to V_{MO}/M_{MO} or V_{NE}, whichever is appropriate with flaps retracted.

(2) 1.3 V_{S1} to V_{FE} with flaps extended.

(c) The design and installation of each airspeed indicating system must provide positive drainage of moisture from the pitot static plumbing.

(d) If certification for instrument flight rules or flight in icing conditions is requested, each airspeed system must have a heated pitot tube or an equivalent means of preventing malfunction due to icing.

(e) In addition, for commuter category airplanes, the airspeed indicating system must be calibrated to determine the system error during the accelerate-takeoff ground run. The ground run calibration must be obtained between 0.8 of the minimum value of V_1, and 1.2 times the maximum value of V_1 considering the approved ranges of altitude and weight. The ground run calibration must be determined assuming an engine failure at the minimum value of V_1.

(f) For commuter category airplanes, where duplicate airspeed indicators are required, their respective pitot tubes must be far enough apart to avoid damage to both tubes in a collision with a bird.

[Amdt. 23–20, 42 FR 36968, July 18, 1977; as amended by Amdt. 23–34, 52 FR 1834, Jan. 15, 1987; 52 FR 34745, Sept. 14, 1987; Amdt. 23–42, 56 FR 354, Jan. 3, 1991; Amdt. 23–49, 61 FR 5168, Feb. 9, 1996]

§23.1325 Static pressure system.

(a) Each instrument provided with static pressure case connections must be so vented that the influence of airplane speed, the opening and closing of windows, airflow variations, moisture, or other foreign matter will least affect the accuracy of the instruments except as noted in paragraph (b)(3) of this section.

(b) If a static pressure system is necessary for the functioning of instruments, systems, or devices, it must comply with the provisions of paragraphs (b) (1) through (3) of this section.

(1) The design and installation of a static pressure system must be such that—

(i) Positive drainage of moisture is provided;

(ii) Chafing of the tubing, and excessive distortion or restriction at bends in the tubing, is avoided; and

(iii) The materials used are durable, suitable for the purpose intended, and protected against corrosion.

(2) A proof test must be conducted to demonstrate the integrity of the static pressure system in the following manner:

(i) *Unpressurized airplanes.* Evacuate the static pressure system to a pressure differential of approximately 1 inch of mercury or to a reading on the altimeter, 1,000 feet above the aircraft elevation at the time of the test. Without additional pumping for a period of 1 minute, the loss of indicated altitude must not exceed 100 feet on the altimeter.

(ii) *Pressurized airplanes.* Evacuate the static pressure system until a pressure differential equivalent to the maximum cabin pressure differential for which the airplane is type certificated is achieved. Without additional pumping for a period of 1 minute, the loss of indicated altitude must not exceed 2 percent of the equivalent altitude of the maximum cabin differential pressure or 100 feet, whichever is greater.

(3) If a static pressure system is provided for any instrument, device, or system required by the operating rules of this chapter, each static pressure port must be designed or located in such a manner that the correlation between air pressure in the static pressure system and true ambient atmospheric static pressure is not altered when the airplane encounters icing conditions. An anti-icing means or an alternate source of static pressure may be used in showing compliance with this requirement. If the reading of the altimeter, when on the alternate static pressure system differs from the reading of the altimeter when on the primary static system by more than 50 feet, a correction card must be provided for the alternate static system.

(c) Except as provided in paragraph (d) of this section, if the static pressure system incorporates both a primary and an alternate static pressure source, the means for selecting one or the other source must be designed so that—

(1) When either source is selected, the other is blocked off; and

(2) Both sources cannot be blocked off simultaneously.

(d) For unpressurized airplanes, paragraph (c)(1) of this section does not apply if it can be demonstrated that the static pressure system calibration, when either static pressure source is selected, is not changed by the other static pressure source being open or blocked.

(e) Each static pressure system must be calibrated in flight to determine the system error. The system error, in indicated pressure altitude, at sea level, with a standard atmosphere, excluding instrument calibration error, may not exceed +/- 30 feet per 100 knot speed for the appropriate configuration in the speed range between 1.3 V_{S0} with flaps extended, and 1.8 V_{S1} with flaps retracted. However, the error need not be less than 30 feet.

(f) [Reserved]

(g) For airplanes prohibited from flight in instrument meteorological or icing conditions, in accordance with §23.1559(b) of this part, paragraph (b)(3) of this section does not apply.

[Amdt. 23–1, 30 FR 8261, June 29, 1965; as amended by Amdt. 23–6, 32 FR 7586, May 24, 1967; 32 FR 13505, Sept. 27, 1967; 32 FR 13714, Sept. 30, 1967; Amdt. 23–20, 42 FR 36968, July 18, 1977; Amdt. 23–34, 52 FR 1834, Jan. 15, 1987; Amdt. 23–42, 56 FR 354, Jan. 3, 1991; Amdt. 23–49, 61 FR 5169, Feb. 9, 1996; Amdt. 23–50, 61 FR 5192, Feb. 9, 1996]

§23.1326 Pitot heat indication systems.

If a flight instrument pitot heating system is installed to meet the requirements specified in §23.1323(d), an indication system must be provided to indicate to the flight crew when that pitot heating system is not operating. The indication system must comply with the following requirements:

(a) The indication provided must incorporate an amber light that is in clear view of a flightcrew member.

(b) The indication provided must be designed to alert the flight crew if either of the following conditions exist:

(1) The pitot heating system is switched "off."

(2) The pitot heating system is switched "on" and any pitot tube heating element is inoperative.

[Docket No. 27806, 61 FR 5169, Feb. 9, 1996]

§23.1327 Magnetic direction indicator.

(a) Except as provided in paragraph (b) of this section—

(1) Each magnetic direction indicator must be installed so that its accuracy is not excessively affected by the airplane's vibration or magnetic fields; and

(2) The compensated installation may not have a deviation in level flight, greater than ten degrees on any heading.

(b) A magnetic nonstabilized direction indicator may deviate more than ten degrees due to the operation of electrically powered systems such as electrically heated windshields if either a magnetic stabilized direction indicator, which does not have a deviation in level flight greater than ten degrees on any heading, or a gyroscopic direction indicator, is installed. Deviations of a magnetic nonstabilized direction indicator of more than 10 degrees must be placarded in accordance with §23.1547(e).

[Amdt. 23–20, 42 FR 36969, July 18, 1977]

§23.1329 Automatic pilot system.

If an automatic pilot system is installed, it must meet the following:

(a) Each system must be designed so that the automatic pilot can—

(1) Be quickly and positively disengaged by the pilots to prevent it from interfering with their control of the airplane; or

(2) Be sufficiently overpowered by one pilot to let him control the airplane.

(b) If the provisions of paragraph (a)(1) of this section are applied, the quick release (emergency) control must be located on the control wheel (both control wheels if the airplane can be operated from either pilot seat) on the side opposite the throttles, or on the stick control, (both stick controls, if the airplane can be operated from either pilot seat) such that it can be operated without moving the hand from its normal position on the control.

(c) Unless there is automatic synchronization, each system must have a means to readily indicate to the pilot the alignment of the actuating device in relation to the control system it operates.

(d) Each manually operated control for the system operation must be readily accessible to the pilot. Each control must operate in the same plane and sense of motion as specified in §23.779 for cockpit controls. The direction of motion must be plainly indicated on or near each control.

(e) Each system must be designed and adjusted so that, within the range of adjustment available to the pilot, it cannot produce hazardous loads on the airplane or create hazardous deviations in the flight path, under any flight condition appropriate to its use, either during normal operation or in the event of a malfunction, assuming that corrective action begins within a reasonable period of time.

(f) Each system must be designed so that a single malfunction will not produce a hardover signal in more than one control axis. If the automatic pilot integrates signals from auxiliary controls or furnishes signals for operation of other equipment, positive interlocks and sequencing of engagement to prevent improper operation are required.

(g) There must be protection against adverse interaction of integrated components, resulting from a malfunction.

(h) If the automatic pilot system can be coupled to airborne navigation equipment, means must be provided to indicate to the flight crew the current mode of operation. Selector switch position is not acceptable as a means of indication.

[Docket No. 4080, 29 FR 17955, Dec. 18, 1964; 30 FR 258, Jan. 9, 1965; as amended by Amdt. 23–23, 43 FR 50593, Oct. 30, 1978; Amdt. 23–43, 58 FR 18976, April 9, 1993; Amdt. 23–49, 61 FR 5169, Feb. 9, 1996]

§23.1331 Instruments using a power source.

For each instrument that uses a power source, the following apply:

(a) Each instrument must have an integral visual power annunciator or separate power indicator to indicate when power is not adequate to sustain proper instrument performance. If a separate indicator is used, it must be located so that the pilot using the instruments can monitor the indicator with minimum head and eye movement. The power must be sensed at or near the point where it enters the instrument. For electric and vacuum/pressure instruments, the power is considered to be adequate when the voltage or the vacuum/pressure, respectively, is within approved limits.

(b) The installation and power supply systems must be designed so that—

(1) The failure of one instrument will not interfere with the proper supply of energy to the remaining instrument; and

(2) The failure of the energy supply from one source will not interfere with the proper supply of energy from any other source.

(c) There must be at least two independent sources of power (not driven by the same engine on multiengine airplanes), and a manual or an automatic means to select each power source.

[Docket No. 26344, 58 FR 18976, April 9, 1993]

§23.1335 Flight director systems.

If a flight director system is installed, means must be provided to indicate to the flight crew its current mode of operation. Selector switch position is not acceptable as a means of indication.

[Amdt. 23–20, 42 FR 36969, July 18, 1977]

§23.1337 Powerplant instruments installation.

(a) *Instruments and instrument lines.*

(1) Each powerplant and auxiliary power unit instrument line must meet the requirements of §23.993.

(2) Each line carrying flammable fluids under pressure must—

(i) Have restricting orifices or other safety devices at the source of pressure to prevent the escape of excessive fluid if the line fails; and

(ii) Be installed and located so that the escape of fluids would not create a hazard.

(3) Each powerplant and auxiliary power unit instrument that utilizes flammable fluids must be installed and located so that the escape of fluid would not create a hazard.

(b) *Fuel quantity indication.* There must be a means to indicate to the flightcrew members the quantity of usable fuel in each tank during flight. An indicator calibrated in appropriate units and clearly marked to indicate those units must be used. In addition:

(1) Each fuel quantity indicator must be calibrated to read "zero" during level flight when the quantity of fuel remaining in the tank is equal to the unusable fuel supply determined under §23.959(a);

(2) Each exposed sight gauge used as a fuel quantity indicator must be protected against damage;

(3) Each sight gauge that forms a trap in which water can collect and freeze must have means to allow drainage on the ground;

(4) There must be a means to indicate the amount of usable fuel in each tank when the airplane is on the ground (such as by a stick gauge);

(5) Tanks with interconnected outlets and airspaces may be considered as one tank and need not have separate indicators; and

(6) No fuel quantity indicator is required for an auxiliary tank that is used only to transfer fuel to other tanks if the relative size of the tank, the rate of fuel transfer, and operating instructions are adequate to—

(i) Guard against overflow; and

(ii) Give the flight crewmembers prompt warning if transfer is not proceeding as planned.

(c) *Fuel flowmeter system.* If a fuel flowmeter system is installed, each metering component must have a means to bypass the fuel supply if malfunctioning of that component severely restricts fuel flow.

(d) *Oil quantity indicator.* There must be a means to indicate the quantity of oil in each tank—

(1) On the ground (such as by a stick gauge); and

(2) In flight, to the flight crew members, if there is an oil transfer system or a reserve oil supply system.

[Docket No. 4080, 29 FR 17955, Dec. 18, 1964; as amended by Amdt. 23–7, 34 FR 13096, Aug. 13, 1969; Amdt. 23–18, 42 FR 15042, Mar. 17, 1977; Amdt. 23–43, 58 FR 18976, April 9, 1993; Amdt. 23–49, 61 FR 5169, Feb. 9, 1996: Amdt. 23–51, 61 FR 5138, Feb. 9, 1996]

Electrical Systems and Equipment

§23.1351 General.

(a) *Electrical system capacity.* Each electrical system must be adequate for the intended use. In addition—

(1) Electric power sources, their transmission cables, and their associated control and protective devices, must be able to furnish the required power at the proper voltage to each load circuit essential for safe operation; and

(2) Compliance with paragraph (a)(1) of this section must be shown as follows—

(i) For normal, utility, and acrobatic category airplanes, by an electrical load analysis or by electrical measurements that account for the electrical loads applied to the electrical system in probable combinations and for probable durations; and

(ii) For commuter category airplanes, by an electrical load analysis that accounts for the electrical loads applied to the electrical system in probable combinations and for probable durations.

(b) *Function.* For each electrical system, the following apply:

(1) Each system, when installed, must be—

(i) Free from hazards in itself, in its method of operation, and in its effects on other parts of the airplane;

(ii) Protected from fuel, oil, water, other detrimental substances, and mechanical damage; and

(iii) So designed that the risk of electrical shock to crew, passengers, and ground personnel is reduced to a minimum.

(2) Electric power sources must function properly when connected in combination or independently.

(3) No failure or malfunction of any electric power source may impair the ability of any remaining source to supply load circuits essential for safe operation.

(4) In addition, for commuter category airplanes, the following apply:

(i) Each system must be designed so that essential load circuits can be supplied in the event of reasonably probable faults or open circuits including faults in heavy current carrying cables;

(ii) A means must be accessible in flight to the flight crewmembers for the individual and collective disconnection of the electrical power sources from the system;

(iii) The system must be designed so that voltage and frequency, if applicable, at the terminals of all essential load equipment can be maintained within the limits for which the equipment is designed during any probable operating conditions;

(iv) If two independent sources of electrical power for particular equipment or systems are required, their electrical energy supply must be ensured by means such as duplicate electrical equipment, throwover switching, or multichannel or loop circuits separately routed; and

(v) For the purpose of complying with paragraph (b)(5) of this section, the distribution system includes the distribution busses, their associated feeders, and each control and protective device.

(c) *Generating system.* There must be at least one generator/alternator if the electrical system supplies power to load circuits essential for safe operation. In addition—

(1) Each generator/alternator must be able to deliver its continuous rated power, or such power as is limited by its regulation system.

(2) Generator/alternator voltage control equipment must be able to dependably regulate the generator/alternator output within rated limits.

(3) Automatic means must be provided to prevent damage to any generator/alternator and adverse effects on the airplane electrical system due to reverse current. A means must also be provided to disconnect each generator/alternator from the battery and other generators/alternators.

(4) There must be a means to give immediate warning to the flight crew of a failure of any generator/alternator.

(5) Each generator/alternator must have an overvoltage control designed and installed to prevent damage to the electrical system, or to equipment supplied by the electrical system that could result if that generator/alternator were to develop an overvoltage condition.

(d) *Instruments.* A means must exist to indicate to appropriate flight crewmembers the electric power system quantities essential for safe operation.

(1) For normal, utility, and acrobatic category airplanes with direct current systems, an ammeter that can be switched into each generator feeder may be used and, if only one generator exists, the ammeter may be in the battery feeder.

(2) For commuter category airplanes, the essential electric power system quantities include the voltage and current supplied by each generator.

(e) *Fire resistance.* Electrical equipment must be so designed and installed that in the event of a fire in the engine compartment, during which the surface of the firewall adjacent to the fire is heated to 2,000°F for 5 minutes or to a lesser temperature substantiated by the applicant, the equipment essential to continued safe operation and located behind the firewall will function satisfactorily and will not create an additional fire hazard.

(f) *External power.* If provisions are made for connecting external power to the airplane, and that external power can be electrically connected to equipment other than that used for engine starting, means must be provided to ensure that no external power supply having a reverse polarity, or a reverse phase sequence, can supply power to the airplane's electrical system. The external power connection must be located so that its use will not result in a hazard to the airplane or ground personnel.

(g) It must be shown by analysis, tests, or both, that the airplane can be operated safely in VFR conditions, for a period of not less than five minutes, with the normal electrical power (electrical power sources excluding the battery and any other standby electrical sources) inoperative, with critical type fuel (from the standpoint of flameout and restart capability), and with the airplane initially at the maximum certificated altitude. Parts of the electrical system may remain on if—

(1) A single malfunction, including a wire bundle or junction box fire, cannot result in loss of the part turned off and the part turned on; and

(2) The parts turned on are electrically and mechanically isolated from the parts turned off.

[Docket No. 4080, 29 FR 17955, Dec. 18, 1964; as amended by Amdt. 23–7, 34 FR 13096, Aug. 13, 1969; Amdt. 23–14, 38 FR 31824, Nov. 19, 1973; Amdt. 23–17, 41 FR 55465, Dec. 20, 1976; Amdt. 23–20, 42 FR 36969, July 18, 1977; Amdt. 23–34, 52 FR 1834, Jan. 15, 1987; 52 FR 34745, Sept. 14, 1987; Amdt. 23–43, 58 FR 18976, April 9, 1993; Amdt. 23–49, 61 FR 5169, Feb. 9, 1996]

§23.1353 Storage battery design and installation.

(a) Each storage battery must be designed and installed as prescribed in this section.

(b) Safe cell temperatures and pressures must be maintained during any probable charging and discharging condition. No uncontrolled increase in cell temperature may result when the battery is recharged (after previous complete discharge)—

(1) At maximum regulated voltage or power;

(2) During a flight of maximum duration; and

(3) Under the most adverse cooling condition likely to occur in service.

(c) Compliance with paragraph (b) of this section must be shown by tests unless experience with similar batteries and installations has shown that maintaining safe cell temperatures and pressures presents no problem.

(d) No explosive or toxic gases emitted by any battery in normal operation, or as the result of any probable malfunction in the charging system or battery installation, may accumulate in hazardous quantities within the airplane.

(e) No corrosive fluids or gases that may escape from the battery may damage surrounding structures or adjacent essential equipment.

(f) Each nickel cadmium battery installation capable of being used to start an engine or auxiliary power unit must have provisions to prevent any hazardous effect on structure or essential systems that may be caused by the maximum amount of heat the battery can generate during a short circuit of the battery or of its individual cells.

(g) Nickel cadmium battery installations capable of being used to start an engine or auxiliary power unit must have—

(1) A system to control the charging rate of the battery automatically so as to prevent battery overheating;

(2) A battery temperature sensing and over-temperature warning system with a means for disconnecting the battery from its charging source in the event of an over-temperature condition; or

(3) A battery failure sensing and warning system with a means for disconnecting the battery from its charging source in the event of battery failure.

(h) In the event of a complete loss of the primary electrical power generating system, the battery must be capable of providing at least 30 minutes of electrical power to those loads that are essential to continued safe flight and landing. The 30 minute time period includes the time needed for the pilots to recognize the loss of generated power and take appropriate load shedding action.

[Docket No. 4080, 29 FR 17955, Dec. 18, 1964; 30 FR 258, Jan. 9, 1965; as amended by Amdt. 23–20, 42 FR 36969, July 18, 1977; Amdt. 23–21, 43 FR 2319, Jan. 16, 1978; Amdt. 23–49, 61 FR 5169, Feb. 9, 1996]

§23.1357 Circuit protective devices.

(a) Protective devices, such as fuses or circuit breakers, must be installed in all electrical circuits other than—

(1) Main circuits of starter motors used during starting only; and

(2) Circuits in which no hazard is presented by their omission.

(b) A protective device for a circuit essential to flight safety may not be used to protect any other circuit.

(c) Each resettable circuit protective device ("trip free" device in which the tripping mechanism cannot be overridden by the operating control) must be designed so that—

(1) A manual operation is required to restore service after tripping; and

(2) If an overload or circuit fault exists, the device will open the circuit regardless of the position of the operating control.

(d) If the ability to reset a circuit breaker or replace a fuse is essential to safety in flight, that circuit breaker or fuse must be so located and identified that it can be readily reset or replaced in flight.

(e) For fuses identified as replaceable in flight—

(1) There must be one spare of each rating or 50 percent spare fuses of each rating, whichever is greater; and

(2) The spare fuse(s) must be readily accessible to any required pilot.

[Docket No. 4080, 29 FR 17955, Dec. 18, 1964; 30 FR 258, Jan. 9, 1965; as amended by Amdt. 23–20, 42 FR 36969, July 18, 1977; Amdt. 23–43, 58 FR 18976, April 9, 1993]

§23.1359 Electrical system fire protection.

(a) Each component of the electrical system must meet the applicable fire protection requirements of §§23.863 and 23.1182.

(b) Electrical cables, terminals, and equipment in designated fire zones that are used during emergency procedures must be fire-resistant.

(c) Insulation on electrical wire and electrical cable must be self-extinguishing when tested at an angle of 60 degrees in accordance with the applicable portions of Appendix F of this part, or other approved equivalent methods. The average burn length must not exceed 3 inches (76 mm) and the average flame time after removal of the flame source must not exceed 30 seconds. Drippings from the test specimen must not continue to flame for more than an average of 3 seconds after falling.

[Docket No. 27806, 61 FR 5169, Feb. 9, 1996]

§23.1361 Master switch arrangement.

(a) There must be a master switch arrangement to allow ready disconnection of each electric power source from power distribution systems, except as provided in paragraph (b) of this section. The point of disconnection must be adjacent to the sources controlled by the switch arrangement. If separate switches are incorporated into the master switch arrangement, a means must be provided for the switch arrangement to be operated by one hand with a single movement.

(b) Load circuits may be connected so that they remain energized when the master switch is open, if the circuits are isolated, or physically shielded, to prevent their igniting flammable fluids or vapors that might be liberated by the leakage or rupture of any flammable fluid system; and

(1) The circuits are required for continued operation of the engine; or

(2) The circuits are protected by circuit protective devices with a rating of five amperes or less adjacent to the electric power source.

(3) In addition, two or more circuits installed in accordance with the requirements of paragraph (b)(2) of this section must not be used to supply a load of more than five amperes.

(c) The master switch or its controls must be so installed that the switch is easily discernible and accessible to a crewmember.

[Docket No. 4080, 29 FR 17955, Dec. 18, 1964; 30 FR 258, Jan. 9, 1965; as amended by Amdt. 23–20, 42 FR 36969, July 18, 1977; Amdt. 23–43, 58 FR 18977, April 9, 1993; Amdt. 23–49, 61 FR 5169, Feb. 9, 1996]

§23.1365 Electrical cables and equipment.

(a) Each electric connecting cable must be of adequate capacity.

(b) Any equipment that is associated with any electrical cable installation and that would overheat in the event of circuit overload or fault must be flame resistant. That equipment and the electrical cables must not emit dangerous quantities of toxic fumes.

(c) Main power cables (including generator cables) in the fuselage must be designed to allow a reasonable degree of deformation and stretching without failure and must—

(1) Be separated from flammable fluid lines; or

(2) Be shrouded by means of electrically insulated flexible conduit, or equivalent, which is in addition to the normal cable insulation.

(d) Means of identification must be provided for electrical cables, terminals, and connectors.

(e) Electrical cables must be installed such that the risk of mechanical damage and/or damage cased by fluids vapors, or sources of heat, is minimized.

(f) Where a cable cannot be protected by a circuit protection device or other overload protection, it must not cause a fire hazard under fault conditions.

[Docket No. 4080, 29 FR 17955, Dec. 18, 1964; as amended by Amdt. 23–14, 38 FR 31824, Nov. 19, 1973; Amdt. 23–43, 58 FR 18977, April 9, 1993; Amdt. 23–49, 61 FR 5169, Feb. 9, 1996]

§23.1367 Switches.

Each switch must be—

(a) Able to carry its rated current;

(b) Constructed with enough distance or insulating material between current carrying parts and the housing so that vibration in flight will not cause shorting;

(c) Accessible to appropriate flight crewmembers; and

(d) Labeled as to operation and the circuit controlled.

Lights

§23.1381 Instrument lights.

The instrument lights must—

(a) Make each instrument and control easily readable and discernible;

(b) Be installed so that their direct rays, and rays reflected from the windshield or other surface, are shielded from the pilot's eyes; and

(c) Have enough distance or insulating material between current carrying parts and the housing so that vibration in flight will not cause shorting.

A cabin dome light is not an instrument light.

§23.1383 Taxi and landing lights.

Each taxi and landing light must be designed and installed so that:

(a) No dangerous glare is visible to the pilots.

(b) The pilot is not seriously affected by halation.

(c) It provides enough light for night operations.

(d) It does not cause a fire hazard in any configuration.

[Docket No. 27806, 61 FR 5169, Feb. 9, 1996]

§23.1385 Position light system installation.

(a) *General.* Each part of each position light system must meet the applicable requirements of this section and each system as a whole must meet the requirements of §§23.1387 through 23.1397.

(b) *Left and right position lights.* Left and right position lights must consist of a red and a green light spaced laterally as far apart as practicable and installed on the airplane such that, with the airplane in the normal flying position, the red light is on the left side and the green light is on the right side.

(c) *Rear position light.* The rear position light must be a white light mounted as far aft as practicable on the tail or on each wing tip.

(d) *Light covers and color filters.* Each light cover or color filter must be at least flame resistant and may not change color or shape or lose any appreciable light transmission during normal use.

[Docket No. 4080, 29 FR 17955, Dec. 18, 1964; as amended by Amdt. 23–17, 41 FR 55465, Dec. 20, 1976; Amdt. 23–43, 58 FR 18977, April 9, 1993]

§23.1387 Position light system dihedral angles.

(a) Except as provided in paragraph (e) of this section, each position light must, as installed, show unbroken light within the dihedral angles described in this section.

(b) Dihedral angle *L* (left) is formed by two intersecting vertical planes, the first parallel to the longitudinal axis of the airplane, and the other at 110 degrees to the left of the first, as viewed when looking forward along the longitudinal axis.

(c) Dihedral angle *R* (right) is formed by two intersecting vertical planes, the first parallel to the longitudinal axis of the airplane, and the other at 110 degrees to the right of the first, as viewed when looking forward along the longitudinal axis.

(d) Dihedral angle *A* (aft) is formed by two intersecting vertical planes making angles of 70 degrees to the right and to the left, respectively, to a vertical plane passing through the longitudinal axis, as viewed when looking aft along the longitudinal axis.

(e) If the rear position light, when mounted as far aft as practicable in accordance with §23.1385(c), cannot show unbroken light within dihedral angle A (as defined in paragraph (d) of this section), a solid angle or angles of obstructed visibility totaling not more than 0.04 steradians is allowable within that dihedral angle, if such solid angle is within a cone whose apex is at the rear position light and whose elements make an angle of 30° with a vertical line passing through the rear position light.

[Docket No. 4080, 29 FR 17955, Dec. 18, 1964; 30 FR 258, Jan. 9, 1965; as amended by Amdt. 23–12, 36 FR 21278, Nov. 5, 1971; Amdt. 23–43, 58 FR 18977, April 9, 1993]

§23.1389 Position light distribution and intensities.

(a) *General.* The intensities prescribed in this section must be provided by new equipment with each light cover and color filter in place. Intensities must be determined with the light source operating at a steady value equal to the average luminous output of the source at the normal operating voltage of the airplane. The light distribution and intensity of each position light must meet the requirements of paragraph (b) of this section.

(b) *Position lights.* The light distribution and intensities of position lights must be expressed in terms of minimum intensities in the horizontal plane, minimum intensities in any vertical plane, and maximum intensities in overlapping beams, within dihedral angles *L*, *R*, and *A*, and must meet the following requirements:

(1) *Intensities in the horizontal plane.* Each intensity in the horizontal plane (the plane containing the longitudinal axis of the airplane and perpendicular to the plane of symmetry of the airplane) must equal or exceed the values in §23.1391.

(2) *Intensities in any vertical plane.* Each intensity in any vertical plane (the plane perpendicular to the horizontal plane) must equal or exceed the appropriate value in §23.1393, where *I* is the minimum intensity prescribed in §23.1391 for the corresponding angles in the horizontal plane.

(3) *Intensities in overlaps between adjacent signals.* No intensity in any overlap between adjacent signals may exceed the values in §23.1395, except that higher intensities in overlaps may be used with main beam intensities substantially greater than the minima specified in §§23.1391 and 23.1393, if the overlap intensities in relation to the main beam intensities do not adversely affect signal clarity. When the peak intensity of the left and right position lights is more than 100 candles, the maximum overlap intensities between them may exceed the values in §23.1395 if the overlap intensity in Area A is not more than 10 percent of peak position light intensity and the overlap intensity in Area B is not more than 2.5 percent of peak position light intensity.

(c) *Rear position light installation.* A single rear position light may be installed in a position displaced laterally from the plane of symmetry of an airplane if—

(1) The axis of the maximum cone of illumination is parallel to the flight path in level flight; and

(2) There is no obstruction aft of the light and between planes 70 degrees to the right and left of the axis of maximum illumination.

[Docket No. 4080, 29 FR 17955, Dec. 18, 1964; as amended by Amdt. 23–43, 58 FR 18977, April 9, 1993]

§23.1391 Minimum intensities in the horizontal plane of position lights.

Each position light intensity must equal or exceed the applicable values in the following table:

Dihedral angle (light included)	Angle from right or left of longitudinal axis, measured from dead ahead	Intensity (candles)
L and R (red and green)	0° to 10°	40
	10° to 20°	30
	20° to 110°	5
A (rear white)	110° to 180°	20

[Docket No. 4080, 29 FR 17955, Dec. 18, 1964; as amended by Amdt. 23–43, 58 FR 18977, April 9, 1993]

§23.1393 Minimum intensities in any vertical plane of position lights.

Each position light intensity must equal or exceed the applicable values in the following table:

Angle above or below the horizontal plane	Intensity, *I*
0°	1.00
0° to 5°	0.90
5° to 10°	0.80
10° to 15°	0.70
15° to 20°	0.50
20° to 30°	0.30
30° to 40°	0.10
40° to 90°	0.05

[Docket No. 4080, 29 FR 17955, Dec. 18, 1964; as amended by Amdt. 23–43, 58 FR 18977, April 9, 1993]

§23.1395 Maximum intensities in overlapping beams of position lights.

No position light intensity may exceed the applicable values in the following equal or exceed the applicable values in §23.1389(b)(3):

Overlaps	Maximum Intensity	
	Area A (candles)	Area B (candles)
Green in dihedral angle L	10	1
Red in dihedral angle R	10	1
Green in dihedral angle A	5	1
Red in dihedral angle A	5	1
Rear white in dihedral angle L	5	1
Rear white in dihedral angle R	5	1

Where—

(a) Area A includes all directions in the adjacent dihedral angle that pass through the light source and intersect the common boundary plane at more than 10 degrees but less than 20 degrees; and

(b) Area B includes all directions in the adjacent dihedral angle that pass through the light source and intersect the common boundary plane at more than 20 degrees.

[Docket No. 4080, 29 FR 17955, Dec. 18, 1964; as amended by Amdt. 23–43, 58 FR 18977, April 9, 1993]

§23.1397 Color specifications.

Each position light color must have the applicable International Commission on Illumination chromaticity coordinates as follows:

(a) *Aviation red*—

"y" is not greater than 0.335; and

"z" is not greater than 0.002.

(b) *Aviation green*—

"x" is not greater than 0.440 – 0.320 y;

"x" is not greater than y – 0.170; and

"y" is not less than 0.390 – 0.170 x.

(c) *Aviation white*—

"x" is not less than 0.300 and not greater than 0.540;

"y" is not less than "x – 0.040" or "y_0 – 0.010," whichever is the smaller; and

"y" is not greater than "x + 0.020" nor "0.636 – 0.400 x";

Where "y_0" is the "y" coordinate of the Planckian radiator for the value of "x" considered.

[Docket No. 4080, 29 FR 17955, Dec. 18, 1964, amended by Amdt. 23–11, 36 FR 12971, July 10, 1971]

§23.1399 Riding light.

(a) Each riding (anchor) light required for a seaplane or amphibian, must be installed so that it can—

(1) Show a white light for at least two miles at night under clear atmospheric conditions; and

(2) Show the maximum unbroken light practicable when the airplane is moored or drifting on the water.

(b) Externally hung lights may be used.

§23.1401 Anticollision light system.

(a) *General.* The airplane must have an anticollision light system that:

(1) Consists of one or more approved anticollision lights located so that their light will not impair the flight crewmembers' vision or detract from the conspicuity of the position lights; and

(2) Meets the requirements of paragraphs (b) through (f) of this section.

(b) *Field of coverage.* The system must consist of enough lights to illuminate the vital areas around the airplane, considering the physical configuration and flight characteristics of the airplane. The field of coverage must extend in each direction within at least 75 degrees above and 75 degrees below the horizontal plane of the airplane, except that there may be solid angles of obstructed visibility totaling not more than 0.5 steradians.

(c) *Flashing characteristics.* The arrangement of the system, that is, the number of light sources, beam width, speed of rotation, and other characteristics, must give an effective flash frequency of not less than 40, nor more than 100, cycles per minute. The effective flash frequency is the frequency at which the airplane's complete anticollision light system is observed from a distance, and applies to each sector of light including any overlaps that exist when the system consists of more than one light source. In overlaps, flash frequencies may exceed 100, but not 180, cycles per minute.

(d) *Color.* Each anticollision light must be either aviation red or aviation white and must meet the applicable requirements of §23.1397.

(e) *Light intensity.* The minimum light intensities in any vertical plane, measured with the red filter (if used) and expressed in terms of "effective" intensities, must meet the requirements of paragraph (f) of this section. The following relation must be assumed:

$$I_e = \frac{\int_{t_1}^{t_2} I(t)dt}{0.2 + (t_2 - t_1)}$$

where:

I_e = effective intensity (candles).

I(t) = instantaneous intensity as a function of time.

$t_2 - t_1$ = flash time interval (seconds).

Normally, the maximum value of effective intensity is obtained when t_2 and t_1 are chosen so that the effective intensity is equal to the instantaneous intensity at t_2 and t_1.

(f) *Minimum effective intensities for anticollision lights.* Each anticollision light effective intensity must equal or exceed the applicable values in the following table.

Angle above or below the horizontal plane	Effective intensity (candles)
0° to 5°	400
5° to 10°	240
10° to 20°	80
20° to 30°	40
30° to 75°	20

[Docket No. 4080, 29 FR 17955, Dec. 18, 1964; as amended by Amdt. 23–11, 36 FR 12972, July 10, 1971; Amdt. 23–20, 42 FR 36969, July 18, 1977; Amdt 23–49, 61 FR 5169, Feb. 9, 1996]

SAFETY EQUIPMENT

§23.1411 General.

(a) Required safety equipment to be used by the flight crew in an emergency, such as automatic liferaft releases, must be readily accessible.

(b) Stowage provisions for required safety equipment must be furnished and must—

(1) Be arranged so that the equipment is directly accessible and its location is obvious; and

(2) Protect the safety equipment from damage caused by being subjected to the inertia loads resulting from the ultimate static load factors specified in §23.561(b)(3) of this part.

[Amdt. 23–17, 41 FR 55465, Dec. 20, 1976; as amended by Amdt. 23–36, 53 FR 30815, Aug. 15, 1988]

§23.1415 Ditching equipment.

(a) Emergency flotation and signaling equipment required by any operating rule in this chapter must be installed so that it is readily available to the crew and passengers.

(b) Each raft and each life preserver must be approved.

(c) Each raft released automatically or by the pilot must be attached to the airplane by a line to keep it alongside the airplane. This line must be weak enough to break before submerging the empty raft to which it is attached.

(d) Each signaling device required by any operating rule in this chapter, must be accessible, function satisfactorily, and must be free of any hazard in its operation.

§23.1416 Pneumatic de-icer boot system.

If certification with ice protection provisions is desired and a pneumatic de-icer boot system is installed—

(a) The system must meet the requirements specified in §23.1419.

(b) The system and its components must be designed to perform their intended function under any normal system operating temperature or pressure, and

(c) Means to indicate to the flight crew that the pneumatic de-icer boot system is receiving adequate pressure and is functioning normally must be provided.

[Amdt. 23–23, 43 FR 50593, Oct. 30, 1978]

§23.1419 Ice protection.

If certification with ice protection provisions is desired, compliance with the requirements of this section and other applicable sections of this part must be shown:

(a) An analysis must be performed to establish, on the basis of the airplane's operational needs, the adequacy of the ice protection system for the various components of the airplane. In addition, tests of the ice protection system must be conducted to demonstrate that the airplane is capable of operating safely in continuous maximum and intermittent maximum icing conditions, as described in appendix C of part 25 of this chapter. As used in this section, "Capable of operating safely," means that airplane performance, controllability, maneuverability, and stability must not be less than that required in part 23, subpart B.

(b) Except as provided by paragraph (c) of this section, in addition to the analysis and physical evaluation prescribed in paragraph (a) of this section, the effectiveness of the ice protection system and its components must be shown by flight tests of the airplane or its components in measured natural atmospheric icing conditions and by one or more of the following tests, as found necessary to determine the adequacy of the ice protection system—

(1) Laboratory dry air or simulated icing tests, or a combination of both, of the components or models of the components.

(2) Flight dry air tests of the ice protection system as a whole, or its individual components.

(3) Flight test of the airplane or its components in measured simulated icing conditions.

(c) If certification with ice protection has been accomplished on prior type certificated airplanes whose designs include components that are thermodynamically and aerodynamically equivalent to those used on a new airplane design, certification of these equivalent components may be accomplished by reference to previously accomplished tests, required in §23.1419 (a) and (b), provided that the applicant accounts for any differences in installation of these components.

(d) A means must be identified or provided for determining the formation of ice on the critical parts of the airplane. Adequate lighting must be provided for the use of this means during night operation. Also, when monitoring of the external surfaces of the airplane by the flight crew is required for operation of the ice protection equipment, external lighting must be provided that is adequate to enable the monitoring to be done at night. Any illumination that is used must be of a type that will not cause glare or reflection that would handicap crewmembers in the performance of their duties. The Airplane Flight Manual or other approved manual material must describe the means of determining ice formation and must contain information for the safe operation of the airplane in icing conditions.

[Docket No. 26344, 58 FR 18977, April 9, 1993]

MISCELLANEOUS EQUIPMENT

§23.1431 Electronic equipment.

(a) In showing compliance with §23.1309(b) (1) and (2) with respect to radio and electronic equipment and their installations, critical environmental conditions must be considered.

(b) Radio and electronic equipment, controls, and wiring must be installed so that operation of any unit or system of units will not adversely affect the simultaneous operation of any other radio or electronic unit, or system of units, required by this chapter.

(c) For those airplanes required to have more than one flightcrew member, or whose operation will require more than one flightcrew member, the cockpit must be evaluated to determine if the flightcrew members, when seated at their duty station, can converse without difficulty under the actual cockpit noise conditions when the airplane is being operated. If the airplane design includes provision for the use of communication headsets, the evaluation must also consider conditions where headsets are being used. If the evaluation shows conditions under which it will be difficult to converse, an intercommunication system must be provided.

(d) If installed communication equipment includes transmitter "off-on" switching, that switching means must be designed to return from the "transmit" to the "off" position when it is released and ensure that the transmitter will return to the off (non transmitting) state.

(e) If provisions for the use of communication headsets are provided, it must be demonstrated that the flightcrew members will receive all aural warnings under the actual cockpit noise conditions when the airplane is being operated when any headset is being used.

[Docket No. 26344, 58 FR 18977, April 9, 1993; as amended by Amdt. 23–49, 61 FR 5169, Feb. 9, 1996]

§23.1435 Hydraulic systems.

(a) *Design.* Each hydraulic system must be designed as follows:

(1) Each hydraulic system and its elements must withstand, without yielding, the structural loads expected in addition to hydraulic loads.

(2) A means to indicate the pressure in each hydraulic system which supplies two or more primary functions must be provided to the flight crew.

(3) There must be means to ensure that the pressure, including transient (surge) pressure, in any part of the system will not exceed the safe limit above design operating pressure and to prevent excessive pressure resulting from fluid volumetric changes in all lines which are likely to remain closed long enough for such changes to occur.

(4) The minimum design burst pressure must be 2.5 times the operating pressure.

(b) *Tests.* Each system must be substantiated by proof pressure tests. When proof tested, no part of any system may fail, malfunction, or experience a permanent set. The proof load of each system must be at least 1.5 times the maximum operating pressure of that system.

(c) *Accumulators.* A hydraulic accumulator or reservoir may be installed on the engine side of any firewall if—

(1) It is an integral part of an engine or propeller system, or

(2) The reservoir is nonpressurized and the total capacity of all such nonpressurized reservoirs is one quart or less.

[Docket No. 4080, 29 FR 17955, Dec. 18, 1964; as amended by Amdt. 23–7, 34 FR 13096, Aug. 13, 1969; Amdt. 23–14, 38 FR 31824, Nov. 19, 1973; Amdt. 23–43, 58 FR 18977, April 9, 1993 Amdt. 23–49, 61 FR 5170, Feb. 9, 1996]

§23.1437 Accessories for multiengine airplanes.

For multiengine airplanes, engine-driven accessories essential to safe operation must be distributed among two or more engines so that the failure of any one engine will not impair safe operation through the malfunctioning of these accessories.

§23.1438 Pressurization and pneumatic systems.

(a) Pressurization system elements must be burst pressure tested to 2.0 times, and proof pressure tested to 1.5 times, the maximum normal operating pressure.

(b) Pneumatic system elements must be burst pressure tested to 3.0 times, and proof pressure tested to 1.5 times, the maximum normal operating pressure.

(c) An analysis, or a combination of analysis and test, may be substituted for any test required by paragraph (a) or (b) of this section if the Administrator finds it equivalent to the required test.

[Amdt. 23–20, 42 FR 36969, July 18, 1977]

§23.1441 Oxygen equipment and supply.

(a) If certification with supplemental oxygen equipment is requested, or the airplane is approved for operations at or above altitudes where oxygen is required to be used by the operating rules, oxygen equipment must be provided that meets the requirements of this section and §§23.1443 through 23.1449. Portable oxygen equipment may be used to meet the requirements of this part if the portable equipment is shown to comply with the applicable requirements, is identified in the airplane type design, and its stowage provisions are found to be in compliance with the requirements of §23.561.

(b) The oxygen system must be free from hazards in itself, in its method of operation, and its effect upon other components.

(c) There must be a means to allow the crew to readily determine, during the flight, the quantity of oxygen available in each source of supply.

(d) Each required flight crewmember must be provided with—

(1) Demand oxygen equipment if the airplane is to be certificated for operation above 25,000 feet.

(2) Pressure demand oxygen equipment if the airplane is to be certificated for operation above 40,000 feet.

(e) There must be a means, readily available to the crew in flight, to turn on and to shut off the oxygen supply at the high pressure source. This shutoff requirement does not apply to chemical oxygen generators.

[Amdt. 23–9, 35 FR 6386, April 21, 1970; as amended by Amdt. 23–43, 58 FR 18978, April 9, 1993]

§23.1443 Minimum mass flow of supplemental oxygen.

(a) If continuous flow oxygen equipment is installed, an applicant must show compliance with the requirements of either paragraphs (a)(1) and (a)(2) or paragraph (a)(3) of this section:

(1) For each passenger, the minimum mass flow of supplemental oxygen required at various cabin pressure alti-

tudes may not be less than the flow required to maintain, during inspiration and while using the oxygen equipment (including masks) provided, the following mean tracheal oxygen partial pressures;

(i) At cabin pressure altitudes above 10,000 feet up to and including 18,500 feet, a mean tracheal oxygen partial pressure of 100 mm. Hg when breathing 15 liters per minute, Body Temperature, Pressure, Saturated (BTPS) and with a tidal volume of 700 cc. with a constant time interval between respirations.

(ii) At cabin pressure altitudes above 18,500 feet up to and including 40,000 feet a mean tracheal oxygen partial pressure of 83.8 mm. Hg when breathing 30 liters per minute, BTPS, and with a tidal volume of 1,100 cc. with a constant time interval between respirations.

(2) For each flight crewmember, the minimum mass flow may not be less than the flow required to maintain, during inspiration, a mean tracheal oxygen partial pressure of 149 mm. Hg when breathing 15 liters per minute, BTPS, and with a maximum tidal volume of 700 cc. with a constant time interval between respirations.

(3) The minimum mass flow of supplemental oxygen supplied for each user must be at a rate not less than that shown in the following figure for each altitude up to and including the maximum operating altitude of the airplane.

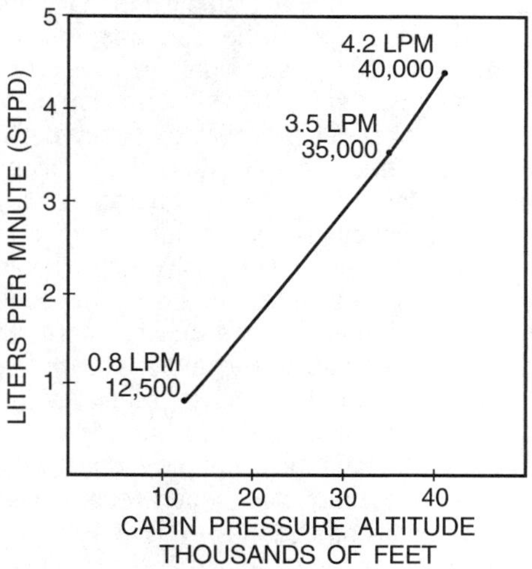

(b) If demand equipment is installed for use by flight crewmembers, the minimum mass flow of supplemental oxygen required for each flight crewmember may not be less than the flow required to maintain, during inspiration, a mean tracheal oxygen partial pressure of 122 mm. Hg up to and including a cabin pressure altitude of 35,000 feet, and 95 percent oxygen between cabin pressure altitudes of 35,000 and 40,000 feet, when breathing 20 liters per minute BTPS. In addition, there must be means to allow the crew to use undiluted oxygen at their discretion.

(c) If first-aid oxygen equipment is installed, the minimum mass flow of oxygen to each user may not be less than 4 liters per minute, STPD. However, there may be a means to decrease this flow to not less than 2 liters per minute, STPD, at any cabin altitude. The quantity of oxygen required is based upon an average flow rate of 3 liters per minute per person for whom first-aid oxygen is required.

(d) As used in this section:

(1) BTPS means Body Temperature, and Pressure, Saturated (which is, 37°C, and the ambient pressure to which the body is exposed, minus 47 mm. Hg, which is the tracheal pressure displaced by water vapor pressure when the breathed air becomes saturated with water vapor at 37°C).

(2) STPD means Standard, Temperature, and Pressure, Dry (which is, 0°C at 760 mm. Hg with no water vapor)

[Docket No. 26344, 58 FR 18978, April 9, 1993]

§23.1445 Oxygen distribution system.

(a) Except for flexible lines from oxygen outlets to the dispensing units, or where shown to be otherwise suitable to the installation, nonmetallic tubing must not be used for any oxygen line that is normally pressurized during flight

(b) Nonmetallic oxygen distribution lines must not be routed where they may be subjected to elevated temperatures, electrical arcing, and released flammable fluids that might result from any probable failure.

[Docket No. 26344, 58 FR 18978, April 9, 1993]

§23.1447 Equipment standards for oxygen dispensing units.

If oxygen dispensing units are installed, the following apply:

(a) There must be an individual dispensing unit for each occupant for whom supplemental oxygen is to be supplied. Each dispensing unit must:

(1) Provide for effective utilization of the oxygen being delivered to the unit.

(2) Be capable of being readily placed into position on the face of the user.

(3) Be equipped with a suitable means to retain the unit in position on the face.

(4) If radio equipment is installed, the flightcrew oxygen dispensing units must be designed to allow the use of that equipment and to allow communication with any other required crew member while at their assigned duty station.

(b) If certification for operation up to and including 18,000 feet (MSL) is requested, each oxygen dispensing unit must:

(1) Cover the nose and mouth of the user; or

(2) Be a nasal cannula, in which case one oxygen dispensing unit covering both the nose and mouth of the user must be available. In addition, each nasal cannula or its connecting tubing must have permanently affixed—

(i) A visible warning against smoking while in use;

(ii) An illustration of the correct method of donning; and

(iii) A visible warning against use with nasal obstructions or head colds with resultant nasal congestion.

(c) If certification for operation above 18,000 feet (MSL) is requested, each oxygen dispensing unit must cover the nose and mouth of the user.

(d) For a pressurized airplane designed to operate at flight altitudes above 25,000 feet (MSL), the dispensing units must meet the following:

(1) The dispensing units for passengers must be connected to an oxygen supply terminal and be immediately available to each occupant wherever seated.

(2) The dispensing units for crewmembers must be automatically presented to each crewmember before the cabin pressure altitude exceeds 15,000 feet, or the units must be

of the quick-donning type, connected to an oxygen supply terminal that is immediately available to crewmembers at their station.

(e) If certification for operation above 30,000 feet is requested, the dispensing units for passengers must be automatically presented to each occupant before the cabin pressure altitude exceeds 15,000 feet.

(f) If an automatic dispensing unit (hose and mask, or other unit) system is installed, the crew must be provided with a manual means to make the dispensing units immediately available in the event of failure of the automatic system.

[Amdt. 23–9, 35 FR 6387, April 21, 1970; as amended by Amdt. 23–20, 42 FR 36969, July 18, 1977; Amdt. 23–30, 49 FR 7340, Feb. 28, 1984; Amdt. 23–43, 58 FR 18978, April 9, 1993; Amdt. 23–49, 61 FR 5170, Feb. 9, 1996]

§23.1449 Means for determining use of oxygen.

There must be a means to allow the crew to determine whether oxygen is being delivered to the dispensing equipment.

[Amdt. 23–9, 35 FR 6387, April 21, 1970]

§23.1450 Chemical oxygen generators.

(a) For the purpose of this section, a chemical oxygen generator is defined as a device which produces oxygen by chemical reaction.

(b) Each chemical oxygen generator must be designed and installed in accordance with the following requirements:

(1) Surface temperature developed by the generator during operation may not create a hazard to the airplane or to its occupants.

(2) Means must be provided to relieve any internal pressure that may be hazardous.

(c) In addition to meeting the requirements in paragraph (b) of this section, each portable chemical oxygen generator that is capable of sustained operation by successive replacement of a generator element must be placarded to show—

(1) The rate of oxygen flow, in liters per minute;

(2) The duration of oxygen flow, in minutes, for the replaceable generator element; and

(3) A warning that the replaceable generator element may be hot, unless the element construction is such that the surface temperature cannot exceed 100°F.

[Amdt. 23–20, 42 FR 36969, July 18, 1977]

§23.1451 Fire protection for oxygen equipment.

Oxygen equipment and lines must:

(a) Not be installed in any designed fire zones.

(b) Be protected from heat that may be generated in, or escape from, any designated fire zone.

(c) Be installed so that escaping oxygen cannot come in contact with and cause ignition of grease, fluid, or vapor accumulations that are present in normal operation or that may result from the failure or malfunction of any other system.

[Docket No. 27806, 61 FR 5170, Feb. 9, 1996]

§23.1453 Protection of oxygen equipment from rupture.

(a) Each element of the oxygen system must have sufficient strength to withstand the maximum pressure and temperature, in combination with any externally applied loads arising from consideration of limit structural loads, that may be acting on that part of the system.

(b) Oxygen pressure sources and the lines between the source and the shutoff means must be:

(1) Protected from unsafe temperatures; and

(2) Located where the probability and hazard of rupture in a crash landing are minimized.

[Docket No. 27806, 61 FR 5170, Feb. 9, 1996]

§23.1457 Cockpit voice recorders.

(a) Each cockpit voice recorder required by the operating rules of this chapter must be approved and must be installed so that it will record the following:

(1) Voice communications transmitted from or received in the airplane by radio.

(2) Voice communications of flight crewmembers on the flight deck.

(3) Voice communications of flight crewmembers on the flight deck, using the airplane's interphone system.

(4) Voice or audio signals identifying navigation or approach aids introduced into a headset or speaker.

(5) Voice communications of flight crewmembers using the passenger loudspeaker system, if there is such a system and if the fourth channel is available in accordance with the requirements of paragraph (c)(4)(ii) of this section.

(b) The recording requirements of paragraph (a)(2) of this section must be met by installing a cockpit-mounted area microphone, located in the best position for recording voice communications originating at the first and second pilot stations and voice communications of other crewmembers on the flight deck when directed to those stations. The microphone must be so located and, if necessary, the preamplifiers and filters of the recorder must be so adjusted or supplemented, so that the intelligibility of the recorded communications is as high as practicable when recorded under flight cockpit noise conditions and played back. Repeated aural or visual playback of the record may be used in evaluating intelligibility.

(c) Each cockpit voice recorder must be installed so that the part of the communication or audio signals specified in paragraph (a) of this section obtained from each of the following sources is recorded on a separate channel:

(1) For the first channel, from each boom, mask, or handheld microphone, headset, or speaker used at the first pilot station.

(2) For the second channel from each boom, mask, or handheld microphone, headset, or speaker used at the second pilot station.

(3) For the third channel—from the cockpit-mounted area microphone.

(4) For the fourth channel from:

(i) Each boom, mask, or handheld microphone, headset, or speaker used at the station for the third and fourth crewmembers.

(ii) If the stations specified in paragraph (c)(4)(i) of this section are not required or if the signal at such a station is picked up by another channel, each microphone on the flight deck that is used with the passenger loudspeaker system, if its signals are not picked up by another channel.

(5) And that as far as is practicable all sounds received by the microphone listed in paragraphs (c) (1), (2), and (4) of this section must be recorded without interruption irrespective of the position of the interphone-transmitter key switch. The design shall ensure that sidetone for the flight crew is produced only when the interphone, public address system, or radio transmitters are in use.

(d) Each cockpit voice recorder must be installed so that:

(1) It receives its electric power from the bus that provides the maximum reliability for operation of the cockpit voice recorder without jeopardizing service to essential or emergency loads.

(2) There is an automatic means to simultaneously stop the recorder and prevent each erasure feature from functioning, within 10 minutes after crash impact; and

(3) There is an aural or visual means for preflight checking of the recorder for proper operation.

(e) The record container must be located and mounted to minimize the probability of rupture of the container as a result of crash impact and consequent heat damage to the record from fire. In meeting this requirement, the record container must be as far aft as practicable, but may not be where aft mounted engines may crush the container during impact. However, it need not be outside of the pressurized compartment.

(f) If the cockpit voice recorder has a bulk erasure device, the installation must be designed to minimize the probability of inadvertent operation and actuation of the device during crash impact.

(g) Each recorder container must:

(1) Be either bright orange or bright yellow;

(2) Have reflective tape affixed to its external surface to facilitate its location underwater; and

(3) Have an underwater locating device, when required by the operating rules of this chapter, on or adjacent to the container which is secured in such manner that they are not likely to be separated during crash impact.

[Amdt. 23–35, 53 FR 26142, July 11, 1988]

§23.1459 Flight recorders.

(a) Each flight recorder required by the operating rules of this chapter must be installed so that:

(1) It is supplied with airspeed, altitude, and directional data obtained from sources that meet the accuracy requirements of §§23.1323, 23.1325, and 23.1327, as appropriate;

(2) The vertical acceleration sensor is rigidly attached, and located longitudinally either within the approved center of gravity limits of the airplane, or at a distance forward or aft of these limits that does not exceed 25 percent of the airplane's mean aerodynamic chord;

(3) It receives its electrical power from the bus that provides the maximum reliability for operation of the flight recorder without jeopardizing service to essential or emergency loads;

(4) There is an aural or visual means for preflight checking of the recorder for proper recording of data in the storage medium.

(5) Except for recorders powered solely by the engine-driven electrical generator system, there is an automatic means to simultaneously stop a recorder that has a data erasure feature and prevent each erasure feature from functioning, within 10 minutes after crash impact; and

(b) Each nonejectable record container must be located and mounted so as to minimize the probability of container rupture resulting from crash impact and subsequent damage to the record from fire. In meeting this requirement the record container must be located as far aft as practicable, but need not be aft of the pressurized compartment, and may not be where aft-mounted engines may crush the container upon impact.

(c) A correlation must be established between the flight recorder readings of airspeed, altitude, and heading and the corresponding readings (taking into account correction factors) of the first pilot's instruments. The correlation must cover the airspeed range over which the airplane is to be operated, the range of altitude to which the airplane is limited, and 360 degrees of heading. Correlation may be established on the ground as appropriate.

(d) Each recorder container must:

(1) Be either bright orange or bright yellow;

(2) Have reflective tape affixed to its external surface to facilitate its location under water; and

(3) Have an underwater locating device, when required by the operating rules of this chapter, on or adjacent to the container which is secured in such a manner that they are not likely to be separated during crash impact.

(e) Any novel or unique design or operational characteristics of the aircraft shall be evaluated to determine if any dedicated parameters must be recorded on flight recorders in addition to or in place of existing requirements.

[Amdt. 23–35, 53 FR 26143, July 11, 1988]

§23.1461 Equipment containing high energy rotors.

(a) Equipment, such as Auxiliary Power Units (APU) and constant speed drive units, containing high energy rotors must meet paragraphs (b), (c), or (d) of this section.

(b) High energy rotors contained in equipment must be able to withstand damage caused by malfunctions, vibration, abnormal speeds, and abnormal temperatures. In addition—

(1) Auxiliary rotor cases must be able to contain damage caused by the failure of high energy rotor blades; and

(2) Equipment control devices, systems, and instrumentation must reasonably ensure that no operating limitations affecting the integrity of high energy rotors will be exceeded in service.

(c) It must be shown by test that equipment containing high energy rotors can contain any failure of a high energy rotor that occurs at the highest speed obtainable with the normal speed control devices inoperative.

(d) Equipment containing high energy rotors must be located where rotor failure will neither endanger the occupants nor adversely affect continued safe flight.

[Amdt. 23–20, 42 FR 36969, July 18, 1977; as amended by Amdt. 23–49, 61 FR 5170, Feb. 9, 1996]

Subpart G—Operating Limitations and Information

§23.1501 General.

(a) Each operating limitation specified in §23.1505 through §23.1527 and other limitations and information necessary for safe operation must be established.

(b) The operating limitations and other information necessary for safe operation must be made available to the crewmembers as prescribed in §§23.1541 through 23.1589.

[Amdt. 23–21, 43 FR 2319, Jan. 16, 1978]

§23.1505 Airspeed limitations.

(a) The never-exceed speed V_{NE} must be established so that it is—

(1) Not less than 0.9 times the minimum value of V_D allowed under §23.335; and

(2) Not more than the lesser of—

(i) 0.9 V_D established under §23.335; or

(ii) 0.9 times the maximum speed shown under §23.251.

(b) The maximum structural cruising speed V_{NO} must be established so that it is—

(1) Not less than the minimum value of V_C allowed under §23.335; and

(2) Not more than the lesser of—

(i) V_C established under §23.335; or

(ii) 0.89 V_{NE} established under paragraph (a) of this section.

(c) Paragraphs (a) and (b) of this section do not apply to turbine airplanes or to airplanes for which a design diving speed V_D/M_D is established under §23.335(b)(4). For those airplanes, a maximum operating limit speed (V_{MO}/M_{MO}-airspeed or Mach number, whichever is critical at a particular altitude) must be established as a speed that may not be deliberately exceeded in any regime of flight (climb, cruise, or descent) unless a higher speed is authorized for flight test or pilot training operations. V_{MO}/M_{MO} must be established so that it is not greater than the design cruising speed V_C/M_C and so that it is sufficiently below V_D/M_D and the maximum speed shown under §23.251 to make it highly improbable that the latter speeds will be inadvertently exceeded in operations. The speed margin between V_{MO}/M_{MO} and V_D/M_D or the maximum speed shown under §23.251 may not be less than the speed margin established between V_C/M_C and V_D/M_D under §23.335(b), or the speed margin found necessary in the flight test conducted under §23.253.

[Docket No. 4080, 29 FR 17955, Dec. 18, 1964; as amended by Amdt. 23–7, 34 FR 13096, Aug. 13, 1969]

§23.1507 Operating maneuvering speed.

The maximum operating maneuvering speed, V_O must be established as an operating limitation. V_O is a selected speed that is not greater than $V_S\sqrt{n}$ established in §23.335(c).

[Docket No. 26269, 58 FR 42165, Aug. 6, 1993]

§23.1511 Flap extended speed.

(a) The flap extended speed V_{FE} must be established so that it is—

(1) Not less than the minimum value of V_F allowed in §23.345(b); and

(2) Not more than V_F established under §23.345(a), (c), and (d).

(i) V_F established under §23.345; or

(ii) V_F established under §23.457.

(b) Additional combinations of flap setting, airspeed, and engine power may be established if the structure has been proven for the corresponding design conditions.

[Docket No. 4080, 29 FR 17955, Dec. 18, 1964; 30 FR 258, Jan. 9, 1965; as amended by Amdt. 23–50, 61 FR 5192, Feb. 9, 1996]

§23.1513 Minimum control speed.

The minimum control speed V_{MC}, determined under §23.149, must be established as an operating limitation.

§23.1519 Weight and center of gravity.

The weight and center of gravity limitations determined under §23.23 must be established as operating limitations.

§23.1521 Powerplant limitations.

(a) *General.* The powerplant limitations prescribed in this section must be established so that they do not exceed the corresponding limits for which the engines or propellers are type certificated. In addition, other powerplant limitations used in determining compliance with this part must be established.

(b) *Takeoff operation.* The powerplant takeoff operation must be limited by—

(1) The maximum rotational speed (rpm);

(2) The maximum allowable manifold pressure (for reciprocating engines);

(3) The maximum allowable gas temperature (for turbine engines);

(4) The time limit for the use of the power or thrust corresponding to the limitations established in paragraphs (b) (1) through (3) of this section; and

(5) The maximum allowable cylinder head (as applicable), liquid coolant and oil temperatures.

(c) *Continuous operation.* The continuous operation must be limited by—

(1) The maximum rotational speed;

(2) The maximum allowable manifold pressure (for reciprocating engines);

(3) The maximum allowable gas temperature (for turbine engines); and

(4) The maximum allowable cylinder head, oil, and liquid coolant temperatures.

(d) *Fuel grade or designation.* The minimum fuel grade (for reciprocating engines), or fuel designation (for turbine engines), must be established so that it is not less than that required for the operation of the engines within the limitations in paragraphs (b) and (c) of this section.

(e) *Ambient temperature.* For all airplanes except reciprocating engine-powered airplanes of 6,000 pounds or less maximum weight, ambient temperature limitations (including limitations for winterization installations if applicable) must be established as the maximum ambient atmospheric temperature at which compliance with the cooling provisions of §§23.1041 through 23.1047 is shown.

[Docket No. 4080, 29 FR 17955, Dec. 18, 1964; 30 FR 258, Jan. 9, 1965; as amended by Amdt. 23–21, 43 FR 2319, Jan. 16, 1978; Amdt. 23–45, 58 FR 42165, Aug. 6, 1993; Amdt. 23–50, 61 FR 5192, Feb. 9, 1996]

§23.1522 Auxiliary power unit limitations.

If an auxiliary power unit is installed. the limitations established for the auxiliary power must be specified in the operating limitations for the airplane.

[Docket No. 26269, 58 FR 42166, Aug. 6, 1993]

§23.1523 Minimum flight crew.

The minimum flight crew must be established so that it is sufficient for safe operation considering—

(a) The workload on individual crewmembers and, in addition for commuter category airplanes, each crewmember workload determination must consider the following:

(1) Flight path control,

(2) Collision avoidance,

(3) Navigation,

(4) Communications,

(5) Operation and monitoring of all essential airplane systems,

(6) Command decisions, and

(7) The accessibility and ease of operation of necessary controls by the appropriate crewmember during all normal and emergency operations when at the crewmember flight station;

(b) The accessibility and ease of operation of necessary controls by the appropriate crewmember; and

(c) The kinds of operation authorized under §23.1525.

[Amdt. 23–21, 43 FR 2319, Jan. 16, 1978; as amended by Amdt. 23–34, 52 FR 1834, Jan. 15, 1987]

§23.1524 Maximum passenger seating configuration.

The maximum passenger seating configuration must be established.

[Amdt. 23–10, 36 FR 2864, Feb. 11, 1971]

§23.1525 Kinds of operation.

The kinds of operation authorized (e.g. VFR, IFR, day or night) and the meteorological conditions (e.g. icing) to which the operation of the airplane is limited or from which it is prohibited, must be established appropriate to the installed equipment.

[Docket No. 26269, 58 FR 42166, Aug. 6, 1993]

§23.1527 Maximum operating altitude.

(a) The maximum altitude up to which operation is allowed, as limited by flight, structural, powerplant, functional or equipment characteristics, must be established.

(b) A maximum operating altitude limitation of not more than 25,000 feet must be established for pressurized airplanes unless compliance with §23.775(e) is shown.

[Docket No. 26269, 58 FR 42166, Aug. 6, 1993]

§23.1529 Instructions for Continued Airworthiness.

The applicant must prepare instructions for Continued Airworthiness in accordance with Appendix G to this part that are acceptable to the Administrator. The instructions may be incomplete at type certification if a program exists to ensure their completion prior to delivery of the first airplane or issuance of a standard certificate of airworthiness, whichever occurs later.

[Amdt. 23–26, 45 FR 60171, Sept. 11, 1980]

Markings and Placards

§23.1541 General.

(a) The airplane must contain—

(1) The markings and placards specified in §§23.1545 through 23.1567; and

(2) Any additional information, instrument markings, and placards required for the safe operation if it has unusual design, operating, or handling characteristics.

(b) Each marking and placard prescribed in paragraph (a) of this section—

(1) Must be displayed in a conspicuous place; and

(2) May not be easily erased, disfigured, or obscured.

(c) For airplanes which are to be certificated in more than one category—

(1) The applicant must select one category upon which the placards and markings are to be based; and

(2) The placards and marking information for all categories in which the airplane is to be certificated must be furnished in the Airplane Flight Manual.

[Docket No. 4080, 29 FR 17955, Dec. 18, 1964; 30 FR 258, Jan. 9, 1965; as amended by Amdt. 23–21, 43 FR 2319, Jan. 16, 1978]

§23.1543 Instrument markings: General.

For each instrument—

(a) When markings are on the cover glass of the instrument, there must be means to maintain the correct alignment of the glass cover with the face of the dial; and

(b) Each arc and line must be wide enough and located to be clearly visible to the pilot.

(c) All related instruments must be calibrated in compatible units.

[Docket No. 4080, 29 FR 17955, Dec. 18, 1964; 30 FR 258, Jan. 9, 1965; as amended by Amdt. 23–50, 61 FR 5192, Feb. 9, 1996]

§23.1545 Airspeed indicator.

(a) Each airspeed indicator must be marked as specified in paragraph (b) of this section, with the marks located at the corresponding indicated airspeeds.

(b) The following markings must be made:

(1) For the never-exceed speed V_{NE}, a radial red line.

(2) For the caution range, a yellow arc extending from the red line specified in paragraph (b)(1) of this section to the upper limit of the green arc specified in paragraph (b)(3) of this section.

(3) For the normal operating range, a green arc with the lower limit at V_{S1} with maximum weight and with landing gear and wing flaps retracted, and the upper limit at the max-

imum structural cruising speed V_{NO} established under §23.1505(b).

(4) For the flap operating range, a white arc with the lower limit at V_{SO} at the maximum weight, and the upper limit at the flaps-extended speed V_{FE} established under §23.1511.

(5) For reciprocating multiengine-powered airplanes of 6,000 pounds or less maximum weight, for the speed at which compliance has been shown with §23.69(b) relating to rate of climb at maximum weight and at sea level, a blue radial line.

(6) For reciprocating multiengine-powered airplanes of 6,000 pounds or less maximum weight, for the maximum value of minimum control speed, V_{MC}, (one-engine-inoperative) determined under §23.149(b), a red radial line.

(c) If V_{NE} or V_{NO} vary with altitude, there must be means to indicate to the pilot the appropriate limitations throughout the operating altitude range.

(d) Paragraphs (b)(1) through (b)(3) and paragraph (c) of this section do not apply to aircraft for which a maximum operating speed V_{MO}/M_{MO} is established under §23.1505(c). For those aircraft there must either be a maximum allowable airspeed indication showing the variation of V_{MO}/M_{MO} with altitude or compressibility limitations (as appropriate), or a radial red line marking for V_{MO}/M_{MO} must be made at lowest value of V_{MO}/M_{MO} established for any altitude up to the maximum operating altitude for the airplane.

[Docket No. 4080, 29 FR 17955, Dec. 18, 1964; as amended by Amdt. 23–3, 30 FR 14240, Nov. 13, 1965; Amdt. 23–7, 34 FR 13097, Aug. 13, 1969; Amdt. 23–23, 43 FR 50593, Oct. 30, 1978; Amdt. 23–50, 61 FR 5193, Feb. 9, 1996]

§23.1547 Magnetic direction indicator.

(a) A placard meeting the requirements of this section must be installed on or near the magnetic direction indicator.

(b) The placard must show the calibration of the instrument in level flight with the engines operating.

(c) The placard must state whether the calibration was made with radio receivers on or off.

(d) Each calibration reading must be in terms of magnetic headings in not more than 30 degree increments.

(e) If a magnetic nonstabilized direction indicator can have a deviation of more than 10 degrees caused by the operation of electrical equipment, the placard must state which electrical loads, or combination of loads, would cause a deviation of more than 10 degrees when turned on.

[Docket No. 4080, 29 FR 17955, Dec. 18, 1964; 30 FR 258, Jan. 9, 1965; as amended by Amdt. 23–20, 42 FR 36969, July 18, 1977]

§23.1549 Powerplant and auxiliary power unit instruments.

For each required powerplant and auxiliary power unit instrument, as appropriate to the type of instruments—

(a) Each maximum and, if applicable, minimum safe operating limit must be marked with a red radial or a red line;

(b) Each normal operating range must be marked with a green arc or green line, not extending beyond the maximum and minimum safe limits;

(c) Each takeoff and precautionary range must be marked with a yellow arc or a yellow line; and

(d) Each engine, auxiliary power unit, or propeller range that is restricted because of excessive vibration stresses must be marked with red arcs or red lines.

[Amdt. 23–12, 41 FR 55466, Dec. 20, 1976; as amended by Amdt. 23–28, 47 FR 13315, Mar. 29, 1982; Amdt. 23–45, 58 FR 42166, Aug. 6, 1993]

§23.1551 Oil quantity indicator.

Each oil quantity indicator must be marked in sufficient increments to indicate readily and accurately the quantity of oil.

§23.1553 Fuel quantity indicator.

A red radial line must be marked on each indicator at the calibrated zero reading, as specified in §23.1337(b)(1).

[Docket No. 27807, 61 FR 5193, Feb. 9, 1996]

§23.1555 Control markings.

(a) Each cockpit control, other than primary flight controls and simple push button type starter switches, must be plainly marked as to its function and method of operation.

(b) Each secondary control must be suitably marked.

(c) For powerplant fuel controls—

(1) Each fuel tank selector control must be marked to indicate the position corresponding to each tank and to each existing cross feed position;

(2) If safe operation requires the use of any tanks in a specific sequence, that sequence must be marked on or near the selector for those tanks;

(3) The conditions under which the full amount of usable fuel in any restricted usage fuel tank can safely be used must be stated on a placard adjacent to the selector valve for that tank; and

(4) Each valve control for any engine of a multiengine airplane must be marked to indicate the position corresponding to each engine controlled.

(d) Usable fuel capacity must be marked as follows:

(1) For fuel systems having no selector controls, the usable fuel capacity of the system must be indicated at the fuel quantity indicator.

(2) For fuel systems having selector controls, the usable fuel capacity available at each selector control position must be indicated near the selector control.

(e) For accessory, auxiliary, and emergency controls—

(1) If retractable landing gear is used, the indicator required by §23.729 must be marked so that the pilot can, at any time, ascertain that the wheels are secured in the extreme positions; and

(2) Each emergency control must be red and must be marked as to method of operation. No control other than an emergency control, or a control that serves an emergency function in addition to its other functions, shall be this color.

[Docket No. 4080, 29 FR 17955, Dec. 18, 1964; 30 FR 258, Jan. 9, 1965; as amended by Amdt. 23–21, 43 FR 2319, Jan. 16, 1978; Amdt. 23–50, 61 FR 5193, Feb. 9, 1996]

§23.1557 Miscellaneous markings and placards.

(a) *Baggage and cargo compartments, and ballast location.* Each baggage and cargo compartment, and each ballast location, must have a placard stating any limitations on contents, including weight, that are necessary under the loading requirements.

(b) *Seats.* If the maximum allowable weight to be carried in a seat is less than 170 pounds, a placard stating the lesser weight must be permanently attached to the seat structure.

(c) *Fuel, oil, and coolant filler openings.* The following apply:

(1) Fuel filter openings must be marked at or near the filler cover with—

(i) For reciprocating engine-powered airplanes—

(A) The word "Avgas"; and

(B) The minimum fuel grade.

(ii) For turbine engine-powered airplanes—

(A) The words "Jet Fuel"; and

(B) The permissible fuel designations, or references to the Airplane Flight Manual (AFM) for permissible fuel designations.

(iii) For pressure fueling systems, the maximum permissible fueling supply pressure and the maximum permissible defueling pressure.

(2) Oil filler openings must be marked at or near the filler cover with the word "Oil" and the permissible oil designations, or references to the Airplane Flight Manual (AFM) for permissible oil designations.

(3) Coolant filler openings must be marked at or near the filler cover with the word "Coolant".

(d) *Emergency exit placards.* Each placard and operating control for each emergency exit must be red. A placard must be near each emergency exit control and must clearly indicate the location of that exit and its method of operation.

(e) The system voltage of each direct current installation must be clearly marked adjacent to its external power connection.

[Docket No. 4080, 29 FR 17955, Dec. 18, 1964; as amended by Amdt. 23–21, 42 FR 15042, Mar. 17, 1977; Amdt. 23–23, 43 FR 50594, Oct. 30, 1978; Amdt. 23–45, 58 FR 42166, Aug. 6, 1993]

§23.1559 Operating limitations placard.

(a) There must be a placard in clear view of the pilot stating—

(1) That the airplane must be operated in accordance with the Airplane Flight Manual; and

(2) The certification category of the airplane to which the placards apply.

(b) For airplanes certificated in more than one category, there must be a placard in clear view of the pilot stating that other limitations are contained in the Airplane Flight Manual.

(c) There must be a placard in clear view of the pilot that specifies the kind of operations to which the operation of the airplane is limited or from which it is prohibited under §23.1525.

[Docket No. 4080, 29 FR 17955, Dec. 18, 1964; 30 FR 258, Jan. 9, 1965; as amended by Amdt. 23–13, 37 FR 20023, Sept. 23, 1972; 37 FR 21320, Oct. 7, 1972; Amdt. 23–21, 43 FR 2319, Jan. 16, 1978; Amdt. 23–50, 61 FR 5193, Feb. 9, 1996]

§23.1561 Safety equipment.

(a) Safety equipment must be plainly marked as to method of operation.

(b) Stowage provisions for required safety equipment must be marked for the benefit of occupants.

§23.1563 Airspeed placards.

There must be an airspeed placard in clear view of the pilot and as close as practicable to the airspeed indicator. This placard must list—

(a) The operating maneuvering speed, V_O; and

(b) The maximum landing gear operating speed V_{LO}.

(c) For reciprocating multiengine-powered airplanes of more than 6,000 pounds maximum weight, and turbine engine-powered airplanes, the maximum value of the minimum control speed, V_{MC} (one-engine-inoperative) determined under §23.149(b).

[Amdt. 23–7, 34 FR 13097, Aug. 13, 1969; as amended by Amdt. 23–45, 58 FR 42166, Aug. 6, 1993; Amdt. 23–50, 61 FR 5193, Feb. 9, 1996]

§23.1567 Flight maneuver placard.

(a) For normal category airplanes, there must be a placard in front of and in clear view of the pilot stating: "No acrobatic maneuvers, including spins, approved."

(b) For utility category airplanes, there must be—

(1) A placard in clear view of the pilot stating: "Acrobatic maneuvers are limited to the following __________" (list approved maneuvers and the recommended entry speed for each); and

(2) For those airplanes that do not meet the spin requirements for acrobatic category airplanes, an additional placard in clear view of the pilot stating: "Spins Prohibited."

(c) For acrobatic category airplanes, there must be a placard in clear view of the pilot listing the approved acrobatic maneuvers and the recommended entry airspeed for each. If inverted flight maneuvers are not approved, the placard must bear a notation to this effect.

(d) For acrobatic category airplanes and utility category airplanes approved for spinning, there must be a placard in clear view of the pilot—

(1) Listing the control actions for recovery from spinning maneuvers; and

(2) Stating that recovery must be initiated when spiral characteristics appear, or after not more than six turns or not more than any greater number of turns for which the airplane has been certificated.

[Docket No. 4080, 29 FR 17955, Dec. 18, 1964; 30 FR 258, Jan. 9, 1965; as amended by Amdt. 23–13, 37 FR 20023, Sept. 23, 1972; Amdt. 23–21, 43 FR 2319, Jan. 16, 1978; Amdt. 23–50, 61 FR 5193, Feb. 9, 1996]

AIRPLANE FLIGHT MANUAL AND APPROVED MANUAL MATERIAL

§23.1581 General.

(a) *Furnishing information.* An Airplane Flight Manual must be furnished with each airplane, and it must contain the following:

(1) Information required by §§23.1583 through 23.1589.

(2) Other information that is necessary for safe operation because of design, operating, or handling characteristics.

(3) Further information necessary to comply with the relevant operating rules.

(b) *Approved information.*

(1) Except as provided in paragraph (b)(2) of this section, each part of the Airplane Flight Manual containing information prescribed in §§23.1583 through 23.1589 must be ap-

proved, segregated, identified and clearly distinguished from each unapproved part of that Airplane Flight Manual.

(2) The requirements of paragraph (b)(1) of this section do not apply to reciprocating engine-powered airplanes of 6,000 pounds or less maximum weight, if the following is met:

(i) Each part of the Airplane Flight Manual containing information prescribed in §23.1583 must be limited to such information, and must be approved, identified, and clearly distinguished from each other part of the Airplane Flight Manual.

(ii) The information prescribed in §§23.1585 through 23.1589 must be determined in accordance with the applicable requirements of this part and presented in its entirety in a manner acceptable to the Administrator.

(3) Each page of the Airplane Flight Manual containing information prescribed in this section must be of a type that is not easily erased, disfigured, or misplaced, and is capable of being inserted in a manual provided by the applicant, or in a folder, or in any other permanent binder.

(c) The units used in the Airplane Flight Manual must be the same as those marked on the appropriate instruments and placards.

(d) All Airplane Flight Manual operational airspeeds, unless otherwise specified, must be presented as indicated airspeeds.

(e) Provision must be made for stowing the Airplane Flight Manual in a suitable fixed container which is readily accessible to the pilot.

(f) *Revisions and amendments.* Each Airplane Flight Manual (AFM) must contain a means for recording the incorporation of revisions and amendments.

[Amdt. 23–21, 43 FR 2319, Jan. 16, 1978; as amended by Amdt. 23–34, 52 FR 1834, Jan. 15, 1987; Amdt. 23–45, 58 FR 42166, Aug. 6, 1993; Amdt. 23–50, 61 FR 5193, Feb. 9, 1996]

§23.1583 Operating limitations.

The Airplane Flight Manual must contain operating limitations determined under this part 23, including the following—

(a) *Airspeed limitations.* The following information must be furnished,

(1) Information necessary for the marking of the airspeed limits on the indicator as required in §23.1545, and the significance of each of those limits and of the color coding used on the indicator.

(2) The speeds V_{MC}, V_O, V_{LE}, and V_{LO}, if established, and their significance.

(3) In addition, for turbine powered commuter category airplanes—

(i) The maximum operating limit speed, V_{MO}/M_{MO} and a statement that this speed must not be deliberately exceeded in any regime of flight (climb, cruise or descent) unless a higher speed is authorized for flight test or pilot training;

(ii) If an airspeed limitation is based upon compressibility effects, a statement to this effect and information as to any symptoms, the probable behavior of the airplane, and the recommended recovery procedures; and

(iii) The airspeed limits must be shown in terms of V_{MO}/M_{MO} instead of V_{NO} and V_{NE}.

(b) *Powerplant limitations.* The following information must be furnished:

(1) Limitations required by §23.1521.

(2) Explanation of the limitations, when appropriate.

(3) Information necessary for marking the instruments required by §§23.1549 through 23.1553.

(c) *Weight.* The airplane flight manual must include—

(1) The maximum weight; and

(2) The maximum landing weight, if the design landing weight selected by the applicant is less than the maximum weight.

(3) For normal, utility, and acrobatic category reciprocating engine-powered airplanes of more than 6,000 pounds maximum weight and for turbine engine-powered airplanes in the normal, utility, and acrobatic category, performance operating limitations as follows—

(i) The maximum takeoff weight for each airport altitude and ambient temperature within the range selected by the applicant at which the airplane complies with the climb requirements of §23.63(c)(1).

(ii) The maximum landing weight for each airport altitude and ambient temperature within the range selected by the applicant at which the airplane complies with the climb requirements of §23.63(c)(2).

(4) For commuter category airplanes, the maximum takeoff weight for each airport altitude and ambient temperature within the range selected by the applicant at which—

(i) The airplane complies with the climb requirements of §23.63(d)(1); and

(ii) The accelerate-stop distance determined under §23.55 is equal to the available runway length plus the length of any stopway, if utilized; and either:

(iii) The takeoff distance determined under §23.59(a) is equal to the available runway length; or

(iv) At the option of the applicant, the takeoff distance determined under §23.59(a) is equal to the available runway length plus the length of any clearway and the takeoff run determined under §23.59(b) is equal to the available runway length.

(5) For commuter category airplanes, the maximum landing weight for each airport altitude within the range selected by the applicant at which—

(i) The airplane complies with the climb requirements of §23.63(d)(2) for ambient temperatures within the range selected by the applicant; and

(ii) The landing distance determined under §23.75 for standard temperatures is equal to the available runway length.

(6) The maximum zero wing fuel weight, where relevant, as established in accordance with §23.343.

(d) *Center of gravity.* The established center of gravity limits.

(e) *Maneuvers.* The following authorized maneuvers, appropriate airspeed limitations, and unauthorized maneuvers, as prescribed in this section.

(1) *Normal category airplanes.* No acrobatic maneuvers, including spins, are authorized.

(2) *Utility category airplanes.* A list of authorized maneuvers demonstrated in the type flight tests, together with recommended entry speeds and any other associated limitations. No other maneuver is authorized.

(3) *Acrobatic category airplanes.* A list of approved flight maneuvers demonstrated in the type flight tests, together with recommended entry speeds and any other associated limitations.

(4) *Acrobatic category airplanes and utility category airplanes approved for spinning.* Spin recovery procedure established to show compliance with §23.221(c).

(5) *Commuter category airplanes.* Maneuvers are limited to any maneuver incident to normal flying, stalls, (except whip stalls) and steep turns in which the angle of bank is not more than 60 degrees.

(f) *Maneuver load factor.* The positive limit load factors in g's, and, in addition, the negative limit load factor for acrobatic category airplanes.

(g) *Minimum flight crew.* The number and functions of the minimum flight crew determined under §23.1523.

(h) *Kinds of operation.* A list of the kinds of operation to which the airplane is limited or from which it is prohibited under §23.1525, and also a list of installed equipment that affects any operating limitation and identification as to the equipment's required operational status for the kinds of operation for which approval has been given.

(i) *Maximum operating altitude.* The maximum altitude established under §23.1527.

(j) *Maximum passenger seating configuration.* The maximum passenger seating configuration.

(k) *Allowable lateral fuel loading.* The maximum allowable lateral fuel loading differential, if less than the maximum possible.

(l) *Baggage and cargo loading.* The following information for each baggage and cargo compartment or zone—

(1) The maximum allowable load; and

(2) The maximum intensity of loading.

(m) *Systems.* Any limitations on the use of airplane systems and equipment.

(n) *Ambient temperatures.* Where appropriate, maximum and minimum ambient air temperatures for operation.

(o) *Smoking.* Any restrictions on smoking in the airplane.

(p) *Types of surface.* A statement of the types of surface on which operations may be conducted. (See §23.45(g) and §23.1587 (a)(4), (c)(2), and (d)(4)).

[Docket No. 4080, 29 FR 17955, Dec. 18, 1964; as amended by Amdt. 23–7, 34 FR 13097, Aug. 13, 1969; Amdt. 23–10, 36 FR 2864, Feb. 11, 1971; Amdt. 23–21, 43 FR 2320, Jan. 16, 1978; Amdt. 23–23, 43 FR 50594, Oct. 30, 1978; Amdt. 23–34, 52 FR 1834, Jan. 15, 1987; Amdt. 23–45, 58 FR 42166, Aug. 6, 1993; Amdt. 23–50, 61 FR 5193, Feb. 9, 1996]

§23.1585 Operating procedures.

(a) For all airplanes, information concerning normal, abnormal (if applicable), and emergency procedures and other pertinent information necessary for safe operation and the achievement of the scheduled performance must be furnished, including—

(1) An explanation of significant or unusual flight or ground handling characteristics;

(2) The maximum demonstrated values of crosswind for takeoff and landing, and procedures and information pertinent to operations in crosswinds;

(3) A recommended speed for flight in rough air. This speed must be chosen to protect against the occurrence, as a result of gusts, of structural damage to the airplane and loss of control (for example, stalling);

(4) Procedures for restarting any turbine engine in flight, including the effects of altitude; and

(5) Procedures, speeds, and configuration(s) for making a normal approach and landing, in accordance with §§23.73 and 23.75, and a transition to the balked landing condition.

(6) For seaplanes and amphibians, water handling procedures and the demonstrated wave height.

(b) In addition to paragraph (a) of this section, for all single-engine airplanes, the procedures, speeds, and configuration(s) for a glide following engine failure, in accordance with §23.71 and the subsequent forced landing, must be furnished.

(c) In addition to paragraph (a) of this section, for all multi-engine airplanes, the following information must be furnished:

(1) Procedures, speeds, and configuration(s) for making an approach and landing with one engine inoperative;

(2) Procedures, speeds, and configuration(s) for making a balked landing with one engine inoperative and the conditions under which a balked landing can be performed safely, or a warning against attempting a balked landing;

(3) The V_{SSE} determined in §23.149; and

(4) Procedures for restarting any engine in flight including the effects of altitude.

(d) In addition to paragraphs (a) and either (b) or (c) of this section, as appropriate, for all normal, utility, and acrobatic category airplanes, the following information must be furnished:

(1) Procedures, speeds, and configuration(s) for making a normal takeoff, in accordance with §23.51 (a) and (b), and §23.53 (a) and (b), and the subsequent climb, in accordance with §23.65 and §23.69(a).

(2) Procedures for abandoning a takeoff due to engine failure or other cause.

(e) In addition to paragraphs (a), (c), and (d) of this section, for all normal, utility, and acrobatic category multiengine airplanes, the information must include the following:

(1) Procedures and speeds for continuing a takeoff following engine failure and the conditions under which takeoff can safely be continued, or a warning against attempting to continue the takeoff.

(2) Procedures, speeds, and configurations for continuing a climb following engine failure, after takeoff, in accordance with §23.67, or enroute, in accordance with §23.69(b).

(f) In addition to paragraphs (a) and (c) of this section, for commuter category airplanes, the information must include the following:

(1) Procedures, speeds, and configuration(s) for making a normal takeoff.

(2) Procedures and speeds for carrying out an accelerate-stop in accordance with §23.55.

(3) Procedures and speeds for continuing a takeoff following engine failure in accordance with §23.59(a)(1) and for following the flight path determined under §23.57 and §23.61(a).

(g) For multiengine airplanes, information identifying each operating condition in which the fuel system independence prescribed in §23.953 is necessary for safety must be furnished, together with instructions for placing the fuel system in a configuration used to show compliance with that section.

(h) For each airplane showing compliance with §23.1353 (g)(2) or (g)(3), the operating procedures for disconnecting the battery from its charging source must be furnished.

(i) Information on the total quantity of usable fuel for each fuel tank, and the effect on the usable fuel quantity, as a result of a failure of any pump, must be furnished.

(j) Procedures for the safe operation of the airplane's systems and equipment, both in normal use and in the event of malfunction, must be furnished.

[Docket No. 27807, 61 FR 5194, Feb. 9, 1996]

§23.1587 Performance information.

Unless otherwise prescribed, performance information must be provided over the altitude and temperature ranges required by §23.45(b).

(a) For all airplanes, the following information must be furnished—

(1) The stalling speeds V_{S0} and V_{S1} with the landing gear and wing flaps retracted, determined at maximum weight under §23.49, and the effect on these stalling speeds of angles of bank up to 60 degrees;

(2) The steady rate and gradient of climb with all engines operating, determined under §23.69(a);

(3) The landing distance, determined under §23.75 for each airport altitude and standard temperature, and the type of surface for which it is valid;

(4) The effect on landing distances of operation on other than smooth hard surfaces, when dry, determined under §23.45(g); and

(5) The effect on landing distances of runway slope and 50 percent of the headwind component and 150 percent of the tailwind component.

(b) In addition to paragraph (a) of this section, for all normal, utility, and acrobatic category reciprocating engine-powered airplanes of 6,000 pounds or less maximum weight, the steady angle of climb/descent, determined under §23.77(a), must be furnished.

(c) In addition to paragraphs (a) and (b) of this section, if appropriate, for normal, utility, and acrobatic category airplanes, the following information must be furnished—

(1) The takeoff distance, determined under §23.53 and the type of surface for which it is valid.

(2) The effect on takeoff distance of operation on other than smooth hard surfaces, when dry, determined under §23.45(g);

(3) The effect on takeoff distance of runway slope and 50 percent of the headwind component and 150 percent of the tailwind component;

(4) For multiengine reciprocating engine-powered airplanes of more than 6,000 pounds maximum weight and multiengine turbine powered airplanes, the one-engine-inoperative takeoff climb/descent gradient, determined under §23.66;

(5) For multiengine airplanes, the enroute rate and gradient of climb/descent with one engine inoperative, determined under §23.69(b); and

(6) For single-engine airplanes, the glide performance determined under §23.71.

(d) In addition to paragraph (a) of this section, for commuter category airplanes, the following information must be furnished—

(1) The accelerate-stop distance determined under §23.55;

(2) The takeoff distance determined under §23.59(a);

(3) At the option of the applicant, the takeoff run determined under §23.59(b);

(4) The effect on accelerate-stop distance, takeoff distance and, if determined, takeoff run, of operation on other than smooth hard surfaces, when dry, determined under §23.45(g);

(5) The effect on accelerate-stop distance, takeoff distance, and if determined, takeoff run, of runway slope and 50 percent of the headwind component and 150 percent of the tailwind component;

(6) The net takeoff flight path determined under §23.61(b);

(7) The enroute gradient of climb/descent with one engine inoperative, determined under §23.69(b);

(8) The effect, on the net takeoff flight path and on the enroute gradient of climb/descent with one engine inoperative, of 50 percent of the headwind component and 150 percent of the tailwind component;

(9) Overweight landing performance information (determined by extrapolation and computed for the range of weights between the maximum landing and maximum takeoff weights) as follows—

(i) The maximum weight for each airport altitude and ambient temperature at which the airplane complies with the climb requirements of §23.63(d)(2); and

(ii) The landing distance determined under §23.75 for each airport altitude and standard temperature.

(10) The relationship between IAS and CAS determined in accordance with §23.1323 (b) and (c).

(11) The altimeter system calibration required by §23.1325(e).

[Amdt. 23–21, 43 FR 2320, Jan. 16, 1978; as amended by Amdt. 23–28, 47 FR 13315, Mar. 29, 1982; Amdt. 23–34, 52 FR 1835, Jan. 15, 1987; Amdt. 23–39, 55 FR 18575, May 2, 1990; Amdt. 23–45, 58 FR 42167, Aug. 6, 1993; 58 FR 51970, Oct. 5, 1993; Amdt. 23–50, 61 FR 5195, Feb. 9, 1996]

§23.1589 Loading information.

The following loading information must be furnished:

(a) The weight and location of each item of equipment that can be easily removed, relocated, or replaced and that is installed when the airplane was weighed under the requirement of §23.25.

(b) Appropriate loading instructions for each possible loading condition between the maximum and minimum weights established under §23.25, to facilitate the center of gravity remaining within the limits established under §23.23.

[Docket No. 4080, 29 FR 17955, Dec. 18, 1964; as amended by Amdt. 23–45, 58 FR 42167, Aug. 6, 1993; Amdt. 23–50, 61 FR 5195, Feb. 9, 1996]

Appendix A to Part 23

Simplified Design Load Criteria

A23.1 General.

(a) The design load criteria in this appendix are an approved equivalent of those in §§23.321 through 23.459 of this subchapter for an airplane having a maximum weight of 6,000 pounds or less and the following configuration:

(1) A single engine excluding turbine powerplants;

(2) A main wing located closer to the airplane's center of gravity than to the aft, fuselage-mounted, empennage;

(3) A main wing that contains a quarter-chord sweep angle of not more than 15 degrees fore or aft;

(4) A main wing that is equipped with trailing-edge controls (ailerons or flaps, or both);
(5) A main wing aspect ratio not greater than 7;
(6) A horizontal tail aspect ratio not greater than 4;
(7) A horizontal tail volume coefficient not less than 0.34;
(8) A vertical tail aspect ratio not greater than 2;
(9) A vertical tail platform area not greater than 10 percent of the wing platform area; and
(10) Symmetrical airfoils must be used in both the horizontal and vertical tail designs.

(b) Appendix A criteria may not be used on any airplane configuration that contains any of the following design features:
(1) Canard, tandem-wing, close-coupled, or tailless arrangements of the lifting surfaces;
(2) Biplane or multiplane wing arrangements;
(3) T-tail, V-tail, or cruciform-tail (+) arrangements;
(4) Highly-swept wing platform (more than 15-degrees of sweep at the quarter-chord), delta planforms, or slatted lifting surfaces; or
(5) Winglets or other wing tip devices, or outboard fins.

A23.3 Special symbols.

n_1 = Airplane Positive Maneuvering Limit Load Factor.
n_2 = Airplane Negative Maneuvering Limit Load Factor.
n_3 = Airplane Positive Gust Limit Load Factor at V_C.
n_4 = Airplane Negative Gust Limit Load Factor at V_C.
n_{flap} = Airplane Positive Limit Load Factor With Flaps Fully Extended at V_F.
$V_{F\,min}$ = Minimum Design Flap Speed =

$$11.0\sqrt{n_1 \mathrm{W/S}}\ \ [kts]$$

$V_{A\,min}$ = Minimum Design Maneuvering Speed =

$$15.0\sqrt{n_1 \mathrm{W/S}}\ \ [kts]$$

$V_{C\,min}$ = Minimum Design Cruising Speed =

$$17.0\sqrt{n_1 \mathrm{W/S}}\ \ [kts]$$

$V_{D\,min}$ = Minimum Design Dive Speed =

$$24.0\sqrt{n_1 \mathrm{W/S}}\ \ [kts]$$

A23.5 Certification in more than one category.

The criteria in this appendix may be used for certification in the normal, utility, and acrobatic categories, or in any combination of these categories. If certification in more than one category is desired, the design category weights must be selected to make the term "n_1 W" constant for all categories or greater for one desired category than for others. The wings and control surfaces (including wing flaps and tabs) need only be investigated for the maximum value of " n_1 W ", or for the category corresponding to the maximum design weight, where " n_1 W " is constant. If the acrobatic category is selected, a special unsymmetrical flight load investigation in accordance with paragraphs A23.9(c)(2) and A23.11(c)(2) of this appendix must be completed. The wing, wing carry-through, and the horizontal tail structures must be checked for this condition. The basic fuselage structure need only be investigated for the highest load factor design category selected. The local supporting structure for dead weight items need only be designed for the highest load factor imposed when the particular items are installed in the airplane. The engine mount, however, must be designed for a higher side load factor, if certification in the acrobatic category is desired, than that required for certification in the normal and utility categories. When designing for landing loads, the landing gear and the airplane as a whole need only be investigated for the category corresponding to the maximum design weight. These simplifications apply to single-engine aircraft of conventional types for which experience is available, and the Administrator may require additional investigations for aircraft with unusual design features.

23

A23.7 Flight loads.

(a) Each flight load may be considered independent of altitude and, except for the local supporting structure for dead weight items, only the maximum design weight conditions must be investigated.

(b) Table 1 and figures 3 and 4 of this appendix must be used to determine values of n_1, n_2, n_3, and n_4, corresponding to the maximum design weights in the desired categories.

(c) Figures 1 and 2 of this appendix must be used to determine values of n_3 and n_4 corresponding to the minimum flying weights in the desired categories, and, if these load factors are greater than the load factors at the design weight, the supporting structure for dead weight items must be substantiated for the resulting higher load factors.

(d) Each specified wing and tail loading is independent of the center of gravity range. The applicant, however, must select a c.g. range, and the basic fuselage structure must be investigated for the most adverse dead weight loading conditions for the c.g. range selected.

(e) The following loads and loading conditions are the minimums for which strength must be provided in the structure:

(1) *Airplane equilibrium.* The aerodynamic wing loads may be considered to act normal to the relative wind, and to have a magnitude of 1.05 times the airplane normal loads (as determined from paragraphs A23.9 (b) and (c) of this appendix) for the positive flight conditions and a magnitude equal to the airplane normal loads for the negative conditions. Each chordwise and normal component of this wing load must be considered.

(2) *Minimum design airspeeds.* The minimum design airspeeds may be chosen by the applicant except that they may not be less than the minimum speeds found by using figure 3 of this appendix. In addition, $V_{C\,min}$ need not exceed values of 0.9 V_H actually obtained at sea level for the lowest design weight category for which certification is desired. In computing these minimum design airspeeds, n_1 may not be less than 3.8.

(3) *Flight load factor.* The limit flight load factors specified in Table 1 of this appendix represent the ratio of the aerodynamic force component (acting normal to the assumed longitudinal axis of the airplane) to the weight of the airplane. A positive flight load factor is an aerodynamic force acting upward, with respect to the airplane.

A23.9 FLIGHT CONDITIONS.

(a) *General.* Each design condition in paragraphs (b) and (c) of this section must be used to assure sufficient strength for each condition of speed and load factor on or within the boundary of a V–n diagram for the airplane similar to the diagram in figure 4 of this appendix. This diagram must also be used to determine the airplane structural operating limitations as specified in §23.1501(c) through §23.1513 and §23.1519.

(b) *Symmetrical flight conditions.* The airplane must be designed for symmetrical flight conditions as follows:

(1) The airplane must be designed for at least the four basic flight conditions, "A", "D", "E", and "G" as noted on the flight envelope of figure 4 of this appendix. In addition, the following requirements apply:

(i) The design limit flight load factors corresponding to conditions "D" and "E" of figure 4 must be at least as great as those specified in Table 1 and figure 4 of this appendix, and the design speed for these conditions must be at least equal to the value of V_D found from figure 3 of this appendix.

(ii) For conditions "A" and "G" of figure 4, the load factors must correspond to those specified in Table 1 of this appendix, and the design speeds must be computed using these load factors with the maximum static lift coefficient C_{NA} determined by the applicant. However, in the absence of more precise computations, these latter conditions may be based on a value of $C_{NA} = \pm 1.35$ and the design speed for condition "A" may be less than $V_{A\,min}$.

(iii) Conditions "C" and "F" of figure 4 need only be investigated when n_3W/S or n_4W/S are greater than n_1W/S or n_2W/S of this appendix, respectively.

(2) If flaps or other high lift devices intended for use at the relatively low airspeed of approach, landing, and takeoff, are installed, the airplane must be designed for the two flight conditions corresponding to the values of limit flap-down factors specified in Table 1 of this appendix with the flaps fully extended at not less than the design flap speed $V_{F\,min}$ from figure 3 of this appendix.

(c) *Unsymmetrical flight conditions.* Each affected structure must be designed for unsymmetrical loadings as follows:

(1) The aft fuselage-to-wing attachment must be designed for the critical vertical surface load determined in accordance with paragraph SA23.11(c) (1) and (2) of this appendix.

(2) The wing and wing carry-through structures must be designed for 100 percent of condition "A" loading on one side of the plane of symmetry and 70 percent on the opposite side for certification in the normal and utility categories, or 60 percent on the opposite side for certification in the acrobatic category.

(3) The wing and wing carry-through structures must be designed for the loads resulting from a combination of 75 percent of the positive maneuvering wing loading on both sides of the plane of symmetry and the maximum wing torsion resulting from aileron displacement. The effect of aileron displacement on wing torsion at V_C or V_A using the basic airfoil moment coefficient modified over the aileron portion of the span, must be computed as follows:

(i) Cm = Cm +0.01δμ (up aileron side) wing basic airfoil.

(ii) Cm = Cm –0.01δμ (down aileron side) wing basic airfoil, where δμ is the up aileron deflection and δd is the down aileron deflection.

(4) Δ critical, which is the sum of δμ + δd must be computed as follows:

(i) Compute Δ_a and Δ_b from the formulas:

$$\Delta_a = \frac{V_A}{V_C} \times \Delta_p \quad \text{and}$$

$$\Delta_b = 0.5\frac{V_A}{V_D} \times \Delta_p$$

Where Δ_p = the maximum total deflection (sum of both aileron deflections) at V_A with V_A, V_C, and V_D described in subparagraph (2) of 23.7(e) of this Appendix.

(ii) Compute K from the formula:

$$K = \frac{(C_m - 0.01\delta_b)V_{D^2}}{(C_m - 0.01\delta_a)V_{C^2}}$$

where δa is the down aileron deflection corresponding to Δa, and db is the down aileron deflection corresponding to Δb as computed in step (i).

(iii) If K is less than 1.0, Δa is Δ critical and must be used to determine δ_u and δd. In this case, V_C is the critical speed which must be used in computing the wing torsion loads over the aileron span.

(iv) If K is equal to or greater than 1.0, Δb is Δ critical and must be used to determine δu and δ_d. In this case, V_d is the critical speed which must be used in computing the wing torsion loads over the aileron span.

(d) *Supplementary conditions; rear lift truss; engine torque; side load on engine mount.* Each of the following supplementary conditions must be investigated:

(1) In designing the rear lift truss, the special condition specified in §23.369 may be investigated instead of condition "G" of figure 4 of this appendix. If this is done, and if certification in more than one category is desired, the value of W/S used in the formula appearing in §23.369 must be that for the category corresponding to the maximum gross weight.

(2) Each engine mount and its supporting structures must be designed for the maximum limit torque corresponding to METO power and propeller speed acting simultaneously with the limit loads resulting from the maximum positive maneuvering flight load factor n_1. The limit torque must be obtained by multiplying the mean torque by a factor of 1.33 for engines with five or more cylinders. For 4, 3, and 2 cylinder engines, the factor must be 2, 3, and 4, respectively.

(3) Each engine mount and its supporting structure must be designed for the loads resulting from a lateral limit load factor of not less than 1.47 for the normal and utility categories, or 2.0 for the acrobatic category.

A23.11 CONTROL SURFACE LOADS.

(a) *General.* Each control surface load must be determined using the criteria of paragraph (b) of this section and must lie within the simplified loadings of paragraph (c) of this section.

(b) *Limit pilot forces.* In each control surface loading condition described in paragraphs (c) through (e) of this section, the airloads on the movable surfaces and the corresponding deflections need not exceed those which could be obtained in flight by employing the maximum limit pilot forces specified in the table in §23.397(b). If the surface loads are limited by these maximum limit pilot forces, the tabs must either be considered to be deflected to their maximum travel in the direction which would assist the pilot or the deflection must correspond to the maximum degree of "out of trim" expected at the speed for the condition under consideration. The tab load, however, need not exceed the value specified in Table 2 of this appendix.

(c) *Surface loading conditions.* Each surface loading condition must be investigated as follows:

(1) Simplified limit surface loadings for the horizontal tail, vertical tail, aileron, wing flaps, and trim tabs are specified in figures 5 and 6 of this appendix.

(i) The distribution of load along the span of the surface, irrespective of the chordwise load distribution, must be assumed proportional to the total chord, except on horn balance surfaces.

(ii) The load on the stabilizer and elevator, and the load on fin and rudder, must be distributed chordwise as shown in figure 7 of this appendix.

(iii) In order to ensure adequate torsional strength and to account for maneuvers and gusts, the most severe loads must be considered in association with every center of pressure position between the leading edge and the half chord of the mean chord of the surface (stabilizer and elevator, or fin and rudder).

(iv) To ensure adequate strength under high leading edge loads, the most severe stabilizer and fin loads must be further considered as being increased by 50 percent over the leading 10 percent of the chord with the loads aft of this appropriately decreased to retain the same total load.

(v) The most severe elevator and rudder loads should be further considered as being distributed parabolically from three times the mean loading of the surface (stabilizer and elevator, or fin and rudder) at the leading edge of the elevator and rudder, respectively, to zero at the trailing edge according to the equation:

$$P(x) = 3(\overline{w})\frac{(c-x)^2}{c_f^2}$$

Where—

P(x) = local pressure at the chordwise stations x,

c = chord length of the tail surface,

c_f = chord length of the elevator and rudder respectively, and

$\overline{w}$ = average surface loading as specified in Figure A5.

(vi) The chordwise loading distribution for ailerons, wing flaps, and trim tabs are specified in Table 2 of this appendix.

(2) If certification in the acrobatic category is desired, the horizontal tail must be investigated for an unsymmetrical load of 100 percent w on one side of the airplane centerline and 50 percent on the other side of the airplane centerline.

(d) *Outboard fins.* Outboard fins must meet the requirements of §23.445.

(e) *Special devices.* Special devices must meet the requirements of §23.459.

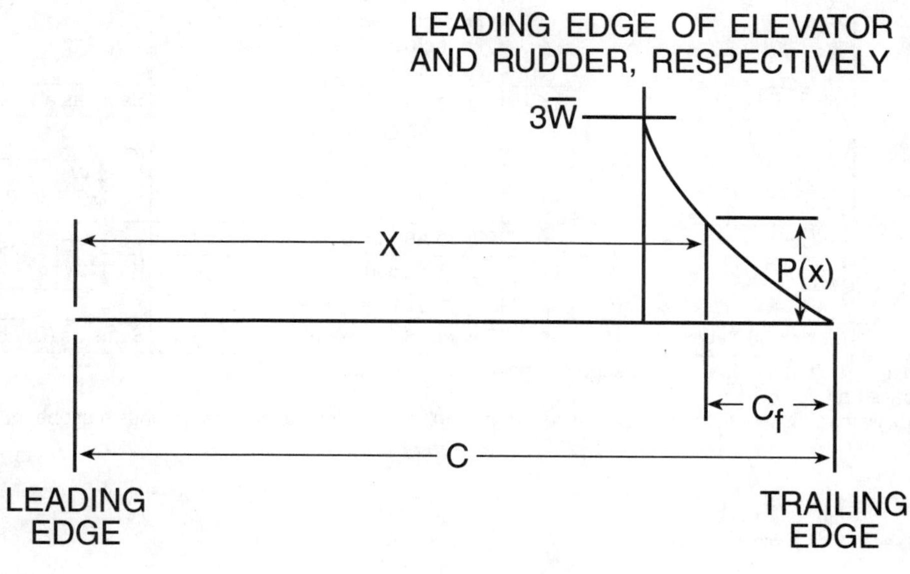

A23.13 Control System Loads.

(a) *Primary flight controls and systems.* Each primary flight control and system must be designed as follows:

(1) The flight control system and its supporting structure must be designed for loads corresponding to 125 percent of the computed hinge moments of the movable control surface in the conditions prescribed in A23.11 of this appendix. In addition—

(i) The system limit loads need not exceed those that could be produced by the pilot and automatic devices operating the controls; and

(ii) The design must provide a rugged system for service use, including jamming, ground gusts, taxiing downwind, control inertia, and friction.

(2) Acceptable maximum and minimum limit pilot forces for elevator, aileron, and rudder controls are shown in the table in §23.397(b). These pilots loads must be assumed to act at the appropriate control grips or pads as they would under flight conditions, and to be reacted at the attachments of the control system to the control surface horn.

(b) *Dual controls.* If there are dual controls, the systems must be designed for pilots operating in opposition, using individual pilot loads equal to 75 percent of those obtained in accordance with paragraph (a) of this section, except that individual pilot loads may not be less than the minimum limit pilot forces shown in the table in §23.397(b).

(c) *Ground gust conditions.* Ground gust conditions must meet the requirements of §23.415.

(d) *Secondary controls and systems.* Secondary controls and systems must meet the requirements of §23.405.

Table 1—Limit Flight Load Factors

Flight load factors	Normal category	Utility category	Acrobatic category
Flaps up:			
n_1	3.8	4.4	6.0
n_2	$-0.5\ n_1$		
n_3	(1)		
n_4	(2)		
Flaps down:			
n flap	$0.5\ n_1$		
n flap	[3] Zero		

[1] Find n_3 from Fig. 1
[2] Find n_4 from Fig. 2
[3] Vertical wing load may be assumed equal to zero and only the flap part of the wing need be checked for this condition.

Table 2—Average Limit Control Surface Loading

Average Limit Control Surface Loading			
Surface	**Direction of Loading**	**Magnitude of Loading**	**Chordwise Distribution**
Horizontal Tail I	(a) Up and Down	Figure A5 Curve (2)	See Figure A7
	(b) Unsymmetrical Loading (Up and Down)	100% $\overline{w}$ on one side of airplane ℄ 65% $\overline{w}$ on other side of airplane ℄ for normal and utility categories. For acrobatic category see A23.11(c)	
Vertical Tail II	Right and Left	Figure A5 Curve (1)	Same as above
Aileron III	(a) Up and Down	Figure A6 Curve (5)	(C) 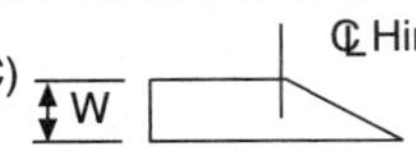
Wing Flap IV	(a) Up	Figure A6 Curve (4)	(D) 
	(b) Down	.25 x Up Load (a)	
Trim Tab V	(a) Up and Down	Figure A6 Curve (3)	Same as (D) above

Note: The surface loading I, II, III, and V above are based on speeds $V_{A\,min}$ and $V_{C\,min}$.
The loading of IV is based on $V_{F\,min}$.
If values of speed *greater* than these minimums are selected for design, the appropriate surface loadings must be multiplied by the ratio

$$\left(\frac{V_{selected}}{V_{minimum}}\right)^2$$

For conditions I, II, III, and V the multiplying factor used must be the higher of

$$\left(\frac{V_A \text{ sel.}}{V_A \text{ min.}}\right)^2 or \left(\frac{V_C \text{ sel.}}{V_C \text{ min.}}\right)^2$$

FIGURE A1—CHART FOR FINDING n_3 FACTOR AT SPEED V_c

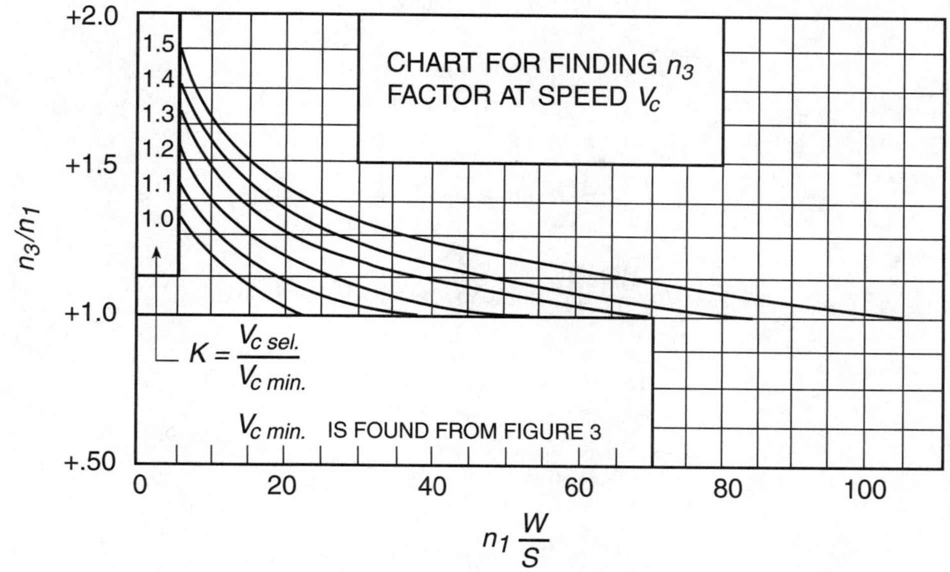

FIGURE A2—CHART FOR FINDING n_4 FACTOR AT SPEED V_c

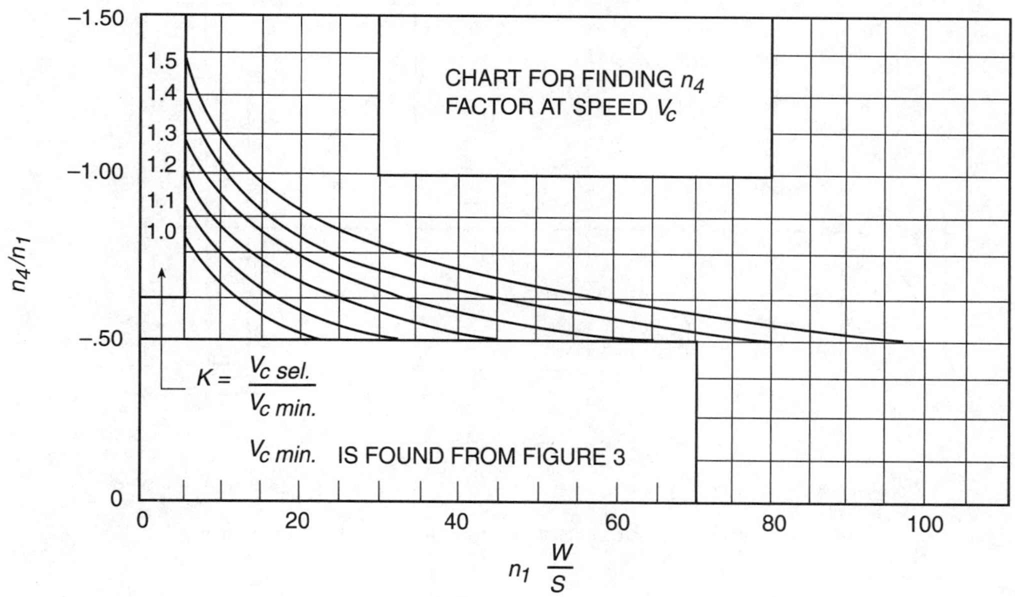

FIGURE A3 — DETERMINATIONS OF MINIMUM DESIGN SPEEDS — EQUATIONS

SPEEDS ARE IN KNOTS

$$V_{D\,\min} = \sqrt{n_1 \frac{W}{S}} \quad \text{but need not exceed} \quad 1.4\sqrt{\frac{n_1}{3.8}}\,V_{C\,\min};$$

$$V_{C\,\min} = 17.0\sqrt{n_1 \frac{W}{S}} \quad \text{but need not exceed} \quad 0.9\,V_H:$$

$$V_{A\,\min} = 15.0\sqrt{n_1 \frac{W}{S}} \quad \text{but need not exceed } V_C \text{ used in design.}$$

$$V_{F\,\min} = 11.0\sqrt{n_1 \frac{W}{S}}$$

FIGURE A4 — FLIGHT ENVELOPE

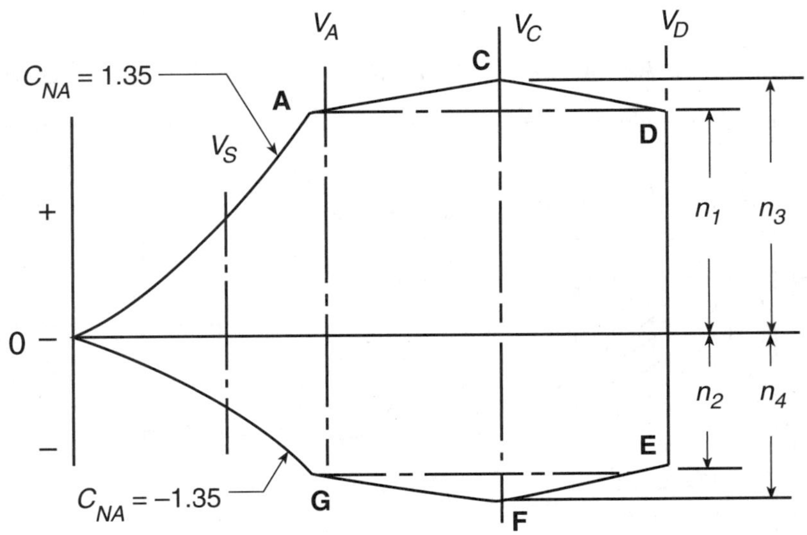

1. Conditions "C" or "F" need only be investigated when $n_3 \frac{W}{S}$ or $n_4 \frac{W}{S}$ is greater than $n_1 \frac{W}{S}$ W/S, respectively.
2. Condition "G" need not be investigated when the supplementary condition specified in §23.369 is investigated.

FIGURE A5 – AVERAGE LIMIT CONTROL SURFACE LOADING

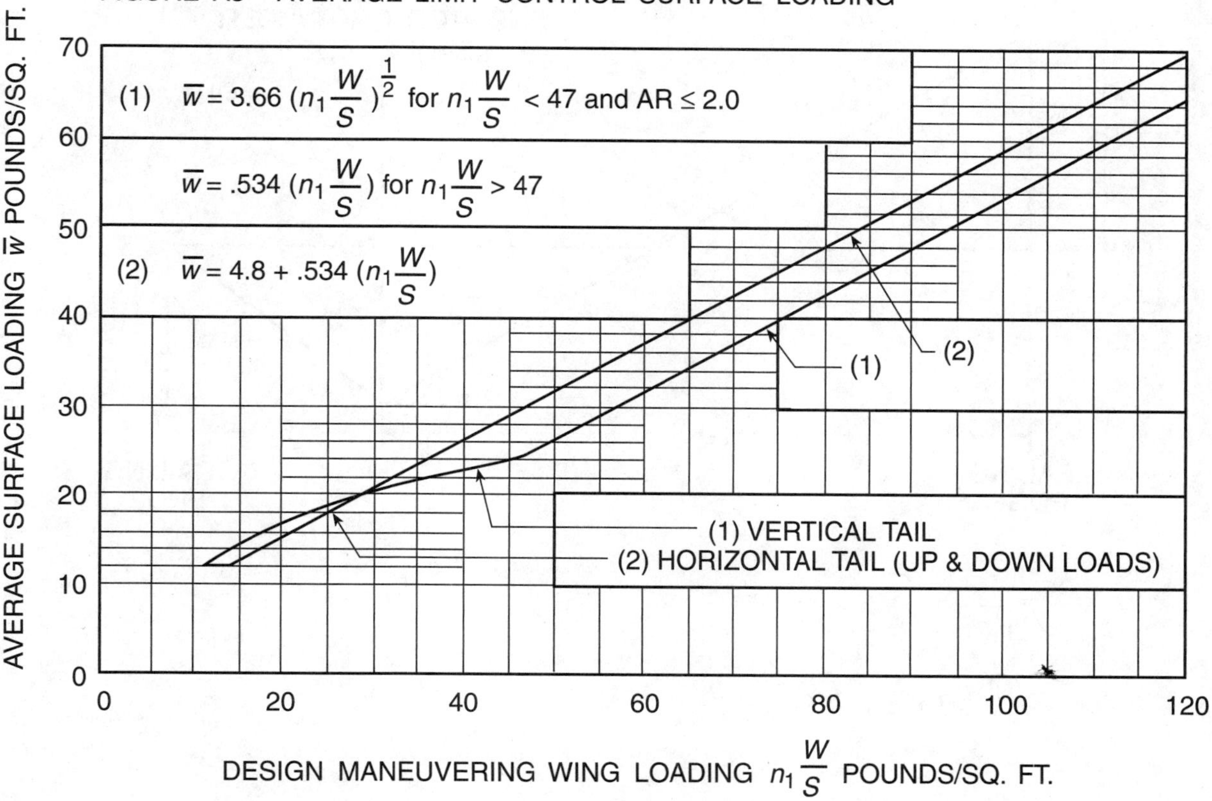

FIGURE A6 – AVERAGE LIMIT CONTROL SURFACE LOADING

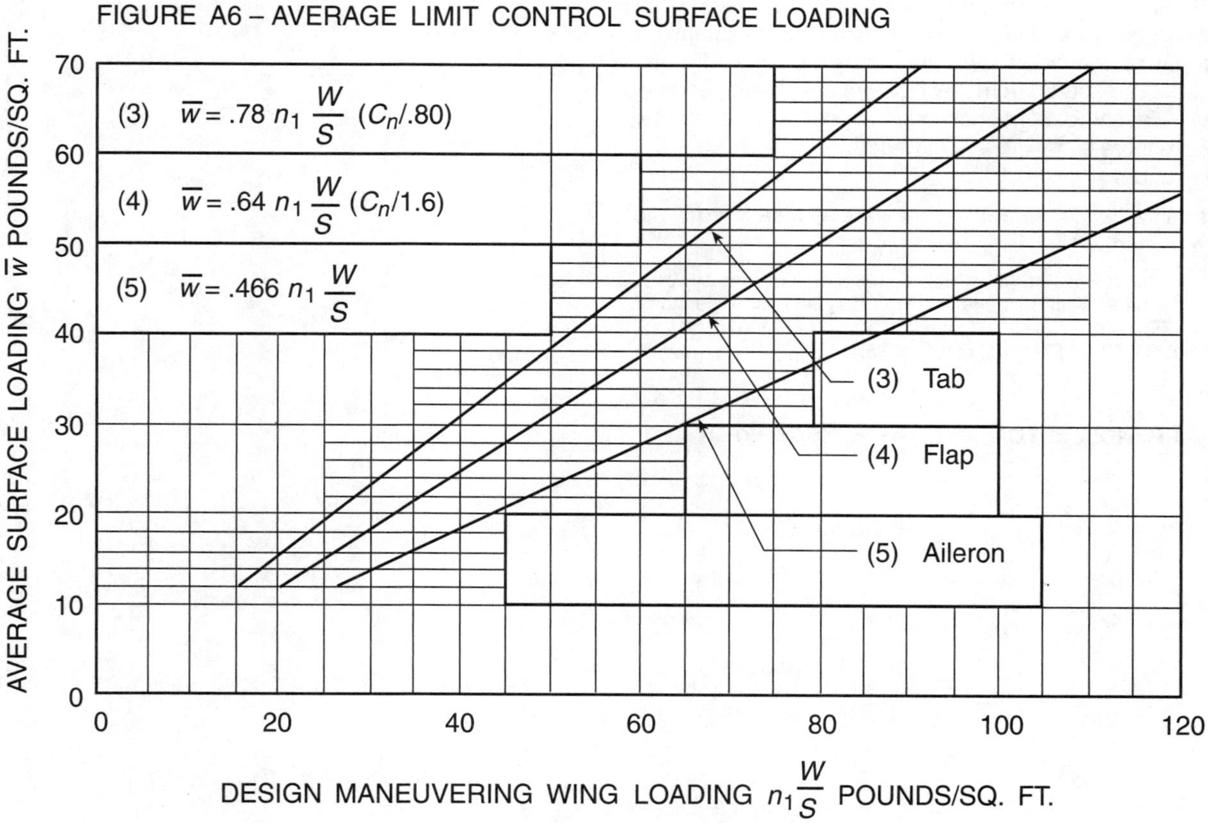

FIGURE A7.—CHORDWISE LOAD DISTRIBUTION FOR STABILIZER AND ELEVATOR OR FIN AND RUDDER

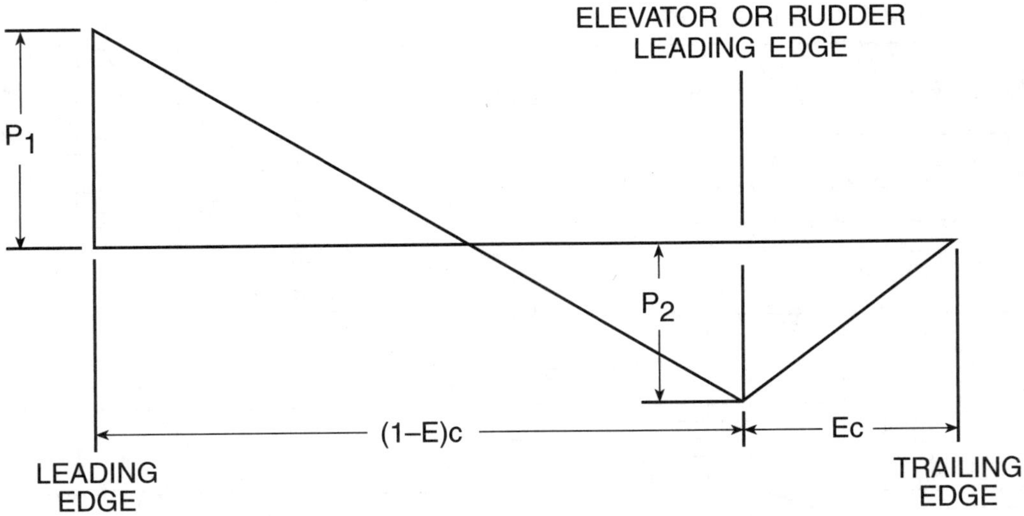

$$P_1 = 2(\overline{w})\frac{(2 - E - 3d')}{(1 - E)}$$

$$P_2 = 2(\overline{w})(3d' + E - 1)$$

where:

$\overline{w}$ = average surface loading (as specified in figure A.5)

E = ratio of elevator (or rudder) chord to total stabilizer and elevator (or fin and rudder) chord.

d' = ratio of distance of center of pressure of a unit spanwise length of combined stabilizer and elevator (or fin and rudder) measured from stabilizer (or fin) leading edge to the local chord. Sign convention is positive when center of pressure is behind leading edge.

c = local chord.

Note: Positive values of $\overline{w}$, P_1 and P_2 are all measured in the same direction.

[Docket No. 4080, 29 FR 17955, Dec. 18, 1964; as amended by Amdt. 23–7, 34 FR 13097, Aug. 13, 1969; 34 FR 14727, Sept. 24, 1969; Amdt. 23–16, 40 FR 2577, Jan. 14, 1975; Amdt. 23–28, 47 FR 13315, Mar. 29, 1982; Amdt. 23–48, 61 FR 5148, Feb. 9, 1996]

APPENDIX B TO PART 23—[RESERVED]

APPENDIX C TO PART 23

BASIC LANDING CONDITIONS

Condition	Tail wheel type		Nose wheel type		
	Level landing	**Tail-down landing**	**Level landing with inclined reactions**	**Level landing with nose wheel just clear of ground**	**Tail-down landing**
Reference section	23.479(a)(1)	23.481(a)(1)	23.479(a)(2)(i)	23.479(a)(2)(ii)	23.481(a)(2) and (b)
Vertical component at c.g.	*nW*	*nW*	*nW*	*nW*	*nW*
Fore and aft component at c.g	*KnW*	0	*KnW*	*KnW*	0
Lateral component in either direction at c.g.	0	0	0	0	0
Shock absorber extension (hydraulic shock absorber)	Note (2)	Note (2)	Note (2)	Note (2)	Note (2)
Shock absorber deflection (rubber or spring shock absorber), percent	100	100	100	100	100
Tire deflection	Static	Static	Static	Static	Static
Main wheel loads (both wheels) *(Vr)*	*(n–L)W*	*(n–L)W* b/d	*(n–L)W* a'/d'	*(n –L)W*	*(n–L)W*
Main wheel loads (both wheels) *(Dr)*	*KnW*	0	*KnW* a'/d'	*KnW*	0
Tail (nose) wheel loads *(Vf)*	0	*(n–L)W* a/d	*(n–L)W* b'/d'	0	0
Tail (nose) wheel loads *(Df)*	0	0	*KnW* b'/d'	0	0
Notes	(1), (3), and (4)	(4)	(1)	(1), (3), and (4)	(3) and (4)

Note (1). *K* may be determined as follows: *K* = 0.25 for *W* = 3,000 pounds or less; *K* = 0.33 for *W* = 6,000 pounds or greater, with linear variation of *K* between these weights.

Note (2). For the purpose of design, the maximum load factor is assumed to occur throughout the shock absorber stroke from 25 percent deflection to 100 percent deflection unless otherwise shown and the load factor must be used with whatever shock absorber extension is most critical for each element of the landing gear.

Note (3). Unbalanced moments must be balanced by a rational or conservative method.

Note (4). *L* is defined in §23.735(b).

Note (5). *n* is the limit inertia load factor, at the c.g. of the airplane, selected under §23.473 (d), (f), and (g).

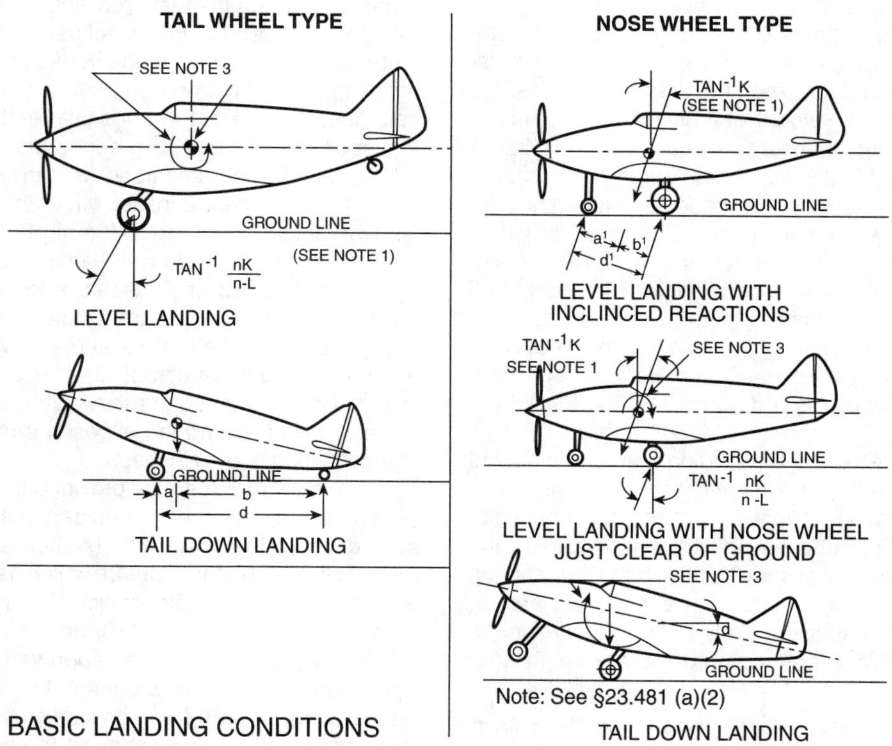

BASIC LANDING CONDITIONS

[Docket No. 4080, 29 FR 17955, Dec. 18, 1964; as amended by Amdt. 23–7, 34 FR 13099, Aug. 13, 1969]

Appendix D to Part 23
Wheel Spin-Up and Spring-Back Loads

D23.1 Wheel spin-up loads.

(a) The following method for determining wheel spin-up loads for landing conditions is based on NACA T.N. 863. However, the drag component used for design may not be less than the drag load prescribed in §23.479(b).

$$F_{Hmax} = 1/r_e \sqrt{2I_w(V_H - V_C)nF_{Vmax}/t_s}$$

where—

F_{Hmax} = maximum rearward horizontal force acting on the wheel (in pounds);

r_e = effective rolling radius of wheel under impact based on recommended operating tire pressure (which may be assumed to be equal to the rolling radius under a static load of $n_j W_e$) in feet;

I_w = rotational mass moment of inertia of rolling assembly (in slug feet);

V_H = linear velocity of airplane parallel to ground at instant of contact (assumed to be 1.2 V_{S0}, in feet per second);

V_c = peripheral speed of tire, if prerotation is used (in feet per second) (there must be a positive means of pre-rotation before pre-rotation may be considered);

n = equals effective coefficient of friction (0.80 may be used);

F_{Vmax} = maximum vertical force on wheel (pounds) = $n_j W_e$, where W_e and n_j are defined in §23.725;

t_s = time interval between ground contact and attainment of maximum vertical force on wheel (seconds). (However, if the value of F_{Vmax}, from the above equation exceeds 0.8 F_{Vmax}, the latter value must be used for F_{Hmax}.)

(b) The equation assumes a linear variation of load factor with time until the peak load is reached and under this assumption, the equation determines the drag force at the time that the wheel peripheral velocity at radius r_e equals the airplane velocity. Most shock absorbers do not exactly follow a linear variation of load factor with time. Therefore, rational or conservative allowances must be made to compensate for these variations. On most landing gears, the time for wheel spin-up will be less than the time required to develop maximum vertical load factor for the specified rate of descent and forward velocity. For exceptionally large wheels, a wheel peripheral velocity equal to the ground speed may not have been attained at the time of maximum vertical gear load. However, as stated above, the drag spin-up load need not exceed 0.8 of the maximum vertical loads.

(c) Dynamic spring-back of the landing gear and adjacent structure at the instant just after the wheels come up to speed may result in dynamic forward acting loads of considerable magnitude. This effect must be determined in the level landing condition, by assuming that the wheel spin-up loads calculated by the methods of this appendix are reversed. Dynamic spring-back is likely to become critical for landing gear units having wheels of large mass or high landing speeds.

[Docket No. 4080, 29 FR 17955, Dec. 18, 1964; as amended by Amdt. 23–45, 58 FR 42167, Aug. 6, 1993]

Appendix E to Part 23—[Reserved]

Appendix F to Part 23
Test Procedure

Acceptable test procedure for self-extinguishing materials for showing compliance with §§23.853, 23.855 and 23.1359.

(a) *Conditioning.* Specimens must be conditioned to 70 degrees F, plus or minus 5 degrees, and at 50 percent plus or minus 5 percent relative humidity until moisture equilibrium is reached or for 24 hours. Only one specimen at a time may be removed from the conditioning environment immediately before subjecting it to the flame.

(b) *Specimen configuration.* Except as provided for materials used in electrical wire and cable insulation and in small parts, materials must be tested either as a section cut from a fabricated part as installed in the airplane or as a specimen simulating a cut section, such as: a specimen cut from a flat sheet of the material or a model of the fabricated part. The specimen may be cut from any location in a fabricated part; however, fabricated units, such as sandwich panels, may not be separated for a test. The specimen thickness must be no thicker than the minimum thickness to be qualified for use in the airplane, except that: (1) Thick foam parts, such as seat cushions, must be tested in ½ inch thickness; (2) when showing compliance with §23.853(d)(3)(v) for materials used in small parts that must be tested, the materials must be tested in no more than ⅛ inch thickness; (3) when showing compliance with §23.1359(c) for materials used in electrical wire and cable insulation, the wire and cable specimens must be the same size as used in the airplane. In the case of fabrics, both the warp and fill direction of the weave must be tested to determine the most critical flammability conditions. When performing the tests prescribed in paragraphs (d) and (e) of this appendix, the specimen must be mounted in a metal frame so that (1) in the vertical tests of paragraph (d) of this appendix, the two long edges and the upper edge are held securely; (2) in the horizontal test of paragraph (e) of this appendix, the two long edges and the edge away from the flame are held securely; (3) the exposed area of the specimen is at least 2 inches wide and 12 inches long, unless the actual size used in the airplane is smaller; and (4) the edge to which the burner flame is applied must not consist of the finished or protected edge of the specimen but must be representative of the actual cross section of the material or part installed in the airplane. When performing the test prescribed in paragraph (f) of this appendix, the specimen must be mounted in metal frame so that all four edges are held securely and the exposed area of the specimen is at least 8 inches by 8 inches.

(c) *Apparatus.* Except as provided in paragraph (g) of this appendix, tests must be conducted in a draft-free cabinet in accordance with Federal Test Method Standard 191 Method 5903 (revised Method 5902) which is available from the General Services Administration, Business Service Center, Region 3, Seventh and D Streets SW, Washington, D.C. 20407, or with some other approved equivalent method. Specimens which are too large for the cabinet must be tested in similar draft-free conditions.

(d) *Vertical test.* A minimum of three specimens must be tested and the results averaged. For fabrics, the direction of weave corresponding to the most critical flammability conditions must be parallel to the longest dimension. Each specimen must be supported vertically. The specimen must be exposed to a Bunsen or Tirrill burner with a nominal ⅜-inch I.D. tube adjusted to give a flame of 1½ inches in height. The minimum flame temperature measured by a calibrated thermocouple pryometer in the center of the flame must be 1550°F. The lower edge of the specimen must be three-fourths inch above the top edge of the burner. The flame must be applied to the center line of the lower edge of the specimen. For materials covered by §§23.853(d)(3)(i) and 23.853(f), the flame must be applied for 60 seconds and then removed. For materials covered by §23.853(d)(3)(ii), the flame must be applied for 12 seconds and then removed. Flame time, burn length, and flaming time of drippings, if any, must be recorded. The burn length determined in accordance with paragraph (h) of this appendix must be measured to the nearest one-tenth inch.

(e) *Horizontal test.* A minimum of three specimens must be tested and the results averaged. Each specimen must be supported horizontally. The exposed surface when installed in the airplane must be face down for the test. The specimen must be exposed to a Bunsen burner or Tirrill burner with a nominal ⅜-inch I.D. tube adjusted to give a flame of 1½ inches in height. The minimum flame temperature measured by a calibrated thermocouple pyrometer in the center of the flame must be 1550°F. The specimen must be positioned so that the edge being tested is three-fourths of an inch above the top of, and on the center line of, the burner. The flame must be applied for 15 seconds and then removed. A minimum of 10 inches of the specimen must be used for timing purposes, approximately 1½ inches must burn before the burning front reaches the timing zone, and the average burn rate must be recorded.

(f) *Forty-five degree test.* A minimum of three specimens must be tested and the results averaged. The specimens must be supported at an angle of 45 degrees to a horizontal surface. The exposed surface when installed in the aircraft must be face down for the test. The specimens must be exposed to a Bunsen or Tirrill burner with a nominal ⅜-inch I.D. tube adjusted to give a flame of 1½ inches in height. The minimum flame temperature measured by a calibrated thermocouple pyrometer in the center of the flame must be 1550°F. Suitable precautions must be taken to avoid drafts. The flame must be applied for 30 seconds with one-third contacting the material at the center of the specimen and then removed. Flame time, glow time, and whether the flame penetrates (passes through) the specimen must be recorded.

(g) *Sixty-degree test.* A minimum of three specimens of each wire specification (make and size) must be tested. The specimen of wire or cable (including insulation) must be placed at an angle of 60 degrees with the horizontal in the cabinet specified in paragraph (c) of this appendix, with the cabinet door open during the test or placed within a chamber approximately 2 feet high x 1 foot x 1 foot, open at the top and at one vertical side (front), that allows sufficient flow of air for complete combustion but is free from drafts. The specimen must be parallel to and approximately 6 inches from the front of the chamber. The lower end of the specimen must be held rigidly clamped. The upper end of the specimen must pass over a pulley or rod and must have an appropriate weight attached to it so that the specimen is held tautly throughout the flammability test. The test specimen span between lower clamp and upper pulley or rod must be 24 inches and must be marked 8 inches from the lower end to indicate the central point for flame application. A flame from a Bunsen or Tirrill burner must be applied for 30 seconds at the test mark. The burner must be mounted underneath the test mark on the specimen, perpendicular to the specimen and at an angle of 30 degrees to the vertical plane of the specimen. The burner must have a nominal bore of three-eighths inch, and must be adjusted to provide a three-inch-high flame with an inner cone approximately one-third of the flame height. The minimum temperature of the hottest portion of the flame, as measured with a calibrated thermocouple pyrometer, may not be less than 1,750°F. The burner must be positioned so that the hottest portion of the flame is applied to the test mark on the wire. Flame time, burn length, and flaming time drippings, if any, must be recorded. The burn length determined in accordance with paragraph (h) of this appendix must be measured to the nearest one-tenth inch. Breaking of the wire specimen is not considered a failure.

(h) *Burn length.* Burn length is the distance from the original edge to the farthest evidence of damage to the test specimen due to flame impingement, including areas of partial or complete consumption, charring, or embrittlement, but not including areas sooted, stained, warped, or discolored, nor areas where material has shrunk or melted away from the heat source.

[Amdt. 23–23, 43 FR 50594, Oct. 30, 1978; Amdt. 23–34, 52 FR 1835, Jan. 15, 1987; 52 FR 34745, Sept. 14, 1987; Amdt. 23–49, 61 FR 5170, Feb. 9, 1996]

APPENDIX G TO PART 23
INSTRUCTIONS FOR CONTINUED AIRWORTHINESS

G23.1 GENERAL.

(a) This appendix specifies requirements for the preparation of Instructions for Continued Airworthiness as required by §23.1529.

(b) The Instructions for Continued Airworthiness for each airplane must include the Instructions for Continued Airworthiness for each engine and propeller (hereinafter designated 'products'), for each appliance required by this chapter, and any required information relating to the interface of those appliances and products with the airplane. If Instructions for Continued Airworthiness are not supplied by the manufacturer of an appliance or product installed in the airplane, the Instructions for Continued Airworthiness for the airplane must include the information essential to the continued airworthiness of the airplane.

(c) The applicant must submit to the FAA a program to show how changes to the Instructions for Continued Airworthiness made by the applicant or by the manufacturers of products and appliances installed in the airplane will be distributed.

G23.2 Format.

(a) The Instructions for Continued Airworthiness must be in the form of a manual or manuals as appropriate for the quantity of data to be provided.

(b) The format of the manual or manuals must provide for a practical arrangement.

G23.3 Content.

The contents of the manual or manuals must be prepared in the English language. The Instructions for Continued Airworthiness must contain the following manuals or sections, as appropriate, and information:

(a) *Airplane maintenance manual or section.*

(1) Introduction information that includes an explanation of the airplane's features and data to the extent necessary for maintenance or preventive maintenance.

(2) A description of the airplane and its systems and installations including its engines, propellers, and appliances.

(3) Basic control and operation information describing how the airplane components and systems are controlled and how they operate, including any special procedures and limitations that apply.

(4) Servicing information that covers details regarding servicing points, capacities of tanks, reservoirs, types of fluids to be used, pressures applicable to the various systems, location of access panels for inspection and servicing, locations of lubrication points, lubricants to be used, equipment required for servicing, tow instructions and limitations, mooring, jacking, and leveling information.

(b) *Maintenance instructions.*

(1) Scheduling information for each part of the airplane and its engines, auxiliary power units, propellers, accessories, instruments, and equipment that provides the recommended periods at which they should be cleaned, inspected, adjusted, tested, and lubricated, and the degree of inspection, the applicable wear tolerances, and work recommended at these periods. However, the applicant may refer to an accessory, instrument, or equipment manufacturer as the source of this information if the applicant shows that the item has an exceptionally high degree of complexity requiring specialized maintenance techniques, test equipment, or expertise. The recommended overhaul periods and necessary cross reference to the Airworthiness Limitations section of the manual must also be included. In addition, the applicant must include an inspection program that includes the frequency and extent of the inspections necessary to provide for the continued airworthiness of the airplane.

(2) Troubleshooting information describing probable malfunctions, how to recognize those malfunctions, and the remedial action for those malfunctions.

(3) Information describing the order and method of removing and replacing products and parts with any necessary precautions to be taken.

(4) Other general procedural instructions including procedures for system testing during ground running, symmetry checks, weighing and determining the center of gravity, lifting and shoring, and storage limitations.

(c) Diagrams of structural access plates and information needed to gain access for inspections when access plates are not provided.

(d) Details for the application of special inspection techniques including radiographic and ultrasonic testing where such processes are specified.

(e) Information needed to apply protective treatments to the structure after inspection.

(f) All data relative to structural fasteners such as identification, discard recommendations, and torque values.

(g) A list of special tools needed.

(h) In addition, for commuter category airplanes, the following information must be furnished:

(1) Electrical loads applicable to the various systems;

(2) Methods of balancing control surfaces;

(3) Identification of primary and secondary structures; and

(4) Special repair methods applicable to the airplane.

G23.4 Airworthiness Limitations Section.

The Instructions for Continued Airworthiness must contain a section titled Airworthiness Limitations that is segregated and clearly distinguishable from the rest of the document. This section must set forth each mandatory replacement time, structural inspection interval, and related structural inspection procedure required for type certification. If the Instructions for Continued Airworthiness consist of multiple documents, the section required by this paragraph must be included in the principal manual. This section must contain a legible statement in a prominent location that reads: "The Airworthiness Limitations section is FAA approved and specifies maintenance required under §§43.16 and 91.403 of the Federal Aviation Regulations unless an alternative program has been FAA approved."

[Amdt. 23–26, 45 FR 60171, Sept. 11, 1980; as amended by Amdt. 23–34, 52 FR 1835, Jan. 15, 1987; 52 FR 34745, Sept. 14, 1987; Amdt. 23–37, 54 FR 34329, Aug. 18, 1989]

Appendix H to Part 23

Installation of an Automatic Power Reserve (APR) System

H23.1 General.

(a) This appendix specifies requirements for installation of an APR engine power control system that automatically advances power or thrust on the operating engine(s) in the event any engine fails during takeoff.

(b) With the APR system and associated systems functioning normally, all applicable requirements (except as provided in this appendix) must be met without requiring any action by the crew to increase power or thrust.

H23.2 Definitions.

(a) *Automatic power reserve system* means the entire automatic system used only during takeoff, including all devices both mechanical and electrical that sense engine failure, transmit signals, actuate fuel controls or power levers on operating engines, including power sources, to achieve the scheduled power increase and furnish cockpit information on system operation.

(b) *Selected takeoff power,* notwithstanding the definition of "Takeoff Power" in Part 1 of the Federal Aviation Regulations, means the power obtained from each initial power setting approved for takeoff

(c) *Critical Time Interval*, as illustrated in figure H1, means that period starting at V_1 minus one second and ending at the intersection of the engine and APR failure flight path line with the minimum performance all engine flight path line. The engine and APR failure flight path line intersects the one-engine inoperative flight path line at 400 feet above the takeoff surface. The engine and APR failure flight path is based on the airplane's performance and must have a positive gradient of at least 0.5 percent at 400 feet above the takeoff surface.

FIGURE H1—CRITICAL TIME INTERVAL ILLUSTRATION

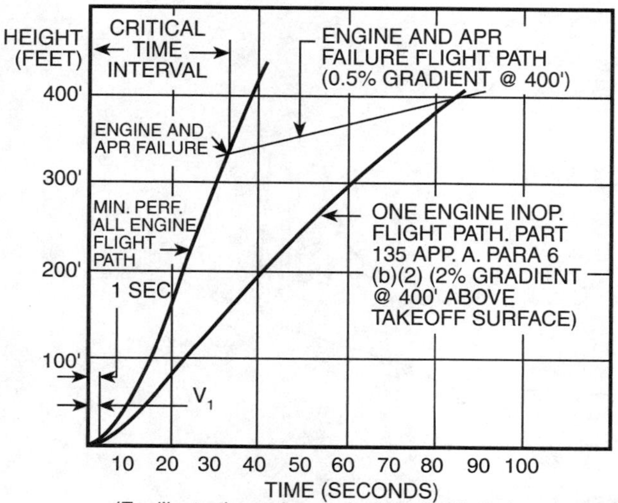

(For illustration only – typical for 120K climb speed)

H23.3 RELIABILITY AND PERFORMANCE REQUIREMENTS.

(a) It must be shown that, during the critical time interval, an APR failure that increases or does not affect power on either engine will not create a hazard to the airplane, or it must be shown that such failures are improbable.

(b) It must be shown that, during the critical time interval, there are no failure modes of the APR system that would result in a failure that will decrease the power on either engine or it must be shown that such failures are extremely improbable.

(c) It must be shown that, during the critical time interval, there will be no failure of the APR system in combination with an engine failure or it must be shown that such failures are extremely improbable.

(d) All applicable performance requirements must be met with an engine failure occurring at the most critical point during takeoff with the APR system functioning normally.

H23.4 POWER SETTING.

The selected takeoff power set on each engine at the beginning of the takeoff roll may not be less than—

(a) The power necessary to attain, at V_1, 90 percent of the maximum takeoff power approved for the airplane for the existing conditions;

(b) That required to permit normal operation of all safety-related systems and equipment that are dependent upon engine power or power lever position; and

(c) That shown to be free of hazardous engine response characteristics when power is advanced from the selected takeoff power level to the maximum approved takeoff power.

H23.5 POWERPLANT CONTROLS—GENERAL.

(a) In addition to the requirements of §23.1141, no single failure or malfunction (or probable combination thereof) of the APR, including associated systems, may cause the failure of any powerplant function necessary for safety.

(b) The APR must be designed to—

(1) Provide a means to verify to the flight crew before takeoff that the APR is in an operating condition to perform its intended function;

(2) Automatically advance power on the operating engines following an engine failure during takeoff to achieve the maximum attainable takeoff power without exceeding engine operating limits;

(3) Prevent deactivation of the APR by manual adjustment of the power levers following an engine failure;

(4) Provide a means for the flight crew to deactivate the automatic function. This means must be designed to prevent inadvertent deactivation; and

(5) Allow normal manual decrease or increase in power up to the maximum takeoff power approved for the airplane under the existing conditions through the use of power levers, as stated in §23.1141(c), except as provided under paragraph (c) of H23.5 of this appendix.

(c) For airplanes equipped with limiters that automatically prevent engine operating limits from being exceeded, other means may be used to increase the maximum level of power controlled by the power levers in the event of an APR failure. The means must be located on or forward of the power levers, must be easily identified and operated under all operating conditions by a single action of any pilot with the hand that is normally used to actuate the power levers, and must meet the requirements of §23.777(a), (b), and (c).

H23.6 POWERPLANT INSTRUMENTS.

In addition to the requirements of §23.1305:

(a) A means must be provided to indicate when the APR is in the armed or ready condition.

(b) If the inherent flight characteristics of the airplane do not provide warning that an engine has failed, a warning system independent of the APR must be provided to give the pilot a clear warning of any engine failure during takeoff.

(c) Following an engine failure at V_1 or above, there must be means for the crew to readily and quickly verify that the APR has operated satisfactorily.

[Docket 26344, 58 FR 18979, April 9, 1993]

Appendix I to Part 23
Seaplane Loads

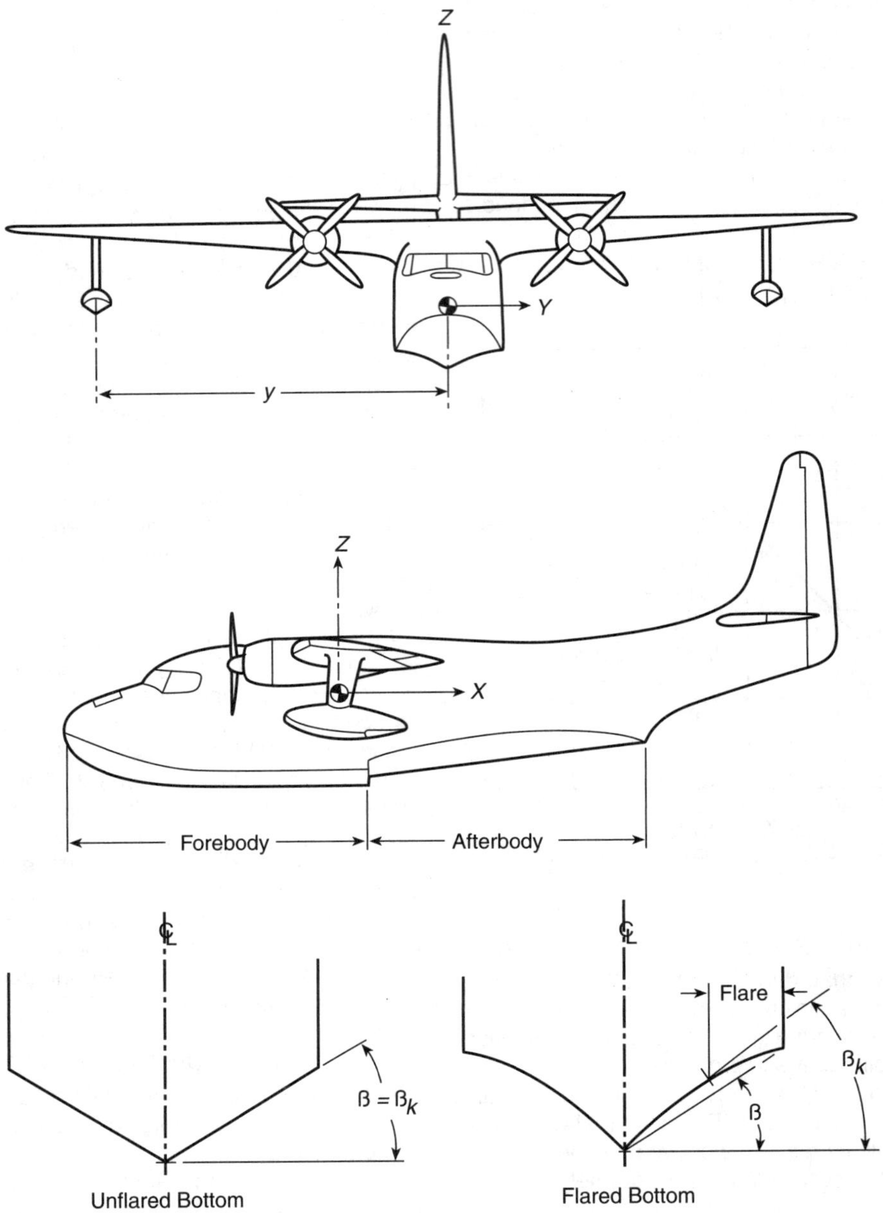

Figure 1. Pictorial definition of angles, dimensions, and directions on a seaplane.

APPENDIX I TO PART 23

(CONTINUED)

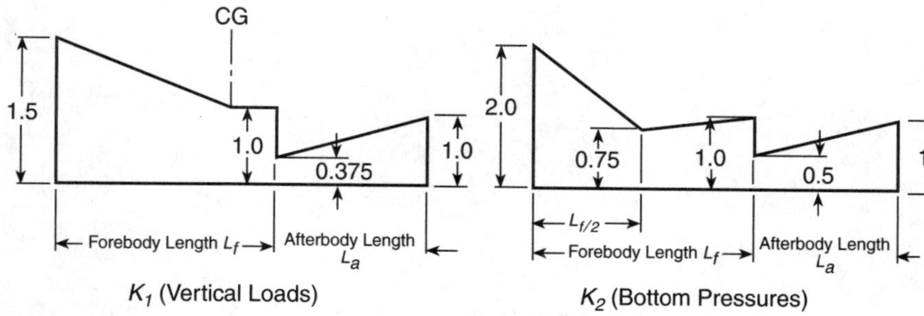

Figure 2. Hull station weighing factor.

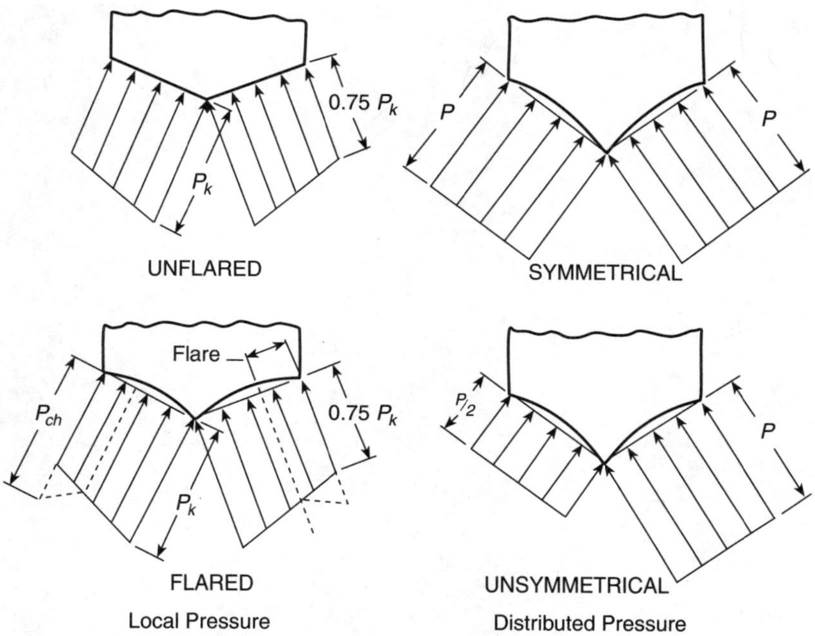

Figure 3. Transverse pressure distributions.

[Amdt. 23–45, 58 FR 42167, Aug. 6, 1993; 58 FR 51970, Oct. 5, 1993]

PART 27

AIRWORTHINESS STANDARDS: NORMAL CATEGORY ROTORCRAFT

Subpart A—General

Sec.
27.1 Applicability.
27.2 Special retroactive requirements.

Subpart B—Flight

GENERAL

27.21 Proof of compliance.
27.25 Weight limits.
27.27 Center of gravity limits.
27.29 Empty weight and corresponding center of gravity.
27.31 Removable ballast.
27.33 Main rotor speed and pitch limits.

PERFORMANCE

27.45 General.
27.51 Takeoff.
27.65 Climb: all engines operating.
27.67 Climb: one engine inoperative.
27.71 Glide performance.
27.73 Performance at minimum operating speed.
27.75 Landing.
27.79 Limiting height-speed envelope.

FLIGHT CHARACTERISTICS

27.141 General.
27.143 Controllability and maneuverability.
27.151 Flight controls.
27.161 Trim control.
27.171 Stability: general.
27.173 Static longitudinal stability.
27.175 Demonstration of static longitudinal stability.
27.177 Static directional stability.

GROUND AND WATER HANDLING CHARACTERISTICS

27.231 General.
27.235 Taxiing condition.
27.239 Spray characteristics.
27.241 Ground resonance.

MISCELLANEOUS FLIGHT REQUIREMENTS

27.251 Vibration.

Subpart C—Strength Requirements

GENERAL

27.301 Loads.
27.303 Factor of safety.
27.305 Strength and deformation.
27.307 Proof of structure.
27.309 Design limitations.

FLIGHT LOADS

27.321 General.
27.337 Limit maneuvering load factor.
27.339 Resultant limit maneuvering loads.
27.341 Gust loads.
27.351 Yawing conditions.
27.361 Engine torque.

CONTROL SURFACE AND SYSTEM LOADS

27.391 General.
27.395 Control system.
27.397 Limit pilot forces and torques.
27.399 Dual control system.
27.411 Ground clearance: tall rotor guard.
27.427 Unsymmetrical loads.

GROUND LOADS

27.471 General.
27.473 Ground loading conditions and assumptions.
27.475 Tires and shock absorbers.
27.477 Landing gear arrangement.
27.479 Level landing conditions.
27.481 Tail-down landing conditions.
27.483 One-wheel landing conditions.
27.485 Lateral drift landing conditions.
27.493 Braked roll conditions.
27.497 Ground loading conditions: Landing gear with tail wheels.
27.501 Ground loading conditions: landing gear with skids.
27.505 Ski landing conditions.

WATER LOADS

27.521 Float landing conditions.

MAIN COMPONENT REQUIREMENTS

27.547 Main rotor structure.
27.549 Fuselage, landing gear, and rotor pylon structures.

EMERGENCY LANDING CONDITIONS

27.561 General.
27.562 Emergency landing dynamic conditions.
27.563 Structural ditching provisions.

FATIGUE EVALUATION

27.571 Fatigue evaluation of flight structure.

Subpart D—Design and Construction

GENERAL

27.601 Design.
27.602 Critical parts.
27.603 Materials.
27.605 Fabrication methods.
27.607 Fasteners.
27.609 Protection of structure.
27.610 Lightning and static electricity protection.
27.611 Inspection provisions.
27.613 Material strength properties and design values.
27.619 Special factors.
27.621 Casting factors.

27.623 Bearing factors.
27.625 Fitting factors.
27.629 Flutter.

Rotors

27.653 Pressure venting and drainage of rotor blades.
27.659 Mass balance.
27.661 Rotor blade clearance.
27.663 Ground resonance prevention means.

Control Systems

27.671 General.
27.672 Stability augmentation, automatic, and power-operated systems.
27.673 Primary flight control.
27.674 Interconnected controls.
27.675 Stops.
27.679 Control system locks.
27.681 Limit load static tests.
27.683 Operation tests.
27.685 Control system details.
27.687 Spring devices.
27.691 Autorotation control mechanism.
27.695 Power boost and power-operated control system.

Landing Gear

27.723 Shock absorption tests.
27.725 Limit drop test.
27.727 Reserve energy absorption drop test.
27.729 Retracting mechanism.
27.731 Wheels.
27.733 Tires.
27.735 Brakes.
27.737 Skis.

Floats and Hulls

27.751 Main float buoyancy.
27.753 Main float design.
27.755 Hulls.

Personnel and Cargo Accommodations

27.771 Pilot compartment.
27.773 Pilot compartment view.
27.775 Windshields and windows.
27.777 Cockpit controls.
27.779 Motion and effect of cockpit controls.
27.783 Doors.
27.785 Seats, berths, litters, safety belts, and harnesses.
27.787 Cargo and baggage compartments.
27.801 Ditching.
27.805 Flight crew emergency exits.
27.807 Emergency exits.
27.831 Ventilation.
27.833 Heaters.

Fire Protection

27.853 Compartment interiors.
27.855 Cargo and baggage compartments.
27.859 Heating systems.
27.861 Fire protection of structure, controls, and other parts.
27.863 Flammable fluid fire protection.

External Loads

27.865 External loads.

Miscellaneous

27.871 Leveling marks.
27.873 Ballast provisions.

Subpart E — Powerplant

General

27.901 Installation.
27.903 Engines.
27.907 Engine vibration.

Rotor Drive System

27.917 Design.
27.921 Rotor brake.
27.923 Rotor drive system and control mechanism tests.
27.927 Additional tests.
27.931 Shafting critical speed.
27.935 Shafting joints.
27.939 Turbine engine operating characteristics.

Fuel System

27.951 General.
27.952 Fuel system crash resistance.
27.953 Fuel system independence.
27.954 Fuel system lightning protection.
27.955 Fuel flow.
27.959 Unusable fuel supply.
27.961 Fuel system hot weather operation.
27.963 Fuel tanks: general.
27.965 Fuel tank tests.
27.967 Fuel tank installation.
27.969 Fuel tank expansion space.
27.971 Fuel tank sump.
27.973 Fuel tank filler connection.
27.975 Fuel tank vents.
27.977 Fuel tank outlet.

Fuel System Components

27.991 Fuel pumps.
27.993 Fuel system lines and fittings.
27.995 Fuel valves.
27.997 Fuel strainer or filter.
27.999 Fuel system drains.

OIL SYSTEM

27.1011 Engines: General.
27.1013 Oil tanks.
27.1015 Oil tank tests.
27.1017 Oil lines and fittings.
27.1019 Oil strainer or filter.
27.1021 Oil system drains.
27.1027 Transmissions and gearboxes: General.

COOLING

27.1041 General.
27.1043 Cooling tests.
27.1045 Cooling test procedures.

INDUCTION SYSTEM

27.1091 Air induction.
27.1093 Induction system icing protection.

EXHAUST SYSTEM

27.1121 General.
27.1123 Exhaust piping.

POWERPLANT CONTROLS AND ACCESSORIES

27.1141 Powerplant controls: general.
27.1143 Engine controls.
27.1145 Ignition switches.
27.1147 Mixture controls.
27.1151 Rotor brake controls.
27.1163 Powerplant accessories.

POWERPLANT FIRE PROTECTION

27.1183 Lines, fittings, and components.
27.1185 Flammable fluids.
27.1187 Ventilation and drainage.
27.1189 Shutoff means.
27.1191 Firewalls.
27.1193 Cowling and engine compartment covering.
27.1194 Other surfaces.
27.1195 Fire detector systems.

Subpart F—Equipment

GENERAL

27.1301 Function and installation.
27.1303 Flight and navigation instruments.
27.1305 Powerplant instruments.
27.1307 Miscellaneous equipment.
27.1309 Equipment, systems, and installations.

INSTRUMENTS: INSTALLATION

27.1321 Arrangement and visibility.
27.1322 Warning, caution, and advisory lights.
27.1323 Airspeed indicating system.
27.1325 Static pressure systems.
27.1327 Magnetic direction indicator.
27.1329 Automatic pilot system.
27.1335 Flight director systems.
27.1337 Powerplant instruments.

ELECTRICAL SYSTEMS AND EQUIPMENT

27.1351 General.
27.1353 Storage battery design and installation.
27.1357 Circuit protective devices.
27.1361 Master switch.
27.1365 Electric cables.
27.1367 Switches.

LIGHTS

27.1381 Instrument lights.
27.1383 Landing lights.
27.1385 Position light system installation.
27.1387 Position light system dihedral angles.
27.1389 Position light distribution and intensities.
27.1391 Minimum intensities in the horizontal plane of forward and rear position lights.
27.1393 Minimum intensities in any vertical plane of forward and rear position lights.
27.1395 Maximum intensities in overlapping beams of forward and rear position lights.
27.1397 Color specifications.
27.1399 Riding light.
27.1401 Anticollision light system.

SAFETY EQUIPMENT

27.1411 General.
27.1413 Safety belts.
27.1415 Ditching equipment.
27.1419 Ice protection.
27.1435 Hydraulic systems.
27.1457 Cockpit voice recorders.
26.1459 Flight recorders.
27.1461 Equipment containing high energy rotors.

Subpart G—Operating Limitations and Information

27.1501 General.

OPERATING LIMITATIONS

27.1503 Airspeed limitations: general.
27.1505 Never-exceed speed.
27.1509 Rotor speed.
27.1519 Weight and center of gravity.
27.1521 Powerplant limitations.
27.1523 Minimum flight crew.
27.1525 Kinds of operations.
27.1527 Maximum operating altitude.
27.1529 Instructions for Continued Airworthiness.

MARKINGS AND PLACARDS

27.1541 General.
27.1543 Instrument markings: general.
27.1545 Airspeed indicator.
27.1547 Magnetic direction indicator.
27.1549 Powerplant instruments.
27.1551 Oil quantity indicator.
27.1553 Fuel quantity indicator.
27.1555 Control markings.
27.1557 Miscellaneous markings and placards.
27.1559 Limitations placard.
27.1561 Safety equipment.
27.1565 Tail rotor.

ROTORCRAFT FLIGHT MANUAL AND APPROVED MANUAL MATERIAL

27.1581 General.
27.1583 Operating limitations.
27.1585 Operating procedures.
27.1587 Performance information.
27.1589 Loading information.

Appendix A to Part 27—Instructions for Continued Airworthiness
Appendix B to Part 27—Airworthiness Criteria for Helicopter Instrument Flight
Appendix C to Part 27—Criteria for Category A

Authority: 49 U.S.C. 106(g), 40113, 44701–44702, 44704.

Source: Docket No. 5074, 29 FR 15695, Nov. 24, 1964, unless otherwise noted.

Subpart A—General

§27.1 Applicability.

(a) This part prescribes airworthiness standards for the issue of type certificates, and changes to those certificates, for normal category rotorcraft with maximum weights of 7,000 pounds or less and nine or less passenger seats.

(b) Each person who applies under Part 21 for such a certificate or change must show compliance with the applicable requirements of this part.

(c) Multiengine rotorcraft may be type certificated as Category A provided the requirements referenced in appendix C of this part are met.

[Docket No. 5074, 29 FR 15695, Nov. 24, 1964; as amended by Amdt. 27–33, 61 FR 21906, May 10, 1996; Amdt. 27–37, 64 FR 45094, Aug. 18, 1999]

§27.2 Special retroactive requirements.

(a) For each rotorcraft manufactured after September 16, 1992, each applicant must show that each occupant's seat is equipped with a safety belt and shoulder harness that meets the requirements of paragraphs (a), (b), and (c) of this section.

(1) Each occupant's seat must have a combined safety belt and shoulder harness with a single-point release. Each pilot's combined safety belt and shoulder harness must allow each pilot, when seated with safety belt and shoulder harness fastened, to perform all functions necessary for flight operations. There must be a means to secure belts and harnesses, when not in use, to prevent interference with the operation of the rotorcraft and with rapid egress in an emergency.

(2) Each occupant must be protected from serious head injury by a safety belt plus a shoulder harness that will prevent the head from contacting any injurious object.

(3) The safety belt and shoulder harness must meet the static and dynamic strength requirements, if applicable, specified by the rotorcraft type certification basis.

(4) For purposes of this section, the date of manufacture is either—

(i) The date the inspection acceptance records, or equivalent, reflect that the rotorcraft is complete and meets the FAA-Approved Type Design Data; or

(ii) The date the foreign civil airworthiness authority certifies that the rotorcraft is complete and issues an original standard airworthiness certificate, or equivalent, in that country.

(b) For rotorcraft with a certification basis established prior to October 18, 1999—

(1) The maximum passenger seat capacity may be increased to eight or nine provided the applicant shows compliance with all the airworthiness requirements of this part in effect on October 18, 1999.

(2) The maximum weight may be increased to greater than 6,000 pounds provided—

(i) The number of passenger seats is not increased above the maximum number certificated on October 18, 1999; or

(ii) The applicant shows compliance with all of the airworthiness requirements of this part in effect on October 18, 1999.

[Docket No. 26078, 58 FR 41051, Aug. 16, 1991; as amended by Amdt. 27–37, 64 FR 45094, Aug. 18, 1999]

Subpart B—Flight

GENERAL

§27.21 Proof of compliance.

Each requirement of this subpart must be met at each appropriate combination of weight and center of gravity within the range of loading conditions for which certification is requested. This must be shown—

(a) By tests upon a rotorcraft of the type for which certification is requested, or by calculations based on, and equal in accuracy to, the results of testing; and

(b) By systematic investigation of each required combination of weight and center of gravity if compliance cannot be reasonably inferred from combinations investigated.

[Docket No. 5074, 29 FR 15695, Nov. 24, 1964; as amended by Amdt. 27–21, 49 FR 44432, Nov. 6, 1984]

§27.25 Weight limits.

(a) *Maximum weight.* The maximum weight (the highest weight at which compliance with each applicable requirement of this part is shown) must be established so that it is—

(1) Not more than—

(i) The highest weight selected by the applicant;

(ii) The design maximum (the highest weight at which compliance with each applicable structural loading condition of this part is shown); or

(iii) The highest weight at which compliance with each applicable flight requirement of this part is shown; and

(2) Not less than the sum of—

(i) The empty weight determined under §27.29; and

(ii) The weight of usable fuel appropriate to the intended operation with full payload;

(iii) The weight of full oil capacity; and

(iv) For each seat, an occupant weight of 170 pounds or any lower weight for which certification is requested.

(b) *Minimum weight.* The minimum weight (the lowest weight at which compliance with each applicable requirement of this part is shown) must be established so that it is—

(1) Not more than the sum of—

(i) The empty weight determined under §27.29; and

(ii) The weight of the minimum crew necessary to operate the rotorcraft, assuming for each crewmember a weight no more than 170 pounds, or any lower weight selected by the applicant or included in the loading instructions; and

(2) Not less than—

(i) The lowest weight selected by the applicant;

(ii) The design minimum weight (the lowest weight at which compliance with each applicable structural loading condition of this part is shown); or

(iii) The lowest weight at which compliance with each applicable flight requirement of this part is shown.

(c) *Total weight with jettisonable external load.* A total weight for the rotorcraft with a jettisonable external load attached that is greater than the maximum weight established under paragraph (a) of this section may be established for any rotorcraft-load combination if—

(1) The rotorcraft-load combination does not include human external cargo,

(2) Structural component approval for external load operations under either §27.865 or under equivalent operational standards is obtained,

(3) The portion of the total weight that is greater than the maximum weight established under paragraph (a) of this section is made up only of the weight of all or part of the jettisonable external load,

(4) Structural components of the rotorcraft are shown to comply with the applicable structural requirements of this part under the increased loads and stresses caused by the weight increase over that established under paragraph (a) of this section, and

(5) Operation of the rotorcraft at a total weight greater than the maximum certificated weight established under paragraph (a) of this section is limited by appropriate operating limitations under §27.865(a) and (d) of this part.

(Secs. 313(a), 601, 603, 604, and 605 of the Federal Aviation Act of 1958 (49 U.S.C. 1354(a), 1421, 1423, 1424, and 1425); and sec. 6(c) of the Dept. of Transportation Act (49 U.S.C. 1655(c)))

[Docket No. 5074, 29 FR 15695, Nov. 29, 1964; as amended by Amdt. 27–11, 41 FR 55468, Dec. 20, 1976; Amdt. 27–42, 43 FR 2324, Jan. 16, 1978; Amdt. 27–36, 64 FR 43019, Aug. 6, 1999]

§27.27 Center of gravity limits.

The extreme forward and aft centers of gravity and, where critical, the extreme lateral centers of gravity must be established for each weight established under §27.25. Such an extreme may not lie beyond—

(a) The extremes selected by the applicant;

(b) The extremes within which the structure is proven; or

(c) The extremes within which compliance with the applicable flight requirements is shown.

[Docket No. 5074, 29 FR 15695, Nov. 24, 1964; as amended by Amdt. 27–2, 33 FR 962, Jan. 26, 1968]

§27.29 Empty weight and corresponding center of gravity.

(a) The empty weight and corresponding center of gravity must be determined by weighing the rotorcraft without the crew and payload, but with—

(1) Fixed ballast;

(2) Unusable fuel; and

(3) Full operating fluids, including—

(i) Oil;

(ii) Hydraulic fluid; and

(iii) Other fluids required for normal operation of rotorcraft systems, except water intended for injection in the engines.

(b) The condition of the rotorcraft at the time of determining empty weight must be one that is well defined and can be easily repeated, particularly with respect to the weights of fuel, oil, coolant, and installed equipment.

(Secs. 313(a), 601, 603, 604, and 605 of the Federal Aviation Act of 1958 (49 U.S.C. 1354(a), 1421, 1423, 1424, and 1425); and sec. 6(c) of the Dept. of Transportation Act (49 U.S.C. 1655(c)))

[Docket No. 5074, 29 FR 15695, Nov. 24, 1964; as amended by Amdt. 27–14, 43 FR 2324, Jan. 16, 1978]

§27.31 Removable ballast.

Removable ballast may be used in showing compliance with the flight requirements of this subpart.

§27.33 Main rotor speed and pitch limits.

(a) *Main rotor speed limits.* A range of main rotor speeds must be established that—

(1) With power on, provides adequate margin to accommodate the variations in rotor speed occurring in any appropriate maneuver, and is consistent with the kind of governor or synchronizer used; and

(2) With power off, allows each appropriate autorotative maneuver to be performed throughout the ranges of airspeed and weight for which certification is requested.

(b) *Normal main rotor high pitch limits (power on).* For rotorcraft, except helicopters required to have a main rotor low speed warning under paragraph (e) of this section. It must be shown, with power on and without exceeding approved engine maximum limitations, that main rotor speeds substantially less than the minimum approved main rotor speed will not occur under any sustained flight condition. This must be met by—

(1) Appropriate setting of the main rotor high pitch stop;

(2) Inherent rotorcraft characteristics that make unsafe low main rotor speeds unlikely; or

(3) Adequate means to warn the pilot of unsafe main rotor speeds.

(c) *Normal main rotor low pitch limits (power off).* It must be shown, with power off, that—

(1) The normal main rotor low pitch limit provides sufficient rotor speed, in any autorotative condition, under the most critical combinations of weight and airspeed; and

(2) It is possible to prevent overspeeding of the rotor without exceptional piloting skill.

(d) *Emergency high pitch.* If the main rotor high pitch stop is set to meet paragraph (b)(1) of this section, and if that stop cannot be exceeded inadvertently, additional pitch may be made available for emergency use.

(e) *Main rotor low speed warning for helicopters.* For each single engine helicopter, and each multiengine helicopter that does not have an approved device that automatically increases power on the operating engines when one engine fails, there must be a main rotor low speed warning which meets the following requirements:

(1) The warning must be furnished to the pilot in all flight conditions, including power-on and power-off flight, when the speed of a main rotor approaches a value that can jeopardize safe flight.

(2) The warning may be furnished either through the inherent aerodynamic qualities of the helicopter or by a device.

(3) The warning must be clear and distinct under all conditions, and must be clearly distinguishable from all other warnings. A visual device that requires the attention of the crew within the cockpit is not acceptable by itself.

(4) If a warning device is used, the device must automatically deactivate and reset when the low-speed condition is corrected. If the device has an audible warning, it must also be equipped with a means for the pilot to manually silence the audible warning before the low-speed condition is corrected.

(Secs. 313(a), 601, 603, 604, and 605 of the Federal Aviation Act of 1958 (49 U.S.C. 1354(a) 1421, 1423, 1424, and 1425); and sec. 6(c) of the Dept. of Transportation Act (49 U.S.C. 1655(c)))

[Docket No. 5074, 29 FR 15695, Nov. 24, 1964; as amended by Amdt. 27–2, 33 FR 962, Jan. 26, 1968; Amdt. 27–14, 43 FR 2324, Jan. 16, 1978]

PERFORMANCE

§27.45 General.

(a) Unless otherwise prescribed, the performance requirements of this subpart must be met for still air and a standard atmosphere.

(b) The performance must correspond to the engine power available under the particular ambient atmospheric conditions, the particular flight condition, and the relative humidity specified in paragraphs (d) or (e) of this section, as appropriate.

(c) The available power must correspond to engine power, not exceeding the approved power, less—

(1) Installation losses; and

(2) The power absorbed by the accessories and services appropriate to the particular ambient atmospheric conditions and the particular flight condition.

(d) For reciprocating engine-powered rotorcraft, the performance, as affected by engine power, must be based on a relative humidity of 80 percent in a standard atmosphere.

(e) For turbine engine-powered rotorcraft, the performance, as affected by engine power, must be based on a relative humidity of—

(1) 80 percent, at and below standard temperature; and

(2) 34 percent, at and above standard temperature plus 50 degrees F. Between these two temperatures, the relative humidity must vary linearly.

(f) For turbine-engine-powered rotorcraft, a means must be provided to permit the pilot to determine prior to takeoff that each engine is capable of developing the power necessary to achieve the applicable rotorcraft performance prescribed in this subpart.

(Secs. 313(a), 601, 603, 604, and 605 of the Federal Aviation Act of 1958 (49 U.S.C. 1354(a) 1421, 1423, 1424, and 1425); and sec. 6(c) of the Dept. of Transportation Act (49 U.S.C. 1655(c)))

[Docket No. 5074, 29 FR 15695, Nov. 24, 1964; as amended by Amdt. 27–14, 43 FR 2324, Jan. 16, 1978; Amdt. 27–21, 49 FR 44432, Nov. 6 1984]

§27.51 Takeoff.

(a) The takeoff, with takeoff power and r.p.m., and with the extreme forward center of gravity—

(1) May not require exceptional piloting skill or exceptionally favorable conditions; and

(2) Must be made in such a manner that a landing can be made safely at any point along the flight path if an engine fails.

(b) Paragraph (a) of this section must be met throughout the ranges of—

(1) Altitude, from standard sea level conditions to the maximum altitude capability of the rotorcraft, or 7,000 feet, whichever is less; and

(2) Weight, from the maximum weight (at sea level) to each lesser weight selected by the applicant for each altitude covered by paragraph (b)(1) of this section.

§27.65 Climb: all engines operating.

(a) For rotorcraft other than helicopters—

(1) The steady rate of climb, at V_Y must be determined—

(i) With maximum continuous power on each engine;

(ii) With the landing gear retracted; and

(iii) For the weights, altitudes, and temperatures for which certification is requested; and

(2) The climb gradient, at the rate of climb determined in accordance with paragraph (a)(1) of this section, must be either—

(i) At least 1:10 if the horizontal distance required to take off and climb over a 50-foot obstacle is determined for each weight, altitude, and temperature within the range for which certification is requested; or

(ii) At least 1:6 under standard sea level conditions.

(b) Each helicopter must meet the following requirements:

(1) V_Y must be determined—

(i) For standard sea level conditions;

(ii) At maximum weight; and

(iii) With maximum continuous power on each engine.

(2) The steady rate of climb must be determined—

(i) At the climb speed selected by the applicant at or below V_{NE};

(ii) Within the range from sea level up to the maximum altitude for which certification is requested;

(iii) For the weights and temperatures that correspond to the altitude range set forth in paragraph (b)(2)(ii) of this section and for which certification is requested; and

(iv) With maximum continuous power on each engine.

(Secs. 313(a), 601, 603, 604, and 605 of the Federal Aviation Act of 1958 (49 U.S.C. 1354(a), 1421, 1423, 1424, and 1425); and sec. 6(c) of the Dept. of Transportation Act (49 U.S.C. 1655(c)))

[Docket No. 5074, 29 FR 15695, Nov. 24, 1964; as amended by Amdt. 27–14, 43 FR 2324, Jan. 16, 1978; Amdt. 27–33, 61 FR 21907, May 10, 1996]

§27.67 Climb: one engine inoperative.

For multiengine helicopters, the steady rate of climb (or descent), at V_Y (or at the speed for minimum rate of descent), must be determined with—

(a) Maximum weight;

(b) The critical engine inoperative and the remaining engines at either—

(1) Maximum continuous power and, for helicopters for which certification for the use of 30-minute OEI power is requested, at 30-minute OEI power; or

(2) Continuous OEI power for helicopters for which certification for the use of continuous OEI power is requested.

(Secs. 313(a), 601, 603, 604, and 605 of the Federal Aviation Act of 1958 (49 U.S.C. 1354(a), 1421, 1423, 1424, and 1425); and sec. 6(c) of the Dept. of Transportation Act (49 U.S.C. 1655(c)))

[Docket No 5074, 29 FR 15695, Nov. 24, 1964; as amended by Amdt. 27–23, 53 FR 34210, Sept. 2 1988]

§27.71 Glide performance.

For single-engine helicopters and multiengine helicopters that do not meet the Category A engine isolation requirements of Part 29 of this chapter, the minimum rate of descent airspeed and the best angle-of-glide airspeed must be determined in autorotation at—

(a) Maximum weight; and

(b) Rotor speed(s) selected by the applicant.

[Docket No. 5074, 29 FR 15695, Nov. 24, 1964; as amended by Amdt. 27–21, 49 FR 44433, Nov. 6, 1984]

§27.73 Performance at minimum operating speed.

(a) For helicopters—

(1) The hovering ceiling must be determined over the ranges of weight, altitude, and temperature for which certification is requested, with—

(i) Takeoff power;

(ii) The landing gear extended; and

(iii) The helicopter in ground effect at a height consistent with normal takeoff procedures; and

(2) The hovering ceiling determined under paragraph (a)(1) of this section must be at least—

(i) For reciprocating engine powered helicopters, 4,000 feet at maximum weight with a standard atmosphere; or

(ii) For turbine engine powered helicopters, 2,500 feet pressure altitude at maximum weight at a temperature of standard +40 degrees F.

(b) For rotorcraft other than helicopters, the steady rate of climb at the minimum operating speed must be determined, over the ranges of weight, altitude, and temperature for which certification is requested, with—

(1) Takeoff power; and

(2) The landing gear extended.

§27.75 Landing.

(a) The rotorcraft must be able to be landed with no excessive vertical acceleration, no tendency to bounce, nose over, ground loop, porpoise, or water loop, and without exceptional piloting skill or exceptionally favorable conditions, with—

(1) Approach or glide speeds appropriate to the type of rotorcraft and selected by the applicant;

(2) The approach and landing made with—

(i) Power off, for single-engine rotorcraft; and

(ii) For multiengine rotorcraft, one engine inoperative and with each operating engine within approved operating limitations; and

(3) The approach and landing entered from steady autorotation.

(b) Multiengine rotorcraft must be able to be landed safely after complete power failure under normal operating conditions.

[Docket No. 5074, 29 FR 15695, Nov. 24, 1964; as amended by Amdt. 27–14, 43 FR 2329, Jan. 16, 1978]

§27.79 Limiting height-speed envelope.

(a) If there is any combination of height and forward speed (including hover) under which a safe landing cannot be made under the applicable power failure condition in paragraph (b) of this section, a limiting height-speed envelope must be established (including all pertinent information) for that condition, throughout the ranges of—

(1) Altitude, from standard sea level conditions to the maximum altitude capability of the rotorcraft, or 7,000 feet, whichever is less; and

(2) Weight, from the maximum weight (at sea level) to the lesser weight selected by the applicant for each altitude covered by paragraph (a)(1) of this section. For helicopters, the weight at altitudes above sea level may not be less than the maximum weight or the highest weight allowing hovering out of ground effect which is lower.

(b) The applicable power failure conditions are—

(1) For single-engine helicopters, full autorotation;

(2) For multiengine helicopters, one engine inoperative (where engine isolation features insure continued operation of the remaining engines), and the remaining engines at the greatest power for which certification is requested, and

(3) For other rotorcraft, conditions appropriate to the type.

(Secs. 313(a), 601, 603, 604, Federal Aviation Act of 1958 (49 U.S.C. 1354(a), 1421, 1423, 1424), sec. 6(c), Dept. of Transportation Act (49 U.S.C. 1655(c)))

[Docket No. 5074, 29 FR 15695, Nov. 24, 1964; as amended by Amdt. 27–14 43 FR 2324, Jan. 16, 1978; Amdt 27–21, 49 FR 44433, Nov. 6, 1984]

FLIGHT CHARACTERISTICS

§27.141 General.

The rotorcraft must—

(a) Except as specifically required in the applicable section, meet the flight characteristics requirements of this subpart—

(1) At the altitudes and temperatures expected in operation;

(2) Under any critical loading condition within the range of weights and centers of gravity for which certification is requested;

(3) For power-on operations, under any condition of speed, power, and rotor r.p.m. for which certification is requested; and

(4) For power-off operations, under any condition of speed and rotor r.p.m. for which certification is requested that is at-

tainable with the controls rigged in accordance with the approved rigging instructions and tolerances;

(b) Be able to maintain any required flight condition and make a smooth transition from any flight condition to any other flight condition without exceptional piloting skill, alertness, or strength, and without danger of exceeding the limit load factor under any operating condition probable for the type, including—

(1) Sudden failure of one engine, for multiengine rotorcraft meeting Transport Category A engine isolation requirements of Part 29 of this chapter;

(2) Sudden, complete power failure for other rotorcraft; and

(3) Sudden, complete control system failures specified in §27.695 of this part; and

(c) Have any additional characteristic required for night or instrument operation, if certification for those kinds of operation is requested. Requirements for helicopter instrument flight are contained in Appendix B of this part.

[Docket No. 5074, 29 FR 15695, Nov. 24, 1964; as amended by Amdt. 27–2, 33 FR 962, Jan. 26, 1968; Amdt. 27–11, 41 FR 55468, Dec. 20, 1976; Amdt. 27–19, 48 FR 4389, Jan. 31, 1983; Amdt. 27–21, 49 FR 44433, Nov. 6, 1984]

§27.143 Controllability and maneuverability.

(a) The rotorcraft must be safely controllable and maneuverable—

(1) During steady flight; and

(2) During any maneuver appropriate to the type, including—

(i) Takeoff;

(ii) Climb;

(iii) Level flight;

(iv) Turning flight;

(v) Glide;

(vi) Landing (power on and power off); and

(vii) Recovery to power-on flight from a balked autorotative approach.

(b) The margin of cyclic control must allow satisfactory roll and pitch control at V_{NE} with—

(1) Critical weight;

(2) Critical center of gravity;

(3) Critical rotor r.p.m.; and

(4) Power off (except for helicopters demonstrating compliance with paragraph (e) of this section) and power on.

(c) A wind velocity of not less than 17 knots must be established in which the rotorcraft can be operated without loss of control on or near the ground in any maneuver appropriate to the type (such as crosswind takeoffs, sideward flight, and rearward flight), with—

(1) Critical weight;

(2) Critical center of gravity;

(3) Critical rotor r.p.m.; and

(4) Altitude, from standard sea level conditions to the maximum altitude capability of the rotorcraft or 7,000 feet, whichever is less.

(d) The rotorcraft, after

(1) failure of one engine in the case of multiengine rotorcraft that meet Transport Category A engine isolation requirements, or

(2) complete engine failure in the case of other rotorcraft, must be controllable over the range of speeds and altitudes for which certification is requested when such power failure occurs with maximum continuous power and critical weight. No corrective action time delay for any condition following power failure may be less than—

(i) For the cruise condition, one second, or normal pilot reaction time (whichever is greater); and

(ii) For any other condition, normal pilot reaction time.

(e) For helicopters for which a V_{NE} (power-off) is established under §27.1505(c), compliance must be demonstrated with the following requirements with critical weight, critical center of gravity, and critical rotor r.p.m.:

(1) The helicopter must be safely slowed to V_{NE} (power-off), without exceptional pilot skill, after the last operating engine is made inoperative at power-on V_{NE}.

(2) At a speed of 1.1 V_{NE} (power-off), the margin of cyclic control must allow satisfactory roll and pitch control with power off.

(Secs. 313(a), 601, 603, 604, and 605 of the Federal Aviation Act of 1958 (49 U.S.C. 1354(a), 1421, 1423, 1424, and 1425); and sec. 6(c) of the Dept. of Transportation Act (49 U.S.C. 1655(c)))

[Docket No. 5074, 29 FR 15695, Nov. 24, 1964; as amended by Amdt. 27–2, 33 FR 963, Jan. 26, 1968; Amdt. 27–14, 43 FR 2325, Jan. 16, 1978; Amdt. 27–21, 49 FR 44433, Nov. 6, 1984]

§27.151 Flight controls.

(a) Longitudinal, lateral, directional, and collective controls may not exhibit excessive breakout force, friction, or preload.

(b) Control system forces and free play may not inhibit a smooth, direct rotorcraft response to control system input.

[Docket No. 5074, 29 FR 15695, Nov. 24, 1964; as amended by Amdt. 27–21, 49 FR 44433, Nov. 6, 1984]

§27.161 Trim control.

The trim control—

(a) Must trim any steady longitudinal, lateral, and collective control forces to zero in level flight at any appropriate speed; and

(b) May not introduce any undesirable discontinuities in control force gradients.

[Docket No. 5074, 29 FR 15695, Nov. 24, 1964; as amended by Amdt. 27–21, 49 FR 44433, Nov. 6, 1984]

§27.171 Stability: general.

The rotorcraft must be able to be flown, without undue pilot fatigue or strain, in any normal maneuver for a period of time as long as that expected in normal operation. At least three landings and takeoffs must be made during this demonstration.

§27.173 Static longitudinal stability.

(a) The longitudinal control must be designed so that a rearward movement of the control is necessary to obtain a speed less than the trim speed, and a forward movement of the control is necessary to obtain a speed more than the trim speed.

(b) With the throttle and collective pitch held constant during the maneuvers specified in §27.175 (a) through (c), the slope of the control position versus speed curve must be positive throughout the full range of altitude for which certification is requested.

(c) During the maneuver specified in §27.175(d), the longitudinal control position versus speed curve may have a negative slope within the specified speed range if the negative motion is not greater than 10 percent of total control travel.

[Docket No. 5074, 29 FR 15695, Nov. 24, 1964; as amended by Amdt. 27–21, 49 FR 44433, Nov. 6, 1984]

§27.175 Demonstration of static longitudinal stability.

(a) *Climb.* Static longitudinal stability must be shown in the climb condition at speeds from 0.85 V_Y to 1.2 V_Y, with—

(1) Critical weight;

(2) Critical center of gravity;

(3) Maximum continuous power;

(4) The landing gear retracted; and

(5) The rotorcraft trimmed at V_Y.

(b) *Cruise.* Static longitudinal stability must be shown in the cruise condition at speeds from 0.7 V_H or 0.7 V_{NE}, whichever is less, to 1.1 V_H or 1.1 V_{NE}, whichever is less, with—

(1) Critical weight;

(2) Critical center of gravity;

(3) Power for level flight at 0.9 V_H or 0.9 V_{NE}, whichever is less;

(4) The landing gear retracted; and

(5) The rotorcraft trimmed at 0.9 V_H or 0.9 V_{NE}, whichever is less.

(c) *Autorotation.* Static longitudinal stability must be shown in autorotation at airspeeds from 0.5 times the speed for minimum rate of descent to V_{NE}, or to 1.1 V_{NE} (power-off) if V_{NE} (power-off) is established under §27.1505(c), and with—

(1) Critical weight;

(2) Critical center of gravity;

(3) Power off;

(4) The landing gear—

(i) Retracted; and

(ii) Extended; and

(5) The rotorcraft trimmed at appropriate speeds found necessary by the Administrator to demonstrate stability throughout the prescribed speed range.

(d) *Hovering.* For helicopters, the longitudinal cyclic control must operate with the sense and direction of motion prescribed in §27.173 between the maximum approved rearward speed and a forward speed of 17 knots with—

(1) Critical weight;

(2) Critical center of gravity;

(3) Power required to maintain an approximate constant height in ground effect;

(4) The landing gear extended; and

(5) The helicopter trimmed for hovering.

(Secs. 313(a), 601, 603, 604, and 605 of the Federal Aviation Act of 1958 (49 U.S.C. 1354(a), 1421, 1423, 1424, and 1425); and sec. 6(c) of the Dept. of Transportation Act (49 U.S.C. 1655(c)))

[Docket No. 5074, 29 FR 15695, Nov. 24, 1964; as amended by Amdt. 27–2, 33 FR 963, Jan. 26, 1968; Amdt. 27–11, 41 FR 55468, Dec. 20, 1976; Amdt. 27–14, 43 FR 2325, Jan. 16, 1978; Amdt. 27–21, 49 FR 44433, Nov. 6, 1984; Amdt. 27–34, 62 FR 46173, Aug. 29, 1997]

§27.177 Static directional stability.

Static directional stability must be positive with throttle and collective controls held constant at the trim conditions specified in §27.175 (a) and (b). This must be shown by steadily increasing directional control deflection for sideslip angles up to ±10° from trim. Sufficient cues must accompany sideslip to alert the pilot when approaching sideslip limits.

[Docket No. 5074, 29 FR 15695, Nov. 24, 1964; as amended by Amdt. 27–21, 49 FR 44433, Nov. 6, 1984]

Ground and Water Handling Characteristics

§27.231 General.

The rotorcraft must have satisfactory ground and water handling characteristics, including freedom from uncontrollable tendencies in any condition expected in operation.

§27.235 Taxiing condition.

The rotorcraft must be designed to withstand the loads that would occur when the rotorcraft is taxied over the roughest ground that may reasonably be expected in normal operation.

§27.239 Spray characteristics.

If certification for water operation is requested, no spray characteristics during taxiing, takeoff, or landing may obscure the vision of the pilot or damage the rotors, propellers, or other parts of the rotorcraft.

§27.241 Ground resonance.

The rotorcraft may have no dangerous tendency to oscillate on the ground with the rotor turning.

Miscellaneous Flight Requirements

§27.251 Vibration.

Each part of the rotorcraft must be free from excessive vibration under each appropriate speed and power condition.

Subpart C— Strength Requirements

General

§27.301 Loads.

(a) Strength requirements are specified in terms of limit loads (the maximum loads to be expected in service) and ultimate loads (limit loads multiplied by prescribed factors of safety). Unless otherwise provided, prescribed loads are limit loads.

(b) Unless otherwise provided, the specified air, ground, and water loads must be placed in equilibrium with inertia forces, considering each item of mass in the rotorcraft. These loads must be distributed to closely approximate or conservatively represent actual conditions.

(c) If deflections under load would significantly change the distribution of external or internal loads, this redistribution must be taken into account.

§27.303 Factor of safety.

Unless otherwise provided, a factor of safety of 1.5 must be used. This factor applies to external and inertia loads unless its application to the resulting internal stresses is more conservative.

§27.305 Strength and deformation.

(a) The structure must be able to support limit loads without detrimental or permanent deformation. At any load up to limit loads, the deformation may not interfere with safe operation.

(b) The structure must be able to support ultimate loads without failure. This must be shown by—

(1) Applying ultimate loads to the structure in a static test for at least three seconds; or

(2) Dynamic tests simulating actual load application.

§27.307 Proof of structure.

(a) Compliance with the strength and deformation requirements of this subpart must be shown for each critical loading condition accounting for the environment to which the structure will be exposed in operation. Structural analysis (static or fatigue) may be used only if the structure conforms to those structures for which experience has shown this method to be reliable. In other cases, substantiating load tests must be made.

(b) Proof of compliance with the strength requirements of this subpart must include—

(1) Dynamic and endurance tests of rotors, rotor drives, and rotor controls;

(2) Limit load tests of the control system, including control surfaces;

(3) Operation tests of the control system;

(4) Flight stress measurement tests;

(5) Landing gear drop tests; and

(6) Any additional test required for new or unusual design features.

(Secs. 604, 605, 72 Stat. 778, 49 U.S.C. 1424, 1425)

[Docket No. 5074, 29 FR 15695, Nov. 24, 1964; as amended by Amdt. 27–3, 33 FR 14105, Sept. 18, 1968; Amdt. 27–26, 55 FR 7999, March 6, 1990]

§27.309 Design limitations.

The following values and limitations must be established to show compliance with the structural requirements of this subpart:

(a) The design maximum weight.

(b) The main rotor r.p.m. ranges power on and power off.

(c) The maximum forward speeds for each main rotor r.p.m. within the ranges determined under paragraph (b) of this section.

(d) The maximum rearward and sideward flight speeds.

(e) The center of gravity limits corresponding to the limitations determined under paragraphs (b), (c), and (d) of this section.

(f) The rotational speed ratios between each powerplant and each connected rotating component.

(g) The positive and negative limit maneuvering load factors.

FLIGHT LOADS

§27.321 General.

(a) The flight load factor must be assumed to act normal to the longitudinal axis of the rotorcraft, and to be equal in magnitude and opposite in direction to the rotorcraft inertia load factor at the center of gravity.

(b) Compliance with the flight load requirements of this subpart must be shown—

(1) At each weight from the design minimum weight to the design maximum weight; and

(2) With any practical distribution of disposable load within the operating limitations in the Rotorcraft Flight Manual.

[Docket No. 5074, 29 FR 15695, Nov. 24, 1964; as amended by Amdt. 27–11, 41 FR 55468, Dec. 20, 1976]

§27.337 Limit maneuvering load factor.

The rotorcraft must be designed for—

(a) A limit maneuvering load factor ranging from a positive limit of 3.5 to a negative limit of -1.0; or

(b) Any positive limit maneuvering load factor not less than 2.0 and any negative limit maneuvering load factor of not less than -0.5 for which—

(1) The probability of being exceeded is shown by analysis and flight tests to be extremely remote; and

(2) The selected values are appropriate to each weight condition between the design maximum and design minimum weights.

[Docket No. 5074, 29 FR 15695, Nov. 24, 1964; as amended by Amdt. 27–26, 55 FR 7999, March 6, 1990]

§27.339 Resultant limit maneuvering loads.

The loads resulting from the application of limit maneuvering load factors are assumed to act at the center of each rotor hub and at each auxiliary lifting surface, and to act in directions, and with distributions of load among the rotors and auxiliary lifting surfaces, so as to represent each critical maneuvering condition, including power-on and power-off flight with the maximum design rotor tip speed ratio. The rotor tip speed ratio is the ratio of the rotorcraft flight velocity component in the plane of the rotor disc to the rotational tip speed of the rotor blades, and is expressed as follows:

$$\mu = \frac{V \cos a}{\Omega R}$$

where—

V = The airspeed along flight path (f.p.s.);

a = The angle between the projection, in the plane of symmetry, of the axis of no feathering and a line perpendicular to the flight path (radians, positive when axis is pointing aft);

omega = The angular velocity of rotor (radians per second); and

R = The rotor radius (ft).

[Docket No. 5074, 29 FR 15695, Nov. 24, 1964; as amended by Amdt. 27–11, 41 FR 55469, Dec. 20, 1976]

§27.341 Gust loads.

The rotorcraft must be designed to withstand, at each critical airspeed including hovering, the loads resulting from a vertical gust of 30 feet per second.

§27.351 Yawing conditions.

(a) Each rotorcraft must be designed for the loads resulting from the maneuvers specified in paragraphs (b) and (c) of this section with—

(1) Unbalanced aerodynamic moments about the center of gravity which the aircraft reacts to in a rational or conservative manner considering the principal masses furnishing the reacting inertia forces; and

(2) Maximum main rotor speed.

(b) To produce the load required in paragraph (a) of this section, in unaccelerated flight with zero yaw, at forward speeds from zero up to 0.6 V_{NE}—

(1) Displace the cockpit directional control suddenly to the maximum deflection limited by the control stops or by the maximum pilot force specified in §27.397(a);

(2) Attain a resulting sideslip angle or 90°, whichever is less; and

(3) Return the directional control suddenly to neutral.

(c) To produce the load required in paragraph (a) of this section, in unaccelerated flight with zero yaw, at forward speeds from 0.6 V_{NE} up to V_{NE} or V_H, whichever is less—

(1) Displace the cockpit directional control suddenly to the maximum deflection limited by the control stops or by the maximum pilot force specified in §27.397(a);

(2) Attain a resulting sideslip angle or 15°, whichever is less, at the lesser speed of V_{NE} or V_H;

(3) Vary the sideslip angles of paragraphs (b)(2) and (c)(2) of this section directly with speed; and

(4) Return the directional control suddenly to neutral.

[Docket No. 5074, 29 FR 15695, Nov. 24, 1964; as amended by Amdt. 27–26, 55 FR 7999, March 6, 1990; Amdt. 27–34, 62 FR 46173, Aug. 29, 1997]

§27.361 Engine torque.

(a) For turbine engines, the limit torque may not be less than the highest of—

(1) The mean torque for maximum continuous power multiplied by 1.25;

(2) The torque required by §27.923;

(3) The torque required by §27.927; or

(4) The torque imposed by sudden engine stoppage due to malfunction or structural failure (such as compressor jamming).

(b) For reciprocating engines, the limit torque may not be less than the mean torque for maximum continuous power multiplied by—

(1) 1.33, for engines with five or more cylinders; and

(2) Two, three, and four, for engines with four, three, and two cylinders, respectively.

[Docket No. 5074, 29 FR 15695, Nov. 24, 1964; as amended by Amdt. 27–23, 53 FR 34210, Sept. 2, 1988]

Control Surface and System Loads

§27.391 General.

Each auxiliary rotor, each fixed or movable stabilizing or control surface, and each system operating any flight control must meet the requirements of §§27.395, 27.397, 27.399, 27.411, and 27.427.

[Docket No. 5074, 29 FR 15695, Nov. 24, 1964; as amended by Amdt. 27–26, 55 FR 7999, March 6, 1990; Amdt. 27–34, 62 FR 46173, Aug. 29, 1997]

§27.395 Control system.

(a) The part of each control system from the pilot's controls to the control stops must be designed to withstand pilot forces of not less than—

(1) The forces specified in §27.397; or

(2) If the system prevents the pilot from applying the limit pilot forces to the system, the maximum forces that the system allows the pilot to apply, but not less than 0.60 times the forces specified in §27.397.

(b) Each primary control system, including its supporting structure, must be designed as follows:

(1) The system must withstand loads resulting from the limit pilot forces prescribed in §27.397.

(2) Notwithstanding paragraph (b)(3) of this section, when power-operated actuator controls or power boost controls are used, the system must also withstand the loads resulting from the force output of each normally energized power device, including any single power boost or actuator system failure.

(3) If the system design or the normal operating loads are such that a part of the system cannot react to the limit pilot forces prescribed in §27.397, that part of the system must be designed to withstand the maximum loads that can be obtained in normal operation. The minimum design loads must, in any case, provide a rugged system for service use, including consideration of fatigue, jamming, ground gusts, control inertia, and friction loads. In the absence of rational analysis, the design loads resulting from 0.60 of the specified limit pilot forces are acceptable minimum design loads.

(4) If operational loads may be exceeded through jamming, ground gusts, control inertia, or friction, the system must withstand the limit pilot forces specified in §27.397, without yielding.

[Docket No. 5074, 29 FR 15695, Nov. 24, 1964; as amended by Amdt. 27–26, 55 FR 7999, March 6, 1990]

§27.397 Limit pilot forces and torques.

(a) Except as provided in paragraph (b) of this section, the limit pilot forces are as follows:

(1) For foot controls, 130 pounds.

(2) For stick controls, 100 pounds fore and aft, and 67 pounds laterally.

(b) For flap, tab, stabilizer, rotor brake, and landing gear operating controls, the follows apply (R = radius in inches):

(1) Crank, wheel, and lever controls, [1+R]/3 x 50 pounds, but not less than 50 pounds nor more than 100 pounds for hand operated controls or 130 pounds for foot operated controls, applied at any angle within 20 degrees of the plane of motion of the control.

(2) Twist controls, 80R inch-pounds.

[Docket No. 5074, 29 FR 15695, Nov. 24, 1964; as amended by Amdt. 27–11, 41 FR 55469, Dec. 20, 1976; Amdt. 27–40, 66 FR 23538, May 9, 2001]

§27.399 Dual control system.

Each dual primary flight control system must be designed to withstand the loads that result when pilot forces of 0.75 times those obtained under §27.395 are applied—

(a) In opposition; and

(b) In the same direction.

§27.411 Ground clearance: tail rotor guard.

(a) It must be impossible for the tail rotor to contact the landing surface during a normal landing.

(b) If a tail rotor guard is required to show compliance with paragraph (a) of this section—

(1) Suitable design loads must be established for the guard; and

(2) The guard and its supporting structure must be designed to withstand those loads.

§27.427 Unsymmetrical loads.

(a) Horizontal tail surfaces and their supporting structure must be designed for unsymmetrical loads arising from yawing and rotor wake effects in combination with the prescribed flight conditions.

(b) To meet the design criteria of paragraph (a) of this section, in the absence of more rational data, both of the following must be met:

(1) One hundred percent of the maximum loading from the symmetrical flight conditions acts on the surface on one side of the plane of symmetry, and no loading acts on the other side.

(2) Fifty percent of the maximum loading from the symmetrical flight conditions acts on the surface on each side of the plane of symmetry but in opposite directions.

(c) For empennage arrangements where the horizontal tail surfaces are supported by the vertical tail surfaces, the vertical tail surfaces and supporting structure must be designed for the combined vertical and horizontal surface loads resulting from each prescribed flight condition, considered separately. The flight conditions must be selected so the maximum design loads are obtained on each surface. In the absence of more rational data, the unsymmetrical horizontal tail surface loading distributions described in this section must be assumed.

[Docket No. 5074, 29 FR 15695, Nov. 24, 1964; as amended by Amdt. 27–26, 55 FR 7999, March 6, 1990; Amdt. 27–27, 55 FR 38966, Sept. 21, 1990]

Ground Loads

§27.471 General.

(a) *Loads and equilibrium.* For limit ground loads—

(1) The limit ground loads obtained in the landing conditions in this part must be considered to be external loads that would occur in the rotorcraft structure if it were acting as a rigid body; and

(2) In each specified landing condition, the external loads must be placed in equilibrium with linear and angular inertia loads in a rational or conservative manner.

(b) *Critical centers of gravity.* The critical centers of gravity within the range for which certification is requested must be selected so that the maximum design loads are obtained in each landing gear element.

§27.473 Ground loading conditions and assumptions.

(a) For specified landing conditions, a design maximum weight must be used that is not less than the maximum weight. A rotor lift may be assumed to act through the center of gravity throughout the landing impact. This lift may not exceed two-thirds of the design maximum weight.

(b) Unless otherwise prescribed, for each specified landing condition, the rotorcraft must be designed for a limit load factor of not less than the limit inertia load factor substantiated under §27.725.

[Docket No. 5074, 29 FR 15695, Nov. 24, 1964; as amended by Amdt. 27–2, 33 FR 963, Jan. 26, 1968]

§27.475 Tires and shock absorbers.

Unless otherwise prescribed, for each specified landing condition, the tires must be assumed to be in their static position and the shock absorbers to be in their most critical position.

§27.477 Landing gear arrangement.

Sections 27.235, 27.479 through 27.485, and 27.493 apply to landing gear with two wheels aft, and one or more wheels forward, of the center of gravity.

§27.479 Level landing conditions.

(a) *Attitudes.* Under each of the loading conditions prescribed in paragraph (b) of this section, the rotorcraft is assumed to be in each of the following level landing attitudes:

(1) An attitude in which all wheels contact the ground simultaneously.

(2) An attitude in which the aft wheels contact the ground with the forward wheels just clear of the ground.

(b) *Loading conditions.* The rotorcraft must be designed for the following landing loading conditions:

(1) Vertical loads applied under §27.471.

(2) The loads resulting from a combination of the loads applied under paragraph (b)(1) of this section with drag loads at each wheel of not less than 25 percent of the vertical load at that wheel.

(3) If there are two wheels forward, a distribution of the loads applied to those wheels under paragraphs (b)(1) and (2) of this section in a ratio of 40:60.

(c) Pitching moments. Pitching moments are assumed to be resisted by—

(1) In the case of the attitude in paragraph (a)(1) of this section, the forward landing gear; and

(2) In the case of the attitude in paragraph (a)(2) of this section, the angular inertia forces.

[Docket No. 5074, 29 FR 15695, Nov. 24, 1964; 29 FR 17885, Dec. 17, 1964]

§27.481 Tail-down landing conditions.

(a) The rotorcraft is assumed to be in the maximum nose-up attitude allowing ground clearance by each part of the rotorcraft.

(b) In this attitude, ground loads are assumed to act perpendicular to the ground.

§27.483 One-wheel landing conditions.

For the one-wheel landing condition, the rotorcraft is assumed to be in the level attitude and to contact the ground on one aft wheel. In this attitude—

(a) The vertical load must be the same as that obtained on that side under §27.479(b)(1); and

(b) The unbalanced external loads must be reacted by rotorcraft inertia.

§27.485 Lateral drift landing conditions.

(a) The rotorcraft is assumed to be in the level landing attitude, with—

(1) Side loads combined with one-half of the maximum ground reactions obtained in the level landing conditions of §27.479 (b)(1); and

(2) The loads obtained under paragraph (a)(1) of this section applied—

(i) At the ground contact point; or

(ii) For full-swiveling gear, at the center of the axle.

(b) The rotorcraft must be designed to withstand, at ground contact—

(1) When only the aft wheels contact the ground, side loads of 0.8 times the vertical reaction acting inward on one side, and 0.6 times the vertical reaction acting outward on the other side, all combined with the vertical loads specified in paragraph (a) of this section; and

(2) When all wheels contact the ground simultaneously—

(i) For the aft wheels, the side loads specified in paragraph (b)(1) of this section; and

(ii) For the forward wheels, a side load of 0.8 times the vertical reaction combined with the vertical load specified in paragraph (a) of this section.

§27.493 Braked roll conditions.

Under braked roll conditions with the shock absorbers in their static positions—

(a) The limit vertical load must be based on a load factor of at least—

(1) 1.33, for the attitude specified in §27.479(a)(1); and

(2) 1.0 for the attitude specified in §27.479(a)(2); and

(b) The structure must be designed to withstand at the ground contact point of each wheel with brakes, a drag load at least the lesser of—

(1) The vertical load multiplied by a coefficient of friction of 0.8; and

(2) The maximum value based on limiting brake torque.

§27.497 Ground loading conditions: Landing gear with tail wheels.

(a) *General.* Rotorcraft with landing gear with two wheels forward, and one wheel aft, of the center of gravity must be designed for loading conditions as prescribed in this section.

(b) *Level landing attitude with only the forward wheels contacting the ground.* In this attitude—

(1) The vertical loads must be applied under §§27.471 through 27.475;

(2) The vertical load at each axle must be combined with a drag load at that axle of not less than 25 percent of that vertical load; and

(3) Unbalanced pitching moments are assumed to be resisted by angular inertia forces.

(c) *Level landing attitude with all wheels contacting the ground simultaneously.* In this attitude, the rotorcraft must be designed for landing loading conditions as prescribed in paragraph (b) of this section.

(d) *Maximum nose-up attitude with only the rear wheel contacting the ground.* The attitude for this condition must be the maximum nose-up attitude expected in normal operation, including autorotative landings. In this attitude—

(1) The appropriate ground loads specified in paragraphs (b)(1) and (2) of this section must be determined and applied, using a rational method to account for the moment arm between the rear wheel ground reaction and the rotorcraft center of gravity; or

(2) The probability of landing with initial contact on the rear wheel must be shown to be extremely remote.

(e) *Level landing attitude with only one forward wheel contacting the ground.* In this attitude, the rotorcraft must be designed for ground loads as specified in paragraphs (b)(1) and (3) of this section.

(f) *Side loads in the level landing attitude.* In the attitudes specified in paragraphs (b) and (c) of this section, the following apply:

(1) The side loads must be combined at each wheel with one-half of the maximum vertical ground reactions obtained for that wheel under paragraphs (b) and (c) of this section. In this condition, the side loads must be

(i) For the forward wheels, 0.8 times the vertical reaction (on one side) acting inward, and 0.6 times the vertical reaction (on the other side) acting outward; and

(ii) For the rear wheel, 0.8 times the vertical reaction.

(2) The loads specified in paragraph (f)(1) of this section must be applied—

(i) At the ground contact point with the wheel in the trailing position (for non-full swiveling landing gear or for full swiveling landing gear with a lock, steering device, or shimmy damper to keep the wheel in the trailing position); or

(ii) At the center of the axle (for full swiveling landing gear without a lock, steering device, or shimmy damper).

(g) *Braked roll conditions in the level landing attitude.* In the attitudes specified in paragraphs (b) and (c) of this section, and with the shock absorbers in their static positions, the rotorcraft must be designed for braked roll loads as follows:

(1) The limit vertical load must be based on a limit vertical load factor of not less than—

(i) 1.0, for the attitude specified in paragraph (b) of this section; and

(ii) 1.33, for the attitude specified in paragraph (c) of this section.

(2) For each wheel with brakes, a drag load must be applied, at the ground contact point, of not less than the lesser of—

(i) 0.8 times the vertical load; and

27

(ii) The maximum based on limiting brake torque.

(h) *Rear wheel turning loads in the static ground attitude.* In the static ground attitude, and with the shock absorbers and tires in their static positions, the rotorcraft must be designed for rear wheel turning loads as follows:

(1) A vertical ground reaction equal to the static load on the rear wheel must be combined with an equal sideload.

(2) The load specified in paragraph (h)(1) of this section must be applied to the rear landing gear—

(i) Through the axle, if there is a swivel (the rear wheel being assumed to be swiveled 90 degrees to the longitudinal axis of the rotorcraft); or

(ii) At the ground contact point, if there is a lock, steering device or shimmy damper (the rear wheel being assumed to be in the trailing position).

(i) *Taxiing condition.* The rotorcraft and its landing gear must be designed for loads that would occur when the rotorcraft is taxied over the roughest ground that may reasonably be expected in normal operation.

§27.501 Ground loading conditions: Landing gear with skids.

(a) *General.* Rotorcraft with landing gear with skids must be designed for the loading conditions specified in this section. In showing compliance with this section, the following apply:

(1) The design maximum weight, center of gravity, and load factor must be determined under §27.471 through 27.475.

(2) Structural yielding of elastic spring members under limit loads is acceptable.

(3) Design ultimate loads for elastic spring members need not exceed those obtained in a drop test of the gear with—

(i) A drop height of 1.5 times that specified in §27.725; and

(ii) An assumed rotor lift of not more than 1.5 times that used in the limit drop tests prescribed in §27.725.

(4) Compliance with paragraphs (b) through (e) of this section must be shown with—

(i) The gear in its most critically deflected position for the landing condition being considered; and

(ii) The ground reactions rationally distributed along the bottom of the skid tube.

(b) *Vertical reactions in the level landing attitude.* In the level attitude, and with the rotorcraft contacting the ground along the bottom of both skids, the vertical reactions must be applied as prescribed in paragraph (a) of this section.

(c) *Drag reactions in the level landing attitude.* In the level attitude, and with the rotorcraft contacting the ground along the bottom of both skids, the following apply:

(1) The vertical reactions must be combined with horizontal drag reactions of 50 percent of the vertical reaction applied at the ground.

(2) The resultant ground loads must equal the vertical load specified in paragraph (b) of this section.

(d) *Sideloads in the level landing attitude.* In the level attitude, and with the rotorcraft contacting the ground along the bottom of both skids, the following apply:

(1) The vertical ground reaction must be—

(i) Equal to the vertical loads obtained in the condition specified in paragraph (b) of this section; and

(ii) Divided equally among the skids.

(2) The vertical ground reactions must be combined with a horizontal sideload of 25 percent of their value.

(3) The total sideload must be applied equally between the skids and along the length of the skids.

(4) The unbalanced moments are assumed to be resisted by angular inertia.

(5) The skid gear must be investigated for—

(i) Inward acting sideloads; and

(ii) Outward acting sideloads.

(e) *One-skid landing loads in the level attitude.* In the level attitude, and with the rotorcraft contacting the ground along the bottom of one skid only, the following apply:

(1) The vertical load on the ground contact side must be the same as that obtained on that side in the condition specified in paragraph (b) of this section.

(2) The unbalanced moments are assumed to be resisted by angular inertia.

(f) *Special conditions.* In addition to the conditions specified in paragraphs (b) and (c) of this section, the rotorcraft must be designed for the following ground reactions:

(1) A ground reaction load acting up and aft at an angle of 45 degrees to the longitudinal axis of the rotorcraft. This load must be—

(i) Equal to 1.33 times the maximum weight;

(ii) Distributed symmetrically among the skids;

(iii) Concentrated at the forward end of the straight part of the skid tube; and

(iv) Applied only to the forward end of the skid tube and its attachment to the rotorcraft.

(2) With the rotorcraft in the level landing attitude, a vertical ground reaction load equal to one-half of the vertical load determined under paragraph (b) of this section. This load must be—

(i) Applied only to the skid tube and its attachment to the rotorcraft; and

(ii) Distributed equally over 33.3 percent of the length between the skid tube attachments and centrally located midway between the skid tube attachments.

[Docket No. 5074, 29 FR 15695, Nov. 24, 1964; as amended by Amdt. 27–2, 33 FR 963, Jan. 26 1968; Amdt. 27–26, 55 FR 8000, March 6, 1990]

§27.505 Ski landing conditions.

If certification for ski operation is requested, the rotorcraft, with skis, must be designed to withstand the following loading conditions (where P is the maximum static weight on each ski with the rotorcraft at design maximum weight, and n is the limit load factor determined under §27.473(b).

(a) Up-load conditions in which—

(1) A vertical load of Pn and a horizontal load of Pn/4 are simultaneously applied at the pedestal bearings; and

(2) A vertical load of 1.33 P is applied at the pedestal bearings.

(b) A side-load condition in which a side load of 0.35 Pn is applied at the pedestal bearings in a horizontal plane perpendicular to the centerline of the rotorcraft.

(c) A torque-load condition in which a torque load of 1.33 P (in foot pounds) is applied to the ski about the vertical axis through the centerline of the pedestal bearings.

WATER LOADS

§27.521 Float landing conditions.

If certification for float operation is requested, the rotorcraft, with floats, must be designed to withstand the following loading conditions (where the limit load factor is determined under §27.473(b) or assumed to be equal to that determined for wheel landing gear):

(a) Up-load conditions in which—

(1) A load is applied so that, with the rotorcraft in the static level attitude, the resultant water reaction passes vertically through the center of gravity; and

(2) The vertical load prescribed in paragraph (a)(1) of this section is applied simultaneously with an aft component of 0.25 times the vertical component.

(b) A side-load condition in which—

(1) A vertical load of 0.75 times the total vertical load specified in paragraph (a)(1) of this section is divided equally among the floats; and

(2) For each float, the load share determined under paragraph (b)(1) of this section, combined with a total side load of 0.25 times the total vertical load specified in paragraph (b)(1) of this section, is applied to that float only.

MAIN COMPONENT REQUIREMENTS

§27.547 Main rotor structure.

(a) Each main rotor assembly (including rotor hubs and blades) must be designed as prescribed in this section.

(b) [Reserved]

(c) The main rotor structure must be designed to withstand the following loads prescribed in §§27.337 through 27.341:

(1) Critical flight loads.

(2) Limit loads occurring under normal conditions of autorotation. For this condition, the rotor r.p.m. must be selected to include the effects of altitude.

(d) The main rotor structure must be designed to withstand loads simulating—

(1) For the rotor blades, hubs, and flapping hinges, the impact force of each blade against its stop during ground operation; and

(2) Any other critical condition expected in normal operation.

(e) The main rotor structure must be designed to withstand the limit torque at any rotational speed, including zero. In addition:

(1) The limit torque need not be greater than the torque defined by a torque limiting device (where provided), and may not be less than the greater of—

(i) The maximum torque likely to be transmitted to the rotor structure in either direction; and

(ii) The limit engine torque specified in §27.361.

(2) The limit torque must be distributed to the rotor blades in a rational manner.

(Secs. 604, 605, 72 Stat. 778, 49 U.S.C. 1424, 1425)

[Docket No. 5074, 29 FR 15695, Nov. 24, 1964; as amended by Amdt. 27–3, 33 FR 14105, Sept. 18, 1968]

§27.549 Fuselage, landing gear, and rotor pylon structures.

(a) Each fuselage, landing gear, and rotor pylon structure must be designed as prescribed in this section. Resultant rotor forces may be represented as a single force applied at the rotor hub attachment point.

(b) Each structure must be designed to withstand—

(1) The critical loads prescribed in §§27.337 through 27.341;

(2) The applicable ground loads prescribed in §§27.235, 27.471 through 27.485, 27.493, 27.497, 27.501, 27.505, and 27.521; and

(3) The loads prescribed in §27.547 (d)(2) and (e).

(c) Auxiliary rotor thrust, and the balancing air and inertia loads occurring under accelerated flight conditions, must be considered.

(d) Each engine mount and adjacent fuselage structure must be designed to withstand the loads occurring under accelerated flight and landing conditions, including engine torque.

(Secs. 604, 605, 72 Stat. 778, 49 U.S.C. 1424, 1425)

[Docket No. 5074, 29 FR 15695, Nov. 24, 1964; as amended by Amdt. 27–3, 33 FR 14105, Sept. 18, 1968]

EMERGENCY LANDING CONDITIONS

§27.561 General.

(a) The rotorcraft, although it may be damaged in emergency landing conditions on land or water, must be designed as prescribed in this section to protect the occupants under those conditions.

(b) The structure must be designed to give each occupant every reasonable chance of escaping serious injury in a crash landing when—

(1) Proper use is made of seats, belts, and other safety design provisions;

(2) The wheels are retracted (where applicable); and

(3) Each occupant and each item of mass inside the cabin that could injure an occupant is restrained when subjected to the following ultimate inertial load factors relative to the surrounding structure:

(i) Upward—4g.

(ii) Forward—16g.

(iii) Sideward—8g.

(iv) Downward—20g, after intended displacement of the seat device.

(v) Rearward—1.5g.

(c) The supporting structure must be designed to restrain, under any ultimate inertial load up to those specified in this paragraph, any item of mass above and/or behind the crew and passenger compartment that could injure an occupant if it came loose in an emergency landing. Items of mass to be considered include, but are not limited to, rotors, transmissions, and engines. The items of mass must be restrained for the following ultimate inertial load factors:

(1) Upward—1.5g.

(2) Forward—12g.

(3) Sideward—6g.

(4) Downward—12g.

(5) Rearward—1.5g.

(d) Any fuselage structure in the area of internal fuel tanks below the passenger floor level must be designed to resist the following ultimate inertial factors and loads and to protect the fuel tanks from rupture when those loads are applied to that area:

(i) Upward—1.5g.

(ii) Forward—4.0g.

(iii) Sideward—2.0g.

(iv) Downward—4.0g.

[Docket No. 5074, 29 FR 15695, Nov. 24, 1964; as amended by Amdt. 27–25, 54 FR 47318, Nov. 13, 1989; Amdt. 27–30, 59 FR 50386, Oct. 3, 1994; Amdt. 27–32, 61 FR 10438, March 13, 1996]

§27.562 Emergency landing dynamic conditions.

(a) The rotorcraft, although it may be damaged in an emergency crash landing, must be designed to reasonably protect each occupant when—

(1) The occupant properly uses the seats, safety belts, and shoulder harnesses provided in the design; and

(2) The occupant is exposed to the loads resulting from the conditions prescribed in this section.

(b) Each seat type design or other seating device approved for crew or passenger occupancy during takeoff and landing must successfully complete dynamic tests or be demonstrated by rational analysis based on dynamic tests of a similar type seat in accordance with the following criteria. The tests must be conducted with an occupant, simulated by a 170-pound anthropomorphic test dummy (ATD), as defined by 49 CFR 572, subpart B, or its equivalent, sitting in the normal upright position.

(1) A change in downward velocity of not less than 30 feet per second when the seat or other seating device is oriented in its nominal position with respect to the rotorcraft's reference system, the rotorcraft's longitudinal axis is canted upward 60° with respect to the impact velocity vector, and the rotorcraft's lateral axis is perpendicular to a vertical plane containing the impact velocity vector and the rotorcraft's longitudinal axis. Peak floor deceleration must occur in not more than 0.031 seconds after impact and must reach a minimum of 30 g's.

(2) A change in forward velocity of not less than 42 feet per second when the seat or other seating device is oriented in its nominal position with respect to the rotorcraft's reference system, the rotorcraft's longitudinal axis is yawed 10° either right or left of the impact velocity vector (whichever would cause the greatest load on the shoulder harness), the rotorcraft's lateral axis is contained in a horizontal plane containing the impact velocity vector, and the rotorcraft's vertical axis is perpendicular to a horizontal plane containing the impact velocity vector. Peak floor deceleration must occur in not more than 0.071 seconds after impact and must reach a minimum of 18.4 g's.

(3) Where floor rails or floor or sidewall attachment devices are used to attach the seating devices to the airframe structure for the conditions of this section, the rails or devices must be misaligned with respect to each other by at least 10° vertically (i.e., pitch out of parallel) and by at least a 10° lateral roll, with the directions optional, to account for possible floor warp.

(c) Compliance with the following must be shown:

(1) The seating device system must remain intact although it may experience separation intended as part of its design.

(2) The attachment between the seating device and the airframe structure must remain intact, although the structure may have exceeded its limit load.

(3) The ATD's shoulder harness strap or straps must remain on or in the immediate vicinity of the ATD's shoulder during the impact.

(4) The safety belt must remain on the ATD's pelvis during the impact.

(5) The ATD's head either does not contact any portion of the crew or passenger compartment, or if contact is made, the head impact does not exceed a head injury criteria (HIC) of 1,000 as determined by this equation.

$$HIC = (t_2 - t_1)\left[\frac{1}{(t_2 - t_1)}\int_{t_1}^{t_2} a(t)dt\right]^{2.5}$$

Where: a(t) is the resultant acceleration at the center of gravity of the head form expressed as a multiple of g (the acceleration of gravity) and $t_2 - t_1$, is the time duration, in seconds, of major head impact, not to exceed 0.05 seconds.

(6) Loads in individual upper torso harness straps must not exceed 1,750 pounds. If dual straps are used for retaining the upper torso, the total harness strap loads must not exceed 2,000 pounds.

(7) The maximum compressive load measured between the pelvis and the lumbar column of the ATD must not exceed 1,500 pounds.

(d) An alternate approach that achieves an equivalent or greater level of occupant protection, as required by this section, must be substantiated on a rational basis.

[Docket No. 5074, 29 FR 15695, Nov. 24, 1964; as amended by Amdt. 27–25, 54 FR 47318, Nov. 13, 1989]

§27.563 Structural ditching provisions.

If certification with ditching provisions is requested, structural strength for ditching must meet the requirements of this section and §27.801(e).

(a) *Forward speed landing conditions.* The rotorcraft must initially contact the most critical wave for reasonably probable water conditions at forward velocities from zero up to 30 knots in likely pitch, roll, and yaw attitudes. The rotorcraft limit vertical descent velocity may not be less than 5 feet per second relative to the mean water surface. Rotor lift may be used to act through the center of gravity throughout the landing impact. This lift may not exceed two-thirds of the design maximum weight. A maximum forward velocity of less than 30 knots may be used in design if it can be demonstrated that the forward velocity selected would not be exceeded in a normal one-engine-out touchdown.

(b) *Auxiliary or emergency float conditions*—

(1) *Floats fixed or deployed before initial water contact.* In addition to the landing loads in paragraph (a) of this section, each auxiliary or emergency float, of its support and attaching structure in the airframe or fuselage, must be designed for the load developed by a fully immersed float unless it can be shown that full immersion is unlikely. If full immersion is

unlikely, the highest likely float buoyancy load must be applied. The highest likely buoyancy load must include consideration of a partially immersed float creating restoring moments to compensate the upsetting moments caused by side wind, unsymmetrical rotorcraft loading, water wave action, rotorcraft inertia, and probable structural damage and leakage considered under §27.801(d). Maximum roll and pitch angles determined from compliance with §27.801(d) may be used, if significant, to determine the extent of immersion of each float. If the floats are deployed in flight, appropriate air loads derived from the flight limitations with the floats deployed shall be used in substantiation of the floats and their attachment to the rotorcraft. For this purpose, the design airspeed for limit load is the float deployed airspeed operating limit multiplied by 1.11.

(2) *Floats deployed after initial water contact.* Each float must be designed for full or partial immersion prescribed in paragraph (b)(1) of this section. In addition, each float must be designed for combined vertical and drag loads using a relative limit speed of 20 knots between the rotorcraft and the water. The vertical load may not be less than the highest likely buoyancy load determined under paragraph (b)(1) of this section.

[Docket No. 5074, 29 FR 15695, Nov. 24, 1964; as amended by Amdt. 27–26, 55 FR 8000, March 6, 1990]

Fatigue Evaluation

§27.571 Fatigue evaluation of flight structure.

(a) *General.* Each portion of the flight structure (the flight structure includes rotors, rotor drive systems between the engines and the rotor hubs, controls, fuselage, landing gear, and their related primary attachments), the failure of which could be catastrophic, must be identified and must be evaluated under paragraph (b), (c), (d), or (e) of this section. The following apply to each fatigue evaluation:

(1) The procedure for the evaluation must be approved.

(2) The locations of probable failure must be determined.

(3) Inflight measurement must be included in determining the following:

(i) Loads or stresses in all critical conditions throughout the range of limitations in §27.309, except that maneuvering load factors need not exceed the maximum values expected in operation.

(ii) The effect of altitude upon these loads or stresses.

(4) The loading spectra must be as severe as those expected in operation including, but not limited to, external cargo operations, if applicable, and ground-air-ground cycles. The loading spectra must be based on loads or stresses determined under paragraph (a)(3) of this section.

(b) *Fatigue tolerance evaluation.* It must be shown that the fatigue tolerance of the structure endures that the probability of catastrophic fatigue failure is extremely remote without establishing replacement times, inspection intervals or other procedures under section A27.4 of Appendix A.

(c) *Replacement time evaluation.* It must be shown that the probability of catastrophic fatigue failure is extremely remote within a replacement time furnished under section A27.4 of Appendix A.

(d) *Fail-safe evaluation.* The following apply to fail-safe evaluation:

(1) It must be shown that all partial failures will become readily detectable under inspection procedures furnished under section A27.4 of Appendix A.

(2) The interval between the time when any partial failure becomes readily detectable under paragraph (d)(1) of this section, and the time when any such failure is expected to reduce the remaining strength of the structure to limit or maximum attainable loads (whichever is less), must be determined.

(3) It must be shown that the interval determined under paragraph (d)(2) of this section is long enough, in relation to the inspection intervals and related procedures furnished under section A27.4 of Appendix A, to provide a probability of detection great enough to ensure that the probability of catastrophic failure is extremely remote.

(e) *Combination of replacement time and failsafe evaluations.* A component may be evaluated under a combination of paragraphs (c) and (d) of this section. For such component it must be shown that the probability of catastrophic failure is extremely remote with an approved combination of replacement time, inspection intervals, and related procedures furnished under section A27.4 of Appendix A.

(Secs. 313(a), 601, 603, 604, and 605, 72 Stat. 752, 775, and 778, (49 U.S.C. 1354(a), 1421, 1423, 1424, and 1425; sec. 6(c), 49 U.S.C. 1655(c)))

[Docket No. 5074, 29 FR 15695, Nov. 24, 1964; as amended by Amdt. 27–3, 33 FR 14106, Sept. 18, 1968; Amdt. 27–12, 42 FR 15044, March 17, 1977; Amdt. 27–18, 45 FR 60177, Sept. 11 1980; Amdt. 27–26, 55 FR 8000, March 6, 1990]

Subpart D— Design and Construction

General

§27.601 Design.

(a) The rotorcraft may have no design features or details that experience has shown to be hazardous or unreliable.

(b) The suitability of each questionable design detail and part must be established by tests.

§27.602 Critical parts.

(a) *Critical part.* A critical part is a part, the failure of which could have a catastrophic effect upon the rotorcraft, and for which critical characteristics have been identified which must be controlled to ensure the required level of integrity.

(b) If the type design includes critical parts, a critical parts list shall be established. Procedures shall be established to define the critical design characteristics, identify processes that affect those characteristics, and identify the design change and process change controls necessary for showing compliance with the quality assurance requirements of part 21 of this chapter.

[Docket No. 29311, 64 FR 46232, Aug. 24, 1999]

§27.603 Materials.

The suitability and durability of materials used for parts, the failure of which could adversely affect safety, must —

(a) Be established on the basis of experience or tests;

(b) Meet approved specifications that ensure their having the strength and other properties assumed in the design data; and

(c) Take into account the effects of environmental conditions, such as temperature and humidity, expected in service.

(Secs. 313(a), 601, 603, 604, Federal Aviation Act of 1958 (49 U.S.C. 1354(a), 1421, 1423, 1424); and sec. 6(c) of the Dept. of Transportation Act (49 U.S.C. 1655(c)))

[Docket No. 5074, 29 FR 15695, Nov. 24, 1964; as amended by Amdt. 27–11, 41 FR 55469, Dec. 20, 1976; Amdt. 27–16, 43 FR 50599, Oct. 30, 1978]

§27.605 Fabrication methods.

(a) The methods of fabrication used must produce consistently sound structures. If a fabrication process (such as gluing, spot welding, or heat-treating) requires close control to reach this objective, the process must be performed according to an approved process specification.

(b) Each new aircraft fabrication method must be substantiated by a test program.

(Secs. 313(a), 601, 603, 604, and 605 of the Federal Aviation Act of 1958 (49 U.S.C. 1354(a), 1421, 1423, 1424 and 1425); sec. 6(c) of the Dept. of Transportation Act (49 U.S.C. 1655(c)))

[Docket No. 5074, 29 FR 15695, Nov. 24, 1964; as amended by Amdt. 27–16, 43 FR 50599, Oct. 30, 1978]

§27.607 Fasteners.

(a) Each removable bolt, screw, nut, pin, or other fastener whose loss could jeopardize the safe operation of the rotorcraft must incorporate two separate locking devices. The fastener and its locking devices may not be adversely affected by the environmental conditions associated with the particular installation.

(b) No self-locking nut may be used on any bolt subject to rotation in operation unless a nonfriction locking device is used in addition to the self-locking device.

[Docket No. 5074, 29 FR 15695, Nov. 24, 1964; as amended by Amdt. 27–4, 33 FR 14533, Sept. 27, 1968]

§27.609 Protection of structure.

Each part of the structure must—

(a) Be suitably protected against deterioration or loss of strength in service due to any cause, including—

(1) Weathering;

(2) Corrosion; and

(3) Abrasion; and

(b) Have provisions for ventilation and drainage where necessary to prevent the accumulation of corrosive, flammable, or noxious fluids.

§27.610 Lightning and static electricity protection.

(a) The rotorcraft must be protected against catastrophic effects from lightning.

(b) For metallic components, compliance with paragraph (a) of this section may be shown by—

(1) Electrically bonding the components properly to the airframe; or

(2) Designing the components so that a strike will not endanger the rotorcraft.

(c) For nonmetallic components, compliance with paragraph (a) of this section may be shown by—

(1) Designing the components to minimize the effect of a strike; or

(2) Incorporating acceptable means of diverting the resulting electrical current so as not to endanger the rotorcraft.

(d) The electrical bonding and protection against lightning and static electricity must—

(1) Minimize the accumulation of electrostatic charge;

(2) Minimize the risk of electric shock to crew, passengers, and service and maintenance personnel using normal precautions;

(3) Provide an electrical return path, under both normal and fault conditions, on rotorcraft having grounded electrical systems; and

(4) Reduce to an acceptable level the effects of lightning and static electricity on the functioning of essential electrical and electronic equipment.

[Docket No. 5074, 29 FR 15695, Nov. 24, 1964; as amended by Amdt. 27–21, 49 FR 44433, Nov. 6, 1984; Amdt. 27–37, 64 FR 45094, Aug. 18, 1999]

§27.611 Inspection provisions.

There must be means to allow the close examination of each part that requires—

(a) Recurring inspection;

(b) Adjustment for proper alignment and functioning; or

(c) Lubrication.

§27.613 Material strength properties and design values.

(a) Material strength properties must be based on enough tests of material meeting specifications to establish design values on a statistical basis.

(b) Design values must be chosen to minimize the probability of structural failure due to material variability. Except as provided in paragraphs (d) and (e) of this section, compliance with this paragraph must be shown by selecting design values that assure material strength with the following probability—

(1) Where applied loads are eventually distributed through a single member within an assembly, the failure of which would result in loss of structural integrity of the component, 99 percent probability with 95 percent confidence; and

(2) For redundant structure, those in which the failure of individual elements would result in applied loads being safely distributed to other load-carrying members, 90 percent probability with 95 percent confidence.

(c) The strength, detail design, and fabrication of the structure must minimize the probability of disastrous fatigue failure, particularly at points of stress concentration.

(d) Design values may be those contained in the following publications (available from the Naval Publications and Forms Center, 5801 Tabor Avenue, Philadelphia, Pennsylvania 19120) or other values approved by the Administrator:

(1) MIL HDBK-5, "Metallic Materials and Elements for Flight Vehicle Structure".

(2) MIL HDBK-17, "Plastics for Flight Vehicles".

(3) ANC-18, "Design of Wood Aircraft Structures".

(4) MIL-HDBK-23, "Composite Construction for Flight Vehicles".

(e) Other design values may be used if a selection of the material is made in which a specimen of each individual item is tested before use and it is determined that the actual strength properties of that particular item will equal or exceed those used in design.

(Secs. 313(a), 601, 603, 604, Federal Aviation Act of 1958 (49 U.S.C. 1354(a), 1421, 1423, 1424), sec. 6(c), Dept. of Transportation Act (49 U.S.C. 1655(c)))

[Docket No. 5074, 29 FR 15695, Nov. 24, 1964; as amended by Amdt. 27–16, 43 FR 50599, Oct. 30, 1978; Amdt. 27–26, 55 FR 8000, March 6, 1990]

§27.619 Special factors.

(a) The special factors prescribed in §§27.621 through 27.625 apply to each part of the structure whose strength is—

(1) Uncertain;

(2) Likely to deteriorate in service before normal replacement; or

(3) Subject to appreciable variability due to—

(i) Uncertainties in manufacturing processes; or

(ii) Uncertainties in inspection methods.

(b) For each part to which §§27.621 through 27.625 apply, the factor of safety prescribed in §27.303 must be multiplied by a special factor equal to—

(1) The applicable special factors prescribed in §§27.621 through 27.625; or

(2) Any other factor great enough to ensure that the probability of the part being understrength because of the uncertainties specified in paragraph (a) of this section is extremely remote.

§27.621 Casting factors.

(a) *General.* The factors, tests, and inspections specified in paragraphs (b) and (c) of this section must be applied in addition to those necessary to establish foundry quality control. The inspections must meet approved specifications. Paragraphs (c) and (d) of this section apply to structural castings except castings that are pressure tested as parts of hydraulic or other fluid systems and do not support structural loads.

(b) *Bearing stresses and surfaces.* The casting factors specified in paragraphs (c) and (d) of this section—

(1) Need not exceed 1.25 with respect to bearing stresses regardless of the method of inspection used; and

(2) Need not be used with respect to the bearing surfaces of a part whose bearing factor is larger than the applicable casting factor.

(c) *Critical castings.* For each casting whose failure would preclude continued safe flight and landing of the rotorcraft or result in serious injury to any occupant, the following apply:

(1) Each critical casting must—

(i) Have a casting factor of not less than 1.25; and

(ii) Receive 100 percent inspection by visual, radiographic, and magnetic particle (for ferromagnetic materials) or penetrant (for nonferromagnetic materials) inspection methods or approved equivalent inspection methods.

(2) For each critical casting with a casting factor less than 1.50, three sample castings must be static tested and shown to meet—

(i) The strength requirements of §27.305 at an ultimate load corresponding to a casting factor of 1.25; and

(ii) The deformation requirements of §27.305 at a load of 1.15 times the limit load.

(d) *Noncritical castings.* For each casting other than those specified in paragraph (c) of this section, the following apply:

(1) Except as provided in paragraphs (d)(2) and (3) of this section, the casting factors and corresponding inspections must meet the following table:

Casting factor	Inspection
2.0 or greater	100 percent visual
Less than 2.0, greater than 1.5	100 percent visual, and magnetic particle (ferromagnetic materials), penetrant (nonferromagnetic materials), or approved equivalent inspection methods.
1.25 through 1.50	100 percent visual, and magnetic particle (ferromagnetic materials), penetrant (nonferromagnetic materials), and radiographic or approved equivalent inspection methods.

(2) The percentage of castings inspected by nonvisual methods may be reduced below that specified in paragraph (d)(1) of this section when an approved quality control procedure is established.

(3) For castings procured to a specification that guarantees the mechanical properties of the material in the casting and provides for demonstration of these properties by test of coupons cut from the castings on a sampling basis—

(i) A casting factor of 1.0 may be used; and

(ii) The castings must be inspected as provided in paragraph (d)(1) of this section for casting factors of "1.25 through 1.50" and tested under paragraph (c)(2) of this section.

[Docket No. 5074, 29 FR 15695, Nov. 24, 1964; as amended by Amdt. 27–34, 62 FR 46173, Aug. 29, 1997]

§27.623 Bearing factors.

(a) Except as provided in paragraph (b) of this section, each part that has clearance (free fit), and that is subject to pounding or vibration, must have a bearing factor large enough to provide for the effects of normal relative motion.

(b) No bearing factor need be used on a part for which any larger special factor is prescribed.

§27.625 Fitting factors.

For each fitting (part or terminal used to join one structural member to another) the following apply:

(a) For each fitting whose strength is not proven by limit and ultimate load tests in which actual stress conditions are simulated in the fitting and surrounding structures, a fitting factor of at least 1.15 must be applied to each part of—

(1) The fitting;

(2) The means of attachment; and

(3) The bearing on the joined members.

(b) No fitting factor need be used—

(1) For joints made under approved practices and based on comprehensive test data (such as continuous joints in metal plating, welded joints, and scarf joints in wood); and

(2) With respect to any bearing surface for which a larger special factor is used.

(c) For each integral fitting, the part must be treated as a fitting up to the point at which the section properties become typical of the member.

(d) Each seat, berth, litter, safety belt, and harness attachment to the structure must be shown by analysis, tests, or both, to be able to withstand the inertia forces prescribed in §27.561(b)(3) multiplied by a fitting factor of 1.33.

[Docket No. 5074, 29 FR 15695, Nov. 24, 1964; as amended by Amdt. 27–35, 63 FR 43285, Aug. 12, 1998]

§27.629 Flutter.

Each aerodynamic surface of the rotorcraft must be free from flutter under each appropriate speed and power condition.

[Docket No. 5074, 29 FR 15695, Nov. 24, 1964; as amended by Amdt. 27–26, 55 FR 8000, March 6, 1990]

Rotors

§27.653 Pressure venting and drainage of rotor blades.

(a) For each rotor blade—

(1) There must be means for venting the internal pressure of the blade;

(2) Drainage holes must be provided for the blade; and

(3) The blade must be designed to prevent water from becoming trapped in it.

(b) Paragraphs (a)(1) and (2) of this section do not apply to sealed rotor blades capable of withstanding the maximum pressure differentials expected in service.

[Docket No. 5074, 29 FR 15695, Nov. 24, 1964; as amended by Amdt. 27–2, 33 FR 963, Jan. 26, 1968]

§27.659 Mass balance.

(a) The rotors and blades must be mass balanced as necessary to—

(1) Prevent excessive vibration; and

(2) Prevent flutter at any speed up to the maximum forward speed.

(b) The structural integrity of the mass balance installation must be substantiated.

[Docket No. 5074, 29 FR 15695, Nov. 24, 1964; as amended by Amdt. 27–2, 33 FR 963, Jan. 26, 1968]

§27.661 Rotor blade clearance.

There must be enough clearance between the rotor blades and other parts of the structure to prevent the blades from striking any part of the structure during any operating condition.

[Docket No. 5074, 29 FR 15695, Nov. 24, 1964; as amended by Amdt. 27–2, 33 FR 963, Jan. 26, 1968]

§27.663 Ground resonance prevention means.

(a) The reliability of the means for preventing ground resonance must be shown either by analysis and tests, or reliable service experience, or by showing through analysis or tests that malfunction or failure of a single means will not cause ground resonance.

(b) The probable range of variations, during service, of the damping action of the ground resonance prevention means must be established and must be investigated during the test required by §27.241.

[Docket No. 5074, 29 FR 15695, Nov. 24, 1964; as amended by Amdt. 27–2, 33 FR 963, Jan. 26, 1968; Amdt. 27–26, 55 FR 8000, March 6, 1990]

Control Systems

§27.671 General.

(a) Each control and control system must operate with the ease, smoothness, and positiveness appropriate to its function.

(b) Each element of each flight control system must be designed, or distinctively and permanently marked, to minimize the probability of any incorrect assembly that could result in the malfunction of the system.

§27.672 Stability augmentation, automatic, and power-operated systems.

If the functioning of stability augmentation or other automatic or power-operated systems is necessary to show compliance with the flight characteristics requirements of this part, such systems must comply with §27.671 of this part and the following:

(a) A warning which is clearly distinguishable to the pilot under expected flight conditions without requiring the pilot's attention must be provided for any failure in the stability augmentation system or in any other automatic or power-operated system which could result in an unsafe condition if the pilot is unaware of the failure. Warning systems must not activate the control systems.

(b) The design of the stability augmentation system or of any other automatic or power-operated system must allow initial counteraction of failures without requiring exceptional pilot skill or strength by overriding the failure by movement of the flight controls in the normal sense and deactivating the failed system.

(c) It must be shown that after any single failure of the stability augmentation system or any other automatic or power-operated system—

(1) The rotorcraft is safely controllable when the failure or malfunction occurs at any speed or altitude within the approved operating limitations;

(2) The controllability and maneuverability requirements of this part are met within a practical operational flight envelope

(for example, speed, altitude, normal acceleration, and rotorcraft configurations) which is described in the Rotorcraft Flight Manual; and

(3) The trim and stability characteristics are not impaired below a level needed to permit continued safe flight and landing.

[Docket No. 5074, 29 FR 15695, Nov. 24, 1964; as amended by Amdt. 27–21, 49 FR 44433, Nov. 6, 1984; 49 FR 47594, Dec. 6, 1984]

§27.673 Primary flight control.

Primary flight controls are those used by the pilot for immediate control of pitch, roll, yaw, and vertical motion of the rotorcraft.

[Docket No. 5074, 29 FR 15695, Nov. 24, 1964; as amended by Amdt. 27–21, 49 FR 44434, Nov. 6, 1984]

§27.674 Interconnected controls.

Each primary flight control system must provide for safe flight and landing and operate independently after a malfunction, failure, or jam of any auxiliary interconnected control.

[Docket No. 5074, 29 FR 15695, Nov. 24, 1964; as amended by Amdt. 27–26, 55 FR 8001, March 6, 990]

§27.675 Stops.

(a) Each control system must have stops that positively limit the range of motion of the pilot's controls.

(b) Each stop must be located in the system so that the range of travel of its control is not appreciably affected by—

(1) Wear;

(2) Slackness; or

(3) Takeup adjustments.

(c) Each stop must be able to withstand the loads corresponding to the design conditions for the system.

(d) For each main rotor blade—

(1) Stops that are appropriate to the blade design must be provided to limit travel of the blade about its hinge points; and

(2) There must be means to keep the blade from hitting the droop stops during any operation other than starting and stopping the rotor.

(Secs. 313(a), 601, 603, 604, Federal Aviation Act of 1958 (49 U.S.C. 1354(a), 1421, 1423, 1424), sec. 6(c), Dept. of Transportation Act (49 U.S.C. 1655(c)))

[Docket No. 5074, 29 FR 15695, Nov. 24, 1964; as amended by Amdt. 27–16, 43 FR 50599, Oct. 30, 1978]

§27.679 Control system locks.

If there is a device to lock the control system with the rotorcraft on the ground or water, there must be means to—

(a) Give unmistakable warning to the pilot when the lock is engaged; and

(b) Prevent the lock from engaging in flight.

§27.681 Limit load static tests.

(a) Compliance with the limit load requirements of this part must be shown by tests in which—

(1) The direction of the test loads produces the most severe loading in the control system; and

(2) Each fitting, pulley, and bracket used in attaching the system to the main structure is included.

(b) Compliance must be shown (by analyses or individual load tests) with the special factor requirements for control system joints subject to angular motion.

§27.683 Operation tests.

It must be shown by operation tests that, when the controls are operated from the pilot compartment with the control system loaded to correspond with loads specified for the system, the system is free from—

(a) Jamming;

(b) Excessive friction; and

(c) Excessive deflection.

§27.685 Control system details.

(a) Each detail of each control system must be designed to prevent jamming, chafing, and interference from cargo, passengers, loose objects or the freezing of moisture.

(b) There must be means in the cockpit to prevent the entry of foreign objects into places where they would jam the system.

(c) There must be means to prevent the slapping of cables or tubes against other parts.

(d) Cable systems must be designed as follows:

(1) Cables, cable fittings, turnbuckles, splices, and pulleys must be of an acceptable kind.

(2) The design of the cable systems must prevent any hazardous change in cable tension throughout the range of travel under any operating conditions and temperature variations.

(3) No cable smaller than three thirty-seconds of an inch diameter may be used in any primary control system.

(4) Pulley kinds and sizes must correspond to the cables with which they are used. The pulley cable combinations and strength values which must be used are specified in Military Handbook MIL-HDBK-5C, Vol. 1 & Vol. 2, Metallic Materials and Elements for Flight Vehicle Structures, (Sept. 15, 1976, as amended through December 15, 1978). This incorporation by reference was approved by the Director of the Federal Register in accordance with 5 U.S.C. section 552(a) and 1 CFR part 51. Copies may be obtained from the Naval Publications and Forms Center, 5801 Tabor Avenue, Philadelphia, Pennsylvania, 19120. Copies may be inspected at the FAA, Rotorcraft Standards Staff, 4400 Blue Mount Road, Fort Worth, Texas, or at the Office of the Federal Register, 800 North Capitol Street, NW, Suite 700, Washington, DC.

(5) Pulleys must have close fitting guards to prevent the cables from being displaced or fouled.

(6) Pulleys must lie close enough to the plane passing through the cable to prevent the cable from rubbing against the pulley flange.

(7) No fairlead may cause a change in cable direction of more than 3°.

(8) No clevis pin subject to load or motion and retained only by cotter pins may be used in the control system.

(9) Turnbuckles attached to parts having angular motion must be installed to prevent binding throughout the range of travel.

(10) There must be means for visual inspection at each fairlead, pulley, terminal, and turnbuckle.

(e) Control system joints subject to angular motion must incorporate the following special factors with respect to the ultimate bearing strength of the softest material used as a bearing:

(1) 3.33 for push-pull systems other than ball and roller bearing systems.

(2) 2.0 for cable systems.

(f) For control system joints, the manufacturer's static, non-Brinell rating of ball and roller bearings must not be exceeded.

[Docket No. 5074, 29 FR 15695, Nov. 24, 1964; as amended by Amdt. 27–11, 41 FR 55469, Dec. 20, 1976; Amdt. 27–26, 55 FR 8001, March 6, 1990]

§27.687 Spring devices.

(a) Each control system spring device whose failure could cause flutter or other unsafe characteristics must be reliable.

(b) Compliance with paragraph (a) of this section must be shown by tests simulating service conditions.

§27.691 Autorotation control mechanism.

Each main rotor blade pitch control mechanism must allow rapid entry into autorotation after power failure.

§27.695 Power boost and power-operated control system.

(a) If a power boost or power-operated control system is used, an alternate system must be immediately available that allows continued safe flight and landing in the event of—

(1) Any single failure in the power portion of the system; or

(2) The failure of all engines.

(b) Each alternate system may be a duplicate power portion or a manually operated mechanical system. The power portion includes the power source (such as hydraulic pumps), and such items as valves, lines, and actuators.

(c) The failure of mechanical parts (such as piston rods and links), and the jamming of power cylinders, must be considered unless they are extremely improbable.

Landing Gear

§27.723 Shock absorption tests.

The landing inertia load factor and the reserve energy absorption capacity of the landing gear must be substantiated by the tests prescribed in §§27.725 and 27.727, respectively. These tests must be conducted on the complete rotorcraft or on units consisting of wheel, tire, and shock absorber in their proper relation.

§27.725 Limit drop test.

The limit drop test must be conducted as follows:

(a) The drop height must be—

(1) 13 inches from the lowest point of the landing gear to the ground; or

(2) Any lesser height, not less than eight inches, resulting in a drop contact velocity equal to the greatest probable sinking speed likely to occur at ground contact in normal power-off landings.

(b) If considered, the rotor lift specified in §27.473(a) must be introduced into the drop test by appropriate energy absorbing devices or by the use of an effective mass.

(c) Each landing gear unit must be tested in the attitude simulating the landing condition that is most critical from the standpoint of the energy to be absorbed by it.

(d) When an effective mass is used in showing compliance with paragraph (b) of this section, the following formula may be used instead of more rational computations:

$$W_e = W \times \frac{h + (1 - L)d}{h + d}; \text{ and}$$

$$n = n_j \frac{W_e}{W} + L$$

where:

W_e = the effective weight to be used in the drop test (lbs.);

$W = W_M$ for main gear units (lbs.), equal to the static reaction on the particular unit with the rotorcraft In the most critical attitude. A rational method may be used In computing a main gear static reaction, taking into consideration the moment arm between the main wheel reaction and the rotorcraft center of gravity.

$W = W_N$ for nose gear units (lbs.), equal to the vertical component of the static reaction that would exist at the nose wheel, assuming that the mass of the rotorcraft acts at the center of gravity and exerts a force of 1.0g downward and 0.25g forward.

$W = W_T$ for tailwheel units (lbs.), equal to whichever of the following is critical:

(1) The static weight on the tailwheel with the rotorcraft resting on all wheels; or

(2) The vertical component of the ground reaction that would occur at the tailwheel, assuming that the mass of the rotorcraft acts at the center of gravity and exerts a force of 1*g* downward with the rotorcraft in the maximum nose-up attitude considered in the nose-up landing conditions.

h = specified free drop height (inches).

L = ration of assumed rotor lift to the rotorcraft weight.

d = deflection under impact of the tire (at the proper inflation pressure) plus the vertical component of the axle travels (inches) relative to the drop mass.

n = limit inertia load factor.

n_j = the load factor developed, during impact, on the mass used in the drop test (i.e., the acceleration dv/dt in g's recorded in the drop test plus 1.0).

§27.727 Reserve energy absorption drop test.

The reserve energy absorption drop test must be conducted as follows:

(a) The drop height must be 1.5 times that specified in §27.725(a).

(b) Rotor lift, where considered in a manner similar to that prescribed in §27.725(b), may not exceed 1.5 times the lift allowed under that paragraph.

(c) The landing gear must withstand this test without collapsing. Collapse of the landing gear occurs when a member of the nose, tail, or main gear will not support the rotorcraft in the proper attitude or allows the rotorcraft structure, other than the landing gear and external accessories, to impact the landing surface.

[Docket No. 5074, 29 FR 15695, Nov. 24, 1964; as amended by Amdt. 27–26, 55 FR 8001, March 6, 1990]

§27.729 Retracting mechanism.

For rotorcraft with retractable landing gear, the following apply:

(a) *Loads.* The landing gear, retracting mechanism, wheel-well doors, and supporting structure must be designed for—

(1) The loads occurring in any maneuvering condition with the gear retracted;

(2) The combined friction, inertia, and air loads occurring during retraction and extension at any airspeed up to the design maximum landing gear operating speed; and

(3) The flight loads, including those in yawed flight, occurring with the gear extended at any airspeed up to the design maximum landing gear extended speed.

(b) *Landing gear lock.* A positive means must be provided to keep the gear extended.

(c) *Emergency operation.* When other than manual power is used to operate the gear, emergency means must be provided for extending the gear in the event of—

(1) Any reasonably probable failure in the normal retraction system; or

(2) The failure of any single source of hydraulic, electric, or equivalent energy.

(d) *Operation tests.* The proper functioning of the retracting mechanism must be shown by operation tests.

(e) *Position indicator.* There must be a means to indicate to the pilot when the gear is secured in the extreme positions.

(f) *Control.* The location and operation of the retraction control must meet the requirements of §§27.777 and 27.779.

(g) *Landing gear warning.* An aural or equally effective landing gear warning device must be provided that functions continuously when the rotorcraft is in a normal landing mode and the landing gear is not fully extended and locked. A manual shutoff capability must be provided for the warning device and the warning system must automatically reset when the rotorcraft is no longer in the landing mode.

[Docket No. 5074, 29 FR 15695, Nov. 24, 1964; as amended by Amdt. 27–21, 49 FR 44434, Nov. 6, 1984]

§27.731 Wheels.

(a) Each landing gear wheel must be approved.

(b) The maximum static load rating of each wheel may not be less than the corresponding static ground reaction with—

(1) Maximum weight; and

(2) Critical center of gravity.

(c) The maximum limit load rating of each wheel must equal or exceed the maximum radial limit load determined under the applicable ground load requirements of this part.

§27.733 Tires.

(a) Each landing gear wheel must have a tire—

(1) That is a proper fit on the rim of the wheel; and

(2) Of the proper rating.

(b) The maximum static load rating of each tire must equal or exceed the static ground reaction obtained at its wheel, assuming—

(1) The design maximum weight; and

(2) The most unfavorable center of gravity.

(c) Each tire installed on a retractable landing gear system must, at the maximum size of the tire type expected in service, have a clearance to surrounding structure and systems that is adequate to prevent contact between the tire and any part of the structure or systems.

[Docket No. 5074, 29 FR 15695, Nov. 24, 1964; as amended by Amdt. 27–11, 41 FR 55469, Dec. 20, 1976]

§27.735 Brakes.

For rotorcraft with wheel-type landing gear, a braking device must be installed that is—

(a) Controllable by the pilot;

(b) Usable during power-off landings; and

(c) Adequate to—

(1) Counteract any normal unbalanced torque when starting or stopping the rotor; and

(2) Hold the rotorcraft parked on a 10-degree slope on a dry, smooth pavement.

[Docket No. 5074, 29 FR 15695, Nov. 24, 1964; as amended by Amdt. 27–21, 49 FR 44434, Nov. 6, 1984]

§27.737 Skis.

The maximum limit load rating of each ski must equal or exceed the maximum limit load determined under the applicable ground load requirements of this part.

Floats and Hulls

§27.751 Main float buoyancy.

(a) For main floats, the buoyancy necessary to support the maximum weight of the rotorcraft in fresh water must be exceeded by—

(1) 50 percent, for single floats; and

(2) 60 percent, for multiple floats.

(b) Each main float must have enough water-tight compartments so that, with any single main float compartment flooded, the main floats will provide a margin of positive stability great enough to minimize the probability of capsizing.

[Docket No. 5074, 29 FR 15695, Nov. 24, 1964; as amended by Amdt. 27–2, 33 FR 963, Jan. 26, 1968]

§27.753 Main float design.

(a) *Bag floats.* Each bag float must be designed to withstand—

(1) The maximum pressure differential that might be developed at the maximum altitude for which certification with that float is requested; and

(2) The vertical loads prescribed in §27.521(a), distributed along the length of the bag over three-quarters of its projected area.

(b) *Rigid floats.* Each rigid float must be able to withstand the vertical, horizontal, and side loads prescribed in §27.521. These loads may be distributed along the length of the float.

§27.755 Hulls.

For each rotorcraft, with a hull and auxiliary floats, that is to be approved for both taking off from and landing on water, the hull and auxiliary floats must have enough watertight compartments so that, with any single compartment flooded, the buoyancy of the hull and auxiliary floats (and wheel tires if used) provides a margin of positive stability great enough to minimize the probability of capsizing.

PERSONNEL AND CARGO ACCOMMODATIONS

§27.771 Pilot compartment.

For each pilot compartment—

(a) The compartment and its equipment must allow each pilot to perform his duties without unreasonable concentration or fatigue;

(b) If there is provision for a second pilot, the rotorcraft must be controllable with equal safety from either pilot seat; and

(c) The vibration and noise characteristics of cockpit appurtenances may not interfere with safe operation.

§27.773 Pilot compartment view.

(a) Each pilot compartment must be free from glare and reflections that could interfere with the pilot's view, and designed so that—

(1) Each pilot's view is sufficiently extensive, clear, and undistorted for safe operation; and

(2) Each pilot is protected from the elements so that moderate rain conditions do not unduly impair his view of the flight path in normal flight and while landing.

(b) If certification for night operation is requested, compliance with paragraph (a) of this section must be shown in night flight tests.

§27.775 Windshields and windows.

Windshields and windows must be made of material that will not break into dangerous fragments.

[Docket No. 5074, 29 FR 15695, Nov. 24, 1964; as amended by Amdt. 27–27, 55 FR 38966, Sept. 21, 1990]

§27.777 Cockpit controls.

Cockpit controls must be—

(a) Located to provide convenient operation and to prevent confusion and inadvertent operation; and

(b) Located and arranged with respect to the pilots' seats so that there is full and unrestricted movement of each control without interference from the cockpit structure or the pilot's clothing when pilots from 5'2" to 6'0" in height are seated.

§27.779 Motion and effect of cockpit controls.

Cockpit controls must be designed so that they operate in accordance with the following movements and actuation:

(a) Flight controls, including the collective pitch control, must operate with a sense of motion which corresponds to the effect on the rotorcraft.

(b) Twist-grip engine power controls must be designed so that, for lefthand operation, the motion of the pilot's hand is clockwise to increase power when the hand is viewed from the edge containing the index finger. Other engine power controls, excluding the collective control, must operate with a forward motion to increase power.

(c) Normal landing gear controls must operate downward to extend the landing gear.

[Docket No. 5074, 29 FR 15695, Nov. 24, 1964; as amended by Amdt. 27–21, 49 FR 44434, Nov. 6, 1984]

§27.783 Doors.

(a) Each closed cabin must have at least one adequate and easily accessible external door.

(b) Each external door must be located where persons using it will not be endangered by the rotors, propellers, engine intakes, and exhausts when appropriate operating procedures are used. If opening procedures are required, they must be marked inside, on or adjacent to the door opening device.

[Docket No. 5074, 29 FR 15695, Nov. 24, 1964; as amended by Amdt. 27–26, 55 FR 8001, March 6, 1990]

§27.785 Seats, berths, litters, safety belts, and harnesses.

(a) Each seat, safety belt, harness, and adjacent part of the rotorcraft at each station designated for occupancy during takeoff and landing must be free of potentially injurious objects, sharp edges, protuberances, and hard surfaces and must be designed so that a person making proper use of these facilities will not suffer serious injury in an emergency landing as a result of the static inertial load factors specified in §27.561(b) and dynamic conditions specified in §27.562.

(b) Each occupant must be protected from serious head injury by a safety belt plus a shoulder harness that will prevent the head from contacting any injurious object except as provided for in §27.562(c)(5). A shoulder harness (upper torso restraint), in combination with the safety belt, constitutes a torso restraint system as described in TSO-C114.

(c) Each occupant's seat must have a combined safety belt and shoulder harness with a single-point release. Each pilot's combined safety belt and shoulder harness must allow each pilot when seated with safety belt and shoulder harness fastened to perform all functions necessary for flight operations. There must be a means to secure belts and harnesses, when not in use, to prevent interference with the operation of the rotorcraft and with rapid egress in an emergency.

(d) If seat backs do not have a firm handhold, there must be hand grips or rails along each aisle to enable the occupants to steady themselves while using the aisle in moderately rough air.

(e) Each projecting object that could injure persons seated or moving about in the rotorcraft in normal flight must be padded.

(f) Each seat and its supporting structure must be designed for an occupant weight of at least 170 pounds considering the maximum load factors, inertial forces, and reactions between occupant, seat, and safety belt or harness corresponding with the applicable flight and ground load conditions, including the emergency landing conditions of §27.561(b). In addition—

(1) Each pilot seat must be designed for the reactions resulting from the application of the pilot forces prescribed in §27.397; and

(2) The inertial forces prescribed in §27.561(b) must be multiplied by a factor of 1.33 in determining the strength of the attachment of—

(i) Each seat to the structure; and

(ii) Each safety belt or harness to the seat or structure.

(g) When the safety belt and shoulder harness are combined, the rated strength of the safety belt and shoulder harness may not be less than that corresponding to the inertial forces specified in §27.561(b), considering the occupant weight of at least 170 pounds, considering the dimensional characteristics of the restraint system installation, and using a distribution of at least a 60-percent load to the safety belt and at least a 40-percent load to the shoulder harness. If the safety belt is capable of being used without the shoulder harness, the inertial forces specified must be met by the safety belt alone.

(h) When a headrest is used, the headrest and its supporting structure must be designed to resist the inertia forces specified in §27.561, with a 1.33 fitting factor and a head weight of at least 13 pounds.

(i) Each seating device system includes the device such as the seat, the cushions, the occupant restraint system, and attachment devices.

(j) Each seating device system may use design features such as crushing or separation of certain parts of the seats to reduce occupant loads for the emergency landing dynamic conditions of §27.562; otherwise, the system must remain intact and must not interfere with rapid evacuation of the rotorcraft.

(k) For the purposes of this section, a litter is defined as a device designed to carry a nonambulatory person, primarily in a recumbent position, into and on the rotorcraft. Each berth or litter must be designed to withstand the load reaction of an occupant weight of at least 170 pounds when the occupant is subjected to the forward inertial factors specified in §27.561(b). A berth or litter installed within 15° or less of the longitudinal axis of the rotorcraft must be provided with a padded end-board, cloth diaphragm, or equivalent means that can withstand the forward load reaction. A berth or litter oriented greater than 15° with the longitudinal axis of the rotorcraft must be equipped with appropriate restraints, such as straps or safety belts, to withstand the forward load reaction. In addition—

(1) The berth or litter must have a restraint system and must not have corners or other protuberances likely to cause serious injury to a person occupying it during emergency landing conditions; and

(2) The berth or litter attachment and the occupant restraint system attachments to the structure must be designed to withstand the critical loads resulting from flight and ground load conditions and from the conditions prescribed in §27.561(b). The fitting factor required by §27.625(d) shall be applied.

[Docket No. 5074, 29 FR 15695, Nov. 24, 1964; as amended by Amdt. 27–21, 49 FR 44434, Nov. 6, 1984, Amdt. 27–25, 54 FR 47319, Nov. 13, 1989; Amdt. 27–35, 63 FR 43285, Aug. 12, 1998]

§27.787 Cargo and baggage compartments.

(a) Each cargo and baggage compartment must be designed for its placarded maximum weight of contents and for the critical load distributions at the appropriate maximum load factors corresponding to the specified flight and ground load conditions, except the emergency landing conditions of §27.561.

(b) There must be means to prevent the contents of any compartment from becoming a hazard by shifting under the loads specified in paragraph (a) of this section.

(c) Under the emergency landing conditions of §27.561, cargo and baggage compartments must—

(1) Be positioned so that if the contents break loose they are unlikely to cause injury to the occupants or restrict any of the escape facilities provided for use after an emergency landing; or

(2) Have sufficient strength to withstand the conditions specified in §27.561 including the means of restraint, and their attachments, required by paragraph (b) of this section. Sufficient strength must be provided for the maximum authorized weight of cargo and baggage at the critical loading distribution.

(d) If cargo compartment lamps are installed, each lamp must be installed so as to prevent contact between lamp bulb and cargo.

[Docket No. 5074, 29 FR 15695, Nov. 24, 1964; as amended by Amdt. 27–11, 41 FR 55469, Dec. 20, 1976; Amdt. 27–27, 55 FR 38966, Sept. 21, 1990]

27

§27.801 Ditching.

(a) If certification with ditching provisions is requested, the rotorcraft must meet the requirements of this section and §§27.807(d), 27.1411 and 27.1415.

(b) Each practicable design measure, compatible with the general characteristics of the rotorcraft, must be taken to minimize the probability that in an emergency landing on water, the behavior of the rotorcraft would cause immediate injury to the occupants or would make it impossible for them to escape.

(c) The probable behavior of the rotorcraft in a water landing must be investigated by model tests or by comparison with rotorcraft of similar configuration for which the ditching characteristics are known. Scoops, flaps, projections, and any other factor likely to affect the hydrodynamic characteristics of the rotorcraft must be considered.

(d) It must be shown that, under reasonably probable water conditions, the flotation time and trim of the rotorcraft will allow the occupants to leave the rotorcraft and enter the life rafts required by §27.1415. If compliance with this provision is shown by buoyancy and trim computations, appropriate allowances must be made for probable structural damage and leakage. If the rotorcraft has fuel tanks (with fuel jettisoning provisions) that can reasonably be expected to withstand a ditching without leakage, the jettisonable volume of fuel may be considered as buoyancy volume.

(e) Unless the effects of the collapse of external doors and windows are accounted for in the investigation of the probable behavior of the rotorcraft in a water landing (as prescribed in paragraphs (c) and (d) of this section), the external doors and windows must be designed to withstand the probable maximum local pressures.

[Docket No. 5074, 29 FR 15695, Nov. 24, 1964; as amended by Amdt. 27–11, 41 FR 55469, Dec. 20, 1976]

§27.805 Flight crew emergency exits.

(a) For rotorcraft with passenger emergency exits that are not convenient to the flight crew, there must be flight crew emergency exits, on both sides of the rotorcraft or as a top hatch in the flight crew area.

(b) Each flight crew emergency exit must be of sufficient size and must be located so as to allow rapid evacuation of the flight crew. This must be shown by test.

(c) Each flight crew emergency exit must not be obstructed by water or flotation devices after an emergency landing on water. This must be shown by test, demonstration, or analysis.

[Docket No. 29247, 64 FR 45094, Aug. 18, 1999]

§27.807 Emergency exits.

(a) *Number and location.*

(1) There must be at least one emergency exit on each side of the cabin readily accessible to each passenger. One of these exits must be usable in any probable attitude that may result from a crash;

(2) Doors intended for normal use may also serve as emergency exits, provided that they meet the requirements of this section; and

(3) If emergency flotation devices are installed, there must be an emergency exit accessible to each passenger on each side of the cabin that is shown by test, demonstration, or analysis to;

(i) Be above the waterline; and

(ii) Open without interference from flotation devices, whether stowed or deployed.

(b) *Type and operation.* Each emergency exit prescribed in paragraph (a) of this section must—

(1) Consist of a movable window or panel, or additional external door, providing an unobstructed opening that will admit a 19- by 26-inch ellipse;

(2) Have simple and obvious methods of opening, from the inside and from the outside, which do not require exceptional effort;

(3) Be arranged and marked so as to be readily located and opened even in darkness; and

(4) Be reasonably protected from jamming by fuselage deformation.

(c) *Tests.* The proper functioning of each emergency exit must be shown by test.

(d) *Ditching emergency exits for passengers.* If certification with ditching provisions is requested, the markings required by paragraph (b)(3) of this section must be designed to remain visible if the rotorcraft is capsized and the cabin is submerged.

[Docket No. 5074, 29 FR 15695, Nov. 24, 1964; as amended by Amdt. 27–2, 33 FR 963, Jan. 26, 1968; Amdt. 27–11, 41 FR 55469, Dec. 20, 1976; Amdt. 27–21, 49 FR 44435, Nov. 6, 1984; Amdt. 27–26, 55 FR 8001, March 6, 1990; Amdt. 27–37, 64 FR 45094, Aug. 18, 1999]

§27.831 Ventilation.

(a) The ventilating system for the pilot and passenger compartments must be designed to prevent the presence of excessive quantities of fuel fumes and carbon monoxide.

(b) The concentration of carbon monoxide may not exceed one part in 20,000 parts of air during forward flight or hovering in still air. If the concentration exceeds this value under other conditions, there must be suitable operating restrictions.

§27.833 Heaters.

Each combustion heater must be approved.

[Docket No. 5074, 29 FR 15695, Nov. 24, 1964; as amended by Amdt. 27–23, 53 FR 34210, Sept. 2, 1988]

Fire Protection

§27.853 Compartment interiors.

For each compartment to be used by the crew or passengers—

(a) The materials must be at least flame-resistant;

(b) [Reserved]

(c) If smoking is to be prohibited, there must be a placard so stating, and if smoking is to be allowed—

(1) There must be an adequate number of self-contained, removable ashtrays; and

(2) Where the crew compartment is separated from the passenger compartment, there must be at least one illuminated sign (using either letters or symbols) notifying all passengers when smoking is prohibited. Signs which notify when smoking is prohibited must—

(i) When illuminated, be legible to each passenger seated in the passenger cabin under all probable lighting conditions; and

(ii) Be so constructed that the crew can turn the illumination on and off.

[Docket No. 5074, 29 FR 15695, Nov. 24, 1964; as amended by Amdt. 27–17, 45 FR 7755, Feb. 4, 1980; Amdt. 27–37, 64 FR 45095, Aug. 18, 1999]

§27.855 Cargo and baggage compartments.

(a) Each cargo and baggage compartment must be constructed of, or lined with, materials that are at least—

(1) Flame resistant, in the case of compartments that are readily accessible to a crewmember in flight; and

(2) Fire resistant, in the case of other compartments.

(b) No compartment may contain any controls, wiring, lines, equipment, or accessories whose damage or failure would affect safe operation, unless those items are protected so that—

(1) They cannot be damaged by the movement of cargo in the compartment; and

(2) Their breakage or failure will not create a fire hazard.

§27.859 Heating systems.

(a) *General.* For each heating system that involves the passage of cabin air over, or close to, the exhaust manifold, there must be means to prevent carbon monoxide from entering any cabin or pilot compartment.

(b) *Heat exchangers.* Each heat exchanger must be—

(1) Of suitable materials;

(2) Adequately cooled under all conditions; and

(3) Easily disassembled for inspection.

(c) *Combustion heater fire protection.* Except for heaters which incorporate designs to prevent hazards in the event of fuel leakage in the heater fuel system, fire within the ventilating air passage, or any other heater malfunction, each heater zone must incorporate the fire protection features of the applicable requirements of §§27.1183, 27.1185, 27.1189, 27.1191, and be provided with—

(1) Approved, quick-acting fire detectors in numbers and locations ensuring prompt detection of fire in the heater region.

(2) Fire extinguisher systems that provide at least one adequate discharge to all areas of the heater region.

(3) Complete drainage of each part of each zone to minimize the hazards resulting from failure or malfunction of any component containing flammable fluids. The drainage means must be—

(i) Effective under conditions expected to prevail when drainage is needed; and

(ii) Arranged so that no discharged fluid will cause an additional fire hazard.

(4) Ventilation, arranged so that no discharged vapors will cause an additional fire hazard.

(d) *Ventilating air ducts.* Each ventilating air duct passing through any heater region must be fireproof.

(1) Unless isolation is provided by fireproof valves or by equally effective means, the ventilating air duct downstream of each heater must be fireproof for a distance great enough to ensure that any fire originating in the heater can be contained in the duct.

(2) Each part of any ventilating duct passing through any region having a flammable fluid system must be so constructed or isolated from that system that the malfunctioning of any component of that system cannot introduce flammable fluids or vapors into the ventilating airstream.

(e) *Combustion air ducts.* Each combustion air duct must be fireproof for a distance great enough to prevent damage from backfiring or reverse flame propagation.

(1) No combustion air duct may connect with the ventilating airstream unless flames from backfires or reverse burning cannot enter the ventilating airstream under any operating condition, including reverse flow or malfunction of the heater or its associated components.

(2) No combustion air duct may restrict the prompt relief of any backfire that, if so restricted, could cause heater failure.

(f) *Heater control: General.* There must be means to prevent the hazardous accumulation of water or ice on or in any heater control component, control system tubing, or safety control.

(g) *Heater safety controls.* For each combustion heater, safety control means must be provided as follows:

(1) Means independent of the components provided for the normal continuous control of air temperature, airflow, and fuel flow must be provided for each heater to automatically shut off the ignition and fuel supply of that heater at a point remote from that heater when any of the following occurs:

(i) The heat exchanger temperature exceeds safe limits.

(ii) The ventilating air temperature exceeds safe limits.

(iii) The combustion airflow becomes inadequate for safe operation.

(iv) The ventilating airflow becomes inadequate for safe operation.

(2) The means of complying with paragraph (g)(1) of this section for any individual heater must—

(i) Be independent of components serving any other heater, the heat output of which is essential for safe operation; and

(ii) Keep the heater off until restarted by the crew.

(3) There must be means to warn the crew when any heater, the heat output of which is essential for safe operation, has been shut off by the automatic means prescribed in paragraph (g)(1) of this section.

(h) *Air intakes.* Each combustion and ventilating air intake must be located so that no flammable fluids or vapors can enter the heater system—

(1) During normal operation; or

(2) As a result of the malfunction of any other component.

(i) *Heater exhaust.* Each heater exhaust system must meet the requirements of §§27.1121 and 27.1123.

(1) Each exhaust shroud must be sealed so that no flammable fluids or hazardous quantities of vapors can reach the exhaust system through joints.

(2) No exhaust system may restrict the prompt relief of any backfire that, if so restricted, could cause heater failure.

(j) *Heater fuel systems.* Each heater fuel system must meet the powerplant fuel system requirements affecting safe heater operation. Each heater fuel system component in the ventilating airstream must be protected by shrouds so that no leakage from those components can enter the ventilating airstream.

(k) *Drains.* There must be means for safe drainage of any fuel that might accumulate in the combustion chamber or the heat exchanger.

(1) Each part of any drain that operates at high temperatures must be protected in the same manner as heater exhausts.

(2) Each drain must be protected against hazardous ice accumulation under any operating condition.

[Docket No. 5074, 29 FR 15695, Nov. 24, 1964; as amended by Amdt. 27–23, 53 FR 34211, Sept. 2, 1988]

§27.861 Fire protection of structure, controls, and other parts.

Each part of the structure, controls, rotor mechanism, and other parts essential to a controlled landing that would be affected by powerplant fires must be fireproof or protected so they can perform their essential functions for at least 5 minutes under any foreseeable powerplant fire conditions.

[Docket No. 5074, 29 FR 15695, Nov. 24, 1964; as amended by Amdt. 27–26, 55 FR 8001, March 6, 1990]

§27.863 Flammable fluid fire protection.

(a) In each area where flammable fluids or vapors might escape by leakage of a fluid system, there must be means to minimize the probability of ignition of the fluids and vapors, and the resultant hazards if ignition does occur.

(b) Compliance with paragraph (a) of this section must be shown by analysis or tests, and the following factors must be considered:

(1) Possible sources and paths of fluid leakage, and means of detecting leakage.

(2) Flammability characteristics of fluids, including effects of any combustible or absorbing materials.

(3) Possible ignition sources, including electrical faults, overheating of equipment, and malfunctioning of protective devices.

(4) Means available for controlling or extinguishing a fire, such as stopping flow of fluids, shutting down equipment, fireproof containment, or use of extinguishing agents.

(5) Ability of rotorcraft components that are critical to safety of flight to withstand fire and heat.

(c) If action by the flight crew is required to prevent or counteract a fluid fire (e.g. equipment shutdown or actuation of a fire extinguisher) quick acting means must be provided to alert the crew.

(d) Each area where flammable fluids or vapors might escape by leakage of a fluid system must be identified and defined.

(Secs. 313(a), 601, 603, 604, Federal Aviation Act of 1958 (49 U.S.C. 1354(a), 1421, 1423, 1424), sec. 6(c), Dept. of Transportation Act (49 U.S.C. 1655(c)))

[Docket No. 5074, 29 FR 15695, Nov. 24, 1964; as amended by Amdt. 27–16, 43 FR 50599, Oct. 30, 1978]

External Loads

§27.865 External loads.

(a) It must be shown by analysis, test, or both, that the rotorcraft external load attaching means for rotorcraft-load combinations to be used for nonhuman external cargo applications can withstand a limit static load equal to 2.5, or some lower load factor approved under §§27.337 through 27.341, multiplied by the maximum external load for which authorization is requested. It must be shown by analysis, test, or both that the rotorcraft external load attaching means and corresponding personnel carrying device system for rotorcraft-load combinations to be used for human external cargo applications can withstand a limit static load equal to 3.5 or some lower load factor, not less than 2.5, approved under §§27.337 through 27.341, multiplied by the maximum external load for which authorization is requested. The load for any rotorcraft-load combination class, for any external cargo type, must be applied in the vertical direction. For jettisonable external loads of any applicable external cargo type, the load must also be applied in any direction making the maximum angle with the vertical that can be achieved in service but not less than 30°. However, the 30° angle may be reduced to a lesser angle if—

(1) An operating limitation is established limiting external load operations to such angles for which compliance with this paragraph has been shown; or

(2) It is shown that the lesser angle cannot be exceeded in service.

(b) The external load attaching means, for jettisonable rotorcraft-load combinations, must include a quick-release system to enable the pilot to release the external load quickly during flight. The quick-release system must consist of a primary quick release subsystem and a backup quick release subsystem that are isolated from one another. The quick-release system, and the means by which it is controlled, must comply with the following:

(1) A control for the primary quick release subsystem must be installed either on one of the pilot's primary controls or in an equivalently accessible location and must be designed and located so that it may be operated by either the pilot or a crewmember without hazardously limiting the ability to control the rotorcraft during an emergency situation.

(2) A control for the backup quick release subsystem, readily accessible to either the pilot or another crewmember, must be provided.

(3) Both the primary and backup quick release subsystems must—

(i) Be reliable, durable, and function properly with all external loads up to and including the maximum external limit load for which authorization is requested.

(ii) Be protected against electromagnetic interference (EMI) from external and internal sources and against lightning to prevent inadvertent load release.

(A) The minimum level of protection required for jettisonable rotorcraft-load combinations used for nonhuman external cargo is a radio frequency field strength of 20 volts per meter.

(B) The minimum level of protection required for jettisonable rotorcraft-load combinations used for human external cargo is a radio frequency field strength of 200 volts per meter.

(iii) Be protected against any failure that could be induced by a failure mode of any other electrical or mechanical rotorcraft system.

(c) For rotorcraft-load combinations to be used for human external cargo applications, the rotorcraft must—

(1) For jettisonable external loads, have a quick-release system that meets the requirements of paragraph (b) of this section and that—

(i) Provides a dual actuation device for the primary quick release subsystem, and

(ii) Provides a separate dual actuation device for the backup quick release subsystem;

(2) Have a reliable, approved personnel carrying device system that has the structural capability and personnel safety features essential for external occupant safety;

(3) Have placards and markings at all appropriate locations that clearly state the essential system operating instructions and, for the personnel carrying device system, the ingress and egress instructions;

(4) Have equipment to allow direct intercommunication among required crewmembers and external occupants; and

(5) Have the appropriate limitations and procedures incorporated in the flight manual for conducting human external cargo operations.

(d) The critically configured jettisonable external loads must be shown by a combination of analysis, ground tests, and flight tests to be both transportable and releasable throughout the approved operational envelope without hazard to the rotorcraft during normal flight conditions. In addition, these external loads must be shown to be releasable without hazard to the rotorcraft during emergency flight conditions.

(e) A placard or marking must be installed next to the external-load attaching means clearly stating any operational limitations and the maximum authorized external load as demonstrated under §27.25 and this section.

(f) The fatigue evaluation of §27.571 of this part does not apply to rotorcraft-load combinations to be used for nonhuman external cargo except for the failure of critical structural elements that would result in a hazard to the rotorcraft. For rotorcraft-load combinations to be used for human external cargo, the fatigue evaluation of §27.571 of this part applies to the entire quick release and personnel carrying device structural systems and their attachments.

[Docket No. 5074, 29 FR 15695, Nov. 24, 1964; as amended by Amdt. 27–11, 41 FR 55469, Dec. 20, 1976; Amdt. 27–26, 55 FR 8001, March 6, 1990; Amdt. 27–36, 64 FR 43019, Aug. 6, 1999]

MISCELLANEOUS

§27.871 Leveling marks.

There must be reference marks for leveling the rotorcraft on the ground.

§27.873 Ballast provisions.

Ballast provisions must be designed and constructed to prevent inadvertent shifting of ballast in flight.

Subpart E—Powerplant

GENERAL

§27.901 Installation.

(a) For the purpose of this part, the powerplant installation includes each part of the rotorcraft (other than the main and auxiliary rotor structures) that—

(1) Is necessary for propulsion;

(2) Affects the control of the major propulsive units; or

(3) Affects the safety of the major propulsive units between normal inspections or overhauls.

(b) For each powerplant installation—

(1) Each component of the installation must be constructed, arranged, and installed to ensure its continued safe operation between normal inspections or overhauls for the range of temperature and altitude for which approval is requested;

(2) Accessibility must be provided to allow any inspection and maintenance necessary for continued airworthiness;

(3) Electrical interconnections must be provided to prevent differences of potential between major components of the installation and the rest of the rotorcraft;

(4) Axial and radial expansion of turbine engines may not affect the safety of the installation; and

(5) Design precautions must be taken to minimize the possibility of incorrect assembly of components and equipment essential to safe operation of the rotorcraft, except where operation with the incorrect assembly can be shown to be extremely improbable.

(c) The installation must comply with—

(1) The installation instructions provided under §33.5 of this chapter; and

(2) The applicable provisions of this subpart.

(Secs. 313(a), 601, and 603, 72 Stat. 752, 775, 49 U.S.C. 1354(a), 1421, and 1423; sec. 6(c), 49 U.S.C. 1655(c))

[Docket No. 5074, 29 FR 15695, Nov. 24, 1964; as amended by Amdt. 27–2, 33 FR 963, Jan. 26, 1968; Amdt. 27–12, 42 FR 15044, March 17, 1977; Amdt. 27–23, 53 FR 34211, Sept. 2, 1988]

§27.903 Engines.

(a) *Engine type certification.* Each engine must have an approved type certificate. Reciprocating engines for use in helicopters must be qualified in accordance with §33.49(d) of this chapter or be otherwise approved for the intended usage.

(b) *Engine or drive system cooling fan blade protection.*

(1) If an engine or rotor drive system cooling fan is installed, there must be a means to protect the rotorcraft and allow a safe landing if a fan blade fails. This must be shown by showing that—

(i) The fan blades are contained in case of failure;

(ii) Each fan is located so that a failure will not jeopardize safety; or

(iii) Each fan blade can withstand an ultimate load of 1.5 times the centrifugal force resulting from operation limited by the following:

(A) For fans driven directly by the engine—

(1) The terminal engine r.p.m. under uncontrolled conditions; or

(2) An overspeed limiting device.

(B) For fans driven by the rotor drive system, the maximum rotor drive system rotational speed to be expected in service, including transients.

(2) Unless a fatigue evaluation under §27.571 is conducted, it must be shown that cooling fan blades are not operating at resonant conditions within the operating limits of the rotorcraft.

(c) *Turbine engine installation.* For turbine engine installations, the powerplant systems associated with engine control devices, systems, and instrumentation must be designed to give reasonable assurance that those engine operating limitations that adversely affect turbine rotor structural integrity will not be exceeded in service.

[Docket No. 5074, 29 FR 15695, Nov. 24, 1964; as amended by Amdt. 27–11, 41 FR 55469, Dec. 20, 1976; Amdt. 27–23, 53 FR 34211, Sept. 2, 1988]

§27.907 Engine vibration.

(a) Each engine must be installed to prevent the harmful vibration of any part of the engine or rotorcraft.

(b) The addition of the rotor and the rotor drive system to the engine may not subject the principal rotating parts of the engine to excessive vibration stresses. This must be shown by a vibration investigation.

(c) No part of the rotor drive system may be subjected to excessive vibration stresses.

ROTOR DRIVE SYSTEM

§27.917 Design.

(a) Each rotor drive system must incorporate a unit for each engine to automatically disengage that engine from the main and auxiliary rotors if that engine fails.

(b) Each rotor drive system must be arranged so that each rotor necessary for control in autorotation will continue to be driven by the main rotors after disengagement of the engine from the main and auxiliary rotors.

(c) If a torque limiting device is used in the rotor drive system, it must be located so as to allow continued control of the rotorcraft when the device is operating.

(d) The rotor drive system includes any part necessary to transmit power from the engines to the rotor hubs. This includes gear boxes, shafting, universal joints, couplings, rotor brake assemblies, clutches, supporting bearings for shafting, any attendant accessory pads or drives, and any cooling fans that are a part of, attached to, or mounted on the rotor drive system.

[Docket No. 5074, 29 FR 15695, Nov. 24, 1964; as amended by Amdt. 27–11, 41 FR 55469, Dec. 20, 1976]

§27.921 Rotor brake.

If there is a means to control the rotation of the rotor drive system independently of the engine, any limitations on the use of that means must be specified, and the control for that means must be guarded to prevent inadvertent operation.

§27.923 Rotor drive system and control mechanism tests.

(a) Each part tested as prescribed in this section must be in a serviceable condition at the end of the tests. No intervening disassembly which might affect test results may be conducted.

(b) Each rotor drive system and control mechanism must be tested for not less than 100 hours. The test must be conducted on the rotorcraft, and the torque must be absorbed by the rotors to be installed, except that other ground or flight test facilities with other appropriate methods of torque absorption may be used if the conditions of support and vibration closely simulate the conditions that would exist during a test on the rotorcraft.

(c) A 60-hour part of the test prescribed in paragraph (b) of this section must be run at not less than maximum continuous torque and the maximum speed for use with maximum continuous torque. In this test, the main rotor controls must be set in the position that will give maximum longitudinal cyclic pitch change to simulate forward flight. The auxiliary rotor controls must be in the position for normal operation under the conditions of the test.

(d) A 30-hour or, for rotorcraft for which the use of either 30-minute OEI power or continuous OEI power is requested, a 25-hour part of the test prescribed in paragraph (b) of this section must be run at not less than 75 percent of maximum continuous torque and the minimum speed for use with 75 percent of maximum continuous torque. The main and auxiliary rotor controls must be in the position for normal operation under the conditions of the test.

(e) A 10-hour part of the test prescribed in paragraph (b) of this section must be run at not less than takeoff torque and the maximum speed for use with takeoff torque. The main and auxiliary rotor controls must be in the normal position for vertical ascent.

(1) For multiengine rotorcraft for which the use of $2\frac{1}{2}$ minute OEI power is requested, 12 runs during the 10-hour test must be conducted as follows:

(i) Each run must consist of at least one period of $2\frac{1}{2}$ minutes with takeoff torque and the maximum speed for use with takeoff torque on all engines.

(ii) Each run must consist of at least one period for each engine in sequence, during which that engine simulates a power failure and the remaining engines are run at $2\frac{1}{2}$ minute OEI torque and the maximum speed for use with $2\frac{1}{2}$ minute OEI torque for $2\frac{1}{2}$ minutes.

(2) For multiengine turbine-powered rotorcraft for which the use of 30-second and 2-minute OEI power is requested, 10 runs must be conducted as follows:

(i) Immediately following a takeoff run of at least 5 minutes, each power source must simulate a failure, in turn, and apply the maximum torque and the maximum speed for use with 30-second OEI power to the remaining affected drive system power inputs for not less than 30 seconds, followed by application of the maximum torque and the maximum speed for use with 2-minute OEI power for not less than 2 minutes. At least one run sequence must be conducted from a simulated "flight idle" condition. When conducted on a bench test, the test sequence must be conducted following stabilization at takeoff power.

(ii) For the purpose of this paragraph, an affected power input includes all parts of the rotor drive system which can be adversely affected by the application of higher or asymmetric torque and speed prescribed by the test.

(iii) This test may be conducted on a representative bench test facility when engine limitations either preclude repeated use of this power or would result in premature engine removal during the test. The loads, the vibration frequency, and the methods of application to the affected rotor drive system components must be representative of rotorcraft conditions. Test components must be those used to show compliance with the remainder of this section.

(f) The parts of the test prescribed in paragraphs (c) and (d) of this section must be conducted in intervals of not less than 30 minutes and may be accomplished either on the ground or in flight. The part of the test prescribed in paragraph (e) of this section must be conducted in intervals of not less than five minutes.

(g) At intervals of not more than five hours during the tests prescribed in paragraphs (c), (d), and (e) of this section, the engine must be stopped rapidly enough to allow the engine and rotor drive to be automatically disengaged from the rotors.

(h) Under the operating conditions specified in paragraph (c) of this section, 500 complete cycles of lateral control, 500 complete cycles of longitudinal control of the main rotors, and 500 complete cycles of control of each auxiliary rotor must be accomplished. A "complete cycle" involves movement of the controls from the neutral position, through both extreme positions, and back to the neutral position, except that control movements need not produce loads or flapping motions exceeding the maximum loads or motions encountered in flight. The cycling may be accomplished during the testing prescribed in paragraph (c) of this section.

(i) At least 200 start-up clutch engagements must be accomplished—

(1) So that the shaft on the driven side of the clutch is accelerated; and

(2) Using a speed and method selected by the applicant.

(j) For multiengine rotorcraft for which the use of 30-minute OEI power is requested, five runs must be made at 30-minute OEI torque and the maximum speed for use with 30-minute OEI torque, in which each engine, in sequence, is made inoperative and the remaining engine(s) is run for a 30-minute period.

(k) For multiengine rotorcraft for which the use of continuous OEI power is requested, five runs must be made at continuous OEI torque and the maximum speed for use with continuous OEI torque, in which each engine, in sequence, is made inoperative and the remaining engine(s) is run for a 1-hour period.

(Secs. 313(a), 601, and 603, 72 Stat. 752, 775, 49 U.S.C. 1354(a), 1421, and 1423; sec. 6(c), 49 U.S.C. 1655(c))

[Docket No. 5074, 29 FR 15695, Nov. 24, 1964; as amended by Amdt. 27–2, 33 FR 963, Jan. 26, 1968; Amdt. 27–12, 42 FR 15044, March 17, 1977; Amdt. 27–23, 53 FR 34212, Sept. 2, 1988; Amdt. 27–29, 59 FR 47767, Sept. 16, 1994]

§27.927 Additional tests.

(a) Any additional dynamic, endurance, and operational tests, and vibratory investigations necessary to determine that the rotor drive mechanism is safe, must be performed.

(b) If turbine engine torque output to the transmission can exceed the highest engine or transmission torque rating limit, and that output is not directly controlled by the pilot under normal operating conditions (such as where the primary engine power control is accomplished through the flight control), the following test must be made:

(1) Under conditions associated with all engines operating, make 200 applications, for 10 seconds each, or torque that is at least equal to the lesser of—

(i) The maximum torque used in meeting §27.923 plus 10 percent; or

(ii) The maximum attainable torque output of the engines, assuming that torque limiting devices, if any, function properly.

(2) For multiengine rotorcraft under conditions associated with each engine, in turn, becoming inoperative, apply to the remaining transmission torque inputs the maximum torque attainable under probable operating conditions, assuming that torque limiting devices, if any, function properly. Each transmission input must be tested at this maximum torque for at least 15 minutes.

(3) The tests prescribed in this paragraph must be conducted on the rotorcraft at the maximum rotational speed intended for the power condition of the test and the torque must be absorbed by the rotors to be installed, except that other ground or flight test facilities with other appropriate methods of torque absorption may be used if the conditions of support and vibration closely simulate the conditions that would exist during a test on the rotorcraft.

(c) It must be shown by tests that the rotor drive system is capable of operating under autorotative conditions for 15 minutes after the loss of pressure in the rotor drive primary oil system.

(Secs. 313(a), 601, and 603, 72 Stat. 752, 775, 49 U.S.C. 1354(a), 1421, and 1423; sec. 6(c), 49 U.S.C. 1655(c))

[Docket No. 5074, 29 FR 15695, Nov. 24, 1964; as amended by Amdt. 27–2, 33 FR 963, Jan. 26, 1968; Amdt. 27–12, 42 FR 15045, March 17, 1977; Amdt. 27–23, 53 FR 34212, Sept. 2, 1988]

§27.931 Shafting critical speed.

(a) The critical speeds of any shafting must be determined by demonstration except that analytical methods may be used if reliable methods of analysis are available for the particular design.

(b) If any critical speed lies within, or close to, the operating ranges for idling, power on, and autorotative conditions, the stresses occurring at that speed must be within safe limits. This must be shown by tests.

(c) If analytical methods are used and show that no critical speed lies within the permissible operating ranges, the margins between the calculated critical speeds and the limits of the allowable operating ranges must be adequate to allow for possible variations between the computed and actual values.

§27.935 Shafting joints.

Each universal joint, slip joint, and other shafting joints whose lubrication is necessary for operation must have provision for lubrication.

§27.939 Turbine engine operating characteristics.

(a) Turbine engine operating characteristics must be investigated in flight to determine that no adverse characteristics (such as stall, surge, or flameout) are present, to a hazardous degree, during normal and emergency operation within the range of operating limitations of the rotorcraft and of the engine.

(b) The turbine engine air inlet system may not, as a result of airflow distortion during normal operation, cause vibration harmful to the engine.

(c) For governor-controlled engines, it must be shown that there exists no hazardous torsional instability of the drive system associated with critical combinations of power, rotational speed, and control displacement.

[Docket No. 5074, 29 FR 15695, Nov. 24, 1964; as amended by Amdt. 27–1, 32 FR 6914, May 5, 1967; Amdt. 27–11, 41 FR 55469, Dec. 20, 1976]

Fuel System

§27.951 General.

(a) Each fuel system must be constructed and arranged to ensure a flow of fuel at a rate and pressure established for proper engine functioning under any likely operating condition, including the maneuvers for which certification is requested.

(b) Each fuel system must be arranged so that—

(1) No fuel pump can draw fuel from more than one tank at a time; or

(2) There are means to prevent introducing air into the system.

(c) Each fuel system for a turbine engine must be capable of sustained operation throughout its flow and pressure range with fuel initially saturated with water at 80° F and having 0.75cc of free water per gallon added and cooled to the most critical condition for icing likely to be encountered in operation.

[Docket No. 5074, 29 FR 15695, Nov. 24, 1964; as amended by Amdt. 27–9, 39 FR 35461, Oct. 1, 1974]

§27.952 Fuel system crash resistance.

Unless other means acceptable to the Administrator are employed to minimize the hazard of fuel fires to occupants following an otherwise survivable impact (crash landing), the fuel systems must incorporate the design features of this section. These systems must be shown to be capable of sustaining the static and dynamic deceleration loads of this section, considered as ultimate loads acting alone, measured at the system component's center of gravity, without structural damage to system components, fuel tanks, or their attachments that would leak fuel to an ignition source.

(a) *Drop test requirements.* Each tank, or the most critical tank, must be drop-tested as follows:

(1) The drop height must be at least 50 feet.

(2) The drop impact surface must be nondeforming.

(3) The tank must be filled with water to 80 percent of the normal, full capacity.

(4) The tank must be enclosed in a surrounding structure representative of the installation unless it can be established that the surrounding structure is free of projections or other design features likely to contribute to rupture of the tank.

(5) The tank must drop freely and impact in a horizontal position ±10°.

(6) After the drop test, there must be no leakage.

(b) *Fuel tank load factors.* Except for fuel tanks located so that tank rupture with fuel release to either significant ignition sources, such as engines, heaters, and auxiliary power units, or occupants is extremely remote, each fuel tank must be designed and installed to retain its contents under the following ultimate inertial load factors, acting alone.

(1) For fuel tanks in the cabin:

(i) Upward—4g.

(ii) Forward—16g.

(iii) Sideward—8g.

(iv) Downward—20g.

(2) For fuel tanks located above or behind the crew or passenger compartment that, if loosened, could injure an occupant in an emergency landing:

(i) Upward—1.5g.

(ii) Forward—8g.

(iii) Sideward—2g.

(iv) Downward—4g.

(3) For fuel tanks in other areas:

(i) Upward—1.5g.

(ii) Forward—4g.

(iii) Sideward—2g.

(iv) Downward—4g.

(c) *Fuel line self-sealing breakaway couplings.* Self-sealing breakaway couplings must be installed unless hazardous relative motion of fuel system components to each other or to local rotorcraft structure is demonstrated to be extremely improbable or unless other means are provided. The couplings or equivalent devices must be installed at all fuel tank-to-fuel line connections, tank-to-tank interconnects, and at other points in the fuel system where local structural deformation could lead to the release of fuel.

(1) The design and construction of self-sealing breakaway couplings must incorporate the following design features:

(i) The load necessary to separate a breakaway coupling must be between 25 and 50 percent of the minimum ultimate failure load (ultimate strength) of the weakest component in the fluid-carrying line. The separation load must in no case be less than 300 pounds, regardless of the size of the fluid line.

(ii) A breakaway coupling must separate whenever its ultimate load (as defined in paragraph (c)(1)(i) of this section) is applied in the failure modes most likely to occur.

(iii) All breakaway couplings must incorporate design provisions to visually ascertain that the coupling is locked together (leak-free) and is open during normal installation and service.

(iv) All breakaway couplings must incorporate design provisions to prevent uncoupling or unintended closing due to operational shocks, vibrations, or accelerations.

(v) No breakaway coupling design may allow the release of fuel once the coupling has performed its intended function.

(2) All individual breakaway couplings, coupling fuel feed systems, or equivalent means must be designed, tested, installed, and maintained so that inadvertent fuel shutoff in flight is improbable in accordance with §27.955(a) and must comply with the fatigue evaluation requirements of §27.571 without leaking.

(3) Alternate, equivalent means to the use of breakaway couplings must not create a survivable impact-induced load on the fuel line to which it is installed greater than 25 to 50 percent of the ultimate load (strength) of the weakest component in the line and must comply with the fatigue requirements of §27.571 without leaking.

(d) *Frangible or deformable structural attachments.* Unless hazardous relative motion of fuel tanks and fuel system components to local rotorcraft structure is demonstrated to be extremely improbable in an otherwise survivable impact, frangible or locally deformable attachments of fuel tanks and fuel system components to local rotorcraft structure must be used. The attachment of fuel tanks and fuel system components to local rotorcraft structure, whether frangible or locally deformable, must be designed such that its separation or relative local deformation will occur without rupture or local tear-out of the fuel tank or fuel system components that will cause fuel leakage. The ultimate strength of frangible or deformable attachments must be as follows:

(1) The load required to separate a frangible attachment from its support structure, or deform a locally deformable attachment relative to its support structure, must be between 25 and 50 percent of the minimum ultimate load (ultimate strength) of the weakest component in the attached system. In no case may the load be less than 300 pounds.

(2) A frangible or locally deformable attachment must separate or locally deform as intended whenever its ultimate load (as defined in paragraph (d)(1) of this section) is applied in the modes most likely to occur.

(3) All frangible or locally deformable attachments must comply with the fatigue requirements of §27.571.

(e) *Separation of fuel and ignition sources.* To provide maximum crash resistance, fuel must be located as far as practicable from all occupiable areas and from all potential ignition sources.

(f) *Other basic mechanical design criteria.* Fuel tanks, fuel lines, electrical wires, and electrical devices must be designed, constructed, and installed, as far as practicable, to be crash resistant.

(g) *Rigid or semirigid fuel tanks.* Rigid or semirigid fuel tank or bladder walls must be impact and tear resistant.

[Docket No. 26352, 59 FR 50386, Oct. 3, 1994]

§27.953 Fuel system independence.

(a) Each fuel system for multiengine rotorcraft must allow fuel to be supplied to each engine through a system independent of those parts of each system supplying fuel to other engines. However, separate fuel tanks need not be provided for each engine.

(b) If a single fuel tank is used on a multiengine rotorcraft, the following must be provided:

(1) Independent tank outlets for each engine, each incorporating a shutoff valve at the tank. This shutoff valve may also serve as the firewall shutoff valve required by §27.995 if the line between the valve and the engine compartment does not contain a hazardous amount of fuel that can drain into the engine compartment.

(2) At least two vents arranged to minimize the probability of both vents becoming obstructed simultaneously.

(3) Filler caps designed to minimize the probability of incorrect installation or inflight loss.

(4) A fuel system in which those parts of the system from each tank outlet to any engine are independent of each part of each system supplying fuel to other engines.

§27.954 Fuel system lightning protection.

The fuel system must be designed and arranged to prevent the ignition of fuel vapor within the system by—

(a) Direct lightning strikes to areas having a high probability of stroke attachment;

(b) Swept lightning strokes to areas where swept strokes are highly probable; or

(c) Corona and streamering at fuel vent outlets.

[Docket No. 5074, 29 FR 15695, Nov. 24, 1964; as amended by Amdt. 27–23, 53 FR 34212, Sept. 2, 1988]

§27.955 Fuel flow.

(a) *General.* The fuel system for each engine must be shown to provide the engine with at least 100 percent of the fuel required under each operating and maneuvering condition to be approved for the rotorcraft including, as applicable, the fuel required to operate the engine(s) under the test conditions required by §27.927. Unless equivalent methods are used, compliance must be shown by test during which the following provisions are met except that combinations of conditions which are shown to be improbable need not be considered.

(1) The fuel pressure, corrected for critical accelerations, must be within the limits specified by the engine type certificate data sheet.

(2) The fuel level in the tank may not exceed that established as the unusable fuel supply for that tank under §27.959, plus the minimum additional fuel necessary to conduct the test.

(3) The fuel head between the tank outlet and the engine inlet must be critical with respect to rotorcraft flight attitudes.

(4) The critical fuel pump (for pump-fed systems) is installed to produce (by actual or simulated failure) the critical restriction to fuel flow to be expected from pump failure.

(5) Critical values of engine rotation speed, electrical power, or other sources of fuel pump motive power must be applied.

(6) Critical values of fuel properties which adversely affect fuel flow must be applied.

(7) The fuel filter required by §27.997 must be blocked to the degree necessary to simulate the accumulation of fuel contamination required to activate the indicator required by §27.1305(q).

(b) *Fuel transfer systems.* If normal operation of the fuel system requires fuel to be transferred to an engine feed tank, the transfer must occur automatically via a system which has been shown to maintain the fuel level in the engine feed tank within acceptable limits during flight or surface operation of the rotorcraft.

(c) *Multiple fuel tanks.* If an engine can be supplied with fuel from more than one tank, the fuel systems must, in addition to having appropriate manual switching capability, be designed to prevent interruption of fuel flow to that engine, without attention by the flightcrew, when any tank supplying fuel to that engine is depleted of usable fuel during normal operation, and any other tank that normally supplies fuel to the engine alone contains usable fuel.

[Docket No. 5074, 29 FR 15695, Nov. 24, 1964; as amended by Amdt. 27–23, 53 FR 34212, Sept. 2, 1988]

§27.959 Unusable fuel supply.

The unusable fuel supply for each tank must be established as not less than the quantity at which the first evidence of malfunction occurs under the most adverse fuel feed condition occurring under any intended operations and flight maneuvers involving that tank.

§27.961 Fuel system hot weather operation.

Each suction lift fuel system and other fuel systems with features conducive to vapor formation must be shown by test to operate satisfactorily (within certification limits) when using fuel at a temperature of 110°F under critical operating conditions including, if applicable, the engine operating conditions defined by §27.927 (b)(1) and (b)(2).

[Docket No. 5074, 29 FR 15695, Nov. 24, 1964; as amended by Amdt. 27–23, 53 FR 34212, Sept. 2, 1988]

§27.963 Fuel tanks: general.

(a) Each fuel tank must be able to withstand, without failure, the vibration, inertia, fluid, and structural loads to which it may be subjected in operation.

(b) Each fuel tank of 10 gallons or greater capacity must have internal baffles, or must have external support to resist surging.

(c) Each fuel tank must be separated from the engine compartment by a firewall. At least one-half inch of clear airspace must be provided between the tank and the firewall.

(d) Spaces adjacent to the surfaces of fuel tanks must be ventilated so that fumes cannot accumulate in the tank compartment in case of leakage. If two or more tanks have interconnected outlets, they must be considered as one tank, and the airspaces in those tanks must be interconnected to prevent the flow of fuel from one tank to another as a result of a difference in pressure between those airspaces.

(e) The maximum exposed surface temperature of any component in the fuel tank must be less, by a safe margin as determined by the Administrator, than the lowest expected autoignition temperature of the fuel or fuel vapor in the tank. Compliance with this requirement must be shown under all operating conditions and under all failure or malfunction conditions of all components inside the tank.

(f) Each fuel tank installed in personnel compartments must be isolated by fume-proof and fuel-proof enclosures that are drained and vented to the exterior of the rotorcraft. The design and construction of the enclosures must provide necessary protection for the tank, must be crash resistant during a survivable impact in accordance with §27.952, and must be adequate to withstand loads and abrasions to be expected in personnel compartments.

(g) Each flexible fuel tank bladder or liner must be approved or shown to be suitable for the particular application and must be puncture resistant. Puncture resistance must be shown by meeting the TSO-C80, paragraph 16.0, requirements using a minimum puncture force of 370 pounds.

(h) Each integral fuel tank must have provisions for inspection and repair of its interior.

[Docket No. 5074, 29 FR 15695, Nov. 24, 1964; as amended by Amdt. 27–23, 53 FR 34213, Sept. 2, 1988; Amdt. 27–30, 59 FR 50387, Oct. 3, 1994]

§27.965 Fuel tank tests.

(a) Each fuel tank must be able to withstand the applicable pressure tests in this section without failure or leakage. If practicable, test pressures may be applied in a manner simulating the pressure distribution in service.

(b) Each conventional metal tank, nonmetallic tank with walls that are not supported by the rotorcraft structure, and integral tank must be subjected to a pressure of 3.5 p.s.i. unless the pressure developed during maximum limit acceleration or emergency deceleration with a full tank exceeds this value, in which case a hydrostatic head, or equivalent test, must be applied to duplicate the acceleration loads as far as possible. However, the pressure need not exceed 3.5 p.s.i. on surfaces not exposed to the acceleration loading.

(c) Each nonmetallic tank with walls supported by the rotorcraft structure must be subjected to the following tests:

(1) A pressure test of at least 2.0 p.s.i. This test may be conducted on the tank alone in conjunction with the test specified in paragraph (c)(2) of this section.

(2) A pressure test, with the tank mounted in the rotorcraft structure, equal to the load developed by the reaction of the contents, with the tank full, during maximum limit acceleration or emergency deceleration. However, the pressure need not exceed 2.0 p.s.i. on surfaces not exposed to the acceleration loading.

(d) Each tank with large unsupported or unstiffened flat areas, or with other features whose failure or deformation could cause leakage, must be subjected to the following test or its equivalent:

(1) Each complete tank assembly and its support must be vibration tested while mounted to simulate the actual installation.

(2) The tank assembly must be vibrated for 25 hours while two-thirds full of any suitable fluid. The amplitude of vibration may not be less than one thirty-second of an inch, unless otherwise substantiated.

(3) The test frequency of vibration must be as follows:

(i) If no frequency of vibration resulting from any r.p.m. within the normal operating range of engine or rotor system speeds is critical, the test frequency of vibration, in number of cycles per minute must, unless a frequency based on a more rational calculation is used, be the number obtained by averaging the maximum and minimum power-on engine speeds (r.p.m.) for reciprocating engine powered rotorcraft or 2,000 c.p.m. for turbine engine powered rotorcraft.

(ii) If only one frequency of vibration resulting from any r.p.m. within the normal operating range of engine or rotor system speeds is critical, that frequency of vibration must be the test frequency.

(iii) If more than one frequency of vibration resulting from any r.p.m. within the normal operating range of engine or rotor system speeds is critical, the most critical of these frequencies must be the test frequency.

(4) Under paragraphs (d)(3)(ii) and (iii) of this section, the time of test must be adjusted to accomplish the same number of vibration cycles as would be accomplished in 25 hours at the frequency specified in paragraph (d)(3)(i) of this section.

(5) During the test, the tank assembly must be rocked at the rate of 16 to 20 complete cycles per minute through an angle of 15 degrees on both sides of the horizontal (30 degrees total), about the most critical axis, for 25 hours. If motion about more than one axis is likely to be critical, the tank must be rocked about each critical axis for 12½ hours.

(Secs. 313(a), 601, and 603, 72 Stat. 752, 775, 49 U.S.C. 1354(9), 1421, and 1423; sec. 6(c), 49 U.S.C. 1655(c))

[Docket No. 5074, 29 FR 15695, Nov. 24, 1964; as amended by Amdt. 27–12, 42 FR 15045, March 17, 1977]

§27.967 Fuel tank installation.

(a) Each fuel tank must be supported so that tank loads are not concentrated on unsupported tank surfaces. In addition—

(1) There must be pads, if necessary, to prevent chafing between each tank and its supports;

(2) The padding must be nonabsorbent or treated to prevent the absorption of fuel;

(3) If flexible tank liners are used, they must be supported so that it is not necessary for them to withstand fluid loads; and

(4) Each interior surface of tank compartments must be smooth and free of projections that could cause wear of the liner unless—

(i) There are means for protection of the liner at those points; or

(ii) The construction of the liner itself provides such protection.

(b) Any spaces adjacent to tank surfaces must be adequately ventilated to avoid accumulation of fuel or fumes in those spaces due to minor leakage. If the tank is in a sealed compartment, ventilation may be limited to drain holes that prevent clogging and excessive pressure resulting from altitude changes. If flexible tank liners are installed, the venting arrangement for the spaces between the liner and its container must maintain the proper relationship to tank vent pressures for any expected flight condition.

(c) The location of each tank must meet the requirements of §27.1185(a) and (c).

(d) No rotorcraft skin immediately adjacent to a major air outlet from the engine compartment may act as the wall of the integral tank.

[Docket No. 26352, 59 FR 50387, Oct. 3, 1994]

§27.969 Fuel tank expansion space.

Each fuel tank or each group of fuel tanks with interconnected vent systems must have an expansion space of not less than 2 percent of the tank capacity. It must be impossible to fill the fuel tank expansion space inadvertently with the rotorcraft in the normal ground attitude.

[Docket No. 5074, 29 FR 15695, Nov. 24, 1964; as amended by Amdt. 27–23, 53 FR 34213, Sept. 2, 1988]

§27.971 Fuel tank sump.

(a) Each fuel tank must have a drainable sump with an effective capacity in any ground attitude to be expected in service of 0.25 percent of the tank capacity or $\frac{1}{16}$ gallon, whichever is greater, unless—

(1) The fuel system has a sediment bowl or chamber that is accessible for preflight drainage and has a minimum capacity of 1 ounce for every 20 gallons of fuel tank capacity; and

(2) Each fuel tank drain is located so that in any ground attitude to be expected in service, water will drain from all parts of the tank to the sediment bowl or chamber.

(b) Each sump, sediment bowl, and sediment chamber drain required by this section must comply with the drain provisions of §27.999(b).

[Docket No. 5074, 29 FR 15695, Nov. 24, 1964; as amended by Amdt. 27–23, 53 FR 34213, Sept. 2, 1988]

§27.973 Fuel tank filler connection.

(a) Each fuel tank filler connection must prevent the entrance of fuel into any part of the rotorcraft other than the tank itself during normal operations and must be crash resistant during a survivable impact in accordance with §27.952(c). In addition—

(1) Each filler must be marked as prescribed in §27.1557(c)(1);

(2) Each recessed filler connection that can retain any appreciable quantity of fuel must have a drain that discharges clear of the entire rotorcraft; and

(3) Each filler cap must provide a fuel-tight seal under the fluid pressure expected in normal operation and in a survivable impact.

(b) Each filler cap or filler cap cover must warn when the cap is not fully locked or seated on the filler connection.

[Docket No. 26352, 59 FR 50387, Oct. 3, 1994]

§27.975 Fuel tank vents.

(a) Each fuel tank must be vented from the top part of the expansion space so that venting is effective under all normal flight conditions. Each vent must minimize the probability of stoppage by dirt or ice.

(b) The venting system must be designed to minimize spillage of fuel through the vents to an ignition source in the event of a rollover during landing, ground operation, or a survivable impact.

[Docket No. 5074, 29 FR 15695, Nov. 24, 1964; as amended by Amdt. 27–23, 53 FR 34213, Sept. 2, 1988; Amdt. 27–30, 59 FR 50387, Oct. 3, 1994; Amdt. 27–35, 63 FR 43285, Aug. 12, 1998]

§27.977 Fuel tank outlet.

(a) There must be a fuel strainer for the fuel tank outlet or for the booster pump. This strainer must—

(1) For reciprocating engine powered rotorcraft, have 8 to 16 meshes per inch; and

(2) For turbine engine powered rotorcraft, prevent the passage of any object that could restrict fuel flow or damage any fuel system component.

(b) The clear area of each fuel tank outlet strainer must be at least five times the area of the outlet line.

(c) The diameter of each strainer must be at least that of the fuel tank outlet.

(d) Each finger strainer must be accessible for inspection and cleaning.

[Docket No. 5074, 29 FR 15695, Nov. 24, 1964; as amended by Amdt. 27–11, 41 FR 55470, Dec. 20, 1976]

Fuel System Components

§27.991 Fuel pumps.

Compliance with §27.955 may not be jeopardized by failure of—

(a) Any one pump except pumps that are approved and installed as parts of a type certificated engine; or

(b) Any component required for pump operation except, for engine driven pumps, the engine served by that pump.

[Docket No. 5074, 29 FR 15695, Nov. 24, 1964; as amended by Amdt. 27–23, 53 FR 34213, Sept. 2, 1988]

§27.993 Fuel system lines and fittings.

(a) Each fuel line must be installed and supported to prevent excessive vibration and to withstand loads due to fuel pressure and accelerated flight conditions.

(b) Each fuel line connected to components of the rotorcraft between which relative motion could exist must have provisions for flexibility.

(c) Flexible hose must be approved.

(d) Each flexible connection in fuel lines that may be under pressure or subjected to axial loading must use flexible hose assemblies.

(e) No flexible hose that might be adversely affected by high temperatures may be used where excessive temperatures will exist during operation or after engine shutdown.

[Docket No. 5074, 29 FR 15695, Nov. 24, 1964; as amended by Amdt. 27–2, 33 FR 964, Jan. 26, 1968]

§27.995 Fuel valves.

(a) There must be a positive, quick-acting valve to shut off fuel to each engine individually.

(b) The control for this valve must be within easy reach of appropriate crewmembers.

(c) Where there is more than one source of fuel supply there must be means for independent feeding from each source.

(d) No shutoff valve may be on the engine side of any firewall.

§27.997 Fuel strainer or filter.

There must be a fuel strainer or filter between the fuel tank outlet and the inlet of the first fuel system component which is susceptible to fuel contamination, including but not limited to the fuel metering device or an engine positive displacement pump, whichever is nearer the fuel tank outlet. This fuel strainer or filter must—

(a) Be accessible for draining and cleaning and must incorporate a screen or element which is easily removable;

(b) Have a sediment trap and drain except that it need not have a drain if the strainer or filter is easily removable for drain purposes;

(c) Be mounted so that its weight is not supported by the connecting lines or by the inlet or outlet connections of the strainer or filter itself, unless adequate strength margins under all loading conditions are provided in the lines and connections; and

(d) Provide a means to remove from the fuel any contaminant which would jeopardize the flow of fuel through rotorcraft or engine fuel system components required for proper rotorcraft fuel system or engine fuel system operation.

[Docket No. 5074, 29 FR 15695, Nov. 24, 1964; as amended by Amdt. 27–9, 39 FR 35461, Oct. 1, 1974; Amdt. 27–20, 49 FR 6849, Feb. 23, 1984; Amdt. 27–23, 53 FR 34213, Sept. 2, 1988]

§27.999 Fuel system drains.

(a) There must be at least one accessible drain at the lowest point in each fuel system to completely drain the system with the rotorcraft in any ground attitude to be expected in service.

(b) Each drain required by paragraph (a) of this section must—

(1) Discharge clear of all parts of the rotorcraft;

(2) Have manual or automatic means to assure positive closure in the off position; and

(3) Have a drain valve—

(i) That is readily accessible and which can be easily opened and closed; and

(ii) That is either located or protected to prevent fuel spillage in the event of a landing with landing gear retracted.

[Docket No. 574, 29 FR 15695, Nov. 24, 1964; as amended by Amdt. 27–11, 41 FR 55470, Dec. 20, 1976; Amdt. 27–23, 53 FR 34213, Sept. 2, 1988]

Oil System

§27.1011 Engines: General.

(a) Each engine must have an independent oil system that can supply it with an appropriate quantity of oil at a temperature not above that safe for continuous operation.

(b) The usable oil capacity of each system may not be less than the product of the endurance of the rotorcraft under critical operating conditions and the maximum oil consumption of the engine under the same conditions, plus a suitable margin to ensure adequate circulation and cooling. Instead of a rational analysis of endurance and consumption, a usable oil capacity of one gallon for each 40 gallons of usable fuel may be used.

(c) The oil cooling provisions for each engine must be able to maintain the oil inlet temperature to that engine at or below the maximum established value. This must be shown by flight tests.

[Docket No. 5074, 29 FR 15695, Nov. 24, 1964; as amended by Amdt. 27–23, 53 FR 34213, Sept. 2, 1988]

§27.1013 Oil tanks.

Each oil tank must be designed and installed so that—

(a) It can withstand, without failure, each vibration, inertia, fluid, and structural load expected in operation;

(b) [Reserved]

(c) Where used with a reciprocating engine, it has an expansion space of not less than the greater of 10 percent of the tank capacity or 0.5 gallon, and where used with a turbine engine, it has an expansion space of not less than 10 percent of the tank capacity.

(d) It is impossible to fill the tank expansion space inadvertently with the rotorcraft in the normal ground attitude;

(e) Adequate venting is provided; and

(f) There are means in the filler opening to prevent oil overflow from entering the oil tank compartment.

[Docket No. 5074, 29 FR 15695, Nov. 24, 1964; as amended by Amdt. 27–9, 39 FR 35461, Oct. 1, 1974]

§27.1015 Oil tank tests.

Each oil tank must be designed and installed so that it can withstand, without leakage, an internal pressure of 5 p.s.i., except that each pressurized oil tank used with a turbine engine must be designed and installed so that it can withstand, without leakage, an internal pressure of 5 p.s.i., plus the maximum operating pressure of the tank.

[Docket No. 5074, 29 FR 15695, Nov. 24, 1964; as amended by Amdt. 27–9, 39 FR 35462, Oct. 1, 1974]

§27.1017 Oil lines and fittings.

(a) Each oil line must be supported to prevent excessive vibration.

(b) Each oil line connected to components of the rotorcraft between which relative motion could exist must have provisions for flexibility.

(c) Flexible hose must be approved.

(d) Each oil line must have an inside diameter of not less than the inside diameter of the engine inlet or outlet. No line may have splices between connections.

§27.1019 Oil strainer or filter.

(a) Each turbine engine installation must incorporate an oil strainer or filter through which all of the engine oil flows and which meets the following requirements:

(1) Each oil strainer or filter that has a bypass must be constructed and installed so that oil will flow at the normal rate through the rest of the system with the strainer or filter completely blocked.

(2) The oil strainer or filter must have the capacity (with respect to operating limitations established for the engine) to ensure that engine oil system functioning is not impaired when the oil is contaminated to a degree (with respect to particle size and density) that is greater than that established for the engine under Part 33 of this chapter.

(3) The oil strainer or filter, unless it is installed at an oil tank outlet, must incorporate a means to indicate contamination before it reaches the capacity established in accordance with paragraph (a)(2) of this section.

(4) The bypass of a strainer or filter must be constructed and installed so that the release of collected contaminants is minimized by appropriate location of the bypass to ensure that collected contaminants are not in the bypass flow path.

(5) An oil strainer or filter that has no bypass, except one that is installed at an oil tank outlet, must have a means to connect it to the warning system required in §27.1305(r).

(b) Each oil strainer or filter in a powerplant installation using reciprocating engines must be constructed and installed so that oil will flow at the normal rate through the rest of the system with the strainer or filter element completely blocked.

[Docket No. 5074, 29 FR 15695, Nov. 24, 1964; as amended by Amdt. 27–9, 39 FR 35462, Oct. 1, 1974; Amdt. 27–20, 49 FR 6849, Feb. 23, 1984; Amdt. 27–23, 53 FR 34213, Sept. 2, 1988]

§27.1021 Oil system drains.

A drain (or drains) must be provided to allow safe drainage of the oil system. Each drain must—

(a) Be accessible; and

(b) Have manual or automatic means for positive locking in the closed position.

[Docket No. 5074, 29 FR 15695, Nov. 24, 1964; as amended by Amdt. 27–20, 49 FR 6849, Feb. 23, 1984]

§27.1027 Transmissions and gearboxes: General.

(a) The lubrication system for components of the rotor drive system that require continuous lubrication must be sufficiently independent of the lubrication systems of the engine(s) to ensure lubrication during autorotation.

(b) Pressure lubrication systems for transmissions and gearboxes must comply with the engine oil system requirements of §§27.1013 (except paragraph (c)), 27.1015, 27.1017, 27.1021, and 27.1337(d).

(c) Each pressure lubrication system must have an oil strainer or filter through which all of the lubricant flows and must—

(1) Be designed to remove from the lubricant any contaminant which may damage transmission and drive system components or impede the flow of lubricant to a hazardous degree;

(2) Be equipped with a means to indicate collection of contaminants on the filter or strainer at or before opening of the bypass required by paragraph (c)(3) of this section; and

(3) Be equipped with a bypass constructed and installed so that—

(i) The lubricant will flow at the normal rate through the rest of the system with the strainer or filter completely blocked; and

(ii) The release of collected contaminants is minimized by appropriate location of the bypass to ensure that collected contaminants are not in the bypass flowpath.

(d) For each lubricant tank or sump outlet supplying lubrication to rotor drive systems and rotor drive system components, a screen must be provided to prevent entrance into the lubrication system of any object that might obstruct the flow of lubricant from the outlet to the filter required by paragraph (c) of this section. The requirements of paragraph (c) do not apply to screens installed at lubricant tank or sump outlets.

(e) Splash-type lubrication systems for rotor drive system gearboxes must comply with §§27.1021 and 27.1337(d).

[Docket No. 5074, 29 FR 15695, Nov. 24, 1964; as amended by Amdt. 27–23, 53 FR 34213, Sept. 2, 1988; Amdt. 27–37, 64 FR 45095, Aug. 18, 1999]

Cooling

§27.1041 General.

(a) Each powerplant cooling system must be able to maintain the temperatures of powerplant components within the limits established for these components under critical surface (ground or water) and flight operating conditions for which certification is required and after normal shutdown. Powerplant components to be considered include but may not be limited to engines, rotor drive system components, auxiliary power units, and the cooling or lubricating fluids used with these components.

(b) Compliance with paragraph (a) of this section must be shown in tests conducted under the conditions prescribed in that paragraph.

[Docket No. 5074, 29 FR 15695, Nov. 24, 1964; as amended by Amdt. 27–23, 53 FR 34213, Sept. 2, 1988]

§27.1043 Cooling tests.

(a) *General.* For the tests prescribed in §27.1041(b), the following apply:

(1) If the tests are conducted under conditions deviating from the maximum ambient atmospheric temperature specified in paragraph (b) of this section, the recorded powerplant temperatures must be corrected under paragraphs (c) and (d) of this section unless a more rational correction method is applicable.

(2) No corrected temperature determined under paragraph (a)(1) of this section may exceed established limits.

(3) For reciprocating engines, the fuel used during the cooling tests must be of the minimum grade approved for the engines, and the mixture settings must be those normally used in the flight stages for which the cooling tests are conducted.

(4) The test procedures must be as prescribed in §27.1045.

(b) *Maximum ambient atmospheric temperature.* A maximum ambient atmospheric temperature corresponding to sea level conditions of at least 100 degrees F must be established. The assumed temperature lapse rate is 3.6 degrees F per thousand feet of altitude above sea level until a temperature of -69.7 degrees F is reached, above which altitude the temperature is considered constant at -69.7 degrees F. However, for winterization installations, the applicant may select a maximum ambient atmospheric temperature corresponding to sea level conditions of less than 100 degrees F.

(c) *Correction factor (except cylinder barrels).* Unless a more rational correction applies, temperatures of engine fluids and powerplant components (except cylinder barrels) for which temperature limits are established, must be corrected by adding to them the difference between the maximum ambient atmospheric temperature and the temperature of the ambient air at the time of the first occurrence of the maximum component or fluid temperature recorded during the cooling test.

(d) *Correction factor for cylinder barrel temperatures.* Cylinder barrel temperatures must be corrected by adding to them 0.7 times the difference between the maximum ambient atmospheric temperature and the temperature of the ambient air at the time of the first occurrence of the maximum cylinder barrel temperature recorded during the cooling test.

(Secs. 313(a), 601, 603, 604, and 605 of the Federal Aviation Act of 1958 (49 U.S.C. 1354(a), 1421, 1423, 1424, and 1425); and sec. 6(c) of the Dept. of Transportation Act (49 U.S.C. 1655(c)))

[Docket No. 5074, 29 FR 15695, Nov. 24, 1964; as amended by Amdt. 27–11, 41 FR 55470, Dec. 20, 1976; Amdt. 27–14, 43 FR 2325, Jan. 16, 1978]

§27.1045 Cooling test procedures.

(a) *General.* For each stage of flight, the cooling tests must be conducted with the rotorcraft—

(1) In the configuration most critical for cooling; and

(2) Under the conditions most critical for cooling.

(b) *Temperature stabilization.* For the purpose of the cooling tests, a temperature is "stabilized" when its rate of change is less than two degrees F per minute. The following component and engine fluid temperature stabilization rules apply:

(1) For each rotorcraft, and for each stage of flight—

(i) The temperatures must be stabilized under the conditions from which entry is made into the stage of flight being investigated; or

(ii) If the entry condition normally does not allow temperatures to stabilize, operation through the full entry condition must be conducted before entry into the stage of flight being investigated in order to allow the temperatures to attain their natural levels at the time of entry.

(2) For each helicopter during the takeoff stage of flight, the climb at takeoff power must be preceded by a period of hover during which the temperatures are stabilized.

(c) *Duration of test.* For each stage of flight the tests must be continued until—

(1) The temperatures stabilize or 5 minutes after the occurrence of the highest temperature recorded, as appropriate to the test condition;

(2) That stage of flight is completed; or

(3) An operating limitation is reached.

[Docket No. 5074, 29 FR 15695, Nov. 24, 1964; as amended by Amdt. 27–23, 53 FR 34214, Sept. 2, 1988]

Induction System

§27.1091 Air induction.

(a) The air induction system for each engine must supply the air required by that engine under the operating conditions and maneuvers for which certification is requested.

(b) Each cold air induction system opening must be outside the cowling if backfire flames can emerge.

(c) If fuel can accumulate in any air induction system, that system must have drains that discharge fuel—

(1) Clear of the rotorcraft; and

(2) Out of the path of exhaust flames.

(d) For turbine engine powered rotorcraft—

(1) There must be means to prevent hazardous quantities of fuel leakage or overflow from drains, vents, or other components of flammable fluid systems from entering the engine intake system; and

(2) The air inlet ducts must be located or protected so as to minimize the ingestion of foreign matter during takeoff, landing, and taxiing.

[Docket No. 5074, 29 FR 15695, Nov. 24, 1964; as amended by Amdt. 27–2, 33 FR 964, Jan. 26, 1968; Amdt. 27–23, 53 FR 34214, Sept. 2, 1988]

§27.1093 Induction system icing protection.

(a) *Reciprocating engines.* Each reciprocating engine air induction system must have means to prevent and eliminate icing. Unless this is done by other means, it must be shown that, in air free of visible moisture at a temperature of 30 degrees F, and with the engines at 75 percent of maximum continuous power—

(1) Each rotorcraft with sea level engines using conventional venturi carburetors has a preheater that can provide a heat rise of 90 degrees F;

(2) Each rotorcraft with sea level engines using carburetors tending to prevent icing has a sheltered alternate source of air, and that the preheat supplied to the alternate air intake is not less than that provided by the engine cooling air downstream of the cylinders;

(3) Each rotorcraft with altitude engines using conventional venturi carburetors has a preheater capable of providing a heat rise of 120 degrees F; and

(4) Each rotorcraft with altitude engines using carburetors tending to prevent icing has a preheater that can provide a heat rise of—

(i) 100 degrees F; or

(ii) If a fluid deicing system is used, at least 40 degrees F.

(b) *Turbine engine.*

(1) It must be shown that each turbine engine and its air inlet system can operate throughout the flight power range of the engine (including idling)—

(i) Without accumulating ice on engine or inlet system components that would adversely affect engine operation or cause a serious loss of power under the icing conditions specified in Appendix C of Part 29 of this chapter; and

(ii) In snow, both falling and blowing, without adverse effect on engine operation, within the limitations established for the rotorcraft.

(2) Each turbine engine must idle for 30 minutes on the ground, with the air bleed available for engine icing protection at its critical condition, without adverse effect, in an at-

mosphere that is at a temperature between 15° and 30°F (between -9° and -1°C) and has a liquid water content not less than 0.3 gram per cubic meter in the form of drops having a mean effective diameter not less than 20 microns, followed by momentary operation at takeoff power or thrust. During the 30 minutes of idle operation, the engine may be run up periodically to a moderate power or thrust setting in a manner acceptable to the Administrator.

(c) *Supercharged reciprocating engines.* For each engine having superchargers to pressurize the air before it enters the carburetor, the heat rise in the air caused by that supercharging at any altitude may be utilized in determining compliance with paragraph (a) of this section if the heat rise utilized is that which will be available, automatically, for the applicable altitude and operating condition because of supercharging.

(Secs. 313(a), 601, and 603, 72 Stat. 752, 775, 49 U.S.C. 1354(a), 1421, and 1423; sec. 6(c), 49 U.S.C. 1655(c))

[Docket No. 5074, 29 FR 15695, Nov. 24, 1964; as amended by Amdt. 27–11, 41 FR 55470, Dec. 20, 1976; Amdt. 27–12, 42 FR 15045, March 17, 1977; Amdt. 27–20, 49 FR 6849, Feb. 23, 1984; Amdt. 27–23, 53 FR 34214, Sept. 2, 1988]

EXHAUST SYSTEM

§27.1121 General.

For each exhaust system—

(a) There must be means for thermal expansion of manifolds and pipes;

(b) There must be means to prevent local hot spots;

(c) Exhaust gases must discharge clear of the engine air intake, fuel system components, and drains;

(d) Each exhaust system part with a surface hot enough to ignite flammable fluids or vapors must be located or shielded so that leakage from any system carrying flammable fluids or vapors will not result in a fire caused by impingement of the fluids or vapors on any part of the exhaust system including shields for the exhaust system;

(e) Exhaust gases may not impair pilot vision at night due to glare;

(f) If significant traps exist, each turbine engine exhaust system must have drains discharging clear of the rotorcraft, in any normal ground and flight attitudes, to prevent fuel accumulation after the failure of an attempted engine start;

(g) Each exhaust heat exchanger must incorporate means to prevent blockage of the exhaust port after any internal heat exchanger failure.

(Secs. 313(a), 601, and 603, 72 Stat. 752, 775, 49 U.S.C. 1354(a), 1421, and 1423; sec. 6(c), 49 U.S.C. 1655(c))

[Docket No. 5074, 29 FR 15695, Nov. 24, 1964 as amended by Amdt. 27–12, 42 FR 15045, March 17, 1977]

§27.1123 Exhaust piping.

(a) Exhaust piping must be heat and corrosion resistant, and must have provisions to prevent failure due to expansion by operating temperatures.

(b) Exhaust piping must be supported to withstand any vibration and inertia loads to which it would be subjected in operations.

(c) Exhaust piping connected to components between which relative motion could exist must have provisions for flexibility.

[Docket No. 5074, 29 FR 15695, Nov. 24, 1964; as amended by Amdt. 27–11, 41 FR 55470, Dec. 20, 1976]

POWERPLANT CONTROLS AND ACCESSORIES

§27.1141 Powerplant controls: general.

(a) Powerplant controls must be located and arranged under §27.777 and marked under §27.1555.

(b) Each flexible powerplant control must be approved.

(c) Each control must be able to maintain any set position without—

(1) Constant attention; or

(2) Tendency to creep due to control loads or vibration.

(d) Controls of powerplant valves required for safety must have—

(1) For manual valves, positive stops or in the case of fuel valves suitable index provisions, in the open and closed position; and

(2) For power-assisted valves, a means to indicate to the flight crew when the valve—

(i) Is in the fully open or fully closed position; or

(ii) Is moving between the fully open and fully closed position.

(e) For turbine engine powered rotorcraft, no single failure or malfunction, or probable combination thereof, in any powerplant control system may cause the failure of any powerplant function necessary for safety.

(Secs. 313(a), 601, and 603, 72 Stat. 752, 775, 49 U.S.C. 1354(a), 1421, and 1423; sec. 6(c), 49 U.S.C. 1655(c))

[Docket No. 5074, 29 FR 15695, Nov. 24, 1964; as amended by Amdt. 27–12, 42 FR 15045, March 17, 1977; Amdt. 27–23, 53 FR 34214, Sept. 2, 1988; Amdt. 27–33, 61 FR 21907, May 10, 1996]

§27.1143 Engine controls.

(a) There must be a separate power control for each engine.

(b) Power controls must be grouped and arranged to allow—

(1) Separate control of each engine; and

(2) Simultaneous control of all engines.

(c) Each power control must provide a positive and immediately responsive means of controlling its engine.

(d) If a power control incorporates a fuel shutoff feature, the control must have a means to prevent the inadvertent movement of the control into the shutoff position. The means must—

(1) Have a positive lock or stop at the idle position; and

(2) Require a separate and distinct operation to place the control in the shutoff position.

(e) For rotorcraft to be certificated for a 30-second OEI power rating, a means must be provided to automatically activate and control the 30-second OEI power and prevent any engine from exceeding the installed engine limits associated with the 30-second OEI power rating approved for the rotorcraft.

[Docket No. 5074, 29 FR 15695, Nov. 24, 1964; as amended by Amdt. 27–11, 41 FR 55470, Dec. 20, 1976; Amdt. 27–23, 53 FR 34214, Sept. 2, 1988; Amdt. 27–29, 59 FR 47767, Sept. 16, 1994]

§27.1145 Ignition switches.

(a) There must be means to quickly shut off all ignition by the grouping of switches or by a master ignition control.

(b) Each group of ignition switches, except ignition switches for turbine engines for which continuous ignition is not required, and each master ignition control must have a means to prevent its inadvertent operation.

(Secs. 313(a), 601, and 603, 72 Stat. 752, 775, 49 U.S.C. 1354(a), 1421, and 1423; sec. 6(c), 49 U.S.C. 1655(c))

[Docket No. 5074, 29 FR 15695, Nov. 24, 1964; as amended by Amdt. 27–12, 42 FR 15045, March 17, 1977]

§27.1147 Mixture controls.

If there are mixture controls, each engine must have a separate control and the controls must be arranged to allow—

(a) Separate control of each engine; and

(b) Simultaneous control of all engines.

§27.1151 Rotor brake controls.

(a) It must be impossible to apply the rotor brake inadvertently in flight.

(b) There must be means to warn the crew if the rotor brake has not been completely released before takeoff.

[Docket No. 28008, 61 FR 21907, May 10, 1996]

§27.1163 Powerplant accessories.

(a) Each engine-mounted accessory must—

(1) Be approved for mounting on the engine involved;

(2) Use the provisions on the engine for mounting; and

(3) Be sealed in such a way as to prevent contamination of the engine oil system and the accessory system.

(b) Unless other means are provided, torque limiting means must be provided for accessory drives located on any component of the transmission and rotor drive system to prevent damage to these components from excessive accessory load.

[Docket No. 5074, 29 FR 15695, Nov. 24, 1964; as amended by Amdt. 27–2, 33 FR 964, Jan. 26, 1968; Amdt. 27–20, 49 FR 6849, Feb. 23, 1984; Amdt. 27–23, 53 FR 34214, Sept. 2, 1988]

Powerplant Fire Protection

§27.1183 Lines, fittings, and components.

(a) Except as provided in paragraph (b) of this section, each line, fitting, and other component carrying flammable fluid in any area subject to engine fire conditions must be fire resistant, except that flammable fluid tanks and supports which are part of and attached to the engine must be fireproof or be enclosed by a fireproof shield unless damage by fire to any non-fireproof part will not cause leakage or spillage of flammable fluid. Components must be shielded or located so as to safeguard against the ignition of leaking flammable fluid. An integral oil sump of less than 25-quart capacity on a reciprocating engine need not be fireproof nor be enclosed by a fireproof shield.

(b) Paragraph (a) does not apply to—

(1) Lines, fittings, and components which are already approved as part of a type certificated engine; and

(2) Vent and drain lines, and their fittings, whose failure will not result in, or add to, a fire hazard.

(c) Each flammable fluid drain and vent must discharge clear of the induction system air inlet.

[Docket No. 5074, 29 FR 15695, Nov. 24, 1964; as amended by Amdt. 27–1, 32 FR 6914, May 5, 1967; Amdt. 27–9, 39 FR 35462, Oct. 1, 1974; Amdt. 27–20, 49 FR 6849, Feb. 23, 1984]

§27.1185 Flammable fluids.

(a) Each fuel tank must be isolated from the engines by a firewall or shroud.

(b) Each tank or reservoir, other than a fuel tank, that is part of a system containing flammable fluids or gases must be isolated from the engine by a firewall or shroud, unless the design of the system, the materials used in the tank and its supports, the shutoff means, and the connections, lines and controls provide a degree of safety equal to that which would exist if the tank or reservoir were isolated from the engines.

(c) There must be at least one-half inch of clear airspace between each tank and each firewall or shroud isolating that tank, unless equivalent means are used to prevent heat transfer from each engine compartment to the flammable fluid.

(d) Absorbent materials close to flammable fluid system components that might leak must be covered or treated to prevent the absorption of hazardous quantities of fluids.

[Docket No. 5074, 29 FR 15695, Nov. 24, 1964; as amended by Amdt. 27–2, 33 FR 964, Jan. 26, 1968; Amdt. 27–11, 41 FR 55470, Dec. 20, 1976; Amdt. 27–37, 64 FR 45095, Aug. 18, 1999]

§27.1187 Ventilation and drainage.

Each compartment containing any part of the powerplant installation must have provision for ventilation and drainage of flammable fluids. The drainage means must be—

(a) Effective under conditions expected to prevail when drainage is needed, and

(b) Arranged so that no discharged fluid will cause an additional fire hazard.

[Docket No. 5074, 29 FR 15695, Nov. 24, 1964; as amended by Amdt. 27–37, 64 FR 45095, Aug. 18, 1999]

§27.1189 Shutoff means.

(a) There must be means to shut off each line carrying flammable fluids into the engine compartment, except—

(1) Lines, fittings, and components forming an integral part of an engine;

(2) For oil systems for which all components of the system, including oil tanks, are fireproof or located in areas not subject to engine fire conditions; and

(3) For reciprocating engine installations only, engine oil system lines in installation using engines of less than 500 cu. in. displacement.

(b) There must be means to guard against inadvertent operation of each shutoff, and to make it possible for the crew to reopen it in flight after it has been closed.

(c) Each shutoff valve and its control must be designed, located, and protected to function properly under any condition likely to result from an engine fire.

[Docket No. 5074, 29 FR 15695, Nov. 24, 1964; as amended by Amdt. 27–2, 33 FR 964, Jan. 26, 1968; Amdt. 27–20, 49 FR 6850, Feb. 23, 1984; Amdt. 27–23, 53 FR 34214, Sept. 2, 1988]

§27.1191 Firewalls.

(a) Each engine, including the combustor, turbine, and tailpipe sections of turbine engines must be isolated by a firewall, shroud, or equivalent means, from personnel compartments, structures, controls, rotor mechanisms, and other parts that are—

(1) Essential to a controlled landing: and

(2) Not protected under §27.861.

(b) Each auxiliary power unit and combustion heater, and any other combustion equipment to be used in flight, must be isolated from the rest of the rotorcraft by firewalls, shrouds, or equivalent means.

(c) In meeting paragraphs (a) and (b) of this section, account must be taken of the probable path of a fire as affected by the airflow in normal flight and in autorotation.

(d) Each firewall and shroud must be constructed so that no hazardous quantity of air, fluids, or flame can pass from any engine compartment to other parts of the rotorcraft.

(e) Each opening in the firewall or shroud must be sealed with close-fitting, fireproof grommets, bushings, or firewall fittings.

(f) Each firewall and shroud must be fireproof and protected against corrosion.

[Docket No. 5074, 29 FR 15695, Nov. 24, 1964; as amended by Amdt. 27–2, 22 FR 964, Jan. 26, 1968]

§27.1193 Cowling and engine compartment covering.

(a) Each cowling and engine compartment covering must be constructed and supported so that it can resist the vibration, inertia, and air loads to which it may be subjected in operation.

(b) There must be means for rapid and complete drainage of each part of the cowling or engine compartment in the normal ground and flight attitudes.

(c) No drain may discharge where it might cause a fire hazard.

(d) Each cowling and engine compartment covering must be at least fire resistant.

(e) Each part of the cowling or engine compartment covering subject to high temperatures due to its nearness to exhaust system parts or exhaust gas impingement must be fireproof.

(f) A means of retaining each openable or readily removable panel, cowling, or engine or rotor drive system covering must be provided to preclude hazardous damage to rotors or critical control components in the event of structural or mechanical failure of the normal retention means, unless such failure is extremely improbable.

[Docket No. 5074, 29 FR 15695, Nov. 24, 1964; as amended by Amdt. 27–23, 53 FR 34214, Sept. 2, 1988]

§27.1194 Other surfaces.

All surfaces aft of, and near, powerplant compartments, other than tail surfaces not subject to heat, flames, or sparks emanating from a powerplant compartment, must be at least fire resistant.

[Docket No. 5074, 29 FR 15695, Nov. 24, 1964; as amended by Amdt. 27–2, 33 FR 964, Jan. 26, 1968]

§27.1195 Fire detector systems.

Each turbine engine powered rotorcraft must have approved quick-acting fire detectors in numbers and locations insuring prompt detection of fire in the engine compartment which cannot be readily observed in flight by the pilot in the cockpit.

[Docket No. 5074, 29 FR 15695, Nov. 24, 1964; as amended by Amdt. 27–5, 36 FR 5493, March 24, 1971]

Subpart F—Equipment

General

§27.1301 Function and installation.

Each item of installed equipment must—

(a) Be of a kind and design appropriate to its intended function;

(b) Be labeled as to its identification, function, or operating limitations, or any applicable combination of these factors;

(c) Be installed according to limitations specified for that equipment; and

(d) Function properly when installed.

§27.1303 Flight and navigation instruments.

The following are the required flight and navigation instruments:

(a) An airspeed indicator.

(b) An altimeter.

(c) A magnetic direction indicator.

§27.1305 Powerplant instruments.

The following are the required powerplant instruments:

(a) A carburetor air temperature indicator, for each engine having a preheater that can provide a heat rise in excess of 60°F.

(b) A cylinder head temperature indicator, for each—

(1) Air cooled engine;

(2) Rotorcraft with cooling shutters; and

(3) Rotorcraft for which compliance with §27.1043 is shown in any condition other than the most critical flight condition with respect to cooling.

(c) A fuel pressure indicator, for each pump-fed engine.

(d) A fuel quantity indicator, for each fuel tank.

(e) A manifold pressure indicator, for each altitude engine.

(f) An oil temperature warning device to indicate when the temperature exceeds a safe value in each main rotor drive gearbox (including any gearboxes essential to rotor phasing) having an oil system independent of the engine oil system.

(g) An oil pressure warning device to indicate when the pressure falls below a safe value in each pressure-lubricated main rotor drive gearbox (including any gearboxes essential to rotor phasing) having an oil system independent of the engine oil system.

(h) An oil pressure indicator for each engine.

(i) An oil quantity indicator for each oil tank.

(j) An oil temperature indicator for each engine.

(k) At least one tachometer to indicate the r.p.m. of each engine and, as applicable—

(1) The r.p.m. of the single main rotor;

(2) The common r.p.m. of any main rotors whose speeds cannot vary appreciably with respect to each other; or

(3) The r.p.m. of each main rotor whose speed can vary appreciably with respect to that of another main rotor.

(l) A low fuel warning device for each fuel tank which feeds an engine. This device must—

(1) Provide a warning to the flightcrew when approximately 10 minutes of usable fuel remains in the tank; and

(2) Be independent of the normal fuel quantity indicating system.

(m) Means to indicate to the flightcrew the failure of any fuel pump installed to show compliance with §27.955.

(n) A gas temperature indicator for each turbine engine.

(o) Means to enable the pilot to determine the torque of each turboshaft engine, if a torque limitation is established for that engine under §27.1521(e).

(p) For each turbine engine, an indicator to indicate the functioning of the powerplant ice protection system.

(q) An indicator for the fuel filter required by §27.997 to indicate the occurrence of contamination of the filter at the degree established by the applicant in compliance with §27.955.

(r) For each turbine engine, a warning means for the oil strainer or filter required by §27.1019, if it has no bypass, to warn the pilot of the occurrence of contamination of the strainer or filter before it reaches the capacity established in accordance with §27.1019(a)(2).

(s) An indicator to indicate the functioning of any selectable or controllable heater used to prevent ice clogging of fuel system components.

(t) For rotorcraft for which a 30-second/2-minute OEI power rating is requested, a means must be provided to alert the pilot when the engine is at the 30-second and the 2-minute OEI power levels, when the event begins, and when the time interval expires.

(u) For each turbine engine utilizing 30-second/2-minute OEI power, a device or system must be provided for use by ground personnel which—

(1) Automatically records each usage and duration of power at the 30-second and 2-minute OEI levels;

(2) Permits retrieval of the recorded data;

(3) Can be reset only by ground maintenance personnel; and

(4) Has a means to verify proper operation of the system or device.

(v) Warning or caution devices to signal to the flight crew when ferromagnetic particles are detected by the chip detector required by §27.1337(e).

[Docket No. 5074, 29 FR 15695, Nov. 24, 1964; as amended by Amdt. 27–9, 39 FR 35462, Oct. 1, 1974; Amdt. 27–23, 53 FR 34214, Sept. 2, 1988; Amdt. 27–29, 59 FR 47767, Sept. 16, 1994; Amdt. 27–37, 64 FR 45095, Aug. 18, 1999]

§27.1307 Miscellaneous equipment.

The following is the required miscellaneous equipment:

(a) An approved seat for each occupant.

(b) An approved safety belt for each occupant.

(c) A master switch arrangement.

(d) An adequate source of electrical energy, where electrical energy is necessary for operation of the rotorcraft.

(e) Electrical protective devices.

§27.1309 Equipment, systems, and installations.

(a) The equipment, systems, and installations whose functioning is required by this subchapter must be designed and installed to ensure that they perform their intended functions under any foreseeable operating condition.

(b) The equipment, systems, and installations of a multiengine rotorcraft must be designed to prevent hazards to the rotorcraft in the event of a probable malfunction or failure.

(c) The equipment, systems, and installations of single-engine rotorcraft must be designed to minimize hazards to the rotorcraft in the event of a probable malfunction or failure.

(d) In showing compliance with paragraph (a), (b), or (c) of this section, the effects of lightning strikes on the rotorcraft must be considered in accordance with §27.610.

[Docket No. 5074, 29 FR 15695, Nov. 24, 1964; as amended by Amdt. 27–21, 49 FR 44435, Nov. 6, 1984]

Instruments: Installation

§27.1321 Arrangement and visibility.

(a) Each flight, navigation, and powerplant instrument for use by any pilot must be easily visible to him.

(b) For each multiengine rotorcraft, identical powerplant instruments must be located so as to prevent confusion as to which engine each instrument relates.

(c) Instrument panel vibration may not damage, or impair the readability or accuracy of, any instrument.

(d) If a visual indicator is provided to indicate malfunction of an instrument, it must be effective under all probable cockpit lighting conditions.

(Secs. 313(a), 601, 603, 604, and 605 of the Federal Aviation Act of 1958 (49 U.S.C. 1354(a), 1421, 1423, 1424, and 1425); and sec. 6(c) of the Dept. of Transportation Act (49 U.S.C. 1655(c)))

[Docket No. 5074, 29 FR 15695, Nov. 24, 1964; 29 FR 17885, Dec. 17, 1964; as amended by Amdt. 27–13, 42 FR 36971, July 18, 1977]

§27.1322 Warning, caution, and advisory lights.

If warning, caution or advisory lights are installed in the cockpit, they must, unless otherwise approved by the Administrator, be—

(a) Red, for warning lights (lights indicating a hazard which may require immediate corrective action):

(b) Amber, for caution lights (lights indicating the possible need for future corrective action);

(c) Green, for safe operation lights; and

(d) Any other color, including white, for lights not described in paragraphs (a) through (c) of this section, provided the color differs sufficiently from the colors prescribed in paragraphs (a) through (c) of this section to avoid possible confusion.

[Docket No. 5074, 29 FR 15695, Nov. 24, 1964; as amended by Amdt. 27–11, 41 FR 55470, Dec. 20, 1976]

§27.1323 Airspeed indicating system.

(a) Each airspeed indicating instrument must be calibrated to indicate true airspeed (at sea level with a standard atmosphere) with a minimum practicable instrument calibration error when the corresponding pitot and static pressures are applied.

(b) The airspeed indicating system must be calibrated in flight at forward speeds of 20 knots and over.

(c) At each forward speed above 80 percent of the climbout speed, the airspeed indicator must indicate true airspeed, at sea level with a standard atmosphere, to within an allowable installation error of not more than the greater of—

(1) ±3 percent of the calibrated airspeed; or

(2) Five knots.

(Secs. 313(a), 601, 603, 604, and 605 of the Federal Aviation Act of 1958 (49 U.S.C. 1354(a), 1421, 1423, 1424, and 1425); and sec. 6(c) of the Dept. of Transportation Act (49 U.S.C. 1655(c)))

[Docket No. 5074, 29 FR 15695, Nov. 24, 1964; as amended by Amdt. 27–13, 42 FR 36972, July 18, 1977]

§27.1325 Static pressure systems.

(a) Each instrument with static air case connections must be vented so that the influence of rotorcraft speed, the opening and closing of windows, airflow variation, and moisture or other foreign matter does not seriously affect its accuracy.

(b) Each static pressure port must be designed and located in such manner that the correlation between air pressure in the static pressure system and true ambient atmospheric static pressure is not altered when the rotorcraft encounters icing conditions. An anti-icing means or an alternate source of static pressure may be used in showing compliance with this requirement. If the reading of the altimeter, when on the alternate static pressure system, differs from the reading of the altimeter when on the primary static system by more than 50 feet, a correction card must be provided for the alternate static system.

(c) Except as provided in paragraph (d) of this section, if the static pressure system incorporates both a primary and an alternate static pressure source, the means for selecting one or the other source must be designed so that—

(1) When either source is selected, the other is blocked off; and

(2) Both sources cannot be blocked off simultaneously.

(d) For unpressurized rotorcraft, paragraph (c)(1) of this section does not apply if it can be demonstrated that the static pressure system calibration, when either static pressure source is selected is not changed by the other static pressure source being open or blocked.

(Secs. 313(a), 601, 603, 604, and 605 of the Federal Aviation Act of 1958 (49 U.S.C. 1354(a), 1421, 1423, 1424, and 1425); and sec. 6(c) of the Dept. of Transportation Act (49 U.S.C. 1655(c)))

[Docket No. 5074, 29 FR 15695, Nov. 24, 1964; as amended by Amdt. 27–13, 42 FR 36972, July 18, 1977]

§27.1327 Magnetic direction indicator.

(a) Except as provided in paragraph (b) of this section—

(1) Each magnetic direction indicator must be installed so that its accuracy is not excessively affected by the rotorcraft's vibration or magnetic fields; and

(2) The compensated installation may not have a deviation, in level fight, greater than 10 degrees on any heading.

(b) A magnetic nonstabilized direction indicator may deviate more than 10 degrees due to the operation of electrically powered systems such as electrically heated windshields if either a magnetic stabilized direction indicator, which does not have a deviation in level flight greater than 10 degrees on any heading, or a gyroscopic direction indicator, is installed. Deviations of a magnetic nonstabilized direction indicator of more than 10 degrees must be placarded in accordance with §27.1547(e).

(Secs. 313(a), 601, 603, 604, and 605 of the Federal Aviation Act of 1958 (49 U.S.C. 1354(a), 1421, 1423, 1424, and 1425); and sec. 6(c) of the Dept. of Transportation Act (49 U.S.C. 1655(c)))

[Docket No. 5074, 29 FR 15695, Nov. 24, 1964; as amended by Amdt. 27–13, 42 FR 36972, July 18, 1977]

§27.1329 Automatic pilot system.

(a) Each automatic pilot system must be designed so that the automatic pilot can—

(1) Be sufficiently overpowered by one pilot to allow control of the rotorcraft; and

(2) Be readily and positively disengaged by each pilot to prevent it from interfering with control of the rotorcraft.

(b) Unless there is automatic synchronization, each system must have a means to readily indicate to the pilot the alignment of the actuating device in relation to the control system it operates.

(c) Each manually operated control for the system's operation must be readily accessible to the pilots.

(d) The system must be designed and adjusted so that, within the range of adjustment available to the pilot, it cannot produce hazardous loads on the rotorcraft or create hazardous deviations in the flight path under any flight condition appropriate to its use, either during normal operation or in the event of a malfunction, assuming that corrective action begins within a reasonable period of time.

(e) If the automatic pilot integrates signals from auxiliary controls or furnishes signals for operation of other equipment, there must be positive interlocks and sequencing of engagement to prevent improper operation.

(f) If the automatic pilot system can be coupled to airborne navigation equipment, means must be provided to indicate to the pilots the current mode of operation. Selector switch position is not acceptable as a means of indication.

[Docket No. 5074, 29 FR 15695, Nov. 24, 1964; as amended by Amdt. 27–21, 49 FR 44435, Nov. 6, 1984; Amdt. 27–35, 63 FR 43285, Aug. 12, 1998]

§27.1335 Flight director systems.

If a flight director system is installed, means must be provided to indicate to the flight crew its current mode of operation. Selector switch position is not acceptable as a means of indication.

(Secs. 313(a), 601, 603, 604, and 605 of the Federal Aviation Act of 1958 (49 U.S.C. 1354(a), 1421, 1423, 1424, and 1425); and sec. 6(c) of the Dept. of Transportation Act (49 U.S.C. 1655(c)))

[Docket No. 5074, 29 FR 15695, Nov. 24, 1964; as amended by Amdt. 27–13, 42 FR 36972, July 18, 1977]

§27.1337 Powerplant instruments.

(a) *Instruments and instrument lines.*

(1) Each powerplant instrument line must meet the requirements of §§27.961 and 27.993.

(2) Each line carrying flammable fluids under pressure must—

(i) Have restricting orifices or other safety devices at the source of pressure to prevent the escape of excessive fluid if the line fails; and

(ii) Be installed and located so that the escape of fluids would not create a hazard.

(3) Each powerplant instrument that utilizes flammable fluids must be installed and located so that the escape of fluid would not create a hazard.

(b) *Fuel quantity indicator.* Each fuel quantity indicator must be installed to clearly indicate to the flight crew the quantity of fuel in each tank in flight. In addition—

(1) Each fuel quantity indicator must be calibrated to read "zero" during level flight when the quantity of fuel remaining in the tank is equal to the unusable fuel supply determined under §27.959;

(2) When two or more tanks are closely interconnected by a gravity feed system and vented, and when it is impossible to feed from each tank separately, at least one fuel quantity indicator must be installed; and

(3) Each exposed sight gauge used as a fuel quantity indicator must be protected against damage.

(c) *Fuel flowmeter system.* If a fuel flowmeter system is installed, each metering component must have a means for bypassing the fuel supply if malfunction of that component severely restricts fuel flow.

(d) *Oil quantity indicator.* There must be means to indicate the quantity of oil in each tank—

(1) On the ground (including during the filling of each tank); and

(2) In flight, if there is an oil transfer system or reserve oil supply system.

(e) Rotor drive system transmissions and gearboxes utilizing ferromagnetic materials must be equipped with chip detectors designed to indicate the presence of ferromagnetic particles resulting from damage or excessive wear. Chip detectors must—

(1) Be designed to provide a signal to the device required by §27.1305(v) and be provided with a means to allow crewmembers to check, in flight, the function of each detector electrical circuit and signal.

(2) [Reserved]

(Secs. 313(a), 601, and 603, 72 Stat. 752, 775, 49 U.S.C. 1354(a), 1421, and 1423; sec. 6(c) 49 U.S.C. 1655(c))

[Docket No. 5074, 29 FR 15695, Nov. 24, 1964; as amended by Amdt. 27–12, 42 FR 15046, March 17, 1977; Amdt. 27–23, 53 FR 34214, Sept. 2, 1988; Amdt. 27–37, 64 FR 45095, Aug. 18, 1999]

Electrical Systems and Equipment

§27.1351 General.

(a) *Electrical system capacity.* Electrical equipment must be adequate for its intended use. In addition—

(1) Electric power sources, their transmission cables, and their associated control and protective devices must be able to furnish the required power at the proper voltage to each load circuit essential for safe operation; and

(2) Compliance with paragraph (a)(1) of this section must be shown by an electrical load analysis, or by electrical measurements that take into account the electrical loads applied to the electrical system, in probable combinations and for probable durations.

(b) *Function.* For each electrical system, the following apply:

(1) Each system, when installed, must be—

(i) Free from hazards in itself, in its method of operation, and in its effects on other parts of the rotorcraft; and

(ii) Protected from fuel, oil, water, other detrimental substances, and mechanical damage.

(2) Electric power sources must function properly when connected in combination or independently.

(3) No failure or malfunction of any source may impair the ability of any remaining source to supply load circuits essential for safe operation.

(4) Each electric power source control must allow the independent operation of each source.

(c) *Generating system.* There must be at least one generator if the system supplies power to load circuits essential for safe operation. In addition—

(1) Each generator must be able to deliver its continuous rated power;

(2) Generator voltage control equipment must be able to dependably regulate each generator output within rated limits;

(3) Each generator must have a reverse current cutout designed to disconnect the generator from the battery and from the other generators when enough reverse current exists to damage that generator; and

(4) Each generator must have an overvoltage control designed and installed to prevent damage to the electrical system, or to equipment supplied by the electrical system, that could result if that generator were to develop an overvoltage condition.

(d) *Instruments.* There must be means to indicate to appropriate crewmembers the electric power system quantities essential for safe operation of the system. In addition—

(1) For direct current systems, an ammeter that can be switched into each generator feeder may be used; and

(2) If there is only one generator, the ammeter may be in the battery feeder.

(e) *External power.* If provisions are made for connecting external power to the rotorcraft, and that external power can be electrically connected to equipment other than that used for engine starting, means must be provided to ensure that no external power supply having a reverse polarity, or a reverse phase sequence, can supply power to the rotorcraft's electrical system.

(Secs. 313(a), 601, 603, 604, and 605 of the Federal Aviation Act of 1958 (49 U.S.C. 1354(a), 1421, 1423, 1424, and 1425); and sec. 6(c) of the Dept. of Transportation Act (49 U.S.C. 1655(c)))

[Docket No. 5074, 29 FR 15695, Nov. 24, 1964; as amended by Amdt. 27–11, 41 FR 55470, Dec. 20, 1976; Amdt. 27–13, 42 FR 36972, July 18, 1977]

§27.1353 Storage battery design and installation.

(a) Each storage battery must be designed and installed as prescribed in this section.

(b) Safe cell temperatures and pressures must be maintained during any probable charging and discharging condition. No uncontrolled increase in cell temperature may result when the battery is recharged (after previous complete discharge)—

(1) At maximum regulated voltage or power;

(2) During a flight of maximum duration; and

(3) Under the most adverse cooling condition likely to occur in service.

(c) Compliance with paragraph (b) of this section must be shown by test unless experience with similar batteries and installations has shown that maintaining safe cell temperatures and pressures presents no problem.

(d) No explosive or toxic gases emitted by any battery in normal operation, or as the result of any probable malfunction in the charging system or battery installation, may accumulate in hazardous quantities within the rotorcraft.

(e) No corrosive fluids or gases that may escape from the battery may damage surrounding structures or adjacent essential equipment.

(f) Each nickel cadmium battery installation capable of being used to start an engine or auxiliary power unit must have provisions to prevent any hazardous effect on structure or essential systems that may be caused by the maximum amount of heat the battery can generate during a short circuit of the battery or of its individual cells.

(g) Nickel cadmium battery installations capable of being used to start an engine or auxiliary power unit must have—

(1) A system to control the charging rate of the battery automatically so as to prevent battery overheating;

(2) A battery temperature sensing and over-temperature warning system with a means for disconnecting the battery from its charging source in the event of an over-temperature condition; or

(3) A battery failure sensing and warning system with a means for disconnecting the battery from its charging source in the event of battery failure.

(Secs. 313(a), 601, 603, 604, and 605 of the Federal Aviation Act of 1958 (49 U.S.C. l354(a), 1421, 1423, 1424, and 1425); and sec. 6(c) of the Dept. of Transportation Act (49 U.S.C. 1655(c)))

[Docket No. 5074, 29 FR 15695, Nov. 24, 1964; as amended by Amdt. 27–13, 42 FR 36972, July 18, 1977; Amdt. 27–14, 43 FR 2325, Jan. 16, 1978]

§27.1357 Circuit protective devices.

(a) Protective devices, such as fuses or circuit breakers, must be installed in each electrical circuit other than—

(1) The main circuits of starter motors; and

(2) Circuits in which no hazard is presented by their omission.

(b) A protective device for a circuit essential to flight safety may not be used to protect any other circuit.

(c) Each resettable circuit protective device ("trip free" device in which the tripping mechanism cannot be overridden by the operating control) must be designed so that—

(1) A manual operation is required to restore service after tripping; and

(2) If an overload or circuit fault exists, the device will open the circuit regardless of the position of the operating control.

(d) If the ability to reset a circuit breaker or replace a fuse is essential to safety in flight, that circuit breaker or fuse must be located and identified so that it can be readily reset or replaced in flight.

(e) If fuses are used, there must be one spare of each rating, or 50 percent spare fuses of each rating, whichever is greater.

(Secs. 313(a), 601, 603, 604, and 605 of the Federal Aviation Act of 1958 (49 U.S.C. 1354(a), 1421, 1423, 1424, and 1425); and sec. 6(c) of the Dept. of Transportation Act (49 U.S.C. 1655(c)))

[Docket No. 5074, 29 FR 15695, Nov. 24, 1964; 29 FR 17885, Dec. 17, 1964; as amended by Amdt. 27–13, 42 FR 36972, July 18, 1977]

§27.1361 Master switch.

(a) There must be a master switch arrangement to allow ready disconnection of each electric power source from the main bus. The point of disconnection must be adjacent to the sources controlled by the switch.

(b) Load circuits may be connected so that they remain energized after the switch is opened, if they are protected by circuit protective devices, rated at five amperes or less, adjacent to the electric power source.

(c) The master switch or its controls must be installed so that the switch is easily discernible and accessible to a crewmember in flight.

§27.1365 Electric cables.

(a) Each electric connecting cable must be of adequate capacity.

(b) Each cable that would overheat in the event of circuit overload or fault must be at least flame resistant and may not emit dangerous quantities of toxic fumes.

(c) Insulation on electrical wire and cable installed in the rotorcraft must be self-extinguishing when tested in accordance with Appendix F, Part I(a)(3), of part 25 of this chapter.

[Docket No. 5074, 29 FR 15695, Nov. 24, 1964; as amended by Amdt. 27–35, 63 FR 43285, Aug. 12, 1998]

§27.1367 Switches.

Each switch must be—

(a) Able to carry its rated current;

(b) Accessible to the crew; and

(c) Labeled as to operation and the circuit controlled.

LIGHTS

§27.1381 Instrument lights.

The instrument lights must—

(a) Make each instrument, switch, and other devices for which they are provided easily readable; and

(b) Be installed so that—

(1) Their direct rays are shielded from the pilot's eyes; and

(2) No objectionable reflections are visible to the pilot.

§27.1383 Landing lights.

(a) Each required landing or hovering light must be approved.

(b) Each landing light must be installed so that—

(1) No objectionable glare is visible to the pilot;

(2) The pilot is not adversely affected by halation; and

(3) It provides enough light for night operation, including hovering and landing.

(c) At least one separate switch must be provided, as applicable—

(1) For each separately installed landing light; and

(2) For each group of landing lights installed at a common location.

§27.1385 Position light system installation.

(a) *General.* Each part of each position light system must meet the applicable requirements of this section, and each system as a whole must meet the requirements of §§27.1387 through 27.1397.

(b) *Forward position lights.* Forward position lights must consist of a red and a green light spaced laterally as far apart as practicable and installed forward on the rotorcraft so that, with the rotorcraft in the normal flying position, the red light is on the left side and the green light is on the right side. Each light must be approved.

(c) *Rear position light.* The rear position light must be a white light mounted as far aft as practicable, and must be approved.

(d) *Circuit.* The two forward position lights and the rear position light must make a single circuit.

(e) *Light covers and color filters.* Each light cover or color filter must be at least flame resistant and may not change color or shape or lose any appreciable light transmission during normal use.

§27.1387 Position light system dihedral angles.

(a) Except as provided in paragraph (e) of this section, each forward and rear position light must, as installed, show unbroken light within the dihedral angles described in this section.

(b) Dihedral angle L (left) is formed by two intersecting vertical planes, the first parallel to the longitudinal axis of the rotorcraft, and the other at 110 degrees to the left of the first, as viewed when looking forward along the longitudinal axis.

(c) Dihedral angle R (right) is formed by two intersecting vertical planes, the first parallel to the longitudinal axis of the rotorcraft, and the other at 110 degrees to the right of the first, as viewed when looking forward along the longitudinal axis.

(d) Dihedral angle A (aft) is formed by two intersecting vertical planes making angles of 70 degrees to the right and to the left, respectively, to a vertical plane passing through the longitudinal axis, as viewed when looking aft along the longitudinal axis.

(e) If the rear position light, when mounted as far aft as practicable in accordance with §25.1385(c), cannot show unbroken light within dihedral angle *A* (as defined in paragraph (d) of this section), a solid angle or angles of obstructed visibility totaling not more than 0.04 steradians is allowable within that dihedral angle, if such solid angle is within a cone whose apex is at the rear position light and whose elements make an angle of 30° with a vertical line passing through the rear position light.

(49 U.S.C. 1655(c))

[Docket No. 5074, 29 FR 15695, Nov. 24, 1964; as amended by Amdt. 27–7, 36 FR 21278, Nov. 5, 1971]

§27.1389 Position light distribution and intensities.

(a) *General.* The intensities prescribed in this section must be provided by new equipment with light covers and color filters in place. Intensities must be determined with the light source operating at a steady value equal to the average luminous output of the source at the normal operating voltage of the rotorcraft. The light distribution and intensity of each position light must meet the requirements of paragraph (b) of this section.

(b) *Forward and rear position lights.* The light distribution and intensities of forward and rear position lights must be expressed in terms of minimum intensities in the horizontal plane, minimum intensities in any vertical plane, and maximum intensities in overlapping beams, within dihedral angles L, R, and A, and must meet the following requirements:

(1) *Intensities in the horizontal plane.* Each intensity in the horizontal plane (the plane containing the longitudinal axis of the rotorcraft and perpendicular to the plane of symmetry of the rotorcraft) must equal or exceed the values in §27.1391.

(2) *Intensities in any vertical plane.* Each intensity in any vertical plane (the plane perpendicular to the horizontal plane) must equal or exceed the appropriate value in §27.1393, where I is the minimum intensity prescribed in §27.1391 for the corresponding angles in the horizontal plane.

(3) *Intensities in overlaps between adjacent signals.* No intensity in any overlap between adjacent signals may exceed the values in §27.1395, except that higher intensities in overlaps may be used with main beam intensities substantially greater than the minima specified in §§27.1391 and 27.1393, if the overlap intensities in relation to the main beam intensities do not adversely affect signal clarity. When the peak intensity of the forward position lights is greater than 100 candles, the maximum overlap intensities between them may exceed the values in §27.1395 if the overlap intensity in Area A is not more than 10 percent of peak position light intensity and the overlap intensity in Area B is not more than 2.5 percent of peak position light intensity.

§27.1391 Minimum intensities in the horizontal plane of forward and rear position lights.

Each position light intensity must equal or exceed the applicable values in the following table:

Dihedral angle (light included)	Angle from right or left of longitudinal axis, measured from dead ahead	Intensity (candles)
L and R (forward red and green)	10° to 10°	40
	10° to 20°	30
	20° to 110°	5
A (rear white)	110° to 180°	20

§27.1393 Minimum intensities in any vertical plane of forward and rear position lights.

Each position light intensity must equal or exceed the applicable values in the following table:

Angle above or below the horizontal plane	Intensity, I
0°	1.00
0° to 5°	0.90
5° to 10°	0.80
10° to 15°	0.70
15° to 20°	0.50
20° to 30°	0.30
30° to 40°	0.10
40° to 90°	0.05

§27.1395 Maximum intensities in overlapping beams of forward and rear position lights.

No position light intensity may exceed the applicable values in the following table, except as provided in §27.1389(b)(3).

Overlaps	Maximum Intensity	
	Area A (candles)	Area B (candles)
Green in dihedral angle L	10	1
Red in dihedral angle R	10	1
Green in dihedral angle A	5	1
Red in dihedral angle A	5	1
Rear white in dihedral angle L	5	1
Rear white in dihedral angle R	5	1

Where—

(a) Area A includes all directions in the adjacent dihedral angle that pass through the light source and intersect the common boundary plane at more than 10 degrees but less than 20 degrees, and

(b) Area B includes all directions in the adjacent dihedral angle that pass through the light source and intersect the common boundary plane at more than 20 degrees.

§27.1397 Color specifications.

Each position light color must have the applicable International Commission on Illumination chromaticity coordinates as follows:

(a) *Aviation red*—

"y" is not greater than 0.335; and
"z" is not greater than 0.002.

(b) *Aviation green*—

"x" is not greater than 0.440—0.320y;
"x" is not greater than y—0.170; and
"y" is not less than 0.390—0.170x.

(c) *Aviation white*—

"x" is not less than 0.300 and not greater than 0.540;
"y" is not less than "x—0.040" or y_c— 0.010", whichever is the smaller; and
"y" is not greater than "x+0.020" nor "0.636—0.400x;

Where "y_c" is the "y" coordinate of the Planckian radiator for the value of "x" considered.

[Docket No. 5074, 29 FR 15695, Nov. 24, 1964; as amended by Amdt. 27–6, 36 FR 12972, July 10, 1971]

§27.1399 Riding light.

(a) Each riding light required for water operation must be installed so that it can—

(1) Show a white light for at least two nautical miles at night under clear atmospheric conditions; and

(2) Show a maximum practicable unbroken light with the rotorcraft on the water.

(b) Externally hung lights may be used.

[Docket No. 5074, 29 FR 15695, Nov. 24, 1964; as amended by Amdt. 27–2, 33 FR 964, Jan. 26, 1968]

§27.1401 Anticollision light system.

(a) *General.* If certification for night operation is requested, the rotorcraft must have an anticollision light system that—

(1) Consists of one or more approved anticollision lights located so that their emitted light will not impair the crew's vision or detract from the conspicuity of the position lights; and

(2) Meets the requirements of paragraphs (b) through (f) of this section.

(b) *Field of coverage.* The system must consist of enough lights to illuminate the vital areas around the rotorcraft, considering the physical configuration and flight characteristics of the rotorcraft. The field of coverage must extend in each direction within at least 30 degrees below the horizontal plane of the rotorcraft, except that there may be solid angles of obstructed visibility totaling not more than 0.5 steradians.

(c) *Flashing characteristics.* The arrangement of the system, that is, the number of light sources, beam width, speed of rotation, and other characteristics, must give an effective flash frequency of not less than 40, nor more than 100, cycles per minute. The effective flash frequency is the frequency at which the rotorcraft's complete anticollision light system is observed from a distance, and applies to each sector of light including any overlaps that exist when the system consists of more than one light source. In overlaps, flash frequencies may exceed 100, but not 180, cycles per minute.

(d) *Color.* Each anticollision light must be aviation red and must meet the applicable requirements of §27.1397.

(e) *Light intensity.* The minimum light intensities in any vertical plane, measured with the red filter (if used) and expressed in terms of "effective" intensities, must meet the requirements of paragraph (f) of this section. The following relation must be assumed:

$$I_e = \frac{\int_{t_1}^{t_2} I(t)dt}{0.2 + (t_2 - t_1)}$$

where:
I_e = effective intensity (candles).
$I(t)$ = instantaneous intensity as a function of time.
$t_2 - t_1$ = flash time interval (seconds).

Normally, the maximum value of effective intensity is obtained when t_2 and t_1, are chosen so that the effective intensity is equal to the instantaneous intensity at t_2 and t_1.

(f) *Minimum effective intensities for anticollision light.* Each anticollision light effective intensity must equal or exceed the applicable values in the following table:

Angle above or below the horizontal plane	Effective intensity (candles)
0° to 5°	150
5° to 10°	90
10° to 20°	30
20° to 30°	15

[Docket No. 5074, 29 FR 15695, Nov. 24, 1964; as amended by Amdt. 27–6, 36 FR 12972, July 10, 1971; Amdt. 27–10, 41 FR 5290, Feb. 5, 1976]

SAFETY EQUIPMENT

§27.1411 General.

(a) Required safety equipment to be used by the crew in an emergency, such as flares and automatic liferaft releases, must be readily accessible.

(b) Stowage provisions for required safety equipment must be furnished and must—

(1) Be arranged so that the equipment is directly accessible and its location is obvious; and

(2) Protect the safety equipment from damage caused by being subjected to the inertia loads specified in §27.561.

[Docket No. 5074, 29 FR 15695, Nov. 24, 1964; as amended by Amdt. 27–11, 41 FR 55470, Dec. 20, 1976]

§27.1413 Safety belts.

Each safety belt must be equipped with a metal to metal latching device.

(Secs. 313, 314, and 601 through 610 of the Federal Aviation Act of 1958 (49 U.S.C. 1354, 1355, and 1421 through 1430) and sec. 6(c), Dept. of Transportation Act (49 U.S.C. 1655(c)))

[Docket No. 5074, 29 FR 15695, Nov. 24, 1964; as amended by Amdt. 27–15, 43 FR 46233, Oct. 5, 1978; Amdt. 27–21, 49 FR 44435, Nov. 6, 1984]

§27.1415 Ditching equipment.

(a) Emergency flotation and signaling equipment required by any operating rule in this chapter must meet the requirements of this section.

(b) Each raft and each life preserver must be approved and must be installed so that it is readily available to the crew and passengers. The storage provisions for life preservers must accommodate one life preserver for each occupant for which certification for ditching is requested.

(c) Each raft released automatically or by the pilot must be attached to the rotorcraft by a line to keep it alongside the rotorcraft. This line must be weak enough to break before submerging the empty raft to which it is attached.

(d) Each signaling device must be free from hazard in its operation and must be installed in an accessible location.

[Docket No. 5074, 29 FR 15695, Nov. 24, 1964; as amended by Amdt. 27–11, 41 FR 55470, Dec. 20, 1976]

§27.1419 Ice protection.

(a) To obtain certification for flight into icing conditions, compliance with this section must be shown.

(b) It must be demonstrated that the rotorcraft can be safely operated in the continuous maximum and intermittent maximum icing conditions determined under Appendix C of Part 29 of this chapter within the rotorcraft altitude envelope. An analysis must be performed to establish, on the basis of the rotorcraft's operational needs, the adequacy of the ice protection system for the various components of the rotorcraft.

(c) In addition to the analysis and physical evaluation prescribed in paragraph (b) of this section, the effectiveness of the ice protection system and its components must be shown by flight tests of the rotorcraft or its components in measured natural atmospheric icing conditions and by one or more of the following tests as found necessary to determine the adequacy of the ice protection system:

(1) Laboratory dry air or simulated icing tests, or a combination of both, of the components or models of the components.

(2) Flight dry air tests of the ice protection system as a whole, or its individual components.

(3) Flight tests of the rotorcraft or its components in measured simulated icing conditions.

(d) The ice protection provisions of this section are considered to be applicable primarily to the airframe. Powerplant installation requirements are contained in Subpart E of this part.

(e) A means must be identified or provided for determining the formation of ice on critical parts of the rotorcraft. Unless otherwise restricted, the means must be available for nighttime as well as daytime operation. The rotorcraft flight manual must describe the means of determining ice formation and must contain information necessary for safe operation of the rotorcraft in icing conditions.

[Docket No. 5074, 29 FR 15695, Nov. 24, 1964; as amended by Amdt. 27–19, 48 FR 4389, Jan. 31, 1983]

§27.1435 Hydraulic systems.

(a) *Design.* Each hydraulic system and its elements must withstand, without yielding, any structural loads expected in addition to hydraulic loads.

(b) *Tests.* Each system must be substantiated by proof pressure tests. When proof tested, no part of any system may fail, malfunction, or experience a permanent set. The proof load of each system must be at least 1.5 times the maximum operating pressure of that system.

(c) *Accumulators.* No hydraulic accumulator or pressurized reservoir may be installed on the engine side of any firewall unless it is an integral part of an engine.

§27.1457 Cockpit voice recorders.

(a) Each cockpit voice recorder required by the operating rules of this chapter must be approved, and must be installed so that it will record the following:

(1) Voice communications transmitted from or received in the rotorcraft by radio.

(2) Voice communications of flight crewmembers on the flight deck.

(3) Voice communications of flight crewmembers on the flight deck, using the rotorcraft's interphone system.

(4) Voice or audio signals identifying navigation or approach aids introduced into a headset or speaker.

(5) Voice communications of flight crewmembers using the passenger loudspeaker system, if there is such a system, and if the fourth channel is available in accordance with the requirements of paragraph (c)(4)(ii) of this section.

(b) The recording requirements of paragraph (a)(2) of this section may be met:

(1) By installing a cockpit-mounted area microphone located in the best position for recording voice communications originating at the first and second pilot stations and voice communications of other crewmembers on the flight deck when directed to those stations; or

(2) By installing a continually energized or voice-actuated lip microphone at the first and second pilot stations.

The microphone specified in this paragraph must be so located and, if necessary, the preamplifiers and filters of the recorder must be adjusted or supplemented so that the recorded communications are intelligible when recorded under flight cockpit noise conditions and played back. The level of intelligibility must be approved by the Administrator. Repeated aural or visual playback of the record may be used in evaluating intelligibility.

(c) Each cockpit voice recorder must be installed so that the part of the communication or audio signals specified in paragraph (a) of this section obtained from each of the following sources is recorded on a separate channel:

(1) For the first channel, from each microphone, headset, or speaker used at the first pilot station.

(2) For the second channel, from each microphone, headset, or speaker used at the second pilot station.

(3) For the third channel, from the cockpit-mounted area microphone, or the continually energized or voice-actuated lip microphone at the first and second pilot stations.

(4) For the fourth channel, from:

(i) Each microphone, headset, or speaker used at the stations for the third and fourth crewmembers; or

(ii) If the stations specified in paragraph (c)(4)(i) of this section are not required or if the signal at such a station is picked up by another channel, each microphone on the flight deck that is used with the passenger loudspeaker system if its signals are not picked up by another channel.

(iii) Each microphone on the flight deck that is used with the rotorcraft's loudspeaker system if its signals are not picked up by another channel.

(d) Each cockpit voice recorder must be installed so that:

(1) It receives its electric power from the bus that provides the maximum reliability for operation of the cockpit voice recorder without jeopardizing service to essential or emergency loads;

(2) There is an automatic means to simultaneously stop the recorder and prevent each erasure feature from functioning, within 10 minutes after crash impact; and

(3) There is an aural or visual means for preflight checking of the recorder for proper operation.

(e) The record container must be located and mounted to minimize the probability of rupture of the container as a result of crash impact and consequent heat damage to the record from fire.

(f) If the cockpit voice recorder has a bulk erasure device, the installation must be designed to minimize the probability of inadvertent operation and actuation of the device during crash impact.

(g) Each recorder container must be either bright orange or bright yellow.

[Docket No. 5074, 29 FR 15695, Nov. 24, 1964; as amended by Amdt. 27–22, 53 FR 26144, July 11, 1988]

§27.1459 Flight recorders.

27

(a) Each flight recorder required by the operating rules of Subchapter G of this chapter must be installed so that:

(1) It is supplied with airspeed, altitude, and directional data obtained from sources that meet the accuracy requirements of §§27.1323, 27.1325, and 27.1327 of this part, as applicable;

(2) The vertical acceleration sensor is rigidly attached, and located longitudinally within the approved center of gravity limits of the rotorcraft;

(3) It receives its electrical power from the bus that provides the maximum reliability for operation of the flight recorder without jeopardizing service to essential or emergency loads;

(4) There is an aural or visual means for preflight checking of the recorder for proper recording of data in the storage medium;

(5) Except for recorders powered solely by the engine-driven electrical generator system, there is an automatic means to simultaneously stop a recorder that has a data erasure feature and prevent each erasure feature from functioning, within 10 minutes after any crash impact; and

(b) Each nonejectable recorder container must be located and mounted so as to minimize the probability of container rupture resulting from crash impact and subsequent damage to the record from fire.

(c) A correlation must be established between the flight recorder readings of airspeed, altitude, and heading and the corresponding readings (taking into account correction factors) of the first pilot's instruments. This correlation must cover the airspeed range over which the aircraft is to be operated, the range of altitude to which the aircraft is limited, and 360 degrees of heading. Correlation may be established on the ground as appropriate.

(d) Each recorder container must:

(1) Be either bright orange or bright yellow;

(2) Have a reflective tape affixed to its external surface to facilitate its location under water; and

(3) Have an underwater locating device, when required by the operating rules of this chapter, on or adjacent to the container which is secured in such a manner that they are not likely to be separated during crash impact.

[Docket No. 5074, 29 FR 15695, Nov. 24, 1964; as amended by Amdt. 27–22, 53 FR 26144, July 11, 1988]

§27.1461 Equipment containing high energy rotors.

(a) Equipment containing high energy rotors must meet paragraph (b), (c), or (d) of this section.

(b) High energy rotors contained in equipment must be able to withstand damage caused by malfunctions, vibration, abnormal speeds, and abnormal temperatures. In addition—

(1) Auxiliary rotor cases must be able to contain damage caused by the failure of high energy rotor blades; and

(2) Equipment control devices, systems, and instrumentation must reasonably ensure that no operating limitations affecting the integrity of high energy rotors will be exceeded in service.

(c) It must be shown by test that equipment containing high energy rotors can contain any failure of a high energy rotor that occurs at the highest speed obtainable with the normal speed control devices inoperative.

(d) Equipment containing high energy rotors must be located where rotor failure will neither endanger the occupants nor adversely affect continued safe flight.

[Docket No. 5074, 29 FR 15695, Nov. 24, 1964; as amended by Amdt. 27–2, 33 FR 964, Jan. 26, 1968]

Subpart G—Operating Limitations and Information

§27.1501 General.

(a) Each operating limitation specified in §§27.1503 through 27.1525 and other limitations and information necessary for safe operation must be established.

(b) The operating limitations and other information necessary for safe operation must be made available to the crewmembers as prescribed in §§27.1541 through 27.1589.

(Secs. 313(a), 601, 603, 604, and 605 of the Federal Aviation Act of 1958 (49 U.S.C. 1354(a), 1421, 1423, 1424, and 1425); and sec. 6(c) of the Dept. of Transportation Act (49 U.S.C. 1655(c)))

[Docket No. 5074, 29 FR 15695, Nov. 24, 1964; as amended by Amdt. 27–14, 43 FR 2325, Jan. 16, 1978]

OPERATING LIMITATIONS

§27.1503 Airspeed limitations: general.

(a) An operating speed range must be established.

(b) When airspeed limitations are a function of weight, weight distribution, altitude, rotor speed, power, or other factors, airspeed limitations corresponding with the critical combinations of these factors must be established.

§27.1505 Never-exceed speed.

(a) The never-exceed speed, V_{NE} must be established so that it is—

(1) Not less than 40 knots (CAS); and

(2) Not more than the lesser of—

(i) 0.9 times the maximum forward speeds established under §27.309;

(ii) 0.9 times the maximum speed shown under §§27.251 and 27.629; or

(iii) 0.9 times the maximum speed substantiated for advancing blade tip mach number effects.

(b) V_{NE} may vary with altitude, r.p.m., temperature, and weight, if—

(1) No more than two of these variables (or no more than two instruments integrating more than one of these variables) are used at one time; and

(2) The ranges of these variables (or of the indications on instruments integrating more than one of these variables) are large enough to allow an operationally practical and safe variation of V_{NE}.

(c) For helicopters, a stabilized power-off V_{NE} denoted as V_{NE} (power-off) may be established at a speed less than V_{NE} established pursuant to paragraph (a) of this section, if the following conditions are met:

(1) V_{NE} (power-off) is not less than a speed midway between the power-on V_{NE} and the speed used in meeting the requirements of—

(i) §27.65(b) for single engine helicopters; and

(ii) §27.67 for multiengine helicopters.

(2) V_{NE} (power-off) is—

(i) A constant airspeed;

(ii) A constant amount less than power-on V_{NE}; or

(iii) A constant airspeed for a portion of the altitude range for which certification is requested, and a constant amount less than power-on V_{NE} for the remainder of the altitude range.

(Secs. 313(a), 601, 603, 604, and 605 of the Federal Aviation Act of 1958 (49 U.S.C. 1354(a), 1421, 1423, 1424, and 1425); and sec. 6(c) of the Dept. of Transportation Act (49 U.S.C. 1655(c)))

[Docket No. 5074, 29 FR 15695, Nov. 24, 1964; as amended by Amdt. 27–2, 33 FR 964, Jan. 26, 1968, and Amdt. 27–14, 43 FR 2325, Jan. 16, 1978; Amdt. 27–21, 49 FR 44435, Nov. 6, 1984]

§27.1509 Rotor speed.

(a) *Maximum power off (autorotation).* The maximum power-off rotor speed must be established so that it does not exceed 95 percent of the lesser of—

(1) The maximum design r.p.m. determined under §27.309(b); and

(2) The maximum r.p.m. shown during the type tests.

(b) *Minimum power off.* The minimum power-off rotor speed must be established so that it is not less than 105 percent of the greater of—

(1) The minimum shown during the type tests; and

(2) The minimum determined by design substantiation.

(c) *Minimum power on.* The minimum power-on rotor speed must be established so that it is—

(1) Not less than the greater of—

(i) The minimum shown during the type tests; and

(ii) The minimum determined by design substantiation; and

(2) Not more than a value determined under §27.33(a)(1) and (b)(1).

§27.1519 Weight and center of gravity.

The weight and center of gravity limitations determined under §§27.25 and 27.27, respectively, must be established as operating limitations.

[Docket No. 5074, 29 FR 15695, Nov. 24, 1964; as amended by Amdt. 27–2, 33 FR 965, Jan. 26, 1968; Amdt. 27–21, 49 FR 44435, Nov. 6, 1984]

§27.1521 Powerplant limitations.

(a) *General.* The powerplant limitations prescribed in this section must be established so that they do not exceed the corresponding limits for which the engines are type certificated.

(b) *Takeoff operation.* The powerplant takeoff operation must be limited by—

(1) The maximum rotational speed, which may not be greater than—

(i) The maximum value determined by the rotor design; or

(ii) The maximum value shown during the type tests;

(2) The maximum allowable manifold pressure (for reciprocating engines);

(3) The time limit for the use of the power corresponding to the limitations established in paragraphs (b)(1) and (2) of this section;

(4) If the time limit in paragraph (b)(3) of this section exceeds two minutes, the maximum allowable cylinder head, coolant outlet, or oil temperatures;

(5) The gas temperature limits for turbine engines over the range of operating and atmospheric conditions for which certification is requested.

(c) *Continuous operation.* The continuous operation must be limited by—

(1) The maximum rotational speed which may not be greater than—

(i) The maximum value determined by the rotor design; or

(ii) The maximum value shown during the type tests;

(2) The minimum rotational speed shown under the rotor speed requirements in §27.1509(c); and

(3) The gas temperature limits for turbine engines over the range of operating and atmospheric conditions for which certification is requested.

(d) *Fuel grade or designation.* The minimum fuel grade (for reciprocating engines), or fuel designation (for turbine engines), must be established so that it is not less than that required for the operation of the engines within the limitations in paragraphs (b) and (c) of this section.

(e) *Turboshaft engine torque.* For rotorcraft with main rotors driven by turboshaft engines, and that do not have a torque limiting device in the transmission system, the following apply:

(1) A limit engine torque must be established if the maximum torque that the engine can exert is greater than—

(i) The torque that the rotor drive system is designed to transmit; or

(ii) The torque that the main rotor assembly is designed to withstand in showing compliance with §27.547(e).

(2) The limit engine torque established under paragraph (e)(1) of this section may not exceed either torque specified in paragraph (e)(1)(i) or (ii) of this section.

(f) *Ambient temperature.* For turbine engines, ambient temperature limitations (including limitations for winterization installations, if applicable) must be established as the maximum ambient atmospheric temperature at which compliance with the cooling provisions of §§27.1041 through 27.1045 is shown.

(g) *Two and one-half-minute OEI power operation.* Unless otherwise authorized, the use of 2½-minute OEI power must be limited to engine failure operation of multiengine, turbine-powered rotorcraft for not longer than 2½ minutes after failure of an engine. The use of 2½-minute OEI power must also be limited by—

(1) The maximum rotational speed, which may not be greater than—

(i) The maximum value determined by the rotor design; or

(ii) The maximum demonstrated during the type tests;

(2) The maximum allowable gas temperature; and

(3) The maximum allowable torque.

(h) *Thirty-minute OEI power operation.* Unless otherwise authorized, the use of 30-minute OEI power must be limited to multiengine, turbine-powered rotorcraft for not longer than 30 minutes after failure of an engine. The use of 30 minute OEI power must also be limited by—

(1) The maximum rotational speed, which may not be greater than—

(i) The maximum value determined by the rotor design; or

(ii) The maximum value demonstrated during the type tests;

(2) The maximum allowable gas temperature; and

(3) The maximum allowable torque.

(i) *Continuous OEI power operation.* Unless otherwise authorized, the use of continuous OEI power must be limited to multiengine, turbine-powered rotorcraft for continued flight after failure of an engine. The use of continuous OEI power must also be limited by—

(1) The maximum rotational speed, which may not be greater than—

(i) The maximum value determined by the rotor design; or

(ii) The maximum value demonstrated during the type tests;

(2) The maximum allowable gas temperature; and

(3) The maximum allowable torque.

(j) *Rated 30-second OEI power operation.* Rated 30-second OEI power is permitted only on multiengine, turbine-powered rotorcraft, also certificated for the use of rated 2-minute OEI power, and can only be used for continued operation of the remaining engine(s) after a failure or precautionary shutdown of an engine. It must be shown that following application of 30-second OEI power, any damage will be readily detectable by the applicable inspections and other related procedures furnished in accordance with Section A27.4 of Appendix A of this part and Section A33.4 of Appendix A of part 33. The use of 30-second OEI power must be limited to not more than 30 seconds for any period in which that power is used, and by—

(1) The maximum rotational speed, which may not be greater than—

(i) The maximum value determined by the rotor design; or

(ii) The maximum value demonstrated during the type tests;

(2) The maximum allowable gas temperature, and

(3) The maximum allowable torque.

(k) *Rated 2-minute OEI power operation.* Rated 2-minute OEI power is permitted only on multiengine, turbine-powered rotorcraft, also certificated for the use of rated 30-second OEI power, and can only be used for continued operation of the remaining engine(s) after a failure or precautionary shutdown of an engine. It must be shown that following application of 2-minute OEI power, any damage will be readily detectable by the applicable inspections and other related procedures furnished in accordance with Section A27.4 of

Appendix A of this part and Section A33.4 of Appendix A of part 33. The use of 2-minute OEI power must be limited to not more than 2 minutes for any period in which that power is used, and by—

(1) The maximum rotational speed, which may not be greater than—

(i) The maximum value determined by the rotor design; or

(ii) The maximum value demonstrated during the type tests;

(2) The maximum allowable gas temperature; and

(3) The maximum allowable torque.

(Secs. 313(a), 601, 603, 604, and 605 of the Federal Aviation Act of 1958 (49 U.S.C. 1354(a), 1421, 1423, 1424, and 1425); and sec. 6(c) of the Dept. of Transportation Act (49 U.S.C. 1655(c)))

[Docket No. 5074, 29 FR 15695, Nov. 24, 1964; as amended by Amdt. 27–14, 43 FR 2325, Jan. 16, 1978; Amdt. 27–23, 53 FR 34214, Sept. 2, 1988; Amdt. 27–29, 59 FR 47767, Sept. 16, 1994]

§27.1523 Minimum flight crew.

The minimum flight crew must be established so that it is sufficient for safe operation, considering—

(a) The workload on individual crewmembers;

(b) The accessibility and ease of operation of necessary controls by the appropriate crewmember; and

(c) The kinds of operation authorized under §27.1525.

§27.1525 Kinds of operations.

The kinds of operations (such as VFR, IFR, day, night, or icing) for which the rotorcraft is approved are established by demonstrated compliance with the applicable certification requirements and by the installed equipment.

[Docket No. 5074, 29 FR 15695, Nov. 24, 1964; as amended by Amdt. 27–21, 49 FR 44435, Nov. 6, 1984]

§27.1527 Maximum operating altitude.

The maximum altitude up to which operation is allowed, as limited by flight, structural, powerplant, functional, or equipment characteristics, must be established.

(Secs. 313(a), 601, 603, 604, and 605 of the Federal Aviation Act of 1958 (49 U.S.C. 1354(a) 1421, 1423, 1424, and 1425); and sec. 6(c) of the Dept. of Transportation Act (49 U.S.C. 1655(C)))

[Docket No. 5074, 29 FR 15695, Nov. 24, 1964; as amended by Amdt. 27–14, 43 FR 2325, Jan. 16, 1978]

§27.1529 Instructions for Continued Airworthiness.

The applicant must prepare Instructions for Continued Airworthiness in accordance with Appendix A to this part that are acceptable to the Administrator. The instructions may be incomplete at type certification if a program exists to ensure their completion prior to delivery of the first rotorcraft or issuance of a standard certificate of airworthiness, whichever occurs later.

[Docket No. 5074, 29 FR 15695, Nov. 24, 1964; as amended by Amdt. 27–18, 45 FR 60177, Sept. 11, 1980]

MARKINGS AND PLACARDS

§27.1541 General.

(a) The rotorcraft must contain—

(1) The markings and placards specified in §§27.1545 through 27.1565, and

(2) Any additional information, instrument markings, and placards required for the safe operation of rotorcraft with unusual design, operating or handling characteristics.

(b) Each marking and placard prescribed in paragraph (a) of this section—

(1) Must be displayed in a conspicuous place; and

(2) May not be easily erased, disfigured, or obscured.

§27.1543 Instrument markings: general.

For each instrument—

(a) When markings are on the cover glass of the instrument, there must be means to maintain the correct alignment of the glass cover with the face of the dial; and

(b) Each arc and line must be wide enough, and located, to be clearly visible to the pilot.

§27.1545 Airspeed indicator.

(a) Each airspeed indicator must be marked as specified in paragraph (b) of this section, with the marks located at the corresponding indicated airspeeds.

(b) The following markings must be made:

(1) A red radial line—

(i) For rotorcraft other than helicopters, at V_{NE}; and

(ii) For helicopters at V_{NE} (power-on).

(2) A red cross-hatched radial line at V_{NE} (power-off) for helicopters, if V_{NE} (power-off) is less than V_{NE} (power-on).

(3) For the caution range, a yellow arc.

(4) For the safe operating range, a green arc.

(Secs. 313(a), 601, 603, 604, and 605 of the Federal Aviation Act of 1958 (49 U.S.C. 1354(a), 1421, 1423, 1424, and 1425); and sec. 6(c) of the Dept. of Transportation Act (49 U.S.C. 1655(c)))

[Docket No. 5074, 29 FR 15695, Nov. 24, 1964; as amended by Amdt. 27–14, 43 FR 2325, Jan. 16, 1978; 43 FR 3900, Jan. 30, 1978; Amdt. 27–16, 43 FR 50599, Oct. 30, 1978]

§27.1547 Magnetic direction indicator.

(a) A placard meeting the requirements of this section must be installed on or near the magnetic direction indicator.

(b) The placard must show the calibration of the instrument in level flight with the engines operating.

(c) The placard must state whether the calibration was made with radio receivers on or off.

(d) Each calibration reading must be in terms of magnetic heading in not more than 45 degree increments.

(e) If a magnetic nonstabilized direction indicator can have a deviation of more than 10 degrees caused by the operation of electrical equipment, the placard must state which electrical loads, or combination of loads, would cause a deviation of more than 10 degrees when turned on.

(Secs. 313(a), 601, 603, 604, and 605 of the Federal Aviation Act of 1958 (49 U.S.C. 1354(a), 1421, 1423, 1424, and 1425); and sec. 6(c) of the Dept. of Transportation Act (49 U.S.C. 1655(c)))

[Docket No. 5074, 29 FR 15695, Nov. 24, 1964; as amended by Amdt. 27–13, 42 FR 36972, July 18, 1977]

§27.1549 Powerplant instruments.

For each required powerplant instrument, as appropriate to the type of instrument—

(a) Each maximum and, if applicable, minimum safe operating limit must be marked with a red radial or a red line;

(b) Each normal operating range must be marked with a green arc or green line, not extending beyond the maximum and minimum safe limits;

(c) Each takeoff and precautionary range must be marked with a yellow arc or yellow line;

(d) Each engine or propeller range that is restricted because of excessive vibration stresses must be marked with red arcs or red lines; and

(e) Each OEI limit or approved operating range must be marked to be clearly differentiated from the markings of paragraphs (a) through (d) of this section except that no marking is normally required for the 30-second OEI limit.

[Docket No. 5074, 29 FR 15695, Nov. 24, 1964; as amended by Amdt. 27–11, 41 FR 55470, Dec. 20, 1976; Amdt. 27–23, 53 FR 34215, Sept. 2, 1988; Amdt. 27–29, 59 FR 47768, Sept. 16, 1994]

§27.1551 Oil quantity indicator.

Each oil quantity indicator must be marked with enough increments to indicate readily and accurately the quantity of oil.

§27.1553 Fuel quantity indicator.

If the unusable fuel supply for any tank exceeds one gallon, or five percent of the tank capacity, whichever is greater, a red arc must be marked on its indicator extending from the calibrated zero reading to the lowest reading obtainable in level flight.

§27.1555 Control markings.

(a) Each cockpit control, other than primary flight controls or control whose function is obvious, must be plainly marked as to its function and method of operation.

(b) For powerplant fuel controls—

(1) Each fuel tank selector control must be marked to indicate the position corresponding to each tank and to each existing cross feed position;

(2) If safe operation requires the use of any tanks in a specific sequence, that sequence must be marked on, or adjacent to, the selector for those tanks; and

(3) Each valve control for any engine of a multiengine rotorcraft must be marked to indicate the position corresponding to each engine controlled.

(c) Usable fuel capacity must be marked as follows:

(1) For fuel systems having no selector controls, the usable fuel capacity of the system must be indicated at the fuel quantity indicator.

(2) For fuel systems having selector controls, the usable fuel capacity available at each selector control position must be indicated near the selector control.

(d) For accessory, auxiliary, and emergency controls—

(1) Each essential visual position indicator, such as those showing rotor pitch or landing gear position, must be marked so that each crewmember can determine at any time the position of the unit to which it relates; and

(2) Each emergency control must be red and must be marked as to method of operation.

(e) For rotorcraft incorporating retractable landing gear, the maximum landing gear operating speed must be displayed in clear view of the pilot.

[Docket No. 5074, 29 FR 15695, Nov. 24, 1964; as amended by Amdt. 27–11, 41 FR 55470, Dec. 20, 1976; Amdt. 27–21, 49 FR 44435, Nov. 6, 1984]

§27.1557 Miscellaneous markings and placards.

(a) *Baggage and cargo compartments, and ballast location.* Each baggage and cargo compartment, and each ballast location must have a placard stating any limitations on contents, including weight, that are necessary under the loading requirements.

(b) *Seats.* If the maximum allowable weight to be carried in a seat is less than 170 pounds, a placard stating the lesser weight must be permanently attached to the seat structure.

(c) *Fuel and oil filler openings.* The following apply:

(1) Fuel filler openings must be marked at or near the filler cover with—

(i) The word "fuel";

(ii) For reciprocating engine powered rotorcraft, the minimum fuel grade;

(iii) For turbine engine powered rotorcraft, the permissible fuel designations; and

(iv) For pressure fueling systems, the maximum permissible fueling supply pressure and the maximum permissible defueling pressure.

(2) Oil filler openings must be marked at or near the filler cover with the word "oil".

(d) *Emergency* exit *placards.* Each placard and operating control for each emergency exit must be red. A placard must be near each emergency exit control and must clearly indicate the location of that exit and its method of operation.

[Docket No. 5074, 29 FR 15695, Nov. 24, 1964, as amended by Amdt 27–11, 41 FR 55471, Dec. 20, 1976]

§27.1559 Limitations placard.

There must be a placard in clear view of the pilot that specifies the kinds of operations (such as VFR, IFR, day, night, or icing) for which the rotorcraft is approved.

[Docket No. 5074, 29 FR 15695, Nov. 24, 1964; as amended by Amdt. 27–21, 49 FR 44435, Nov. 6, 1984]

§27.1561 Safety equipment.

(a) Each safety equipment control to be operated by the crew in emergency, such as controls for automatic liferaft releases, must be plainly marked as to its method of operation.

(b) Each location, such as a locker or compartment, that carries any fire extinguishing, signaling, or other life saving equipment, must be so marked.

§27.1565 Tail rotor.

Each tail rotor must be marked so that its disc is conspicuous under normal daylight ground conditions.

[Docket No. 5074, 29 FR 15695, Nov. 24, 1964; as amended by Amdt. 27–2, 33 FR 965, Jan. 26, 1968]

Rotorcraft Flight Manual and Approved Manual Material

§27.1581 General.

(a) *Furnishing information.* A Rotorcraft Flight Manual must be furnished with each rotorcraft, and it must contain the following:

(1) Information required by §§27.1583 through 27.1589.

(2) Other information that is necessary for safe operation because of design, operating, or handling characteristics.

(b) *Approved information.* Each part of the manual listed in §§27.1583 through 27.1589, that is appropriate to the rotorcraft, must be furnished, verified, and approved, and must be segregated, identified, and clearly distinguished from each unapproved part of that manual.

(c) [Reserved]

(d) *Table of contents.* Each Rotorcraft Flight Manual must include a table of contents if the complexity of the manual indicates a need for it.

(Secs. 313(a), 601, 603, 604, and 605 of the Federal Aviation Act of 1958 (49 U.S.C. 1354(a), 1421, 1423, 1424, and 1425); and sec. 6(c) of the Dept. of Transportation Act (49 U.S.C. 1655(c)))

[Docket No. 5074, 29 FR 15695, Nov. 24, 1964; as amended by Amdt. 27–14, 43 FR 2325, Jan. 16, 1978]

§27.1583 Operating limitations.

(a) *Airspeed and rotor limitations.* Information necessary for the marking of airspeed and rotor limitations on, or near, their respective indicators must be furnished. The significance of each limitation and of the color coding must be explained.

(b) *Powerplant limitations. The* following information must be furnished:

(1) Limitations required by §27.1521.

(2) Explanation of the limitations, when appropriate.

(3) Information necessary for marking the instruments required by §§27.1549 through 27.1553.

(c) *Weight and loading distribution.* The weight and center of gravity limits required by §§27.25 and 27.27, respectively, must be furnished. If the variety of possible loading conditions warrants, instructions must be included to allow ready observance of the limitations.

(d) *Flight crew.* When a flight crew of more than one is required, the number and functions of the minimum flight crew determined under §27.1523 must be furnished.

(e) *Kinds of operation.* Each kind of operation for which the rotorcraft and its equipment installations are approved must be listed.

(f) [Reserved]

(g) *Altitude.* The altitude established under §27.1527 and an explanation of the limiting factors must be furnished.

(Secs. 313(a), 601, 603, 604, and 605 of the Federal Aviation Act of 1958 (49 U.S C 1354(a), 1421, 1423, 1424, and 1425); and sec. 6(c) of the Dept. of Transportation Act (49 U.S.C. 1655(c)))

[Docket No. 5074, 29 FR 15695, Nov. 24, 1964; as amended by Amdt. 27–2, 33 FR 965, Jan. 26, 1968; Amdt. 27–14, 43 FR 2325, Jan. 16, 1978; Amdt. 27–16, 43 FR 50599, Oct. 30, 1978]

§27.1585 Operating procedures.

(a) Parts of the manual containing operating procedures must have information concerning any normal and emergency procedures and other information necessary for safe operation, including takeoff and landing procedures and associated airspeeds. The manual must contain any pertinent information including—

(1) The kind of takeoff surface used in the tests and each appropriate climbout speed; and

(2) The kind of landing surface used in the tests and appropriate approach and glide airspeeds.

(b) For multiengine rotorcraft, information identifying each operating condition in which the fuel system independence prescribed in §27.953 is necessary for safety must be furnished, together with instructions for placing the fuel system in a configuration used to show compliance with that section.

(c) For helicopters for which a V_{NE} (power-off) is established under §27.1505(c), information must be furnished to explain the V_{NE} (power-off) and the procedures for reducing airspeed to not more than the V_{NE} (power-off) following failure of all engines.

(d) For each rotorcraft showing compliance with §27.1353 (g)(2) or (g)(3), the operating procedures for disconnecting the battery from its charging source must be furnished.

(e) If the unusable fuel supply in any tank exceeds five percent of the tank capacity, or one gallon, whichever is greater, information must be furnished which indicates that when the fuel quantity indicator reads "zero" in level fight, any fuel remaining in the fuel tank cannot be used safely in flight.

(f) Information on the total quantity of usable fuel for each fuel tank must be furnished.

(g) The airspeeds and rotor speeds for minimum rate of descent and best glide angle as prescribed in §27.71 must be provided.

(Secs. 313(a), 601, 603, 604, and 605 of the Federal Aviation Act of 1958 (49 U.S.C. 1354(a), 1421, 1423, 1424, and 1425); and sec. 6(c) of the Dept. of Transportation Act (49 U.S.C. 1655(c)))

[Docket No. 5074, 29 FR 15695, Nov. 24, 1964; as amended by Amdt. 27–1, 32 FR 6914, May 5, 1967; Amdt. 27–14, 43 FR 2326, Jan. 16, 1978; Amdt. 27–16, 43 FR 50599, Oct. 30, 1978; Amdt. 27–21, 49 FR 44435, Nov. 6, 1984]

§27.1587 Performance information.

(a) The rotorcraft must be furnished with the following information, determined in accordance with §§27.51 through 27.79 and 27.143(c):

(1) Enough information to determine the limiting height-speed envelope.

(2) Information relative to—

(i) The hovering ceilings and the steady rates of climb and descent, as affected by any pertinent factors such as airspeed, temperature, and altitude;

(ii) The maximum safe wind for operation near the ground. If there are combinations of weight, altitude, and temperature for which performance information is provided and at which the rotorcraft cannot land and takeoff safely with the maximum wind value, those portions of the operating envelope and the appropriate safe wind conditions shall be identified in the flight manual;

(iii) For reciprocating engine-powered rotorcraft, the maximum atmospheric temperature at which compliance with the cooling provisions of §§27.1041 through 27.1045 is shown; and

(iv) Glide distance as a function of altitude when autorotating at the speeds and conditions for minimum rate of descent and best glide as determined in §27.71.

(b) The Rotorcraft Flight Manual must contain—

(1) In its performance information section any pertinent information concerning the takeoff weights and altitudes used in compliance with §27.51; and

(i) Any pertinent information concerning the takeoff procedure, including the kind of takeoff surface used in the tests and each appropriate climbout speed; and

(ii) Any pertinent landing procedures, including the kind of landing surface used in the tests and appropriate approach and glide airspeeds; and

(2) The horizontal takeoff distance determined in accordance with §27.65(a)(2)(i).

(Secs. 313(a), 601, 603, 604, and 605 of the Federal Aviation Act of 1958 (49 U.S.C. 1354(a), 1421, 1423, 1424, and 1425); and sec. 6(c) of the Dept. of Transportation Act (49 U.S.C. 1655(c)))

[Docket No. 5074, 29 FR 15695, Nov. 24, 1964; as amended by Amdt. 27–14, 43 FR 2326, Jan. 16, 1978; Amdt. 27–21, 49 FR 44435, Nov. 6, 1984]

§27.1589 Loading information.

There must be loading instructions for each possible loading condition between the maximum and minimum weights determined under §27.25 that can result in a center of gravity beyond any extreme prescribed in §27.27, assuming any probable occupant weights.

Appendix A to Part 27

Instructions For Continued Airworthiness

A27.1 General.

(a) This appendix specifies requirements for the preparation of Instructions for Continued Airworthiness as required by §27.1529.

(b) The Instructions for Continued Airworthiness for each rotorcraft must include the Instructions for Continued Airworthiness for each engine and rotor (hereinafter designated "products"), for each appliance required by this chapter, and any required information relating to the interface of those appliances and products with the rotorcraft. If Instructions for Continued Airworthiness are not supplied by the manufacturer of an appliance or product installed in the rotorcraft, the Instructions for Continued Airworthiness for the rotorcraft must include the information essential to the continued airworthiness of the rotorcraft.

(c) The applicant must submit to the FAA a program to show how changes to the Instructions for Continued Airworthiness made by the applicant or by the manufacturers of products and appliances installed in the rotorcraft will be distributed.

A27.2 Format.

(a) The Instructions for Continued Airworthiness must be in the form of a manual or manuals as appropriate for the quantity of data to be provided.

(b) The format of the manual or manuals must provide for a practical arrangement.

A27.3 Content.

The contents of the manual or manuals must be prepared in the English language. The Instructions for Continued Airworthiness must contain the following manuals or sections, as appropriate, and information:

(a) *Rotorcraft maintenance manual or section.*

(1) Introduction information that includes an explanation of the rotorcraft's features and data to the extent necessary for maintenance or preventive maintenance.

(2) A description of the rotorcraft and its systems and installations including its engines, rotors, and appliances.

(3) Basic control and operation information describing how the rotorcraft components and systems are controlled and how they operate, including any special procedures and limitations that apply.

(4) Servicing information that covers details regarding servicing points, capacities of tanks, reservoirs, types of fluids to be used, pressures applicable to the various systems, location of access panels for inspection and servicing, locations of lubrication points, the lubricants to be used, equipment required for servicing, tow instructions and limitations, mooring, jacking, and leveling information.

(b) *Maintenance instructions.*

(1) Scheduling information for each part of the rotorcraft and its engines, auxiliary power units, rotors, accessories, instruments and equipment that provides the recommended periods at which they should be cleaned, inspected, adjusted, tested, and lubricated, and the degree of inspection, the applicable wear tolerances, and work recommended at these periods. However, the applicant may refer to an accessory, instrument, or equipment manufacturer as the source of this information if the applicant shows the item has an exceptionally high degree or complexity requiring specialized maintenance techniques, test equipment, or expertise. The recommended overhaul periods and necessary cross references to the Airworthiness Limitations section of the manual must also be included. In addition, the applicant must include an inspection program that includes the frequency and extent of the inspections necessary to provide for the continued airworthiness of the rotorcraft.

(2) Troubleshooting information describing problem malfunctions, how to recognize those malfunctions, and the remedial action for those malfunctions.

(3) Information describing the order and method of removing and replacing products and parts with any necessary precautions to be taken.

(4) Other general procedural instructions including procedures for system testing during ground running, symmetry checks, weighing and determining the center of gravity, lifting and shoring, and storage limitations.

(c) Diagrams or structural access plates and information needed to gain access for inspections when access plates are not provided.

(d) Details for the application of special inspection techniques including radiographic and ultrasonic testing where such processes are specified.

(e) Information needed to apply protective treatments to the structure after inspection.

(f) All data relative to structural fasteners such as identification, discarded recommendations, and torque values.

(g) A list of special tools needed.

A27.4 Airworthiness Limitations Section.

The Instructions for Continued Airworthiness must contain a section, titled Airworthiness Limitations that is segregated and clearly distinguishable from the rest of the document. This section must set forth each mandatory replacement time, structural inspection interval, and related structural inspection procedure approved under §27.571. If the Instructions for Continued Airworthiness consist of multiple documents, the section required by this paragraph must be included in the principal manual. This section must contain a legible statement in a prominent location that reads: "The Airworthiness Limitations section is FAA approved and specifies inspections and other maintenance required under §§43.16 and 91.403 of the Federal Aviation Regulations unless an alternative program has been FAA approved."

[Docket No. 5074, 29 FR 15695, Nov. 24, 1964; as amended by Amdt. 27–17, 45 FR 60178, Sept. 11, 1980; Amdt. 27–24, 54 FR 34329, Aug. 18, 1989]

Appendix B to Part 27

Airworthiness Criteria For Helicopter Instrument Flight

I. *General.* A normal category helicopter may not be type certificated for operation under the instrument flight rules (IFR) of this chapter unless it meets the design and installation requirements contained in this appendix.

II. *Definitions.*

(a) V_{YI} means instrument climb speed, utilized instead of V_Y for compliance with the climb requirements for instrument flight.

(b) V_{NEI} means instrument flight never exceed speed, utilized instead of V_{NE} for compliance with maximum limit speed requirements for instrument flight.

(c) V_{MINI} means instrument flight minimum speed, utilized in complying with minimum limit speed requirements for instrument flight.

III. *Trim.* It must be possible to trim the cyclic, collective, and directional control forces to zero at all approved IFR airspeeds, power settings, and configurations appropriate to the type.

IV. *Static longitudinal stability.*

(a) *General.* The helicopter must possess positive static longitudinal control force stability at critical combinations of weight and center of gravity at the conditions specified in paragraph IV (b) or (c) of this appendix, as appropriate. The stick force must vary with speed so that any substantial speed change results in a stick force clearly perceptible to the pilot. For single-pilot approval the airspeed must return to within 10 percent of the trim speed when the control force is slowly released for each trim condition specified in paragraph IV(b) of the this appendix.

(b) *For single-pilot approval:*

(1) *Climb.* Stability must be shown in climb throughout the speed range 20 knots either side of trim with—

(i) The helicopter trimmed at V_{YI};

(ii) Landing gear retracted (if retractable); and

(iii) Power required for limit climb rate (at least 1,000 fpm) at V_{YI} or maximum continuous power whichever is less.

(2) *Cruise.* Stability must be shown throughout the speed range from 0.7 to 1.1 V_H or V_{NEI}, whichever is lower not to exceed ±20 knots from trim with—

(i) The helicopter trimmed and power adjusted for level flight at 0.9 V_H or 0.9 V_{NEI} whichever is lower; and

(ii) Landing gear retracted (if retractable).

(3) *Slow cruise.* Stability must be shown throughout the speed range from 0.9 V_{MINI} to 1.3 V_{MINI} or 20 knots above trim speed whichever is greater with—

(i) the helicopter trimmed and power adjusted for level flight at 1.1 V_{MINI}; and

(ii) Landing gear retracted (if retractable).

(4) *Descent.* Stability must be shown throughout the speed range *20* knots either side of trim with—

(i) The helicopter trimmed at 0.8 V_H or 0.8 V_{NEI} (or 0.8 V_{LE} for the landing gear extended case) whichever is lower;

(ii) Power required for 1,000 fpm descent at trim speed; and

(iii) Landing gear extended and retracted if applicable.

(5) *Approach.* Stability must be shown throughout the speed range from 0.7 times the minimum recommended approach speed to 20 knots above the maximum recommended approach speed with—

(i) The helicopter trimmed at the recommended approach speed or speeds;

(ii) Landing gear extended and retracted if applicable; and

(iii) Power required to maintain a 3° glide path and power required to maintain the steepest approach gradient for which approval is requested.

(c) Helicopters approved for a minimum crew of two pilots must comply with the provisions of paragraphs IV(b)(2) and IV(b)(5) of this appendix.

V. *Static lateral-directional stability.*

(a) Static directional stability must be positive throughout the approved ranges of airspeed, power, and vertical speed. In straight, steady sideslips up to ±10° from trim, directional control position must increase in approximately constant proportion to angle of sideslip. At greater angles up to the maximum sideslip angle appropriate to the type increased directional control position must produce increased angle of sideslip.

(b) During sideslips up to ±10° from trim throughout the approved ranges of airspeed, power, and vertical speed, there must be no negative dihedral stability perceptible to the pilot through lateral control motion or force. Longitudinal cyclic movement with sideslip must not be excessive.

VI. *Dynamic stability.*

(a) For single-pilot approval—

(1) Any oscillation having a period of less than 5 seconds must damp to ½ amplitude in not more than one cycle.

(2) Any oscillation having a period of 5 seconds or more but less than 10 seconds must damp to ½ amplitude in not more than two cycles.

(3) Any oscillation having a period of 10 seconds or more but less than 20 seconds must be damped.

(4) Any oscillation having a period of 20 seconds or more may not achieve double amplitude in less than 20 seconds.

(5) Any aperiodic response may not achieve double amplitude in less than 6 seconds.

(b) For helicopters approved with a minimum crew of two pilots—

(1) Any oscillation having a period of less than 5 seconds must damp to ½ amplitude in not more than two cycles.

(2) Any oscillation having a period of 5 seconds or more but less than 10 seconds must be damped.

(3) Any oscillation having a period of 10 seconds or more may not achieve double amplitude in less than 10 seconds.

VII. *Stability augmentation system (SAS).*

(a) If a SAS is used the reliability of the SAS must be related to the effects of its failure. The occurrence of any failure condition which would prevent continued safe flight and landing must be extremely improbable. For any failure condition of the SAS which is not shown to be extremely improbable—

(1) The helicopter must be safely controllable and capable of prolonged Instrument flight without undue pilot effort. Additional unrelated probable failures affecting the control system must be considered; and

(2) The flight characteristics requirements in Subpart B of Part 27 must be met throughout a practical flight envelope.

(b) The SAS must be designed so that it cannot create a hazardous deviation In flight path or produce hazardous loads on the helicopter during normal operation or in the event of malfunction or failure assuming corrective action begins within an appropriate period of time. Where multiple systems are installed subsequent malfunction conditions must be considered in sequence unless their occurrence is shown to be improbable.

VIII. *Equipment, systems, and installation.* The basic equipment and installation must comply with §§29.1303, 29.1431, and 29.1433 through Amendment 29–14, with the following exceptions and additions:

(a) *Flight and Navigation Instruments.*

(1) *A* magnetic gyro-stabilized direction indicator instead of a gyroscopic direction indicator required by §29.1303(h); and

(2) A standby attitude indicator which meets the requirements of §§29.1303(g)(1) through (7) instead of a rate-of-turn indicator required by §29.1303(g). For two-pilot configurations, one pilot's primary indicator may be designated for this purpose. If standby batteries are provided, they may be charged from the aircraft electrical system if adequate isolation is incorporated.

(b) *Miscellaneous requirements.*

(1) Instrument systems and other systems essential for IFR flight that could be adversely affected by icing must be adequately protected when exposed to the continuous and intermittent maximum icing conditions defined in Appendix C of Part 29 of this chapter, whether or not the rotorcraft is certificated for operation in icing conditions.

(2) There must be means in the generating system to automatically de-energize and disconnect from the main bus any power source developing hazardous overvoltage.

(3) Each required flight instrument using a power supply (electric, vacuum, etc.) must have a visual means integral with the Instrument to indicate the adequacy of the power being supplied.

(4) When multiple systems performing like functions are required, each system must be grouped, routed, and spaced so that physical separation between systems is provided to ensure that a single malfunction will not adversely affect more than one system.

(5) For systems that operate the required flight instruments at each pilot's station—

(i) Only the required flight Instruments for the first pilot may be connected to that operating system;

(ii) Additional instruments, systems, or equipment may not be connected to an operating system for a second pilot unless provisions are made to ensure the continued normal functioning of the required instruments in the event of any malfunction of the additional instruments, systems, or equipment which is not shown to be extremely improbable;

(iii) The equipment, systems, and installations must be designed so that one display of the information essential to the safety of flight which is provided by the instruments will remain available to a pilot, without additional crewmember action, after any single failure or combination of failures that is not shown to be extremely improbable; and

(iv) For single-pilot configurations, instruments which require a static source must be provided with a means of selecting an alternate source and that source must be calibrated.

IX. *Rotorcraft Flight Manual.* A Rotorcraft Flight Manual or Rotorcraft Flight Manual IFR Supplement must be provided and must contain—

(a) *Limitations.* The approved IFR flight envelope, the IFR flightcrew composition, the revised kinds of operation, and the steepest IFR precision approach gradient for which the helicopter is approved;

(b) *Procedures.* Required information for proper operation of IFR systems and the recommended procedures in the event of stability augmentation or electrical system failures; and

(c) *Performance.* If V_{YI} differs from V_Y, climb performance at V_{YI} and with maximum continuous power throughout the ranges of weight, altitude, and temperature for which approval is requested.

[Docket No. 5074, 29 FR 15695, Nov. 24, 1964; as amended by Amdt. 27–19, 48 FR 4389, Jan. 31, 1983]

Appendix C to Part 27

Criteria for Category A

C27.1 General.

A small multiengine rotorcraft may not be type certificated for Category A operation unless it meets the design installation and performance requirements contained in this appendix in addition to the requirements of this part.

C27.2 Applicable Part 29 Sections.

The following sections of part 29 of this chapter must be met in addition to the requirements of this part:

29.45(a) and (b)(2)—General.
29.49(a)—Performance at minimum operating speed.
29.51—Takeoff data: General.
29.53—Takeoff: Category A.
29.55—Takeoff decision point: Category A.
29.59—Takeoff Path: Category A.
29.60—Elevated heliport takeoff path: Category A.
29.61—Takeoff distance: Category A.
29.62—Rejected takeoff: Category A.
29.64—Climb: General.
29.65(a)—Climb: AEO.
29.67(a)—Climb: OEI.
29.75—Landing: General.
29.77—Landing decision point: Category A.
29.79—Landing: Category A.
29.81—Landing distance (Ground level sites): Category A.
29.85—Balked landing: Category A.
29.87(a)—Height-velocity envelope.
29.547(a) and (b)—Main and tail rotor structure.
29.861(a)—Fire protection of structure, controls, and other parts.
29.901(c)—Powerplant: Installation.
29.903(b), (c) and (e)—Engines.
29.908(a)—Cooling fans.
29.917(b) and (c)(1)—Rotor drive system: Design.
29.927(c)(1)—Additional tests.
29.953(a)—Fuel system independence.
29.1027(a)—Transmission and gearboxes: General.
29.1045(a)(1), (b), (c), (d), and (f)—Climb cooling test procedures.
29.1047(a)—Takeoff cooling test procedures.
29.1181(a)—Designated fire zones: Regions included.
29.1187(e)—Drainage and ventilation of fire zones.
29.1189(c)—Shutoff means.
29.1191(a)(1)—Firewalls.
29.1193(e)—Cowling and engine compartment covering.
29.1195(a) and (d)—Fire extinguishing systems (one shot).
29.1197—Fire extinguishing agents.
29.1199—Extinguishing agent containers.
29.1201—Fire extinguishing system materials.
29.1305(a)(6) and (b)—Powerplant instruments.
29.1309(b)(2)(i) and (d)—Equipment, systems, and installations.
29.1323(c)(1)—Airspeed indicating system.
29.1331(b)—Instruments using a power supply.
29.1351(d)(2)—Electrical systems and equipment: General (operation without normal electrical power).
29.1587(a)—Performance information.

Note: In complying with the paragraphs listed in paragraph C27.2 above, relevant material in the AC "Certification of Transport Category Rotorcraft" should be used.

[Docket No. 28008, 61 FR 21907, May 10, 1996]

PART 33
AIRWORTHINESS STANDARDS: AIRCRAFT ENGINES

Subpart A — General

Sec.
33.1 Applicability.
33.3 General.
33.4 Instructions for Continued Airworthiness.
33.5 Instruction manual for installing and operating the engine.
33.7 Engine ratings and operating limitations.
33.8 Selection of engine power and thrust ratings.

Subpart B — Design and Construction: General

33.11 Applicability.
33.13 [Reserved]
33.14 Start-stop cyclic stress (low-cycle fatigue).
33.15 Materials.
33.17 Fire prevention.
33.19 Durability.
33.21 Engine cooling.
33.23 Engine mounting attachments and structure.
33.25 Accessory attachments.
33.27 Turbine, compressor, fan, and turbosupercharger rotors.
33.28 Electrical and electronic engine control systems.
33.29 Instrument connection.

Subpart C — Design and Construction: Reciprocating Aircraft Engines

33.31 Applicability.
33.33 Vibration.
33.35 Fuel and induction system.
33.37 Ignition system.
33.39 Lubrication system.

Subpart D — Block Tests: Reciprocating Aircraft Engines

33.41 Applicability.
33.42 General.
33.43 Vibration test.
33.45 Calibration tests.
33.47 Detonation test.
33.49 Endurance test.
33.51 Operation test.
33.53 Engine component tests.
33.55 Teardown inspection.
33.57 General conduct of block tests.

Subpart E — Design and Construction: Turbine Aircraft Engines

33.61 Applicability.
33.62 Stress analysis.
33.63 Vibration.
33.65 Surge and stall characteristics.
33.66 Bleed air system.
33.67 Fuel system.
33.68 Induction system icing.
33.69 Ignitions system.
33.71 Lubrication system.
33.72 Hydraulic actuating systems.
33.73 Power or thrust response.
33.74 Continued rotation.
33.75 Safety analysis.
33.76 Bird ingestion.
33.77 Foreign object ingestion — ice.
33.78 Rain and hail ingestion.
33.79 Fuel burning thrust augmentor.

Subpart F — Block Tests: Turbine Aircraft Engines

33.81 Applicability.
33.82 General.
33.83 Vibration test.
33.85 Calibration tests.
33.87 Endurance test.
33.88 Engine overtemperature test.
33.89 Operation test.
33.90 Initial maintenance inspection.
33.91 Engine component tests.
33.92 Rotor locking tests.
33.93 Teardown inspection.
33.94 Blade containment and rotor unbalance tests.
33.95 Engine-propeller systems tests.
33.96 Engine tests in auxiliary power unit (APU) mode.
33.97 Thrust reversers.
33.99 General conduct of block tests.

Appendix A to Part 33 — Instructions for Continued Airworthiness
Appendix B to Part 33 — Certification Standard Atmospheric Concentrations of Rain and Hail

Authority: 49 U.S.C. 106(g), 40113, 44701–44702, 44704.

Source: Docket No. 3025, 29 FR 7453, June 10, 1964, unless otherwise noted.

Note: For miscellaneous amendments to cross references in this Part 33, see Amdt. 33–2, 31 FR 9211, July 6, 1966.

Subpart A—General

§33.1 Applicability.

(a) This part prescribes airworthiness standards for the issue of type certificates and changes to those certificates, for aircraft engines.

(b) Each person who applies under part 21 for such a certificate or change must show compliance with the applicable requirements of this part and the applicable requirements of part 34 of this chapter.

[Amdt. 33–7, 41 FR 55474, Dec. 20, 1976, as amended by Amdt. 33–14, 55 FR 32861, Aug. 10, 1990]

§33.3 General.

Each applicant must show that the aircraft engine concerned meets the applicable requirements of this part.

§33.4 Instructions for Continued Airworthiness.

The applicant must prepare Instructions for Continued Airworthiness in accordance with Appendix A to this part that are acceptable to the Administrator. The instructions may be incomplete at type certification if a program exists to ensure their completion prior to delivery of the first aircraft with the engine installed, or upon issuance of a standard certificate of airworthiness for the aircraft with the engine installed, whichever occurs later.

[Amdt. 33–9, 45 FR 60181, Sept. 11, 1980]

§33.5 Instruction manual for installing and operating the engine.

Each applicant must prepare and make available to the Administrator prior to the issuance of the type certificate, and to the owner at the time of delivery of the engine, approved instructions for installing and operating the engine. The instructions must include at least the following:

(a) *Installation instructions.*

(1) The location of engine mounting attachments, the method of attaching the engine to the aircraft, and the maximum allowable load for the mounting attachments and related structure.

(2) The location and description of engine connections to be attached to accessories, pipes, wires, cables, ducts, and cowling.

(3) An outline drawing of the engine including overall dimensions.

(b) *Operation instructions.*

(1) The operating limitations established by the Administrator.

(2) The power or thrust ratings and procedures for correcting for nonstandard atmosphere.

(3) The recommended procedures, under normal and extreme ambient conditions for—

(i) Starting;

(ii) Operating on the ground; and

(iii) Operating during flight.

[Amdt. 33–6, 39 FR 35463, Oct. 1, 1974, as amended by Amdt. 33–9, 45 FR 60181, Sept. 11, 1980]

§33.7 Engine ratings and operating limitations.

(a) Engine ratings and operating limitations are established by the Administrator and included in the engine certificate data sheet specified in §21.41 of this chapter, including ratings and limitations based on the operating conditions and information specified in this section, as applicable, and any other information found necessary for safe operation of the engine.

(b) For reciprocating engines, ratings and operating limitations are established relating to the following:

(1) Horsepower or torque, r.p.m., manifold pressure, and time at critical pressure altitude and sea level pressure altitude for—

(i) Rated maximum continuous power (relating to unsupercharged operation or to operation in each supercharger mode as applicable); and

(ii) Rated takeoff power (relating to unsupercharged operation or to operation in each supercharger mode as applicable).

(2) Fuel grade or specification.

(3) Oil grade or specification.

(4) Temperature of the—

(i) Cylinder;

(ii) Oil at the oil inlet; and

(iii) Turbosupercharger turbine wheel inlet gas.

(5) Pressure of—

(i) Fuel at the fuel inlet; and

(ii) Oil at the main oil gallery.

(6) Accessory drive torque and overhang moment.

(7) Component life.

(8) Turbosupercharger turbine wheel r.p.m.

(c) For turbine engines, ratings and operating limitations are established relating to the following:

(1) Horsepower, torque, or thrust, r.p.m., gas temperature, and time for—

(i) Rated maximum continuous power or thrust (augmented);

(ii) Rated maximum continuous power or thrust (unaugmented);

(iii) Rated takeoff power or thrust (augmented);

(iv) Rated takeoff power or thrust (unaugmented);

(v) Rated 30-minute OEI power;

(vi) Rated $2\frac{1}{2}$ minute OEI power;

(vii) Rated continuous OEI power; and

(viii) Rated 2-minute OEI power;

(ix) Rated 30-second OEI power; and

(x) Auxiliary power unit (APU) mode of operation.

(2) Fuel designation or specification.

(3) Oil grade or specification.

(4) Hydraulic fluid specification.

(5) Temperature of—

(i) Oil at a location specified by the applicant;

(ii) Induction air at the inlet face of a supersonic engine, including steady state operation and transient over-temperature and time allowed;

(iii) Hydraulic fluid of a supersonic engine;

(iv) Fuel at a location specified by the applicant; and

(v) External surfaces of the engine, if specified by the applicant.

(6) Pressure of—

(i) Fuel at the fuel inlet;

(ii) Oil at a location specified by the applicant;

(iii) Induction air at the inlet face of a supersonic engine, including steady state operation and transient overpressure and time allowed; and

(iv) Hydraulic fluid.

(7) Accessory drive torque and overhang moment.

(8) Component life.

(9) Fuel filtration.

(10) Oil filtration.

(11) Bleed air.

(12) The number of start-stop stress cycles approved for each rotor disc and spacer.

(13) Inlet air distortion at the engine inlet.

(14) Transient rotor shaft overspeed r.p.m., and number of overspeed occurrences.

(15) Transient gas overtemperature, and number of overtemperature occurrences.

(16) For engines to be used in supersonic aircraft, engine rotor windmilling rotational r.p.m.

[Amdt. 33–6, 39 FR 35463, Oct. 1, 1974, as amended by Amdt. 33–10, 49 FR 6850, Feb. 23, 1984; Amdt. 33–11, 51 FR 10346, Mar. 25, 1986; Amdt. 33–12, 53 FR 34220, Sept. 2, 1988; Amdt. 33–18, 61 FR 31328, June 19, 1996]

§33.8 Selection of engine power and thrust ratings.

(a) Requested engine power and thrust ratings must be selected by the applicant.

(b) Each selected rating must be for the lowest power or thrust that all engines of the same type may be expected to produce under the conditions used to determine that rating.

[Amdt. 33–3, 32 FR 3736, Mar. 4, 1967]

Subpart B— Design and Construction: General

§33.11 Applicability.

This subpart prescribes the general design and construction requirements for reciprocating and turbine aircraft engines.

§33.13 [Reserved]

§33.14 Start-stop cyclic stress (low-cycle fatigue).

By a procedure approved by the FAA, operating limitations must be established which specify the maximum allowable number of start-stop stress cycles for each rotor structural part (such as discs, spacers, hubs, and shafts of the compressors and turbines), the failure of which could produce a hazard to the aircraft. A start-stop stress cycle consists of a flight cycle profile or an equivalent representation of engine usage. It includes starting the engine, accelerating to maximum rated power or thrust, decelerating, and stopping. For each cycle, the rotor structural parts must reach stabilized temperature during engine operation at a maximum rate power or thrust and after engine shutdown, unless it is shown that the parts undergo the same stress range without temperature stabilization.

[Amdt. 33–10, 49 FR 6850, Feb. 23, 1984]

§33.15 Materials.

The suitability and durability of materials used in the engine must—

(a) Be established on the basis of experience or tests; and

(b) Conform to approved specifications (such as industry or military specifications) that ensure their having the strength and other properties assumed in the design data.

(Secs. 313(a), 601, and 603, 72 Stat. 759, 775, 49 U.S.C. 1354(a), 1421, and 1423; sec. 6(c), 49 U.S.C. 1655(c))

[Amdt. 33–8, 42 FR 15047, Mar. 17, 1977, as amended by Amdt. 33–10, 49 FR 6850, Feb. 23, 1984]

§33.17 Fire prevention.

(a) The design and construction of the engine and the materials used must minimize the probability of the occurrence and spread of fire. In addition, the design and construction of turbine engines must minimize the probability of the occurrence of an internal fire that could result in structural failure, overheating, or other hazardous conditions.

(b) Except as provided in paragraphs (c), (d), and (e) of this section, each external line, fitting, and other component, which contains or conveys flammable fluid must be fire resistant. Components must be shielded or located to safeguard against the ignition of leaking flammable fluid.

(c) Flammable fluid tanks and supports which are part of and attached to the engine must be fireproof or be enclosed by a fireproof shield unless damage by fire to any non-fireproof part will not cause leakage or spillage of flammable fluid. For a reciprocating engine having an integral oil sump of less than 25-quart capacity, the oil sump need not be fireproof nor be enclosed by fireproof shield.

(d) For turbine engines type certificated for use in supersonic aircraft, each external component which conveys or contains flammable fluid must be fireproof.

(e) Unwanted accumulation of flammable fluid and vapor must be prevented by draining and venting.

(Secs. 313(a), 601, and 603, 72 Stat. 759, 775, 49 U.S.C. 1354(a), 1421, and 1423; sec. 6(c), 49 U.S.C. 1655(c))

[Amdt. 33–6, 39 FR 35464, Oct. 1, 1974, as amended by Amdt. 33–8, 42 FR 15047, Mar. 17, 1977; Amdt. 33–10, 49 FR 6850, Feb. 23, 1984]

§33.19 Durability.

(a) Engine design and construction must minimize the development of an unsafe condition of the engine between overhaul periods. The design of the compressor and turbine rotor cases must provide for the containment of damage from rotor blade failure. Energy levels and trajectories of fragments resulting from rotor blade failure that lie outside the compressor and turbine rotor cases must be defined.

(b) Each component of the propeller blade pitch control system which is a part of the engine type design must meet the requirements of §35.42 of this chapter.

[Docket No. 3025, 29 FR 7453, June 10, 1964, as amended by Amdt. 33–9, 45 FR 60181, Sept. 11, 1980; Amdt. 33–10, 49 FR 6851, Feb. 23, 1984]

§33.21 Engine cooling.

Engine design and construction must provide the necessary cooling under conditions in which the airplane is expected to operate.

§33.23 Engine mounting attachments and structure.

(a) The maximum allowable limit and ultimate loads for engine mounting attachments and related engine structure must be specified.

(b) The engine mounting attachments and related engine structure must be able to withstand—

(1) The specified limit loads without permanent deformation; and

(2) The specified ultimate loads without failure, but may exhibit permanent deformation.

[Amdt. 33–10, 49 FR 6851, Feb. 23, 1984]

§33.25 Accessory attachments.

The engine must operate properly with the accessory drive and mounting attachments loaded. Each engine accessory drive and mounting attachment must include provisions for sealing to prevent contamination of, or unacceptable leakage from, the engine interior. A drive and mounting attachment requiring lubrication for external drive splines, or coupling by engine oil, must include provisions for sealing to prevent unacceptable loss of oil and to prevent contamination from sources outside the chamber enclosing the drive connection. The design of the engine must allow for the examination, adjustment, or removal of each accessory required for engine operation.

[Amdt. 33–10, 49 FR 6851, Feb. 23, 1984]

§33.27 Turbine, compressor, fan, and turbosupercharger rotors.

(a) Turbine, compressor, fan, and turbosupercharger rotors must have sufficient strength to withstand the test conditions specified in paragraph (c) of this section.

(b) The design and functioning of engine control devices, systems, and instruments must give reasonable assurance that those engine operating limitations that affect turbine, compressor, fan, and turbosupercharger rotor structural integrity will not be exceeded in service.

(c) The most critically stressed rotor component (except blades) of each turbine, compressor, and fan, including integral drum rotors and centrifugal compressors in an engine or turbosupercharger, as determined by analysis or other acceptable means, must be tested for a period of 5 minutes—

(1) At its maximum operating temperature, except as provided in paragraph (c)(2)(iv) of this section; and

(2) At the highest speed of the following, as applicable:

(i) 120 percent of its maximum permissible r.p.m. if tested on a rig and equipped with blades or blade weights.

(ii) 115 percent of its maximum permissible r.p.m. if tested on an engine.

(iii) 115 percent of its maximum permissible r.p.m. if tested on turbosupercharger driven by a hot gas supply from a special burner rig.

(iv) 120 percent of the r.p.m. at which, while cold spinning, it is subject to operating stresses that are equivalent to those induced at the maximum operating temperature and maximum permissible r.p.m.

(v) 105 percent of the highest speed that would result from failure of the most critical component or system in a representative installation of the engine.

(vi) The highest speed that would result from the failure of any component or system in a representative installation of the engine, in combination with any failure of a component or system that would not normally be detected during a routine preflight check or during normal flight operation.

Following the test, each rotor must be within approved dimensional limits for an overspeed condition and may not be cracked.

[Amdt. 33–10, 49 FR 6851, Feb. 23, 1984]

§33.28 Electrical and electronic engine control systems.

Each control system which relies on electrical and electronic means for normal operation must:

(a) Have the control system description, the percent of available power or thrust controlled in both normal operation and failure conditions, and the range of control of other controlled functions, specified in the instruction manual required by §33.5 for the engine;

(b) Be designed and constructed so that any failure of aircraft-supplied power or data will not result in an unacceptable change in power or thrust, or prevent continued safe operation of the engine;

(c) Be designed and constructed so that no single failure or malfunction, or probable combination of failures of electrical or electronic components of the control system, results in an unsafe condition;

(d) Have environmental limits, including transients caused by lightning strikes, specified in the instruction manual; and

(e) Have all associated software designed and implemented to prevent errors that would result in an unacceptable loss of power or thrust, or other unsafe condition, and have the method used to design and implement the software approved by the Administrator.

[Docket No. 24466, 58 FR 29095, May 18, 1993]

§33.29 Instrument connection.

(a) Unless it is constructed to prevent its connection to an incorrect instrument, each connection provided for powerplant instruments required by aircraft airworthiness regulations or necessary to insure operation of the engine in compliance with any engine limitation must be marked to identify it with its corresponding instrument.

(b) A connection must be provided on each turbojet engine for an indicator system to indicate rotor system unbalance.

(c) Each rotorcraft turbine engine having a 30-second OEI rating and a 2-minute OEI rating must have a provision for a means to:

(1) Alert the pilot when the engine is at the 30-second OEI and the 2-minute OEI power levels, when the event begins, and when the time interval expires;

(2) Determine, in a positive manner, that the engine has been operated at each rating; and

(3) Automatically record each usage and duration of power at each rating.

[Amdt. 33–5, 39 FR 1831, Jan. 15, 1974, as amended by Amdt. 33–6, 39 FR 35465, Oct. 1, 1974; Amdt. 33–18, 61 FR 31328, June 19, 1996]

Subpart C— Design and Construction: Reciprocating Aircraft Engines

§33.31 Applicability.

This subpart prescribes additional design and construction requirements for reciprocating aircraft engines.

§33.33 Vibration.

The engine must be designed and constructed to function throughout its normal operating range of crankshaft rotational speeds and engine powers without inducing excessive stress in any of the engine parts because of vibration and without imparting excessive vibration forces to the aircraft structure.

§33.35 Fuel and induction system.

(a) The fuel system of the engine must be designed and constructed to supply an appropriate mixture of fuel to the cylinders throughout the complete operating range of the engine under all flight and atmospheric conditions.

(b) The intake passages of the engine through which air or fuel in combination with air passes for combustion purposes must be designed and constructed to minimize the danger of ice accretion in those passages. The engine must be designed and constructed to permit the use of a means for ice prevention.

(c) The type and degree of fuel filtering necessary for protection of the engine fuel system against foreign particles in the fuel must be specified. The applicant must show that foreign particles passing through the prescribed filtering means will not critically impair engine fuel system functioning.

(d) Each passage in the induction system that conducts a mixture of fuel and air must be self-draining, to prevent a liquid lock in the cylinders, in all attitudes that the applicant establishes as those the engine can have when the aircraft in which it is installed is in the static ground attitude.

(e) If provided as part of the engine, the applicant must show for each fluid injection (other than fuel) system and its controls that the flow of the injected fluid is adequately controlled.

[Docket No. 3025, 29 FR 7453, June 10, 1964; as amended by Amdt. 33–10, 49 FR 6851, Feb. 23, 1984]

§33.37 Ignition system.

Each spark ignition engine must have a dual ignition system with at least two spark plugs for each cylinder and two separate electric circuits with separate sources of electrical energy, or have an ignition system of equivalent in-flight reliability.

§33.39 Lubrication system.

(a) The lubrication system of the engine must be designed and constructed so that it will function properly in all flight attitudes and atmospheric conditions in which the airplane is expected to operate. In wet sump engines, this requirement must be met when only one-half of the maximum lubricant supply is in the engine.

(b) The lubrication system of the engine must be designed and constructed to allow installing a means of cooling the lubricant.

(c) The crankcase must be vented to the atmosphere to preclude leakage of oil from excessive pressure in the crankcase.

Subpart D— Block Tests: Reciprocating Aircraft Engines

§33.41 Applicability.

This subpart prescribes the block tests and inspections for reciprocating aircraft engines.

§33.42 General.

Before each endurance test required by this subpart, the adjustment setting and functioning characteristic of each component having an adjustment setting and a functioning characteristic that can be established independent of installation on the engine must be established and recorded.

[Amdt. 33–6, 39 FR 35465, Oct. 1, 1974]

§33.43 Vibration test.

(a) Each engine must undergo a vibration survey to establish the torsional and bending vibration characteristics of the crankshaft and the propeller shaft or other output shaft, over the range of crankshaft speed and engine power, under steady state and transient conditions, from idling speed to either 110 percent of the desired maximum continuous speed rating or 103 percent of the maximum desired takeoff speed rating, whichever is higher. The survey must be conducted using, for airplane engines, the same configuration of the propeller type which is used for the endurance test, and using, for other engines, the same configuration of the loading device type which is used for the endurance test.

(b) The torsional and bending vibration stresses of the crankshaft and the propeller shaft or other output shaft may not exceed the endurance limit stress of the material from which the shaft is made. If the maximum stress in the shaft cannot be shown to be below the endurance limit by measurement, the vibration frequency and amplitude must be measured. The peak amplitude must be shown to produce a stress below the endurance limit; if not, the engine must be run at the condition producing the peak amplitude until, for steel shafts, 10 million stress reversals have been sustained without fatigue failure and, for other shafts, until it is shown that fatigue will not occur within the endurance limit stress of the material.

(c) Each accessory drive and mounting attachment must be loaded, with the loads imposed by each accessory used only for an aircraft service being the limit load specified by the applicant for the drive or attachment point.

(d) The vibration survey described in paragraph (a) of this section must be repeated with that cylinder not firing which has the most adverse vibration effect, in order to establish the conditions under which the engine can be operated safely in that abnormal state. However, for this vibration survey, the engine speed range need only extend from idle to the maximum desired takeoff speed, and compliance with paragraph (b) of this section need not be shown.

[Amdt. 33–6, 39 FR 35465, Oct. 1, 1974, as amended by Amdt. 33–10, 49 FR 6851, Feb. 23, 1984]

§33.45 Calibration tests.

(a) Each engine must be subjected to the calibration tests necessary to establish its power characteristics and the conditions for the endurance test specified in §33.49. The results of the power characteristics calibration tests form the basis for establishing the characteristics of the engine over its entire operating range of crankshaft rotational speeds, manifold pressures, fuel/air mixture settings, and altitudes. Power ratings are based upon standard atmospheric conditions with only those accessories installed which are essential for engine functioning.

(b) A power check at sea level conditions must be accomplished on the endurance test engine after the endurance test. Any change in power characteristics which occurs during the endurance test must be determined. Measurements taken during the final portion of the endurance test may be used in showing compliance with the requirements of this paragraph.

[Docket No. 3025, 29 FR 7453, June 10, 1964, as amended by Amdt. 33–6, 39 FR 35465, Oct. 1, 1974]

§33.47 Detonation test.

Each engine must be tested to establish that the engine can function without detonation throughout its range of intended conditions of operation.

§33.49 Endurance test.

(a) *General.* Each engine must be subjected to an endurance test that includes a total of 150 hours of operation (except as provided in paragraph (e)(1)(iii) of this section) and, depending upon the type and contemplated use of the engine, consists of one of the series of runs specified in paragraphs (b) through (e) of this section, as applicable. The runs must be made in the order found appropriate by the Administrator for the particular engine being tested. During the endurance test the engine power and the crankshaft rotational speed must be kept within ±3 percent of the rated values. During the runs at rated takeoff power and for at least 35 hours at rated maximum continuous power, one cylinder must be operated at not less than the limiting temperature, the other cylinders must be operated at a temperature not lower than 50 degrees F below the limiting temperature, and the oil inlet temperature must be maintained within ±10 degrees F of the limiting temperature. An engine that is equipped with a propeller shaft must be fitted for the endurance test with a propeller that thrust-loads the engine to the maximum thrust which the engine is designed to resist at each applicable operating condition specified in this section. Each accessory drive and mounting attachment must be loaded. During operation at rated takeoff power and rated maximum continuous power, the load imposed by each accessory used only for an aircraft service must be the limit load specified by the applicant for the engine drive or attachment point.

(b) *Unsupercharged engines and engines incorporating a gear-driven single-speed supercharger.* For engines not incorporating a supercharger and for engines incorporating a gear-driven single-speed supercharger the applicant must conduct the following runs:

(1) A 30-hour run consisting of alternate periods of 5 minutes at rated takeoff power with takeoff speed, and 5 minutes at maximum best economy cruising power or maximum recommended cruising power.

(2) A 20-hour run consisting of alternate periods of 1½ hours at rated maximum continuous power with maximum continuous speed, and ½ hour at 75 percent rated maximum continuous power and 91 percent maximum continuous speed.

(3) A 20-hour run consisting of alternate periods of 1½ hours at rated maximum continuous power with maximum continuous speed, and ½ hour at 70 percent rated maximum continuous power and 89 percent maximum continuous speed.

(4) A 20-hour run consisting of alternate periods of 1½ hours at rated maximum continuous power with maximum continuous speed, and ½ hour at 65 percent rated maximum continuous power and 87 percent maximum continuous speed.

(5) A 20-hour run consisting of alternate periods of 1½ hours at rated maximum continuous power with maximum continuous speed, and ½ hour at 60 percent rated maximum continuous power and 84.5 percent maximum continuous speed.

(6) A 20-hour run consisting of alternate periods of 1½ hours at rated maximum continuous power with maximum continuous speed, and ½ hour at 50 percent rated maximum continuous power and 79.5 percent maximum continuous speed.

(7) A 20-hour run consisting of alternate periods of 2½ hours at rated maximum continuous power with maximum continuous speed, and 2½ hours at maximum best economy cruising power or at maximum recommended cruising power.

(c) *Engines incorporating a gear-driven two-speed supercharger.* For engines incorporating a gear-driven two-speed supercharger the applicant must conduct the following runs:

(1) A 30-hour run consisting of alternate periods in the lower gear ratio of 5 minutes at rated takeoff power with takeoff speed, and 5 minutes at maximum best economy cruising power or at maximum recommended cruising power. If a takeoff power rating is desired in the higher gear ratio, 15 hours of the 30-hour run must be made in the higher gear ratio in alternate periods of 5 minutes at the observed horsepower obtainable with the takeoff critical altitude manifold pressure and takeoff speed, and 5 minutes at 70 percent high ratio rated maximum continuous power and 89 percent high ratio maximum continuous speed.

(2) A 15-hour run consisting of alternate periods in the lower gear ratio of 1 hour at rated maximum continuous power with maximum continuous speed, and ½ hour at 75 percent rated maximum continuous power and 91 percent maximum continuous speed.

(3) A 15-hour run consisting of alternate periods in the lower gear ratio of 1 hour at rated maximum continuous power with maximum continuous speed, and ½ hour at 70

percent rated maximum continuous power and 89 percent maximum continuous speed.

(4) A 30-hour run in the higher gear ratio at rated maximum continuous power with maximum continuous speed.

(5) A 5-hour run consisting of alternate periods of 5 minutes in each of the supercharger gear ratios. The first 5 minutes of the test must be made at maximum continuous speed in the higher gear ratio and the observed horsepower obtainable with 90 percent of maximum continuous manifold pressure in the higher gear ratio under sea level conditions. The condition for operation for the alternate 5 minutes in the lower gear ratio must be that obtained by shifting to the lower gear ratio at constant speed.

(6) A 10-hour run consisting of alternate periods in the lower gear ratio of 1 hour at rated maximum continuous power with maximum continuous speed, and 1 hour at 65 percent rated maximum continuous power and 87 percent maximum continuous speed.

(7) A 10-hour run consisting of alternate periods in the lower gear ratio of 1 hour at rated maximum continuous power with maximum continuous speed, and 1 hour at 60 percent rated maximum continuous power and 84.5 percent maximum continuous speed.

(8) A 10-hour run consisting of alternate periods in the lower gear ratio of 1 hour at rated maximum continuous power with maximum continuous speed, and 1 hour at 50 percent rated maximum continuous power and 79.5 percent maximum continuous speed.

(9) A 20-hour run consisting of alternate periods in the lower gear ratio of 2 hours at rated maximum continuous power with maximum continuous speed, and 2 hours at maximum best economy cruising power and speed or at maximum recommended cruising power.

(10) A 5-hour run in the lower gear ratio at maximum best economy cruising power and speed or at maximum recommended cruising power and speed.

Where simulated altitude test equipment is not available when operating in the higher gear ratio, the runs may be made at the observed horsepower obtained with the critical altitude manifold pressure or specified percentages thereof, and the fuel-air mixtures may be adjusted to be rich enough to suppress detonation.

(d) *Helicopter engines.* To be eligible for use on a helicopter each engine must either comply with paragraphs (a) through (j) of §29.923 of this chapter, or must undergo the following series of runs:

(1) A 35-hour run consisting of alternate periods of 30 minutes each at rated takeoff power with takeoff speed, and at rated maximum continuous power with maximum continuous speed.

(2) A 25-hour run consisting of alternate periods of 2½ hours each at rated maximum continuous power with maximum continuous speed, and at 70 percent rated maximum continuous power with maximum continuous speed.

(3) A 25-hour run consisting of alternate periods of 2½ hours each at rated maximum continuous power with maximum continuous speed, and at 70 percent rated maximum continuous power with 80 to 90 percent maximum continuous speed.

(4) A 25-hour run consisting of alternate periods of 2½ hours each at 30 percent rated maximum continuous power with takeoff speed, and at 30 percent rated maximum continuous power with 80 to 90 percent maximum continuous speed.

(5) A 25-hour run consisting of alternate periods of 2½ hours each at 80 percent rated maximum continuous power with takeoff speed, and at either rated maximum continuous power with 110 percent maximum continuous speed or at rated takeoff power with 103 percent takeoff speed, whichever results in the greater speed.

(6) A 15-hour run at 105 percent rated maximum continuous power with 105 percent maximum continuous speed or at full throttle and corresponding speed at standard sea level carburetor entrance pressure, if 105 percent of the rated maximum continuous power is not exceeded.

(e) *Turbosupercharged engines.* For engines incorporating a turbosupercharger the following apply except that altitude testing may be simulated provided the applicant shows that the engine and supercharger are being subjected to mechanical loads and operating temperatures no less severe than if run at actual altitude conditions:

(1) For engines used in airplanes the applicant must conduct the runs specified in paragraph (b) of this section, except—

(i) The entire run specified in paragraph (b)(1) of this section must be made at sea level altitude pressure;

(ii) The portions of the runs specified in paragraphs (b)(2) through (7) of this section at rated maximum continuous power must be made at critical altitude pressure, and the portions of the runs at other power must be made at 8,000 feet altitude pressure; and

(iii) The turbosupercharger used during the 150-hour endurance test must be run on the bench for an additional 50 hours at the limiting turbine wheel inlet gas temperature and rotational speed for rated maximum continuous power operation unless the limiting temperature and speed are maintained during 50 hours of the rated maximum continuous power operation.

(2) For engines used in helicopters the applicant must conduct the runs specified in paragraph (d) of this section, except—

(i) The entire run specified in paragraph (d)(1) of this section must be made at critical altitude pressure;

(ii) The portions of the runs specified in paragraphs (d)(2) and (3) of this section at rated maximum continuous power must be made at critical altitude pressure and the portions of the runs at other power must be made at 8,000 feet altitude pressure;

(iii) The entire run specified in paragraph (d)(4) of this section must be made at 8,000 feet altitude pressure;

(iv) The portion of the runs specified in paragraph (d)(5) of this section at 80 percent of rated maximum continuous power must be made at 8,000 feet altitude pressure and the portions of the runs at other power must be made at critical altitude pressure;

(v) The entire run specified in paragraph (d)(6) of this section must be made at critical altitude pressure; and

(vi) The turbosupercharger used during the endurance test must be run on the bench for 50 hours at the limiting turbine wheel inlet gas temperature and rotational speed for rated maximum continuous power operation unless the limiting temperature and speed are maintained during 50 hours of the rated maximum continuous power operation.

[Amdt. 33–3, 32 FR 3736, Mar. 4, 1967, as amended by Amdt. 33–6, 39 FR 35465, Oct. 1, 1974; Amdt. 33–10, 49 FR 6851, Feb. 23, 1984]

§33.51 Operation test.

The operation test must include the testing found necessary by the Administrator to demonstrate backfire characteristics, starting, idling, acceleration, overspeeding, functioning of propeller and ignition, and any other operational characteristic of the engine. If the engine incorporates a multispeed supercharger drive, the design and construction must allow the supercharger to be shifted from operation at the lower speed ratio to the higher and the power appropriate to the manifold pressure and speed settings for rated maximum continuous power at the higher supercharger speed ratio must be obtainable within five seconds.

[Docket No. 3025, 29 FR 7453, June 10, 1964, as amended by Amdt. 33–3, 32 FR 3737, Mar. 4, 1967]

§33.53 Engine component tests.

(a) For each engine that cannot be adequately substantiated by endurance testing in accordance with §33.49, the applicant must conduct additional tests to establish that components are able to function reliably in all normally anticipated flight and atmospheric conditions.

(b) Temperature limits must be established for each component that requires temperature controlling provisions in the aircraft installation to assure satisfactory functioning, reliability, and durability.

§33.55 Teardown inspection.

After completing the endurance test—

(a) Each engine must be completely disassembled;

(b) Each component having an adjustment setting and a functioning characteristic that can be established independent of installation on the engine must retain each setting and functioning characteristic within the limits that were established and recorded at the beginning of the test; and

(c) Each engine component must conform to the type design and be eligible for incorporation into an engine for continued operation, in accordance with information submitted in compliance with §33.4.

[Amdt. 33–6, 39 FR 35466, Oct. 1, 1974, as amended by Amdt. 33–9, 45 FR 60181, Sept. 11, 1980]

§33.57 General conduct of block tests.

(a) The applicant may, in conducting the block tests, use separate engines of identical design and construction in the vibration, calibration, detonation, endurance, and operation tests, except that, if a separate engine is used for the endurance test it must be subjected to a calibration check before starting the endurance test.

(b) The applicant may service and make minor repairs to the engine during the block tests in accordance with the service and maintenance instructions submitted in compliance with §33.4. If the frequency of the service is excessive, or the number of stops due to engine malfunction is excessive, or a major repair, or replacement of a part is found necessary during the block tests or as the result of findings from the teardown inspection, the engine or its parts may be subjected to any additional test the Administrator finds necessary.

(c) Each applicant must furnish all testing facilities, including equipment and competent personnel, to conduct the block tests.

[Docket No. 3025, 29 FR 7453, June 10, 1964, as amended by Amdt. 33–6, 39 FR 35466, Oct. 1, 1974; Amdt. 33–9, 45 FR 60181, Sept. 11, 1980]

Subpart E— Design and Construction: Turbine Aircraft Engines

§33.61 Applicability.

This subpart prescribes additional design and construction requirements for turbine aircraft engines.

§33.62 Stress analysis.

A stress analysis must be performed on each turbine engine showing the design safety margin of each turbine engine rotor, spacer, and rotor shaft.

[Amdt. 33–6, 39 FR 35466, Oct. 1, 1974]

§33.63 Vibration.

Each engine must be designed and constructed to function throughout its declared flight envelope and operating range of rotational speeds and power/thrust, without inducing excessive stress in any engine part because of vibration and without imparting excessive vibration forces to the aircraft structure.

[Docket No. 28107, 61 FR 28433, June 4, 1996]

§33.65 Surge and stall characteristics.

When the engine is operated in accordance with operating instructions required by §33.5(b), starting, a change of power or thrust, power or thrust augmentation, limiting inlet air distortion, or inlet air temperature may not cause surge or stall to the extent that flameout, structural failure, overtemperature, or failure of the engine to recover power or thrust will occur at any point in the operating envelope.

[Amdt. 33–6, 39 FR 35466, Oct. 1, 1974]

§33.66 Bleed air system.

The engine must supply bleed air without adverse effect on the engine, excluding reduced thrust or power output, at all conditions up to the discharge flow conditions established as a limitation under §33.7(c)(11). If bleed air used for engine anti-icing can be controlled, provision must be made for a means to indicate the functioning of the engine ice protection system.

[Amdt. 33–10, 49 FR 6851, Feb. 23, 1984]

§33.67 Fuel system.

(a) With fuel supplied to the engine at the flow and pressure specified by the applicant, the engine must function properly under each operating condition required by this part. Each fuel control adjusting means that may not be manipulated while the fuel control device is mounted on the engine must be secured by a locking device and sealed, or otherwise be inaccessible. All other fuel control adjusting means must be accessible and marked to indicate the function of the adjustment unless the function is obvious.

(b) There must be a fuel strainer or filter between the engine fuel inlet opening and the inlet of either the fuel metering device or the engine-driven positive displacement pump whichever is nearer the engine fuel inlet. In addition, the following provisions apply to each strainer or filter required by this paragraph (b):

(1) It must be accessible for draining and cleaning and must incorporate a screen or element that is easily removable.

(2) It must have a sediment trap and drain except that it need not have a drain if the strainer or filter is easily removable for drain purposes.

(3) It must be mounted so that its weight is not supported by the connecting lines or by the inlet or outlet connections of the strainer or filter, unless adequate strength margins under all loading conditions are provided in the lines and connections.

(4) It must have the type and degree of fuel filtering specified as necessary for protection of the engine fuel system against foreign particles in the fuel. The applicant must show:

(i) That foreign particles passing through the specified filtering means do not impair the engine fuel system functioning; and

(ii) That the fuel system is capable of sustained operation throughout its flow and pressure range with the fuel initially saturated with water at 80°F (27°C) and having 0.025 fluid ounces per gallon (0.20 milliliters per liter) of free water added and cooled to the most critical condition for icing likely to be encountered in operation. However, this requirement may be met by demonstrating the effectiveness of specified approved fuel anti-icing additives, or that the fuel system incorporates a fuel heater which maintains the fuel temperature at the fuel strainer or fuel inlet above 32°F (0°C) under the most critical conditions.

(5) The applicant must demonstrate that the filtering means has the capacity (with respect to engine operating limitations) to ensure that the engine will continue to operate within approved limits, with fuel contaminated to the maximum degree of particle size and density likely to be encountered in service. Operation under these conditions must be demonstrated for a period acceptable to the Administrator, beginning when indication of impending filter blockage is first given by either:

(i) Existing engine instrumentation; or

(ii) Additional means incorporated into the engine fuel system.

(6) Any strainer or filter bypass must be designed and constructed so that the release of collected contaminants is minimized by appropriate location of the bypass to ensure that collected contaminants are not in the bypass flow path.

(c) If provided as part of the engine, the applicant must show for each fluid injection (other than fuel) system and its controls that the flow of the injected fluid is adequately controlled.

(d) Engines having a 30-second OEI rating must incorporate means for automatic availability and automatic control of a 30-second OEI power.

[Amdt. 33–6, 39 FR 35466, Oct. 1, 1974, as amended by Amdt. 33–10, 49 FR 6851, Feb. 23, 1984; Amdt. 33–18, 61 FR 31328, June 19, 1996]

§33.68 Induction system icing.

Each engine, with all icing protection systems operating, must—

(a) Operate throughout its flight power range (including idling) without the accumulation of ice on the engine components that adversely affects engine operation or that causes a serious loss of power or thrust in continuous maximum and intermittent maximum icing conditions as defined in Appendix C of Part 25 of this chapter; and

(b) Idle for 30 minutes on the ground, with the available air bleed for icing protection at its critical condition, without adverse effect, in an atmosphere that is at a temperature between 15° and 30° F (between –9° and –1°C) and has a liquid water content not less than 0.3 grams per cubic meter in the form of drops having a mean effective diameter not less than 20 microns, followed by a momentary operation at takeoff power or thrust. During the 30 minutes of idle operation the engine may be run up periodically to a moderate power or thrust setting in a manner acceptable to the Administrator.

[Amdt. 33–6, 39 FR 35466, Oct. 1, 1974, as amended by Amdt. 33–10, 49 FR 6852, Feb. 23, 1984]

§33.69 Ignitions system.

Each engine must be equipped with an ignition system for starting the engine on the ground and in flight. An electric ignition system must have at least two igniters and two separate secondary electric circuits, except that only one igniter is required for fuel burning augmentation systems.

[Amdt. 33–6, 39 FR 35466, Oct. 1, 1974]

§33.71 Lubrication system.

(a) *General.* Each lubrication system must function properly in the flight attitudes and atmospheric conditions in which an aircraft is expected to operate.

(b) *Oil strainer or filter.* There must be an oil strainer or filter through which all of the engine oil flows. In addition:

(1) Each strainer or filter required by this paragraph that has a bypass must be constructed and installed so that oil will flow at the normal rate through the rest of the system with the strainer or filter element completely blocked.

(2) The type and degree of filtering necessary for protection of the engine oil system against foreign particles in the oil must be specified. The applicant must demonstrate that foreign particles passing through the specified filtering means do not impair engine oil system functioning.

(3) Each strainer or filter required by this paragraph must have the capacity (with respect to operating limitations established for the engine) to ensure that engine oil system functioning is not impaired with the oil contaminated to a degree (with respect to particle size and density) that is greater

than that established for the engine in paragraph (b)(2) of this section.

(4) For each strainer or filter required by this paragraph, except the strainer or filter at the oil tank outlet, there must be means to indicate contamination before it reaches the capacity established in accordance with paragraph (b)(3) of this section.

(5) Any filter bypass must be designed and constructed so that the release of collected contaminants is minimized by appropriate location of the bypass to ensure that the collected contaminants are not in the bypass flow path.

(6) Each strainer or filter required by this paragraph that has no bypass, except the strainer or filter at an oil tank outlet or for a scavenge pump, must have provisions for connection with a warning means to warn the pilot of the occurrence of contamination of the screen before it reaches the capacity established in accordance with paragraph (b)(3) of this section.

(7) Each strainer or filter required by this paragraph must be accessible for draining and cleaning.

(c) *Oil tanks.*

(1) Each oil tank must have an expansion space of not less than 10 percent of the tank capacity.

(2) It must be impossible to inadvertently fill the oil tank expansion space.

(3) Each recessed oil tank filler connection that can retain any appreciable quantity of oil must have provision for fitting a drain.

(4) Each oil tank cap must provide an oil-tight seal.

(5) Each oil tank filler must be marked with the word "oil."

(6) Each oil tank must be vented from the top part of the expansion space, with the vent so arranged that condensed water vapor that might freeze and obstruct the line cannot accumulate at any point.

(7) There must be means to prevent entrance into the oil tank or into any oil tank outlet, of any object that might obstruct the flow of oil through the system.

(8) There must be a shutoff valve at the outlet of each oil tank, unless the external portion of the oil system (including oil tank supports) is fireproof.

(9) Each unpressurized oil tank may not leak when subjected to a maximum operating temperature and an internal pressure of 5 p.s.i., and each pressurized oil tank may not leak when subjected to maximum operating temperature and an internal pressure that is not less than 5 p.s.i. plus the maximum operating pressure of the tank.

(10) Leaked or spilled oil may not accumulate between the tank and the remainder of the engine.

(11) Each oil tank must have an oil quantity indicator or provisions for one.

(12) If the propeller feathering system depends on engine oil—

(i) There must be means to trap an amount of oil in the tank if the supply becomes depleted due to failure of any part of the lubricating system other than the tank itself;

(ii) The amount of trapped oil must be enough to accomplish the feathering operation and must be available only to the feathering pump; and

(iii) Provision must be made to prevent sludge or other foreign matter from affecting the safe operation of the propeller feathering system.

(d) *Oil drains.* A drain (or drains) must be provided to allow safe drainage of the oil system. Each drain must—

(1) Be accessible; and

(2) Have manual or automatic means for positive locking in the closed position.

(e) *Oil radiators.* Each oil radiator must withstand, without failure, any vibration, inertia, and oil pressure load to which it is subjected during the block tests.

[Amdt. 33–6, 39 FR 35466, Oct. 1, 1974, as amended by Amdt. 33–10, 49 FR 6852, Feb. 23, 1984]

§33.72 Hydraulic actuating systems.

Each hydraulic actuating system must function properly under all conditions in which the engine is expected to operate. Each filter or screen must be accessible for servicing and each tank must meet the design criteria of §33.71.

[Amdt. 33–6, 39 FR 35467, Oct. 1, 1974]

§33.73 Power or thrust response.

The design and construction of the engine must enable an increase—

(a) From minimum to rated takeoff power or thrust with the maximum bleed air and power extraction to be permitted in an aircraft, without overtemperature, surge, stall, or other detrimental factors occurring to the engine whenever the power control lever is moved from the minimum to the maximum position in not more than 1 second, except that the Administrator may allow additional time increments for different regimes of control operation requiring control scheduling; and

(b) From the fixed minimum flight idle power lever position when provided, or if not provided, from not more than 15 percent of the rated takeoff power or thrust available to 95 percent rated takeoff power or thrust in not over 5 seconds. The 5-second power or thrust response must occur from a stabilized static condition using only the bleed air and accessories loads necessary to run the engine. This takeoff rating is specified by the applicant and need not include thrust augmentation.

[Amdt. 33–1, 36 FR 5493, March 24, 1971]

§33.74 Continued rotation.

If any of the engine main rotating systems will continue to rotate after the engine is shutdown for any reason while in flight, and where means to prevent that continued rotation are not provided; then any continued rotation during the maximum period of flight, and in the flight conditions expected to occur with that engine inoperative, must not result in any condition described in §33.75(a) through (c).

[Docket No. 28107, 61 FR 28433, June 4, 1996]

§33.75 Safety analysis.

It must be shown by analysis that any probable malfunction or any probable single or multiple failure, or any probable improper operation of the engine will not cause the engine to—

(a) Catch fire;

(b) Burst (release hazardous fragments through the engine case);

(c) Generate loads greater than those ultimate loads specified in §33.23(a); or

(d) Lose the capability of being shut down.

[Amdt. 33–6, 39 FR 35467, Oct. 1, 1974, as amended by Amdt. 33–10, 49 FR 6852, Feb. 23, 1984]

§33.76 Bird ingestion.

(a) *General.* Compliance with paragraphs (b) and (c) of this section shall be in accordance with the following:

(1) All ingestion tests shall be conducted with the engine stabilized at no less than 100-percent takeoff power or thrust, for test day ambient conditions prior to the ingestion. In addition, the demonstration of compliance must account for engine operation at sea level takeoff conditions on the hottest day that a minimum engine can achieve maximum rated takeoff thrust or power.

(2) The engine inlet throat area as used in this section to determine the bird quantity and weights will be established by the applicant and identified as a limitation in the installation instructions required under §33.5.

(3) The impact to the front of the engine from the single large bird and the single largest medium bird which can enter the inlet must be evaluated. It must be shown that the associated components when struck under the conditions prescribed in paragraphs (b) or (c) of this section, as applicable, will not affect the engine to the extent that it cannot comply with the requirements of paragraphs (b)(3) and (c)(6) of this section.

(4) For an engine that incorporates an inlet protection device, compliance with this section shall be established with the device functioning. The engine approval will be endorsed to show that compliance with the requirements has been established with the device functioning.

(5) Objects that are accepted by the Administrator may be substituted for birds when conducting the bird ingestion tests required by paragraphs (b) and (c) of this section.

(6) If compliance with the requirements of this section is not established, the engine type certification documentation will show that the engine shall be limited to aircraft installations in which it is shown that a bird cannot strike the engine, or be ingested into the engine, or adversely restrict airflow into the engine.

(b) *Large birds.* Compliance with the large bird ingestion requirements shall be in accordance with the following:

(1) The large bird ingestion test shall be conducted using one bird of a weight determined from Table 1 aimed at the most critical exposed location on the first stage rotor blades and ingested at a bird speed of 200-knots for engines to be installed on airplanes, or the maximum airspeed for normal rotorcraft flight operations for engines to be installed on rotorcraft.

(2) Power lever movement is not permitted within 15 seconds following ingestion of the large bird.

(3) Ingestion of a single large bird tested under the conditions prescribed in this section may not cause the engine to:

(i) Catch fire;

(ii) Release hazardous fragments through the engine casing;

(iii) Generate loads greater than those ultimate loads specified under §33.23(a); or

(iv) Lose the ability to be shut down.

(4) Compliance with the large bird ingestion requirements of this paragraph may be shown by demonstrating that the requirements of §33.94(a) constitute a more severe demonstration of blade containment and rotor unbalance than the requirements of this paragraph.

Table 1 to §33.76.—Large Bird Weight Requirements

Engine Inlet Throat Area (A)—Square-meters (square-inches)	Bird weight kg. (lb.)
1.35 (2,092) > A	1.85 (4.07) minimum, unless a smaller bird is determined to be a more severe demonstration.
1.35 (2,092) ≤ A < 3.90 (6,045)	2.75 (6.05)
3.90 (6,045) ≤ A	3.65 (8.03)

(c) *Small and medium birds.* Compliance with the small and medium bird ingestion requirements shall be in accordance with the following:

(1) Analysis or component test, or both, acceptable to the Administrator, shall be conducted to determine the critical ingestion parameters affecting power loss and damage. Critical ingestion parameters shall include, but are not limited to, the effects of bird speed, critical target location, and first stage rotor speed. The critical bird ingestion speed should reflect the most critical condition within the range of airspeeds used for normal flight operations up to 1,500 feet above ground level, but not less than V_1 minimum for airplanes.

(2) Medium bird engine tests shall be conducted so as to simulate a flock encounter, and will use the bird weights and quantities specified in Table 2. When only one bird is specified, that bird will be aimed at the engine core primary flow path; the other critical locations on the engine face area must be addressed, as necessary, by appropriate tests or analysis, or both. When two or more birds are specified in Table 2, the largest of those birds must be aimed at the engine core primary flow path, and a second bird must be aimed at the most critical exposed location on the first stage rotor blades. Any remaining birds must be evenly distributed over the engine face area.

(3) In addition, except for rotorcraft engines, it must also be substantiated by appropriate tests or analysis or both, that when the full fan assembly is subjected to the ingestion of the quantity and weights of bird from Table 3, aimed at the fan assembly's most critical location outboard of the primary core flowpath, and in accordance with the applicable test conditions of this paragraph, that the engine can comply with the acceptance criteria of this paragraph.

(4) A small bird ingestion test is not required if the prescribed number of medium birds pass into the engine rotor blades during the medium bird test.

(5) Small bird ingestion tests shall be conducted so as to simulate a flock encounter using one 85 gram (0.187 lb.) bird for each 0.032 square-meter (49.6 square-inches) of inlet area, or fraction thereof, up to a maximum of 16 birds. The birds will be aimed so as to account for any critical exposed locations on the first stage rotor blades, with any remaining birds evenly distributed over the engine face area.

(6) Ingestion of small and medium birds tested under the conditions prescribed in this paragraph may not cause any of the following:

(i) More than a sustained 25-percent power or thrust loss;

(ii) The engine to be shut down during the required run-on demonstration prescribed in paragraphs (c)(7) or (c)(8) of this section;

(iii) The conditions defined in paragraph (b)(3) of this section.

(iv) Unacceptable deterioration of engine handling characteristics.

(7) Except for rotorcraft engines, the following test schedule shall be used:

(i) Ingestion so as to simulate a flock encounter, with approximately 1 second elapsed time from the moment of the first bird ingestion to the last.

(ii) Followed by 2 minutes without power lever movement after the ingestion.

(iii) Followed by 3 minutes at 75-percent of the test condition.

(iv) Followed by 6 minutes at 60-percent of the test condition.

(v) Followed by 6 minutes at 40-percent of the test condition.

(vi) Followed by 1 minute at approach idle.

(vii) Followed by 2 minutes at 75-percent of the test condition.

(viii) Followed by stabilizing at idle and engine shut down.

(ix) The durations specified are times at the defined conditions with the power being changed between each condition in less than 10 seconds.

(8) For rotorcraft engines, the following test schedule shall be used:

(i) Ingestion so as to simulate a flock encounter within approximately 1 second elapsed time between the first ingestion and the last.

(ii) Followed by 3 minutes at 75-percent of the test condition.

(iii) Followed by 90 seconds at descent flight idle.

(iv) Followed by 30 seconds at 75-percent of the test condition.

(v) Followed by stabilizing at idle and engine shut down.

(vi) The duration specified are times at the defined conditions with the power being changed between each condition in less than 10 seconds.

(9) Engines intended for use in multi-engine rotorcraft are not required to comply with the medium bird ingestion portion of this section, providing that the appropriate type certificate documentation is so endorsed.

(10) If any engine operating limit(s) is exceeded during the initial 2 minutes without power lever movement, as provided by paragraph (c)(7)(ii) of this section, then it shall be established that the limit exceedence will not result in an unsafe condition.

Table 2 to §33.76—Medium Flocking Bird Weight and Quantity Requirements

Engine Inlet Throat Area (A)—Square-meters (square-inches)	Bird quantity	Bird weight kg. (lb.)
0.05 (77.5) > A	none	
0.05 (77.5) ≤ A < 0.10 (155)	1	0.35 (0.77)
0.10 (155) ≤ A < 0.20 (310)	1	0.45 (0.99)
0.20 (310) ≤ A < 0.40 (620)	2	0.45 (0.99)
0.40 (620) ≤ A < 0.60 (930)	2	0.70 (1.54)
0.60 (930) ≤ A < 1.00 (1,550)	3	0.70 (1.54)
1.00 (1,550) ≤ A < 1.35 (2,092)	4	0.70 (1.54)
1.35 (2,092) ≤ A < 1.70 (2,635)	1 plus 3	1.15 (2.53) 0.70 (1.54)
1.70 (2,635) ≤ A < 2.10 (3,255)	1 plus 4	1.15 (2.53) 0.70 (1.54)
2.10 (3,255) ≤ A < 2.50 (3,875)	1 plus 5	1.15 (2.53) 0.70 (1.54)
2.50 (3,875) ≤ A < 3.90 < 3.90 (6045)	1 plus 6	1.15 (2.53) 0.70 (1.54)
3.90 (6045) ≤ A < 4.50 (6975)	3	1.15 (2.53)
4.50 (6975) ≤ A	4	1.15 (2.53)

Table 3 to §33.76—Additional Integrity Assessment

Engine Inlet Throat Area (A)—square-meters (square-inches)	Bird quantity	Bird weight kg. (lb.)
1.35 (2,092) > A	none	
1.35 (2,092) ≤ A < 2.90 (4,495)	1	1.15 (2.53)
2.90 (4,495) ≤ A < 3.90 (6,045)	2	1.15 (2.53)
3.90 (6,045) ≤ A	1 plus 6	1.15 (2.53) 0.70 (1.54)

[Docket No. FAA–1998–4815, Amdt. 33–20, 65 FR 55854, Sept. 14, 2000; as amended by Amdt. 33–20, 68 FR 75391, Dec. 31, 2003]

§33.77 Foreign object ingestion — ice.

(a) [Reserved]

(b) [Reserved]

(c) Ingestion of ice under the conditions of paragraph (e) of this section may not—

(1) Cause a sustained power or thrust loss; or

(2) require the engine to be shutdown.

(d) For an engine that incorporates a protection device, compliance with this section need not be demonstrated with respect to foreign objects to be ingested under the conditions prescribed in paragraph (e) of this section if it is shown that—

(1) Such foreign objects are of a size that will not pass through the protective device;

(2) The protective device will withstand the impact of the foreign objects; and

(3) The foreign object, or objects, stopped by the protective device will not obstruct the flow of induction air into the engine with a resultant sustained reduction in power or thrust greater than those values required by paragraph (c) of this section.

(e) Compliance with paragraph (c) of this section must be shown by engine test under the following ingestion conditions:

(1) Ice quantity will be the maximum accumulation on a typical inlet cowl and engine face resulting from a 2-minute delay in actuating the anti-icing system; or a slab of ice which is comparable in weight or thickness for that size engine.

(2) The ingestion velocity will simulate ice being sucked into the engine inlet.

(3) Engine operation will be maximum cruise power or thrust.

(4) The ingestion will simulate a continuous maximum icing encounter at 25 degrees Fahrenheit.

[Amdt. 33–10, 49 FR 6852, Feb. 23, 1984; as amended by Amdt. 33–19, 63 FR 14798, March 26, 1998; Amdt. 33–19, 63 FR 53278, Oct. 5, 1998; Amdt. 33–20, 65 FR 55856, Sept. 14, 2000]

§33.78 Rain and hail ingestion.

(a) All engines.

(1) The ingestion of large hailstones (0.8 to 0.9 specific gravity) at the maximum true air speed, up to 15,000 feet (4,500 meters), associated with a representative aircraft operating in rough air, with the engine at maximum continuous power, may not cause unacceptable mechanical damage or unacceptable power or thrust loss after the ingestion, or require the engine to be shut down. One-half the number of hailstones shall be aimed randomly over the inlet face area and the other half aimed at the critical inlet face area. The hailstones shall be ingested in a rapid sequence to simulate a hailstone encounter and the number and size of the hailstones shall be determined as follows:

(i) One 1-inch (25 millimeters) diameter hailstone for engines with inlet areas of not more than 100 square inches (0.0645 square meters).

(ii) One 1-inch (25 millimeters) diameter and one 2-inch (50 millimeters) diameter hailstone for each 150 square inches (0.0968 square meters) of inlet area, or fraction thereof, for engines with inlet areas of more than 100 square inches (0.0645 square meters).

(2) In addition to complying with paragraph (a)(1) of this section and except as provided in paragraph (b) of this section, it must be shown that each engine is capable of acceptable operation throughout its specified operating envelope when subjected to sudden encounters with the certification standard concentrations of rain and hail, as defined in appendix B to this part. Acceptable engine operation precludes flameout, run down, continued or nonrecoverable surge or stall, or loss of acceleration and deceleration capability, during any three minute continuous period in rain and during any 30 second continuous period in hail. It must also be shown after the ingestion that there is no unacceptable mechanical damage, unacceptable power or thrust loss, or other adverse engine anomalies.

(b) Engines for rotorcraft. As an alternative to the requirements specified in paragraph (a)(2) of this section, for rotorcraft turbine engines only, it must be shown that each engine is capable of acceptable operation during and after the ingestion of rain with an overall ratio of water droplet flow to airflow, by weight, with a uniform distribution at the inlet plane, of at least four percent. Acceptable engine operation precludes flameout, run down, continued or nonrecoverable surge or stall, or loss of acceleration and deceleration capability. It must also be shown after the ingestion that there is no unacceptable mechanical damage, unacceptable power loss, or other adverse engine anomalies. The rain ingestion must occur under the following static ground level conditions:

(1) A normal stabilization period at take-off power without rain ingestion, followed immediately by the suddenly commencing ingestion of rain for three minutes at takeoff power, then

(2) Continuation of the rain ingestion during subsequent rapid deceleration to minimum idle, then

(3) Continuation of the rain ingestion during three minutes at minimum idle power to be certified for flight operation, then

(4) Continuation of the rain ingestion during subsequent rapid acceleration to takeoff power.

(c) Engines for supersonic airplanes. In addition to complying with paragraphs (a)(1) and (a)(2) of this section, a separate test for supersonic airplane engines only, shall be conducted with three hailstones ingested at supersonic cruise velocity. These hailstones shall be aimed at the engine's critical face area, and their ingestion must not cause unacceptable mechanical damage or unacceptable power or thrust loss after the ingestion or require the engine to be shut down. The size of these hailstones shall be determined from the linear variation in diameter from 1-inch (25 millimeters) at 35,000 feet (10,500 meters) to ¼-inch (6 millimeters) at 60,000 feet (18,000 meters) using the diameter corresponding to the lowest expected supersonic cruise altitude. Alternatively, three larger hailstones may be ingested at subsonic velocities such that the kinetic energy of these larger hailstones is equivalent to the applicable supersonic ingestion conditions.

(d) For an engine that incorporates or requires the use of a protection device, demonstration of the rain and hail ingestion capabilities of the engine, as required in paragraphs (a), (b), and (c) of this section, may be waived wholly or in part by the Administrator if the applicant shows that:

(1) The subject rain and hail constituents are of a size that will not pass through the protection device;

(2) The protection device will withstand the impact of the subject rain and hail constituents; and

(3) The subject of rain and hail constituents, stopped by the protection device, will not obstruct the flow of induction air into the engine, resulting in damage, power or thrust loss, or other adverse engine anomalies in excess of what would be accepted in paragraphs (a), (b), and (c) of this section.

[Docket No. 28652, 63 FR 14799, March 26, 1998]

§33.79 Fuel burning thrust augmentor.

Each fuel burning thrust augmentor, including the nozzle, must—

(a) Provide cutoff of the fuel burning thrust augmentor;

(b) Permit on-off cycling;

(c) Be controllable within the intended range of operation;

(d) Upon a failure or malfunction of augmentor combustion, not cause the engine to lose thrust other than that provided by the augmentor; and

(e) Have controls that function compatibly with the other engine controls and automatically shut off augmentor fuel flow if the engine rotor speed drops below the minimum rotational speed at which the augmentor is intended to function.

[Amdt. 33–6, 39 FR 35468, Oct. 1, 1974]

Subpart F—Block Tests: Turbine Aircraft Engines

§33.81 Applicability.

This subpart prescribes the block tests and inspections for turbine engines.

[Docket 3025, 29 FR 7453, June 10, 1964, as amended by Amdt. 33–6, 39 FR 35468, Oct. 1, 1974]

§33.82 General.

Before each endurance test required by this subpart, the adjustment setting and functioning characteristic of each component having an adjustment setting and a functioning characteristic that can be established independent of installation on the engine must be established and recorded.

[Amdt. 36–6, 39 FR 35468, Oct. 1, 1974]

§33.83 Vibration test.

(a) Each engine must undergo vibration surveys to establish that the vibration characteristics of those components that may be subject to mechanically or aerodynamically induced vibratory excitations are acceptable throughout the declared flight envelope. The engine surveys shall be based upon an appropriate combination of experience, analysis, and component test and shall address, as a minimum, blades, vanes, rotor discs, spacers, and rotor shafts.

(b) The surveys shall cover the ranges of power or thrust, and both the physical and corrected rotational speeds for each rotor system, corresponding to operations throughout the range of ambient conditions in the declared flight envelope, from the minimum rotational speed up to 103 percent of the maximum physical and corrected rotational speed permitted for rating periods of two minutes or longer, and up to 100 percent of all other permitted physical and corrected rotational speeds, including those that are overspeeds. If there is any indication of a stress peak arising at the highest of those required physical or corrected rotational speeds, the surveys shall be extended sufficiently to reveal the maximum stress values present, except that the extension need not cover more than a further 2 percentage points increase beyond those speeds.

(c) Evaluations shall be made of the following:

(1) The effects on vibration characteristics of operating with scheduled changes (including tolerances) to variable vane angles, compressor bleeds, accessory loading, the most adverse inlet air flow distortion pattern declared by the manufacturer, and the most adverse conditions in the exhaust duct(s); and

(2) The aerodynamic and aeromechanical factors which might induce or influence flutter in those systems susceptible to that form of vibration.

(d) Except as provided by paragraph (e) of this section, the vibration stresses associated with the vibration characteristics determined under this section, when combined with the appropriate steady stresses, must be less than the endurance limits of the materials concerned, after making due allowances for operating conditions for the permitted variations in properties of the materials. The suitability of these stress margins must be justified for each part evaluated. If it is determined that certain operating conditions, or ranges, need to be limited, operating and installation limitations shall be established.

(e) The effects on vibration characteristics of excitation forces caused by fault conditions (such as, but not limited to, out-of-balance, local blockage or enlargement of stator vane passages, fuel nozzle blockage, incorrectly schedule compressor variables, etc.) shall be evaluated by test or analysis, or by reference to previous experience and shall be shown not to create a hazardous condition.

(f) Compliance with this section shall be substantiated for each specific installation configuration that can affect the vibration characteristics of the engine. If these vibration effects cannot be fully investigated during engine certification, the methods by which they can be evaluated and methods by which compliance can be shown shall be substantiated and defined in the installation instructions required by §33.5.

[Docket No. 28107, 61 FR 28433, June 4, 1996]

§33.85 Calibration tests.

(a) Each engine must be subjected to those calibration tests necessary to establish its power characteristics and the conditions for the endurance test specified §33.87. The results of the power characteristics calibration tests form the basis for establishing the characteristics of the engine over its entire operating range of speeds, pressures, temperatures, and altitudes. Power ratings are based upon standard atmospheric conditions with no airbleed for aircraft services and with only those accessories installed which are essential for engine functioning.

(b) A power check at sea level conditions must be accomplished on the endurance test engine after the endurance test and any change in power characteristics which occurs during the endurance test must be determined. Measurements taken during the final portion of the endurance test may be used in showing compliance with the requirements of this paragraph.

(c) In showing compliance with this section, each condition must stabilize before measurements are taken, except as permitted by paragraph (d) of this section.

(d) In the case of engines having 30-second OEI, and 2-minute OEI ratings, measurements taken during the applicable endurance test prescribed in §33.87(f) (1) through (8) may be used in showing compliance with the requirements of this section for these OEI ratings.

[Docket No. 3025, 29 FR 7453, June 10, 1964, as amended by Amdt. 33–6, 39 FR 35468, Oct. 1, 1974; Amdt. 33–18, 61 FR 31328, June 19, 1996]

§33.87 Endurance test.

(a) *General.* Each engine must be subjected to an endurance test that includes a total of at least 150 hours of operation and, depending upon the type and contemplated use of the engine, consists of one of the series of runs specified in paragraphs (b) through (g) of this section, as applicable. For engines tested under paragraphs (b), (c), (d), (e) or (g) of this section, the prescribed 6-hour test sequence must be conducted 25 times to complete the required 150 hours of operation. Engines for which the 30-second OEI and 2-minute OEI ratings are desired must be further tested under paragraph (f) of this section. The following test requirements apply:

(1) The runs must be made in the order found appropriate by the Administrator for the particular engine being tested.

(2) Any automatic engine control that is part of the engine must control the engine during the endurance test except for operations where automatic control is normally overridden by manual control or where manual control is otherwise specified for a particular test run.

(3) Except as provided in paragraph (a)(5) of this section, power or thrust, gas temperature, rotor shaft rotational speed, and, if limited, temperature of external surfaces of the engine must be at least 100 percent of the value associated with the particular engine operation being tested. More than one test may be run if all parameters cannot be held at the 100 percent level simultaneously.

(4) The runs must be made using fuel, lubricants and hydraulic fluid which conform to the specifications specified in complying with §33.7(c).

(5) Maximum air bleed for engine and aircraft services must be used during at least one-fifth of the runs. However, for these runs, the power or thrust or the rotor shaft rotational speed may be less than 100 percent of the value associated with the particular operation being tested if the Administrator finds that the validity of the endurance test is not compromised.

(6) Each accessory drive and mounting attachment must be loaded. The load imposed by each accessory used only for aircraft service must be the limit load specified by the applicant for the engine drive and attachment point during rated maximum continuous power or thrust and higher output. The endurance test of any accessory drive and mounting attachment under load may be accomplished on a separate rig if the validity of the test is confirmed by an approved analysis.

(7) During the runs at any rated power or thrust the gas temperature and the oil inlet temperature must be maintained at the limiting temperature except where the test periods are not longer than 5 minutes and do not allow stabilization. At least one run must be made with fuel, oil, and hydraulic fluid at the minimum pressure limit and at least one run must be made with fuel, oil, and hydraulic fluid at the maximum pressure limit with fluid temperature reduced as necessary to allow maximum pressure to be attained.

(8) If the number of occurrences of either transient rotor shaft overspeed or transient gas overtemperature is limited, that number of the accelerations required by paragraphs (b) through (g) of this section must be made at the limiting overspeed or overtemperature. If the number of occurrences is not limited, half the required accelerations must be made at the limiting overspeed or overtemperature.

(9) For each engine type certificated for use on supersonic aircraft the following additional test requirements apply:

(i) To change the thrust setting, the power control lever must be moved from the initial position to the final position in not more than one second except for movements into the fuel burning thrust augmentor augmentation position if additional time to confirm ignition is necessary.

(ii) During the runs at any rated augmented thrust the hydraulic fluid temperature must be maintained at the limiting temperature except where the test periods are not long enough to allow stabilization.

(iii) During the simulated supersonic runs the fuel temperature and induction air temperature may not be less than the limiting temperature.

(iv) The endurance test must be conducted with the fuel burning thrust augmentor installed, with the primary and secondary exhaust nozzles installed, and with the variable area exhaust nozzles operated during each run according to the methods specified in complying with §33.5(b).

(v) During the runs at thrust settings for maximum continuous thrust and percentages thereof, the engine must be operated with the inlet air distortion at the limit for those thrust settings.

(b) *Engines other than certain rotorcraft engines.* For each engine except a rotorcraft engine for which a rating is desired under paragraph (c), (d), or (e) of this section, the applicant must conduct the following runs:

(1) *Takeoff and idling.* One hour of alternate five-minute periods at rated takeoff power and thrust and at idling power and thrust. The developed powers and thrusts at takeoff and idling conditions and their corresponding rotor speed and gas temperature conditions must be as established by the power control in accordance with the schedule established by the manufacturer. The applicant may, during any one period, manually control the rotor speed, power, and thrust while taking data to check performance. For engines with augmented takeoff power ratings that involve increases in turbine inlet temperature, rotor speed, or shaft power, this period of running at takeoff must be at the augmented rating. For engines with augmented takeoff power ratings that do not materially increase operating severity, the amount of running conducted at the augmented rating is determined by the Administrator. In changing the power setting after each period, the power-control lever must be moved in the manner prescribed in paragraph (b)(5) of this section.

(2) *Rated maximum continuous and takeoff power and thrust.* Thirty minutes at—

(i) Rated maximum continuous power and thrust during fifteen of the twenty-five 6-hour endurance test cycles; and

(ii) Rated takeoff power and thrust during ten of the twenty-five 6-hour endurance test cycles.

(3) *Rated maximum continuous power and thrust.* One hour and 30 minutes at rated maximum continuous power and thrust.

(4) *Incremental cruise power and thrust.* Two hours and 30 minutes at the successive power lever positions corresponding to at least 15 approximately equal speed and time increments between maximum continuous engine rotational speed and ground or minimum idle rotational speed. For engines operating at constant speed, the thrust and power may be varied in place of speed. If there is significant peak vibration anywhere between ground idle and maximum continuous conditions, the number of increments chosen may be changed to increase the amount of running made while subject to the peak vibrations up to not more than 50 percent of the total time spent in incremental running.

(5) *Acceleration and deceleration runs.* 30 minutes of accelerations and decelerations, consisting of six cycles from idling power and thrust to rated takeoff power and thrust and maintained at the takeoff power lever position for 30 seconds

and at the idling power lever position for approximately four and one-half minutes. In complying with this paragraph, the power-control lever must be moved from one extreme position to the other in not more than one second, except that, if different regimes of control operations are incorporated necessitating scheduling of the power-control lever motion in going from one extreme position to the other, a longer period of time is acceptable, but not more than two seconds.

(6) *Starts*. One hundred starts must be made, of which 25 starts must be preceded by at least a two-hour engine shutdown. There must be at least 10 false engine starts, pausing for the applicant's specified minimum fuel drainage time, before attempting a normal start. There must be at least 10 normal restarts with not longer than 15 minutes since engine shutdown. The remaining starts may be made after completing the 150 hours of endurance testing.

(c) *Rotorcraft engines for which a 30-minute OEI power rating is desired.* For each rotorcraft engine for which a 30-minute OEI power rating is desired, the applicant must conduct the following series of tests:

(1) *Takeoff and idling*. One hour of alternate 5-minute periods at rated takeoff power and at idling power. The developed powers at takeoff and idling conditions and their corresponding rotor speed and gas temperature conditions must be as established by the power control in accordance with the schedule established by the manufacturer. During any one period, the rotor speed and power may be controlled manually while taking data to check performance. For engines with augmented takeoff power ratings that involve increases in turbine inlet temperature, rotor speed, or shaft power, this period of running at rated takeoff power must be at the augmented power rating. In changing the power setting after each period, the power control lever must be moved in the manner prescribed in paragraph (c)(5) of this section.

(2) *Rated 30-minute OEI power.* Thirty minutes at rated 30-minute OEI power.

(3) *Rated maximum continuous power.* Two hours at rated maximum continuous power.

(4) *Incremental cruise power.* Two hours at the successive power lever positions corresponding with not less than 12 approximately equal speed and time increments between maximum continuous engine rotational speed and ground or minimum idle rotational speed. For engines operating at constant speed, power may be varied in place of speed. If there are significant peak vibrations anywhere between ground idle and maximum continuous conditions, the number of increments chosen must be changed to increase the amount of running conducted while being subjected to the peak vibrations up to not more than 50 percent of the total time spent in incremental running.

(5) *Acceleration and deceleration runs.* Thirty minutes of accelerations and decelerations, consisting of six cycles from idling power to rated takeoff power and maintained at the takeoff power lever position for 30 seconds and at the idling power lever position for approximately $4\frac{1}{2}$ minutes. In complying with this paragraph, the power control lever must be moved from one extreme position to the other in not more than 1 second, except that if different regimes of control operations are incorporated necessitating scheduling of the power control lever motion in going from one extreme position to the other, a longer period of time is acceptable, but not more than 2 seconds.

(6) *Starts*. One hundred starts, of which 25 starts must be preceded by at least a two-hour engine shutdown. There must be at least 10 false engine starts, pausing for the applicant's specified minimum fuel drainage time, before attempting a normal start. There must be at least 10 normal restarts with not longer than 15 minutes since engine shutdown. The remaining starts may be made after completing the 150 hours of endurance testing.

(d) *Rotorcraft engines for which a continuous OEI rating is desired.* For each rotorcraft engine for which a continuous OEI power rating is desired, the applicant must conduct the following series of tests:

(1) *Takeoff and idling.* One hour of alternate 5-minute periods at rated takeoff power and at idling power. The developed powers at takeoff and idling conditions and their corresponding rotor speed and gas temperature conditions must be as established by the power control in accordance with the schedule established by the manufacturer. During any one period the rotor speed and power may be controlled manually while taking data to check performance. For engines with augmented takeoff power ratings that involve increases in turbine inlet temperature, rotor speed, or shaft power, this period of running at rated takeoff power must be at the augmented power rating. In changing the power setting after each period, the power control lever must be moved in the manner prescribed in paragraph (c)(5) of this section.

(2) *Rated maximum continuous and takeoff power.* Thirty minutes at—

(i) Rated maximum continuous power during fifteen of the twenty-five 6-hour endurance test cycles; and

(ii) Rated takeoff power during ten of the twenty-five 6-hour endurance test cycles.

(3) *Rated continuous OEI power.* One hour at rated continuous OEI power.

(4) *Rated maximum continuous power.* One hour at rated maximum continuous power.

(5) *Incremental cruise power.* Two hours at the successive power lever positions corresponding with not less than 12 approximately equal speed and time increments between maximum continuous engine rotational speed and ground or minimum idle rotational speed. For engines operating at constant speed, power may be varied in place of speed. If there are significant peak vibrations anywhere between ground idle and maximum continuous conditions, the number of increments chosen must be changed to increase the amount of running conducted while being subjected to the peak vibrations up to not more than 50 percent of the total time spent in incremental running.

(6) *Acceleration and deceleration runs.* Thirty minutes of accelerations and decelerations, consisting of six cycles from idling power to rated takeoff power and maintained at the takeoff power lever position for 30 seconds and at the idling power lever position for approximately $4\frac{1}{2}$ minutes. In complying with this paragraph, the power control lever must be moved from one extreme position to the other in not more than 1 second, except that if different regimes of control operations are incorporated necessitating scheduling of the power control lever motion in going from one extreme posi-

tion to the other, a longer period of time is acceptable, but not more than 2 seconds.

(7) *Starts.* One hundred starts, of which 25 starts must be preceded by at least a 2-hour engine shutdown. There must be at least 10 false engine starts, pausing for the applicant's specified minimum fuel drainage time, before attempting a normal start. There must be at least 10 normal restarts with not longer than 15 minutes since engine shutdown. The remaining starts may be made after completing the 150 hours of endurance testing.

(e) *Rotorcraft engines for which a 2½-minute OEI power rating is desired.* For each rotorcraft engine for which a 2½-minute OEI power rating is desired, the applicant must conduct the following series of tests:

(1) *Takeoff, 2½-minute OEI, and idling.* One hour of alternate 5-minute periods at rated takeoff power and at idling power except that, during the third and sixth takeoff power periods, only 2½ minutes need be conducted at rated takeoff power, and the remaining 2½ minutes must be conducted at rated 2½-minute OEI power. The developed powers at takeoff, 2½-minute OEI, and idling conditions and their corresponding rotor speed and gas temperature conditions must be as established by the power control in accordance with the schedule established by the manufacturer. The applicant may, during any one period, control manually the rotor speed and power while taking data to check performance. For engines with augmented takeoff power ratings that involve increases in turbine inlet temperature, rotor speed, or shaft power, this period of running at rated takeoff power must be at the augmented rating. In changing the power setting after or during each period, the power control lever must be moved in the manner prescribed in paragraph (d)(6) of this section.

(2) The tests required in paragraphs (b)(2) through (b)(6), or (c)(2) through (c)(6), or (d)(2) through (d)(7) of this section, as applicable, except that in one of the 6-hour test sequences, the last 5 minutes of the 30 minutes at takeoff power test period of paragraph (b)(2) of this section, or of the 30 minutes at 30-minute OEI power test period of paragraph (c)(2) of this section, or of the 1 hour at continuous OEI power test period of paragraph (d)(3) of this section, must be run at 2½ minute OEI power.

(f) *Rotorcraft engines for which 30-second OEI and 2-minute OEI ratings are desired.* For each rotorcraft engine for which 30-second OEI and 2-minute OEI power ratings are desired, and following completion of the tests under paragraphs (b), (c), (d), or (e) of this section, the applicant may disassemble the tested engine to the extent necessary to show compliance with the requirements of §33.93(a). The tested engine must then be reassembled using the same parts used during the test runs of paragraphs (b), (c), (d), or (e) of this section, except those parts described as consumables in the Instructions for Continued Airworthiness. The applicant must then conduct the following test sequence four times, for a total time of not less than 120 minutes:

(1) *Takeoff power.* Three minutes at rated takeoff power.

(2) *30-second OEI power.* Thirty seconds at rated 30-second OEI power.

(3) *2-minute OEI power.* Two minutes at rated 2-minute OEI power.

(4) *30-minute OEI power, continuous OEI power, or maximum continuous power.* Five minutes at rated 30-minute OEI power, rated continuous OEI power, or rated maximum continuous power, whichever is greatest, except that, during the first test sequence, this period shall be 65 minutes.

(5) *50 percent takeoff power.* One minute at 50 percent takeoff power.

(6) *30-second OEI power.* Thirty seconds at rated 30-second OEI power.

(7) *2-minute OEI power.* Two minutes at rated 2-minute OEI power.

(8) *Idle.* One minute at idle.

(g) *Supersonic aircraft engines.* For each engine type certificated for use on supersonic aircraft the applicant must conduct the following:

(1) *Subsonic test under sea level ambient atmospheric conditions.* Thirty runs of one hour each must be made, consisting of—

(i) Two periods of 5 minutes at rated takeoff augmented thrust each followed by 5 minutes at idle thrust;

(ii) One period of 5 minutes at rated takeoff thrust followed by 5 minutes at not more than 15 percent of rated takeoff thrust;

(iii) One period of 10 minutes at rated takeoff augmented thrust followed by 2 minutes at idle thrust, except that if rated maximum continuous augmented thrust is lower than rated takeoff augmented thrust, 5 of the 10-minute periods must be at rated maximum continuous augmented thrust; and

(iv) Six periods of 1 minute at rated takeoff augmented thrust each followed by 2 minutes, including acceleration and deceleration time, at idle thrust.

(2) *Simulated supersonic test.* Each run of the simulated supersonic test must be preceded by changing the inlet air temperature and pressure from that attained at subsonic condition to the temperature and pressure attained at supersonic velocity, and must be followed by a return to the temperature attained at subsonic condition. Thirty runs of 4 hours each must be made, consisting of—

(i) One period of 30 minutes at the thrust obtained with the power control lever set at the position for rated maximum continuous augmented thrust followed by 10 minutes at the thrust obtained with the power control lever set at the position for 90 percent of rated maximum continuous augmented thrust. The end of this period in the first five runs must be made with the induction air temperature at the limiting condition of transient overtemperature, but need not be repeated during the periods specified in paragraphs (g)(2)(ii) through (iv) of this section;

(ii) One period repeating the run specified in paragraph (g)(2)(i) of this section, except that it must be followed by 10 minutes at the thrust obtained with the power control lever set at the position for 80 percent of rated maximum continuous augmented thrust;

(iii) One period repeating the run specified in paragraph (g)(2)(i) of this section, except that it must be followed by 10 minutes at the thrust obtained with the power control lever set at the position for 60 percent of rated maximum continuous augmented thrust and then 10 minutes at not more than 15 percent of rated takeoff thrust;

(iv) One period repeating the runs specified in paragraphs (g)(2)(i) and (ii) of this section; and

(v) One period of 30 minutes with 25 of the runs made at the thrust obtained with the power control lever set at the position for rated maximum continuous augmented thrust, each followed by idle thrust and with the remaining 5 runs at the thrust obtained with the power control lever set at the position for rated maximum continuous augmented thrust for 25 minutes each, followed by subsonic operation at not more than 15 percent or rated takeoff thrust and accelerated to rated takeoff thrust for 5 minutes using hot fuel.

(3) *Starts.* One hundred starts must be made, of which 25 starts must be preceded by an engine shutdown of at least 2 hours. There must be at least 10 false engine starts, pausing for the applicant's specified minimum fuel drainage time before attempting a normal start. At least 10 starts must be normal restarts, each made no later than 15 minutes after engine shutdown. The starts may be made at any time, including the period of endurance testing.

[Docket No. 3025, 29 FR 7453, June 10, 1964, as amended by Amdt. 33–3, 32 FR 3737, Mar. 4, 1967; Amdt. 33–6, 39 FR 35468, Oct. 1, 1974; Amdt. 33–10, 49 FR 6853, Feb. 23, 1984; Amdt. 33–12, 53 FR 34220, Sept. 2, 1988; Amdt. 33–18, 61 FR 31328, June 19, 1996]

§33.88 Engine overtemperature test.

(a) Each engine must run for 5 minutes at maximum permissible rpm with the gas temperature at least 75° F (42° C) higher than the maximum rating's steady-state operating limit, excluding maximum values of rpm and gas temperature associated with the 30-second OEI and 2-minute OEI ratings. Following this run, the turbine assembly must be within serviceable limits.

(b) Each engine for which 30-second OEI and 2-minute OEI ratings are desired, that does not incorporate a means to limit temperature, must be run for a period of 5 minutes at the maximum power-on rpm with the gas temperature at least 75° F (42° C) higher than the 30-second OEI rating operating limit. Following this run, the turbine assembly may exhibit distress beyond the limits for an overtemperature condition provided the engine is shown by analysis or test, as found necessary by the Administrator, to maintain the integrity of the turbine assembly.

(c) Each engine for which 30-second OEI and 2-minute OEI ratings are desired, that incorporates a means to limit temperature, must be run for a period of 4 minutes at the maximum power-on rpm with the gas temperature at least 35° F (20° C) higher than the maximum operating limit. Following this run, the turbine assembly may exhibit distress beyond the limits for an overtemperature condition provided the engine is shown by analysis or test, as found necessary by the Administrator, to maintain the integrity of the turbine assembly.

(d) A separate test vehicle may be used for each test condition.

[Docket No. 26019, 61 FR 31329, June 19, 1996]

§33.89 Operation test.

(a) The operation test must include testing found necessary by the Administrator to demonstrate—

(1) Starting, idling, acceleration, overspeeding, ignition, functioning of the propeller (if the engine is designated to operate with a propeller);

(2) Compliance with the engine response requirements of §33.73; and

(3) The minimum power or thrust response time to 95 percent rated takeoff power or thrust, from power lever positions representative of minimum idle and of minimum flight idle, starting from stabilized idle operation, under the following engine load conditions:

(i) No bleed air and power extraction for aircraft use.

(ii) Maximum allowable bleed air and power extraction for aircraft use.

(iii) An intermediate value for bleed air and power extraction representative of that which might be used as a maximum for aircraft during approach to a landing.

(4) If testing facilities are not available, the determination of power extraction required in paragraph (a)(3)(ii) and (iii) of this section may be accomplished through appropriate analytical means.

(b) The operation test must include all testing found necessary by the Administrator to demonstrate that the engine has safe operating characteristics throughout its specified operating envelope.

[Amdt. 33–4, 36 FR 5493, Mar. 24, 1971, as amended by Amdt. 33–6, 39 FR 35469, Oct. 1, 1974; Amdt. 33–10, 49 FR 6853, Feb. 23, 1984]

§33.90 Initial maintenance inspection.

Each engine, except engines being type certificated through amendment of an existing type certificate or through supplemental type certification procedures, must undergo an approved test run that simulates the conditions in which the engine is expected to operate in service, including typical start-stop cycles, to establish when the initial maintenance inspection is required. The test run must be accomplished on an engine which substantially conforms to the final type design.

[Amdt. 33–10, 49 FR 6854, Feb. 23, 1984]

§33.91 Engine component tests.

(a) For those systems that cannot be adequately substantiated by endurance testing in accordance with the provisions of §33.87, additional tests must be made to establish that components are able to function reliably in all normally anticipated flight and atmospheric conditions.

(b) Temperature limits must be established for those components that require temperature controlling provisions in the aircraft installation to assure satisfactory functioning, reliability, and durability.

(c) Each unpressurized hydraulic fluid tank may not fail or leak when subjected to maximum operating temperature and an internal pressure of 5 p.s.i., and each pressurized hydraulic fluid tank may not fail or leak when subjected to maximum operating temperature and an internal pressure not less than 5 p.s.i. plus the maximum operating pressure of the tank.

(d) For an engine type certificated for use in supersonic aircraft, the systems, safety devices, and external components that may fail because of operation at maximum and minimum operating temperatures must be identified and tested at maximum and minimum operating temperatures and while temperature and other operating conditions are cycled between maximum and minimum operating values.

[Docket No. 3025, 29 FR 7453, June 10, 1964, as amended by Amdt. 33–6, 39 FR 35469, Oct. 1, 1974]

§33.92 Rotor locking tests.

If continued rotation is prevented by a means to lock the rotor(s), the engine must be subjected to a test that includes 25 operations of this means under the following conditions:

(a) The engine must be shut down from rated maximum continuous thrust or power; and

(b) The means for stopping and locking the rotor(s) must be operated as specified in the engine operating instructions while being subjected to the maximum torque that could result from continued flight in this condition; and

(c) Following rotor locking, the rotor(s) must be held stationary under these conditions for five minutes for each of the 25 operations.

[Docket No. 28107, 61 FR 28433, June 4, 1996]

§33.93 Teardown inspection.

(a) After completing the endurance testing of §33.87 (b), (c), (d), (e), or (g) of this part, each engine must be completely disassembled, and

(1) Each component having an adjustment setting and a functioning characteristic that can be established independent of installation on the engine must retain each setting and functioning characteristic within the limits that were established and recorded at the beginning of the test; and

(2) Each engine part must conform to the type design and be eligible for incorporation into an engine for continued operation, in accordance with information submitted in compliance with §33.4.

(b) After completing the endurance testing of §33.87(f), each engine must be completely disassembled, and

(1) Each component having an adjustment setting and a functioning characteristic that can be established independent of installation on the engine must retain each setting and functioning characteristic within the limits that were established and recorded at the beginning of the test; and

(2) Each engine may exhibit deterioration in excess of that permitted in paragraph (a)(2) of this section including some engine parts or components that may be unsuitable for further use. The applicant must show by analysis and/or test, as found necessary by the Administrator, that structural integrity of the engine including mounts, cases, bearing supports, shafts, and rotors, is maintained; or

(c) In lieu of compliance with paragraph (b) of this section, each engine for which the 30-second OEI and 2-minute OEI ratings are desired, may be subjected to the endurance testing of §§33.87 (b), (c), (d), or (e) of this part, and followed by the testing of §33.87(f) without intervening disassembly and inspection. However, the engine must comply with paragraph (a) of this section after completing the endurance testing of §33.87(f).

[Docket No. 26019, 61 FR 31329, June 19, 1996]

§33.94 Blade containment and rotor unbalance tests.

(a) Except as provided in paragraph (b) of this section, it must be demonstrated by engine tests that the engine is capable of containing damage without catching fire and without failure of its mounting attachments when operated for at least 15 seconds, unless the resulting engine damage induces a self shutdown, after each of the following events:

(1) Failure of the most critical compressor or fan blade while operating at maximum permissible r.p.m. The blade failure must occur at the outermost retention groove or, for integrally-bladed rotor discs, at least 80 percent of the blade must fail.

(2) Failure of the most critical turbine blade while operating at maximum permissible r.p.m. The blade failure must occur at the outermost retention groove or, for integrally-bladed rotor discs, at least 80 percent of the blade must fail. The most critical turbine blade must be determined by considering turbine blade weight and the strength of the adjacent turbine case at case temperatures and pressures associated with operation at maximum permissible r.p.m.

(b) Analysis based on rig testing, component testing, or service experience may be substitute for one of the engine tests prescribed in paragraphs (a)(1) and (a)(2) of this section if—

(1) That test, of the two prescribed, produces the least rotor unbalance; and

(2) The analysis is shown to be equivalent to the test.

(Secs. 313(a), 601, and 603, Federal Aviation Act of 1958 (49 U.S.C. 1354(a), 1421, and 1423); and 49 U.S.C. 106(g) Revised, Pub. L. 97–449, Jan. 12, 1983)

[Amdt. 33–10, 49 FR 6854, Feb. 23, 1984]

§33.95 Engine-propeller systems tests.

If the engine is designed to operate with a propeller, the following tests must be made with a representative propeller installed by either including the tests in the endurance run or otherwise performing them in a manner acceptable to the Administrator:

(a) Feathering operation: 25 cycles.

(b) Negative torque and thrust system operation: 25 cycles from rated maximum continuous power.

(c) Automatic decoupler operation: 25 cycles from rated maximum continuous power (if repeated decoupling and recoupling in service is the intended function of the device).

(d) Reverse thrust operation: 175 cycles from the flight-idle position to full reverse and 25 cycles at rated maximum continuous power from full forward to full reverse thrust. At the end of each cycle the propeller must be operated in reverse pitch for a period of 30 seconds at the maximum rotational speed and power specified by the applicant for reverse pitch operation.

[Docket No. 3025, 29 FR 7453, June 10, 1964, as amended by Amdt. 33–3, 32 FR 3737, Mar. 4, 1967]

§33.96 Engine tests in auxiliary power unit (APU) mode.

If the engine is designed with a propeller brake which will allow the propeller to be brought to a stop while the gas generator portion of the engine remains in operation, and remain stopped during operation of the engine as an auxiliary power unit ("APU mode"), in addition to the requirements of §33.87, the applicant must conduct the following tests:

(a) Ground locking*:* A total of 45 hours with the propeller brake engaged in a manner which clearly demonstrates its ability to function without adverse effects on the complete engine while the engine is operating in the APU mode under the maximum conditions of engine speed, torque, temperature, air bleed, and power extraction as specified by the applicant.

(b) Dynamic braking*:* A total of 400 application-release cycles of brake engagements must be made in a manner which clearly demonstrates its ability to function without adverse effects on the complete engine under the maximum conditions of engine acceleration/deceleration rate, speed, torque, and temperature as specified by the applicant. The propeller must be stopped prior to brake release.

(c) One hundred engine starts and stops with the propeller brake engaged.

(d) The tests required by paragraphs (a), (b), and (c) of this section must be performed on the same engine, but this engine need not be the same engine used for the tests required by §33.87.

(e) The tests required by paragraphs (a), (b), and (c) of this section must be followed by engine disassembly to the extent necessary to show compliance with the requirements of §33.93(a) and §33.93(b).

[Amdt. 33–11, 51 FR 10346, Mar. 25, 1986]

§33.97 Thrust reversers.

(a) If the engine incorporates a reverser, the endurance calibration, operation, and vibration tests prescribed in this subpart must be run with the reverser installed. In complying with this section, the power control lever must be moved from one extreme position to the other in not more than one second except, if regimes of control operations are incorporated necessitating scheduling of the power-control lever motion in going from one extreme position to the other, a longer period of time is acceptable but not more than three seconds. In addition, the test prescribed in paragraph (b) of this section must be made. This test may be scheduled as part of the endurance run.

(b) 175 reversals must be made from flight-idle forward thrust to maximum reverse thrust and 25 reversals must be made from rated takeoff thrust to maximum reverse thrust. After each reversal the reverser must be operated at full reverse thrust for a period of one minute, except that, in the case of a reverser intended for use only as a braking means on the ground, the reverser need only be operated at full reverse thrust for 30 seconds.

[Docket No. 3025, 29 FR 7453, June 10, 1964, as amended by Amdt. 33–3, 32 FR 3737, Mar. 4, 1967]

§33.99 General conduct of block tests.

(a) Each applicant may, in making a block test, use separate engines of identical design and construction in the vibration, calibration, endurance, and operation tests, except that, if a separate engine is used for the endurance test it must be subjected to a calibration check before starting the endurance test.

(b) Each applicant may service and make minor repairs to the engine during the block tests in accordance with the service and maintenance instructions submitted in compliance with §33.4. If the frequency of the service is excessive, or the number of stops due to engine malfunction is excessive, or a major repair, or replacement of a part is found necessary during the block tests or as the result of findings from the teardown inspection, the engine or its parts must be subjected to any additional tests the Administrator finds necessary.

(c) Each applicant must furnish all testing facilities, including equipment and competent personnel, to conduct the block tests.

[Docket No. 3025, 29 FR 7453, June 10, 1964, as amended by Amdt. 33–6, 39 FR 35470, Oct. 1, 1974; Amdt. 33–9, 45 FR 60181, Sept. 11, 1980]

Appendix A to Part 33

Instructions for Continued Airworthiness

A33.1 General

(a) This appendix specifies requirements for the preparation of Instructions for Continued Airworthiness as required by §33.4.

(b) The Instructions for Continued Airworthiness for each engine must include the Instructions for Continued Airworthiness for all engine parts. If Instructions for Continued Airworthiness are not supplied by the engine part manufacturer for an engine part, the Instructions for Continued Airworthiness for the engine must include the information essential to the continued airworthiness of the engine.

(c) The applicant must submit to the FAA a program to show how changes to the Instructions for Continued Airworthiness made by the applicant or by the manufacturers of engine parts will be distributed.

A33.2 Format

(a) The Instructions for Continued Airworthiness must be in the form of a manual or manuals as appropriate for the quantity of data to be provided.

(b) The format of the manual or manuals must provide for a practical arrangement.

A33.3 Content

The contents of the manual or manuals must be prepared in the English language. The Instructions for Continued Airworthiness must contain the following manuals or sections, as appropriate, and information:

(a) *Engine Maintenance Manual or Section.*

(1) Introduction information that includes an explanation of the engine's features and data to the extent necessary for maintenance or preventive maintenance.

(2) A detailed description of the engine and its components, systems, and installations.

(3) Installation instructions, including proper procedures for uncrating, deinhibiting, acceptance checking, lifting, and attaching accessories, with any necessary checks.

(4) Basic control and operating information describing how the engine components, systems, and installations operate, and information describing the methods of starting, running, testing, and stopping the engine and its parts including any special procedures and limitations that apply.

(5) Servicing information that covers details regarding servicing points, capacities of tanks, reservoirs, types of fluids to be used, pressures applicable to the various systems, locations of lubrication points, lubricants to be used, and equipment required for servicing.

(6) Scheduling information for each part of the engine that provides the recommended periods at which it should be cleaned, inspected, adjusted, tested, and lubricated, and the degree of inspection the applicable wear tolerances, and work recommended at these periods. However, the applicant may refer to an accessory, instrument, or equipment manufacturer as the source of this information if the applicant shows that the item has an exceptionally high degree of complexity requiring specialized maintenance techniques, test equipment, or expertise. The recommended overhaul periods and necessary cross references to the Airworthiness Limitations section of the manual must also be included. In addition, the applicant must include an inspection program that includes the frequency and extent of the inspections necessary to provide for the continued airworthiness of the engine.

(7) Troubleshooting information describing probable malfunctions, how to recognize those malfunctions, and the remedial action for those malfunctions.

(8) Information describing the order and method of removing the engine and its parts and replacing parts, with any necessary precautions to be taken. Instructions for proper ground handling, crating, and shipping must also be included.

(9) A list of the tools and equipment necessary for maintenance and directions as to their method of use.

(b) *Engine Overhaul Manual or Section.*

(1) Disassembly information including the order and method of disassembly for overhaul.

(2) Cleaning and inspection instructions that cover the materials and apparatus to be used and methods and precautions to be taken during overhaul. Methods of overhaul inspection must also be included.

(3) Details of all fits and clearances relevant to overhaul.

(4) Details of repair methods for worn or otherwise substandard parts and components along with the information necessary to determine when replacement is necessary.

(5) The order and method of assembly at overhaul.

(6) Instructions for testing after overhaul.

(7) Instructions for storage preparation, including any storage limits.

(8) A list of tools needed for overhaul.

A33.4 Airworthiness Limitations Section

The Instructions for Continued Airworthiness must contain a section titled Airworthiness Limitations that is segregated and clearly distinguishable from the rest of the document. This section must set forth each mandatory replacement time, inspection interval, and related procedure required for type certification. If the Instructions for Continued Airworthiness consist of multiple documents, the section required by this paragraph must be included in the principal manual. This section must contain a legible statement in a prominent location that reads: "The Airworthiness Limitations section is FAA approved and specifies maintenance required under §§43.16 and 91.403 of the Federal Aviation Regulations unless an alternative program has been FAA approved."

[Amdt. 33–9, 45 FR 60181, Sept. 11, 1980, as amended by Amdt. 33–13, 54 FR 34330, Aug. 18, 1989]

Appendix B to Part 33

Certification Standard Atmospheric Concentrations of Rain and Hail

Figure B1, Table B1, Table B2, Table B3, and Table B4 specify the atmospheric concentrations and size distributions of rain and hail for establishing certification, in accordance with the requirements of §33.78(a)(2). In conducting tests, normally by spraying liquid water to simulate rain conditions and by delivering hail fabricated from ice to simulate hail conditions, the use of water droplets and hail having shapes, sizes and distributions of sizes other than those defined in this appendix B, or the use of a single size or shape for each water droplet or hail, can be accepted, provided that applicant shows that the substitution does not reduce the severity of the test.

[See Figure B1 on the next page.]

FIGURE B1 – Illustration of Rain and Hail Threats. Certification concentrations are obtained using Tables B1 and B2.

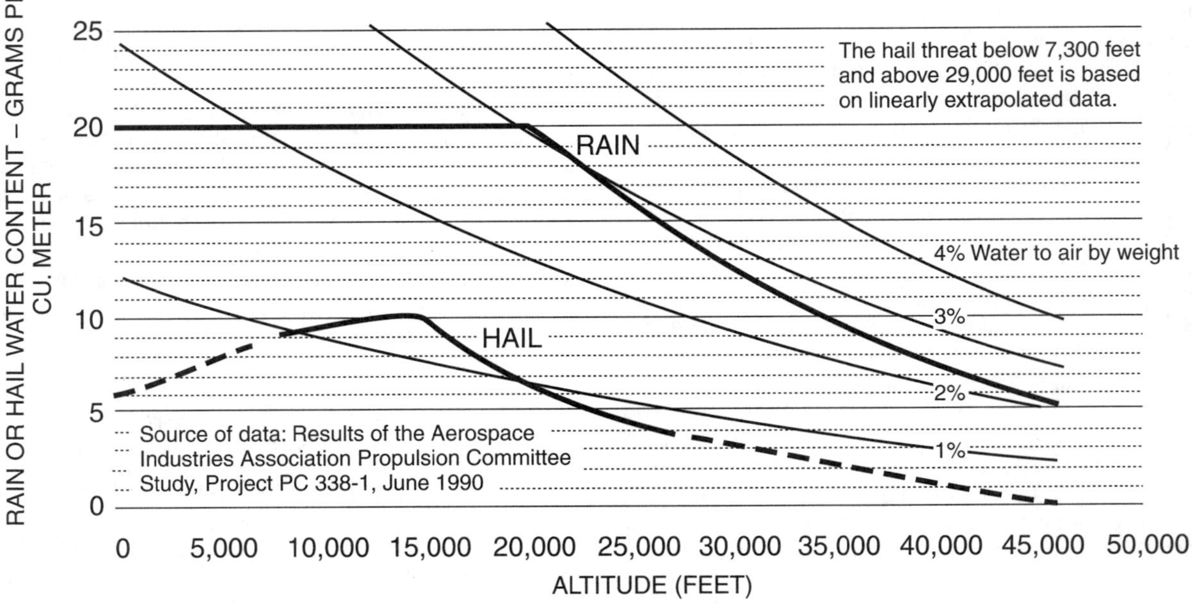

TABLE B1.
CERTIFICATION STANDARD ATMOSPHERIC RAIN CONCENTRATIONS

Altitude (feet)	Rain water content (RWC) (grams water/meter³ air)
0	20.0
20,000	20.0
26,300	15.2
32,700	10.8
39,300	7.7
46,000	5.2

RWC values at other altitudes may be determined by linear interpolation.

Note: Source of data – Results of the Aerospace Industries Association (AIA) Propulsion Committee Study, Project PC 338–1, June 1990.

TABLE B2.
CERTIFICATION STANDARD ATMOSPHERIC HAIL CONCENTRATIONS

Altitude (feet)	Hail water content (HWC) (grams water/meter³ air)
0	6.0
7,300	8.9
8,500	9.4
10,000	9.9
12,000	10.0
15,000	10.0
16,000	8.9
17,700	7.8
19,300	6.6
21,500	5.6
24,300	4.4
29,000	3.3
46,000	0.2

HWC values at other altitudes may be determined by linear interpolation. The hail threat below 7,300 feet and above 29,000 feet is based on linearly extrapolated data.

Note: Source of data – Results of the Aerospace Industries Association (AIA) Propulsion Committee (PC) Study, Project PC 338–1, June 1990.

TABLE B3.
CERTIFICATION STANDARD ATMOSPHERIC
RAIN DROPLET SIZE DISTRIBUTION

Rain droplet diameter (mm)	Contribution total RWC (%)
0–0.49	0
0.50–0.99	2.25
1.00–1.49	8.75
1.50–1.99	16.25
2.00–2.49	19.00
2.50–2.99	17.75
3.00–3.49	13.50
3.50–3.99	9.50
4.00–4.49	6.00
4.50–4.99	3.00
5.00–5.49	2.00
5.50–5.99	1.25
6.00–6.49	0.50
6.50–7.00	0.25
Total	100.00

Median diameter of rain droplets is 2.66 mm.

Note: Source of data–Results of the Aerospace Industries Association (AIA) Propulsion Committee (PC) Study, Project PC 338–1, June 1990.

TABLE B4.
CERTIFICATION STANDARD ATMOSPHERIC
HAIL SIZE DISTRIBUTION

Hail diameter (mm)	Contribution total HWC (%)
0–4.9	0
5.0–9.9	17.00
10.0–14.9	25.00
15.0–19.9	22.50
20.0–24.9	16.00
25.0–29.9	9.75
30.0–34.9	4.75
35.0–39.9	2.50
40.0–44.9	1.50
45.0–49.9	0.75
50.0–55.0	0.25
Total	100.00

Median diameter of hail is 16 mm.

Note: Source of data–Results of the Aerospace Industries Association (AIA) Propulsion Committee (PC) Study, Project PC 338–1, June 1990.

[Docket No. 28652, 63 FR 14799, March 26, 1998]

PART 34
FUEL VENTING AND EXHAUST EMISSION REQUIREMENTS FOR TURBINE ENGINE POWERED AIRPLANES

Subpart A—General Provisions

Sec.
34.1 Definitions.
34.2 Abbreviations.
34.3 General requirements.
34.4 [Reserved]
34.5 Special test procedures.
34.6 Aircraft safety.
34.7 Exemptions.

Subpart B—
Engine Fuel Venting Emissions
(New and In-Use Aircraft Gas Turbine Engines)

34.10 Applicability.
34.11 Standard for fuel venting emissions.

Subpart C—
Exhaust Emissions (New Aircraft Gas Turbine Engines)

34.20 Applicability.
34.21 Standards for exhaust emissions.

Subpart D—
Exhaust Emissions
(In-Use Aircraft Gas Turbine Engines)

34.30 Applicability.
34.31 Standards for exhaust emissions.

Subpart E–F [Reserved]

Subpart G—
Test Procedures for Engine Exhaust Gaseous Emissions (Aircraft and Aircraft Gas Turbine Engines)

34.60 Introduction.
34.61 Turbine fuel specifications.
34.62 Test procedure (propulsion engines).
34.63 [Reserved]
34.64 Sampling and analytical procedures for measuring gaseous exhaust emissions.
34.65–34.70 [Reserved]
34.71 Compliance with gaseous emission standards.

Subpart H—
Test Procedures for Engine Smoke Emissions
(Aircraft Gas Turbine Engines)

34.80 Introduction.
34.81 Fuel specifications.
34.82 Sampling and analytical procedures for measuring smoke exhaust emissions.
34.83–34.88 [Reserved]
34.89 Compliance with smoke emission standards.

Authority: 42 U.S.C. 4321 et seq., 7572; 49 U.S.C. 106(g), 40113, 44701–44702, 44704, 44714.

Source: Docket No. 25613, 55 FR 32861, Aug. 10, 1990, unless otherwise noted.

Subpart A—General Provisions

§34.1 Definitions.

As used in this part, all terms not defined herein shall have the meaning given them in the Clean Air Act, as amended (42 U.S.C. 7401 et. seq.):

Act means the Clean Air Act, as amended (42 U.S.C. 7401 et. seq.).

Administrator means the Administrator of the Federal Aviation Administration or any person to whom he has delegated his authority in the matter concerned.

Administrator of the EPA means the Administrator of the Environmental Protection Agency and any other officer or employee of the Environmental Protection Agency to whom the authority involved may be delegated.

Aircraft as used in this part means any airplane as defined in 14 CFR part 1 for which a U.S. standard airworthiness certificate or equivalent foreign airworthiness certificate is issued.

Aircraft engine means a propulsion engine which is installed in, or which is manufactured for installation in, an aircraft.

Aircraft gas turbine engine means a turboprop, turbofan, or turbojet aircraft engine.

Class TP means all aircraft turboprop engines.

Class TF means all turbofan or turbojet aircraft engines or aircraft engines designed for applications that otherwise would have been fulfilled by turbojet and turbofan engines except engines of class T3, T8, and TSS.

Class T3 means all aircraft gas turbine engines of the JT3D model family.

Class T8 means all aircraft gas turbine engines of the JT8D model family.

Class TSS means all aircraft gas turbine engines employed for propulsion of aircraft designed to operate at supersonic flight speeds.

Commercial aircraft engine means any aircraft engine used or intended for use by an "air carrier" (including those engaged in "intrastate air transportation") or a "commercial operator" (including those engaged in "intrastate air transportation") as these terms are defined in the Federal Aviation Act and the Federal Aviation Regulations.

Commercial aircraft gas turbine engine means a turboprop, turbofan, or turbojet commercial aircraft engine.

Date of manufacture of an engine is the date the inspection acceptance records reflect that the engine is complete and meets the FAA approved type design.

Emission measurement system means all of the equipment necessary to transport the emission sample and measure the level of emissions. This includes the sample system and the instrumentation system.

Engine model means all commercial aircraft turbine engines which are of the same general series, displacement, and design characteristics and are approved under the same type certificate.

Exhaust emissions means substances emitted into the atmosphere from the exhaust discharge nozzle of an aircraft or aircraft engine.

Fuel venting emissions means raw fuel, exclusive of hydrocarbons in the exhaust emissions, discharged from aircraft gas turbine engines during all normal ground and flight operations.

In-use aircraft gas turbine engine means an aircraft gas turbine engine which is in service.

New aircraft turbine engine means an aircraft gas turbine engine which has never been in service.

Power setting means the power or thrust output of an engine in terms of kilonewtons thrust for turbojet and turbofan engines or shaft power in terms of kilowatts for turboprop engines.

Rated output (rO) means the maximum power/thrust available for takeoff at standard day conditions as approved for the engine by the Federal Aviation Administration, including reheat contribution where applicable, but excluding any contribution due to water injection and excluding any emergency power/thrust rating.

Rated pressure ratio (rPR) means the ratio between the combustor inlet pressure and the engine inlet pressure achieved by an engine operation at rated output.

Reference day conditions means the reference ambient conditions to which the gaseous emissions (HC and smoke) are to be corrected. The reference day conditions are as follows: Temperature=15°C, specific humidity=0.00629 kg H_2O/kg of dry air, and pressure=101325 Pa.

Sample system means the system which provides for the transportation of the gaseous emission sample from the sample probe to the inlet of the instrumentation system.

Shaft power means only the measured shaft power output of a turboprop engine.

Smoke means the matter in exhaust emissions which obscures the transmission of light.

Smoke number (SN) means the dimensionless term quantifying smoke emissions.

Standard day conditions means standard ambient conditions as described in the United States Standard Atmosphere 1976, (i.e., temperature=15°C, specific humidity=0.00 kg H_2O/kg dry air, and pressure=101325 Pa.)

Taxi/idle (in) means those aircraft operations involving taxi and idle between the time of landing roll-out and final shutdown of all propulsion engines.

Taxi/idle (out) means those aircraft operations involving taxi and idle between the time of initial starting of the propulsion engine(s) used for the taxi and the turn onto the duty runway.

[Docket No. 25613, 55 FR 32861, Aug. 10, 1990; 55 FR 37287, Sept. 10, 1990; as amended by Amdt. 34–3, 64 FR 5558, Feb. 3, 1999]

§34.2 Abbreviations.

The abbreviations used in this part have the following meanings in both upper and lower case:

CO	Carbon Monoxide
EPA	United States Environmental Protection Agency
FAA	Federal Aviation Administration, United States Department of Transportation
HC	Hydrocarbon(s)
HP	Horsepower
hr	Hour(s)
H_2O	Water
kg	Kilogram(s)
kJ	Kilojoule(s)
LTO	Landing and takeoff
min	Minute(s)
NO_X	Oxides of Nitrogen
Pa	Pascal(s)
rO	Rated output
rPR	Rated pressure ratio
sec	Second(s)
SP	Shaft power
SN	Smoke number
T	Temperature, degrees Kelvin
TIM	Time in mode
W	Watt(s)
°C	Degrees Celsius
%	Percent

[Docket No. 25613, 55 FR 32861, Aug. 10, 1990; as amended by Amdt. 34–3, 64 FR 5559, Feb. 3, 1999]

§34.3 General requirements.

(a) This part provides for the approval or acceptance by the Administrator or the Administrator of the EPA of testing and sampling methods, analytical techniques, and related equipment not identical to those specified in this part. Before either approves or accepts any such alternate, equivalent, or otherwise nonidentical procedures or equipment, the Administrator or the Administrator of the EPA shall consult with the other in determining whether or not the action requires rulemaking under sections 231 and 232 of the Clean Air Act, as amended, consistent with the responsibilities of the Administrator of the EPA and the Secretary of Transportation under sections 231 and 232 of the Clean Air Act.

(b) Under section 232 of the Act, the Secretary of Transportation issues regulations to ensure compliance with 40 CFR part 87. This authority has been delegated to the Administrator of the FAA (49 CFR 1.47).

(c) *U.S. airplanes.* This Federal Aviation Regulation (FAR) applies to civil airplanes that are powered by aircraft gas turbine engines of the classes specified herein and that have U.S. standard airworthiness certificates.

(d) *Foreign airplanes.* Pursuant to the definition of "aircraft" in 40 CFR 87.1(c), this FAR applies to civil airplanes that are powered by aircraft gas turbine engines of the classes specified herein and that have foreign airworthiness certificates that are equivalent to U.S. standard airworthiness certificates. This FAR applies only to those foreign civil airplanes that, if registered in the United States, would be required by applicable Federal Aviation Regulations to have a U.S. standard airworthiness certificate in order to conduct the operations intended for the airplane. Pursuant to 40 CFR 87.3(c), this FAR does not apply where it would be inconsistent with an obligation assumed by the United States to a foreign country in a treaty, convention, or agreement.

(e) Reference in this regulation to 40 CFR part 87 refers to title 40 of the Code of Federal Regulations, chapter I—Environmental Protection Agency, part 87, Control of Air Pollution from Aircraft and Aircraft Engines (40 CFR part 87).

(f) This part contains regulations to ensure compliance with certain standards contained in 40 CFR part 87. If EPA takes any action, including the issuance of an exemption or issuance of a revised or alternate procedure, test method, or other regulation, the effect of which is to relax or delay the effective date of any provision of 40 CFR part 87 that is made applicable to an aircraft under this FAR, the Administrator of FAA will grant a general administrative waiver of its more stringent requirements until this FAR is amended to reflect the more relaxed requirements prescribed by EPA.

(g) Unless otherwise stated, all terminology and abbreviations in this FAR that are defined in 40 CFR part 87 have the meaning specified in that part, and all terms in 40 CFR part 87 that are not defined in that part but that are used in this FAR have the meaning given them in the Clean Air Act, as amended by Public Law 91–604.

(h) All interpretations of 40 CFR part 87 that are rendered by the EPA also apply to this FAR.

(i) If the EPA, under 40 CFR 87.3(a), approves or accepts any testing and sampling procedures or methods, analytical techniques, or related equipment not identical to those specified in that part, this FAR requires an applicant to show that such alternate, equivalent, or otherwise nonidentical procedures have been complied with, and that such alternate equipment was used to show compliance, unless the applicant elects to comply with those procedures, methods, techniques, and equipment specified in 40 CFR part 87.

(j) If the EPA, under 40 CFR 87.5, prescribes special test procedures for any aircraft or aircraft engine that is not susceptible to satisfactory testing by the procedures in 40 CFR part 87, the applicant must show the Administrator that those special test procedures have been complied with.

(k) Wherever 40 CFR part 87 requires agreement, acceptance, or approval by the Administrator of the EPA, this FAR requires a showing that such agreement or approval has been obtained.

(l) Pursuant to 42 U.S.C. 7573, no state or political subdivision thereof may adopt or attempt to enforce any standard respecting emissions of any air pollutant from any aircraft or engine thereof unless that standard is identical to a standard made applicable to the aircraft by the terms of this FAR.

(m) If EPA, by regulation or exemption, relaxes a provision of 40 CFR part 87 that is implemented in this FAR, no state or political subdivision thereof may adopt or attempt to enforce the terms of this FAR that are superseded by the relaxed requirement.

(n) If any provision of this FAR is rendered inapplicable to a foreign aircraft as provided in 40 CFR 87.3(c) (international agreements), and §34.3(d) of this FAR, that provision may not be adopted or enforced against that foreign aircraft by a state or political subdivision thereof.

(o) For exhaust emissions requirements of this FAR that apply beginning February 1, 1974, January 1, 1976, January 1, 1978, January 1, 1984, and August 9, 1985, continued compliance with those requirements is shown for engines for which the type design has been shown to meet those requirements, if the engine is maintained in accordance with applicable maintenance requirements for 14 CFR chapter I. All methods of demonstrating compliance and all model designations previously found acceptable to the Administrator shall be deemed to continue to be an acceptable demonstration of compliance with the specific standards for which they were approved.

(p) Each applicant must allow the Administrator to make, or witness, any test necessary to determine compliance with the applicable provisions of this FAR.

[Docket No. 25613, 55 FR 32861, Aug. 10, 1990; 55 FR 37287, Sept. 10, 1990]

§34.4 [Reserved]

§34.5 Special test procedures.

The Administrator or the Administrator of the EPA may, upon written application by a manufacturer or operator of aircraft or aircraft engines, approve test procedures for any aircraft or aircraft engine that is not susceptible to satisfactory testing by the procedures set forth herein. Prior to taking action on any such application, the Administrator or the Administrator of the EPA shall consult with the other.

§34.6 Aircraft safety.

(a) The provisions of this part will be revised if at any time the Administrator determines that an emission standard cannot be met within the specified time without creating a safety hazard.

(b) Consistent with 40 CFR 87.6, if the FAA Administrator determines that any emission control regulation in this part cannot be safely applied to an aircraft, that provision may not be adopted or enforced against that aircraft by any state or political subdivision thereof.

§34.7 Exemptions.

Notwithstanding part 11 of the Federal Aviation Regulations (14 CFR part 11), all petitions for rulemaking involving either the substance of an emission standard or test procedure prescribed by the EPA that is incorporated in this FAR, or the compliance date for such standard or procedure, must be submitted to the EPA. Information copies of such petitions are invited by the FAA. Petitions for rulemaking or exemption involving provisions of this FAR that do not affect the substance or the compliance date of an emission standard or test procedure that is prescribed by the EPA, and petitions for exemptions under the provisions for which the EPA has specifically granted exemption authority to the Secretary of Transportation are subject to part 11 of the Federal Aviation Regulations (14 CFR part 11). Petitions for rulemaking or exemptions involving these FARs must be submitted to the FAA.

(a) *Exemptions based on flights for short durations at infrequent intervals.* The emission standards of this part do not apply to engines which power aircraft operated in the United States for short durations at infrequent intervals. Such operations are limited to:

(1) Flights of an aircraft for the purpose of export to a foreign country, including any flights essential to demonstrate the integrity of an aircraft prior to a flight to a point outside the United States.

(2) Flights to a base where repairs, alterations or maintenance are to be performed, or to a point of storage, or for the purpose of returning an aircraft to service.

(3) Official visits by representatives of foreign governments.

(4) Other flights the Administrator determines, after consultation with the Administrator of the EPA, to be for short

34

durations at infrequent intervals. A request for such a determination shall be made before the flight takes place.

(b) *Exemptions for very low production engine models.* The emissions standards of this part do not apply to engines of very low production after the date of applicability. For the purpose of this part, "very low production" is limited to a maximum total production for United States civil aviation applications of no more than 200 units covered by the same type certificate after January 1, 1984. Engines manufactured under this provision must be reported to the FAA by serial number on or before the date of manufacture and exemptions granted under this provision are not transferable to any other engine.

(c) *Exemptions for new engines in other categories.* The emissions standards of this part do not apply to engines for which the Administrator determines, with the concurrence of the Administrator of the EPA, that application of any standard under §34.21 is not justified, based upon consideration of—

(1) Adverse economic impact on the manufacturer;

(2) Adverse economic impact on the aircraft and airline industries at large;

(3) Equity in administering the standards among all economically competing parties;

(4) Public health and welfare effects; and

(5) Other factors which the Administrator, after consultation with the Administrator of the EPA, may deem relevant to the case in question.

(d) *Time-limited exemptions for in-use engines.* The emissions standards of this part do not apply to aircraft or aircraft engines for time periods which the Administrator determines, with the concurrence of the Administrator of the EPA, that any applicable standard under §34.11(a), or §34.31(a), should not be applied based upon consideration of—

(1) Documentation demonstrating that all good faith efforts to achieve compliance with such standard have been made;

(2) Documentation demonstrating that the inability to comply with such standard is due to circumstances beyond the control of the owner or operator of the aircraft; and

(3) A plan in which the owner or operator of the aircraft shows that he will achieve compliance in the shortest time which is feasible.

(e) Applications for exemption from this part shall be submitted in duplicate to the Administrator in accordance with the procedures established by the Administrator in part 11.

(f) The Administrator shall publish in the Federal Register the name of the organization to whom exemptions are granted and the period of such exemptions.

(g) No state or political subdivision thereof may attempt to enforce a standard respecting emissions from an aircraft or engine if such aircraft or engine has been exempted from such standard under this part.

Subpart B— Engine Fuel Venting Emissions (New and In-Use Aircraft Gas Turbine Engines)

§34.10 Applicability.

(a) The provisions of this subpart are applicable to all new aircraft gas turbine engines of classes T3, T8, TSS, and TF equal to or greater than 36 kilonewtons (8090 pounds) rated output, manufactured on or after January 1, 1974, and to all in-use aircraft gas turbine engines of classes T3, T8, TSS, and TF equal to or greater than 36 kilonewtons (8090 pounds) rated output manufactured after February 1, 1974.

(b) The provisions of this subpart are also applicable to all new aircraft gas turbine engines of class TF less than 36 kilonewtons (8090 pounds) rated output and class TP manufactured on or after January 1, 1975, and to all in-use aircraft gas turbine engines of class TF less than 36 kilonewtons (8090 pounds) rated output and class TP manufactured after January 1, 1975.

§34.11 Standard for fuel venting emissions.

(a) No fuel venting emissions shall be discharged into the atmosphere from any new or in-use aircraft gas turbine engine subject to the subpart. This paragraph is directed at the elimination of intentional discharge to the atmosphere of fuel drained from fuel nozzle manifolds after engines are shut down and does not apply to normal fuel seepage from shaft seals, joints, and fittings.

(b) Conformity with the standard set forth in paragraph (a) of this section shall be determined by inspection of the method designed to eliminate these emissions.

(c) As applied to an airframe or an engine, any manufacturer or operator may show compliance with the fuel venting and emissions requirements of this section that were effective beginning February 1, 1974 or January 1, 1975, by any means that prevents the intentional discharge of fuel from fuel nozzle manifolds after the engines are shut down. Acceptable means of compliance include one of the following:

(1) Incorporation of an FAA-approved system that recirculates the fuel back into the fuel system.

(2) Capping or securing the pressurization and drain valve.

(3) Manually draining the fuel from a holding tank into a container.

Subpart C— Exhaust Emissions (New Aircraft Gas Turbine Engines)

§34.20 Applicability.

The provisions of this subpart are applicable to all aircraft gas turbine engines of the classes specified beginning on the dates specified in §34.21.

§34.21 Standards for exhaust emissions.

(a) Exhaust emissions of smoke from each new aircraft gas turbine engine of class T8 manufactured on or after February 1, 1974, shall not exceed a smoke number (SN) of 30.

(b) Exhaust emissions of smoke from each new aircraft gas turbine engine of class TF and of rated output of 129 kilonewtons (29,000 pounds) thrust or greater, manufactured on or after January 1, 1976, shall not exceed

SN = $83.6(rO)^{-0.274}$ (rO is in kilonewtons).

(c) Exhaust emission of smoke from each new aircraft gas turbine engine of class T3 manufactured on or after January 1, 1978, shall not exceed a smoke number (SN) of 25.

(d) Gaseous exhaust emissions from each new aircraft gas turbine engine shall not exceed:

(1) For Classes TF, T3, T8 engines greater than 26.7 kilonewtons (6000 pounds) rated output:

(i) Engines manufactured on or after January 1, 1984:

Hydrocarbons: 19.6 grams/kilonewton rO.

(ii) Engines manufactured on or after July 7, 1997.

Carbon Monoxide: 118 grams/kilonewton rO.

(iii) Engines of a type or model of which the date of manufacture of the first individual production model was on or before December 31, 1995, and for which the date of manufacture of the individual engine was on or before December 31, 1999:

Oxides of Nitrogen: (40+2(rPR)) grams/kilonewtons rO.

(iv) Engines of a type or model of which the date of manufacture of the first individual production model was after December 31, 1995, or for which the date of manufacture of the individual engine was after December 31, 1999:

Oxides of Nitrogen: (32+1.6 (rPR)) grams/kilonewtons rO.

(v) The emission standards prescribed in paragraphs (d)(1)(iii) and (iv) of this section apply as prescribed beginning July 7, 1997.

(2) For Class TSS Engines manufactured on or after January 1, 1984:

Hydrocarbons = $140 (0.92)^{rPR}$ grams/kilonewtons rO.

(e) Smoke exhaust emissions from each gas turbine engine of the classes specified below shall not exceed:

(1) Class TF of rated output less than 26.7 kilonewtons (6000 pounds) manufactured on or after August 9, 1985:

SN = $83.6(rO)^{-0.274}$ (rO is in kilonewtons) not to exceed a maximum of SN = 50.

(2) Classes T3, T8, TSS, and TF of rated output equal to or greater than 26.7 kilonewtons (6000 pounds) manufactured on or after January 1, 1984

SN = $83.6(rO)^{-0.274}$ (rO is in kilonewtons) not to exceed a maximum of SN = 50.

(3) For Class TP of rated output equal to or greater than 1,000 kilowatts manufactured on or after January 1, 1984:

SN=$187(rO)^{-0.168}$ (rO is in kilowatts).

(f) The standards set forth in paragraphs (a), (b), (c), (d), and (e) of this section refer to a composite gaseous emission sample representing the operating cycles set forth in the applicable sections of subpart G of this part, and exhaust smoke emissions emitted during operations of the engine as specified in the applicable sections of subpart H of this part, measured and calculated in accordance with the procedures set forth in those subparts.

[Docket No. 25613, 55 FR 32861, Aug. 10, 1990; 55 FR 37287, Sept. 10, 1990; as amended by Amdt. 34–3, 64 FR 5559, Feb. 3, 1999]

Subpart D— Exhaust Emissions (In-Use Aircraft Gas Turbine Engines)

§34.30 Applicability.

The provisions of this subpart are applicable to all in-use aircraft gas turbine engines certificated for operation within the United States of the classes specified, beginning on the dates specified in §34.31.

§34.31 Standards for exhaust emissions.

(a) Exhaust emissions of smoke from each in-use aircraft gas turbine engine of Class T8, beginning February 1, 1974, shall not exceed a smoke number (SN) of 30.

(b) Exhaust emissions of smoke from each in-use aircraft gas turbine engine of Class TF and of rated output of 129 kilonewtons (29,000 pounds) thrust or greater, beginning January 1, 1976, shall not exceed

SN = $83.6(rO)^{-0.274}$ (rO is in kilonewtons).

(c) The standards set forth in paragraphs (a) and (b) of this section refer to exhaust smoke emissions emitted during operations of the engine as specified in the applicable section of subpart H of this part, and measured and calculated in accordance with the procedure set forth in this subpart.

Subpart E—F [Reserved]

Subpart G—Test Procedures for Engine Exhaust Gaseous Emissions (Aircraft and Aircraft Gas Turbine Engines)

§34.60 Introduction.

(a) Except as provided under §34.5, the procedures described in this subpart shall constitute the test program used to determine the conformity of new aircraft gas turbine engines with the applicable standards set forth in this part.

(b) The test consists of operating the engine at prescribed power settings on an engine dynamometer (for engines producing primarily shaft power) or thrust measuring test stand (for engines producing primarily thrust). The exhaust gases generated during engine operation must be sampled continuously for specific component analysis through the analytical train.

(c) The exhaust emission test is designed to measure concentrations of hydrocarbons, carbon monoxide, carbon dioxide, and oxides of nitrogen, and to determine mass emissions through calculations during a simulated aircraft landing-takeoff cycle (LTO). The LTO cycle is based on time in mode data during high activity periods at major airports. The test for propulsion engines consists of at least the following four modes of engine operation: taxi/idle, takeoff, climbout, and approach. The mass emission for the modes are combined to yield the reported values.

(d) When an engine is tested for exhaust emissions on an engine dynamometer or test stand, the complete engine (with all accessories which might reasonably be expected to influence emissions to the atmosphere installed and functioning), shall be used if not otherwise prohibited by §34.62(a)(2). Use of service air bleed and shaft power extraction to power auxiliary, gearbox-mounted components required to drive aircraft systems is not permitted.

(e) Other gaseous emissions measurement systems may be used if shown to yield equivalent results and if approved in advance by the Administrator or the Administrator of the EPA.

[Docket No. 25613, 55 FR 32861, Aug. 10, 1990; as amended by Amdt. 34–3, 64 FR 5559, Feb. 3, 1999]

§34.61 Turbine fuel specifications.

For exhaust emission testing, fuel that meets the specifications listed in this section shall be used. Additives used for the purpose of smoke suppression (such as organometallic compounds) shall not be present.

SPECIFICATION FOR FUEL TO BE USED IN AIRCRAFT TURBINE ENGINE EMISSION TESTING

Property	Allowable range of values
Density at 15°C	780–820
Distillation Temperature, °C 10% Boiling Point	155–201
Final Boiling Point	235–285
Net Heat of Combustion, MJ/Kg	42.86–43.50
Aromatics, Volume %	15–23
Naphthalenes, Volume %	1.0–3.5
Smoke point, mm	20–28
Hydrogen, Mass %	13.4–14.1
Sulphur, Mass %	Less than 0.3%
Kinematic viscosity at—20°C, mm^2/sec.	2.5–6.5

[Docket No. 25613, 55 FR 32861, Aug. 10, 1990; 55 FR 37287, Sept. 10, 1990; as amended by Amdt. 34–3, 64 FR 5559, Feb. 3, 1999]

§34.62 Test procedure (propulsion engines).

(a)(1) The engine shall be tested in each of the following engine operating modes which simulate aircraft operation to determine its mass emission rates. The actual power setting, when corrected to standard day conditions, should correspond to the following percentages of rated output. Analytical correction for variations from reference day conditions and minor variations in actual power setting should be specified and/or approved by the Administrator:

Mode	Class		
	TP	TF, T3, T8	TSS
Taxi/idle	(*)	(*)	(*)
Takeoff	100	100	100
Climbout	90	85	65
Descent	NA	NA	15
Approach	30	30	34

*See paragraph (a) of this section.

(2) The taxi/idle operating modes shall be carried out at a power setting of 7% rated thrust unless the Administrator determines that the unique characteristics of an engine model undergoing certification testing at 7% would result in substantially different HC and CO emissions than if the engine model were tested at the manufacturers recommended idle power setting. In such cases the Administrator shall specify an alternative test condition.

(3) The times in mode (TIM) shall be as specified below:

Mode	Class		
	TP	TF, T3, T8	TSS
Taxi/idle	26.0 Min.	26.0 Min.	26.0 Min.
Takeoff	0.5	0.7	1.2
Climbout	2.5	2.2	2.0
Descent	N/A	N/A	1.2
Approach	4.5	4.0	2.3

(b) Emissions testing shall be conducted on warmed-up engines which have achieved a steady operating temperature.

[Docket No. 25613, 55 FR 32861, Aug. 10, 1990; 55 FR 37287, Sept. 10, 1990; as amended by Amdt. 34–3, 64 FR 5559, Feb. 3, 1999]

§34.63 [Reserved]

§34.64 Sampling and analytical procedures for measuring gaseous exhaust emissions.

The system and procedures for sampling and measurement of gaseous emissions shall be as specified in Appendices 3 and 5 to the International Civil Aviation Organization (ICAO) Annex 16, Environmental Protection, Volume II, Aircraft Engine Emissions, Second Edition, July 1993, effective March 20, 1997. This incorporation by reference was approved by the Director of the Federal Register in accordance with 5 U.S.C. 552(a) and 1 CFR part 51. This document can be obtained from the International Civil Aviation Organization (ICAO), Document Sales Unit, P.O. Box 400, Succursale: Place de L'Aviation Internationale, 1000 Sherbrooke Street West, Suite 400, Montreal, Quebec, Canada H3A 2R2. Copies may be reviewed at the FAA Office of the Chief Counsel, Rules Docket, Room 916, Federal Aviation Administration Headquarters Building, 800 Independence Avenue SW, Washington, DC, or at the FAA New England Regional Office, 12 New England Executive Park, Burlington, Massachusetts, or at the Office of the Federal Register, 800 North Capitol Street NW, Suite 700, Washington, DC.

[Docket No. 25613, 55 FR 32861, Aug. 10, 1990; 55 FR 37287, Sept. 10, 1990; as amended by Amdt. No. 34–1, 60 FR 34077, June 29, 1995; Amdt. 34–3, 64 FR 5559, Feb. 3, 1999]

§§34.65 – 34.70 [Reserved]

§34.71 Compliance with gaseous emission standards.

Compliance with each gaseous emission standard by an aircraft engine shall be determined by comparing the pollutant level in grams/kilonewton/thrust/cycle or grams/kilowatt/cycle as calculated in §34.64 with the applicable emission standard under this part. An acceptable alternative to testing every engine is described in Appendix 6 to ICAO Annex 16, Environmental Protection, Volume II, Aircraft Engine Emissions, Second Edition, July 1993, effective July 26, 1993. This incorporation by reference was approved by the Director of the Federal Register in accordance with 5 U.S.C. 552(a) and 1 CFR part 51. This document can be obtained from, and copies may be reviewed at, the respective addresses listed in §34.64. Other methods of demonstrating compliance may be approved by the FAA Administrator with the concurrence of the Administrator of the EPA.

[Docket No. 27686, 60 FR 34077, June 29, 1995; as amended by Amdt. 34–3, 64 FR 5559, Feb. 3, 1999]

Subpart H—Test Procedures for Engine Smoke Emissions (Aircraft Gas Turbine Engines)

§34.80 Introduction.

Except as provided under §34.5, the procedures described in this subpart shall constitute the test program to be used to determine the conformity of new and in-use gas turbine engines with the applicable standards set forth in this part. The test is essentially the same as that described in §§34.60–34.62, except that the test is designed to determine the smoke emission level at various operating points representative of engine usage in aircraft. Other smoke measurement systems may be used if shown to yield equivalent results and if approved in advance by the Administrator or the Administrator of the EPA.

§34.81 Fuel specifications.

Fuel having specifications as provided in §34.61 shall be used in smoke emission testing.

§34.82 Sampling and analytical procedures for measuring smoke exhaust emissions.

The system and procedures for sampling and measurement of smoke emissions shall be as specified in Appendix 2 to ICAO Annex 16, Volume II, Environmental Protection, Aircraft Engine Emissions, Second Edition, July 1993, effective July 26, 1993. This incorporation by reference was approved by the Director of the Federal Register in accordance with 5 U.S.C. 552(a) and 1 CFR part 51. This document can be obtained from, and copies may be reviewed at, the respective addresses listed in §34.64.

[Docket No. 25613, 55 FR 32861, Aug. 10, 1990; 55 FR 37287, Sept. 10, 1990; as amended by Amdt. No. 34–1, 60 FR 34077, June 29, 1995; Amdt. 34–3, 64 FR 5560, Feb. 3, 1999]

§§34.83 – 34.88 [Reserved]

§34.89 Compliance with smoke emission standards.

Compliance with each smoke emission standard shall be determined by comparing the plot of SN as a function of power setting with the applicable emission standard under this part. The SN at every power setting must be such that there is a high degree of confidence that the standard will not be exceeded by any engine of the model being tested. An acceptable alternative to testing every engine is described in Appendix 6 to ICAO Annex 16, Environmental Protection, Volume II, Aircraft Engine Emissions, Second Edition, July 1993, effective July 26, 1993. This incorporation by reference was approved by the Director of the Federal Register in accordance with 5 U.S.C. 552(a) and 1 CFR part 51. This document can be obtained from the address listed in §34.64. Other methods of demonstrating compliance may be approved by the Administrator with the concurrence of the Administrator of the EPA.

[Docket No. 25613, 55 FR 32861, Aug. 10, 1990; as amended by Amdt. 34–1, 60 FR 34077, June 29, 1995; Amdt. 34–3, 64 FR 5560, Feb. 3, 1999]

PART 35
AIRWORTHINESS STANDARDS: PROPELLERS

Subpart A — General

Sec.
35.1 Applicability.
35.3 Instruction manual for installing and operating the propeller.
35.4 Instructions for Continued Airworthiness.
35.5 Propeller operating limitations.

Subpart B — Design and Construction

35.11 Applicability.
35.13 General.
35.15 Design features.
35.17 Materials.
35.19 Durability.
35.21 Reversible propellers.
35.23 Pitch control and indication.

Subpart C — Tests and Inspections

35.31 Applicability.
35.33 General.
35.35 Blade retention test.
35.37 Fatigue limit tests.
35.39 Endurance test.
35.41 Functional test.
35.42 Blade pitch control system component test.
35.43 Special tests.
35.45 Teardown inspection.
35.47 Propeller adjustments and parts replacements.

Appendix A to Part 35 — Instructions for Continued Airworthiness

Authority: 49 U.S.C. 106(g), 40113, 44701–44702, 44704.

Source: Docket No. 2095, 29 FR 7458, June 10, 1964, unless otherwise noted.

Subpart A — General

§35.1 Applicability.

(a) This part prescribes airworthiness standards for the issue of type certificates and changes to those certificates, for propellers.

(b) Each person who applies under Part 21 for such a certificate or change must show compliance with the applicable requirements of this part.

[Amdt. 35–3, 41 FR 55475, Dec. 20, 1976]

§35.3 Instruction manual for installing and operating the propeller.

Each applicant must prepare and make available an approved manual or manuals containing instructions for installing and operating the propeller.

[Amdt. 35–5, 45 FR 60181, Sept. 11, 1980]

§35.4 Instructions for Continued Airworthiness.

The applicant must prepare Instructions for Continued Airworthiness in accordance with Appendix A to this part that are acceptable to the Administrator. The instructions may be incomplete at type certification if a program exists to ensure their completion prior to delivery of the first aircraft with the propeller installed, or upon issuance of a standard certificate of airworthiness for an aircraft with the propeller installed, whichever occurs later.

[Amdt. 35–5, 45 FR 60181, Sept. 11, 1980]

§35.5 Propeller operating limitations.

Propeller operating limitations are established by the Administrator, are included in the propeller type certificate data sheet specified in §21.41 of this chapter, and include limitations based on the operating conditions demonstrated during the tests required by this part and any other information found necessary for the safe operation of the propeller.

[Amdt. 35–5, 45 FR 60182, Sept. 11, 1980]

Subpart B — Design and Construction

§35.11 Applicability.

This subpart prescribes the design and construction requirements for propellers.

§35.13 General.

Each applicant must show that the propeller concerned meets the design and construction requirements of this subpart.

§35.15 Design features.

The propeller may not have design features that experience has shown to be hazardous or unreliable. The suitability of each questionable design detail or part must be established by tests.

§35.17 Materials.

The suitability and durability of materials used in the propeller must —

(a) Be established on the basis of experience or tests; and

(b) Conform to approved specifications (such as industry or military specifications, or Technical Standard Orders) that ensure their having the strength and other properties assumed in the design data.

(Secs. 313(a), 601, and 603, 72 Stat. 752, 775, 49 U.S.C. 1354(a), 1421, and 1423; sec. 6(c), 49 U.S.C. 1655(c))

[Amdt. 35–4, 42 FR 15047, Mar. 17, 1977]

§35.19 Durability.

Each part of the propeller must be designed and constructed to minimize the development of any unsafe condition of the propeller between overhaul periods.

§35.21 Reversible propellers.

A reversible propeller must be adaptable for use with a reversing system in an airplane so that no single failure or malfunction in that system during normal or emergency operation will result in unwanted travel of the propeller blades to a position substantially below the normal flight low-pitch stop. Failure of structural elements need not be considered if the occurrence of such a failure is expected to be extremely remote. For the purposes of this section the term "reversing system" means that part of the complete reversing system that is in the propeller itself and those other parts that are supplied by the applicant for installation in the aircraft.

§35.23 Pitch control and indication.

(a) No loss of normal propeller pitch control may cause hazardous overspeeding of the propeller under intended operating conditions.

(b) Each pitch control system that is within the propeller, or supplied with the propeller, and that uses engine oil for feathering, must incorporate means to override or bypass the normally operative hydraulic system components so as to allow feathering if those components fail or malfunction.

(c) Each propeller approved for installation on a turbopropeller engine must incorporate a provision for an indicator to indicate when the propeller blade angle is below the flight low pitch position. The provision must directly sense the blade position and be arranged to cause an indicator to indicate that the blade angle is below the flight low pitch position before the blade moves more than 8° below the flight low pitch stop.

[Amdt. 35–2, 32 FR 3737, Mar. 4, 1967, as amended by Amdt. 35–5, 45 FR 60182, Sept. 11, 1980]

Subpart C— Tests and Inspections

§35.31 Applicability.

This subpart prescribes the tests and inspections for propellers and their essential accessories.

§35.33 General.

(a) Each applicant must show that the propeller concerned and its essential accessories complete the tests and inspections of this subpart without evidence of failure or malfunction.

(b) Each applicant must furnish testing facilities, including equipment, and competent personnel, to conduct the required tests.

§35.35 Blade retention test.

The hub and blade retention arrangement of propellers with detachable blades must be subjected to a centrifugal load of twice the maximum centrifugal force to which the propeller would be subjected during operations within the limitations established for the propeller. This may be done by either a whirl test or a static pull test.

(Secs. 313(a), 601, and 603, 72 Stat. 752, 775, 49 U.S.C. 1354(a), 1421, and 1423; sec. 6(c), 49 U.S.C. 1655(c))

[Amdt. 35–4, 42 FR 15047, Mar. 17, 1977]

§35.37 Fatigue limit tests.

A fatigue evaluation must be made and the fatigue limits determined for each metallic hub and blade, and each primary load carrying metal component of nonmetallic blades. The fatigue evaluation must include consideration of all reasonably foreseeable vibration load patterns. The fatigue limits must account for the permissible service deterioration (such as nicks, grooves, galling, bearing wear, and variations in material properties).

[Amdt. 35–5, 45 FR 60182, Sept. 11, 1980]

§35.39 Endurance test.

(a) *Fixed-pitch wood propellers.* Fixed-pitch wood propellers must be subjected to one of the following tests:

(1) A 10-hour endurance block test on an engine with a propeller of the greatest pitch and diameter for which certification is sought at the rated rotational speed.

(2) A 50-hour flight test in level flight or in climb. At least five hours of this flight test must be with the propeller operated at the rated rotational speed, and the remainder of the 50 hours must be with the propeller operated at not less than 90 percent of the rated rotational speed. This test must be conducted on a propeller of the greatest diameter for which certification is requested.

(3) A 50-hour endurance block test on an engine at the power and propeller rotational speed for which certification is sought. This test must be conducted on a propeller of the greatest diameter for which certification is requested.

(b) *Fixed-pitch metal propellers and ground adjustable-pitch propellers.* Each fixed-pitch metal propeller or ground adjustable-pitch propeller must be subjected to the test prescribed in either paragraph (a)(2) or (a)(3) of this section.

(c) *Variable-pitch propellers.* Compliance with this paragraph must be shown for a propeller of the greatest diameter for which certification is requested. Each variable-pitch propeller (a propeller the pitch setting of which can be changed by the flight crew or by automatic means while the propeller is rotating) must be subjected to one of the following tests:

(1) A 100-hour test on a representative engine with the same or higher power and rotational speed and the same or more severe vibration characteristics as the engine with which the propeller is to be used. Each test must be made at the maximum continuous rotational speed and power rating of the propeller. If a takeoff rating greater than the maximum continuous rating is to be established, and additional 10-hour block test must be made at the maximum power and rotational speed for the takeoff rating.

(2) Operation of the propeller throughout the engine endurance tests prescribed in Part 33 of this subchapter.

[Docket No. 2095, 29 FR 7458, June 10, 1964, as amended by Amdt. 35–2, 32 FR 3737, Mar. 4, 1967; Amdt. 35–3, 41 FR 55475, Dec. 20, 1976]

§35.41 Functional test.

(a) Each variable-pitch propeller must be subjected to the applicable functional tests of this section. The same propeller used in the endurance test must be used in the functional tests and must be driven by an engine on a test stand or on an aircraft.

(b) *Manually controllable propellers.* 500 complete cycles of control must be made throughout the pitch and rotational speed ranges.

(c) *Automatically controllable propellers.* 1,500 complete cycles of control must be made throughout the pitch and rotational speed ranges.

(d) *Feathering propellers.* 50 cycles of feathering operation must be made.

(e) *Reversible-pitch propellers.* Two hundred complete cycles of control must be made from lowest normal pitch to maximum reverse pitch, and, while in maximum reverse pitch, during each cycle, the propeller must be run for 30 seconds at the maximum power and rotational speed selected by the applicant for maximum reverse pitch.

[Docket No. 2095, 29 FR 7458, June 10, 1964, as amended by Amdt. 35–3, 41 FR 55475, Dec. 20, 1976]

§35.42 Blade pitch control system component test.

The following durability requirements apply to propeller blade pitch control system components:

(a) Except as provided in paragraph (b) of this section, each propeller blade pitch control system component, including governors, pitch change assemblies, pitch locks, mechanical stops, and feathering system components, must be subjected in tests to cyclic loadings that simulate the frequency and amplitude those to which the component would be subjected during 1,000 hours of propeller operation.

(b) Compliance with paragraph (a) of this section may be shown by a rational analysis based on the results of tests on similar components.

[Amdt. 35–5, 45 FR 60182, Sept. 11, 1980]

§35.43 Special tests.

The Administrator may require any additional tests he finds necessary to substantiate the use of any unconventional features of design, material, or construction.

§35.45 Teardown inspection.

(a) After completion of the tests prescribed in this subpart, the propeller must be completely disassembled and a detailed inspection must be made of the propeller parts for cracks, wear, distortion, and any other unusual conditions.

(b) After the inspection the applicant must make any changes to the design or any additional tests that the Administrator finds necessary to establish the airworthiness of the propeller.

[Docket No. 3095, 29 FR 7458, June 10, 1964, as amended by Amdt. 35–3, 41 FR 55475, Dec. 20, 1976]

§35.47 Propeller adjustments and parts replacements.

The applicant may service and make minor repairs to the propeller during the tests. If major repairs or replacement of parts are found necessary during the tests or in the teardown inspection, the parts in question must be subjected to any additional tests the Administrator finds necessary.

Appendix A to Part 35

Instructions for Continued Airworthiness

A35.1 General

(a) This appendix specifies requirements for the preparation of Instructions for Continued Airworthiness as required by §35.4.

(b) The Instructions for Continued Airworthiness for each propeller must include the Instructions for Continued Airworthiness for all propeller parts. If Instructions for Continued Airworthiness are not supplied by the propeller part manufacturer for a propeller part, the Instructions for Continued Airworthiness for the propeller must include the information essential to the continued airworthiness of the propeller.

(c) The applicant must submit to the FAA a program to show how changes to the Instructions for Continued Airworthiness made by the applicant or by the manufacturers of propeller parts will be distributed.

A35.2 Format

(a) The Instructions for Continued Airworthiness must be in the form of a manual or manuals as appropriate for the quantity of data to be provided.

(b) The format of the manual or manuals must provide for a practical arrangement.

A35.3 Content

The contents of the manual must be prepared in the English language. The Instructions for Continued Airworthiness must contain the following sections and information:

(a) *Propeller Maintenance Section.*

(1) Introduction information that includes an explanation of the propeller's features and data to the extent necessary for maintenance or preventive maintenance.

(2) A detailed description of the propeller and its systems and installations.

(3) Basic control and operation information describing how the propeller components and systems are controlled and how they operate, including any special procedures that apply.

(4) Instructions for uncrating, acceptance checking, lifting, and installing the propeller.

(5) Instructions for propeller operational checks.

(6) Scheduling information for each part of the propeller that provides the recommended periods at which it should be cleaned, adjusted, and tested, the applicable wear tolerances, and the degree of work recommended at these periods. However, the applicant may refer to an accessory, instrument, or equipment manufacturer as the source of this information if it shows that the item has an exceptionally high degree of complexity requiring specialized maintenance techniques, test equipment, or expertise. The recommended overhaul periods and necessary cross-references to the Airworthiness Limitations section of the manual must also be included. In addition, the applicant must include an inspection program that includes the frequency and extent of the in-

spections necessary to provide for the continued airworthiness of the propeller.

(7) Troubleshooting information describing probable malfunctions, how to recognize those malfunctions, and the remedial action for those malfunctions.

(8) Information describing the order and method of removing and replacing propeller parts with any necessary precautions to be taken.

(9) A list of the special tools needed for maintenance other than for overhauls.

(b) *Propeller Overhaul Section.*

(1) Disassembly information including the order and method of disassembly for overhaul.

(2) Cleaning and inspection instructions that cover the materials and apparatus to be used and methods and precautions to be taken during overhaul. Methods of overhaul inspection must also be included.

(3) Details of all fits and clearances relevant to overhaul.

(4) Details of repair methods for worn or otherwise substandard parts and components along with information necessary to determine when replacement is necessary.

(5) The order and method of assembly at overhaul.

(6) Instructions for testing after overhaul.

(7) Instructions for storage preparation including any storage limits.

(8) A list of tools needed for overhaul.

A35.4 Airworthiness Limitations Section

The Instructions for Continued Airworthiness must contain a section titled Airworthiness Limitations that is segregated and clearly distinguishable from the rest of the document. This section must set forth each mandatory replacement time, inspection interval, and related procedure required for type certification. This section must contain a legible statement in a prominent location that reads: "The Airworthiness Limitations section is FAA approved and specifies maintenance required under §§43.16 and 91.403 of the Federal Aviation Regulations unless an alternative program has been FAA approved."

[Amdt. 35–5, 45 FR 60182, Sept. 11, 1980, as amended by Amdt. 35–6, 54 FR 34330, Aug. 18, 1989]

PART 39
AIRWORTHINESS DIRECTIVES

Sec.

39.1 Purpose of this regulation.
39.3 Definition of airworthiness directives.
39.5 When does FAA issue airworthiness directives?
39.7 What is the legal effect of failing to comply with an airworthiness directive?
39.9 What if I operate an aircraft or use a product that does not meet the requirements of an airworthiness directive?
39.11 What actions do airworthiness directives require?
39.13 Are airworthiness directives part of the Code of Federal Regulations?
39.15 Does an airworthiness directive apply if the product has been changed?
39.17 What must I do if a change in a product affects my ability to accomplish the actions required in an airworthiness directive?
39.19 May I address the unsafe condition in a way other than that set out in the airworthiness directive?
39.21 Where can I get information about FAA-approved alternative methods of compliance?
39.23 May I fly my aircraft to a repair facility to do the work required by an airworthiness directive?
39.25 How do I get a special flight permit?
39.27 What do I do if the airworthiness directive conflicts with the service document on which it is based?

Authority: 49 U.S.C. 106(g), 40113, 44701.

Source: Docket No. FAA–2000–8460, 67 FR 48003, July 22, 2002 unless otherwise noted.

§39.1 Purpose of this regulation.

The regulations in this part provide a legal framework for FAA's system of Airworthiness Directives.

§39.3 Definition of airworthiness directives.

FAA's airworthiness directives are legally enforceable rules that apply to the following products: aircraft, aircraft engines, propellers, and appliances.

§39.5 When does FAA issue airworthiness directives?

FAA issues an airworthiness directive addressing a product when we find that:

(a) An unsafe condition exists in the product; and

(b) The condition is likely to exist or develop in other products of the same type design.

§39.7 What is the legal effect of failing to comply with an airworthiness directive?

Anyone who operates a product that does not meet the requirements of an applicable airworthiness directive is in violation of this section.

§39.9 What if I operate an aircraft or use a product that does not meet the requirements of an airworthiness directive?

If the requirements of an airworthiness directive have not been met, you violate §39.7 each time you operate the aircraft or use the product.

§39.11 What actions do airworthiness directives require?

Airworthiness directives specify inspections you must carry out, conditions and limitations you must comply with, and any actions you must take to resolve an unsafe condition.

§39.13 Are airworthiness directives part of the Code of Federal Regulations?

Yes, airworthiness directives are part of the Code of Federal Regulations, but they are not codified in the annual edition. FAA publishes airworthiness directives in full in the Federal Register as amendments to §39.13.

§39.15 Does an airworthiness directive apply if the product has been changed?

Yes, an airworthiness directive applies to each product identified in the airworthiness directive, even if an individual product has been changed by modifying, altering, or repairing it in the area addressed by the airworthiness directive.

§39.17 What must I do if a change in a product affects my ability to accomplish the actions required in an airworthiness directive?

If a change in a product affects your ability to accomplish the actions required by the airworthiness directive in any way, you must request FAA approval of an alternative method of compliance. Unless you can show the change eliminated the unsafe condition, your request should include the specific actions that you propose to address the unsafe condition. Submit your request in the manner described in §39.19.

§39.19 May I address the unsafe condition in a way other than that set out in the airworthiness directive?

Yes, anyone may propose to FAA an alternative method of compliance or a change in the compliance time, if the proposal provides an acceptable level of safety. Unless FAA authorizes otherwise, send your proposal to your principal inspector. Include the specific actions you are proposing to address the unsafe condition. The principal inspector may add comments and will send your request to the manager of the office identified in the airworthiness directive (manager). You may send a copy to the manager at the same time you send it to the principal inspector. If you do not have a principal inspector send your proposal directly to the manager. You may use the alternative you propose only if the manager approves it.

§39.21 Where can I get information about FAA-approved alternative methods of compliance?

Each airworthiness directive identifies the office responsible for approving alternative methods of compliance. That office can provide information about alternatives it has already approved.

§39.23 May I fly my aircraft to a repair facility to do the work required by an airworthiness directive?

Yes, the operations specifications giving some operators authority to operate include a provision that allow them to fly their aircraft to a repair facility to do the work required by an airworthiness directive. If you do not have this authority, the local Flight Standards District Office of FAA may issue you a special flight permit unless the airworthiness directive states otherwise. To ensure aviation safety, FAA may add special requirements for operating your aircraft to a place where the repairs or modifications can be accomplished. FAA may also decline to issue a special flight permit in particular cases if we determine you cannot move the aircraft safely.

§39.25 How do I get a special flight permit?

Apply to FAA for a special flight permit following the procedures in 14 CFR §21.199.

§39.27 What do I do if the airworthiness directive conflicts with the service document on which it is based?

In some cases an airworthiness directive incorporates by reference a manufacturer's service document. In these cases, the service document becomes part of the airworthiness directive. In some cases the directions in the service document may be modified by the airworthiness directive. If there is a conflict between the service document and the airworthiness directive, you must follow the requirements of the airworthiness directive.

PART 43
MAINTENANCE, PREVENTIVE MAINTENANCE, REBUILDING, AND ALTERATION

Sec.
43.1 Applicability.
43.2 Records of overhaul and rebuilding.
43.3 Persons authorized to perform maintenance, preventive maintenance, rebuilding, and alterations.
43.5 Approval for return to service after maintenance, preventive maintenance, rebuilding, or alteration.
43.7 Persons authorized to approve aircraft, airframes, aircraft engines, propellers, appliances, or component parts for return to service after maintenance, preventive maintenance, rebuilding, or alteration.
43.9 Content, form, and disposition of maintenance, preventive maintenance, rebuilding, and alteration records (except inspections performed in accordance with Part 91, Part 125, §135.411(a)(1), and §135.419 of this chapter).
43.10 Disposition of life-limited aircraft parts.
43.11 Content, form, and disposition of records for inspections conducted under Parts 91 and 125 and §§135.411(a)(1) and 135.419 of this chapter.
43.12 Maintenance records: Falsification, reproduction, or alteration.
43.13 Performance rules (general).
43.15 Additional performance rules for inspections.
43.16 Airworthiness Limitations.
***43.17 Maintenance, preventive maintenance, and alterations performed on U.S. aeronautical products by certain Canadian persons.**

Appendix A to Part 43— Major Alterations, Major Repairs, and Preventive Maintenance
Appendix B to Part 43— Recording of Major Repairs and Major Alterations
Appendix C to Part 43—[Reserved]
Appendix D to Part 43— Scope and Detail of Items (as Applicable to the Particular Aircraft) to be included in Annual and 100-Hour Inspections
Appendix E to Part 43— Altimeter System Test and Inspection
Appendix F to Part 43— ATC Transponder Tests and Inspections

Authority: 49 U.S.C. 106(g), 40113, 44701, 44703, 44705, 44707, 44711, 44713, 44717, 44725.

Source: Docket No. 1993, 29 FR 5451, April 23, 1964, unless otherwise noted.

Editorial Note: For miscellaneous technical amendments to this Part 43, see Amdt. 43–3, 31 FR 3336, March 3, 1966, and Amdt. 43–6, 31 FR 9211, July 6, 1966.

§43.1 Applicability.

(a) Except as provided in paragraphs (b) and (d) of this section, this part prescribes rules governing the maintenance, preventive maintenance, rebuilding, and alteration of any—

(1) Aircraft having a U.S. airworthiness certificate;

(2) Foreign-registered civil aircraft used in common carriage or carriage of mail under the provisions of Part 121 or 135 of this chapter; and

(3) Airframe, aircraft engines, propellers, appliances, and component parts of such aircraft.

(b) This part does not apply to any aircraft for which the FAA has issued an experimental certificate, unless the FAA has previously issued a different kind of airworthiness certificate for that aircraft.

(c) This part applies to all life-limited parts that are removed from a type certificated product, segregated, or controlled as provided in §43.10.

(d) This part applies to any aircraft issued a special airworthiness certificate in the light-sport category except:

(1) The repair or alteration form specified in §§43.5(b) and 43.9(d) is not required to be completed for products not produced under an FAA approval;

(2) Major repairs and major alterations for products not produced under an FAA approval are not required to be recorded in accordance with appendix B of this part; and

(3) The listing of major alterations and major repairs specified in paragraphs (a) and (b) of appendix A of this part is not applicable to products not produced under an FAA approval.

[Docket No. 1993, 29 FR 5451, April 23, 1964; as amended by Amdt. 43–23, 47 FR 41084, Sept. 16, 1982; Amdt. 43–37, 66 FR 21066, April 27, 2001; Amdt. No. 43–38, 67 FR 2109, Jan. 15, 2002; Amdt. 43–39, 69 FR 44863, July 27, 2004]

§43.2 Records of overhaul and rebuilding.

(a) No person may describe in any required maintenance entry or form an aircraft, airframe, aircraft engine, propeller, appliance, or component part as being overhauled unless—

(1) Using methods, techniques, and practices acceptable to the Administrator, it has been disassembled, cleaned, inspected, repaired as necessary, and reassembled; and

(2) It has been tested in accordance with approved standards and technical data, or in accordance with current standards and technical data acceptable to the Administrator, which have been developed and documented by the holder of the type certificate, supplemental type certificate, or a material, part, process, or applicance approval under §21.305 of this chapter.

(b) No person may describe in any required maintenance entry or form an aircraft, airframe, aircraft engine, propeller, appliance, or component part as being rebuilt unless it has been disassembled, cleaned, inspected, repaired as necessary, reassembled, and tested to the same tolerances and limits as a new item, using either new parts or used parts that either conform to new part tolerances and limits or to approved oversized or undersized dimensions.

[Docket No. 1993, 29 FR 5451, April 23, 1964; as amended by Amdt. 43–23, 47 FR 41084, Sept. 16, 1982]

43

§43.3 Persons authorized to perform maintenance, preventive maintenance, rebuilding, and alterations.

(a) Except as provided in this section and §43.17, no person may maintain, rebuild, alter, or perform preventive maintenance on an aircraft, airframe, aircraft engine, propeller, appliance, or component part to which this part applies. Those items, the performance of which is a major alteration, a major repair, or preventive maintenance, are listed in Appendix A.

(b) The holder of a mechanic certificate may perform maintenance, preventive maintenance, and alterations as provided in Part 65 of this chapter.

(c) The holder of a repairman certificate may perform maintenance, preventive maintenance, and alterations as provided in part 65 of this chapter.

(d) A person working under the supervision of a holder of a mechanic or repairman certificate may perform the maintenance, preventive maintenance, and alterations that his supervisor is authorized to perform, if the supervisor personally observes the work being done to the extent necessary to ensure that it is being done properly and if the supervisor is readily available, in person, for consultation. However, this paragraph does not authorize the performance of any inspection required by Part 91 or Part 125 of this chapter or any inspection performed after a major repair or alteration.

(e) The holder of a repair station certificate may perform maintenance, preventive maintenance, and alterations as provided in Part 145 of this chapter.

(f) The holder of an air carrier operating certificate or an operating certificate issued under Part 121 or 135, may perform maintenance, preventive maintenance, and alterations as provided in Part 121 or 135.

(g) Except for holders of a sport pilot certificate, the holder of a pilot certificate issued under part 61 may perform preventive maintenance on any aircraft owned or operated by that pilot which is not used under part 121, 129, or 135 of this chapter. The holder of a sport pilot certificate may perform preventive maintenance on an aircraft owned or operated by that pilot and issued a special airworthiness certificate in the light-sport category.

(h) Notwithstanding the provisions of paragraph (g) of this section, the Administrator may approve a certificate holder under Part 135 of this chapter, operating rotorcraft in a remote area, to allow a pilot to perform specific preventive maintenance items provided—

(1) The items of preventive maintenance are a result of a known or suspected mechanical difficulty or malfunction that occurred en route to or in a remote area;

(2) The pilot has satisfactorily completed an approved training program and is authorized in writing by the certificate holder for each item of preventive maintenance that the pilot is authorized to perform;

(3) There is no certificated mechanic available to perform preventive maintenance;

(4) The certificate holder has procedures to evaluate the accomplishment of a preventive maintenance item that requires a decision concerning the airworthiness of the rotorcraft; and

(5) The items of preventive maintenance authorized by this section are those listed in paragraph (c) of Appendix A of this part.

(i) Notwithstanding the provisions of paragraph (g) of this section, in accordance with an approval issued to the holder of a certificate issued under part 135 of this chapter, a pilot of an aircraft type-certificated for 9 or fewer passenger seats, excluding any pilot seat, may perform the removal and reinstallation of approved aircraft cabin seats, approved cabin-mounted stretchers, and when no tools are required, approved cabin-mounted medical oxygen bottles, provided—

(1) The pilot has satisfactorily completed an approved training program and is authorized in writing by the certificate holder to perform each task; and

(2) The certificate holder has written procedures available to the pilot to evaluate the accomplishment of the task.

(j) A manufacturer may —

(1) Rebuild or alter any aircraft, aircraft engine, propeller, or appliance manufactured by him under a type or production certificate;

(2) Rebuild or alter any appliance or part of aircraft, aircraft engines, propellers, or appliances manufactured by him under a Technical Standard Order Authorization, an FAA-Parts Manufacturer Approval, or Product and Process Specification issued by the Administrator; and

(3) Perform any inspection required by Part 91 or Part 125 of this chapter on aircraft it manufacturers, while currently operating under a production certificate or under a currently approved production inspection system for such aircraft.

[Docket No. 1993, 29 FR 5451, April 23, 1964; as amended by Amdt. 43–4, 31 FR 5249, April 1, 1966; Amdt. 43–23, 47 FR 41084, Sept. 16, 1982; Amdt. 43–25, 51 FR 40702, Nov. 7, 1986; Amdt. 43–36, 61 FR 19501, May 1, 1996; Amdt. 43–37, 66 FR 21066, April 27, 2001; Amdt. 43–39, 69 FR 44863, July 27, 2004]

§43.5 Approval for return to service after maintenance, preventive maintenance, rebuilding, or alteration.

No person may approve for return to service any aircraft, airframe, aircraft engine, propeller, or appliance, that has undergone maintenance, preventive maintenance, rebuilding, or alteration unless—

(a) The maintenance record entry required by §43.9 or §43.11, as appropriate, has been made;

(b) The repair or alteration form authorized by or furnished by the Administrator has been executed in a manner prescribed by the Administrator; and

(c) If a repair or an alteration results in any change in the aircraft operating limitations or flight data contained in the approved aircraft flight manual, those operating limitations or flight data are appropriately revised and set forth as prescribed in §91.9 of this chapter.

[Docket No. 1993, 29 FR 5451, April 23, 1964; as amended by Amdt. 43–23, 47 FR 41084, Sept. 16, 1982; Amdt. 43–31, 54 FR 34330, Aug. 18, 1989]

§43.7 Persons authorized to approve aircraft, airframes, aircraft engines, propellers, appliances, or component parts for return to service after maintenance, preventive maintenance, rebuilding, or alteration.

(a) Except as provided in this section and §43.17, no person, other than the Administrator, may approve an aircraft, airframe, aircraft engine, propeller, appliance, or component part for return to service after it has undergone maintenance, preventive maintenance, rebuilding, or alteration.

(b) The holder of a mechanic certificate or an inspection authorization may approve an aircraft, airframe, aircraft engine, propeller, appliance, or component part for return to service as provided in Part 65 of this chapter.

(c) The holder of a repair station certificate may approve an aircraft, airframe, aircraft engine, propeller, appliance, or component part for return to service as provided in Part 145 of this chapter.

(d) A manufacturer may approve for return to service any aircraft, airframe, aircraft engine, propeller, appliance, or component part which that manufacturer has worked on under §43.3(j). However, except for minor alterations, the work must have been done in accordance with technical data approved by the Administrator.

(e) The holder of an air carrier operating certificate or an operating certificate issued under Part 121 or 135, may approve an aircraft, airframe, aircraft engine, propeller, appliance, or component part for return to service as provided in Part 121 or 135 of this chapter, as applicable.

(f) A person holding at least a private pilot certificate may approve an aircraft for return to service after performing preventive maintenance under the provisions of §43.3(g).

(g) The holder of a repairman certificate (light-sport aircraft) with a maintenance rating may approve an aircraft issued a special airworthiness certificate in light-sport category for return to service, as provided in part 65 of this chapter.

(h) The holder of at least a sport pilot certificate may approve an aircraft owned or operated by that pilot and issued a special airworthiness certificate in the light-sport category for return to service after performing preventive maintenance under the provisions of §43.3(g).

[Docket No. 1993, 29 FR 5451, April 23, 1964; as amended by Amdt. 43–23, 47 FR 41084, Sept. 16, 1982; Amdt. 43–36, 61 FR 19501, May 1, 1996; Amdt. 43–37, 66 FR 21066, April 27, 2001; Amdt. 43–39, 69 FR 44863, July 27, 2004]

§43.9 Content, form, and disposition of maintenance, preventive maintenance, rebuilding, and alteration records (except inspections performed in accordance with Part 91, Part 125, §135.411(a)(1), and §135.419 of this chapter).

(a) *Maintenance record entries.* Except as provided in paragraphs (b) and (c) of this section, each person who maintains, performs preventive maintenance, rebuilds, or alters an aircraft, airframe, aircraft engine, propeller, appliance, or component part shall make an entry in the maintenance record of that equipment containing the following information:

(1) A description (or reference to data acceptable to the Administrator) of work performed.

(2) The date of completion of the work performed.

(3) The name of the person performing the work if other than the person specified in paragraph (a)(4) of this section.

(4) If the work performed on the aircraft, airframe, aircraft engine, propeller, appliance, or component part has been performed satisfactorily, the signature, certificate number, and kind of certificate held by the person approving the work. The signature constitutes the approval for return to service only for the work performed.

(b) Each holder of an air carrier operating certificate or an operating certificate issued under Part 121 or 135, that is required by its approved operations specifications to provide for a continuous airworthiness maintenance program, shall make a record of the maintenance, preventive maintenance, rebuilding, and alteration, on aircraft, airframes, aircraft engines, propellers, appliances, or component parts which it operates in accordance with the applicable provisions of Part 121 or 135 of this chapter, as appropriate.

(c) This section does not apply to persons performing inspections in accordance with Part 91, 125, §135.411(a)(1), or §135.419 of this chapter.

(d) In addition to the entry required by paragraph (a) of this section, major repairs and major alterations shall be entered on a form, and the form disposed of, in the manner prescribed in appendix B, by the person performing the work.

[Docket No. 1993, 29 FR 5451, April 23, 1964; as amended by Amdt. 43–23, 47 FR 41085, Sept. 16, 1982; Amdt. 43–37, 66 FR 21066, April 27, 2001; Amdt. 43–39, 69 FR 44863, July 27, 2004]

§43.10 Disposition of life-limited aircraft parts.

(a) *Definitions used in this section.* For the purposes of this section the following definitions apply.

Life-limited part means any part for which a mandatory replacement limit is specified in the type design, the Instructions for Continued Airworthiness, or the maintenance manual.

Life status means the accumulated cycles, hours, or any other mandatory replacement limit of a life-limited part.

(b) *Temporary removal of parts from type-certificated products.* When a life-limited part is temporarily removed and reinstalled for the purpose of performing maintenance, no disposition under paragraph (c) of this section is required if—

(1) The life status of the part has not changed;

(2) The removal and reinstallation is performed on the same serial numbered product; and

(3) That product does not accumulate time in service while the part is removed.

(c) *Disposition of parts removed from type-certificated products.* Except as provided in paragraph (b) of this section, after April 15, 2002 each person who removes a life-limited part from a type-certificated product must ensure that the part is controlled using one of the methods in this paragraph. The method must deter the installation of the part after it has reached its life limit. Acceptable methods include:

(1) *Record keeping system.* The part may be controlled using a record keeping system that substantiates the part number, serial number, and current life status of the part.

43

Each time the part is removed from a type certificated product, the record must be updated with the current life status. This system may include electronic, paper, or other means of record keeping.

(2) *Tag or record attached to part.* A tag or other record may be attached to the part. The tag or record must include the part number, serial number, and current life status of the part. Each time the part is removed from a type certificated product, either a new tag or record must be created, or the existing tag or record must be updated with the current life status.

(3) *Non-permanent marking.* The part may be legibly marked using a non-permanent method showing its current life status. The life status must be updated each time the part is removed from a type certificated product, or if the mark is removed, another method in this section may be used. The mark must be accomplished in accordance with the instructions under §45.16 of this chapter in order to maintain the integrity of the part.

(4) *Permanent marking.* The part may be legibly marked using a permanent method showing its current life status. The life status must be updated each time the part is removed from a type certificated product. Unless the part is permanently removed from use on type certificated products, this permanent mark must be accomplished in accordance with the instructions under §45.16 of this chapter in order to maintain the integrity of the part.

(5) *Segregation.* The part may be segregated using methods that deter its installation on a type-certificated product. These methods must include, at least—

(i) Maintaining a record of the part number, serial number, and current life status, and

(ii) Ensuring the part is physically stored separately from parts that are currently eligible for installation.

(6) *Mutilation.* The part may be mutilated to deter its installation in a type certificated produce. The mutilation must render the part beyond repair and incapable of being reworked to appear to be airworthy.

(7) *Other methods.* Any other method approved or accepted by the FAA.

(d) *Transfer of life-limited parts.* Each person who removes a life-limited part from a type certificated product and later sells or otherwise transfers that part must transfer with the part the mark, tag, or other record used to comply with this section, unless the part is mutilated before it is sold or transferred.

[Docket No. FAA–2000–8017, 67 FR 2110, Jan. 15, 2002]

§43.11 Content, form, and disposition of records for inspections conducted under Parts 91 and 125 and §§135.411(a)(1) and 135.419 of this chapter.

(a) *Maintenance record entries.* The person approving or disapproving for return to service an aircraft, airframe, aircraft engine, propeller, appliance, or component part after any inspection performed in accordance with Part 91, 123, 125, §§135.411(a)(1), or 135.419 shall make an entry in the maintenance record of that equipment containing the following information:

(1) The type of inspection and a brief description of the extent of the inspection.

(2) The date of the inspection and aircraft total time in service.

(3) The signature, the certificate number, and kind of certificate held by the person approving or disapproving for return to service the aircraft, airframe, aircraft engine, propeller, appliance, component part, or portions thereof.

(4) Except for progressive inspections, if the aircraft is found to be airworthy and approved for return to service, the following or a similarly worded statement—"I certify that this aircraft has been inspected in accordance with (insert type) inspection and was determined to be in airworthy condition."

(5) Except for progressive inspections, if the aircraft is not approved for return to service because of needed maintenance, noncompliance with applicable specifications, airworthiness directives, or other approved data, the following or a similarly worded statement—"I certify that this aircraft has been inspected in accordance with (insert type) inspection and a list of discrepancies and unairworthy items dated (date) has been provided for the aircraft owner or operator."

(6) For progressive inspections, the following or a similarly worded statement—"I certify that in accordance with a progressive inspection program, a routine inspection of (identify whether aircraft or components) and a detailed inspection of (identify components) were performed and the (aircraft or components) are (approved or disapproved) for return to service." If disapproved, the entry will further state "and a list of discrepancies and unairworthy items dated (date) has been provided to the aircraft owner or operator."

(7) If an inspection is conducted under an inspection program provided for in Part 91, 123, 125, or §135.411(a)(1), the entry must identify the inspection program, that part of the inspection program accomplished, and contain a statement that the inspection was performed in accordance with the inspections and procedures for that particular program.

(b) *Listing of discrepancies and placards.* If the person performing any inspection required by Part 91 or 125 or §135.411(a)(1) of this chapter finds that the aircraft is unairworthy or does not meet the applicable type certificate data, airworthiness directives, or other approved data upon which its airworthiness depends, that persons must give the owner or lessee a signed and dated list of those discrepancies. For those items permitted to be inoperative under §91.213(d)(2) of this chapter, that person shall place a placard, that meets the aircraft's airworthiness certification regulations, on each inoperative instrument and the cockpit control of each item of inoperative equipment, marking it "Inoperative," and shall add the items to the signed and dated list of discrepancies given to the owner or lessee.

[Amdt. 43–23, 47 FR 41085, Sept. 16, 1982; as amended by Amdt. 43–30, 53 FR 50195, Dec. 13, 1988; Amdt. 43–36, 61 FR 19501, May 1, 1996]

§43.12 Maintenance records: Falsification, reproduction, or alteration.

(a) No person may make or cause to be made:

(1) Any fraudulent or intentionally false entry in any record or report that is required to be made, kept, or used to show compliance with any requirement under this part;

(2) Any reproduction, for fraudulent purpose, of any record or report under this part; or

(3) Any alteration, for fraudulent purpose, of any record or report under this part.

(b) The commission by any person of an act prohibited under paragraph (a) of this section is a basis for suspending or revoking the applicable airman, operator, or production certificate, Technical Standard Order Authorization, FAA-Parts Manufacturer Approval, or Product and Process Specification issued by the Administrator and held by that person.

[Amdt. 43–19, 43 FR 22639, May 25, 1978; as amended by Amdt. 43–23, 47 FR 41085, Sept. 16, 1982]

§43.13 Performance rules (general).

(a) Each person performing maintenance, alteration, or preventive maintenance on an aircraft, engine, propeller, or appliance shall use the methods, techniques, and practices prescribed in the current manufacturer's maintenance manual or Instructions for Continued Airworthiness prepared by its manufacturer, or other methods, techniques, and practices acceptable to the Administrator, except as noted in §43.16. He shall use the tools, equipment, and test apparatus necessary to assure completion of the work in accordance with accepted industry practices. If special equipment or test apparatus is recommended by the manufacturer involved, he must use that equipment or apparatus or its equivalent acceptable to the Administrator.

(b) Each person maintaining or altering, or performing preventive maintenance, shall do that work in such a manner and use materials of such a quality, that the condition of the aircraft, airframe, aircraft engine, propeller, or appliance worked on will be at least equal to its original or properly altered condition (with regard to aerodynamic function, structural strength, resistance to vibration and deterioration, and other qualities affecting airworthiness).

(c) *Special provisions for holders of air carrier operating certificates and operating certificates issued under the provisions of Part 121 or 135 and Part 129 operators holding operations specifications.* Unless otherwise notified by the administrator, the methods, techniques, and practices contained in the maintenance manual or the maintenance part of the manual of the holder of an air carrier operating certificate or an operating certificate under Part 121 or 135 and Part 129 operators holding operations specifications (that is required by its operating specifications to provide a continuous airworthiness maintenance and inspection program) constitute acceptable means of compliance with this section.

[Docket No. 1993, 29 FR 5451, April 23, 1964; as amended by Amdt. 43–20, 45 FR 60182, Sept. 11, 1980; Amdt. 43–23, 47 FR 41085, Sept. 16, 1982; Amdt. 43–28, 52 FR 20028, June 16, 1987; Amdt. 43–37, 66 FR 21066, April 27, 2001]

§43.15 Additional performance rules for inspections.

(a) *General.* Each person performing an inspection required by Part 91, 123, 125, or 135 of this chapter, shall—

(1) Perform the inspection so as to determine whether the aircraft, or portion(s) thereof under inspection, meets all applicable airworthiness requirements; and

(2) If the inspection is one provided for in Part 123, 125, 135, or §91.409(e) of this chapter, perform the inspection in accordance with the instructions and procedures set forth in the inspection program for the aircraft being inspected.

(b) *Rotorcraft.* Each person performing an inspection required by Part 91 on a rotorcraft shall inspect the following systems in accordance with the maintenance manual or Instructions for Continued Airworthiness of the manufacturer concerned:

(1) The drive shafts or similar systems.

(2) The main rotor transmission gear box for obvious defects.

(3) The main rotor and center section (or the equivalent area).

(4) The auxiliary rotor on helicopters.

(c) *Annual and 100-hour inspections.*

(1) Each person performing an annual or 100-hour inspection shall use a checklist while performing the inspection. The checklist may be of the person's own design, one provided by the manufacturer of the equipment being inspected or one obtained from another source. This checklist must include the scope and detail of the items contained in Appendix D to this part and paragraph (b) of this section.

(2) Each person approving a reciprocating-engine-powered aircraft for return to service after an annual or 100-hour inspection shall, before that approval, run the aircraft engine or engines to determine satisfactory performance in accordance with the manufacturer's recommendations of—

(i) Power output (static and idle r.p.m.);

(ii) Magnetos;

(iii) Fuel and oil pressure; and

(iv) Cylinder and oil temperature.

(3) Each person approving a turbine-engine-powered aircraft for return to service after an annual, 100-hour, or progressive inspection shall, before that approval, run the aircraft engine or engines to determine satisfactory performance in accordance with the manufacturer's recommendations.

(d) *Progressive inspection.*

(1) Each person performing a progressive inspection shall, at the start of a progressive inspection system, inspect the aircraft completely. After this initial inspection, routine and detailed inspections must be conducted as prescribed in the progressive inspection schedule. Routine inspections consist of visual examination or check of the appliances, the aircraft, and its components and systems, insofar as practicable without disassembly. Detailed inspections consist of a thorough examination of the appliances, the aircraft, and its components and systems, with such disassembly as is necessary. For the purposes of this subparagraph, the overhaul of a component or system is considered to be a detailed inspection.

(2) If the aircraft is away from the station where inspections are normally conducted, an appropriately rated mechanic, a certificated repair station, or the manufacturer of the aircraft may perform inspections in accordance with the procedures and using the forms of the person who would otherwise perform the inspection.

[Docket No. 1993, 29 FR 5451, April 23, 1964; as amended by Amdt. 43–23, 47 FR 41086, Sept. 16, 1982; Amdt. 43–25, 51 FR 40702, Nov. 7, 1986; Amdt. 43–31, 54 FR 34330, Aug. 18, 1989]

§43.16 Airworthiness Limitations.

Each person performing an inspection or other maintenance specified in an Airworthiness Limitations section of a manufacturer's maintenance manual or Instructions for Continued Airworthiness shall perform the inspection or other maintenance in accordance with that section, or in accordance with operations specifications approved by the Administrator under Parts 121, 123, or 135, or an inspection program approved under §91.409(e).

[Amdt. 43–20, 45 FR 60183, Sept. 11, 1980; as amended by Amdt. 43–23, 47 FR 41086, Sept. 16, 1982; Amdt. 43–31, 54 FR 34330, Aug. 18, 1989; Amdt. 43–37, 66 FR 21066, April 27, 2001]

§43.17 Maintenance, preventive maintenance, and alterations performed on U.S. aeronautical products by certain Canadian persons.

(a) *Definitions.* For purposes of this section:

Aeronautical product means any civil aircraft or airframe, aircraft engine, propeller, appliance, component, or part to be installed thereon.

Canadian aeronautical product means any aeronautical product under airworthiness regulation by Transport Canada Civil Aviation.

U.S. aeronautical product means any aeronautical product under airworthiness regulation by the FAA.

(b) *Applicability.* This section does not apply to any U.S. aeronautical products maintained or altered under any bilateral agreement made between Canada and any country other than the United States.

(c) *Authorized persons.*

(1) A person holding a valid Transport Canada Civil Aviation Maintenance Engineer license and appropriate ratings may, with respect to a U.S.-registered aircraft located in Canada, perform maintenance, preventive maintenance, and alterations in accordance with the requirements of paragraph (d) of this section and approve the affected aircraft for return to service in accordance with the requirements of paragraph (e) of this section.

(2) A Transport Canada Civil Aviation Approved Maintenance Organization (AMO) holding appropriate ratings may, with respect to a U.S.-registered aircraft or other U.S. aeronautical products located in Canada, perform maintenance, preventive maintenance, and alterations in accordance with the requirements of paragraph (d) of this section and approve the affected products for return to service in accordance with the requirements of paragraph (e) of this section.

(d) *Performance requirements.* A person authorized in paragraph (c) of this section may perform maintenance (including any inspection required by §91.409 of this chapter, except an annual inspection), preventive maintenance, and alterations, provided—

(1) The person performing the work is authorized by Transport Canada Civil Aviation to perform the same type of work with respect to Canadian aeronautical products;

(2) The maintenance, preventive maintenance, or alteration is performed in accordance with a Bilateral Aviation Safety Agreement between the United States and Canada and associated Maintenance Implementation Procedures that provide a level of safety equivalent to that provided by the provisions of this chapter;

(3) The maintenance, preventive maintenance, or alteration is performed such that the affected product complies with the applicable requirements of part 36 of this chapter; and

(4) The maintenance, preventive maintenance, or alteration is recorded in accordance with a Bilateral Aviation Safety Agreement between the United States and Canada and associated Maintenance Implementation Procedures that provide a level of safety equivalent to that provided by the provisions of this chapter.

(e) *Approval requirements.*

(1) To return an affected product to service, a person authorized in paragraph (c) of this section must approve (certify) maintenance, preventive maintenance, and alterations performed under this section, except that an Aircraft Maintenance Engineer may not approve a major repair or major alteration.

(2) An AMO whose system of quality control for the maintenance, preventive maintenance, alteration, and inspection of aeronautical products has been approved by Transport Canada Civil Aviation, or an authorized employee performing work for such an AMO, may approve (certify) a major repair or major alteration performed under this section if the work was performed in accordance with technical data approved by the FAA.

(f) No person may operate in air commerce an aircraft, airframe, aircraft engine, propeller, or appliance on which maintenance, preventive maintenance, or alteration has been performed under this section unless it has been approved for return to service by a person authorized in this section.

[Docket No. 1993, 29 FR 5451, April 23, 1964; as amended by Amdt. 43–33, 56 FR 57571, Nov. 12, 1991; Amdt. 43–40, 70 FR 40877, July 14, 2005]

APPENDIX A TO PART 43

MAJOR ALTERATIONS, MAJOR REPAIRS, AND PREVENTIVE MAINTENANCE

(a) *Major alterations*—

(1) *Airframe major alterations.* Alterations of the following parts and alterations of the following types, when not listed in the aircraft specifications issued by the FAA, are airframe major alterations:

(i) Wings.

(ii) Tail surfaces.

(iii) Fuselage.

(iv) Engine mounts.

(v) Control system.

(vi) Landing gear.

(vii) Hull or floats.

(viii) Elements of an airframe including spars, ribs, fittings, shock absorbers, bracing, cowling, fairings, and balance weights.

(ix) Hydraulic and electrical actuating system of components.

(x) Rotor blades.

(xi) Changes to the empty weight or empty balance which result in an increase in the maximum certificated weight or center of gravity limits of the aircraft.

(xii) Changes to the basic design of the fuel, oil, cooling, heating, cabin pressurization, electrical, hydraulic, de-icing, or exhaust systems.

(xiii) Changes to the wing or to fixed or movable control surfaces which affect flutter and vibration characteristics.

(2) *Powerplant major alterations.* The following alterations of a powerplant when not listed in the engine specifications issued by the FAA, are powerplant major alterations.

(i) Conversion of an aircraft engine from one approved model to another, involving any changes in compression ratio, propeller reduction gear, impeller gear ratios or the substitution of major engine parts which requires extensive rework and testing of the engine.

(ii) Changes to the engine by replacing aircraft engine structural parts with parts not supplied by the original manufacturer or parts not specifically approved by the Administrator.

(iii) Installation of an accessory which is not approved for the engine.

(iv) Removal of accessories that are listed as required equipment on the aircraft or engine specification.

(v) Installation of structural parts other than the type of parts approved for the installation.

(vi) Conversions of any sort for the purpose of using fuel of a rating or grade other than that listed in the engine specifications.

(3) *Propeller major alterations.* The following alterations of a propeller when not authorized in the propeller specifications issued by the FAA are propeller major alterations:

(i) Changes in blade design.

(ii) Changes in hub design.

(iii) Changes in the governor or control design.

(iv) Installation of a propeller governor or feathering system.

(v) Installation of propeller de-icing system.

(vi) Installation of parts not approved for the propeller.

(4) *Appliance major alterations.* Alterations of the basic design not made in accordance with recommendations of the appliance manufacturer or in accordance with an FAA Airworthiness Directive are appliance major alterations. In addition, changes in the basic design of radio communication and navigation equipment approved under type certification or a Technical Standard Order that have an effect on frequency stability, noise level, sensitivity, selectivity, distortion, spurious radiation, AVC characteristics, or ability to meet environmental test conditions and other changes that have an effect on the performance of the equipment are also major alterations.

(b) *Major repairs—*

(1) *Airframe major repairs.* Repairs to the following parts of an airframe and repairs of the following types, involving the strengthening, reinforcing, splicing, and manufacturing of primary structural members or their replacement, when replacement is by fabrication such as riveting or welding, are airframe major repairs.

(i) Box beams.

(ii) Monocoque or semimonocoque wings or control surfaces.

(iii) Wing stringers or chord members.

(iv) Spars.

(v) Spar flanges.

(vi) Members of truss-type beams.

(vii) Thin sheet webs of beams.

(viii) Keel and chine members of boat hulls or floats.

(ix) Corrugated sheet compression members which act as flange material of wings or tail surfaces.

(x) Wing main ribs and compression members.

(xi) Wing or tail surface brace struts.

(xii) Engine mounts.

(xiii) Fuselage longerons.

(xiv) Members of the side truss, horizontal truss, or bulkheads.

(xv) Main seat support braces and brackets.

(xvi) Landing gear brace struts.

(xvii) Axles.

(xviii) Wheels.

(xix) Skis, and ski pedestals.

(xx) Parts of the control system such as control columns, pedals, shafts, brackets, or horns.

(xxi) Repairs involving the substitution of material.

(xxii) The repair of damaged areas in metal or plywood stressed covering exceeding six inches in any direction.

(xxiii) The repair of portions of skin sheets by making additional seams.

(xxiv) The splicing of skin sheets.

(xxv) The repair of three or more adjacent wing or control surface ribs or the leading edge of wings and control surfaces, between such adjacent ribs.

(xxvi) Repair of fabric covering involving an area greater than that required to repair two adjacent ribs.

(xxvii) Replacement of fabric on fabric covered parts such as wings, fuselages, stabilizers, and control surfaces.

(xxviii) Repairing, including rebottoming, of removable or integral fuel tanks and oil tanks.

(2) *Powerplant major repairs.* Repairs of the following parts of an engine and repairs of the following types, are powerplant major repairs:

(i) Separation or disassembly of a crankcase or crankshaft of a reciprocating engine equipped with an integral supercharger.

(ii) Separation or disassembly of a crankcase or crankshaft of a reciprocating engine equipped with other than spur-type propeller reduction gearing.

(iii) Special repairs to structural engine parts by welding, plating, metalizing, or other methods.

(3) *Propeller major repairs.* Repairs of the following types to a propeller are propeller major repairs:

(i) Any repairs to, or straightening of steel blades.

(ii) Repairing or machining of steel hubs.

(iii) Shortening of blades.

(iv) Retipping of wood propellers.

(v) Replacement of outer laminations on fixed pitch wood propellers.

(vi) Repairing elongated bolt holes in the hub of fixed pitch wood propellers.

(vii) Inlay work on wood blades.

(viii) Repairs to composition blades.

(ix) Replacement of tip fabric.

(x) Replacement of plastic covering.

(xi) Repair of propeller governors.

(xii) Overhaul of controllable pitch propellers.

(xiii) Repairs to deep dents, cuts, scars, nicks, etc., and straightening of aluminum blades.

(xiv) The repair or replacement of internal elements of blades.

(4) *Appliance major repairs.* Repairs of the following types to appliances are appliance major repairs:

(i) Calibration and repair of instruments.

(ii) Calibration of radio equipment.

(iii) Rewinding the field coil of an electrical accessory.

(iv) Complete disassembly of complex hydraulic power valves.

(v) Overhaul of pressure type carburetors, and pressure type fuel, oil and hydraulic pumps.

(c) *Preventive maintenance.* Preventive maintenance is limited to the following work, provided it does not involve complex assembly operations:

(1) Removal, installation, and repair of landing gear tires.

(2) Replacing elastic shock absorber cords on landing gear.

(3) Servicing landing gear shock struts by adding oil, air, or both.

(4) Servicing landing gear wheel bearings, such as cleaning and greasing.

(5) Replacing defective safety wiring or cotter keys.

(6) Lubrication not requiring disassembly other than removal of nonstructural items such as cover plates, cowlings, and fairings.

(7) Making simple fabric patches not requiring rib stitching or the removal of structural parts or control surfaces. In the case of balloons, the making of small fabric repairs to envelopes (as defined in, and in accordance with, the balloon manufacturers' instructions) not requiring load tape repair or replacement.

(8) Replenishing hydraulic fluid in the hydraulic reservoir.

(9) Refinishing decorative coating of fuselage, balloon baskets, wings tail group surfaces (excluding balanced control surfaces), fairings, cowlings, landing gear, cabin, or cockpit interior when removal or disassembly of any primary structure or operating system is not required.

(10) Applying preservative or protective material to components where no disassembly of any primary structure or operating system is involved and where such coating is not prohibited or is not contrary to good practices.

(11) Repairing upholstery and decorative furnishings of the cabin, cockpit, or balloon basket interior when the repairing does not require disassembly of any primary structure or operating system or interfere with an operating system or affect the primary structure of the aircraft.

(12) Making small simple repairs to fairings, nonstructural cover plates, cowlings, and small patches and reinforcements not changing the contour so as to interfere with proper air flow.

(13) Replacing side windows where that work does not interfere with the structure or any operating system such as controls, electrical equipment, etc.

(14) Replacing safety belts.

(15) Replacing seats or seat parts with replacement parts approved for the aircraft, not involving disassembly of any primary structure or operating system.

(16) Trouble shooting and repairing broken circuits in landing light wiring circuits.

(17) Replacing bulbs, reflectors, and lenses of position and landing lights.

(18) Replacing wheels and skis where no weight and balance computation is involved.

(19) Replacing any cowling not requiring removal of the propeller or disconnection of flight controls.

(20) Replacing or cleaning spark plugs and setting of spark plug gap clearance.

(21) Replacing any hose connection except hydraulic connections.

(22) Replacing prefabricated fuel lines.

(23) Cleaning or replacing fuel and oil strainers or filter elements.

(24) Replacing and servicing batteries.

(25) Cleaning of balloon burner pilot and main nozzles in accordance with the balloon manufacturer's instructions.

(26) Replacement or adjustment of nonstructural standard fasteners incidental to operations.

(27) The interchange of balloon baskets and burners on envelopes when the basket or burner is designated as interchangeable in the balloon type certificate data and the baskets and burners are specifically designed for quick removal and installation.

(28) The installations of anti-misfueling devices to reduce the diameter of fuel tank filler openings provided the specific device has been made a part of the aircraft type certificate data by the aircraft manufacturer, the aircraft manufacturer has provided FAA-approved instructions for installation of the specific device, and installation does not involve the disassembly of the existing tank filler opening.

(29) Removing, checking, and replacing magnetic chip detectors.

(30) The inspection and maintenance tasks prescribed and specifically identified as preventive maintenance in a primary category aircraft type certificate or supplemental type certificate holder's approved special inspection and preventive maintenance program when accomplished on a primary category aircraft provided:

(i) They are performed by the holder of at least a private pilot certificate issued under part 61 who is the registered owner (including co-owners) of the affected aircraft and who holds a certificate of competency for the affected aircraft (1) issued by a school approved under §147.21(e) of this chapter; (2) issued by the holder of the production certificate for that primary category aircraft that has a special training program approved under §21.24 of this subchapter; or (3) issued by another entity that has a course approved by the Administrator; and

(ii) The inspections and maintenance tasks are performed in accordance with instructions contained by the special inspection and preventive maintenance program approved as part of the aircraft's type design or supplemental type design.

(31) Removing and replacing self-contained, front instrument panel-mounted navigation and communication devices that employ tray-mounted connectors that connect the unit when the unit is installed into the instrument panel, (excluding automatic flight control systems, transponders, and microwave frequency distance measuring equipment (DME)). The approved unit must be designed to be readily and repeatedly removed and replaced, and pertinent instructions must be provided. Prior to the unit's intended use, an opera-

tional check must be performed in accordance with the applicable sections of part 91 of this chapter.

(32) Updating self-contained, front instrument panel-mounted Air Traffic Control (ATC) navigational software data bases (excluding those of automatic flight control systems, transponders, and microwave frequency distance measuring equipment (DME)) provided no disassembly of the unit is required and pertinent instructions are provided. Prior to the unit's intended use, an operational check must be performed in accordance with applicable sections of part 91 of this chapter.

(Secs. 313, 601 through 610, and 1102, Federal Aviation Act of 1958 as amended (49 U.S.C. 1354, 1421 through 1430 and 1502); (49 U.S.C. 106(g) (Revised Pub. L. 97–449, Jan. 21, 1983); and 14 CFR 11.45)

[Docket No. 1993, 29 FR 5451, April 23, 1964; as amended by Amdt. 43–14, 37 FR 14291, June 19, 1972; Amdt. 43–23, 47 FR 41086, Sept. 16, 1982; Amdt. 43–24, 49 FR 44602, Nov. 7, 1984; Amdt. 43–25, 51 FR 40703, Nov. 7, 1986; Amdt. 43–27, 52 FR 17277, May 6, 1987; Amdt. 43–34, 57 FR 41369, Sept. 9, 1992; Amdt. No. 43–36, 61 FR 19501, May 1, 1996]

Appendix B to Part 43
Recording of Major Repairs and Major Alterations

(a) Except as provided in paragraphs (b), (c), and (d) of this appendix, each person performing a major repair or major alteration shall—

(1) Execute FAA Form 337 at least in duplicate;

(2) Give a signed copy of that form to the aircraft owner; and

(3) Forward a copy of that form to the local Flight Standards District Office within 48 hours after the aircraft, airframe, aircraft engine, propeller, or appliance is approved for return to service.

(b) For major repairs made in accordance with a manual or specifications acceptable to the Administrator, a certificated repair station may, in place of the requirements of paragraph (a)—

(1) Use the customer's work order upon which the repair is recorded;

(2) Give the aircraft owner a signed copy of the work order and retain a duplicate copy for at least two years from the date of approval for return to service of the aircraft, airframe, aircraft engine, propeller, or appliance;

(3) Give the aircraft owner a maintenance release signed by an authorized representative of the repair station and incorporating the following information:

(i) Identity of the aircraft, airframe, aircraft engine, propeller or appliance.

(ii) If an aircraft, the make, model, serial number, nationality and registration marks, and location of the repaired area.

(iii) If an airframe, aircraft engine, propeller, or appliance, give the manufacturer's name, name of the part, model, and serial numbers (if any); and

(4) Include the following or a similarly worded statement—

"The aircraft, airframe, aircraft engine, propeller, or appliance identified above was repaired and inspected in accordance with current Regulations of the Federal Aviation Agency and is approved for return to service.

Pertinent details of the repair are on file at this repair station under Order No. ____________
Date ____________
Signed ____________
(For signature of authorized representative)

(Repair station name)
(Certificate No.) ____________."
(Address)

(c) For a major repair or major alteration made by a person authorized in §43.17, the person who performs the major repair or major alteration and the person authorized by §43.17 to approve that work shall execute a FAA Form 337 at least in duplicate. A completed copy of that form shall be—

(1) Given to the aircraft owner; and

(2) Forwarded to the Federal Aviation Administration, Aircraft Registration Branch, Post Office Box 25082, Oklahoma City, Okla. 73125, within 48 hours after the work is inspected.

(d) For extended-range fuel tanks installed within the passenger compartment or a baggage compartment, the person who performs the work and the person authorized to approve the work by §43.7 of this part shall execute an FAA Form 337 in at least triplicate. One (1) copy of the FAA Form 337 shall be placed on board the aircraft as specified in §91.417 of this chapter. The remaining forms shall be distributed as required by paragraph (a)(2) and (3) or (c)(1) and (2) of this paragraph as appropriate.

(Secs. 101, 610, 72 Stat. 737, 780, 49 U.S.C. 1301, 1430)

[Docket No. 1993, 29 FR 5451, April 23, 1964; as amended by Amdt. 43–10, 33 FR 15989, Oct. 31, 1968; Amdt. 43–29, 52 FR 34101, Sept. 9, 1987; Amdt. 43–31, 54 FR 34330, Aug. 18, 1989]

Appendix C to Part 43—[Reserved]

Appendix D to Part 43
Scope and Detail of Items (as Applicable to the Particular Aircraft) To Be Included in Annual and 100-Hour Inspections

(a) Each person performing an annual or 100-hour inspection shall, before that inspection, remove or open all necessary inspection plates, access doors, fairing, and cowling. He shall thoroughly clean the aircraft and aircraft engine.

(b) Each person performing an annual or 100-hour inspection shall inspect (where applicable) the following components of the fuselage and hull group:

(1) Fabric and skin—for deterioration, distortion, other evidence of failure, and defective or insecure attachment of fittings.

(2) Systems and components—for improper installation, apparent defects, and unsatisfactory operation.

(3) Envelope, gas bags, ballast tanks, and related parts—for poor condition.

43

(c) Each person performing an annual or 100-hour inspection shall inspect (where applicable) the following components of the cabin and cockpit group:

(1) Generally—for uncleanliness and loose equipment that might foul the controls.

(2) Seats and safety belts—for poor condition and apparent defects.

(3) Windows and windshields—for deterioration and breakage.

(4) Instruments—for poor condition, mounting, marking, and (where practicable) improper operation.

(5) Flight and engine controls—for improper installation and improper operation.

(6) Batteries—for improper installation and improper charge.

(7) All systems—for improper installation, poor general condition, apparent and obvious defects, and insecurity of attachment.

(d) Each person performing an annual or 100-hour inspection shall inspect (where applicable) components of the engine and nacelle group as follows:

(1) Engine section—for visual evidence of excessive oil, fuel, or hydraulic leaks, and sources of such leaks.

(2) Studs and nuts—for improper torquing and obvious defects.

(3) Internal engine—for cylinder compression and for metal particles or foreign matter on screens and sump drain plugs. If there is weak cylinder compression, for improper internal condition and improper internal tolerances.

(4) Engine mount—for cracks, looseness of mounting, and looseness of engine to mount.

(5) Flexible vibration dampeners—for poor condition and deterioration.

(6) Engine controls—for defects, improper travel, and improper safetying.

(7) Lines, hoses, and clamps—for leaks, improper condition and looseness.

(8) Exhaust stacks—for cracks, defects, and improper attachment.

(9) Accessories—for apparent defects in security of mounting.

(10) All systems—for improper installation, poor general condition, defects, and insecure attachment.

(11) Cowling—for cracks, and defects.

(e) Each person performing an annual or 100-hour inspection shall inspect (where applicable) the following components of the landing gear group:

(1) All units—for poor condition and insecurity of attachment.

(2) Shock absorbing devices—for improper oleo fluid level.

(3) Linkages, trusses, and members—for undue or excessive wear fatigue, and distortion.

(4) Retracting and locking mechanism—for improper operation.

(5) Hydraulic lines—for leakage.

(6) Electrical system—for chafing and improper operation of switches.

(7) Wheels—for cracks, defects, and condition of bearings.

(8) Tires—for wear and cuts.

(9) Brakes—for improper adjustment.

(10) Floats and skis—for insecure attachment and obvious or apparent defects.

(f) Each person performing an annual or 100-hour inspection shall inspect (where applicable) all components of the wing and center section assembly for poor general condition, fabric or skin deterioration, distortion, evidence of failure, and insecurity of attachment.

(g) Each person performing an annual or 100-hour inspection shall inspect (where applicable) all components and systems that make up the complete empennage assembly for poor general condition, fabric or skin deterioration, distortion, evidence of failure, insecure attachment, improper component installation, and improper component operation.

(h) Each person performing an annual or 100-hour inspection shall inspect (where applicable) the following components of the propeller group:

(1) Propeller assembly—for cracks, nicks, binds, and oil leakage.

(2) Bolts—for improper torquing and lack of safetying.

(3) Anti-icing devices—for improper operations and obvious defects.

(4) Control mechanisms—for improper operation, insecure mounting, and restricted travel.

(i) Each person performing an annual or 100-hour inspection shall inspect (where applicable) the following components of the radio group:

(1) Radio and electronic equipment—for improper installation and insecure mounting.

(2) Wiring and conduits—for improper routing, insecure mounting, and obvious defects.

(3) Bonding and shielding—for improper installation and poor condition.

(4) Antenna including trailing antenna—for poor condition, insecure mounting, and improper operation.

(j) Each person performing an annual or 100-hour inspection shall inspect (where applicable) each installed miscellaneous item that is not otherwise covered by this listing for improper installation and improper operation.

Appendix E to Part 43

Altimeter System Test and Inspection

Each person performing the altimeter system tests and inspections required by §91.411 shall comply with the following:

(a) *Static pressure system:*

(1) Ensure freedom from entrapped moisture and restrictions.

(2) Determine that leakage is within the tolerances established in §23.1325 or §25.1325, whichever is applicable.

(3) Determine that the static port heater, if installed, is operative.

(4) Ensure that no alterations or deformations of the airframe surface have been made that would affect the relationship between air pressure in the static pressure system and true ambient static air pressure for any flight condition.

(b) *Altimeter:*

(1) Test by an appropriately rated repair facility in accordance with the following subparagraphs. Unless otherwise specified, each test for performance may be conducted with the instrument subjected to vibration. When tests are con-

ducted with the temperature substantially different from ambient temperature of approximately 25 degrees C., allowance shall be made for the variation from the specified condition.

(i) *Scale error.* With the barometric pressure scale at 29.92 inches of mercury, the altimeter shall be subjected successively to pressures corresponding to the altitude specified in Table I up to the maximum normally expected operating altitude of the airplane in which the altimeter is to be installed. The reduction in pressure shall be made at a rate not in excess of 20,000 feet per minute to within approximately 2,000 feet of the test point. The test point shall be approached at a rate compatible with the test equipment. The altimeter shall be kept at the pressure corresponding to each test point for at least 1 minute, but not more than 10 minutes, before a reading is taken. The error at all test points must not exceed the tolerances specified in Table I.

(ii) *Hysteresis.* The hysteresis test shall begin not more than 15 minutes after the altimeter's initial exposure to the pressure corresponding to the upper limit of the scale error test prescribed in subparagraph (i); and while the altimeter is at this pressure, the hysteresis test shall commence. Pressure shall be increased at a rate simulating a descent in altitude at the rate of 5,000 to 20,000 feet per minute until within 3,000 feet of the first test point (50 percent of maximum altitude). The test point shall then be approached at a rate of approximately 3,000 feet per minute. The altimeter shall be kept at this pressure for at least 5 minutes, but not more than 15 minutes, before the test reading is taken. After the reading has been taken, the pressure shall be increased further, in the same manner as before, until the pressure corresponding to the second test point (40 percent of maximum altitude) is reached. The altimeter shall be kept at this pressure for at least 1 minute, but not more than 10 minutes, before the test reading is taken. After the reading has been taken, the pressure shall be increased further, in the same manner as before, until atmospheric pressure is reached. The reading of the altimeter at either of the two test points shall not differ by more than the tolerance specified in Table II from the reading of the altimeter for the corresponding altitude recorded during the scale error test prescribed in paragraph (b)(i).

(iii) *After effect.* Not more than 5 minutes after the completion of the hysteresis test prescribed in paragraph (b)(ii), the reading of the altimeter (corrected for any change in atmospheric pressure) shall not differ from the original atmospheric pressure reading by more than the tolerance specified in Table II.

(iv) *Friction.* The altimeter shall be subjected to a steady rate of decrease of pressure approximating 750 feet per minute. At each altitude listed in Table III, the change in reading of the pointers after vibration shall not exceed the corresponding tolerance listed in Table III.

(v) *Case leak.* The leakage of the altimeter case, when the pressure within it corresponds to an altitude of 18,000 feet, shall not change the altimeter reading by more than the tolerance shown in Table II during an interval of 1 minute.

(vi) *Barometric scale error.* At constant atmospheric pressure, the barometric pressure scale shall be set at each of the pressures (falling within its range of adjustment) that are listed in Table IV, and shall cause the pointer to indicate the equivalent altitude difference shown in Table IV with a tolerance of 25 feet.

(2) Altimeters which are the air data computer type with associated computing systems, or which incorporate air data correction internally, may be tested in a manner and to specifications developed by the manufacturer which are acceptable to the Administrator.

(c) Automatic Pressure Altitude Reporting Equipment and ATC Transponder System Integration Test. The test must be conducted by an appropriately rated person under the conditions specified in paragraph (a). Measure the automatic pressure altitude at the output of the installed ATC transponder when interrogated on Mode C at a sufficient number of test points to ensure that the altitude reporting equipment, altimeters, and ATC transponders perform their intended functions as installed in the aircraft. The difference between the automatic reporting output and the altitude displayed at the altimeter shall not exceed 125 feet.

(d) Records: Comply with the provisions of §43.9 of this chapter as to content, form, and disposition of the records. The person performing the altimeter tests shall record on the altimeter the date and maximum altitude to which the altimeter has been tested and the persons approving the airplane for return to service shall enter that data in the airplane log or other permanent record.

43

Table I

Altitude	Equivalent pressure (inches of mercury)	Tolerance ± (feet)
-1,000	31.018	20
0	29.921	20
500	29.385	20
1,000	28.856	20
1,500	28.335	25
2,000	27.821	30
3,000	26.817	30
4,000	25.842	35
6,000	23.978	40
8,000	22.225	60
10,000	20.577	80
12,000	19.029	90
14,000	17.577	100
16,000	16.216	110
18,000	14.942	120
20,000	13.750	130
22,000	12.636	140
25,000	11.104	155
30,000	8.885	180
35,000	7.041	205
40,000	5.538	230
45,000	4.355	255
50,000	3.425	280

Table II — Test Tolerances

Test	Tolerance (feet)
Case Leak Test	±100
Hysteresis Test:	
First Test Point (50 percent of maximum altitude)	75
Second Test Point (40 percent of maximum altitude)	75
After Effect Test	30

Table III — Friction

Altitude (feet)	Tolerance (feet)
1,000	±70
2,000	70
3,000	70
5,000	70
10,000	80
15,000	90
20,000	100
25,000	120
30,000	140
35,000	160
40,000	180
50,000	250

Table IV — Pressure-Altitude Difference

Pressure (inches of Hg)	Altitude difference (feet)
28.10	-1,727
28.50	-1,340
29.00	-863
29.50	-392
29.92	0
30.50	+531
30.90	+893
30.99	+974

(Secs. 313, 314, and 601 through 610 of the Federal Aviation Act of 1958 (49 U.S.C. 1354, 1355, and 1421 through 1430) and sec. 6(c), Dept. of Transportation Act (49 U.S.C. 1655(c)))

[Amdt. 43–2, 30 FR 8262, June 29, 1965; as amended by Amdt. 43–7, 32 FR 7587, May 24, 1967; Amdt. 43–19, 43 FR 22639, May 25, 1978; Amdt. 43–23, 47 FR 41086, Sept. 16, 1982; Amdt. 43–31, 54 FR 34330, Aug. 18, 1989]

APPENDIX F TO PART 43

ATC TRANSPONDER TESTS AND INSPECTIONS

The ATC transponder tests required by §91.413 of this chapter may be conducted using a bench check or portable test equipment and must meet the requirements prescribed in paragraphs (a) through (j) of this appendix. If portable test equipment with appropriate coupling to the aircraft antenna system is used, operate the test equipment for ATCRBS transponders at a nominal rate of 235 interrogations per second to avoid possible ATCRBS interference. Operate the test equipment at a nominal rate of 50 Mode S interrogations per second for Mode S. An additional 3 dB loss is allowed to compensate for antenna coupling errors during receiver sensitivity measurements conducted in accordance with paragraph (c)(1) when using portable test equipment.

(a) Radio Reply Frequency:

(1) For all classes of ATCRBS transponders, interrogate the transponder and verify that the reply frequency is 1090±3 Megahertz (MHz).

(2) For classes 1B, 2B, and 3B Mode S transponders, interrogate the transponder and verify that the reply frequency is 1090±3 MHz.

(3) For classes 1B, 2B, and 3B Mode S transponders that incorporate the optional 1090±1 MHz reply frequency, interrogate the transponder and verify that the reply frequency is correct.

(4) For classes 1A, 2A, 3A, and 4 Mode S transponders, interrogate the transponder and verify that the reply frequency is 1090±1 MHz.

(b) Suppression: When Classes 1B and 2B ATCRBS Transponders, or Classes 1B, 2B, and 3B Mode S transponders are interrogated Mode 3/A at an interrogation rate between 230 and 1,000 interrogations per second; or when Classes 1A and 2A ATCRBS Transponders, or Classes 1B, 2A, 3A, and 4 Mode S transponders are interrogated at a rate between 230 and 1,200 Mode 3/A interrogations per second:

(1) Verify that the transponder does not respond to more than 1 percent of ATCRBS interrogations when the amplitude of P_2 pulse is equal to the P_1 pulse.

(2) Verify that the transponder replies to at least 90 percent of ATCRBS interrogations when the amplitude of the P_2 pulse is 9 dB less than the P_1 pulse. If the test is conducted with a radiated test signal, the interrogation rate shall be 235±5 interrogations per second unless a higher rate has been approved for the test equipment used at that location.

(c) Receiver Sensitivity:

(1) Verify that for any class of ATCRBS Transponder, the receiver minimum triggering level (MTL) of the system is –73 ±4 dbm, or that for any class of Mode S transponder the receiver MTL for Mode S format (P6 type) interrogations is –74 ±3 dbm by use of a test set either:

(i) Connected to the antenna end of the transmission line;

(ii) Connected to the antenna terminal of the transponder with a correction for transmission line loss; or

(iii) Utilized radiated signal.

(2) Verify that the difference in Mode 3/A and Mode C receiver sensitivity does not exceed 1 db for either any class of ATCRBS transponder or any class of Mode S transponder.

(d) Radio Frequency (RF) Peak Output Power:

(1) Verify that the transponder RF output power is within specifications for the class of transponder. Use the same conditions as described in (c)(1) (i), (ii), and (iii) above.

(i) For Class 1A and 2A ATCRBS transponders, verify that the minimum RF peak output power is at least 21.0 dbw (125 watts).

(ii) For Class 1B and 2B ATCRBS Transponders, verify that the minimum RF peak output power is at least 18.5 dbw (70 watts).

(iii) For Class 1A, 2A, 3A, and 4 and those Class 1B, 2B, and 3B Mode S transponders that include the optional high RF peak output power, verify that the minimum RF peak output power is at least 21.0 dbw (125 watts).

(iv) For Classes 1B, 2B, and 3B Mode S transponders, verify that the minimum RF peak output power is at least 18.5 dbw (70 watts).

(v) For any class of ATCRBS or any class of Mode S transponders, verify that the maximum RF peak output power does not exceed 27.0 dbw (500 watts).

Note: The tests in (e) through (j) apply only to Mode S transponders.

(e) Mode S Diversity Transmission Channel Isolation: For any class of Mode S transponder that incorporates diversity operation, verify that the RF peak output power transmitted from the selected antenna exceeds the power transmitted from the nonselected antenna by at least 20 db.

(f) Mode S Address: Interrogate the Mode S transponder and verify that it replies only to its assigned address. Use the correct address and at least two incorrect addresses. The interrogations should be made at a nominal rate of 50 interrogations per second.

(g) Mode S Formats: Interrogate the Mode S transponder with uplink formats (UF) for which it is equipped and verify that the replies are made in the correct format. Use the surveillance formats UF=4 and 5. Verify that the altitude reported in the replies to UF=4 are the same as that reported in a valid ATCRBS Mode C reply. Verify that the identity reported in the replies to UF=5 are the same as that reported in a valid ATCRBS Mode 3/A reply. If the transponder is so equipped, use the communication formats UF=20, 21, and 24.

(h) Mode S All-Call Interrogations: Interrogate the Mode S transponder with the Mode S-only all-call format UF=11, and the ATCRBS/Mode S all-call formats (1.6 microsecond P_4 pulse) and verify that the correct address and capability are reported in the replies (downlink format DF=11).

(i) ATCRBS-Only All-Call Interrogation: Interrogate the Mode S transponder with the ATCRBS-only all-call interrogation (0.8 microsecond P_4 pulse) and verify that no reply is generated.

(j) Squitter: Verify that the Mode S transponder generates a correct squitter approximately once per second.

(k) Records: Comply with the provisions of §43.9 of this chapter as to content, form, and disposition of the records.

[Amdt. 43–26, 52 FR 3390, Feb. 3, 1987; 52 FR 6651, March 4, 1987; as amended by Amdt. 43–31, 54 FR 34330, Aug. 18, 1989]

PART 45
IDENTIFICATION AND REGISTRATION MARKING

Subpart A — General

Sec.
45.1 Applicability.

Subpart B — Identification of Aircraft and Related Products

45.11 General.
45.13 Identification data.
45.14 Identification of critical components.
45.15 Replacement and modification parts.
45.16 Marking of life-limited parts.

Subpart C — Nationality and Registration Marks

45.21 General.
45.22 Exhibition, antique, and other aircraft: Special rules.
45.23 Display of marks; general.
45.25 Location of marks on fixed-wing aircraft.
45.27 Location of marks; nonfixed-wing aircraft.
45.29 Size of marks.
45.31 Marking of export aircraft.
45.33 Sale of aircraft; removal of marks.

Authority: 49 U.S.C. 106(g), 40103, 40109, 40113–40114, 44101–44105, 44107–44108, 44110–44111, 44504, 44701, 44708–44709, 44711–44713, 44725, 45302–45303, 46104, 46304, 46306, 47122.

Source: Docket No. 2047, 29 FR 3223, March 11, 1964, unless otherwise noted.

Subpart A — General

§45.1 Applicability.

This part prescribes the requirements for—

(a) Identification of aircraft, and identification of aircraft engines and propellers that are manufactured under the terms of a type or production certificate:

(b) Identification of certain replacement and modified parts produced for installation on type certificated products; and

(c) Nationality and registration marking of U.S. registered aircraft.

[Docket No. 2047, 29 FR 3223, March 11, 1964; as amended by Amdt. 45–3, 32 FR 188, Jan. 10, 1967]

Subpart B — Identification of Aircraft and Related Products

§45.11 General.

(a) *Aircraft and aircraft engines.* Aircraft covered under §21.182 of this chapter must be identified, and each person who manufacturers an aircraft engine under a type or production certificate shall identify that engine, by means of a fireproof plate that has the information specified in §45.13 of this part marked on it by etching, stamping, engraving, or other approved method of fireproof marking. The identification plate for aircraft must be secured in such a manner that it will not likely be defaced or removed during normal service, or lost or destroyed in an accident. Except as provided in paragraphs (c), (d), and (e) of this section, the aircraft identification plate must be secured to the aircraft fuselage exterior so that it is legible to a person on the ground, and must be either adjacent to and aft of the rear-most entrance door or on the fuselage surface near the tail surfaces. For aircraft engines, the identification plate must be affixed to the engine at an accessible location in such a manner that it will not likely be defaced or removed during normal service, or lost or destroyed in an accident.

(b) *Propellers and propeller blades and hubs.* Each person who manufactures a propeller, propeller blade, or propeller hub under the terms of a type or production certificate shall identify his product by means of a plate, stamping, engraving, etching, or other approved method of fireproof identification that is placed on it on a noncritical surface, contains the information specified in §45.13, and will not be likely to be defaced or removed during normal service or lost or destroyed in an accident.

(c) For manned free balloons, the identification plate prescribed in paragraph (a) of this section must be secured to the balloon envelope and must be located, if practicable, where it is legible to the operator when the balloon is inflated. In addition, the basket and heater assembly must be permanently and legibly marked with the manufacturer's name, part number (or equivalent) and serial number (or equivalent).

(d) On aircraft manufactured before March 7, 1988, the identification plate required by paragraph (a) of this section may be secured at an accessible exterior or interior location near an entrance, if the model designation and builder's serial number are also displayed on the aircraft fuselage exterior. The model designation and builder's serial number must be legible to a person on the ground and must be located either adjacent to and aft of the rear-most entrance door or on the fuselage near the tail surfaces. The model designation and builder's serial number must be displayed in such a manner that they are not likely to be defaced or removed during normal service.

(e) For powered parachutes and weight-shift-control aircraft, the identification plate prescribed in paragraph (a) of this section must be secured to the aircraft fuselage exterior so that it is legible to a person on the ground.

[Amdt. 45–3, 32 FR 188, Jan. 10, 1967; as amended by Amdt. 45–7, 33 FR 14402, Sept. 25, 1968; Amdt. 45–12, 45 FR 60183, Sept. 11, 1980; 45 FR 85597, Dec. 29, 1980; Amdt. 45–17, 52 FR 34101, Sept. 9, 1987; 52 FR 36566, Sept. 30, 1987; Amdt. 45–24, 69 FR 44863, July 27, 2004]

§45.13 Identification data.

(a) The identification required by §45.11 (a) and (b) shall include the following information:

(1) Builder's name.

(2) Model designation.

(3) Builder's serial number.

(4) Type certificate number, if any.

(5) Production certificate number, if any.

(6) For aircraft engines, the established rating.

(7) On or after January 1, 1984, for aircraft engines specified in part 34 of this chapter, the date of manufacture as de-

fined in §34.1 of that part, and a designation, approved by the Administrator of the FAA, that indicates compliance with the applicable exhaust emission provisions of part 34 and 40 CFR part 87. Approved designations include COMPLY, EXEMPT, and NON-US as appropriate.

(i) The designation COMPLY indicates that the engine is in compliance with all of the applicable exhaust emissions provisions of part 34. For any engine with a rated thrust in excess of 26.7 kilonewtons (6000 pounds) which is not used or intended for use in commercial operations and which is in compliance with the applicable provisions of part 34, but does not comply with the hydrocarbon emissions standard of §34.21(d), the statement "May not be used as a commercial aircraft engine" must be noted in the permanent powerplant record that accompanies the engine at the time of manufacture of the engine.

(ii) The designation EXEMPT indicates that the engine has been granted an exemption pursuant to the applicable provision of §34.7 (a)(1), (a)(4), (b), (c), or (d), and an indication of the type of exemption and the reason for the grant must be noted in the permanent powerplant record that accompanies the engine from the time of manufacture of the engine.

(iii) The designation NON-US indicates that the engine has been granted an exemption pursuant to §34.7(a)(1), and the notation "This aircraft may not be operated within the United States", or an equivalent notation approved by the Administrator of the FAA, must be inserted in the aircraft logbook, or alternate equivalent document, at the time of installation of the engine.

(8) Any other information the Administrator finds appropriate.

(b) Except as provided in paragraph (d)(1) of this section, no person may remove, change, or place identification information required by paragraph (a) of this section, on any aircraft, aircraft engine, propeller, propeller blade, or propeller hub, without the approval of the Administrator.

(c) Except as provided in paragraph (d)(2) of this section, no person may remove or install any identification plate required by §45.11 of this part, without the approval of the Administrator.

(d) Persons performing work under the provisions of Part 43 of this chapter may, in accordance with methods, techniques, and practices acceptable to the Administrator—

(1) Remove, change, or place the identification information required by paragraph (a) of this section on any aircraft, aircraft engine, propeller, propeller blade, or propeller hub; or

(2) Remove an identification plate required by §45.11 when necessary during maintenance operations.

(e) No person may install an identification plate removed in accordance with paragraph (d)(2) of this section on any aircraft, aircraft engine, propeller, propeller blade, or propeller hub other than the one from which it was removed.

[Amdt. 45–3, 32 FR 188, Jan. 10, 1967; as amended by Amdt. 45–10, 44 FR 45379, Aug. 2, 1979; Amdt. 45–12, 45 FR 60183, Sept. 11, 1980; Amdt. 45–20, 55 FR 32861, Aug. 10, 1990; 55 FR 37287, Sept. 10, 1990]

§45.14 Identification of critical components.

Each person who produces a part for which a replacement time, inspection interval, or related procedure is specified in the Airworthiness Limitations section of a manufacturer's maintenance manual or Instructions for Continued Airworthiness shall permanently and legibly mark that component with a part number (or equivalent) and a serial number (or equivalent).

[Amdt. 45–16, 51 FR 40703, Nov. 7, 1986]

§45.15 Replacement and modification parts.

(a) Except as provided in paragraph (b) of this section, each person who produces a replacement or modification part under a Parts Manufacturer Approval issued under §21.303 of this chapter shall permanently and legibly mark the part with—

(1) The letters "FAA-PMA";

(2) The name, trademark, or symbol of the holder of the Parts Manufacturer Approval;

(3) The part number; and

(4) The name and model designation of each type certificated product on which the part is eligible for installation.

(b) If the Administrator finds that a part is too small or that it is otherwise impractical to mark a part with any of the information required by paragraph (a) of this section, a tag attached to the part or its container must include the information that could not be marked on the part. If the marking required by paragraph (a)(4) of this section is so extensive that to mark it on a tag is impractical, the tag attached to the part or the container may refer to a specific readily available manual or catalog for part eligibility information.

[Amdt. 45–8, 37 FR 10660, May 26, 1972; as amended by Amdt. 45–14, 47 FR 13315, March 29, 1982]

§45.16 Marking of life-limited parts.

When requested by a person required to comply with §43.10 of this chapter, the holder of a type certificate or design approval for a life-limited part must provide marking instructions, or must state that the part cannot be practicably marked without compromising its integrity. Compliance with this paragraph may be made by providing marking instructions in readily available documents, such as the maintenance manual or the Instructions for Continued Airworthiness.

[Docket No. FAA–2000–8017, 67 FR 2110, Jan. 15, 2002]

Subpart C—Nationality and Registration Marks

§45.21 General.

(a) Except as provided in §45.22, no person may operate a U.S.-registered aircraft unless that aircraft displays nationality and registration marks in accordance with the requirements of this section and §§45.23 through 45.33.

(b) Unless otherwise authorized by the Administrator, no person may place on any aircraft a design, mark, or symbol that modifies or confuses the nationality and registration marks.

(c) Aircraft nationality and registration marks must—

(1) Except as provided in paragraph (d) of this section, be painted on the aircraft or affixed by any other means insuring a similar degree of permanence;

(2) Have no ornamentation;

(3) Contrast in color with the background; and

(4) Be legible.

(d) The aircraft nationality and registration marks may be affixed to an aircraft with readily removable material if—

(1) It is intended for immediate delivery to a foreign purchaser;

(2) It is bearing a temporary registration number; or

(3) It is marked temporarily to meet the requirements of §45.22(c)(1) or §45.29(h) of this part, or both.

[Docket No. 8093, Amdt. 45–5, 33 FR 450, Jan 12, 1968; as amended by Amdt. 45–17, 52 FR 34102, Sept. 9, 1987]

§45.22 Exhibition, antique, and other aircraft: Special rules.

(a) When display of aircraft nationality and registration marks in accordance with §§45.21 and 45.23 through 45.33 would be inconsistent with exhibition of that aircraft, a U.S.-registered aircraft may be operated without displaying those marks anywhere on the aircraft if:

(1) It is operated for the purpose of exhibition, including a motion picture or television production, or an airshow;

(2) Except for practice and test fights necessary for exhibition purposes, it is operated only at the location of the exhibition, between the exhibition locations, and between those locations and the base of operations of the aircraft; and

(3) For each flight in the United States:

(i) It is operated with the prior approval of the Flight Standards District Office, in the case of a flight within the lateral boundaries of the surface areas of Class B, Class C, Class D, or Class E airspace designated for the takeoff airport, or within 4.4 nautical miles of that airport if it is within Class G airspace; or

(ii) It is operated under a flight plan filed under either §91.153 or §91.169 of this chapter describing the marks it displays, in the case of any other flight.

(b) A small U.S.-registered aircraft built at least 30 years ago or a U.S.-registered aircraft for which an experimental certificate has been issued under §21.191(d) or 21.191(g) for operation as an exhibition aircraft or as an amateur-built aircraft and which has the same external configuration as an aircraft built at least 30 years ago may be operated without displaying marks in accordance with §§45.21 and 45.23 through 45.33 if:

(1) It displays in accordance with §45.21(c) marks at least 2 inches high on each side of the fuselage or vertical tail surface consisting of the Roman capital letter "N" followed by:

(i) The U.S. registration number of the aircraft; or

(ii) The symbol appropriate to the airworthiness certificate of the aircraft ("C", standard; "R", restricted; "L", limited; or "X", experimental) followed by the U.S. registration number of the aircraft; and

(2) It displays no other mark that begins with the letter "N" anywhere on the aircraft, unless it is the same mark that is displayed under paragraph (b)(1) of this section.

(c) No person may operate an aircraft under paragraph (a) or (b) of this section—

(1) In an ADIZ or DEWIZ described in Part 99 of this chapter unless it temporarily bears marks in accordance with §§45.21 and 45.23 through 45.33;

(2) In a foreign country unless that country consents to that operation; or

(3) In any operation conducted under Part 121, 133, 135, or 137 of this chapter.

(d) If, due to the configuration of an aircraft, it is impossible for a person to mark it in accordance with §§45.21 and 45.23 through 45.33, he may apply to the Administrator for a different marking procedure.

[Docket No. 8093, Amdt. 45–5, 33 FR 450, Jan. 12, 1968; as amended by Amdt. 45–13, 46 FR 48603, Oct. 1, 1981; Amdt. 45–19, 54 FR 39291, Sept. 25, 1989; Amdt. 45–18, 54 FR 34330, Aug. 18, 1989; Amdt. 45–21, 56 FR 65653, Dec. 17, 1991; Amdt. 45–22, 66 FR 21066, April 27, 2001]

§45.23 Display of marks; general.

(a) Each operator of an aircraft shall display on that aircraft marks consisting of the Roman capital letter "N" (denoting United States registration) followed by the registration number of the aircraft. Each suffix letter used in the marks displayed must also be a Roman capital letter.

(b) When marks include only the Roman capital letter "N" and the registration number is displayed on limited, restricted or light-sport category aircraft or experimental or provisionally certificated aircraft, the operator must also display on that aircraft near each entrance to the cabin, cockpit, or pilot station, in letters not less than 2 inches nor more than 6 inches high, the words "limited," "restricted," "light-sport," "experimental," or "provisional," as applicable.

[Docket No. 8093, Amdt. 45–5, 33 FR 450, Jan. 12, 1968; as amended by Amdt. 45–9, 42 FR 41102, Aug. 15, 1977; Amdt. 45–24, 69 FR 44863, July 27, 2004]

§45.25 Location of marks on fixed-wing aircraft.

(a) The operator of a fixed-wing aircraft shall display the required marks on either the vertical tail surfaces or the sides of the fuselage, except as provided in §45.29(f).

(b) The marks required by paragraph (a) of this section shall be displayed as follows:

(1) If displayed on the vertical tail surfaces, horizontally on both surfaces, horizontally on both surfaces of a single vertical tail or on the outer surfaces of a multivertical tail. However, on aircraft on which marks at least 3 inches high may be displayed in accordance with §45.29(b)(1), the marks may be displayed vertically on the vertical tail surfaces.

(2) If displayed on the fuselage surfaces, horizontally on both sides of the fuselage between the trailing edge of the wing and the leading edge of the horizontal stabilizer. However, if engine pods or other appurtenances are located in this area and are an integral part of the fuselage side surfaces, the operator may place the marks on those pods or appurtenances.

[Amdt. 45–9 42 FR 41102, Aug. 15,1977]

§45.27 Location of marks; nonfixed-wing aircraft.

(a) *Rotorcraft.* Each operator of a rotorcraft shall display on that rotorcraft horizontally on both surfaces of the cabin, fuselage, boom, or tail the marks required by §45.23.

(b) *Airships.* Each operator of an airship shall display on that airship the marks required by §45.23, horizontally on—

(1) The upper surface of the right horizontal stabilizer and on the under surface of the left horizontal stabilizer with the top of the marks toward the leading edge of each stabilizer; and

(2) Each side of the bottom half of the vertical stabilizer.

(c) *Spherical balloons.* Each operator of a spherical balloon shall display the marks required by §45.23 in two places diametrically opposite and near the maximum horizontal circumference of that balloon.

(d) *Nonspherical balloons.* Each operator of a nonspherical balloon shall display the marks required by §45.23 on each side of the balloon near its maximum cross section and immediately above either the rigging band or the points of attachment of the basket or cabin suspension cables.

(e) *Powered parachute and weight-shift-control aircraft.* Each operator of a powered parachute or a weight-shift-control aircraft must display the marks required by §45.23. The marks must be displayed horizontally and in two diametrically opposite positions on any fuselage structural member.

[Docket No. 2047, 29 FR 3223, March 11, 1964; as amended by Amdt. 45–15, 48 FR 11392, March 17, 1983; Amdt. 45–24, 69 FR 44863, July 27, 2004]

§45.29 Size of marks.

(a) Except as provided in paragraph (f) of this section, each operator of an aircraft shall display marks on the aircraft meeting the size requirements of this section.

(b) *Height.* Except as provided in paragraph (h) of this part, the nationality and registration marks must be of equal height and on—

(1) Fixed-wing aircraft, must be at least 12 inches high, except that:

(i) An aircraft displaying marks at least 2 inches high before November 1, 1981 and an aircraft manufactured after November 2, 1981, but before January 1, 1983, may display those marks until the aircraft is repainted or the marks are repainted, restored, or changed;

(ii) Marks at least 3 inches high may be displayed on a glider;

(iii) Marks at least 3 inches high may be displayed on an aircraft for which the FAA has issued an experimental certificate under §21.191(d), §21.191(g), or §21.191(i) of this chapter to operate as an exhibition aircraft, an amateur-built aircraft, or a light-sport aircraft when the maximum cruising speed of the aircraft does not exceed 180 knots CAS; and

(iv) Marks may be displayed on an exhibition, antique, or other aircraft in accordance with §45.22.

(2) Airships, spherical balloons, nonspherical balloons, powered parachutes, and weight-shift-control aircraft must be at least 3 inches high; and

(3) Rotorcraft, must be at least 12 inches high, except that rotorcraft displaying before April 18, 1983, marks required by §45.29(b)(3) in effect on April 17, 1983, and rotorcraft manufactured on or after April 18, 1983, but before December 31, 1983, may display those marks until the aircraft is repainted or the marks are repainted, restored, or changed.

(c) *Width.* Characters must be two-thirds as wide as they are high, except the number "1", which must be one-sixth as wide as it is high, and the letters "M" and "W" which may be as wide as they are high.

(d) *Thickness.* Characters must be formed by solid lines one-sixth as thick as the character is high.

(e) *Spacing.* The space between each character may not be less than one-fourth of the character width.

(f) If either one of the surfaces authorized for displaying required marks under §45.25 is large enough for display of marks meeting the size requirements of this section and the other is not, full-size marks shall be placed on the larger surface. If neither surface is large enough for full-size marks, marks as large as practicable shall be displayed on the larger of the two surfaces. If any surface authorized to be marked by §45.27 is not large enough for full-size marks, marks as large as practicable shall be placed on the largest of the authorized surfaces.

(g) *Uniformity.* The marks required by this part for fixed-wing aircraft must have the same height, width, thickness, and spacing on both sides of the aircraft.

(h) After March 7, 1988, each operator of an aircraft penetrating an ADIZ or DEWIZ shall display on that aircraft temporary or permanent nationality and registration marks at least 12 inches high.

[Docket No. 2047, 29 FR 3223, March 11, 1964; as amended by Amdt. 45–2, 31 FR 9863, July 21, 1966; Amdt. 45–9, 42 FR 41102, Aug. 15, 1977; Amdt. 45–13, 46 FR 48604, Oct. 1, 1981; Amdt. 45–15, 48 FR 11392, March 17, 1983: Amdt. 45–17, 52 FR 34102, Sept. 9, 1987; 52 FR 36566, Sept. 30, 1987; Amdt. 45–24, 69 FR 44863, July 27, 2004]

§45.31 Marking of export aircraft.

A person who manufactures an aircraft in the United States for delivery outside thereof may display on that aircraft any marks required by the State of registry of the aircraft. However, no person may operate an aircraft so marked within the United States, except for test and demonstration flights for a limited period of time, or while in necessary transit to the purchaser.

§45.33 Sale of aircraft; removal of marks.

When an aircraft that is registered in the United States is sold, the holder of the Certificate of Aircraft Registration shall remove, before its delivery to the purchaser, all United States marks from the aircraft, unless the purchaser is—

(a) A citizen of the United States;

(b) An individual citizen of a foreign country who is lawfully admitted for permanent residence in the United States; or

(c) When the aircraft is to be based and primarily used in the United States, a corporation (other than a corporation which is a citizen of the United States) lawfully organized and doing business under the laws of the United States or any State thereof.

[Amdt. 45–11, 44 FR 61938. Oct. 29, 1979]

PART 47
AIRCRAFT REGISTRATION

Subpart A — General

Sec.
***47.1 Applicability.**
***47.2 Definitions.**
***47.3 Registration required.**
***47.5 Applicants.**
***47.7 United States citizens and resident aliens.**
***47.8 Voting trusts.**
***47.9 Corporations not U.S. citizens.**
47.11 Evidence of ownership.
***47.13 Signatures and instruments made by representatives.**
47.15 Identification number.
47.16 Temporary registration numbers.
47.17 Fees.
***47.19 FAA Aircraft Registry.**

Subpart B — Certificates of Aircraft Registration

47.31 Application.
***47.33 Aircraft not previously registered anywhere.**
***47.35 Aircraft last previously registered in the United States.**
***47.37 Aircraft last previously registered in a foreign country.**
47.39 Effective date of registration.
47.41 Duration and return of Certificate.
***47.43 Invalid registration.**
47.45 Change of address.
***47.47 Cancellation of Certificate for export purpose.**
47.49 Replacement of Certificate.
47.51 Triennial aircraft registration report.

Subpart C — Dealers' Aircraft Registration Certificate

47.61 Dealers' Aircraft Registration Certificates.
47.63 Application.
***47.65 Eligibility.**
47.67 Evidence of ownership.
47.69 Limitations.
47.71 Duration of Certificate; change of status.

Authority: 4 U.S.T. 1830; Pub. L. 108-297, 118 Stat. 1095 (49 U.S.C. 40101 note, 49 U.S.C. 44101 note); 49 U.S.C. 106(g), 40113–40114, 44101–44108, 44110–44113, 44703–44704, 44713, 45302, 46104, 46301.

Source: Docket No. 7190, 31 FR 4495, March 17, 1966, unless otherwise noted.

Subpart A — General

§47.1 Applicability.

This part prescribes the requirements for registering aircraft under 49 U.S.C. 44101-44104. Subpart B applies to each applicant for, and holder of, a Certificate of Aircraft Registration. Subpart C applies to each applicant for and holder of, a Dealers' Aircraft Registration Certificate.

[Docket No. FAA–2004–19944, 70 FR 244, Jan. 3, 2005]

§47.2 Definitions.

The following are definitions of terms used in this part:

Resident alien means an individual citizen of a foreign country lawfully admitted for permanent residence in the United States as an immigrant in conformity with the regulations of the Immigration and Naturalization Service of the Department of Justice (8 CFR Chapter 1).

U.S. citizen means one of the following:

(1) An individual who is a citizen of the United States or one of its possessions.

(2) A partnership of which each member is such an individual.

(3) A corporation or association created or organized under the laws of the United States or of any State, Territory, or possession of the United States, of which the president and two-thirds or more of the board of directors and other managing officers thereof are such individuals and in which at least 75 percent of the voting interest is owned or controlled by persons who are citizens of the United States or of one of its possessions.

[Docket No. 7190, 31 FR 4495, March 17, 1966; as amended by Amdt. 47–20, 44 FR 61939, Oct. 29, 1979; Amdt. 47–27, 70 FR 244, Jan. 3, 2005]

47

§47.3 Registration required.

(a) An aircraft may be registered under 49 U.S.C. 44103 only when the aircraft is—

(1) Not registered under the laws of a foreign country and is owned by—

(i) A citizen of the United States;

(ii) An individual citizen of a foreign country lawfully admitted for permanent residence in the United States; or

(iii) A corporation not a citizen of the United States when the corporation is organized and doing business under the laws of the United States or a State, and the aircraft is based and primarily used in the United States; or

(2) An aircraft of—

(i) The United States Government; or

(ii) A State, the District of Columbia, a territory or possession of the United States, or a political subdivision of a State, territory, or possession.

(b) No person may operate an aircraft that is eligible for registration under 49 U.S.C. 44101-44104, unless the aircraft—

(1) Has been registered by its owner;

(2) Is carrying aboard the temporary authorization required by §47.31(b); or

(3) Is an aircraft of the Armed Forces.

(c) Governmental units are those named in paragraph (a) of this section and Puerto Rico.

[Docket No. 7190, 31 FR 4495, March 17, 1966; as amended by Amdt. 47–20, 44 FR 61939, Oct. 29, 1979; Amdt. 47–27, 70 FR 244, Jan. 3, 2005]

§47.5 Applicants.

(a) A person who wishes to register an aircraft in the United States must submit an Application for Aircraft Registration under this part.

(b) An aircraft may be registered only by and in the legal name of its owner.

(c) 49 U.S.C. 44103(c) provides that registration is not evidence of ownership of aircraft in any proceeding in which ownership by a particular person is in issue. The FAA does not issue any certificate of ownership or endorse any information with respect to ownership on a Certificate of Aircraft Registration. The FAA issues a Certificate of Aircraft Registration to the person who appears to be the owner on the basis of the evidence of ownership submitted pursuant to §47.11 with the Application for Aircraft Registration, or recorded at the FAA Aircraft Registry.

(d) In this part, "owner" includes a buyer in possession, a bailee, or a lessee of an aircraft under a contract of conditional sale, and the assignee of that person.

[Docket No. 7190, 31 FR 4495, March 17, 1966; as amended by Amdt. 47–20, 44 FR 61939, Oct. 29, 1979; Amdt. 47–27, 70 FR 244, Jan. 3, 2005]

§47.7 United States citizens and resident aliens.

(a) *U.S. citizens.* An applicant for aircraft registration under this part who is a U.S. citizen must certify to this in the application.

(b) *Resident aliens.* An applicant for aircraft registration under 49 U.S.C. 44102 who is a resident alien must furnish a representation of permanent residence and the applicant's alien registration number issued by the Immigration and Naturalization Service.

(c) *Trustees.* An applicant for aircraft registration under 49 U.S.C. 44102 that holds legal title to an aircraft in trust must comply with the following requirements:

(1) Each trustee must be either a U.S. citizen or a resident alien.

(2) The applicant must submit with the application—

(i) A copy of each document legally affecting a relationship under the trust;

(ii) If each beneficiary under the trust, including each person whose security interest in the aircraft is incorporated in the trust, is either a U.S. citizen or a resident alien, an affidavit by the applicant to that effect; and

(iii) If any beneficiary under the trust, including any person whose security interest in the aircraft is incorporated in the trust, is not a U.S. citizen or resident alien, an affidavit from each trustee stating that the trustee is not aware of any reason, situation, or relationship (involving beneficiaries or other persons who are not U.S. citizens or resident aliens) as a result of which those persons together would have more than 25 percent of the aggregate power to influence or limit the exercise of the trustee's authority.

(3) If persons who are neither U.S. citizens nor resident aliens have the power to direct or remove a trustee, either directly or indirectly through the control of another person, the trust instrument must provide that those persons together may not have more than 25 percent of the aggregate power to direct or remove a trustee. Nothing in this paragraph prevents those persons from having more than 25 percent of the beneficial interest in the trust.

(d) *Partnerships.* A partnership may apply for a Certificate of Aircraft Registration under 49 U.S.C. 44102 only if each partner, whether a general or limited partner, is a citizen of the United States. Nothing in this section makes ineligible for registration an aircraft which is not owned as a partnership asset but is co-owned by—

(1) Resident aliens; or

(2) One or more resident aliens and one or more U.S. citizens.

[Docket No. 7190, 31 FR 4495, March 17, 1966; as amended by Amdt. 47–20, 44 FR 61939, Oct. 29, 1979; Amdt. 47–27, 70 FR 244, Jan. 3, 2005]

§47.8 Voting trusts.

(a) If a voting trust is used to qualify a domestic corporation as a U.S. citizen, the corporate applicant must submit to the FAA Aircraft Registry—

(1) A true copy of the fully executed voting trust agreement, which must identify each voting interest of the applicant, and which must be binding upon each voting trustee, the applicant corporation, all foreign stockholders, and each other party to the transaction; and

(2) An affidavit executed by each person designated as voting trustee in the voting trust agreement, in which each affiant represents—

(i) That each voting trustee is a citizen of the United States within the meaning of 49 U.S.C 40102(a)(15);

(ii) That each voting trustee is not a past, present, or prospective director, officer, employee, attorney, or agent of any other party to the trust agreement;

(iii) That each voting trustee is not a present or prospective beneficiary, creditor, debtor, supplier or contractor of any other party to the trust agreement;

(iv) That each voting trustee is not aware of any reason, situation, or relationship under which any other party to the agreement might influence the exercise of the voting trustee's totally independent judgment under the voting trust agreement.

(b) Each voting trust agreement submitted under paragraph (a)(1) of this section must provide for the succession of a voting trustee in the event of death, disability, resignation, termination of citizenship, or any other event leading to the replacement of any voting trustee. Upon succession, the replacement voting trustee shall immediately submit to the FAA Aircraft Registry the affidavit required by paragraph (a)(2) of this section.

(c) If the voting trust terminates or is modified, and the result is less than 75 percent control of the voting interest in the corporation by citizens of the United States, a loss of citizenship of the holder of the registration certificate occurs, and §47.41(a)(5) of this part applies.

(d) A voting trust agreement may not empower a trustee to act through a proxy.

[Docket No. 7190, 31 FR 4495, March 17, 1966; as amended by Amdt. 47–20, 44 FR 61939, Oct. 29, 1979; Amdt. 47–27, 70 FR 245, Jan. 3, 2005]

§47.9 Corporations not U.S. citizens.

(a) Each corporation applying for registration of an aircraft under 49 U.S.C. 44102 must submit to the FAA Registry with the application—

(1) A certified copy of its certificate of incorporation;

(2) A certification that it is lawfully qualified to do business in one or more States;

(3) A certification that the aircraft will be based and primarily used in the United States; and

(4) The location where the records required by paragraph (e) of this section will be maintained.

(b) For the purposes of registration, an aircraft is based and primarily used in the United States if the flight hours accumulated within the United States amount to at least 60 percent of the total flight hours of the aircraft during—

(1) For aircraft registered on or before January 1, 1980, the 6-calendar month period beginning on January 1, 1980, and each 6-calendar month period thereafter; and

(2) For aircraft registered after January 1, 1980, the period consisting in the remainder of the registration month and the succeeding 6 calendar months and each 6-calendar month period thereafter.

(c) For the purpose of this section, only those flight hours accumulated during non-stop (except for stops in emergencies or for purposes of refueling) flight between two points in the United States, even if the aircraft is outside of the United States during part of the flight, are considered flight hours accumulated within the United States.

(d) In determining compliance with this section, any periods during which the aircraft is not validly registered in the United States are disregarded.

(e) The corporation that registers an aircraft pursuant to 49 U.S.C. 44102 shall maintain, and make available for inspection by the Administrator upon request, records containing the total flight hours in the United States of the aircraft for three calendar years after the year in which the flight hours were accumulated.

(f) The corporation that registers an aircraft pursuant to 49 U.S.C. 44102 shall send to the FAA Aircraft Registry, at the end of each period of time described in paragraphs (b)(1) and (2) of this section, either—

(1) A signed report containing—

(i) The total time in service of the airframe as provided in §91.417(a)(2)(i), accumulated during that period; and

(ii) The total flight hours in the United States of the aircraft accumulated during that period; or

(2) A signed statement that the total flight hours of the aircraft, while registered in the United States during that period, have been exclusively within the United States.

[Amdt. No. 47–20, 44 FR 61940, Oct. 29, 1979; as amended by Amdt. 47–24, 54 FR 34330, Aug. 18, 1989; Amdt. 47–27, 70 FR 245, Jan. 3, 2005]

Editorial Note: For documents relating to the effective date of reporting requirements in §47.9 and the correction of certain reporting periods, see 46 FR 35491, July 9, 1981 and 47 FR 8158, February 25, 1982.

§47.11 Evidence of ownership.

Except as provided in §§47.33 and 47.35, each person that submits an Application for Aircraft Registration under this part must also submit the required evidence of ownership, recordable under §§49.13 and 49.17 of this chapter, as follows:

(a) The buyer in possession, the bailee, or the lessee of an aircraft under a contract of conditional sale must submit the contract. The assignee under a contract of conditional sale must submit both the contract (unless it is already recorded at the FAA Aircraft Registry), and his assignment from the original buyer, bailee, lessee, or prior assignee.

(b) The repossessor of an aircraft must submit—

(1) A certificate of repossession on FAA Form 8050-4, or its equivalent, signed by the applicant and stating that the aircraft was repossessed or otherwise seized under the security agreement involved and applicable local law;

(2) The security agreement (unless it is already recorded at the FAA Aircraft Registry), or a copy thereof certified as true under §49.21 of this chapter; and

(3) When repossession was through foreclosure proceedings resulting in sale, a bill of sale signed by the sheriff, auctioneer, or other authorized person who conducted the sale, and stating that the sale was made under applicable local law.

(c) The buyer of an aircraft at a judicial sale, or at a sale to satisfy a lien or charge, must submit a bill of sale signed by the sheriff, auctioneer, or other authorized person who conducted the sale, and stating that the sale was made under applicable local law.

(d) The owner of an aircraft, the title to which has been in controversy and has been determined by a court, must submit a certified copy of the decision of the court.

(e) The executor or administrator of the estate of the deceased former owner of an aircraft must submit a certified copy of the letters testamentary or letters of administration appointing him executor or administrator. The Certificate of Aircraft Registration is issued to the applicant as executor or administrator.

(f) The buyer of an aircraft from the estate of a deceased former owner must submit both a bill of sale, signed for the estate by the executor or administrator, and a certified copy of the letters testamentary or letters of administration. When no executor or administrator has been or is to be appointed, the applicant must submit both a bill of sale, signed by the heir-at-law of the deceased former owner, and an affidavit of the heir-at-law stating that no application for appointment of an executor or administrator has been made, that so far as he can determine none will be made, and that he is the person entitled to, or having the right to dispose of, the aircraft under applicable local law.

(g) The guardian of another person's property that includes an aircraft must submit a certified copy of the order of the court appointing him guardian. The Certificate of Aircraft Registration is issued to the applicant as guardian.

(h) The trustee of property that includes an aircraft, as described in §47.7(c), must submit either a certified copy of the order of the court appointing the trustee, or a complete and true copy of the instrument creating the trust. If there is more than one trustee, each trustee must sign the application. The Certificate of Aircraft Registration is issued to a single applicant as trustee, or to several trustees jointly as co-trustees.

[Docket No. 7190, 31 FR 4495, March 17, 1966; as amended by Amdt. 47–20, 44 FR 61940, Oct. 29, 1979; Amdt. 47–23, 53 FR 1915, Jan. 25, 1988]

§47.13 Signatures and instruments made by representatives.

(a) Each signature on an Application for Aircraft Registration, on a request for cancellation of a Certificate of Aircraft Registration or on a document submitted as supporting evidence under this part, must be in ink.

(b) When one or more persons doing business under a trade name submits an Application for Aircraft Registration or a request for cancellation of a Certificate of Aircraft Registration, the application or request must be signed by, or in behalf of, each person who shares title to the aircraft.

(c) When an agent submits an Application for Aircraft Registration or a request for cancellation of a Certificate of Aircraft Registration in behalf of the owner, he must—

(1) State the name of the owner on the application or request;

(2) Sign as agent or attorney-in-fact on the application or request; and

(3) Submit a signed power of attorney, or a true copy thereof certified under §49.21 of this chapter, with the application or request.

(d) When a corporation submits an Application for Aircraft Registration or a request for cancellation of a Certificate of Aircraft Registration, it must—

(1) Have an authorized person sign the application or request;

(2) Show the title of the signer's office on the application or request; and

(3) Submit a copy of the authorization from the board of directors to sign for the corporation, certified as true under §49.21 of this chapter by a corporate officer or other person in a managerial position therein, with the application or request, unless—

(i) The signer of the application or request is a corporate officer or other person in a managerial position in the corporation and the title of his office is stated in connection with his signature; or

(ii) A valid authorization to sign is on file at the FAA Aircraft Registry.

(4) The provisions of paragraph (d)(3) do not apply to an irrevocable deregistration and export request authorization when an irrevocable deregistration and export request authorization under the Cape Town Treaty is signed by a corporate officer and is filed with the FAA Aircraft Registry.

(e) When a partnership submits an Application for Aircraft Registration or a request for cancellation of a Certificate of Aircraft Registration, it must—

(1) State the full name of the partnership on the application or request;

(2) State the name of each general partner on the application or request; and

(3) Have a general partner sign the application or request.

(f) When co-owners, who are not engaged in business as partners, submit an Application for Aircraft Registration or a request for cancellation of a Certificate of Aircraft Registration, each person who shares title to the aircraft under the arrangement must sign the application or request.

(g) A power of attorney or other evidence of a person's authority to sign for another, submitted under this part, is valid for the purposes of this section, unless sooner revoked, until—

(1) Its expiration date stated therein; or

(2) If an expiration date is not stated therein, for not more than 3 years after the date—

(i) It is signed; or

(ii) The grantor (a corporate officer or other person in a managerial position therein, where the grantor is a corporation) certifies in writing that the authority to sign shown by the power of attorney or other evidence is still in effect.

[Docket No. 7190, 31 FR 4495, March 17, 1966; as amended by Amdt. 47–2, 31 FR 15349, Dec. 8, 1966; Amdt. 47–3, 32 FR 6554, April 28, 1967; Amdt. 47–12, 36 FR 8661, May 11, 1971; Amdt. 47–27, 70 FR 245, Jan. 3, 2005]

§47.15 Identification number.

(a) *Number required.* An applicant for Aircraft Registration must place a U.S. identification number (registration mark) on his Aircraft Registration Application, AC Form 8050-1, and on any evidence submitted with the application. There is no charge for the assignment of numbers provided in this paragraph. This paragraph does not apply to an aircraft manufacturer who applies for a group of U.S. identification numbers under paragraph (c) of this section; a person who applies for a special identification number under paragraphs (d) through (g) of this section; or a holder of a Dealer's Aircraft Registration Certificate who applies for a temporary registration number under §47.16.

(1) *Aircraft not previously registered anywhere.* The applicant must obtain the U.S. identification number from the FAA Aircraft Registry by request in writing describing the aircraft by make, type, model, and serial number (or, if it is amateur-built, as provided in §47.33(b)) and stating that the aircraft has not previously been registered anywhere. If the aircraft was brought into the United States from a foreign country, the applicant must submit evidence that the aircraft has never been registered in a foreign country.

(2) *Aircraft last previously registered in the United States.* Unless he applies for a different number under paragraphs (d) through (g) of this section, the applicant must place the U.S. identification number that is already assigned to the aircraft on his application and the supporting evidence.

(3) *Aircraft last previously registered in a foreign country.* Whether or not the foreign registration has ended, the applicant must obtain a U.S. identification number from the FAA Aircraft Registry for an aircraft last previously registered in a foreign country, by request in writing describing the aircraft by make, model, and serial number, accompanied by—

(i) Evidence of termination of foreign registration in accordance with §47.37(b) or the applicant's affidavit showing that foreign registration has ended; or

(ii) If foreign registration has not ended, the applicant's affidavit stating that the number will not be placed on the aircraft until foreign registration has ended.

Authority to use the identification number obtained under paragraph (a)(1) or (3) of this section expires 90 days after the date it is issued unless the applicant submits an Aircraft Registration Application, AC Form 8050-1, and complies with §47.33 or §47.37, as applicable, within that period of time. However, the applicant may obtain an extension of this 90-day period from the FAA Aircraft Registry if he shows that his delay in complying with that section is due to circumstances beyond his control.

(b) A U.S. identification number may not exceed five symbols in addition to the prefix letter "N". These symbols may be all numbers (N10000), one to four numbers and one suffix letter (N 1000A), or one to three numbers and two suffix letters (N 100AB). The letters "I" and "O" may not be used. The first zero in a number must always be preceded by at least one of the numbers 1 through 9.

(c) An aircraft manufacturer may apply to the FAA Aircraft Registry for enough U.S. identification numbers to supply his estimated production for the next 18 months. There is no charge for this assignment of numbers.

(d) Any unassigned U.S. identification number may be assigned as a special identification number. An applicant who wants a special identification number or wants to change the identification number of his aircraft may apply for it to the FAA Aircraft Registry. The fee required by §47.17 must accompany the application.

(e) [Reserved]

(f) The FAA Aircraft Registry assigns a special identification number on AC Form 8050-64. Within 5 days after he affixes the special identification number to his aircraft, the owner must complete and sign the receipt contained in AC Form 8050-64, state the date he affixed the number to his aircraft, and return the original form to the FAA Aircraft Registry. The owner shall carry the duplicate of AC Form 8050-64 and the present Certificate of Aircraft Registration in the aircraft as temporary authority to operate it. This temporary authority is valid until the date the owner receives the revised Certificate of Aircraft Registration issued by the FAA Aircraft Registry.

(g) [Reserved]

(h) A special identification number may be reserved for no more than 1 year. If a person wishes to renew his reservation from year to year, he must apply to the FAA Aircraft Registry for renewal and submit the fee required by §47.17 for a special identification number.

[Docket No. 7190, 31 FR 4495, March 17, 1966; as amended by Amdt. 47–1, 31 FR 13314, Oct. 14, 1966; Amdt. 47–5, 32 FR 13505, Sept. 27, 1967; Amdt. 47–7, 34 FR 2480, Feb. 21, 1969; Amdt. 47–13, 36 FR 16187, Aug. 20, 1971; Amdt. 47–15, 37 FR 21528, Oct. 12, 1972; Amdt. 47–16, 37 FR 25487, Dec. 1, 1972; Amdt. 47–17, 39 FR 1353, Jan. 8, 1974; Amdt. 47–22, 47 FR 12153, March 22, 1982]

§47.16 Temporary registration numbers.

(a) Temporary registration numbers are issued by the FAA to manufacturers, distributors, and dealers who are holders of Dealer's Aircraft Registration Certificates for temporary display on aircraft during flight allowed under Subpart C of this part.

(b) The holder of a Dealer's Aircraft Registration Certificate may apply to the FAA Aircraft Registry for as many temporary registration numbers as are necessary for his business. The application must be in writing and include—

(1) Sufficient information to justify the need for the temporary registration numbers requested; and

(2) The number of each Dealer's Aircraft Registration Certificate held by the applicant.

There is no charge for these numbers.

(c) The use of temporary registration numbers is subject to the following conditions:

(1) The numbers may be used and reused—

(i) Only in connection with the holder's Dealer's Aircraft Registration Certificate;

(ii) Within the limitations of §47.69 where applicable, including the requirements of §47.67; and

(iii) On aircraft not registered under Subpart B of this part or in a foreign country, and not displaying any other identification markings.

(2) A temporary registration number may not be used on more than one aircraft in flight at the same time.

(3) Temporary registration numbers may not be used to fly aircraft into the United States for the purpose of importation.

(d) The assignment of any temporary registration number to any person lapses upon the expiration of all of his Dealer's Aircraft Registration Certificates. When a temporary registration number is used on a flight outside the United States for delivery purposes, the holder shall record the assignment of that number to the aircraft and shall keep that record for at least 1 year after the removal of the number from that aircraft. Whenever the owner of an aircraft bearing a temporary registration number applies for an airworthiness certificate under Part 21 of this chapter he shall furnish that number in the application. The temporary registration number must be removed from the aircraft not later than the date on which either title or possession passes to another person.

[Amdt. 47–4, 32 FR 12556, Aug. 30, 1967]

§47.17 Fees.

(a) The fees for applications under this part are as follows:

(1) Certificate of Aircraft Registration (each aircraft)................$5.00

(2) Dealer's Aircraft Registration Certificate............................10.00

(3) Additional Dealer's Aircraft Registration Certificate (issued to same dealer) 2.00

(4) Special identification number (each number) 10.00

(5) Changed, reassigned, or reserved identification number...10.00

(6) Duplicate Certificate of Registration 2.00

(b) Each application must be accompanied by the proper fee, that may be paid by check or money order to the Federal Aviation Administration.

[Docket No. 7190, 31 FR 4495, March 17, 1966; 31 FR 5483, April 7, 1966, as amended by Docket No. 8084, 32 FR 5769, April 11, 1967]

§47.19 FAA Aircraft Registry.

Each application, request, notification, or other communication sent to the FAA under this Part must be mailed to the FAA Aircraft Registry, Department of Transportation, Post Office Box 25504, Oklahoma City, Oklahoma 73125-0504, or delivered to the Registry at 6425 S. Denning Ave., Oklahoma City, Oklahoma 73169.

[Docket No. FAA–2004–19944, 70 FR 245, Jan. 3, 2005]

Subpart B—Certificates of Aircraft Registration

§47.31 Application.

(a) Each applicant for a Certificate of Aircraft Registration must submit the following to the FAA Aircraft Registry—

(1) The original (white) and one copy (green) of the Aircraft Registration Application, AC Form 8050-1;

(2) The original Aircraft Bill of Sale, ACC Form 8050-2, or other evidence of ownership authorized by §§47.33, 47.35, or 47.37 (unless already recorded at the FAA Aircraft Registry); and

(3) The fee required by §47.17.

The FAA rejects an application when any form is not completed, or when the name and signature of the applicant are not the same throughout.

(b) After he complies with paragraph (a) of this section, the applicant shall carry the second duplicate copy (pink) of the Aircraft Registration Application, AC Form 8050-1, in the aircraft as temporary authority to operate it without registration. This temporary authority is valid until the date the applicant receives the certificate of the Aircraft Registration, AC Form 8050-3, or until the date the FAA denies the application, but in no case for more than 90 days after the date the applicant signs the application. If by 90 days after the date the applicant signs the application, the FAA has neither issued the Certificate of Aircraft Registration nor denied the application, the FAA Aircraft Registry issues a letter of extension that serves as authority to continue to operate the aircraft without registration while it is carried in the aircraft.

(c) Paragraph (b) of this section applies to each application submitted under paragraph (a) of this section, and signed after October 5, 1967. If, after that date, an applicant signs an application and the second duplicate copy (pink) of the Aircraft Registration Application, AC Form 8050-1, bears an obsolete statement limiting its validity to 30 days, the applicant may strike out the number "30" on that form, and insert the number "90" in place thereof.

[Docket No. 7190, 31 FR 4495, March 17, 1966; 31 FR 5483, April 7, 1966; as amended by Amdt. 47–6, 33 FR 11, Jan. 3, 1968; Amdt. 47–15, 37 FR 21528, Oct. 12, 1972; Amdt. 47–16, 37 FR 25487, Dec. 1, 1972]

§47.33 Aircraft not previously registered anywhere.

(a) A person who is the owner of an aircraft that has not been registered under 49 U.S.C. 44101-44104, under other law of the United States, or under foreign law, may register it under this part if he—

(1) Complies with §§47.3, 47.7, 47.8, 47.9, 47.11, 47.13, 47.15, and 47.17, as applicable; and

(2) Submits with his application an aircraft Bill of Sale, AC Form 8050-2, signed by the seller, an equivalent bill of sale, or other evidence of ownership authorized by §47.11.

(b) If, for good reason, the applicant cannot produce the evidence of ownership required by paragraph (a) of this section, he must submit other evidence that is satisfactory to the Administrator. This other evidence may be an affidavit stating why he cannot produce the required evidence, accompanied by whatever further evidence is available to prove the transaction.

(c) The owner of an amateur-built aircraft who applies for registration under paragraphs (a) and (b) of this section must describe the aircraft by class (airplane, rotorcraft, glider, or balloon), serial number, number of seats, type of engine installed, (reciprocating, turbopropeller, turbojet, or other), number of engines installed, and make, model, and serial number of each engine installed; and must state whether the aircraft is built for land or water operation. Also, he must submit as evidence of ownership an affidavit giving the U.S. identification number, and stating that the aircraft was built from parts and that he is the owner. If he built the aircraft from a kit, the applicant must also submit a bill of sale from the manufacturer of the kit.

(d) The owner, other than the holder of the type certificate, of an aircraft that he assembles from parts to conform to the approved type design, must describe the aircraft and engine in the manner required by paragraph (c) of this section, and also submit evidence of ownership satisfactory to the Administrator, such as bills of sale, for all major components of the aircraft.

[Docket No. 7190, 31 FR 4495, March 17, 1966; 31 FR 5483, April 7, 1966; as amended by Amdt. 47–16, 37 FR 25487, Dec. 1, 1972; Amdt. 47–20, 44 FR 61940, Oct. 29, 1979; Amdt. 47–27, 70 FR 245, Jan. 3, 2005]

§47.35 Aircraft last previously registered in the United States.

(a) A person who is the owner of an aircraft last previously registered under 49 U.S.C. Sections 44101-44104, or under other law of the United States, may register it under this part if he complies with §§47.3, 47.7, 47.8, 47.9, 47.11, 47.13, 47.15, and 47.17, as applicable and submits with his application an Aircraft Bill of Sale, AC Form 8050-2, signed by the seller or an equivalent conveyance, or other evidence of ownership authorized by §47.11.

(1) If the applicant bought the aircraft from the last registered owner, the conveyance must be from that owner to the applicant.

(2) If the applicant did not buy the aircraft from the last registered owner, he must submit conveyances or other instruments showing consecutive transactions from the last registered owner through each intervening owner to the applicant.

(b) If, for good reason, the applicant cannot produce the evidence of ownership required by paragraph (a) of this section, he must submit other evidence that is satisfactory to the Administrator. This other evidence may be an affidavit stating why he cannot produce the required evidence, accompanied by whatever further evidence is available to prove the transaction.

[Docket No. 7190, 31 FR 4495, March 17, 1966; as amended by Amdt. 47–16, 37 FR 25487, Dec. 1, 1972; Amdt. 47–20, 44 FR 61940, Oct. 29, 1979; Amdt. 47–27, 70 FR 245, Jan. 3, 2005]

§47.37 Aircraft last previously registered in a foreign country.

(a) A person who is the owner of an aircraft last previously registered under the law of a foreign country may register it under this part if the owner—

(1) Complies with §§47.3, 47.7, 47.8, 47.9, 47.11, 47.13, 47.15, and 47.17, as applicable;

(2) Submits with his application a bill of sale from the foreign seller or other evidence satisfactory to the FAA that he owns the aircraft; and

(3) Submits evidence satisfactory to the FAA that—

(i) If the country in which the aircraft was registered has not ratified the Convention on the International Recognition of Rights in Aircraft (4 U.S.T. 1830), (the Geneva Convention), or the Convention on International Interests in Mobile Equipment, as modified by the Protocol to the Convention on International Interests in Mobile Equipment on Matters Specific to Aircraft Equipment (the Cape Town Treaty), the foreign registration has ended or is invalid; or

(ii) If that country has ratified the Geneva Convention, but has not ratified the Cape Town Treaty, the foreign registration has ended or is invalid, and each holder of a recorded right against the aircraft has been satisfied or has consented to the transfer, or ownership in the country of export has been ended by a sale in execution under the terms of the Geneva Convention; or

(iii) If that country has ratified the Cape Town Treaty and the aircraft is subject to the Treaty, that the foreign registration has ended or is invalid, and that all interests ranking in priority have been discharged or that the holders of such interests have consented to the deregistration and export of the aircraft.

(iv) Nothing under (a)(3)(iii) affects rights established prior to the Treaty entering into force with respect to the country in which the aircraft was registered.

(b) For the purposes of paragraph (a)(3) of this section, satisfactory evidence of termination of the foreign registration may be—

(1) A statement, by the official having jurisdiction over the national aircraft registry of the foreign country, that the registration has ended or is invalid, and showing the official's name and title and describing the aircraft by make, model, and serial number; or

(2) A final judgment or decree of a court of competent jurisdiction of the foreign country, determining that, under the laws of that country, the registration has become invalid.

[Docket No. 7190, 31 FR 4495, March 17, 1966; as amended by Amdt. 47–20, 44 FR 61940, Oct. 29,1979; Amdt. 47–26, 68 FR 10317, March 4, 2003; Amdt. 47–27, 70 FR 245, Jan. 3, 2005]

§47.39 Effective date of registration.

(a) Except for an aircraft last previously registered in a foreign country, an aircraft is registered under this subpart on the date and at the time the FAA Aircraft Registry receives the documents required by §47.33 or §47.35.

(b) An aircraft last previously registered in a foreign country is registered under this subpart on the date and at the time the FAA Aircraft Registry issues the Certificate of Aircraft Registration, AC Form 8050-3, after the documents required by §47.37 have been received and examined.

[Docket No. 7190, 31 FR 4495, March 17, 1966; as amended by Amdt. 47–16, 37 FR 25487, Dec. 1, 1972]

§47.41 Duration and return of Certificate.

(a) Each Certificate of Aircraft Registration issued by the FAA under this subpart is effective, unless suspended or revoked, until the date upon which—

(1) Subject to the Convention on the International Recognition of Rights in Aircraft when applicable, the aircraft is registered under the laws of a foreign country;

(2) The registration is canceled at the written request of the holder of the certificate;

(3) The aircraft is totally destroyed or scrapped;

(4) Ownership of the aircraft is transferred;

(5) The holder of the certificate loses his U.S. citizenship;

(6) 30 days have elapsed since the death of the holder of the certificate;

(7) The owner, if an individual who is not a citizen of the United States, loses status as a resident alien, unless that person becomes a citizen of the United States at the same time; or

(8) If the owner is a corporation other than a corporation which is a citizen of the United States—

(i) The corporation ceases to be lawfully organized and doing business under the laws of the United States or any State thereof; or

(ii) A period described in §47.9(b) ends and the aircraft was not based and primarily used in the United States during that period.

(9) If the trustee in whose name the aircraft is registered—

(i) Loses U.S. citizenship;

(ii) Loses status as a resident alien and does not become a citizen of the United States at the same time; or

(iii) In any manner ceases to act as trustee and is not immediately replaced by another who meets the requirements of §47.7(c).

(b) The Certificate of Aircraft Registration, with the reverse side completed, must be returned to the FAA Aircraft Registry—

(1) In case of registration under the laws of a foreign country, by the person who was the owner of the aircraft before foreign registration;

(2) Within 60 days after the death of the holder of the certificate, by the administrator or executor of his estate, or by his heir-at-law if no administrator or executor has been or is to be appointed; or

(3) Upon the termination of the registration, by the holder of the Certificate of Aircraft Registration in all other cases mentioned in paragraph (a) of this section.

[Docket No. 7190, 31 FR 4495, March 17, 1966; 31 FR 5483, April 7, 1966; as amended by Amdt. 47–20, 44 FR 61940, Oct. 29, 1979]

§47.43 Invalid registration.

(a) The registration of an aircraft is invalid if, at the time it is made—

(1) The aircraft is registered in a foreign country;

(2) The applicant is not the owner;

(3) The applicant is not qualified to submit an application under this part; or

47

(4) The interest of the applicant in the aircraft was created by a transaction that was not entered into in good faith, but rather was made to avoid (with or without the owner's knowledge) compliance with 49 U.S.C. 44101-44104.

(b) If the registration of an aircraft is invalid under paragraph (a) of this section, the holder of the invalid Certificate of Aircraft Registration shall return it as soon as possible to the FAA Aircraft Registry.

[Docket No. 7190, 31 FR 4495, March 17, 1966; 31 FR 5483, April 7, 1966; as amended by Amdt. 47–20, 44 FR 61940, Oct. 29, 1979; Amdt. 47–27, 70 FR 245, Jan. 3, 2005]

§47.45 Change of address.

Within 30 days after any change in his permanent mailing address, the holder of a Certificate of Aircraft Registration for an aircraft shall notify the FAA Aircraft Registry of his new address. A revised Certificate of Aircraft Registration is then issued, without charge.

§47.47 Cancellation of Certificate for export purpose.

(a) The holder of a Certificate of Aircraft Registration or the holder of an irrevocable deregistration and export request authorization recognized under the Cape Town Treaty and filed with FAA who wishes to cancel the Certificate for the purpose of export must submit to the FAA Aircraft Registry—

(1) A written request for cancellation of the Certificate describing the aircraft by make, model, and serial number, stating the U.S. identification number and the country to which the aircraft will be exported;

(2)(i) For an aircraft not subject to the Cape Town Treaty, evidence satisfactory to the FAA that each holder of a recorded right has been satisfied or has consented to the transfer; or

(ii) For an aircraft subject to the Cape Town Treaty, evidence satisfactory to the FAA that each holder of a recorded right established prior to the date the Treaty entered into force with respect to the United States has been satisfied or has consented to the transfer; and

(3) A written certification that all registered interests ranking in priority to that of the requestor have been discharged or that the holders of such interests have consented to the cancellation for export purposes.

(b) If the aircraft is subject to the Cape Town Treaty and an irrevocable deregistration and export request authorization has been filed with the FAA Aircraft Registry, the FAA Registry will honor a request for cancellation only if an authorized party makes the request.

(c) The FAA Aircraft Registry notifies the country to which the aircraft is to be exported of the cancellation.

[Docket No. FAA–2004–19944, 70 FR 245, Jan. 3, 2005]

§47.49 Replacement of Certificate.

(a) If a Certificate of Aircraft Registration is lost, stolen, or mutilated, the holder of the Certificate of Aircraft Registration may apply to the FAA Aircraft Registry for a duplicate certificate, accompanying his application with the fee required by §47.17.

(b) If the holder has applied and has paid the fee for a duplicate Certificate of Aircraft Registration and needs to operate his aircraft before receiving it, he may request a temporary certificate. The FAA Aircraft Registry issues a temporary certificate, by a collect telegram, to be carried in the aircraft. This temporary certificate is valid until he receives the duplicate Certificate of Aircraft Registration.

§47.51 Triennial aircraft registration report.

(a) Unless one of the registration activities listed in paragraph (b) of this section has occurred within the preceding 36 calendar months, the holder of each Certificate of Aircraft Registration issued under this subpart shall submit, on the form provided by the FAA Aircraft Registry and in the manner described in paragraph (c) of this section, a Triennial Aircraft Registration Report, certifying—

(1) The current identification number (registration mark) assigned to the aircraft;

(2) The name and permanent mailing address of the certificate holder;

(3) The name of the manufacturer of the aircraft and its model and serial number;

(4) Whether the certificate holder is—

(i) A citizen of the United States;

(ii) An individual citizen of a foreign country who has lawfully been admitted for permanent residence in the United States; or

(iii) A corporation (other than a corporation which is a citizen of the United States) lawfully organized and doing business under the laws of the United States or any State thereof; and

(5) Whether the aircraft is currently registered under the laws of any foreign country.

(b) The FAA Aircraft Registry will forward a Triennial Aircraft Registration Report to each holder of a Certificate of Aircraft Registration whenever 36 months has expired since the latest of the following registration activities occurred with respect to the certificate holder's aircraft:

(1) The submission of an Application for Aircraft Registration.

(2) The submission of a report or statement required by §47.9(f).

(3) The filing of a notice of change of permanent mailing address.

(4) The filing of an application for a duplicate Certificate of Aircraft Registration.

(5) The filing of an application for a change of aircraft identification number.

(6) The submission of an Aircraft Registration Eligibility, Identification, and Activity Report, Part 1, AC Form 8050-73, under former §47.44.

(7) The submission of a Triennial Aircraft Registration Report under this section.

(c) The holder of the Certificate of Aircraft Registration shall return the Triennial Aircraft Registration Report to the FAA Aircraft Registry within 60 days after issuance by the FAA Aircraft Registry. The report must be dated, legibly executed, and signed by the certificate holder in the manner prescribed by §47.13, except that any co-owner may sign for all co-owners.

(d) Refusal or failure to submit the Triennial Aircraft Registration Report with the information required by this section may be cause for suspension or revocation of the Certificate of Aircraft Registration in accordance with Part 13 of this chapter.

[Amdt. 47–21, 45 FR 20773, March 31, 1980]

Subpart C—Dealers' Aircraft Registration Certificate

§47.61 Dealers' Aircraft Registration Certificates.

(a) The FAA issues a Dealers' Aircraft Registration Certificate, AC Form 8050-6, to manufacturers and dealers so as to—

(1) Allow manufacturers to make any required flight tests of aircraft.

(2) Facilitate operating, demonstrating, and merchandising aircraft by the manufacturer or dealer without the burden of obtaining a Certificate of Aircraft Registration for each aircraft with each transfer of ownership, under Subpart B of this part.

(b) A Dealers' Aircraft Registration Certificate is an alternative for the Certificate of Aircraft Registration issued under Subpart B of this part. A dealer may, under this subpart, obtain one or more Dealers' Aircraft Registration Certificates in addition to his original certificate, and he may use a Dealer's Aircraft Registration Certificate for any aircraft he owns.

[Docket No. 7190, 31 FR 4495, March 17, 1966; as amended by Amdt. 47–9, 35 FR 802, Jan. 21, 1970; Amdt. 47–16, 37 FR 25487, Dec. 1, 1972]

§47.63 Application.

A manufacturer or dealer that wishes to obtain a Dealers' Aircraft Registration Certificate, AC Form 8050-6, must submit—

(a) An Application for Dealers' Aircraft Registration Certificates, AC Form 8050-5; and

(b) The fee required by §47.17.

[Docket No. 7190, 31 FR 4495, March 17, 1966; as amended by Amdt. 47–16, 37 FR 25487, Dec. 1, 1972]

§47.65 Eligibility.

To be eligible for a Dealer's Aircraft Registration Certificate, a person must have an established place of business in the United States, must be substantially engaged in manufacturing or selling aircraft, and must be a citizen of the United States, as defined by 49 U.S.C. 40102(a)(15).

[Docket No. FAA–2004–19944, 70 FR 245, Jan. 3, 2005]

§47.67 Evidence of ownership.

Before using his Dealer's Aircraft Registration Certificate for operating an aircraft, the holder of the certificate (other than a manufacturer) must send to the FAA Aircraft Registry evidence satisfactory to the Administrator that he is the owner of that aircraft. An Aircraft Bill of Sale, or its equivalent, may be used as evidence of ownership. There is no recording fee.

§47.69 Limitations.

A Dealer's Aircraft Registration Certificate is valid only in connection with use of aircraft—

(a) By the owner of the aircraft to whom it was issued, his agent or employee, or a prospective buyer, and in the case of a dealer other than a manufacturer, only after he has complied with §47.67;

(b) Within the United States, except when used to deliver to a foreign purchaser an aircraft displaying a temporary registration number and carrying an airworthiness certificate on which that number is written;

(c) While a certificate is carried within the aircraft; and

(d) On a flight that is—

(1) For required flight testing of aircraft; or

(2) Necessary for, or incident to, sale of the aircraft.

However, a prospective buyer may operate an aircraft for demonstration purposes only while he is under the direct supervision of the holder of the Dealer's Aircraft Registration Certificate or his agent.

[Docket No. 7190 31 FR 4495, March 17, 1966; 31 FR 5483, April 7, 1966; as amended by Amdt. 47–4, 32 FR 12556, Aug. 30, 1967]

§47.71 Duration of Certificate; change of status.

(a) A Dealer's Aircraft Registration Certificate expires 1 year after the date it is issued. Each additional certificate expires on the date the original certificate expires.

(b) The holder of a Dealer's Aircraft Registration Certificate shall immediately notify the FAA Aircraft Registry of any of the following—

(1) A change of his name;

(2) A change of his address;

(3) A change that affects his status as a citizen of the United States; or

(4) The discontinuance of his business.

47

PART 65

CERTIFICATION: AIRMEN OTHER THAN FLIGHT CREWMEMBERS

SPECIAL FEDERAL AVIATION REGULATIONS

SFAR No. 58
***SFAR No. 100-1**
***SFAR No. 103**

Subpart A—General

Sec.
65.1 Applicability.
65.3 Certification of foreign airmen other than flight crewmembers.
65.11 Application and issue.
65.12 Offenses involving alcohol or drugs.
65.13 Temporary certificate.
65.14 Security disqualification.
65.15 Duration of certificates.
65.16 Change of name: Replacement of lost or destroyed certificate.
65.17 Tests: General procedure.
65.18 Written tests: Cheating or other unauthorized conduct.
65.19 Retesting after failure.
65.20 Applications, certificates, logbooks reports, and records: Falsification, reproduction, or alteration.
65.21 Change of address.
65.23 Refusal to submit to a drug or alcohol test.

Subpart B—Air Traffic Control Tower Operators

65.31 Required certificates, and rating or qualification.
65.33 Eligibility requirements: General.
65.35 Knowledge requirements.
65.37 Skill requirements: Operating positions.
65.39 Practical experience requirements: Facility rating.
65.41 Skill requirements: Facility ratings.
65.43 Rating privileges and exchange.
65.45 Performance of duties.
65.46 Use of prohibited drugs.
65.46a Misuse of alcohol.
65.46b Testing for alcohol.
65.47 Maximum hours.
65.49 General operating rules.
65.50 Currency requirements.

Subpart C—Aircraft Dispatchers

65.51 Certificate required.
65.53 Eligibility requirements: General.
65.55 Knowledge requirements.
65.57 Experience or training requirements.
65.59 Skill requirements.
65.61 Aircraft dispatcher certification courses: Content and minimum hours.
65.63 Aircraft dispatcher certification courses: Application, duration, and other general requirements.
65.65 Aircraft dispatcher certification courses: Training facilities.
65.67 Aircraft dispatcher certification courses: Personnel.
65.70 Aircraft dispatcher certification courses: Records.

Subpart D—Mechanics

65.71 Eligibility requirements: General.
65.73 Ratings.
65.75 Knowledge requirements.
65.77 Experience requirements.
65.79 Skill requirements.
65.80 Certificated aviation maintenance technician school students.
65.81 General privileges and limitations.
65.83 Recent experience requirements.
65.85 Airframe rating; additional privileges.
65.87 Powerplant rating; additional privileges.
65.89 Display of certificate.
65.91 Inspection authorization.
65.92 Inspection authorization: Duration.
65.93 Inspection authorization: Renewal.
65.95 Inspection authorization: Privileges and limitations.

Subpart E—Repairmen

65.101 Eligibility requirements: General.
65.103 Repairman certificate: Privileges and limitations.
65.104 Repairman certificate—experimental aircraft builder—Eligibility, privileges and limitations.
65.105 Display of certificate.
65.107 Repairman certificate (light-sport aircraft): Eligibility, privileges, and limits.

Subpart F—Parachute Riggers

65.111 Certificate required.
65.113 Eligibility requirements: General.
65.115 Senior parachute rigger certificate: Experience, knowledge, and skill requirements.
65.117 Military riggers or former military riggers: Special certification rule.
65.119 Master parachute rigger certificate: Experience, knowledge, and skill requirements.
65.121 Type ratings.
65.123 Additional type ratings: Requirements.
65.125 Certificates: Privileges.
65.127 Facilities and equipment.
65.129 Performance standards.
65.131 Records.
65.133 Seal.

Appendix A to Part 65—Aircraft Dispatcher Courses

Authority: 5 U.S.C. 8335(a); 49 U.S.C. 106(g); 49 U.S.C. 40113; 49 U.S.C. 44701–44703; 49 U.S.C. 44707; 49 U.S.C. 44709–44711; 49 U.S.C. 45102–45103; 49 U.S.C. 45301–45302.

Source: Docket No. 1179, 27 FR 7973, Aug. 10, 1962, unless otherwise noted.

65

SPECIAL FEDERAL AVIATION REGULATIONS

SFAR No. 58 to Part 65

ADVANCED QUALIFICATION PROGRAM

Section

1. Purpose and eligibility
2. Definitions
3. Required Curriculums
4. Indoctrination Curriculums
5. Qualification Curriculums
6. Continuing Qualification Curriculums
7. Other Requirements
8. Certification
9. Training Devices and Simulators
10. Approval of Advanced Qualification Program
11. Approval of Training, Qualification, or Evaluation by a Person Who Provides Training by Arrangement
12. Recordkeeping requirements
13. Expiration

Contrary provisions of parts 61, 63, 65, 121, and 135 of the Federal Aviation Regulations notwithstanding—

1. *Purpose and Eligibility.*

(a) This Special Federal Aviation Regulation provides for approval of an alternate method (known as "Advanced Qualification Program" or "AQP") for qualifying, training, certifying, and otherwise ensuring competency of crewmembers, aircraft dispatchers, other operations personnel, instructors, and evaluators who are required to be trained or qualified under parts 121 and 135 of the FAR or under this SFAR.

(b) A certificate holder is eligible under this Special Federal Aviation Regulation if the certificate holder is required to have an approved training program under §121.401 or §135.341 of the FAR, or elects to have an approved training program under §135.341.

(c) A certificate holder obtains approval of each proposed curriculum under this AQP as specified in section 10 of this SFAR.

(d) A curriculum approved under the AQP may include elements of present Part 121 and Part 135 training programs. Each curriculum must specify the make, model, and series aircraft (or variant) and each crewmember position or other positions to be covered by that curriculum. Positions to be covered by the AQP must include all flight crewmember positions, instructors, and evaluators and may include other positions, such as flight attendants, aircraft dispatchers, and other operations personnel.

(e) Each certificate holder that obtains approval of an AQP under this SFAR shall comply with all of the requirements of that program.

2. *Definitions.* As used in this SFAR:

Curriculum means a portion of an Advanced Qualification Program that covers one of three program areas: (1) indoctrination, (2) qualification, or (3) continuing qualification. A qualification or continuing qualification curriculum addresses the required training and qualification activities for a specific make, model, and series aircraft (or variant) and for a specific duty position.

Evaluator means a person who has satisfactorily completed training and evaluation that qualifies that person to evaluate the performance of crewmembers, instructors, other evaluators, aircraft dispatchers, and other operations personnel.

Facility means the physical environment required for training and qualification (e.g., buildings, classrooms).

Training center means an organization certificated under part 142 of this chapter or an organization approved by the Administrator to operate under the terms of this SFAR to provide training as described in section 1(b) of SFAR 58.

Variant means a specifically configured aircraft for which the FAA has identified training and qualification requirements that are significantly different from those applicable to other aircraft of the same make, model and series.

3. *Required Curriculums.* Each AQP must have separate curriculums for indoctrination, qualification, and continuing qualification as specified in sections 4, 5, and 6 of this SFAR.

4. *Indoctrination Curriculums.* Each indoctrination curriculum must include the following:

(a) For newly hired persons being trained under an AQP: Company policies and operating practices and general operational knowledge.

(b) For newly hired flight crewmembers and air dispatchers: General aeronautical knowledge.

(c) For instructors: The fundamental principles of the teaching and learning process; methods and theories of instruction; and the knowledge necessary to use aircraft flight training devices, flight simulators, and other training equipment in advanced qualification curriculums.

(d) For evaluators: Evaluation requirements specified in each approved curriculum; methods of evaluating crewmembers and aircraft dispatchers and other operations personnel; and policies and practices used to conduct the kinds of evaluations particular to an advanced qualification curriculum.(e.g., proficiency and online).

5. *Qualification Curriculums.* Each qualification curriculum must include the following:

(a) The certificate holder's planned hours of training, evaluation, and supervised operating experience.

(b) A list of and text describing the training, qualification and certification activities, as applicable for specific positions subject to the AQP, as follows:

(1) *Crewmembers, aircraft dispatchers, and other operations personnel.* Training, evaluation and certification activities which are aircraft- and equipment-specific to qualify a person for a particular duty position on, or duties related to the operation of a specific make, model, and series aircraft (or variant); a list of and text describing the knowledge requirements, subject materials, job skills, and each maneuver procedure to be trained and evaluated; the practical test requirements in addition to or in place of the requirements of parts 61, 63, and 65; and a list of and text describing supervised operating experience.

(2) *Instructors.* Training and evaluation to qualify a person to impart instruction on how to operate, or on how to ensure the safe operation of a particular make, model and series aircraft (or variant).

(3) *Evaluators.* Training, evaluation, and certification activities that are aircraft and equipment specific to qualify a person to evaluate the performance of persons who operate or who ensure the safe operation of, a particular make, model, and series aircraft (or variant).

6. *Continuing Qualification Curriculums.* Continuing qualification curriculums must comply with the following requirements:

(a) *General.* A continuing qualification curriculum must be based on—

(1) A continuing qualification cycle that ensures that during each cycle each person qualified under an AQP, including instructors and evaluators, will receive a balanced mix of training and evaluation on all events and subjects necessary to ensure that each person maintains the minimum proficiency levels of knowledge, skills and attitudes required for original qualification: and

(2) If applicable, flight crewmember or aircraft dispatcher recency of experience requirements.

(b) *Continuing Qualification Cycle Content.* Each continuing qualification cycle must include at least the following:

(1) *Evaluation period.* An evaluation period during which each person qualified under an AQP must receive at least one training session and a proficiency evaluation at a training facility. The number and frequency of training sessions must be approved by the Administrator. A training session, including any proficiency evaluation completed at that session, that occurs any time during the two calendar months before the last date for completion of an evaluation period can be considered by the certificate holder to be completed in the last calendar month.

(2) *Training.* Continuing qualification must include training in all events and major subjects required for original qualification, as follows:

(i) For pilots in command, seconds in command, flight engineers, and instructors and evaluators: Ground training including a general review of knowledge and skills covered in qualification training, updated information on newly developed procedures, and safety information.

(ii) For crewmembers, aircraft dispatchers, instructors, evaluators, and other operation personnel who conduct their duties in flight; Proficiency training in an aircraft, flight training device, or flight simulator on normal, abnormal, and emergency flight procedures and maneuvers.

(iii) For instructors and evaluators who are limited to conducting their duties in flight simulators and flight training devices: Proficiency training in a flight training device and/or flight simulator regarding operation of this training equipment and in operational flight procedures and maneuvers (normal, abnormal, and emergency).

(3) *Evaluations.* Continuing qualification must include evaluation in all events and major subjects required for original qualification, and online evaluations for pilots in command and other eligible flight crewmembers. Each person qualified under an AQP must successfully complete a proficiency evaluation and, if applicable, an online evaluation during each evaluation period. An individual's proficiency evaluation may be accomplished over several training sessions if a certificate holder provides more than one training session in an evaluation period. The following evaluation requirements apply:

(i) Proficiency evaluations as follows:

(A) For pilots in command, seconds in command, and flight engineers: A proficiency evaluation, portions of which may be conducted in an aircraft flight simulator, or flight training device as approved in the certificate holder's curriculum which must be completed during each evaluation period.

(B) For any other persons covered by an AQP a means to evaluate their proficiency in the performance of their duties in their assigned tasks in an operational setting.

(ii) Online evaluations as follows:

(A) For pilots in command: An online evaluation conducted in an aircraft during actual flight operations under part 121 or part 135 or during operationally (line) oriented flights or proving flights. An online evaluation in an aircraft must be completed in the calendar month that includes the midpoint of the evaluation period. An online evaluation that is satisfactorily completed in the calendar month after the calendar month in which it becomes due is considered to have been completed during the calendar month it became due. However, in no case is an evaluation under this paragraph required more often than once during an evaluation period.

(B) During the online evaluations required under paragraph (b)(3)(ii)(A) of this section, each person performing duties as a pilot in command, second in command, or flight engineer for that flight, must be individually evaluated to determine whether he or she—

(1) Remains adequately trained and currently proficient with respect to the particular aircraft, crew position, and type of operation in which he or she serves; and

(2) Has sufficient knowledge and skills to operate effectively as part of the crew.

(4) *Recency of experience.* For pilots in command and seconds in command and if the certificate holder elects, flight engineers and flight dispatchers, approved recency of experience requirements.

(c) *Duration periods.* Initially the continuing qualification cycle approved for an AQP may not exceed 26 calendar months and the evaluation period may not exceed 13 calendar months. Thereafter, upon demonstration by a certificate holder that an extension is warranted, the Administrator may approve extensions of the continuing qualification cycle and the evaluation period in increments not exceeding 3 calendar months. However, a continuing qualification cycle may not exceed 39 calendar months and an evaluation period may not exceed 26 calendar months.

(d) *Requalification.* Each continuing qualification curriculum must include a curriculum segment that covers the requirements for requalifying a crewmember, aircraft dispatcher, or other operations personnel who has not maintained continuing qualification.

7. *Other Requirements.* In addition to the requirements of sections 4, 5, and 6, each AQP qualification and continuing qualification curriculum must include the following requirements:

(a) Approved Cockpit Resource Management (CRM) Training applicable to each position for which training is provided under an AQP.

(b) Approved training on an evaluation of skills and proficiency of each person being trained under an AQP to use their cockpit resource management skills and technical (piloting or other) skills in an actual or simulated operations scenario. For flight crew members this training and evaluation must be conducted in an approved flight training device or flight simulator.

(c) Data collection procedures that will ensure that the certificate holder provides information from its crew members, instructors, and evaluators that will enable the FAA to determine whether the training and evaluations are working to accomplish the overall objectives of the curriculum.

8. *Certification.* A person enrolled in an AQP is eligible to receive a commercial or airline transport pilot, flight engineer, aircraft dispatcher certificate or appropriate rating based on the successful completion of training and evaluation events accomplished under that program if the following requirements are met:

(a) Training and evaluation of required knowledge and skills under the AQP must meet minimum certification and rating criteria established by the Administrator in parts 61, 63, or 65. The Administrator may accept substitutes for the practical test requirements of parts 61, 63, or 65, as applicable.

(b) The applicant satisfactorily completes the appropriate qualification curriculum.

(c) The applicant shows competence in required technical knowledge and skills (e.g., piloting) and cockpit resource management knowledge and skills in scenarios that test both types of knowledge and skills together.

(d) the applicant is otherwise eligible under the applicable requirements of part 61, 63, or 65.

9. *Training Devices and Simulators.*

(a) *Qualification and approval of flight training devices and flight simulators.*

(1) Any training device or simulator that will be used in an AQP for one of the following purposes must be evaluated by the Administrator for assignment of a flight training device or flight simulator qualification level:

(i) Required evaluation of individual or crew proficiency.

(ii) Training activities that determine if an individual or crew is ready for a proficiency evaluation.

(iii) Activities used to meet recency of experience requirements.

(iv) Line Operations Simulations (LOS).

(2) To be eligible to request evaluation for a qualification level of a flight training device or flight simulator an applicant must—

(i) Hold an operating certificate; or

(ii) Be a training center that has applied for authorization to the administrator or has been authorized by the Administrator to conduct training or qualification under an AQP.

(3) Each flight training device or flight simulator to be used by a certificate holder or training center for any of the purposes set forth in paragraph (a)(1) of this section must—

(i) Be, or have been, evaluated against a set of criteria established by the Administrator for a particular qualification level of simulation;

(ii) Be approved for its intended use in a specified AQP, and

(iii) Be part of a flight simulator or flight training device continuing qualification program approved by the Administrator.

(b) *Approval of other Training Equipment.*

(1) Any training device that is intended to be used in an AQP for purposes other than those set forth in paragraph (a)(1) of this section must be approved by the Administrator for its intended use.

(2) An applicant for approval of a training device under this paragraph must identify the device by its nomenclature and describe its intended use.

(3) Each training device approved for use in an AQP must be part of a continuing program to provide for its serviceability and fitness to perform its intended function as approved by the Administrator.

10. *Approval of Advanced Qualification Program.*

(a) *Approval Process.* Each applicant for approval of an AQP curriculum under this SFAR shall apply for approval of that curriculum. Application for approval is made to the certificate holder's FAA Flight Standards District Office.

(b) *Approval Criteria.* An application for approval of an AQP curriculum will be approved if the program meets the following requirements:

(1) It must be submitted in a form and manner acceptable to the Administrator.

(2) It must meet all of the requirements of this SFAR.

(3) It must indicate specifically the requirements of parts 61, 63, 65, 121 or 135, as applicable, that would be replaced by an AQP curriculum. If a requirement of parts 61, 63, 65, 121, or 135 is replaced by an AQP curriculum, the certificate holder must show how the AQP curriculum provides an equivalent level of safety for each requirement that is replaced. Each applicable requirement of parts 61, 63, 65, 121 or 135 that is not specifically addressed in an AQP curriculum continues to apply to the certificate holder.

(c) *Application and Transition.* Each certificate holder that applies for one or more advanced qualification curriculums or for a revision to a previously approved curriculum must comply with §121.405 or §135.325, as applicable, and must include as part of its application a proposed transition plan (containing a calendar of events) for moving from its present approved training to the advanced qualification training.

(d) *Advanced Qualification Program Revisions or Rescissions of Approval.* If after a certificate holder begins operations under an AQP, the Administrator finds that the certificate holder is not meeting the provisions of its approved AQP, the Administrator may require the certificate holder to make revisions in accordance with §121.405 or §135.325, as applicable, or to submit and obtain approval for a plan (containing a schedule of events) that the certificate holder must comply with and use to transition to an approved part 121 or part 135 training program, as appropriate.

11. *Approval of Training, Qualification, or Evaluation by a Person who Provides Training by Arrangement.*

(a) A certificate holder under part 121 or part 135 may arrange to have AQP required training, qualification, or evaluation functions performed by another person (a *training center*) if the following requirements are met:

(1) The training center's training and qualification curriculums, curriculum segments, or portions of curriculum segments must be provisionally approved by the Administrator. A training center may apply for provisional approval independently or in conjunction with a certificate holder's application for AQP approval. Application for provisional approval must be made to the FAA's Flight Standards District Office that has responsibility for the training center.

(2) The specific use of provisionally approved curriculums, curriculum segments, or portions of curriculum segments in

a certificate holder's AQP must be approved by the Administrator as set forth in section 10 of this SFAR.

(b) An applicant for provisional approval of a curriculum, curriculum segment, or portion of a curriculum segment under this paragraph must show that the following requirements are met:

(1) The applicant must have a curriculum for the qualification and continuing qualification of each instructor or evaluator employed by the applicant.

(2) The applicant's facilities must be found by the Administrator to be adequate for any planned training, qualification, or evaluation for a part 121 or part 135 certificate holder.

(3) Except for indoctrination curriculums, the curriculum, curriculum segment, or portion of a curriculum segment must identify the specific make, model, and series aircraft (or variant) and crewmember or other positions for which it is designed.

(c) A certificate holder who wants approval to use a training center's provisionally approved curriculum, curriculum segment, or portion of a curriculum segment in its AQP, must show that the following requirements are met:

(1) Each instructor or evaluator used by the training center must meet all of the qualification and continuing qualification requirements that apply to employees of the certificate holder that has arranged for the training, including knowledge of the certificate holder's operations.

(2) Each provisionally approved curriculum, curriculum segment, or portion of a curriculum segment must be approved by the Administrator for use in the certificate holder's AQP. The Administrator will either provide approval or require modifications to ensure that each curriculum, curriculum segment, or portion of a curriculum segment is applicable to the certificate holder's AQP.

(d) Approval for the training, qualification, or evaluation by a person who provides training by arrangement authorized by this section expires on August 3, 1998 unless that person meets the eligibility requirements specified under §121.402 or §135.324 of this chapter. After August 2, 1998 approval for the training, qualification, or evaluation, by a person who provides training by arrangement authorized by this section, shall be granted only to persons who meet the eligibility requirements specified under §121.402 or §135.234 of this chapter.

12. *Recordkeeping Requirements.* Each certificate holder and each training center holding AQP provisional approval shall show that it will establish and maintain records in sufficient detail to establish the training, qualification, and certification of each person qualified under an AQP in accordance with the training, qualification, and certification requirements of this SFAR.

13. *Expiration.* This Special Federal Aviation Regulation terminates on October 2, 2005, unless sooner terminated.

[SFAR 58, 55 FR 40275, Oct. 2, 1990; as amended by 60 FR 51851, Oct. 3, 1995; SFAR 58–2, 61 FR 34560, July 2, 1996; Amdt. 121–280, 65 FR 60336, Oct. 10, 2000]

SFAR No. 100-1 to Part 65

Relief for U.S. Military and Civilian Personnel Who are Assigned Outside the United States in Support of U.S. Armed Forces Operations

1. Applicability. Flight Standards District Offices are authorized to accept from an eligible person, as described in paragraph 2 of this SFAR, the following:

(a) An expired flight instructor certificate to show eligibility for renewal of a flight instructor certificate under §61.197, or an expired written test report to show eligibility under part 61 to take a practical test;

(b) An expired written test report to show eligibility under §§63.33 and 63.57 to take a practical test; and

(c) An expired written test report to show eligibility to take a practical test required under part 65 or an expired inspection authorization to show eligibility for renewal under §65.93.

2. Eligibility. A person is eligible for the relief described in paragraph 1 of this SFAR if:

(a) The person served in a U.S. military or civilian capacity outside the United States in support of the U.S. Armed Forces' operation during some period of time from September 11, 2001, through June 20, 2010;

(b) The person's flight instructor certificate, airman written test report, or inspection authorization expired some time between September 11, 2001, and 6 calendar months after returning to the United States, or June 20, 2010, whichever is earlier; and

(c) The person complies with §61.197 or §65.93 of this chapter, as appropriate, or completes the appropriate practical test within 6 calendar months after returning to the United States, or June 20, 2010, whichever is earlier.

3. Required documents. The person must send the Airman Certificate and/or Rating Application (FAA Form 8710-1) to the appropriate Flight Standards District Office. The person must include with the application one of the following documents, which must show the date of assignment outside the United States and the date of return to the United States:

(a) An official U.S. Government notification of personnel action, or equivalent document, showing the person was a civilian on official duty for the U.S. Government outside the United States and was assigned to a U.S. Armed Forces' operation some time between September 11, 2001, through June 20, 2010;

(b) Military orders showing the person was assigned to duty outside the United States and was assigned to a U.S. Armed Forces' operation some time between September 11, 2001 through June 20, 2010; or

(c) A letter from the person's military commander or civilian supervisor providing the dates during which the person served outside the United States and was assigned to a U.S. Armed Forces' operation some time between September 11, 2001 through June 20, 2010.

65

4. Expiration date. This Special Federal Aviation Regulation No.100-1 expires June 20, 2010, unless sooner superseded or rescinded.

[Docket No. FAA–2005–15431, SFAR No. 100–1, 70 FR 37948, June 30, 2005]

SFAR No. 103 to Part 65

Process for Requesting Waiver of Mandatory Separation Age for a Federal Aviation Administration Air Traffic Control Specialist In Flight Service Stations, Enroute or Terminal Facilities, and the David J. Hurley Air Traffic Control System Command Center

1. ***To whom does this SFAR apply?*** This Special Federal Aviation Regulation (SFAR) applies to you if you are an air traffic control specialist (ATCS) employed by the FAA in flight service stations, enroute facilities, terminal facilities, or at the David J. Hurley Air Traffic Control System Command Center who wishes to obtain a waiver of the mandatory separation age as provided by 5 U.S.C. section 8335(a).

2. ***When must I file for a waiver?*** No earlier than the beginning of the twelfth month before, but no later than the beginning of the sixth month before, the month in which you turn 56, your official chain-of-command must receive your written request asking for a waiver of mandatory separation.

3. ***What if I do not file a request before six months before the month in which I turn 56?*** If your official chain-of-command does not receive your written request for a waiver of mandatory separation before the beginning of the sixth month before the month in which you turn 56, your request will be denied.

4. ***How will the FAA determine if my request meets the filing time requirements of this SFAR?***

a. We consider your request to be filed in a timely manner under this SFAR if your official chain-of-command receives it or it is postmarked:

i. After 12 a.m. on the first day of the twelfth month before the month in which you turn 56; and

ii. Before 12 a.m. of the first day of the sixth month before the month in which you turn 56.

b. If you file your request by mail and the postmark is not legible, we will consider it to comply with paragraph a.2 of this section if we receive it by 12 p.m. of the fifth day of the sixth month before the month in which you turn 56.

c. If the last day of the time period specified in paragraph a.2 or paragraph b falls on a Saturday, Sunday, or Federal holiday, we will consider the time period to end at 12 p.m. of the next business day.

5. ***Where must I file my request for waiver and what must it include?***

a. You must file your request for waiver of mandatory separation in writing with the Air Traffic Manager in flight service stations, enroute facilities, terminal facilities, or the David J. Hurley Air Traffic Control System Command Center in which you are employed.

b. Your request for waiver must include all of the following:

i. Your name.

ii. Your current facility.

iii. Your starting date at the facility.

iv. A list of positions at the facility that you are certified in and how many hours it took to achieve certification at the facility.

v. Your area of specialty at the facility.

vi. Your shift schedule.

vii. Your statement that you have not been involved in an operational error, operational deviation or runway incursion in the last 5 years while working a control position;

viii. A list of all facilities where you have worked as a certified professional controller (CPC) including facility level and dates at each facility;

ix. Evidence of your exceptional skills and experience as a controller; and

x. Your signature.

6. ***How will my waiver request be reviewed?***

a. Upon receipt of your request for waiver, the Air Traffic Manager of your facility will make a written recommendation that the Administrator either approve or deny your request. If the manager recommends approval of your request, he or she will certify in writing the accuracy of the information you provided as evidence of your exceptional skills and experience as a controller.

b. The Air Traffic Manager will then forward the written recommendation with a copy of your request to the senior executive manager in the Air Traffic Manager's regional chain-of-command.

c. The senior executive manager in the regional chain-of-command will make a written recommendation that the Administrator either approve or deny your request. If the senior executive manager recommends approval of your request, he or she will certify in writing the accuracy of the information you have provided as evidence of exceptional skills and experience.

d. The senior executive manager in the regional chain-of-command will then forward his or her recommendation with a copy of your request to the appropriate Vice President at FAA Headquarters. Depending on the facility in which you are employed, the request will be forwarded to either the Vice President for Flight Services, the Vice President for Enroute and Oceanic Services, the Vice President for Terminal Services or the Vice President for Systems Operations. For example, if you work at a flight service station at the time that you request a waiver, the request will be forwarded to the Vice President for Flight Services.

e. The appropriate Vice President will review your request and make a written recommendation that the Administrator either approve or deny your request, which will be forwarded to the Administrator.

f. The Administrator will issue the final decision on your request.

7. ***If I am granted a waiver, when will it expire?***

a. Waivers will be granted for a period of one year.

b. No later than 90-days prior to expiration of a waiver, you may request that the waiver be extended using the same process identified in section 6.

c. If you timely request an extension of the waiver and it is denied, you will receive a 60-day advance notice of your separation date simultaneously with notification of the denial.

d. If you do not request an extension of the waiver granted, you will receive a 60-day advance notice of your separation date.

e. Action to separate you from your covered position becomes effective on the last day of the month in which the 60-day notice expires.

8. *Under what circumstances may my waiver be terminated?*

a. The FAA/DOT may terminate your waiver under the following circumstances:

i. The needs of the FAA; or

ii. If you are identified as a primary contributor to an operational error/deviation or runway incursion.

b. If the waiver is terminated for either of the reasons identified in paragraph 1 of this section, the air traffic control specialist will receive a 60-day advance notice.

c. Action to separate you from your covered position becomes effective on the last day of the month in which the 60-day notice expires.

9. *Appeal of denial or termination of waiver request:* The denial or termination of a waiver of mandatory separation request is neither appealable nor grievable.

[Docket No. FAA–2004–17334; SFAR No. 103, 70 FR 1636, Jan. 7, 2005]

Subpart A—General

§65.1 Applicability.

This part prescribes the requirements for issuing the following certificates and associated ratings and the general operating rules for the holders of those certificates and ratings:

(a) Air-traffic control-tower operators.

(b) Aircraft dispatchers.

(c) Mechanics.

(d) Repairmen.

(e) Parachute riggers.

§65.3 Certification of foreign airmen other than flight crewmembers.

A person who is neither a U.S. citizen nor a resident alien is issued a certificate under subpart D of this part, outside the United States, only when the Administrator finds that the certificate is needed for the operation or continued airworthiness of a U.S.-registered civil aircraft.

[Docket 65–28, FR 35693, Aug. 16, 1982]

§65.11 Application and issue.

(a) Application for a certificate and appropriate class rating, or for an additional rating, under this part must be made on a form and in a manner prescribed by the Administrator. Each person who is neither a U.S. citizen nor a resident alien and who applies for a written or practical test to be administered outside the United States or for any certificate or rating issued under this part must show evidence that the fee prescribed in appendix A of part 187 of this chapter has been paid.

(b) An applicant who meets the requirements of this part is entitled to an appropriate certificate and rating.

(c) Unless authorized by the Administrator, a person whose air traffic control tower operator, mechanic, or parachute rigger certificate is suspended may not apply for any rating to be added to that certificate during the period of suspension.

(d) Unless the order of revocation provides otherwise—

(1) A person whose air traffic control tower operator, aircraft dispatcher, or parachute rigger certificate is revoked may not apply for the same kind of certificate for 1 year after the date of revocation; and

(2) A person whose mechanic or repairman certificate is revoked may not apply for either of those kinds of certificates for 1 year after the date of revocation.

[Docket No. 1179, 27 FR 7973, Aug. 10, 1962; as amended by Amdt. 65–9, 31 FR 13524, Oct. 20, 1966; Amdt. 65–28, 47 FR 35693, Aug. 16, 1982]

§65.12 Offenses involving alcohol or drugs.

(a) A conviction for the violation of any Federal or state statute relating to the growing, processing, manufacture, sale, disposition, possession, transportation, or importation of narcotic drugs, marihuana, or depressant or stimulant drugs or substances is grounds for—

(1) Denial of an application for any certificate or rating issued under this part for a period of up to 1 year after the date of final conviction; or

(2) Suspension or revocation of any certificate or rating issued under this part.

(b) The commission of an act prohibited by §91.19(a) of this chapter is grounds for—

(1) Denial of an application for a certificate or rating issued under this part for a period of up to 1 year after the date of that act; or

(2) Suspension or revocation of any certificate or rating issued under this part.

[Docket No. 21956, 50 FR 15379, April 17, 1985; as amended by Amdt. 65–34, 54 FR 34330, Aug. 18, 1989]

§65.13 Temporary certificate.

A certificate and ratings effective for a period of not more than 120 days may be issued to a qualified applicant, pending review of his application and supplementary documents and the issue of the certificate and ratings for which he applied.

[Docket No. 1179, 27 FR 7973, Aug. 10, 1962; as amended by Amdt. 65–23, 43 FR 22640, May 25, 1978]

§65.14 Security disqualification.

(a) *Eligibility standard.* No person is eligible to hold a certificate, rating, or authorization issued under this part when the Transportation Security Administration (TSA) has notified the FAA in writing that the person poses a security threat.

(b) *Effect of the issuance by the TSA of an Initial Notification of Threat Assessment.*

(1) The FAA will hold in abeyance pending the outcome of the TSA's final threat assessment review an application for any certificate, rating, or authorization under this part by any person who has been issued an Initial Notification of Threat Assessment by the TSA.

(2) The FAA will suspend any certificate, rating, or authorization issued under this part after the TSA issues to the holder an Initial Notification of Threat Assessment.

(c) *Effect of the issuance by the TSA of a Final Notification of Threat Assessment.*

(1) The FAA will deny an application for any certificate, rating, or authorization under this part to any person who has been issued a Final Notification of Threat Assessment.

(2) The FAA will revoke any certificate, rating, or authorization issued under this part after the TSA has issued to the holder a Final Notification of Threat Assessment.

[Docket No. FAA–2003–14293, 68 FR 3775, Jan. 24, 2003]

§65.15 Duration of certificates.

(a) Except for repairman certificates, a certificate or rating issued under this part is effective until it is surrendered, suspended, or revoked.

(b) Unless it is sooner surrendered, suspended, or revoked, a repairman certificate is effective until the holder is relieved from the duties for which the holder was employed and certificated.

(c) The holder of a certificate issued under this part that is suspended, revoked, or no longer effective shall return it to the Administrator.

[Docket No. 22052, 47 FR 35693, Aug. 16, 1982]

§65.16 Change of name: Replacement of lost or destroyed certificate.

(a) An application for a change of name on a certificate issued under this part must be accompanied by the applicant's current certificate and the marriage license, court order, or other document verifying the change. The documents are returned to the applicant after inspection.

(b) An application for a replacement of a lost or destroyed certificate is made by letter to the Department of Transportation, Federal Aviation Administration, Airman Certification Branch, Post Office Box 25082, Oklahoma City, OK 73125. The letter must—

(1) Contain the name in which the certificate was issued, the permanent mailing address (including zip code), social security number (if any), and date and place of birth of the certificate holder, and any available information regarding the grade, number, and date of issue of the certificate, and the ratings on it; and

(2) Be accompanied by a check or money order for $2, payable to the Federal Aviation Administration.

(c) An application for a replacement of a lost or destroyed medical certificate is made by letter to the Department of Transportation, Federal Aviation Administration, Civil Aeromedical Institute, Aeromedical Certification Branch, Post Office Box 25082, Oklahoma City, OK 73125, accompanied by a check or money order for $2.00.

(d) A person whose certificate issued under this part or medical certificate, or both, has been lost may obtain a telegram from the FAA confirming that it was issued. The telegram may be carried as a certificate for a period not to exceed 60 days pending his receiving a duplicate certificate under paragraph (b) or (c) of this section, unless he has been notified that the certificate has been suspended or revoked. The request for such a telegram may be made by prepaid telegram, stating the date upon which a duplicate certificate was requested, or including the request for a duplicate and a money order for the necessary amount. The request for a telegraphic certificate should be sent to the office prescribed in paragraph (b) or (c) of this section, as appropriate. However, a request for both at the same time should be sent to the office prescribed in paragraph (b) of this section.

[Docket No. 7258, 31 FR 13524, Oct. 20, 1966; as amended by Docket No. 8084, 32 FR 5769, Apr. 11, 1967; Amdt. 65–16, 35 FR 14075, Sept. 4, 1970; Amdt. 65–17, 36 FR 2865, Feb. 11, 1971]

§65.17 Tests: General procedure.

(a) Tests prescribed by or under this part are given at times and places, and by persons, designated by the Administrator.

(b) The minimum passing grade for each test is 70 percent.

§65.18 Written tests: Cheating or other unauthorized conduct.

(a) Except as authorized by the Administrator, no person may—

(1) Copy, or intentionally remove, a written test under this part;

(2) Give to another, or receive from another, any part or copy of that test;

(3) Give help on that test to, or receive help on that test from, any person during the period that test is being given;

(4) Take any part of that test in behalf of another person;

(5) Use any material or aid during the period that test is being given; or

(6) Intentionally cause, assist, or participate in any act prohibited by this paragraph.

(b) No person who commits an act prohibited by paragraph (a) of this section is eligible for any airman or ground instructor certificate or rating under this chapter for a period of 1 year after the date of that act. In addition, the commission of that act is a basis for suspending or revoking any airman or ground instructor certificate or rating held by that person.

[Docket No. 4086, 30 FR 2196, Feb. 18, 1965]

§65.19 Retesting after failure.

An applicant for a written, oral, or practical test for a certificate and rating, or for an additional rating under this part, may apply for retesting—

(a) After 30 days after the date the applicant failed the test; or

(b) Before the 30 days have expired if the applicant presents a signed statement from an airman holding the certificate and rating sought by the applicant, certifying that the airman has given the applicant additional instruction in each of the subjects failed and that the airman considers the applicant ready for retesting.

[Docket No. 16383, 43 FR 22640, May 25, 1978]

§65.20 Applications, certificates, logbooks, reports, and records: Falsification, reproduction, or alteration.

(a) No person may make or cause to be made—

(1) Any fraudulent or intentionally false statement on any application for a certificate or rating under this part;

(2) Any fraudulent or intentionally false entry in any logbook, record, or report that is required to be kept, made, or used, to show compliance with any requirement for any certificate or rating under this part;

(3) Any reproduction, for fraudulent purpose, of any certificate or rating under this part; or

(4) Any alteration of any certificate or rating under this part.

(b) The commission by any person of an act prohibited under paragraph (a) of this section is a basis for suspending or revoking any airman or ground instructor certificate or rating held by that person.

[Docket No. 4086, 30 FR 2196, Feb. 18, 1965]

§65.21 Change of address.

Within 30 days after any change in his permanent mailing address, the holder of a certificate issued under this part shall notify the Department of Transportation, Federal Aviation Administration, Airman Certification Branch, Post Office Box 25082, Oklahoma City, OK 73125, in writing, of his new address.

[Docket No. 10536, 35 FR 14075, Sept. 4, 1970]

§65.23 Refusal to submit to a drug or alcohol test.

(a) *General.* This section applies to an employee who performs a function listed in appendix I or appendix J to part 121 of this chapter directly or by contract for a part 121 certificate holder, a part 135 certificate holder, an operator as defined in §135.1(c) of this chapter, or an air traffic control facility not operated by the FAA or the U.S. military.

(b) Refusal by the holder of a certificate issued under this part to take a drug test required under the provisions of appendix I to part 121 or an alcohol test required under the provisions of appendix J to part 121 is grounds for—

(1) Denial of an application for any certificate or rating issued under this part for a period of up to 1 year after the date of such refusal; and

(2) Suspension or revocation of any certificate or rating issued under this part.

[Docket No. 25148, 53 FR 47056, Nov. 21, 1988; 54 FR 1289, Jan. 12, 1989; as amended by Amdt. 65–33, 54 FR 15152, April 14, 1989; Amdt. 65–37, 59 FR 7389, Feb. 15, 1994]

Subpart B— Air Traffic Control Tower Operators

Source: Docket No. 10193, 35 FR 12326, Aug. 1, 1970, unless otherwise noted.

§65.31 Required certificates, and rating or qualification.

No person may act as an air traffic control tower operator at an air traffic control tower in connection with civil aircraft unless he—

(a) Holds an air traffic control tower operator certificate issued to him under this subpart;

(b) Holds a facility rating for that control tower issued to him under this subpart, or has qualified for the operating position at which he acts and is under the supervision of the holder of a facility rating for that control tower; and

For the purpose of this subpart, *operating position* means an air traffic control function performed within or directly associated with the control tower;

(c) Except for a person employed by the FAA or employed by, or on active duty with, the Department of the Air Force, Army, or Navy or the Coast Guard, holds at least a second-class medical certificate issued under part 67 of this chapter.

[Docket No. 10193, 35 FR 12326, Aug. 1, 1970; as amended by Amdt. 65–25, 45 FR 18911, Mar. 24, 1980; Amdt. 65–31, 52 FR 17518, May 8, 1987]

§65.33 Eligibility requirements: General.

To be eligible for an air traffic control tower operator certificate a person must—

(a) Be at least 18 years of age;

(b) Be of good moral character;

(c) Be able to read, write, and understand the English language and speak it without accent or impediment of speech that would interfere with two-way radio conversation;

(d) Except for a person employed by the FAA or employed by, or on active duty with, the Department of the Air Force, Army, or Navy or the Coast Guard, holds at least a second-class medical certificate issued under part 67 of this chapter within the 12 months before the date application is made; and

(e) Comply with §65.35.

[Docket No. 10193, 35 FR 12326, Aug. 1, 1970; as amended by Amdt. 65–25, 45 FR 18911, March 24, 1980; Amdt. 65–31, 52 FR 17518, May 8, 1987]

§65.35 Knowledge requirements.

Each applicant for an air traffic control tower operator certificate must pass a written test on—

(a) The flight rules in part 91 of this chapter:

(b) Airport traffic control procedures, and this subpart:

(c) En route traffic control procedures;

(d) Communications operating procedures;

(e) Flight assistance service;

(f) Air navigation, and aids to air navigation; and

(g) Aviation weather.

§65.37 Skill requirements: Operating positions.

No person may act as an air traffic control tower operator at any operating position unless he has passed a practical test on—

(a) Control tower equipment and its use;

(b) Weather reporting procedures and use of reports;

(c) Notices to Airmen, and use of the Airman's Information Manual;

(d) Use of operational forms;

(e) Performance of noncontrol operational duties; and

(f) Each of the following procedures that is applicable to that operating position and is required by the person performing the examination:

(1) The airport, including rules, equipment, runways, taxiways, and obstructions.

(2) The terrain features, visual check-points, and obstructions within the lateral boundaries of the surface areas of Class B, Class C, Class D, or Class E airspace designated for the airport.

(3) Traffic patterns and associated procedures for use of preferential runways and noise abatement.

(4) Operational agreements.

(5) The center, alternate airports, and those airways, routes, reporting points, and air navigation aids used for terminal air traffic control.

(6) Search and rescue procedures.

(7) Terminal air traffic control procedures and phraseology.

(8) Holding procedures, prescribed instrument approach, and departure procedures.

(9) Radar alignment and technical operation.

(10) The application of the prescribed radar and nonradar separation standard, as appropriate.

[Docket No. 10193, 35 FR 12326, Aug. 1, 1991; as amended by Amdt. 65–36, 56 FR 65653, Dec. 17, 1991]

§65.39 Practical experience requirements: Facility rating.

Each applicant for a facility rating at any air traffic control tower must have satisfactorily served—

(a) As an air traffic control tower operator at that control tower without a facility rating for at least 6 months; or

(b) As an air traffic control tower operator with a facility rating at a different control tower for at least 6 months before the date he applies for the rating.

However, an applicant who is a member of an Armed Force of the United States meets the requirements of this section if he has satisfactorily served as an air traffic control tower operator for at least 6 months.

[Docket No. 1179, 27 FR 7973, Aug. 10, 1962; as amended by Amdt. 65–19, 36 FR 21280, Nov. 5, 1971]

§65.41 Skill requirements: Facility ratings.

Each applicant for a facility rating at an air traffic control tower must have passed a practical test on each item listed in §65.37 of this part that is applicable to each operating position at the control tower at which the rating is sought.

§65.43 Rating privileges and exchange.

(a) The holder of a senior rating on August 31, 1970, may at any time after that date exchange his rating for a facility rating at the same air traffic control tower. However, if he does not do so before August 31, 1971, he may not thereafter exercise the privileges of his senior rating at the control tower concerned until he makes the exchange.

(b) The holder of a junior rating on August 31, 1970, may not control air traffic, at any operating position at the control tower concerned, until he has met the applicable requirements of §65.37 of this part. However, before meeting those requirements he may control air traffic under the supervision, where required, of an operator with a senior rating (or facility rating) in accordance with §65.41 of this part in effect before August 31, 1970.

§65.45 Performance of duties.

(a) An air traffic control tower operator shall perform his duties in accordance with the limitations on his certificate and the procedures and practices prescribed in air traffic control manuals of the FAA, to provide for the safe, orderly, and expeditious flow of air traffic.

(b) An operator with a facility rating may control traffic at any operating position at the control tower at which he holds a facility rating. However, he may not issue an air traffic clearance for IFR flight without authorization from the appropriate facility exercising IFR control at that location.

(c) An operator who does not hold a facility rating for a particular control tower may act at each operating position for which he has qualified, under the supervision of an operator holding a facility rating for that control tower.

[Docket No. 10193, 35 FR 12326, Aug. 1, 1970; as amended by Amdt. 65–16, 35 FR 14075, Sept. 4, 1970]

§65.46 Use of prohibited drugs.

(a) The following definitions apply for the purposes of this section:

(1) An *employee* is a person who performs an air traffic control function for an employer. For the purpose of this section, a person who performs such a function pursuant to a contract with an employer is considered to be performing that function for the employer.

(2) An "employer" means an air traffic control facility not operated by the FAA or by or under contract to the U.S. military that employs a person to perform an air traffic control function.

(b) Each employer shall provide each employee performing a function listed in appendix I to part 121 of this chapter and his or her supervisor with the training specified in that appendix. No employer may use any contractor to perform an air traffic control function unless that contractor provides each of its employees and his or her supervisor with the training specified in that appendix.

(c) No employer may knowingly use any person to perform, nor may any person perform for an employer, either directly or by contract, any air traffic control function while that person has a prohibited drug, as defined in appendix I to part 121 of this chapter, in his or her system.

(d) No employer shall knowingly use any person to perform, nor may any person perform for an employer, either directly or by contract, any air traffic control function if the person has a verified positive drug test result on or has refused to submit to a drug test required by appendix I to part 121 of this chapter and the person has not met the requirements of appendix I to part 121 of this chapter for returning to the performance of safety-sensitive duties.

(e) Each employer shall test each of its employees who perform any air traffic control function in accordance with appendix I to part 121 of this chapter. No employer may use any contractor to perform any air traffic control function unless that contractor tests each employee performing such a function for the employer in accordance with that appendix.

[Docket No. 25148, 53 FR 47056, Nov. 21, 1988; as amended by Amdt. 65–38, 59 FR 42977, Aug. 19, 1994]

§65.46a Misuse of alcohol.

(a) This section applies to employees who perform air traffic control duties directly or by contract for an employer that is an air traffic control facility not operated by the FAA or the U.S. military *(covered employees).*

(b) *Alcohol concentration.* No covered employee shall report for duty or remain on duty requiring the performance of safety-sensitive functions while having an alcohol concentration of 0.04 or greater. No employer having actual knowledge that an employee has an alcohol concentration of 0.04 or greater shall permit the employee to perform or continue to perform safety-sensitive functions.

(c) *On-duty use.* No covered employee shall use alcohol while performing safety-sensitive functions. No employer having actual knowledge that a covered employee is using alcohol while performing safety-sensitive functions shall permit the employee to perform or continue to perform safety-sensitive functions.

(d) *Pre-duty use.* No covered employees shall perform air traffic control duties within 8 hours after using alcohol. No employer having actual knowledge that such an employee has used alcohol within 8 hours shall permit the employee to perform or continue to perform air traffic control duties.

(e) *Use following an accident.* No covered employee who has actual knowledge of an accident involving an aircraft for which he or she performed a safety-sensitive function at or near the time of the accident shall use alcohol for 8 hours following the accident, unless he or she has been given a post-accident test under appendix J to part 121 of this chapter, or the employer has determined that the employee's performance could not have contributed to the accident.

(f) *Refusal to submit to a required alcohol test.* No covered employee shall refuse to submit to a post-accident, random, reasonable suspicion, or follow-up alcohol test required under appendix J to part 121 of this chapter. No employer shall permit an employee who refuses to submit to such a test to perform or continue to perform safety-sensitive functions.

[Docket No. 27065, 59 FR 7389, Feb. 15, 1994]

§65.46b Testing for alcohol.

(a) Each air traffic control facility not operated by the FAA or the U.S. military (hereinafter *employer*) must establish an alcohol misuse prevention program in accordance with the provisions of appendix J to part 121 of this chapter.

(b) No employer shall use any person who meets the definition of *covered employee* in appendix J to part 121 to perform a safety-sensitive function listed in that appendix unless such person is subject to testing for alcohol misuse in accordance with the provisions of appendix J.

[Docket No. 27065, 59 FR 7389, Feb. 15, 1994]

§65.47 Maximum hours.

Except in an emergency, a certificated air traffic control tower operator must be relieved of all duties for at least 24 consecutive hours at least once during each 7 consecutive days. Such an operator may not serve or be required to serve—

(a) For more than 10 consecutive hours; or

(b) For more than 10 hours during a period of 24 consecutive hours, unless he has had a rest period of at least 8 hours at or before the end of the 10 hours of duty.

§65.49 General operating rules.

(a) Except for a person employed by the FAA or employed by, or on active duty with, the Department of the Air Force, Army, or Navy, or the Coast Guard, no person may act as an air traffic control tower operator under a certificate issued to him or her under this part unless he or she has in his or her personal possession an appropriate current medical certificate issued under part 67 of this chapter.

(b) Each person holding an air traffic control tower operator certificate shall keep it readily available when performing duties in an air traffic control tower, and shall present that certificate or his medical certificate or both for inspection upon the request of the Administrator or an authorized representative of the National Transportation Safety Board, or of any Federal, State, or local law enforcement officer.

(c) A certificated air traffic control tower operator who does not hold a facility rating for a particular control tower may not act at any operating position at the control tower concerned unless there is maintained at that control tower, readily available to persons named in paragraph (b) of this section, a current record of the operating positions at which he has qualified.

(d) An air traffic control tower operator may not perform duties under his certificate during any period of known physical deficiency that would make him unable to meet the physical requirements for his current medical certificate. However, if the deficiency is temporary, he may perform duties that are not affected by it whenever another certificated and qualified operator is present and on duty.

(e) A certificated air traffic control tower operator may not control air traffic with equipment that the Administrator has found to be inadequate.

(f) The holder of an air traffic control tower operator certificate, or an applicant for one, shall, upon the reasonable request of the Administrator, cooperate fully in any test that is made of him.

[Docket No. 1179, 27 FR 7973, Aug. 10, 1962; as amended by Amdt. 65–31, 52 FR 17519, May 8, 1987]

§65.50 Currency requirements.

The holder of an air traffic control tower operator certificate may not perform any duties under that certificate unless—

(a) He has served for at least three of the preceding 6 months as an air traffic control tower operator at the control tower to which his facility rating applies, or at the operating positions for which he has qualified; or

(b) He has shown that he meets the requirements for his certificate and facility rating at the control tower concerned, or for operating at positions for which he has previously qualified.

Subpart C—Aircraft Dispatchers

Source: Docket No. FAA–1998–4553, 64 FR 68923, Dec. 8, 1999, unless otherwise noted.

§65.51 Certificate required.

(a) No person may act as an aircraft dispatcher (exercising responsibility with the pilot in command in the operational control of a flight) in connection with any civil aircraft in air commerce unless that person has in his or her personal possession an aircraft dispatcher certificate issued under this subpart.

(b) Each person who holds an aircraft dispatcher certificate must present it for inspection upon the request of the Administrator or an authorized representative of the National Transportation Safety Board, or of any Federal, State, or local law enforcement officer.

§65.53 Eligibility requirements: General.

(a) To be eligible to take the aircraft dispatcher knowledge test, a person must be at least 21 years of age.

(b) To be eligible for an aircraft dispatcher certificate, a person must—

(1) Be at least 23 years of age;

(2) Be able to read, speak, write, and understand the English language;

(3) Pass the required knowledge test prescribed by §65.55 of this part;

(4) Pass the required practical test prescribed by §65.59 of this part; and

(5) Comply with the requirements of §65.57 of this part.

§65.55 Knowledge requirements.

(a) A person who applies for an aircraft dispatcher certificate must pass a knowledge test on the following aeronautical knowledge areas:

(1) Applicable Federal Aviation Regulations of this chapter that relate to airline transport pilot privileges, limitations, and flight operations;

(2) Meteorology, including knowledge of and effects of fronts, frontal characteristics, cloud formations, icing, and upper-air data;

(3) General system of weather and NOTAM collection, dissemination, interpretation, and use;

(4) Interpretation and use of weather charts, maps, forecasts, sequence reports, abbreviations, and symbols;

(5) National Weather Service functions as they pertain to operations in the National Airspace System;

(6) Windshear and microburst awareness, identification, and avoidance;

(7) Principles of air navigation under instrument meteorological conditions in the National Airspace System;

(8) Air traffic control procedures and pilot responsibilities as they relate to enroute operations, terminal area and radar operations, and instrument departure and approach procedures;

(9) Aircraft loading, weight and balance, use of charts, graphs, tables, formulas, and computations, and their effect on aircraft performance;

(10) Aerodynamics relating to an aircraft's flight characteristics and performance in normal and abnormal flight regimes;

(11) Human factors;

(12) Aeronautical decision making and judgment; and

(13) Crew resource management, including crew communication and coordination.

(b) The applicant must present documentary evidence satisfactory to the administrator of having passed an aircraft dispatcher knowledge test within the preceding 24 calendar months.

§65.57 Experience or training requirements.

An applicant for an aircraft dispatcher certificate must present documentary evidence satisfactory to the Administrator that he or she has the experience prescribed in paragraph (a) of this section or has accomplished the training described in paragraph (b) of this section as follows:

(a) A total of at least 2 years experience in the 3 years before the date of application, in any one or in any combination of the following areas:

(1) In military aircraft operations as a—

(i) Pilot;

(ii) Flight navigator; or

(iii) Meteorologist.

(2) In aircraft operations conducted under part 121 of this chapter as—

(i) An assistant in dispatching air carrier aircraft, under the direct supervision of a dispatcher certificated under this subpart;

(ii) A pilot;

(iii) A flight engineer; or

(iv) A meteorologist.

(3) In aircraft operations as—

(i) An Air Traffic Controller; or

(ii) A Flight Service Specialist.

(4) In aircraft operations, performing other duties that the Administrator finds provide equivalent experience.

(b) A statement of graduation issued or revalidated in accordance with §65.70(b) of this part, showing that the person has successfully completed an approved aircraft dispatcher course.

§65.59 Skill requirements.

An applicant for an aircraft dispatcher certificate must pass a practical test given by the Administrator, with respect to any one type of large aircraft used in air carrier operations. The practical test must be based on the aircraft dispatcher practical test standards, as published by the FAA, on the items outlined in appendix A of this part.

§65.61 Aircraft dispatcher certification courses: Content and minimum hours.

(a) An approved aircraft dispatcher certification course must:

(1) Provide instruction in the areas of knowledge and topics listed in appendix A of this part;

(2) Include a minimum of 200 hours of instruction.

(b) An applicant for approval of an aircraft dispatcher course must submit an outline that describes the major topics and subtopics to be covered and the number of hours proposed for each.

(c) Additional subject headings for an aircraft dispatcher certification course may also be included, however the hours proposed for any subjects not listed in appendix A of this part must be in addition to the minimum 200 course hours required in paragraph (a) of this section.

(d) For the purpose of completing an approved course, a student may substitute previous experience or training for a portion of the minimum 200 hours of training. The course operator determines the number of hours of credit based on an evaluation of the experience or training to determine if it is comparable to portions of the approved course curriculum. The credit allowed, including the total hours and the basis for it, must be placed in the student's record required by §65.70(a) of this part.

§65.63 Aircraft dispatcher certification courses: Application, duration, and other general requirements.

(a) Application. Application for original approval of an aircraft dispatcher certification course or the renewal of approval of an aircraft dispatcher certification course under this part must be:

(1) Made in writing to the Administrator;

(2) Accompanied by two copies of the course outline required under §65.61(b) of this part, for which approval is sought;

(3) Accompanied by a description of the equipment and facilities to be used; and

(4) Accompanied by a list of the instructors and their qualifications.

(b) Duration. Unless withdrawn or canceled, an approval of an aircraft dispatcher certification course of study expires:

(1) On the last day of the 24th month from the month the approval was issued; or

(2) Except as provided in paragraph (f) of this section, on the date that any change in ownership of the school occurs.

(c) Renewal. Application for renewal of an approved aircraft dispatcher certification course must be made within 30 days preceding the month the approval expires, provided the course operator meets the following requirements:

(1) At least 80 percent of the graduates from that aircraft dispatcher certification course, who applied for the practical test required by §65.59 of this part, passed the practical test on their first attempt; and

(2) The aircraft dispatcher certification course continues to meet the requirements of this subpart for course approval.

(d) Course revisions. Requests for approval of a revision of the course outline, facilities, or equipment must be in accordance with paragraph (a) of this section. Proposed revisions of the course outline or the description of facilities and equipment must be submitted in a format that will allow an entire page or pages of the approved outline or description to be removed and replaced by any approved revision. The list of instructors may be revised at any time without request for approval, provided the minimum requirements of §65.67 of this part are maintained and the Administrator is notified in writing.

(e) Withdrawal or cancellation of approval. Failure to continue to meet the requirements of this subpart for the approval or operation of an approved aircraft dispatcher certification course is grounds for withdrawal of approval of the course. A course operator may request cancellation of course approval by a letter to the Administrator. The operator must forward any records to the FAA as requested by the Administrator.

(f) Change in ownership. A change in ownership of a part 65, appendix A-approved course does not terminate that aircraft dispatcher certification course approval if, within 10 days after the date that any change in ownership of the school occurs:

(1) Application is made for an appropriate amendment to the approval; and

(2) No change in the facilities, personnel, or approved aircraft dispatcher certification course is involved.

(g) Change in name or location. A change in name or location of an approved aircraft dispatcher certification course does not invalidate the approval if, within 10 days after the date that any change in name or location occurs, the course operator of the part 65, appendix A-approved course notifies the Administrator, in writing, of the change.

§65.65 Aircraft dispatcher certification courses: Training facilities.

An applicant for approval of authority to operate an aircraft dispatcher course of study must have facilities, equipment, and materials adequate to provide each student the theoretical and practical aspects of aircraft dispatching. Each room, training booth, or other space used for instructional purposes must be temperature controlled, lighted, and ventilated to conform to local building, sanitation, and health codes. In addition, the training facility must be so located that the students in that facility are not distracted by the instruction conducted in other rooms.

§65.67 Aircraft dispatcher certification courses: Personnel.

(a) Each applicant for an aircraft dispatcher certification course must meet the following personnel requirements:

(1) Each applicant must have adequate personnel, including one instructor who holds an aircraft dispatcher certificate and is available to coordinate all training course instruction.

(2) Each applicant must not exceed a ratio of 25 students for one instructor.

(b) The instructor who teaches the practical dispatch applications area of the appendix A course must hold an aircraft dispatchers certificate.

§65.70 Aircraft dispatcher certification courses: Records.

(a) The operator of an aircraft dispatcher course must maintain a record for each student, including a chronological log of all instructors, subjects covered, and course examinations and results. The record must be retained for at least 3 years after graduation. The course operator also must prepare, for its records, and transmit to the Administrator not later than January 31 of each year, a report containing the following information for the previous year:

(1) The names of all students who graduated, together with the results of their aircraft dispatcher certification courses.

(2) The names of all the students who failed or withdrew, together with the results of their aircraft dispatcher certification courses or the reasons for their withdrawal.

(b) Each student who successfully completes the approved aircraft dispatcher certification course must be given a written statement of graduation, which is valid for 90 days. After 90 days, the course operator may revalidate the graduation certificate for an additional 90 days if the course operator determines that the student remains proficient in the subject areas listed in appendix A of this part.

Subpart D—Mechanics

§65.71 Eligibility requirements: General.

(a) To be eligible for a mechanic certificate and associated ratings, a person must—

(1) Be at least 18 years of age;

(2) Be able to read, write, speak, and understand the English language, or in the case of an applicant who does not meet this requirement and who is employed outside of the United States by a U.S. air carrier, have his certificate endorsed "Valid only outside the United States";

(3) Have passed all of the prescribed tests within a period of 24 months; and

(4) Comply with the sections of this subpart that apply to the rating he seeks.

(b) A certificated mechanic who applies for an additional rating must meet the requirements of §65.77 and, within a period of 24 months, pass the tests prescribed by §§65.75 and 65.79 for the additional rating sought.

[Docket No. 1179, 27 FR 7973, Aug. 10, 1962; as amended by Amdt. 65–6, 31 FR 5950, Apr. 19, 1966]

§65.73 Ratings.

(a) The following ratings are issued under this subpart:

(1) Airframe.

(2) Powerplant.

(b) A mechanic certificate with an aircraft or aircraft engine rating, or both, that was issued before, and was valid on, June 15, 1952, is equal to a mechanic certificate with an airframe or powerplant rating, or both, as the case may be, and may be exchanged for such a corresponding certificate and rating or ratings.

§65.75 Knowledge requirements.

(a) Each applicant for a mechanic certificate or rating must, after meeting the applicable experience requirements of §65.77, pass a written test covering the construction and maintenance of aircraft appropriate to the rating he seeks, the regulations in this subpart, and the applicable provisions of parts 43 and 91 of this chapter. The basic principles covering the installation and maintenance of propellers are included in the powerplant test.

(b) The applicant must pass each section of the test before applying for the oral and practical tests prescribed by §65.79. A report of the written test is sent to the applicant.

[Docket No. 1179, 27 FR 7973, Aug. 10, 1962; as amended by Amdt. 65–1, 27 FR 10410, Oct. 25, 1962; Amdt. 65–6, 31 FR 5950, April 19, 1966]

§65.77 Experience requirements.

Each applicant for a mechanic certificate or rating must present either an appropriate graduation certificate or certificate of completion from a certificated aviation maintenance technician school or documentary evidence, satisfactory to the Administrator, of—

(a) At least 18 months of practical experience with the procedures, practices, materials, tools, machine tools, and equipment generally used in constructing, maintaining, or altering airframes, or powerplants appropriate to the rating sought; or

(b) At least 30 months of practical experience concurrently performing the duties appropriate to both the airframe and powerplant ratings.

[Docket No. 1179, 27 FR, 7973, Aug. 10, 1962; as amended by Amdt. 65–14, 35 FR, 5533, April 3, 1970]

§65.79 Skill requirements.

Each applicant for a mechanic certificate or rating must pass an oral and a practical test on the rating he seeks. The tests cover the applicant's basic skill in performing practical projects on the subjects covered by the written test for that rating. An applicant for a powerplant rating must show his ability to make satisfactory minor repairs to, and minor alterations of, propellers.

§65.80 Certificated aviation maintenance technician school students.

Whenever an aviation maintenance technician school certificated under part 147 of this chapter shows to an FAA inspector that any of its students has made satisfactory progress at the school and is prepared to take the oral and practical tests prescribed by §65.79, that student may take those tests during the final subjects of his training in the approved curriculum, before he meets the applicable experience requirements of §65.77 and before he passes each section of the written test prescribed by §65.75.

[Amdt. 65–14, 35 FR, 5533, Apr. 3, 1970]

§65.81 General privileges and limitations.

(a) A certificated mechanic may perform or supervise the maintenance, preventive maintenance or alteration of an aircraft or appliance, or a part thereof, for which he is rated (but excluding major repairs to, and major alterations of, propellers, and any repair to, or alteration of, instruments), and may perform additional duties in accordance with §§65.85, 65.87, and 65.95. However, he may not supervise the maintenance, preventive maintenance, or alteration of, or approve and return to service, any aircraft or appliance, or part thereof, for which he is rated unless he has satisfactorily performed the work concerned at an earlier date. If he has not so performed that work at an earlier date, he may show his ability to do it by performing it to the satisfaction of the Administrator or under the direct supervision of a certificated and appropriately rated mechanic, or a certificated repairman, who has had previous experience in the specific operation concerned.

(b) A certificated mechanic may not exercise the privileges of his certificate and rating unless he understands the current instructions of the manufacturer, and the maintenance manuals, for the specific operation concerned.

[Docket No. 1179, 27 FR 7973, Aug. 10, 1962; as amended by Amdt. 65–2, 29 FR 5451, April 23, 1964; Amdt. 65–26, 45 FR 46737, July 10, 1980]

§65.83 Recent experience requirements.

A certificated mechanic may not exercise the privileges of his certificate and rating unless, within the preceding 24 months—

(a) The Administrator has found that he is able to do that work; or

(b) He has, for at least 6 months—

(1) Served as a mechanic under his certificate and rating;

(2) Technically supervised other mechanics;

(3) Supervised, in an executive capacity, the maintenance or alteration of aircraft; or

(4) Been engaged in any combination of paragraph (b)(1), (2), or (3) of this section.

§65.85 Airframe rating; additional privileges.

(a) Except as provided in paragraph (b) of this section, a certificated mechanic with an airframe rating may approve and return to service an airframe, or any related part or appliance, after he has performed, supervised, or inspected its maintenance or alteration (excluding major repairs and major alterations). In addition, he may perform the 100-hour inspection required by part 91 of this chapter on an airframe, or any related part or appliance, and approve and return it to service.

(b) A certificated mechanic with an airframe rating can approve and return to service an airframe, or any related part or appliance, of an aircraft with a special airworthiness certificate in the light-sport category after performing and inspecting a major repair or major alteration for products that are not produced under an FAA approval provided the work was performed in accordance with instructions developed by the manufacturer or a person acceptable to the FAA.

[Docket No. 1179, 27 FR 7973, Aug. 10, 1962; as amended by Amdt. 65–10, 32 FR 5770, April 11, 1967; Amdt. 65–45, 69 FR 44879, July 27, 2004]

§65.87 Powerplant rating; additional privileges.

(a) Except as provided in paragraph (b) of this section, a certificated mechanic with a powerplant rating may approve and return to service a powerplant or propeller or any related part or appliance, after he has performed, supervised, or inspected its maintenance or alteration (excluding major repairs and major alterations). In addition, he may perform the 100-hour inspection required by part 91 of this chapter on a powerplant or propeller, or any part thereof, and approve and return it to service.

(b) A certificated mechanic with a powerplant rating can approve and return to service a powerplant or propeller, or any related part or appliance, of an aircraft with a special airworthiness certificate in the light-sport category after performing and inspecting a major repair or major alteration for products that are not produced under an FAA approval, provided the work was performed in accordance with instructions developed by the manufacturer or a person acceptable to the FAA.

[Docket No. 1179, 27 FR 7973, Aug. 10, 1962; as amended by Amdt. 65–10, 32 FR 5770, April 11, 1967; Amdt. 65–45, 69 FR 44879, July 27, 2004]

§65.89 Display of certificate.

Each person who holds a mechanic certificate shall keep it within the immediate area where he normally exercises the privileges of the certificate and shall present it for inspection upon the request of the Administrator or an authorized representative of the National Transportation Safety Board, or of any Federal, State, or local law enforcement officer.

[Docket No. 7258, 31 FR 13524, Oct. 20, 1966, as amended by Docket No. 8084, 32 FR 5769, Apr. 11, 1967]

§65.91 Inspection authorization.

(a) An application for an inspection authorization is made on a form and in a manner prescribed by the Administrator.

(b) An applicant who meets the requirements of this section is entitled to an inspection authorization.

(c) To be eligible for an inspection authorization, an applicant must—

(1) Hold a currently effective mechanic certificate with both an airframe rating and a powerplant rating, each of which is currently effective and has been in effect for a total of at least 3 years;

(2) Have been actively engaged, for at least the 2-year period before the date he applies, in maintaining aircraft certificated and maintained in accordance with this chapter;

(3) Have a fixed base of operations at which he may be located in person or by telephone during a normal working week but it need not be the place where he will exercise his inspection authority;

(4) Have available to him the equipment, facilities, and inspection data necessary to properly inspect airframes, powerplants, propellers, or any related part or appliance; and

(5) Pass a written test on his ability to inspect according to safety standards for returning aircraft to service after major repairs and major alterations and annual and progressive inspections performed under part 43 of this chapter.

An applicant who fails the test prescribed in paragraph (c)(5) of this section may not apply for retesting until at least 90 days after the date he failed the test.

[Docket No. 1179, 27 FR 7973, Aug. 10, 1962; as amended by Amdt. 65–5, 31 FR 3337, March 3, 1966; Amdt. 65–22, 42 FR 46279, Sept. 15, 1977; Amdt. 65–30, 50 FR 15700, April 19, 1985]

§65.92 Inspection authorization: Duration.

(a) Each inspection authorization expires on March 31 of each year. However, the holder may exercise the privileges of that authorization only while he holds a currently effective mechanic certificate with both a currently effective airframe rating and a currently effective powerplant rating.

(b) An inspection authorization ceases to be effective whenever any of the following occurs:

(1) The authorization is surrendered, suspended, or revoked.

(2) The holder no longer has a fixed base of operation.

(3) The holder no longer has the equipment, facilities, and inspection data required by §65.91(c) (3) and (4) for issuance of his authorization.

(c) The holder of an inspection authorization that is suspended or revoked shall, upon the Administrator's request, return it to the Administrator.

[Docket No. 12537, 42 FR 46279, Sept. 15, 1977]

§65.93 Inspection authorization: Renewal.

(a) To be eligible for renewal of an inspection authorization for a 1-year period an applicant must present evidence annually, during the month of March, at an FAA Flight Standards District Office or an International Field Office that the applicant still meets the requirements of §65.91(c)(1) through (4) and must show that, during the current period that the applicant held the inspection authorization, the applicant—

(1) Has performed at least one annual inspection for each 90 days that the applicant held the current authority; or

(2) Has performed inspections of at least two major repairs or major alterations for each 90 days that the applicant held the current authority; or

(3) Has performed or supervised and approved at least one progressive inspection in accordance with standards prescribed by the Administrator; or

(4) Has attended and successfully completed a refresher course, acceptable to the Administrator, of not less than 8 hours of instruction during the 12-month period preceding the application for renewal; or

(5) Has passed on oral test by an FAA inspector to determine that the applicant's knowledge of applicable regulations and standards is current.

(b) The holder of an inspection authorization that has been in effect for less than 90 days before the expiration date need not comply with paragraphs (a) (1) through (5) of this section.

[Docket No. 18241, 45 FR 46738, July 10, 1980; as amended by Amdt. 65–35, 54 FR 39292, Sept. 25, 1989]

§65.95 Inspection authorization: Privileges and limitations.

(a) The holder of an inspection authorization may—

(1) Inspect and approve for return to service any aircraft or related part or appliance (except any aircraft maintained in accordance with a continuous airworthiness program under part 121 of this chapter) after a major repair or major alteration to it in accordance with part 43 [New] of this chapter, if the work was done in accordance with technical data approved by the Administrator; and

(2) Perform an annual, or perform or supervise a progressive inspection according to §§43.13 and 43.15 of this chapter.

(b) When he exercises the privileges of an inspection authorization the holder shall keep it available for inspection by the aircraft owner, the mechanic submitting the aircraft, repair, or alteration for approval (if any), and shall present it upon the request of the Administrator or an authorized representative of the National Transportation Safety Board, or of any Federal, State, or local law enforcement officer.

(c) If the holder of an inspection authorization changes his fixed base of operation, he may not exercise the privileges of the authorization until he has notified the FAA Flight Standards District Office or International Field Office for the area in which the new base is located, in writing, of the change.

[Docket No. 1179, 27 FR 7973, Aug. 10, 1962; as amended by Amdt. 65–2, 29 FR 5451, April 23, 1964; Amdt. 65–4, 30 FR 3638, March 14, 1965; Amdt. 65–5, 31 FR 3337, March 3, 1966; Amdt. 65–9, 31 FR 13524, Oct. 20, 1966; 32 FR 5769, April 11, 1967; Amdt. 65–35, 54 FR 39292, Sept. 25, 1989; Amdt. 65–41, 66 FR 21066, April 27, 2001]

Subpart E—Repairmen

§65.101 Eligibility requirements: General.

(a) To be eligible for a repairman certificate a person must—

(1) Be at least 18 years of age;

(2) Be specially qualified to perform maintenance on aircraft or components thereof, appropriate to the job for which he is employed;

(3) Be employed for a specific job requiring those special qualifications by a certificated repair station, or by a certificated commercial operator or certificated air carrier, that is required by its operating certificate or approved operations specifications to provide a continuous airworthiness maintenance program according to its maintenance manuals;

(4) Be recommended for certification by his employer, to the satisfaction of the Administrator, as able to satisfactorily maintain aircraft or components, appropriate to the job for which he is employed;

(5) Have either—

(i) At least 18 months of practical experience in the procedures, practices, inspection methods, materials, tools, machine tools, and equipment generally used in the maintenance duties of the specific job for which the person is to be employed and certificated; or

(ii) Completed formal training that is acceptable to the Administrator and is specifically designed to qualify the applicant for the job on which the applicant is to be employed; and

(6) Be able to read, write, speak, and understand the English language, or, in the case of an applicant who does not meet this requirement and who is employed outside the United States by a certificated repair station, a certificated U.S. commercial operator, or a certificated U.S. air carrier, described in paragraph (c) of this section, have his certificate endorsed "Valid only outside the United States."

(b) This section does not apply to the issuance of a repairman certificate (experimental aircraft builder) under §65.104 or to a repairman certificate (light-sport aircraft) under §65.107.

[Docket No. 1179, 27 FR 7973, Aug. 10, 1962; as amended by Amdt. 65–11, 32 FR 13506, Sept. 27, 1967; Amdt. 65–24, 44 FR 46781, Aug. 9, 1979; Amdt. 65–27, 47 FR 13316, March 29, 1982; Amdt. 65–45, 69 FR 44879, July 27, 2004]

§65.103 Repairman certificate: Privileges and limitations.

(a) A certificated repairman may perform or supervise the maintenance, preventive maintenance, or alteration of aircraft or aircraft components appropriate to the job for which the repairman was employed and certificated, but only in connection with duties for the certificate holder by whom the repairman was employed and recommended.

(b) A certificated repairman may not perform or supervise duties under the repairman certificate unless the repairman understands the current instructions of the certificate holder by whom the repairman is employed and the manufacturer's instructions for continued airworthiness relating to the specific operations concerned.

(c) This section does not apply to the holder of a repairman certificate (light-sport aircraft) while that repairman is performing work under that certificate.

[Docket No. 18241, 45 FR 46738, July 10, 1980; Amdt. 65–45, 69 FR 44879, July 27, 2004]

§65.104 Repairman certificate—experimental aircraft builder—Eligibility, privileges and limitations.

(a) To be eligible for a repairman certificate (experimental aircraft builder), an individual must—

(1) Be at least 18 years of age;

(2) Be the primary builder of the aircraft to which the privileges of the certificate are applicable;

(3) Show to the satisfaction of the Administrator that the individual has the requisite skill to determine whether the aircraft is in a condition for safe operations; and

(4) Be a citizen of the United States or an individual citizen of a foreign country who has lawfully been admitted for permanent residence in the United States.

(b) The holder of a repairman certificate (experimental aircraft builder) may perform condition inspections on the aircraft constructed by the holder in accordance with the operating limitations of that aircraft.

(c) Section 65.103 does not apply to the holder of a repairman certificate (experimental aircraft builder) while performing under that certificate.

[Docket No. 18739, 44 FR 46781, Aug. 9, 1979]

§65.105 Display of certificate.

Each person who holds a repairman certificate shall keep it within the immediate area where he normally exercises the privileges of the certificate and shall present it for inspection upon the request of the Administrator or an authorized representative of the National Transportation Safety Board, or of any Federal, State, or local law enforcement officer.

[Docket No. 7258, 31 FR 13524, Oct. 20, 1966, as amended by Docket No. 8084, 32 FR 5769, Apr. 11, 1967]

§65.107 Repairman certificate (light-sport aircraft): Eligibility, privileges, and limits.

(a) Use the following table to determine your eligibility for a repairman certificate (light-sport aircraft) and appropriate rating:

To be eligible for…	You must…
(1) A repairman certificate (light-sport aircraft),	(i) Be at least 18 years old, (ii) Be able to read, speak, write, and understand English. If for medical reasons you cannot meet one of these requirements, the FAA may place limits on your repairman certificate necessary to safely perform the actions authorized by the certificate and rating, (iii) Demonstrate the requisite skill to determine whether a light-sport aircraft is in a condition for safe operation, and (iv) Be a citizen of the United States, or a citizen of a foreign country who has been lawfully admitted for permanent residence in the United States.
(2) A repairman certificate (light-sport aircraft) with an inspection rating,	(i) Meet the requirements of paragraph (a)(1) of this section, and (ii) Complete a 16-hour training course acceptable to the FAA on inspecting the particular class of experimental light-sport aircraft for which you intend to exercise the privileges of this rating.
(3) A repairman certificate (light-sport aircraft) with a maintenance rating,	(i) Meet the requirements of paragraph (a)(1) of this section, and (ii) Complete a training course acceptable to the FAA on maintaining the particular class of light-sport aircraft for which you intend to exercise the privileges of this rating. The training course must, at a minimum, provide the following number of hours of instruction: (A) For airplane class privileges—120-hours, (B) For weight-shift control aircraft class privileges—104 hours, (C) For powered parachute class privileges—104 hours, (D) For lighter than air class privileges—80 hours, (E) For glider class privileges—80 hours.

(b) The holder of a repairman certificate (light-sport aircraft) with an inspection rating may perform the annual condition inspection on a light-sport aircraft:

(1) That is owned by the holder;

(2) That has been issued an experimental certificate for operating a light-sport aircraft under §21.191 (i) of this chapter; and

(3) That is in the same class of light-sport-aircraft for which the holder has completed the training specified in paragraph (a)(2)(ii) of this section.

(c) The holder of a repairman certificate (light-sport aircraft) with a maintenance rating may—

(1) Approve and return to service an aircraft that has been issued a special airworthiness certificate in the light-sport category under §21.190 of this chapter, or any part thereof,

after performing or inspecting maintenance (to include the annual condition inspection and the 100-hour inspection required by §91.327 of this chapter), preventive maintenance, or an alteration (excluding a major repair or a major alteration on a product produced under an FAA approval);

(2) Perform the annual condition inspection on a light-sport aircraft that has been issued an experimental certificate for operating a light-sport aircraft under §21.191(i) of this chapter; and

(3) Only perform maintenance, preventive maintenance, and an alteration on a light-sport aircraft that is in the same class of light-sport aircraft for which the holder has completed the training specified in paragraph (a)(3)(ii) of this section. Before performing a major repair, the holder must complete additional training acceptable to the FAA and appropriate to the repair performed.

(d) The holder of a repairman certificate (light-sport aircraft) with a maintenance rating may not approve for return to service any aircraft or part thereof unless that person has previously performed the work concerned satisfactorily. If that person has not previously performed that work, the person may show the ability to do the work by performing it to the satisfaction of the FAA, or by performing it under the direct supervision of a certificated and appropriately rated mechanic, or a certificated repairman, who has had previous experience in the specific operation concerned. The repairman may not exercise the privileges of the certificate unless the repairman understands the current instructions of the manufacturer and the maintenance manuals for the specific operation concerned.

[Docket No. FAA-2001-11133, 69 FR 44879, July 27, 2004]

Subpart F—Parachute Riggers

§65.111 Certificate required.

(a) No person may pack, maintain, or alter any personnel-carrying parachute intended for emergency use in connection with civil aircraft of the United States (including the reserve parachute of a dual parachute system to be used for intentional parachute jumping) unless that person holds an appropriate current certificate and type rating issued under this subpart and complies with §§65.127 through 65.133.

(b) No person may pack, maintain, or alter any main parachute of a dual-parachute system to be used for intentional parachute jumping in connection with civil aircraft of the United States unless that person—

(1) Has an appropriate current certificate issued under this subpart;

(2) Is under the supervision of a current certificated parachute rigger;

(3) Is the person making the next parachute jump with that parachute in accordance with §105.43(a) of this chapter; or

(4) Is the parachutist in command making the next parachute jump with that parachute in a tandem parachute operation conducted under §105.45(b)(1) of this chapter.

(c) Each person who holds a parachute rigger certificate shall present it for inspection upon the request of the Administrator or an authorized representative of the National Transportation Safety Board, or of any Federal, State, or local law enforcement officer.

(d) The following parachute rigger certificates are issued under this part:

(1) Senior parachute rigger.

(2) Master parachute rigger.

(e) Sections 65.127 through 65.133 do not apply to parachutes packed, maintained, or altered for the use of the armed forces.

[Docket No. 1179, 27 FR 7973, Aug. 10, 1962; as amended by Amdt. 65–9, 31 FR 13524, Oct. 20, 1966; 32 FR 5769, April 11, 1967; Amdt. No. 65–42, 66 FR 23553, May 9, 2001]

§65.113 Eligibility requirements: General.

(a) To be eligible for a parachute rigger certificate, a person must—

(1) Be at least 18 years of age;

(2) Be able to read, write, speak, and understand the English language, or, in the case of a citizen of Puerto Rico, or a person who is employed outside of the United States by a U.S. air carrier, and who does not meet this requirement, be issued a certificate that is valid only in Puerto Rico or while he is employed outside of the United States by that air carrier, as the case may be; and

(3) Comply with the sections of this subpart that apply to the certificate and type rating he seeks.

(b) Except for a master parachute rigger certificate, a parachute rigger certificate that was issued before, and was valid on, October 31, 1962, is equal to a senior parachute rigger certificate, and may be exchanged for such a corresponding certificate.

§65.115 Senior parachute rigger certificate: Experience, knowledge, and skill requirements.

Except as provided in §65.117, an applicant for a senior parachute rigger certificate must—

(a) Present evidence satisfactory to the Administrator that he has packed at least 20 parachutes of each type for which he seeks a rating, in accordance with the manufacturer's instructions and under the supervision of a certificated parachute rigger holding a rating for that type or a person holding an appropriate military rating;

(b) Pass a written test, with respect to parachutes in common use, on—

(1) Their construction, packing, and maintenance;

(2) The manufacturer's instructions;

(3) The regulations of this subpart; and

(c) Pass an oral and practical test showing his ability to pack and maintain at least one type of parachute in common use, appropriate to the type rating he seeks.

[Docket No. 10468, 37 FR 13251, July 6, 1972]

§65.117 Military riggers or former military riggers: Special certification rule.

In place of the procedure in §65.115, an applicant for a senior parachute rigger certificate is entitled to it if he passes a written test on the regulations of this subpart and presents satisfactory documentary evidence that he—

(a) Is a member or civilian employee of an Armed Force of the United States, is a civilian employee of a regular armed force of a foreign country, or has, within the 12 months before he applies, been honorably discharged or released from any status covered by this paragraph;

(b) Is serving, or has served within the 12 months before he applies, as a parachute rigger for such an Armed Force; and

(c) Has the experience required by §65.115(a).

§65.119 Master parachute rigger certificate: Experience, knowledge, and skill requirements.

An applicant for a master parachute rigger certificate must meet the following requirements:

(a) Present evidence satisfactory to the Administrator that he has had at least 3 years of experience as a parachute rigger and has satisfactorily packed at least 100 parachutes of each of two types in common use, in accordance with the manufacturer's instructions—

(1) While a certificated and appropriately rated senior parachute rigger; or

(2) While under the supervision of a certificated and appropriately rated parachute rigger or a person holding appropriate military ratings.

An applicant may combine experience specified in paragraphs (a) (1) and (2) of this section to meet the requirements of this paragraph.

(b) If the applicant is not the holder of a senior parachute rigger certificate, pass a written test, with respect to parachutes in common use, on—

(1) Their construction, packing, and maintenance;

(2) The manufacturer's instructions; and

(3) The regulations of this subpart.

(c) Pass an oral and practical test showing his ability to pack and maintain two types of parachutes in common use, appropriate to the type ratings he seeks.

[Docket No. 10468, 37 FR 13252, July 6, 1972]

§65.121 Type ratings.

(a) The following type ratings are issued under this subpart:

(1) Seat.

(2) Back.

(3) Chest.

(4) Lap.

(b) The holder of a senior parachute rigger certificate who qualifies for a master parachute rigger certificate is entitled to have placed on his master parachute rigger certificate the ratings that were on his senior parachute rigger certificate.

§65.123 Additional type ratings: Requirements.

A certificated parachute rigger who applies for an additional type rating must—

(a) Present evidence satisfactory to the Administrator that he has packed at least 20 parachutes of the type for which he seeks a rating, in accordance with the manufacturer's instructions and under the supervision of a certificated parachute rigger holding a rating for that type or a person holding an appropriate military rating; and

(b) Pass a practical test, to the satisfaction of the Administrator, showing his ability to pack and maintain the type of parachute for which he seeks a rating.

[Docket No. 1179, 27 FR 7973, Aug. 10, 1962; as amended by Amdt. 65–20, 37 FR 13251, July 6, 1972]

§65.125 Certificates: Privileges.

(a) A certificated senior parachute rigger may—

(1) Pack or maintain (except for major repair) any type of parachute for which he is rated; and

(2) Supervise other persons in packing any type of parachute for which that person is rated in accordance with §105.43(a) or §105.45(b)(1) of this chapter.

(b) A certificated master parachute rigger may—

(1) Pack, maintain, or alter any type of parachute for which he is rated; and

(2) Supervise other persons in packing, maintaining, or altering any type of parachute for which the certificated parachute rigger is rated in accordance with §105.43(a) or §105.45(b)(1) of this chapter.

(c) A certificated parachute rigger need not comply with §§65.127 through 65.133 (relating to facilities, equipment, performance standards, records, recent experience, and seal) in packing, maintaining, or altering (if authorized) the main parachute of a dual parachute pack to be used for intentional jumping.

[Docket No. 1179, 27 FR 7973, Aug. 10, 1962; as amended by Amdt. 65–20, 37 FR 13252, July 6, 1972; Amdt. No. 65–42, 66 FR 23553, May 9, 2001]

§65.127 Facilities and equipment.

No certificated parachute rigger may exercise the privileges of his certificate unless he has at least the following facilities and equipment available to him:

(a) A smooth top table at least three feet wide by 40 feet long.

(b) Suitable housing that is adequately heated, lighted, and ventilated for drying and airing parachutes.

(c) Enough packing tools and other equipment to pack and maintain the types of parachutes that he services.

(d) Adequate housing facilities to perform his duties and to protect his tools and equipment.

[Docket No. 1179, 27 FR 7973, Aug. 10, 1962; as amended by Amdt. 65–27, 47 FR 13316, March 29, 1982]

§65.129 Performance standards.

No certificated parachute rigger may—

(a) Pack, maintain, or alter any parachute unless he is rated for that type;

(b) Pack a parachute that is not safe for emergency use;

(c) Pack a parachute that has not been thoroughly dried and aired;

(d) Alter a parachute in a manner that is not specifically authorized by the Administrator or the manufacturer;

(e) Pack, maintain, or alter a parachute in any manner that deviates from procedures approved by the Administrator or the manufacturer of the parachute; or

(f) Exercise the privileges of his certificate and type rating unless he understands the current manufacturer's instructions for the operation involved and has—

(1) Performed duties under his certificate for at least 90 days within the preceding 12 months; or

(2) Shown the Administrator that he is able to perform those duties.

§65.131 Records.

(a) Each certificated parachute rigger shall keep a record of the packing, maintenance, and alteration of parachutes performed or supervised by him. He shall keep in that record, with respect to each parachute worked on, a statement of—

(1) Its type and make;

(2) Its serial number;

(3) The name and address of its owner;

(4) The kind and extent of the work performed;

(5) The date when and place where the work was performed; and

(6) The results of any drop tests made with it.

(b) Each person who makes a record under paragraph (a) of this section shall keep it for at least 2 years after the date it is made.

(c) Each certificated parachute rigger who packs a parachute shall write, on the parachute packing record attached to the parachute, the date and place of the packing and a notation of any defects he finds on inspection. He shall sign that record with his name and the number of his certificate.

§65.133 Seal.

Each certificated parachute rigger must have a seal with an identifying mark prescribed by the Administrator, and a seal press. After packing a parachute he shall seal the pack with his seal in accordance with the manufacturer's recommendation for that type of parachute.

Appendix A to Part 65

Aircraft Dispatcher Courses

Source: Docket No. FAA–1998–4553, 64 FR 68925, Dec. 8, 1999, unless otherwise noted.

Overview

This appendix sets forth the areas of knowledge necessary to perform dispatcher functions. The items listed below indicate the minimum set of topics that must be covered in a training course for aircraft dispatcher certification. The order of coverage is at the discretion of the approved school. For the latest technological advancements refer to the Practical Test Standards as published by the FAA.

I. Regulations

A. Subpart C of this part;

B. Parts 1, 25, 61, 71, 91, 121, 139, and 175, of this chapter;

C. 49 CFR part 830;

D. General Operating Manual.

II. Meteorology

A. Basic Weather Studies

(1) The earth's motion and its effects on weather.

(2) Analysis of the following regional weather types, characteristics, and structures, or combinations thereof:

(a) Maritime.

(b) Continental.

(c) Polar.

(d) Tropical.

(3) Analysis of the following local weather types, characteristics, and structures or combinations thereof:

(a) Coastal.

(b) Mountainous.

(c) Island.

(d) Plains.

(4) The following characteristics of the atmosphere:

(a) Layers.

(b) Composition.

(c) Global Wind Patterns.

(d) Ozone.

(5) Pressure:

(a) Units of Measure.

(b) Weather Systems Characteristics.

(c) Temperature Effects on Pressure.

(d) Altimeters.

(e) Pressure Gradient Force.

(f) Pressure Pattern Flying Weather.

(6) Wind:

(a) Major Wind Systems and Coriolis Force.

(b) Jetstreams and their Characteristics.

(c) Local Wind and Related Terms.

(7) States of Matter:

(a) Solids, Liquid, and Gases.

(b) Causes of change of state.

(8) Clouds:

(a) Composition, Formation, and Dissipation.

(b) Types and Associated Precipitation.

(c) Use of Cloud Knowledge in Forecasting.

(9) Fog:

(a) Causes, Formation, and Dissipation.

(b) Types.

(10) Ice:

(a) Causes, Formation, and Dissipation.

(b) Types.

(11) Stability/Instability:

(a) Temperature Lapse Rate, Convection.

(b) Adiabatic Processes.

(c) Lifting Processes.

(d) Divergence.

(e) Convergence.

(12) Turbulence:

(a) Jetstream Associated.

(b) Pressure Pattern Recognition.

(c) Low Level Windshear.

(d) Mountain Waves.

(e) Thunderstorms.

(f) Clear Air Turbulence.

(13) Airmasses:

(a) Classification and Characteristics.

(b) Source Regions.

(c) Use of Airmass Knowledge in Forecasting.

(14) Fronts:

(a) Structure and Characteristics, Both Vertical and Horizontal.

(b) Frontal Types.
(c) Frontal Weather Flying.
(15) Theory of Storm Systems:
(a) Thunderstorms.
(b) Tornadoes.
(c) Hurricanes and Typhoons.
(d) Microbursts.
(e) Causes, Formation, and Dissipation.
B. Weather, Analysis, and Forecasts
(1) Observations:
(a) Surface Observations.
(i) Observations made by certified weather observer.
(ii) Automated Weather Observations.
(b) Terminal Forecasts.
(c) Significant En route Reports and Forecasts.
(i) Pilot Reports.
(ii) Area Forecasts.
(iii) Sigmets, Airmets.
(iv) Center Weather Advisories.
(d) Weather Imagery.
(i) Surface Analysis.
(ii) Weather Depiction.
(iii) Significant Weather Prognosis.
(iv) Winds and Temperature Aloft.
(v) Tropopause Chart.
(vi) Composite Moisture Stability Chart.
(vii) Surface Weather Prognostic Chart.
(viii) Radar Meteorology.
(ix) Satellite Meteorology.
(x) Other charts as applicable.
(e) Meteorological Information Data Collection Systems.
(2) Data Collection, Analysis, and Forecast Facilities.
(3) Service Outlets Providing Aviation Weather Products.
C. Weather Related Aircraft Hazards
(1) Crosswinds and Gusts.
(2) Contaminated Runways.
(3) Restrictions to Surface Visibility.
(4) Turbulence and Windshear.
(5) Icing.
(6) Thunderstorms and Microburst.
(7) Volcanic Ash.

III. Navigation

A. Study of the Earth
(1) Time reference and location (0 Longitude, UTC).
(2) Definitions.
(3) Projections.
(4) Charts.
B. Chart Reading, Application, and Use.
C. National Airspace Plan.
D. Navigation Systems.
E. Airborne Navigation Instruments.
F. Instrument Approach Procedures.
(1) Transition Procedures.
(2) Precision Approach Procedures.
(3) Non-precision Approach Procedures.
(4) Minimums and the relationship to weather.
G. Special Navigation and Operations.
(1) North Atlantic.
(2) Pacific.
(3) Global Differences.

IV. Aircraft

A. Aircraft Flight Manual.
B. Systems Overview.
(1) Flight controls.
(2) Hydraulics.
(3) Electrical.
(4) Air Conditioning and Pressurization.
(5) Ice and Rain protection.
(6) Avionics, Communication, and Navigation.
(7) Powerplants and Auxiliary Power Units.
(8) Emergency and Abnormal Procedures.
(9) Fuel Systems and Sources.
C. Minimum Equipment List/Configuration Deviation List (MEL/CDL) and Applications.
D. Performance.
(1) Aircraft in general.
(2) Principles of flight:
(a) Group one aircraft.
(b) Group two aircraft.
(3) Aircraft Limitations.
(4) Weight and Balance.
(5) Flight instrument errors.
(6) Aircraft performance:
(a) Take-off performance.
(b) En route performance.
(c) Landing performance.

V. Communications

A. Regulatory requirements.
B. Communication Protocol.
C. Voice and Data Communications.
D. Notice to Airmen (NOTAMs).
E. Aeronautical Publications.
F. Abnormal Procedures.

VI. Air Traffic Control

A. Responsibilities.
B. Facilities and Equipment.
C. Airspace classification and route structure.
D. Flight Plans.
(1) Domestic.
(2) International.
E. Separation Minimums.
F. Priority Handling.
G. Holding Procedures.
H. Traffic Management.

VII. Emergency and Abnormal Procedures

A. Security measures on the ground.
B. Security measures in the air.
C. FAA responsibility and services.
D. Collection and dissemination of information on overdue or missing aircraft.
E. Means of declaring an emergency.
F. Responsibility for declaring an emergency.
G. Required reporting of an emergency.
H. NTSB reporting requirements.

VIII. Practical Dispatch Applications

A. Human Factors.
(1) Decisionmaking:
(a) Situation Assessment.
(b) Generation and Evaluation of Alternatives.
(i) Tradeoffs and Prioritization.
(ii) Contingency Planning.
(c) Support Tools and Technologies.
(2) Human Error:
(a) Causes.
(i) Individual and Organizational Factors.
(ii) Technology-Induced Error.
(b) Prevention.
(c) Detection and Recovery.
(3) Teamwork:
(a) Communication and Information Exchange.
(b) Cooperative and Distributed Problem-Solving.
(c) Resource Management.
(i) Air Traffic Control (ATC) activities and workload.
(ii) Flightcrew activities and workload.
(iii) Maintenance activities and workload.
(iv) Operations Control Staff activities and workload.
B. Applied Dispatching.
(1) Briefing techniques, Dispatcher, Pilot.
(2) Preflight:
(a) Safety.
(b) Weather Analysis.
(i) Satellite imagery.
(ii) Upper and lower altitude charts.
(iii) Significant en route reports and forecasts.
(iv) Surface charts.
(v) Surface observations.
(vi) Terminal forecasts and orientation to Enhanced Weather Information System (EWINS).
(c) NOTAMs and airport conditions.
(d) Crew.
(i) Qualifications.
(ii) Limitations.
(e) Aircraft.
(i) Systems.
(ii) Navigation instruments and avionics systems.
(iii) Flight instruments.
(iv) Operations manuals and MEL/CDL.
(v) Performance and limitations.
(f) Flight Planning.
(i) Route of flight.
1. Standard Instrument Departures and Standard Terminal Arrival Routes.
2. En route charts.
3. Operational altitude.
4. Departure and arrival charts.
(ii) Minimum departure fuel.
1. Climb.
2. Cruise.
3. Descent.
(g) Weight and balance.
(h) Economics of flight overview (Performance, Fuel Tankering).
(i) Decision to operate the flight.
(j) ATC flight plan filing.
(k) Flight documentation.
(i) Flight plan.
(ii) Dispatch release.
(3) Authorize flight departure with concurrence of pilot in command.
(4) In-flight operational control:
(a) Current situational awareness.
(b) Information exchange.
(c) Amend original flight release as required.
(5) Post-Flight:
(a) Arrival verification.
(b) Weather debrief.
(c) Flight irregularity reports as required.

SUBCHAPTER F
AIR TRAFFIC AND GENERAL OPERATING RULES

PART 91
GENERAL OPERATING AND FLIGHT RULES

SPECIAL FEDERAL AVIATION REGULATIONS

SFAR No. 50–2
SFAR No. 60
***SFAR No. 65–1 [Removed]**
SFAR No. 71
SFAR No. 77
SFAR No. 79
SFAR No. 87
SFAR No. 94
SFAR No. 97
SFAR No. 104

Subpart A—General

Sec.
91.1 Applicability.
91.3 Responsibility and authority of the pilot in command.
91.5 Pilot in command of aircraft requiring more than one required pilot.
91.7 Civil aircraft airworthiness.
91.9 Civil aircraft flight manual, marking, and placard requirements.
91.11 Prohibition on interference with crewmembers.
91.13 Careless or reckless operation.
91.15 Dropping objects.
91.17 Alcohol or drugs.
91.19 Carriage of narcotic drugs, marihuana, and depressant or stimulant drugs or substances.
91.21 Portable electronic devices.
91.23 Truth-in-leasing clause requirement in leases and conditional sales contracts.
91.25 Aviation Safety Reporting Program: Prohibition against use of reports for enforcement purposes.
91.27–91.99 [Reserved]

Subpart B—Flight Rules

GENERAL

91.101 Applicability.
91.103 Preflight action.
91.105 Flight crewmembers at stations.
91.107 Use of safety belts, shoulder harnesses, and child restraint systems.
91.109 Flight instruction; Simulated instrument flight and certain flight tests.
91.111 Operating near other aircraft.
91.113 Right-of-way rules: Except water operations.
91.115 Right-of-way rules: Water operations.
91.117 Aircraft speed.
91.119 Minimum safe altitudes: General.
91.121 Altimeter settings.
91.123 Compliance with ATC clearances and instructions.
91.125 ATC light signals.
91.126 Operating on or in the vicinity of an airport in Class G airspace.
91.127 Operating on or in the vicinity of an airport in Class E airspace.
91.129 Operations in Class D airspace.
91.130 Operations in Class C airspace.
91.131 Operations in Class B airspace.
91.133 Restricted and prohibited areas.
91.135 Operations in Class A airspace.
91.137 Temporary flight restrictions.
91.138 Temporary flight restrictions in national disaster areas in the State of Hawaii.
91.139 Emergency air traffic rules.
91.141 Flight restrictions in the proximity of the Presidential and other parties.
***91.143 Flight limitation in the proximity of space flight operations.**
91.144 Temporary restriction on flight operations during abnormally high barometric pressure conditions.
91.145 Management of aircraft operations in the vicinity of aerial demonstrations and major sporting events.
91.146–91.149 [Reserved]

VISUAL FLIGHT RULES

91.151 Fuel requirements for flight in VFR conditions.
91.153 VFR flight plan: Information required.
91.155 Basic VFR weather minimums.
91.157 Special VFR weather minimums.
91.159 VFR cruising altitude or flight level.
91.161–91.165 [Reserved]

INSTRUMENT FLIGHT RULES

91.167 Fuel requirements for flight in IFR conditions.
91.169 IFR flight plan: Information required.
91.171 VOR equipment check for IFR operations.
91.173 ATC clearance and flight plan required.
91.175 Takeoff and landing under IFR.
91.177 Minimum altitudes for IFR operations.
91.179 IFR cruising altitude or flight level.
91.180 Operations within airspace designated as Reduced Vertical Separation Minimum airspace.
91.181 Course to be flown.
91.183 IFR radio communications.
91.185 IFR operations: Two-way radio communications failure.
91.187 Operation under IFR in controlled airspace: Malfunction reports.
91.189 Category II and III operations: General operating rules.
91.191 Category II and Category III manual.
91.193 Certificate of authorization for certain Category II operations.
91.195–91.199 [Reserved]

Subpart C— Equipment, Instrument, and Certificate Requirements

91.201 [Reserved]
91.203 Civil aircraft: Certifications required.
***91.205 Powered civil aircraft with standard category U.S. airworthiness certificates: Instrument and equipment requirements.**
91.207 Emergency locator transmitters.
91.209 Aircraft lights.
91.211 Supplemental oxygen.
91.213 Inoperative instruments and equipment.
91.215 ATC transponder and altitude reporting equipment and use.
91.217 Data correspondence between automatically reported pressure altitude data and the pilot's altitude reference.
91.219 Altitude alerting system or device: Turbojet-powered civil airplanes.
91.221 Traffic alert and collision avoidance system equipment and use.
91.223 Terrain awareness and warning system.
91.224–91.299 [Reserved]

Subpart D—Special Flight Operations

91.301 [Reserved]
91.303 Aerobatic flight.
91.305 Flight test areas.
91.307 Parachutes and parachuting.
91.309 Towing: Gliders and unpowered ultralight vehicles.
91.311 Towing: Other than under §91.309.
91.313 Restricted category civil aircraft: Operating limitations.
91.315 Limited category civil aircraft: Operating limitations.
91.317 Provisionally certificated civil aircraft: Operating limitations.
91.319 Aircraft having experimental certificates: Operating limitations.
***91.321 Carriage of candidates in elections.**
91.323 Increased maximum certificated weights for certain airplanes operated in Alaska.
91.325 Primary category aircraft: Operating limitations.
91.326 [Reserved]
91.327 Aircraft having a special airworthiness certificate in the light-sport category: Operating limitations.
91.328–91.399 [Reserved]

Subpart E— Maintenance, Preventive Maintenance, and Alterations

91.401 Applicability.
91.403 General.
91.405 Maintenance required.
91.407 Operation after maintenance, preventive maintenance, rebuilding, or alteration.
91.409 Inspections.
91.410 Special maintenance program requirements.
91.411 Altimeter system and altitude reporting equipment tests and inspections.
91.413 ATC transponder tests and inspections.
91.415 Changes to aircraft inspection programs.
91.417 Maintenance records.
91.419 Transfer of maintenance records.
91.421 Rebuilt engine maintenance records.
91.423–91.499 [Reserved]

Subpart F— Large and Turbine-Powered Multiengine Airplanes and Fractional Ownership Program Aircraft

91.501 Applicability.
91.503 Flying equipment and operating information.
91.505 Familiarity with operating limitations and emergency equipment.
91.507 Equipment requirements: Over-the-top or night VFR operations.
91.509 Survival equipment for overwater operations.
91.511 Radio equipment for overwater operations.
91.513 Emergency equipment.
91.515 Flight altitude rules.
91.517 Passenger information.
91.519 Passenger briefing.
91.521 Shoulder harness.
91.523 Carry-on baggage.
91.525 Carriage of cargo.
91.527 Operating in icing conditions.
91.529 Flight engineer requirements.
91.531 Second in command requirements.
91.533 Flight attendant requirements.
91.535 Stowage of food, beverage, and passenger service equipment during aircraft movement on the surface, takeoff, and landing.
91.537–91.599 [Reserved]

Subpart G— Additional Equipment and Operating Requirements for Large and Transport Category Aircraft

91.601 Applicability.
91.603 Aural speed warning device.
91.605 Transport category civil airplane weight limitations.
91.607 Emergency exits for airplanes carrying passengers for hire.
91.609 Flight recorders and cockpit voice recorders.
91.611 Authorization for ferry flight with one engine inoperative.
91.613 Materials for compartment interiors.
91.615–91.699 [Reserved]

Subpart H— Foreign Aircraft Operations and Operations of U.S.-Registered Civil Aircraft Outside of the United States; and Rules Governing Persons On Board Such Aircraft

91.701 Applicability.
91.702 Persons on board.
91.703 Operations of civil aircraft of U.S. registry outside of the United States.
91.705 Operations within airspace designated as Minimum Navigation Performance Specifications Airspace.
91.706 Operations within airspace designated as Reduced Vertical Separation Minimum Airspace.
91.707 Flights between Mexico or Canada and the United States.
91.709 Operations to Cuba.

91.711 Special rules for foreign civil aircraft.
91.713 Operation of civil aircraft of Cuban registry.
91.715 Special flight authorizations for foreign civil aircraft.
91.717–91.799 [Reserved]

Subpart I—Operating Noise Limits

91.801 Applicability: Relation to part 36.
91.803 Part 125 operators: Designation of applicable regulations.
91.805 Final compliance: Subsonic airplanes.
91.807–91.813 [Reserved]
91.815 Agricultural and fire fighting airplanes: Noise operating limitations.
91.817 Civil aircraft sonic boom.
91.819 Civil supersonic airplanes that do not comply with Part 36.
91.821 Civil supersonic airplanes: Noise limits.
91.823–91.849 [Reserved]
***91.851 Definitions.**
***91.853 Final compliance: Civil subsonic airplanes.**
***91.855 Entry and nonaddition rule.**
91.857 Stage 2 operations outside of the 48 contiguous United States.
91.858 Special flight authorizations for non-revenue Stage 2 operations.
***91.859 Modification to meet Stage 3 or Stage 4 noise levels.**
91.861 Base level.
91.863 Transfers of Stage 2 airplanes with base level.
91.865 Phased compliance for operators with base level.
91.867 Phased compliance for new entrants.
91.869 Carry-forward compliance.
91.871 Waivers from interim compliance requirements.
91.873 Waivers from final compliance.
91.875 Annual progress reports.
91.877 Annual reporting of Hawaiian operations.
91.878–91.899 [Reserved]

Subpart J—Waivers

91.901 [Reserved]
91.903 Policy and procedures.
91.905 List of rules subject to waivers.
91.907–91.999 [Reserved]

Subpart K—Fractional Ownership Operations

91.1001 Applicability.
***91.1002 Compliance date.**
91.1003 Management contract between owner and program manager.
91.1005 Prohibitions and limitations.
91.1007 Flights conducted under part 121 or part 135 of this chapter.
91.1009 Clarification of operational control.
91.1011 Operational control responsibilities and delegation.
91.1013 Operational control briefing and acknowledgment.
91.1014 Issuing or denying management specifications.
91.1015 Management specifications.
91.1017 Amending program manager's management specifications.
91.1019 Conducting tests and inspections.
91.1021 Internal safety reporting and incident/accident response.
91.1023 Program operating manual requirements.
91.1025 Program operating manual contents.
91.1027 Recordkeeping.
91.1029 Flight scheduling and locating requirements.
91.1031 Pilot in command or second in command: Designation required.
91.1033 Operating information required.
91.1035 Passenger awareness.
91.1037 Large transport category airplanes: Turbine engine powered; Limitations; Destination and alternate airports.
91.1039 IFR takeoff, approach and landing minimums.
91.1041 Aircraft proving and validation tests.
91.1043 [Reserved]
91.1045 Additional equipment requirements.
91.1047 Drug and alcohol misuse education program.
91.1049 Personnel.
91.1051 Pilot safety background check.
91.1053 Crewmember experience.
91.1055 Pilot operating limitations and pairing requirement.
91.1057 Flight, duty and rest time requirements; All crewmembers.
91.1059 Flight time limitations and rest requirements: One or two pilot crews.
91.1061 Augmented flight crews.
91.1062 Duty periods and rest requirements: Flight attendants.
91.1063 Testing and training: Applicability and terms used.
91.1065 Initial and recurrent pilot testing requirements.
91.1067 Initial and recurrent flight attendant crewmember testing requirements.
91.1069 Flight crew: Instrument proficiency check requirements.
91.1071 Crewmember: Tests and checks, grace provisions, training to accepted standards.
91.1073 Training program: General.
91.1075 Training program: Special rules.
91.1077 Training program and revision: Initial and final approval.
91.1079 Training program: Curriculum.
91.1081 Crewmember training requirements.
91.1083 Crewmember emergency training.
91.1085 Hazardous materials recognition training.
91.1087 Approval of aircraft simulators and other training devices.
91.1089 Qualifications: Check pilots (aircraft) and check pilots (simulator).
91.1091 Qualifications: Flight instructors (aircraft) and flight instructors (simulator).
91.1093 Initial and transition training and checking: Check pilots (aircraft), check pilots (simulator).
91.1095 Initial and transition training and checking: Flight instructors (aircraft), flight instructors (simulator).

91.1097 Pilot and flight attendant crewmember training programs.
91.1099 Crewmember initial and recurrent training requirements.
91.1101 Pilots: Initial, transition, and upgrade ground training.
91.1103 Pilots: Initial, transition, upgrade, requalification, and differences flight training.
91.1105 Flight attendants: Initial and transition ground training.
91.1107 Recurrent training.
91.1109 Aircraft maintenance: Inspection program.
91.1111 Maintenance training.
91.1113 Maintenance recordkeeping.
91.1115 Inoperable instruments and equipment.
91.1411 Continuous airworthiness maintenance program use by fractional ownership program manager.
91.1413 CAMP: Responsibility for airworthiness.
91.1415 CAMP: Mechanical reliability reports.
91.1417 CAMP: Mechanical interruption summary report.
91.1423 CAMP: Maintenance organization.
91.1425 CAMP: Maintenance, preventive maintenance, and alteration programs.
91.1427 CAMP: Manual requirements.
91.1429 CAMP: Required inspection personnel.
91.1431 CAMP: Continuing analysis and surveillance.
91.1433 CAMP: Maintenance and preventive maintenance training program.
91.1435 CAMP: Certificate requirements.
91.1437 CAMP: Authority to perform and approve maintenance.
91.1439 CAMP: Maintenance recording requirements.
91.1441 CAMP: Transfer of maintenance records.
91.1443 CAMP: Airworthiness release or aircraft maintenance log entry.

Appendices to Part 91

Appendix A—Category II Operations: Manual, Instruments, Equipment, and Maintenance
Appendix B—Authorizations to Exceed Mach 1 (Section 91.817)
Appendix C—Operations in the North Atlantic (NAT) Minimum Navigation Performance Specifications (MNPS) Airspace
Appendix D—Airports/Locations: Special Operating Restrictions
Appendix E—Airplane Flight Recorder Specifications
Appendix F—Helicopter Flight Recorder Specifications
Appendix G—Operations in Reduced Vertical Separation Minimum (RVSM) Airspace

Authority: 49 U.S.C. 106(g), 40103, 40113, 40120, 44101, 44111, 44701, 44709, 44711, 44712, 44715, 44716, 44717, 44722, 46306, 46315, 46316, 46502, 46504, 46506–46507, 47122, 47508, 47528–47531, Articles 12 and 29 of the Convention on International Civil Aviation (61 Stat. 1180). 902; 49 U.S.C. 106(g).

Special Federal Aviation Regulations

SFAR No. 50–2 to Part 91

Special Flight Rules in the Vicinity of the Grand Canyon National Park, AZ

Section 1. *Applicability.* This rule prescribes special operating rules for all persons operating aircraft in the following airspace, designated as the Grand Canyon National Park Special Flight Rules Area:

That airspace extending upward from the surface up to but not including 14,500 feet MSL within an area bounded by a line beginning at lat. 36°09'30" N., long. 114°03'00" W.; northeast to lat. 36°14'00" N., long. 113°09'50" W.; thence northeast along the boundary of the Grand Canyon National Park to lat. 36°24'47" N., long. 112°52'00" W.; to lat. 36°30'30" N., long. 112°36'15" W. to lat. 36°21'30" N., long. 112°00'00" W. to lat. 36°35'30" N., long. 111°53'10" W., to lat. 36°53'00" N., long. 111°36'45" W. to lat. 36°53'00" N., long. 111°33'00" W.; to lat. 36°19'00" N., long. 111°50'50" W.; to lat. 36°17'00" N., long. 111°42'00" W.; to lat. 35°59'30" N., long. 111°42'00" W.; to lat. 35°57'30" N., long. 112°03'55" W.; thence counterclockwise via the 5 statute mile radius of the Grand Canyon Airport airport reference point (lat. 35°57'09" N., long. 112°08'47" W.) to lat. 35°57'30" N., long. 112°14'00" W.; to lat. 35°57'30" N., long. 113°11'00" W.; to lat. 35°42'30" N., long. 113°11'00" W.; to 35°38'30" N.; long. 113°27'30" W.; thence counterclockwise via the 5 statute mile radius of the Peach Springs VORTAC to lat. 35°41'20" N., long. 113°36'00" W.; to lat. 35°55'25" N., long. 113°49'10" W.; to lat. 35°57'45" N., 113°45'20" W.; thence northwest along the park boundary to lat. 36°02'20" N., long. 113°50'15" W.; to 36°00'10" N., long. 113°53'45" W.; thence to the point of beginning.

Section 3. *Aircraft operations: general.* Except in an emergency, no person may operate an aircraft in the Special Flight Rules, Area under VFR on or after September 22, 1988, or under IFR on or after April 6, 1989, unless the operation—

(a) Is conducted in accordance with the following procedures:

Note: The following procedures do not relieve the pilot from see-and-avoid responsibility or compliance with FAR 91.119.

(1) Unless necessary to maintain a safe distance from other aircraft or terrain—

(i) Remain clear of the areas described in Section 4; and

(ii) Remain at or above the following altitudes in each sector of the canyon:

Eastern section from Lees Ferry to North Canyon and North Canyon to Boundary Ridge: as prescribed in Section 5.

Boundary Ridge to Supai Point (Yumtheska Point): 10,000 feet MSL.

Western section from Diamond Creek to the Grant Wash Cliffs: 8,000 feet MSL.

(2) Proceed through the four flight corridors describe in Section 4 at the following altitudes unless otherwise authorized in writing by the Flight Standards District Office:

Northbound
11,500 or
13,500 feet MSL

Southbound
>10,500 or
>12,500 feet MSL

(b) Is authorized in writing by the Flight Standards District Office and is conducted in compliance with the conditions contained in that authorization. Normally authorization will be granted for operation in the areas described in Section 4 or below the altitudes listed in Section 5 only for operations of aircraft necessary for law enforcement, firefighting, emergency medical treatment/evacuation of persons in the vicinity of the Park; for support of Park maintenance or activities; or for aerial access to and maintenance of other property located within the Special Flight Rules Area. Authorization may be issued on a continuing basis.

(c)(1) Prior to November 1, 1988, is conducted in accordance with a specific authorization to operate in that airspace incorporated in the operator's part 135 operations specifications in accordance with the provisions of SFAR 50–1, notwithstanding the provisions of Sections 4 and 5; and

(2) On or after November 1, 1988, is conducted in accordance with a specific authorization to operate in that airspace incorporated in the operated in the operator's operations specifications and approved by the Flight Standards District Office in accordance with the provisions of SFAR 50–2.

(d) Is a search and rescue mission directed by the U.S. Air Force Rescue Coordination Center.

(e) Is conducted within 3 nautical miles of Whitmore Airstrip, Pearce Ferry Airstrip, North Rim Airstrip, Cliff Dwellers Airstrip, or Marble Canyon Airstrip at an altitudes less than 3,000 feet above airport elevation, for the purpose of landing at or taking off from that facility. Or

(f) Is conducted under an IFR clearance and the pilot is acting in accordance with ATC instructions. An IFR flight plan may not be filed on a route or at an altitude that would require operation in an area described in Section 4.

Section 4. *Flight-free zones.* Except in an emergency or if otherwise necessary for safety of flight, or unless otherwise authorized by the Flight Standards District Office for a purpose listed in Section 3(b), no person may operate an aircraft in the Special Flight Rules Area within the following areas:

(a) Desert View Flight-Free Zone. Within an area bounded by a line beginning at Lat. 35°59'30" N., Long. 111°46'20" W. to 35°59'30" N., Long. 111°52'45" W.; to Lat. 36°04'50" N., Long. 111°52'00" W.; to Lat. 36°06'00" N., Long. 111°46'20" W.; to the point of origin; but not including the airspace at and above 10,500 feet MSL within 1 mile of the western boundary of the zone. The area between the Desert View and Bright Angel Flight-Free Zones is designated the "Zuni Point Corridor."

(b) Bright Angel Flight-Free Zone. Within an area bounded by a line beginning at Lat. 35°59'30" N., Long. 111°55'30" W.; to Lat. 35°59'30" N., Long. 112°04'00" W.; thence counterclockwise via the 5 statute mile radius of the Grand Canyon Airport point (Lat. 35°57'09" N., Long. 112°08'47" W.) to Lat. 36°01'30" N., Long. 112°11'00" W.; to Lat. 36°06'15" N., Long. 112°12'50" W.; to Lat. 36°14'40" N., Long. 112°08'50" W.; to Lat. 36°14'40" N., Long. 111°57'30" W.; to Lat. 36°12'30" N., Long. 111°53'50" W.; to the point of origin; but not including the airspace at and above 10,500 feet MSL within 1 mile of the eastern boundary between the southern boundary and Lat. 36°04'50" N. or the airspace at and above 10,500 feet MSL within 2 miles of the northwest boundary. The area bounded by the Bright Angel and Shinumo Flight-Free Zones is designated the "Dragon Corridor."

(c) Shinumo Flight-Free Zone. Within an area bounded by a line beginning at Lat. 36°04'00" N., Long. 112°16'40" W.; northwest along the park boundary to a point at Lat. 36°12'47" N., Long. 112°30'53" W.; to Lat. 36°21'15" N., Long. 112°20'20" W.; east along the park boundary to Lat. 36°21'15" N., Long. 112°13'55" W.; to Lat. 36°14'40" N., Long. 112°11'25" W.; to the point of origin. The area between the Thunder River/Toroweap and Shinumo Flight Free Zones is designated the "Fossil Canyon Corridor."

(d) Toroweap/Thunder River Flight-Free Zone. Within an area bounded by a line beginning at Lat. 36°22'45" N., Long. 112°20'35" W.; thence northwest along the boundary of the Grand Canyon National Park to Lat. 36°17'48" N., Long. 113°03'15" W.; to Lat. 36°15'00" N., Long. 113°07'10" W.; to Lat. 36°10'30" N., Long. 113°07'10" W.; thence east along the Colorado River to the confluence of Havasu Canyon (Lat. 36°18'40" N., Long. 112°45'45" W.;) including that area within a 1.5 nautical mile radius of Toroweap Overlook (Lat. 36°12'45" N., Long. 113°03'30" W.); to the point of origin; but not including the following airspace designated as the "Tuckup Corridor": at or above 10,500 feet MSL within 2 nautical miles either side of a line extending between Lat. 36°24'47" N., Long. 112°48'50" W. and Lat. 36°17'10" N., Long. 112°48'50" W.; to the point of origin.

Section 5. *Minimum flight altitudes.* Except in an emergency or if otherwise necessary for safety of flight, or unless otherwise authorized by the Flight Standards District Office for a purpose listed in Section 3(b), no person may operate an aircraft in the Special Flight Rules Area at an altitude lower than the following:

(a) Eastern section from Lees Ferry to North Canyon: 5,000 feet MSL.

(b) Eastern section from North Canyon to Boundary Ridge: 6,000 feet MSL.

(c) Boundary Ridge to Supai (Yumtheska) Point: 7,500 feet MSL.

(d) Supai Point to Diamond Creek: 6,500 feet MSL.

(e) Western section from Diamond Creek to the Grand Wash Cliffs: 5,000 feet MSL.

[Editorial Note: Sections 6–8 are intentionally omitted by the FAA]

Section 9. *Termination date.* Section 1. Applicability, Section 4, Flight-free zones, and Section 5. Minimum flight altitudes, expire on April 19, 2001.

Note: An informational map of the special flight rules areas defined by SFAR 50–2 is available on the Office of Rulemaking's website at:
http://www.faa.gov/avr/armhome.htm
A paper copy is available from the Office of Rulemaking by calling Linda Williams at (202) 267-9685.

[Docket No. FAA–1999–5926, 66 FR 1003, Jan. 4, 2001; as amended by FAA–2001–9218, 66 FR 16584, March 26, 2001]

SFAR No. 60 to Part 91

Air Traffic Control System Emergency Operation

Section 1. Each person shall, before conducting any operation under the Federal Aviation Regulations (14 CFR chapter I), be familiar with all available information concerning that operation, including Notices to Airmen issued under §91.139 and, when activated, the provisions of the National Air Traffic Reduced Complement Operations Plan available for inspection at operating air traffic facilities and Regional air traffic division offices, and the General Aviation Reservation Program. No operator may change the designated airport of intended operation for any flight contained in the October 1, 1990, OAG.

Section 2. Notwithstanding any provision of the Federal Aviation Regulations to the contrary, no person may operate an aircraft in the Air Traffic Control System:

a. Contrary to any restriction, prohibition, procedure or other action taken by the Director of the Office of Air Traffic Systems Management (Director) pursuant to paragraph 3 of this regulation and announced in a Notice to Airmen pursuant to §91.139 of the Federal Aviation Regulations.

b. When the National Air Traffic Reduced Complement Operations Plan is activated pursuant to paragraph 4 of this regulation, except in accordance with the pertinent provisions of the National Air Traffic Reduced Complement Operations Plan.

Section 3. Prior to or in connection with the implementation of the RCOP, and as conditions warrant, the Director is authorized to:

a. Restrict, prohibit, or permit VFR and/or IFR operations at any airport, Class B airspace area, Class C airspace area, or other class of controlled airspace.

b. Give priority at any airport to flights that are of military necessity, or are medical emergency flights, Presidential flights, and flights transporting critical Government employees.

c. Implement, at any airport, traffic management procedures, that may include reduction of flight operations. Reduction of flight operations will be accomplished, to the extent practical, on a pro rata basis among and between air carrier, commercial operator, and general aviation operations. Flights canceled under this SFAR at a high density traffic airport will be considered to have been operated for purposes of part 93 of the Federal Aviation Regulations.

Section 4. The Director may activate the National Air Traffic Reduced Complement Operations Plan at any time he finds that it is necessary for the safety and efficiency of the National Airspace System. Upon activation of the RCOP and notwithstanding any provision of the FAR to the contrary, the Director is authorized to suspend or modify any airspace designation.

Section 5. Notice of restrictions, prohibitions, procedures and other actions taken by the Director under this regulation with respect to the operation of the Air Traffic Control system will be announced in Notices to Airmen issued pursuant to §91.139 of the Federal Aviation Regulations.

Section 6. The Director may delegate his authority under this regulation to the extent he considers necessary for the safe and efficient operation of the National Air Traffic Control System.

Authority: 49 U.S.C. app. 1301(7), 1303, 1344, 1348, 1352 through 1355, 1401, 1421 through 1431, 1471, 1472, 1502, 1510, 1522, and 2121 through 2125; articles 12, 29, 31, and 32(a) of the Convention on International Civil Aviation (61 stat. 1180); 42 U.S.C. 4321 et seq.; E.O. 11514, 35 FR 4247, 3 CFR, 1966–1970 Comp., p. 902; 49 U.S.C. 106(g).

[Docket No. 26351, 55 FR 40760, Oct. 4, 1990; as amended by Amdt. 91–227, 56 FR 65652, Dec. 17, 1991]

SFAR No. 71 to Part 91

Special Operating Rules for Air Tour Operators in the State of Hawaii

Section 1. *Applicability.* This Special Federal Aviation Regulation prescribes operating rules for airplane and helicopter visual flight rules air tour flights conducted in the State of Hawaii under 14 CFR parts 91, 121, and 135. This rule does not apply to:

(a) Operations conducted under 14 CFR part 121 in airplanes with a passenger seating configuration of more than 30 seats or a payload capacity of more than 7,500 pounds.

(b) Flights conducted in gliders or hot air balloons.

Section 2. *Definitions.* For the purposes of this SFAR:

"Air tour" means any sightseeing flight conducted under visual flight rules in an airplane or helicopter for compensation or hire.

"Air tour operator" means any person who conducts an air tour.

Section 3. *Helicopter flotation equipment.* No person may conduct an air tour in Hawaii in a single-engine helicopter beyond the shore of any island, regardless of whether the helicopter is within gliding distance of the shore, unless:

(a) The helicopter is amphibious or is equipped with floats adequate to accomplish a safe emergency ditching and approved flotation gear is easily accessible for each occupant; or

(b) Each person on board the helicopter is wearing approved flotation gear.

Section 4. *Helicopter performance plan.* Each operator must complete a performance plan before each helicopter air tour flight. The performance plan must be based on the information in the Rotorcraft Flight Manual (RFM), considering the maximum density altitude for which the operation is planned for the flight to determine the following:

(a) Maximum gross weight and center of gravity (CG) limitations for hovering in ground effect;

(b) Maximum gross weight and CG limitations for hovering out of ground effect; and,

(c) Maximum combination of weight, altitude, and temperature for which height velocity information in the RFM, is valid.

The pilot in command (PIC) must comply with the performance plan.

Section 5. *Helicopter operating limitations.* Except for approach to and transition from a hover, the PIC shall operate the helicopter at a combination of height and forward speed (including hover) that would permit a safe landing in event of engine power loss, in accordance with the height-speed envelope for that helicopter under current weight and aircraft altitude.

Section 6. *Minimum flight altitudes.* Except when necessary for takeoff and landing, or operating in compliance with an air traffic control clearance, or as otherwise authorized by the Administrator, no person may conduct an air tour in Hawaii:

(a) Below an altitude of 1,500 feet above the surface over all areas of the State of Hawaii, and,

(b) Closer than 1,500 feet to any person or property; or

(c) Below any altitude prescribed by federal statute or regulation.

Section 7. *Passenger briefing.* Before takeoff, each PIC of an air tour flight of Hawaii with a flight segment beyond the ocean shore of any island shall ensure that each passenger has been briefed on the following, in addition to requirements set forth in 14 CFR 91.107, 121.571, or 135.117:

(a) Water ditching procedures;

(b) Use of required flotation equipment; and

(c) Emergency egress from the aircraft in event of a water landing.

Section 8. *Termination date.* This SFAR No. 71 shall remain in effect until further notice.

[SFAR 71, 59 FR 49145, Sept. 26, 1994; as amended by 60 FR 65913, Dec. 20, 1995; 62 FR 58859, Oct. 30, 1997; 65 FR 58612, Sept. 29, 2000; 68 FR 60839, Oct. 23, 2003]

SFAR No. 77 to Part 91

Prohibition Against Certain Flights Within the Territory and Airspace of Iraq

1. *Applicability.* This rule applies to the following persons:

(a) All U.S. air carriers or commercial operators;

(b) All persons exercising the privileges of an airman certificate issued by the FAA except such persons operating U.S.-registered aircraft for a foreign air carrier; or

(c) All operators of aircraft registered in the United States except where the operator of such aircraft is a foreign air carrier.

2. *Flight prohibition.* No person may conduct flight operations over or within the territory of Iraq except as provided in paragraphs 3 and 4 of this SFAR or except as follows:

(a) Overflights of Iraq may be conducted above flight level (FL) 200 subject to the approval of, and in accordance with the conditions established by, the appropriate authorities of Iraq.

(b) Flights departing from countries adjacent to Iraq whose climb performance will not permit operation above FL200 prior to Iraqi airspace may operate at altitudes below FL200 within Iraq to the extent necessary to permit a climb above FL200, subject to the approval of, and in accordance with the conditions established by, the appropriate authorities of Iraq.

(c) [Reserved]

3. *Permitted operations.* This SFAR does not prohibit persons described in paragraph 1 from conducting flight operations within the territory and airspace of Iraq when such operations are authorized either by another agency of the United States Government with the approval of the FAA or by an exemption issued by the Administrator.

4. *Emergency situations.* In an emergency that requires immediate decision and action for the safety of the flight, the pilot in command of an aircraft may deviate from this SFAR to the extent required by that emergency. Except for U.S. air carriers or commercial operators that are subject to the requirements of 14 CFR parts 119, 121, or 135, each person who deviates from this rule shall, within ten (10) days of the deviation, excluding Saturdays, Sundays, and Federal holidays, submit to the nearest FAA Flight Standards District Office a complete report of the operations of the aircraft involved in the deviation including a description of the deviation and the reasons therefore.

5. *Expiration.* This Special Federal Aviation Regulation will remain in effect until further notice.

[Docket No. FAA–2003–14766, SFAR 77; 69 FR 21953, April 23, 2004]

SFAR No. 79 to Part 91

Prohibition Against Certain Flights within the Flight Information Region (FIR) of the Democratic People's Republic of Korea (DPRK)

Section 1. *Applicability.* This rule applied to the following persons:

(a) All U.S. air carriers or commercial operators.

(b) All persons exercising the privileges of an airman certificate issued by the FAA, except such persons operating U.S.-registered aircraft for a foreign air carrier.

(c) All operators of aircraft registered in the United States except where the operator of such aircraft is a foreign air carrier.

Section 2. *Flight Prohibition.* Except as provided in paragraphs 3 and 4 of this SFAR, no person described in paragraph 1 may conduct flight operations through the Pyongyang FIR west of 132 degrees east longitude.

Section 3. *Permitted Operations.* This SFAR does not prohibit persons described in paragraph 1 from conducting flight operations within the Pyongyang FIR west of 132 degrees east longitude where such operations are authorized either by exemption issued by the Administrator or by another agency of the United States Government with FAA approval.

Section 4. *Emergency situations.* In an emergency that requires immediate decision and action for the safety of the flight, the pilot in command on an aircraft may deviate from this SFAR to the extend required by that emergency. Except for U.S. air carriers and commercial operators that are subject to the requirements of 14 CFR parts 121, 125, or 135, each person who deviates from this rule shall, within ten (10) days of the deviation, excluding Saturdays, Sundays, and Federal holidays, submit to the nearest FAA Flight Standards District Office a complete report of the operations of the aircraft involved in the deviation, including a description of the deviation and the reasons therefore.

Section 5. *Expiration.* This Special Federal Aviation Regulation No. 79 will remain in effect until further notice.

[Docket No. 28831, 62 FR 20077, April 24, 1997; as amended by 63 FR 8017, Feb. 17, 1998; 63 FR 19286, April 17, 1998]

SFAR No. 87 to Part 91

Prohibition Against Certain Flights Within the Territory and Airspace of Ethiopia

1. *Applicability.* This Special Federal Aviation Regulation (SFAR) No. 87 applies to all U.S. air carriers or commercial operators, all persons exercising the privileges of an airman certificate issued by the FAA unless that person is engaged in the operation of a U.S.-registered aircraft for a foreign air carrier, and all operators using aircraft registered in the United States except where the operator of such aircraft is a foreign air carrier.

2. *Flight prohibition.* Except as provided in paragraphs 3 and 4 of this SFAR, no person described in paragraph 1 may conduct flight operations within the territory and airspace of Ethiopia north of 12 degrees north latitude.

3. *Permitted operations.* This SFAR does not prohibit persons described in paragraph 1 from conducting flight operations within the territory and airspace of Ethiopia where such operations are authorized either by exemption issued by the Administrator or by an authorization issued by another agency of the United States Government with the approval of the FAA.

4. *Emergency situations.* In an emergency that requires immediate decision and action for the safety of the flight, the pilot in command of an aircraft may deviate from this SFAR to the extent required by that emergency. Except for U.S. air carriers and commercial operators that are subject to the requirements of 14 CFR 121.557, 121.559, or 135.19, each person who deviates from this rule shall, within ten (10) days of the deviation, excluding Saturdays, Sundays, and Federal holidays, submit to the nearest FAA Flight Standards District Office a complete report of the operations of the aircraft involved in the deviation, including a description of the deviation and the reasons therefor.

5. *Expiration.* This Special Federal Aviation Regulation shall remain in effect until further notice.

[Docket No. FAA–2000–7360, 65 FR 31215, May 16, 2000]

SFAR No. 94 to Part 91

Enhanced Security Procedures for Operations at Certain Airports in the Washington, DC Metropolitan Area Special Flight Rules Area

1. *Applicability.* This Special Federal Aviation Regulation (SFAR) establishes rules for all persons operating an aircraft to or from the following airports located within the airspace designated as the Washington, DC Metropolitan Area Special Flight Rules Area:

(a) College Park Airport (CGS).

(b) Potomac Airfield (VKX).

(c) Washington Executive/Hyde Field (W32).

2. *Definitions.* For the purposes of this SFAR the following definitions apply:

Administrator means the Federal Aviation Administrator, the Under Secretary of Transportation for Security, or any person delegated the authority of the Federal Aviation Administrator or Under Secretary of Transportation for Security.

Washington, DC Metropolitan Area Special Flight Rules Area means that airspace within an area from the surface up to but not including Flight Level 180, bounded by a line beginning at the Washington (DCA) VOR/DME 300 degree radial at 15 nautical miles (Lat. 38°56'55" N., Long. 77°20'08" W.); thence clockwise along the DCA 15 nautical mile arc to the DCA 022 degree radial at 15 nautical miles (Lat. 39°06'11" N., Long 76°57'51" W.); thence southeast via a line drawn to the DCA 049 degree radial at 14 nautical miles (Lat. 39°02'18" N., Long. 76°50'38" W.); thence south via a line drawn to the DCA 064 degree radial at 13 nautical miles (Lat. 38°59'01" N., Long. 76°48'32" W.); thence clockwise along the DCA 13 nautical mile arc to the DCA 282 degree radial at 13 nautical miles (Lat. 38°52'14" N., Long 77°18'48" W.); thence north via a line drawn to the point of the beginning; excluding the airspace within a one nautical mile radius of Freeway Airport (W00), Mitchellville, MD.

3. *Operating requirements.*

(a) Except as specified in paragraph 3(c) of this SFAR, no person may operate an aircraft to or from an airport to which this SFAR applies unless security procedures that meet the provisions of paragraph 4 of this SFAR have been approved by the Administrator for operations at that airport.

(b) Except as specified in paragraph 3(c) of this SFAR, each person serving as a required flightcrew member of an aircraft operating to or from an airport to which this SFAR applies must:

(1) Prior to obtaining authorization to operate to or from the airport, present to the Administrator the following:

(i) A current and valid airman certificate;

(ii) A current medical certificate;

(iii) One form of Government issued picture identification; and

(iv) A list containing the make, model, and registration number of each aircraft that the pilot intends to operate to or from the airport;

(2) Successfully complete a background check by a law enforcement agency, which may include submission of fingerprints and the conduct of a criminal history, records check.

(3) Attend a briefing acceptable to the Administrator that describes procedures for operating to or from the airport;

(4) Not have been convicted or found not guilty by reason of insanity, in any jurisdiction, during the 10 years prior to being authorized to operate to or from the airport, or while authorized to operate to or from the airport, of those crimes specified in §108.229 (d) of this chapter;

(5) Not have a record on file with the FAA of:

(i) A violation of a prohibited area designated under part 73 of this chapter, a flight restriction established under §91.141 of this chapter, or special security instructions issued under §99.7 of this chapter; or

(ii) More than one violation of a restricted area designated under part 73 of this chapter, emergency air traffic rules issued under §91.139 of this chapter, a temporary flight restriction designated under §91.137, §91.138, or §91.145 of this chapter, an area designated under §91.143 of this chapter, or any combination thereof;

(6) Be authorized by the Administrator to conduct operations to or from the airport;

(7) Protect from unauthorized disclosure any identification information issued by the Administrator for the conduct of operations to or from the airport;

(8) Operate an aircraft that is authorized by the Administrator for operations to or from the airport;

(9) File an IFR or VFR flight plan telephonically with Leesburg AFSS prior to departure and obtain an ATC clearance prior to entering the Washington, DC Metropolitan Area Special Flight Rules Area;

(10) Operate the aircraft in accordance with an open IFR or VFR flight plan while in the Washington, DC Metropolitan Area Special Flight Rules Area, unless otherwise authorized by ATC;

(11) Maintain two-way communications with an appropriate ATC facility while in the Washington, DC Metropolitan Area Special Flight Rules Area;

(12) Ensure that the aircraft is equipped with an operable transponder with altitude reporting capability and use an assigned discrete beacon code while operating in the Washington, DC Metropolitan Area Special Flight Rules Area;

(13) Comply with any instructions issued by ATC for the flight;

(14) Secure the aircraft after returning to the airport from any flight;

(15) Comply with all additional safety and security requirements specified in applicable NOTAMs; and

(16) Comply with any Transportation Security Administration, or law enforcement requirements to operate to or from the airport.

(c) A person may operate a U.S. Armed Forces, law enforcement, or aeromedical services aircraft to or from an affected airport provided the operator complies with paragraphs 3(b)(10) through 3(b)(16) of this SFAR and any additional procedures specified by the Administrator necessary to provide for the security of aircraft operations to or from the airport.

4. *Airport Security Procedures.*

(a) Airport security procedures submitted to the Administrator for approval must:

(1) Identify and provide contact information for the airport manager who is responsible for ensuring that the security procedures at the airport are implemented and maintained;

(2) Contain procedures to identify those aircraft eligible to be authorized for operations to or from the airport;

(3) Contain procedures to ensure that a current record of those persons authorized to conduct operations to or from the airport and the aircraft in which the person is authorized to conduct those operations is maintained at the airport;

(4) Contain airport arrival and departure route descriptions, air traffic control clearance procedures, flight plan requirements, communications procedures, and procedures for transponder use;

(5) Contain procedures to monitor the security of aircraft at the airport during operational and non-operational hours and to alert aircraft owners and operators, airport operators, and the Administrator of unsecured aircraft;

(6) Contain procedures to ensure that security awareness procedures are implemented and maintained at the airport;

(7) Contain procedures to ensure that a copy of the approved security procedures is maintained at the airport and can be made available for inspection upon request of the Administrator;

(8) Contain procedures to provide the Administrator with the means necessary to make any inspection to determine compliance with the approved security procedures; and

(9) Contain any additional procedures necessary to provide for the security of aircraft operations to or from the airport.

(b) Airport security procedures are approved without an expiration date and remain in effect unless the Administrator makes a determination that operations at the airport have not been conducted in accordance with those procedures or that those procedures must be amended in accordance with paragraph 4(a)(9) of this SFAR.

5. *Waivers.* The Administrator may permit an operation to or from an airport to which this SFAR applies, in deviation from the provisions of this SFAR if the Administrator finds that such action is in the public interest, provides the level of security required by this SFAR, and the operation can be conducted safely under the terms of the waiver.

6. *Delegation.* The authority of the Administrator under this SFAR is also exercised by the Associate Administrator for Civil Aviation Security and the Deputy Associate Administrator for Civil Aviation Security. This authority may be further delegated.

7. *Expiration.* This Special Federal Aviation Regulation shall remain in effect until February 13, 2005.

[Docket No. FAA–2002–11580, 67 FR 7544, Feb. 19, 2002; as amended by Docket No. FAA–2002–11580, Feb. 14, 2003]

SFAR No. 97 to Part 91

Special Operating Rules for the Conduct of Instrument Flight Rules (IFR) Area Navigation (RNAV) Operations using Global Positioning Systems (GPS) in Alaska

Those persons identified in Section 1 may conduct IFR en route RNAV operations in the State of Alaska and its airspace on published air traffic routes using TSO C145a/C146a navigation systems as the only means of IFR navigation. Despite contrary provisions of parts 71, 91, 95, 121, 125, and 135 of this chapter, a person may operate aircraft in accordance with this SFAR if the following requirements are met.

Section 1. Purpose, use, and limitations

a. This SFAR permits TSO C145a/C146a GPS (RNAV) systems to be used for IFR en route operations in the United States airspace over and near Alaska (as set forth in paragraph c of this section) at Special Minimum En Route Altitudes (MEA) that are outside the operational service volume of ground-based navigation aids, if the aircraft operation also meets the requirements of sections 3 and 4 of this SFAR.

b. Certificate holders and part 91 operators may operate aircraft under this SFAR provided that they comply with the requirements of this SFAR.

c. Operations conducted under this SFAR are limited to United States Airspace within and near the State of Alaska as defined in the following area description:

From 62°00'00.000"N, Long. 141°00'00.00"W.;
to Lat. 59°47'54.11"N., Long. 135°28'38.34"W.;

to Lat. 56°00'04.11"N., Long. 130°00'07.80"W.;
to Lat. 54°43'00.00"N., Long. 130°37'00.00"W.;
to Lat. 51°24'00.00"N., Long. 167°49'00.00"W.;
to Lat. 50°08'00.00"N., Long. 176°34'00.00"W.;
to Lat. 45°42'00.00"N., Long. -162°55'00.00"E.;
to Lat. 50°05'00.00"N., Long. -159°00'00.00"E.;
to Lat. 54°00'00.00"N., Long. -169°00'00.00"E.;
to Lat. 60°00 00.00"N., Long. -180°00' 00.00"E;
to Lat. 65°00'00.00"N., Long. 168°58'23.00"W.;
to Lat. 90°00'00.00"N., Long. 00°00'0.00"W.;
to Lat. 62°00'00.000"N, Long. 141°00'00.00"W.

(d) No person may operate an aircraft under IFR during the en route portion of flight below the standard MEA or at the special MEA unless the operation is conducted in accordance with sections 3 and 4 of this SFAR.

Section 2. Definitions and abbreviations

For the purposes of this SFAR, the following definitions and abbreviations apply.

Area navigation (RNAV). RNAV is a method of navigation that permits aircraft operations on any desired flight path.

Area navigation (RNAV) route. RNAV route is a published route based on RNAV that can be used by suitably equipped aircraft.

Certificate holder. A certificate holder means a person holding a certificate issued under part 119 or part 125 of this chapter or holding operations specifications issued under part 129 of this chapter.

Global Navigation Satellite System (GNSS). GNSS is a world-wide position and time determination system that uses satellite ranging signals to determine user location. It encompasses all satellite ranging technologies, including GPS and additional satellites. Components of the GNSS include GPS, the Global Orbiting Navigation Satellite System, and WAAS satellites.

Global Positioning System (GPS). GPS is a satellite-based radio navigational, positioning, and time transfer system. The system provides highly accurate position and velocity information and precise time on a continuous global basis to properly equipped users.

Minimum crossing altitude (MCA). The minimum crossing altitude (MCA) applies to the operation of an aircraft proceeding to a higher minimum en route altitude when crossing specified fixes.

Required navigation system. Required navigation system means navigation equipment that meets the performance requirements of TSO C145a/C146a navigation systems certified for IFR en route operations.

Route segment. Route segment is a portion of a route bounded on each end by a fix or NAVAID.

Special MEA. Special MEA refers to the minimum en route altitudes, using required navigation systems, on published routes outside the operational service volume of ground-based navigation aids and are depicted on the published Low Altitude and High Altitude En Route Charts using the color blue and with the suffix "G." For example, a GPS MEA of 4000 feet MSL would be depicted using the color blue, as 4000G.

Standard MEA. Standard MEA refers to the minimum en route IFR altitude on published routes that uses ground-based navigation aids and are depicted on the published Low Altitude and High Altitude En Route Charts using the color black.

Station referenced. Station referenced refers to radio navigational aids or fixes that are referenced by ground based navigation facilities such as VOR facilities.

Wide Area Augmentation System (WAAS). WAAS is an augmentation to GPS that calculates GPS integrity and correction data on the ground and uses geo-stationary satellites to broadcast GPS integrity and correction data to GPS/WAAS users and to provide ranging signals. It is a safety critical system consisting of a ground network of reference and integrity monitor data processing sites to assess current GPS performance, as well as a space segment that broadcasts that assessment to GNSS users to support en route through precision approach navigation. Users of the system include all aircraft applying the WAAS data and ranging signal.

Section 3. Operational Requirements

To operate an aircraft under this SFAR, the following requirements must be met:

a. Training and qualification for operations and maintenance personnel on required navigation equipment used under this SFAR.

b. Use authorized procedures for normal, abnormal, and emergency situations unique to these operations, including degraded navigation capabilities, and satellite system outages.

c. For certificate holders, training of flight crewmembers and other personnel authorized to exercise operational control on the use of those procedures specified in paragraph b of this section.

d. Part 129 operators must have approval from the State of the operator to conduct operations in accordance with this SFAR.

e. In order to operate under this SFAR, a certificate holder must be authorized in operations specifications.

Section 4. Equipment Requirements

a. The certificate holder must have properly installed, certificated, and functional dual required navigation systems as defined in section 2 of this SFAR for the en route operations covered under this SFAR.

b. When the aircraft is being operated under part 91, the aircraft must be equipped with at least one properly installed, certificated, and functional required navigation system as defined in section 2 of this SFAR for the en route operations covered under this SFAR.

Section 5. Expiration date

This Special Federal Aviation Regulation will remain in effect until rescinded.

[Docket FAA-2003-14305, SFAR No. 97; 68 FR 14077, March 21, 2003]

SFAR No. 104 to Part 91

Prohibition Against Certain Flights by Syrian Air Carriers to the United States

1. *Applicability.* This Special Federal Aviation Regulation (SFAR) No. 104 applies to any air carrier owned or controlled by Syria that is engaged in scheduled international air services.

2. *Special flight restrictions.* Except as provided in paragraphs 3 and 4 of this SFAR No. 104, no air carrier described in paragraph 1 may take off from or land in the territory of the United States.

3. *Permitted operations.* This SFAR does not prohibit overflights of the territory of the United States by any air carrier described in paragraph 1.

4. *Emergency situations.* In an emergency that requires immediate decision and action for the safety of the flight, the pilot in command of an aircraft of any air carrier described in paragraph 1 may deviate from this SFAR to the extent required by that emergency. Each person who deviates from this rule must, within 10 days of the deviation, excluding Saturdays, Sundays, and Federal holidays, submit to the nearest FAA Flight Standards District Office a complete report of the operations or the aircraft involved in the deviation, including a description of the deviation and the reasons therefor.

5. *Duration.* This SFAR No. 104 will remain in effect until further notice.

[Docket No. FAA–2004–17763, SFAR No. 104, 69 FR 31718, June 4, 2004]

Subpart A—General

Source: Docket No. 18334, 54 FR 34292, Aug. 18, 1989, unless otherwise noted.

§91.1 Applicability.

(a) Except as provided in paragraphs (b) and (c) of this section and §§91.701 and 91.703, this part prescribes rules governing the operation of aircraft (other than moored balloons, kites, unmanned rockets, and unmanned free balloons, which are governed by part 101 of this chapter, and ultralight vehicles operated in accordance with part 103 of this chapter) within the United States, including the waters within 3 nautical miles of the U.S. coast.

(b) Each person operating an aircraft in the airspace overlying the waters between 3 and 12 nautical miles from the coast of the United States must comply with §§91.1 through 91.21; §§91.101 through 91.143; §§91.151 through 91.159; §§91.167 through 91.193; §91.203; §91.205; §§ 91.209 through 91.217; §91.221; §§91.303 through 91.319; §§91.323 through 91.327; §91.605; §91.609; §§91.703 through 91.715; and §91.903.

(c) This part applies to each person on board an aircraft being operated under this part, unless otherwise specified.

[Docket No. 18334, 54 FR 34292, Aug. 18, 1989; as amended by Amdt. 91–257, 64 FR 1079, Jan. 7, 1999; Amdt. 91–282, 69 FR 44880, July 27, 2004]

§91.3 Responsibility and authority of the pilot in command.

(a) The pilot in command of an aircraft is directly responsible for, and is the final authority as to, the operation of that aircraft.

(b) In an in-flight emergency requiring immediate action, the pilot in command may deviate from any rule of this part to the extent required to meet that emergency.

(c) Each pilot in command who deviates from a rule under paragraph (b) of this section shall, upon the request of the Administrator, send a written report of that deviation to the Administrator.

(Approved by the Office of Management and Budget under control number 2120–0005)

§91.5 Pilot in command of aircraft requiring more than one required pilot.

No person may operate an aircraft that is type certificated for more than one required pilot flight crewmember unless the pilot in command meets the requirements of §61.58 of this chapter.

§91.7 Civil aircraft airworthiness.

(a) No person may operate a civil aircraft unless it is in an airworthy condition.

(b) The pilot in command of a civil aircraft is responsible for determining whether that aircraft is in condition for safe flight. The pilot in command shall discontinue the flight when unairworthy mechanical, electrical, or structural conditions occur.

§91.9 Civil aircraft flight manual, marking, and placard requirements.

(a) Except as provided in paragraph (d) of this section, no person may operate a civil aircraft without complying with the operating limitations specified in the approved Airplane or Rotorcraft Flight Manual, markings, and placards, or as otherwise prescribed by the certificating authority of the country of registry.

(b) No person may operate a U.S.-registered civil aircraft—

(1) For which an Airplane or Rotorcraft Flight Manual is required by §21.5 of this chapter unless there is available in the aircraft a current, approved Airplane or Rotorcraft Flight Manual or the manual provided for in §121.141(b); and

(2) For which an Airplane or Rotorcraft Flight Manual is not required by §21.5 of this chapter, unless there is available in the aircraft a current approved Airplane or Rotorcraft Flight Manual, approved manual material, markings, and placards, or any combination thereof.

(c) No person may operate a U.S.-registered civil aircraft unless that aircraft is identified in accordance with part 45 of this chapter.

(d) Any person taking off or landing a helicopter certificated under part 29 of this chapter at a heliport constructed over water may make such momentary flight as is necessary for takeoff or landing through the prohibited range of the limiting height-speed envelope established for the helicopter if that flight through the prohibited range takes place over water on which a safe ditching can be accomplished and if the helicopter is amphibious or is equipped with floats or other emergency flotation gear adequate to accomplish a safe emergency ditching on open water.

§91.11 Prohibition on interference with crewmembers.

No person may assault, threaten, intimidate, or interfere with a crewmember in the performance of the crewmember's duties aboard an aircraft being operated.

[Docket No. 18334, 54 FR 34292, Aug. 18, 1989; as amended by Amdt. 91–257, 64 FR 1079, Jan. 7, 1999]

§91.13 Careless or reckless operation.

(a) *Aircraft operations for the purpose of air navigation.* No person may operate an aircraft in a careless or reckless manner so as to endanger the life or property of another.

(b) *Aircraft operations other than for the purpose of air navigation.* No person may operate an aircraft, other than for the purpose of air navigation, on any part of the surface of an airport used by aircraft for air commerce (including areas used by those aircraft for receiving or discharging persons or cargo), in a careless or reckless manner so as to endanger the life or property of another.

§91.15 Dropping objects.

No pilot in command of a civil aircraft may allow any object to be dropped from that aircraft in flight that creates a hazard to persons or property. However, this section does not prohibit the dropping of any object if reasonable precautions are taken to avoid injury or damage to persons or property.

§91.17 Alcohol or drugs.

(a) No person may act or attempt to act as a crewmember of a civil aircraft—

(1) Within 8 hours after the consumption of any alcoholic beverage;

(2) While under the influence of alcohol;

(3) While using any drug that affects the person's faculties in any way contrary to safety; or

(4) While having .04 percent by weight or more alcohol in the blood.

(b) Except in an emergency, no pilot of a civil aircraft may allow a person who appears to be intoxicated or who demonstrates by manner or physical indications that the individual is under the influence of drugs (except a medical patient under proper care) to be carried in that aircraft.

(c) A crewmember shall do the following:

(1) On request of a law enforcement officer, submit to a test to indicate the percentage by weight of alcohol in the blood, when—

(i) The law enforcement officer is authorized under State or local law to conduct the test or to have the test conducted; and

(ii) The law enforcement officer is requesting submission to the test to investigate a suspected violation of State or local law governing the same or substantially similar conduct prohibited by paragraph (a)(1), (a)(2), or (a)(4) of this section.

(2) Whenever the Administrator has a reasonable basis to believe that a person may have violated paragraph (a)(1), (a)(2), or (a)(4) of this section, that person shall, upon request by the Administrator, furnish the Administrator, or authorize any clinic, hospital, doctor, or other person to release to the Administrator, the results of each test taken within 4 hours after acting or attempting to act as a crewmember that indicates percentage by weight of alcohol in the blood.

(d) Whenever the Administrator has a reasonable basis to believe that a person may have violated paragraph (a)(3) of this section, that person shall, upon request by the Administrator, furnish the Administrator, or authorize any clinic, hospital, doctor, or other person to release to the Administrator, the results of each test taken within 4 hours after acting or attempting to act as a crewmember that indicates the presence of any drugs in the body.

(e) Any test information obtained by the Administrator under paragraph (c) or (d) of this section may be evaluated in determining a person's qualifications for any airman certificate or possible violations of this chapter and may be used as evidence in any legal proceeding under section 602, 609, or 901 of the Federal Aviation Act of 1958.

§91.19 Carriage of narcotic drugs, marihuana, and depressant or stimulant drugs or substances.

(a) Except as provided in paragraph (b) of this section, no person may operate a civil aircraft within the United States with knowledge that narcotic drugs, marihuana, and depressant or stimulant drugs or substances as defined in Federal or State statutes are carried in the aircraft.

(b) Paragraph (a) of this section does not apply to any carriage of narcotic drugs, marihuana, and depressant or stimulant drugs or substances authorized by or under any Federal or State statute or by any Federal or State agency.

§91.21 Portable electronic devices.

(a) Except as provided in paragraph (b) of this section, no person may operate, nor may any operator or pilot in command of an aircraft allow the operation of, any portable electronic device on any of the following U.S.-registered civil aircraft:

(1) Aircraft operated by a holder of an air carrier operating certificate or an operating certificate; or

(2) Any other aircraft while it is operated under IFR.

(b) Paragraph (a) of this section does not apply to—

(1) Portable voice recorders;

(2) Hearing aids;

(3) Heart pacemakers;

(4) Electric shavers; or

(5) Any other portable electronic device that the operator of the aircraft has determined will not cause interference with the navigation or communication system of the aircraft on which it is to be used.

(c) In the case of an aircraft operated by a holder of an air operating certificate or an operating certificate, the determination required by paragraph (b)(5) of this section shall be made by that operator of the aircraft on which the particular device is to be used. In the case of other aircraft, the determination may be made by the pilot in command or other operator of the aircraft.

§91.23 Truth-in-leasing clause requirement in leases and conditional sales contracts.

(a) Except as provided in paragraph (b) of this section, the parties to a lease or contract of conditional sale involving a U.S.-registered large civil aircraft and entered into after January 2, 1973, shall execute a written lease or contract and include therein a written truth-in-leasing clause as a concluding paragraph in large print, immediately preceding the space for the signature of the parties, which contains the following with respect to each such aircraft:

(1) Identification of the Federal Aviation Regulations under which the aircraft has been maintained and inspected during the 12 months preceding the execution of the lease or contract of conditional sale, and certification by the parties thereto regarding the aircraft's status of compliance with applicable maintenance and inspection requirements in this part for the operation to be conducted under the lease or contract of conditional sale.

(2) The name and address (printed or typed) and the signature of the person responsible for operational control of the aircraft under the lease or contract of conditional sale, and certification that each person understands that person's responsibilities for compliance with applicable Federal Aviation Regulations.

(3) A statement that an explanation of factors bearing on operational control and pertinent Federal Aviation Regulations can be obtained from the nearest FAA Flight Standards district office.

(b) The requirements of paragraph (a) of this section do not apply—

(1) To a lease or contract of conditional sale when—

(i) The party to whom the aircraft is furnished is a foreign air carrier or certificate holder under part 121, 125, 135, or 141 of this chapter, or

(ii) The party furnishing the aircraft is a foreign air carrier or a person operating under part 121, 125, and 141 of this chapter, or a person operating under part 135 of this chapter having authority to engage in on-demand operations with large aircraft.

(2) To a contract of conditional sale, when the aircraft involved has not been registered anywhere prior to the execution of the contract, except as a new aircraft under a dealer's aircraft registration certificate issued in accordance with §47.61 of this chapter.

(c) No person may operate a large civil aircraft of U.S. registry that is subject to a lease or contract of conditional sale to which paragraph (a) of this section applies, unless—

(1) The lessee or conditional buyer, or the registered owner if the lessee is not a citizen of the United States, has mailed a copy of the lease or contract that complies with the requirements of paragraph (a) of this section, within 24 hours of its execution, to the Aircraft Registration Branch, Attn: Technical Section, P.O. Box 25724, Oklahoma City, OK 73125;

(2) A copy of the lease or contract that complies with the requirements of paragraph (a) of this section is carried in the aircraft. The copy of the lease or contract shall be made available for review upon request by the Administrator, and

(3) The lessee or conditional buyer, or the registered owner if the lessee is not a citizen of the United States, has notified by telephone or in person the FAA Flight Standards district office nearest the airport where the flight will originate. Unless otherwise authorized by that office, the notification shall be given at least 48 hours before takeoff in the case of the first flight of that aircraft under that lease or contract and inform the FAA of—

(i) The location of the airport of departure;

(ii) The departure time; and

(iii) The registration number of the aircraft involved.

(d) The copy of the lease or contract furnished to the FAA under paragraph (c) of this section is commercial or financial information obtained from a person. It is, therefore, privileged and confidential and will not be made available by the FAA for public inspection or copying under 5 U.S.C. 552(b)(4) unless recorded with the FAA under part 49 of this chapter.

(e) For the purpose of this section, a lease means any agreement by a person to furnish an aircraft to another person for compensation or hire, whether with or without flight crewmembers, other than an agreement for the sale of an aircraft and a contract of conditional sale under section 101 of the Federal Aviation Act of 1958. The person furnishing the aircraft is referred to as the lessor, and the person to whom it is furnished the lessee.

(Approved by the Office of Management and Budget under control number 2120–0005)

[Docket No. 18334, 54 FR 34292, Aug. 18, 1989; as amended by Amdt. 91–212, 54 FR 39293, Sept. 25, 1989; Amdt. 91–253, 62 FR 13253, March 19, 1997; Amdt. 91–267, 66 FR 21066, April 27, 2001]

§91.25 Aviation Safety Reporting Program: Prohibition against use of reports for enforcement purposes.

The Administrator of the FAA will not use reports submitted to the National Aeronautics and Space Administration under the Aviation Safety Reporting Program (or information derived therefrom) in any enforcement action except information concerning accidents or criminal offenses which are wholly excluded from the Program.

§91.27 – 91.99 [Reserved]

Subpart B—Flight Rules

Source: Docket No. 18334, 54 FR 34294, Aug. 18, 1989, unless otherwise noted.

General

§91.101 Applicability.

This subpart prescribes flight rules governing the operation of aircraft within the United States and within 12 nautical miles from the coast of the United States.

§91.103 Preflight action.

Each pilot in command shall, before beginning a flight, become familiar with all available information concerning that flight. This information must include—

(a) For a flight under IFR or a flight not in the vicinity of an airport, weather reports and forecasts, fuel requirements, alternatives available if the planned flight cannot be completed, and any known traffic delays of which the pilot in command has been advised by ATC;

(b) For any flight, runway lengths at airports of intended use, and the following takeoff and landing distance information:

(1) For civil aircraft for which an approved Airplane or Rotorcraft Flight Manual containing takeoff and landing distance data is required, the takeoff and landing distance data contained therein; and

(2) For civil aircraft other than those specified in paragraph (b)(1) of this section, other reliable information appropriate to the aircraft, relating to aircraft performance under expected values of airport elevation and runway slope, aircraft gross weight, and wind and temperature.

§91.105 Flight crewmembers at stations.

(a) During takeoff and landing, and while en route, each required flight crewmember shall—

(1) Be at the crewmember station unless the absence is necessary to perform duties in connection with the operation of the aircraft or in connection with physiological needs; and

(2) Keep the safety belt fastened while at the crewmember station.

(b) Each required flight crewmember of a U.S.-registered civil aircraft shall, during takeoff and landing, keep the shoulder harness fastened while at his or her assigned duty station. This paragraph does not apply if—

(1) The seat at the crewmember's station is not equipped with a shoulder harness; or

(2) The crewmember would be unable to perform required duties with the shoulder harness fastened.

[Docket No. 18334, 54 FR 34294, Aug. 18, 1989; as amended by Amdt. 91–231, 57 FR 42671, Sept. 15, 1992]

§91.107 Use of safety belts, shoulder harnesses, and child restraint systems.

(a) Unless otherwise authorized by the Administrator—

(1) No pilot may take off a U.S.-registered civil aircraft (except a free balloon that incorporates a basket or gondola, or an airship type certificated before November 2, 1987) unless the pilot in command of that aircraft ensures that each person on board is briefed on how to fasten and unfasten that person's safety belt and, if installed, shoulder harness.

(2) No pilot may cause to be moved on the surface, take off, or land a U.S.-registered civil aircraft (except a free balloon that incorporates a basket or gondola, or an airship certificated before November 2, 1987) unless the pilot in command of that aircraft ensures that each person on board has been notified to fasten his or her safety belt and, if installed, his or her shoulder harness.

(3) Except as provided in this paragraph, each person on board a U.S.-registered civil aircraft (except a free balloon that incorporates a basket or gondola or an airship certificated before November 2, 1987) must occupy an approved seat or berth with a safety belt and, if installed, shoulder harness, properly secured about him or her during movement on the surface, takeoff and landing. For seaplane and float equipped rotorcraft operations during movement on the surface, the person pushing off the seaplane or rotorcraft from the dock and the person mooring the seaplane or rotor craft at the dock are excepted from the preceding seating and safety belt requirements. Notwithstanding the preceding requirements of this paragraph, a person may:

(i) Be held by an adult who is occupying an approved seat or berth, provided that the person being held has not reached his or her second birthday and does not occupy or use any restraining device;

(ii) Use the floor of the aircraft as a seat, provided that the person is on board for the purpose of engaging in sport parachuting; or

(iii) Notwithstanding any other requirement of this chapter, occupy an approved child restraint system furnished by the operator or one of the persons described in paragraph (a)(3)(iii)(A) of this section provided that:

(A) The child is accompanied by a parent, guardian, or attendant designated by the child's parent or guardian to attend to the safety of the child during flight;

(B) Except as provided in paragraph (a)(3)(iii)(B)(*4*) of this action, the approved child restraint system bears one or more labels as follows:

(1) Seats manufactured to U.S. standards between January 1, 1981, and February 25, 1985, must bear the label: "This child restraint system conforms to all applicable Federal motor vehicle safety standards.";

(2) Seats manufactured to U.S. standards on or after February 26, 1985, must bear two labels:

(i) "This child restraint system conforms to all applicable Federal motor vehicle safety standards;" and

(ii) "THIS RESTRAINT IS CERTIFIED FOR USE IN MOTOR VEHICLES AND AIRCRAFT" in red lettering;

(3) Seats that do not qualify under paragraphs (a)(3)(iii)(B)(*1*) and (a)(3)(iii)(B)(*2*) of this section must bear either a label showing approval of a foreign government or a label showing that the seat was manufactured under the standards of the United Nations;

(4) Notwithstanding any other provision of this section, booster-type child restraint systems (as defined in Federal Motor Vehicle Safety Standard No. 213 (49 CFR 571.213)), vest- and harness-type child restraint systems, and lap held child restraints are not approved for use in aircraft; and

(C) The operator complies with the following requirements:

(1) The restraint system must be properly secured to an approved forward-facing seat or berth:

(2) The child must be properly secured in the restraint system and must not exceed the specified weight limit for the restraint system; and

(3) The restraint system must bear the appropriate label(s).

(b) Unless otherwise stated, this section does not apply to operations conducted under part 121, 125, or 135 of this chapter. Paragraph (a)(3) of this section does not apply to person subject to §91.105.

[Docket No. 26142, 57 FR 42671, Sept. 15, 1992; as amended by Amdt. 91–250, 61 FR 28421, June 4, 1996]

§91.109 Flight instruction; Simulated instrument flight and certain flight tests.

(a) No person may operate a civil aircraft (except a manned free balloon) that is being used for flight instruction unless that aircraft has fully functioning dual controls. However, instrument flight instruction may be given in a single-engine airplane equipped with a single, functioning throwover control wheel in place of fixed, dual controls of the elevator and ailerons when—

(1) The instructor has determined that the flight can be conducted safely; and

(2) The person manipulating the controls has at least a private pilot certificate with appropriate category and class ratings.

(b) No person may operate a civil aircraft in simulated instrument flight unless—

(1) The other control seat is occupied by a safety pilot who possesses at least a private pilot certificate with category and class ratings appropriate to the aircraft being flown.

(2) The safety pilot has adequate vision forward and to each side of the aircraft, or a competent observer in the aircraft adequately supplements the vision of the safety pilot; and

(3) Except in the case of lighter-than-air aircraft, that aircraft is equipped with fully functioning dual controls. However, simulated instrument flight may be conducted in a single-engine airplane, equipped with a single, functioning, throwover control wheel, in place of fixed, dual controls of the elevator and ailerons, when—

(i) The safety pilot has determined that the flight can be conducted safely; and

(ii) The person manipulating the controls has at least a private pilot certificate with appropriate category and class ratings.

(c) No person may operate a civil aircraft that is being used for a flight test for an airline transport pilot certificate or a class or type rating on that certificate, or for a part 121 proficiency flight test, unless the pilot seated at the controls, other than the pilot being checked, is fully qualified to act as pilot in command of the aircraft.

§91.111 Operating near other aircraft.

(a) No person may operate an aircraft so close to another aircraft as to create a collision hazard.

(b) No person may operate an aircraft in formation flight except by arrangement with the pilot in command of each aircraft in the formation.

(c) No person may operate an aircraft, carrying passengers for hire, in formation flight.

§91.113 Right-of-way rules: Except water operations.

(a) *Inapplicability.* This section does not apply to the operation of an aircraft on water.

(b) *General.* When weather conditions permit, regardless of whether an operation is conducted under instrument flight rules or visual flight rules, vigilance shall be maintained by each person operating an aircraft so as to see and avoid other aircraft. When a rule of this section gives another aircraft the right-of-way, the pilot shall give way to that aircraft and may not pass over, under, or ahead of it unless well clear.

(c) *In distress.* An aircraft in distress has the right-of-way over all other air traffic.

(d) *Converging.* When aircraft of the same category are converging at approximately the same altitude (except head-on, or nearly so), the aircraft to the other's right has the right-of-way. If the aircraft are of different categories—

(1) A balloon has the right-of-way over any other category of aircraft;

(2) A glider has the right-of-way over an airship, powered parachute, weight-shift-control aircraft, airplane, or rotorcraft.

(3) An airship has the right-of-way over a powered parachute, weight-shift-control aircraft, airplane, or rotorcraft.

However, an aircraft towing or refueling other aircraft has the right-of-way over all other engine-driven aircraft.

(e) *Approaching head-on.* When aircraft are approaching each other head-on, or nearly so, each pilot of each aircraft shall alter course to the right.

(f) *Overtaking.* Each aircraft that is being overtaken has the right-of-way and each pilot of an overtaking aircraft shall alter course to the right to pass well clear.

(g) *Landing.* Aircraft, while on final approach to land or while landing, have the right-of-way over other aircraft in flight or operating on the surface, except that they shall not take advantage of this rule to force an aircraft off the runway surface which has already landed and is attempting to make way for an aircraft on final approach. When two or more aircraft are approaching an airport for the purpose of landing, the aircraft at the lower altitude has the right-of-way, but it shall not take advantage of this rule to cut in front of another which is on final approach to land or to overtake that aircraft.

[Docket No. 18334, 54 FR 34294, Aug. 18, 1989; as amended by Amdt. 91–282, 69 FR 44880, July 27, 2004]

§91.115 Right-of-way rules: Water operations.

(a) *General.* Each person operating an aircraft on the water shall, insofar as possible, keep clear of all vessels and avoid impeding their navigation, and shall give way to any vessel or other aircraft that is given the right-of-way by any rule of this section.

(b) *Crossing.* When aircraft, or an aircraft and a vessel, are on crossing courses, the aircraft or vessel to the other's right has the right-of-way.

(c) *Approaching head-on.* When aircraft, or an aircraft and a vessel, are approaching head-on, or nearly so, each shall alter its course to the right to keep well clear.

(d) *Overtaking.* Each aircraft or vessel that is being overtaken has the right-of-way, and the one overtaking shall alter course to keep well clear.

(e) *Special circumstances.* When aircraft, or an aircraft and a vessel, approach so as to involve risk of collision, each aircraft or vessel shall proceed with careful regard to existing circumstances, including the limitations of the respective craft.

§91.117 Aircraft speed.

(a) Unless otherwise authorized by the Administrator, no person may operate an aircraft below 10,000 feet MSL at an indicated airspeed of more than 250 knots (288 m.p.h.).

(b) Unless otherwise authorized or required by ATC, no person may operate an aircraft at or below 2,500 feet above the surface within 4 nautical miles of the primary airport of a Class C or Class D airspace area at an indicated airspeed of more than 200 knots (230 m.p.h.). This paragraph (b) does not apply to any operations within a Class B airspace area. Such operations shall comply with paragraph (a) of this section.

(c) No person may operate an aircraft in the airspace underlying a Class B airspace area designated for an airport or in a VFR corridor designated through such a Class B airspace area, at an indicated airspeed of more than 200 knots (230 mph).

(d) If the minimum safe airspeed for any particular operation is greater than the maximum speed prescribed in this section, the aircraft may be operated at that minimum speed.

[Docket No. 18334, 54 FR 34292, Aug. 18, 1989; as amended by Amdt. 91–219, 55 FR 34708, Aug. 24, 1990; Amdt. 91–227, 56 FR 65657, Dec. 17, 1991; Amdt. 91–233, 58 FR 43554, Aug. 17, 1993]

§91.119 Minimum safe altitudes: General.

Except when necessary for takeoff or landing, no person may operate an aircraft below the following altitudes:

(a) *Anywhere.* An altitude allowing, if a power unit fails, an emergency landing without undue hazard to persons or property on the surface.

(b) *Over congested areas.* Over any congested area of a city, town, or settlement, or over any open air assembly of persons, an altitude of 1,000 feet above the highest obstacle within a horizontal radius of 2,000 feet of the aircraft.

(c) *Over other than congested areas.* An altitude of 500 feet above the surface, except over open water or sparsely populated areas. In those cases, the aircraft may not be operated closer than 500 feet to any person, vessel, vehicle, or structure.

(d) *Helicopters.* Helicopters may be operated at less than the minimums prescribed in paragraph (b) or (c) of this section if the operation is conducted without hazard to persons or property on the surface. In addition, each person operating a helicopter shall comply with any routes or altitudes specifically prescribed for helicopters by the Administrator.

§91.121 Altimeter settings.

(a) Each person operating an aircraft shall maintain the cruising altitude or flight level of that aircraft, as the case may be, by reference to an altimeter that is set, when operating—

(1) Below 18,000 feet MSL, to—

(i) The current reported altimeter setting of a station along the route and within 100 nautical miles of the aircraft;

(ii) If there is no station within the area prescribed in paragraph (a)(1)(i) of this section, the current reported altimeter setting of an appropriate available station; or

(iii) In the case of an aircraft not equipped with a radio, the elevation of the departure airport or an appropriate altimeter setting available before departure; or

(2) At or above 18,000 feet MSL, to 29.92" Hg.

(b) The lowest usable flight level is determined by the atmospheric pressure in the area of operation as shown in the following table:

Current altimeter setting	Lowest usable flight level
29.92 (or higher)	180
29.91 through 29.42	185
29.41 through 28.92	190
28.91 through 28.42	195
28.41 through 27.92	200
27.91 through 27.42	205
27.41 through 26.92	210

(c) To convert minimum altitude prescribed under §§91.119 and 91.177 to the minimum flight level, the pilot shall take the flight level equivalent of the minimum altitude in feet and add the appropriate number of feet specified below, according to the current reported altimeter setting:

Current altimeter setting	Adjustment factor
29.92 (or higher)	None
29.91 through 29.42	500
29.41 through 28.92	1,000
28.91 through 28.42	1,500
28.41 through 27.92	2,000
27.91 through 27.42	2,500
27.41 through 26.92	3,000

§91.123 Compliance with ATC clearances and instructions.

(a) When an ATC clearance has been obtained, no pilot in command may deviate from that clearance unless an amended clearance is obtained, an emergency exists, or the deviation is in response to a traffic alert and collision avoidance system resolution advisory. However, except in Class A airspace, a pilot may cancel an IFR flight plan if the operation is being conducted in VFR weather conditions. When a pilot is uncertain of an ATC clearance, that pilot shall immediately request clarification from ATC.

(b) Except in an emergency, no person may operate an aircraft contrary to an ATC instruction in an area in which air traffic control is exercised.

(c) Each pilot in command who, in an emergency, or in response to a traffic alert and collision avoidance system resolution advisory, deviates from an ATC clearance or instruction shall notify ATC of that deviation as soon as possible.

(d) Each pilot in command who (though not deviating from a rule of this subpart) is given priority by ATC in an emergency, shall submit a detailed report of that emergency within 48 hours to the manager of that ATC facility, if requested by ATC.

(e) Unless otherwise authorized by ATC, no person operating an aircraft may operate that aircraft according to any clearance or instruction that has been issued to the pilot of another aircraft for radar air traffic control purposes.

(Approved by the Office of Management and Budget under control number 2120–0005)

[Docket No. 18834, 54 FR 34294, Aug. 18, 1989; as amended by Amdt. 91–227, 56 FR 65658, Dec. 17, 1991; Amdt. 91–244, 60 FR 50679, Sept. 29, 1995]

§91.125 ATC light signals.

ATC light signals have the meaning shown in the following table:

Color and type of signal	Meaning with respect to aircraft on the surface	Meaning with respect to aircraft in flight
Steady green	Cleared for takeoff	Cleared to land
Flashing green	Cleared to taxi	Return for landing (to be followed by steady green at proper time)
Steady red	Stop	Give way to other aircraft and continue circling
Flashing red	Taxi clear of runway in use	Airport unsafe — do not land
Flashing white	Return to starting point on airport	Not applicable
Alternating red and green	Exercise extreme caution	Exercise extreme caution

§91.126 Operating on or in the vicinity of an airport in Class G airspace.

(a) *General.* Unless otherwise authorized or required, each person operating an aircraft on or in the vicinity of an airport in a Class G airspace area must comply with the requirements of this section.

(b) *Direction of turns.* When approaching to land at an airport without an operating control tower in Class G airspace—

(1) Each pilot of an airplane must make all turns of that airplane to the left unless the airport displays approved light signals or visual markings indicating that turns should be made to the right, in which case the pilot must make all turns to the right; and

(2) Each pilot of a helicopter or a powered parachute must avoid the flow of fixed-wing aircraft.

(c) *Flap settings.* Except when necessary for training or certification, the pilot in command of a civil turbojet-powered aircraft must use, as a final flap setting, the minimum certificated landing flap setting set forth in the approved performance information in the Airplane Flight Manual for the applicable conditions. However, each pilot in command has the final authority and responsibility for the safe operation of the pilot's airplane, and may use a different flap setting for that airplane if the pilot determines that it is necessary in the interest of safety.

(d) *Communications with control towers.* Unless otherwise authorized or required by ATC, no person may operate an aircraft to, from, through, or on an airport having an operational control tower unless two-way radio communications are maintained between that aircraft and the control tower. Communications must be established prior to 4 nautical miles from the airport, up to and including 2,500 feet AGL. However, if the aircraft radio fails in flight, the pilot in command may operate that aircraft and land if weather conditions are at or above basic VFR weather minimums, visual contact with the tower is maintained, and a clearance to land is received. If the aircraft radio fails while in flight under IFR, the pilot must comply with §91.185.

[Docket No. 24458, 56 FR 65658, Dec. 17, 1991; as amended by Amdt. 91–239, 59 FR 11693, March 11, 1994; Amdt. 91–282, 69 FR 44880, July 27, 2004]

§91.127 Operating on or in the vicinity of an airport in Class E airspace.

(a) Unless otherwise required by part 93 of this chapter or unless otherwise authorized or required by the ATC facility having jurisdiction over the Class E airspace area, each person operating an aircraft on or in the vicinity of an airport in a Class E airspace area must comply with the requirements of §91.126.

(b) *Departures.* Each pilot of an aircraft must comply with any traffic patterns established for that airport in part 93 of this chapter.

(c) *Communications with control towers.* Unless otherwise authorized or required by ATC, no person may operate an aircraft to, from, through, or on an airport having an operational control tower unless two-way radio communications are maintained between that aircraft and the control tower. Communications must be established prior to 4 nautical miles from the airport, up to and including 2,500 feet AGL. However, if the aircraft radio fails in flight, the pilot in command may operate that aircraft and land if weather conditions are at or above basic VFR weather minimums, visual contact with the tower is maintained, and a clearance to land is received. If the aircraft radio fails while in flight under IFR, the pilot must comply with §91.185.

[Docket No. 24458, 56 FR 65658, Dec. 17, 1991; as amended by Amdt. 91–239, 59 FR 11693, March 11, 1994]

§91.129 Operations in Class D airspace.

(a) *General.* Unless otherwise authorized or required by the ATC facility having jurisdiction over the Class D airspace area, each person operating an aircraft in Class D airspace must comply with the applicable provisions of this section. In addition, each person must comply with §§91.126 and 91.127. For the purpose of this section, the primary airport is the airport for which the Class D airspace area is designated. A satellite airport is any other airport within the Class D airspace area.

(b) *Deviations.* An operator may deviate from any provision of this section under the provisions of an ATC authorization issued by the ATC facility having jurisdiction over the airspace concerned. ATC may authorize a deviation on a continuing basis or for an individual flight, as appropriate.

(c) *Communications.* Each person operating an aircraft in Class D airspace must meet the following two-way radio communications requirements:

(1) *Arrival or through flight.* Each person must establish two-way radio communications with the ATC facility (including foreign ATC in the case of foreign airspace designated in the United States) providing air traffic services prior to enter-

ing that airspace and thereafter maintain those communications while within that airspace.

(2) *Departing flight.* Each person—

(i) From the primary airport or satellite airport with an operating control tower must establish and maintain two-way radio communications with the control tower, and thereafter as instructed by ATC while operating in the Class D airspace area; or

(ii) From a satellite airport without an operating control tower, must establish and maintain two-way radio communications with the ATC facility having jurisdiction over the Class D airspace area as soon as practicable after departing.

(d) *Communications failure.* Each person who operates an aircraft in a Class D airspace area must maintain two-way radio communications with the ATC facility having jurisdiction over that area.

(1) If the aircraft radio fails in flight under IFR, the pilot must comply with §91.185 of the part.

(2) If the aircraft radio fails in flight under VFR, the pilot in command may operate that aircraft and land if—

(i) Weather conditions are at or above basic VFR weather minimums;

(ii) Visual contact with the tower is maintained; and

(iii) A clearance to land is received.

(e) *Minimum altitudes.* When operating to an airport in Class D airspace, each pilot of—

(1) A large or turbine-powered airplane shall, unless otherwise required by the applicable distance from cloud criteria, enter the traffic pattern at an altitude of at least 1,500 feet above the elevation of the airport and maintain at least 1,500 feet until further descent is required for a safe landing.

(2) A large or turbine-powered airplane approaching to land on a runway served by an instrument landing system (ILS), if the airplane is ILS equipped, shall fly that airplane at an altitude at or above the glide slope between the outer marker (or point of interception of glide slope, if compliance with the applicable distance from cloud criteria requires interception closer in) and the middle marker; and

(3) An airplane approaching to land on a runway served by a visual approach slope indicator shall maintain an altitude at or above the glide slope until a lower altitude is necessary for a safe landing.

Paragraphs (e)(2) and (e)(3) of this section do not prohibit normal bracketing maneuvers above or below the glide slope that are conducted for the purpose of remaining on the glide slope.

(f) *Approaches.* Except when conducting a circling approach under Part 97 of this chapter or unless otherwise required by ATC, each pilot must—

(1) Circle the airport to the left, if operating an airplane; or

(2) Avoid the flow of fixed-wing aircraft, if operating a helicopter.

(g) *Departures.* No person may operate an aircraft departing from an airport except in compliance with the following:

(1) Each pilot must comply with any departure procedures established for that airport by the FAA.

(2) Unless otherwise required by the prescribed departure procedure for that airport or the applicable distance from clouds criteria, each pilot of a turbine-powered airplane and each pilot of a large airplane must climb to an altitude of 1,500 feet above the surface as rapidly as practicable.

(h) *Noise abatement.* Where a formal runway use program has been established by the FAA, each pilot of a large or turbine-powered airplane assigned a noise abatement runway by ATC must use that runway. However, consistent with the final authority of the pilot in command concerning the safe operation of the aircraft as prescribed in §91.3(a), ATC may assign a different runway if requested by the pilot in the interest of safety.

(i) *Takeoff, landing, taxi clearance.* No person may, at any airport with an operating control tower, operate an aircraft on a runway or taxiway, or take off or land an aircraft, unless an appropriate clearance is received from ATC. A clearance to "taxi to" the takeoff runway assigned to the aircraft is not a clearance to cross that assigned takeoff runway, or to taxi on that runway at any point, but is a clearance to cross other runways that intersect the taxi route to that assigned takeoff runway. A clearance to "taxi to" any point other than an assigned takeoff runway is clearance to cross all runways that intersect the taxi route to that point.

[Docket No. 24458, 56 FR 65658, Dec. 17, 1991; as amended by Amdt. 91–234, 58 FR 48793, Sept. 20, 1993]

§91.130 Operations in Class C airspace.

(a) *General.* Unless otherwise authorized by ATC each aircraft operation in Class C airspace must be conducted in compliance with this section and §91.129. For the purpose of this section, the primary airport is the airport for which the Class C airspace area is designated. A satellite airport is any other airport within the Class C airspace area.

(b) *Traffic patterns.* No person may take off or land an aircraft at a satellite airport within a Class C airspace area except in compliance with FAA arrival and departure traffic patterns.

(c) *Communications.* Each person operating an aircraft in Class C airspace must meet the following two-way radio communications requirements:

(1) *Arrival or through flight.* Each person must establish two-way radio communications with the ATC facility (including foreign ATC in the case of foreign airspace designated in the United States) providing air traffic services prior to entering that airspace and thereafter maintain those communications while within that airspace.

(2) *Departing flight.* Each person—

(i) From the primary airport or satellite airport with an operating control tower must establish and maintain two-way radio communications with the control tower, and thereafter as instructed by ATC while operating in the Class C airspace area; or

(ii) From a satellite airport without an operating control tower, must establish and maintain two-way radio communications with the ATC facility having jurisdiction over the Class C airspace area as soon as practicable after departing.

(d) *Equipment requirements.* Unless otherwise authorized by the ATC having jurisdiction over the Class C airspace area, no person may operate an aircraft within a Class C airspace area designated for an airport unless that aircraft is equipped with the applicable equipment specified in §91.215.

(e) *Deviations.* An operator may deviate from any provision of this section under the provisions of an ATC authorization issued by the ATC facility having jurisdiction over the airspace concerned. ATC may authorize a deviation on a continuing basis or for an individual flight, as appropriate.

[Docket No. 24458, 56 FR 65659, Dec. 17, 1991; as amended by Amdt. 91–232, 58 FR 40736, July 30, 1993; Amdt. 91–239, 59 FR 11693, March 11, 1994]

§91.131 Operations in Class B airspace.

(a) *Operating rules.* No person may operate an aircraft within a Class B airspace area except in compliance with §91.129 and the following rules:

(1) The operator must receive an ATC clearance from the ATC facility having jurisdiction for that area before operating an aircraft in that area.

(2) Unless otherwise authorized by ATC, each person operating a large turbine engine-powered airplane to or from a primary airport for which a Class B airspace area is designated must operate at or above the designated floors of the Class B airspace area while within the lateral limits of that area.

(3) Any person conducting pilot training operations at an airport within a Class B airspace area must comply with any procedures established by ATC for such operations in that area.

(b) *Pilot requirements.*

(1) No person may take off or land a civil aircraft at an airport within a Class B airspace area or operate a civil aircraft within a Class B airspace area unless—

(i) The pilot in command holds at least a private pilot certificate;

(ii) The pilot in command holds a recreational pilot certificate and has met—

(A) The requirements of §61.101(d) of this chapter; or

(B) The requirements for a student pilot seeking a recreational pilot certificate in §61.94 of this chapter;

(iii) The pilot in command holds a sport pilot certificate and has met—

(A) The requirements of §61.325 of this chapter; or

(B) The requirements for a student pilot seeking a recreational pilot certificate in §61.94 of this chapter; or

(iv) The aircraft is operated by a student pilot who has met the requirements of §61.94 or §61.95 of this chapter, as applicable.

(2) Notwithstanding the provisions of paragraphs (b)(1)(ii), (b)(1)(iii) and (b)(1)(iv) of this section, no person may take off or land a civil aircraft at those airports listed in section 4 of appendix D to this part unless the pilot in command holds at least a private pilot certificate.

(c) *Communications and navigation equipment requirements.* Unless otherwise authorized by ATC, no person may operate an aircraft within a Class B airspace area unless that aircraft is equipped with—

(1) For IFR operation. An operable VOR or TACAN receiver; and

(2) For all operations. An operable two-way radio capable of communications with ATC on appropriate frequencies for that Class B airspace area.

(d) *Transponder requirements.* No person may operate an aircraft in a Class B airspace area unless the aircraft is equipped with the applicable operating transponder and automatic altitude reporting equipment specified in paragraph (a) of §91.215, except as provided in paragraph (d) of that section.

[Docket No. 24458, 56 FR 65658, Dec. 17, 1991; Amdt. 91–282, 69 FR 44880, July 27, 2004]

§91.133 Restricted and prohibited areas.

(a) No person may operate an aircraft within a restricted area (designated in part 73) contrary to the restrictions imposed, or within a prohibited area, unless that person has the permission of the using or controlling agency, as appropriate.

(b) Each person conducting, within a restricted area, an aircraft operation (approved by the using agency) that creates the same hazards as the operations for which the restricted area was designated may deviate from the rules of this subpart that are not compatible with the operation of the aircraft.

§91.135 Operations in Class A airspace.

Except as provided in paragraph (d) of this section, each person operating an aircraft in Class A airspace must conduct that operation under instrument flight rules (IFR) and in compliance with the following:

(a) *Clearance.* Operations may be conducted only under an ATC clearance received prior to entering the airspace.

(b) *Communications.* Unless otherwise authorized by ATC, each aircraft operating in Class A airspace must be equipped with a two-way radio capable of communicating with ATC on a frequency assigned by ATC. Each pilot must maintain two-way radio communications with ATC while operating in Class A airspace.

(c) *Transponder requirement.* Unless otherwise authorized by ATC, no person may operate an aircraft within Class A airspace unless that aircraft is equipped with the applicable equipment specified in §91.215.

(d) *ATC authorizations.* An operator may deviate from any provision of this section under the provisions of an ATC authorization issued by the ATC facility having jurisdiction of the airspace concerned. In the case of an inoperative transponder, ATC may immediately approve an operation within a Class A airspace area allowing flight to continue, if desired, to the airport of ultimate destination, including any intermediate stops, or to proceed to a place where suitable repairs can be made, or both. Requests for deviation from any provision of this section must be submitted in writing, at least 4 days before the proposed operation. ATC may authorize a deviation on a continuing basis or for an individual flight.

[Docket No. 24458, 56 FR 65659, Dec. 17, 1991]

§91.137 Temporary flight restrictions in the vicinity of disaster/hazard areas.

(a) The Administrator will issue a Notice to Airmen (NOTAM) designating an area within which temporary flight restrictions apply and specifying the hazard or condition requiring their imposition, whenever he determines it is necessary in order to—

(1) Protect persons and property on the surface or in the air from a hazard associated with an incident on the surface;

(2) Provide a safe environment for the operation of disaster relief aircraft; or

(3) Prevent an unsafe congestion of sightseeing and other aircraft above an incident or event which may generate a high degree of public interest.

The Notice to Airmen will specify the hazard or condition that requires the imposition of temporary flight restrictions.

(b) When a NOTAM has been issued under paragraph (a)(1) of this section, no person may operate an aircraft within the designated area unless that aircraft is participating in the hazard relief activities and is being operated under the direction of the official in charge of on scene emergency response activities.

(c) When a NOTAM has been issued under paragraph (a)(2) of this section, no person may operate an aircraft within the designated area unless at least one of the following conditions are met:

(1) The aircraft is participating in hazard relief activities and is being operated under the direction of the official in charge of on scene emergency response activities.

(2) The aircraft is carrying law enforcement officials.

(3) The aircraft is operating under the ATC approved IFR flight plan.

(4) The operation is conducted directly to or from an airport within the area, or is necessitated by the impracticability of VFR flight above or around the area due to weather, or terrain; notification is given to the Flight Service Station (FSS) or ATC facility specified in the NOTAM to receive advisories concerning disaster relief aircraft operations; and the operation does not hamper or endanger relief activities and is not conducted for the purpose of observing the disaster.

(5) The aircraft is carrying properly accredited news representatives, and, prior to entering the area, a flight plan is filed with the appropriate FAA or ATC facility specified in the Notice to Airmen and the operation is conducted above the altitude used by the disaster relief aircraft, unless otherwise authorized by the official in charge of on scene emergency response activities.

(d) When a NOTAM has been issued under paragraph (a)(3) of this section, no person may operate an aircraft within the designated area unless at least one of the following conditions is met:

(1) The operation is conducted directly to or from an airport within the area, or is necessitated by the impracticability of VFR flight above or around the area due to weather or terrain, and the operation is not conducted for the purpose of observing the incident or event.

(2) The aircraft is operating under an ATC approved IFR flight plan.

(3) The aircraft is carrying incident or event personnel, or law enforcement officials.

(4) The aircraft is carrying properly accredited news representatives and, prior to entering that area, a flight plan is filed with the appropriate FSS or ATC facility specified in the NOTAM.

(e) Flight plans filed and notifications made with an FSS or ATC facility under this section shall include the following information:

(1) Aircraft identification, type and color.

(2) Radio communications frequencies to be used.

(3) Proposed times of entry of, and exit from, the designated area.

(4) Name of news media or organization and purpose of flight.

(5) Any other information requested by ATC.

[Docket No. 26476, 56 FR 23178, May 20, 1991; as amended by Amdt. 91–270, 66 FR 47377, Sept. 11, 2001]

§91.138 Temporary flight restrictions in national disaster areas in the State of Hawaii.

(a) When the Administrator has determined, pursuant to a request and justification provided by the Governor of the State of Hawaii, or the Governor's designee, that an inhabited area within a declared national disaster area in the State of Hawaii is in need of protection for humanitarian reasons, the Administrator will issue a Notice to Airmen (NOTAM) designating an area within which temporary flight restrictions apply. The Administrator will designate the extent and duration of the temporary flight restrictions necessary to provide for the protection of persons and property on the surface.

(b) When a NOTAM has been issued in accordance with this section, no person may operate an aircraft within the designated area unless at least one of the following conditions is met:

(1) That person has obtained authorization from the official in charge of associated emergency or disaster relief response activities, and is operating the aircraft under the conditions of that authorization.

(2) The aircraft is carrying law enforcement officials.

(3) The aircraft is carrying persons involved in an emergency or a legitimate scientific purpose.

(4) The aircraft is carrying properly accredited newspersons, and that prior to entering the area, a flight plan is filed with the appropriate FAA or ATC facility specified in the NOTAM and the operation is conducted in compliance with the conditions and restrictions established by the official in charge of on-scene emergency response activities.

(5) The aircraft is operating in accordance with an ATC clearance or instruction.

(c) A NOTAM issued under this section is effective for 90 days or until the national disaster area designation is terminated, whichever comes first, unless terminated by notice or extended by the Administrator at the request of the Governor of the State of Hawaii or the Governor's designee.

[Docket No. 26476, 56 FR 23178, May 20, 1991; as amended by Amdt. 91–270, 66 FR 47377, Sept. 11, 2001]

§91.139 Emergency air traffic rules.

(a) This section prescribes a process for utilizing Notices to Airmen (NOTAMs) to advise of the issuance and operations under emergency air traffic rules and regulations and designates the official who is authorized to issue NOTAMs on behalf of the Administrator in certain matters under this section.

(b) Whenever the Administrator determines that an emergency condition exists, or will exist, relating to the FAA's ability to operate the air traffic control system and during which normal flight operations under this chapter cannot be conducted consistent with the required levels of safety and efficiency—

(1) The Administrator issues an immediately effective air traffic rule or regulation in response to that emergency condition; and

(2) The Administrator or the Associate Administrator for Air Traffic may utilize the NOTAM system to provide notification of the issuance of the rule or regulation.

Those NOTAMs communicate information concerning the rules and regulations that govern flight operations, the use of navigation facilities, and designation of that airspace in which the rules and regulations apply.

(c) When a NOTAM has been issued under this section, no person may operate an aircraft, or other device governed by the regulation concerned, within the designated airspace except in accordance with the authorizations, terms, and conditions prescribed in the regulation covered by the NOTAM.

§91.141 Flight restrictions in the proximity of the Presidential and other parties.

No person may operate an aircraft over or in the vicinity of any area to be visited or traveled by the President, the Vice President, or other public figures contrary to the restrictions established by the Administrator and published in a Notice to Airmen (NOTAM).

§91.143 Flight limitation in the proximity of space flight operations.

When a Notice to Airmen (NOTAM) is issued in accordance with this section, no person may operate any aircraft of U.S. registry, or pilot any aircraft under the authority of an airman certificate issued by the Federal Aviation Administration, within areas designated in a NOTAM for space flight operation except when authorized by ATC.

[Docket No. FAA–2004–19246, 69 FR 59753, Oct. 5, 2004]

§91.144 Temporary restriction on flight operations during abnormally high barometric pressure conditions.

(a) *Special flight restrictions.* When any information indicates that barometric pressure on the route of flight currently exceeds or will exceed 31 inches of mercury, no person may operate an aircraft or initiate a flight contrary to the requirements established by the Administrator and published in a Notice to Airmen issued under this section.

(b) *Waivers.* The administrator is authorized to waive any restriction issued under paragraph (a) of this section to permit emergency supply, transport, or medical services to be delivered to isolated communities, where the operation can be conducted with an acceptable level of safety.

[Docket No. 26806, 59 FR 17452, April 12, 1994; as amended by Amdt. 91–240, 59 FR 37669, July 25, 1994]

§91.145 Management of aircraft operations in the vicinity of aerial demonstrations and major sporting events.

(a) The FAA will issue a Notice to Airmen (NOTAM) designating an area of airspace in which a temporary flight restriction applies when it determines that a temporary flight restriction is necessary to protect persons or property on the surface or in the air, to maintain air safety and efficiency, or to prevent the unsafe congestion of aircraft in the vicinity of an aerial demonstration or major sporting event. These demonstrations and events may include:

(1) United States Naval Flight Demonstration Team (Blue Angels);

(2) United States Air Force Air Demonstration Squadron (Thunderbirds);

(3) United States Army Parachute Team (Golden Knights);

(4) Summer/Winter Olympic Games;

(5) Annual Tournament of Roses Football Game;

(6) World Cup Soccer;

(7) Major League Baseball All-Star Game;

(8) World Series;

(9) Kodak Albuquerque International Balloon Fiesta;

(10) Sandia Classic Hang Gliding Competition;

(11) Indianapolis 500 Mile Race;

(12) Any other aerial demonstration or sporting event the FAA determines to need a temporary flight restriction in accordance with paragraph (b) of this section.

(b) In deciding whether a temporary flight restriction is necessary for an aerial demonstration or major sporting event not listed in paragraph (a) of this section, the FAA considers the following factors:

(1) Area where the event will be held.

(2) Effect flight restrictions will have on known aircraft operations.

(3) Any existing ATC airspace traffic management restrictions.

(4) Estimated duration of the event.

(5) Degree of public interest.

(6) Number of spectators.

(7) Provisions for spectator safety.

(8) Number and types of participating aircraft.

(9) Use of mixed high and low performance aircraft.

(10) Impact on non-participating aircraft.

(11) Weather minimums.

(12) Emergency procedures that will be in effect.

(c) A NOTAM issued under this section will state the name of the aerial demonstration or sporting event and specify the effective dates and times, the geographic features or coordinates, and any other restrictions or procedures governing flight operations in the designated airspace.

(d) When a NOTAM has been issued in accordance with this section, no person may operate an aircraft or device, or engage in any activity within the designated airspace area, except in accordance with the authorizations, terms, and conditions of the temporary flight restriction published in the NOTAM, unless otherwise authorized by:

(1) Air traffic control; or

(2) A Flight Standards Certificate of Waiver or Authorization issued for the demonstration or event.

(e) For the purpose of this section:

(1) Flight restricted airspace area for an aerial demonstration—

The amount of airspace needed to protect persons and property on the surface or in the air, to maintain air safety and efficiency, or to prevent the unsafe congestion of aircraft will vary depending on the aerial demonstration and the factors listed in paragraph (b) of this section. The restricted airspace area will normally be limited to a 5 nautical mile radius from the center of the demonstration and an altitude 17,000 mean sea level (for high performance aircraft) or 13,000 feet above the surface (for certain parachute operations), but will be no greater than the minimum airspace necessary for the management of aircraft operations in the vicinity of the specified area.

(2) Flight restricted area for a major sporting event—

The amount of airspace needed to protect persons and property on the surface or in the air, to maintain air safety and efficiency, or to prevent the unsafe congestion of aircraft will vary depending on the size of the event and the factors listed in paragraph (b) of this section. The restricted airspace will normally be limited to a 3 nautical mile radius from the center of the event and 2,500 feet above the surface but will not be greater than the minimum airspace necessary for the management of aircraft operations in the vicinity of the specified area.

(f) A NOTAM issued under this section will be issued at least 30 days in advance of an aerial demonstration or a major sporting event, unless the FAA finds good cause for a shorter period and explains this in the NOTAM.

(g) When warranted, the FAA Administrator may exclude the following flights from the provisions of this section:

(1) Essential military.

(2) Medical and rescue.

(3) Presidential and Vice Presidential.

(4) Visiting heads of state.

(5) Law enforcement and security.

(6) Public health and welfare.

[Docket No. FAA–2000–8274, 66 FR 47378, Sept. 11, 2001]

§91.146 – 91.149 [Reserved]

Visual Flight Rules

§91.151 Fuel requirements for flight in VFR conditions.

(a) No person may begin a flight in an airplane under VFR conditions unless (considering wind and forecast weather conditions) there is enough fuel to fly to the first point of intended landing and, assuming normal cruising speed—

(1) During the day, to fly after that for at least 30 minutes; or

(2) At night, to fly after that for at least 45 minutes.

(b) No person may begin a flight in a rotorcraft under VFR conditions unless (considering wind and forecast weather conditions) there is enough fuel to fly to the first point of intended landing and, assuming normal cruising speed, to fly after that for at least 20 minutes.

§91.153 VFR flight plan: Information required.

(a) *Information required.* Unless otherwise authorized by ATC, each person filing a VFR flight plan shall include in it the following information:

(1) The aircraft identification number and, if necessary, its radio call sign.

(2) The type of the aircraft or, in the case of a formation flight, the type of each aircraft and the number of aircraft in the formation.

(3) The full name and address of the pilot in command or, in the case of a formation flight, the formation commander.

(4) The point and proposed time of departure.

(5) The proposed route, cruising altitude (or flight level), and true airspeed at that altitude.

(6) The point of first intended landing and the estimated elapsed time until over that point.

(7) The amount of fuel on board (in hours).

(8) The number of persons in the aircraft, except where that information is otherwise readily available to the FAA.

(9) Any other information the pilot in command or ATC believes is necessary for ATC purposes.

(b) *Cancellation.* When a flight plan has been activated, the pilot in command, upon canceling or completing the flight under the flight plan, shall notify an FAA Flight Service Station or ATC facility.

§91.155 Basic VFR weather minimums.

(a) Except as provided in paragraph (b) of this section and §91.157, no person may operate an aircraft under VFR when the flight visibility is less, or at a distance from clouds that is less, than that prescribed for the corresponding altitude and class of airspace in the following table:

Airspace	Flight visibility	Distance from clouds
Class A	Not applicable	Not applicable.
Class B	3 statute miles	Clear of clouds.
Class C	3 statute miles	500 feet below. 1,000 feet above. 2,000 feet horizontal.
Class D	3 statute miles	500 feet below. 1,000 feet above. 2,000 feet horizontal.
Class E: Less than 10,000 feet MSL	3 statute miles	500 feet below. 1,000 feet above. 2,000 feet horizontal.
At or above 10,000 feet MSL	5 statute miles	1,000 feet below. 1,000 feet above. 1 statute mile horizontal.
Class G: 1,200 feet or less above the surface (regardless of MSL altitude)		
Day, except as provided in §91.155(b)	1 statute mile	Clear of clouds.
Night, except as provided in §91.155(b)	3 statute miles	500 feet below. 1,000 feet above. 2,000 feet horizontal.
More than 1,200 feet above the surface but less than 10,000 feet MSL		
Day	1 statute mile	500 feet below. 1,000 feet above. 2,000 feet horizontal.
Night	3 statute miles	500 feet below. 1,000 feet above. 2,000 feet horizontal.
More than 1,200 feet above the surface and at or above 10,000 feet MSL	5 statute miles	1,000 feet below. 1,000 feet above. 1 statute mile horizontal.

(b) *Class G Airspace.* Notwithstanding the provisions of paragraph (a) of this section, the following operations may be conducted in Class G airspace below 1,200 feet above the surface:

(1) *Helicopter.* A helicopter may be operated clear of clouds if operated at a speed that allows the pilot adequate opportunity to see any air traffic or obstruction in time to avoid a collision.

(2) *Airplane, powered parachute, or weight-shift-control aircraft.* If the visibility is less than 3 statute miles but not less than 1 statute mile during night hours and you are operating in an airport traffic pattern within 1/2 mile of the runway, you may operate an airplane, powered parachute, or weight-shift-control aircraft clear of clouds.

(c) Except as provided in §91.157, no person may operate an aircraft beneath the ceiling under VFR within the lateral boundaries of controlled airspace designated to the surface for an airport when the ceiling is less than 1,000 feet.

(d) Except as provided in §91.157 of this part, no person may take off or land an aircraft, or enter the traffic pattern of an airport, under VFR, within the lateral boundaries of the surface areas of Class B, Class C, Class D, or Class E airspace designated for an airport—

(1) Unless ground visibility at that airport is at least 3 statute miles; or

(2) If ground visibility is not reported at that airport, unless flight visibility during landing or takeoff, or while operating in the traffic pattern is at least 3 statute miles.

(e) For the purpose of this section, an aircraft operating at the base altitude of a Class E airspace area is considered to be within the airspace directly below that area.

[Docket No. 24458, 56 FR 65660, Dec. 17, 1991; as amended by Amdt. 91–235, 58 FR 51968, Oct. 5, 1993; Amdt. 91–282, 69 FR 44880, July 27, 2004]

§91.157 Special VFR weather minimums.

(a) Except as provided in Appendix D, section 3, of this part, special VFR operations may be conducted under the weather minimums and requirements of this section, instead of those contained in §91.155, below 10,000 feet MSL within the airspace contained by the upward extension of the lateral boundaries of the controlled airspace designated to the surface for an airport.

(b) Special VFR operations may only be conducted—

(1) With an ATC clearance;

(2) Clear of clouds;

(3) Except for helicopters, when flight visibility is at least 1 statute mile; and

(4) Except for helicopters, between sunrise and sunset (or in Alaska, when the sun is 6 degrees or more below the horizon) unless—

(i) The person being granted the ATC clearance meets the applicable requirements for instrument flight under part 61 of this chapter;

(ii) The aircraft is equipped as required in Part 91.205(d).

(c) No person may take off or land an aircraft (other than a helicopter) under special VFR—

(1) Unless ground visibility is at least 1 statute mile; or

(2) If ground visibility is not reported, unless flight visibility is at least 1 statute mile. For the purposes of this paragraph, the term flight visibility includes the visibility from the cockpit of an aircraft in takeoff position if:

(i) The flight is conducted under this Part 91; and

(ii) The airport at which the aircraft is located is a satellite airport that does not have weather reporting capabilities.

(d) The determination of visibility by a pilot in accordance with paragraph (c)(2) of this section is not an official weather report or an official ground visibility report.

[Docket No. 18334, 54 FR 34294, Aug. 18, 1989; as amended by Amdt. 91–235, 58 FR 51968, Oct. 5, 1993; Amdt. 91–247, 60 FR 66875, Dec. 27, 1995; Amdt. 91–262, 65 FR 16116, March 24, 2000]

§91.159 VFR cruising altitude or flight level.

Except while holding in a holding pattern of 2 minutes or less, or while turning, each person operating an aircraft under VFR in level cruising flight more than 3,000 feet above the surface shall maintain the appropriate altitude or flight level prescribed below, unless otherwise authorized by ATC:

(a) When operating below 18,000 feet MSL and—

(1) On a magnetic course of zero degrees through 179 degrees, any odd thousand foot MSL altitude +500 feet (such as 3,500, 5,500, or 7,500); or

(2) On a magnetic course of 180 degrees through 359 degrees, any even thousand foot MSL altitude +500 feet (such as 4,500, 6,500, or 8,500).

(b) When operating above 18,000 feet MSL, maintain the altitude or flight level assigned by ATC.

[Docket No. 18334, 54 FR 34294, Aug. 18, 1989; as amended by Amdt. 91–276, 68 FR 61321, Oct. 27, 2003; Amdt. 91–276, 68 FR 70133, Dec. 17, 2003]

§91.161 – 91.165 [Reserved]

INSTRUMENT FLIGHT RULES

§91.167 Fuel requirements for flight in IFR conditions.

(a) No person may operate a civil aircraft in IFR conditions unless it carries enough fuel (considering weather reports and forecasts and weather conditions) to—

(1) Complete the flight to the first airport of intended landing;

(2) Except as provided in paragraph (b) of this section, fly from that airport to the alternate airport; and

(3) Fly after that for 45 minutes at normal cruising speed or, for helicopters, fly after that for 30 minutes at normal cruising speed.

(b) Paragraph (a)(2) of this section does not apply if:

(1) Part 97 of this chapter prescribes a standard instrument approach procedure to, or a special instrument approach procedure has been issued by the Administrator to the operator for, the first airport of intended landing; and

(2) Appropriate weather reports or weather forecasts, or a combination of them, indicate the following:

(i) *For aircraft other than helicopters.* For at least 1 hour before and for 1 hour after the estimated time of arrival, the ceiling will be at least 2,000 feet above the airport elevation and the visibility will be at least 3 statute miles.

(ii) *For helicopters.* At the estimated time of arrival and for 1 hour after the estimated time of arrival, the ceiling will be at least 1,000 feet above the airport elevation, or at least 400 feet above the lowest applicable approach minima, whichever is higher, and the visibility will be at least 2 statute miles.

[Docket No. 18334, 54 FR 34294, Aug. 18, 1989; as amended by Amdt. 91–259, 65 FR 3546, Jan. 21, 2000]

§91.169 IFR flight plan: Information required.

(a) *Information required.* Unless otherwise authorized by ATC, each person filing an IFR flight plan must include in it the following information:

(1) Information required under §91.153(a) of this part.

(2) Except as provided in paragraph (b) of this section, an alternate airport.

(b) Paragraph (a)(2) of this section does not apply if:

(1) Part 97 of this chapter prescribes a standard instrument approach procedure to, or a special instrument approach procedure has been issued by the Administrator to the operator for, the first airport of intended landing; and

(2) Appropriate weather reports or weather forecasts, or a combination of them, indicate the following:

(i) *For aircraft other than helicopters.* For at least 1 hour before and for 1 hour after the estimated time of arrival, the ceiling will be at least 2,000 feet above the airport elevation and the visibility will be at least 3 statute miles.

(ii) *For helicopters.* At the estimated time of arrival and for 1 hour after the estimated time of arrival, the ceiling will be at least 1,000 feet above the airport elevation, or at least 400 feet above the lowest applicable approach minima, whichever is higher, and the visibility will be at least 2 statute miles.

(c) *IFR alternate airport weather minimums.* Unless otherwise authorized by the Administrator, no person may include an alternate airport in an IFR flight plan unless appropriate weather reports or forecasts, or a combination of them, indicate that, at the estimated time of arrival at the alternate airport, the ceiling and visibility at that airport will be at or above the following weather minima:

(1) If an instrument approach procedure has been published in part 97 of this chapter, or a special instrument approach procedure has been issued by the Administrator to the operator, for that airport, the following minima:

(i) *For aircraft other than helicopters.* The alternate airport minima specified in that procedure, or if none are specified the following standard approach minima:

(A) *For a precision approach procedure.* Ceiling 600 feet and visibility 2 statute miles.

(B) *For a nonprecision approach procedure.* Ceiling 800 feet and visibility 2 statute miles.

(ii) *For helicopters.* Ceiling 200 feet above the minimum for the approach to be flown, and visibility at least 1 statute mile but never less than the minimum visibility for the approach to be flown, and

(2) If no instrument approach procedure has been published in part 97 of this chapter and no special instrument approach procedure has been issued by the Administrator to the operator, for the alternate airport, the ceiling and visibility minima are those allowing descent from the MEA, approach, and landing under basic VFR.

(d) *Cancellation.* When a flight plan has been activated, the pilot in command, upon canceling or completing the flight under the flight plan, shall notify an FAA Flight Service Station or ATC facility.

[Docket No. 18334, 54 FR 34294, Aug. 18, 1989; as amended by Amdt. 91–259, 65 FR 3546, Jan. 21, 2000]

§91.171 VOR equipment check for IFR operations.

(a) No person may operate a civil aircraft under IFR using the VOR system of radio navigation unless the VOR equipment of that aircraft—

(1) Is maintained, checked, and inspected under an approved procedure; or

(2) Has been operationally checked within the preceding 30 days, and was found to be within the limits of the permissible indicated bearing error set forth in paragraph (b) or (c) of this section.

(b) Except as provided in paragraph (c) of this section, each person conducting a VOR check under paragraph (a)(2) of this section shall—

(1) Use, at the airport of intended departure, an FAA-operated or approved test signal or a test signal radiated by a certificated and appropriately rated radio repair station or, outside the United States, a test signal operated or approved by an appropriate authority to check the VOR equipment (the maximum permissible indicated bearing error is plus or minus 4 degrees); or

(2) Use, at the airport of intended departure, a point on the airport surface designated as a VOR system checkpoint by the Administrator, or, outside the United States, by an appropriate authority (the maximum permissible bearing error is plus or minus 4 degrees);

(3) If neither a test signal nor a designated checkpoint on the surface is available, use an airborne checkpoint designated by the Administrator or, outside the United States, by an appropriate authority (the maximum permissible bearing error is plus or minus 6 degrees); or

(4) If no check signal or point is available, while in flight—

(i) Select a VOR radial that lies along the centerline of an established VOR airway;

(ii) Select a prominent ground point along the selected radial preferably more than 20 nautical miles from the VOR ground facility and maneuver the aircraft directly over the point at a reasonably low altitude; and

(iii) Note the VOR bearing indicated by the receiver when over the ground point (the maximum permissible variation between the published radial and the indicated bearing is 6 degrees).

(c) If dual system VOR (units independent of each other except for the antenna) is installed in the aircraft, the person checking the equipment may check one system against the other in place of the check procedures specified in paragraph (b) of this section. Both systems shall be tuned to the same VOR ground facility and note the indicated bearings to that station. The maximum permissible variation between the two indicated bearings is 4 degrees.

(d) Each person making the VOR operational check, as specified in paragraph (b) or (c) of this section, shall enter the date, place, bearing error, and sign the aircraft log or other record. In addition, if a test signal radiated by a repair station, as specified in paragraph (b)(1) of this section, is used, an entry must be made in the aircraft log or other record by the repair station certificate holder or the certificate holder's representative certifying to the bearing transmitted by the repair station for the check and the date of transmission.

(Approved by the Office of Management and Budget under control number 2120–0005)

§91.173 ATC clearance and flight plan required.

No person may operate an aircraft in controlled airspace under IFR unless that person has—

(a) Filed an IFR flight plan; and

(b) Received an appropriate ATC clearance.

§91.175 Takeoff and landing under IFR.

(a) *Instrument approaches to civil airports.* Unless otherwise authorized by the Administrator, when an instrument letdown to a civil airport is necessary, each person operating an aircraft, except a military aircraft of the United States, shall use a standard instrument approach procedure prescribed for the airport in part 97 of this chapter.

(b) *Authorized DH or MDA.* For the purpose of this section, when the approach procedure being used provides for and requires the use of a DH or MDA, the authorized DH or MDA is the highest of the following:

(1) The DH or MDA prescribed by the approach procedure.

(2) The DH or MDA prescribed for the pilot in command.

(3) The DH or MDA for which the aircraft is equipped.

(c) Operation below DH or MDA. Except as provided in paragraph (l) of this section, where a DH or MDA is applicable, no pilot may operate an aircraft, except a military aircraft of the United States, at any airport below the authorized MDA or continue an approach below the authorized DH unless—

(1) The aircraft is continuously in a position from which a descent to a landing on the intended runway can be made at a normal rate of descent using normal maneuvers, and for operations conducted under part 121 or part 135 unless that descent rate will allow touchdown to occur within the touchdown zone of the runway of intended landing;

(2) The flight visibility is not less than the visibility prescribed in the standard instrument approach being used; and

(3) Except for a Category II or Category III approach where any necessary visual reference requirements are specified by the Administrator, at least one of the following visual references for the intended runway is distinctly visible and identifiable to the pilot:

(i) The approach light system, except that the pilot may not descend below 100 feet above the touchdown zone elevation using the approach lights as a reference unless the red terminating bars or the red side row bars are also distinctly visible and identifiable.

(ii) The threshold.

(iii) The threshold markings.

(iv) The threshold lights.

(v) The runway end identifier lights.

(vi) The visual approach slope indicator.

(vii) The touchdown zone or touchdown zone markings.

(viii) The touchdown zone lights.

(ix) The runway or runway markings.

(x) The runway lights.

(d) *Landing.* No pilot operating an aircraft, except a military aircraft of the United States, may land that aircraft when—

(1) For operations conducted under paragraph (l) of this section, the requirements of (l)(4) of this section are not met; or

(2) For all other part 91 operations and parts 121, 125, 129, and 135 operations, the flight visibility is less than the visibility prescribed in the standard instrument approach procedure being used.

(e) *Missed approach procedures.* Each pilot operating an aircraft, except a military aircraft of the United States, shall immediately execute an appropriate missed approach procedure when either of the following conditions exist:

(1) Whenever operating an aircraft pursuant to paragraph (c) or (l) of this section and the requirements of that paragraph are not met at either of the following times:

(i) When the aircraft is being operated below MDA; or

(ii) Upon arrival at the missed approach point, including a DH where a DH is specified and its use is required, and at any time after that until touchdown.

(2) Whenever an identifiable part of the airport is not distinctly visible to the pilot during a circling maneuver at or above MDA, unless the inability to see an identifiable part of the airport results only from a normal bank of the aircraft during the circling approach.

(f) *Civil airport takeoff minimums.* Unless otherwise authorized by the Administrator, no pilot operating an aircraft under parts 121, 125, 129, or 135 of this chapter may take off from a civil airport under IFR unless weather conditions are at or above the weather minimum for IFR takeoff prescribed for that airport under part 97 of this chapter. If takeoff minimums are not prescribed under part 97 of this chapter for a particular airport, the following minimums apply to takeoffs under IFR for aircraft operating under those parts:

(1) For aircraft, other than helicopters, having two engines or less—1 statute mile visibility.

(2) For aircraft having more than two engines—½-statute mile visibility.

(3) For helicopters—½-statute mile visibility.

(g) *Military airports.* Unless otherwise prescribed by the Administrator, each person operating a civil aircraft under IFR into or out of a military airport shall comply with the instrument approach procedures and the takeoff and landing minimum prescribed by the military authority having jurisdiction of that airport.

(h) *Comparable values of RVR and ground visibility.*

(1) Except for Category II or Category III minimums, if RVR minimums for takeoff or landing are prescribed in an instrument approach procedure, but RVR is not reported for the runway of intended operation, the RVR minimum shall be converted to ground visibility in accordance with the table in paragraph (h)(2) of this section and shall be the visibility minimum for takeoff or landing on that runway.

(2)

RVR (feet)	Visibility (statute miles)
1,600	1/4
2,400	1/2
3,200	5/8
4,000	3/4
4,500	7/8
5,000	1
6,000	$1\frac{1}{4}$

(i) *Operations on unpublished routes and use of radar in instrument approach procedures.* When radar is approved at certain locations for ATC purposes, it may be used not only for surveillance and precision radar approaches, as applicable, but also may be used in conjunction with instrument approach procedures predicated on other types of radio navigational aids. Radar vectors may be authorized to provide course guidance through the segments of an approach to the final course or fix. When operating on an unpublished route or while being radar vectored, the pilot, when an approach clearance is received, shall, in addition to complying with §91.177, maintain the last altitude assigned to that pilot until the aircraft is established on a segment of a published route or instrument approach procedure unless a different altitude is assigned by ATC. After the aircraft is so established, published altitudes apply to descent within each succeeding route or approach segment unless a different altitude is assigned by ATC. Upon reaching the final approach course or fix, the pilot may either complete the instrument approach in accordance with a procedure approved for the facility or continue a surveillance or precision radar approach to a landing.

(j) *Limitation on procedure turns.* In the case of a radar vector to a final approach course or fix, a timed approach from a holding fix, or an approach for which the procedure specifies "No PT," no pilot may make a procedure turn unless cleared to do so by ATC.

(k) *ILS components.* The basic ground components of an ILS are the localizer, glide slope, outer marker, middle marker, and, when installed for use with Category II or Category III instrument approach procedures, an inner marker. A compass locator or precision radar may be substituted for the outer or middle marker. DME, VOR, or nondirectional beacon fixes authorized in the standard instrument approach procedure or surveillance radar may be substituted for the outer marker. Applicability of, and substitution for, the inner marker for Category II or III approaches is determined by the appropriate part 97 approach procedure, letter of authorization, or operations specification pertinent to the operations.

(l) Approach to straight-in landing operations below DH, or MDA using an enhanced flight vision system (EFVS). For straight-in instrument approach procedures other than Category II or Category III, no pilot operating under this section or §§121.651, 125.381, and 135.225 of this chapter may operate an aircraft at any airport below the authorized MDA or continue an approach below the authorized DH and land unless—

(1) The aircraft is continuously in a position from which a descent to a landing on the intended runway can be made at a normal rate of descent using normal maneuvers, and, for operations conducted under part 121 or part 135 of this chapter, the descent rate will allow touchdown to occur within the touchdown zone of the runway of intended landing;

(2) The pilot determines that the enhanced flight visibility observed by use of a certified enhanced flight vision system is not less than the visibility prescribed in the standard instrument approach procedure being used;

(3) The following visual references for the intended runway are distinctly visible and identifiable to the pilot using the enhanced flight vision system:

(i) The approach light system (if installed); or

(ii) The following visual references in both paragraphs (l)(3)(ii)(A) and (B) of this section:

(A) The runway threshold, identified by at least one of the following:

(1) The beginning of the runway landing surface;

(2) The threshold lights; or

(3) The runway end identifier lights.

(B) The touchdown zone, identified by at least one of the following:

(1) The runway touchdown zone landing surface;

(2) The touchdown zone lights;

(3) The touchdown zone markings; or

(4) The runway lights.

(4) At 100 feet above the touchdown zone elevation of the runway of intended landing and below that altitude, the flight visibility must be sufficient for the following to be distinctly visible and identifiable to the pilot without reliance on the enhanced flight vision system to continue to a landing:

(i) The lights or markings of the threshold; or

(ii) The lights or markings of the touchdown zone;

(5) The pilot(s) is qualified to use an EFVS as follows—

(i) For parts 119 and 125 certificate holders, the applicable training, testing and qualification provisions of parts 121, 125, and 135 of this chapter;

(ii) For foreign persons, in accordance with the requirements of the civil aviation authority of the State of the operator; or

(iii) For persons conducting any other operation, in accordance with the applicable currency and proficiency requirements of part 61 of this chapter;

(6) For parts 119 and 125 certificate holders, and part 129 operations specifications holders, their operations specifications authorize use of EFVS; and

(7) The aircraft is equipped with, and the pilot uses, an enhanced flight vision system, the display of which is suitable for maneuvering the aircraft and has either an FAA type design approval or, for a foreign-registered aircraft, the EFVS complies with all of the EFVS requirements of this chapter.

(m) For purposes of this section, "enhanced flight vision system" (EFVS) is an installed airborne system comprised of the following features and characteristics:

(1) An electronic means to provide a display of the forward external scene topography (the natural or manmade features of a place or region especially in a way to show their relative positions and elevation) through the use of imaging sensors, such as a forward-looking infrared, millimeter wave radiometry, millimeter wave radar, and low-light level image intensifying;

(2) The EFVS sensor imagery and aircraft flight symbology (i.e., at least airspeed, vertical speed, aircraft attitude, heading, altitude, command guidance as appropriate for the approach to be flown, path deviation indications, and flight path vector, and flight path angle reference cue) are presented on a head-up display, or an equivalent display, so that they are clearly visible to the pilot flying in his or her normal position and line of vision and looking forward along the flight path, to include:

(i) The displayed EFVS imagery, attitude symbology, flight path vector, and flight path angle reference cue, and other cues, which are referenced to this imagery and external scene topography, must be presented so that they are aligned with and scaled to the external view; and

(ii) The flight path angle reference cue must be displayed with the pitch scale, selectable by the pilot to the desired descent angle for the approach, and suitable for monitoring the vertical flight path of the aircraft on approaches without vertical guidance; and

(iii) The displayed imagery and aircraft flight symbology do not adversely obscure the pilot's outside view or field of view through the cockpit window;

(3) The EFVS includes the display element, sensors, computers and power supplies, indications, and controls. It may receive inputs from an airborne navigation system or flight guidance system; and

(4) The display characteristics and dynamics are suitable for manual control of the aircraft.

[Docket No. 18334, 54 FR 34294, Aug. 18, 1989; as amended by Amdt. 91-267, 66 FR 21066, April 27, 2001; Amdt. 91–281, 69 FR 1640, Jan. 9, 2004]

§91.177 Minimum altitudes for IFR operations.

(a) *Operation of aircraft at minimum altitudes.* Except when necessary for takeoff or landing, no person may operate an aircraft under IFR below—

(1) The applicable minimum altitudes prescribed in parts 95 and 97 of this chapter; or

(2) If no applicable minimum altitude is prescribed in those parts—

(i) In the case of operations over an area designated as a mountainous area in part 95, an altitude of 2,000 feet above the highest obstacle within a horizontal distance of 4 nautical miles from the course to be flown; or

(ii) In any other case, an altitude of 1,000 feet above the highest obstacle within a horizontal distance of 4 nautical miles from the course to be flown.

However, if both a MEA and a MOCA are prescribed for a particular route or route segment, a person may operate an aircraft below the MEA down to, but not below, the MOCA, when within 22 nautical miles of the VOR concerned (based on the pilot's reasonable estimate of that distance).

(b) *Climb.* Climb to a higher minimum IFR altitude shall begin immediately after passing the point beyond which that minimum altitude applies, except that when ground obstructions intervene, the point beyond which that higher minimum altitude applies shall be crossed at or above the applicable MCA.

§91.179 IFR cruising altitude or flight level.

(a) *In controlled airspace.* Each person operating an aircraft under IFR in level cruising flight in controlled airspace shall maintain the altitude or flight level assigned that aircraft by ATC. However, if the ATC clearance assigns "VFR conditions on-top," that person shall maintain an altitude or flight level as prescribed by §91.159.

(b) *In uncontrolled airspace.* Except while in a holding pattern of 2 minutes or less or while turning, each person operating an aircraft under IFR in level cruising flight in uncontrolled airspace shall maintain an appropriate altitude as follows:

(1) When operating below 18,000 feet MSL and—

(i) On a magnetic course of zero degrees through 179 degrees, any odd thousand foot MSL altitude (such as 3,000, 5,000, or 7,000); or

(ii) On a magnetic course of 180 degrees through 359 degrees, any even thousand foot MSL altitude (such as 2,000, 4,000, or 6,000).

(2) When operating at or above 18,000 feet MSL but below flight level 290, and—

(i) On a magnetic course of zero degrees through 179 degrees, any odd flight level (such as 190, 210, or 230); or

(ii) On a magnetic course of 180 degrees through 359 degrees, any even flight level (such as 180, 200, or 220).

(3) When operating at flight level 290 and above in non-RVSM airspace, and—

(i) On a magnetic course of zero degrees through 179 degrees, any flight level, at 4,000-foot intervals, beginning at and including flight level 290 (such as flight level 290, 330, or 370); or

(ii) On a magnetic course of 180 degrees through 359 degrees, any flight level, at 4,000-foot intervals, beginning at and including flight level 310 (such as flight level 310, 350, or 390).

(4) When operating at flight level 290 and above in airspace designated as Reduced Vertical Separation Minimum (RVSM) airspace and—

(i) On a magnetic course of zero degrees through 179 degrees, any odd flight level, at 2,000-foot intervals beginning at and including flight level 290 (such as flight level 290, 310, 330, 350, 370, 390, 410); or

(ii) On a magnetic course of 180 degrees through 359 degrees, any even flight level, at 2000-foot intervals beginning at and including flight level 300 (such as 300, 320, 340, 360, 380, 400).

[Docket No. 18334, 54 FR 34294, Aug. 18, 1989; as amended by Amdt. 91–276, 68 FR 61321, Oct. 27, 2003; Amdt. 91–276, 68 FR 70133, Dec. 17, 2003]

§91.180 Operations within airspace designated as Reduced Vertical Separation Minimum airspace.

(a) Except as provided in paragraph (b) of this section, no person may operate a civil aircraft in airspace designated as Reduced Vertical Separation Minimum (RVSM) airspace unless:

(1) The operator and the operator's aircraft comply with the minimum standards of appendix G of this part; and

(2) The operator is authorized by the Administrator or the country of registry to conduct such operations.

(b) The Administrator may authorize a deviation from the requirements of this section.

[Docket No. FAA–2002–12261, 68 FR 61321, Oct. 27, 2003; as amended by Amdt. 91–276, 68 FR 70133, Dec. 17, 2003]

§91.181 Course to be flown.

Unless otherwise authorized by ATC, no person may operate an aircraft within controlled airspace under IFR except as follows:

(a) On a Federal airway, along the centerline of that airway.

(b) On any other route, along the direct course between the navigational aids or fixes defining that route. However, this section does not prohibit maneuvering the aircraft to pass well clear of other air traffic or the maneuvering of the aircraft in VFR conditions to clear the intended flight path both before and during climb or descent.

§91.183 IFR radio communications.

The pilot in command of each aircraft operated under IFR in controlled airspace shall have a continuous watch maintained on the appropriate frequency and shall report by radio as soon as possible—

(a) The time and altitude of passing each designated reporting point, or the reporting points specified by ATC, except that while the aircraft is under radar control, only the passing of those reporting points specifically requested by ATC need be reported;

(b) Any unforecast weather conditions encountered; and

(c) Any other information relating to the safety of flight.

§91.185 IFR operations: Two-way radio communications failure.

(a) *General.* Unless otherwise authorized by ATC, each pilot who has two-way radio communications failure when operating under IFR shall comply with the rules of this section.

(b) *VFR conditions.* If the failure occurs in VFR conditions, or if VFR conditions are encountered after the failure, each pilot shall continue the flight under VFR and land as soon as practicable.

(c) *IFR conditions.* If the failure occurs in IFR conditions, or if paragraph (b) of this section cannot be complied with, each pilot shall continue the flight according to the following:

(1) *Route.*

(i) By the route assigned in the last ATC clearance received;

(ii) If being radar vectored, by the direct route from the point of radio failure to the fix, route, or airway specified in the vector clearance;

(iii) In the absence of an assigned route, by the route that ATC has advised may be expected in a further clearance; or

(iv) In the absence of an assigned route or a route that ATC has advised may be expected in a further clearance, by the route filed in the flight plan.

(2) *Altitude.* At the highest of the following altitudes or flight levels for the route segment being flown:

(i) The altitude or flight level assigned in the last ATC clearance received;

(ii) The minimum altitude (converted, if appropriate, to minimum flight level as prescribed in §91.121(c)) for IFR operations; or

(iii) The altitude or flight level ATC has advised may be expected in a further clearance.

(3) *Leave clearance limit.*

(i) When the clearance limit is a fix from which an approach begins, commence descent or descent and approach as close as possible to the expect-further-clearance time if one has been received, or if one has not been received, as close as possible to the estimated time of arrival as calculated from the filed or amended (with ATC) estimated time en route.

(ii) If the clearance limit is not a fix from which an approach begins, leave the clearance limit at the expect-further-clearance time if one has been received, or if none has been received, upon arrival over the clearance limit, and proceed to a fix from which an approach begins and commence descent or descent and approach as close as possible to the estimated time of arrival as calculated from the filed or amended (with ATC) estimated time en route.

[Docket No. 18334, 54 FR 34294, Aug. 18, 1989; as amended by Amdt. 91–211, 54 FR 41211, Oct. 5, 1989]

§91.187 Operation under IFR in controlled airspace: Malfunction reports.

(a) The pilot in command of each aircraft operated in controlled airspace under IFR shall report as soon as practical to ATC any malfunctions of navigational, approach, or communication equipment occurring in flight.

(b) In each report required by paragraph (a) of this section, the pilot in command shall include the—

(1) Aircraft identification;

(2) Equipment affected;

(3) Degree to which the capability of the pilot to operate under IFR in the ATC system is impaired; and

(4) Nature and extent of assistance desired from ATC.

§91.189 Category II and III operations: General operating rules.

(a) No person may operate a civil aircraft in a Category II or III operation unless—

(1) The flight crew of the aircraft consists of a pilot in command and a second in command who hold the appropriate authorizations and ratings prescribed in §61.3 of this chapter;

(2) Each flight crewmember has adequate knowledge of, and familiarity with, the aircraft and the procedures to be used; and

(3) The instrument panel in front of the pilot who is controlling the aircraft has appropriate instrumentation for the type of flight control guidance system that is being used.

(b) Unless otherwise authorized by the Administrator, no person may operate a civil aircraft in a Category II or Category III operation unless each ground component required for that operation and the related airborne equipment is installed and operating.

(c) *Authorized DH.* For the purpose of this section, when the approach procedure being used provides for and requires the use of a DH, the authorized DH is the highest of the following:

(1) The DH prescribed by the approach procedure.
(2) The DH prescribed for the pilot in command.
(3) The DH for which the aircraft is equipped.

(d) Unless otherwise authorized by the Administrator, no pilot operating an aircraft in a Category II or Category III approach that provides and requires use of a DH may continue the approach below the authorized decision height unless the following conditions are met:

(1) The aircraft is in a position from which a descent to a landing on the intended runway can be made at a normal rate of descent using normal maneuvers, and where that descent rate will allow touchdown to occur within the touchdown zone of the runway of intended landing.

(2) At least one of the following visual references for the intended runway is distinctly visible and identifiable to the pilot:

(i) The approach light system, except that the pilot may not descend below 100 feet above the touchdown zone elevation using the approach lights as a reference unless the red terminating bars or the red side row bars are also distinctly visible and identifiable.
(ii) The threshold.
(iii) The threshold markings.
(iv) The threshold lights.
(v) The touchdown zone or touchdown zone markings.
(vi) The touchdown zone lights.

(e) Unless otherwise authorized by the Administrator, each pilot operating an aircraft shall immediately execute an appropriate missed approach whenever, prior to touchdown, the requirements of paragraph (d) of this section are not met.

(f) No person operating an aircraft using a Category III approach without decision height may land that aircraft except in accordance with the provisions of the letter of authorization issued by the Administrator.

(g) Paragraphs (a) through (f) of this section do not apply to operations conducted by certificate holders operating under part 121, 125, 129, or 135 of this chapter, or holders of management specifications issued in accordance with subpart K of this part. Holders of operations specifications or management specifications may operate a civil aircraft in a Category II or Category III operation only in accordance with their operations specifications or management specifications, as applicable.

[Docket No. 18334, 54 FR 34294, Aug. 18, 1989; as amended by Amdt. 91–280, 68 FR 54560, Sept. 17, 2003]

§91.191 Category II and Category III manual.

(a) Except as provided in paragraph (c) of this section, after August 4, 1997, no person may operate a U.S.-registered civil aircraft in a Category II or a Category III operation unless—

(1) There is available in the aircraft a current and approved Category II or Category III manual, as appropriate, for that aircraft;

(2) The operation is conducted in accordance with the procedures, instructions, and limitations in the appropriate manual; and

(3) The instruments and equipment listed in the manual that are required for a particular Category II or Category III operation have been inspected and maintained in accordance with the maintenance program contained in the manual.

(b) Each operator must keep a current copy of each approved manual at its principal base of operations and must make each manual available for inspection upon request by the Administrator.

(c) This section does not apply to operations conducted by a certificate holder operating under part 121 or part 135 of this chapter or a holder of management specifications issued in accordance with subpart K of this part.

[Docket No. 26933, 61 FR 34560, July 2, 1996; as amended by Amdt. 91–280, 68 FR 54560, Sept. 17, 2003]

§91.193 Certificate of authorization for certain Category II operations.

The Administrator may issue a certificate of authorization authorizing deviations from the requirements of §§91.189, 91.191, and 91.205(f) for the operation of small aircraft identified as Category A aircraft in §97.3 of this chapter in Category II operations if the Administrator finds that the proposed operation can be safely conducted under the terms of the certificate. Such authorization does not permit operation of the aircraft carrying persons or property for compensation or hire.

§91.195 – 91.199 [Reserved]

Subpart C— Equipment, Instrument, and Certificate Requirements

Source: Docket No. 18334, 54 FR 34304, Aug. 18, 1989, unless otherwise noted.

§91.201 [Reserved]

§91.203 Civil aircraft: Certifications required.

(a) Except as provided in §91.715, no person may operate a civil aircraft unless it has within it the following:

(1) An appropriate and current airworthiness certificate. Each U.S. airworthiness certificate used to comply with this subparagraph (except a special flight permit, a copy of the applicable operations specifications issued under §21.197(c) of this chapter, appropriate sections of the air carrier manual required by parts 121 and 135 of this chapter containing that portion of the operations specifications issued under §21.197(c), or an authorization under §91.611) must have on it the registration number assigned to the aircraft under part 47 of this chapter. However, the airworthiness certificate need not have on it an assigned special identification number before 10 days after that number is first affixed to the aircraft. A revised airworthiness certificate having on it an assigned special identification number, that has been affixed to an aircraft, may only be obtained upon application to an FAA Flight Standards district office.

(2) An effective U.S. registration certificate issued to its owner or, for operation within the United States, the second duplicate copy (pink) of the Aircraft Registration Application as provided for in §47.31(b), or a registration certificate issued under the laws of a foreign country.

(b) No person may operate a civil aircraft unless the airworthiness certificate required by paragraph (a) of this section or a special flight authorization issued under §91.715 is displayed at the cabin or cockpit entrance so that it is legible to passengers or crew.

(c) No person may operate an aircraft with a fuel tank installed within the passenger compartment or a baggage compartment unless the installation was accomplished pursuant to part 43 of this chapter, and a copy of FAA Form 337 authorizing that installation is on board the aircraft.

(d) No person may operate a civil airplane (domestic or foreign) into or out of an airport in the United States unless it complies with the fuel venting and exhaust emissions requirements of part 34 of this chapter.

[Docket No. 18334, 54 FR 34292, Aug. 18, 1989; as amended by Amdt. 91–218, 55 FR 32861, Aug. 10, 1990]

§91.205 Powered civil aircraft with standard category U.S. airworthiness certificates: Instrument and equipment requirements.

(a) *General.* Except as provided in paragraphs (c)(3) and (e) of this section, no person may operate a powered civil aircraft with a standard category U.S. airworthiness certificate in any operation described in paragraphs (b) through (f) of this section unless that aircraft contains the instruments and equipment specified in those paragraphs (or FAA-approved equivalents) for that type of operation, and those instruments and items of equipment are in operable condition.

(b) *Visual-flight rules (day).* For VFR flight during the day, the following instruments and equipment are required:

(1) Airspeed indicator.

(2) Altimeter.

(3) Magnetic direction indicator.

(4) Tachometer for each engine.

(5) Oil pressure gauge for each engine using pressure system.

(6) Temperature gauge for each liquid-cooled engine.

(7) Oil temperature gauge for each air-cooled engine.

(8) Manifold pressure gauge for each altitude engine.

(9) Fuel gauge indicating the quantity of fuel in each tank.

(10) Landing gear position indicator, if the aircraft has a retractable landing gear.

(11) For small civil airplanes certificated after March 11, 1996, in accordance with part 23 of this chapter, an approved aviation red or aviation white anticollision light system. In the event of failure of any light of the anticollision light system, operation of the aircraft may continue to a location where repairs or replacement can be made.

(12) If the aircraft is operated for hire over water and beyond power-off gliding distance from shore, approved flotation gear readily available to each occupant and, unless the aircraft is operating under part 121 of this subchapter, at least one pyrotechnic signaling device. As used in this section, "shore" means that area of the land adjacent to the water which is above the high water mark and excludes land areas which are intermittently under water.

(13) An approved safety belt with an approved metal-to-metal latching device for each occupant 2 years of age or older.

(14) For small civil airplanes manufactured after July 18, 1978, an approved shoulder harness for each front seat. The shoulder harness must be designed to protect the occupant from serious head injury when the occupant experiences the ultimate inertia forces specified in §23.561(b)(2) of this chapter. Each shoulder harness installed at a flight crewmember station must permit the crewmember, when seated and with the safety belt and shoulder harness fastened, to perform all functions necessary for flight operations. For purposes of this paragraph—

(i) The date of manufacture of an airplane is the date the inspection acceptance records reflect that the airplane is complete and meets the FAA-approved type design data; and

(ii) A front seat is a seat located at a flight crewmember station or any seat located alongside such a seat.

(15) An emergency locator transmitter, if required by §91.207.

(16) For normal, utility, and acrobatic category airplanes with a seating configuration, excluding pilot seats, of 9 or less, manufactured after December 12, 1986, a shoulder harness for—

(i) Each front seat that meets the requirements of §23.785 (g) and (h) of this chapter in effect on December 12, 1985;

(ii) Each additional seat that meets the requirements of §23.785(g) of this chapter in effect on December 12, 1985.

(17) For rotorcraft manufactured after September 16, 1992, a shoulder harness for each seat that meets the requirements of §27.2 or §29.2 of this chapter in effect on September 16, 1991.

(c) *Visual flight rules (night).* For VFR flight at night, the following instruments and equipment are required:

(1) Instruments and equipment specified in paragraph (b) of this section.

(2) Approved position lights.

(3) An approved aviation red or aviation white anticollision light system on all U.S.-registered civil aircraft. Anticollision light systems initially installed after August 11, 1971, on aircraft for which a type certificate was issued or applied for before August 11, 1971, must at least meet the anticollision light standards of part 23, 25, 27, or 29 of this chapter, as applicable, that were in effect on August 10, 1971, except that the color may be either aviation red or aviation white. In the event of failure of any light of the anticollision light system, operations with the aircraft may be continued to a stop where repairs or replacement can be made.

(4) If the aircraft is operated for hire, one electric landing light.

(5) An adequate source of electrical energy for all installed electrical and radio equipment.

(6) One spare set of fuses, or three spare fuses of each kind required, that are accessible to the pilot in flight.

(d) *Instrument flight rules.* For IFR flight, the following instruments and equipment are required:

(1) Instruments and equipment specified in paragraph (b) of this section, and, for night flight, instruments and equipment specified in paragraph (c) of this section.

(2) Two-way radio communications system and navigational equipment appropriate to the ground facilities to be used.

(3) Gyroscopic rate-of-turn indicator, except on the following aircraft:

(i) Airplanes with a third attitude instrument system usable through flight attitudes of 360 degrees of pitch and roll and installed in accordance with the instrument requirements prescribed in §121.305(j) of this chapter; and

(ii) Rotorcraft with a third attitude instrument system usable through flight attitudes of ±80 degrees of pitch and ±120 degrees of roll and installed in accordance with §29.1303(g) of this chapter.

(4) Slip-skid indicator.

(5) Sensitive altimeter adjustable for barometric pressure.

(6) A clock displaying hours, minutes, and seconds with a sweep-second pointer or digital presentation.

(7) Generator or alternator of adequate capacity.

(8) Gyroscopic pitch and bank indicator (artificial horizon).

(9) Gyroscopic direction indicator (directional gyro or equivalent).

(e) *Flight at and above 24,000 ft. MSL (FL 240).* If VOR navigational equipment is required under paragraph (d)(2) of this section, no person may operate a U.S.-registered civil aircraft within the 50 states and the District of Columbia at or above FL 240 unless that aircraft is equipped with approved distance measuring equipment (DME). When DME required by this paragraph fails at and above FL 240, the pilot in command of the aircraft shall notify ATC immediately, and then may continue operations at and above FL 240 to the next airport of intended landing at which repairs or replacement of the equipment can be made.

(f) *Category II operations.* The requirements for Category II operations are the instruments and equipment specified in—

(1) Paragraph (d) of this section; and

(2) Appendix A to this part.

(g) *Category III operations.* The instruments and equipment required for Category III operations are specified in paragraph (d) of this section.

(h) *Exclusions.* Paragraphs (f) and (g) of this section do not apply to operations conducted by a holder of a certificate issued under part 121 or part 135 of this chapter.

[Docket No. 18334, 54 FR 34292, Aug. 18, 1989; as amended by Amdt. 91–220, 55 FR 43310, Oct. 26, 1990; Amdt. 91–223, 56 FR 41052, Aug. 16, 1991; Amdt. 91–231, 57 FR 42672, Sept. 15, 1992; Amdt. 91–247, 61 FR 5171, Feb. 9, 1996; Amdt. 91–251, 61 FR 34560, July 2, 1996; Amdt. 91–285, 69 FR 77599, Dec. 27, 2004]

§91.207 Emergency locator transmitters.

(a) Except as provided in paragraphs (e) and (f) of this section, no person may operate a U.S. registered civil airplane unless—

(1) There is attached to the airplane an approved automatic type emergency locator transmitter that is in operable condition for the following operations, except that after June 21, 1995, an emergency locator transmitter that meets the requirements of TSO-C91 may not be used for new installations:

(i) Those operations governed by the supplemental air carrier and commercial operator rules of parts 121 and 125;

(ii) Charter flights governed by the domestic and flag air carrier rules of part 121 of this chapter; and

(iii) Operations governed by part 135 of this chapter; or

(2) For operations other than those specified in paragraph (a)(1) of this section, there must be attached to the airplane an approved personal type or an approved automatic type emergency locator transmitter that is in operable condition, except that after June 21, 1995, an emergency locator transmitter that meets the requirements of TSO-C91 may not be used for new installations.

(b) Each emergency locator transmitter required by paragraph (a) of this section must be attached to the airplane in such a manner that the probability of damage to the transmitter in the event of crash impact is minimized. Fixed and deployable automatic type transmitters must be attached to the airplane as far aft as practicable.

(c) Batteries used in the emergency locator transmitters required by paragraphs (a) and (b) of this section must be replaced (or recharged, if the batteries are rechargeable)—

(1) When the transmitter has been in use for more than 1 cumulative hour; or

(2) When 50 percent of their useful life (or, for rechargeable batteries, 50 percent of their useful life of charge) has expired, as established by the transmitter manufacturer under its approval. The new expiration date for replacing (or recharging) the battery must be legibly marked on the outside of the transmitter and entered in the aircraft maintenance record. Paragraph (c)(2) of this section does not apply to batteries (such as water-activated batteries) that are essentially unaffected during probable storage intervals.

(d) Each emergency locator transmitter required by paragraph (a) of this section must be inspected within 12 calendar months after the last inspection for—

(1) Proper installation;

(2) Battery corrosion;

(3) Operation of the controls and crash sensor; and

(4) The presence of a sufficient signal radiated from its antenna.

(e) Notwithstanding paragraph (a) of this section, a person may—

(1) Ferry a newly acquired airplane from the place where possession of it was taken to a place where the emergency locator transmitter is to be installed; and

(2) Ferry an airplane with an inoperative emergency locator transmitter from a place where repairs or replacements cannot be made to a place where they can be made.

No person other than required crewmembers may be carried aboard an airplane being ferried under paragraph (e) of this section.

(f) Paragraph (a) of this section does not apply to—

(1) Before January 1, 2004, turbojet-powered aircraft;

(2) Aircraft while engaged in scheduled flights by scheduled air carriers;

(3) Aircraft while engaged in training operations conducted entirely within a 50-nautical mile radius of the airport from which such local flight operations began;

(4) Aircraft while engaged in flight operations incident to design and testing;

(5) New aircraft while engaged in flight operations incident to their manufacture, preparation, and delivery;

(6) Aircraft while engaged in flight operations incident to the aerial application of chemicals and other substances for agricultural purposes;

(7) Aircraft certificated by the Administrator for research and development purposes;

(8) Aircraft while used for showing compliance with regulations, crew training, exhibition, air racing, or market surveys;

(9) Aircraft equipped to carry not more than one person.

(10) An aircraft during any period for which the transmitter has been temporarily removed for inspection, repair, modification, or replacement, subject to the following:

(i) No person may operate the aircraft unless the aircraft records contain an entry which includes the date of initial removal, the make, model, serial number, and reason for removing the transmitter, and a placard located in view of the pilot to show "ELT not installed."

(ii) No person may operate the aircraft more than 90 days after the ELT is initially removed from the aircraft; and

(11) On and after January 1, 2004, aircraft with a maximum payload capacity of more than 18,000 pounds when used in air transportation.

[Docket No. 18334, 54 FR 34304, Aug. 18, 1989; as amended by Amdt. 91–242, 59 FR 32057, June 21, 1994; 59 FR 34578, July 6, 1994; Amdt. 91–265, 65 FR 81318, Dec. 22, 2000]

§91.209 Aircraft lights.

No person may:

(a) During the period from sunset to sunrise (or, in Alaska, during the period a prominent unlighted object cannot be seen from a distance of 3 statute miles or the sun is more than 6 degrees below the horizon)—

(1) Operate an aircraft unless it has lighted position lights;

(2) Park or move an aircraft in, or in dangerous proximity to, a night flight operations area of an airport unless the aircraft—

(i) Is clearly illuminated;

(ii) Has lighted position lights; or

(iii) is in an area that is marked by obstruction lights;

(3) Anchor an aircraft unless the aircraft—

(i) Has lighted anchor lights; or

(ii) Is in an area where anchor lights are not required on vessels; or

(b) Operate an aircraft that is equipped with an anticollision light system, unless it has lighted anticollision lights. However, the anticollision lights need not be lighted when the pilot-in-command determines that, because of operating conditions, it would be in the interest of safety to turn the lights off.

[Docket No. 27806, 61 FR 5171, Feb. 9, 1996]

§91.211 Supplemental oxygen.

(a) *General.* No person may operate a civil aircraft of U.S. registry—

(1) At cabin pressure altitudes above 12,500 feet (MSL) up to and including 14,000 feet (MSL) unless the required minimum flight crew is provided with and uses supplemental oxygen for that part of the flight at those altitudes that is of more than 30 minutes duration;

(2) At cabin pressure altitudes above 14,000 feet (MSL) unless the required minimum flight crew is provided with and uses supplemental oxygen during the entire flight time at those altitudes; and

(3) At cabin pressure altitudes above 15,000 feet (MSL) unless each occupant of the aircraft is provided with supplemental oxygen.

(b) *Pressurized cabin aircraft.*

(1) No person may operate a civil aircraft of U.S. registry with a pressurized cabin—

(i) At flight altitudes above flight level 250 unless at least a 10-minute supply of supplemental oxygen, in addition to any oxygen required to satisfy paragraph (a) of this section, is available for each occupant of the aircraft for use in the event that a descent is necessitated by loss of cabin pressurization; and

(ii) At flight altitudes above flight level 350 unless one pilot at the controls of the airplane is wearing and using an oxygen mask that is secured and sealed and that either supplies oxygen at all times or automatically supplies oxygen whenever the cabin pressure altitude of the airplane exceeds 14,000 feet (MSL), except that the one pilot need not wear and use an oxygen mask while at or below flight level 410 if there are two pilots at the controls and each pilot has a quick-donning type of oxygen mask that can be placed on the face with one hand from the ready position within 5 seconds, supplying oxygen and properly secured and sealed.

(2) Notwithstanding paragraph (b)(1)(ii) of this section, if for any reason at any time it is necessary for one pilot to leave the controls of the aircraft when operating at flight altitudes above flight level 350, the remaining pilot at the controls shall put on and use an oxygen mask until the other pilot has returned to that crewmember's station.

§91.213 Inoperative instruments and equipment.

(a) Except as provided in paragraph (d) of this section, no person may take off an aircraft with inoperative instruments or equipment installed unless the following conditions are met:

(1) An approved Minimum Equipment List exists for that aircraft.

(2) The aircraft has within it a letter of authorization, issued by the FAA Flight Standards district office having jurisdiction over the area in which the operator is located, authorizing operation of the aircraft under the Minimum Equipment List. The letter of authorization may be obtained by written request of the airworthiness certificate holder. The Minimum Equipment List and the letter of authorization constitute a supplemental type certificate for the aircraft.

(3) The approved Minimum Equipment List must—

(i) Be prepared in accordance with the limitations specified in paragraph (b) of this section; and

(ii) Provide for the operation of the aircraft with the instruments and equipment in an inoperable condition.

(4) The aircraft records available to the pilot must include an entry describing the inoperable instruments and equipment.

(5) The aircraft is operated under all applicable conditions and limitations contained in the Minimum Equipment List and the letter authorizing the use of the list.

(b) The following instruments and equipment may not be included in a Minimum Equipment List:

(1) Instruments and equipment that are either specifically or otherwise required by the airworthiness requirements under which the aircraft is type certificated and which are essential for safe operations under all operating conditions.

(2) Instruments and equipment required by an airworthiness directive to be in operable condition unless the airworthiness directive provides otherwise.

(3) Instruments and equipment required for specific operations by this part.

(c) A person authorized to use an approved Minimum Equipment List issued for a specific aircraft under subpart K of this part, part 121, 125, or 135 of this chapter must use that Minimum Equipment List to comply with the requirements in this section.

(d) Except for operations conducted in accordance with paragraph (a) or (c) of this section, a person may takeoff an aircraft in operations conducted under this part with inoperative instruments and equipment without an approved Minimum Equipment List provided—

(1) The flight operation is conducted in a—

(i) Rotorcraft, non-turbine-powered airplane, glider, lighter-than-air aircraft, powered parachute, or weight-shift-control aircraft, for which a master minimum equipment list has not been developed; or

(ii) Small rotorcraft, nonturbine-powered small airplane, glider, or lighter-than-air aircraft for which a Master Minimum Equipment List has been developed; and

(2) The inoperative instruments and equipment are not—

(i) Part of the VFR-day type certification instruments and equipment prescribed in the applicable airworthiness regulations under which the aircraft was type certificated;

(ii) Indicated as required on the aircraft's equipment list, or on the Kinds of Operations Equipment List for the kind of flight operation being conducted;

(iii) Required by §91.205 or any other rule of this part for the specific kind of flight operation being conducted; or

(iv) Required to be operational by an airworthiness directive; and

(3) The inoperative instruments and equipment are—

(i) Removed from the aircraft, the cockpit control placarded, and the maintenance recorded in accordance with §43.9 of this chapter; or

(ii) Deactivated and placarded "Inoperative." If deactivation of the inoperative instrument or equipment involves maintenance, it must be accomplished and recorded in accordance with part 43 of this chapter; and

(4) A determination is made by a pilot, who is certificated and appropriately rated under part 61 of this chapter, or by a person, who is certificated and appropriately rated to perform maintenance on the aircraft, that the inoperative instrument or equipment does not constitute a hazard to the aircraft.

An aircraft with inoperative instruments or equipment as provided in paragraph (d) of this section is considered to be in a properly altered condition acceptable to the Administrator.

(e) Notwithstanding any other provision of this section, an aircraft with inoperable instruments or equipment may be operated under a special flight permit issued in accordance with §§21.197 and 21.199 of this chapter.

[Docket No. 26933, 61 FR 34560, July 2, 1996; as amended by Amdt. 91–280, 68 FR 54560, Sept. 17, 2003; Amdt. 91–282, 69 FR 44880, July 27, 2004]

§91.215 ATC transponder and altitude reporting equipment and use.

(a) *All airspace: U.S.-registered civil aircraft.* For operations not conducted under part 121 or 135 of this chapter, ATC transponder equipment installed must meet the performance and environmental requirements of any class of TSO-C74b (Mode A) or any class of TSO-C74c (Mode A with altitude reporting capability) as appropriate, or the appropriate class of TSO-C112 (Mode S).

(b) *All airspace.* Unless otherwise authorized or directed by ATC, no person may operate an aircraft in the airspace described in paragraphs (b)(1) through (b)(5) of this section, unless that aircraft is equipped with an operable coded radar beacon transponder having either Mode 3/A 4096 code capability, replying to Mode 3/A interrogations with the code specified by ATC, or a Mode S capability, replying to Mode 3/A interrogations with the code specified by ATC and intermode and Mode S interrogations in accordance with the applicable provisions specified in TSO-C112, and that aircraft is equipped with automatic pressure altitude reporting equipment having a Mode C capability that automatically replies to Mode C interrogations by transmitting pressure altitude information in 100-foot increments. This requirement applies—

(1) *All aircraft.* In Class A, Class B, and Class C airspace areas;

(2) *All aircraft.* In all airspace within 30 nautical miles of an airport listed in Appendix D, section 1 of this part from the surface upward to 10,000 feet MSL;

(3) Notwithstanding paragraph (b)(2) of this section, any aircraft which was not originally certificated with an engine-driven electrical system or which has not subsequently been certified with such a system installed, balloon or glider may conduct operations in the airspace within 30 nautical miles of an airport listed in Appendix D, section 1 of this part provided such operations are conducted—

(i) Outside any Class A, Class B, or Class C airspace area; and

(ii) Below the altitude of the ceiling of a Class B or Class C airspace area designated for an airport or 10,000 feet MSL, whichever is lower; and

(4) All aircraft in all airspace above the ceiling and within the lateral boundaries of a Class B or Class C airspace area designated for an airport upward to 10,000 feet MSL; and

(5) All aircraft except any aircraft which was not originally certificated with an engine-driven electrical system or which has not subsequently been certified with such a system installed, balloon, or glider—

(i) In all airspace of the 48 contiguous states and the District of Columbia at and above 10,000 feet MSL, excluding the airspace at and below 2,500 feet above the surface; and

(ii) In the airspace from the surface to 10,000 feet MSL within a 10-nautical-mile radius of any airport listed in Appendix D, section 2 of this part, excluding the airspace below 1,200 feet outside of the lateral boundaries of the surface area of the airspace designated for that airport.

(c) *Transponder-on operation.* While in the airspace as specified in paragraph (b) of this section or in all controlled airspace, each person operating an aircraft equipped with an operable ATC transponder maintained in accordance with §91.413 of this part shall operate the transponder, including Mode C equipment if installed, and shall reply on the appropriate code or as assigned by ATC.

(d) *ATC authorized deviations.* Requests for ATC authorized deviations must be made to the ATC facility having jurisdiction over the concerned airspace within the time periods specified as follows:

(1) For operation of an aircraft with an operating transponder but without operating automatic pressure altitude report-

ing equipment having a Mode C capability, the request may be made at any time.

(2) For operation of an aircraft with an inoperative transponder to the airport of ultimate destination, including any intermediate stops, or to proceed to a place where suitable repairs can be made or both, the request may be made at any time.

(3) For operation of an aircraft that is not equipped with a transponder, the request must be made at least one hour before the proposed operation.

(Approved by the Office of Management and Budget under control number 2120–0005)

[Docket No. 18334, 54 FR 34304, Aug. 18, 1989; as amended by Amdt. 91–221, 56 FR 469, Jan. 4, 1991; Amdt. 91–227, 56 FR 65660, Dec. 17, 1991; Amdt. 91–227, 7 FR 328, Jan. 3, 1992; Amdt. 91–229, 57 FR 34618, Aug. 5, 1992; Amdt. 91–267, 66 FR 21066, April 27, 2001]

§91.217 Data correspondence between automatically reported pressure altitude data and the pilot's altitude reference.

No person may operate any automatic pressure altitude reporting equipment associated with a radar beacon transponder—

(a) When deactivation of that equipment is directed by ATC;

(b) Unless, as installed, that equipment was tested and calibrated to transmit altitude data corresponding within 125 feet (on a 95 percent probability basis) of the indicated or calibrated datum of the altimeter normally used to maintain flight altitude, with that altimeter referenced to 29.92 inches of mercury for altitudes from sea level to the maximum operating altitude of the aircraft; or

(c) Unless the altimeters and digitizers in that equipment meet the standards of TSO-C10b and TSO-C88, respectively.

§91.219 Altitude alerting system or device: Turbojet-powered civil airplanes.

(a) Except as provided in paragraph (d) of this section, no person may operate a turbojet-powered U.S.-registered civil airplane unless that airplane is equipped with an approved altitude alerting system or device that is in operable condition and meets the requirements of paragraph (b) of this section.

(b) Each altitude alerting system or device required by paragraph (a) of this section must be able to—

(1) Alert the pilot—

(i) Upon approaching a preselected altitude in either ascent or descent, by a sequence of both aural and visual signals in sufficient time to establish level flight at that preselected altitude; or

(ii) Upon approaching a preselected altitude in either ascent or descent, by a sequence of visual signals in sufficient time to establish level flight at that preselected altitude, and when deviating above and below that preselected altitude, by an aural signal;

(2) Provide the required signals from sea level to the highest operating altitude approved for the airplane in which it is installed;

(3) Preselect altitudes in increments that are commensurate with the altitudes at which the aircraft is operated;

(4) Be tested without special equipment to determine proper operation of the alerting signals; and

(5) Accept necessary barometric pressure settings if the system or device operates on barometric pressure. However, for operation below 3,000 feet AGL, the system or device need only provide one signal, either visual or aural, to comply with this paragraph. A radio altimeter may be included to provide the signal if the operator has an approved procedure for its use to determine DH or MDA, as appropriate.

(c) Each operator to which this section applies must establish and assign procedures for the use of the altitude alerting system or device and each flight crewmember must comply with those procedures assigned to him.

(d) Paragraph (a) of this section does not apply to any operation of an airplane that has an experimental certificate or to the operation of any airplane for the following purposes:

(1) Ferrying a newly acquired airplane from the place where possession of it was taken to a place where the altitude alerting system or device is to be installed.

(2) Continuing a flight as originally planned, if the altitude alerting system or device becomes inoperative after the airplane has taken off; however, the flight may not depart from a place where repair or replacement can be made.

(3) Ferrying an airplane with any inoperative altitude alerting system or device from a place where repairs or replacements cannot be made to a place where it can be made.

(4) Conducting an airworthiness flight test of the airplane.

(5) Ferrying an airplane to a place outside the United States for the purpose of registering it in a foreign country.

(6) Conducting a sales demonstration of the operation of the airplane.

(7) Training foreign flight crews in the operation of the airplane before ferrying it to a place outside the United States for the purpose of registering it in a foreign country.

§91.221 Traffic alert and collision avoidance system equipment and use.

(a) *All airspace: U.S.-registered civil aircraft.* Any traffic alert and collision avoidance system installed in a U.S.-registered civil aircraft must be approved by the Administrator.

(b) *Traffic alert and collision avoidance system, operation required.* Each person operating an aircraft equipped with an operable traffic alert and collision avoidance system shall have that system on and operating.

§91.223 Terrain awareness and warning system.

(a) *Airplanes manufactured after March 29, 2002.* Except as provided in paragraph (d) of this section, no person may operate a turbine-powered U.S.-registered airplane configured with six or more passenger seats, excluding any pilot seat, unless that airplane is equipped with an approved terrain awareness and warning system that as a minimum meets the requirements for Class B equipment in Technical Standard Order (TSO)–C151.

(b) *Airplanes manufactured on or before March 29, 2002.* Except as provided in paragraph (d) of this section, no person may operate a turbine-powered U.S.-registered airplane configured with six or more passenger seats, excluding any pilot seat, after March 29, 2005, unless that airplane is equipped with an approved terrain awareness and warning system that as a minimum meets the requirements for Class B equipment in Technical Standard Order (TSO)–C151.

(Approved by the Office of Management and Budget under control number 2120-0631)

(c) *Airplane Flight Manual.* The Airplane Flight Manual shall contain appropriate procedures for—

(1) The use of the terrain awareness and warning system; and

(2) Proper flight crew reaction in response to the terrain awareness and warning system audio and visual warnings.

(d) *Exceptions.* Paragraphs (a) and (b) of this section do not apply to—

(1) Parachuting operations when conducted entirely within a 50 nautical mile radius of the airport from which such local flight operations began.

(2) Firefighting operations.

(3) Flight operations when incident to the aerial application of chemicals and other substances.

[Docket No. 29312, 65 FR 16755, March 29, 2000]

§91.224 – 91.299 [Reserved]

Subpart D— Special Flight Operations

Source: Docket No. 18334, 54 FR 34308, Aug. 18, 1989, unless otherwise noted.

§91.301 [Reserved]

§91.303 Aerobatic flight.

No person may operate an aircraft in aerobatic flight—

(a) Over any congested area of a city, town, or settlement;

(b) Over an open air assembly of persons;

(c) Within the lateral boundaries of the surface areas of Class B, Class C, Class D, or Class E airspace designated for an airport;

(d) Within 4 nautical miles of the center line of any Federal airway;

(e) Below an altitude of 1,500 feet above the surface; or

(f) When flight visibility is less than 3 statute miles.

For the purposes of this section, aerobatic flight means an intentional maneuver involving an abrupt change in an aircraft's attitude, an abnormal attitude, or abnormal acceleration, not necessary for normal flight.

[Docket No. 18834, 54 FR 34308, Aug. 18, 1989; as amended by Amdt. 91–227, 56 FR 65661, Dec. 17, 1991]

§91.305 Flight test areas.

No person may flight test an aircraft except over open water, or sparsely populated areas, having light air traffic.

§91.307 Parachutes and parachuting.

(a) No pilot of a civil aircraft may allow a parachute that is available for emergency use to be carried in that aircraft unless it is an approved type and—

(1) If a chair type (canopy in back), it has been packed by a certificated and appropriately rated parachute rigger within the preceding 120 days; or

(2) If any other type, it has been packed by a certificated and appropriately rated parachute rigger—

(i) Within the preceding 120 days, if its canopy, shrouds, and harness are composed exclusively of nylon, rayon, or other similar synthetic fiber or materials that are substantially resistant to damage from mold, mildew, or other fungi and other rotting agents propagated in a moist environment; or

(ii) Within the preceding 60 days, if any part of the parachute is composed of silk, pongee, or other natural fiber, or materials not specified in paragraph (a)(2)(i) of this section.

(b) Except in an emergency, no pilot in command may allow, and no person may conduct, a parachute operation from an aircraft within the United States except in accordance with part 105 of this chapter.

(c) Unless each occupant of the aircraft is wearing an approved parachute, no pilot of a civil aircraft carrying any person (other than a crewmember) may execute any intentional maneuver that exceeds—

(1) A bank of 60 degrees relative to the horizon; or

(2) A nose-up or nose-down attitude of 30 degrees relative to the horizon.

(d) Paragraph (c) of this section does not apply to—

(1) Flight tests for pilot certification or rating; or

(2) Spins and other flight maneuvers required by the regulations for any certificate or rating when given by—

(i) A certificated flight instructor; or

(ii) An airline transport pilot instructing in accordance with §61.67 of this chapter.

(e) For the purposes of this section, *approved parachute* means—

(1) A parachute manufactured under a type certificate or a technical standard order (C-23 series); or

(2) A personnel-carrying military parachute identified by an NAF, AAF, or AN drawing number, an AAF order number, or any other military designation or specification number.

[Docket No. 18334, 54 FR 34308, Aug. 18, 1989; as amended by Amdt. 91–255, 62 FR 68137, Dec. 30, 1997; Amdt. 91–268, 66 FR 23553, May 9, 2001]

§91.309 Towing: Gliders and unpowered ultralight vehicles.

(a) No person may operate a civil aircraft towing a glider or unpowered ultralight vehicle unless—

(1) The pilot in command of the towing aircraft is qualified under §61.69 of this chapter;

(2) The towing aircraft is equipped with a tow-hitch of a kind, and installed in a manner, that is approved by the Administrator;

(3) The towline used has breaking strength not less than 80 percent of the maximum certificated operating weight of the glider or unpowered ultralight vehicle and not more than twice this operating weight. However, the towline used may have a breaking strength more than twice the maximum cer-

tificated operating weight of the glider or unpowered ultralight vehicle if—

(i) A safety link is installed at the point of attachment of the towline to the glider or unpowered ultralight vehicle with a breaking strength not less than 80 percent of the maximum certificated operating weight of the glider or unpowered ultralight vehicle and not greater than twice this operating weight;

(ii) A safety link is installed at the point of attachment of the towline to the towing aircraft with a breaking strength greater, but not more than 25 percent greater, than that of the safety link at the towed glider or unpowered ultralight vehicle end of the towline and not greater than twice the maximum certificated operating weight of the glider or unpowered ultralight vehicle;

(4) Before conducting any towing operation within the lateral boundaries of the surface areas of Class B, Class C, Class D, or Class E airspace designated for an airport, or before making each towing flight within such controlled airspace if required by ATC, the pilot in command notifies the control tower. If a control tower does not exist or is not in operation, the pilot in command must notify the FAA flight service station serving that controlled airspace before conducting any towing operations in that airspace; and

(5) The pilots of the towing aircraft and the glider or unpowered ultralight vehicle have agreed upon a general course of action, including takeoff and release signals, airspeeds, and emergency procedures for each pilot.

(b) No pilot of a civil aircraft may intentionally release a towline, after release of a glider or unpowered ultralight vehicle, in a manner that endangers the life or property of another.

[Docket No. 18834, 54 FR 34308, Aug. 18, 1989; as amended by Amdt. 91–227, 56 FR 65661, Dec. 17, 1991; Amdt. 91–282, 69 FR 44880, July 27, 2004]

§91.311 Towing: Other than under §91.309.

No pilot of a civil aircraft may tow anything with that aircraft (other than under §91.309) except in accordance with the terms of a certificate of waiver issued by the Administrator.

§91.313 Restricted category civil aircraft: Operating limitations.

(a) No person may operate a restricted category civil aircraft—

(1) For other than the special purpose for which it is certificated; or

(2) In an operation other than one necessary to accomplish the work activity directly associated with that special purpose.

(b) For the purpose of paragraph (a) of this section, operating a restricted category civil aircraft to provide flight crewmember training in a special purpose operation for which the aircraft is certificated is considered to be an operation for that special purpose.

(c) No person may operate a restricted category civil aircraft carrying persons or property for compensation or hire. For the purposes of this paragraph, a special purpose operation involving the carriage of persons or material necessary to accomplish that operation, such as crop dusting, seeding, spraying, and banner towing (including the carrying of required persons or material to the location of that operation), and operation for the purpose of providing flight crewmember training in a special purpose operation, are not considered to be the carriage of persons or property for compensation or hire.

(d) No person may be carried on a restricted category civil aircraft unless that person—

(1) Is a flight crewmember;

(2) Is a flight crewmember trainee;

(3) Performs an essential function in connection with a special purpose operation for which the aircraft is certificated; or

(4) Is necessary to accomplish the work activity directly associated with that special purpose.

(e) Except when operating in accordance with the terms and conditions of a certificate of waiver or special operating limitations issued by the Administrator, no person may operate a restricted category civil aircraft within the United States—

(1) Over a densely populated area;

(2) In a congested airway; or

(3) Near a busy airport where passenger transport operations are conducted.

(f) This section does not apply to nonpassenger-carrying civil rotorcraft external-load operations conducted under part 133 of this chapter.

(g) No person may operate a small restricted-category civil airplane manufactured after July 18, 1978, unless an approved shoulder harness is installed for each front seat. The shoulder harness must be designed to protect each occupant from serious head injury when the occupant experiences the ultimate inertia forces specified in §23.561(b)(2) of this chapter. The shoulder harness installation at each flight crewmember station must permit the crewmember, when seated and with the safety belt and shoulder harness fastened, to perform all functions necessary for flight operation. For purposes of this paragraph—

(1) The date of manufacture of an airplane is the date the inspection acceptance records reflect that the airplane is complete and meets the FAA-approved type design data; and

(2) A front seat is a seat located at a flight crewmember station or any seat located alongside such a seat.

§91.315 Limited category civil aircraft: Operating limitations.

No person may operate a limited category civil aircraft carrying persons or property for compensation or hire.

§91.317 Provisionally certificated civil aircraft: Operating limitations.

(a) No person may operate a provisionally certificated civil aircraft unless that person is eligible for a provisional airworthiness certificate under §21.213 of this chapter.

(b) No person may operate a provisionally certificated civil aircraft outside the United States unless that person has specific authority to do so from the Administrator and each foreign country involved.

(c) Unless otherwise authorized by the Director, Flight Standards Service, no person may operate a provisionally certificated civil aircraft in air transportation.

(d) Unless otherwise authorized by the Administrator, no person may operate a provisionally certificated civil aircraft except—

(1) In direct conjunction with the type or supplemental type certification of that aircraft;

(2) For training flight crews, including simulated air carrier operations;

(3) Demonstration flight by the manufacturer for prospective purchasers;

(4) Market surveys by the manufacturer;

(5) Flight checking of instruments, accessories, and equipment that do not affect the basic airworthiness of the aircraft; or

(6) Service testing of the aircraft.

(e) Each person operating a provisionally certificated civil aircraft shall operate within the prescribed limitations displayed in the aircraft or set forth in the provisional aircraft flight manual or other appropriate document. However, when operating in direct conjunction with the type or supplemental type certification of the aircraft, that person shall operate under the experimental aircraft limitations of §21.191 of this chapter and when flight testing, shall operate under the requirements of §91.305 of this part.

(f) Each person operating a provisionally certificated civil aircraft shall establish approved procedures for—

(1) The use and guidance of flight and ground personnel in operating under this section; and

(2) Operating in and out of airports where takeoffs or approaches over populated areas are necessary. No person may operate that aircraft except in compliance with the approved procedures.

(g) Each person operating a provisionally certificated civil aircraft shall ensure that each flight crewmember is properly certificated and has adequate knowledge of, and familiarity with, the aircraft and procedures to be used by that crewmember.

(h) Each person operating a provisionally certificated civil aircraft shall maintain it as required by applicable regulations and as may be specially prescribed by the Administrator.

(i) Whenever the manufacturer, or the Administrator, determines that a change in design, construction, or operation is necessary to ensure safe operation, no person may operate a provisionally certificated civil aircraft until that change has been made and approved. Section 21.99 of this chapter applies to operations under this section.

(j) Each person operating a provisionally certificated civil aircraft—

(1) May carry in that aircraft only persons who have a proper interest in the operations allowed by this section or who are specifically authorized by both the manufacturer and the Administrator; and

(2) Shall advise each person carried that the aircraft is provisionally certificated.

(k) The Administrator may prescribe additional limitations or procedures that the Administrator considers necessary, including limitations on the number of persons who may be carried in the aircraft.

(Approved by the Office of Management and Budget under control number 2120–0005)

[Docket No. 18334, 54 FR 34308, Aug. 18, 1989; as amended by Amdt. 91–212, 54 FR 39293, Sept. 25, 1989]

§91.319 Aircraft having experimental certificates: Operating limitations.

(a) No person may operate an aircraft that has an experimental certificate—

(1) For other than the purpose for which the certificate was issued; or

(2) Carrying persons or property for compensation or hire.

(b) No person may operate an aircraft that has an experimental certificate outside of an area assigned by the Administrator until it is shown that—

(1) The aircraft is controllable throughout its normal range of speeds and throughout all the maneuvers to be executed; and

(2) The aircraft has no hazardous operating characteristics or design features.

(c) Unless otherwise authorized by the Administrator in special operating limitations, no person may operate an aircraft that has an experimental certificate over a densely populated area or in a congested airway. The Administrator may issue special operating limitations for particular aircraft to permit takeoffs and landings to be conducted over a densely populated area or in a congested airway, in accordance with terms and conditions specified in the authorization in the interest of safety in air commerce.

(d) Each person operating an aircraft that has an experimental certificate shall—

(1) Advise each person carried of the experimental nature of the aircraft;

(2) Operate under VFR, day only, unless otherwise specifically authorized by the Administrator; and

(3) Notify the control tower of the experimental nature of the aircraft when operating the aircraft into or out of airports with operating control towers.

(e) No person may operate an aircraft that is issued an experimental certificate under §21.191(i) of this chapter for compensation or hire, except a person may operate an aircraft issued an experimental certificate under §21.191 (i)(1) for compensation or hire to—

(1) Tow a glider that is a light-sport aircraft or unpowered ultralight vehicle in accordance with §91.309; or

(2) Conduct flight training in an aircraft which that person provides prior to January 31, 2010.

(f) No person may lease an aircraft that is issued an experimental certificate under §21.191(i) of this chapter, except in accordance with paragraph (e)(1) of this section.

(g) No person may operate an aircraft issued an experimental certificate under §21.191(i)(1) of this chapter to tow a glider that is a light-sport aircraft or unpowered ultralight vehicle for compensation or hire or to conduct flight training for compensation or hire in an aircraft which that persons provides unless within the preceding 100 hours of time in service the aircraft has—

(1) Been inspected by a certificated repairman (light-sport aircraft) with a maintenance rating, an appropriately rated mechanic, or an appropriately rated repair station in accor-

91

dance with inspection procedures developed by the aircraft manufacturer or a person acceptable to the FAA; or

(2) Received an inspection for the issuance of an airworthiness certificate in accordance with part 21 of this chapter.

(h) The FAA may issue deviation authority providing relief from the provisions of paragraph (a) of this section for the purpose of conducting flight training. The FAA will issue this deviation authority as a letter of deviation authority.

(1) The FAA may cancel or amend a letter of deviation authority at any time.

(2) An applicant must submit a request for deviation authority to the FAA at least 60 days before the date of intended operations. A request for deviation authority must contain a complete description of the proposed operation and justification that establishes a level of safety equivalent to that provided under the regulations for the deviation requested.

(i) The Administrator may prescribe additional limitations that the Administrator considers necessary, including limitations on the persons that may be carried in the aircraft.

[Docket No. 18334, 54 FR 34308, Aug. 18, 1989; as amended by Amdt. 91–282, 69 FR 44881, July 27, 2004; Amdt. 91–282, 69 FR 51162, Aug. 18, 2004]

§91.321 Carriage of candidates in elections.

(a) As an aircraft operator, you may receive payment for carrying a candidate, agent of a candidate, or person traveling on behalf of a candidate, running for Federal, State, or local election, without having to comply with the rules in parts 121, 125 or 135 of this chapter, under the following conditions:

(1) Your primary business is not as an air carrier or commercial operator;

(2) You carry the candidate, agent, or person traveling on behalf of a candidate, under the rules of part 91; and

(3) By Federal, state or local law, you are required to receive payment for carrying the candidate, agent, or person traveling on behalf of a candidate. For federal elections, the payment may not exceed the amount required by the Federal Election Commission. For a state or local election, the payment may not exceed the amount required under the applicable state or local law.

(b) For the purposes of this section, for Federal elections, the terms candidate and election have the same meaning as set forth in the regulations of the Federal Election Commission. For State or local elections, the terms candidate and election have the same meaning as provided by the applicable State or local law and those terms relate to candidates for election to public office in State and local government elections.

[Docket No. FAA–2005–20168, 70 FR 4982, Jan. 31, 2005]

§91.323 Increased maximum certificated weights for certain airplanes operated in Alaska.

(a) Notwithstanding any other provision of the Federal Aviation Regulations, the Administrator will approve, as provided in this section, an increase in the maximum certificated weight of an airplane type certificated under Aeronautics Bulletin No. 7–A of the U.S. Department of Commerce dated January 1, 1931, as amended, or under the normal category of part 4a of the former Civil Air Regulations (14 CFR part 4a, 1964 ed.) if that airplane is operated in the State of Alaska by—

(1) A certificate holder conducting operations under part 121 or part 135 of this chapter; or

(2) The U.S. Department of Interior in conducting its game and fish law enforcement activities or its management, fire detection, and fire suppression activities concerning public lands.

(b) The maximum certificated weight approved under this section may not exceed—

(1) 12,500 pounds;

(2) 115 percent of the maximum weight listed in the FAA aircraft specifications;

(3) The weight at which the airplane meets the positive maneuvering load factor requirement for the normal category specified in §23.337 of this chapter; or

(4) The weight at which the airplane meets the climb performance requirements under which it was type certificated.

(c) In determining the maximum certificated weight, the Administrator considers the structural soundness of the airplane and the terrain to be traversed.

(d) The maximum certificated weight determined under this section is added to the airplane's operation limitations and is identified as the maximum weight authorized for operations within the State of Alaska.

[Docket No. 18334, 54 FR 34308, Aug. 18, 1989; as amended by Amdt. 91–211, 54 FR 41211, Oct. 5, 1989; Amdt. 91–253, 62 FR 13253, March 19, 1997]

§91.325 Primary category aircraft: Operating limitations.

(a) No person may operate a primary category aircraft carrying passengers or property for compensation or hire.

(b) No person may operate a primary category aircraft that is maintained by the pilot-owner under an approved special inspection and maintenance program except—

(1) The pilot-owner; or

(2) A designee of the pilot-owner, provided that the pilot-owner does not receive compensation for the use of the aircraft.

[Docket No. 23345, 57 FR 41370, Sept. 9, 1992]

§91.326 [Reserved]

§91.327 Aircraft having a special airworthiness certificate in the light-sport category: Operating limitations.

(a) No person may operate an aircraft that has a special airworthiness certificate in the light-sport category for compensation or hire except—

(1) To tow a glider or an unpowered ultralight vehicle in accordance with §91.309 of this chapter; or

(2) To conduct flight training.

(b) No person may operate an aircraft that has a special airworthiness certificate in the light-sport category unless—

(1) The aircraft is maintained by a certificated repairman with a light-sport aircraft maintenance rating, an appropriately rated mechanic, or an appropriately rated repair station in accordance with the applicable provisions of part 43 of this chapter and maintenance and inspection procedures

developed by the aircraft manufacturer or a person acceptable to the FAA;

(2) A condition inspection is performed once every 12 calendar months by a certificated repairman (light-sport aircraft) with a maintenance rating, an appropriately rated mechanic, or an appropriately rated repair station in accordance with inspection procedures developed by the aircraft manufacturer or a person acceptable to the FAA;

(3) The owner or operator complies with all applicable airworthiness directives;

(4) The owner or operator complies with each safety directive applicable to the aircraft that corrects an existing unsafe condition. In lieu of complying with a safety directive an owner or operator may—

(i) Correct the unsafe condition in a manner different from that specified in the safety directive provided the person issuing the directive concurs with the action; or

(ii) Obtain an FAA waiver from the provisions of the safety directive based on a conclusion that the safety directive was issued without adhering to the applicable consensus standard;

(5) Each alteration accomplished after the aircraft's date of manufacture meets the applicable and current consensus standard and has been authorized by either the manufacturer or a person acceptable to the FAA;

(6) Each major alteration to an aircraft product produced under a consensus standard is authorized, performed and inspected in accordance with maintenance and inspection procedures developed by the manufacturer or a person acceptable to the FAA; and

(7) The owner or operator complies with the requirements for the recording of major repairs and major alterations performed on type-certificated products in accordance with §43.9(d) of this chapter, and with the retention requirements in §91.417.

(c) No person may operate an aircraft issued a special airworthiness certificate in the light-sport category to tow a glider or unpowered ultralight vehicle for compensation or hire or conduct flight training for compensation or hire in an aircraft which that persons provides unless within the preceding 100 hours of time in service the aircraft has—

(1) Been inspected by a certificated repairman with a light-sport aircraft maintenance rating, an appropriately rated mechanic, or an appropriately rated repair station in accordance with inspection procedures developed by the aircraft manufacturer or a person acceptable to the FAA and been approved for return to service in accordance with part 43 of this chapter; or

(2) Received an inspection for the issuance of an airworthiness certificate in accordance with part 21 of this chapter.

(d) Each person operating an aircraft issued a special airworthiness certificate in the light-sport category must operate the aircraft in accordance with the aircraft's operating instructions, including any provisions for necessary operating equipment specified in the aircraft's equipment list.

(e) Each person operating an aircraft issued a special airworthiness certificate in the light-sport category must advise each person carried of the special nature of the aircraft and that the aircraft does not meet the airworthiness requirements for an aircraft issued a standard airworthiness certificate.

(f) The FAA may prescribe additional limitations that it considers necessary.

[Docket No. FAA–2001–11133, 69 FR 44881, July 27, 2004]

§91.328 – 91.399 [Reserved]

Subpart E—Maintenance, Preventive Maintenance, and Alterations

Source: Docket No. 18334, 54 FR 34311, Aug. 18, 1989, unless otherwise noted.

§91.401 Applicability.

(a) This subpart prescribes rules governing the maintenance, preventive maintenance, and alterations of U.S.-registered civil aircraft operating within or outside of the United States.

(b) Sections 91.405, 91.409, 91.411, 91.417, and 91.419 of this subpart do not apply to an aircraft maintained in accordance with a continuous airworthiness maintenance program as provided in part 121, 129, or §§91.1411 or 135.411(a)(2) of this chapter.

(c) Sections 91.405 and 91.409 of this part do not apply to an airplane inspected in accordance with part 125 of this chapter.

[Docket No. 18334, 54 FR 34311, Aug. 18, 1989; as amended by Amdt. 91–267, 66 FR 21066, April 27, 2001; Amdt. 91–280, 68 FR 54560, Sept. 17, 2003]

§91.403 General.

(a) The owner or operator of an aircraft is primarily responsible for maintaining that aircraft in an airworthy condition, including compliance with part 39 of this chapter.

(b) No person may perform maintenance, preventive maintenance, or alterations on an aircraft other than as prescribed in this subpart and other applicable regulations, including part 43 of this chapter.

(c) No person may operate an aircraft for which a manufacturer's maintenance manual or instructions for continued airworthiness has been issued that contains an airworthiness limitations section unless the mandatory replacement times, inspection intervals, and related procedures specified in that section or alternative inspection intervals and related procedures set forth in an operations specification approved by the Administrator under part 121 or 135 of this chapter or in accordance with an inspection program approved under §91.409(e) have been complied with.

[Docket No. 18334, 54 FR 34311, Aug. 18, 1989; as amended by Amdt. 91–267, 66 FR 21066, April 27, 2001]

§91.405 Maintenance required.

Each owner or operator of an aircraft—

(a) Shall have that aircraft inspected as prescribed in subpart E of this part and shall between required inspections, except as provided in paragraph (c) of this section, have discrepancies repaired as prescribed in part 43 of this chapter;

(b) Shall ensure that maintenance personnel make appropriate entries in the aircraft maintenance records indicating the aircraft has been approved for return to service;

(c) Shall have any inoperative instrument or item of equipment, permitted to be inoperative by §91.213(d)(2) of this part, repaired, replaced, removed, or inspected at the next required inspection; and

(d) When listed discrepancies include inoperative instruments or equipment, shall ensure that a placard has been installed as required by §43.11 of this chapter.

§91.407 Operation after maintenance, preventive maintenance, rebuilding, or alteration.

(a) No person may operate any aircraft that has undergone maintenance, preventive maintenance, rebuilding, or alteration unless—

(1) It has been approved for return to service by a person authorized under §43.7 of this chapter; and

(2) The maintenance record entry required by §43.9 or §43.11, as applicable, of this chapter has been made.

(b) No person may carry any person (other than crewmembers) in an aircraft that has been maintained, rebuilt, or altered in a manner that may have appreciably changed its flight characteristics or substantially affected its operation in flight until an appropriately rated pilot with at least a private pilot certificate flies the aircraft, makes an operational check of the maintenance performed or alteration made, and logs the flight in the aircraft records.

(c) The aircraft does not have to be flown as required by paragraph (b) of this section if, prior to flight, ground tests, inspection, or both show conclusively that the maintenance, preventive maintenance, rebuilding, or alteration has not appreciably changed the flight characteristics or substantially affected the flight operation of the aircraft.

(Approved by the Office of Management and Budget under control number 2120–0005)

§91.409 Inspections.

(a) Except as provided in paragraph (c) of this section, no person may operate an aircraft unless, within the preceding 12 calendar months, it has had—

(1) An annual inspection in accordance with part 43 of this chapter and has been approved for return to service by a person authorized by §43.7 of this chapter; or

(2) An inspection for the issuance of an airworthiness certificate in accordance with part 21 of this chapter.

No inspection performed under paragraph (b) of this section may be substituted for any inspection required by this paragraph unless it is performed by a person authorized to perform annual inspections and is entered as an "annual" inspection in the required maintenance records.

(b) Except as provided in paragraph (c) of this section, no person may operate an aircraft carrying any person (other than a crewmember) for hire, and no person may give flight instruction for hire in an aircraft which that person provides, unless within the preceding 100 hours of time in service the aircraft has received an annual or 100-hour inspection and been approved for return to service in accordance with part 43 of this chapter or has received an inspection for the issuance of an airworthiness certificate in accordance with part 21 of this chapter. The 100-hour limitation may be exceeded by not more than 10 hours while en route to reach a place where the inspection can be done. The excess time used to reach a place where the inspection can be done must be included in computing the next 100 hours of time in service.

(c) Paragraphs (a) and (b) of this section do not apply to—

(1) An aircraft that carries a special flight permit, a current experimental certificate, or a light-sport or provisional airworthiness certificate;

(2) An aircraft inspected in accordance with an approved aircraft inspection program under part 125 or 135 of this chapter and so identified by the registration number in the operations specifications of the certificate holder having the approved inspection program;

(3) An aircraft subject to the requirements of paragraph (d) or (e) of this section; or

(4) Turbine-powered rotorcraft when the operator elects to inspect that rotorcraft in accordance with paragraph (e) of this section.

(d) *Progressive inspection.* Each registered owner or operator of an aircraft desiring to use a progressive inspection program must submit a written request to the FAA Flight Standards district office having jurisdiction over the area in which the applicant is located, and shall provide—

(1) A certificated mechanic holding an inspection authorization, a certificated airframe repair station, or the manufacturer of the aircraft to supervise or conduct the progressive inspection;

(2) A current inspection procedures manual available and readily understandable to pilot and maintenance personnel containing, in detail—

(i) An explanation of the progressive inspection, including the continuity of inspection responsibility, the making of reports, and the keeping of records and technical reference material;

(ii) An inspection schedule, specifying the intervals in hours or days when routine and detailed inspections will be performed and including instructions for exceeding an inspection interval by not more than 10 hours while en route and for changing an inspection interval because of service experience;

(iii) Sample routine and detailed inspection forms and instructions for their use; and

(iv) Sample reports and records and instructions for their use;

(3) Enough housing and equipment for necessary disassembly and proper inspection of the aircraft; and

(4) Appropriate current technical information for the aircraft.

The frequency and detail of the progressive inspection shall provide for the complete inspection of the aircraft within each 12 calendar months and be consistent with the manufacturer's recommendations, field service experience, and the kind of operation in which the aircraft is engaged. The progressive inspection schedule must ensure that the aircraft, at all times, will be airworthy and will conform to all applicable FAA aircraft specifications, type certificate data sheets, airworthiness directives, and other approved data. If the progressive inspection is discontinued, the owner or operator shall immediately notify the local FAA Flight Standards district office, in writing, of the discontinuance. After the discontinuance, the first annual inspection under §91.409(a)(1) is due within 12 calendar months after the last complete inspection of the aircraft under the progressive inspection. The 100-hour inspection under §91.409(b) is due within 100 hours after that complete inspection. A complete inspection of the aircraft, for the purpose of determining when the annual and 100-hour inspections are due, requires a detailed inspection of the aircraft and all its components in accordance with the progressive inspection. A routine inspection of the aircraft and a detailed inspection of several components is not considered to be a complete inspection.

(e) *Large airplanes (to which part 125 is not applicable), turbojet multiengine airplanes, turbopropeller-powered multiengine airplanes, and turbine-powered rotorcraft.* No person may operate a large airplane, turbojet multiengine airplane, turbopropeller-powered multiengine airplane, or turbine-powered rotorcraft unless the replacement times for life-limited parts specified in the aircraft specifications, type data sheets, or other documents approved by the Administrator are complied with and the airplane or turbine-powered rotorcraft, including the airframe, engines, propellers, rotors, appliances, survival equipment, and emergency equipment, is inspected in accordance with an inspection program selected under the provisions of paragraph (f) of this section, except that, the owner or operator of a turbine-powered rotorcraft may elect to use the inspection provisions of §91.409(a), (b), (c), or (d) in lieu of an inspection option of §91.409(f).

(f) *Selection of inspection program under paragraph (e) of this section.* The registered owner or operator of each airplane or turbine-powered rotorcraft described in paragraph (e) of this section must select, identify in the aircraft maintenance records, and use one of the following programs for the inspection of the aircraft:

(1) A continuous airworthiness inspection program that is part of a continuous airworthiness maintenance program currently in use by a person holding an air carrier operating certificate or an operating certificate issued under part 121 or 135 of this chapter and operating that make and model aircraft under part 121 of this chapter or operating that make and model under part 135 of this chapter and maintaining it under §135.411(a)(2) of this chapter.

(2) An approved aircraft inspection program approved under §135.419 of this chapter and currently in use by a person holding an operating certificate issued under part 135 of this chapter.

(3) A current inspection program recommended by the manufacturer.

(4) Any other inspection program established by the registered owner or operator of that airplane or turbine-powered rotorcraft and approved by the Administrator under paragraph (g) of this section. However, the Administrator may require revision of this inspection program in accordance with the provisions of §91.415.

Each operator shall include in the selected program the name and address of the person responsible for scheduling the inspections required by the program and make a copy of that program available to the person performing inspections on the aircraft and, upon request, to the Administrator.

(g) *Inspection program approved under paragraph (e) of this section.* Each operator of an airplane or turbine-powered rotorcraft desiring to establish or change an approved inspection program under paragraph (f)(4) of this section must submit the program for approval to the local FAA Flight Standards district office having jurisdiction over the area in which the aircraft is based. The program must be in writing and include at least the following information:

(1) Instructions and procedures for the conduct of inspections for the particular make and model airplane or turbine-powered rotorcraft, including necessary tests and checks. The instructions and procedures must set forth in detail the parts and areas of the airframe, engines, propellers, rotors, and appliances, including survival and emergency equipment required to be inspected.

(2) A schedule for performing the inspections that must be performed under the program expressed in terms of the time in service, calendar time, number of system operations, or any combination of these.

(h) *Changes from one inspection program to another.* When an operator changes from one inspection program under paragraph (f) of this section to another, the time in service, calendar times, or cycles of operation accumulated under the previous program must be applied in determining inspection due times under the new program.

(Approved by the Office of Management and Budget under control number 2120–0005)

[Docket No. 18334, 54 FR 34311, Aug. 18, 1989; as amended by Amdt. 91–211, 54 FR 41211, Oct. 5, 1989; Amdt. 91–267, 66 FR 21066, April 27, 2001; Amdt. 91–282, 69 FR 44882, July 27, 2004]

§91.410 Special maintenance program requirements.

(a) No person may operate an Airbus Model A300 (excluding the –600 series), British Aerospace Model BAC 1–11, Boeing Model 707, 720, 727, 737 or 747, McDonnell Douglas Model DC–8, DC–9/MD–80 or DC–10, Fokker Model F28, or Lockheed Model L–1011 airplane beyond applicable flight cycle implementation time specified below, or May 25, 2001, whichever occurs later, unless repair assessment guidelines applicable to the fuselage pressure boundary (fuselage skin, door skin, and bulkhead webs) that have been approved by the FAA Aircraft Certification Office (ACO), or office of the Transport Airplane Directorate, having cognizance over the type certificate for the affected airplane are incorporated within its inspection program:

(1) For the Airbus Model A300 (excluding the –600 series), the flight cycle implementation time is:

(i) Model B2: 36,000 flights.

(ii) Model B4–100 (including Model B4–2C): 30,000 flights above the window line, and 36,000 flights below the window line.

(iii) Model B4–200: 25,500 flights above the window line, and 34,000 flights below the window line.

(2) For all models of the British Aerospace BAC 1–11, the flight cycle implementation time is 60,000 flights.

(3) For all models of the Boeing 707, the flight cycle implementation time is 15,000 flights.

(4) For all models of the Boeing 720, the flight cycle implementation time is 23,000 flights.

(5) For all models of the Boeing 727, the flight cycle implementation time is 45,000 flights.

(6) For all models of the Boeing 737, the flight cycle implementation time is 60,000 flights.

(7) For all models of the Boeing 747, the flight cycle implementation time is 15,000 flights.

(8) For all models of the McDonnell Douglas DC–8, the flight cycle implementation time is 30,000 flights.

(9) For all models of the McDonnell Douglas DC–9/MD–80, the flight cycle implementation time is 60,000 flights.

(10) For all models of the McDonnell Douglas DC–10, the flight cycle implementation time is 30,000 flights.

(11)For all models of the Lockheed L–1011, the flight cycle implementation time is 27,000 flights.

(12) For the Fokker F–28 Mark 1000, 2000, 3000, and 4000, the flight cycle implementation time is 60,000 flights.

(b) After December 16, 2008, no person may operate a turbine-powered transport category airplane with a type certificate issued after January 1, 1958, and either a maximum type certificated passenger capacity of 30 or more, or a maximum type certificated payload capacity of 7,500 pounds or more, unless instructions for maintenance and inspection of the fuel tank system are incorporated into its inspection program. These instructions must address the actual configuration of the fuel tank systems of each affected airplane, and must be approved by the FAA Aircraft Certification Office (ACO), or office of the Transport Airplane Directorate, having cognizance over the type certificate for the affected airplane. Operators must submit their request through the cognizant Flight Standards District Office, who may add comments and then send it to the manager of the appropriate office. Thereafter, the approved instructions can be revised only with the approval of the FAA Aircraft Certification Office (ACO), or office of the Transport Airplane Directorate, having cognizance over the type certificate for the affected airplane. Operators must submit their request for revisions through the cognizant Flight Standards District Office, who may add comments and then send it to the manager of the appropriate office.

[Docket No. 29104, 65 FR 24125, April 25, 2000; as amended by Amdt. 91–264, 65 FR 50744, Aug. 21, 2000; Amdt. 91–266, 66 FR 23130, May 7, 2001; Amdt. 91–277, 67 FR 72834, Dec. 9, 2002; Amdt. 91–283, 69 FR 45941, July 30, 2004; Amdt. 91–283, 69 FR 51940, Aug. 23, 2004]

§91.411 Altimeter system and altitude reporting equipment tests and inspections.

(a) No person may operate an airplane, or helicopter, in controlled airspace under IFR unless—

(1) Within the preceding 24 calendar months, each static pressure system, each altimeter instrument, and each automatic pressure altitude reporting system has been tested and inspected and found to comply with Appendix E of part 43 of this chapter;

(2) Except for the use of system drain and alternate static pressure valves, following any opening and closing of the static pressure system, that system has been tested and inspected and found to comply with paragraph (a), appendices E and F, of part 43 of this chapter; and

(3) Following installation or maintenance on the automatic pressure altitude reporting system of the ATC transponder where data correspondence error could be introduced, the integrated system has been tested, inspected, and found to comply with paragraph (c), Appendix E, of part 43 of this chapter.

(b) The tests required by paragraph (a) of this section must be conducted by—

(1) The manufacturer of the airplane, or helicopter, on which the tests and inspections are to be performed;

(2) A certificated repair station properly equipped to perform those functions and holding—

(i) An instrument rating, Class I;

(ii) A limited instrument rating appropriate to the make and model of appliance to be tested;

(iii) A limited rating appropriate to the test to be performed;

(iv) An airframe rating appropriate to the airplane, or helicopter, to be tested; or

(3) A certificated mechanic with an airframe rating (static pressure system tests and inspections only).

(c) Altimeter and altitude reporting equipment approved under Technical Standard Orders are considered to be tested and inspected as of the date of their manufacture.

(d) No person may operate an airplane, or helicopter, in controlled airspace under IFR at an altitude above the maximum altitude at which all altimeters and the automatic altitude reporting system of that airplane, or helicopter, have been tested.

[Docket No. 18334, 54 FR 34311, Aug. 18, 1989; as amended by Amdt. 91–269, 66 FR 41116, Aug. 6, 2001]

§91.413 ATC transponder tests and inspections.

(a) No persons may use an ATC transponder that is specified in §§91.215(a), 121.345(c), or 135.143(c) of this chapter unless, within the preceding 24 calendar months, the ATC transponder has been tested and inspected and found to comply with Appendix F of part 43 of this chapter; and

(b) Following any installation or maintenance on an ATC transponder where data correspondence error could be introduced, the integrated system has been tested, inspected, and found to comply with paragraph (c), Appendix E, of part 43 of this chapter.

(c) The tests and inspections specified in this section must be conducted by—

(1) A certificated repair station properly equipped to perform those functions and holding—

(i) A radio rating, Class III;

(ii) A limited radio rating appropriate to the make and model transponder to be tested;

(iii) A limited rating appropriate to the test to be performed;

(2) A holder of a continuous airworthiness maintenance program as provided in part 121 or §135.411(a)(2) of this chapter; or

(3) The manufacturer of the aircraft on which the transponder to be tested is installed, if the transponder was installed by that manufacturer.

Docket No. 18334, 54 FR 34311, Aug. 18, 1989; as amended by Amdt. 91–267, 66 FR 21066, April 27, 2001; Amdt. 91–269, 66 FR 41116, Aug. 6, 2001

§91.415 Changes to aircraft inspection programs.

(a) Whenever the Administrator finds that revisions to an approved aircraft inspection program under §91.409(f)(4) or §91.1109 are necessary for the continued adequacy of the program, the owner or operator must, after notification by the Administrator, make any changes in the program found to be necessary by the Administrator.

(b) The owner or operator may petition the Administrator to reconsider the notice to make any changes in a program in accordance with paragraph (a) of this section.

(c) The petition must be filed with the Director, Flight Standards Service within 30 days after the certificate holder or fractional ownership program manager receives the notice.

(d) Except in the case of an emergency requiring immediate action in the interest of safety, the filing of the petition stays the notice pending a decision by the Administrator.

[Docket No. 18334, 54 FR 34311, Aug. 18, 1989; as amended by Amdt. 91–280, 68 FR 54560, Sept. 17, 2003]

§91.417 Maintenance records.

(a) Except for work performed in accordance with §§91.411 and 91.413, each registered owner or operator shall keep the following records for the periods specified in paragraph (b) of this section:

(1) Records of the maintenance, preventive maintenance, and alteration and records of the 100-hour, annual, progressive, and other required or approved inspections, as appropriate, for each aircraft (including the airframe) and each engine, propeller, rotor, and appliance of an aircraft. The records must include—

(i) A description (or reference to data acceptable to the Administrator) of the work performed; and

(ii) The date of completion of the work performed; and

(iii) The signature, and certificate number of the person approving the aircraft for return to service.

(2) Records containing the following information:

(i) The total time in service of the airframe, each engine, each propeller, and each rotor.

(ii) The current status of life-limited parts of each airframe, engine, propeller, rotor, and appliance.

(iii) The time since last overhaul of all items installed on the aircraft which are required to be overhauled on a specified time basis.

(iv) The current inspection status of the aircraft, including the time since the last inspection required by the inspection program under which the aircraft and its appliances are maintained.

(v) The current status of applicable airworthiness directives (AD) including, for each, the method of compliance, the AD number, and revision date. If the AD involves recurring action, the time and date when the next action is required.

(vi) Copies of the forms prescribed by §43.9(a) of this chapter for each major alteration to the airframe and currently installed engines, rotors, propellers, and appliances.

(b) The owner or operator shall retain the following records for the periods prescribed:

(1) The records specified in paragraph (a)(1) of this section shall be retained until the work is repeated or superseded by other work or for 1 year after the work is performed.

(2) The records specified in paragraph (a)(2) of this section shall be retained and transferred with the aircraft at the time the aircraft is sold.

(3) A list of defects furnished to a registered owner or operator under §43.11 of this chapter shall be retained until the defects are repaired and the aircraft is approved for return to service.

(c) The owner or operator shall make all maintenance records required to be kept by this section available for inspection by the Administrator or any authorized representative of the National Transportation Safety Board (NTSB). In addition, the owner or operator shall present Form 337 described in paragraph (d) of this section for inspection upon request of any law enforcement officer.

(d) When a fuel tank is installed within the passenger compartment or a baggage compartment pursuant to part 43 of this chapter, a copy of FAA Form 337 shall be kept on board the modified aircraft by the owner or operator.

(Approved by the Office of Management and Budget under control number 2120–0005)

§91.419 Transfer of maintenance records.

Any owner or operator who sells a U.S.-registered aircraft shall transfer to the purchaser, at the time of sale, the following records of that aircraft, in plain language form or in coded form at the election of the purchaser, if the coded form provides for the preservation and retrieval of information in a manner acceptable to the Administrator:

(a) The records specified in §91.417(a)(2).

(b) The records specified in §91.417(a)(1) which are not included in the records covered by paragraph (a) of this section, except that the purchaser may permit the seller to keep physical custody of such records. However, custody of records by the seller does not relieve the purchaser of the responsibility under §91.417(c) to make the records available for inspection by the Administrator or any authorized representative of the National Transportation Safety Board (NTSB).

§91.421 Rebuilt engine maintenance records.

(a) The owner or operator may use a new maintenance record, without previous operating history, for an aircraft engine rebuilt by the manufacturer or by an agency approved by the manufacturer.

(b) Each manufacturer or agency that grants zero time to an engine rebuilt by it shall enter in the new record—

(1) A signed statement of the date the engine was rebuilt;

(2) Each change made as required by airworthiness directives; and

(3) Each change made in compliance with manufacturer's service bulletins, if the entry is specifically requested in that bulletin.

(c) For the purposes of this section, a rebuilt engine is a used engine that has been completely disassembled, inspected, repaired as necessary, reassembled, tested, and approved in the same manner and to the same tolerances and limits as a new engine with either new or used parts. However, all parts used in it must conform to the production drawing tolerances and limits for new parts or be of approved oversized or undersized dimensions for a new engine.

§91.423 – 91.499 [Reserved]

Subpart F— Large and Turbine-Powered Multiengine Airplanes and Fractional Ownership Program Aircraft

Source: Docket No. 18334, 54 FR 34314, Aug. 18, 1989, unless otherwise noted.

§91.501 Applicability.

(a) This subpart prescribes operating rules, in addition to those prescribed in other subparts of this part, governing the operation of large airplanes of U.S. registry, turbojet-powered multiengine civil airplanes of U.S. registry, and fractional ownership program aircraft of U.S. registry that are operating under subpart K of this part in operations not involving common carriage. The operating rules in this subpart do not apply to those aircraft when they are required to be operated under parts 121, 125, 129, 135, and 137 of this chapter. (Section 91.409 prescribes an inspection program for large and for turbine-powered (turbojet and turboprop) multiengine airplanes and turbine-powered rotorcraft of U.S. registry when they are operated under this part or part 129 or 137.)

(b) Operations that may be conducted under the rules in this subpart instead of those in parts 121, 129, 135, and 137 of this chapter when common carriage is not involved, include—

(1) Ferry or training flights;

(2) Aerial work operations such as aerial photography or survey, or pipeline patrol, but not including fire fighting operations;

(3) Flights for the demonstration of an airplane to prospective customers when no charge is made except for those specified in paragraph (d) of this section;

(4) Flights conducted by the operator of an airplane for his personal transportation, or the transportation of his guests when no charge, assessment, or fee is made for the transportation;

(5) Carriage of officials, employees, guests, and property of a company on an airplane operated by that company, or the parent or a subsidiary of the company or a subsidiary of the parent, when the carriage is within the scope of, and incidental to, the business of the company (other than transportation by air) and no charge, assessment or fee is made for the carriage in excess of the cost of owning, operating, and maintaining the airplane, except that no charge of any kind may be made for the carriage of a guest of a company, when the carriage is not within the scope of, and incidental to, the business of that company;

(6) The carriage of company officials, employees, and guests of the company on an airplane operated under a time sharing, interchange, or joint ownership agreement as defined in paragraph (c) of this section;

(7) The carriage of property (other than mail) on an airplane operated by a person in the furtherance of a business or employment (other than transportation by air) when the carriage is within the scope of, and incidental to, that business or employment and no charge, assessment, or fee is made for the carriage other than those specified in paragraph (d) of this section;

(8) The carriage on an airplane of an athletic team, sports group, choral group, or similar group having a common purpose or objective when there is no charge, assessment, or fee of any kind made by any person for that carriage; and

(9) The carriage of persons on an airplane operated by a person in the furtherance of a business other than transportation by air for the purpose of selling them land, goods, or property, including franchises or distributorships, when the carriage is within the scope of, and incidental to, that business and no charge, assessment, or fee is made for that carriage.

(10) Any operation identified in paragraphs (b)(1) through (b)(9) of this section when conducted—

(i) By a fractional ownership program manager, or

(ii) By a fractional owner in a fractional ownership program aircraft operated under subpart K of this part, except that a flight under a joint ownership arrangement under paragraph (b)(6) of this section may not be conducted. For a flight under an interchange agreement under paragraph (b)(6) of this section, the exchange of equal time for the operation must be properly accounted for as part of the total hours associated with the fractional owner's share of ownership.

(c) As used in this section—

(1) *A time sharing agreement* means an arrangement whereby a person leases his airplane with flight crew to another person, and no charge is made for the flights conducted under that arrangement other than those specified in paragraph (d) of this section;

(2) *An interchange agreement* means an arrangement whereby a person leases his airplane to another person in exchange for equal time, when needed, on the other person's airplane, and no charge, assessment, or fee is made, except that a charge may be made not to exceed the difference between the cost of owning, operating, and maintaining the two airplanes;

(3) *A joint ownership agreement* means an arrangement whereby one of the registered joint owners of an airplane employs and furnishes the flight crew for that airplane and each of the registered joint owners pays a share of the charge specified in the agreement.

(d) The following may be charged, as expenses of a specific flight, for transportation as authorized by paragraphs (b)(3) and (7) and (c)(1) of this section:

(1) Fuel, oil, lubricants, and other additives.

(2) Travel expenses of the crew, including food, lodging, and ground transportation.

(3) Hangar and tie-down costs away from the aircraft's base of operation.

(4) Insurance obtained for the specific flight.

(5) Landing fees, airport taxes, and similar assessments.

(6) Customs, foreign permit, and similar fees directly related to the flight.

(7) In flight food and beverages.

(8) Passenger ground transportation.

(9) Flight planning and weather contract services.

(10) An additional charge equal to 100 percent of the expenses listed in paragraph (d)(1) of this section.

[Docket No. 18334, 54 FR 34314, Aug. 18, 1989; as amended by Amdt. 91–280, 68 FR 54560, Sept. 17, 2003]

§91.503 Flying equipment and operating information.

(a) The pilot in command of an airplane shall ensure that the following flying equipment and aeronautical charts and data, in current and appropriate form, are accessible for each flight at the pilot station of the airplane:

(1) A flashlight having at least two size "D" cells, or the equivalent, that is in good working order.

(2) A cockpit checklist containing the procedures required by paragraph (b) of this section.

(3) Pertinent aeronautical charts.

(4) For IFR, VFR over-the-top, or night operations, each pertinent navigational en route, terminal area, and approach and letdown chart.

(5) In the case of multiengine airplanes, one-engine inoperative climb performance data.

(b) Each cockpit checklist must contain the following procedures and shall be used by the flight crewmembers when operating the airplane:

(1) Before starting engines.

(2) Before takeoff.

(3) Cruise.

(4) Before landing.

(5) After landing.

(6) Stopping engines.

(7) Emergencies.

(c) Each emergency cockpit checklist procedure required by paragraph (b)(7) of this section must contain the following procedures, as appropriate:

(1) Emergency operation of fuel, hydraulic, electrical, and mechanical systems.

(2) Emergency operation of instruments and controls.

(3) Engine inoperative procedures.

(4) Any other procedures necessary for safety.

(d) The equipment, charts, and data prescribed in this section shall be used by the pilot in command and other members of the flight crew, when pertinent.

§91.505 Familiarity with operating limitations and emergency equipment.

(a) Each pilot in command of an airplane shall, before beginning a flight, become familiar with the Airplane Flight Manual for that airplane, if one is required, and with any placards, listings, instrument markings, or any combination thereof, containing each operating limitation prescribed for that airplane by the Administrator, including those specified in §91.9(b).

(b) Each required member of the crew shall, before beginning a flight, become familiar with the emergency equipment installed on the airplane to which that crewmember is assigned and with the procedures to be followed for the use of that equipment in an emergency situation.

§91.507 Equipment requirements: Over-the-top or night VFR operations.

No person may operate an airplane over-the-top or at night under VFR unless that airplane is equipped with the instruments and equipment required for IFR operations under §91.205(d) and one electric landing light for night operations. Each required instrument and item of equipment must be in operable condition.

§91.509 Survival equipment for overwater operations.

(a) No person may take off an airplane for a flight over water more than 50 nautical miles from the nearest shore unless that airplane is equipped with a life preserver or an approved flotation means for each occupant of the airplane.

(b) Except as provided in paragraph (c) of this section, no person may take off an airplane for flight over water more than 30 minutes flying time or 100 nautical miles from the nearest shore, whichever is less, unless it has on board the following survival equipment:

(1) A life preserver, equipped with an approved survivor locator light, for each occupant of the airplane.

(2) Enough liferafts (each equipped with an approved survival locator light) of a rated capacity and buoyancy to accommodate the occupants of the airplane.

(3) At least one pyrotechnic signaling device for each liferaft.

(4) One self-buoyant, water-resistant, portable emergency radio signaling device that is capable of transmission on the appropriate emergency frequency or frequencies and not dependent upon the airplane power supply.

(5) A lifeline stored in accordance with §25.1411(g) of this chapter.

(c) A fractional ownership program manager under subpart K of this part may apply for a deviation from paragraphs (b)(2) through (5) of this section for a particular over water operation or the Administrator may amend the management specifications to require the carriage of all or any specific items of the equipment listed in paragraphs (b)(2) through (5) of this section.

(d) The required life rafts, life preservers, and signaling devices must be installed in conspicuously marked locations and easily accessible in the event of a ditching without appreciable time for preparatory procedures.

(e) A survival kit, appropriately equipped for the route to be flown, must be attached to each required life raft.

(f) As used in this section, the term shore means that area of the land adjacent to the water that is above the high water mark and excludes land areas that are intermittently under water.

[Docket No. 18334, 54 FR 34314, Aug. 18, 1989; as amended by Amdt. 91–280, 68 FR 54561, Sept. 17, 2003]

§91.511 Radio equipment for overwater operations.

(a) Except as provided in paragraphs (c), (d), and (f) of this section, no person may take off an airplane for a flight over water more than 30 minutes flying time or 100 nautical miles from the nearest shore unless it has at least the following operable equipment:

(1) Radio communication equipment appropriate to the facilities to be used and able to transmit to, and receive from, any place on the route, at least one surface facility:

(i) Two transmitters.

(ii) Two microphones.

(iii) Two headsets or one headset and one speaker.

(iv) Two independent receivers.

(2) Appropriate electronic navigational equipment consisting of at least two independent electronic navigation units capable of providing the pilot with the information necessary to navigate the airplane within the airspace assigned by air traffic control. However, a receiver that can receive both communications and required navigational signals may be used in place of a separate communications receiver and a separate navigational signal receiver or unit.

(b) For the purposes of paragraphs (a)(1)(iv) and (a)(2) of this section, a receiver or electronic navigation unit is independent if the function of any part of it does not depend on the functioning of any part of another receiver or electronic navigation unit.

(c) Notwithstanding the provisions of paragraph (a) of this section, a person may operate an airplane on which no passengers are carried from a place where repairs or replacement cannot be made to a place where they can be made, if not more than one of each of the dual items of radio communication and navigational equipment specified in paragraphs (a)(1)(i) through (iv) and (a)(2) of this section malfunctions or becomes inoperative.

(d) Notwithstanding the provisions of paragraph (a) of this section, when both VHF and HF communications equipment are required for the route and the airplane has two VHF transmitters and two VHF receivers for communications, only one HF transmitter and one HF receiver is required for communications.

(e) As used in this section, the term *shore* means that area of the land adjacent to the water which is above the high-water mark and excludes land areas which are intermittently under water.

(f) Notwithstanding the requirements in paragraph (a)(2) of this section, a person may operate in the Gulf of Mexico, the Caribbean Sea, and the Atlantic Ocean west of a line which extends from 44° 47'00" N / 67° 00'00" W to 39° 00'00" N / 67° 00'00" W to 38° 30'00" N / 60° 00'00" W south along the 60° 00'00" W longitude line to the point where the line intersects with the northern coast of South America, when:

(1) A single long-range navigation system is installed, operational, and appropriate for the route; and

(2) Flight conditions and the aircraft's capabilities are such that no more than a 30-minute gap in two-way radio very high frequency communications is expected to exist.

[Docket No. 18334, 54 FR 34314, Aug. 18, 1989; as amended by Amdt. 91–249, 61 FR 7190, Feb. 26, 1996]

§91.513 Emergency equipment.

(a) No person may operate an airplane unless it is equipped with the emergency equipment listed in this section.

(b) Each item of equipment—

(1) Must be inspected in accordance with §91.409 to ensure its continued serviceability and immediate readiness for its intended purposes;

(2) Must be readily accessible to the crew;

(3) Must clearly indicate its method of operation; and

(4) When carried in a compartment or container, must have that compartment or container marked as to contents and date of last inspection.

(c) Hand fire extinguishers must be provided for use in crew, passenger, and cargo compartments in accordance with the following:

(1) The type and quantity of extinguishing agent must be suitable for the kinds of fires likely to occur in the compartment where the extinguisher is intended to be used.

(2) At least one hand fire extinguisher must be provided and located on or near the flight deck in a place that is readily accessible to the flight crew.

(3) At least one hand fire extinguisher must be conveniently located in the passenger compartment of each airplane accommodating more than six but less than 31 passengers, and at least two hand fire extinguishers must be conveniently located in the passenger compartment of each airplane accommodating more than 30 passengers.

(4) Hand fire extinguishers must be installed and secured in such a manner that they will not interfere with the safe operation of the airplane or adversely affect the safety of the crew and passengers. They must be readily accessible and, unless the locations of the fire extinguishers are obvious, their stowage provisions must be properly identified.

(d) First aid kits for treatment of injuries likely to occur in flight or in minor accidents must be provided.

(e) Each airplane accommodating more than 19 passengers must be equipped with a crash axe.

(f) Each passenger-carrying airplane must have a portable battery-powered megaphone or megaphones readily accessible to the crewmembers assigned to direct emergency evacuation, installed as follows:

(1) One megaphone on each airplane with a seating capacity of more than 60 but less than 100 passengers, at the most rearward location in the passenger cabin where it would be readily accessible to a normal flight attendant seat. However, the Administrator may grant a deviation from the requirements of this subparagraph if the Administrator finds that a different location would be more useful for evacuation of persons during an emergency.

(2) On each airplane with a seating capacity of 100 or more passengers, one megaphone installed at the forward end and one installed at the most rearward location where it would be readily accessible to a normal flight attendant seat.

§91.515 Flight altitude rules.

(a) Notwithstanding §91.119, and except as provided in paragraph (b) of this section, no person may operate an airplane under VFR at less than—

(1) One thousand feet above the surface, or 1,000 feet from any mountain, hill, or other obstruction to flight, for day operations; and

(2) The altitudes prescribed in §91.177, for night operations.

(b) This section does not apply—

(1) During takeoff or landing;

(2) When a different altitude is authorized by a waiver to this section under subpart J of this part; or

(3) When a flight is conducted under the special VFR weather minimums of §91.157 with an appropriate clearance from ATC.

§91.517 Passenger information.

(a) Except as provided in paragraph (b) of this section, no person may operate an airplane carrying passengers unless it is equipped with signs that are visible to passengers and flight attendants to notify them when smoking is prohibited and when safety belts must be fastened. The signs must be so constructed that the crew can turn them on and off. They must be turned on during airplane movement on the surface, for each takeoff, for each landing, and when otherwise considered to be necessary by the pilot in command.

(b) The pilot in command of an airplane that is not required, in accordance with applicable aircraft and equipment requirements of this chapter, to be equipped as provided in paragraph (a) of this section shall ensure that the passengers are notified orally each time that it is necessary to fasten their safety belts and when smoking is prohibited.

(c) If passenger information signs are installed, no passenger or crewmember may smoke while any "no smoking" sign is lighted nor may any passenger or crewmember smoke in any lavatory.

(d) Each passenger required by §91.107 (a) (3) to occupy a seat or berth shall fasten his or her safety belt about him or her and keep it fastened while any "fasten seat belt" sign is lighted.

(e) Each passenger shall comply with instructions given him or her by crewmembers regarding compliance with paragraphs (b), (c), and (d) of this section.

[Docket No. 26142, 57 FR 42672, Sept. 15, 1992]

§91.519 Passenger briefing.

(a) Before each takeoff the pilot in command of an airplane carrying passengers shall ensure that all passengers have been orally briefed on—

(1) *Smoking.* Each passenger shall be briefed on when, where, and under what conditions smoking is prohibited. This briefing shall include a statement, as appropriate, that the Federal Aviation Regulations require passenger compliance with lighted passenger information signs and no smoking placards, prohibit smoking in the lavatories, and require compliance with crewmember instructions with regard to these items;

(2) *Use of safety belts and shoulder harnesses.* Each passenger shall be briefed on when, where, and under what conditions it is necessary to have his or her safety belt and, if installed, his or her shoulder harness fastened about him or her. The briefing shall include a statement, as appropriate, that Federal Aviation Regulations require passenger compliance with the lighted passenger sign and/or crewmember instructions with regard to these items;

(3) Location and means for opening the passenger entry door and emergency exits;

(4) Location of survival equipment;

(5) Ditching procedures and the use of flotation equipment required under §91.509 for a flight over water; and

(6) The normal and emergency use of oxygen equipment installed on the airplane.

(b) The oral briefing required by paragraph (a) of this section shall be given by the pilot in command or a member of the crew, but need not be given when the pilot in command determines that the passengers are familiar with the contents of the briefing. It may be supplemented by printed cards for the use of each passenger containing—

(1) A diagram of, and methods of operating, the emergency exits; and

(2) Other instructions necessary for use of emergency equipment.

(c) Each card used under paragraph (b) must be carried in convenient locations on the airplane for the use of each passenger and must contain information that is pertinent only to the type and model airplane on which it is used.

(d) For operations under subpart K of this part, the passenger briefing requirements of §91.1035 apply, instead of the requirements of paragraphs (a) through (c) of this section.

[Docket No. 18334, 54 FR 34314, Aug. 18, 1989; as amended by Amdt. 91–231, 57 FR 42672, Sept. 15, 1992; Amdt. 91–280, 68 FR 54561, Sept. 17, 2003]

§91.521 Shoulder harness.

(a) No person may operate a transport category airplane that was type certificated after January 1, 1958, unless it is equipped at each seat at a flight deck station with a combined safety belt and shoulder harness that meets the applicable requirements specified in §25.785 of this chapter, except that—

(1) Shoulder harnesses and combined safety belt and shoulder harnesses that were approved and installed before March 6, 1980, may continue to be used; and

(2) Safety belt and shoulder harness restraint systems may be designed to the inertia load factors established under the certification basis of the airplane.

(b) No person may operate a transport category airplane unless it is equipped at each required flight attendant seat in the passenger compartment with a combined safety belt and shoulder harness that meets the applicable requirements specified in §25.785 of this chapter, except that—

(1) Shoulder harnesses and combined safety belt and shoulder harnesses that were approved and installed before March 6, 1980, may continue to be used; and

(2) Safety belt and shoulder harness restraint systems may be designed to the inertia load factors established under the certification basis of the airplane.

§91.523 Carry-on baggage.

No pilot in command of an airplane having a seating capacity of more than 19 passengers may permit a passenger to stow baggage aboard that airplane except—

(a) In a suitable baggage or cargo storage compartment, or as provided in §91.525; or

(b) Under a passenger seat in such a way that it will not slide forward under crash impacts severe enough to induce the ultimate inertia forces specified in §25.561(b)(3) of this chapter, or the requirements of the regulations under which the airplane was type certificated. Restraining devices must also limit sideward motion of under-seat baggage and be designed to withstand crash impacts severe enough to induce sideward forces specified in §25.561(b)(3) of this chapter.

§91.525 Carriage of cargo.

(a) No pilot in command may permit cargo to be carried in any airplane unless—

(1) It is carried in an approved cargo rack, bin, or compartment installed in the airplane;

(2) It is secured by means approved by the Administrator; or

(3) It is carried in accordance with each of the following:

(i) It is properly secured by a safety belt or other tiedown having enough strength to eliminate the possibility of shifting under all normally anticipated flight and ground conditions.

(ii) It is packaged or covered to avoid possible injury to passengers.

(iii) It does not impose any load on seats or on the floor structure that exceeds the load limitation for those components.

(iv) It is not located in a position that restricts the access to or use of any required emergency or regular exit, or the use of the aisle between the crew and the passenger compartment.

(v) It is not carried directly above seated passengers.

(b) When cargo is carried in cargo compartments that are designed to require the physical entry of a crewmember to extinguish any fire that may occur during flight, the cargo must be loaded so as to allow a crewmember to effectively reach all parts of the compartment with the contents of a hand fire extinguisher.

§91.527 Operating in icing conditions.

(a) No pilot may take off an airplane that has—

(1) Frost, snow, or ice adhering to any propeller, windshield, or powerplant installation or to an airspeed, altimeter, rate of climb, or flight attitude instrument system;

(2) Snow or ice adhering to the wings or stabilizing or control surfaces; or

(3) Any frost adhering to the wings or stabilizing or control surfaces, unless that frost has been polished to make it smooth.

(b) Except for an airplane that has ice protection provisions that meet the requirements in section 34 of Special Federal Aviation Regulation No. 23, or those for transport category airplane type certification, no pilot may fly—

(1) Under IFR into known or forecast moderate icing conditions; or

(2) Under VFR into known light or moderate icing conditions unless the aircraft has functioning de-icing or anti-icing equipment protecting each propeller, windshield, wing, stabilizing or control surface, and each airspeed, altimeter, rate of climb, or flight attitude instrument system.

(c) Except for an airplane that has ice protection provisions that meet the requirements in section 34 of Special Federal Aviation Regulation No. 23, or those for transport category airplane type certification, no pilot may fly an airplane into known or forecast severe icing conditions.

(d) If current weather reports and briefing information relied upon by the pilot in command indicate that the forecast icing conditions that would otherwise prohibit the flight will not be encountered during the flight because of changed weather conditions since the forecast, the restrictions in paragraphs (b) and (c) of this section based on forecast conditions do not apply.

§91.529 Flight engineer requirements.

(a) No person may operate the following airplanes without a flight crewmember holding a current flight engineer certificate:

(1) An airplane for which a type certificate was issued before January 2, 1964, having a maximum certificated takeoff weight of more than 80,000 pounds.

(2) An airplane type certificated after January 1, 1964, for which a flight engineer is required by the type certification requirements.

(b) No person may serve as a required flight engineer on an airplane unless, within the preceding 6 calendar months, that person has had at least 50 hours of flight time as a flight engineer on that type airplane or has been checked by the Administrator on that type airplane and is found to be familiar and competent with all essential current information and operating procedures.

§91.531 Second in command requirements.

(a) Except as provided in paragraph (b) and (d) of this section, no person may operate the following airplanes without a pilot who is designated as second in command of that airplane:

(1) A large airplane, except that a person may operate an airplane certificated under SFAR 41 without a pilot who is designated as second in command if that airplane is certificated for operation with one pilot.

(2) A turbojet-powered multiengine airplane for which two pilots are required under the type certification requirements for that airplane.

(3) A commuter category airplane, except that a person may operate a commuter category airplane notwithstanding paragraph (a)(1) of this section, that has a passenger seating configuration, excluding pilot seats, of nine or less without a pilot who is designated as second in command if that airplane is type certificated for operations with one pilot.

(b) The Administrator may issue a letter of authorization for the operation of an airplane without compliance with the requirements of paragraph (a) of this section if that airplane is designed for and type certificated with only one pilot station. The authorization contains any conditions that the Administrator finds necessary for safe operation.

(c) No person may designate a pilot to serve as second in command, nor may any pilot serve as second in command, of an airplane required under this section to have two pilots unless that pilot meets the qualifications for second in command prescribed in §61.55 of this chapter.

(d) No person may operate an aircraft under subpart K of this part without a pilot who is designated as second in command of that aircraft in accordance with §91.1049(d). The second in command must meet the experience requirements of §91.1053.

[Docket No. 18334, 54 FR 34314, Aug. 18, 1989; as amended by Amdt. 91–280, 68 FR 54561, Sept. 17, 2003]

§91.533 Flight attendant requirements.

(a) No person may operate an airplane unless at least the following number of flight attendants are on board the airplane:

(1) For airplanes having more than 19 but less than 51 passengers on board, one flight attendant.

(2) For airplanes having more than 50 but less than 101 passengers on board, two flight attendants.

(3) For airplanes having more than 100 passengers on board, two flight attendants plus one additional flight attendant for each unit (or part of a unit) of 50 passengers above 100.

(b) No person may serve as a flight attendant on an airplane when required by paragraph (a) of this section unless that person has demonstrated to the pilot in command familiarity with the necessary functions to be performed in an emergency or a situation requiring emergency evacuation and is capable of using the emergency equipment installed on that airplane.

§91.535 Stowage of food, beverage, and passenger service equipment during aircraft movement on the surface, takeoff, and landing.

(a) No operator may move an aircraft on the surface, takeoff or land when any food, beverage, or tableware furnished by the operator is located at any passenger seat.

(b) No operator may move an aircraft on the surface, takeoff, or land unless each food and beverage tray is secured in its stowed position.

(c) No operator may permit an aircraft to move on the surface, takeoff, or land unless each passenger serving cart is secured in its stowed position.

(d) No operator may permit an aircraft to move on the surface, takeoff, or land unless each movie screen that extends into the aisle is stowed.

(e) Each passenger shall comply with instructions given by a crewmember with regard to compliance with this section.

[Docket No. 26142, 57 FR 42672, Sept. 15, 1992]

§91.537 – 91.599 [Reserved]

Subpart G—Additional Equipment and Operating Requirements for Large and Transport Category Aircraft

Source: Docket No. 18334, 54 FR 34318, Aug. 18, 1989, unless otherwise noted.

§91.601 Applicability.

This subpart applies to operation of large and transport category U.S.-registered civil aircraft.

§91.603 Aural speed warning device.

No person may operate a transport category airplane in air commerce unless that airplane is equipped with an aural speed warning device that complies with §25.1303(c)(1).

§91.605 Transport category civil airplane weight limitations.

(a) No person may take off any transport category airplane (other than a turbine-engine-powered airplane certificated after September 30, 1958) unless—

(1) The takeoff weight does not exceed the authorized maximum takeoff weight for the elevation of the airport of takeoff;

(2) The elevation of the airport of takeoff is within the altitude range for which maximum takeoff weights have been determined;

(3) Normal consumption of fuel and oil in flight to the airport of intended landing will leave a weight on arrival not in excess of the authorized maximum landing weight for the elevation of that airport; and

(4) The elevations of the airport of intended landing and of all specified alternate airports are within the altitude range for which the maximum landing weights have been determined.

(b) No person may operate a turbine-engine-powered transport category airplane certificated after September 30, 1958, contrary to the Airplane Flight Manual, or take off that airplane unless—

(1) The takeoff weight does not exceed the takeoff weight specified in the Airplane Flight Manual for the elevation of the airport and for the ambient temperature existing at the time of takeoff;

(2) Normal consumption of fuel and oil in flight to the airport of intended landing and to the alternate airports will leave a weight on arrival not in excess of the landing weight specified in the Airplane Flight Manual for the elevation of each of the airports involved and for the ambient temperatures expected at the time of landing;

(3) The takeoff weight does not exceed the weight shown in the Airplane Flight Manual to correspond with the minimum distances required for takeoff, considering the elevation of the airport, the runway to be used, the effective runway gradient, and the ambient temperature and wind component at the time of takeoff, and, if operating limitations exist for the minimum distances required for takeoff from wet runways, the runway surface condition (dry or wet). Wet runway distances associated with grooved or porous friction course runways, if provided in the Airplane Flight Manual, may be used only for runways that are grooved or treated with a porous friction course (PFC) overlay, and that the operator determines are designed, constructed, and maintained in a manner acceptable to the Administrator.

(4) Where the takeoff distance includes a clearway, the clearway distance is not greater than one-half of—

(i) The takeoff run, in the case of airplanes certificated after September 30, 1958, and before August 30, 1959; or

(ii) The runway length, in the case of airplanes certificated after August 29, 1959.

(c) No person may take off a turbine-engine-powered transport category airplane certificated after August 29,

1959, unless, in addition to the requirements of paragraph (b) of this section—

(1) The accelerate-stop distance is no greater than the length of the runway plus the length of the stopway (if present); and

(2) The takeoff distance is no greater than the length of the runway plus the length of the clearway (if present); and

(3) The takeoff run is no greater than the length of the runway.

[Docket No. 18334, 54 FR 34318, Aug. 18, 1989; as amended by Amdt. 91–256, 63 FR 8321, Feb. 18, 1998]

§91.607 Emergency exits for airplanes carrying passengers for hire.

(a) Notwithstanding any other provision of this chapter, no person may operate a large airplane (type certificated under the Civil Air Regulations effective before April 9, 1957) in passenger-carrying operations for hire, with more than the number of occupants—

(1) Allowed under Civil Air Regulations §4b.362 (a), (b), and (c) as in effect on December 20, 1951; or

(2) Approved under Special Civil Air Regulations SR–387, SR–389, SR–389A, or SR–389B, or under this section as in effect.

However, an airplane type listed in the following table may be operated with up to the listed number of occupants (including crewmembers) and the corresponding number of exits (including emergency exits and doors) approved for the emergency exit of passengers or with an occupant-exit configuration approved under paragraph (b) or (c) of this section.

Airplane type	Maximum number of occupants including all crewmembers	Corresponding number of exits authorized for passenger use
B-307	61	4
B-377	96	9
C-46	67	4
CV-240	53	6
CV-340 and CV-440	53	6
DC-3	35	4
DC-3 (Super)	39	5
DC-4	86	5
DC-6	87	7
DC-6B	112	11
L-18	17	3
L-049, L-649, L-749	87	7
L-1049 series	96	9
M-202	53	6
M-404	53	7
Viscount 700 series	53	7

(b) Occupants in addition to those authorized under paragraph (a) of this section may be carried as follows:

(1) For each additional floor-level exit at least 24 inches wide by 48 inches high, with an unobstructed 20-inch-wide access aisleway between the exit and the main passenger aisle, 12 additional occupants.

(2) For each additional window exit located over a wing that meets the requirements of the airworthiness standards under which the airplane was type certificated or that is large enough to inscribe an ellipse 19 X 26 inches, eight additional occupants.

(3) For each additional window exit that is not located over a wing but that otherwise complies with paragraph (b)(2) of this section, five additional occupants.

(4) For each airplane having a ratio (as computed from the table in paragraph (a) of this section) of maximum number of occupants to number of exits greater than 14:1, and for each airplane that does not have at least one full-size, door-type exit in the side of the fuselage in the rear part of the cabin, the first additional exit must be a floor-level exit that complies with paragraph (b)(1) of this section and must be located in the rear part of the cabin on the opposite side of the fuselage from the main entrance door. However, no person may operate an airplane under this section carrying more than 115 occupants unless there is such an exit on each side of the fuselage in the rear part of the cabin.

(c) No person may eliminate any approved exit except in accordance with the following:

(1) The previously authorized maximum number of occupants must be reduced by the same number of additional occupants authorized for that exit under this section.

(2) Exits must be eliminated in accordance with the following priority schedule: First, non-over-wing window exits; second, over-wing window exits; third, floor-level exits located in the forward part of the cabin; and fourth, floor-level exits located in the rear of the cabin.

(3) At least one exit must be retained on each side of the fuselage regardless of the number of occupants.

(4) No person may remove any exit that would result in a ratio of maximum number of occupants to approved exits greater than 14:1.

(d) This section does not relieve any person operating under part 121 of this chapter from complying with §121.291.

§91.609 Flight recorders and cockpit voice recorders.

(a) No holder of an air carrier operating certificate or an operating certificate may conduct any operation under this part with an aircraft listed in the holder's operations specifications or current list of aircraft used in air transportation unless that aircraft complies with any applicable flight recorder and cockpit voice recorder requirements of the part under which its certificate is issued except that the operator may—

(1) Ferry an aircraft with an inoperative flight recorder or cockpit voice recorder from a place where repair or replacement cannot be made to a place where they can be made;

(2) Continue a flight as originally planned, if the flight recorder or cockpit voice recorder becomes inoperative after the aircraft has taken off;

(3) Conduct an airworthiness flight test during which the flight recorder or cockpit voice recorder is turned off to test it

or to test any communications or electrical equipment installed in the aircraft; or

(4) Ferry a newly acquired aircraft from the place where possession of it is taken to a place where the flight recorder or cockpit voice recorder is to be installed.

(b) Notwithstanding paragraphs (c) and (e) of this section, an operator other than the holder of an air carrier or a commercial operator certificate may—

(1) Ferry an aircraft with an inoperative flight recorder or cockpit voice recorder from a place where repair or replacement cannot be made to a place where they can be made;

(2) Continue a flight as originally planned if the flight recorder or cockpit voice recorder becomes inoperative after the aircraft has taken off;

(3) Conduct an airworthiness flight test during which the flight recorder or cockpit voice recorder is turned off to test it or to test any communications or electrical equipment installed in the aircraft;

(4) Ferry a newly acquired aircraft from a place where possession of it was taken to a place where the flight recorder or cockpit voice recorder is to be installed; or

(5) Operate an aircraft:

(i) For not more than 15 days while the flight recorder and/or cockpit voice recorder is inoperative and/or removed for repair provided that the aircraft maintenance records contain an entry that indicates the date of failure, and a placard is located in view of the cockpit to show that the flight recorder or pilot voice recorder is inoperative.

(ii) For not more than an additional 15 days, provided that the requirements in paragraph (b)(5)(i) are met and that a certified pilot, or a certified person authorized to return an aircraft to service under §43.7 of this chapter certifies in the aircraft maintenance records that additional time is required to complete repairs or obtain a replacement unit.

(c) No person may operate a U.S. civil registered, multiengine, turbine-powered airplane or rotorcraft having a passenger seating configuration, excluding any pilot seats of 10 or more that has been manufactured after October 11, 1991, unless it is equipped with one or more approved flight recorders that utilize a digital method of recording and storing data and a method of readily retrieving that data from the storage medium, that are capable of recording the data specified in Appendix E to this part, for an airplane, or Appendix F to this part, for a rotorcraft, of this part within the range, accuracy, and recording interval specified, and that are capable of retaining no less than 8 hours of aircraft operation.

(d) Whenever a flight recorder, required by this section, is installed, it must be operated continuously from the instant the airplane begins the takeoff roll or the rotorcraft begins lift-off until the airplane has completed the landing roll or the rotorcraft has landed at its destination.

(e) Unless otherwise authorized by the Administrator, after October 11, 1991, no person may operate a U.S. civil registered multiengine, turbine-powered airplane or rotorcraft having a passenger seating configuration of six passengers or more and for which two pilots are required by type certification or operating rule unless it is equipped with an approved cockpit voice recorder that:

(1) Is installed in compliance with §23.1457(a) (1) and (2), (b), (c), (d), (e), (f), and (g); §25.1457(a) (1) and (2), (b), (c), (d), (e), (f), and (g); §27.1457(a) (1) and (2), (b), (c), (d), (e), (f), and (g); or §29.1457(a) (1) and (2), (b), (c), (d), (e), (f), and (g) of this chapter, as applicable; and

(2) Is operated continuously from the use of the checklist before the flight to completion of the final checklist at the end of the flight.

(f) In complying with this section, an approved cockpit voice recorder having an erasure feature may be used, so that at any time during the operation of the recorder, information recorded more than 15 minutes earlier may be erased or otherwise obliterated.

(g) In the event of an accident or occurrence requiring immediate notification to the National Transportation Safety Board under part 830 of its regulations that results in the termination of the flight, any operator who has installed approved flight recorders and approved cockpit voice recorders shall keep the recorded information for at least 60 days or, if requested by the Administrator or the Board, for a longer period. Information obtained from the record is used to assist in determining the cause of accidents or occurrences in connection with the investigation under part 830. The Administrator does not use the cockpit voice recorder record in any civil penalty or certificate action.

[Docket No. 18334, 54 FR 34318, Aug. 18, 1989; as amended by Amdt. 91–226, 56 FR 51621, Oct. 11, 1991; Amdt. 91–228, 57 FR 19353, May 5, 1992]

§91.611 Authorization for ferry flight with one engine inoperative.

(a) *General.* The holder of an air carrier operating certificate or an operating certificate issued under part 125 may conduct a ferry flight of a four-engine airplane or a turbine-engine-powered airplane equipped with three engines, with one engine inoperative, to a base for the purpose of repairing that engine subject to the following:

(1) The airplane model has been test flown and found satisfactory for safe flight in accordance with paragraph (b) or (c) of this section, as appropriate. However, each operator who before November 19, 1966, has shown that a model of airplane with an engine inoperative is satisfactory for safe flight by a test flight conducted in accordance with performance data contained in the applicable Airplane Flight Manual under paragraph (a)(2) of this section need not repeat the test flight for that model.

(2) The approved Airplane Flight Manual contains the following performance data and the flight is conducted in accordance with that data:

(i) Maximum weight.

(ii) Center of gravity limits.

(iii) Configuration of the inoperative propeller (if applicable).

(iv) Runway length for takeoff (including temperature accountability).

(v) Altitude range.

(vi) Certificate limitations.

(vii) Ranges of operational limits.

(viii) Performance information.

(ix) Operating procedures.

(3) The operator has FAA approved procedures for the safe operation of the airplane, including specific requirements for—

(i) Limiting the operating weight on any ferry flight to the minimum necessary for the flight plus the necessary reserve fuel load;

(ii) A limitation that takeoffs must be made from dry runways unless, based on a showing of actual operating takeoff techniques on wet runways with one engine inoperative, takeoffs with full controllability from wet runways have been approved for the specific model aircraft and included in the Airplane Flight Manual:

(iii) Operations from airports where the runways may require a takeoff or approach over populated areas; and

(iv) Inspection procedures for determining the operating condition of the operative engines.

(4) No person may take off an airplane under this section if—

(i) The initial climb is over thickly populated areas; or

(ii) Weather conditions at the takeoff or destination airport are less than those required for VFR flight.

(5) Persons other than required flight crewmembers shall not be carried during the flight.

(6) No person may use a flight crewmember for flight under this section unless that crewmember is thoroughly familiar with the operating procedures for one-engine inoperative ferry flight contained in the certificate holder's manual and the limitations and performance information in the Airplane Flight Manual.

(b) *Flight tests: reciprocating-engine-powered airplanes.* The airplane performance of a reciprocating-engine-powered airplane with one engine inoperative must be determined by flight test as follows:

(1) A speed not less than 1.3 V_{S1} must be chosen at which the airplane may be controlled satisfactorily in a climb with the critical engine inoperative (with its propeller removed or in a configuration desired by the operator and with all other engines operating at the maximum power determined in paragraph (b)(3) of this section.

(2) The distance required to accelerate to the speed listed in paragraph (b)(1) of this section and to climb to 50 feet must be determined with—

(i) The landing gear extended;

(ii) The critical engine inoperative and its propeller removed or in a configuration desired by the operator; and

(iii) The other engines operating at not more than maximum power established under paragraph (b)(3) of this section.

(3) The takeoff, flight and landing procedures, such as the approximate trim settings, method of power application, maximum power, and speed must be established.

(4) The performance must be determined at a maximum weight not greater than the weight that allows a rate of climb of at least 400 feet per minute in the en route configuration set forth in §25.67(d) of this chapter in effect on January 31, 1977, at an altitude of 5,000 feet.

(5) The performance must be determined using temperature accountability for the takeoff field length, computed in accordance with §25.61 of this chapter in effect on January 31, 1977.

(c) *Flight tests: Turbine-engine-powered airplanes.* The airplane performance of a turbine-engine-powered airplane with one engine inoperative must be determined by flight tests, including at least three takeoff tests, in accordance with the following:

(1) Takeoff speeds V_R and V_2, not less than the corresponding speeds under which the airplane was type certificated under §25.107 of this chapter, must be chosen at which the airplane may be controlled satisfactorily with the critical engine inoperative (with its propeller removed or in a configuration desired by the operator, if applicable) and with all other engines operating at not more than the power selected for type certification as set forth in §25.101 of this chapter.

(2) The minimum takeoff field length must be the horizontal distance required to accelerate and climb to the 35-foot height at V_2 speed (including any additional speed increment obtained in the tests) multiplied by 115 percent and determined with—

(i) The landing gear extended;

(ii) The critical engine inoperative and its propeller removed or in a configuration desired by the operator (if applicable); and

(iii) The other engine operating at not more than the power selected for type certification as set forth in §25.101 of this chapter.

(3) The takeoff, flight, and landing procedures such as the approximate trim setting, method of power application, maximum power, and speed must be established. The airplane must be satisfactorily controllable during the entire takeoff run when operated according to these procedures.

(4) The performance must be determined at a maximum weight not greater than the weight determined under §25.121(c) of this chapter but with—

(i) The actual steady gradient of the final takeoff climb requirement not less than 1.2 percent at the end of the takeoff path with two critical engines inoperative; and

(ii) The climb speed not less than the two-engine inoperative trim speed for the actual steady gradient of the final takeoff climb prescribed by paragraph (c)(4)(i) of this section.

(5) The airplane must be satisfactorily controllable in a climb with two critical engines inoperative. Climb performance may be shown by calculations based on, and equal in accuracy to, the results of testing.

(6) The performance must be determined using temperature accountability for takeoff distance and final takeoff climb computed in accordance with §25.101 of this chapter.

For the purpose of paragraphs (c)(4) and (5) of this section, *two critical engines* means two adjacent engines on one side of an airplane with four engines, and the center engine and one outboard engine on an airplane with three engines.

§91.613 Materials for compartment interiors.

(a) No person may operate an airplane that conforms to an amended or supplemental type certificate issued in accordance with SFAR No. 41 for a maximum certificated takeoff weight in excess of 12,500 pounds unless within 1 year after issuance of the initial airworthiness certificate under that SFAR the airplane meets the compartment interior requirements set forth in §25.853 (a), (b), (b-1), (b-2), and (b-3) of this chapter in effect on September 26, 1978.

(b) Thermal/acoustic insulation materials. For transport category airplanes type certificated after January 1, 1958:

(1) For airplanes manufactured before September 2, 2005, when thermal/acoustic insulation materials are in-

stalled in the fuselage as replacements after September 2, 2005, those materials must meet the flame propagation requirements of §25.856 of this chapter, effective September 2, 2003.

(2) For airplanes manufactured after September 2, 2005, thermal/acoustic insulation materials installed in the fuselage must meet the flame propagation requirements of §25.856 of this chapter, effective September 2, 2003.

[Docket No. 18334, 54 FR 34318, Aug. 18, 1989; as amended by Docket No. FAA–2000–7909; Amdt. 91–279, 68 FR 45083, July 31, 2003]

§91.615 – 91.699 [Reserved]

Subpart H— Foreign Aircraft Operations and Operations of U.S.-Registered Civil Aircraft Outside of the United States; and Rules Governing Persons On Board Such Aircraft

Source: Docket No. 18334, 54 FR 34320, Aug. 18, 1989, unless otherwise noted.

§91.701 Applicability.

(a) This subpart applies to the operations of civil aircraft of U.S. registry outside of the United States and the operations of foreign civil aircraft within the United States.

(b) Section 91.702 of this subpart also applies to each person on board an aircraft operated as follows:

(1) A U.S. registered civil aircraft operated outside the United States;

(2) Any aircraft operated outside the United States—

(i) That has its next scheduled destination or last place of departure in the United States if the aircraft next lands in the United States; or

(ii) If the aircraft lands in the United States with the individual still on the aircraft regardless of whether it was a scheduled or otherwise planned landing site.

[Docket No. 18334, 54 FR 34320, Aug. 18, 1989; as amended by Amdt. 91–257, 64 FR 1079, Jan. 7, 1999]

§91.702 Persons on board.

Section 91.11 of this part (Prohibitions on interference with crewmembers) applies to each person on board an aircraft.

[Docket No. 18334, 54 FR 34320, Aug. 18, 1989; as amended by Amdt. 91–257, 64 FR 1079, Jan. 7, 1999]

§91.703 Operations of civil aircraft of U.S. registry outside of the United States.

(a) Each person operating a civil aircraft of U.S. registry outside of the United States shall—

(1) When over the high seas, comply with annex 2 (Rules of the Air) to the Convention on International Civil Aviation and with §§91.117(c), 91.127, 91.129, and 91.131;

(2) When within a foreign country, comply with the regulations relating to the flight and maneuver of aircraft there in force;

(3) Except for §§91.307(b), 91.309, 91.323, and 91.711, comply with this part so far as it is not inconsistent with applicable regulations of the foreign country where the aircraft is operated or annex 2 of the Convention on International Civil Aviation; and

(4) When operating within airspace designated as Minimum Navigation Performance Specifications (MNPS) airspace, comply with §91.705. When operating within airspace designated as Reduced Vertical Separation Minimum (RVSM) airspace, comply with §91.706.

(b) Annex 2 to the Convention on International Civil Aviation, Ninth Edition—July 1990, with Amendments through Amendment 32 effective February 19, 1996, to which reference is made in this part, is incorporated into this part and made a part hereof as provided in 5 U.S.C. §552 and pursuant to 1 CFR part 51. Annex 2 (including a complete historic file of changes thereto) is available for public inspection at the Rules Docket, AGC–200, Federal Aviation Administration, 800 Independence Avenue SW, Washington, DC 20591; or at the Office of the Federal Register, 800 North Capitol Street NW., Suite 700, Washington DC. In addition, Annex 2 may be purchased from the International Civil Aviation Organization (Attention: Distribution Officer), P.O. Box 400, Succursale, Place de L'Aviation Internationale, 1000 Sherbrooke Street West, Montreal, Quebec, Canada H3A 2R2.

[Docket No. 18834, 54 FR 34320, Aug. 18, 1989; as amended by Amdt. 91–227, 56 FR 65661, Dec. 17, 1991; Amdt. 91–254, 62 FR 17487, April 9, 1997]

§91.705 Operations within airspace designated as Minimum Navigation Performance Specification Airspace.

(a) Except as provided in paragraph (b) of this section, no person may operate a civil aircraft of U.S. registry in airspace designated as Minimum Navigation Performance Specifications airspace unless—

(1) The aircraft has approved navigation performance capability that complies with the requirements of Appendix C of this part; and

(2) The operator is authorized by the Administrator to perform such operations.

(b) The Administrator may authorize a deviation from the requirements of this section in accordance with Section 3 of Appendix C to this part.

[Docket No. 28870, 62 FR 17487, April 9, 1997]

§91.706 Operations within airspace designated as Reduced Vertical Separation Minimum Airspace.

(a) Except as provided in paragraph (b) of this section, no person may operate a civil aircraft of U.S. registry in airspace designated as Reduced Vertical Separation Minimum (RVSM) airspace unless—

(1) The operator and the operator's aircraft comply with the requirements of Appendix G of this part; and

(2) The operator is authorized by the Administrator to conduct such operations.

(b) The Administrator may authorize a deviation from the requirements of this section in accordance with Section 5 of Appendix G to this part.

[Docket No. 28870, 62 FR 17487, April 9, 1997]

§91.707 Flights between Mexico or Canada and the United States.

Unless otherwise authorized by ATC, no person may operate a civil aircraft between Mexico or Canada and the United States without filing an IFR or VFR flight plan, as appropriate.

§91.709 Operations to Cuba.

No person may operate a civil aircraft from the United States to Cuba unless—

(a) Departure is from an international airport of entry designated in §6.13 of the Air Commerce Regulations of the Bureau of Customs (19 CFR 6.13); and

(b) In the case of departure from any of the 48 contiguous States or the District of Columbia, the pilot in command of the aircraft has filed—

(1) A DVFR or IFR flight plan as prescribed in §99.11 or §99.13 of this chapter; and

(2) A written statement, within 1 hour before departure, with the Office of Immigration and Naturalization Service at the airport of departure, containing—

(i) All information in the flight plan;

(ii) The name of each occupant of the aircraft;

(iii) The number of occupants of the aircraft; and

(iv) A description of the cargo, if any.

This section does not apply to the operation of aircraft by a scheduled air carrier over routes authorized in operations specifications issued by the Administrator.

(Approved by the Office of Management and Budget under control number 2120–0005)

§91.711 Special rules for foreign civil aircraft.

(a) *General.* In addition to the other applicable regulations of this part, each person operating a foreign civil aircraft within the United States shall comply with this section.

(b) *VFR.* No person may conduct VFR operations which require two-way radio communications under this part unless at least one crewmember of that aircraft is able to conduct two-way radio communications in the English language and is on duty during that operation.

(c) *IFR.* No person may operate a foreign civil aircraft under IFR unless—

(1) That aircraft is equipped with—

(i) Radio equipment allowing two-way radio communication with ATC when it is operated in controlled airspace; and

(ii) Radio navigational equipment appropriate to the navigational facilities to be used;

(2) Each person piloting the aircraft—

(i) Holds a current United States instrument rating or is authorized by his foreign airman certificate to pilot under IFR; and

(ii) Is thoroughly familiar with the United States en route, holding, and letdown procedures; and

(3) At least one crewmember of that aircraft is able to conduct two-way radiotelephone communications in the English language and that crewmember is on duty while the aircraft is approaching, operating within, or leaving the United States.

(d) *Over water.* Each person operating a foreign civil aircraft over water off the shores of the United States shall give flight notification or file a flight plan in accordance with the Supplementary Procedures for the ICAO region concerned.

(e) *Flight at and above FL 240.* If VOR navigational equipment is required under paragraph (c)(1)(ii) of this section, no person may operate a foreign civil aircraft within the 50 States and the District of Columbia at or above FL 240, unless the aircraft is equipped with distance measuring equipment (DME) capable of receiving and indicating distance information from the VORTAC facilities to be used. When DME required by this paragraph fails at and above FL 240, the pilot in command of the aircraft shall notify ATC immediately and may then continue operations at and above FL 240 to the next airport of intended landing at which repairs or replacement of the equipment can be made. However, paragraph (e) of this section does not apply to foreign civil aircraft that are not equipped with DME when operated for the following purposes and if ATC is notified prior to each takeoff:

(1) Ferry flights to and from a place in the United States where repairs or alterations are to be made.

(2) Ferry flights to a new country of registry.

(3) Flight of a new aircraft of U.S. manufacture for the purpose of—

(i) Flight testing the aircraft;

(ii) Training foreign flight crews in the operation of the aircraft; or

(iii) Ferrying the aircraft for export delivery outside the United States.

(4) Ferry, demonstration, and test flight of an aircraft brought to the United States for the purpose of demonstration or testing the whole or any part thereof.

[Docket No. 18834, 54 FR 34320, Aug. 18, 1989; as amended by Amdt. 91–227, 56 FR 65661, Dec. 17, 1991]

§91.713 Operation of civil aircraft of Cuban registry.

No person may operate a civil aircraft of Cuban registry except in controlled airspace and in accordance with air traffic clearance or air traffic control instructions that may require use of specific airways or routes and landings at specific airports.

§91.715 Special flight authorizations for foreign civil aircraft.

(a) Foreign civil aircraft may be operated without airworthiness certificates required under §91.203 if a special flight authorization for that operation is issued under this section. Application for a special flight authorization must be made to the Flight Standards Division Manager or Aircraft Certification Directorate Manager of the FAA region in which the applicant is located or to the region within which the U.S. point of entry is located. However, in the case of an aircraft to be operated in the U.S. for the purpose of demonstration at an airshow, the application may be made to the Flight Standards Division Manager or Aircraft Certification Directorate Manager of the FAA region in which the airshow is located.

(b) The Administrator may issue a special flight authorization for a foreign civil aircraft subject to any conditions and limitations that the Administrator considers necessary for safe operation in the U.S. airspace.

(c) No person may operate a foreign civil aircraft under a special flight authorization unless that operation also complies with part 375 of the Special Regulations of the Department of Transportation (14 CFR part 375).

(Approved by the Office of Management and Budget under control number 2120–0005)

[Docket No. 18334, 54 FR 34320, Aug. 18, 1989; as amended by Amdt. 91–212, 54 FR 39293, Sept. 25, 1989]

§91.717 – 91.799 [Reserved]

Subpart I— Operating Noise Limits

Source: Docket No. 18334, 54 FR 34321, Aug. 18, 1989, unless otherwise noted.

§91.801 Applicability: Relation to part 36.

(a) This subpart prescribes operating noise limits and related requirements that apply, as follows, to the operation of civil aircraft in the United States.

(1) Sections 91.803, 91.805, 91.807, 91.809, and 91.811 apply to civil subsonic jet (turbojet) airplanes with maximum weights of more than 75,000 pounds and—

(i) If U.S. registered, that have standard airworthiness certificates; or

(ii) If foreign registered, that would be required by this chapter to have a U.S. standard airworthiness certificate in order to conduct the operations intended for the airplane were it registered in the United States. Those sections apply to operations to or from airports in the United States under this part and parts 121, 125, 129, and 135 of this chapter.

(2) Section 91.813 applies to U.S. operators of civil subsonic jet (turbojet) airplanes covered by this subpart. This section applies to operators operating to or from airports in the United States under this part and parts 121, 125, and 135, but not to those operating under part 129 of this chapter.

(3) Sections 91.803, 91.819, and 91.821 apply to U.S.-registered civil supersonic airplanes having standard airworthiness certificates and to foreign-registered civil supersonic airplanes that, if registered in the United States, would be required by this chapter to have U.S. standard airworthiness certificates in order to conduct the operations intended for the airplane. Those sections apply to operations under this part and under parts 121, 125, 129, and 135 of this chapter.

(b) Unless otherwise specified, as used in this subpart "part 36" refers to 14 CFR part 36, including the noise levels under Appendix C of that part, notwithstanding the provisions of that part excepting certain airplanes from the specified noise requirements. For purposes of this subpart, the various stages of noise levels, the terms used to describe airplanes with respect to those levels, and the terms "subsonic airplane" and "supersonic airplane" have the meanings specified under part 36 of this chapter. For purposes of this subpart, for subsonic airplanes operated in foreign air commerce in the United States, the Administrator may accept compliance with the noise requirements under annex 16 of the International Civil Aviation Organization when those requirements have been shown to be substantially compatible with, and achieve results equivalent to those achievable under, part 36 for that airplane. Determinations made under these provisions are subject to the limitations of §36.5 of this chapter as if those noise levels were part 36 noise levels.

(c) Sections 91.851 through 91.877 of this subpart prescribe operating noise limits and related requirements that apply to any civil subsonic turbojet airplane (for which an airworthiness certificate other than an experimental certificate has been issued by the Administrator) with a maximum certificated takeoff weight of more than 75,000 pounds operating to or from an airport in the 48 contiguous United States and the District of Columbia under this part, parts 121, 125, 129, or 135 of this chapter on and after September 25, 1991.

(d) Section 91.877 prescribes reporting requirements that apply to any civil subsonic jet (turbojet) airplane with a maximum weight of more than 75,000 pounds operated by an air carrier or foreign air carrier between the contiguous United States and the State of Hawaii, between the State of Hawaii and any point outside of the 48 contiguous United States, or between the islands of Hawaii in turnaround service, under part 121 or 129 of this chapter on or after November 5, 1990.

[Docket No. 18334, 54 FR 34321, Aug. 18, 1989; as amended by Amdt. 91–211, 54 FR 41211, Oct. 5, 1989, Amdt. 91–225, 56 FR 48658, Sept. 25, 1991; Amdt. 91–252, 61 FR 66185, Dec. 16, 1996; Amdt. 91–275, 67 FR 45237, July 8, 2002; Amdt. 91–276, 67 FR 46571, July 15, 2002]

§91.803 Part 125 operators: Designation of applicable regulations.

For airplanes covered by this subpart and operated under part 125 of this chapter, the following regulations apply as specified:

(a) For each airplane operation to which requirements prescribed under this subpart applied before November 29, 1980, those requirements of this subpart continue to apply.

(b) For each subsonic airplane operation to which requirements prescribed under this subpart did not apply before November 29, 1980, because the airplane was not operated in the United States under this part or part 121, 129, or 135 of this chapter, the requirements prescribed under §91.805 of this subpart apply.

(c) For each supersonic airplane operation to which requirements prescribed under this subpart did not apply before November 29, 1980, because the airplane was not operated in the United States under this part or part 121, 129, or 135 of this chapter, the requirements of §§91.819 and 91.821 of this subpart apply.

(d) For each airplane required to operate under part 125 for which a deviation under that part is approved to operate, in whole or in part, under this part or part 121, 129, or 135 of this chapter, notwithstanding the approval, the requirements prescribed under paragraphs (a), (b), and (c) of this section continue to apply.

[Docket No. 18334, 54 FR 34321, Aug. 18, 1989; as amended by Amdt. 91–276, 67 FR 46571, July 15, 2002

§91.805 Final compliance: Subsonic airplanes.

Except as provided in §§91.809 and 91.811, on and after January 1, 1985, no person may operate to or from an airport in the United States any subsonic airplane covered by this subpart unless that airplane has been shown to comply with Stage 2 or Stage 3 noise levels under part 36 of this chapter.

§91.807–91.813 [Reserved]

§91.815 Agricultural and fire fighting airplanes: Noise operating limitations.

(a) This section applies to propeller-driven, small airplanes having standard airworthiness certificates that are designed for "agricultural aircraft operations" (as defined in §137.3 of this chapter, as effective on January 1, 1966) or for dispensing fire fighting materials.

(b) If the Airplane Flight Manual, or other approved manual material information, markings, or placards for the airplane indicate that the airplane has not been shown to comply with the noise limits under part 36 of this chapter, no person may operate that airplane, except—

(1) To the extent necessary to accomplish the work activity directly associated with the purpose for which it is designed;

(2) To provide flight crewmember training in the special purpose operation for which the airplane is designed; and

(3) To conduct "nondispensing aerial work operations" in accordance with the requirements under §137.29(c) of this chapter.

§91.817 Civil aircraft sonic boom.

(a) No person may operate a civil aircraft in the United States at a true flight Mach number greater than 1 except in compliance with conditions and limitations in an authorization to exceed Mach 1 issued to the operator under Appendix B of this part.

(b) In addition, no person may operate a civil aircraft for which the maximum operating limit speed M_{MO} exceeds a Mach number of 1, to or from an airport in the United States, unless—

(1) Information available to the flight crew includes flight limitations that ensure that flights entering or leaving the United States will not cause a sonic boom to reach the surface within the United States; and

(2) The operator complies with the flight limitations prescribed in paragraph (b)(1) of this section or complies with conditions and limitations in an authorization to exceed Mach 1 issued under Appendix B of this part.

(Approved by the Office of Management and Budget under control number 2120–0005)

§91.819 Civil supersonic airplanes that do not comply with part 36.

(a) *Applicability.* This section applies to civil supersonic airplanes that have not been shown to comply with the Stage 2 noise limits of part 36 in effect on October 13, 1977, using applicable trade-off provisions, and that are operated in the United States, after July 31, 1978.

(b) *Airport use.* Except in an emergency, the following apply to each person who operates a civil supersonic airplane to or from an airport in the United States:

(1) Regardless of whether a type design change approval is applied for under part 21 of this chapter, no person may land or take off an airplane covered by this section for which the type design is changed, after July 31, 1978, in a manner constituting an "acoustical change" under §21.93 unless the acoustical change requirements of part 36 are complied with.

(2) No flight may be scheduled, or otherwise planned, for takeoff or landing after 10 p.m. and before 7 a.m. local time.

§91.821 Civil supersonic airplanes: Noise limits.

Except for Concorde airplanes having flight time before January 1, 1980, no person may operate in the United States, a civil supersonic airplane that does not comply with Stage 2 noise limits of part 36 in effect on October 13, 1977, using applicable trade-off provisions.

§91.823 – 91.849 [Reserved]

§91.851 Definitions.

For the purposes of §§91.851 through 91.877 of this subpart:

Chapter 4 noise level means a noise level at or below the maximum noise level prescribed in Chapter 4, Paragraph 4.4, Maximum Noise Levels, of the International Civil Aviation Organization (ICAO) Annex 16, Volume I, Amendment 7, effective March 21, 2002. The Director of the Federal Register in accordance with 5 U.S.C. 552(a) and 1 CFR part 51 approved the incorporation by reference of this document, which can be obtained from the International Civil Aviation Organization (ICAO), Document Sales Unit, 999 University Street, Montreal, Quebec H3C 5H7, Canada. Also, you may obtain documents on the Internet at http://www.ICAO.int/eshop/index.cfm. Copies may be reviewed at the U.S. Department of Transportation, Docket Management System, 400 7th Street, SW., Room PL 401, Washington, DC or at the National Archives and Records Administration (NARA). For information on the availability of this material at NARA, call 202-741-6030, or go to:
http://www.archives.gov/federal_register/code_of_federal_regulations/ibr_locations.html

Contiguous United States means the area encompassed by the 48 contiguous United States and the District of Columbia.

Fleet means those civil subsonic jet (turbojet) airplanes with a maximum certificated weight of more than 75,000 pounds that are listed on an operator's operations specifications as eligible for operation in the contiguous United States.

Import means a change in ownership of an airplane from a non-U.S. person to a U.S. person when the airplane is brought into the United States for operation.

Operations specifications means an enumeration of airplanes by type, model, series, and serial number operated by the operator or foreign air carrier on a given day, regardless of how or whether such airplanes are formally listed or designated by the operator.

Owner means any person that has indicia of ownership sufficient to register the airplane in the United States pursuant to part 47 of this chapter.

New entrant means an air carrier or foreign air carrier that, on or before November 5, 1990, did not conduct operations under part 121 or 129 of this chapter using an airplane covered by this subpart to or from any airport in the contiguous United States, but that initiates such operation after that date.

Stage 2 noise levels mean the requirements for Stage 2 noise levels as defined in part 36 of this chapter in effect on November 5, 1990.

Stage 3 noise levels mean the requirements for Stage 3 noise levels as defined in part 36 of this chapter in effect on November 5, 1990.

Stage 4 noise level means a noise level at or below the Stage 4 noise limit prescribed in part 36 of this chapter.

Stage 2 airplane means a civil subsonic jet (turbojet) airplane with a maximum certificated weight of 75,000 pounds or more that complies with Stage 2 noise levels as defined in part 36 of this chapter.

Stage 3 airplane means a civil subsonic jet (turbojet) airplane with a maximum certificated weight of 75,000 pounds or more that complies with Stage 3 noise levels as defined in part 36 of this chapter.

Stage 4 airplane means an airplane that has been shown not to exceed the Stage 4 noise limit prescribed in part 36 of this chapter. A Stage 4 airplane complies with all of the noise operating rules of this part.

[Docket No. 26433, 56 FR 48658, Sept. 25, 1991; as amended by Amdt. 91–252, 61 FR 66185, Dec. 16, 1996; Amdt. 91–275, 67 FR 45237, July 8, 2002; Amdt. 91–288, 70 FR 38749, July 5, 2005]

§91.853 Final compliance: Civil subsonic airplanes.

Except as provided in §91.873, after December 31, 1999, no person shall operate to or from any airport in the contiguous United States any airplane subject to §91.801(c) of this subpart, unless that airplane has been shown to comply with Stage 3 or Stage 4 noise levels.

[Docket No. 26433, 56 FR 48658, Sept. 25, 1991; as amended by Amdt. 91–288, 70 FR 38749, July 5, 2005]

§91.855 Entry and nonaddition rule.

No person may operate any airplane subject to §91.801(c) of this subpart to or from an airport in the contiguous United States unless one or more of the following apply:

(a) The airplane complies with Stage 3 or Stage 4 noise levels.

(b) The airplane complies with Stage 2 noise levels and was owned by a U.S. person on and since November 5, 1990. Stage 2 airplanes that meet these criteria and are leased to foreign airlines are also subject to the return provisions of paragraph (e) of this section.

(c) The airplane complies with Stage 2 noise levels, is owned by a non-U.S. person, and is the subject of a binding lease to a U.S. person effective before and on September 25, 1991. Any such airplane may be operated for the term of the lease in effect on that date, and any extensions thereof provided for in that lease.

(d) The airplane complies with Stage 2 noise levels and is operated by a foreign air carrier.

(e) The airplane complies with Stage 2 noise levels and is operated by a foreign operator other than for the purpose of foreign air commerce.

(f) The airplane complies with Stage 2 noise levels and—

(1) On November 5, 1990, was owned by:

(i) A corporation, trust, or partnership organized under the laws of the United States or any State (including individual States, territories, possessions, and the District of Columbia);

(ii) An individual who is a citizen of the United States; or

(iii) An entity owned or controlled by a corporation, trust, partnership, or individual described in paragraph (f)(1) (i) or (ii) of this section; and

(2) Enters into the United States not later than 6 months after the expiration of a lease agreement (including any extensions thereof) between an owner described in paragraph (f)(1) of this section and a foreign airline.

(g) The airplane complies with Stage 2 noise levels and was purchased by the importer under a written contract executed before November 5, 1990.

(h) Any Stage 2 airplane described in this section is eligible for operation in the contiguous United States only as provided under §§91.865 or 91.867.

[Docket No. 26433, 56 FR 48658, Sept. 25, 1991; 56 FR 51167, Oct. 10, 1991; as amended by Amdt. 91–288, 70 FR 38749, July 5, 2005]

§ 91.857 Stage 2 operations outside of the 48 contiguous United States.

An operator of a Stage 2 airplane that is operating only between points outside the contiguous United States on or after November 5, 1990, must include in its operations specifications a statement that such airplane may not be used to provide air transportation to or from any airport in the contiguous United States.

[Docket No. FAA–2002–12771, 67 FR 46571, July 15, 2002]

§ 91.858 Special flight authorizations for non-revenue Stage 2 operations.

(a) After December 31, 1999, any operator of a Stage 2 airplane over 75,000 pounds may operate that airplane in nonrevenue service in the contiguous United States only for the following purposes:

(1) Sell, lease, or scrap the airplane;

(2) Obtain modifications to meet Stage 3 noise levels;

(3) Obtain scheduled heavy maintenance or significant modifications;

(4) Deliver the airplane to a lessee or return it to a lessor;

(5) Park or store the airplane; and

(6) Prepare the airplane for any of the purposes listed in paragraph (a)(1) through (a)(5) of this section.

(b) An operator of a Stage 2 airplane that needs to operate in the contiguous United States for any of the purposes listed above may apply to FAA's Office of Environment and Energy for a special flight authorization. The applicant must file in advance. Applications are due 30 days in advance of the planned flight and must provide the information necessary for the FAA to determine that the planned flight is within the limits prescribed in the law.

[Docket No. FAA–2002–12771, 67 FR 46571, July 15, 2002]

§91.859 Modification to meet Stage 3 or Stage 4 noise levels.

For an airplane subject to §91.801(c) of this subpart and otherwise prohibited from operation to or from an airport in the contiguous United States by §91.855, any person may apply for a special flight authorization for that airplane to operate in the contiguous United States for the purpose of obtaining modifications to meet Stage 3 or Stage 4 noise levels.

[Docket No. FAA–2003–16526, 70 FR 38750, July 5, 2005]

§91.861 Base level.

(a) *U.S. Operators.* The base level of a U.S. operator is equal to the number of owned or leased Stage 2 airplanes subject to §91.801(c) of this subpart that were listed on that operator's operations specifications for operations to or from airports in the contiguous United States on any one day selected by the operator during the period January 1, 1990, through July 1, 1991, plus or minus adjustments made pursuant to paragraphs (a)(1) and (2).

(1) The base level of a U.S. operator shall be increased by a number equal to the total of the following—

(i) The number of Stage 2 airplanes returned to service in the United States pursuant to §91.855(f);

(ii) The number of Stage 2 airplanes purchased pursuant to §91.855(g); and

(iii) Any U.S. operator base level acquired with a Stage 2 airplane transferred from another person under §91.863.

(2) The base level of a U.S. operator shall be decreased by the amount of U.S. operator base level transferred with the corresponding number of Stage 2 airplanes to another person under §91.863.

(b) Foreign air carriers. The base level of a foreign air carrier is equal to the number of owned or leased Stage 2 airplanes that were listed on that carrier's U.S. operations specifications on any one day during the period January 1, 1990, through July 1, 1991, plus or minus any adjustments to the base levels made pursuant to paragraphs (b)(1) and (2).

(1) The base level of a foreign air carrier shall be increased by the amount of foreign air carrier base level acquired with a Stage 2 airplane from another person under §91.863.

(2) The base level of a foreign air carrier shall be decreased by the amount of foreign air carrier base level transferred with a Stage 2 airplane to another person under §91.863.

(c) New entrants do not have a base level.

[Docket No. 26433, 56 FR 48659, Sept. 25, 1991; 56 FR 51167, Oct. 10, 1991]

§91.863 Transfers of Stage 2 airplanes with base level.

(a) Stage 2 airplanes may be transferred with or without the corresponding amount of base level. Base level may not be transferred without the corresponding number of Stage 2 airplanes.

(b) No portion of a U.S. operator's base level established under §91.861(a) may be used for operations by a foreign air carrier. No portion of a foreign air carrier's base level established under §91.861(b) may be used for operations by a U.S. operator.

(c) Whenever a transfer of Stage 2 airplanes with base level occurs, the transferring and acquiring parties shall, within 10 days, jointly submit written notification of the transfer to the FAA, Office of Environment and Energy. Such notification shall state:

(1) The names of the transferring and acquiring parties;

(2) The name, address, and telephone number of the individual responsible for submitting the notification on behalf of the transferring and acquiring parties;

(3) The total number of Stage 2 airplanes transferred, listed by airplane type, model, series, and serial number;

(4) The corresponding amount of base level transferred and whether it is U.S. operator or foreign air carrier base level; and

(5) The effective date of the transaction.

(d) If, taken as a whole, a transaction or series of transactions made pursuant to this section does not produce an increase or decrease in the number of Stage 2 airplanes for either the acquiring or transferring operator, such transaction or series of transactions may not be used to establish compliance with the requirements of §91.865.

[Docket No. 26433, 56 FR 48659, Sept. 25, 1991]

§91.865 Phased compliance for operators with base level.

Except as provided in paragraph (a) of this section, each operator that operates an airplane under part 91, 121, 125, 129, or 135 of this chapter, regardless of the national registry of the airplane, shall comply with paragraph (b) or (d) of this section at each interim compliance date with regard to its subsonic airplane fleet covered by §91.801(c) of this subpart.

(a) This section does not apply to new entrants covered by §91.867 or to foreign operators not engaged in foreign air commerce.

(b) Each operator that chooses to comply with this paragraph pursuant to any interim compliance requirement shall reduce the number of Stage 2 airplanes it operates that are eligible for operation in the contiguous United States to a maximum of:

(1) After December 31, 1994, 75 percent of the base level held by the operator;

(2) After December 31, 1996, 50 percent of the base level held by the operator;

(3) After December 31, 1998, 25 percent of the base level held by the operator.

(c) Except as provided under §91.871, the number of Stage 2 airplanes that must be reduced at each compliance date contained in paragraph (b) of this section shall be determined by reference to the amount of base level held by the operator on that compliance date, as calculated under §91.861.

(d) Each operator that chooses to comply with this paragraph pursuant to any interim compliance requirement shall operate a fleet that consists of:

(1) After December 31, 1994, not less than 55 percent Stage 3 airplanes;

(2) After December 31, 1996, not less than 65 percent Stage 3 airplanes;

(3) After December 31, 1998, not less than 75 percent Stage 3 airplanes.

(e) Calculations resulting in fractions may be rounded to permit the continued operation of the next whole number of Stage 2 airplanes.

[Docket No. 26433, 56 FR 48659, Sept. 25, 1991]

§91.867 Phased compliance for new entrants.

(a) New entrant U.S. air carriers.

(1) A new entrant initiating operations under part 121 of this chapter on or before December 31, 1994, may initiate service without regard to the percentage of its fleet composed of Stage 3 airplanes.

(2) After December 31, 1994, at least 25 percent of the fleet of a new entrant must comply with Stage 3 noise levels.

(3) After December 31, 1996, at least 50 percent of the fleet of a new entrant must comply with Stage 3 noise levels.

(4) After December 31, 1998, at least 75 percent of the fleet of a new entrant must comply with Stage 3 noise levels.

(b) New entrant foreign air carriers.

(1) A new entrant foreign air carrier initiating part 129 operations on or before December 31, 1994, may initiate service without regard to the percentage of its fleet composed of Stage 3 airplanes.

(2) After December 31, 1994, at least 25 percent of the fleet on U.S. operations specifications of a new entrant foreign air carrier must comply with Stage 3 noise levels.

(3) After December 31, 1996, at least 50 percent of the fleet on U.S. operations specifications of a new entrant foreign air carrier must comply with Stage 3 noise levels.

(4) After December 31, 1998, at least 75 percent of the fleet on U.S. operations specifications of a new entrant foreign air carrier must comply with Stage 3 noise levels.

(c) Calculations resulting in fractions may be rounded to permit the continued operation of the next whole number of Stage 2 airplanes.

[Docket No. 26433, 56 FR 48659, Sept. 25, 1991; as amended by Amdt. 91–252, 61 FR 66185, Dec. 16, 1996]

§91.869 Carry-forward compliance.

(a) Any operator that exceeds the requirements of paragraph (b) of §91.865 of this part on or before December 31, 1994, or on or before December 31, 1996, may claim a credit that may be applied at a subsequent interim compliance date.

(b) Any operator that eliminates or modifies more Stage 2 airplanes pursuant to §91.865(b) than required as of December 31, 1994, or December 31, 1996, may count the number of additional Stage 2 airplanes reduced as a credit toward—

(1) The number of Stage 2 airplanes it would otherwise be required to reduce following a subsequent interim compliance date specified in §91.865(b); or

(2) The number of Stage 3 airplanes it would otherwise be required to operate in its fleet following a subsequent interim compliance date to meet the percentage requirements specified in §91.865(d).

[Docket No. 26433, 56 FR 48659, Sept. 25, 1991; 56 FR 65783, Dec. 18, 1991]

§91.871 Waivers from interim compliance requirements.

(a) Any U.S. operator or foreign air carrier subject to the requirements of §§91.865 or 91.867 of this subpart may request a waiver from any individual compliance requirement.

(b) Applications must be filed with the Secretary of Transportation at least 120 days prior to the compliance date from which the waiver is requested.

(c) Applicants must show that a grant of waiver would be in the public interest, and must include in its application its plans and activities for modifying its fleet, including evidence of good faith efforts to comply with the requirements of §§91.865 or 91.867. The application should contain all information the applicant considers relevant, including, as appropriate, the following:

(1) The applicant's balance sheet and cash flow positions;

(2) The composition of the applicant's current fleet; and

(3) The applicant's delivery position with respect to new airplanes or noise-abatement equipment.

(d) Waivers will be granted only upon a showing by the applicant that compliance with the requirements of §91.865 or 91.867 at a particular interim compliance date is financially onerous, physically impossible, or technologically infeasible, or that it would have an adverse effect on competition or on service to small communities.

(e) The conditions of any waiver granted under this section shall be determined by the circumstances presented in the application, but in no case may the term extend beyond the next interim compliance date.

(f) A summary of any request for a waiver under this section will be published in the Federal Register, and public comment will be invited. Unless the Secretary finds that circumstances require otherwise, the public comment period will be at least 14 days.

[Docket No. 26433, 56 FR 48660, Sept. 25, 1991]

§91.873 Waivers from final compliance.

(a) A U.S. air carrier or a foreign air carrier may apply for a waiver from the prohibition contained in §91.853 of this part for its remaining Stage 2 airplanes, provided that, by July 1, 1999, at least 85 percent of the airplanes used by the carrier to provide service to or from an airport in the contiguous United States will comply with the Stage 3 noise levels.

(b) An application for the waiver described in paragraph (a) of this section must be filed with the Secretary of Transportation no later than January 1, 1999, or, in the case of a foreign air carrier, no later than April 20, 2000. Such application must include a plan with firm orders for replacing or modifying all airplanes to comply with Stage 3 noise levels at the earliest practicable time.

(c) To be eligible to apply for the waiver under this section, a new entrant U.S. air carrier must initiate service no later than January 1, 1999, and must comply fully with all provisions of this section.

(d) The Secretary may grant a waiver under this section if the Secretary finds that granting such waiver is in the public interest. In making such a finding, the Secretary shall include consideration of the effect of granting such waiver on competition in the air carrier industry and the effect on small community air service, and any other information submitted by the applicant that the Secretary considers relevant.

(e) The term of any waiver granted under this section shall be determined by the circumstances presented in the application, but in no case will the waiver permit the operation of any Stage 2 airplane covered by this subchapter in the contiguous United States after December 31, 2003.

(f) A summary of any request for a waiver under this section will be published in the Federal Register, and public comment will be invited. Unless the secretary finds that circumstances require otherwise, the public comment period will be at least 14 days.

[Docket No. 26433, 56 FR 48660, Sept. 25, 1991; 56 FR 51167 Oct. 10, 1991; as amended by Amdt. 91–276, 67 FR 46571, July 15, 2002]

§91.875 Annual progress reports.

(a) Each operator subject to §91.865 or §91.867 of this chapter shall submit an annual report to the FAA, Office of Environment and Energy, on the progress it has made toward complying with the requirements of that section. Such reports shall be submitted no later than 45 days after the end of a calendar year. All progress reports must provide the information through the end of the calendar year, be certified by the operator as true and complete (under penalty of 18 U.S.C. 1001), and include the following information:

(1) The name and address of the operator;

(2) The name, title, and telephone number of the person designated by the operator to be responsible for ensuring the accuracy of the information in the report;

(3) The operator's progress during the reporting period toward compliance with the requirements of §91.853, §91.865 or §91.867. For airplanes on U.S. operations specifications, each operator shall identify the airplanes by type, model, series, and serial number.

(i) Each Stage 2 airplane added or removed from operation or U.S. operations specifications (grouped separately by those airplanes acquired with and without base level);

(ii) Each Stage 2 airplane modified to Stage 3 noise levels (identifying the manufacturer and model of noise abatement retrofit equipment;

(iii) Each Stage 3 airplane on U.S. operations specifications as of the last day of the reporting period; and

(iv) For each Stage 2 airplane transferred or acquired, the name and address of the recipient or transferor; and, if base level was transferred, the person to or from whom base level was transferred or acquired pursuant to Section 91.863 along with the effective date of each base level transaction, and the type of base level transferred or acquired.

(b) Each operator subject to §91.865 or §91.867 of this chapter shall submit an initial progress report covering the period from January 1, 1990, through December 31, 1991, and provide:

(1) For each operator subject to §91.865:

(i) The date used to establish its base level pursuant to §91.861(a); and

(ii) A list of those Stage 2 airplanes (by type, model, series and serial number) in its base level, including adjustments made pursuant to §91.861 after the date its base level was established.

(2) For each U.S. operator:

(i) A plan to meet the compliance schedules in §91.865 or §91.867 and the final compliance date of §91.853, including the schedule for delivery of replacement Stage 3 airplanes or the installation of noise abatement retrofit equipment; and

(ii) A separate list (by type, model, series, and serial number) of those airplanes included in the operator's base level, pursuant to §91.861(a)(1) (i) and (ii), under the categories "returned" or "purchased," along with the date each was added to its operations specifications.

(c) Each operator subject to §91.865 or §91.867 of this chapter shall submit subsequent annual progress reports covering the calendar year preceding the report and including any changes in the information provided in paragraphs (a) and (b) of this section; including the use of any carry-forward credits pursuant to §91.869.

(d) An operator may request, in any report, that specific planning data be considered proprietary.

(e) If an operator's actions during any reporting period cause it to achieve compliance with §91.853, the report should include a statement to that effect. Further progress reports are not required unless there is any change in the information reported pursuant to paragraph (a) of this section.

(f) For each U.S. operator subject to §91.865, progress reports submitted for calendar years 1994, 1996, and 1998, shall also state how the operator achieved compliance with the requirements of that section, i.e.—

(1) By reducing the number of Stage 2 airplanes in its fleet to no more than the maximum permitted percentage of its base level under §91.865(b), or

(2) By operating a fleet that consists of at least the minimum required percentage of Stage 3 airplanes under §91.865(d).

(Approved by the Office of Management and Budget under control number 2120–0553)

[Docket No. 26433, 56 FR 48660, Sept. 25, 1991; 56 FR 51168, Oct. 10, 1991; 57 FR 5977, Feb. 19, 1992]

§91.877 Annual reporting of Hawaiian operations.

(a) Each air carrier or foreign air carrier subject to §91.865 or §91.867 of this part that conducts operations between the contiguous United States and the State of Hawaii, between the State of Hawaii and any point outside of the contiguous United States, or between the islands of Hawaii in turnaround service, on or since November 5, 1990, shall include in its annual report the information described in paragraph (c) of this section.

(b) Each air carrier or foreign air carrier not subject to §91.865 or §91.867 of this part that conducts operations between the contiguous U.S. and the State of Hawaii, between the State of Hawaii and any point outside of the contiguous United States, or between the islands of Hawaii in turnaround service, on or since November 5, 1990, shall submit an annual report to the FAA, Office of Environment and Energy, on its compliance with the Hawaiian operations provisions of 49 U.S.C. 47528. Such reports shall be submitted no later than 45 days after the end of a calendar year. All progress reports must provide the information through the end of the calendar year, be certified by the operator as true and complete (under penalty of 18 U.S.C. 1001), and include the following information—

(1) The name and address of the air carrier or foreign air carrier;

(2) The name, title, and telephone number of the person designated by the air carrier or foreign air carrier to be responsible for ensuring the accuracy of the information in the report; and

(3) The information specified in paragraph (c) of this section.

(c) The following information must be included in reports filed pursuant to this section—

(1) For operations conducted between the contiguous United States and the State of Hawaii—

(i) The number of Stage 2 airplanes used to conduct such operations as of November 5, 1990;

(ii) Any change to that number during the calendar year being reported, including the date of such change;

(2) For air carriers that conduct inter-island turnaround service in the State of Hawaii—

(i) The number of Stage 2 airplanes used to conduct such operations as of November 5, 1990;

(ii) Any change to that number during the calendar year being reported, including the date of such change;

(iii) For an air carrier that provided inter-island turnaround service within the State of Hawaii on November 5, 1990, the number reported under paragraph (c)(2)(i) of this section may include all Stage 2 airplanes with a maximum certificated takeoff weight of more than 75,000 pounds that were owned or leased by the air carrier on November 5, 1990, regardless of whether such airplanes were operated by that air carrier or foreign air carrier on that date.

(3) For operations conducted between the State of Hawaii and a point outside the contiguous United States—

(i) The number of Stage 2 airplanes used to conduct such operations as of November 5, 1990; and

(ii) Any change to that number during the calendar year being reported, including the date of such change.

(d) Reports or amended reports for years predating this regulation are required to be filed concurrently with the next annual report.

[Docket No. 28213, 61 FR 66185, Dec. 16, 1996]

§91.878 – 91.899 [Reserved]

Subpart J—Waivers

§91.901 [Reserved]

§91.903 Policy and procedures.

(a) The Administrator may issue a certificate of waiver authorizing the operation of aircraft in deviation from any rule listed in this subpart if the Administrator finds that the proposed operation can be safely conducted under the terms of that certificate of waiver.

(b) An application for a certificate of waiver under this part is made on a form and in a manner prescribed by the Administrator and may be submitted to any FAA office.

(c) A certificate of waiver is effective as specified in that certificate of waiver.

[Docket No. 18334, 54 FR 34325, Aug. 18, 1989]

§91.905 List of rules subject to waivers.

Sec.

91.107 Use of safety belts.
91.111 Operating near other aircraft.
91.113 Right-of-way rules: Except water operations.
91.115 Right-of-way rules: Water operations.
91.117 Aircraft speed.
91.119 Minimum safe altitudes: General.
91.121 Altimeter settings.
91.123 Compliance with ATC clearances and instructions.
91.125 ATC light signals.
91.126 Operating on or in the vicinity of an airport in Class G airspace.
91.127 Operating on or in the vicinity of an airport in Class E airspace.
91.129 Operations in Class D airspace.
91.130 Operations in Class C airspace.
91.131 Operations in Class B airspace.
91.133 Restricted and prohibited areas.
91.135 Operations in Class A airspace.
91.137 Temporary flight restrictions.
91.141 Flight restrictions in the proximity of the Presidential and other parties.
91.143 Flight limitation in the proximity of space flight operations.
91.153 VFR flight plan: Information required.
91.155 Basic VFR weather minimums
91.157 Special VFR weather minimums.
91.159 VFR cruising altitude or flight level.
91.169 IFR flight plan: Information required.
91.173 ATC clearance and flight plan required.
91.175 Takeoff and landing under IFR.
91.177 Minimum altitudes for IFR operations.
91.179 IFR cruising altitude or flight level.
91.181 Course to be flown.
91.183 IFR radio communications.
91.185 IFR operations: Two-way radio communications failure.
91.187 Operation under IFR in controlled airspace: Malfunction reports.
91.209 Aircraft lights.
91.303 Aerobatic flights.
91.305 Flight test areas.
91.311 Towing: Other than under §91.309.
91.313(e) Restricted category civil aircraft: Operating limitations.
91.515 Flight altitude rules.
91.705 Operations within the North Atlantic Minimum Navigation Performance Specifications Airspace.
91.707 Flights between Mexico or Canada and the United States.
91.713 Operation of civil aircraft of Cuban registry.

[Docket No. 18334, 54 FR 34325, Aug. 18, 1989; as amended by Amdt. 91–227, 56 FR 65661, Dec. 17, 1991]

§91.907 – 91.999 [Reserved]

Subpart K—Fractional Ownership Operations

Source: Docket No. FAA–2001–10047, 68 FR 54561, Sept. 17, 2003 unless otherwise noted.

§91.1001 Applicability.

(a) This subpart prescribes rules, in addition to those prescribed in other subparts of this part, that apply to fractional owners and fractional ownership program managers governing—

(1) The provision of program management services in a fractional ownership program;

(2) The operation of a fractional ownership program aircraft in a fractional ownership program; and

(3) The operation of a program aircraft included in a fractional ownership program managed by an affiliate of the manager of the program to which the owner belongs.

(b) As used in this part—

(1) ***Affiliate of a program manager*** means a manager that, directly, or indirectly, through one or more intermediaries, controls, is controlled by, or is under common control with, another program manager. The holding of at least forty percent (40 percent) of the equity and forty percent (40 percent) of the voting power of an entity will be presumed to constitute control for purposes of determining an affiliation under this subpart.

(2) A ***dry-lease aircraft exchange*** means an arrangement, documented by the written program agreements, under which the program aircraft are available, on an as needed basis without crew, to each fractional owner.

(3) A ***fractional owner or owner*** means an individual or entity that possesses a minimum fractional ownership interest in a program aircraft and that has entered into the applicable program agreements; provided, however, that in the case of the flight operations described in paragraph (b)(6)(ii) of this section, and solely for purposes of requirements pertaining to those flight operations, the fractional owner operating the aircraft will be deemed to be a fractional owner in the program managed by the affiliate.

(4) A ***fractional ownership interest*** means the ownership of an interest or holding of a multi-year leasehold interest and/or a multi-year leasehold interest that is convertible into an ownership interest in a program aircraft.

(5) A ***fractional ownership program or program*** means any system of aircraft ownership and exchange that consists of all of the following elements:

(i) The provision for fractional ownership program management services by a single fractional ownership program manager on behalf of the fractional owners.

(ii) Two or more airworthy aircraft.

(iii) One or more fractional owners per program aircraft, with at least one program aircraft having more than one owner.

(iv) Possession of at least a minimum fractional ownership interest in one or more program aircraft by each fractional owner.

(v) A dry-lease aircraft exchange arrangement among all of the fractional owners.

(vi) Multi-year program agreements covering the fractional ownership, fractional ownership program management services, and dry-lease aircraft exchange aspects of the program.

(6) A ***fractional ownership program aircraft or program aircraft*** means:

(i) An aircraft in which a fractional owner has a minimal fractional ownership interest and that has been included in the dry-lease aircraft exchange pursuant to the program agreements, or

(ii) In the case of a fractional owner from one program operating an aircraft in a different fractional ownership program managed by an affiliate of the operating owner's program manager, the aircraft being operated by the fractional owner, so long as the aircraft is:

(A) Included in the fractional ownership program managed by the affiliate of the operating owner's program manager, and

(B) Included in the operating owner's program's dry-lease aircraft exchange pursuant to the program agreements of the operating owner's program.

(iii) An aircraft owned in whole or in part by the program manager that has been included in the dry-lease aircraft exchange and is used to supplement program operations.

(7) A ***Fractional Ownership Program Flight or Program Flight*** means a flight under this subpart when one or more passengers or property designated by a fractional owner are on board the aircraft.

(8) ***Fractional ownership program management services or program management services*** mean administrative and aviation support services furnished in accordance with the applicable requirements of this subpart or provided by the program manager on behalf of the fractional owners, including, but not limited to, the—

(i) Establishment and implementation of program safety guidelines;

(ii) Employment, furnishing, or contracting of pilots and other crewmembers;

(iii) Training and qualification of pilots and other crewmembers and personnel;

(iv) Scheduling and coordination of the program aircraft and crews;

(v) Maintenance of program aircraft;

(vi) Satisfaction of recordkeeping requirements;

(vii) Development and use of a program operations manual and procedures; and

(viii) Application for and maintenance of management specifications and other authorizations and approvals.

(9) A ***fractional ownership program manager or program manager*** means the entity that offers fractional ownership program management services to fractional owners, and is designated in the multi-year program agreements referenced in paragraph (b)(1)(v) of this section to fulfill the requirements of this chapter applicable to the manager of the program containing the aircraft being flown. When a fractional owner is operating an aircraft in a fractional ownership program managed by an affiliate of the owner's program manager, the references in this subpart to the flight-related responsibilities of the program manager apply, with respect

to that particular flight, to the affiliate of the owner's program manager rather than to the owner's program manager.

(10) A ***minimum fractional ownership interest*** means—

(i) A fractional ownership interest equal to, or greater than, one-sixteenth (1/16) of at least one subsonic, fixed-wing or powered-lift program aircraft; or

(ii) A fractional ownership interest equal to, or greater than, one-thirty-second (1/32) of at least one rotorcraft program aircraft.

(c) The rules in this subpart that refer to a fractional owner or a fractional ownership program manager also apply to any person who engages in an operation governed by this subpart without the management specifications required by this subpart.

§91.1002 Compliance date.

No person that conducted flights before November 17, 2003 under a program that meets the definition of fractional ownership program in §91.1001 may conduct such flights after February 17, 2005 unless it has obtained management specifications under this subpart.

[Docket No. FAA–2001–10047, 68 FR 54561, Sept. 17, 2003; as amended by Amdt. 91–274, 69 FR 74413, Dec. 14, 2004]

§91.1003 Management contract between owner and program manager.

Each owner must have a contract with the program manager that—

(a) Requires the program manager to ensure that the program conforms to all applicable requirements of this chapter.

(b) Provides the owner the right to inspect and to audit, or have a designee of the owner inspect and audit, the records of the program manager pertaining to the operational safety of the program and those records required to show compliance with the management specifications and all applicable regulations. These records include, but are not limited to, the management specifications, authorizations, approvals, manuals, log books, and maintenance records maintained by the program manager.

(c) Designates the program manager as the owner's agent to receive service of notices pertaining to the program that the FAA seeks to provide to owners and authorizes the FAA to send such notices to the program manager in its capacity as the agent of the owner for such service.

(d) Acknowledges the FAA's right to contact the owner directly if the Administrator determines that direct contact is necessary.

§91.1005 Prohibitions and limitations.

(a) Except as provided in §91.321 or §91.501, no owner may carry persons or property for compensation or hire on a program flight.

(b) During the term of the multi-year program agreements under which a fractional owner has obtained a minimum fractional ownership interest in a program aircraft, the flight hours used during that term by the owner on program aircraft must not exceed the total hours associated with the fractional owner's share of ownership.

(c) No person may sell or lease an aircraft interest in a fractional ownership program that is smaller than that prescribed in the definition of "minimum fractional ownership interest" in §91.1001(b)(10) unless flights associated with that interest are operated under part 121 or 135 of this chapter and are conducted by an air carrier or commercial operator certificated under part 119 of this chapter.

§91.1007 Flights conducted under part 121 or part 135 of this chapter.

(a) Except as provided in §91.501(b), when a nonprogram aircraft is used to substitute for a program flight, the flight must be operated in compliance with part 121 or part 135 of this chapter, as applicable.

(b) A program manager who holds a certificate under part 119 of this chapter may conduct a flight for the use of a fractional owner under part 121 or part 135 of this chapter if the aircraft is listed on that certificate holder's operations specifications for part 121 or part 135, as applicable.

(c) The fractional owner must be informed when a flight is being conducted as a program flight or is being conducted under part 121 or part 135 of this chapter.

Operational Control

§91.1009 Clarification of operational control.

(a) An owner is in operational control of a program flight when the owner—

(1) Has the rights and is subject to the limitations set forth in §§91.1003 through 91.1013;

(2) Has directed that a program aircraft carry passengers or property designated by that owner; and

(3) The aircraft is carrying those passengers or property.

(b) An owner is not in operational control of a flight in the following circumstances:

(1) A program aircraft is used for a flight for administrative purposes such as demonstration, positioning, ferrying, maintenance, or crew training, and no passengers or property designated by such owner are being carried; or

(2) The aircraft being used for the flight is being operated under part 121 or 135 of this chapter.

§91.1011 Operational control responsibilities and delegation.

(a) Each owner in operational control of a program flight is ultimately responsible for safe operations and for complying with all applicable requirements of this chapter, including those related to airworthiness and operations in connection with the flight. Each owner may delegate some or all of the performance of the tasks associated with carrying out this responsibility to the program manager, and may rely on the program manager for aviation expertise and program management services. When the owner delegates performance of tasks to the program manager or relies on the program manager's expertise, the owner and the program manager are jointly and individually responsible for compliance.

(b) The management specifications, authorizations, and approvals required by this subpart are issued to, and in the sole name of, the program manager on behalf of the fractional owners collectively. The management specifications, authorizations, and approvals will not be affected by any change in ownership of a program aircraft, as long as the aircraft remains a program aircraft in the identified program.

§91.1013 Operational control briefing and acknowledgment.

(a) Upon the signing of an initial program management services contract, or a renewal or extension of a program management services contract, the program manager must brief the fractional owner on the owner's operational control responsibilities, and the owner must review and sign an acknowledgment of these operational control responsibilities. The acknowledgment must be included with the program management services contract. The acknowledgment must define when a fractional owner is in operational control and the owner's responsibilities and liabilities under the program. These include:

(1) Responsibility for compliance with the management specifications and all applicable regulations.

(2) Enforcement actions for any noncompliance.

(3) Liability risk in the event of a flight-related occurrence that causes personal injury or property damage.

(b) The fractional owner's signature on the acknowledgment will serve as the owner's affirmation that the owner has read, understands, and accepts the operational control responsibilities described in the acknowledgment.

(c) Each program manager must ensure that the fractional owner or owner's representatives have access to the acknowledgments for such owner's program aircraft. Each program manager must ensure that the FAA has access to the acknowledgments for all program aircraft.

Program Management

§91.1014 Issuing or denying management specifications.

(a) A person applying to the Administrator for management specifications under this subpart must submit an application—

(1) In a form and manner prescribed by the Administrator; and

(2) Containing any information the Administrator requires the applicant to submit.

(b) Management specifications will be issued to the program manager on behalf of the fractional owners if, after investigation, the Administrator finds that the applicant:

(1) Meets the applicable requirements of this subpart; and

(2) Is properly and adequately equipped in accordance with the requirements of this chapter and is able to conduct safe operations under appropriate provisions of part 91 of this chapter and management specifications issued under this subpart.

(c) An application for management specifications will be denied if the Administrator finds that the applicant is not properly or adequately equipped or is not able to conduct safe operations under this part.

§91.1015 Management specifications.

(a) Each person conducting operations under this subpart or furnishing fractional ownership program management services to fractional owners must do so in accordance with management specifications issued by the Administrator to the fractional ownership program manager under this subpart. Management specifications must include:

(1) The current list of all fractional owners and types of aircraft, registration markings and serial numbers;

(2) The authorizations, limitations, and certain procedures under which these operations are to be conducted,

(3) Certain other procedures under which each class and size of aircraft is to be operated;

(4) Authorization for an inspection program approved under §91.1109, including the type of aircraft, the registration markings and serial numbers of each aircraft to be operated under the program. No person may conduct any program flight using any aircraft not listed.

(5) Time limitations, or standards for determining time limitations, for overhauls, inspections, and checks for airframes, engines, propellers, rotors, appliances, and emergency equipment of aircraft.

(6) The specific location of the program manager's principal base of operations and, if different, the address that will serve as the primary point of contact for correspondence between the FAA and the program manager and the name and mailing address of the program manager's agent for service;

(7) Other business names the program manager may use;

(8) Authorization for the method of controlling weight and balance of aircraft;

(9) Any authorized deviation and exemption granted from any requirement of this chapter; and

(10) Any other information the Administrator determines is necessary.

(b) The program manager may keep the current list of all fractional owners required by paragraph (a)(1) of this section at its principal base of operation or other location approved by the Administrator and referenced in its management specifications. Each program manager shall make this list of owners available for inspection by the Administrator.

(c) Management specifications issued under this subpart are effective unless—

(1) The management specifications are amended as provided in §91.1017; or

(2) The Administrator suspends or revokes the management specifications.

(d) At least 30 days before it proposes to establish or change the location of its principal base of operations, its main operations base, or its main maintenance base, a program manager must provide written notification to the Flight Standards District Office that issued the program manager's management specifications.

(e) Each program manager must maintain a complete and separate set of its management specifications at its principal base of operations, or at a place approved by the Administrator, and must make its management specifications available for inspection by the Administrator and the fractional owner(s) to whom the program manager furnishes its services for review and audit.

(f) Each program manager must insert pertinent excerpts of its management specifications, or references thereto, in its program manual and must—

(1) Clearly identify each such excerpt as a part of its management specifications; and

(2) State that compliance with each management specifications requirement is mandatory.

(g) Each program manager must keep each of its employees and other persons who perform duties material to its operations informed of the provisions of its management specifications that apply to that employee's or person's duties and responsibilities.

§91.1017 Amending program manager's management specifications.

(a) The Administrator may amend any management specifications issued under this subpart if—

(1) The Administrator determines that safety and the public interest require the amendment of any management specifications; or

(2) The program manager applies for the amendment of any management specifications, and the Administrator determines that safety and the public interest allows the amendment.

(b) Except as provided in paragraph (e) of this section, when the Administrator initiates an amendment of a program manager's management specifications, the following procedure applies:

(1) The Flight Standards District Office that issued the program manager's management specifications will notify the program manager in writing of the proposed amendment.

(2) The Flight Standards District Office that issued the program manager's management specifications will set a reasonable period (but not less than 7 days) within which the program manager may submit written information, views, and arguments on the amendment.

(3) After considering all material presented, the Flight Standards District Office that issued the program manager's management specifications will notify the program manager of—

(i) The adoption of the proposed amendment,

(ii) The partial adoption of the proposed amendment, or

(iii) The withdrawal of the proposed amendment.

(4) If the Flight Standards District Office that issued the program manager's management specifications issues an amendment of the management specifications, it becomes effective not less than 30 days after the program manager receives notice of it unless—

(i) The Flight Standards District Office that issued the program manager's management specifications finds under paragraph (e) of this section that there is an emergency requiring immediate action with respect to safety; or

(ii) The program manager petitions for reconsideration of the amendment under paragraph (d) of this section.

(c) When the program manager applies for an amendment to its management specifications, the following procedure applies:

(1) The program manager must file an application to amend its management specifications—

(i) At least 90 days before the date proposed by the applicant for the amendment to become effective, unless a shorter time is approved, in cases such as mergers, acquisitions of operational assets that require an additional showing of safety (for example, proving tests or validation tests), and resumption of operations following a suspension of operations as a result of bankruptcy actions.

(ii) At least 15 days before the date proposed by the applicant for the amendment to become effective in all other cases.

(2) The application must be submitted to the Flight Standards District Office that issued the program manager's management specifications in a form and manner prescribed by the Administrator.

(3) After considering all material presented, the Flight Standards District Office that issued the program manager's management specifications will notify the program manager of—

(i) The adoption of the applied for amendment;

(ii) The partial adoption of the applied for amendment; or

(iii) The denial of the applied for amendment. The program manager may petition for reconsideration of a denial under paragraph (d) of this section.

(4) If the Flight Standards District Office that issued the program manager's management specifications approves the amendment, following coordination with the program manager regarding its implementation, the amendment is effective on the date the Administrator approves it.

(d) When a program manager seeks reconsideration of a decision of the Flight Standards District Office that issued the program manager's management specifications concerning the amendment of management specifications, the following procedure applies:

(1) The program manager must petition for reconsideration of that decision within 30 days of the date that the program manager receives a notice of denial of the amendment of its management specifications, or of the date it receives notice of an FAA-initiated amendment of its management specifications, whichever circumstance applies.

(2) The program manager must address its petition to the Director, Flight Standards Service.

(3) A petition for reconsideration, if filed within the 30-day period, suspends the effectiveness of any amendment issued by the Flight Standards District Office that issued the program manager's management specifications unless that District Office has found, under paragraph (e) of this section, that an emergency exists requiring immediate action with respect to safety.

(4) If a petition for reconsideration is not filed within 30 days, the procedures of paragraph (c) of this section apply.

(e) If the Flight Standards District Office that issued the program manager's management specifications finds that an emergency exists requiring immediate action with respect to safety that makes the procedures set out in this section impracticable or contrary to the public interest—

(1) The Flight Standards District Office amends the management specifications and makes the amendment effective on the day the program manager receives notice of it; and

(2) In the notice to the program manager, the Flight Standards District Office will articulate the reasons for its finding that an emergency exists requiring immediate action with respect to safety or that makes it impracticable or contrary to the public interest to stay the effectiveness of the amendment.

§91.1019 Conducting tests and inspections.

(a) At any time or place, the Administrator may conduct an inspection or test, other than an en route inspection, to determine whether a program manager under this subpart is complying with title 49 of the United States Code, applicable regulations, and the program manager's management specifications.

(b) The program manager must—

(1) Make available to the Administrator at the program manager's principal base of operations, or at a place approved by the Administrator, the program manager's management specifications; and

(2) Allow the Administrator to make any test or inspection, other than an en route inspection, to determine compliance respecting any matter stated in paragraph (a) of this section.

(c) Each employee of, or person used by, the program manager who is responsible for maintaining the program manager's records required by or necessary to demonstrate compliance with this subpart must make those records available to the Administrator.

(d) The Administrator may determine a program manager's continued eligibility to hold its management specifications on any grounds listed in paragraph (a) of this section, or any other appropriate grounds.

(e) Failure by any program manager to make available to the Administrator upon request, the management specifications, or any required record, document, or report is grounds for suspension of all or any part of the program manager's management specifications.

§91.1021 Internal safety reporting and incident/accident response.

(a) Each program manager must establish an internal anonymous safety reporting procedure that fosters an environment of safety without any potential for retribution for filing the report.

(b) Each program manager must establish procedures to respond to an aviation incident/accident.

§91.1023 Program operating manual requirements.

(a) Each program manager must prepare and keep current a program operating manual setting forth procedures and policies acceptable to the Administrator. The program manager's management, flight, ground, and maintenance personnel must use this manual to conduct operations under this subpart. However, the Administrator may authorize a deviation from this paragraph if the Administrator finds that, because of the limited size of the operation, part of the manual is not necessary for guidance of management, flight, ground, or maintenance personnel.

(b) Each program manager must maintain at least one copy of the manual at its principal base of operations.

(c) No manual may be contrary to any applicable U.S. regulations, foreign regulations applicable to the program flights in foreign countries, or the program manager's management specifications.

(d) The program manager must make a copy of the manual, or appropriate portions of the manual (and changes and additions), available to its maintenance and ground operations personnel and must furnish the manual to—

(1) Its crewmembers; and

(2) Representatives of the Administrator assigned to the program manager.

(e) Each employee of the program manager to whom a manual or appropriate portions of it are furnished under paragraph (d)(1) of this section must keep it up-to-date with the changes and additions furnished to them.

(f) Except as provided in paragraph (h) of this section, the appropriate parts of the manual must be carried on each aircraft when away from the principal operations base. The appropriate parts must be available for use by ground or flight personnel.

(g) For the purpose of complying with paragraph (d) of this section, a program manager may furnish the persons listed therein with all or part of its manual in printed form or other form, acceptable to the Administrator, that is retrievable in the English language. If the program manager furnishes all or part of the manual in other than printed form, it must ensure there is a compatible reading device available to those persons that provides a legible image of the maintenance information and instructions, or a system that is able to retrieve the maintenance information and instructions in the English language.

(h) If a program manager conducts aircraft inspections or maintenance at specified facilities where the approved aircraft inspection program is available, the program manager is not required to ensure that the approved aircraft inspection program is carried aboard the aircraft en route to those facilities.

(i) Program managers that are also certificated to operate under part 121 or 135 of this chapter may be authorized to use the operating manual required by those parts to meet the manual requirements of subpart K, provided:

(1) The policies and procedures are consistent for both operations, or

(2) When policies and procedures are different, the applicable policies and procedures are identified and used.

§91.1025 Program operating manual contents.

Each program operating manual must have the date of the last revision on each revised page. Unless otherwise authorized by the Administrator, the manual must include the following:

(a) Procedures for ensuring compliance with aircraft weight and balance limitations;

(b) Copies of the program manager's management specifications or appropriate extracted information, including area of operations authorized, category and class of aircraft authorized, crew complements, and types of operations authorized;

(c) Procedures for complying with accident notification requirements;

(d) Procedures for ensuring that the pilot in command knows that required airworthiness inspections have been made and that the aircraft has been approved for return to service in compliance with applicable maintenance requirements;

(e) Procedures for reporting and recording mechanical irregularities that come to the attention of the pilot in command before, during, and after completion of a flight;

(f) Procedures to be followed by the pilot in command for determining that mechanical irregularities or defects reported for previous flights have been corrected or that correction of certain mechanical irregularities or defects have been deferred;

(g) Procedures to be followed by the pilot in command to obtain maintenance, preventive maintenance, and servicing of the aircraft at a place where previous arrangements have not been made by the program manager or owner, when the pilot is authorized to so act for the operator;

(h) Procedures under §91.213 for the release of, and continuation of flight if any item of equipment required for the particular type of operation becomes inoperative or unserviceable en route;

(i) Procedures for refueling aircraft, eliminating fuel contamination, protecting from fire (including electrostatic protection), and supervising and protecting passengers during refueling;

(j) Procedures to be followed by the pilot in command in the briefing under §91.1035.

(k) Procedures for ensuring compliance with emergency procedures, including a list of the functions assigned each category of required crewmembers in connection with an emergency and emergency evacuation duties;

(l) The approved aircraft inspection program, when applicable;

(m) Procedures for the evacuation of persons who may need the assistance of another person to move expeditiously to an exit if an emergency occurs;

(n) Procedures for performance planning that take into account take off, landing and en route conditions;

(o) An approved Destination Airport Analysis, when required by §91.1037(c), that includes the following elements, supported by aircraft performance data supplied by the aircraft manufacturer for the appropriate runway conditions—

(1) Pilot qualifications and experience;

(2) Aircraft performance data to include normal, abnormal and emergency procedures as supplied by the aircraft manufacturer;

(3) Airport facilities and topography;

(4) Runway conditions (including contamination);

(5) Airport or area weather reporting;

(6) Appropriate additional runway safety margins, if required;

(7) Airplane inoperative equipment;

(8) Environmental conditions; and

(9) Other criteria that affect aircraft performance.

(p) A suitable system (which may include a coded or electronic system) that provides for preservation and retrieval of maintenance recordkeeping information required by §91.1113 in a manner acceptable to the Administrator that provides—

(1) A description (or reference to date acceptable to the Administrator) of the work performed:

(2) The name of the person performing the work if the work is performed by a person outside the organization of the program manager; and

(3) The name or other positive identification of the individual approving the work.

(q) Flight locating and scheduling procedures; and

(r) Other procedures and policy instructions regarding program operations that are issued by the program manager or required by the Administrator.

§91.1027 Recordkeeping.

(a) Each program manager must keep at its principal base of operations or at other places approved by the Administrator, and must make available for inspection by the Administrator all of the following:

(1) The program manager's management specifications.

(2) A current list of the aircraft used or available for use in operations under this subpart, the operations for which each is equipped (for example, MNPS, RNP5/10, RVSM.).

(3) An individual record of each pilot used in operations under this subpart, including the following information:

(i) The full name of the pilot.

(ii) The pilot certificate (by type and number) and ratings that the pilot holds.

(iii) The pilot's aeronautical experience in sufficient detail to determine the pilot's qualifications to pilot aircraft in operations under this subpart.

(iv) The pilot's current duties and the date of the pilot's assignment to those duties.

(v) The effective date and class of the medical certificate that the pilot holds.

(vi) The date and result of each of the initial and recurrent competency tests and proficiency checks required by this subpart and the type of aircraft flown during that test or check.

(vii) The pilot's flight time in sufficient detail to determine compliance with the flight time limitations of this subpart.

(viii) The pilot's check pilot authorization, if any.

(ix) Any action taken concerning the pilot's release from employment for physical or professional disqualification; and

(x) The date of the satisfactory completion of initial, transition, upgrade, and differences training and each recurrent training phase required by this subpart.

(4) An individual record for each flight attendant used in operations under this subpart, including the following information:

(i) The full name of the flight attendant, and

(ii) The date and result of training required by §91.1063, as applicable.

(5) A current list of all fractional owners and associated aircraft. This list or a reference to its location must be included in the management specifications and should be of sufficient detail to determine the minimum fractional ownership interest of each aircraft.

(b) Each program manager must keep each record required by paragraph (a)(2) of this section for at least 6 months, and must keep each record required by paragraphs (a)(3) and (a)(4) of this section for at least 12 months. When an employee is no longer employed or affiliated with the program manager or fractional owner, each record required by paragraphs (a)(3) and (a)(4) of this section must be retained for at least 12 months.

(c) Each program manager is responsible for the preparation and accuracy of a load manifest in duplicate containing information concerning the loading of the aircraft. The manifest must be prepared before each takeoff and must include—

(1) The number of passengers;
(2) The total weight of the loaded aircraft;
(3) The maximum allowable takeoff weight for that flight;
(4) The center of gravity limits;
(5) The center of gravity of the loaded aircraft, except that the actual center of gravity need not be computed if the aircraft is loaded according to a loading schedule or other approved method that ensures that the center of gravity of the loaded aircraft is within approved limits. In those cases, an entry must be made on the manifest indicating that the center of gravity is within limits according to a loading schedule or other approved method;
(6) The registration number of the aircraft or flight number;
(7) The origin and destination; and
(8) Identification of crewmembers and their crew position assignments.

(d) The pilot in command of the aircraft for which a load manifest must be prepared must carry a copy of the completed load manifest in the aircraft to its destination. The program manager must keep copies of completed load manifest for at least 30 days at its principal operations base, or at another location used by it and approved by the Administrator.

(e) Each program manager is responsible for providing a written document that states the name of the entity having operational control on that flight and the part of this chapter under which the flight is operated. The pilot in command of the aircraft must carry a copy of the document in the aircraft to its destination. The program manager must keep a copy of the document for at least 30 days at its principal operations base, or at another location used by it and approved by the Administrator.

(f) Records may be kept either in paper or other form acceptable to the Administrator.

(g) Program managers that are also certificated to operate under part 121 or 135 of this chapter may satisfy the recordkeeping requirements of this section and of §91.1113 with records maintained to fulfill equivalent obligations under part 121 or 135 of this chapter.

§91.1029 Flight scheduling and locating requirements.

(a) Each program manager must establish and use an adequate system to schedule and release program aircraft.

(b) Except as provided in paragraph (d) of this section, each program manager must have adequate procedures established for locating each flight, for which a flight plan is not filed, that—

(1) Provide the program manager with at least the information required to be included in a VFR flight plan;
(2) Provide for timely notification of an FAA facility or search and rescue facility, if an aircraft is overdue or missing; and
(3) Provide the program manager with the location, date, and estimated time for reestablishing radio or telephone communications, if the flight will operate in an area where communications cannot be maintained.

(c) Flight locating information must be retained at the program manager's principal base of operations, or at other places designated by the program manager in the flight locating procedures, until the completion of the flight.

(d) The flight locating requirements of paragraph (b) of this section do not apply to a flight for which an FAA flight plan has been filed and the flight plan is canceled within 25 nautical miles of the destination airport.

§91.1031 Pilot in command or second in command: Designation required.

(a) Each program manager must designate a—

(1) Pilot in command for each program flight; and
(2) Second in command for each program flight requiring two pilots.

(b) The pilot in command, as designated by the program manager, must remain the pilot in command at all times during that flight.

§91.1033 Operating information required.

(a) Each program manager must, for all program operations, provide the following materials, in current and appropriate form, accessible to the pilot at the pilot station, and the pilot must use them—

(1) A cockpit checklist;
(2) For multiengine aircraft or for aircraft with retractable landing gear, an emergency cockpit checklist containing the procedures required by paragraph (c) of this section, as appropriate;
(3) At least one set of pertinent aeronautical charts; and
(4) For IFR operations, at least one set of pertinent navigational en route, terminal area, and instrument approach procedure charts.

(b) Each cockpit checklist required by paragraph (a)(1) of this section must contain the following procedures:

(1) Before starting engines;
(2) Before takeoff;
(3) Cruise;
(4) Before landing;
(5) After landing; and
(6) Stopping engines.

(c) Each emergency cockpit checklist required by paragraph (a)(2) of this section must contain the following procedures, as appropriate:

(1) Emergency operation of fuel, hydraulic, electrical, and mechanical systems.
(2) Emergency operation of instruments and controls.
(3) Engine inoperative procedures.
(4) Any other emergency procedures necessary for safety.

§91.1035 Passenger awareness.

(a) Prior to each takeoff, the pilot in command of an aircraft carrying passengers on a program flight must ensure that all passengers have been orally briefed on—

(1) ***Smoking:*** Each passenger must be briefed on when, where, and under what conditions smoking is prohibited. This briefing must include a statement, as appropriate, that the regulations require passenger compliance with lighted passenger information signs and no smoking placards, prohibit smoking in lavatories, and require compliance with crewmember instructions with regard to these items;
(2) ***Use of safety belts, shoulder harnesses, and child restraint systems:*** Each passenger must be briefed on when, where and under what conditions it is necessary to

have his or her safety belt and, if installed, his or her shoulder harness fastened about him or her, and if a child is being transported, the appropriate use of child restraint systems, if available. This briefing must include a statement, as appropriate, that the regulations require passenger compliance with the lighted passenger information sign and/or crewmember instructions with regard to these items;

(3) The placement of seat backs in an upright position before takeoff and landing;

(4) Location and means for opening the passenger entry door and emergency exits;

(5) Location of survival equipment;

(6) Ditching procedures and the use of flotation equipment required under §91.509 for a flight over water;

(7) The normal and emergency use of oxygen installed in the aircraft; and

(8) Location and operation of fire extinguishers.

(b) Prior to each takeoff, the pilot in command of an aircraft carrying passengers on a program flight must ensure that each person who may need the assistance of another person to move expeditiously to an exit if an emergency occurs and that person's attendant, if any, has received a briefing as to the procedures to be followed if an evacuation occurs. This paragraph does not apply to a person who has been given a briefing before a previous leg of that flight in the same aircraft.

(c) Prior to each takeoff, the pilot in command must advise the passengers of the name of the entity in operational control of the flight.

(d) The oral briefings required by paragraphs (a), (b), and (c) of this section must be given by the pilot in command or another crewmember.

(e) The oral briefing required by paragraph (a) of this section may be delivered by means of an approved recording playback device that is audible to each passenger under normal noise levels.

(f) The oral briefing required by paragraph (a) of this section must be supplemented by printed cards that must be carried in the aircraft in locations convenient for the use of each passenger. The cards must—

(1) Be appropriate for the aircraft on which they are to be used;

(2) Contain a diagram of, and method of operating, the emergency exits; and

(3) Contain other instructions necessary for the use of emergency equipment on board the aircraft.

§91.1037 Large transport category airplanes: Turbine engine powered; Limitations; Destination and alternate airports.

(a) No program manager or any other person may permit a turbine engine powered large transport category airplane on a program flight to take off that airplane at a weight that (allowing for normal consumption of fuel and oil in flight to the destination or alternate airport) the weight of the airplane on arrival would exceed the landing weight in the Airplane Flight Manual for the elevation of the destination or alternate airport and the ambient temperature expected at the time of landing.

(b) Except as provided in paragraph (c) of this section, no program manager or any other person may permit a turbine engine powered large transport category airplane on a program flight to take off that airplane unless its weight on arrival, allowing for normal consumption of fuel and oil in flight (in accordance with the landing distance in the Airplane Flight Manual for the elevation of the destination airport and the wind conditions expected there at the time of landing), would allow a full stop landing at the intended destination airport within 60 percent of the effective length of each runway described below from a point 50 feet above the intersection of the obstruction clearance plane and the runway. For the purpose of determining the allowable landing weight at the destination airport, the following is assumed:

(1) The airplane is landed on the most favorable runway and in the most favorable direction, in still air.

(2) The airplane is landed on the most suitable runway considering the probable wind velocity and direction and the ground handling characteristics of that airplane, and considering other conditions such as landing aids and terrain.

(c) A program manager or other person flying a turbine engine powered large transport category airplane on a program flight may permit that airplane to take off at a weight in excess of that allowed by paragraph (b) of this section if all of the following conditions exist:

(1) The operation is conducted in accordance with an approved Destination Airport Analysis in that person's program operating manual that contains the elements listed in §91.1025(o).

(2) The airplane's weight on arrival, allowing for normal consumption of fuel and oil in flight (in accordance with the landing distance in the Airplane Flight Manual for the elevation of the destination airport and the wind conditions expected there at the time of landing), would allow a full stop landing at the intended destination airport within 80 percent of the effective length of each runway described below from a point 50 feet above the intersection of the obstruction clearance plane and the runway. For the purpose of determining the allowable landing weight at the destination airport, the following is assumed:

(i) The airplane is landed on the most favorable runway and in the most favorable direction, in still air.

(ii) The airplane is landed on the most suitable runway considering the probable wind velocity and direction and the ground handling characteristics of that airplane, and considering other conditions such as landing aids and terrain.

(3) The operation is authorized by management specifications.

(d) No program manager or other person may select an airport as an alternate airport for a turbine engine powered large transport category airplane unless (based on the assumptions in paragraph (b) of this section) that airplane, at the weight expected at the time of arrival, can be brought to a full stop landing within 80 percent of the effective length of the runway from a point 50 feet above the intersection of the obstruction clearance plane and the runway.

(e) Unless, based on a showing of actual operating landing techniques on wet runways, a shorter landing distance (but never less than that required by paragraph (b) or (c) of this section) has been approved for a specific type and model airplane and included in the Airplane Flight Manual, no person may take off a turbojet airplane when the appropriate weather reports or forecasts, or any combination of them, indicate that the runways at the destination or alternate airport may be wet or slippery at the estimated time of arrival unless the effective runway length at the destination airport is at least 115 percent of the runway length required under paragraph (b) or (c) of this section.

§91.1039 IFR takeoff, approach and landing minimums.

(a) No pilot on a program aircraft operating a program flight may begin an instrument approach procedure to an airport unless—

(1) Either that airport or the alternate airport has a weather reporting facility operated by the U.S. National Weather Service, a source approved by the U.S. National Weather Service, or a source approved by the Administrator; and

(2) The latest weather report issued by the weather reporting facility includes a current local altimeter setting for the destination airport. If no local altimeter setting is available at the destination airport, the pilot must obtain the current local altimeter setting from a source provided by the facility designated on the approach chart for the destination airport.

(b) For flight planning purposes, if the destination airport does not have a weather reporting facility described in paragraph (a)(1) of this section, the pilot must designate as an alternate an airport that has a weather reporting facility meeting that criteria.

(c) The MDA or Decision Altitude and visibility landing minimums prescribed in part 97 of this chapter or in the program manager's management specifications are increased by 100 feet and 1/2 mile respectively, but not to exceed the ceiling and visibility minimums for that airport when used as an alternate airport, for each pilot in command of a turbine-powered aircraft who has not served at least 100 hours as pilot in command in that type of aircraft.

(d) No person may take off an aircraft under IFR from an airport where weather conditions are at or above takeoff minimums but are below authorized IFR landing minimums unless there is an alternate airport within one hour's flying time (at normal cruising speed, in still air) of the airport of departure.

(e) Each pilot making an IFR takeoff or approach and landing at an airport must comply with applicable instrument approach procedures and take off and landing weather minimums prescribed by the authority having jurisdiction over the airport. In addition, no pilot may, at that airport take off when the visibility is less than 600 feet.

§91.1041 Aircraft proving and validation tests.

(a) No program manager may permit the operation of an aircraft, other than a turbojet aircraft, for which two pilots are required by the type certification requirements of this chapter for operations under VFR, if it has not previously proved such an aircraft in operations under this part in at least 25 hours of proving tests acceptable to the Administrator including—

(1) Five hours of night time, if night flights are to be authorized;

(2) Five instrument approach procedures under simulated or actual conditions, if IFR flights are to be authorized; and

(3) Entry into a representative number of en route airports as determined by the Administrator.

(b) No program manager may permit the operation of a turbojet airplane if it has not previously proved a turbojet airplane in operations under this part in at least 25 hours of proving tests acceptable to the Administrator including—

(1) Five hours of night time, if night flights are to be authorized;

(2) Five instrument approach procedures under simulated or actual conditions, if IFR flights are to be authorized; and

(3) Entry into a representative number of en route airports as determined by the Administrator.

(c) No program manager may carry passengers in an aircraft during proving tests, except those needed to make the tests and those designated by the Administrator to observe the tests. However, pilot flight training may be conducted during the proving tests.

(d) Validation testing is required to determine that a program manager is capable of conducting operations safely and in compliance with applicable regulatory standards. Validation tests are required for the following authorizations:

(1) The addition of an aircraft for which two pilots are required for operations under VFR or a turbojet airplane, if that aircraft or an aircraft of the same make or similar design has not been previously proved or validated in operations under this part.

(2) Operations outside U.S. airspace.

(3) Class II navigation authorizations.

(4) Special performance or operational authorizations.

(e) Validation tests must be accomplished by test methods acceptable to the Administrator. Actual flights may not be required when an applicant can demonstrate competence and compliance with appropriate regulations without conducting a flight.

(f) Proving tests and validation tests may be conducted simultaneously when appropriate.

(g) The Administrator may authorize deviations from this section if the Administrator finds that special circumstances make full compliance with this section unnecessary.

§91.1043 [Reserved]

§91.1045 Additional equipment requirements.

No person may operate a program aircraft on a program flight unless the aircraft is equipped with the following—

(a) Airplanes having a passenger-seat configuration of more than 30 seats or a payload capacity of more than 7,500 pounds:

(1) A cockpit voice recorder as required by §121.359 of this chapter as applicable to the aircraft specified in that section.

(2) A flight recorder as required by §121.343 or §121.344 of this chapter as applicable to the aircraft specified in that section.

(3) A terrain awareness and warning system as required by §121.354 of this chapter as applicable to the aircraft specified in that section.

(4) A traffic alert and collision avoidance system as required by §121.356 of this chapter as applicable to the aircraft specified in that section.

(5) Airborne weather radar as required by §121.357 of this chapter, as applicable to the aircraft specified in that section.

(b) Airplanes having a passenger-seat configuration of 30 seats or fewer, excluding each crewmember, and a payload capacity of 7,500 pounds or less, and any rotorcraft (as applicable):

(1) A cockpit voice recorder as required by §135.151 of this chapter as applicable to the aircraft specified in that section.

(2) A flight recorder as required by §135.152 of this chapter as applicable to the aircraft specified in that section.

(3) A terrain awareness and warning system as required by §135.154 of this chapter as applicable to the aircraft specified in that section.

(4) A traffic alert and collision avoidance system as required by §135.180 of this chapter as applicable to the aircraft specified in that section.

(5) As applicable to the aircraft specified in that section, either:

(i) Airborne thunderstorm detection equipment as required by §135.173 of this chapter; or

(ii) Airborne weather radar as required by §135.175 of this chapter.

§91.1047 Drug and alcohol misuse education program.

(a) Each program manager must provide each direct employee performing flight crewmember, flight attendant, flight instructor, or aircraft maintenance duties with drug and alcohol misuse education.

(b) No program manager may use any contract employee to perform flight crewmember, flight attendant, flight instructor, or aircraft maintenance duties for the program manager unless that contract employee has been provided with drug and alcohol misuse education.

(c) Program managers must disclose to their owners and prospective owners the existence of a company drug and alcohol misuse testing program. If the program manager has implemented a company testing program, the program manager's disclosure must include the following:

(1) Information on the substances that they test for, for example, alcohol and a list of the drugs;

(2) The categories of employees tested, the types of tests, for example, pre-employment, random, reasonable cause/suspicion, post accident, return to duty and follow-up; and

(3) The degree to which the program manager's company testing program is comparable to the federally mandated drug and alcohol misuse prevention program required under part 121, appendices I and J, of this chapter, regarding the information in paragraphs (c)(1) and (c)(2) of this section.

(d) If a program aircraft is operated on a program flight into an airport at which no maintenance personnel are available that are subject to the requirements of paragraphs (a) or (b) of this section and emergency maintenance is required, the program manager may use persons not meeting the requirements of paragraphs (a) or (b) of this section to provide such emergency maintenance under both of the following conditions:

(1) The program manager must notify the Drug Abatement Program Division, AAM-800, 800 Independence Avenue, SW., Washington, DC 20591 in writing within 10 days after being provided emergency maintenance in accordance with this paragraph. The program manager must retain copies of all such written notifications for two years.

(2) The aircraft must be reinspected by maintenance personnel who meet the requirements of paragraph (a) or (b) of this section when the aircraft is next at an airport where such maintenance personnel are available.

(e) For purposes of this section, emergency maintenance means maintenance that—

(1) Is not scheduled, and

(2) Is made necessary by an aircraft condition not discovered prior to the departure for that location.

(f) Notwithstanding paragraphs (a) and (b) of this section, drug and alcohol misuse education conducted under an FAA-approved drug and alcohol misuse prevention program may be used to satisfy these requirements.

§91.1049 Personnel.

(a) Each program manager and each fractional owner must use in program operations on program aircraft flight crews meeting §91.1053 criteria and qualified under the appropriate regulations. The program manager must provide oversight of those crews.

(b) Each program manager must employ (either directly or by contract) an adequate number of pilots per program aircraft. Flight crew staffing must be determined based on the following factors, at a minimum:

(1) Number of program aircraft.

(2) Program manager flight, duty, and rest time considerations, and in all cases within the limits set forth in §§91.1057 through 91.1061.

(3) Vacations.

(4) Operational efficiencies.

(5) Training.

(6) Single pilot operations, if authorized by deviation under paragraph (d) of this section.

(c) Each program manager must publish pilot and flight attendant duty schedules sufficiently in advance to follow the flight, duty, and rest time limits in §§91.1057 through 91.1061 in program operations.

(d) Unless otherwise authorized by the Administrator, when any program aircraft is flown in program operations with passengers onboard, the crew must consist of at least two qualified pilots employed or contracted by the program manager or the fractional owner.

(e) The program manager must ensure that trained and qualified scheduling or flight release personnel are on duty to schedule and release program aircraft during all hours that such aircraft are available for program operations.

§91.1051 Pilot safety background check.

Within 90 days of an individual beginning service as a pilot, the program manager must request the following information:

(a) FAA records pertaining to—

(1) Current pilot certificates and associated type ratings.

(2) Current medical certificates.

(3) Summaries of legal enforcement actions resulting in a finding by the Administrator of a violation.

(b) Records from all previous employers during the five years preceding the date of the employment application where the applicant worked as a pilot. If any of these firms are in bankruptcy, the records must be requested from the trustees in bankruptcy for those employees. If the previous employer is no longer in business, a documented good faith effort must be made to obtain the records. Records from previous employers must include, as applicable—

(1) Crew member records.

(2) Drug testing—collection, testing, and rehabilitation records pertaining to the individual.

(3) Alcohol misuse prevention program records pertaining to the individual.

(4) The applicant's individual record that includes certifications, ratings, aeronautical experience, effective date and class of the medical certificate.

§91.1053 Crewmember experience.

(a) No program manager or owner may use any person, nor may any person serve, as a pilot in command or second in command of a program aircraft, or as a flight attendant on a program aircraft, in program operations under this subpart unless that person has met the applicable requirements of part 61 of this chapter and has the following experience and ratings:

(1) Total flight time for all pilots:

(i) Pilot in command—A minimum of 1,500 hours.

(ii) Second in command—A minimum of 500 hours.

(2) For multi-engine turbine-powered fixed-wing and powered-lift aircraft, the following FAA certification and ratings requirements:

(i) Pilot in command—Airline transport pilot and applicable type ratings.

(ii) Second in command—Commercial pilot and instrument ratings.

(iii) Flight attendant (if required or used)—Appropriately trained personnel.

(3) For all other aircraft, the following FAA certification and rating requirements:

(i) Pilot in command—Commercial pilot and instrument ratings.

(ii) Second in command—Commercial pilot and instrument ratings.

(iii) Flight attendant (if required or used)—Appropriately trained personnel.

(b) The Administrator may authorize deviations from paragraph (a)(1) of this section if the Flight Standards District Office that issued the program manager's management specifications finds that the crewmember has comparable experience, and can effectively perform the functions associated with the position in accordance with the requirements of this chapter. Grants of deviation under this paragraph may be granted after consideration of the size and scope of the operation, the qualifications of the intended personnel and the circumstances set forth in §91.1055(b)(1) through (3). The Administrator may, at any time, terminate any grant of deviation authority issued under this paragraph.

§91.1055 Pilot operating limitations and pairing requirement.

(a) If the second in command of a fixed-wing program aircraft has fewer than 100 hours of flight time as second in command flying in the aircraft make and model and, if a type rating is required, in the type aircraft being flown, and the pilot in command is not an appropriately qualified check pilot, the pilot in command shall make all takeoffs and landings in any of the following situations:

(1) Landings at the destination airport when a Destination Airport Analysis is required by §91.1037(c); and

(2) In any of the following conditions:

(i) The prevailing visibility for the airport is at or below 3/4 mile.

(ii) The runway visual range for the runway to be used is at or below 4,000 feet.

(iii) The runway to be used has water, snow, slush, ice or similar contamination that may adversely affect aircraft performance.

(iv) The braking action on the runway to be used is reported to be less than "good."

(v) The crosswind component for the runway to be used is in excess of 15 knots.

(vi) Windshear is reported in the vicinity of the airport.

(vii) Any other condition in which the pilot in command determines it to be prudent to exercise the pilot in command's authority.

(b) No program manager may release a program flight under this subpart unless, for that aircraft make or model and, if a type rating is required, for that type aircraft, either the pilot in command or the second in command has at least 75 hours of flight time, either as pilot in command or second in command. The Administrator may, upon application by the program manager, authorize deviations from the requirements of this paragraph by an appropriate amendment to the management specifications in any of the following circumstances:

(1) A newly authorized program manager does not employ any pilots who meet the minimum requirements of this paragraph.

(2) An existing program manager adds to its fleet a new category and class aircraft not used before in its operation.

(3) An existing program manager establishes a new base to which it assigns pilots who will be required to become qualified on the aircraft operated from that base.

(c) No person may be assigned in the capacity of pilot in command in a program operation to more than two aircraft types that require a separate type rating.

§91.1057 Flight, duty and rest time requirements: All crewmembers.

(a) For purposes of this subpart—

Augmented flight crew means at least three pilots.

Calendar day means the period of elapsed time, using Coordinated Universal Time or local time that begins at midnight and ends 24 hours later at the next midnight.

Duty period means the period of elapsed time between reporting for an assignment involving flight time and release from that assignment by the program manager. All time between these two points is part of the duty period, even if flight time is interrupted by nonflight-related duties. The time is calculated using either Coordinated Universal Time or local time to reflect the total elapsed time.

Extension of flight time means an increase in the flight time because of circumstances beyond the control of the program manager or flight crewmember (such as adverse weather) that are not known at the time of departure and that prevent the flightcrew from reaching the destination within the planned flight time.

Flight attendant means an individual, other than a flight crewmember, who is assigned by the program manager, in accordance with the required minimum crew complement under the program manager's management specifications or in addition to that minimum complement, to duty in an aircraft during flight time and whose duties include but are not necessarily limited to cabin-safety-related responsibilities.

Multi-time zone flight means an easterly or westerly flight or multiple flights in one direction in the same duty period that results in a time zone difference of 5 or more hours and is conducted in a geographic area that is south of 60 degrees north latitude and north of 60 degrees south latitude.

Reserve status means that status in which a flight crewmember, by arrangement with the program manager: Holds himself or herself fit to fly to the extent that this is within the control of the flight crewmember; remains within a reasonable response time of the aircraft as agreed between the flight crewmember and the program manager; and maintains a ready means whereby the flight crewmember may be contacted by the program manager. Reserve status is not part of any duty period or rest period.

Rest period means a period of time required pursuant to this subpart that is free of all responsibility for work or duty prior to the commencement of, or following completion of, a duty period, and during which the flight crewmember or flight attendant cannot be required to receive contact from the program manager. A rest period does not include any time during which the program manager imposes on a flight crewmember or flight attendant any duty or restraint, including any actual work or present responsibility for work should the occasion arise.

Standby means that portion of a duty period during which a flight crewmember is subject to the control of the program manager and holds himself or herself in a condition of readiness to undertake a flight. Standby is not part of any rest period.

(b) A program manager may assign a crewmember and a crewmember may accept an assignment for flight time only when the applicable requirements of this section and §§91.1059–91.1062 are met.

(c) No program manager may assign any crewmember to any duty during any required rest period.

(d) Time spent in transportation, not local in character, that a program manager requires of a crewmember and provides to transport the crewmember to an airport at which he or she is to serve on a flight as a crewmember, or from an airport at which he or she was relieved from duty to return to his or her home station, is not considered part of a rest period.

(e) A flight crewmember may continue a flight assignment if the flight to which he or she is assigned would normally terminate within the flight time limitations, but because of circumstances beyond the control of the program manager or flight crewmember (such as adverse weather conditions), is not at the time of departure expected to reach its destination within the planned flight time. The extension of flight time under this paragraph may not exceed the maximum time limits set forth in §91.1059.

(f) Each flight assignment must provide for at least 10 consecutive hours of rest during the 24-hour period that precedes the completion time of the assignment.

(g) The program manager must provide each crewmember at least 13 rest periods of at least 24 consecutive hours each in each calendar quarter.

(h) A flight crewmember may decline a flight assignment if, in the flight crewmember's determination, to do so would not be consistent with the standard of safe operation required under this subpart, this part, and applicable provisions of this title.

(i) Any rest period required by this subpart may occur concurrently with any other rest period.

(j) If authorized by the Administrator, a program manager may use the applicable unscheduled flight time limitations, duty period limitations, and rest requirements of part 121 or part 135 of this chapter instead of the flight time limitations, duty period limitations, and rest requirements of this subpart.

§91.1059 Flight time limitations and rest requirements: One or two pilot crews.

(a) No program manager may assign any flight crewmember, and no flight crewmember may accept an assignment, for flight time as a member of a one- or two-pilot crew if that crewmember's total flight time in all commercial flying will exceed—

(1) 500 hours in any calendar quarter;

(2) 800 hours in any two consecutive calendar quarters;

(3) 1,400 hours in any calendar year.

(b) Except as provided in paragraph (c) of this section, during any 24 consecutive hours the total flight time of the assigned flight, when added to any commercial flying by that flight crewmember, may not exceed—

(1) 8 hours for a flight crew consisting of one pilot; or

(2) 10 hours for a flight crew consisting of two pilots qualified under this subpart for the operation being conducted.

(c) No program manager may assign any flight crewmember, and no flight crewmember may accept an assignment, if that crewmember's flight time or duty period will exceed, or rest time will be less than—

	Normal duty	Extension of flight time
(1) Minimum Rest Immediately Before Duty	10 Hours	10 Hours
(2) Duty Period	Up to 14 Hours	Up to 14 Hours
(3) Flight Time For 1 Pilot	Up to 8 Hours	Exceeding 8 Hours up to 9 Hours
(4) Flight Time For 2 Pilots	Up to 10 Hours	Exceeding 10 Hours up to 12 Hours
(5) Minimum After Duty Rest	10 Hours	12 Hours
(6) Minimum After Duty Rest Period for Multi-Time Zone Flights	14 Hours	18 Hours

§91.1061 Augmented flight crews.

(a) No program manager may assign any flight crewmember, and no flight crewmember may accept an assignment, for flight time as a member of an augmented crew if that crewmember's total flight time in all commercial flying will exceed—

(1) 500 hours in any calendar quarter;

(2) 800 hours in any two consecutive calendar quarters;

(3) 1,400 hours in any calendar year.

(b) No program manager may assign any pilot to an augmented crew, unless the program manager ensures:

(1) Adequate sleeping facilities are installed on the aircraft for the pilots.

(2) No more than 8 hours of flight deck duty is accrued in any 24 consecutive hours.

(3) For a three-pilot crew, the crew must consist of at least the following:

(i) A pilot in command (PIC) who meets the applicable flight crewmember requirements of this subpart and §61.57 of this chapter.

(ii) A PIC qualified pilot who meets the applicable flight crewmember requirements of this subpart and §61.57(c) and (d) of this chapter.

(iii) A second in command (SIC) who meets the SIC qualifications of this subpart. For flight under IFR, that person must also meet the recent instrument experience requirements of part 61 of this chapter.

(4) For a four-pilot crew, at least three pilots who meet the conditions of paragraph (b)(3) of this section, plus a fourth pilot who meets the SIC qualifications of this subpart. For flight under IFR, that person must also meet the recent instrument experience requirements of part 61 of this chapter.

(c) No program manager may assign any flight crewmember, and no flight crewmember may accept an assignment, if that crewmember's flight time or duty period will exceed, or rest time will be less than—

	3-Pilot crew	4-Pilot crew
(1) Minimum Rest Immediately Before Duty	10 Hours	10 Hours
(2) Duty Period	Up to 16 Hours	Up to 18 Hours
(3) Flight Time	Up to 12 Hours	Up to 16 Hours
(4) Minimum After Duty Rest	12 Hours	18 Hours
(5) Minimum After Duty Rest Period for Multi-Time Zone Flights	18 hours	24 hours

§91.1062 Duty periods and rest requirements: Flight attendants.

(a) Except as provided in paragraph (b) of this section, a program manager may assign a duty period to a flight attendant only when the assignment meets the applicable duty period limitations and rest requirements of this paragraph.

(1) Except as provided in paragraphs (a)(4), (a)(5), and (a)(6) of this section, no program manager may assign a flight attendant to a scheduled duty period of more than 14 hours.

(2) Except as provided in paragraph (a)(3) of this section, a flight attendant scheduled to a duty period of 14 hours or less as provided under paragraph (a)(1) of this section must be given a scheduled rest period of at least 9 consecutive hours. This rest period must occur between the completion of the scheduled duty period and the commencement of the subsequent duty period.

(3) The rest period required under paragraph (a)(2) of this section may be scheduled or reduced to 8 consecutive hours if the flight attendant is provided a subsequent rest period of at least 10 consecutive hours; this subsequent rest period must be scheduled to begin no later than 24 hours after the beginning of the reduced rest period and must occur between the completion of the scheduled duty period and the commencement of the subsequent duty period.

(4) A program manager may assign a flight attendant to a scheduled duty period of more than 14 hours, but no more than 16 hours, if the program manager has assigned to the flight or flights in that duty period at least one flight attendant in addition to the minimum flight attendant complement required for the flight or flights in that duty period under the program manager's management specifications.

(5) A program manager may assign a flight attendant to a scheduled duty period of more than 16 hours, but no more than 18 hours, if the program manager has assigned to the flight or flights in that duty period at least two flight attendants in addition to the minimum flight attendant complement required for the flight or flights in that duty period under the program manager's management specifications.

(6) A program manager may assign a flight attendant to a scheduled duty period of more than 18 hours, but no more than 20 hours, if the scheduled duty period includes one or more flights that land or take off outside the 48 contiguous states and the District of Columbia, and if the program manager has assigned to the flight or flights in that duty period at least three flight attendants in addition to the minimum flight attendant complement required for the flight or flights in that duty period under the program manager's management specifications.

(7) Except as provided in paragraph (a)(8) of this section, a flight attendant scheduled to a duty period of more than 14 hours but no more than 20 hours, as provided in paragraphs (a)(4), (a)(5), and (a)(6) of this section, must be given a scheduled rest period of at least 12 consecutive hours. This rest period must occur between the completion of the scheduled duty period and the commencement of the subsequent duty period.

(8) The rest period required under paragraph (a)(7) of this section may be scheduled or reduced to 10 consecutive hours if the flight attendant is provided a subsequent rest period of at least 14 consecutive hours; this subsequent rest period must be scheduled to begin no later than 24 hours after the beginning of the reduced rest period and must occur between the completion of the scheduled duty period and the commencement of the subsequent duty period.

(9) Notwithstanding paragraphs (a)(4), (a)(5), and (a)(6) of this section, if a program manager elects to reduce the rest period to 10 hours as authorized by paragraph (a)(8) of this section, the program manager may not schedule a flight attendant for a duty period of more than 14 hours during the 24-hour period commencing after the beginning of the reduced rest period.

(b) Notwithstanding paragraph (a) of this section, a program manager may apply the flight crewmember flight time and duty limitations and rest requirements of this part to flight attendants for all operations conducted under this part provided that the program manager establishes written procedures that—

(1) Apply to all flight attendants used in the program manager's operation;

(2) Include the flight crewmember rest and duty requirements of §§91.1057, 91.1059, and 91.1061, as appropriate to the operation being conducted, except that rest facilities on board the aircraft are not required;

(3) Include provisions to add one flight attendant to the minimum flight attendant complement for each flight crewmember who is in excess of the minimum number required in the aircraft type certificate data sheet and who is assigned to the aircraft under the provisions of §91.1061; and

(4) Are approved by the Administrator and described or referenced in the program manager's management specifications.

§91.1063 Testing and training: Applicability and terms used.

(a) Sections 91.1065 through 91.1107:

(1) Prescribe the tests and checks required for pilots and flight attendant crewmembers and for the approval of check pilots in operations under this subpart;

(2) Prescribe the requirements for establishing and maintaining an approved training program for crewmembers, check pilots and instructors, and other operations personnel employed or used by the program manager in program operations;

(3) Prescribe the requirements for the qualification, approval and use of aircraft simulators and flight training devices in the conduct of an approved training program; and

(4) Permits training center personnel authorized under part 142 of this chapter who meet the requirements of §91.1075 to conduct training, testing and checking under contract or other arrangements to those persons subject to the requirements of this subpart.

(b) If authorized by the Administrator, a program manager may comply with the applicable training and testing sections of subparts N and O of part 121 of this chapter instead of §§91.1065 through 91.1107, except for the operating experience requirements of §121.434 of this chapter.

(c) If authorized by the Administrator, a program manager may comply with the applicable training and testing sections of subparts G and H of part 135 of this chapter instead of §§91.1065 through 91.1107, except for the operating experience requirements of §135.244 of this chapter.

(d) For the purposes of this subpart, the following terms and definitions apply:

(1) ***Initial training.*** The training required for crewmembers who have not qualified and served in the same capacity on an aircraft.

(2) ***Transition training.*** The training required for crewmembers who have qualified and served in the same capacity on another aircraft.

(3) ***Upgrade training.*** The training required for crewmembers who have qualified and served as second in command on a particular aircraft type, before they serve as pilot in command on that aircraft.

(4) ***Differences training.*** The training required for crewmembers who have qualified and served on a particular type aircraft, when the Administrator finds differences training is necessary before a crewmember serves in the same capacity on a particular variation of that aircraft.

(5) ***Recurrent training.*** The training required for crewmembers to remain adequately trained and currently proficient for each aircraft crewmember position, and type of operation in which the crewmember serves.

(6) ***In flight.*** The maneuvers, procedures, or functions that will be conducted in the aircraft.

(7) ***Training center.*** An organization governed by the applicable requirements of part 142 of this chapter that conducts training, testing, and checking under contract or other arrangement to program managers subject to the requirements of this subpart.

(8) ***Requalification training.*** The training required for crewmembers previously trained and qualified, but who have become unqualified because of not having met within the required period any of the following:

(i) Recurrent crewmember training requirements of §91.1107.

(ii) Instrument proficiency check requirements of §91.1069.

(iii) Testing requirements of §91.1065.

(iv) Recurrent flight attendant testing requirements of §91.1067.

§91.1065 Initial and recurrent pilot testing requirements.

(a) No program manager or owner may use a pilot, nor may any person serve as a pilot, unless, since the beginning of the 12th month before that service, that pilot has passed either a written or oral test (or a combination), given by the Administrator or an authorized check pilot, on that pilot's knowledge in the following areas—

(1) The appropriate provisions of parts 61 and 91 of this chapter and the management specifications and the operating manual of the program manager;

(2) For each type of aircraft to be flown by the pilot, the aircraft powerplant, major components and systems, major appliances, performance and operating limitations, standard and emergency operating procedures, and the contents of the accepted operating manual or equivalent, as applicable;

(3) For each type of aircraft to be flown by the pilot, the method of determining compliance with weight and balance limitations for takeoff, landing and en route operations;

(4) Navigation and use of air navigation aids appropriate to the operation or pilot authorization, including, when applicable, instrument approach facilities and procedures;

(5) Air traffic control procedures, including IFR procedures when applicable;

(6) Meteorology in general, including the principles of frontal systems, icing, fog, thunderstorms, and windshear, and, if appropriate for the operation of the program manager, high altitude weather;

(7) Procedures for—

(i) Recognizing and avoiding severe weather situations;

(ii) Escaping from severe weather situations, in case of inadvertent encounters, including low-altitude windshear (except that rotorcraft aircraft pilots are not required to be tested on escaping from low-altitude windshear); and

(iii) Operating in or near thunderstorms (including best penetration altitudes), turbulent air (including clear air turbulence), icing, hail, and other potentially hazardous meteorological conditions; and

(8) New equipment, procedures, or techniques, as appropriate.

(b) No program manager or owner may use a pilot, nor may any person serve as a pilot, in any aircraft unless, since the beginning of the 12th month before that service, that pilot has passed a competency check given by the Administrator or an authorized check pilot in that class of aircraft, if single-engine aircraft other than turbojet, or that type of aircraft, if rotorcraft, multiengine aircraft, or turbojet airplane, to determine the pilot's competence in practical skills and techniques in that aircraft or class of aircraft. The extent of the competency check will be determined by the Administrator or authorized check pilot conducting the competency check. The competency check may include any of the maneuvers and procedures currently required for the original issuance of the particular pilot certificate required for the operations authorized and appropriate to the category, class and type of aircraft involved. For the purposes of this paragraph, type, as to an airplane, means any one of a group of airplanes determined by the Administrator to have a similar means of propulsion, the same manufacturer, and no significantly different handling or flight characteristics. For the purposes of this paragraph, type, as to a rotorcraft, means a basic make and model.

(c) The instrument proficiency check required by §91.1069 may be substituted for the competency check required by this section for the type of aircraft used in the check.

(d) For the purpose of this subpart, competent performance of a procedure or maneuver by a person to be used as a pilot requires that the pilot be the obvious master of the aircraft, with the successful outcome of the maneuver never in doubt.

(e) The Administrator or authorized check pilot certifies the competency of each pilot who passes the knowledge or flight check in the program manager's pilot records.

(f) All or portions of a required competency check may be given in an aircraft simulator or other appropriate training device, if approved by the Administrator.

§91.1067 Initial and recurrent flight attendant crewmember testing requirements.

No program manager or owner may use a flight attendant crewmember, nor may any person serve as a flight attendant crewmember unless, since the beginning of the 12th month before that service, the program manager has determined by appropriate initial and recurrent testing that the person is knowledgeable and competent in the following areas as appropriate to assigned duties and responsibilities—

(a) Authority of the pilot in command;

(b) Passenger handling, including procedures to be followed in handling deranged persons or other persons whose conduct might jeopardize safety;

(c) Crewmember assignments, functions, and responsibilities during ditching and evacuation of persons who may need the assistance of another person to move expeditiously to an exit in an emergency;

(d) Briefing of passengers;

(e) Location and operation of portable fire extinguishers and other items of emergency equipment;

(f) Proper use of cabin equipment and controls;

(g) Location and operation of passenger oxygen equipment;

(h) Location and operation of all normal and emergency exits, including evacuation slides and escape ropes; and

(i) Seating of persons who may need assistance of another person to move rapidly to an exit in an emergency as prescribed by the program manager's operations manual.

§91.1069 Flight crew: Instrument proficiency check requirements.

(a) No program manager or owner may use a pilot, nor may any person serve, as a pilot in command of an aircraft under IFR unless, since the beginning of the 6th month before that service, that pilot has passed an instrument proficiency check under this section administered by the Administrator or an authorized check pilot.

(b) No program manager or owner may use a pilot, nor may any person serve, as a second command pilot of an aircraft under IFR unless, since the beginning of the 12th month before that service, that pilot has passed an instrument proficiency check under this section administered by the Administrator or an authorized check pilot.

(c) No pilot may use any type of precision instrument approach procedure under IFR unless, since the beginning of the 6th month before that use, the pilot satisfactorily demonstrated that type of approach procedure. No pilot may use any type of nonprecision approach procedure under IFR unless, since the beginning of the 6th month before that use, the pilot has satisfactorily demonstrated either that type of approach procedure or any other two different types of nonprecision approach procedures. The instrument approach procedure or procedures must include at least one straight-in approach, one circling approach, and one missed approach. Each type of approach procedure demonstrated must be conducted to published minimums for that procedure.

(d) The instrument proficiency checks required by paragraphs (a) and (b) of this section consists of either an oral or written equipment test (or a combination) and a flight check under simulated or actual IFR conditions. The equipment test includes questions on emergency procedures, engine operation, fuel and lubrication systems, power settings, stall speeds, best engine-out speed, propeller and supercharger operations, and hydraulic, mechanical, and electrical systems, as appropriate. The flight check includes navigation by instruments, recovery from simulated emergencies, and standard instrument approaches involving navigational facilities which that pilot is to be authorized to use.

(e) Each pilot taking the instrument proficiency check must show that standard of competence required by §91.1065(d).

(1) The instrument proficiency check must—

(i) For a pilot in command of an aircraft requiring that the PIC hold an airline transport pilot certificate, include the procedures and maneuvers for an airline transport pilot certificate in the particular type of aircraft, if appropriate; and

(ii) For a pilot in command of a rotorcraft or a second in command of any aircraft requiring that the SIC hold a commercial pilot certificate include the procedures and maneuvers for a commercial pilot certificate with an instrument rating and, if required, for the appropriate type rating.

(2) The instrument proficiency check must be given by an authorized check pilot or by the Administrator.

(f) If the pilot is assigned to pilot only one type of aircraft, that pilot must take the instrument proficiency check required by paragraph (a) of this section in that type of aircraft.

(g) If the pilot in command is assigned to pilot more than one type of aircraft, that pilot must take the instrument proficiency check required by paragraph (a) of this section in each type of aircraft to which that pilot is assigned, in rotation, but not more than one flight check during each period described in paragraph (a) of this section.

(h) If the pilot in command is assigned to pilot both single-engine and multiengine aircraft, that pilot must initially take the instrument proficiency check required by paragraph (a) of this section in a multiengine aircraft, and each succeeding check alternately in single-engine and multiengine aircraft, but not more than one flight check during each period described in paragraph (a) of this section.

(i) All or portions of a required flight check may be given in an aircraft simulator or other appropriate training device, if approved by the Administrator.

§91.1071 Crewmember: Tests and checks, grace provisions, training to accepted standards.

(a) If a crewmember who is required to take a test or a flight check under this subpart, completes the test or flight check in the month before or after the month in which it is required, that crewmember is considered to have completed the test or check in the month in which it is required.

(b) If a pilot being checked under this subpart fails any of the required maneuvers, the person giving the check may give additional training to the pilot during the course of the check. In addition to repeating the maneuvers failed, the person giving the check may require the pilot being checked to repeat any other maneuvers that are necessary to determine the pilot's proficiency. If the pilot being checked is unable to demonstrate satisfactory performance to the person conducting the check, the program manager may not use the pilot, nor may the pilot serve, as a flight crewmember in operations under this subpart until the pilot has satisfactorily completed the check. If a pilot who demonstrates unsatisfactory performance is employed as a pilot for a certificate holder operating under part 121, 125, or 135 of this chapter, he or she must notify that certificate holder of the unsatisfactory performance.

§91.1073 Training program: General.

(a) Each program manager must have a training program and must:

(1) Establish, obtain the appropriate initial and final approval of, and provide a training program that meets this subpart and that ensures that each crewmember, including each flight attendant if the program manager uses a flight attendant crewmember, flight instructor, check pilot, and each person assigned duties for the carriage and handling of hazardous materials (as defined in 49 CFR 171.8) is adequately trained to perform these assigned duties.

(2) Provide adequate ground and flight training facilities and properly qualified ground instructors for the training required by this subpart.

(3) Provide and keep current for each aircraft type used and, if applicable, the particular variations within the aircraft type, appropriate training material, examinations, forms, instructions, and procedures for use in conducting the training and checks required by this subpart.

(4) Provide enough flight instructors, check pilots, and simulator instructors to conduct required flight training and flight checks, and simulator training courses allowed under this subpart.

(b) Whenever a crewmember who is required to take recurrent training under this subpart completes the training in the month before, or the month after, the month in which that training is required, the crewmember is considered to have completed it in the month in which it was required.

(c) Each instructor, supervisor, or check pilot who is responsible for a particular ground training subject, segment of flight training, course of training, flight check, or competence check under this subpart must certify as to the proficiency and knowledge of the crewmember, flight instructor, or check pilot concerned upon completion of that training or check. That certification must be made a part of the crewmember's record. When the certification required by this paragraph is made by an entry in a computerized recordkeeping system, the certifying instructor, supervisor, or check pilot, must be identified with that entry. However, the signature of the certifying instructor, supervisor, or check pilot is not required for computerized entries.

(d) Training subjects that apply to more than one aircraft or crewmember position and that have been satisfactorily completed during previous training while employed by the program manager for another aircraft or another crewmember position, need not be repeated during subsequent training other than recurrent training.

(e) Aircraft simulators and other training devices may be used in the program manager's training program if approved by the Administrator.

(f) Each program manager is responsible for establishing safe and efficient crew management practices for all phases of flight in program operations including crew resource management training for all crewmembers used in program operations.

(g) If an aircraft simulator has been approved by the Administrator for use in the program manager's training program, the program manager must ensure that each pilot annually completes at least one flight training session in an approved simulator for at least one program aircraft. The training session may be the flight training portion of any of the pilot training or check requirements of this subpart, including the initial, transition, upgrade, requalification, differences, or recurrent training, or the accomplishment of a competency check or instrument proficiency check. If there is no approved simulator for that aircraft type in operation, then all flight training and checking must be accomplished in the aircraft.

§91.1075 Training program: Special rules.

Other than the program manager, only the following are eligible under this subpart to conduct training, testing, and checking under contract or other arrangement to those persons subject to the requirements of this subpart.

(a) Another program manager operating under this subpart:

(b) A training center certificated under part 142 of this chapter to conduct training, testing, and checking required by this subpart if the training center—

(1) Holds applicable training specifications issued under part 142 of this chapter;

(2) Has facilities, training equipment, and courseware meeting the applicable requirements of part 142 of this chapter;

(3) Has approved curriculums, curriculum segments, and portions of curriculum segments applicable for use in training courses required by this subpart; and

(4) Has sufficient instructors and check pilots qualified under the applicable requirements of §§91.1089 through 91.1095 to conduct training, testing, and checking to persons subject to the requirements of this subpart.

(c) A part 119 certificate holder operating under part 121 or part 135 of this chapter.

(d) As authorized by the Administrator, a training center that is not certificated under part 142 of this chapter.

§91.1077 Training program and revision: Initial and final approval.

(a) To obtain initial and final approval of a training program, or a revision to an approved training program, each program manager must submit to the Administrator—

(1) An outline of the proposed or revised curriculum, that provides enough information for a preliminary evaluation of the proposed training program or revision; and

(2) Additional relevant information that may be requested by the Administrator.

(b) If the proposed training program or revision complies with this subpart, the Administrator grants initial approval in writing after which the program manager may conduct the training under that program. The Administrator then evaluates the effectiveness of the training program and advises the program manager of deficiencies, if any, that must be corrected.

(c) The Administrator grants final approval of the proposed training program or revision if the program manager shows that the training conducted under the initial approval in paragraph (b) of this section ensures that each person who successfully completes the training is adequately trained to perform that person's assigned duties.

(d) Whenever the Administrator finds that revisions are necessary for the continued adequacy of a training program that has been granted final approval, the program manager must, after notification by the Administrator, make any changes in the program that are found necessary by the Administrator. Within 30 days after the program manager receives the notice, it may file a petition to reconsider the notice with the Administrator. The filing of a petition to reconsider stays the notice pending a decision by the Administrator. However, if the Administrator finds that there is an emergency that requires immediate action in the interest of safety, the Administrator may, upon a statement of the reasons, require a change effective without stay.

§91.1079 Training program: Curriculum.

(a) Each program manager must prepare and keep current a written training program curriculum for each type of aircraft for each crewmember required for that type aircraft. The curriculum must include ground and flight training required by this subpart.

(b) Each training program curriculum must include the following:

(1) A list of principal ground training subjects, including emergency training subjects, that are provided.

(2) A list of all the training devices, mock-ups, systems trainers, procedures trainers, or other training aids that the program manager will use.

(3) Detailed descriptions or pictorial displays of the approved normal, abnormal, and emergency maneuvers, procedures and functions that will be performed during each flight training phase or flight check, indicating those maneuvers, procedures and functions that are to be performed during the inflight portions of flight training and flight checks.

§91.1081 Crewmember training requirements.

(a) Each program manager must include in its training program the following initial and transition ground training as appropriate to the particular assignment of the crewmember:

(1) Basic indoctrination ground training for newly hired crewmembers including instruction in at least the—

(i) Duties and responsibilities of crewmembers as applicable;

(ii) Appropriate provisions of this chapter;

(iii) Contents of the program manager's management specifications (not required for flight attendants); and

(iv) Appropriate portions of the program manager's operating manual.

(2) The initial and transition ground training in §§91.1101 and 91.1105, as applicable.

(3) Emergency training in §91.1083.

(b) Each training program must provide the initial and transition flight training in §91.1103, as applicable.

(c) Each training program must provide recurrent ground and flight training as provided in §91.1107.

(d) Upgrade training in §§91.1101 and 91.1103 for a particular type aircraft may be included in the training program for crewmembers who have qualified and served as second in command on that aircraft.

(e) In addition to initial, transition, upgrade and recurrent training, each training program must provide ground and flight training, instruction, and practice necessary to ensure that each crewmember—

(1) Remains adequately trained and currently proficient for each aircraft, crewmember position, and type of operation in which the crewmember serves; and

(2) Qualifies in new equipment, facilities, procedures, and techniques, including modifications to aircraft.

§91.1083 Crewmember emergency training.

(a) Each training program must provide emergency training under this section for each aircraft type, model, and configuration, each crewmember, and each kind of operation conducted, as appropriate for each crewmember and the program manager.

(b) Emergency training must provide the following:

(1) Instruction in emergency assignments and procedures, including coordination among crewmembers.

(2) Individual instruction in the location, function, and operation of emergency equipment including—

(i) Equipment used in ditching and evacuation;

(ii) First aid equipment and its proper use; and

(iii) Portable fire extinguishers, with emphasis on the type of extinguisher to be used on different classes of fires.

(3) Instruction in the handling of emergency situations including—

(i) Rapid decompression;

(ii) Fire in flight or on the surface and smoke control procedures with emphasis on electrical equipment and related circuit breakers found in cabin areas;

(iii) Ditching and evacuation;

(iv) Illness, injury, or other abnormal situations involving passengers or crewmembers; and

(v) Hijacking and other unusual situations.

(4) Review and discussion of previous aircraft accidents and incidents involving actual emergency situations.

(c) Each crewmember must perform at least the following emergency drills, using the proper emergency equipment and procedures, unless the Administrator finds that, for a particular drill, the crewmember can be adequately trained by demonstration:

(1) Ditching, if applicable.

(2) Emergency evacuation.

(3) Fire extinguishing and smoke control.

(4) Operation and use of emergency exits, including deployment and use of evacuation slides, if applicable.

(5) Use of crew and passenger oxygen.

(6) Removal of life rafts from the aircraft, inflation of the life rafts, use of lifelines, and boarding of passengers and crew, if applicable.

(7) Donning and inflation of life vests and the use of other individual flotation devices, if applicable.

(d) Crewmembers who serve in operations above 25,000 feet must receive instruction in the following:

(1) Respiration.

(2) Hypoxia.

(3) Duration of consciousness without supplemental oxygen at altitude.

(4) Gas expansion.

(5) Gas bubble formation.

(6) Physical phenomena and incidents of decompression.

§91.1085 Hazardous materials recognition training.

No program manager may use any person to perform, and no person may perform, any assigned duties and responsibilities for the handling or carriage of hazardous materials (as defined in 49 CFR 171.8), unless that person has received training in the recognition of hazardous materials.

§91.1087 Approval of aircraft simulators and other training devices.

(a) Training courses using aircraft simulators and other training devices may be included in the program manager's training program if approved by the Administrator.

(b) Each aircraft simulator and other training device that is used in a training course or in checks required under this subpart must meet the following requirements:

(1) It must be specifically approved for—

(i) The program manager; and

(ii) The particular maneuver, procedure, or crewmember function involved.

(2) It must maintain the performance, functional, and other characteristics that are required for approval.

(3) Additionally, for aircraft simulators, it must be—

(i) Approved for the type aircraft and, if applicable, the particular variation within type for which the training or check is being conducted; and

(ii) Modified to conform with any modification to the aircraft being simulated that changes the performance, functional, or other characteristics required for approval.

(c) A particular aircraft simulator or other training device may be used by more than one program manager.

(d) In granting initial and final approval of training programs or revisions to them, the Administrator considers the training devices, methods, and procedures listed in the program manager's curriculum under §91.1079.

§91.1089 Qualifications: Check pilots (aircraft) and check pilots (simulator).

(a) For the purposes of this section and §91.1093:

(1) A check pilot (aircraft) is a person who is qualified to conduct flight checks in an aircraft, in a flight simulator, or in a flight training device for a particular type aircraft.

(2) A check pilot (simulator) is a person who is qualified to conduct flight checks, but only in a flight simulator, in a flight training device, or both, for a particular type aircraft.

(3) Check pilots (aircraft) and check pilots (simulator) are those check pilots who perform the functions described in §91.1073(a)(4) and (c).

(b) No program manager may use a person, nor may any person serve as a check pilot (aircraft) in a training program established under this subpart unless, with respect to the aircraft type involved, that person—

(1) Holds the pilot certificates and ratings required to serve as a pilot in command in operations under this subpart;

(2) Has satisfactorily completed the training phases for the aircraft, including recurrent training, that are required to serve as a pilot in command in operations under this subpart;

(3) Has satisfactorily completed the proficiency or competency checks that are required to serve as a pilot in command in operations under this subpart;

(4) Has satisfactorily completed the applicable training requirements of §91.1093;

(5) Holds at least a Class III medical certificate unless serving as a required crewmember, in which case holds a Class I or Class II medical certificate as appropriate; and

(6) Has been approved by the Administrator for the check pilot duties involved.

(c) No program manager may use a person, nor may any person serve as a check pilot (simulator) in a training program established under this subpart unless, with respect to the aircraft type involved, that person meets the provisions of paragraph (b) of this section, or—

(1) Holds the applicable pilot certificates and ratings, except medical certificate, required to serve as a pilot in command in operations under this subpart;

(2) Has satisfactorily completed the appropriate training phases for the aircraft, including recurrent training, that are required to serve as a pilot in command in operations under this subpart;

(3) Has satisfactorily completed the appropriate proficiency or competency checks that are required to serve as a pilot in command in operations under this subpart;

(4) Has satisfactorily completed the applicable training requirements of §91.1093; and

(5) Has been approved by the Administrator for the check pilot (simulator) duties involved.

(d) Completion of the requirements in paragraphs (b)(2), (3), and (4) or (c)(2), (3), and (4) of this section, as applicable, must be entered in the individual's training record maintained by the program manager.

(e) A check pilot who does not hold an appropriate medical certificate may function as a check pilot (simulator), but may not serve as a flightcrew member in operations under this subpart.

(f) A check pilot (simulator) must accomplish the following—

(1) Fly at least two flight segments as a required crewmember for the type, class, or category aircraft involved within the 12-month period preceding the performance of any check pilot duty in a flight simulator; or

(2) Before performing any check pilot duty in a flight simulator, satisfactorily complete an approved line-observation program within the period prescribed by that program.

(g) The flight segments or line-observation program required in paragraph (f) of this section are considered to be completed in the month required if completed in the month before or the month after the month in which they are due.

§91.1091 Qualifications: Flight instructors (aircraft) and flight instructors (simulator).

(a) For the purposes of this section and §91.1095:

(1) A flight instructor (aircraft) is a person who is qualified to instruct in an aircraft, in a flight simulator, or in a flight training device for a particular type, class, or category aircraft.

(2) A flight instructor (simulator) is a person who is qualified to instruct in a flight simulator, in a flight training device, or in both, for a particular type, class, or category aircraft.

(3) Flight instructors (aircraft) and flight instructors (simulator) are those instructors who perform the functions described in §91.1073(a)(4) and (c).

(b) No program manager may use a person, nor may any person serve as a flight instructor (aircraft) in a training program established under this subpart unless, with respect to the type, class, or category aircraft involved, that person—

(1) Holds the pilot certificates and ratings required to serve as a pilot in command in operations under this subpart or part 121 or 135 of this chapter;

(2) Has satisfactorily completed the training phases for the aircraft, including recurrent training, that are required to serve as a pilot in command in operations under this subpart;

(3) Has satisfactorily completed the proficiency or competency checks that are required to serve as a pilot in command in operations under this subpart;

(4) Has satisfactorily completed the applicable training requirements of §91.1095; and

(5) Holds at least a Class III medical certificate.

(c) No program manager may use a person, nor may any person serve as a flight instructor (simulator) in a training program established under this subpart, unless, with respect to the type, class, or category aircraft involved, that person meets the provisions of paragraph (b) of this section, or—

(1) Holds the pilot certificates and ratings, except medical certificate, required to serve as a pilot in command in operations under this subpart or part 121 or 135 of this chapter;

(2) Has satisfactorily completed the appropriate training phases for the aircraft, including recurrent training, that are required to serve as a pilot in command in operations under this subpart;

(3) Has satisfactorily completed the appropriate proficiency or competency checks that are required to serve as a pilot in command in operations under this subpart; and

(4) Has satisfactorily completed the applicable training requirements of §91.1095.

(d) Completion of the requirements in paragraphs (b)(2), (3), and (4) or (c)(2), (3), and (4) of this section, as applicable, must be entered in the individual's training record maintained by the program manager.

(e) A pilot who does not hold a medical certificate may function as a flight instructor in an aircraft if functioning as a non-required crewmember, but may not serve as a flightcrew member in operations under this subpart.

(f) A flight instructor (simulator) must accomplish the following—

(1) Fly at least two flight segments as a required crewmember for the type, class, or category aircraft involved within the 12-month period preceding the performance of any flight instructor duty in a flight simulator; or

(2) Satisfactorily complete an approved line-observation program within the period prescribed by that program and that must precede the performance of any check pilot duty in a flight simulator.

(g) The flight segments or line-observation program required in paragraph (f) of this section are considered completed in the month required if completed in the month before, or in the month after, the month in which they are due.

§91.1093 Initial and transition training and checking: Check pilots (aircraft), check pilots (simulator).

(a) No program manager may use a person nor may any person serve as a check pilot unless—

(1) That person has satisfactorily completed initial or transition check pilot training; and

(2) Within the preceding 24 months, that person satisfactorily conducts a proficiency or competency check under the observation of an FAA inspector or an aircrew designated examiner employed by the program manager. The observation check may be accomplished in part or in full in an aircraft, in a flight simulator, or in a flight training device.

(b) The observation check required by paragraph (a)(2) of this section is considered to have been completed in the month required if completed in the month before or the month after the month in which it is due.

(c) The initial ground training for check pilots must include the following:

(1) Check pilot duties, functions, and responsibilities.

(2) The applicable provisions of the Code of Federal Regulations and the program manager's policies and procedures.

(3) The applicable methods, procedures, and techniques for conducting the required checks.

(4) Proper evaluation of student performance including the detection of—

(i) Improper and insufficient training; and

(ii) Personal characteristics of an applicant that could adversely affect safety.

(5) The corrective action in the case of unsatisfactory checks.

(6) The approved methods, procedures, and limitations for performing the required normal, abnormal, and emergency procedures in the aircraft.

(d) The transition ground training for a check pilot must include the approved methods, procedures, and limitations for performing the required normal, abnormal, and emergency procedures applicable to the aircraft to which the check pilot is in transition.

(e) The initial and transition flight training for a check pilot (aircraft) must include the following—

(1) The safety measures for emergency situations that are likely to develop during a check;

(2) The potential results of improper, untimely, or nonexecution of safety measures during a check;

(3) Training and practice in conducting flight checks from the left and right pilot seats in the required normal, abnormal, and emergency procedures to ensure competence to conduct the pilot flight checks required by this subpart; and

(4) The safety measures to be taken from either pilot seat for emergency situations that are likely to develop during checking.

(f) The requirements of paragraph (e) of this section may be accomplished in full or in part in flight, in a flight simulator, or in a flight training device, as appropriate.

(g) The initial and transition flight training for a check pilot (simulator) must include the following:

(1) Training and practice in conducting flight checks in the required normal, abnormal, and emergency procedures to ensure competence to conduct the flight checks required by this subpart. This training and practice must be accomplished in a flight simulator or in a flight training device.

(2) Training in the operation of flight simulators, flight training devices, or both, to ensure competence to conduct the flight checks required by this subpart.

§91.1095 Initial and transition training and checking: Flight instructors (aircraft), flight instructors (simulator).

(a) No program manager may use a person nor may any person serve as a flight instructor unless—

(1) That person has satisfactorily completed initial or transition flight instructor training; and

(2) Within the preceding 24 months, that person satisfactorily conducts instruction under the observation of an FAA inspector, a program manager check pilot, or an aircrew designated examiner employed by the program manager. The observation check may be accomplished in part or in full in an aircraft, in a flight simulator, or in a flight training device.

(b) The observation check required by paragraph (a)(2) of this section is considered to have been completed in the month required if completed in the month before, or the month after, the month in which it is due.

(c) The initial ground training for flight instructors must include the following:

(1) Flight instructor duties, functions, and responsibilities.

(2) The applicable Code of Federal Regulations and the program manager's policies and procedures.

(3) The applicable methods, procedures, and techniques for conducting flight instruction.

(4) Proper evaluation of student performance including the detection of—

(i) Improper and insufficient training; and

(ii) Personal characteristics of an applicant that could adversely affect safety.

(5) The corrective action in the case of unsatisfactory training progress.

(6) The approved methods, procedures, and limitations for performing the required normal, abnormal, and emergency procedures in the aircraft.

(7) Except for holders of a flight instructor certificate—

(i) The fundamental principles of the teaching-learning process;

(ii) Teaching methods and procedures; and

(iii) The instructor-student relationship.

(d) The transition ground training for flight instructors must include the approved methods, procedures, and limitations for performing the required normal, abnormal, and emergency procedures applicable to the type, class, or category aircraft to which the flight instructor is in transition.

(e) The initial and transition flight training for flight instructors (aircraft) must include the following—

(1) The safety measures for emergency situations that are likely to develop during instruction;

(2) The potential results of improper or untimely safety measures during instruction;

(3) Training and practice from the left and right pilot seats in the required normal, abnormal, and emergency maneuvers to ensure competence to conduct the flight instruction required by this subpart; and

(4) The safety measures to be taken from either the left or right pilot seat for emergency situations that are likely to develop during instruction.

(f) The requirements of paragraph (e) of this section may be accomplished in full or in part in flight, in a flight simulator, or in a flight training device, as appropriate.

(g) The initial and transition flight training for a flight instructor (simulator) must include the following:

(1) Training and practice in the required normal, abnormal, and emergency procedures to ensure competence to conduct the flight instruction required by this subpart. These maneuvers and procedures must be accomplished in full or in part in a flight simulator or in a flight training device.

(2) Training in the operation of flight simulators, flight training devices, or both, to ensure competence to conduct the flight instruction required by this subpart.

§91.1097 Pilot and flight attendant crewmember training programs.

(a) Each program manager must establish and maintain an approved pilot training program, and each program manager who uses a flight attendant crewmember must establish and maintain an approved flight attendant training program, that is appropriate to the operations to which each pilot and flight attendant is to be assigned, and will ensure that they are adequately trained to meet the applicable knowledge and practical testing requirements of §§91.1065 through 91.1071.

(b) Each program manager required to have a training program by paragraph (a) of this section must include in that program ground and flight training curriculums for—

(1) Initial training;

(2) Transition training;

(3) Upgrade training;

(4) Differences training;

(5) Recurrent training; and

(6) Requalification training.

(c) Each program manager must provide current and appropriate study materials for use by each required pilot and flight attendant.

(d) The program manager must furnish copies of the pilot and flight attendant crewmember training program, and all changes and additions, to the assigned representative of the Administrator. If the program manager uses training facilities of other persons, a copy of those training programs or appropriate portions used for those facilities must also be furnished. Curricula that follow FAA published curricula may be cited by reference in the copy of the training program furnished to the representative of the Administrator and need not be furnished with the program.

§91.1099 Crewmember initial and recurrent training requirements.

No program manager may use a person, nor may any person serve, as a crewmember in operations under this subpart unless that crewmember has completed the appropriate initial or recurrent training phase of the training program appropriate to the type of operation in which the crewmember is to serve since the beginning of the 12th month before that service.

§91.1101 Pilots: Initial, transition, and upgrade ground training.

Initial, transition, and upgrade ground training for pilots must include instruction in at least the following, as applicable to their duties:

(a) General subjects—

(1) The program manager's flight locating procedures;

(2) Principles and methods for determining weight and balance, and runway limitations for takeoff and landing;

(3) Enough meteorology to ensure a practical knowledge of weather phenomena, including the principles of frontal systems, icing, fog, thunderstorms, windshear and, if appropriate, high altitude weather situations;

(4) Air traffic control systems, procedures, and phraseology;

(5) Navigation and the use of navigational aids, including instrument approach procedures;

(6) Normal and emergency communication procedures;

(7) Visual cues before and during descent below Decision Altitude or MDA; and

(8) Other instructions necessary to ensure the pilot's competence.

(b) For each aircraft type—

(1) A general description;

(2) Performance characteristics;

(3) Engines and propellers;

(4) Major components;

(5) Major aircraft systems (that is, flight controls, electrical, and hydraulic), other systems, as appropriate, principles of normal, abnormal, and emergency operations, appropriate procedures and limitations;

(6) Knowledge and procedures for—

(i) Recognizing and avoiding severe weather situations;

(ii) Escaping from severe weather situations, in case of inadvertent encounters, including low-altitude windshear (except that rotorcraft pilots are not required to be trained in escaping from low-altitude windshear);

(iii) Operating in or near thunderstorms (including best penetration altitudes), turbulent air (including clear air turbulence), inflight icing, hail, and other potentially hazardous meteorological conditions; and

(iv) Operating airplanes during ground icing conditions, (that is, any time conditions are such that frost, ice, or snow may reasonably be expected to adhere to the aircraft), if the program manager expects to authorize takeoffs in ground icing conditions, including:

(A) The use of holdover times when using deicing/anti-icing fluids;

(B) Airplane deicing/anti-icing procedures, including inspection and check procedures and responsibilities;

(C) Communications;

(D) Airplane surface contamination (that is, adherence of frost, ice, or snow) and critical area identification, and knowledge of how contamination adversely affects airplane performance and flight characteristics;

(E) Types and characteristics of deicing/anti-icing fluids, if used by the program manager;

(F) Cold weather preflight inspection procedures;

(G) Techniques for recognizing contamination on the airplane;

(7) Operating limitations;

(8) Fuel consumption and cruise control;
(9) Flight planning;
(10) Each normal and emergency procedure; and
(11) The approved Aircraft Flight Manual or equivalent.

§91.1103 Pilots: Initial, transition, upgrade, requalification, and differences flight training.

(a) Initial, transition, upgrade, requalification, and differences training for pilots must include flight and practice in each of the maneuvers and procedures contained in each of the curriculums that are a part of the approved training program.

(b) The maneuvers and procedures required by paragraph (a) of this section must be performed in flight, except to the extent that certain maneuvers and procedures may be performed in an aircraft simulator, or an appropriate training device, as allowed by this subpart.

(c) If the program manager's approved training program includes a course of training using an aircraft simulator or other training device, each pilot must successfully complete—

(1) Training and practice in the simulator or training device in at least the maneuvers and procedures in this subpart that are capable of being performed in the aircraft simulator or training device; and

(2) A flight check in the aircraft or a check in the simulator or training device to the level of proficiency of a pilot in command or second in command, as applicable, in at least the maneuvers and procedures that are capable of being performed in an aircraft simulator or training device.

§91.1105 Flight attendants: Initial and transition ground training.

Initial and transition ground training for flight attendants must include instruction in at least the following—

(a) General subjects—

(1) The authority of the pilot in command; and

(2) Passenger handling, including procedures to be followed in handling deranged persons or other persons whose conduct might jeopardize safety.

(b) For each aircraft type—

(1) A general description of the aircraft emphasizing physical characteristics that may have a bearing on ditching, evacuation, and inflight emergency procedures and on other related duties;

(2) The use of both the public address system and the means of communicating with other flight crewmembers, including emergency means in the case of attempted hijacking or other unusual situations; and

(3) Proper use of electrical galley equipment and the controls for cabin heat and ventilation.

§91.1107 Recurrent training.

(a) Each program manager must ensure that each crewmember receives recurrent training and is adequately trained and currently proficient for the type aircraft and crewmember position involved.

(b) Recurrent ground training for crewmembers must include at least the following:

(1) A quiz or other review to determine the crewmember's knowledge of the aircraft and crewmember position involved.

(2) Instruction as necessary in the subjects required for initial ground training by this subpart, as appropriate, including low-altitude windshear training and training on operating during ground icing conditions, as prescribed in §91.1097 and described in §91.1101, and emergency training.

(c) Recurrent flight training for pilots must include, at least, flight training in the maneuvers or procedures in this subpart, except that satisfactory completion of the check required by §91.1065 within the preceding 12 months may be substituted for recurrent flight training.

§91.1109 Aircraft maintenance: Inspection program.

Each program manager must establish an aircraft inspection program for each make and model program aircraft and ensure each aircraft is inspected in accordance with that inspection program.

(a) The inspection program must be in writing and include at least the following information:

(1) Instructions and procedures for the conduct of inspections for the particular make and model aircraft, including necessary tests and checks. The instructions and procedures must set forth in detail the parts and areas of the airframe, engines, propellers, rotors, and appliances, including survival and emergency equipment required to be inspected.

(2) A schedule for performing the inspections that must be accomplished under the inspection program expressed in terms of the time in service, calendar time, number of system operations, or any combination thereof.

(3) The name and address of the person responsible for scheduling the inspections required by the inspection program. A copy of the inspection program must be made available to the person performing inspections on the aircraft and, upon request, to the Administrator.

(b) Each person desiring to establish or change an approved inspection program under this section must submit the inspection program for approval to the Flight Standards District Office that issued the program manager's management specifications. The inspection program must be derived from one of the following programs:

(1) An inspection program currently recommended by the manufacturer of the aircraft, aircraft engines, propellers, appliances, and survival and emergency equipment;

(2) An inspection program that is part of a continuous airworthiness maintenance program currently in use by a person holding an air carrier or operating certificate issued under part 119 of this chapter and operating that make and model aircraft under part 121 or 135 of this chapter;

(3) An aircraft inspection program approved under §135.419 of this chapter and currently in use under part 135 of this chapter by a person holding a certificate issued under part 119 of this chapter; or

(4) An airplane inspection program approved under §125.247 of this chapter and currently in use under part 125 of this chapter.

(5) An inspection program that is part of the program manager's continuous airworthiness maintenance program under §§91.1411 through 91.1443.

(c) The Administrator may require revision of the inspection program approved under this section in accordance with the provisions of §91.415.

§91.1111 Maintenance training.

The program manager must ensure that all employees who are responsible for maintenance related to program aircraft undergo appropriate initial and annual recurrent training and are competent to perform those duties.

§91.1113 Maintenance recordkeeping.

Each fractional ownership program manager must keep (using the system specified in the manual required in §91.1025) the records specified in §91.417(a) for the periods specified in §91.417(b).

§91.1115 Inoperable instruments and equipment.

(a) No person may take off an aircraft with inoperable instruments or equipment installed unless the following conditions are met:

(1) An approved Minimum Equipment List exists for that aircraft.

(2) The program manager has been issued management specifications authorizing operations in accordance with an approved Minimum Equipment List. The flight crew must have direct access at all times prior to flight to all of the information contained in the approved Minimum Equipment List through printed or other means approved by the Administrator in the program manager's management specifications. An approved Minimum Equipment List, as authorized by the management specifications, constitutes an approved change to the type design without requiring recertification.

(3) The approved Minimum Equipment List must:

(i) Be prepared in accordance with the limitations specified in paragraph (b) of this section.

(ii) Provide for the operation of the aircraft with certain instruments and equipment in an inoperable condition.

(4) Records identifying the inoperable instruments and equipment and the information required by (a)(3)(ii) of this section must be available to the pilot.

(5) The aircraft is operated under all applicable conditions and limitations contained in the Minimum Equipment List and the management specifications authorizing use of the Minimum Equipment List.

(b) The following instruments and equipment may not be included in the Minimum Equipment List:

(1) Instruments and equipment that are either specifically or otherwise required by the airworthiness requirements under which the airplane is type certificated and that are essential for safe operations under all operating conditions.

(2) Instruments and equipment required by an airworthiness directive to be in operable condition unless the airworthiness directive provides otherwise.

(3) Instruments and equipment required for specific operations by this part.

(c) Notwithstanding paragraphs (b)(1) and (b)(3) of this section, an aircraft with inoperable instruments or equipment may be operated under a special flight permit under §§21.197 and 21.199 of this chapter.

(d) A person authorized to use an approved Minimum Equipment List issued for a specific aircraft under part 121, 125, or 135 of this chapter must use that Minimum Equipment List to comply with this section.

§91.1411 Continuous airworthiness maintenance program use by fractional ownership program manager.

Fractional ownership program aircraft may be maintained under a continuous airworthiness maintenance program (CAMP) under §§91.1413 through 91.1443. Any program manager who elects to maintain the program aircraft using a continuous airworthiness maintenance program must comply with §§91.1413 through 91.1443.

§91.1413 CAMP: Responsibility for airworthiness.

(a) For aircraft maintained in accordance with a Continuous Airworthiness Maintenance Program, each program manager is primarily responsible for the following:

(1) Maintaining the airworthiness of the program aircraft, including airframes, aircraft engines, propellers, rotors, appliances, and parts.

(2) Maintaining its aircraft in accordance with the requirements of this chapter.

(3) Repairing defects that occur between regularly scheduled maintenance required under part 43 of this chapter.

(b) Each program manager who maintains program aircraft under a CAMP must—

(1) Employ a Director of Maintenance or equivalent position. The Director of Maintenance must be a certificated mechanic with airframe and powerplant ratings who has responsibility for the maintenance program on all program aircraft maintained under a continuous airworthiness maintenance program. This person cannot also act as Chief Inspector.

(2) Employ a Chief Inspector or equivalent position. The Chief Inspector must be a certificated mechanic with airframe and powerplant ratings who has overall responsibility for inspection aspects of the CAMP. This person cannot also act as Director of Maintenance.

(3) Have the personnel to perform the maintenance of program aircraft, including airframes, aircraft engines, propellers, rotors, appliances, emergency equipment and parts, under its manual and this chapter; or make arrangements with another person for the performance of maintenance. However, the program manager must ensure that any maintenance, preventive maintenance, or alteration that is performed by another person is performed under the program manager's operating manual and this chapter.

§91.1415 CAMP: Mechanical reliability reports.

(a) Each program manager who maintains program aircraft under a CAMP must report the occurrence or detection of each failure, malfunction, or defect in an aircraft concerning—

(1) Fires during flight and whether the related fire-warning system functioned properly;

(2) Fires during flight not protected by related fire-warning system;

(3) False fire-warning during flight;

(4) An exhaust system that causes damage during flight to the engine, adjacent structure, equipment, or components;

(5) An aircraft component that causes accumulation or circulation of smoke, vapor, or toxic or noxious fumes in the crew compartment or passenger cabin during flight;

(6) Engine shutdown during flight because of flameout;

(7) Engine shutdown during flight when external damage to the engine or aircraft structure occurs;

(8) Engine shutdown during flight because of foreign object ingestion or icing;

(9) Shutdown of more than one engine during flight;

(10) A propeller feathering system or ability of the system to control overspeed during flight;

(11) A fuel or fuel-dumping system that affects fuel flow or causes hazardous leakage during flight;

(12) An unwanted landing gear extension or retraction or opening or closing of landing gear doors during flight;

(13) Brake system components that result in loss of brake actuating force when the aircraft is in motion on the ground;

(14) Aircraft structure that requires major repair;

(15) Cracks, permanent deformation, or corrosion of aircraft structures, if more than the maximum acceptable to the manufacturer or the FAA; and

(16) Aircraft components or systems that result in taking emergency actions during flight (except action to shut down an engine).

(b) For the purpose of this section, ***during flight*** means the period from the moment the aircraft leaves the surface of the earth on takeoff until it touches down on landing.

(c) In addition to the reports required by paragraph (a) of this section, each program manager must report any other failure, malfunction, or defect in an aircraft that occurs or is detected at any time if, in the manager's opinion, the failure, malfunction, or defect has endangered or may endanger the safe operation of the aircraft.

(d) Each program manager must send each report required by this section, in writing, covering each 24-hour period beginning at 0900 hours local time of each day and ending at 0900 hours local time on the next day to the Flight Standards District Office that issued the program manager's management specifications. Each report of occurrences during a 24-hour period must be mailed or transmitted to that office within the next 72 hours. However, a report that is due on Saturday or Sunday may be mailed or transmitted on the following Monday and one that is due on a holiday may be mailed or transmitted on the next workday. For aircraft operated in areas where mail is not collected, reports may be mailed or transmitted within 72 hours after the aircraft returns to a point where the mail is collected.

(e) The program manager must transmit the reports required by this section on a form and in a manner prescribed by the Administrator, and must include as much of the following as is available:

(1) The type and identification number of the aircraft.

(2) The name of the program manager.

(3) The date.

(4) The nature of the failure, malfunction, or defect.

(5) Identification of the part and system involved, including available information pertaining to type designation of the major component and time since last overhaul, if known.

(6) Apparent cause of the failure, malfunction or defect (for example, wear, crack, design deficiency, or personnel error).

(7) Other pertinent information necessary for more complete identification, determination of seriousness, or corrective action.

(f) A program manager that is also the holder of a type certificate (including a supplemental type certificate), a Parts Manufacturer Approval, or a Technical Standard Order Authorization, or that is the licensee of a type certificate need not report a failure, malfunction, or defect under this section if the failure, malfunction, or defect has been reported by it under §21.3 of this chapter or under the accident reporting provisions of part 830 of the regulations of the National Transportation Safety Board.

(g) No person may withhold a report required by this section even when not all information required by this section is available.

(h) When the program manager receives additional information, including information from the manufacturer or other agency, concerning a report required by this section, the program manager must expeditiously submit it as a supplement to the first report and reference the date and place of submission of the first report.

§91.1417 CAMP: Mechanical interruption summary report.

Each program manager who maintains program aircraft under a CAMP must mail or deliver, before the end of the 10th day of the following month, a summary report of the following occurrences in multiengine aircraft for the preceding month to the Flight Standards District Office that issued the management specifications:

(a) Each interruption to a flight, unscheduled change of aircraft en route, or unscheduled stop or diversion from a route, caused by known or suspected mechanical difficulties or malfunctions that are not required to be reported under §91.1415.

(b) The number of propeller featherings in flight, listed by type of propeller and engine and aircraft on which it was installed. Propeller featherings for training, demonstration, or flight check purposes need not be reported.

§91.1423 CAMP: Maintenance organization.

(a) Each program manager who maintains program aircraft under a CAMP that has its personnel perform any of its maintenance (other than required inspections), preventive maintenance, or alterations, and each person with whom it arranges for the performance of that work, must have an organization adequate to perform the work.

(b) Each program manager who has personnel perform any inspections required by the program manager's manual under §91.1427(b) (2) or (3), (in this subpart referred to as required inspections), and each person with whom the program manager arranges for the performance of that work, must have an organization adequate to perform that work.

(c) Each person performing required inspections in addition to other maintenance, preventive maintenance, or alterations, must organize the performance of those functions so as to separate the required inspection functions from the other maintenance, preventive maintenance, or alteration functions. The separation must be below the level of administrative control at which overall responsibility for the required inspection functions and other maintenance, preventive maintenance, or alterations is exercised.

§91.1425 CAMP: Maintenance, preventive maintenance, and alteration programs.

Each program manager who maintains program aircraft under a CAMP must have an inspection program and a program covering other maintenance, preventive maintenance, or alterations that ensures that—

(a) Maintenance, preventive maintenance, or alterations performed by its personnel, or by other persons, are performed under the program manager's manual;

(b) Competent personnel and adequate facilities and equipment are provided for the proper performance of maintenance, preventive maintenance, or alterations; and

(c) Each aircraft released to service is airworthy and has been properly maintained for operation under this part.

§91.1427 CAMP: Manual requirements.

(a) Each program manager who maintains program aircraft under a CAMP must put in the operating manual the chart or description of the program manager's organization required by §91.1423 and a list of persons with whom it has arranged for the performance of any of its required inspections, and other maintenance, preventive maintenance, or alterations, including a general description of that work.

(b) Each program manager must put in the operating manual the programs required by §91.1425 that must be followed in performing maintenance, preventive maintenance, or alterations of that program manager's aircraft, including airframes, aircraft engines, propellers, rotors, appliances, emergency equipment, and parts, and must include at least the following:

(1) The method of performing routine and nonroutine maintenance (other than required inspections), preventive maintenance, or alterations.

(2) A designation of the items of maintenance and alteration that must be inspected (required inspections) including at least those that could result in a failure, malfunction, or defect endangering the safe operation of the aircraft, if not performed properly or if improper parts or materials are used.

(3) The method of performing required inspections and a designation by occupational title of personnel authorized to perform each required inspection.

(4) Procedures for the reinspection of work performed under previous required inspection findings (buy-back procedures).

(5) Procedures, standards, and limits necessary for required inspections and acceptance or rejection of the items required to be inspected and for periodic inspection and calibration of precision tools, measuring devices, and test equipment.

(6) Procedures to ensure that all required inspections are performed.

(7) Instructions to prevent any person who performs any item of work from performing any required inspection of that work.

(8) Instructions and procedures to prevent any decision of an inspector regarding any required inspection from being countermanded by persons other than supervisory personnel of the inspection unit, or a person at the level of administrative control that has overall responsibility for the management of both the required inspection functions and the other maintenance, preventive maintenance, or alterations functions.

(9) Procedures to ensure that maintenance (including required inspections), preventive maintenance, or alterations that are not completed because of work interruptions are properly completed before the aircraft is released to service.

(c) Each program manager must put in the manual a suitable system (which may include an electronic or coded system) that provides for the retention of the following information—

(1) A description (or reference to data acceptable to the Administrator) of the work performed;

(2) The name of the person performing the work if the work is performed by a person outside the organization of the program manager; and

(3) The name or other positive identification of the individual approving the work.

(d) For the purposes of this part, the program manager must prepare that part of its manual containing maintenance information and instructions, in whole or in part, in a format acceptable to the Administrator, that is retrievable in the English language.

§91.1429 CAMP: Required inspection personnel.

(a) No person who maintains an aircraft under a CAMP may use any person to perform required inspections unless the person performing the inspection is appropriately certificated, properly trained, qualified, and authorized to do so.

(b) No person may allow any person to perform a required inspection unless, at the time the work was performed, the person performing that inspection is under the supervision and control of the chief inspector.

(c) No person may perform a required inspection if that person performed the item of work required to be inspected.

(d) Each program manager must maintain, or must ensure that each person with whom it arranges to perform required inspections maintains, a current listing of persons who have been trained, qualified, and authorized to conduct required inspections. The persons must be identified by name, occupational title, and the inspections that they are authorized to perform. The program manager (or person with whom it arranges to perform its required inspections) must give written information to each person so authorized, describing the extent of that person's responsibilities, authorities, and inspectional limitations. The list must be made available for inspection by the Administrator upon request.

§91.1431 CAMP: Continuing analysis and surveillance.

(a) Each program manager who maintains program aircraft under a CAMP must establish and maintain a system for the continuing analysis and surveillance of the performance and effectiveness of its inspection program and the program covering other maintenance, preventive maintenance, and alterations and for the correction of any deficiency in those programs, regardless of whether those programs are carried out by employees of the program manager or by another person.

(b) Whenever the Administrator finds that the programs described in paragraph (a) of this section does not contain adequate procedures and standards to meet this part, the program manager must, after notification by the Administrator, make changes in those programs requested by the Administrator.

(c) A program manager may petition the Administrator to reconsider the notice to make a change in a program. The petition must be filed with the Director, Flight Standards Service, within 30 days after the program manager receives the notice. Except in the case of an emergency requiring immediate action in the interest of safety, the filing of the petition stays the notice pending a decision by the Administrator.

§91.1433 CAMP: Maintenance and preventive maintenance training program.

Each program manager who maintains program aircraft under a CAMP or a person performing maintenance or preventive maintenance functions for it must have a training program to ensure that each person (including inspection personnel) who determines the adequacy of work done is fully informed about procedures and techniques and new equipment in use and is competent to perform that person's duties.

§91.1435 CAMP: Certificate requirements.

(a) Except for maintenance, preventive maintenance, alterations, and required inspections performed by repair stations located outside the United States certificated under the provisions of part 145 of this chapter, each person who is directly in charge of maintenance, preventive maintenance, or alterations for a CAMP, and each person performing required inspections for a CAMP must hold an appropriate airman certificate.

(b) For the purpose of this section, a person "directly in charge" is each person assigned to a position in which that person is responsible for the work of a shop or station that performs maintenance, preventive maintenance, alterations, or other functions affecting airworthiness. A person who is directly in charge need not physically observe and direct each worker constantly but must be available for consultation and decision on matters requiring instruction or decision from higher authority than that of the person performing the work.

§91.1437 CAMP: Authority to perform and approve maintenance.

A program manager who maintains program aircraft under a CAMP may employ maintenance personnel, or make arrangements with other persons to perform maintenance and preventive maintenance as provided in its maintenance manual. Unless properly certificated, the program manager may not perform or approve maintenance for return to service.

§91.1439 CAMP: Maintenance recording requirements.

(a) Each program manager who maintains program aircraft under a CAMP must keep (using the system specified in the manual required in §91.1427) the following records for the periods specified in paragraph (b) of this section:

(1) All the records necessary to show that all requirements for the issuance of an airworthiness release under §91.1443 have been met.

(2) Records containing the following information:

(i) The total time in service of the airframe, engine, propeller, and rotor.

(ii) The current status of life-limited parts of each airframe, engine, propeller, rotor, and appliance.

(iii) The time since last overhaul of each item installed on the aircraft that are required to be overhauled on a specified time basis.

(iv) The identification of the current inspection status of the aircraft, including the time since the last inspections required by the inspection program under which the aircraft and its appliances are maintained.

(v) The current status of applicable airworthiness directives, including the date and methods of compliance, and, if the airworthiness directive involves recurring action, the time and date when the next action is required.

(vi) A list of current major alterations and repairs to each airframe, engine, propeller, rotor, and appliance.

(b) Each program manager must retain the records required to be kept by this section for the following periods:

(1) Except for the records of the last complete overhaul of each airframe, engine, propeller, rotor, and appliance the records specified in paragraph (a)(1) of this section must be retained until the work is repeated or superseded by other work or for one year after the work is performed.

(2) The records of the last complete overhaul of each airframe, engine, propeller, rotor, and appliance must be retained until the work is superseded by work of equivalent scope and detail.

(3) The records specified in paragraph (a)(2) of this section must be retained as specified unless transferred with the aircraft at the time the aircraft is sold.

(c) The program manager must make all maintenance records required to be kept by this section available for inspection by the Administrator or any representative of the National Transportation Safety Board.

§91.1441 CAMP: Transfer of maintenance records.

When a U.S.-registered fractional ownership program aircraft maintained under a CAMP is removed from the list of program aircraft in the management specifications, the program manager must transfer to the purchaser, at the time of the sale, the following records of that aircraft, in plain language form or in coded form that provides for the preservation and retrieval of information in a manner acceptable to the Administrator:

(a) The records specified in §91.1439(a)(2).

(b) The records specified in §91.1439(a)(1) that are not included in the records covered by paragraph (a) of this section, except that the purchaser may allow the program manager to keep physical custody of such records. However, custody of records by the program manager does not relieve the purchaser of its responsibility under §91.1439(c) to make the records available for inspection by the Administrator or any representative of the National Transportation Safety Board.

§91.1443 CAMP: Airworthiness release or aircraft maintenance log entry.

(a) No program aircraft maintained under a CAMP may be operated after maintenance, preventive maintenance, or alterations are performed unless qualified, certificated personnel employed by the program manager prepare, or cause the person with whom the program manager arranges for the performance of the maintenance, preventive maintenance, or alterations, to prepare—

(1) An airworthiness release; or

(2) An appropriate entry in the aircraft maintenance log.

(b) The airworthiness release or log entry required by paragraph (a) of this section must—

(1) Be prepared in accordance with the procedure in the program manager's manual;

(2) Include a certification that—

(i) The work was performed in accordance with the requirements of the program manager's manual;

(ii) All items required to be inspected were inspected by an authorized person who determined that the work was satisfactorily completed;

(iii) No known condition exists that would make the aircraft unairworthy;

(iv) So far as the work performed is concerned, the aircraft is in condition for safe operation; and

(3) Be signed by an authorized certificated mechanic.

(c) Notwithstanding paragraph (b)(3) of this section, after maintenance, preventive maintenance, or alterations performed by a repair station certificated under the provisions of part 145 of this chapter, the approval for return to service or log entry required by paragraph (a) of this section may be signed by a person authorized by that repair station.

(d) Instead of restating each of the conditions of the certification required by paragraph (b) of this section, the program manager may state in its manual that the signature of an authorized certificated mechanic or repairman constitutes that certification.

Appendix A to Part 91
Category II Operations: Manual, Instruments, Equipment, and Maintenance

1. Category II Manual

(a) *Application for approval.* An applicant for approval of a Category II manual or an amendment to an approved Category II manual must submit the proposed manual or amendment to the Flight Standards District Office having jurisdiction of the area in which the applicant is located. If the application requests an evaluation program, it must include the following:

(1) The location of the aircraft and the place where the demonstrations are to be conducted; and

(2) The date the demonstrations are to commence (at least 10 days after filing the application).

(b) *Contents.* Each Category II manual must contain:

(1) The registration number, make, and model of the aircraft to which it applies;

(2) A maintenance program as specified in section 4 of this appendix; and

(3) The procedures and instructions related to recognition of decision height, use of runway visual range information, approach monitoring, the decision region (the region between the middle marker and the decision height), the maximum permissible deviations of the basic ILS indicator within the decision region, a missed approach, use of airborne low approach equipment, minimum altitude for the use of the autopilot, instrument and equipment failure warning systems, instrument failure, and other procedures, instructions, and limitations that may be found necessary by the Administrator.

2. Required Instruments and Equipment

The instruments and equipment listed in this section must be installed in each aircraft operated in a Category II operation. This section does not require duplication of instruments and equipment required by §91.205 or any other provisions of this chapter.

(a) *Group I.*

(1) Two localizer and glide slope receiving systems. Each system must provide a basic ILS display and each side of the instrument panel must have a basic ILS display. However, a single localizer antenna and a single glide slope antenna may be used.

(2) A communications system that does not affect the operation of at least one of the ILS systems.

(3) A marker beacon receiver that provides distinctive aural and visual indications of the outer and the middle markers.

(4) Two gyroscopic pitch and bank indicating systems.

(5) Two gyroscopic direction indicating systems.

(6) Two airspeed indicators.

(7) Two sensitive altimeters adjustable for barometric pressure, each having a placarded correction for altimeter scale error and for the wheel height of the aircraft. After June 26, 1979, two sensitive altimeters adjustable for barometric pressure, having markings at 20-foot intervals and each having a placarded correction for altimeter scale error and for the wheel height of the aircraft.

(8) Two vertical speed indicators.

(9) A flight control guidance system that consists of either an automatic approach coupler or a flight director system. A flight director system must display computed information as steering command in relation to an ILS localizer and, on the same instrument, either computed information as pitch command in relation to an ILS glide slope or basic ILS glide slope information. An automatic approach coupler must provide at least automatic steering in relation to an ILS localizer. The flight control guidance system may be operated from one of the receiving systems required by subparagraph (1) of this paragraph.

(10) For Category II operations with decision heights below 150 feet either a marker beacon receiver providing aural and visual indications of the inner marker or a radio altimeter.

(b) *Group II.*

(1) Warning systems for immediate detection by the pilot of system faults in items (1), (4), (5), and (9) of Group I and, if installed for use in Category III operations, the radio altimeter and autothrottle system.

(2) Dual controls.

(3) An externally vented static pressure system with an alternate static pressure source.

(4) A windshield wiper or equivalent means of providing adequate cockpit visibility for a safe visual transition by either pilot to touchdown and rollout.

(5) A heat source for each airspeed system pitot tube installed or an equivalent means of preventing malfunctioning due to icing of the pitot system.

3. *Instruments and Equipment Approval*

(a) *General.* The instruments and equipment required by section 2 of this appendix must be approved as provided in this section before being used in Category II operations. Before presenting an aircraft for approval of the instruments and equipment, it must be shown that since the beginning of the 12th calendar month before the date of submission—

(1) The ILS localizer and glide slope equipment were bench checked according to the manufacturer's instructions and found to meet those standards specified in RTCA Paper 23–63/DO–117 dated March 14, 1963, "Standard Adjustment Criteria for Airborne Localizer and Glide Slope Receivers," which may be obtained from the RTCA Secretariat, 1425 K St. NW., Washington, DC 20005.

(2) The altimeters and the static pressure systems were tested and inspected in accordance with Appendix E to part 43 of this chapter; and

(3) All other instruments and items of equipment specified in section 2(a) of this appendix that are listed in the proposed maintenance program were bench checked and found to meet the manufacturer's specifications.

(b) *Flight control guidance system.* All components of the flight control guidance system must be approved as installed by the evaluation program specified in paragraph (e) of this section if they have not been approved for Category III operations under applicable type or supplemental type certification procedures. In addition, subsequent changes to make, model, or design of the components must be approved under this paragraph. Related systems or devices, such as the autothrottle and computed missed approach guidance system, must be approved in the same manner if they are to be used for Category II operations.

(c) *Radio altimeter.* A radio altimeter must meet the performance criteria of this paragraph for original approval and after each subsequent alteration.

(1) It must display to the flight crew clearly and positively the wheel height of the main landing gear above the terrain.

(2) It must display wheel height above the terrain to an accuracy of plus or minus 5 feet or 5 percent, whichever is greater, under the following conditions:

(i) Pitch angles of zero to plus or minus 5 degrees about the mean approach attitude.

(ii) Roll angles of zero to 20 degrees in either direction.

(iii) Forward velocities from minimum approach speed up to 200 knots.

(iv) Sink rates from zero to 15 feet per second at altitudes from 100 to 200 feet.

(3) Over level ground, it must track the actual altitude of the aircraft without significant lag or oscillation.

(4) With the aircraft at an altitude of 200 feet or less, any abrupt change in terrain representing no more than 10 percent of the aircraft's altitude must not cause the altimeter to unlock, and indicator response to such changes must not exceed 0.1 seconds and, in addition, if the system unlocks for greater changes, it must reacquire the signal in less than 1 second.

(5) Systems that contain a push-to-test feature must test the entire system (with or without an antenna) at a simulated altitude of less than 500 feet.

(6) The system must provide to the flight crew a positive failure warning display any time there is a loss of power or an absence of ground return signals within the designed range of operating altitudes.

(d) *Other instruments and equipment.* All other instruments and items of equipment required by §2 of this appendix must be capable of performing as necessary for Category II operations. Approval is also required after each subsequent alteration to these instruments and items of equipment.

(e) *Evaluation program*—

(1) *Application.* Approval by evaluation is requested as a part of the application for approval of the Category II manual.

(2) *Demonstrations.* Unless otherwise authorized by the Administrator, the evaluation program for each aircraft requires the demonstrations specified in this paragraph. At least 50 ILS approaches must be flown with at least five approaches on each of three different ILS facilities and no more than one half of the total approaches on any one ILS facility. All approaches shall be flown under simulated instrument conditions to a 100-foot decision height and 90 percent of the total approaches made must be successful. A successful approach is one in which—

(i) At the 100-foot decision height, the indicated airspeed and heading are satisfactory for a normal flare and landing (speed must be plus or minus 5 knots of programmed airspeed, but may not be less than computed threshold speed if autothrottles are used);

(ii) The aircraft at the 100-foot decision height, is positioned so that the cockpit is within, and tracking so as to remain within, the lateral confines of the runway extended;

(iii) Deviation from glide slope after leaving the outer marker does not exceed 50 percent of full-scale deflection as displayed on the ILS indicator;

(iv) No unusual roughness or excessive attitude changes occur after leaving the middle marker; and

(v) In the case of an aircraft equipped with an approach coupler, the aircraft is sufficiently in trim when the approach coupler is disconnected at the decision height to allow for the continuation of a normal approach and landing.

(3) *Records.* During the evaluation program the following information must be maintained by the applicant for the aircraft with respect to each approach and made available to the Administrator upon request:

(i) Each deficiency in airborne instruments and equipment that prevented the initiation of an approach.

(ii) The reasons for discontinuing an approach, including the altitude above the runway at which it was discontinued.

(iii) Speed control at the 100-foot decision height if auto throttles are used.

(iv) Trim condition of the aircraft upon disconnecting the auto coupler with respect to continuation to flare and landing.

(v) Position of the aircraft at the middle marker and at the decision height indicated both on a diagram of the basic ILS display and a diagram of the runway extended to the middle marker. Estimated touchdown point must be indicated on the runway diagram.

(vi) Compatibility of flight director with the auto coupler, if applicable.

(vii) Quality of overall system performance.

(4) *Evaluation.* A final evaluation of the flight control guidance system is made upon successful completion of the demonstrations. If no hazardous tendencies have been displayed or are otherwise known to exist, the system is approved as installed.

4. Maintenance program

(a) Each maintenance program must contain the following:

(1) A list of each instrument and item of equipment specified in §2 of this appendix that is installed in the aircraft and approved for Category II operations, including the make and model of those specified in §2(a).

(2) A schedule that provides for the performance of inspections under subparagraph (5) of this paragraph within 3 calendar months after the date of the previous inspection. The inspection must be performed by a person authorized by part 43 of this chapter, except that each alternate inspection may be replaced by a functional flight check. This functional flight check must be performed by a pilot holding a Category II pilot authorization for the type aircraft checked.

(3) A schedule that provides for the performance of bench checks for each listed instrument and item of equipment that is specified in section 2(a) within 12 calendar months after the date of the previous bench check.

(4) A schedule that provides for the performance of a test and inspection of each static pressure system in accordance with Appendix E to part 43 of this chapter within 12 calendar months after the date of the previous test and inspection.

(5) The procedures for the performance of the periodic inspections and functional flight checks to determine the ability of each listed instrument and item of equipment specified in section 2(a) of this appendix to perform as approved for Category II operations including a procedure for recording functional flight checks.

(6) A procedure for assuring that the pilot is informed of all defects in listed instruments and items of equipment.

(7) A procedure for assuring that the condition of each listed instrument and item of equipment upon which maintenance is performed is at least equal to its Category II approval condition before it is returned to service for Category II operations.

(8) A procedure for an entry in the maintenance records required by §43.9 of this chapter that shows the date, airport, and reasons for each discontinued Category II operation because of a malfunction of a listed instrument or item of equipment.

(b) *Bench check.* A bench check required by this section must comply with this paragraph.

(1) It must be performed by a certificated repair station holding one of the following ratings as appropriate to the equipment checked:

(i) An instrument rating.

(ii) A radio rating.

(2) It must consist of removal of an instrument or item of equipment and performance of the following:

(i) A visual inspection for cleanliness, impending failure, and the need for lubrication, repair, or replacement of parts;

(ii) Correction of items found by that visual inspection; and

(iii) Calibration to at least the manufacturer's specifications unless otherwise specified in the approved Category II manual for the aircraft in which the instrument or item of equipment is installed.

(c) *Extensions.* After the completion of one maintenance cycle of 12 calendar months, a request to extend the period for checks, tests, and inspections is approved if it is shown that the performance of particular equipment justifies the requested extension.

[Docket No. 18334, 54 FR 34325, Aug. 18, 1989; as amended by Amdt. 91–269, 66 FR 41116, Aug. 6, 2001]

Appendix B to Part 91

Authorizations to Exceed Mach 1 (Section 91.817)

Section 1. Application

(a) An applicant for an authorization to exceed Mach 1 must apply in a form and manner prescribed by the Administrator and must comply with this appendix.

(b) In addition, each application for an authorization to exceed Mach 1 covered by section 2(a) of this appendix must contain all information requested by the Administrator necessary to assist him in determining whether the designation of a particular test area or issuance of a particular authorization is a "major Federal action significantly affecting the quality of the human environment" within the meaning of the National Environmental Policy Act of 1969 (42 U.S.C. 4321 et seq.), and to assist him in complying with that act and with related Executive Orders, guidelines, and orders prior to such action.

(c) In addition, each application for an authorization to exceed Mach 1 covered by section 2(a) of this appendix must contain—

(1) Information showing that operation at a speed greater than Mach 1 is necessary to accomplish one or more of the purposes specified in section 2(a) of this appendix, including

a showing that the purpose of the test cannot be safely or properly accomplished by overocean testing;

(2) A description of the test area proposed by the applicant, including an environmental analysis of that area meeting the requirements of paragraph (b) of this section; and

(3) Conditions and limitations that will ensure that no measurable sonic boom overpressure will reach the surface outside of the designated test area.

(d) An application is denied if the Administrator finds that such action is necessary to protect or enhance the environment.

SECTION 2. ISSUANCE

(a) For a flight in a designated test area, an authorization to exceed Mach 1 may be issued when the Administrator has taken the environmental protective actions specified in section 1(b) of this appendix and the applicant shows one or more of the following:

(1) The flight is necessary to show compliance with airworthiness requirements.

(2) The flight is necessary to determine the sonic boom characteristics of the airplane or to establish means of reducing or eliminating the effects of sonic boom.

(3) The flight is necessary to demonstrate the conditions and limitations under which speeds greater than a true flight Mach number of 1 will not cause a measurable sonic boom overpressure to reach the surface.

(b) For a flight outside of a designated test area, an authorization to exceed Mach 1 may be issued if the applicant shows conservatively under paragraph (a)(3) of this section that—

(1) The flight will not cause a measurable sonic boom overpressure to reach the surface when the aircraft is operated under conditions and limitations demonstrated under paragraph (a)(3) of this section; and

(2) Those conditions and limitations represent all foreseeable operating conditions.

SECTION 3. DURATION

(a) An authorization to exceed Mach 1 is effective until it expires or is surrendered, or until it is suspended or terminated by the Administrator. Such an authorization may be amended or suspended by the Administrator at any time if the Administrator finds that such action is necessary to protect the environment. Within 30 days of notification of amendment, the holder of the authorization must request reconsideration or the amendment becomes final. Within 30 days of notification of suspension, the holder of the authorization must request reconsideration or the authorization is automatically terminated. If reconsideration is requested within the 30-day period, the amendment or suspension continues until the holder shows why the authorization should not be amended or terminated. Upon such showing, the Administrator may terminate or amend the authorization if the Administrator finds that such action is necessary to protect the environment, or he may reinstate the authorization without amendment if he finds that termination or amendment is not necessary to protect the environment.

(b) Findings and actions by the Administrator under this section do not affect any certificate issued under title VI of the Federal Aviation Act of 1958.

[Docket No. 18334, 54 FR 34327, Aug. 18, 1989]

APPENDIX C TO PART 91
OPERATIONS IN THE NORTH ATLANTIC (NAT) MINIMUM NAVIGATION PERFORMANCE SPECIFICATIONS (MNPS) AIRSPACE

SECTION 1

NAT MNPS airspace is that volume of airspace between FL 285 and FL 420 extending between latitude 27 degrees north and the North Pole, bounded in the east by the eastern boundaries of control areas Santa Maria Oceanic, Shanwick Oceanic, and Reykjavik Oceanic and in the west by the western boundary of Reykjavik Oceanic Control Area, the western boundary of Gander Oceanic Control Area, and the western boundary of New York Oceanic Control Area, excluding the areas west of 60 degrees west and south of 38 degrees 30 minutes north.

SECTION 2

The navigation performance capability required for aircraft to be operated in the airspace defined in section 1 of this appendix is as follows:

(a) The standard deviation of lateral track errors shall be less than 6.3 NM (11.7 Km). Standard deviation is a statistical measure of data about a mean value. The mean is zero nautical miles. The overall form of data is such that the plus and minus 1 standard deviation about the mean encompasses approximately 68 percent of the data and plus or minus 2 deviations encompasses approximately 95 percent.

(b) The proportion of the total flight time spent by aircraft 30 NM (55.6 Km) or more off the cleared track shall be less than 5.3×10^{-4} (less than 1 hour in 1,887 flight hours).

(c) The proportion of the total flight time spent by aircraft between 50 NM and 70 NM (92.6 Km and 129.6 Km) off the cleared track shall be less than 13×10^{-5} (less than 1 hour in 7,693 flight hours.)

SECTION 3

Air traffic control (ATC) may authorize an aircraft operator to deviate from the requirements of §91.705 for a specific flight if, at the time of flight plan filing for that flight, ATC determines that the aircraft may be provided appropriate separation and that the flight will not interfere with, or impose a burden upon, the operations of other aircraft which meet the requirements of §91.705.

[Docket No. 18334, 54 FR 34327, Aug. 18, 1989; as amended by Amdt. 91–254, 62 FR 17487, April 9, 1997]

Appendix D to Part 91

Airports/Locations: Special Operating Restrictions

Section 1. Locations at which the requirements of §91.215(b)(2) apply.

The requirements of §91.215(b)(2) apply below 10,000 feet above the surface within a 30-nautical-mile radius of each location in the following list:

Atlanta, GA
(The William B. Hartsfield Atlanta International Airport)
Baltimore, MD
(Baltimore Washington International Airport)
Boston, MA
(General Edward Lawrence Logan International Airport)
Chantilly, VA
(Washington Dulles International Airport)
Charlotte, NC
(Charlotte/Douglas International Airport)
Chicago, IL
(Chicago-O'Hare International Airport)
Cleveland, OH
(Cleveland-Hopkins International Airport)
Covington, KY (Cincinnati Northern Kentucky International Airport)
Dallas, TX (Dallas/Fort Worth Regional Airport)
Denver, CO (Denver International Airport)
Detroit, MI (Metropolitan Wayne County Airport)
Honolulu, HI (Honolulu International Airport)
Houston, TX (George Bush Intercontinental Airport/ Houston)
Kansas City, KS (Mid-Continent International Airport)
Las Vegas, NV (McCarran International Airport)
Los Angeles, CA (Los Angeles International Airport)
Memphis, TN (Memphis International Airport)
Miami, FL (Miami International Airport)
Minneapolis, MN
(Minneapolis-St. Paul International Airport)
Newark, NJ (Newark International Airport)
New Orleans, LA
(New Orleans International Airport—Moisant Field)
New York, NY (John F. Kennedy International Airport)
New York, NY (LaGuardia Airport)
Orlando, FL (Orlando International Airport)
Philadelphia, PA (Philadelphia International Airport)
Phoenix, AZ (Phoenix Sky Harbor International Airport)
Pittsburgh, PA (Greater Pittsburgh International Airport)
St. Louis, MO (Lambert-St. Louis International Airport)
Salt Lake City, UT (Salt Lake City International Airport)
San Diego, CA (San Diego International Airport)
San Francisco, CA (San Francisco International Airport)
Seattle, WA (Seattle-Tacoma International Airport)
Tampa, FL (Tampa International Airport)
Washington, DC (Ronald Reagan Washington National Airport and Andrews Air Force Base, MD)

Section 2. Airports at which the requirements of §91.215(b)(5)(ii) apply. *[Reserved]*

Section 3. Locations at which fixed-wing Special VFR operations are prohibited.

The Special VFR weather minimums of §91.157 do not apply to the following airports:

Atlanta, GA
(The William B. Hartsfield Atlanta International Airport)
Baltimore, MD
(Baltimore/Washington International Airport)
Boston, MA (General Edward Lawrence Logan International Airport)
Buffalo, NY (Greater Buffalo International Airport)
Chicago, IL (Chicago-O'Hare International Airport)
Cleveland, OH (Cleveland-Hopkins International Airport)
Columbus, OH (Port Columbus International Airport)
Covington, KY (Cincinnati Northern Kentucky International Airport)
Dallas, TX (Dallas/Fort Worth Regional Airport)
Dallas, TX (Love Field)
Denver, CO (Denver International Airport)
Detroit, MI (Metropolitan Wayne County Airport)
Honolulu, HI (Honolulu International Airport)
Houston, TX (George Bush Intercontinental Airport/ Houston)
Indianapolis, IN (Indianapolis International Airport)
Los Angeles, CA (Los Angeles International Airport)
Louisville, KY (Standiford Field)
Memphis, TN (Memphis International Airport)
Miami, FL (Miami International Airport)
Minneapolis, MN
(Minneapolis-St. Paul International Airport)
Newark, NJ (Newark International Airport)
New York, NY (John F. Kennedy International Airport)
New York, NY (LaGuardia Airport)
New Orleans, LA
(New Orleans International Airport—Moisant Field)
Philadelphia, PA (Philadelphia International Airport)
Pittsburgh, PA (Greater Pittsburgh International Airport)
Portland, OR (Portland International Airport)
San Francisco, CA (San Francisco International Airport)
Seattle, WA (Seattle-Tacoma International Airport)
St. Louis, MO (Lambert-St. Louis International Airport)
Tampa, FL (Tampa International Airport)
Washington, DC (Ronald Reagan Washington National Airport and Andrews Air Force Base, MD)

Section 4. Locations at which solo student, sport, and recreational pilot activity is not permitted.

Pursuant to §91.131(b)(2), solo student, sport, and recreational pilot operations are not permitted at any of the following airports.

Atlanta, GA
(The William B. Hartsfield Atlanta International Airport)
Boston, MA
(General Edward Lawrence Logan International Airport)
Chicago, IL (Chicago-O'Hare International Airport)
Dallas, TX (Dallas/Fort Worth Regional Airport)
Los Angeles, CA (Los Angeles International Airport)
Miami, FL (Miami International Airport)
Newark, NJ (Newark International Airport)
New York, NY (John F. Kennedy International Airport)
New York, NY (LaGuardia Airport)
San Francisco, CA (San Francisco International Airport)
Washington, DC (Ronald Reagan Washington National Airport)
Andrews Air Force Base, MD

[Docket No. 24458, Amdt. 91–227, 56 FR 65661, Dec. 17, 1991; as amended by Amdt. 91–237, 59 FR 6547, Feb. 11, 1994; 59 FR 37667, July 25, 1994; Amdt. 91–258, 64 FR 66769, Nov. 30, 1999; Amdt. 91–282, 69 FR 44882, July 27, 2004]

Appendix E to Part 91

Airplane Flight Recorder Specifications

Parameters	Range	Installed system[1] minimum accuracy (to recovered data)	Sampling interval (per second)	Resolution[4] read out
Relative Time (From Recorded on Prior to Takeoff)	8 hr minimum	±0.125% per hour	1	1 sec.
Indicated Airspeed	V_{S0} to V_D (KIAS)	±5% or ±10 kts., whichever is greater. Resolution 2 kts. below 175 KIAS.	1	1%[3]
Altitude	−1,000 ft. to max cert. alt. of A/C	±100 to ±700 ft. (see Table 1. TSO C51-a)	11	25 to 150 ft.
Magnetic Heading	360°	±5°	1	1°
Vertical Acceleration	−3g to +6g	±0.2g in addition to ±0.3g maximum datum	4 (or 1 per second where peaks, ref. to 1g are recorded)	0.03g
Longitudinal Acceleration	±1.0g	±1.5% max. range excluding datum error of ±5%	2	0.01g
Pitch Attitude	100% of usable	±2°	1	0.8°
Roll Attitude	±60° of 100% of usable range, whichever is greater	±2°	1	0.8°
Stabilizer Trim Position, or Pitch Control Position	Full Range	±3% unless higher uniquely required	1	1%[3]
Engine Power, Each Engine: Fan or N[1] Speed or EPR or cockpit indications used for aircraft certification OR Prop. speed and Torque (sample once/sec as close together as practicable)	Full Range Maximum Range —	±3% unless higher uniquely required ±5% —	1 1 1 (prop speed) 1 (torque)	1%[3] 1%[3] 1%[3] 1%[3]
Altitude Rate[2] (need depends on altitude resolution)	±8,000 fpm	±10%. Resolution 250 fpm below 12,000 ft. indicated	1	250 fpm below 12,000
Angle of Attack[2] (need depends on altitude resolution)	−20° to 40° or 100% of usable range	±2°	1	0.8%[3]
Radio Transmitter Keying (Discrete)	On/Off	—	1	—
TE Flaps (Discrete or Analog)	Each discrete position (U.D. T/O. AAP) OR	—	1	—
LE Flaps (Discrete or Analog)	Analog 0–100% range Each discrete position (U.D. T/O, AAP) OR	±3% —	1 1	1%[3] —
Thrust Reverser, Each Engine (Discrete)	Analog 0–100% range Stowed or full reverse	±3° —	1 —	1%[3]
Spoiler/Speed brake (Discrete)	Stowed or out	—	1	—
Autopilot Engaged (Discrete)	Engaged or Disengaged	—	1	—

[1] When data sources are aircraft instruments (except altimeters) of acceptable quality to fly the aircraft the recording system excluding these sensors (but including all other characteristics of the recording system) shall contribute no more than half of the values in this column.

[2] If data from the altitude encoding altimeter (100 ft. resolution) is used, then either one of these parameters should also be recorded. If however, altitude is recorded at a minimum resolution of 25 feet, then these two parameters can be omitted.

[3] Percent of full range.

[4] This column applies to aircraft manufactured after October 11, 1991.

[Docket No. 18334, 54 FR 34327, Aug. 18, 1989]

Appendix F to Part 91

Helicopter Flight Recorder Specifications

Parameters	Range	Installed system[1] minimum accuracy (to recovered data)	Sampling interval (per second)	Resolution[3] read out
Relative Time (from recorded on prior to takeoff)	4 hr minimum	±0.125% per hour	1	1 sec.
Indicated Airspeed	V_{min} to V_D (KIAS) (minimum airspeed signal attainable with installed pilot-static system)	±5% or ±10 kts., whichever is greater	1	1 kt.
Altitude	−1,000 ft. to 20,000 ft. pressure altitude	±100 to ±700 ft. (see Table 1. TSO C51-a)	1	25 to 150 ft.
Magnetic Heading	360°	±5°	1	1°
Vertical Acceleration	−3g to +6g	±0.2g in addition to ±0.3g maximum datum	4 (or 1 per second where peaks, ref. to 1g are recorded)	0.05g
Longitudinal Acceleration	±1.0g	±1.5% max. range excluding datum error of ±5%	2	0.03g
Pitch Attitude	100% of usable range	±2°	1	0.8°
Roll Attitude	±60 or 100% of usable range, whichever is greater	±2°	1	0.8°
Altitude Rate	±8,000 fpm	±10% Resolution 250 fpm below 12,000 ft. indicated	1	250 fpm below 12,000
Engine Power, Each Engine:				
Main Rotor Speed	Maximum Range	±5%	1	1%[2]
Free or Power Turbine	Maximum Range	±5%	1	1%[2]
Engine Torque	Maximum Range	±5%	1	1%[2]
Flight Control Hydraulic Pressure:				
Primary (Discrete)	High / Low		1	
Secondary – if applicable (Discrete)	High / Low		1	
Radio Transmitter Keying (Discrete)	On / Off		1	
Autopilot Engaged (Discrete)	Engaged or Disengaged		1	
SAS Status – Engaged (Discrete)	Engaged or Disengaged		1	
SAS Fault Status (Discrete)	Fault / OK		1	
Flight Controls:				
Collective	Full range	±3%	2	1%[2]
Pedal Position	Full range	±3%	2	1%[2]
Lat. Cyclic	Full range	±3%	2	1%[2]
Long. Cyclic	Full range	±3%	2	1%[2]
Controllable Stabilator Position	Full range	±3%	2	1%[2]

[1] When data sources are aircraft instruments (except altimeters) of acceptable quality to fly the aircraft the recording system excluding these sensors (but including all other characteristics of the recording system) shall contribute no more than half of the values in this column.

[2] Percent of full range.

[3] This column applies to aircraft manufactured after October 11, 1991.

[Docket No. 18334, 54 FR 34328, Aug. 18, 1989; 54 FR 41211, Oct. 5, 1989; 54 FR 53036, Dec. 26, 1989]

91

Appendix G to Part 91

Operations in Reduced Vertical Separation Minimum (RVSM) Airspace

Section 1. Definitions

Reduced Vertical Separation Minimum (RVSM) Airspace. Within RVSM airspace, air traffic control (ATC) separates aircraft by a minimum of 1,000 feet vertically between flight level (FL) 290 and FL 410 inclusive. RVSM airspace is special qualification airspace; the operator and the aircraft used by the operator must be approved by the Administrator. Air-traffic control notifies operators of RVSM by providing route planning information. Section 8 of this appendix identifies airspace where RVSM may be applied.

RVSM Group Aircraft. Aircraft within a group of aircraft, approved as a group by the Administrator, in which each of the aircraft satisfy each of the following:

(a) The aircraft have been manufactured to the same design, and have been approved under the same type certificate, amended type certificate, or supplemental type certificate.

(b) The static system of each aircraft is installed in a manner and position that is the same as those of the other aircraft in the group. The same static source error correction is incorporated in each aircraft of the group.

(c) The avionics units installed in each aircraft to meet the minimum RVSM equipment requirements of this appendix are:

(1) Manufactured to the same manufacturer specification and have the same part number; or

(2) Of a different manufacturer or part number, if the applicant demonstrates that the equipment provides equivalent system performance.

RVSM Nongroup Aircraft. An aircraft that is approved for RVSM operations as an individual aircraft.

RVSM Flight envelope. An RVSM flight envelope includes the range of Mach number, weight divided by atmospheric pressure ratio, and altitudes over which an aircraft is approved to be operated in cruising flight within RVSM airspace. RVSM flight envelopes are defined as follows:

(a) The *full RVSM flight envelope* is bounded as follows:

(1) The altitude flight envelope extends from FL 290 upward to the lowest altitude of the following:

(i) FL 410 (the RVSM altitude limit);

(ii) The maximum certificated altitude for the aircraft; or

(iii) The altitude limited by cruise thrust, buffet, or other flight limitations.

(2) The airspeed flight envelopes extends:

(i) From the airspeed of the slats/flaps-up maximum endurance (holding) airspeed, or the maneuvering airspeed, whichever is lower;

(ii) To the maximum operating airspeed (V_{MO}/M_{MO}), or airspeed limited by cruise thrust buffet, or other flight limitations, whichever is lower.

(3) All permissible gross weights within the flight envelopes defined in paragraphs (1) and (2) of this definition.

(b) The *basic RVSM flight envelope* is the same as the full RVSM flight envelope except that the airspeed flight envelope extends:

(1) From the airspeed of the slats/flaps-up maximum endurance (holding) airspeed, or the maneuver airspeed, whichever is lower;

(2) To the upper Mach/airspeed boundary defined for the full RVSM flight envelope, or a specified lower value not less than the long-range cruise Mach number plus .04 Mach, unless further limited by available cruise thrust, buffet, or other flight limitations.

Section 2. Aircraft Approval

(a) An operator may be authorized to conduct RVSM operations if the Administrator finds that its aircraft comply with this section.

(b) The application for authorization shall submit the appropriate data package for aircraft approval. The package must consist of at least the following:

(1) An identification of the RVSM aircraft group or the non-group aircraft;

(2) A definition of the RVSM flight envelopes applicable to the subject aircraft;

(3) Documentation that establishes compliance with the applicable RVSM aircraft requirements of this section; and

(4) The conformity tests used to ensure that aircraft approved with the data package meet the RVSM aircraft requirements.

(c) *Altitude-keeping equipment: All aircraft.* To approve an aircraft group or a nongroup aircraft, the Administrator must find that the aircraft meets the following requirements:

(1) The aircraft must be equipped with two operational independent altitude measurement systems.

(2) The aircraft must be equipped with at least one automatic altitude control system that controls the aircraft altitude—

(i) Within a tolerance band of ±65 feet about an acquired altitude when the aircraft is operated in straight and level flight under nonturbulent, nongust conditions; or

(ii) Within a tolerance band of ±130 feet under nonturbulent, nongust conditions for aircraft for which application for type certification occurred on or before April 9, 1997 that are equipped with an automatic altitude control system with flight management/performance system inputs.

(3) The aircraft must be equipped with an altitude alert system that signals an alert when the altitude displayed to the flight crew deviates from the selected altitude by more than:

(i) ±300 feet for aircraft for which application for type certification was made on or before April 9, 1997; or

(ii) ±200 feet for aircraft for which application for type certification is made after April 9, 1997.

(d) *Altimetry system error containment: Group aircraft for which application for type certification was made on or before April 9, 1997.* To approve group aircraft for which application for type certification was made on or before April 9, 1997, the Administrator must find that the altimetry system error (ASE) is contained as follows:

(1) At the point in the basic RVSM flight envelope where mean ASE reaches its largest absolute value, the absolute value may not exceed 80 feet.

(2) At the point in the basic RVSM flight envelope where mean ASE plus three standard deviations reaches its largest absolute value, the absolute value may not exceed 200 feet.

(3) At the point in the full RVSM flight envelope where mean ASE reaches its largest absolute value, the absolute value may not exceed 120 feet.

(4) At the point in the full RVSM flight envelope where mean ASE plus three standard deviations reaches its largest absolute value, the absolute value may not exceed 245 feet.

(5) *Necessary operating restrictions.* If the applicant demonstrates that its aircraft otherwise comply with the ASE containment requirements, the Administrator may establish an operating restriction on that applicant's aircraft to restrict the aircraft from operating in areas of the basic RVSM flight envelope where the absolute value of mean ASE exceeds 80 feet, and/or the absolute value of mean ASE plus three standard deviations exceeds 200 feet; or from operating in areas of the full RVSM flight envelope where the absolute value of the mean ASE exceeds 120 feet and/or the absolute value of the mean ASE plus three standard deviations exceeds 245 feet.

(e) *Altimetry system error containment: Group aircraft for which application for type certification is made after April 9, 1997.* To approve group aircraft for which application for type certification is made after April 9, 1997, the Administrator must find that the altimetry system error (ASE) is contained as follows:

(1) At the point in the full RVSM flight envelope where mean ASE reaches its largest absolute value, the absolute value may not exceed 80 feet.

(2) At the point in the full RVSM flight envelope where mean ASE plus three standard deviations reaches its largest absolute value, the absolute value may not exceed 200 feet.

(f) *Altimetry system error containment: Nongroup aircraft.* To approve a nongroup aircraft, the Administrator must find that the altimetry system error (ASE) is contained as follows:

(1) For each condition in the basic RVSM flight envelope, the largest combined absolute value for residual static source error plus the avionics error may not exceed 160 feet.

(2) For each condition in the full RVSM flight envelope, the largest combined absolute value for residual static source error plus the avionics error may not exceed 200 feet.

(g) Traffic Alert and Collision Avoidance System (TCAS) Compatibility With RVSM Operations: All aircraft. After March 31, 2002, unless otherwise authorized by the Administrator, if you operate an aircraft that is equipped with TCAS II in RVSM airspace, it must be a TCAS II that meets TSO C-119b (Version 7.0), or a later version.

(h) If the Administrator finds that the applicant's aircraft comply with this section, the Administrator notifies the applicant in writing.

Section 3. Operator Authorization

(a) Authority for an operator to conduct flight in airspace where RVSM is applied is issued in operations specifications, a Letter of Authorization, or management specifications issued under subpart K of this part, as appropriate. To issue an RVSM authorization, the Administrator must find that the operator's aircraft have been approved in accordance with Section 2 of this appendix and the operator complies with this section.

(b) An applicant for authorization to operate within RVSM airspace shall apply in a form and manner prescribed by the Administrator. The application must include the following:

(1) An approved RVSM maintenance program outlining procedures to maintain RVSM aircraft in accordance with the requirements of this appendix. Each program must contain the following:

(i) Periodic inspections, functional flight tests, and maintenance and inspection procedures, with acceptable maintenance practices, for ensuring continued compliance with the RVSM aircraft requirements.

(ii) A quality assurance program for ensuring continuing accuracy and reliability of test equipment used for testing aircraft to determine compliance with the RVSM aircraft requirements.

(iii) Procedures for returning noncompliant aircraft to service.

(2) For an applicant who operates under part 121 or 135 of this chapter or under subpart K of this part, initial and recurring pilot training requirements.

(3) Policies and procedures: An applicant who operates under part 121 or 135 of this chapter or under subpart K of this part must submit RVSM policies and procedures that will enable it to conduct RVSM operations safely.

(c) Validation and Demonstration. In a manner prescribed by the Administrator, the operator must provide evidence that:

(1) It is capable to operate and maintain each aircraft or aircraft group for which it applies for approval to operate in RVSM airspace; and

(2) Each pilot has an adequate knowledge of RVSM requirements, policies, and procedures.

Section 4. RVSM Operations

(a) Each person requesting a clearance to operate within RVSM airspace shall correctly annotate the flight plan filed with air traffic control with the status of the operator and aircraft with regard to RVSM approval. Each operator shall verify RVSM applicability for the flight planned route through the appropriate flight planning information sources.

(b) No person may show, on the flight plan filed with air traffic control, an operator or aircraft as approved for RVSM operations, or operate on a route or in an area where RVSM approval is required, unless:

(1) The operator is authorized by the Administrator to perform such operations; and

(2) The aircraft has been approved and complies with the requirements of Section 2 of this appendix.

Section 5. Deviation Authority Approval

The Administrator may authorize an aircraft operator to deviate from the requirements of §91.180 or §91.706 for a specific flight in RVSM airspace if that operator has not been approved in accordance with Section 3 of this appendix if:

(a) The operator submits a request in a time and manner acceptable to the Administrator; and

(b) At the time of filing the flight plan for that flight, ATC determines that the aircraft may be provided appropriate separation and that the flight will not interfere with, or impose a burden on, the operations of operators who have been approved for RVSM operations in accordance with Section 3 of this appendix.

Section 6. Reporting altitude-Keeping Errors

Each operator shall report to the Administrator each event in which the operator's aircraft has exhibited the following altitude-keeping performance:

(a) Total vertical error of 300 feet or more;

(b) Altimetry system error of 245 feet or more; or

(c) Assigned altitude deviation of 300 feet or more.

Section 7. Removal or Amendment of Authority

The Administrator may amend operations specifications or management specifications issued under subpart K of this part to revoke or restrict an RVSM authorization, or may revoke or restrict an RVSM letter of authorization, if the Administrator determines that the operator is not complying, or is unable to comply, with this appendix or subpart H of this part. Examples of reasons for amendment, revocation, ore restriction include, but are not limited to, an operator's:

(a) Committing one of more altitude-keeping errors in RVSM airspace;

(b) Failing to make an effective and timely response to identify and correct an altitude-keeping error; or

(c) Failing to report an altitude-keeping error.

Section 8. Airspace Designation

(a) RVSM in the North Atlantic.

(1) RVSM may be applied in the NAT in the following ICAO Flight Information Regions (FIRs): New York Oceanic, Gander Oceanic, Sondrestrom FIR, Reykjavik Oceanic, Shanwick Oceanic, and Santa Maria Oceanic.

(2) RVSM may be effective in the Minimum Navigation Performance Specification (MNPS) airspace within the NAT. The MNPS airspace within the NAT is defined by the volume of airspace FL285 and FL420 (inclusive) extending between latitude 27 degrees north and the North Pole, bounded in the east by the eastern boundaries of control areas Santa Maria Oceanic, Shanwick Oceanic, and Reykjavik Oceanic and in the west by the western boundaries of control areas Reykjavik Oceanic, Gander Oceanic, and New York Oceanic, excluding the areas west of 60 degrees west and south of 38 degrees 30 minutes north.

(b) RVSM in the Pacific.

(1) RVSM may be applied in the Pacific in the following ICAO Flight Information Regions (FIRs): Anchorage Arctic, Anchorage Continental, Anchorage Oceanic, Auckland Oceanic, Brisbane, Edmonton, Honiara, Los Angeles, Melbourne, Nadi, Naha, Nauru, New Zealand, Oakland, Oakland Oceanic, Port Moresby, Seattle, Tahiti, Tokyo, Ujung Pandang and Vancouver.

(c) RVSM in the West Atlantic Route System (WATRS). RVSM may be applied in the New York FIR portion of the West Atlantic Route System (WATRS). The area is defined as beginning at a point 38°30' N/60°00'W direct to 38°30'N/ 69°15' W direct to 38°20' N/69°57' W direct to 37°31' N/ 71°41' W direct to 37°13' N/72°40' W direct to 35°05' N/ 72°40' W direct to 34°54' N/72°57' W direct to 34°29' N/ 73°34' W direct to 34°33' N/73°41' W direct to 34°19' N/ 74°02' W direct to 34°14' N/73°57' W direct to 32°12' N/ 76°49' W direct to 32°20' N/77°00' W direct to 28°08' N/ 77°00' W direct to 27°50' N/76°32' W direct to 27°50' N/ 74°50' W direct to 25°00' N/73°21' W direct to 25°00'05" N/ 69°13'06" W direct to 25°00' N/69°07' W direct to 23°30' N/ 68°40' W direct to 23°30' N/60°00' W to the point of beginning.

(d) RVSM in the United States. RVSM may be applied in the airspace of the 48 contiguous states, District of Columbia, and Alaska, including that airspace overlying the waters within 12 nautical miles of the coast.

(e) RVSM in the Gulf of Mexico. RVSM may be applied in the Gulf of Mexico in the following areas: Gulf of Mexico High Offshore Airspace, Houston Oceanic ICAO FIR and Miami Oceanic ICAO FIR.

(f) RVSM in Atlantic High Offshore Airspace and the San Juan FIR. RVSM may be applied in Atlantic High Offshore Airspace and in the San Juan ICAO FIR.

[Docket No. 28870, 62 FR 17487, April 9, 1997; as amended by Amdt. 91–261, 65 FR 5942, Feb. 7, 2000; Amdt. 91–271, 66 FR 63895, Dec. 10, 2001; Amdt. 91–280, 68 FR 54584, Sept. 17, 2003; Amdt. 91–276, 68 FR 61321, Oct. 27, 2003; Amdt. 91–276, 68 FR 70133, Dec. 17, 2003]

SUBCHAPTER G

AIR CARRIERS AND OPERATORS FOR COMPENSATION OR HIRE: CERTIFICATION AND OPERATIONS

PART 119

CERTIFICATION: AIR CARRIERS AND COMMERCIAL OPERATORS

SPECIAL FEDERAL AVIATION REGULATION

SFAR No. 78 [Note]

Subpart A—General

Sec.

119.1 Applicability.
119.3 Definitions.
119.5 Certifications, authorizations, and prohibitions.
119.7 Operations specifications.
119.9 Use of business names.

Subpart B— Applicability of Operating Requirements to Different Kinds of Operations Under Parts 121, 125, and 135 of this Chapter

119.21 Commercial operators engaged in intrastate common carriage and direct air carriers.
119.23 Operators engaged in passenger-carrying operations, cargo operations, or both with airplanes when common carriage is not involved.
119.25 Rotorcraft operations: Direct air carriers and commercial operators.

Subpart C—Certification, Operations Specifications, and Certain Other Requirements for Operations Conducted Under Part 121 or Part 135 of this Chapter

119.31 Applicability.
119.33 General requirements.
119.35 Certificate application requirements for all operators.
119.36 Additional certificate application requirements for commercial operators.
119.37 Contents of an Air Carrier Certificate or Operating Certificate.
119.39 Issuing or denying a certificate.
119.41 Amending a certificate.
119.43 Certificate holder's duty to maintain operations specifications.
119.45 [Reserved]
119.47 Maintaining a principal base of operations, main operations base, and main maintenance base; change of address.
119.49 Contents of operations specifications.
119.51 Amending operations specifications.
119.53 Wet leasing of aircraft and other arrangements for transportation by air.
119.55 Obtaining deviation authority to perform operations under a U.S. military contract.
119.57 Obtaining deviation authority to perform an emergency operation.
119.59 Conducting tests and inspections.
119.61 Duration and surrender of certificate and operations specifications.
119.63 Recency of operation.
119.65 Management personnel required for operations conducted under part 121 of this chapter.
119.67 Management personnel: Qualifications for operations conducted under part 121 of this chapter.
119.69 Management personnel required for operations conducted under part 135 of this chapter.
119.71 Management personnel: Qualifications for operations conducted under part 135 of this chapter.
***119.72 [Removed]**

Authority: 49 U.S.C. 106(g), 1153, 40101, 40102, 40103, 40113, 44105, 44106, 44111, 44701–44717, 44722, 44901, 44903, 44904, 44906, 44912, 44914, 44936, 44938, 46103, 46105.

Source: Docket No. 28154, 60 FR 65913, Dec. 20, 1995, unless otherwise noted.

SPECIAL FEDERAL AVIATION REGULATION

SFAR No. 78 to Part 119

SPECIAL OPERATING RULES FOR COMMERCIAL AIR TOUR OPERATORS IN THE VICINITY OF THE ROCKY MOUNTAIN NATIONAL PARK

Editorial Note: For the text of SFAR No. 78, see Part 91 of this chapter.

Subpart A—General

§119.1 Applicability.

(a) This part applies to each person operating or intending to operate civil aircraft—

(1) As an air carrier or commercial operator, or both, in air commerce or

(2) When common carriage is not involved, in operations of U.S.-registered civil airplanes with a seat configuration of 20 or more passengers, or a maximum payload capacity of 6,000 pounds or more.

(b) This part prescribes —

(1) The types of air operator certificates issued by the Federal Aviation Administration, including air carrier certificates and operating certificates;

(2) The certification requirements an operator must meet in order to obtain and hold a certificate authorizing operations under part 121, 125, or 135 of this chapter and operations specifications for each kind of operation to be conducted and each class and size of aircraft to be operated under part 121 or 135 of this chapter;

(3) The requirements an operator must meet to conduct operations under part 121, 125, or 135 of this chapter and in operating each class and size of aircraft authorized in its operations specifications;

(4) Requirements affecting wet leasing of aircraft and other arrangements for transportation by air;

(5) Requirements for obtaining deviation authority to perform operations under a military contract and obtaining deviation authority to perform an emergency operation; and

(6) Requirements for management personnel for operations conducted under part 121 or part 135 of this chapter.

(c) Persons subject to this part must comply with the other requirements of this chapter, except where those requirements are modified by or where additional requirements are imposed by part 119, 121, 125, or 135 of this chapter.

(d) This part does not govern operations conducted under part 91, subpart K (when common carriage is not involved) nor does it govern operations conducted under part 129, 133, 137, or 139 of this chapter.

(e) Except for operations when common carriage is not involved conducted with airplanes having a passenger-seat configuration of 20 seats or more, excluding any required crewmember seat, or a payload capacity of 6,000 pounds or more, this part does not apply to—

(1) Student instruction;

(2) Nonstop sightseeing flights conducted with aircraft having a passenger seat configuration of 30 or fewer, excluding each crewmember seat, and a payload capacity of 7,500 pounds or less, that begin and end at the same airport, and are conducted within a 25 statute mile radius of that airport; however, for nonstop sightseeing flights for compensation or hire conducted in the vicinity of the Grand Canyon National Park, Arizona, the requirements of SFAR 50–2 of this part or 14 CFR part 119, as applicable, apply;

(3) Ferry or training flights;

(4) Aerial work operations, including—

(i) Crop dusting, seeding, spraying, and bird chasing;

(ii) Banner towing;

(iii) Aerial photography or survey;

(iv) Fire fighting;

(v) Helicopter operations in construction or repair work (but it does apply to transportation to and from the site of operations); and

(vi) Powerline or pipeline patrol;

(5) Sightseeing flights conducted in hot air balloons;

(6) Nonstop flights conducted within a 25-statute-mile radius of the airport of takeoff carrying persons or objects for the purpose of conducting intentional parachute operations.

(7) Helicopter flights conducted within a 25 statute mile radius of the airport of takeoff if—

(i) Not more than two passengers are carried in the helicopter in addition to the required flightcrew;

(ii) Each flight is made under day VFR conditions;

(iii) The helicopter used is certificated in the standard category and complies with the 100-hour inspection requirements of part 91 of this chapter;

(iv) The operator notifies the FAA Flight Standards District Office responsible for the geographic area concerned at least 72 hours before each flight and furnishes any essential information that the office requests;

(v) The number of flights does not exceed a total of six in any calendar year;

(vi) Each flight has been approved by the Administrator; and

(vii) Cargo is not carried in or on the helicopter;

(8) Operations conducted under part 133 of this chapter or 375 of this title;

(9) Emergency mail service conducted under 49 U.S.C. 41906; or

(10) Operations conducted under the provisions of §91.321 of this chapter.

[Docket No. 28154, 60 FR 65913, Dec. 20, 1995; as amended by Amdt. 119–4, 66 FR 23557, May 9, 2001; Amdt. 119–5, 67 FR 9554, March 1, 2002; Amdt. 119–7, 68 FR 54584, Sept. 17, 2003]

§119.3 Definitions.

For the purpose of subchapter G of this chapter, the term—

All-cargo operation means any operation for compensation or hire that is other than a passenger-carrying operation or, if passengers are carried, they are only those specified in §§121.583(a) or 135.85 of this chapter.

Certificate-holding district office means the Flight Standards District Office that has responsibility for administering the certificate and is charged with the overall inspection of the certificate holder's operations.

Commuter operation means any scheduled operation conducted by any person operating one of the following types of aircraft with a frequency of operations of at least five round trips per week on at least one route between two or more points according to the published flight schedules:

(1) Airplanes, other than turbojet powered airplanes, having a maximum passenger-seat configuration of 9 seats or less, excluding each crew-member seat, and a maximum payload capacity of 7,500 pounds or less; or

(2) Rotorcraft.

Direct air carrier means a person who provides or offers to provide air transportation and who has control over the operational functions performed in providing that transportation.

DOD commercial air carrier evaluator means a qualified Air Mobility Command, Survey and Analysis Office (AMC/DOB) cockpit evaluator performing the duties specified in Public Law 99-661 when the evaluator is flying on an air carrier that is contracted or pursuing a contract with the U.S. Department of Defense (DOD).

Domestic operation means any scheduled operation conducted by any person operating any airplane described in paragraph (1) of this definition at locations described in paragraph (2) of this definition:

(1) Airplanes:

(i) Turbojet-powered airplanes;

(ii) Airplanes having a passenger-seat configuration of more than 9 passenger seats, excluding each crewmember seat; or

(iii) Airplanes having a payload capacity of more than 7,500 pounds.

(2) Locations:

(i) Between any points within the 48 contiguous States of the United States or the District of Columbia; or

(ii) Operations solely within the 48 contiguous States of the United States or the District of Columbia; or

(iii) Operations entirely within any State, territory, or possession of the United States; or

(iv) When specifically authorized by the Administrator, operations between any point within the 48 contiguous States of the United States or the District of Columbia and any specifically authorized point located outside the 48 contiguous States of the United States or the District of Columbia.

Empty weight means the weight of the airframe, engines, propellers, rotors, and fixed equipment. Empty weight excludes the weight of the crew and payload, but includes the weight of all fixed ballast, unusable fuel supply, undrainable oil, total quantity of engine coolant, and total quantity of hydraulic fluid.

Flag operation means any scheduled operation conducted by any person operating any airplane described in paragraph (1) of this definition at the locations described in paragraph (2) of this definition:

(1) Airplanes:

(i) Turbojet-powered airplanes;

(ii) Airplanes having a passenger-seat configuration of more than 9 passenger seats, excluding each crewmember seat; or

(iii) Airplanes having a payload capacity of more than 7,500 pounds.

(2) Locations:

(i) Between any point within the State of Alaska or the State of Hawaii or any territory or possession of the United States and any point outside the State of Alaska or the State of Hawaii or any territory or possession of the United States, respectively; or

(ii) Between any point within the 48 contiguous States of the United States or the District of Columbia and any point outside the 48 contiguous States of the United States and the District of Columbia.

(iii) Between any point outside the U.S. and another point outside the U.S.

Justifiable aircraft equipment means any equipment necessary for the operation of the aircraft. It does not include equipment or ballast specifically installed, permanently or otherwise, for the purpose of altering the empty weight of an aircraft to meet the maximum payload capacity.

Kind of operation means one of the various operations a certificate holder is authorized to conduct, as specified in its operations specifications, i.e., domestic, flag, supplemental, commuter, or on-demand operations.

Maximum payload capacity means:

(1) For an aircraft for which a maximum zero fuel weight is prescribed in FAA technical specifications, the maximum zero fuel weight, less empty weight, less all justifiable aircraft equipment, and less the operating load (consisting of minimum flightcrew, foods and beverages, and supplies and equipment related to foods and beverages, but not including disposable fuel or oil).

(2) For all other aircraft, the maximum certificated takeoff weight of an aircraft, less the empty weight, less all justifiable aircraft equipment, and less the operating load (consisting of minimum fuel load, oil, and flightcrew). The allowance for the weight of the crew, oil, and fuel is as follows:

(i) Crew—for each crewmember required by the Federal Aviation Regulations—

(A) For male flight crewmembers—180 pounds.

(B) For female flight crewmembers—140 pounds.

(C) For male flight attendants—180 pounds.

(D) For female flight attendants—130 pounds.

(E) For flight attendants not identified by gender—140 pounds.

(ii) Oil—350 pounds or the oil capacity as specified on the Type Certificate Data Sheet.

(iii) Fuel—the minimum weight of fuel required by the applicable Federal Aviation Regulations for a flight between domestic points 174 nautical miles apart under VFR weather conditions that does not involve extended overwater operations.

Maximum zero fuel weight means the maximum permissible weight of an aircraft with no disposable fuel or oil. The zero fuel weight figure may be found in either the aircraft type certificate data sheet, the approved Aircraft Flight Manual, or both.

Noncommon carriage means an aircraft operation for compensation or hire that does not involve a holding out to others.

On-demand operation means any operation for compensation or hire that is one of the following:

(1) Passenger-carrying operations conducted as a public charter under part 380 of this title or any operations in which the departure time, departure location, and arrival location are specifically negotiated with the customer or the customer's representative that are any of the following types of operations:

(i) Common carriage operations conducted with airplanes, including turbojet-powered airplanes, having a passenger-seat configuration of 30 seats or fewer, excluding each crewmember seat, and a payload capacity of 7,500 pounds or less, except that operations using a specific airplane that is also used in domestic or flag operations and that is so listed in the operations specifications as required by §119.49(a)(4) for those operations are considered supplemental operations;

(ii) Noncommon or private carriage operations conducted with airplanes having a passenger-seat configuration of less than 20 seats, excluding each crewmember seat, and a payload capacity of less than 6,000 pounds; or

(iii) Any rotorcraft operation.

(2) Scheduled passenger-carrying operations conducted with one of the following types of aircraft with a frequency of operations of less than five round trips per week on at least one route between two or more points according to the published flight schedules:

(i) Airplanes, other than turbojet powered airplanes, having a maximum passenger-seat configuration of 9 seats or less, excluding each crew-member seat, and a maximum payload capacity of 7,500 pounds or less; or

(ii) Rotorcraft.

(3) All-cargo operations conducted with airplanes having a payload capacity of 7,500 pounds or less, or with rotorcraft.

Passenger-carrying operation means any aircraft operation carrying any person, unless the only persons on the aircraft are those identified in §§121.583(a) or 135.85 of this chapter, as applicable. An aircraft used in a passenger-carrying operation may also carry cargo or mail in addition to passengers.

Principal base of operations means the primary operating location of a certificate holder as established by the certificate holder.

Provisional airport means an airport approved by the Administrator for use by a certificate holder for the purpose of providing service to a community when the regular airport used by the certificate holder is not available.

Regular airport means an airport used by a certificate holder in scheduled operations and listed in its operations specifications.

Scheduled operation means any common carriage passenger-carrying operation for compensation or hire conducted by an air carrier or commercial operator for which the certificate holder or its representative offers in advance the departure location, departure time, and arrival location. It does not include any passenger-carrying operation that is conducted as a public charter operation under part 380 of this title.

Supplemental operation means any common carriage operation for compensation or hire conducted with any airplane described in paragraph (1) of this definition that is a type of operation described in paragraph (2) of this definition:

(1) Airplanes:

(i) Airplanes having a passenger-seat configuration of more than 30 seats, excluding each crewmember seat;

(ii) Airplanes having a payload capacity of more than 7,500 pounds; or

(iii) Each propeller-powered airplane having a passenger-seat configuration of more than 9 seats and less than 31 seats, excluding each crewmember seat, that is also used in domestic or flag operations and that is so listed in the operations specifications as required by §119.49(a)(4) for those operations; or

(iv) Each turbojet powered airplane having a passenger seat configuration of 1 or more and less than 31 seats, excluding each crewmember seat, that is also used in domestic or flag operations and that is so listed in the operations specifications as required by §119.49(a)(4) for those operations.

(2) Types of operation:

(i) Operations for which the departure time, departure location, and arrival location are specifically negotiated with the customer or the customer's representative;

(ii) All-cargo operations; or

(iii) Passenger-carrying public charter operations conducted under part 380 of this title.

Wet lease means any leasing arrangement whereby a person agrees to provide an entire aircraft and at least one crewmember. A wet lease does not include a code-sharing arrangement.

When common carriage is not involved or operations not involving common carriage means any of the following:

(1) Noncommon carriage.

(2) Operations in which persons or cargo are transported without compensation or hire.

(3) Operations not involving the transportation of persons or cargo.

(4) Private carriage.

Years in service means the calendar time elapsed since an aircraft was issued its first U.S. or first foreign airworthiness certificate.

[Docket No. 28154, 60 FR 65913, Dec. 28, 1995; as amended by Amdt. 119–1, 61 FR 2609, Jan. 26, 1996; Amdt. 119–2, 61 FR 30433, June 14, 1996; Amdt. 119–3, 62 FR 13253, March 19, 1997; Amdt. 119–8, 68 FR 41217, July 10, 2003; Amdt. 119–6, 67 FR 72761, Dec. 6, 2002]

§119.5 Certifications, authorizations, and prohibitions.

(a) A person authorized by the Administrator to conduct operations as a direct air carrier will be issued an Air Carrier Certificate.

(b) A person who is not authorized to conduct direct air carrier operations, but who is authorized by the Administrator to conduct operations as a U.S. commercial operator, will be issued an Operating Certificate.

(c) A person who is not authorized to conduct direct air carrier operations, but who is authorized by the Administrator to conduct operations when common carriage is not involved as an operator of U.S.-registered civil airplanes with a seat configuration of 20 or more passengers, or a maximum payload capacity of 6,000 pounds or more, will be issued an Operating Certificate.

(d) A person authorized to engage in common carriage under part 121 or part 135 of this chapter, or both, shall be issued only one certificate authorizing such common carriage, regardless of the kind of operation or the class or size of aircraft to be operated.

(e) A person authorized to engage in noncommon or private carriage under part 125 or part 135 of this chapter, or both, shall be issued only one certificate authorizing such carriage, regardless of the kind of operation or the class or size of aircraft to be operated.

(f) A person conducting operations under more than one paragraph of §§119.21, 119.23, or 119.25 shall conduct those operations in compliance with—

(1) The requirements specified in each paragraph of those sections for the kind of operation conducted under that paragraph; and

(2) The appropriate authorizations, limitations, and procedures specified in the operations specifications for each kind of operation.

(g) No person may operate as a direct air carrier or as a commercial operator without, or in violation of, an appropriate certificate and appropriate operations specifications. No person may operate as a direct air carrier or as a commercial operator in violation of any deviation or exemption authority, if issued to that person or that person's representative.

(h) A person holding an Operating Certificate authorizing noncommon or private carriage operations shall not conduct any operations in common carriage. A person holding an Air Carrier Certificate or Operating Certificate authorizing common carriage operations shall not conduct any operations in noncommon carriage.

(i) No person may operate as a direct air carrier without holding appropriate economic authority from the Department of Transportation.

(j) A certificate holder under this part may not operate aircraft under part 121 or part 135 of this chapter in a geographical area unless its operations specifications specifically authorize the certificate holder to operate in that area.

(k) No person may advertise or otherwise offer to perform an operation subject to this part unless that person is authorized by the Federal Aviation Administration to conduct that operation.

(l) No person may operate an aircraft under this part, part 121 of this chapter, or part 135 of this chapter in violation of an air carrier operating certificate, operating certificate, or appropriate operations specifications issued under this part.

[Docket No. 28154, 60 FR 65913, Dec. 20, 1995; as amended by Amdt. 119–3, 62 FR 13253, March 19, 1997]

§119.7 Operations specifications.

(a) Each certificate holder's operations specifications must contain—

(1) The authorizations, limitations, and certain procedures under which each kind of operation, if applicable, is to be conducted; and

(2) Certain other procedures under which each class and size of aircraft is to be operated.

(b) Except for operations specifications paragraphs identifying authorized kinds of operations, operations specifications are not a part of a certificate.

§119.9 Use of business names.

(a) A certificate holder under this part may not operate an aircraft under part 121 or part 135 of this chapter using a business name other than a business name appearing in the certificate holder's operations specifications.

(b) No person may operate an aircraft under part 121 or part 135 of this chapter unless the name of the certificate holder who is operating the aircraft, or the air carrier or operating certificate number of the certificate holder who is operating the aircraft, is legibly displayed on the aircraft and is clearly visible and readable from the outside of the aircraft to a person standing on the ground at any time except during flight time. The means of displaying the name on the aircraft and its readability must be acceptable to the Administrator.

[Docket No. 28154, 60 FR 65913, Dec. 20, 1995; as amended by Amdt. 119–3, 62 FR 13253, March 19, 1997]

Subpart B— Applicability of Operating Requirements to Different Kinds of Operations Under Parts 121, 125, and 135 of this Chapter

§119.21 Commercial operators engaged in intrastate common carriage and direct air carriers.

(a) Each person who conducts airplane operations as a commercial operator engaged in intrastate common carriage of persons or property for compensation or hire in air commerce, or as a direct air carrier, shall comply with the certification and operations specifications requirements in subpart C of this part, and shall conduct its:

(1) Domestic operations in accordance with the applicable requirements of part 121 of this chapter, and shall be issued operations specifications for those operations in accordance with those requirements. However, based on a showing of safety in air commerce, the Administrator may permit persons who conduct domestic operations between any point located within any of the following Alaskan islands and any point in the State of Alaska to comply with the requirements applicable to flag operations contained in subpart U of part 121 of this chapter:

(i) The Aleutian Islands.

(ii) The Pribilof Islands.

(iii) The Shumagin Islands.

(2) Flag operations in accordance with the applicable requirements of part 121 of this chapter, and shall be issued operations specifications for those operations in accordance with those requirements.

(3) Supplemental operations in accordance with the applicable requirements of part 121 of this chapter, and shall be issued operations specifications for those operations in accordance with those requirements. However, based on a determination of safety in air commerce, the Administrator may authorize or require those operations to be conducted under paragraph (a)(1) or (a)(2) of this section:

(i) Passenger-carrying operations which are conducted between points that are also served by the certificate holder's domestic or flag operations.

(ii) All-cargo operations which are conducted regularly and frequently between the same two points.

(4) Commuter operations in accordance with the applicable requirements of part 135 of this chapter, and shall be issued operations specifications for those operations in accordance with those requirements.

(5) On-demand operations in accordance with the applicable requirements of part 135 of this chapter, and shall be issued operations specifications for those operations in accordance with those requirements.

(b) Persons who are subject to the requirements of paragraph (a)(4) of this section may conduct those operations in accordance with the requirements of paragraph (a)(1) or (a)(2) of this section, provided they obtain authorization from the Administrator.

(c) Persons who are subject to the requirements of paragraph (a)(5) of this section may conduct those operations in accordance with the requirements of paragraph (a)(3) of this section, provided they obtain authorization from the Administrator.

[Docket No. 28154, 60 FR 65913, Dec. 20, 1995; as amended by Amdt. 119–2, 61 FR 30433, June 14, 1996; Amdt. 119–3, 62 FR 13254, March 19, 1997]

§119.23 Operators engaged in passenger-carrying operations, cargo operations, or both with airplanes when common carriage is not involved.

(a) Each person who conducts operations when common carriage is not involved with airplanes having a passenger-seat configuration of 20 seats or more, excluding each crewmember seat, or a payload capacity of 6,000 pounds or more, shall, unless deviation authority is issued—

(1) Comply with the certification and operations specifications requirements of part 125 of this chapter;

(2) Conduct its operations with those airplanes in accordance with the requirements of part 125 of this chapter; and

(3) Be issued operations specifications in accordance with those requirements.

(b) Each person who conducts noncommon carriage (except as provided in §91.501(b) of this chapter) or private carriage operations for compensation or hire with airplanes having a passenger-seat configuration of less than 20 seats, excluding each crewmember seat, and a payload capacity of less than 6,000 pounds shall—

(1) Comply with the certification and operations specifications requirements in subpart C of this part;

(2) Conduct those operations in accordance with the requirements of part 135 of this chapter, except for those requirements applicable only to commuter operations; and

(3) Be issued operations specifications in accordance with those requirements.

[Docket No. 28154, 60 FR 65913, Dec. 20, 1995; as amended by Amdt. 119–2, 61 FR 30434, June 14, 1996]

§119.25 Rotorcraft operations: Direct air carriers and commercial operators.

Each person who conducts rotorcraft operations for compensation or hire must comply with the certification and operations specifications requirements of Subpart C of this part, and shall conduct its:

(a) Commuter operations in accordance with the applicable requirements of part 135 of this chapter, and shall be issued operations specifications for those operations in accordance with those requirements.

(b) On-demand operations in accordance with the applicable requirements of part 135 of this chapter, and shall be issued operations specifications for those operations in accordance with those requirements.

Subpart C— Certification, Operations Specifications, and Certain Other Requirements for Operations Conducted Under Part 121 or Part 135 of this Chapter

§119.31 Applicability.

This subpart sets out certification requirements and prescribes the content of operations specifications and certain other requirements for operations conducted under part 121 or part 135 of this chapter.

§119.33 General requirements.

(a) A person may not operate as a direct air carrier unless that person—

(1) Is a citizen of the United States;

(2) Obtains an Air Carrier Certificate; and

(3) Obtains operations specifications that prescribe the authorizations, limitations, and procedures under which each kind of operation must be conducted.

(b) A person other than a direct air carrier may not conduct any commercial passenger or cargo aircraft operation for compensation or hire under part 121 or part 135 of this chapter unless that person—

(1) Is a citizen of the United States;

(2) Obtains an Operating Certificate; and

(3) Obtains operations specifications that prescribe the authorizations, limitations, and procedures under which each kind of operation must be conducted.

(c) Each applicant for a certificate under this part and each applicant for operations specifications authorizing a new kind of operation that is subject to §121.163 or §135.145 of this chapter shall conduct proving tests as authorized by the Administrator during the application process for authority to conduct operations under part 121 or part 135 of this chapter. All proving tests must be conducted under the appropriate operating and maintenance requirements of part 121 or 135 of this chapter that would apply if the applicant were fully certificated. The Administrator will issue a letter of authorization to each person stating the various authorities under which the proving tests shall be conducted.

[Docket No. 28154, 60 FR 65913, Dec. 20, 1995; as amended by Amdt. 119–2, 61 FR 30434, June 14, 1996]

§119.35 Certificate application requirements for all operators.

(a) A person applying to the Administrator for an Air Carrier Certificate or Operating Certificate under this part (applicant) must submit an application—

(1) In a form and manner prescribed by the Administrator; and

(2) Containing any information the Administrator requires the applicant to submit.

(b) Each applicant must submit the application to the Administrator at least 90 days before the date of intended operation.

[Docket No. 28154, 62 FR 13254, March 19, 1997; as amended by Amdt. 119–3, 62 FR 15570, April 1, 1997]

§119.36 Additional certificate application requirements for commercial operators.

(a) Each applicant for the original issue of an operating certificate for the purpose of conducting intrastate common carriage operations under part 121 or part 135 of this chapter must submit an application in a form and manner prescribed by the Administrator to the Flight Standards District Office in whose area the applicant proposes to establish or has established his or her principal base of operations.

(b) Each application submitted under paragraph (a) of this section must contain a signed statement showing the following:

(1) For corporate applicants:

(i) The name and address of each stockholder who owns 5 percent or more of the total voting stock of the corporation, and if that stockholder is not the sole beneficial owner of the stock, the name and address of each beneficial owner. An individual is considered to own the stock owned, directly or indirectly, by or for his or her spouse, children, grandchildren, or parents.

(ii) The name and address of each director and each officer and each person employed or who will be employed in a management position described in §§119.65 and 119.69, as applicable.

(iii) The name and address of each person directly or indirectly controlling or controlled by the applicant and each person under direct or indirect control with the applicant.

(2) For non-corporate applicants:

(i) The name and address of each person having a financial interest therein and the nature and extent of that interest.

(ii) The name and address of each person employed or who will be employed in a management position described in §§119.65 and 119.69, as applicable.

(c) In addition, each applicant for the original issue of an operating certificate under paragraph (a) of this section must submit with the application a signed statement showing—

(1) The nature and scope of its intended operation, including the name and address of each person, if any, with whom the applicant has a contract to provide services as a commercial operator and the scope, nature, date, and duration of each of those contracts; and

(2) For applicants intending to conduct operations under part 121 of this chapter, the financial information listed in paragraph (e) of this section.

(d) Each applicant for, or holder of, a certificate issued under paragraph (a) of this section, shall notify the Administrator within 10 days after—

(1) A change in any of the persons, or the names and addresses of any of the persons, submitted to the Administrator under paragraph (b)(1) or (b)(2) of this section; or

(2) For applicants intending to conduct operations under part 121 of this chapter, a change in the financial information submitted to the Administrator under paragraph (e) of this section that occurs while the application for the issue is pending before the FAA and that would make the applicant's financial situation substantially less favorable than originally reported.

(e) Each applicant for the original issue of an operating certificate under paragraph (a) of this section who intends to conduct operations under part 121 of this chapter must submit the following financial information:

(1) A balance sheet that shows assets, liabilities, and net worth, as of a date not more than 60 days before the date of application.

(2) An itemization of liabilities more than 60 days past due on the balance sheet date, if any, showing each creditor's name and address, a description of the liability, and the amount and due date of the liability.

(3) An itemization of claims in litigation, if any, against the applicant as of the date of application showing each claimant's name and address and a description and the amount of the claim.

(4) A detailed projection of the proposed operation covering 6 complete months after the month in which the certificate is expected to be issued including—

(i) Estimated amount and source of both operating and nonoperating revenue, including identification of its existing and anticipated income producing contracts and estimated revenue per mile or hour of operation by aircraft type;

(ii) Estimated amount of operating and nonoperating expenses by expense objective classification; and

(iii) Estimated net profit or loss for the period.

(5) An estimate of the cash that will be needed for the proposed operations during the first 6 months after the month in which the certificate is expected to be issued, including—

(i) Acquisition of property and equipment (explain);

(ii) Retirement of debt (explain);

(iii) Additional working capital (explain);

(iv) Operating losses other than depreciation and amortization (explain); and

(v) Other (explain).

(6) An estimate of the cash that will be available during the first 6 months after the month in which the certificate is expected to be issued, from—

(i) Sale of property or flight equipment (explain);

(ii) New debt (explain);

(iii) New equity (explain);

(iv) Working capital reduction (explain);

(v) Operations (profits) (explain);

(vi) Depreciation and amortization (explain); and

(vii) Other (explain).

(7) A schedule of insurance coverage in effect on the balance sheet date showing insurance companies; policy numbers; types, amounts, and period of coverage; and special conditions, exclusions, and limitations.

(8) Any other financial information that the Administrator requires to enable him or her to determine that the applicant has sufficient financial resources to conduct his or her operations with the degree of safety required in the public interest.

(f) Each financial statement containing financial information required by paragraph (e) of this section must be based on accounts prepared and maintained on an accrual basis in accordance with generally accepted accounting principles applied on a consistent basis, and must contain the name and address of the applicant's public accounting firm, if any.

Information submitted must be signed by an officer, owner, or partner of the applicant or certificate holder.

[Docket No. 28154, 62 FR 133254, March 19, 1999; as amended by Amdt. 119–3, 62 FR 15570, April 1, 1997]

§119.37 Contents of an Air Carrier Certificate or Operating Certificate.

The Air Carrier Certificate or Operating Certificate includes—

(a) The certificate holder's name;

(b) The location of the certificate holder's principal base of operations;

(c) The certificate number;

(d) The certificate's effective date; and

(e) The name or the designator of the certificate-holding district office.

§119.39 Issuing or denying a certificate.

(a) An applicant may be issued an Air Carrier Certificate or Operating Certificate if, after investigation, the Administrator finds that the applicant—

(1) Meets the applicable requirements of this part;

(2) Holds the economic authority applicable to the kinds of operations to be conducted, issued by the Department of Transportation, if required; and

(3) Is properly and adequately equipped in accordance with the requirements of this chapter and is able to conduct a safe operation under appropriate provisions of part 121 or part 135 of this chapter and operations specifications issued under this part.

(b) An application for a certificate may be denied if the Administrator finds that—

(1) The applicant is not properly or adequately equipped or is not able to conduct safe operations under this subchapter;

(2) The applicant previously held an Air Carrier Certificate or Operating Certificate which was revoked;

(3) The applicant intends to or fills a key management position listed in §119.65(a) or §119.69(a), as applicable, with an individual who exercised control over or who held the same or a similar position with a certificate holder whose certificate was revoked, or is in the process of being revoked, and that individual materially contributed to the circumstances causing revocation or causing the revocation process;

(4) An individual who will have control over or have a substantial ownership interest in the applicant had the same or similar control or interest in a certificate holder whose certificate was revoked, or is in the process of being revoked, and that individual materially contributed to the circumstances causing revocation or causing the revocation process; or

(5) In the case of an applicant for an Operating Certificate for intrastate common carriage, that for financial reasons the applicant is not able to conduct a safe operation.

§119.41 Amending a certificate.

(a) The Administrator may amend any certificate issued under this part if—

(1) The Administrator determines, under 49 U.S.C. 44709 and part 13 of this chapter, that safety in air commerce and the public interest requires the amendment; or

(2) The certificate holder applies for the amendment and the certificate-holding district office determines that safety in air commerce and the public interest allows the amendment.

(b) When the Administrator proposes to issue an order amending, suspending, or revoking all or part of any certificate, the procedure in §13.19 of this chapter applies.

(c) When the certificate holder applies for an amendment of its certificate, the following procedure applies:

(1) The certificate holder must file an application to amend its certificate with the certificate-holding district office at least 15 days before the date proposed by the applicant for the amendment to become effective, unless the administrator approves filing within a shorter period; and

(2) The application must be submitted to the certificate-holding district office in the form and manner prescribed by the Administrator.

(d) When a certificate holder seeks reconsideration of a decision from the certificate-holding district office concerning amendments of a certificate, the following procedure applies:

(1) The petition for reconsideration must be made within 30 days after the certificate holder receives the notice of denial; and

(2) The certificate holder must petition for reconsideration to the Director, Flight Standards Service.

§119.43 Certificate holder's duty to maintain operations specifications.

(a) Each certificate holder shall maintain a complete and separate set of its operations specifications at its principal base of operations.

(b) Each certificate holder shall insert pertinent excerpts of its operations specifications, or references thereto, in its manual and shall—

(1) Clearly identify each such excerpt as a part of its operations specifications; and

(2) State that compliance with each operations specifications requirement is mandatory.

(c) Each certificate holder shall keep each of its employees and other persons used in its operations informed of the provisions of its operations specifications that apply to that employee's or person's duties and responsibilities.

§119.45 [Reserved]

§119.47 Maintaining a principal base of operations, main operations base, and main maintenance base; change of address.

(a) Each certificate holder must maintain a principal base of operations. Each certificate holder may also establish a main operations base and a main maintenance base which may be located at either the same location as the principal base of operations or at separate locations.

(b) At least 30 days before it proposes to establish or change the location of its principal base of operations, its main operations base, or its main maintenance base, a certificate holder must provide written notification to its certificate-holding district office.

§119.49 Contents of operations specifications.

(a) Each certificate holder conducting domestic, flag, or commuter operations must obtain operations specifications containing all of the following:

(1) The specific location of the certificate holder's principal base of operations and, if different, the address that shall serve as the primary point of contact for correspondence between the FAA and the certificate holder and the name and mailing address of the certificate holder's agent for service.

(2) Other business names under which the certificate holder may operate.

(3) Reference to the economic authority issued by the Department of Transportation, if required.

(4) Type of aircraft, registration markings, and serial numbers of each aircraft authorized for use, each regular and alternate airport to be used in scheduled operations, and, except for commuter operations, each provisional and refueling airport.

(i) Subject to the approval of the Administrator with regard to form and content, the certificate holder may incorporate by reference the items listed in paragraph (a)(4) of this section into the certificate holder's operations specifications by maintaining a current listing of those items and by referring to the specific list in the applicable paragraph of the operations specifications.

(ii) The certificate holder may not conduct any operation using any aircraft or airport not listed.

(5) Kinds of operations authorized.

(6) Authorization and limitations for routes and areas of operations.

(7) Airport limitations.

(8) Time limitations, or standards for determining time limitations, for overhauling, inspecting, and checking airframes, engines, propellers, rotors, appliances, and emergency equipment.

(9) Authorization for the method of controlling weight and balance of aircraft.

(10) Interline equipment interchange requirements, if relevant.

(11) Aircraft wet lease information required by §119.53(c).

(12) Any authorized deviation and exemption granted from any requirement of this chapter.

(13) Any other item the Administrator determines is necessary.

(b) Each certificate holder conducting supplemental operations must obtain operations specifications containing all of the following:

(1) The specific location of the certificate holder's principal base of operations, and, if different, the address that shall serve as the primary point of contact for correspondence between the FAA and the certificate holder and the name and mailing address of the certificate holder's agent for service.

(2) Other business names under which the certificate holder may operate.

(3) Reference to the economic authority issued by the Department of Transportation, if required.

(4) Type of aircraft, registration markings, and serial number of each aircraft authorized for use.

(i) Subject to the approval of the Administrator with regard to form and content, the certificate holder may incorporate by reference the items listed in paragraph (b)(4) of this section into the certificate holder's operations specifications by maintaining a current listing of those items and by referring to the specific list in the applicable paragraph of the operations specifications.

(ii) The certificate holder may not conduct any operation using any aircraft not listed.

(5) Kinds of operations authorized.

(6) Authorization and limitations for routes and areas of operations.

(7) Special airport authorizations and limitations.

(8) Time limitations, or standards for determining time limitations, for overhauling, inspecting, and checking airframes, engines, propellers, appliances, and emergency equipment.

(9) Authorization for the method of controlling weight and balance of aircraft.

(10) Aircraft wet lease information required by §119.53(c).

(11) Any authorization or requirement to conduct supplemental operations as provided by §119.21(a)(3)(i) or (ii).

(12) Any authorized deviation or exemption from any requirement of this chapter.

(13) Any other item the Administrator determines is necessary.

(c) Each certificate holder conducting on-demand operations must obtain operations specifications containing all of the following:

(1) The specific location of the certificate holder's principal base of operations, and if different, the address that shall serve as the primary point of contact for correspondence between the FAA and the name and mailing address of the certificate holder's agent for service.

(2) Other business names under which the certificate holder may operate.

(3) Reference to the economic authority issued by the Department of Transportation, if required.

(4) Kind and area of operations authorized.

(5) Category and class of aircraft that may be used in those operations.

(6) Type of aircraft, registration markings, and serial number of each aircraft that is subject to an airworthiness maintenance program required by §135.411(a)(2) of this chapter.

(i) Subject to the approval of the Administrator with regard to form and content, the certificate holder may incorporate by reference the items listed in paragraph (c)(6) of this section into the certificate holder's operations specifications by maintaining a current listing of those items and by referring to the specific list in the applicable paragraph of the operations specifications.

(ii) The certificate holder may not conduct any operation using any aircraft not listed.

(7) Registration markings of each aircraft that is to be inspected under an approved aircraft inspection program under §135.419 of this chapter.

(8) Time limitations or standards for determining time limitations, for overhauls, inspections, and checks for airframes, engines, propellers, rotors, appliances, and emergency equipment of aircraft that are subject to an airworthiness maintenance program required by §135.411(a)(2) of this chapter.

(9) Additional maintenance items required by the Administrator under §135.421 of this chapter.

(10) Aircraft wet lease information required by §119.53(c).

119

(11) Any authorized deviation or exemption from any requirement of this chapter.

(12) Any other item the Administrator determines is necessary.

§119.51 Amending operations specifications.

(a) The Administrator may amend any operations specifications issued under this part if—

(1) The Administrator determines that safety in air commerce and the public interest require the amendment; or

(2) The certificate holder applies for the amendment, and the Administrator determines that safety in air commerce and the public interest allows the amendment.

(b) Except as provided in paragraph (e) of this section, when the Administrator initiates an amendment to a certificate holder's operations specifications, the following procedure applies:

(1) The certificate-holding district office notifies the certificate holder in writing of the proposed amendment.

(2) The certificate-holding district office sets a reasonable period (but not less than 7 days) within which the certificate holder may submit written information, views, and arguments on the amendment.

(3) After considering all material presented, the certificate-holding district office notifies the certificate holder of—

(i) The adoption of the proposed amendment;

(ii) The partial adoption of the proposed amendment; or

(iii) The withdrawal of the proposed amendment.

(4) If the certificate-holding district office issues an amendment to the operations specifications, it becomes effective not less than 30 days after the certificate holder receives notice of it unless—

(i) The certificate-holding district office finds under paragraph (e) of this section that there is an emergency requiring immediate action with respect to safety in air commerce; or

(ii) The certificate holder petitions for reconsideration of the amendment under paragraph (d) of this section.

(c) When the certificate holder applies for an amendment to its operations specifications, the following procedure applies:

(1) The certificate holder must file an application to amend its operations specifications—

(i) At least 90 days before the date proposed by the applicant for the amendment to become effective, unless a shorter time is approved, in cases of mergers; acquisitions of airline operational assets that require an additional showing of safety (e.g., proving tests); changes in the kind of operation as defined in §119.3; resumption of operations following a suspension of operations as a result of bankruptcy actions; or the initial introduction of aircraft not before proven for use in air carrier or commercial operator operations.

(ii) At least 15 days before the date proposed by the applicant for the amendment to become effective in all other cases.

(2) The application must be submitted to the certificate-holding district office in a form and manner prescribed by the Administrator.

(3) After considering all material presented, the certificate-holding district office notifies the certificate holder of—

(i) The adoption of the applied for amendment;

(ii) The partial adoption of the applied for amendment; or

(iii) The denial of the applied for amendment. The certificate holder may petition for reconsideration of a denial under paragraph (d) of this section.

(4) If the certificate-holding district office approves the amendment, following coordination with the certificate holder regarding its implementation, the amendment is effective on the date the Administrator approves it.

(d) When a certificate holder seeks reconsideration of a decision from the certificate-holding district office concerning the amendment of operations specifications, the following procedure applies:

(1) The certificate holder must petition for reconsideration of that decision within 30 days of the date that the certificate holder receives a notice of denial of the amendment to its operations specifications, or of the date it receives notice of an FAA-initiated amendment to its operations specifications, whichever circumstance applies.

(2) The certificate holder must address its petition to the Director, Flight Standards Service.

(3) A petition for reconsideration, if filed within the 30-day period, suspends the effectiveness of any amendment issued by the certificate-holding district office unless the certificate-holding district office has found, under paragraph (e) of this section, that an emergency exists requiring immediate action with respect to safety in air transportation or air commerce.

(4) If a petition for reconsideration is not filed within 30 days, the procedures of paragraph (c) of this section apply.

(e) If the certificate-holding district office finds that an emergency exists requiring immediate action with respect to safety in air commerce or air transportation that makes the procedures set out in this section impracticable or contrary to the public interest:

(1) The certificate-holding district office amends the operations specifications and makes the amendment effective on the day the certificate holder receives notice of it.

(2) In the notice to the certificate holder, the certificate-holding district office articulates the reasons for its finding that an emergency exists requiring immediate action with respect to safety in air transportation or air commerce or that makes it impracticable or contrary to the public interest to stay the effectiveness of the amendment.

§119.53 Wet leasing of aircraft and other arrangements for transportation by air.

(a) Unless otherwise authorized by the Administrator, prior to conducting operations involving a wet lease, each certificate holder under this part authorized to conduct common carriage operations under this subchapter shall provide the Administrator with a copy of the wet lease to be executed which would lease the aircraft to any other person engaged in common carriage operations under this subchapter, including foreign air carriers, or to any other foreign person engaged in common carriage wholly outside the United States.

(b) No certificate holder under this part may wet lease from a foreign air carrier or any other foreign person or any person not authorized to engage in common carriage.

(c) Upon receiving a copy of a wet lease, the Administrator determines which party to the agreement has operational control of the aircraft and issues amendments to the operations specifications of each party to the agreement, as needed. The lessor must provide the following information to be incorporated into the operations specifications of both parties, as needed.

(1) The names of the parties to the agreement and the duration thereof.

(2) The nationality and registration markings of each aircraft involved in the agreement.

(3) The kind of operation (e.g., domestic, flag, supplemental, commuter, or on-demand).

(4) The airports or areas of operation.

(5) A statement specifying the party deemed to have operational control and the times, airports, or areas under which such operational control is exercised.

(d) In making the determination of paragraph (c) of this section, the Administrator will consider the following:

(1) Crewmembers and training.

(2) Airworthiness and performance of maintenance.

(3) Dispatch.

(4) Servicing the aircraft.

(5) Scheduling.

(6) Any other factor the Administrator considers relevant.

(e) Other arrangements for transportation by air: Except as provided in paragraph (f) of this section, a certificate holder under this part operating under part 121 or 135 of this chapter may not conduct any operation for another certificate holder under this part or a foreign air carrier under part 129 of this chapter or a foreign person engaged in common carriage wholly outside the United States unless it holds applicable Department of Transportation economic authority, if required, and is authorized under its operations specifications to conduct the same kinds of operations (as defined in §119.3). The certificate holder conducting the substitute operation must conduct that operation in accordance with the same operations authority held by the certificate holder arranging for the substitute operation. These substitute operations must be conducted between airports for which the substitute certificate holder holds authority for scheduled operations or within areas of operations for which the substitute certificate holder has authority for supplemental or on-demand operations.

(f) A certificate holder under this part may, if authorized by the Department of Transportation under §380.3 of this title and the Administrator in the case of interstate commuter, interstate domestic, and flag operations, or the Administrator in the case of scheduled intrastate common carriage operations, conduct one or more flights for passengers who are stranded because of the cancellation of their scheduled flights. These flights must be conducted under the rules of part 121 or part 135 of this chapter applicable to supplemental or on-demand operations.

§119.55 Obtaining deviation authority to perform operations under a U.S. military contract.

(a) The Administrator may authorize a certificate holder that is authorized to conduct supplemental or on-demand operations to deviate from the applicable requirements of this part, part 121, or part 135 of this chapter in order to perform operations under a U.S. military contract.

(b) A certificate holder that has a contract with the U.S. Department of Defense's Air Mobility Command (AMC) must submit a request for deviation authority to AMC. AMC will review the requests, then forward the carriers' consolidated requests, along with AMC's recommendations, to the FAA for review and action.

(c) The Administrator may authorize a deviation to perform operations under a U.S. military contract under the following conditions—

(1) The Department of Defense certifies to the Administrator that the operation is essential to the national defense;

(2) The Department of Defense further certifies that the certificate holder cannot perform the operation without deviation authority;

(3) The certificate holder will perform the operation under a contract or subcontract for the benefit of a U.S. armed service; and

(4) The Administrator finds that the deviation is based on grounds other than economic advantage either to the certificate holder or to the United States.

(d) In the case where the Administrator authorizes a deviation under this section, the Administrator will issue an appropriate amendment to the certificate holder's operations specifications.

(e) The Administrator may, at any time, terminate any grant of deviation authority issued under this section.

§119.57 Obtaining deviation authority to perform an emergency operation.

(a) In emergency conditions, the Administrator may authorize deviations if—

(1) Those conditions necessitate the transportation of persons or supplies for the protection of life or property; and

(2) The Administrator finds that a deviation is necessary for the expeditious conduct of the operations.

(b) When the Administrator authorizes deviations for operations under emergency conditions—

(1) The Administrator will issue an appropriate amendment to the certificate holder's operations specifications; or

(2) If the nature of the emergency does not permit timely amendment of the operations specifications—

(i) The Administrator may authorize the deviation orally; and

(ii) The certificate holder shall provide documentation describing the nature of the emergency to the certificate-holding district office within 24 hours after completing the operation.

§119.59 Conducting tests and inspections.

(a) At any time or place, the Administrator may conduct an inspection or test to determine whether a certificate holder under this part is complying with title 49 of the United States Code, applicable regulations, the certificate, or the certificate holder's operations specifications.

(b) The certificate holder must—

(1) Make available to the Administrator at the certificate holder's principal base of operations—

(i) The certificate holder's Air Carrier Certificate or the certificate holder's Operating Certificate and the certificate holder's operations specifications; and

(ii) A current listing that will include the location and persons responsible for each record, document, and report required to be kept by the certificate holder under title 49 of the

United States Code applicable to the operation of the certificate holder.

(2) Allow the Administrator to make any test or inspection to determine compliance respecting any matter stated in paragraph (a) of this section.

(c) Each employee of, or person used by, the certificate holder who is responsible for maintaining the certificate holder's records must make those records available to the Administrator.

(d) The Administrator may determine a certificate holder's continued eligibility to hold its certificate and/or operations specifications on any grounds listed in paragraph (a) of this section, or any other appropriate grounds.

(e) Failure by any certificate holder to make available to the Administrator upon request, the certificate, operations specifications, or any required record, document, or report is grounds for suspension of all or any part of the certificate holder's certificate and operations specifications.

(f) In the case of operators conducting intrastate common carriage operations, these inspections and tests include inspections and tests of financial books and records.

§119.61 Duration and surrender of certificate and operations specifications.

(a) An Air Carrier Certificate or Operating Certificate issued under this part is effective until—

(1) The certificate holder surrenders it to the Administrator; or

(2) The Administrator suspends, revokes, or otherwise terminates the certificate.

(b) Operations specifications issued under this part, part 121, or part 135 of this chapter are effective unless—

(1) The Administrator suspends, revokes, or otherwise terminates the certificate;

(2) The operations specifications are amended as provided in §119.51;

(3) The certificate holder does not conduct a kind of operation for more than the time specified in §119.63 and fails to follow the procedures of §119.63 upon resuming that kind of operation; or

(4) The Administrator suspends or revokes the operations specifications for a kind of operation.

(c) Within 30 days after a certificate holder terminates operations under part 135 of this chapter, the operating certificate and operations specifications must be surrendered by the certificate holder to the certificate-holding district office.

§119.63 Recency of operation.

(a) Except as provided in paragraph (b) of this section, no certificate holder may conduct a kind of operation for which it holds authority in its operations specifications unless the certificate holder has conducted that kind of operation within the preceding number of consecutive calendar days specified in this paragraph:

(1) For domestic, flag, or commuter operations—30 days.

(2) For supplemental or on-demand operations—90 days, except that if the certificate holder has authority to conduct domestic, flag, or commuter operations, and has conducted domestic, flag or commuter operations within the previous 30 days, this paragraph does not apply.

(b) If a certificate holder does not conduct a kind of operation for which it is authorized in its operations specifications within the number of calendar days specified in paragraph (a) of this section, it shall not conduct such kind of operation unless—

(1) It advises the Administrator at least 5 consecutive calendar days before resumption of that kind of operation; and

(2) It makes itself available and accessible during the 5 consecutive calendar day period in the event that the FAA decides to conduct a full inspection reexamination to determine whether the certificate holder remains properly and adequately equipped and able to conduct a safe operation.

[Docket No. 28154, 60 FR 65913, Dec. 20, 1995; as amended by Amdt. 119–2, 61 FR 30434, June 14, 1996]

§119.65 Management personnel required for operations conducted under part 121 of this chapter.

(a) Each certificate holder must have sufficient qualified management and technical personnel to ensure the highest degree of safety in its operations. The certificate holder must have qualified personnel serving full-time in the following or equivalent positions:

(1) Director of Safety.

(2) Director of Operations.

(3) Chief Pilot.

(4) Director of Maintenance.

(5) Chief Inspector.

(b) The Administrator may approve positions or numbers of positions other than those listed in paragraph (a) of this section for a particular operation if the certificate holder shows that it can perform the operation with the highest degree of safety under the direction of fewer or different categories of management personnel due to—

(1) The kind of operation involved;

(2) The number and type of airplanes used; and

(3) The area of operations.

(c) The title of the positions required under paragraph (a) of this section or the title and number of equivalent positions approved under paragraph (b) of this section shall be set forth in the certificate holder's operations specifications.

(d) The individuals who serve in the positions required or approved under paragraph (a) or (b) of this section and anyone in a position to exercise control over operations conducted under the operating certificate must—

(1) Be qualified through training, experience, and expertise;

(2) To the extent of their responsibilities, have a full understanding of the following materials with respect to the certificate holder's operation—

(i) Aviation safety standards and safe operating practices;

(ii) 14 CFR Chapter I (Federal Aviation Regulations);

(iii) The certificate holder's operations specifications;

(iv) All appropriate maintenance and airworthiness requirements of this chapter (e.g., parts 1, 21, 23, 25, 43, 45, 47, 65, 91, and 121 of this chapter); and

(v) The manual required by §121.133 of this chapter; and

(3) Discharge their duties to meet applicable legal requirements and to maintain safe operations.

(e) Each certificate holder must:

(1) State in the general policy provisions of the manual required by §121.133 of this chapter, the duties, responsibilities, and authority of personnel required under paragraph (a) of this section;

(2) List in the manual the names and business addresses of the individuals assigned to those positions; and

(3) Notify the certificate-holding district office within 10 days of any change in personnel or any vacancy in any position listed.

§119.67 Management personnel: Qualifications for operations conducted under part 121 of this chapter.

(a) To serve as Director of Operations under §119.65(a) a person must—

(1) Hold an airline transport pilot certificate;

(2) Have at least 3 years supervisory or managerial experience within the last 6 years in a position that exercised operational control over any operations conducted with large airplanes under part 121 or part 135 of this chapter, or if the certificate holder uses only small airplanes in its operations, the experience may be obtained in large or small airplanes; and

(3) In the case of a person becoming a Director of Operations—

(i) For the first time ever, have at least 3 years experience, within the past 6 years, as pilot in command of a large airplane operated under part 121 or part 135 of this chapter, if the certificate holder operates large airplanes. If the certificate holder uses only small airplanes in its operation, the experience may be obtained in either large or small airplanes.

(ii) In the case of a person with previous experience as a Director of Operations, have at least 3 years experience as pilot in command of a large airplane operated under part 121 or part 135 of this chapter, if the certificate holder operates large airplanes. If the certificate holder uses only small airplanes in its operation, the experience may be obtained in either large or small airplanes.

(b) To serve as Chief Pilot under §119.65(a) a person must hold an airline transport pilot certificate with appropriate ratings for at least one of the airplanes used in the certificate holder's operation and:

(1) In the case of a person becoming a Chief Pilot for the first time ever, have at least 3 years experience, within the past 6 years, as pilot in command of a large airplane operated under part 121 or part 135 of this chapter, if the certificate holder operates large airplanes. If the certificate holder uses only small airplanes in its operation, the experience may be obtained in either large or small airplanes.

(2) In the case of a person with previous experience as a Chief Pilot, have at least 3 years experience, as pilot in command of a large airplane operated under part 121 or part 135 of this chapter, if the certificate holder operates large airplanes. If the certificate holder uses only small airplanes in its operation, the experience may be obtained in either large or small airplanes.

(c) To serve as Director of Maintenance under §119.65(a) a person must—

(1) Hold a mechanic certificate with airframe and powerplant ratings;

(2) Have 1 year of experience in a position responsible for returning airplanes to service;

(3) Have at least 1 year of experience in a supervisory capacity under either paragraph (c)(4)(i) or (c)(4)(ii) of this section maintaining the same category and class of airplane as the certificate holder uses; and

(4) Have 3 years experience within the past 6 years in one or a combination of the following—

(i) Maintaining large airplanes with 10 or more passenger seats, including at the time of appointment as Director of Maintenance, experience in maintaining the same category and class of airplane as the certificate holder uses; or

(ii) Repairing airplanes in a certificated airframe repair station that is rated to maintain airplanes in the same category and class of airplane as the certificate holder uses.

(d) To serve as Chief Inspector under §119.65(a) a person must—

(1) Hold a mechanic certificate with both airframe and powerplant ratings, and have held these ratings for at least 3 years;

(2) Have at least 3 years of maintenance experience on different types of large airplanes with 10 or more passenger seats with an air carrier or certificated repair station, 1 year of which must have been as maintenance inspector; and

(3) Have at least 1 year of experience in a supervisory capacity maintaining the same category and class of aircraft as the certificate holder uses.

(e) A certificate holder may request a deviation to employ a person who does not meet the appropriate airman experience, managerial experience, or supervisory experience requirements of this section if the Manager of the Air Transportation Division, AFS–200, or the Manager of the Aircraft Maintenance Division, AFS–300, as appropriate, finds that the person has comparable experience, and can effectively perform the functions associated with the position in accordance with the requirements of this chapter and the procedures outlined in the certificate holder's manual. Grants of deviation under this paragraph may be granted after consideration of the size and scope of the operation and the qualifications of the intended personnel. The Administrator may, at any time, terminate any grant of deviation authority issued under this paragraph.

[Docket No. 28154, 60 FR 65913, Dec. 20, 1995; as amended by Amdt. 119–2, 61 FR 30434, June 14, 1996; Amdt. 119–3, 62 FR 13255, March 19, 1997]

§119.69 Management personnel required for operations conducted under part 135 of this chapter.

(a) Each certificate holder must have sufficient qualified management and technical personnel to ensure the safety of its operations. Except for a certificate holder using only one pilot in its operations, the certificate holder must have qualified personnel serving in the following or equivalent positions:

(1) Director of Operations.

(2) Chief Pilot.

(3) Director of Maintenance.

(b) The Administrator may approve positions or numbers of positions other than those listed in paragraph (a) of this section for a particular operation if the certificate holder shows that it can perform the operation with the highest degree of safety under the direction of fewer or different categories of management personnel due to—

(1) The kind of operation involved;

(2) The number and type of aircraft used; and

(3) The area of operations.

(c) The title of the positions required under paragraph (a) of this section or the title and number of equivalent positions approved under paragraph (b) of this section shall be set forth in the certificate holder's operations specifications.

(d) The individuals who serve in the positions required or approved under paragraph (a) or (b) of this section and anyone in a position to exercise control over operations conducted under the operating certificate must—

(1) Be qualified through training, experience, and expertise;

(2) To the extent of their responsibilities, have a full understanding of the following material with respect to the certificate holder's operation—

(i) Aviation safety standards and safe operating practices;

(ii) 14 CFR Chapter I (Federal Aviation Regulations);

(iii) The certificate holder's operations specifications;

(iv) All appropriate maintenance and airworthiness requirements of this chapter (e.g., parts 1, 21, 23, 25, 43, 45, 47, 65, 91, and 135 of this chapter); and

(v) The manual required by §135.21 of this chapter; and

(3) Discharge their duties to meet applicable legal requirements and to maintain safe operations.

(e) Each certificate holder must—

(1) State in the general policy provisions of the manual required by §135.21 of this chapter, the duties, responsibilities, and authority of personnel required or approved under paragraph (a) or (b), respectively, of this section;

(2) List in the manual the names and business addresses of the individuals assigned to those positions; and

(3) Notify the certificate-holding district office within 10 days of any change in personnel or any vacancy in any position listed.

§119.71 Management personnel: Qualifications for operations conducted under part 135 of this chapter.

(a) To serve as Director of Operations under §119.69(a) for a certificate holder conducting any operations for which the pilot in command is required to hold an airline transport pilot certificate a person must hold an airline transport pilot certificate and either:

(1) Have at least 3 years supervisory or managerial experience within the last 6 years in a position that exercised operational control over any operations conducted under part 121 or part 135 of this chapter; or

(2) In the case of a person becoming Director of Operations—

(i) For the first time ever, have at least 3 years experience, within the past 6 years, as pilot in command of an aircraft operated under part 121 or part 135 of this chapter.

(ii) In the case of a person with previous experience as a Director of Operations, have at least 3 years experience, as pilot in command of an aircraft operated under part 121 or part 135 of this chapter.

(b) To serve as Director of Operations under §119.69(a) for a certificate holder that only conducts operations for which the pilot in command is required to hold a commercial pilot certificate, a person must hold at least a commercial pilot certificate. If an instrument rating is required for any pilot in command for that certificate holder, the Director of Operations must also hold an instrument rating. In addition, the Direction of Operations must either—

(1) Have at least 3 years supervisory or managerial experience within the last 6 years in a position that exercised operational control over any operations conducted under part 121 or part 135 of this chapter; or

(2) In the case of a person becoming Director of Operations—

(i) For the first time ever, have at least 3 years experience, within the past 6 years, as pilot in command of an aircraft operated under part 121 or part 135 of this chapter.

(ii) In the case of a person with previous experience as a Director of Operations, have at least 3 years experience as pilot in command of an aircraft operated under part 121 or part 135 of this chapter.

(c) To serve as Chief Pilot under §119.69(a) for a certificate holder conducting any operation for which the pilot in command is required to hold an airline transport pilot certificate a person must hold an airline transport pilot certificate with appropriate ratings and be qualified to serve as pilot in command in at least one aircraft used in the certificate holder's operation and:

(1) In the case of a person becoming a Chief Pilot for the first time ever, have at least 3 years experience, within the past 6 years, as pilot in command of an aircraft operated under part 121 or part 135 of this chapter.

(2) In the case of a person with previous experience as a Chief Pilot, have at least 3 years experience as pilot in command of an aircraft operated under part 121 or part 135 of this chapter.

(d) To serve as Chief Pilot under §119.69(a) for a certificate holder that only conducts operations for which the pilot in command is required to hold a commercial pilot certificate, a person must hold at least a commercial pilot certificate. If an instrument rating is required for any pilot in command for that certificate holder, the Chief Pilot must also hold an instrument rating. The Chief Pilot must be qualified to serve as pilot in command in at least one aircraft used in the certificate holder's operation. In addition, the Chief Pilot must:

(1) In the case of a person becoming a Chief Pilot for the first time ever, have at least 3 years experience, within the past 6 years, as pilot in command of an aircraft operated under part 121 or part 135 of this chapter.

(2) In the case of a person with previous experience as a Chief Pilot, have at least 3 years experience as pilot in command of an aircraft operated under part 121 or part 135 of this chapter.

(e) To serve as Director of Maintenance under §119.69(a) a person must hold a mechanic certificate with airframe and powerplant ratings and either:

(1) Have 3 years of experience within the past 3 years maintaining aircraft as a certificated mechanic, including, at the time of appointment as Director of Maintenance, experience in maintaining the same category and class of aircraft as the certificate holder uses; or

(2) Have 3 years of experience within the past 3 years repairing aircraft in a certificated airframe repair station, including 1 year in the capacity of approving aircraft for return to service.

(f) A certificate holder may request a deviation to employ a person who does not meet the appropriate airmen experience requirements, managerial experience requirements, or supervisory experience requirements of this section if the Manager of the Air Transportation Division, AFS–200, or the Manager of the Aircraft Maintenance Division, AFS–300, as appropriate, find that the person has comparable experience, and can effectively perform the functions associated with the position in accordance with the requirements of this chapter and the procedures outlined in the certificate holder's manual. Grants of deviation under this paragraph may be granted after consideration of the size and scope of the operation and the qualifications of the intended personnel. The Administrator may, at any time, terminate any grant of deviation authority issued under this paragraph.

[Docket No. 28154, 60 FR 65913, Dec. 20, 1995; as amended by Amdt. 119–3, 62 FR 13255, March 19, 1997]

SUBCHAPTER G AIR CARRIERS FOR COMPENSATION OR HIRE: CERTIFICATION AND OPERATIONS

PART 121

OPERATING REQUIREMENTS: DOMESTIC, FLAG, AND SUPPLEMENTAL OPERATIONS

Subpart J—
Special Airworthiness Requirements

121.211 Applicability.
121.213 [Reserved]
121.215 Cabin interiors.
121.217 Internal doors.
121.219 Ventilation.
121.221 Fire precautions.
121.223 Proof of compliance with §121.221.
121.225 Propeller deicing fluid.
121.227 Pressure cross-feed arrangements.
121.229 Location of fuel tanks.
121.231 Fuel system lines and fittings.
121.233 Fuel lines and fittings in designated fire zones.
121.235 Fuel valves.
121.237 Oil lines and fittings in designated fire zones.
121.239 Oil valves.
121.241 Oil system drains.
121.243 Engine breather lines.
121.245 Fire walls.
121.247 Fire-wall construction.
121.249 Cowling.
121.251 Engine accessory section diaphragm.
121.253 Powerplant fire protection.
121.255 Flammable fluids.
121.257 Shutoff means.
121.259 Lines and fittings.
121.261 Vent and drain lines.
121.263 Fire-extinguishing systems.
121.265 Fire-extinguishing agents.
121.267 Extinguishing agent container pressure relief.
121.269 Extinguishing agent container compartment temperature.
121.271 Fire-extinguishing system materials.
121.273 Fire-detector systems.
121.275 Fire detectors.
121.277 Protection of other airplane components against fire.
121.279 Control of engine rotation.
121.281 Fuel system independence.
121.283 Induction system ice prevention.
121.285 Carriage of cargo in passenger compartments.
121.287 Carriage of cargo in cargo compartments.
121.289 Landing gear: Aural warning device.
***121.291 Demonstration of emergency evacuation procedures.**
121.293 Special airworthiness requirements for nontransport category airplanes type certificated after December 31, 1964.

Subpart L—
Maintenance, Preventive Maintenance, and Alterations

121.361 Applicability.
121.363 Responsibility for airworthiness.
121.365 Maintenance, preventive maintenance, and alteration organization.
121.367 Maintenance, preventive maintenance, and alterations programs.
***121.368 Aging airplane inspections and records reviews.**
121.369 Manual requirements.
121.370 Special maintenance program requirements.
***121.370a Supplemental inspections.**
121.371 Required inspection personnel.
121.373 Continuing analysis and surveillance.
121.375 Maintenance and preventive maintenance training program.
121.377 Maintenance and preventive maintenance personnel duty time limitations.
121.378 Certificate requirements.
121.379 Authority to perform and approve maintenance, preventive maintenance, and alterations.
121.380 Maintenance recording requirements.
121.380a Transfer of maintenance records.

Subpart J— Special Airworthiness Requirements

Source: Docket No. 6258, 29 FR 19202, Dec. 31, 1964, unless otherwise noted.

§121.211 Applicability.

(a) This subpart prescribes special airworthiness requirements applicable to certificate holders as stated in paragraphs (b) through (e) of this section.

(b) Except as provided in paragraph (d) of this section, each airplane type certificated under Aero Bulletin 7A or part 04 of the Civil Air Regulations in effect before November 1, 1946 must meet the special airworthiness requirements in §§121.215 through 121.283.

(c) Each certificate holder must comply with the requirements of §§121.285 through 121.291.

(d) If the Administrator determines that, for a particular model of airplane used in cargo service, literal compliance with any requirement under paragraph (b) of this section would be extremely difficult and that compliance would not contribute materially to the objective sought, he may require compliance only with those requirements that are necessary to accomplish the basic objectives of this part.

(e) No person may operate under this part a nontransport category airplane type certificated after December 31, 1964,

121

unless the airplane meets the special airworthiness requirements in §121.293.

[Docket No. 6258, 29 FR 19202, Dec. 31, 1964; as amended by Amdt. 121–251, 60 FR 65928, Dec. 20, 1995]

§121.213 [Reserved]

§121.215 Cabin interiors.

(a) Except as provided in §121.312, each compartment used by the crew or passengers must meet the requirements of this section.

(b) Materials must be at least flash resistant.

(c) The wall and ceiling linings and the covering of upholstering, floors, and furnishings must be flame resistant.

(d) Each compartment where smoking is to be allowed must be equipped with self-contained ash trays that are completely removable and other compartments must be placarded against smoking.

(e) Each receptacle for used towels, papers, and wastes must be of fire-resistant material and must have a cover or other means of containing possible fires started in the receptacles.

[Docket No. 6258, 29 FR 19202, Dec. 31, 1964; as amended by Amdt. 121–84, 37 FR 3974, Feb. 24, 1972]

§121.217 Internal doors.

In any case where internal doors are equipped with louvres or other ventilating means, there must be a means convenient to the crew for closing the flow of air through the door when necessary.

§121.219 Ventilation.

Each passenger or crew compartment must be suitably ventilated. Carbon monoxide concentration may not be more than one part in 20,000 parts of air, and fuel fumes may not be present. In any case where partitions between compartments have louvres or other means allowing air to flow between compartments, there must be a means convenient to the crew for closing the flow of air through the partitions, when necessary.

§121.221 Fire precautions.

(a) Each compartment must be designed so that, when used for storing cargo or baggage, it meets the following requirements:

(1) No compartment may include controls, wiring, lines, equipment, or accessories that would upon damage or failure, affect the safe operation of the airplane unless the item is adequately shielded, isolated, or otherwise protected so that it cannot be damaged by movement of cargo in the compartment and so that damage to or failure of the item would not create a fire hazard in the compartment.

(2) Cargo or baggage may not interfere with the functioning of the fire-protective features of the compartment.

(3) Materials used in the construction of the compartments, including tie-down equipment, must be at least flame resistant.

(4) Each compartment must include provisions for safeguarding against fires according to the classifications set forth in paragraphs (b) through (f) of this section.

(b) *Class A.* Cargo and baggage compartments are classified in the "A" category if—

(1) A fire therein would be readily discernible to a member of the crew while at his station; and

(2) All parts of the compartment are easily accessible in flight.

There must be a hand fire extinguisher available for each Class A compartment.

(c) *Class B.* Cargo and baggage compartments are classified in the "B" category if enough access is provided while in flight to enable a member of the crew to effectively reach all of the compartment and its contents with a hand fire extinguisher and the compartment is so designed that, when the access provisions are being used, no hazardous amount of smoke, flames, or extinguishing agent enters any compartment occupied by the crew or passengers. Each Class B compartment must comply with the following:

(1) It must have a separate approved smoke or fire detector system to give warning at the pilot or flight engineer station.

(2) There must be a hand fire extinguisher available for the compartment.

(3) It must be lined with fire-resistant material, except that additional service lining of flame-resistant material may be used.

(d) *Class C.* Cargo and baggage compartments are classified in the "C" category if they do not conform with the requirements for the "A," "B," "D," or "E" categories. Each Class C compartment must comply with the following:

(1) It must have a separate approved smoke or fire detector system to give warning at the pilot or flight engineer station.

(2) It must have an approved built-in fire-extinguishing system controlled from the pilot or flight engineer station.

(3) It must be designed to exclude hazardous quantities of smoke, flames, or extinguishing agents from entering into any compartment occupied by the crew or passengers.

(4) It must have ventilation and draft controlled so that the extinguishing agent provided can control any fire that may start in the compartment.

(5) It must be lined with fire-resistant material, except that additional service lining of flame-resistant material may be used.

(e) *Class D.* Cargo and baggage compartments are classified in the "D" category if they are so designed and constructed that a fire occurring therein will be completely confined without endangering the safety of the airplane or the occupants. Each Class D compartment must comply with the following:

(1) It must have a means to exclude hazardous quantities of smoke, flames, or noxious gases from entering any compartment occupied by the crew or passengers.

(2) Ventilation and drafts must be controlled within each compartment so that any fire likely to occur in the compartment will not progress beyond safe limits.

(3) It must be completely lined with fire-resistant material.

(4) Consideration must be given to the effect of heat within the compartment on adjacent critical parts of the airplane.

(f) *Class E.* On airplanes used for the carriage of cargo only, the cabin area may be classified as a Class "E" compartment. Each Class E compartment must comply with the following:

(1) It must be completely lined with fire-resistant material.

(2) It must have a separate system of an approved type smoke or fire detector to give warning at the pilot or flight engineer station.

(3) It must have a means to shut off the ventilating air flow to or within the compartment and the controls for that means must be accessible to the flight crew in the crew compartment.

(4) It must have a means to exclude hazardous quantities of smoke, flames, or noxious gases from entering the flight crew compartment.

(5) Required crew emergency exits must be accessible under all cargo loading conditions.

§121.223 Proof of compliance with §121.221.

Compliance with those provisions of §121.221 that refer to compartment accessibility, the entry of hazardous quantities of smoke or extinguishing agent into compartments occupied by the crew or passengers, and the dissipation of the extinguishing agent in Class "C" compartments must be shown by tests in flight. During these tests it must be shown that no inadvertent operation of smoke or fire detectors in other compartments within the airplane would occur as a result of fire contained in any one compartment, either during the time it is being extinguished, or thereafter, unless the extinguishing system floods those compartments simultaneously.

§121.225 Propeller deicing fluid.

If combustible fluid is used for propeller deicing, the certificate holder must comply with §121.255.

§121.227 Pressure cross-feed arrangements.

(a) Pressure cross-feed lines may not pass through parts of the airplane used for carrying persons or cargo unless—

(1) There is a means to allow crewmembers to shut off the supply of fuel to these lines; or

(2) The lines are enclosed in a fuel and fume-proof enclosure that is ventilated and drained to the exterior of the airplane.

However, such an enclosure need not be used if those lines incorporate no fittings on or within the personnel or cargo areas and are suitably routed or protected to prevent accidental damage.

(b) Lines that can be isolated from the rest of the fuel system by valves at each end must incorporate provisions for relieving excessive pressures that may result from exposure of the isolated line to high temperatures.

§121.229 Location of fuel tanks.

(a) Fuel tanks must be located in accordance with §121.255.

(b) No part of the engine nacelle skin that lies immediately behind a major air outlet from the engine compartment may be used as the wall of an integral tank.

(c) Fuel tanks must be isolated from personnel compartments by means of fume- and fuel-proof enclosures.

§121.231 Fuel system lines and fittings.

(a) Fuel lines must be installed and supported so as to prevent excessive vibration and so as to be adequate to withstand loads due to fuel pressure and accelerated flight conditions.

(b) Lines connected to components of the airplanes between which there may be relative motion must incorporate provisions for flexibility.

(c) Flexible connections in lines that may be under pressure and subject to axial loading must use flexible hose assemblies rather than hose clamp connections.

(d) Flexible hose must be of an acceptable type or proven suitable for the particular application.

§121.233 Fuel lines and fittings in designated fire zones.

Fuel lines and fittings in each designated fire zone must comply with §121.259.

§121.235 Fuel valves.

Each fuel valve must—

(a) Comply with §121.257;

(b) Have positive stops or suitable index provisions in the "on" and "off" positions; and

(c) Be supported so that loads resulting from its operation or from accelerated flight conditions are not transmitted to the lines connected to the valve.

§121.237 Oil lines and fittings in designated fire zones.

Oil line and fittings in each designated fire zone must comply with §121.259.

§121.239 Oil valves.

(a) Each oil valve must—

(1) Comply with §121.257;

(2) Have positive stops or suitable index provisions in the "on" and "off" positions; and

(3) Be supported so that loads resulting from its operation or from accelerated flight conditions are not transmitted to the lines attached to the valve.

(b) The closing of an oil shutoff means must not prevent feathering the propeller, unless equivalent safety provisions are incorporated.

§121.241 Oil system drains.

Accessible drains incorporating either a manual or automatic means for positive locking in the closed position, must be provided to allow safe drainage of the entire oil system.

§121.243 Engine breather lines.

(a) Engine breather lines must be so arranged that condensed water vapor that may freeze and obstruct the line cannot accumulate at any point.

(b) Engine breathers must discharge in a location that does not constitute a fire hazard in case foaming occurs and so that oil emitted from the line does not impinge upon the pilots' windshield.

(c) Engine breathers may not discharge into the engine air induction system.

§121.245 Fire walls.

Each engine, auxiliary power unit, fuel-burning heater, or other item of combustion equipment that is intended for operation in flight must be isolated from the rest of the airplane by means of firewalls or shrouds, or by other equivalent means.

§121.247 Fire-wall construction.

Each fire wall and shroud must—

(a) Be so made that no hazardous quantity of air, fluids, or flame can pass from the engine compartment to other parts of the airplane;

(b) Have all openings in the fire wall or shroud sealed with close-fitting fire-proof grommets, bushings, or firewall fittings;

(c) Be made of fireproof material; and

(d) Be protected against corrosion.

§121.249 Cowling.

(a) Cowling must be made and supported so as to resist the vibration inertia, and air loads to which it may be normally subjected.

(b) Provisions must be made to allow rapid and complete drainage of the cowling in normal ground and flight attitudes. Drains must not discharge in locations constituting a fire hazard. Parts of the cowling that are subjected to high temperatures because they are near exhaust system parts or because of exhaust gas impingement must be made of fireproof material. Unless otherwise specified in these regulations all other parts of the cowling must be made of material that is at least fire resistant.

§121.251 Engine accessory section diaphragm.

Unless equivalent protection can be shown by other means, a diaphragm that complies with §121.247 must be provided on air-cooled engines to isolate the engine power section and all parts of the exhaust system from the engine accessory compartment.

§121.253 Powerplant fire protection.

(a) Designated fire zones must be protected from fire by compliance with §§121.255 through 121.261.

(b) Designated fire zones are—

(1) Engine accessory sections;

(2) Installations where no isolation is provided between the engine and accessory compartment; and

(3) Areas that contain auxiliary power units, fuel-burning heaters, and other combustion equipment.

§121.255 Flammable fluids.

(a) No tanks or reservoirs that are a part of a system containing flammable fluids or gases may be located in designated fire zones, except where the fluid contained, the design of the system, the materials used in the tank, the shutoff means, and the connections, lines, and controls provide equivalent safety.

(b) At least one-half inch of clear airspace must be provided between any tank or reservoir and a firewall or shroud isolating a designated fire zone.

§121.257 Shutoff means.

(a) Each engine must have a means for shutting off or otherwise preventing hazardous amounts of fuel, oil, deicer, and other flammable fluids from flowing into, within, or through any designated fire zone. However, means need not be provided to shut off flow in lines that are an integral part of an engine.

(b) The shutoff means must allow an emergency operating sequence that is compatible with the emergency operation of other equipment, such as feathering the propeller, to facilitate rapid and effective control of fires.

(c) Shutoff means must be located outside of designated fire zones, unless equivalent safety is provided, and it must be shown that no hazardous amount of flammable fluid will drain into any designated fire zone after a shut off.

(d) Adequate provisions must be made to guard against inadvertent operation of the shutoff means and to make it possible for the crew to reopen the shutoff means after it has been closed.

§121.259 Lines and fittings.

(a) Each line, and its fittings, that is located in a designated fire zone, if it carries flammable fluids or gases under pressure, or is attached directly to the engine, or is subject to relative motion between components (except lines and fittings forming an integral part of the engine), must be flexible and fire-resistant with fire-resistant, factory-fixed, detachable, or other approved fire-resistant ends.

(b) Lines and fittings that are not subject to pressure or to relative motion between components must be of fire-resistant materials.

§121.261 Vent and drain lines.

All vent and drain lines and their fittings, that are located in a designated fire zone must, if they carry flammable fluids or gases, comply with §121.259, if the Administrator finds that the rupture or breakage of any vent or drain line may result in a fire hazard.

§121.263 Fire-extinguishing systems.

(a) Unless the certificate holder shows that equivalent protection against destruction of the airplane in case of fire is provided by the use of fireproof materials in the nacelle and other components that would be subjected to flame, fire-extinguishing systems must be provided to serve all designated fire zones.

(b) Materials in the fire-extinguishing system must not react chemically with the extinguishing agent so as to be a hazard.

§121.265 Fire-extinguishing agents.

Only methyl bromide, carbon dioxide, or another agent that has been shown to provide equivalent extinguishing action may be used as a fire-extinguishing agent. If methyl bromide or any other toxic extinguishing agent is used, provisions must be made to prevent harmful concentrations of fluid or fluid vapors from entering any personnel compartment either because of leakage during normal operation of the airplane or because of discharging the fire extinguisher on the ground or in flight when there is a defect in the extinguishing system. If a methyl bromide system is used, the containers must be charged with dry agent and sealed by the fire-extinguisher manufacturer or some other person using satisfactory recharging equipment. If carbon dioxide is used, it must not be possible to discharge enough gas into the personnel compartments to create a danger of suffocating the occupants.

§121.267 Extinguishing agent container pressure relief.

Extinguishing agent containers must be provided with a pressure relief to prevent bursting of the container because of excessive internal pressures. The discharge line from the relief connection must terminate outside the airplane in a place convenient for inspection on the ground. An indicator must be provided at the discharge end of the line to provide a visual indication when the container has discharged.

§121.269 Extinguishing agent container compartment temperature.

Precautions must be taken to insure that the extinguishing agent containers are installed in places where reasonable temperatures can be maintained for effective use of the extinguishing system.

§121.271 Fire-extinguishing system materials.

(a) Except as provided in paragraph (b) of this section, each component of a fire-extinguishing system that is in a designated fire zone must be made of fireproof materials.

(b) Connections that are subject to relative motion between components of the airplane must be made of flexible materials that are at least fire-resistant and be located so as to minimize the probability of failure.

§121.273 Fire-detector systems.

Enough quick-acting fire detectors must be provided in each designated fire zone to assure the detection of any fire that may occur in that zone.

§121.275 Fire detectors.

Fire detectors must be made and installed in a manner that assures their ability to resist, without failure, all vibration, inertia, and other loads to which they may be normally subjected. Fire detectors must be unaffected by exposure to fumes, oil, water, or other fluids that may be present.

§121.277 Protection of other airplane components against fire.

(a) Except as provided in paragraph (b) of this section, all airplane surfaces aft of the nacelles in the area of one nacelle diameter on both sides of the nacelle centerline must be made of material that is at least fire resistant.

(b) Paragraph (a) of this section does not apply to tail surfaces lying behind nacelles unless the dimensional configuration of the airplane is such that the tail surfaces could be affected readily by heat, flames, or sparks emanating from a designated fire zone or from the engine compartment of any nacelle.

§121.279 Control of engine rotation.

(a) Except as provided in paragraph (b) of this section, each airplane must have a means of individually stopping and restarting the rotation of any engine in flight.

(b) In the case of turbine engine installations, a means of stopping the rotation need be provided only if the Administrator finds that rotation could jeopardize the safety of the airplane.

§121.281 Fuel system independence.

(a) Each airplane fuel system must be arranged so that the failure of any one component does not result in the irrecoverable loss of power of more than one engine.

(b) A separate fuel tank need not be provided for each engine if the certificate holder shows that the fuel system incorporates features that provide equivalent safety.

§121.283 Induction system ice prevention.

A means for preventing the malfunctioning of each engine due to ice accumulation in the engine air induction system must be provided for each airplane.

§121.285 Carriage of cargo in passenger compartments.

(a) Except as provided in paragraph (b), (c), or (d) or this section, no certificate holder may carry cargo in the passenger compartment of an airplane.

(b) Cargo may be carried anywhere in the passenger compartment if it is carried in an approved cargo bin that meets the following requirements:

(1) The bin must withstand the load factors and emergency landing conditions applicable to the passenger seats of the airplane in which the bin is installed, multiplied by a factor of 1.15, using the combined weight of the bin and the maximum weight of cargo that may be carried in the bin.

(2) The maximum weight of cargo that the bin is approved to carry and any instructions necessary to insure proper weight distribution within the bin must be conspicuously marked on the bin.

(3) The bin may not impose any load on the floor or other structure of the airplane that exceeds the load limitations of that structure.

(4) The bin must be attached to the seat tracks or to the floor structure of the airplane, and its attachment must withstand the load factors and emergency landing conditions applicable to the passenger seats of the airplane in which the bin is installed, multiplied by either the factor 1.15 or the seat attachment factor specified for the airplane, whichever is greater, using the combined weight of the bin and the maximum weight of cargo that may be carried in the bin.

(5) The bin may not be installed in a position that restricts access to or use of any required emergency exit, or of the aisle in the passenger compartment.

(6) The bin must be fully enclosed and made of material that is at least flame resistant.

(7) Suitable safeguards must be provided within the bin to prevent the cargo from shifting under emergency landing conditions.

(8) The bin may not be installed in a position that obscures any passenger's view of the "seat belt" sign "no smoking" sign, or any required exit sign, unless an auxiliary sign or other approved means for proper notification of the passenger is provided.

(c) Cargo may be carried aft of a bulkhead or divider in any passenger compartment provided the cargo is restrained to the load factors in §25.561(b)(3) and is loaded as follows:

(1) It is properly secured by a safety belt or other tiedown having enough strength to eliminate the possibility of shifting under all normally anticipated flight and ground conditions.

(2) It is packaged or covered in a manner to avoid possible injury to passengers and passenger compartment occupants.

(3) It does not impose any load on seats or the floor structure that exceeds the load limitation for those components.

(4) Its location does not restrict access to or use of any required emergency or regular exit, or of the aisle in the passenger compartment.

(5) Its location does not obscure any passenger's view of the "seat belt" sign, "no smoking" sign, or required exit sign, unless an auxiliary sign or other approved means for proper notification of the passenger is provided.

(d) Cargo, including carry-on baggage, may be carried anywhere in the passenger compartment of a nontransport category airplane type certificated after December 31, 1964, if it is carried in an approved cargo rack, bin, or compartment installed in or on the airplane, if it is secured by an approved means, or if it is carried in accordance with each of the following:

(1) For cargo, it is properly secured by a safety belt or other tie-down having enough strength to eliminate the possibility of shifting under all normally anticipated flight and ground conditions, or for carry-on baggage, it is restrained so as to prevent its movement during air turbulence.

(2) It is packaged or covered to avoid possible injury to occupants.

(3) It does not impose any load on seats or in the floor structure that exceeds the load limitation for those components.

(4) It is not located in a position that obstructs the access to, or use of, any required emergency or regular exit, or the use of the aisle between the crew and the passenger compartment, or is located in a position that obscures any passenger's view of the "seat belt" sign, "no smoking" sign or placard, or any required exit sign, unless an auxiliary sign or other approved means for proper notification of the passengers is provided.

(5) It is not carried directly above seated occupants.

(6) It is stowed in compliance with this section for takeoff and landing.

(7) For cargo-only operations, paragraph (d)(4) of this section does not apply if the cargo is loaded so that at least one emergency or regular exit is available to provide all occupants of the airplane a means of unobstructed exit from the airplane if an emergency occurs.

[Docket No. 6258, 29 FR 19202, Dec. 31, 1964; as amended by Amdt. 121–179, 47 FR 33390, Aug. 2, 1982; Amdt. 121–251, 60 FR 65928, Dec. 20, 1995]

§121.287 Carriage of cargo in cargo compartments.

When cargo is carried in cargo compartments that are designed to require the physical entry of a crewmember to extinguish any fire that may occur during flight, the cargo must be loaded so as to allow a crewmember to effectively reach all parts of the compartment with the contents of a hand fire extinguisher.

§121.289 Landing gear: Aural warning device.

(a) Except for airplanes that comply with the requirements of §25.729 of this chapter on or after January 6, 1992, each airplane must have a landing gear aural warning device that functions continuously under the following conditions:

(1) For airplanes with an established approach wing-flap position, whenever the wing flaps are extended beyond the maximum certificated approach climb configuration position in the Airplane Flight Manual and the landing gear is not fully extended and locked.

(2) For airplanes without an established approach climb wing-flap position, whenever the wing flaps are extended beyond the position at which landing gear extension is normally performed and the landing gear is not fully extended and locked.

(b) The warning system required by paragraph (a) of this section—

(1) May not have a manual shutoff;

(2) Must be in addition to the throttle-actuated device installed under the type certification airworthiness requirements; and

(3) May utilize any part of the throttle-actuated system including the aural warning device.

(c) The flap position sensing unit may be installed at any suitable place in the airplane.

[Docket No. 6258, 29 FR 19202, Dec. 31, 1964; as amended by Amdt. 121–3, 30 FR 3638, March 19, 1965; Amdt. 121–130, 41 FR 47229, Oct. 28, 1976; Amdt. 121–227, 56 FR 63762, Dec. 5, 1991; Amdt. 121–251, 60 FR 65929, Dec. 20, 1995]

§121.291 Demonstration of emergency evacuation procedures.

(a) Except as provided in paragraph (a)(1) of this section, each certificate holder must conduct an actual demonstration of emergency evacuation procedures in accordance with paragraph (a) of appendix D to this part to show that each type and model of airplane with a seating capacity of more than 44 passengers to be used in its passenger-carrying operations allows the evacuation of the full capacity, including crewmembers, in 90 seconds or less.

(1) An actual demonstration need not be conducted if that airplane type and model has been shown to be in compliance with this paragraph in effect on or after October 24, 1967, or, if during type certification, with §25.803 of this chapter in effect on or after December 1, 1978.

(2) Any actual demonstration conducted after September 27, 1993, must be in accordance with paragraph (a) of Appendix D to this part in effect on or after that date or with §25.803 in effect on or after that date.

(b) Each certificate holder conducting operations with airplanes with a seating capacity of more than 44 passengers must conduct a partial demonstration of emergency evacuation procedures in accordance with paragraph (c) of this section upon:

(1) Initial introduction of a type and model of airplane into passenger-carrying operation;

(2) Changing the number, location, or emergency evacuation duties or procedures of flight attendants who are required by §121.391; or

(3) Changing the number, location, type of emergency exits, or type of opening mechanism on emergency exits available for evacuation.

(c) In conducting the partial demonstration required by paragraph (b) of this section, each certificate holder must:

(1) Demonstrate the effectiveness of its crewmember emergency training and evacuation procedures by conducting a demonstration, not requiring passengers and observed by the Administrator, in which the flight attendants for that type and model of airplane, using that operator's line operating procedures, open 50 percent of the required floor-level emergency exits and 50 percent of the required non-floor-level emergency exits whose opening by a flight attendant is defined as an emergency evacuation duty under §121.397, and deploy 50 percent of the exit slides. The exits and slides will be selected by the administrator and must be ready for use within 15 seconds;

(2) Apply for and obtain approval from the certificate-holding district office before conducting the demonstration;

(3) Use flight attendants in this demonstration who have been selected at random by the Administrator, have completed the certificate holder's FAA-approved training program for the type and model of airplane, and have passed a written or practical examination on the emergency equipment and procedures; and

(4) Apply for and obtain approval from the certificate-holding district office before commencing operations with this type and model airplane.

(d) Each certificate holder operating or proposing to operate one or more landplanes in extended overwater operations, or otherwise required to have certain equipment under §121.339, must show, by simulated ditching conducted in accordance with paragraph (b) of appendix D to this part, that it has the ability to efficiently carry out its ditching procedures. For certificate holders subject to §121.2(a)(1), this paragraph applies only when a new type or model airplane is introduced into the certificate holder's operations after January 19, 1996.

(e) For a type and model airplane for which the simulated ditching specified in paragraph (d) has been conducted by a part 121 certificate holder, the requirements of paragraphs (b)(2), (b)(4), and (b)(5) of appendix D to this part are complied with if each life raft is removed from stowage, one life raft is launched and inflated (or one slide life raft is inflated) and crewmembers assigned to the inflated life raft display and describe the use of each item of required emergency equipment. The life raft or slide life raft to be inflated will be selected by the Administrator.

[Docket No. 21269, 46 FR 61453, Dec. 17, 1981; as amended by Amdt. 121–233, 58 FR 45230, Aug. 26, 1993; Amdt. 121–251, 60 FR 65929, Dec. 20, 1995; Amdt. 121–307, 69 FR 67499, Nov. 17, 2004]

§121.293 Special airworthiness requirements for nontransport category airplanes type certificated after December 31, 1964.

No certificate holder may operate a nontransport category airplane manufactured after December 20, 1999, unless the airplane contains a takeoff warning system that meets the requirements of 14 CFR 25.703. However, the takeoff warning system does not have to cover any device for which it has been demonstrated that takeoff with that device in the most adverse position would not create a hazardous condition.

[Docket No. 28154, 60 FR 65929, Dec. 20, 1995]

Subpart L— Maintenance, Preventive Maintenance, and Alterations

Source: Docket No. 6258, 29 FR 19210, Dec. 31, 1964, unless otherwise noted.

§121.361 Applicability.

(a) Except as provided by paragraph (b) of this section, this subpart prescribes requirements for maintenance, preventive maintenance, and alternations for all certificate holders.

(b) The Administrator may amend a certificate holder's operations specifications to permit deviation from those provisions of this subpart that would prevent the return to service and use of airframe components, powerplants, appliances, and spare parts thereof because those items have been maintained, altered, or inspected by persons employed outside the United States who do not hold U.S. airman certificates. Each certificate holder who uses parts under this deviation must provide for surveillance of facilities and practices to assure that all work performed on these parts is accomplished in accordance with the certificate holder's manual.

[Docket No. 8754, 33 FR 14406, Sept. 25, 1968]

§121.363 Responsibility for airworthiness.

(a) Each certificate holder is primarily responsible for—

(1) The airworthiness of its aircraft, including airframes, aircraft engines, propellers, appliances, and parts thereof; and

(2) The performance of the maintenance, preventive maintenance, and alteration of its aircraft, including airframes, aircraft engines, propellers, appliances, emergency equipment, and parts thereof, in accordance with its manual and the regulations of this chapter.

(b) A certificate holder may make arrangements with another person for the performance of any maintenance, preventive maintenance, or alterations. However, this does not relieve the certificate holder of the responsibility specified in paragraph (a) of this section.

[Docket No. 6258, 29 FR 19210, Dec. 31, 1964; as amended by Amdt. 121–106, 38 FR 22378, Aug. 20, 1973]

§121.365 Maintenance, preventive maintenance, and alteration organization.

(a) Each certificate holder that performs any of its maintenance (other than required inspections), preventive maintenance, or alterations, and each person with whom it arranges for the performance of that work must have an organization adequate to perform the work.

(b) Each certificate holder that performs any inspections required by its manual in accordance with §121.369(b)(2) or (3) (in this subpart referred to as *required inspections*) and each person with whom it arranges for the performance of that work must have an organization adequate to perform that work.

(c) Each person performing required inspections in addition to other maintenance, preventive maintenance, or alterations, shall organize the performance of those functions so as to separate the required inspection functions from the other maintenance, preventive maintenance, and alteration functions. The separation shall be below the level of administrative control at which overall responsibility for the required inspection functions and other maintenance, preventive maintenance, and alteration functions are exercised.

[Docket No. 6258, 29 FR 19210, Dec. 31, 1964; as amended by Amdt. 121–3, 30 FR 3639, March 19, 1965]

§121.367 Maintenance, preventive maintenance, and alterations programs.

Each certificate holder shall have an inspection program and a program covering other maintenance, preventive maintenance, and alterations that ensures that—

(a) Maintenance, preventive maintenance, and alterations performed by it, or by other persons, are performed in accordance with the certificate holder's manual;

(b) Competent personnel and adequate facilities and equipment are provided for the proper performance of maintenance, preventive maintenance, and alterations; and

(c) Each aircraft released to service is airworthy and has been properly maintained for operation under this part.

[Docket No. 6258, 29 FR 19210, Dec. 31, 1964; as amended by Amdt. 121–100, 37 FR 28053, Dec. 20, 1972]

§121.368 Aging airplane inspections and records reviews.

(a) *Applicability.* This section applies to all airplanes operated by a certificate holder under this part, except for those airplanes operated between any point within the State of Alaska and any other point within the State of Alaska.

(b) *Operation after inspection and records review.* After the dates specified in this paragraph, a certificate holder may not operate an airplane under this part unless the Administrator has notified the certificate holder that the Administrator has completed the aging airplane inspection and records review required by this section. During the inspection and records review, the certificate holder must demonstrate to the Administrator that the maintenance of age-sensitive parts and components of the airplane has been adequate and timely enough to ensure the highest degree of safety.

(1) Airplanes exceeding 24 years in service on December 8, 2003; initial and repetitive inspections and records reviews. For an airplane that has exceeded 24 years in service on December 8, 2003, no later than December 5, 2007, and thereafter at intervals not to exceed 7 years.

(2) Airplanes exceeding 14 years in service but not 24 years in service on December 8, 2003; initial and repetitive inspections and records reviews. For an airplane that has exceeded 14 years in service but not 24 years in service on December 8, 2003, no later than December 4, 2008, and thereafter at intervals not to exceed 7 years.

(3) Airplanes not exceeding 14 years in service on December 8, 2003; initial and repetitive inspections and records reviews. For an airplane that has not exceeded 14 years in service on December 8, 2003, no later than 5 years after the start of the airplane's 15th year in service and thereafter at intervals not to exceed 7 years.

(c) *Unforeseen schedule conflict.* In the event of an unforeseen scheduling conflict for a specific airplane, the Administrator may approve an extension of up to 90 days beyond an interval specified in paragraph (b) of this section.

(d) *Airplane and records availability.* The certificate holder must make available to the Administrator each airplane for which an inspection and records review is required under this section, in a condition for inspection specified by the Administrator, together with records containing the following information:

(1) Total years in service of the airplane;

(2) Total time in service of the airframe;

(3) Total flight cycles of the airframe;

(4) Date of the last inspection and records review required by this section;

(5) Current status of life-limited parts of the airframe;

(6) Time since the last overhaul of all structural components required to be overhauled on a specific time basis;

(7) Current inspection status of the airplane, including the time since the last inspection required by the inspection program under which the airplane is maintained;

(8) Current status of applicable airworthiness directives, including the date and methods of compliance, and if the airworthiness directive involves recurring action, the time and date when the next action is required;

(9) A list of major structural alterations; and

(10) A report of major structural repairs and the current inspection status for those repairs.

(e) *Notification to Administrator.* Each certificate holder must notify the Administrator at least 60 days before the date on which the airplane and airplane records will be made available for the inspection and records review.

[Docket No. FAA–1999–5401, 67 FR 72761, Dec. 6, 2002; as amended by Amdt. 121–284, 70 FR 5532, Feb. 2, 2005; Amdt. 121–310, 70 FR 23936, May 6, 2005]

§121.369 Manual requirements.

(a) The certificate holder shall put in its manual a chart or description of the certificate holder's organization required by §121.365 and a list of persons with whom it has arranged for the performance of any of its required inspections, other maintenance, preventive maintenance, or alterations, including a general description of that work.

(b) The certificate holder's manual must contain the programs required by §121.367 that must be followed in performing maintenance, preventive maintenance, and alterations of that certificate holder's airplanes, including airframes, aircraft engines, propellers, appliances, emergency equipment, and parts thereof, and must include at least the following:

(1) The method of performing routine and nonroutine maintenance (other than required inspections), preventive maintenance, and alterations.

(2) A designation of the items of maintenance and alteration that must be inspected (required inspections), including at least those that could result in a failure, malfunction, or defect endangering the safe operation of the aircraft, if not performed properly or if improper parts or materials are used.

(3) The method of performing required inspections and a designation by occupational title of personnel authorized to perform each required inspection.

(4) Procedures for the reinspection of work performed pursuant to previous required inspection findings (*buy-back procedures*).

(5) Procedures, standards, and limits necessary for required inspections and acceptance or rejection of the items required to be inspected and for periodic inspection and calibration of precision tools, measuring devices, and test equipment.

(6) Procedures to ensure that all required inspections are performed.

(7) Instructions to prevent any person who performs any item of work from performing any required inspection of that work.

(8) Instructions and procedures to prevent any decision of an inspector, regarding any required inspection from being countermanded by persons other than supervisory personnel of the inspection unit, or a person at that level of administrative control that has overall responsibility for the management of both the required inspection functions and the other maintenance, preventive maintenance, and alterations functions.

(9) Procedures to ensure that required inspections, other maintenance, preventive maintenance, and alterations that are not completed as a result of shift changes or similar work interruptions are properly completed before the aircraft is released to service.

(c) The certificate holder must set forth in its manual a suitable system (which may include a coded system) that provides for preservation and retrieval of information in a manner acceptable to the Administrator and that provides—

(1) A description (or reference to data acceptable to the Administrator) of the work performed;

(2) The name of the person performing the work if the work is performed by a person outside the organization of the certificate holder; and

(3) The name or other positive identification of the individual approving the work.

[Docket No. 6258, 29 FR 19210, Dec. 31, 1964; as amended by Amdt. 121–94, 37 FR 15983, Aug. 9, 1972; Amdt. 121–106, 38 FR 22378, Aug. 20, 1973]

§121.370 Special maintenance program requirements.

(a) No certificate holder may operate an Airbus Model A300 (excluding the –600 series), British Aerospace Model BAC 1–11, Boeing Model 707, 720, 727, 737, or 747, McDonnell Douglas Model DC–8, DC–9/MD–80 or DC–10, Fokker Model F28, or Lockheed Model L–1011 airplane beyond the applicable fflight cycle implementation time specified below, or May 25, 2001, whichever occurs later, unless operations specifications have been issued to reference repair assessment guidelines applicable to the fuselage pressure boundary (fuselage skin, door skin, and bulkhead webs), and those guidelines are incorporated in its maintenance program. The repair assessment guidelines must be approved by the FAA Aircraft Certification Office (ACO), or office of the Transport Airplane Directorate, having cognizance over the type certificate for the affected airplane.

(1) For the Airbus Model A300 (excluding the –600 series), the flight cycle implementation time is:

(i) Model B2: 36,000 flights.

(ii) Model B4–100 (including Model B4–2C): 30,000 flights above the window line, and 36,000 flights below the window line.

(iii) Model B4–200: 25,500 flights above the window line, and 34,000 flights below the window line.

(2) For all models of the British Aerospace BAC 1–11, the flight cycle implementation time is 60,000 flights.

(3) For all models of the Boeing 707, the flight cycle implementation time is 15,000 flights.

(4) For all models of the Boeing 720, the flight cycle implementation time is 23,000 flights.

(5) For all models of the Boeing 727, the flight cycle implementation time is 45,000 flights.

(6) For all models of the Boeing 737, the flight cycle implementation time is 60,000 flights.

(7) For all models of the Boeing 747, the flight cycle implementation time is 15,000 flights.

(8) For all models of the McDonnell Douglas DC–8, the flight cycle implementation time is 30,000 flights.

(9) For all models of the McDonnell Douglas DC–9/MD–80, the flight cycle implementation time is 60,000 flights.

(10) For all models of the McDonnell Douglas DC–10, the flight cycle implementation time is 30,000 flights.

(11) For all models of the Lockheed L–1011, the flight cycle implementation time is 27,000 flights.

(12) For the Fokker F–28 Mark 1000, 2000, 3000, and 4000, the flight cycle implementation time is 60,000 flights.

(b) After December 16, 2008, no certificate holder may operate a turbine-powered transport category airplane with a type certificate issued after January 1, 1958, and either a maximum type certificated passenger capacity of 30 or more, or a maximum type certificated payload capacity of 7,500 pounds or more, unless instructions for maintenance and inspection of the fuel tank system are incorporated in its maintenance program. These instructions must address the actual configuration of the fuel tank systems of each affected airplane and must be approved by the FAA Aircraft Certification Office (ACO), or office of the Transport Airplane Directorate, having cognizance over the type certificate for the affected airplane. Operators must submit their request through an appropriate FAA Principal Maintenance Inspector, who may add comments and then send it to the manager of the appropriate office. Thereafter, the approved instructions can be revised only with the approval of the FAA Aircraft Certification Office (ACO), or office of the Transport Airplane Directorate, having cognizance over the type certificate for the affected airplane. Operators must submit their requests for revisions through an appropriate FAA Principal Maintenance Inspector, who may add comments and then send it to the manager of the appropriate office.

[Docket No. 29104, 65 FR 24125, April 25, 2000; as amended by Amdt. 121–275, 65 FR 50744, Aug. 21, 2000; Amdt. 121–282, 66 FR 23130, May 7, 2001; Amdt. 121–285, 67 FR 72834, Dec. 9, 2002; Amdt. 121–305, 69 FR 45942, July 30, 2004]

§121.370a Supplemental inspections.

(a) ***Applicability.*** Except as specified in paragraph (b) of this section, this section applies to transport category, turbine powered airplanes with a type certificate issued after January 1, 1958, that as a result of original type certification or later increase in capacity have—

(1) A maximum type certificated passenger seating capacity of 30 or more; or

(2) A maximum payload capacity of 7,500 pounds or more.

(b) ***Exception.*** This section does not apply to an airplane operated by a certificate holder under this part between any point within the State of Alaska and any other point within the State of Alaska.

(c) ***General requirements.*** After December 20, 2010, a certificate holder may not operate an airplane under this part unless the following requirements have been met:

(1) The maintenance program for the airplane includes FAA-approved damage-tolerance-based inspections and procedures for airplane structure susceptible to fatigue cracking that could contribute to a catastrophic failure. These inspections and procedures must take into account the adverse affects repairs, alterations, and modifications may have on fatigue cracking and the inspection of this airplane structure.

(2) The damage-tolerance-based inspections and procedures identified in this section and any revisions to these inspections and procedures must be approved by the Aircraft Certification Office or office of the Transport Airplane Directorate with oversight responsibility for the relevant type certificate or supplemental type certificate, as determined by the Administrator. The certificate holder must include the damage-tolerance-based inspections and procedures in the certificate holder's FAA-approved maintenance program.

[Docket No. FAA–1999–5401, 70 FR 5532, Feb. 2, 2005]

§121.371 Required inspection personnel.

(a) No person may use any person to perform required inspections unless the person performing the inspection is appropriately certificated, properly trained, qualified, and authorized to do so.

(b) No person may allow any person to perform a required inspection unless, at that time, the person performing that inspection is under the supervision and control of an inspection unit.

(c) No person may perform a required inspection if he performed the item of work required to be inspected.

(d) Each certificated holder shall maintain, or shall determine that each person with whom it arranges to perform its required inspections maintains, a current listing of persons who have been trained, qualified, and authorized to conduct required inspections. The persons must be identified by name, occupational title, and the inspections that they are authorized to perform. The certificated holder (or person with whom it arranges to perform its required inspections) shall give written information to each person so authorized describing the extent of his responsibilities authorities, and inspectional limitations. The list shall be made available for inspection by the Administrator upon request.

§121.373 Continuing analysis and surveillance.

(a) Each certificate holder shall establish and maintain a system for the continuing analysis and surveillance of the performance and effectiveness of its inspection program and the program covering other maintenance, preventive maintenance, and alterations and for the correction of any deficiency in those programs, regardless of whether those programs are carried out by the certificate holder or by another person.

(b) Whenever the Administrator finds that either or both of the programs described in paragraph (a) of this section does not contain adequate procedures and standards to meet the requirements of this part, the certificate holder shall, after notification by the Administrator, make any changes in those programs that are necessary to meet those requirements.

(c) A certificate holder may petition the Administrator to reconsider the notice to make a change in a program. The petition must be filed with the FAA certificate-holding district office charged with the overall inspection of the certificate holder's operations within 30 days after the certificate holder receives the notice. Except in the case of an emergency requiring immediate action in the interest of safety, the filing of the petition stays the notice pending a decision by the Administrator.

[Docket No. 6258, 29 FR 19210, Dec. 31, 1964; as amended by Amdt. 121–207, 54 FR 39293, Sept. 25, 1989; Amdt. 121–253, 61 FR, Jan. 26, 1996]

§121.375 Maintenance and preventive maintenance training program.

Each certificate holder or person performing maintenance or preventive maintenance functions for it shall have a training program to ensure that each person (including inspection personnel) who determines the adequacy of work done is fully informed about procedures and techniques and new equipment in use and is competent to perform his duties.

§121.377 Maintenance and preventive maintenance personnel duty time limitations.

Within the United States, each certificate holder (or person performing maintenance or preventive maintenance functions for it) shall relieve each person performing maintenance or preventive maintenance from duty for a period of at least 24 consecutive hours during any seven consecutive days, or the equivalent thereof within any one calendar month.

§121.378 Certificate requirements.

(a) Except for maintenance, preventive maintenance, alterations, and required inspections performed by a certificated repair station that is located outside the United States, each person who is directly in charge of maintenance, preventive maintenance, or alterations, and each person performing required inspections must hold an appropriate airman certificate.

(b) For the purposes of this section, a person *directly in charge* is each person assigned to a position in which he is responsible for the work of a shop or station that performs maintenance, preventive maintenance, alterations, or other functions affecting aircraft airworthiness. A person who is *directly in charge* need not physically observe and direct each worker constantly but must be available for consultation and decision on matters requiring instruction or decision from higher authority than that of the persons performing the work.

[Docket No. 6258, 29 FR 19210, Dec. 31, 1964; as amended by Amdt. 121–21, 31 FR 10618, Aug. 9, 1966; Amdt. 121–286, 66 FR 41116, Aug. 6, 2001]

§121.379 Authority to perform and approve maintenance, preventive maintenance, and alterations.

(a) A certificate holder may perform, or it may make arrangements with other persons to perform, maintenance, preventive maintenance, and alterations as provided in its continuous airworthiness maintenance program and its maintenance manual. In addition, a certificate holder may perform these functions for another certificate holder as provided in the continuous airworthiness maintenance program and maintenance manual of the other certificate holder.

(b) A certificate holder may approve any aircraft, airframe, aircraft engine, propeller, or appliance for return to service after maintenance, preventive maintenance, or alterations that are performed under paragraph (a) of this section. However, in the case of a major repair or major alteration, the work must have been done in accordance with technical data approved by the Administrator.

[Docket No. 10289, 35 FR 16793, Oct. 30, 1970]

§121.380 Maintenance recording requirements.

(a) Each certificate holder shall keep (using the system specified in the manual required in §121.369) the following records for the periods specified in paragraph (c) of this section:

(1) All the records necessary to show that all requirements for the issuance of an airworthiness release under §121.709 have been met.

(2) Records containing the following information:

(i) The total time in service of the airframe.

(ii) Except as provided in paragraph (b) of this section, the total time in service of each engine and propeller.

(iii) The current status of life-limited parts of each airframe, engine, propeller, and appliance.

(iv) The time since last overhaul of all items installed on the aircraft which are required to be overhauled on a specified time basis.

(v) The identification of the current inspection status of the aircraft, including the times since the last inspections required by the inspection program under which the aircraft and its appliances are maintained.

(vi) The current status of applicable airworthiness directives, including the date and methods of compliance, and, if the airworthiness directive involves recurring action, the time and date when the next action is required.

(vii) A list of current major alterations to each airframe, engine, propeller, and appliance.

(b) A certificate holder need not record the total time in service of an engine or propeller on a transport category airplane that has a passenger seat configuration of more than 30 seats or a nontransport category airplane type certificated before January 1, 1958, until the following, whichever occurs first:

(1) March 20, 1997; or

(2) The date of the first overhaul of the engine or propeller, as applicable, after January 19, 1996

(c) Each certificate holder shall retain the records required to be kept by this section for the following periods:

(1) Except for the records of the last complete overhaul of each airframe, engine, propeller, and appliance, the records specified in paragraph (a)(1) of this section shall be retained until the work is repeated or superseded by other work or for one year after the work is performed.

(2) The records of the last complete overhaul of each airframe, engine, propeller, and appliance shall be retained until the work is superseded by work of equivalent scope and detail.

(3) The records specified in paragraph (a)(2) of this section shall be retained and transferred with the aircraft at the time the aircraft is sold.

(d) The certificate holder shall make all maintenance records required to be kept by this section available for inspection by the Administrator or any authorized representative of the National Transportation Safety Board (NTSB).

[Docket No. 10658, 37 FR 15983, Aug. 9, 1972; amended by Amdt. 121–251, 60 FR 65933, Dec. 20, 1995]

§121.380a Transfer of maintenance records.

Each certificate holder who sells a U.S. registered aircraft shall transfer to the purchaser, at the time of sale, the following records of that aircraft, in plain language form or in coded form at the election of the purchaser, if the coded form provides for the preservation and retrieval of information in a manner acceptable to the Administrator:

(a) The record specified in §121.380(a)(2).

(b) The records specified in §121.380(a)(1) which are not included in the records covered by paragraph (a) of this section, except that the purchaser may permit the seller to keep physical custody of such records. However, custody of records in the seller does not relieve the purchaser of his responsibility under §121.380(c) to make the records available for inspection by the Administrator or any authorized representative of the National Transportation Safety Board (NTSB).

[Docket No. 10658, 37 FR 15984, August 9, 1972]

PART 125
CERTIFICATION AND OPERATIONS: AIRPLANES HAVING A SEATING CAPACITY OF 20 OR MORE PASSENGERS OR A MAXIMUM PAYLOAD CAPACITY OF 6,000 POUNDS OR MORE; AND RULES GOVERNING PERSONS ON BOARD SUCH AIRCRAFT

EDITOR'S NOTE: EFFECTIVE NOVEMBER 18, 2004, THE TSA IS REQUIRING PART 125 OPERATORS USING AIRCRAFT OVER 12,500 POUNDS NOT ALREADY OPERATING UNDER A TSA SECURITY PROGRAM TO MEET THE REQUIREMENTS OF 49 CFR 1544.101 (E) AND (F).

SPECIAL FEDERAL AVIATION REGULATIONS

SFAR No. 89 [Note]
SFAR No. 97 [Note]

Subpart A—General

Sec.
125.1 Applicability.
125.3 Deviation authority.
125.5 Operating certificate and operations specifications required.
125.7 Display of certificate.
125.9 Definitions.
125.11 Certificate eligibility and prohibited operations.

Subpart B— Certification Rules and Miscellaneous Requirements

125.21 Application for operating certificate.
125.23 Rules applicable to operations subject to this part.
125.25 Management personnel required.
125.27 Issue of certificate.
125.29 Duration of certificate.
125.31 Contents of certificate and operations specifications.
125.33 Operations specifications not a part of certificate.
125.35 Amendment of operations specifications.
125.37 Duty period limitations.
125.39 Carriage of narcotic drugs, marihuana, and depressant or stimulant drugs or substances.
125.41 Availability of certificate and operations specifications.
125.43 Use of operations specifications.
125.45 Inspection authority.
125.47 Change of address.
125.49 Airport requirements.
125.51 En route navigational facilities.
125.53 Flight locating requirements.

Subpart C—Manual Requirements

125.71 Preparation.
125.73 Contents.
125.75 Airplane flight manual.

Subpart D—Airplane Requirements

125.91 Airplane requirements: General.
125.93 Airplane limitations.

Subpart E— Special Airworthiness Requirements

125.111 General.
125.113 Cabin interiors.
125.115 Internal doors.
125.117 Ventilation.
125.119 Fire precautions.
125.121 Proof of compliance with §125.119.
125.123 Propeller deicing fluid.
125.125 Pressure cross-feed arrangements.
125.127 Location of fuel tanks.
125.129 Fuel system lines and fittings.
125.131 Fuel lines and fittings in designated fire zones.
125.133 Fuel valves.
125.135 Oil lines and fittings in designated fire zones.
125.137 Oil valves.
125.139 Oil system drains.
125.141 Engine breather lines.
125.143 Firewalls.
125.145 Firewall construction.
125.147 Cowling.
125.149 Engine accessory section diaphragm.
125.151 Powerplant fire protection.
125.153 Flammable fluids.
125.155 Shutoff means.
125.157 Lines and fittings.
125.159 Vent and drain lines.
125.161 Fire-extinguishing systems.
125.163 Fire-extinguishing agents.
125.165 Extinguishing agent container pressure relief.
125.167 Extinguishing agent container compartment temperature.
125.169 Fire-extinguishing system materials.
125.171 Fire-detector systems.
125.173 Fire detectors.
125.175 Protection of other airplane components against fire.
125.177 Control of engine rotation.
125.179 Fuel system independence.
125.181 Induction system ice prevention.
125.183 Carriage of cargo in passenger compartments.
125.185 Carriage of cargo in cargo compartments.
125.187 Landing gear: Aural warning device.
125.189 Demonstration of emergency evacuation procedures.

Subpart F— Instrument and Equipment Requirements

125.201 Inoperable instruments and equipment.
125.203 Radio and navigational equipment.
125.204 Portable electronic devices.
125.205 Equipment requirements: Airplanes under IFR.
125.206 Pitot heat indication systems.
125.207 Emergency equipment requirements.
125.209 Emergency equipment: Extended overwater operations.

125.211 Seat and safety belts.
125.213 Miscellaneous equipment.
125.215 Operating information required.
125.217 Passenger information.
125.219 Oxygen for medical use by passengers.
125.221 Icing conditions: Operating limitations.
125.223 Airborne weather radar equipment requirements.
125.224 Collision avoidance system.
125.225 Flight recorders.
125.226 Digital flight data recorders.
125.227 Cockpit voice recorders.

Subpart G — Maintenance

125.241 Applicability.
125.243 Certificate holder's responsibilities.
125.245 Organization required to perform maintenance, preventive maintenance, and alteration.
125.247 Inspection programs and maintenance.
125.248 Special maintenance program requirements.
125.249 Maintenance manual requirements.
125.251 Required inspection personnel.

Subpart H — Airman and Crewmember Requirements

125.261 Airman: Limitations on use of services.
125.263 Composition of flightcrew.
125.265 Flight engineer requirements.
125.267 Flight navigator and long-range navigation equipment.
125.269 Flight attendants.
125.271 Emergency and emergency evacuation duties.

Subpart I — Flight Crewmember Requirements

125.281 Pilot-in-command qualifications.
125.283 Second-in-command qualifications.
125.285 Pilot qualifications: Recent experience.
125.287 Initial and recurrent pilot testing requirements.
125.289 Initial and recurrent flight attendant crewmember testing requirements.
125.291 Pilot in command: Instrument proficiency check requirements.
125.293 Crewmember: Tests and checks, grace provisions, accepted standards.
125.295 Check airman authorization: Application and issue.
125.296 Training, testing, and checking conducted by training centers: Special rules.
125.297 Approval of flight simulators and flight training devices.

Subpart J — Flight Operations

125.311 Flight crewmembers at controls.
125.313 Manipulation of controls when carrying passengers.
125.315 Admission to flight deck.
125.317 Inspector's credentials: Admission to pilots' compartment: Forward observer's seat.
125.319 Emergencies.
125.321 Reporting potentially hazardous meteorological conditions and irregularities of ground and navigation facilities.
125.323 Reporting mechanical irregularities.
125.325 Instrument approach procedures and IFR landing minimums.
125.327 Briefing of passengers before flight.
125.328 Prohibition on crew interference.
125.329 Minimum altitudes for use of autopilot.
125.331 Carriage of persons without compliance with the passenger-carrying provisions of this part.
125.333 Stowage of food, beverage, and passenger service equipment during airplane movement on the surface, takeoff, and landing.

Subpart K — Flight Release Rules

125.351 Flight release authority.
125.353 Facilities and services.
125.355 Airplane equipment.
125.357 Communication and navigation facilities.
125.359 Flight release under VFR.
125.361 Flight release under IFR or over-the-top.
125.363 Flight release over water.
125.365 Alternate airport for departure.
125.367 Alternate airport for destination: IFR or over-the-top.
125.369 Alternate airport weather minimums.
125.371 Continuing flight in unsafe conditions.
125.373 Original flight release or amendment of flight release.
125.375 Fuel supply: Nonturbine and turbopropeller-powered airplanes.
125.377 Fuel supply: Turbine-engine-powered airplanes other than turbopropeller.
125.379 Landing weather minimums: IFR.
125.381 Takeoff and landing weather minimums: IFR.
125.383 Load manifest.

Subpart L — Records and Reports

125.401 Crewmember record.
125.403 Flight release form.
125.405 Disposition of load manifest, flight release, and flight plans.
125.407 Maintenance log: Airplanes.
125.409 Service difficulty reports (operational).
125.410 Service difficulty reports (structural).
125.411 Airworthiness release or maintenance record entry.

Appendix A — Additional Emergency Equipment
Appendix B — Criteria for Demonstration of Emergency Evacuation Procedures Under §125.189
Appendix C — Ice Protection
Appendix D — Airplane Flight Recorder Specifications
Appendix E — Airplane Flight Recorder Specifications

Authority: 49 U.S.C. 106(g), 40113, 44701–44702, 44705, 44710–44711, 44713, 44716–44717, 44722.

Source: Docket No. 19779, 45 FR 67235, Oct. 9, 1980, unless otherwise noted.

Special Federal Aviation Regulations

SFAR No. 89 to Part 125

Suspension of Certain Flight Data Recorder Requirements

Editorial Note: For the text of SFAR No. 89, see Part 135 of this chapter.

SFAR No. 97 to Part 125

Special Operating Rules for the Conduct of Instrument Flight Rules (IFR) Area Navigation (RNAV) Operations using Global Positioning Systems (GPS) in Alaska

Editorial Note: For the text of SFAR No. 97, see Part 91 of this chapter.

Subpart A — General

§125.1 Applicability.

(a) Except as provided in paragraphs (b), (c) and (d) of this section, this part prescribes rules governing the operations of U.S.-registered civil airplanes which have a seating configuration of 20 or more passengers or a maximum payload capacity of 6,000 pounds or more when common carriage is not involved.

(b) The rules of this part do not apply to the operations of airplanes specified in paragraph (a) of this section, when—

(1) They are required to be operated under part 121, 129, 135, or 137 of this chapter;

(2) They have been issued restricted, limited, or provisional airworthiness certificates, special flight permits, or experimental certificates;

(3) They are being operated by a part 125 certificate holder without carrying passengers or cargo under part 91 for training, ferrying, positioning, or maintenance purposes;

(4) They are being operated under part 91 by an operator certificated to operate those airplanes under the rules of parts 121, 135, or 137 of this chapter, they are being operated under the applicable rules of part 121 or part 135 of this chapter by an applicant for a certificate under part 119 of this chapter or they are being operated by a foreign air carrier or a foreign person engaged in common carriage solely outside the United States under part 91 of this chapter;

(5) They are being operated under a deviation authority issued under §125.3;

(6) They are being operated under part 91, subpart K by a fractional owner as defined in §91.1001 of this chapter; or

(7) They are being operated by a fractional ownership program manager as defined in §91.1001 of this chapter, for training, ferrying, positioning, maintenance, or demonstration purposes under part 91 of this chapter and without carrying passengers or cargo for compensation or hire except as permitted for demonstration flights under §91.501(b)(3) of this chapter.

(c) The rules of this part, except §125.247, do not apply to the operation of airplanes specified in paragraph (a) when they are operated outside the United States by a person who is not a citizen of the United States.

(d) The provisions of this part apply to each person on board an aircraft being operated under this part, unless otherwise specified.

[Docket No. 19779, 45 FR 67235, Oct. 9, 1980; as amended by Amdt. 125–4, 47 FR 44719, Oct. 12, 1982; Amdt. 125–5, 49 FR 34816, Sept. 4, 1984; Amdt. 125–6, 51 FR 873, Jan. 8, 1986; Amdt. 125–9, 52 FR 20028, May 28, 1987; Amdt. 125–23, 60 FR 65937, Dec. 20, 1995; Amdt. 125–31, 64 FR 1080, Jan. 7, 1999; Amdt. 125–44, 68 FR 54584, Sept. 17, 2003]

§125.3 Deviation authority.

(a) The Administrator may, upon consideration of the circumstances of a particular operation, issue deviation authority providing relief from specified sections of part 125. This deviation authority will be issued as a Letter of Deviation Authority.

(b) A Letter of Deviation Authority may be terminated or amended at any time by the Administrator.

(c) A request for deviation authority must be submitted to the nearest Flight Standards District Office, not less than 60 days prior to the date of intended operations. A request for deviation authority must contain a complete statement of the circumstances and justification for the deviation requested.

[Docket No. 19779, 45 FR 67235, Oct. 9, 1980; as amended by Amdt. 125–13, 54 FR 39294, Sept. 25, 1989]

§125.5 Operating certificate and operations specifications required.

(a) After February 3, 1981, no person may engage in operations governed by this part unless that person holds a certificate and operations specification or appropriate deviation authority.

(b) Applicants who file an application before June 1, 1981 shall continue to operate under the rules applicable to their operations on February 2, 1981 until the application for an operating certificate required by this part has been denied or the operating certificate and operations specifications required by this part have been issued.

(c) The rules of this part which apply to a certificate holder also apply to any person who engages in any operation governed by this part without an appropriate certificate and operations specifications required by this part or a Letter of Deviation Authority issued under §125.3.

[Docket No. 19779, 45 FR 67235, Oct. 9, 1980; as amended by Amdt. 125–1A, 46 FR 10903, Feb. 5, 1981]

§125.7 Display of certificate.

(a) The certificate holder must display a true copy of the certificate in each of its aircraft.

(b) Each operator holding a Letter of Deviation Authority issued under this part must carry a true copy in each of its airplanes.

§125.9 Definitions.

(a) For the purposes of this part, *maximum payload capacity* means:

(1) For an airplane for which a maximum zero fuel weight is prescribed in FAA technical specifications, the maximum zero fuel weight, less empty weight, less all justifiable airplane equipment, and less the operating load (consisting of minimum flightcrew, foods and beverages and supplies and equipment related to foods and beverages, but not including disposable fuel or oil):

(2) For all other airplanes, the maximum certificated takeoff weight of an airplane, less the empty weight, less all justifiable airplane equipment, and less the operating load (consisting of minimum fuel load, oil, and flightcrew). The allowance for the weight of the crew, oil, and fuel is as follows:

(i) Crew—200 pounds for each crewmember required under this chapter

(ii) Oil—350 pounds.

(iii) Fuel—the minimum weight of fuel required under this chapter for a flight between domestic points 174 nautical miles apart under VFR weather conditions that does not involve extended overwater operations.

(b) For the purposes of this part, *empty weight* means the weight of the airframe, engines, propellers, and fixed equipment. Empty weight excludes the weight of the crew and payload, but includes the weight of all fixed ballast, unusable fuel supply, undrainable oil, total quantity of engine coolant, and total quantity of hydraulic fluid.

(c) For the purposes of this part, *maximum zero fuel weight* means the maximum permissible weight of an airplane with no disposable fuel or oil. The zero fuel weight figure may be found in either the airplane type certificate data sheet or the approved Airplane Flight Manual, or both.

(d) For the purposes of this section, *justifiable airplane equipment* means any equipment necessary for the operation of the airplane. It does not include equipment or ballast specifically installed, permanently or otherwise, for the purpose of altering the empty weight of an airplane to meet the maximum payload capacity.

§125.11 Certificate eligibility and prohibited operations.

(a) No person is eligible for a certificate or operations specifications under this part if the person holds the appropriate operating certificate and/or operations specifications necessary to conduct operations under part 121, 129 or 135 of this chapter.

(b) No certificate holder may conduct any operation which results directly or indirectly from any person's holding out to the public to furnish transportation.

(c) No person holding operations specifications under this part may operate or list on its operations specifications any aircraft listed on any operations specifications or other required aircraft listing under part 121, 129, or 135 of this chapter.

[Docket No. 19779, 45 FR 67235, Oct. 9, 1980; as amended by Amdt. 125–9, 52 FR 20028, May 28, 1987]

Subpart B— Certification Rules and Miscellaneous Requirements

§125.21 Application for operating certificate.

(a) Each applicant for the issuance of an operating certificate must submit an application in a form and manner prescribed by the Administrator to the FAA Flight Standards district office in whose area the applicant proposes to establish or has established its principal operations base. The application must be submitted at least 60 days before the date of intended operations.

(b) Each application submitted under paragraph (a) of this section must contain a signed statement showing the following:

(1) The name and address of each director and each officer or person employed or who will be employed in a management position described in §125.25.

(2) A list of flight crewmembers with the type of airman certificate held, including ratings and certificate numbers.

§125.23 Rules applicable to operations subject to this part.

Each person operating an airplane in operations under this part shall—

(a) While operating inside the United States, comply with the applicable rules in part 91 of this chapter; and

(b) While operating outside the United States, comply with Annex 2, Rules of the Air, to the Convention on International Civil Aviation or the regulations of any foreign country, whichever applies, and with any rules of parts 61 and 91 of this chapter and this part that are more restrictive than that Annex or those regulations and that can be complied with without violating that Annex or those regulations. Annex 2 is incorporated by reference in §91.703(b) of this chapter.

[Docket No. 19779, 45 FR 67235, Oct. 9, 1980; as amended by Amdt. 125–12, 54 FR 34331, Aug. 18, 1989]

§125.25 Management personnel required.

(a) Each applicant for a certificate under this part must show that it has enough management personnel, including at least a director of operations, to assure that its operations are conducted in accordance with the requirements of this part.

(b) Each applicant shall—

(1) Set forth the duties, responsibilities, and authority of each of its management personnel in the general policy section of its manual;

(2) List in the manual the names and addresses of each of its management personnel;

(3) Designate a person as responsible for the scheduling of inspections required by the manual and for the updating of the approved weight and balance system on all airplanes.

(c) Each certificate holder shall notify the FAA Flight Standards district office charged with the overall inspection of the certificate holder of any change made in the assignment of persons to the listed positions within 10 days, excluding Saturdays, Sundays, and Federal holidays, of such change.

§125.27 Issue of certificate.

(a) An applicant for a certificate under this subpart is entitled to a certificate if the Administrator finds that the applicant is properly and adequately equipped and able to conduct a safe operation in accordance with the requirements of this part and the operations specifications provided for in this part.

(b) The Administrator may deny an application for a certificate under this subpart if the Administrator finds—

(1) That an operating certificate required under this part or part 121, 123, or 135 of this chapter previously issued to the applicant was revoked; or

(2) That a person who was employed in a management position under §125.25 of this part with (or has exercised control with respect to) any certificate holder under part 121, 123, 125, or 135 of this chapter whose operating certificate has been revoked, will be employed in any of those positions or a similar position with the applicant and that the person's employment or control contributed materially to the reasons for revoking that certificate.

§125.29 Duration of certificate.

(a) A certificate issued under this part is effective until surrendered, suspended, or revoked.

(b) The Administrator may suspend or revoke a certificate under section 609 of the Federal Aviation Act of 1958 and the applicable procedures of part 13 of this chapter for any cause that, at the time of suspension or revocation, would have been grounds for denying an application for a certificate.

(c) If the Administrator suspends or revokes a certificate or it is otherwise terminated, the holder of that certificate shall return it to the Administrator.

§125.31 Contents of certificate and operations specifications.

(a) Each certificate issued under this part contains the following:

(1) The holder's name.

(2) A description of the operations authorized.

(3) The date it is issued.

(b) The operations specifications issued under this part contain the following:

(1) The kinds of operations authorized.

(2) The types and registration numbers of airplanes authorized for use.

(3) Approval of the provisions of the operator's manual relating to airplane inspections, together with necessary conditions and limitations.

(4) Registration numbers of airplanes that are to be inspected under an approved airplane inspection program under §125.247.

(5) Procedures for control of weight and balance of airplanes.

(6) Any other item that the Administrator determines is necessary to cover a particular situation.

§125.33 Operations specifications not a part of certificate.

Operations specifications are not a part of an operating certificate.

§125.35 Amendment of operations specifications.

(a) The FAA Flight Standards district office charged with the overall inspection of the certificate holder may amend any operations specifications issued under this part if—

(1) It determines that safety in air commerce requires that amendment; or

(2) Upon application by the holder, that district office determines that safety in air commerce allows that amendment.

(b) The certificate holder must file an application to amend operations specifications at least 15 days before the date proposed by the applicant for the amendment to become effective, unless a shorter filing period is approved. The application must be on a form and in a manner prescribed by the Administrator and be submitted to the FAA Flight Standards district office charged with the overall inspection of the certificate holder.

(c) Within 30 days after a notice of refusal to approve a holder's application for amendment is received, the holder may petition the Director, Flight Standards Service, to reconsider the refusal to amend.

(d) When the FAA Flight Standards district office charged with the overall inspection of the certificate holder amends operations specifications, that district office gives notice in writing to the holder of a proposed amendment to the operations specifications, fixing a period of not less than 7 days within which the holder may submit written information, views, and arguments concerning the proposed amendment. After consideration of all relevant matter presented, that district office notifies the holder of any amendment adopted, or a rescission of the notice. That amendment becomes effective not less than 30 days after the holder receives notice of the adoption of the amendment, unless the holder petitions the Director, Flight Standards Service, for reconsideration of the amendment. In that case, the effective date of the amendment is stayed pending a decision by the Director. If the Director finds there is an emergency requiring immediate action as to safety in air commerce that makes the provisions of this paragraph impracticable or contrary to the public interest, the Director notifies the certificate holder that the amendment is effective on the date of receipt, without previous notice.

[Docket No. 19779, 45 FR 67235, Oct. 9, 1980; as amended by Amdt. 125–13, 54 FR 39294, Sept. 25, 1989]

§125.37 Duty period limitations.

(a) Each flight crewmember and flight attendant must be relieved from all duty for at least 8 consecutive hours during any 24-hour period.

(b) The Administrator may specify rest, flight time, and duty time limitations in the operations specifications that are other than those specified in paragraph (a) of this section.

[Docket No. 19779, 45 FR 67235, Oct. 9, 1980; as amended by Amdt. 125–21, 59 FR 42993, Aug. 19, 1994]

§125.39 Carriage of narcotic drugs, marihuana, and depressant or stimulant drugs or substances.

If the holder of a certificate issued under this part permits any airplane owned or leased by that holder to be engaged in any operation that the certificate holder knows to be in violation of §91.19(a) of this chapter, that operation is a basis for suspending or revoking the certificate.

[Docket No. 19779, 45 FR 67235, Oct. 9, 1980; as amended by Amdt. 125–12, 54 FR 34331, Aug. 18, 1989]

§125.41 Availability of certificate and operations specifications.

Each certificate holder shall make its operating certificate and operations specifications available for inspection by the Administrator at its principal operations base.

§125.43 Use of operations specifications.

(a) Each certificate holder shall keep each of its employees informed of the provisions of its operations specifications that apply to the employee's duties and responsibilities.

(b) Each certificate holder shall maintain a complete and separate set of its operations specifications. In addition, each certificate holder shall insert pertinent excerpts of its operations specifications, or reference thereto, in its manual in such a manner that they retain their identity as operations specifications.

§125.45 Inspection authority.

Each certificate holder shall allow the Administrator, at any time or place, to make any inspections or tests to determine its compliance with the Federal Aviation Act of 1958, the Federal Aviation Regulations, its operating certificate and operations specifications, its letter of deviation authority, or its eligibility to continue to hold its certificate or its letter of deviation authority.

§125.47 Change of address.

Each certificate holder shall notify the FAA Flight Standards district office charged with the overall inspection of its operations, in writing, at least 30 days in advance, of any change in the address of its principal business office, its principal operations base, or its principal maintenance base.

§125.49 Airport requirements.

(a) No certificate holder may use any airport unless it is adequate for the proposed operation, considering such items as size, surface, obstructions, and lighting.

(b) No pilot of an airplane carrying passengers at night may take off from, or land on, an airport unless—

(1) That pilot has determined the wind direction from an illuminated wind direction indicator or local ground communications, or, in the case of takeoff, that pilot's personal observations; and

(2) The limits of the area to be used for landing or takeoff are clearly shown by boundary or runway marker lights.

(c) For the purposes of paragraph (b) of this section, if the area to be used for takeoff or landing is marked by flare pots or lanterns, their use must be approved by the Administrator.

§125.51 En route navigational facilities.

(a) Except as provided in paragraph (b) of this section, no certificate holder may conduct any operation over a route unless nonvisual ground aids are—

(1) Available over the route for navigating airplanes within the degree of accuracy required for ATC; and

(2) Located to allow navigation to any airport of destination, or alternate airport, within the degree of accuracy necessary for the operation involved.

(b) Nonvisual ground aids are not required for—

(1) Day VFR operations that can be conducted safely by pilotage because of the characteristics of the terrain;

(2) Night VFR operations on routes that the Administrator determines have reliable landmarks adequate for safe operation; or

(3) Operations where the use of celestial or other specialized means of navigation, such as an inertial navigation system, is approved.

§125.53 Flight locating requirements.

(a) Each certificate holder must have procedures established for locating each flight for which an FAA flight plan is not filed that—

(1) Provide the certificate holder with at least the information required to be included in a VFR flight plan;

(2) Provide for timely notification of an FAA facility or search and rescue facility, if an airplane is overdue or missing; and

(3) Provide the certificate holder with the location, date, and estimated time for reestablishing radio or telephone communications, if the flight will operate in an area where communications cannot be maintained.

(b) Flight locating information shall be retained at the certificate holder's principal operations base, or at other places designated by the certificate holder in the flight locating procedures, until the completion of the flight.

(c) Each certificate holder shall furnish the representative of the Administrator assigned to it with a copy of its flight locating procedures and any changes or additions, unless those procedures are included in a manual required under this part.

Subpart C— Manual Requirements

§125.71 Preparation.

(a) Each certificate holder shall prepare and keep current a manual setting forth the certificate holder's procedures and policies acceptable to the Administrator. This manual must be used by the certificate holder's flight, ground, and maintenance personnel in conducting its operations. However, the Administrator may authorize a deviation from this paragraph if the Administrator finds that, because of the limited size of the operation, all or part of the manual is not necessary for guidance of flight, ground, or maintenance personnel.

(b) Each certificate holder shall maintain at least one copy of the manual at its principal operations base.

(c) The manual must not be contrary to any applicable Federal regulations, foreign regulation applicable to the certificate holder's operations in foreign countries, or the certificate holder's operating certificate or operations specifications.

(d) A copy of the manual, or appropriate portions of the manual (and changes and additions) shall be made available to maintenance and ground operations personnel by the certificate holder and furnished to—

(1) Its flight crewmembers; and

(2) The FAA Flight Standards district office charged with the overall inspection of its operations.

(e) Each employee of the certificate holder to whom a manual or appropriate portions of it are furnished under paragraph (d)(1) of this section shall keep it up to date with the changes and additions furnished to them.

(f) For the purpose of complying with paragraph (d) of this section, a certificate holder may furnish the persons listed therein with the maintenance part of its manual in printed form or other form, acceptable to the Administrator, that is retrievable in the English language. If the certificate holder furnishes the maintenance part of the manual in other than printed form, it must ensure there is a compatible reading device available to those persons that provides a legible image of the maintenance information and instructions or a system that is able to retrieve the maintenance information and instructions in the English language.

(g) If a certificate holder conducts airplane inspections or maintenance at specified stations where it keeps the approved inspection program manual, it is not required to carry the manual aboard the airplane en route to those stations.

[Docket No. 19779, 45 FR 67235, Oct. 9, 1980; as amended by Amdt. 125–28, 62 FR 13257, March 19, 1997]

§125.73 Contents.

Each manual shall have the date of the last revision and revision number on each revised page. The manual must include—

(a) The name of each management person who is authorized to act for the certificate holder, the person's assigned area of responsibility, and the person's duties, responsibilities, and authority;

(b) Procedures for ensuring compliance with airplane weight and balance limitations;

(c) Copies of the certificate holder's operations specifications or appropriate extracted information, including area of operations authorized, category and class of airplane authorized, crew complements, and types of operations authorized;

(d) Procedures for complying with accident notification requirements;

(e) Procedures for ensuring that the pilot in command knows that required airworthiness inspections have been made and that the airplane has been approved for return to service in compliance with applicable maintenance requirements;

(f) Procedures for reporting and recording mechanical irregularities that come to the attention of the pilot in command before, during, and after completion of a flight;

(g) Procedures to be followed by the pilot in command for determining that mechanical irregularities or defects reported for previous flights have been corrected or that correction has been deferred;

(h) Procedures to be followed by the pilot in command to obtain maintenance, preventive maintenance, and servicing of the airplane at a place where previous arrangements have not been made by the operator, when the pilot is authorized to so act for the operator;

(i) Procedures for the release for, or continuation of, flight if any item of equipment required for the particular type of operation becomes inoperative or unserviceable en route;

(j) Procedures for refueling airplanes, eliminating fuel contamination, protecting from fire (including electrostatic protection), and supervising and protecting passengers during refueling;

(k) Procedures to be followed by the pilot in command in the briefing under §125.327;

(l) Flight locating procedures, when applicable;

(m) Procedures for ensuring compliance with emergency procedures, including a list of the functions assigned each category of required crewmembers in connection with an emergency and emergency evacuation;

(n) The approved airplane inspection program;

(o) Procedures and instructions to enable personnel to recognize hazardous materials, as defined in title 49 CFR, and if these materials are to be carried, stored, or handled, procedures and instructions for—

(1) Accepting shipment of hazardous material required by title 49 CFR, to assure proper packaging, marking, labeling, shipping documents, compatibility of articles, and instructions on their loading, storage, and handling;

(2) Notification and reporting hazardous material incidents as required by title 49 CFR; and

(3) Notification of the pilot in command when there are hazardous materials aboard, as required by title 49 CFR;

(p) Procedures for the evacuation of persons who may need the assistance of another person to move expeditiously to an exit if an emergency occurs;

(q) The identity of each person who will administer tests required by this part, including the designation of the tests authorized to be given by the person; and

(r) Other procedures and policy instructions regarding the certificate holder's operations that are issued by the certificate holder.

§125.75 Airplane flight manual.

(a) Each certificate holder shall keep a current approved Airplane Flight Manual or approved equivalent for each type airplane that it operates.

(b) Each certificate holder shall carry the approved Airplane Flight Manual or the approved equivalent aboard each airplane it operates. A certificate holder may elect to carry a combination of the manuals required by this section and §125.71. If it so elects, the certificate holder may revise the operating procedures sections and modify the presentation of performance from the applicable Airplane Flight Manual if the revised operating procedures and modified performance data presentation are approved by the Administrator.

Subpart D— Airplane Requirements

§125.91 Airplane requirements: General.

(a) No certificate holder may operate an airplane governed by this part unless it—

(1) Carries an appropriate current airworthiness certificate issued under this chapter; and

(2) Is in an airworthy condition and meets the applicable airworthiness requirements of this chapter, including those relating to identification and equipment.

(b) No person may operate an airplane unless the current empty weight and center of gravity are calculated from the values established by actual weighing of the airplane within the preceding 36 calendar months.

(c) Paragraph (b) of this section does not apply to airplanes issued an original airworthiness certificate within the preceding 36 calendar months.

§125.93 Airplane limitations.

No certificate holder may operate a land airplane (other than a DC-3, C-46, CV-240, CV-340, CV-440, CV-580, CV-600, CV-640, or Martin 404) in an extended overwater operation unless it is certificated or approved as adequate for ditching under the ditching provisions of part 25 of this chapter.

Subpart E—Special Airworthiness Requirements

§125.111 General.

(a) Except as provided in paragraph (b) of this section, no certificate holder may use an airplane powered by airplane engines rated at more than 600 horsepower each for maximum continuous operation unless that airplane meets the requirements of §§125.113 through 125.181.

(b) If the Administrator determines that, for a particular model of airplane used in cargo service, literal compliance with any requirement under paragraph (a) of this section would be extremely difficult and that compliance would not contribute materially to the objective sought, the Administrator may require compliance with only those requirements that are necessary to accomplish the basic objectives of this part.

(c) This section does not apply to any airplane certificated under—

(1) Part 4b of the Civil Air Regulations in effect after October 31, 1946;

(2) Part 25 of this chapter; or

(3) Special Civil Air Regulation 422, 422A, or 422B.

§125.113 Cabin interiors.

(a) Upon the first major overhaul of an airplane cabin or refurbishing of the cabin interior, all materials in each compartment used by the crew or passengers that do not meet the following requirements must be replaced with materials that meet these requirements:

(1) For an airplane for which the application for the type certificate was filed prior to May 1, 1972, §25.853 in effect on April 30, 1972.

(2) For an airplane for which the application for the type certificate was filed on or after May 1, 1972, the materials requirement under which the airplane was type certificated.

(b) Except as provided in paragraph (a) of this section, each compartment used by the crew or passengers must meet the following requirements:

(1) Materials must be at least flash resistant.

(2) The wall and ceiling linings and the covering of upholstering, floors, and furnishings must be flame resistant.

(3) Each compartment where smoking is to be allowed must be equipped with self-contained ash trays that are completely removable and other compartments must be placarded against smoking.

(4) Each receptacle for used towels, papers, and wastes must be of fire-resistant material and must have a cover or other means of containing possible fires started in the receptacles.

(c) Thermal/acoustic insulation materials. For transport category airplanes type certificated after January 1, 1958:

(1) For airplanes manufactured before September 2, 2005, when thermal/acoustic insulation materials are installed in the fuselage as replacements after September 2, 2005, those materials must meet the flame propagation requirements of §25.856 of this chapter, effective September 2, 2003.

(2) For airplanes manufactured after September 2, 2005, thermal/acoustic insulation materials installed in the fuselage must meet the flame propagation requirements of §25.856 of this chapter, effective September 2, 2003.

[Docket No. FAA–2000–7909; as amended by Amdt. 125–43, 68 FR 45084, July 31, 2003]

§125.115 Internal doors.

In any case where internal doors are equipped with louvres or other ventilating means, there must be a means convenient to the crew for closing the flow of air through the door when necessary.

§125.117 Ventilation.

Each passenger or crew compartment must be suitably ventilated. Carbon monoxide concentration may not be more than one part in 20,000 parts of air, and fuel fumes may not be present. In any case where partitions between compartments have louvres or other means allowing air to flow between compartments, there must be a means convenient to the crew for closing the flow of air through the partitions when necessary.

§125.119 Fire precautions.

(a) Each compartment must be designed so that, when used for storing cargo or baggage, it meets the following requirements:

(1) No compartment may include controls, wiring, lines, equipment, or accessories that would upon damage or failure, affect the safe operation of the airplane unless the item is adequately shielded, isolated, or otherwise protected so that it cannot be damaged by movement of cargo in the compartment and so that damage to or failure of the item would not create a fire hazard in the compartment.

(2) Cargo or baggage may not interfere with the functioning of the fire-protective features of the compartment.

(3) Materials used in the construction of the compartments, including tie-down equipment, must be at least flame resistant.

(4) Each compartment must include provisions for safeguarding against fires according to the classifications set forth in paragraphs (b) through (f) of this section.

(b) *Class A.* Cargo and baggage compartments are classified in the "A" category if a fire therein would be readily discernible to a member of the crew while at that crewmember's station, and all parts of the compartment are easily accessible in flight. There must be a hand fire extinguisher available for each Class A compartment.

(c) *Class B.* Cargo and baggage compartments are classified in the "B" category if enough access is provided while in flight to enable a member of the crew to effectively reach all of the compartment and its contents with a hand fire extinguisher and the compartment is so designed that, when the access provisions are being used, no hazardous amount of smoke, flames, or extinguishing agent enters any compartment occupied by the crew or passengers. Each Class B compartment must comply with the following:

(1) It must have a separate approved smoke or fire detector system to give warning at the pilot or flight engineer station.

(2) There must be a hand-held fire extinguisher available for the compartment.

(3) It must be lined with fire-resistant material, except that additional service lining of flame-resistant material may be used.

(d) *Class C.* Cargo and baggage compartments are classified in the "C" category if they do not conform with the requirements for the "A", "B", "D", or "E" categories. Each Class C compartment must comply with the following:

(1) It must have a separate approved smoke or fire detector system to give warning at the pilot or flight engineer station.

(2) It must have an approved built-in fire-extinguishing system controlled from the pilot or flight engineer station.

(3) It must be designed to exclude hazardous quantities of smoke, flames, or extinguishing agents from entering into any compartment occupied by the crew or passengers.

(4) It must have ventilation and draft control so that the extinguishing agent provided can control any fire that may start in the compartment.

(5) It must be lined with fire-resistant material, except that additional service lining of flame-resistant material may be used.

(e) *Class D.* Cargo and baggage compartments are classified in the "D" category if they are so designed and constructed that a fire occurring therein will be completely confined without endangering the safety of the airplane or the occupants. Each Class D compartment must comply with the following:

(1) It must have a means to exclude hazardous quantities of smoke, flames, or noxious gases from entering any compartment occupied by the crew or passengers.

(2) Ventilation and drafts must be controlled within each compartment so that any fire likely to occur in the compartment will not progress beyond safe limits.

(3) It must be completely lined with fire-resistant material.

(4) Consideration must be given to the effect of heat within the compartment on adjacent critical parts of the airplane.

(f) *Class E.* On airplanes used for the carriage of cargo only, the cabin area may be classified as a Class "E" compartment. Each Class E compartment must comply with the following:

(1) It must be completely lined with fire-resistant material.

(2) It must have a separate system of an approved type smoke or fire detector to give warning at the pilot or flight engineer station.

(3) It must have a means to shut off the ventilating air flow to or within the compartment and the controls for that means must be accessible to the flightcrew in the crew compartment.

(4) It must have a means to exclude hazardous quantities of smoke, flames, or noxious gases from entering the flightcrew compartment.

(5) Required crew emergency exits must be accessible under all cargo loading conditions.

§125.121 Proof of compliance with §125.119.

Compliance with those provisions of §125.119 that refer to compartment accessibility, the entry of hazardous quantities of smoke or extinguishing agent into compartment occupied by the crew or passengers, and the dissipation of the extinguishing agent in Class "C" compartments must be shown by tests in flight. During these tests it must be shown that no inadvertent operation of smoke or fire detectors in other compartments within the airplane would occur as a result of fire contained in any one compartment, either during the time it is being extinguished, or thereafter, unless the extinguishing system floods those compartments simultaneously.

§125.123 Propeller deicing fluid.

If combustible fluid is used for propeller deicing, the certificate holder must comply with §125.153.

§125.125 Pressure cross-feed arrangements.

(a) Pressure cross-feed lines may not pass through parts of the airplane used for carrying persons or cargo unless there is a means to allow crewmembers to shut off the supply of fuel to these lines or the lines are enclosed in a fuel and fume-proof enclosure that is ventilated and drained to the exterior of the airplane. However, such an enclosure need not be used if those lines incorporate no fittings on or within the personnel or cargo areas and are suitably routed or protected to prevent accidental damage.

(b) Lines that can be isolated from the rest of the fuel system by valves at each end must incorporate provisions for relieving excessive pressures that may result from exposure of the isolated line to high temperatures.

§125.127 Location of fuel tanks.

(a) Fuel tanks must be located in accordance with §125.153.

(b) No part of the engine nacelle skin that lies immediately behind a major air outlet from the engine compartment may be used as the wall of an integral tank.

(c) Fuel tanks must be isolated from personnel compartments by means of fume- and fuel-proof enclosures.

§125.129 Fuel system lines and fittings.

(a) Fuel lines must be installed and supported so as to prevent excessive vibration and so as to be adequate to withstand loads due to fuel pressure and accelerated flight conditions.

(b) Lines connected to components of the airplane between which there may be relative motion must incorporate provisions for flexibility.

(c) Flexible connections in lines that may be under pressure and subject to axial loading must use flexible hose assemblies rather than hose clamp connections.

(d) Flexible hoses must be of an acceptable type or proven suitable for the particular application.

§125.131 Fuel lines and fittings in designated fire zones.

Fuel lines and fittings in each designated fire zone must comply with §125.157.

§125.133 Fuel valves.

Each fuel valve must—

(a) Comply with §125.155;

(b) Have positive stops or suitable index provisions in the "on" and "off" positions; and

(c) Be supported so that loads resulting from its operation or from accelerated flight conditions are not transmitted to the lines connected to the valve.

§125.135 Oil lines and fittings in designated fire zones.

Oil lines and fittings in each designated fire zone must comply with §125.157.

§125.137 Oil valves.

(a) Each oil valve must—

(1) Comply with §125.155;

(2) Have positive stops or suitable index provisions in the "on" and "off" positions; and

(3) Be supported so that loads resulting from its operation or from accelerated flight conditions are not transmitted to the lines attached to the valve.

(b) The closing of an oil shutoff means must not prevent feathering the propeller, unless equivalent safety provisions are incorporated.

§125.139 Oil system drains.

Accessible drains incorporating either a manual or automatic means for positive locking in the closed position must be provided to allow safe drainage of the entire oil system.

§125.141 Engine breather lines.

(a) Engine breather lines must be so arranged that condensed water vapor that may freeze and obstruct the line cannot accumulate at any point.

(b) Engine breathers must discharge in a location that does not constitute a fire hazard in case foaming occurs and so that oil emitted from the line does not impinge upon the pilots' windshield.

(c) Engine breathers may not discharge into the engine air induction system.

§125.143 Firewalls.

Each engine, auxiliary power unit, fuel-burning heater, or other item of combusting equipment that is intended for operation in flight must be isolated from the rest of the airplane by means of firewalls or shrouds, or by other equivalent means.

§125.145 Firewall construction.

Each firewall and shroud must—

(a) Be so made that no hazardous quantity of air, fluids, or flame can pass from the engine compartment to other parts of the airplane;

(b) Have all openings in the firewall or shroud sealed with close-fitting fireproof grommets, bushings, or firewall fittings;

(c) Be made of fireproof material; and

(d) Be protected against corrosion.

§125.147 Cowling.

(a) Cowling must be made and supported so as to resist the vibration, inertia, and air loads to which it may be normally subjected.

(b) Provisions must be made to allow rapid and complete drainage of the cowling in normal ground and flight attitudes. Drains must not discharge in locations constituting a fire hazard. Parts of the cowling that are subjected to high temperatures because they are near exhaust system parts or because of exhaust gas impingement must be made of fireproof material. Unless otherwise specified in these regulations, all other parts of the cowling must be made of material that is at least fire resistant.

§125.149 Engine accessory section diaphragm.

Unless equivalent protection can be shown by other means, a diaphragm that complies with §125.145 must be provided on air-cooled engines to isolate the engine power section and all parts of the exhaust system from the engine accessory compartment.

§125.151 Powerplant fire protection.

(a) Designated fire zones must be protected from fire by compliance with §§125.153 through 125.159.

(b) Designated fire zones are—

(1) Engine accessory sections;

(2) Installations where no isolation is provided between the engine and accessory compartment; and

(3) Areas that contain auxiliary power units, fuel-burning heaters, and other combustion equipment.

§125.153 Flammable fluids.

(a) No tanks or reservoirs that are a part of a system containing flammable fluids or gases may be located in designated fire zones, except where the fluid contained, the design of the system, the materials used in the tank, the shutoff means, and the connections, lines, and controls provide equivalent safety.

(b) At least one-half inch of clear airspace must be provided between any tank or reservoir and a firewall or shroud isolating a designated fire zone.

§125.155 Shutoff means.

(a) Each engine must have a means for shutting off or otherwise preventing hazardous amounts of fuel, oil, deicer, and other flammable fluids from flowing into, within, or through any designated fire zone. However, means need not be provided to shut off flow in lines that are an integral part of an engine.

(b) The shutoff means must allow an emergency operating sequence that is compatible with the emergency operation of other equipment, such as feathering the propeller, to facilitate rapid and effective control of fires.

(c) Shutoff means must be located outside of designated fire zones, unless equivalent safety is provided, and it must be shown that no hazardous amount of flammable fluid will drain into any designated fire zone after a shutoff.

(d) Adequate provisions must be made to guard against inadvertent operation of the shutoff means and to make it possible for the crew to reopen the shutoff means after it has been closed.

§125.157 Lines and fittings.

(a) Each line, and its fittings, that is located in a designated fire zone, if it carries flammable fluids or gases under pressure, or is attached directly to the engine, or is subject to relative motion between components (except lines and fittings forming an integral part of the engine), must be flexible and fire-resistant with fire-resistant, factory-fixed, detachable, or other approved fire-resistant ends.

(b) Lines and fittings that are not subject to pressure or to relative motion between components must be of fire-resistant materials.

§125.159 Vent and drain lines.

All vent and drain lines, and their fittings, that are located in a designated fire zone must, if they carry flammable fluids or gases, comply with §125.157, if the Administrator finds that the rupture or breakage of any vent or drain line may result in a fire hazard.

§125.161 Fire-extinguishing systems.

(a) Unless the certificate holder shows that equivalent protection against destruction of the airplane in case of fire is provided by the use of fireproof materials in the nacelle and other components that would be subjected to flame, fire-extinguishing systems must be provided to serve all designated fire zones.

(b) Materials in the fire-extinguishing system must not react chemically with the extinguishing agent so as to be a hazard.

§125.163 Fire-extinguishing agents.

Only methyl bromide, carbon dioxide, or another agent that has been shown to provide equivalent extinguishing action may be used as a fire-extinguishing agent. If methyl bromide or any other toxic extinguishing agent is used, provisions must be made to prevent harmful concentrations of fluid or fluid vapors from entering any personnel compartment either because of leakage during normal operation of the airplane or because of discharging the fire extinguisher on the ground or in flight when there is a defect in the extinguishing system. If a methyl bromide system is used, the containers must be charged with dry agent and sealed by the fire-extinguisher manufacturer or some other person using satisfactory recharging equipment. If carbon dioxide is used, it must not be possible to discharge enough gas into the personnel compartments to create a danger of suffocating the occupants.

§125.165 Extinguishing agent container pressure relief.

Extinguishing agent containers must be provided with a pressure relief to prevent bursting of the container because of excessive internal pressures. The discharge line from the relief connection must terminate outside the airplane in a place convenient for inspection on the ground. An indicator must be provided at the discharge end of the line to provide a visual indication when the container has discharged.

§125.167 Extinguishing agent container compartment temperature.

Precautions must be taken to ensure that the extinguishing agent containers are installed in places where reasonable temperatures can be maintained for effective use of the extinguishing system.

§125.169 Fire-extinguishing system materials.

(a) Except as provided in paragraph (b) of this section, each component of a fire-extinguishing system that is in a designated fire zone must be made of fireproof materials.

(b) Connections that are subject to relative motion between components of the airplane must be made of flexible materials that are at least fire-resistant and be located so as to minimize the probability of failure.

§125.171 Fire-detector systems.

Enough quick-acting fire detectors must be provided in each designated fire zone to assure the detection of any fire that may occur in that zone.

§125.173 Fire detectors.

Fire detectors must be made and installed in a manner that assures their ability to resist, without failure, all vibration, inertia, and other loads to which they may be normally subjected. Fire detectors must be unaffected by exposure to fumes, oil, water, or other fluids that may be present.

§125.175 Protection of other airplane components against fire.

(a) Except as provided in paragraph (b) of this section, all airplane surfaces aft of the nacelles in the area of one nacelle diameter on both sides of the nacelle centerline must be made of material that is at least fire resistant.

(b) Paragraph (a) of this section does not apply to tail surfaces lying behind nacelles unless the dimensional configuration of the airplane is such that the tail surfaces could be affected readily by heat, flames, or sparks emanating from a designated fire zone or from the engine from a designated fire zone or from the engine compartment of any nacelle.

§125.177 Control of engine rotation.

(a) Except as provided in paragraph (b) of this section, each airplane must have a means of individually stopping and restarting the rotation of any engine in flight.

(b) In the case of turbine engine installations, a means of stopping rotation need be provided only if the Administrator finds that rotation could jeopardize the safety of the airplane.

§125.179 Fuel system independence.

(a) Each airplane fuel system must be arranged so that the failure of any one component does not result in the irrecoverable loss of power of more than one engine.

(b) A separate fuel tank need not be provided for each engine if the certificate holder shows that the fuel system incorporates features that provide equivalent safety.

§125.181 Induction system ice prevention.

A means for preventing the malfunctioning of each engine due to ice accumulation in the engine air induction system must be provided for each airplane.

§125.183 Carriage of cargo in passenger compartments.

(a) Except as provided in paragraph (b) or (c) of this section, no certificate holder may carry cargo in the passenger compartment of an airplane.

(b) Cargo may be carried aft of the foremost seated passengers if it is carried in an approved cargo bin that meets the following requirements:

(1) The bin must withstand the load factors and emergency landing conditions applicable to the passenger seats of the airplane in which the bin is installed, multiplied by a factor of 1.15, using the combined weight of the bin and the maximum weight of cargo that may be carried in the bin.

(2) The maximum weight of cargo that the bin is approved to carry and any instructions necessary to ensure proper weight distribution within the bin must be conspicuously marked on the bin.

(3) The bin may not impose any load on the floor or other structure of the airplane that exceeds the load limitations of that structure.

(4) The bin must be attached to the seat tracks or to the floor structure of the airplane, and its attachment must withstand the load factors and emergency landing conditions applicable to the passenger seats of the airplane in which the bin is installed, multiplied by either the factor 1.15 or the seat attachment factor specified for the airplane, whichever is greater, using the combined weight of the bin and the maximum weight of cargo that may be carried in the bin.

(5) The bin may not be installed in a position that restricts access to or use of any required emergency exit, or of the aisle in the passenger compartment.

(6) The bin must be fully enclosed and made of material that is at least flame-resistant.

(7) Suitable safeguards must be provided within the bin to prevent the cargo from shifting under emergency landing conditions.

(8) The bin may not be installed in a position that obscures any passenger's view of the "seat belt" sign, "no smoking" sign, or any required exit sign, unless an auxiliary sign or other approved means for proper notification of the passenger is provided.

(c) All cargo may be carried forward of the foremost seated passengers and carry-on baggage may be carried alongside the foremost seated passengers if the cargo (including carry-on baggage) is carried either in approved bins as specified in paragraph (b) of this section or in accordance with the following:

(1) It is properly secured by a safety belt or other tie down having enough strength to eliminate the possibility of shifting under all normally anticipated flight and ground conditions.

(2) It is packaged or covered in a manner to avoid possible injury to passengers.

(3) It does not impose any load on seats or the floor structure that exceeds the load limitation for those components.

(4) Its location does not restrict access to or use of any required emergency or regular exit, or of the aisle in the passenger compartment.

(5) Its location does not obscure any passenger's view of the "seat belt" sign, "no smoking" sign, or required exit sign, unless an auxiliary sign or other approved means for proper notification of the passenger is provided.

§125.185 Carriage of cargo in cargo compartments.

When cargo is carried in cargo compartments that are designed to require the physical entry of a crewmember to extinguish any fire that may occur during flight, the cargo must be loaded so as to allow a crewmember to effectively reach all parts of the compartment with the contents of a hand-held fire extinguisher.

§125.187 Landing gear: Aural warning device.

(a) Except for airplanes that comply with the requirements of §25.729 of this chapter on or after January 6, 1992, each airplane must have a landing gear aural warning device that functions continuously under the following conditions:

(1) For airplanes with an established approach wing-flap position, whenever the wing flaps are extended beyond the maximum certificated approach climb configuration position in the Airplane Flight Manual and the landing gear is not fully extended and locked.

(2) For airplanes without an established approach climb wing-flap position, whenever the wing flaps are extended beyond the position at which landing gear extension is normally performed and the landing gear is not fully extended and locked.

(b) The warning system required by paragraph (a) of this section—

(1) May not have a manual shutoff;

(2) Must be in addition to the throttle-actuated device installed under the type certification airworthiness requirements; and

(3) May utilize any part of the throttle-actuated system including the aural warning device.

(c) The flap position sensing unit may be installed at any suitable place in the airplane.

[Docket No. 19779, 45 FR 67235, Oct. 9, 1980; as amended by Amdt. 125–16, 56 FR 63762, Dec. 5, 1991]

§125.189 Demonstration of emergency evacuation procedures.

(a) Each certificate holder must show, by actual demonstration conducted in accordance with paragraph (a) of appendix B of this part, that the emergency evacuation procedures for each type and model of airplane with a seating of more than 44 passengers, that is used in its passenger-carrying operations, allow the evacuation of the full seating capacity, including crewmembers, in 90 seconds or less, in each of the following circumstances:

(1) A demonstration must be conducted by the certificate holder upon the initial introduction of a type and model of airplane into passenger-carrying operations. However, the demonstration need not be repeated for any airplane type or model that has the same number and type of exits, the same cabin configuration, and the same emergency equipment as any other airplane used by the certificate holder in successfully demonstrating emergency evacuation in compliance with this paragraph.

(2) A demonstration must be conducted—

(i) Upon increasing by more than 5 percent the passenger seating capacity for which successful demonstration has been conducted; or

(ii) Upon a major change in the passenger cabin interior configuration that will affect the emergency evacuation of passengers.

(b) If a certificate holder has conducted a successful demonstration required by §121.291(a) in the same type airplane as a part 121 or part 123 certificate holder, it need not conduct a demonstration under this paragraph in that type airplane to achieve certification under part 125.

(c) Each certificate holder operating or proposing to operate one or more landplanes in extended overwater operations, or otherwise required to have certain equipment under §125.209, must show, by a simulated ditching conducted in accordance with paragraph (b) of appendix B of this part, that it has the ability to efficiently carry out its ditching procedures.

(d) If a certificate holder has conducted a successful demonstration required by §121.291(b) in the same type airplane as a part 121 or part 123 certificate holder, it need not conduct a demonstration under this paragraph in that type airplane to achieve certification under part 125.

Subpart F—Instrument and Equipment Requirements

§125.201 Inoperable instruments and equipment.

(a) No person may take off an airplane with inoperable instruments or equipment installed unless the following conditions are met:

(1) An approved Minimum Equipment List exists for that airplane.

(2) The Flight Standards District Office having certification responsibility has issued the certificate holder operations specifications authorizing operations in accordance with an approved Minimum Equipment List. The flight crew shall have direct access at all times prior to flight to all of the information contained in the approved Minimum Equipment List through printed or other means approved by the Administrator in the certificate holders operations specifications. An approved Minimum Equipment List, as authorized by the operations specifications, constitutes an approved change to the type design without requiring recertification.

(3) The approved Minimum Equipment List must:

(i) Be prepared in accordance with the limitations specified in paragraph (b) of this section.

(ii) Provide for the operation of the airplane with certain instruments and equipment in an inoperable condition.

(4) Records identifying the inoperable instruments and equipment and the information required by paragraph (a)(3)(ii) of this section must be available to the pilot.

(5) The airplane is operated under all applicable conditions and limitations contained in the Minimum Equipment List and the operations specifications authorizing use of the Minimum Equipment List.

(b) The following instruments and equipment may not be included in the Minimum Equipment List:

(1) Instruments and equipment that are either specifically or otherwise required by the airworthiness requirements under which the airplane is type certificated and which are essential for safe operations under all operating conditions.

(2) Instruments and equipment required by an airworthiness directive to be in operable condition unless the airworthiness directive provides otherwise.

(3) Instruments and equipment required for specific operations by this part.

(c) Notwithstanding paragraphs (b)(1) and (b)(3) of this section, an airplane with inoperable instruments or equipment may be operated under a special flight permit under §§21.197 and 21.199 of this chapter.

[Docket No. 25780, 56 FR 12310, Mar. 22, 1991]

§125.203 Radio and navigational equipment.

(a) No person may operate an airplane unless it has two-way radio communications equipment able, at least in flight, to transmit to, and receive from, ground facilities 25 miles away.

(b) No person may operate an airplane over-the-top unless it has radio navigational equipment able to receive radio signals from the ground facilities to be used.

(c) Except as provided in paragraph (e) of this section, no person may operate an airplane carrying passengers under IFR or in extended overwater operations unless it has at least the following radio communication and navigational equipment appropriate to the facilities to be used which are capable of transmitting to, and receiving from, at any place on the route to be flown, at least one ground facility:

(1) Two transmitters, (2) two microphones, (3) two headsets or one headset and one speaker (4) a marker beacon receiver, (5) two independent receivers for navigation, and (6) two independent receivers for communications.

(d) For the purposes of paragraphs (c)(5) and (c)(6) of this section, a receiver is independent if the function of any part of it does not depend on the functioning of any part of another receiver. However, a receiver that can receive both communications and navigational signals may be used in place of a separate communications receiver and a separate navigational signal receiver.

(e) Notwithstanding the requirements of paragraph (c) of this section, installation and use of a single long-range navigation system and a single long-range communication system for extended overwater operations in certain geographic areas may be authorized by the Administrator and approved in the certificate holder's operations specifications. The following are among the operational factors the Administrator may consider in granting an authorization:

(1) The ability of the flightcrew to reliably fix the position of the airplane within the degree of accuracy required by ATC,

(2) The length of the route being flown, and

(3) The duration of the very high frequency communications gap.

[Docket No. 19779, 45 FR 67235, Oct. 9, 1980; as amended by Amdt. 125–25, 61 FR 7191, Feb. 26, 1996]

§125.204 Portable electronic devices.

(a) Except as provided in paragraph (b) of this section, no person may operate, nor may any operator or pilot in command of an aircraft allow the operation of, any portable electronic device on any U.S.-registered civil aircraft operating under this part.

(b) Paragraph (a) of this section does not apply to—

(1) Portable voice recorders;

(2) Hearing aids;

(3) Heart pacemakers;

(4) Electric shavers; or

(5) Any other portable electronic device that the Part 125 certificate holder has determined will not cause interference with the navigation or communication system of the aircraft on which it is to be used.

(c) The determination required by paragraph (b)(5) of this section shall be made by that Part 125 certificate holder operating the particular device to be used.

[Docket No. 19779, 45 FR 67235, Oct. 9, 1980; as amended by Amdt. 125–31, 64 FR 1080, Jan. 7, 1999]

§125.205 Equipment requirements: Airplanes under IFR.

No person may operate an airplane under IFR unless it has—

(a) A vertical speed indicator;

(b) A free-air temperature indicator;

(c) A heated pitot tube for each airspeed indicator;

(d) A power failure warning device or vacuum indicator to show the power available for gyroscopic instruments from each power source;

(e) An alternate source of static pressure for the altimeter and the airspeed and vertical speed indicators;

(f) At least two generators each of which is on a separate engine, or which any combination of one-half of the total number are rated sufficiently to supply the electrical loads of all required instruments and equipment necessary for safe emergency operation of the airplane; and

(g) Two independent sources of energy (with means of selecting either), of which at least one is an engine-driven pump or generator, each of which is able to drive all gyroscopic instruments and installed so that failure of one instrument or source does not interfere with the energy supply to the remaining instruments or the other energy source. For the purposes of this paragraph, each engine-driven source of energy must be on a different engine.

(h) For the purposes of paragraph (f) of this section, a continuous inflight electrical load includes one that draws current continuously during flight, such as radio equipment, electrically driven instruments, and lights, but does not include occasional intermittent loads.

(i) An airspeed indicating system with heated pitot tube or equivalent means for preventing malfunctioning due to icing.

(j) A sensitive altimeter.

(k) Instrument lights providing enough light to make each required instrument, switch, or similar instrument easily readable and installed so that the direct rays are shielded from the flight crewmembers' eyes and that no objectionable reflections are visible to them. There must be a means of controlling the intensity of illumination unless it is shown that nondimming instrument lights are satisfactory.

§125.206 Pitot heat indication systems.

(a) Except as provided in paragraph (b) of this section, after April 12, 1981, no person may operate a transport category airplane equipped with a flight instrument pitot heating system unless the airplane is equipped with an operable pitot heat indication system that complies with §25.1326 of this chapter in effect on April 12, 1978.

(b) A certificate holder may obtain an extension of the April 12, 1981, compliance date specified in paragraph (a) of this section, but not beyond April 12, 1983, from the Director, Flight Standards Service if the certificate holder—

(1) Shows that due to circumstances beyond its control it cannot comply by the specified compliance date; and

(2) Submits by the specified compliance date a schedule for compliance acceptable to the Director, indicating that compliance will be achieved at the earliest practicable date.

[Docket No. 18904, 46 FR 43806, Aug. 31, 1981; as amended by Amdt. 125–13, 54 FR 39294, Sept. 25, 1989]

§125.207 Emergency equipment requirements.

(a) No person may operate an airplane having a seating capacity of 20 or more passengers unless it is equipped with the following emergency equipment:

(1) One approved first aid kit for treatment of injuries likely to occur in flight or in a minor accident, which meets the following specifications and requirements:

(i) Each first aid kit must be dust and moisture proof and contain only materials that either meet Federal Specifications GGK-391a, as revised, or as approved by the Administrator.

(ii) Required first aid kits must be readily accessible to the cabin flight attendants.

(iii) Except as provided in paragraph (a)(1)(iv) of this section, at time of takeoff, each first aid kit must contain at least the following or other contents approved by the Administrator:

Contents	Quantity
Adhesive bandage compressors, 1 in	16
Antiseptic swabs	20
Ammonia inhalants	10
Bandage compressors, 4 in	8
Triangular bandage compressors, 40 in	5
Arm splint, noninflatable	1
Leg splint, noninflatable	1
Roller bandage, 4 in	4
Adhesive tape, 1-in standard roll	2
Bandage scissors	1
Protective latex gloves or equivalent nonpermeable gloves	1 Pair

(iv) Protective latex gloves or equivalent nonpermeable gloves may be placed in the first aid kit or in a location that is readily accessible to crewmembers.

(2) A crash axe carried so as to be accessible to the crew but inaccessible to passengers during normal operations.

(3) Signs that are visible to all occupants to notify them when smoking is prohibited and when safety belts should be fastened. The signs must be so constructed that they can be turned on and off by a crewmember. They must be turned on for each takeoff and each landing and when otherwise considered to be necessary by the pilot in command.

(4) The additional emergency equipment specified in appendix A of this part.

(b) *Megaphones.* Each passenger-carrying airplane must have a portable battery-powered megaphone or megaphones readily accessible to the crewmembers assigned to direct emergency evacuation, installed as follows:

(1) One megaphone on each airplane with a seating capacity of more than 60 and less than 100 passengers, at the most rearward location in the passenger cabin where it would be readily accessible to a normal flight attendant seat. However, the Administrator may grant a deviation from the requirements of this paragraph if the Administrator finds that a different location would be more useful for evacuation of persons during an emergency.

(2) Two megaphones in the passenger cabin on each airplane with a seating capacity of more than 99 and less than 200 passengers, one installed at the forward end and the other at the most rearward location where it would be readily accessible to a normal flight attendant seat.

(3) Three megaphones in the passenger cabin on each airplane with a seating capacity of more than 199 passengers, one installed at the forward end, one installed at the most rearward location where it would be readily accessible to a normal flight attendant seat, and one installed in a readily accessible location in the mid-section of the airplane.

[Docket No. 19779, 45 FR 67235, Oct. 9, 1980; as amended by Amdt. 125–19, 59 FR 1781, Jan. 12, 1994; Amdt. 125–22, 59 FR 52643, Oct. 18, 1994; Amdt. 125–22, 59 FR 55208, Nov. 4, 1994]

§125.209 Emergency equipment: Extended overwater operations.

(a) No person may operate an airplane in extended overwater operations unless it carries, installed in conspicuously marked locations easily accessible to the occupants if a ditching occurs, the following equipment:

(1) An approved life preserver equipped with an approved survivor locator light, or an approved flotation means, for each occupant of the aircraft. The life preserver or other flotation means must be easily accessible to each seated occupant. If a flotation means other than a life preserver is used, it must be readily removable from the airplane.

(2) Enough approved life rafts (with proper buoyancy) to carry all occupants of the airplane, and at least the following equipment for each raft clearly marked for easy identification—

(i) One canopy (for sail, sunshade, or rain catcher);

(ii) One radar reflector (or similar device);

(iii) One life raft repair kit;

(iv) One bailing bucket;

(v) One signaling mirror;

(vi) One police whistle;

(vii) One raft knife;

(viii) One CO_2, bottle for emergency inflation;

(ix) One inflation pump;

(x) Two oars;

(xi) One 75-foot retaining line;

(xii) One magnetic compass;

(xiii) One dye marker;

(xiv) One flashlight having at least two size "D" cells or equivalent;

(xv) At least one approved pyrotechnic signaling device;

(xvi) A 2-day supply of emergency food rations supplying at least 1,000 calories a day for each person;

(xvii) One sea water desalting kit for each two persons that raft is rated to carry, or two pints of water for each person the raft is rated to carry;

(xviii) One fishing kit; and

(xix) One book on survival appropriate for the area in which the airplane is operated.

(b) No person may operate an airplane in extended overwater operations unless there is attached to one of the life rafts required by paragraph (a) of this section, an approved survival type emergency locator transmitter. Batteries used in this transmitter must be replaced (or recharged, if the batteries are rechargeable) when the transmitter has been in use for more than one cumulative hour, or, when 50 percent of their useful life (or for rechargeable batteries, 50 percent of their useful life of charge) has expired, as established by the transmitter manufacturer under its approval. The new expiration date for replacing (or recharging) the battery must be legibly marked on the outside of the transmitter. The battery useful life (or useful life of charge) requirements of this paragraph do not apply to batteries (such as water-activated batteries) that are essentially unaffected during probable storage intervals.

[Docket No. 19779, 45 FR 67235, Oct. 9, 1980; as amended by Amdt. 125–20, 59 FR 32058, June 21, 1994]

§125.211 Seat and safety belts.

(a) No person may operate an airplane unless there are available during the takeoff, en route flight, and landing—

(1) An approved seat or berth for each person on board the airplane who is at least 2 years old; and

(2) An approved safety belt for separate use by each person on board the airplane who is at least 2 years old, except that two persons occupying a berth may share one approved safety belt and two persons occupying a multiple lounge or divan seat may share one approved safety belt during en route flight only.

(b) Except as provided in paragraphs (b)(1) and (b)(2) of this section, each person on board an airplane operated under this part shall occupy an approved seat or berth with a separate safety belt properly secured about him or her during movement on the surface, takeoff, and landing. A safety belt provided for the occupant of a seat may not be used for more than one person who has reached his or her second birthday. Notwithstanding the preceding requirements, a child may:

(1) Be held by an adult who is occupying an approved seat or berth, provided the child has not reached his or her second birthday and the child does not occupy or use any restraining device; or

(2) Notwithstanding any other requirement of this chapter, occupy an approved child restraint system furnished by the certificate holder or one of the persons described in paragraph (b)(2)(i) of this section, provided:

(i) The child is accompanied by a parent, guardian, or attendant designated by the child's parent or guardian to attend to the safety of the child during the flight;

(ii) Except as provided in paragraph (b)(2)(ii)(D) of this section, the approved child restraint system bears one or more labels as follows:

(A) Seats manufactured to U.S. standards between January 1, 1981, and February 25, 1985, must bear the label: "This child restraint system conforms to all applicable Federal motor vehicle safety standards.";

(B) Seats manufactured to U.S. standards on or after February 26, 1985, must bear two labels:

(1) "This child restraint system conforms to all applicable Federal motor vehicle safety standards"; and

(2) "This restraint is certified for use in motor vehicles and aircraft" in red lettering;

(C) Seats that do not qualify under paragraphs (b)(2)(ii)(A) and (b)(2)(ii)(B) of this section must bear either a label showing approval of a foreign government or a label showing that the seat was manufactured under the standards of the United Nations;

(D) Notwithstanding any other provisions of this section, booster-type child restraint systems (as defined in Federal Motor Vehicle Standard No. 213 (49 CFR 571.213)), vest- and harness-type child restraint systems, and lap held child restraints are not approved for use in aircraft; and

(iii) The certificate holder complies with the following requirements:

(A) The restraint system must be properly secured to an approved forward-facing seat or berth;

(B) The child must be properly secured in the restraint system and must not exceed the specified weight limit for the restraint system; and

(C) The restraint system must bear the appropriate label(s).

(c) Except as provided in paragraph (c)(3) of this section, the following prohibitions apply to certificate holders:

(1) No certificate holder may permit a child, in an aircraft, to occupy a booster-type child restraint system, a vest-type child restraint system, a harness-type child restraint system, or a lap held child restraint system during take off, landing, and movement on the surface.

(2) Except as required in paragraph (c)(1) of this section, no certificate holder may prohibit a child, if requested by the child's parent, guardian, or designated attendant, from occupying a child restraint system furnished by the child's parent, guardian, or designated attendant provided:

(i) The child holds a ticket for an approved seat or berth or such seat or berth is otherwise made available by the certificate holder for the child's use;

(ii) The requirements of paragraph (b)(2)(i) of this section are met;

(iii) The requirements of paragraph (b)(2)(iii) of this section are met; and

(iv) The child restraint system has one or more of the labels described in paragraphs (b)(2)(ii)(A) through (b)(2)(ii)(C) of this section.

(3) This section does not prohibit the certificate holder from providing child restraint systems authorized by this section or, consistent with safe operating practices, determining the most appropriate passenger seat location for the child restraint system.

(d) Each sideward facing seat must comply with the applicable requirements of §25.785(c) of this chapter.

(e) No certificate holder may take off or land an airplane unless each passenger seat back is in the upright position. Each passenger shall comply with instructions given by a crewmember in compliance with this paragraph. This paragraph does not apply to seats on which cargo or persons who are unable to sit erect for a medical reason are carried in accordance with procedures in the certificate holder's manual if the seat back does not obstruct any passenger's access to the aisle or to any emergency exit.

(f) Each occupant of a seat equipped with a shoulder harness must fasten the shoulder harness during takeoff and landing, except that, in the case of crewmembers, the shoulder harness need not be fastened if the crewmember cannot perform his required duties with the shoulder harness fastened.

[Docket No. 19799, 45 FR 67235, Oct. 9, 1980; as amended by Amdt. 125–17, 57 FR 42674, Sept. 15, 1992; Amdt. 125–26, 61 FR 28422, June 4, 1996]

§125.213 Miscellaneous equipment.

No person may conduct any operation unless the following equipment is installed in the airplane:

(a) If protective fuses are installed on an airplane, the number of spare fuses approved for the airplane and appropriately described in the certificate holder's manual.

(b) A windshield wiper or equivalent for each pilot station.

(c) A power supply and distribution system that meets the requirements of §§25.1309, 25.1331, 25.1351 (a) and (b) (1) through (4), 25.1353, 25.1355, and 25.1431(b) or that is able to produce and distribute the load for the required instruments and equipment, with use of an external power supply if any one power source or component of the power distribution system fails. The use of common elements in the system may be approved if the Administrator finds that they are designed to be reasonably protected against malfunctioning. Engine-driven sources of energy, when used, must be on separate engines.

(d) A means for indicating the adequacy of the power being supplied to required flight instruments.

(e) Two independent static pressure systems, vented to the outside atmospheric pressure so that they will be least affected by air flow variation or moisture or other foreign matter, and installed so as to be airtight except for the vent. When a means is provided for transferring an instrument from its primary operating system to an alternative system, the means must include a positive positioning control and must be marked to indicate clearly which system is being used.

(f) A placard on each door that is the means of access to a required passenger emergency exit to indicate that it must be open during takeoff and landing.

(g) A means for the crew, in an emergency, to unlock each door that leads to a compartment that is normally accessible to passengers and that can be locked by passengers.

§125.215 Operating information required.

(a) The operator of an airplane must provide the following materials, in current and appropriate form, accessible to the pilot at the pilot station, and the pilot shall use them:

(1) A cockpit checklist.

(2) An emergency cockpit checklist containing the procedures required by paragraph (c) of this section, as appropriate.

(3) Pertinent aeronautical charts.

(4) For IFR operations, each pertinent navigational en route, terminal area, and approach and letdown chart;

(5) One-engine-inoperative climb performance data and, if the airplane is approved for use in IFR or over-the-top operations, that data must be sufficient to enable the pilot to determine that the airplane is capable of carrying passengers over-the-top or in IFR conditions at a weight that will allow it to climb, with the critical engine inoperative, at least 50 feet a minute when operating at the MEA's of the route to be flown or 5,000 feet MSL, whichever is higher.

(b) Each cockpit checklist required by paragraph (a)(1) of this section must contain the following procedures:

(1) Before starting engines;

(2) Before take-off;

(3) Cruise;

(4) Before landing;

(5) After landing;

(6) Stopping engines.

(c) Each emergency cockpit checklist required by paragraph (a)(2) of this section must contain the following procedures, as appropriate:

(1) Emergency operation of fuel, hydraulic, electrical, and mechanical systems.

(2) Emergency operation of instruments and controls.

(3) Engine inoperative procedures.

(4) Any other emergency procedures necessary for safety.

§125.217 Passenger information.

(a) Except as provided in paragraph (b) of this section, no person may operate an airplane carrying passengers unless it is equipped with signs that meet the requirements of §25.791 of this chapter and that are visible to passengers and flight attendants to notify them when smoking is prohibited and when safety belts must be fastened. The signs must be so constructed that the crew can turn them on and off. They must be turned on during airplane movement on the surface, for each takeoff, for each landing, and when otherwise considered to be necessary by the pilot in command.

(b) No passenger or crewmember may smoke while any "No Smoking" sign is lighted nor may any passenger or crewmember smoke in any lavatory.

(c) Each passenger required by §125.211(b) to occupy a seat or berth shall fasten his or her safety belt about him or her and keep it fastened while any "Fasten Seat Belt" sign is lighted.

(d) Each passenger shall comply with instructions given him or her by crewmembers regarding compliance with paragraphs (b) and (c) of this section.

[Docket No. 26142, 57 FR 42675, Sept. 15, 1992]

§125.219 Oxygen for medical use by passengers.

(a) Except as provided in paragraphs (d) and (e) of this section, no certificate holder may allow the carriage or operation of equipment for the storage, generation or dispensing of medical oxygen unless the unit to be carried is constructed so that all valves, fittings, and gauges are protected from damage during that carriage or operation and unless the following conditions are met:

(1) The equipment must be—

(i) Of an approved type or in conformity with the manufacturing, packaging, marking, labeling, and maintenance requirements of title 49 CFR parts 171, 172, and 173, except §173.24(a)(1);

(ii) When owned by the certificate holder, maintained under the certificate holder's approved maintenance program;

(iii) Free of flammable contaminants on all exterior surfaces; and

(iv) Appropriately secured.

(2) When the oxygen is stored in the form of a liquid, the equipment must have been under the certificate holder's approved maintenance program since its purchase new or since the storage container was last purged.

(3) When the oxygen is stored in the form of a compressed gas as defined in title 49 CFR 173.300(a)—

(i) When owned by the certificate holder, it must be maintained under its approved maintenance program; and

(ii) The pressure in any oxygen cylinder must not exceed the rated cylinder pressure.

(4) The pilot in command must be advised when the equipment is on board and when it is intended to be used.

(5) The equipment must be stowed, and each person using the equipment must be seated so as not to restrict access to or use of any required emergency or regular exit or of the aisle in the passenger compartment.

(b) When oxygen is being used, no person may smoke and no certificate holder may allow any person to smoke within 10 feet of oxygen storage and dispensing equipment carried under paragraph (a) of this section.

(c) No certificate holder may allow any person other than a person trained in the use of medical oxygen equipment to connect or disconnect oxygen bottles or any other ancillary component while any passenger is aboard the airplane.

(d) Paragraph (a)(1)(i) of this section does not apply when that equipment is furnished by a professional or medical emergency service for use on board an airplane in a medical emergency when no other practical means of transportation (including any other properly equipped certificate holder) is reasonably available and the person carried under the medical emergency is accompanied by a person trained in the use of medical oxygen.

(e) Each certificate holder who, under the authority of paragraph (d) of this section, deviates from paragraph (a)(1)(i) of this section under a medical emergency shall, within 10 days, excluding Saturdays, Sundays, and Federal holidays, after the deviation, send to the FAA Flight Standards district office charged with the overall inspection of the certificate holder a complete report of the operation involved, including a description of the deviation and the reasons for it.

§125.221 Icing conditions: Operating limitations.

(a) No pilot may take off an airplane that has frost, ice, or snow adhering to any propeller, windshield, wing, stabilizing or control surface, to a powerplant installation, or to an airspeed, altimeter, rate of climb, or flight attitude instrument system, except under the following conditions:

(1) Takeoffs may be made with frost adhering to the wings, or stabilizing or control surfaces, if the frost has been polished to make it smooth.

(2) Takeoffs may be made with frost under the wing in the area of the fuel tanks if authorized by the Administrator.

(b) No certificate holder may authorize an airplane to take off and no pilot may take off an airplane any time conditions are such that frost, ice, or snow may reasonably be expected to adhere to the airplane unless the pilot has completed the testing required under §125.287(a)(9) and unless one of the following requirements is met:

(1) A pretakeoff contamination check, that has been established by the certificate holder and approved by the Administrator for the specific airplane type, has been completed within 5 minutes prior to beginning takeoff. A pretakeoff contamination check is a check to make sure the wings and control surfaces are free of frost, ice, or snow.

(2) The certificate holder has an approved alternative procedure and under that procedure the airplane is determined to be free of frost, ice, or snow.

(3) The certificate holder has an approved deicing/anti-icing program that complies with §121.629(c) of this chapter and the takeoff complies with that program.

(c) Except for an airplane that has ice protection provisions that meet appendix C of this part or those for transport category airplane type certification, no pilot may fly—

(1) Under IFR into known or forecast light or moderate icing conditions; or

(2) Under VFR into known light or moderate icing conditions, unless the airplane has functioning deicing or anti-icing equipment protecting each propeller, windshield, wing, stabilizing or control surface, and each airspeed, altimeter, rate of climb, or flight attitude instrument system.

(d) Except for an airplane that has ice protection provisions that meet appendix C of this part or those for transport category airplane type certification, no pilot may fly an airplane into known or forecast severe icing conditions.

(e) If current weather reports and briefing information relied upon by the pilot in command indicate that the forecast icing condition that would otherwise prohibit the flight will not be encountered during the flight because of changed weather conditions since the forecast, the restrictions in paragraphs (b) and (c) of this section based on forecast conditions do not apply.

[45 FR 67235, Oct. 9, 1980; as amended by Amdt. 125–18, 58 FR 69629, Dec. 30, 1993]

§125.223 Airborne weather radar equipment requirements.

(a) No person may operate an airplane governed by this part in passenger-carrying operations unless approved airborne weather radar equipment is installed in the airplane.

(b) No person may begin a flight under IFR or night VFR conditions when current weather reports indicate that thunderstorms, or other potentially hazardous weather conditions that can be detected with airborne weather radar equipment, may reasonably be expected along the route to be flown, unless the airborne weather radar equipment required by paragraph (a) of this section is in satisfactory operating condition.

(c) If the airborne weather radar equipment becomes inoperative en route, the airplane must be operated under the instructions and procedures specified for that event in the manual required by §125.71.

(d) This section does not apply to airplanes used solely within the State of Hawaii, within the State of Alaska, within that part of Canada west of longitude 130 degrees W, between latitude 70 degrees N, and latitude 53 degrees N, or during any training, test, or ferry flight.

(e) Without regard to any other provision of this part, an alternate electrical power supply is not required for airborne weather radar equipment.

§125.224 Collision avoidance system.

(a) After December 30, 1993, no person may operate a large airplane that has a passenger seating configuration, excluding any pilot seat, of more than 30 seats unless it is equipped with an approved TCAS II traffic alert and collision avoidance system and the appropriate class of Mode S transponder.

(b) The manual required by §125.71 of this part shall contain the following information on the TCAS II system required by this section.

(1) Appropriate procedures for—

(i) The operation of the equipment; and

(ii) Proper flightcrew action with respect to the equipment.

(2) An outline of all input sources that must be operating for the TCAS II to function properly.

(c) Effective May 1, 2003, if TCAS II is installed in an airplane for the first time after April 30, 2003, and before January 1, 2005, no person may operate that airplane without TCAS II that meets TSO C-119b (version 7.0), or a later version.

[Docket No. 25355, 54 FR 951, Jan. 10, 1989, as amended by Amdt. 125–14, 55 FR 13247, Apr. 9, 1990; Amdt. 125–41, 68 FR 15903, April 1, 2003]

§125.224 Collision avoidance system.

Effective January 1, 2005, any airplane you operate under this part 125 must be equipped and operated according to the following table:

COLLISION AVOIDANCE SYSTEMS

If you operate any—	Then you must operate that airplane with:
(a) Turbine-powered airplane of more than 33,000 pounds maximum certificated takeoff weight.	(1) An appropriate class of Mode S transponder that meets Technical Standard Order (TSO) C-112, or a later version, and one of the following approved units: (i) TCAS II that meets TSO C-119b (version 7.0), or a later version. (ii) TCAS II that meets TSO C-119a (version 6.04A Enhanced) that was installed in that airplane before May 1, 2003. If that TCAS II version 6.04A Enhanced no longer can be repaired to TSO C-119a standards, it must be replaced with a TCAS II that meets TSO C-119b (version 7.0), or a later version. (iii) A collision avoidance system equivalent to TSO C-119b (version 7.0), or a later version, capable of coordinating with units that meet TSO C-119a (version 6.04A Enhanced), or a later version.
(b) Piston-powered airplane of more 33,000 pounds maximum certificated takeoff weight.	(1) TCAS I that meets TSO C-118, or a later version, or (2) A collision avoidance system equivalent to TSO C-118, or a later version, or (1)(3) A collision avoidance system and Mode S transponder that meet paragraph (a)(1) of this section.

[Docket No. FAA–2001–10910, 68 FR 15903, April 1, 2003]

§125.225 Flight recorders.

(a) Except as provided in paragraph (d) of this section, after October 11, 1991, no person may operate a large airplane type certificated before October 1, 1969, for operations above 25,000 feet altitude, nor a multiengine, turbine powered airplane type certificated before October 1, 1969, unless it is equipped with one or more approved flight recorders that utilize a digital method of recording and storing data and a method of readily retrieving that data from the storage medium. The following information must be able to be determined within the ranges, accuracies, resolution, and recording intervals specified in appendix D of this part:

(1) Time;

(2) Altitude;

(3) Airspeed;

(4) Vertical acceleration;

(5) Heading;

(6) Time of each radio transmission to or from air traffic control;

(7) Pitch attitude;

(8) Roll attitude;

(9) Longitudinal acceleration;

(10) Control column or pitch control surface position; and

(11) Thrust of each engine.

(b) Except as provided in paragraph (d) of this section, after October 11, 1991, no person may operate a large airplane type certificated after September 30, 1969, for operations above 25,000 feet altitude, nor a multiengine, turbine powered airplane type certificated after September 30, 1969, unless it is equipped with one or more approved flight recorders that utilize a digital method of recording and storing data and a method of readily retrieving that data from the storage medium. The following information must be able to be determined within the ranges, accuracies, resolutions, and recording intervals specified in appendix D of this part:

(1) Time;

(2) Altitude;

(3) Airspeed;

(4) Vertical acceleration;

(5) Heading;

(6) Time of each radio transmission either to or from air traffic control;

(7) Pitch attitude;

(8) Roll attitude;

(9) Longitudinal acceleration;

(10) Pitch trim position;

(11) Control column or pitch control surface position;

(12) Control wheel or lateral control surface position;

(13) Rudder pedal or yaw control surface position;

(14) Thrust of each engine;

(15) Position of each trust reverser;

(16) Trailing edge flap or cockpit flap control position; and

(17) Leading edge flap or cockpit flap control position.

(c) After October 11, 1991, no person may operate a large airplane equipped with a digital data bus and ARINC 717 digital flight data acquisition unit (DFDAU) or equivalent unless it is equipped with one or more approved flight recorders that utilize a digital method of recording and storing data and a method of readily retrieving that data from the storage medium. Any parameters specified in appendix D of this part that are available on the digital data bus must be recorded within the ranges, accuracies, resolutions, and sampling intervals specified.

(d) No person may operate under this part an airplane that is manufactured after October 11, 1991, unless it is equipped with one or more approved flight recorders that utilize a digital method of recording and storing data and a method of readily retrieving that data from the storage medium. The parameters specified in appendix D of this part must be recorded within the ranges, accuracies, resolutions and sampling intervals specified. For the purpose of this section, "manufactured" means the point in time at which the airplane inspection acceptance records reflect that the airplane is complete and meets the FAA-approved type design data.

(e) Whenever a flight recorder required by this section is installed, it must be operated continuously from the instant the airplane begins the takeoff roll until it has completed the landing roll at an airport.

(f) Except as provided in paragraph (g) of this section, and except for recorded data erased as authorized in this paragraph, each certificate holder shall keep the recorded data prescribed in paragraph (a), (b), (c), or (d) of this section, as applicable, until the airplane has been operated for at least 25 hours of the operating time specified in §125.227(a) of this chapter. A total of 1 hour of recorded data may be erased for the purpose of testing the flight recorder or the flight recorder system. Any erasure made in accordance with this paragraph must be of the oldest recorded data accumulated at the time of testing. Except as provided in paragraph (g) of this section, no record need be kept more than 60 days.

(g) In the event of an accident or occurrence that requires immediate notification of the National Transportation Safety Board under 49 CFR part 830 and that results in termination of the flight, the certificate holder shall remove the recording media from the airplane and keep the recorded data required by paragraph (a), (b), (c), or (d) of this section, as applicable, for at least 60 days or for a longer period upon the request of the Board or the Administrator.

(h) Each flight recorder required by this section must be installed in accordance with the requirements of §25.1459 of this chapter in effect on August 31, 1977. The correlation required by §25.1459(c) of this chapter need be established only on one airplane of any group of airplanes.

(1) That are of the same type;

(2) On which the flight recorder models and their installations are the same; and

(3) On which there are no differences in the type design with respect to the installation of the first pilot's instruments associated with the flight recorder. The most recent instrument calibration, including the recording medium from which this calibration is derived, and the recorder correlation must be retained by the certificate holder.

(i) Each flight recorder required by this section that records the data specified in paragraphs (a), (b), (c), or (d) of this section must have an approved device to assist in locating that recorder under water.

[Docket No. 25530, 53 FR 26148, July 11, 1988; 53 FR 30906, Aug. 16, 1988]

§125.226 Digital flight data recorders.

(a) Except as provided in paragraph (l) of this section, no person may operate under this part a turbine-engine-powered transport category airplane unless it is equipped with one or more approved flight recorders that use a digital method of recording and storing data and a method of readily retrieving that data from the storage medium. The operational parameters required to be recorded by digital flight data recorders required by this section are as follows: the phrase "when an information source is installed" following a parameter indicates that recording of that parameter is not intended to require a change in installed equipment:

(1) Time;
(2) Pressure altitude;
(3) Indicated airspeed;
(4) Heading—primary flight crew reference (if selectable, record discrete, true or magnetic);
(5) Normal acceleration (Vertical);
(6) Pitch attitude;
(7) Roll attitude;
(8) Manual radio transmitter keying, or CVR/DFDR synchronization reference;
(9) Thrust/power of each engine—primary flight crew reference;
(10) Autopilot engagement status;
(11) Longitudinal acceleration;
(12) Pitch control input;
(13) Lateral control input;
(14) Rudder pedal input;
(15) Primary pitch control surface position;
(16) Primary lateral control surface position;
(17) Primary yaw control surface position;
(18) Lateral acceleration;
(19) Pitch trim surface position or parameters of paragraph (a)(82) of this section if currently recorded;
(20) Trailing edge flap or cockpit flap control selection (except when parameters of paragraph (a)(85) of this section apply);
(21) Leading edge flap or cockpit flap control selection (except when parameters of paragraph (a)(86) of this section apply);
(22) Each Thrust reverser position (or equivalent for propeller airplane);
(23) Ground spoiler position or speed brake selection (except when parameters of paragraph (a)(87) of this section apply);
(24) Outside or total air temperature;
(25) Automatic Flight Control System (AFCS) modes and engagement status, including auto-throttle;
(26) Radio altitude (when an information source is installed);
(27) Localizer deviation, MLS Azimuth;
(28) Glideslope deviation, MLS Elevation;
(29) Marker beacon passage;
(30) Master warning;
(31) Air/ground sensor (primary airplane system reference nose or main gear);
(32) Angle of attack (when information source is installed);
(33) Hydraulic pressure low (each system);
(34) Ground speed (when an information source is installed);

(35) Ground proximity warning system;
(36) Landing gear position or landing gear cockpit control selection;
(37) Drift angle (when an information source is installed);
(36) Wind speed and direction (when an information source is installed);
(39) Latitude and longitude (when an information source is installed);
(40) Stick shaker/pusher (when an information source is installed);
(41) Windshear (when an information source is installed);
(42) Throttle/power lever position;
(43) Additional engine parameters (as designed in appendix E of this part);
(44) Traffic alert and collision avoidance system;
(45) DME 1 and 2 distances;
(46) Nav 1 and 2 selected frequency;
(47) Selected barometric setting (when an information source is installed);
(48) Selected altitude (when an information source is installed);
(49) Selected speed (when an information source is installed);
(50) Selected mach (when an information source is installed);
(51) Selected vertical speed (when an information source is installed);
(52) Selected heading (when an information source is installed);
(53) Selected flight path (when an information source is installed);
(54) Selected decision height (when an information source is installed);
(55) EFIS display format;
(56) Multi-function/engine/alerts display format;
(57) Thrust command (when an information source is installed);
(58) Thrust target (when an information source is installed);
(59) Fuel quantity in CG trim tank (when an information source is installed);
(60) Primary Navigation System Reference;
(61) Icing (when an information source is installed);
(62) Engine warning each engine vibration (when an information source is installed);
(63) Engine warning each engine over temp. (when an information source is installed);
(64) Engine warning each engine oil pressure low (when an information source is installed);
(65) Engine warning each engine over speed (when an information source is installed);
(66) Yaw trim surface position;
(67) Roll trim surface position;
(68) Brake pressure (selected system);
(69) Brake pedal application (left and right);
(70) Yaw of sideslip angle (when an information source is installed);
(71) Engine bleed valve position (when an information source is installed);
(72) De-icing or anti-icing system selection (when an information source is installed);
(73) Computed center of gravity (when an information source is installed);
(74) AC electrical bus status;
(75) DC electrical bus status;
(76) APU bleed valve position (when an information source is installed);
(77) Hydraulic pressure (each system);
(78) Loss of cabin pressure;
(79) Computer failure;
(80) Heads-up display (when an information source is installed);
(81) Para-visual display (when an information source is installed);
(82) Cockpit trim control input position—pitch;
(83) Cockpit trim control input position—roll;
(84) Cockpit trim control input position—yaw;
(85) Trailing edge flap and cockpit flap control position;
(86) Leading edge flap and cockpit flap control position;
(87) Ground spoiler position and speed brake selection; and
(88) All cockpit flight control input forces (control wheel, control column, rudder pedal).

(b) For all turbine-engine powered transport category airplanes manufactured on or before October 11, 1991, by August 20, 2001—

(1) For airplanes not equipped as of July 16, 1996, with a flight data acquisition unit (FDAU), the parameters listed in paragraphs (a)(1) through (a)(18) of this section must be recorded within the ranges and accuracies specified in Appendix D of this part, and—

(i) For airplanes with more than two engines, the parameter described in paragraph (a)(18) is not required unless sufficient capacity is available on the existing recorder to record that parameter.

(ii) Parameters listed in paragraphs (a)(12) through (a)(17) each may be recorded from a single source.

(2) For airplanes that were equipped as of July 16, 1996, with a flight data acquisition unit (FDAU), the parameters listed in paragraphs (a)(1) through (a)(22) of this section must be recorded within the ranges, accuracies, and recording intervals specified in Appendix E of this part. Parameters listed in paragraphs (a)(12) through (a)(17) each may be recorded from a single source.

(3) The approved flight recorder required by this section must be installed at the earliest time practicable, but no later than the next heavy maintenance check after August 18, 1999 and no later than August 20, 2001. A heavy maintenance check is considered to be any time an airplane is scheduled to be out of service for 4 or more days and is scheduled to include access to major structural components.

(c) For all turbine-engine-powered transport category airplanes manufactured on or before October 11, 1991—

(1) That were equipped as of July 16, 1996, with one or more digital data bus(es) and an ARINC 717 digital flight data acquisition unit (DFDAU) or equivalent, the parameters specified in paragraphs (a)(1) through (a)(22) of this section must be recorded within the ranges, accuracies, resolutions, and sampling intervals specified in Appendix E of this part by August 20, 2001. Parameters listed in paragraphs (a)(12) through (a)(14) each may be recorded from a single source.

125

(2) Commensurate with the capacity of the recording system (DFDAU or equivalent and the DFDR), all additional parameters for which information sources are installed and which are connected to the recording system must be recorded within the ranges, accuracies, resolutions, and sampling intervals specified in Appendix E of this part by August 20, 2001.

(3) That were subject to §125.225(e) of this part, all conditions of §125.225(c) must continue to be met until compliance with paragraph (c)(1) of this section is accomplished.

(d) For all turbine-engine-powered transport category airplanes that were manufactured after October 11, 1991—

(1) The parameters listed in paragraphs (a)(1) through (a)(34) of this section must be recorded within the ranges, accuracies, resolutions, and recording intervals specified in Appendix E of this part by August 20, 2001. Parameters listed in paragraphs (a)(12) through (a)(14) each may be recorded from a single source.

(2) Commensurate with the capacity of the recording system, all additional parameters for which information sources are installed and which are connected to the recording system, must be recorded within the ranges, accuracies, resolutions, and sampling intervals specified in Appendix E of this part by August 20, 2001.

(e) For all turbine-engine-powered transport category airplanes that are manufactured after August 18, 2000—

(1) The parameters listed in paragraph (a) (1) through (57) of this section must be recorded within the ranges, accuracies, resolutions, and recording intervals specified in Appendix E of this part.

(2) Commensurate with the capacity of the recording system, all additional parameters for which information sources are installed and which are connected to the recording system, must be recorded within the ranges, accuracies, resolutions, and sampling intervals specified in Appendix E of this part.

(f) For all turbine-engine-powered transport category airplanes that are manufactured after August 19, 2002 parameters listed in paragraph (a)(1) through (a)(88) of this section must be recorded within the ranges, accuracies, resolutions, and recording intervals specified in Appendix E of this part.

(g) Whenever a flight data recorder required by this section is installed, it must be operated continuously from the instant the airplane begins its takeoff roll until it has completed its landing roll.

(h) Except as provided in paragraph (i) of this section, and except for recorded data erased as authorized in this paragraph, each certificate holder shall keep the recorded data prescribed by this section, as appropriate, until the airplane has been operated for at least 25 hours of the operating time specified in §121.359(a) of this part. A total of 1 hour of recorded data may be erased for the purpose of testing the flight recorder or the flight recorder system. Any erasure made in accordance with this paragraph must be of the oldest recorded data accumulated at the time of testing. Except as provided in paragraph (i) of this section, no record need to be kept more than 60 days.

(i) In the event of an accident or occurrence that requires immediate notification of the National Transportation Safety Board under 49 CFR 830 of its regulations and that results in termination of the flight, the certificate holder shall remove the recorder from the airplane and keep the recorder data prescribed by this section, as appropriate, for at least 60 days or for a longer period upon the request of the Board or the Administrator.

(j) Each flight data recorder system required by this section must be installed in accordance with the requirements of §25.1459 (a), (b), (d), and (e) of this chapter. A correlation must be established between the values recorded by the flight data recorder and the corresponding values being measured. The correlation must contain a sufficient number of correlation points to accurately establish the conversion from the recorded values to engineering units or discrete state over the full operating range of the parameter. Except for airplanes having separate altitude and airspeed sensors that are an integral part of the flight data recorder system, a single correlation may be established for any group of airplanes—

(1) That are of the same type;

(2) On which the flight recorder system and its installation are the same; and

(3) On which there is no difference in the type design with respect to the installation of those sensors associated with the flight data recorder system. Documentation sufficient to convert recorded data into the engineering units and discrete values specified in the applicable appendix must be maintained by the certificate holder.

(k) Each flight data recorder required by this section must have an approved device to assist in locating that recorder under water.

(l) The following airplanes that were manufactured before August 18, 1997 need not comply with this section, but must continue to comply with applicable paragraphs of §125.225 of this chapter, as appropriate:

(1) Airplanes that meet the Stage 2 noise levels of part 36 of this chapter and are subject to §91.801(c) of this chapter, until January 1, 2000. On and after January 1, 2000, any Stage 2 airplane otherwise allowed to be operated under Part 91 of this chapter must comply with the applicable flight data recorder requirements of this section for that airplane.

(2) British Aerospace 1-11, General Dynamics Convair 580, General Dynamics Convair 600, General Dynamics Convair 640, deHavilland Aircraft Company Ltd. DHC-7, Fairchild Industries FH 227, Fokker F-27 (except Mark 50), F-28 Mark 1000 and Mark 4000, Gulfstream Aerospace G-159, Jetstream 4100 Series, Lockheed Aircraft Corporation Electra 10-A, Lockheed Aircraft Corporation Electra 10-B, Lockheed Aircraft Corporation Electra 10-E, Lockheed Aircraft Corporation Electra L-188, Lockheed Martin Model 382 (L-100) Hercules, Maryland Air Industries, Inc. F27, Mitsubishi Heavy Industries, Ltd. YS-11, Short Bros. Limited SD3-30, Short Bros. Limited SD3-60.

[Docket No. 28109, 62 FR 38387, July 17, 1997; 62 FR 48135, Sept. 12, 1997; as amended by Amdt. 125–42, 68 FR 42937, July 18, 2003; Amdt. 125–42, 68 FR 50069, Aug. 20, 2003]

§125.227 Cockpit voice recorders.

(a) No certificate holder may operate a large turbine engine powered airplane or a large pressurized airplane with four reciprocating engines unless an approved cockpit voice recorder is installed in that airplane and is operated continuously from the start of the use of the checklist (before starting engines for the purpose of flight) to completion of the final checklist at the termination of the flight.

(b) Each certificate holder shall establish a schedule for completion, before the prescribed dates, of the cockpit voice recorder installations required by paragraph (a) of this section. In addition, the certificate holder shall identify any airplane specified in paragraph (a) of this section he intends to discontinue using before the prescribed dates.

(c) The cockpit voice recorder required by this section must also meet the following standards:

(1) The requirements of part 25 of this chapter in effect after October 11, 1991.

(2) After September 1, 1980, each recorder container must—

(i) Be either bright orange or bright yellow;

(ii) Have reflective tape affixed to the external surface to facilitate its location under water; and

(iii) Have an approved underwater locating device on or adjacent to the container which is secured in such a manner that it is not likely to be separated during crash impact, unless the cockpit voice recorder and the flight recorder, required by §125.225 of this chapter, are installed adjacent to each other in such a manner that they are not likely to be separated during crash impact.

(d) In complying with this section, an approved cockpit voice recorder having an erasure feature may be used so that, at any time during the operation of the recorder, information recorded more than 30 minutes earlier may be erased or otherwise obliterated.

(e) For those aircraft equipped to record the uninterrupted audio signals received by a boom or a mask microphone the flight crewmembers are required to use the boom microphone below 18,000 feet mean sea level. No person may operate a large turbine engine powered airplane or a large pressurized airplane with four reciprocating engines manufactured after October 11, 1991, or on which a cockpit voice recorder has been installed after October 11, 1991, unless it is equipped to record the uninterrupted audio signal received by a boom or mask microphone in accordance with §25.1457(c)(5) of this chapter.

(f) In the event of an accident or occurrence requiring immediate notification of the National Transportation Safety Board under 49 CFR part 830 of its regulations, which results in the termination of the flight, the certificate holder shall keep the recorded information for at least 60 days or, if requested by the Administrator or the Board, for a longer period. Information obtained from the record is used to assist in determining the cause of accidents or occurrences in connection with investigations under 49 CFR part 830. The Administrator does not use the record in any civil penalty or certificate action.

[Docket No. 25530, 53 FR 26149, July 11, 1988]

Subpart G—Maintenance

§125.241 Applicability.

This subpart prescribes rules, in addition to those prescribed in other parts of this chapter, for the maintenance of airplanes, airframes, aircraft engines, propellers, appliances, each item of survival and emergency equipment, and their component parts operated under this part.

§125.243 Certificate holder's responsibilities.

(a) With regard to airplanes, including airframes, aircraft engines, propellers, appliances, and survival and emergency equipment, operated by a certificate holder, that certificate holder is primarily responsible for—

(1) Airworthiness;

(2) The performance of maintenance, preventive maintenance, and alteration in accordance with applicable regulations and the certificate holder's manual;

(3) The scheduling and performance of inspections required by this part; and

(4) Ensuring that maintenance personnel make entries in the airplane maintenance log and maintenance records which meet the requirements of part 43 of this chapter and the certificate holder's manual, and which indicate that the airplane has been approved for return to service after maintenance, preventive maintenance, or alteration has been performed.

§125.245 Organization required to perform maintenance, preventive maintenance, and alteration.

The certificate holder must ensure that each person with whom it arranges for the performance of maintenance, preventive maintenance, alteration, or required inspection items identified in the certificate holder's manual in accordance with §125.249(a)(3)(ii) must have an organization adequate to perform that work.

§125.247 Inspection programs and maintenance.

(a) No person may operate an airplane subject to this part unless

(1) The replacement times for life-limited parts specified in the aircraft type certificate data sheets, or other documents approved by the Administrator, are complied with;

(2) Defects disclosed between inspections, or as a result of inspection, have been corrected in accordance with part 43 of this chapter; and

(3) The airplane, including airframe, aircraft engines, propellers, appliances, and survival and emergency equipment, and their component parts, is inspected in accordance with an inspection program approved by the Administrator.

(b) The inspection program specified in paragraph (a)(3) of this section must include at least the following:

(1) Instructions, procedures, and standards for the conduct of inspections for the particular make and model of airplane, including necessary tests and checks. The instructions and procedures must set forth in detail the parts and areas of the airframe, aircraft engines, propellers, appliances, and survival and emergency equipment required to be inspected.

(2) A schedule for the performance of inspections that must be performed under the program, expressed in terms of the time in service, calendar time, number of system operations, or any combination of these.

(c) No person may be used to perform the inspections required by this part unless that person is authorized to perform maintenance under part 43 of this chapter.

(d) No person may operate an airplane subject to this part unless—

(1) The installed engines have been maintained in accordance with the overhaul periods recommended by the manufacturer or a program approved by the Administrator; and

(2) The engine overhaul periods are specified in the inspection programs required by §125.247(a)(3).

(e) Inspection programs which may be approved for use under this part include, but are not limited to—

(1) A continuous inspection program which is a part of a current continuous airworthiness program approved for use by a certificate holder under part 121 or part 135 of this chapter;

(2) Inspection programs currently recommended by the manufacturer of the airplane, aircraft engines, propellers, appliances, or survival and emergency equipment; or

(3) An inspection program developed by a certificate holder under this part.

[Docket No. 19779, 45 FR 67235, Oct. 9, 1980; as amended by Amdt. 125–2, 46 FR 24409, April 30, 1981]

§ 125.248 Special maintenance program requirements.

(a) No person may operate an Airbus Model A300 (excluding the –600 series), British Aerospace Model BAC 1–11, Boeing Model 707, 720, 727, 737 or 747, McDonnell Douglas Model DC–8, DC–9/MD–80 or DC–10, Fokker Model F28, or Lockheed Model L–1011 beyond the applicable flight cycle implementation time specified below, or May 25, 2001, whichever occurs later, unless operations specifications have been issued to reference repair assessment guidelines applicable to the fuselage pressure boundary (fuselage skin, door skin, and bulkhead webs), and those guidelines are incorporated in its maintenance program. The repair assessment guidelines must be approved by the FAA Aircraft Certification Office (ACO), or office of the Transport Airplane Directorate, having cognizance over the type certificate for the affected airplane.

(1) For the Airbus Model A300 (excluding the –600 series), the flight cycle implementation time is:

(i) Model B2: 36,000 flights.

(ii) Model B4–100 (including Model B4–2C): 30,000 flights above the window line, and 36,000 flights below the window line.

(iii) Model B4–200: 25,500 flights above the window line, and 34,000 flights below the window line.

(2) For all models of the British Aerospace BAC 1–11, the flight cycle implementation time is 60,000 flights.

(3) For all models of the Boeing 707, the flight cycle implementation time is 15,000 flights.

(4) For all models of the Boeing 720, the flight cycle implementation time is 23,000 flights.

(5) For all models of the Boeing 727, the flight cycle implementation time is 45,000 flights.

(6) For all models of the Boeing 737, the flight cycle implementation time is 60,000 flights.

(7) For all models of the Boeing 747, the flight cycle implementation time is 15,000 flights.

(8) For all models of the McDonnell Douglas DC–8, the flight cycle implementation time is 30,000 flights.

(9) For all models of the McDonnell Douglas DC–9/MD–80, the flight cycle implementation time is 60,000 flights.

(10) For all models of the McDonnell Douglas DC–10, the flight cycle implementation time is 30,000 flights.

(11) For all models of the Lockheed L–1011, the flight cycle implementation time is 27,000 flights.

(12) For the Fokker F–28 Mark 1000, 2000, 3000, and 4000, the flight cycle implementation time is 60,000 flights.

(b) After December 16, 2008, no certificate holder may operate a turbine-powered transport category airplane with a type certificate issued after January 1, 1958, and either a maximum type certificated passenger capacity of 30 or more, or a maximum type certificated payload capacity of 7,500 pounds or more unless instructions for maintenance and inspection of the fuel tank system are incorporated in its inspection program. These instructions must address the actual configuration of the fuel tank systems of each affected airplane and must be approved by the FAA Aircraft Certification Office (ACO), or office of the Transport Airplane Directorate, having cognizance over the type certificate for the affected airplane. Operators must submit their request through an appropriate FAA Principal Maintenance Inspector, who may add comments and then send it to the manager of the appropriate office. Thereafter, the approved instructions can be revised only with the approval of the FAA Aircraft Certification Office (ACO), or office of the Transport Airplane Directorate, having cognizance over the type certificate for the affected airplane. Operators must submit their requests for revisions through an appropriate FAA Principal Maintenance Inspector, who may add comments and then send it to the manager of the appropriate office.

[Docket No. 29104, 65 FR 24126, April 25, 2000; as amended by Amdt. 125–33, 65 FR 50744, Aug. 21, 2000; Amdt. 125–36, 66 FR 23131, May 7, 2001; Amdt. 125–40, 67 FR 72834, Dec. 9, 2002; Amdt. 125–46, 69 FR 45942, July 30, 2004; Amdt. 125–46, 69 FR 51940, Aug. 23, 2004]

§125.249 Maintenance manual requirements.

(a) Each certificate holder's manual required by §125.71 of this part shall contain, in addition to the items required by §125.73 of this part, at least the following:

(1) A description of the certificate holders maintenance organization, when the certificate holder has such an organization.

(2) A list of those persons with whom the certificate holder has arranged for performance of inspections under this part. The list shall include the persons' names and addresses.

(3) The inspection programs required by §125.247 of this part to be followed in the performance of inspections under this part including—

(i) The method of performing routine and nonroutine inspections (other than required inspections);

(ii) The designation of the items that must be inspected (required inspections), including at least those which if improperly accomplished could result in a failure, malfunction, or defect endangering the safe operation of the airplane;

(iii) The method of performing required inspections;

(iv) Procedures for the inspection of work performed under previously required inspection findings ("buy-back procedures");

(v) Procedures, standards, and limits necessary for required inspections and acceptance or rejection of the items required to be inspected;

(vi) Instructions to prevent any person who performs any item of work from performing any required inspection of that work; and

(vii) Procedures to ensure that work interruptions do not adversely affect required inspections and to ensure required inspections are properly completed before the airplane is released to service.

(b) In addition, each certificate holder's manual shall contain a suitable system which may include a coded system that provides for the retention of the following:

(1) A description (or reference to data acceptable to the Administrator) of the work performed.

(2) The name of the person performing the work and the person's certificate type and number.

(3) The name of the person approving the work and the person's certificate type and number.

§125.251 Required inspection personnel.

(a) No person may use any person to perform required inspections unless the person performing the inspection is appropriately certificated, properly trained, qualified, and authorized to do so.

(b) No person may perform a required inspection if that person performed the item of work required to be inspected.

Subpart H—Airman and Crewmember Requirements

§125.261 Airman: Limitations on use of services.

(a) No certificate holder may use any person as an airman nor may any person serve as an airman unless that person—

(1) Holds an appropriate current airman certificate issued by the FAA;

(2) Has any required appropriate current airman and medical certificates in that person's possession while engaged in operations under this part; and

(3) Is otherwise qualified for the operation for which that person is to be used.

(b) Each airman covered by paragraph (a) of this section shall present the certificates for inspection upon the request of the Administrator.

§125.263 Composition of flightcrew.

(a) No certificate holder may operate an airplane with less than the minimum flightcrew specified in the type certificate and the Airplane Flight Manual approved for that type airplane and required by this part for the kind of operation being conducted.

(b) In any case in which this part requires the performance of two or more functions for which an airman certificate is necessary, that requirement is not satisfied by the performance of multiple functions at the same time by one airman.

(c) On each flight requiring a flight engineer, at least one flight crewmember, other than the flight engineer, must be qualified to provide emergency performance of the flight engineer's functions for the safe completion of the flight if the flight engineer becomes ill or is otherwise incapacitated. A pilot need not hold a flight engineer's certificate to perform the flight engineer's functions in such a situation.

§125.265 Flight engineer requirements.

(a) No person may operate an airplane for which a flight engineer is required by the type certification requirements without a flight crewmember holding a current flight engineer certificate.

(b) No person may serve as a required flight engineer on an airplane unless, within the preceding 6 calendar months, that person has had at least 50 hours of flight time as a flight engineer on that type airplane, or the Administrator has checked that person on that type airplane and determined that person is familiar and competent with all essential current information and operating procedures.

§125.267 Flight navigator and long-range navigation equipment.

(a) No certificate holder may operate an airplane outside the 48 conterminous States and the District of Columbia when its position cannot be reliably fixed for a period of more than 1 hour, without—

(1) A flight crewmember who holds a current flight navigator certificate; or

(2) Two independent, properly functioning, and approved long-range means of navigation which enable a reliable determination to be made of the position of the airplane by each pilot seated at that person's duty station.

(b) Operations where a flight navigator or long-range navigation equipment, or both, are required are specified in the operations specifications of the operator.

§125.269 Flight attendants.

(a) Each certificate holder shall provide at least the following flight attendants on each passenger-carrying airplane used:

(1) For airplanes having more than 19 but less than 51 passengers—one flight attendant.

(2) For airplanes having more than 50 but less than 101 passengers—two flight attendants.

(3) For airplanes having more than 100 passengers—two flight attendants plus one additional flight attendant for each unit (or part of a unit) of 50 passengers above 100 passengers.

(b) The number of flight attendants approved under paragraphs (a) and (b) of this section are set forth in the certificate holder's operations specifications.

(c) During takeoff and landing, flight attendants required by this section shall be located as near as practicable to required floor level exits and shall be uniformly distributed throughout the airplane to provide the most effective egress of passengers in event of an emergency evacuation.

§125.271 Emergency and emergency evacuation duties.

(a) Each certificate holder shall, for each type and model of airplane, assign to each category of required crewmember, as appropriate, the necessary functions to be performed in an emergency or a situation requiring emergency evacuation. The certificate holder shall show those functions are realistic, can be practically accomplished, and will meet any reasonably anticipated emergency, including the possible incapacitation of individual crewmembers or their inability to reach the passenger cabin because of shifting cargo in combination cargo-passenger airplanes.

(b) The certificate holder shall describe in its manual the functions of each category of required crewmembers under paragraph (a) of this section.

Subpart I—Flight Crewmember Requirements

§125.281 Pilot-in-command qualifications.

No certificate holder may use any person, nor may any person serve, as pilot in command of an airplane unless that person—

(a) Holds at least a commercial pilot certificate, an appropriate category, class, and type rating, and an instrument rating; and

(b) Has had at least 1,200 hours of flight time as a pilot, including 500 hours of cross-country flight time, 100 hours of night flight time, including at least 10 night takeoffs and landings, and 75 hours of actual or simulated instrument flight time, at least 50 hours of which were actual flight.

§125.283 Second-in-command qualifications.

No certificate holder may use any person, nor may any person serve, as second in command of an airplane unless that person—

(a) Holds at least a commercial pilot certificate with appropriate category and class ratings, and an instrument rating; and

(b) For flight under IFR, meets the recent instrument experience requirements prescribed for a pilot in command in part 61 of this chapter.

§125.285 Pilot qualifications: Recent experience.

(a) No certificate holder may use any person, nor may any person serve, as a required pilot flight crewmember unless within the preceding 90 calendar days that person has made at least three takeoffs and landings in the type airplane in which that person is to serve. The takeoffs and landings required by this paragraph may be performed in a flight simulator if the flight simulator is qualified and approved by the Administrator for such purpose. However, any person who fails to qualify for a 90-consecutive-day period following the date of that person's last qualification under this paragraph must reestablish recency of experience as provided in paragraph (b) of this section.

(b) A required pilot flight crewmember who has not met the requirements of paragraph (a) of this section may reestablish recency of experience by making at least three takeoffs and landings under the supervision of an authorized check airman, in accordance with the following:

(1) At least one takeoff must be made with a simulated failure of the most critical powerplant.

(2) At least one landing must be made from an ILS approach to the lowest ILS minimums authorized for the certificate holder.

(3) At least one landing must be made to a complete stop.

(c) A required pilot flight crewmember who performs the maneuvers required by paragraph (b) of this section in a qualified and approved flight simulator, as prescribed in paragraph (a) of this section, must—

(1) Have previously logged 100 hours of flight time in the same type airplane in which the pilot is to serve; and

(2) Be observed on the first two landings made in operations under this part by an authorized check airman who acts as pilot in command and occupies a pilot seat. The landings must be made in weather minimums that are not less than those contained in the certificate holder's operations specifications for Category I operations and must be made within 45 days following completion of simulator testing.

(d) An authorized check airman who observes the takeoffs and landings prescribed in paragraphs (b) and (c)(3) of this section shall certify that the person being observed is proficient and qualified to perform flight duty in operations under this part, and may require any additional maneuvers that are determined necessary to make this certifying statement.

[Docket No. 19779, 45 FR 67235, Oct. 9, 1980; as amended by Amdt. 125–27, 61 FR 34561, July 2, 1996]

§125.287 Initial and recurrent pilot testing requirements.

(a) No certificate holder may use any person, nor may any person serve as a pilot, unless, since the beginning of the 12th calendar month before that service, that person has passed a written or oral test, given by the Administrator or an authorized check airman on that person's knowledge in the following areas—

(1) The appropriate provisions of parts 61, 91, and 125 of this chapter and the operations specifications and the manual of the certificate holder;

(2) For each type of airplane to be flown by the pilot, the airplane powerplant, major components and systems, major appliances, performance and operating limitations, standard and emergency operating procedures, and the contents of the approved Airplane Flight Manual or approved equivalent, as applicable;

(3) For each type of airplane to be flown by the pilot, the method of determining compliance with weight and balance limitations for takeoff, landing, and en route operations;

(4) Navigation and use of air navigation aids appropriate to the operation of pilot authorization, including, when applicable, instrument approach facilities and procedures;

(5) Air traffic control procedures, including IFR procedures when applicable;

(6) Meteorology in general, including the principles of frontal systems, icing, fog, thunderstorms, and windshear, and, if appropriate for the operation of the certificate holder, high altitude weather;

(7) Procedures for avoiding operations in thunderstorms and hail, and for operating in turbulent air or in icing conditions;

(8) New equipment, procedures, or techniques, as appropriate;

(9) Knowledge and procedures for operating during ground icing conditions, (i.e., any time conditions are such

that frost, ice, or snow may reasonably be expected to adhere to the airplane), if the certificate holder expects to authorize takeoffs in ground icing conditions, including:

(i) The use of holdover times when using deicing/anti-icing fluids.

(ii) Airplane deicing/anti-icing procedures, including inspection and check procedures and responsibilities.

(iii) Communications.

(iv) Airplane surface contamination (i.e., adherence of frost, ice, or snow) and critical area identification, and knowledge of how contamination adversely affects airplane performance and flight characteristics.

(v) Types and characteristics of deicing/anti-icing fluids, if used by the certificate holder.

(vi) Cold weather preflight inspection procedures.

(vii) Techniques for recognizing contamination on the airplane.

(b) No certificate holder may use any person, nor may any person serve, as a pilot in any airplane unless, since the beginning of the 12th calendar month before that service, that person has passed a competency check given by the Administrator or an authorized check airman in that type of airplane to determine that person's competence in practical skills and techniques in that airplane or type of airplane. The extent of the competency check shall be determined by the Administrator or authorized check airman conducting the competency check. The competency check may include any of the maneuvers and procedures currently required for the original issuance of the particular pilot certificate required for the operations authorized and appropriate to the category, class, and type of airplane involved. For the purposes of this paragraph, type, as to an airplane, means any one of a group of airplanes determined by the Administrator to have a similar means of propulsion, the same manufacturer, and no significantly different handling or flight characteristics.

(c) The instrument proficiency check required by §125.291 may be substituted for the competency check required by this section for the type of airplane used in the check.

(d) For the purposes of this part, competent performance of a procedure or maneuver by a person to be used as a pilot requires that the pilot be the obvious master of the airplane with the successful outcome of the maneuver never in doubt.

(e) The Administrator or authorized check airman certifies the competency of each pilot who passes the knowledge or flight check in the certificate holder's pilot records.

(f) Portions of a required competency check may be given in an airplane simulator or other appropriate training device, if approved by the Administrator.

[45 FR 67235, Oct. 9, 1980; as amended by Amdt. 125–18, 58 FR 69629, Dec. 30, 1993]

§125.289 Initial and recurrent flight attendant crewmember testing requirements.

No certificate holder may use any person, nor may any person serve, as a flight attendant crewmember, unless, since the beginning of the 12th calendar month before that service, the certificate holder has determined by appropriate initial and recurrent testing that the person is knowledgeable and competent in the following areas as appropriate to assigned duties and responsibilities:

(a) Authority of the pilot in command;

(b) Passenger handling, including procedures to be followed in handling deranged persons or other persons whose conduct might jeopardize safety;

(c) Crewmember assignments, functions, and responsibilities during ditching and evacuation of persons who may need the assistance of another person to move expeditiously to an exit in an emergency;

(d) Briefing of passengers;

(e) Location and operation of portable fire extinguishers and other items of emergency equipment;

(f) Proper use of cabin equipment and controls;

(g) Location and operation of passenger oxygen equipment;

(h) Location and operation of all normal and emergency exits, including evacuation chutes and escape ropes; and

(i) Seating of persons who may need assistance of another person to move rapidly to an exit in an emergency as prescribed by the certificate holder's operations manual.

§125.291 Pilot in command: Instrument proficiency check requirements.

(a) No certificate holder may use any person, nor may any person serve, as a pilot in command of an airplane under IFR unless, since the beginning of the sixth calendar month before that service, that person has passed an instrument proficiency check and the Administrator or an authorized check airman has so certified in a letter of competency.

(b) No pilot may use any type of precision instrument approach procedure under IFR unless, since the beginning of the sixth calendar month before that use, the pilot has satisfactorily demonstrated that type of approach procedure and has been issued a letter of competency under paragraph (g) of this section. No pilot may use any type of nonprecision approach procedure under IFR unless, since the beginning of the sixth calendar month before that use, the pilot has satisfactorily demonstrated either that type of approach procedure or any other two different types of nonprecision approach procedures and has been issued a letter of competency under paragraph (g) of this section. The instrument approach procedure or procedures must include at least one straight-in approach, one circling approach, and one missed approach. Each type of approach procedure demonstrated must be conducted to published minimums for that procedure.

(c) The instrument proficiency check required by paragraph (a) of this section consists of an oral or written equipment test and a flight check under simulated or actual IFR conditions. The equipment test includes questions on emergency procedures, engine operation, fuel and lubrication systems, power settings, stall speeds, best engine-out speed, propeller and supercharge operations, and hydraulic, mechanical, and electrical systems, as appropriate. The flight check includes navigation by instruments, recovery from simulated emergencies, and standard instrument approaches involving navigational facilities which that pilot is to be authorized to use.

(1) For a pilot in command of an airplane, the instrument proficiency check must include the procedures and maneuvers for a commercial pilot certificate with an instrument rating and, if required, for the appropriate type rating.

(2) The instrument proficiency check must be given by an authorized check airman or by the Administrator.

(d) If the pilot in command is assigned to pilot only one type of airplane, that pilot must take the instrument proficiency check required by paragraph (a) of this section in that type of airplane.

(e) If the pilot in command is assigned to pilot more than one type of airplane, that pilot must take the instrument proficiency check required by paragraph (a) of this section in each type of airplane to which that pilot is assigned, in rotation, but not more than one flight check during each period described in paragraph (a) of this section.

(f) Portions of a required flight check may be given in an airplane simulator or other appropriate training device, if approved by the Administrator.

(g) The Administrator or authorized check airman issues a letter of competency to each pilot who passes the instrument proficiency check. The letter of competency contains a list of the types of instrument approach procedures and facilities authorized.

§125.293 Crewmember: Tests and checks, grace provisions, accepted standards.

(a) If a crewmember who is required to take a test or a flight check under this part completes the test or flight check in the calendar month before or after the calendar month in which it is required, that crewmember is considered to have completed the test or check in the calendar month in which it is required.

(b) If a pilot being checked under this subpart fails any of the required maneuvers, the person giving the check may give additional training to the pilot during the course of the check. In addition to repeating the maneuvers failed, the person giving the check may require the pilot being checked to repeat any other maneuvers that are necessary to determine the pilot's proficiency. If the pilot being checked is unable to demonstrate satisfactory performance to the person conducting the check, the certificate holder may not use the pilot, nor may the pilot serve, in the capacity for which the pilot is being checked in operations under this part until the pilot has satisfactorily completed the check.

§125.295 Check airman authorization: Application and issue.

Each certificate holder desiring FAA approval of a check airman shall submit a request in writing to the FAA Flight Standards district office charged with the overall inspection of the certificate holder. The Administrator may issue a letter of authority to each check airman if that airman passes the appropriate oral and flight test. The letter of authority lists the tests and checks in this part that the check airman is qualified to give, and the category, class and type airplane, where appropriate, for which the check airman is qualified.

§125.296 Training, testing, and checking conducted by training centers: Special rules.

A crewmember who has successfully completed training, testing, or checking in accordance with an approved training program that meets the requirements of this part and that is conducted in accordance with an approved course conducted by a training center certificated under part 142 of this chapter, is considered to meet applicable requirements of this part.

[Docket No. 26933, 61 FR 34561, July 2, 1996]

§125.297 Approval of flight simulators and flight training devices.

(a) Flight simulators and flight training devices approved by the Administrator may be used in training, testing, and checking required by this subpart.

(b) Each flight simulator and flight training device that is used in training, testing, and checking required under this subpart must be used in accordance with an approved training course conducted by a training center certificated under part 142 of this chapter, or meet the following requirements:

(1) It must be specifically approved for—

(i) The certificate holder;

(ii) The type airplane and, if applicable, the particular variation within type for which the check is being conducted; and

(iii) The particular maneuver, procedure, or crewmember function involved.

(2) It must maintain the performance, functional, and other characteristics that are required for approval.

(3) It must be modified to conform with any modification to the airplane being simulated that changes the performance, functional, or other characteristics required for approval.

[Docket No. 19779, 45 FR 67235, Oct. 9, 1980; as amended by Amdt. 125–27, 61 FR 34561, July 2, 1996]

Subpart J—Flight Operations

§125.311 Flight crewmembers at controls.

(a) Except as provided in paragraph (b) of this section, each required flight crewmember on flight deck duty must remain at the assigned duty station with seat belt fastened while the airplane is taking off or landing and while it is en route.

(b) A required flight crewmember may leave the assigned duty station—

(1) If the crewmember's absence is necessary for the performance of duties in connection with the operation of the airplane;

(2) If the crewmember's absence is in connection with physiological needs; or

(3) If the crewmember is taking a rest period and relief is provided—

(i) In the case of the assigned pilot in command, by a pilot qualified to act as pilot in command.

(ii) In the case of the assigned second in command, by a pilot qualified to act as second in command of that airplane during en route operations. However, the relief pilot need not meet the recent experience requirements of §125.285.

§125.313 Manipulation of controls when carrying passengers.

No pilot in command may allow any person to manipulate the controls of an airplane while carrying passengers during flight, nor may any person manipulate the controls while carrying passengers during flight, unless that person is a qualified pilot of the certificate holder operating that airplane.

§125.315 Admission to flight deck.

(a) No person may admit any person to the flight deck of an airplane unless the person being admitted is—

(1) A crewmember;

(2) An FAA inspector or an authorized representative of the National Transportation Safety Board who is performing official duties; or

(3) Any person who has the permission of the pilot in command.

(b) No person may admit any person to the flight deck unless there is a seat available for the use of that person in the passenger compartment, except—

(1) An FAA inspector or an authorized representative of the Administrator or National Transportation Safety Board who is checking or observing flight operations; or

(2) A certificated airman employed by the certificate holder whose duties require an airman certificate.

§125.317 Inspector's credentials: Admission to pilots' compartment: Forward observer's seat.

(a) Whenever, in performing the duties of conducting an inspection, an FAA inspector presents an Aviation Safety Inspector credential, FAA Form 110A, to the pilot in command of an airplane operated by the certificate holder, the inspector must be given free and uninterrupted access to the pilot compartment of that airplane. However, this paragraph does not limit the emergency authority of the pilot in command to exclude any person from the pilot compartment in the interest of safety.

(b) A forward observer's seat on the flight deck, or forward passenger seat with headset or speaker, must be provided for use by the Administrator while conducting en route inspections. The suitability of the location of the seat and the headset or speaker for use in conducting en route inspections is determined by the Administrator.

§125.319 Emergencies.

(a) In an emergency situation that requires immediate decision and action, the pilot in command may take any action considered necessary under the circumstances. In such a case, the pilot in command may deviate from prescribed operations, procedures and methods, weather minimums, and this chapter, to the extent required in the interests of safety.

(b) In an emergency situation arising during flight that requires immediate decision and action by appropriate management personnel in the case of operations conducted with a flight following service and which is known to them, those personnel shall advise the pilot in command of the emergency, shall ascertain the decision of the pilot in command, and shall have the decision recorded. If they cannot communicate with the pilot, they shall declare an emergency and take any action that they consider necessary under the circumstances.

(c) Whenever emergency authority is exercised, the pilot in command or the appropriate management personnel shall keep the appropriate ground radio station fully informed of the progress of the flight. The person declaring the emergency shall send a written report of any deviation, through the operator's director of operations, to the Administrator within 10 days, exclusive of Saturdays, Sundays, and Federal holidays, after the flight is completed or, in the case of operations outside the United States, upon return to the home base.

§125.321 Reporting potentially hazardous meteorological conditions and irregularities of ground and navigation facilities.

Whenever the pilot in command encounters a meteorological condition or an irregularity in a ground or navigational facility in flight, the knowledge of which the pilot in command considers essential to the safety of other flights, the pilot in command shall notify an appropriate ground station as soon as practicable.

§125.323 Reporting mechanical irregularities.

The pilot in command shall ensure that all mechanical irregularities occurring during flight are entered in the maintenance log of the airplane at the next place of landing. Before each flight, the pilot in command shall ascertain the status of each irregularity entered in the log at the end of the preceding flight.

§125.325 Instrument approach procedures and IFR landing minimums.

No person may make an instrument approach at an airport except in accordance with IFR weather minimums and unless the type of instrument approach procedure to be used is listed in the certificate holder's operations specifications.

§125.327 Briefing of passengers before flight.

(a) Before each takeoff, each pilot in command of an airplane carrying passengers shall ensure that all passengers have been orally briefed on—

(1) *Smoking.* Each passenger shall be briefed on when, where, and under what conditions smoking is prohibited. This briefing shall include a statement that the Federal Aviation Regulations require passenger compliance with the lighted passenger information signs, posted placards, areas designated for safety purposes as no smoking areas, and crewmember instructions with regard to these items.

(2) *The use of safety belts, including instructions on how to fasten and unfasten the safety belts.* Each passenger shall be briefed on when, where, and under what conditions the safety belt must be fastened about him or her. This briefing shall include a statement that the Federal Aviation Regulations require passenger compliance with lighted passenger information signs and crewmember instructions concerning the use of safety belts.

(3) The placement of seat backs in an upright position before takeoff and landing;

(4) Location and means for opening the passenger entry door and emergency exits;

(5) Location of survival equipment;

(6) If the flight involves extended overwater operation, ditching procedures and the use of required flotation equipment;

(7) If the flight involves operations above 12,000 feet MSL, the normal and emergency use of oxygen; and

(8) Location and operation of fire extinguishers.

(b) Before each takeoff, the pilot in command shall ensure that each person who may need the assistance of another person to move expeditiously to an exit if an emergency occurs and that person's attendant, if any, has received a briefing as to the procedures to be followed if an evacuation occurs. This paragraph does not apply to a person who has been given a briefing before a previous leg of a flight in the same airplane.

(c) The oral briefing required by paragraph (a) of this section shall be given by the pilot in command or a member of the crew. It shall be supplemented by printed cards for the use of each passenger containing—

(1) A diagram and method of operating the emergency exits; and

(2) Other instructions necessary for the use of emergency equipment on board the airplane.

Each card used under this paragraph must be carried in the airplane in locations convenient for the use of each passenger and must contain information that is appropriate to the airplane on which it is to be used.

(d) The certificate holder shall describe in its manual the procedure to be followed in the briefing required by paragraph (a) of this section.

(e) If the airplane does not proceed directly over water after takeoff, no part of the briefing required by paragraph (a)(6) of this section has to be given before takeoff but the briefing required by paragraph (a)(6) must be given before reaching the overwater part of the flight.

[Docket No. 19779, 45 FR 67235, Oct. 9, 1980; as amended by Amdt. 125–17, 57 FR 42675, Sept. 15, 1992]

§125.328 Prohibition on crew interference.

No person may assault, threaten, intimidate, or interfere with a crewmember in the performance of the crewmember's duties aboard an aircraft being operated under this part.

[Docket No. 19779, 45 FR 67235, Oct. 9, 1980; as amended by Amdt. 125–31, 64 FR 1080, Jan. 7, 1999]

§125.329 Minimum altitudes for use of autopilot.

(a) Except as provided in paragraphs (b), (c), (d), and (e) of this section, no person may use an autopilot at an altitude above the terrain which is less than 500 feet or less than twice the maximum altitude loss specified in the approved Airplane Flight Manual or equivalent for a malfunction of the autopilot, whichever is higher.

(b) When using an instrument approach facility other than ILS, no person may use an autopilot at an altitude above the terrain that is less than 50 feet below the approved minimum descent altitude for that procedure, or less than twice the maximum loss specified in the approved Airplane Flight Manual or equivalent for a malfunction of the autopilot under approach conditions, whichever is higher.

(c) For ILS approaches when reported weather conditions are less than the basic weather conditions in §91.155 of this chapter, no person may use an autopilot with an approach coupler at an altitude above the terrain that is less than 50 feet above the terrain, or the maximum altitude loss specified in the approved Airplane Flight Manual or equivalent for the malfunction of the autopilot with approach coupler, whichever is higher.

(d) Without regard to paragraph (a), (b), or (c) of this section, the Administrator may issue operations specifications to allow the use, to touchdown, of an approved flight control guidance system with automatic capability, if—

(1) The system does not contain any altitude loss (above zero) specified in the approved Airplane Flight Manual or equivalent for malfunction of the autopilot with approach coupler; and

(2) The Administrator finds that the use of the system to touchdown will not otherwise adversely affect the safety standards of this section.

(e) Notwithstanding paragraph (a) of this section, the Administrator issues operations specifications to allow the use of an approved autopilot system with automatic capability during the take-off and initial climb phase of flight provided:

(1) The Airplane Flight Manual specifies a minimum altitude engagement certification restriction;

(2) The system is not engaged prior to the minimum engagement certification restriction specified in the Airplane Flight Manual or an altitude specified by the Administrator, whichever is higher; and

(3) The Administrator finds that the use of the system will not otherwise affect the safety standards required by this section.

[Docket No. 19779, 45 FR 67325, Oct. 9, 1980; as amended by Amdt. 125–12, 54 FR 34332, Aug. 18, 1989; Amdt. 125–29, 62 FR 27922, May 21, 1997]

§125.331 Carriage of persons without compliance with the passenger-carrying provisions of this part.

The following persons may be carried aboard an airplane without complying with the passenger-carrying requirements of this part:

(a) A crewmember.

(b) A person necessary for the safe handling of animals on the airplane.

(c) A person necessary for the safe handling of hazardous materials (as defined in subchapter C of title 49 CFR).

(d) A person performing duty as a security or honor guard accompanying a shipment made by or under the authority of the U.S. Government.

(e) A military courier or a military route supervisor carried by a military cargo contract operator if that carriage is specifically authorized by the appropriate military service.

(f) An authorized representative of the Administrator conducting an en route inspection.

(g) A person authorized by the Administrator.

§125.333 Stowage of food, beverage, and passenger service equipment during airplane movement on the surface, takeoff, and landing.

(a) No certificate holder may move an airplane on the surface, takeoff, or land when any food, beverage, or tableware furnished by the certificate holder is located at any passenger seat.

(b) No certificate holder may move an airplane on the surface, takeoff, or land unless each food and beverage tray and seat back tray table is secured in its stowed position.

(c) No certificate holder may permit an airplane to move on the surface, takeoff, or land unless each passenger serving cart is secured in its stowed position.

(d) Each passenger shall comply with instructions given by a crewmember with regard to compliance with this section.

[Docket No. 26142, 57 FR 42675, Sept. 15, 1992]

Subpart K— Flight Release Rules

§125.351 Flight release authority.

(a) No person may start a flight without authority from the person authorized by the certificate holder to exercise operational control over the flight.

(b) No person may start a flight unless the pilot in command or the person authorized by the certificate holder to exercise operational control over the flight has executed a flight release setting forth the conditions under which the flight will be conducted. The pilot in command may sign the flight release only when both the pilot in command and the person authorized to exercise operational control believe the flight can be made safely, unless the pilot in command is authorized by the certificate holder to exercise operational control and execute the flight release without the approval of any other person.

(c) No person may continue a flight from an intermediate airport without a new flight release if the airplane has been on the ground more than 6 hours.

§125.353 Facilities and services.

During a flight, the pilot in command shall obtain any additional available information of meteorological conditions and irregularities of facilities and services that may affect the safety of the flight.

§125.355 Airplane equipment.

No person may release an airplane unless it is airworthy and is equipped as prescribed.

§125.357 Communication and navigation facilities.

No person may release an airplane over any route or route segment unless communication and navigation facilities equal to those required by §125.51 are in satisfactory operating condition.

§125.359 Flight release under VFR.

No person may release an airplane for VFR operation unless the ceiling and visibility en route, as indicated by available weather reports or forecasts, or any combination thereof, are and will remain at or above applicable VFR minimums until the airplane arrives at the airport or airports specified in the flight release.

§125.361 Flight release under IFR or over-the-top.

Except as provided in §125.363, no person may release an airplane for operations under IFR or over-the-top unless appropriate weather reports or forecasts, or any combination thereof, indicate that the weather conditions will be at or above the authorized minimums at the estimated time of arrival at the airport or airports to which released.

§125.363 Flight release over water.

(a) No person may release an airplane for a flight that involves extended overwater operation unless appropriate weather reports or forecasts, or any combination thereof, indicate that the weather conditions will be at or above the authorized minimums at the estimated time of arrival at any airport to which released or to any required alternate airport.

(b) Each certificate holder shall conduct extended overwater operations under IFR unless it shows that operating under IFR is not necessary for safety.

(c) Each certificate holder shall conduct other overwater operations under IFR if the Administrator determines that operation under IFR is necessary for safety.

(d) Each authorization to conduct extended overwater operations under VFR and each requirement to conduct other overwater operations under IFR will be specified in the operations specifications.

§125.365 Alternate airport for departure.

(a) If the weather conditions at the airport of takeoff are below the landing minimums in the certificate holder's operations specifications for that airport, no person may release an airplane from that airport unless the flight release specifies an alternate airport located within the following distances from the airport of takeoff:

(1) *Airplanes having two engines.* Not more than 1 hour from the departure airport at normal cruising speed in still air with one engine inoperative.

(2) *Airplanes having three or more engines.* Not more than 2 hours from the departure airport at normal cruising speed in still air with one engine inoperative.

(b) For the purposes of paragraph (a) of this section, the alternate airport weather conditions must meet the requirements of the certificate holder's operations specifications.

(c) No person may release an airplane from an airport unless that person lists each required alternate airport in the flight release.

§125.367 Alternate airport for destination: IFR or over-the-top.

(a) Except as provided in paragraph (b) of this section, each person releasing an airplane for operation under IFR or over-the-top shall list at least one alternate airport for each destination airport in the flight release.

(b) An alternate airport need not be designated for IFR or over-the-top operations where the airplane carries enough fuel to meet the requirements of §§125.375 and 125.377 for flights outside the 48 conterminous States and the District of Columbia over routes without an available alternate airport for a particular airport of destination.

(c) For the purposes of paragraph (a) of this section, the weather requirements at the alternate airport must meet the requirements of the operator's operations specifications.

(d) No person may release a flight unless that person lists each required alternate airport in the flight release.

§125.369 Alternate airport weather minimums.

No person may list an airport as an alternate airport in the flight release unless the appropriate weather reports or forecasts, or any combination thereof, indicate that the weather conditions will be at or above the alternate weather minimums specified in the certificate holder's operations specifications for that airport when the flight arrives.

§125.371 Continuing flight in unsafe conditions.

(a) No pilot in command may allow a flight to continue toward any airport to which it has been released if, in the opinion of the pilot in command, the flight cannot be completed safely, unless, in the opinion of the pilot in command, there is no safer procedure. In that event, continuation toward that airport is an emergency situation.

§125.373 Original flight release or amendment of flight release.

(a) A certificate holder may specify any airport authorized for the type of airplane as a destination for the purpose of original release.

(b) No person may allow a flight to continue to an airport to which it has been released unless the weather conditions at an alternate airport that was specified in the flight release are forecast to be at or above the alternate minimums specified in the operations specifications for that airport at the time the airplane would arrive at the alternate airport. However, the flight release may be amended en route to include any alternate airport that is within the fuel range of the airplane as specified in §125.375 or §125.377.

(c) No person may change an original destination or alternate airport that is specified in the original flight release to another airport while the airplane is en route unless the other airport is authorized for that type of airplane.

(d) Each person who amends a flight release en route shall record that amendment.

§125.375 Fuel supply: Nonturbine and turbopropeller-powered airplanes.

(a) Except as provided in paragraph (b) of this section, no person may release for flight or take off a nonturbine or turbopropeller-powered airplane unless, considering the wind and other weather conditions expected, it has enough fuel—

(1) To fly to and land at the airport to which it is released;

(2) Thereafter, to fly to and land at the most distant alternate airport specified in the flight release; and

(3) Thereafter, to fly for 45 minutes at normal cruising fuel consumption.

(b) If the airplane is released for any flight other than from one point in the conterminous United States to another point in the conterminous United States, it must carry enough fuel to meet the requirements of paragraphs (a) (1) and (2) of this section and thereafter fly for 30 minutes plus 15 percent of the total time required to fly at normal cruising fuel consumption to the airports specified in paragraphs (a) (1) and (2) of this section, or fly for 90 minutes at normal cruising fuel consumption, whichever is less.

(c) No person may release a nonturbine or turbopropeller-powered airplane to an airport for which an alternate is not specified under §125.367(b) unless it has enough fuel, considering wind and other weather conditions expected, to fly to that airport and thereafter to fly for 3 hours at normal cruising fuel consumption.

§125.377 Fuel supply: Turbine-engine-powered airplanes other than turbo-propeller.

(a) Except as provided in paragraph (b) of this section, no person may release for flight or takeoff a turbine-powered airplane (other than a turbopropeller-powered airplane) unless, considering the wind and other weather conditions expected, it has enough fuel—

(1) To fly to and land at the airport to which it is released;

(2) Thereafter, to fly to and land at the most distant alternate airport specified in the flight release; and

(3) Thereafter, to fly for 45 minutes at normal cruising fuel consumption.

(b) For any operation outside the 48 conterminous United States and the District of Columbia, unless authorized by the Administrator in the operations specifications, no person may release for flight or take off a turbine-engine powered airplane (other than a turbopropeller-powered airplane) unless, considering wind and other weather conditions expected, it has enough fuel—

(1) To fly and land at the airport to which it is released;

(2) After that, to fly for a period of 10 percent of the total time required to fly from the airport of departure and land at the airport to which it was released;

(3) After that, to fly to and land at the most distant alternate airport specified in the flight release, if an alternate is required; and

(4) After that, to fly for 30 minutes at holding speed at 1,500 feet above the alternate airport (or the destination airport if no alternate is required) under standard temperature conditions.

(c) No person may release a turbine-engine-powered airplane (other than a turbopropeller airplane) to an airport for which an alternate is not specified under §125.367(b) unless it has enough fuel, considering wind and other weather conditions expected, to fly to that airport and thereafter to fly for at least 2 hours at normal cruising fuel consumption.

(d) The Administrator may amend the operations specifications of a certificate holder to require more fuel than any of the minimums stated in paragraph (a) or (b) of this section if the Administrator finds that additional fuel is necessary on a particular route in the interest of safety.

§125.379 Landing weather minimums: IFR.

(a) If the pilot in command of an airplane has not served 100 hours as pilot in command in the type of airplane being operated, the MDA or DH and visibility landing minimums in the certificate holder's operations specification are increased by 100 feet and one-half mile (or the RVR equivalent). The MDA or DH and visibility minimums need not be increased above those applicable to the airport when used as an alternate airport, but in no event may the landing minimums be less than a 300-foot ceiling and 1 mile of visibility.

(b) The 100 hours of pilot-in-command experience required by paragraph (a) may be reduced (not to exceed 50 percent) by substituting one landing in operations under this part in the type of airplane for 1 required hour of pilot-in-command experience if the pilot has at least 100 hours as pilot in command of another type airplane in operations under this part.

(c) Category II minimums, when authorized in the certificate holder's operations specifications, do not apply until the pilot in command subject to paragraph (a) of this section meets the requirements of that paragraph in the type of airplane the pilot is operating.

§125.381 Takeoff and landing weather minimums: IFR.

(a) Regardless of any clearance from ATC, if the reported weather conditions are less than that specified in the certificate holder's operations specifications, no pilot may—

(1) Take off an airplane under IFR; or

(2) Except as provided in paragraph (c) of this section, land an airplane under IFR.

(b) Except as provided in paragraph (c) of this section, no pilot may execute an instrument approach procedure if the latest reported visibility is less than the landing minimums specified in the certificate holder's operations specifications.

(c) If a pilot initiates an instrument approach procedure based on a weather report that indicates that the specified visibility minimums exist and subsequently receives another weather report that indicates that conditions are below the minimum requirements, then the pilot may continue with the approach only if, the requirements of §91.175(l) of this chapter, or both of the following conditions are met—

(1) The later weather report is received when the airplane is in one of the following approach phases:

(i) The airplane is on a ILS approach and has passed the final approach fix;

(ii) The airplane is on an ASR or PAR final approach and has been turned over to the final approach controller; or

(iii) The airplane is on a nonprecision final approach and the airplane—

(A) Has passed the appropriate facility or final approach fix; or

(B) Where a final approach fix is not specified, has completed the procedure turn and is established inbound toward the airport on the final approach course within the distance prescribed in the procedure; and

(2) The pilot in command finds, on reaching the authorized MDA, or DH, that the actual weather conditions are at or above the minimums prescribed for the procedure being used.

[Docket No. 19779, 45 FR 67235, Oct. 9, 1980; as amended by Amdt. 125–2, 46 FR 24409, Apr. 30, 1981; Amdt. 125–45, 69 FR 1641, Jan. 9, 2004]

§125.383 Load manifest.

(a) Each certificate holder is responsible for the preparation and accuracy of a load manifest in duplicate containing information concerning the loading of the airplane. The manifest must be prepared before each takeoff and must include—

(1) The number of passengers;

(2) The total weight of the loaded airplane;

(3) The maximum allowable takeoff and landing weights for that flight;

(4) The center of gravity limits;

(5) The center of gravity of the loaded airplane, except that the actual center of gravity need not be computed if the airplane is loaded according to a loading schedule or other approved method that ensures that the center of gravity of the loaded airplane is within approved limits. In those cases, an entry shall be made on the manifest indicating that the center of gravity is within limits according to a loading schedule or other approved method:

(6) The registration number of the airplane;

(7) The origin and destination; and

(8) Names of passengers.

(b) The pilot in command of an airplane for which a load manifest must be prepared shall carry a copy of the completed load manifest in the airplane to its destination. The certificate holder shall keep copies of completed load manifests for at least 30 days at its principal operations base, or at another location used by it and approved by the Administrator.

Subpart L— Records and Reports

§125.401 Crewmember record.

(a) Each certificate holder shall—

(1) Maintain current records of each crewmember that show whether or not that crewmember complies with this chapter (e.g., proficiency checks, airplane qualifications, any required physical examinations, and flight time records); and

(2) Record each action taken concerning the release from employment or physical or professional disqualification of any flight crewmember and keep the record for at least 6 months thereafter.

(b) Each certificate holder shall maintain the records required by paragraph (a) of this section at its principal operations base, or at another location used by it and approved by the Administrator.

(c) Computer record systems approved by the Administrator may be used in complying with the requirements of paragraph (a) of this section.

§125.403 Flight release form.

(a) The flight release may be in any form but must contain at least the following information concerning each flight:

(1) Company or organization name.

(2) Make, model, and registration number of the airplane being used.

(3) Date of flight.

(4) Name and duty assignment of each crewmember.

(5) Departure airport, destination airports, alternate airports, and route.

(6) Minimum fuel supply (in gallons or pounds).

(7) A statement of the type of operation (e.g., IFR, VFR).

(b) The airplane flight release must contain, or have attached to it, weather reports, available weather forecasts, or a combination thereof.

§125.405 Disposition of load manifest, flight release, and flight plans.

(a) The pilot in command of an airplane shall carry in the airplane to its destination the original or a signed copy of the—

(1) Load manifest required by §125.383;

(2) Flight release;

(3) Airworthiness release; and

(4) Flight plan, including route.

(b) If a flight originates at the principal operations base of the certificate holder, it shall retain at that base a signed copy of each document listed in paragraph (a) of this section.

(c) Except as provided in paragraph (d) of this section, if a flight originates at a place other than the principal operations base of the certificate holder, the pilot in command (or another person not aboard the airplane who is authorized by the operator) shall, before or immediately after departure of the flight, mail signed copies of the documents listed in paragraph (a) of this section to the principal operations base.

(d) If a flight originates at a place other than the principal operations base of the certificate holder and there is at that place a person to manage the flight departure for the operator who does not depart on the airplane, signed copies of the documents listed in paragraph (a) of this section may be retained at that place for not more than 30 days before being sent to the principal operations base of the certificate holder. However, the documents for a particular flight need not be further retained at that place or be sent to the principal operations base, if the originals or other copies of them have been previously returned to the principal operations base.

(e) The certificate holder shall:

(1) Identify in its operations manual the person having custody of the copies of documents retained in accordance with paragraph (d) of this section; and

(2) Retain at its principal operations base either the original or a copy of the records required by this section for at least 30 days.

§125.407 Maintenance log: Airplanes.

(a) Each person who takes corrective action or defers action concerning a reported or observed failure or malfunction of an airframe, aircraft engine, propeller, or appliance shall record the action taken in the airplane maintenance log in accordance with part 43 of this chapter.

(b) Each certificate holder shall establish a procedure for keeping copies of the airplane maintenance log required by this section in the airplane for access by appropriate personnel and shall include that procedure in the manual required by §125.249.

THE FOLLOWING SECTION IS EFFECTIVE UNTIL JANUARY 30, 2006

§125.409 Reports of defects or unairworthy conditions.

(a) Each certificate holder shall report the occurrence or detection of each failure, malfunction, or defect, in a form and manner prescribed by the Administrator.

(b) The report must be made within 72 hours to the FAA Flight Standards district office in whose area the certificate holder has its principal operations base. The procedures to be used in complying with this section must be made a part of the manual procedures required by §125.73(f).

THE FOLLOWING SECTION BECOMES EFFECTIVE JANUARY 30, 2006

§125.409 Service difficulty reports (operational).

(a) Each certificate holder shall report the occurrence or detection of each failure, malfunction, or defect concerning—

(1) Any fire and, when monitored by a related fire-warning system, whether the fire-warning system functioned properly;

(2) Any false warning of fire or smoke;

(3) An engine exhaust system that causes damage to the engine, adjacent structure, equipment, or components;

(4) An aircraft component that causes the accumulation or circulation of smoke, vapor, or toxic or noxious fumes;

(5) Any engine flameout or shutdown during flight or ground operations;

(6) A propeller feathering system or ability of the system to control overspeed;

(7) A fuel or fuel-dumping system that affects fuel flow or causes hazardous leakage;

(8) A landing gear extension or retraction, or the opening or closing of landing gear doors during flight;

(9) Any brake system component that results in any detectable loss of brake actuating force when the aircraft is in motion on the ground;

(10) Any aircraft component or system that results in a rejected takeoff after initiation of the takeoff roll or the taking of emergency actions, as defined by the Aircraft Flight Manual or Pilot's Operating Handbook;

(11) Any emergency evacuation system or component including any exit door, passenger emergency evacuation lighting system, or evacuation equipment found to be defective or that fails to perform the intended function during an actual emergency or during training, testing, maintenance, demonstrations, or inadvertent deployments; and

(12) Autothrottle, autoflight, or flight control systems or components of these systems.

(b) For the purposes of this section, "during flight" means the period from the moment the aircraft leaves the surface of the earth on takeoff until it touches down on landing.

(c) In addition to the reports required by paragraph (a) of this section, each certificate holder shall report any other failure, malfunction, or defect in an aircraft, system, component, or powerplant that occurs or is detected at any time if that failure, malfunction, or defect has endangered or may endanger the safe operation of an aircraft.

(d) Each certificate holder shall submit each report required by this section, covering each 24-hour period beginning at 0900 local time of each day and ending at 0900 local time on the next day, to a centralized collection point as specified by the Administrator. Each report of occurrences during a 24-hour period shall be submitted to the FAA within the next 96 hours. However, a report due on Saturday or Sunday may be submitted on the following Monday, and a report due on a holiday may be submitted on the next workday. For aircraft operating in areas where mail is not collected, reports may be submitted within 24 hours after the aircraft returns to a point where the mail is collected. Each certificate holder also shall make the report data available for 30 days for examination by the certificate-holding district office in a form and manner acceptable to the Administrator.

(e) The certificate holder shall submit the reports required by this section on a form or in another format acceptable to the Administrator. The reports shall include the following information:

(1) The manufacturer, model, and serial number of the aircraft, engine, or propeller;

(2) The registration number of the aircraft;

(3) The operator designator;

(4) The date on which the failure, malfunction, or defect was discovered;

(5) The stage of flight or ground operation during which the failure, malfunction, or defect was discovered;

(6) The nature of the failure, malfunction, or defect;

(7) The applicable Joint Aircraft System/Component Code;

(8) The total cycles, if applicable, and total time of the aircraft, aircraft engine, propeller, or component;

(9) The manufacturer, manufacturer part number, part name, serial number, and location of the component that failed, malfunctioned, or was defective, if applicable;

(10) The manufacturer, manufacturer part number, part name, serial number, and location of the part that failed, malfunctioned, or was defective, if applicable;

(11) The precautionary or emergency action taken;

(12) Other information necessary for a more complete analysis of the cause of the failure, malfunction, or defect, including available information pertaining to type designation of the major component and the time since the last maintenance overhaul, repair, or inspection; and

(13) A unique control number for the occurrence, in a form acceptable to the Administrator.

(f) A certificate holder that also is the holder of a Type Certificate (including a Supplemental Type Certificate), a Parts Manufacturer Approval, or a Technical Standard Order authorization, or that is a licensee of a Type Certificate holder, need not report a failure, malfunction, or defect under this section if the failure, malfunction, or defect has been reported by that certificate holder under §21.3 of this chapter or under the accident reporting provisions of 49 CFR part 830.

(g) A report required by this section may be submitted by a certificated repair station when the reporting task has been assigned to that repair station by a part 125 certificate holder. However, the part 125 certificate holder remains primarily responsible for ensuring compliance with the provisions of this section. The part 125 certificate holder shall receive a copy of each report submitted by the repair station.

(h) No person may withhold a report required by this section although all information required by this section is not available.

(i) When a certificate holder gets supplemental information to complete the report required by this section, the certificate holder shall expeditiously submit that information as a supplement to the original report and use the unique control number from the original report.

[Docket No. 28293, 65 FR 56203, Sept. 15, 2000; as amended by Amdt. 125–37, 66 FR 21626, April 30, 2001; Docket FAA–2000–7952, 66 FR 58912, Nov. 23, 2001; FAA–2000–7952, 67 FR 78970, Dec. 27, 2002; FAA–2000–7952, 68 FR 75116, Dec. 30, 2003]

THE FOLLOWING NEW SECTION BECOMES EFFECTIVE JANUARY 30, 2006

§ 125.410 Service difficulty reports (structural).

(a) Each certificate holder shall report the occurrence or detection of each failure or defect related to—

(1) Corrosion, cracks, or disbonding that requires replacement of the affected part;

(2) Corrosion, cracks, or disbonding that requires rework or blendout because the corrosion, cracks, or disbonding exceeds the manufacturer's established allowable damage limits;

(3) Cracks, fractures, or disbonding in a composite structure that the equipment manufacturer has designated as a primary structure or a principal structural element; or

(4) Repairs made in accordance with approved data not contained in the manufacturer's maintenance manual.

(b) In addition to the reports required by paragraph (a) of this section, each certificate holder shall report any other failure or defect in aircraft structure that occurs or is detected at any time if that failure or defect has endangered or may endanger the safe operation of an aircraft.

(c) Each certificate holder shall submit each report required by this section, covering each 24-hour period beginning at 0900 local time of each day and ending at 0900 local time on the next day, to a centralized collection point as specified by the Administrator. Each report of occurrences during a 24-hour period shall be submitted to the FAA within the next 96 hours. However, a report due on Saturday or Sunday may be submitted on the following Monday, and a report due on a holiday may be submitted on the next workday. For aircraft operating in areas where mail is not collected, reports may be submitted within 24 hours after the aircraft returns to a point where the mail is collected. Each certificate holder also shall make the report data available for 30 days for examination by the certificate-holding district office in a form and manner acceptable to the Administrator.

(d) The certificate holder shall submit the reports required by this section on a form or in another format acceptable to the Administrator. The reports shall include the following information:

(1) The manufacturer, model, serial number, and registration number of the aircraft;

(2) The operator designator;

(3) The date on which the failure or defect was discovered;

(4) The stage of ground operation during which the failure or defect was discovered;

(5) The part name, part condition, and location of the failure or defect;

(6) The applicable Joint Aircraft System/Component Code;

(7) The total cycles, if applicable, and total time of the aircraft;

(8) Other information necessary for a more complete analysis of the cause of the failure or defect, including corrosion classification, if applicable, or crack length and available information pertaining to type designation of the major component and the time since the last maintenance overhaul, repair, or inspection; and

(9) A unique control number for the occurrence, in a form acceptable to the Administrator.

(e) A certificate holder that also is the holder of a Type Certificate (including a Supplemental Type Certificate), a Parts Manufacturer Approval, or a Technical Standard Order authorization, or that is a licensee of a Type Certificate holder, need not report a failure or defect under this section if the failure or defect has been reported by that certificate holder under §21.3 of this chapter or under the accident reporting provisions of 49 CFR part 830.

(f) A report required by this section may be submitted by a certificated repair station when the reporting task has been assigned to that repair station by the part 125 certificate holder. However, the part 125 certificate holder remains primarily responsible for ensuring compliance with the provisions of this section. The part 125 certificate holder shall receive a copy of each report submitted by the repair station.

(g) No person may withhold a report required by this section although all information required by this section is not available.

(h) When a certificate holder gets supplemental information to complete the report required by this section, the certificate holder shall expeditiously submit that information as a supplement to the original report and use the unique control number from the original report.

[Docket No. 28293, 65 FR 56204, Sept. 15, 2000; as amended by Amdt. 125–37, 66 FR 21626, April 30, 2001; Docket FAA–2000–7952, 66 FR 58912, Nov. 23, 2001; FAA–2000–7972, 67 FR 78970, Dec. 27, 2002; FAA–2000–7952, 68 FR 75116, Dec. 30, 2003]

§125.411 Airworthiness release or maintenance record entry.

(a) No certificate holder may operate an airplane after maintenance, preventive maintenance, or alteration is performed on the airplane unless the person performing that maintenance, preventive maintenance, or alteration prepares or causes to be prepared—

(1) An airworthiness release; or

(2) An entry in the aircraft maintenance records in accordance with the certificate holder's manual.

(b) The airworthiness release or maintenance record entry required by paragraph (a) of this section must—

(1) Be prepared in accordance with the procedures set forth in the certificate holder's manual;

(2) Include a certification that—

(i) The work was performed in accordance with the requirements of the certificate holder's manual;

(ii) All items required to be inspected were inspected by an authorized person who determined that the work was satisfactorily completed;

(iii) No known condition exists that would make the airplane unairworthy; and

(iv) So far as the work performed is concerned, the airplane is in condition for safe operation; and

(3) Be signed by a person authorized in part 43 of this chapter to perform maintenance, preventive maintenance, and alteration.

(c) When an airworthiness release form is prepared, the certificate holder must give a copy to the pilot in command and keep a record of it for at least 60 days.

(d) Instead of restating each of the conditions of the certification required by paragraph (b) of this section, the certificate holder may state in its manual that the signature of a person authorized in part 43 of this chapter constitutes that certification.

Appendix A to Part 125

Additional Emergency Equipment

(a) *Means for emergency evacuation.* Each passenger-carrying landplane emergency exit (other than over-the-wing) that is more than 6 feet from the ground with the airplane on the ground and the landing gear extended must have an approved means to assist the occupants in descending to the ground. The assisting means for a floor level emergency exit must meet the requirements of §25.809(f)(1) of this chapter in effect on April 30, 1972, except that, for any airplane for which the application for the type certificate was filed after that date, it must meet the requirements under which the airplane was type certificated. An assisting means that deploys automatically must be armed during taxiing, takeoffs, and landings. However, if the Administrator finds that the design of the exit makes compliance impractical, the Administrator may grant a deviation from the requirement of automatic deployment if the assisting means automatically erects upon deployment and, with respect to required emergency exits, if an emergency evacuation demonstration is conducted in accordance with §125.189. This paragraph does not apply to the rear window emergency exit of DC-3 airplanes operated with less than 36 occupants, including crewmembers, and less than five exits authorized for passenger use.

(b) *Interior emergency exit marking.* The following must be complied with for each passenger-carrying airplane:

(1) Each passenger emergency exit, its means of access, and means of opening must be conspicuously marked. The identity and location of each passenger emergency exit must be recognizable from a distance equal to the width of the cabin. The location of each passenger emergency exit must be indicated by a sign visible to occupants approaching along the main passenger aisle. There must be a locating sign—

(i) Above the aisle near each over-the-wing passenger emergency exit, or at another ceiling location if it is more practical because of low headroom;

(ii) Next to each floor level passenger emergency exit, except that one sign may serve two such exits if they both can be seen readily from that sign; and

(iii) On each bulkhead or divider that prevents fore and aft vision along the passenger cabin, to indicate emergency exits beyond and obscured by it, except that if this is not possible the sign may be placed at another appropriate location.

(2) Each passenger emergency exit marking and each locating sign must meet the following:

(i) For an airplane for which the application for the type certificate was filed prior to May 1, 1972, each passenger emergency exit marking and each locating sign must be manufactured to meet the requirements of §25.812(b) of this chapter in effect on April 30, 1972. On these airplanes, no sign may continue to be used if its luminescence (brightness) decreases to below 100 microlamberts. The colors may be reversed if it increases the emergency illumination of the passenger compartment. However, the Administrator may authorize deviation from the 2-inch background requirements if the Administrator finds that special circumstances exist that make compliance impractical and that the proposed deviation provides an equivalent level of safety.

(ii) For an airplane for which the application for the type certificate was filed on or after May 1, 1972, each passenger emergency exit marking and each locating sign must be manufactured to meet the interior emergency exit marking requirements under which the airplane was type certificated. On these airplanes, no sign may continue to be used if its luminescence (brightness) decreases to below 250 microlamberts.

(c) *Lighting for interior emergency exit markings.* Each passenger-carrying airplane must have an emergency lighting system, independent of the main lighting system. However, sources of general cabin illumination may be common to both the emergency and the main lighting systems if the power supply to the emergency lighting system is independent of the power supply to the main lighting system. The emergency lighting system must—

(1) Illuminate each passenger exit marking and locating sign; and

(2) Provide enough general lighting in the passenger cabin so that the average illumination, when measured at 40-inch intervals at seat armrest height, on the centerline of the main passenger aisle, is at least 0.05 foot-candles.

(d) *Emergency light operation.* Except for lights forming part of emergency lighting subsystems provided in compliance with §25.812(g) of this chapter (as prescribed in paragraph (h) of this section) that serve no more than one assist means, are independent of the airplane's main emergency lighting systems, and are automatically activated when the assist means is deployed, each light required by paragraphs (c) and (h) must comply with the following:

(1) Each light must be operable manually and must operate automatically from the independent lighting system—

(i) In a crash landing; or

(ii) Whenever the airplane's normal electric power to the light is interrupted.

(2) Each light must—

(i) Be operable manually from the flightcrew station and from a point in the passenger compartment that is readily accessible to a normal flight attendant seat;

(ii) Have a means to prevent inadvertent operation of the manual controls; and

(iii) When armed or turned on at either station, remain lighted or become lighted upon interruption of the airplane's normal electric power.

Each light must be armed or turned on during taxiing, takeoff, and landing. In showing compliance with this paragraph, a transverse vertical separation of the fuselage need not be considered.

(3) Each light must provide the required level of illumination for at least 10 minutes at the critical ambient conditions after emergency landing.

(e) *Emergency exit operating handles.*

(1) For a passenger-carrying airplane for which the application for the type certificate was filed prior to May 1, 1972, the location of each passenger emergency exit operating handle and instructions for opening the exit must be shown by a marking on or near the exit that is readable from a distance of 30 inches. In addition, for each Type I and Type II emergency exit with a locking mechanism released by rotary motion of the handle, the instructions for opening must be shown by—

(i) A red arrow with a shaft at least $\frac{3}{4}$-inch wide and a head twice the width of the shaft, extending along at least 70 degrees of arc at a radius approximately equal to $\frac{3}{4}$ of the handle length; and

(ii) The word "open" in red letters 1 inch high placed horizontally near the head of the arrow.

(2) For a passenger-carrying airplane for which the application for the type certificate was filed on or after May 1, 1972, the location of each passenger emergency exit operating handle and instructions for opening the exit must be shown in accordance with the requirements under which the airplane was type certificated. On these airplanes, no operating handle or operating handle cover may continue to be used if its luminescence (brightness) decreases to below 100 microlamberts.

(f) *Emergency exit access.* Access to emergency exits must be provided as follows for each passenger-carrying airplane:

(1) Each passageway between individual passenger areas, or leading to a Type I or Type II emergency exit, must be unobstructed and at least 20 inches wide.

(2) There must be enough space next to each Type I or Type II emergency exit to allow a crewmember to assist in the evacuation of passengers without reducing the unobstructed width of the passageway below that required in paragraph (f)(1) of this section. However, the Administrator may authorize deviation from this requirement for an airplane certificated under the provisions of part 4b of the Civil Air Regulations in effect before December 20, 1951, if the Administrator finds that special circumstances exist that provide an equivalent level of safety.

(3) There must be access from the main aisle to each Type III and Type IV exit. The access from the aisle to these exits must not be obstructed by seats, berths, or other protrusions in a manner that would reduce the effectiveness of the exit. In addition—

(i) For an airplane for which the application for the type certificate was filed prior to May 1, 1972, the access must meet the requirements of §25.813(c) of this chapter in effect on April 30, 1972; and

(ii) For an airplane for which the application for the type certificate was filed on or after May 1, 1972, the access must meet the emergency exit access requirements under which the airplane was certificated.

(4) If it is necessary to pass through a passageway between passenger compartments to reach any required emergency exit from any seat in the passenger cabin, the passageway must not be obstructed. However, curtains may be used if they allow free entry through the passageway.

(5) No door may be installed in any partition between passenger compartments.

(6) If it is necessary to pass through a doorway separating the passenger cabin from other areas to reach any required emergency exit from any passenger seat, the door must have a means to latch it in open position, and the door must be latched open during each takeoff and landing. The latching means must be able to withstand the loads imposed upon it when the door is subjected to the ultimate inertia forces, relative to the surrounding structure, listed in §25.561(b) of this chapter.

(g) *Exterior exit markings.* Each passenger emergency exit and the means of opening that exit from the outside must be marked on the outside of the airplane. There must be a 2-inch colored band outlining each passenger emergency exit on the side of the fuselage. Each outside marking, including the band, must be readily distinguishable from the surrounding fuselage area by contrast in color. The markings must comply with the following:

(1) If the reflectance of the darker color is 15 percent or less, the reflectance of the lighter color must be at least 45 percent. "Reflectance" is the ratio of the luminous flux reflected by a body to the luminous flux it receives.

(2) If the reflectance of the darker color is greater than 15 percent, at least a 30 percent difference between its reflectance and the reflectance of the lighter color must be provided.

(3) Exits that are not in the side of the fuselage must have the external means of opening and applicable instructions marked conspicuously in red or, if red is inconspicuous against the background color, in bright chrome yellow and, when the opening means for such an exit is located on only one side of the fuselage, a conspicuous marking to that effect must be provided on the other side.

(h) *Exterior emergency lighting and escape route.*

(1) Each passenger-carrying airplane must be equipped with exterior lighting that meets the following requirements:

(i) For an airplane for which the application for the type certificate was filed prior to May 1, 1972, the requirements of §25.812(f) and (g) of this chapter in effect on April 30, 1972.

(ii) For an airplane for which the application for the type certificate was filed on or after May 1, 1972, the exterior emergency lighting requirements under which the airplane was type certificated.

(2) Each passenger-carrying airplane must be equipped with a slip-resistant escape route that meets the following requirements:

(i) For an airplane for which the application for the type certificate was filed prior to May 1, 1972, the requirements of §25.803(e) of this chapter in effect on April 30, 1972.

(ii) For an airplane for which the application for the type certificate was filed on or after May 1, 1972, the slip-resistant escape route requirements under which the airplane was type certificated.

(i) *Floor level exits.* Each floor level door or exit in the side of the fuselage (other than those leading into a cargo or baggage compartment that is not accessible from the passenger cabin) that is 44 or more inches high and 20 or more inches wide, but not wider than 46 inches, each passenger ventral exit (except the ventral exits on M-404 and CV-240 airplanes) and each tail cone exit must meet the requirements of this section for floor level emergency exits. However, the Administrator may grant a deviation from this paragraph if the Administrator finds that circumstances make full compliance impractical and that an acceptable level of safety has been achieved.

(j) *Additional emergency exits.* Approved emergency exits in the passenger compartments that are in excess of the minimum number of required emergency exits must meet all of the applicable provisions of this section except paragraph (f), (1), (2), and (3) and must be readily accessible.

(k) On each large passenger-carrying turbojet-powered airplane, each ventral exit and tailcone exit must be—

(1) Designed and constructed so that it cannot be opened during flight; and

(2) Marked with a placard readable from a distance of 30 inches and installed at a conspicuous location near the means of opening the exit, stating that the exit has been designed and constructed so that it cannot be opened during flight.

Appendix B to Part 125

Criteria for Demonstration of Emergency Evacuation Procedures Under §125.189

(a) *Aborted takeoff demonstration.*

(1) The demonstration must be conducted either during the dark of the night or during daylight with the dark of the night simulated. If the demonstration is conducted indoors during daylight hours, it must be conducted with each window covered and each door closed to minimize the daylight effect. Illumination on the floor or ground may be used, but it must be kept low and shielded against shining into the airplane's windows or doors.

(2) The airplane must be in a normal ground attitude with landing gear extended.

(3) Stands or ramps may be used for descent from the wing to the ground. Safety equipment such as mats or inverted life rafts may be placed on the ground to protect participants. No other equipment that is not part of the airplane's emergency evacuation equipment may be used to aid the participants in reaching the ground.

(4) The airplane's normal electric power sources must be deenergized.

(5) All emergency equipment for the type of passenger-carrying operation involved must be installed in accordance with the certificate holder's manual.

(6) Each external door and exit and each internal door or curtain must be in position to simulate a normal takeoff.

(7) A representative passenger load of persons in normal health must be used. At least 30 percent must be females. At least 5 percent must be over 60 years of age with a proportionate number of females. At least 5 percent, but not more than 10 percent, must be children under 12 years of age, prorated through that age group. Three life-size dolls, not included as part of the total passenger load, must be carried by passengers to simulate live infants 2 years old or younger. Crewmembers, mechanics, and training personnel who maintain or operate the airplane in the normal course of their duties may not be used as passengers.

(8) No passenger may be assigned a specific seat except as the Administrator may require. Except as required by item (12) of this paragraph, no employee of the certificate holder may be seated next to an emergency exit.

(9) Seat belts and shoulder harnesses (as required) must be fastened.

(10) Before the start of the demonstration, approximately one-half of the total average amount of carry-on baggage, blankets, pillows, and other similar articles must be distributed at several locations in the aisles and emergency exit access ways to create minor obstructions.

(11) The seating density and arrangement of the airplane must be representative of the highest capacity passenger version of that airplane the certificate holder operates or proposes to operate.

(12) Each crewmember must be a member of a regularly scheduled line crew, must be seated in that crewmember's normally assigned seat for takeoff, and must remain in that seat until the signal for commencement of the demonstration is received.

(13) No crewmember or passenger may be given prior knowledge of the emergency exits available for the demonstration.

(14) The certificate holder may not practice, rehearse, or describe the demonstration for the participants nor may any participant have taken part in this type of demonstration within the preceding 6 months.

(15) The pretakeoff passenger briefing required by §125.327 may be given in accordance with the certificate holder's manual. The passengers may also be warned to follow directions of crewmembers, but may not be instructed on the procedures to be followed in the demonstration.

(16) If safety equipment as allowed by item (3) of this section is provided, either all passenger and cockpit windows must be blacked out or all of the emergency exits must have safety equipment to prevent disclosure of the available emergency exits.

(17) Not more than 50 percent of the emergency exits in the sides of the fuselage of an airplane that meet all of the requirements applicable to the required emergency exits for that airplane may be used for the demonstration. Exits that are not to be used in the demonstration must have the exit handle deactivated or must be indicated by red lights, red tape or other acceptable means, placed outside the exits to indicate fire or other reason that they are unusable. The exits to be used must be representative of all of the emergency exits on the airplane and must be designated by the certificate holder, subject to approval by the Administrator. At least one floor level exit must be used.

(18) All evacuees, except those using an over-the-wing exit, must leave the airplane by a means provided as part of the airplane's equipment.

(19) The certificate holder's approved procedures and all of the emergency equipment that is normally available, including slides, ropes, lights, and megaphones, must be fully utilized during the demonstration.

(20) The evacuation time period is completed when the last occupant has evacuated the airplane and is on the ground. Evacuees using stands or ramps allowed by item (3) above are considered to be on the ground when they are on the stand or ramp: *Provided*, That the acceptance rate of the stand or ramp is no greater than the acceptance rate of the means available on the airplane for descent from the wing during an actual crash situation.

(b) *Ditching demonstration.* The demonstration must assume that daylight hours exist outside the airplane and that all required crewmembers are available for the demonstration.

(1) If the certificate holder's manual requires the use of passengers to assist in the launching of liferafts, the needed passengers must be aboard the airplane and participate in the demonstration according to the manual.

(2) A stand must be placed at each emergency exit and wing with the top of the platform at a height simulating the water level of the airplane following a ditching.

(3) After the ditching signal has been received, each evacuee must don a life vest according to the certificate holder's manual.

(4) Each liferaft must be launched and inflated according to the certificate holder's manual and all other required emergency equipment must be placed in rafts.

(5) Each evacuee must enter a liferaft and the crewmembers assigned to each liferaft must indicate the location of emergency equipment aboard the raft and describe its use.

(6) Either the airplane, a mockup of the airplane, or a floating device simulating a passenger compartment must be used.

(i) If a mockup of the airplane is used, it must be a life-size mockup of the interior and representative of the airplane currently used by or proposed to be used by the certificate holder and must contain adequate seats for use of the evacuees. Operation of the emergency exits and the doors must closely simulate that on the airplane. Sufficient wing area must be installed outside the over-the-wing exits to demonstrate the evacuation.

(ii) If a floating device simulating a passenger compartment is used, it must be representative, to the extent possible, of the passenger compartment of the airplane used in operations. Operation of the emergency exits and the doors must closely simulate operation on that airplane. Sufficient wing area must be installed outside the over-the-wing exits to demonstrate the evacuation. The device must be equipped with the same survival equipment as is installed on the airplane, to accommodate all persons participating in the demonstration.

Appendix C to Part 125

Ice Protection

If certification with ice protection provisions is desired, compliance with the following must be shown:

(a) The recommended procedures for the use of the ice protection equipment must be set forth in the Airplane Flight Manual.

(b) An analysis must be performed to establish, on the basis of the airplane's operational needs, the adequacy of the ice protection system for the various components of the airplane. In addition, tests of the ice protection system must be conducted to demonstrate that the airplane is capable of operating safely in continuous maximum and intermittent maximum icing conditions as described in appendix C of part 25 of this chapter.

(c) Compliance with all or portions of this section may be accomplished by reference, where applicable because of similarity of the designs, to analyses and tests performed by the applicant for a type certificated model.

Appendix D to Part 125
Airplane Flight Recorder Specification

Parameters	Range	Accuracy sensor input to DFDR readout	Sampling interval (per second)	Resolution[4] readout
Time (GMT or Frame Counter) (range 0 to 4095, sampled 1 per frame)	24 Hrs	±0.125% per hour	0.25 (1 per 4 seconds)	1 sec.
Altitude	–1,000 ft to max certificated altitude of aircraft	±100 to ±700 ft (See Table 1, TSO–C51a)	1	5' to 35'[1]
Airspeed	50 KIAS to V_{S0}, and V_{S0} to 1.2 V_D	±5%, ±3%	1	1 kt.
Heading	360°	±2°	1	0.5°
Normal Acceleration (Vertical)	–3g to +6g	±1% of max range excluding datum error of ±5%	8	0.01g
Pitch Attitude	±75°	±2°	1	0.5°
Roll Attitude	±180°	±2°	1	0.5°
Radio Transmitter Keying	On-Off (Discrete)		1	
Thrust/Power on Each Engine	Full range forward	±2°	1	0.2%[2]
Trailing Edge Flap or Cockpit Control Selection	Full range or each discrete position	±3° or as pilot's indicator	0.5	0.5%[2]
Leading Edge Flap or Cockpit Control Selection	Full range or each discrete position	±3° or as pilot's indicator	0.5	0.5%[2]
Thrust Reverser Position	Stowed, in transit, and reverse (Discrete)		1 (per 4 seconds per engine)	
Ground Spoiler Position/Speed Brake Selection	Full range or each discrete position	±2% unless higher accuracy uniquely required	1	0.2%[2]
Marker Beacon Passage	Discrete		1	
Autopilot Engagement	Discrete		1	
Longitudinal Acceleration	±1g	±1.5% max range excluding datum error of ±5%	4	0.01g
Pilot Input and/or Surface Position—Primary Controls (Pitch, Roll, Yaw)[3]	Full range	±2° unless higher accuracy uniquely required	1	0.2%[2]
Lateral Acceleration	±1g	±1.5% max range excluding datum error of ±5%	4	0.01g
Pitch Trim Position	Full Range	±3% unless higher accuracy uniquely required	1	0.3%[2]
Glideslope Deviation	±400 Microamps	±3%	1	0.3%[2]
Localizer Deviation	±400 Microamps	±3%	1	0.3%[2]
AFCS Mode and Engagement Status	Discrete		1	
Radio Altitude	–20 ft to 2,500 ft	±2 Ft or ±3% whichever is greater below 500 ft and ±5% above 500 ft	1	1 ft + 5%[2] above 500'
Master Warning	Discrete		1	
Main Gear Squat Switch Status	Discrete		1	
Angle of Attack (if recorded directly)	As installed	As installed	2	0.3%[2]
Outside Air Temperature or Total Air Temperature	–50°C to +90°C	±2°C	0.5	0.3°C
Hydraulics, Each System Low Pressure	Discrete		0.5	or 0.5%[2]
Groundspeed	As installed	Most accurate systems installed (IMS equipped aircraft only)	1	0.2%[2]

Appendix D to Part 125
Airplane Flight Recorder Specification (*Continued*)

If additional recording capacity is available, recording of the following parameters is recommended. The parameters are listed in order of significance:

Parameters	Range	Accuracy sensor input to DFDR readout	Sampling interval (per second)	Resolution[4] readout
Drift Angle	When available, As installed	As installed	4	
Wind Speed and Direction	When available, As installed	As installed	4	
Latitude and Longitude	When available, As installed	As installed	4	
Brake pressure / Brake pedal position	As installed	As installed	1	
Additional engine parameters: EPR N[1] N[2] EGT	 As installed As installed As installed As installed	 As installed As installed As installed As installed	 1 (per engine) 1 (per engine 1 (per engine) 1 (per engine)	
Throttle Lever Position	As installed	As installed	1 (per engine)	
Fuel Flow	As installed	As installed	1 (per engine)	
TCAS: TA RA Sensitivity level (as selected by crew)	 As installed As installed As installed	 As installed As installed As installed	 1 1 2	
GPWS (ground proximity warning system)	Discrete		1	
Landing gear or gear selector position	Discrete		0.25 (1 per 4 seconds)	
DME 1 and 2 Distance	0–200 NM	As installed	0.25	1 mi.
Nav 1 and 2 Frequency Selection	Full range	As installed	0.25	

[1] When altitude rate is recorded. Altitude rate must have sufficient resolution and sampling to permit the derivation of altitude to 5 feet.

[2] Percent of full range.

[3] For airplanes that can demonstrate the capability of deriving either the control input on control movement (one from the other) for all modes of operation and flight regimes, the "or" applies. For airplanes with non-mechanical control systems (fly-by-wire) the "and" applies. In airplanes with split surfaces, suitable combination of inputs is acceptable in lieu of recording each surface separately.

[4] This column applies to aircraft manufactured after October 11, 1991.

[Docket No. 25530, 53 FR 26150, July 11, 1988; 53 FR 30906, Aug. 16, 1988]

125

Appendix E to Part 125
Airplane Flight Recorder Specifications

The recorded values must meet the designated range, resolution, and accuracy requirements during dynamic and static conditions. All data recorded must be correlated in time to within one second.

Parameters	Range	Accuracy (sensor input)	Seconds per sampling interval	Resolution	Remarks
1. Time or Relative Times Counts [1]	24 Hrs, 0 to 4095	±0.125% Per Hour	4	1 sec	UTC time preferred when available. Count increments each 4 seconds of system operation.
2. Pressure Altitude	–1000 ft to max certificated altitude of aircraft. +5000 ft.	±100 to ±700 ft (see table, TSO C124a or TSO C51a)	1	5' to 35'	Data should be obtained from the air data computer when practicable.
3. Indicated airspeed or Calibrated airspeed	50 KIAS or minimum value to Max V_{SO} to 1.2 V_D	±5% and ±3%	1	1 kt	Data should be obtained from the air data computer when practicable.
4. Heading (Primary flight crew reference)	0–360° and Discrete "true" or "mag"	±2°	1	0.5°	When true or magnetic heading can be selected as the primary heading reference, a discrete indicating selection must be recorded.
5. Normal Acceleration (Vertical)[9]	–3g to +6g	±1% of max range excluding datum error of ±5%	0.125	0.004g	—
6. Pitch Attitude	±75°	±2°	1 or 0.25 for airplanes operated under §125.226(f)	0.5°	A sampling rate of 0.25 is recommended.
7. Roll Attitude [2]	±180°	±2°	1 or 0.5 for airplanes operated under §125.226(f)	0.5°	A sampling rate of 0.5 is recommended.
8. Manual Radio Transmitter Keying or CVR/DFDR synchronization reference	On-Off (Discrete) None	—	1	—	Preferably each crewmember but one discrete acceptable for all transmission provided the CVR/FDR system complies with TSO C124a CVR synchronization requirements (paragraph 4.2.1 ED-55).
9. Thrust/Power on each engine — primary flight crew reference	Full Range Forward	±2%	1 (per engine)	0.3% of full range	Sufficient parameters (e.g. EPR, N1 or Torque, NP) as appropriate to the particular engine be recorded to determine power in forward and reverse thrust, including potential overspeed condition.
10. Autopilot Engagement	Discrete "on" or "off"	—	1	—	—
11. Longitudinal Acceleration	±1g	±1.5% max. range excluding datum error of ±5%	0.25	0.004g	—
12a. Pitch Control(s) position (non-fly-by-wire systems)	Full Range	±2% Unless Higher Accuracy Uniquely Required	0.5 or 0.25 for airplanes operated under §125.226(f)	0.5% of full range	For airplanes that have a flight control break away capability that allows either pilot to operate the controls independently, record both control inputs. The control inputs may be sampled alternately once per second to produce the sampling interval of 0.5 or 0.25, as applicable.

Appendix E to Part 125
Airplane Flight Recorder Specifications (Continued)

The recorded values must meet the designated range, resolution, and accuracy requirements during dynamic and static conditions. All data recorded must be correlated in time to within one second.

Parameters	Range	Accuracy (sensor input)	Seconds per sampling interval	Resolution	Remarks
12b. Pitch Control(s) position (fly-by-wire systems) [3]	Full Range	±2° Unless Higher Accuracy Uniquely Required	0.5 or 0.25 for airplanes operated under §125.226(f)	0.2% of full range	—
13a. Lateral Control position(s) (non-fly-by-wire)	Full Range	±2° Unless Higher Accuracy Uniquely Required	0.5 or 0.25 for airplanes operated under §125.226(f)	0.2% of full range	For airplanes that have a flight control break away capability that allows either pilot to operate the controls independently, record both control inputs. The control inputs may be sampled alternately once per second to produce the sampling interval of 0.5 or 0.25, as applicable.
13b. Lateral Control position(s) (fly-by-wire) [4]	Full Range	±2° Unless Higher Accuracy Uniquely Required	0.5 or 0.25 for airplanes operated under §125.226(f)	0.2% of full range	—
14a. Yaw Control position(s) (non-fly-by-wire) [5]	Full Range	±2° Unless Higher Accuracy Uniquely Required	0.5	0.3% of full range	For airplanes that have a flight control break away capability that allows either pilot to operate the controls independently, record both control inputs. The control inputs may be sampled alternately once per second to produce the sampling interval of 0.5.
14b. Yaw Control position(s) (fly-by-wire)	Full Range	±2° Unless Higher Accuracy Uniquely Required	0.5	0.2% of full range	—
15. Pitch Control Surface(s) Position [6]	Full Range	±2° Unless Higher Accuracy Uniquely Required	0.5 or 0.25 for airplanes operated under §125.226(f)	0.3% of full range	For airplanes fitted with multiple or split surfaces, a suitable combination of inputs is acceptable in lieu of recording each surface separately. The control surfaces may be sampled alternately to produce the sampling interval of 0.5 or 0.25.
16. Lateral Control Surface(s) Position [7]	Full Range	±2° Unless Higher Accuracy Uniquely Required	0.5 or 0.25 for airplanes operated under §125.226(f)	0.3% of full range	A suitable combination of surface position sensors is acceptable in lieu of recording each surface separately. The control surfaces may be sampled alternately to produce the sampling interval of 0.5 or 0.25.
17. Yaw Control Surface(s) Position [8]	Full Range	±2° Unless Higher Accuracy Uniquely Required	0.5	0.2% of full range	For airplanes with multiple or split surfaces, a suitable combination of surface position sensors is acceptable in lieu of recording each surface separately. The control surfaces may be sampled alternately to produce the sampling interval of 0.5.
18. Lateral Acceleration	±1g	±1.5% max. range excluding datum error of ± 5%	0.25	0.004g	—
19. Pitch Trim Surface Position	Full Range	±3° Unless Higher Accuracy Uniquely Required	1	0.6% of full range	—

125

Appendix E to Part 125
Airplane Flight Recorder Specifications (Continued)

The recorded values must meet the designated range, resolution, and accuracy requirements during dynamic and static conditions. All data recorded must be correlated in time to within one second.

Parameters	Range	Accuracy (sensor input)	Seconds per sampling interval	Resolution	Remarks
20. Trailing Edge Flap or Cockpit Control Selection[10]	Full Range or Each Position (discrete)	±3° or as Pilot's indicator	2	0.5% of full range	Flap position and cockpit control may each be sampled alternately at 4 second intervals, to give a data point every 2 seconds.
21. Leading Edge Flap or Cockpit Control Selection[11]	Full Range or Each Discrete Position	±3° or as Pilot's indicator and sufficient to determine each discrete position	2	0.5% of full range	Left and right sides, or flap position and cockpit control may each be sampled at 4 second intervals, so as to give a data point every 2 seconds.
22. Each Thrust Reverser Position (or equivalent for propeller airplane)	Stowed, In Transit, and Reverse (Discrete)	—	1 (per engine)	—	Turbo-jet – 2 discretes enable the 3 states to be determined. Turbo-prop – 1 discrete.
23. Ground Spoiler Position or Speed Brake Selection[12]	Full Range or Each Position (discrete)	±2° Unless Higher Accuracy Uniquely Required	1 or 0.5 for airplanes operated under §125.226(f)	0.5% of full range	—
24. Outside Air Temperature or Total Air Temperature[13]	−50°C to +90°C	±2°C	2	0.3°C	—
25. Autopilot/Autothrottle/ AFCS Mode and Engagement Status	A suitable combination of discretes	—	1	—	Discretes should show which systems are engaged and which primary modes are controlling the flight path and speed of the aircraft.
26. Radio Altitude[14]	–20 ft to 2,500 ft	±2 ft or ±3% Whichever is Greater Below 500 ft and ±5% Above 500 ft	1	1 ft + 5% above 500 ft	For autoland/category 3 operations. Each radio altimeter should be recorded, but arranged so that at least one is recorded each second.
27. Localizer Deviation, MLS Azimuth, or GPS Latitude Deviation	±400 Microamps or available sensor range as installed ±62°	As installed ±3% recommended	1	0.3% of full range	For autoland/category 3 operations. Each system should be recorded, but arranged so that at least one is recorded each second. It is not necessary to record ILS and MLS at the same time, only the approach aid in use need be recorded.
28. Glideslope Deviation, MLS Elevation, or GPS Vertical Deviation	±400 Microamps or available sensor range as installed 0.9 to +30°	As installed ±3% recommended	1	0.3% of full range	For autoland/category 3 operations. Each system should be recorded, but arranged so that at least one is recorded each second. It is not necessary to record ILS and MLS at the same time, only the approach aid in use need be recorded.
29. Marker Beacon Passage	Discrete "on" or "off"		1	—	A single discrete is acceptable for all markers.
30. Master Warning	Discrete	—	1	—	Record the master warning and record each "red" warning that cannot be determined from other parameters or from the cockpit voice recorder.
31. Air/ground sensor (primary airplane system reference nose or main gear)	Discrete "air" or "ground"	—	1 (0.25 recommended)	—	—

Appendix E to Part 125
Airplane Flight Recorder Specifications (Continued)

The recorded values must meet the designated range, resolution, and accuracy requirements during dynamic and static conditions. All data recorded must be correlated in time to within one second.

Parameters	Range	Accuracy (sensor input)	Seconds per sampling interval	Resolution	Remarks
32. Angle of Attack (if measured directly)	As installed	As installed	2 or 0.5 for airplanes operated under §125.226(f)	0.3% of full range	If left and right sensors are available, each may be recorded at 4 or 1 second intervals, as appropriate, so as to give a data point at 2 seconds or 0.5 second, as required.
33. Hydraulic Pressure Low, Each System	Discrete or available sensor range, "low" or "normal"	±5%	2	0.5% of full range	—
34. Groundspeed	As installed	Most Accurate Systems Installed	1	0.2% of full range	—
35. GPWS (ground proximity warning system)	Discrete "warning" or "off"	—	1	—	A suitable combination of discretes unless recorder capacity is limited in which case a single discrete for all modes is acceptable.
36. Landing Gear Position or Landing gear cockpit control selection	Discrete	—	4	—	A suitable combination of discretes should be recorded.
37. Drift Angle [15]	As installed	As installed	4	0.1°	—
38. Wind Speed and Direction	As installed	As installed	4	1 knot, and 1.0°	—
39. Latitude and Longitude	As installed	As installed	4	0.002°, or as installed	Provided by the Primary Navigation System Reference. Where capacity permits latitude/longitude resolution should be 0.0002°.
40. Stick shaker and pusher activation	Discrete(s) "on" or "off"	—	1	—	A suitable combination of discretes to determine activation.
41. Windshear Detection	Discrete "warning" or "off"	—	1	—	—
42. Throttle/power lever position [16]	Full Range	±2%	1 for each lever	2% of full range	For airplanes with non-mechanically linked cockpit engine controls.
43. Additional Engine Parameters	As installed	As installed	Each engine, each second	2% of full range	Where capacity permits, the preferred priority is indicated vibration level, N2, EGT, Fuel Flow, Fuel Cut-off lever position and N3, unless engine manufacturer recommends otherwise.
44. Traffic Alert and Collision Avoidance System (TCAS)	Discretes	As installed	1	—	A suitable combination of discretes should be recorded to determine the status of – Combined Control, Vertical Control, Up Advisory, and Down Advisory. (ref. ARINC Characteristic 735 Attachment 6E, TCAS VERTICAL RA DATA OUTPUT WORD.)
45. DME 1 and 2 Distance	0–200 NM	As installed	4	1 NM	1 mile
46. Nav 1 and 2 Selected Frequency	Full Range	As installed	4	—	Sufficient to determine selected frequency.

Appendix E to Part 125
Airplane Flight Recorder Specifications (Continued)

The recorded values must meet the designated range, resolution, and accuracy requirements during dynamic and static conditions. All data recorded must be correlated in time to within one second.

Parameters	Range	Accuracy (sensor input)	Seconds per sampling interval	Resolution	Remarks
47. Selected barometric setting	Full Range	±5%	(1 per 64 sec.)	0.2% of full range	—
48. Selected altitude	Full Range	±5%	1	100 ft	—
49. Selected speed	Full Range	±5%	1	1 knot	—
50. Selected Mach	Full Range	±5%	1	.01	—
51. Selected vertical speed	Full Range	±5%	1	100 ft/min	—
52. Selected heading	Full Range	±5%	1	1°	—
53. Selected flight path	Full Range	±5%	1	1°	—
54. Selected decision height	Full Range	±5%	64	1 ft	—
55. EFIS display format	Discrete(s)	—	4	—	Discretes should show the display system status (e.g., off, normal, fail, composite, sector, plan, nav aids, weather radar, range, copy).
56. Multi-function/Engine Alerts Display format	Discrete(s)	—	4	—	Discretes should show the display system status (e.g., off, normal, fail, and the identity of display pages for emergency procedures, need not be recorded.)
57. Thrust command[17]	Full Range	±2%	2	2% of full range	—
58. Thrust target	Full Range	±2%	4	2% of full range	—
59. Fuel quantity in CG trim tank	Full Range	±5%	(1 per 64 sec.)	1% of full range	—
60. Primary Navigation System Reference	Discrete GPS, INS, VOR/ DME, MLS, Loran C, Omega, Localizer Glideslope	—	4	—	A suitable combination of discretes to determine the Primary Navigation System reference.
61. Ice Detection	Discrete "ice" or "no ice"	—	4	—	—
62. Engine warning each engine vibration	Discrete	—	1	—	—
63. Engine warning each engine over temp	Discrete	—	1	—	—
64. Engine warning each engine oil pressure low	Discrete	—	1	—	—
65. Engine warning each engine over speed	Discrete	—	1	—	—

Appendix E to Part 125
Airplane Flight Recorder Specifications (Continued)

The recorded values must meet the designated range, resolution, and accuracy requirements during dynamic and static conditions. All data recorded must be correlated in time to within one second.

Parameters	Range	Accuracy (sensor input)	Seconds per sampling interval	Resolution	Remarks
66. Yaw Trim Surface Position	Full Range	±3% Unless Higher Accuracy Uniquely Required	2	0.3% of full range	—
67. Roll Trim Surface Position	Full Range	±3% Unless Higher Accuracy Uniquely Required	2	0.3% of full range	—
68. Brake Pressure (left and right)	As installed	±5%	1	—	To determine braking effort applied by pilots or by autobrakes.
69. Brake Pedal Application (left and right)	Discrete or Analog "applied" or "off"	±5% (Analog)	1	—	To determine braking applied by pilots.
70. Yaw or sideslip angle	Full Range	±5%	1	0.5°	—
71. Engine bleed valve position	Discrete "open" or "closed"	—	4	—	—
72. De-icing or anti-icing system selection	Discrete "on" or "off"	—	4	—	—
73. Computed center of gravity	Full Range	±5%	(1 per 64 sec.)	1% of full range	—
74. AC electrical bus status	Discrete "power" or "off"	—	4	—	Each bus.
75. DC electrical bus status	Discrete "power" or "off"	—	4	—	Each bus.
76. APU bleed valve position	Discrete "open" or "closed"	—	4	—	—
77. Hydraulic Pressure (each system)	Full Range	±5%	2	100 psi	—
78. Loss of cabin pressure	Discrete "loss" or "normal"	—	1	—	—
79. Computer failure (critical flight and engine control systems)	Discrete "fail" or "normal"	—	4	—	—
80. Heads-up display (when an information source is installed)	Discrete(s) "on" or "off"	—	4	—	—
81. Para-visual display (when an information source is installed)	Discrete(s) "on" or "off"	—	1	—	—
82. Cockpit trim control input position – pitch	Full Range	±5%	1	0.2% of full range	Where mechanical means for control inputs are not available, cockpit display trim positions should be recorded.

125

Appendix E to Part 125
Airplane Flight Recorder Specifications (Continued)

The recorded values must meet the designated range, resolution, and accuracy requirements during dynamic and static conditions. All data recorded must be correlated in time to within one second.

Parameters	Range	Accuracy (sensor input)	Seconds per sampling interval	Resolution	Remarks
83. Cockpit trim control input position – roll	Full Range	±5%	1	0.7% of full range	Where mechanical means for control inputs are not available, cockpit display trim position should be recorded.
84. Cockpit trim control input position – yaw	Full Range	±5%	1	0.3% of full range	Where mechanical means for control input are not available, cockpit display trim positions should be recorded.
85. Trailing edge flap and cockpit flap control position	Full Range	±5%	2	0.5% of full range	Trailing edge flaps and cockpit flap control position may each be sampled alternately at 4 second intervals to provide a sample each 0.5 second.
86. Leading edge flap and cockpit flap control position	Full Range or Discrete	±5%	1	0.5% of full range	—
87. Ground spoiler position and speed brake selection	Full Range or Discrete	±5%	0.5	0.3% of full range	—
88. All cockpit flight control input forces (control wheel, control column, rudder pedal)	Full Range Control wheel ±70 lbs Control column ±85 lbs Rudder pedal ±165 lbs	±5%	1	0.3% of full range	For fly-by-wire flight control systems, where flight control surface position is a function of the displacement of the control input device only, it is not necessary to record this parameter. For airplanes that have a flight control break away capability that allows either pilot to operate the control independently, record both control force inputs. The control force inputs may be sampled alternately once per 2 seconds to produce the sampling interval of 1.

[1] For A300 B2/B4 airplanes, resolution = 6 seconds.
[2] For A330/A340 series airplanes, resolution = 0.703°.
[3] For A318/A319/A320/A321 series airplanes, resolution = 0.275% (0.088° > 0.064°).
For A330/A340 series airplanes, resolution = 2.20% (0.703° > 0.064°).
[4] For A318/A319/A320/A321 series airplanes, resolution = 0.22% (0.088° > 0.080°).
For A330/A340 series airplanes, resolution = 1.76% (0.703° > 0.080°).
[5] For A330/A340 series airplanes, resolution = 1.18% (0.703° > 0.120°).
[6] For A330/A340 series airplanes, resolution = 0.783% (0.352° > 0.090°).
[7] For A330/A340 series airplanes, aileron resolution = 0.704% (0.352° > 0.100°).
For A330/A340 series airplanes, spoiler resolution = 1.406% (0.703° > 0.100°).
[8] For A330/A340 series airplanes, resolution = 0.30% (0.176° > 0.12°).
For A330/A340 series airplanes, seconds per sampling interval = 1.
[9] For B-717 series airplanes, resolution = .005g.
For Dassault F900C/F900EX airplanes, resolution = .007g.
[10] For A330/A340 series airplanes, resolution = 1.05% (0.250° > 0.120°).
[11] For A330/A340 series airplanes, resolution = 1.05% (0.250° > 0.120°).
For A330 B2/B4 series airplanes, resolution = 0.92% (0.230° > 0.125°).
[12] For A330/A340 series airplanes, spoiler resolution = 1.406% (0.703° > 0.100°).
[13] For A330/A340 series airplanes, resolution = 0.5°C.
[14] For Dassault F900C/F900EX airplanes, Radio Altitude resolution = 1.25 ft.
[15] For A330/A340 series airplanes, resolution = 0.352°.
[16] For A318/A319/A320/A321 series airplanes, resolution = 4.32%.
For A330/A340 series airplanes, resolution is 3.27% of full range for throttle lever angle (TLA); for reverse thrust, reverse throttle lever angle (RLA) resolution is nonlinear over the active reverse thrust range, which is 51.54° to 96.14°. The resolved element is 2.8° uniformly over the entire active reverse thrust range, or 2.9% of the full range value of 96.14°.
[17] For A318/A319/A320/A321 series airplanes, with IAE engines, resolution = 2.58%.

[Docket No. 28109, 62 FR 38390, July 17, 1997; 62 FR 48135, Sept. 12, 1997; Amdt. 125–32, 64 FR 46121, Aug. 24, 1999; Amdt. 125–34, 65 FR 51745, Aug. 24, 2000; Amdt. 125–39, 67 FR 54323, Aug. 21, 2002; Amdt. 125–42, 68 FR 42937, July 18, 2003; Amdt. 125–42, 68 FR 50069, Aug. 20, 2003]

PART 135

OPERATING REQUIREMENTS: COMMUTER AND ON-DEMAND OPERATIONS AND RULES GOVERNING PERSONS ON BOARD SUCH AIRCRAFT

SPECIAL FEDERAL AVIATION REGULATIONS

SFAR No. 36
SFAR No. 50–2 [Note]
SFAR No. 58
SFAR No. 71 [Note]
SFAR No. 78 [Note]
SFAR No. 89
SFAR No. 93
SFAR No. 97 [Note]

Subpart A — General

Sec.

135.1 Applicability.
135.2 Compliance schedule for operators that transition to part 121 of this chapter; certain new entrant operators
135.3 Rules applicable to operations subject to this part.
135.4 Applicability of rules for eligible on-demand operations.
135.7 Applicability of rules to unauthorized operators.
135.12 Previously trained crewmembers.
135.19 Emergency operations.
135.21 Manual requirements.
135.23 Manual contents.
135.25 Aircraft requirements.
135.41 Carriage of narcotic drugs, marihuana, and depressant or stimulant drugs or substances.
135.43 Crewmember certificates: International operations.

Subpart B — Flight Operations

135.61 General.
135.63 Recordkeeping requirements.
135.64 Retention of contracts and amendments: Commercial operators who conduct intrastate operations for compensation or hire.
135.65 Reporting mechanical irregularities.
135.67 Reporting potentially hazardous meteorological conditions and irregularities of communications or navigation facilities.
135.69 Restriction or suspension of operations: Continuation of flight in an emergency.
135.71 Airworthiness check.
135.73 Inspections and tests.
135.75 Inspectors credentials: Admission to pilots' compartment: Forward observer's seat.
135.76 DOD Commercial Air Carrier Evaluator's Credentials: Admission to pilots' compartment: Forward observer's seat.
135.77 Responsibility for operational control.
135.79 Flight locating requirements.
135.81 Informing personnel of operational information and appropriate changes.
135.83 Operating information required.
135.85 Carriage of persons without compliance with the passenger-carrying provisions of this part.
135.87 Carriage of cargo including carry-on baggage.
135.89 Pilot requirements: Use of oxygen.
135.91 Oxygen for medical use by passengers.
135.93 Autopilot: Minimum altitudes for use.
135.95 Airmen: Limitations on use of services.
135.97 Aircraft and facilities for recent flight experience.
135.99 Composition of flight crew.
135.100 Flight crewmember duties.
135.101 Second in command required under IFR.
135.103 [Reserved]
135.105 Exception to second in command requirement: Approval for use of autopilot system.
135.107 Flight attendant crewmember requirement.
135.109 Pilot in command or second in command: Designation required.
135.111 Second in command required in Category II operations.
135.113 Passenger occupancy of pilot seat.
135.115 Manipulation of controls.
135.117 Briefing of passengers before flight.
135.119 Prohibition against carriage of weapons.
135.120 Prohibition on interference with crewmembers.
135.121 Alcoholic beverages.
135.122 Stowage of food, beverage, and passenger service equipment during aircraft movement on the surface, takeoff, and landing.
135.123 Emergency and emergency evacuation duties.
135.125 Airplane security.
135.127 Passenger information requirements and smoking prohibitions.
135.128 Use of safety belts and child restraint systems.
135.129 Exit seating.

Subpart C — Aircraft and Equipment

135.141 Applicability.
135.143 General requirements.
135.144 Portable electronic devices.
135.145 Aircraft proving and validation tests.
135.147 Dual controls required.
135.149 Equipment requirements: General.
135.150 Public address and crewmember interphone systems.
135.151 Cockpit voice recorders.
135.152 Flight recorders.
135.153 Ground proximity warning system.
135.154 Terrain awareness and warning system.
135.155 Fire extinguishers: Passenger-carrying aircraft.
135.157 Oxygen equipment requirements.
135.158 Pitot heat indication systems.
135.159 Equipment requirements: Carrying passengers under VFR at night or under VFR over-the-top conditions.
135.161 Radio and navigational equipment: Carrying passengers under VFR at night or under VFR over-the-top.
135.163 Equipment requirements: Aircraft carrying passengers under IFR.
135.165 Radio and navigational equipment: Extended overwater or IFR operations.

135.167 Emergency equipment: Extended overwater operations.
135.168 Supplemental inspections.
135.169 Additional airworthiness requirements.
135.170 Materials for compartment interiors.
135.171 Shoulder harness installation at flight crewmember stations.
135.173 Airborne thunderstorm detection equipment requirements.
135.175 Airborne weather radar equipment requirements.
135.177 Emergency equipment requirements for aircraft having a passenger seating configuration of more than 19 passengers.
135.178 Additional emergency equipment.
135.179 Inoperable instruments and equipment.
135.180 Traffic Alert and Collision Avoidance System.
135.181 Performance requirements: Aircraft operated over-the-top or in IFR conditions.
135.183 Performance requirements: Land aircraft operated over water.
135.185 Empty weight and center of gravity: Currency requirement.

Subpart D — VFR/IFR Operating Limitations and Weather Requirements

135.201 Applicability.
135.203 VFR: Minimum altitudes.
135.205 VFR: Visibility requirements.
135.207 VFR: Helicopter surface reference requirements.
135.209 VFR: Fuel supply.
135.211 VFR: Over-the-top carrying passengers: Operating limitations.
135.213 Weather reports and forecasts.
135.215 IFR: Operating limitations.
135.217 IFR: Takeoff limitations.
135.219 IFR: Destination airport weather minimums.
135.221 IFR: Alternate airport weather minimums.
135.223 IFR: Alternate airport requirements.
135.225 IFR: Takeoff, approach and landing minimums.
135.227 Icing conditions: Operating limitations.
135.229 Airport requirements.

Subpart E — Flight Crewmember Requirements

135.241 Applicability.
135.243 Pilot in command qualifications.
135.244 Operating experience.
135.245 Second in command qualifications.
135.247 Pilot qualifications: Recent experience.
135.249 Use of prohibited drugs.
135.251 Testing for prohibited drugs.
135.253 Misuse of alcohol.
135.255 Testing for alcohol.

Subpart F — Crewmember Flight Time and Duty Period Limitations and Rest Requirements

135.261 Applicability.
135.263 Flight time limitations and rest requirements: All certificate holders.
135.265 Flight time limitations and rest requirements: Scheduled operations.
135.267 Flight time limitations and rest requirements: Unscheduled one- and two-pilot crews.
135.269 Flight time limitations and rest requirements: Unscheduled three- and four-pilot crews.
135.271 Helicopter hospital emergency medical evacuation service (HEMES).
135.273 Duty period limitations and rest time requirements.

Subpart G — Crewmember Testing Requirements

135.291 Applicability.
135.293 Initial and recurrent pilot testing requirements.
135.295 Initial and recurrent flight attendant crewmember testing requirements.
135.297 Pilot in command: Instrument proficiency check requirements.
135.299 Pilot in command: Line checks: Routes and airports.
135.301 Crewmember: Tests and checks, grace provisions, training to accepted standards.

Subpart H — Training

135.321 Applicability and terms used.
135.323 Training program: General.
135.324 Training program: Special rules.
135.325 Training program and revision: Initial and final approval.
135.327 Training program: Curriculum.
135.329 Crewmember training requirements.
135.331 Crewmember emergency training.
135.333 Training requirements: Handling and carriage of hazardous materials.
135.335 Approval of aircraft simulators and other training devices.
135.337 Qualifications: Check airmen (aircraft) and check airmen (simulator).
135.338 Qualifications: Flight instructors (aircraft) and flight instructors (simulator).
135.339 Initial and transition training and checking: Check airmen (aircraft), check airmen (simulator).
135.340 Initial and transition training and checking: Flight instructors (aircraft), flight instructors (simulator).
135.341 Pilot and flight attendant crewmember training programs.
135.343 Crewmember initial and recurrent training requirements.
135.345 Pilots: Initial, transition, and upgrade ground training.
135.347 Pilots: Initial, transition, upgrade, and differences flight training.
135.349 Flight attendants: Initial and transition ground training.
135.351 Recurrent training.
135.353 Prohibited drugs.

Subpart I— Airplane Performance Operating Limitations

135.361 Applicability.
135.363 General.
135.365 Large transport category airplanes: Reciprocating engine powered: Weight limitations.
135.367 Large transport category airplanes: Reciprocating engine powered: Takeoff limitations.
135.369 Large transport category airplanes: Reciprocating engine powered: En route limitations: All engines operating.
135.371 Large transport category airplanes: Reciprocating engine powered: En route limitations: One engine inoperative.
135.373 Part 25 transport category airplanes with four or more engines: Reciprocating engine powered: En route limitations: Two engines inoperative.
135.375 Large transport category airplanes: Reciprocating engine powered: Landing limitations: Destination airports.
135.377 Large transport category airplanes: Reciprocating engine powered: Landing limitations: Alternate airports.
135.379 Large transport category airplanes: Turbine engine powered: Takeoff limitations.
135.381 Large transport category airplanes: Turbine engine powered: En route limitations: One engine inoperative.
135.383 Large transport category airplanes: Turbine engine powered: En route limitations: Two engines inoperative.
135.385 Large transport category airplanes: Turbine engine powered: Landing limitations: Destination airports.
135.387 Large transport category airplanes: Turbine engine powered: Landing limitations: Alternate airports.
135.389 Large nontransport category airplanes: Takeoff limitations.
135.391 Large nontransport category airplanes: En route limitations: One engine inoperative.
135.393 Large nontransport category airplanes: Landing limitations: Destination airports.
135.395 Large nontransport category airplanes: Landing limitations: Alternate airports.
135.397 Small transport category airplane performance operating limitations.
135.398 Commuter category airplanes performance operating limitations.
135.399 Small nontransport category airplane performance operating limitations.

Subpart J— Maintenance, Preventive Maintenance, and Alterations

***135.411 Applicability.**
135.413 Responsibility for airworthiness.
135.415 Service difficulty reports (operational).
135.416 Service difficulty reports (structural).
135.417 Mechanical interruption summary report.
135.419 Approved aircraft inspection program.
135.421 Additional maintenance requirements.
***135.422 Aging airplane inspections and records reviews for multiengine airplanes certificated with nine or fewer passenger seats.**
***135.423 Maintenance, preventive maintenance, and alteration organization.**
135.425 Maintenance, preventive maintenance, and alteration programs.
135.427 Manual requirements.
135.429 Required inspection personnel.
135.431 Continuing analysis and surveillance.
135.433 Maintenance and preventive maintenance training program.
135.435 Certificate requirements.
135.437 Authority to perform and approve maintenance, preventive maintenance, and alterations.
135.439 Maintenance recording requirements.
135.441 Transfer of maintenance records.
135.443 Airworthiness release or aircraft maintenance log entry.

Appendices to Part 135

Appendix A—Additional Airworthiness Standards for 10 or More Passenger Airplanes
Appendix B—Airplane Flight Recorder Specifications
Appendix C—Helicopter Flight Recorder Specifications
Appendix D—Airplane Flight Recorder Specifications
Appendix E—Helicopter Flight Recorder Specifications
Appendix F—Airplane Flight Recorder Specifications
***Appendix G—[Removed]**

Authority: 49 U.S.C. 106(g), 41706, 44113, 44701–44702, 44705, 44709, 44711–44713, 44715–44717, 44722.

Source: Docket No. 16097, 43 FR 46783, Oct. 10, 1978, unless otherwise noted.

Special Federal Aviation Regulations

SFAR No. 36 to Part 135

1. *Definitions.* For purposes of this Special Federal Aviation Regulation—

(a) A product is an aircraft, airframe, aircraft engine, propeller, or appliance;

(b) An article is an airframe, powerplant, propeller, instrument, radio, or accessory; and

(c) A component is a part of a product or article.

2. *General.*

(a) Contrary provisions of §121.379(b) and §135.437(b) of this chapter notwithstanding, the holder of an air carrier certificate or operating certificate, that operates large aircraft, and that has been issued operations specifications for operations required to be conducted in accordance with 14 CFR part 121 or 135, may perform a major repair on a product as described in §121.379(b) or §135.437(a), using technical data that have not been approved by the Administrator, and approve that product for return to service, if authorized in accordance with this Special Federal Aviation Regulation.

(b) Reserved.

(c) Contrary provisions of §145.201(c)(2) notwithstanding, the holder of a repair station certificate under 14 CFR part

145 that is located in the United States may perform a major repair on an article for which it is rated using technical data not approved by the FAA and approve that article for return to service, if authorized in accordance with this Special Federal Aviation Regulation. If the certificate holder holds a rating limited to a component of a product or article, the holder may not, by virtue of this Special Federal Aviation Regulation, approve that product or article for return to service.

3. *Major Repair Data and Return to Service.*

(a) As referenced in section 2 of this Special Federal Aviation Regulation, a certificate holder may perform a major repair on a product or article using technical data that have not been approved by the Administrator, and approve that product or article for return to service, if the certificate holder—

(1) Has been issued an authorization under, and a procedures manual that complies with, Special Federal Aviation Regulation No. 36–8, effective on January 23, 1999;

(2) Has developed the technical data in accordance with the procedures manual;

(3) Has developed the technical data specifically for the product or article being repaired; and

(4) Has accomplished the repair in accordance with the procedures manual and the procedures approved by the Administrator for the certificate.

(b) For purposes of this section, an authorization holder may develop technical data to perform a major repair on a product or article and use that data to repair a subsequent product or article of the same type as long as the holder—

(1) Evaluates each subsequent repair and the technical data to determine that performing the subsequent repair with the same data will return the product or article to its original or properly altered condition, and that the repaired product or article conforms with applicable airworthiness requirements; and

(2) Records each evaluation in the records referenced in paragraph (a) of section 13 of this Special Federal Aviation Regulation.

4. *Application.* The applicant for an authorization under this Special Federal Aviation Regulation must submit an application, in writing, and signed by an officer of the applicant, to the FAA Certificate Holding District Office charged with the overall inspection of the applicant's operations under its certificate. The application must contain—

(a) If the applicant is

(1) The holder of an air carrier operating or commercial operating certificate, or the holder of an air taxi operating certificate that operates large aircraft, the—

(i) The applicant's certificate number; and

(ii) The specific product(s) the applicant is authorized to maintain under its certificate, operations specifications, and maintenance manual; or

(2) The holder of a domestic repair station certificate—

(i) The applicant's certificate number;

(ii) A copy of the applicant's operations specifications; and

(iii) The specific article(s) for which the applicant is rated;

(b) The name, signature, and title of each person for whom authorization to approve, on behalf of the authorization holder, the use of technical data for major repairs is requested; and

(c) The qualifications of the applicant's staff that show compliance with section 5 of this Special Federal Aviation Regulation.

5. *Eligibility.*

(a) To be eligible for an authorization under this Special Federal Aviation Regulation, the applicant, in addition to having the authority to repair products or articles must—

(1) Hold an air carrier certificate or operating certificate, operate large aircraft, and have been issued operations specifications for operations required to be conducted in accordance with 14 CFR part 121 or 135, or hold a domestic repair station certificate under 14 CFR part 145;

(2) Have an adequate number of sufficiently trained personnel in the United States to develop data and repair the products that the applicant is authorized to maintain under its operating certificate or the articles for which it is rated under its domestic repair station certificate;

(3) Employ, or have available, a staff of engineering personnel that can determine compliance with the applicable airworthiness requirements of the Federal Aviation Regulations.

(b) At least one member of the staff required by paragraph (a)(3) of this section must—

(1) Have a thorough working knowledge of the applicable requirements of the Federal Aviation Regulations;

(2) Occupy a position on the applicant's staff that has the authority to establish a repair program that ensures that each repaired product or article meets the applicable requirements of the Federal Aviation Regulations;

(3) Have at least one year of satisfactory experience in processing engineering work, in direct contact with the FAA, for type certification or major repair projects; and

(4) Have at least eight years of aeronautical engineering experience (which may include the one year of experience in processing engineering work for type certification or major repair projects).

(c) The holder of an authorization issued under this Special Federal Aviation Regulation shall notify the Administrator within 48 hours of any change (including a change of personnel) that could affect the ability of the holder to meet the requirements of this Special Federal Aviation Regulation.

6. *Procedures Manual.*

(a) A certificate holder may not approve a product or article for return to service under section 2 of this Special Federal Aviation Regulation unless the holder—

(1) Has a procedures manual that has been approved by the Administrator as complying with paragraph (b) of this section; and

(2) Complies with the procedures contained in this procedures manual.

(b) The approved procedures manual must contain—

(1) The procedures for developing and determining the adequacy of technical data for major repairs;

(2) The identification (names, signatures, and responsibilities) of officials and of each staff member described in section 5 of this Special Federal Aviation Regulation who—

(i) Has the authority to make changes in procedures that require a revision to the procedures manual; and

(ii) Prepares or determines the adequacy of technical data, plans or conducts tests, and approves, on behalf of the authorization holder, test results; and

(3) A "log of revisions" page that identifies each revised item, page, and date of revision, and contains the signature of the person approving the change for the Administrator.

(c) The holder of an authorization issued under this Special Federal Aviation Regulation may not approve a product or article for return to service after a change in staff necessary to meet the requirements of section 5 of this regulation or a change in procedures from those approved under paragraph (a) of this section, unless that change has been approved by the FAA and entered in the procedures manual.

7. *Duration of Authorization.* Each authorization issued under this Special Federal Aviation Regulation is effective from the date of issuance until January 23, 2009, unless it is earlier surrendered, suspended, revoked, or otherwise terminated. Upon termination of such authorization, the terminated authorization holder must:

(a) Surrender to the FAA all data developed pursuant to Special Federal Aviation Regulation No. 36; or

(b) Maintain indefinitely all data developed pursuant to Special Federal Aviation Regulation No. 36, and make that data available to the FAA for inspection upon request.

8. *Transferability.* An authorization issued under this Special Federal Aviation Regulation is not transferable.

9. *Inspections.* Each holder of an authorization issued under this Special Federal Aviation Regulation and each applicant for an authorization must allow the Administrator to inspect its personnel, facilities, products and articles, and records upon request.

10. *Limits of Applicability.* An authorization issued under this Special Federal Aviation Regulation applies only to—

(a) A product that the air carrier, commercial, or air taxi operating certificate holder is authorized to maintain pursuant to its continuous airworthiness maintenance program or maintenance manual; or

(b) An article for which the domestic repair station certificate holder is rated. If the certificate holder is rated for a component of an article, the holder may not, in accordance with this Special Federal Aviation Regulation, approve that article for return to service.

11. *Additional Authorization Limitations.* Each holder of an authorization issued under this Special Federal Aviation Regulation must comply with any additional limitations prescribed by the Administrator and made a part of the authorization.

12. *Data Review and Service Experience.* If the Administrator finds that a product or article has been approved for return to service after a major repair has been performed under this Special Federal Aviation Regulation, that the product or article may not conform to the applicable airworthiness requirements or that an unsafe feature or characteristic of the product or article may exist, and that the nonconformance or unsafe feature or characteristic may be attributed to the repair performed, the holder of the authorization, upon notification by the Administrator, shall—

(a) Investigate the matter;

(b) Report to the Administrator the results of the investigation and any action proposed or taken; and

(c) If notified that an unsafe condition exists, provide within the time period stated by the Administrator, the information necessary for the FAA to issue an airworthiness directive under part 39 of the Federal Aviation Regulations.

13. *Current Records.* Each holder of an authorization issued under this Special Federal Aviation Regulation shall maintain, at its facility, current records containing—

(a) For each product or article for which it has developed and used major repair data, a technical data file that includes all data and amendments thereto (including drawings, photographs, specifications, instructions, and reports) necessary to accomplish the major repair;

(b) A list of products or articles by make, model, manufacturer's serial number (including specific part numbers and serial numbers of components) and, if applicable, FAA Technical Standard Order (TSO) or Parts Manufacturer Approval (PMA) identification, that have been repaired under the authorization; and

(c) A file of information from all available sources on difficulties experienced with products and articles repaired under the authorization.

This Special Federal Aviation Regulation terminates January 23, 2009.

[SFAR 36–6, 59 FR 3940, Jan. 27, 1994; SFAR 36–7, 64 FR 960, Jan. 6, 1999; SFAR 36–7, 66 FR 41116, Aug. 6, 2001; SFAR 36–8, 68 FR 65378, Nov. 19, 2003]

SFAR No. 50–2 to Part 135

Special Flight Rules in the Vicinity of the Grand Canyon National Park, AZ

Editorial Note: For the text of SFAR No. 50–2, see Part 91 of this chapter.

SFAR No. 58 to Part 135

Advanced Qualification Program

Section

1. Purpose and eligibility
2. Definitions
3. Required Curriculums
4. Indoctrination Curriculums
5. Qualification Curriculums
6. Continuing Qualification Curriculums
7. Other Requirements
8. Certification
9. Training Devices and Simulators
10. Approval of Advanced Qualification Program
11. Approval of Training, Qualification, or Evaluation by a Person Who Provides Training by Arrangement
12. Recordkeeping requirements
13. Expiration

Contrary provisions of parts 61, 63, 65, 121, and 135 of the Federal Aviation Regulations notwithstanding—

1. *Purpose and Eligibility.*

(a) This Special Federal Aviation Regulation provides for approval of an alternate method (known as "Advanced Qualification Program" or "AQP") for qualifying, training, certifying, and otherwise ensuring competency of crewmembers, aircraft dispatchers, other operations personnel, instructors, and evaluators who are required to be trained or qualified under parts 121 and 135 of the FAR or under this SFAR.

(b) A certificate holder is eligible under this Special Federal Aviation Regulation if the certificate holder is required to have an approved training program under §121.401 or §135.341 of the FAR, or elects to have an approved training program under §135.341.

(c) A certificate holder obtains approval of each proposed curriculum under this AQP as specified in section 10 of this SFAR.

(d) A curriculum approved under the AQP may include elements of present Part 121 and Part 135 training programs. Each curriculum must specify the make, model, and series aircraft (or variant) and each crewmember position or other positions to be covered by that curriculum. Positions to be covered by the AQP must include all flight crewmember positions, instructors, and evaluators and may include other positions, such as flight attendants, aircraft dispatchers, and other operations personnel.

(e) Each certificate holder that obtains approval of an AQP under this SFAR shall comply with all of the requirements of that program.

2. *Definitions.* As used in this SFAR:

Curriculum means a portion of an Advanced Qualification Program that covers one of three program areas: (1) indoctrination, (2) qualification, or (3) continuing qualification. A qualification or continuing qualification curriculum addresses the required training and qualification activities for a specific make, model, and series aircraft (or variant) and for a specific duty position.

Evaluator means a person who has satisfactorily completed training and evaluation that qualifies that person to evaluate the performance of crewmembers, instructors, other evaluators, aircraft dispatchers, and other operations personnel.

Facility means the physical environment required for training and qualification (e.g., buildings, classrooms).

Training center means an organization certificated under part 142 of this chapter or an organization approved by the Administrator to operate under the terms of this SFAR to provide training as described in section 1(b) of SFAR 58.

Variant means a specifically configured aircraft for which the FAA has identified training and qualification requirements that are significantly different from those applicable to other aircraft of the same make, model and series.

3. *Required Curriculums.* Each AQP must have separate curriculums for indoctrination, qualification, and continuing qualification as specified in sections 4, 5, and 6 of this SFAR.

4. *Indoctrination Curriculums.* Each indoctrination curriculum must include the following:

(a) For newly hired persons being trained under an AQP: Company policies and operating practices and general operational knowledge.

(b) For newly hired flight crewmembers and air dispatchers: General aeronautical knowledge.

(c) For instructors: The fundamental principles of the teaching and learning process; methods and theories of instruction; and the knowledge necessary to use aircraft flight training devices, flight simulators, and other training equipment in advanced qualification curriculums.

(d) For evaluators: Evaluation requirements specified in each approved curriculum; methods of evaluating crewmembers and aircraft dispatchers and other operations personnel; and policies and practices used to conduct the kinds of evaluations particular to an advanced qualification curriculum.(e.g., proficiency and online).

5. *Qualification Curriculums.* Each qualification curriculum must include the following:

(a) The certificate holder's planned hours of training, evaluation, and supervised operating experience.

(b) A list of and text describing the training, qualification and certification activities, as applicable for specific positions subject to the AQP, as follows:

(1) *Crewmembers, aircraft dispatchers, and other operations personnel.* Training, evaluation and certification activities which are aircraft- and equipment-specific to qualify a person for a particular duty position on, or duties related to the operation of a specific make, model, and series aircraft (or variant); a list of and text describing the knowledge requirements, subject materials, job skills, and each maneuver procedure to be trained and evaluated; the practical test requirements in addition to or in place of the requirements of parts 61, 63, and 65; and a list of and text describing supervised operating experience.

(2) *Instructors.* Training and evaluation to qualify a person to impart instruction on how to operate, or on how to ensure the safe operation of a particular make, model and series aircraft (or variant).

(3) *Evaluators.* Training, evaluation, and certification activities that are aircraft and equipment specific to qualify a person to evaluate the performance of persons who operate or who ensure the safe operation of, a particular make, model, and series aircraft (or variant).

6. *Continuing Qualification Curriculums.* Continuing qualification curriculums must comply with the following requirements:

(a) *General.* A continuing qualification curriculum must be based on—

(1) A continuing qualification cycle that ensures that during each cycle each person qualified under an AQP, including instructors and evaluators, will receive a balanced mix of training and evaluation on all events and subjects necessary to ensure that each person maintains the minimum proficiency levels of knowledge, skills and attitudes required for original qualification: and

(2) If applicable, flight crewmember or aircraft dispatcher recency of experience requirements.

(b) *Continuing Qualification Cycle Content.* Each continuing qualification cycle must include at least the following:

(1) *Evaluation period.* An evaluation period during which each person qualified under an AQP must receive at least one training session and a proficiency evaluation at a training facility. The number and frequency of training sessions must be approved by the Administrator. A training session, including any proficiency evaluation completed at that session, that occurs any time during the two calendar months before the last date for completion of an evaluation period can be considered by the certificate holder to be completed in the last calendar month.

(2) *Training.* Continuing qualification must include training in all events and major subjects required for original qualification, as follows:

(i) For pilots in command, seconds in command, flight engineers, and instructors and evaluators: Ground training including a general review of knowledge and skills covered in qualification training, updated information on newly developed procedures, and safety information.

(ii) For crewmembers, aircraft dispatchers, instructors, evaluators, and other operation personnel who conduct their duties in flight; Proficiency training in an aircraft, flight training device, or flight simulator on normal, abnormal, and emergency flight procedures and maneuvers.

(iii) For instructors and evaluators who are limited to conducting their duties in flight simulators and flight training devices: Proficiency training in a flight training device and/or flight simulator regarding operation of this training equipment and in operational flight procedures and maneuvers (normal, abnormal, and emergency).

(3) *Evaluations.* Continuing qualification must include evaluation in all events and major subjects required for original qualification, and online evaluations for pilots in command and other eligible flight crewmembers. Each person qualified under an AQP must successfully complete a proficiency evaluation and, if applicable, an online evaluation during each evaluation period. An individual's proficiency evaluation may be accomplished over several training sessions if a certificate holder provides more than one training session in an evaluation period. The following evaluation requirements apply:

(i) Proficiency evaluations as follows:

(A) For pilots in command, seconds in command, and flight engineers: A proficiency evaluation, portions of which may be conducted in an aircraft flight simulator, or flight training device as approved in the certificate holder's curriculum which must be completed during each evaluation period.

(B) For any other persons covered by an AQP a means to evaluate their proficiency in the performance of their duties in their assigned tasks in an operational setting.

(ii) Online evaluations as follows:

(A) For pilots in command: An online evaluation conducted in an aircraft during actual flight operations under part 121 or part 135 or during operationally (line) oriented flights or proving flights. An online evaluation in an aircraft must be completed in the calendar month that includes the midpoint of the evaluation period. An online evaluation that is satisfactorily completed in the calendar month after the calendar month in which it becomes due is considered to have been completed during the calendar month it became due. However, in no case is an evaluation under this paragraph required more often than once during an evaluation period.

(B) During the online evaluations required under paragraph (b)(3)(ii)(A) of this section, each person performing duties as a pilot in command, second in command, or flight engineer for that flight, must be individually evaluated to determine whether he or she—

(1) Remains adequately trained and currently proficient with respect to the particular aircraft, crew position, and type of operation in which he or she serves; and

(2) Has sufficient knowledge and skills to operate effectively as part of the crew.

(4) *Recency of experience.* For pilots in command and seconds in command and if the certificate holder elects, flight engineers and flight dispatchers, approved recency of experience requirements.

(c) *Duration periods.* Initially the continuing qualification cycle approved for an AQP may not exceed 26 calendar months and the evaluation period may not exceed 13 calendar months. Thereafter, upon demonstration by a certificate holder that an extension is warranted, the Administrator may approve extensions of the continuing qualification cycle and the evaluation period in increments not exceeding 3 calendar months. However, a continuing qualification cycle may not exceed 39 calendar months and an evaluation period may not exceed 26 calendar months.

(d) *Requalification.* Each continuing qualification curriculum must include a curriculum segment that covers the requirements for requalifying a crewmember, aircraft dispatcher, or other operations personnel who has not maintained continuing qualification.

7. *Other Requirements.* In addition to the requirements of sections 4, 5, and 6, each AQP qualification and continuing qualification curriculum must include the following requirements:

(a) Approved Cockpit Resource Management (CRM) Training applicable to each position for which training is provided under an AQP.

(b) Approved training on an evaluation of skills and proficiency of each person being trained under an AQP to use their cockpit resource management skills and technical (piloting or other) skills in an actual or simulated operations scenario. For flight crew members this training and evaluation must be conducted in an approved flight training device or flight simulator.

(c) Data collection procedures that will ensure that the certificate holder provides information from its crew members, instructors, and evaluators that will enable the FAA to determine whether the training and evaluations are working to accomplish the overall objectives of the curriculum.

8. *Certification.* A person enrolled in an AQP is eligible to receive a commercial or airline transport pilot, flight engineer, aircraft dispatcher certificate or appropriate rating based on the successful completion of training and evaluation events accomplished under that program if the following requirements are met:

(a) Training and evaluation of required knowledge and skills under the AQP must meet minimum certification and rating criteria established by the Administrator in parts 61, 63, or 65. The Administrator may accept substitutes for the practical test requirements of parts 61, 63, or 65, as applicable.

(b) The applicant satisfactorily completes the appropriate qualification curriculum.

(c) The applicant shows competence in required technical knowledge and skills (e.g., piloting) and cockpit resource management knowledge and skills in scenarios that test both types of knowledge and skills together.

(d) the applicant is otherwise eligible under the applicable requirements of part 61, 63, or 65.

9. *Training Devices and Simulators.*

(a) *Qualification and approval of flight training devices and flight simulators.*

(1) Any training device or simulator that will be used in an AQP for one of the following purposes must be evaluated by the Administrator for assignment of a flight training device or flight simulator qualification level:

(i) Required evaluation of individual or crew proficiency.

(ii) Training activities that determine if an individual or crew is ready for a proficiency evaluation.

(iii) Activities used to meet recency of experience requirements.

(iv) Line Operations Simulations (LOS).

(2) To be eligible to request evaluation for a qualification level of a flight training device or flight simulator an applicant must—

(i) Hold an operating certificate; or

(ii) Be a training center that has applied for authorization to the administrator or has been authorized by the Administrator to conduct training or qualification under an AQP.

(3) Each flight training device or flight simulator to be used by a certificate holder or training center for any of the purposes set forth in paragraph (a)(1) of this section must—

(i) Be, or have been, evaluated against a set of criteria established by the Administrator for a particular qualification level of simulation;

(ii) Be approved for its intended use in a specified AQP, and

(iii) Be part of a flight simulator or flight training device continuing qualification program approved by the Administrator.

(b) *Approval of other Training Equipment.*

(1) Any training device that is intended to be used in an AQP for purposes other than those set forth in paragraph (a)(1) of this section must be approved by the Administrator for its intended use.

(2) An applicant for approval of a training device under this paragraph must identify the device by its nomenclature and describe its intended use.

(3) Each training device approved for use in an AQP must be part of a continuing program to provide for its serviceability and fitness to perform its intended function as approved by the Administrator.

10. *Approval of Advanced Qualification Program.*

(a) *Approval Process.* Each applicant for approval of an AQP curriculum under this SFAR shall apply for approval of that curriculum. Application for approval is made to the certificate holder's FAA Flight Standards District Office.

(b) *Approval Criteria.* An application for approval of an AQP curriculum will be approved if the program meets the following requirements:

(1) It must be submitted in a form and manner acceptable to the Administrator.

(2) It must meet all of the requirements of this SFAR.

(3) It must indicate specifically the requirements of parts 61, 63, 65, 121 or 135, as applicable, that would be replaced by an AQP curriculum. If a requirement of parts 61, 63, 65, 121, or 135 is replaced by an AQP curriculum, the certificate holder must show how the AQP curriculum provides an equivalent level of safety for each requirement that is replaced. Each applicable requirement of parts 61, 63, 65, 121 or 135 that is not specifically addressed in an AQP curriculum continues to apply to the certificate holder.

(c) *Application and Transition.* Each certificate holder that applies for one or more advanced qualification curriculums or for a revision to a previously approved curriculum must comply with §121.405 or §135.325, as applicable, and must include as part of its application a proposed transition plan (containing a calendar of events) for moving from its present approved training to the advanced qualification training.

(d) *Advanced Qualification Program Revisions or Rescissions of Approval.* If after a certificate holder begins operations under an AQP, the Administrator finds that the certificate holder is not meeting the provisions of its approved AQP, the Administrator may require the certificate holder to make revisions in accordance with §121.405 or §135.325, as applicable, or to submit and obtain approval for a plan (containing a schedule of events) that the certificate holder must comply with and use to transition to an approved part 121 or part 135 training program, as appropriate.

11. *Approval of Training, Qualification, or Evaluation by a Person who Provides Training by Arrangement.*

(a) A certificate holder under part 121 or part 135 may arrange to have AQP required training, qualification, or evaluation functions performed by another person (a *training center*) if the following requirements are met:

(1) The training center's training and qualification curriculums, curriculum segments, or portions of curriculum segments must be provisionally approved by the Administrator. A training center may apply for provisional approval independently or in conjunction with a certificate holder's application for AQP approval. Application for provisional approval must be made to the FAA's Flight Standards District Office that has responsibility for the training center.

(2) The specific use of provisionally approved curriculums, curriculum segments, or portions of curriculum segments in a certificate holder's AQP must be approved by the Administrator as set forth in section 10 of this SFAR.

(b) An applicant for provisional approval of a curriculum, curriculum segment, or portion of a curriculum segment under this paragraph must show that the following requirements are met:

(1) The applicant must have a curriculum for the qualification and continuing qualification of each instructor or evaluator employed by the applicant.

(2) The applicant's facilities must be found by the Administrator to be adequate for any planned training, qualification, or evaluation for a part 121 or part 135 certificate holder.

(3) Except for indoctrination curriculums, the curriculum, curriculum segment, or portion of a curriculum segment must identify the specific make, model, and series aircraft (or variant) and crewmember or other positions for which it is designed.

(c) A certificate holder who wants approval to use a training center's provisionally approved curriculum, curriculum segment, or portion of a curriculum segment in its AQP, must show that the following requirements are met:

(1) Each instructor or evaluator used by the training center must meet all of the qualification and continuing qualification requirements that apply to employees of the certificate holder that has arranged for the training, including knowledge of the certificate holder's operations.

(2) Each provisionally approved curriculum, curriculum segment, or portion of a curriculum segment must be approved by the Administrator for use in the certificate holder's AQP. The Administrator will either provide approval or require modifications to ensure that each curriculum, curriculum segment, or portion of a curriculum segment is applicable to the certificate holder's AQP.

(d) Approval for the training, qualification, or evaluation by a person who provides training by arrangement authorized by this section expires on August 3, 1998 unless that person meets the eligibility requirements specified under §121.402 or §135.324 of this chapter. After August 2, 1998 approval for the training, qualification, or evaluation, by a person who provides training by arrangement authorized by this section, shall be granted only to persons who meet the eligibility requirements specified under §121.402 or §135.234 of this chapter.

12. *Recordkeeping Requirements.* Each certificate holder and each training center holding AQP provisional approval shall show that it will establish and maintain records in sufficient detail to establish the training, qualification, and certification of each person qualified under an AQP in accordance with the training, qualification, and certification requirements of this SFAR.

13. *Expiration.* This Special Federal Aviation Regulation terminates on October 2, 2005, unless sooner terminated.

[SFAR 58, 55 FR 40275, Oct. 2, 1990; as amended by 60 FR 51851, Oct. 3, 1995; SFAR 58–2, 61 FR 34560, July 2, 1996; Amdt. 121–280, 65 FR 60336, Oct. 10, 2000]

SFAR No. 71 to Part 135

Special Operating Rules for Air Tour Operators in the State of Hawaii

Editorial Note: For the text of SFAR No. 71, see Part 91 of this chapter.

SFAR No. 78 to Part 135

Special Operating Rules for Commercial Air Tour Operators in the Vicinity of the Rocky Mountain National Park

Editorial Note: For the text of SFAR No. 78, see Part 91 of this chapter.

SFAR No. 89 to Part 135

Suspension of Certain Flight Data Recorder Requirements

1. *Applicability.* This Special Federal Aviation Regulation provides relief to operators of the airplanes listed in paragraph 2 of this regulation. Relief under this regulation is limited to suspension of the resolution requirements only as listed in appendix M to part 121, appendix E to part 125, or appendix F to part 135, for the flight data recorder parameters noted for individual airplane models.

2. *Airplanes Affected.*

(a) Boeing model 717 airplanes—resolution requirement of appendix M to Part 121 or appendix E to part 125 for parameter number 5. Normal Acceleration (Vertical);

(b) Boeing model 757 airplanes—resolution requirements of appendix M to Part 121 or appendix E to part 125 for parameter number 12a. Pitch Control(s) position (non-fly-by-wire systems); number 14a. Yaw Control position(s) (non-fly-by-wire); number 19. Pitch Trim Surface Position; and number 23. Ground Spoiler Position or Speed Brake Selection.

(c) Boeing Model 767 airplanes—resolution requirements of appendix M to Part 121 or appendix E to part 125 for parameter number 12a. Pitch Control(s) position (non-fly-by-wire systems); number 14a. Yaw Control position(s) (non-fly-by-wire); number 16. Lateral Control Surface(s) Position (for inboard aileron(s) only); number 19. Pitch Trim Surface Position; and number 23. Ground Spoiler Position or Speed Brake Selection.

(d) Dassault Model Falcon 900 EX and Model Mystere-Falcon 900 (with modification M1975 or M2695 installed) airplanes—resolution requirements of appendix M to Part 121, appendix E to part 125 or appendix F to part 135 for parameter number 5. Normal Acceleration (Vertical); and number 26. Radio Altitude.

(e) Other airplanes for which notification under paragraph 3(b) of this regulation is made to the FAA regarding flight data recorder resolution requirement noncompliance.

3. *Requirements for use.*

(a) An operator of an airplane described in paragraphs 2(a) through 2(d) of this regulation may make immediate use of the relief granted by this SFAR.

(b) An operator seeking relief for another airplane model under paragraph 2(e) of this SFAR must notify the FAA immediately in writing as to the nature and extent of the resolution problem found, and must comply with all other requirements of this SFAR, including the report required in paragraph 3(d) of this SFAR. Operators may make immediate use of this relief, but relief may be withdrawn by the FAA after a review of the information filed. Additional information may be required.

(c) An operator of an affected airplane must continue to record all affected parameters to the maximum resolution possible using the installed equipment; that equipment must be maintained in proper working order.

(d) An operator of an affected airplane must, within 30 days of using the relief granted by this regulation, report the following information:

(1) The operator's name and address, and the name and phone number of a contact person for the information reported;

(2) The model and registration number of each affected airplane;

(3) For each affected airplane, the parameter(s) for which resolution relief is being used, and the actual resolution being recorded;

(4) Any additional information requested by the FAA.

(e) Reports must be filed with the FAA Flight Standards Service, Denise Cashmere, Administrative Officer, AFS-200, 800 Independence Ave. SW, Washington, DC 20591. Additionally, each operator must file a copy of the report with its Principal Avionics Inspector or Principal Operations Inspector, as appropriate.

4. *Expiration.* This Special Federal Aviation Regulation expires on August 18, 2003.

[Docket No. FAA–2001–10428, SFAR 89, 66 FR 44273, Aug. 22, 2001]

SFAR No. 93 to Part 135

Temporary Extension of Time To Allow for Certain Training and Testing

1. *Applicability.* This SFAR applies to all part 121 and 135 check airmen (simulator) and flight instructors (simulator), part 121 aircraft dispatchers, and part 142 training center instructors who were required to complete qualification requirements, an inflight line observation program, or operating familiarization in September 2001 to become qualified, or remain qualified, to perform their assigned duties. It also applies to persons who have satisfactorily accomplished the part 61 aeronautical knowledge test or the part 63 written test, either one of which has an expiration date of September 2001 for pilot, flight instructor, or flight engineer certification.

2. *Special Qualification Requirements.* The sections of 14 CFR that prescribes these requirements are sections 61.39(a)(1); 63.35(d); 121.411(f); 121.412(f); 121.463(a)(2); 121.463(c); 135.337(f); 135.338(f); 142.53(b)(2) and (b)(3).

3. *Extension of Time to Fulfill Certain Qualification Requirements.* Persons identified in paragraph 1 of this SFAR who had until the end of September 2001 to complete the specified qualification requirements in September 2001 will be deemed to have completed those requirements in September 2001 provided they satisfactorily complete those requirements by November 30, 2001. For those persons identified in paragraph 1, who are qualifying for the first time to be a check airmen (simulator), flight instructor (simulator), aircraft dispatcher, or training center instructor, they must fulfill the applicable qualification requirements before they may serve as a check airmen (simulator), flight instructor (simulator), aircraft dispatcher, or training center instructor, as appropriate. This extension does not change the 12-calendar-month requirement for aircraft dispatchers or the anniversary month for check airmen, flight instructors and training center instructors. Therefore, if you were due for qualification in September 2001 you will be due for qualification September 2002, regardless of this extension for 2001.

4. *Termination Date.* This Special Federal Aviation Regulation expires November 30, 2001.

[Docket No. FAA–2001–10797; 66 FR 52279, Oct. 12, 2001]

SFAR No. 97 to Part 135

Special Operating Rules for the Conduct of Instrument Flight Rules (IFR) Area Navigation (RNAV) Operations using Global Positioning Systems (GPS) in Alaska

Editorial Note: For the text of SFAR No. 97, see Part 91 of this chapter.

Subpart A — General

§135.1 Applicability.

(a) This part prescribes rules governing—

(1) The commuter or on-demand operations of each person who holds or is required to hold an Air Carrier Certificate or Operating Certificate under part 119 of this chapter.

(2) Each person employed or used by a certificate holder conducting operations under this part including the maintenance, preventative maintenance and alteration of an aircraft.

(3) The transportation of mail by aircraft conducted under a postal service contract awarded under 39 U.S.C. 5402c.

(4) Each person who applies for provisional approval of an Advanced Qualification Program curriculum, curriculum segment, or portion of a curriculum segment under SFAR No. 58 of 14 CFR part 121 and each person employed or used by an air carrier or commercial operator under this part to perform training, qualification, or evaluation functions under an Advanced Qualification Program under SFAR No. 58 of 14 CFR part 121.

(5) Nonstop sightseeing flights for compensation or hire that begin and end at the same airport, and are conducted within a 25 statute mile radius of that airport; however, except for operations subject to SFAR 50–2, these operations, when conducted for compensation or hire, must comply only with §§135.249, 135.251, 135.253, 135.255, and 135.353.

(6) Each person who is on board an aircraft being operated under this part.

(7) Each person who is an applicant for an Air Carrier Certificate or an Operating Certificate under 119 of this chapter, when conducting proving tests.

(b) [Reserved]

(c) For the purpose of §§135.249, 135.251, 135.253, 135.255, and 135.353, *operator* means any person or entity conducting non-stop sightseeing flights for compensation or hire in an airplane or rotorcraft that begin and end at the same airport and are conducted within a 25 statute mile radius of that airport.

(d) Notwithstanding the provisions of this part and appendices I and J to part 121 of this chapter, an operator who does not hold a part 121 or part 135 certificate is permitted to use a person who is otherwise authorized to perform aircraft maintenance or preventive maintenance duties and who is not subject to FAA-approved anti-drug and alcohol misuse prevention programs to perform—

(1) Aircraft maintenance or preventive maintenance on the operator's aircraft if the operator would otherwise be required to transport the aircraft more than 50 nautical miles further than the repair point closest to operator's principal place of operation to obtain these services; or

(2) Emergency repairs on the operator's aircraft if the aircraft cannot be safely operated to a location where an employee subject to FAA-approved programs can perform the repairs.

[Docket No. 16097, 43 FR 46783, Oct. 10, 1978; as amended by Amdt. 135–5, 45 FR 43162, June 26, 1980; Amdt. 135–7, 45 FR 67235, Oct. 9, 1980; Amdt. 135–20, 51 FR 40709, Nov. 7, 1986; Amdt. 135–28, 53 FR 47060, Nov. 21, 1988; Amdt. 135–32, 54 FR 34332, Aug. 18, 1989; Amdt. 135–37, 55 FR 40278, Oct. 2, 1990; Amdt. 135–41, 56 FR 43976, Sept. 5, 1991; Amdt. 135–48, 59 FR 7396, Feb. 15, 1994; Amdt. 135–58, 60 FR 65938, Dec. 20, 1995]

§135.2 Compliance schedule for operators that transition to part 121 of this chapter; certain new entrant operators.

(a) *Applicability.* This section applies to the following:

(1) Each certificate holder that was issued an air carrier or operating certificate and operations specifications under the requirements of part 135 of this chapter or under SFAR No. 38–2 of 14 CFR part 121 before January 19, 1996, and that conducts scheduled passenger-carrying operations with:

(i) Nontransport category turbopropeller powered airplanes type certificated after December 31, 1964, that have a passenger seat configuration of 10–19 seats;

(ii) Transport category turbopropeller powered airplanes that have a passenger seat configuration of 20–30 seats; or

(iii) Turbojet engine powered airplanes having a passenger seat configuration of 1–30 seats.

(2) Each person who, after January 19, 1996, applies for or obtains an initial air carrier or operating certificate and operations specifications to conduct scheduled passenger-carrying operations in the kinds of airplanes described in paragraphs (a)(1)(i), (a)(1)(ii), or paragraph (a)(1)(iii) of this section.

(b) *Obtaining operations specifications.* A certificate holder described in paragraph (a)(1) of this section may not, after March 20, 1997, operate an airplane described in paragraphs (a)(1)(i), (a)(1)(ii), or (a)(1)(iii) of this section in scheduled passenger-carrying operations, unless it obtains operations specifications to conduct its scheduled operations under part 121 of this chapter on or before March 20, 1997.

(c) *Regular or accelerated compliance.* Except as provided in paragraphs (d) and (e) of this section, each certificate holder described in paragraphs (a)(1) of this section shall comply with each applicable requirement of part 121 of this chapter on and after March 20, 1997 or on and after the date on which the certificate holder is issued operations specifications under this part, whichever occurs first. Except as provided in paragraphs (d) and (e) of this section, each person described in paragraph (a)(2) of this section shall comply with each applicable requirement of part 121 of this chapter on and after the date on which that person is issued a certificate and operations specifications under part 121 of this chapter.

(d) *Delayed compliance dates.* Unless paragraph (e) of this section specifies an earlier compliance date, no certificate holder that is covered by paragraph (a) of this section may operate an airplane in 14 CFR part 121 operations on or after a date listed in this paragraph unless that airplane meets the applicable requirement of this paragraph:

(1) *Nontransport category turbopropeller powered airplanes type certificated after December 31, 1964, that have a passenger seat configuration of 10–19 seats.* No certificate holder may operate under this part an airplane that is described in paragraph (a)(1)(i) of this section on or after a date listed in paragraph (d)(1) of this section unless that airplane meets the applicable requirement listed in paragraph (d)(1) of this section:

(i) December 20, 1997:

(A) Section 121.289, Landing gear aural warning.

(B) Section 121.308, Lavatory fire protection.

(C) Section 121.310(e), Emergency exit handle illumination.

(D) Section 121.337(b)(8), Protective breathing equipment.

(E) Section 121.340, Emergency flotation means.

(ii) December 20, 1999: Section 121.342, Pitot heat indication system.

(iii) December 20, 2010:

(A) For airplanes described in §121.157(f), the Airplane Performance Operating Limitations in §§121.189 through 121.197.

(B) Section 121.161(b), Ditching approval.

(C) Section 121.305(j), Third attitude indicator.

(D) Section 121.312(c), Passenger seat cushion flammability.

(iv) March 12, 1999: Section 121.310(b)(1), Interior emergency exit locating sign.

(2) *Transport category turbopropeller powered airplanes that have a passenger seat configuration of 20–30 seats.* No certificate holder may operate under this part an airplane that is described in paragraph (a)(1)(ii) of this section on or after a date listed in paragraph (d)(2) of this section unless that airplane meets the applicable requirement listed in paragraph (d)(2) of this section:

(i) December 20, 1997:

(A) Section 121.308, Lavatory fire protection.

(B) Section 121.337(b)(8) and (9), Protective breathing equipment.

(C) Section 121.340, Emergency flotation means.

(ii) December 20, 2010: Section 121.305(j), Third attitude indicator.

(e) *Newly manufactured airplanes.* No certificate holder that is described in paragraph (a) of this section may operate under part 121 of this chapter an airplane manufactured on or after a date listed in this paragraph (e) unless that airplane meets the applicable requirement listed in this paragraph (e).

(1) For nontransport category turbopropeller powered airplanes type certificated after December 31, 1964, that have a passenger seat configuration of 10–19 seats:

(i) Manufactured on or after March 20, 1997:

(A) Section 121.305(j), Third attitude indicator.

(B) Section 121.311(f), Safety belts and shoulder harnesses.

(ii) Manufactured on or after December 20, 1997: Section 121.317(a), Fasten seat belt light.

(iii) Manufactured on or after December 20, 1999: Section 121.293, Takeoff warning system.

(iv) Manufactured on or after March 12, 1999: Section 121.310(b)(1), Interior emergency exit locating sign.

(2) For transport category turbopropeller powered airplanes that have a passenger seat configuration of 20–30 seats manufactured on or after March 20, 1997: Section 121.305(j), Third attitude indicator.

(f) *New type certification requirements.* No person may operate an airplane for which the application for a type certificate was filed after March 29, 1995, in 14 CFR part 121 operations unless that airplane is type certificated under part 25 of this chapter.

(g) *Transition plan.* Before March 19, 1996, each certificate holder described in paragraph (a)(1) of this section must submit to the FAA a transition plan (containing a calendar of events) for moving from conducting its scheduled operations under the commuter requirements of part 135 of this chapter to the requirements for domestic or flag operations under part 121 of this chapter. Each transition plan must contain details on the following:

(1) Plans for obtaining new operations specifications authorizing domestic or flag operations;

(2) Plans for being in compliance with the applicable requirements of part 121 of this chapter on or before March 20, 1997; and

(3) Plans for complying with the compliance date schedules contained in paragraphs (d) and (e) of this section.

[Docket. No. 28154, 60 FR 65938, Dec. 20, 1995; as amended by Amdt. 135–65, 61 FR 30435, June 14, 1996; Amdt. 135–66, 62 FR 13257, March 19, 1997]

§135.3 Rules applicable to operations subject to this part.

(a) Each person operating an aircraft in operations under this part shall—

(1) While operating inside the United States, comply with the applicable rules of this chapter; and

(2) While operating outside the United States, comply with Annex 2, Rules of the Air, to the Convention on International Civil Aviation or the regulations of any foreign country, whichever applies, and with any rules of parts 61 and 91 of this chapter and this part that are more restrictive than that Annex or those regulations and that can be complied with without violating that Annex or those regulations. Annex 2 is incorporated by reference in §91.703(b) of this chapter.

(b) After March 19, 1997, each certificate holder that conducts commuter operations under this part with airplanes in which two pilots are required by the type certification rules of this chapter shall comply with subparts N and O of part 121 of this chapter instead of the requirements of subparts E, G, and H of this part. Each affected certificate holder must submit to the Administrator and obtain approval of a transition plan (containing a calendar of events) for moving from its present part 135 training, checking, testing, and qualification requirements to the requirements of part 121 of this chapter. Each transition plan must be submitted by March 19, 1996, and must contain details on how the certificate holder plans to be in compliance with subparts N and O of part 121 on or before March 19, 1997.

(c) If authorized by the Administrator upon application, each certificate holder that conducts operations under this part to which paragraph (b) of this section does not apply, may comply with the applicable sections of subparts N and O of part 121 instead of the requirements of subparts E, G, and H of this part, except that those authorized certificate holders may choose to comply with the operating experience requirements of §135.244, instead of the requirements of §121.434 of this chapter.

[Docket No. 27993, 60 FR 65949, Dec. 20, 1995; as amended by Amdt. 135–65, 61 FR 30435, June 14, 1996]

§135.4 Applicability of rules for eligible on-demand operations.

(a) An "eligible on-demand operation" is an on-demand operation conducted under this part that meets the following requirements:

(1) ***Two-pilot crew.*** The flightcrew must consist of at least two qualified pilots employed or contracted by the certificate holder.

(2) ***Flight crew experience.*** The crewmembers must have met the applicable requirements of part 61 of this chapter and have the following experience and ratings:

(i) Total flight time for all pilots:

(A) Pilot in command—A minimum of 1,500 hours.

(B) Second in command—A minimum of 500 hours.

(ii) For multi-engine turbine-powered fixed-wing and powered-lift aircraft, the following FAA certification and ratings requirements:

(A) Pilot in command—Airline transport pilot and applicable type ratings.

(B) Second in command—Commercial pilot and instrument ratings.

(iii) For all other aircraft, the following FAA certification and rating requirements:

(A) Pilot in command—Commercial pilot and instrument ratings.

(B) Second in command—Commercial pilot and instrument ratings.

(3) ***Pilot operating limitations.*** If the second in command of a fixed-wing aircraft has fewer than 100 hours of flight time as second in command flying in the aircraft make and model and, if a type rating is required, in the type aircraft being flown, and the pilot in command is not an appropriately qualified check pilot, the pilot in command shall make all takeoffs and landings in any of the following situations:

(i) Landings at the destination airport when a Destination Airport Analysis is required by §135.385(f); and

(ii) In any of the following conditions:

(A) The prevailing visibility for the airport is at or below 3/4 mile.

(B) The runway visual range for the runway to be used is at or below 4,000 feet.

(C) The runway to be used has water, snow, slush, ice, or similar contamination that may adversely affect aircraft performance.

(D) The braking action on the runway to be used is reported to be less than "good."

(E) The crosswind component for the runway to be used is in excess of 15 knots.

(F) Windshear is reported in the vicinity of the airport.

(G) Any other condition in which the pilot in command determines it to be prudent to exercise the pilot in command's authority.

(4) ***Crew pairing.*** Either the pilot in command or the second in command must have at least 75 hours of flight time in that aircraft make or model and, if a type rating is required, for that type aircraft, either as pilot in command or second in command.

(b) The Administrator may authorize deviations from paragraphs (a)(2)(i) or (a)(4) of this section if the Flight Standards District Office that issued the certificate holder's operations specifications finds that the crewmember has comparable experience, and can effectively perform the functions associated with the position in accordance with the requirements of this chapter. The Administrator may, at any time, terminate any grant of deviation authority issued under this paragraph. Grants of deviation under this paragraph may be granted after consideration of the size and scope of the operation, the qualifications of the intended personnel and the following circumstances:

(1) A newly authorized certificate holder does not employ any pilots who meet the minimum requirements of paragraphs (a)(2)(i) or (a)(4) of this section.

(2) An existing certificate holder adds to its fleet a new category and class aircraft not used before in its operation.

(3) An existing certificate holder establishes a new base to which it assigns pilots who will be required to become qualified on the aircraft operated from that base.

(c) An eligible on-demand operation may comply with alternative requirements specified in §§135.225(b), 135.385(f), and 135.387(b) instead of the requirements that apply to other on-demand operations.

[Docket No. FAA–2001–10047, 68 FR 54585, Sept. 17, 2003]

§135.7 Applicability of rules to unauthorized operators.

The rules in this part which apply to a person certificated under part 119 of this chapter also apply to a person who engages in any operation governed by this part without an appropriate certificate and operations specifications required by part 119 of this chapter.

[Docket No. 16097, 43 FR 46783, Oct. 10, 1978; as amended by Amdt. 135–58, 60 FR 65939, Dec. 20, 1995]

§135.12 Previously trained crewmembers.

A certificate holder may use a crewmember who received the certificate holder's training in accordance with subparts E, G, and H of this part before March 19, 1997, without complying with initial training and qualification requirements of subparts N and O of part 121 of this chapter. The crewmember must comply with the applicable recurrent training requirements of part 121 of this chapter.

[Docket No. 27993, 60 FR 65950, Dec. 20, 1995]

§135.19 Emergency operations.

(a) In an emergency involving the safety of persons or property, the certificate holder may deviate from the rules of this part relating to aircraft and equipment and weather minimums to the extent required to meet that emergency.

(b) In an emergency involving the safety of persons or property, the pilot in command may deviate from the rules of this part to the extent required to meet that emergency.

(c) Each person who, under the authority of this section, deviates from a rule of this part shall, within 10 days, excluding Saturdays, Sundays, and Federal holidays, after the deviation, send to the FAA Flight Standards District Office charged with the overall inspection of the certificate holder a complete report of the aircraft operation involved, including a description of the deviation and reasons for it.

§135.21 Manual requirements.

(a) Each certificate holder, other than one who uses only one pilot in the certificate holder's operations, shall prepare and keep current a manual setting forth the certificate holder's procedures and policies acceptable to the Administrator. This manual must be used by the certificate holder's flight, ground, and maintenance personnel in conducting its operations. However, the Administrator may authorize a deviation from this paragraph if the Administrator finds that, because of the limited size of the operation, all or part of the manual is not necessary for guidance of flight, ground, or maintenance personnel.

(b) Each certificate holder shall maintain at least one copy of the manual at its principal base of operations.

(c) The manual must not be contrary to any applicable Federal regulations, foreign regulation applicable to the certificate holder's operations in foreign countries, or the certificate holder's operating certificate or operations specifications.

(d) A copy of the manual, or appropriate portions of the manual (and changes and additions) shall be made available to maintenance and ground operations personnel by the certificate holder and furnished to—

(1) Its flight crewmembers; and

(2) Representatives of the Administrator assigned to the certificate holder.

(e) Each employee of the certificate holder to whom a manual or appropriate portions of it are furnished under paragraph (d)(1) of this section shall keep it up to date with the changes and additions furnished to them.

(f) Except as provided in paragraph (h) of this section, each certificate holder must carry appropriate parts of the manual on each aircraft when away from the principal operations base. The appropriate parts must be available for use by ground or flight personnel.

(g) For the purpose of complying with paragraph (d) of this section, a certificate holder may furnish the persons listed therein with all or part of its manual in printed form or other form, acceptable to the Administrator, that is retrievable in the English language. If the certificate holder furnishes all or part of the manual in other than printed form, it must ensure there is a compatible reading device available to those persons that provides a legible image of the information and instructions, or a system that is able to retrieve the information and instructions in the English language.

(h) If a certificate holder conducts aircraft inspections or maintenance at specified stations where it keeps the approved inspection program manual, it is not required to carry the manual aboard the aircraft en route to those stations.

[Docket No. 16097, 43 FR 46783, Oct. 10, 1978; as amended by Amdt. 135–18, 47 FR 33396, Aug. 2, 1982; Amdt. 135–58, 60 FR 65939, Dec. 20, 1995; Amdt. 135–66, 62 FR 13257, March 19, 199; Amdt. 135–91, 68 FR 54585, Sept. 17, 2003]

§135.23 Manual contents.

Each manual shall have the date of the last revision on each revised page. The manual must include—

(a) The name of each management person required under §119.69(a) of this chapter who is authorized to act for the certificate holder, the person's assigned area of responsibility, the person's duties, responsibilities, and authority, and the name and title of each person authorized to exercise operational control under §135.77;

(b) Procedures for ensuring compliance with aircraft weight and balance limitations and, for multiengine aircraft, for determining compliance with §135.185;

(c) Copies of the certificate holder's operations specifications or appropriate extracted information, including area of operations authorized, category and class of aircraft authorized, crew complements, and types of operations authorized;

(d) Procedures for complying with accident notification requirements;

(e) Procedures for ensuring that the pilot in command knows that required airworthiness inspections have been made and that the aircraft has been approved for return to service in compliance with applicable maintenance requirements;

(f) Procedures for reporting and recording mechanical irregularities that come to the attention of the pilot in command before, during, and after completion of a flight;

(g) Procedures to be followed by the pilot in command for determining that mechanical irregularities or defects reported for previous flights have been corrected or that correction has been deferred;

(h) Procedures to be followed by the pilot in command to obtain maintenance, preventive maintenance, and servicing of the aircraft at a place where previous arrangements have not been made by the operator, when the pilot is authorized to so act for the operator;

(i) Procedures under §135.179 for the release for, or continuation of, flight if any item of equipment required for the particular type of operation becomes inoperative or unserviceable en route;

(j) Procedures for refueling aircraft, eliminating fuel contamination, protecting from fire (including electrostatic protection), and supervising and protecting passengers during refueling;

(k) Procedures to be followed by the pilot in command in the briefing under §135.117;

(l) Flight locating procedures, when applicable;

(m) Procedures for ensuring compliance with emergency procedures, including a list of the functions assigned each category of required crewmembers in connection with an emergency and emergency evacuation duties under §135.123;

(n) En route qualification procedures for pilots, when applicable;

(o) The approved aircraft inspection program, when applicable;

(p) Procedures and instructions to enable personnel to recognize hazardous materials, as defined in title 49 CFR, and if these materials are to be carried, stored, or handled, procedures and instructions for—

(1) Accepting shipment of hazardous material required by title 49 CFR, to assure proper packaging, marking, labeling, shipping documents, compatibility of articles, and instructions on their loading, storage, and handling;

(2) Notification and reporting hazardous material incidents as required by title 49 CFR; and

(3) Notification of the pilot in command when there are hazardous materials aboard, as required by title 49 CFR;

(q) Procedures for the evacuation of persons who may need the assistance of another person to move expeditiously to an exit if an emergency occurs; and

(r) If required by §135.385, an approved Destination Airport Analysis establishing runway safety margins at destination airports, taking into account the following factors as supported by published aircraft performance data supplied by the aircraft manufacturer for the appropriate runway conditions—

(1) Pilot qualifications and experience;

(2) Aircraft performance data to include normal, abnormal and emergency procedures as supplied by the aircraft manufacturer;

(3) Airport facilities and topography;

(4) Runway conditions (including contamination);

(5) Airport or area weather reporting;

(6) Appropriate additional runway safety margins, if required;

(7) Airplane inoperative equipment;

(8) Environmental conditions; and

(9) Other criteria affecting aircraft performance.

(s) Other procedures and policy instructions regarding the certificate holder's operations issued by the certificate holder.

[Docket No. 16097, 43 FR 46783, Oct. 10, 1978; as amended by Amdt. 135–20, 51 FR 40709, Nov. 7, 1986; Amdt. 135–58, 60 FR 65939, Dec. 20, 1995; Amdt. 135–91, 68 FR 54586, Sept. 17, 2003]

§135.25 Aircraft requirements.

(a) Except as provided in paragraph (d) of this section, no certificate holder may operate an aircraft under this part unless that aircraft—

(1) Is registered as a civil aircraft of the United States and carries an appropriate and current airworthiness certificate issued under this chapter; and

(2) Is in an airworthy condition and meets the applicable airworthiness requirements of this chapter, including those relating to identification and equipment.

(b) Each certificate holder must have the exclusive use of at least one aircraft that meets the requirements for at least one kind of operation authorized in the certificate holder's operations specifications. In addition, for each kind of operation for which the certificate holder does not have the exclusive use of an aircraft, the certificate holder must have available for use under a written agreement (including arrangements for performing required maintenance) at least one aircraft that meets the requirements for that kind of operation. However, this paragraph does not prohibit the operator from using or authorizing the use of the aircraft for other than operations under this part and does not require the certificate holder to have exclusive use of all aircraft that the certificate holder uses.

(c) For the purposes of paragraph (b) of this section, a person has exclusive use of an aircraft if that person has the sole possession, control, and use of it for flight, as owner, or has a written agreement (including arrangements for performing required maintenance), in effect when the aircraft is operated, giving the person that possession, control, and use for at least 6 consecutive months.

(d) A certificate holder may operate in common carriage, and for the carriage of mail, a civil aircraft which is leased or chartered to it without crew and is registered in a country which is a party to the Convention on International Civil Aviation if—

(1) The aircraft carries an appropriate airworthiness certificate issued by the country of registration and meets the registration and identification requirements of that country;

(2) The aircraft is of a type design which is approved under a U.S. type certificate and complies with all of the requirements of this chapter (14 CFR chapter 1) that would be applicable to that aircraft were it registered in the United States, in-

cluding the requirements which must be met for issuance of a U.S. standard airworthiness certificate (including type design conformity, condition for safe operation, and the noise, fuel venting, and engine emission requirements of this chapter), except that a U.S. registration certificate and a U.S. standard airworthiness certificate will not be issued for the aircraft;

(3) The aircraft is operated by U.S.-certificated airmen employed by the certificate holder; and

(4) The certificate holder files a copy of the aircraft lease or charter agreement with the FAA Aircraft Registry, Department of Transportation, 6400 South MacArthur Boulevard, Oklahoma City, OK (Mailing address: P.O. Box 25504, Oklahoma City, OK 73125).

[Docket No. 16097, 43 FR 46783, Oct. 10, 1978; as amended by Amdt. 135–8, 45 FR 68649, Oct. 16, 1980; Amdt. 135–66, 62 FR 13257, March 19, 1997]

§135.41 Carriage of narcotic drugs, marihuana, and depressant or stimulant drugs or substances.

If the holder of a certificate operating under this part allows any aircraft owned or leased by that holder to be engaged in any operation that the certificate holder knows to be in violation of §91.19(a) of this chapter, that operation is a basis for suspending or revoking the certificate.

[Docket No. 28154, 60 FR 65939, Dec. 20, 1995]

§135.43 Crewmember certificates: International operations.

(a) This section describes the certificates that were issued to United States citizens who were employed by air carriers at the time of issuance as flight crewmembers on United States registered aircraft engaged in international air commerce. The purpose of the certificate is to facilitate the entry and clearance of those crewmembers into ICAO contracting states. They were issued under Annex 9, as amended, to the Convention on International Civil Aviation.

(b) The holder of a certificate issued under this section, or the air carrier by whom the holder is employed, shall surrender the certificate for cancellation at the nearest FAA Flight Standards District Office at the termination of the holder's employment with that air carrier.

[Docket No. 28154, 61 FR 30435, June 14, 1996]

Subpart B—Flight Operations

§135.61 General.

This subpart prescribes rules, in addition to those in part 91 of this chapter, that apply to operations under this part.

§135.63 Recordkeeping requirements.

(a) Each certificate holder shall keep at its principal business office or at other places approved by the Administrator, and shall make available for inspection by the Administrator the following—

(1) The certificate holder's operating certificate;

(2) The certificate holder's operations specifications;

(3) A current list of the aircraft used or available for use in operations under this part and the operations for which each is equipped;

(4) An individual record of each pilot used in operations under this part, including the following information:

(i) The full name of the pilot.

(ii) The pilot certificate (by type and number) and ratings that the pilot holds.

(iii) The pilot's aeronautical experience in sufficient detail to determine the pilot's qualifications to pilot aircraft in operations under this part.

(iv) The pilot's current duties and the date of the pilot's assignment to those duties.

(v) The effective date and class of the medical certificate that the pilot holds.

(vi) The date and result of each of the initial and recurrent competency tests and proficiency and route checks required by this part and the type of aircraft flown during that test or check.

(vii) The pilot's flight time in sufficient detail to determine compliance with the flight time limitations of this part.

(viii) The pilot's check pilot authorization, if any.

(ix) Any action taken concerning the pilot's release from employment for physical or professional disqualification.

(x) The date of the completion of the initial phase and each recurrent phase of the training required by this part; and

(5) An individual record for each flight attendant who is required under this part, maintained in sufficient detail to determine compliance with the applicable portions of §135.273 of this part.

(b) Each certificate holder must keep each record required by paragraph (a)(3) of this section for at least 6 months, and must keep each record required by paragraphs (a)(4) and (a)(5) of this section for at least 12 months.

(c) For multiengine aircraft, each certificate holder is responsible for the preparation and accuracy of a load manifest in duplicate containing information concerning the loading of the aircraft. The manifest must be prepared before each takeoff and must include:

(1) The number of passengers;

(2) The total weight of the loaded aircraft;

(3) The maximum allowable takeoff weight for that flight;

(4) The center of gravity limits;

(5) The center of gravity of the loaded aircraft, except that the actual center of gravity need not be computed if the aircraft is loaded according to a loading schedule or other approved method that ensures that the center of gravity of the loaded aircraft is within approved limits. In those cases, an entry shall be made on the manifest indicating that the center of gravity is within limits according to a loading schedule or other approved method;

(6) The registration number of the aircraft or flight number;

(7) The origin and destination; and

(8) Identification of crew members and their crew position assignments.

(d) The pilot in command of an aircraft for which a load manifest must be prepared shall carry a copy of the completed load manifest in the aircraft to its destination. The certificate holder shall keep copies of completed load manifests for at least 30 days at its principal operations base, or at another location used by it and approved by the Administrator.

[Docket No. 16097, 43 FR 46783, Oct. 10, 1978; as amended by Amdt. 135–52, 59 FR 42993, Aug. 19, 1994]

§135.64 Retention of contracts and amendments: Commercial operators who conduct intrastate operations for compensation or hire.

Each commercial operator who conducts intrastate operations for compensation or hire shall keep a copy of each written contract under which it provides services as a commercial operator for a period of at least one year after the date of execution of the contract. In the case of an oral contract, it shall keep a memorandum stating its elements, and of any amendments to it, for a period of at least one year after the execution of that contract or change.

[Docket No. 28154, 60 FR 65939, Dec. 20, 1995; as amended by Amdt. 135–65, 61 FR 30435, June 14, 1996; Amdt. 135–66, 62 FR 13257, March 19, 1997]

§135.65 Reporting mechanical irregularities.

(a) Each certificate holder shall provide an aircraft maintenance log to be carried on board each aircraft for recording or deferring mechanical irregularities and their correction.

(b) The pilot in command shall enter or have entered in the aircraft maintenance log each mechanical irregularity that comes to the pilot's attention during flight time. Before each flight, the pilot in command shall, if the pilot does not already know, determine the status of each irregularity entered in the maintenance log at the end of the preceding flight.

(c) Each person who takes corrective action or defers action concerning a reported or observed failure or malfunction of an airframe, powerplant, propeller, rotor, or appliance, shall record the action taken in the aircraft maintenance log under the applicable maintenance requirements of this chapter.

(d) Each certificate holder shall establish a procedure for keeping copies of the aircraft maintenance log required by this section in the aircraft for access by appropriate personnel and shall include that procedure in the manual required by §135.21.

§135.67 Reporting potentially hazardous meteorological conditions and irregularities of communications or navigation facilities.

Whenever a pilot encounters a potentially hazardous meteorological condition or an irregularity in a ground communications or navigational facility in flight, the knowledge of which the pilot considers essential to the safety of other flights, the pilot shall notify an appropriate ground radio station as soon as practicable.

[Docket No. 16097, 43 FR 46783, Oct. 1, 1978; as amended by Amdt. 135–1, 44 FR 26737, May 7, 1979]

§135.69 Restriction or suspension of operations: Continuation of flight in an emergency.

(a) During operations under this part, if a certificate holder or pilot in command knows of conditions, including airport and runway conditions, that are a hazard to safe operations, the certificate holder or pilot in command, as the case may be, shall restrict or suspend operations as necessary until those conditions are corrected.

(b) No pilot in command may allow a flight to continue toward any airport of intended landing under the conditions set forth in paragraph (a) of this section, unless, in the opinion of the pilot in command, the conditions that are a hazard to safe operations may reasonably be expected to be corrected by the estimated time of arrival or, unless there is no safer procedure. In the latter event, the continuation toward that airport is an emergency situation under §135.19.

§135.71 Airworthiness check.

The pilot in command may not begin a flight unless the pilot determines that the airworthiness inspections required by §91.409 of this chapter, or §135.419, whichever is applicable, have been made.

[Docket No. 16097, 43 FR 46783, Oct. 10, 1978; as amended by Amdt. 135–32, 54 FR 34332, Aug. 18, 1989]

§135.73 Inspections and tests.

Each certificate holder and each person employed by the certificate holder shall allow the Administrator, at any time or place, to make inspections or tests (including en route inspections) to determine the holder's compliance with the Federal Aviation Act of 1958, applicable regulations, and the certificate holder's operating certificate, and operations specifications.

§135.75 Inspectors credentials: Admission to pilots' compartment: Forward observer's seat.

(a) Whenever, in performing the duties of conducting an inspection, an FAA inspector presents an Aviation Safety Inspector credential, FAA Form 110A, to the pilot in command of an aircraft operated by the certificate holder, the inspector must be given free and uninterrupted access to the pilot compartment of that aircraft. However, this paragraph does not limit the emergency authority of the pilot in command to exclude any person from the pilot compartment in the interest of safety.

(b) A forward observer's seat on the flight deck, or forward passenger seat with headset or speaker must be provided for use by the Administrator while conducting en route inspections. The suitability of the location of the seat and the headset or speaker for use in conducting en route inspections is determined by the Administrator.

§135.76 DOD Commercial Air Carrier Evaluator's Credentials: Admission to pilots compartment: Forward observer's seat.

(a) Whenever, in performing the duties of conducting an evaluation, a DOD commercial air carrier evaluator presents S&A Form 110B, "DOD Commercial Air Carrier Evaluator's Credential," to the pilot in command of an aircraft operated by the certificate holder, the evaluator must be given free and uninterrupted access to the pilot's compartment of that aircraft. However, this paragraph does not limit the emergency authority of the pilot in command to exclude any person from the pilot compartment in the interest of safety.

(b) A forward observer's seat on the flight deck or forward passenger seat with headset or speaker must be provided for use by the evaluator while conducting en route evaluations. The suitability of the location of the seat and the headset or speaker for use in conducting en route evaluations is determined by the FAA.

[Docket No. FAA–2003–15571, 68 FR 41218, July 10, 2003]

§135.77 Responsibility for operational control.

Each certificate holder is responsible for operational control and shall list, in the manual required by §135.21, the name and title of each person authorized by it to exercise operational control.

§135.79 Flight locating requirements.

(a) Each certificate holder must have procedures established for locating each flight, for which an FAA flight plan is not filed, that—

(1) Provide the certificate holder with at least the information required to be included in a VFR flight plan;

(2) Provide for timely notification of an FAA facility or search and rescue facility, if an aircraft is overdue or missing; and

(3) Provide the certificate holder with the location, date, and estimated time for reestablishing radio or telephone communications, if the flight will operate in an area where communications cannot be maintained.

(b) Flight locating information shall be retained at the certificate holder's principal place of business, or at other places designated by the certificate holder in the flight locating procedures, until the completion of the flight.

(c) Each certificate holder shall furnish the representative of the Administrator assigned to it with a copy of its flight locating procedures and any changes or additions, unless those procedures are included in a manual required under this part.

§135.81 Informing personnel of operational information and appropriate changes.

Each certificate holder shall inform each person in its employment of the operations specifications that apply to that person's duties and responsibilities and shall make available to each pilot in the certificate holder's employ the following materials in current form:

(a) Airman's Information Manual (Alaska Supplement in Alaska and Pacific Chart Supplement in Pacific-Asia Regions) or a commercial publication that contains the same information.

(b) This part and part 91 of this chapter.

(c) Aircraft Equipment Manuals, and Aircraft Flight Manual or equivalent.

(d) For foreign operations, the International Flight Information Manual or a commercial publication that contains the same information concerning the pertinent operational and entry requirements of the foreign country or countries involved.

§135.83 Operating information required.

(a) The operator of an aircraft must provide the following materials, in current and appropriate form, accessible to the pilot at the pilot station, and the pilot shall use them:

(1) A cockpit checklist.

(2) For multiengine aircraft or for aircraft with retractable landing gear, an emergency cockpit checklist containing the procedures required by paragraph (c) of this section, as appropriate.

(3) Pertinent aeronautical charts.

(4) For IFR operations, each pertinent navigational en route, terminal area, and approach and letdown chart.

(5) For multiengine aircraft, one-engine-inoperative climb performance data and if the aircraft is approved for use in IFR or over-the-top operations, that data must be sufficient to enable the pilot to determine compliance with §135.181(a)(2).

(b) Each cockpit checklist required by paragraph (a)(1) of this section must contain the following procedures:

(1) Before starting engines;

(2) Before takeoff;

(3) Cruise;

(4) Before landing;

(5) After landing;

(6) Stopping engines.

(c) Each emergency cockpit checklist required by paragraph (a)(2) of this section must contain the following procedures, as appropriate:

(1) Emergency operation of fuel, hydraulic, electrical, and mechanical systems.

(2) Emergency operation of instruments and controls.

(3) Engine inoperative procedures.

(4) Any other emergency procedures necessary for safety.

§135.85 Carriage of persons without compliance with the passenger-carrying provisions of this part.

The following persons may be carried aboard an aircraft without complying with the passenger-carrying requirements of this part:

(a) A crewmember or other employee of the certificate holder.

(b) A person necessary for the safe handling of animals on the aircraft.

(c) A person necessary for the safe handling of hazardous materials (as defined in subchapter C of title 49 CFR).

(d) A person performing duty as a security or honor guard accompanying a shipment made by or under the authority of the U.S. Government.

(e) A military courier or a military route supervisor carried by a military cargo contract air carrier or commercial operator in operations under a military cargo contract, if that carriage is specifically authorized by the appropriate military service.

(f) An authorized representative of the Administrator conducting an en route inspection.

(g) A person, authorized by the Administrator, who is performing a duty connected with a cargo operation of the certificate holder.

(h) A DOD commercial air carrier evaluator conducting an en route evaluation.

[Docket No. 16097, 43 FR 46783, Oct. 10, 1978; as amended by Amdt. 135–88, 68 FR 41218, July 10, 2003

§135.87 Carriage of cargo including carry-on baggage.

No person may carry cargo, including carry-on baggage, in or on any aircraft unless—

(a) It is carried in an approved cargo rack, bin, or compartment installed in or on the aircraft;

(b) It is secured by an approved means; or

(c) It is carried in accordance with each of the following:

(1) For cargo, it is properly secured by a safety belt or other tie-down having enough strength to eliminate the possibility of shifting under all normally anticipated flight and ground conditions, or for carry-on baggage, it is restrained so as to prevent its movement during air turbulence.

(2) It is packaged or covered to avoid possible injury to occupants.

(3) It does not impose any load on seats or on the floor structure that exceeds the load limitation for those components.

(4) It is not located in a position that obstructs the access to, or use of, any required emergency or regular exit, or the use of the aisle between the crew and the passenger compartment, or located in a position that obscures any passenger's view of the "seat belt" sign, "no smoking" sign, or any required exit sign, unless an auxiliary sign or other approved means for proper notification of the passengers is provided.

(5) It is not carried directly above seated occupants.

(6) It is stowed in compliance with this section for takeoff and landing.

(7) For cargo only operations, paragraph (c)(4) of this section does not apply if the cargo is loaded so that at least one emergency or regular exit is available to provide all occupants of the aircraft a means of unobstructed exit from the aircraft if an emergency occurs.

(d) Each passenger seat under which baggage is stowed shall be fitted with a means to prevent articles of baggage stowed under it from sliding under crash impacts severe enough to induce the ultimate inertia forces specified in the emergency landing condition regulations under which the aircraft was type certificated.

(e) When cargo is carried in cargo compartments that are designed to require the physical entry of a crewmember to extinguish any fire that may occur during flight, the cargo must be loaded so as to allow a crewmember to effectively reach all parts of the compartment with the contents of a hand fire extinguisher.

§135.89 Pilot requirements: Use of oxygen.

(a) *Unpressurized aircraft.* Each pilot of an unpressurized aircraft shall use oxygen continuously when flying—

(1) At altitudes above 10,000 feet through 12,000 feet MSL for that part of the flight at those altitudes that is of more than 30 minutes duration; and

(2) Above 12,000 feet MSL.

(b) *Pressurized aircraft.*

(1) Whenever a pressurized aircraft is operated with the cabin pressure altitude more than 10,000 feet MSL, each pilot shall comply with paragraph (a) of this section.

(2) Whenever a pressurized aircraft is operated at altitudes above 25,000 feet through 35,000 feet MSL, unless each pilot has an approved quick-donning type oxygen mask—

(i) At least one pilot at the controls shall wear, secured and sealed, an oxygen mask that either supplies oxygen at all times or automatically supplies oxygen whenever the cabin pressure altitude exceeds 12,000 feet MSL; and

(ii) During that flight, each other pilot on flight deck duty shall have an oxygen mask, connected to an oxygen supply, located so as to allow immediate placing of the mask on the pilot's face sealed and secured for use.

(3) Whenever a pressurized aircraft is operated at altitudes above 35,000 feet MSL, at least one pilot at the controls shall wear, secured and sealed, an oxygen mask required by paragraph (b)(2)(i) of this section.

(4) If one pilot leaves a pilot duty station of an aircraft when operating at altitudes above 25,000 feet MSL, the remaining pilot at the controls shall put on and use an approved oxygen mask until the other pilot returns to the pilot duty station of the aircraft.

§135.91 Oxygen for medical use by passengers.

(a) Except as provided in paragraphs (d) and (e) of this section, no certificate holder may allow the carriage or operation of equipment for the storage, generation or dispensing of medical oxygen unless the unit to be carried is constructed so that all valves, fittings, and gauges are protected from damage during that carriage or operation and unless the following conditions are met—

(1) The equipment must be—

(i) Of an approved type or in conformity with the manufacturing, packaging, marking, labeling, and maintenance requirements of title 49 CFR parts 171, 172, and 173, except §173.24(a)(1);

(ii) When owned by the certificate holder, maintained under the certificate holder's approved maintenance program;

(iii) Free of flammable contaminants on all exterior surfaces; and

(iv) Appropriately secured.

(2) When the oxygen is stored in the form of a liquid, the equipment must have been under the certificate holder's approved maintenance program since its purchase new or since the storage container was last purged.

(3) When the oxygen is stored in the form of a compressed gas as defined in title 49 CFR 173.300(a)—

(i) When owned by the certificate holder, it must be maintained under its approved maintenance program; and

(ii) The pressure in any oxygen cylinder must not exceed the rated cylinder pressure.

(4) The pilot in command must be advised when the equipment is on board, and when it is intended to be used.

(5) The equipment must be stowed, and each person using the equipment must be seated, so as not to restrict access to or use of any required emergency or regular exit, or of the aisle in the passenger compartment.

(b) No person may smoke and no certificate holder may allow any person to smoke within 10 feet of oxygen storage and dispensing equipment carried under paragraph (a) of this section.

(c) No certificate holder may allow any person other than a person trained in the use of medical oxygen equipment to connect or disconnect oxygen bottles or any other ancillary component while any passenger is aboard the aircraft.

(d) Paragraph (a)(1)(i) of this section does not apply when that equipment is furnished by a professional or medical emergency service for use on board an aircraft in a medical emergency when no other practical means of transportation (including any other properly equipped certificate holder) is reasonably available and the person carried under the medical emergency is accompanied by a person trained in the use of medical oxygen.

(e) Each certificate holder who, under the authority of paragraph (d) of this section, deviates from paragraph (a)(1)(i) of this section under a medical emergency shall, within 10 days, excluding Saturdays, Sundays, and Federal holidays, after the deviation, send to the certificate-holding district office a complete report of the operation involved, including a description of the deviation and the reasons for it.

[Docket No. 16097, 43 FR 46783, Oct. 10, 1978; as amended by Amdt. 135–60, 61 FR 2616, Jan. 26, 1996]

§135.93 Autopilot: Minimum altitudes for use.

(a) Except as provided in paragraphs (b), (c), (d), and (e) of this section, no person may use an autopilot at an altitude above the terrain which is less than 500 feet or less than twice the maximum altitude loss specified in the approved Aircraft Flight Manual or equivalent for a malfunction of the autopilot, whichever is higher.

(b) When using an instrument approach facility other than ILS, no person may use an autopilot at an altitude above the terrain that is less than 50 feet below the approved minimum descent altitude for that procedure, or less than twice the maximum loss specified in the approved Airplane Flight Manual or equivalent for a malfunction of the autopilot under approach conditions, whichever is higher.

(c) For ILS approaches, when reported weather conditions are less than the basic weather conditions in §91.155 of this chapter, no person may use an autopilot with an approach coupler at an altitude above the terrain that is less than 50 feet above the terrain, or the maximum altitude loss specified in the approved Airplane Flight Manual or equivalent for the malfunction of the autopilot with approach coupler, whichever is higher.

(d) Without regard to paragraph (a), (b), or (c) of this section, the Administrator may issue operations specifications to allow the use, to touchdown, of an approved flight control guidance system with automatic capability, if—

(1) The system does not contain any altitude loss (above zero) specified in the approved Aircraft Flight Manual or equivalent for malfunction of the autopilot with approach coupler; and

(2) The Administrator finds that the use of the system to touchdown will not otherwise adversely affect the safety standards of this section.

(e) Notwithstanding paragraph (a) of this section, the Administrator issues operations specifications to allow the use of an approved autopilot system with automatic capability during the takeoff and initial climb phase of flight provided:

(1) The Airplane Flight Manual specifies a minimum altitude engagement certification restriction;

(2) The system is not engaged prior to the minimum engagement certification restriction specified in the Airplane Flight Manual or an altitude specified by the Administrator, whichever is higher; and

(3) The Administrator finds that the use of the system will not otherwise affect the safety standards required by this section.

(f) This section does not apply to operations conducted in rotorcraft.

[Docket No. 16097, 43 FR 46783, Oct. 10, 1978; as amended by Amdt. 135–32, 54 FR 34332, Aug. 18, 1989; Amdt. 135–68, 62 FR 27923, May 21, 1997]

§135.95 Airmen: Limitations on use of services.

No certificate holder may use the services of any person as an airman unless the person performing those services—

(a) Holds an appropriate and current airman certificate; and

(b) Is qualified, under this chapter, for the operation for which the person is to be used.

§135.97 Aircraft and facilities for recent flight experience.

Each certificate holder shall provide aircraft and facilities to enable each of its pilots to maintain and demonstrate the pilot's ability to conduct all operations for which the pilot is authorized.

§135.99 Composition of flight crew.

(a) No certificate holder may operate an aircraft with less than the minimum flight crew specified in the aircraft operating limitations or the Aircraft Flight Manual for that aircraft and required by this part for the kind of operation being conducted.

(b) No certificate holder may operate an aircraft without a second in command if that aircraft has a passenger seating configuration, excluding any pilot seat, of ten seats or more.

§135.100 Flight crewmember duties.

(a) No certificate holder shall require, nor may any flight crewmember perform, any duties during a critical phase of flight except those duties required for the safe operation of the aircraft. Duties such as company required calls made for such nonsafety related purposes as ordering galley supplies and confirming passenger connections, announcements made to passengers promoting the air carrier or pointing out sights of interest, and filling out company payroll and related records are not required for the safe operation of the aircraft.

(b) No flight crewmember may engage in, nor may any pilot in command permit, any activity during a critical phase of flight which could distract any flight crewmember from the performance of his or her duties or which could interfere in any way with the proper conduct of those duties. Activities such as eating meals, engaging in nonessential conversations within the cockpit and nonessential communications between the cabin and cockpit crews, and reading publications not related to the proper conduct of the flight are not required for the safe operation of the aircraft.

(c) For the purposes of this section, critical phases of flight includes all ground operations involving taxi, takeoff and landing, and all other flight operations conducted below 10,000 feet, except cruise flight.

Note: Taxi is defined as "movement of an airplane under its own power on the surface of an airport."

[Docket No. 20661, 46 FR 5502, Jan. 19, 1981]

§135.101 Second in command required under IFR.

Except as provided in §§135.105, no person may operate an aircraft carrying passengers under IFR unless there is a second in command in the aircraft.

[Docket No. 28743, 62 FR 42374, Aug. 6, 1997]

§135.103 [Reserved]

§135.105 Exception to second in command requirement: Approval for use of autopilot system.

(a) Except as provided in §§135.99 and 135.111, unless two pilots are required by this chapter for operations under VFR, a person may operate an aircraft without a second in command, if it is equipped with an operative approved autopilot system and the use of that system is authorized by appropriate operations specifications. No certificate holder may use any person, nor may any person serve, as a pilot in command under this section of an aircraft operated in a commuter operation, as defined in part 119 of this chapter unless that person has at least 100 hours pilot in command flight time in the make and model of aircraft to be flown and has met all other applicable requirements of this part.

(b) The certificate holder may apply for an amendment of its operations specifications to authorize the use of an autopilot system in place of a second in command.

(c) The Administrator issues an amendment to the operations specifications authorizing the use of an autopilot system, in place of a second in command, if—

(1) The autopilot is capable of operating the aircraft controls to maintain flight and maneuver it about the three axes; and

(2) The certificate holder shows, to the satisfaction of the Administrator, that operations using the autopilot system can be conducted safely and in compliance with this part.

The amendment contains any conditions or limitations on the use of the autopilot system that the Administrator determines are needed in the interest of safety.

[Docket No. 16097, 43 FR 46783, Oct. 10, 1978; as amended by Amdt. 135–3, 45 FR 7542, Feb. 4, 1980; Amdt. 135–58, 60 FR 65939, Dec. 20, 1995]

§135.107 Flight attendant crewmember requirement.

No certificate holder may operate an aircraft that has a passenger seating configuration, excluding any pilot seat, of more than 19 unless there is a flight attendant crewmember on board the aircraft.

§135.109 Pilot in command or second in command: Designation required.

(a) Each certificate holder shall designate a—

(1) Pilot in command for each flight; and

(2) Second in command for each flight requiring two pilots.

(b) The pilot in command, as designated by the certificate holder, shall remain the pilot in command at all times during that flight.

§135.111 Second in command required in Category II operations.

No person may operate an aircraft in a Category II operation unless there is a second in command of the aircraft.

§135.113 Passenger occupancy of pilot seat.

No certificate holder may operate an aircraft type certificated after October 15, 1971, that has a passenger seating configuration, excluding any pilot seat, of more than eight seats if any person other than the pilot in command, a second in command, a company check airman, or an authorized representative of the Administrator, the National Transportation Safety Board, or the United States Postal Service occupies a pilot seat.

§135.115 Manipulation of controls.

No pilot in command may allow any person to manipulate the flight controls of an aircraft during flight conducted under this part, nor may any person manipulate the controls during such flight unless that person is—

(a) A pilot employed by the certificate holder and qualified in the aircraft; or

(b) An authorized safety representative of the Administrator who has the permission of the pilot in command, is qualified in the aircraft, and is checking flight operations.

§135.117 Briefing of passengers before flight.

(a) Before each takeoff each pilot in command of an aircraft carrying passengers shall ensure that all passengers have been orally briefed on—

(1) *Smoking.* Each passenger shall be briefed on when, where, and under what conditions smoking is prohibited (including, but not limited to, any applicable requirements of part 252 of this title). This briefing shall include a statement that the Federal Aviation Regulations require passenger compliance with the lighted passenger information signs (if such signs are required), posted placards, areas designated for safety purposes as no smoking areas, and crewmember instructions with regard to these items. The briefing shall also include a statement (if the aircraft is equipped with a lavatory) that Federal law prohibits: tampering with, disabling, or destroying any smoke detector installed in an aircraft lavatory; smoking in lavatories; and when applicable, smoking in passenger compartments.

(2) Use of safety belts, including instructions on how to fasten and unfasten the safety belts. Each passenger shall be briefed on when, where and under what conditions the safety belt must be fastened about that passenger. This briefing shall include a statement that the Federal Aviation Regulations require passenger compliance with lighted passenger information signs and crewmember instructions concerning the use of safety belts.

(3) The placement of seat backs in an upright position before takeoff and landing;

(4) Location and means for opening the passenger entry door and emergency exits;

(5) Location of survival equipment;

(6) If the flight involves extended overwater operation, ditching procedures and the use of required flotation equipment;

(7) If the flight involves operations above 12,000 feet MSL, the normal and emergency use of oxygen; and

(8) Location and operation of fire extinguishers.

(b) Before each takeoff the pilot in command shall ensure that each person who may need the assistance of another person to move expeditiously to an exit if an emergency occurs and that person's attendant, if any, has received a briefing as to the procedures to be followed if an evacuation occurs. This paragraph does not apply to a person who has been given a briefing before a previous leg of a flight in the same aircraft.

(c) The oral briefing required by paragraph (a) of this section shall be given by the pilot in command or a crewmember.

(d) Notwithstanding the provisions of paragraph (c) of this section, for aircraft certificated to carry 19 passengers or less, the oral briefing required by paragraph (a) of this section shall be given by the pilot in command, a crewmember, or other qualified person designated by the certificate holder and approved by the Administrator.

(e) The oral briefing required by paragraph (a) of this section must be supplemented by printed cards which must be carried in the aircraft in locations convenient for the use of each passenger. The cards must—

(1) Be appropriate for the aircraft on which they are to be used;

(2) Contain a diagram of, and method of operating, the emergency exits;

(3) Contain other instructions necessary for the use of emergency equipment on board the aircraft; and

(4) No later than June 12, 2005, for scheduled Commuter passenger-carrying flights, include the sentence, "Final assembly of this aircraft was completed in [INSERT NAME OF COUNTRY]."

(f) The briefing required by paragraph (a) may be delivered by means of an approved recording playback device that is audible to each passenger under normal noise levels.

[Docket No. 16097, 43 FR 46783, Oct. 10, 1978; as amended by Amdt. 135–9, 51 FR 40709, Nov. 7, 1986; Amdt. 135–25, 53 FR 12362, Apr. 13, 1988; Amdt. 135–44, 57 FR 42675, Sept. 15, 1992; 57 FR 43776, Sept. 22, 1992; Docket No. FAA–2004–18477, 69 FR 39294, June 29, 2004; Amdt. 135–98, 70 FR 36020, June 22, 2005]

§135.119 Prohibition against carriage of weapons.

No person may, while on board an aircraft being operated by a certificate holder, carry on or about that person a deadly or dangerous weapon, either concealed or unconcealed. This section does not apply to—

(a) Officials or employees of a municipality or a State, or of the United States, who are authorized to carry arms; or

(b) Crewmembers and other persons authorized by the certificate holder to carry arms.

§135.120 Prohibition on interference with crewmembers.

No person may assault, threaten, intimidate, or interfere with a crewmember in the performance of the crewmember's duties aboard an aircraft being operated under this part.

[Docket No. 16097, 43 FR 46783, Oct. 10, 1978; as amended by Amdt. 135–73, 64 FR 1080, Jan. 7, 1999]

§135.121 Alcoholic beverages.

(a) No person may drink any alcoholic beverage aboard an aircraft unless the certificate holder operating the aircraft has served that beverage.

(b) No certificate holder may serve any alcoholic beverage to any person aboard its aircraft if that person appears to be intoxicated.

(c) No certificate holder may allow any person to board any of its aircraft if that person appears to be intoxicated.

§135.122 Stowage of food, beverage, and passenger service equipment during aircraft movement on the surface, takeoff, and landing.

(a) No certificate holder may move an aircraft on the surface, takeoff, or land when any food, beverage, or tableware furnished by the certificate holder is located at any passenger seat.

(b) No certificate holder may move an aircraft on the surface, takeoff, or land unless each food and beverage tray and seat back tray table is secured in its stowed position.

(c) No certificate holder may permit an aircraft to move on surface, takeoff or land unless each passenger serving cart is secured in its stowed position.

(d) Each passenger shall comply with instructions given by a crewmember with regard to compliance with this section.

[Docket No. 26142, 57 FR 42675, Sept. 15, 1992]

§135.123 Emergency and emergency evacuation duties.

(a) Each certificate holder shall assign to each required crewmember for each type of aircraft as appropriate, the necessary functions to be performed in an emergency or in a situation requiring emergency evacuation. The certificate holder shall ensure that those functions can be practicably accomplished, and will meet any reasonably anticipated emergency including incapacitation of individual crewmembers or their inability to reach the passenger cabin because of shifting cargo in combination cargo-passenger aircraft.

(b) The certificate holder shall describe in the manual required under §135.21 the functions of each category of required crewmembers assigned under paragraph (a) of this section.

§135.125 Airplane security.

Certificate holders conducting operations under this part shall comply with the applicable security requirements in 49 CFR chapter XII.

[Docket No. TSA–2002–11602, 67 FR 8350, Feb. 22, 2002]

§135.127 Passenger information requirements and smoking prohibitions.

(a) No person may conduct a scheduled flight on which smoking is prohibited by part 252 of this title unless the "No Smoking" passenger information signs are lighted during the entire flight, or one or more "No Smoking" placards meeting the requirements of §25.1541 of this chapter are posted during the entire flight. If both the lighted signs and the placards are used, the signs must remain lighted during the entire flight segment.

(b) No person may smoke while a "No Smoking" sign is lighted or while "No Smoking" placards are posted, except as follows:

(1) *On-demand operations.* The pilot in command of an aircraft engaged in an on-demand operation may authorize smoking on the flight deck (if it is physically separated from any passenger compartment), except in any of the following situations:

(i) During aircraft movement on the surface or during takeoff or landing;

(ii) During scheduled passenger-carrying public charter operations conducted under part 380 of this title;

(iii) During on-demand operations conducted interstate that meet paragraph (2) of the definition "On-demand operation" in §119.3 of this chapter, unless permitted under paragraph (b)(2) of this section; or

(iv) During any operation where smoking is prohibited by part 252 of this title or by international agreement.

(2) *Certain intrastate commuter operations and certain intrastate on-demand operations.* Except during aircraft movement on the surface or during takeoff or landing, a pilot in command of an aircraft engaged in a commuter operation or an on-demand operation that meets paragraph (2) of the definition of "On-demand operation" in §119.3 of this chapter may authorize smoking on the flight deck (if it is physically separated from the passenger compartment, if any) if—

(i) Smoking on the flight deck is not otherwise prohibited by part 252 of this title;

(ii) The flight is conducted entirely within the same State of the United States (a flight from one place in Hawaii to another place in Hawaii through the airspace over a place outside Hawaii is not entirely within the same State); and

(iii) The aircraft is either not turbojet-powered or the aircraft is not capable of carrying at least 30 passengers.

(c) No person may smoke in any aircraft lavatory.

(d) No person may operate an aircraft with a lavatory equipped with a smoke detector unless there is in that lavatory a sign or placard which reads: "Federal law provides for a penalty of up to $2,000 for tampering with the smoke detector installed in this lavatory."

(e) No person may tamper with, disable, or destroy any smoke detector installed in any aircraft lavatory.

(f) On flight segments other than those described in paragraph (a) of this section, the "No Smoking" signs required by §135.177(a)(3) of this part must be turned on during any movement of the aircraft on the surface, for each takeoff and landing, and at any other time considered necessary by the pilot in command.

(g) The passenger information requirements prescribed in §91.517(b) and (d) of this chapter are in addition to the requirements prescribed in this section.

(h) Each passenger shall comply with instructions given him or her by crewmembers regarding compliance with paragraphs (b), (c), and (e) of this section.

[Docket No. 25590, 55 FR 8367, March 7, 1990; as amended by Amdt. 135–35, 55 FR 20135, May 15, 1990; Amdt. 135–44, 57 FR 42675, Sept. 15, 1992; Amdt. 135–60, 61 FR 2616, Jan. 26, 1996; Amdt. 135–76, 65 FR 36780, June 9, 2000]

§135.128 Use of safety belts and child restraint systems.

(a) Except as provided in this paragraph, each person on board an aircraft operated under this part shall occupy an approved seat or berth with a separate safety belt properly secured about him or her during movement on the surface, takeoff and landing. For seaplane and float equipped rotorcraft operations during movement on the surface, the person pushing off the seaplane or rotorcraft from the dock and the person mooring the seaplane or rotorcraft at the dock are excepted from the preceding seating and safety belt requirements. A safety belt provided for the occupant of a seat may not be used by more than one person who has reached his or her second birthday. Not withstanding the preceding requirements, a child may:

(1) Be held by an adult who is occupying an approved seat or berth, provided the child has not reached his or her second birthday and the child does not occupy or use any restraining device; or

(2) Notwithstanding any other requirement of this chapter, occupy an approved child restraint system furnished by the certificate holder or one of the persons described in paragraph (a)(2)(i) of this section, provided:

(i) The child is accompanied by a parent, guardian, or attendant designated by the child's parent or guardian to attend to the safety of the child during flight;

(ii) Except as provided in paragraph (a)(2)(ii)(D) of this section, the approved child restraint system bears one or more labels as follows:

(A) Seats manufactured to U.S. standards between January 1, 1981, and February 25, 1985, must bear the label: "This child restraint system conforms to all applicable Federal motor vehicle safety standards";

(B) Seats manufactured to U.S. standards on or after February 26, 1985, must bear two labels:

(*1*) "This child restraint system conforms to all applicable Federal motor vehicle safety standards"; and

(*2*) "THIS RESTRAINT IS CERTIFIED FOR USE IN MOTOR VEHICLES AND AIRCRAFT" in red lettering;

(C) Seats that do not qualify under paragraphs (a)(2)(ii)(A) and (a)(2)(ii)(B) of this section must bear either a label showing approval of a foreign government or a label showing that the seat was manufactured under the standards of the United Nations;

(D) Notwithstanding any other provisions of this section, booster-type child restraint systems (as defined in Federal Motor Vehicle Standard No. 213 (49 CFR 571.213)), vest- and harness-type child restraint systems, and lap held child restraints are not approved for use in aircraft; and

(iii) The certificate holder complies with the following requirements:

(A) The restraint system must be properly secured to an approved forward-facing seat or berth;

(B) The child must be properly secured in the restraint system and must not exceed the specified weight limit for the restraint system; and

(C) The restraint system must bear the appropriate label(s).

(b) Except as provided in paragraph (b)(3) of this section, the following prohibitions apply to certificate holders:

(1) No certificate holder may permit a child, in an aircraft, to occupy a booster-type child restraint system, a vest-type child restraint system, a harness-type child restraint system, or a lap held child restraint system during take off, landing, or movement on the surface.

(2) Except as required in paragraph (b)(1) of this section, no certificate holder may prohibit a child, if requested by the child's parent, guardian, or designated attendant, from occupying a child restraint system furnished by the child's parent, guardian, or designated attendant provided:

(i) The child holds a ticket for an approved seat or berth or such seat or berth is otherwise made available by the certificate holder for the child's use;

(ii) The requirements of paragraph (a)(2)(i) of this section are met;

(iii) The requirements of paragraph (a)(2)(iii) of this section are met; and

(iv) The child restraint system has one or more of the labels described in paragraphs (a)(2)(ii)(A) through (a)(2)(ii)(C) of this section.

(3) This section does not prohibit the certificate holder from providing child restraint systems authorized by this or, consistent with safe operating practices, determining the most appropriate passenger seat location for the child restraint system.

[Docket No. 26142, 57 FR 42676, Sept. 15, 1992; as amended by Amdt. 135–62, 61 FR 28422, June 4, 1996]

§135.129 Exit seating.

(a)(1) *Applicability.* This section applies to all certificate holders operating under this part, except for on-demand operations with aircraft having 19 or fewer passenger seats and commuter operations with aircraft having 9 or fewer passenger seats.

(2) *Duty to make determination of suitability.* Each certificate holder shall determine, to the extent necessary to perform the applicable functions of paragraph (d) of this section, the suitability of each person it permits to occupy an exit seat. For the purpose of this section—

(i) *Exit seat* means—

(A) Each seat having direct access to an exit; and

(B) Each seat in a row of seats through which passengers would have to pass to gain access to an exit, from the first seat inboard of the exit to the first aisle inboard of the exit.

(ii) A passenger seat having *direct access* means a seat from which a passenger can proceed directly to the exit without entering an aisle or passing around an obstruction.

(3) *Persons designated to make determination.* Each certificate holder shall make the passenger exit seating determinations required by the paragraph in a non-discriminatory manner consistent with the requirements of this section, by persons designated in the certificate holder's required operations manual.

(4) *Submission of designation for approval.* Each certificate holder shall designate the exit seats for each passenger seating configuration in its fleet in accordance with the definitions in this paragraph and submit those designations for approval as part of the procedures required to be submitted for approval under paragraphs (n) and (p) of this section.

(b) No certificate holder may seat a person in a seat affected by this section if the certificate holder determines that it is likely that the person would be unable to perform one or more of the applicable functions listed in paragraph (d) of this section because—

(1) The person lacks sufficient mobility, strength, or dexterity in both arms and hands, and both legs:

(i) To reach upward, sideways, and downward to the location of emergency exit and exit-slide operating mechanisms;

(ii) To grasp and push, pull, turn, or otherwise manipulate those mechanisms;

(iii) To push, shove, pull, or otherwise open emergency exits;

(iv) To lift out, hold, deposit on nearby seats, or maneuver over the seatbacks to the next row objects the size and weight of over-wing window exit doors;

(v) To remove obstructions of size and weight similar over-wing exit doors;

(vi) To reach the emergency exit expeditiously;

(vii) To maintain balance while removing obstructions;

(viii) To exit expeditiously;

(ix) To stabilize an escape slide after deployment; or

(x) To assist others in getting off an escape slide;

(2) The person is less than 15 years of age or lacks the capacity to perform one or more of the applicable functions listed in paragraph (d) of this section without the assistance of an adult companion, parent, or other relative;

(3) The person lacks the ability to read and understand instructions required by this section and related to emergency evacuation provided by the certificate holder in printed or graphic form or the ability to understand oral crew commands.

(4) The person lacks sufficient visual capacity to perform one or more of the applicable functions in paragraph (d) of this section without the assistance of visual aids beyond contact lenses or eyeglasses;

(5) The person lacks sufficient aural capacity to hear and understand instructions shouted by flight attendants, without assistance beyond a hearing aid;

(6) The person lacks the ability adequately to impart information orally to other passengers; or,

(7) The person has:

(i) A condition or responsibilities, such as caring for small children, that might prevent the person from performing one or more of the applicable functions listed in paragraph (d) of this section; or

(ii) A condition that might cause the person harm if he or she performs one or more of the applicable functions listed in paragraph (d) of this section.

(c) Each passenger shall comply with instructions given by a crewmember or other authorized employee of the certificate holder implementing exit seating restrictions established in accordance with this section.

(d) Each certificate holder shall include on passenger information cards, presented in the languages in which briefings and oral commands are given by the crew, at each exit seat affected by this section, information that, in the event of an emergency in which a crewmember is not available to assist, a passenger occupying an exit row seat may use if called upon to perform the following functions:

(1) Locate the emergency exit;

(2) Recognize the emergency exit opening mechanism;

(3) Comprehend the instructions for operating the emergency exit;

(4) Operate the emergency exit;

(5) Assess whether opening the emergency exit will increase the hazards to which passengers may be exposed;

(6) Follow oral directions and hand signals given by a crewmember;

(7) Stow or secure the emergency exit door so that it will not impede use of the exit;

(8) Assess the condition of an escape slide, activate the slide, and stabilize the slide after deployment to assist others in getting off the slide;

(9) Pass expeditiously through the emergency exit; and

(10) Assess, select, and follow a safe path away from the emergency exit.

(e) Each certificate holder shall include on passenger information cards, at each exit seat—

(1) In the primary language in which emergency commands are given by the crew, the selection criteria set forth in paragraph (b) of this section, and a request that a passenger identify himself or herself to allow reseating if he or she—

(i) Cannot meet the selection criteria set forth in paragraph (b) of this section;

(ii) Has a nondiscernible condition that will prevent him or her from performing the applicable functions listed in paragraph (d) of this section;

(iii) May suffer bodily harm as the result of performing one or more of those functions; or,

(iv) Does not wish to perform those functions; and,

(2) In each language used by the certificate holder for passenger information cards, a request that a passenger identify himself or herself to allow reseating if he or she lacks the ability to read, speak, or understand the language or the graphic form in which instructions required by this section and related to emergency evacuation are provided by the certificate holder, or the ability to understand the specified language in which crew commands will be given in an emergency;

(3) May suffer bodily harm as the result of performing one or more of those functions; or,

(4) Does not wish to perform those functions.

A certificate holder shall not require the passenger to disclose his or her reason for needing reseating.

(f) Each certificate holder shall make available for inspection by the public at all passenger loading gates and ticket counters at each airport where it conducts passenger operations, written procedures established for making determinations in regard to exit row seating.

(g) No certificate holder may allow taxi or pushback unless at least one required crewmember has verified that no exit row seat is occupied by a person the crewmember determines is likely to be unable to perform the applicable functions listed in paragraph (d) of this section.

(h) Each certificate holder shall include in its passenger briefings a reference to the passenger information cards, required by paragraphs (d) and (e), the selection criteria set forth in paragraph (b), and the functions to be performed, set forth in paragraph (d) of this section.

(i) Each certificate holder shall include in its passenger briefings a request that a passenger identify himself or herself to allow reseating if he or she—

(1) Cannot meet the selection criteria set forth in paragraph (b) of this section;

(2) Has a nondiscernible condition that will prevent him or her from performing the applicable functions listed in paragraph (d) of this section;

(3) May suffer bodily harm as the result of performing one or more of those functions; or,

(4) Does not wish to perform those functions.

A certificate holder shall not require the passenger to disclose his or her reason for needing reseating.

(j) [Reserved]

(k) In the event a certificate holder determines in accordance with this section that it is likely that a passenger assigned to an exit row seat would be unable to perform the functions listed in paragraph (d) of this section or a passenger requests a non-exit seat, the certificate holder shall expeditiously relocate the passenger to a non-exit seat.

(l) In the event of full booking in the non-exit seats, and if necessary to accommodate a passenger being relocated from an exit seat, the certificate holder shall move a passenger who is willing and able to assume the evacuation functions that may be required, to an exit seat.

(m) A certificate holder may deny transportation to any passenger under this section only because—

(1) The passenger refuses to comply with instructions given by a crewmember or other authorized employee of the certificate holder implementing exit seating restrictions established in accordance with this section, or

(2) The only seat that will physically accommodate the person's handicap is an exit seat.

(n) In order to comply with this section certificate holders shall—

(1) Establish procedures that address:

(i) The criteria listed in paragraph (b) of this section;

(ii) The functions listed in paragraph (d) of this section;

(iii) The requirements for airport information, passenger information cards, crewmember verification of appropriate seating in exit rows, passenger briefings, seat assignments, and denial of transportation as set forth in this section;

(iv) How to resolve disputes arising from implementation of this section, including identification of the certificate holder employee on the airport to whom complaints should be addressed for resolution; and,

(2) Submit their procedures for preliminary review and approval to the principal operations inspectors assigned to them at the certificate-holding district office.

(o) Certificate holders shall assign seats prior to boarding consistent with the criteria listed in paragraph (b) and the functions listed in paragraph (d) of this section, to the maximum extent feasible.

(p) The procedures required by paragraph (n) of this section will not become effective until final approval is granted by the Director, Flight Standards Service, Washington, DC. Approval will be based solely upon the safety aspects of the certificate holder's procedures.

[Docket No. 25821, 55 FR 8073, March 6, 1990; as amended by Amdt. 135–45, 57 FR 48664, Oct. 27, 1992; as Amdt. 135–50, 59 FR 33603, June 29, 1994; Amdt. 135–60, 61 FR 2616, Jan. 26, 1996]

Subpart C— Aircraft and Equipment

§135.141 Applicability.

This subpart prescribes aircraft and equipment requirements for operations under this part. The requirements of this subpart are in addition to the aircraft and equipment requirements of part 91 of this chapter. However, this part does not require the duplication of any equipment required by this chapter.

§135.143 General requirements.

(a) No person may operate an aircraft under this part unless that aircraft and its equipment meet the applicable regulations of this chapter.

(b) Except as provided in §135.179, no person may operate an aircraft under this part unless the required instruments and equipment in it have been approved and are in an operable condition.

(c) ATC transponder equipment installed within the time periods indicated below must meet the performance and environmental requirements of the following TSOs:

(1) *Through January 1, 1992:*

(i) Any class of TSO-C74b or any class of TSO-C74c as appropriate, provided that the equipment was manufactured before January 1, 1990; or

(ii) The appropriate class of TSO-C112 (Mode S).

(2) *After January 1, 1992:* The appropriate class of TSO-C112 (Mode S). For purposes of paragraph (c)(2) of this section, "installation" does not include—

(i) Temporary installation of TSO-C74b or TSO-C74c substitute equipment, as appropriate, during maintenance of the permanent equipment;

(ii) Reinstallation of equipment after temporary removal for maintenance; or

(iii) For fleet operations, installation of equipment in a fleet aircraft after removal of the equipment for maintenance from another aircraft in the same operator's fleet.

[Docket No. 16097, 43 FR 46783, Oct. 10, 1978; as amended by Amdt. 135–22, 52 FR 3392, Feb. 3, 1987]

§135.144 Portable electronic devices.

(a) Except as provided in paragraph (b) of this section, no person may operate, nor may any operator or pilot in command of an aircraft allow the operation of, any portable electronic device on any U.S.-registered civil aircraft operating under this part.

(b) Paragraph (a) of this section does not apply to—

(1) Portable voice recorders;

(2) Hearing aids;

(3) Heart pacemakers;

(4) Electric shavers; or

(5) Any other portable electronic device that the part 119 certificate holder has determined will not cause interference with the navigation or communication system of the aircraft on which it is to be used.

(c) The determination required by paragraph (b)(5) of this section shall be made by that part 119 certificate holder operating the aircraft on which the particular device is to be used.

[Docket No. 16097, 43 FR 46783, Oct. 10, 1978; as amended by Amdt. 135–73, 64 FR 1080, Jan. 7, 1999]

§135.145 Aircraft proving and validation tests.

(a) No certificate holder may operate an aircraft, other than a turbojet aircraft, for which two pilots are required by this chapter for operations under VFR, if it has not previously proved such an aircraft in operations under this part in at least 25 hours of proving tests acceptable to the Administrator including—

(1) Five hours of night time, if night flights are to be authorized;

(2) Five instrument approach procedures under simulated or actual conditions, if IFR flights are to be authorized; and

(3) Entry into a representative number of en route airports as determined by the Administrator.

(b) No certificate holder may operate a turbojet airplane if it has not previously proved a turbojet airplane in operations under this part in at least 25 hours of proving tests acceptable to the Administrator including—

(1) Five hours of night time, if night flights are to be authorized;

(2) Five instrument approach procedures under simulated or actual conditions, if IFR flights are to be authorized; and

(3) Entry into a representative number of en route airports as determined by the Administrator.

(c) No certificate holder may carry passengers in an aircraft during proving tests, except those needed to make the tests and those designated by the Administrator to observe the tests. However, pilot flight training may be conducted during the proving tests.

(d) Validation testing is required to determine that a certificate holder is capable of conducting operations safely and in compliance with applicable regulatory standards. Validation tests are required for the following authorizations:

(1) The addition of an aircraft for which two pilots are required for operations under VFR or a turbojet airplane, if that aircraft or an aircraft of the same make or similar design has not been previously proved or validated in operations under this part.

(2) Operations outside U.S. airspace.

(3) Class II navigation authorizations.

(4) Special performance or operational authorizations.

(e) Validation tests must be accomplished by test methods acceptable to the Administrator. Actual flights may not be required when an applicant can demonstrate competence and compliance with appropriate regulations without conducting a flight.

(f) Proving tests and validation tests may be conducted simultaneously when appropriate.

(g) The Administrator may authorize deviations from this section if the Administrator finds that special circumstances make full compliance with this section unnecessary.

[Docket No. FAA–2001–10047, 68 FR 54586, Sept. 17, 2003]

§135.147 Dual controls required.

No person may operate an aircraft in operations requiring two pilots unless it is equipped with functioning dual controls. However, if the aircraft type certification operating limitations do not require two pilots, a throwover control wheel may be used in place of two control wheels.

§135.149 Equipment requirements: General.

No person may operate an aircraft unless it is equipped with—

(a) A sensitive altimeter that is adjustable for barometric pressure;

(b) Heating or deicing equipment for each carburetor or, for a pressure carburetor, an alternate air source;

(c) For turbojet airplanes, in addition to two gyroscopic bank-and-pitch indicators (artificial horizons) for use at the pilot stations, a third indicator that is installed in accordance with the instrument requirements prescribed in §121.305(j) of this chapter.

(d) [Reserved]

(e) For turbine powered aircraft, any other equipment as the Administrator may require.

[Docket No. 16097, 43 FR 46783, Oct. 10, 1978; as amended by Amdt. 135–1, 44 FR 26737, May 7, 1979; Amdt. 135–34, 54 FR 43926, Oct. 27, 1989; Amdt. 135–38, 55 FR 43310, Oct. 26, 1990]

§135.150 Public address and crewmember interphone systems.

No person may operate an aircraft having a passenger seating configuration, excluding any pilot seat, of more than 19 unless it is equipped with—

(a) A public address system which—

(1) Is capable of operation independent of the crewmember interphone system required by paragraph (b) of this section, except for handsets, headsets, microphones, selector switches, and signaling devices;

(2) Is approved in accordance with §21.305 of this chapter;

(3) Is accessible for immediate use from each of two flight crewmember stations in the pilot compartment;

(4) For each required floor-level passenger emergency exit which has an adjacent flight attendant seat, has a microphone which is readily accessible to the seated flight attendant, except that one microphone may serve more than one exit, provided the proximity of the exits allows unassisted verbal communication between seated flight attendants;

(5) Is capable of operation within 10 seconds by a flight attendant at each of those stations in the passenger compartment from which its use is accessible;

(6) Is audible at all passenger seats, lavatories, and flight attendant seats and work stations; and

(7) For transport category airplanes manufactured on or after November 27, 1990, meets the requirements of §25.1423 of this chapter.

(b) A crewmember interphone system which—

(1) Is capable of operation independent of the public address system required by paragraph (a) of this section, except for handsets, headsets, microphones, selector switches, and signaling devices;

(2) Is approved in accordance with §21.305 of this chapter;

(3) Provides a means of two-way communication between the pilot compartment and—

(i) Each passenger compartment; and

(ii) Each galley located on other than the main passenger deck level;

(4) Is accessible for immediate use from each of two flight crewmember stations in the pilot compartment;

(5) Is accessible for use from at least one normal flight attendant station in each passenger compartment;

(6) Is capable of operation within 10 seconds by a flight attendant at each of those stations in each passenger compartment from which its use is accessible; and

(7) For large turbojet-powered airplanes—

(i) Is accessible for use at enough flight attendant stations so that all floor-level emergency exits (or entryways to those exits in the case of exits located within galleys) in each passenger compartment are observable from one or more of those stations so equipped;

(ii) Has an alerting system incorporating aural or visual signals for use by flight crewmembers to alert flight attendants and for use by flight attendants to alert flight crewmembers;

(iii) For the alerting system required by paragraph (b)(7)(ii) of this section, has a means for the recipient of a call to determine whether it is a normal call or an emergency call; and

(iv) When the airplane is on the ground, provides a means of two-way communication between ground personnel and either of at least two flight crewmembers in the pilot compartment. The interphone system station for use by ground personnel must be so located that personnel using the system may avoid visible detection from within the airplane.

[Docket No. 24995, 54 FR 43926, Oct. 27, 1989]

§135.151 Cockpit voice recorders.

(a) No person may operate a multiengine, turbine-powered airplane or rotorcraft having a passenger seating configuration of six or more and for which two pilots are required by certification or operating rules unless it is equipped with an approved cockpit voice recorder that:

(1) Is installed in compliance with §23.1457(a) (1) and (2), (b), (c), (d), (e), (f), and (g); §25.1457(a) (1) and (2), (b), (c), (d), (e), (f), and (g); §27.1457(a) (1) and (2), (b), (c), (d), (e), (f), and (g); or §29.1457(a) (1) and (2), (b), (c), (d), (e), (f), and (g) of this chapter, as applicable; and

(2) Is operated continuously from the use of the check list before the flight to completion of the final check list at the end of the flight.

(b) No person may operate a multiengine, turbine-powered airplane or rotorcraft having a passenger seating configuration of 20 or more seats unless it is equipped with an approved cockpit voice recorder that—

(1) Is installed in compliance with §23.1457, §25.1457, §27.1457 or §29.1457 of this chapter, as applicable; and

(2) Is operated continuously from the use of the check list before the flight to completion of the final check list at the end of the flight.

(c) In the event of an accident, or occurrence requiring immediate notification of the National Transportation Safety Board which results in termination of the flight, the certificate holder shall keep the recorded information for at least 60 days or, if requested by the Administrator or the Board, for a longer period. Information obtained from the record may be used to assist in determining the cause of accidents or occurrences in connection with investigations. The Administrator does not use the record in any civil penalty or certificate action.

(d) For those aircraft equipped to record the uninterrupted audio signals received by a boom or a mask microphone the flight crewmembers are required to use the boom microphone below 18,000 feet mean sea level. No person may operate a large turbine engine powered airplane manufactured after October 11, 1991, or on which a cockpit voice recorder has been installed after October 11, 1991, unless it is equipped to record the uninterrupted audio signal received by a boom or mask microphone in accordance with §25.1457(c)(5) of this chapter.

(e) In complying with this section, an approved cockpit voice recorder having an erasure feature may be used, so that during the operation of the recorder, information:

(1) Recorded in accordance with paragraph (a) of this section and recorded more than 15 minutes earlier; or

(2) Recorded in accordance with paragraph (b) of this section and recorded more than 30 minutes earlier; may be erased or otherwise obliterated.

[Docket No. 16097, 43 FR 46783, Oct. 10, 1978; as amended by Amdt. 135–23, 52 FR 9637, March 25, 1987; Amdt. 135–26, 53 FR 26151, July 11, 1988; Amdt. 135–60, 61 FR 2616, Jan. 26, 1996]

§135.152 Flight recorders.

(a) Except as provided in paragraph (k) of this section, no person may operate under this part a multi-engine, turbine-engine powered airplane or rotorcraft having a passenger seating configuration, excluding any required crewmember seat, of 10 to 19 seats, that was either brought onto the U.S. register after, or was registered outside the United States and added to the operator's U.S. operations specifications after, October 11, 1991, unless it is equipped with one or more approved flight recorders that use a digital method of recording and storing data and a method of readily retrieving that data from the storage medium. The parameters specified in either Appendix B or C of this part, as applicable must be recorded within the range, accuracy, resolution, and recording intervals as specified. The recorder shall retain no less than 25 hours of aircraft operation.

(b) After October 11, 1991, no person may operate a multiengine, turbine-powered airplane having a passenger seating configuration of 20 to 30 seats or a multiengine, turbine-powered rotorcraft having a passenger seating configuration of 20 or more seats unless it is equipped with one or more approved flight recorders that utilize a digital method of recording and storing data, and a method of readily retrieving that data from the storage medium. The parameters in Appendix D or E of this part, as applicable, that are set forth below, must be recorded within the ranges, accuracies, resolutions, and sampling intervals as specified.

(1) Except as provided in paragraph (b)(3) of this section for aircraft type certificated before October 1, 1969, the following parameters must be recorded:

(i) Time;

(ii) Altitude;

(iii) Airspeed;

(iv) Vertical acceleration;

(v) Heading;

(vi) Time of each radio transmission to or from air traffic control;

(vii) Pitch attitude;

(viii) Roll attitude;

(ix) Longitudinal acceleration;

(x) Control column or pitch control surface position; and

(xi) Thrust of each engine.

(2) Except as provided in paragraph (b)(3) of this section for aircraft type certificated after September 30, 1969, the following parameters must be recorded:

(i) Time;

(ii) Altitude;

(iii) Airspeed;

(iv) Vertical acceleration;

(v) Heading;

(vi) Time of each radio transmission either to or from air traffic control;

(vii) Pitch attitude;

(viii) Roll attitude;

(ix) Longitudinal acceleration;

(x) Pitch trim position;

(xi) Control column or pitch control surface position;

(xii) Control wheel or lateral control surface position;

(xiii) Rudder pedal or yaw control surface position;

(xiv) Thrust of each engine;

(xv) Position of each thrust reverser;

(xvi) Trailing edge flap or cockpit flap control position; and

(xvii) Leading edge flap or cockpit flap control position.

(3) For aircraft manufactured after October 11, 1991, all of the parameters listed in Appendix D or E of this part, as applicable, must be recorded.

(c) Whenever a flight recorder required by this section is installed, it must be operated continuously from the instant the airplane begins the takeoff roll or the rotorcraft begins the lift-off until the airplane has completed the landing roll or the rotorcraft has landed at its destination.

(d) Except as provided in paragraph (c) of this section, and except for recorded data erased as authorized in this paragraph, each certificate holder shall keep the recorded data prescribed in paragraph (a) of this section until the aircraft has been operating for at least 25 hours of the operating time specified in paragraph (c) of this section. In addition, each certificate holder shall keep the recorded data prescribed in paragraph (b) of this section for an airplane until the airplane has been operating for at least 25 hours, and for a rotorcraft until the rotorcraft has been operating for at least 10 hours, of the operating time specified in paragraph (c) of this section. A total of 1 hour of recorded data may be erased for the purpose of testing the flight recorder or the flight recorder system. Any erasure made in accordance with this paragraph must be of the oldest recorded data accumulated at the time of testing. Except as provided in paragraph

(c) of this section, no record need be kept more than 60 days.

(e) In the event of an accident or occurrence that requires the immediate notification of the National Transportation Safety Board under 49 CFR part 830 of its regulations and that results in termination of the flight, the certificate holder shall remove the recording media from the aircraft and keep the recorded data required by paragraphs (a) and (b) of this section for at least 60 days or for a longer period upon request of the Board or the Administrator.

(f)(1) For airplanes manufactured on or before August 18, 2000, and all other aircraft, each flight recorder required by this section must be installed in accordance with the requirements of §23.1459, 25.1459, 27.1459, or 29.1459, as appropriate, of this chapter. The correlation required by paragraph (c) of §23.1459, 25.1459, 27.1459, or 29.1459, as appropriate, of this chapter need be established only on one aircraft of a group of aircraft:

(i) That are of the same type;

(ii) On which the flight recorder models and their installations are the same; and

(iii) On which there are no differences in the type designs with respect to the installation of the first pilot's instruments associated with the flight recorder. The most recent instrument calibration, including the recording medium from which this calibration is derived, and the recorder correlation must be retained by the certificate holder.

(f)(2) For airplanes manufactured after August 18, 2000, each flight data recorder system required by this section must be installed in accordance with the requirements of §23.1459 (a), (b), (d) and (e) of this chapter, or §25.1459 (a), (b), (d), and (e) of this chapter. A correlation must be established between the values recorded by the flight data recorder and the corresponding values being measured. The correlation must contain a sufficient number of correlation points to accurately establish the conversion from the recorded values to engineering units or discrete state over the full operating range of the parameter. Except for airplanes having separate altitude and airspeed sensors that are an integral part of the flight data recorder system, a single correlation may be established for any group of airplanes—

(i) That are of the same type;

(ii) On which the flight recorder system and its installation are the same; and

(iii) On which there is no difference in the type design with respect to the installation of those sensors associated with the flight data recorder system. Documentation sufficient to convert recorded data into the engineering units and discrete values specified in the applicable appendix must be maintained by the certificate holder.

(g) Each flight recorder required by this section that records the data specified in paragraphs (a) and (b) of this section must have an approved device to assist in locating that recorder under water.

(h) The operational parameters required to be recorded by digital flight data recorders required by paragraphs (i) and (j) of this section are as follows, the phrase "when an information source is installed" following a parameter indicates that recording of that parameter is not intended to require a change in installed equipment.

(1) Time;

(2) Pressure altitude;

(3) Indicated airspeed;

(4) Heading—primary flight crew reference (if selectable, record discrete, true or magnetic);

(5) Normal acceleration (Vertical);

(6) Pitch attitude;

(7) Roll attitude;

(8) Manual radio transmitter keying, or CVR/DFDR synchronization reference;

(9) Thrust/power of each engine—primary flight crew reference;

(10) Autopilot engagement status;

(11) Longitudinal acceleration;

(12) Pitch control input;

(13) Lateral control input;

(14) Rudder pedal input;

(15) Primary pitch control surface position;

(16) Primary lateral control surface position;

(17) Primary yaw control surface position;

(18) Lateral acceleration;

(19) Pitch trim surface position or parameters of paragraph (h)(82) of this section if currently recorded;

(20) Trailing edge flap or cockpit flap control selection (except when parameters of paragraph (h)(85) of this section apply);

(21) Leading edge flap or cockpit flap control selection (except when parameters of paragraph (h)(86) of this section apply);

(22) Each Thrust reverser position (or equivalent for propeller airplane);

(23) Ground spoiler position or speed brake selection (except when parameters of paragraph (h)(87) of this section apply);

(24) Outside or total air temperature;

(25) Automatic Flight Control System (AFCS) modes and engagement status, including autothrottle;

(26) Radio altitude (when an information source is installed);

(27) Localizer deviation, MLS Azimuth;

(28) Glideslope deviation, MLS Elevation;

(29) Marker beacon passage;

(30) Master warning;

(31) Air/ground sensor (primary airplane system reference nose or main gear);

(32) Angle of attack (when information source is installed);

(33) Hydraulic pressure low (each system);

(34) Ground speed (when an information source is installed);

(35) Ground proximity warning system;

(36) Landing gear position or landing gear cockpit control selection;

(37) Drift angle (when an information source is installed);

(38) Wind speed and direction (when an information source is installed);

(39) Latitude and longitude (when an information source is installed);

(40) Stick shaker/pusher (when an information source is installed);

(41) Windshear (when an information source is installed);

(42) Throttle/power lever position;

(43) Additional engine parameters (as designated in Appendix F of this part);
(44) Traffic alert and collision avoidance system;
(45) DME 1 and 2 distances;
(46) Nav 1 and 2 selected frequency;
(47) Selected barometric setting (when an information source is installed);
(48) Selected altitude (when an information source is installed);
(49) Selected speed (when an information source is installed);
(50) Selected mach (when an information source is installed);
(51) Selected vertical speed (when an information source is installed);
(52) Selected heading (when an information source is installed);
(53) Selected flight path (when an information source is installed);
(54) Selected decision height (when an information source is installed);
(55) EFIS display format;
(56) Multi-function/engine/alerts display format;
(57) Thrust command (when an information source is installed);
(58) Thrust target (when an information source is installed);
(59) Fuel quantity in CG trim tank (when an information source is installed);
(60) Primary Navigation System Reference;
(61) Icing (when an information source is installed);
(62) Engine warning each engine vibration (when an information source is installed);
(63) Engine warning each engine over temp. (when an information source is installed);
(64) Engine warning each engine oil pressure low (when an information source is installed);
(65) Engine warning each engine over speed (when an information source is installed;
(66) Yaw trim surface position;
(67) Roll trim surface position;
(68) Brake pressure (selected system);
(69) Brake pedal application (left and right);
(70) Yaw or sideslip angle (when an information source is installed);
(71) Engine bleed valve position (when an information source is installed);
(72) De-icing or anti-icing system selection (when an information source is installed);
(73) Computed center of gravity (when an information source is installed);
(74) AC electrical bus status;
(75) DC electrical bus status;
(76) APU bleed valve position (when an information source is installed);
(77) Hydraulic pressure (each system);
(78) Loss of cabin pressure;
(79) Computer failure;
(80) Heads-up display (when an information source is installed);
(81) Para-visual display (when an information source is installed);
(82) Cockpit trim control input position—pitch;
(83) Cockpit trim control input position—roll;
(84) Cockpit trim control input position—yaw;
(85) Trailing edge flap and cockpit flap control position;
(86) Leading edge flap and cockpit flap control position;
(87) Ground spoiler position and speed brake selection; and
(88) All cockpit flight control input forces (control wheel, control column, rudder pedal).

(i) For all turbine-engine powered airplanes with a seating configuration, excluding any required crewmember seat, of 10 to 30 passenger seats, manufactured after August 18, 2000—

(1) The parameters listed in paragraphs (h)(1) through (h)(57) of this section must be recorded within the ranges, accuracies, resolutions, and recording intervals specified in Appendix F of this part.

(2) Commensurate with the capacity of the recording system, all additional parameters for which information sources are installed and which are connected to the recording system must be recorded within the ranges, accuracies, resolutions, and sampling intervals specified in Appendix F of this part.

(j) For all turbine-engine-powered airplanes with a seating configuration, excluding any required crewmember seat, of 10 to 30 passenger seats, that are manufactured after August 19, 2002 the parameters listed in paragraph (a)(1) through (a)(88) of this section must be recorded within the ranges, accuracies, resolutions, and recording intervals specified in Appendix F of this part.

(k) For aircraft manufactured before August 18, 1997, the following aircraft types need not comply with this section: Bell 212, Bell 214ST, Bell 412, Bell 412SP, Boeing Chinook (BV-234), Boeing/Kawasaki Vertol 107 (BV/KV-107-II), deHavilland DHC-6, Eurocopter Puma 330J, Sikorsky 58, Sikorsky 61N, Sikorsky 76A.

[Docket No. 25530, 53 FR 26151, July 11, 1988; as amended by Amdt. 135–69, 62 FR 38396, July 17, 1997; Amdt. 135–69, 62 FR 48135, Sept. 12, 1997; Amdt. 135–84, 68 FR 42939, July 18, 2003]

§135.153 Ground proximity warning system.

(a) No person may operate a turbine-powered airplane having a passenger seat configuration of 10 seats or more, excluding any pilot seat, unless it is equipped with an approved ground proximity warning system.

(b) [Reserved]

(c) For a system required by this section, the Airplane Flight Manual shall contain—

(1) Appropriate procedures for—

(i) The use of the equipment;

(ii) Proper flight crew action with respect to the equipment; and

(iii) Deactivation for planned abnormal and emergency conditions; and

(2) An outline of all input sources that must be operating.

(d) No person may deactivate a system required by this section except under procedures in the Airplane Flight Manual.

(e) Whenever a system required by this section is deactivated, an entry shall be made in the airplane maintenance record that includes the date and time of deactivation.

(f) This section expires on March 29, 2005.

[Docket No. 26202, 57 FR 9951, March 20, 1992; as amended by Amdt. 135–60, 61 FR 2616, Jan. 26, 1996; Amdt. 135–66, 62 FR 13257, March 19, 1997; Amdt. 135–75, 65 FR 16755, March 29, 2000]

§135.154 Terrain awareness and warning system.

(a) *Airplanes manufactured after March 29, 2002:*

(1) No person may operate a turbine-powered airplane configured with 10 or more passenger seats, excluding any pilot seat, unless that airplane is equipped with an approved terrain awareness and warning system that meets the requirements for Class A equipment in Technical Standard Order (TSO)–C151. The airplane must also include an approved terrain situational awareness display.

(2) No person may operate a turbine-powered airplane configured with 6 to 9 passenger seats, excluding any pilot seat, unless that airplane is equipped with an approved terrain awareness and warning system that meets as a minimum the requirements for Class B equipment in Technical Standard Order (TSO)–C151.

(b) *Airplanes manufactured on or before March 29, 2002:*

(1) No person may operate a turbine-powered airplane configured with 10 or more passenger seats, excluding any pilot seat, after March 29, 2005, unless that airplane is equipped with an approved terrain awareness and warning system that meets the requirements for Class A equipment in Technical Standard Order (TSO)–C151. The airplane must also include an approved terrain situational awareness display.

(2) No person may operate a turbine-powered airplane configured with 6 to 9 passenger seats, excluding any pilot seat, after March 29, 2005, unless that airplane is equipped with an approved terrain awareness and warning system that meets as a minimum the requirements for Class B equipment in Technical Standard Order (TSO)–C151.

(Approved by the Office of Management and Budget under control number 2120-0631)

(c) *Airplane Flight Manual.* The Airplane Flight Manual shall contain appropriate procedures for—

(1) The use of the terrain awareness and warning system; and

(2) Proper flight crew reaction in response to the terrain awareness and warning system audio and visual warnings.

[Docket No. 29312, 65 FR 16755, March 29, 2000]

§135.155 Fire extinguishers: Passenger-carrying aircraft.

No person may operate an aircraft carrying passengers unless it is equipped with hand fire extinguishers of an approved type for use in crew and passenger compartments as follows—

(a) The type and quantity of extinguishing agent must be suitable for the kinds of fires likely to occur;

(b) At least one hand fire extinguisher must be provided and conveniently located on the flight deck for use by the flight crew; and

(c) At least one hand fire extinguisher must be conveniently located in the passenger compartment of each aircraft having a passenger seating configuration, excluding any pilot seat, of at least 10 seats but less than 31 seats.

§135.157 Oxygen equipment requirements.

(a) *Unpressurized aircraft.* No person may operate an unpressurized aircraft at altitudes prescribed in this section unless it is equipped with enough oxygen dispensers and oxygen to supply the pilots under §135.89(a) and to supply, when flying—

(1) At altitudes above 10,000 feet through 15,000 feet MSL, oxygen to at least 10 percent of the occupants of the aircraft, other than the pilots, for that part of the flight at those altitudes that is of more than 30 minutes duration; and

(2) Above 15,000 feet MSL, oxygen to each occupant of the aircraft other than the pilots.

(b) *Pressurized aircraft.* No person may operate a pressurized aircraft—

(1) At altitudes above 25,000 feet MSL, unless at least a 10-minute supply of supplemental oxygen is available for each occupant of the aircraft, other than the pilots, for use when a descent is necessary due to loss of cabin pressurization; and

(2) Unless it is equipped with enough oxygen dispensers and oxygen to comply with paragraph (a) of this section whenever the cabin pressure altitude exceeds 10,000 feet MSL and, if the cabin pressurization fails, to comply with §135.89(a) or to provide a 2-hour supply for each pilot, whichever is greater, and to supply when flying—

(i) At altitudes above 10,000 feet through 15,000 feet MSL, oxygen to at least 10 percent of the occupants of the aircraft, other than the pilots, for that part of the flight at those altitudes that is of more than 30 minutes duration; and

(ii) Above 15,000 feet MSL, oxygen to each occupant of the aircraft, other than the pilots, for one hour unless, at all times during flight above that altitude, the aircraft can safely descend to 15,000 feet MSL within four minutes, in which case only a 30-minute supply is required.

(c) The equipment required by this section must have a means—

(1) To enable the pilots to readily determine, in flight, the amount of oxygen available in each source of supply and whether the oxygen is being delivered to the dispensing units; or

(2) In the case of individual dispensing units, to enable each user to make those determinations with respect to that person's oxygen supply and delivery; and

(3) To allow the pilots to use undiluted oxygen at their discretion at altitudes above 25,000 feet MSL.

§135.158 Pitot heat indication systems.

(a) Except as provided in paragraph (b) of this section, after April 12, 1981, no person may operate a transport category airplane equipped with a flight instrument pitot heating system unless the airplane is also equipped with an operable pitot heat indication system that complies with §25.1326 of this chapter in effect on April 12, 1978.

(b) A certificate holder may obtain an extension of the April 12, 1981, compliance date specified in paragraph (a) of this section, but not beyond April 12, 1983, from the Director, Flight Standards Service if the certificate holder—

(1) Shows that due to circumstances beyond its control it cannot comply by the specified compliance date; and

(2) Submits by the specified compliance date a schedule for compliance, acceptable to the Director, indicating that compliance will be achieved at the earliest practicable date.

[Docket No. 18094, Amdt. 135–17, 46 FR 48306, Aug. 31, 1981; as amended by Amdt. 135–33, 54 FR 39294, Sept. 25, 1989]

§135.159 Equipment requirements: Carrying passengers under VFR at night or under VFR over-the-top conditions.

No person may operate an aircraft carrying passengers under VFR at night or under VFR over-the-top, unless it is equipped with—

(a) A gyroscopic rate-of-turn indicator except on the following aircraft:

(1) Airplanes with a third attitude instrument system usable through flight attitudes of 360 degrees of pitch-and-roll and installed in accordance with the instrument requirements prescribed in §121.305(j) of this chapter.

(2) Helicopters with a third attitude instrument system usable through flight attitudes of ±80 degrees of pitch and ±120 degrees of roll and installed in accordance with §29.1303(g) of this chapter.

(3) Helicopters with a maximum certificated takeoff weight of 6,000 pounds or less.

(b) A slip skid indicator.

(c) A gyroscopic bank-and-pitch indicator.

(d) A gyroscopic direction indicator.

(e) A generator or generators able to supply all probable combinations of continuous in-flight electrical loads for required equipment and for recharging the battery.

(f) For night flights—

(1) An anticollision light system;

(2) Instrument lights to make all instruments, switches, and gauges easily readable, the direct rays of which are shielded from the pilots' eyes; and

(3) A flashlight having at least two size "D" cells or equivalent.

(g) For the purpose of paragraph (e) of this section, a continuous in-flight electrical load includes one that draws current continuously during flight, such as radio equipment and electrically driven instruments and lights, but does not include occasional intermittent loads.

(h) Notwithstanding provisions of paragraphs (b), (c), and (d), helicopters having a maximum certificated takeoff weight of 6,000 pounds or less may be operated until January 6, 1988, under visual flight rules at night without a slip skid indicator, a gyroscopic bank-and-pitch indicator, or a gyroscopic direction indicator.

[Docket No. 24550, 51 FR 40709, Nov. 7, 1986; as amended by Amdt. 135–38, 55 FR 43310, Oct. 26, 1990]

§135.161 Radio and navigational equipment: Carrying passengers under VFR at night or under VFR over-the-top.

(a) No person may operate an aircraft carrying passengers under VFR at night, or under VFR over-the-top, unless it has two-way radio communications equipment able, at least in flight, to transmit to, and receive from, ground facilities 25 miles away.

(b) No person may operate an aircraft carrying passengers under VFR over-the-top unless it has radio navigational equipment able to receive radio signals from the ground facilities to be used.

(c) No person may operate an airplane carrying passengers under VFR at night unless it has radio navigational equipment able to receive radio signals from the ground facilities to be used.

§135.163 Equipment requirements: Aircraft carrying passengers under IFR.

No person may operate an aircraft under IFR, carrying passengers, unless it has—

(a) A vertical speed indicator;

(b) A free-air temperature indicator;

(c) A heated pitot tube for each airspeed indicator;

(d) A power failure warning device or vacuum indicator to show the power available for gyroscopic instruments from each power source;

(e) An alternate source of static pressure for the altimeter and the airspeed and vertical speed indicators;

(f) For a single-engine aircraft:

(1) Two independent electrical power generating sources each of which is able to supply all probable combinations of continuous inflight electrical loads for required instruments and equipment; or

(2) In addition to the primary electrical power generating source, a standby battery or an alternate source of electric power that is capable of supplying 150% of the electrical loads of all required instruments and equipment necessary for safe emergency operation of the aircraft for at least one hour;

(g) For multi-engine aircraft, at least two generators or alternators each of which is on a separate engine, of which any combination of one-half of the total number are rated sufficiently to supply the electrical loads of all required instruments and equipment necessary for safe emergency operation of the aircraft except that for multi-engine helicopters, the two required generators may be mounted on the main rotor drive train; and

(h) Two independent sources of energy (with means of selecting either) of which at least one is an engine-driven pump or generator, each of which is able to drive all required gyroscopic instruments powered by, or to be powered by, that particular source and installed so that failure of one instrument or source, does not interfere with the energy supply to the remaining instruments or the other energy source unless, for single-engine aircraft in all cargo operations only, the rate of turn indicator has a source of energy separate from the bank and pitch and direction indicators. For the purpose of this paragraph, for multi-engine aircraft, each engine-driven source of energy must be on a different engine.

(i) For the purpose of paragraph (f) of this section, a continuous inflight electrical load includes one that draws current continuously during flight, such as radio equipment, electrically driven instruments, and lights, but does not include occasional intermittent loads.

[Docket No. 16097, 43 FR 46783, Oct. 10, 1978; as amended by Amdt. 135–70, 62 FR 42374, Aug. 6, 1997; Amdt. 135–73, 63 FR 25573, May 8, 1998]

§135.165 Radio and navigational equipment: Extended overwater or IFR operations.

(a) No person may operate a turbojet airplane having a passenger seating configuration, excluding any pilot seat, of 10 seats or more, or a multiengine airplane in a commuter operation, as defined in part 119 of this chapter, under IFR or in extended overwater operations unless it has at least the following radio communication and navigational equipment appropriate to the facilities to be used which are capable of transmitting to, and receiving from, at any place on the route to be flown, at least one ground facility:

(1) Two transmitters, (2) two microphones, (3) two headsets or one headset and one speaker, (4) a marker beacon receiver, (5) two independent receivers for navigation, and (6) two independent receivers for communications.

(b) No person may operate an aircraft other than that specified in paragraph (a) of this section, under IFR or in extended overwater operations unless it has at least the following radio communication and navigational equipment appropriate to the facilities to be used and which are capable of transmitting to, and receiving from, at any place on the route, at least one ground facility:

(1) A transmitter, (2) two microphones, (3) two headsets or one headset and one speaker, (4) a marker beacon receiver, (5) two independent receivers for navigation, (6) two independent receivers for communications, and (7) for extended overwater operations only, an additional transmitter.

(c) For the purpose of paragraphs (a)(5), (a)(6), (b)(5), and (b)(6) of this section, a receiver is independent if the function of any part of it does not depend on the functioning of any part of another receiver. However, a receiver that can receive both communications and navigational signals may be used in place of a separate communications receiver and a separate navigational signal receiver.

(d) Notwithstanding the requirements of paragraphs (a) and (b) of this section, installation and use of a single long-range navigation system and a single long-range communication system, for extended overwater operations, may be authorized by the Administrator and approved in the certificate holder's operations specifications. The following are among the operational factors the Administrator may consider in granting an authorization:

(1) The ability of the flightcrew to reliably fix the position of the airplane within the degree of accuracy required by ATC,

(2) The length of the route being flown, and

(3) The duration of the very high frequency communications gap.

[Docket No. 16097, 43 FR 46073, Oct. 10, 1978; as amended by Amdt. 135–58, 60 FR 65939, Dec. 20, 1995; Amdt. 135–61, 61 FR 7191, Feb. 26, 1996]

§135.167 Emergency equipment: Extended overwater operations.

(a) Except where the Administrator, by amending the operations specifications of the certificate holder, requires the carriage of all or any specific items of the equipment listed below for any overwater operation, or, upon application of the certificate holder, the Administrator allows deviation for a particular extended overwater operation, no person may operate an aircraft in extended overwater operations unless it carries, installed in conspicuously marked locations easily accessible to the occupants if a ditching occurs, the following equipment:

(1) An approved life preserver equipped with an approved survivor locator light for each occupant of the aircraft. The life preserver must be easily accessible to each seated occupant.

(2) Enough approved liferafts of a rated capacity and buoyancy to accommodate the occupants of the aircraft.

(b) Each liferaft required by paragraph (a) of this section must be equipped with or contain at least the following:

(1) One approved survivor locator light.

(2) One approved pyrotechnic signaling device.

(3) Either—

(i) One survival kit, appropriately equipped for the route to be flown; or

(ii) One canopy (for sail, sunshade, or rain catcher);

(iii) One radar reflector;

(iv) One liferaft repair kit;

(v) One bailing bucket;

(vi) One signaling mirror;

(vii) One police whistle;

(viii) One raft knife;

(ix) One CO_2 bottle for emergency inflation;

(x) One inflation pump;

(xi) Two oars;

(xii) One 75-foot retaining line;

(xiii) One magnetic compass;

(xiv) One dye marker;

(xv) One flashlight having at least two size "D" cells or equivalent;

(xvi) A 2-day supply of emergency food rations supplying at least 1,000 calories per day for each person;

(xvii) For each two persons the raft is rated to carry, two pints of water or one sea water desalting kit;

(xviii) One fishing kit; and

(xix) One book on survival appropriate for the area in which the aircraft is operated.

(c) No person may operate an airplane in extended overwater operations unless there is attached to one of the life rafts required by paragraph (a) of this section, an approved survival type emergency locator transmitter. Batteries used in this transmitter must be replaced (or recharged, if the batteries are rechargeable) when the transmitter has been in use for more than 1 cumulative hour, or, when 50 percent of their useful life (or for rechargeable batteries, 50 percent of their useful life of charge) has expired, as established by the transmitter manufacturer under its approval. The new expiration date for replacing (or recharging) the battery must be legibly marked on the outside of the transmitter. The battery useful life (or useful life of charge) requirements of this paragraph do not apply to batteries (such as water-activated batteries) that are essentially unaffected during probable storage intervals.

[Docket No. 16097, 43 FR 46783, Oct. 10, 1978; as amended by Amdt. 135–4, 45 FR 38348, June 30, 1980; Amdt. 135–20, 51 FR 40710, Nov. 7, 1986; Amdt. 135–49, 59 FR 32058, June 21, 1994; Amdt. 135–91, 68 FR 54586, Sept. 17, 2003]

§135.168 Supplemental inspections.

(a) *Applicability.* This section applies to each multiengine airplane operated by a certificate holder in scheduled operations under this part, except for those operations conducted between any point within the State of Alaska and any other point within the State of Alaska.

(b) *Multiengine airplanes with 10 or more passenger seats.* After December 5, 2007, a certificate holder may not operate, in scheduled operations under this part, a multiengine airplane initially type certificated with 10 or more passenger seats unless the maintenance program for that airplane includes damage-tolerance-based inspections and procedures. Paragraphs (d), (e), and (f) of this section list the exceptions to this requirement.

(c) *Multiengine airplanes with nine or fewer passenger seats.* After December 20, 2010, a certificate holder may not operate, in scheduled operations under this part, a multiengine airplane initially type certificated with nine or fewer passenger seats unless the inspection program for that airplane includes service-history-based inspections and procedures. Paragraph (e) of this section lists the exception to this requirement.

(d) *New model added through type certificate amendment.* This paragraph applies to each U.S.-registered multiengine airplane initially type certificated with 10 or more passenger seats added to a type certificate after December 8, 2003, that has a certification basis that does not include a requirement for damage-tolerance-based inspections and procedures. A certificate holder may not operate that airplane, in scheduled operations, more than 4 years after the date of the type certificate amendment unless the maintenance program for that airplane includes damage-tolerance-based inspections and procedures.

(e) *Design-life goal airplanes.* If on or after December 5, 2007, the time in service of the airplane reaches the design-life goal listed in appendix G to this part the certificate holder may operate that airplane in scheduled operations until the date the airplane's time in service reaches the design-life goal or until December 20, 2010, whichever occurs sooner. After that date, the certificate holder may not operate the airplane in scheduled operations unless it complies with paragraph (b) or paragraph (c) of this section.

(f) *Airworthiness directive-mandated service-history-based inspections.* Until December 20, 2010, a certificate holder may operate an airplane for which an airworthiness directive requires the maintenance program to include service-history-based inspections and procedures. After that date, the certificate holder may not operate the airplane unless the maintenance program for that airplane includes damage-tolerance-based inspections and procedures.

(g) *Approvals.* The inspections and procedures required by this section to be included in the certificate holder's maintenance program for an airplane must be approved by the FAA Aircraft Certification Office or office of the Small Aircraft Directorate or Transport Airplane Directorate having cognizance over the type certificate for the affected airplane.

[Docket No. FAA–1999–5401, 67 FR 72764, Dec. 6, 2002]

§135.169 Additional airworthiness requirements.

(a) Except for commuter category airplanes, no person may operate a large airplane unless it meets the additional airworthiness requirements of §§121.213 through 121.283 and 121.307 of this chapter.

(b) No person may operate a reciprocating-engine or turbopropeller-powered small airplane that has a passenger seating configuration, excluding pilot seats, of 10 seats or more unless it is type certificated—

(1) In the transport category;

(2) Before July 1, 1970, in the normal category and meets special conditions issued by the Administrator for airplanes intended for use in operations under this part;

(3) Before July 19, 1970, in the normal category and meets the additional airworthiness standards in Special Federal Aviation Regulation No. 23;

(4) In the normal category and meets the additional airworthiness standards in Appendix A;

(5) In the normal category and complies with section 1.(a) of Special Federal Aviation Regulation No. 41;

(6) In the normal category and complies with section 1.(b) of Special Federal Aviation Regulation No. 41; or

(7) In the commuter category.

(c) No person may operate a small airplane with a passenger seating configuration, excluding any pilot seat, of 10 seats or more, with a seating configuration greater than the maximum seating configuration used in that type airplane in operations under this part before August 19, 1977. This paragraph does not apply to—

(1) An airplane that is type certificated in the transport category; or

(2) An airplane that complies with—

(i) Appendix A of this part provided that its passenger seating configuration, excluding pilot seats, does not exceed 19 seats; or

(ii) Special Federal Aviation Regulation No. 41.

(d) Cargo or baggage compartments:

(1) After March 20, 1991, each Class C or D compartment, as defined in §25.857 of part 25 of this chapter, greater than 200 cubic feet in volume in a transport category airplane type certificated after January 1, 1958, must have ceiling and sidewall panels which are constructed of:

(i) Glass fiber reinforced resin;

(ii) Materials which meet the test requirements of part 25, Appendix F, part III of this chapter; or

(iii) In the case of liner installations approved prior to March 20, 1989, aluminum.

(2) For compliance with this paragraph, the term "liner" includes any design feature, such as a joint or fastener, which would affect the capability of the liner to safely contain a fire.

[Docket No. 16097, 43 FR 46783, Oct. 10, 1978; as amended by Amdt. 135–2, 44 FR 53731, Sept. 17, 1979; Amdt. 135–21, 52 FR 1836, Jan. 15, 1987; 52 FR 34745, Sept. 14, 1987; Amdt. 135–31, 54 FR 7389, Feb. 17, 1989; Amdt. 135–55, 60 FR 6628, Feb. 2, 1995]

§135.170 Materials for compartment interiors.

(a) No person may operate an airplane that conforms to an amended or supplemental type certificate issued in accordance with SFAR No. 41 for a maximum certificated takeoff weight in excess of 12,500 pounds unless within one year after issuance of the initial airworthiness certificate under that SFAR, the airplane meets the compartment interior requirements set forth in §25.853(a) in effect March 6, 1995 (formerly §25.853(a), (b), (b-1), (b-2), and (b-3) of this chapter in effect on September 26, 1978).

(b) Except for commuter category airplanes and airplanes certificated under Special Federal Aviation Regulation No. 41, no person may operate a large airplane unless it meets the following additional airworthiness requirements:

(1) Except for those materials covered by paragraph (b)(2) of this section, all materials in each compartment used by the crewmembers or passengers must meet the requirements of §25.853 of this chapter in effect as follows or later amendment thereto:

(i) Except as provided in paragraph (b)(1)(iv) of this section, each airplane with a passenger capacity of 20 or more and manufactured after August 19, 1988, but prior to August 20, 1990, must comply with the heat release rate testing provisions of §25.853(d) in effect March 6, 1995 (formerly §25.853(a-1) in effect on August 20, 1986), except that the total heat release over the first 2 minutes of sample exposure rate must not exceed 100 kilowatt minutes per square meter and the peak heat release rate must not exceed 100 kilowatts per square meter.

(ii) Each airplane with a passenger capacity of 20 or more and manufactured after August 19, 1990, must comply with the heat release rate and smoke testing provisions of §25.853(d) in effect March 6, 1995 (formerly §25.83(a-1) in effect on September 26, 1988).

(iii) Except as provided in paragraph (b)(1)(v) or (vi) of this section, each airplane for which the application for type certificate was filed prior to May 1, 1972, must comply with the provisions of §25.853 in effect on April 30, 1972, regardless of the passenger capacity, if there is a substantially complete replacement of the cabin interior after April 30, 1972.

(iv) Except as provided in paragraph (b)(1)(v) or (vi) of this section, each airplane for which the application for type certificate was filed after May 1, 1972, must comply with the material requirements under which the airplane was type certificated regardless of the passenger capacity if there is a substantially complete replacement of the cabin interior after that date.

(v) Except as provided in paragraph (b)(1)(vi) of this section, each airplane that was type certificated after January 1, 1958, must comply with the heat release testing provisions of §25.853(d) in effect March 6, 1995 (formerly §25.853(a-1) in effect on August 20, 1986), if there is a substantially complete replacement of the cabin interior components identified in that paragraph on or after that date, except that the total heat release over the first 2 minutes of sample exposure shall not exceed 100 kilowatt-minutes per square meter and the peak heat release rate shall not exceed 100 kilowatts per square meter.

(vi) Each airplane that was type certificated after January 1, 1958, must comply with the heat release rate and smoke testing provisions of §25.853(d) in effect March 6, 1995 (formerly §25.853(a-1) in effect on August 20, 1986), if there is a substantially complete replacement of the cabin interior components identified in that paragraph after August 19, 1990.

(vii) Contrary provisions of this section notwithstanding, the Manager of the Transport Airplane Directorate, Aircraft Certification Service, Federal Aviation Administration, may authorize deviation from the requirements of paragraph (b)(1)(i), (b)(1)(ii), (b)(1)(v), or (b)(1)(vi) of this section for specific components of the cabin interior that do not meet applicable flammability and smoke emission requirements, if the determination is made that special circumstances exist that make compliance impractical. Such grants of deviation will be limited to those airplanes manufactured within 1 year after the applicable date specified in this section and those airplanes in which the interior is replaced within 1 year of that date. A request for such grant of deviation must include a thorough and accurate analysis of each component subject to §25.853(d) in effect March 6, 1995 (formerly §25.853(a-1) in effect on August 20, 1986), the steps being taken to achieve compliance, and for the few components for which timely compliance will not be achieved, credible reasons for such noncompliance.

(viii) Contrary provisions of this section notwithstanding, galley carts and standard galley containers that do not meet the flammability and smoke emission requirements of §25.853(d) in effect March 6, 1995 (formerly §25.853(a-1) in effect on August 20, 1986), may be used in airplanes that must meet the requirements of paragraph (b)(1)(i), (b)(1)(ii), (b)(1)(iv) or (b)(1)(vi) of this section provided the galley carts or standard containers were manufactured prior to March 6, 1995.

(2) For airplanes type certificated after January 1, 1958, seat cushions, except those on flight crewmember seats, in any compartment occupied by crew or passengers must comply with the requirements pertaining to fire protection of seat cushions in §25.853(c) effective November 26, 1984.

(c) Thermal/acoustic insulation materials. For transport category airplanes type certificated after January 1, 1958:

(1) For airplanes manufactured before September 2, 2005, when thermal/acoustic insulation materials are installed in the fuselage as replacements after September 2, 2005, those materials must meet the flame propagation requirements of §25.856 of this chapter, effective September 2, 2003.

(2) For airplanes manufactured after September 2, 2005, thermal/acoustic insulation materials installed in the fuselage must meet the flame propagation requirements of §25.856 of this chapter, effective September 2, 2003.

[Docket No. 26192, 60 FR 6628, Feb. 2, 1995; as amended by Amdt. 135–55, 60 FR 11194, March 1, 1995; Amdt. 135–56, 60 FR 13011, March 9, 1995; Amdt. 135–90, 68 FR 45084, July 31, 2003]

§135.171 Shoulder harness installation at flight crewmember stations.

(a) No person may operate a turbojet aircraft or an aircraft having a passenger seating configuration, excluding any pilot seat, of 10 seats or more unless it is equipped with an approved shoulder harness installed for each flight crewmember station.

(b) Each flight crewmember occupying a station equipped with a shoulder harness must fasten the shoulder harness during takeoff and landing, except that the shoulder harness may be unfastened if the crewmember cannot perform the required duties with the shoulder harness fastened.

§135.173 Airborne thunderstorm detection equipment requirements.

(a) No person may operate an aircraft that has a passenger seating configuration, excluding any pilot seat, of 10 seats or more in passenger-carrying operations, except a helicopter operating under day VFR conditions, unless the aircraft is equipped with either approved thunderstorm detection equipment or approved airborne weather radar equipment.

(b) No person may operate a helicopter that has a passenger seating configuration, excluding any pilot seat, of 10 seats or more in passenger-carrying operations, under night VFR when current weather reports indicate that thunderstorms or other potentially hazardous weather conditions that can be detected with airborne thunderstorm detection equipment may reasonably be expected along the route to be flown, unless the helicopter is equipped with either approved thunderstorm detection equipment or approved airborne weather radar equipment.

(c) No person may begin a flight under IFR or night VFR conditions when current weather reports indicate that thunderstorms or other potentially hazardous weather conditions that can be detected with airborne thunderstorm detection equipment, required by paragraph (a) or (b) of this section, may reasonably be expected along the route to be flown, unless the airborne thunderstorm detection equipment is in satisfactory operating condition.

(d) If the airborne thunderstorm detection equipment becomes inoperative en route, the aircraft must be operated under the instructions and procedures specified for that event in the manual required by §135.21.

(e) This section does not apply to aircraft used solely within the State of Hawaii, within the State of Alaska, within that part of Canada west of longitude 130 degrees W, between latitude 70 degrees N, and latitude 53 degrees N, or during any training, test, or ferry flight.

(f) Without regard to any other provision of this part, an alternate electrical power supply is not required for airborne thunderstorm detection equipment.

[Docket No. 16097, 43 FR 46783, Oct. 10, 1978; as amended by Amdt. 135–20, 51 FR 40710, Nov. 7, 1986; Amdt. 135–60, 61 FR 2616, Jan. 26, 1996]

§135.175 Airborne weather radar equipment requirements.

(a) No person may operate a large, transport category aircraft in passenger-carrying operations unless approved airborne weather radar equipment is installed in the aircraft.

(b) No person may begin a flight under IFR or night VFR conditions when current weather reports indicate that thunderstorms, or other potentially hazardous weather conditions that can be detected with airborne weather radar equipment, may reasonably be expected along the route to be flown, unless the airborne weather radar equipment required by paragraph (a) of this section is in satisfactory operating condition.

(c) If the airborne weather radar equipment becomes inoperative en route, the aircraft must be operated under the instructions and procedures specified for that event in the manual required by §135.21.

(d) This section does not apply to aircraft used solely within the State of Hawaii, within the State of Alaska, within that part of Canada west of longitude 130 degrees W, between latitude 70 degrees N, and latitude 53 degrees N, or during any training, test, or ferry flight.

(e) Without regard to any other provision of this part, an alternate electrical power supply is not required for airborne weather radar equipment.

§135.177 Emergency equipment requirements for aircraft having a passenger seating configuration of more than 19 passengers.

(a) No person may operate an aircraft having a passenger seating configuration, excluding any pilot seat, of more than 19 seats unless it is equipped with the following emergency equipment:

(1) At least one approved first-aid kit for treatment of injuries likely to occur in flight or in a minor accident that must:

(i) Be readily accessible to crewmembers.

(ii) Be stored securely and kept free from dust, moisture, and damaging temperatures.

(iii) Contain at least the following appropriately maintained contents in the specified quantities:

Contents	Quantity
Adhesive bandage compressors, 1-inch	16
Antiseptic swabs	20
Ammonia inhalants	10
Bandage compresses, 4-inch	8
Triangular bandage compresses, 40-inch	5
Arm splint, noninflatable	1
Leg splint, noninflatable	1
Roller bandage, 4-inch	4
Adhesive tape, 1-inch standard roll	2
Bandage scissors	1
Protective nonpermeable gloves or equivalent	1 Pair

(iv) Protective latex gloves or equivalent nonpermeable gloves may be placed in the first aid kit or in a location that is readily accessible to crewmembers.

(2) A crash axe carried so as to be accessible to the crew but inaccessible to passengers during normal operations.

(3) Signs that are visible to all occupants to notify them when smoking is prohibited and when safety belts must be fastened. The signs must be constructed so that they can be turned on during any movement by the aircraft on the surface, for each takeoff and landing, and at other times considered necessary by the pilot in command. "No smoking" signs shall be turned on when required by §135.127.

(4) [Reserved]

(b) Each item of equipment must be inspected regularly under inspection periods established in the operations specifications to ensure its condition for continued serviceability and immediate readiness to perform its intended emergency purposes.

[Docket No. 16097, 43 FR 46783, Oct. 10, 1978; as amended by Amdt. 135–25, 53 FR 12362, April 13, 1988; Amdt. 135–43, 57 FR 19245, May 4, 1992; Amdt. 135–44, 57 FR 42676, Sept. 15, 1992; Amdt. 135–47, 59 FR 1781, Jan. 12, 1994; Amdt. 135–53, 59 FR 52643, Oct. 18, 1994, 59 FR 55208, Nov. 4, 1994; Amdt. 135–80, 66 FR 19045, April 12, 2001]

§135.178 Additional emergency equipment.

No person may operate an airplane having a passenger seating configuration of more than 19 seats, unless it has the additional emergency equipment specified in paragraphs (a) through (l) of this section.

(a) *Means for emergency evacuation.* Each passenger-carrying landplane emergency exit (other than over-the-wing) that is more than 6 feet from the ground, with the airplane on the ground and the landing gear extended, must have an approved means to assist the occupants in descending to the ground. The assisting means for a floor-level emergency exit must meet the requirements of §25.809(f)(1) of this chapter in effect on April 30, 1972, except that, for any airplane for which the application for the type certificate was filed after the date, it must meet the requirements under which the airplane was type certificated. An assisting means that deploys automatically must be armed during taxiing, takeoffs, and landings; however, the Administrator may grant a deviation from the requirement of automatic deployment if he finds that the design of the exit makes compliance impractical, if the assisting means automatically erects upon deployment and, with respect to require emergency exits, if an emergency evacuation demonstration is conducted in accordance with §121.291(a) of this chapter. This paragraph does not apply to the rear window emergency exit of Douglas DC-3 airplanes operated with fewer than 36 occupants, including crewmembers, and fewer than five exits authorized for passenger use.

(b) *Interior emergency exit marking.* The following must be complied with for each passenger-carrying airplane:

(1) Each passenger emergency exit, its means of access, and its means of opening must be conspicuously marked. The identity and locating of each passenger emergency exit must be recognizable from a distance equal to the width of the cabin. The location of each passenger emergency exit must be indicated by a sign visible to occupants approaching along the main passenger aisle. There must be a locating sign—

(i) Above the aisle near each over-the-wing passenger emergency exit, or at another ceiling location if it is more practical because of low headroom;

(ii) Next to each floor level passenger emergency exit, except that one sign may serve two such exits if they both can be seen readily from that sign; and

(iii) On each bulkhead or divider that prevents fore and aft vision along the passenger cabin, to indicate emergency exits beyond and obscured by it, except that if this is not possible, the sign may be placed at another appropriate location.

(2) Each passenger emergency exit marking and each locating sign must meet the following:

(i) For an airplane for which the application for the type certificate was filed prior to May 1, 1972, each passenger emergency exit marking and each locating sign must be manufactured to meet the requirements of §25.812(b) of this chapter in effect on April 30, 1972. On these airplanes, no sign may continue to be used if its luminescence (brightness) decreases to below 100 microlamberts. The colors may be reversed if it increases the emergency illumination of the passenger compartment. However, the Administrator may authorize deviation from the 2-inch background requirements if he finds that special circumstances exist that make compliance impractical and that the proposed deviation provides an equivalent level of safety.

(ii) For an airplane for which the application for the type certificate was filed on or after May 1, 1972, each passenger emergency exit marking and each locating sign must be manufactured to meet the interior emergency exit marking requirements under which the airplane was type certificated. On these airplanes, no sign may continue to be used if its luminescence (brightness) decreases to below 250 microlamberts.

(c) *Lighting for interior emergency exit markings.* Each passenger-carrying airplane must have an emergency lighting system, independent of the main lighting system; however, sources of general cabin illumination may be common to both the emergency and the main lighting systems if the power supply to the emergency lighting system is independent of the power supply to the main lighting system. The emergency lighting system must—

(1) Illuminate each passenger exit marking and locating sign;

(2) Provide enough general lighting in the passenger cabin so that the average illumination when measured at 40-inch intervals at seat armrest height, on the centerline of the main passenger aisle, is at least 0.05 foot-candles; and

(3) For airplanes type certificated after January 1, 1958, include floor proximity emergency escape path marking which meets the requirements of §25.812(e) of this chapter in effect on November 26, 1984.

(d) *Emergency light operation.* Except for lights forming part of emergency lighting subsystems provided in compliance with §25.812(h) of this chapter (as prescribed in paragraph (h) of this section) that serve no more than one assist means, are independent of the airplane's main emergency lighting systems, and are automatically activated when the assist means is deployed, each light required by paragraphs (c) and (h) of this section must:

(1) Be operable manually both from the flightcrew station and from a point in the passenger compartment that is readily accessible to a normal flight attendant seat;

(2) Have a means to prevent inadvertent operation of the manual controls;

(3) When armed or turned on at either station, remain lighted or become lighted upon interruption of the airplane's normal electric power;

(4) Be armed or turned on during taxiing, takeoff, and landing. In showing compliance with this paragraph, a transverse vertical separation of the fuselage need not be considered;

(5) Provide the required level of illumination for at least 10 minutes at the critical ambient conditions after emergency landing; and

(6) Have a cockpit control device that has an "on," "off," and "armed" position.

(e) *Emergency exit operating handles.*

(1) For a passenger-carrying airplane for which the application for the type certificate was filed prior to May 1, 1972,

the location of each passenger emergency exit operating handle, and instructions for opening the exit, must be shown by a marking on or near the exit that is readable from a distance of 30 inches. In addition, for each Type I and Type II emergency exit with a locking mechanism released by rotary motion of the handle, the instructions for opening must be shown by—

(i) A red arrow with a shaft at least three-fourths inch wide and a head twice the width of the shaft, extending along at least 70° of arc at a radius approximately equal to three-fourths of the handle length; and

(ii) The word "open" in red letters 1 inch high placed horizontally near the head of the arrow.

(2) For a passenger-carrying airplane for which the application for the type certificate was filed on or after May 1, 1972, the location of each passenger emergency exit operating handle and instructions for opening the exit must be shown in accordance with the requirements under which the airplane was type certificated. On these airplanes, no operating handle or operating handle cover may continue to be used if its luminescence (brightness) decreases to below 100 microlamberts.

(f) *Emergency exit access.* Access to emergency exits must be provided as follows for each passenger-carrying airplane:

(1) Each passageway between individual passenger areas, or leading to a Type I or Type II emergency exit, must be unobstructed and at least 20 inches wide.

(2) There must be enough space next to each Type I or Type II emergency exit to allow a crewmember to assist in the evacuation of passengers without reducing the unobstructed width of the passageway below that required in paragraph (f)(1) of this section; however, the Administrator may authorize deviation from this requirement for an airplane certificated under the provisions of part 4b of the Civil Air Regulations in effect before December 20, 1951, if he finds that special circumstances exist that provide an equivalent level of safety.

(3) There must be access from the main aisle to each Type III and Type IV exit. The access from the aisle to these exits must not be obstructed by seats, berths, or other protrusions in a manner that would reduce the effectiveness of the exit. In addition, for a transport category airplane type certificated after January 1, 1958, there must be placards installed in accordance with §25.813(c)(3) of this chapter for each Type III exit after December 3, 1992.

(4) If it is necessary to pass through a passageway between passenger compartments to reach any required emergency exit from any seat in the passenger cabin, the passageway must not be obstructed. Curtains may, however, be used if they allow free entry through the passageway.

(5) No door may be installed in any partition between passenger compartments.

(6) If it is necessary to pass through a doorway separating the passenger cabin from other areas to reach a required emergency exit from any passenger seat, the door must have a means to latch it in the open position, and the door must be latched open during each takeoff and landing. The latching means must be able to withstand the loads imposed upon it when the door is subjected to the ultimate inertia forces, relative to the surrounding structure, listed in §25.561(b) of this chapter.

(g) *Exterior exit markings.* Each passenger emergency exit and the means of opening that exit from the outside must be marked on the outside of the airplane. There must be a 2-inch colored band outlining each passenger emergency exit on the side of the fuselage. Each outside marking, including the band, must be readily distinguishable from the surrounding fuselage area by contrast in color. The markings must comply with the following:

(1) If the reflectance of the darker color is 15 percent or less, the reflectance of the lighter color must be at least 45 percent.

(2) If the reflectance of the darker color is greater than 15 percent, at least a 30 percent difference between its reflectance and the reflectance of the lighter color must be provided.

(3) Exits that are not in the side of the fuselage must have the external means of opening and applicable instructions marked conspicuously in red or, if red is inconspicuous against the background color, in bright chrome yellow and, when the opening means for such an exit is located on only one side of the fuselage, a conspicuous marking to that effect must be provided on the other side. "Reflectance" is the ratio of the luminous flux reflected by a body to the luminous flux it receives.

(h) *Exterior emergency lighting and escape route.*

(1) Each passenger-carrying airplane must be equipped with exterior lighting that meets the following requirements:

(i) For an airplane for which the application for the type certificate was filed prior to May 1, 1972, the requirements of §25.812(f) and (g) of this chapter in effect on April 30, 1972.

(ii) For an airplane for which the application for the type certificate was filed on or after May 1, 1972, the exterior emergency lighting requirements under which the airplane was type certificated.

(2) Each passenger-carrying airplane must be equipped with a slip-resistant escape route that meets the following requirements:

(i) For an airplane for which the application for the type certificate was filed prior to May 1, 1972, the requirements of §25.803(e) of this chapter in effect on April 30, 1972.

(ii) For an airplane for which the application for the type certificate was filed on or after May 1, 1972, the slip-resistant escape route requirements under which the airplane was type certificated.

(i) *Floor level exits.* Each floor level door or exit in the side of the fuselage (other than those leading into a cargo or baggage compartment that is not accessible from the passenger cabin) that is 44 or more inches high and 20 or more inches wide, but not wider than 46 inches, each passenger ventral exit (except the ventral exits on Martin 404 and Convair 240 airplanes), and each tail cone exit, must meet the requirements of this section for floor level emergency exits. However, the Administrator may grant a deviation from this paragraph if he finds that circumstances make full compliance impractical and that an acceptable level of safety has been achieved.

(j) *Additional emergency exits.* Approved emergency exits in the passenger compartments that are in excess of the minimum number of required emergency exits must meet all of the applicable provisions of this section, except paragraphs (f)(1), (2), and (3) of this section, and must be readily accessible.

(k) On each large passenger-carrying turbojet-powered airplane, each ventral exit and tailcone exit must be—

(1) Designed and constructed so that it cannot be opened during flight; and

(2) Marked with a placard readable from a distant of 30 inches and installed at a conspicuous location near the means of opening the exit, stating that the exit has been designed and constructed so that it cannot be opened during flight.

(l) *Portable lights.* No person may operate a passenger-carrying airplane unless it is equipped with flashlight stowage provisions accessible from each flight attendant seat.

[Docket No. 26530, 57 FR 19245, May 4, 1992; 57 FR 29120, June 30, 1992; as amended by 57 FR 34682, Aug. 6, 1992]

§135.179 Inoperable instruments and equipment.

(a) No person may take off an aircraft with inoperable instruments or equipment installed unless the following conditions are met:

(1) An approved Minimum Equipment List exists for that aircraft.

(2) The certificate-holding district office has issued the certificate holder operations specifications authorizing operations in accordance with an approved Minimum Equipment List. The flight crew shall have direct access at all times prior to flight to all of the information contained in the approved Minimum Equipment List through printed or other means approved by the Administrator in the certificate holder's operations specifications. An approved Minimum Equipment List, as authorized by the operations specifications, constitutes an approved change to the type design without requiring recertification.

(3) The approved Minimum Equipment List must:

(i) Be prepared in accordance with the limitations specified in paragraph (b) of this section.

(ii) Provide for the operation of the aircraft with certain instruments and equipment in an inoperable condition.

(4) Records identifying the inoperable instruments and equipment and the information required by (a)(3)(ii) of this section must be available to the pilot.

(5) The aircraft is operated under all applicable conditions and limitations contained in the Minimum Equipment List and the operations specifications authorizing use of the Minimum Equipment List.

(b) The following instruments and equipment may not be included in the Minimum Equipment List:

(1) Instruments and equipment that are either specifically or otherwise required by the airworthiness requirements under which the airplane is type certificated and which are essential for safe operations under all operating conditions.

(2) Instruments and equipment required by an airworthiness directive to be in operable condition unless the airworthiness directive provides otherwise.

(3) Instruments and equipment required for specific operations by this part.

(c) Notwithstanding paragraphs (b)(1) and (b)(3) of this section, an aircraft with inoperable instruments or equipment may be operated under a special flight permit under §§21.197 and 21.199 of this chapter.

[Docket No. 25780, 56 FR 12311, March 22, 1991; 56 FR 14920, April 8, 1991; as amended by Amdt. 135–60, 61 FR 2616, Jan. 26, 1996; Amdt. 135–91, 68 FR 54586, Sept. 17, 2003]

§135.180 Traffic Alert and Collision Avoidance System.

(a) Unless otherwise authorized by the Administrator, after December 31, 1995, no person may operate a turbine powered airplane that has a passenger seat configuration, excluding any pilot seat, of 10 to 30 seats unless it is equipped with an approved traffic alert and collision avoidance system. If a TCAS II system is installed, it must be capable of coordinating with TCAS units that meet TSO C-119.

(b) The airplane flight manual required by §135.21 of this part shall contain the following information on the TCAS I system required by this section:

(1) Appropriate procedures for—

(i) The use of the equipment; and

(ii) Proper flightcrew action with respect to the equipment operation.

(2) An outline of all input sources that must be operating for the TCAS to function properly.

[Docket No. 25355, 54 FR 951, Jan. 10, 1989; as amended by Amdt. 135–54, 59 FR 67587, Dec. 29, 1994]

§135.181 Performance requirements: Aircraft operated over-the-top or in IFR conditions.

(a) Except as provided in paragraphs (b) and (c) of this section, no person may—

(1) Operate a single-engine aircraft carrying passengers over-the-top; or

(2) Operate a multiengine aircraft carrying passengers over-the-top or in IFR conditions at a weight that will not allow it to climb, with the critical engine inoperative, at least 50 feet a minute when operating at the MEAs of the route to be flown or 5,000 feet MSL, whichever is higher.

(b) Notwithstanding the restrictions in paragraph (a)(2) of this section, multiengine helicopters carrying passengers offshore may conduct such operations in over-the-top or in IFR conditions at a weight that will allow the helicopter to climb at least 50 feet per minute with the critical engine inoperative when operating at the MEA of the route to be flown or 1,500 feet MSL, whichever is higher.

(c) Without regard to paragraph (a) of this section, if the latest weather reports or forecasts, or any combination of them, indicate that the weather along the planned route (including takeoff and landing) allows flight under VFR under the ceiling (if a ceiling exists) and that the weather is forecast to remain so until at least 1 hour after the estimated time of arrival at the destination, a person may operate an aircraft over-the-top.

(d) Without regard to paragraph (a) of this section, a person may operate an aircraft over-the-top under conditions allowing—

(1) For multiengine aircraft, descent or continuance of the flight under VFR if its critical engine fails; or

(2) For single-engine aircraft, descent under VFR if its engine fails.

[Docket No. 16097, 43 FR 46783, Oct. 10, 1978; as amended by Amdt. 135–20, 51 FR 40710, Nov. 7, 1986; Amdt. 135–70, 62 FR 42374, Aug. 6, 1997]

§135.183 Performance requirements: Land aircraft operated over water.

No person may operate a land aircraft carrying passengers over water unless—

(a) It is operated at an altitude that allows it to reach land in the case of engine failure;

(b) It is necessary for takeoff or landing;

(c) It is a multiengine aircraft operated at a weight that will allow it to climb, with the critical engine inoperative, at least 50 feet a minute, at an altitude of 1,000 feet above the surface; or

(d) It is a helicopter equipped with helicopter flotation devices.

§135.185 Empty weight and center of gravity: Currency requirement.

(a) No person may operate a multiengine aircraft unless the current empty weight and center of gravity are calculated from values established by actual weighing of the aircraft within the preceding 36 calendar months.

(b) Paragraph (a) of this section does not apply to—

(1) Aircraft issued an original airworthiness certificate within the preceding 36 calendar months; and

(2) Aircraft operated under a weight and balance system approved in the operations specifications of the certificate holder.

Subpart D— VFR/IFR Operating Limitations and Weather Requirements

§135.201 Applicability.

This subpart prescribes the operating limitations for VFR/IFR flight operations and associated weather requirements for operations under this part.

§135.203 VFR: Minimum altitudes.

Except when necessary for takeoff and landing, no person may operate under VFR—

(a) An airplane—

(1) During the day, below 500 feet above the surface or less than 500 feet horizontally from any obstacle; or

(2) At night, at an altitude less than 1,000 feet above the highest obstacle within a horizontal distance of 5 miles from the course intended to be flown or, in designated mountainous terrain, less than 2,000 feet above the highest obstacle within a horizontal distance of 5 miles from the course intended to be flown; or

(b) A helicopter over a congested area at an altitude less than 300 feet above the surface.

§135.205 VFR: Visibility requirements.

(a) No person may operate an airplane under VFR in uncontrolled airspace when the ceiling is less than 1,000 feet unless flight visibility is at least 2 miles.

(b) No person may operate a helicopter under VFR in Class G airspace at an altitude of 1,200 feet or less above the surface or within the lateral boundaries of the surface areas of Class B, Class C, Class D, or Class E airspace designated for an airport unless the visibility is at least—

(1) During the day—½ mile; or

(2) At night—1 mile.

[Docket No. 16097, 43 FR 46783, Oct. 10, 1978; as amended by Amdt. 135–41, 56 FR 65663, Dec. 17, 1991]

§135.207 VFR: Helicopter surface reference requirements.

No person may operate a helicopter under VFR unless that person has visual surface reference or, at night, visual surface light reference, sufficient to safely control the helicopter.

§135.209 VFR: Fuel supply.

(a) No person may begin a flight operation in an airplane under VFR unless, considering wind and forecast weather conditions, it has enough fuel to fly to the first point of intended landing and, assuming normal cruising fuel consumption—

(1) During the day, to fly after that for at least 30 minutes; or

(2) At night, to fly after that for at least 45 minutes.

(b) No person may begin a flight operation in a helicopter under VFR unless, considering wind and forecast weather conditions, it has enough fuel to fly to the first point of intended landing and, assuming normal cruising fuel consumption, to fly after that for at least 20 minutes.

§135.211 VFR: Over-the-top carrying passengers: Operating limitations.

Subject to any additional limitations in §135.181, no person may operate an aircraft under VFR over-the-top carrying passengers, unless—

(a) Weather reports or forecasts, or any combination of them, indicate that the weather at the intended point of termination of over-the-top flight—

(1) Allows descent to beneath the ceiling under VFR and is forecast to remain so until at least 1 hour after the estimated time of arrival at that point; or

(2) Allows an IFR approach and landing with flight clear of the clouds until reaching the prescribed initial approach altitude over the final approach facility, unless the approach is made with the use of radar under §91.175(f) of this chapter; or

(b) It is operated under conditions allowing—

(1) For multiengine aircraft, descent or continuation of the flight under VFR if its critical engine fails; or

(2) For single-engine aircraft, descent under VFR if its engine fails.

[Docket No. 16097, 43 FR 46783, Oct. 10, 1978; as amended by Amdt. 135–32, 54 FR 34332, Aug. 18, 1989]

§135.213 Weather reports and forecasts.

(a) Whenever a person operating an aircraft under this part is required to use a weather report or forecast, that person shall use that of the U.S. National Weather Service, a source approved by the U.S. National Weather Service, or a source approved by the Administrator. However, for operations under VFR, the pilot in command may, if such a report is not available, use weather information based on that pilot's own observations or on those of other persons competent to supply appropriate observations.

(b) For the purposes of paragraph (a) of this section, weather observations made and furnished to pilots to conduct IFR operations at an airport must be taken at the airport where those IFR operations are conducted, unless the Administrator issues operations specifications allowing the use of weather observations taken at a location not at the airport where the IFR operations are conducted. The Administrator issues such operations specifications when, after investigation by the U.S. National Weather Service and the certificate-holding district office, it is found that the standards of safety for that operation would allow the deviation from this paragraph for a particular operation for which an air carrier operating certificate or operating certificate has been issued.

[Docket No. 16097, 43 FR 46783, Oct. 10, 1978; as amended by Amdt. 135–60, 61 FR 2616, Jan. 26, 1996]

§135.215 IFR: Operating limitations.

(a) Except as provided in paragraphs (b), (c) and (d) of this section, no person may operate an aircraft under IFR outside of controlled airspace or at any airport that does not have an approved standard instrument approach procedure.

(b) The Administrator may issue operations specifications to the certificate holder to allow it to operate under IFR over routes outside controlled airspace if—

(1) The certificate holder shows the Administrator that the flight crew is able to navigate, without visual reference to the ground, over an intended track without deviating more than 5 degrees or 5 miles, whichever is less, from that track; and

(2) The Administrator determines that the proposed operations can be conducted safely.

(c) A person may operate an aircraft under IFR outside of controlled airspace if the certificate holder has been approved for the operations and that operation is necessary to—

(1) Conduct an instrument approach to an airport for which there is in use a current approved standard or special instrument approach procedure; or

(2) Climb into controlled airspace during an approved missed approach procedure; or

(3) Make an IFR departure from an airport having an approved instrument approach procedure.

(d) The Administrator may issue operations specifications to the certificate holder to allow it to depart at an airport that does not have an approved standard instrument approach procedure when the Administrator determines that it is necessary to make an IFR departure from that airport and that the proposed operations can be conducted safely. The approval to operate at that airport does not include an approval to make an IFR approach to that airport.

§135.217 IFR: Takeoff limitations.

No person may takeoff an aircraft under IFR from an airport where weather conditions are at or above takeoff minimums but are below authorized IFR landing minimums unless there is an alternate airport within 1 hour's flying time (at normal cruising speed, in still air) of the airport of departure.

§135.219 IFR: Destination airport weather minimums.

No person may takeoff an aircraft under IFR or begin an IFR or over-the-top operation unless the latest weather reports or forecasts, or any combination of them, indicate that weather conditions at the estimated time of arrival at the next airport of intended landing will be at or above authorized IFR landing minimums.

§135.221 IFR: Alternate airport weather minimums.

No person may designate an alternate airport unless the weather reports or forecasts, or any combination of them, indicate that the weather conditions will be at or above authorized alternate airport landing minimums for that airport at the estimated time of arrival.

§135.223 IFR: Alternate airport requirements.

(a) Except as provided in paragraph (b) of this section, no person may operate an aircraft in IFR conditions unless it carries enough fuel (considering weather reports or forecasts or any combination of them) to—

(1) Complete the flight to the first airport of intended landing;

(2) Fly from that airport to the alternate airport; and

(3) Fly after that for 45 minutes at normal cruising speed or, for helicopters, fly after that for 30 minutes at normal cruising speed.

(b) Paragraph (a)(2) of this section does not apply if part 97 of this chapter prescribes a standard instrument approach procedure for the first airport of intended landing and, for at least one hour before and after the estimated time of arrival, the appropriate weather reports or forecasts, or any combination of them, indicate that—

(1) The ceiling will be at least 1,500 feet above the lowest circling approach MDA; or

(2) If a circling instrument approach is not authorized for the airport, the ceiling will be at least 1,500 feet above the lowest published minimum or 2,000 feet above the airport elevation, whichever is higher; and

(3) Visibility for that airport is forecast to be at least three miles, or two miles more than the lowest applicable visibility minimums, whichever is the greater, for the instrument approach procedure to be used at the destination airport.

[Docket No. 16097, 43 FR 46783, Oct. 10, 1978; as amended by Amdt. 135–20, 51 FR 40710, Nov. 7, 1986]

§135.225 IFR: Takeoff, approach and landing minimums.

(a) Except to the extent permitted by paragraph (b) of this section, no pilot may begin an instrument approach procedure to an airport unless—

(1) That airport has a weather reporting facility operated by the U.S. National Weather Service, a source approved by U.S. National Weather Service, or a source approved by the Administrator; and

(2) The latest weather report issued by that weather reporting facility indicates that weather conditions are at or above the authorized IFR landing minimums for that airport.

(b) A pilot conducting an eligible on-demand operation may begin an instrument approach procedure to an airport that does not have a weather reporting facility operated by the U.S. National Weather Service, a source approved by the U.S. National Weather Service, or a source approved by the Administrator if—

(1) The alternate airport has a weather reporting facility operated by the U.S. National Weather Service, a source approved by the U.S. National Weather Service, or a source approved by the Administrator; and

(2) The latest weather report issued by the weather reporting facility includes a current local altimeter setting for the destination airport. If no local altimeter setting for the destination airport is available, the pilot may use the current altimeter setting provided by the facility designated on the approach chart for the destination airport.

(c) If a pilot has begun the final approach segment of an instrument approach to an airport under paragraph (b) of this section, and the pilot receives a later weather report indicating that conditions have worsened to below the minimum requirements, then the pilot may continue the approach only if the requirements of §91.175(l) of this chapter, or both of the following conditions, are met—

(1) The later weather report is received when the aircraft is in one of the following approach phases:

(i) The aircraft is on an ILS final approach and has passed the final approach fix;

(ii) The aircraft is on an ASR or PAR final approach and has been turned over to the final approach controller; or

(iii) The aircraft is on a nonprecision final approach and the aircraft—

(A) Has passed the appropriate facility or final approach fix; or

(B) Where a final approach fix is not specified, has completed the procedure turn and is established inbound toward the airport on the final approach course within the distance prescribed in the procedure; and

(2) The pilot in command finds, on reaching the authorized MDA or DH, that the actual weather conditions are at or above the minimums prescribed for the procedure being used.

(d) If a pilot has begun the final approach segment of an instrument approach to an airport under paragraph (c) of this section and a later weather report indicating below minimum conditions is received after the aircraft is—

(1) On an ILS final approach and has passed the final approach fix; or

(2) On an ASR or PAR final approach and has been turned over to the final approach controller; or

(3) On a final approach using a VOR, NDB, or comparable approach procedure; and the aircraft—

(i) Has passed the appropriate facility or final approach fix; or

(ii) Where a final approach fix is not specified, has completed the procedure turn and is established inbound toward the airport on the final approach course within the distance prescribed in the procedure; the approach may be continued and a landing made if the pilot finds, upon reaching the authorized MDA or DH, that actual weather conditions are at least equal to the minimums prescribed for the procedure.

(e) The MDA or DH and visibility landing minimums prescribed in part 97 of this chapter or in the operator's operations specifications are increased by 100 feet and ½ mile respectively, but not to exceed the ceiling and visibility minimums for that airport when used as an alternate airport, for each pilot in command of a turbine-powered airplane who has not served at least 100 hours as pilot in command in that type of airplane.

(f) Each pilot making an IFR takeoff or approach and landing at a military or foreign airport shall comply with applicable instrument approach procedures and weather minimums prescribed by the authority having jurisdiction over that airport. In addition, no pilot may, at that airport—

(1) Take off under IFR when the visibility is less than 1 mile; or

(2) Make an instrument approach when the visibility is less than ½ mile.

(g) If takeoff minimums are specified in part 97 of this chapter for the takeoff airport, no pilot may take off an aircraft under IFR when the weather conditions reported by the facility described in paragraph (a)(1) of this section are less than the takeoff minimums specified for the takeoff airport in part 97 or in the certificate holder's operations specifications.

(h) Except as provided in paragraph (i) of this section, if takeoff minimums are not prescribed in part 97 of this chapter for the takeoff airport, no pilot may takeoff an aircraft under IFR when the weather conditions reported by the facility described in paragraph (a)(1) of this section are less than that prescribed in part 91 of this chapter or in the certificate holder's operations specifications.

(i) At airports where straight-in instrument approach procedures are authorized, a pilot may take off an aircraft under IFR when the weather conditions reported by the facility described in paragraph (a)(1) of this section are equal to or better than the lowest straight-in landing minimums, unless otherwise restricted, if—

(1) The wind direction and velocity at the time of takeoff are such that a straight-in instrument approach can be made to the runway served by the instrument approach;

(2) The associated ground facilities upon which the landing minimums are predicated and the related airborne equipment are in normal operation; and

(3) The certificate holder has been approved for such operations.

[Docket No. 16097, 43 FR 46783, Oct. 10, 1978; as amended by Amdt. 135–91, 68 FR 54586, Sept. 17, 2003; Amdt. 135–93, 69 FR 1641, Jan. 9, 2004]

§135.227 Icing conditions: Operating limitations.

(a) No pilot may take off an aircraft that has frost, ice, or snow adhering to any rotor blade, propeller, windshield, wing, stabilizing or control surface, to a powerplant installation, or to an airspeed, altimeter, rate of climb, or flight attitude instrument system, except under the following conditions:

(1) Takeoffs may be made with frost adhering to the wings, or stabilizing or control surfaces, if the frost has been polished to make it smooth.

(2) Takeoffs may be made with frost under the wing in the area of the fuel tanks if authorized by the Administrator.

(b) No certificate holder may authorize an airplane to take off and no pilot may take off an airplane any time conditions are such that frost, ice, or snow may reasonably be expected to adhere to the airplane unless the pilot has completed all applicable training as required by §135.341 and unless one of the following requirements is met:

(1) A pretakeoff contamination check, that has been established by the certificate holder and approved by the Administrator for the specific airplane type, has been completed within 5 minutes prior to beginning takeoff. A pretakeoff contamination check is a check to make sure the wings and control surfaces are free of frost, ice, or snow.

(2) The certificate holder has an approved alternative procedure and under that procedure the airplane is determined to be free of frost, ice, or snow.

(3) The certificate holder has an approved deicing/anti-icing program that complies with §121.629(c) of this chapter and the takeoff complies with that program.

(c) Except for an airplane that has ice protection provisions that meet section 34 of Appendix A, or those for transport category airplane type certification, no pilot may fly—

(1) Under IFR into known or forecast light or moderate icing conditions; or

(2) Under VFR into known light or moderate icing conditions; unless the aircraft has functioning deicing or anti-icing equipment protecting each rotor blade, propeller, windshield, wing, stabilizing or control surface, and each airspeed, altimeter, rate of climb, or flight attitude instrument system.

(d) No pilot may fly a helicopter under IFR into known or forecast icing conditions or under VFR into known icing conditions unless it has been type certificated and appropriately equipped for operations in icing conditions.

(e) Except for an airplane that has ice protection provisions that meet section 34 of Appendix A, or those for transport category airplane type certification, no pilot may fly an aircraft into known or forecast severe icing conditions.

(f) If current weather reports and briefing information relied upon by the pilot in command indicate that the forecast icing condition that would otherwise prohibit the flight will not be encountered during the flight because of changed weather conditions since the forecast, the restrictions in paragraphs (c), (d), and (e) of this section based on forecast conditions do not apply.

[Docket No. 16097, 43 FR 46783, Oct. 10, 1978; as amended by Amdt. 133–20, 51 FR 40710, Nov. 7, 1986; Amdt. 135–46, 58 FR 69629, Dec. 30, 1993; Amdt. 135–46, 58 FR 69629, Dec. 30, 1993; Amdt. 135–60, 61 FR, Jan. 26, 1996]

§135.229 Airport requirements.

(a) No certificate holder may use any airport unless it is adequate for the proposed operation, considering such items as size, surface, obstructions, and lighting.

(b) No pilot of an aircraft carrying passengers at night may take off from, or land on, an airport unless—

(1) That pilot has determined the wind direction from an illuminated wind direction indicator or local ground communications or, in the case of takeoff, that pilot's personal observations; and

(2) The limits of the area to be used for landing or takeoff are clearly shown—

(i) For airplanes, by boundary or runway marker lights;

(ii) For helicopters, by boundary or runway marker lights or reflective material.

(c) For the purpose of paragraph (b) of this section, if the area to be used for takeoff or landing is marked by flare pots or lanterns, their use must be approved by the Administrator.

Subpart E—Flight Crewmember Requirements

§135.241 Applicability.

Except as provided in §135.3, this subpart prescribes the flight crewmember requirements for operations under this part.

[Docket No. 16097, 43 FR 46783, Oct. 10, 1978; as amended by Amdt. 135–57, 60 FR 65950, Dec. 20, 1995]

§135.243 Pilot in command qualifications.

(a) No certificate holder may use a person, nor may any person serve, as pilot in command in passenger-carrying operations—

(1) Of a turbojet airplane, of an airplane having a passenger-seat configuration, excluding each crewmember seat, of 10 seats or more, or of a multiengine airplane in a commuter operation as defined in part 119 of this chapter, unless that person holds an airline transport pilot certificate with appropriate category and class ratings and, if required, an appropriate type rating for that airplane.

(2) Of a helicopter in a scheduled interstate air transportation operation by an air carrier within the 48 contiguous states unless that person holds an airline transport pilot certificate, appropriate type ratings, and an instrument rating.

(b) Except as provided in paragraph (a) of this section, no certificate holder may use a person, nor may any person serve, as pilot in command of an aircraft under VFR unless that person—

(1) Holds at least a commercial pilot certificate with appropriate category and class ratings and, if required, an appropriate type rating for that aircraft; and

(2) Has had at least 500 hours of flight time as a pilot, including at least 100 hours of cross-country flight time, at least 25 hours of which were at night; and

(3) For an airplane, holds an instrument rating or an airline transport pilot certificate with an airplane category rating; or

(4) For helicopter operations conducted VFR over-the-top, holds a helicopter instrument rating, or an airline transport pilot certificate with a category and class rating for that aircraft, not limited to VFR.

(c) Except as provided in paragraph (a) of this section, no certificate holder may use a person, nor may any person serve, as pilot in command of an aircraft under IFR unless that person—

(1) Holds at least a commercial pilot certificate with appropriate category and class ratings and, if required, an appropriate type rating for that aircraft; and

(2) Has had at least 1,200 hours of flight time as a pilot, including 500 hours of cross country flight time, 100 hours of night flight time, and 75 hours of actual or simulated instrument time at least 50 hours of which were in actual flight; and

(3) For an airplane, holds an instrument rating or an airline transport pilot certificate with an airplane category rating; or

(4) For a helicopter, holds a helicopter instrument rating, or an airline transport pilot certificate with a category and class rating for that aircraft, not limited to VFR.

(d) Paragraph (b)(3) of this section does not apply when—

(1) The aircraft used is a single reciprocating-engine-powered airplane;

(2) The certificate holder does not conduct any operation pursuant to a published flight schedule which specifies five or more round trips a week between two or more points and places between which the round trips are performed, and does not transport mail by air under a contract or contracts with the United States Postal Service having total amount estimated at the beginning of any semiannual reporting period (January 1–June 30; July 1–December 31) to be in excess of $20,000 over the 12 months commencing with the beginning of the reporting period;

(3) The area, as specified in the certificate holder's operations specifications, is an isolated area, as determined by the Flight Standards district office, if it is shown that—

(i) The primary means of navigation in the area is by pilotage, since radio navigational aids are largely ineffective; and

(ii) The primary means of transportation in the area is by air;

(4) Each flight is conducted under day VFR with a ceiling of not less than 1,000 feet and visibility not less than 3 statute miles;

(5) Weather reports or forecasts, or any combination of them, indicate that for the period commencing with the planned departure and ending 30 minutes after the planned arrival at the destination the flight may be conducted under VFR with a ceiling of not less than 1,000 feet and visibility of not less than 3 statute miles, except that if weather reports and forecasts are not available, the pilot in command may use that pilot's observations or those of other persons competent to supply weather observations if those observations indicate the flight may be conducted under VFR with the ceiling and visibility required in this paragraph;

(6) The distance of each flight from the certificate holder's base of operation to destination does not exceed 250 nautical miles for a pilot who holds a commercial pilot certificate with an airplane rating without an instrument rating, provided the pilot's certificate does not contain any limitation to the contrary; and

(7) The areas to be flown are approved by the certificate-holding FAA Flight Standards district office and are listed in the certificate holder's operations specifications.

[Docket No. 16097, 43 FR 46783, Oct. 10, 1978; as amended by Amdt. 135–1, 43 FR 49975, Oct. 26, 1978; Amdt. 135–15, 46 FR 30971, June 11, 1981; Amdt. 135–58, 60 FR 65939, Dec. 20, 1995; 63 FR 53804, Oct. 7, 1998]

§135.244 Operating experience.

(a) No certificate holder may use any person, nor may any person serve, as a pilot in command of an aircraft operated in a commuter operation, as defined in part 119 of this chapter, unless that person has completed, prior to designation as pilot in command, on that make and basic model aircraft and in that crewmember position, the following operating experience in each make and basic model of aircraft to be flown:

(1) Aircraft, single engine—10 hours.

(2) Aircraft multiengine, reciprocating engine-powered—15 hours.

(3) Aircraft multiengine, turbine engine-powered—20 hours.

(4) Airplane, turbojet-powered—25 hours.

(b) In acquiring the operating experience, each person must comply with the following:

(1) The operating experience must be acquired after satisfactory completion of the appropriate ground and flight training for the aircraft and crewmember position. Approved provisions for the operating experience must be included in the certificate holder's training program.

(2) The experience must be acquired in flight during commuter passenger-carrying operations under this part. However, in the case of an aircraft not previously used by the certificate holder in operations under this part, operating experience acquired in the aircraft during proving flights or ferry flights may be used to meet this requirement.

(3) Each person must acquire the operating experience while performing the duties of a pilot in command under the supervision of a qualified check pilot.

(4) The hours of operating experience may be reduced to not less than 50 percent of the hours required by this section by the substitution of one additional takeoff and landing for each hour of flight.

[Docket No. 20011, 45 FR 7541, Feb. 4, 1980; as amended by Amdt. 135–9, 45 FR 80461, Dec. 14, 1980; Amdt. 135–58, 60 FR 65940, Dec. 20, 1995]

§135.245 Second in command qualifications.

(a) Except as provided in paragraph (b), no certificate holder may use any person, nor may any person serve, as second in command of an aircraft unless that person holds at least a commercial pilot certificate with appropriate category and class ratings and an instrument rating. For flight under IFR, that person must meet the recent instrument experience requirements of part 61 of this chapter.

(b) A second in command of a helicopter operated under VFR, other than over-the-top, must have at least a commercial pilot certificate with an appropriate aircraft category and class rating.

[44 FR 26738, May 7, 1979]

§135.247 Pilot qualifications: Recent experience.

(a) No certificate holder may use any person, nor may any person serve, as pilot in command of an aircraft carrying passengers unless, within the preceding 90 days, that person has—

(1) Made three takeoffs and three landings as the sole manipulator of the flight controls in an aircraft of the same category and class and, if a type rating is required, of the same type in which that person is to serve; or

(2) For operation during the period beginning 1 hour after sunset and ending 1 hour before sunrise (as published in the Air Almanac), made three takeoffs and three landings during that period as the sole manipulator of the flight controls in an aircraft of the same category and class and, if a type rating is required, of the same type in which that person is to serve.

A person who complies with paragraph (a)(2) of this section need not comply with paragraph (a)(1) of this section.

(3) Paragraph (a)(2) of this section does not apply to a pilot in command of a turbine-powered airplane that is type certificated for more than one pilot crewmember, provided that pilot has complied with the requirements of paragraph (a)(3)(i) or (ii) of this section:

(i) The pilot in command must hold at least a commercial pilot certificate with the appropriate category, class, and type rating for each airplane that is type certificated for more than one pilot crewmember that the pilot seeks to operate under this alternative, and:

(A) That pilot must have logged at least 1,500 hours of aeronautical experience as a pilot;

(B) In each airplane that is type certificated for more than one pilot crewmember that the pilot seeks to operate under this alternative, that pilot must have accomplished and logged the daytime takeoff and landing recent flight experience of paragraph (a) of this section, as the sole manipulator of the flight controls;

(C) Within the preceding 90 days prior to the operation of that airplane that is type certificated for more than one pilot crewmember, the pilot must have accomplished and logged at least 15 hours of flight time in the type of airplane that the pilot seeks to operate under this alternative; and

(D) That pilot has accomplished and logged at least 3 takeoffs and 3 landings to a full stop, as the sole manipulator of the flight controls, in a turbine-powered airplane that requires more than one pilot crewmember. The pilot must have performed the takeoffs and landings during the period beginning 1 hour after sunset and ending 1 hour before sunrise within the preceding 6 months prior to the month of the flight.

(ii) The pilot in command must hold at least a commercial pilot certificate with the appropriate category, class, and type rating for each airplane that is type certificated for more than one pilot crewmember that the pilot seeks to operate under this alternative, and:

(A) That pilot must have logged at least 1,500 hours of aeronautical experience as a pilot;

(B) In each airplane that is type certificated for more than one pilot crewmember that the pilot seeks to operate under this alternative, that pilot must have accomplished and logged the daytime takeoff and landing recent flight experience of paragraph (a) of this section, as the sole manipulator of the flight controls;

(C) Within the preceding 90 days prior to the operation of that airplane that is type certificated for more than one pilot crewmember, the pilot must have accomplished and logged at least 15 hours of flight time in the type of airplane that the pilot seeks to operate under this alternative; and

(D) Within the preceding 12 months prior to the month of the flight, the pilot must have completed a training program that is approved under part 142 of this chapter. The approved training program must have required and the pilot must have performed, at least 6 takeoffs and 6 landings to a full stop as the sole manipulator of the controls in a flight simulator that is representative of a turbine-powered airplane that requires more than one pilot crewmember. The flight simulator's visual system must have been adjusted to represent the period beginning 1 hour after sunset and ending 1 hour before sunrise.

(b) For the purpose of paragraph (a) of this section, if the aircraft is a tailwheel airplane, each takeoff must be made in a tailwheel airplane and each landing must be made to a full stop in a tailwheel airplane.

[Docket No. 16097, 43 FR 46783, Oct. 10, 1978; as amended by Amdt. 135–91, 68 FR 54587, Sept. 17, 2003]

§ 135.249 Use of prohibited drugs.

(a) This section applies to persons who perform a function listed in Appendix I to part 121 of this chapter for a certificate holder or an operator. For the purpose of this section, a person who performs such a function pursuant to a contract with the certificate holder or the operator is considered to be performing that function for the certificate holder or the operator.

(b) No certificate holder or operator may knowingly use any person to perform, nor may any person perform for a certificate holder or an operator, either directly or by contract, any function listed in Appendix I to part 121 of this chapter while that person has a prohibited drug, as defined in that appendix, in his or her system.

(c) No certificate holder or operator shall knowingly use any person to perform, nor shall any person perform for a certificate holder or operator, either directly or by contract, any safety-sensitive function if the person has a verified positive drug test result on or has refused to submit to a drug test required by Appendix I to part 121 of this chapter and the person has not met the requirements of Appendix I to part 121 of this chapter for returning to the performance of safety-sensitive duties.

[Docket No. 25148, 53 FR 47061, Nov. 21, 1988; as amended by Amdt. 135–51, 59 FR 42933, Aug. 19, 1994]

§ 135.251 Testing for prohibited drugs.

(a) Each certificate holder or operator shall test each of its employees who performs a function listed in Appendix I to part 121 of this chapter in accordance with that appendix.

(b) Except as provided in paragraph (c) of this section, no certificate holder or operator may use any contractor to perform a function listed in appendix I part 121 of this chapter unless that contractor tests each employee performing such a function for the certificate holder or operator in accordance with that appendix.

(c) If a certificate holder conducts an on-demand operation into an airport at which no maintenance providers are available that are subject to the requirements of appendix I to part 121 and emergency maintenance is required, the certificate holder may use persons not meeting the requirements of paragraph (b) of this section to provide such emergency maintenance under both of the following conditions:

(1) The certificate holder must give written notification of the emergency maintenance to the Drug Abatement Program Division, AAM-800, 800 Independence Avenue, Washington, DC, 20591, within 10 days after being provided same

in accordance with this paragraph. A certificate holder must retain copies of all such written notifications for two years.

(2) The aircraft must be reinspected by maintenance personnel who meet the requirements of paragraph (b) of this section when the aircraft is next at an airport where such maintenance personnel are available.

(d) For purposes of this section, emergency maintenance means maintenance that—

(1) Is not scheduled and

(2) Is made necessary by an aircraft condition not discovered prior to the departure for that location.

[Docket No. 25148, 53 FR 47061, Nov. 21, 1988; as amended by Amdt. 135–91, 68 FR 54587, Sept. 17, 2003]

§135.253 Misuse of alcohol.

(a) This section applies to employees who perform a function listed in Appendix J to part 121 of this chapter for a certificate holder or operator (*covered employees*). For the purpose of this section, a person who meets the definition of covered employee in Appendix J is considered to be performing the function for the certificate holder or operator.

(b) *Alcohol concentration.* No covered employee shall report for duty or remain on duty requiring the performance of safety-sensitive functions while having an alcohol concentration of 0.04 or greater. No certificate holder or operator having actual knowledge that an employee has an alcohol concentration of 0.04 or greater shall permit the employee to perform or continue to perform safety-sensitive functions.

(c) *On-duty use.* No covered employee shall use alcohol while performing safety-sensitive functions. No certificate holder or operator having actual knowledge that a covered employee is using alcohol while performing safety-sensitive functions shall permit the employee to perform or continue to perform safety-sensitive functions.

(d) *Pre-duty use.*

(1) No covered employee shall perform flight crewmember or flight attendant duties within 8 hours after using alcohol. No certificate holder or operator having actual knowledge that such an employee has used alcohol within 8 hours shall permit the employee to perform or continue to perform the specified duties.

(2) No covered employee shall perform safety-sensitive duties other than those specified in paragraph (d)(1) of this section within 4 hours after using alcohol. No certificate holder or operator having actual knowledge that such an employee has used alcohol within 4 hours shall permit the employee to perform or continue to perform safety-sensitive functions.

(e) *Use following an accident.* No covered employee who has actual knowledge of an accident involving an aircraft for which he or she performed a safety-sensitive function at or near the time of the accident shall use alcohol for 8 hours following the accident, unless he or she has been given a post-accident test under Appendix J of part 121 of this chapter, or the employer has determined that the employee's performance could not have contributed to the accident.

(f) *Refusal to submit to a required alcohol test.* No covered employee shall refuse to submit to a post-accident, random, reasonable suspicion, or follow-up alcohol test required under Appendix J to part 121 of this chapter. No operator or certificate holder shall permit a covered employee who refuses to submit to such a test to perform or continue to perform safety-sensitive functions.

[Docket No. 16097, 43 FR 46783, Oct. 10, 1978; as amended by Amdt. 135–48, 59 FR 7396, Feb. 15, 1994]

§135.255 Testing for alcohol.

(a) Each certificate holder and operator must establish an alcohol misuse prevention program in accordance with the provisions of Appendix J to part 121 of this chapter.

(b) Except as provided in paragraph (c) of this section, no certificate holder or operator may use any person who meets the definition of "covered employee" in appendix J to part 121 of this chapter to perform a safety-sensitive function listed in that appendix unless such person is subject to testing for alcohol misuse in accordance with the provisions of appendix J.

(c) If a certificate holder conducts an on-demand operation into an airport at which no maintenance providers are available that are subject to the requirements of appendix J to part 121 of this chapter and emergency maintenance is required, the certificate holder may use persons not meeting the requirements of paragraph (b) of this section to provide such emergency maintenance under both of the following conditions:

(1) The certificate holder must give written notification of the emergency maintenance to the Drug Abatement Program Division, AAM-800, 800 Independence Avenue, Washington, DC, 20591, within 10 days after being provided same in accordance with this paragraph. A certificate holder must retain copies of all such written notifications for two years.

(2) The aircraft must be reinspected by maintenance personnel who meet the requirements of paragraph (b) of this section when the aircraft is next at an airport where such maintenance personnel are available.

(d) For purposes of this section, emergency maintenance means maintenance that—

(1) Is not scheduled, and

(2) Is made necessary by an aircraft condition not discovered prior to the departure for that location.

[Docket No. 16097, 43 FR 46783, Oct. 10, 1978; as amended by Amdt. 135–48, 59 FR 7397, Feb. 15, 1994; Amdt. 135–91, 68 FR 54587, Sept. 17, 2003]

Subpart F— Crewmember Flight Time and Duty Period Limitations and Rest Requirements

Source: Docket No. 23634, 50 FR 29320, July 18, 1985, unless otherwise noted.

§135.261 Applicability.

Sections 135.263 through 135.273 of this part prescribe flight time limitations, duty period limitations, and rest requirements for operations conducted under this part as follows:

(a) Section 135.263 applies to all operations under this subpart.

(b) Section 135.265 applies to:

(1) Scheduled passenger-carrying operations except those conducted solely within the state of Alaska. "Scheduled passenger-carrying operations" means passenger-carrying operations that are conducted in accordance with a published schedule which covers at least five round trips per week on at least one route between two or more points, includes dates or times (or both), and is openly advertised or otherwise made readily available to the general public, and

(2) Any other operation under this part, if the operator elects to comply with §135.265 and obtains an appropriate operations specification amendment.

(c) Sections 135.267 and 135.269 apply to any operation that is not a scheduled passenger-carrying operation and to any operation conducted solely within the State of Alaska, unless the operator elects to comply with §135.265 as authorized under paragraph (b)(2) of this section.

(d) Section 135.271 contains special daily flight time limits for operations conducted under the helicopter emergency medical evacuation service (HEMES).

(e) Section 135.273 prescribes duty period limitations and rest requirements for flight attendants in all operations conducted under this part.

[Docket No. 23634, 50 FR 29320, July 18, 1985; as amended by Amdt. 135–52, 59 FR 42993, Aug. 19, 1994]

§135.263 Flight time limitations and rest requirements: All certificate holders.

(a) A certificate holder may assign a flight crewmember and a flight crewmember may accept an assignment for flight time only when the applicable requirements of §§135.263 through 135.271 are met.

(b) No certificate holder may assign any flight crewmember to any duty with the certificate holder during any required rest period.

(c) Time spent in transportation, not local in character, that a certificate holder requires of a flight crewmember and provides to transport the crewmember to an airport at which he is to serve on a flight as a crewmember, or from an airport at which he was relieved from duty to return to his home station, is not considered part of a rest period.

(d) A flight crewmember is not considered to be assigned flight time in excess of flight time limitations if the flights to which he is assigned normally terminate within the limitations, but due to circumstances beyond the control of the certificate holder or flight crewmember (such as adverse weather conditions), are not at the time of departure expected to reach their destination within the planned flight time.

§135.265 Flight time limitations and rest requirements: Scheduled operations.

(a) No certificate holder may schedule any flight crewmember, and no flight crewmember may accept an assignment, for flight time in scheduled operations or in other commercial flying if that crewmember's total flight time in all commercial flying will exceed—

(1) 1,200 hours in any calendar year.

(2) 120 hours in any calendar month.

(3) 34 hours in any 7 consecutive days.

(4) 8 hours during any 24 consecutive hours for a flight crew consisting of one pilot.

(5) 8 hours between required rest periods for a flight crew consisting of two pilots qualified under this part for the operation being conducted.

(b) Except as provided in paragraph (c) of this section, no certificate holder may schedule a flight crewmember, and no flight crewmember may accept an assignment, for flight time during the 24 consecutive hours preceding the scheduled completion of any flight segment without a scheduled rest period during that 24 hours of at least the following:

(1) 9 consecutive hours of rest for less than 8 hours of scheduled flight time.

(2) 10 consecutive hours of rest for 8 or more but less than 9 hours of scheduled flight time.

(3) 11 consecutive hours of rest for 9 or more hours of scheduled flight time.

(c) A certificate holder may schedule a flight crewmember for less than the rest required in paragraph (b) of this section or may reduce a scheduled rest under the following conditions:

(1) A rest required under paragraph (b)(1) of this section may be scheduled for or reduced to a minimum of 8 hours if the flight crewmember is given a rest period of at least 10 hours that must begin no later than 24 hours after the commencement of the reduced rest period.

(2) A rest required under paragraph (b)(2) of this section may be scheduled for or reduced to a minimum of 8 hours if the flight crewmember is given a rest period of at least 11 hours that must begin no later than 24 hours after the commencement of the reduced rest period.

(3) A rest required under paragraph (b)(3) of this section may be scheduled for or reduced to a minimum of 9 hours if the flight crewmember is given a rest period of at least 12 hours that must begin no later than 24 hours after the commencement of the reduced rest period.

(d) Each certificate holder shall relieve each flight crewmember engaged in scheduled air transportation from all further duty for at least 24 consecutive hours during any 7 consecutive days.

§135.267 Flight time limitations and rest requirements: Unscheduled one- and two-pilot crews.

(a) No certificate holder may assign any flight crewmember, and no flight crewmember may accept an assignment, for flight time as a member of a one- or two-pilot crew if that crewmember's total flight time in all commercial flying will exceed—

(1) 500 hours in any calendar quarter.

(2) 800 hours in any two consecutive calendar quarters.

(3) 1,400 hours in any calendar year.

(b) Except as provided in paragraph (c) of this section, during any 24 consecutive hours the total flight time of the assigned flight when added to any other commercial flying by that flight crewmember may not exceed—

(1) 8 hours for a flight crew consisting of one pilot; or

(2) 10 hours for a flight crew consisting of two pilots qualified under this part for the operation being conducted.

(c) A flight crewmember's flight time may exceed the flight time limits of paragraph (b) of this section if the assigned flight time occurs during a regularly assigned duty period of no more than 14 hours and—

(1) If this duty period is immediately preceded by and followed by a required rest period of at least 10 consecutive hours of rest;

(2) If flight time is assigned during this period, that total flight time when added to any other commercial flying by the flight crewmember may not exceed—

(i) 8 hours for a flight crew consisting of one pilot; or

(ii) 10 hours for a flight crew consisting of two pilots; and

(3) If the combined duty and rest periods equal 24 hours.

(d) Each assignment under paragraph (b) of this section must provide for at least 10 consecutive hours of rest during the 24-hour period that precedes the planned completion time of the assignment.

(e) When a flight crewmember has exceeded the daily flight time limitations in this section, because of circumstances beyond the control of the certificate holder or flight crewmember (such as adverse weather conditions), that flight crewmember must have a rest period before being assigned or accepting an assignment for flight time of at least—

(1) 11 consecutive hours of rest if the flight time limitation is exceeded by not more than 30 minutes;

(2) 12 consecutive hours of rest if the flight time limitation is exceeded by more than 30 minutes, but not more than 60 minutes; and

(3) 16 consecutive hours of rest if the flight time limitation is exceeded by more than 60 minutes.

(f) The certificate holder must provide each flight crewmember at least 13 rest periods of at least 24 consecutive hours each in each calendar quarter.

[Docket No. 23634, 50 FR 29320, July 18, 1989; as amended by Amdt. 135–33, 54 FR 39294, Sept. 25, 1989; Amdt. 135–60, 61 FR 2616, Jan. 26, 1996]

§135.269 Flight time limitations and rest requirements: Unscheduled three- and four-pilot crews.

(a) No certificate holder may assign any flight crewmember, and no flight crewmember may accept an assignment, for flight time as a member of a three- or four-pilot crew if that crewmember's total flight time in all commercial flying will exceed—

(1) 500 hours in any calendar quarter.

(2) 800 hours in any two consecutive calendar quarters.

(3) 1,400 hours in any calendar year.

(b) No certificate holder may assign any pilot to a crew of three or four pilots, unless that assignment provides—

(1) At least 10 consecutive hours of rest immediately preceding the assignment;

(2) No more than 8 hours of flight deck duty in any 24 consecutive hours;

(3) No more than 18 duty hours for a three-pilot crew or 20 duty hours for a four-pilot crew in any 24 consecutive hours;

(4) No more than 12 hours aloft for a three-pilot crew or 16 hours aloft for a four-pilot crew during the maximum duty hours specified in paragraph (b)(3) of this section;

(5) Adequate sleeping facilities on the aircraft for the relief pilot;

(6) Upon completion of the assignment, a rest period of at least 12 hours;

(7) For a three-pilot crew, a crew which consists of at least the following:

(i) A pilot in command (PIC) who meets the applicable flight crewmember requirements of subpart E of part 135;

(ii) A PIC who meets the applicable flight crewmember requirements of subpart E of part 135, except those prescribed in §§135.244 and 135.247; and

(iii) A second in command (SIC) who meets the SIC qualifications of §135.245.

(8) For a four-pilot crew, at least three pilots who meet the conditions of paragraph (b)(7) of this section, plus a fourth pilot who meets the SIC qualifications of §135.245.

(c) When a flight crewmember has exceeded the daily flight deck duty limitation in this section by more than 60 minutes, because of circumstances beyond the control of the certificate holder or flight crewmember, that flight crewmember must have a rest period before the next duty period of at least 16 consecutive hours.

(d) A certificate holder must provide each flight crewmember at least 13 rest periods of at least 24 consecutive hours each in each calendar quarter.

§135.271 Helicopter hospital emergency medical evacuation service (HEMES).

(a) No certificate holder may assign any flight crewmember, and no flight crewmember may accept an assignment for flight time if that crewmember's total flight time in all commercial flight will exceed—

(1) 500 hours in any calendar quarter.

(2) 800 hours in any two consecutive calendar quarters.

(3) 1,400 hours in any calendar year.

(b) No certificate holder may assign a helicopter flight crewmember, and no flight crewmember may accept an assignment, for hospital emergency medical evacuation service helicopter operations unless that assignment provides for at least 10 consecutive hours of rest immediately preceding reporting to the hospital for availability for flight time.

(c) No flight crewmember may accrue more than 8 hours of flight time during any 24-consecutive hour period of a HEMES assignment, unless an emergency medical evacuation operation is prolonged. Each flight crewmember who exceeds the daily 8 hour flight time limitation in this paragraph must be relieved of the HEMES assignment immediately upon the completion of that emergency medical evacuation operation and must be given a rest period in compliance with paragraph (h) of this section.

(d) Each flight crewmember must receive at least 8 consecutive hours of rest during any 24 consecutive hour period of a HEMES assignment. A flight crewmember must be relieved of the HEMES assignment if he or she has not or cannot receive at least 8 consecutive hours of rest during any 24 consecutive hour period of a HEMES assignment.

(e) A HEMES assignment may not exceed 72 consecutive hours at the hospital.

(f) An adequate place of rest must be provided at, or in close proximity to, the hospital at which the HEMES assignment is being performed.

(g) No certificate holder may assign any other duties to a flight crewmember during a HEMES assignment.

(h) Each pilot must be given a rest period upon completion of the HEMES assignment and prior to being assigned any further duty with the certificate holder of—

(1) At least 12 consecutive hours for an assignment of less than 48 hours.

(2) At least 16 consecutive hours for an assignment of more than 48 hours.

(i) The certificate holder must provide each flight crewmember at least 13 rest periods of at least 24 consecutive hours each in each calendar quarter.

§135.273 Duty period limitations and rest time requirements.

(a) For purposes of this section—

Calendar day means the period of elapsed time, using Coordinated Universal Time or local time, that begins at midnight and ends 24 hours later at the next midnight.

Duty period means the period of elapsed time between reporting for an assignment involving flight time and release from that assignment by the certificate holder. The time is calculated using either Coordinated Universal Time or local time to reflect the total elapsed time.

Flight attendant means an individual, other than a flight crewmember, who is assigned by the certificate holder, in accordance with the required minimum crew complement under the certificate holder's operations specifications or in addition to that minimum complement, to duty in an aircraft during flight time and whose duties include but are not necessarily limited to cabin-safety-related responsibilities.

Rest period means the period free of all responsibility for work or duty should the occasion arise.

(b) Except as provided in paragraph (c) of this section, a certificate holder may assign a duty period to a flight attendant only when the applicable duty period limitations and rest requirements of this paragraph are met.

(1) Except as provided in paragraphs (b)(4), (b)(5), and (b)(6) of this section, no certificate holder may assign a flight attendant to a scheduled duty period of more than 14 hours.

(2) Except as provided in paragraph (b)(3) of this section, a flight attendant scheduled to a duty period of 14 hours or less as provided under paragraph (b)(1) of this section must be given a scheduled rest period of at least 9 consecutive hours. This rest period must occur between the completion of the scheduled duty period and the commencement of the subsequent duty period.

(3) The rest period required under paragraph (b)(2) of this section may be scheduled or reduced to 8 consecutive hours if the flight attendant is provided a subsequent rest period of at least 10 consecutive hours; this subsequent rest period must be scheduled to begin no later than 24 hours after the beginning of the reduced rest period and must occur between the completion of the scheduled duty period and the commencement of the subsequent duty period.

(4) A certificate holder may assign a flight attendant to a scheduled duty period of more than 14 hours, but no more than 16 hours, if the certificate holder has assigned to the flight or flights in that duty period at least one flight attendant in addition to the minimum flight attendant complement required for the flight or flights in that duty period under the certificate holder's operations specifications.

(5) A certificate holder may assign a flight attendant to a scheduled duty period of more than 16 hours, but no more than 18 hours, if the certificate holder has assigned to the flight or flights in that duty period at least two flight attendants in addition to the minimum flight attendant complement required for the flight or flights in that duty period under the certificate holder's operations specifications.

(6) A certificate holder may assign a flight attendant to a scheduled duty period of more than 18 hours, but no more than 20 hours, if the scheduled duty period includes one or more flights that land or take off outside the 48 contiguous states and the District of Columbia, and if the certificate holder has assigned to the flight or flights in that duty period at least three flight attendants in addition to the minimum flight attendant complement required for the flight or flights in that duty period under the certificate holder's operations specifications.

(7) Except as provided in paragraph (b)(8) of this section, a flight attendant scheduled to a duty period of more than 14 hours but no more than 20 hours, as provided in paragraphs (b)(4), (b)(5), and (b)(6) of this section, must be given a scheduled rest period of at least 12 consecutive hours. This rest period must occur between the completion of the scheduled duty period and the commencement of the subsequent duty period.

(8) The rest period required under paragraph (b)(7) of this section may be scheduled or reduced to 10 consecutive hours if the flight attendant is provided a subsequent rest period of at least 14 consecutive hours; this subsequent rest period must be scheduled to begin no later than 24 hours after the beginning of the reduced rest period and must occur between the completion of the scheduled duty period and the commencement of the subsequent duty period.

(9) Notwithstanding paragraphs (b)(4), (b)(5), and (b)(6) of this section, if a certificate holder elects to reduce the rest period to 10 hours as authorized by paragraph (b)(8) of this section, the certificate holder may not schedule a flight attendant for a duty period of more than 14 hours during the 24-hour period commencing after the beginning of the reduced rest period.

(10) No certificate holder may assign a flight attendant any duty period with the certificate holder unless the flight attendant has had at least the minimum rest required under this section.

(11) No certificate holder may assign a flight attendant to perform any duty with the certificate holder during any required rest period.

(12) Time spent in transportation, not local in character, that a certificate holder requires of a flight attendant and provides to transport the flight attendant to an airport at which that flight attendant is to serve on a flight as a crewmember, or from an airport at which the flight attendant was relieved from duty to return to the flight attendant's home station, is not considered part of a rest period.

(13) Each certificate holder must relieve each flight attendant engaged in air transportation from all further duty for at least 24 consecutive hours during any 7 consecutive calendar days.

(14) A flight attendant is not considered to be scheduled for duty in excess of duty period limitations if the flights to which the flight attendant is assigned are scheduled and nor-

mally terminate within the limitations but due to circumstances beyond the control of the certificate holder (such as adverse weather conditions) are not at the time of departure expected to reach their destination within the scheduled time.

(c) Notwithstanding paragraph (b) of this section, a certificate holder may apply the flight crewmember flight time and duty limitations and rest requirements of this part to flight attendants for all operations conducted under this part provided that—

(1) The certificate holder establishes written procedures that—

(i) Apply to all flight attendants used in the certificate holder's operation;

(ii) Include the flight crewmember requirements contained in subpart F of this part, as appropriate to the operation being conducted, except that rest facilities on board the aircraft are not required; and

(iii) Include provisions to add one flight attendant to the minimum flight attendant complement for each flight crewmember who is in excess of the minimum number required in the aircraft type certificate data sheet and who is assigned to the aircraft under the provisions of subpart F of this part, as applicable.

(iv) Are approved by the Administrator and described or referenced in the certificate holder's operations specifications; and

(2) Whenever the Administrator finds that revisions are necessary for the continued adequacy of duty period limitation and rest requirement procedures that are required by paragraph (c)(1) of this section and that had been granted final approval, the certificate holder must, after notification by the Administrator, make any changes in the procedures that are found necessary by the Administrator. Within 30 days after the certificate holder receives such notice, it may file a petition to reconsider the notice with the certificate-holding district office. The filing of a petition to reconsider stays the notice, pending decision by the Administrator. However, if the Administrator finds that there is an emergency that requires immediate action in the interest of safety, the Administrator may, upon a statement of the reasons, require a change effective without stay.

[Docket No. 23634, 50 FR 29320, July 18, 1985; as amended by Amdt. 135–52, 59 FR 42993, Aug. 19, 1994; Amdt. 135–60, 61 FR 2616, Jan. 26, 1996]

Subpart G—Crewmember Testing Requirements

§135.291 Applicability.

Except as provided in §135.3, this subpart—

(a) Prescribes the tests and checks required for pilot and flight attendant crewmembers and for the approval of check pilots in operations under this part; and

(b) Permits training center personnel authorized under part 142 of this chapter who meet the requirements of §§135.337 and 135.339 to conduct training, testing, and checking under contract or other arrangement to those persons subject to the requirements of this subpart.

[Docket No. 26933, 61 FR 34561, July 2, 1996; as amended by Amdt. 135–91, 68 FR 54587, Sept. 17, 2003]

§135.293 Initial and recurrent pilot testing requirements.

(a) No certificate holder may use a pilot, nor may any person serve as a pilot, unless, since the beginning of the 12th calendar month before that service, that pilot has passed a written or oral test, given by the Administrator or an authorized check pilot, on that pilot's knowledge in the following areas—

(1) The appropriate provisions of parts 61, 91, and 135 of this chapter and the operations specifications and the manual of the certificate holder;

(2) For each type of aircraft to be flown by the pilot, the aircraft powerplant, major components and systems, major appliances, performance and operating limitations, standard and emergency operating procedures, and the contents of the approved Aircraft Flight Manual or equivalent, as applicable;

(3) For each type of aircraft to be flown by the pilot, the method of determining compliance with weight and balance limitations for takeoff, landing and en route operations;

(4) Navigation and use of air navigation aids appropriate to the operation or pilot authorization, including, when applicable, instrument approach facilities and procedures;

(5) Air traffic control procedures, including IFR procedures when applicable;

(6) Meteorology in general, including the principles of frontal systems, icing, fog, thunderstorms, and windshear, and, if appropriate for the operation of the certificate holder, high altitude weather;

(7) Procedures for—

(i) Recognizing and avoiding severe weather situations;

(ii) Escaping from severe weather situations, in case of inadvertent encounters, including low-altitude windshear (except that rotorcraft pilots are not required to be tested on escaping from low-altitude windshear); and

(iii) Operating in or near thunderstorms (including best penetrating altitudes), turbulent air (including clear air turbulence), icing, hail, and other potentially hazardous meteorological conditions; and

(8) New equipment, procedures, or techniques, as appropriate.

(b) No certificate holder may use a pilot, nor may any person serve as a pilot, in any aircraft unless, since the beginning of the 12th calendar month before that service, that pilot has passed a competency check given by the Administrator or an authorized check pilot in that class of aircraft, if single-engine airplane other than turbojet, or that type of aircraft, if helicopter, multiengine airplane, or turbojet airplane, to determine the pilot's competence in practical skills and techniques in that aircraft or class of aircraft. The extent of the competency check shall be determined by the Administrator or authorized check pilot conducting the competency check. The competency check may include any of the maneuvers and procedures currently required for the original issuance of the particular pilot certificate required for the operations authorized and appropriate to the category, class and type of aircraft involved. For the purposes of this paragraph, type, as to an airplane, means any one of a group of airplanes determined by the Administrator to have a similar means of propulsion, the same manufacturer, and no significantly different handling or flight characteristics. For the purposes of this paragraph, type, as to a helicopter, means a basic make and model.

(c) The instrument proficiency check required by §135.297 may be substituted for the competency check required by this section for the type of aircraft used in the check.

(d) For the purpose of this part, competent performance of a procedure or maneuver by a person to be used as a pilot requires that the pilot be the obvious master of the aircraft, with the successful outcome of the maneuver never in doubt.

(e) The Administrator or authorized check pilot certifies the competency of each pilot who passes the knowledge or flight check in the certificate holder's pilot records.

(f) Portions of a required competency check may be given in an aircraft simulator or other appropriate training device, if approved by the Administrator.

[Docket No. 16097, 43 FR 46783, Oct. 10, 1978; as amended by Amdt. 135–27, 53 FR 37697, Sept. 27, 1988]

§135.295 Initial and recurrent flight attendant crewmember testing requirements.

No certificate holder may use a flight attendant crewmember, nor may any person serve as a flight attendant crewmember unless, since the beginning of the 12th calendar month before that service, the certificate holder has determined by appropriate initial and recurrent testing that the person is knowledgeable and competent in the following areas as appropriate to assigned duties and responsibilities—

(a) Authority of the pilot in command;

(b) Passenger handling, including procedures to be followed in handling deranged persons or other persons whose conduct might jeopardize safety;

(c) Crewmember assignments, functions, and responsibilities during ditching and evacuation of persons who may need the assistance of another person to move expeditiously to an exit in an emergency;

(d) Briefing of passengers;

(e) Location and operation of portable fire extinguishers and other items of emergency equipment;

(f) Proper use of cabin equipment and controls;

(g) Location and operation of passenger oxygen equipment;

(h) Location and operation of all normal and emergency exits, including evacuation chutes and escape ropes; and

(i) Seating of persons who may need assistance of another person to move rapidly to an exit in an emergency as prescribed by the certificate holder's operations manual.

§135.297 Pilot in command: Instrument proficiency check requirements.

(a) No certificate holder may use a pilot, nor may any person serve, as a pilot in command of an aircraft under IFR unless, since the beginning of the 6th calendar month before that service, that pilot has passed an instrument proficiency check under this section administered by the Administrator or an authorized check pilot.

(b) No pilot may use any type of precision instrument approach procedure under IFR unless, since the beginning of the 6th calendar month before that use, the pilot satisfactorily demonstrated that type of approach procedure. No pilot may use any type of nonprecision approach procedure under IFR unless, since the beginning of the 6th calendar month before that use, the pilot has satisfactorily demonstrated either that type of approach procedure or any other two different types of nonprecision approach procedures. The instrument approach procedure or procedures must include at least one straight-in approach, one circling approach, and one missed approach. Each type of approach procedure demonstrated must be conducted to published minimums for that procedure.

(c) The instrument proficiency check required by paragraph (a) of this section consists of an oral or written equipment test and a flight check under simulated or actual IFR conditions. The equipment test includes questions on emergency procedures, engine operation, fuel and lubrication systems, power settings, stall speeds, best engine-out speed, propeller and supercharger operations, and hydraulic, mechanical, and electrical systems, as appropriate. The flight check includes navigation by instruments, recovery from simulated emergencies, and standard instrument approaches involving navigational facilities which that pilot is to be authorized to use. Each pilot taking the instrument proficiency check must show that standard of competence required by §135.293(d).

(1) The instrument proficiency check must—

(i) For a pilot in command of an airplane under §135.243(a), include the procedures and maneuvers for an airline transport pilot certificate in the particular type of airplane, if appropriate; and

(ii) For a pilot in command of an airplane or helicopter under §135.243(c), include the procedures and maneuvers for a commercial pilot certificate with an instrument rating and, if required, for the appropriate type rating.

(2) The instrument proficiency check must be given by an authorized check airman or by the Administrator.

(d) If the pilot in command is assigned to pilot only one type of aircraft, that pilot must take the instrument proficiency check required by paragraph (a) of this section in that type of aircraft.

(e) If the pilot in command is assigned to pilot more than one type of aircraft, that pilot must take the instrument proficiency check required by paragraph (a) of this section in each type of aircraft to which that pilot is assigned, in rotation, but not more than one flight check during each period described in paragraph (a) of this section.

(f) If the pilot in command is assigned to pilot both single-engine and multiengine aircraft, that pilot must initially take the instrument proficiency check required by paragraph (a) of this section in a multiengine aircraft, and each succeeding check alternately in single-engine and multiengine aircraft, but not more than one flight check during each period described in paragraph (a) of this section. Portions of a required flight check may be given in an aircraft simulator or other appropriate training device, if approved by the Administrator.

(g) If the pilot in command is authorized to use an autopilot system in place of a second in command, that pilot must show, during the required instrument proficiency check, that the pilot is able (without a second in command) both with and without using the autopilot to—

(1) Conduct instrument operations competently; and

(2) Properly conduct air-ground communications and comply with complex air traffic control instructions.

(3) Each pilot taking the autopilot check must show that, while using the autopilot, the airplane can be operated as proficiently as it would be if a second in command were present to handle air-ground communications and air traffic control instructions. The autopilot check need only be demonstrated once every 12 calendar months during the instrument proficiency check required under paragraph (a) of this section.

[Docket No. 16097, 43 FR 46783, Oct. 10, 1978; as amended by Amdt. 135–15, 46 FR 30971, June 11, 1981]

§135.299 Pilot in command: Line checks: Routes and airports.

(a) No certificate holder may use a pilot, nor may any person serve, as a pilot in command of a flight unless, since the beginning of the 12th calendar month before that service, that pilot has passed a flight check in one of the types of aircraft which that pilot is to fly. The flight check shall—

(1) Be given by an approved check pilot or by the Administrator;

(2) Consist of at least one flight over one route segment; and

(3) Include takeoffs and landings at one or more representative airports. In addition to the requirements of this paragraph, for a pilot authorized to conduct IFR operations, at least one flight shall be flown over a civil airway, an approved off-airway route, or a portion of either of them.

(b) The pilot who conducts the check shall determine whether the pilot being checked satisfactorily performs the duties and responsibilities of a pilot in command in operations under this part, and shall so certify in the pilot training record.

(c) Each certificate holder shall establish in the manual required by §135.21 a procedure which will ensure that each pilot who has not flown over a route and into an airport within the preceding 90 days will, before beginning the flight, become familiar with all available information required for the safe operation of that flight.

§135.301 Crewmember: Tests and checks, grace provisions, training to accepted standards.

(a) If a crewmember who is required to take a test or a flight check under this part, completes the test or flight check in the calendar month before or after the calendar month in which it is required, that crewmember is considered to have completed the test or check in the calendar month in which it is required.

(b) If a pilot being checked under this subpart fails any of the required maneuvers, the person giving the check may give additional training to the pilot during the course of the check. In addition to repeating the maneuvers failed, the person giving the check may require the pilot being checked to repeat any other maneuvers that are necessary to determine the pilot's proficiency. If the pilot being checked is unable to demonstrate satisfactory performance to the person conducting the check, the certificate holder may not use the pilot, nor may the pilot serve, as a flight crewmember in operations under this part until the pilot has satisfactorily completed the check.

Subpart H—Training

§135.321 Applicability and terms used.

(a) Except as provided in §135.3, this subpart prescribes the requirements applicable to—

(1) A certificate holder under this part which contracts with, or otherwise arranges to use the services of a training center certificated under part 142 to perform training, testing, and checking functions;

(2) Each certificate holder for establishing and maintaining an approved training program for crewmembers, check airmen and instructors, and other operations personnel employed or used by that certificate holder; and

(3) Each certificate holder for the qualification, approval, and use of aircraft simulators and flight training devices in the conduct of the program.

(b) For the purposes of this subpart, the following terms and definitions apply:

(1) ***Initial training.*** The training required for crewmembers who have not qualified and served in the same capacity on an aircraft.

(2) ***Transition training.*** The training required for crewmembers who have qualified and served in the same capacity on another aircraft.

(3) ***Upgrade training.*** The training required for crewmembers who have qualified and served as second in command on a particular aircraft type, before they serve as pilot in command on that aircraft.

(4) ***Differences training.*** The training required for crewmembers who have qualified and served on a particular type aircraft, when the Administrator finds differences training is necessary before a crewmember serves in the same capacity on a particular variation of that aircraft.

(5) ***Recurrent training.*** The training required for crewmembers to remain adequately trained and currently proficient for each aircraft, crewmember position, and type of operation in which the crewmember serves.

(6) ***In flight.*** The maneuvers, procedures, or functions that must be conducted in the aircraft.

(7) ***Training center.*** An organization governed by the applicable requirements of part 142 of this chapter that conducts training, testing, and checking under contract or other arrangement to certificate holders subject to the requirements of this part.

(8) ***Requalification training.*** The training required for crewmembers previously trained and qualified, but who have become unqualified due to not having met within the required period the—

(i) Recurrent pilot testing requirements of §135.293;

(ii) Instrument proficiency check requirements of §135.297; or

(iii) Line checks required by §135.299.

[Docket No. 16097, 43 FR 46783, Oct. 10, 1978; as amended by Amdt. 135–57, 60 FR 65950, Dec. 20, 1995; Amdt. 135–63, 61 FR 34561, July 2, 1996; Amdt. 135–91, 68 FR 54588, Sept. 17, 2003]

§135.323 Training program: General.

(a) Each certificate holder required to have a training program under §135.341 shall:

(1) Establish, obtain the appropriate initial and final approval of, and provide a training program that meets this subpart and that ensures that each crewmember, flight instructor, check airman, and each person assigned duties for the carriage and handling of hazardous materials (as defined in 49 CFR 171.8) is adequately trained to perform their assigned duties.

(2) Provide adequate ground and flight training facilities and properly qualified ground instructors for the training required by this subpart.

(3) Provide and keep current for each aircraft type used and, if applicable, the particular variations within the aircraft type, appropriate training material, examinations, forms, instructions, and procedures for use in conducting the training and checks required by this subpart.

(4) Provide enough flight instructors, check airmen, and simulator instructors to conduct required flight training and flight checks, and simulator training courses allowed under this subpart.

(b) Whenever a crewmember who is required to take recurrent training under this subpart completes the training in the calendar month before, or the calendar month after, the month in which that training is required, the crewmember is considered to have completed it in the calendar month in which it was required.

(c) Each instructor, supervisor, or check airman who is responsible for a particular ground training subject, segment of flight training, course of training, flight check, or competence check under this part shall certify as to the proficiency and knowledge of the crewmember, flight instructor, or check airman concerned upon completion of that training or check. That certification shall be made a part of the crewmember's record. When the certification required by this paragraph is made by an entry in a computerized recordkeeping system, the certifying instructor, supervisor, or check airman, must be identified with that entry. However, the signature of the certifying instructor, supervisor, or check airman, is not required for computerized entries.

(d) Training subjects that apply to more than one aircraft or crewmember position and that have been satisfactorily completed during previous training while employed by the certificate holder for another aircraft or another crewmember position, need not be repeated during subsequent training other than recurrent training.

(e) Aircraft simulators and other training devices may be used in the certificate holder's training program if approved by the Administrator.

§135.324 Training program: Special rules.

(a) Other than the certificate holder, only another certificate holder certificated under this part or a training center certificated under part 142 of this chapter is eligible under this subpart to conduct training, testing, and checking under contract or other arrangement to those persons subject to the requirements of this subpart.

(b) A certificate holder may contract with, or otherwise arrange to use the services of, a training center certificated under part 142 of this chapter to conduct training, testing, and checking required by this part only if the training center—

(1) Holds applicable training specifications issued under part 142 of this chapter;

(2) Has facilities, training equipment, and course-ware meeting the applicable requirements of part 142 of this chapter;

(3) Has approved curriculums, curriculum segments, and portions of curriculum segments applicable for use in training courses required by this subpart; and

(4) Has sufficient instructor and check airmen qualified under the applicable requirements of §§135.337 through 135.340 to provide training, testing, and checking to persons subject to the requirements of this subpart.

[Docket No. 26933, 61 FR 34562, July 2, 1996; as amended by Amdt. 135–67, 62 FR 13791, March 21, 1997; Amdt. 135–91, 68 FR 54588, Sept. 17, 2003]

§135.325 Training program and revision: Initial and final approval.

(a) To obtain initial and final approval of a training program, or a revision to an approved training program, each certificate holder must submit to the Administrator—

(1) An outline of the proposed or revised curriculum, that provides enough information for a preliminary evaluation of the proposed training program or revision; and

(2) Additional relevant information that may be requested by the Administrator.

(b) If the proposed training program or revision complies with this subpart, the Administrator grants initial approval in writing after which the certificate holder may conduct the training under that program. The Administrator then evaluates the effectiveness of the training program and advises the certificate holder of deficiencies, if any, that must be corrected.

(c) The Administrator grants final approval of the proposed training program or revision if the certificate holder shows that the training conducted under the initial approval in paragraph (b) of this section ensures that each person who successfully completes the training is adequately trained to perform that person's assigned duties.

(d) Whenever the Administrator finds that revisions are necessary for the continued adequacy of a training program that has been granted final approval, the certificate holder shall, after notification by the Administrator, make any changes in the program that are found necessary by the Administrator. Within 30 days after the certificate holder receives the notice, it may file a petition to reconsider the notice with the Administrator. The filing of a petition to reconsider stays the notice pending a decision by the Administrator. However, if the Administrator finds that there is an emergency that requires immediate action in the interest of safety, the Administrator may, upon a statement of the reasons, require a change effective without stay.

§135.327 Training program: Curriculum.

(a) Each certificate holder must prepare and keep current a written training program curriculum for each type of aircraft for each crewmember required for that type aircraft. The curriculum must include ground and flight training required by this subpart.

(b) Each training program curriculum must include the following:

(1) A list of principal ground training subjects, including emergency training subjects, that are provided.

(2) A list of all the training devices, mockups, systems trainers, procedures trainers, or other training aids that the certificate holder will use.

(3) Detailed descriptions or pictorial displays of the approved normal, abnormal, and emergency maneuvers, procedures and functions that will be performed during each flight training phase or flight check, indicating those maneuvers, procedures and functions that are to be performed during the inflight portions of flight training and flight checks.

§135.329 Crewmember training requirements.

(a) Each certificate holder must include in its training program the following initial and transition ground training as appropriate to the particular assignment of the crewmember:

(1) Basic indoctrination ground training for newly hired crewmembers including instruction in at least the—

(i) Duties and responsibilities of crewmembers as applicable;

(ii) Appropriate provisions of this chapter;

(iii) Contents of the certificate holder's operating certificate and operations specifications (not required for flight attendants); and

(iv) Appropriate portions of the certificate holder's operating manual.

(2) The initial and transition ground training in §§135.345 and 135.349, as applicable.

(3) Emergency training in §135.331.

(b) Each training program must provide the initial and transition flight training in §135.347, as applicable.

(c) Each training program must provide recurrent ground and flight training in §135.351.

(d) Upgrade training in §§135.345 and 135.347 for a particular type aircraft may be included in the training program for crewmembers who have qualified and served as second in command on that aircraft.

(e) In addition to initial, transition, upgrade and recurrent training, each training program must provide ground and flight training, instruction, and practice necessary to ensure that each crewmember—

(1) Remains adequately trained and currently proficient for each aircraft, crewmember position, and type of operation in which the crewmember serves; and

(2) Qualifies in new equipment, facilities, procedures, and techniques, including modifications to aircraft.

§135.331 Crewmember emergency training.

(a) Each training program must provide emergency training under this section for each aircraft type, model, and configuration, each crewmember, and each kind of operation conducted, as appropriate for each crewmember and the certificate holder.

(b) Emergency training must provide the following:

(1) Instruction in emergency assignments and procedures, including coordination among crewmembers.

(2) Individual instruction in the location, function, and operation of emergency equipment including—

(i) Equipment used in ditching and evacuation;

(ii) First aid equipment and its proper use; and

(iii) Portable fire extinguishers, with emphasis on the type of extinguisher to be used on different classes of fires.

(3) Instruction in the handling of emergency situations including—

(i) Rapid decompression;

(ii) Fire in flight or on the surface and smoke control procedures with emphasis on electrical equipment and related circuit breakers found in cabin areas;

(iii) Ditching and evacuation;

(iv) Illness, injury, or other abnormal situations involving passengers or crewmembers; and

(v) Hijacking and other unusual situations.

(4) Review of the certificate holder's previous aircraft accidents and incidents involving actual emergency situations.

(c) Each crewmember must perform at least the following emergency drills, using the proper emergency equipment and procedures, unless the Administrator finds that, for a particular drill, the crewmember can be adequately trained by demonstration:

(1) Ditching, if applicable.

(2) Emergency evacuation.

(3) Fire extinguishing and smoke control.

(4) Operation and use of emergency exits, including deployment and use of evacuation chutes, if applicable.

(5) Use of crew and passenger oxygen.

(6) Removal of life rafts from the aircraft, inflation of the life rafts, use of life lines, and boarding of passengers and crew, if applicable.

(7) Donning and inflation of life vests and the use of other individual flotation devices, if applicable.

(d) Crewmembers who serve in operations above 25,000 feet must receive instruction in the following:

(1) Respiration.

(2) Hypoxia.

(3) Duration of consciousness without supplemental oxygen at altitude.

(4) Gas expansion.

(5) Gas bubble formation.

(6) Physical phenomena and incidents of decompression.

§135.333 Training requirements: Handling and carriage of hazardous materials.

(a) Except as provided in paragraph (d) of this section, no certificate holder may use any person to perform, and no person may perform, any assigned duties and responsibilities for the handling or carriage of hazardous materials (as defined in 49 CFR 171.8), unless within the preceding 12 calendar months that person has satisfactorily completed initial or recurrent training in an appropriate training program established by the certificate holder, which includes instruction regarding—

(1) The proper shipper certification, packaging, marking, labeling, and documentation for hazardous materials; and

(2) The compatibility, loading, storage, and handling characteristics of hazardous materials.

(b) Each certificate holder shall maintain a record of the satisfactory completion of the initial and recurrent training given to crewmembers and ground personnel who perform assigned duties and responsibilities for the handling and carriage of hazardous materials.

(c) Each certificate holder that elects not to accept hazardous materials shali ensure that each crewmember is adequately trained to recognize those items classified as hazardous materials.

(d) If a certificate holder operates into or out of airports at which trained employees or contract personnel are not available, it may use persons not meeting the requirements of paragraphs (a) and (b) of this section to load, offload, or otherwise handle hazardous materials if these persons are supervised by a crewmember who is qualified under paragraphs (a) and (b) of this section.

§135.335 Approval of aircraft simulators and other training devices.

(a) Training courses using aircraft simulators and other training devices may be included in the certificate holder's training program if approved by the Administrator.

(b) Each aircraft simulator and other training device that is used in a training course or in checks required under this subpart must meet the following requirements:

(1) It must be specifically approved for—

(i) The certificate holder; and

(ii) The particular maneuver, procedure, or crewmember function involved.

(2) It must maintain the performance, functional, and other characteristics that are required for approval.

(3) Additionally, for aircraft simulators, it must be—

(i) Approved for the type aircraft and, if applicable, the particular variation within type for which the training or check is being conducted; and

(ii) Modified to conform with any modification to the aircraft being simulated that changes the performance, functional, or other characteristics required for approval.

(c) A particular aircraft simulator or other training device may be used by more than one certificate holder.

(d) In granting initial and final approval of training programs or revisions to them, the Administrator considers the training devices, methods and procedures listed in the certificate holder's curriculum under §135.327.

[Docket No. 16907, 43 FR 46783, Oct. 10, 1978; as amended by Amdt. 135–1, 44 FR 26738, May 7, 1979]

§135.337 Qualifications: Check airmen (aircraft) and check airmen (simulator).

(a) For the purposes of this section and §135.339:

(1) A check airman (aircraft) is a person who is qualified to conduct flight checks in an aircraft, in a flight simulator, or in a flight training device for a particular type aircraft.

(2) A check airman (simulator) is a person who is qualified to conduct flight checks, but only in a flight simulator, in a flight training device, or both, for a particular type aircraft.

(3) Check airmen (aircraft) and check airmen (simulator) are those check airmen who perform the functions described in §§135.321(a) and 135.323(a)(4) and (c).

(b) No certificate holder may use a person, nor may any person serve as a check airman (aircraft) in a training program established under this subpart unless, with respect to the aircraft type involved, that person—

(1) Holds the airman certificates and ratings required to serve as a pilot in command in operations under this part;

(2) Has satisfactorily completed the training phases for the aircraft, including recurrent training, that are required to serve as a pilot in command in operations under this part;

(3) Has satisfactorily completed the proficiency or competency checks that are required to serve as a pilot in command in operations under this part;

(4) Has satisfactorily completed the applicable training requirements of §135.339;

(5) Holds at least a Class III medical certificate unless serving as a required crewmember, in which case holds a Class I or Class II medical certificate as appropriate.

(6) Has satisfied the recency of experience requirements of §135.247; and

(7) Has been approved by the Administrator for the check airman duties involved.

(c) No certificate holder may use a person, nor may any person serve as a check airman (simulator) in a training program established under this subpart unless, with respect to the aircraft type involved, that person meets the provisions of paragraph (b) of this section, or—

(1) Holds the applicable airman certificates and ratings, except medical certificate, required to serve as a pilot in command in operations under this part;

(2) Has satisfactorily completed the appropriate training phases for the aircraft, including recurrent training, that are required to serve as a pilot in command in operations under this part;

(3) Has satisfactorily completed the appropriate proficiency or competency checks that are required to serve as a pilot in command in operations under this part;

(4) Has satisfactorily completed the applicable training requirements of §135.339; and

(5) Has been approved by the Administrator for the check airman (simulator) duties involved.

(d) Completion of the requirements in paragraphs (b)(2), (3), and (4) or (c)(2), (3), and (4) of this section, as applicable, shall be entered in the individual's training record maintained by the certificate holder.

(e) Check airmen who do not hold an appropriate medical certificate may function as check airmen (simulator), but may not serve as flightcrew members in operations under this part.

(f) A check airman (simulator) must accomplish the following—

(1) Fly at least two flight segments as a required crewmember for the type, class, or category aircraft involved within the 12-month preceding the performance of any check airman duty in a flight simulator; or

(2) Satisfactorily complete an approved line-observation program within the period prescribed by that program and that must precede the performance of any check airman duty in a flight simulator.

(g) The flight segments or line-observation program required in paragraph (f) of this section are considered to be completed in the month required if completed in the calendar month before or the calendar month after the month in which they are due.

[Docket No. 28471, 61 FR 30744, June 17, 1996]

§135.338 Qualifications: Flight instructors (aircraft) and flight instructors (simulator).

(a) For the purposes of this section and §135.340:

(1) A flight instructor (aircraft) is a person who is qualified to instruct in an aircraft, in a flight simulator, or in a flight training device for a particular type, class, or category aircraft.

(2) A flight instructor (simulator) is a person who is qualified to instruct in a flight simulator, in a flight training device, or in both, for a particular type, class, or category aircraft.

(3) Flight instructors (aircraft) and flight instructors (simulator) are those instructors who perform the functions described in §§135.321(a) and 135.323 (a)(4) and (c).

(b) No certificate holder may use a person, nor may any person serve as a flight instructor (aircraft) in a training program established under this subpart unless, with respect to the type, class, or category aircraft involved, that person—

(1) Holds the airman certificates and ratings required to serve as a pilot in command in operations under this part;

(2) Has satisfactorily completed the training phases for the aircraft, including recurrent training, that are required to serve as a pilot in command in operations under this part;

(3) Has satisfactorily completed the proficiency or competency checks that are required to serve as a pilot in command in operations under this part;

(4) Has satisfactorily completed the applicable training requirements of §135.340;

(5) Holds at least a Class III medical certificate; and

(6) Has satisfied the recency of experience requirements of §135.247.

(c) No certificate holder may use a person, nor may any person serve as a flight instructor (simulator) in a training program established under this subpart, unless, with respect to the type, class, or category aircraft involved, that person meets the provisions of paragraph (b) of this section, or—

(1) Holds the airman certificates and ratings, except medical certificate, required to serve as a pilot in command in operations under this part except before March 19, 1997 that person need not hold a type rating for the type, class, or category of aircraft involved.

(2) Has satisfactorily completed the appropriate training phases for the aircraft, including recurrent training, that are required to serve as a pilot in command in operations under this part;

(3) Has satisfactorily completed the appropriate proficiency or competency checks that are required to serve as a pilot in command in operations under this part; and

(4) Has satisfactorily completed the applicable training requirements of §135.340.

(d) Completion of the requirements in paragraphs (b) (2), (3), and (4) or (c) (2), (3), and (4) of this section, as applicable, shall be entered in the individual's training record maintained by the certificate holder.

(e) An airman who does not hold a medical certificate may function as a flight instructor in an aircraft if functioning as a non-required crewmember, but may not serve as a flightcrew member in operations under this part.

(f) A flight instructor (simulator) must accomplish the following—

(1) Fly at least two flight segments as a required crewmember for the type, class, or category aircraft involved within the 12-month period preceding the performance of any flight instructor duty in a flight simulator; or

(2) Satisfactorily complete an approved line-observation program within the period prescribed by that program and that must precede the performance of any check airman duty in a flight simulator.

(g) The flight segments or line-observation program required in paragraph (f) of this section are considered completed in the month required if completed in the calendar month before, or in the calendar month after, the month in which they are due.

[Docket No. 28471, 61 FR 30744, June 17, 1996; as amended by Amdt. 135–64, 62 FR 3739, Jan. 24, 1997]

§135.339 Initial and transition training and checking: Check airmen (aircraft), check airmen (simulator).

(a) No certificate holder may use a person nor may any person serve as a check airman unless—

(1) That person has satisfactorily completed initial or transition check airman training; and

(2) Within the preceding 24 calendar months, that person satisfactorily conducts a proficiency or competency check under the observation of an FAA inspector or an aircrew designated examiner employed by the operator. The observation check may be accomplished in part or in full in an aircraft, in a flight simulator, or in a flight training device. This paragraph applies after March 19, 1997.

(b) The observation check required by paragraph (a)(2) of this section is considered to have been completed in the month required if completed in the calendar month before or the calendar month after the month in which it is due.

(c) The initial ground training for check airmen must include the following:

(1) Check airman duties, functions, and responsibilities.

(2) The applicable Code of Federal Regulations and the certificate holder's policies and procedures.

(3) The applicable methods, procedures, and techniques for conducting the required checks.

(4) Proper evaluation of student performance including the detection of—

(i) Improper and insufficient training; and

(ii) Personal characteristics of an applicant that could adversely affect safety.

(5) The corrective action in the case of unsatisfactory checks.

(6) The approved methods, procedures, and limitations for performing the required normal, abnormal, and emergency procedures in the aircraft.

(d) The transition ground training for check airmen must include the approved methods, procedures, and limitations for performing the required normal, abnormal, and emergency procedures applicable to the aircraft to which the check airman is in transition.

(e) The initial and transition flight training for check airmen (aircraft) must include the following—

(1) The safety measures for emergency situations that are likely to develop during a check;

(2) The potential results of improper, untimely, or nonexecution of safety measures during a check;

(3) Training and practice in conducting flight checks from the left and right pilot seats in the required normal, abnormal, and emergency procedures to ensure competence to conduct the pilot flight checks required by this part; and

(4) The safety measures to be taken from either pilot seat for emergency situations that are likely to develop during checking.

(f) The requirements of paragraph (e) of this section may be accomplished in full or in part in flight, in a flight simulator, or in a flight training device, as appropriate.

(g) The initial and transition flight training for check airmen (simulator) must include the following:

(1) Training and practice in conducting flight checks in the required normal, abnormal, and emergency procedures to ensure competence to conduct the flight checks required by this part. This training and practice must be accomplished in a flight simulator or in a flight training device.

(2) Training in the operation of flight simulators, flight training devices, or both, to ensure competence to conduct the flight checks required by this part.

[Docket No. 28471, 61 FR 30745, June 17, 1996; as amended by Amdt. 135–64, 62 FR 3739, Jan. 24, 1997]

§135.340 Initial and transition training and checking: Flight instructors (aircraft), flight instructors (simulator).

(a) No certificate holder may use a person nor may any person serve as a flight instructor unless—

(1) That person has satisfactorily completed initial or transition flight instructor training; and

(2) Within the preceding 24 calendar months, that person satisfactorily conducts instruction under the observation of an FAA inspector, an operator check airman, or an aircrew designated examiner employed by the operator. The observation check may be accomplished in part or in full in an aircraft, in a flight simulator, or in a flight training device. This paragraph applies after March 19, 1997.

(b) The observation check required by paragraph (a)(2) of this section is considered to have been completed in the month required if completed in the calendar month before, or the calendar month after, the month in which it is due.

(c) The initial ground training for flight instructors must include the following:

(1) Flight instructor duties, functions, and responsibilities.

(2) The applicable Code of Federal Regulations and the certificate holder's policies and procedures.

(3) The applicable methods, procedures, and techniques for conducting flight instruction.

(4) Proper evaluation of student performance including the detection of—

(i) Improper and insufficient training; and

(ii) Personal characteristics of an applicant that could adversely affect safety.

(5) The corrective action in the case of unsatisfactory training progress.

(6) The approved methods, procedures, and limitations for performing the required normal, abnormal, and emergency procedures in the aircraft.

(7) Except for holders of a flight instructor certificate—

(i) The fundamental principles of the teaching-learning process;

(ii) Teaching methods and procedures; and

(iii) The instructor-student relationship.

(d) The transition ground training for flight instructors must include the approved methods, procedures, and limitations for performing the required normal, abnormal, and emergency procedures applicable to the type, class, or category aircraft to which the flight instructor is in transition.

(e) The initial and transition flight training for flight instructors (aircraft) must include the following—

(1) The safety measures for emergency situations that are likely to develop during instruction;

(2) The potential results of improper or untimely safety measures during instruction;

(3) Training and practice from the left and right pilot seats in the required normal, abnormal, and emergency maneuvers to ensure competence to conduct the flight instruction required by this part; and

(4) The safety measures to be taken from either the left or right pilot seat for emergency situations that are likely to develop during instruction.

(f) The requirements of paragraph (e) of this section may be accomplished in full or in part in flight, in a flight simulator, or in a flight training device, as appropriate.

(g) The initial and transition flight training for a flight instructor (simulator) must include the following:

(1) Training and practice in the required normal, abnormal, and emergency procedures to ensure competence to conduct the flight instruction required by this part. These maneuvers and procedures must be accomplished in full or in part in a flight simulator or in a flight training device.

(2) Training in the operation of flight simulators, flight training devices, or both, to ensure competence to conduct the flight instruction required by this part.

[Docket No. 28471, 61 FR 30745, June 17, 1996; as amended by Amdt. 135–64, 62 FR 3739, Jan. 24, 1997]

§135.341 Pilot and flight attendant crewmember training programs.

(a) Each certificate holder, other than one who uses only one pilot in the certificate holder's operations, shall establish and maintain an approved pilot training program, and each certificate holder who uses a flight attendant crewmember shall establish and maintain an approved flight attendant training program, that is appropriate to the operations to which each pilot and flight attendant is to be assigned, and will ensure that they are adequately trained to meet the applicable knowledge and practical testing requirements of §§135.293 through 135.301. However, the Administrator may authorize a deviation from this section if the Administrator finds that, because of the limited size and scope of the operation, safety will allow a deviation from these requirements.

(b) Each certificate holder required to have a training program by paragraph (a) of this section shall include in that program ground and flight training curriculums for—

(1) Initial training;

(2) Transition training;
(3) Upgrade training;
(4) Differences training; and
(5) Recurrent training.

(c) Each certificate holder required to have a training program by paragraph (a) of this section shall provide current and appropriate study materials for use by each required pilot and flight attendant.

(d) The certificate holder shall furnish copies of the pilot and flight attendant crewmember training program, and all changes and additions, to the assigned representative of the Administrator. If the certificate holder uses training facilities of other persons, a copy of those training programs or appropriate portions used for those facilities shall also be furnished. Curricula that follow FAA published curricula may be cited by reference in the copy of the training program furnished to the representative of the Administrator and need not be furnished with the program.

[Docket No. 16097, 43 FR 46783, Oct. 10, 1978; as amended by Amdt. 135–18, 47 FR 33396, Aug. 2, 1982]

§135.343 Crewmember initial and recurrent training requirements.

No certificate holder may use a person, nor may any person serve, as a crewmember in operations under this part unless that crewmember has completed the appropriate initial or recurrent training phase of the training program appropriate to the type of operation in which the crewmember is to serve since the beginning of the 12th calendar month before that service. This section does not apply to a certificate holder that uses only one pilot in the certificate holder's operations.

[Docket No. 16097, 43 FR 46783, Oct. 10, 1978; as amended by Amdt. 135–18, 47 FR 33396, Aug. 2, 1982]

§135.345 Pilots: Initial, transition, and upgrade ground training.

Initial, transition, and upgrade ground training for pilots must include instruction in at least the following, as applicable to their duties:

(a) General subjects—

(1) The certificate holder's flight locating procedures;

(2) Principles and methods for determining weight and balance, and runway limitations for takeoff and landing;

(3) Enough meteorology to ensure a practical knowledge of weather phenomena, including the principles of frontal systems, icing, fog, thunderstorms, windshear and, if appropriate, high altitude weather situations;

(4) Air traffic control systems, procedures, and phraseology;

(5) Navigation and the use of navigational aids, including instrument approach procedures;

(6) Normal and emergency communication procedures;

(7) Visual cues before and during descent below DH or MDA; and

(8) Other instructions necessary to ensure the pilot's competence.

(b) For each aircraft type—

(1) A general description;

(2) Performance characteristics;

(3) Engines and propellers;

(4) Major components;

(5) Major aircraft systems (i.e., flight controls, electrical, and hydraulic), other systems, as appropriate, principles of normal, abnormal, and emergency operations, appropriate procedures and limitations;

(6) Knowledge and procedures for—

(i) Recognizing and avoiding severe weather situations;

(ii) Escaping from severe weather situations, in case of inadvertent encounters, including low-altitude windshear (except that rotorcraft pilots are not required to be trained in escaping from low-altitude windshear);

(iii) Operating in or near thunderstorms (including best penetrating altitudes), turbulent air (including clear air turbulence), icing, hail, and other potentially hazardous meteorological conditions; and

(iv) Operating airplanes during ground icing conditions, (i.e., any time conditions are such that frost, ice, or snow may reasonably be expected to adhere to the airplane), if the certificate holder expects to authorize takeoffs in ground icing conditions, including:

(A) The use of holdover times when using deicing/anti-icing fluids:

(B) Airplane deicing/anti-icing procedures, including inspection and check procedures and responsibilities.

(C) Communications;

(D) Airplane surface contamination (i.e., adherence of frost, ice, or snow) and critical area identification, and knowledge of how contamination adversely affects airplane performance and flight characteristics;

(E) Types and characteristics of deicing/anti-icing fluids, if used by the certificates holder;

(F) Cold weather preflight inspection procedures;

(G) Techniques for recognizing contamination on the airplane;

(7) Operating limitations;

(8) Fuel consumption and cruise control;

(9) Flight planning;

(10) Each normal and emergency procedure; and

(11) The approved Aircraft Flight Manual, or equivalent.

[Docket No. 16097, 43 FR 46783, Oct. 10, 1978; as amended by Amdt. 135–27, 53 FR 37697, Sept. 27, 1988; Amdt. 135–46, 58 FR 69630, Dec. 30, 1993]

§135.347 Pilots: Initial, transition, upgrade, and differences flight training.

(a) Initial, transition, upgrade, and differences training for pilots must include flight and practice in each of the maneuvers and procedures in the approved training program curriculum.

(b) The maneuvers and procedures required by paragraph (a) of this section must be performed in flight, except to the extent that certain maneuvers and procedures may be performed in an aircraft simulator, or an appropriate training device, as allowed by this subpart.

(c) If the certificate holder's approved training program includes a course of training using an aircraft simulator or other training device, each pilot must successfully complete—

(1) Training and practice in the simulator or training device in at least the maneuvers and procedures in this subpart that

are capable of being performed in the aircraft simulator or training device; and

(2) A flight check in the aircraft or a check in the simulator or training device to the level of proficiency of a pilot in command or second in command, as applicable, in at least the maneuvers and procedures that are capable of being performed in an aircraft simulator or training device.

§135.349 Flight attendants: Initial and transition ground training.

Initial and transition ground training for flight attendants must include instruction in at least the following—

(a) General subjects—

(1) The authority of the pilot in command; and

(2) Passenger handling, including procedures to be followed in handling deranged persons or other persons whose conduct might jeopardize safety.

(b) For each aircraft type—

(1) A general description of the aircraft emphasizing physical characteristics that may have a bearing on ditching, evacuation, and inflight emergency procedures and on other related duties;

(2) The use of both the public address system and the means of communicating with other flight crewmembers, including emergency means in the case of attempted hijacking or other unusual situations; and

(3) Proper use of electrical galley equipment and the controls for cabin heat and ventilation.

§135.351 Recurrent training.

(a) Each certificate holder must ensure that each crewmember receives recurrent training and is adequately trained and currently proficient for the type aircraft and crewmember position involved.

(b) Recurrent ground training for crewmembers must include at least the following:

(1) A quiz or other review to determine the crewmember's knowledge of the aircraft and crewmember position involved.

(2) Instruction as necessary in the subjects required for initial ground training by this subpart, as appropriate, including low-altitude windshear training and training on operating during ground icing conditions, as prescribed in §135.341 and described in §135.345, and emergency training.

(c) Recurrent flight training for pilots must include, at least, flight training in the maneuvers or procedures in this subpart, except that satisfactory completion of the check required by §135.293 within the preceding 12 calendar months may be substituted for recurrent flight training.

[Docket No. 16097, 43 FR 46783, Oct. 10, 1978; as amended by Amdt. 135–27, 53 FR 37698, Sept. 27, 1988; Amdt. 135–46, 58 FR 69630, Dec. 30, 1993]

§135.353 Prohibited drugs.

(a) Each certificate holder or operator shall provide each employee performing a function listed in Appendix I to part 121 of this chapter and his or her supervisor with the training specified in that appendix.

(b) No certificate holder or operator may use any contractor to perform a function specified in Appendix I to part 121 of this chapter unless that contractor provides each of its employees performing that function for the certificate holder or the operator and his or her supervisor with the training specified in that appendix.

[Docket No. 25148, 53 FR 47061, Nov. 21, 1988]

Subpart I— Airplane Performance Operating Limitations

§135.361 Applicability.

(a) This subpart prescribes airplane performance operating limitations applicable to the operation of the categories of airplanes listed in §135.363 when operated under this part.

(b) For the purpose of this subpart, *effective length of the runway,* for landing means the distance from the point at which the obstruction clearance plane associated with the approach end of the runway intersects the centerline of the runway to the far end of the runway.

(c) For the purpose of this subpart, *obstruction clearance plane* means a plane sloping upward from the runway at a slope of 1:20 to the horizontal, and tangent to or clearing all obstructions within a specified area surrounding the runway as shown in a profile view of that area. In the plan view, the centerline of the specified area coincides with the centerline of the runway, beginning at the point where the obstruction clearance plane intersects the centerline of the runway and proceeding to a point at least 1,500 feet from the beginning point. After that the centerline coincides with the takeoff path over the ground for the runway (in the case of takeoffs) or with the instrument approach counterpart (for landings), or, where the applicable one of these paths has not been established, it proceeds consistent with turns of at least 4,000-foot radius until a point is reached beyond which the obstruction clearance plane clears all obstructions. This area extends laterally 200 feet on each side of the centerline at the point where the obstruction clearance plane intersects the runway and continues at this width to the end of the runway; then it increases uniformly to 500 feet on each side of the centerline at a point 1,500 feet from the intersection of the obstruction clearance plane with the runway; after that it extends laterally 500 feet on each side of the centerline.

§135.363 General.

(a) Each certificate holder operating a reciprocating engine powered large transport category airplane shall comply with §§135.365 through 135.377.

(b) Each certificate holder operating a turbine engine powered large transport category airplane shall comply with §§135.379 through 135.387, except that when it operates a turbopropeller-powered large transport category airplane certificated after August 29, 1959, but previously type certificated with the same number of reciprocating engines, it may comply with §§135.365 through 135.377.

(c) Each certificate holder operating a large nontransport category airplane shall comply with §§135.389 through 135.395 and any determination of compliance must be based only on approved performance data. For the purpose of this subpart, a large nontransport category airplane is an airplane that was type certificated before July 1, 1942.

(d) Each certificate holder operating a small transport category airplane shall comply with §135.397.

(e) Each certificate holder operating a small nontransport category airplane shall comply with §135.399.

(f) The performance data in the Airplane Flight Manual applies in determining compliance with §§135.365 through 135.387. Where conditions are different from those on which the performance data is based, compliance is determined by interpolation or by computing the effects of change in the specific variables, if the results of the interpolation or computations are substantially as accurate as the results of direct tests.

(g) No person may take off a reciprocating engine powered large transport category airplane at a weight that is more than the allowable weight for the runway being used (determined under the runway takeoff limitations of the transport category operating rules of this subpart) after taking into account the temperature operating correction factors in section 4a.749a-T or section 4b.117 of the Civil Air Regulations in effect on January 31, 1965, and in the applicable Airplane Flight Manual.

(h) The Administrator may authorize in the operations specifications deviations from this subpart if special circumstances make a literal observance of a requirement unnecessary for safety.

(i) The 10-mile width specified in §§135.369 through 135.373 may be reduced to 5 miles, for not more than 20 miles, when operating under VFR or where navigation facilities furnish reliable and accurate identification of high ground and obstructions located outside of 5 miles, but within 10 miles, on each side of the intended track.

(j) Each certificate holder operating a commuter category airplane shall comply with §135.398.

[Docket No. 16097, 43 FR 46783, Oct. 10, 1978; as amended by Amdt. 135–21, 52 FR 1836, Jan. 15, 1987]

§135.365 Large transport category airplanes: Reciprocating engine powered: Weight limitations.

(a) No person may take off a reciprocating engine powered large transport category airplane from an airport located at an elevation outside of the range for which maximum takeoff weights have been determined for that airplane.

(b) No person may take off a reciprocating engine powered large transport category airplane for an airport of intended destination that is located at an elevation outside of the range for which maximum landing weights have been determined for that airplane.

(c) No person may specify, or have specified, an alternate airport that is located at an elevation outside of the range for which maximum landing weights have been determined for the reciprocating engine powered large transport category airplane concerned.

(d) No person may take off a reciprocating engine powered large transport category airplane at a weight more than the maximum authorized takeoff weight for the elevation of the airport.

(e) No person may take off a reciprocating engine powered large transport category airplane if its weight on arrival at the airport of destination will be more than the maximum authorized landing weight for the elevation of that airport, allowing for normal consumption of fuel and oil en route.

§135.367 Large transport category airplanes: Reciprocating engine powered: Takeoff limitations.

(a) No person operating a reciprocating engine powered large transport category airplane may take off that airplane unless it is possible—

(1) To stop the airplane safely on the runway, as shown by the accelerate-stop distance data, at any time during takeoff until reaching critical-engine failure speed;

(2) If the critical engine fails at any time after the airplane reaches critical-engine failure speed V_1, to continue the takeoff and reach a height of 50 feet, as indicated by the takeoff path data, before passing over the end of the runway; and

(3) To clear all obstacles either by at least 50 feet vertically (as shown by the takeoff path data) or 200 feet horizontally within the airport boundaries and 300 feet horizontally beyond the boundaries, without banking before reaching a height of 50 feet (as shown by the takeoff path data) and after that without banking more than 15 degrees.

(b) In applying this section, corrections must be made for any runway gradient. To allow for wind effect, takeoff data based on still air may be corrected by taking into account not more than 50 percent of any reported headwind component and not less than 150 percent of any reported tailwind component.

§135.369 Large transport category airplanes: Reciprocating engine powered: En route limitations: All engines operating.

(a) No person operating a reciprocating engine powered large transport category airplane may take off that airplane at a weight, allowing for normal consumption of fuel and oil, that does not allow a rate of climb (in feet per minute), with all engines operating, of at least 6.90 V_{S0} (that is, the number of feet per minute obtained by multiplying the number of knots by 6.90) at an altitude of a least 1,000 feet above the highest ground or obstruction within ten miles of each side of the intended track.

(b) This section does not apply to large transport category airplanes certificated under part 4a of the Civil Air Regulations.

§135.371 Large transport category airplanes: Reciprocating engine powered: En route limitations: One engine inoperative.

(a) Except as provided in paragraph (b) of this section, no person operating a reciprocating engine powered large transport category airplane may take off that airplane at a weight, allowing for normal consumption of fuel and oil, that does not allow a rate of climb (in feet per minute), with one engine inoperative, of at least (0.079-0.106/N) V_{S0}^2 (where N is the number of engines installed and V_{S0} is expressed in knots) at an altitude of least 1,000 feet above the highest ground or obstruction within 10 miles of each side of the intended track. However, for the purposes of this paragraph the rate of climb for transport category airplanes certificated under part 4a of the Civil Air Regulations is 0.026 V_{SO}^2.

(b) In place of the requirements of paragraph (a) of this section, a person may, under an approved procedure, operate a reciprocating engine powered large transport category airplane at an all-engines-operating altitude that allows the airplane to continue, after an engine failure, to an alternate airport where a landing can be made under §135.377, allowing for normal consumption of fuel and oil. After the assumed failure, the flight path must clear the ground and any obstruction within five miles on each side of the intended track by at least 2,000 feet.

(c) If an approved procedure under paragraph (b) of this section is used, the certificate holder shall comply with the following:

(1) The rate of climb (as prescribed in the Airplane Flight Manual for the appropriate weight and altitude) used in calculating the airplane's flight path shall be diminished by an amount in feet per minute, equal to (0.079-0.106/N) V_{SO}^2 (when N is the number of engines installed and V_{SO} is expressed in knots) for airplanes certificated under part 25 of this chapter and by 0.026 V_{SO}^2 for airplanes certificated under part 4a of the Civil Air Regulations.

(2) The all-engines-operating altitude shall be sufficient so that in the event the critical engine becomes inoperative at any point along the route, the flight will be able to proceed to a predetermined alternate airport by use of this procedure. In determining the takeoff weight, the airplane is assumed to pass over the critical obstruction following engine failure at a point no closer to the critical obstruction than the nearest approved radio navigational fix, unless the Administrator approves a procedure established on a different basis upon finding that adequate operational safeguards exist.

(3) The airplane must meet the provisions of paragraph (a) of this section at 1,000 feet above the airport used as an alternate in this procedure.

(4) The procedure must include an approved method of accounting for winds and temperatures that would otherwise adversely affect the flight path.

(5) In complying with this procedure, fuel jettisoning is allowed if the certificate holder shows that it has an adequate training program, that proper instructions are given to the flight crew, and all other precautions are taken to ensure a safe procedure.

(6) The certificate holder and the pilot in command shall jointly elect an alternate airport for which the appropriate weather reports or forecasts, or any combination of them, indicate that weather conditions will be at or above the alternate weather minimum specified in the certificate holder's operations specifications for that airport when the flight arrives.

§135.373 Part 25 transport category airplanes with four or more engines: Reciprocating engine powered: En route limitations: Two engines inoperative.

(a) No person may operate an airplane certificated under part 25 and having four or more engines unless—

(1) There is no place along the intended track that is more than 90 minutes (with all engines operating at cruising power) from an airport that meets §135.377; or

(2) It is operated at a weight allowing the airplane, with the two critical engines inoperative, to climb at 0.013 V_{SO}^2 feet per minute (that is, the number of feet per minute obtained by multiplying the number of knots squared by 0.013) at an altitude of 1,000 feet above the highest ground or obstruction within 10 miles on each side of the intended track, or at an altitude of 5,000 feet, whichever is higher.

(b) For the purposes of paragraph (a)(2) of this section, it is assumed that—

(1) The two engines fail at the point that is most critical with respect to the takeoff weight;

(2) Consumption of fuel and oil is normal with all engines operating up to the point where the two engines fail with two engines operating beyond that point;

(3) Where the engines are assumed to fail at an altitude above the prescribed minimum altitude, compliance with the prescribed rate of climb at the prescribed minimum altitude need not be shown during the descent from the cruising altitude to the prescribed minimum altitude, if those requirements can be met once the prescribed minimum altitude is reached, and assuming descent to be along a net flight path and the rate of descent to be 0.013 V_{SO}^2 greater than the rate in the approved performance data; and

(4) If fuel jettisoning is provided, the airplane's weight at the point where the two engines fail is considered to be not less than that which would include enough fuel to proceed to an airport meeting §135.377 and to arrive at an altitude of at least 1,000 feet directly over that airport.

§135.375 Large transport category airplanes: Reciprocating engine powered: Landing limitations: Destination airports.

(a) Except as provided in paragraph (b) of this section, no person operating a reciprocating engine powered large transport category airplane may take off that airplane, unless its weight on arrival, allowing for normal consumption of fuel and oil in flight, would allow a full stop landing at the intended destination within 60 percent of the effective length of each runway described below from a point 50 feet directly above the intersection of the obstruction clearance plane and the runway. For the purposes of determining the allowable landing weight at the destination airport the following is assumed:

(1) The airplane is landed on the most favorable runway and in the most favorable direction in still air.

(2) The airplane is landed on the most suitable runway considering the probable wind velocity and direction (forecast for the expected time of arrival), the ground handling characteristics of the type of airplane, and other conditions such as landing aids and terrain, and allowing for the effect of the landing path and roll of not more than 50 percent of the headwind component or not less than 150 percent of the tailwind component.

(b) An airplane that would be prohibited from being taken off because it could not meet paragraph (a)(2) of this section may be taken off if an alternate airport is selected that meets all of this section except that the airplane can accomplish a full stop landing within 70 percent of the effective length of the runway.

§135.377 Large transport category airplanes: Reciprocating engine powered: Landing limitations: Alternate airports.

No person may list an airport as an alternate airport in a flight plan unless the airplane (at the weight anticipated at the time of arrival at the airport), based on the assumptions in §135.375(a)(1) and (2), can be brought to a full stop landing within 70 percent of the effective length of the runway.

§135.379 Large transport category airplanes: Turbine engine powered: Takeoff limitations.

(a) No person operating a turbine engine powered large transport category airplane may take off that airplane at a weight greater than that listed in the Airplane Flight Manual for the elevation of the airport and for the ambient temperature existing at take off.

(b) No person operating a turbine engine powered large transport category airplane certificated after August 26, 1957, but before August 30, 1959 (SR422, 422A), may take off that airplane at a weight greater than that listed in the Airplane Flight Manual for the minimum distance required for takeoff. In the case of an airplane certificated after September 30, 1958 (SR422A, 422B), the takeoff distance may include a clearway distance but the clearway distance included may not be greater than one-half of the takeoff run.

(c) No person operating a turbine engine powered large transport category airplane certificated after August 29, 1959 (SR422B), may take off that airplane at a weight greater than that listed in the Airplane Flight Manual at which compliance with the following may be shown:

(1) The accelerate-stop distance, as defined in §25.109 of this chapter, must not exceed the length of the runway plus the length of any stopway.

(2) The takeoff distance must not exceed the length of the runway plus the length of any clearway except that the length of any clearway included must not be greater than one-half the length of the runway.

(3) The takeoff run must not be greater than the length of the runway.

(d) No person operating a turbine engine powered large transport category airplane may take off that airplane at a weight greater than that listed in the Airplane Flight Manual—

(1) For an airplane certificated after August 26, 1957, but before October 1, 1958 (SR422), that allows a takeoff path that clears all obstacles either by at least (35+0.01 D) feet vertically (D is the distance along the intended flight path from the end of the runway in feet), or by at least 200 feet horizontally within the airport boundaries and by at least 300 feet horizontally after passing the boundaries; or

(2) For an airplane certificated after September 30, 1958 (SR422A, 422B), that allows a net takeoff flight path that clears all obstacles either by a height of at least 35 feet vertically, or by at least 200 feet horizontally within the airport boundaries and by at least 300 feet horizontally after passing the boundaries.

(e) In determining maximum weights, minimum distances, and flight paths under paragraphs (a) through (d) of this section, correction must be made for the runway to be used, the elevation of the airport, the effective runway gradient, the ambient temperature and wind component at the time of takeoff, and, if operating limitations exist for the minimum distances required for takeoff from wet runways, the runway surface condition (dry or wet). Wet runway distances associated with grooved or porous friction course runways, if provided in the Airplane Flight Manual, may be used only for runways that are grooved or treated with a porous friction course (PFC) overlay, and that the operator determines are designed, constructed, and maintained in a manner acceptable to the Administrator.

(f) For the purposes of this section, it is assumed that the airplane is not banked before reaching a height of 50 feet, as shown by the takeoff path or net takeoff flight path data (as appropriate) in the Airplane Flight Manual, and after that the maximum bank is not more than 15 degrees.

(g) For the purposes of this section, the terms, takeoff distance, takeoff run, net takeoff flight path, have the same meanings as set forth in the rules under which the airplane was certificated.

[Docket No. 16097, 43 FR 46783, Oct. 10, 1978; as amended by Amdt. 135–71, 63 FR 8321, Feb. 18, 1998]

§135.381 Large transport category airplanes: Turbine engine powered: En route limitations: One engine inoperative.

(a) No person operating a turbine engine powered large transport category airplane may take off that airplane at a weight, allowing for normal consumption of fuel and oil, that is greater than that which (under the approved, one engine inoperative, en route net flight path data in the Airplane Flight Manual for that airplane) will allow compliance with paragraph (a) (1) or (2) of this section, based on the ambient temperatures expected en route.

(1) There is a positive slope at an altitude of at least 1,000 feet above all terrain and obstructions within five statute miles on each side of the intended track, and, in addition, if that airplane was certificated after August 29, 1958 (SR422B), there is a positive slope at 1,500 feet above the airport where the airplane is assumed to land after an engine fails.

(2) The net flight path allows the airplane to continue flight from the cruising altitude to an airport where a landing can be made under §135.387 clearing all terrain and obstructions within five statute miles of the intended track by at least 2,000 feet vertically and with a positive slope at 1,000 feet above the airport where the airplane lands after an engine fails, or, if that airplane was certificated after September 30, 1958 (SR422A, 422B), with a positive slope at 1,500 feet above the airport where the airplane lands after an engine fails.

(b) For the purpose of paragraph (a)(2) of this section, it is assumed that—

(1) The engine fails at the most critical point en route;

(2) The airplane passes over the critical obstruction, after engine failure at a point that is no closer to the obstruction than the approved radio navigation fix, unless the Administrator authorizes a different procedure based on adequate operational safeguards;

(3) An approved method is used to allow for adverse winds;

(4) Fuel jettisoning will be allowed if the certificate holder shows that the crew is properly instructed, that the training program is adequate, and that all other precautions are taken to ensure a safe procedure;

(5) The alternate airport is selected and meets the prescribed weather minimums; and

(6) The consumption of fuel and oil after engine failure is the same as the consumption that is allowed for in the approved net flight path data in the Airplane Flight Manual.

§135.383 Large transport category airplanes: Turbine engine powered: En route limitations: Two engines inoperative.

(a) Airplanes certificated after August 26, 1957, but before October 1, 1958 (SR422). No person may operate a turbine engine powered large transport category airplane along an intended route unless that person complies with either of the following:

(1) There is no place along the intended track that is more than 90 minutes (with all engines operating at cruising power) from an airport that meets §135.387.

(2) Its weight, according to the two-engine-inoperative, en route, net flight path data in the Airplane Flight Manual, allows the airplane to fly from the point where the two engines are assumed to fail simultaneously to an airport that meets §135.387, with a net flight path (considering the ambient temperature anticipated along the track) having a positive slope at an altitude of at least 1,000 feet above all terrain and obstructions within five statute miles on each side of the intended track, or at an altitude of 5,000 feet, whichever is higher.

For the purposes of paragraph (a)(2) of this section, it is assumed that the two engines fail at the most critical point en route, that if fuel jettisoning is provided, the airplane's weight at the point where the engines fail includes enough fuel to continue to the airport and to arrive at an altitude of at least 1,000 feet directly over the airport, and that the fuel and oil consumption after engine failure is the same as the consumption allowed for in the net flight path data in the Airplane Flight Manual.

(b) Airplanes certificated after September 30, 1958, but before August 30, 1959 (SR422A). No person may operate a turbine engine powered large transport category airplane along an intended route unless that person complies with either of the following:

(1) There is no place along the intended track that is more than 90 minutes (with all engines operating at cruising power) from an airport that meets §135.387.

(2) Its weight, according to the two-engine-inoperative, en route, net flight path data in the Airplane Flight Manual allows the airplane to fly from the point where the two engines are assumed to fail simultaneously to an airport that meets §135.387 with a net flight path (considering the ambient temperatures anticipated along the track) having a positive slope at an altitude of at least 1,000 feet above all terrain and obstructions within five statute miles on each side of the intended track, or at an altitude of 2,000 feet, whichever is higher.

For the purpose of paragraph (b)(2) of this section, it is assumed that the two engines fail at the most critical point en route, that the airplane's weight at the point where the engines fail includes enough fuel to continue to the airport, to arrive at an altitude of at least 1,500 feet directly over the airport, and after that to fly for 15 minutes at cruise power or thrust, or both, and that the consumption of fuel and oil after engine failure is the same as the consumption allowed for in the net flight path data in the Airplane Flight Manual.

(c) Aircraft certificated after August 29, 1959 (SR422B). No person may operate a turbine engine powered large transport category airplane along an intended route unless that person complies with either of the following:

(1) There is no place along the intended track that is more than 90 minutes (with all engines operating at cruising power) from an airport that meets §135.387.

(2) Its weight, according to the two-engine-inoperative, en route, net flight path data in the Airplane Flight Manual, allows the airplane to fly from the point where the two engines are assumed to fail simultaneously to an airport that meets §135.387, with the net flight path (considering the ambient temperatures anticipated along the track) clearing vertically by at least 2,000 feet all terrain and obstructions within five statute miles on each side of the intended track. For the purposes of this paragraph, it is assumed that—

(i) The two engines fail at the most critical point en route;

(ii) The net flight path has a positive slope at 1,500 feet above the airport where the landing is assumed to be made after the engines fail;

(iii) Fuel jettisoning will be approved if the certificate holder shows that the crew is properly instructed, that the training program is adequate, and that all other precautions are taken to ensure a safe procedure;

(iv) The airplane's weight at the point where the two engines are assumed to fail provides enough fuel to continue to the airport, to arrive at an altitude of at least 1,500 feet directly over the airport, and after that to fly for 15 minutes at cruise power or thrust, or both; and

(v) The consumption of fuel and oil after the engines fail is the same as the consumption that is allowed for in the net flight path data in the Airplane Flight Manual.

§135.385 Large transport category airplanes: Turbine engine powered: Landing limitations: Destination airports.

(a) No person operating a turbine engine powered large transport category airplane may take off that airplane at a weight that (allowing for normal consumption of fuel and oil in flight to the destination or alternate airport) the weight of the airplane on arrival would exceed the landing weight in the Airplane Flight Manual for the elevation of the destination or alternate airport and the ambient temperature anticipated at the time of landing.

(b) Except as provided in paragraph (c), (d), (e), or (f) of this section, no person operating a turbine engine powered large transport category airplane may take off that airplane unless its weight on arrival, allowing for normal consumption of fuel and oil in flight (in accordance with the landing distance in the Airplane Flight Manual for the elevation of the destination airport and the wind conditions expected there at the time of landing), would allow a full stop landing at the intended destination airport within 60 percent of the effective length of each runway described below from a point 50 feet above the intersection of the obstruction clearance plane and the runway. For the purpose of determining the allowable landing weight at the destination airport the following is assumed:

(1) The airplane is landed on the most favorable runway and in the most favorable direction, in still air.

(2) The airplane is landed on the most suitable runway considering the probable wind velocity and direction and the ground handling characteristics of the airplane, and considering other conditions such as landing aids and terrain.

(c) A turbopropeller powered airplane that would be prohibited from being taken off because it could not meet paragraph (b)(2) of this section, may be taken off if an alternate airport is selected that meets all of this section except that the airplane can accomplish a full stop landing within 70 percent of the effective length of the runway.

(d) Unless, based on a showing of actual operating landing techniques on wet runways, a shorter landing distance (but never less than that required by paragraph (b) of this section) has been approved for a specific type and model airplane and included in the Airplane Flight Manual, no person may take off a turbojet airplane when the appropriate weather reports or forecasts, or any combination of them, indicate that the runways at the destination airport may be wet or slippery at the estimated time of arrival unless the effective runway length at the destination airport is at least 115 percent of the runway length required under paragraph (b) of this section.

(e) A turbojet airplane that would be prohibited from being taken off because it could not meet paragraph (b)(2) of this section may be taken off if an alternate airport is selected that meets all of paragraph (b) of this section.

(f) An eligible on-demand operator may take off a turbine engine powered large transport category airplane on an on-demand flight if all of the following conditions exist:

(1) The operation is permitted by an approved Destination Airport Analysis in that person's operations manual.

(2) The airplane's weight on arrival, allowing for normal consumption of fuel and oil in flight (in accordance with the landing distance in the Airplane Flight Manual for the elevation of the destination airport and the wind conditions expected there at the time of landing), would allow a full stop landing at the intended destination airport within 80 percent of the effective length of each runway described below from a point 50 feet above the intersection of the obstruction clearance plane and the runway. For the purpose of determining the allowable landing weight at the destination airport, the following is assumed:

(i) The airplane is landed on the most favorable runway and in the most favorable direction, in still air.

(ii) The airplane is landed on the most suitable runway considering the probable wind velocity and direction and the ground handling characteristics of the airplane, and considering other conditions such as landing aids and terrain.

(3) The operation is authorized by operations specifications.

[Docket No. 16097, 43 FR 46783, Oct. 10, 1978; as amended by Amdt. 135–91, 68 FR 54588, Sept. 17, 2003]

§135.387 Large transport category airplanes: Turbine engine powered: Landing limitations: Alternate airports.

(a) Except as provided in paragraph (b) of this section, no person may select an airport as an alternate airport for a turbine engine powered large transport category airplane unless (based on the assumptions in §135.385(b)) that airplane, at the weight expected at the time of arrival, can be brought to a full stop landing within 70 percent of the effective length of the runway for turbo-propeller-powered airplanes and 60 percent of the effective length of the runway for turbojet airplanes, from a point 50 feet above the intersection of the obstruction clearance plane and the runway.

(b) Eligible on-demand operators may select an airport as an alternate airport for a turbine engine powered large transport category airplane if (based on the assumptions in §135.385(f)) that airplane, at the weight expected at the time of arrival, can be brought to a full stop landing within 80 percent of the effective length of the runway from a point 50 feet above the intersection of the obstruction clearance plane and the runway.

[Docket No. FAA–2001–10047, 68 FR 54588, Sept. 17, 2003]

§135.389 Large nontransport category airplanes: Takeoff limitations.

(a) No person operating a large nontransport category airplane may take off that airplane at a weight greater than the weight that would allow the airplane to be brought to a safe stop within the effective length of the runway, from any point during the takeoff before reaching 105 percent of minimum control speed (the minimum speed at which an airplane can be safely controlled in flight after an engine becomes inoperative) or 115 percent of the power off stalling speed in the takeoff configuration, whichever is greater.

(b) For the purposes of this section—

(1) It may be assumed that takeoff power is used on all engines during the acceleration;

(2) Not more than 50 percent of the reported headwind component, or not less than 150 percent of the reported tailwind component, may be taken into account;

(3) The average runway gradient (the difference between the elevations of the endpoints of the runway divided by the total length) must be considered if it is more than one-half of one percent;

(4) It is assumed that the airplane is operating in standard atmosphere; and

(5) For takeoff, *effective length of the runway* means the distance from the end of the runway at which the takeoff is started to a point at which the obstruction clearance plane associated with the other end of the runway intersects the runway centerline.

§135.391 Large nontransport category airplanes: En route limitations: One engine inoperative.

(a) Except as provided in paragraph (b) of this section, no person operating a large nontransport category airplane may take off that airplane at a weight that does not allow a rate of climb of at least 50 feet a minute, with the critical engine inoperative, at an altitude of at least 1,000 feet above the highest obstruction within five miles on each side of the intended track, or 5,000 feet, whichever is higher.

(b) Without regard to paragraph (a) of this section, if the Administrator finds that safe operations are not impaired, a person may operate the airplane at an altitude that allows the airplane, in case of engine failure, to clear all obstructions within five miles on each side of the intended track by 1,000 feet. If this procedure is used, the rate of descent for the appropriate weight and altitude is assumed to be 50 feet a minute greater than the rate in the approved performance data. Before approving such a procedure, the Administrator considers the following for the route, route segment, or area concerned:

(1) The reliability of wind and weather forecasting.

(2) The location and kinds of navigation aids.

(3) The prevailing weather conditions, particularly the frequency and amount of turbulence normally encountered.

(4) Terrain features.

(5) Air traffic problems.

(6) Any other operational factors that affect the operations.

(c) For the purposes of this section, it is assumed that—

(1) The critical engine is inoperative;

(2) The propeller of the inoperative engine is in the minimum drag position;

(3) The wing flaps and landing gear are in the most favorable position;

(4) The operating engines are operating at the maximum continuous power available;

(5) The airplane is operating in standard atmosphere; and

(6) The weight of the airplane is progressively reduced by the anticipated consumption of fuel and oil.

§135.393 Large nontransport category airplanes: Landing limitations: Destination airports.

(a) No person operating a large nontransport category airplane may take off that airplane at a weight that—

(1) Allowing for anticipated consumption of fuel and oil, is greater than the weight that would allow a full stop landing within 60 percent of the effective length of the most suitable runway at the destination airport; and

(2) Is greater than the weight allowable if the landing is to be made on the runway—

(i) With the greatest effective length in still air; and

(ii) Required by the probable wind, taking into account not more than 50 percent of the headwind component or not less than 150 percent of the tailwind component.

(b) For the purpose of this section, it is assumed that—

(1) The airplane passes directly over the intersection of the obstruction clearance plane and the runway at a height of 50 feet in a steady gliding approach at a true indicated airspeed of at least 1.3 V_{S0};

(2) The landing does not require exceptional pilot skill; and

(3) The airplane is operating in standard atmosphere.

§135.395 Large nontransport category airplanes: Landing limitations: Alternate airports.

No person may select an airport as an alternate airport for a large nontransport category airplane unless that airplane (at the weight anticipated at the time of arrival), based on the assumptions in §135.393(b), can be brought to a full stop landing within 70 percent of the effective length of the runway.

§135.397 Small transport category airplane performance operating limitations.

(a) No person may operate a reciprocating engine powered small transport category airplane unless that person complies with the weight limitations in §135.365, the takeoff limitations in §135.367 (except paragraph (a)(3)), and the landing limitations in §§135.375 and 135.377.

(b) No person may operate a turbine engine powered small transport category airplane unless that person complies with the takeoff limitations in §135.379 (except paragraphs (d) and (f)) and the landing limitations in §§135.385 and 135.387.

§135.398 Commuter category airplanes performance operating limitations.

(a) No person may operate a commuter category airplane unless that person complies with the takeoff weight limitations in the approved Airplane Flight Manual.

(b) No person may take off an airplane type certificated in the commuter category at a weight greater than that listed in the Airplane Flight Manual that allows a net takeoff flight path that clears all obstacles either by a height of at least 35 feet vertically, or at least 200 feet horizontally within the airport boundaries and by at least 300 feet horizontally after passing the boundaries.

(c) No person may operate a commuter category airplane unless that person complies with the landing limitations prescribed in §§135.385 and 135.387 of this part. For purposes of this paragraph, §§135.385 and 135.387 are applicable to all commuter category airplanes notwithstanding their stated applicability to turbine-engine-powered large transport category airplanes.

(d) In determining maximum weights, minimum distances and flight paths under paragraphs (a) through (c) of this section, correction must be made for the runway to be used, the elevation of the airport, the effective runway gradient, and ambient temperature, and wind component at the time of takeoff.

(e) For the purposes of this section, the assumption is that the airplane is not banked before reaching a height of 50 feet as shown by the net takeoff flight path data in the Airplane Flight Manual and thereafter the maximum bank is not more than 15 degrees.

[Docket No. 23516, 52 FR 1836, Jan. 15, 1987]

§135.399 Small nontransport category airplane performance operating limitations.

(a) No person may operate a reciprocating engine or turbopropeller-powered small airplane that is certificated under §135.169(b) (2), (3), (4), (5), or (6) unless that person complies with the takeoff weight limitations in the approved Airplane Flight Manual or equivalent for operations under this part, and, if the airplane is certificated under §135.169(b) (4) or (5) with the landing weight limitations in the Approved Airplane Flight Manual or equivalent for operations under this part.

(b) No person may operate an airplane that is certificated under §135.169(b)(6) unless that person complies with the landing limitations prescribed in §§135.385 and 135.387 of this part. For purposes of this paragraph, §§135.385 and 135.387 are applicable to reciprocating and turbopropeller-powered small airplanes notwithstanding their stated applicability to turbine engine powered large transport category airplanes.

[44 FR 53731, Sept. 17, 1979]

Subpart J— Maintenance, Preventive Maintenance, and Alterations

§135.411 Applicability.

(a) This subpart prescribes rules in addition to those in other parts of this chapter for the maintenance, preventive maintenance, and alterations for each certificate holder as follows:

(1) Aircraft that are type certificated for a passenger seating configuration, excluding any pilot seat, of nine seats or less, shall be maintained under parts 91 and 43 of this chapter and §§135.415, 135.416, 135.417, 135.421 and 135.422. An approved aircraft inspection program may be used under §135.419.

(2) Aircraft that are type certificated for a passenger seating configuration, excluding any pilot seat, of ten seats or more, shall be maintained under a maintenance program in §§135.415, 135.416, 135.417, and 135.423 through 135.443.

(b) A certificate holder who is not otherwise required, may elect to maintain its aircraft under paragraph (a)(2) of this section.

(c) Single engine aircraft used in passenger-carrying IFR operations shall also be maintained in accordance with §135.421 (c), (d), and (e).

[Docket No. 16097, 43 FR 46783, Oct. 10, 1978; as amended by Amdt. 135–70, 62 FR 42374, Aug. 6, 1997; Amdt. 135–78, 65 FR 60556, Oct. 11, 2000; Amdt. 135–92, 68 FR 69308, Dec. 12, 2003; Amdt. 135–81, 70 FR 5533, Feb. 2, 2005]

§135.413 Responsibility for airworthiness.

(a) Each certificate holder is primarily responsible for the airworthiness of its aircraft, including airframes, aircraft engines, propellers, rotors, appliances, and parts, and shall have its aircraft maintained under this chapter, and shall have defects repaired between required maintenance under part 43 of this chapter.

(b) Each certificate holder who maintains its aircraft under §135.411(a)(2) shall—

(1) Perform the maintenance, preventive maintenance, and alteration of its aircraft, including airframe, aircraft engines, propellers, rotors, appliances, emergency equipment and parts, under its manual and this chapter; or

(2) Make arrangements with another person for the performance of maintenance, preventive maintenance, or alteration. However, the certificate holder shall ensure that any maintenance, preventive maintenance, or alteration that is performed by another person is performed under the certificate holder's manual and this chapter.

THE FOLLOWING SECTION IS EFFECTIVE UNTIL JANUARY 30, 2006

§135.415 Mechanical reliability reports.

(a) Each certificate holder shall report the occurrence or detection of each failure, malfunction, or defect in an aircraft concerning—

(1) Fires during flight and whether the related fire-warning system functioned properly;

(2) Fires during flight not protected by related fire-warning system;

(3) False fire-warning during flight;

(4) An exhaust system that causes damage during flight to the engine, adjacent structure, equipment, or components;

(5) An aircraft component that causes accumulation or circulation of smoke, vapor, or toxic or noxious fumes in the crew compartment or passenger cabin during flight;

(6) Engine shutdown during flight because of flameout;

(7) Engine shutdown during flight when external damage to the engine or aircraft structure occurs;

(8) Engine shutdown during flight due to foreign object ingestion or icing;

(9) Shutdown of more than one engine during flight;

(10) A propeller feathering system or ability of the system to control overspeed during flight;

(11) A fuel or fuel-dumping system that affects fuel flow or causes hazardous leakage during flight;

(12) An unwanted landing gear extension or retraction or opening or closing of landing gear doors during flight;

(13) Brake system components that result in loss of brake actuating force when the aircraft is in motion on the ground;

(14) Aircraft structure that requires major repair;

(15) Cracks, permanent deformation, or corrosion of aircraft structures, if more than the maximum acceptable to the manufacturer or the FAA; and

(16) Aircraft components or systems that result in taking emergency actions during flight (except action to shut-down an engine).

(b) For the purpose of this section, *during flight* means the period from the moment the aircraft leaves the surface of the earth on takeoff until it touches down on landing.

(c) In addition to the reports required by paragraph (a) of this section, each certificate holder shall report any other failure, malfunction, or defect in an aircraft that occurs or is detected at any time if, in its opinion, the failure, malfunction, or defect has endangered or may endanger the safe operation of the aircraft.

(d) Each certificate holder shall send each report required by this section, in writing, covering each 24-hour period beginning at 0900 hours local time of each day and ending at 0900 hours local time on the next day to the FAA Flight Standards District Office charged with the overall inspection of the certificate holder. Each report of occurrences during a 24-hour period must be mailed or delivered to that office within the next 72 hours. However, a report that is due on Saturday or Sunday may be mailed or delivered on the following Monday and one that is due on a holiday may be mailed or delivered on the next work day. For aircraft operated in areas where mail is not collected, reports may be mailed or delivered within 72 hours after the aircraft returns to a point where the mail is collected.

(e) The certificate holder shall transmit the reports required by this section on a form and in a manner prescribed by the Administrator, and shall include as much of the following as is available:

(1) The type and identification number of the aircraft.

(2) The name of the operator.

(3) The date.

(4) The nature of the failure, malfunction, or defect.

(5) Identification of the part and system involved, including available information pertaining to type designation of the major component and time since last overhaul, if known.

(6) Apparent cause of the failure, malfunction or defect (e.g., wear, crack, design deficiency, or personnel error).

(7) Other pertinent information necessary for more complete identification, determination of seriousness, or corrective action.

(f) A certificate holder that is also the holder of a type certificate (including a supplemental type certificate), a Parts Manufacturer Approval, or a Technical Standard Order Authorization, or that is the licensee of a type certificate need not report a failure, malfunction, or defect under this section if the failure, malfunction, or defect has been reported by it under §21.3 or §37.17 of this chapter or under the accident reporting provisions of part 830 of the regulations of the National Transportation Safety Board.

(g) No person may withhold a report required by this section even though all information required by this section is not available.

(h) When the certificate holder gets additional information, including information from the manufacturer or other agency, concerning a report required by this section, it shall expeditiously submit it as a supplement to the first report and reference the date and place of submission of the first report.

THE FOLLOWING SECTION BECOMES EFFECTIVE JANUARY 30, 2006

§135.415 Service difficulty reports (operational).

(a) Each certificate holder shall report the occurrence or detection of each failure, malfunction, or defect concerning—

(1) Any fire and, when monitored by a related fire-warning system, whether the fire-warning system functioned properly;

(2) Any false warning of fire or smoke;

(3) An engine exhaust system that causes damage to the engine, adjacent structure, equipment, or components;

(4) An aircraft component that causes the accumulation or circulation of smoke, vapor, or toxic or noxious fumes;

(5) Any engine flameout or shutdown during flight or ground operations;

(6) A propeller feathering system or ability of the system to control overspeed;

(7) A fuel or fuel-dumping system that affects fuel flow or causes hazardous leakage;

(8) A landing gear extension or retraction, or the opening or closing of landing gear doors during flight;

(9) Any brake system component that results in any detectable loss of brake actuating force when the aircraft is in motion on the ground;

(10) Any aircraft component or system that results in a rejected takeoff after initiation of the takeoff roll or the taking of emergency action, as defined by the Aircraft Flight Manual or Pilot's Operating Handbook;

(11) Any emergency evacuation system or component including any exit door, passenger emergency evacuation lighting system, or evacuation equipment found to be defective, or that fails to perform the intended function during an actual emergency or during training, testing, maintenance, demonstrations, or inadvertent deployments; and

(12) Autothrottle, autoflight, or flight control systems or components of these systems.

(b) For the purpose of this section, *during flight* means the period from the moment the aircraft leaves the surface of the earth on takeoff until it touches down on landing.

(c) In addition to the reports required by paragraph (a) of this section, each certificate holder shall report any other failure, malfunction, or defect in an aircraft, system, component, or powerplant that occurs or is detected at any time if that failure, malfunction, or defect has endangered or may endanger the safe operation of an aircraft.

(d) Each certificate holder shall submit each report required by this section, covering each 24-hour period beginning at 0900 local time of each day and ending at 0900 local time on the next day, to a centralized collection point as specified by the Administrator. Each report of occurrences during a 24-hour period shall be submitted to the FAA within the next 96 hours. However, a report due on Saturday or Sunday may be submitted on the following Monday, and a report due on a holiday may be submitted on the next workday. For aircraft operating in areas where mail is not collected, reports may be submitted within 24 hours after the aircraft returns to a point where the mail is collected. Each certificate holder also shall make the report data available for 30 days for examination by the certificate-holding district office in a form and manner acceptable to the Administrator.

(e) The certificate holder shall submit the reports required by this section on a form or in another format acceptable to the Administrator. The reports shall include the following information:

(1) The manufacturer, model, and serial number of the aircraft, engine, or propeller;

(2) The registration number of the aircraft;

(3) The operator designator;

(4) The date on which the failure, malfunction, or defect was discovered;

(5) The stage of flight or ground operation during which the failure, malfunction, or defect was discovered;

(6) The nature of the failure, malfunction, or defect;

(7) The applicable Joint Aircraft System/Component Code;

(8) The total cycles, if applicable, and total time of the aircraft, aircraft engine, propeller, or component;

(9) The manufacturer, manufacturer part number, part name, serial number, and location of the component that failed, malfunctioned, or was defective, if applicable;

(10) The manufacturer, manufacturer part number, part name, serial number, and location of the part that failed, malfunctioned, or was defective, if applicable;

(11) The precautionary or emergency action taken;

(12) Other information necessary for more complete analysis of the cause of the failure, malfunction, or defect, including available information pertaining to type designation of the major component and the time since the last maintenance overhaul, repair, or inspection; and

(13) A unique control number for the occurrence, in a form acceptable to the Administrator.

(f) A certificate holder that also is the holder of a Type Certificate (including a Supplemental Type Certificate), a Parts Manufacturer Approval, or a Technical Standard Order authorization, or that is a licensee of a Type Certificate holder, need not report a failure, malfunction, or defect under this section if the failure, malfunction, or defect has been reported by that certificate holder under §21.3 of this chapter or under the accident reporting provisions of 49 CFR part 830.

(g) A report required by this section may be submitted by a certificated repair station when the reporting task has been assigned to that repair station by a part 135 certificate holder. However, the part 135 certificate holder remains primarily responsible for ensuring compliance with the provisions of this section. The part 135 certificate holder shall receive a copy of each report submitted by the repair station.

(h) No person may withhold a report required by this section although all information required by this section is not available.

(i) When a certificate holder gets supplemental information to complete the report required by this section, the certificate holder shall expeditiously submit that information as a supplement to the original report and use the unique control number from the original report.

[Docket No. 16097, 43 FR 46783, Oct. 10, 1978; as amended by Amdt. 135–77, 65 FR 56204, Sept. 15, 2000; Amdt. 135–81, 66 FR 21626, April 30, 2001; Docket FAA–2000–7952, 66 FR 58912, Nov. 23, 2001; FAA–2000–7952, 67 FR 78970, Dec. 27, 2002; FAA–2000–7952, 68 FR 75116, Dec. 30, 2003]

THE FOLLOWING NEW SECTION BECOMES EFFECTIVE JANUARY 30, 2006

§135.416 Service difficulty reports (structural).

(a) Each certificate holder shall report the occurrence or detection of each failure or defect related to—

(1) Corrosion, cracks, or disbonding that requires replacement of the affected part;

(2) Corrosion, cracks, or disbonding that requires rework or blendout because the corrosion, cracks, or disbonding exceeds the manufacturer's established allowable damage limits;

(3) Cracks, fractures, or disbonding in a composite structure that the equipment manufacturer has designated as a primary structure or a principal structural element; or

(4) Repairs made in accordance with approved data not contained in the manufacturer's maintenance manual.

(b) In addition to the reports required by paragraph (a) of this section, each certificate holder shall report any other failure or defect in aircraft structure that occurs or is detected at any time if that failure or defect has endangered or may endanger the safe operation of an aircraft.

(c) Each certificate holder shall submit each report required by this section, covering each 24-hour period beginning at 0900 local time of each day and ending at 0900 local time on the next day, to a centralized collection point as specified by the Administrator. Each report of occurrences during a 24-hour period shall be submitted to the FAA within the next 96 hours. However, a report due on Saturday or Sunday may be submitted on the following Monday, and a report due on a holiday may be submitted on the next workday. For aircraft operating in areas where mail is not collected, reports may be submitted within 24 hours after the aircraft returns to a point where the mail is collected. Each certificate holder also shall make the report data available for 30 days for examination by the certificate-holding district office in a form and manner acceptable to the Administrator.

(d) The certificate holder shall submit the reports required by this section on a form or in another format acceptable to the Administrator. The reports shall include the following information:

(1) The manufacturer, model, serial number, and registration number of the aircraft;

(2) The operator designator;

(3) The date on which the failure or defect was discovered;

(4) The stage of ground operation during which the failure or defect was discovered;

(5) The part name, part condition, and location of the failure or defect;

(6) The applicable Joint Aircraft System/Component Code;

(7) The total cycles, if applicable, and total time of the aircraft;

(8) Other information necessary for a more complete analysis of the cause of the failure or defect, including corrosion classification, if applicable, or crack length and available information pertaining to type designation of the major component and the time since the last maintenance overhaul, repair, or inspection; and

(9) A unique control number for the occurrence, in a form acceptable to the Administrator.

(e) A certificate holder that also is the holder of a Type Certificate (including a Supplemental Type Certificate), a Parts Manufacturer Approval, or a Technical Standard Order authorization, or that is a licensee of a Type Certificate holder, need not report a failure or defect under this section if the failure or defect has been reported by that certificate holder under §21.3 of this chapter or under the accident reporting provisions of 49 CFR part 830.

(f) A report required by this section may be submitted by a certificated repair station when the reporting task has been assigned to that repair station by the part 135 certificate holder. However, the part 135 certificate holder remains primarily responsible for ensuring compliance with the provisions of this section. The part 135 certificate holder shall receive a copy of each report submitted by the repair station.

(g) No person may withhold a report required by this section although all information required by this section is not available.

(h) When a certificate holder gets supplemental information to complete the report required by this section, the certificate holder shall expeditiously submit that information as a supplement to the original report and use the unique control number from the original report.

[Docket No. 28293, 65 FR 56205, Sept. 15, 2000; Amdt. 135–81, 66 FR 21626, April 30, 2001; Docket FAA–2000–7952, 66 FR 58912, Nov. 23, 2001; FAA–2000–7952, 67 FR 78970, Dec. 27, 2002; FAA–2000–7952, 68 FR 75116, Dec. 30, 2003]

THE FOLLOWING SECTION IS EFFECTIVE UNTIL JANUARY 30, 2006

§135.417 Mechanical interruption summary report.

Each certificate holder shall mail or deliver, before the end of the 10th day of the following month, a summary report of the following occurrences in multiengine aircraft for the preceding month to the certificate-holding district office:

(a) Each interruption to a flight, unscheduled change of aircraft en route, or unscheduled stop or diversion from a route, caused by known or suspected mechanical difficulties or malfunctions that are not required to be reported under §135.415.

(b) The number of propeller featherings in flight, listed by type of propeller and engine and aircraft on which it was installed. Propeller featherings for training, demonstration, or flight check purposes need not be reported.

[Docket No. 16097, 43 FR 46783, Oct. 10, 1978; as amended by Amdt. 135–60, 61 FR 2616, Jan. 26, 1996]

THE FOLLOWING SECTION BECOMES EFFECTIVE JANUARY 30, 2006

§135.417 Mechanical interruption summary report.

Each certificate holder shall submit to the Administrator, before the end of the 10th day of the following month, a summary report for the previous month of each interruption to a flight, unscheduled change of aircraft en route, unscheduled stop or diversion from a route, or unscheduled engine removal caused by known or suspected mechanical difficulties or malfunctions that are not required to be reported under §135.415 or §135.416 of this part.

[Docket No. 28293, 65 FR 56205, Sept. 15, 2000; Amdt. 135–81, 66 FR 21626, April 30, 2001; Docket FAA–2000–7952, 66 FR 58912, Nov. 23, 2001; FAA–2000–7952, 67 FR 78970, Dec. 27, 2002; FAA–2000–7952, 68 FR 75116, Dec. 30, 2003]

§135.419 Approved aircraft inspection program.

(a) Whenever the Administrator finds that the aircraft inspections required or allowed under part 91 of this chapter are not adequate to meet this part, or upon application by a certificate holder, the Administrator may amend the certificate holder's operations specifications under §135.17, to require or allow an approved aircraft inspection program for any make and model aircraft of which the certificate holder has the exclusive use of at least one aircraft (as defined in §135.25(b)).

(b) A certificate holder who applies for an amendment of its operations specifications to allow an approved aircraft inspection program must submit that program with its application for approval by the Administrator.

(c) Each certificate holder who is required by its operations specifications to have an approved aircraft inspection program shall submit a program for approval by the Administrator within 30 days of the amendment of its operations specifications or within any other period that the Administrator may prescribe in the operations specifications.

(d) The aircraft inspection program submitted for approval by the Administrator must contain the following:

(1) Instructions and procedures for the conduct of aircraft inspections (which must include necessary tests and checks), setting forth in detail the parts and areas of the airframe, engines, propellers, rotors, and appliances, including emergency equipment, that must be inspected.

(2) A schedule for the performance of the aircraft inspections under paragraph (d)(1) of this section expressed in terms of the time in service, calendar time, number of system operations, or any combination of these.

(3) Instructions and procedures for recording discrepancies found during inspections and correction or deferral of discrepancies including form and disposition of records.

(e) After approval, the certificate holder shall include the approved aircraft inspection program in the manual required by §135.21.

(f) Whenever the Administrator finds that revisions to an approved aircraft inspection program are necessary for the continued adequacy of the program, the certificate holder shall, after notification by the Administrator, make any changes in the program found by the Administrator to be necessary. The certificate holder may petition the Administrator to reconsider the notice to make any changes in a program. The petition must be filed with the representatives of the Administrator assigned to it within 30 days after the certificate holder receives the notice. Except in the case of an emergency requiring immediate action in the interest of safety, the filing of the petition stays the notice pending a decision by the Administrator.

(g) Each certificate holder who has an approved aircraft inspection program shall have each aircraft that is subject to the program inspected in accordance with the program.

(h) The registration number of each aircraft that is subject to an approved aircraft inspection program must be included in the operations specifications of the certificate holder.

§135.421 Additional maintenance requirements.

(a) Each certificate holder who operates an aircraft type certificated for a passenger seating configuration, excluding any pilot seat, of nine seats or less, must comply with the manufacturer's recommended maintenance programs, or a program approved by the Administrator, for each aircraft engine, propeller, rotor, and each item of emergency equipment required by this chapter.

(b) For the purpose of this section, a manufacturer's maintenance program is one which is contained in the maintenance manual or maintenance instructions set forth by the manufacturer as required by this chapter for the aircraft, aircraft engine, propeller, rotor or item of emergency equipment.

(c) For each single engine aircraft to be used in passenger-carrying IFR operations, each certificate holder must incorporate into its maintenance program either:

(1) the manufacturer's recommended engine trend monitoring program, which includes an oil analysis, if appropriate, or

(2) an FAA approved engine trend monitoring program that includes an oil analysis at each 100 hour interval or at the manufacturer's suggested interval, whichever is more frequent.

(d) For single engine aircraft to be used in passenger-carrying IFR operations, written maintenance instructions containing the methods, techniques, and practices necessary to maintain the equipment specified in §§135.105, and 135.163 (f) and (h) are required.

(e) No certificate holder may operate a single engine aircraft under IFR, carrying passengers, unless the certificate holder records and maintains in the engine maintenance records the results of each test, observation, and inspection required by the applicable engine trend monitoring program specified in (c)(1) and (c)(2) of this section.

[Docket No. 16097, 43 FR 46783, Oct. 10, 1978; as amended by Amdt. 135–70, 62 FR 42374, Aug. 6, 1997]

§135.422 Aging airplane inspections and records reviews for multiengine airplanes certificated with nine or fewer passenger seats.

(a) ***Applicability.*** This section applies to multiengine airplanes certificated with nine or fewer passenger seats, operated by a certificate holder in a scheduled operation under this part, except for those airplanes operated by a certificate holder in a scheduled operation between any point within the State of Alaska and any other point within the State of Alaska.

(b) ***Operation after inspections and records review.*** After the dates specified in this paragraph, a certificate holder may not operate a multiengine airplane in a scheduled operation under this part unless the Administrator has notified the certificate holder that the Administrator has completed the aging airplane inspection and records review required by this section. During the inspection and records review, the certificate holder must demonstrate to the Administrator that the maintenance of age-sensitive parts and components of the airplane has been adequate and timely enough to ensure the highest degree of safety.

(1) Airplanes exceeding 24 years in service on December 8, 2003; initial and repetitive inspections and records reviews. For an airplane that has exceeded 24 years in service on December 8, 2003, no later than December 5, 2007, and thereafter at intervals not to exceed 7 years.

(2) Airplanes exceeding 14 years in service but not 24 years in service on December 8, 2003; initial and repetitive inspections and records reviews. For an airplane that has exceeded 14 years in service, but not 24 years in service, on December 8, 2003, no later than December 4, 2008, and thereafter at intervals not to exceed 7 years.

(3) Airplanes not exceeding 14 years in service on December 8, 2003; initial and repetitive inspections and records reviews. For an airplane that has not exceeded 14 years in service on December 8, 2003, no later than 5 years after the start of the airplane's 15th year in service and thereafter at intervals not to exceed 7 years.

(c) ***Unforeseen schedule conflict.*** In the event of an unforeseen scheduling conflict for a specific airplane, the Administrator may approve an extension of up to 90 days beyond an interval specified in paragraph (b) of this section.

(d) ***Airplane and records availability.*** The certificate holder must make available to the Administrator each airplane for which an inspection and records review is required under this section, in a condition for inspection specified by the Administrator, together with the records containing the following information:

(1) Total years in service of the airplane;

(2) Total time in service of the airframe;

(3) Date of the last inspection and records review required by this section;

(4) Current status of life-limited parts of the airframe;

(5) Time since the last overhaul of all structural components required to be overhauled on a specific time basis;

(6) Current inspection status of the airplane, including the time since the last inspection required by the inspection program under which the airplane is maintained;

(7) Current status of applicable airworthiness directives, including the date and methods of compliance, and, if the airworthiness directive involves recurring action, the time and date when the next action is required;

(8) A list of major structural alterations; and

(9) A report of major structural repairs and the current inspection status for these repairs.

(e) ***Notification to the Administrator.*** Each certificate holder must notify the Administrator at least 60 days before the date on which the airplane and airplane records will be made available for the inspection and records review.

[Docket No. FAA–1999–5401, 70 FR 5533, Feb. 2, 2005]

§135.423 Maintenance, preventive maintenance, and alteration organization.

(a) Each certificate holder that performs any of its maintenance (other than required inspections), preventive maintenance, or alterations, and each person with whom it arranges for the performance of that work, must have an organization adequate to perform the work.

(b) Each certificate holder that performs any inspections required by its manual under §135.427(b) (2) or (3), (in this subpart referred to as *required inspections*), and each person with whom it arranges for the performance of that work, must have an organization adequate to perform that work.

(c) Each person performing required inspections in addition to other maintenance, preventive maintenance, or alterations, shall organize the performance of those functions so as to separate the required inspection functions from the other maintenance, preventive maintenance, and alteration functions. The separation shall be below the level of administrative control at which overall responsibility for the required inspection functions and other maintenance, preventive maintenance, and alteration functions is exercised.

[Docket No. FAA–1999–5401; Amdt. 135–81, 67 FR 72764, Dec. 6, 2002; as amended by Amdt. 135–81, 70 FR 5533, Feb. 2, 2005]

§135.425 Maintenance, preventive maintenance, and alteration programs.

Each certificate holder shall have an inspection program and a program covering other maintenance, preventive maintenance, and alterations, that ensures that—

(a) Maintenance, preventive maintenance, and alterations performed by it, or by other persons, are performed under the certificate holder's manual;

(b) Competent personnel and adequate facilities and equipment are provided for the proper performance of maintenance, preventive maintenance, and alterations; and

(c) Each aircraft released to service is airworthy and has been properly maintained for operation under this part.

§135.427 Manual requirements.

(a) Each certificate holder shall put in its manual the chart or description of the certificate holder's organization required by §135.424 and a list of persons with whom it has arranged for the performance of any of its required inspections, other maintenance, preventive maintenance, or alterations, including a general description of that work.

(b) Each certificate holder shall put in its manual the programs required by §135.425 that must be followed in performing maintenance, preventive maintenance, and alterations of that certificate holder's aircraft, including airframes, aircraft engines, propellers, rotors, appliances, emergency equipment, and parts, and must include at least the following:

(1) The method of performing routine and nonroutine maintenance (other than required inspections), preventive maintenance, and alterations.

(2) A designation of the items of maintenance and alteration that must be inspected (required inspections) including at least those that could result in a failure, malfunction, or defect endangering the safe operation of the aircraft, if not performed properly or if improper parts or materials are used.

(3) The method of performing required inspections and a designation by occupational title of personnel authorized to perform each required inspection.

(4) Procedures for the reinspection of work performed under previous required inspection findings (*buy-back procedures*).

(5) Procedures, standards, and limits necessary for required inspections and acceptance or rejection of the items required to be inspected and for periodic inspection and calibration of precision tools, measuring devices, and test equipment.

(6) Procedures to ensure that all required inspections are performed.

(7) Instructions to prevent any person who performs any item of work from performing any required inspection of that work.

(8) Instructions and procedures to prevent any decision of an inspector regarding any required inspection from being countermanded by persons other than supervisory personnel of the inspection unit, or a person at the level of administrative control that has overall responsibility for the management of both the required inspection functions and the other maintenance, preventive maintenance, and alterations functions.

(9) Procedures to ensure that required inspections, other maintenance, preventive maintenance, and alterations that are not completed as a result of work interruptions are properly completed before the aircraft is released to service.

(c) Each certificate holder shall put in its manual a suitable system (which may include a coded system) that provides for the retention of the following information—

(1) A description (or reference to data acceptable to the Administrator) of the work performed;

(2) The name of the person performing the work if the work is performed by a person outside the organization of the certificate holder; and

(3) The name or other positive identification of the individual approving the work.

(d) For the purposes of this part, the certificate holder must prepare that part of its manual containing maintenance information and instructions, in whole or in part, in printed form or other form, acceptable to the Administrator, that is retrievable in the English language.

[Docket No. 16097, 43 FR 46783, Oct. 10, 1978; as amended by Amdt. 135–66, 62 FR 13257, March 19, 1997; Docket No. FAA–2004–17119, 69 FR 18472, April 8, 2004]

§135.429 Required inspection personnel.

(a) No person may use any person to perform required inspections unless the person performing the inspection is appropriately certificated, properly trained, qualified, and authorized to do so.

(b) No person may allow any person to perform a required inspection unless, at the time, the person performing that inspection is under the supervision and control of an inspection unit.

(c) No person may perform a required inspection if that person performed the item of work required to be inspected.

(d) In the case of rotorcraft that operate in remote areas or sites, the Administrator may approve procedures for the performance of required inspection items by a pilot when no other qualified person is available, provided—

(1) The pilot is employed by the certificate holder;

(2) It can be shown to the satisfaction of the Administrator that each pilot authorized to perform required inspections is properly trained and qualified;

(3) The required inspection is a result of a mechanical interruption and is not a part of a certificate holder's continuous airworthiness maintenance program;

(4) Each item is inspected after each flight until the item has been inspected by an appropriately certificated mechanic other than the one who originally performed the item of work; and

(5) Each item of work that is a required inspection item that is part of the flight control system shall be flight tested and reinspected before the aircraft is approved for return to service.

(e) Each certificate holder shall maintain, or shall determine that each person with whom it arranges to perform its required inspections maintains, a current listing of persons who have been trained, qualified, and authorized to conduct required inspections. The persons must be identified by name, occupational title and the inspections that they are authorized to perform. The certificate holder (or person with whom it arranges to perform its required inspections) shall give written information to each person so authorized, describing the extent of that person's responsibilities, authorities, and inspectional limitations. The list shall be made available for inspection by the Administrator upon request.

[Docket No. 16097, 43 FR 46783, Oct. 10, 1978; as amended by Amdt. 135–20, 51 FR 40710, Nov. 7, 1986]

§135.431 Continuing analysis and surveillance.

(a) Each certificate holder shall establish and maintain a system for the continuing analysis and surveillance of the performance and effectiveness of its inspection program and the program covering other maintenance, preventive maintenance, and alterations and for the correction of any deficiency in those programs, regardless of whether those programs are carried out by the certificate holder or by another person.

(b) Whenever the Administrator finds that either or both of the programs described in paragraph (a) of this section does not contain adequate procedures and standards to meet this part, the certificate holder shall, after notification by the Administrator, make changes in those programs requested by the Administrator.

(c) A certificate holder may petition the Administrator to reconsider the notice to make a change in a program. The petition must be filed with the certificate-holding district office within 30 days after the certificate holder receives the notice. Except in the case of an emergency requiring immediate action in the interest of safety, the filing of the petition stays the notice pending a decision by the Administrator.

[Docket No. 16097, 43 FR 46783, Oct. 10, 1978; as amended by Amdt. 135–60, 61 FR 2617, Jan. 26, 1996]

§135.433 Maintenance and preventive maintenance training program.

Each certificate holder or a person performing maintenance or preventive maintenance functions for it shall have a training program to ensure that each person (including inspection personnel) who determines the adequacy of work done is fully informed about procedures and techniques and new equipment in use and is competent to perform that person's duties.

§135.435 Certificate requirements.

(a) Except for maintenance, preventive maintenance, alterations and required inspections performed by a certificated repair station that is located outside the United States, each person who is directly in charge of maintenance, preventive maintenance, or alterations, and each person performing required inspections must hold an appropriate airman certificate.

(b) For the purpose of this section, a person *directly in charge* is each person assigned to a position in which that person is responsible for the work of a shop or station that performs maintenance, preventive maintenance, alterations, or other functions affecting airworthiness. A person who is *directly in charge* need not physically observe and direct each worker constantly but must be available for consultation and decision on matters requiring instruction or decision from higher authority than that of the person performing the work.

[Docket No. 16097, 43 FR 46783, Oct. 10, 1978; as amended by Amdt. 135–82, 66 FR 41117, Aug. 6, 2001]

§135.437 Authority to perform and approve maintenance, preventive maintenance, and alterations.

(a) A certificate holder may perform or make arrangements with other persons to perform maintenance, preventive maintenance, and alterations as provided in its maintenance manual. In addition, a certificate holder may perform these functions for another certificate holder as provided in the maintenance manual of the other certificate holder.

(b) A certificate holder may approve any airframe, aircraft engine, propeller, rotor, or appliance for return to service after maintenance, preventive maintenance, or alterations that are performed under paragraph (a) of this section. However, in the case of a major repair or alteration, the work must have been done in accordance with technical data approved by the Administrator.

§135.439 Maintenance recording requirements.

(a) Each certificate holder shall keep (using the system specified in the manual required in §135.427) the following records for the periods specified in paragraph (b) of this section:

(1) All the records necessary to show that all requirements for the issuance of an airworthiness release under §135.443 have been met.

(2) Records containing the following information:

(i) The total time in service of the airframe, engine, propeller, and rotor.

(ii) The current status of life-limited parts of each airframe, engine, propeller, rotor, and appliance.

(iii) The time since last overhaul of each item installed on the aircraft which are required to be overhauled on a specified time basis.

(iv) The identification of the current inspection status of the aircraft, including the time since the last inspections required by the inspection program under which the aircraft and its appliances are maintained.

(v) The current status of applicable airworthiness directives, including the date and methods of compliance, and, if the airworthiness directive involves recurring action, the time and date when the next action is required.

(vi) A list of current major alterations and repairs to each airframe, engine, propeller, rotor, and appliance.

(b) Each certificate holder shall retain the records required to be kept by this section for the following periods:

(1) Except for the records of the last complete overhaul of each airframe, engine, propeller, rotor, and appliance the records specified in paragraph (a)(1) of this section shall be retained until the work is repeated or superseded by other work or for one year after the work is performed.

(2) The records of the last complete overhaul of each airframe, engine, propeller, rotor, and appliance shall be retained until the work is superseded by work of equivalent scope and detail.

(3) The records specified in paragraph (a)(2) of this section shall be retained and transferred with the aircraft at the time the aircraft is sold.

(c) The certificate holder shall make all maintenance records required to be kept by this section available for inspection by the Administrator or any representative of the National Transportation Safety Board.

[Docket No. 16097, 43 FR 46783, Oct. 10, 1978; 43 FR 49975, Oct. 26, 1978]

§135.441 Transfer of maintenance records.

Each certificate holder who sells a United States registered aircraft shall transfer to the purchaser, at the time of the sale, the following records of that aircraft, in plain language form or in coded form which provides for the preservation and retrieval of information in a manner acceptable to the Administrator:

(a) The records specified in §135.439(a)(2).

(b) The records specified in §135.439(a)(1) which are not included in the records covered by paragraph (a) of this section, except that the purchaser may allow the seller to keep physical custody of such records. However, custody of records by the seller does not relieve the purchaser of its responsibility under §135.439(c) to make the records available for inspection by the Administrator or any representative of the National Transportation Safety Board.

§135.443 Airworthiness release or aircraft maintenance log entry.

(a) No certificate holder may operate an aircraft after maintenance, preventive maintenance, or alterations are performed on the aircraft unless the certificate holder prepares, or causes the person with whom the certificate holder arranges for the performance of the maintenance, preventive maintenance, or alterations, to prepare—

(1) An airworthiness release; or

(2) An appropriate entry in the aircraft maintenance log.

(b) The airworthiness release or log entry required by paragraph (a) of this section must—

(1) Be prepared in accordance with the procedure in the certificate holder's manual;

(2) Include a certification that—

(i) The work was performed in accordance with the requirements of the certificate holder's manual;

(ii) All items required to be inspected were inspected by an authorized person who determined that the work was satisfactorily completed;

(iii) No known condition exists that would make the aircraft unairworthy; and

(iv) So far as the work performed is concerned, the aircraft is in condition for safe operation; and

(3) Be signed by an authorized certificated mechanic or repairman, except that a certificated repairman may sign the release or entry only for the work for which that person is employed and for which that person is certificated.

(c) Notwithstanding paragraph (b)(3) of this section, after maintenance, preventive maintenance, or alterations performed by a repair station located outside the United States, the airworthiness release or log entry required by paragraph (a) of this section may be signed by a person authorized by that repair station.

(d) Instead of restating each of the conditions of the certification required by paragraph (b) of this section, the certificate holder may state in its manual that the signature of an authorized certificated mechanic or repairman constitutes that certification.

[Docket No. 16097, 43 FR 46783, Oct. 10, 1978; as amended by Amdt. 135–29, 53 FR 47375, Nov. 22, 1988; Amdt. 135–82, 66 FR 41117, Aug. 6, 2001]

Appendix A to Part 135

Additional Airworthiness Standards For 10 or More Passenger Airplanes

Applicability

1. *Applicability.* This appendix prescribes the additional airworthiness standards required by §135.169.

2. *References.* Unless otherwise provided, references in this appendix to specific sections of part 23 of the Federal Aviation Regulations (FAR part 23) are to those sections of part 23 in effect on March 30, 1967.

Flight Requirements

3. *General.* Compliance must be shown with the applicable requirements of subpart B of FAR part 23, as supplemented or modified in §§4 through 10.

Performance

4. *General.*

(a) Unless otherwise prescribed in this appendix, compliance with each applicable performance requirement in sections 4 through 7 must be shown for ambient atmospheric conditions and still air.

(b) The performance must correspond to the propulsive thrust available under the particular ambient atmospheric conditions and the particular flight condition. The available propulsive thrust must correspond to engine power or thrust, not exceeding the approved power or thrust less—

(1) Installation losses; and

(2) The power or equivalent thrust absorbed by the accessories and services appropriate to the particular ambient atmospheric conditions and the particular flight condition.

(c) Unless otherwise prescribed in this appendix, the applicant must select the takeoff, en route, and landing configurations for the airplane.

(d) The airplane configuration may vary with weight, altitude, and temperature, to the extent they are compatible with the operating procedures required by paragraph (e) of this section.

(e) Unless otherwise prescribed in this appendix, in determining the critical engine inoperative takeoff performance, the accelerate-stop distance, takeoff distance, changes in the airplane's configuration, speed, power, and thrust must be made under procedures established by the applicant for operation in service.

(f) Procedures for the execution of balked landings must be established by the applicant and included in the Airplane Flight Manual.

(g) The procedures established under paragraphs (e) and (f) of this section must—

(1) Be able to be consistently executed in service by a crew of average skill;

(2) Use methods or devices that are safe and reliable; and

(3) Include allowance for any time delays in the execution of the procedures, that may reasonably be expected in service.

5. *Takeoff*—

(a) *General.* Takeoff speeds the accelerate-stop distance, the takeoff distance, and the one-engine-inoperative takeoff flight path data (described in paragraphs (b), (c), (d), and (f) of this section), must be determined for—

(1) Each weight, altitude, and ambient temperature within the operational limits selected by the applicant;

(2) The selected configuration for takeoff;

(3) The center of gravity in the most unfavorable position;

(4) The operating engine within approved operating limitations; and

(5) Takeoff data based on smooth, dry, hard-surface runway.

(b) *Takeoff speeds.*

(1) The decision speed V_1 is the calibrated airspeed on the ground at which, as a result of engine failure or other reasons, the pilot is assumed to have made a decision to continue or discontinue the takeoff. The speed V_1 must be selected by the applicant but may not be less than—

(i) 1.10 V_{S1};

(ii) 1.10 V_{MC};

(iii) A speed that allows acceleration to V_1 and stop under paragraph (c) of this section; or

(iv) A speed at which the airplane can be rotated for takeoff and shown to be adequate to safely continue the takeoff, using normal piloting skill, when the critical engine is suddenly made inoperative.

(2) The initial climb out speed V_2 in terms of calibrated airspeed, must be selected by the applicant so as to allow the gradient of climb required in section 6(b)(2), but it must not be less than V_1 or less than 1.2 V_{S1}.

(3) Other essential take off speeds necessary for safe operation of the airplane.

(c) *Accelerate-stop distance.*

(1) The accelerate-stop distance is the sum of the distances necessary to—

(i) Accelerate the airplane from a standing start to V_1; and

(ii) Come to a full stop from the point at which V_1 is reached assuming that in the case of engine failure, failure of the critical engine is recognized by the pilot at the speed V_1.

(2) Means other than wheel brakes may be used to determine the accelerate-stop distance if that means is available with the critical engine inoperative and—

(i) Is safe and reliable;

(ii) Is used so that consistent results can be expected under normal operating conditions; and

(iii) Is such that exceptional skill is not required to control the airplane.

(d) *All engines operating takeoff distance.* The all engine operating takeoff distance is the horizontal distance required to takeoff and climb to a height of 50 feet above the takeoff surface under the procedures in FAR 23.51(a).

(e) *One-engine-inoperative takeoff.* Determine the weight for each altitude and temperature within the operational limits established for the airplane, at which the airplane has the capability, after failure of the critical engine at V_1 determined under paragraph (b) of this section, to take off and climb at not less than V_2, to a height 1,000 feet above the takeoff surface and attain the speed and configuration at which compliance is shown with the en route one engine-inoperative gradient of climb specified in section 6(c).

(f) *One-engine-inoperative takeoff flight path data.* The one-engine-inoperative takeoff flight path data consist of takeoff flight paths extending from a standing start to a point in the takeoff at which the airplane reaches a height 1,000 feet above the takeoff surface under paragraph (e) of this section.

6. *Climb*—

(a) *Landing climb: All-engines operating.* The maximum weight must be determined with the airplane in the landing configuration, for each altitude, and ambient temperature within the operational limits established for the airplane, with the most unfavorable center of gravity, and out-of-ground effect in free air, at which the steady gradient of climb will not be less than 3.3 percent, with:

(1) The engines at the power that is available 8 seconds after initiation of movement of the power or thrust controls from the minimum flight idle to the takeoff position.

(2) A climb speed not greater than the approach speed established under section 7 and not less than the greater of 1.05 V_{MC} or 1.10 V_{S1}.

(b) *Takeoff climb: one-engine-inoperative.* The maximum weight at which the airplane meets the minimum climb performance specified in paragraphs (1) and (2) of this paragraph must be determined for each altitude and ambient temperature within the operational limits established for the airplane, out of ground effect in free air, with the airplane in the takeoff configuration, with the most unfavorable center of gravity, the critical engine inoperative, the remaining engines at the maximum takeoff power or thrust, and the propeller of the inoperative engine windmilling with the propeller controls in the normal position except that, if an approved automatic feathering system is installed, the propellers may be in the feathered position:

(1) *Takeoff: landing gear extended.* The minimum steady gradient of climb must be measurably positive at the speed V_1.

(2) *Takeoff: landing gear retracted.* The minimum steady gradient of climb may not be less than 2 percent at speed V_2. For airplanes with fixed landing gear this requirement must be met with the landing gear extended.

(c) *En route climb: one-engine-inoperative.* The maximum weight must be determined for each altitude and ambient temperature within the operational limits established for the airplane, at which the steady gradient of climb is not less 1.2 percent at an altitude 1,000 feet above the takeoff surface, with the airplane in the en route configuration, the critical engine inoperative, the remaining engine at the maximum continuous power or thrust, and the most unfavorable center of gravity.

7. *Landing.*

(a) The landing field length described in paragraph (b) of this section must be determined for standard atmosphere at each weight and altitude within the operational limits established by the applicant.

(b) The landing field length is equal to the landing distance determined under FAR 23.75(a) divided by a factor of 0.6 for the destination airport and 0.7 for the alternate airport. Instead of the gliding approach specified in FAR 23.75(a)(1), the landing may be preceded by a steady approach down to the 50-foot height at a gradient of descent not greater than 5.2 percent (3°) at a calibrated airspeed not less than 1.3 V_{S1}.

TRIM

8. *Trim*

(a) *Lateral and directional trim.* The airplane must maintain lateral and directional trim in level flight at a speed of V_H or V_{MO}/M_{MO}, whichever is lower, with landing gear and wing flaps retracted.

(b) *Longitudinal trim.* The airplane must maintain longitudinal trim during the following conditions, except that it need not maintain trim at a speed greater than V_{MO}/M_{MO}.

(1) In the approach conditions specified in FAR 23.161(c)(3) through (5), except that instead of the speeds specified in those paragraphs, trim must be maintained with a stick force of not more than 10 pounds down to a speed used in showing compliance with section 7 or 1.4 V_{S1} whichever is lower.

(2) In level flight at any speed from V_H or V_{MO}/M_{MO}, whichever is lower, to either V_X or 1.4 V_{S1}, with the landing gear and wing flaps retracted.

STABILITY

9. *Static longitudinal stability.*

(a) In showing compliance with FAR 23.175(b) and with paragraph (b) of this section, the airspeed must return to within ±7½ percent of the trim speed.

(b) *Cruise stability.* The stick force curve must have a stable slope for a speed range of ±50 knots from the trim speed except that the speeds need not exceed V_{FC}/M_{FC} or be less than 1.4 V_{S1}. This speed range will be considered to begin at the outer extremes of the friction band and the stick force may not exceed 50 pounds with—

(1) Landing gear retracted;

(2) Wing flaps retracted;

(3) The maximum cruising power as selected by the applicant as an operating limitation for turbine engines or 75 percent of maximum continuous power for reciprocating engines except that the power need not exceed that required at V_{MO}/M_{MO};

(4) Maximum takeoff weight; and

(5) The airplane trimmed for level flight with the power specified in paragraph (3) of this paragraph.

V_{FC}/M_{FC} may not be less than a speed midway between V_{MO}/M_{MO} and V_{DF}/M_{DF}, except that, for altitudes where Mach number is the limiting factor, M_{FC} need not exceed the Mach number at which effective speed warning occurs.

(c) *Climb stability (turbopropeller powered airplanes only).* In showing compliance with FAR 23.175(a), an applicant must, instead of the power specified in FAR 23.175(a)(4), use the maximum power or thrust selected by the applicant as an operating limitation for use during climb at the best rate of climb speed, except that the speed need not be less than 1.4 V_{S1}.

STALLS

10. *Stall warning.* If artificial stall warning is required to comply with FAR 23.207, the warning device must give clearly distinguishable indications under expected conditions of flight. The use of a visual warning device that requires the attention of the crew within the cockpit is not acceptable by itself.

CONTROL SYSTEMS

11. *Electric trim tabs.* The airplane must meet FAR 23.677 and in addition it must be shown that the airplane is safely controllable and that a pilot can perform all the maneuvers and operations necessary to effect a safe landing following any probable electric trim tab runaway which might be reasonably expected in service allowing for appropriate time delay after pilot recognition of the runaway. This demonstration must be conducted at the critical airplane weights and center of gravity positions.

INSTRUMENTS: INSTALLATION

12. *Arrangement and visibility.* Each instrument must meet FAR 23.1321 and in addition:

(a) Each flight, navigation, and powerplant instrument for use by any pilot must be plainly visible to the pilot from the pilot's station with the minimum practicable deviation from the pilot's normal position and line of vision when the pilot is looking forward along the flight path.

(b) The flight instruments required by FAR 23.1303 and by the applicable operating rules must be grouped on the instrument panel and centered as nearly as practicable about the vertical plane of each pilot's forward vision. In addition—

(1) The instrument that most effectively indicates the attitude must be in the panel in the top center position;

(2) The instrument that most effectively indicates the airspeed must be on the panel directly to the left of the instrument in the top center position;

(3) The instrument that most effectively indicates altitude must be adjacent to and directly to the right of the instrument in the top center position; and

(4) The instrument that most effectively indicates direction of flight must be adjacent to and directly below the instrument in the top center position.

13. *Airspeed indicating system.* Each airspeed indicating system must meet FAR 23.1323 and in addition:

(a) Airspeed indicating instruments must be of an approved type and must be calibrated to indicate true airspeed at sea level in the standard atmosphere with a minimum practicable instrument calibration error when the corresponding pitot and static pressures are supplied to the instruments.

(b) The airspeed indicating system must be calibrated to determine the system error, i.e., the relation between IAS and CAS, in flight and during the accelerate-takeoff ground run. The ground run calibration must be obtained between 0.8 of the minimum value of V_1 and 1.2 times the maximum value of V_1, considering the approved ranges of altitude and weight. The ground run calibration is determined assuming an engine failure at the minimum value of V_1.

(c) The airspeed error of the installation excluding the instrument calibration error, must not exceed 3 percent or 5 knots whichever is greater, throughout the speed range from V_{MO} to 1.3 V_{S1} with flaps retracted and from 1.3 V_{S0} to V_{FE} with flaps in the landing position.

(d) Information showing the relationship between IAS and CAS must be shown in the Airplane Flight manual.

14. *Static air vent system.* The static air vent system must meet FAR 23.1325. The altimeter system calibration must be determined and shown in the Airplane Flight Manual.

OPERATING LIMITATIONS AND INFORMATION

15. *Maximum operating limit speed V_{MO}/M_{MO}.* Instead of establishing operating limitations based on V_{NE} and V_{NO}. the applicant must establish a maximum operating limit speed V_{MO}/M_{MO} as follows:

(a) The maximum operating limit speed must not exceed the design cruising speed V_C and must be sufficiently below V_D/M_D or V_{DF}/M_{DF} to make it highly improbable that the latter speeds will be inadvertently exceeded in flight.

(b) The speed V_{MO} must not exceed 0.8 V_D/M_D or 0.8 V_{DF}/M_{DF} unless flight demonstrations involving upsets as specified by the Administrator indicates a lower speed margin will not result in speeds exceeding V_D/M_D or V_{DF}. Atmospheric variations, horizontal gusts, system and equipment errors, and airframe production variations are taken into account.

16. *Minimum flight crew.* In addition to meeting FAR 23.1523, the applicant must establish the minimum number and type of qualified flight crew personnel sufficient for safe operation of the airplane considering—

(a) Each kind of operation for which the applicant desires approval;

(b) The workload on each crewmember considering the following:

(1) Flight path control.

(2) Collision avoidance.

(3) Navigation.

(4) Communications.

(5) Operation and monitoring of all essential aircraft systems.

(6) Command decisions; and

(c) The accessibility and ease of operation of necessary controls by the appropriate crewmember during all normal and emergency operations when at the crewmember flight station.

17. *Airspeed indicator.* The airspeed indicator must meet FAR 23.1545 except that, the airspeed notations and markings in terms of V_{NO} and V_{NH} must be replaced by the V_{MO}/M_{MO} notations. The airspeed indicator markings must be easily read and understood by the pilot. A placard adjacent to the airspeed indicator is an acceptable means of showing compliance with FAR 23.1545(c).

AIRPLANE FLIGHT MANUAL

18. *General.* The Airplane Flight Manual must be prepared under FARs 23.1583 and 23.1587, and in addition the operating limitations and performance information in sections 19 and 20 must be included.

19. *Operating limitations.* The Airplane Flight Manual must include the following limitations—

(a) *Airspeed limitations.*

(1) The maximum operating limit speed V_{MO}/M_{MO} and a statement that this speed limit may not be deliberately exceeded in any regime of flight (climb. cruise, or descent) unless a higher speed is authorized for flight test or pilot training;

(2) If an airspeed limitation is based upon compressibility effects, a statement to this effect and information as to any symptoms the probable behavior of the airplane, and the recommended recovery procedures; and

(3) The airspeed limits, shown in terms of V_{MO}/M_{MO} instead of V_{NO} and V_{NE}.

(b) *Takeoff weight limitations.* The maximum takeoff weight for each airport elevation, ambient temperature, and available takeoff runway length within the range selected by the applicant may not exceed the weight at which—

(1) The all-engine-operating takeoff distance determined under section 5(b) or the accelerate-stop distance determined under section 5(c), whichever is greater, is equal to the available runway length;

(2) The airplane complies with the one-engine-inoperative takeoff requirements specified in section 5(e); and

(3) The airplane complies with the one-engine-inoperative takeoff and en route climb requirements specified in sections 6 (b) and (c).

(c) *Landing weight limitations.* The maximum landing weight for each airport elevation (standard temperature) and available landing runway length, within the range selected by the applicant. This weight may not exceed the weight at which the landing field length determined under section 7(b) is equal to the available runway length. In showing compliance with this operating limitation, it is acceptable to assume that the landing weight at the destination will be equal to the takeoff weight reduced by the normal consumption of fuel and oil en route.

20. *Performance information.* The Airplane Flight Manual must contain the performance information determined under the performance requirements of this appendix. The information must include the following:

(a) Sufficient information so that the takeoff weight limits specified in section 19(b) can be determined for all temperatures and altitudes within the operation limitations selected by the applicant.

(b) The conditions under which the performance information was obtained, including the airspeed at the 50-foot height used to determine landing distances.

(c) The performance information (determined by extrapolation and computed for the range of weights between the maximum landing and takeoff weights) for—

(1) Climb in the landing configuration; and

(2) Landing distance.

(d) Procedure established under section 4 related to the limitations and information required by this section in the form of guidance material including any relevant limitations or information.

(e) An explanation of significant or unusual flight or ground handling characteristics of the airplane.

(f) Airspeeds, as indicated airspeeds, corresponding to those determined for takeoff under section 5(b).

21. *Maximum operating altitudes.* The maximum operating altitude to which operation is allowed, as limited by flight, structural, powerplant, functional, or equipment characteristics, must be specified in the Airplane Flight Manual.

22. *Stowage provision for airplane flight manual.* Provision must be made for stowing the Airplane Flight Manual in a suitable fixed container which is readily accessible to the pilot.

23. *Operating procedures.* Procedures for restarting turbine engines in flight (including the effects of altitude) must be set forth in the Airplane Flight Manual.

AIRFRAME REQUIREMENTS

FLIGHT LOADS

24. *Engine torque.*

(a) Each turbopropeller engine mount and its supporting structure must be designed for the torque effects of:

(1) The conditions in FAR 23.361(a).

(2) The limit engine torque corresponding to takeoff power and propeller speed multiplied by a factor accounting for propeller control system malfunction, including quick feathering action, simultaneously with 1g level flight loads. In the absence of a rational analysis, a factor of 1.6 must be used.

(b) The limit torque is obtained by multiplying the mean torque by a factor of 1.25.

25. *Turbine engine gyroscopic loads.* Each turbopropeller engine mount and its supporting structure must be designed for the gyroscopic loads that result, with the engines at maximum continuous r.p.m., under either—

(a) The conditions in FARs 23.351 and 23.423; or

(b) All possible combinations of the following:

(1) A yaw velocity of 2.5 radians per second.

(2) A pitch velocity of 1.0 radians per second.

(3) A normal load factor of 2.5.

(4) Maximum continuous thrust.

26. *Unsymmetrical loads due to engine failure.*

(a) Turbopropeller powered airplanes must be designed for the unsymmetrical loads resulting from the failure of the critical engine including the following conditions in combination with a single malfunction of the propeller drag limiting system, considering the probable pilot corrective action on the flight controls:

(1) At speeds between V_{MO} and V_D, the loads resulting from power failure because of fuel flow interruption are considered to be limit loads.

(2) At speeds between V_{MO} and V_C, the loads resulting from the disconnection of the engine compressor from the turbine or from loss of the turbine blades are considered to be ultimate loads.

(3) The time history of the thrust decay and drag buildup occurring as a result of the prescribed engine failures must be substantiated by test or other data applicable to the particular engine-propeller combination.

(4) The timing and magnitude of the probable pilot corrective action must be conservatively estimated, considering the characteristics of the particular engine-propeller-airplane combination.

(b) Pilot corrective action may be assumed to be initiated at the time maximum yawing velocity is reached, but not earlier than 2 seconds after the engine failure. The magnitude of the corrective action may be based on the control forces in FAR 23.397 except that lower forces may be assumed where it is shown by analysis or test that these forces can control the yaw and roll resulting from the prescribed engine failure conditions.

GROUND LOADS

27. *Dual wheel landing gear units.* Each dual wheel landing gear unit and its supporting structure must be shown to comply with the following:

(a) *Pivoting.* The airplane must be assumed to pivot about one side of the main gear with the brakes on that side locked. The limit vertical load factor must be 1.0 and the coefficient of friction 0.8. This condition need apply only to the main gear and its supporting structure.

(b) *Unequal tire inflation.* A 60–40 percent distribution of the loads established under FAR 23.471 through FAR 23.483 must be applied to the dual wheels.

(c) *Flat tire.*

(1) Sixty percent of the loads in FAR 23.471 through FAR 23.483 must be applied to either wheel in a unit.

(2) Sixty percent of the limit drag and side loads and 100 percent of the limit vertical load established under FARs 23.493 and 23.485 must be applied to either wheel in a unit except that the vertical load need not exceed the maximum vertical load in paragraph (c)(1) of this section.

FATIGUE EVALUATION

28. *Fatigue evaluation of wing and associated structure.* Unless it is shown that the structure, operating stress levels, materials and expected use are comparable from a fatigue standpoint to a similar design which has had substantial satisfactory service experience, the strength, detail design, and the fabrication of those parts of the wing, wing carry through, and attaching structure whose failure would be catastrophic must be evaluated under either—

(a) A fatigue strength investigation in which the structure is shown by analysis, tests, or both to be able to withstand the repeated loads of variable magnitude expected in service, or

(b) A fail-safe strength investigation in which it is shown by analysis, tests, or both that catastrophic failure of the structure is not probable after fatigue, or obvious partial failure, of a principal structural element, and that the remaining structure is able to withstand a static ultimate load factor of 75 percent of the critical limit load factor at V_C. These loads must be multiplied by a factor of 1.15 unless the dynamic effects of failure under static load are otherwise considered.

DESIGN AND CONSTRUCTION

29. *Flutter.* For multiengine turbopropeller powered airplanes, a dynamic evaluation must be made and must include—

(a) The significant elastic, inertia, and aerodynamic forces associated with the rotations and displacements of the plane of the propeller; and

(b) Engine-propeller-nacelle stiffness and damping variations appropriate to the particular configuration.

LANDING GEAR

30. *Flap operated landing gear warning device.* Airplanes having retractable landing gear and wing flaps must be equipped with a warning device that functions continuously when the wing flaps are extended to a flap position that activates the warning device to give adequate warning before landing, using normal landing procedures, if the landing gear is not fully extended and locked. There may not be a manual shut off for this warning device. The flap position sensing unit may be installed at any suitable location. The system for this device may use any part of the system (including the aural warning device) provided for other landing gear warning devices.

PERSONNEL AND CARGO ACCOMMODATIONS

31. *Cargo and baggage compartments.* Cargo and baggage compartments must be designed to meet FAR 23.787 (a) and (b), and in addition means must be provided to protect passengers from injury by the contents of any cargo or baggage compartment when the ultimate forward inertia force is 9g.

32. *Doors and exits.* The airplane must meet FAR 23.783 and FAR 23.807 (a)(3), (b), and (c), and in addition:

(a) There must be a means to lock and safeguard each external door and exit against opening in flight either inadvertently by persons, or as a result of mechanical failure. Each external door must be operable from both the inside and the outside.

(b) There must be means for direct visual inspection of the locking mechanism by crewmembers to determine whether external doors and exits, for which the initial opening movement is outward, are fully locked. In addition, there must be a visual means to signal to crewmembers when normally used external doors are closed and fully locked.

(c) The passenger entrance door must qualify as a floor level emergency exit. Each additional required emergency exit except floor level exits must be located over the wing or must be provided with acceptable means to assist the occupants in descending to the ground. In addition to the passenger entrance door:

(1) For a total seating capacity of 15 or less, an emergency exit as defined in FAR 23.807(b) is required on each side of the cabin.

(2) For a total seating capacity of 16 through 23, three emergency exits as defined in FAR 23.807(b) are required with one on the same side as the door and two on the side opposite the door.

(d) An evacuation demonstration must be conducted utilizing the maximum number of occupants for which certification is desired. It must be conducted under simulated night conditions utilizing only the emergency exits on the most critical side of the aircraft. The participants must be representative of average airline passengers with no previous practice or rehearsal for the demonstration. Evacuation must be completed within 90 seconds.

(e) Each emergency exit must be marked with the word "Exit" by a sign which has white letters 1 inch high on a red background 2 inches high, be self-illuminated or independently internally electrically illuminated, and have a minimum luminescence (brightness) of at least 160 microlamberts. The colors may be reversed if the passenger compartment illumination is essentially the same.

(f) Access to window type emergency exits must not be obstructed by seats or seat backs.

(g) The width of the main passenger aisle at any point between seats must equal or exceed the values in the following table:

	Minimum main passenger aisle width	
Total seating capacity	Less than 25 inches from floor	25 inches and more from floor
10 through 23	9 inches	15 inches

MISCELLANEOUS

33. *Lightning strike protection.* Parts that are electrically insulated from the basic airframe must be connected to it through lightning arrestors unless a lightning strike on the insulated part—

(a) Is improbable because of shielding by other parts; or

(b) Is not hazardous.

34. *Ice protection.* If certification with ice protection provisions is desired, compliance with the following must be shown:

(a) The recommended procedures for the use of the ice protection equipment must be set forth in the Airplane Flight Manual.

(b) An analysis must be performed to establish, on the basis of the airplane's operational needs, the adequacy of the ice protection system for the various components of the airplane. In addition, tests of the ice protection system must be conducted to demonstrate that the airplane is capable of operating safely in continuous maximum and intermittent maximum icing conditions as described in Appendix C of part 25 of this chapter.

(c) Compliance with all or portions of this section may be accomplished by reference, where applicable because of similarity of the designs, to analysis and tests performed by the applicant for a type certificated model.

35. *Maintenance information.* The applicant must make available to the owner at the time of delivery of the airplane the information the applicant considers essential for the proper maintenance of the airplane. That information must include the following:

(a) Description of systems, including electrical, hydraulic, and fuel controls.

(b) Lubrication instructions setting forth the frequency and the lubricants and fluids which are to be used in the various systems.

(c) Pressures and electrical loads applicable to the various systems.

(d) Tolerances and adjustments necessary for proper functioning.

(e) Methods of leveling, raising, and towing.

(f) Methods of balancing control surfaces.

(g) Identification of primary and secondary structures.

(h) Frequency and extent of inspections necessary to the proper operation of the airplane.

(i) Special repair methods applicable to the airplane.

(j) Special inspection techniques, such as X-ray, ultrasonic, and magnetic particle inspection.

(k) List of special tools.

PROPULSION

GENERAL

36. *Vibration characteristics.* For turbopropeller powered airplanes, the engine installation must not result in vibration characteristics of the engine exceeding those established during the type certification of the engine.

37. *In flight restarting of engine.* If the engine on turbopropeller powered airplanes cannot be restarted at the maximum cruise altitude, a determination must be made of the altitude below which restarts can be consistently accomplished. Restart information must be provided in the Airplane Flight Manual.

38. *Engines.*

(a) *For turbopropeller powered airplanes.* The engine installation must comply with the following:

(1) *Engine isolation.* The powerplants must be arranged and isolated from each other to allow operation, in at least one configuration, so that the failure or malfunction of any engine, or of any system that can affect the engine, will not—

(i) Prevent the continued safe operation of the remaining engines; or

(ii) Require immediate action by any crewmember for continued safe operation.

(2) *Control of engine rotation.* There must be a means to individually stop and restart the rotation of any engine in flight except that engine rotation need not be stopped if continued rotation could not jeopardize the safety of the airplane. Each component of the stopping and restarting system on the engine side of the firewall, and that might be exposed to fire, must be at least fire resistant. If hydraulic propeller feathering systems are used for this purpose, the feathering lines must be at least fire resistant under the operating conditions that may be expected to exist during feathering.

(3) *Engine speed and gas temperature control devices.* The powerplant systems associated with engine control devices, systems, and instrumentation must provide reasonable assurance that those engine operating limitations that adversely affect turbine rotor structural integrity will not be exceeded in service.

(b) *For reciprocating engine powered airplanes.* To provide engine isolation, the powerplants must be arranged and isolated from each other to allow operation, in at least one configuration, so that the failure or malfunction of any engine, or of any system that can affect that engine, will not—

(1) Prevent the continued safe operation of the remaining engines: or

(2) Require immediate action by any crewmember for continued safe operation.

39. *Turbopropeller reversing systems.*

(a) Turbopropeller reversing systems intended for ground operation must be designed so that no single failure or malfunction of the system will result in unwanted reverse thrust under any expected operating condition. Failure of structural elements need not be considered if the probability of this kind of failure is extremely remote.

(b) Turbopropeller reversing systems intended for in flight use must be designed so that no unsafe condition will result during normal operation of the system, or from any failure (or reasonably likely combination of failures) of the reversing system, under any anticipated condition of operation of the airplane. Failure of structural elements need not be considered if the probability of this kind of failure is extremely remote.

(c) Compliance with this section may be shown by failure analysis, testing, or both for propeller systems that allow propeller blades to move from the flight low-pitch position to a position that is substantially less than that at the normal flight low-pitch stop position. The analysis may include or be supported by the analysis made to show compliance with the type certification of the propeller and associated installation components. Credit will be given for pertinent analysis and testing completed by the engine and propeller manufacturers.

40. *Turbopropeller drag-limiting systems.* Turbopropeller drag-limiting systems must be designed so that no single failure or malfunction of any of the systems during normal or emergency operation results in propeller drag in excess of that for which the airplane was designed. Failure of structural elements of the drag-limiting systems need not be considered if the probability of this kind of failure is extremely remote.

41. *Turbine engine powerplant operating characteristics.* For turbopropeller powered airplanes, the turbine engine powerplant operating characteristics must be investigated in flight to determine that no adverse characteristics (such as stall, surge, or flameout) are present to a hazardous degree, during normal and emergency operation within the range of operating limitations of the airplane and of the engine.

42. *Fuel flow.*

(a) For turbopropeller powered airplanes—

(1) The fuel system must provide for continuous supply of fuel to the engines for normal operation without interruption due to depletion of fuel in any tank other than the main tank; and

(2) The fuel flow rate for turbopropeller engine fuel pump systems must not be less than 125 percent of the fuel flow required to develop the standard sea level atmospheric conditions takeoff power selected and included as an operating limitation in the Airplane Flight Manual.

(b) For reciprocating engine powered airplanes, it is acceptable for the fuel flow rate for each pump system (main and reserve supply) to be 125 percent of the takeoff fuel consumption of the engine.

FUEL SYSTEM COMPONENTS

43. *Fuel pumps.* For turbopropeller powered airplanes, a reliable and independent power source must be provided for each pump used with turbine engines which do not have provisions for mechanically driving the main pumps. It must be demonstrated that the pump installations provide a reliability and durability equivalent to that in FAR 23.991(a).

44. *Fuel strainer or filter.* For turbopropeller powered airplanes, the following apply:

(a) There must be a fuel strainer or filter between the tank outlet and the fuel metering device of the engine. In addition, the fuel strainer or filter must be—

(1) Between the tank outlet and the engine-driven positive displacement pump inlet, if there is an engine-driven positive displacement pump;

(2) Accessible for drainage and cleaning and, for the strainer screen, easily removable; and

(3) Mounted so that its weight is not supported by the connecting lines or by the inlet or outlet connections of the strainer or filter itself.

(b) Unless there are means in the fuel system to prevent the accumulation of ice on the filter, there must be means to automatically maintain the fuel-flow if ice-clogging of the filter occurs; and

(c) The fuel strainer or filter must be of adequate capacity (for operating limitations established to ensure proper service) and of appropriate mesh to insure proper engine operation, with the fuel contaminated to a degree (for particle size and density) that can be reasonably expected in service. The degree of fuel filtering may not be less than that established for the engine type certification.

45. *Lightning strike protection.* Protection must be provided against the ignition of flammable vapors in the fuel vent system due to lightning strikes.

Cooling

46. *Cooling test procedures for turbopropeller powered airplanes.*

(a) Turbopropeller powered airplanes must be shown to comply with FAR 23.1041 during takeoff, climb, en route, and landing stages of flight that correspond to the applicable performance requirements. The cooling tests must be conducted with the airplane in the configuration, and operating under the conditions that are critical relative to cooling during each stage of flight. For the cooling tests a temperature is "stabilized" when its rate of change is less than 2°F per minute.

(b) Temperatures must be stabilized under the conditions from which entry is made into each stage of flight being investigated unless the entry condition is not one during which component and engine fluid temperatures would stabilize, in which case, operation through the full entry condition must be conducted before entry into the stage of flight being investigated to allow temperatures to reach their natural levels at the time of entry. The takeoff cooling test must be preceded by a period during which the powerplant component and engine fluid temperatures are stabilized with the engines at ground idle.

(c) Cooling tests for each stage of flight must be continued until—

(1) The component and engine fluid temperatures stabilize;

(2) The stage of flight is completed; or

(3) An operating limitation is reached.

Induction System

47. *Air induction.* For turbopropeller powered airplanes—

(a) There must be means to prevent hazardous quantities of fuel leakage or overflow from drains, vents, or other components of flammable fluid systems from entering the engine intake systems; and

(b) The air inlet ducts must be located or protected so as to minimize the ingestion of foreign matter during takeoff, landing, and taxiing.

48. *Induction system icing protection.* For turbopropeller powered airplanes, each turbine engine must be able to operate throughout its flight power range without adverse effect on engine operation or serious loss of power or thrust, under the icing conditions specified in Appendix C of part 25 of this chapter. In addition, there must be means to indicate to appropriate flight crewmembers the functioning of the powerplant ice protection system.

49. *Turbine engine bleed air systems.* Turbine engine bleed air systems of turbopropeller powered airplanes must be investigated to determine—

(a) That no hazard to the airplane will result if a duct rupture occurs. This condition must consider that a failure of the duct can occur anywhere between the engine port and the airplane bleed service; and

(b) That, if the bleed air system is used for direct cabin pressurization, it is not possible for hazardous contamination of the cabin air system to occur in event of lubrication system failure.

Exhaust System

50. *Exhaust system drains.* Turbopropeller engine exhaust systems having low spots or pockets must incorporate drains at those locations. These drains must discharge clear of the airplane in normal and ground attitudes to prevent the accumulation of fuel after the failure of an attempted engine start.

Powerplant Controls and Accessories

51. *Engine controls.* If throttles or power levers for turbopropeller powered airplanes are such that any position of these controls will reduce the fuel flow to the engine(s) below that necessary for satisfactory and safe idle operation of the engine while the airplane is in flight, a means must be provided to prevent inadvertent movement of the control into this position. The means provided must incorporate a positive lock or stop at this idle position and must require a separate and distinct operation by the crew to displace the control from the normal engine operating range.

52. *Reverse thrust controls.* For turbopropeller powered airplanes, the propeller reverse thrust controls must have a means to prevent their inadvertent operation. The means must have a positive lock or stop at the idle position and must require a separate and distinct operation by the crew to displace the control from the flight regime.

53. *Engine ignition systems.* Each turbopropeller airplane ignition system must be considered an essential electrical load.

54. *Powerplant accessories.* The powerplant accessories must meet FAR 23.1163, and if the continued rotation of any accessory remotely driven by the engine is hazardous when malfunctioning occurs, there must be means to prevent rotation without interfering with the continued operation of the engine.

Powerplant Fire Protection

55. *Fire detector system.* For turbopropeller powered airplanes, the following apply:

(a) There must be a means that ensures prompt detection of fire in the engine compartment. An overtemperature switch in each engine cooling air exit is an acceptable method of meeting this requirement.

(b) Each fire detector must be constructed and installed to withstand the vibration, inertia, and other loads to which it may be subjected in operation.

(c) No fire detector may be affected by any oil, water, other fluids, or fumes that might be present.

(d) There must be means to allow the flight crew to check, in flight, the functioning of each fire detector electric circuit.

(e) Wiring and other components of each fire detector system in a fire zone must be at least fire resistant.

56. *Fire protection, cowling and nacelle skin.* For reciprocating engine powered airplanes, the engine cowling must be designed and constructed so that no fire originating in the engine compartment can enter either through openings or by burn through, any other region where it would create additional hazards.

57. *Flammable fluid fire protection.* If flammable fluids or vapors might be liberated by the leakage of fluid systems in areas other than engine compartments, there must be means to—

(a) Prevent the ignition of those fluids or vapors by any other equipment; or

(b) Control any fire resulting from that ignition.

Equipment

58. *Powerplant instruments.*

(a) The following are required for turbopropeller airplanes:

(1) The instruments required by FAR 23.1305 (a)(1) through (4), (b)(2) and (4).

(2) A gas temperature indicator for each engine.

(3) Free air temperature indicator.

(4) A fuel flowmeter indicator for each engine.

(5) Oil pressure warning means for each engine.

(6) A torque indicator or adequate means for indicating power output for each engine.

(7) Fire warning indicator for each engine.

(8) A means to indicate when the propeller blade angle is below the low-pitch position corresponding to idle operation in flight.

(9) A means to indicate the functioning of the ice protection system for each engine.

(b) For turbopropeller powered airplanes, the turbopropeller blade position indicator must begin indicating when the blade has moved below the flight low-pitch position.

(c) The following instruments are required for reciprocating engine powered airplanes:

(1) The instruments required by FAR 23.1305.

(2) A cylinder head temperature indicator for each engine.

(3) A manifold pressure indicator for each engine.

Systems and Equipment

General

59. *Function and installation.* The systems and equipment of the airplane must meet FAR 23.1301, and the following:

(a) Each item of additional installed equipment must—

(1) Be of a kind and design appropriate to its intended function;

(2) Be labeled as to its identification, function, or operating limitations, or any applicable combination of these factors, unless misuse or inadvertent actuation cannot create a hazard

(3) Be installed according to limitations specified for that equipment; and

(4) Function properly when installed.

(b) Systems and installations must be designed to safeguard against hazards to the aircraft in the event of their malfunction or failure.

(c) Where an installation, the functioning of which is necessary in showing compliance with the applicable requirements, requires a power supply, that installation must be considered an essential load on the power supply, and the power sources and the distribution system must be capable of supplying the following power loads in probable operation combinations and for probable durations:

(1) All essential loads after failure of any prime mover, power converter, or energy storage device.

(2) All essential loads after failure of any one engine on two-engine airplanes.

(3) In determining the probable operating combinations and durations of essential loads for the power failure conditions described in paragraphs (1) and (2) of this paragraph, it is permissible to assume that the power loads are reduced in accordance with a monitoring procedure which is consistent with safety in the types of operations authorized.

60. *Ventilation.* The ventilation system of the airplane must meet FAR 23.831, and in addition, for pressurized aircraft, the ventilating air in flight crew and passenger compartments must be free of harmful or hazardous concentrations of gases and vapors in normal operation and in the event of reasonably probable failures or malfunctioning of the ventilating, heating, pressurization, or other systems, and equipment. If accumulation of hazardous quantities of smoke in the cockpit area is reasonably probable, smoke evacuation must be readily accomplished.

Electrical Systems and Equipment

61. *General.* The electrical systems and equipment of the airplane must meet FAR 23.1351, and the following:

(a) *Electrical system capacity.* The required generating capacity, and number and kinds of power sources must—

(1) Be determined by an electrical load analysis; and

(2) Meet FAR 23.1301.

(b) *Generating system.* The generating system includes electrical power sources, main power busses, transmission cables, and associated control, regulation and protective devices. It must be designed so that—

(1) The system voltage and frequency (as applicable) at the terminals of all essential load equipment can be maintained within the limits for which the equipment is designed, during any probable operating conditions;

(2) System transients due to switching, fault clearing, or other causes do not make essential loads inoperative, and do not cause a smoke or fire hazard;

(3) There are means, accessible in flight to appropriate crewmembers, for the individual and collective disconnection of the electrical power sources from the system; and

(4) There are means to indicate to appropriate crewmembers the generating system quantities essential for the safe operation of the system, including the voltage and current supplied by each generator.

62. *Electrical equipment and installation.* Electrical equipment, controls, and wiring must be installed so that operation of any one unit or system of units will not adversely affect the simultaneous operation of any other electrical unit or system essential to the safe operation.

63. *Distribution system.*

(a) For the purpose of complying with this section, the distribution system includes the distribution busses, their associated feeders, and each control and protective device.

(b) Each system must be designed so that essential load circuits can be supplied in the event of reasonably probable faults or open circuits, including faults in heavy current carrying cables.

(c) If two independent sources of electrical power for particular equipment or systems are required under this appendix, their electrical energy supply must be ensured by means such as duplicate electrical equipment, throwover switching, or multichannel or loop circuits separately routed.

64. *Circuit protective devices.* The circuit protective devices for the electrical circuits of the airplane must meet FAR 23.1357, and in addition circuits for loads which are essential to safe operation must have individual and exclusive circuit protection.

Appendix B to Part 135

Airplane Flight Recorder Specifications

Parameters	Range	Installed system[1] minimum accuracy (to recovered data)	Sampling interval (per second)	Resolution[4] readout
Relative time (from recorded on prior to takeoff)	25 hr minimum	±0.125% per hour	1	1 sec.
Indicated airspeed	V_{SO} to V_D (KIAS)	±5% or ±10 knots, whichever is greater. Resolution 2 knots below 175 KIAS	1	1%[3]
Altitude	–1,000 feet to max cert. alt of A/C	±100 to ±700 feet (see Table 1, TSO C51-a)	1	25 to 150
Magnetic heading	360°	±5°	1	1°
Vertical acceleration	–3g to +6g	±0.2g in addition to ±0.3g maximum datum	4 (or 1 per second where peaks, ref. to 1g are recorded)	0.03g
Longitudinal acceleration	±1.0g	±1.5% max. range excluding datum error of ±5%	2	0.01g
Pitch attitude	100% of usable	±2°	1	0.8°
Roll attitude	±60° or 100% of usable range, whichever is greater	±2°	1	0.8°
Stabilizer trim position Or	Full range	±3% unless higher uniquely required	1	1%[3]
Pitch control position	Full range	±3% unless higher uniquely required	1	1%[3]
Engine Power, Each Engine Fan or N_1 speed or EPR or cockpit indications used for aircraft certification Or	Maximum range	±5%	1	1%[3]
Prop. speed and torque (sample once/sec as close together as practicable)			1 (prop speed), 1 (torque)	
Altitude rate[2] (need depends on altitude resolution)	±8,000 fpm	±10%. Resolution 250 fpm below 12,000 feet indicated	1	250 fpm below 12,000
Angle of attack[2] (need depends on altitude resolution)	–20° to 40° or of usable range	±2°	1	0.8%[3]
Radio transmitter keying (discrete)	On/off		1	
TE flaps (discrete or analog)	Each discrete position (U, D, T/O, AAP) Or Analog 0–100% range	±3°	1 1	1%[3]
LE flaps (discrete or analog)	Each discrete position (U, D, T/O, AAP) Or Analog 0–100% range	±3°	1 1	1%[3]
Thrust reverser, each engine (discrete)	Stowed or full reverse		1	
Spoiler/speedbrake (discrete)	Stowed or out		1	
Autopilot engaged (discrete)	Engaged or disengaged		1	

[1] When data sources are aircraft instruments (except altimeters) of acceptable quality to fly the aircraft the recording system excluding these sensors (but including all other characteristics of the recording system) shall contribute no more than half of the values in this column.

[2] If data from the altitude encoding altimeter (100 ft. resolution) is used, then either one of these parameters should also be recorded. If however, altitude is recorded at a minimum resolution of 25 feet, then these two parameters can be omitted.

[3] Percent of full range.

[4] This column applies to aircraft manufacturing after October 11, 1991.

[Docket No. 25530, 53 FR 26152, July 11, 1988; 53 FR 30906, Aug. 16, 1988; as amended by Amdt. 135-69, 62 FR 38397, July 17, 1997]

Appendix C to Part 135

Helicopter Flight Recorder Specifications

Parameters	Range	Installed system[1] minimum accuracy (to recovered data)	Sampling interval (per second)	Resolution[3] readout
Relative time (from recorded on prior to takeoff)	25 hr minimum	±0.125% per hour	1	1 sec.
Indicated airspeed	V_{MIN} to V_D (KIAS) (minimum airspeed signal attainable with installed pilot-static system)	±5% or ±10 kts, whichever is greater	1	1 kt.
Altitude	−1,000 feet to 20,000 ft pressure altitude	±100 to ±700 ft (see Table 1, TSO C51-a)	1	25 to 150 ft.
Magnetic heading	360°	±5°	1	1°
Vertical acceleration	−3g to +6g	±0.2g in addition to ±0.3g maximum datum	4 (or 1 per second where peaks, ref. to 1g are recorded)	0.05g
Longitudinal acceleration	±1.0g	±1.5% max. range excluding datum error of ±5%	2	0.03g
Pitch attitude	100% of usable range	±2°	1	0.8°
Roll attitude	±60° or 100% of usable range, whichever is greater	±2°	1	0.8°
Altitude rate	±8,000 fpm	±10%. Resolution 250 fpm below 12,000 ft indicated	1	250 fpm below 12,000
Engine Power, Each Engine				
Main rotor speed	Maximum range	±5%	1	1%[2]
Free or power turbine	Maximum range	±5%	1	1%[2]
Engine torque	Maximum range	±5%	1	1%[2]
Flight Control— Hydraulic Pressure				
Primary (discrete)	High/low		1	
Secondary—if applicable (discrete)	High/low		1	
Radio transmitter keying (discrete)	On/off		1	
Autopilot engaged (discrete)	Engaged or disengaged		1	
SAS status—engaged (discrete)	Engaged/disengaged		1	
SAS fault status (discrete)	Fault/OK		1	
Flight Controls				
Collective	Full range	±3%	2	1%[2]
Pedal position	Full range	±3%	2	1%[2]
Lat. cyclic	Full range	±3%	2	1%[2]
Long. cyclic	Full range	±3%	2	1%[2]
Controllable stabilator position	Full range	±3%	2	1%[2]

[1] When data sources are aircraft instruments (except altimeters) of acceptable quality to fly the aircraft the recording system excluding these sensors (but including all other characteristics of the recording system) shall contribute no more than half of the values in this column.

[2] Percent of full range.

[3] This column applies to aircraft manufactured after October 11, 1991.

[Docket No. 25530, 53 FR 26152, July 11, 1988; 53 FR 30906, Aug. 16, 1988; as amended by Amdt. 135-69, 62 FR 38397, July 17, 1997]

135

APPENDIX D TO PART 135

AIRPLANE FLIGHT RECORDER SPECIFICATIONS

Parameters	Range	Accuracy sensor input to DFDR readout	Sampling interval (per second)	Resolution[4] readout
Time (GMT or Frame Counter) (range 0 to 4095, sampled 1 per frame)	24 Hrs	±0.125% per hour	0.25 (1 per 4 seconds)	1 sec.
Altitude	–1,000 ft to max certificated altitude of aircraft	±100 to ±700 ft (See Table 1, TSO–C51a)	1	5' to 35'[1]
Airspeed	50 KIAS to V_{S0}, and V_{S0} to 1.2 V_D	±5%, ±3%	1	1 kt.
Heading	360°	±2°	1	0.5°
Normal Acceleration (Vertical)	–3g to +6g	±1% of max range excluding datum error of ±5%	8	0.01g
Pitch Attitude	±75°	±2°	1	0.5°
Roll Attitude	±180°	±2°	1	0.5°
Radio Transmitter Keying	On-Off (Discrete)		1	
Thrust / Power on Each Engine	Full range forward	±2°	1 (per engine)	0.2%[2]
Trailing Edge Flap or Cockpit Control Selection	Full range or each discrete position	±3° or as pilot's indicator	0.5	0.5%[2]
Leading Edge Flap or Cockpit Control Selection	Full range or each discrete position	±3° or as pilot's indicator	0.5	0.5%[2]
Thrust Reverser Position	Stowed, in transit, and reverse (discretion)		1 (per 4 seconds per engine)	
Ground Spoiler Position / Speed Brake Selection	Full range or each discrete position	±2% unless higher accuracy uniquely required	1	0.2%[2]
Marker Beacon Passage	Discrete		1	
Autopilot Engagement	Discrete		1	
Longitudinal Acceleration	±1g	±1.5% max range excluding datum error of ±5%	4	0.01g
Pilot Input and/or Surface Position — Primary Controls (Pitch, Roll, Yaw)[3]	Full Range	±2° unless higher accuracy uniquely required	1	0.2%[2]
Lateral Acceleration	±1g	±1.5% max range excluding datum error of ±5%	4	0.01g
Pitch Trim Position	Full Range	±3% unless higher accuracy uniquely required	1	0.3%[2]
Glideslope Deviation	±400 Microamps	±3%	1	0.3%[2]
Localizer Deviation	±400 Microamps	±3%	1	0.3%[2]
AFCS Mode and Engagement Status	Discrete		1	
Radio Altitude	–20 ft to 2,500 ft	±2 Ft or ±3% whichever is greater below 500 ft and ±5% above 500 ft	1	1 ft + 5%[2] above 500'
Master Warning	Discrete		1	
Main Gear Squat Switch Status	Discrete		1	
Angle of Attack (if recorded directly)	As installed	As installed	2	0.3%[2]
Outside Air Temperature or Total Air Temperature	–50°C to +90°C	±2°C	0.5	0.3°C
Hydraulics, Each System Low Pressure	Discrete		0.5	or 0.5%[2]
Groundspeed	As installed	Most accurate systems installed (IMS equipped aircraft only)	1	0.2%[2]

Appendix D to Part 135

Airplane Flight Recorder Specifications (*Continued*)

If additional recording capacity is available, recording of the following parameters is recommended. The parameters are listed in order of significance:

Parameters	Range	Accuracy sensor input to DFDR readout	Sampling interval (per second)	Resolution[4] readout
Drift Angle	When available, As installed	As installed	4	
Wind Speed and Direction	When available, As installed	As installed	4	
Latitude and Longitude	When available, As installed	As installed	4	
Brake pressure / Brake pedal position	As installed	As installed	1	
Additional engine parameters: EPR N[1] N[2] EGT	 As installed As installed As installed As installed	 As installed As installed As installed As installed	 1 (per engine) 1 (per engine 1 (per engine) 1 (per engine)	
Throttle Lever Position	As installed	As installed	1 (per engine)	
Fuel Flow	As installed	As installed	1 (per engine)	
TCAS: TA RA Sensitivity level (as selected by crew)	 As installed As installed As installed	 As installed As installed As installed	 1 1 2	
GPWS (ground proximity warning system)	Discrete		1	
Landing gear or gear selector position	Discrete		0.25 (1 per 4 seconds)	
DME 1 and 2 Distance	0–200 NM	As installed	0.25	1 mi.
Nav 1 and 2 Frequency Selection	Full range	As installed	0.25	

[1] When altitude rate is recorded. Altitude rate must have sufficient resolution and sampling to permit the derivation of altitude to 5 feet.

[2] Percent of full range

[3] For airplanes that can demonstrate the capability of deriving either the control input on control movement (one from the other) for all modes of operation and flight regimes, the "or" applies. For airplanes with non-mechanical control systems (fly-by-wire) the "and" applies. In airplanes with split surfaces, suitable combination of inputs is acceptable in lieu of recording each surface separately.

[4] This column applies to aircraft manufactured after October 11, 1991.

[Docket No. 25530, 53 FR 26153, July 11, 1988; 53 FR 30906, Aug. 16, 1988]

Appendix E to Part 135

Helicopter Flight Recorder Specifications

Parameters	Range	Installed system[1] minimum accuracy (to recovered data)	Sampling interval (per second)	Resolution[2] read out
Time (GMT)	24 Hrs	±0.125% per hour	0.25 (1 per 4 seconds)	1 sec
Altitude	−1,000 ft to max certificated altitude of aircraft	±100 to ±700 ft (see Table 1. TSO C51-a)	1	5' to 30'
Airspeed	As the installed measuring system	±3%	1	1 kt
Heading	360°	±2°	1	0.5°
Normal Acceleration (vertical)	−3g to +6g	±1% of max range excluding datum error of ±5%	8	0.01g
Pitch Attitude	±75°	±2°	2	0.5°
Roll Attitude	±180°	±2°	2	0.5°
Radio Transmitter Keying	On-Off (Discrete)		1	0.25 sec
Power in Each Engine: Free Power Turbine Speed *and* Engine Torque	0–130% (power Turbine Speed) Full range (Torque)	±2%	1 speed 1 torque (per engine)	0.2%[1] to 0.4%[1]
Main Rotor Speed	0–130%	±2%	2	0.3%[1]
Altitude Rate	±6,000 ft/min	As installed	2	0.2%[1]
Pilot input—Primary Controls (Collective, Longitudinal Cyclic, Lateral Cyclic, Pedal)	Full Range	±3%	2	0.5%[1]
Flight Control Hydraulic Pressure Low	Discrete, each circuit		1	
Flight Control Hydraulic Pressure Selector Switch Position, 1st and 2nd stage	Discrete		1	
AFCS Mode and Engagement Status	Discrete (5 bits necessary)		1	
Stability Augmentation System Engage	Discrete		1	
SAS Fault Status	Discrete		0.25	
Main Gearbox Temperature Low	As installed	As installed	0.25	0.5%[1]
Main Gearbox Temperature High	As installed	As installed	0.5	0.5%[1]
Controllable Stabilator Position	Full range ±3%		2	0.4%[1]
Longitudinal Acceleration	±1g	±1.5% max range excluding datum of ±5%	4	0.01g
Lateral Acceleration	±1g	±1.5% max range excluding datum of ±5%		0.01g
Master Warning	Discrete		1	
Nav 1 and 2 Frequency Selection	Full range	As installed	0.25	
Outside Air Temperature	−50°C to +90°C	±2°C	0.5	0.3°C

[1] Percent of full range.
[2] This column applies to aircraft manufactured after October 11, 1991.

[Docket No. 25530, 53 FR 26154, July 11, 1988; 53 FR 30906, Aug. 16, 1988]

Appendix F to Part 135
Airplane Flight Recorder Specifications

The recorded values must meet the designated range, resolution, and accuracy requirements during dynamic and static conditions. All data recorded must be correlated in time to within one second.

Parameters	Range	Accuracy (sensor input)	Seconds per sampling interval	Resolution	Remarks
1. Time or Relative Time Counts[1]	24 Hrs, 0 to 4095	±0.125% Per Hour	4	1 sec	UTC time preferred when available. Counter increments each 4 seconds of system operation.
2. Pressure Altitude	–1000 ft to max certificated altitude of aircraft. +5000 ft.	±100 to ±700 ft (see table, TSO C124a or TSO C51a)	1	5' to 35'	Data should be obtained from the air data computer when practicable.
3. Indicated airspeed or Calibrated airspeed	50 KIAS or minimum value to Max V_{SO} to 1.2 V_D	±5% and ±3%	1	1 kt	Data should be obtained from the air data computer when practicable.
4. Heading (Primary flight crew reference)	0–360° and Discrete "true" or "mag"	±2°	1	0.5°	When true or magnetic heading can be selected as the primary heading reference, a discrete indicating selection must be recorded.
5. Normal Acceleration (Vertical)[9]	–3g to +6g	±1% of max range excluding datum error of ±5%	0.125	0.004g	—
6. Pitch Attitude	±75°	±2°	1 or 0.25 for airplanes operated under §135.152(j)	0.5°	A sampling rate of 0.25 is recommended.
7. Roll Attitude[2]	±180°	±2°	1 or 0.5 for airplanes operated under §135.152(j)	0.5°	A sampling rate of 0.5 is recommended.
8. Manual Radio Transmitter Keying or CVR/DFDR synchronization reference	On-Off (Discrete) None	—	1	—	Preferably each crewmember but one discrete acceptable for all transmission provided the CVR/FDR system complies with TSO C124a CVR synchronization requirements (paragraph 4.2.1 ED-55).
9. Thrust/Power on each engine—primary flight crew reference	Full Range Forward	±2%	1 (per engine)	0.3% of full range	Sufficient parameters (e.g. EPR, N1 or Torque, NP) as appropriate to the particular engine be recorded to determine power in forward and reverse thrust, including potential overspeed conditions.
10. Autopilot Engagement	Discrete "on" or "off"	—	1	—	—
11. Longitudinal Acceleration	±1g	±1.5% max. range excluding datum error of ±5%	0.25	0.004g	—
12a. Pitch Control(s) position (non-fly-by-wire systems)	Full Range	±2° Unless Higher Accuracy Uniquely Required	0.5 or 0.25 for airplanes operated under §135.152(j)	0.5% of full range	For airplanes that have a flight control break away capability that allows either pilot to operate the controls independently, record both control inputs. The control inputs may be sampled alternately once per second to produce the sampling interval of 0.5 or 0.25, as applicable.

135

Appendix F to Part 135
Airplane Flight Recorder Specifications (Continued)

The recorded values must meet the designated range, resolution, and accuracy requirements during dynamic and static conditions. All data recorded must be correlated in time to within one second.

Parameters	Range	Accuracy (sensor input)	Seconds per sampling interval	Resolution	Remarks
12b. Pitch Control(s) position (fly-by-wire systems)[3]	Full Range	±2° Unless Higher Accuracy Uniquely Required	0.5 or 0.25 for airplanes operated under §135.152(j)	0.2% of full range	—
13a. Lateral Control position(s) (non-fly-by-wire)	Full Range	±2° Unless Higher Accuracy Uniquely Required	0.5 or 0.25 for airplanes operated under §135.152(j)	0.2% of full range	For airplanes that have a flight control break away capability that allows either pilot to operate the controls independently, record both control inputs. The control inputs may be sampled alternately once per second to produce the sampling interval of 0.5 or 0.25, as applicable.
13b. Lateral Control position(s) (fly-by-wire)[4]	Full Range	±2° Unless Higher Accuracy Uniquely Required	0.5 or 0.25 for airplanes operated under §135.152(j)	0.2% of full range	—
14a. Yaw Control position(s) (non-fly-by-wire)[5]	Full Range	±2° Unless Higher Accuracy Uniquely Required	0.5 or 0.25 for airplanes operated under §135.152(j)	0.3% of full range	For airplanes that have a flight control break away capability that allows either pilot to operate the controls independently, record both control inputs. The control inputs may be sampled alternately once per second to produce the sampling interval of 0.5.
14b. Yaw Control position(s) (fly-by-wire)	Full Range	±2° Unless Higher Accuracy Uniquely Required	0.5	0.2% of full range	—
15. Pitch Control Surface(s) Position[6]	Full Range	±2° Unless Higher Accuracy Uniquely Required	0.5 or 0.25 for airplanes operated under §135.152(j)	0.3% of full range	For airplanes fitted with multiple or split surfaces, a suitable combination of inputs is acceptable in lieu of recording each surface separately. The control surfaces may be sampled alternately to produce the sampling interval of 0.5 or 0.25.
16. Lateral Control Surface(s) Position[7]	Full Range	±2° Unless Higher Accuracy Uniquely Required	0.5 or 0.25 for airplanes operated under §135.152(j)	0.2% of full range	A suitable combination of surface position sensors is acceptable in lieu of recording each surface separately. The control surfaces may be sampled alternately to produce the sampling interval of 0.5 or 0.25.
17. Yaw Control Surface(s) Position[8]	Full Range	±2° Unless Higher Accuracy Uniquely Required	0.5	0.2% of full range	For airplanes with multiple or split surfaces, a suitable combination of surface position sensors is acceptable in lieu of recording each surface separately. The control surfaces may be sampled alternately to produce the sampling interval of 0.5.
18. Lateral Acceleration	±1g	±1.5% max. range excluding datum error of ± 5%	0.25	0.004g	—

Appendix F to Part 135
Airplane Flight Recorder Specifications (Continued)

The recorded values must meet the designated range, resolution, and accuracy requirements during dynamic and static conditions. All data recorded must be correlated in time to within one second.

Parameters	Range	Accuracy (sensor input)	Seconds per sampling interval	Resolution	Remarks
19. Pitch Trim Surface Position	Full Range	±3° Unless Higher Accuracy Uniquely Required	1	0.6% of full range	—
20. Trailing Edge Flap or Cockpit Control Selection[10]	Full Range or Each Position (discrete)	±3° or as Pilot's indicator	2	0.5% of full range	Flap position and cockpit control may each be sampled alternately at 4 second intervals, to give a data point every 2 seconds.
21. Leading Edge Flap or Cockpit Control Selection[11]	Full Range or Each Discrete Position	±3° or as Pilot's Indicator and sufficient to determine each discrete position	2	0.5% of full range	Left and right sides of flap position and cockpit control may each be sampled at 4 second intervals, so as to give a data point every 2 seconds.
22. Each Thrust Reverser Position (or equivalent for propeller airplane)	Stowed, In Transit, and Reverse (Discrete)	—	1 (per engine)	—	Turbo-jet – 2 discretes enable the 3 states to be determined. Turbo-prop – 1 discrete.
23. Ground Spoiler Position or Speed Brake Selection[12]	Full Range or Each Position (discrete)	±2° Unless Higher Accuracy Uniquely Required	1 or 0.5 for airplanes operated under §135.152(j)	0.5% of full range	—
24. Outside Air Temperature or Total Air Temperature[13]	−50°C to +90°C	±2°C	2	0.3°C	—
25. Autopilot/Autothrottle/ AFCS Mode and Engagement Status	A suitable combination of discretes	—	1	—	Discretes should show which systems are engaged and which primary modes are controlling the flight path and speed of the aircraft.
26. Radio Altitude[14]	–20 ft to 2,500 ft	±2 ft or ±3% whichever is greater below 500 ft & ±5% above 500 ft	1	1 ft + 5% above 500 ft	For autoland/category 3 operations. Each radio altimeter should be recorded, but arranged so that at least one is recorded each second.
27. Localizer Deviation, MLS Azimuth, or GPS Latitude Deviation	±400 Microamps or available sensor range as installed ±62°	As installed ±3% recommended	1	0.3% of full range	For autoland/category 3 operations. Each system should be recorded, but arranged so that at least one is recorded each second. It is not necessary to record ILS and MLS at the same time, only the approach aid in use need be recorded.
28. Glideslope Deviation, MLS Elevation, or GPS Vertical Deviation	±400 Microamps or available sensor range as installed 0.9 to +30°	As installed ±3% recommended	1	0.3% of full range	For autoland/category 3 operations. Each system should be recorded, but arranged so that at least one is recorded each second. It is not necessary to record ILS and MLS at the same time, only the approach aid in use need be recorded.
29. Marker Beacon Passage	Discrete "on" or "off"		1	—	A single discrete is acceptable for all markers.
30. Master Warning	Discrete	—	1	—	Record the master warning and record each "red" warning that cannot be determined from other parameters or from the cockpit voice recorder.

Appendix F to Part 135
Airplane Flight Recorder Specifications (Continued)

The recorded values must meet the designated range, resolution, and accuracy requirements during dynamic and static conditions. All data recorded must be correlated in time to within one second.

Parameters	Range	Accuracy (sensor input)	Seconds per sampling interval	Resolution	Remarks
31. Air/ground sensor (primary airplane system reference nose or main gear)	Discrete "air" or "ground"	—	1 (0.25 recommended)	—	—
32. Angle of Attack (if measured directly)	As installed	As installed	2 or 0.5 for airplanes operated under §135.152(j)	0.3% of full range	If left and right sensors are available, each may be recorded at 4 or 1 second intervals, as appropriate, so as to give a data point at 2 seconds or 0.5 second, as required.
33. Hydraulic Pressure Low, Each System	Discrete or available sensor range, "low" or "normal"	±5%	2	0.5% of full range	—
34. Groundspeed	As installed	Most Accurate Systems Installed	1	0.2% of full range	—
35. GPWS (ground proximity warning system)	Discrete "warning" or "off"	—	1	—	A suitable combination of discretes unless recorder capacity is limited in which case a single discrete for all modes is acceptable.
36. Landing Gear Position or Landing gear cockpit control selection	Discrete	—	4	—	A suitable combination of discretes should be recorded.
37. Drift Angle[15]	As installed	As installed	4	0.1°	—
38. Wind Speed and Direction	As installed	As installed	4	1 knot, and 1.0°	—
39. Latitude and Longitude	As installed	As installed	4	0.002°, or as installed	Provided by the Primary Navigation System Reference. Where capacity permits latitude/longitude resolution should be 0.0002°.
40. Stick shaker and pusher activation	Discrete(s) "on" or "off"	—	1	—	A suitable combination of discretes to determine activation.
41. Windshear Detection	Discrete "warning" or "off"	—	1	—	—
42. Throttle/power lever position[16]	Full Range	±2%	1 for each lever	2% of full range	For airplanes with non-mechanically linked cockpit engine controls.
43. Additional Engine Parameters	As installed	As installed	Each engine, each second	2% of full range	Where capacity permits, the preferred priority is indicated vibration level, N2, EGT, Fuel Flow, Fuel Cut-off lever position and N3, unless engine manufacturer recommends otherwise.

Appendix F to Part 135
Airplane Flight Recorder Specifications (Continued)

The recorded values must meet the designated range, resolution, and accuracy requirements during dynamic and static conditions. All data recorded must be correlated in time to within one second.

Parameters	Range	Accuracy (sensor input)	Seconds per sampling interval	Resolution	Remarks
44. Traffic Alert and Collision Avoidance System (TCAS)	Discretes	As installed	1	—	A suitable combination of discretes should be recorded to determine the status of – Combined Control, Vertical Control, Up Advisory, and Down Advisory. (ref. ARINC Characteristic 735 Attachment 6E, TCAS VERTICAL RA DATA OUTPUT WORD.)
45. DME 1 and 2 Distance	0–200 NM	As installed	4	1 NM	1 mile
46. Nav 1 and 2 Selected Frequency	Full Range	As installed	4	—	Sufficient to determine selected frequency.
47. Selected barometric setting	Full Range	±5%	(1 per 64 sec.)	0.2% of full range	—
48. Selected altitude	Full Range	±5%	1	100 ft	—
49. Selected speed	Full Range	±5%	1	1 knot	—
50. Selected Mach	Full Range	±5%	1	.01	—
51. Selected vertical speed	Full Range	±5%	1	100 ft/min	—
52. Selected heading	Full Range	±5%	1	1°	—
53. Selected flight path	Full Range	±5%	1	1°	—
54. Selected decision height	Full Range	±5%	64	1 ft	—
55. EFIS display format	Discrete(s)	—	4	—	Discretes should show the display system status (e.g., off, normal, fail, composite, sector, plan, nav aids, weather radar, range, copy).
56. Multi-function/Engine Alerts Display format	Discrete(s)	—	4	—	Discretes should show the display system status (e.g., off, normal, fail, and the identity of display pages for emergency procedures, need not be recorded.)
57. Thrust command[17]	Full Range	±2%	2	2% of full range	—
58. Thrust target	Full Range	±2%	4	2% of full range	—
59. Fuel quantity in CG trim tank	Full Range	±5%	(1 per 64 sec.)	1% of full range	—
60. Primary Navigation System Reference	Discrete GPS, INS, VOR/DME, MLS, Loran C, Omega, Localizer Glideslope	—	4	—	A suitable combination of discretes to determine the Primary Navigation System reference.

135

Appendix F to Part 135
Airplane Flight Recorder Specifications (Continued)

The recorded values must meet the designated range, resolution, and accuracy requirements during dynamic and static conditions. All data recorded must be correlated in time to within one second.

Parameters	Range	Accuracy (sensor input)	Seconds per sampling interval	Resolution	Remarks
61. Ice Detection	Discrete "ice" or "no ice"	—	4	—	—
62. Engine warning each engine vibration	Discrete	—	1	—	—
63. Engine warning each engine over temp	Discrete	—	1	—	—
64. Engine warning each engine oil pressure low	Discrete	—	1	—	—
65. Engine warning each engine over speed	Discrete	—	1	—	—
66. Yaw Trim Surface Position	Full Range	±3% Unless Higher Accuracy Uniquely Required	2	0.3% of full range	—
67. Roll Trim Surface Position	Full Range	±3% Unless Higher Accuracy Uniquely Required	2	0.3% of full range	—
68. Brake Pressure (left and right)	As installed	±5%	1	—	To determine braking effort applied by pilots or by autobrakes.
69. Brake Pedal Application (left and right)	Discrete or Analog "applied" or "off"	±5% (Analog)	1	—	To determine braking applied by pilots.
70. Yaw or sideslip angle	Full Range	±5%	1	0.5°	—
71. Engine bleed valve position	Discrete "open" or "closed"	—	4	—	—
72. De-icing or anti-icing system selection	Discrete "on" or "off"	—	4	—	—
73. Computed center of gravity	Full Range	±5%	(1 per 64 sec.)	1% of full range	—
74. AC electrical bus status	Discrete "power" or "off"	—	4	—	Each bus.
75. DC electrical bus status	Discrete "power" or "off"	—	4	—	Each bus.
76. APU bleed valve position	Discrete "open" or "closed"	—	4	—	—
77. Hydraulic Pressure (each system)	Full Range	±5%	2	100 psi	—
78. Loss of cabin pressure	Discrete "loss" or "normal"	—	1	—	—

Appendix F to Part 135
Airplane Flight Recorder Specifications (Continued)

The recorded values must meet the designated range, resolution, and accuracy requirements during dynamic and static conditions. All data recorded must be correlated in time to within one second.

Parameters	Range	Accuracy (sensor input)	Seconds per sampling interval	Resolution	Remarks
79. Computer failure (critical flight and engine control systems)	Discrete "fail" or "normal"	—	4	—	—
80. Heads-up display (when an information source is installed)	Discrete(s) "on" or "off"	—	4	—	—
81. Para-visual display (when an information source is installed)	Discrete(s) "on" or "off"	—	1	—	—
82. Cockpit trim control input position – pitch	Full Range	±5%	1	0.2% of full range	Where mechanical means for control inputs are not available, cockpit display trim positions should be recorded.
83. Cockpit trim control input position – roll	Full Range	±5%	1	0.7% of full range	Where mechanical means for control inputs are not available, cockpit display trim position should be recorded.
84. Cockpit trim control input position – yaw	Full Range	±5%	1	0.3% of full range	Where mechanical means for control input are not available, cockpit display trim positions should be recorded.
85. Trailing edge flap and cockpit flap control position	Full Range	±5%	2	0.5% of full range	Trailing edge flaps and cockpit flap control position may each be sampled alternately at 4 second intervals to provide a sample each 0.5 second.
86. Leading edge flap and cockpit flap control position	Full Range or Discrete	±5%	1	0.5% of full range	—
87. Ground spoiler position and speed brake selection	Full Range or Discrete	±5%	0.5	0.3% of full range	—
88. All cockpit flight control input forces (control wheel, control column, rudder pedal)	Full Range Control wheel ±70 lbs Control column ±85 lbs Rudder pedal ±165 lbs	±5%	1	0.3% of full range	For fly-by-wire flight control systems, where flight control surface position is a function of the displacement of the control input device only, it is not necessary to record this parameter. For airplanes that have a flight control break away capability that allows either pilot to operate the control independently, record both control force inputs. The control force inputs may be sampled alternately once per 2 seconds to produce the sampling interval of 1.

135

[1] For A300 B2/B4 airplanes, resolution = 6 seconds.
[2] For A330/A340 series airplanes, resolution = 0.703°.
[3] For A318/A319/A320/A321 series airplanes, resolution = 0.275% (0.088°>0.064°).
For A330/A340 series airplanes, resolution = 2.20% (0.703°>0.064°).
[4] For A318/A319/A320/A321 series airplanes, resolution = 0.22% (0.088°>0.080°).
For A330/A340 series airplanes, resolution = 1.76% (0.703°>0.080°).
[5] For A330/A340 series airplanes, resolution = 1.18% (0.703°>0.120°).
[6] For A330/A340 series airplanes, resolution = 0.783% (0.352°>0.090°).
[7] For A330/A340 series airplanes, aileron resolution = 0.704% (0.352°>0.100°).
For A330/A340 series airplanes, spoiler resolution = 1.406% (0.703°>0.100°).
[8] For A330/A340 series airplanes, resolution = 0.30% (0.176°>0.12°).
For A330/A340 series airplanes, seconds per sampling interval = 1.
[9] For B-717 series airplanes, resolution = .005g.
For Dassault F900C/F900EX airplanes, resolution = .007g.
[10] For A330/A340 series airplanes, resolution = 1.05% (0.250°>0.120°).
[11] For A330/A340 series airplanes, resolution = 1.05% (0.250°>0.120°).
For A300 B2/B4 series airplanes, resolution = 0.92% (0.230°>0.125°).
[12] For A330/A340 series airplanes, spoiler resolution = 1.406% (0.703°>0.100°).
[13] For A330/A340 series airplanes, resolution = 0.5° C.
[14] For Dassault F900C/F900EX airplanes, Radio Altitude resolution = 1.25 ft.
[15] For A330/A340 series airplanes, resolution = 0.352 degrees.
[16] For A318/A319/A320/A321 series airplanes, resolution = 4.32%.
For A330/A340 series airplanes, resolution is 3.27% of full range for throttle lever angle (TLA); for reverse thrust, reverse throttle lever angle (RLA) resolution is nonlinear over the active reverse thrust range, which is 51.54 degrees to 96.14 degrees. The resolved element is 2.8 degrees uniformly over the entire active reverse thrust range, or 2.9% of the full range value of 96.14 degrees.
[17] For A318/A319/A320/A321 series airplanes, with IAE engines, resolution = 2.58%.

[Docket No. 28109, 62 FR 38396, July 17, 1997, as amended by Amdt. 135–69, 62 FR 48135, Sept. 12, 1997; Amdt. 135–85, 67 FR 54323, Aug. 21, 2002; Amdt. 135–84, 68 FR 42939, July 18, 2003; Amdt. 135–84, 68 FR 50069, Aug. 20, 2003]

Appendix G to Part 135 [Removed]

[Docket No. FAA–1999–5401, 67 FR 72764, Dec. 6, 2002; as amended by Amdt. 135–81, 70 FR 5533, Feb. 2, 2005]

PART 145
REPAIR STATIONS

SPECIAL FEDERAL AVIATION REGULATION

SFAR No. 36 [Note]

Subpart A — General

Sec.
145.1 Applicability.
145.3 Definition of terms.
145.5 Certificate and operations specifications requirements.

Subpart B — Certification

145.51 Application for certificate.
145.53 Issue of certificate.
145.55 Duration and renewal of certificate.
145.57 Amendment to or transfer of certificate.
145.59 Ratings.
145.61 Limited ratings.

Subpart C — Housing, Facilities, Equipment, Materials, and Data

145.101 General.
145.103 Housing and facilities requirements.
145.105 Change of location, housing, or facilities.
145.107 Satellite repair stations.
145.109 Equipment, materials, and data requirements.

Subpart D — Personnel

145.151 Personnel requirements.
145.153 Supervisory personnel requirements.
145.155 Inspection personnel requirements.
145.157 Personnel authorized to approve an article for return to service.
145.159 Recommendation of a person for certification as a repairman.
145.161 Records of management, supervisory, and inspection personnel.
***145.163 Training requirements.**

Subpart E — Operating Rules

145.201 Privileges and limitations of certificate.
145.203 Work performed at another location.
145.205 Maintenance, preventive maintenance, and alterations performed for certificate holders under parts 121, 125, and 135, and for foreign air carriers or foreign persons operating a U.S.-registered aircraft in common carriage under part 129.
145.207 Repair station manual.
145.209 Repair station manual contents.
145.211 Quality control system.
145.213 Inspection of maintenance, preventive maintenance, or alterations.
145.215 Capability list.
145.217 Contract maintenance.
145.219 Recordkeeping.
145.221 Reports of failures, malfunctions, or defects.
145.223 FAA inspections.

Authority: 49 U.S.C. 106(g), 40113, 44701–44702, 44707, 44709, 44717.

Source: Docket No. FAA–1999–5836; 66 FR 41117, August 6, 2001, unless otherwise noted.

SPECIAL FEDERAL AVIATION REGULATION

SFAR NO. 36 TO PART 145

EDITORIAL NOTE: FOR THE TEXT OF SFAR NO. 36, SEE PART 135 OF THIS CHAPTER.

Subpart A — General

§145.1 Applicability.

This part describes how to obtain a repair station certificate. This part also contains the rules a certificated repair station must follow related to its performance of maintenance, preventive maintenance, or alterations of an aircraft, airframe, aircraft engine, propeller, appliance, or component part to which part 43 applies. It also applies to any person who holds, or is required to hold, a repair station certificate issued under this part.

§145.3 Definition of terms.

For the purposes of this part, the following definitions apply:

(a) *Accountable manager* means the person designated by the certificated repair station who is responsible for and has the authority over all repair station operations that are conducted under part 145, including ensuring that repair station personnel follow the regulations and serving as the primary contact with the FAA.

(b) *Article* means an aircraft, airframe, aircraft engine, propeller, appliance, or component part.

(c) *Directly in charge* means having the responsibility for the work of a certificated repair station that performs maintenance, preventive maintenance, alterations, or other functions affecting aircraft airworthiness. A person directly in charge does not need to physically observe and direct each worker constantly but must be available for consultation on matters requiring instruction or decision from higher authority.

(d) *Line maintenance* means—

(1) Any unscheduled maintenance resulting from unforeseen events; or

(2) Scheduled checks that contain servicing and/or inspections that do not require specialized training, equipment, or facilities.

§145.5 Certificate and operations specifications requirements.

(a) No person may operate as a certificated repair station without, or in violation of, a repair station certificate, ratings, or operations specifications issued under this part.

(b) The certificate and operations specifications issued to a certificated repair station must be available on the premises for inspection by the public and the FAA.

Subpart B—Certification

§145.51 Application for certificate.

(a) An application for a repair station certificate and rating must be made in a format acceptable to the FAA and must include the following:

(1) A repair station manual acceptable to the FAA as required by §145.207;

(2) A quality control manual acceptable to the FAA as required by §145.211(c);

(3) A list by type, make, or model, as appropriate, of each article for which the application is made;

(4) An organizational chart of the repair station and the names and titles of managing and supervisory personnel;

(5) A description of the housing and facilities, including the physical address, in accordance with §145.103;

(6) A list of the maintenance functions, for approval by the FAA, to be performed for the repair station under contract by another person in accordance with §145.217; and

(7) A training program for approval by the FAA in accordance with §145.163.

(b) The equipment, personnel, technical data, and housing and facilities required for the certificate and rating, or for an additional rating must be in place for inspection at the time of certification or rating approval by the FAA. An applicant may meet the equipment requirement of this paragraph if the applicant has a contract acceptable to the FAA with another person to make the equipment available to the applicant at the time of certification and at any time that it is necessary when the relevant work is being performed by the repair station.

(c) In addition to meeting the other applicable requirements for a repair station certificate and rating, an applicant for a repair station certificate and rating located outside the United States must meet the following requirements:

(1) The applicant must show that the repair station certificate and/or rating is necessary for maintaining or altering the following:

(i) U.S.-registered aircraft and articles for use on U.S.-registered aircraft, or

(ii) Foreign-registered aircraft operated under the provisions of part 121 or part 135, and articles for use on these aircraft.

(2) The applicant must show that the fee prescribed by the FAA has been paid.

(d) An application for an additional rating, amended repair station certificate, or renewal of a repair station certificate must be made in a format acceptable to the FAA. The application must include only that information necessary to substantiate the change or renewal of the certificate.

§145.53 Issue of certificate.

(a) Except as provided in paragraph (b) of this section, a person who meets the requirements of this part is entitled to a repair station certificate with appropriate ratings prescribing such operations specifications and limitations as are necessary in the interest of safety.

(b) If the person is located in a country with which the United States has a bilateral aviation safety agreement, the FAA may find that the person meets the requirements of this part based on a certification from the civil aviation authority of that country. This certification must be made in accordance with implementation procedures signed by the Administrator or the Administrator's designee.

§145.55 Duration and renewal of certificate.

(a) A certificate or rating issued to a repair station located in the United States is effective from the date of issue until the repair station surrenders it or the FAA suspends or revokes it.

(b) A certificate or rating issued to a repair station located outside the United States is effective from the date of issue until the last day of the 12th month after the date of issue unless the repair station surrenders the certificate or the FAA suspends or revokes it. The FAA may renew the certificate or rating for 24 months if the repair station has operated in compliance with the applicable requirements of part 145 within the preceding certificate duration period.

(c) A certificated repair station located outside the United States that applies for a renewal of its repair station certificate must—

(1) Submit its request for renewal no later than 30 days before the repair station's current certificate expires. If a request for renewal is not made within this period, the repair station must follow the application procedures in §145.51.

(2) Send its request for renewal to the FAA office that has jurisdiction over the certificated repair station.

(d) The holder of an expired, surrendered, suspended, or revoked certificate must return it to the FAA.

§145.57 Amendment to or transfer of certificate.

(a) The holder of a repair station certificate must apply for a change to its certificate in a format acceptable to the FAA. A change to the certificate is necessary if the certificate holder—

(1) Changes the location of the repair station, or

(2) Requests to add or amend a rating.

(b) If the holder of a repair station certificate sells or transfers its assets, the new owner must apply for an amended certificate in accordance with §145.51.

§145.59 Ratings.

The following ratings are issued under this subpart:

(a) *Airframe ratings.*

(1) Class 1: Composite construction of small aircraft.

(2) Class 2: Composite construction of large aircraft.

(3) Class 3: All-metal construction of small aircraft.

(4) Class 4: All-metal construction of large aircraft.

(b) *Powerplant ratings.*

(1) Class 1: Reciprocating engines of 400 horsepower or less.

(2) Class 2: Reciprocating engines of more than 400 horsepower.

(3) Class 3: Turbine engines.

(c) *Propeller ratings.*

(1) Class 1: Fixed-pitch and ground-adjustable propellers of wood, metal, or composite construction.

(2) Class 2: Other propellers, by make.

(d) *Radio ratings.*

(1) Class 1: Communication equipment. Radio transmitting and/or receiving equipment used in an aircraft to send or receive communications in flight, regardless of carrier frequency or type of modulation used. This equipment includes auxiliary and related aircraft interphone systems, amplifier systems, electrical or electronic intercrew signaling devices, and similar equipment. This equipment does not include equipment used for navigating or aiding navigation of aircraft, equipment used for measuring altitude or terrain clearance, other measuring equipment operated on radio or radar principles, or mechanical, electrical, gyroscopic, or electronic instruments that are a part of communications radio equipment.

(2) Class 2: Navigational equipment. A radio system used in an aircraft for en route or approach navigation. This does not include equipment operated on radar or pulsed radio frequency principles, or equipment used for measuring altitude or terrain clearance.

(3) Class 3: Radar equipment. An aircraft electronic system operated on radar or pulsed radio frequency principles.

(e) *Instrument ratings.*

(1) Class 1: Mechanical. A diaphragm, bourdon tube, aneroid, optical, or mechanically driven centrifugal instrument used on aircraft or to operate aircraft, including tachometers, airspeed indicators, pressure gauges drift sights, magnetic compasses, altimeters, or similar mechanical instruments.

(2) Class 2: Electrical. Self-synchronous and electrical-indicating instruments and systems, including remote indicating instruments, cylinder head temperature gauges, or similar electrical instruments.

(3) Class 3: Gyroscopic. An instrument or system using gyroscopic principles and motivated by air pressure or electrical energy, including automatic pilot control units, turn and bank indicators, directional gyros, and their parts, and flux gate and gyrosyn compasses.

(4) Class 4: Electronic. An instrument whose operation depends on electron tubes, transistors, or similar devices, including capacitance type quantity gauges, system amplifiers, and engine analyzers.

(f) *Accessory ratings.*

(1) Class 1: A mechanical accessory that depends on friction, hydraulics, mechanical linkage, or pneumatic pressure for operation, including aircraft wheel brakes, mechanically driven pumps, carburetors, aircraft wheel assemblies, shock absorber struts and hydraulic servo units.

(2) Class 2: An electrical accessory that depends on electrical energy for its operation, and a generator, including starters, voltage regulators, electric motors, electrically driven fuel pumps magnetos, or similar electrical accessories.

(3) Class 3: An electronic accessory that depends on the use of an electron tube transistor, or similar device, including supercharger, temperature, air conditioning controls, or similar electronic controls.

§145.61 Limited ratings.

(a) The FAA may issue a limited rating to a certificated repair station that maintains or alters only a particular type of airframe, powerplant, propeller, radio, instrument, or accessory, or part thereof, or performs only specialized maintenance requiring equipment and skills not ordinarily performed under other repair station ratings. Such a rating may be limited to a specific model aircraft, engine, or constituent part, or to any number of parts made by a particular manufacturer.

(b) The FAA issues limited ratings for—

(1) Airframes of a particular make and model;

(2) Engines of a particular make and model;

(3) Propellers of a particular make and model;

(4) Instruments of a particular make and model;

(5) Radio equipment of a particular make and model;

(6) Accessories of a particular make and model;

(7) Landing gear components;

(8) Floats, by make;

(9) Nondestructive inspection, testing, and processing;

(10) Emergency equipment;

(11) Rotor blades, by make and model; and

(12) Aircraft fabric work.

(c) For a limited rating for specialized services, the operations specifications of the repair station must contain the specification used to perform the specialized service. The specification may be—

(1) A civil or military specification currently used by industry and approved by the FAA, or

(2) A specification developed by the applicant and approved by the FAA.

Subpart C— Housing, Facilities, Equipment, Materials, and Data

§145.101 General.

A certificated repair station must provide housing, facilities, equipment, materials, and data that meet the applicable requirements for the issuance of the certificate and ratings the repair station holds.

§145.103 Housing and facilities requirements.

(a) Each certificated repair station must provide—

(1) Housing for the facilities, equipment, materials, and personnel consistent with its ratings.

(2) Facilities for properly performing the maintenance, preventive maintenance, or alterations of articles or the specialized services for which it is rated. Facilities must include the following:

(i) Sufficient work space and areas for the proper segregation and protection of articles during all maintenance, preventive maintenance, or alterations;

(ii) Segregated work areas enabling environmentally hazardous or sensitive operations such as painting, cleaning, welding, avionics work, electronic work, and machining to be done properly and in a manner that does not adversely affect other maintenance or alteration articles or activities;

(iii) Suitable racks, hoists, trays, stands, and other segregation means for the storage and protection of all articles undergoing maintenance, preventive maintenance, or alterations;

(iv) Space sufficient to segregate articles and materials stocked for installation from those articles undergoing maintenance, preventive maintenance, or alterations; and

(v) Ventilation, lighting, and control of temperature, humidity, and other climatic conditions sufficient to ensure personnel perform maintenance, preventive maintenance, or alterations to the standards required by this part.

(b) A certificated repair station with an airframe rating must provide suitable permanent housing to enclose the largest type and model of aircraft listed on its operations specifications.

(c) A certificated repair station may perform maintenance, preventive maintenance, or alterations on articles outside of its housing if it provides suitable facilities that are acceptable to the FAA and meet the requirements of §145.103(a) so that the work can be done in accordance with the requirements of part 43 of this chapter.

§145.105 Change of location, housing, or facilities.

(a) A certificated repair station may not change the location of its housing without written approval from the FAA.

(b) A certificated repair station may not make any changes to its housing or facilities required by §145.103 that could have a significant effect on its ability to perform the maintenance, preventive maintenance, or alterations under its repair station certificate and operations specifications without written approval from the FAA.

(c) The FAA may prescribe the conditions, including any limitations, under which a certificated repair station must operate while it is changing its location, housing, or facilities.

§145.107 Satellite repair stations.

(a) A certificated repair station under the managerial control of another certificated repair station may operate as a satellite repair station with its own certificate issued by the FAA. A satellite repair station—

(1) May not hold a rating not held by the certificated repair station with managerial control;

(2) Must meet the requirements for each rating it holds;

(3) Must submit a repair station manual acceptable to the FAA as required by §145.207; and

(4) Must submit a quality control manual acceptable to the FAA as required by §145.211(c).

(b) Unless the FAA indicates otherwise, personnel and equipment from the certificated repair station with managerial control and from each of the satellite repair stations may be shared. However, inspection personnel must be designated for each satellite repair station and available at the satellite repair station any time a determination of airworthiness or return to service is made. In other circumstances, inspection personnel may be away from the premises but must be available by telephone, radio, or other electronic means.

(c) A satellite repair station may not be located in a country other than the domicile country of the certificated repair station with managerial control.

§145.109 Equipment, materials, and data requirements.

(a) Except as otherwise prescribed by the FAA, a certificated repair station must have the equipment, tools, and materials necessary to perform the maintenance, preventive maintenance, or alterations under its repair station certificate and operations specifications in accordance with part 43. The equipment, tools, and material must be located on the premises and under the repair station's control when the work is being done.

(b) A certificated repair station must ensure all test and inspection equipment and tools used to make airworthiness determinations on articles are calibrated to a standard acceptable to the FAA.

(c) The equipment, tools, and material must be those recommended by the manufacturer of the article or must be at least equivalent to those recommended by the manufacturer and acceptable to the FAA.

(d) A certificated repair station must maintain, in a format acceptable to the FAA, the documents and data required for the performance of maintenance, preventive maintenance, or alterations under its repair station certificate and operations specifications in accordance with part 43. The following documents and data must be current and accessible when the relevant work is being done:

(1) Airworthiness directives,

(2) Instructions for continued airworthiness,

(3) Maintenance manuals,

(4) Overhaul manuals,

(5) Standard practice manuals,

(6) Service bulletins, and

(7) Other applicable data acceptable to or approved by the FAA.

Subpart D—Personnel

§145.151 Personnel requirements.

Each certificated repair station must—

(a) Designate a repair station employee as the accountable manager;

(b) Provide qualified personnel to plan, supervise, perform, and approve for return to service the maintenance, preventive maintenance, or alterations performed under the repair station certificate and operations specifications;

(c) Ensure it has a sufficient number of employees with the training or knowledge and experience in the performance of maintenance, preventive maintenance, or alterations authorized by the repair station certificate and operations specifications to ensure all work is performed in accordance with part 43; and

(d) Determine the abilities of its noncertificated employees performing maintenance functions based on training, knowledge, experience, or practical tests.

§145.153 Supervisory personnel requirements.

(a) A certificated repair station must ensure it has a sufficient number of supervisors to direct the work performed under the repair station certificate and operations specifications. The supervisors must oversee the work performed by any individuals who are unfamiliar with the methods, techniques, practices, aids, equipment, and tools used to perform the maintenance, preventive maintenance, or alterations.

(b) Each supervisor must—

(1) If employed by a repair station located inside the United States, be certificated under part 65.

(2) If employed by a repair station located outside the United States—

(i) Have a minimum of 18 months of practical experience in the work being performed; or

(ii) Be trained in or thoroughly familiar with the methods, techniques, practices, aids, equipment, and tools used to perform the maintenance, preventive maintenance, or alterations.

(c) A certificated repair station must ensure its supervisors understand, read, and write English.

§145.155 Inspection personnel requirements.

(a) A certificated repair station must ensure that persons performing inspections under the repair station certificate and operations specifications are—

(1) Thoroughly familiar with the applicable regulations in this chapter and with the inspection methods, techniques, practices, aids, equipment, and tools used to determine the airworthiness of the article on which maintenance, preventive maintenance, or alterations are being performed; and

(2) Proficient in using the various types of inspection equipment and visual inspection aids appropriate for the article being inspected; and

(b) A certificated repair station must ensure its inspectors understand, read, and write English.

§145.157 Personnel authorized to approve an article for return to service.

(a) A certificated repair station located inside the United States must ensure each person authorized to approve an article for return to service under the repair station certificate and operations specifications is certificated under part 65.

(b) A certificated repair station located outside the United States must ensure each person authorized to approve an article for return to service under the repair station certificate and operations specifications is—

(1) Trained in or has 18 months practical experience with the methods, techniques, practices, aids, equipment, and tools used to perform the maintenance, preventive maintenance, or alterations; and

(2) Thoroughly familiar with the applicable regulations in this chapter and proficient in the use of the various inspection methods, techniques, practices, aids, equipment, and tools appropriate for the work being performed and approved for return to service.

(c) A certificated repair station must ensure each person authorized to approve an article for return to service understands, reads, and writes English.

§145.159 Recommendation of a person for certification as a repairman.

A certificated repair station that chooses to use repairmen to meet the applicable personnel requirements of this part must certify in a format acceptable to the FAA that each person recommended for certification as a repairman—

(a) Is employed by the repair station, and

(b) Meets the eligibility requirements of §65.101.

§145.161 Records of management, supervisory, and inspection personnel.

(a) A certificated repair station must maintain and make available in a format acceptable to the FAA the following:

(1) A roster of management and supervisory personnel that includes the names of the repair station officials who are responsible for its management and the names of its supervisors who oversee maintenance functions.

(2) A roster with the names of all inspection personnel.

(3) A roster of personnel authorized to sign a maintenance release for approving a maintained or altered article for return to service.

(4) A summary of the employment of each individual whose name is on the personnel rosters required by paragraphs (a)(1) through (a)(3) of this section. The summary must contain enough information on each individual listed on the roster to show compliance with the experience requirements of this part and must include the following:

(i) Present title,

(ii) Total years of experience and the type of maintenance work performed,

(iii) Past relevant employment with names of employers and periods of employment,

(iv) Scope of present employment, and

(v) The type of mechanic or repairman certificate held and the ratings on that certificate, if applicable.

(b) Within 5 business days of the change, the rosters required by this section must reflect changes caused by termination, reassignment, change in duties or scope of assignment, or addition of personnel.

§145.163 Training requirements.

(a) A certificated repair station must have an employee training program approved by the FAA that consists of initial and recurrent training. For purposes of meeting the requirements of this paragraph, beginning **April 6, 2006**—

(1) An applicant for a repair station certificate must submit a training program for approval by the FAA as required by §145.51(a)(7).

(2) A repair station certificated before that date must submit its training program to the FAA for approval by the last day of the month in which its repair station certificate was issued.

(b) The training program must ensure each employee assigned to perform maintenance, preventive maintenance, or alterations, and inspection functions is capable of performing the assigned task.

(c) A certificated repair station must document, in a format acceptable to the FAA, the individual employee training required under paragraph (a) of this section. These training records must be retained for a minimum of 2 years.

(d) A certificated repair station must submit revisions to its training program to its certificate holding district office in accordance with the procedures required by §145.209(e).

[Docket No. FAA–1999–5836, 66 FR 41117, Aug. 6, 2001; as amended by Amdt. 145–27, 68 FR 12541, March 14, 2003; 70 FR 15583, March 28, 2005]

Subpart E—Operating Rules

§145.201 Privileges and limitations of certificate.

(a) A certificated repair station may—

(1) Perform maintenance, preventive maintenance, or alterations in accordance with part 43 on any article for which it is rated and within the limitations in its operations specifications.

(2) Arrange for another person to perform the maintenance, preventive maintenance, or alterations of any article for which the certificated repair station is rated. If that person is not certificated under part 145, the certificated repair station must ensure that the noncertificated person follows a quality control system equivalent to the system followed by the certificated repair station.

(3) Approve for return to service any article for which it is rated after it has performed maintenance, preventive maintenance, or an alteration in accordance with part 43.

(b) A certificated repair station may not maintain or alter any article for which it is not rated, and may not maintain or alter any article for which it is rated if it requires special technical data, equipment, or facilities that are not available to it.

(c) A certificated repair station may not approve for return to service—

(1) Any article unless the maintenance, preventive maintenance, or alteration was performed in accordance with the applicable approved technical data or data acceptable to the FAA.

(2) Any article after a major repair or major alteration unless the major repair or major alteration was performed in accordance with applicable approved technical data; and

(3) Any experimental aircraft after a major repair or major alteration performed under §43.1(b) unless the major repair or major alteration was performed in accordance with methods and applicable technical data acceptable to the FAA.

§145.203 Work performed at another location.

A certificated repair station may temporarily transport material, equipment, and personnel needed to perform maintenance, preventive maintenance, alterations, or certain specialized services on an article for which it is rated to a place other than the repair station's fixed location if the following requirements are met:

(a) The work is necessary due to a special circumstance, as determined by the FAA; or

(b) It is necessary to perform such work on a recurring basis, and the repair station's manual includes the procedures for accomplishing maintenance, preventive maintenance, alterations, or specialized services at a place other than the repair station's fixed location.

§145.205 Maintenance, preventive maintenance, and alterations performed for certificate holders under parts 121, 125, and 135, and for foreign air carriers or foreign persons operating a U.S.-registered aircraft in common carriage under part 129.

(a) A certificated repair station that performs maintenance, preventive maintenance, or alterations for an air carrier or commercial operator that has a continuous airworthiness maintenance program under part 121 or part 135 must follow the air carrier's or commercial operator's program and applicable sections of its maintenance manual.

(b) A certificated repair station that performs inspections for a certificate holder conducting operations under part 125 must follow the operator's FAA-approved inspection program.

(c) A certificated repair station that performs maintenance, preventive maintenance, or alterations for a foreign air carrier or foreign person operating a U.S.-registered aircraft under part 129 must follow the operator's FAA-approved maintenance program.

(d) Notwithstanding the housing requirement of §145.103(b), the FAA may grant approval for a certificated repair station to perform line maintenance for an air carrier certificated under part 121 or part 135, or a foreign air carrier or foreign person operating a U.S.-registered aircraft in common carriage under part 129 on any aircraft of that air carrier or person, provided—

(1) The certificated repair station performs such line maintenance in accordance with the operator's manual, if applicable, and approved maintenance program;

(2) The certificated repair station has the necessary equipment, trained personnel, and technical data to perform such line maintenance; and

(3) The certificated repair station's operations specifications include an authorization to perform line maintenance.

§145.207 Repair station manual.

(a) A certificated repair station must prepare and follow a repair station manual acceptable to the FAA.

(b) A certificated repair station must maintain a current repair station manual.

(c) A certificated repair station's current repair station manual must be accessible for use by repair station personnel required by subpart D of this part.

(d) A certificated repair station must provide to its certificate holding district office the current repair station manual in a format acceptable to the FAA.

(e) A certificated repair station must notify its certificate holding district office of each revision of its repair station manual in accordance with the procedures required by §145.209(j).

§145.209 Repair station manual contents.

A certificated repair station's manual must include the following:

(a) An organizational chart identifying—

(1) Each management position with authority to act on behalf of the repair station,

(2) The area of responsibility assigned to each management position, and

(3) The duties, responsibilities, and authority of each management position;

(b) Procedures for maintaining and revising the rosters required by §145.161;

(c) A description of the certificated repair station's operations, including the housing, facilities, equipment, and materials as required by subpart C of this part;

(d) Procedures for—

(1) Revising the capability list provided for in §145.215 and notifying the certificate holding district office of revisions to the list, including how often the certificate holding district office will be notified of revisions; and

(2) The self-evaluation required under §145.215(c) for revising the capability list, including methods and frequency of such evaluations, and procedures for reporting the results to the appropriate manager for review and action;

(e) Procedures for revising the training program required by §145.163 and submitting revisions to the certificate holding district office for approval;

(f) Procedures to govern work performed at another location in accordance with §145.203;

(g) Procedures for maintenance, preventive maintenance, or alterations performed under §145.205;

(h) Procedures for—

(1) Maintaining and revising the contract maintenance information required by §145.217(a)(2)(i), including submitting revisions to the certificate holding district office for approval; and

(2) Maintaining and revising the contract maintenance information required by §145.217(a)(2)(ii) and notifying the certificate holding district office of revisions to this information, including how often the certificate holding district office will be notified of revisions;

(i) A description of the required records and the recordkeeping system used to obtain, store, and retrieve the required records;

(j) Procedures for revising the repair station's manual and notifying its certificate holding district office of revisions to the manual, including how often the certificate holding district office will be notified of revisions; and

(k) A description of the system used to identify and control sections of the repair station manual.

§145.211 Quality control system.

(a) A certificated repair station must establish and maintain a quality control system acceptable to the FAA that ensures the airworthiness of the articles on which the repair station or any of its contractors performs maintenance, preventive maintenance, or alterations.

(b) Repair station personnel must follow the quality control system when performing maintenance, preventive maintenance, or alterations under the repair station certificate and operations specifications.

(c) A certificated repair station must prepare and keep current a quality control manual in a format acceptable to the FAA that includes the following:

(1) A description of the system and procedures used for—

(i) Inspecting incoming raw materials to ensure acceptable quality;

(ii) Performing preliminary inspection of all articles that are maintained;

(iii) Inspecting all articles that have been involved in an accident for hidden damage before maintenance, preventive maintenance, or alteration is performed;

(iv) Establishing and maintaining proficiency of inspection personnel;

(v) Establishing and maintaining current technical data for maintaining articles;

(vi) Qualifying and surveilling noncertificated persons who perform maintenance, prevention maintenance, or alterations for the repair station;

(vii) Performing final inspection and return to service of maintained articles;

(viii) Calibrating measuring and test equipment used in maintaining articles, including the intervals at which the equipment will be calibrated; and

(ix) Taking corrective action on deficiencies;

(2) References, where applicable, to the manufacturer's inspection standards for a particular article, including reference to any data specified by that manufacturer;

(3) A sample of the inspection and maintenance forms and instructions for completing such forms or a reference to a separate forms manual; and

(4) Procedures for revising the quality control manual required under this section and notifying the certificate holding district office of the revisions, including how often the certificate holding district office will be notified of revisions.

(d) A certificated repair station must notify its certificate holding district office of revisions to its quality control manual.

§145.213 Inspection of maintenance, preventive maintenance, or alterations.

(a) A certificated repair station must inspect each article upon which it has performed maintenance, preventive maintenance, or alterations as described in paragraphs (b) and (c) of this section before approving that article for return to service.

(b) A certificated repair station must certify on an article's maintenance release that the article is airworthy with respect to the maintenance, preventive maintenance, or alterations performed after—

(1) The repair station performs work on the article; and

(2) An inspector inspects the article on which the repair station has performed work and determines it to be airworthy with respect to the work performed.

(c) For the purposes of paragraphs (a) and (b) of this section, an inspector must meet the requirements of §145.155.

(d) Except for individuals employed by a repair station located outside the United States, only an employee certificated under part 65 is authorized to sign off on final inspections and maintenance releases for the repair station.

§145.215 Capability list.

(a) A certificated repair station with a limited rating may perform maintenance, preventive maintenance, or alterations on an article if the article is listed on a current capability list acceptable to the FAA or on the repair station's operations specifications.

(b) The capability list must identify each article by make and model or other nomenclature designated by the article's manufacturer and be available in a format acceptable to the FAA.

(c) An article may be listed on the capability list only if the article is within the scope of the ratings of the repair station's certificate, and only after the repair station has performed a self-evaluation in accordance with the procedures under §145.209(d)(2). The repair station must perform this self-evaluation to determine that the repair station has all of the housing, facilities, equipment, material, technical data, processes, and trained personnel in place to perform the work on the article as required by part 145. The repair station must retain on file documentation of the evaluation.

(d) Upon listing an additional article on its capability list, the repair station must provide its certificate holding district office with a copy of the revised list in accordance with the procedures required in §145.209(d)(1).

§145.217 Contract maintenance.

(a) A certificated repair station may contract a maintenance function pertaining to an article to an outside source provided—

(1) The FAA approves the maintenance function to be contracted to the outside source; and

(2) The repair station maintains and makes available to its certificate holding district office, in a format acceptable to the FAA, the following information:

(i) The maintenance functions contracted to each outside facility; and

(ii) The name of each outside facility to whom the repair station contracts maintenance functions and the type of certificate and ratings, if any, held by each facility.

(b) A certificated repair station may contract a maintenance function pertaining to an article to a noncertificated person provided—

(1) The noncertificated person follows a quality control system equivalent to the system followed by the certificated repair station;

(2) The certificated repair station remains directly in charge of the work performed by the noncertificated person; and

(3) The certificated repair station verifies, by test and/or inspection, that the work has been performed satisfactorily by the noncertificated person and that the article is airworthy before approving it for return to service.

(c) A certificated repair station may not provide only approval for return to service of a complete type-certificated product following contract maintenance, preventive maintenance, or alterations.

§145.219 Recordkeeping.

(a) A certificated repair station must retain records in English that demonstrate compliance with the requirements of part 43. The records must be retained in a format acceptable to the FAA.

(b) A certificated repair station must provide a copy of the maintenance release to the owner or operator of the article on which the maintenance, preventive maintenance, or alteration was performed.

(c) A certificated repair station must retain the records required by this section for at least 2 years from the date the article was approved for return to service.

(d) A certificated repair station must make all required records available for inspection by the FAA and the National Transportation Safety Board.

§145.221 Reports of failures, malfunctions, or defects.

(a) A certificated repair station must report to the FAA within 96 hours after it discovers any serious failure, malfunction, or defect of an article. The report must be in a format acceptable to the FAA.

(b) The report required under paragraph (a) of this section must include as much of the following information as is available:

(1) Aircraft registration number;

(2) Type, make, and model of the article;

(3) Date of the discovery of the failure, malfunction, or defect;

(4) Nature of the failure, malfunction, or defect;

(5) Time since last overhaul, if applicable;

(6) Apparent cause of the failure, malfunction, or defect; and

(7) Other pertinent information that is necessary for more complete identification, determination of seriousness, or corrective action.

(c) The holder of a repair station certificate that is also the holder of a part 121, 125, or 135 certificate; type certificate (including a supplemental type certificate); parts manufacturer approval; or technical standard order authorization, or that is the licensee of a type certificate holder, does not need to report a failure, malfunction, or defect under this section if the failure, malfunction, or defect has been reported under parts 21, 121, 125, or 135 of this chapter.

(d) A certificated repair station may submit a service difficulty report (operational or structural) for the following:

(1) A part 121 certificate holder, provided the report meets the requirements of part 121 of this chapter, as appropriate.

(2) A part 125 certificate holder, provided the report meets the requirements of part 125 of this chapter, as appropriate.

(3) A part 135 certificate holder, provided the report meets the requirements of part 135 of the chapter, as appropriate.

(e) A certificated repair station authorized to report a failure, malfunction, or defect under paragraph (d) of this section must not report the same failure, malfunction, or defect under paragraph (a) of this section. A copy of the report submitted under paragraph (d) of this section must be forwarded to the certificate holder.

[Docket No. FAA–1999–5836; 66 FR 41117, August 6, 2001; as amended by Docket No. FAA–2003–16772; Amdt. 22, 68 FR 75382, Dec. 30, 2003]

§145.223 FAA inspections.

(a) A certificated repair station must allow the FAA to inspect that repair station at any time to determine compliance with this chapter.

(b) A certificated repair station may not contract for the performance of a maintenance function on an article with a noncertificated person unless it provides in its contract with the noncertificated person that the FAA may make an inspection and observe the performance of the noncertificated person's work on the article.

(c) A certificated repair station may not return to service any article on which a maintenance function was performed by a noncertificated person if the noncertificated person does not permit the FAA to make the inspection described in paragraph (b) of this section.

PART 147
AVIATION MAINTENANCE TECHNICIAN SCHOOLS

Subpart A — General

Sec.
147.1 Applicability.
147.3 Certificate required.
147.5 Application and issue.
147.7 Duration of certificates.

Subpart B — Certification Requirements

147.11 Ratings.
147.13 Facilities, equipment, and material requirements.
147.15 Space requirements.
147.17 Instructional equipment requirements.
147.19 Materials, special tools, and shop equipment requirements.
147.21 General curriculum requirements.
147.23 Instructor requirements.

Subpart C — Operating Rules

147.31 Attendance and enrollment, tests and credit for prior instruction or experience.
147.33 Records.
147.35 Transcripts and graduation certificates.
147.36 Maintenance of instructor requirements.
147.37 Maintenance of facilities, equipment and material.
147.38 Maintenance of curriculum requirements.
147.38a Quality of instruction.
147.39 Display of certificate.
147.41 Change of location.
147.43 Inspection.
147.45 Advertising.

APPENDIX A to Part 147 — Curriculum Requirements
APPENDIX B to Part 147 — General Curriculum Subjects
APPENDIX C to Part 147 — Airframe Curriculum Subjects
APPENDIX D to Part 147 — Powerplant Curriculum Subjects

Authority: 49 U.S.C. 106(g), 40113, 44701–44702, 44707–44709.

Source: Docket No. 1157, 27 FR 6669 July 13, 1962, unless otherwise noted.

Subpart A — General

§147.1 Applicability.

This part prescribes the requirements for issuing aviation maintenance technician school certificates and associated ratings and the general operating rules for the holders of those certificates and ratings.

§147.3 Certificate required.

No person may operate as a certificated aviation maintenance technician school without, or in violation of, an aviation maintenance technician school certificate issued under this part.

[Docket No. 15196, 41 FR 47230, Oct. 28, 1976]

§147.5 Application and issue.

(a) An application for a certificate and rating, or for an additional rating, under this part is made on a form and in a manner prescribed by the Administrator, and submitted with —

(1) A description of the proposed curriculum;

(2) A list of the facilities and materials to be used;

(3) A list of its instructors, including the kind of certificate and ratings held and the certificate numbers; and

(4) A statement of the maximum number of students it expects to teach at any one time.

(b) An applicant who meets the requirements of this part is entitled to an aviation maintenance technician school certificate and associated ratings prescribing such operations specifications and limitations as are necessary in the interests of safety.

[Docket No. 1157, 27 FR 6669, July 13, 1962, as amended by Amdt. 147–5, 57 FR 28959, June 29, 1992]

§147.7 Duration of certificates.

(a) An aviation maintenance technician school certificate or rating is effective until it is surrendered, suspended, or revoked.

(b) The holder of a certificate that is surrendered, suspended, or revoked, shall return it to the Administrator.

[Docket No. 1157, 27 FR 6669, July 19, 1962, as amended by Amdt. 147–3, 41 FR 47230, Oct. 28, 1976]

Subpart B — Certification Requirements

§147.11 Ratings.

The following ratings are issued under this part:

(a) Airframe.

(b) Powerplant.

(c) Airframe and powerplant.

§147.13 Facilities, equipment, and material requirements.

An applicant for an aviation maintenance technician school certificate and rating, or for an additional rating, must have at least the facilities, equipment, and materials specified in §§147.15 to 147.19 that are appropriate to the rating he seeks.

§147.15 Space requirements.

An applicant for an aviation maintenance technician school certificate and rating, or for an additional rating, must have such of the following properly heated, lighted, and ventilated facilities as are appropriate to the rating he seeks and as the Administrator determines are appropriate for the maximum number of students expected to be taught at any time:

(a) An enclosed classroom suitable for teaching theory classes.

(b) Suitable facilities, either central or located in training areas, arranged to assure proper separation from the working space, for parts, tools, materials, and similar articles.

(c) Suitable area for application of finishing materials, including paint spraying.

(d) Suitable areas equipped with washtank and degreasing equipment with air pressure or other adequate cleaning equipment.

(e) Suitable facilities for running engines.

(f) Suitable area with adequate equipment, including benches, tables, and test equipment, to disassemble, service, and inspect.

(1) Ignition, electrical equipment, and appliances;

(2) Carburetors and fuel systems; and

(3) Hydraulic and vacuum systems for aircraft, aircraft engines, and their appliances.

(g) Suitable space with adequate equipment, including tables, benches, stands, and jacks, for disassembling, inspecting, and rigging aircraft.

(h) Suitable space with adequate equipment for disassembling, inspecting, assembling, troubleshooting, and timing engines.

[Amdt. 147–2, 35 FR 5533, Apr. 3, 1970, as amended by Amdt. 147–5, 57 FR 28959, June 29, 1992]

§147.17 Instructional equipment requirements.

(a) An applicant for a mechanic school certificate and rating, or for an additional rating, must have such of the following instructional equipment as is appropriate to the rating he seeks:

(1) Various kinds of airframe structures, airframe systems and components, powerplants, and powerplant systems and components (including propellers), of a quantity and type suitable to complete the practical projects required by its approved curriculums.

(2) At least one aircraft of a type currently certificated by FAA for private or commercial operation, with powerplant, propeller, instruments, navigation and communications equipment, landing lights, and other equipment and accessories on which a maintenance technician might be required to work and with which the technician should be familiar.

(b) The equipment required by paragraph (a) of this section need not be in an airworthy condition. However, if it was damaged, it must have been repaired enough for complete assembly.

(c) Airframes, powerplants, propellers, appliances, and components thereof, on which instruction is to be given, and from which practical working experience is to be gained, must be so diversified as to show the different methods of construction, assembly, inspection, and operation when installed in an aircraft for use. There must be enough units so that not more than eight students will work on any one unit at a time.

(d) If the aircraft used for instructional purposes does not have retractable landing gear and wing flaps, the school must provide training aids, or operational mock-ups of them.

[Docket No. 1157, 27 FR 6669, July 19, 1962, as amended by Amdt. 147–5, 57 FR 28959, June 29, 1992]

§147.19 Materials, special tools, and shop equipment requirements.

An applicant for an aviation maintenance technician school certificate and rating, or for an additional rating, must have an adequate supply of material, special tools, and such of the shop equipment as are appropriate to the approved curriculum of the school and are used in constructing and maintaining aircraft, to assure that each student will be properly instructed. The special tools and shop equipment must be in satisfactory working condition for the purpose for which they are to be used.

[Amdt. 147–5, 57 FR 28959, June 29, 1992]

§147.21 General curriculum requirements.

(a) An applicant for an aviation maintenance technician school certificate and rating, or for an additional rating, must have an approved curriculum that is designed to qualify his students to perform the duties of a mechanic for a particular rating or ratings.

(b) The curriculum must offer at least the following number of hours of instruction for the rating shown, and the instruction unit hour shall not be less than 50 minutes in length—

(1) Airframe—1,150 hours (400 general plus 750 airframe).

(2) Powerplant—1,150 hours (400 general plus 750 powerplant).

(3) Combined airframe and powerplant—1,900 hours (400 general plus 750 airframe and 750 powerplant).

(c) The curriculum must cover the subjects and items prescribed in appendixes B, C, or D, as applicable. Each item must be taught to at least the indicated level of proficiency, as defined in appendix A.

(d) The curriculum must show—

(1) The required practical projects to be completed;

(2) For each subject, the proportions of theory and other instruction to be given; and

(3) A list of the minimum required school tests to be given.

(e) Notwithstanding the provisions of paragraphs (a) through (d) of this section and §147.11, the holder of a certificate issued under subpart B of this part may apply for and receive approval of special courses in the performance of special inspection and preventive maintenance programs for a primary category aircraft type certificated under §21.24(b) of this chapter. The school may also issue certificates of competency to persons successfully completing such courses provided that all other requirements of this part are met and the certificate of competency specifies the aircraft make and model to which the certificate applies.

[Docket No. 1157, 27 FR 6669, July 13, 1962 as amended by Amdt. 147–1, 32 FR 5770 Apr. 11, 1967; Amdt. 147–5, 57 FR 28959, June 29, 1992; Amdt. 147–6, 57 FR 41370, Sept. 9, 1992]

§147.23 Instructor requirements.

An applicant for an aviation maintenance technician school certificate and rating, or for an additional rating, must provide the number of instructors holding appropriate mechanic certificates and rating that the Administrator determines necessary to provide adequate instruction and supervision of the students, including at least one such instructor for each 25 students in each shop class. However, the applicant may provide specialized instructors, who are not certificated mechanics, to teach mathematics, physics, basic electricity, basic hydraulics, drawing, and similar subjects. The applicant is required to maintain a list of the names and qualifications of specialized instructors, and upon request, provide a copy of the list to the FAA.

[Amdt. 147–5, 57 FR 28959, June 29, 1992]

Subpart C—Operating Rules

§147.31 Attendance and enrollment, tests, and credit for prior instruction or experience.

(a) A certificated aviation maintenance technician school may not require any student to attend classes of instruction more than 8 hours in any day or more than 6 days or 40 hours in any 7-day period.

(b) Each school shall give an appropriate test to each student who completes a unit of instruction as shown in that school's approved curriculum.

(c) A school may not graduate a student unless he has completed all of the appropriate curriculum requirements. However, the school may credit a student with instruction or previous experience as follows:

(1) A school may credit a student with instruction satisfactorily completed at—

(i) An accredited university, college, junior college;

(ii) An accredited vocational, technical, trade or high school;

(iii) A military technical school;

(iv) A certificated aviation maintenance technician school.

(2) A school may determine the amount of credit to be allowed—

(i) By an entrance test equal to one given to the students who complete a comparable required curriculum subject at the crediting school;

(ii) By an evaluation of an authenticated transcript from the student's former school; or

(iii) In the case of an applicant from a military school, only on the basis of an entrance test.

(3) A school may credit a student with previous aviation maintenance experience comparable to required curriculum subjects. It must determine the amount of credit to be allowed by documents verifying that experience, and by giving the student a test equal to the one given to students who complete the comparable required curriculum subject at the school.

(4) A school may credit a student seeking an additional rating with previous satisfactory completion of the general portion of an AMTS curriculum.

(d) A school may not have more students enrolled than the number stated in its application for a certificate, unless it amends its application and has it approved.

(e) A school shall use an approved system for determining final course grades and for recording student attendance. The system must show hours of absence allowed and show how the missed material will be made available to the student.

[Amdt. 147–2, 35 FR 5534, Apr. 3, 1970, as amended by Amdt. 147–4, 43 FR 22643, May 25, 1978; Amdt. 147–5, 57 FR 28959, June 29, 1992]

§147.33 Records.

(a) Each certificated aviation maintenance technician school shall keep a current record of each student enrolled, showing—

(1) His attendance, tests, and grades received on the subjects required by this part;

(2) The instruction credited to him under §147.31(c), if any; and

(3) The authenticated transcript of his grades from that school.

It shall retain the record for at least two years after the end of the student's enrollment, and shall make each record available for inspection by the Administrator during that period.

(b) Each school shall keep a current progress chart or individual progress record for each of its students, showing the practical projects or laboratory work completed, or to be completed, by the student in each subject.

[Docket No. 1157, 27 FR 6669, July 13, 1962]

§147.35 Transcripts and graduation certificates.

(a) Upon request, each certificated aviation maintenance technician school shall provide a transcript of the student's grades to each student who is graduated from that school or who leaves it before being graduated. An official of the school shall authenticate the transcript. The transcript must state the curriculum in which the student was enrolled, whether the student satisfactorily completed that curriculum, and the final grades the student received.

(b) Each school shall give a graduation certificate or certificate of completion to each student that it graduates. An official of the school shall authenticate the certificate. The certificate must show the date of graduation and the approved curriculum title.

[Docket No. 1157, 27 FR 6669, July 13, 1962, as amended by Amdt. 147–5, 57 FR 28959, June 29, 1992]

§147.36 Maintenance of instructor requirements.

Each certificated aviation maintenance technician school shall, after certification or addition of a rating, continue to provide the number of instructors holding appropriate mechanic certificates and ratings that the Administrator determines necessary to provide adequate instruction to the students, including at least one such instructor for each 25 students in each shop class. The school may continue to provide specialized instructors who are not certificated mechanics to teach mathematics, physics, drawing, basic electricity, basic hydraulics, and similar subjects.

[Amdt. 147–5, 57 FR 28959, June 29, 1992]

§147.37 Maintenance of facilities, equipment, and material.

(a) Each certificated aviation maintenance technician school shall provide facilities, equipment, and material equal to the standards currently required for the issue of the certificate and rating that it holds.

(b) A school may not make a substantial change in facilities, equipment, or material that have been approved for a particular curriculum, unless that change is approved in advance.

§147.38 Maintenance of curriculum requirements.

(a) Each certificated aviation maintenance technician school shall adhere to its approved curriculum. With FAA approval, curriculum subjects may be taught at levels exceeding those shown in appendix A of this part.

(b) A school may not change its approved curriculum unless the change is approved in advance.

[Amdt. 147–2, 35 FR 5534, Apr. 3, 1970, as amended by Amdt. 147–5, 57 FR 28960, June 29, 1992]

§147.38a Quality of instruction.

Each certificated aviation maintenance technician school shall provide instruction of such quality that, of its graduates of a curriculum for each rating who apply for a mechanic certificate or additional rating within 60 days after they are graduated, the percentage of those passing the applicable FAA written tests on their first attempt during any period of 24 calendar months is at least the percentage figured as follows:

(a) For a school graduating fewer than 51 students during that period—the national passing norm minus the number 20.

(b) For a school graduating at least 51, but fewer than 201, students during that period—the national passing norm minus the number 15.

(c) For a school graduating more than 200 students during that period—the national passing norm minus the number 10.

As used in this section, "national passing norm" is the number representing the percentage of all graduates (of a curriculum for a particular rating) of all certificated aviation maintenance technician schools who apply for a mechanic certificate or additional rating within 60 days after they are graduated and pass the applicable FAA written tests on their first attempt during the period of 24 calendar months described in this section.

[Amdt. 147–2, 35 FR 5534, Apr. 3, 1970, as amended by Amdt. 147–3, 41 FR 47230, Oct. 28, 1976]

§147.39 Display of certificate.

Each holder of an aviation maintenance technician school certificate and ratings shall display them at a place in the school that is normally accessible to the public and is not obscured. The certificate must be available for inspection by the Administrator.

§147.41 Change of location.

The holder of an aviation maintenance technician school certificate may not make any change in the school's location unless the change is approved in advance. If the holder desires to change the location he shall notify the Administrator, in writing, at least 30 days before the date the change is contemplated. If he changes its location without approval, the certificate is revoked.

§147.43 Inspection.

The Administrator may, at any time, inspect an aviation maintenance technician school to determine its compliance with this part. Such an inspection is normally made once each six months to determine if the school continues to meet the requirements under which it was originally certificated. After such an inspection is made, the school is notified, in writing, of any deficiencies found during the inspection. Other informal inspections may be made from time to time.

§147.45 Advertising.

(a) A certificated aviation maintenance technician school may not make any statement relating to itself that is false or is designed to mislead any person considering enrollment therein.

(b) Whenever an aviation maintenance technician school indicates in advertising that it is a certificated school, it shall clearly distinguish between its approved courses and those that are not approved.

Appendix A to Part 147

Curriculum Requirements

This appendix defines terms used in appendices B, C, and D of this part, and describes the levels of proficiency at which items under each subject in each curriculum must be taught, as outlined in Appendices B, C, and D.

(a) *Definitions.* As used in Appendices B, C, and D:

(1) "Inspect" means to examine by sight and touch.

(2) "Check" means to verify proper operation.

(3) "Troubleshoot" means to analyze and identify malfunctions.

(4) "Service" means to perform functions that assure continued operation.

(5) "Repair" means to correct a defective condition. Repair of an airframe or powerplant system includes component replacement and adjustment, but not component repair.

(6) "Overhaul" means to disassemble, inspect, repair as necessary, and check.

(b) *Teaching levels.*

(1) Level 1 requires:

(i) Knowledge of general principles, but no practical application.

(ii) No development of manipulative skill.

(iii) Instruction by lecture, demonstration, and discussion.

(2) Level 2 requires:

(i) Knowledge of general principles, and limited practical application.

(ii) Development of sufficient manipulative skill to perform basic operations.

(iii) Instruction by lecture, demonstration, discussion, and limited practical application.

(3) Level 3 requires:

(i) Knowledge of general principles, and performance of a high degree of practical application.

(ii) Development of sufficient manipulative skills to simulate return to service.

(iii) Instruction by lecture, demonstration, discussion, and a high degree of practical application.

(c) Teaching materials and equipment. The curriculum may be presented utilizing currently accepted educational materials and equipment, including, but not limited to: calculators, computers, and audio-visual equipment.

[Amdt. 147–2, 35 FR 5534, Apr. 3, 1970, as amended by Amdt. 147–5, 57 FR 28960, June 29, 1992]

Appendix B to Part 147

General Curriculum Subjects

This appendix lists the subjects required in at least 400 hours in general curriculum subjects.

The number in parentheses before each item listed under each subject heading indicates the level of proficiency at which that item must be taught.

Teaching level

A. BASIC ELECTRICITY

(2) 1. Calculate and measure capacitance and inductance.

(2) 2. Calculate and measure electrical power.

(3) 3. Measure voltage, current, resistance and continuity.

(3) 4. Determine the relationship of voltage, current, and resistance in electrical circuits.

(3) 5. Read and interpret aircraft electrical circuit diagrams, including solid state devices and logic functions.

(3) 6. Inspect and service batteries

B. AIRCRAFT DRAWINGS

(2) 7. Use aircraft drawings, symbols, and system schematics.

(3) 8. Draw sketches of repairs and alterations.

(3) 9. Use blueprint information.

(3) 10. Use graphs and charts.

C. WEIGHT AND BALANCE

(2) 11. Weigh aircraft.

(3) 12. Perform complete weight-and-balance check and record data.

D. FLUID LINES AND FITTINGS

(3) 13. Fabricate and install rigid and flexible fluid lines and fittings.

E. MATERIALS AND PROCESSES

(1) 14. Identify and select appropriate nondestructive testing methods.

(2) 15. Perform dye penetrant, eddy current, ultrasonic, and magnetic particle inspections.

(1) 16. Perform basic heat-treating processes.

(3) 17. Identify and select aircraft hardware and materials.

(3) 18. Inspect and check welds.

(3) 19. Perform precision measurements.

F. GROUND OPERATION AND SERVICING

(2) 20. Start, ground operate, move, service, and secure aircraft and identify typical ground operation hazards.

(2) 21. Identify and select fuels.

G. CLEANING AND CORROSION CONTROL

(3) 22. Identify and select cleaning materials.

(3) 23. Inspect, identify, remove, and treat aircraft corrosion and perform aircraft cleaning.

H. MATHEMATICS

(3) 24. Extract roots and raise numbers to a given power.

(3) 25. Determine areas and volumes of various geometrical shapes.

(3) 26. Solve ratio, proportion, and percentage problems.

(3) 27. Perform algebraic operations involving addition, subtraction, multiplication, and division of positive and negative numbers.

I. MAINTENANCE FORMS AND RECORDS

(3) 28. Write descriptions of work performed including aircraft discrepancies and corrective actions using typical aircraft maintenance records.

(3) 29. Complete required maintenance forms, records, and inspection reports.

J. BASIC PHYSICS

(2) 30. Use and understand the principles of simple machines; sound, fluid, and heat dynamics; basic aerodynamics; aircraft structures; and theory of flight.

K. MAINTENANCE PUBLICATIONS

(3) 31. Demonstrate ability to read, comprehend, and apply information contained in FAA and manufacturers' aircraft maintenance specifications, data sheets, manuals, publications, and related Federal Aviation Regulations, Airworthiness Directives, and Advisory material.

(3) 32. Read technical data.

L. MECHANIC PRIVILEGES AND LIMITATIONS

(3) 33. Exercise mechanic privileges within the limitations prescribed by part 65 of this chapter.

[Amdt. 147–2, 35 FR 5534, Apr. 3, 1970, as amended by Amdt. 147–5, 57 FR 28960, June 29, 1992]

Appendix C to Part 147

Airframe Curriculum Subjects

This appendix lists the subjects required in at least 750 hours of each airframe curriculum, in addition to at least 400 hours in general curriculum subjects.

The number in parentheses before each item listed under each subject heading indicates the level of proficiency at which that item must be taught.

I. Airframe Structures

Teaching level

A. WOOD STRUCTURES

(1) 1. Service and repair wood structures.
(1) 2. Identify wood defects
(1) 3. Inspect wood structures

B. AIRCRAFT COVERING

(1) 4. Select and apply fabric and fiberglass covering materials
(1) 5. Inspect, test, and repair fabric and fiberglass.

C. AIRCRAFT FINISHES

(1) 6. Apply trim, letters, and touchup paint.
(2) 7. Identify and select aircraft finishing materials.
(2) 8. Apply finishing materials.
(2) 9. Inspect finishes and identify defects.

D. SHEET METAL AND NON-METALLIC STRUCTURES

(2) 10. Select, install, and remove special fasteners for metallic, bonded, and composite structures.
(2) 11. Inspect bonded structures.
(2) 12. Inspect, test, and repair fiberglass, plastics, honeycomb, composite, and laminated primary and secondary structures.
(2) 13. Inspect, check, service, and repair windows, doors, and interior furnishings.
(3) 14. Inspect and repair sheet-metal structures.
(3) 15. Install conventional rivets.
(3) 16. Form, lay out, and bend sheet metal.

E. WELDING

(1) 17. Weld magnesium and titanium.
(1) 18. Solder stainless steel.
(1) 19. Fabricate tubular structures.
(2) 20. Solder, braze, gas-weld, and arc-weld steel.
(1) 21. Weld aluminum and stainless steel.

F. ASSEMBLY AND RIGGING

(1) 22. Rig rotary-wing aircraft.
(2) 23. Rig fixed-wing aircraft.
(2) 24. Check alignment of structures.
(3) 25. Assemble aircraft components, including flight control surfaces.
(3) 26. Balance, rig, and inspect movable primary and secondary flight control surfaces.
(3) 27. Jack aircraft.

G. AIRFRAME INSPECTION

(3) 28. Perform airframe conformity and airworthiness inspections.

II. Airframe Systems and Components

Teaching level

A. AIRCRAFT LANDING GEAR SYSTEMS

(3) 29. Inspect, check, service, and repair landing gear, retraction systems, shock struts, brakes, wheels, tires, and steering systems.

B. HYDRAULIC AND PNEUMATIC POWER SYSTEMS

(2) 30. Repair hydraulic and pneumatic power system components.
(3) 31. Identify and select hydraulic fluids.
(3) 32. Inspect, check, service, troubleshoot, and repair hydraulic and pneumatic power systems.

C. CABIN ATMOSPHERE CONTROL SYSTEMS

(1) 33. Inspect, check, troubleshoot, service, and repair heating, cooling, air conditioning, pressurization systems, and air cycle machines.
(1) 34. Inspect, check, troubleshoot, service, and repair heating, cooling, air-conditioning, and pressurization systems.
(2) 35. Inspect, check, troubleshoot, service and repair oxygen systems.

D. AIRCRAFT INSTRUMENT SYSTEMS

(1) 36. Inspect, check, service, troubleshoot and repair electronic flight instrument systems and both mechanical and electrical heading, speed, altitude, temperature, pressure, and position indicating systems to include the use of built-in test equipment.
(2) 37. Install instruments and perform a static pressure system leak test.

E. COMMUNICATION AND NAVIGATION SYSTEMS

(1) 38. Inspect, check, and troubleshoot autopilot servos and approach coupling systems.

(1) 39. Inspect, check, and service aircraft electronic communications and navigation systems, including VHF passenger address interphones and static discharge devices, aircraft VOR, ILS, LORAN, Radar beacon transponders, flight management computers, and GPWS.

(2) 40. Inspect and repair antenna and electronic equipment installations.

F. AIRCRAFT FUEL SYSTEMS

(1) 41. Check and service fuel dump systems.

(1) 42. Perform fuel management transfer, and defueling.

(1) 43. Inspect, check, and repair pressure fueling systems.

(2) 44. Repair aircraft fuel systems components.

(2) 45. Inspect and repair fluid quantity indicating systems.

(2) 46. Troubleshoot, service, and repair fluid pressure and temperature warning systems.

(3) 47. Inspect, check, service, troubleshoot, and repair aircraft fuel systems.

G. AIRCRAFT ELECTRICAL SYSTEMS

(2) 48. Repair and inspect aircraft electrical system components; crimp and splice wiring to manufacturers' specifications; and repair pins and sockets of aircraft connectors.

(3) 49. Install, check, and service airframe electrical wiring, controls, switches, indicators, and protective devices.

(3) 50.a. Inspect, check, troubleshoot, service and repair alternating and direct current electrical systems.

(1) 50.b. Inspect, check, and troubleshoot constant speed and integrated speed drive generators.

H. POSITION AND WARNING SYSTEMS

(2) 51. Inspect, check and service speed and configuration warning systems, electrical brake controls, and anti-skid systems.

(3) 52. Inspect, check, troubleshoot, and service landing gear position indicating and warning systems.

I. ICE AND RAIN CONTROL SYSTEMS

(2) 53. Inspect, check, troubleshoot, service, and repair airframe ice and rain control systems.

J. FIRE PROTECTION SYSTEMS

(1) 54. Inspect, check, and service smoke and carbon monoxide detection systems.

(3) 55. Inspect, check, service, troubleshoot, and repair aircraft fire detection and extinguishing systems.

[Amdt. 147–2, 35 FR 5535, Apr. 3, 1970, as amended by Amdt. 147–5, 57 FR 28960, June 29, 1992]

APPENDIX D TO PART 147

POWERPLANT CURRICULUM SUBJECTS

This appendix lists the subjects required in at least 750 hours of each powerplant curriculum, in addition to at least 400 hours in general curriculum subjects.

The number in parentheses before each item listed under each subject heading indicates the level of proficiency at which that item must be taught.

I. Powerplant Theory and Maintenance

Teaching level

A. RECIPROCATING ENGINES

(1) 1. Inspect and repair a radial engine.

(2) 2. Overhaul reciprocating engine.

(3) 3. Inspect, check, service, and repair reciprocating engines and engine installations.

(3) 4. Install, troubleshoot, and remove reciprocating engines.

B. TURBINE ENGINES

(2) 5. Overhaul turbine engine.

(3) 6. Inspect, check, service, and repair turbine engines and turbine engine installations.

(3) 7. Install, troubleshoot, and remove turbine engines.

C. ENGINE INSPECTION

(3) 8. Perform powerplant conformity and air worthiness inspections.

II. Powerplant Systems and Components

Teaching level

A. ENGINE INSTRUMENT SYSTEMS

(2) 9. Troubleshoot, service, and repair electrical and mechanical fluid rate-of-flow indicating systems.

(3) 10. Inspect, check, service, troubleshoot, and repair electrical and mechanical engine temperature, pressure, and r.p.m. indicating systems.

B. ENGINE FIRE PROTECTION SYSTEMS

(3) 11. Inspect, check, service, troubleshoot, and repair engine fire detection and extinguishing systems.

C. ENGINE ELECTRICAL SYSTEMS

(2) 12. Repair engine electrical system components.

(3) 13. Install, check, and service engine electrical wiring, controls, switches, indicators, and protective devices.

D. LUBRICATION SYSTEMS

(2) 14. Identify and select lubricants.

(2) 15. Repair engine lubrication system components.

(3) 16. Inspect, check, service, troubleshoot, and repair engine lubrication systems.

E. IGNITION AND STARTING SYSTEMS

(2) 17. Overhaul magneto and ignition harness.

(2) 18. Inspect, service, troubleshoot, and repair reciprocating and turbine engine ignition systems and components.

(3) 19.a. Inspect, service, troubleshoot, and repair turbine engine electrical starting systems.

(1) 19.b. Inspect, service, and troubleshoot turbine engine pneumatic starting systems.

F. FUEL METERING SYSTEMS

(1) 20. Troubleshoot and adjust turbine engine fuel metering systems and electronic engine fuel controls.

(2) 21. Overhaul carburetor.

(2) 22. Repair engine fuel metering components.

(3) 23. Inspect, check, service, troubleshoot, and repair reciprocating and turbine engine fuel metering systems.

G. ENGINE FUEL SYSTEMS

(2) 24. Repair engine fuel system components.

(3) 25. Inspect, check, service, troubleshoot, and repair engine fuel systems.

H. INDUCTION AND ENGINE AIRFLOW SYSTEMS

(2) 26. Inspect, check, troubleshoot, service and repair engine ice and rain control systems.

(1) 27. Inspect, check, service, troubleshoot and repair heat exchangers, superchargers and turbine engine airflow and temperature control systems.

(3) 28. Inspect, check, service, and repair carburetor air intake and induction manifolds.

I. ENGINE COOLING SYSTEMS

(2) 29. Repair engine cooling system components.

(3) 30. Inspect, check, troubleshoot, service, and repair engine cooling systems.

J. ENGINE EXHAUST AND REVERSER SYSTEMS

(2) 31. Repair engine exhaust system components.

(3) 32.a. Inspect, check, troubleshoot, service, and repair engine exhaust systems.

(1) 32.b. Troubleshoot and repair engine thrust reverser systems and related components.

K. PROPELLERS

(1) 33. Inspect, check, service, and repair propeller synchronizing and ice control systems.

(2) 34. Identify and select propeller lubricants.

(1) 35. Balance propellers.

(2) 36. Repair propeller control system components.

(3) 37. Inspect, check, service, and repair fixed-pitch, constant-speed, and feathering propellers, and propeller governing systems.

(3) 38. Install, troubleshoot, and remove propellers.

(3) 39. Repair aluminum alloy propeller blades.

L. UNDUCTED FANS

(1) 40. Inspect and troubleshoot unducted fan systems and components.

M. AUXILIARY POWER UNITS

(1) 41. Inspect, check, service, and troubleshoot turbine-driven auxiliary power units.

(Sec. 6(c), Dept. of Transportation Act; 49 U.S.C. 1655(c)))

[Amdt. 147–2, 35 FR 5535, Apr. 3, 1970, as amended by Amdt. 147–5, 57 FR 28961, June 29, 1992]

SUBCHAPTER K
ADMINISTRATIVE REGULATIONS

PART 183
REPRESENTATIVES OF THE ADMINISTRATOR

Subpart A — General

Sec.
183.1 Scope.

Subpart B — Certification of Representatives

183.11 Selection.
183.13 Certification.
183.15 Duration of certificates.
183.17 Reports.

Subpart C — Kinds of Designations: Privileges

183.21 Aviation Medical Examiners.
183.23 Pilot examiners.
183.25 Technical personnel examiners.
183.27 Designated aircraft maintenance inspectors.
183.29 Designated engineering representatives.
183.31 Designated manufacturing inspection representatives.
183.33 Designated Airworthiness Representative.

Authority: 31 U.S.C. 9701; 49 U.S.C. 106(g), 40113, 44702, 45303.

Source: Docket No. 1151, 27 FR 4951, May 26, 1962, unless otherwise noted.

Editorial Note: For miscellaneous amendments to cross references in this part 183, see Amdt. 183–1, 31 FR 9211, July 6, 1966.

Subpart A — General

§183.1 Scope.

This part describes the requirements for designating private persons to act as representatives of the Administrator in examining, inspecting, and testing persons and aircraft for the purpose of issuing airman and aircraft certificates. In addition, it states the privileges of those representatives and prescribes rules for their exercising of those privileges.

Subpart B — Certification of Representatives

§183.11 Selection.

(a) The Federal Air Surgeon, or his authorized representative within the FAA, may select Aviation Medical Examiners from qualified physicians who apply. In addition, the Federal Air Surgeon may designate qualified forensic pathologists to assist in the medical investigation of aircraft accidents.

(b) Any local Flight Standards Inspector may select a pilot examiner, technical personnel examiner, or a designated aircraft maintenance inspector whenever he determines there is a need for one.

(c)(1) The Manager, Aircraft Certification Office, or the Manager's designee, may select Designated Engineering Representatives from qualified persons who apply by a letter accompanied by a "Statement of Qualifications of Designated Engineering Representative."

(2) The Manager, Aircraft Certification Directorate, or the Manager's designee, may select Designated Manufacturing Inspection Representatives from qualified persons who apply by a letter accompanied by a "Statement of Qualifications of Designated Manufacturing Inspection Representative."

(d) The Associate Administrator for Air Traffic, may select Air Traffic Control Tower Operator Examiners.

(e) The Director, Aircraft Certification Service, or the Director's designee, may select Designated Airworthiness Representatives from qualified persons who apply by a letter accompanied by a "Statement of Qualifications of Designated Airworthiness Representative."

(Approved by the Office of Management and Budget under control number 2120-0035)

(Secs. 313(a), 314, 601, 603, 605, and 1102, Federal Aviation Act of 1958, as amended (49 U.S.C. 1354(a), 1355, 1421, 1423, 1425, and 1502); sec. 6(c) Department of Transportation Act (49 U.S.C. 1655(c)))

[Docket No. 1151, 27 FR 4951, May 26, 1962, as amended by Amdt. 183–7, 45 FR 32669, May 19, 1980; Amdt. 183–8, 48 FR 16179, April 14, 1983; Amdt. 183–9, 54 FR 39296, Sept. 25, 1989]

§183.13 Certification.

(a) A "Certificate of Designation" and an appropriate Identification Card is issued to each Aviation Medical Examiner and to each forensic pathologist designated under §183.11(a).

(b) A "Certificate of Authority" specifying the kinds of designation for which the person concerned is qualified and stating an expiration date is issued to each Flight Standards Designated Representative, along with a "Certificate of Designation" for display purposes, designating the holder as a Flight Standards Representative and specifying the kind of designation for which he is qualified.

(c) A "Certificate of Authority," stating the specific functions which the person concerned is authorized to perform and stating an expiration date, is issued to each Designated Airworthiness Representative, along with a "Certificate of Designation" for display purposes.

(Secs. 601 and 602, 72 Stat. 752, 49 U.S.C. 1421–1422; secs. 313(a), 314, 601, 603, 605, and 1102, Federal Aviation Act of 1958, as amended (49 U.S.C. 1354(a), 1355, 1421, 1423, 1425, and 1502); sec. 6(c) Department of Transportation Act (49 U.S.C. 1655(c)))

[Docket No. 1151, 27 FR 4951, May 26, 1962, as amended by Amdt. 183–2, 32 FR 46, Jan. 5, 1967; Amdt. 183–8, 48 FR 16179, April 14, 1983]

§183.15 Duration of certificates.

(a) Unless sooner terminated under paragraph (d) of this section, a designation as an Aviation Medical Examiner is effective for 1 year after the date it is issued, and may be renewed for additional periods of 1 year in the Federal Air Surgeon's discretion. A renewal is effected by a letter and issuance of a new identification card specifying the renewal period.

(b) Unless sooner terminated under paragraph (d) of this section, a designation as a Flight Standards and Aircraft Certification Service Designated Representative is effective for one year after the date it is issued and may be renewed for additional periods of one year in the Administrator's discretion.

(c) Unless sooner terminated under paragraph (d) of this section, a designation as a Designated Airworthiness Representative is effective until the expiration date shown on the Certificate of Authority.

(d) A designation made under this subpart terminates—

(1) Upon the written request of the representative;

(2) Upon the written request of the employer in any case in which the recommendation of the employer is required for the designation;

(3) Upon the representative being separated from the employment of the employer who recommended him for certification;

(4) Upon a finding by the Administrator that the representative has not properly performed his duties under the designation;

(5) Upon the assistance of the representative being no longer needed by the Administrator; or

(6) For any reason the Administration considers appropriate.

(Secs. 313(a), 314, 601, 603, 605, and 1102, Federal Aviation Act of 1958, as amended (49 U.S.C. 1354(a), 1355, 1421, 1423, 1425, and 1502); sec. 6(c) Department of Transportation Act (49 U.S.C. 1655(c)))

[Docket No. 1151, 27 FR 4951, May 26, 1962, as amended by Amdt. 183–3, 33 FR 1072, Jan. 27, 1968; Amdt. 183–8, 48 FR 16179, April 14, 1983; Amdt. 183–9, 54 FR 39296, Sept. 25, 1989]

§183.17 Reports.

Each representative designated under this part shall make such reports as are prescribed by the Administrator.

Subpart C—Kinds of Designations: Privileges

§183.21 Aviation Medical Examiners.

An Aviation Medical Examiner may—

(a) Accept applications for physical examinations necessary for issuing medical certificates under part 67 of this chapter;

(b) Under the general supervision of the Federal Air Surgeon or the appropriate senior regional flight surgeon, conduct those physical examinations;

(c) Issue or deny medical certificates in accordance with part 67 of this chapter, subject to reconsideration by the Federal Air Surgeon or his authorized representatives within the FAA;

(d) Issue student pilot certificates as specified in §61.85 of this chapter; and

(e) As requested, participate in investigating aircraft accidents.

(Secs. 601 and 602, 72 Stat. 752, 49 U.S.C. 1421–1422)

[Docket No. 1151, 27 FR 4951, May 26, 1962, as amended by Amdt. 183–2, 32 FR 46, Jan. 5, 1967; Amdt. 183–5, 38 FR 12203, May 10, 1973]

§183.23 Pilot examiners.

Any pilot examiner, instrument rating examiner, or airline transport pilot examiner may—

(a) As authorized in his designation, accept applications for flight tests necessary for issuing pilot certificates and ratings under this chapter;

(b) Under the general supervision of the appropriate local Flight Standards Inspector, conduct those tests; and

(c) In the discretion of the appropriate local Flight Standards Inspector, issue temporary pilot certificates and ratings to qualified applicants.

§183.25 Technical personnel examiners.

(a) A designated mechanic examiner (DME) (airframe and power plant) may—

(1) Accept applications for, and conduct, mechanic, oral and practical tests necessary for issuing mechanic certificates under part 65 of this chapter; and

(2) In the discretion of the appropriate local Flight Standards Inspector, issue temporary mechanic certificates to qualified applicants.

(b) A designated parachute rigger examiner (DPRE) may—

(1) Accept applications for, and conduct, oral and practical tests necessary for issuing parachute rigger certificates under part 65 of this chapter; and

(2) In the discretion of the appropriate local Flight Standards Inspector, issue temporary parachute rigger certificates to qualified applicants.

(c) An air traffic control tower operator examiner may—

(1) Accept applications for, and conduct, written and practical tests necessary for issuing control tower operator certificates under part 65 of this chapter; and

(2) In the discretion of the Associate Administrator for Air Traffic issue temporary control tower operator certificates to qualified applicants.

(d) A designated flight engineer examiner (DFEE) may—

(1) Accept applications for, and conduct, oral and practical tests necessary for issuing flight engineer certificates under part 63 of this chapter; and

(2) In the discretion of the appropriate local Flight Standards Inspector, issue temporary flight engineer certificates to qualified applicants.

(e) A designated flight navigator examiner (DFNE) may—

(1) Accept applications for, and conduct, oral and practical tests necessary for issuing flight navigator certificates under part 63 of this chapter; and

(2) In the discretion of the appropriate local Flight Standards Inspector, issue temporary flight navigator certificates to qualified applicants.

(f) A designated aircraft dispatcher examiner (DADE) may—

(1) Accept applications for, and conduct, written and practical tests necessary for issuing aircraft dispatcher certificates under part 65 of this chapter; and

(2) In the discretion of the appropriate local Flight Standards Inspector, issue temporary aircraft dispatcher certificates to qualified applicants.

[Docket No. 1151, 27 FR 4951, May 26, 1962, as amended by Amdt. 183–9, 54 FR 39296, Sept. 25, 1989]

§183.27 Designated aircraft maintenance inspectors.

A designated aircraft maintenance inspector (DAMI) may approve maintenance on civil aircraft used by United States military flying clubs in foreign countries.

§183.29 Designated engineering representatives.

(a) A structural engineering representative may approve structural engineering information and other structural considerations within limits prescribed by and under the general supervision of the Administrator, whenever the representative determines that information and other structural considerations comply with the applicable regulations of this chapter.

(b) A power plant engineering representative may approve information relating to power plant installations within limitations prescribed by and under the general supervision of the Administrator whenever the representative determines that information complies with the applicable regulations of this chapter.

(c) A systems and equipment engineering representative may approve engineering information relating to equipment and systems, other than those of a structural, powerplant, or radio nature, within limits prescribed by and under the general supervision of the Administrator, whenever the representative determines that information complies with the applicable regulations of this chapter.

(d) A radio engineering representative may approve engineering information relating to the design and operating characteristics of radio equipment, within limits prescribed by and under the general supervision of the Administrator whenever the representative determines that information complies with the applicable regulations of this chapter.

(e) An engine engineering representative may approve engineering information relating to engine design, operation and service, within limits prescribed by and under the general supervision of the Administrator, whenever the representative determines that information complies with the applicable regulations of this chapter.

(f) A propeller engineering representative may approve engineering information relating to propeller design, operation, and maintenance, within limits prescribed by and under the general supervision of the Administrator whenever the representative determines that information complies with the applicable regulations of this chapter.

(g) A flight analyst representative may approve flight test information, within limits prescribed by and under the general supervision of the Administrator, whenever the representative determines that information complies with the applicable regulations of this chapter.

(h) A flight test pilot representative may make flight tests, and prepare and approve flight test information relating to compliance with the regulations of this chapter, within limits prescribed by and under the general supervision of the Administrator.

(i) An acoustical engineering representative may witness and approve aircraft noise certification tests and approve measured noise data and evaluated noise data analyses, within the limits prescribed by, and under the general supervision of, the Administrator, whenever the representative determines that the noise test, test data, and associated analyses are in conformity with the applicable regulations of this chapter. Those regulations include, where appropriate, the methodologies and any equivalencies previously approved by the Director of Environment and Energy, for that noise test series. No designated acoustical engineering representative may determine that a type design change is not an acoustical change, or approve equivalencies to prescribed noise procedures or standards.

[Docket No. 1151, 27 FR 4951, May 26, 1962, as amended by Amdt. 183–7, 45 FR 32669, May 19, 1980; Amdt. 183–9, 54 FR 39296, Sept. 25, 1989]

§183.31 Designated manufacturing inspection representatives.

A designated manufacturing inspection representative (DMIR) may, within limits prescribed by, and under the general supervision of, the Administrator, do the following:

(a) Issue—

(1) Original airworthiness certificates for aircraft and airworthiness approvals for engines, propellers, and product parts that conform to the approved design requirements and are in a condition for safe operation;

(2) Export certificates of airworthiness and airworthiness approval tags in accordance with subpart L of part 21 of this chapter;

(3) Experimental certificates for aircraft for which the manufacturer holds the type certificate and which have undergone changes to the type design requiring a flight test; and

(4) Special flight permits to export aircraft.

(b) Conduct any inspections that may be necessary to determine that—

(1) Prototype products and related parts conform to design specifications; and

(2) Production products and related parts conform to the approved type design and are in condition for safe operation.

(c) Perform functions authorized by this section for the manufacturer, or the manufacturer's supplier, at any location authorized by the FAA.

[Docket No. 16622, 45 FR 1416, Jan. 7, 1980]

§183.33 Designated Airworthiness Representative.

A Designated Airworthiness Representative (DAR) may, within limits prescribed by and under the general supervision of the Administrator, do the following:

(a) Perform examination, inspection, and testing services necessary to issue, and to determine the continuing effectiveness of, certificates, including issuing certificates, as authorized by the Director of Flight Standards Service in the area of maintenance or as authorized by the Director of Aircraft Certification Service in the areas of manufacturing and engineering.

(b) Charge a fee for his or her services.

(c) Perform authorized functions at any authorized location.

(Secs. 313(a), 314, 601, 603, 605, and 1102, Federal Aviation Act of 1958, as amended (49 U.S.C. 1354(a), 1355, 1421, 1423, 1425, and 1502); sec. 6(c) Department of Transportation Act (49 U.S.C. 1655(c)))

[Docket No. 23140, 48 FR 16179, Apr. 14, 1983, as amended by Amdt. 183–9, 54 FR 39296, Sept. 25, 1989; Amdt. 183–11, 67 FR 72766, Dec. 6, 2002]

Advisory Circulars

Page

AC 20-62D Eligibility, Quality, and Identification of Approved Aeronautical Replacement Parts .... 641 .... 20-62D

AC 20-109A Service Difficulty Program (General Aviation) .... 651 .... 20-109A

AC 21-12B Application for U.S. Airworthiness Certificate, FAA Form 8130-6 .... 665 .... 21-12B

AC 39-7C Airworthiness Directives .... 693 .... 39-7C

AC 43-9C Maintenance Records .... 699 .... 43-9C

AC 43.9-1E Instructions for Completion of FAA Form 337 (OMB 2120-0020), Major Repair and Alteration (Airframe, Powerplant, Propeller, or Appliance) .... 711 .... 43.9-1E

AC 65-30A Overview of the Aviation Maintenance Profession .... 721 .... 65-30A

FAA-G-8082-11A Inspection Authorization Knowledge Test Guide .... 741 .... 8082-11A

U.S. Department of Transportation
Federal Aviation Administration

Advisory Circular 20-62D

Subject: **Eligibility, Quality, and Identification of Aeronautical Replacement Parts**
Date: 5/24/96 Initiated by: AFS-340

1. **PURPOSE.** This advisory circular (AC) provides information and guidance for use in determining the quality, eligibility and traceability of aeronautical parts and materials intended for installation on U.S. type-certificated products and to enable compliance with the applicable regulations.

2. **CANCELLATION.** AC 20-62C, Eligibility, Quality, and Identification of Approved Aeronautical Replacement Parts, dated August 26, 1976, is canceled.

3. **RELATED REGULATORY SECTIONS.** (Title 14 of the Code of Federal Regulations (14 CFR)):

   a. Part 1, Definitions and Abbreviations.

   b. Part 21, Certification Procedures for Products and Parts.

   c. Part 39, Airworthiness Directives.

   d. Part 43, Maintenance, Preventative Maintenance, Rebuilding, and Alteration.

   e. Part 45, Identification and Registration Marking.

   f. Part 91, General Operating and Flight Rules.

   g. Part 119, Certification: Air Carriers and Commercial Operators.

   h. Part 121, Certification and Operations: Domestic, Flag and Supplemental Air Carriers and Commercial Operators of Large Aircraft.

   i. Part 125, Certification and Operation: Airplanes having a seating capacity of 20 or more passengers or a maximum payload capacity of 6,000 pounds or more.

   j. Part 135, Air Taxi Operators and Commercial Operators.

   k. Part 145, Repair Stations.

4. **DEFINITIONS.** The following definitions apply to this AC:

   a. ***Federal Aviation Administration (FAA)-Approved Parts.*** Under 14 CFR part 21, section 21.305, parts which were produced under an FAA-approved production system and conform with FAA-approved data, may be approved under the following:

   (1) A Parts Manufacturer Approval (PMA) issued under section 21.303.

   (2) A Technical Standard Order Authorization (TSOA) issued by the Administrator.

   (3) In conjunction with type certification procedures for a product.

   (4) In any manner approved by the Administrator, such as part 21, subpart F, Parts Produced Under a Type Certificate (TC), and subpart G, Production Certificate (PC). In addition, subpart N provides for the acceptance of a new part produced in a country with which the United States has an agreement for the acceptance of parts for export and import. The part is approved when the country of manufacture issues a certificate of airworthiness for export for the part.

b. ***Acceptable Parts.*** The following parts may be found to be acceptable for installation on a type-certificated product:

(1) Standard parts (such as nuts and bolts) conforming to an established industry or U.S. specification.

(2) Parts produced by an owner or operator for maintaining or altering their own product and which are shown to conform with FAA-approved data.

(3) Parts for which inspections and tests have been accomplished by appropriately certificated persons authorized to determine conformity to FAA-approved design data.

c. ***Class I Product.*** A complete aircraft, aircraft engine, or propeller that has been type-certificated in accordance with the applicable regulations, and for which Federal Aviation Specifications or TC data sheets have been issued.

d. ***Class II Product.*** A major component of a Class I product (e.g., wings, fuselages, empennage assemblies, landing gears, power transmissions, or control surfaces, etc.), the failure of which would jeopardize the safety of a Class I product; or any part, material, or appliance, approved and manufactured under the Technical Standard Order (TSO) system in the "C" series.

e. ***Class III Product.*** Any part or component that is not a Class I or Class II product, including standard parts. Class III products are considered to be parts.

f. ***Standard Part.*** Is a part manufactured in complete compliance with an established U.S. Government or industry-accepted specification which includes design, manufacturing, and uniform identification requirements. The specification must include all information necessary to produce and conform the part. The specification must be published so that any party may manufacture the part. Examples include, but are not limited to, National Aerospace Standards (NAS), Air Force-Navy Aeronautical Standard (AN), Society of Automotive Engineers (SAE), SAE Aerospace Standard (AS), Military Standard (MS), etc.

g. ***New.*** A product, accessory, part, or material that has no operating time or cycles.

NOTE: There could be time/cycles on a newly type-certificated product (e.g., use of a manufacturer's test cell or certification requirements).

h. ***Surplus.*** Describes a product, assembly, part, or material that has been released as surplus by the military, manufacturers, owners/operators, repair facilities, or any other parts supplier. These products should show traceability to an FAA-approved manufacturing procedure.

i. ***Overhauled.*** Describes an airframe, aircraft engine, propeller, appliance, or component part using methods, techniques, and practices acceptable to the Administrator, which has undergone the following:

(1) Has been disassembled, cleaned, inspected, repaired when necessary, and reassembled to the extent possible.

(2) Has been tested in accordance with approved standards and technical data, or current standards and technical data acceptable to the Administrator (i.e., manufacturer's data), which have been developed and documented by the holder of one of the following:

(a) TC.

(b) Supplemental Type Certificate (STC), or material, part, process, or appliance approval under section 21.305.

(c) PMA.

j. ***Rebuilt.*** Describes an aircraft, airframe, aircraft engine, propeller, or appliance, using new or used parts that conform to new part tolerances and limits or to approved oversized or undersized dimensions that has undergone the following:

(1) Has been disassembled, cleaned, inspected, repaired as necessary, and reassembled to the extent possible.

(2) Has been tested to the same tolerances and limits as a new item.

k. ***Return to Service Inspection Records.*** The person approving or disapproving for return to service a type-certificated product must ensure that the required maintenance record entries comply with 14 CFR part 43, and therefore must include the following information:

(1) Type of inspection and a brief description of the extent of the inspection.

(2) Date.

(3) Product hours, cycles, or life limits as applicable.

(4) Signature, certificate number, and kind of certificate held by the person approving or disapproving for return to service.

(5) The appropriate certifying statement that the product or part thereof, is approved or disapproved for return to service, as applicable.

l. ***As Is.*** Describes any airframe, aircraft engine, propeller, appliance, component part, or material, the condition of which is unknown.

m. ***Appropriately Certificated Person.*** As related to return to service after maintenance, preventative maintenance, rebuilding, or alteration, can include the holder of a:

(1) Mechanic certificate. May perform maintenance, preventative maintenance, and alterations as provided in 14 CFR part 65.

(2) Inspection authorization. May inspect and approve for return to service any aircraft or related part or appliance (except aircraft maintained in accordance with a continuous airworthiness program under part 121 or 127) after a major repair or alteration as provided in part 43 if the work was done in accordance with technical data approved by the administrator. Perform an annual, or supervise a progressive inspection according to 14 CFR part 43, sections 43.13 and 43.15.

(3) Repair station certificate under 14 CFR part 145. May perform maintenance, preventative maintenance, or alterations as provided in part 145.

(4) Air carriers operating may perform maintenance, preventative maintenance, or alterations as provided 14 CFR part 119, 121, 127, 129, or 135.

(5) Private pilot certificate (for performing preventative maintenance). May perform preventative maintenance described in part 43, appendix A on any aircraft operated by the pilot except, those aircraft operated under part 119, 121, 125, 127, 129, or 135.

(6) Manufacturer's type or production certificate. May rebuild or alter any aircraft, aircraft engine, or propeller, or appliance manufactured by him under a TSOA, PMA, or Product or Parts Specification, or perform any inspection required under 14 CFR part 91 or 125 while currently operating under a production certificate or approved production inspection system.

n. ***Owner/Operator Produced Part.*** Parts that were produced by an owner/operator for installation on their own aircraft (e.g., by a certificated air carrier). An owner/operator is considered a producer of a part, if the owner participated in controlling the design, manufacture, or quality of the part. Participating in the design of the part can include supervising the manufacture of the part or providing the manufacturer with the following: the design data, the materials with which to make the part, the fabrication processes, assembly methods, or the quality control procedures.

5. RELATED READING MATERIALS.

a. Copies of current editions of the following publications may be obtained free of charge from the U.S. Department of Transportation, Subsequent Distribution Office, Ardmore East Business Center, 3341 Q 75th Avenue, Landover, MD 20785.

(1) AC 21-13, Standard Airworthiness Certification of Surplus Military Aircraft and Aircraft Built from Spare and Surplus Parts.

(2) AC 21-20, Supplier Surveillance Procedures.

(3) AC 21-23, Airworthiness Certification of Civil Aircraft, Engines, Propellers, and Related Products Imported to the United States.

(4) AC 21-29, Detecting and Reporting Suspected Unapproved Parts.

(5) AC 21-38, Disposition of Unsalvageable Aircraft Parts and Materials.

(6) AC 43-9, Maintenance Records.

(7) FAA Order 8000.50, Repair Station Production of Replacement or Modification Parts.

(8) FAA Order 8130.21, Procedures for Completion and Use of FAA Form 8130-3 Airworthiness Approval Tag.

(9) FAA Order 8120.10, Suspected Unapproved Part Program.

(10) FAA Order 8120.2, Production Approval And Surveillance Procedures.

b. Copies of current editions of the following AC's may be purchased from the Superintendent of Documents. Make check or money order payable to the Superintendent of Documents.

(1) AC 21-2, Export Airworthiness Approval Procedures.

(2) AC 21-6, Production Under Type Certificate Only.

(3) AC 21-18, Bilateral Airworthiness Agreements.

(4) AC 43.13-1, Acceptable Methods, Techniques and Practices — Aircraft Inspection and Repair.

(5) AC 43.13-2, Acceptable Methods, Techniques and Practices — Aircraft Alterations.

6. DISCUSSION. The FAA continues to receive reports of replacement parts being offered for sale as aircraft quality when the quality and origin of the parts are unknown or questionable. Such parts may be advertised or presented as "unused," "like new," or "remanufactured." These imply that the quality of the parts is equal to an acceptable part. Purchasers of these parts may not be aware of the potential hazards involved with replacement parts for which acceptability for installation on a type-certificated product has not been established.

a. The performance rules for replacement of parts and materials used in the maintenance, preventive maintenance, and alteration of aircraft that have (or have had) a U.S. airworthiness certificate, and components thereof, are specified in 14 CFR parts 43 and 145, sections 43.13 and 145.57. These rules require that the installer of a part use methods, techniques, and practices acceptable to the FAA. Additionally, the installer of a part must accomplish the work in such a manner and use materials of such quality, that the product or appliance worked on will be at least equal to its original or properly altered condition with respect to the qualities affecting airworthiness.

b. The continued airworthiness of an aircraft, which includes the replacement of parts, is the responsibility of the owner/operator, as specified in 14 CFR parts 91, 119, 121, 125, and 135, sections 91.403, 121.363, 125.243, and 135.413. These rules require that the installer determine that a part is acceptable for installation on a product or component prior to returning that product or component to service with the part installed. Those rules also require that the installation of a part must be accomplished in accordance with data approved by the FAA, if the installation constitutes a major repair or alteration.

c. As part of determining whether installation of a part conforms with all applicable regulations, the installer should establish that the part was manufactured under a production approval pursuant to part 21, that an originally acceptable part has been maintained in accordance with part 43, or that the part is otherwise acceptable for installation (e.g., has been found to conform to data approved by the FAA). This AC addresses means to help the installer make the required determinations.

7. IDENTIFICATION OF REPLACEMENT PARTS. Acceptable replacement parts should be identified using one of the following methods:

*a. **Airworthiness Approval Tag.*** FAA Form 8130-3, Airworthiness Approval Tag, identifies a part or group of parts for export approval and conformity determination from production approval holders. It also serves as approval for return to service after maintenance or alteration by an authorized part 145 Repair Station, or a U.S. Air Carrier having an approved Continuous Airworthiness Maintenance Program under part 135.

*b. **Foreign Manufactured Replacement Parts.*** New foreign manufactured parts for use on U.S. type-certificated products may be imported when there is a bilateral airworthiness agreement between the country of manufacture and the United States and the part meets the requirements under section 21.502.

(1) The certification may be verified on a form similar to the FAA Form 8130-3, (i.e., Joint Aviation Authority (JAA), JAA Form One), used by European member countries of the JAA with which the U.S. has a bilateral airworthiness agreement. The JAA is an organization of European member nations that has the responsibility to develop JAA regulations and policy. The procedures and the countries with which the U.S. has bilateral airworthiness agreements and the condition of the agreements, are contained in AC 21-23.

(2) Used parts may be identified by the records required for approval for return to service as set forth in section 43.9. FAA Form 8130-3 may be used for this purpose if the requirements of section 43.9 are contained in or attached to the form and approved for return to service by a U.S. FAA-certificated repair station or U.S. air carrier under the requirement of their Continuous Airworthiness Maintenance Program. There is no set format or form required for a maintenance or alteration record. However, the data or information used to identify a part must be traceable to a person authorized to perform and approve for return to service maintenance and alteration under part 43. The records must contain as a minimum those data that set forth in section 43.9

(3) The use of an authorization tag does not approve the installation of a part on a type-certificated product. Additional substantiated authorization for compliance with part 43 and the FAA-approved data for major repairs and alterations may be required for installation on a type-certificated product.

*c. **FAA TSO Markings.*** TSOA is issued under section 21.607, subpart O. A TSOA must be permanently and legibly marked with the following:

(1) Name and address of the manufacturer.

(2) The name, type, part number, or model designation of the article.

(3) The serial number or the date of manufacture of the article or both.

(4) The applicable TSO number.

d. ***FAA-PMA Symbol.*** An FAA-PMA is issued under section 21.303. Each PMA part should be marked with the letters, "FAA-PMA," in accordance with 14 CFR part 45, section 45.15:

(1) The name.

(2) Trademark, or symbol.

(3) Part number.

(4) Name and model designation of each certificated product on which the part is eligible for installation.

NOTE: Parts that are too small or otherwise impractical to be marked may, as an alternative, be marked showing the above information on an attached tag or labeled container. If the marking on the tag is too extensive to be practical, the tag attached to a part or container may refer to a readily available manual or catalog for part eligibility information. Under a licensing agreement, when the applicant has been given the right to use the TC holder's design, which includes the part number, and a replacement part is produced under that agreement, the part number may be identical to that of the TC holder, provided that the PMA holder includes the letters, "FAA-PMA," and the PMA holder's identification symbol is on the part. In all other cases, the PMA holder's part number must be different from that of the TC holder.

e. ***Shipping Ticket, Invoice, or Other Production Approval Holder's (PAH) Documents or Markings.*** These may provide evidence that a part was produced by a manufacturer holding an FAA-approved manufacturing process.

f. ***Direct Ship Authority.*** In order for U.S. manufactured parts, with "direct ship" authority to be recognized as being produced under a manufacturer's FAA production approval, the manufacturer must specifically authorize the shipping supplier, in writing, and must establish procedures to ensure that the shipped parts conform to the approved design and are in condition for safe operation. A statement to the supplier from the certificate holder authorizing direct shipment and date of authorization, should be included on the shipping ticket, invoice, or other transfer document. It should contain a declaration that the individual part was produced under a production certificate.

g. ***Maintenance Release Document.*** A release, signed by an appropriately certificated person, qualified for the relevant function that signifies that the item has been returned to service, after a maintenance or test function has been completed. This type of documentation could be in the form of a repair station tag, containing adequate information (section 43.9), work order, FAA Form 337, FAA Form 8130-3, or a maintenance record entry, which must include an appropriate description of the maintenance work performed, including the recording requirements of section 43.9 and Appendix B.

NOTE: When a noncertificated person certifies that they are shipping the correct part ordered, the only thing they are stating is that the part number agrees with the purchase order, not the status of FAA acceptability of the part.

8. INFORMATION RELEVANT TO USED PARTS. The following information may be useful when assessing maintenance records and part status.

a. ***Documentation.*** If the part has been rebuilt, overhauled, inspected, modified, or repaired, the records should include a maintenance release, return to service tag, repaired parts tag, or similar documentation from an FAA-certificated person. Documentation describing the maintenance performed and parts replaced must be made for the part (i.e., FAA Form 8130-3 or FAA Repair Station work order). (Reference section 43.9 and Appendix B).

b. ***Information that should be obtained.*** The records should include information, either directly or by reference, to support documentation that may be helpful to the user or installer in making a final determination as to the airworthiness and eligibility of the part. Listed are examples of information that should be obtained, as applicable:

(1) AD status.

(2) Compliance or noncompliance with service bulletins.

(3) Life/cycle limited parts status (i.e., time, time since overhaul, cycles, history) should be substantiated. If the part is serialized and life-limited, then both operational time and/or cycles (where applicable) must be indicated. Historical records that clearly establish and substantiate time and cycles must be provided as evidence.

(4) Shelf-life data, including manufacturing date or cure date.

(5) Return to service date.

(6) Shortages applicable to assemblies or kits.

(7) Import or export certification documents.

(8) The name of the person who removed the part.

(9) FAA Form 337, Major Repair or Alteration.

(10) Maintenance Manual standards used for performing maintenance.

c. ***Unusual Circumstances.*** If a particular part was obtained from any of the following, then it should be so identified by some type of documentation (i.e., maintenance record entries, removal entries, overhaul records).

(1) Noncertificated aircraft (aircraft without airworthiness certificate, i.e., public use, non-U.S., and military surplus aircraft).

(2) Aircraft, aircraft engines, propellers or appliances subjected to extreme stress, sudden stoppage, heat, major failure or accident.

(3) Salvaged aircraft or aircraft components.

d. ***Seller's Designation.*** The seller may be able to provide documentation that shows traceability to an FAA-approved manufacturing procedure for one of the following:

(1) Parts produced by an FAA PAH by TC, PC, PMA, TSOA.

(2) Parts produced by a foreign manufacturer (in accordance with part 21, subpart N).

(3) Standard parts produced by a named manufacturer.

(4) Parts distributed with direct ship authority.

(5) Parts produced, for the work being accomplished, by a repair station to accomplish a repair or alteration on a specific type-certificated product.

(6) Parts produced by an owner or operator for installation on the owner's or operator's aircraft (e.g., by a certificated air carrier).

(7) Parts with removal records showing traceability to a U.S.-certificated aircraft, signed by an appropriately certificated person.

e. ***Manufactured.*** The manufacturer of the part should be identified; if not identified it may be difficult to prove that the part is acceptable for installation on a type-certificated product.

f. ***Certificates and Approvals Held.***

(1) Manufacturers – The certificate or approval held by the manufacturer, TC, PC, TSOA, or PMA may be listed; if not known, state as unknown.

(2) Air Agencies – The certificate held by the Air Agencies, part 145 may be listed; if not known, state as unknown.

(3) Air Operator – The certificate held by Air Operators, parts 119, 121, 125, and 135.

g. ***Part Description.*** Indicate the part's physical description for positive identification.

h. ***Part Number.*** Document the manufacturer's part number or, if the part has been modified, the amended part number.

i. ***Serial Number.*** Document the specific part's serial number, if so marked. Determine if serialized part has any life or overhaul limitations.

9. SURPLUS. Many materials, parts, appliances, and components that have been released as surplus by the military service or by manufacturers may originate from obsolete or overstocked items. Parts obtained from surplus sources may be used, provided it is established that they meet the standards to which they were manufactured, interchangeability with the original part can be established, and they are in compliance with all applicable AD's. Such items, although advertised as "remanufactured," "high quality," "like new," "unused," or "looks good," should be carefully evaluated before they are purchased. The storage time, storage conditions, or shelf life of surplus parts and materials are not usually known.

10. CONDITION FOR SAFE OPERATION. Parts and materials should be properly stored, protected, and maintained to ensure airworthiness. The following factors should be considered when determining airworthiness:

a. ***Composite Materials.*** Generally, most composite materials (thermoset polymers) have a refrigeration shelf-life recommended by the manufacturer. Composite materials must be kept refrigerated in accordance with the manufacturer's recommended temperature range and out-of-refrigeration time (out-time) limitations. Records must be maintained of the cumulative total of material out-time to prevent exceeding shelf-life.

b. ***Anti-friction Bearings.*** Anti-friction bearings that have been in storage for a long period of time, or have been improperly stored, are subject to the deteriorating effects of time and elements, unless they were hermetically sealed. Such parts should be completely inspected and lubricated before being placed in service.

c. ***Aircraft Fabric.*** Fabric and prefabricated covers should be used only if they are identifiable as meeting aircraft standards. All fabric should be examined or tested for freedom from deterioration, as determined by an appropriately certificated person.

d. ***Dope, Paint, Sealants, and Adhesives.*** These items advertised as aircraft quality may have deteriorated due to age or environmental conditions, while in storage, and may require testing before use.

e. ***Parts with Internal Seals.*** Internal seals on parts such as pumps, valves, actuators, motors, generators, and alternators are subject to deterioration from long-term storage and are susceptible to early failure in service. A procedure should be established for control of shelf-life items in order to prevent possible premature failures of the parts/components, unless other preventive procedures are in place.

f. ***Rotating Components.*** Rotating components, such as propellers, engine parts, and rotor blades, may have a life-limit or retirement life. Maintenance records should reflect a complete continuity of service time and repair history. Information that indicates whether the component has exceeded the life limit may, in some cases, be obtained from the manufacturer or from an FAA-approved repair station that may have affixed a logo, decal, or some other identification.

g. ***Heat and Fire.*** Parts that may have been exposed to heat or fire can be seriously affected and are likely unserviceable.

h. ***Corrosives.*** Foreign or corrosive liquids can also be detrimental on aircraft parts. Parts, appliances, and components that have been submerged in salt water may be unserviceable parts.

i. ***Manufacturing Rejects.*** Parts that failed the manufacturers quality assurance inspection criteria for conformity to type design, may be offered for sale by the manufacturers as scrap without being mutilated or destroyed rendering them unusable, and are unacceptable for installation.

j. ***Damaged Aircraft.*** Parts removed from aircraft involved in an accident may have been subjected to undue stresses that may have seriously effected structural integrity and rendered them permanently unstable.

k. ***Rebuilt Engines.*** Only engines that are rebuilt by a manufacturer holding an FAA production approval, an agency approved by the PAH, or an appropriately rated FAA-certificated agency can be considered as zero-timed (reference section 91.421).

11. ELECTRICAL PARTS AND INSTRUMENTS.

a. ***Electronic Kits.*** Kits assembled by noncertificated individuals are not eligible for installation on type-certificated aircraft, until the part is certified as airworthy and found eligible for installation, in accordance with parts 21 and 43. During and after assembly, these kits should receive documented conformity inspections, by properly certificated persons, to ensure that they meet all applicable airworthiness requirements, for use on the specific aircraft on which they are to be installed. The installation of these approved units should be accomplished by or under the supervision of a properly certificated person or agency in accordance with parts 21 and 43. When the installation is a major alteration, the kit data and the data used for the alteration of the product must be approved by a representative of the Administrator. An appropriately certificated person must complete the maintenance records to ensure that the aircraft is approved and airworthy for return to service.

b. ***Discrete Electrical and Electronic Component Parts.*** Electrical and electronic parts, such as resistors, capacitors, diodes, and transistors, if not specifically marked by the equipment manufacturers part number or marking scheme, may be substituted or used as replacement parts, provided that such parts are tested or it is determined that they meet their published performance specifications and do not adversely affect the performance of the equipment or article into or onto which they are installed. The performance of such equipment or article must be equal to its original or properly altered or repaired condition. Integrated circuits such as hybrids, large scale integrated circuits (LSIC), programmable logic devices, gate arrays, application specific integrated circuits (ASIC), memories, CPU's etc., are not included because their highly specialized functionality does not readily lend itself to substitution.

c. ***Aircraft Instruments.*** Instruments advertised as "high quality," "looks good," or "remanufactured" or that were acquired from aircraft involved in an accident should not be put in service unless they are inspected, tested, and/or overhauled as necessary, by an appropriately rated FAA-certificated repair station, and the installer establishes that (for the aircraft in which) the instrument installed will comply with the applicable regulations.

NOTE: Instruments are highly susceptible to hidden damage caused by rough handling or improper storage conditions; therefore, instruments that have been sitting on a shelf for a period of time that cannot be established, should be tested by an appropriately rated FAA-certificated person.

12. KNOW YOUR SUPPLIERS.

a. ***Used and Repaired Parts.*** In addition to unapproved parts, used or repaired parts may be offered for sale as "like new," "near new," and "remanufactured." Such terms do not aid the purchaser in positively determining whether the part is acceptable for installation on a type-certificated product and do not constitute the legal serviceability and condition of aircraft parts.

b. ***Caution.*** It is the installer's responsibility to ensure airworthiness. Aircraft parts distributors, aircraft supply companies or aircraft electronic parts distributors, unless they are a PAH, cannot certify the airworthiness of the parts they advertise and/or sell; therefore, it is the installer's responsibility to request documentation establishing traceability to a PAH.

13. REPORTING SUSPECTED UNAPPROVED PARTS (SUP).

a. ***SUP.*** SUP's are parts, components, or materials that may not be approved or acceptable, as described in paragraphs 4a and 4b. Some appear to be as good as the part manufactured from an FAA-approved source; however, there may be manufacturing processes that were not performed in accordance with FAA-approved data or possibly not performed at all, and would not be readily apparent to the purchaser (e.g., heat treating, plating, or various tests and inspections).

b. Persons with possible knowledge of safety violations or other circumstances that may affect aviation safety are encouraged to report them in accordance with AC 21-29, Detecting and Reporting Suspected Unapproved Parts. This AC includes procedures for referral of such reports to the appropriate FAA office. Reports may be filed by using FAA Form 8120-11, Suspected Unapproved Parts Notification, or by calling the toll free FAA Aviation Safety Hotline at 1-800-255-1111.

14. SUMMARY. The approval for return to service after maintenance of aircraft, engines, propellers, appliances, and materials and parts thereof, is the responsibility of the person who performs the maintenance and who signs the record for approval for return to service. The owner/operator (as noted in paragraph 6b) is responsible for the continued airworthiness of the aircraft. To ensure continued safety in civil aviation, it is essential that appropriate data is used when inspecting, testing, and determining the acceptability of all parts and materials. Particular caution should be exercised when the origin of parts, materials, and appliances cannot be established or when their origin is in doubt.

William J. White
Deputy Director, Flight Standards Service

U.S. Department of Transportation
Federal Aviation Administration

Advisory Circular 20-109A

Subject: **Service Difficulty Program (General Aviation)**
Date: 4/8/93 **Initiated by:** AFS-640

1. **PURPOSE.** This advisory circular (AC) describes the Service Difficulty Program as it applies to general aviation activities. Instructions for completion of the revised FAA Form 8010-4 (10-92), Malfunction or Defect Report, are provided. This AC also solicits the participation of the aviation community in the Service Difficulty Program and their cooperation in improving the quality of FAA Form 8010-4.

2. **CANCELLATION.** AC 20-109, Service Difficulty Program (General Aviation), dated 1/8/79, is canceled.

3. **FORMS.** FAA Form 8010-4 (10-92), Malfunction or Defect Report, (National Stock Number (NSN) 0052-00-039-1005, Unit of Issue "BK" (25 forms per book), is available free from Flight Standards District Offices (FSDO's). See appendix 1 for directions on completing FAA Form 8010-4.

4. **DISCUSSION.** The Service Difficulty Program is an information system designed to provide assistance to aircraft owners, operators, maintenance organizations, manufacturers, and the Federal Aviation Administration (FAA) in identifying aircraft problems encountered during service. The Service Difficulty Program provides for the collection, organization, analysis, and dissemination of aircraft service information to improve service reliability of aeronautical products. The primary sources of this information are the aircraft maintenance facilities, owners, and operators. General aviation aircraft service difficulty information is normally submitted to the FAA by use of FAA Form 8010-4. However, information will be accepted in any form or format when FAA Form 8010-4 is not readily available for use.

5. **INPUT.** All of the FAA Forms 8010-4 are received by local FSDO's or Certificate Management Offices (CMO's). All the FAA Forms 8010-4 are reviewed for immediate impact items, and then forwarded for processing to the Flight Standards Service, Safety Data Analysis Section (AFS-643), in Oklahoma City, Oklahoma.

   The information contained in the FAA Form 8010-4 is stored in a computerized data bank for retrieval and analysis. Items potentially hazardous to flight are telephoned directly to AFS-643 personnel by FAA Aviation Safety Inspectors in FSDO's. These items are immediately referred to, and expeditiously handled by, the appropriate FAA offices.

   a. **Certain owners, operators, certificate holders, and certificated repair stations are required by the Federal Aviation Regulations (FAR) to submit reports of defects, unairworthy conditions, and mechanical reliability problems to the FAA.** However, success of the Service Difficulty Program is enhanced by submission of service difficulty information by all of the aviation community regardless of whether required by regulation. Voluntary submission of service difficulty information is strongly encouraged.

   b. **Additional service difficulty information is collected by FAA Aviation Safety Inspectors** in the performance of routine aircraft and maintenance surveillance, accident and incident investigations, during the operation of rental aircraft, and during pilot certification flights.

c. **All service difficulty information is retained in the computer data bank** for a period of 5 years providing a base for the detection of trends and failure rates. If necessary, data in excess of 5 years may be retrieved through the archives.

6. **THE INFORMATION MANAGEMENT SECTION, AFS-624, IS AN INFORMATION CENTER.** AFS-624 personnel responds to individual requests from the aviation community concerning service difficulty information. Further details regarding computer-generated service difficulty information, may be obtained by telephoning (405) 954-4173 or by writing to:

FAA
Flight Standards Service
Attn: Information Management Section (AFS-624)
P.O. Box 25082
Oklahoma City, OK 73125-5012

7. **PUBLICATIONS PRODUCED BY AFS-643.** Analysis of service difficulty information is primarily done by AFS-643. When trends are detected, they are made available to pertinent FAA field personnel for their information and possible investigation. AFS-643 produces the following publications.

a. **The Flight Standards Service Difficulty Reports (General and Commercial)**, known as the weekly summary, contains all information obtained from FAA Forms 8010-4 and those service difficulties which were reported by telephone. Reports of a significant nature are highlighted with a "star" border, while reports which are of an "URGENT AIRWORTHINESS CONCERN" are highlighted with a "black and white slashed" border. These highly significant items are sometimes obtained from sources other than FAA Forms 8010-4. This publication is distributed to FSDO's, Manufacturing Inspection District Offices (MIDO's), and Aircraft Certification Offices (ACO's). This publication is also made available to the public free of charge by telephoning (405) 954-4171 or by writing to AFS-643 at the following address:

FAA
Flight Standards Service
Attn: Safety Data Analysis Section (AFS-643)
P.O. Box 25082
Oklahoma City, OK 73125-5029

b. **AC 43-16, General Aviation Airworthiness Alerts**, contains information that is of assistance to maintenance and inspection personnel in the performance of their duties. These items are developed from submitted FAA Form 8010-4 and articles pertaining to aviation. This publication is made available to the public free of charge by telephoning (405) 954-4171 or by writing to AFS-643 (see the address given in paragraph 7a).

8. **IMPORTANCE OF REPORTING.** The FAA requests the cooperation of all aircraft owners, operators, mechanics, pilots, and others in reporting service difficulties experienced with airframes, powerplants, propellers, or appliances/components.

a. **FAA Forms 8010-4 provide the FAA and industry with a very essential service record** of mechanical difficulties encountered in aircraft operations. Such reports contribute to the correction of conditions or situations which otherwise will continue to prove costly and/or adversely affect the airworthiness of aircraft.

b. **When a system component or part of an aircraft (powerplants, propellers, or appliances) functions badly or fails to operate in the normal or usual manner**, it has malfunctioned and should be reported. Also, if a system, component, or part has a flaw or imperfection which impairs function or which may impair future function, it is defective and should be reported. While at first sight it appears this will generate numerous insignificant reports, the Service Difficulty Program is designed to detect trends. Any report can be very constructive in evaluating design or maintenance reliability.

c. **When preparing FAA Form 8010-4**, furnish as much information as possible. Any attachments such as photographs and sketches of defective parts are appreciated. However, do not send parts to AFS-643. AFS-643 does not have storage facilities for defective parts.

d. **Public cooperation in submitting service difficulty information is greatly appreciated** by the FAA and others who have an interest in safety. The quantity of service difficulty reports received precludes individual acknowledgement of each report.

Thomas C. Accardi
Director, Flight Standards Service

Appendix 1.
Instructions for Completing the Revised FAA Form 8010-4 (10-92) Malfunction or Defect Report

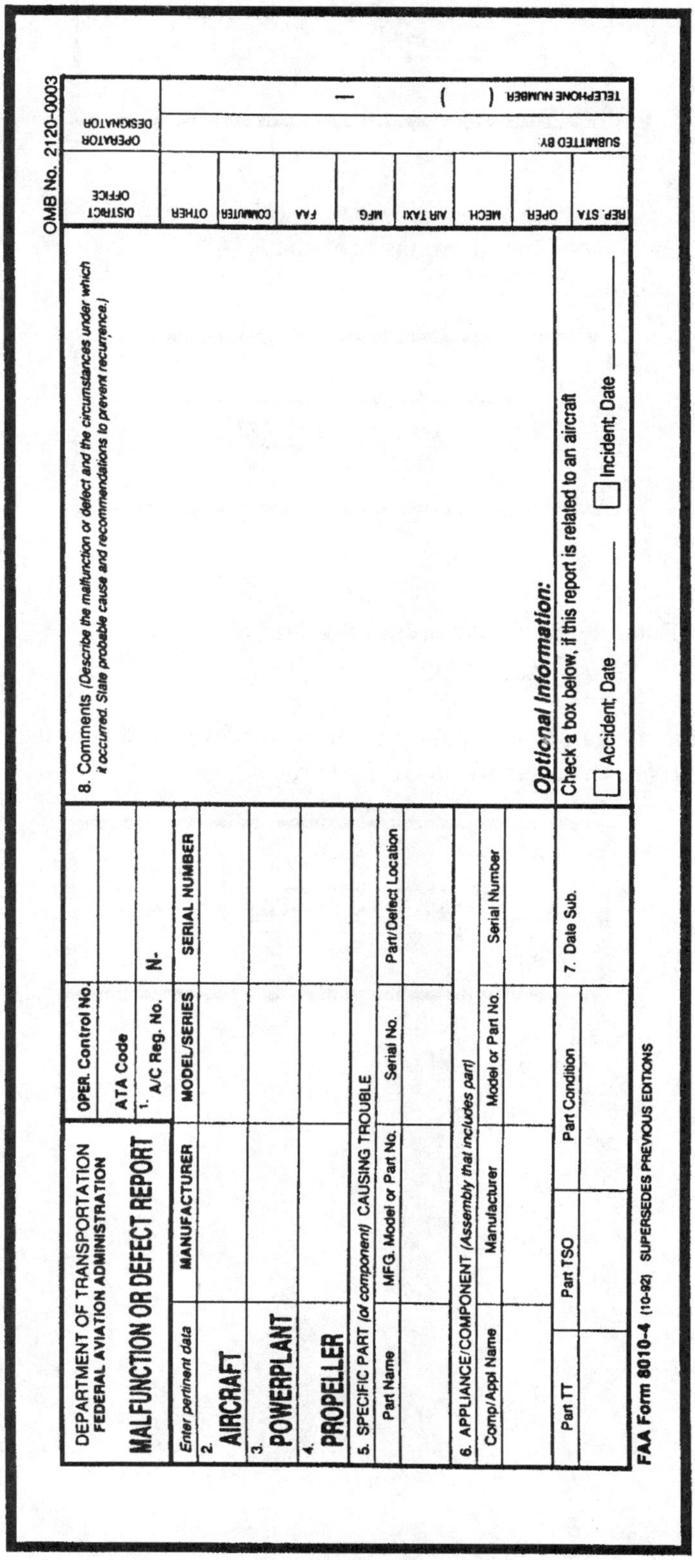

OMB No. 2120-0003

DEPARTMENT OF TRANSPORTATION
FEDERAL AVIATION ADMINISTRATION

MALFUNCTION OR DEFECT REPORT

OPER. Control No.	
ATA Code	
1. A/C Reg. No.	N-

Enter pertinent data	MANUFACTURER	MODEL/SERIES	SERIAL NUMBER
2. **AIRCRAFT**			
3. **POWERPLANT**			
4. **PROPELLER**			

5. SPECIFIC PART *(of component)* CAUSING TROUBLE

Part Name	MFG. Model or Part No.	Serial No.	Part/Defect Location

6. APPLIANCE/COMPONENT *(Assembly that includes part)*

Comp/Appl Name	Manufacturer	Model or Part No.	Serial Number

Part TT	Part TSO	Part Condition	7. Date Sub.

8. Comments *(Describe the malfunction or defect and the circumstances under which it occurred. State probable cause and recommendations to prevent recurrence.)*

Optional Information:
Check a box below, if this report is related to an aircraft
☐ Accident; Date ________ ☐ Incident; Date ________

DISTRICT OFFICE	OPERATOR DESIGNATOR

REP. STA. | OPER. | MECH. | AIR TAXI | MFG. | FAA | COMMUTER | OTHER

SUBMITTED BY

TELEPHONE NUMBER ( ) –

FAA Form 8010-4 (10-92) SUPERSEDES PREVIOUS EDITIONS

ITEM. **OPER. Control No.:** Primarily to be used for FAR Part 135 and 121 operators.
Example: ABCD9212345, BCDE1235436

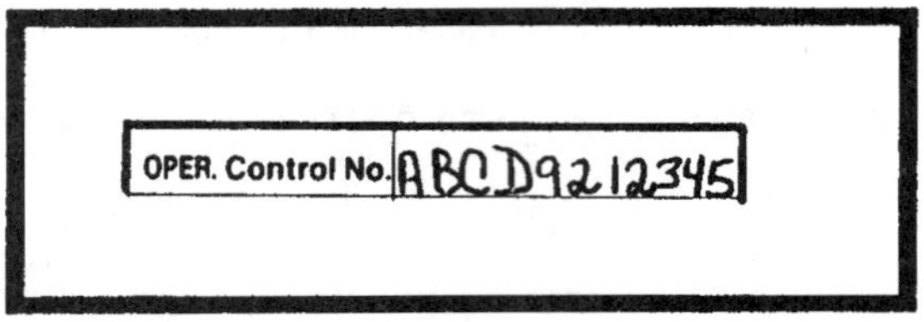

ITEM. **ATA Code:** Four-digit code used primarily by the FAA.
Example: 7200, 8300

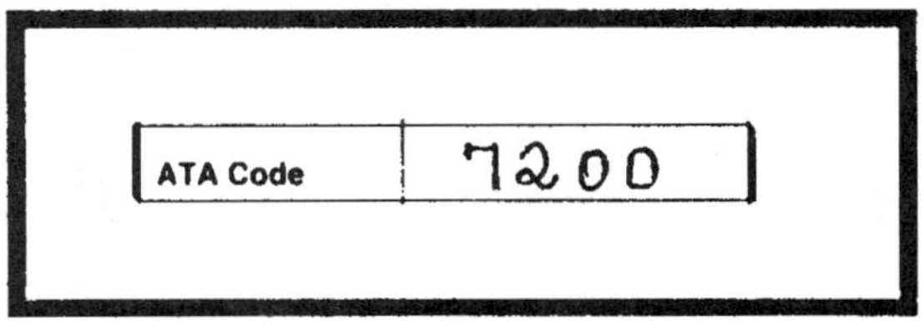

ITEM 1. **A/C Reg. No.:** Enter the complete aircraft registration number.
Example: 7523Q, 8304Q

NOTE: The registration number is not mandatory; however, it is of use when there is a need to trace the aircraft model by series.

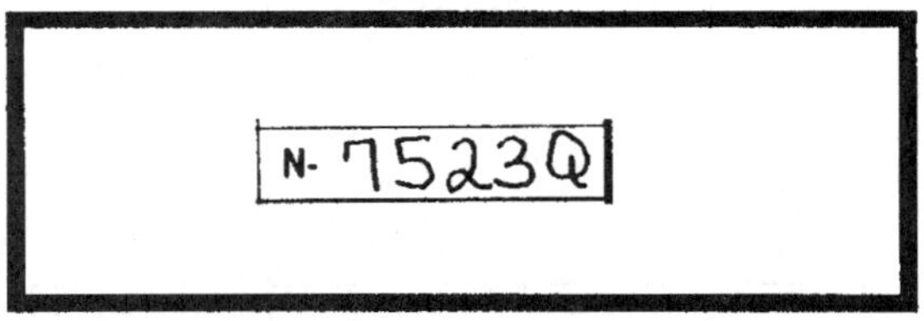

ITEM 2. AIRCRAFT:

NOTE: Always supply aircraft data if available.

MANUFACTURER: Enter the aircraft manufacturer's name.
Any meaningful abbreviation will be acceptable.
Example: Beech, Cessna

MODEL / SERIES: Enter aircraft model as identified on the aircraft data plate.
Example: 172A, 180

SERIAL NUMBER: Enter the serial number assigned by the manufacturer.
Example: 81RK, 94RK

Enter pertinent data	MANUFACTURER	MODEL/SERIES	SERIAL NUMBER
2. AIRCRAFT	Beech	172A	81RK

ITEM 3. POWERPLANT:

MANUFACTURER: Enter the engine manufacturer's name.
Any meaningful abbreviation will be acceptable.
Example: Lyc., Cont.

MODEL / SERIES: Enter engine model as identified on the engine data plate.
Example: IO-540, O-470R

SERIAL NUMBER: Enter the serial number assigned by the engine manufacturer.
Example: 4700, 2300

Enter pertinent data	MANUFACTURER	MODEL/SERIES	SERIAL NUMBER
3. POWERPLANT	Lyc.	IO-540	4700

ITEM 4. PROPELLER: Complete only if pertinent to the problem being reported.

MANUFACTURER: Enter the manufacturer's name.
Any meaningful abbreviation will be acceptable.
Example: Hartzl., Hamstd.

MODEL / SERIES: Enter propeller model as identified in FAA type certificate data sheet/propeller specifications.
Example: DHCC2Y, M74CC

SERIAL NUMBER: Enter the serial number assigned by the propeller manufacturer.
Example: D800, D900

Enter pertinent data	MANUFACTURER	MODEL/SERIES	SERIAL NUMBER
4. PROPELLER	Hartzl.	DHCC2Y	D 800

ITEM 5. SPECIFIC PART (of component) CAUSING TROUBLE:

Part Name: Enter the name of the specific part causing the problem. The appliance or component is the assembly which includes the part. For instance: When the part is a burned wire, the component would be the system using the wire, such as VHF communication system. When the part is a bearing, the appliance should be the unit using the bearing, such as starter, alternator, generator, etc. When the part is a stringer, the component name should be fuselage, wing, or stabilizer, etc.

Example: crankcase, wire

MFG. Model or Part No.: Enter the manufacturer's part number.

Example: 14542, 23893

NOTE: If same as aircraft engine, or propeller, leave blank.

NOTE: If the aircraft, engine, or propeller manufacturer is the component manufacturer, leave blank.

Serial No.: Enter the serial number assigned by the manufacturer.

Example: N/A, W5489

Part / Defect Location: Enter the location.

Example: left half, right wing

5. SPECIFIC PART *(of component)* CAUSING TROUBLE			
Part Name	MFG. Model or Part No.	Serial No.	Part/Defect Location
CranKcase	14542	N/A	left half

ITEM 6. APPLIANCE / COMPONENT (Assembly that includes part):

Comp/Appl Name: Enter the manufacturer's nomenclature for the component or appliance of the specific part causing the problem.
Example: engine, starter

Manufacturer: Enter the part manufacturer's name.
Example: Lyc., Lear

Model or Part No.: If supplied by the manufacturer.
Example: O-362YK-1, O-473GH-2

Serial Number: If supplied by the manufacturer.
Example: CH9693, DE8549

Part TT: Enter the service time of the part in whole hours. (If Part TT is unknown, use aircraft, engine, propeller, or appliance/component total time, whichever is applicable.)
Example: 02756, 04278

Part TSO: Enter the service time of the part since it was last overhauled, in whole hours. (If part TSO is unknown, use an aircraft, engine, propeller, or appliance/component time since last overhaul, whichever is applicable.)
Example: 00351, 00427

Part Condition: Enter the word(s) which best describe the part condition.
Example: cracked, disintegrated

6. APPLIANCE COMPONENT *(Assembly that includes part)*

Comp/Appl Name	Manufacturer	Model or Part No.	Serial Number
engine	Lyc.	O-362YK-1	CH9693

Part TT	Part TSO	Part Condition
02756	00351	cracked

ITEM 7. Date Sub: Enter the date of submission, day, month, year.
Example: 08/15/92, 11/15/92

7. Date Sub.
08/15/92

ITEM 8. **Comments** (Describe the malfunction or defect and the circumstances under which it occurred. State probable cause and recommendations to prevent recurrence.):

Continue on reverse side if needed. Powerplant TT and TSO should be shown in this box when it is a secondary item.

Example: (See the following typed example.)

NOTE: It is requested that submitters make their comments as legible as possible (preferably typed). Information vital to the FAA and the aviation industry may be lost when it is not possible to contact the submitter of an illegible report.

8. Comments *(Describe the malfunction or defect and the circumstances under which it occurred. State probable cause and recommendations to prevent recurrence.)*

```
During a scheduled inspection of the
landing gear, the mechanic found the
left main landing gear support was
broken completely in half.

It is suspected that fatigue or an
unreported hard landing could be the
cause.
```

Optional Information:

Check a box below, if this report is related to an aircraft

☐ Accident; Date ________ ☑ Incident; Date 01/14/93

ITEM. **Optional Information:**

Accident; Date: Accident where substantial damage to aircraft or property and/or serious injury. Enter the date of the accident (day, month, and year).

Example: 01/22/93, 02/13/93

Incident; Date: Anything less than an accident. Enter the date of the incident (day, month, and year).

Example: 01/14/93, 02/12/93

NOTE: This information may be used to trace data to accident or incident records.

ITEM. **DISTRICT OFFICE:** District Office Flight Standards District Office Code.
Example: DAL, LAX

NOTE: FAA Aviation Safety Inspectors reviewing this report should show their FSDO symbol in this box.

ITEM. **SUBMITTED BY:** Enter the name (and certificate number if appropriate) of the person submitting the report. This is not mandatory, but is extremely important when further information is required. Information such as names, telephone numbers, etc., are dealt with strict confidentiality to protect the submitter. However, the report will be entered in the system even if unsigned.
Example: (See the following hand-written example.)

NOTE: Check the appropriate box to identify the organization/person initiating the report.

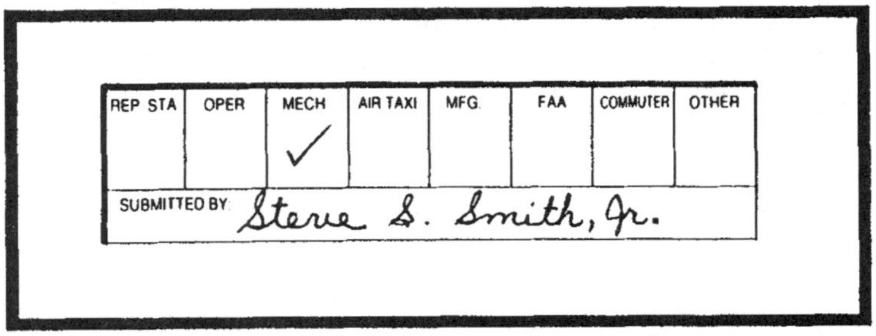

ITEM. **TELEPHONE NUMBER:** Enter the telephone number of the person submitting the report.
Example: (See the following hand-written example.)

NOTE: This is not mandatory, but is of use when further information is required.

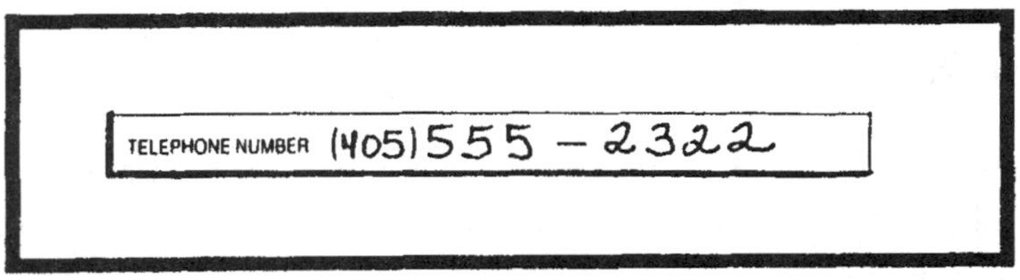

ITEM. **OPERATOR DESIGNATOR:** Enter four-letter designator assigned by the FAA, as appropriate. <u>Example: DXRA, UMNA</u>

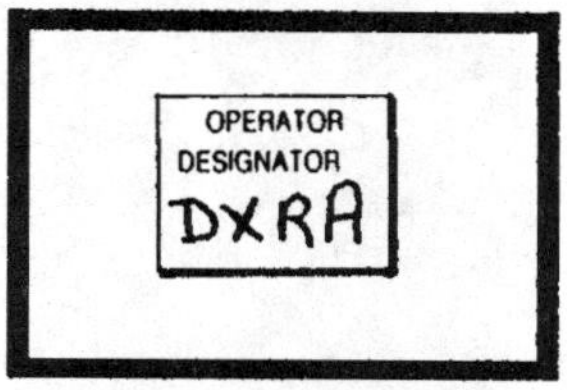

U.S. Department
of Transportation
Federal Aviation Administration

Advisory Circular 21-12B

Subject: **Application for U.S. Airworthiness Certificate FAA Form 8130-6**

Date: 11/06/01 Initiated by: AIR-210

1. **PURPOSE.** This advisory circular (AC) provides guidance and information on the preparation and submittal of Federal Aviation Administration (FAA) Form 8130-6, Application for Airworthiness Certificate. This application is completed to obtain an airworthiness certificate and for an amendment or modification to a current airworthiness certificate. Form 8130-6 is not required for the issuance of a replacement airworthiness certificate.

2. **CANCELLATION.** AC 21-12A, Application for U.S. Airworthiness Certificate, FAA Form 8130-6 (OMB 2120-0018), dated March 26, 1987, is cancelled.

3. **PRINCIPAL CHANGES.**

a. Instructions for completing Form 8130-6 have been updated and revised to reflect minor changes to the new version of Form 8130-6, dated May 2001.

b. Appendix 1, Listing of FAA Regional Offices, has been removed and reference information for contacting these offices has been added to the AC.

c. Title 14 Code of Federal Regulations (14 CFR) references have been revised and the text reworded for clarification.

4. **RELATED READING MATERIAL.**

a. Title 14 Code of Federal Regulations:

(1) 14 CFR part 21, Certification Procedures for Products and Parts (part 21).

(2) 14 CFR part 39, Airworthiness Directives (part 39).

(3) 14 CFR part 43, Maintenance, Preventive Maintenance, Rebuilding, and Alteration (part 43).

(4) 14 CFR part 45, Identification and Registration Marking (part 45).

(5) 14 CFR part 47, Aircraft Registration (part 47).

(6) 14 CFR part 91, General Operating and Flight Rules (part 91).

b. FAA Order 8130.2, Airworthiness Certification of Aircraft and Related Products.

c. FAA Advisory Circulars:

(1) AC 20-27, Certification and Operation of Amateur-Built Aircraft.

(2) AC 20-65, U.S. Airworthiness Certificates and Authorization for Operation of Domestic and Foreign Aircraft.

(3) AC 20-126, Aircraft Certification Service Field Office Listing.

(4) AC 21-4, Special Flight Permits for Operation of Overweight Aircraft.

(5) AC 21-37, Primary Category Aircraft.

(6) AC 39-7, Airworthiness Directives.

5. INFORMATION. The current version of Form 8130-6 (dated May 2001) may be obtained free of charge at any Manufacturing Inspection District Office (MIDO) or Flight Standards District Office (FSDO). Applicants may continue to use Form 8130-6 (dated November 1988) while the newer form is distributed for availability. A geographic listing of the location, phone number, and FAX number of the nearest MIDO can be found in AC 20-126, Aircraft Certification Service Field Office Listing. Similar information for FSDO's can be found by accessing the FAA website at: www.faa.gov.

6. INSTRUCTIONS FOR COMPLETING FORM 8130-6. The applicant, or the applicant's agent, should complete sections I through IV when submitting an application for an airworthiness certificate. If submitting an application for a special flight permit, only sections II and VI, or II and VII, as applicable, are required. The following instructions apply to the corresponding items on the form:

a. Section I. Aircraft Description.

NOTE: Do not complete this section when application is being submitted for a special flight permit.

(1) **Registration Mark.** Enter the United States (U.S.) nationality designator letter "N" followed by the registration marks as shown on the aircraft registration certificate. (Reference part 45, subpart C.)

(2) **Aircraft Builder's Name (Make).** Enter the name of the manufacturer or builder as it appears on the aircraft identification (ID) plate. (Reference section 45.13(a)(1).)

(a) For amateur-built aircraft, the aircraft make is the name of the builder. When two or more persons are involved, enter only the name of the individual that is listed first on the aircraft's ID plate.

(b) For aircraft built from spare and/or surplus parts, the aircraft make is that of the Type Certificate (TC) holder (as it appears on the applicable aircraft listing, specification, or Type Certificate Data Sheet (TCDS)) together with the name of the builder (for example, Bell-Jackson).

(c) For surplus military aircraft (not assembled from spare and/or surplus parts), the builder's name will be as listed on the TCDS.

(3) **Aircraft Model Designation.** Enter the model designation as shown on the aircraft ID plate. Trade names should not be used. (Reference section 45.13(a)(2).)

(a) For amateur-built aircraft, the model may be any arbitrary designation selected by the builder. For aircraft purchased as a kit, the model designation assigned by the kit manufacturer should be used.

(b) For aircraft built from spare and/or surplus parts, the model designation will be the civil model shown on the TCDS to which the applicant shows conformity.

(c) For surplus military aircraft having a civil model counterpart, enter the civil model designation along with the military model designation in parentheses. If the TC was issued under section 21.27, the military model designation becomes the civil model designation.

(d) For surplus military aircraft type certificated under the provisions of section 21.25(a)(2) in the restricted category, only the military designation will be entered.

(4) **Year of Manufacture.** Enter the year of manufacture if shown on the aircraft ID plate or as reflected in the aircraft's records.

(a) For aircraft eligible for standard airworthiness certificates, the year of manufacture is the date (entered by the manufacturer) the aircraft was completed and met the FAA-approved type design data. Inspection records reflect the date of aircraft completion.

(b) For aircraft other than the above, the year of manufacture is the date entered by the builder in the inspection records or logbook, establishing that the aircraft is airworthy and eligible for the certificate requested.

(5) **Aircraft Serial Number.** Enter the serial number as shown on the aircraft ID plate. (Reference section 45.13(a)(3).)

(a) For amateur-built aircraft fabricated and assembled from the builder's own design, the serial number may be any arbitrary number assigned by the builder. For any aircraft fabricated and assembled from a kit or plans, the aircraft identification information provided by the kit manufacturer or plans designer should be used.

(b) For aircraft built from spare and/or surplus parts, enter the serial number assigned by the builder. That number should not be confused with the serial numbers assigned by an original manufacturer who builds the same type aircraft under a production approval. It is suggested that a letter prefix or suffix, such as the builder's name or initials, be used with the serial number to provide positive identification.

(c) For surplus military aircraft, enter the manufacturer's civil serial number. The military serial number should be placed in parentheses following the civil serial number. If no civil serial number exists, enter the military serial number.

(6) **Engine Builder's Name (Make).** The engine make is the name of the manufacturer as it appears on the engine ID plate. Abbreviations may be used (for example, "P&W," "G.E.," etc.). When engines are not installed, as in the case of a glider or balloon, enter "not applicable" or "N/A." (Reference section 45.13(a)(1).)

(7) **Engine Model Designation.** When engine(s) are installed, enter the complete designation as shown on the engine ID plate (for example, "O-320-A1B," "PT6A-20A," "CFM-56-3C-1," etc.). (Reference section 45.13(a)(2).)

(8) Number of Engines. When applicable, enter the quantity of engines installed on the aircraft.

(9) Propeller Builder's Name (Make). Enter the name of the manufacturer as shown on the propeller identification marking. Enter "not applicable" or "N/A" if propellers are not installed. (Reference section 45.13(a)(1).)

(10) Propeller Model Designation. When applicable, enter the model designation as shown on the propeller identification marking. For amateur-built aircraft having a propeller not identified in accordance with section 45.13(a)(1), enter the propeller diameter times (X) pitch in lieu of propeller model designation. (Reference section 45.13(a)(2).)

(11) Aircraft is Import. This block should be checked only if the aircraft was manufactured outside the U.S. and certified under the provisions of section 21.29, and the applicant is seeking airworthiness certification under the provisions of section 21.183(c).

b. Section II. Certification Requested. The following paragraphs refer to the applicable 14 CFR for standard and special airworthiness certificates used to aid in the completion of Form 8130-6 (see Appendix 1, figures 1-17, for illustrated examples of a completed Form 8130-6).

(1) Item A. Standard Airworthiness Certificate. This certificate is issued to type certificated aircraft in the normal, utility, acrobatic, transport, commuter, and manned free balloon categories; and for special classes of aircraft. Special class aircraft include gliders, airships, and other non-conventional aircraft. Special class application is indicated by marking the standard and other blocks (section II (A) of the application), and entering the type, (for example, glider, very light aircraft, airship, etc.) in the blank space directly above the category blocks. For aircraft type certificated prior to the adoption of categories, enter in the open space above the category blocks, the basis for certification as shown in that aircraft's TCDS or specification sheet (for example, Category N/A—Certification basis CAR 04 A (Civil Air Regulations part 4a)). Applicable regulations are as follows:

(a) Section 21.183(a), New aircraft manufactured under a production certificate.

(b) Section 21.183(b), New aircraft manufactured under a type certificate only.

(c) Section 21.183(c), Import aircraft.

(d) Section 21.183(d), Other aircraft.

(2) Item B. Special Airworthiness Certificate. This certificate is issued to aircraft not meeting the requirements for a standard airworthiness certificate. Special airworthiness certificates are identified as primary, limited, provisional, restricted, experimental, and special flight permit. Applicable regulations are as follows:

(a) Primary Airworthiness Certificate.

1. Section 21.184(a), New primary category aircraft manufactured under a production certificate.

2. Section 21.184(b), Imported aircraft.

3. Section 21.184(c), Aircraft having a current standard airworthiness certificate.

4. Section 21.184(d), Other aircraft.

(b) **Limited Airworthiness Certificate.** Section 21.189, Issue of airworthiness certificate for limited category aircraft.

(c) **Provisional Airworthiness Certificate.**

1. Section 21.221, Class I provisional airworthiness certificates. (May be issued for all categories.)

2. Section 21.223, Class II provisional airworthiness certificates. (Transport category only.)

(d) **Restricted Airworthiness Certificate.**

1. Section 21.185(a), Aircraft manufactured under a production certificate or type certificate only.

2. Section 21.185(b), Other aircraft (surplus U.S. military aircraft or one previously type certificated in another category).

3. Section 21.185(c), Import aircraft (type certificated in the restricted category in accordance with section 21.29).

(e) **Experimental Certificate.**

1. Section 21.191(a), Research and development.

2. Section 21.191(b), Showing compliance with regulations.

3. Section 21.191(c), Crew training.

4. Section 21.191(d), Exhibition.

5. Section 21.191(e), Air racing.

6. Section 21.191(f), Market surveys.

7. Section 21.191(g), Operating amateur-built aircraft.

8. Section 21.191(h), Operating kit-built aircraft (primary category aircraft assembled by a person(s) without the supervision and quality control of the production certificate holder).

(f) **Special Flight Permit.**

1. Section 21.197(a)(1), Flying the aircraft to a base where repairs, alterations, or maintenance are to be performed, or to a point of storage.

2. Section 21.197(a)(2), Delivering or exporting the aircraft.

3. Section 21.197(a)(3), Production flight testing new production aircraft.

4. Section 21.197(a)(4), Evacuating aircraft from areas of impending danger.

5. Section 21.197(a)(5), Conducting customer demonstration flights in new production aircraft that have satisfactorily completed production flight tests.

6. Section 21.197(b), Operation of an aircraft at a weight in excess of its maximum certificated takeoff weight.

(3) Item C. Multiple Airworthiness Certificates. These certificates are issued to an applicant in the restricted category and one or more other categories except the primary category. Section 21.187 identifies the requirements an applicant must comply with before multiple airworthiness certificates are issued.

c. Section III. Owner's Certification. Do not complete this section when application is being submitted for a special flight permit.

(1) Item A. Registered Owner.

(a) Enter the name and address exactly as shown on the aircraft registration certificate. (Reference part 47.)

(b) If Dealer, Check Here. This block should be checked ONLY if the aircraft is registered under an aircraft dealer's aircraft registration certificate. (Reference part 47, subpart C.)

(2) Item B. Aircraft Certification Basis.

(a) Aircraft Specification or TCDS and/or Aircraft Listing Block. This item should be completed when an application is submitted for a standard, primary, limited, provisional, restricted, or multiple airworthiness certificates.

(b) When application is submitted for multiple airworthiness certificates, the certification basis for each certificate should be entered.

(c) When a TCDS or specification for a new aircraft or model HAS BEEN APPROVED BUT NOT PUBLISHED, enter the date of approval, TC or specification number, and the word "preliminary." This item is not applicable when submitting an application for an experimental certificate, therefore, "N/A" should be entered.

(d) Airworthiness Directives. This block should be checked to indicate compliance with all applicable Airworthiness Directives (AD). Enter the number of the last biweekly supplement to the Summary of Airworthiness Directives available as of the date of application. (For example, Biweekly Supplement 97-06 was published on March 24, 1997.)

NOTE: Each AD contains an applicability statement specifying the product to which it applies. Some aircraft owners and operators mistakenly assume that AD's are not applicable to aircraft certificated in certain categories such as experimental or restricted. AD's, unless specifically limited apply to the make and model set forth in the applicability statement regardless of category. The type certificate and airworthiness certification categories are used to identify the product affected. (Reference AC 39-7.)

(e) Supplemental Type Certificate (STC). This block is applicable to all standard airworthiness certification; and special airworthiness certification in the restricted, limited, provisional, and primary categories, and should be completed at the time of application. The number of each installed STC should be entered. If more space is required, an attachment may be used. (Reference part 21, subpart E.)

(3) Item C. Aircraft Operation and Maintenance Records.

(a) Maintenance records shall comply with section 91.417. This block is applicable to all aircraft and should be checked to indicate that the recordkeeping requirements of section 91.417 have been met. For example, section 91.417(a)(2)(i), requires the total service time of the airframe, each engine, propeller, and rotor. Compliance to section 91.417(a)(2)(ii), requires a maintenance record of the current status of life-limited parts of each airframe, engine, propeller, rotor, and appliance. All entries should be written in English and not with erasable materials such as lead/carbon pencils.

(b) Total Airframe Hours. The total service time of the aircraft, including production flight test time, should be entered.

(c) Experimental Only. When submitting an application for renewal of an experimental certificate, or when requesting a change back to a standard certificate, the hours flown since the previous experimental certificate was issued or renewed should be entered. If the application is for an original issuance of an experimental certificate, zero hours should be entered.

(4) Item D. Certification. If the signature is the owner's agent, a notarized letter from the registered owner authorizing the agent to act on the owner's behalf is required.

NOTE: The term AIRWORTHY, as stated in FAA Order 8130.2, Airworthiness Certification of Aircraft and Related Products, means (1) the aircraft conforms to its type design and (2) the aircraft is in a condition for safe operation. In the case of an application for an aircraft in the experimental category, only the "AIRCRAFT IS IN A CONDITION FOR SAFE OPERATION" portion of the definition would apply for the purpose of this application.

d. Section IV. Inspection Agency Verification. This section should be completed only if the application is for a standard airworthiness certificate in accordance with section 21.183(d). This section should be left blank for all other certification actions.

e. Section V. FAA Representative Certification. Applicants should not make any entries in this section. This information will be entered by the FAA Inspector/Designee who inspects the aircraft and issues the certificate.

f. Section VI. Production Flight Testing. This section should be completed ONLY BY A MANUFACTURER applying for a special flight permit for the purpose of flight testing production aircraft. (Reference section 21.197(a)(3).)

g. Section VII. Special Flight Permit Purposes other than Production Flight Test.

(1) Item A. Description of Aircraft. Entries in this section should be the same as the corresponding data recorded on the aircraft's registration certificate and, as applicable, on the aircraft's identification plate.

(2) Item B. Description of Flight. Enter the present location of the aircraft in the From box and the aircraft's intended destination in the To box.

(a) The Via block should contain the name of an airport or city at some intermediate flight point to provide a general description of the route flown. For example, a flight from Kansas City, Missouri to Dallas, Texas may be flown via Wichita, Kansas and Oklahoma City, Oklahoma. (Reference section 21.199(a)(2).)

(b) The Duration entry should reflect the overall duration of the special flight permit. Factors such as fueling stops, weather conditions, overnight stops, or any other reasonable condition should be given consideration when establishing the duration. (Reference section 21.199(a)(2).)

(3) **Item C. Crew Required to Operate the Aircraft and its Equipment.** Self-explanatory.

(4) **Item D. The Aircraft Does Not Meet the Applicable Airworthiness Requirements as Follows.** This entry should contain in detail the conditions, if any, in which the aircraft does not comply with the applicable airworthiness requirements. (Reference section 21.199(a)(4).)

(5) **Item E. The Following Restrictions are Considered Necessary for Safe Operation.** This entry should contain in detail any restrictions the applicant considers necessary for safe operation of the aircraft (for example, reduced airspeed or operating weight, turbulence avoidance, crew limitations or qualifications, etc.). After review of the application, the FAA may prescribe additional conditions and/or limitations deemed necessary for safe operation. (Reference section 21.199(a)(5) and (6).)

(6) **Item F. Certification.** Self-explanatory.

h. Section VIII. Airworthiness Documentation. This section will be completed by the FAA Inspector/Designee who inspects the aircraft and issues the airworthiness certificate, and is not required when the applicant is submitting an application for a special flight permit.

7. INSTRUCTIONS FOR SUBMITTING THE COMPLETED FAA FORM 8130-6. When the applicant has completed the applicable sections and has signed the Form 8130-6, it should be submitted to the local MIDO or FSDO. The nearest MIDO or FSDO location can be determined by referencing the information in paragraph 5 of this AC. Other material may be required by the regulations for the final airworthiness certification. In the case of a manufacturer holding a FAA production approval, an application may be submitted to an authorized Designated Airworthiness Representative or Designated Manufacturing Inspection Representative.

8. HOW TO OBTAIN THE REFERENCED PUBLICATIONS.

a. The CFR and those ACs for which a fee is charged may be obtained from the Superintendent of Documents, P.O. Box 371954, Pittsburgh, PA 15250-7954. A listing of the CFR and current prices is located in AC 00-44, Status of Federal Aviation Regulations, and a listing of all ACs is located in AC 00-2, Advisory Circular Checklist.

b. To be placed on the FAA's mailing list for free ACs, contact: U.S. Department of Transportation, Subsequent Distribution Office, SVC-121.23, Ardmore East Business Center, 3341Q 75th Avenue, Landover, MD 20785.

c. The FAA website at: www.faa.gov.

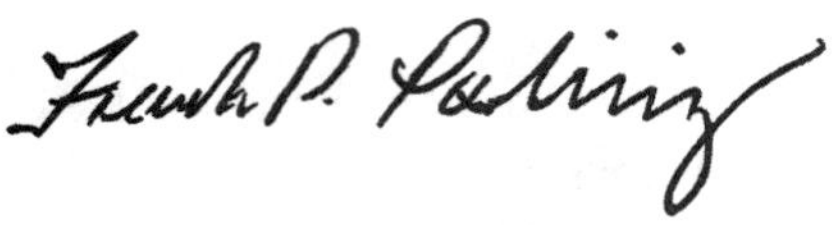

Frank P. Paskiewicz
Manager, Production and Airworthiness Division, AIR-200

APPENDIX 1. SAMPLES OF FORM 8130-6, APPLICATION FOR AIRWORTHINESS CERTIFICATE

Figure 1. Sample FAA Form 8130-6, Application for a Standard Airworthiness Certificate — Very Light Aircraft Produced Under Section 21.183(a) (Face Side Only)

OMB. No. 2120-0018

U.S. Department of Transportation **Federal Aviation Administration**	**APPLICATION FOR AIRWORTHINESS CERTIFICATE**	**INSTRUCTIONS** - Print or type. Do not write in shaded areas; these are for FAA use only. Submit original only to an authorized FAA Representative. If additional space is required, use attachment. For special flight permits complete Sections II, VI, and VII as applicable.

I. AIRCRAFT DESCRIPTION

1. REGISTRATION MARK N 18CE	2. AIRCRAFT BUILDER'S NAME *(Make)* Lite-Flight Corp	3. AIRCRAFT MODEL DESIGNATION LF-1-A	4. YR. MFR. 96	FAA CODING
5. AIRCRAFT SERIAL NO. LF 010	6. ENGINE BUILDER'S NAME *(Make)* Rotax	7. ENGINE MODEL DESIGNATION 912		
8. NUMBER OF ENGINES One	9. PROPELLER BUILDER'S NAME *(Make)* Wood Built	10. PROPELLER MODEL DESIGNATION Good-1	11. AIRCRAFT IS *(Check if applicable)* IMPORT	

II. CERTIFICATION REQUESTED

APPLICATION IS HEREBY MADE FOR: *(Check applicable items)* Very Light Aircraft

A	1	X	*STANDARD AIRWORTHINESS CERTIFICATE (Indicate category)*		NORMAL		UTILITY		ACROBATIC		TRANSPORT		COMMUTER	BALLOON	X OTHER

B — *SPECIAL AIRWORTHINESS CERTIFICATE (Check appropriate items)*

7	PRIMARY			
2	LIMITED			
5	PROVISIONAL *(Indicate class)*	1 CLASS I 2 CLASS II		
3	RESTRICTED *(Indicate operation(s) to be conducted)*	1 AGRICULTURE AND PEST CONTROL	2 AERIAL	3 AERIAL ADVERTISING
		4 FOREST *(Wildlife conservation)*	5 PATROLLING	6 WEATHER CONTROL
		0 OTHER *(Specify)*		
4	EXPERIMENTAL *(Indicate operation(s) to be conducted)*	1 RESEARCH AND DEVELOPMENT	2 AMATEUR BUILT	3 EXHIBITION
		4 AIR RACING	5 CREW TRAINING	6 MARKET SURVEY
		0 TO SHOW COMPLIANCE WITH THE CFR	7 OPERATING *(Primary Category)* KIT BUILT AIRCRAFT	
8	SPECIAL FLIGHT PERMIT *(Indicate operation to be conducted, then complete Section VI or VII as applicable on reverse side)*	1 FERRY FLIGHT FOR REPAIRS, ALTERATIONS, MAINTENANCE, OR STORAGE		
		2 EVACUATE FROM AREA OF IMPENDING DANGER		
		3 OPERATION IN EXCESS OF MAXIMUM CERTIFICATED TAKE-OFF WEIGHT		
		4 DELIVERING OR EXPORTING	5 PRODUCTION FLIGHT TESTING	
		6 CUSTOMER DEMONSTRATION FLIGHTS		

C 6 — MULTIPLE AIRWORTHINESS CERTIFICATE *(Check ABOVE "Restricted Operation" and "Standard" or "Limited" as applicable.)*

III. OWNER'S CERTIFICATION

A. REGISTERED OWNER (As shown on certificate of aircraft registration) — IF DEALER, CHECK HERE

NAME Lite Flight Corp	ADDRESS 1801 Airport Rd Wichita, KS 67209

B. AIRCRAFT CERTIFICATION BASIS (Check applicable blocks and complete items as indicated)

X	AIRCRAFT SPECIFICATION OR TYPE CERTIFICATE DATA SHEET *(Give No. and Revision No.)* A2WI Rev-1	X	AIRWORTHINESS DIRECTIVES *(Check if all applicable AD's complied with and give the number of the last AD SUPPLEMENT available in the biweekly series as of the date of application)* 96-23
	AIRCRAFT LISTING (Give page number(s)) N/A		SUPPLEMENTAL TYPE CERTIFICATE (List number of each STC incorporated) N/A

C. AIRCRAFT OPERATION AND MAINTENANCE RECORDS

X	CHECK IF RECORDS IN COMPLIANCE WITH 14 CFR section 91.417	TOTAL AIRFRAME HOURS 2.0	3	EXPERIMENTAL ONLY *(Enter hours flown since last certificate issued or renewed)* 0

D. CERTIFICATION - I hereby certify that I am the registered owner (or his agent) of the aircraft described above, that the aircraft is registered with the Federal Aviation Administration in accordance with Title 49 of the United States Code 44101 et seq. and applicable Federal Aviation Regulations, and that the aircraft has been inspected and is airworthy and eligible for the airworthiness certificate requested.

DATE OF APPLICATION 11/25/98	NAME AND TITLE (Print or type) K.D. Good, Director QA	SIGNATURE *K.D. Good*

IV. INSPECTION AGENCY VERIFICATION

A. THE AIRCRAFT DESCRIBED ABOVE HAS BEEN INSPECTED AND FOUND AIRWORTHY BY: (Complete this section only if 14 CFR part 21.183(d) applies).

2	14 CFR part 121 CERTIFICATE HOLDER *(Give Certificate No.)*	3	CERTIFICATED MECHANIC *(Give Certificate No.)*	6	CERTIFICATED REPAIR STATION *(Give Certificate No.)*
5	AIRCRAFT MANUFACTURER (Give name or firm)				

DATE	TITLE	SIGNATURE

V. FAA REPRESENTATIVE CERTIFICATION

(Check ALL applicable blocks in items A and B)
A. I find that the aircraft described in Section I or VII meets requirements for

	THE CERTIFICATE REQUESTED
4	AMENDMENT OR MODIFICATION OF CURRENT AIRWORTHINESS CERTIFICATE

B. Inspection for a special flight permit under Section VII was conducted by:

FAA INSPECTOR	FAA DESIGNEE		
CERTIFICATE HOLDER UNDER	14 CFR part 65	14 CFR part 121 OR 135	14 CFR part 145

DATE	DISTRICT OFFICE	4	DESIGNEE'S SIGNATURE AND NO.	1	FAA INSPECTOR'S SIGNATURE

FAA Form 8130-6 (5-01) Supersedes Previous Edition — NSN: 0052-00-024-7006

21-12B

AC

Figure 2. Sample FAA Form 8130-6, Application for a Standard Airworthiness Certificate — Aircraft Produced in the Transport Category (Face Side Only)

O.M.B. No. 2120-00180

U.S. Department of Transportation
Federal Aviation Administration

APPLICATION FOR AIRWORTHINESS CERTIFICATE

INSTRUCTIONS - Print or type. Do not write in shaded areas; these are for FAA use only. Submit original only to an authorized FAA Representative. If additional space is required, use attachment. For special flight permits complete Sections II, VI, and VII as applicable.

I. AIRCRAFT DESCRIPTION

1. REGISTRATION MARK N12345	2. AIRCRAFT BUILDER'S NAME *(Make)* BOEING	3. AIRCRAFT MODEL DESIGNATION 737-200	4. YR. MFR. 1968	FAA CODING
5. AIRCRAFT SERIAL NO. 19714	6. ENGINE BUILDER'S NAME *(Make)* Pratt & Whitney	7. ENGINE MODEL DESIGNATION JT8D-9		
8. NUMBER OF ENGINES 2	9. PROPELLER BUILDER'S NAME *(Make)* N/A	10. PROPELLER MODEL DESIGNATION N/A	11. AIRCRAFT IS *(Check if applicable)*	IMPORT

II. CERTIFICATION REQUESTED

APPLICATION IS HEREBY MADE FOR: *(Check applicable items)*

A | 1 | X | *STANDARD AIRWORTHINESS CERTIFICATE (Indicate category)* | NORMAL | UTILITY | ACROBATIC | X TRANSPORT | COMMUTER | BALLOON | OTHER

B | *SPECIAL AIRWORTHINESS CERTIFICATE (Check appropriate items)*

7	PRIMARY		
2	LIMITED		
5	PROVISIONAL *(Indicate class)*	1	CLASS I
		2	CLASS II
3	RESTRICTED *(Indicate operation(s) to be conducted)*	1	AGRICULTURE AND PEST CONTROL; 2 AERIAL; 3 AERIAL ADVERTISING
		4	FOREST *(Wildlife conservation)*; 5 PATROLLING; 6 WEATHER CONTROL
		0	OTHER *(Specify)*
4	EXPERIMENTAL *(Indicate operation(s) to be conducted)*	1	RESEARCH AND DEVELOPMENT; 2 AMATEUR BUILT; 3 EXHIBITION
		4	AIR RACING; 5 CREW TRAINING; 6 MARKET SURVEY
		0	TO SHOW COMPLIANCE WITH THE CFR; 7 OPERATING *(Primary Category)* KIT BUILT AIRCRAFT
8	SPECIAL FLIGHT PERMIT *(Indicate operation to be conducted, then complete Section VI or VII as applicable on reverse side)*	1	FERRY FLIGHT FOR REPAIRS, ALTERATIONS, MAINTENANCE, OR STORAGE
		2	EVACUATE FROM AREA OF IMPENDING DANGER
		3	OPERATION IN EXCESS OF MAXIMUM CERTIFICATED TAKE-OFF WEIGHT
		4	DELIVERING OR EXPORTING; 5 PRODUCTION FLIGHT TESTING
		6	CUSTOMER DEMONSTRATION FLIGHTS

C | 6 | MULTIPLE AIRWORTHINESS CERTIFICATE *(Check ABOVE "Restricted Operation" and "Standard" or "Limited" as applicable.)*

III. OWNER'S CERTIFICATION

A. REGISTERED OWNER (As shown on certificate of aircraft registration) — **IF DEALER, CHECK HERE** ______

NAME	ADDRESS
Shorthaul Airlines, Inc	111 Airport Way, St Louis, Missouri 58010

B. AIRCRAFT CERTIFICATION BASIS (Check applicable blocks and complete items as indicated)

X	AIRCRAFT SPECIFICATION OR TYPE CERTIFICATE DATA SHEET *(Give No. and Revision No.)* A16WE	X	AIRWORTHINESS DIRECTIVES *(Check if all applicable AD's complied with and give the number of the last AD SUPPLEMENT available in the biweekly series as of the date of application)* 96-23
	AIRCRAFT LISTING (Give page number(s))		SUPPLEMENTAL TYPE CERTIFICATE (List number of each STC incorporated)

C. AIRCRAFT OPERATION AND MAINTENANCE RECORDS

X	CHECK IF RECORDS IN COMPLIANCE WITH 14 CFR section 91.417	TOTAL AIRFRAME HOURS 8:45	3	EXPERIMENTAL ONLY *(Enter hours flown since last certificate issued or renewed)* N/A

D. CERTIFICATION - I hereby certify that I am the registered owner (or his agent) of the aircraft described above, that the aircraft is registered with the Federal Aviation Administration in accordance with Title 49 of the United States Code 44101 et seq. and applicable Federal Aviation Regulations, and that the aircraft has been inspected and is airworthy and eligible for the airworthiness certificate requested.

DATE OF APPLICATION	NAME AND TITLE (Print or type)	SIGNATURE
11/25/96	John Doe, VP Operations	John Doe

IV. INSPECTION AGENCY VERIFICATION

A. THE AIRCRAFT DESCRIBED ABOVE HAS BEEN INSPECTED AND FOUND AIRWORTHY BY: (Complete this section only if 14 CFR part 21.183(d) applies).

2	14 CFR part 121 CERTIFICATE HOLDER *(Give Certificate No.)*	3	CERTIFICATED MECHANIC *(Give Certificate No.)*	6	CERTIFICATED REPAIR STATION *(Give Certificate No.)*
5	AIRCRAFT MANUFACTURER (Give name or firm)				

DATE	TITLE	SIGNATURE

V. FAA REPRESENTATIVE CERTIFICATION

(Check ALL applicable blocks in items A and B)
A. I find that the aircraft described in Section I or VII meets requirements for — THE CERTIFICATE REQUESTED; 4 AMENDMENT OR MODIFICATION OF CURRENT AIRWORTHINESS CERTIFICATE

B. Inspection for a special flight permit under Section VII was conducted by: FAA INSPECTOR; FAA DESIGNEE; CERTIFICATE HOLDER UNDER 14 CFR part 65; 14 CFR part 121 OR 135; 14 CFR part 145

DATE	DISTRICT OFFICE	4	DESIGNEE'S SIGNATURE AND NO.	1	FAA INSPECTOR'S SIGNATURE

FAA Form 8130-6 (5-01) Supersedes Previous Edition NSN: 0052-00-024-7006

Figure 3. Sample FAA Form 8130-6, Application for a Standard Airworthiness Certificate — Import Glider (Face Side Only)

O.M.B. No. 2120-0018

U.S. Department of Transportation
Federal Aviation Administration

APPLICATION FOR AIRWORTHINESS CERTIFICATE

INSTRUCTIONS - Print or type. Do not write in shaded areas; these are for FAA use only. Submit original only to an authorized FAA Representative. If additional space is required, use attachment. For special flight permits complete Sections II, VI, and VII as applicable.

I. AIRCRAFT DESCRIPTION

1. REGISTRATION MARK N53B	2. AIRCRAFT BUILDER'S NAME *(Make)* Schleicher	3. AIRCRAFT MODEL DESIGNATION AS-K13	4. YR. MFR. 1984	FAA CODING
5. AIRCRAFT SERIAL NO. 101	6. ENGINE BUILDER'S NAME *(Make)* N/A	7. ENGINE MODEL DESIGNATION N/A		
8. NUMBER OF ENGINES N/A	9. PROPELLER BUILDER'S NAME *(Make)* N/A	10. PROPELLER MODEL DESIGNATION N/A	11. AIRCRAFT IS *(Check if applicable)* X IMPORT	

II. CERTIFICATION REQUESTED

APPLICATION IS HEREBY MADE FOR: *(Check applicable items)* Import Glider

A	1	X	*STANDARD AIRWORTHINESS CERTIFICATE (Indicate category)* ☐ NORMAL ☐ UTILITY ☐ ACROBATIC ☐ TRANSPORT ☐ COMMUTER ☐ BALLOON X OTHER
B			*SPECIAL AIRWORTHINESS CERTIFICATE (Check appropriate items)*
	7		PRIMARY
	2		LIMITED
	5		PROVISIONAL *(Indicate class)*: 1 CLASS I; 2 CLASS II
	3		RESTRICTED *(Indicate operation(s) to be conducted)*: 1 AGRICULTURE AND PEST CONTROL; 2 AERIAL; 3 AERIAL ADVERTISING; 4 FOREST *(Wildlife conservation)*; 5 PATROLLING; 6 WEATHER CONTROL; 0 OTHER *(Specify)*
	4		EXPERIMENTAL *(Indicate operation(s) to be conducted)*: 1 RESEARCH AND DEVELOPMENT; 2 AMATEUR BUILT; 3 EXHIBITION; 4 AIR RACING; 5 CREW TRAINING; 6 MARKET SURVEY; 0 TO SHOW COMPLIANCE WITH THE CFR; 7 OPERATING *(Primary Category)* KIT BUILT AIRCRAFT
	8		SPECIAL FLIGHT PERMIT *(Indicate operation to be conducted, then complete Section VI or VII as applicable on reverse side)*: 1 FERRY FLIGHT FOR REPAIRS, ALTERATIONS, MAINTENANCE, OR STORAGE; 2 EVACUATE FROM AREA OF IMPENDING DANGER; 3 OPERATION IN EXCESS OF MAXIMUM CERTIFICATED TAKE-OFF WEIGHT; 4 DELIVERING OR EXPORTING; 5 PRODUCTION FLIGHT TESTING; 6 CUSTOMER DEMONSTRATION FLIGHTS
C	6		MULTIPLE AIRWORTHINESS CERTIFICATE *(Check ABOVE "Restricted Operation" and "Standard" or "Limited" as applicable.)*

III. OWNER'S CERTIFICATION

A. REGISTERED OWNER (As shown on certificate of aircraft registration) — IF DEALER, CHECK HERE ———

NAME Elmer E. Jones	ADDRESS 1601 E. 6th Street San Diego, california 95472

B. AIRCRAFT CERTIFICATION BASIS (Check applicable blocks and complete items as indicated)

X	AIRCRAFT SPECIFICATION OR TYPE CERTIFICATE DATA SHEET *(Give No. and Revision No.)* G15EU	X	AIRWORTHINESS DIRECTIVES *(Check if all applicable AD's complied with and give the number of the last AD SUPPLEMENT available in the biweekly series as of the date of application)* 96-23
	AIRCRAFT LISTING (Give page number(s)) N/A		SUPPLEMENTAL TYPE CERTIFICATE (List number of each STC incorporated) N/A

C. AIRCRAFT OPERATION AND MAINTENANCE RECORDS

X	CHECK IF RECORDS IN COMPLIANCE WITH 14 CFR section 91.417	TOTAL AIRFRAME HOURS 320	3	EXPERIMENTAL ONLY *(Enter hours flown since last certificate issued or renewed)* N/A

D. CERTIFICATION - I hereby certify that I am the registered owner (or his agent) of the aircraft described above, that the aircraft is registered with the Federal Aviation Administration in accordance with Title 49 of the United States Code 44101 et seq. and applicable Federal Aviation Regulations, and that the aircraft has been inspected and is airworthy and eligible for the airworthiness certificate requested.

DATE OF APPLICATION 11/25/96	NAME AND TITLE (Print or type) Elmer E. Jones, Owner	SIGNATURE Elmer E. Jones

IV. INSPECTION AGENCY VERIFICATION

A. THE AIRCRAFT DESCRIBED ABOVE HAS BEEN INSPECTED AND FOUND AIRWORTHY BY: (Complete this section only if 14 CFR part 21 .183(d) applies).

2	14 CFR part 121 CERTIFICATE HOLDER *(Give Certificate No.)*	3	CERTIFICATED MECHANIC *(Give Certificate No.)*
6	CERTIFICATED REPAIR STATION *(Give Certificate No.)*	5	AIRCRAFT MANUFACTURER (Give name or firm)

DATE	TITLE	SIGNATURE

V. FAA REPRESENTATIVE CERTIFICATION

(Check ALL applicable blocks in items A and B)

A. I find that the aircraft described in Section I or VII meets requirements for — THE CERTIFICATE REQUESTED; 4 AMENDMENT OR MODIFICATION OF CURRENT AIRWORTHINESS CERTIFICATE

B. Inspection for a special flight permit under Section VII was conducted by: FAA INSPECTOR; FAA DESIGNEE; CERTIFICATE HOLDER UNDER: 14 CFR part 65; 14 CFR part 121 OR 135; 14 CFR part 145

DATE	DISTRICT OFFICE	4	DESIGNEE'S SIGNATURE AND NO.	1	FAA INSPECTOR'S SIGNATURE

FAA Form 8130-6 (5-01) Supersedes Previous Edition — NSN: 0052-00-024-7006

Figure 4. Sample FAA Form 8130-6, Application for a Standard Airworthiness Certificate — Surplus Military Aircraft (Face Side Only)

O.M.B. No. 2120-0018

U.S. Department of Transportation **Federal Aviation Administration**	**APPLICATION FOR AIRWORTHINESS CERTIFICATE**	**INSTRUCTIONS** - Print or type. Do not write in shaded areas; these are for FAA use only. Submit original only to an authorized FAA Representative. If additional space is required, use attachment. For special flight permits complete Sections II, VI, and VII as applicable.

I. AIRCRAFT DESCRIPTION

1. REGISTRATION MARK N34582	2. AIRCRAFT BUILDER'S NAME *(Make)* Hughes	3. AIRCRAFT MODEL DESIGNATION 369A	4. YR. MFR. 1966	FAA CODING
5. AIRCRAFT SERIAL NO. 1332	6. ENGINE BUILDER'S NAME *(Make)* Allison	7. ENGINE MODEL DESIGNATION 250-C10B		
8. NUMBER OF ENGINES 1	9. PROPELLER BUILDER'S NAME *(Make)* N/A	10. PROPELLER MODEL DESIGNATION N/A	11. AIRCRAFT IS *(Check if applicable)* IMPORT	

II. CERTIFICATION REQUESTED

APPLICATION IS HEREBY MADE FOR: *(Check applicable items)*

A	1	X	*STANDARD AIRWORTHINESS CERTIFICATE (Indicate category)*	X NORMAL; UTILITY; ACROBATIC; TRANSPORT; COMMUTER; BALLOON; OTHER	
B			*SPECIAL AIRWORTHINESS CERTIFICATE (Check appropriate items)*		
	7		PRIMARY		
	2		LIMITED		
	5		PROVISIONAL *(Indicate class)*	1 CLASS I; 2 CLASS II	
	3		RESTRICTED *(Indicate operation(s) to be conducted)*	1 AGRICULTURE AND PEST CONTROL; 2 AERIAL; 3 AERIAL ADVERTISING; 4 FOREST *(Wildlife conservation)*; 5 PATROLLING; 6 WEATHER CONTROL; 0 OTHER *(Specify)*	
	4		EXPERIMENTAL *(Indicate operation(s) to be conducted)*	1 RESEARCH AND DEVELOPMENT; 2 AMATEUR BUILT; 3 EXHIBITION; 4 AIR RACING; 5 CREW TRAINING; 6 MARKET SURVEY; 0 TO SHOW COMPLIANCE WITH THE CFR; 7 OPERATING *(Primary Category)* KIT BUILT AIRCRAFT	
	8		SPECIAL FLIGHT PERMIT *(Indicate operation to be conducted, then complete Section VI or VII as applicable on reverse side)*	1 FERRY FLIGHT FOR REPAIRS, ALTERATIONS, MAINTENANCE, OR STORAGE; 2 EVACUATE FROM AREA OF IMPENDING DANGER; 3 OPERATION IN EXCESS OF MAXIMUM CERTIFICATED TAKE-OFF WEIGHT; 4 DELIVERING OR EXPORTING; 5 PRODUCTION FLIGHT TESTING; 6 CUSTOMER DEMONSTRATION FLIGHTS	
C			MULTIPLE AIRWORTHINESS CERTIFICATE *(Check ABOVE "Restricted Operation" and "Standard" or "Limited" as applicable.)*		

III. OWNER'S CERTIFICATION

A. REGISTERED OWNER (As shown on certificate of aircraft registration) — **IF DEALER, CHECK HERE** ______

NAME Helicopter Operations, Inc	ADDRESS 2345 Perimeter Drive Stockton, California 94044

B. AIRCRAFT CERTIFICATION BASIS (Check applicable blocks and complete items as indicated)

X	AIRCRAFT SPECIFICATION OR TYPE CERTIFICATE DATA SHEET *(Give No. and Revision No.)* H3WE Rev 2	X	AIRWORTHINESS DIRECTIVES *(Check if all applicable AD's complied with and give the number of the last AD SUPPLEMENT available in the biweekly series as of the date of application)* 96-23
	AIRCRAFT LISTING (Give page number(s)) N/A		SUPPLEMENTAL TYPE CERTIFICATE (List number of each STC incorporated) N/A

C. AIRCRAFT OPERATION AND MAINTENANCE RECORDS

X	CHECK IF RECORDS IN COMPLIANCE WITH 14 CFR section 91.417	TOTAL AIRFRAME HOURS 2852:00	3	EXPERIMENTAL ONLY *(Enter hours flown since last certificate issued or renewed)* N/A

D. CERTIFICATION - I hereby certify that I am the registered owner (or his agent) of the aircraft described above, that the aircraft is registered with the Federal Aviation Administration in accordance with Title 49 of the United States Code 44101 et seq. and applicable Federal Aviation Regulations, and that the aircraft has been inspected and is airworthy and eligible for the airworthiness certificate requested.

DATE OF APPLICATION 11/25/96	NAME AND TITLE (Print or type) James J. Jones, General Manager	SIGNATURE *James J. Jones*

IV. INSPECTION AGENCY VERIFICATION

A. THE AIRCRAFT DESCRIBED ABOVE HAS BEEN INSPECTED AND FOUND AIRWORTHY BY: (Complete this section only if 14 CFR part 21.183(d) applies).

2	14 CFR part 121 CERTIFICATE HOLDER *(Give Certificate No.)*	3	CERTIFICATED MECHANIC *(Give Certificate No.)*	6	CERTIFICATED REPAIR STATION *(Give Certificate No.)*
5	AIRCRAFT MANUFACTURER (Give name or firm)				

DATE	TITLE	SIGNATURE

V. FAA REPRESENTATIVE CERTIFICATION

(Check ALL applicable blocks in items A and B) A. I find that the aircraft described in Section I or VII meets requirements for		THE CERTIFICATE REQUESTED
	4	AMENDMENT OR MODIFICATION OF CURRENT AIRWORTHINESS CERTIFICATE
B. Inspection for a special flight permit under Section VII was conducted by:		FAA INSPECTOR; FAA DESIGNEE
		CERTIFICATE HOLDER UNDER; 14 CFR part 65; 14 CFR part 121 OR 135; 14 CFR part 145

DATE	DISTRICT OFFICE	4	DESIGNEE'S SIGNATURE AND NO.	1	FAA INSPECTOR'S SIGNATURE

FAA Form 8130-6 (5-01) Supersedes Previous Edition

NSN: 0052-00-024-7006

Figure 5. Sample FAA Form 8130-6, Application for a Standard Airworthiness Certificate — Aircraft Built From Spare and Surplus Parts (No Previous U.S. Airworthiness Certificate Issued) (Face Side Only)

O.M.B. No. 2120-0018

U.S. Department of Transportation Federal Aviation Administration	**APPLICATION FOR AIRWORTHINESS CERTIFICATE**	**INSTRUCTIONS** - Print or type. Do not write in shaded areas; these are for FAA use only. Submit original only to an authorized FAA Representative. If additional space is required, use attachment. For special flight permits complete Sections II, VI, and VII as applicable.

I. AIRCRAFT DESCRIPTION

1. REGISTRATION MARK N 6934M	2. AIRCRAFT BUILDER'S NAME *(Make)* Smith	3. AIRCRAFT MODEL DESIGNATION C-172M	4. YR. MFR. 1980	FAA CODING
5. AIRCRAFT SERIAL NO. Smith 001	6. ENGINE BUILDER'S NAME *(Make)* Lycoming	7. ENGINE MODEL DESIGNATION 0-320-B		
8. NUMBER OF ENGINES One	9. PROPELLER BUILDER'S NAME *(Make)* McCauley	10. PROPELLER MODEL DESIGNATION 1C160/CTM	11. AIRCRAFT IS *(Check if applicable)* IMPORT	

II. CERTIFICATION REQUESTED

APPLICATION IS HEREBY MADE FOR: *(Check applicable items)*

A	1	X	*STANDARD AIRWORTHINESS CERTIFICATE (Indicate category)*	X NORMAL · UTILITY · ACROBATIC · TRANSPORT · COMMUTER · BALLOON · OTHER		
B			*SPECIAL AIRWORTHINESS CERTIFICATE (Check appropriate items)*			
	7		PRIMARY			
	2		LIMITED			
	5		PROVISIONAL *(Indicate class)*	1 CLASS I		
				2 CLASS II		
	3		RESTRICTED *(Indicate operation(s) to be conducted)*	1 AGRICULTURE AND PEST CONTROL	2 AERIAL	3 AERIAL ADVERTISING
				4 FOREST *(Wildlife conservation)*	5 PATROLLING	6 WEATHER CONTROL
				0 OTHER *(Specify)*		
	4		EXPERIMENTAL *(Indicate operation(s) to be conducted)*	1 RESEARCH AND DEVELOPMENT	2 AMATEUR BUILT	3 EXHIBITION
				4 AIR RACING	5 CREW TRAINING	6 MARKET SURVEY
				0 TO SHOW COMPLIANCE WITH THE CFR	7 OPERATING *(Primary Category)* KIT BUILT AIRCRAFT	
	8		SPECIAL FLIGHT PERMIT *(Indicate operation to be conducted, then complete Section VI or VII as applicable on reverse side)*	1 FERRY FLIGHT FOR REPAIRS, ALTERATIONS, MAINTENANCE, OR STORAGE		
				2 EVACUATE FROM AREA OF IMPENDING DANGER		
				3 OPERATION IN EXCESS OF MAXIMUM CERTIFICATED TAKE-OFF WEIGHT		
				4 DELIVERING OR EXPORTING	5 PRODUCTION FLIGHT TESTING	
				6 CUSTOMER DEMONSTRATION FLIGHTS		
C			MULTIPLE AIRWORTHINESS CERTIFICATE *(Check ABOVE "Restricted Operation" and "Standard" or "Limited" as applicable.)*			

III. OWNER'S CERTIFICATION

A. REGISTERED OWNER (As shown on certificate of aircraft registration)	IF DEALER, CHECK HERE
NAME John R. Smith	ADDRESS 6224 Arbor Way Springfield, Tennessee 70653

B. AIRCRAFT CERTIFICATION BASIS (Check applicable blocks and complete items as indicated)

X	AIRCRAFT SPECIFICATION OR TYPE CERTIFICATE DATA SHEET *(Give No. and Revision No.)* H-1, Rev. 36	X	AIRWORTHINESS DIRECTIVES *(Check if all applicable AD's complied with and give the number of the last AD SUPPLEMENT available in the biweekly series as of the date of application)* 96-23
	AIRCRAFT LISTING (Give page number(s)) N/A		SUPPLEMENTAL TYPE CERTIFICATE (List number of each STC incorporated) N/A

C. AIRCRAFT OPERATION AND MAINTENANCE RECORDS

X	CHECK IF RECORDS IN COMPLIANCE WITH 14 CFR section 91.417	TOTAL AIRFRAME HOURS 6.5	3	EXPERIMENTAL ONLY *(Enter hours flown since last certificate issued or renewed)* N/A

D. CERTIFICATION - I hereby certify that I am the registered owner (or his agent) of the aircraft described above, that the aircraft is registered with the Federal Aviation Administration in accordance with Title 49 of the United States Code 44101 et seq. and applicable Federal Aviation Regulations, and that the aircraft has been inspected and is airworthy and eligible for the airworthiness certificate requested.

DATE OF APPLICATION 11/25/96	NAME AND TITLE (Print or type) John R. Smith, Owner	SIGNATURE *John R. Smith*

IV. INSPECTION AGENCY VERIFICATION

A. THE AIRCRAFT DESCRIBED ABOVE HAS BEEN INSPECTED AND FOUND AIRWORTHY BY: (Complete this section only if 14 CFR part 21.183(d) applies).

2	14 CFR part 121 CERTIFICATE HOLDER *(Give Certificate No.)*	3	CERTIFICATED MECHANIC *(Give Certificate No.)*	6	CERTIFICATED REPAIR STATION *(Give Certificate No.)*
5	AIRCRAFT MANUFACTURER (Give name or firm)				
DATE		TITLE		SIGNATURE	

V. FAA REPRESENTATIVE CERTIFICATION

(Check ALL applicable blocks in items A and B) A. I find that the aircraft described in Section I or VII meets requirements for		THE CERTIFICATE REQUESTED		
	4	AMENDMENT OR MODIFICATION OF CURRENT AIRWORTHINESS CERTIFICATE		
B. Inspection for a special flight permit under Section VII was conducted by:		FAA INSPECTOR	FAA DESIGNEE	
		CERTIFICATE HOLDER UNDER	14 CFR part 65 · 14 CFR part 121 OR 135	14 CFR part 145
DATE	DISTRICT OFFICE	4 DESIGNEE'S SIGNATURE AND NO.	1 FAA INSPECTOR'S SIGNATURE	

FAA Form 8130-6 (5-01) Supersedes Previous Edition

NSN: 0052-00-024-7006

21-12B

AC

Figure 6. Sample FAA Form 8130-6, Application for a Special Airworthiness Certificate — Primary Category Aircraft Certificated Under Section 21.184(a) (Face Side Only)

OMB No. 2120-0018

U.S. Department of Transportation
Federal Aviation Administration

APPLICATION FOR AIRWORTHINESS CERTIFICATE

INSTRUCTIONS - Print or type. Do not write in shaded areas; these are for FAA use only. Submit original only to an authorized FAA Representative. If additional space is required, use attachment. For special flight permits complete Sections II, VI, and VII as applicable.

I. AIRCRAFT DESCRIPTION

1. REGISTRATION MARK N2EZ	2. AIRCRAFT BUILDER'S NAME *(Make)* Flight Corp.	3. AIRCRAFT MODEL DESIGNATION F-C-1A	4. YR. MFR. 96	FAA CODING
5. AIRCRAFT SERIAL NO. F0002	6. ENGINE BUILDER'S NAME *(Make)* TCM	7. ENGINE MODEL DESIGNATION 10-360-ES		
8. NUMBER OF ENGINES One	9. PROPELLER BUILDER'S NAME *(Make)* McCauley	10. PROPELLER MODEL DESIGNATION 2A34C 209	11. AIRCRAFT IS *(Check if applicable)* IMPORT	

II. CERTIFICATION REQUESTED

APPLICATION IS HEREBY MADE FOR: *(Check applicable items)*

A	1		*STANDARD AIRWORTHINESS CERTIFICATE (Indicate category)*	NORMAL / UTILITY / ACROBATIC / TRANSPORT / COMMUTER / BALLOON / OTHER		
B		X	*SPECIAL AIRWORTHINESS CERTIFICATE (Check appropriate items)*			
	7	X	PRIMARY			
	2		LIMITED			
	5		PROVISIONAL *(Indicate class)*	1		CLASS I
				2		CLASS II
	3		RESTRICTED *(Indicate operation(s) to be conducted)*	1		AGRICULTURE AND PEST CONTROL; 2 AERIAL; 3 AERIAL ADVERTISING
				4		FOREST *(Wildlife conservation)*; 5 PATROLLING; 6 WEATHER CONTROL
				0		OTHER *(Specify)*
	4		EXPERIMENTAL *(Indicate operation(s) to be conducted)*	1		RESEARCH AND DEVELOPMENT; 2 AMATEUR BUILT; 3 EXHIBITION
				4		AIR RACING; 5 CREW TRAINING; 6 MARKET SURVEY
				0		TO SHOW COMPLIANCE WITH THE CFR; 7 OPERATING *(Primary Category)* KIT BUILT AIRCRAFT
	8		SPECIAL FLIGHT PERMIT *(Indicate operation to be conducted, then complete Section VI or VII as applicable on reverse side)*	1		FERRY FLIGHT FOR REPAIRS, ALTERATIONS, MAINTENANCE, OR STORAGE
				2		EVACUATE FROM AREA OF IMPENDING DANGER
				3		OPERATION IN EXCESS OF MAXIMUM CERTIFICATED TAKE-OFF WEIGHT
				4		DELIVERING OR EXPORTING; 5 PRODUCTION FLIGHT TESTING
				6		CUSTOMER DEMONSTRATION FLIGHTS
C			MULTIPLE AIRWORTHINESS CERTIFICATE *(Check ABOVE "Restricted Operation" and "Standard" or "Limited" as applicable.)*			

III. OWNER'S CERTIFICATION

A. REGISTERED OWNER (As shown on certificate of aircraft registration) — IF DEALER, CHECK HERE

NAME Flight Corp.	ADDRESS 10 Lane Ave Doby, TX 78907

B. AIRCRAFT CERTIFICATION BASIS (Check applicable blocks and complete items as indicated)

X	AIRCRAFT SPECIFICATION OR TYPE CERTIFICATE DATA SHEET *(Give No. and Revision No.)* CE785	X	AIRWORTHINESS DIRECTIVES *(Check if all applicable AD's complied with and give the number of the last AD SUPPLEMENT available in the biweekly series as of the date of application)* 96-23
	AIRCRAFT LISTING (Give page number(s)) N/A		SUPPLEMENTAL TYPE CERTIFICATE (List number of each STC incorporated) N/A

C. AIRCRAFT OPERATION AND MAINTENANCE RECORDS

X	CHECK IF RECORDS IN COMPLIANCE WITH 14 CFR section 91.417	TOTAL AIRFRAME HOURS 2.1	3	EXPERIMENTAL ONLY *(Enter hours flown since last certificate issued or renewed)*

D. CERTIFICATION - I hereby certify that I am the registered owner (or his agent) of the aircraft described above, that the aircraft is registered with the Federal Aviation Administration in accordance with Title 49 of the United States Code 44101 et seq. and applicable Federal Aviation Regulations, and that the aircraft has been inspected and is airworthy and eligible for the airworthiness certificate requested.

DATE OF APPLICATION 11/25/96	NAME AND TITLE (Print or type) Joe Quality, Director QA	SIGNATURE *Joe Quality*

IV. INSPECTION AGENCY VERIFICATION

A. THE AIRCRAFT DESCRIBED ABOVE HAS BEEN INSPECTED AND FOUND AIRWORTHY BY: (Complete this section only if 14 CFR part 21.183(d) applies).

2	14 CFR part 121 CERTIFICATE HOLDER *(Give Certificate No.)*	3	CERTIFICATED MECHANIC *(Give Certificate No.)*
6	CERTIFICATED REPAIR STATION *(Give Certificate No.)*	5	AIRCRAFT MANUFACTURER (Give name or firm)

DATE	TITLE	SIGNATURE

V. FAA REPRESENTATIVE CERTIFICATION

(Check ALL applicable blocks in items A and B)
A. I find that the aircraft described in Section I or VII meets requirements for

		THE CERTIFICATE REQUESTED
4		AMENDMENT OR MODIFICATION OF CURRENT AIRWORTHINESS CERTIFICATE

B. Inspection for a special flight permit under Section VII was conducted by:

FAA INSPECTOR	FAA DESIGNEE		
CERTIFICATE HOLDER UNDER	14 CFR part 65	14 CFR part 121 OR 135	14 CFR part 145

DATE	DISTRICT OFFICE	4	DESIGNEE'S SIGNATURE AND NO.	1	FAA INSPECTOR'S SIGNATURE

FAA Form 8130-6 (5-01) Supersedes Previous Edition — NSN: 0052-00-024-7006

Figure 7. Sample FAA Form 8130-6, Application for a Special Airworthiness Certificate — Limited Category (Face Side Only)

O.M.B. No. 2120-0018

U.S. Department of Transportation Federal Aviation Administration **APPLICATION FOR AIRWORTHINESS CERTIFICATE**	**INSTRUCTIONS** - Print or type. Do not write in shaded areas; these are for FAA use only. Submit original only to an authorized FAA Representative. If additional space is required, use attachment. For special flight permits complete Sections II, VI, and VII as applicable.

I. AIRCRAFT DESCRIPTION

1. REGISTRATION MARK N1256	2. AIRCRAFT BUILDER'S NAME *(Make)* Martin	3. AIRCRAFT MODEL DESIGNATION B-26C	4. YR. MFR. 1943	FAA CODING
5. AIRCRAFT SERIAL NO. 2256	6. ENGINE BUILDER'S NAME *(Make)* P&W	7. ENGINE MODEL DESIGNATION R-2800-83AMB		
8. NUMBER OF ENGINES Two	9. PROPELLER BUILDER'S NAME *(Make)* Hamilton Standard	10. PROPELLER MODEL DESIGNATION 42E60-7/6895-8	11. AIRCRAFT IS *(Check if applicable)* IMPORT	

II. CERTIFICATION REQUESTED

APPLICATION IS HEREBY MADE FOR: *(Check applicable items)*

A	1		*STANDARD AIRWORTHINESS CERTIFICATE (Indicate category)*		NORMAL / UTILITY / ACROBATIC / TRANSPORT / COMMUTER / BALLOON / OTHER
B		X	*SPECIAL AIRWORTHINESS CERTIFICATE (Check appropriate items)*		
	7		PRIMARY		
	2	X	LIMITED		
	5		PROVISIONAL *(Indicate class)*	1	CLASS I
				2	CLASS II
	3		RESTRICTED *(Indicate operation(s) to be conducted)*	1	AGRICULTURE AND PEST CONTROL; 2 AERIAL; 3 AERIAL ADVERTISING
				4	FOREST *(Wildlife conservation)*; 5 PATROLLING; 6 WEATHER CONTROL
				0	OTHER *(Specify)*
	4		EXPERIMENTAL *(Indicate operation(s) to be conducted)*	1	RESEARCH AND DEVELOPMENT; 2 AMATEUR BUILT; 3 EXHIBITION
				4	AIR RACING; 5 CREW TRAINING; 6 MARKET SURVEY
				0	TO SHOW COMPLIANCE WITH THE CFR; 7 OPERATING *(Primary Category)* KIT BUILT AIRCRAFT
	8		SPECIAL FLIGHT PERMIT *(Indicate operation to be conducted, then complete Section VI or VII as applicable on reverse side)*	1	FERRY FLIGHT FOR REPAIRS, ALTERATIONS, MAINTENANCE, OR STORAGE
				2	EVACUATE FROM AREA OF IMPENDING DANGER
				3	OPERATION IN EXCESS OF MAXIMUM CERTIFICATED TAKE-OFF WEIGHT
				4	DELIVERING OR EXPORTING; 5 PRODUCTION FLIGHT TESTING
				6	CUSTOMER DEMONSTRATION FLIGHTS
C			MULTIPLE AIRWORTHINESS CERTIFICATE *(Check ABOVE "Restricted Operation" and "Standard" or "Limited" as applicable.)*		

III. OWNER'S CERTIFICATION

A. REGISTERED OWNER (As shown on certificate of aircraft registration) — IF DEALER, CHECK HERE

NAME Gas Transmission Company	ADDRESS 1216 West 48th Street Dallas, Texas 64072

B. AIRCRAFT CERTIFICATION BASIS (Check applicable blocks and complete items as indicated)

X	AIRCRAFT SPECIFICATION OR TYPE CERTIFICATE DATA SHEET *(Give No. and Revision No.)* AL-33 Rev.1	X	AIRWORTHINESS DIRECTIVES *(Check if all applicable AD's complied with and give the number of the last AD SUPPLEMENT available in the biweekly series as of the date of application)* 96-23
	AIRCRAFT LISTING (Give page number(s)) N/A		SUPPLEMENTAL TYPE CERTIFICATE (List number of each STC incorporated) N/A

C. AIRCRAFT OPERATION AND MAINTENANCE RECORDS

X	CHECK IF RECORDS IN COMPLIANCE WITH 14 CFR section 91.417	TOTAL AIRFRAME HOURS 12,632	3	EXPERIMENTAL ONLY *(Enter hours flown since last certificate issued or renewed)* N/A

D. CERTIFICATION - I hereby certify that I am the registered owner (or his agent) of the aircraft described above, that the aircraft is registered with the Federal Aviation Administration in accordance with Title 49 of the United States Code 44101 et seq. and applicable Federal Aviation Regulations, and that the aircraft has been inspected and is airworthy and eligible for the airworthiness certificate requested.

DATE OF APPLICATION 11/20/96	NAME AND TITLE (Print or type) George Brown, President	SIGNATURE George Brown

IV. INSPECTION AGENCY VERIFICATION

A. THE AIRCRAFT DESCRIBED ABOVE HAS BEEN INSPECTED AND FOUND AIRWORTHY BY: (Complete this section only if 14 CFR part 21.183(d) applies).

2	14 CFR part 121 CERTIFICATE HOLDER *(Give Certificate No.)*	3	CERTIFICATED MECHANIC *(Give Certificate No.)*	6	CERTIFICATED REPAIR STATION *(Give Certificate No.)*
5	AIRCRAFT MANUFACTURER (Give name or firm)				

DATE	TITLE	SIGNATURE

V. FAA REPRESENTATIVE CERTIFICATION

(Check ALL applicable blocks in items A and B)

A. I find that the aircraft described in Section I or VII meets requirements for		THE CERTIFICATE REQUESTED	
	4	AMENDMENT OR MODIFICATION OF CURRENT AIRWORTHINESS CERTIFICATE	
B. Inspection for a special flight permit under Section VII was conducted by:		FAA INSPECTOR	FAA DESIGNEE
		CERTIFICATE HOLDER UNDER	14 CFR part 65 / 14 CFR part 121 OR 135 / 14 CFR part 145

DATE	DISTRICT OFFICE	4 DESIGNEE'S SIGNATURE AND NO.	1 FAA INSPECTOR'S SIGNATURE

FAA Form 8130-6 (5-01) Supersedes Previous Edition — NSN: 0052-00-024-7006

Figure 8. Sample FAA Form 8130-6, Application for a Special Airworthiness Certificate — Provisional Category (Face Side Only)

O.M.B. No. 2120-0018

U.S. Department of Transportation Federal Aviation Administration **APPLICATION FOR AIRWORTHINESS CERTIFICATE**	**INSTRUCTIONS** - Print or type. Do not write in shaded areas; these are for FAA use only. Submit original only to an authorized FAA Representative. If additional space is required, use attachment. For special flight permits complete Sections II, VI, and VII as applicable.

I. AIRCRAFT DESCRIPTION

1. REGISTRATION MARK N 502A	2. AIRCRAFT BUILDER'S NAME *(Make)* Lockheed-Georgia Co.	3. AIRCRAFT MODEL DESIGNATION 382G	4. YR. MFR. 1996	FAA CODING
5. AIRCRAFT SERIAL NO. 4387	6. ENGINE BUILDER'S NAME *(Make)* Allison	7. ENGINE MODEL DESIGNATION 501-D22A		
8. NUMBER OF ENGINES Four	9. PROPELLER BUILDER'S NAME *(Make)* Hamilton-Standard	10. PROPELLER MODEL DESIGNATION 54H60-91/54H60-117	11. AIRCRAFT IS *(Check if applicable)* IMPORT	

II. CERTIFICATION REQUESTED

APPLICATION IS HEREBY MADE FOR: *(Check applicable items)*

A	1		STANDARD AIRWORTHINESS CERTIFICATE *(Indicate category)*	NORMAL / UTILITY / ACROBATIC / TRANSPORT / COMMUTER / BALLOON / OTHER			
B		X	SPECIAL AIRWORTHINESS CERTIFICATE *(Check appropriate items)*				
	7		PRIMARY				
	2		LIMITED				
	5	X	PROVISIONAL *(Indicate class)*	1	X	CLASS I	
				2		CLASS II	
	3		RESTRICTED *(Indicate operation(s) to be conducted)*	1		AGRICULTURE AND PEST CONTROL	2 AERIAL; 3 AERIAL ADVERTISING
				4		FOREST *(Wildlife conservation)*	5 PATROLLING; 6 WEATHER CONTROL
				0		OTHER *(Specify)*	
	4		EXPERIMENTAL *(Indicate operation(s) to be conducted)*	1		RESEARCH AND DEVELOPMENT	2 AMATEUR BUILT; 3 EXHIBITION
				4		AIR RACING	5 CREW TRAINING; 6 MARKET SURVEY
				0		TO SHOW COMPLIANCE WITH THE CFR	7 OPERATING *(Primary Category)* KIT BUILT AIRCRAFT
	8		SPECIAL FLIGHT PERMIT *(Indicate operation to be conducted, then complete Section VI or VII as applicable on reverse side)*	1		FERRY FLIGHT FOR REPAIRS, ALTERATIONS, MAINTENANCE, OR STORAGE	
				2		EVACUATE FROM AREA OF IMPENDING DANGER	
				3		OPERATION IN EXCESS OF MAXIMUM CERTIFICATED TAKE-OFF WEIGHT	
				4		DELIVERING OR EXPORTING	5 PRODUCTION FLIGHT TESTING
				6		CUSTOMER DEMONSTRATION FLIGHTS	
C			MULTIPLE AIRWORTHINESS CERTIFICATE *(Check ABOVE "Restricted Operation" and "Standard" or "Limited" as applicable.)*				

III. OWNER'S CERTIFICATION

A. REGISTERED OWNER (As shown on certificate of aircraft registration) — IF DEALER, CHECK HERE

NAME Lockheed Georgia Co.	ADDRESS Marietta, Georgia 30060

B. AIRCRAFT CERTIFICATION BASIS (Check applicable blocks and complete items as indicated)

X	AIRCRAFT SPECIFICATION OR TYPE CERTIFICATE DATA SHEET *(Give No. and Revision No.)* A1SO	X	AIRWORTHINESS DIRECTIVES *(Check if all applicable AD's complied with and give the number of the last AD SUPPLEMENT available in the biweekly series as of the date of application)* 96-23
	AIRCRAFT LISTING (Give page number(s)) N/A		SUPPLEMENTAL TYPE CERTIFICATE (List number of each STC incorporated) N/A

C. AIRCRAFT OPERATION AND MAINTENANCE RECORDS

X	CHECK IF RECORDS IN COMPLIANCE WITH 14 CFR section 91.417	TOTAL AIRFRAME HOURS 10.2	3	EXPERIMENTAL ONLY *(Enter hours flown since last certificate issued or renewed)* N/A

D. CERTIFICATION - I hereby certify that I am the registered owner (or his agent) of the aircraft described above, that the aircraft is registered with the Federal Aviation Administration in accordance with Title 49 of the United States Code 44101 et seq. and applicable Federal Aviation Regulations, and that the aircraft has been inspected and is airworthy and eligible for the airworthiness certificate requested.

DATE OF APPLICATION 11/25/96	NAME AND TITLE (Print or type) James A. Jones Vice President Engineering	SIGNATURE *James A. Jones*

IV. INSPECTION AGENCY VERIFICATION

A. THE AIRCRAFT DESCRIBED ABOVE HAS BEEN INSPECTED AND FOUND AIRWORTHY BY: (Complete this section only if 14 CFR part 21.183(d) applies).

2	14 CFR part 121 CERTIFICATE HOLDER *(Give Certificate No.)*	3	CERTIFICATED MECHANIC *(Give Certificate No.)*	6	CERTIFICATED REPAIR STATION *(Give Certificate No.)*
5	AIRCRAFT MANUFACTURER (Give name or firm)				

DATE	TITLE	SIGNATURE

V. FAA REPRESENTATIVE CERTIFICATION

(Check ALL applicable blocks in items A and B)

A. I find that the aircraft described in Section I or VII meets requirements for		THE CERTIFICATE REQUESTED
	4	AMENDMENT OR MODIFICATION OF CURRENT AIRWORTHINESS CERTIFICATE
B. Inspection for a special flight permit under Section VII was conducted by:	FAA INSPECTOR	FAA DESIGNEE
	CERTIFICATE HOLDER UNDER	14 CFR part 65 / 14 CFR part 121 OR 135 / 14 CFR part 145

DATE	DISTRICT OFFICE	4	DESIGNEE'S SIGNATURE AND NO.	1	FAA INSPECTOR'S SIGNATURE

FAA Form 8130-6 (5-01) Supersedes Previous Edition NSN:0052-00-024-7006

Figure 9. Sample FAA Form 8130-6, Application for a Special Airworthiness Certificate — Restricted Category (Face Side Only)

O.M.B. No. 2120-0018

U.S. Department of Transportation **Federal Aviation Administration**	**APPLICATION FOR AIRWORTHINESS CERTIFICATE**	**INSTRUCTIONS** - Print or type. Do not write in shaded areas; these are for FAA use only. Submit original only to an authorized FAA Representative. If additional space is required, use attachment. For special flight permits complete Sections II, VI, and VII as applicable.

I. AIRCRAFT DESCRIPTION

1. REGISTRATION MARK N7777	2. AIRCRAFT BUILDER'S NAME *(Make)* North American Rockwell	3. AIRCRAFT MODEL DESIGNATION S2R	4. YR. MFR. 1950	FAA CODING
5. AIRCRAFT SERIAL NO. 1916R	6. ENGINE BUILDER'S NAME *(Make)* P&W	7. ENGINE MODEL DESIGNATION R1340AN1(S3H1)		
8. NUMBER OF ENGINES One	9. PROPELLER BUILDER'S NAME *(Make)* Hamilton Standard	10. PROPELLER MODEL DESIGNATION 12D40-305/EAC/AG 100-2	11. AIRCRAFT IS *(Check if applicable)* IMPORT	

II. CERTIFICATION REQUESTED

APPLICATION IS HEREBY MADE FOR: *(Check applicable items)*

A	1		*STANDARD AIRWORTHINESS CERTIFICATE (Indicate category)*	NORMAL / UTILITY / ACROBATIC / TRANSPORT / COMMUTER / BALLOON / OTHER			
B		X	*SPECIAL AIRWORTHINESS CERTIFICATE (Check appropriate items)*				
	7		PRIMARY				
	2		LIMITED				
	5		PROVISIONAL *(Indicate class)*	1		CLASS I	
				2		CLASS II	
	3	X	RESTRICTED *(Indicate operation(s) to be conducted)*	1	X	AGRICULTURE AND PEST CONTROL	2 AERIAL; 3 AERIAL ADVERTISING
				4		FOREST *(Wildlife conservation)*	5 PATROLLING; 6 WEATHER CONTROL
				0		OTHER *(Specify)*	
	4		EXPERIMENTAL *(Indicate operation(s) to be conducted)*	1		RESEARCH AND DEVELOPMENT	2 AMATEUR BUILT; 3 EXHIBITION
				4		AIR RACING	5 CREW TRAINING; 6 MARKET SURVEY
				0		TO SHOW COMPLIANCE WITH THE CFR	7 OPERATING *(Primary Category)* KIT BUILT AIRCRAFT
	8		SPECIAL FLIGHT PERMIT *(Indicate operation to be conducted, then complete Section VI or VII as applicable on reverse side)*	1		FERRY FLIGHT FOR REPAIRS, ALTERATIONS, MAINTENANCE, OR STORAGE	
				2		EVACUATE FROM AREA OF IMPENDING DANGER	
				3		OPERATION IN EXCESS OF MAXIMUM CERTIFICATED TAKE-OFF WEIGHT	
				4		DELIVERING OR EXPORTING	5 PRODUCTION FLIGHT TESTING
				6		CUSTOMER DEMONSTRATION FLIGHTS	
C			MULTIPLE AIRWORTHINESS CERTIFICATE *(Check ABOVE "Restricted Operation" and "Standard" or "Limited" as applicable.)*				

III. OWNER'S CERTIFICATION

A. REGISTERED OWNER (As shown on certificate of aircraft registration) — IF DEALER, CHECK HERE

NAME John J Jones, R.B. Jones DBA Crop Dusters, Inc.	ADDRESS Rt. 5 Greenville, Mississippi 38701

B. AIRCRAFT CERTIFICATION BASIS (Check applicable blocks and complete items as indicated)

X	AIRCRAFT SPECIFICATION OR TYPE CERTIFICATE DATA SHEET *(Give No. and Revision No.)* A4SW Rev. 5	X	AIRWORTHINESS DIRECTIVES *(Check if all applicable AD's complied with and give the number of the last AD SUPPLEMENT available in the biweekly series as of the date of application)* 96-23
	AIRCRAFT LISTING (Give page number(s)) N/A		SUPPLEMENTAL TYPE CERTIFICATE (List number of each STC incorporated) N/A

C. AIRCRAFT OPERATION AND MAINTENANCE RECORDS

X	CHECK IF RECORDS IN COMPLIANCE WITH 14 CFR section 91.417	TOTAL AIRFRAME HOURS 2105	3	EXPERIMENTAL ONLY *(Enter hours flown since last certificate issued or renewed)* N/A

D. CERTIFICATION - I hereby certify that I am the registered owner (or his agent) of the aircraft described above, that the aircraft is registered with the Federal Aviation Administration in accordance with Title 49 of the United States Code 44101 et seq. and applicable Federal Aviation Regulations, and that the aircraft has been inspected and is airworthy and eligible for the airworthiness certificate requested.

DATE OF APPLICATION 11/25/96	NAME AND TITLE (Print or type) John J. Jones, Co-Owner	SIGNATURE *John J. Jones*

IV. INSPECTION AGENCY VERIFICATION

A. THE AIRCRAFT DESCRIBED ABOVE HAS BEEN INSPECTED AND FOUND AIRWORTHY BY: (Complete this section only if 14 CFR part 21.183(d) applies).

2	14 CFR part 121 CERTIFICATE HOLDER *(Give Certificate No.)*	3	CERTIFICATED MECHANIC *(Give Certificate No.)*	6	CERTIFICATED REPAIR STATION *(Give Certificate No.)*
5	AIRCRAFT MANUFACTURER (Give name or firm)				

DATE	TITLE	SIGNATURE

V. FAA REPRESENTATIVE CERTIFICATION

(Check ALL applicable blocks in items A and B)

A. I find that the aircraft described in Section I or VII meets requirements for	4	THE CERTIFICATE REQUESTED	
		AMENDMENT OR MODIFICATION OF CURRENT AIRWORTHINESS CERTIFICATE	
B. Inspection for a special flight permit under Section VII was conducted by:		FAA INSPECTOR	FAA DESIGNEE
		CERTIFICATE HOLDER UNDER	14 CFR part 65 / 14 CFR part 121 OR 135 / 14 CFR part 145

DATE	DISTRICT OFFICE	4	DESIGNEE'S SIGNATURE AND NO.	1	FAA INSPECTOR'S SIGNATURE

FAA Form 8130-6 (5-01) Supersedes Previous Edition

NSN: 0052-00-024-7006

Figure 10. Sample FAA Form 8130-6, Application for a Special Airworthiness Certificate — Experimental Category Amateur-Built (Face Side Only)

O.M.B. No. 2120-0018

U.S. Department of Transportation
Federal Aviation Administration

APPLICATION FOR AIRWORTHINESS CERTIFICATE

INSTRUCTIONS - Print or type. Do not write in shaded areas; these are for FAA use only. Submit original only to an authorized FAA Representative. If additional space is required, use attachment. For special flight permits complete Sections II, VI, and VII as applicable.

I. AIRCRAFT DESCRIPTION

1. REGISTRATION MARK N1234	2. AIRCRAFT BUILDER'S NAME *(Make)* Pratt	3. AIRCRAFT MODEL DESIGNATION B-3	4. YR. MFR. 1996	FAA CODING
5. AIRCRAFT SERIAL NO. 001	6. ENGINE BUILDER'S NAME *(Make)* CMC	7. ENGINE MODEL DESIGNATION A-65		
8. NUMBER OF ENGINES One	9. PROPELLER BUILDER'S NAME *(Make)* Sensenich	10. PROPELLER MODEL DESIGNATION N76AM-2-50	11. AIRCRAFT IS *(Check if applicable)* IMPORT	

II. CERTIFICATION REQUESTED

APPLICATION IS HEREBY MADE FOR: *(Check applicable items)*

A	1		*STANDARD AIRWORTHINESS CERTIFICATE (Indicate category)*	NORMAL / UTILITY / ACROBATIC / TRANSPORT / COMMUTER / BALLOON / OTHER		
B		X	*SPECIAL AIRWORTHINESS CERTIFICATE (Check appropriate items)*			
	7		PRIMARY			
	2		LIMITED			
	5		PROVISIONAL *(Indicate class)*	1	CLASS I	
				2	CLASS II	
	3		RESTRICTED *(Indicate operation(s) to be conducted)*	1	AGRICULTURE AND PEST CONTROL	2 AERIAL; 3 AERIAL ADVERTISING
				4	FOREST *(Wildlife conservation)*	5 PATROLLING; 6 WEATHER CONTROL
				0	OTHER *(Specify)*	
	4	X	EXPERIMENTAL *(Indicate operation(s) to be conducted)*	1	RESEARCH AND DEVELOPMENT	2 X AMATEUR BUILT; 3 EXHIBITION
				4	AIR RACING	5 CREW TRAINING; MARKET SURVEY
				0	TO SHOW COMPLIANCE WITH THE CFR	OPERATING *(Primary Category)* KIT BUILT AIRCRAFT
	8		SPECIAL FLIGHT PERMIT *(Indicate operation to be conducted, then complete Section VI or VII as applicable on reverse side)*	1	FERRY FLIGHT FOR REPAIRS, ALTERATIONS, MAINTENANCE, OR STORAGE	
				2	EVACUATE FROM AREA OF IMPENDING DANGER	
				3	OPERATION IN EXCESS OF MAXIMUM CERTIFICATED TAKE-OFF WEIGHT	
				4	DELIVERING OR EXPORTING	5 PRODUCTION FLIGHT TESTING
				6	CUSTOMER DEMONSTRATION FLIGHTS	
C			MULTIPLE AIRWORTHINESS CERTIFICATE *(Check ABOVE "Restricted Operation" and "Standard" or "Limited" as applicable.)*			

III. OWNER'S CERTIFICATION

A. REGISTERED OWNER (As shown on certificate of aircraft registration) — IF DEALER, CHECK HERE ______

NAME Howard D. Pratt John J Smith Co-Owner	ADDRESS 1120 West Street ST Louis, Missouri 41346

B. AIRCRAFT CERTIFICATION BASIS (Check applicable blocks and complete items as indicated)

	AIRCRAFT SPECIFICATION OR TYPE CERTIFICATE DATA SHEET *(Give No. and Revision No.)* N/A	X	AIRWORTHINESS DIRECTIVES *(Check if all applicable AD's complied with and give the number of the last AD SUPPLEMENT available in the biweekly series as of the date of application)* 96-23
	AIRCRAFT LISTING (Give page number(s))		SUPPLEMENTAL TYPE CERTIFICATE (List number of each STC incorporated)

C. AIRCRAFT OPERATION AND MAINTENANCE RECORDS

X	CHECK IF RECORDS IN COMPLIANCE WITH 14 CFR section 91.417	TOTAL AIRFRAME HOURS 0.0	3	EXPERIMENTAL ONLY *(Enter hours flown since last certificate issued or renewed)* 0.0

D. CERTIFICATION - I hereby certify that I am the registered owner (or his agent) of the aircraft described above, that the aircraft is registered with the Federal Aviation Administration in accordance with Title 49 of the United States Code 44101 et seq. and applicable Federal Aviation Regulations, and that the aircraft has been inspected and is airworthy and eligible for the airworthiness certificate requested.

DATE OF APPLICATION 11/25/96	NAME AND TITLE (Print or type) Howard D. Pratt, Co Owner	SIGNATURE *Howard D. Pratt*

IV. INSPECTION AGENCY VERIFICATION

A. THE AIRCRAFT DESCRIBED ABOVE HAS BEEN INSPECTED AND FOUND AIRWORTHY BY: (Complete this section only if 14 CFR part 21.183(d) applies).

2	14 CFR part 121 CERTIFICATE HOLDER *(Give Certificate No.)*	3	CERTIFICATED MECHANIC *(Give Certificate No.)*	6	CERTIFICATED REPAIR STATION *(Give Certificate No.)*
5	AIRCRAFT MANUFACTURER (Give name or firm)				
DATE		TITLE		SIGNATURE	

V. FAA REPRESENTATIVE CERTIFICATION

(Check ALL applicable blocks in items A and B) A. I find that the aircraft described in Section I or VII meets requirements for	4	THE CERTIFICATE REQUESTED AMENDMENT OR MODIFICATION OF CURRENT AIRWORTHINESS CERTIFICATE	
B. Inspection for a special flight permit under Section VII was conducted by:		FAA INSPECTOR CERTIFICATE HOLDER UNDER	FAA DESIGNEE 14 CFR part 65 / 14 CFR part 121 OR 135 / 14 CFR part 145

DATE	DISTRICT OFFICE	4 DESIGNEE'S SIGNATURE AND NO.	1 FAA INSPECTOR'S SIGNATURE

FAA Form 8130-6 (5-01) Supersedes Previous Edition NSN: 0052-00-024-7006

Figure 11. Sample FAA Form 8130-6, Application for a Special Airworthiness Certificate — Experimental Category, No Previous Experimental Certificate Issued (Face Side Only)

O.M.B. No. 2120-0018

U.S. Department of Transportation **Federal Aviation Administration**	**APPLICATION FOR AIRWORTHINESS CERTIFICATE**	**INSTRUCTIONS** - Print or type. Do not write in shaded areas; these are for FAA use only. Submit original only to an authorized FAA Representative. If additional space is required, use attachment. For special flight permits complete Sections II, VI, and VII as applicable.

I. AIRCRAFT DESCRIPTION

1. REGISTRATION MARK N5216	2. AIRCRAFT BUILDER'S NAME *(Make)* Boeing	3. AIRCRAFT MODEL DESIGNATION 727-228	4. YR. MFR. 1968	FAA CODING
5. AIRCRAFT SERIAL NO. 20540	6. ENGINE BUILDER'S NAME *(Make)* P&W	7. ENGINE MODEL DESIGNATION JT8D-7		
8. NUMBER OF ENGINES Three	9. PROPELLER BUILDER'S NAME *(Make)* N/A	10. PROPELLER MODEL DESIGNATION N/A	11. AIRCRAFT IS *(Check if applicable)* IMPORT	

II. CERTIFICATION REQUESTED

APPLICATION IS HEREBY MADE FOR: *(Check applicable items)*

A	1		*STANDARD AIRWORTHINESS CERTIFICATE (Indicate category)*	NORMAL	UTILITY	ACROBATIC	TRANSPORT	COMMUTER	BALLOON	OTHER	
B		X	*SPECIAL AIRWORTHINESS CERTIFICATE (Check appropriate items)*								
	7		PRIMARY								
	2		LIMITED								
	5		PROVISIONAL *(Indicate class)*	1		CLASS I					
				2		CLASS II					
	3		RESTRICTED *(Indicate operation(s) to be conducted)*	1		AGRICULTURE AND PEST CONTROL	2	AERIAL	3	AERIAL ADVERTISING	
				4		FOREST *(Wildlife conservation)*	5	PATROLLING	6	WEATHER CONTROL	
				0		OTHER *(Specify)*					
	4	X	EXPERIMENTAL *(Indicate operation(s) to be conducted)*	1		RESEARCH AND DEVELOPMENT	2	AMATEUR BUILT	3	EXHIBITION	
				4		AIR RACING	5	CREW TRAINING	6	MARKET SURVEY	
				0	X	TO SHOW COMPLIANCE WITH THE CFR	7	OPERATING *(Primary Category)* KIT BUILT AIRCRAFT			
	8		SPECIAL FLIGHT PERMIT *(Indicate operation to be conducted, then complete Section VI or VII as applicable on reverse side)*	1		FERRY FLIGHT FOR REPAIRS, ALTERATIONS, MAINTENANCE, OR STORAGE					
				2		EVACUATE FROM AREA OF IMPENDING DANGER					
				3		OPERATION IN EXCESS OF MAXIMUM CERTIFICATED TAKE-OFF WEIGHT					
				4		DELIVERING OR EXPORTING	5	PRODUCTION FLIGHT TESTING			
				6		CUSTOMER DEMONSTRATION FLIGHTS					
C			MULTIPLE AIRWORTHINESS CERTIFICATE *(Check ABOVE "Restricted Operation" and "Standard" or "Limited" as applicable.)*								

III. OWNER'S CERTIFICATION

A. REGISTERED OWNER (As shown on certificate of aircraft registration) — **IF DEALER, CHECK HERE**

NAME The Boeing Company	ADDRESS PO Box 3707 Seattle, Washington 98124

B. AIRCRAFT CERTIFICATION BASIS (Check applicable blocks and complete items as indicated)

	AIRCRAFT SPECIFICATION OR TYPE CERTIFICATE DATA SHEET *(Give No. and Revision No.)* N/A	X	AIRWORTHINESS DIRECTIVES *(Check if all applicable AD's complied with and give the number of the last AD SUPPLEMENT available in the biweekly series as of the date of application)* 96-23
	AIRCRAFT LISTING (Give page number(s)) N/A		SUPPLEMENTAL TYPE CERTIFICATE (List number of each STC incorporated)

C. AIRCRAFT OPERATION AND MAINTENANCE RECORDS

X	CHECK IF RECORDS IN COMPLIANCE WITH 14 CFR section 91.417	TOTAL AIRFRAME HOURS 5.51	3	EXPERIMENTAL ONLY *(Enter hours flown since last certificate issued or renewed)* 0.0

D. CERTIFICATION - I hereby certify that I am the registered owner (or his agent) of the aircraft described above, that the aircraft is registered with the Federal Aviation Administration in accordance with Title 49 of the United States Code 44101 et seq. and applicable Federal Aviation Regulations, and that the aircraft has been inspected and is airworthy and eligible for the airworthiness certificate requested.

DATE OF APPLICATION 11/25/96	NAME AND TITLE (Print or type) R.B. Smith, Airworthiness Certification Manager	SIGNATURE R.B. Smith

IV. INSPECTION AGENCY VERIFICATION

A. THE AIRCRAFT DESCRIBED ABOVE HAS BEEN INSPECTED AND FOUND AIRWORTHY BY: (Complete this section only if 14 CFR part 21.183(d) applies).

2		14 CFR part 121 CERTIFICATE HOLDER *(Give Certificate No.)*	3	CERTIFICATED MECHANIC *(Give Certificate No.)*	6		CERTIFICATED REPAIR STATION *(Give Certificate No.)*
5		AIRCRAFT MANUFACTURER (Give name or firm)					

DATE	TITLE	SIGNATURE

V. FAA REPRESENTATIVE CERTIFICATION

(Check ALL applicable blocks in items A and B)

A. I find that the aircraft described in Section I or VII meets requirements for		THE CERTIFICATE REQUESTED			
	4	AMENDMENT OR MODIFICATION OF CURRENT AIRWORTHINESS CERTIFICATE			
B. Inspection for a special flight permit under Section VII was conducted by:		FAA INSPECTOR	FAA DESIGNEE		
		CERTIFICATE HOLDER UNDER	14 CFR part 65	14 CFR part 121 OR 135	14 CFR part 145

DATE	DISTRICT OFFICE	4	DESIGNEE'S SIGNATURE AND NO.	1	FAA INSPECTOR'S SIGNATURE

FAA Form 8130-6 (5-01) Supersedes Previous Edition — NSN: 0052-00-024-7006

21-12B

AC

Figure 12. Sample FAA Form 8130-6, Application for a Special Airworthiness Certificate — Experimental Category (Face Side Only)

O.M.B. No. 2120-0018

U.S. Department of Transportation Federal Aviation Administration	**APPLICATION FOR AIRWORTHINESS CERTIFICATE**	**INSTRUCTIONS** - Print or type. Do not write in shaded areas; these are for FAA use only. Submit original only to an authorized FAA Representative. If additional space is required, use attachment. For special flight permits complete Sections II, VI, and VII as applicable.

I. AIRCRAFT DESCRIPTION

1. REGISTRATION MARK N51CA	2. AIRCRAFT BUILDER'S NAME *(Make)* Cessna	3. AIRCRAFT MODEL DESIGNATION 551	4. YR. MFR. 1992	FAA CODING
5. AIRCRAFT SERIAL NO. 551-0004	6. ENGINE BUILDER'S NAME *(Make)* UACL	7. ENGINE MODEL DESIGNATION JT 15D-4		
8. NUMBER OF ENGINES Two	9. PROPELLER BUILDER'S NAME *(Make)* N/A	10. PROPELLER MODEL DESIGNATION N/A	11. AIRCRAFT IS *(Check if applicable)* IMPORT	

II. CERTIFICATION REQUESTED

APPLICATION IS HEREBY MADE FOR: *(Check applicable items)*

A	1		*STANDARD AIRWORTHINESS CERTIFICATE (Indicate category)*		NORMAL / UTILITY / ACROBATIC / TRANSPORT / COMMUTER / BALLOON / OTHER
B		X	*SPECIAL AIRWORTHINESS CERTIFICATE (Check appropriate items)*		
	7		PRIMARY		
	2		LIMITED		
	5		PROVISIONAL *(Indicate class)*	1	CLASS I
				2	CLASS II
	3		RESTRICTED *(Indicate operation(s) to be conducted)*	1	AGRICULTURE AND PEST CONTROL; 2 AERIAL; 3 AERIAL ADVERTISING
				4	FOREST *(Wildlife conservation)*; 5 PATROLLING; 6 WEATHER CONTROL
				0	OTHER *(Specify)*
	4	X	EXPERIMENTAL *(Indicate operation(s) to be conducted)*	1 X	RESEARCH AND DEVELOPMENT; 2 AMATEUR BUILT; 3 EXHIBITION
				4	AIR RACING; 5 CREW TRAINING; 6 MARKET SURVEY
				0	TO SHOW COMPLIANCE WITH THE CFR; 7 OPERATING *(Primary Category)* KIT BUILT AIRCRAFT
	8		SPECIAL FLIGHT PERMIT *(Indicate operation to be conducted, then complete Section VI or VII as applicable on reverse side)*	1	FERRY FLIGHT FOR REPAIRS, ALTERATIONS, MAINTENANCE, OR STORAGE
				2	EVACUATE FROM AREA OF IMPENDING DANGER
				3	OPERATION IN EXCESS OF MAXIMUM CERTIFICATED TAKE-OFF WEIGHT
				4	DELIVERING OR EXPORTING; 5 PRODUCTION FLIGHT TESTING
				6	CUSTOMER DEMONSTRATION FLIGHTS
C			MULTIPLE AIRWORTHINESS CERTIFICATE *(Check ABOVE "Restricted Operation" and "Standard" or "Limited" as applicable.)*		

III. OWNER'S CERTIFICATION

A. REGISTERED OWNER (As shown on certificate of aircraft registration) — IF DEALER, CHECK HERE

NAME Cessna Aircraft Company	ADDRESS Wichita, Kansas 67277-7704

B. AIRCRAFT CERTIFICATION BASIS (Check applicable blocks and complete items as indicated)

	AIRCRAFT SPECIFICATION OR TYPE CERTIFICATE DATA SHEET *(Give No. and Revision No.)* N/A	X	AIRWORTHINESS DIRECTIVES *(Check if all applicable AD's complied with and give the number of the last AD SUPPLEMENT available in the biweekly series as of the date of application)* 96-23
	AIRCRAFT LISTING (Give page number(s)) N/A		SUPPLEMENTAL TYPE CERTIFICATE (List number of each STC incorporated) N/A

C. AIRCRAFT OPERATION AND MAINTENANCE RECORDS

X	CHECK IF RECORDS IN COMPLIANCE WITH 14 CFR section 91.417	TOTAL AIRFRAME HOURS 2509	3	EXPERIMENTAL ONLY *(Enter hours flown since last certificate issued or renewed)* 22.0

D. CERTIFICATION - I hereby certify that I am the registered owner (or his agent) of the aircraft described above, that the aircraft is registered with the Federal Aviation Administration in accordance with Title 49 of the United States Code 44101 et seq. and applicable Federal Aviation Regulations, and that the aircraft has been inspected and is airworthy and eligible for the airworthiness certificate requested.

DATE OF APPLICATION 11/25/96	NAME AND TITLE (Print or type) A.D. Smith, Quality Control Manager	SIGNATURE *A.D. Smith*

IV. INSPECTION AGENCY VERIFICATION

A. THE AIRCRAFT DESCRIBED ABOVE HAS BEEN INSPECTED AND FOUND AIRWORTHY BY: (Complete this section only if 14 CFR part 21.183(d) applies).

2	14 CFR part 121 CERTIFICATE HOLDER *(Give Certificate No.)*	3	CERTIFICATED MECHANIC *(Give Certificate No.)*
6	CERTIFICATED REPAIR STATION *(Give Certificate No.)*	5	AIRCRAFT MANUFACTURER (Give name or firm)

DATE	TITLE	SIGNATURE

V. FAA REPRESENTATIVE CERTIFICATION

(Check ALL applicable blocks in items A and B)

A. I find that the aircraft described in Section I or VII meets requirements for — THE CERTIFICATE REQUESTED; 4 AMENDMENT OR MODIFICATION OF CURRENT AIRWORTHINESS CERTIFICATE

E. Inspection for a special flight permit under Section VII was conducted by: FAA INSPECTOR; FAA DESIGNEE; CERTIFICATE HOLDER UNDER; 14 CFR part 65; 14 CFR part 121 OR 135; 14 CFR part 145

DATE	DISTRICT OFFICE	4	DESIGNEE'S SIGNATURE AND NO.	1	FAA INSPECTOR'S SIGNATURE

FAA Form 8130-6 (5-01) Supersedes Previous Edition NSN: 0052-00-024-7006

Figure 13. Sample FAA Form 8130-6, Application for a Primary Category Certificate — Aircraft Certificated Under Section 21.191(h) (Face Side Only)

O.M.B. No. 2120-0018

U.S. Department of Transportation Federal Aviation Administration	**APPLICATION FOR AIRWORTHINESS CERTIFICATE**	**INSTRUCTIONS** - Print or type. Do not write in shaded areas; these are for FAA use only. Submit original only to an authorized FAA Representative. If additional space is required, use attachment. For special flight permits complete Sections II, VI, and VII as applicable.

I. AIRCRAFT DESCRIPTION

1. REGISTRATION MARK N654GL	2. AIRCRAFT BUILDER'S NAME *(Make)* Night	3. AIRCRAFT MODEL DESIGNATION N7-xray	4. YR. MFR. 1996	FAA CODING
5. AIRCRAFT SERIAL NO. NX09	6. ENGINE BUILDER'S NAME *(Make)* TCM	7. ENGINE MODEL DESIGNATION 10-360-ES		
8. NUMBER OF ENGINES One	9. PROPELLER BUILDER'S NAME *(Make)* McCauley	10. PROPELLER MODEL DESIGNATION 2A34C 209	11. AIRCRAFT IS *(Check if applicable)* IMPORT	

II. CERTIFICATION REQUESTED

APPLICATION IS HEREBY MADE FOR: *(Check applicable items)*

A	1		*STANDARD AIRWORTHINESS CERTIFICATE (Indicate category)*		NORMAL / UTILITY / ACROBATIC / TRANSPORT / COMMUTER / BALLOON / OTHER
B		X	*SPECIAL AIRWORTHINESS CERTIFICATE (Check appropriate items)*		
	7		PRIMARY		
	2		LIMITED		
	5		PROVISIONAL *(Indicate class)*	1	CLASS I
				2	CLASS II
	3		RESTRICTED *(Indicate operation(s) to be conducted)*	1	AGRICULTURE AND PEST CONTROL; 2 AERIAL; 3 AERIAL ADVERTISING
				4	FOREST *(Wildlife conservation)*; 5 PATROLLING; 6 WEATHER CONTROL
				0	OTHER *(Specify)*
	4	X	EXPERIMENTAL *(Indicate operation(s) to be conducted)*	1	RESEARCH AND DEVELOPMENT; 2 AMATEUR BUILT; 3 EXHIBITION
				4	AIR RACING; 5 CREW TRAINING; 6 MARKET SURVEY
				0	TO SHOW COMPLIANCE WITH THE CFR; 7 X OPERATING *(Primary Category)* KIT BUILT AIRCRAFT
	8		SPECIAL FLIGHT PERMIT *(Indicate operation to be conducted, then complete Section VI or VII as applicable on reverse side)*	1	FERRY FLIGHT FOR REPAIRS, ALTERATIONS, MAINTENANCE, OR STORAGE
				2	EVACUATE FROM AREA OF IMPENDING DANGER
				3	OPERATION IN EXCESS OF MAXIMUM CERTIFICATED TAKE-OFF WEIGHT
				4	DELIVERING OR EXPORTING; 5 PRODUCTION FLIGHT TESTING
				6	CUSTOMER DEMONSTRATION FLIGHTS
C			MULTIPLE AIRWORTHINESS CERTIFICATE *(Check ABOVE "Restricted Operation" and "Standard" or "Limited" as applicable.)*		

III. OWNER'S CERTIFICATION

A. REGISTERED OWNER (As shown on certificate of aircraft registration) — IF DEALER, CHECK HERE

NAME Mary Test	ADDRESS 78 China Drive Jumping, Texas 89765

B. AIRCRAFT CERTIFICATION BASIS (Check applicable blocks and complete items as indicated)

X	AIRCRAFT SPECIFICATION OR TYPE CERTIFICATE DATA SHEET *(Give No. and Revision No.)* A1W1	X	AIRWORTHINESS DIRECTIVES *(Check if all applicable AD's complied with and give the number of the last AD SUPPLEMENT available in the biweekly series as of the date of application)* 96-23
	AIRCRAFT LISTING (Give page number(s)) N/A		SUPPLEMENTAL TYPE CERTIFICATE (List number of each STC incorporated) N/A

C. AIRCRAFT OPERATION AND MAINTENANCE RECORDS

X	CHECK IF RECORDS IN COMPLIANCE WITH 14 CFR section 91.417	TOTAL AIRFRAME HOURS 2.2	3	EXPERIMENTAL ONLY *(Enter hours flown since last certificate issued or renewed)* 0.0

D. CERTIFICATION - I hereby certify that I am the registered owner (or his agent) of the aircraft described above, that the aircraft is registered with the Federal Aviation Administration in accordance with Title 49 of the United States Code 44101 et seq. and applicable Federal Aviation Regulations, and that the aircraft has been inspected and is airworthy and eligible for the airworthiness certificate requested.

DATE OF APPLICATION 11/25/96	NAME AND TITLE (Print or type) Mary Test, Owner	SIGNATURE *Mary Test*

IV. INSPECTION AGENCY VERIFICATION

A. THE AIRCRAFT DESCRIBED ABOVE HAS BEEN INSPECTED AND FOUND AIRWORTHY BY: (Complete this section only if 14 CFR part 21 .183(d) applies).

2	14 CFR part 121 CERTIFICATE HOLDER *(Give Certificate No.)*	3	CERTIFICATED MECHANIC *(Give Certificate No.)*	6	CERTIFICATED REPAIR STATION *(Give Certificate No.)*
5	AIRCRAFT MANUFACTURER (Give name or firm)				

DATE	TITLE	SIGNATURE

V. FAA REPRESENTATIVE CERTIFICATION

(Check ALL applicable blocks in items A and B) A. I find that the aircraft described in Section I or VII meets requirements for		THE CERTIFICATE REQUESTED
	4	AMENDMENT OR MODIFICATION OF CURRENT AIRWORTHINESS CERTIFICATE
B. Inspection for a special flight permit under Section VII was conducted by:	FAA INSPECTOR	FAA DESIGNEE
	CERTIFICATE HOLDER UNDER	14 CFR part 65 / 14 CFR part 121 OR 135 / 14 CFR part 145

DATE	DISTRICT OFFICE	4	DESIGNEE'S SIGNATURE AND NO.	1	FAA INSPECTOR'S SIGNATURE

FAA Form 8130-6 (5-01) Supersedes Previous Edition — NSN: 0052-00-024-7006

21-12B

AC

Figure 14. Sample FAA Form 8130-6, Application for a Special Airworthiness Certificate — Special Flight Permit for Ferry Flight in Excess of Maximum Take-off Weight (Face Side)

O.M.B. No. 2120-0018

U.S. Department of Transportation
Federal Aviation Administration

APPLICATION FOR AIRWORTHINESS CERTIFICATE

INSTRUCTIONS - Print or type. Do not write in shaded areas; these are for FAA use only. Submit original only to an authorized FAA Representative. If additional space is required, use attachment. For special flight permits complete Sections II, VI, and VII as applicable.

I. AIRCRAFT DESCRIPTION

1. REGISTRATION MARK	2. AIRCRAFT BUILDER'S NAME *(Make)*	3. AIRCRAFT MODEL DESIGNATION	4. YR. MFR.	FAA CODING
5. AIRCRAFT SERIAL NO.	6. ENGINE BUILDER'S NAME *(Make)*	7. ENGINE MODEL DESIGNATION		
8. NUMBER OF ENGINES	9. PROPELLER BUILDER'S NAME *(Make)*	10. PROPELLER MODEL DESIGNATION	11. AIRCRAFT IS *(Check if applicable)*	IMPORT

II. CERTIFICATION REQUESTED

APPLICATION IS HEREBY MADE FOR: *(Check applicable items)*

A	1		*STANDARD AIRWORTHINESS CERTIFICATE (Indicate category)*	NORMAL / UTILITY / ACROBATIC / TRANSPORT / COMMUTER / BALLOON / OTHER		
B		X	*SPECIAL AIRWORTHINESS CERTIFICATE (Check appropriate items)*			
	7		PRIMARY			
	2		LIMITED			
	5		PROVISIONAL *(Indicate class)*	1		CLASS I
				2		CLASS II
	3		RESTRICTED *(Indicate operation(s) to be conducted)*	1		AGRICULTURE AND PEST CONTROL; 2 AERIAL; 3 AERIAL ADVERTISING
				4		FOREST *(Wildlife conservation)*; 5 PATROLLING; 6 WEATHER CONTROL
				0		OTHER *(Specify)*
	4		EXPERIMENTAL *(Indicate operation(s) to be conducted)*	1		RESEARCH AND DEVELOPMENT; 2 AMATEUR BUILT; 3 EXHIBITION
				4		AIR RACING; 5 CREW TRAINING; 6 MARKET SURVEY
				0		TO SHOW COMPLIANCE WITH THE CFR; 7 OPERATING *(Primary Category)* KIT BUILT AIRCRAFT
	8	X	SPECIAL FLIGHT PERMIT *(Indicate operation to be conducted, then complete Section VI or VII as applicable on reverse side)*	1		FERRY FLIGHT FOR REPAIRS, ALTERATIONS, MAINTENANCE, OR STORAGE
				2		EVACUATE FROM AREA OF IMPENDING DANGER
				3	X	OPERATION IN EXCESS OF MAXIMUM CERTIFICATED TAKE-OFF WEIGHT
				4		DELIVERING OR EXPORTING; 5 PRODUCTION FLIGHT TESTING
				6		CUSTOMER DEMONSTRATION FLIGHTS
C			MULTIPLE AIRWORTHINESS CERTIFICATE *(Check ABOVE "Restricted Operation" and "Standard" or "Limited" as applicable.)*			

III. OWNER'S CERTIFICATION

A. REGISTERED OWNER (As shown on certificate of aircraft registration) — IF DEALER, CHECK HERE ———

NAME	ADDRESS

B. AIRCRAFT CERTIFICATION BASIS (Check applicable blocks and complete items as indicated)

AIRCRAFT SPECIFICATION OR TYPE CERTIFICATE DATA SHEET *(Give No. and Revision No.)*	AIRWORTHINESS DIRECTIVES *(Check if all applicable AD's complied with and give the number of the last AD SUPPLEMENT available in the biweekly series as of the date of application)*
AIRCRAFT LISTING (Give page number(s))	SUPPLEMENTAL TYPE CERTIFICATE (List number of each STC incorporated)

C. AIRCRAFT OPERATION AND MAINTENANCE RECORDS

CHECK IF RECORDS IN COMPLIANCE WITH 14 CFR section 91.417	TOTAL AIRFRAME HOURS	3 — EXPERIMENTAL ONLY *(Enter hours flown since last certificate issued or renewed)*

D. CERTIFICATION - I hereby certify that I am the registered owner (or his agent) of the aircraft described above, that the aircraft is registered with the Federal Aviation Administration in accordance with Title 49 of the United States Code 44101 et seq. and applicable Federal Aviation Regulations, and that the aircraft has been inspected and is airworthy and eligible for the airworthiness certificate requested.

DATE OF APPLICATION	NAME AND TITLE (Print or type)	SIGNATURE

IV. INSPECTION AGENCY VERIFICATION

A. THE AIRCRAFT DESCRIBED ABOVE HAS BEEN INSPECTED AND FOUND AIRWORTHY BY: (Complete this section only if 14 CFR part 21.183(d) applies).

2 — 14 CFR part 121 CERTIFICATE HOLDER *(Give Certificate No.)*	3 — CERTIFICATED MECHANIC *(Give Certificate No.)*	6 — CERTIFICATED REPAIR STATION *(Give Certificate No.)*
5 — AIRCRAFT MANUFACTURER (Give name or firm)		
DATE	TITLE	SIGNATURE

V. FAA REPRESENTATIVE CERTIFICATION

(Check ALL applicable blocks in items A and B)
A. I find that the aircraft described in Section I or VII meets requirements for

	THE CERTIFICATE REQUESTED
4	AMENDMENT OR MODIFICATION OF CURRENT AIRWORTHINESS CERTIFICATE

B. Inspection for a special flight permit under Section VII was conducted by:

FAA INSPECTOR	FAA DESIGNEE		
CERTIFICATE HOLDER UNDER	14 CFR part 65	14 CFR part 121 OR 135	14 CFR part 145

DATE	DISTRICT OFFICE	4 — DESIGNEE'S SIGNATURE AND NO.	1 — FAA INSPECTOR'S SIGNATURE

FAA Form 8130-6 (5-01) Supersedes Previous Edition

NSN: 0052-00-024-7006

Figure 14. Sample FAA Form 8130-6, Application for a Special Airworthiness Certificate — Special Flight Permit for Ferry Flight in Excess of Maximum Take-off Weight (Reverse Side) (cont'd)

VI. PRODUCTION FLIGHT TESTING

A. MANUFACTURER

NAME	ADDRESS

B. PRODUCTION BASIS *(Check applicable item)*

- [ ] PRODUCTION CERTIFICATE *(Give production certificate number)*
- [ ] TYPE CERTIFICATE ONLY
- [ ] APPROVED PRODUCTION INSPECTION SYSTEM

C. GIVE QUANTITY OF CERTIFICATES REQUIRED FOR OPERATING NEEDS ______

DATE OF APPLICATION	NAME AND TITLE *(Print or type)*	SIGNATURE

VII. SPECIAL FLIGHT PERMIT PURPOSES OTHER THAN PRODUCTION FLIGHT TEST

A. DESCRIPTION OF AIRCRAFT

REGISTERED OWNER Weldon H. Jackson	ADDRESS P.O. Box 945, Maui, Hawaii 96782
BUILDER (Make) Piper	MODEL PA 23-250
SERIAL NUMBER 27-647	REGISTRATION MARK N4588P

B. DESCRIPTION OF FLIGHT — CUSTOMER DEMONSTRATION FLIGHTS [ ] *(Check if applicable)*

FROM El Paso Texas	TO Maui, Hawaii	
VIA San Jose, California	DEPARTURE DATE 11/30/96	DURATION 30 Days

C. CREW REQUIRED TO OPERATE THE AIRCRAFT AND ITS EQUIPMENT

X	PILOT	X	CO-PILOT		FLIGHT ENGINEER	OTHER *(Specify)*

D. THE AIRCRAFT DOES NOT MEET THE APPLICABLE AIRWORTHINESS REQUIREMENTS AS FOLLOWS:

Temporary Ferry Fuel Ststem installed in accordance with FAA Form 337, "Major Repair and Alteration" dated 12/88.

Gross weight not to exceed 110% of certified maximun weight.

E. THE FOLLOWING RESTRICTIONS ARE CONSIDERED NECESSARY FOR SAFE OPERATION: *(Use attachment if necessary)*

1. When the aircraft is in an overweight condition, the design cruise speed should not exceed 162 MPH.
2. The fuel quantity should not exceed 140 gallons in the forward tank and 35 gallons in the aft tank.
3. The sequence of use of the ferry tanks shall be as shown by a temporary placard installed in full view of the pilot.

F. CERTIFICATION - I hereby certify that I am the registered owner (or his agent) of the aircraft described above; that the aircraft is registered with the Federal Aviation Administration in accordance with Title 49 of the United States Code 44101 et seq. and applicable Federal Aviation Regulations; and that the aircraft has been inspected and is airworthy for the flight described.

DATE	NAME AND TITLE *(Print or type)*	SIGNATURE
11/25/96	Don Brown, Agent	Don Brown

VIII. AIRWORTHINESS DOCUMENTATION (FAA/DESIGNEE use only)

	A. Operating Limitations and Markings in Compliance with 14 CFR section 91.9, as Applicable		G. Statement of Conformity, FAA Form 8130-9 *(Attach when required)*
	B. Current Operating Limitations Attached		H. Foreign Airworthiness Certification for Import Aircraft *(Attach when required)*
	C. Data, Drawings, Photographs, etc. *(Attach when required)*		I. Previous Airworthiness Certificate Issued in Accordance with
	D. Current Weight and Balance Information Available in Aircraft		14 CFR Section ______ CAR ______ *(Original Attached)*
	E. Major Repair and Alteration, FAA Form 337 *(Attach when required)*		J. Current Airworthiness Certificate Issued in Accordance with
	F. This inspection Recorded in Aircraft Records		14 CFR Section *(Copy attached)*

FAA Form 8130-6 (5-01) Supersedes Previous Edition

NSN: 0052-00-024-7006

21-12B

AC

Figure 15. Sample FAA Form 8130-6, Application for a Special Airworthiness Certificate — Special Flight Permit for Ferry Flight (Face Side)

O.M.B. No. 2120-0018

U.S. Department of Transportation
Federal Aviation Administration

APPLICATION FOR AIRWORTHINESS CERTIFICATE

INSTRUCTIONS - Print or type. Do not write in shaded areas; these are for FAA use only. Submit original only to an authorized FAA Representative. If additional space is required, use attachment. For special flight permits complete Sections II, VI, and VII as applicable.

I. AIRCRAFT DESCRIPTION

1. REGISTRATION MARK	2. AIRCRAFT BUILDER'S NAME *(Make)*	3. AIRCRAFT MODEL DESIGNATION	4. YR. MFR.	FAA CODING
5. AIRCRAFT SERIAL NO.	6. ENGINE BUILDER'S NAME *(Make)*	7. ENGINE MODEL DESIGNATION		
8. NUMBER OF ENGINES	9. PROPELLER BUILDER'S NAME *(Make)*	10. PROPELLER MODEL DESIGNATION	11. AIRCRAFT IS *(Check if applicable)*	IMPORT

II. CERTIFICATION REQUESTED

APPLICATION IS HEREBY MADE FOR: *(Check applicable items)*

A	1		*STANDARD AIRWORTHINESS CERTIFICATE (Indicate category)*	NORMAL	UTILITY	ACROBATIC	TRANSPORT	COMMUTER / BALLOON / OTHER
B		X	*SPECIAL AIRWORTHINESS CERTIFICATE (Check appropriate items)*					
	7		PRIMARY					
	2		LIMITED					
	5		PROVISIONAL *(Indicate class)*	1	CLASS I			
				2	CLASS II			
	3		RESTRICTED *(Indicate operation(s) to be conducted)*	1	AGRICULTURE AND PEST CONTROL	2 AERIAL	3 AERIAL ADVERTISING	
				4	FOREST *(Wildlife conservation)*	5 PATROLLING	6 WEATHER CONTROL	
				0	OTHER *(Specify)*			
	4		EXPERIMENTAL *(Indicate operation(s) to be conducted)*	1	RESEARCH AND DEVELOPMENT	2 AMATEUR BUILT	3 EXHIBITION	
				4	AIR RACING	5 CREW TRAINING	6 MARKET SURVEY	
				0	TO SHOW COMPLIANCE WITH THE CFR	7 OPERATING *(Primary Category)* KIT BUILT AIRCRAFT		
	8	X	SPECIAL FLIGHT PERMIT *(Indicate operation to be conducted, then complete Section VI or VII as applicable on reverse side)*	1 X	FERRY FLIGHT FOR REPAIRS, ALTERATIONS, MAINTENANCE, OR STORAGE			
				2	EVACUATE FROM AREA OF IMPENDING DANGER			
				3	OPERATION IN EXCESS OF MAXIMUM CERTIFICATED TAKE-OFF WEIGHT			
				4	DELIVERING OR EXPORTING	5 PRODUCTION FLIGHT TESTING		
				6	CUSTOMER DEMONSTRATION FLIGHTS			
C			MULTIPLE AIRWORTHINESS CERTIFICATE *(Check ABOVE "Restricted Operation" and "Standard" or "Limited" as applicable.)*					

III. OWNER'S CERTIFICATION

A. REGISTERED OWNER (As shown on certificate of aircraft registration) — IF DEALER, CHECK HERE

NAME	ADDRESS

B. AIRCRAFT CERTIFICATION BASIS (Check applicable blocks and complete items as indicated)

AIRCRAFT SPECIFICATION OR TYPE CERTIFICATE DATA SHEET *(Give No. and Revision No.)*	AIRWORTHINESS DIRECTIVES *(Check if all applicable AD's complied with and give the number of the last AD SUPPLEMENT available in the biweekly series as of the date of application)*
AIRCRAFT LISTING (Give page number(s))	SUPPLEMENTAL TYPE CERTIFICATE (List number of each STC incorporated)

C. AIRCRAFT OPERATION AND MAINTENANCE RECORDS

CHECK IF RECORDS IN COMPLIANCE WITH 14 CFR section 91.417	TOTAL AIRFRAME HOURS	3	EXPERIMENTAL ONLY *(Enter hours flown since last certificate issued or renewed)* N/A

D. CERTIFICATION - I hereby certify that I am the registered owner (or his agent) of the aircraft described above, that the aircraft is registered with the Federal Aviation Administration in accordance with Title 49 of the United States Code 44101 et seq. and applicable Federal Aviation Regulations, and that the aircraft has been inspected and is airworthy and eligible for the airworthiness certificate requested.

DATE OF APPLICATION	NAME AND TITLE (Print or type)	SIGNATURE

IV. INSPECTION AGENCY VERIFICATION

A. THE AIRCRAFT DESCRIBED ABOVE HAS BEEN INSPECTED AND FOUND AIRWORTHY BY: (Complete this section only if 14 CFR part 21.183(d) applies).

2	14 CFR part 121 CERTIFICATE HOLDER *(Give Certificate No.)*	3	CERTIFICATED MECHANIC *(Give Certificate No.)*	6	CERTIFICATED REPAIR STATION *(Give Certificate No.)*
5	AIRCRAFT MANUFACTURER (Give name or firm)				

DATE	TITLE	SIGNATURE

V. FAA REPRESENTATIVE CERTIFICATION

(Check ALL applicable blocks in items A and B)

A. I find that the aircraft described in Section I or VII meets requirements for		THE CERTIFICATE REQUESTED	
	4	AMENDMENT OR MODIFICATION OF CURRENT AIRWORTHINESS CERTIFICATE	
B. Inspection for a special flight permit under Section VII was conducted by:		FAA INSPECTOR	FAA DESIGNEE
		CERTIFICATE HOLDER UNDER	14 CFR part 65 / 14 CFR part 121 OR 135 / 14 CFR part 145

DATE	DISTRICT OFFICE	4	DESIGNEE'S SIGNATURE AND NO.	1	FAA INSPECTOR'S SIGNATURE

FAA Form 8130-6 (5-01) Supersedes Previous Edition

NSN: 0052-00-024-7006

Figure 15. Sample FAA Form 8130-6, Application for a Special Airworthiness Certificate — Special Flight Permit for Ferry Flight (Reverse Side) (cont'd)

VI. PRODUCTION FLIGHT TESTING

A. MANUFACTURER		
NAME	ADDRESS	
B. PRODUCTION BASIS *(Check applicable item)*		
☐ PRODUCTION CERTIFICATE *(Give production certificate number)*		
☐ TYPE CERTIFICATE ONLY		
☐ APPROVED PRODUCTION INSPECTION SYSTEM		
C. GIVE QUANTITY OF CERTIFICATES REQUIRED FOR OPERATING NEEDS ______		
DATE OF APPLICATION	NAME AND TITLE *(Print or type)*	SIGNATURE

VII. SPECIAL FLIGHT PERMIT PURPOSES OTHER THAN PRODUCTION FLIGHT TEST

A. DESCRIPTION OF AIRCRAFT

REGISTERED OWNER Robert F. Turner	ADDRESS 4623 Mountainview Drive, Waterloo, Iowa 50701	
BUILDER (Make) Bellancia	MODEL 14-19-2	
SERIAL NUMBER 4099	REGISTRATION MARK N254B	
B. DESCRIPTION OF FLIGHT	CUSTOMER DEMONSTRATION FLIGHTS ☐ *(Check if applicable)*	
FROM Waterloo, Iowa	TO Des Moines, Iowa	
VIA Direct	DEPARTURE DATE 11/30/96	DURATION 12/03/96

C. CREW REQUIRED TO OPERATE THE AIRCRAFT AND ITS EQUIPMENT

X PILOT ☐ CO-PILOT ☐ FLIGHT ENGINEER ☐ OTHER *(Specify)*

D. THE AIRCRAFT DOES NOT MEET THE APPLICABLE AIRWORTHINESS REQUIREMENTS AS FOLLOWS:

Aircraft damaged in landing accident. Temporary repairs have been made for one flight to repair shop at Des Moines - Dodge Airport, where permanent repairs will be made.

E. THE FOLLOWING RESTRICTIONS ARE CONSIDERED NECESSARY FOR SAFE OPERATION: *(Use attachment if necessary)*

1. Airspeed should not exceed 115 MPH.
2. Landing gear should not be retracted.
3. No passengers or cargo should be carried.

F. CERTIFICATION - I hereby certify that I am the registered owner (or his agent) of the aircraft described above; that the aircraft is registered with the Federal Aviation Administration in accordance with Title 49 of the United States Code 44101 et seq. and applicable Federal Aviation Regulations; and that the aircraft has been inspected and is airworthy for the flight described.

DATE	NAME AND TITLE *(Print or type)*	SIGNATURE
11/25/96	Robert F. Turner, Owner	Robert F. Turner

VIII. AIRWORTHINESS DOCUMENTATION (FAA/DESIGNEE use only)

☐ A. Operating Limitations and Markings in Compliance with 14 CFR section 91.9, as Applicable	☐ G. Statement of Conformity, FAA Form 8130-9 *(Attach when required)*
☐ B. Current Operating Limitations Attached	☐ H. Foreign Airworthiness Certification for Import Aircraft *(Attach when required)*
☐ C. Data, Drawings, Photographs, etc. *(Attach when required)*	☐ I. Previous Airworthiness Certificate Issued in Accordance with
☐ D. Current Weight and Balance Information Available in Aircraft	14 CFR Section ______ CAR ______ *(Original Attached)*
☐ E. Major Repair and Alteration, FAA Form 337 *(Attach when required)*	☐ J. Current Airworthiness Certificate Issued in Accordance with
☐ F. This inspection Recorded in Aircraft Records	14 CFR Section ______ *(Copy attached)*

FAA Form 8130-6 (5-01) Supersedes Previous Edition

NSN: 0052-00-024-7006

Figure 16. Sample FAA Form 8130-6, Application for a Special Airworthiness Certificate — Special Flight Permit for Production Flight Testing (Face Side)

O.M.B. No. 2120-0018

U.S. Department of Transportation
Federal Aviation Administration

APPLICATION FOR AIRWORTHINESS CERTIFICATE

INSTRUCTIONS - Print or type. Do not write in shaded areas; these are for FAA use only. Submit original only to an authorized FAA Representative. If additional space is required, use attachment. For special flight permits complete Sections II, VI, and VII as applicable.

I. AIRCRAFT DESCRIPTION

1. REGISTRATION MARK	2. AIRCRAFT BUILDER'S NAME *(Make)*	3. AIRCRAFT MODEL DESIGNATION	4. YR. MFR.	FAA CODING
5. AIRCRAFT SERIAL NO.	6. ENGINE BUILDER'S NAME *(Make)*	7. ENGINE MODEL DESIGNATION		
8. NUMBER OF ENGINES	9. PROPELLER BUILDER'S NAME *(Make)*	10. PROPELLER MODEL DESIGNATION	11. AIRCRAFT IS *(Check if applicable)*	IMPORT

II. CERTIFICATION REQUESTED

APPLICATION IS HEREBY MADE FOR: *(Check applicable items)*

A	1		*STANDARD AIRWORTHINESS CERTIFICATE (Indicate category)*	NORMAL	UTILITY	ACROBATIC	TRANSPORT	COMMUTER	BALLOON	OTHER
B		X	*SPECIAL AIRWORTHINESS CERTIFICATE (Check appropriate items)*							
	7		PRIMARY							
	2		LIMITED							
	5		PROVISIONAL *(Indicate class)*	1	CLASS I					
				2	CLASS II					
	3		RESTRICTED *(Indicate operation(s) to be conducted)*	1	AGRICULTURE AND PEST CONTROL	2	AERIAL	3	AERIAL ADVERTISING	
				4	FOREST *(Wildlife conservation)*	5	PATROLLING	6	WEATHER CONTROL	
				0	OTHER *(Specify)*					
	4		EXPERIMENTAL *(Indicate operation(s) to be conducted)*	1	RESEARCH AND DEVELOPMENT	2	AMATEUR BUILT	3	EXHIBITION	
				4	AIR RACING	5	CREW TRAINING	6	MARKET SURVEY	
				0	TO SHOW COMPLIANCE WITH THE CFR	7	OPERATING *(Primary Category)* KIT BUILT AIRCRAFT			
	8	x	SPECIAL FLIGHT PERMIT *(Indicate operation to be conducted, then complete Section VI or VII as applicable on reverse side)*	1	FERRY FLIGHT FOR REPAIRS, ALTERATIONS, MAINTENANCE, OR STORAGE					
				2	EVACUATE FROM AREA OF IMPENDING DANGER					
				3	OPERATION IN EXCESS OF MAXIMUM CERTIFICATED TAKE-OFF WEIGHT					
				4	DELIVERING OR EXPORTING	5	x	PRODUCTION FLIGHT TESTING		
				6	CUSTOMER DEMONSTRATION FLIGHTS					
C	6		MULTIPLE AIRWORTHINESS CERTIFICATE *(Check ABOVE "Restricted Operation" and "Standard" or "Limited" as applicable.)*							

III. OWNER'S CERTIFICATION

A. REGISTERED OWNER (As shown on certificate of aircraft registration) — IF DEALER, CHECK HERE

NAME	ADDRESS

B. AIRCRAFT CERTIFICATION BASIS (Check applicable blocks and complete items as indicated)

	AIRCRAFT SPECIFICATION OR TYPE CERTIFICATE DATA SHEET *(Give No. and Revision No.)*		AIRWORTHINESS DIRECTIVES *(Check if all applicable AD's complied with and give the number of the last AD SUPPLEMENT available in the biweekly series as of the date of application)*
	AIRCRAFT LISTING (Give page number(s))		SUPPLEMENTAL TYPE CERTIFICATE (List number of each STC incorporated)

C. AIRCRAFT OPERATION AND MAINTENANCE RECORDS

	CHECK IF RECORDS IN COMPLIANCE WITH 14 CFR section 91.417	TOTAL AIRFRAME HOURS	3	EXPERIMENTAL ONLY *(Enter hours flown since last certificate issued or renewed)*

D. CERTIFICATION - I hereby certify that I am the registered owner (or his agent) of the aircraft described above, that the aircraft is registered with the Federal Aviation Administration in accordance with Title 49 of the United States Code 44101 et seq. and applicable Federal Aviation Regulations, and that the aircraft has been inspected and is airworthy and eligible for the airworthiness certificate requested.

DATE OF APPLICATION	NAME AND TITLE (Print or type)	SIGNATURE

IV. INSPECTION AGENCY VERIFICATION

A. THE AIRCRAFT DESCRIBED ABOVE HAS BEEN INSPECTED AND FOUND AIRWORTHY BY: (Complete this section only if 14 CFR part 21.183(d) applies).

2		14 CFR part 121 CERTIFICATE HOLDER *(Give Certificate No.)*	3		CERTIFICATED MECHANIC *(Give Certificate No.)*	6	CERTIFICATED REPAIR STATION *(Give Certificate No.)*
5		AIRCRAFT MANUFACTURER (Give name or firm)					

DATE	TITLE	SIGNATURE

V. FAA REPRESENTATIVE CERTIFICATION

(Check ALL applicable blocks in items A and B)

A. I find that the aircraft described in Section I or VII meets requirements for			THE CERTIFICATE REQUESTED
	4		AMENDMENT OR MODIFICATION OF CURRENT AIRWORTHINESS CERTIFICATE

B. Inspection for a special flight permit under Section VII was conducted by:		FAA INSPECTOR		FAA DESIGNEE	
		CERTIFICATE HOLDER UNDER	14 CFR part 65	14 CFR part 121 OR 135	14 CFR part 145

DATE	DISTRICT OFFICE	4	DESIGNEE'S SIGNATURE AND NO.	1	FAA INSPECTOR'S SIGNATURE

FAA Form 8130-6 (5-01) Supersedes Previous Edition — NSN: 0052-00-024-7006

Figure 16. Sample FAA Form 8130-6, Application for a Special Airworthiness Certificate — Special Flight Permit for Production Flight Testing (Reverse Side) (cont'd)

VI. PRODUCTION FLIGHT TESTING

A. MANUFACTURER

NAME	ADDRESS
ABC Aircraft Company	509 Moreland Blvd, Paloma New York 20101

B. PRODUCTION BASIS *(Check applicable item)*

X	PRODUCTION CERTIFICATE *(Give production certificate number)* PC# 700
	TYPE CERTIFICATE ONLY
	APPROVED PRODUCTION INSPECTION SYSTEM

C. GIVE QUANTITY OF CERTIFICATES REQUIRED FOR OPERATING NEEDS ____________

DATE OF APPLICATION	NAME AND TITLE *(Print or type)*	SIGNATURE
11/25/96	John C. Burns, President	*John C. Burns*

VII. SPECIAL FLIGHT PERMIT PURPOSES OTHER THAN PRODUCTION FLIGHT TEST

A. DESCRIPTION OF AIRCRAFT

REGISTERED OWNER	ADDRESS
BUILDER (Make)	MODEL
SERIAL NUMBER	REGISTRATION MARK

B. DESCRIPTION OF FLIGHT CUSTOMER DEMONSTRATION FLIGHTS ☐ *(Check if applicable)*

FROM	TO	
VIA	DEPARTURE DATE	DURATION

C. CREW REQUIRED TO OPERATE THE AIRCRAFT AND ITS EQUIPMENT

☐ PILOT ☐ CO-PILOT ☐ FLIGHT ENGINEER ☐ OTHER *(Specify)*

D. THE AIRCRAFT DOES NOT MEET THE APPLICABLE AIRWORTHINESS REQUIREMENTS AS FOLLOWS:

E. THE FOLLOWING RESTRICTIONS ARE CONSIDERED NECESSARY FOR SAFE OPERATION: *(Use attachment if necessary)*

F. CERTIFICATION - I hereby certify that I am the registered owner (or his agent) of the aircraft described above; that the aircraft is registered with the Federal Aviation Administration in accordance with Title 49 of the United States Code 44101 et seq. and applicable Federal Aviation Regulations; and that the aircraft has been inspected and is airworthy for the flight described.

DATE	NAME AND TITLE *(Print or type)*	SIGNATURE

VIII. AIRWORTHINESS DOCUMENTATION (FAA/DESIGNEE use only)

	A. Operating Limitations and Markings in Compliance with 14 CFR section 91.9, as Applicable		G. Statement of Conformity, FAA Form 8130-9 *(Attach when required)*
	B. Current Operating Limitations Attached		H. Foreign Airworthiness Certification for Import Aircraft *(Attach when required)*
	C. Data, Drawings, Photographs, etc. *(Attach when required)*		I. Previous Airworthiness Certificate Issued in Accordance with
	D. Current Weight and Balance Information Available in Aircraft		14 CFR Section ____________ CAR ____________ *(Original Attached)*
	E. Major Repair and Alteration, FAA Form 337 *(Attach when required)*		J. Current Airworthiness Certificate Issued in Accordance with
	F. This inspection Recorded in Aircraft Records		14 CFR Section *(Copy attached)*

FAA Form 8130-6 (5-01) Supersedes Previous Edition

NSN: 0052-00-024-7006

Figure 17. Sample FAA Form 8130-6, Application for a Multiple Airworthiness Certificate (Face Side Only)

Form Approved
O.M.B. No. 2120-0018

U.S. Department of Transportation
Federal Aviation Administration

APPLICATION FOR AIRWORTHINESS CERTIFICATE

INSTRUCTIONS - Print or type. Do not write in shaded areas; these are for FAA use only. Submit original only to an authorized FAA Representative. If additional space is required, use attachment. For special flight permits complete Sections II, VI, and VII as applicable.

I. AIRCRAFT DESCRIPTION

1. REGISTRATION MARK N54321	2. AIRCRAFT BUILDER'S NAME *(Make)* Piper	3. AIRCRAFT MODEL DESIGNATION PA18A-150	4. YR. MFR. 1951	FAA CODING
5. AIRCRAFT SERIAL NO. 18-3792	6. ENGINE BUILDER'S NAME *(Make)* Lycoming	7. ENGINE MODEL DESIGNATION 0-320		
8. NUMBER OF ENGINES One	9. PROPELLER BUILDER'S NAME *(Make)* Sensenich	10. PROPELLER MODEL DESIGNATION M74DM	11. AIRCRAFT IS *(Check if applicable)* IMPORT	

II. CERTIFICATION REQUESTED

APPLICATION IS HEREBY MADE FOR: *(Check applicable items)*

A	1	X	*STANDARD AIRWORTHINESS CERTIFICATE (Indicate category)*	X NORMAL, X UTILITY, ACROBATIC, TRANSPORT, COMMUTER, BALLOON, OTHER	
B			*SPECIAL AIRWORTHINESS CERTIFICATE (Check appropriate items)*		
	7		PRIMARY		
	2		LIMITED		
	5		PROVISIONAL *(Indicate class)*	1 CLASS I; 2 CLASS II	
	3	X	RESTRICTED *(Indicate operation(s) to be conducted)*	1 x AGRICULTURE AND PEST CONTROL; 2 AERIAL; 3 AERIAL ADVERTISING; 4 FOREST *(Wildlife conservation)*; 5 PATROLLING; 6 WEATHER CONTROL; 0 OTHER *(Specify)*	
	4		EXPERIMENTAL *(Indicate operation(s) to be conducted)*	7 RESEARCH AND DEVELOPMENT; 2 AMATEUR BUILT; 3 EXHIBITION; 4 AIR RACING; 5 CREW TRAINING; 6 MARKET SURVEY; 0 TO SHOW COMPLIANCE WITH THE CFR; 7 OPERATING *(Primary Category)* KIT BUILT AIRCRAFT	
	8		SPECIAL FLIGHT PERMIT *(Indicate operation to be conducted, then complete Section VI or VII as applicable on reverse side)*	1 FERRY FLIGHT FOR REPAIRS, ALTERATIONS, MAINTENANCE, OR STORAGE; 2 EVACUATE FROM AREA OF IMPENDING DANGER; 3 OPERATION IN EXCESS OF MAXIMUM CERTIFICATED TAKE-OFF WEIGHT; 4 DELIVERING OR EXPORTING; 5 PRODUCTION FLIGHT TESTING; 5 CUSTOMER DEMONSTRATION FLIGHTS	
C		X	MULTIPLE AIRWORTHINESS CERTIFICATE *(Check ABOVE "Restricted Operation" and "Standard" or "Limited" as applicable.)*		

III. OWNER'S CERTIFICATION

A. REGISTERED OWNER (As shown on certificate of aircraft registration) — IF DEALER, CHECK HERE ______

NAME North Central Airplane Corp.	ADDRESS Rt. 1 Box 502 Cutback, Minn. 43692

B. AIRCRAFT CERTIFICATION BASIS (Check applicable blocks and complete items as indicated)

X	AIRCRAFT SPECIFICATION OR TYPE CERTIFICATE DATA SHEET *(Give No. and Revision No.)* 1A2 Rev. 33, AR-7 Rev. 9	X	AIRWORTHINESS DIRECTIVES *(Check if all applicable AD's complied with and give the number of the last AD SUPPLEMENT available in the biweekly series as of the date of application)* 96-23
	AIRCRAFT LISTING (Give page number(s)) N/A		SUPPLEMENTAL TYPE CERTIFICATE (List number of each STC incorporated)

C. AIRCRAFT OPERATION AND MAINTENANCE RECORDS

X	CHECK IF RECORDS IN COMPLIANCE WITH 14 CFR section 91.417	TOTAL AIRFRAME HOURS 12,050	3	EXPERIMENTAL ONLY *(Enter hours flown since last certificate issued or renewed)* N/A

D. CERTIFICATION - I hereby certify that I am the registered owner (or his agent) of the aircraft described above, that the aircraft is registered with the Federal Aviation Administration in accordance with Title 49 of the United States Code 44101 et seq. and applicable Federal Aviation Regulations, and that the aircraft has been inspected and is airworthy and eligible for the airworthiness certificate requested.

DATE OF APPLICATION 11/21/96	NAME AND TITLE (Print or type) John Jones, President	SIGNATURE *John Jones*

IV. INSPECTION AGENCY VERIFICATION

A. THE AIRCRAFT DESCRIBED ABOVE HAS BEEN INSPECTED AND FOUND AIRWORTHY BY: (Complete this section only if 14 CFR part 21.183(d) applies).

2	14 CFR part 121 CERTIFICATE HOLDER *(Give Certificate No.)*	3	CERTIFICATED MECHANIC *(Give Certificate No.)*	6	CERTIFICATED REPAIR STATION *(Give Certificate No.)*
5	AIRCRAFT MANUFACTURER (Give name or firm)				

DATE	TITLE	SIGNATURE

V. FAA REPRESENTATIVE CERTIFICATION

(Check ALL applicable blocks in items A and B)
A. I find that the aircraft described in Section I or VII meets requirements for

	THE CERTIFICATE REQUESTED
4	AMENDMENT OR MODIFICATION OF CURRENT AIRWORTHINESS CERTIFICATE

B. Inspection for a special flight permit under Section VII was conducted by:

FAA INSPECTOR	FAA DESIGNEE		
CERTIFICATE HOLDER UNDER	14 CFR part 65	14 CFR part 121 OR 135	14 CFR part 145

DATE	DISTRICT OFFICE	4	DESIGNEE'S SIGNATURE AND NO.	1	FAA INSPECTOR'S SIGNATURE

FAA Form 8130-6 (5-01) Supersedes Previous Edition

NSN: 0052-00-024-7006

U.S. Department
of Transportation
Federal Aviation
Administration

Advisory Circular 39-7C

Subject: **Airworthiness Directives**
Date: 11/16/95 Initiated by: AFS-340

1. **PURPOSE.** This advisory circular (AC) provides guidance and information to owners and operators of aircraft concerning their responsibility for complying with airworthiness directives (AD) and recording AD compliance in the appropriate maintenance records.

2. **CANCELLATION.** AC 39-7B, Airworthiness Directives, dated April 8, 1987, is canceled.

3. **PRINCIPAL CHANGES.** References to specific Federal Aviation Regulations have been updated and text reworded for clarification throughout this document.

4. **RELATED FEDERAL AVIATION REGULATIONS.** 14 Code of Federal Regulations (CFR) part 39; part 43, §§ 43.9 and 43.11; part 91, §§ 91.403, 91.417, and 91.419.

5. **BACKGROUND.** The authority for the role of the Federal Aviation Administration (FAA) regarding the promotion of safe flight for civil aircraft may be found generally at Title 49 of the United State Code (USC) § 44701 et. seq. (formerly, Title VI of the Federal Aviation Act of 1958 and related statutes). One of the ways the FAA has implemented its authority is through 14 CFR part 39, Airworthiness Directives. Pursuant to its authority, the FAA issues AD's when an unsafe condition is found to exist in a product (aircraft, aircraft engine, propeller, or appliance) of a particular type design. AD's are used by the FAA to notify aircraft owners and operators of unsafe conditions and to require their correction. AD's prescribe the conditions and limitations, including inspection, repair, or alteration under which the product may continue to be operated. AD's are authorized under part 39 and issued in accordance with the public rulemaking procedures of the Administrative Procedure Act, 5 USC 553, and FAA procedures in part 11.

6. **AD CATEGORIES.** AD's are published in the Federal Register as amendments to part 39. Depending on the urgency, AD's are issued as follows:

   a. Normally a notice of proposed rulemaking (NPRM) for an AD is issued and published in the Federal Register when an unsafe condition is found to exist in a product. Interested persons are invited to comment on the NPRM by submitting such written data, views, contained in the notice may be changed or withdrawn in light of comments received. When the final rule, resulting from the NPRM, is adopted, it is published in the Federal Register, printed and distributed by first class mail to the registered owners and certain known operators of the product(s) affected.

39-7C

AC

b. Emergency AD's. AD's of an urgent nature may be adopted without prior notice (without an NPRM) under emergency procedures as immediately adopted rules. The AD's normally become effective in less than 30 days after publication in the Federal Register and are distributed by first class mail, telegram, or other electronic methods to the registered owners and certain known operators of the product affected. In addition, notification is also provided to special interest groups, other government agencies, and Civil Aviation Authorities of certain foreign countries.

7. AD's WHICH APPLY TO PRODUCTS OTHER THAN AIRCRAFT. AD's may be issued which apply to aircraft engines, propellers, or appliances installed on multiple makes or models of aircraft. When the product can be identified as being installed on a specific make or model aircraft, the AD is distributed by first class mail to the registered owners of those aircraft. However, there are times when such a determination cannot be made, and direct distribution to registered owners is impossible. For this reason, aircraft owners and operators are urged to subscribe to the Summary of Airworthiness Directives which contains all previously published AD's and a biweekly supplemental service. Advisory Circular 39-6, Announcement of Availability — Summary of Airworthiness Directives, provides ordering information and subscription prices on these publications. The most recent copy of AC 39-6 may be obtained, without cost, from the U.S. Department of Transportation, General Services Section, M-483.1, Washington, D.C. 20590. Information concerning the Summary of Airworthiness Directives may also be obtained by contacting the FAA, Manufacturing Standards Section (AFS-613), P.O. Box 26460, Oklahoma City, Oklahoma 73125-0460. Telephone (405) 954-4103, FAX (405) 954-4104.

8. APPLICABILITY OF AD's. Each AD contains an applicability statement specifying the product (aircraft, aircraft engine, propeller, or appliance) to which it applies. Some aircraft owners and operators mistakenly assume that AD's do not apply to aircraft with other than standard airworthiness certificates, i.e., special airworthiness certificates in the restricted, limited, or experimental category. Unless specifically stated, AD's apply to the make and model set forth in the applicability statement regardless of the classification or category of the airworthiness certificate issued for the aircraft. Type certificate and airworthiness certification information are used to identify the product affected. Limitations may be placed on applicability by specifying the serial number or number series to which the AD is applicable. When there is no reference to serial numbers, all serial numbers are affected. The following are examples of AD applicability statements:

a. "Applies to Smith (Formerly Robin Aero) RA-15-150 series airplanes, certificated in any category." This statement, or one similarly worded, makes the AD applicable to all airplanes of the model listed, regardless of the type of airworthiness certificate issued to the aircraft.

b. "Applies to Smith (Formerly Robin Aero) RA-15-150 Serial Numbers 15-1081 through 15-1098." This statement, or one similarly worded, specifies certain aircraft by serial number within a specific model and series regardless of the type of airworthiness certificate issued to the aircraft.

c. "Applies to Smith (Formerly Robin Aero) RA-15-150 series aircraft certificated in all categories excluding experimental aircraft." This statement, or one similarly worded, makes the AD applicable to all airplanes except those issued experimental airworthiness certificates.

d. "Applicability: Smith (Formerly Robin Aero) RA-15-150 series airplanes; Cessna Models 150, 170, 172, and 175 series airplanes; and Piper PA-28-140 airplanes; certificated in any category, that have been modified in accordance with STC SA807NM using ABLE INDUSTRIES, Inc., (Part No. 1234) muffler kits." This statement, or one similarly worded, makes the AD applicable to all airplanes listed when altered by the supplemental type certificate listed, regardless of the type of airworthiness certificate issued to the aircraft.

e. Every AD applies to each product identified in the applicability statement, regardless of whether it has been modified, altered, or repaired in the area subject to the requirements of the AD. For products that have been modified, altered, or repaired so that performance of the requirements of the AD is affected, the owner/operator must use the authority provided in the alternative methods of compliance provision of the AD (see paragraph 12) to request approval from the FAA. This approval may address either no action, if the current configuration eliminates the unsafe condition; or, different actions necessary to address the unsafe condition described in the AD. In no case, does the presence of any alteration, modification, or repair remove any product from the applicability of this AD. Performance of the requirements of the AD is "affected" if an operator is unable to perform those requirements in the manner described in the AD. In short, either the requirements of the AD can be performed as specified in the AD and the specified results can be achieved, or they cannot.

9. **AD COMPLIANCE.** AD's are regulations issued under part 39. Therefore, no person may operate a product to which an AD applies, except in accordance with the requirements of that AD. Owners and operators should understand that to "operate" not only means piloting the aircraft, but also causing or authorizing the product to be used for the purpose of air navigation, with or without the right of legal control as owner, lessee, or otherwise. Compliance with emergency AD's can be a problem for operators of leased aircraft because the FAA has no legal requirement for notification of other than registered owners. Therefore, it is important that the registered owner(s) of leased aircraft make the AD information available to the operators leasing their aircraft as expeditiously as possible, otherwise the lessee may not be aware of the AD and safety may be jeopardized.

10. COMPLIANCE TIME OR DATE.

a. The belief that AD compliance is only required at the time of a required inspection, e.g., at a 100-hour or annual inspection is not correct. The required compliance time is specified in each AD, and no person may operate the affected product after expiration of that stated compliance time.

b. Compliance requirements specified in AD's are established for safety reasons and may be stated in various ways. Some AD's are of such a serious nature they require compliance before further flight, for example: "To prevent uncommanded engine shutdown with the inability to restart the engine, prior to further flight, inspect…" Other AD's express compliance time in terms of a specific number of hours in operation, for example: "Compliance is required within the next 50 hours time in service after the effective date of this AD." Compliance times may also be expressed in operational terms, such as: "Within the next 10 landings after the effective date of this AD…" For turbine engines, compliance times are often expressed in terms of cycles. A cycle normally consists of an engine start, takeoff operation, landing, and engine shutdown.

c. When a direct relationship between airworthiness and calendar time is identified, compliance time may be expressed as a calendar date. For example, if the compliance time is specified as "within 12 months after the effective date of this AD…" with an effective date of July 15, 1995, the deadline for compliance is July 15, 1996.

d. In some instances, the AD may authorize flight after the compliance date has passed, provided that a special flight permit is obtained. Special flight authorization may be granted only when the AD specifically permits such operation. Another aspect of compliance times to be emphasized is that not all AD's have a one-time compliance requirement. Repetitive inspections at specified intervals after initial compliance may be required in lieu of, or until a permanent solution for the unsafe condition is developed.

11. ADJUSTMENTS IN COMPLIANCE REQUIREMENTS. In some instances, a compliance time other than the compliance time specified in the AD may be advantageous to an aircraft owner or operator. In recognition of this need, and when an acceptable level of safety can be shown, flexibility may be provided by a statement in the AD allowing adjustment of the specified interval. When adjustment authority is provided in an AD, owners or operators desiring to make an adjustment are required to submit data substantiating their proposed adjustment to their local FAA Flight Standards District Office or other FAA office for consideration as specified in the AD. The FAA office or person authorized to approve adjustments in compliance requirements is normally identified in the AD.

12. ALTERNATIVE METHODS OF COMPLIANCE. Many AD's indicate the acceptability of one or more alternative methods of compliance. Any alternative method of compliance or adjustment of compliance time other than that listed in the AD must be substantiated and approved by the FAA before it may be used. Normally the office or person authorized to approve an alternative method of compliance is indicated in the AD.

13. RESPONSIBILITY FOR AD COMPLIANCE AND RECORDATION. The owner or operator of an aircraft is primarily responsible for maintaining that aircraft in an airworthy condition, including compliance with AD's.

a. This responsibility may be met by ensuring that properly certificated and appropriately rated maintenance person(s) accomplish the requirements of the AD and properly record this action in the appropriate maintenance records. This action must be accomplished within the compliance time specified in the AD or the aircraft may not be operated.

b. Maintenance persons may also have direct responsibility for AD compliance, aside from the times when AD compliance is the specific work contracted for by the owner or operator. When a 100-hour, annual, progressive, or any other inspection required under parts 91, 121, 125, or 135 is accomplished, § 43.15 (a) requires the person performing the inspection to determine that all applicable airworthiness requirements are met, including compliance with AD's.

c. Maintenance persons should note even though an inspection of the complete aircraft is not made, if the inspection conducted is a progressive inspection, determination of AD compliance is required for those portions of the aircraft inspected.

d. For aircraft being inspected in accordance with a continuous inspection program (§ 91.409), the person performing the inspection must ensure that an AD is complied with only when the portion of the inspection program being handled by that person involves an area covered by a particular AD. The program may require a determination of AD compliance for the entire aircraft by a general statement, or compliance with AD's applicable only to portions of the aircraft being inspected, or it may not require compliance at all. This does not mean AD compliance is not required at the compliance time or date specified in the AD. It only means that the owner or operator has elected to handle AD compliance apart from the inspection program. The owner or operator remains fully responsible for AD compliance.

e. The person accomplishing the AD is required by § 43.9 to record AD compliance. The entry must include those items specified in § 43.9 (a)(1) through (a)(4). The owner or operator is required by § 91.405 to ensure that maintenance personnel make appropriate entries and, by § 91.417, to maintain those records. Owners and operators should note that there is a difference between the records required to be kept by the owner under § 91.417 and those § 43.9 requires maintenance personnel to make. In either case, the owner or operator is responsible for maintaining proper records.

f. Pilot Performed AD Checks. Certain AD's permit pilots to perform checks of some items under specific conditions. AD's allowing this action will include specific direction regarding recording requirements. However, if the AD does not include recording requirements for the pilot, § 43.9 requires persons complying with an AD to make an entry in the maintenance record of that product. § 91.417 (a) and (b) requires the owner or operator to keep and retain certain minimum records for a specific time. The person who accomplished the action, the person who returned the aircraft to service, and the status of AD compliance are the items of information required to be kept in those records.

14. RECURRING/PERIODIC AD's. Some AD's require repetitive or periodic inspection. In order to provide for flexibility in administering such AD's, an AD may provide for adjustment of the inspection interval to coincide with inspections required by part 91, or other regulations. The conditions and approval requirements under which adjustments may be allowed are stated in the AD. If the AD does not contain such provisions, adjustments are usually not permitted. However, amendment, modification, or adjustment of the terms of the AD may be requested by contacting the office that issued the AD or by following the petition procedures provided in part 11.

15. DETERMINING REVISION DATES. The revision date required by § 91.417 (a)(2)(v) is the effective date of the latest amendment to the AD and may be found in the last sentence of the body of each AD. For example: "This amendment becomes effective on July 10, 1995." Similarly, the revision date for an emergency AD distributed by telegram or priority mail is the date it was issued. For example: "Priority Letter AD 95-11-09, issued May 25, 1995, becomes effective upon receipt." Each emergency AD is normally followed by a final rule version that will reflect the final status and amendment number of the regulation including any changes in the effective date.

16. SUMMARY. The registered owner or operator of an aircraft is responsible for compliance with AD's applicable to the airframe, engine, propeller, appliances, and parts and components thereof for all aircraft it owns or operates. Maintenance personnel are responsible for determining that all applicable airworthiness requirements are met when they accomplish an inspection in accordance with part 43.

Thomas C. Accardi
Director, Flight Standards Service

U.S. Department
of Transportation
**Federal Aviation
Administration**

Advisory Circular 43-9C

Subject: **Maintenance Records**

Date: June 8, 1998 Initiated by: AFS-340

1. **PURPOSE.** This advisory circular (AC) describes methods, procedures and practices that have been determined to be acceptable means of showing compliance with the general aviation maintenance record making and record keeping requirements of Title 14 of the Code of Federal Regulations (14 CFR) parts 43 and 91. This material is not mandatory, nor is it regulatory and acknowledges that the Federal Aviation Administration (FAA) will consider other methods that may be presented. It is issued for guidance purposes and outlines several methods of compliance with the regulations.

   NOTE: The information in this AC does not apply to air carrier maintenance records made and retained in accordance with 14 CFR part 121.

2. **CANCELLATION.** AC 43-9B, Maintenance Records, dated January 9, 1984, is canceled.

3. **RELATED REGULATIONS.** 14 CFR parts 1, 43, 91, and 145.

4. **DISCUSSION.** The Code of Federal Regulations state that a U.S. standard airworthiness certificate is effective until it is surrendered, suspended, revoked, or a termination date is otherwise established by the Administrator. In addition to those terms, a U.S. standard airworthiness certificate is effective only as long as the maintenance, preventive maintenance, and alterations are performed in accordance with part 43 and 91, and the aircraft are registered in the United States. These terms and conditions are further restated, in block 6, on the front of FAA Form 8100–2, Standard Airworthiness Certificate. Qualified persons, who perform the maintenance, preventive maintenance and alterations, shall make a record entry of this accomplishment, thus maintaining the validity of the certificate of airworthiness. Adequate aircraft records provide tangible evidence that the aircraft complies with the appropriate airworthiness requirements. In accordance with the terms and conditions listed in block 6 of the Standard Airworthiness Certificate, insufficient or non-existent aircraft records may render that standard airworthiness certificate invalid.

5. MAINTENANCE RECORD REQUIREMENTS.

a. **Responsibilities.** 14 CFR part 91, section 91.417 states that an aircraft owner/operator shall keep and maintain aircraft maintenance records. 14 CFR part 43, sections 43.9 and 43.11 state that maintenance personnel, however, are required to make the record entries.

b. **Maintenance Records That Are to Be Retained.** Section 91.405 requires each owner or operator to ensure that maintenance personnel make appropriate entries in the maintenance records to indicate that the aircraft has been approved for return to service. Section 91.417(a) sets forth the content requirements and retention requirements for maintenance records. Maintenance records may be kept in any format that provides record continuity; includes required contents; lends itself to the addition of new entries; provides for signature entry; and, is intelligible. Section 91.417(b) requires records of maintenance, alterations, and required or approved inspections to be retained until the work is repeated, superseded by other work, or for one year. It also requires the records, specified in section 91.417(a)(2), to be retained and transferred with the aircraft at the time of sale.

NOTE: Section 91.417(a) contains an exception regarding work accomplished in accordance with section 91.411. This does not exclude the making of entries for this work, but applies to the retention period of the records for work done in accordance with this section. The exclusion is necessary since the retention period of one year is inconsistent with the 24-month interval of test and inspection specified in section 91.411. Entries for work done per this section are to be retained for 24 months or until the work is repeated or superseded.

c. **Section 91.417(a)(1).** Requires a record of maintenance, for each aircraft (including the airframe) and each engine, propeller, rotor, and appliance of an aircraft. This does not require separate or individual records for each of these items. It does require the information specified in sections 91.417(a)(1) through 91.417(a)(2)(vi) to be kept for each item as appropriate. As a practical matter, many owners and operators find it advantageous to keep separate or individual records since it facilitates transfer of the record with the item when ownership changes. Section 91.417(a)(1) has no counterpart in section 43.9 or section 43.11.

d. **Section 91.417(a)(1)(i).** Requires the maintenance record entry to include "a description of the work performed." The description should be in sufficient detail to permit a person unfamiliar with the work to understand what was done, and the methods and procedures used in doing it. When the work is extensive, this results in a voluminous record. To provide for this contingency, the rule permits reference to technical data acceptable to the Administrator in lieu of making the detailed entry. Manufacturer's manuals, service letters, bulletins, work orders, FAA AC's, and others, which accurately describe what was done, or how it was done, may be referenced. Except for the documents mentioned, which are in common usage, referenced documents are to be made a part of the maintenance records and retained in accordance with section 91.417(b).

NOTE: Certificated repair stations frequently work on components shipped to them without the maintenance records. To provide for this situation, repair stations should supply owners and operators with copies of work orders written for the work, in lieu of maintenance record entries. The work order copy must include the information, required by section 91.417(a)(1) through section 91.417(a)(1)(iii), be made a part of the maintenance record, and retained per section 91.417(b). This procedure is not the same as that for maintenance releases discussed in paragraph 16, and it may not be used when maintenance records are available. Section 91.417(a)(1)(i) is identical to its counterpart, section 43.9(a)(1), which imposes the same requirements on maintenance personnel.

e. Section 91.417(a)(1)(ii). Is identical to section 43.9(a)(2) and requires entries to contain the date the work was completed. This is normally the date upon which the work is approved for return to service. However, when work is accomplished by one person and approved for return to service by another, the dates may differ. Two signatures may also appear under this circumstance; however, a single entry in accordance with section 43.9(a)(3) is acceptable.

f. Section 91.417(a)(1)(iii). Differs slightly from section 43.9(a)(4) in that it requires the entry to indicate only the signature and certificate number of the person approving the work for return to service, and does not require the type of certificate being exercised to be indicated as does section 43.9(a)(4). This is a new requirement of section 43.9(a)(4), which assists owners and operators in meeting their responsibilities. Maintenance personnel may indicate the type of certificate exercised by using airframe (A), powerplant (P), airframe & powerplant (A&P), inspection authorization (IA), or certificated repair station (CRS).

g. Section 91.417(a)(2). Require six items to be made a part of the maintenance record and maintained as such. Section 43.9 does not require maintenance personnel to enter these items. Section 43.11 requires some of them to be part of entries made for inspections, but they are all the responsibility of the owner or operator. The six items are discussed as follows:

(1) Section 91.417(a)(2)(i). Requires a record of total time-in-service to be kept for the airframe, each engine, and each propeller. Part 1, section 1.1, Definitions, defines time in service, with respect to maintenance time records, as that time from the moment an aircraft leaves the surface of the earth until it touches down at the next point of landing. Section 43.9 does not require this to be part of the entries for maintenance, preventive maintenance, rebuilding, or alterations. However, section 43.11 requires maintenance personnel to make it a part of the entries for inspections made under parts 91, 125, and time-in-service in all entries.

(a) Some circumstances impact the owner's or operator's ability to comply with section 91.417(a)(2)(i). For example, in the case of rebuilt engines, the owner or operator would not have a way of knowing the total time-in-service, since section 91.421 permits the maintenance record to be discontinued and the engine time to be started at zero. In this case, the maintenance record and time-in-service, subsequent to the rebuild, comprise a satisfactory record.

(b) Many components, presently in-service, were put into service before the requirements to keep maintenance records on them. Propellers are probably foremost in this group. In these instances, practicable procedures for compliance with the record requirements must be used. For example, total time-in-service may be derived using the procedures described in paragraph 12; or if records prior to the regulatory requirements are just not available from any source, time-in-service may be kept since last complete overhaul. Neither of these procedures is acceptable when life-limited parts status is involved or when airworthiness directive (AD) compliance is a factor. Only the actual record since new may be used in these instances.

(c) Sometimes engines are assembled from modules (turbojet and some turbopropeller engines) and a true total time-in-service for the total engine is not kept. If owners and operators wish to take advantage of this modular design, then total time-in-service and a maintenance record for each module is to be maintained. The maintenance records specified in section 91.417(a)(2) are to be kept with the module.

(2) **Section 91.417(a)(2)(ii).** Requires the current status of life-limited parts to be part of the maintenance record. If total time-in-service of the aircraft, engine, propeller, etc., is entered in the record when a life-limited part is installed and the time-in-service of the life-limited part is included, the normal record of time-in-service automatically meets this requirement.

(3) **Section 91.417(a)(2)(iii).** Requires the maintenance record to indicate the time since last overhaul of all items installed on the aircraft that are required to be overhauled on a specified time basis. The explanation in paragraph 5g (2) also applies to this requirement.

(4) **Section 91.417(a)(2)(iv).** Deals with the current inspection status and requires it to be reflected in the maintenance record. Again, the explanation in paragraph 5g (2) is appropriate even though section 43.11(a)(2) requires maintenance persons to determine time-in-service of the item being inspected and to include it as part of the inspection entry.

(5) **Section 91.417(a)(2)(v).** Requires the current status of applicable AD's to be a part of the maintenance record. The record is to include, at minimum, the method used to comply with the AD, the AD number, and revision date; and if the AD has requirements for recurring action, the time-in-service and the date when that action is required. When AD's are accomplished, maintenance persons are required to include the items specified in section 43.9(a)(2), (3), and (4) in addition to those required by section 91.417(a)(2)(v). An example of a maintenance record format for AD compliance is contained in Appendix 1.

(6) Section 91.417(a)(2)(vi). In the past, the owner or operator has been permitted to maintain a list of current major alterations to the airframe, engine(s), propeller(s), rotor(s), or appliances. This procedure did not produce a record of value to the owner/operator or to maintenance persons in determining the continued airworthiness of the alteration since such a record was not sufficient detail. This section of the rule has now been changed. It now prescribes that copies of FAA Form 337, issued for the alteration, be made a part of the maintenance record.

6. PREVENTIVE MAINTENANCE.

a. Preventive maintenance is defined in part 1, section 1.1. Part 43, appendix A, paragraph (c) lists those items which a pilot may accomplish under section 43.3(g). Section 43.7 authorizes appropriately rated repair stations and mechanics, and persons holding at least a private pilot certificate to approve an aircraft for return to service after they have performed preventive maintenance. All of these persons must record preventive maintenance accomplished in accordance with the requirements of section 43.9. AC 43-12, Preventive Maintenance, current edition, contains further information on this subject.

b. The type of certificate exercised when maintenance or preventive maintenance is accomplished must be indicated in the maintenance record. Pilots may use private pilot (PP), commercial pilot (CP), or air transport pilot (ATP) to indicate private, commercial, or airline transport pilot certificate, respectively, in approving preventive maintenance for return to service. Pilots are not authorized by section 43.3(g) to perform preventive maintenance on aircraft when they are operated under part 121, 127, 129, or 135. Pilots may only approve for return to service preventive maintenance that they themselves have accomplished.

7. REBUILT ENGINE MAINTENANCE RECORDS.

a. Section 91.421 provides that zero time may be granted to an engine that has been rebuilt by a manufacturer or an agency approved by the manufacturer. When this is done, the owner/operator may use a new maintenance record without regard to previous operating history.

b. The manufacturer or an agency approved by the manufacturer that rebuilds and grants zero time to an engine is required by section 91.421 to provide a signed statement containing: 1) the date the engine was rebuilt; 2) each change made, as required by an AD; and 3) each change made in compliance with service bulletins, when the service bulletin specifically requests an entry to be made.

c. Section 43.2(b) prohibits the use of the term rebuilt in describing work accomplished in required maintenance records or forms unless the component worked on has had specific work functions accomplished. These functions are listed in section 43.2(b) and, except for testing requirements, are the same as those set forth in section 91.421(c). When terms such as remanufactured, reconditioned, or other terms coined by various aviation enterprises are used in maintenance records, owners and operators cannot assume that the functions outlined in section 43.2(b) have been done.

8. RECORDING TACHOMETERS.

a. Time-in-service recording devices sense such things as electrical power on, oil pressure, wheels on the ground, etc., and from these conditions provide an indication of time-in-service. With the exception of those that sense aircraft lift-off and touchdown, the indications are approximate.

b. Some owners and operators mistakenly believe these devices may be used in lieu of keeping time-in-service in the maintenance record. While they are of great assistance in arriving at the time-in-service, such instruments, alone, do not meet the requirements of section 91.417. For example, when the device fails and requires change, it is necessary to enter time-in-service and the instrument reading at the change. Otherwise, record continuity is lost.

9. MAINTENANCE RECORDS FOR AD COMPLIANCE. This subject is covered in AC 39-7, Airworthiness Directives for General Aviation Aircraft, current edition. A separate AD record may be kept for the airframe and each engine, propeller, rotor, and appliance, but is not required. This would facilitate record searches when inspection is needed, and when an engine, propeller, rotor, or appliance is removed, the record may be transferred with it. Such records may be used as a schedule for recurring inspections. The format, shown in Appendix 1, is a suggested one, and adherence is not mandatory. Owners should be aware that they may be responsible for non-compliance with AD's when their aircraft are leased to foreign operators. They should, therefore, ensure that leases should be drafted to deal with this subject.

10. MAINTENANCE RECORDS FOR REQUIRED INSPECTIONS.

a. Section 43.11 contains the requirement for inspection entries. While these requirements are imposed on maintenance personnel, owners and operators should become familiar with them in order to meet their responsibilities under section 91.405.

b. The maintenance record requirements of section 43.11 apply to the 100-hour, annual, and progressive inspections under part 91; inspection programs under parts 91 and 125; approved airplane inspection programs under part 135; and the 100-hour and annual inspections under section 135.411(a)(1).

c. Appropriately rated mechanics are authorized to conduct these inspections and make the required entries. Particular attention should be given to section 43.11(a)(7) in that it now requires a more specific statement than previously required under section 43.9. The entry, in addition to other items, must identify the inspection program used; identify the portion or segment of the inspection program accomplished; and contain a statement that the inspection was performed in accordance with the instructions and procedures for that program.

d. Questions continue regarding multiple entries for 100-hour/annual inspections. As discussed in paragraph 5c, neither part 43 nor part 91 requires separate records to be kept. Section 43.11, however, requires persons approving or disapproving equipment for return to service, after any required inspection, to make an entry in the record of that equipment. Therefore, when an owner maintains a single record, the entry of the 100-hour or annual inspections is made in that record. If the owner maintains separate records for the airframe, powerplants, and propellers, the entry for the 100-hour inspection is entered in each, while the annual inspection is only required to be entered into the airframe record.

11. DISCREPANCY LISTS.

a. Before October 15, 1982, issuance of discrepancy lists (or lists of defects) to owners or operators was appropriate only in connection with annual inspections under part 91; inspections under section 135.411(a)(1); inspection programs under part 125; and inspections under section 91.217. Now, section 43.11 requires that a discrepancy list be prepared by a person performing any inspection required by parts 91, 125, or section 135.411(a)(1).

b. When a discrepancy list is provided to an owner or operator, it says in effect, except for these discrepancies, the item inspected is airworthy. It is imperative, therefore, that inspections be complete and that all discrepancies appear in the list. When circumstances dictate that an inspection be terminated before it is completed, the maintenance record should clearly indicate that the inspection was discontinued. The entry should meet all the other requirements of section 43.11.

c. It is no longer a requirement that copies of discrepancy lists be forwarded to the local Flight Standards District Office (FSDO).

d. Discrepancy lists (or lists of defects) are part of the maintenance record and the owner/operator is responsible to maintain that record in accordance with section 91.417(b)(3). The entry made by maintenance personnel in the maintenance record should reference the discrepancy list when a list is issued.

12. LOST OR DESTROYED RECORDS. Occasionally, the records for an aircraft are lost or destroyed. In order to re-construct them, it is necessary to establish the total time-in-service of the airframe. This can be done by reference to other records that reflect the time-in-service; research of records maintained by repair facilities; and reference to records maintained by individual mechanics, etc. When these things have been done and the record is still incomplete, the owner/operator may make a notarized statement in the new record describing the loss and establishing the time-in-service based on the research and the best estimate of time-in-service.

a. The current status of applicable AD's may present a more formidable problem. This may require a detailed inspection by maintenance personnel to establish that the applicable AD's have been complied with. It can readily be seen that this could entail considerable time, expense, and in some instances, might require recompliance with the AD.

b. Other items required by section 91.417(a)(2), such as the current status of life-limited parts, time since last overhaul, current inspection status, and current list of major alterations, may present difficult problems. Some items may be easier to reestablish than others, but all are problems. Losing maintenance records can be troublesome, costly, and time consuming. Safekeeping of the records is an integral part of a good record keeping system.

13. COMPUTERIZED RECORDS. There is a growing trend toward computerized maintenance records. Many of these systems are offered to owners/operators on a commercial basis. While these are excellent scheduling systems, alone they normally do not meet the requirements of section 43.9 or 91.417. The owner/operator who used such a system is required to ensure that it provides the information required by section 91.417, including signatures. If not, modification to make them complete is the owner's/operator's responsibility and that responsibility may not be delegated.

14. PUBLIC AIRCRAFT. Prospective purchasers of aircraft that have been used as public aircraft, should be aware that public aircraft may not be subject to the certification and maintenance requirements in Title 14 of the Code of Federal Regulations and may not have records that meet the requirements of section 91.417. Considerable research may be involved in establishing the required records when these aircraft are purchased and brought into civil aviation. The aircraft may not be certificated or used without such records.

15. LIFE-LIMITED PARTS.

a. Present day aircraft and powerplants commonly have life-limited parts installed. These life limits may be referred to as retirement times, service life limitations, parts retirement limitations, retirement life limits, life limitations, or other such terminology and may be expressed in hours, cycles of operation, or calendar time. They are set forth in type certificate data sheets (TCDS), AD's, or the limitations section of FAA-approved airplane or rotorcraft flight manuals. Additionally, instructions for continued airworthiness, which require life-limits be specified, may apply (See CFR 23 Appendix G and CFR 27 Appendix A).

b. Section 91.417(a)(2)(ii) requires the owner or operator of an aircraft with such parts installed to have records containing the current status of these parts. Many owners/operators have found it advantageous to have a separate record for such parts showing the name of the part, part number, serial number, date of installation, total time-in-service, date removed, and signature and certificate number of the person installing or removing the part. A separate record, as described, facilitates transferring the record with the part in the event the part is removed and later reinstalled or installed on another aircraft or engine. If a separate record is not kept, the aircraft record must contain sufficient information to clearly establish the status of the life-limited parts installed.

16. MAINTENANCE RELEASE.

a. In addition to those requirements discussed previously, section 43.9 requires that major repairs and alterations be recorded as indicated in appendix B of part 43, (i.e., on FAA Form 337). An exception is provided in paragraph (b) of that appendix, which allows repair stations certificated under part 145 to use a maintenance release in lieu of the form for major repairs (and only major repairs).

b. The maintenance release must contain the information specified in paragraph (b)(1), (2) and (3), appendix B of part 43, be made a part of the aircraft maintenance record, and retained by the owner/operator as specified in section 91.417. The maintenance release is usually a special document (normally a tag) and is attached to the product when it is approved for return to service. The maintenance release may, however, be on a copy of the work order written for the product. When this is done (**for major repairs only**) the entry on the work order must meet paragraph (b)(1), (2), and (3) of the appendix. That is to say that the Repair Station is required to give the owner: (1) the customers work order upon which the repair is recorded; (2) a signed copy of the work order; and (3) a maintenance release which has been signed by an authorized representative of the company. In some cases, a work order and a maintenance release may be a different document. Both must be supplied to the customer.

c. Some repair stations use what they call a maintenance release for other than major repairs. This is sometimes a tag and sometimes information on a work order. When this is done, all of the requirements of section 43.9 must be met (paragraph (b)(3), appendix B, not applicable) and the document is to be made and retained as part of the maintenance records under section 91.417 per discussion in paragraph 5c.

17. FAA FORM 337, MAJOR REPAIR AND ALTERATION.

a. Major repairs and alterations are to be recorded on FAA Form 337, as stated in paragraph 16. This form is executed by the person making the repair or alteration. Provisions are made on the form for a person other than that person performing the work to approve the repair or alteration for return to service.

b. These forms are now required to be made part of the maintenance record of the product repaired or altered and retained in accordance with section 91.417.

c. Detailed instructions for use of this form are contained in AC 43.9-1, Instructions for Completion of FAA Form 337, current edition.

d. Some manufacturers have initiated a policy of indicating, on their service letters and bulletins, and other documents dealing with changes to their aircraft, whether or not the changes constitute major repairs or alterations. Some manufacturers also indicate that the responsibility for completing FAA Form 337 lies with the person accomplishing the repairs or alterations and cannot be delegated. When there is a question, it is advisable to contact the local FSDO for guidance.

18. TESTS AND INSPECTIONS FOR ALTIMETER SYSTEMS, ALTITUDE REPORTING EQUIPMENT, AND AIR TRAFFIC CONTROL (ATC) TRANSPONDERS.
The recordation requirements for these tests and inspections are the same as for other maintenance. There are essentially three tests and inspections (the altimeter system, the transponder system, and the data correspondence test), each of which may be subdivided relative to who may perform specific portions of the test. The basic authorization for performing these tests and inspections, found in section 43.3, is supplemented by sections 91.411 and 91.413. When multiple persons are involved in the performance of tests and inspections, care must be exercised to insure proper authorization under these three sections and compliance with sections 43.9 and 43.9(a)(3) in particular.

19. BEFORE YOU BUY. This is the proper time to take a close look at the maintenance records of any used aircraft you expect to purchase. A well-kept set of maintenance records, which properly identifies all previously performed maintenance, alterations, and AD compliances, is generally a good indicator of the aircraft condition. This is not always the case, but in any event, before you buy, require the owner to produce the maintenance records for your examination, and require correction of any discrepancies found on the aircraft or in the records. Many prospective owners have found it advantageous to have a reliable unbiased maintenance person examine the maintenance records, as well as the aircraft, before negotiations have progressed too far. If the aircraft is purchased, take the time to review and learn the system of the previous owner to ensure compliance and continuity when you modify or continue that system.

Thomas E. Stuckey
Acting Director, Flight Standards Service

Appendix 1. Airworthiness Directive Compliance Record (suggested format)

AD Number and Amendment Number	Date Received	Subject	Compliance Due Date Hours/Other	Date of Compliance	Airframe Total Time-in-Service at Compliance	One-Time	Recurring	Next Compliance Due Date Hours/Other	Authorized Signature, Certificate, Type and Number	Remarks

*Aircraft, Engine, Propeller, Rotor, or Appliance: Make ________ Model ________ S.N. ________ N ________

U.S. Department
of Transportation
**Federal Aviation
Administration**

Advisory Circular 43.9-1E

Subject: Instructions for Completion of FAA Form 337 (OMB No. 2120-0020)
MAJOR REPAIR AND ALTERATION
(Airframe, Powerplant, Propeller, or Appliance)

Date: 5/21/87 Initiated by: AFS-340

1. PURPOSE. This advisory circular (AC) provides instructions for completing Federal Aviation Administration (FAA) Form 337, Major Repair and Alteration (Airframe, Powerplant, Propeller, or Appliance).

2. CANCELLATION. AC 43.9-1D, Instructions for Completion of FAA Form 337 (OMB 04-R0060), Major Repair and Alteration (Airframe, Powerplant, Propeller, or Appliance), dated 9/5/79, is canceled.

3. RELATED FEDERAL AVIATION REGULATIONS (FAR) SECTIONS. FAR Part 43, Sections 43.5, 43.7, 43.9, and Appendix B.

4. INFORMATION. FAA Form 337 is furnished free of charge and is available at all FAA Air Carrier (ACDO), General Aviation (GADO), Manufacturing Inspection (MIDO), and Flight Standards (FSDO) district offices, and at all International Field Offices (IFO). The form serves two main purposes; one is to provide aircraft owners and operators with a record of major repairs or alterations indicting details and approval, and the other is to provide the FAA with a copy of the form for inclusion in the aircraft records at the FAA Aircraft Registration Branch, Oklahoma City, Oklahoma.

5. INSTRUCTIONS FOR COMPLETING FAA FORM 337. The person who performs or supervises a major repair or major alteration should prepare FAA Form 337. The form is executed at least in duplicate and is used to record major repairs and major alterations made to an aircraft, an airframe, powerplant, propeller, appliance, or spare part. The following instructions apply to corresponding items 1 through 8 of the form as illustrated in Appendix 1.

   a. Item 1 – Aircraft. Information to complete the "Make," "Model," and "Serial Number" blocks will be found on the aircraft manufacturer's identification plate. The "Nationality and Registration Mark" is the same as shown on AC Form 8050-3, Certificate of Aircraft Registration.

   b. Item 2 – Owner. Enter the aircraft owner's complete name and address as shown on AC Form 8050-3.

Note: When a major repair or alteration is made to a spare part or appliance, items 1 and 2 will be left blank, and the original and duplicate copy of the form will remain with the part until such time as it is installed on an aircraft. The person installing the part will then enter the required information in blocks 1 and 2, give the original of the form to the aircraft owner/operator, and forward the duplicate copy to the local FAA district office within 48 hours after the work is inspected.

c. Item 3 – For FAA Use Only. Approval may be indicated in Item 3 when the FAA determines that data to be used in performing a major alteration or a major repair complies with accepted industry practices and all applicable FAR. Approval is indicated in one of the following methods. (See paragraph 6b for further details.)

(1) Approval by examination of data only – one aircraft only: "The data identified herein complies with the applicable airworthiness requirements and is approved for the above described aircraft, subject to conformity inspection by a person authorized in FAR Part 43, Section 43.7."

(2) Approval by physical inspection, demonstration, testing, etc., of the data and aircraft – one aircraft only: "The alteration (or repair) identified herein complies with the applicable airworthiness requirements and is approved for the above described aircraft, subject to conformity inspection by a person authorized in FAR Part 43, Section 43.7."

(3) Approval by examination of data only – duplication on identical aircraft. "The alteration identified herein complies with the applicable airworthiness requirements and is approved for duplication on identical aircraft make, model, and altered configuration by the original modifier."

d. 4 – Unit Identification. The information blocks under item 4 are used to identify the airframe, powerplant, propeller, or appliance repaired or altered. It is only necessary to complete the blocks for the unit repaired or altered.

e. Item 5 – Type. Enter a checkmark in the appropriate column to indicate if the unit was repaired or altered.

f. Item 6 – Conformity Statement.

(1) "A" – Agency's Name and Address. Enter name of the mechanic, repair station, or manufacturer accomplishing the repair or alteration. Mechanics should enter their name and permanent mailing address. Manufacturers and repair stations should enter the name and address under which they do business.

(2) "B" – Kind of Agency. Check the appropriate box to indicate the type of person or organization who performed the work.

(3) "C" – Certificate Number. Mechanics should enter their mechanic certificate number in this block, e.g., 1305888. Repair stations should enter their air agency certificate number and the rating or ratings under which the work was performed, e.g., 1234, Airframe Class 3. Manufacturers should enter their type production or Supplemental Type Certificate (STC) number. Manufacturers of Technical Standard Orders (TSO) appliances altering these appliances should enter the TSO number of the appliance altered.

(4) "D" – Compliance Statement: This space is used to certify that the repair or alteration was made in accordance with the FAR. When work was performed or supervised by certificated mechanics not employed by a manufacturer or repair station, they should enter the date the repair or alteration was completed and sign their full name. Repair stations are permitted to authorize persons in their employ to date and sign this conformity statement.

g. Item 7 – Approval for Return to Service. FAR Part 43 establishes the conditions under which major repairs or alterations to airframes, powerplants, propellers, and/or appliances may be approved for return to service. This portion of the form is used to indicate approval or rejection of the repair or alteration of the unit involved and to identify the person or agency making the airworthiness inspection. Check the "approved" or "rejected" box to indicate the finding. Additionally, check the appropriate box to indicate who made the finding. Use the box labeled "other" to indicate a finding by a person other than those listed. Enter the date the finding was made. The authorized person who made the finding should sign the form and enter the appropriate certificate or designation number.

h. Item 8 – Description of Work Accomplished. A clear, concise, and legible statement describing the work accomplished should be entered in item 8 on the reverse side of FAA Form 337. It is important that the location of the repair or alteration, relative to the aircraft or component, be described. The approved data used as the basis for approving the major repair or alteration for return to service should be identified and described in this area.

(1) For example, if a repair was made to a buckled spar, the description entered in this part might begin by stating "Removed wing from aircraft and removed skin from outer 6 feet. Repaired buckled spar 49 inches from tip in accordance with…" and continue with a description of the repair. The description should refer to applicable FAR sections and to the FAA-approved data used to substantiate the airworthiness of the repair or alteration. If the repair or alteration is subject to being covered by skin or other structure, a statement should be made certifying that a precover inspection was made and that covered areas were found satisfactory.

(2) Data used as a basis for approving major repairs or alterations for return to service must be FAA-approved prior to its use for that purpose and includes: FAR (e.g., airworthiness directives), AC's (e.g., AC 43.13-1A under certain circumstances), TSO's parts manufacturing approval (PMA), FAA-approved manufacturer's instructions, kits and service handbooks, type certificate data sheets, and aircraft specifications. Other forms of approved data would be those approved by a designated engineering representative (DER), a manufacturer holding a delegation option authorization (DOA), STC's, and, with certain limitations, previous FAA field approvals. Supporting data such as stress analyses, test reports, sketches, or photographs should be submitted with the FAA Form 337. These supporting data will be returned to the applicant by the local FAA district office since only FAA Form 337 is retained as a part of the aircraft records at Oklahoma City.

(3) If additional space is needed to describe the repair or alteration, attach sheets bearing the aircraft nationality and registration mark and the date work was completed.

(4) Showing weight and balance computations under this item is not required; however, it may be done. In all cases where weight and balance of the aircraft are affected, the changes should be entered in the aircraft weight and balance records with the date, signature, and reference to the work performed on the FAA Form 337 that required the changes.

6. ADMINISTRATIVE PROCESSING. At least an original and one duplicate copy of the FAA Form 337 will be executed. FAA district office processing of the forms and their supporting data will depend upon whether previously approved or non-previously approved data was used as follows:

a. Previously Approved Data. The forms will be completed as instructed in this AC ensuring that item 7, "Approval for Return to Service," has been properly executed. Give the original of the form to the aircraft owner or operator, and send the duplicate copy to the local FAA district office within 48 hours after the work is inspected.

b. Non-previously Approved Data. The forms will be completed as instructed in this AC, leaving item 7, "Approval for Return to Service," blank. Both copies of the form, with supporting data, will be sent to the local FAA district office. When the FAA determines that the major repair or alteration data complies with applicable regulations and is in conformity with accepted industry practices, data approval will be recorded by entering an appropriate statement in item 3, "For FAA Use Only." Both forms and supporting data will be returned to the applicant who will complete item 7, "Approval for Return to Service." The applicant will give the original of the form, with its supporting data, to the aircraft owner or operator and return the duplicate copy to the local FAA district office who will, in turn, forward it to the FAA Aircraft Registration Branch, Oklahoma City, Oklahoma, for inclusion in the aircraft records.

c. Signatures on FAA Form 337 have limited purposes:

(1) A signature in item 3, "For FAA Use Only," indicates approval of the data described in that section for use in accomplishing the work described under item 8 on the reverse of FAA Form 337.

(2) A signature in item 6, "Conformity Statement," is a certification by the person performing the work that it was accomplished in accordance with applicable FAR and FAA-approved data. The certification is only applicable to that work described under item 8 on the reverse of FAA Form 337.

Note: Neither of these signatures (subparagraph c(1) and c(2)) indicate FAA approval of the work described under item 8 for return to service.

(3) A signature in item 7, "Approval for Return to Service," does not signify FAA approval unless the box to the left of "FAA Flight Standards Inspector" or "FAA Designee" is checked. The other persons listed in item 7, are authorized to "approve for return to service" if the repair or alteration is accomplished using FAA-approved data, is performed in accordance with applicable FAR, and found to conform.

d. FAA Form 337 is not authorized for use on other than U.S.-registered aircraft. If a foreign civil air authority requests the form, as a record of work performed, it may be provided. The form should be executed in accordance with the FAR and this AC. The foreign authority should be notified on the form that it is not an official record and that it will not be recorded by the FAA Aircraft Registration Branch, Oklahoma City, Oklahoma.

e. FAR Part 43, Appendix B, Paragraph (b) authorizes FAA certificated repair stations to use a work order, in lieu of FAA Form 337, for only major repairs. Such work orders should contain all the information provided on the form and in no less detail; that is, the data used as a basis of approval should be identified, a certification that the work was accomplished using that data and in accordance with the FAR, a description of the work performed (as required in item 8 of the FAA Form 337), and approval for return to service must be indicated by an authorized person. Signature, kind of certificate, and certificate number must also appear in the record (reference FAR Section 43.9).

William T. Brennan
Acting Director of Flight Standards

APPENDIX 1.
FAA Form 337 (front)
Major Repair and Alteration (Airframe, Powerplant, Propeller, or Appliance)

US Department of Transportation
Federal Aviation Administration

MAJOR REPAIR AND ALTERATION
(Airframe, Powerplant, Propeller, or Appliance)

Form Approved
OMB No. 2120-0020

For FAA Use Only
Office Identification

INSTRUCTIONS: Print or type all entries. See FAR 43.9, FAR 43 Appendix B, and AC 43.9-1 (or subsequent revision thereof) for instructions and disposition of this form. This report is required by law (49 U.S.C. 1421). Failure to report can result in a civil penalty not to exceed $1,000 for each such violation (Section 901 Federal Aviation Act of 1958).

1. Aircraft	Make: Cessna	Model: 182
	Serial No.: 15-10521	Nationality and Registration Mark: N-3763
2. Owner	Name (As shown on registration certificate): William Taylor	Address (As shown on registration certificate): 36 Main Street, Cambria, Pennsylvania 15946

3. For FAA Use Only

The data identified herein complies with the applicable airworthiness requirements and is approved for the above described aircraft, subject to conformity inspection by a person authorized by FAR Part 43, Section 43.7.

AEA-GADO-19 — District Office
April 5, 1986 — Date
Ralph Burlingame — Signature of FAA Inspector

4. Unit Identification / **5. Type**

Unit	Make	Model	Serial No.	Repair	Alteration
AIRFRAME	(As described in Item 1 above)			X	
POWERPLANT					
PROPELLER					
APPLIANCE	Type				
	Manufacturer				

6. Conformity Statement

A. Agency's Name and Address	B. Kind of Agency	C. Certificate No.
George Morris High Street Johnstown, Pennsylvania 15236	X U.S. Certificated Mechanic Foreign Certificated Mechanic Certificated Repair Station Manufacturer	1305888

D. I certify that the repair and/or alteration made to the unit(s) identified in item 4 above and described on the reverse or attachments hereto have been made in accordance with the requirements of Part 43 of the U.S. Federal Aviation Regulations and that the information furnished herein is true and correct to the best of my knowledge.

Date	Signature of Authorized Individual
March 19, 1987	George Morris

7. Approval for Return To Service

Pursuant to the authority given persons specified below, the unit identified in item 4 was inspected in the manner prescribed by the Administrator of the Federal Aviation Administration and is ☒ APPROVED ☐ REJECTED

BY			
FAA Flt. Standards Inspector	Manufacturer	X Inspection Authorization	Other (Specify)
FAA Designee	Repair Station	Person Approved by Transport Canada Airworthiness Group	

Date of Approval or Rejection	Certificate or Designation No.	Signature of Authorized Individual
April 9, 1987	237412	Donald Pauley

FAA Form 337 (4-87)

FAA Form 337 (back)
Major Repair and Alteration (Airframe, Powerplant, Propeller, or Appliance)

NOTICE

Weight and balance or operating limitation changes shall be entered in the appropriate aircraft record. An alteration must be compatible with all previous alterations to assure continued conformity with the applicable airworthiness requirements.

8. Description of Work Accomplished
(If more space is required, attach additional sheets. Identify with aircraft nationality and registration mark and date work completed.)

1. Removed right wing from aircraft and removed skin from outer 6 feet. Repaired buckled spar 49 inches from tip in accordance with attached photographs and figure 1 of drawing dated March 6, 1987.

   DATE: March 15, 1987, inspected splice in Item 1 and found it to be in accordance with data indicated. Splice is okay to cover. Inspected internal and external wing assembly for hidden damage and condition.

   Donald Pauley

   Donald Pauley, A&P 237412 IA

2. Primed interior wing structure and replaced skin P/Ns 63-0085, 63-0086, and 63-00878 with same material, 2024-T3, .025 inches thick. Rivet size and spacing all the same as original and using procedures in Chapter 2, Section 3, of AC 43.13-1A, dated 1972.

3. Replaced stringers as required and installed 6 splices as per attached drawing and photographs.

4. Installed wing, rigged aileron, and operationally checked in accordance with manufacturer's maintenance manual.

5. No change in weight or balance.

END

☐ Additional Sheets Are Attached

Appendix 1.
Airworthiness Directive Compliance Record (suggested format)

APPENDIX 1. AIRWORTHINESS DIRECTIVE COMPLIANCE RECORD

*Aircraft, Engine, Propeller, Rotor, or Appliance: Make ________ Model ________ Ser. No. ________ N ________

AD Number and Amendment Number	Date Received	Subject	Compliance Due Date Hours/Other	Method of Compliance	Date of Compliance	Airframe Total Time-in-Service at Compliance	Component Total Time-in-Service at Compliance	One-Time	Recurring	Next Compliance Due Date Hours/Other	Authorized Signature, Certificate, Type and Number	Remarks

*Suggest providing a page for each category.

U.S. Department
of Transportation
Federal Aviation Administration

Advisory Circular 65-30A

Subject: **Overview of the Aviation Maintenance Profession**

Date: **11/09/01**
Initiated By: **AFS-305**

AC No: **65-30A**
Change:

1. **PURPOSE.** This advisory circular (AC) was prepared by the Federal Aviation Administration (FAA) Flight Standards Service to provide information to prospective airframe and powerplant mechanics and other persons interested in the certification of mechanics. It contains information about the certificate requirements, application procedures, and the mechanic written, oral, and practical tests.

2. **CANCELLATION.** AC 65-30, Overview of the Aviation Maintenance Profession, dated June 27, 2000, and AC 65-11B, Airframe and Power Plant Mechanics Certification Information, revised in 1987, are canceled.

3. **RELATED 14 CFR REFERENCES.** Title 14 of the Code of Federal Regulations (14 CFR).
   a. Part 65, Certification: Airmen other than Flight Crewmembers.
   b. Part 145, Repair Stations.
   c. Part 147, Aviation Maintenance Technician Schools.
   d. Part 187, Fees.

4. **RELATED READING MATERIAL.**
   a. To obtain a directory of names and school locations that are FAA certified under the provision of 14 CFR part 147, write to: U.S. Department of Transportation; Subsequent Distribution Office; Ardmore East Business Center; 3341 Q. 75th Ave.; Landover, MD 20785. Request AC 147-2EE, Directory of FAA Certificated Aviation Maintenance Technician Schools. This AC is a free publication.
   b. For educational assistance, contact the Department of Education, Office of Student Financial Assistance, 400 Maryland Ave, S.W., Washington D.C. 20202.
   c. A comprehensive list of all airlines, repair stations, manufacturers, and fixed base operators (FBO) can be found in the World Aviation Directory at the reference section of your local library. This resource document will provide you with a number of job contacts in the location and maintenance field in which you wish to work.
   d. Federal aviation regulations, other related ACs, FAA Inspectors' Handbooks, and additional aviation subjects are available on the FAA website at http://www.mmac.jccbi.gov/afs/afs600/.

5. **BACKGROUND.**

   a. Aviation maintenance personnel work in a number of highly technical specialty occupations such as airframe and powerplants, maintenance, avionics (e.g., navigation, communication, and other electronic based or depended systems), and instrument repair (e.g., navigation, flight, and engine). These individuals hold the very important responsibility of keeping our fleet of U.S.-registered aircraft operating safely and efficiently. To accomplish this goal of a 100% reliability that aviation industry and the flying public demands, these maintenance professionals maintain, service, repair, and overhaul aircraft components and systems.

   b. Aviation maintenance is a dynamic career field. It has changed a great deal since Charles Taylor, the first aircraft mechanic, helped design, build, and maintain the engine for the 1903 Wright Brothers' Flyer. Now and in the future, aircraft maintenance will continue to change. This is due to the introduction of new designs and materials in aircraft construction and the interface between complex space-age systems, such as navigation computers, fly-by-wire and solid state fuel controls, and improvements in the time proven systems such as hydraulics, flight controls, and propellers.

6. **OUTLOOK FOR THE FUTURE.** The long-term employment picture for aviation maintenance is bright. A well-trained, certificated individual with a strong background in technical subjects will have little trouble finding a life-time career in aviation.

7. **WHERE THE JOBS ARE.** The scheduled airlines employ approximately 50,000 mechanics at terminals and overhaul bases throughout the United States and overseas. The major overhaul facilities are in New York, NY; Los Angeles, CA; San Francisco, CA; Denver, CO; Atlanta, GA; Kansas City, MO; Tulsa, OK; and Minneapolis, MN. When you enter this career field most likely you will start at a major overhaul center to learn the aircraft and the airline's maintenance procedures. Once you have acquired enough seniority, you can "bid out" to work at the line station of your choice. These line stations are located at every airport the airline services.

   a. Approximately 37,000 mechanics are employed in general aviation. These mechanics work in the large metropolitan cities on 35 million dollar plus corporate jets to radial engine powered agricultural aircraft operating from grass strips. FAA part 145 repair stations are another segment of the aviation maintenance industry that hires mechanics. These repair stations (approximately 4,600) perform maintenance on aircraft from those as small and simple as the two-place, Piper J3 cub to major overhauls on air carrier aircraft of 400 seats or more.

   b. The U.S. Government also employs many civilian aircraft mechanics and avionics technicians to work on military aircraft at Army, Navy, Marine Corps, and Air Force installations in the states and overseas. Another government employer is the FAA. Most of the FAA maintenance personnel work on flight inspection aircraft at the FAA main overhaul base in Oklahoma City, OK. State and local governments also employ mechanics to maintain and service aircraft used for government, emergency medical, or police activities.

8. **WORKING CONDITIONS.** The majority of mechanics and avionics technicians work in hangars, on flight lines, or repair stations located on or near large airports. They use hand and power tools as well as sophisticated test equipment. The noise level both indoors and on the flight line can be very high. Those mechanics and technicians performing flight line maintenance often work in all kinds of weather and temperatures.

a. All aircraft mechanics and technicians must perform moderate to heavy physical activity, from climbing ladders to crawling under wings, the physical demands can be arduous. Frequent lifts or pulls of up to 50 pounds in weight are not uncommon.

b. Stress is another factor that aircraft mechanics and technicians must deal with. Working for a scheduled airline, the pressure to meet a gate time, or to meet a deadline for a corporation aircraft can be high. However, a mechanic or a technician must never sacrifice the high standards of workmanship and public trust just to meet a schedule.

9. WAGES AND BENEFITS. The aviation maintenance industry is broken down into two separate areas: Air Carrier and General Aviation.

a. Air Carriers.

(1) Air Carriers offer mechanics and technicians a starting yearly salary between $20,000 and $27,000 for a 40-hour week. Mechanics with a strong avionics background usually start between $25,000 and $30,000 a year. Maintenance is performed around the clock, seven days a week. New mechanics and technicians should expect to work nights and weekends. Within five years the salary for a mechanic with an Airframe and Powerplant Rating (A & P), should be between $35,000 and $45,000 a year. An avionics technician should earn between $38,000 and $48,000 a year.

(2) Air carriers offer paid holidays, vacations, insurance plans, retirement programs, sick leave, and free or reduced cost air travel within the airline's route structure. There are also opportunities to bid for maintenance positions at other locations the airline serves. With a larger work force, the opportunities for advancement may be greater with an air carrier than with other segments of the aviation maintenance industry, because of the high numbers of aircraft in the air carrier's fleet and the large number of cities served.

b. General Aviation.

(1) General Aviation is composed of many different types of organizations. These organizations are involved in all kinds of aviation activities from corporate transportation to agricultural application. Many aviation mechanics and technicians work for small FBOs or FAA part 145 Repair Stations that service and maintain the private/corporate aircraft fleet. The starting salary for these mechanics range between $18,000 and $24,000 a year. For avionics technicians the starting salary is between $22,000 and $28,000 a year. After 5 years a mechanic's salary range is between $25,000 and $30,000 a year. An avionics technicians salary is between $28,000 and $35,000 a year.

(2) Normal general aviation working hours are weekdays from 8:00 a.m. to 4:30 p.m. However, working nights, weekends, or working overtime is not uncommon in this industry.

(3) General Aviation benefits packages vary greatly, depending on the organization that one works for. Many general aviation corporations' operations rival the compensation packages of large air carriers, while other general aviation maintenance operations offer little in the way of health or retirement benefits.

(4) Some individuals are drawn to general aviation despite a lower pay scale and less generous benefits package because most of the general aviation jobs are found at the local airport or in smaller cities, where the quality of life is less hectic and the cost of living is less than working at the large hub airports.

10. MAINTENANCE OCCUPATIONS. There are two types of maintenance technicians: non-certificated mechanics and FAA-certificated mechanics.

a. Non-Certificated.

(1) A non-certificated mechanic can work only under the supervision of a certificated person. Non-certificated mechanics work in manufacturing, FAA Repair Stations, Air Carriers, and FBOs.

(2) Since these mechanics are not certificated by the FAA, there are no Federal certification requirements to meet. However, a job applicant must still meet the employer's requirements. As a non-certificated mechanic, he or she cannot sign off a maintenance record "approving the aircraft or component for return to service." Because of this limitation, a non-certificated mechanic is restricted in the scope, function, and duties he or she can perform. This limited level of ability also reduces the chances of advancement in the maintenance career field.

b. FAA-Certificated Mechanics and Repairmen. The FAA certificates aviation maintenance personnel in two ways: a mechanic certificate and a repairman certificate.

(1) Certificated Mechanic Requirements.

(a) The vast majority of technicians are certificated as FAA mechanics. Under an FAA mechanic's certificate there are two ratings: Airframe and Powerplant. Although most certificated mechanics hold both ratings and are referred to in the industry as an "A & P," there are many mechanics certificated only with an airframe (A) rating, or only a powerplant (P) rating.

(b) To become an FAA-certificated mechanic an applicant must:

1. Be 18 years of age or older.
2. Be able to read, write, and understand English.
3. Document 18 months of practical experience in either one of the ratings sought, or 30 months of practical experience working concurrently on airframes and power plants, or graduate from an FAA-approved part 147 Aviation Maintenance Technician School.
4. Must pass a written examination, an oral test, and a practical test for each rating.
5. Pass all the prescribed tests within 24 months.

(c) Additional certification requirements for foreign applicants located outside of the United States at the time of the examination:

1. The applicant must demonstrate that a mechanic certificate is needed to maintain U.S.-registered civil aircraft and that the applicant is neither a U.S. citizen or a resident alien.
2. Positive identification of the applicant must be established. (i.e., passport).
3. Applicant must provide a signed and detailed statement (original copy only, no duplicate copies will be accepted) from their employer substantiating specific type and duration of maintenance performed on each aircraft.
4. The applicant must provide a letter obtained from the foreign airworthiness authority of the country in which the experience was gained or from an advisor of the International Civil Aviation Organization (ICAO) that will validate their maintenance experience.

5. All documents must be signed, dated originals, and traceable to the initiator.
6. A fee for the document review will be charged in accordance with 14 CFR part 187.
7. Applicants who do not meet the English requirements of 14 CFR part 65, section 65.71(a)(2) will have their certificates endorsed: "Valid only outside of the U.S."

(2) Repairman Requirements.

(a) Repairman are maintenance technicians that are certificated by the FAA for only one or two specific tasks. Because they are limited by function, they can only exercise the privileges of the repairman certificate by being under the supervision of FAA-approved Repair Stations, commercial operators, or air carriers where these specific tasks are routinely accomplished on a daily basis. It is the repair station, commercial operator, or air carrier who recommend an individual to be a repairman. The individual must meet the following requirements.

(b) To be eligible for a repairman certificate an applicant must be:

1. At least 18 years of age.
2. Able to read, write, and understand the English language.

NOTE: This may be waived for a repairman living outside the United States.

3. Specially qualified to perform maintenance on aircraft or components.
4. Employed for a specific job requiring the special qualifications by an FAA-certificated Repair Station, or a certificated commercial operator, or a certificated air carrier.
5. Recommended for the repairman certificate by his or her employer.
6. Have either 18 months practical experience in the specific job function (i.e., Industry X-Ray technician) or complete a formal training course acceptable to the FAA.

c. Avionics Occupations. Avionics technicians work on some of the most advanced electronic equipment outside of an electronic research and development laboratory. It is not uncommon for the avionics bay of an air carrier aircraft to hold eight to ten million dollars worth of "black boxes" all of which need a highly qualified person to maintain them.

(1) An individual who holds an FAA mechanic certificate with an airframe rating is authorized under his rating to maintain avionics equipment. But this privilege is allowed only if that individual is properly trained, qualified, and has the proper tools and equipment to perform the work.

(2) There are also un-certificated individuals working for air carrier avionics departments or FAA-certificated avionics repair stations. These individuals have gained experience in avionics repairs from serving in the military, working for avionics manufacturers, and other related industries.

11. PRACTICAL EXPERIENCE QUALIFICATION REQUIREMENTS. Individuals who wish to become FAA-certificated aircraft mechanics can choose one of three paths to meet the experience requirements for the FAA Airframe and Power Plant Certificate.

a. An individual can work for an FAA Repair Station or FBO under the supervision of an A & P mechanic for 18 months, for each individual airframe or powerplant rating, or 30 months for both ratings. The FAA considers a "month of practical experience" to contain at least 160 hours. This practical experience must be documented. Some acceptable forms of documentation are: Pay receipts, a record of work (log book) signed by the supervising mechanic, a notarized statement stating that the applicant has at least the required number of hours for the rating(s) requested from a certificated air carrier, repair station, or a certificated mechanic or repairman who supervised the work.

b. An individual can join one of the armed services and obtain valuable training and experience in aircraft maintenance. Care must be taken that an individual enters a military occupational specialty (MOS) that is one the FAA credits for practical experience for the mechanics certificate. A list of these acceptable MOS positions that was current as of March 2001 can be found in Appendix A.

NOTE: Before requesting credit for a specific MOS or before joining the military, the individual should get a *current list* of the acceptable MOS codes from the local FAA Flight Standards District Office (FSDO) and compare it against the MOS that he or she has or is applying for (see Appendix B for a list of the FSDOs). When the 18/30 month requirement is satisfied the applicant should ensure that the MOS code is properly identified on his or her DD-214 Form, Certificate of Release or Discharge from Active Duty.

(1) In addition to the MOS code on the DD-214 form the applicant must have a letter from the applicant's executive officer, maintenance officer, or classification officer that certifies the applicant's length of military service, the amount of time the applicant worked in each MOS, the make and model of the aircraft and/or engine on which the applicant acquired the practical experience, and where the experience was obtained.

(2) Time spent in training for the MOS is NOT credited toward the 18/30 month practical experience requirement. As with experience obtained from civilian employment the applicant that is using military experience to qualify must set aside additional study time to prepare for the written and oral/practical tests. Having an acceptable MOS does not mean the applicant will get the credit for practical experience. Only after a complete review of the applicant's paperwork, and a satisfactory interview with an FAA Airworthiness inspector to ensure that the applicant did satisfy part 65, subpart D, will the authorization be granted.

c. An individual can attend one of the 170 FAA 14 CFR part 147 Aviation Maintenance Technician Schools nationwide. These schools offer training for one mechanic's rating or both. Many schools offer avionics courses that cover electronics and instrumentation.

(1) A high school diploma or a General Education Diploma (GED) is usually an entrance requirement for most schools. The length of the FAA-approved course varies between 12 months and 24 months, but the period of training is normally shorter than the FAA requirements for on-the-job training.

(2) Upon graduation from the school, the individual is qualified to take the FAA exams. A positive benefit of attending a part 147 school is that the starting salary is sometimes higher for a graduate than for an individual who earns his certification strictly on military or civilian experience.

d. To apply to take the mechanic written test, the applicant must first present his or her part 147 certificate of graduation or completion, or proof of civilian or military practical experience, to an FAA inspector at the local FSDO.

(1) Once the FAA inspector is satisfied that the applicant is eligible for the rating(s) requested, the inspector signs FAA Form 8610-2, Airman Certificate and/or Rating Application. There are three kinds of written tests: Aviation Mechanic General (AMG), Aviation Mechanic Airframe (AMA), and Aviation Mechanic Powerplant (AMP).

(2) The applicant must then make an appointment for testing at one of the many computer testing facilities world-wide. Contact the nearest FSDO for the nearest computer testing facility. The tests are provided on a cost basis but test results are immediate. If an applicant fails a test, then he or she must wait 30 days to either retake the test or provide the testing facility with documentation from a certificated person that the applicant has received instruction in each of the subject areas previously failed, or have the bottom portion of AC Form 8080-2, Airman Written Test Report, properly filled out and signed. The retest covers all subject areas in the failed section. All written tests must be completed within a 24-month period.

(3) For a list of computer testing locations contact the nearest FSDO or access the internet at http://www.fedworld.gov. A list of sample general airframe and powerplant test questions are also available at the same internet site.

e. Oral and Practical Skill Test Requirements. These tests are given on a fee for services basis by a Designated Mechanic Examiner (DME). A list of the DMEs is available at the local FSDO. The oral and practical tests cover all 43 technical and regulatory subject areas and combine oral questions with demonstration of technical skill. A test for a single rating (airframe or powerplant) commonly requires 8 hours to complete.

(1) If a portion of the test is failed, he or she will have to wait 30 days to retest. However, the applicant can be retested in less than 30 days if the applicant presents a letter to the DME showing that the applicant has received additional instruction in the areas that he or she has failed, a retest can be administered covering only the subject(s) failed in the original test.

(2) When all tests are satisfactorily completed within a 24-month period, the successful applicant receives a copy of FAA Form 8060-4, Temporary Airman Certificate, which is valid for 120 days or until the FAA Airmen Certification Branch in Oklahoma issues the mechanic a permanent certificate.

/s/ Louis C. Cusimano for
Ava L. Mims
Acting Director, Flight Standards Service

APPENDIX A

Military Occupational Specialty Codes

Following are both the updated, new, and the older MOS codes for the U.S. Army, Air Force, Navy, Marine Corps, and Coast Guard dated March 2001. The new codes are used for active duty time after January 1990. The older codes are still valid for persons wishing to credit their military aviation maintenance experience toward meeting the requirements of the FAA airframe and powerplant mechanic certificate.

U.S. Army Codes

Updated MOS Codes	New MOS Codes	Title	Creditable Experience
67G 10/20/30/40		Utility Aircraft Repairer	Airframe & Powerplant
67H 10/20/30/40		Observation Aircraft Repairer	Airframe & Powerplant
67N 10/20/30/40		Utility Helicopter Repairer	Airframe & Powerplant
67R 10/20/30/40		AH-64 Helicopter Repairer	Airframe & Powerplant
67S 10/20/30/40		Scout Helicopter Repairer	Airframe & Powerplant
67T 10/20/30/40		Tact/Transport Helicopter Repairer	Airframe & Powerplant
67U 10/20/30/40		Medium Helicopter Repairer	Airframe & Powerplant
67V 10/20/30/40		Observe/Scout Helicopter Repairer	Airframe & Powerplant
67X 10/20/30/40		Heavy Lift Helicopter Repairer	Airframe & Powerplant
67Y 10/20/30/40		AH-1 Helicopter Repairer	Airframe & Powerplant
67Z 50		Aircraft Maintenance Sr. Sergeant	Airframe & Powerplant
68B 10/20/30		Aircraft Powerplant Repairer	Powerplant
68D 10/20/30		Aircraft Powertrain Repairer	Powerplant
68G 10/20/30		Aircraft Structural Repairer	Airframe
68K 40		Aircraft Components Repair Supervision	Airframe & Powerplant

U.S. Air Force Codes

Current MOS Codes	1992-MOS Codes	Prior to 1992 MOS Code	Title	Creditable Experience
2A333	45234	43131	Tactical Aircraft Main. Apprentice	Airframe
2A353	45254	43151	Tactical Aircraft Main. Journeyman	Airframe & Powerplant
2A373	45274	43171	Tactical Aircraft Main. Craftsman	Airframe & Powerplant
2A390	45299	43191, 43199	Tactical Aircraft Main. Superintendent	Airframe & Powerplant
2A531	45730, 45732	43131, 43132, 43133, 45333	Aerospace Maintenance Apprentice	Airframe
2A551	45750, 45752	43151, 43152, 43153, 45353	Aerospace Maintenance Journeyman	Airframe & Powerplant
2A571	45770, 45772	43171, 43172, 43173, 45373	Aerospace Maintenance Craftsman	Airframe & Powerplant
2A590	45799	43191, 43199	Aerospace Maintenance Superintendent	Airframe & Powerplant
2A532	45731	43130	Helicopter Maintenance Apprentice	Airframe
2A552	45751	43150	Helicopter Maintenance Journeyman	Airframe & Powerplant
2A572	45771	43170	Helicopter Maintenance Craftsman	Airframe & Powerplant
2A590	45791	43190, 43199	Helicopter Maintenance Superintendent	Airframe & Powerplant
2A631	45430	42632, 42644, 43132	Aerospace Propulsion Apprentice	Powerplant
2A651	45450	42652, 42653, 43152	Aerospace Propulsion Journeyman	Powerplant
2A671	45470	42672, 42673, 43172	Aerospace Propulsion Craftsman	Powerplant
2A690	45490	42692, 42693, 43192	Aerospace Propulsion Superintendent	Powerplant
2A635	45434	42334	AC Pneudraulic System Maintenance Apprentice	Airframe
2A655	45454	42354	AC Pneudraulic System Maintenance Journeyman	Airframe
2A675	45474	42374	AC Pneudraulic System Maintenance Craftsman	Airframe
2A690	45494	42396	AC Pneudraulic System Maintenance Superintendent	Airframe
2A636	45235, 45435, 45436	42330, 42331	AC Electrical & Environmental System Apprentice	Airframe
2A656	45255, 45455, 45456	42350, 42351	AC Electrical & Environmental System Journeyman	Airframe
2A676	45275, 45475, 45476	42370, 42371	AC Electrical & Environmental System Craftsman	Airframe

U.S. Air Force Codes (Continued)

Current MOS Codes	1992-MOS Codes	Prior to 1992 MOS Code	Title	Creditable Experience
2A690	45295, 45495, 45496	42390	AC Electrical & Environmental System Superintendent	Airframe
2A733	45832	42731, 42735	Aircraft Structural Main. Apprentice	Airframe
2A753	45852	42751,42755	Aircraft Structural Main. Journeyman	Airframe
2A773	45872	42771, 42775	Aircraft Structural Main. Craftsman	Airframe
2A793	45899	42799	Aircraft Structural Main. Superintendent	Airframe

U.S. Coast Guard Codes

OLD MOS Codes	New MOS Codes	Title	Creditable Experience
AD		Aviation Machinist Mate	Airframe & Powerplant
AE		Aviation Electrician	Airframe
AM		Aviation Structural Mechanic	Airframe & Powerplant
AMT		Aviation Maintenance Technician	Airframe & Powerplant

U.S. Navy Codes

Current MOS Codes	Title	Creditable Experience
AD-6402	Reciprocating Engine Technician	Powerplant
AD-6409	J-57 Turbojet Engine Mechanic	Powerplant
AD-6410	F-110 Turbofan Jet Engine Technician	Powerplant
AD-6414	TF-41 Turbofan Jet Engine Technician	Powerplant
AD-6415	TF-30 Turbofan Jet Engine Mechanic	Powerplant
AD-6416	J-52 Turbojet Engine Mechanic	Powerplant
AD-6417	T-400 Turboshaft Jet Engine Mechanic	Powerplant
AD-6418	T-56 Turboprop Engine Mechanic	Powerplant
AD-6419	T-58 Turbofan Jet Engine Mechanic	Powerplant
AD-6420	T-404 Turbofan Jet Engine Mechanic	Powerplant
AD-6421	TF-34 Turbofan Jet Engine Mechanic	Powerplant
AD-6422	Test Cell Operator Maintainer	Powerplant
AD-6423	T-56-425/426 Turboprop Engine and Propeller Mechanic	Powerplant
AD-6424	T-64 Turboshaft Jet Engine and Propeller Mechanic	Powerplant
AD-6426	T-700 Turboshaft Jet Engine Mechanic	Powerplant
AD-6428	J-85 Turboshaft Engine Mechanic	Powerplant

U.S. Navy Codes (Continued)

Current MOS Codes	Title	Creditable Experience
AM-7232	Structural Repair Technician	Airframe

NOTE: The following NECs may qualify for both an A and/or P rating. FSDOs will need to evaluate individual to determine appropriate rating:

8235	E-6 Flight Engineer	Airframe and/or Powerplant
8251	P-3 Flight Engineer	Airframe and/or Powerplant
8252	C-130 Flight Engineer	Airframe and/or Powerplant

NOTE: The following NECs are aircraft specific and are awarded to individuals advancing from the AD (powerplant), AM (structure), AE (electronics), or AT (avionics). The only individuals that should be given consideration for an A and/or P rating are ones who have held an AM or AD rating. Therefore, the FSDO needs to determine individuals' background to ascertain if they have held an AM or AD rating. If so, then the FSDO can determine, through the interview process, on whether the individual meets the qualifications for an A and/or P rating:

8303	CH/MH-53E Systems Organizational Main. Tech.	Airframe OR Powerplant
8305	C2/E2 Systems Organizational Main. Tech.	Airframe OR Powerplant
8306	E-2C Group II Systems Organizational Main. Tech.	Airframe OR Powerplant
8318	C-130 Systems Organizational Main. Tech.	Airframe OR Powerplant
8319	P-3 Systems Organizational Main. Tech.	Airframe OR Powerplant
8332	EA-6B Systems Organizational Main. Tech.	Airframe OR Powerplant
8335	F-14B/D Systems Organizational Main. Tech.	Airframe OR Powerplant
8341	F/A-18E/F Systems Organizational Main. Tech.	Airframe OR Powerplant
8342	F/A 18 Systems Organizational Main. Tech.	Airframe OR Powerplant
8343	E-6A Systems Organizational Main. Tech.	Airframe OR Powerplant
8345	F-14 Systems Organizational Main. Tech.	Airframe OR Powerplant
8346	S-3A Systems Organizational Main. Tech.	Airframe OR Powerplant
8378	H-60 Systems Organizational Main. Tech.	Airframe OR Powerplant
8379	H-46 Systems Organizational Main. Tech.	Airframe OR Powerplant
8380	UH-1N Systems Organizational Main. Tech.	Airframe OR Powerplant

U.S. Marine Corps Codes

Updated MOS Codes	New MOS Codes	Title	Creditable Experience
6012		Aircraft Mechanic	Airframe
6013	6213	Aircraft Mechanic	Airframe
6014		Aircraft Mechanic	Airframe
6015	6212	Aircraft Mechanic	Airframe
6016	6216	Aircraft Mechanic	Airframe
6017	6217	Aircraft Mechanic	Airframe
6018		Aircraft Mechanic	Airframe
6019		Aircraft Maintenance Chief	Airframe & Powerplant
6022	6223	Aircraft Powerplant Mechanic J-52	Powerplant
6024		Aircraft Powerplant Mechanic T-76	Powerplant
6025	6222	Aircraft Powerplant Mechanic–Rolls Royce Pegasus	Powerplant
6026	6226	Aircraft Powerplant Mechanic T-56	Powerplant
6027	6227	Aircraft Powerplant Mechanic F-404	Powerplant
6028		Aircraft Powerplant Mechanic	Powerplant
6029		Aircraft Powerplant Mechanic	Powerplant
6053	6253	Aircraft Structures Mechanic	Airframe
6055	6252	Aircraft Structures Mechanic	Airframe
6056	6256	Aircraft Structures Mechanic	Airframe
6057	6257	Aircraft Structures Mechanic	Airframe
6059	6019	Aircraft Airframe Maintenance Chief	Airframe
6112		Helicopter Mechanic	Airframe
6113		Helicopter Mechanic	Airframe
6114		Helicopter Mechanic	Airframe
6119	6019	Helicopter Maintenance Chief	Airframe & Powerplant
6122		Helicopter Powerplant Mechanic T-58	Powerplant
6123		Helicopter Powerplant Mechanic T-58	Powerplant
6152A		Aircraft Structures Mechanic	Airframe
6153A		Aircraft Structures Mechanic	Airframe
6154A		Aircraft Structures Mechanic	Airframe
6155A	6156	Aircraft Structures Mechanic	Airframe
6172		Helicopter Crew Chief CH-46	Airframe & Powerplant
6173		Helicopter Crew Chief CH-53	Airframe & Powerplant
6174		Helicopter Crew Chief H-1/AH-1	Airframe & Powerplant
6175		Tilt Rotor Crew Chief V-22	Airframe & Powerplant
	6116	Tilt Rotor Mechanic	Airframe
	6124	Helicopter Powerplant Mech. T-400/T-700	Powerplant
	6178	Presidential Helicopter Crew Chief VH-60N	Airframe & Powerplant
	6179	Presidential Helicopter Crew Chief VH-3D	Airframe & Powerplant

APPENDIX B
Flight Standards District Office's Addresses

ALASKAN REGION

ANCHORAGE FSDO–03
4510 W. International Airport Road
Anchorage, AK 99502-1088
COM: (907) 271-2000
FAX: (907) 271-4777

FAIRBANKS FSDO–01
6450 Airport Way, Suite 2
Fairbanks, AK 99709
COM: (907) 457-0276
FAX: (907) 479-9650

JUNEAU FSDO–05
1873 Shell Simmons Drive
Juneau, AK 99801
COM: (907) 586-7532
FAX: (907) 586-8833

CENTRAL REGION

DES MOINES, FSDO
3021 Army Post Road
Des Moines, IA 50321
COM: (515) 285-9895
FAX: (515) 285-7595

SAINT LOUIS FSDO–03
10801 Pear Tree Lane, Suite 200
St. Ann, MO 63074
COM: (314) 429-1006
FAX: (314) 429-6367

KANSAS CITY FSDO–05
10015 N. Executive Hills Blvd.
Kansas City, MO 64153
COM: (816) 891-2100
FAX: (816) 891-2155

WICHITA FSDO–07
1801 Airport Road
Mid-Continent Airport
FAA Building, Room 103
Wichita, KS 67209
COM: (316) 941-1200
FAX: (316) 946-4420

LINCOLN FSDO–09
3841 Aviation Rd., Suite 120
Lincoln, NE 68524
COM: (402) 475-1738
FAX: (402) 474-7013

EASTERN REGION

ALBANY FSDO–1
7 Airport Park Blvd.
Latham, NY 12110
COM: (518) 785-5660
FAX: (518) 785-7165

ALLEGHENY FSDO–03
Graham Building, Suite 300
3000 Lebanon Church Rd
West Mifflin, PA 15122-2630
COM: (412) 466-5357
FAX: (412) 466-3749

ALLENTOWN FSDO–5
961 Marcon Blvd, Suite 111
Allentown, PA 18103
COM: (610) 264-2888
FAX: (610) 264-3179

BALTIMORE FSDO–07
890 Airport Park Rd., Suite 101
Glen Burnie, MD 21061-2559
COM: (410) 787-0040
FAX: (410) 787-8708

CHARLESTON FSDO–09
301 Eagle Mountain Road
Yeager Airport, Room 144
Charleston, WV 25311-1093
COM: (304) 347-5199
FAX: (304) 343-2011

FARMINGDALE FSDO–11
Administration Bldg, Suite 235
Route 110, Republic Airport
Farmingdale, NY 11735-1583
COM: (631) 755-1300
FAX: (631) 694-5516

HARRISBURG FSDO–13
Room 101, Administration Bldg.
400 Airport Drive
New Cumberland, PA 17070-2489
COM: (717) 774-8271 x206
FAX: (717) 774-8327

PHILADELPHIA FSDO–17
2 International Plaza, Suite 110
Philadelphia, PA 19113-1504
COM: (610) 595-1500
FAX: (610) 595-1519

RICHMOND FSDO–21
5707 Huntsman Rd, Suite 100
Richmond Int'l Airport, VA 23250-2415
COM: (804) 222-7494
FAX: (804) 222-4843

ROCHESTER FSDO–23
1 Airport Way, Suite 110
Rochester, NY 14624
COM: (716) 436-3880
FAX: (716) 436-2322

TETERBORO FSDO–25
150 Fred Wehran Drive, Room 1
Teterboro Airport
Teterboro, NJ 07608
COM: (201) 393-6700
FAX: (201) 288-7308

WASHINGTON DC FSDO–27
PO Box 17325
Washington FSDO–27
Washington/Dulles Int'l Airport
Washington, DC 20041-0325
COM: (703) 661-8160
FAX: (703) 661-8744
Mailing address: 600 W. Service Rd
Chantilly, VA 22021

GREAT LAKES REGION

DUPAGE FSDO–03
31W 775 N. Avenue
DuPage Airport
West Chicago, IL 60185-1056
COM: (630) 443-3100
FAX: (630) 443-3155

CINCINNATI FSDO–05
Lunken Airport, Executive Bldg.
4240 Airport Road, Ground Floor
Cincinnati, OH 45226
COM: (513) 533-8110
FAX: (513) 533-8420

COLUMBUS FSDO, GL-07
3939 Int'l Gateway, 2nd Floor
Port Columbus Int'l Airport
Columbus, OH 43219
COM: (614) 237-1039
FAX: (614) 231-0920

GRAND RAPIDS FSDO–09
PO Box 888879
Grand Rapids, MI 49588-8879
COM: (616) 954-6657
FAX: (616) 940-3140

INDIANAPOLIS FSDO–11
8303 W. Southern Avenue
Indianapolis, IN 46241
COM: (317) 487-2400
FAX: (317) 487-2429

MILWAUKEE FSDO–13
4915 South Howell Avenue
Milwaukee, WI 53207
COM: (414) 486-2920
FAX: (414) 486-2921

MINNEAPOLIS FSDO–15
6020 28th Ave. South, Room 201
Minneapolis-St. Paul Int'l Airport
Minneapolis, MN 55450
COM: (612) 713-4211
FAX: (612) 713-4195

SOUTH BEND FSDO–17
1843 Commerce Drive
South Bend, IN 46628
COM: (219) 245-4600
FAX: (219) 233-9387

SPRINGFIELD FSDO–19
1250 North Airport Drive, Suite 1
Springfield, IL 62707-8417
COM: (217) 744-1910
FAX: (217) 744-1947

FARGO FSDO–21
1801 23rd Avenue N, Room 216
Fargo, ND 58102
COM: (701) 232-8949
FAX: (701) 235-2863

DETROIT FSDO–23
Willow Run Airport, East Side
800 Beck Road, Room 6
Belleville, MI 48111
COM: (734) 487-7222
FAX: (734) 487-7221

CLEVELAND FSDO–25
Great Northern Technology Park II
25249 Country Club Blvd
North Olmstead, OH 44070
COM: (440) 686-2001
FAX: (440) 686-2080

RAPID CITY FSDO–27
Flight Standards District Office
909 St. Joseph St, Suite 700
Rapid City, SD 57701-2699
COM: (605) 737-3050
FAX: (605) 737-3069

MINNEAPOLIS CMO–01
6020 28th Avenue S., Room 202
Minneapolis, MN 55450
COM: (612) 713-4211
FAX: (612) 713-4204

NEW ENGLAND REGION

BEDFORD FSDO–01
Civil Air Terminal, 2nd floor
Hanscom Field
Bedford, MA 01730-2616
COM: (781) 274-7130
FAX: (781) 274-6725

WINDSOR LOCKS FSDO–03
Building 85-214, 1st Floor
Bradley International Airport
Windsor Locks, CT 06096-1009
COM: (860) 654-1000
FAX: (860) 654-1009

PORTLAND FSDO–05
Portland International Jetport
2 Al McKay Avenue
Portland, ME 04102-1999
COM: (207) 780-3263
FAX: (207) 780-3296

NORTHWEST MOUNTAIN REGION

SEATTLE FSDO–01
1601 Lind Ave SW
Renton, WA 98055-4056
COM: (1-800) 354-1940
FAX: (425) 227-1810

DENVER FSDO–03
26805 E. 68th Ave, Suite 200
Denver, CO 80249-6361
COM: (303) 342-110
FAX: (303) 342-1176

CASPER FSDO–04
905 Werner Court, Suite 320
Casper, WY 82601-1312
COM: (307) 261-5425
FAX: (307) 261-5424

HELENA FSDO–05
2725 Skyway Drive, Suite 1
Helena Regional Airport
Helena, MT 59601
COM: (406) 449-5270
FAX: (406) 449-5275

SALT LAKE CITY FSDO–07
116 North 2400 West
Salt Lake City, UT 84116
COM: (800) 532-00268
FAX: (801) 524-5329

PORTLAND FSDO–09
Portland-Hillsboro Airport
1800 NE 25th Avenue, Suite 15
Hillsboro, OR 97124
COM: (503) 681-5500
FAX: (503) 681-5555

BOISE FSDO–11
3295 Elder Street
Airport Plaza, Suite 350
Boise, ID 83705-4712
COM: (208) 334-1238
FAX: (208) 334-9261

SPOKANE FSDO–13
6133 E. Rutter Avenue
Spokane, WA 99212
COM: (509) 353-2434
FAX: (509) 353-2122

SOUTHERN REGION

LOUISVILLE, FSDO–01
Watterson Tower, 11th Floor
1930 Bishop Lane
Louisville, KY 40218-1921
COM: (502) 582-5941
FAX: (502) 582-6735

NASHVILLE, FSDO–03
2 Int'l Plaza Dr., Suite 700
Nashville, TN 37217
COM: (615) 781-5430
FAX: (615) 781-5436

GREENSBORO FSDO–05
6433 Bryan Blvd
Greensboro, NC 27409
COM: (336) 662-1000
FAX: (336) 662-1080

JACKSON, FSDO–07
120 N Hangar Drive, Suite C
Jackson, MS 39208
COM: (601) 965-4633
FAX: (601) 965-4636

BIRMINGHAM FSDO 09
1500 Urban Center Dr, Suite 250
Vestavia Hills, AL 35242
COM: (205) 731-1557
FAX: (205) 731-0939

ATLANTA, FSDO–11
1701 Columbia Avenue
(Campus Building 2-110)
College Park, GA 30337
COM: (404) 305-7200
FAX: (404) 305-7215

COLUMBIA, FSDO–13
125-B Summer Lake Dr.
West Columbia, SC 29170
COM: (803) 765-5931
FAX: (404) 253-3999

ORLANDO, FSDO–15
Citadel International, Suite 500
5950 Hazeltine National Dr.
Orlando, FL 32822-5023
COM: (407) 816-0000
FAX: (407) 816-0507

FT. LAUDERDALE, FSDO–17
1050 Lee Wagener Blvd., Suite 201
Ft. Lauderdale, FL 33315
COM: (954) 356-7520
FAX: (954) 356-7531

MIAMI, FSDO–19
8600 NW 36th Street, Room 201
Miami, FL 33166
COM: (305) 716-3400
FAX: (305) 716-3455

SAN JUAN, FSDO–21
Suite 901, La Torre De Las Americas
525 F.D. Roosevelt Avenue
Hato Rey, PR 00918-1198
COM: (787) 764-2538
FAX: (787) 764-2641

MEMPHIS FSDO–25
3385 Airways Blvd, Suite 30
Memphis, TN 38116
COM: (901) 544-3801
FAX: (901) 544-4205

CHARLOTTE, FSDO–33
4700 Yorkmont Road, Room 203
Charlotte, NC 28208
COM: (704) 344-6488
FAX: (704) 344-6485

TAMPA FSDO–35
5601 Mariner St, Suite 310
Tampa, FL 33609
COM: (813) 639-1540
FAX: (813) 639-1551

SOUTHWEST REGION

ALBUQUERQUE FSDO–01
ABQ International Airport
1601 Randolph Rd SE, Suite 200N
Albuquerque, NM 87106
COM: (505) 764-1200
FAX: (505) 764-1233

BATON-ROUGE FSDO–03
FAA Building, Ryan Airport
9191 Plank Road
Baton Rouge, LA 70811
COM: (504) 358-6800
FAX: (504) 358-6875

DALLAS-FSDO–05
3300 Love Field Drive
Dallas, TX 75235
COM: (214) 902-1800
FAX: (214) 902-1872

HOUSTON FSDO–09
13100 Space Center Blvd, Suite 5400
Houston, TX 77059-3598
COM: (713) 212-9700
FAX: (713) 212-9759

LITTLE ROCK FSDO–11
1701 Bond St, Adams Field
Little Rock, AR 72202-5733
COM: (501) 918-4400
FAX: (501) 918-4403

LUBBOCK FSDO–13
Lubbock Airport
Route 3, Box 51
Lubbock, TX 79401-9712
COM: (806) 740-3800
FAX: (806) 740-3809

OKLAHOMA FSDO–15
The Parkway Building
1300 S. Meridan, Suite 601
Oklahoma City, OK 73108
COM: (405) 951-4200
FAX: (405) 951-4282

SAN ANTONIO FSDO–17
International Airport
10100 Reunion Place, Suite 200
San Antonio, TX 78216
COM: (210) 308-3300
FAX: (210) 308-3399

FORT WORTH FSDO–19
Fort Worth Alliance Airport
2260 Alliance Boulevard
Fort Worth, TX 76177
COM: (817) 491-5000
FAX: (817) 491-5014

WESTERN PACIFIC REGION

VAN NUYS FSDO–1
16501 Sherman Way, Suite 330
Van Nuys, CA 91406
COM: (818) 904-6291
FAX: (818) 786-9732

LONG BEACH FSDO–05
5001 Airport Plaza Dr, Suite 100
Long Beach, CA 90815
COM: (562) 420-1755
FAX: (562) 420-6765

SCOTTDALE FSDO–7
17777 N. Perimeter Drive, Suite 101
Scottsdale, AZ 85255
COM: (480) 419-0111
FAX: (480) 419-0800

SAN DIEGO FSDO–9
8525 Gibbs Drive, Suite 120
San Diego, CA 92123
COM: (619) 557-5281
FAX: (619) 279-3241

RENO FSDO–11
4900 Energy Way
Reno, NV 89502
COM: (702) 858-7700
FAX: (702) 858-7737

HONOLULU FSDO–13
135 Nakolo Place
Honolulu, HI 96819-1845
COM: (808) 837-8307
FAX: (808) 837-8399

SAN JOSE FSDO–15
1250 Aviation Avenue, Suite 295
San Jose, CA 95110-1130
COM: (408) 291-7681
FAX: (408) 279-5448

FRESNO, FSDO–17
Fresno Air Terminal
4955 E. Anderson, Suite 110
Fresno, CA 93827
COM: (559) 487-5306
FAX: (559) 454-8808

LAS VEGAS FSDO–19
7181 Amigo St, Suite 180
Las Vegas, NV 89119
COM: (702) 269-1445
FAX: (702) 269 8013

RIVERSIDE FSDO–21
6961 Flight Road
Riverside Municipal Airport
Riverside, CA 92504-1991
COM: (909) 276-6701
FAX: (909) 689-4309

LOS ANGELES FSDO–23
2250 E. Imperial, Suite 140
El Sequendo, CA 90245
COM: (310) 215-2150
FAX: (310) 645-3768

SACRAMENTO FSDO–25
6650 Belleau Wood Lane
Sacramento, CA 95822
COM: (916) 422-0272
FAX: (916) 422-0462

OAKLAND FSDO–27
8517 Earhart Road, Suite 100
Oakland, CA 94621-4500
COM: (510) 273-7155
FAX: (510) 632-4773

FAA-G-8082-11A

Inspection Authorization Knowledge Test Guide

INSPECTION
IA
AUTHORIZATION

U.S. Department of Transportation
Federal Aviation Administration

8082-11A

AC

Inspection Authorization Knowledge Test Guide

2004

U.S. Department of Transportation
Federal Aviation Administration
Flight Standards Service

8082-11A

AC

Preface

FAA-G-8082-11A, Inspection Authorization Knowledge Test Guide, provides information for preparing to take the Inspection Authorization Knowledge Test. Appendix 1 provides sample forms. Appendix 2 provides publication and technical data. Appendix 3 provides lists of reference materials and subject matter knowledge codes.

Changes to the subject matter knowledge codes will be published in AC 60-25, Reference Materials and Subject Matter Knowledge Codes for Airman Knowledge Testing.

The current Flight Standards Service subject matter knowledge codes for all airman certificates and ratings can be obtained from the Regulatory Support Division, AFS-600, home page on the Internet.

The Regulatory Support Division's Internet address is: http://afs600.faa.gov

FAA-G-8082-11A supersedes FAA-G-8082-11, dated 1999.

Comments regarding this guide should be sent in e-mail form to AFS630Comments@faa.gov.

Contents

Preface ... iii
Contents ... v
Introduction ... 1
Knowledge Test Eligibility Requirements ... 1
Knowledge Areas on the Test ... 1
Description of the Test ... 2
Process for Taking a Knowledge Test ... 2
Use of Test Aids and Materials ... 4
Cheating or Other Unauthorized Conduct ... 5
Retesting Procedures ... 5
Basic Functions of an IA ... 6
General ... 6
Approving Major Repairs and Major Alterations ... 6
Annual and Progressive Inspections ... 8
Aircraft Records ... 12
Maintenance Records ... 12
Completion of FAA Form 337, Major Repair and Alteration (Airframe, Powerplant, Propeller, or Appliance) ... 12
Weight and Balance ... 13
Suggestions for Developing Good Owner / IA Relations ... 14
Sample Test Questions and Answers ... 16
Suggestions for Studying for the IA Test ... 19

Appendix 1—Sample Forms

FIGURE 1. FAA Form 8610-1, Mechanic's Application for Inspection Authorization ... 1-1
FIGURE 2. FAA Form 8310-5, Inspection Authorization, (front and back view) ... 1-2
FIGURE 3. FAA Form 337, Major Repair and Alteration (Airframe, Powerplant, Propeller, or Appliance), (front view) ... 1-3
FIGURE 4. FAA Form 337, Major Repair and Alteration (Airframe, Powerplant, Propeller, or Appliance), (back view) ... 1-4
FIGURE 5. Example of a maintenance record entry ... 1-5
FIGURE 6. Airworthiness Directive compliance record (suggested format) ... 1-6
FIGURE 7. FAA Form 8010-4, Malfunction or Defect Report, (revised 10-92) ... 1-7
FIGURE 8. Example of an operating limitations placard ... 1-8
FIGURE 9. Example of a record entry for an annual inspection in which the aircraft was found to be unairworthy ... 1-8
FIGURE 10. Example of a discrepancy list to be provided to an aircraft owner when reporting an aircraft with unairworthy items after completing an annual inspection ... 1-9
FIGURE 11. Example of a weight and balance revision for a typical light, single-engine aircraft ... 1-10
FIGURE 12. Example of a one-time Airworthiness Directive compliance entry ... 1-11
FIGURE 13. Example of a recurrent Airworthiness Directive compliance entry ... 1-11

Appendix 2 — Publications and Technical Data

1. Title 14 of the Code of Federal Regulations (CFR) 2-1
2. Type Certificate Data Sheets and Specifications 2-2
3. Summary of Airworthiness Directives for Small Aircraft and Rotorcraft (ADs) 2-3
4. Advisory Circulars 2-3
5. How to Order Publications 2-4
6. Additional Sources of Inspection Data 2-4

Appendix 3 — List of Reference Materials and Subject Matter Knowledge Codes

List of Reference Materials and Subject Matter Knowledge Codes 3-1

Inspection Authorization Knowledge Test Guide

Introduction

The Federal Aviation Administration (FAA) initiated the issuance of the Inspection Authorization (IA) more than 35 years ago. This system of allowing qualified mechanics the privilege of performing certain inspections has served well in the maintenance of the U.S. Civil Fleet. The attainment of an IA and performance of the duties of that certificate greatly enhance the privileges and responsibilities of the aircraft mechanic. The IA permits the airframe and powerplant (A&P) mechanic to perform a greater variety of maintenance and alterations than any other single maintenance entity.

The determination of airworthiness during an inspection is a serious responsibility. For many general aviation aircraft, the annual inspection could be the only in-depth inspection it receives throughout the year. In view of the wide ranging authority conveyed with the authorization, the test examines a broader field of knowledge than required for the A&P certificate and reflects the emphasis that is placed on the holder of the certificate in perpetuating air safety.

This guide is not offered as an easy way to obtain the necessary information for passing the inspection authorization knowledge test. Rather, the intent of this guide is to define and narrow the field of study to the required knowledge areas included in the test.

Knowledge Test Eligibility Requirements

Eligibility is established at the local FAA Flight Standards District Office (FSDO) prior to taking the Inspection Authorization Knowledge Test.

You are eligible for the Inspection Authorization Knowledge Test if you meet the requirements of Title 14 of the Code of Federal Regulations (14 CFR) Part 65, section 65.91(c).

"Sec. 65.91 Inspection Authorization…

(1) Hold a currently effective mechanic certificate with both an airframe rating and a powerplant rating, each of which is currently effective and has been in effect for a total of at least 3 years;

(2) Have been actively engaged, for at least the 2-year period before the date he applies, in maintaining aircraft certificated and maintained in accordance with this chapter;

(3) Have a fixed base of operations at which he may be located in person or by telephone during a normal working week, but it need not be the place where he will exercise his inspection authority;

(4) Have available to him the equipment, facilities, and inspection data necessary to properly inspect airframes, powerplants, propellers, or any related part or appliance; and

(5) Pass a written test on his ability to inspect according to safety standards for returning aircraft to service after major repairs and major alterations and annual and progressive inspection performed under Part 43 of this chapter…"

Knowledge Areas on the Test

The Inspection Authorization Knowledge Test is comprehensive as it must test your knowledge in many subject areas. When applying for an IA you should review 14 CFR Part 65, section 65.91(c)(5) for the knowledge areas on the test.

Description of the Test

All test questions are the objective, multiple-choice type. The test contains 50 questions, numbered 1 through 50. Each question can be answered by the selection of a single response. Each test question is independent of other questions; therefore, a correct response to one does not depend upon, or influence the correct response to another.

The maximum time allowed for the test is 3 hours. The allotted time is based on previous experience and educational statistics. This amount of time is considered more than adequate if you have prepared properly.

The Inspection Authorization Knowledge Test has been considered by some as an open book test because of the use of reference material during the test. To view the test in this manner is a misconception. There has always been a core knowledge requirement for which no reference material was provided. Therefore, it should be noted that, during the tests, there are subject areas for which reference material is not included in the test supplement. These areas will draw on skills acquired as an airframe and powerplant mechanic and which are necessary to properly inspect work performed by others.

The IA test supplement provides appropriate segments of Title 14 of the Code of Federal Regulations, all necessary charts, graphs, and technical data necessary to solve problems contained in the test. Prior to taking the test, you should take a few minutes to look through the supplement to determine what is included.

You should carefully read the information and instructions given with the tests, as well as the statements in each test item.

When taking a test, you should keep the following points in mind:

1. Answer each question in accordance with the latest regulations and procedures.
2. Read each question carefully before looking at the possible answers. You should clearly understand the problem before attempting to solve it.
3. After formulating an answer, determine which of the alternatives most nearly corresponds with that answer. The answer chosen should completely resolve the problem.
4. From the answers given, it may appear that there is more than one possible answer; however, there is only one answer that is correct and complete. The other answers are either incomplete or are derived from popular misconceptions.
5. If a certain question is difficult for you, it is best to mark it for review and proceed to the other questions. After you answer the less difficult questions, return to those which you marked for review and answer them. The review marking procedure will be explained to you prior to starting the test. When you have finished taking the test, make sure an answer has been recorded for each question. However, the computer will alert you to all unanswered questions. This procedure will enable you to use the available time to the maximum advantage.
6. When solving a calculation problem, select the answer nearest your solution. The problem has been checked with various types of calculators; therefore, if you have solved it correctly, your answer will be closer to the correct answer than any of the other choices.

Process for Taking a Knowledge Test

The first step in taking the Inspection Authorization Knowledge Test is to contact your local FSDO to make an appointment to interview with an Aviation Safety Inspector (ASI) (airworthiness) to determine eligibility before registering for the knowledge test. At the interview, the inspector will ask you to complete an FAA Form 8610-1, Mechanic's Application for Inspection Authorization (refer to appendix 1, figure 1) and provide positive proof of identification. An acceptable identification document includes your current photograph, signature, and actual residential address, if different from the mailing address. This information may be presented in more than one form of identification.

Acceptable forms of identification include, but are not limited to, drivers' licenses, government identification cards, passports, alien residency cards, and military identification cards. Other forms of identification that meet the requirements of this paragraph are acceptable. Some applicants may not possess the identification documentation described. In any case, you should always check with your local FSDO if you are unsure of what kind of authorization to bring to the interview.

During the interview, you will be asked to demonstrate to the inspector's satisfaction that you meet the requirements for the authorization as specified in 14 CFR Part 65, section 65.91(c)(1) through (4).

The inspector will interview to the extent necessary to determine that you clearly understand the inspection authorization privileges, limitations, responsibilities, and the functions in the aviation community. Once your qualifications have been demonstrated, the inspector will sign the 8610-1 form you completed. You must present this form at the test site in order to take the test.

The next step is the actual registration process. This may be done in either of two ways, you may contact the computer testing designees (CTDs) through their national 1-800 number. LaserGrade's phone number is 1-800-211-2753. CATS phone number is 1-800-947-4228. A complete listing of test centers may be found on the Internet at the web address: afs600.faa.gov, and under the heading "Airman Testing Standards (AFS-630)." Once a site is selected you should ensure that the site provides this test, most do, but not all. You will then need to schedule a test date, and make financial arrangements for test payment. You may register for tests several weeks in advance, and you may cancel your appointment according to the CTD's cancellation policy. If you do not follow the CTD's cancellation policies, you could be subject to a cancellation fee.

You will not need to take any of your IA reference material to the test center; however, you will need proper identification.

Before you take the actual test, you will have the option to take a sample test. The actual test is time limited; however, you should have sufficient time to complete and review your test.

Upon completion of the test, you will receive your Airman Test Report, with the testing center's embossed seal, which reflects your score.

The Airman Test Report lists the subject matter knowledge codes for questions answered incorrectly. The total number of subject matter knowledge codes shown on the Airman Test Report is not necessarily an indication of the total number of questions answered incorrectly. These codes refer to a list of subject matter knowledge areas, which can be found in appendix 3 of this guide. Study the subject matter knowledge code references to increase your knowledge of the subject.

The minimum passing score is 70; however, if the test is failed, there will be a 90-day waiting period before retesting is allowed. An attempt to retest prior to the waiting period is contrary to 14 CFR Part 65, and could result in revocation of any airman certificates that you hold.

Do not lose the Airman Test Report as you will need to present it at the FSDO if you obtain a passing score to receive your IA, or if the test is failed, it must be presented at the test proctor when you are ready to retest after the 90-day waiting period. Should you require a duplicate Airman Test Report due to loss or destruction of the original, send a signed request accompanied by a check or money order for $1 payable to the FAA. Your request should be sent to the Federal Aviation Administration, Airmen Certification Branch, AFS-760, P.O. 25082, Oklahoma City, OK 73125.

After passing the test, present your Airman Test Report to an ASI (A/W) at the FSDO where you interviewed. It is best to return to the original interviewer if possible; however, any available ASI can complete the authorization process. At that time, the ASI will again review your application and discuss any questions you have. When the ASI is satisfied that all requirements are met, the certificate will be issued.

Use of Test Aids and Materials

Airman knowledge tests require applicants to analyze the relationship between variables needed to solve aviation problems, in addition to testing for accuracy of a mathematical calculation. The intent is that all applicants are tested on concepts rather than rote calculation ability. It is permissible to use certain calculating devices when taking airman knowledge tests, provided they are used within the following guidelines. The term "calculating devices" is interchangeable with such items as calculators, computers, or any similar devices designed for aviation-related activities.

When taking a knowledge test, you may use aids, reference materials, and test materials within the guidelines listed below, if actual test questions or answers are not revealed. All models of aviation-oriented calculators may be used, including small electronic calculators that perform only arithmetic functions (add, subtract, multiply, and divide). Simple programmable memories, which allow addition to, subtraction from, or retrieval of one number from the memory, are permissible. Also, simple functions such as square root and percent keys are permissible. The following guidelines apply.

1. You may use any reference materials provided with the test. In addition, you may use scales, straightedges, protractors, plotters, navigation computers and electronic or mechanical calculators that are directly related to the test.
2. Manufacturer's permanently inscribed instructions on the front and back of such aids, e.g., formulas, conversions, regulations, and weight and balance formulas are permissible.
3. Testing centers may provide a calculator to you and/or deny you use of your personal calculator based on the following limitations.
    a. Prior to, and upon completion of the test, while in the presence of the proctor, you must actuate the ON/OFF switch and perform any other function that ensures erasure of any data stored in memory circuits.
    b. The use of electronic calculators incorporating permanent or continuous type memory circuits without erasure capability is prohibited. The testing center may refuse the use of your calculator when unable to determine the calculator's erasure capability.
    c. Printouts of data must be surrendered at the completion of the test if the calculator incorporates this design feature.
    d. The use of magnetic cards, magnetic tapes, modules, computer chips, or any other device upon which pre-written programs or information related to the test can be stored and retrieved is prohibited.
    e. You are not permitted to use any booklet or manual containing instructions related to use of test aids.
4. Dictionaries are not allowed in the testing area.
5. The testing center makes the final determination relating to test materials and personal possessions you may take into the testing area.
6. Guidelines for dyslexic applicant's use of test aids and materials. A dyslexic applicant may request approval from the local Flight Standards District Office (FSDO) to take an airman knowledge test using one of the three options listed in preferential order:
    a. Option One. Use current testing facilities and procedures whenever possible.
    b. Option Two. Applicants may use Franklin Speaking Wordmaster© to facilitate the testing process. The Wordmaster© is a self-contained electronic thesaurus that audibly pronounces typed in words and presents them on a display screen. It has a built-in headphone jack for private listening. The headphone feature will be used during testing to avoid disturbing others.
    c. Option Three. Applicants who do not choose to use the first or second option may request a test proctor to assist in reading specific words or terms from the test questions and supplement material. In the interest of preventing compromise of the testing process, the test proctor should be someone who is nonaviation oriented. The test proctor will provide reading assistance only, with no explanation of words or terms. The Airman Testing Standards Branch, AFS-630, will assist in the selection of a test site and test proctor.

Cheating or Other Unauthorized Conduct

Computer testing centers follow strict security procedures to avoid test compromise. These procedures are established by the FAA and are covered in FAA Order 8080.6, Conduct of Airman Knowledge Tests. The FAA has directed all testing centers to terminate a test at any time a test proctor suspects a cheating incident has occurred. An FAA investigation will then follow. If the investigation determines that cheating or other unauthorized conduct has occurred, any airman certificate that you hold may be revoked, and you may not be allowed to take a test for 1 year.

Retesting Procedures

If you fail the Inspection Authorization Knowledge Test, you may not apply for retesting until 90 days after the date that you failed the test. Any attempt to retest prior to the 90-day waiting period is contrary to 14 CFR Part 65, and could result in revocation of any airman certificates that you hold.

After the 90-day waiting period simply present the failed Airman Test Report along with required ID at the test center to retest. There is no need to return to the FSDO until the test is passed.

Basic Functions of an IA

General

The basic functions of the holder of an Inspection Authorization (IA) are set forth in 14 CFR Part 65, section 65.95. With the exception of aircraft maintained in accordance with a Continuous Airworthiness Maintenance Program, an IA may inspect and approve for return to service any aircraft or related part or appliance after a major repair or major alteration. Also, the holder of an IA may perform an annual inspection and he or she may supervise or perform a progressive inspection.

Approving Major Repairs and Major Alterations

A primary responsibility of the holder of an IA is to determine airworthiness by inspecting repairs or alterations for conformity to approved data, and assuring that the aircraft is in a condition for safe operation. During inspection of major repairs or major alterations, the holder of an IA must also determine that they are compatible with previous repairs and alterations that have been made to the aircraft.

The holder of an IA must personally perform the inspection. The Code of Federal Regulations (CFRs) do not provide for delegation of this responsibility.

Approving major repairs and major alterations is a serious responsibility. The approval action should consist of a detailed investigation to establish, at least that:

1. All replacement parts installed conform to approved design and/or have traceability to the original equipment manufacturer (OEM) (14 CFR section 21.303).
2. As installed, the installation conforms to approved data that is applicable to the installation.
3. Workmanship meets the requirements of 14 CFR Part 43, section 43.13 (the aircraft or product is equal to its original or properly altered condition).
4. The data used is appropriate to the aircraft certification rule (e.g. CAR 3, 14 CFR Part 23).
5. Work is complete and compatible with other structures or systems.
6. The holder of an IA CANNOT approve the DATA for major repairs or major alterations. He/she may, however, inspect to see that alterations conform to data previously approved by the Administrator (14 CFR Part 65, section 65.95). This means the holder of an IA ensures that approved data is available and is used as the basis for the approval. This availability determination should be made prior to beginning the repair or alteration. If data is unavailable, or if the holder of an IA is unsure of the acceptability of the available data, the local Aviation Safety Inspector (ASI) should be consulted. The ASI may, as the circumstances warrant, be able to:

   a. establish an acceptable basis for approval;

   b. approve the data; or

   c. recommend application for a supplemental type certificate.

Quite often major repairs are performed that are eventually covered by fabric, metal skin, or another structure. When this situation exists, the holder of an IA should have a clear understanding with the mechanic performing the repair that a precover inspection is necessary. The inspection should assure that the repair was made in accordance with acceptable methods, techniques, and practices prescribed by 14 CFR Part 43 and that the structure to be covered is free from defects, corrosion, or wood rot, and is protected from the elements. In addition, the holder of an IA should inspect other affected areas for hidden damage, if the aircraft has been involved in an accident or incident. An entry is required to be made in the maintenance record and FAA Form 337, Major Repair and Alteration, be completed. (Refer to appendix 1, figure 4, showing typical entries on the back of FAA Form 337.)

Minor deviation from approved data is permissible if the change is one that could be approved as a minor alteration when considered by itself. Be sure to list the deviations on FAA Form 337 and make an entry in the maintenance record when completing the aircraft records. When in doubt, contact the local ASI who may decide the change is not minor and would need specific approval or an amendment of the original approval.

Approved data to be used for major repairs and major alterations may be one or more of the following.

1. Type Certificate Data Sheets
2. Aircraft Specifications
3. Supplemental Type Certificates (STCs)
4. Airworthiness Directives (ADs)
5. Manufacturer's FAA Approved Data (DOA)
6. Designated Engineering Representative (DER)
7. Approved Data With FAA Form 8110-3, Statement of Compliance (Note: This type of data usually requires additional approval.)
8. Designated Alteration Station (DAS) Approved Data
9. Appliance Manufacturer's Manuals (Excluding Installation Instructions)
10. FAA-approved chapters of the Structural Repair Manuals.

AC 43.13-1A, Acceptable Methods, Techniques, and Practices — Aircraft Inspection and Repair is acceptable to the Administrator for the inspection and repair of nonpressurized areas of civil aircraft, only when there are no manufacturer repair or maintenance instructions. This data generally pertains to minor repairs. The repairs identified in this AC may also be used as a basis for major repairs. The repair data may also be used as approved data, and the AC chapter, page, and paragraph listed in block 8 of FAA Form 337 when:

1. the user has determined that it is appropriate to the product being repaired;
2. it is directly applicable to the repair being made; and
3. it is not contrary to manufacturer's data.

FAA FIELD APPROVAL (FAA FORM 337) issued for duplication of identical aircraft may be used as approved data only when the identical alteration is performed on an aircraft of identical make, model, and series by the original modifier. FAA Form 337s approved prior to Oct. 1, 1955 may be used as approved data.

Inspecting repairs or alterations consists of these basic operations.

1. Determine that the repair or alteration data has FAA approval.
2. Inspect the configuration of the repair or alteration for conformity to the approved data and the performance standards of 14 CFR Part 43. At the same time, the aircraft should still comply with applicable airworthiness requirements, and the repair or alteration be compatible with all other installations.
3. All operating limitations affected by an alteration should be appropriately revised. Sometimes limitations are in the form of flight manual supplements, instrument range markings, placards, or combinations of these. See the local ASI for limitations on changes which can be made.
4. Determine that aircraft record entries have been made and the weight and balance data and equipment list have been revised, when appropriate. There should be a statement on the FAA Form 337 to the effect that the weight and balance data and equipment list have been revised. When an alteration results in a change in the center-of-gravity (CG) position, the affected CG limit should be investigated under adverse loading conditions unless the new CG falls within an approved empty CG range. For instance, if the CG has shifted aft, the loading conditions should be computed to see that the aircraft does not exceed the aft CG limit. It is the pilot's responsibility to have the aircraft correctly loaded. However, when approving an alteration, it is the IA's responsibility to see that weight and balance data have been revised. The aircraft record entries may

refer to the FAA Form 337 for details, such as: "Installed STOL kit in accordance with STC SA 940 CE drawing number 5084 dated April 24, 2002. See FAA Form 337, this date, for details."

5. Indicate approval in block 7 of FAA Form 337, and return both copies to the person who performed the work, for disposition in accordance with 14 CFR Part 43, appendix B.

Annual and Progressive Inspections

The procedures and scope for annual inspections are set forth in 14 CFR Part 43, appendix D, and should be followed in detail. The scope and detail for a progressive inspection is established by the owner or operator in accordance with 14 CFR Part 91, section 91.409(d). There are additional requirements for annual and progressive inspections listed in 14 CFR Part 43, section 43.15. The scope and detail of 100-hour and annual inspections are the same. Record entries are very important as they are the only evidence an aircraft owner has to show compliance with the inspection requirements of 14 CFR Part 91, section 91.409 (refer to appendix 1, figure 5).

The following reminders should help in determining that the aircraft complies with all airworthiness requirements (Refer to 14 CFR Part 43, section 43.15(a)).

Configuration

The aircraft should conform to the aircraft specification or type certificate data sheet, any changes by supplemental type certificates and/or its properly altered condition. When the aircraft does not conform, use the procedures for "unairworthy" items listed in 14 CFR Part 43, section 43.11(a)(5).

1. Alterations to the product may have changed some of the operating limitations.
2. Unrecorded alterations or repairs may have been made in the past and warrant one of the following:
    a. Contact owner for pertinent information.
    b. If approved data is available, conduct inspection and personally approve for return to service by completing FAA Form 337.
    c. Contact local ASI for assistance.
3. The aircraft specification or type certificate data sheet indicates when a flight manual is required. It also identifies limitations which must be displayed in the form of markings and placards.
4. Unlike the specifications, type certificate data sheets do not contain a list of equipment approved for a particular aircraft. The list of required and optional equipment can be found in the equipment list furnished by the manufacturer of the aircraft. Sometimes a later issue of the list is needed to cover recently approved items. Serial number eligibility should always be considered.

Condition

The holder of an IA may use the checklist in 14 CFR Part 43 (appendix D), the manufacturer's inspection sheets, or a checklist designed by the holder of an IA, that includes the scope and detail of the items listed in appendix D, to check the condition of the entire aircraft. This includes checks of the various systems listed in 14 CFR Part 43, section 43.15.

1. Routine servicing is NOT a part of the annual inspection. The inspection itself is essentially a visual evaluation of the condition of the aircraft and its components and certain operational checks. The manufacturer may recommend certain services to be performed at various operating intervals. These can often be done conveniently during an annual inspection, and in fact should be done, but are not considered to be a part of the inspection itself.
2. It is very important that the holder of an IA be familiar with the manufacturer's service manuals, bulletins, and letters for the product being inspected. Use these publications to avoid overlooking problem areas.

3. AC 43-16, Aviation Maintenance Alerts, is also an important source of service experience. The articles for the alerts are taken from selected service difficulties reported to the FAA on FAA Form 8010-4, Malfunction or Defect Reports. Monthly copies of the alerts are provided on the Internet at http://av-info.faa.gov. Select from "Aircraft Information" heading, then select the subheading "General Aviation Airworthiness Alerts." Comments may be sent by letter, with name and address typed or legibly printed to the Federal Aviation Administration, Aviation Systems Data Branch, AFS-620, P.O. Box 25082, Oklahoma City, OK 73125.
4. When the holder of an IA approves an aircraft for return to service, he or she will be held responsible for the condition of the aircraft AS OF THE TIME OF APPROVAL.

Minimum Equipment List

The minimum equipment list (MEL) is intended to permit operations with certain inoperative items of equipment for the minimum period of time necessary until repairs can be accomplished. It is important that repairs are accomplished at the earliest opportunity in order to return the aircraft to its design level of safety and reliability.

1. When inspecting aircraft operating with an MEL, the holder of an IA should review the document where inoperative items are recorded, (aircraft maintenance record, logbook, discrepancy record, etc.) to determine the state of airworthiness with regard to those recorded discrepancies. Inspections of aircraft with approved MELs will be in accordance with 14 CFR under which the MEL was issued.
2. Those MELs specifying repair intervals through the use of A, B, C, D codes require repairs of deferred items at or prior to the repair times established by the letter designated category. In such instances, some items previously deferred may not be eligible for continued deference at the inspection or may require additional maintenance. Where repair intervals are not specified by codes in the MEL, all MEL-authorized inoperative instruments and/or equipment should be repaired or inspected and deferred before approval for return to service.
3. Aircraft established on a progressive inspection program require that all MEL-authorized inoperative items be repaired or inspected and deferred at each inspection whether or not the item is encompassed in that particular segment.

Deferring Inoperative Instruments or Equipment

1. When inspecting aircraft operating without an MEL, the rule "14 CFR Part 91, section 91.213(d)," allows certain aircraft not having an approved MEL to be flown with inoperative instruments and/or equipment. These aircraft may be presented for annual or progressive inspection with such items previously deferred or may have inoperative instruments and equipment deferred during an inspection. In either case, the holder of an IA is required by 14 CFR Part 43, section 43.13(b) to determine that:
   a. the deferrals are eligible within the guidelines of that rule.
   b. all conditions for deferral are met, including proper recordation in accordance with 14 CFR Part 43, sections 43.9 and 43.11; and
   c. deferral of any item or combination of items will not affect the intended function of any other operable instruments and/or equipment, or in any manner constitute a hazard to the aircraft. When these requirements are met, such an aircraft is considered to be in a properly altered condition with regard to those deferred items.

Airworthiness Directives

The holder of an IA is required by 14 CFR Part 43, section 43.13, to determine that all applicable airworthiness directives (ADs) for aircraft, powerplants, propellers, instruments, and appliances have been accomplished.

1. If the maintenance records indicate compliance with an AD, the holder of an IA should make a reasonable attempt to verify the compliance. It is not uncommon for a component to have compliance with an AD accomplished and properly recorded then later be replaced by another component on which the AD has not been accomplished. The holder of an IA is not expected to disassemble major components such as cylinders, crankcases, etc., if adequate records of compliance exist.

2. When the maintenance records DO NOT contain indications of AD compliance, the holder of an IA should:
   a. make the AD an item on a discrepancy list provided to the owner, in accordance with 14 CFR Part 43, section 43.11(b);
   b. with the owner's concurrence, do whatever disassembly is required to determine the status of compliance; or
   c. obtain concurrence of the owner to comply with the AD.
3. Often, an AD calls for an inspection at one time with a modification or inspection required at a later date. It is very important to identify, in the maintenance record entry, the portion of the AD complied with and the exact method of compliance.
4. 14 CFR section 91.417(a)(2)(v) requires each registered owner or operator to keep a record of the current status of applicable ADs. This status includes, for each, the method of compliance, AD number, and revision date. If the AD involves recurring action, the time and date should be recorded when the next action is required. As a vital part of the services performed, the holder of an IA may wish to provide the owner with information he/she is expected to keep. (Refer to appendix 1, figure 6.)
5. The owner should also be informed of any subsequent requirements of an AD or whether a reinspection is required at operating intervals other than at annual inspections. Often, the subsequent requirements are at 100-hour intervals and will need to be done whether or not the aircraft is required to have 100-hour inspections. Where a progressive inspection is involved, the approved program should state how and when the AD review will be accomplished. However, as a mechanic or IA, you should be aware of an AD that is pending or due, and is not in the area you are inspecting. It is good customer relations to inform the owner or pilot of the situation.

Malfunction or Defect Reports

All malfunctions or defects that come to the attention of the holder of an IA should be reported on FAA Form 8010-4. (Refer to appendix 1, figure 7.) Copies of the self-addressed form are available at all Flight Standards District Offices (FSDOs), easy to fill out and require no postage. Prompt reporting will contribute much toward improving air safety by helping correct unsafe conditions.

Paperwork Review

The owner or operator is responsible for maintaining the equipment list, CG and weight distribution computations, and loading schedules, if necessary.

1. The holder of an IA, as required by 14 CFR Part 43, section 43.13, determines that the required placards and documents set forth in the aircraft specification or type certificate data sheet are available and current. The aircraft should be reported as being in an unairworthy condition if these placards and documents are not available. Missing, incorrect, or improperly located placards are regarded as an unairworthy item, and the owner or operator should be informed that, under the requirements of 14 CFR Part 91, section 91.9, the aircraft may not be operated until they are available.
2. The holder of an IA should refer to the registration and airworthiness certificates for the owner's name and address; the aircraft make, model, registration, and serial numbers needed for recording purposes. Be sure not to use manufacturers' trade names as they do not always coincide with the actual model designation (Cessna Skylane is 182, Piper Seneca III is PA 34 220T, etc.). If registration and airworthiness certificates are not available, the aircraft does not need to be reported in unairworthy condition; however, the owner or operator should be informed that the documents required by 14 CFR Part 91, section 91.203(a)(i)(2)(b), should be in the aircraft and the airworthiness certificate displayed, WHEN THE AIRCRAFT IS OPERATED.
3. On aircraft for which no approved flight manual is required, the operating limitations prescribed during original certification, and as required by 14 CFR Part 91, section 91.9, must be carried in or be affixed to the aircraft. Range markings on the instruments, placards, and listings are required to be worded and located as specified in the type certificate data sheet. (Refer to appendix 1, figure 8.)

Aircraft Markings

Required aircraft identification markings are discussed in 14 CFR Part 45. It is the owner's or operator's responsibility to have the nationality and registration markings properly displayed on the aircraft (14 CFR Part 91, section 91.9(c)). The holder of an IA can, and should, offer advisory service to owners and operators in regard to any deficiencies in markings; however, such deficiencies are not cause to report an aircraft in "unairworthy" condition.

Aircraft with Discrepancies or Unairworthy Conditions

If the aircraft is not approved for return to service after a required inspection, use the procedures specified in 14 CFR Part 43, section 43.11. This will permit an owner to assume responsibility for having the discrepancies corrected prior to operating the aircraft.

1. The discrepancies can be cleared by a person who is authorized by 14 CFR Part 43 to do the work. Preventive maintenance items could be cleared by a pilot who owns or operates the aircraft, provided the aircraft is not used under 14 CFR parts 121, 129, or 135; except that approval may be granted to allow a pilot operating a rotorcraft in a remote area under 14 CFR Part 135 to perform preventive maintenance.
2. The owner may want the aircraft flown to another location to have repairs completed, in which case the owner should be advised that the issuance of FAA Form 8130-7, Special Flight Permit, is required. This form is commonly called a ferry permit and is detailed in 14 CFR Part 21, section 21.197. The certificate may be obtained in person or by fax at the local FSDO or from a Designated Airworthiness Representative.
3. If the aircraft is found to be in an unairworthy condition, an entry will be made in the maintenance records that the inspection was completed and a list of unairworthy items was provided to the owner. When all unairworthy items are corrected by a person authorized to perform maintenance and that person makes an entry in the maintenance record for the correction of those items, the aircraft is approved for return to service. (Refer to appendix 1, figures 9 and 10.)

Incomplete Inspection

If an annual inspection is not completed, the holder of an IA should:

1. Indicate any discrepancies found in the aircraft records.
2. NOT indicate that an annual inspection was conducted.
3. Indicate the extent of the inspection and all work accomplished in the aircraft records.

Aircraft Records

Maintenance Records

The holder of an IA and other maintenance personnel or agencies are required to record maintenance, inspections, or alterations performed or approved in accordance with the requirements of 14 CFR Part 43, sections 43.9 and 43.11. The owner or operator is required by 14 CFR Part 91, section 91.417 to keep maintenance records. The holder of an IA is also required to indicate the total aircraft time in service when a required inspection is done.

Significance of Maintenance Record Entries

Responsibility for maintenance work performed rests with the person whose signature and certificate number is entered on the appropriate maintenance record and/or forms. The responsibility for annual and progressive inspections and approval for return to service of major repairs or major alterations is assumed by the holder of an IA whose signature and certificate number appears on the appropriate maintenance records.

Completion of FAA Form 337, Major Repair and Alteration (Airframe, Powerplant, Propeller, or Appliance)

FAA Form 337, Major Repair and Alteration (Airframe, Powerplant, Propeller, or Appliance), serves two purposes. One is to provide owners and operators a record of major repairs and major alterations indicating details and approval. The other purpose is to provide the FAA with a copy for the aircraft records. An example of a typical completed FAA Form 337 is provided in appendix 1, figures 3 and 4.

1. The person who performed or supervised the major repair or major alteration prepares the original FAA Form 337 (two copies). The holder of an IA then further processes the forms when they are presented for approval.
2. Instructions for the completion of FAA Form 337 appear in AC 43.9-1E, Instructions for Completion of FAA Form 337, Major Repair and Alteration (Airframe, Powerplant, Propeller, or Appliance).
3. Disposition of FAA Form 337.
    a. The holder of an IA who has found a major alteration or a major repair to be in conformity with FAA-approved data should review the FAA Form 337 for completeness and accuracy, and complete item 7.
    b. The person performing a major repair or major alteration shall in accordance with 14 CFR Part 43:
        (1) Give a signed copy of FAA Form 337 to the aircraft owner.
        (2) Make the proper entry in the maintenance records.
        (3) Forward the duplicate copy to the local FAA FSDO within 48 hours after the form is signed.
    c. The holder of an IA should ensure that the duplicate copy is an exact and legible reproduction of the original. The signatures should not be carbon copies but original signatures written in ink.
    d. If the FAA Form 337 is completed for extended-range fuel tanks installed within the passenger compartment or a baggage compartment, the person who performs the work and the person authorized to approve the work by 14 CFR section 43.7 shall execute an FAA Form 337 in at least triplicate, as required by 14 CFR Part 43, appendix B. One (1) copy of the FAA Form 337 shall be placed on board the aircraft as specified in 14 CFR section 91.417 of the rules. The remaining forms shall be distributed as previously noted.
    e. If FAA Form 337 has been completed for engines, propellers, spare parts or components, both copies of the form, with the approval portion completed, should be attached to the part or component until it is installed on an aircraft.
        (1) The mechanic who makes the installation will, in accordance with 14 CFR Part 43, section 43.9(a)(4), complete both copies of FAA Form 337 by filling in blocks 1 and 2 and sign for the installation in the aircraft records, making reference to the FAA Form 337 in the record entry.
        (2) Give a copy to the owner and forward a copy to the FAA FSDO for the area where the installing mechanic is operating.

Weight and Balance

Weight and balance data are no longer required to be entered on FAA Form 337. However, it is imperative that weight and balance checks and computations be made very carefully. Since practically every aircraft manufacturer uses a different method of weight and balance control, it would be impossible to provide a universally adaptable method. The example provided in appendix 1, figure 11, of this guide is general in nature and can be modified or revised as needed to fit the aircraft involved. When revising weight and balance data, these general guidelines should be followed.

1. The weight and balance data should be kept together in the aircraft records.
2. When making revisions, use a permanent easily identified method, with full-size sheets of paper large enough to contain complete computations and minimize the possibility of becoming detached or lost.
3. Each page should be identified with the aircraft by make, model, serial number, and registration number.
4. The pages should be signed and dated by the person making the revision.
5. The nature of the weight change should be described.
6. The old weight and balance data should be marked "superseded" and dated.
7. A new page should show the date of the old figures it supersedes.
8. Appropriate fore and/or aft extreme loading conditions should be investigated and the computations shown.
9. Example loading computations may be helpful.
10. On large aircraft, be careful to distinguish between empty weight and operating weights that may include items, such as commissary supplies, spare parts, lavatory water, etc.
11. On small aircraft, it is often convenient to post a placard in the aircraft indicating the empty weight, useful load, and empty CG, along with example loadings or general instructions, to cover the most likely loading conditions. (Refer to 14 CFR section 91.9(b)(2).) AC 120-27, Aircraft Weight and Balance Control, and FAA-H-8083-1, Aircraft Weight and Balance Handbook contain useful information applicable to the functions performed by the holder of an IA on general aviation aircraft.

Get It Straight

Be sure to come to a mutual agreement with the aircraft owner concerning exactly what work is to be performed. Misunderstandings usually result from a lack of clear communication. Attention to the following details will usually avoid the ill will a later disagreement may generate.

Suggestions for Developing Good Owner/IA Relations

1. Itemize the work to be done so the owner will have a clear understanding of the work order.
2. Establish a firm understanding about the cost, or range of cost, anticipated for the job.
3. If an annual inspection is involved, indicate that certain maintenance is required to perform the inspection, such as:
   a. Removing cowling and fairing, opening inspection plates, etc.
   b. Cleaning the aircraft and engine.
   c. Disassembling wheels and other components to determine their condition.
4. Advise the owner that an annual inspection involves determination of compliance with aircraft specifications and airworthiness directives (ADs).
5. Agree whether routine servicing is to be included as part of the inspection or if it is to be performed separately. Such servicing is not a part of the inspection, but may be conveniently done while conducting the inspection. Such items might be:
   a. Cleaning spark plugs.
   b. Servicing landing gear shock struts.
   c. Changing oil.
   d. Making minor adjustments.
   e. Servicing brakes.
   f. Dressing nicked propeller blades.
   g. Lubricating where necessary.
   h. Stop-drilling small cracks and minor patching of cowling and baffles.
6. The owner should be made aware that the annual or progressive inspection does not include correction of discrepancies or unairworthy items and that such maintenance will be additional to the inspection. Maintenance and repairs may be accomplished simultaneously with the inspection by a person authorized to perform maintenance if agreed on by the owner and holder of the IA. This method would result in an aircraft that is approved for return to service with the completion of the inspection. A written list of discrepancies and unairworthy items not repaired concurrently with the inspection must be made and given to the owner. Record uncorrected discrepancies and unairworthy items in the maintenance records. The owner must make arrangement for correction or deferral of items on the list of discrepancies and unairworthy items with a person authorized to perform maintenance prior to returning the aircraft to service. The holder of the IA ensures that any item permitted to be inoperative by a MEL or under 14 CFR Part 91, section 91.213(d)(2) are properly placarded and any maintenance for deferral has been carried out. Any deferred item are to be included on the list of discrepancies and unairworthy items. The owner should be informed that the aircraft should not be operated until the discrepancies and unairworthy items are corrected or are appropriately deferred.
7. Establish a reasonable time frame to accomplish the inspection.
8. Request the owner to supply the complete aircraft records (airframe, engines, and propellers) for study, review, and entries. Point out that this is necessary to properly conduct an annual inspection.
9. Complete the inspection as soon as practicable. Often, an aircraft will sit around the shops waiting for parts, even though the inspection has actually been completed. In this cases, it is advisable to officially report the aircraft unairworthy. (Refer to 14 CFR Part 43, section 43.11(a)(5).) When the parts arrive, the repairs can be completed and the aircraft approved for return to service in the usual manner by the person who makes the repairs. The time lapse may represent several weeks, or even months, and things can deteriorate on the aircraft. Also, there is the chance that an AD involving some part of the aircraft may have been issued in the interim. In these cases, it might be unwise to complete the repairs originally intended and sign off the aircraft as "airworthy" without doing another complete inspection.

10. Complete the aircraft record entries as required by 14 CFR Part 43, sections 43.9 and 43.11 and provide sufficient information for the owner to comply with 14 CFR Part 91, section 91.417(a)(2)(i). Make adequate descriptions of repairs or alterations if accomplished along with the inspection.
11. Record compliance with all ADs actually accomplished. Provide sufficient information for the owner to comply with 14 CFR Part 91, section 91.417(a)(2)(v). A general statement, such as "All ADs complied with" is NOT an adequate entry and should be avoided. Many owners keep a separate record of AD compliance in the back of the logbook or in a section specifically provided for this record. This is a good place to identify the ADs of a recurring nature and show when the next compliance is required. (Refer to appendix 1, figures 12 and 13, for typical entries.)
12. When approving repairs and alterations, the holder of an IA should be available as work progresses on major jobs. In this way, affected areas and structures can be seen more readily than after completion of the entire job. In many cases, the workmanship can be inspected and improved easier during the process of the job rather than having to redo it later.
13. Remind the owners or operators that they are responsible for operational requirements, such as:
    a. VOR equipment checked in accordance with 14 CFR Part 91, section 91.171.
    b. Altimeter and altitude reporting equipment test and inspections in accordance with 14 CFR Part 91, section 91.411.
    c. ATC transponder inspection in accordance with 14 CFR Part 91, section 91.413. These tests and inspections are not part of the annual inspection.
    d. ELT inspection in accordance with 14 CFR Part 91, section 91.207.

Sample Test Questions and Answers

1. What ignition system is approved for a Lycoming engine model 0-540-A4A5?

A— Bendix magneto model D6LN-3031.
B— Slick magnetos models 662 and 663.
C— Bendix magnetos models S6LN-20 and S6LN-21.

Answer C—Subject Matter Knowledge Code: Y303. Type Certificate Data Sheet No. E-295, Note 8.

2. A lower horizontal stabilizer streamlined brace is to be repaired by welding. The brace size is 1-1/4 inch. The repair should be accomplished using which of the following materials?

A— A round insert tube of the same material, one gauge thicker than the original streamlined tube and a minimum length of 5.01 inch.
B— An outside sleeve of at least the same gauge with a minimum length of 9.128 inches.
C— An inside sleeve of the same streamlined tubing as original with a maximum insert length of 6.43 inches.

Answer B—Subject Matter Knowledge Code: K49. AC 43.13-1B, Chapter 2, Paragraph 81; and figure 2.13.

3. Use Airworthiness Directive (AD) AD 80-10-02 to answer this question.

Known Information: Messerschmitt-Bolkow-Blohm Model BO-105 helicopter with tail rotor blade grips P/N 105-31722 installed.

While performing a progressive inspection on this helicopter, you note in the aircraft's records that the last compliance with AD 80-10-02 was at an aircraft time of 5402 hours. The records further indicate that the tail rotor blade grips were replaced at an aircraft time of 4902. What action is required at this inspection with a time of 5502?

A— Compliance is required for paragraph (c)(1)(2).
B— Compliance is required for paragraph (e).
C— Compliance is required for paragraphs (b)(d) and (e).

Answer C—Subject Matter Knowledge Code: A14. AD80-10-02.

4. Where can the major items to be inspected be found that must be included in a checklist used while performing an annual inspection on a fixed-wing aircraft?

A— FAA Form 8130-10.
B— 14 CFR Part 43, Appendix D.
C— Advisory Circular 43.13-1B.

Answer B—Subject Matter Knowledge Code: K49. 14 CFR Part 43, section 43.15(c) states:

"Sec. 43.15 Additional performance rules for inspections…

(c) Annual and 100-hour inspections.

(1) Each person performing an annual or 100-hour inspection shall use a checklist while performing the inspection. The checklist may be of the person's own design, one provided by the manufacturer of the equipment being inspected or one obtained from another source. This checklist must include the scope and detail of the items contained in appendix D to this part and paragraph (b) of this section...."

5. Airworthiness Approval Tags (FAA Form 8130-3) may be used by which maintenance entity for approving products for return to service after maintenance or alteration?

A— Inspection Authorizations.
B— 14 CFR Part 145, Certified Repair Stations.
C— Either A or B.

Answer B—Subject Matter Knowledge Code K05. Order 8130.21C.

The work must be accomplished by a certificate holder under 14 CFR Part 121 or 135, having a continuous airworthiness maintenance program or by a repair station certificated under Part 145.

6. When installing additional equipment in an aircraft, if not otherwise specified, the ultimate load factor used in the static load test is

A— four times the weight of the equipment.
B— variable, depending on the direction of applied force.
C— the limit load factor multiplied by 1.5.

Answer C—Subject Matter Knowledge Code: K50. AC 43.13-2A, Chapter 1, Paragraph 3.

Ultimate load factors are limit load factors multiplied by a 1.5 safety factor.

7. Which Code of Federal Regulations (CFRs) provides for the fabrication of aircraft replacement and modification parts?

A— 14 CFR Part 21.303.
B— 14 CFR Part 23, appendix B.
C— 14 CFR Part 45.21.

Answer A—Subject Matter Knowledge Code A112. 14 CFR Part 21, subpart K, section 21.303, defines who may produce modification and replacement parts for sale and those persons to which the part does not apply.

8. A proposed airframe alteration will require a section of Mil-H-8788-10 hydraulic hose to flex through 60° of travel. The system will operate at 210° centigrade and 1200 psi. What is the minimum bend radius for this installation?

A— 3-1/4 inches.
B— 5-1/2 inches.
C— 7-3/4 inches.

Answer B—Subject Matter Knowledge Code: K49. Acceptable Methods, Techniques, and Practices – Aircraft Inspection and Repair, Chapter 10, Paragraph d; and figure 10.5.

9. Where would you find the marking and placards required for Cessna Model 208, serial number 20800044?

A— Type Certificate Data Sheet No. A37CE.
B— Airplane Flight Manual, Cessna P/N D1286-13PH.
C— Model 208 Series Maintenance Manual.

Answer B—Subject Matter Knowledge Code: A157. 14 CFR Part 23, Subpart G "Operating limitations and Information."

10. Which of the following aircraft, operating under 14 CFR Part 91, could the holder of an inspection authorization approve for return-to-service after a major alteration has been made in accordance with technical data approved by the administrator?

A— A commuter category, multiengine, turbopeller airplane.
B— A transport category, multiengine, turbojet airplane.
C— Either A or B.

Answer C—Subject Matter Knowledge Code: A45. 14 CFR Part 65, section 65.95(a).

"Sec. 65.95 Inspection authorization: privileges and limitations.

(a) The holder of an inspection authorization may—

(1) Inspect and approve for return to service any aircraft or related part or appliance (except any aircraft maintained in accordance with a continuous airworthiness program under Part 121 or 127 of this chapter) after a major repair or major alteration to it in accordance with Part 43 of this chapter, if the work was done in accordance with technical data approved by the Administrator; and

(2) Perform an annual or perform or supervise a progressive inspection according to §§43.13 and 43.15 of this chapter."

Suggestions for Studying for the IA Test

The following should not be considered to be an all inclusive study outline. It is intended only to highlight some major areas. The test draws on the entire spectrum of aircraft technology, with emphasis on maintenance and inspection.

1. Be familiar with the parts of Title 14 Code of Federal Regulations (14 CFR) as listed in appendix 2.
2. Study 14 CFR parts 91 and 135 aircraft maintenance and inspection requirements.
3. Be familiar with aircraft type certificate data sheets and specifications. This should include the differences and history of these documents. Applicant should know how revisions are noted.
4. Study 14 CFR Part 43, appendixes A, B, and D for detailed information regarding major repairs, major alterations, and annual inspections.
5. Learn to use the graphs and tables in AC 43.13-1B, (or most current revision) Acceptable Methods, Techniques and Practices – Aircraft Inspection and Repair; and AC 43.13-2A, (or most current revision) Acceptable Methods, Techniques, and Practices – Aircraft Alterations.
6. Be familiar with airworthiness directives for small aircraft and rotorcraft. This should include knowledge of the rule, 14 CFR Part 39.
7. Be familiar with the completion of FAA Form 337 (Major Repair and Alteration – Airframe, Powerplant, Propeller, or Appliance). Guidance in this area is provided in AC 43.9-1E, Instructions for Completion of FAA Form 337, Major Repair and Alteration (Airframe, Powerplant, Propeller, or Appliance).
8. Know the requirements for maintenance and inspection record entries for 14 CFR parts 43, and 91. Guidance in this area is provided in AC 43.9C, Maintenance Records; also AC 39-7C, Airworthiness Directives.
9. Be familiar with minimum equipment list for general aviation aircraft. Guidance in this area is provided in AC 91-67, Minimum Equipment Requirements for General Aviation Operations under FAR Part 91.
10. Be familiar with all aspects of weight and balance computations. Applicant must be able to:
    a. calculate basic empty weight and center of gravity in both inches and percent of mean aerodynamic chord (MAC).
    b. conduct adverse loading checks for extreme forward and rearward CG positions.

Applicants should practice making changes to an aircraft weight and balance report by simulating installing or removing equipment and then computing the forward, aft, and empty weight center of gravity (CG). Guidance in this area is provided in AC 65-9, Airframe and Powerplant Mechanics General Handbook and FAA-H-8083-1, Aircraft Weight and Balance Handbook. Also, many commercial publications are available on this subject.

NOTE: You should use the most current versions of the referenced documents.

Appendix 1
Sample Forms

8082-11A

AC

No certificate may be issued unless a completed application form has been received (14 C.F.R. 65).

U.S. DEPARTMENT OF TRANSPORTATION FEDERAL AVIATION ADMINISTRATION **MECHANIC'S APPLICATION FOR INSPECTION AUTHORIZATION**	*Form Approved:* *OMB No. 04-R0110*

1. NAME *(Last, first, middle)*	2. MECHANIC CERTIFICATE NO.
Doe, John J.	A&P 123455678

3. MAILING ADDRESS *(Number, street, city, State/County; ZIP Code) (Place at which you desire to receive Airworthiness Directives, etc.)*	4a. FIXED BASE OF OPERATIONS PLACE AT WHICH YOU MAY BE LOCATED IN PERSON DURING NORMAL WORKING WEEK	4b. TELEPHONE NO. PLACE AT WHICH YOU MAY BE LOCATED BY TELEPHONE DURING NORMAL WORKING WEEK
1450 E. Cheltenham Ave. Cleveland County Oklahoma City, OK 73098	Meridian Aviation Downtown Airpark 5060 S. Western Oklahoma City, OK 73452	(405) 555-1842

	YES	NO
5. HAVE YOU HELD A MECHANIC CERTIFICATE WITH BOTH AIRFRAME AND POWERPLANT RATINGS FOR THE 3 YEARS PRECEDING THE DATE OF THIS APPLICATION?	X	
6. HAVE YOU BEEN ACTIVELY ENGAGED, FOR AT LEAST THE 2-YEAR PERIOD BEFORE THE DATE OF APPLICATION IN MAINTAINING AIRCRAFT CERTIFICATED AND MAINTAINED IN ACCORDANCE WITH THE FARS?	X	
7. HAS YOUR MECHANIC CERTIFICATE AND/OR RATINGS BEEN REVOKED OR SUSPENDED DURING THE 3-YEAR PERIOD PRECEDING THIS APPLICATION?		X
8. HAS AN INSPECTION AUTHORIZATION BEEN DENIED YOU WITHIN 90 DAYS PREVIOUS TO THIS APPLICATION? IF ANSWER IS "YES", EXPLAIN IN REMARKS.		X
9. HAVE YOU MET THE MINIMUM REQUIREMENTS FOR RENEWAL OF INSPECTION AUTHORIZATION? *(For Renewal Only)*		

10. BASIS FOR RENEWAL *(Number Performed)*

ALTERATIONS	REPAIRS	ANNUAL INSPECTIONS	PROGRESSIVE INSPECTIONS	RECENT ISSUANCE-IN EFFECT LESS THAN 90 DAYS BEFORE EXPIRATION DATE

11. AIRCRAFT MAINTENANCE ACTIVITY DURING LAST 2 YEARS

DATES	NAME AND ADDRESS OF REPAIR STATION, FACILITY, MANUFACTURER, OPERATOR, ETC.	DESCRIPTION OF ACTIVITY
FROM June 12, 20XX TO PRESENT	Meridian Aviation Downtown Airpark 5060 S. Western Oklahoma City, OK 73452	Inspection, repair and overhaul of single-engine and multiengine aircraft.
FROM TO		
FROM TO		
FROM TO		

12. REMARKS

13. CERTIFICATION: *I certify that the statements made above and in all attachments hereto are correct and true.*

DATE	SIGNATURE OF APPLICANT
March 19, 20XX	John Doe

14. RECORD OF ACTION *(For FAA Use Only)*

☐ ISSUANCE ☐ VOLUNTARY SURRENDER ☐ ENDORSEMENT ☐ RENEWAL	INSPECTOR'S SIGNATURE	OFFICE IDENTIFICATION

FAA Form 8610-1 (2-78) SUPERSEDES PREVIOUS EDITION

Figure 1.—FAA Form 8610-1, Mechanic's Application for Inspection Authorization.

8082-11A

AC

UNITED STATES OF AMERICA
DEPARTMENT OF TRANSPORTATION
FEDERAL AVIATION ADMINISTRATION

INSPECTION AUTHORIZATION

This certifies that Robert D. Burge
holder of Mechanic Certificate No. 123456789
has been authorized to exercise the privileges of Federal Aviation Regulation 65.95.
This authority expires March 31, 20XX unless sooner revoked by the Administrator of the Federal Aviation Administration or extended by endorsement on the reverse of this card.

DATE ISSUED	SIGNATURE, FLT. STDS. INSPECTOR
03-16-20XX	JOHN J. DOE John Doe

FAA FORM 8310-5 (8-80) SUPERSEDES PREVIOUS EDITION

SIGNATURE OF AUTHORIZED MECHANIC: Robert D. Burge

Front view showing initial date of authorization.

Authority to exercise the privileges of FAR 65.95 has been endorsed or renewed to expire on the date shown below.

EXPIRATION DATE	ENDORSED BY INSPECTOR	FAA OFFICE
03-30-20XX	John Doe	SW-FSDO-2

Back view showing new expiration.

Figure 2.—FAA Form 8310-5, Inspection Authorization, (front and back view).

U.S. Department of Transportation
Federal Aviation Administration

MAJOR REPAIR AND ALTERATION
(Airframe, Powerplant, Propeller, or Appliance)

Form Approved
OMB No. 2120-0020

For FAA Use Only
Office Identification

INSTRUCTIONS: Print or type all entries. See FAR 43.9, FAR 43 Appendix B, and AC 43.9-1 (or subsequent revision thereof) for instructions and disposition of this form. This report is required by law (49 U.S.C. 1421). Failure to report can result in a civil penalty not to exceed $1,000 for each violation (Section 901 Federal Aviation Act of 1958).

1. Aircraft	Make: Cessna	Model: 182L
	Serial No.: 18259080	Nationality and Registration Mark: N42565
2. Owner	Name *(As shown on registration certificate)*: B.J. & P., Inc.	Address *(As shown on registration certificate)*: 1888 N.W. 92 St. Oklahoma City, OK 73405

3. For FAA Use Only

The data identified herein complies with the applicable airworthiness requirements and is approved for the above described aircraft, subject to conformity inspection by a person authorized by 14 CFR Part 43, Section 43.7.

SW-FSDO-23	April 6, 20XX	John J. Doe
District Office	Date	Signature of FAA Inspector

4. Unit Identification

Unit	Make	Model	Serial No.	Repair	Alteration
AIRFRAME	~~~ *(As described in item 1 above)* ~~~			X	
POWERPLANT					
PROPELLER					
APPLIANCE	Type Manufacturer				

6. Conformity Statement

A. Agency's Name and Address	B. Kind of Agency	C. Certificate No.
Katy M. Johnson 411 Riverview Dr. Norman, OK 72091	X U.S. Certificated Mechanic Foreign Certificated Mechanic Certificated Repair Station Manufacturer	130598865

D. I certify that the repair and/or alteration made to the unit(s) identified in item 4 above and described on the reverse or attachments hereto have been made in accordance with the requirements of Part 43 of the U.S. Federal Aviation Regulations and that the information furnished herein is true and correct to the best of my knowledge.

Date	Signature of Authorized Individual
March 23, 20XX	*Katy M. Johnson* Katy M. Johnson

7. Approval for Return To Service

Pursuant to the authority given persons specified below, the unit identified in item 4 was inspected in the manner prescribed by the Administrator of the Federal Aviation Administration and is ☒ APPROVED ☐ REJECTED

BY				
☐ FAA Flt. Standards Inspector	☐ Manufacturer	X Inspection Authorization	Other (Specify)
☐ FAA Designee	☐ Repair Station	☐ Person Approved by Transport Canada Airworthiness Group	

Date of Approval or Rejection	Certificate or Designation No.	Signature of Authorized Individual
April 12, 20XX	233346566	Mike J. Woodham *Mike J Woodham*

FAA Form 337 (12-88)

FIGURE 3.—FAA Form 337, Major Repair and Alteration (Airframe, Powerplant, Propeller, or Appliance), (front view).

NOTE: The FAA inspector's data approval for a major repair (block 3). Detailed instructions for the use of FAA Form 337 are in 14 CFR part 43, and AC 43.9-1E.

NOTICE

Weight and balance or operating limitation changes shall be entered in the appropriate aircraft record. An alteration must be compatible with all previous alterations to assure continued conformity with the applicable airworthiness requirements.

8. Description of Work Accomplished
(If more space is required, attach additional sheets. Identify with aircraft nationality and registration mark and date work completed.)

N42565
April 12, 20XX
Aircraft Total Time 4,218 hours

1. Removed right wing from aircraft and removed skin from outer 6 feet. Repaired buckled spar 49 inches from tip in accordance with attached photographs and figure 1 of drawing dated March 23, 1998.

   DATE: March 26, 20XX, inspected splice in Item 1 and found it to be in accordance with data indicated. Splice is okay to cover. Inspected internal wing assembly for hidden damage and condition.

   Mike J Woodham

   Mike J. Woodham, A&P 233346566 IA

2. Primed interior wing structure and replaced skin P/N's 63-0085,63-0086, and 63-00878 with same skin 2024-T3, .025 inches thick. Rivet size and spacing all the same as original and using procedures in Chapter 2, Section 3, of AC 43.13-1A, dated 1972.

3. Replaced stringers as required and installed 6 splices as per attached drawing and photographs.

4. Installed wing, rigged aileron, and operationally checked in accordance with manufacturer's maintenance manual.

5. No change in weight or balance.

END

☐ *Additional Sheets Are Attached*

Figure 4.—FAA Form 337, Major Repair and Alteration (Airframe, Powerplant, Propeller, or Appliance), (back view).

NOTE: Please note the specific references which identify FAA approved or acceptable data. Also note entry regarding inspection of the repair by the holder of an IA prior to the cover being applied and an inspection of the wing assembly for hidden damage and condition.

March 22, 2002 Total Aircraft Time 1502.0 Hours Tach Time 972.4 Hours I certify that this aircraft has been inspected in accordance with an annual inspection as per Air Tractor AT502 owner's manual and was determined to be in an airworthy condition. Joseph P. Kline A&P 123456789 IA

Figure 5.—Example of a maintenance record entry.

NOTE: This is an example of a record entry for an **annual inspection** determining the aircraft to be in "airworthy" condition. The date, aircraft total time, and tach or recorder reading are included. The tach or recorder readings should not be confused with the total time and should only be shown in **addition** to the total time entry. The mechanic's certificate number is suffixed by the letters "IA" indicating that the mechanic is the holder of an inspection authorization. Maintenance done in conjunction with the inspection should be entered as a separate entry.

AD NOTES COMPLIANCE RECORD

Page 2 of 3 Date ________

Reg # N1234 A/C Make/Model CESSNA C-182-L S/N 18266080

A/C Cert. Date 4-21-68 Eng. Model CONT. 0470R Prop. Model McCAULEY 2A34-66N

S/N 1022 S/N 6297

AD#	Rev. Date	Applicable S.B. # & Subject	Date & Hours @ Comp.	Method of Compliance	One Time	Recurring	Next Comp. @ Hrs/Date	Authorized Signature & Number
79-08-03		ELEC. SYSTEM FAILURE	11-4-79 2176 HRS	C/W PER PART A3	X			Joe Kline 32977112
79-10-14		FUEL VENTING	10-1-80 2421 HRS	LT + RT VENTED FUEL CAPS INSTALLED	X			Joe Kline 32977117
83-13-01		FUEL QUANTITY INDICATORS	6-26-83 2930 HRS	INSPECT FUEL CAP SEALS		X	EACH ANNUAL	Bill Johnson 91162915
83-17-06		ROBERTSON STOL INST.	NA	NOT INSTALLED ON A/C				Bill Johnson 91162915
84-10-01	R1	INSPECT FUEL BLADDERS	11-10-84 3110 HRS	C/W PARAGRAPHS (A) (B) + (C)			NO FURTHER ACTION REQ	Mike White 66295677

FIGURE 6.—Airworthiness Directive compliance record (suggested format).

OMB No. 2120-0003

DEPARTMENT OF TRANSPORTATION FEDERAL AVIATION ADMINISTRATION **MALFUNCTION OR DEFECT REPORT**	OPER. Control No.	
	ATA Code	8120
	1. A/C Reg. No	695J

Enter pertinent data	MANUFACTURER	MODEL/SERIES	SERIAL NUMBER
2. **AIRCRAFT**	Cessna	421B	421B79485
3. **POWERPLANT**	Continental	GTSIO520L	C216977
4. **PROPELLER**	McCauley	3AF34C92	42279

5. SPECIFIC PART *(of component)* CAUSING TROUBLE

Part Name	MFG. Model or Part No.	Serial No.	Part/Defect Location
Wastegate shaft	Garrett PN4166952	NA	Left engine wastegate

6. APPLIANCE/COMPONENT *(Assembly that includes part)*

Comp/Appl Name	Manufacturer	Model or Part No.	Serial Number
Wastegate	Garrett	480164-10	1121

Part TT	Part TSO	Part Condition	7.Date Sub.
1222 hrs	NA	warped	1-22-98

FAA Form 8010-4 (10-92) SUPERSEDES PREVIOUS EDITIONS

8. Comments *(Describe the malfunction or defect and the circumstances under which it occurred. State probable cause and recommendations to prevent recurrence.)*

Pilot reported loss in aircraft's critical altitiude. Inspection revealed the left engine's wastegate shaft warped and binding. The shaft's freedom of travel was also found to be partially restricted due to carbon buildup in the bearings. This is possibly a contributing factor in the warping. Recommend lubricating wastegate valve with approved lubricant such as Mouse Milk or WD-40 when shaft is cool.

Optional Information:

Check a box below, if this report is related to an aircraft

☐ Accident; Date ________ ☐ Incident; Date ________

DISTRICT OFFICE	OPERATOR DESIGNATOR
OTHER	
COMMUTER	
FAA	
MFG.	
AIR TAXI	
MECH.	X
OPER.	
REP. STA	

SUBMITTED BY: Mike Merritt

TELEPHONE NUMBER: (429) 555-6219

FIGURE 7.—FAA Form 8010-4, Malfunction or Defect Report, (revised 10-92).

NOTE: This is a typical FAA Form 8010-4 (revised 10-92). The holder of an IA is urged to use this form for all malfunctions or defects that cannot be attributed to poor maintenance procedures. Provide the information requested on the form. Note that item 8 requests information concerning how the defect can be corrected.

Operating Limitations:	Zeph-Air 63-1A N40023
RPM	Do not exceed 2300
Oil temperature	212° max.
Airspeed limits do not exceed:	
Level flight or climb	95 MPH
Glide or dive	129 MPH
Gross weight	1,200 lbs
Empty CG	14.4" aft of datum
Useful load	453 lb
Kinds of operation	VFR-Day
	40 lb solo front
	20 lb solo rear

FIGURE 8.—Example of an operating limitations placard.

NOTE: Example operating limitations placard for a typical light aircraft certified under 14 CFR part 23.

March 30, 2002

Total Aircraft Time 1853.00 Hours

Tach Reading 975.80

I certify that this aircraft has been inspected in accordance with an annual inspection and a list of discrepancies and unairworthy items dated March 30, 2002, have been provided for the aircraft owner.

Joseph P. Kline
A&P 123456789 IA

FIGURE 9.—Example of a record entry for an annual inspection in which the aircraft was found to be unairworthy.

Academy Aviation
Hangar 4
North Philadelphia Airport
Philadelphia, PA 19114

Mr. Morris McCall
1450 W. Cheltenham Ave.
Philadelphia, PA 19125

Dear Mr. McCall:

This is to certify that on March 30, 2002, I completed an annual inspection on your aircraft, Condor 191B, S/N 3945, N1234, and found the following unairworthy items:

1. Compression in No. 3 cylinder read 30 over 80, which is below the manufacturer's recommended limits.

2. The muffler has a broken baffle plate which is blocking the engine exhaust outlet.

3. There is a 6-inch crack on bottom of left wing just aft of main landing gear attach point.

Jospeh P. Kline
A&P 123456789 IA

FIGURE 10.—Example of a discrepancy list to be provided to an aircraft owner when reporting an aircraft with unairworthy items after completing an annual inspection.

Weight & Balance
Cessna 182L
N42565
S/N18259080

Date: 04/22/20XX

Supersedes Computations of FAA Form 337, dated 10/02/90.

Removed the following equipment:

	Weight	Arm	Moment
1. Turn Coordinator P/N C661003-0201	2.5 lbs	15	37.5
2. Directional Gyro P/N 0706000	3.12 lbs	13.5	42.12
TOTAL	5.62		79.62
	1709.60	35.26	60282.2
	-5.62		-79.62
Aircraft after removal:	1703.98	35.3	60202.58

Installed the following equipment:

	Weight	Arm	Moment
1. S-Tec 40 Autopilot system, includes Turn Coordinator and Directional Gyro.	13 lbs	32.7	425.13
	1703.98		60202.20
	+13.00		+425.13
***REVISED LICENSED EMPTY WEIGHT**	**1716.98**	**35.31**	**60627.71**

NEW USEFUL LOAD 1083.02

Forward Check (Limit +38.4)

	Wt.	Arm	Moment
A/C Empty	1716.98	35.31	60627.21
Fwd. Seats	170.00	36.00	6120.00
Aft. Seats			
Fuel (min.)	115.00	48.00	5520.00
Oil	22.00	-15.00	-330.00
Baggage			
	2023.98	35.5	71937.71

Rearward Check (Limit +47.4)

	Wt.	Arm	Moment
A/C Empty	1716.98	35.31	60627.21
Fwd. Seats	170.00	36.00	6120.00
Aft. Seats	340.00	71.00	24140.00
Fuel (max.)	360.00	48.00	17280.00
Oil	22.00	-15.00	-330.00
Baggage	120.00	97.0	11640.00
	2728.98	43.78	119477.71

Joseph P. Kline

Joseph P. Kline
A& P 123456789

Figure 11.—Example of a weight and balance revision for a typical light, single-engine aircraft.

NOTE: Computations are shown. Form is signed, dated, and identifies the computations or figures it supersedes. It is recommended that manufacturer's weight and balance data forms be used for specific aircraft.

March 30, 2002 Aircraft Total Time 1520 Hours Complied with AD 90-06-03R1, effective date March 27, 20XX. Modified the airplane by compliance with paragraph (b) of AD. Installed Cessna Service Kit SK 172-10A. No recurring action required. Bill Quinlan A&P 143298671

Figure 12.—Example of a one-time Airworthiness Directive compliance entry.

April 1, 2002 Engine Total Time 720 Hours Complied with AD 82-27-03, Roto-Masters Turbo Chargers by inspection as required by paragraph (b) through (g) of the AD. Turbine housing found satisfactory, next inspection due at 920 hours. Joe Knight A&P 279862423

Figure 13.—Example of a recurrent Airworthiness Directive compliance entry.

Appendix 2
Publications and Technical Data

Publications and Technical Data

The following publications and technical data provide information for aircraft inspection.

1. Title 14 of the Code of Federal Regulations (CFR).

The Code of Federal Regulations is a codification of the general and permanent rules published in the Federal Register by the Executive departments and agencies of the Federal Government. The Code is divided into 50 titles, which represent broad areas subject to Federal regulation. Each title is divided into chapters, which usually bear the name of the issuing agency. Title 14—Aeronautics and Space is composed of four chapters. Chapter I of this title is the Federal Aviation Administration, Department of Transportation (DOT). This chapter contains parts 1–199.

The following CFR parts are of particular interest to the holder of an inspection authorization.

CFR Part Number	Title
1	Definitions and Abbreviations
11	General Rulemaking Procedures
21	Certification Procedures for Products and Parts
23	Airworthiness Standards: Normal, Utility, Acrobatic, and Commuter Category Airplanes
25	Airworthiness Standards: Transport Category Airplanes
27	Airworthiness Standards: Normal Category Rotorcraft
29	Airworthiness Standards: Transport Category Rotorcraft
31	Airworthiness Standards: Manned Free Balloons
33	Airworthiness Standards: Aircraft Engines
35	Airworthiness Standards: Propellers
39	Airworthiness Directives
43	Maintenance, Preventive Maintenance, Rebuilding, and Alteration
45	Identification and Registration Marking
47	Aircraft Registration
65	Certification: Airmen Other Than Flight Crewmembers
91	General Operating and Flight Rules
119	Certification: Air Carriers and Commercial Operators
125	Certification and Operations: Airplanes Having a Seating Capacity of 20 or More Passengers or a Maximum Payload Capacity of 6,000 Pounds or More
135	Operating Requirements: Commuter and On-Demand Operations and Rules Governing Persons on Board Such Aircraft
183	Representatives of the Administrator

The Code of Federal Regulations may be obtained in either official paper or official electronic copies.

Paper copies are available from the following.

U.S. Government Printing Office (GPO)
Mail Stop: SDE
732 N. Capitol Street, NW
Washington, DC 20401
Toll Free: 888-293-6498

Electronic copies of the Code of Federal Regulations may be found on the Internet at the following addresses.

- www.airweb.faa.gov/rgl
(Regulatory and Guidance Library) — The official FAA Copy
- www.faa.gov
(Federal Aviation Administration)
- www.access.gpo.gov
(Government Printing Office)
- www.gpo.gov/nara/cfr/index.html
(National Archives and Records Administration)

2. Type Certificate Data Sheets and Specifications.

Type Certificate Data Sheets and Specifications (TCDS) set forth essential factors and other conditions, which are necessary for U.S. airworthiness certification. Aircraft, engines, and propellers which conform to a U.S. type certificate (TC) are eligible for U.S. airworthiness certification when found to be in a condition for safe operation and ownership requisites are fulfilled.

TCDS background information.

There are two kinds of certification documents contained in the TCDS file:

(1) Type Certificate Data Sheets

(2) Specifications

"**Type Certificate Data Sheets**" were originated and first published in January 1958. CFR subpart 21.41 indicates they are part of the type certificate. As such, a type certificate data sheet is evidence the product has been type certificated. Generally, type certificate data sheets are compiled from details supplied by the type certificate holder; however, FAA may request and incorporate additional details when conditions warrant.

"**Specifications**" were originated during implementation of the Air Commerce Act of 1926. Specifications are FAA recordkeeping document issued for both type certificated and non-type certificated products which have been found eligible for U.S. airworthiness certification. Although they are no longer issued, specifications remain in effect and will be further amended. Specifications covering type certificated products may be converted to type certificate data sheets at the option of the type certificate holder. However, to do so requires the type certificate holder to provide an equipment list. A specification is not part of a type certificate.

The official FAA copy in electronic version is available on the Internet at the FAA web site titled "Regulatory and Guidance Library" at www.airweb.faa.gov/rgl. This is a free service.

3. Summary of Airworthiness Directives for Small Aircraft And Rotorcraft (ADs).

An airworthiness directive (AD) contains information regarding an unsafe condition that exists in an aircraft, aircraft engine, propeller, or appliance when that condition is likely to exist or develop in other products of the same type design. No person may operate a product to which an AD applies, except in accordance with the requirements of the AD. All ADs are summarized and issued by the FAA. New and revised ADs are published bi-weekly and mailed to registered owners of effected equipment and subscription holders. Airworthiness directives are issued in two weight categories:

1. Small aircraft with a maximum certificated takeoff weight aircraft of 12,500 pounds or less, and all rotorcraft regardless of weight.
2. Large aircraft over 12,500 pounds maximum certificated takeoff weight.

Each of these categories is presented in three books. Included in these books are the airframe ADs and the ADs applicable to the engines, propellers, and appliances of the category.

These books may be purchased from:

U.S. Government Printing Office (GPO)
Mail Stop: SDE
732 N. Capitol Street, NW
Washington, DC 20401
Toll Free: 888-293-6498

The official FAA copy in electronic version is available on the Internet at the FAA web site titled "Regulatory and Guidance Library" (RGL) at www.airweb.faa.gov/rgl.

The ADs are totally searchable and easily located. The individual airworthiness directives and the AD biweeklies on the RGL website are considered official FAA copy and may be used in lieu of purchasing paper copies. This is a free service. Questions concerning the RGL may be directed to the Delegation & Airworthiness Programs Branch (AIR-140) at (405) 954-4103.

4. Advisory Circulars.

The Federal Aviation Administration issues advisory circulars to inform the aviation public in a systematic way of nonregulatory material. Unless incorporated into a regulation by reference, the contents of an advisory circular are not binding on the public. Advisory circulars are issued in a numbered-subject system corresponding to the numerical part of the subject regulation (AC 39-7 would therefore deal with a subject related to CFR Part 39 or Airworthiness Directives).

An advisory circular is issued to provide guidance and information in a designated subject area or to show a method acceptable to the Administrator for complying with a related Federal Aviation Regulation. Electronic versions are available on the Internet at the FAA web site.

- AC 39-7C, Airworthiness Directives. (FREE)
- AC 43-4A, Corrosion Control for Aircraft. (FOR SALE)
- AC 43-11, Reciprocating Engine Overhaul Terminology and Standards. (FREE)
- AC 43.13-1B, Acceptable Methods, Techniques and Practices – Aircraft Inspection and Repair. (FOR SALE)
- AC 43.13-2A, Acceptable Methods, Techniques, and Practices – Aircraft Alterations. (FOR SALE)
- AC 43-9C, Maintenance Records. (FREE)
- AC 43.9-1E, Instructions for Completion of FAA Form 337 Major Repair and Alteration (Airframe, Powerplant, Propeller, or Appliance). (FREE)
- AC 91-67, Minimum Equipment Requirements for General Aviation Operations Under FAR Part 91. (FREE)

ADDITIONAL INFORMATION of particular interest to the holder of an inspection authorization.

- FAA-H-8083-1, Aircraft Weight and Balance Handbook (FOR SALE)

5. How to Order Publications.

Refer to AC 00-2.13, Advisory Circular Checklist, for ordering instructions for both free and sale advisory circulars (ACs). AC 00-2.13 also gives stock numbers and prices for ACs sold by the Superintendent of Documents. The checklist is available on the Internet at: http://www.faa.gov/aba/html_policies/ac00_2.html

6. Additional Sources of Inspection Data.

Several commercial publishers offer subscription services that include the Airworthiness Directives, Advisory Circulars, and Type Certificate Data Sheets along with other inspection data. They may be found in aviation trade paper and magazines.

Appendix 3
List of Reference Materials and Subject Matter Knowledge Codes

8082-11A

AC

List of Reference Materials and Subject Matter Knowledge Codes

The publications listed in the following pages are documents that are used as references in preparing the inspection authorization knowledge tests. The official FAA copy in electronic format is available on the FAA web site titled "Regulatory and Guidance Library (RGL)." (www.airweb.faa.gov/rgl) All of these publications can be purchased through U.S. Government Bookstores, commercial aviation supply houses, or industry organizations. The latest revision of the listed references should be requested. Additional study material is also available through these sources that may be helpful in preparing for knowledge tests.

The subject matter knowledge codes establish the specific reference for the knowledge standard. When reviewing results of your knowledge test, you should compare the subject matter knowledge code(s) on your Airman Test Report to the ones found below.

Title 14 of the Code of Federal Regulations (14 CFR)

Part 1 — Definitions and Abbreviations

A01 General Definitions
A02 Abbreviations and Symbols

14 CFR Part 21 — Certification Procedures for Products and Parts

A100 General
A102 Type Certificates
A104 Supplemental Type Certificates
A108 Airworthiness Certificates
A110 Approval of Materials, Parts, Processes, and Appliances
A112 Export Airworthiness Approvals
A117 Technical Standard Order Authorizations

14 CFR Part 23 — Airworthiness Standards: Normal, Utility, Acrobatic and Commuter Category Airplanes

A150 General
A151 Flight
A152 Structure
A153 Design and Construction
A154 Powerplant
A155 Equipment
A157 Operating Limitations and Information
A159 Appendix G: Instructions for Continued Airworthiness

8082-11A

AC

14 CFR Part 27 — Airworthiness Standards: Normal Category Rotorcraft

A250 General
A253 Flight
A255 Strength Requirements
A257 Design and Construction
A259 Powerplant
A261 Equipment
A263 Operating Limitations and Information
A265 Appendix A: Instructions for Continued Airworthiness

14 CFR Part 39 — Airworthiness Directives

A13 Airworthiness Directives

14 CFR Part 43 — Maintenance, Preventive Maintenance, Rebuilding, and Alteration

A15 Maintenance, Preventive Maintenance, Rebuilding, and Alteration
A16 Appendixes

14 CFR Part 45 — Identification and Registration Marking

A400 General
A401 Identification of Aircraft and Related Products
A402 Nationality and Registration Marks

14 CFR Part 65 — Certification: Airmen Other Than Flight Crewmembers

A40 General
A45 Mechanics
A46 Repairmen

14 CFR Part 91 — General Operating and Flight Rules

B07 General
B11 Equipment, Instrument, and Certificate Requirements
B12 Special Flight Operations
B13 Maintenance, Preventive Maintenance, and Alterations

14 CFR Part 125 — Certification and Operations: Airplanes Having a Seating Capacity of 20 or More Passengers or a Maximum Payload Capacity of 6,000 Pounds or More; and Rules Governing Persons on Board Such Aircraft

D30 General
D36 Maintenance

14 CFR Part 135 — Operating Requirements: Commuter and on Demand Operations and Rules Governing Persons on Board Such Aircraft

E03 Aircraft and Equipment
E09 Airplane Performance Operating Limitations
E10 Maintenance, Preventive Maintenance, and Alterations
E12 Special Federal Aviation Regulations SFAR No. 36

14 CFR Part 183 — Representatives of the Administrator

E150 General
E151 Certification of Representatives
E152 Kinds of Designations: Privileges

FAA-H-8083-1 — Aircraft Weight and Balance Handbook

H108 Equipment for Weighing
H109 Preparation for Weighing
H110 Determining the Center of Gravity
H111 Empty-Weight Center of Gravity Formulas
H112 Determining the Loaded Weight and CG
H113 Multiengine Airplane Weight and Balance Computations
H114 Determining the Loaded CG
H115 Equipment List
H116 Weight and Balance Revision Record
H117 Weight Changes Caused by a Repair or Alteration
H118 Empty-Weight CG Range
H119 Adverse-Loaded CG Checks
H120 Ballast
H121 Weighing Requirements
H122 Locating and Monitoring Weight and CG Location
H123 Determining the Correct Stabilizer Trim Setting
H124 Determining CG Changes Caused by Modifying the Cargo
H125 Determining Cargo Pallet Loads with Regard to Floor Loading Limits
H126 Determining the Maximum Amount of Payload That Can Be carried
H127 Determining the Landing Weight
H128 Determining the Minutes of Fuel Dump Time
H129 Weight and Balance of Commuter Category Airplanes
H130 Determining the Loaded CG of a Helicopter
H131 Using an Electronic Calculator to Solve Weight and Balance Problems
H132 Using an E6-B Flight Computer to Solve Weight and Balance Problems
H133 Using a Dedicated Electronic Computer to Solve Weight and Balance Problems
H134 Typical Weight and Balance Problems
H135 Glossary

Additional Advisory Circulars

K03 AC 00-34, Aircraft Ground Handling and Servicing
K12 AC 20-32, Carbon Monoxide (CO) Contamination in Aircraft — Detection and Prevention
K13 AC 20-43, Aircraft Fuel Control
K20 AC 20-103, Aircraft Engine Crankshaft Failure
K45 AC 39-7, Airworthiness Directives
K46 AC 43-9, Maintenance Records
K47 AC 43.9-1, Instructions for Completion of FAA Form 337
K48 AC 43-11, Reciprocating Engine Overhaul Terminology and Standards
K49 AC 43.13-1, Acceptable Methods, Techniques, and Practices — Aircraft Inspection and Repair
K50 AC 43.13-2, Acceptable Methods, Techniques, and Practices — Aircraft Alterations
L25 FAA-G-8082-11, Inspection Authorization Knowledge Test Guide
L70 AC 91-67, Minimum Equipment Requirements for General Aviation Operations Under FAR Part 91
M02 AC 120-27, Aircraft Weight and Balance Control
M52 AC 00-2, Advisory Circular Checklist

Type Certificate Data Sheets and Specifications

Y300 Type Certificate Data Sheets and Specifications Alphabetical Index and Users Guide
Y301 Type Certificate Data Sheet No. 2A13 Piper
Y302 Type Certificate Data Sheet No. 3A19 Cessna
Y303 Type Certificate Data Sheet No. E-295 Textron Lycoming
Y304 Type Certificate Data Sheet No. A7CE Cessna
Y305 Type Certificate Data Sheet No. 3A13 Cessna
Y306 Type Certificate Data Sheet No. A7S0 Piper
Y307 Type Certificate Data Sheet No. A11EA Tiger Aircraft LLC
Y308 Type Certificate Data Sheet No. E-273 Teledyne Continental
Y309 Aircraft Specification No. 1A6 Piper
Y310 Type Certificate Data Sheet No. P57GL McCauley
Y311 Type Certificate Data Sheet No. P-920 Hartzell
Y312 Type Certificate Data Sheet No. 2A4 Twin Commander
Y313 Type Certificate Data Sheet No. E-284 Textron Lycoming

NOTE: AC 00-2, Advisory Circular Checklist, transmits the status of all FAA advisory circulars (ACs), as well as FAA internal publications and miscellaneous flight information, such as Aeronautical Information Manual, Airport/Facility Directory, knowledge test guides, practical test standards, and other material directly related to a certificate or rating. The checklist is available on the Internet at: http://www.airweb.faa.gov/rgl

Please submit terms you think should be added to the Index, including the FAR section number, to:
asa@asa2fly.com *~Thank you!*

A

Abbreviations and symbols *§1.2, 34.2*....8, 286
Accelerate-stop distance *§23.55*....95
Accessibility provisions *§23.611*....126
Accessories for multiengine airplanes *§23.1437*....176
Accessory (appliance), defined *§1.1*....1
Accessory attachments *§33.25*....263
Acrobatic maneuvers *§23.151*....101
Additional airworthiness requirements, under Part 135 *§135.169*....555
Additional airworthiness standards, under Part 135 *Part 135 Appendix A*....594
Additional maintenance requirements *§135.421*....590
Administrative actions *§13.11*....14
Administrative disposition of certain violations *§13.11*....14
Administrative law judge
  argument before *§13.231*....37
  defined *§13.202*....28
  judges *§13.205*....29
Administrator, defined *§1.1*....1
Admission to flight deck *§125.315*....503
Advertising *§147.45*....630
Aerial demonstrations and major sporting events
  aircraft operations management *§91.145*....369
Aerobatic flight *§91.303*....383
Aerobatics, parachutes required *§91.307*....383
Aerodynamic coefficients, defined *§1.1*....1
Aging airplane, inspection and review *§121.368, §135.422, §135.423*....470, 591
Agricultural and fire fighting airplanes
  noise operating limitations *§91.815*....404
Ailerons *§23.455*....116
Air carrier
  defined *§1.1*....1
  foreign, defined *§1.1*....3
  United States, defined *§1.1*....8
Air commerce
  defined *§1.1*....1
  overseas air commerce, defined *§1.1*....5
  overseas air transportation, defined *§1.1*....5
Air induction system *§23.1091, 27.1091*....157, 240
Air taxi, commercial operators *§135.1*....532
Air taxi operations
  alternate airport requirements *§135.223*....562
  alternate airport weather minimums *§135.221*....562
  destination airport weather minimums *§135.219*....562
  takeoff, approach, and landing minimums *§135.225*....562
Air taxi operators
  aircraft requirements *§135.25*....536
  drugs, carriage of *§135.41*....537
  manual contents *§135.23*....535
  manual requirements *§135.21*....535
Air traffic
  defined *§1.1*....1
  emergency rules *§91.139*....368
Air traffic clearance, defined *§1.1*....1

Air traffic control
- clearance light signals *§91.125* ... 365
- compliance with clearances *§91.123* ... 364
- defined *§1.1* ... 1

Air traffic control tower operators
- currency *§65.50* ... 337
- drugs and alcohol *§65.46–65.46b* ... 336–337
- duties *§65.45* ... 336
- eligibility, knowledge, skill and other requirements for certificate *§65.31–65.43* ... 335–336
- facility ratings, exchange of *§65.43* ... 336
- facility ratings *§65.39, 65.41* ... 336
- maximum hours on duty *§65.47* ... 337
- operating positions *§65.37* ... 335
- operating rules *§65.49* ... 337

Air Traffic Service (ATS) route, defined *§1.1* ... 1

Air transportation
- defined *§1.1* ... 1
- foreign air transportation, defined *§1.1* ... 3

Airborne weather radar equipment requirements *§125.223, 135.175* ... 492, 557

Aircraft
- and equipment requirements *§135.141–135.180* ... 547–560
- defined *§1.1* ... 1
- engine, defined *§1.1* ... 1
- flight manual, marking, and placard requirements *§91.9* ... 359
- identification *§21.182* ... 60
- large aircraft, defined *§1.1* ... 4
- lights required *§91.209* ... 380
- proving tests *§135.145* ... 547
- registration proceedings *§13.27* ... 21
- safety *§34.6* ... 287
- speed *§91.117* ... 363

Aircraft dispatchers
- certificate required *§65.51* ... 338
- certification course
  - content, hours *§65.61* ... 338
  - facilities *§65.65* ... 339
  - general *§65.63* ... 339
- courses *Part 65 Appendix A* ... 346
- eligibility *§65.53* ... 338
- experience required *§65.57* ... 338
- knowledge required *§65.55* ... 338
- personnel requirements *§65.67* ... 339
- skill required *§65.59* ... 338
- student records *§65.70* ... 339
- training required *§65.57* ... 338

Aircraft performance
- operating limitations *§135.361–135.399* ... 580–587

Aircraft registration
Cape Town Treaty, and *§47.47* 324
certificates of aircraft registration
application *§47.31* 322
cancellation, for export purpose *§47.47* 324
change of address *§47.45* 324
duration, return of certificate *§47.41* 323
effective date of registration *§47.39* 323
invalid registration *§47.43* 323
not previously registered anywhere *§47.33* 322
previously registered in foreign country *§47.37* 323
previously registered in United States *§47.35* 322
replacement, certificate *§47.49* 324
triennial report *§47.51* 324
dealers' certificate
application *§47.63* 325
certificate *§47.61* 325
duration, change of status *§47.71* 325
eligibility *§47.65* 325
evidence of ownership *§47.67* 325
limitations *§47.69* 325
general
applicability *§47.1* 317
applicants *§47.5* 318
corporations not U.S. citizens *§47.9* 319
definitions *§47.2* 317
evidence of ownership *§47.11* 319
FAA aircraft registry *§47.19* 321
fees *§47.17* 321
identification number *§47.15* 320
registration required *§47.3* 317
signatures and instruments made by representatives *§47.13* 320
temporary registration numbers *§47.16* 321
United States citizens and resident aliens *§47.7* 318
voting trusts *§47.8* 318
Aircraft requirements
for flight instruction *§91.109* 362
Part 135 operations *§135.25* 536
Aircraft simulators and other training devices *§135.335* 576
Airframe curriculum subjects *Part 147 Appendix C* 632
Airframe, defined *§1.1* 1
Airmen
limitations on use of services *§125.261, 135.95* 499, 541
other than flight crewmembers, temporary certificate *§65.13* 333
Airplane
categories *§23.3* 92
defined *§1.1* 1
flight manual *§125.75* 482
level position *§23.871* 145
limitations *§125.93* 482
or rotorcraft flight manual *§21.5* 46
requirements, general *§125.91* 482
Airplane components
fire protection *§121.277* 467
Airplane performance
operating limitations *§135.361–135.399* 580–586
Airplanes, years in service *§121.368, §135.422, §135.423* 470, 591
Airport traffic area
airspeed limits *§91.117* 363

Airport(s)
- defined *§1.1* ... 1
- operating on or in vicinity of *§91.126–91.131* ... 365–367
- requirements *§125.49, 135.229* ... 480, 564

Airship, defined *§1.1* ... 1

Airspace
- airport radar service areas, *See* Class C *§91.130* ... 366

Airspeed
- indicating system *§23.1323, 27.1323* ... 167, 244
- indicator *§23.1545, 27.1545* ... 181, 254
- limitations *§23.1505, 27.1503* ... 180, 252
- maximums in controlled airspace *§91.117* ... 363
- placard *§23.1563* ... 183

Airworthiness
- approval tags *§21.271* ... 67
- certificates
  - classification *§21.175* ... 59
  - other than experimental *§21.273* ... 67
  - required for civil aircraft *§91.203* ... 377
- check, pilot-in-command *§135.71* ... 538
- civil aircraft *§91.7* ... 359
- criteria for helicopter instrument flight *Part 27 Appendix B* ... 258
- directive *§39.1–39.27* ... 297–298
- directives
  - alternative method of compliance *§39.17* ... 297
  - compliance *§39.7* ... 297
  - conflicts with other documents *§39.27* ... 298
- limitations, in manufacturer's maintenance manuals *§21.50* ... 51
- maintenance limitations *§43.16* ... 304
- owner, operator responsibility *§91.403* ... 387
- release, maintenance performed *§135.443* ... 594
- release or maintenance record entry *§125.411* ... 510
- requirements *§135.169* ... 555
- responsibility for *§135.413* ... 587

Airworthiness Standards—Aircraft Engines
- block tests
  - reciprocating aircraft engines *§33.41–33.57* ... 265–268
  - turbine aircraft engines *§33.81–33.99* ... 274–278
- design and construction
  - general *§33.11–33.29* ... 263–264
  - reciprocating aircraft engines *§33.31–33.39* ... 265
  - turbine aircraft engines *§33.61–33.79* ... 268–273
- general
  - applicability *§33.1* ... 261
  - engine power and thrust ratings, selection of *§33.8* ... 263
  - engine ratings, operating limitations *§33.7* ... 262
  - instruction manual, installing and operating the engine *§33.5* ... 262
  - instructions for continued airworthiness *§33.4* ... 262

Airworthiness Standards—Normal Category Rotorcraft
- design and construction
  - control systems *§27.671–27.695* ... 222–224
  - external loads *§27.865* ... 230
  - fire protection *§27.853–27.863* ... 228–230
  - floats and hulls *§27.751–27.755* ... 225
  - general *§27.601–27.629* ... 219–222
  - landing gear *§27.723–27.737* ... 224–225
  - personnel and cargo accommodations *§27.771–27.833* ... 226–228
  - rotors *§27.653–27.663* ... 222
- equipment
  - electrical systems and equipment *§27.1351–27.1367* ... 246–247
  - general *§27.1301–27.1309* ... 243–244
  - instruments, installation of *§27.1321–27.1337* ... 244–245

lights §27.1381–27.1401 ... 247–249
safety equipment §27.1411–27.1461 ... 250–252
flight
flight characteristics §27.141–27.177 ... 209–211
general §27.21–27.33 ... 206–207
ground and water handling characteristics §27.231–27.241 ... 211
miscellaneous flight requirements §27.251 ... 211
performance §27.45–27.79 ... 208–209
operating limitations and information
general §27.1501 ... 252
markings and placards §27.1541–27.1565 ... 254–255
operating limitations §27.1503–27.1529 ... 252–254
rotorcraft flight manual, approved manual material §27.1581–27.1589 ... 256–257
powerplant
controls and accessories §27.1141–27.1163 ... 241–242
cooling §27.1041, 27.1043, 27.1045 ... 239, 240
exhaust system §27.1121, 27.1123 ... 241
fire protection §27.1183–27.1195 ... 242–243
fuel system components §27.991–27.999 ... 237–238
fuel system §27.951–27.977 ... 233–237
general §27.901, 27.903, 27.907 ... 231
induction system §27.1091, 27.1093 ... 240
oil system §27.1011–27.1027 ... 238–239
rotor drive system §27.917–27.939 ... 231–233
special retroactive requirements §27.2 ... 206
strength requirements
control surface and system loads §27.391–27.427 ... 213–214
emergency landing conditions §27.561, 27.562, 27.563 ... 217, 218
fatigue evaluation §27.571 ... 219
flight loads §27.321–27.361 ... 212–213
general §27.301–27.309 ... 211–212
ground loads §27.471–27.505 ... 214–216
main component requirements §27.547, 27.549 ... 217
water loads §27.521 ... 217
Airworthiness Standards—Normal, Utility, Acrobatic, and Commuter Category Airplanes
airplane categories §23.3 ... 92
applicability §23.1 ... 92
design and construction
control surfaces §23.651–23.659 ... 128
control systems §23.671–23.703 ... 128–131
electrical bonding and lightning protection §23.867 ... 145
fabrication methods §23.605 ... 125
fasteners §23.607 ... 125
fatigue strength §23.627 ... 127
fire protection §23.851–23.865 ... 142–145
floats and hulls §23.751–23.757 ... 134
flutter §23.629 ... 127
general §23.601 ... 125
landing gear §23.721–23.745 ... 131–133
leveling means §23.871 ... 145
personnel and cargo accommodations §23.771–23.831 ... 134–142
pressurization §23.841, 23.843 ... 142
wings §23.641 ... 128
equipment
electrical systems and equipment §23.1351–23.1367 ... 170–172
general §23.1301–23.1309 ... 164–166
instruments, installation of §23.1311–23.1337 ... 166–170
lights §23.1381–23.1401 ... 172–174
safety equipment §23.1411–23.1419 ... 175
flight
characteristics §23.141 ... 99
controllability and maneuverability §23.143–23.157 ... 99–102
general §23.21–23.33 ... 92–93
ground and water handling characteristics §23.231–23.239 ... 106

high-speed characteristics *§23.251, 23.253* ... 106
performance *§23.45–23.77* ... 94–99
spinning *§23.221* ... 105
stability *§23.171–23.181* ... 102–104
stalls *§23.201–23.207* ... 104–105
trim *§23.161* ... 102
vibration and buffeting *§23.251* ... 106
operating limitations and information
airplane flight manual, approved manual material *§23.1581–23.1589* ... 183–186
general *§23.1501–23.1529* ... 180–181
markings and placards *§23.1541–23.1567* ... 181–183
powerplant
cooling *§23.1041–23.1047* ... 156–157
exhaust system *§23.1121, 23.1123, 23.1125* ... 159, 160
fuel system components *§23.991–23.1001* ... 153–154
fuel system *§23.951–23.979* ... 149–152
general *§23.901–23.943* ... 145–149
induction system *§23.1091–23.1111* ... 157–159
liquid cooling *§23.1061, 23.1063* ... 157
oil system *§23.1011–23.1027* ... 154–156
powerplant controls, accessories *§23.1141–23.1165* ... 160–161
powerplant fire protection *§23.1181–23.1203* ... 162–164
special retroactive requirements *§23.2* ... 92
structure
ailerons and special devices *§23.455, 23.459* ... 116
control surface and system loads *§23.391–23.415* ... 112–113
emergency landing conditions *§23.561, 23.562* ... 122
fatigue evaluation *§23.571–23.575* ... 123–125
flight loads *§23.321–23.373* ... 107–111
general *§23.301–23.307* ... 106–107
ground loads *§23.471–23.511* ... 116–119
horizontal stabilizing and balancing surfaces *§23.421–23.427* ... 113–114
vertical surfaces *§23.441, 23.443, 23.445* ... 114, 115
water loads *§23.521–23.537* ... 119–122
Airworthiness Standards—Propellers
design and construction
applicability *§35.11* ... 293
design features *§35.15* ... 293
durability *§35.19* ... 293
general *§35.13* ... 293
materials *§35.17* ... 293
pitch control indication *§35.23* ... 294
reversible propellers *§35.21* ... 294
general
applicability *§35.1* ... 293
instruction manual, installing and operating *§35.3* ... 293
instructions for continued airworthiness *§35.4* ... 293
operating limitations *§35.5* ... 293
tests and inspections
blade pitch control system component test *§35.42* ... 295
blade retention *§35.35* ... 294
endurance *§35.39* ... 294
fatigue limit *§35.37* ... 294
functional *§35.41* ... 294
general *§35.33* ... 294
propeller adjustments, parts replacements *§35.47* ... 295
special tests *§35.43* ... 295
teardown inspection *§35.45* ... 295
Aisle, width of *§23.815* ... 142
Alaska, increased maximum certificated weights allowed *§91.323* ... 386

Alcohol
level, in the blood §91.17 ... 360
misuse of §65.46a, 135.253 ... 337, 567
testing for §65.46b, 135.255 ... 337, 567
Alcohol or drugs §65.12, 91.17 ... 333, 360
Alcoholic beverages §135.121 ... 543
Alert Area, defined §1.1 ... 1
Alteration
major alteration, defined §1.1 ... 5
minor alteration, defined §1.1 ... 5
Alternate airport(s)
defined §1.1 ... 1
fuel requirements §91.167 ... 371
general §125.365–125.369 ... 505–506
IFR flight plan requirements §91.169 ... 372
IFR weather minima §91.169 ... 372
Altimeter settings §91.121 ... 364
Altimeter system, altitude reporting equipment
tests and inspections Part 43 Appendix E, §91.411 ... 308, 390
Altitude
after communications failure §91.185 ... 376
during aerobatic flight §91.303 ... 383
minimum for helicopters §91.119 ... 364
minimum safe §91.119 ... 364
minimum VFR §135.203 ... 561
over congested areas §91.119 ... 364
over other than congested areas §91.119 ... 364
rules, for large and turbine-powered aircraft §91.515 ... 394
use of oxygen §91.211 ... 380
Altitude alerting system
turbojet aircraft §91.219 ... 382
Altitude engine, defined §1.1 ... 1
Altitude reporting equipment
tests and inspections §91.411 ... 390
Amendment of notice and answer §13.45 ... 23
Annual inspections §91.409 ... 388
Anticollision light system §23.1401, 27.1401 ... 174, 249
Appeals, under FAA Civil Penalty Actions §13.83, 13.233 ... 26, 38
Appearances, under FAA Civil Penalty Actions and Hearings §13.33, 13.204 ... 23, 29
Appliance, defined §1.1 ... 1
Application, falsification of §21.2 ... 45
Approval of
flight simulators and flight training devices §125.297 ... 502
major changes in type design §21.97 ... 55
materials, parts, processes, and appliances §21.305 ... 69
minor changes in type design §21.95 ... 55
Approved aircraft inspection program §135.419 ... 590
Approved, defined §1.1 ... 1
Area navigation (RNAV), defined §1.1 ... 1
Armed Forces, defined §1.1 ... 1
Artificial stall barrier system §23.691 ... 130
ATC clearances
compliance with §91.123 ... 364
light signals §91.125 ... 365
ATC transponder
and altitude reporting equipment §91.215 ... 381
Attendance and enrollment, tests and credit §147.31 ... 629
Aural speed warning device §91.603 ... 397
Aural warning device §121.289 ... 468

Authorizations to exceed Mach 1 *Part 91 Appendix B*.....438
Automatic pilot system *§23.1329, 27.1329*.....169, 245
Automatic power reserve (APR) system *§23.904, Part 23 Appendix H*.....147, 198
Autopilot
  minimum altitudes for use of *§125.329*.....504
  use of *§135.93, 135.105*.....541, 542
Autorotation control mechanism *§27.691*.....224
Autorotation, defined *§1.1*.....1
Auxiliary float loads *§23.535*.....121
Auxiliary floats *§23.757*.....134
Auxiliary power unit
  controls *§23.1142*.....160
  limitations *§23.1522*.....181
Auxiliary rotor, defined *§1.1*.....1
Aviation Maintenance Technician Schools
  certification requirements
    facilities, equipment, and material *§147.13*.....627
    general curriculum *§147.21*.....628
    instructional equipment *§147.17*.....628
    instructor *§147.23*.....628
    materials, special tools, and shop equipment *§147.19*.....628
    ratings *§147.11*.....627
    space *§147.15*.....627
  curriculum
    airframe subjects *Part 147 Appendix C*.....632
    general subjects *Part 147 Appendix B*.....631
    powerplant subjects *Part 147 Appendix D*.....633
    requirements *Part 147 Appendix A*.....630
  general
    applicability *§147.1*.....627
    application and issue *§147.5*.....627
    certificate required *§147.3*.....629
    duration of certificates *§147.7*.....627
  operating rules
    advertising *§147.45*.....630
    attendance and enrollment, tests and credit for prior instruction or experience *§147.31*.....629
    change of location *§147.41*.....630
    display of certificate *§147.39*.....630
    inspection *§147.43*.....630
    maintenance of curriculum requirements *§147.38*.....630
    maintenance of facilities, equipment and material *§147.37*.....629
    maintenance of instructor requirements *§147.36*.....629
    quality of instruction *§147.38a*.....630
    records *§147.33*.....629
    transcripts and graduation certificates *§147.35*.....629
  students from certificated schools *§65.80*.....340
Aviation Medical Examiners *§183.21*.....636
Aviation Safety Reporting Program
  prohibition against use of reports for enforcement purposes *§91.25*.....361

B

Baggage, cargo compartments *§23.787*.....138
Balancing loads *§23.421*.....113
Ballast provisions *§27.873*.....231
Balloon, defined *§1.1*.....1
Basic landing conditions *Part 23 Appendix C*.....195
Basic VFR weather minimums *§91.155*.....370
Batteries, in emergency locator transmitters *§91.207*.....379
Bearing factors *§23.623, 27.623*.....127, 221
Bird ingestion *§33.76*.....271
Blade containment, rotor unbalance tests *§33.94*.....279

Blade pitch control system component test *§35.42* ... 295
Blade retention test *§35.35* ... 294
Bleed air system *§33.66* ... 268
Block tests, general conduct of *§33.57, 33.99* ... 268, 280
Blood alcohol level *§91.17* ... 360
Blood test, submission to *§91.17* ... 360
Brake horsepower, defined *§1.1* ... 1
Braked roll conditions *§23.493, 27.493* ... 117, 215
Brakes *§23.735, 27.735* ... 133, 225
Briefing of passengers before flight *§125.327, 135.117* ... 503, 542
Business names, use of *§119.9* ... 451

C

Cabin interiors *§121.215, 125.113* ... 464, 482
Cable systems *§23.689* ... 129
Calendar day, defined *§135.273* ... 570
Calibrated airspeed, defined *§1.1* ... 1
Calibration tests *§33.45, 33.85* ... 266, 274
Canada, flights to *§91.707* ... 402
Canard configuration, defined *§1.1* ... 1
Canard, defined *§1.1* ... 1
Canard or tandem wing configuration *§23.302* ... 107
Cancellation of certificate for export purpose *§47.47* ... 324
Capability list, repair station *§145.215* ... 624
Carburetor air
- preheater design *§23.1101* ... 158
- temperature controls *§23.1157* ... 161

Carburetor deicing fluid
- flow rate *§23.1095* ... 158
- system capacity *§23.1097* ... 158
- system detail design *§23.1099* ... 158

Cargo and baggage compartments *§27.787, 27.855* ... 227, 228
Cargo, carriage of
- in cargo compartments *§121.287, 125.185* ... 468, 486
- in passenger compartments *§121.285, 125.183* ... 467, 486

Cargo, carry-on baggage
- on large and turbine-powered aircraft *§91.523, 91.525* ... 396

Carriage of candidates in elections *§91.321* ... 386
Carriage of cargo
- carry-on baggage *§135.87* ... 540
- in cargo compartments *§121.287, 125.185* ... 468, 486
- in passenger compartments *§121.285, 125.183* ... 467, 486

Carriage of persons, without compliance with passenger-carrying requirements *§125.331, 135.85* ... 504, 539
Casting factors *§23.621, 27.621* ... 126, 221
CAT II and III manual requirements *§91.191* ... 377
CAT II and III operations *§91.189* ... 376
Category, defined *§1.1* ... 1
Category A, defined *§1.1* ... 2
Category B, defined *§1.1* ... 2
Category II operations
- certificate of authorization for *§91.193* ... 377
- defined *§1.1* ... 2
- second-in-command *§135.111* ... 542

Category II operations *Part 91 Appendix A* ... 436
Category III operations, defined *§1.1* ... 2
Category IIIa operations, defined *§1.1* ... 2
Category IIIb operations, defined *§1.1* ... 2
Category IIIc operations, defined *§1.1* ... 2

Ceiling, defined *§1.1* 2
Center of gravity limits *§27.27* 207
Certificate
  action, legal enforcement *§13.19* 19
  and operations specifications *§125.31, 125.41* 479, 480
  change of address *§65.21* 335
  change of name, replacement of lost *§65.16* 334
  display of *§65.89, 65.105* 341, 343
  duration of *§65.15* 334
  eligibility and prohibited operations *§125.11* 478
  holder's responsibilities *§125.243* 497
  lost or destroyed *§65.16* 334
  requirements, maintenance *§135.435* 593
Certificate(s)
  amending *§119.41* 454
  issuing or denying *§119.39* 454
  surrender of *§119.61* 458
  under Part 119 *§119.35, 119.36* 452, 453
Certificates and ratings
  airmen other than flight crewmembers *§65.1* 333
  foreign airmen other than flight crewmembers *§65.3* 333
Certificates, Type
  applicable regulations *§21.17* 47
  application for *§21.15* 47
  calibration report *§21.39* 51
  eligibility *§21.13* 47
  flight test pilot *§21.37* 51
  flight tests *§21.35* 50
  inspections and tests *§21.33* 50
  issue of *§21.21–21.29* 48–50
  privileges *§21.45* 51
  special conditions *§21.16* 47
Certification and Operations
  airman and crewmember requirements *§125.261–125.271* 499
  airplane requirements *§125.91, 125.93* 482
  certification rules and miscellaneous requirements *§125.21–125.53* 478–480
  flight crewmember requirements *§125.281–125.297* 500–502
  flight operations *§125.311–125.333* 502–504
  flight release rules *§125.351–125.383* 505–507
  general
    applicability *§125.1* 477
    certificate *§125.5–125.11* 477–478
    definitions *§125.9* 478
    deviation authority *§125.3* 477
  instrument and equipment requirements *§125.201–125.227* 487–496
  maintenance *§125.241–125.251* 497–499
  manual requirements *§125.71–125.75* 481–482
  records and reports *§125.401–125.411* 507–510
  special airworthiness requirements *§125.111–125.189* 482–487
Certification of foreign repair stations, special requirements *§145.51, 145.53* 618

Certification procedures for products and parts
airplane or rotorcraft flight manual *§21.5* ... 46
airworthiness approvals, exports *§21.321–21.339* ... 69–72
airworthiness certificates
aircraft identification *§21.182* ... 60
applicability *§21.171* ... 59
classification *§21.175* ... 59
eligibility *§21.173* ... 59
experimental certificates
aircraft to be used for market surveys, etc. *§21.195* ... 63
general *§21.191, 21.193* ... 63
issuance of airworthiness certificates
for limited category aircraft *§21.189* ... 62
for primary category aircraft *§21.184* ... 61
for restricted category aircraft *§21.185* ... 61
multiple *§21.187* ... 62
provisional *§21.211–21.225* ... 64–65
special flight permits *§21.197, 21.199* ... 64
applicability *§21.1* ... 45
approval of imports *§21.500, 21.502* ... 75
delegation option authorization procedures *§21.231–21.293* ... 66–68
designated alteration station, authorization procedures *§21.431–21.493* ... 73–74
falsification of applications, reports or records *§21.2* ... 45
production certificates
display *§21.161* ... 59
eligibility *§21.133* ... 58
inspections and tests *§21.157* ... 59
manufacturing facilities, location of *§21.137* ... 58
production limitation record *§21.151* ... 58
quality control *§21.139* ... 58
requirements for issuance *§21.135* ... 58
responsibility of holder *§21.165* ... 59
reporting of failures, malfunctions, and defects *§21.3* ... 46
TSO authorizations *§21.601–21.621* ... 75–77
type certificate only, production under
conformity, statement of *§21.130* ... 57
production inspection system
Materials Review Board *§21.125* ... 57
tests *§21.127–21.129* ... 57
type certificates
application for type certificate *§21.15* ... 47
availability *§21.49* ... 51
certificate *§21.41* ... 51
changes requiring a new type certificate *§21.19* ... 48
changes to *§21.91–21.101* ... 54–55
conformity, statement of *§21.53* ... 52
designation of applicable regulations *§21.17* ... 47
duration *§21.51* ... 52
eligibility *§21.13* ... 47
flight test instrument calibration and correction report *§21.39* ... 51
flight test pilot *§21.37* ... 51
flight tests *§21.35* ... 50
inspections and tests *§21.33* ... 50
instructions for continued airworthiness *§21.50* ... 51
issuance of
import products *§21.29* ... 50
primary category aircraft *§21.24* ... 48
restricted category aircraft *§21.25* ... 48
surplus aircraft of the Armed Forces *§21.27* ... 49
manufacturer's maintenance manuals *§21.50* ... 51
manufacturing facilities, location of *§21.43* ... 51
privileges *§21.45* ... 51
special conditions *§21.16* ... 47
supplemental *§21.111–21.119* ... 56

transferability §21.47 ... 51
type design §21.31 ... 50
type certificates, provisional
application §21.75 ... 52
duration §21.77 ... 52
eligibility §21.73 ... 52
requirements for issue and amendment of
Class I §21.81 ... 52
Class II §21.83 ... 53
Change
location or facilities §145.105, 147.41 ... 620, 630
of address §47.45, 65.21, 119.47, 125.47 ... 324, 335, 454, 480
or renewal of certificates §145.55, 145.57 ... 618
Check airmen
authorization, application and issue §125.295 ... 502
qualifications §135.337 ... 576
training of §135.339 ... 577
Checklist
required, Part 135 operations §135.83 ... 539
Chemical oxygen generators §23.1450 ... 178
Circuit protective devices §23.1357, 27.1357 ... 171, 247
Civil aircraft
certificates, documents required §91.203 ... 377
defined §1.1 ... 2
Civil penalties §13.14, 13.15, 13.16, 13.18, 13.29 ... 15, 18, 22
Class, defined §1.1 ... 2
Class A airspace
operations in §91.135 ... 367
transponder requirement §91.135 ... 367
Class B airspace
airspeed limits §91.117 ... 364
operations in §91.131 ... 367
Class C airspace, operations in §91.130 ... 366
Class C, D airspace, airspeed limits §91.117 ... 363
Class D airspace
communications in, requirements §91.129 ... 365
operations in §91.129 ... 365
special VFR weather minimums §91.157 ... 371
Class E airspace
equipment requirements §91.127 ... 365
operations in §91.127 ... 365
pilot requirements §91.127 ... 365
Class G airspace
equipment requirements §91.126 ... 365
operations in §91.126 ... 365
Clearance
compliance with §91.123 ... 364
Clearway, defined §1.1 ... 2
Climb
all engines operating §23.65, 27.65 ... 97, 208
and descent, en route §23.69 ... 98
general §23.63 ... 96
one engine inoperative §23.67, 27.67 ... 97, 209
Climbout speed, defined §1.1 ... 2
Clouds, distance from
special VFR weather minimums §91.157 ... 371
Cockpit controls §23.777–23.781, 27.777, 27.779 ... 135–136, 226
Cockpit voice recorder, required §135.151 ... 548
Cockpit voice recorders §23.1457, 27.1457, 91.609 ... 178, 250, 398
Collision avoidance system §125.224 ... 493

Collision avoidance *§91.111* ... 363
Color specifications *§23.1397, 27.1397* ... 174, 249
Commercial operations
  carriage of narcotic drugs, marijuana, depressant or stimulant drugs or substances *§135.41* ... 537
  manual
    contents *§135.23* ... 535
    requirements *§135.21* ... 535
Commercial operator, defined *§1.1* ... 2
Commercial operators *§135.1* ... 532
Communication and navigation facilities *§125.357* ... 505
Communications
  Class D airspace, requirements *§91.129* ... 365
  failure, under IFR *§91.185* ... 376
  with control tower *§91.129* ... 366
Commuter or on-demand operations *§135.1* ... 532
Compartment interiors
  fire protection *§27.853* ... 228
  materials allowed *§135.170* ... 556
Compliance with
  §125.119, proof of *§125.121* ... 483
  airworthiness standards, proof of *§23.21, 27.21* ... 92, 206
  gaseous emission standards *§34.71* ... 291
  smoke emission standards *§34.89* ... 292
Composition of flight crew *§125.263, 135.99* ... 499, 541
Consensus standard, defined *§1.1* ... 2
Consent orders *§13.13* ... 14
Continued airworthiness
  §21.50, Part 23 App. G, App. A to Parts 27, 33, 35 ... 51, 197, 254, 257, 280, 295
Continuous airworthiness maintenance program (CAMP) *§91.1411–§91.1443* ... 432–436
Contract maintenance *§145.217* ... 624
Contracts, retention of *§135.64* ... 538
Control markings *§23.1555, 27.1555* ... 182, 255
Control surface loads *§23.391* ... 112
Control system
  details *§23.685, 27.685* ... 129, 223
  joints *§23.693* ... 130
  loads *§23.395, 27.395* ... 112, 213
  locks *§23.679, 27.679* ... 129, 223
  stops *§23.675* ... 128
Control tower
  operations in Class D airspace *§91.129* ... 366
  required communications *§91.129* ... 366
Controllability and maneuverability *§27.143* ... 210
Controlled airspace, defined *§1.1* ... 2
Controlled Firing Area, defined *§1.1* ... 2
Coolant tank tests *§23.1063* ... 157
Cooling test procedures *§23.1045, 23.1047, 27.1045* ... 156, 157, 240
Cooling tests *§23.1043, 27.1043* ... 156, 239
Cowling and engine compartment covering *§27.1193* ... 243
Cowling and nacelle *§23.1193* ... 163
Cowling *§121.249, 125.147* ... 466, 484
Crew
  PIC designation required *§135.109* ... 542
  qualifications *§135.243–135.247* ... 564–565
  requirements, Part 135 operations *§135.99* ... 541
Crew pairing *§135.4* ... 534
Crewmember record *§125.401* ... 507

Crewmember(s)
at stations in flight *§91.105* 362
defined *§1.1* 2
duties *§135.100* 541
emergency training *§135.331* 575
flight time limitations, rest required *§135.261* 567
initial and recurrent training requirements *§135.343* 579
interference with *§91.11* 360
previously trained *§135.12* 535
requirements, large and turbine-powered aircraft *§91.529–91.533* 396–397
testing requirements *§135.291* 571
tests and checks, grace provisions, training to accepted standards *§125.293, 135.301* 502, 573
training requirements *§135.329* 575
Criminal penalties *§13.23* 21
Criteria for Category A *Part 27 Appendix C* 260
Critical altitude, defined *§1.1* 2
Critical engine, defined *§1.1* 2
Critical part, defined *§27.602* 219
Cruising altitudes
IFR *§91.179* 375
VFR *§91.159* 371
Cuba, operations to *§91.709* 402
Currency requirements
Part 135 operations *§135.247* 565
Curriculum requirements
definitions, teaching levels *Part 147 Appendix A* 630
maintenance of *§147.38* 630

D

Damage tolerance, fatigue evaluation of structure *§23.573* 124
Damage-tolerance-based inspections *§121.370a* 472
Dealers' aircraft registration certificate *§47.61* 325
Decision height, defined *§1.1* 2
Defects, reporting of *§21.3* 46
Depositions, FAA hearings and investigations *§13.53, 13.125* 24, 28
Design
airspeeds *§23.335* 108
features *§35.15* 293
fuel loads *§23.343* 109
limitations *§27.309* 212
weights, center of gravity positions *§23.523* 119
Design load criteria *Part 23 Appendix A* 186
Design *§21.99, 27.601, 27.917* 55, 219, 231
Designated
aircraft maintenance inspectors *§183.27* 637
airworthiness representative *§183.33* 638
engineering representatives *§183.29* 637
fire zones *§23.1181* 162
manufacturing inspection representatives *§183.31* 638
Design-life goal, airplane *§121.370a, §135.168, Part 135, App. G.* 555
Destination Airport Analysis *§135.4* 534
Destination Airport Analysis *§91.1037* 417
Deviation authority
for an emergency operation *§119.57* 457
for operations under U.S. military contract *§119.55* 457
Digital flight data recorders *§125.226* 494

Direct air carrier
certificate, application requirements *§119.35* 452
certificate, contents of *§119.37* 454
intrastate common carriage *§119.21* 451
requirements *§119.33* 452
Directional and lateral control *§23.147* 100
Directional stability and control *§23.233* 106
Display of certificate *§21.161, 65.89, 65.105, 125.7, 145.5, 147.39* 59, 341, 343, 477, 617, 630
Display of marks, general *§45.23* 315
Disposition of load manifest, flight release, flight plans *§125.405* 508
Ditching equipment *§23.1415, 27.1415* 175, 250
Ditching *§27.801* 227
Documents
data required for repair stations *§145.109* 620
service and filing *§13.43* 23
Doors
external *§23.783, 27.783* 137, 226
internal *§121.217* 464
Dropping objects *§91.15* 360
Drug or alcohol test, refusal to submit to *§65.23* 335
Drugs or alcohol *§91.17* 360
Drugs, prohibited, use of *§135.249* 566
Dry-lease aircraft exchange *§91.1001* 410
Dual control system *§23.399, 27.399* 112, 214
Dual controls requirement *§135.147* 548
Durability *§33.19, 35.19* 263, 293
Duration of certificates *§145.55* 618
Duty period
defined *§135.273* 570
limitations and rest requirements *§125.37, 135.273* 479, 570
Dynamic stability *§23.181* 104

E

Electrical
cables and equipment *§23.1365, 27.1365* 172, 247
system fire protection *§23.1359* 171
Electronic
device, portable *§91.21* 360
display instrument systems *§23.1311* 166
equipment *§23.1431* 175
Elevator control force in maneuvers *§23.155* 101
Eligible on-demand operation *§135.4* 534
ELT (emergency locator transmitter) *§91.207* 379
Emergencies *§125.319* 503
Emergency
authority of PIC *§91.3* 359
continuation of flight in *§135.69* 538
deviation from ATC clearance *§91.123* 364
equipment *§135.167, 135.177, 135.178* 554, 557, 558
evacuation procedures, demonstration *§121.291* 468
Emergency air traffic rules *§91.139* 368
Emergency and evacuation duties *§125.271, 135.123* 499, 543
Emergency equipment
extended overwater operations *§125.209, 135.167* 489, 554, 555
requirements *§125.207* 489
Emergency evacuation procedures,
demonstration of *§121.291, 125.189, Part 125 Appendix B* 468, 487, 512
Emergency evacuation *§23.803* 139

Emergency exit
access *§23.813* ...141
exit marking *§23.811* ...140
exits *§23.807, 27.807* ...139, 228
flightcrew *§23.805* ...139
for airplanes carrying passengers for hire *§91.607* ...398
lighting *§23.812* ...141
Emergency landing dynamic conditions *§23.562, 27.562* ...122, 218
Emergency locator transmitters *§91.207* ...379
Emergency medical evacuation service (HEMES), crew rest required *§135.271* ...569
Emergency operations
obtaining deviation authority *§119.57* ...457
Emergency operations *§135.19* ...535
Emergency training for crewmembers *§135.331* ...575
Empty weight, defined *§119.3* ...449
Empty weight and center of gravity, currency requirement *§135.185* ...561
Empty weight and corresponding center of gravity *§23.29, 27.29* ...93, 207
En route inspections *§135.75* ...538
Endorsement(s), maintenance records *§91.417* ...391
Endurance test *§33.49, 33.87, 35.39* ...266, 274, 294
Engine
accessory compartment diaphragm *§23.1192* ...163
breather lines *§121.243* ...465
component tests *§33.53, 33.91* ...268, 278
control systems, electrical and electronic *§33.28* ...264
controls *§23.1143, 27.1143* ...160, 241
cooling *§33.21* ...263
general *§23.903, 27.903, 27.1011* ...146, 231, 238
ice protection *§23.929* ...148
ignition systems *§23.1165* ...161
mounting attachments and structure *§33.23* ...263
overtemperature test *§33.88* ...278
power and thrust ratings, selection of *§33.8* ...263
ratings and operating limitations *§33.7* ...262
rotation *§121.279* ...467
tests in APU mode *§33.96* ...280
torque *§23.361* ...110
vibration *§27.907* ...231
Engine accessory section diaphragm *§121.251* ...466
Engine failure, reports required *§135.417* ...590
Engine Powered Airplanes
test procedure (propulsion engines)
compliance with gaseous emission standards *§34.71* ...291
Engine-propeller system tests *§33.95* ...279
Enhanced flight visibility (EFV), defined *§1.1* ...3
Enhanced flight vision system (EFVS), defined *§1.1* ...3
Equipment
and materials requirements *§145.109* ...620
containing high energy rotors *§23.1461, 27.1461* ...179, 252
function and installation *§23.1301, 27.1301* ...164, 243
instrument, and certificate requirements *§91.203–91.221* ...377–382
standards for oxygen dispensing units *§23.1447* ...177
systems, and installations *§23.1309, 27.1309* ...165, 244
Equipment requirements
airplanes under IFR *§125.205* ...488
carrying passengers, under IFR *§135.163* ...553
commuter and on-demand operations *§135.141–135.180* ...547–560
extended overwater or IFR operations *§135.165* ...554
Equivalent airspeed, defined *§1.1* ...3

Equivalent safety provisions, under certification procedures *§21.261* 67
Evidence, public disclosure of *§13.226* 36
Exemptions *§34.7* 287
Exhaust
emissions, standards for *§34.21, 34.31* 289
heat exchanger *§23.1125* 160
piping *§27.1123* 241
system *§23.1123* 160
Exhibition, antique, and other aircraft, special rules *§45.22* 315
Exit row seating *§135.129* 545
Experimental aircraft
operating limitations *§91.319* 385
Experimental certificates
aircraft to be used for market surveys, etc. *§21.195* 63
general *§21.193* 63
Experimental certificates *§21.191, 21.275* 63, 67
Expert or opinion witnesses *§13.227* 37
Export aircraft, marking of *§45.31* 316
Export airworthiness approvals, under certification procedures *§21.269* 67
Extended over-water operation, defined *§1.1* 3
External load attaching means *§27.865* 230
External load, defined *§1.1* 3
External loads *§27.865* 230
External-load attaching, defined *§1.1* 3
Extinguishing agent containers *§23.1199* 164

F

FAA Aircraft Registry *§47.19* 321
FAA civil penalty actions, definitions *§13.202* 28
FAA civil penalty actions, rules of practice in
appeals *§13.219, 13.233, 13.234* 34, 38, 39
applicability *§13.201* 28
decisions, initial and final *§13.232–13.235* 37–39
documents (type of, filing, waivers, notices, amendments, records)
§13.207–13.211, 13.214–13.216, 13.230 ..... 30–31, 31–32, 37
hearings, procedures for *§13.218, 13.220–13.231* 32, 34–37
time and scheduling *§13.212, 13.213, 13.217* 31, 32
FAA hearings, rules of practice for
appearances *§13.33* 23
applicability *§13.31* 23
depositions *§13.53* 24
hearing officer *§13.37, 13.39* 23
motions *§13.43, 13.49* 23
notice of hearing *§13.45, 13.55* 23, 24
request for hearing *§13.35, 13.47* 23
specific rules of practice *§13.44, 13.51, 13.57, 13.59, 13.61, 13.63* 23, 24, 25
FAA inspection of repair stations *§145.223* 625
Fabrication methods *§23.605, 27.605* 125, 220
Facilities and services *§125.353* 505
Facilities, equipment, and material requirements *§147.13* 627
Failure
mechanical, reports required *§125.409, 135.415* 508, 588
Falsification, reproduction, or alteration
maintenance records *§43.12* 302
of applications, certificates, logbooks, reports *§21.2, 43.12, 65.20* 45, 302, 334
Fasteners *§23.607, 27.607* 125, 220

Fatigue
evaluation *§23.574, 27.571* ... 125, 219
limit tests *§35.37* ... 294
strength *§23.627* ... 127
Federal airway
IFR routing *§91.181* ... 376
Ferry flight, authorization for *§91.611* ... 399
Final takeoff speed, defined *§1.1* ... 3
Fire detector systems
§23.1203, 27.1195, 121.273, 121.275, 125.171 ... 164, 243, 467, 486
Fire extinguishers
requirements *§23.851, 135.155* ... 142, 552
Fire extinguishing
agent container compartment temperature *§121.269* ... 467
agent container pressure relief *§121.267* ... 467
agents *§23.1197, 121.265, 125.163* ... 163, 466, 485
system materials *§23.1201, 121.271, 125.169* ... 164, 467, 485
systems *§23.1195, 121.263, 125.161* ... 163, 466, 485
Fire precautions *§121.221* ... 464
Fire prevention *§33.17* ... 263
Fire protection
cargo and baggage *§23.855* ... 144
combustion heater *§23.859* ... 144
flammable fluid *§23.863* ... 145
flight controls, engine mounts, other *§23.865* ... 145
for oxygen equipment *§23.1451* ... 178
of structure, controls, and other parts *§27.861* ... 229
Fire protection *§27.853–27.863* ... 228–229
Fire resistant, defined *§1.1* ... 3
Fire walls *§27.1191, 121.245, 121.247, 125.143* ... 243, 466, 484
Fireproof, defined *§1.1* ... 3
Fitting factors *§23.625, 27.625* ... 127, 222
Flame resistant, defined *§1.1* ... 3
Flammable, defined *§1.1* ... 3
Flammable fluid fire protection *§23.863, 27.863* ... 145, 229
Flammable fluids *§27.1185, 121.225, 121.255, 125.153* ... 242, 465, 466, 485
Flap extended speed, defined *§1.1* ... 3
Flap extended speed *§23.1511* ... 180
Flash resistant, defined *§1.1* ... 3
Flight
locating requirements *§125.53, 135.79* ... 480
maneuver placard *§23.1567* ... 183
navigator and long-range navigation equipment *§125.267* ... 499
Flight and navigation instruments *§23.1303, 27.1303* ... 164, 243
Flight attendant
crewmember requirement *§125.269, 135.107* ... 499, 542
crewmember testing requirements *§135.295* ... 572
defined *§135.273* ... 570
initial and transition ground training *§135.349* ... 580
Flight controls
characteristics *§27.151* ... 210
primary *§23.673* ... 128
Flight crew
composition of *§125.263, 135.99* ... 499, 541
use of oxygen *§91.211* ... 380

Flight crewmember
at controls *§125.311* ... 502
at station *§91.105* ... 362
defined *§1.1* ... 3
duties *§135.100* ... 541
requirements *§135.241* ... 564
Flight cycle implementation time *§91.410, 121.370, 125.248* ... 389, 471, 498
Flight data recorder
suspension of certain requirements *SFAR 89 to Part 135* ... 531
Flight director systems *§23.1335, 27.1335* ... 169, 245
Flight envelope *§23.333* ... 107
Flight instruction
simulated IFR flight and certain flight tests *§91.109* ... 362
Flight instructor
qualifications *§135.338* ... 577
training of *§135.340* ... 578
Flight levels
defined *§1.1* ... 3
lowest usable (table) *§91.121* ... 364
Flight locating requirements *§135.79* ... 539
Flight manual
requirements for aircraft *§91.9* ... 359
Flight operations *§135.61* ... 537
Flight plan
defined *§1.1* ... 3
IFR, information required *§91.169* ... 372
required for IFR *§91.173* ... 373
Flight recorders and cockpit voice recorders *§91.609* ... 398
Flight recorders *§23.1459, 27.1459, 125.225, 135.152* ... 179, 251, 493, 549
Flight release
form *§125.403* ... 507
over water *§125.363* ... 505
under IFR or over-the-top *§125.361* ... 505
under VFR *§125.359* ... 505
Flight restrictions
in proximity of Presidential and other parties *§91.141* ... 369
temporary *§91.137, 91.138, 91.145* ... 367, 368, 369
Flight simulators, flight training devices *§125.297* ... 502
Flight test
areas *§91.305* ... 383
instrument calibration and correction report *§21.39* ... 51
pilot *§21.37* ... 51
Flight tests *§21.35* ... 50
Flight time, defined *§1.1* ... 3
Flight time limitations
general *§135.263* ... 568
rest requirements *§135.261–135.269* ... 567–569
scheduled operations *§135.265* ... 568
unscheduled 1-2 pilot crews *§135.267* ... 568
unscheduled 3-4 pilot crews *§135.269* ... 569
Flight time requirements, Part 135 operations *§135.243* ... 564
Flight visibility, defined *§1.1* ... 3
Float landing conditions *§27.521* ... 217
Floats and hulls *§27.751, 27.753, 27.755* ... 225, 226
Floats, auxiliary *§23.757* ... 134
Flutter *§23.629, 27.629* ... 127, 222
Foreign air carrier, defined *§1.1* ... 3
Foreign air commerce, defined *§1.1* ... 3
Foreign air transportation, defined *§1.1* ... 3

Foreign aircraft operations
operations of U.S.-registered aircraft outside of the U.S. §91.701–91.715 401–402
Foreign object ingestion
birds §33.76 271
ice §33.77 272
Formal complaints §13.5 13
Formation flight
prohibitions §91.111 363
requirements for §91.111 363
Forward wing, defined §1.1 3
Fractional ownership operations §91.1001–§91.1443 410–436
Fractional ownership operations
additional equipment §91.1045 418
aircraft maintenance §91.1109 431
CAMP (continuous airworthiness maintenance program) §91.1411–§91.1443 432–436
CAMP—certificate requirements §91.1435 435
compliance date §91.1002 411
crew qualifications §91.1089–§91.1101 427–431
crewmember experience §91.1053 420
crewmember testing and training requirements §91.1067–§91.1087 424–427
definition §91.1001 410
flight, duty and rest time §91.1057–§91.1062 420–423
flight scheduling §91.1029 416
IFR minimums §91.1039 418
internal safety reporting §91.1021 414
management contract §91.1003 411
operating manual §91.1025 414
operational control §91.1009–§91.1013 411–412
passengers §91.1035 416
pilot testing and training §91.1063 423
program management §91.1014–§91.1443 412–436
recordkeeping §91.1027 415
required operating information §91.1033 416
tests and inspections §91.1019 413
turbine-powered large transport category airplanes §91.1037 417
validation tests §91.1041 418
Fuel and induction system §33.35 265
Fuel burning thrust augmentor §33.79 273
Fuel flow §23.955, 27.955 ..... 149, 235
Fuel jettisoning system §23.1001 154
Fuel pumps §23.991, 27.991 ..... 153, 237
Fuel quantity indicator §23.1553, 27.1553 ..... 182, 255
Fuel requirements
IFR conditions §91.167 371
Part 135 operations §135.209 561
VFR conditions §91.151 370
Fuel specifications §34.81 291
Fuel strainer or filter §23.997, 27.997 ..... 153, 238
Fuel supply
nonturbine and turbopropeller-powered airplanes §125.375 506
turbine-engine-powered airplanes other than turbopropeller §125.377 506
Fuel system
components §23.994 153
crash resistance §27.952 234
design, turbine aircraft engines §33.67 269
drains §23.999, 27.999 ..... 154, 238
hot weather operation §23.961, 27.961 ..... 150, 235
independence §23.953, 27.953, 121.281, 125.179 ..... 149, 235, 467, 486
lightning protection §23.954, 27.954 ..... 149, 235

lines and fittings §23.993, 27.993, 121.231, 125.129 .... 153, 237, 465, 484
Fuel tank
carburetor vapor vents §23.975 152
expansion space §23.969, 27.969 .... 152, 237
filler connection §23.973, 27.973 .... 152, 237
general §23.963, 27.963 .... 150, 235
installation §23.967, 27.967 .... 151, 236
location of §121.229 465
outlet §23.977, 27.977 .... 152, 237
sump §23.971, 27.971 .... 152, 237
tests §23.965, 27.965 .... 150, 236
vents §27.975 237
Fuel tank system
instructions for maintenance and inspection §91.410, 121.370, 125.248 .... 390, 471, 498
Fuel valves and controls §23.995 153
Fuel valves §27.995, 121.235, 125.133 .... 238, 465, 484
Fuel Venting and Exhaust Emission Requirements, Turbine Engine Powered Airplanes
engine fuel venting emissions (new and in-use aircraft gas turbine engines)
applicability §34.10 288
standard for fuel venting emissions §34.11 288
exhaust emissions
in-use aircraft gas turbine engines §34.30, 34.31 289
new aircraft gas turbine engines §34.20, 34.21 289
general provisions
abbreviations §34.2 286
aircraft safety §34.6 287
definitions §34.1 285
exemptions §34.7 287
general requirements §34.3 286
special test procedures §34.5 287
test procedure (propulsion engines)
compliance with gaseous emission standards §34.71 291
sampling and analytical procedures §34.64 291
test procedure (propulsion engines) §34.62 290
test procedures, engine exhaust gaseous emissions (aircraft and aircraft gas turbine engines)
introduction §34.60 290
turbine fuel specifications §34.61 290
test procedures, engine smoke emissions (aircraft gas turbine engines)
compliance with smoke emission standards §34.89 292
fuel specifications §34.81 291
introduction §34.80 291
sampling and analytical procedures §34.82 291
Fuel venting emissions, standard for §34.11 288
Functional test, propellers §35.41 295
Fuselage, landing gear, rotor pylon structures §27.549 217
Fuselage pressure boundary §91.410, 121.370, 125.248 .... 389, 471, 498

G

General curriculum requirements §147.21, Part 147 Appendix B 628, 631
Glide
performance §27.71 209
single-engine airplanes §23.71 98
Glide slope
use of by turbine-powered or large aircraft §91.129 366
Glider(s)
defined §1.1 3
towing, requirements §91.309 383
Go-around power or thrust setting, defined §1.1 3
Ground clearance, tail rotor guard §27.411 214
Ground gust conditions §23.415 113

Ground load
dynamic tests *§23.726* 132
unsymmetrical loads *§23.511* 119
Ground loading conditions
assumptions *§27.473* 214
landing gear with skids *§27.501* 216
landing gear with tail wheels *§27.497* 215
Ground proximity warning system
required for turbine-powered aircraft *§135.153* 551
Ground resonance prevention means *§27.663* 222
Ground resonance *§27.241* 211
Ground visibility, defined *§1.1* 3
Gust loads factors *§23.341* 109
Gust loads *§23.425, 23.443, 27.341* 114, 115, 213
Gyrodyne, defined *§1.1* 4
Gyroplane, defined *§1.1* 4
Gyroscopic and aerodynamic loads *§23.371* 111

H

Hazardous materials
training requirements *§135.333* 575
violations *§13.16* 16
Hazardous Materials Transportation Act
applicability *§13.71* 25
Hazardous Materials Transportation Act, orders of compliance under
appeal *§13.83* 26
applicability *§13.71* 25
compliance *§13.73, 13.77, 13.81* 25
hearing *§13.75, 13.79* 25
time extension, filing service and computation of *§13.85, 13.87* 26
Hearing Officer
disqualification of *§13.39* 23
final order of *§13.27* 21
powers of *§13.37* 23
Heaters *§27.833* 228
Heating systems *§27.859* 228
Helicopter
defined *§1.1* 4
minimum visibility, Part 135 operations *§135.207* 561
surface reference requirements, Part 135 operations *§135.207* 561
Helicopter (HEMES) crew rest required *§135.271* 569
Heliport, defined *§1.1* 4
High lift devices *§23.345* 110
High speed characteristics *§23.253* 106
Hinges *§23.657* 128
Housing, facilities requirements, repair stations *§145.103* 619
Hull and main float
bottom pressures *§23.533* 120
landing conditions *§23.529* 120
load factors *§23.527* 119
takeoff condition *§23.531* 120
Hulls *§23.755, 27.755* 134, 226
Hydraulic actuating systems *§33.72* 270
Hydraulic systems *§23.1435, 27.1435* 176, 250

I

Ice protection *§23.1419, 27.1419, Part 125 Appendix C* 175, 250, 513
Icing conditions, operating limitations *§125.221, 135.227* 492, 563
Icing conditions, operation in *§91.527* 396
Identification and Registration Marking
  identification of aircraft and related products
    identification data *§45.11, 45.13* 313
    identification of critical components *§45.14* 314
    nationality and registration marks
      display, general *§45.23* 315
      exhibition, antique, and other aircraft, special rules *§45.22* 315
      general *§45.21* 314
      location, fixed-wing aircraft *§45.25* 315
      location, nonfixed-wing aircraft *§45.27* 315
      location on *§45.23* 315
      marking of export aircraft *§45.31* 316
      sale of aircraft, removal of marks *§45.33* 316
      size *§45.29* 316
    replacement and modification parts *§45.15* 314
Idle thrust, defined *§1.1* 4
IFR
  alternate airport requirements *§91.169, 135.223* 372, 562
  cancellation *§91.169* 372
  Category II and III operations *§91.189* 376
  clearance and flight plan required *§91.173* 373
  conditions, defined *§1.1* 4
  course to be flown *§91.181* 376
  cruising altitude, flight level *§91.179* 375
  equipment requirements *§135.163* 553
  flight plan, information required *§91.169* 372
  flight, safety pilot required *§91.109* 363
  fuel requirements *§91.167* 371
  instruments required *§91.205* 378
  minimum altitudes for operations *§91.177* 375
  missed approach procedures *§91.175* 373
  operating limitations *§135.215* 562
  operations
    equipment required *§135.165* 554
    malfunctions reporting *§91.187* 376
  Part 135 operations *§135.181* 560
  radio communications *§91.183* 376
  second-in-command required *§135.101* 542
  takeoff and landing *§91.175* 373
  takeoff limitations *§135.217* 562
  two-way communications failure *§91.185* 376
  VOR equipment check *§91.171* 372
  weather minimums, alternate airport *§135.221* 562
  weather minimums, destination airport *§135.219* 562
IFR approaches
  minimum altitudes (DH or MDA) *§91.175* 373
IFR over-the-top, defined *§1.1* 4
Ignition switches *§23.1145, 27.1145* 161, 242
Ignition system *§33.37, 33.69* 265, 269
Indicated airspeed, defined *§1.1* 4

Induction system
ducts *§23.1103*....159
filters *§23.1107*....159
ice prevention *§121.283*....467
icing protection *§23.1093, 27.1093*.... 158, 240
icing *§33.68*....269
screens *§23.1105*....159
Initial and recurrent flight attendant crewmember testing requirements *§125.289, 135.295*.... 501, 572
Initial and recurrent pilot testing requirements *§125.287, 135.293*.... 500, 571
Inoperable instruments and equipment *§91.213, 135.179*.... 380, 560
Inspection
changes to aircraft inspection programs *§91.415*....391
continuing analysis and surveillance *§135.431*....593
provisions *§27.611*....220
required inspection personnel *§121.371, 125.251, 135.429*....472, 499, 592
Inspection and review, aging airplane *§121.368, §135.422, §135.423*.... 470, 591
Inspection authority *§125.45*....480
Inspection authorization
application, requirements, eligibility *§65.91–65.95*.... 341–342
Inspection personnel requirements *§145.155*....621
Inspection program(s)
and maintenance *§125.247*....497
required *§135.419*....590
Inspection(s)
airworthiness certificate *§91.409*....388
altimeter system, altitude reporting equipment *§91.411*....390
annual or 100-hour *§91.409*....388
FAA *§145.223, 147.43*.... 625, 630
of work performed, repair stations *§145.155, 145.157, 145.213*.... 621, 623
progressive *§91.409*....388
Inspections
damage-tolerance-based *§121.370a*....472
service-history-based *§135.168*....555
supplemental *§121.370a*....472
Inspections and tests *§21.33, 21.157, 21.249, 23.575, 135.73*....50, 59, 66, 125, 538
Inspectors' credentials, admission to pilots' compartment *§125.317, 135.75*.... 503, 538
Installation *§23.655, 23.901, 23.1061, 27.901*.... 128, 145, 157, 231
Instruction manual, installing and operating engine *§33.5*....262
Instruction manual, installing and operating propeller *§35.3*....293
Instruction, quality of *§147.38a*....630
Instructional equipment requirements *§147.17*....628
Instructor requirements, maintenance of *§147.36*....629
Instructor requirements *§147.23*....628
Instrument
connections *§33.29*....264
defined *§1.1*....4
lights *§23.1381, 27.1381*.... 172, 247
markings, general *§23.1543, 27.1543*.... 181, 254
Instrument and equipment requirements
VFR and IFR *§91.205*....378
Instrument and equipment requirements *§135.149, 135.159*.... 548, 553
Instrument approach procedures, IFR landing minimums *§125.325*....503
Instrument approaches, to civil airports *§91.175*....373
Instruments
and equipment, inoperative *§91.213*....380
arrangement and visibility *§23.1321, 27.1321*.... 167, 244
using a power source *§23.1331*....169
Interconnected controls *§27.674*....223

Interconnected tanks, flow between *§23.957* 150
Interference with crewmembers *§91.1* 360
Interstate air commerce, defined *§1.1* 4
Interstate air transportation, defined *§1.1* 4
Intrastate air transportation, defined *§1.1* 4
Intrastate operations
  retention of contracts *§135.64* 538
Invalid registration *§47.43* 324
Investigation, formal fact-finding
  applicability *§13.101* 26
  noncompliance with the investigative process *§13.113* 27
  other procedures, witnesses, depositions, reports
    §13.111, 13.115, 13.117, 13.121, 13.123–13.131 .... 27, 28
  procedures, initial *§13.3, 13.103–13.109* 13, 26–27
  rights of persons against self-incrimination *§13.119* 27
Investigative procedures
  formal complaints *§13.5* 13
  investigations, general *§13.3* 13
  records, documents and reports *§13.7* 14
  reports of violations *§13.1* 13
Investigative proceeding or deposition, conduct of *§13.117* 27
Issuance of
  airworthiness certificate for limited category aircraft *§21.189* 62
  airworthiness certificates for restricted category aircraft *§21.185* 61
  certificate *§125.273* 479
  multiple airworthiness certification *§21.187* 62
  special airworthiness certificates for primary category aircraft *§21.184* 61
  special flight permits *§21.199* 64
  standard airworthiness certificates for normal, utility, acrobatic, commuter, and
    transport category aircraft, manned free balloons, and special classes of aircraft *§21.183* 60
  supplemental type certificates *§21.117* 56
  type certificate
    import products *§21.29* 50
    normal, utility, acrobatic, commuter, and transport category aircraft, manned free balloons,
      special classes of aircraft, aircraft engines, propellers *§21.21* 48
    primary category aircraft *§21.24* 48
    restricted category aircraft *§21.25* 48
    surplus aircraft of the Armed Forces *§21.27* 49

J

Jacking loads *§23.507* 118
Joints *§23.693* 130

K

Kite, defined *§1.1* 4
Knowledge tests, cheating or other unauthorized conduct *§65.18* 334

L

Landing
balked *§23.77* 99
conditions, basic *Part 23 Appendix C* 195
control during *§23.153* 101
distance *§23.75* 98
general *§27.75* 209
weather minimums, IFR *§125.379* 506
Landing gear
airworthiness standards, airplane *§23.721–23.745* 131–134
airworthiness standards, rotorcraft *§27.723–27.737* 224–225
arrangement *§23.477, 27.477* 116, 214
aural warning device *§121.289, 125.187* 468, 487
extended speed, defined *§1.1* 4
extension and retraction system *§23.729, 27.729* 132, 225
operating speed, defined *§1.1* 4
Landing lights *§27.1383* 247
Large and transport category aircraft
additional equipment and operating requirements for *§91.601–91.613* 397–400
Large and turbine-powered aircraft
emergency equipment *§91.513* 394
equipment and operating information *§91.501* 393
Large nontransport category airplanes
en route limitations *§135.391* 585
landing limitations, alternate *§135.395* 586
landing limitations, destination *§135.393* 586
takeoff limitations *§135.389* 585
Large transport category airplanes
en route limitations *§135.369* 581
landing limitations, alternate *§135.377* 583
landing limitations, destination *§135.375* 582
takeoff limitations *§135.367* 581
turbine, en route limitations *§135.381* 583
turbine, landing limitations
alternate *§135.387* 585
destination *§135.385* 584
turbine, takeoff limitations *§135.379* 583
weight limitations *§135.365* 581
Lateral drift landing conditions *§27.485* 215
Lease or sale, large aircraft *§91.23* 361
Legal enforcement actions
certificate action *§13.19* 19
civil penalties
streamlined enforcement procedures *§13.29* 22
compliance, cease and desist, denial and other orders *§13.20* 20
consent orders *§13.13* 14
criminal penalties *§13.23* 21
final order, hearing officer *§13.27* 21
injunctions *§13.25* 21
military personnel *§13.21* 21
seizure of aircraft *§13.17* 18
Level landing conditions *§23.479, 27.479* 116, 214
Leveling marks *§27.871* 231
Leveling means *§23.871* 145
Light signals *§91.125* 365
Lighted position lights
requirements for use of *§91.209* 380
Lighter-than-air aircraft, defined *§1.1* 4

Lightning and static electricity
protection against §23.867 145
Lightning protection §27.610 220
Lights
required §91.209 380
warning, caution, and advisory §23.1322, 27.1322 .... 167, 244
Light-sport aircraft §43.7 301
Light-sport aircraft
consensus standard, defined §1.1 2
defined §1.1 4
inspection §65.107 343
operating §21.191 63
powered parachute, defined §1.1 5
repairman certificate §65.107 .... 343, 386
special airworthiness certificate for §21.190 62
weight-shift-control aircraft, defined §1.1 8
Light-sport aircraft category, airframe rating §65.85 341
Limit control forces and torques §23.397 112
Limit drop test §23.725, 27.725 .... 131, 224
Limit load static tests §23.681, 27.681 .... 129, 223
Limit maneuvering load factor §23.337, 27.337 .... 109, 212
Limit pilot forces and torques §27.397 213
Limitation placard §27.1559 255
Limiting height—speed envelope §27.79 209
Line checks §135.299 573
Lines and fittings
fuel and other, requirements §121.231, 121.233, 121.237, 121.259 .... 465, 466
Lines, fittings, and components §23.1183, 27.1183 .... 162, 242
Load distribution limits §23.23 92
Load factor, defined §1.1 4
Load manifest §125.383 507
Loading information §23.1589, 27.1589 .... 186, 257
Loads, application of §23.525 119
Loads parallel to hinge line §23.393 112
Loads §23.301, 27.301 .... 106, 211
Location of marks
fixed-wing aircraft §45.25 315
nonfixed-wing aircraft §45.27 316
Logbooks
false entries §21.2, 43.12, 65.20 .... 45, 302, 334
Longitudinal control §23.145 99
Longitudinal stability and control §23.231 106
Long-range communication system (LRCS), defined §1.1 4
Long-range navigation system (LRNS), defined §1.1 4
Lubrication system §33.39, 33.71 .... 265, 269

M

Mach number, defined §1.1 5
Magnetic direction indicator §23.1327, 23.1547, 27.1327, 27.1547 .... 168, 182, 245, 254
Mail, transportation of §135.1 532
Main float
buoyancy §23.751, 27.751 .... 134, 225
design §23.753, 27.753 .... 134, 225
Main rotor
defined §1.1 5
speed and pitch limits §27.33 207
structure §27.547 217

Maintenance
approval to return to service *§43.5* ... 300
authority to perform *§43.3, 135.437* ... 300, 593
defined *§1.1* ... 5
inspection, initial *§33.90* ... 278
manual requirements *§125.249, 135.427* ... 498, 592
operational check *§91.407* ... 388
records, requirements *§135.439* ... 593
required inspection personnel *§135.429* ... 592
Maintenance and preventive maintenance
training program *§135.433* ... 593
Maintenance log, airplanes *§125.407* ... 508
Maintenance, preventive maintenance, alterations, and required inspections, certificates required *§135.435* ... 593
Maintenance, preventive maintenance, and alterations
airworthiness release, or aircraft log entry *§135.443* ... 594
authority to perform and approve *§135.437* ... 593
domestic, flag, and supplemental operations *§121.361–121.380a* ... 469–473
general *§91.401–91.421* ... 387–391
organization for *§135.423* ... 591
Part 121 operations
airworthiness responsibility *§121.363* ... 469
analysis and surveillance *§121.373* ... 472
authority to perform and approve *§121.379* ... 473
certificate requirements *§121.378* ... 472
duty time limitations *§121.377* ... 472
inspection personnel *§121.371* ... 472
manual requirements *§121.369* ... 470
organization *§121.365* ... 470
programs *§121.367, 121.375* ... 470, 472
records *§121.380, 121.380a* ... 473
programs for *§135.425* ... 591
rules for *§135.411* ... 587
Maintenance program, special requirements *§91.410, 121.370, 125.248* ... 389, 471, 498
Maintenance records
content, form, and disposition of *§43.9, 43.11* ... 301, 302
content *§43.9, 43.11, 43.12* ... 301, 302
general *§91.417* ... 391
rebuilt engine *§43.2, 91.421* ... 299, 391
transfer of *§91.419* ... 391
Maintenance requirements, additional *§135.421* ... 590
Major alteration, defined *§1.1* ... 5
Major repair, defined *§1.1* ... 5
Major repairs, rebuilding and alteration *§21.289* ... 68
Malfunction reports, under IFR *§91.187* ... 376
Malfunction reports *§125.409, 135.415* ... 508, 588
Malfunctions
reporting of *§21.3* ... 46
Management personnel
qualifications *§119.67, 119.71* ... 459, 460
required *§119.65, 119.69, 125.25* ... 458, 459, 478
Maneuvering loads *§23.423, 23.441* ... 113, 114
Manifest
recordkeeping requirements *§135.63* ... 537
Manifold pressure, defined *§1.1* ... 5
Manipulation of controls *§125.313, 135.115* ... 502, 542
Manual contents, Part 135 operations *§135.23* ... 535

Manual(s)
required for CAT II and III *§91.191* 377
requirements, for maintenance *§135.427* 592
requirements, Part 121 maintenance *§121.369* 470
requirements, Part 135 operations *§135.21* 535
Manufacturing facilities, location of *§21.43, 21.137* 51, 58
Marks, size of *§45.29* 316
Mass balance *§23.659, 27.659* 128, 222
Master parachute rigger, certificate requirements *§65.119* 345
Material strength properties, design values *§23.613, 27.613* 126, 220
Materials and workmanship *§23.603* 125
Materials Review Board *§21.125* 57
Materials, special tools, shop equipment requirements *§147.19* 628
Materials *§27.603, 33.15, 35.17* 220, 263
Maximum
airspeeds *§91.117* 363
operating altitude *§23.1527, 27.1527* 181, 254
passenger seating configuration *§23.1524* 181
Maximum payload capacity, defined *§119.3* 449
Maximum speed for stability characteristics, V_{FC}/M_{FC}, defined *§1.1* 5
Maximum zero fuel weight, defined *§119.3* 449
Mechanical interruption summary report *§135.417* 590
Mechanical irregularities, reporting *§135.65* 538
Mechanics
airframe rating *§65.85* 341
eligibility requirements *§65.71* 340
experience requirements *§65.77* 340
inspection authorization, duration *§65.92* 341
inspection authorization, privileges and limitations *§65.95* 342
inspection authorization, renewal *§65.93* 342
inspection authorization *§65.91* 341
knowledge requirements *§65.75* 340
powerplant rating *§65.87* 341
privileges and limitations *§65.81* 340
ratings *§65.73* 340
recent experience requirements *§65.83* 341
skill requirements *§65.79* 340
Medical certificate, defined *§1.1* 5
Metallic damage tolerance, fatigue evaluation, commuter category airplanes *§23.574* 125
Metallic pressurized cabin structures *§23.571* 123
Metallic wing, empennage, and associated structures *§23.572* 124
Mexico, flights to *§91.707* 402
Military operations area, defined *§1.1* 5
Military parachute riggers (or former)
special certification rule *§65.117* 344
Military personnel, legal enforcement procedures *§13.21* 21
Minimum altitudes
for helicopters *§91.119* 364
IFR operations *§91.177* 375
large or turbine-powered aircraft *§91.129* 366
on IFR approaches *§91.175* 373
over congested areas *§91.119* 364
use of autopilot *§135.93* 541
Minimum Navigation Performance Specification airspace (MNPS), operations in *§91.705* 401

Minimum(s)
- control speed *§23.149, 23.1513* 100, 180
- descent altitude, defined *§1.1* 5
- equipment list *§91.213, 135.179* 380, 560
- flight crew *§23.1523, 27.1523* 181, 254
- for aerobatic flight *§91.303* 383
- safe altitudes, general *§91.119* 364
- special VFR weather minimums *§91.157* 371

Minor alteration, defined *§1.1* 5
Minor repair, defined *§1.1* 5
Missed approach procedures *§91.175* 373
Mixture controls *§23.1147, 27.1147* 161, 242
MNPSA operations *§91.705, Part 91 Appendix C* 401, 439
Mode C capability, equipment requirements *§91.215* 381
Motions, in FAA hearings
- general *§13.49* 23
- in civil penalty actions *§13.218* 32
- service and filing *§13.43* 23

Multiengine aircraft, Part 135 operations *§135.181* 560

N

Nacelle areas behind firewalls *§23.1182* 162
Narcotics, testing for *§135.251* 566
NASA, Aviation Safety Reporting Program *§91.25* 361
Navigable airspace, defined *§1.1* 5
Navigational facilities, en route *§125.51* 480
Negative acceleration *§23.943* 149
Never-exceed speed *§27.1505* 252
Night currency requirements *§135.247* 566
Night, defined *§1.1* 5
Night flight, use of aircraft lights *§91.209* 380
Night operations
- (or VFR over-the-top), equipment required under Part 135 *§135.159* 553

Noise operating limitations
- base levels *§91.861* 406
- definitions *§91.851* 404
- final compliance *§91.805* 404
- Part 125 operators *§91.803* 403
- phased compliance for new entrants *§91.867* 407
- phased compliance for operators with base level *§91.865* 406
- sonic boom *§91.817* 404
- Stage 2 noise levels *§91.851* 405
- Stage 3 noise levels *§91.851* 405
- Stage 4 noise levels *§91.851* 405
- waivers from interim compliance requirements *§91.871* 407

Noncommon carriage, defined *§119.3* 449
Nonprecision approach procedure, defined *§1.1* 5
Nontransport category airplanes
- special airworthiness requirements *§121.293* 469

Nose/tail wheel steering *§23.745* 133

O

Objects, dropping §91.15 ... 360
Obstacle clearance, under IFR §91.177 ... 375
Oil
- lines and fittings §23.1017, 27.1017 ... 155, 238
- quantity indicator §23.1551, 27.1551 ... 182, 255
- radiators §23.1023 ... 156
- strainer or filter §23.1019, 27.1019 ... 155, 239
- system drains §23.1021, 27.1021, 121.241, 125.139 ... 156, 239, 465, 484
- tank tests §23.1015, 27.1015 ... 155, 238
- tanks §23.1013, 27.1013 ... 155, 238

On-demand operations
- crew pairing §135.4 ... 534
- eligible §135.4 ... 534
- flight time §135.4 ... 534

One-wheel landing conditions §23.483, 27.483 ... 117, 215
Operate, defined §1.1 ... 5
Operating
- experience §135.244 ... 565
- information required, checklists §125.215, 135.83 ... 491, 539
- near other aircraft §91.111 ... 363
- on or in the vicinity of an airport, general rules §91.127 ... 365

Operating certificate
- maneuvering speed §23.1507 ... 180
- operations specifications required §125.5 ... 477
- procedures §23.1585, 27.1585 ... 185, 256

Operating limitations
- aircraft performance §135.361 ... 580
- commuter category airplanes §135.398 ... 586
- manual information required §23.1583, 27.1583 ... 184, 256
- on-demand operations §135.4 ... 534
- placard §23.1559 ... 183
- restricted category civil aircraft §91.313 ... 384
- restricted, limited, and other aircraft categories §91.313–91.319 ... 384–385
- small nontransport category airplanes §135.399 ... 586
- small transport category airplanes §135.397 ... 586
- VFR over-the-top carrying passengers §135.211 ... 561

Operating limitations, types of §23.1525, 27.1525 ... 181, 254
Operating noise limits and related requirements §91.801–91.877 ... 403–408
Operating rules
- large and turbine-powered multiengine airplanes §91.501–91.535 ... 392–397

Operation
- on water §23.237 ... 106
- tests §23.683, 27.683, 33.51, 33.89 ... 129, 223, 268, 278

Operational control, defined §1.1 ... 5
Operations
- after maintenance, preventive maintenance, rebuilding, or alteration §91.407 ... 388
- aircraft requirements §135.25 ... 536
- alternate airport requirements §135.223 ... 562
- autopilot, minimum altitudes for use §135.93 ... 541
- commercial, air taxi §135.1 ... 532
- continuation of flight in an emergency §135.69 ... 538
- equipment requirements, night or VFR over-the-top §135.159 ... 553
- flight time limitations, rest requirements §135.263 ... 568
- IFR, takeoff, approach, landing minimums §135.225 ... 562
- in Class D airspace §91.129 ... 365
- in critical phases of flight §135.100 ... 541
- limitations, icing conditions §135.227 ... 563
- on unpaved surfaces §23.235 ... 106

Operations specifications
amendment of *§119.51, 125.35* 456, 479
contents *§119.49* 455
duty to maintain *§119.43* 454
manual
contents *§135.23* 535
requirements *§135.21* 535
not a part of certificate *§125.33* 479
recordkeeping requirements *§135.63* 537
use of *§125.43* 480
Order of investigation *§13.103* 26
Orders
compliance, HAZMAT *§13.81* 25
final, of Hearing Officer *§13.27* 21
of compliance, cease and desist orders, orders of denial and other orders *§13.20* 20
Outboard fins or winglets *§23.455* 115
Over water operations *§135.183* 561
Overhauled engines
maintenance records *§43.2, 91.421* 299, 391
Overseas air commerce, defined *§1.1* 5
Overseas air transportation, defined *§1.1* 5
Overtaking another aircraft
right-of-way rules *§91.113* 363
Over-the-top, defined *§1.1* 5
Owner, operator responsibilities
airworthiness *§91.403* 387
Oxygen
distribution system *§23.1445* 177
equipment and supply *§23.1441* 176
equipment requirements *§135.157* 552
means for determining use of *§23.1449* 178
medical use by passengers *§125.219, 135.91* 491, 540
requirements for use *§91.211* 380
use of by pilot *§135.89* 540

P

Parachute, defined *§1.1* 5
Parachute riggers
certificate privileges *§65.125* 345
certification required *§65.111* 344
eligibility *§65.113* 344
facilities and equipment *§65.127* 345
master certificate requirements *§65.119* 345
military or former military, special certification rule *§65.117* 344
performance standards *§65.129* 345
records *§65.131* 346
seal *§65.133* 346
senior parachute rigger certificate *§65.115* 344
type ratings *§65.121, 65.123* 345
Parachute rigging *§91.307* 383
Parachutes and parachuting *§91.307* 383
Part 119 definitions *§119.3* 448

Passenger
and crew compartment interiors *§23.853* ... 143
briefing required, large and turbine-powered aircraft *§91.519* ... 395
information required, large and turbine-powered aircraft *§91.517* ... 395
information signs *§23.791* ... 139
intoxicated *§91.17* ... 360
service equipment, stowage of during aircraft movement *§91.535* ... 397
signs and information, required *§135.127* ... 544
Passenger information, smoking *§135.127* ... 544
Penalties
civil *§13.14, 13.15, 13.16, 13.18, 13.29* ... 15, 18, 22
criminal *§13.23* ... 21
Performance
at minimum operating speed *§27.73* ... 209
information *§23.1587, 27.1587* ... 186, 256
Performance requirements
aircraft operated over-the-top or in IFR conditions *§135.181* ... 560
Person, defined *§1.1* ... 5
Personnel
repair station requirements *§145.151–145.163* ... 620–621
Personnel and cargo accommodations *§27.771–27.833* ... 226–228
Persons authorized to perform maintenance, preventive maintenance, rebuilding, and alterations *§43.3* ... 300
Pilot
reporting hazards *§135.67* ... 538
requirements, use of oxygen *§135.89* ... 540
Pilot compartment *§23.771, 23.773, 27.771, 27.773* ... 134, 226
Pilot examiners *§183.23* ... 636
Pilot qualifications, recent experience *§135.247* ... 565
Pilot seat, passenger occupancy of *§135.113* ... 542
Pilot testing requirements *§135.293* ... 571
Pilotage, defined *§1.1* ... 5
Pilot-in-command
aircraft requiring more than one pilot *§91.5* ... 359
airworthiness check *§135.71* ... 538
defined *§1.1* ... 5
designation required *§135.109* ... 542
familiarity with operating limitations, emergency equipment *§91.505* ... 393
instrument proficiency check requirements *§125.291, 135.297* ... 501, 572
line checks, routes and airports *§135.299* ... 573
preflight action *§91.103* ... 361
qualifications *§125.281, 135.243* ... 500, 564
recent experience *§125.285, 135.247* ... 500, 565
responsibility and authority *§91.3* ... 359
Pitch control and indication *§35.23* ... 294
Pitch setting, defined *§1.1* ... 5
Pitot heat indication systems *§23.1326, 125.206, 135.158* ... 168, 488, 552
Placarding, marking, requirements for aircraft *§91.9* ... 359
Pleadings, service and filing *§13.43* ... 23
Pneumatic de-icer boot system *§23.1416* ... 175
Portable electronic devices *§91.21* ... 360
Position light
distribution and intensities *§23.1389–23.1395, 27.1389–27.1395* ... 173–174, 248–249
system installation *§23.1385, 27.1385* ... 172, 248
Position light system
dihedral angles *§23.1387, 27.1387* ... 172, 248
Positive control, defined *§1.1* ... 5
Power boost and power-operated control system *§27.695* ... 224
Power or thrust response *§33.73* ... 270

Powered parachute, defined *§1.1* 5
Powered parachute *§45.11, 45.27* 313, 316
Powered-lift, defined *§1.1* 5
Powerplant
accessories *§23.1163, 27.1163* 161, 242
controls, general *§23.1141, 27.1141* 160, 241
curriculum subjects *Part 147 Appendix D* 633
fire protection *§121.253* 466
instrument installation *§23.1337* 169
instruments *§23.1305, 23.1549, 27.1305, 27.1337, 27.1549* 165, 182, 243, 245, 255
limitations *§23.1521, 27.1521* 180, 253
operating characteristics *§23.939* 148
Precision approach procedure, defined *§1.1* 5
Preflight action *§91.103* 361
Preflight, required information for flight *§91.103* 361
Pressure
cross-feed *§121.227* 465
fueling systems *§23.979* 152
venting and drainage of rotor blades *§27.653* 222
Pressurization and pneumatic systems *§23.1438* 176
Pressurization tests *§23.843* 142
Pressurized cabins *§23.365, 23.841* 111, 142
Preventive maintenance, defined *§1.1* 6
Primary category aircraft *§91.325* 386
Primary flight controls *§23.673, 27.673* 128, 223
Privileges *§21.45, 21.119, 21.163* 51, 56, 59
Production
certificates *§21.267* 67
inspection system, Materials Review Board *§21.125* 57
limitation record *§21.151* 58
under type certificate *§21.123* 56
Prohibited area, defined *§1.1* 6
Prohibited drugs
testing for *§135.251* 566
training against use of *§135.353* 580
Proof of compliance
with section 121.221 *§121.223* 465
Propeller
adjustments and parts replacements *§35.47* 295
clearance *§23.925* 147
defined *§1.1* 6
feathering controls *§23.1153* 161
feathering system *§23.1027* 156
general *§23.905* 147
operating limitations *§35.5* 293
speed and pitch controls *§23.1149* 161
speed and pitch limits *§23.33* 93
turbopropeller-drag limiting systems *§23.937* 148
vibration *§23.907* 147
Propeller deicing fluid *§121.225* 465
Protection of
oxygen equipment from rupture *§23.1453* 178
structure *§23.609, 27.609* 125, 220
Provisional airport, defined *§119.3* 450
Public address, crewmember interphone systems required *§135.150* 548
Public aircraft, defined *§1.1* 6

Q

Qualifications
flight instructors §135.338, 135.340 ... 577, 578
second-in-command §125.283, 135.245 ... 500, 565
Quality control system, changes in §21.147 ... 58
Quality control §21.139, 21.143 ... 58

R

Radar
weather avoidance equipment requirements §135.173 ... 557
weather radar requirements §135.175 ... 557
Radio and navigational equipment
requirements §125.203, 135.161 ... 488, 553
Radio communications
failure, under IFR §91.185 ... 376
under IFR §91.183 ... 376
Radio equipment, overwater operations §91.511 ... 393
Rate of roll §23.157 ... 101
Rated 2-1/2-minute OEI power, defined §1.1 ... 7
Rated 2-minute OEI power, defined §1.1 ... 7
Rated 30-minute OEI power, defined §1.1 ... 7
Rated 30-second OEI power, defined §1.1 ... 7
Rated continuous OEI power, defined §1.1 ... 6
Rated maximum continuous augmented thrust, defined §1.1 ... 6
Rated maximum continuous power, defined §1.1 ... 6
Rated maximum continuous thrust, defined §1.1 ... 6
Rated takeoff augmented thrust, defined §1.1 ... 6
Rated takeoff power, defined §1.1 ... 6
Rated takeoff thrust, defined §1.1 ... 6
Ratings requirements §135.243 ... 564
Rear lift truss §23.369 ... 111
Recency of operation, under Part 119 §119.63 ... 458
Reciprocating engine-powered airplanes, cooling test procedures for §23.1047 ... 157
Recommendation of persons for certification as repairmen §145.159 ... 621
Records
investigative procedures §13.7 ... 14
logbooks, aircraft and engine §91.417 ... 391
of overhaul and rebuilding §43.2 ... 299
recordkeeping requirements §135.63 ... 537
supervisory and inspection personnel §145.161 ... 621
Recurrent training §135.351 ... 580
Reduced Vertical Separation Minimum (RVSM) airspace, operations in §91.706 ... 401
Reference landing approach speed §23.73 ... 98
Reference landing speed, defined §1.1 ... 7
Removable ballast §23.31, 27.31 ... 93, 207
Renewal of certificates §145.55 ... 618
Repair station manual contents §145.209 ... 623
Repair stations
application and issue §145.51, 145.53 ... 618
certificate required §145.5 ... 617
certification
duration and renewal of certificates §145.55, 145.57 ... 618
certification of foreign repair stations §145.51 ... 618
certification §145.51–145.61 ... 618–619
change of location or facilities §145.105 ... 620
change or renewal of certificates §145.55, 145.57 ... 618
display of certificate §145.5 ... 617
duration of certificates §145.55 ... 618

equipment requirements *§145.109* 620
general *§145.1–145.5* 617
housing and facilities *§145.101–145.109* 619–620
inspection *§145.223* 625
operating rules *§145.201–145.223* 622–625
performance of maintenance, preventive maintenance, alterations and required inspections, air carrier, commercial operator *§145.205* 622
personnel authorized, approval of article for return to service *§145.157* 621
personnel *§145.151–145.163* 620–621
quality control system *§145.211* 623
Repairmen
eligibility, certificate *§65.101* 342
experimental aircraft builder *§65.104* 343
privileges, limitations *§65.103* 343
Replacement
and modification parts *§21.303, 45.15* 68, 314
of certificate *§47.49* 324
Reporting
mechanical irregularities *§125.323, 135.65* 503, 538
of failures, malfunctions, defects *§21.3* 46
of potentially hazardous meteorological conditions *§125.321, 135.67* 503, 538
Reporting point, defined *§1.1* 7
Reports
malfunctions *§91.187* 376
of defects or unairworthy conditions *§145.221* 624
of emergency operations *§135.19* 535
reporting points, IFR *§91.183* 376
Representatives of the Administrator
certification of representatives
certification *§183.13* 635
duration of certificates *§183.15* 636
selection *§183.11* 635
designations, privileges *§183.21–183.33* 636–638
general *§183.1* 635
reports *§183.17* 636
Required inspection personnel *§121.371, 125.251, 135.429* 472, 499, 592
Requirement of supplemental type certificate *§21.113* 56
Reserve energy absorption drop test *§23.727, 27.727* 132, 224
Responsibility and authority of the pilot-in-command *§91.3* 359
Responsibility of holder *§21.165* 59
Rest period, defined *§135.273* 570
Restricted area, defined *§1.1* 7
Restricted category civil aircraft *§91.313* 384
Resultant limit maneuvering loads *§27.339* 212
Retracting mechanism *§27.729* 225
Reversible propellers *§35.21* 294
Reversing systems *§23.933, 23.934* 148
Riding light *§23.1399, 27.1399* 174, 249
Right-of-way rules
aircraft categories *§91.113* 363
operations, except on water *§91.113* 363
water operations *§91.115* 363
Rights of persons against self-incrimination *§13.119* 27
Rocket, defined *§1.1* 7
Rolling conditions *§23.349* 110
Rotor blade clearance *§27.661* 222
Rotor brake *§27.921, 27.1151* 232, 242
Rotor drive system, control mechanism tests *§27.923* 232
Rotor locking tests *§33.92* 279
Rotor speed *§27.1509* 252

Rotorcraft, defined §1.1 ... 7
Rotorcraft operations
direct air carriers and commercial operators §119.25 ... 452
Rotorcraft-load combination, defined §1.1 ... 7
Rotors §27.653–27.663 ... 222
Route segment, defined §1.1 ... 7
Routing, after communications failure §91.185 ... 376
Rules of construction, defined §1.1 ... 9
Rules, Part 135 operations §135.3 ... 534
RVSM airspace §91.706, Part 91 Appendix G ... 401, 444

S

Safety analysis §33.75 ... 270
Safety belts
child restraint systems, use of §135.128 ... 544
use of §91.107 ... 362
Safety equipment §23.1561, 27.1561 ... 183, 255
Safety factor §23.303, 27.303 ... 107, 212
Safety pilot, required for simulated instrument flight §91.109 ... 363
Sale of aircraft, removal of marks §45.33 ... 316
Sampling and analytical procedures §34.64, 34.82 ... 291
Satellite repair stations §145.107 ... 620
Sea level engine, defined §1.1 ... 7
Seaplane loads §23.521–23.537, Part 23 Appendix I ... 119–122, 200
Seat and safety belts §125.211 ... 490
Seats and berths safety belts, and harnesses §23.785, 27.785 ... 138, 226
Seawing loads §23.537 ... 122
Secondary control system §23.405 ... 112
Second-in-command
CAT II operations §135.111 ... 542
defined §1.1 ... 7
qualifications §125.283, 135.245 ... 500, 565
required under IFR §135.101 ... 542
requirements §91.5, 91.531 ... 359, 396
Security disqualification §65.14 ... 333
Seizure of aircraft §13.15, 13.17 ... 18
Self-extinguishing materials, test procedures Part 23 Appendix F ... 196
Senior parachute rigger certificate
experience, knowledge, and skill requirements §65.115 ... 344
Service difficulty reports
operational §125.409, 135.415 ... 508, 588
structural §125.410, 135.416 ... 509, 589
Service-history-based inspections §135.168 ... 555
Shafting critical speed §27.931 ... 233
Shafting joints §27.935 ... 233
Shock absorption tests §23.723, 27.723 ... 131, 224
Shoulder harness
installation at flight crewmember stations §135.171 ... 556
use of by crew §91.105 ... 362
Show, defined §1.1 ... 7
Shutoff means §23.1189, 27.1189, 121.257, 125.155 ... 162, 242, 466, 485
Side load conditions §23.485 ... 117
Side load on engine mount §23.363 ... 111
Simplified design load criteria Part 23 Appendix A ... 186
Ski landing conditions §27.505 ... 216
Skis, limit load rating §23.737, 27.737 ... 133, 225
Small aircraft, defined §1.1 ... 7
Smoking and safety belts signs §91.517 ... 395

Special
conditions §21.16 47
flight operations §91.303–91.325 383–386
flight permits §21.197 64
retroactive requirements §23.2, 27.2 .... 92, 206
tests and test procedures §34.5, 35.43 287
VFR conditions, defined §1.1 7
VFR operations, defined §1.1 7
VFR weather minimums §91.157 371
Special airworthiness requirements
Part 125 operations §121.211–121.293 463–469
Special flight permit §39.23 298
Speed
control devices §23.373 111
limits §91.117 363
reference landing approach §23.73 98
warning device, aural §91.603 397
Spinning §23.221 105
Sport pilot certificate §43.7 301
Sport pilot repairman certificate §43.3 300
Sporting events, major, and aerial demonstrations
aircraft operations management §91.145 369
Spray characteristics §23.239, 27.239 .... 106, 211
Spring devices §23.687, 27.687 .... 129, 224
Stability augmentation, automatic and power-operated systems §23.672, 27.672 .... 128, 222
Stability, general §27.171 210
Stage 4 noise level, defined §91.851 404
Stall warning §23.207 105
Stalling §23.49 94
Standard atmosphere, defined §1.1 7
Start-stop cyclic stress (low-cycle fatigue) §33.14 263
Statement of conformity §21.53, 21.130 .... 52, 57
Static
directional and lateral stability §23.177, 27.177 .... 103, 211
longitudinal stability, demonstration of §23.175, 27.175 .... 103, 211
longitudinal stability §23.173, 27.173 .... 103, 210
Static pressure system §23.1325, 27.1325 .... 168, 245
Stopway, defined §1.1 7
Storage battery design and installation §23.1353, 27.1353 .... 171, 246
Strength
and deformation §23.305, 27.305 .... 107, 212
proof of §23.641, 23.651 128
Stress analysis §33.62 268
Structural ditching provisions §27.563 218
Structure, proof of §23.307, 27.307 .... 107, 212
Subpoenas §13.57, 13.111, 13.228 ....24, 27, 37
Supplemental inspections §121.370a 472
Supplemental oxygen, minimum mass flow of §23.1443 176
Supplemental oxygen §91.211 380
Surge and stall characteristics §33.65 268
Survival equipment, overwater operations §91.509 393
Symmetrical flight conditions §23.331 107
Synthetic vision, defined §1.1 7
Synthetic vision system, defined §1.1 7

T

Tabs *§23.409* 113
Tail down landing conditions *§23.481, 27.481* 117, 215
Tail rotor *§27.1565* 255
Takeoff
  climb, one engine inoperative *§23.66* 97
  distance and takeoff run *§23.59* 96
  flight path *§23.61* 96
  path *§23.57* 96
  performance *§23.53, 27.51* 95, 208
  power, defined *§1.1* 7
  safety speed, defined *§1.1* 8
  speeds *§23.51* 95
  thrust, defined *§1.1* 8
  warning system *§23.703* 131
Takeoff and landing
  recent experience *§135.247* 565
  under IFR *§91.175* 373
  use of safety belts *§91.107* 362
  weather minimums, IFR *§125.381* 507
Takeoff limitations, large aircraft *§135.367* 581
Tandem wing configuration, defined *§1.1* 8
Taxi and landing lights *§23.1383* 172
Taxiing condition *§27.235* 211
TCAS I, defined *§1.1* 8
TCAS II, defined *§1.1* 8
TCAS III, defined *§1.1* 8
Teardown inspection *§33.55, 33.93, 35.45* 268, 279, 295
Technical personnel examiners *§183.25* 636
Technical Standard Order (TSO)-C151 *§91.223, 135.154* 382, 552
Temporary flight restrictions *§91.137, 91.138, 91.145* 367, 368, 369
Temporary registration numbers *§47.16* 321
Terminal control areas
  See Class B airspace *§91.131* 367
Terrain awareness and warning system *§91.223, 135.154* 382, 552
Test procedure, propulsion engines *§34.62* 290
Tests
  additional *§27.927* 233
  aircraft engines *§21.128* 57
  aircraft *§21.127* 57
  cheating *§65.18* 334
  failure, additional training after *§135.301* 573
  flight line checks *§135.299* 573
  general *§65.17* 334
  initial and recurrent pilot, flight attendant testing *§135.293, 135.295* 571, 572
  instrument proficiency checks *§135.297* 572
  pressurization *§23.843* 142
  propellers *§21.129* 57
  retesting after failure *§65.19* 334
Threat assessment
  initial notification of *§65.14* 333
Thrust reversers *§33.97* 280
Thunderstorm detection equipment, requirements *§135.173* 557
Time in service, defined *§1.1* 8
Tires
  and shock absorbers *§27.475* 214
  general *§23.733, 27.733* 133, 225
  loads, ratings *§23.733* 133
Tower light signals *§91.125* 365

Towing
general requirements §91.311 384
loads §23.509 118
Traffic alert and collision avoidance system (TCAS)
equipment and use §91.221 382
requirements, large turbine-powered aircraft §135.180 560
Traffic pattern
defined §1.1 8
general rules §91.127 365
right-of-way rules §91.113 363
Training
aircraft simulators and other training devices §135.335 576
flight attendants, initial and transition ground §135.349 580
for emergencies §135.331 575
hazardous materials §135.333 575
initial and recurrent for crewmembers §135.343 579
initial, transition, and upgrade for pilots §135.345 579
of check airmen §135.339 577
pilots, initial, transition, upgrade, and differences flight training §135.347 579
recurrent §135.351 580
Training, definitions of terms §135.321 573
Training program
check airmen qualifications §135.337 576
curriculum §135.327 575
maintenance or preventive maintenance §135.433 593
pilot and flight attendant crewmember §135.341 578
requirements §135.323 574
revision of §135.325 574
special rules §135.324 574
Transcripts and graduation certificates §147.35 629
Transfer of maintenance records at time of sale §135.441 594
Transmission and gearboxes, general §27.1027 239
Transponder
requirements and use §91.215 381
testing and calibration §91.217 382
tests and inspections §91.413 390
Transportation Security Administration (TSA) §65.14 333
Triennial aircraft registration report §47.51 324
Trim
control §23.161, 27.161 .... 102, 210
systems §23.677 129
tab effects §23.407 113
True airspeed, defined §1.1 8
Truth-in-leasing clause
requirements, in lease or sale of large aircraft §91.23 361
Turbine, compressor, fan, and turbosupercharger rotors §33.27 264
Turbine engine
bleed air system §23.1111 159
operating characteristics §27.939 233
reverse thrust and propeller pitch settings below the flight regime §23.1155 161
Turbine engine-powered airplanes, cooling test procedures for §23.1045 156
Turbine fuel specifications §34.61 290
Turbine-powered aircraft
ground proximity warning system §135.153 551
Turbocharger bleed air system §23.1109 159
Turbocharger systems §23.909 147
Turning flight and accelerated turning stalls §23.203 104
Turns, in traffic pattern §91.126 365
Type, defined §1.1 8

Type certificates
application §21.15, 21.75, 21.253 47, 52, 67
changes requiring new §21.19 48
general §21.41 51
issue §21.257 67
provisional §21.81, 21.83, 21.85, 21.225 52, 53, 65
supplemental §21.111–21.119 56
Type design, classification of changes in §21.93 54
Type design §21.31 50

U

Unauthorized operators, applicability of rules to §135.7 535
United States
air carrier, defined §1.1 8
citizens and resident aliens §47.7 318
defined §1.1 8
Unpowered ultralights
towing, requirements §91.309 383
Unsafe conditions
resolving §39.11, 39.19 297
Unsafe conditions, continuing flight in §125.371 506
Unsymmetrical
flight conditions §23.347 110
loads, due to engine failure §23.367 111
loads §23.427, 27.427 114, 214
Unusable fuel supply §23.959, 27.959 150, 235

V

Valves
fuel and oil, requirements §121.235, 121.239, 121.257 465, 466
Vent and drain lines §121.261 466
Ventilation §23.831, 27.831, 27.1187, 121.219, 125.117 142, 228, 242, 464, 482
VFR
cruising altitude, flight level §91.159 371
flight plan, information required §91.153 370
fuel requirements §91.151 370
fuel supply §135.209 561
instruments required §91.205 378
minimum altitudes §135.203 561
visibility requirements §135.205 561
weather minimums §91.155 370
VFR over-the-top, defined §1.1 8
Vibration and buffeting §23.251 106
Vibration test §33.43, 33.83 265, 274
Vibration §27.251, 33.33, 33.63 211, 265, 268
Violations
administrative disposition of §13.11 14
reports of §13.1 13
Visibility requirements §135.205 561
Visibility §91.157 371
VOR equipment
check, for IFR operations §91.171 372
Voting trusts §47.8 318

W

Waivers
- policy and procedures *§91.903* 409
- rules subject to *§91.905* 409

Warning area, defined *§1.1* 8
Water load conditions *§23.521* 119
Water operations, right-of-way rules *§91.115* 363
Weapons, prohibition against carriage of *§135.119* 543
Weather minimums, special VFR *§91.157* 371
Weather reports, forecasts *§135.213* 562
Weight and balance
- multiengine aircraft *§135.185* 561

Weight and center of gravity *§23.1519, 27.1519* 180, 252
Weight limitations
- large aircraft *§135.365* 581
- transport category aircraft *§91.605* 397

Weight limits *§23.25, 27.25* 93, 206
Weight-shift-control aircraft, defined *§1.1* 8
Weight-shift-control aircraft *§45.11, 45.27* 313, 316
Wet lease, defined *§119.3* 450
Wet leasing
- of aircraft, other arrangements for air transportation *§119.53* 456

Wheel spin-up, spring-back loads *Part 23 Appendix D* 196
Wheels
- limit load rating *§23.731* 133

Wheels *§23.731, 27.731* 133, 225
Windshields and windows *§23.775, 27.775* 134, 226
Wing flap
- control *§23.697* 130
- interconnection *§23.701* 131
- position indicator *§23.699* 130

Winglet or tip fin, defined *§1.1* 8
Wings level stall *§23.201* 104
Witness fees *§13.57, 13.121, 13.229* 24, 27, 37
Written (or, Knowledge) tests
- cheating or other unauthorized conduct *§65.18* 334

Y

Yawing conditions *§23.351, 27.351* 110, 213

Notes

Notes

Flight Library CD-ROM

Fast, simple access to a world of aviation information

The leader in FAR/AIM and aviation information resources brings you the most complete CD-ROM reference library available—the ASA Flight Library Series. The program uses Folio Version 4.2 which provides the easiest, fastest, and most thorough search engine available!

Using the powerful search engine and the unique Query Wizard you can easily and quickly search a single document or the entire CD-ROM for a particular word, phrase, or topic. Visit the ASA website for a free Demo!

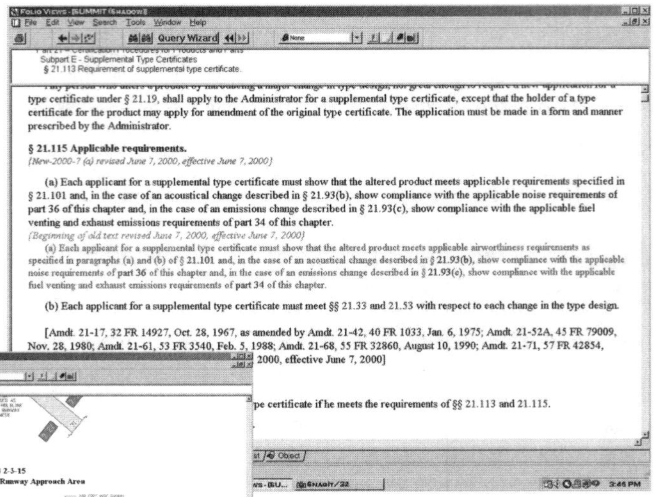

Easily navigate through any document: Page Up or Down, use the arrow keys, or jump from word link to word link to review the information you need.

Pro-Flight Library CD includes:

- All 14 CFR (FAR) Regulations (Parts 1 through 499)
- Practical Test Standards
- FAA reprints and handbooks
- Advisory Circulars
- Dictionary of Aeronautical Terms
- Hazardous materials (Hazmat) regulations
- EPA and NTSB regulations
- Airworthiness Directives (ADs)
- General Aviation Airworthiness Alerts
- Over 850 publications, and over 6,000 graphics!

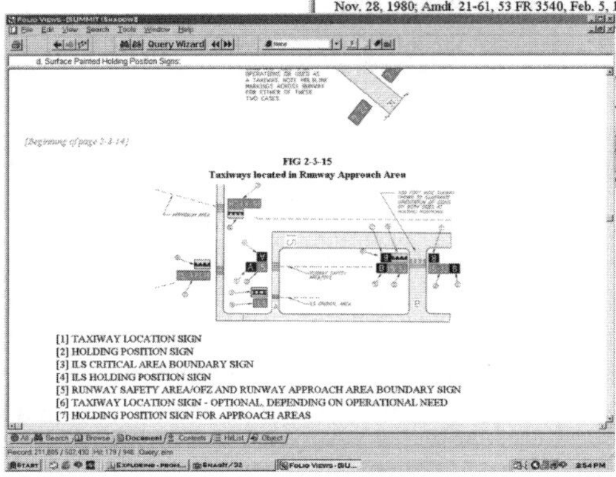

View or print hundreds of graphics from the aviation publications.

Nondestructive & Ultrasonic Testing for Aircraft

Preparation, procedures, inspections, applications, and testing methods are discussed in this reprint of two FAA Advisory Circulars.

Aircraft Inspection, Repair & Alterations

The "bible" for AMTs and aircraft owners alike, this book outlines standards for acceptable methods, techniques, and practices for the inspection, repair and alteration of aircraft. Includes both Part 1B and Part 2A (September 1998); includes Part 1B Change 1.

Call **1-800-ASA-2-FLY** (1-800-272-2-359)
for the retailer nearest you.

Visit our website: **www.asa2fly.com**

Aviation Supplies & Academics, Inc.
7005 132nd Place SE
Newcastle, Washington 98059-3153

Reader Response

Your feedback is invaluable to us. Please take a moment to provide us with your comments and suggestions. Thank you—*Aviation Supplies & Academics, Inc.*

Please print clearly.

Name ______________________________

Title *(Student, Instructor, Pilot, other)* ______________________________

Business/School ______________________________

Address ______________________________

City ______________________________

State ______________________________ Zip/Postal Code ______________

Country ______________________________

Telephone ______________________________

E-mail ______________________________

Where did you purchase this book? ______________________________

Was the text recommended to you? ______________________________

By whom? ______________________________

Please tell us what you liked or disliked about the text:
Does this book meet your needs? (if no, please explain)
Would you like to see certain regulations added or removed? (list each Part number)
Is there anything you'd like to see different regarding the book content or organization?

General comments and suggestions ______________________________

❑ **Please send me an ASA Catalog**

Mail or fax this form to:

Aviation Supplies & Academics, Inc.
7005 132nd Place SE
Newcastle, WA 98059-3153
Fax: 425.235.0128

Visit ASA's website: asa2fly.com

06-FAR-AMT